EXCHANGE ARRANGEMENTS
AND
EXCHANGE RESTRICTIONS

ANNUAL REPORT 1995

Price: US$76.00
(US$38.00 to full-time university faculty members and students)

Address orders to:
International Monetary Fund
Publication Services
Washington, D.C. 20431
U.S.A.
Internet: publications@imf.org

The Library of Congress has cataloged this serial publication as follows:

International Monetary Fund.
  Annual report on exchange arrangements and exchange restrictions.
1979—

Continues: International Monetary Fund. Annual report on exchange
restrictions, 1950–1978
 1. Foreign exchange — Law and legislation — Periodicals. 2. Foreign
exchange — Control — Periodicals. I. Title.
K4440.A13 I57 [date] 341.7'51 79-644506
ISSN 0250-7366
ISBN 1-55775-509-4

Letter of Transmittal to Members
and Governors of the Fund

August 10, 1995

Dear Sir:

I have the honor to transmit to you a copy of the International Monetary Fund's *Annual Report on Exchange Arrangements and Exchange Restrictions, 1995,* which has been prepared in accordance with the provisions of Article XIV, Section 3 of the Articles of Agreement.

On behalf of the Executive Board, I should like to express our appreciation of the cooperation of the countries in the preparation of the Report.

Sincerely yours,

Michel Camdessus
Chairman of the Executive Board
and Managing Director

CONTENTS

Page

Preface vii
Introduction 1

	Page		*Page*
Afghanistan, Islamic State of	3	Dominican Republic	148
Albania	6	Ecuador	150
Algeria	8	Egypt	153
Angola	12	El Salvador	156
Antigua and Barbuda	15	Equatorial Guinea	158
Argentina	17	Eritrea	161
Armenia	20	Estonia	164
Aruba	23	Ethiopia	166
Australia	25	Fiji	170
Austria	29	Finland	174
Azerbaijan	31	France	176
Bahamas, The	34	Gabon	181
Bahrain	38	Gambia, The	185
Bangladesh	40	Georgia	187
Barbados	45	Germany	189
Belarus	49	Ghana	192
Belgium and Luxembourg	53	Greece	196
Belize	55	Grenada	199
Benin	57	Guatemala	201
Bhutan	61	Guinea	203
Bolivia	62	Guinea-Bissau	206
Botswana	65	Guyana	208
Brazil	68	Haiti	211
Bulgaria	75	Honduras	213
Burkina Faso	78	Hong Kong	215
Burundi	83	Hungary	217
Cambodia	86	Iceland	222
Cameroon	88	India	225
Canada	93	Indonesia	234
Cape Verde	96	Iran, Islamic Republic of	239
Central African Republic	98	Iraq	242
Chad	102	Ireland	245
Chile	106	Israel	247
China	110	Italy	250
Colombia	116	Jamaica	252
Comoros	120	Japan	255
Congo	122	Jordan	258
Costa Rica	126	Kazakhstan	262
Côte d'Ivoire	129	Kenya	265
Croatia	133	Kiribati	269
Cyprus	136	Korea	270
Czech Republic	140	Kuwait	275
Denmark	143	Kyrgyz Republic	278
Djibouti	145	Lao People's Democratic Republic	280
Dominica	146	Latvia	282

	Page
Lebanon	284
Lesotho	286
Liberia	288
Libyan Arab Jamahiriya	290
Lithuania	293
Macedonia, former Yugoslav Republic of	295
Madagascar	298
Malawi	302
Malaysia	305
Maldives	310
Mali	312
Malta	315
Marshall Islands	319
Mauritania	320
Mauritius	323
Mexico	325
Micronesia, Federated States of	328
Moldova	329
Mongolia	331
Morocco	333
Mozambique	339
Myanmar	341
Namibia	345
Nepal	347
Netherlands	350
Netherlands Antilles	353
New Zealand	355
Nicaragua	358
Niger	360
Nigeria	364
Norway	368
Oman	371
Pakistan	373
Panama	380
Papua New Guinea	382
Paraguay	385
Peru	387
Philippines	389
Poland	395
Portugal	400
Qatar	402
Romania	404
Russian Federation	407
Rwanda	412
St. Kitts and Nevis	415
St. Lucia	417
St. Vincent and the Grenadines	419
San Marino	421
São Tomé and Príncipe	423

	Page
Saudi Arabia	425
Senegal	427
Seychelles	431
Sierra Leone	433
Singapore	436
Slovak Republic	438
Slovenia	441
Solomon Islands	443
Somalia	445
South Africa	448
Spain	452
Sri Lanka	455
Sudan	461
Suriname	466
Swaziland	470
Sweden	472
Switzerland	474
Syrian Arab Republic	476
Tajikistan	480
Tanzania	482
Thailand	485
Togo	488
Tonga	492
Trinidad and Tobago	494
Tunisia	496
Turkey	502
Turkmenistan	507
Uganda	509
Ukraine	511
United Arab Emirates	514
United Kingdom	516
United States	518
Uruguay	523
Uzbekistan	525
Vanuatu	527
Venezuela	529
Viet Nam	532
Western Samoa	536
Yemen, Republic of	538
Zaïre	541
Zambia	546
Zimbabwe	549
Appendix. EU: Trade Measures Introduced and Eliminated During 1994	554
Summary Features of Exchange and Trade Systems in Member Countries	562
Definition of Acronyms	569

Note: The term "country," as used in this publication, does not in all cases refer to a territorial entity that is a state as understood by international law and practice; the term also covers some territorial entities that are not states but for which statistical data are maintained and provided internationally on a separate and independent basis.

PREFACE

The *Annual Report on Exchange Arrangements and Exchange Restrictions* has been published annually by the IMF since 1950. It draws on information available to the IMF from a number of sources, including that provided in the course of official visits to member countries, and it has been prepared in close consultation with national authorities.

The project is coordinated in the Exchange Regime and Market Operations Division of the Monetary and Exchange Affairs Department. It draws on the specialized contributions of staff of that Department (for specific countries), with assistance from staff members of the IMF's seven Area Departments, together with staff of other Departments. The report was edited and its production coordinated by Gail Berre of the External Relations Department. Design and composition were done by the IMF Graphics Section.

INTRODUCTION

The Report provides a detailed description of the exchange and trade systems of individual member countries, including the nonmetropolitan territory of Hong Kong, for which the United Kingdom has accepted the IMF's Articles of Agreement, and Aruba and the Netherlands Antilles, for which the Kingdom of the Netherlands has accepted the IMF's Articles of Agreement.

In general, the description relates to the exchange and trade systems as of the end of 1994, but in appropriate cases reference is made to significant developments that took place in early 1995.

A standardized approach has been followed, under which the description of each system is broken down into similar headings, and the coverage for each country includes a final section that lists chronologically the more significant changes during 1994 and in early 1995.

The description of the exchange and trade system is not necessarily confined to those aspects involving exchange restrictions or exchange controls. As in previous Reports, questions of definition and jurisdiction have not been raised, and an attempt has been made to describe exchange and trade systems in their entirety, except for the tariff structure and, in most cases, direct taxes on exports and imports. Thus, the coverage extends to such features as import licensing, advance import deposit requirements, import surcharges, travel taxes, export licensing, and export incentive schemes. Similarly, the section *Changes During 1994* (and 1995) includes references to certain developments that may have a direct impact on international transactions, such as major revisions of import tariffs or developments in regional cooperation, but are not necessarily reflected in the body of the country descriptions.

The description given in the section *Exchange Arrangement* is in line with the notification of exchange arrangements that member countries have furnished to the IMF under Article IV, Section 2(*a*). The structure of exchange markets is described, and the official exchange rate is given. The rates quoted are those effective on December 31, 1994, unless stated otherwise.

Under *Administration of Control*, some indication is given of the authorities responsible for policy and administration of the controls and of the extent to which their powers are delegated for working purposes.

The section on *Prescription of Currency* describes the requirements affecting the selection of the currency and method of settlement for transactions with other countries. When a country has concluded payments agreements with other countries, the terms of these agreements often lead to prescription of the currency for specified categories of payments to and from the countries concerned. The countries with which bilateral payments agreements are in force are listed either in the text or in a footnote.

Under *Resident/Nonresident Accounts*, and, in some instances, *External Accounts* or *Foreign Currency Accounts*, a description is given of the manner in which the country treats accounts, if any, maintained in its currency by account holders who are residents or not regarded as residents of that country, and the facilities and limitations attached to such accounts. When there is more than one type of resident/nonresident account, the nature and operation of the various types are also described.

In the section on *Imports and Import Payments*, import-licensing requirements are described briefly, and details are given of other requirements imposed on payments for imports and of any advance deposit requirements. The term "open general license" indicates arrangements whereby certain imports or other international transactions are exempt from the restrictive application of licensing requirements, in contrast to an "individual license," which may be given either freely or restrictively according to administrative decisions.

Under *Payments for Invisibles*, the procedures for permitting payments abroad for current transactions in invisibles are described briefly, together with any limitations on the exportation of foreign and domestic banknotes. For some countries that do not impose limitations on payments for invisibles, this section is combined with the section on *Proceeds from Invisibles* (see below).

Export-licensing requirements and procedures are described under *Exports and Export Proceeds*, with an outline of the requirements that may be imposed on the handling of proceeds from exports. The expression "exchange receipts must be surrendered" indicates that the recipient is required by the regulations to sell any foreign exchange proceeds in return for local currency, usually at the official rate, to the central bank, commercial banks, or exchange dealers authorized for this purpose. In some countries, there is a requirement that such exchange or part thereof be sold in a free market.

Under *Proceeds from Invisibles*, any regulations governing exchange derived from transactions in invisibles are given, and any limitations on the importation of foreign and domestic banknotes are described.

In the section on *Capital*, the special arrangements or limitations attached to international capital movements are described. When regulations on foreign capital also cover the income thereon, they are usually dealt with in this section rather than in the sections on *Payments for Invisibles* and *Proceeds from Invisibles*.

The section on *Gold* gives a summary of the principal regulations that govern the holding, negotiation, importation, and exportation of gold coins and gold in other forms.

ISLAMIC STATE OF AFGHANISTAN

(Position as of December 31, 1994)

Exchange Arrangement

The currency of the Islamic State of Afghanistan is the Afghani. Da Afghanistan Bank (the central bank) maintains an official rate defined in terms of the U.S. dollar. The official rate is applied to (1) a few transactions of the central Government (mainly debt-service payments); and (2) certain foreign currency income earned in Afghanistan (see section on Proceeds from Invisibles, below). On December 31, 1994, the official buying and selling exchange rates for the U.S. dollar were Af 1,000 and Af 1,025, respectively, per US$1.

Almost all other official transactions are conducted at a commercial rate set by the Government. A free market, in the form of a money bazaar, is also operative.

Between May and December 1989, the previously complex multiple exchange rate system was simplified significantly. Different mixed rates that had applied to proceeds in convertible currencies for nine principal exports were abolished, and proceeds from exports in convertible currencies were shifted to the commercial exchange rate. In December 1989, most public sector transactions, with the exception of debt servicing, were also moved to the commercial exchange rate. The commercial exchange rate was, however, not closely linked to the free market rate. Between December 1989 and February 1991, it was closely linked to the free market rate. In February 1991, it was maintained at Af 734 per US$1, and subsequently a significant premium developed between the commercial and free market exchange rates. The central bank limited sales of foreign exchange to five essential commodities (tea, vegetable oil, medicines, powdered milk, and soap) in March 1991. The official exchange rate now applies to no more than 10 percent of convertible currency transactions. Exchange rates for trade under bilateral payments agreements are determined under each agreement (see section on Prescription of Currency, below). The exchange rate applied to transactions of international organizations is set at 80 percent of the level of the commercial exchange rate.

Da Afghanistan Bank posts rates for deutsche mark, French franc, Indian rupees, Pakistani rupees, pounds sterling, and Swiss francs. It charges commissions ranging from 0.10 percent to 0.375 percent on exchange transactions. There are no arrangements for forward cover against exchange rate risk operating in the official or the commercial banking sector.

Administration of Control

Foreign exchange transactions are controlled by the Government through Da Afghanistan Bank. No official restrictions are applied to transactions in the free exchange market.

Prescription of Currency

Settlements with countries with which Afghanistan maintains bilateral payments agreements[1] are made in bilateral accounting dollars in accordance with the procedures set forth in these agreements. Some of these have been inactive for several years and others are being phased out. The proceeds from exports of karakul to all countries must be obtained in convertible currencies. There are no other prescription of currency requirements.

Imports and Import Payments

Imports are not subject to license, but import transactions must be registered before orders are placed abroad. The importation of a few items (e.g., certain drugs, liquor, arms, and ammunition) is prohibited on grounds of public policy or for security reasons; in some instances, however, special permission to import these goods may be granted. The importation of certain other goods (e.g., a few textiles and selected nonessential consumer goods) is also prohibited. There are no quantitative restrictions on other imports. Most bilateral agreements, however, specify quantities (and sometimes prices) for commodities to be traded. An annual import program drawn up by the Ministry of Commerce covers both public and private sector imports. Adjustments in the public sector import plan are made as circumstances change. The import plan for the private sector, drawn up on the basis of proposals submitted by the Chamber of Commerce, is indicative. The importation of petroleum products was a state monopoly until late 1992. In light of recent oil shortages, however, the private sector has been allowed to import and distribute petroleum.

---

[1]Bulgaria, China, the Czech Republic, Hungary, the Russian Federation, and the Slovak Republic.

The present customs tariff structure, promulgated in June 1974, changed little until May 1989. At that time, tariff rates on most consumer items were adjusted upward to 30–50 percent from their former range of about 20–35 percent.

Payments for imports through the banking system to payments agreement countries may usually be made only under letters of credit. Payments to other countries may be made under letters of credit, against bills for collection, or against an undertaking by the importer to import goods of at least equivalent value to the payment made through the banking system. Except for public sector imports under the government budget, all importers are required to lodge minimum import deposits with banks when they open letters of credit. In January 1990, the deposit ratios, based on the c.i.f. value of imports, were adjusted downward to 20 percent from 25 percent for essential products and upward to a range of 30–60 percent from a range of 20–50 percent for other products.

Payments for Invisibles

The maximum amount that can be taken out of the country for tourist travel abroad is the equivalent of $1,000 a trip, except for travel to India, for which the limit is the equivalent of $700. On application, foreign exchange is allocated for business travel and for medical treatment abroad, and the amounts are determined by Da Afghanistan Bank; normally, the limits are $15,000 for business and $2,500 for medical treatment. Foreign exchange for other private purposes may be acquired in the money bazaar. The central bank levies a charge of Af 0.75 per US$1 and 1 percent of hard currency for permits that approve the exportation of convertible currency by authorized travelers. For medical treatment and business travel, the central bank levies Af 0.75 per US$1. Travelers may take out not more than Af 2,000 in domestic banknotes and Af 50 in coins.

Exports and Export Proceeds

Exports (other than gold) are not subject to license, but export transactions must be registered. The exportation of a few products (e.g., opium and museum pieces) is prohibited. Otherwise, control is exercised only over exports to bilateral agreement countries (see section on Imports and Import Payments, above). Export proceeds from bilateral accounts may be retained in bilateral clearing dollar accounts with Da Afghanistan Bank. These retained proceeds may be either used directly by the original exporter or sold to other importers. In either case,

the retained proceeds are converted at the clearing rate applicable to that particular bilateral arrangement.

In the case of exports to countries trading in convertible currencies, export proceeds may be retained abroad for 3, 6, or 12 months, depending on the country of destination. During the relevant period, the exporter may use these funds to import any goods not included on the list of prohibited goods. Alternatively, at the end of the relevant holding period limit, foreign exchange holdings abroad must be repatriated and held in a foreign currency account with a bank in Afghanistan or sold at the commercial exchange rate. However, proceeds from seven items (raisins, fresh fruits, animal casings, skins, licorice roots, medicinal herbs, and wool) must be surrendered immediately at the commercial exchange rate.

Proceeds from Invisibles

Sixty percent of the foreign currency salaries of foreign employees working in the Afghan public and private sectors must be converted into afghanis at the official rate. Travelers entering Afghanistan are required to spend a minimum of the equivalent of $26 a day in foreign exchange. They may bring in any amount of foreign currency but must declare it when entering the country if they intend to take out any unspent amount on departure, subject to the above minimum conversion requirement. Travelers may bring in no more than Af 2,000 in domestic bank notes and Af 50 in coins.

Capital

Foreign investment in Afghanistan requires prior approval and is administered by the Investment Committee. The Foreign and Domestic Private Investment Law No. 1353 (issued on July 4, 1974), which is currently under revision, has a number of provisions, including (1) income tax exemption for four years (six years outside Kabul province), beginning with the date of the first sale of products resulting from the new investment; (2) exemption from import duties on essential imports (mainly of capital goods); (3) exemption from taxes on dividends for four years after the first distribution of dividends, but not more than seven years after the approval of the investment; (4) exemption from personal income and corporate taxes on interest on foreign loans that constitute part of an approved investment; (5) exemption from export duties, provided that the products are not among the prohibited exports; and (6) mandatory procurement by government agencies and departments from enterprises established under the law as long as the prices are not more than 15 percent higher than those of foreign suppliers. The law stipulates that foreign investment in Afghanistan can take place only through joint ventures, with foreign participation not exceeding 49 percent, and that an investment approved by the Investment Committee shall require no further license in order to operate in Afghanistan.

Payments of principal and interest on loans from abroad may be remitted freely to the extent of the legal obligation involved. Profits may be repatriated freely, and capital may be repatriated after five years at an annual rate not exceeding 20 percent of the total registered capital.

Gold

Residents may freely purchase, hold, and sell domestically gold in any form. Imports and re-exports of gold are permitted, subject to regulations. Exports of gold bullion, silver, and jewelry require permission from Da Afghanistan Bank and the Ministry of Finance. Commercial exports of gold and silver jewelry and other articles containing minor quantities of gold or silver do not require a license. Customs duties are payable on imports and exports of silver in any form, unless the transaction is made by or on behalf of the monetary authorities.

Changes During 1994

No significant changes occurred in the exchange and trade system.

ALBANIA

(Position as of December 31, 1994)

Exchange Arrangement

The currency of Albania is the Lek. The exchange rate of the lek is determined on the basis of underlying demand and supply conditions in the domestic market. Exchange rates for other currencies are determined on the basis of the cross-rate relationship between the U.S. dollar and the currencies concerned in the international market. The Bank of Albania calculates and announces the daily average exchange rates for the U.S. dollar and other major currencies. No margins are set between buying and selling rates for the official exchange rate. Government transactions are conducted at market rates. However, the commercial banks charge commissions ranging from 0.5 percent to 1.5 percent, depending on the amount, for cashing traveler's checks.[1] On December 31, 1994, the official (middle) rate for the U.S. dollar was lek 95.39 per US$1. There are no taxes or subsidies on purchases or sales of foreign exchange. There are no arrangements for forward exchange cover against exchange rate risk operating in the official or the commercial banking sector.

Administration of Control

The foreign exchange market is governed by new regulations issued on May 1, 1994 by the Bank of Albania, under the authority of Decree No. 127 of March 25, 1994 of the Council of Ministers. The Bank of Albania is vested with the powers to administer exchange controls.

All commercial banks are authorized to conduct foreign exchange transactions and hold accounts abroad. The Bank of Albania may (1) authorize banks and other dealers to conduct foreign exchange operations; (2) define the limits of their activities; and (3) supervise foreign exchange operations to prevent any participant from dominating the market. It charges licensed banks and foreign exchange bureaus and dealers with ensuring that their operations comply with foreign exchange regulations. There is a reporting requirement by banks and exchange dealers for transactions above $15,000 or equivalent.

Arrears are maintained with respect to external payments.

Prescription of Currency

All merchandise trade is conducted in convertible currencies. All transactions under bilateral payments agreements were suspended in 1992, and the settlement of clearing accounts is pending the outcome of negotiations.[2] Resident individual juridical persons are not permitted to open accounts with banks and financial institutions abroad without the prior written approval of the Bank of Albania.

Resident and Nonresident Accounts

Resident and nonresident natural and juridical persons are permitted to hold accounts in domestic and foreign currencies with commercial banks. Residents and nonresidents may freely receive payments and make payments abroad for current transactions. Authorized banks must maintain 90 percent cover on the foreign deposits placed with them, of which 10 percent represents the reserve requirement. Commercial banks may conduct foreign exchange transactions and hold accounts abroad. There are no restrictions on withdrawals of foreign exchange from foreign exchange accounts by residents or nonresidents. Interest rates paid on foreign currency accounts are determined by banks.

Imports and Exports

All state and private enterprises, individuals, and juridical persons are free to engage in foreign trade activities. The lists of products subject to export and import licenses are issued by the Ministry of Industry and Trade. Licenses are required to import hazardous materials and arms. At the end of 1994, four categories of export products were subject to licensing requirements. Applicants for export licenses must pay a service fee of $5 for each license.

---

[1]The commercial banks are free to determine the margins on purchases and sales of foreign banknotes, but they do not charge commissions.

[2]At the end of 1994, Albania maintained bilateral payments agreements in nonconvertible currencies with Bulgaria, Cuba, the Czech Republic, Hungary, the Democratic People's Republic of Korea, Romania, the Slovak Republic, and Viet Nam. Albania also maintained bilateral payments agreements in convertible currencies with Algeria, Bulgaria, China, Cuba, the Czech Republic, Egypt, Greece, the Democratic People's Republic of Korea, Romania, the Slovak Republic, Turkey, Viet Nam, and some of the countries of the former Socialist Federal Republic of Yugoslavia.

There are no surrender requirements, but all private and public companies or individuals operating in the export sector are required to repatriate their foreign exchange receipts to Albania. They are free to retain these proceeds in or outside the banking system or to convert them into leks.

There are four customs duty rates ranging from zero (for raw materials, intermediate and investment goods, and some foodstuffs) to 30 percent (for certain consumer goods) that are applied to both private and public sector imports. In addition, a surcharge of 5 percent, based on the c.i.f. value, is levied on all imports except wheat, flour, and investment goods.

Payments for and Proceeds from Invisibles

Payments for current invisible transactions are free of restrictions. There is no restriction on transfers of dividends and profits. Proceeds from invisibles are subject to the same repatriation as those from merchandise exports.

Capital

With certain exceptions, capital transfers are subject to the prior written approval of the Bank of Albania. The following capital transfers may be made freely: (1) inward capital transfers by residents or nonresidents; (2) outward transfers representing recorded capital inflows; (3) transfers of proceeds or withdrawal of nonresident deposits; (4) transfers undertaken in accordance with the law on foreign investment, Law No. 7764, November 1993, providing for the free repatriation of capital liquidation proceeds; and (5) transfers of the proceeds of the liquidation of Albanian assets by an emigrant on departure from Albania. Foreign direct investment into Albania is free of registration or preapproval requirements for most sectors. All requests for establishing joint ventures with government entities involving over $50,000 in foreign capital must be approved by the Council of Ministers. Similar requests from financial institutions are approved by the Bank of Albania. Profits of joint ventures may be subject to tax rates of up to 50 percent, depending on the activity of the enterprise; profits are not subject to any tax during the first two years of operation for long-term (at least ten-year) investment projects. Enterprises are eligible for reduced tax rates when they reinvest profits in Albania.

Gold

There are no restrictions on gold holdings. Precious metal exports are prohibited by Council of Ministers (COM) Decree No. 135, March 29, 1994.

Changes During 1994

Administration of Control

March 25. COM Decree No. 288 of July 1, 1992 on the regulation of the foreign exchange market was abolished and replaced by Decree No. 127, which granted authority to the Bank of Albania to govern exchange market regulations. New regulations removing currency restrictions on current transactions were issued by the Bank of Albania on May 1, 1994.

Imports and Exports

March 25. The regulation that export proceeds must be repatriated within 30 days of receipt was abolished.

March 29. Export licensing requirements were reduced to four product groups from eight product groups.

September 22. The temporary export taxes of 25–70 percent on fish and tobacco were abolished.

Payments for and Proceeds from Invisibles

May 1. Limits on foreign exchange allowance for travel abroad were abolished.

ALGERIA

(Position as of December 31, 1994)

Exchange Arrangement

The currency of Algeria is the Algerian Dinar. Daily buying and selling rates for the U.S. dollar, the intervention currency, and other specified currencies[1] are established by the Bank of Algeria (the central bank) in fixing sessions with the participation of commercial banks. A margin of DA 0.015 has been established between the buying and selling rates of the dinar in terms of the U.S. dollar. On December 31, 1994, the buying and selling rates for the U.S. dollar were DA 42.8132 and DA 42.8280, respectively, per US$1.

Foreign exchange reserves are centralized in the Bank of Algeria; authorized banks must clear their foreign currency position with their foreign correspondents at the end of each day but, under certain conditions, they are permitted to hold cover for documentary credits outside Algeria.

Under Regulation No. 91/07, residents may obtain from their commercial banks forward cover against exchange rate risk in the form of forward contracts to buy or sell foreign exchange. Payment for future delivery of foreign exchange may be effected either at the date the contract is made, in which case the spot exchange rate applies, or at the time the foreign exchange is delivered, in which case a forward rate quoted by the Bank of Algeria applies. The Bank of Algeria quotes 3-month, 6-month, 9-month, 12-month, 2-year, and 3-year forward exchange rates for specified currencies (listed in footnote 1). In April 1994, the Bank of Algeria ceased to offer forward cover but will continue to honor outstanding forward contracts.

Administration of Control

The Bank of Algeria has general jurisdiction over exchange control. It formulates exchange legislation and regulations and is responsible for their application by the authorized banks. Authority for a number of exchange control procedures has been delegated to five commercial banks and the Postal Administration.

Prescription of Currency

Settlements with countries with which no payments agreements are in force are made in convertible currencies.[2] Payments under foreign supply contracts (*contrats de fourniture*) can be made in either the currency in use at the headquarters of the supplier or that of the country of origin of the merchandise, except that transactions with Morocco can be effected in U.S. dollars through special clearing accounts maintained at the central banks of the respective countries. Foreign holders of servicing contracts are required to open local nonresident accounts to which payments are made by the Algerian contracting party; such accounts must be closed within six months of the end of the contract; beyond this date, these accounts may not be used for purposes unrelated to the contracts.

Nonresident Accounts

Most nonresident accounts are foreign accounts in convertible dinars or internal nonresident accounts. There are at present four types of accounts, as follows:

Individual Suspense Accounts may be opened without authorization and may be credited with payments from any country. Balances in such accounts opened before January 1, 1975 by nonresident natural persons of foreign nationality have been released for transfer abroad.

Foreign Accounts in Foreign Currency. Under Regulation No. 91/02, juridical and natural persons of foreign nationality may open accounts denominated in the convertible currency of their choice. Such accounts may be credited with (1) banknotes and other means of payment denominated in foreign currency; and (2) other dinar-denominated funds that meet all requirements for transfers abroad. They may be debited without restriction (1) to make transfers abroad, (2) to export through withdrawals of foreign banknotes, and (3) to make dinar payments in Algeria. These accounts pay interest and may not show a net debit position.

Final Departure Accounts may be opened, without prior authorization, in the name of any natural person residing in Algeria, not of Algerian nationality,

---

[1]Austrian schillings, Belgian francs, Canadian dollars, Danish kroner, deutsche mark, Finnish markkaa, French francs, Italian lire, Japanese yen, Netherlands guilders, Norwegian kroner, pounds sterling, Spanish pesetas, Swedish kronor, and Swiss francs.

[2]Specified noncommercial settlements with Morocco and Tunisia are channeled through a dirham account at the Bank of Morocco and an account in Tunisian dinars at the Bank of Tunisia.

who intends to leave Algeria to return to his or her country of origin. These accounts may be credited freely with (1) an amount equivalent to the holdings on October 20, 1963 of the person concerned; (2) the proceeds from sales of real estate by the account holder, provided that the funds are paid directly by a ministerial officer; (3) the proceeds of the sale of securities through a bank; and (4) any other payments, up to DA 2,000. These accounts may be debited without prior approval for certain payments in Algeria on behalf of the account holder. Outward transfers require individual approval.

Foreign Currency Accounts may be opened by natural and juridical Algerian nationals residing in Algeria or by nonresident Algerian nationals who have resided for more than six months in a foreign country. Such accounts may be freely credited with (1) book transfers of convertible currencies from abroad using either postal or banking facilities, (2) imported convertible foreign currencies that were declared at the time of the account holder's entry into the country, and (3) domestic bank-to-bank book transfers between accounts held by individuals. The accounts may be freely debited for book transfers abroad but only through the banking system; they may also be debited for purchases of dinars, for book transfers in dinars, and for purchases of convertible foreign currencies to be physically exported by the account holder. The interest rate payable on deposits in these accounts is fixed quarterly by the Bank of Algeria. Since 1990, economic entities have also been able to open foreign currency accounts for receiving and making foreign currency transfers, including the retained proportion of their export proceeds. They may transfer funds in these accounts to other foreign currency accounts or use them to make payments in Algeria or to make foreign payments for goods and services pertaining to their business.

Imports and Import Payments

Imports from Israel are prohibited. Certain imports are prohibited, regardless of origin.

All import licenses have been abolished. Any juridical and natural persons licensed under the Commercial Register (including concessionaires and wholesalers) may import goods that are not prohibited or restricted without any prior authorization. All these imports are subject to obligatory domiciliation at an authorized intermediary bank, which an importer must establish by submitting a commercial contract or pro forma invoice. Import payments may be made freely but only through the domiciled bank, which effects payments in foreign exchange

and debits the importer's account with corresponding amounts in dinars valued at the official exchange rate. Before import payments are effected, domiciled banks may require from the importer a deposit in dinars up to the full value of the imports. Importers maintaining foreign currency accounts at authorized intermediary banks may use them to pay for imports. Payments for imports of gold, other precious metals, and precious stones must be made from foreign currency accounts.

External borrowing by importers for import financing purposes must be arranged through the authorized intermediary banks. External borrowing may not exceed the import value.

Instruction No. 20/94 of the Bank of Algeria stipulates that the commercial credits used to finance imports of capital goods valued at more than $500,000 must have at least a three-year maturity.

Except as otherwise indicated by the Bank of Algeria, down payments for import payments may not exceed 15 percent of the total value of imports. In accordance with Law No. 80–07 of August 3, 1980, imports must be insured by Algerian insurers. When a public agency, public enterprise, or ministry is effecting expenditures for imports deemed to be urgent or exceptional, the bank may effect payments before exchange and trade control formalities have been completed.

Payments for Invisibles

The Bank of Algeria must approve all payments for invisibles to all countries. When supporting documents are presented, however, approval may be granted by authorized banks, or sometimes by the Postal Administration, either freely or up to specified limits for certain payments, such as (1) those relating to approved trade transactions and maritime contracts, (2) business or official travel expenses, (3) transfers of salaries and wages, (4) educational expenses, and (5) advertising expenses. For payments for which the approval authority has not been delegated, the central bank or the Ministry of Economy must authorize the granting of exchange.

Residents of other countries working in Algeria under technical cooperation programs for public enterprises and agencies or for certain mixed companies may transfer abroad a percentage of their net salaries.

Foreign exchange allocations for tourism abroad by Algerian residents were suspended in October 1986. Residents requiring medical treatment abroad are entitled to a foreign exchange allowance based on need. Emigrant Algerian workers who take their vacations in Algeria may, when returning abroad, re-export foreign exchange that was freely imported and duly declared on their arrival in Algeria.

Pilgrims traveling to Saudi Arabia receive an allowance in Saudi Arabian riyals; the amount is fixed for each pilgrimage and may be furnished in the form of checks that may be cashed on arrival for those traveling by air or by sea. Resident travelers may take out Algerian dinar banknotes up to DA 200 a person. Foreign nonresident travelers may also re-export any foreign currency they declared upon entry. Travel tickets that are bought by nonresidents for travel abroad must be paid for with imported foreign exchange.

Exports and Export Proceeds

All exports to Israel are prohibited. Certain exports are prohibited for social or cultural reasons regardless of destination. All proceeds from exports of crude and refined hydrocarbons, by-products from gas, and mineral products must be surrendered. Exporters of other products may retain 50 percent of their export earnings in a foreign currency account. Entities may use these funds for imports or other payments pertaining to their business or they may transfer the funds to another foreign currency account. Exports other than hydrocarbons benefit from certain incentive measures granted by the Government, including exemption from the tax on industrial and commercial profits and the flat rate levy on the wage bill.

Sales on consignment must be authorized by the Ministry of Economy and must always be registered before customs clearance. Export proceeds must be repatriated within 120 days of collection. Those petroleum companies that hold mineral rights must repatriate to Algeria the proceeds from their exports of hydrocarbons, calculated on the basis of a contractual price for each barrel, which is fixed by agreement with the companies concerned. The petroleum company that holds mineral rights, however, has different repatriation requirements.

Proceeds from Invisibles

Proceeds from invisibles must be repatriated, and 50 percent of the proceeds must be surrendered. There are no restrictions on the importation of foreign banknotes, coins (except gold coins), checks, and letters of credit, but nonresidents, including those of Algerian nationality, must declare such holdings when they enter Algeria. Resident travelers may reimport Algerian dinar banknotes up to DA 200 a person. Nonresident travelers are not permitted to bring in Algerian banknotes.

Capital

Residents are obliged to repatriate and surrender capital assets (or the sales proceeds thereof) held or acquired outside Algeria. Capital transfers to any destination abroad are subject to individual license.

Foreign direct investment is freely permitted, except in certain specified sectors, provided that it conforms to the laws and regulations governing regulated activities and that prior declaration is made to the authorities. The Law of Money and Credit of April 14, 1990 and Legislative Decree No. 93–12 on Investment Promotion provide guarantees on foreign direct investments in accordance with international codes that have been ratified by Algeria. Repatriation in respect of the sale or liquidation proceeds from invested foreign capital is guaranteed. The law also stipulates that profit remittances on such investments will be permitted, provided that documentation requirements on tax payments are met. Tax facilities may be granted, and investments of more than DA 5 million may be given exclusive rights in a specified geographic area and may be accorded tariff protection. Remittances of profits and retransfers of capital are permitted only in respect of investments approved under the code. Legislative Decree No. 93–12 provides for various tax and other incentives for foreign investment for periods of up to five years.

Algerian banks offer three-year interest-free bonds in dinars, which entitle the subscriber to exchange 20 percent of the placement value annually into a convertible currency at the official exchange rate.

Gold

Residents may purchase, hold, and sell gold coins in Algeria for numismatic purposes. Under Ordinance No. 70–6 of January 16, 1970, unworked gold for industrial and professional use is distributed by the Agence nationale pour la distribution et la transformation de l'or et des autres métaux précieux (AGENOR). This agency is also authorized to purchase in Algeria, and to hold, process, and distribute any other precious metal, and, within the exchange control regulations, to import and export any precious metal, including gold. Gold for use by dentists and goldsmiths is imported by AGENOR. Gold and other precious metals are included on the list of items importable by concessionaires.

Changes During 1994

Exchange Arrangement

March 31. The exchange rate of the Algerian dinar was devalued by 7.3 percent to DA 25.9 per US$1.

April 10. The exchange rate of the Algerian dinar was devalued by 28.1 percent to DA 36 per US$1. In conjunction with the devaluation, the system of forward cover provided by the Bank of Algeria was abolished.

October 1. The exchange rate of the Algerian dinar was devalued by 12.2 percent to DA 41 per US$1. Weekly fixing sessions organized by the Bank of Algeria with the participation of the commercial banks began to be held.

Imports and Import Payments

April 12. The *comité ad hoc* as well as the *cahier des charges* were eliminated. All imports were freed, except for a small list of products for which the importers must meet criteria ensuring professionalism, and a negative list of products whose importation is prohibited. The enforcement of the regulations concerning imports valued at more than $100,000 was delegated to the commercial banks.

In addition, the requirement to use own foreign exchange for certain imports was abolished except for private cars. Commercial banks were permitted to provide foreign exchange freely for all importers on the basis of their bona fide requests. Import financing and external borrowing were liberalized, but minimum maturity requirements were maintained temporarily for imports of capital goods.

August 24. The negative list of imports was further reduced.

Exports and Export Proceeds

April 12. All restrictions on exports were eliminated, with the exception of items of historical or archaeological significance. The surrender requirement ratios applicable to all export receipts, except hydrocarbon and mineral exports, were unified and lowered to 50 percent.

ANGOLA

(Position as of December 31, 1994)

Exchange Arrangement

The currency of Angola is the New Kwanza. The official exchange rate is determined in foreign exchange auctions conducted three times a week by the Banco National de Angola (BNA), the central bank. Commercial banks are permitted to participate in these auctions, but are free to set their own exchange rates in transactions with customers. Exchange rates for 17 other currencies[1] are established using the weekly average cross rates of the currencies concerned on the Brussels, Frankfurt, London, New York, Paris, and Zurich markets.

Two sets of exchange rates are published weekly by the BNA, one for transactions between the BNA and the commercial banks and the other for transactions between the commercial banks and economic agents. The BNA applies a margin of 0.25 percent to its buying and selling transactions with economic agents. Buying and selling margins for cash transactions are set at 3–4 percent, depending on the currency.

There are no taxes or subsidies on purchases or sales of foreign exchange. There are no arrangements for forward cover against exchange rate risk operating in the official or the commercial banking sector.

Administration of Control

The Organic Law of the BNA and the Financial Institutions Law, promulgated on April 20, 1991, established the BNA and the commercial banks as the financial institutions that are legally authorized to conduct exchange transactions with foreign parties. The BNA has delegated authority to banks to license and execute permitted invisible foreign exchange transactions.

Commercial banks and foreign exchange dealers licensed by the BNA are authorized to deal in foreign exchange at the floating and the parallel exchange market rates. The BNA uses the floating rate in its dealings with financial institutions.

All imports and exports are subject to licensing. Foreign exchange transactions are effected through the BNA's commercial department, the Banco de Poupança e Crédito (BPC), and the Banco do Comércio e Indústria (BCI), of which the latter two are commercial banks authorized to deal in foreign exchange under the Organic Law of the BNA and the Financial Institutions Law. The BNA's commercial department was established to facilitate the transition from the centralized banking system to the two-tier banking system. Accordingly, the BNA serves both as the central bank and as a commercial bank.

Financial institutions must deposit with the central bank all amounts required for payment of taxes and import duties made by foreign enterprises and all proceeds from exports by domestic enterprises, including those credited to accounts abroad.

Arrears are maintained with respect to external payments.

Prescription of Currency

The BNA prescribes the currency to be used for imports, which depends upon the country with which the transactions are to be carried out. The currency is usually that of the exporting country or the U.S. dollar. Bilateral settlement arrangements, which do not contain bilateral payments features, are maintained with Brazil, Portugal, and Spain. These arrangements use single accounts whose monthly balances can be used without restriction for transactions with third parties.

Resident and Nonresident Accounts

Individual resident juridical persons may maintain demand and fixed-term foreign exchange accounts with Angolan financial institutions. These accounts are remunerated at current interest rates. Checkbooks may not be issued against these accounts. The opening of and transactions through these accounts are not subject to prior authorization from the BNA. These accounts may be credited only through delivery of foreign currency in cash, traveler's checks, or foreign payment orders, and for interest accrued; they may be debited only through conversion into domestic currency or issuance of any instrument normally accepted on the international financial market, in settlement of imports of goods and current invisibles or of capital export operations carried out by the depositor. Transfers between accounts are forbidden.

---

[1]Austrian schillings, Belgian francs, Canadian dollars, Danish kroner, deutsche mark, ECUs, Finnish markkaa, French francs, Italian lire, Japanese yen, Netherlands guilders, Norwegian kroner, Portuguese escudos, pounds sterling, Spanish pesetas, Swedish kronor, and Swiss francs.

Nonresidents may hold accounts in new kwanzas, subject to authorization from the BNA. These accounts may be opened and credited only through the sale of foreign means of payment and with deposits of proceeds from the account holder's activities in Angola; they may be debited only through the issuance of orders of withdrawal for payment of local expenditures or through purchase of foreign means of payment.

Nonresidents may also hold foreign exchange accounts, subject to authorization from the BNA. These accounts may be opened and credited only through the importation of foreign means of payment or the deposit of proceeds from the account holder's activities in Angola; they may be debited only through the sale of foreign means of payment or repatriation of all or part of the existing credit balance.

Former residents may also hold accounts in new kwanzas, but they may withdraw funds from these accounts only to cover expenses during their stay in Angola.

Imports and Import Payments

All imports are subject to licensing, according to a positive list with pre-established limits determined under the import plan, and are also subject to the availability of foreign exchange, except for imports of spare parts, accessories or similar goods, medicines, equipment, and raw materials, up to a quarterly maximum of $50,000 (or its equivalent). Enterprises buying foreign exchange must submit the exporter's pro forma invoices (which may include insurance and freight). For imports exceeding $10,000, enterprises must submit an import registration bulletin within eight days of completion of the operation under penalty of being excluded from future foreign exchange auctions.

Licenses are granted only to registered enterprises of proven technical, commercial, and financial capacity and are issued on the basis of a foreign exchange allocation and restricted to imports of goods for which the enterprise is registered. To obtain a license, enterprises must present offers of three foreign suppliers to the sectoral ministries and the Ministry of Commerce. The approved offer may be considered for an import license application, which, in turn, must be approved by the same ministries. Import licenses specify the importer, supplier, intermediary, product (Brussels Nomenclature Classification, volume, and unit price), shipping and insurance companies, cost, and method and currency of payment. Once the importation of merchandise is approved, the BNA issues the credit document, with a copy for the import license applicant, stating that, before shipment to Angola, the goods must be examined by the international agencies for compliance with international standards for merchandise transactions. Import licenses are valid for 180 days after issuance and may be extended once for an additional 180 days. If an import transaction is not fully effected within this period, the original merchandise transaction is deemed to have become a capital transaction. A license fee of 0.1 percent of the import value is levied. Import licenses are also required for statistical purposes even if foreign exchange is not requested. Imports of capital goods must be financed partly by medium-term foreign financing.

Payments for Invisibles

Service contracts with nonresidents are subject to licensing. Preferential treatment is given to domestic air and sea transportation companies, and imports not insured domestically are approved only in exceptional cases.

Exchange allowances for private travel are granted at the floating rate; for medical treatment abroad, up to $5,000 is provided through the National Health Board at the official rate. A maximum monthly allowance of $2,500 is granted to residents who spend up to 90 days abroad for educational, scientific, or cultural purposes.

Up to the equivalent of $1,500 a month may be granted to Angolans or foreigners residing abroad who are direct ascendants or descendants of, and financially dependent on, residents in Angola, provided that (1) they are minor descendants under 18 years or, if of legal age, they can demonstrate that they are students or are incapable of working; or (2) they are ascendants over 60 years or, if younger, they can demonstrate they are incapable of working.

Education travel expenses are normally expected to be covered by scholarships, but an additional foreign exchange amount may be granted at the floating rate.

Resident nationals who wish to travel abroad may, upon presentation of their passport and airline tickets, where applicable purchase foreign exchange from financial institutions as follows: (1) children up to the age of 16 years, up to $500 a person a trip to neighboring countries and up to $1,000 a trip to other countries; and (2) individuals over 16 years, up to $1,500 a person a trip to neighboring countries and up to $3,000 a trip to other countries. Companies may purchase foreign exchange from financial institutions to cover their employees' travel expenses abroad on trips of up to 30 days, for business, service, or training, with the following daily limits: (1) president or equivalent, $350; (2) vice president or equivalent, $300; and (3) department director or equivalent, $200. If a person returns to Angola earlier than expected, the remaining foreign exchange must be resold to a financial institution. All these transactions take place at the floating rate.

The exportation of domestic currency is prohibited. When departing Angola, nonresidents visiting the country for purposes of tourism or business are permitted, upon presentation of the corresponding sales vouchers, to repurchase up to 50 percent of the foreign exchange they sold to institutions accredited to deal in foreign exchange.

Exports and Export Proceeds

Exports of certain goods are prohibited.[2] Reexports of goods other than capital goods and personal belongings are also prohibited. Restrictions apply to the exportation of products that are in short domestic supply. All other exports are subject to prior licensing. Proceeds from exports must be collected within 30 days of shipment. Oil exporters must surrender all proceeds to the BNA, while exporters of all other products may also sell their proceeds to commercial banks.

Proceeds from Invisibles

Service contracts with nonresidents must be approved by the BNA. The sectoral ministries supervise the execution of contracts. All proceeds must be surrendered to the BNA within 30 days of receipt.

There are no limits on the amount of foreign banknotes or traveler's checks in foreign exchange that a person may bring into the country, but any amount exceeding the equivalent of $10,000 must be declared upon arrival. Residents are permitted to leave the country with more than $5,000 in foreign exchange only if they present exchange purchase documents; nonresidents must present such documents when the amount exceeds $10,000. The importation of domestic currency is prohibited.

Capital

All capital transfers are subject to licensing and control. The Foreign Investment Law of 1994 (Law No. 15/94 of September 23, 1994) prohibits investment in strategic sectors.[3] Direct investments in the oil sector are encouraged. Dividends and capital may be repatriated upon liquidation with the prior approval of the Ministry of Finance. Transfers of personal capital, such as inheritances, dowries, savings from wages and salaries, and proceeds from sales of personal property, are permitted only on a case-by-case basis.

Gold

The importation and exportation of gold are a monopoly of the BNA. Residents are permitted to hold gold only in the form of jewelry.

Changes During 1994

Exchange Arrangement

April 25. An exchange rate system was introduced, under which the official exchange rate is determined in foreign exchange auctions conducted by the BNA. Commercial banks would be allowed to participate in the auctions and would be free to set their own exchange rates in transactions with their customers.

---

[2]Arms and ammunition, ethnological collections, ships, ostrich products, cattle, and ivory products. Special export regimes apply to aircraft, animals and animal products, historical objects, minerals and mineral products, toxic substances, cotton, rice, pork, coffee, cereals, wood and wood products, tobacco, and petroleum.

---

[3]Defense, law and order, education, health, utilities, communications, and transport infrastructure.

ANTIGUA AND BARBUDA

(Position as of December 31, 1994)

Exchange Arrangement

The currency of Antigua and Barbuda is the Eastern Caribbean Dollar,[1] which is issued by the Eastern Caribbean Central Bank (ECCB). The Eastern Caribbean dollar is pegged to the U.S. dollar, the intervention currency, at EC$2.70 per US$1. On December 31, 1994, the buying and selling rates for the U.S. dollar quoted by the ECCB in its transactions with commercial banks were EC$2.6949 and EC$2.7084, respectively, per US$1. The ECCB also quotes daily rates for the Canadian dollar and the pound sterling. There are no arrangements for forward cover against exchange risks operating in the official or the commercial banking sector.

Antigua and Barbuda formally accepted the obligations of Article VIII, Sections 2, 3, and 4 of the Fund Agreement, as from November 22, 1983.

Administration of Control

Exchange control applies to all currencies and is administered by the Ministry of Finance. Export licenses are required for a range of products, particularly those subject to export duties. Import licenses are issued by the Collector of Customs in the Ministry of Finance and by the Ministry of Trade, Industry, and Commerce, depending on the type of commodity. Arrears are maintained with respect to external payments.

Prescription of Currency

Settlements with residents of member countries of the Caribbean Common Market (CARICOM)[2] must be made either in the currency of the CARICOM country concerned or in Eastern Caribbean dollars. Settlements with residents of other countries may be made in any foreign currency or in Eastern Caribbean dollars.

Nonresident Accounts

External accounts may be opened for nonresidents with the approval of the Ministry of Finance and may be maintained in any currency. With the approval of the Ministry of Finance, such accounts may also be opened by resident individuals or firms, especially in tourist-oriented industries or export trade, whose receipts are primarily in foreign currency and a large number of inputs are imported or financed in foreign currency. External accounts can be credited with receipts from sales of merchandise (whether from export-oriented or local production) or from remittances. Commercial banks are required to report external accounts operations to the Ministry of Finance on a monthly basis.

Imports and Import Payments

Most goods may be freely imported under open general licenses granted by the Ministry of Trade, Industry, and Commerce. Certain other commodities require individual licenses, unless imported from CARICOM countries. Antigua and Barbuda follows the CARICOM rules of origin adopted in June 1981. Payments for authorized imports are permitted upon application and submission of documentary evidence.

Imports exempt from import duties include basic foods and agricultural imports. All other exemptions for machinery, equipment, and raw materials are granted on a case-by-case basis, generally under the Fiscal Incentives Act of 1975 and the Hotel Incentives Act.

Payments for Invisibles

Payments for invisibles related to authorized imports are not restricted. Upon presentation of supporting documents, and with the authorization of the Ministry of Finance, residents may purchase foreign exchange, including CARICOM traveler's checks (which are denominated in Trinidad and Tobago currency) for each trip outside the ECCB area. Foreign exchange allowances for education, family maintenance, medical treatment, and remittances of earnings by foreign workers are approved on a case-by-case basis. Profits on foreign direct investment may be remitted in full, subject to confirmation by the Commission of Inland Revenue of registration for corporate income tax purposes.

---

[1] The Eastern Caribbean dollar is also the currency of Anguilla, Dominica, Grenada, Montserrat, St. Kitts and Nevis, St. Lucia, and St. Vincent and the Grenadines.

[2] The CARICOM countries are Antigua and Barbuda, The Bahamas, Barbados, Belize, Dominica, Grenada, Guyana, Jamaica, Montserrat, St. Kitts and Nevis, St. Lucia, St. Vincent and the Grenadines, and Trinidad and Tobago. Exports to Jamaica are settled in U.S. dollars.

There are no limits on the amount of local currency that may be taken out of the country.

Exports and Export Proceeds

No export licenses are required for certain commodities to any destination. Surrender of export proceeds is not required, and re-exports are not subject to any tax if transactions take place within the bonded area.

Proceeds from Invisibles

Travelers to Antigua and Barbuda may freely bring in notes and coins denominated in Eastern Caribbean dollars or in any foreign currency. Foreign currency coins are not normally exchanged. Checks and drafts in U.S. and Canadian currency can be tendered up to US$1,000 without restriction; for amounts over US$1,000, approval from the Ministry of Finance must be obtained. Levy exemptions for transfers, especially for charitable purposes, are usually granted.

Capital

There are no legislated restrictions on capital movements. Foreign investment is granted the same incentives as domestic investment under the Fiscal Incentives Law and the Hotel Incentives Act. Large transfers abroad for investment purposes can be phased over time by the Financial Secretary.

Gold

There are no restrictions on the importation of gold.

Changes During 1994

No significant changes occurred in the exchange and trade system.

ARGENTINA

(Position as of January 31, 1995)

Exchange Arrangement

The currency of Argentina is the Peso, the external value of which is pegged to the U.S. dollar. On December 31, 1994, the middle rate of the peso in terms of the U.S. dollar was Arg$0.999 per US$1. Exchange rates of other currencies are based on the buying and selling rates for the U.S. dollar in markets abroad. Swap transactions and forward exchange operations are permitted in any currency, and the rates may be freely negotiated. Since January 12, 1995, the Central Bank of the Republic of Argentina (BCRA) has been converting pesos into U.S. dollars, and U.S. dollars into pesos, at a rate of Arg$1 to US$1. Deposits denominated in pesos and maintained by the financial institutions at the Central Bank to meet cash reserve requirements are automatically converted into U.S. dollars.

Argentina formally accepted the obligations of Article VIII, Sections 2, 3, and 4 of the Fund Agreement, as from May 14, 1968.

Administration of Control

All exchange transactions are carried out through entities authorized expressly for this purpose with no restrictions on the purchase or sale of foreign exchange at market prices. These authorized entities include banks, exchange agencies, exchange houses, exchange offices, and financial companies; each type of institution is subject to separate regulations. Credit funds and mortgage savings and loan companies may also effect certain foreign exchange transactions, on the condition that they meet certain additional capital requirements.

Prescription of Currency

Within the framework of the multilateral clearing system of the Latin American Integration Association (LAIA), payments between Argentina and Brazil, Chile, Colombia, Ecuador, Mexico, Paraguay, Peru, Uruguay, and Venezuela are settled voluntarily through payment agreements and a reciprocal credit mechanism. All payments between Argentina and Bolivia and the Dominican Republic must be effected through the accounts specified in the agreements. Argentina has also signed similar agreements with Bulgaria, Cuba, Hungary, Malaysia, and the Russian Federation. Payments between Argentina and these countries are settled on a voluntary basis through the accounts maintained by the Central Bank of Argentina and the central banks concerned, with the exception of Bolivia, Cuba, and the Dominican Republic, where settlement through the accounts specified in the agreements is obligatory. Transactions with other countries must be settled in freely usable currencies.

Resident and Nonresident Accounts

Authorized banks may open accounts in pesos or foreign exchange in the name of residents or non-residents who have met certain identification requirements that are aimed at, among other things, preventing money laundering. Accounts in foreign exchange must be denominated in convertible currencies and may be credited only with cash or with remittances from abroad in the following currencies: U.S. dollars for current accounts, savings, and fixed-term deposits; and deutsche mark and other currencies that the BCRA explicitly authorizes at the request of financial institutions for deposits in savings and fixed-term accounts. Both resident and nonresident holders of demand or time foreign currency accounts may use their credit balances freely in Argentina or abroad. Transfers between accounts may be made freely. Use of checking accounts denominated in U.S. dollars is allowed for domestic transactions.[1]

Imports and Import Payments

Import payments may be effected in convertible currencies. Payments for imports may be freely settled by authorized financial entities.

The Treaty of Asunción, signed in 1991, became effective in January 1995. It established the Southern Cone Common Market (MERCOSUR) between Argentina, Brazil, Paraguay, and Uruguay and implemented a 47 percent reduction in tariffs on goods traded among MERCOSUR countries, retroac-

---

[1]Since January 12, 1995, the minimum cash requirements for deposits and other obligations in pesos must be covered in U.S. dollars. Financial institutions accepting savings and fixed-term deposits in foreign currencies must limit them to no more than six times the liabilities included in the computation of capital, and the resulting lending capacity must be applied mainly to financing productive activities and external trade. Any funds not used for these purposes may be placed in alternative investments expressly allowed by law and by the BCRA (government securities, sight placements in the New York branch of the Banco de la Nación Argentina, etc.).

tive to June 30, 1991. Thereafter, tariff reductions were implemented until they were completed at the end of 1994; the tariff positions exempted from these reductions were also eliminated during this period. Tariffs were reduced at a rate of 7 percent every six months. At the end of 1994, a substantial portion of intra-MERCOSUR trade was conducted at a zero tariff rate and the nontariff barriers listed in the Schedule of the 1991 Asunción Treaty were also removed.

In accordance with Decision No. 5/94 of the MERCOSUR Council of Ministers, the member countries may maintain tariffs for some items in intra-MERCOSUR trade. Argentina applies tariffs to certain textiles, paper, and iron and steel products. This regime will be in force until the end of 1998, at which time tariffs will be reduced to zero.

Since January 1, 1995, Argentina and the MERCOSUR countries have been applying a common external tariff (CET) to imports from the rest of the world that encompasses all products, with certain exceptions (Argentina has 300 exceptions) that are subject to a transitional regime until 2001 and 2006. CET rates currently range from zero to 20 percent. At the end of the transitional period in 2001, the CET will be 14 percent for capital goods, and in 2006, the CET will be 16 percent for computer and telecommunications equipment.

Argentina applies a special regime to automobile and sugar imports with the authorization of MERCOSUR, pending agreement on a common regime for these sectors. Quantitative restrictions are applied to the automobile sector and to some paper products. Other restrictions are in force solely for security, hygiene, and public health reasons.

A statistical tax of 3 percent is applied to imports from all countries, except those from MERCOSUR. This tax is waived for capital goods, fuel, and sensitive goods from the paper, computer, and telecommunications sectors.

Payments for Invisibles

Neither payments for invisibles nor the exportation of domestic and foreign banknotes is restricted.

Exports and Export Proceeds

Export proceeds are not required to be repatriated.

Until the end of 1994, the rates of export rebates were equal to the import duties applied to the products concerned (Decree No. 1239/92). On January 1, 1995, rebate rates were changed when MERCOSUR became effective (Decree No. 2275/94), and the applicable rates were reduced (Resolution ME&OSP No. 310/95 of March 20, 1995). At present, the rebates range from 3 percent to 15 percent.

Other export promotion measures involving rebates are the regime for exporting turnkey plants, under which exports of industrial plants and engineering operations sold under turnkey contracts benefit from the highest effective rebate rate of 15 percent; and the regime for Puerto Patagónicos, under which exports through the ports and customs posts located on the Colorado River received an additional rebate ranging from 7 percent to 12 percent until the end of 1994. (Since January 1, 1995, these rates are being reduced by 1 percent a year.)

The drawback regime is in addition to the export rebates, and it allows exporters to receive refunds of import duties, the statistical tax, and the value-added tax (VAT) that are levied on inputs used in the processing of products for export. To be eligible for drawback, the exporter must be a direct importer of inputs. Since March 10, 1995, the drawback regime has been adapted to the new MERCOSUR terms, distinguishing between the treatment of exports to member countries of MERCOSUR and those to nonmember countries (Resolution ME&OSP No. 288/95).

The temporary admission regime permits the importation, free of consumer and statistical taxes, of merchandise for industrial processing, provided that such goods are exported in their new form within 180 days, which may be extended for a further 180 days. To benefit from the temporary admission regime, the exporter must be the direct user of the merchandise subject to temporary importation. Temporary admission is an alternative to the drawback system, and both cannot be used simultaneously.

Quantitative restrictions on exports are maintained only on arms, protected animal species, and products subject to international agreements.

The financing system for promoted exports has been suspended by Communication "A" 1807 of March 8, 1991, except with respect to those products that were in the process of exportation at that time. Under Communication "A" 1994 of August 31, 1992, this system was transferred to the Banco de Inversión y Comercio Exterior (Investment and Foreign Trade Bank).

Proceeds from Invisibles

Proceeds from invisible transactions of the private sector need not be repatriated. The importation of domestic and foreign banknotes is not subject to exchange control.

Capital

Beneficiaries of loans in foreign currencies are not required to convert them into domestic currency in the exchange market. Foreign borrowing by the public sector is regulated by Law No. 24.156 of October 29, 1992.

Decree Law No. 1853 of September 1993 governs foreign investment, combining in one law the liberalization measures contained in the Economic Emergency and State Reform Acts of 1989 and the Foreign Investment Law of 1993. This law allows foreign companies to invest in Argentina, without prior government approval, on an equal footing with domestic firms, thus effectively applying national treatment to foreign investors. Foreign investors are entitled to the same rights and subject to the same obligations as domestic investors, and may enter into any area of economic activity on their own, because no law or regulation forces them to be associated with local partners.

There are no approvals or procedures required to effect foreign investment. Regardless of the amount or the area of economic activity in which they are made, foreign investments may be made without any prior approval. This principle applies even in cases where a foreign investment results in full foreign ownership of a domestic company.

In the banking and insurance sectors, where special statutes require all operators to apply for licenses, foreign and domestic investors are guaranteed access to such licenses on an equal footing. The principle of nondiscrimination applied to banking laws is extended to eliminate the traditional reciprocity requirement when considering a foreign bank application to do business in Argentina, which effectively gives foreign banks full legal equality with their domestic counterparts.

Foreign investors are entitled to repatriate their capital and transfer abroad their realized earnings at any time, without any approval or authorization. Foreign investors may repatriate the full amount of their invested capital at any time, irrespective of the duration of investment. Their access to the foreign exchange market is also unrestricted. These rights assisting foreign investors have been further established under international law by means of over 30 Investment Promotion and Protection Agreements, including all countries where foreign investment usually originates, such as Canada, France, Germany, Italy, Spain, Sweden, Switzerland, the United Kingdom, and the United States. Argentina is a member of the Multilateral Investment Guarantee Agency and the International Center for the Settlement of Investment Disputes and maintains a valid and active agreement with the Overseas Private Investment Corporation.

Swaps of bonds for eligible debts agreed to under the Brady Plan by Argentina and foreign creditor banks were completed in 1994.

Gold

Residents may hold gold coins and gold in any other form in Argentina or abroad. Financial institutions, exchange houses, and exchange agencies may buy or sell gold in the form of coins or good delivery bars among themselves and may buy such gold from their clients as well as other precious metals whose market value is based on the daily list prices of major transactions. The importation of gold coins and good delivery bars is not restricted. Gold exports must be paid for in convertible currencies. Imports of gold by industrial users are subject to a statistical duty of 0.6 percent, and those by other users are also subject to a sales tax. Institutions may carry out arbitrage operations with their clients in gold coins or good delivery gold against foreign banknotes. Authorized institutions may export gold to entities abroad.

Changes During 1994

Imports and Import Payments

January 1. Tariff preferences vis-à-vis MERCOSUR trading partners were increased to 82 percent from 75 percent.

July 1. Tariff preferences vis-à-vis MERCOSUR trading partners were increased to 89 percent from 82 percent.

December 31. The 10 percent statistical tax was abolished.

Capital

April 28. Swaps of bonds for eligible debts agreed to under the Brady Plan by Argentina and foreign creditor banks were completed.

Changes During 1995

Imports and Import Payments

January 1. Tariffs vis-à-vis MERCOSUR trading partners were eliminated (except for a number of products), and a common external tariff (CET) ranging from zero to 20 percent (with 11 different positions) would apply to most products from non-MERCOSUR countries.

ARMENIA

(Position as of May 1, 1995)

Exchange Arrangement

The currency of the Republic of Armenia is the Dram,[1] which is the sole legal tender. The exchange rate against the U.S. dollar is determined on the basis of foreign exchange auctions held by the Yerevan Stock Exchange three times a week and auctions held by Givmri twice a month. Only banks may participate in the auctions (based on marginal pricing). Enterprises may buy and sell at the auction only through banks. On April 28, 1995, the average noncash auction rate was dram 407.8 per US$1.

The Central Bank of Armenia quotes official rates in terms of U.S. dollars three times a week on the basis of the average rate prevailing at the latest foreign exchange auctions. This rate must be used for accounting valuation of all foreign exchange transactions of all economic agents. Exchange rates for other major currencies are calculated either on the basis of quotations on the Yerevan Stock Exchange where applicable, or solely on the basis of the quotation for the U.S. dollar in major interbank markets against the currencies concerned.

Enterprises or any other physical or juridical persons (including state enterprises) are free to buy and sell foreign exchange without restriction through authorized institutions.

Forward transactions, futures, and options in foreign exchange are permitted.

Administration of Control

Central Bank of Armenia Decision No. 33 of May 17, 1994 sets out the principles and procedures for foreign exchange and currency transactions between residents and nonresidents. The Central Bank of Armenia has overall responsibility for regulating financial relations between Armenia and other countries in close collaboration with the Ministry of Finance.

Banks are granted two types of foreign exchange licenses. A general license gives a bank authority to conduct any type of foreign exchange transaction, including those with nonresidents abroad, excluding gold transactions, which are licensed separately.

Banks with a general license may offer a full range of currency transactions. A second, more restricted form of activity, included in licenses to operate as a bank in Armenia, allows banks only to buy and sell foreign exchange, only on behalf of their clients.

Prescription of Currency

Settlements with the Baltic countries, the Russian Federation, and the other countries of the former Soviet Union are made through a system of correspondent accounts maintained by the central banks of these countries but can also be made through other channels. Settlements with countries with which Armenia maintains bilateral payments agreements are effected in accordance with the terms of the agreements.[2] Settlements with all other countries may be made in convertible currencies.

Resident and Nonresident Accounts

Under Central Bank Decision No. 30 of May 16, 1994, residents may only open, maintain, and use loan accounts and foreign exchange bank accounts in banks abroad. Regulations pertaining to the transfer to these accounts of Russian ruble balances held in Armenia have not yet been formulated. Residents may also open, maintain, and use foreign currency accounts at licensed banks in Armenia. There are no limits on the amount of foreign currency banknotes that can be purchased with drams from banks, and banknotes can be deposited in a foreign exchange account or used for transactions with nonresidents. Resident enterprises may maintain and use foreign exchange accounts in banks abroad with the authorization of the Central Bank of Armenia. The opening and use of domestic foreign exchange accounts are not restricted, except that residents may not transfer these balances to other residents.

Nonresident natural and juridical persons may open and use foreign exchange accounts with licensed domestic banks, provided that they are reg-

---

[1]The dram became the sole legal tender with effect from March 1, 1994.

[2]At the end of 1994, Armenia maintained bilateral payments agreements with the Russian Federation and Turkmenistan and bilateral clearing agreements with the Baltic countries and the other countries of the former Soviet Union, but the latter have become largely inoperative.

istered with the local authorities. Balances in these accounts may be transferred abroad or sold to licensed domestic banks for drams. Legislation is being drafted to allow nonresident juridical persons to open accounts in drams and use them for domestic transactions. Foreign governments and international institutions may open dram accounts with authorization from the Central Bank of Armenia.

Imports and Exports

Imports of a number of products are prohibited for public health, national security, and environmental reasons. A license from the Ministry of Agriculture and the Ministry of Health is required and granted on a case-by-case basis to import medicinal preparations and chemical agents for plant protection (pesticides). Imports of weapons, military equipment and parts, and explosives require special authorization from the Government. The Agreement on Creation of a Free Trade Zone, signed in April 1994, establishes the legal framework for the signing of free trade agreements between Armenia and the other countries of the Commonwealth of Independent States (CIS). Bilateral free trade agreements have been signed with the Kyrgyz Republic, Moldova, Tajikistan, the Russian Federation, and Ukraine (to date, only the agreement with the Russian Federation has been ratified), and customs tariffs are thus exempt only for products from the Russian Federation. Government Decree No. 39, passed on January 27, 1995, established new tariff duties. This decree sets five rates for import duties, from zero, 5, 10, 30, and 50 percent; the rate for most imports is zero. There are no export duties.

According to Government Decision No. 17 of January 17, 1995, export licenses are required for three product groups: medicine, wild animals and plants, and textile products exported to the European Union (EU). In addition, special government permission is required for the export of nuclear technology, nuclear waste, and related nonnuclear products having direct military applications. Minimum threshold prices for the export of ferrous and nonferrous metals and foreign produced goods thereof remain in force. By Government Decree No. 615, passed on December 10, 1994, all restrictions on barter trade have been removed. Proceeds from exports must be repatriated within 30 days of receipt, and, as of January 1, 1995, 30 percent of the proceeds are required to be surrendered. Expenses, commissions, and taxes paid abroad relating to exports may be deducted from export proceeds prior

to repatriation. As of April 1, 1995, export receipts are no longer subject to the surrender requirement.

Payments for and Proceeds from Invisibles

Resident persons and enterprises may freely purchase foreign exchange or use foreign exchange balances in their foreign exchange accounts with domestic banks to conduct invisible transactions. Verification procedures are being formulated by the Central Bank of Armenia. There are no limits on foreign exchange allowances for travel.

Proceeds from cultural activities performed abroad are exempt from the repatriation requirement. Proceeds from other invisibles are subject to the same regulations as those applicable to proceeds from merchandise exports.

The importation of foreign banknotes is not restricted. The exportation of foreign banknotes is also not restricted, although a declaration needs to be completed for amounts exceeding the equivalent of $500.

Capital

Foreign investors, including joint ventures, are not required to obtain authorization to undertake investment in Armenia. A foreign investment law passed on July 31, 1994 reflects current international practices and is liberal in its treatment of foreign direct investment. Other inward and outward capital transfers require approval from the Ministry of Finance.

Gold

A license is required to conduct trade in gold. There are no regulations currently in force governing domestic trade in gold, and regulations on purchasing, selling, and holding gold and precious metals by banks have been prepared by the Central Bank of Armenia. The modalities of its implementation are expected to enter into force in May 1995.

Changes During 1994

Exchange Arrangement

March 1. The dram became the sole legal tender in the Republic of Armenia.

Administration of Control

December 1. Banks with a general foreign exchange license were required to offer at least a minimum set of international transaction services.

Capital

July 31. A foreign investment law was passed.

Changes During 1995

Imports and Exports

January 1. The surrender requirement for export proceeds was reduced to 30 percent from 50 percent.

January 10. The number of categories for which export licenses are required was reduced to three product groups from nine product groups.

January 15. The new customs law reduced the number of tariff rates to five, with most imports being zero rated.

April 1. The surrender requirement for export proceeds was abolished.

ARUBA

(Position as of December 31, 1994)

Exchange Arrangement

The currency of Aruba is the Aruban Florin, which is pegged to the U.S. dollar at Af. 1.7900 per US$1. The Centrale Bank van Aruba deals with local commercial banks within margins of 0.00279 percent on either side of parity. On December 30, 1994, the official buying and selling rates for the U.S. dollar were Af. 1.77 and Af. 1.80, respectively, per US$1. Official buying and selling rates for other currencies[1] are set daily on the basis of U.S. dollar rates on the international exchange market. A foreign exchange commission of 1.3 percent is levied on all payments made by residents to nonresidents, except when settled in Netherlands Antillean guilders. Purchases of foreign exchange by resident companies with nonresident status for foreign exchange control purposes are exempted from the commission.

There are no taxes or subsidies on purchases or sales of foreign exchange. There are no arrangements for forward cover against exchange rate risk operating in the official or the commercial banking sector.

Administration of Control

Foreign exchange controls are administered by the Central Bank. Import licenses, when required, are issued by the Department of Economic Affairs, Commerce, and Industry.

Prescription of Currency

Payments to and receipts from nonresidents may be made in any convertible currency, except in the legal tender of Aruba. For purposes of the compilation of the balance of payments, all payments made by residents to nonresidents, as well as receipts through local banks and banks abroad, must be reported to the Central Bank.

Nonresident Accounts

Nonresidents may freely open accounts in any foreign currency and are also permitted to hold accounts in Aruban florins up to Af. 200,000.

Resident Foreign Bank Accounts

Residents are obligated to report in writing to the Central Bank the opening of foreign bank accounts.

Imports and Import Payments

Imports other than eggs are not subject to any quantitative restrictions. The restriction on the importation of eggs, however, is administered liberally, depending on the domestic supply situation. Payments for imports may be made freely.

Payments for Invisibles

Most payments for invisibles exceeding Af. 50,000 a quarter require a license from the Central Bank. Allowances for education remittances for family maintenance and allowances for medical treatment are granted liberally. Residents may buy foreign exchange for travel purposes, up to a maximum amount equivalent to Af. 400 for each day of travel, Af. 8,000 a trip, or Af. 15,000 a calendar year, without a special permit, and up to a maximum amount equivalent to Af. 2,500 without presenting travel documents. Transfers of profits and dividends require a license from the Central Bank. The exportation of Aruban banknotes is prohibited, and that of foreign currencies requires a license.

Exports and Export Proceeds

Exports do not require a license. Unless specifically exempted, export proceeds must be converted into local currency within eight working days and credited to a foreign currency account with a local bank or with a foreign bank with the approval of the Central Bank.

Proceeds from Invisibles

The regulations governing export proceeds also apply to proceeds from invisibles. Nonresidents may bring in any amount of checks, traveler's checks, or banknotes denominated in foreign currency.

Capital

The following transactions require a license from the Central Bank: (1) purchases from and sales to nonresidents of domestic and officially listed securities (a resident natural person must obtain a li-

---

[1]Canadian dollars, deutsche mark, European currency units, French francs, Italian lire, Japanese yen, Netherlands guilders, Netherlands Antillean guilders, pounds sterling, and Swiss francs.

cense if values exceed Af. 200,000 a year); (2) purchases from and sales to nonresidents of domestic and foreign real estate (a resident natural person must obtain a license if values exceed Af. 200,000 a year); (3) proceeds from the liquidation of direct foreign investments; (4) loans received from, and extended to, nonresidents; and (5) other short- and long-term investments by residents abroad, or of nonresidents in Aruba (a resident natural person must obtain a license if values exceed Af. 200,000 a year).

Changes During 1994

No significant changes occurred in the exchange and trade system.

AUSTRALIA

(Position as of December 31, 1994)

Exchange Arrangement

The currency of Australia is the Australian Dollar.[1] The Australian authorities do not maintain margins in respect of exchange transactions; spot and forward exchange rates are determined on the basis of demand and supply conditions in the exchange market, but the Reserve Bank of Australia retains discretionary power to intervene in the foreign exchange market. There is no official exchange rate for the Australian dollar. The Reserve Bank of Australia publishes an indicative rate for the Australian dollar based on market observation at 4 p.m. daily. On December 31, 1994, the indicative rate in terms of the U.S. dollar was $A 1.2873 per US$1. There are no taxes or subsidies on purchases or sales of foreign exchange.

Authorized foreign exchange dealers may deal among themselves, with their customers, and with overseas counterparties at mutually negotiated rates for both spot and forward transactions in any currency, in respect of trade- and nontrade-related transactions. The Reserve Bank sets a limit for each dealer's net open overnight foreign exchange exposure.

Australia formally accepted the obligations of Article VIII, Sections 2, 3, and 4 of the Fund Agreement, as from July 1, 1965.

Administration of Control

The only restrictions on external payments and transfers are those introduced to give effect to UN Security Council Resolutions imposing sanctions against transfers to the governments and nationals of Iraq, the Federal Republic of Yugoslavia (Serbia/Montenegro), Libya, and the Republic of Bosnia and Herzegovina.

Prescription of Currency

Both outward and inward payments may be settled in Australian currency or in any foreign currency,[2] but purchases and sales of foreign currency by persons in Australia must be undertaken with an authorized foreign exchange dealer.

Nonresident Accounts

Nonresidents may establish and operate accounts without formality and may repatriate funds without restriction. Accounts may be denominated in foreign currency, but purchases and sales of foreign currency in Australia must be handled through authorized dealers. Special requirements apply to interest-bearing investments by foreign government monetary authorities (see section on Capital, below).

Imports and Import Payments

There are no import-licensing requirements or quotas on imports other than tariff quotas, which apply to cheese and curd. Australia is not a signatory of the Multifiber Arrangement. For some products, imports are allowed only if written authorization is obtained from the relevant authorities or if certain regulations are complied with. Among the goods subject to control are narcotic, psychotropic, and therapeutic substances; firearms and certain weapons; particular chemicals; certain primary commodities; some glazed ceramic ware; and various dangerous goods. These controls are maintained mainly to meet health and safety requirements; to meet certain requirements for labeling, packaging, or technical specifications; and to satisfy certain obligations arising from Australia's membership in international commodity agreements.

Almost all tariff rates have been subject to a tariff-reduction program in recent years. In 1991–92, the import-weighted average tariff rate (i.e., total duty paid divided by the f.o.b. value of all imports) was 6.5 percent. Under the tariff-reduction program announced in 1988, tariff rates above 15 percent were gradually reduced to 15 percent by July 1992, and tariff rates higher than 10 percent but lower than 15 percent were phased down to 10 percent over the same period. Proportional reductions were made to those tariffs not expressed in ad valorem terms. In the tariff reduction plan announced in March 1991, most specific duty rates were converted to ad valorem rates as from July 1993. The March 1991 plan called for most tariffs to be reduced to a maximum level of 5 percent by July 1996. The exceptions in these two tariff-reduction programs are for passenger automobiles and the textile, clothing, and footwear sectors, where tariffs have been relatively high, especially in effective terms. Under the 1988 program, tariffs on passenger automobiles were reduced

---

[1]The Australian dollar also circulates in several other countries, including Kiribati, Nauru, and Tuvalu.

[2]Foreign currencies are defined as all currencies other than the Australian dollar.

to 35 percent by July 1992, and tariff quotas in the textile, clothing, and footwear sectors were eliminated since March 1993. The March 1991 program calls for further phased tariff reductions to 15 percent in the passenger motor vehicle industry and to a maximum of 25 percent in the textile, footwear, and clothing sectors by the year 2000.

Australia's antidumping procedures were simplified under the revised Customs Tariff (Antidumping) Act of 1988. They provide for stricter conditions for demonstrating the causal link between dumping and material injury to domestic industries. Antidumping duties and undertakings will lapse automatically after five years, although domestic industries may renew the antidumping petition. In special circumstances, antidumping actions may be introduced retrospectively or in anticipation of the arrival of dumped or subsidized goods. The Antidumping Authority was established to advise the Government on these actions, although the Australian Customs Service remains responsible for the preliminary investigation of a complaint. In March 1991, the Government announced plans to strengthen the antidumping procedures, including accelerating the complaint process and extending the injury test to cover upstream agricultural industry. In December 1991, the Government announced it would reduce the time taken to process complaints and change the way in which dumping duties are levied. Australia's antidumping and countervailing legislation was amended on December 6, 1994, to come into effect on January 1, 1995 in line with Uruguay Round changes to the GATT texts on antidumping and countervailing. Some of the major areas of change included (1) a requirement for a set level of support by the Australian industry before an investigation can be initiated; (2) the inclusion of prescribed methodologies to establish dumping margins; and (3) a requirement that investigations will be terminated promptly where it is established that the margins of dumping (or level of subsidization) are de minimis or there are negligible volumes of dumped (or subsidized) imports. A combination of company-specific and residual rates of duty to apply to exporters from subject countries were introduced. The legislation also provided detailed guidelines on what constitutes a countervailable subsidy, giving preferential treatment to developing countries in the consideration of countervailing duties. Specific criteria are listed for making a determination regarding the existence of threat of material injury. The legislation now requires greater levels of evidence from interested parties and notification by authorities.

Under the terms of the Australia-New Zealand Closer Economic Relations and Trade Agreement (ANZCERTA), trade in goods across the Tasman became free from July 1, 1990 (five years ahead of schedule). Imports of motor vehicles from New Zealand were subject to a customs tariff until January 1, 1990. The provision for antidumping actions against imports from New Zealand ceased after July 1, 1990, and domestic trade practices legislation was amended at the same time to provide redress for unfair competition from New Zealand.

The South Pacific Regional Trade and Economic Cooperation Agreement (SPARTECA) provides for duty-free and unrestricted access to Australian and New Zealand markets on a nonreciprocal basis for most of the products exported by the member countries. In the case of Papua New Guinea, although it obtains trade concessions from New Zealand under SPARTECA, its trade and commercial relations with Australia are covered by the Agreement on Trade and Commercial Relations between Australia and Papua New Guinea.[3]

Developing countries obtain tariff preferences on their exports to Australia under the Australian System of Tariff Preference for Developing Countries. Since 1986, a uniform preferential margin of 5 percentage points on dutiable goods has applied to all developing countries; if the general tariff rate is below 5 percent, imports from developing countries enter duty free. From July 1, 1993, the developing countries' preferences have been phased out for Hong Kong, the Republic of Korea, and Taiwan Province of China, and margins applicable to certain industries, including textiles, clothing and footwear, chemicals, vegetable and fruit preparations, tuna, and sugar have been removed for all but the least-developed countries and the South Pacific Island Territories. The preferential rates for these specified industries will be frozen until the General Tariff rate falls to the preference rate; the General Tariff rate will then apply. Both the 1991 and 1993 decisions came into effect on July 1, 1993.

Payments for Invisibles

Payments for invisibles are unrestricted, except for certain transactions involving Iraq, the Federal Republic of Yugoslavia (Serbia/Montenegro), Libya, and the Republic of Bosnia and Herzegovina. There is no restriction on the amount of Austra-

---

[3] The areas covered by this agreement are those constituting the South Pacific Forum (in addition to Australia and New Zealand)—Cook Islands, Fiji, Kiribati, Nauru, Niue, Papua New Guinea, Solomon Islands, Tonga, Tuvalu, Vanuatu, and Western Samoa.

lian or foreign currency that can be taken out of Australia, so long as the foreign currency was purchased from an authorized dealer. Travelers who are not residents of Australia may also take out any foreign currency that they brought into Australia.

Persons leaving Australia with cash (banknotes and coins) in any currency totaling $A 5,000 or more must complete a report for the Australian Transaction Reports and Analysis Center (AUSTRAC); the report forms are available at ports or airports from the Australian customs authorities.

ANZCERTA also provides, through a protocol, for a progressive liberalization of the trade in services between Australia and New Zealand, subject to the foreign investment policies of both countries. In addition, certain service activities are excluded from the agreement. Among Australia's exclusions are the areas of telecommunications, banking (removed after the Martin report), airport services and aviation, coastal shipping, media, and postal services. The protocol was reviewed in 1990 and 1992 and will be reviewed again in 1994 with a view to liberalizing currently exempted services.

Exports and Export Proceeds

The export regime is designed to encourage the relatively unrestricted exportation of Australian products. Bounties are paid to producers of a limited number of products, some of which may be exported. Export prohibitions and restrictions in effect are designed to ensure quality control over specified goods; administer trade embargoes and meet obligations under international arrangements; restrict the exportation of certain defense goods; regulate the exportation of goods that involve high technology and have dual civilian and military applications;[4] and maintain adequate measures of control over designated cultural property, resources, and flora and fauna. There are no formalities regulating the disposal of export proceeds.

The Government also exercises export controls to secure national conservation objectives and to respond to specific market distortions abroad that have an impact on the export prices of certain products. The Government has abolished or amended export controls on many mineral and petroleum products. Remaining controls on primary products apply mainly to food and agricultural products.

The Government monitors trade in the bauxite, alumina, coal, and iron ore sectors and retains authority to withhold export approval for shipments at prices not in line with market conditions. Export controls apply to uranium to ensure compliance with the Government's commercial and nonproliferation policy obligations. Restrictions also apply to the exportation of certain other nuclear and related materials.

Licenses are required for the exportation of unprocessed wood, including wood chips. Licensing requirements are intended to ensure compliance with the Government's policy regarding environmental protection, elimination of market distortions, and promotion of further processing in Australia.

Australia participates in several voluntary restraint agreements (VRAs) or similar restraint agreements affecting its exports. These comprise limits on exports of the meat of sheep and goats as well as high-quality "Hilton" beef to the European Union (EU), and bovine meat and steel products to the United States. The Australian Dairy Corporation administers export control powers in relation to prescribed dairy products under the provisions of the Dairy Produce Act. All exporters of controlled dairy products must be licensed. This system allows the control of exports to markets where quantitative restrictions apply and ensures that export prices do not fall below minimum prices agreed to under the GATT for these products. Exports of red meat and livestock can be made only by persons or firms licensed by the Australian Meat and Livestock Corporation (AMLC). The AMLC has the power to engage in export trading in its own right and may introduce arrangements to control Australian exports to that market to observe quantitative restrictions in any particular market. Other Commonwealth statutory marketing authorities that have export control powers are the Australian Horticultural Corporation, the Australian Honey Board, the Australian Wheat Board, and the Australian Wine and Brandy Corporation. The Australian Wheat Board's powers make it the sole exporter of Australian wheat.

Proceeds from Invisibles

Earnings from invisibles in foreign currencies may be retained or sold for Australian dollars. Travelers may bring in any amount in Australian or foreign currency, subject to completion of an AUSTRACT report for cash amounts totaling $A 5,000 (notes and coins) or more. (See section on Payments for Invisibles, above.)

Capital

The vast majority of transactions involving transfers of interest-bearing capital from Australia and nonresident investments in Australia may be undertaken without formality. The only exceptions are

---

[4]Australia became a participant in the Coordinating Committee for Multilateral Export Controls (COCOM), effective May 1989.

foreign governments, their agencies, and international organizations. These entities are barred from issuing bearer bonds and, when borrowing in the Australian capital market, must advise the Treasury or Reserve Bank of the details of each borrowing after its completion. Although there are no limits on the interest-bearing investments of international organizations or of foreign central banks and other monetary authorities, the Reserve Bank may determine an amount up to which the investment of foreign government monetary institutions (which also undertake commercial investments) will be regarded as having been undertaken for official foreign reserve management purposes. All investing agencies are expected to be stable holders of Australian dollar assets and to keep the Reserve Bank informed of their Australian dollar portfolios. Interest-bearing investments of a foreign government's official foreign reserves are exempt from taxation consistent with the principle of sovereign immunity. Income derived by a foreign government from the conduct of commercial operations is not exempt from Australian taxation.

The Government recognizes the substantial contribution foreign investment makes to the development of Australia's industries and resources and has framed its policies so as to encourage direct investment in line with the needs of the community. Under Australia's foreign investment policy, certain types of proposals by foreign investors for acquisition or investment of more than $A 50 million are subject to full examination. These include (1) acquisitions of substantial interests in existing Australian businesses; and (2) proposals for the establishment of new businesses. Proposals for investments in the following areas are subject to examination irrespective of size: (1) investment in the media; (2) direct investment by foreign governments or their agencies; and (3) acquisition of residential real estate (unless exempt under the regulations). Foreign investors may acquire residential real estate within a designated integrated tourist resort (ITR) without obtaining approval under the foreign investment guidelines.

In most industry sectors, the Government approves proposals to establish new businesses involving total investments of $A 10 million or more and those to acquire existing businesses with total assets valued at $A 5 million or more ($A 3 million or more if more than half of the assets of the business are attributable to rural land) unless judged to be contrary to the national interest.

Certain restrictions apply to proposed acquisitions of real estate, but approval is normally granted to (1) acquisitions of real estate for development;

(2) purchases of vacant residential land (on condition that development occurs within 12 months) and home units and townhouses that are "off the plan" or under construction (on condition that no more than half of the units in any one development are sold to foreign interests); and (3) acquisitions of developed nonresidential commercial real estate valued at over $A 5 million (acquisitions of developed nonresidential commercial real estate valued at less than $A 5 million do not require approval).

In applying the policy, the authorities make every effort to avoid unnecessary interference in normal commercial processes and recognize the special characteristics and circumstances that may arise in individual cases. The policy is nondiscriminatory as to the country of origin of investors, and the Foreign Investment Review Board, which acts as an independent advisor to the Government on foreign investment matters, stands ready to assist and advise foreign investors in formulating their proposals.

In February 1992, the Government decided to permit foreign banks authorized under the Banking Act to operate as wholesale banks in the form of a branch (previously, foreign banks were authorized as incorporated subsidiaries). All foreign corporations seeking authorization to conduct banking business in Australia must satisfy the Reserve Bank of their willingness and capacity to adhere to high standards of prudential management. Foreign bank branches are not required to maintain "endowed capital" in Australia and, consequently, the Reserve Bank does not impose any capital-based large exposure limits on these branches.

Gold

Australia has no restrictions applying to owning, buying, selling, importing, or exporting gold and gold coins. If the exportation or importation of coins (together with any notes) exceeds $A 5,000, it must be reported to AUSTRAC.

Changes During 1994

Administration of Control

April 4. Changes arising from the 1992 CER Review of Rule of Origin were put into effect. The technical and administrative changes from the CER agreement were at the same time applied to all other preference arrangements.

Imports and Import Payments

December 1. Antidumping and countervailing legislation was amended in line with changes that were made to the GATT as a result of the Uruguay Round.

AUSTRIA

(Position as of February 1, 1995)

Exchange Arrangement

The currency of Austria is the Austrian Schilling. Austria participates with Belgium, Denmark, France, Germany, Ireland, Luxembourg, the Netherlands, Portugal, and Spain in the exchange rate mechanism (ERM) of the European Monetary System (EMS).[1] In accordance with this agreement, Austria maintains the spot exchange rates between the schilling and the currencies of the other participants within margins of 15 percent above and below the cross rates based on the central rates expressed in European currency units (ECUs)[2] and continues to keep the schilling's external value consistent against the deutsche mark.

The arrangements imply that the Oesterreichische Nationalbank (the central bank) stands ready to buy or sell the currencies of the other participating states in unlimited amounts at specified intervention rates. On January 9, 1995, these rates were as follows:

Specified Intervention Rates per:	Austrian Schilling	
	Upper limit	Lower limit
100 Belgian or Luxembourg francs	39.40890	29.37670
100 Danish kroner	214.17400	158.84100
100 Deutsche mark	816.92700	605.87700
100 French francs	243.58600	190.65400
1 Irish pound	19.89710	14.60820
100 Netherlands guilders	726.06600	537.74000
100 Portuguese escudos[3]	8.26800	6.12520
100 Spanish pesetas[4]	10.32590	7.65811

The participants in the EMS do not maintain the exchange rates for other currencies within fixed limits. However, to ensure a proper functioning of the system, they intervene in concert with the other EMS members to smooth out fluctuations in exchange rates, the intervention currencies being each other's and the U.S. dollar.

Forward transactions are permitted. Forward premiums and discounts are left to the interplay of market forces, and the Oesterreichische Nationalbank does not intervene in the forward market or provide cover for the forward positions of commercial banks. On December 31, 1994, the authorized banks' buying and selling rates for the U.S. dollar were S 11.045 and S 11.145, respectively, per US$1. There are no exchange taxes or subsidies.

Austria formally accepted the obligations of Article VIII, Sections 2, 3, and 4 of the Fund Agreement, as from August 1, 1962.

Administration of Control

Most exchange transactions are effected through Austrian banks authorized by the central bank. Certain restrictions on payments and transfers for current international transactions to the Government of Iraq are still in force.

In accordance with the Fund's Executive Board Decision No. 144–(52/51), adopted on August 14, 1952, Austria notified the Fund on July 7, 1992 that, in compliance with United Nations Security Council Resolution No. 757 (1992), certain restrictions had been imposed on the making of payments and transfers for current international transactions in respect of the Federal Republic of Yugoslavia (Serbia/Montenegro). Restrictions are imposed on certain current payments and transfers to Libya in accordance with UN Security Council Resolution No. 833 (1993).

Export and import licenses required under the Foreign Trade Act of 1984 and its amendments must be issued by the Federal Ministry for Economic Affairs for industrial products and by the Federal Ministry of Agriculture and Forestry for agricultural products. In instances where the customs authorities are authorized to issue import and export licenses on behalf of these ministries, the licenses are granted without delay or formal application (automatic licensing) when the goods clear customs.

Prescription of Currency

Settlements with all countries may be made either in foreign currencies or through free schilling accounts.

---

[1]Austria became a member of the European Union on January 1, 1995 and joined the ERM of the EMS on January 9, 1995.

[2]Effective August 2, 1993, the intervention thresholds of the currencies participating in the ERM of the EMS, except those of the deutsche mark and the Netherlands guilder, were widened to ±15 percent from ±2.25 percent around the bilateral central exchange rates; the fluctuation band of the deutsche mark and the Netherlands guilder remained unchanged at ±2.25 percent.

[3]Effective March 6, 1995, the upper and lower limits were changed to 7.97000 and 5.910866.

[4]Effective March 6, 1995, the upper and lower limits were changed to 9.60338 and 7.1200.

Nonresident Accounts

There is only one category of nonresident account in schillings, namely, free schilling accounts. These accounts may be freely opened by Austrian banks on behalf of nonresidents and are not subject to restrictions. Balances may be freely converted into any foreign currency. Transfers between these accounts are free.

Nonresidents may also maintain nonresident accounts in foreign currencies. These are subject to the same conditions as free schilling accounts.

Imports and Import Payments

As a member of the European Union, Austria applies the Common Import Regimes. Payments for imports are not restricted.

Payments for Invisibles

Residents are permitted to conclude transactions with nonresidents involving payments for invisibles without restriction. Residents traveling abroad for purposes of tourism may purchase foreign exchange from authorized banks or obtain short-term advances from nonresidents without limitation.

Exports and Export Proceeds

Licenses for exports regulated under the Foreign Trade Law must be obtained from the relevant ministry or, at the time of clearance, from the customs authorities. For most exports, licenses are not required. Export licenses are issued with due consideration for the provisions of relevant EU trade agreements and the fulfillment of quotas established in accordance with such agreements, and the needs of the Austrian economy.

Proceeds from Invisibles

Proceeds from invisibles may be deposited without restriction. Persons entering Austria may import unlimited Austrian or foreign banknotes and coins.

Capital

The acquisition by nonresidents of Austrian securities and shares and participation by nonresidents in Austrian companies are unrestricted. The acquisition of real estate is subject to approval by local authorities. Nonresidents are permitted to issue bonds on the domestic market.

Foreign banks are not permitted to establish branches in Austria. In the auditing and legal profession, the transport sector, and the electric power generation sector, there are certain restrictions for investments by nonresidents and Austrian residents who are not nationals of one of the countries of the European Economic Area.

Residents and nonresidents may export capital freely without a license. Nonresidents' direct investments in Austria and the purchases of Austrian or foreign equities do not require approval.

The transfer of funds owned by emigrants and payments due to nonresidents on account of dowries, inheritances, and settlements under certain agreements between heirs are permitted. Residents may also grant loans to nonresidents, as well as to foreign banks and financial institutions.

Residents may acquire participation rights in foreign companies, associations, and other enterprises; earnings accrued from such investment may be freely used. Residents are permitted to acquire real estate abroad and to purchase from nonresidents securities denominated in Austrian and foreign currencies without restriction. Residents are also permitted to open bank accounts and issue bonds abroad.

Gold

Residents may freely hold gold in any form and may trade with residents and nonresidents both at home and abroad. Imports and exports of gold in any form by residents and nonresidents are unrestricted and free of license.

Changes During 1994

Administration of Control

January 1. The European Economic Area (EEA) came into operation, extending the freedom of movement of goods, services, capital, and persons within the EU to Austria.

March 1. Terms for Austria's accession to the EU were agreed.

Changes During 1995

Administration of Control

January 1. Austria became a member of the European Union.

Exchange Arrangements

January 9. Austria joined the exchange rate mechanism of the European Monetary System.

(See Appendix for a summary of trade measures introduced and eliminated on an EU-wide basis during 1994, page 554.)

AZERBAIJAN

(Position as of December 31, 1994)

Exchange Arrangement

The currency of the Republic of Azerbaijan is the Manat, the external value of which is determined in weekly auctions. Auctions of foreign exchange (noncash) are held weekly at the Baku Interbank Currency Exchange (BICEX). Participation in the auctions is restricted to the commercial banks that are licensed to deal in foreign exchange bidding on behalf of their customers.[1] Since December 15, 1994, the official exchange rate has been set on the basis of the outcome of the foreign exchange auctions. It is used for official transactions and as an accounting rate to value the foreign exchange assets of state-owned enterprises and banks and is applied to proceeds surrendered from exports of services (50 percent of the proceeds). Authorized banks are free to set buying and selling rates for cash transactions. These rates are published weekly at the International Bank. On January 1, 1995, the official exchange rate was Manat 4,182 per US$1, and the exchange rate for cash transactions was Manat 4,300 per US$1 buying and Manat 4,360 per US$1 selling. No commission is assessed on purchases of foreign exchange by the International Bank, but a commission of 2–3 percent is added for sales of foreign exchange.

Differential buying rates arise from the operation of partial surrender requirements in connection with export proceeds, which are converted at highly appreciated exchange rates (see section on Imports and Exports, below).[2]

There are no taxes or subsidies on purchases or sales of foreign exchange. There are no arrangements for forward cover against exchange rate risk operating in the official or the commercial banking sector.

Administration of Control

Foreign exchange transactions are regulated by the Azerbaijan National Bank Law, which gives the

ANB responsibility for regulating the exchange rate of the manat, conducting foreign currency operations, and administering gold and convertible currency reserve holdings. The ANB also has overall responsibility for issuing licenses to deal in foreign exchange; for regulating foreign exchange operations, including implementing and monitoring compliance with the law; and for establishing prudential rules governing foreign exchange operations.

Foreign trade is regulated under the Foreign Economic Activity Law by the Ministry of Foreign Economic Relations (MFER). The customs service law regulates the organization and operation of the customs service. Enterprises engaged in foreign trade must register with the Ministry of Justice. Trade licenses for petroleum, cotton, and other goods considered strategic are issued by the MFER, and minimum export quotas are determined by the Ministry of Economy.[3]

Foreign private investment in joint ventures must be registered with the MFER and the Ministry of Finance. Investment abroad by both Azeri nationals and companies is regulated by a state decree that limits the opening of foreign exchange accounts in foreign countries. A license must be obtained from the ANB as well as permission from the Cabinet of Ministers to open such accounts.

Arrears are maintained with respect to external payments.

Prescription of Currency

Residents of Azerbaijan may, once a transaction is approved, make and receive payments and transfers in any convertible currency. Settlements with the Baltic countries and the other countries of the former U.S.S.R. other than the Russian Federation are effected through correspondent accounts of the commercial banks in these states or through correspondent accounts of the respective central banks. Settlements with the Russian Federation are carried out mostly through the correspondent accounts of the respective central banks, although commercial banks are being licensed to open such accounts with banks in the Russian Federation. Azerbaijan maintains a bilateral payments arrangement with

---

[1]The convertible currencies commercial banks are authorized to deal in are Australian dollars, Austrian schillings, Belgian francs, Canadian dollars, deutsche mark, Finnish markkaa, French francs, Italian lire, Japanese yen, Netherlands guilders, Norwegian kroner, pounds sterling, Swedish kronor, Swiss francs, Turkish liras, and U.S. dollars. An official exchange rate against the ECU is also posted.

[2]The system of surrender requirements at appreciated exchange rates was abolished in March 1995. Exporters are required to sell a maximum of 30 percent of their proceeds to the BICEX at auction exchange rates.

[3]Under the state planning system, minimum export quotas were determined to ensure a minimum supply of foreign exchange to the Unified Foreign Exchange Fund.

the Islamic Republic of Iran. The balance on account earns interest at LIBOR plus 0.75 percent. At the end of three months, the outstanding balance is settled in convertible currencies within 25 days.

Resident and Nonresident Accounts

Resident persons or enterprises may open and use foreign exchange bank accounts at banks abroad subject to authorization by the ANB. Residents may freely open and use foreign currency accounts maintained at licensed banks in Azerbaijan. No declaration of the origin of the foreign exchange is required for individuals. Individuals may transfer a limited amount of foreign exchange held in these accounts upon authorization to the holder's bank account abroad or may freely convert it into domestic currency. Enterprises may use the foreign exchange held in these accounts to pay for imports or convert it freely into domestic currency through the BICEX.

Nonresident persons and enterprises are free to open foreign exchange accounts with licensed domestic banks. Foreign exchange in these accounts may be transferred abroad or sold to the banks for manats. Nonresident enterprises may also open and operate accounts in manats and use them for domestic transactions in accordance with instructions issued by the ANB. Foreign governments and international institutions may open and operate manat accounts with specific authorization from the ANB.

Imports and Exports

Payments for imports from the Baltic countries, Russia, and the other countries of the former Soviet Union may be made in any mutually agreeable currency, including banknotes, or through the system of correspondent accounts operated by the ANB and the commercial banks. Payments for imports from the rest of the world are made in accordance with normal commercial practices. There are no restrictions on the use of foreign exchange for import payments from enterprises' own accounts.

There are no licensing requirements for imports. However, imports are largely controlled through bilateral trade agreements with the Baltic countries, Russia, and the other countries of the former Soviet Union or through a system of contract registration. For imports from the rest of the world, volume and price are constrained by export licenses and contracts in the originating state. A few imports are banned for health, environmental, or security reasons.

Duties are levied on imports in accordance with Resolution No. 252 of June 27, 1994 of the Cabinet of Ministers. Duty rates vary by product but do not distinguish between imports from the Baltic countries, Russia, and the other countries of the former Soviet Union and those from other countries. A customs fee of 0.15 percent is levied on imports from all sources.

Resident persons and enterprises are required to repatriate proceeds from exports within three months and transfer them to a licensed bank in Azerbaijan within ten days of receipt unless specifically exempted by the Government. Expenses, commissions, and taxes paid abroad relating to economic activities may be deducted from the proceeds prior to transfer to a licensed bank. After transfer to a licensed bank, export proceeds are distributed among the exporter's foreign exchange accounts and the Unified Foreign Exchange Fund (UFEF)[4] in accordance with Presidential Decree No. 77 of April 25, 1994.

Surrender requirements range from zero to 75 percent, with rates ranging from 50 percent to 70 percent for major export commodities such as energy products and cotton. The surrender requirement ratios for exports to the Baltic countries, Russia, and the other countries of the former Soviet Union are one-half of the surrender requirements for exports to other countries. The values of foreign exchange subject to surrender requirements are calculated as follows: (1) exporters of goods, the prices of which are officially controlled, receive the domestic currency counterpart to surrendered foreign exchange earnings, calculated as the export volume times the domestic currency price of the commodity; (2) exporters of all other goods are compensated for surrendered foreign exchange at the cost price plus a 15 percent profit margin (enterprises are required to submit information concerning their prices to the ANB); and (3) surrendered foreign exchange originating from foreign exchange exports of services are valued at 50 percent of the official exchange rate.[5] Exports of strategic goods must be licensed by the Ministry of Foreign Economic Relations, and they are subject to global quotas set for each product by the Ministry of Economy based on an estimation of production and domestic consumption. Sub-quotas are set for exports to the Bal-

---

[4]The UFEF, sometimes called the Republican Hard Currency Fund, aims at centralizing a part of the country's foreign exchange earnings in order to finance essential imports and to service external debt. It includes a stabilization fund that the ANB can use to support the manat, subject to presidential approval.

[5]This system of surrender requirements at appreciated exchange rates and the UFEF was abolished in March 1995.

tic countries, Russia, and the other countries of the former Soviet Union, in accordance with bilateral agreements. The MFER issues licenses freely for exports within quota limits, subject to verification of the contract. No licenses are required for other exports, although contracts must be registered with the MFER. Some export bans exist, mainly on defense equipment.

Export duties are assessed in accordance with Resolution No. 252 of June 27, 1994 of the Cabinet of Ministers. Duty rates vary by commodity but do not distinguish between exports destined for the Baltic countries, Russia, and the other countries of the former Soviet Union and those for other countries. However, higher rates are assessed on goods exported under barter trade agreements with Azerbaijan. Duties are payable in foreign exchange received from exports or in manats for goods traded under barter agreements.

A customs fee of 0.15 percent is levied on exports to all destinations.

Payments for and Proceeds from Invisibles

There are no restrictions on the availability of foreign exchange for invisible payments by resident individuals, but documentation is required.

The exportation of foreign banknotes is regulated by the ANB and the Ministry of Finance, in conformity with customs regulations.

Proceeds from invisibles must be repatriated within three months and transferred to a licensed bank within ten days of receipt. The importation of foreign banknotes is regulated by the ANB and the Ministry of Finance in conformity with customs regulations.

Capital

Inward private capital transfers are not restricted, and borrowing abroad by the Government is subject to an annual ceiling determined by Parliament. Foreign exchange transactions of private investors are protected by the Protection of Foreign Investment Law adopted on January 15, 1992. Under this law, the treatment of foreign investment cannot be less favorable than that extended to domestic investment, and foreign investment may receive preferential treatment.

Foreign investment is protected from nationalization and expropriation unless state interests or force majeure is involved. If nationalization or expropriation occurs, adequate compensation is paid. Profits may be reinvested in local currency, held in Azerbaijan, or converted into foreign currency and transferred without restriction. Foreign investors are granted certain privileges: enterprises or joint ventures with foreign equity capital ownership of more than 30 percent are entitled to a two-year holiday on profit taxes; imports and exports of goods and services may be undertaken without licenses; and exporters of manufactured goods are allowed to retain 100 percent of their exchange earnings.

Gold

A license is required to conduct international trade in gold. There are no regulations governing domestic trade in gold.

Changes During 1994

Exchange Arrangement

January 1. The manat became sole legal tender.

May 24. The official exchange rate began to be set on the basis of the weighted average of commercial bank rates.

June 27. All purchases and sales of foreign currency outside the BICEX were prohibited (Decree No. 251 of the Cabinet of Ministers).

Exports and Export Proceeds

April 25. Regulations governing surrender requirements for exports to the Baltic countries, Russia, and the other countries of the former Soviet Union were changed to one-half of those applicable to exports to other countries. The method of calculating the values of foreign exchange subject to surrender requirements was changed as follows: (1) exporters of goods whose prices are officially controlled would receive the domestic currency counterpart to surrendered foreign exchange earnings, calculated as the export volume times the domestic currency price of the commodity; (2) exporters of all other goods would be compensated for surrendered foreign exchange at the cost price plus a 15 percent profit margin (enterprises are required to submit information concerning their prices to the ANB); and (3) surrendered foreign exchange originating from foreign exchange exports of services would be valued at 50 percent of the official exchange rate.

December 15. The official exchange rate began to be set on the basis of the outcome of the foreign exchange auctions held at the BICEX.

Payments for and Proceeds from Invisibles

May 2. Restrictions on the availability of foreign exchange for travel abroad were eliminated by Resolution No. 136 of the Cabinet of Ministers.

THE BAHAMAS

(Position as of December 31, 1994)

Exchange Arrangement

The currency of The Bahamas is the Bahamian Dollar, which is pegged to the U.S. dollar, the intervention currency, at B$1 per US$1. The U.S. dollar circulates concurrently with the Bahamian dollar. The official buying and selling rates for the U.S. dollar are B$1.0025 and B$1.0040, respectively, per US$1. Buying and selling rates for the pound sterling are also officially quoted, with the buying rate based on the rate in the New York market; the selling rate is 0.5 percent above the buying rate. The Central Bank of The Bahamas deals only with commercial banks. For transactions with the public, commercial banks are authorized to charge a commission of 0.50 percent buying and 0.75 percent selling per US$1, and 0.50 percent buying or selling per £1. A stamp tax of 1.5 percent is applied to all outward remittances.

There is also a market in which investment currency[1] may be negotiated between residents through the Central Bank at freely determined rates, usually attracting a premium above the official market rate.

Commercial banks may provide forward cover for residents of The Bahamas when the resident is due to receive or must pay foreign currency under a contractual commitment. Commercial banks may not, however, sell foreign currency spot to be held on account in cover of future requirements without the Central Bank's permission. Authorized dealers may deal in foreign currency forward with nonresidents without prior approval from the Central Bank. Commercial banks may deal forward among themselves at market rates and must ensure when carrying out all forward cover arrangements that their open spot or forward position does not exceed the equivalent of B$500,000 long or short. There are no forward cover arrangements in the official sector.

The Bahamas formally accepted the obligations of Article VIII, Sections 2, 3, and 4 of the Fund Agreement, as from December 5, 1973.

Administration of Control

Exchange control is administered by the Central Bank, which delegates to authorized dealers the authority to approve allocations of foreign exchange for certain current payments, including payments for imports up to B$100,000; approval authority for cash gifts is not delegated, except in the Family Islands.[2] Import and export licenses are not required except for crawfish, conch, arms and ammunition, and, in certain cases, industrial gold. The Department of Agriculture and Fisheries issues export licenses for crawfish and conch, and the police department issues import and export licenses for arms and ammunition.

Prescription of Currency

The exchange control system of The Bahamas makes no distinction between foreign territories. Settlements with residents of foreign countries may be made in any foreign currency[3] or in Bahamian dollars through an external account.

Nonresident Accounts

Authorized banks may freely open external accounts denominated in Bahamian dollars for winter residents and for persons with residency permits who are not gainfully employed in The Bahamas. With the prior approval of the Central Bank, authorized banks may also open external accounts in Bahamian dollars for nonresident companies that have local expenses in The Bahamas and for nonresident investors. External accounts in Bahamian dollars are normally funded entirely from foreign currency originating outside The Bahamas, but income on registered investments may also be credited to these accounts with the approval of the Central Bank. Balances may be converted freely into foreign currency and transferred abroad.[4]

Accounts credited with funds that may not be placed at the free disposal of nonresidents are des-

---

[1]Foreign currency that the Central Bank permits to be retained and used or disposed of as investment currency. Such permission may exist for foreign currency accruing to residents of The Bahamas from the sale or redemption of foreign currency securities; the sale, liquidation, redemption, or realization of property; or direct investments outside The Bahamas. The use of investment currency is prescribed for the purchase of foreign currency securities from nonresidents and the making of direct investments outside The Bahamas. In 1994, total purchases amounted to B$251,061, and total sales to B$227,132.

[2]Beginning in June 1988, the Central Bank established a branch of its Exchange Control Department in Grand Bahama to serve the foreign exchange needs of residents in that area.

[3]Foreign currencies comprise all currencies other than the Bahamian dollar.

[4]Persons of foreign nationality who have been granted temporary resident status are treated in some respects as nonresidents but are not permitted to hold external accounts in Bahamian dollars.

ignated blocked accounts and are held mainly by emigrants. When the value of an emigrant's assets exceeds B$25,000, the excess is credited to a blocked account. Balances on blocked accounts are transferable through the official exchange market after four years or through the investment currency market at any time; they may also be invested, with the approval of the Central Bank, in certain resident-held assets, or they may be spent locally for any other purpose.

Imports and Import Payments

The importation of certain commodities is prohibited or controlled for social, humanitarian, or health reasons. All other goods may be imported without a license. Prior approval from the Central Bank is required to make payments for imports exceeding B$100,000, irrespective of origin;[5] this approval is normally given automatically upon submission of pro forma invoices or other relevant documents proving the existence of a purchase contract. Import duties vary from zero to 300 percent, depending on the type of goods, and stamp duties on imports vary from 2 percent to 22 percent. For all imports of agricultural products, a permit must be obtained from the Ministry of Agriculture. Customs entries are subject to a stamp tax at a rate of 1.5 percent.

Payments for Invisibles

There are no restrictions on current payments. Authorized dealers may make payments to nonresidents on behalf of residents for certain services and other invisibles, such as commissions, royalties, education, freight, ships' disbursements, and insurance premiums within specified limits. On application to the Central Bank, residents are entitled to a foreign exchange allowance for tourist travel equivalent to B$1,000 a person above the age of 18 years and B$500 a person up to the age of 18 years a trip; B$10,000 a person a year for business or professional travel; B$3,000 for educational travel; B$1,000 for travel for medical reasons. The allowance for tourist travel excludes the cost of fares and travel services, which are normally obtained against payment in Bahamian dollars to a travel agent in The Bahamas. Applications for foreign exchange in excess of the official amounts must be referred to the Central Bank, which approves bona fide applications. Foreign exchange obtained for travel may not be retained abroad or used abroad for purposes other than travel; any unused balance must be surren-

dered within a week of issue or, if the traveler is still abroad, within one week of return to The Bahamas.

Subject to adequate documentary evidence, an education allowance is granted without a limit. Temporary residents may, with the approval of the Central Bank, remit up to 50 percent of their wages and salaries, but if commitments outside The Bahamas are more than 50 percent of wages and salaries, additional amounts may be remitted. Temporary residents may also repatriate all of their accumulated savings resulting from their employment in The Bahamas.

A traveler may export Bahamian banknotes not exceeding B$70 in value; Bahamian travelers may not export the banknotes of any other country, except with specific approval from the Central Bank.

Exports and Export Proceeds

Export licenses are not required except for crawfish, conch, and arms and ammunition. The proceeds of exports must be offered for sale to an authorized dealer as soon as the goods have reached their destination or within six months of shipment; alternatively, export proceeds may be used in any manner acceptable to the Central Bank.

Proceeds from Invisibles

Residents are obliged to collect without delay all amounts due to them from nonresidents and to offer the foreign currency proceeds for sale to an authorized dealer without delay, but these requirements are seldom enforced. There are no restrictions on the importation of foreign banknotes. The importation of domestic banknotes is subject to the approval of the Central Bank.

Capital

All capital transfers to countries outside The Bahamas require exchange control approval, and outflows of resident-owned capital are restricted. Inward transfers by nonresidents do not require exchange control approval, although the subsequent use of the funds in The Bahamas may require authorization. The permission of the Central Bank is required for any action whereby nonresidents acquire control of or participate in an incorporated company controlled by residents. Resident individuals and companies require the specific permission of the Central Bank to maintain foreign currency bank accounts abroad.[6]

---

[5]Except in the Family Islands, where this authority is delegated to clearing bank branches.

[6]Banks and trusts established in The Bahamas are exempt from certain exchange control regulations, particularly with regard to their offshore operations.

The use of official exchange for direct investment abroad is limited to B$100,000 or 30 percent of the total cost of the investment (whichever is greater) for investments from which the additional benefits expected to accrue to the balance of payments from export receipts, profits, or other earnings within 18 months of the investment will at least equal the total amount of investment and will continue thereafter. Investments abroad that do not meet the above criteria may be financed by foreign currency borrowed on suitable terms subject to individual approval from the Central Bank, by foreign currency purchased in the investment currency market, or by the retained profits of foreign subsidiary companies. Permission is not given for investments that are likely to have adverse effects on the balance of payments.

In principle, inward investment by nonresidents is unrestricted. However, the consent of the Central Bank is required for the issue or transfer of shares in a Bahamian company to a nonresident and for the transfer of control of a Bahamian company to a nonresident. Foreigners intending to purchase land for commercial purposes or property larger than five acres in size must obtain a permit from the Foreign Investment Board, under the provisions of the International Landholding Act. If such an application is approved, payment for the purchase may be made either in Bahamian dollars from an external source or in foreign currency. Nonresidents wishing to purchase property for residential purposes may do so without prior approval but are required to obtain a Certificate of Registration from the Foreign Investment Board on completion of the transaction.

For all investments with approved status, permission is given upon application for the transfer of profits and dividends representing earned trading profits and investment income. In the event of a sale or liquidation, nonresident investors are permitted to repatriate the proceeds, including any capital appreciation, through the official foreign exchange market.

Residents require the specific approval of the Central Bank to buy property outside The Bahamas; such purchases, if for personal use, may be made only with investment currency, and approval is limited to one property a family. Incidental expenses connected with the purchase of property for personal use may normally be met with investment currency. Expenditures necessary for the maintenance of the property or arising directly from its ownership may, with permission, be met with foreign currency bought at the current market rate in the official foreign exchange market.

The transfer of legacies and inheritances to nonresident beneficiaries under the wills or intestacies of persons who were Bahamian residents at the time of their death is permitted.

Residents may make cash gifts to nonresidents not exceeding a total of B$1,000 a donor each year. This amount may be exceeded, with permission, in special circumstances.

Foreign nationals domiciled in The Bahamas, even if considered residents for exchange control purposes, may be eligible for a measure of exemption from certain exchange control obligations, notably with respect to the mandatory deposit of foreign currency securities and the surrender of certain other foreign capital assets.

Nonresident buyers of Bahamian securities must pay for such purchases in Bahamian dollars from an external account, in funds eligible for credit to an external account, or in Bahamian dollars obtained by selling foreign currency in the official foreign exchange market. Interest, dividends, and capital payments on such securities may not be remitted outside The Bahamas unless the holdings have been properly acquired by nonresidents. Bahamian residents are not permitted to purchase foreign currency securities with official exchange, export proceeds, or other current earnings; payment must be made with investment currency. All purchases, sales, and swaps of foreign currency securities in The Bahamas and all swaps in foreign currency securities by Bahamian residents, wherever the swap takes place, require permission from the Central Bank, and all transactions must take place through authorized agents.[7]

All foreign securities purchased by residents of The Bahamas must be held by or to the order of an authorized agent. Securities of other former Sterling Area countries are considered foreign currency securities. Sale proceeds from such resident-held foreign currency securities, if registered at the Central Bank by December 31, 1972, are eligible for sale in the investment currency market. Unregistered securities may be offered for sale at the official rate of exchange.

Residents leaving the country with the intention of residing permanently outside The Bahamas are redesignated upon departure as nonresidents. Generally, they may transfer, at the current market rate in the official foreign exchange market, up to B$25,000 of their Bahamian dollar assets to the new country of residence and may also take their house-

---

[7]Thirteen banks and trust companies are authorized to deal in Bahamian and foreign currency securities and to receive securities as deposits.

hold and personal effects with them. When the total value of their Bahamian dollar assets is over B$25,000, the excess is transferable through the official exchange market after four years or through the investment currency market at any time. Once a person is redesignated a nonresident, income accruing from assets remaining in The Bahamas is remittable at the current market rate in the official foreign exchange market.

Residents other than authorized banks must obtain permission to borrow foreign currency from nonresidents, and authorized dealers are subject to exchange control direction of their foreign currency loans to residents. Residents must also obtain permission to pay interest on, and to repay the principal of, foreign currency loans by conversion of Bahamian dollars. When permission is granted for residents to accept foreign currency loans, it is conditional upon the currency being offered for sale without delay to an authorized dealer unless the funds are required to meet payments to nonresidents for which permission has been specifically given.

A resident company wholly owned by nonresidents is not allowed to raise working capital in Bahamian dollars unless such funds are a small proportion of the total investment. If the company is partly owned by residents, the amount of local currency borrowing is determined in relation to the resident interest in the equity of the company. Banks and other lenders resident in The Bahamas must have permission to extend loans in domestic currency to any corporate body (other than a bank) that is also resident in The Bahamas but is controlled by any means, whether directly or indirectly, by nonresidents. However, companies set up by nonresidents primarily to import and distribute products manufactured outside The Bahamas are not allowed to borrow Bahamian dollars from residents for either fixed or working capital. Instead, they must provide all their financing in foreign currency, and foreign currency loans are normally permitted on application.

Gold

Residents of The Bahamas, other than authorized dealers, are not permitted to hold or deal in gold bullion. However, residents who are known users of gold for industrial purposes may, with the approval of the Central Bank, meet their current industrial requirements. Authorized dealers are not required to obtain licenses for bullion or coins, and no import duty is imposed on these items. Commercial imports of gold jewelry do not require a license but are subject to an import duty of 35 percent. A 1.5 percent stamp tax payable to customs is also payable on commercial shipments of gold jewelry from any source. There is no restriction on residents' acquisition or retention of gold coins. The Bahamas has issued commemorative coins in denominations of B$10, B$20, B$50, B$100, B$150, B$200, B$250, B$1,000, and B$2,500 in gold, and B$10 and B$25 in silver; these are legal tender but do not circulate.

Changes During 1994

No significant changes occurred in the exchange and trade system.

BAHRAIN

(Position as of December 31, 1994)

Exchange Arrangement

The currency of Bahrain is the Bahrain Dinar, which is pegged to the SDR at the rate of BD 0.46190 per SDR 1. The exchange rate for the Bahrain dinar in terms of the SDR may be set within margins of ± 7.25 percent of this fixed relationship. In practice, however, the Bahrain dinar has maintained a relatively stable relationship with the U.S. dollar, the intervention currency; since December 1980, the exchange rate has remained unchanged at BD 1 per US$2.6596. The middle rate of the Bahrain dinar for the U.S. dollar is quoted by the Bahrain Monetary Agency (BMA) and has remained unchanged since December 1980.

The BMA provides daily recommended rates to banks dealing with the public for amounts up to BD 1,000 in U.S. dollars, pounds sterling, and deutsche mark, based on the latest available U.S. dollar rates against those currencies. The BMA does not deal with the public. On December 31, 1994, the BMA's buying and selling rates for the U.S. dollar were BD 0.375 and BD 0.377, respectively, per US$1. In their dealings with the public, commercial banks are required to use the BMA's rates for U.S. dollars, pounds sterling, and deutsche mark, but they are authorized to charge an exchange commission of 2 per mil (special rates of commission apply for transactions up to BD 1,000). The banks' rates for other currencies are based on the BMA's U.S. dollar rates and the New York market rates against the U.S. dollar.

There are no taxes or subsidies on purchases or sales of foreign exchange. There are no arrangements for forward cover against exchange rate risk operating in the official sector. The BMA monitors the forward exchange transactions of commercial banks through the open position of the banks' monthly returns.

Bahrain formally accepted the obligations of Article VIII, Sections 2, 3, and 4 of the Fund Agreement, as from March 20, 1973.

Administration of Control

The BMA is the exchange control authority, but there is no exchange control legislation in Bahrain. No import or export licenses are required (except for arms, ammunition, and alcoholic beverages). However, importers and exporters must be registered with the commercial registry maintained by the Ministry of Commerce and Agriculture and must be members of the Bahrain Chamber of Commerce and Industry.

Prescription of Currency

All settlements with Israel are prohibited. Otherwise, no requirements are imposed on exchange payments or receipts.

Nonresident Accounts

A distinction is made between accounts held by residents and those held by nonresidents. Offshore banking units are not normally permitted to hold resident accounts.

Imports and Import Payments

All imports from Israel are prohibited. Imports of a few commodities are prohibited from all sources for reasons of health, public policy, or security. Imports of cultured pearls are prohibited. In practice, rice is imported mainly by the Bahrain Import-Export Company.

The rates of customs tariffs range between 5 percent and 10 percent on most commodities, but the rate is 20 percent on vehicles, 50 percent on tobacco, and 125 percent on alcoholic beverages. Mandatory government procurements give preference to goods produced in Bahrain and member countries of the Cooperation Council for the Arab States of the Gulf (GCC), provided that the quality and prices of these goods are within specified margins of the prices of imported substitutes (10 percent for goods produced in Bahrain and 5 percent for goods produced in member countries of the GCC). Foreign exchange for payments in respect of permitted imports may be obtained freely.

Exports and Export Proceeds

All exports to Israel are prohibited. Otherwise, all products may be exported freely. No requirements are attached to receipts from exports or re-exports; the proceeds need not be repatriated or surrendered, and they may be disposed of freely, regardless of the currency involved.

Payments for and Proceeds from Invisibles

Payments for and proceeds from invisibles are not restricted, except that payments must not be made to or received from Israel. Travelers may bring in or take out of Bahrain any amount in domestic or foreign banknotes.

Capital

No exchange control requirements are imposed on capital receipts or payments by residents or nonresidents, but payments may not be made to or received from Israel. Profits from foreign investments in Bahrain may be transferred abroad freely, except that, under Article 72 of the Monetary Agency Law, the banks are subject to special rules regarding the payment of dividends and the remittance of profits. Licensed offshore banking units may freely engage in transactions with nonresidents, although transactions with residents are not normally permitted. The stock exchange began operations on January 2, 1989, and trading on the floor of the exchange began on June 17, 1989.

Gold

Residents may freely purchase, hold, and sell gold in any form, at home or abroad. Imports and exports of gold in any form are freely permitted and do not require a license. Imports of gold jewelry are subject to a 10 percent customs duty, but gold ingots are exempt. Brokers doing business in gold and other commodities must obtain approval from the BMA before they can register with the Ministry of Commerce and Agriculture. Such businesses are subject to a minimum deposit requirement equivalent, in the case of gold, to BD 3,000 or 10 percent of the contract value, whichever is higher.

Changes During 1994

No significant changes occurred in the exchange and trade system.

BANGLADESH

(Position as of December 31, 1994)

Exchange Arrangement

The currency of Bangladesh is the Bangladesh Taka. The value of the taka in terms of the U.S. dollar, the intervention currency, is determined with reference to a weighted basket consisting of the currencies of the country's major trading partners. On December 31, 1994, Bangladesh Bank's (spot) middle rate of the taka in terms of the U.S. dollar was Tk 40.25 per US$1, and the spot buying and selling rates of Bangladesh Bank (the central bank) for authorized dealers were Tk 40.15 and Tk 40.55, respectively, per US$1. Bangladesh Bank deals with authorized domestic banks only in U.S. dollars and the currencies of the member countries of the Asian Clearing Union (ACU).[1] Authorized banks are free to set their own buying and selling rates for the U.S. dollar and the rates for other currencies based on cross rates in international markets.

Forward contracts are available from authorized banks, covering periods of up to six months for export proceeds and import payments and covering up to three months for remittances of surplus collection of foreign shipping companies and airlines. For the currencies of ACU member countries, the authorized banks may, in turn, take forward cover from Bangladesh Bank against transactions entered into through forward contracts with their customers.

Authorized banks are permitted to retain working balances with their foreign correspondents. Currency swaps and forward exchange transactions are permitted when they are against underlying approved commercial transactions.

Bangladesh formally accepted the obligations of Article VIII, Sections 2, 3, and 4 of the Fund Agreement, as from April 11, 1994.

Administration of Control

Exchange control is administered by Bangladesh Bank in accordance with general policy formulated in consultation with the Ministry of Finance. The commercial banks and specialized financial institutions are issued licenses as authorized dealers (authorized banks) in foreign exchange. The Chief Controller of Imports and Exports of the Ministry of Commerce is responsible for registering exporters and importers and for issuing the Import Policy Order (IPO). Registered importers can make their imports in terms of the IPO against letters of credit. Letters of credit authorization forms are issued by authorized dealers and do not require a separate import license. Certain trade transactions are conducted through state-owned agencies, including the Trading Corporation of Bangladesh (TCB).

Prescription of Currency

Settlements normally take place in convertible currencies, and in some cases through nonresident taka accounts. Settlements with ACU member countries are required to be effected through the ACU in terms of the Asian monetary unit (AMU).[2] There are commodity exchange agreements with a few countries.[3] Settlements for trade under these agreements are effected through special nonconvertible U.S. dollar accounts.[4] Payments for imports may be made to the country of origin of the goods or to any other country (with the exception of those countries from which importation is prohibited). They may be made (1) in taka for credit in Bangladesh to a nonresident bank account of the country concerned; (2) in the currency of the country concerned; or (3) in any freely convertible currency. Export proceeds must be received in freely convertible foreign exchange or in taka from a nonresident taka account. All settlements with Israel, Iraq, and the Federal Republic of Yugoslavia (Serbia/Montenegro) are prohibited.

Resident and Nonresident Accounts

The accounts of individuals, firms, or companies residing in countries outside Bangladesh are designated nonresident accounts. All such accounts are regarded for exchange control purposes as accounts related to the country in which the account holder is a permanent resident.[5] Nonresident foreign cur-

---

[1]Members of the Asian Clearing Union are Bangladesh, India, the Islamic Republic of Iran, Myanmar, Nepal, Pakistan, and Sri Lanka.

[2]The AMU is equivalent in value to the SDR and is used for recording transactions through the ACU.

[3]Bulgaria, Czech Republic, Hungary, and Democratic People's Republic of Korea.

[4]Bangladesh is committed to settling promptly any outstanding liability on these accounts.

[5]The accounts of the United Nations and its agencies are treated as resident accounts.

rency accounts may be opened by authorized dealers without prior approval from Bangladesh Bank for Bangladeshi nationals and foreign nationals who reside abroad and for foreign firms operating abroad. Specified debits and credits to these accounts may be made in the account holder's absence by authorized dealers without prior approval from Bangladesh Bank. Certain other debits and credits may be made without prior approval from Bangladesh Bank but are subject to ex post reporting.

Convertible taka accounts. All diplomatic missions operating in Bangladesh, their diplomatic officers, home-based members of the mission staffs, international nonprofit organizations (including charitable organizations functioning in Bangladesh and their respective personnel), foreign oil companies engaged in oil exploration in Bangladesh and their expatriate employees, UN organizations and other international organizations, foreign contractors and consultants engaged in specific projects, and foreign nationals residing in Bangladesh (regardless of their status) are allowed to maintain convertible taka accounts. These accounts may be credited freely with the proceeds of inward remittances in convertible foreign exchange and may be debited freely at any time for local disbursements in taka, as well as for remittances abroad in convertible currencies. Transfers between convertible taka accounts are freely permitted. Foreign missions and embassies, their expatriate personnel, foreign airline and shipping companies, and international nonprofit organizations in Bangladesh may open interest-bearing accounts, but the interest earned can be disbursed only in local currency.

Foreign currency accounts of Bangladeshi nationals working abroad. Bangladeshi nationals and persons of Bangladeshi origin who are working abroad are permitted to open foreign currency accounts denominated in pounds sterling or U.S. dollars. These accounts may be credited with (1) remittances in convertible currencies received from abroad through normal banking and postal channels; (2) proceeds of convertible currencies (banknotes, traveler's checks, drafts, etc.) brought into Bangladesh by the account holders, provided that amounts exceeding $5,000 have been declared to customs upon arrival in Bangladesh; (3) transfers from other foreign currency accounts opened under the former Wage Earners' Scheme (WES); and (4) transfers from nonresident foreign currency deposit accounts. The accounts may be debited without restriction, but debits for the following purposes must be reported to Bangladesh Bank: (1) all local disbursements; (2) transfers to other foreign currency accounts opened under the WES;

(3) payments for imports of specified goods against letters of credit; (4) payments of bank commissions and other bank charges connected with imports; and (5) travel expenditures up to prescribed limits abroad for business or private purposes.

Nonresident foreign currency deposit accounts. Bangladeshi nationals residing abroad; foreign nationals, companies, and firms registered or incorporated abroad; banks and other financial institutions, including institutional investors; officers and staff of Bangladeshi missions and government institutions; autonomous bodies; and commercial banks may open interest-bearing nonresident foreign currency deposit accounts denominated in pounds sterling or U.S. dollars. These accounts, whose terms range from one month to one year, may be credited in initial minimum amounts of $1,000 or £500 ($25,000 for foreigners), with remittances in convertible currencies and transfers from existing foreign currency deposit accounts maintained by Bangladeshi nationals abroad. The balance, including interest earned, may be transferred in foreign exchange by the account holder to any country or to any foreign currency deposit account maintained by Bangladeshi nationals abroad. The balances in the accounts, which are freely convertible into taka, must be reported monthly by banks to Bangladesh Bank.

Nonresident Bangladeshis who do not open or maintain a foreign currency deposit account while abroad may open a nonresident foreign currency deposit with foreign exchange brought in from abroad within six months of the date of their return to take up permanent residence in Bangladesh.

Resident foreign currency deposit (RFCD) accounts. Resident Bangladeshis, at the time of their return from travel abroad, may bring in any amount of foreign currency with a declaration and up to $5,000 or the equivalent without a declaration and may maintain an RFCD account with the foreign exchange brought in. However, proceeds of exports of goods and services from Bangladesh or commissions arising from business deals in Bangladesh are not allowed to be credited to such accounts. Balances in these accounts are freely transferable abroad and may be used for travel in the usual manner. These accounts may be opened in U.S. dollars and pounds sterling. Exporters and local joint-venture firms executing projects financed by a foreign donor or international agency may open foreign currency accounts. Foreign currency accounts may also be opened in the names of diplomatic missions in Bangladesh, their expatriates, and diplomatic bonded warehouses (duty-free shops).

Imports and Import Payments

Imports are financed either from Bangladesh's own resources or from foreign aid, loans, and barter arrangements. Imports are guided by a two-year IPO announced by the Government. The controlled list contains 107 items in about 1,400 categories at the four-digit level of the Harmonized System Codes. The importation of these items is restricted or prohibited either for social or religious reasons or because similar items are produced locally. Up to 26 items are restricted purely for trade purposes. Items not specified in the control list of the IPO are freely importable, provided that the importer has a valid import registration certificate. Imports from Israel are prohibited.

All importers (including all government departments with the exception of the Ministry of Defense) are required to obtain letter of credit authorization forms (LCAFs) for all imports. Under the authority of the IPO issued by the Chief Controller, importers are allowed to effect imports against LCAFs issued by authorized dealer banks without an import license. Single-country LCAFs are issued for imports under bilateral trade or payments agreements and for imports under tied-aid programs. LCAFs are otherwise valid worldwide, except that imports from Israel and imports transported on flag vessels of Israel are prohibited. Goods must be shipped within 17 months of the date of issuance of LCAFs in the case of machinery and spare parts and 9 months in the case of all other items.

Payment against imports is generally permissible only under cover of irrevocable letters of credit. Recognized export-oriented ready-made garments and specialized textile and hosiery units operating under the bonded warehouse system may effect imports of their raw and packing materials by opening back-to-back letters of credit on a deferred-payment basis of up to 180 days against export letters of credit received by them. Public sector importers may import on a cash-against-documents basis, subject to authorization from Bangladesh Bank.

Imports of specified raw materials and packing materials by industrial consumers are governed by an entitlement system, based on the requirements for various industries during each import program period established by the Board of Investment. Firms in the industrial sector are given an entitlement to import specified raw materials and packing materials, and letter of credit authorization forms are issued on the basis of the entitlement. The entitlement system does not apply to raw materials and packing materials that are freely importable but does apply to items appearing on the controlled list. Separately, industrial consumers may be issued with LCAFs for parts and accessories of machinery. Goods imported against LCAFs issued to industrial consumers must be used in the industry concerned and must not be sold or transferred without prior approval.

Authorized dealers may establish letters of credit on an f.o.b. basis without the approval of Bangladesh Bank, subject to the following conditions: (1) cost of goods, cost of freight, and insurance will be accommodated within the amount recorded in the LCAF issued in favor of the importer; (2) cost of freight will be paid locally out of the LCAF value in local currency; and (3) other directives of the IPO will be duly complied with. Foreign exchange for authorized imports is provided automatically by authorized dealers when payments are due. Advance payments for imports require approval from Bangladesh Bank, which is normally given only for specialized or capital goods.

Payments for Invisibles

Payments for invisibles connected with authorized trade transactions are generally not restricted. Applications for foreign exchange for family maintenance and education abroad are accepted upon verification of their bona fide nature. For medical treatment, up to $10,000 can be obtained without prior approval; for larger amounts, the total amount required is granted, subject to the approval of Bangladesh Bank. The indicative allowance for personal travel by resident Bangladeshi nationals to countries other than Bhutan, India, Maldives, Myanmar, Nepal, Pakistan, and Sri Lanka is $2,500 a year; the allowance for air travel to these seven countries is $500 a person a year. Larger amounts are available upon verification by Bangladesh Bank of the bona fide nature of the request. Business travelers may obtain up to $6,000 without prior authorization and more upon verification of bona fides. Exporters maintaining retention accounts may use the funds on these accounts to cover travel expenses abroad without prior approval from Bangladesh Bank. Foreign nationals working in Bangladesh may freely remit up to 50 percent of net salary in terms of service contracts approved by the Government; the entire amount of their leave salaries and savings can also be remitted freely. No prior permission is required for the remittance of royalties and technical fees of up to 6 percent of sales; training and consultancy fees of up to 1 percent of sales; and fees for undergraduate, postgraduate, and some professional courses.

Nonresident travelers may take out the foreign currency and traveler's checks they brought in and declared on entry or up to $5,000 or the equivalent brought in without declaration. They may also, without obtaining the approval of Bangladesh Bank, reconvert taka notes up to Tk 6,000 into convertible foreign currencies at the time of their departure. Resident travelers may take out foreign currency and traveler's checks up to the amount of any travel allocation they are granted. A Bangladeshi or a foreign national may take out Tk 500 in domestic currency; otherwise, the exportation of Bangladeshi currency notes and coins is prohibited.

Authorized dealers are allowed to remit dividends to nonresident shareholders without the prior approval of Bangladesh Bank on receipt of applications from the companies concerned; applications must be supported by an audited balance sheet and profit-and-loss account, a board resolution declaring dividends out of profit derived from the normal business activities of the company, and an auditor's certificate that tax liabilities are covered. Authorized dealers may remit profits of foreign firms, banks, insurance companies, and other financial institutions operating in Bangladesh to their head office on receipt of applications supported by documentation. These remittances are, however, subject to ex post checking by Bangladesh Bank.

Exports and Export Proceeds

Exports to Israel are prohibited. Proceeds from exports must be received within four months of shipment unless otherwise allowed by Bangladesh Bank. Exporters are permitted to retain 5 percent of products with a low value added and 15 percent of other products of the proceeds from exports; they may use retained earnings for bona fide business purposes, such as business travel abroad, participation in trade fairs and seminars, and imports of raw materials, spare parts, and capital goods. They may also be used to set up offices abroad without prior permission from Bangladesh Bank.

Joint ventures, other than in the garment industry, located in export processing zones (EPZs) are allowed to retain 70 percent of their export earnings in a foreign currency deposit account and place the remaining 30 percent in a bank account in domestic currency.

Proceeds from Invisibles

Exporters of services are permitted to retain 5 percent of the proceeds and use retained earnings for bona fide business purposes. Bangladeshi nationals working abroad may retain their earnings in foreign currency accounts or in nonresident foreign currency deposit accounts. Unless specifically exempted by Bangladesh Bank, all Bangladeshi nationals who reside in Bangladesh must surrender any foreign exchange coming into their possession, whether held in Bangladesh or abroad, to an authorized dealer within one month of the date of acquisition. However, returning residents may keep, on hand or in a foreign currency account opened in their name, up to $5,000 without declaration.

Foreign nationals residing in Bangladesh continuously for more than six months are required to surrender within one month of the date of acquisition any foreign exchange representing their earnings in respect of business conducted in Bangladesh or services rendered while in Bangladesh. Foreign exchange held abroad or in Bangladesh by foreign diplomats and by foreign nationals employed in embassies and missions of foreign countries in Bangladesh is, however, exempt from this requirement.

The importation of Bangladeshi currency notes and coins exceeding Tk 500 is prohibited. Foreign currency traveler's checks and foreign currency notes may be brought in up to $5,000 without declaration and up to any amount without limit, provided the amount brought in is declared to customs upon arrival in Bangladesh.

Capital

All outward transfers of capital require approval, which is not normally granted for resident-owned capital. Inward capital transfers other than portfolio investment and direct investment in the industrial sector also require approval. Movable and immovable assets, including foreign exchange, owned in any country other than Bangladesh must be declared to Bangladesh Bank by resident Bangladeshi nationals. However, Bangladeshi residents may continue to maintain foreign currency accounts opened during their stay abroad. There is no restriction on the importation of securities into Bangladesh. The issuing and transfer of shares and securities in favor of nonresidents against foreign investment or inward remittance are allowed without the prior permission of Bangladesh Bank. The transfer of Bangladeshi shares and securities from one nonresident holder to another nonresident holder also does not require prior approval from Bangladesh Bank. Nonresident persons and institutions, including nonresident Bangladeshis, may buy Bangladeshi shares and securities through stock exchanges in Bangladesh against freely convertible foreign currency remitted from abroad through the banking channels. Proceeds from sales including capital gains and dividends earned on the shares or securities bought in this manner may be remitted abroad in freely convertible currency.

Authorized dealers may obtain short-term loans and overdrafts from overseas branches and correspondents for a period not exceeding seven days at a time. Private sector industrial units in Bangladesh may borrow funds from abroad without the approval of the Board of Investment if the interest rate does not exceed 4 percent above the LIBOR, the repayment period is not less than seven years, and the down payment is not more than 10 percent; industrial units in the export promotion zones, including foreign-owned and joint ventures, may obtain short-term foreign loans without prior approval. Local currency loans to enterprises controlled by foreigners or residents do not require Bangladesh Bank approval. Lending by authorized dealers in local currency against overseas or collateral outside Bangladesh requires approval from Bangladesh Bank. Authorized dealers may grant, without reference to Bangladesh Bank and according to banking practice, loans without a specific limit in domestic currency to foreign-owned manufacturing companies located in Bangladesh. Authorized dealers may also approve loans, overdrafts, or credit facilities against goods intended for exportation from Bangladesh to companies controlled by persons residing outside Bangladesh. Authorized dealers must obtain approval before making any loans in foreign currencies to residents or nonresidents, whether secured or unsecured. They are not normally permitted to hold short-term foreign assets other than small working balances.

When their work in Bangladesh is finished, expatriate workers may transfer their savings abroad, provided that their salaries and benefits were initially certified by the Board of Investment.

Foreign private investment is governed by the Foreign Private Investment (Promotion and Protection) Act of 1980 and is permitted in collaboration with both the Government and private entrepreneurs. The act provides for the protection and equitable treatment of foreign private investment, indemnification, protection against expropriation and nationalization, and guarantee for repatriation

of investment. With the exception of a few reserved sectors, private foreign investment is freely allowed.

There is no ceiling on private investment. Tax holidays are granted for periods of up to nine years, depending on the location. There is no upper limit on the foreign equity portion of an industrial investment, and there is no prior approval requirement for investments, which should, however, be registered with the Investment Board. Nonresidents must also obtain the permission of Bangladesh Bank to continue to operate or to establish an office or branch in Bangladesh for the purpose of trading or for commercial activities. Dividends on foreign capital may be remitted freely after payment of taxes.

Gold

The importation and exportation of gold and silver are prohibited without special permission. However, adult female passengers are free to bring in or take out any amount of gold jewelry without prior approval from Bangladesh Bank. Exports of gold jewelry are also allowed under the Jewelry Export Scheme. There are no restrictions on the internal sale, purchase, or possession of gold or silver ornaments (including coins) and jewelry, but there is a prohibition on the holding of gold and silver in all other forms except by licensed industrialists or dentists.

Changes During 1994

Exchange Arrangement

April 11. Bangladesh accepted the obligations of Article VIII, Sections 2, 3, and 4 of the Fund Articles of Agreement.

Payments for Invisibles

March 28. Business travelers were permitted to obtain foreign exchange in excess of $6,000 upon providing verification of the bona fide nature of travel.

March 28. Applications for foreign exchange for family maintenance abroad would be approved upon verification that the need was bona fide.

BARBADOS

(Position as of December 31, 1994)

Exchange Arrangement

The currency of Barbados is the Barbados Dollar, which is pegged to the U.S. dollar, the intervention currency, at BDS$2 per US$1. On December 31, 1994, the official buying and selling rates for the U.S. dollar were BDS$1.9975 and BDS$2.0350, respectively, per US$1. Buying and selling rates for the Canadian dollar, the deutsche mark, and the pound sterling are also officially quoted on the basis of their cross-rate relationships to the U.S. dollar. The quoted rates include commission charges of 0.125 percent buying and 1.75 percent selling against the U.S. dollar, and 0.1875 percent buying and 1.8125 percent selling against the Canadian dollar, the deutsche mark, and the pound sterling.

Under clearing arrangements with regional monetary authorities, the Central Bank of Barbados currently sells currencies of only three Caribbean Common Market (CARICOM) countries;[1] these are the Guyana dollar, the Eastern Caribbean dollar, and the Belize dollar. The Trinidad and Tobago dollar and the Jamaica dollar now float against the U.S. dollar, and the Central Bank fixes daily selling rates based on rates supplied by the monetary authorities of these countries. These rates are applicable only to government transactions. All selling rates fixed by the Central Bank in respect of CARICOM currencies include a commission of 0.125 percent. The Central Bank purchases Eastern Caribbean dollar notes only. The rate applied mutually for the purchase of currency notes is the parity rate between each pair of currencies determined on the basis of the U.S. dollar rate. The Central Bank regulates the commission that the commercial banks may charge their customers for CARICOM currencies. Purchases of foreign exchange for private sector remittances abroad (except for remittances for payment of imports, travel allowances, education, and nontrade payments up to BDS$500, and certain other items) are subject to a levy collected in the approval process by the Central Bank at the rate of 1 percent of the value of the transaction.

The Central Bank periodically obtains forward cover in the international foreign exchange market to cover or hedge its own or the central Government's exchange risks associated with foreign exchange loans that are not denominated in U.S. dollars. Commercial banks are allowed to obtain forward cover in the international markets. The Central Bank and commercial banks enter into swap transactions in U.S. dollars, while commercial banks may freely switch between nonregional currencies.

Barbados formally accepted the obligations of Article VIII, Sections 2, 3, and 4 of the Fund Agreement, as from November 3, 1993.

Administration of Control

Exchange control applies to all countries and is administered by the Central Bank, which delegates to authorized dealers the authority to approve normal import payments and the allocation of foreign exchange for certain other current payments and for cash gifts. The exchange control system stipulates that foreign exchange should normally be surrendered to an authorized dealer. Trade controls are administered by the Ministry of Industry, Commerce, and Business Development.

Prescription of Currency

Settlements with residents of countries outside the CARICOM area may be made in any foreign currency,[2] or through an external account in Barbados dollars. Settlements with residents of CARICOM countries, other than Jamaica and Trinidad and Tobago, must be made either through external accounts (in Barbados dollars) or in the currency of the CARICOM country concerned, except that commercial banks may issue U.S. dollar traveler's checks to Barbadian residents traveling to other CARICOM countries, within the approved limits for travel allowances. With effect from September 21, 1991 and April 13, 1993, the Bank of Jamaica and the Central Bank of Trinidad and Tobago abolished exchange control in Jamaica and Trinidad and Tobago, respectively; as a result, settlements with residents of Jamaica and Trinidad and Tobago are made in U.S. dollars.

---

[1]The CARICOM countries are Antigua and Barbuda, The Bahamas, Barbados, Belize, Dominica, Grenada, Guyana, Jamaica, Montserrat, St. Kitts and Nevis, St. Lucia, St. Vincent and the Grenadines, and Trinidad and Tobago.

[2]Foreign currencies comprise all currencies other than the Barbados dollar.

Resident and Nonresident Accounts

With the permission of the Central Bank, authorized dealers may maintain in foreign currencies foreign currency accounts in the names of residents of Barbados and of other countries. Approval for opening these accounts is given on the basis of the anticipated frequency of receipts and payments in foreign currency. Certain receipts and payments may be credited and debited to foreign currency accounts under the conditions of approval established at the time the account is opened. Other credits and debits require individual approval.

Authorized dealers may open external accounts for nonresidents without consulting the Central Bank. These accounts, maintained in Barbados dollars, may be credited with proceeds from the sale of foreign currencies, with transfers from other external accounts, with bank interest (payable on external accounts or blocked accounts), and with payments by residents for which the Central Bank has given general or specific permission. They may be debited for payments to residents of Barbados, for the cost of foreign exchange required for travel or business purposes, and for any other payment covered by delegated authority to authorized dealers. Other debits and any overdrafts require individual approval.

The Exchange Control Act of 1967 (as amended) empowers the Central Bank to require certain payments in favor of nonresidents that are ineligible for transfer to be credited to blocked accounts. Balances in blocked accounts may not be withdrawn without approval, other than for the purchase of approved securities.

Imports and Import Payments

Certain imports require individual licenses. However, not all goods that are subject to import licensing are subject to quantitative restrictions or import surcharges. Some items on the import-licensing list may be freely imported throughout the year, while others are subject to temporary restrictions (particularly agricultural products, which tend to be subject to seasonal restrictions). Individual licenses are also required for imports of commodities that are subject to the provisions of the Oils and Fats Agreement between the governments of Barbados, Dominica, Grenada, Guyana, St. Lucia, St. Vincent and the Grenadines, and Trinidad and Tobago, whether the goods are being imported from CARICOM countries or from elsewhere. Special licensing arrangements have been made for the regulation of trade between Barbados and other CARICOM countries in 22 agricultural commodities.

The customs duty rates on most goods range from 5 percent to 35 percent, the same range as the Common External Tariff (CET) of the CARICOM region.[3] Import surcharges in the form of stamp duties, consumption taxes, and luxury taxes amount to a total of up to 203 percent.

Payments for authorized imports are permitted upon application and submission of documentary evidence (invoices and customs warrants) to authorized dealers; payments for imports of crude oil and its derivatives are subject to the prior approval of the Central Bank. Authorized dealers may release foreign currency up to the equivalent of BDS$20,000 (c.i.f.) for advance payments for imports into Barbados. Other advance payments require the prior approval of the Central Bank.

Payments for Invisibles

Payments for invisibles require exchange control approval. Payments for all commercial transactions are permitted freely when the application is supported by appropriate documentary evidence.

Authority has been delegated to authorized dealers to provide basic allocations of foreign exchange for certain personal and sundry payments. These include foreign travel, for which up to BDS$5,000 a person a calendar year may be allocated for private travel inside or outside the CARICOM area; BDS$500 a day for business travel, up to BDS$4,000 a person a calendar year; expenses for education abroad, BDS$20,000 a person a year; remittances of cash gifts not exceeding BDS$1,000 a donor a year; subscriptions to newspapers and magazines, BDS$5,000 a person a year; remittances for medical purposes, up to BDS$50,000 a year; and income tax refunds, official payments, and life insurance premiums. Applications for additional amounts or for purposes for which there is no basic allocation are approved by the authorities, provided that no unauthorized transfer of capital appears to be involved. The cost of transportation to any destination may be settled in domestic currency and is not deducted from the travel allocation.

Any person traveling to a destination outside Barbados may take out foreign currency notes and coins up to the value of BDS$500 and Barbados notes up to BDS$200. Nonresident visitors may freely export any foreign currency they previously brought in.

---

[3]The maximum tariff is expected to be lowered to 30 percent on April 1, 1995.

Exports and Export Proceeds

Specific licenses are required for the exportation of certain goods to any country, including rice, cane sugar, rum, molasses, and certain other food products, sewing machines, portland cement, and petroleum products. All other goods may be exported without license. The collection of export proceeds is supervised by the Central Bank to ensure that foreign exchange proceeds are surrendered to authorized dealers within six months of the date of shipment. Exports of sugar to the United Kingdom and the United States are subject to bilateral export quotas, as are exports of rum to the European Union.

Proceeds from Invisibles

Foreign currency proceeds from invisibles must be sold to authorized dealers. Travelers to Barbados may freely bring in notes and coins denominated in Barbados dollars or in any foreign currency. Residents returning to Barbados are required to sell their holdings of foreign currencies to an authorized dealer.

Capital

All outward capital transfers, including direct investments by residents and the purchase by residents of foreign currency securities and real estate abroad, require exchange control approval. Certificates of title to foreign currency securities held by residents must be lodged with an authorized depository in Barbados, and earnings on these securities must be repatriated and surrendered to an authorized dealer.

Personal capital transfers, such as inheritances due to nonresidents, require exchange control approval. Transfers in respect of inheritances are restricted to BDS$30,000 a year for each nonresident beneficiary. Dowries in the form of settlements and cash gifts may be transferred to nonresidents under delegated authority, normally up to BDS$1,000 a donor a year. Emigrating Barbadian nationals are granted settling-in allowances from their declared assets at the rate of BDS$30,000 a family unit a year. The Central Bank also considers applications from foreign nationals who have resided in Barbados and are proceeding to take up permanent residence abroad, provided that they declare the assets they hold in Barbados.

Direct investment by nonresidents may be made with exchange control approval. The remittance of earnings on, and liquidation of proceeds from, such investment is permitted, provided that evidence documenting the validity of the remittance is sub-mitted, all liabilities related to the investment have been discharged, and the original investment was registered with the Central Bank.

The issuance and transfer to nonresidents of securities registered in Barbados require exchange control approval, which is freely given provided that an adequate amount of foreign currency is brought in for their purchase. Proceeds from the realization of these securities may be remitted when it is established that the original investment was financed from foreign currency sources. Nonresidents may acquire real estate in Barbados for private purposes with funds from foreign currency sources; local currency financing is not ordinarily permitted. Proceeds from the realization of such investments equivalent to the amount of foreign currency brought in may be repatriated freely. Capital sums realized in excess of this amount may be repatriated freely on the basis of a calculated rate of return on the original foreign investment, as follows: for the last five years, at 8 percent a year; for the five years immediately preceding the last five years, at 5 percent; and for any period preceding the last ten years, at 4 percent. Amounts in excess of the sum so derived are restricted to the remittance of BDS$24,000 a year.

The approval of the Central Bank is required for residents to borrow abroad or for nonresidents to borrow in Barbados. Authorized dealers may assume short-term liability positions in foreign currencies for the financing of approved transfers in respect of both trade and nontrade transactions. They may also freely accept deposits from nonresidents. Any borrowing abroad by authorized dealers to finance their domestic operations requires the approval of the Central Bank.

A 6 percent tax is levied on portfolio investments of pension funds with foreign companies that are not registered with the Barbados Supervisor of Insurance.

Gold

Gold coins with face values of BDS$50, BDS$100, BDS$150, BDS$200, and BDS$500 are legal tender and are in limited circulation. Residents who are private persons are permitted to acquire and hold gold coins for numismatic purposes only. Otherwise, any gold acquired in Barbados must be surrendered to an authorized dealer unless exchange control approval is obtained for its retention. Residents other than the monetary authorities, authorized dealers, and industrial users are not permitted to hold or acquire gold in any form other than jewelry or coins for numismatic purposes. The importation of gold by residents is permitted for industrial purposes and is subject to customs duties and charges. Licenses to import gold are issued by the Ministry of Industry, Commerce, and Business Development; no license is required to export gold, but exchange control permission is required to do so.

Changes During 1994

Administration of Control

March 17. Barbados lifted economic sanctions against South Africa.

Imports and Import Payments

February 10. Quantitative restrictions and licenses were eliminated on a number of items. A surcharge of 100 percent was imposed on imported products for which locally produced goods can be substituted.

October 1. All taxes on inputs used in the agricultural and manufacturing sectors were eliminated.

Payments for Invisibles

April 5. Authorized dealers were allowed to release foreign exchange as follows: (1) for remittances for cash gift purposes, BDS$1,000 a donor a year; (2) for advertising, legal fees, commissions, dividends, subscriptions, film processing, insurance payments, and personal loan payments, up to BDS$5,000; (3) for advance payments for imports into Barbados, up to BDS$50,000 c.i.f. against specified documentary evidence; (4) for medical treatment outside Barbados, up to BDS$50,000 against specified documentary evidence; and (5) foreign exchange for foreign travels as follows (i) from Barbados to other countries, at the rate of BDS$5,000 a person a calendar year; (ii) business travel from Barbados to other countries, at the rate of BDS$500 a day, up to a maximum of BDS$40,000 a person a calendar year.

Capital

April 5. The annual allowance allowed for remittances under a legacy was raised to BDS$30,000 a person from BDS$20,000.

April 25. (1) The annual allowance for Barbadian national emigrants was increased to BDS$30,000 a person, or family unit from BDS$20,000, and (2) the amount allowed for excess capital gains was raised to BDS$30,000 a year from BDS$24,000.

BELARUS

(Position as of December 31, 1994)

Exchange Arrangements

The currency of Belarus is the Rubel.[1] Restrictions on conversion of noncash rubels into cash (and vice versa) have been abolished effective December 31, 1994. This has eliminated the differentiation that existed between cash and noncash rubels against foreign currencies. The exchange rates of the rubel against the U.S. dollar, the deutsche mark, the Russian ruble, and the Ukrainian karbovanets are established twice weekly, at the Minsk Currency Exchange, with participation of the commercial banks licensed to conduct foreign currency operations and the National Bank of Belarus (NBB). On December 31, 1994, the market exchange rate was Rbl 9,680 per US$1.

The official exchange rates are set on the basis of the auction rate and are used for accounting purposes, for all foreign exchange transactions for the government, for transactions related to exports and imports, and for most current transfers and capital account transactions.

By resolution of the Board of the NBB of October 5, 1994, restrictions on conducting cash transactions on the foreign currency exchange have been lifted. By NBB Board Resolution of November 23, 1994, commercial banks with the required foreign exchange license are permitted to trade at the currency auction for their own account.

Foreign investors must pay a 15 percent tax in convertible currency on income received as a result of the profit remittances. There are no arrangements for forward cover against exchange risk in the official or the commercial banking sector.

Administration of Control

The Parliament is responsible for legislating exchange control regulations and the NBB for administering them. The country's official foreign exchange reserves are controlled by the Council of Ministers and the NBB. Local governments control the local foreign exchange funds. Foreign exchange for official import payments is administratively allocated through state and local government foreign exchange funds. Foreign exchange regulations to vest the NBB with greater authority to control official foreign exchange reserves and to implement exchange rate policy are under preparation.

Only banks may obtain licenses to engage in foreign exchange transactions. Enterprises may obtain permission to open foreign exchange offices, sell goods, and render services for freely convertible currency within Belarus.

Prescription of Currency

Payments with countries with which Belarus has bilateral payments agreements are effected in the currencies specified in these agreements and in accordance with their regulations.[2] The agreements with the Baltic countries, Russia, and the other countries of the former Soviet Union provide for settlement through bilateral clearing accounts held with central banks or authorized commercial banks. Settlement is to take place in convertible currencies, national currencies, or rubels; a number of countries of the former Soviet Union have signed an agreement (in October 1992) that they will use only the ruble in nonbarter transactions among themselves. Foreign trade payments outside this sphere are made in convertible currency. A significant share of trade is conducted in the framework of barter agreements. An attempt is being made to balance the trade with a cash trading partner, but if an imbalance emerges, it is settled, in principle, with deliveries of goods or in convertible currency. Since September 9, 1992, barter trade of certain goods has required approval from the Commission of the Council of Ministers on the Issuance of Authorization to Engage in Commodity-Exchange Operations.

Payments in foreign currency for goods and services (including wage payments) transactions among residents are prohibited.

Resident and Nonresident Accounts

Without declaring the sources of their foreign exchange, residents may open foreign currency ac-

[1]Prior to August 20, 1994, the Russian ruble also served as legal tender in Belarus. Effective August 20, 1994, the rubel replaced the Belarussian ruble and became the sole legal tender. The conversion from the Belarussian ruble to the rubel took place at the rate of 10 Belarussian rubles per Rbl 1.

[2]At the end of 1994, Belarus maintained bilateral trade and/or payments agreements with Bulgaria, China, Cuba, the former Czech and Slovak Federal Republic, Finland, Hungary, the Democratic People's Republic of Korea, Mongolia, Poland, Slovenia, and Viet Nam. Bilateral clearing accounts have been established with all of the Baltic countries, Russia, and the other countries of the former Soviet Union.

counts at commercial banks in Belarus authorized to handle foreign exchange (authorized banks). Residents may maintain bank accounts abroad only with the permission of the NBB. Foreign exchange received by resident juridical persons as a result of foreign economic activities must be repatriated to accounts of authorized banks in Belarus, unless otherwise authorized by the NBB.

Nonresident juridical persons may maintain foreign exchange accounts with authorized banks in Belarus. These accounts may be credited with funds from abroad, proceeds from sales of goods and services in the ruble area to residents and nonresidents, debt-service payments, interest earned on balances in the accounts, funds from other foreign exchange accounts of nonresidents in Belarus, and earnings from investments in the Baltic countries, Russia, and the other countries of the former Soviet Union. These accounts may be debited for purchases of goods and services and for investments in the Baltic countries, Russia, and the other countries of the former Soviet Union, as well as for payments to residents and nonresidents. Funds from these accounts may be freely repatriated or exchanged for Belarussian rubels at the unified exchange rate through the authorized banks.

Nonresident juridical persons may also open two types of accounts in the official currency of Belarus at authorized commercial banks. The first type, "L" Accounts, may be credited with the rubel counterpart of foreign exchange sold to the NBB or authorized banks; dividends from foreign-owned enterprises or joint ventures; returns on securities; and from sales of such securities within Belarus. Funds from these accounts are freely usable in the ruble area and may be converted into foreign currency at the unified exchange rate. The second type, "N" Accounts, may be funded by proceeds from the sale of goods produced in Belarus or received from residents. Balances in these accounts may be used only for business travel expenses; to purchase inputs used for production of goods for export from Belarus; to purchase foreign exchange at the free exchange rate at auctions (up to the limit of nonresidents' initial investment plus proceeds from sales of their output in Belarus); for payment of wages; and for investment purposes according to the procedures established by legislation.

Imports and Exports

Trade with the Baltic countries, Russia, and the other countries of the former Soviet Union is conducted (1) under intergovernmental agreements; (2) through intermediation by former ministries or other agencies involved in resource distribution; (3) through enterprise deals; and (4) through commodity exchanges.

The bilateral trade agreements Belarus maintains with other countries include an appendix that specifies in volume terms the amounts of about 150 products to be delivered during the period covered by the agreement. The signatory governments guarantee that the specified volumes will be provided to the partner country. In most cases, the guarantee takes the form of state orders if corresponding state orders are in effect in the partner country.[3] Defense-related goods are excluded from trade agreements.

Trade in these products that exceeds the volume specified in the appendices and trade in products not included in the appendices of the trade agreements are mainly conducted as follows. The ministries, agencies, or self-financing wholesale trade organizations involved in controlling resource distribution periodically collect information on the demand and supply conditions regarding the products that fall in their respective areas of responsibility. They submit this information to their counterparts in the other countries to match with their lists. When trade takes place, the individual enterprises and organizations negotiate the terms of delivery.

Fifty percent of proceeds from exports in convertible currencies are subject to surrender requirements. Nonconvertible currency proceeds must be repatriated and deposited in special accounts with Belarussian banks and used for payments of imports. If deposits are not used within 20 days, they must be sold through auctions held by the NBB. By NBB Board Resolution of October 5, 1994, the 100 percent surrender requirement for export earnings received in Russian rubles has been lowered to 50 percent. Also, by the same resolution, enterprises and individuals have been permitted to open bank accounts in Russian rubles.

Resident natural and juridical persons must obtain a license to engage in foreign economic activities (licenses are issued by the Committee on Foreign Economic Relations). With the exception of goods on a short negative list (comprising mainly arms and drugs), these licensed agents may trade in any product.

Residents do not need a license or approval from the NBB to conduct foreign exchange operations related to trade, except for (1) down payments for imports or services exceeding $100,000 or the equivalent that represent more than 30 percent of the value of the goods or services imported;

---

[3]Enterprises that produce for state orders have priority access to products imported under trade agreements.

(2) import payments or export receipts not effected within 180 days of the date of shipment;[4] and (3) interest payments to nonresidents on returned down payments when an original contract is not fulfilled. Licenses or approvals for these exceptions are granted by the NBB on a case-by-case basis.

Imports of the following products require a license: medicines, herbicides, industrial waste, movie films, and imports conducted in the framework of intergovernmental trade agreements. By Resolution of the Council of Ministers of December 2, 1994, all export taxes, export licenses, and quotas have been abolished, with the exception of those mandated by international and bilateral commitments, including the customs union arrangement with the Russian Federation.

A new import tax structure was introduced on October 6, 1993 with Resolution No. 672 of the Council of Ministers. Taxes are levied on products traded under barter arrangements and on a cash basis. The rates range from 10 percent to 90 percent. The highest rate is applicable to some old automobiles, and the 80 percent rate is charged on whiskey, gin, and some other alcoholic beverages. Unprocessed leather and intermediate leather products are taxed at 30 percent and 15 percent, respectively.

Payments for and Proceeds from Invisibles

Resident individuals may purchase annually foreign exchange for tourist travel up to an amount equivalent to 25 times the minimum wage at the free market exchange rate; for travel to the Baltic countries, Russia, and the other countries of the former Soviet Union, the limit is 50 times the minimum wage. Larger amounts may be taken out with customs declaration proof that they were brought into Belarus or with a certificate from an authorized bank that they were exchanged legally. Purchases of foreign exchange for education, medical treatment, family maintenance, repatriation of salaries and wages, payments of insurance premiums, profit remittances, and purchases exceeding $10,000 require approval from the NBB. Salaries and wages earned by foreign nationals employed in joint-venture enterprises may be remitted abroad without restriction.

Post-1992 Russian banknotes up to Rub 500 may be taken abroad or brought into the country when traveling to the Baltic countries, Russia, and the other countries of the former Soviet Union; a similar restriction applies to the importation and exportation of rubel banknotes, for which the limit is Rbl 100,000 for travel to the Baltic countries and other countries. Residents of the Baltic countries, Russia, and the other countries of the former Soviet Union may pay for air and train tickets as well as hotel expenses in Russian rubles; nonresidents may be required to pay for these expenses in convertible currency.

Capital

The properties owned by foreign investors in Belarus are protected from expropriation.[5] Foreign investors are guaranteed full freedom to repatriate their initial investment capital and profits earned in Belarus. Repatriation of profits is subject to a tax of 15 percent payable in convertible currency. Foreign investment must be registered with the Committee on Foreign Economic Relations and, in the case of financial institutions, also at the NBB. At the time of registration, the enterprise obtains a license to engage in activities in a particular area of specialization and may not pursue other activities. The proportion of equity capital share by nonresidents in direct investments is not restricted, except in the financial sector, where it cannot exceed 50 percent. Joint-venture enterprises are free to set their own product prices. They may participate in foreign exchange auctions and commodity exchange transactions through authorized banks.

Nonresidents may take part in auctions of state property with their own funds. However, special coefficients that raise the price of state property for nonresidents are set by the Committee of State Property. Other coefficients are set by the Council of Ministers, or their local agencies, and the Ministry of Finance and are announced to participants before auctions take place.

Enterprises with more than 30 percent foreign capital ownership are permitted to export a certain proportion of their output and import inputs necessary for their production without restriction. These enterprises are exempted from the profit tax for three years from the first year the enterprise reports a profit. If the enterprise is deemed to be essential for the economy of Belarus by the Council of Ministers, the profit tax rate may be reduced by 50 percent for an additional three-year period.

External borrowing by residents must be registered with the Ministry of Finance, and the opening of bank accounts abroad requires approval from the NBB.

---

[4]This exception also applies to cosignatory agreements, barter and compensatory deals, and re-exports.

[5]The law on Foreign Investment of the Supreme Soviet (dated November 14, 1991) guarantees that terms offered to foreign investors would remain unchanged for at least five years.

Gold

A license is required for the exportation of gold, which is on the short list of products (together with arms, radioactive materials, and narcotics) under the strictest licensing requirements.

Changes During 1994

Exchange Arrangement

August 20. The Russian ruble ceased to be legal tender.

December 31. The use of foreign currency in local transactions was prohibited.

Imports and Exports

October 5. The ratio of surrender requirement for exports received in Russian rubles was reduced to 50 percent from 100 percent.

October 19. The surrender requirement for proceeds from exports in convertible currencies was set at 50 percent.

December 2. All export taxes, licenses, and quotas, except those mandated by international or bilateral commitments, including the customs union arrangement with the Russian Federation, were abolished.

BELGIUM AND LUXEMBOURG

(Position as of December 31, 1994)

Exchange Arrangement

The currency of Belgium is the Belgian Franc, and the currency of Luxembourg is the Luxembourg Franc. Belgium and Luxembourg are linked in a monetary association, and the Luxembourg franc is at par with the Belgian franc. Belgium and Luxembourg participate with Austria, Denmark, France, Germany, Ireland, the Netherlands, Portugal, and Spain in the exchange rate and intervention mechanism (ERM) of the European Monetary System (EMS).[1] In accordance with this agreement, Belgium and Luxembourg maintain spot exchange rates between their currencies and the currencies of the other participants within margins of 15 percent above or below the cross rates derived from the central rates expressed in European currency units (ECUs).[2]

The agreement implies that the National Bank of Belgium stands ready to buy or sell the currencies of the other participating states in unlimited amounts at specified intervention rates. On December 31, 1994, these rates were as follows:

Specified Intervention Rates per:	Belgian Francs or Luxemburg Francs	
	Upper limit	Lower limit
100 Danish kroner	627.8800	465.6650
100 Deutsche mark	2,395.2000	1,776.2000
100 French francs	714.0300	529.6600
1 Irish pound	57.7445	42.8260
100 Netherlands guilders	2,125.6000	1,576.4500
100 Portuguese escudos[3]	24.2120	17.9570
100 Spanish pesetas[4]	30.2715	22.4510

The participants in the EMS do not maintain the exchange rates for other currencies within fixed limits. However, to ensure a proper functioning of the system, they intervene in concert to smooth out fluctuations in exchange rates, the intervention currencies being each other's and the U.S. dollar.

There are no taxes or subsidies on purchases or sales of foreign exchange. On December 31, 1994, the indicative middle rate for the U.S. dollar was BF 31.87 per US$1.

Banks are allowed to engage in spot and forward exchange transactions in any currency, and they may deal among themselves and with residents and nonresidents in foreign notes and coins.

Belgium and Luxembourg formally accepted the obligations of Article VIII, Sections 2, 3, and 4 of the Fund Agreement, as from February 15, 1961.

Administration of Control

There are no exchange controls. The Belgian-Luxembourg Administrative Commission has the authority to license trade transactions; it determines import and export policy but has delegated authority to issue import and export licenses to the licensing offices of the Belgian-Luxembourg Economic Union (BLEU), one of which is located in each country. Bank supervision in Belgium is exercised by the Banking and Finance Commission and in Luxembourg, by the Luxembourg Monetary Institute (LMI).

For purposes of compiling balance of payments statistics, residents are required to transmit to the Belgian-Luxembourg Exchange Institute (BLEI) the following information on all of their professional transactions with foreign countries: amount, currency, economic nature, and country of residence of the foreign party in the transaction. For foreign payments executed or received through a bank in Belgium or Luxembourg, residents provide this information to the BLEI through their banks; for all other professional foreign transactions, residents report to the BLEI directly on a monthly basis.

Prescription of Currency

No prescription of currency requirements are in force.

Imports and Import Payments

Payments for imports may be made freely. Individual licenses are required for (1) all imports from Albania, Bulgaria, China, the Democratic People's Republic of Korea, Mongolia, the Baltic countries, Russia, and the other countries of the former Soviet

---

[1]Austria became a member of the European Union on January 1, 1995 and joined the ERM of the EMS on January 9, 1995.

[2]Effective August 2, 1993, the intervention thresholds of the currencies participating in the ERM of the EMS, except those of the deutsche mark and the Netherlands guilder, were widened from ±2.25 percent to ±15 percent around the bilateral central exchange rates; the fluctuation band of the deutsche mark and the Netherlands guilder remained unchanged at ±2.25 percent.

[3]Effective March 6, 1995, the upper and lower limits were changed to 23.3645 and 17.3285.

[4]Effective March 6, 1995, the upper and lower limits were changed to 28.1526 and 20.8795.

Union, and Viet Nam;[5] and (2) certain specified imports from all other countries,[6] including many textile and steel products, certain agricultural products and foodstuffs, coal and petroleum products, diamonds, semiprocessed gold, and weapons. All other commodities are free of license. Many commodities subject to individual licensing are also admitted without quantitative restriction. Along with other EU countries, the BLEU applies quotas on a number of textile products from non-EU countries in the framework of the Multifiber Arrangement (MFA) and also applies a system of minimum import prices to foreign steel products.

Imports from non-EU countries of most products covered by the Common Agricultural Policy (CAP) of the EU are subject to import levies, which have replaced all previous barriers to imports. Common EU regulations are also applied to imports of most other agricultural and livestock products from non-EU countries.

Payments for Invisibles

All payments for invisibles may be made freely. Domestic and foreign banknotes and coins and other means of payment may be exported freely.

Exports and Export Proceeds

Export licenses are required only for a few products, mostly of a strategic character, and for some agricultural and iron and steel products.

Foreign exchange proceeds from exports do not have to be surrendered and may be used for all payments.

Proceeds from Invisibles

There are no restrictions on the receipt of payments for services rendered to nonresidents. Domestic and foreign notes and coins and other means of payment may be imported freely.

Capital

Residents and nonresidents may export capital freely. Investments, whether direct or portfolio, may be freely made in the BLEU by nonresidents or abroad by residents. There are no restrictions on transactions in Belgian or Luxembourg francs or foreign currency securities, which may be exported or imported without formality. Banks may freely accept foreign currency deposits from residents or nonresidents.

The prior approval of the Ministry of Finance is required for issues of securities on the Belgian capital market by nonresidents and for public bids by nonresidents for the purchase or exchange of shares issued by Belgian companies.[7]

Bonds denominated in Belgium or Luxembourg francs may be issued freely on the Luxembourg capital market. After they are issued, they are reported to the LMI, mainly for statistical purposes.

Gold

Residents may freely purchase, hold, and sell gold coins and bars, at home or abroad. Imports and exports of gold in these forms by residents and nonresidents are unrestricted and free of license; licenses are required for imports of semiprocessed gold. Settlements of gold may be made freely. Imports and transactions in monetary gold are subject to a 1 percent value-added tax in Belgium.

Changes During 1994

No significant changes occurred in the exchange and trade system.

(See Appendix for a summary of trade measures introduced and eliminated on an EU-wide basis during 1994, page 554.)

---

[5]Import licenses are issued freely for a large number of products that originate in and are shipped from these countries.

[6]Most imports do not require an import license when imported from the member countries of the European Union (EU).

[7]Since January 1, 1991, this approval is no longer needed if the foreign company or individual involved is a resident of an EU country.

BELIZE

(Position as of December 31, 1994)

Exchange Arrangement

The currency of Belize is the Belize Dollar, which is pegged to the U.S. dollar, the intervention currency, at a rate of BZ$1 per US$0.50. The buying and selling rates for transactions between the Central Bank of Belize and the commercial banks are BZ$1.9937 and BZ$2.0063, respectively, per US$1. On December 31, 1994, the buying and selling rates in transactions between the banks and members of the public were BZ$2.69 and BZ$2.71, respectively, per US$1. The Central Bank quotes daily rates for the Canadian dollar, the pound sterling, and a number of currencies of member countries of CARICOM.[1] A stamp duty of 1.25 percent is levied on all conversions from the Belize dollar to a foreign currency.

Belize accepted the obligations of Article VIII, Sections 2, 3, and 4 of the Fund Agreement as from June 14, 1983.

Administration of Control

The Central Bank is responsible for administering exchange control, which applies to all countries. Authority covering a wide range of operations is delegated to the commercial banks in their capacity as authorized dealers. Only in exceptional cases or in applications involving substantial amounts is reference made directly to the Central Bank. However, all applications for foreign exchange processed by authorized dealers are regularly forwarded to the Central Bank for audit and record keeping. The Ministry of Commerce and Industry administers trade controls.

Prescription of Currency

The only prescription of currency requirement relates to a specified list of currencies[2] in which authorized intermediaries are permitted to deal with the public. Payments to a CARICOM member country must be made in the currency of that country.

Nonresident Accounts

Banks must have permission from the Central Bank to open external or foreign currency accounts. The Central Bank may also stipulate that sums to be credited or paid to foreign residents be credited to a blocked account.

Imports and Import Payments

Payments for imports require authorization from the Central Bank; in most cases such authorization is delegated to the commercial banks. For reasons of health, standardization, and protection of domestic industries, import licenses from the Ministry of Commerce and Industry are required for a number of goods—mostly food and agricultural products, and certain household and construction products; such licenses are liberally administered. There are no quota limits or other quantitative restrictions for balance of payments reasons. Most imports are subject to a stamp duty of 14 percent of the c.i.f. value. Imports by most of the public sector and by certain nonprofit entities, imports of an emergency or humanitarian nature, and goods for re-export are exempt from import duties; goods originating from the CARICOM area are also exempt.

Payments for Invisibles

There are no restrictions on payments for invisibles. Authorized dealers have the power to provide foreign exchange for such payments within certain limits. The following limits are applied to purchases of foreign exchange: (1) nonbusiness travel by residents, up to BZ$5,000 a person a calendar year; (2) business travel by residents, BZ$500 a day a person, up to a maximum of BZ$20,000 a year; (3) business or nonbusiness travel by nonresidents, BZ$500 a person a year unless payment is made from an external account or from proceeds of foreign currency; and (4) gifts, BZ$100 a donor. Requests in excess of these amounts are referred to the Central Bank, which grants all bona fide requests. Foreign exchange is provided for payment of correspondence courses by the authorized dealers when applications are properly documented.

Exports of foreign and domestic banknotes and currency are subject to limits as follows: each traveler may carry domestic banknotes up to BZ$100 and the equivalent of BZ$400 in foreign currency,

---

[1]The CARICOM countries are Antigua and Barbuda, The Bahamas, Barbados, Belize, Dominica, Grenada, Guyana, Jamaica, Montserrat, St. Kitts and Nevis, St. Lucia, St. Vincent and the Grenadines, and Trinidad and Tobago. The Central Bank quotes exchange rates for Barbados dollars, Eastern Caribbean dollars, Guyana dollars, and Trinidad and Tobago dollars.

[2]Barbados dollars, Canadian dollars, Eastern Caribbean dollars, Guyana dollars, pounds sterling, Trinidad and Tobago dollars, and U.S. dollars.

except that a visitor may take out such notes up to the amount imported. Amounts beyond these limits require the approval of the Central Bank, which is liberally granted when justified.

Exports and Export Proceeds

Export licenses are required for most export products. Export proceeds must be surrendered to authorized dealers not later than six months after the date of shipment, unless directed otherwise by the Central Bank. A small number of items are subject to an ad valorem export duty of 5 percent.[3] Re-exports and transshipments are subject to a 3 percent customs administration fee.

Proceeds from Invisibles

Foreign currency proceeds from invisibles must be sold to an authorized dealer. Travelers to Belize are free to bring in notes and coins denominated in

---

[3]The items are lobster, shrimp, conch, fish, turtles, mahogany, and wild animals. For sugar, the export duty is 2 percent.

Belize dollars up to BZ$100 a person, but imports of foreign currency are not restricted. Resident travelers are required to sell their excess holdings of foreign currencies to an authorized dealer upon returning to Belize.

Capital

All capital transfers require the approval of the Central Bank, but control is liberally administered. Foreign direct investment is encouraged, and investors benefit from a number of fiscal incentives.

Gold

Residents may not hold gold except with specific authorization from the Central Bank. Gold may be neither imported nor exported without the approval of the Central Bank.

Changes During 1994

No significant changes occurred in the exchange and trade system.

BENIN

(Position as of December 31, 1994)

Exchange Arrangement

The currency of Benin is the CFA Franc,[1] which is pegged to the French franc, the intervention currency, at the fixed rate of CFAF 1 per F 0.01. The official buying and selling rate is CFAF 100 per F 1. Exchange rates for other currencies are derived from the rate for the currency concerned in the Paris exchange market and the fixed rate between the French franc and the CFA franc. They include a bank commission of 2.5 per mil on transfers to all countries outside the West African Monetary Union (WAMU), which must be surrendered in its entirety to the Treasury. There are no taxes or subsidies on purchases or sales of foreign exchange. Forward exchange contracts may be arranged with the prior authorization of the Minister of Finance. The maturity period cannot be extended.

With the exception of those relating to gold and the repatriation of export proceeds, Benin's exchange control measures do not apply to (1) France (and its overseas departments and territories) and Monaco; and (2) all other countries whose bank of issue is linked with the French Treasury by an Operations Account (Burkina Faso, Cameroon, Central African Republic, Chad, Comoros, Congo, Côte d'Ivoire, Equatorial Guinea, Gabon, Mali, Niger, Senegal, and Togo). Hence, all payments to these countries may be made freely. All other countries are considered foreign countries. For certain controls relating to capital flows, the countries specified in this paragraph are also regarded as foreign countries.

Administration of Control

Exchange control is administered by the Directorate of Monetary and Banking Affairs in the Ministry of Finance, in conjunction with the Directorate of External Commerce in the Ministry of Commerce and Tourism. The Ministry of Finance, however, in collaboration with the BCEAO, draws up the exchange control regulations. The BCEAO is authorized to collect, either directly or through banks, financial institutions, and the Postal Administration, any information necessary to compile balance of payments statistics. All exchange transactions relating to foreign countries must be carried out by authorized intermediaries. Import licenses for goods from the African, Caribbean, and Pacific (ACP) State signatories to the Lomé Convention and from member countries of European Union (EU) and Operations Account countries have been abolished. Upon the recommendation of the Directorate of Monetary and Financial Affairs of the Ministry of Finance, exports of diamonds and other precious or semiprecious metals require authorization from the Directorate of External Commerce.

Arrears are maintained with respect to external payments.

Prescription of Currency

Because Benin is linked to the French Treasury through an Operations Account, settlements with France (as defined above), Monaco, and other countries linked to the French Treasury through an Operations Account are made in CFA francs, French francs, or the currency of any other Operations Account country. Current payments to or from The Gambia, Ghana, Guinea, Guinea-Bissau, Liberia, Mauritania, Nigeria, and Sierra Leone are normally made through the West African Clearing House. Settlements with all other countries are usually effected through correspondent banks in France, in any of the currencies of those countries or in French francs through foreign accounts in francs. There is an inoperative payment agreement with Hungary.

Nonresident Accounts

Because the BCEAO has suspended the repurchase of banknotes circulating outside the territories of the CFA franc zone, nonresident accounts may not be credited or debited with BCEAO banknotes. These accounts may not be overdrawn without the prior authorization of the Ministry of Finance. Transfers of funds between nonresident accounts are not restricted.

Imports and Import Payments

Certain imports, such as narcotics, are prohibited from all sources. Certain agencies have an import monopoly over specified commodities.

Imports of goods originating in the EU, the Operations Account countries, and countries belonging to the ACP group are free of import-licensing re-

---

[1]The CFA franc is issued by the Central Bank of West African States (BCEAO) and is the common currency in Benin, Burkina Faso, Côte d'Ivoire, Mali, Niger, Senegal, and Togo.

quirements. All merchandise imports originating in other countries are subject to prior authorization from the Directorate of Foreign Trade. Before shipment, goods from all sources are subject to inspection for quality and price.

All imports valued at more than CFAF 500,000 must be domiciled with an authorized intermediary bank. Importers may not purchase foreign exchange to pay for imports earlier than eight days before suppliers ship the goods if a documentary credit is opened, and only on the due date of payment if the goods have already been imported.

Customs duties consist of four bands (i.e., 5, 10, 15, and 20 percent).

Payments for Invisibles

Payments for invisibles to France (as defined above), Monaco, and countries linked to the French Treasury through an Operations Account are permitted freely; those to other countries are subject to the approval of the Directorate of Monetary and Financial Affairs of the Ministry of Finance, but for many types of invisibles the approval authority has been delegated to authorized intermediary banks. Authorized banks and the Postal Administration have been empowered to make payments abroad freely on behalf of residents, up to CFAF 50,000 a transfer. Payments for invisibles related to trade are permitted freely when the basic trade transaction has been approved or does not require authorization. Transfers of income accruing to nonresidents in the form of profits, dividends, and royalties are subject to prior authorization.

Residents traveling for tourism or business purposes to countries in the franc zone other than WAMU member countries are allowed to take out the equivalent of CFAF 2 million in banknotes other than the CFA franc; amounts in excess of this limit may be taken out in the form of means of payment other than banknotes. The allowances for travel to countries outside the franc zone are subject to the following regulations: (1) for tourist travel, CFAF 500,000 without limit on the number of trips or differentiation by the age of the traveler; (2) for business travel, CFAF 75,000 a day for up to one month, corresponding to a maximum of CFAF 2.25 million (business travel allowances may be combined with tourist allowances); (3) allowances in excess of these limits are subject to the authorization of the respective ministries of finance or, by delegation, the BCEAO; and (4) credit cards, which must be issued by resident financial intermediaries approved by the Ministry of Finance, may be used up to the ceilings indicated above for tourist and business travel. Returning resident travelers are required to declare all means of payment in their possession upon arrival at customs and surrender within eight days all means of payment exceeding the equivalent of CFAF 25,000. Upon departure, all residents traveling to countries that are not members of the WAMU must declare in writing all means of payment at their disposal. Nonresident travelers may re-export all means of payment other than banknotes issued abroad and registered in their name, subject to documentation that they had used funds drawn from a foreign account in CFA francs or other foreign exchange to purchase these means of payment. The re-exportation of foreign banknotes is allowed up to the equivalent of CFAF 250,000; the re-exportation of foreign banknotes above these ceilings requires documentation demonstrating either the importation of the foreign banknotes or their purchase against other means of payment registered in the name of the traveler or through the use of nonresident deposits lodged in local banks.

Upon presentation of an appropriate pay voucher, a residence permit, and documents indicating family situation, foreigners working in Benin may transfer up to 50 percent of their net salary abroad if they live with their family in Benin, or up to 80 percent if their family is living abroad.

Exports and Export Proceeds

Exports to all foreign countries, including those in the Operations Account area, must be domiciled with an authorized intermediary bank when valued at more than CFAF 500,000. Exports are permitted on the basis of a simple authorization from the Directorate of Foreign Trade. Exports of gold, diamonds, and all other precious metals, however, are subject to prior authorization from the Ministry of Finance, with the exception of articles with a small gold content, travelers' personal effects weighing less than 500 grams, and coins (fewer than ten pieces, irrespective of their face value and denomination). Prior authorization for exports of these three product categories is granted by the Directorate of Monetary and Financial Affairs of the Ministry of Finance. Receipts from exports must be collected within 180 days of the arrival of the shipment at its destination. Proceeds must be repatriated to Benin through the BCEAO and sold to authorized banks within 30 days of the contractual due date.

Proceeds from Invisibles

Proceeds from transactions in invisibles with France (as defined above), Monaco, and countries maintaining Operations Accounts with the French

Treasury may be retained. All amounts due from residents of other countries in respect of services and all income earned in those countries from foreign assets must be collected and surrendered. Resident and nonresident travelers may bring in any amount of banknotes and coins issued by the BCEAO, the Bank of France, or a bank of issue maintaining an Operations Account with the French Treasury, as well as any amount of foreign banknotes and coins (except gold coins) of countries outside the Operations Account area.[2] Residents bringing in foreign banknotes and foreign currency traveler's checks exceeding the equivalent of CFAF 25,000 must declare them to customs upon entry and sell them to an authorized intermediary bank within eight days.

Capital

Capital movements between Benin and France (as defined above), Monaco, and countries linked to the French Treasury through an Operations Account are free of exchange control; most capital transfers to all other countries require prior approval from the Minister of Finance and are restricted, but capital receipts from such countries are permitted freely.

Special controls (additional to any exchange control requirements that may be applicable) are maintained over borrowing abroad; over inward foreign direct investment and all outward investment in foreign countries; and over the issuing, advertising, or offering for sale of foreign securities in Benin. Such operations require prior authorization from the Minister of Finance. Exempt from authorization, however, are operations in connection with (1) loans backed by a guarantee from the Beninese Government, and (2) shares that are similar to, or may be substituted for, securities whose issuance or sale in Benin has already been authorized. With the exception of controls over foreign securities, these measures do not apply to France (as defined above), Monaco, member countries of the WAMU, and the countries linked to the French Treasury through an Operations Account. Special controls are also maintained over imports and exports of gold, over the soliciting of funds for deposit or investment with foreign private persons and foreign firms and institutions, and over publicity aimed at placing funds abroad or at subscribing to real estate and building operations abroad; these special controls also apply to France (as defined above), Monaco, and countries maintaining Operations Accounts.

All investments abroad by residents of Benin require prior authorization from the Minister of Finance; at least 75 percent of the investments must be financed from foreign borrowing.[3] Foreign direct investments in Benin[4] must be declared to the Minister before they are made. The Minister may request postponement of the operations within a period of two months. The full or partial liquidation of either type of investment also requires declaration. Both the making and the liquidation of investments, whether these are Beninese investments abroad or foreign investments in Benin, must be reported to the Minister and to the BCEAO within 20 days of each operation. Direct investments are defined as those that imply control of a company or enterprise. Investment that does not exceed 20 percent of the capital of a company whose shares are quoted on a stock exchange is not considered direct investment.

Borrowing by residents from nonresidents requires prior authorization from the Minister of Finance. The following are, however, exempt from this authorization: (1) loans constituting a direct investment, which are subject to prior declaration, as indicated above; (2) loans taken up by industrial firms to finance operations abroad, by international merchanting and export-import firms (approved by the Minister of Finance) to finance transit trade, or by any type of firm to finance imports and exports; (3) loans contracted by authorized intermediary banks; and (4) subject to certain conditions, loans other than those mentioned above, when the total amount outstanding of these loans, including the new borrowing, does not exceed CFAF 50 million for any one borrower. The repayment of loans not constituting a direct investment requires the special authorization of the Minister of Finance, if the loan itself was subject to such approval, but is exempt if the loan was exempt from special authorization. Lending abroad is subject to prior authorization from the Minister of Finance.

The Investment Code (Law No. 90–002 of May 9, 1990) stipulates that preferential status may be granted to foreign and domestic investments in industry, mining, fisheries, agriculture, and tourism that are deemed to contribute to national development. Fiscal benefits are extended to approved in-

---

[2]Effective August 1, 1993, the repurchase of CFAF notes of the BCEAO in circulation outside member countries of the WAMU was suspended.

[3]Including those made through foreign companies that are directly or indirectly controlled by persons in Benin and those made by branches or subsidiaries abroad of companies in Benin.

[4]Including those made by companies in Benin that are directly or indirectly under foreign control and those made by branches or subsidiaries of foreign companies in Benin.

vestors under two regimes: the preferential and the special regimes. The preferential regime consists of three categories: A, B, and C. Category A applies to small and medium-size enterprises; Category B, to large enterprises; and Category C, to very large enterprises.

Enterprises falling under Category A must have investments valued at between CFAF 20 million and CFAF 500 million and employ at least five permanent Beninese workers. These enterprises are exempt from customs duties and levies on equipment and materials during the investment period (excluding the local roads and statistical taxes), as well as from income tax for five to nine years, depending on the geographic location of their investment in Benin. Enterprises qualifying for Category B must undertake investments valued at more than CFAF 500 million (but less than CFAF 3 billion) and employ at least 20 Beninese workers. These enterprises are exempt from virtually all border taxes on imports of equipment and materials for the period the investment is being undertaken, and, for the duration of the investment, they are exempt from export taxes and from taxes on profits. Enterprises qualifying for Category C benefits must undertake investments in excess of CFAF 3 billion. They enjoy the same tax and duty privileges as Category B enterprises. In addition, enterprises in this category are guaranteed stability of tax status for the duration of the agreement.

Enterprises qualifying under the special regime are those with investments valued at between CFAF 5 million and CFAF 20 million that provide services in health, education, or public works. They benefit from a 75 percent reduction in the applicable border taxes (excluding the local roads and sta-tistical taxes) on imported equipment and materials related to their operations. The modalities of implementing this legislation are set out in Decree No. 91-2 of January 4, 1991.

Gold

Authorization from the Directorate of External Commerce, issued after a favorable ruling by the Directorate of Monetary and Financial Affairs of the Ministry of Finance, is required to hold, sell, import, export, or deal in raw diamonds and precious and semiprecious materials. In practice, residents are free to hold, acquire, and dispose of gold in any form in Benin. Imports and exports of gold from or to any other country require prior authorization from the Ministry of Finance, which is seldom granted. Exempt from this requirement are (1) imports and exports by or on behalf of the Treasury or the BCEAO; (2) imports and exports of manufactured articles containing a minor quantity of gold (such as gold-filled or gold-plated articles); and (3) imports and exports by travelers of gold articles up to a maximum weight to be determined by an Order of the Minister. Both licensed and exempt imports of gold are subject to customs declaration.

Changes During 1994

Exchange Arrangement

January 12. The CFA franc was devalued to CFAF 100 per F 1 from CFAF 50 per F 1.

Imports and Import Payments

February 1. The number of tariff bands was changed to four (5, 10, 15, and 20 percent).

BHUTAN

(Position as of December 31, 1994)

Exchange Arrangement

The currency of Bhutan is the Ngultrum, the external value of which is pegged to the Indian rupee. Indian rupees also circulate in Bhutan at a rate of Nu 1 per Rs 1. The rates for currencies other than Indian rupees are determined on the basis of the prevailing quotations by the Reserve Bank of India for those currencies. If no large transactions are involved, exchange rates for other currencies may be determined on the basis of the most recent quotations by the Reserve Bank of India. No other exchange rates apply to international transactions, and there are no subsidies or taxes on exchange transactions. On December 31, 1994, the buying and selling rates of the ngultrum for the U.S. dollar (cash) were Nu 30.85 and Nu 31.85, respectively, per US$1; the buying and selling rates of the ngultrum for the U.S. dollar (traveler's checks) were Nu 31.00 and Nu 31.70, respectively, per US$1. There are no arrangements for forward cover against exchange rate risk operating in the official or the commercial banking sector.

Administration of Control

The Ministry of Finance controls external transactions and provides foreign exchange for most current and capital transactions. The Ministry of Finance has delegated to the Royal Monetary Authority the authority to release foreign exchange (other than Indian rupees) for current transactions. The Royal Monetary Authority is charged with implementing the surrender requirements for proceeds from merchandise exports and approving the use of foreign exchange for imports.

Prescription of Currency

There are no regulations prescribing the use of specific currencies in external receipts and payments.

Imports and Import Payments

Except for imports of large capital goods for which clearance by the Ministry of Finance is required, there are no restrictions on payments or transfers relating to any current account transaction with India. Clearance by the Ministry of Finance is required for the importation of capital and intermediate goods from third countries. The release of foreign exchange is managed separately by the Royal Monetary Authority upon recommendation by the Ministry of Finance. The Royal Monetary Authority does not provide foreign exchange to importers of consumer goods; the latter must make their own arrangements to obtain the foreign exchange before an import license is issued.

Customs duties are levied on imports other than those from India.

Exports and Export Proceeds

There are no export taxes. Exports to countries other than India receive a rebate at one of four rates ranging from 5 percent to 20 percent of the c.i.f. value, with the lowest rate applying to unprocessed primary products and the highest rate applying to processed products. Exports of antiques of Bhutanese origin require government approval. Proceeds of exports in currencies other than the Indian rupee must be surrendered to the Royal Monetary Authority either directly or through the Bank of Bhutan within 90 days.

Payments for and Proceeds from Invisibles

Most invisible payments, other than those made in Indian rupees, must be approved by the Royal Monetary Authority. All receipts from invisible transactions in currencies other than the Indian rupee must be surrendered to the Royal Monetary Authority.

Capital

All capital transactions must be approved by the Ministry of Finance.

Gold

There are no specific regulations on transactions in gold.

Changes During 1994

No significant changes occurred in the exchange and trade system.

BOLIVIA

(Position as of December 31, 1994)

Exchange Arrangement

The currency of Bolivia is the Boliviano. The exchange rate (the official selling rate) is determined at auctions held daily by the Central Bank of Bolivia. This official exchange rate applies to all foreign exchange operations in Bolivia. The auctions are conducted by the Committee for Exchange and Reserves (Comité de Cambio y Reservas) in the Central Bank. Before each auction, the Committee decides on the amount of foreign exchange to be auctioned and a floor price below which the Central Bank will not accept any bids. This floor price is the official exchange rate and is based on the exchange rates of the deutsche mark, Japanese yen, pound sterling, and U.S. dollar. The Central Bank is required to offer in all auctions unitary lots of US$5,000 or multiples of this amount; the minimum allowable bid is US$5,000. Successful bidders are charged the exchange rate specified in their bid. In general, the spreads between the maximum and minimum bids have been less than 2 percent. On December 31, 1994, the official selling rate was Bs 4.70 per US$1.

Sales of foreign exchange by the Central Bank to the public are subject to a commission of Bs 0.01 per US$1 over its buying rate. Except for the requirement to surrender the net proceeds from the exportation of goods and services, all banks, exchange houses, companies, and individuals may buy and sell foreign exchange freely. Successful bids channeled through the banking system are voided if the banking institution submitting the bid is not complying with the legal reserve requirement on deposits at the time of the auction. However, banks must maintain a balanced spot position in foreign exchange at all times and sell to the Central Bank any excess balance at the end of each day. All public sector institutions, including public enterprises, must purchase foreign exchange for imports of goods and services through the Central Bank auction market.

There is a parallel but tolerated exchange market, in which the buying and selling exchange rates on December 31, 1994, were Bs 4.69 and Bs 4.71, respectively, per US$1. There are no arrangements for forward cover against exchange rate risk operating in the official or the commercial banking sector.

Bolivia formally accepted the obligations of Article VIII, Sections 2, 3, and 4 of the Fund Agreement, as from June 5, 1967.

Administration of Control

The Central Bank is in charge of operating the auction market for foreign exchange. It is also the enforcing agency for export surrender requirements as well as for other exchange control regulations. The Ministry of Finance, together with the Central Bank, is in charge of approving public sector purchases of foreign exchange for debt-service payments.

Prescription of Currency

There are no prescription of currency requirements. Settlements are usually made in U.S. dollars or other convertible currencies. Payments between Bolivia and Argentina, Brazil, Chile, Colombia, Ecuador, Mexico, Paraguay, Peru, Uruguay, and Venezuela must be made through accounts maintained with each other by the Central Bank of Bolivia and the central bank of the country concerned, within the framework of the multilateral clearing system of the Latin American Integration Association (LAIA).

Imports and Import Payments

All goods may be freely imported, with the exception of those controlled for reasons of public health or national security. Restrictions on imports of sugar were eliminated on October 13, 1992.

Bolivia has a general uniform tariff of 10 percent. A tariff rate of 5 percent is applied to capital goods, and a rate of 2 percent is applied to imports of books and printed material. Wheat and investment-related products covered by the Investment Code and the Hydrocarbons Law are exempt from the import tariff.[1]

Payments for Invisibles

There are no restrictions on payments for invisibles. Profit remittances abroad are subject to a 12.5 percent tax (which is computed as equivalent to the 25 percent income tax times the presumed net profit of 50 percent of the amount remitted). Residents traveling by air to neighboring countries are required to pay a travel tax of Bs 100; the tax on travel to other foreign destinations is Bs 150. Public

---

[1]Effective February 14, 1992, the charge on capital goods was raised to 5 percent for the following two years.

sector purchases of foreign exchange for debt service must be approved by the Ministry of Finance and the Central Bank. Outward remittances of profit are governed by the provisions of Decision Nos. 24 and 80 of the Cartagena Agreement.

Exports and Export Proceeds

All goods may be freely exported. All proceeds from exports of the public and private sectors must be sold to the Central Bank at the official exchange rate within three days of receipt, with the exception of reasonable amounts deducted for foreign exchange expenditures undertaken to effect the export transaction. Exports other than hydrocarbons are subject to an inspection fee of 1.55 percent for nontraditional products and 1.6 percent for traditional products. A system of tax rebates reimburses exporters for indirect taxes and import duty paid on inputs of exported goods and services, including the duty component of depreciation of capital goods used. Exporters of small items whose value in Bolivia's annual exports is less than $3 million receive tax rebates of 2 percent or 4 percent of the f.o.b. export value under a simplified procedure, and other exporters receive tax and import duty rebates based on annually determined coefficients that reflect their documented cost structure. All exports of goods and services must be effected through documentary letters of credit drawn on domestic banks.

Proceeds from Invisibles

Banks, exchange houses, hotels, and travel agencies may retain the proceeds from their foreign exchange purchases from invisible transactions, including those from tourism. They are required, however, to report daily their purchases on account of these transactions.

Capital

Foreign exchange for outward capital transfers by residents or nonresidents can be purchased only from the commercial banks or from the Central Bank. Inward capital transfers may be made freely, but government receipts of transfers and grants and all proceeds of borrowings from foreign public sector agencies must be surrendered to the Central Bank. All foreign credits, including suppliers' credits, to government agencies and autonomous entities, and credits to the private sector with official guarantees are subject to prior authorization by the Ministry of Finance and to control by the Central Bank. Under Supreme Decree No. 19732 of August 11, 1983, finan-

cial institutions in Bolivia may make loans in the form of credits denominated in foreign currency for imports of capital goods and inputs for the external sector with resources from international financial institutions, foreign government agencies, or external lines of credit. Under Supreme Decree No. 21060 of August 29, 1985, banks are authorized to conduct foreign trade operations, such as letters of credit, bonds and guarantees, advances and acceptances, loans for required financing with their correspondents abroad, and other operations generally accepted in international banking, in favor of the country's exporters and importers.

Banks are allowed to hold foreign exchange positions up to the value of their net worth minus fixed assets.

Foreign investments in Bolivia, except those involving petroleum and mining, are governed by the provisions of the Investment Law. In September 1990, the Investment Law of December 14, 1981 was replaced by another investment law, under which domestic and foreign investors are treated equally (Law No. 1182 on Investment). The law is administered by the National Investment Institute. Investments in petroleum and mining are governed by the Hydrocarbons Law and the Mining Law. Certain foreign investments are subject to Decision Nos. 24 and 103 of the Cartagena Agreement.

Gold

Under Supreme Decree No. 21060 of August 29, 1985, gold may be traded freely, subject to a tax of 3 percent on the gross value of sale of gold bullion (Supreme Decree No. 23394, February 3, 1993).

Changes During 1994

Payments for Invisibles

January 1. Profit remittances abroad were subject to a 12.5 percent tax, which is computed as equivalent to the 25 percent income tax times the presumed net profit of 50 percent of the amount remitted (Law No. 1606: Modifications of Tax System Law No. 843, December 22, 1994).

Exports and Export Proceeds

December 12 (and *January 30, 1995*). The system of indirect tax and duty drawback was revised. Exporters of small items whose value in Bolivia's annual exports is less than $3 million receive tax rebates of 2 percent or 4 percent of the f.o.b. export value under a simplified procedure, and other exporters receive tax and import duty rebates based on annually determined coefficients that reflect their documented cost structure (Supreme Decree No. 23899 of December 12, 1994 and Supreme Decree No. 23944 of January 30, 1995).

Capital

June 5. New regulations on foreign exchange position were introduced, specifying that banks may hold foreign exchange positions up to the value of their net worth minus fixed assets.

BOTSWANA

(Position as of December 31, 1994)

Exchange Arrangement

The currency of Botswana is the Botswana Pula. Its external value in terms of the U.S. dollar, the intervention currency, is determined with reference to a weighted basket of currencies comprising the SDR and currencies of the country's major trading partners. On December 31, 1994, the closing middle rate for the U.S. dollar was P 2.7174 per US$1; on the same date, the rate for the SDR was P 3.9635 per SDR 1. Buying and selling rates for certain other dealing currencies[1] are quoted on the basis of their rates against the U.S. dollar in international markets. For information only, middle rates are quoted for certain other currencies.[2] There are no taxes or subsidies on purchases or sales of foreign exchange.

External loans undertaken by parastatals before October 1, 1990 have been protected from exchange rate movements under a Foreign Exchange Risk-Sharing Scheme; the scheme does not apply to new loans undertaken by parastatals subsequent to October 1, 1990. At the end of 1994, the scheme applied to 37 outstanding loans. Under the scheme, risks associated with exchange rate fluctuations up to 4 percent are fully borne by the borrower, while the next 6 percent and the following 5 percent of fluctuations are shared between the borrower and the Government on a 50:50 and 25:75 basis, respectively. Risks associated with exchange rate fluctuations in excess of 15 percent are fully borne by the Government. The scheme is symmetrical in that the borrower and the Government share any gains from an appreciation in the external value of the pula on the same basis. Forward exchange cover is also offered by the commercial banks. Forward cover may be given in respect of the foreign currency proceeds derived from the exportation of goods for at least three months and, in some cases, for up to six months.

Administration of Control

Exchange control is applicable to transactions with all countries. The Minister of Finance and Development Planning has delegated most of the administration of exchange controls to the Bank of Botswana (the central bank). The latter, in turn, has delegated considerable powers to banks appointed as authorized dealers. Since January 1, 1994, remittances for payments of imports of goods and services have been handled by the commercial banks without reference to the Bank of Botswana.

Prescription of Currency

Payments to or from residents of foreign countries must normally be made or received in a foreign currency or through a nonresident-held pula account in Botswana.

Imports and Import Payments

Botswana is a member of the Southern African Customs Union (SACU) with Lesotho, Namibia, South Africa, and Swaziland, and there are generally no import restrictions on goods moving among the five countries. The arrangement provides for the free movement of goods and the right of transit among members, as well as a common external tariff. Certain imported goods, including firearms, ammunition, fresh meat, and some agricultural and horticultural products, require permits regardless of the country of supply. There are no restrictions on payments for authorized imports. Goods of domestic origin may move freely between Botswana and Zimbabwe by virtue of a customs agreement of 1956, provided they meet certain local value-added requirements and are not intended for re-export. Import shipments exceeding P 2,500 require documentation before foreign exchange is released.

Applications for forward purchases of foreign currency to cover payment for imports when the contract covers a period exceeding six months must be referred to the Bank of Botswana.

Exports and Export Proceeds

Certain exports are subject to licensing, mainly for revenue reasons. Proceeds from exports must be received in a foreign currency or from a nonresident pula account within six months of the date of exportation. Retention of export proceeds for up to one year to finance certain transactions may be permitted by the Bank of Botswana on a case-by-case basis. The value of goods that can be given as gifts to nonresidents is limited to P 3,000 per year. A few

---

[1]Deutsche mark, pounds sterling, South African rand, Swiss francs, and Zimbabwe dollars.

[2]Australian dollars, Canadian dollars, French francs, Japanese yen, Netherlands guilders, Norwegian kroner, Swedish kronor, European Currency Units, and SDRs.

items, such as precious and semiprecious stones, require permits before they can be exported.

Payments for and Proceeds from Invisibles

Payments to nonresidents for current transactions, although subject to control, are not restricted. Authority to approve a range of current payments within limits (i.e., basic exchange allowances) is delegated to commercial banks; any remittances in excess of basic exchange allowances must be referred to the Bank of Botswana for prior approval. Once the bona fide nature of applications has been established and all other requirements have been fulfilled by the applicant, remittances are approved. The basic exchange allowance for tourist travel by permanent residents is the equivalent of P 24,000 a calendar year for an adult (P 12,000 for a child). The allowance for business travel by permanent and temporary residents is P 1,000 a day, up to a maximum of P 70,000 a calendar year. Permanent residents may use credit cards in Botswana for settlement of both pula and foreign currency liabilities; airline tickets may be purchased directly from travel agents or be remitted from abroad, and they are not counted as part of the annual travel allowance. The amount of unused foreign currency for travel that a resident may retain for future travel use is the equivalent of P 2,000 in currency or traveler's checks; any excess amount must be surrendered within six months of the date of return. The basic foreign study allowance for permanent residents to cover maintenance and incidental expenses other than fees or tuition is P 5,000 a month a person and P 7,500 a month a family, with a vacation travel allowance of P 2,000 a year. A temporary resident employed on a contractual basis may remit abroad annually, without reference to the Bank of Botswana, P 25,000 or 65 percent of total eligible earnings, whichever is greater; the limit applicable to a self-employed temporary resident is P 50,000. The period during which temporary residents are allowed to remit their earnings abroad is a block of 36 months, or the period of employment, whichever is shorter. Separately, travelers residing in Botswana may take out domestic banknotes and foreign currency in amounts of P 2,000 and P 5,000 a trip, respectively, and may freely bring in any amount of domestic banknotes and coins. Visitors may take out any foreign currency that they brought in with them in addition to a maximum of P 500 a trip in domestic currency.

The Bank of Botswana may authorize residents to maintain foreign currency accounts with banks abroad in cases where there is a proven commercial need for such a facility.

Capital

Pension and life insurance funds may invest up to one-half of their funds abroad, subject to the requirement of 12 month's advance notification to Bank of Botswana of intention to repatriate funds. Applications for investment abroad of other funds are treated on their merits and in light of possible benefits to Botswana. Foreign inward direct investment in new or existing businesses is generally encouraged but must be financed with funds from external sources. On disinvestment by a nonresident, the Bank of Botswana allows immediate repatriation of proceeds up to a maximum of P 50 million. The excess may be required to be repatriated in installments over a period not exceeding three years. Authorized dealers may approve remittances of dividends/profits without referring to the Bank of Botswana. Remittances of interim dividends are permitted only for companies listed in the Botswana Share Market. Inward portfolio investment is also permitted in shares issued by companies quoted in the Botswana Share Market, provided the funds for financing the acquisitions originate with a nonresident source. Nonresident-controlled companies incorporated in Botswana may make similar investments (referred to as internal portfolio investments), which need not be financed with funds from external sources. In the case of both inward and internal portfolio investments, a shareholder or his nominee may not acquire an interest in excess of 5 percent of the company's paid-up stock. Total portfolio holdings by nonresidents, including nonresident-controlled companies, may not exceed 49 percent of the "free stock" of a local company, that is, total stock issued and paid up less stock held by direct investors. Nonresident-controlled companies may also invest with domestic currency funds in any securities issued by the Bank of Botswana. Nonresident-controlled companies (including branches of foreign companies) are permitted to borrow locally from all sources up to P 500,000. Applications for local finance in excess of P 500,000 by non-resident-controlled companies may be considered by the Bank of Botswana, provided that the resulting debt-equity ratio does not exceed 4:1. Borrowed funds may be used for working capital purposes or for acquisition of new fixed assets (e.g., plant, machinery, equipment, and buildings); these funds may not be used to acquire financial assets. Equity is defined as paid-up capital, reserves, and retained earnings. The 4:1 limit may be exceeded by nonresident-controlled manufacturing companies, if there is evidence that the project will provide a specialist skill to Botswana or will create significant employment. Any external borrowing by a local business must have at least a three-month grace period. Departing temporary residents are entitled to a basic remittable terminal allowance of up to P 25,000. Double taxation agreements exist between Botswana and South Africa, Sweden, and the United Kingdom.

Permanent residents are eligible for an emigration allowance of up to P 150,000 in addition to household and personal effects whose value does not exceed P 75,000. Applications for remittances in excess of these amounts are dealt with by the Bank of Botswana. Such remittances are normally authorized if the amount is not too large; if the amount is excessive, remittances may be permitted in installments over three years.

Nonresident-controlled companies are allowed to invest domestically generated funds in pula as well as those from external sources in any securities issued by the Bank of Botswana.

Self-employed temporary residents may remit abroad up to 65 percent of the previous year's taxable income, or P 50,000, whichever is greater.

Changes During 1994

No significant changes occurred in the exchange and trade system.

BRAZIL

(Position as of December 31, 1994)

Exchange Arrangement

The currency of Brazil is the Real (R$), the external value of which is determined by demand and supply in the interbank exchange market, although the Central Bank has set a floor for the external value of the real in the commercial market at a rate of R$1 per US$1.[1] Transactions in the exchange market are carried out by banks, brokers, and tourist agencies authorized to deal in foreign exchange; the tourist agencies and brokers deal only in banknotes and traveler's checks. The exchange rates are freely negotiated between the authorized institutions and their clients in all operations. On December 31, 1994, the buying and selling rates in the interbank exchange market were R$0.844 and R$0.846, respectively, per US$1. The same exchange rates apply to "agreement dollars" used for settlements with bilateral agreement countries. Rates for other currencies are based on the U.S. dollar rates in Brazil and the rates for the currencies concerned in the international market.

A "financial transactions tax" (*imposto sobre operações de crédito, câmbio e seguro, e sobre operações relativas a títulos e valores mobiliarios* (IOF)) of 25 percent is levied on exchange operations effected for the payment of imports of services.

Limits for the short position of banks are determined according to the size of the bank's total net assets indicated in the financial demonstrations of June and December. No limit is imposed on the long position, but authorized banks must deposit overnight, at the Central Bank, the amounts needed to eliminate overbought positions that exceed the equivalent of US$50 million. The limit for the long position of brokers is fixed at US$1 million; they may not maintain a short position. The banks are permitted to buy and sell foreign exchange to each other without restriction; such transactions may be carried out either on a spot basis by cable or on a forward basis and must be settled within 2 working days for spot transactions or within 180 days for forward transactions. Banks may pay their clients a premium, corresponding to the expected variation of the domestic currency in relation to the currency subject of negotiation, by reason of forward operations. In addition, when an exchange contract for forward settlement is concluded, banks can provide short-term financing to exporters by providing domestic currency in advance, before or after the shipment of goods.

Administration of Control

The National Monetary Council is responsible for formulating overall foreign exchange policy. In accordance with the guidelines established by the council, exchange controls, regulations affecting foreign capital, and the management of international reserves are under the jurisdiction of the Central Bank. The Ministry of Planning enforces limits on foreign borrowing by the public sector.

The foreign trade policy is formulated by the Ministry of Industry, Trade, and Tourism, implemented by the Secretariat of Foreign Trade (SECEX) and carried out by the Technical Department of Commercial Interchange (DTIC).

The Technical Department of Tariffs (DTT) of the Ministry of Industry, Trade, and Tourism is responsible for formulating guidelines for tariff policy. The DTT also decides on changes in customs duties under the provisions of existing legislation. The Ministry of Finance coordinates public sector import policy.

Prescription of Currency

In principle, prescription of currency is related to the country of origin of imports or the country of final destination of exports, unless otherwise prescribed or authorized. Settlements with bilateral payments agreement countries[2] are made in clearing dollars through the relevant agreement account. Payments between Brazil and Argentina, Bolivia, Chile, Colombia, the Dominican Republic, Ecuador, Mexico, Paraguay, Peru, Uruguay, and Venezuela can be made through special central bank accounts within the framework of the multilateral clearing system of the Latin American Integration Association (LAIA). Settlements with countries with which Brazil has no payments agreements and no special payments arrangements are made in U.S. dollars or other freely usable currencies.

---

[1] The real replaced the cruzeiro real at a conversion rate of 2,750 cruzeiros real to R$1 on July 1, 1994.

[2] Bilateral accounts are also maintained with Hungary and Romania, but settlements are made in third-country currencies every 90 days, and interest rates payable on balances are based on those in the international capital market.

Imports and Import Payments

All importers must be registered with the SECEX, and goods may be imported only by registered firms or persons. Imports are grouped into the following three broad categories: (1) imports that do not require prior administrative documentation, including samples without commercial value and certain educational materials; (2) imports that require an import certificate issued by the DTIC; and (3) prohibited imports (luxury boats with an initial sale price of US$3,500 or more, agrochemical products not authorized under Brazilian regulations, and certain drugs that are not licensed for reasons of security, health, morality, or industrial policy). Importers are permitted to purchase foreign exchange in the exchange market within 180 days of the settlement date.

There is also a limit on the direct importation and purchase on the domestic market of consumer goods by the public sector (the Government, autonomous agencies, and public enterprises).[3]

Most imports require prior approval from the DTIC, which is usually given promptly to registered importers of nonprohibited items.[4] The DTIC is authorized to levy a processing fee of up to 0.9 percent on the value of import certificates; as a rule, certificates are valid for 60 days, 90 days, or 180 days, depending on the product. The DTIC issues clearance certificates for certain groups of commodities to special bonded warehouse importers. Import certificates for a number of specified imports may be obtained after the commodities have been landed but before they clear customs.

The importation of certain products requires the approval of the Ministry of Science and Technology. For some products, eligibility for exemption from import duties may be precluded by the existence of satisfactory domestic equivalents (*similares nacionais*).

Goods imported into the Manaus and Tabatinga free zones are subject to an annual quota. Foreign goods up to the equivalent of US$600 imported into the Manaus free trade zone can be transferred to other parts of Brazil (as a passenger's baggage) free of import taxes.

The SECEX may approve applications for payment for imports of any goods at terms of up to 720 days from the date of shipment without prior authorization from the Central Bank. External financing at terms in excess of 720 days for imports must be authorized by the Central Bank, which will evaluate them in the light of foreign debt policy. Payment of the amount financed and accrued interest may be made only upon presentation of a certificate of authorization and a payment schedule issued by the Department of Foreign Capital (FIRCE) of the Central Bank. On October 19, 1994, the time to settle anticipatory settlements for critical imports was set at 30 days.

Exchange contracts may be settled within 180 days. The drafts, or letters of credit, relative to such contracts must be settled on maturity against the presentation of the appropriate documents by the importer. Official education and research institutions and the Ministry of Health may settle contracts within 360 days following the same rules. Exchange contracts for imports financed under letters of credit must be closed on the date of settlement or two working days before the maturity date of the letters of credit. Official education and research institutions and the Ministry for Health may settle exchange contracts up to 360 days prior to the maturity date.

Payments for Invisibles

Payments for current invisibles related to income from foreign capital, royalties, and technical assistance are governed by the provisions of the Foreign Investment Law, Law No. 4131 of September 3, 1962. In addition to certain restrictions on remittances stipulated in that law, limits are placed on remittances of all royalties and technical assistance fees (see below). Payments for current invisibles not covered by current regulations require approval from the Central Bank's Exchange Department (DECAM) or the FIRCE; remittances are authorized freely, subject to the presentation of supporting documents as evidence that a bona fide current transaction is involved.

Prior to October 1994, Brazilian residents temporarily staying abroad were permitted to purchase foreign exchange up to the equivalent of US$4,000 a month in the foreign exchange market; this limit was eliminated on October 19, 1994.

Remittances abroad of income from foreign direct investments and reinvestments and remittances in respect of royalties and technical assistance are governed by Decree No. 55762 of February 17, 1965, which contains the regulations implementing the

---

[3]Under instructions issued by the Economic Development Council, federal ministries and subordinate agencies and public enterprises are required to submit, for approval by the president, an annual investment program specifying their expected import requirements.

[4]Selected imports are exempt from the prior approval requirement, including imports to the free trade zone of Manaus, wheat and petroleum imports, imports under the drawback scheme, and imports of goods included in trade agreements negotiated with LAIA member countries.

Foreign Investment Law. Remittances are allowed only when the foreign capital concerned, including reinvestments, and the contracts for patents and trademarks and for technical, scientific, and administrative assistance are registered with the FIRCE in accordance with the established rules (see section on Capital, below). The registration of contracts or deeds for technical assistance or the use of patents or trademarks is subject to approval by the National Institute of Industrial Property. Remittances of interest on loans and credits and of related amortization payments are permitted freely in accordance with the terms stipulated in the respective contract and recorded in the certificate of registration. Profit remittances are subject to the withholding income tax at a rate of 15 percent or at the rate determined by the agreements concluded with the country concerned for the purpose of avoiding double taxation. Amounts due as royalties for patents or for the use of trademarks, as well as for technical, scientific, and administrative assistance and the like, may be deducted from income tax liability to determine the taxable income, up to the limit of 5 percent of gross receipts in the first five years of the company's operation; amounts exceeding this limit are considered profits. The percentages are the same as those established in Brazil's tax laws for determining the maximum permissible deductions for such expenses.

Purchasers of foreign exchange for a number of current invisibles are subject to the financial transaction tax of 25 percent. The financial transaction tax applicable to purchases of foreign exchange for payments of contracts involving transfers of technology that are registered with the National Institute of Industrial Property was reduced to zero from 25 percent in 1994.

Travelers may take out domestic and foreign banknotes without restriction but must declare to customs any amount over US$10,000 or the equivalent in other currencies. Foreign tourists leaving Brazil may buy foreign currency up to 50 percent of the amount exchanged into domestic currency during the visit.

Exports and Export Proceeds

Exports of certain goods require the prior approval of the SECEX, while exports of others, such as hides of wild animals in any form, are prohibited. Exports requiring approval include those effected through bilateral accounts, exports without exchange cover, exports on consignment, re-exports, commodities for which minimum export prices are fixed by the SECEX, and exports re-

quiring prior authorization from government agencies. In January 1993, the authorities introduced a computerized system of export-licensing customs clearance and exchange clearance controls. This Integrated Foreign Trade System (*Sistema Integrado de Comércio Exterior*—SISCOMEX), introduced by Decree No. 660, dated September 25, 1992 and implemented on January 4, 1993, integrates the activities related to registration, monitoring, and control of foreign trade operations in a single computerized flow of information. The SISCOMEX comprises, basically, two subsystems (exports and imports). The exports subsystem has eliminated, for more than 90 percent of Brazilian exports, all paperwork (forms, licenses, and certificates), allowing exporters, carriers, banks, and brokers to register the various stages of an export process directly through the interlinked computers of the SECEX, customs, and the Central Bank. The import subsystem is being developed.

Prior to October 1994, foreign exchange contracts covering transactions could be concluded either 180 days before the goods were shipped or within 180 days of shipment and needed to be settled within 5 working days of payment abroad. Pre-export financing could be obtained either through a local bank against exchange contracts up to a maximum period of 180 days or through the foreign supplier, who could prepay for imports before the goods arrived. On October 19, 1994, the regulations governing anticipatory export settlements were tightened, and export prefinancing was banned in respect of operations with terms exceeding 720 days. The time for anticipatory settlements was reduced to 90 days from 180 days for large exporters (exporting more than US$10 million a year) and to 150 days for small exporters.

Proceeds from Invisibles

Exchange proceeds from current invisibles must be sold to the authorized banks at the prevailing market rate. Travelers may freely bring in domestic and foreign currency notes but must declare to customs any values over US$10,000 or the equivalent in other currencies.

Capital

Brazilian banks are permitted to sell foreign exchange to Brazilian investors in MERCOSUR countries in the exchange market.

Capital inflows in the form of financial loans under National Monetary Council Resolution No. 63, as amended, or under the provision of Law No. 4131 on foreign investment, require prior approval from the Central Bank. Prior approval from the Central Bank is required for borrowing by the private or public sector when the foreign funds originate from official financial institutions abroad; when the transaction is to be guaranteed by the national Treasury or, on its behalf, by any official credit institution; and for other foreign borrowing by the public sector (that is, the Government, autonomous agencies, and public enterprises). In addition, prior approval from the Central Bank is required for borrowing by the private sector when the funds originate abroad. Proceeds of foreign borrowing converted into domestic currency are subject to a financial transaction tax of 7 percent (increased from 3 percent on October 19, 1994). Otherwise, inward transfers are unrestricted and free of control, although subsequent use of the proceeds for the acquisition of certain domestic assets may be restricted.

There is a separate regime for inward portfolio investment. Portfolio investment by foreign investors in fixed-income instruments is restricted to a single class of fixed-income funds, and these instruments are subject to a transaction tax of 9 percent (increased from 5 percent on October 19, 1994). For the purposes of the repatriation and remittance of income, however, inward transfers of foreign capital and the reinvestment of profits on foreign capital must be registered with the FIRCE. Foreign capital is defined for this purpose as (1) goods, machinery, and equipment used to produce goods or render services that have entered the country without an initial corresponding expenditure of foreign exchange; and (2) financial and monetary resources brought into the country for investment in economic pursuits, provided that, in either case, the owner is a person or firm residing or domiciled abroad or with headquarters abroad.

Foreign capital other than capital invested in Brazilian securities is classified, for purposes of registration, as direct investments or loans and includes reinvested profits from foreign capital. Direct investment is defined as the foreign capital that constitutes part of the corporate capital and participates directly in the risk inherent in an economic undertaking. Foreign capital that is not part of the corporate capital of any enterprise is considered to be a loan, except portfolio investments. Any loan obtained to purchase capital goods abroad is considered import financing, whether financed by the manufacturer (suppliers' credit) or by a third party.

Basically, foreign investments in the Brazilian capital market may be made through one of the five alternatives established under National Monetary Council Resolution 1289, Annexes I–V, dated March 20, 1987. Investment Companies (Annex I) are open to natural persons and companies, and residents domiciled or headquartered abroad. Such companies take the form of authorized capital corporations whose objective is to invest in diversified securities portfolios. They are managed by investment banks, brokerage firms, or securities and exchange dealers. Investment Funds (Annex II) are open to natural persons and companies, and residents domiciled or headquartered abroad, as well as to funds or other foreign collective investment entities. The funds originate from a fund of resources to be invested in a securities and exchange portfolio, established as an open fund without legal representation. Annex III is a Diversified Stock Portfolio managed by an investment bank, a brokerage firm, or a securities and exchange dealer, headquartered in Brazil and owned jointly with a foreign institution. The minimum participation in investment companies by foreign firms or individuals is US$1,000. Portfolio investments may also be made through the purchase of quotas of the Investment Fund—Foreign Capital. The minimum participation in this fund is US$5,000, and invested capital may be repatriated freely. Funds and other collective investment entities established abroad (including pension funds, portfolios belonging to financial institutions and insurance companies, and mutual investment funds) may maintain portfolios of bonds and other securities in Brazil once the constitutions and administrations of these entities have been approved by the Central Bank and the Securities and Exchange Commission (Annex IV). Through the mechanism of Depository Receipts (Annex V), it is possible to purchase abroad certificates representing stocks of a domestic public company (open capital). These papers represent the securitizations of the stocks of an issuing company. The depository receipts are issued abroad when a foreign importer or a Brazilian investor acquires stocks of a Brazilian company and deposits them, on custody, in a local custodian bank, which then instructs the depository bank abroad to issue the corresponding depository receipts. Portfolio investment in fixed-income instruments may be made through the purchase of quotas of the Investment Fund Foreign Capital. Portfolio investments are exempt from the capital gains tax, but profits earned by foreign investors are subject to a 15 percent income tax. Invested capital may be repatriated freely. In October 1994, a financial transaction tax of 1 percent was imposed on new foreign investment in the stock market. The issuance of debentures that can be converted into stocks in domestic enterprises is permitted. Externally financed nonprofit organizations are permitted to undertake debt-for-nature swaps.

Investments made in the form of goods are subject to approval and registration at the Central Bank. To register loans made in a foreign currency, the interest rate must correspond to that prevailing in the loan's original market; the amortization schedule must not be disproportionately heavy in the early stages of repayment.

Reinvestments are defined as the profits of companies established in Brazil and accruing to persons or companies residing abroad when they have been reinvested in the same companies that produced them or in another sector of the Brazilian economy. The registration of reinvested profits is made simultaneously in Brazilian currency and the currency of the country to which the profits could have been remitted. The conversion is calculated at the average exchange rate prevailing on the date the profits are reinvested. Special regulations govern borrowing abroad. Under National Monetary Council Resolution No. 63 (as amended), private, commercial, investment, and development banks and the Banco Nacional de Desenvolvimento Econômico e Social may be authorized to take up foreign currency credits abroad for domestic re-lending in order to finance working capital. Safeguards against excessive use of such credits include limitations on the foreign obligations that each bank may assume (related to the terms of the credit and the size of the bank) and the provision that the ultimate borrower must agree to bear the exchange risk. Financial and nonfinancial institutions are authorized to obtain resources from abroad by issuing commercial papers, notes, and bonds, including securities, that can be converted into stocks. Brazilian banks located abroad are allowed to issue medium- and long-term certificates of deposit, and exporters are allowed to issue medium-term debt instruments secured with future export receipts. All other financial loans in foreign currency are governed by the general provisions of Law No. 4131 on foreign investment. Loans contracted under this law also require prior authorization from the Central Bank, but the Central Bank does not undertake to provide specific exchange cover for them. Loans contracted under Resolution No. 63 and Law No. 4131 must have a minimum term of 36 months. Loans are authorized only if the amount and the maturity conform to requirements established from time to time by the Central Bank, which permits the total of loans outstanding to rise only to the extent that the servicing commitments on Brazil's total external indebtedness do not depart from the guidelines set by the National Monetary Council. As of the end of 1992, the Central Bank's minimum acceptable maturity was set at 30 months. However, provided that the full amount of the foreign exchange remains committed to Brazil for the minimum specified maturity, loans to the final borrower in Brazil, as well as loans to banks under Resolution No. 63, may be made on terms shorter than the final maturity of the debt abroad, and these funds may subsequently be re-lent to the same or to a second borrower.

Remittances of proceeds from sales of property and inheritance have been permitted since October 19, 1994.

Outward transfers other than capital may be made directly through authorized banks upon presentation by the remitters of the appropriate documentation. Outward transfers not included in public regulations need prior authorization from the Central Bank.

The private sector and both the financial and nonfinancial public sector are allowed access to foreign exchange for the purpose of servicing their debts, including those owed to nonresident banks.

Gold

Since the adoption of the Federal Constitution in 1988, gold transactions in Brazil have been delivered in two separate markets: the financial and commercial markets. Over 50 percent of transactions occur in the financial market, which is regulated by the Central Bank. The first domestic negotiation of newly mined gold on this market is subject to a 1 percent financial transactions tax. Rules regarding gold transactions for industrial purposes are defined separately by the federal states, which also establish different rates for the commercial tax levied on them. The Central Bank and authorized institutions are empowered to buy and sell gold on the domestic and international markets (Law No. 4595 of December 31, 1964 and Law No. 7766 of May 11, 1989). Purchases of gold are made at current domestic and international prices; the international price is considered a target price. Imports of gold are subject to the issuance of an import certificate by the SECEX. Exports of gold are subject to the same procedures as those that are applied through the SECEX in respect of other products.

Changes During 1994

Exchange Arrangement

March 1. The authorities introduced a new unit of account (the Unit of Real Value or URV) equivalent to US$1 and sought to establish the use of the URV in the denomination of contracts and prices. The URV would be adjusted daily in light of estimated inflation to keep the exchange rate between the cruzeiro real and the U.S. dollar constant.

June 21. The financial transactions tax for purchases of foreign exchange for payment of contracts involving transfers of technology that are registered with the National Institute of Industrial Property was reduced to zero from 25 percent.

July 1. A new currency, the real (R$), was introduced to replace the cruzeiro real and the URV at the conversion rate of 2,750 cruzeiro real to R$1. All contracts denominated in URVs were converted to reais at a conversion rate of 1:1. The Central Bank would set a floor of R$1 per US$1 in the commercial market and be committed to use its international reserves to maintain the floor for an indefinite period. Otherwise, the exchange rate would be determined by market forces.

Imports and Import Payments

August 31. The 80 percent prefinancing requirement of imports with financing greater than 360 days was abolished (Carta-Circular Form No. 2486).

Payments for Invisibles

March 2. The transfer abroad of national currency was required to be supported by documents (Circular No. 2409 of the Central Bank of Brazil).

October 19. The limit on the foreign exchange allowance for travel abroad was eliminated (Circular No. 2494 of the Central Bank of Brazil).

Exports and Export Proceeds

October 19. The regulations governing anticipatory exports settlements were tightened. The period during which to effect these settlements was reduced to 90 days from 180 days for large exporters (who export more than US$10 million a year) and to 150 days for small exporters (in early February 1995, the distinction between small and large exporters was eliminated).

October 19. Anticipatory settlements were subjected to a 15 percent reserve requirement on credit operations (without interest remuneration).

Capital

January 13. National Monetary Council Resolution No. 2042 authorized certain institutions to conduct swap operations involving gold, exchange rates, interest rates, and price indices in the over-the-counter market.

January 19. National Monetary Council Resolution No. 2046 modified the provisions of Regulation No. 1289 of March 20, 1987 concerning the constitution, operation, and administration of foreign capital, investment companies, and stock and bond portfolios maintained in the country by foreign institutional investors.

February 28. The regulations on the financial transactions tax were revised whereby up to 25 percent may be applied on the issue of bonds abroad and on foreign investments in fixed-income securities, when the Government considers it necessary to raise the tax rates from the current levels of 3 percent and 5 percent, respectively.

March 2. Automatic authorization for issuing bonds, commercial paper, and other fixed-income instruments abroad was terminated. Circular No. 2410 altered the provisions that govern the prior authorization and registration of foreign credits through issues of securities on the international market. Circular No. 2411 permitted foreign currency deposits resulting from excess exchange buyer positions to be made in cash.

April 15. Brazil completed arrangements to reschedule its external debts to commercial bank creditors.

June 15. National Monetary Council Resolution No. 2079 modified the provisions of Regulation No. 1289 of March 20, 1987, concerning the constitution, operation, and administration of foreign investment companies and stock and securities portfolios.

July 1. The minimum period for external export prefinancing was extended to two years.

August 31. Prepayment of foreign borrowing and import financing was permitted (Resolution No. 2105). The 20 percent limit for import financing down payments was eliminated (Circular Letter No. 2486).

September 22. The constitution and operation of Foreign Investment Funds were regulated by Resolution No. 2111 and Circular No. 2485.

October 5. Inflows of resources in the form of advances for future capital increases and bridge investment in anticipation of future conversions of debts into investment were prohibited (Circular No. 2487).

October 19. National Monetary Council Resolution No. 2115 altered the provisions of Regulations No. 1289 of March 20, 1987 pertaining to the constitution, operation, and administration of foreign investment companies and stock and securities portfolios.

October 19. The financial transaction tax on foreign investment in fixed-income instruments was increased to 9 percent from 5 percent.

October 19. (1) The financial transaction tax was levied on foreign investment in stocks at the rate of 1 percent; (2) inflows of resources through operations involving anticipated payment of exports were suspended; and (3) the financial transaction tax on foreign borrowing was increased to 7 percent from 3 percent.

BULGARIA

(Position as of December 31, 1994)

Exchange Arrangement

The currency of Bulgaria is the Lev. The Bulgarian National Bank quotes daily the exchange rate of the lev in terms of the U.S. dollar based on the weighted average of transactions in the interbank exchange market during the previous trading day. This rate is called the central exchange rate. Exchange rates for other currencies are determined by their cross rate relationships with the U.S. dollar in the international exchange market. On December 31, 1994, the exchange rate quoted by the Bulgarian National Bank in terms of the U.S. dollar was Leva 65.015 per US$1. Exchange bureaus are allowed to conduct foreign exchange transactions in cash only. There are no taxes or subsidies on purchases or sales of foreign exchange. There are no arrangements for forward cover against exchange rate risk operating in the official or the commercial banking sector.

Administration of Control

Exchange controls are administered by the Ministry of Finance and the Bulgarian National Bank. The Bulgarian National Bank is responsible for implementing the exchange rate policy. Twenty commercial banks, 2 branches of foreign banks, and 1 financial institution conduct foreign exchange (forex) transactions. Another 13 banks are authorized to open bank accounts for settlement of payments abroad.

Arrears are maintained with respect to certain external payments.

Prescription of Currency

Payments to and from countries with which Bulgaria maintains bilateral agreements are made in the currencies and in accordance with the procedures set forth in those agreements.[1] Transactions are generally settled through clearing accounts. Balances in these accounts (annual and multiyear) are generally to be settled in goods during the six

---

[1]At the end of 1994, Bulgaria maintained bilateral clearing and barter agreements with the Islamic State of Afghanistan, Bangladesh, Cambodia, China, Ethiopia, Ghana, Guinea, Guyana, India, the Islamic Republic of Iran, the Democratic People's Republic of Korea, the Lao People's Democratic Republic, Mozambique, Nicaragua, Pakistan, Romania, the Russian Federation, Syria, and Tanzania. Bulgaria has outstanding transferable ruble accounts with Cuba, Germany, Hungary, Mongolia, Poland, Romania, and the Russian Federation.

months after the agreement has been terminated; thereafter, they are settled in convertible currencies.

Resident and Nonresident Accounts

Residents may maintain foreign currency deposit accounts in Bulgaria, which may be credited without restriction, and from which transfers abroad may be made with permission from the Ministry of Finance and the Bulgarian National Bank (pursuant to the provisions of Decree No. 15 of the Council of Ministers of 1991). Balances on these accounts earn interest at international market rates. Nonresidents may maintain accounts in foreign currencies and leva without authorization, limitation, or restriction for purposes of making transactions in Bulgaria. The crediting and debiting of foreign currency accounts are not subject to any regulations, and transfers abroad from these accounts are free of restriction.

Imports and Exports

Imports of some sensitive goods are subject to registration at the Ministry of Trade. Imports of ice cream are subject to a quota. Imports of certain goods are restricted for health and security reasons. Import tariff rates range from 5 percent to 55 percent. Tariffs are calculated on the transaction values (actual invoice price paid) in foreign currency and converted to leva. An import surcharge of 3 percent was introduced in August 1993, was reduced to 2 percent effective January 1, 1994, and is to be reduced to 1 percent effective January 1, 1995. The surcharge is waived for the importation of certain energy products, pharmaceuticals, and facilities for environmental protection. Under Government Decree No. 241 (January 1, 1994), certain goods in these categories are exempt from customs duty or are subject to ceilings for duty-free imports or reduced-duty imports.

Proceeds from exports must be repatriated within one month but do not have to be surrendered; they may be retained in foreign currencies or sold in the interbank exchange market. Under Government Decree No. 241, export taxes are levied on certain types of timber, hides, wool, sunflower oil, grain, and some copper products. The export tax is quoted in U.S. dollars but paid in leva. Exports and imports of tobacco products, coal, petroleum, livestock and meat, dairy products, certain grains, textiles, ferrous metals and alloys, and imports of flat glass are required to be registered.

Special licenses are required for transactions under barter and clearing arrangements, for exports proceeds to be received in leva; exports under government credits and exports subject to quotas and voluntary export restraint agreements; imports and exports of military hardware and related technologies; endangered flora and fauna; radioactive and hazardous materials; crafts and antiques; pharmaceuticals; herbicides; pesticides; flour; unbottled alcohol; intellectual property; jewelry; and rare and precious metals. Licenses are normally granted within two working days. Exports of ferrous and nonferrous scrap metal, female livestock, and grains were prohibited until the end of 1994. The exportation of goods received as humanitarian aid and of human blood and plasma is prohibited.

Payments for and Proceeds from Invisibles

Foreign exchange allowances for business travel are granted without restriction. Allowances for tourist travel are limited to the leva equivalent of up to $2,000 a person a year for people without foreign currency deposits. Resident holders of foreign exchange deposits may use balances on these deposit accounts without restriction.

Commercial banks may sell foreign exchange freely to resident individuals or resident legal persons if proper documentation certifies that foreign exchange is needed for (1) authorized imports of goods and services; (2) transportation and other expenses related to the conveyance of goods and passengers carried out by nonresidents; (3) interest and amortization with respect to credits approved by the Bulgarian National Bank; (4) business travel in compliance with the established procedures; (5) insurance fees; (6) banking commissions; (7) education and training; (8) health care; (9) diplomatic, consular, and other government agencies of Bulgaria abroad; (10) commercial representative offices of Bulgarian traders abroad; (11) commissions, advertising fees, and other expenses related to economic activities (including fairs and exhibitions); (12) membership fees in international organizations; and (13) participation in international contests and festivals.

Nonresidents may purchase foreign currency from Bulgarian commercial banks to transfer abroad (1) investment income received in leva; (2) compensation received following nationalization of investment enterprises; (3) proceeds from liquidation of investment; (4) proceeds from sales of investment enterprises received in leva; and (5) amounts re-

ceived in leva under judicial settlement of guaranteed claims. Transfers abroad in compliance with the above cases may be effected upon presentation of documents that certify that outstanding liabilities have been paid. Remittances of earnings by foreign workers and remittances for family maintenance are not explicitly mentioned in Decree No. 15 (of February 8, 1991), which governs foreign exchange control, but they have been treated implicitly as transfers abroad that are not related to merchandise imports. The following transfers abroad require prior permission from the Bulgarian National Bank in consultation with the Ministry of Finance as stipulated by the Decree No. 15: (1) indirect investments; (2) official credits extended to and received from abroad; (3) investments abroad; and (4) free transfers in foreign currency when they are not connected with imports of goods and services.

Proceeds from invisibles must be repatriated within one month but do not have to be surrendered and may be retained in foreign currencies or sold in the interbank exchange market.

Residents and nonresidents may take out or bring in Bulgarian banknotes and coins up to Leva 10,000; permission from the Bulgarian National Bank is required to import or export amounts exceeding this limit. Residents may take out foreign currency notes up to the equivalent of $1,000 without restriction. There is no limit on foreign currency notes nonresidents may bring into the country but the amount must be declared, and they may take out unspent foreign currency notes upon departure.

Capital

Licensed banks may borrow abroad without the authorization of the Bulgarian National Bank. The forex-licensed commercial banks, however, may borrow abroad only if they do not request a guarantee from the Government of Bulgaria and if their borrowing complies with the prudential regulations set up by the Bulgarian National Bank. They may also extend foreign currency and lev loans to residents and nonresidents.

Foreign direct investments in Bulgaria are governed by the Law on the Economic Activity of Foreign Persons and Protection of Foreign Investments (State Gazette No. 8/1992). Foreign direct investments must be registered with the Ministry of Finance and require authorization only if they are undertaken in sectors that are considered sensitive. Foreign direct investments are guaranteed against expropriation, except for nationalization through legal process. Foreign firms are granted the same status as domestic firms; they may, under certain conditions, benefit from preferential treatment, including reduced taxation and access to judicial appeal outside the system of state arbitration. In general, fully owned foreign firms are subject to a profit tax of 40 percent, and joint ventures are subject to a profit tax of 30 percent; all other firms with foreign participation are subject to the same profit tax as domestic firms (40 percent). Repatriation of liquidated capital and after-tax profits is not restricted, and transfers of profits in domestic currency do not require a special authorization.

Gold

The Ministry of Finance controls the acquisition, possession, processing, and disposal of gold, silver, and platinum. The Bulgarian National Bank is the only institution entitled to purchase, sell, hold, import, or export gold for monetary and nonmonetary purposes. All domestic transactions for industrial purposes must be conducted at current prices through the Bulgarian National Bank. Commercial banks are not authorized to deal or speculate (on their own or on their customers' behalf) in precious metals, with the exception that the Bulgarian Foreign Trade Bank is licensed to deal in precious metals. Resident individuals may hold gold but may not trade or deal in it. The amount of gold and jewelry products that they may import is limited. Nonresidents are permitted to bring in and take out their jewelry but may not trade. Nonresidents must have permission from the Ministry of Finance, the Bulgarian National Bank, and the Ministry of Industry and Commerce to buy gold, silver, and platinum products.

Changes During 1994

Administration of Control

January 1. Government Decree No. 241 on import and export regulations was issued.

February 11. A new currency regulation governing the exportation and importation of Bulgarian banknotes and coins, foreign currency notes, and other financial assets was issued.

December 20. Government Decree No. 307 on imports and exports was issued, replacing Government Decree No. 241.

Imports and Exports

January 1. The import surcharge was reduced to 2 percent.

May 15. The prohibition on exports of female livestock was extended until December 31, 1994.

June 6. Exports of meat and livestock were allowed with licenses.

October 15. The prohibition on exports of grains was extended from the end of September 1994 to December 1994.

BURKINA FASO

(Position as of December 31, 1994)

Exchange Arrangement

The currency of Burkina Faso is the CFA Franc,[1] the external value of which is pegged to the French franc, the intervention currency, at the fixed rate of CFAF 1 per F 0.01. The official buying and selling rate is CFAF 100 per F 1. Exchange rates for other currencies are derived from the rate in the Paris exchange market and the fixed rate between the French franc and the CFA franc. Banks levy a commission of 2.5 per mil on transfers to all countries outside the West African Monetary Union (WAMU), all of which must be surrendered to the Treasury.[2] There are no taxes or subsidies on purchases or sales of foreign exchange.[3]

In the official and commercial banking sectors, forward exchange cover may be arranged only by residents for settlements with respect to imports of goods on certain lists. All contracts for forward exchange cover must be denominated in the currency of payment stipulated in the contract and are subject to prior authorization by the Minister of Finance. Nonrenewable forward exchange contracts may be concluded for one month. For certain products, the maturity period of forward exchange cover may be renewed once for three months.

With the exception of measures relating to gold, the repatriation of export proceeds, the issuing, advertising or offering for sale of securities and capital assets, and the soliciting of funds for investments abroad, Burkina Faso's exchange controls do not apply to (1) France (and its overseas departments and territories) and Monaco; and (2) all countries whose bank of issue is linked with the French Treasury by an Operations Account (Benin, Cameroon, Central African Republic, Chad, Comoros, Congo, Côte d'Ivoire, Equatorial Guinea, Gabon, Mali, Niger, Senegal, and Togo). All payments to these countries may be made freely. All other countries are considered foreign countries.

Administration of Control

Exchange control is administered by the Directorate of the Treasury in the Ministry of Finance. The approval authority for exchange control (except for imports and exports of gold, forward exchange cover, and the opening of external accounts in foreign currency) has been delegated to the BCEAO and, within limits specified in the exchange control regulations, to its authorized intermediaries. The BCEAO is also authorized to collect, either directly or through banks, financial institutions, the Postal Administration, and judicial agents, any information necessary to compile balance of payments statistics. All exchange transactions relating to foreign countries must be effected through authorized banks, the Postal Administration, or the BCEAO. Import and export licenses are issued by the Directorate-General of Foreign Trade in the Ministry of Industry, Commerce, and Mines. Import certificates for liberalized commodities and export attestations are made out by the importer or exporter and, when settlement takes place with a country outside the Operations Account Area, are visaed by the customs administration.

Arrears are maintained with respect to external payments.

Prescription of Currency

Because Burkina Faso is an Operations Account country, settlements with France (as defined above), Monaco, and other Operations Account countries are made in CFA francs, French francs, or the currency of Operations Account countries. Current transactions with The Gambia, Ghana, Guinea, Guinea-Bissau, Liberia, Mauritania, Nigeria, and Sierra Leone are settled through the West African Clearing House. Certain settlements are channeled through special accounts.[4] Settlements with all other countries are usually effected either through correspondent banks in France or the country concerned in any of the currencies of those countries, or in French francs or other currencies of the Operations Account Area through foreign accounts in francs.

---

[1]The CFA franc is issued by the Central Bank of West African States (BCEAO) and is the common currency in Benin, Burkina Faso, Côte d'Ivoire, Mali, Niger, Senegal, and Togo.

[2]Banks are free to determine and collect a commission on transfers between member countries of the WAMU.

[3]Banks may levy a commission of 2 percent on the exchange of CFAF banknotes for French franc notes.

[4]A bilateral agreement maintained with Ghana is inoperative.

Nonresident Accounts

The crediting to nonresident accounts of BCEAO banknotes, French banknotes, or banknotes issued by any other institute of issue that maintains an Operations Account with the French Treasury is prohibited. These accounts may not be overdrawn without prior authorization.

Imports and Import Payments

Imports of goods originating in or shipped from any country for commercial purposes and under any customs regulations may be made freely; prior acquisition of an official import document is necessary for imports exceeding values of CFAF 250,000. A special import license (*autorisation spéciale d'importation* (ASI)) is required for imports of sugar, rice, explosives, arms, munitions, and military paraphernalia.

A technical import visa (*cerificat de conformité*) is required for the following products: sugar, selected pharmaceutical products (tables R06, R6, R20), insecticides, printed fabric and bleached and tinted threads, wheat and cereal flour, tomato paste, tires and inner tubes for motorcycles, and mats and bags of polyethylene and polypropylene. Imports of certain other products, a list of which is established by decree, may be exempted from the import document requirement. The Minister of Industry, Commerce, and Mines may, on the basis of criteria established by the ministry, waive the prescribed formalities for imports from countries with which Burkina Faso has concluded a customs union or free trade area agreement. All imports, with a few exceptions, are subject to customs duties of 5 percent; the rates on cereals range from 4 percent to 26 percent, and a statistical tax of 4 percent.

All imports from outside the Economic Community of West African States (ECOWAS) are subject to a solidarity communal levy of 1 percent, and imports of certain goods that are also locally produced are subject to a protection tax ranging from 10 percent to 30 percent.

Imports of the following products are prohibited: oil-carrying tank trucks, used coaches and buses, moped inner tubes, bicycle tires and inner tubes, and wheat flour from countries other than those of the West African Economic Community (WAEC), as well as ivory and fishing nets with a mesh not greater than 3 square centimeters.

All import transactions with a value of more than CFAF 500,000 effected with foreign countries must be domiciled with an authorized bank. Import licenses or prior import authorizations entitle importers to purchase the necessary exchange not earlier than eight days before shipment if a documentary credit is opened, on the due date for payment if the commodities have already been imported, or at the time of the payment on account if such a payment must be made before importation.

Payments for Invisibles

Payments for invisibles to France (as defined above), Monaco, and other Operations Account countries are permitted freely. Those to other countries are subject to exchange control approval, which, for many invisibles, has been delegated to authorized intermediaries. Authorized intermediary banks and the Postal Administration are empowered to make payments of up to CFAF 50,000 a transfer to foreign countries on behalf of residents without requiring justification. Payments for invisibles related to trade are permitted freely when the basic trade transaction has been approved or does not require authorization. Transfers of income accruing to nonresidents in the form of profits, dividends, and royalties are also permitted.

Residents traveling for tourism or business purposes to countries in the franc zone that are not members of the WAMU are allowed to take out banknotes other than CFAF banknotes up to the equivalent of CFAF 2 million; amounts in excess of this limit may be taken out in the form of other means of payment. The allowances for travel to countries outside the franc zone are subject to the following regulations: (1) for tourist travel, CFAF 500,000 without limit on the number of trips or differentiation by the age of the traveler; (2) for business travel, CFAF 75,000 a day within the limit of one month, corresponding to a maximum of CFAF 2.25 million (business travel allowances may be cumulated with tourist allowances); (3) allowances in excess of these limits are subject to the authorization of the respective ministries of finance or, by delegation, the BCEAO; and (4) the use of credit cards, which must be issued by resident financial intermediaries and specifically authorized by the respective ministries of finance, is limited to the ceilings indicated above for tourist and business travel. Returning resident travelers are required to declare all means of payment in their possession upon arrival at customs and to surrender within eight days all means of payment exceeding the equivalent of CFAF 25,000. All resident travelers, when traveling to countries that are not members of the WAMU, must declare in writing all means of payment at their disposal at the time of departure. The re-exportation by nonresident travelers of means of payment other than banknotes issued abroad and registered in the name of the nonresident traveler is not restricted, subject to documentation that they had been purchased with funds drawn from a foreign account in CFA francs or with other foreign exchange. The re-exportation of foreign banknotes is allowed up to the equivalent of CFAF 250,000; the re-exportation of foreign banknotes above these ceilings requires documentation demonstrating either the importation of foreign banknotes or their purchase against other means of payment registered in the name of the traveler or through the use of nonresident deposits lodged in local banks.

Exports and Export Proceeds

Exports and re-exports from Burkina Faso may be made freely. However, for the purpose of monitoring, exports or re-exports of certain products may require prior official authorization from the relevant services of the Ministry of Industry, Commerce, and Mines, except in the case of certain goods, a list of which is established by decree. In accordance with criteria defined by the Minister of Industry, Commerce, and Mines, exports of ivory are subject to special regulations (*autorisation spéciale d'exportation* (ASE)). Exports to Ghana are also subject to special regulations. Export proceeds must be surrendered within one month of the date on which the payment falls due (the due date stipulated in the commercial contract must not, in principle, be more than 180 days after the goods arrive at their destination). All export transactions of more than CFAF 500,000 relating to foreign countries, including countries in the Operations Account Area, must be domiciled with an authorized bank. The exporter must sign a foreign exchange commitment and submit an export attestation form. Most exports are subject to a customs stamp tax of 6 percent and a statistical duty of 3 percent.

Proceeds from Invisibles

Proceeds from transactions in invisibles with France (as defined above), Monaco, and the Operations Account countries may be retained. All amounts due from residents of other countries in respect of services and all income earned in those countries from foreign assets must be collected and surrendered within two months of the due date. Resident and nonresident travelers may bring in any amount of banknotes and coins issued by the BCEAO, the Bank of France, or any bank of issue maintaining an Operations Account with the French Treasury, as well as any amount of foreign banknotes and coins (except gold coins) of coun-

tries outside the Operations Account Area. Resident travelers must declare to customs any foreign means of payment in excess of CFAF 25,000 that they bring in and must surrender these to an authorized bank within eight days of their return.

Capital

Capital movements between Burkina Faso and France (as defined above), Monaco, and the Operations Account countries are free of exchange control; capital transfers to all other countries require exchange control approval and are restricted, but capital receipts from such countries are permitted freely.

Special controls in addition to any exchange control requirements that may be applicable are maintained over borrowing abroad, over inward direct investment and all outward investment, and over the issuing, advertising, or offering for sale of foreign securities in Burkina Faso. Such operations require prior authorization from the Minister of Finance. Exempt from authorization, however, are operations in connection with (1) loans backed by a guarantee from the Burkinabé Government; and (2) shares that are similar to or may be substituted for securities whose issue, advertising, or sale in Burkina Faso has already been authorized. With the exception of controls over foreign securities, these measures do not apply to France (as defined above), Monaco, member countries of the WAMU, and the Operations Account countries. Special controls are also maintained over imports and exports of gold, over the soliciting of funds for deposit with foreign firms, institutions, and private individuals, as well as over publicity aimed at placing funds abroad or at subscribing to real estate and building operations abroad. These special controls also apply to France, Monaco, and the Operations Account countries. All special provisions described in this paragraph apply only to transactions and not to the associated payments or collections.

All investments abroad by residents of Burkina Faso require prior authorization from the Minister of Finance[5] and, unless the Minister specifically exempts them, 75 percent of such investments must be financed from borrowing abroad. Foreign direct investments in Burkina Faso[6] must be declared to

---

[5]Including those made through foreign companies that are directly or indirectly controlled by persons residing in Burkina Faso and those made by branches or subsidiaries abroad of companies having their headquarters in Burkina Faso.

[6]Including those made by companies operating in Burkina Faso that are directly or indirectly under foreign control and those made by branches or subsidiaries in Burkina Faso of foreign companies.

the Minister of Finance before they are made. The Minister has a period of two months from receipt of the declaration to request postponement of the project. The full or partial liquidation of either type of investment also requires prior declaration to the Minister. Both the making and the liquidation of investments, whether these are Burkinabé investments abroad or foreign investments in Burkina Faso, must be reported to the Minister of Finance. Direct investments constitute investments implying control of a company or enterprise. Mere participation is not considered direct investment, provided that it does not exceed 20 percent of the capital of a company whose shares are quoted on a stock exchange. Foreign firms operating in Burkina Faso in vital or priority sectors are required to have Burkinabé participation in their capital of at least 51 percent and of at least 35 percent in all other sectors. The sale to residents of Burkina Faso of securities of foreign companies operating in Burkina Faso requires prior authorization from the Minister of Finance, who establishes the sale value.

Borrowing by residents from nonresidents also requires prior authorization from the Minister of Finance. The following are, however, exempt from this authorization: (1) loans constituting a direct investment, which are subject to prior declaration, as indicated above; (2) loans taken up by industrial firms to finance operations abroad, by any type of firm to finance imports into or exports from Burkina Faso, or by international trading houses approved by the Minister of Finance to finance international merchanting transactions; (3) loans contracted by authorized banks; and (4) loans other than those mentioned above, when the total amount of these loans outstanding—including the new borrowing—does not exceed CFAF 100 million for any one borrower, the annual interest rate does not exceed the normal market rate, and the proceeds are immediately surrendered by the sale of foreign currency on the exchange market or debited to a foreign account in francs. The repayment of loans not constituting a direct investment requires the special authorization of the Minister of Finance if the loan itself is subject to such approval but is exempt if the loan is exempt from special authorization. Lending abroad is subject only to exchange control authorization by the BCEAO acting on behalf of the Minister of Finance.

The Investment Code provides preferential treatment for foreign investment in Burkina Faso, except for enterprises whose capital stock belongs entirely to foreigners. Three preferential categories (A, B, and C) are established, in accordance with which special guarantees and tax and customs incentives

may be granted for up to eight years to any enterprise that undertakes to create or considerably expand activities likely to contribute to the country's economic and social development. Enterprises that the Government deems to be of a priority nature may also be given privileged treatment.

Gold

Residents are free to hold, acquire, and dispose of gold in any form in Burkina Faso. Imports and exports of gold from or to any other country require prior authorization from the Minister of Finance. Exempt from this requirement are (1) imports and exports by or on behalf of the Treasury or the BCEAO; (2) imports and exports of manufactured articles containing a minor quantity of gold (such as gold-filled or gold-plated articles); and (3) imports and exports by travelers of gold objects up to a combined weight of 500 grams. Both licensed and exempt imports of gold are subject to customs declaration.

The Comptoir burkinabé des métaux précieux (CBMP) has a monopoly on exports of gold from Burkina Faso.

Changes During 1994

Exchange Arrangement

January 12. The CFA franc was devalued to CFAF 100 per F 1 from CFAF 50 per F 1.

Payments for Invisibles

January 18. Residents traveling for tourism or business purposes to countries in the franc zone that are not members of the WAMU are allowed to take out banknotes, other than CFAF banknotes, up to the equivalent of CFAF 2 million; amounts in excess of this limit may be taken out in the form of other means of payment. (Prior to this decree, the limit applied to BCEAO banknotes for travel to countries in the BEAC zone was equivalent to CFAF 2 million, and the limit for travel to France and Comoros was the equivalent to CFAF million in banknotes other than CFA notes.)

Administration of Control

January 11. The treaty establishing the West African Economic and Monetary Union (WAEMU), complementing the West African Monetary Union (WAMU), was signed by the following seven countries: Benin, Burkina Faso, Côte d'Ivoire, Mali, Niger, Senegal, and Togo. One of the objectives of this union would be to create a common market among the member countries, based on free movement of persons, goods, services, and capital; a common external tariff; and a common trade policy.

March 15. The WAEC was dissolved.

May 6. Law No. 17/94 establishing relations with foreign countries as part of the reform of exchange regulations within WAEMU was adopted.

BURUNDI

(Position as of December 31, 1994)

Exchange Arrangement

The currency of Burundi is the Burundi Franc, the external value of which has been pegged since May 14, 1992 to a basket of currencies that reflects the pattern of Burundi's international trade. On December 31, 1994, the official buying and selling rates for the U.S. dollar were FBu 244.96 and FBu 248.92, respectively, per US$1. Exchange rates for 18 currencies[1] and for 2 units of account, European currency units (ECUs), and units of account of the Common Market for Eastern and Southern Africa, are quoted by the Bank of the Republic of Burundi (the central bank) on the basis of the Burundi franc-U.S. dollar rate and the transaction value of these currencies and units in terms of the U.S. dollar. Commercial banks are authorized to buy and sell foreign exchange on their own account and on behalf of their customers at rates within maximum margins of 1 percent on either side of the middle rate established by the central bank. Commercial banks are allowed to borrow foreign exchange to hedge against exchange rate risks. Exporters of coffee are also allowed to borrow foreign exchange through their banks or from their customers for purposes of crop financing and hedging against exchange risks.

Administration of Control

Control over foreign exchange transactions and foreign trade is vested in the central bank; authority to carry out some transactions is delegated to six authorized banks.

Prescription of Currency

Settlements relating to trade with Rwanda and Zaïre in products specified in the commercial agreements between these countries are effected through SDR accounts maintained with the central bank and authorized banks of each signatory country. With these exceptions, outgoing payments may be made and receipts may be obtained in any convertible currency.

---

[1]Austrian schillings, Belgian francs, Canadian dollars, Danish kroner, deutsche mark, French francs, Italian lire, Japanese yen, Kenya shillings, Netherlands guilders, Norwegian kroner, pounds sterling, Rwanda francs, Swedish kronor, Swiss francs, Tanzania shillings, Uganda shillings, and U.S. dollars.

Nonresident (Foreign Currency Convertible Burundi Franc) Accounts

Accounts in convertible Burundi francs may be maintained by (1) natural persons of foreign nationality (such as staff of diplomatic missions) who are temporarily established in Burundi, (2) juridical persons of foreign nationality with special status (such as diplomatic missions and international organizations), and (3) any other natural or juridical persons authorized by the central bank. These accounts may be credited freely with any convertible currency, and they may be debited freely for withdrawals of Burundi francs or for conversion into foreign exchange. Up to FBu 20,000 in foreign currency may be withdrawn in banknotes upon presentation of travel documents (a passport and an airline ticket) for an unlimited number of trips. Withdrawals of banknotes in excess of this amount are subject to the prior authorization of the central bank. These accounts may bear interest freely and must not be overdrawn.

Certain nonresidents whose main activities are outside Burundi may maintain accounts in foreign currencies with an authorized bank. These accounts may be maintained by (1) natural and juridical persons of foreign nationality who reside abroad, (2) enterprises authorized to operate in the free trade zone, (3) exporters of nontraditional products, who are authorized to retain 30 percent of their export proceeds, (4) Burundi nationals resident abroad, and (5) any other natural or juridical persons authorized by the central bank.

These accounts may be credited freely with any convertible currency received from abroad. They may be debited freely for (1) conversion into Burundi francs for payments in Burundi; and (2) payments abroad for travel and representation or for the purchase of foreign goods, except for banknotes. These accounts must not be overdrawn. However, they may bear interest freely. The related bank charges and commissions must be settled in foreign exchange; and (3) as in the case of accounts in convertible Burundi francs, up to FBu 20,000 may be withdrawn in banknotes upon presentation of travel documents. Withdrawals in excess of this amount are subject to the prior authorization of the central bank. If no deposits are made to the foreign account within three months of its opening, the account must be closed.

Imports and Import Payments

Imports are fully liberalized, except for a limited number of goods the importation of which is restricted mainly for health or security reasons. All goods imported into Burundi must be insured by approved Burundi insurers, and premiums must be paid in Burundi francs. All consignments of imports exceeding FBu 1 million in value (f.o.b.) may be subject to preshipment inspection with regard to quality and price by an international supervising and oversight organization on behalf of the Burundi authorities.

In principle, foreign exchange is made available either at the time the goods are shipped on the basis of the shipping documents or after the goods are imported. All imports are subject to a service tax of 4 percent ad valorem in addition to any applicable customs duties and fiscal duties.

Payments for Invisibles

All payments for invisibles require approval. Shipping insurance on coffee exports normally must be taken out in Burundi francs with a Burundi insurer. Upon presentation of evidence of payment of taxes, foreign nationals residing and working in Burundi are permitted to transfer abroad up to 70 percent of their net annual income (80 percent in the case of foreign nationals working for companies that export at least 50 percent of their production). Private joint-stock companies may freely and immediately transfer 100 percent of the return on foreign capital and of the share allocated to foreign directors after payment of taxes. Airlines are authorized to transfer abroad 100 percent of their earnings after deduction of local expenses.

Persons leaving Burundi permanently are authorized to transfer abroad their holdings of Burundi francs that consist of unremitted savings or the sale proceeds of their personal effects. Transfer of rental income from foreign owners of new commercial, industrial, office, and residential buildings is permitted up to 50 percent of net rental income (after payment of taxes and a deduction of 20 percent for maintenance expenses) in any one-year period; the remainder, plus any accrued interest, may be transferred in full after one year provided that the funds have been held on deposit with a domestic financial institution for two years for commercial, industrial, and office buildings, and for three years for residential buildings.

Residents may apply for foreign exchange needed for foreign travel. The foreign exchange allowance for business travel is $200 a person a day or its equivalent ($250 for exporters), subject to a maximum limit of 15 days a trip. These limits may be increased for travel requiring a longer stay abroad. There is no limit on the number of trips a person may take. All travelers may take out up to FBu 5,000 in Burundi banknotes.

Exports and Export Proceeds

All exports are fully liberalized. Export proceeds must be collected within 30 days of the date of export declaration at customs for shipment by air or within 90 days for all other shipments.

Exporters operating in the free trade area are not required to surrender their export proceeds to an authorized bank.

Deadlines for the collection of proceeds from exports of nontraditional products are set by individual banks. All proceeds from traditional exports must be surrendered to an authorized bank. Exporters of nontraditional products may retain up to 30 percent of proceeds. Exports of mineral products, coffee, and hides are subject to export duties as are exports of all goods that do not qualify for export promotion. Duties paid on raw materials at the time of importation may be refunded, provided that the manufactured products are exported and the proceeds collected. In the case of fully paid exports of nontraditional primary products, the refund will cover 10 percent of the value of such payments.

Proceeds from Invisibles

Exchange receipts from invisibles must be surrendered to authorized banks. Travelers may bring in any amount of foreign currency quoted by the central bank and traveler's checks and up to FBu 5,000 in Burundi banknotes.

Nonresidents staying in a hotel or guest house in Burundi must pay their hotel bills by selling convertible currencies or by using a credit card. Payment in Burundi francs is, however, acceptable in the case of guests for whom a resident company or individual has assumed responsibility with prior authorization from the central bank and in the case of nationals of Rwanda or Zaïre who produce declarations of means of payment issued under the auspices of the Economic Community of the Great Lakes Countries (CEPGL).

Capital

Under the Investment Code introduced on January 14, 1987, new investments that fulfill specified conditions as to amount and economic importance may be granted priority status to which specified privileges are attached, mainly in the form of exemptions from import duties and from taxes on income from the investment. Import duties and taxes may be reduced or suspended for goods and equipment needed for starting a particular project and, during a period of five years, for other merchandise needed for the manufacturing process or for the upkeep of the original investment. Taxes on profits and real estate may likewise be reduced or suspended for up to eight years. Enterprises accorded priority status may be granted a reduction or suspension of export taxes and import taxes on equipment and raw materials for renewable periods of five years. In addition to these privileges, companies undertaking investments that are considered to be of prime importance to Burundi's economic development may be granted, under a separate agreement, a guarantee that direct taxes on their activities will not be increased for ten years. An investment commission under the Ministry of Development Planning and Reconstruction is responsible for examining requests for priority status and granting the necessary authorization. In addition, Burundi guarantees each foreign investor the right to move into the country; foreign investors are also assured an allocation of foreign exchange for the purchase of raw materials abroad as well as for the repayment of loans taken out under the investment agreement.

Capital transfers by residents and transfers of foreign capital on which a repatriation guarantee has been granted require individual authorization. The guarantee is furnished for foreign exchange imported by resident enterprises to provide working capital in foreign exchange; it applies to any of the currencies quoted by the central bank; and the retransfer may take place as soon as the funds to be transferred are available and with no time limitation. The guarantee provides for the transfer of the amount received from abroad. The repatriation of invested capital in the event of sale or shutdown of the business is also guaranteed.

Gold

All natural or juridical persons holding gold mining permits issued by the ministers responsible for mining and customs may open purchasing houses for gold mined by artisans in Burundi. Gold produced by artisans may be sold only to approved houses. Exports of gold must be declared in Burundi francs at the average daily rates communicated by the central bank. Gold exports are authorized jointly by the mining and customs departments.

Changes During 1994

No significant changes occurred in the exchange and trade system.

CAMBODIA

(Position as of December 31, 1994)

Exchange Arrangement

The currency of Cambodia is the Cambodian Riel. The exchange rate system comprises two rates: the official and the market rates. Adjustments to the official exchange rate are made daily by the National Bank of Cambodia so as to limit the spread between the official and parallel market rates to no more than 1 percent since June 1994. The official exchange rate applies mainly to external transactions conducted by the Government and state-owned enterprises. On December 31, 1994, the official exchange rate was CR 2,588 per US$1, and the market rate was CR 2,605 per US$1.

The National Bank is responsible for quoting daily official rates, at which the Foreign Trade Bank of Cambodia and the Phnom Penh Municipal Bank (two state-owned commercial banks) buy and sell foreign exchange. Other commercial banks are free to buy foreign exchange and sell it at their own rates. Exchange transactions take place at the rate prevailing in the market. Foreign exchange dealers are permitted to buy only banknotes and traveler's checks and are required by law to conduct their transactions at the official rate; in practice, however, these transactions take place at the market rate. There are no taxes or subsidies on purchases or sales of foreign exchange.

There are no arrangements for forward cover against exchange rate risk operating in the official or the commercial banking sector.

Administration of Control

The exchange control regime is defined by the 1991 Law on the Management of Foreign Exchange, Precious Metals, and Stones. This law vests responsibility for the management of foreign exchange (as well as precious metals and stones) with the Ministry of Economy and Finance and the National Bank. The National Bank is authorized to license commercial banks and other agents to engage in foreign exchange transactions and to regulate current and capital transactions. State-owned enterprises must be authorized by the Ministry of Economy and Finance to engage in export/import trade or in any other businesses generating foreign exchange and are required to repatriate foreign exchange earnings. Registered trading companies are not required to have a license to engage in foreign trade activities. New foreign exchange legislation that eliminates the foreign exchange restrictions contained in the 1991 law is expected to be presented to the National Assembly by May 1995.

Prescription of Currency

There are no prescription of currency requirements. Cambodia does not maintain operative bilateral payments agreements.

Resident and Nonresident Accounts

Residents and nonresidents are permitted to maintain foreign currency accounts with commercial banks. Although there are no limits on the balances of these accounts, under the 1991 law, the funds may not be used to settle domestic transactions but must be converted into domestic currency. In practice, however, such transactions are allowed to be settled through foreign currency accounts.

Imports and Import Payments

Trade policy is formulated by the Ministry of Commerce, in consultation with the Ministry of Finance.

Imports undertaken by registered trading companies require no license and there are no quantitative restrictions on imports, although imports of certain products are subject to control or are prohibited for reasons of national security, health, environmental well-being, or public morality.

Payments for Invisibles

Payments for invisibles related to trade are not restricted, but are regulated by the Law on Investment in the Kingdom of Cambodia of August 1994. The repatriation of profits is permitted in accordance with the relevant laws and regulations issued by the National Bank of Cambodia.

Under the 1991 law, an exchange allowance for travel of $3,000 a person is granted at the official rate for Cambodians going abroad for all types of travel, irrespective of the length of stay; in practice, however, there are no limits on the use of foreign exchange for travel abroad. Amounts in excess of this limit may be approved by the National Bank. There are no officially established limits on other invisible payments.

Exports and Export Proceeds

Exports of most products by registered trading companies may be undertaken without a license. Exports of a limited list of goods by both state-owned and private sector entities must be licensed by the Ministry of Commerce. Export licenses are required for sawed timber and logs. Exports of rice, gems, and sawed timber are subject to a quota. There are also export restrictions on gold, silver, and antiquities. All proceeds from exports by state-owned enterprises must be repatriated and sold to or deposited with the Foreign Trade Bank of Cambodia (FTBC); private sector entities must repatriate and hold export proceeds in accounts with commercial banks.

Proceeds from Invisibles

Proceeds from invisibles received by private sector entities are not subject to the repatriation or surrender requirement. Proceeds from invisibles earned by state-owned enterprises are subject to the same regulations as those governing proceeds from merchandise exports.

Capital

Borrowing abroad is permitted only with the approval of the Ministry of Economy and Finance. Foreign investors are required to submit investment applications to the Cambodia Investment Board at the Council for Development of Cambodia for review and approval. Foreign direct investment inflows must also be approved by the Cambodian Investment Board and are governed by the Law on Investment. A recently adopted investment law eliminated foreign exchange restrictions applying to investors in Cambodia.

Changes During 1994

Exchange Arrangement

September 1. The spread between the official rate and the market rate was narrowed to less than 1 percent.

Capital

August 4. An investment law eliminating foreign exchange restrictions applying to investors in Cambodia was adopted.

CAMEROON

(Position as of December 31, 1994)

Exchange Arrangement

The currency of Cameroon is the CFA Franc,[1] which is pegged to the French franc, the intervention currency, at the fixed rate of CFAF 1 per F 0.01. The official buying and selling rate is CFAF 100 per F 1. Exchange transactions in French francs between the BEAC and commercial banks take place at the same rate. Buying and selling rates for certain other foreign currencies are also officially posted, with quotations based on the fixed rate for the French franc and the rates in the Paris exchange market for the currencies concerned. A commission of 0.25 percent is levied on transfers to countries that are not members of the BEAC, except transfers in respect of central and local government operations, payments for imports covered by a duly issued license domiciled with a bank, scheduled repayments on loans properly obtained abroad, travel allowances and official representation expenses paid by the Government and its agencies for official missions, and payments of reinsurance premiums. There are no taxes or subsidies on purchases or sales of foreign exchange.

With the exception of those relating to gold, Cameroon's exchange control measures generally do not apply to (1) France (and its overseas departments and territories) and Monaco; and (2) all other countries whose bank of issue is linked with the French Treasury by an Operations Account (Benin, Burkina Faso, Central African Republic, Chad, Comoros, Congo, Côte d'Ivoire, Equatorial Guinea, Gabon, Mali, Niger, Senegal, and Togo). Hence, all payments to these countries may be made freely, but all financial transfers in excess of CFAF 500,000 to the Operations Account countries must be declared to the authorities for statistical purposes.

Forward exchange cover requires the prior authorization of the exchange control authorities. It must be denominated in the currency of settlement prescribed in the contract, and the maturity period must not be less than three months or more than nine months. Settlements must be effected within eight days of the maturity date of the forward contract.

---

[1]The CFA franc circulating in Cameroon is issued by the Bank of Central African States (BEAC) and is also legal tender in the Central African Republic, Chad, Congo, Equatorial Guinea, and Gabon.

Administration of Control

Exchange control is administered by the Directorate of Economic Controls and External Finance of the Ministry of Finance. Exchange transactions relating to all countries must be effected through authorized intermediaries—that is, the Postal Administration and authorized banks. Import licenses for goods other than gold are issued by the Ministry of Commerce and Industry, and those for gold by the Ministry of Mines, Water, and Energy. Export licenses are issued by the Ministry of Finance.

Arrears are maintained with respect to external payments.

Prescription of Currency

Since Cameroon is an Operations Account country, settlements with France (as defined above), Monaco, and the Operations Account countries are made in CFA francs, French francs, or the currency of any other Operations Account country. Settlements with all other countries are usually made through correspondent banks in France in any of the currencies of those countries or in French francs through foreign accounts in francs.

Resident and Nonresident Accounts

The regulations pertaining to nonresident accounts are based on those applied in France. As the BEAC has suspended the repurchase of BEAC banknotes circulating outside the territories of the CFA franc zone, BEAC banknotes received by the foreign correspondents of authorized banks and mailed to the BEAC agency in Yaounde may not be credited to foreign accounts in francs. Nonresidents are allowed to maintain bank accounts in convertible francs. These accounts, held mainly by diplomatic missions, international institutions, and their nonresident employees, may be credited only with (1) proceeds of spot or forward sales of foreign currencies transferred from abroad by account owners; (2) transfers from other nonresident convertible franc accounts; and (3) payments by residents in accordance with exchange regulations. These accounts may be debited only for (1) purchases of foreign currencies; (2) transfers to other nonresident convertible franc accounts; and (3) payments to residents in accordance with exchange regulations. Nonresidents may not maintain accounts in CFA francs abroad or accounts in foreign currency in Cameroon. Residents are not permitted to maintain accounts abroad or accounts in foreign currency in Cameroon.

Imports and Import Payments

Certain imports are prohibited for ecological, health, or safety reasons. Surcharges apply to imports from countries outside the Central African Customs and Economic Union (UDEAC) and imports of maize meal, trailers, iron reinforcing bars, and cement.

All import transactions valued at more than CFAF 500,000 must be domiciled with an authorized bank if the goods are not considered to be in transit. Transactions involving goods in transit must be domiciled with a foreign bank. Advance import deposits are permitted if underlying contracts stipulate them.

Payments for Invisibles

Payments in excess of CFAF 500,000 for invisibles to France (as defined above), Monaco, and the Operations Account countries require prior declaration and are subject to presentation of relevant invoices. Payments for invisibles related to trade follow the same regime as basic trade transactions, as do transfers of income accruing to nonresidents in the form of profits, dividends, and royalties.

Residents traveling for tourism or business purposes to countries other than France (as defined above), Monaco, and the Operations Account countries may be granted foreign exchange allowances subject to the following regulations: (1) for tourist travel, CFAF 100,000 a day, with a maximum of CFAF 2 million a trip; (2) for business travel, CFAF 250,000 a day, with a maximum of CFAF 5 million a trip; (3) allowances in excess of these limits are subject to the authorization of the Ministry of Finance or, by delegation, the BEAC; and (4) the use of credit cards, which must be issued by resident financial intermediaries and approved by the Ministry of Finance is limited to the ceilings indicated above for tourism and business travel. Returning resident travelers are required to declare all means of payment in their possession upon arrival at customs and to surrender within eight days all means of payment exceeding the equivalent of CFAF 25,000. All resident travelers, regardless of destination, must declare in writing all means of payment at their disposal at the time of departure. The re-exportation by nonresident travelers of means of payment, other than banknotes, issued abroad and registered in the name of the nonresident traveler is not restricted, subject to documentation that they were purchased with funds drawn from an account in CFA francs or with other foreign exchange. The re-exportation of foreign banknotes is allowed up to the equivalent of CFAF 250,000; re-exportation above this ceiling requires documentation showing either the importation of foreign banknotes or their purchase against other means of payment registered in the name of the traveler or through the use of deposits lodged in local banks.

The transfer of rent from real property owned in Cameroon by foreign nationals is limited, in principle, to up to 50 percent of the income declared for taxation purposes, net of repair costs and tax payments. Remittances for current repair and management of real property abroad are normally limited to the equivalent of CFAF 200,000 every two or three years. The transfer of up to 50 percent of the salary of a foreigner working in Cameroon, depending on the number of dependents abroad, is permitted upon presentation of the appropriate pay voucher, provided that the transfer takes place within one month of the pay period concerned. Except in the case of foreigners working in Cameroon temporarily who have been insured previously, residents and nonresidents are not allowed to contract insurance abroad when the same services are available in Cameroon. However, payments of premiums for authorized contracts are not restricted.

Exports and Export Proceeds

Export transactions valued at CFAF 500,000 or more must be domiciled with an authorized bank. Exports to all countries are subject to domiciliation requirements for the appropriate documents. Proceeds from exports to all countries must be repatriated within 30 days of the payment date stipulated in the sales contract, and proceeds received in currencies other than those of France or an Operations Account country must be surrendered within a month of collection.

Proceeds from Invisibles

All receipts from services and all income earned abroad must be collected within a month of the due date, and foreign currency receipts must be surrendered within a month of collection. Resident and nonresident travelers may bring into Cameroon any amount of banknotes and coins issued by the Bank of France, or a bank of issue maintaining an Operations Account with the French Treasury, as well as any amount of foreign banknotes and coins (except gold coins) of countries outside the Operations Account Area.

Capital

Capital transactions between Cameroon and France (as defined above), Monaco, and the Operations Account countries are free of exchange control. Outward capital transfers to all other countries require exchange control approval and are restricted. Inward capital transfers are free of restrictions, except for foreign direct investments and borrowing, which are subject to registration and authorization. Provided they have met their tax obligations, emigrants to countries outside the Operations Account Area may transfer abroad their full savings.

Direct investments abroad[2] require the prior approval of the Ministry of Finance, unless they take the form of a capital increase resulting from the reinvestment of undistributed profits or do not exceed 20 percent of the fair market value of the company being purchased. The full or partial liquidation of such investments requires only a report to the Minister of Finance, unless the operation involves the relinquishing of a participation that had previously been approved as constituting a direct investment abroad. Foreign direct investments in Cameroon[3] require prior declaration to the Minister of Finance, unless they take the form of a capital increase resulting from reinvestment of undistributed profits; the Minister has a period of two months from receipt of the declaration during which he may request postponement. The full or partial liquidation of direct investments in Cameroon requires only a report to the Minister of Finance, unless the operation involves the relinquishing of a participation that had previously been approved as constituting a direct investment in Cameroon. Both the making and the liquidation of direct investments, whether Cameroonian investments abroad or foreign investments in Cameroon, must be reported to the Minister of Finance within 20 days of each operation. (Direct investments are defined as investments implying control of a company or enterprise. Mere participation is not considered direct investment, provided that it does not exceed 20 percent of the capital of a company whose shares are quoted on a stock exchange.)

The issuing, advertising, or offering for sale of foreign securities in Cameroon requires prior authorization from the Minister of Finance and must subsequently be reported to him. Exempt from authorization, however, and subject only to a report after the fact, are operations in connection with (1) loans backed by a guarantee from the Cameroonian Government, and (2) shares similar to securities, when their issuing, advertising, or offering for sale in Cameroon has already been authorized. All foreign securities and titles embodying claims on nonresidents must be deposited with an authorized intermediary and are classified as foreign, whether they belong to residents or nonresidents.

Borrowing abroad by natural and juridical persons, whether public or private, whose normal residence or registered office is in Cameroon, or by branches or subsidiaries in Cameroon of juridical persons whose registered office is abroad, requires prior authorization from the Minister of Finance and must subsequently be reported to him. The following are, however, exempt from this authorization and require only a report: (1) loans directly connected with the rendering of services abroad by the persons or firms mentioned above, or with the financing of commercial transactions either between Cameroon and countries abroad or between foreign countries, in which these persons or firms take part; and (2) loans contracted by registered banks and credit institutions.

Lending abroad by natural and juridical persons, whether public or private, whose normal residence or registered office is in Cameroon, or by branches or subsidiaries in Cameroon of juridical persons whose registered office is abroad, requires prior authorization from the Minister of Finance and must subsequently be reported to him. The following are, however, exempt from prior authorization and require only a report: (1) loans constituting a direct investment abroad for which prior approval has been obtained, as indicated above; (2) loans directly connected with the rendering of services abroad by the persons or firms mentioned above, or with the financing of commercial transactions either between Cameroon and countries abroad or between foreign countries, in which these persons or firms take part; and (3) loans not exceeding CFAF 500,000, provided the maturity does not exceed two years and the rate of interest does not exceed 6 percent a year.

The Investment Code of November 1990 aims to promote the development of natural resources, job creation, production, and exportation (especially of manufactures), and the transfer of appropriate technology. Under the code, generalized fiscal benefits are provided to encourage exports and the development of natural resources, and further benefits are

---

[2]Including those made through foreign companies that are directly or indirectly controlled by persons in Cameroon and those made by branches or subsidiaries abroad of companies in Cameroon.

[3]Including those made by companies in Cameroon that are directly or indirectly under foreign control and those made by branches or subsidiaries of foreign companies in Cameroon.

provided to enterprises qualifying for inclusion in one of the five regimes described below.

The generalized fiscal benefits include an exemption from export duties and taxes on insurance and transportation for exports and a deduction of 5 percent of the value of exports from the exporter's taxable income. In addition, firms are exempted under certain conditions from all duties and purchase taxes on raw materials or intermediate inputs produced in Cameroon or the UDEAC region. The new code grants fiscal benefits to domestic and foreign firms undertaking new projects in the raw material processing, mining, forestry, agriculture, fishing, food, construction, equipment maintenance, industrial research, and tourism sectors. These benefits are provided as follows: (1) The basic regime applies to firms whose investment is labor intensive (defined as one job for each CFAF 10 million investment), export-oriented firms, and firms that use domestic natural resources. During a three-year installation phase, firms under this regime are entitled to a reduced tax rate of 15 percent, including their fiscal and customs duties, internal turnover tax, and all other import taxes relating to imported inputs; in addition, these firms are entitled to certain fiscal exemptions. During a five-year exploitation phase, certain tax exemptions are maintained. (2) The small and medium-size enterprise regime applies to firms that are labor intensive (defined as one job for each CFAF 5 million investment), whose investment is of modest size (less than CFAF 1.5 billion), and whose level of Cameroonian participation is at least 35 percent of capital. The benefits under this regime are the same as those under the basic regime, except that during the exploitation phase of seven years, firms may deduct from taxable income 25 percent of salaries paid to Cameroonian nationals. (3) The strategic regime applies to enterprises declared strategic by the Cameroonian authorities and fulfilling certain other conditions. This regime provides the same benefits as those under the basic regime during the installation phase, which is five years, and the same benefits as those available under the small and medium-size enterprise regime during the exploitation phase, which is 12 years. (4) The free trade zone regime is available to enterprises devoted exclusively to exporting; terms are fixed by individual agreements. (5) Firms that expand by more than 20 percent or that satisfy certain other conditions are eligible for benefits under the reinvestment regime. For three years, firms are subject to a reduced tax rate of 15 percent, which includes their fiscal and customs duties, internal turnover tax, and all other import taxes relating to imported inputs; in addi-

tion, these firms are entitled to certain fiscal exemptions.

Law No. 90/19 of August 10, 1990 provides that Cameroonian interests should hold at least one-third of the share capital of each banking institution. This law also requires banks with foreign majority participation to submit to the monetary authorities information on all current transactions abroad and to obtain prior approval for any changes in the structure of their equity holdings. Foreign managers must be approved by the monetary authorities and reside in Cameroon.

Gold

Residents are free to hold, acquire, and dispose of gold jewelry in Cameroon. They require the approval of the Ministry of Mines, Water, and Energy to hold gold in any other form. Such approval is normally given only to industrial users, including jewelers. Newly mined gold must be declared to the Ministry of Mines, Water, and Energy, which authorizes either its exportation or its sale to domestic industrial users; exports are made only to France. Imports and exports of gold require prior authorization from the Ministry of Mines, Water, and Energy and the Minister of Finance, although such authorization is seldom granted for imports. Exempt from this requirement are (1) imports and exports by or on behalf of the monetary authorities, and (2) imports and exports of manufactured articles containing a small quantity of gold (such as gold-filled or gold-plated articles). Both licensed and exempt imports of gold are subject to customs declaration.

Changes During 1994

Exchange Arrangement

January 12. The CFA franc was devalued to CFAF 100 per F 1 from CFAF 50 per F 1.

Imports and Import Payments

January 24. All quantitative restrictions were eliminated. The range of tariff rates was changed to 5–30 percent from 0–200 percent. Duties from the member countries of UDEAC were set at 20 percent of the corresponding rate applicable to imports from other countries.

September 1. A 30 percent temporary import surcharge was introduced on maize meal.

November 1. A 20 percent temporary import surcharge on trailers, iron reinforcing bars, and cement was introduced.

Capital

January 24. The Investment Code was revised to withdraw the exemption from customs duties on imports and from recording taxes that was granted to foreign firms, and this benefit was replaced by a 50 percent reduction in the corporate profit tax.

CANADA

(Position as of December 31, 1994)

Exchange Arrangement

The currency of Canada is the Canadian Dollar. The Canadian authorities do not maintain margins in respect of exchange transactions, and exchange rates are determined on the basis of demand and supply conditions in the exchange market; however, the authorities intervene from time to time to maintain orderly conditions in that market. The principal intervention currency is the U.S. dollar. The closing exchange rate (midpoint) for the U.S. dollar on December 31, 1994 was Can$1.4028 per US$1. Forward exchange rates are similarly determined in the market, and it is not the practice of the authorities to intervene. There are no taxes or subsidies on purchases or sales of foreign exchange.

On March 25, 1952, Canada notified the Fund that it was prepared to accept the obligations of Article VIII, Sections 2, 3, and 4 of the Fund Agreement.

Administration of Control

There are no exchange controls. The licensing of imports and exports, when required, is handled mostly by the Department of Foreign Affairs and International Trade, but other departments also issue licenses in specialized fields.

In accordance with the Fund's Executive Board Decision No. 144–(52/51) adopted on August 14, 1952, Canada notified the Fund on July 23, 1992 that in compliance with UN Security Council Resolution No. 757 (1992), certain restrictions had been imposed on the making of payments and transfers for current international transactions in respect of the Federal Republic of Yugoslavia (Serbia/Montenegro). Canada has also imposed restrictions on financial transactions with Bosnia and Herzegovina in accordance with UN Resolution No. 942.

Prescription of Currency

No prescription of currency requirements are in force.

Imports and Import Payments

Import permits are required for only a few agricultural items, certain textile products and clothing, certain endangered species of fauna and flora, natural gas, and material and equipment for the production or use of atomic energy. In 1994, permits were required for the importation of controlled substances classified as dangerous drugs and firearms for military use. In addition, Health Canada does not permit the importation of drugs not registered with it. Import permits are required for carbon and specialty steel products for monitoring purposes only. Permits are rarely issued for some agricultural items, such as butter and milk, while other agricultural items may be subject to a quota. Commercial imports of certain products, primarily margarine and used motor vehicles (less than 15 years old) have been generally prohibited. However, the prohibition on imports of used vehicles from the United States was phased out over a five-year period that began in 1989, and the prohibition on imports of used vehicles from Mexico will be phased out by January 1, 2019. The prohibition on imports of margarine expired on January 1, 1995. Imports of some clothing and certain textile products, usually in the form of bilateral restraint agreements (Memoranda of Understanding) concluded under the Multifiber Arrangement negotiated within the framework of the General Agreement on Tariffs and Trade (GATT), are also subject to quantitative restrictions. As a result of the commitments made under the Uruguay Round Agreement, Canada has agreed to replace all agricultural import restrictions with tariff rate quotas and to ensure import access levels as negotiated in the Uruguay Round. These changes will be effective on either January 1, 1995 or August 1, 1995 depending on the product. In accordance with the provisions of the Uruguay Round Agreement on textiles and clothing, Canada's system of import controls on textiles and clothing will be liberalized in stages over a ten-year period beginning January 1, 1995.

Exports and Export Proceeds

To support their export sales, exporters may have access to financing and insurance services provided by the Export Development Corporation.

The surrender of proceeds from exports is not required and exchange receipts are freely disposable. The principal legal instrument governing export controls is the Export and Import Permits Act, which controls trade through the Export Control List and Area Control List. The Export Control List identifies all goods that are controlled in order to implement intergovernmental arrangements, maintain supplies, or ensure security. It includes all items identified in the International Munitions List, the International Industrial List, and the International Atomic Energy List. In addition, controls are maintained over a broad range of items controlled for nonproliferation purposes (chemical, biological, and nuclear weapons and their delivery systems).

The Area Control List includes a limited number of countries to which all exports are controlled. At present, the following countries are on the Area Control List: Angola, Bosnia and Herzegovina, the Libyan Arab Jamahiriya, and the Federal Republic of Yugoslavia (Serbia/Montenegro).

Permits are required for the exportation of listed goods to all countries except, in most cases, the United States as well as for all goods destined to countries on the Area Control List.

Payments for and Proceeds from Invisibles

No exchange control requirements are imposed on exchange payments for or exchange receipts from invisibles.

Capital

No exchange control requirements are imposed on capital receipts or payments by residents or nonresidents. Specific restrictions exist on inward direct investments in the broadcasting, telecommunication, transportation, fishery, and energy sectors. As a result of the Uruguay Round Agreement, Canada has eliminated the few remaining restrictions in the financial services sector. Specifically, the 10 percent individual, and 25 percent collective, limitations on the foreign ownership of Canadian-controlled, federally regulated financial institutions, and the 12 percent asset ceiling on the size of the foreign bank sector in Canada were eliminated. This became effective on December 15, 1994, when amendments to the Bank Act, the Trust and Loan Companies Act, the Insurance Companies Act, the Cooperative Insurance Companies Act, and the Investment Companies Act received Royal Assent as part of the World Trade Organization Agreement Implementation Act. These restrictions had already been lifted in the North American Free Trade Agreement (NAFTA). In addition, under the provisions of the Investment Canada Act, new foreign investments are in general subject to notification requirements but not to review requirements. By the end of 1994, only direct acquisitions of businesses with assets exceeding Can$160 million were subject to review. As a result of NAFTA, indirect acquisitions are no longer subject to review. This provision was multilateralized as part of Canada's implementation of the Uruguay Round results. In

addition, acquisitions below these limits and investments to establish new businesses in culturally sensitive sectors may be reviewed. Investments subject to review are required only to pass a test proving that they will yield a net benefit to Canada. There are no controls on outward direct investment or on inward or outward portfolio investment.

Gold

Residents may freely purchase, hold, and sell gold in any form, at home or abroad. Gold of U.S. origin requires a permit when re-exported to all countries except the United States. Commercial imports of articles containing minor quantities of gold, such as watches, are unrestricted and free of license. Legal tender gold coins with a face value of Can$100 have been issued annually since 1976, and Can$50 "bullion" coins, containing 1 ounce of gold, have also been issued since 1979. In 1982, Can$5 and Can$10 coins containing $\frac{1}{10}$ and $\frac{1}{4}$ of an ounce of gold, respectively, were issued; in 1986, a coin containing $\frac{1}{2}$ of an ounce of gold with a face value of Can$50 was issued.

Changes During 1994

Administration of Control

January 1. The North American Free Trade Agreement between Canada, the United States, and Mexico came into force. NAFTA replaced the Canada-United States Free Trade Agreement and extended the benefits of the agreement to Mexico.

December 11. Chile was invited by Canada and the other two NAFTA signatories to join in preaccession negotiations with a view to having Chile become the fourth member of the trade agreement.

December 15. The Canadian Parliament passed an act to implement the agreement establishing the World Trade Organization, which took effect on January 1, 1995 implementing Canada's obligations resulting from the Uruguay Round.

Imports and Import Payments

During 1994, the injury findings in respect of sour cherries, delicious apples, and malt beverages (beer) imported from the United States ended, as did the undertakings in respect of aluminum wedge clamps and steel grinding balls from the United States. The injury finding in respect of the dumping of electric motors also expired. There were injury findings in respect of the dumping of carbon steel plate, 12-gauge shotgun shells and corrosion-resistant steel, each from various countries, as well as an injury finding in respect of the subsidizing and the dumping of black granite memorials from India.

March 31. The Canadian General Preferential Tariff was extended to June 30, 2004, and a review of the scheme was announced.

May 6. The 25 percent surtax on boneless beef levied on imports of more than 72,021 metric tons from countries other than the United States and Mexico was liberalized and would be levied on imports of more than 85,021 metric tons.

October 6. Certain cuts of boneless beef were excluded from the application of the 25 percent surtax on imports from countries other than the United States and Mexico.

December 31. The 25 percent surtax on certain imports of boneless beef lapsed.

CAPE VERDE

(Position as of December 31, 1994)

Exchange Arrangement

The currency of Cape Verde is the Cape Verde Escudo, which is pegged to a weighted basket of currencies issued by the nine countries (other than the United States) that are the most important suppliers of imports and emigrant remittances. The exchange rate of the Cape Verde escudo in terms of the U.S. dollar, the intervention currency, is fixed daily on the basis of quotations for the U.S. dollar and the other currencies included in the basket. On December 31, 1994, the buying and selling rates for the U.S. dollar were C.V. Esc 80.85 and C.V. Esc 81.42, respectively, per US$1. Most dealings in foreign exchange with the general public are conducted by the two commercial banks (BCA and CECV), which are allowed net foreign exchange positions of up to the equivalent of US$1.5 million and US$1 million, respectively. In addition to the two commercial banks, hotels and tourist agencies are authorized to buy foreign exchange from the public. There are no taxes or subsidies on purchases or sales of foreign exchange. There are no arrangements for forward cover against exchange rate risk operating in the official or the commercial banking sector.

Administration of Control

All foreign exchange transactions are under the control of the Bank of Cape Verde (the central bank). Certain categories of imports, exports, and re-exports exceeding specified limits are subject to licensing.

Arrears are maintained with respect to external payments.

Prescription of Currency

Export proceeds must be repatriated in convertible currencies. Cape Verde maintains bilateral payments agreements with Angola and São Tomé and Príncipe, both of which are currently inoperative.

Nonresident Accounts

Nonresidents may open demand deposit accounts in local currency. These accounts may be credited only with the proceeds from the sale or surrender of receipts of convertible currencies and may be debited for payment of any obligations in Cape Verde. Outward transfers of balances from such accounts may be made freely. Embassies and foreign officials of embassies are required to open special accounts in foreign currency and in local currency; such accounts must be replenished exclusively with foreign exchange. Foreign enterprises may maintain accounts in foreign currency.

Special Accounts (Emigrants)

Three types of special interest-bearing deposit accounts are available for emigrants: (1) foreign exchange deposit accounts, (2) savings-credit deposit accounts, and (3) special accounts in Cape Verde escudos. These accounts may be credited only with convertible foreign currencies. Holders of savings-credit deposit accounts can benefit from loans on special terms for financing small-scale projects.

Imports and Import Payments

Imports with a value of less than C.V. Esc 100,000 are exempt from the licensing requirement. Imports of goods exceeding C.V. Esc 100,000 and not involving payments from the country's foreign exchange resources are subject to the preregistration requirement. The importation of maize, rice, sugar, and cooking oil is a government monopoly.

Licenses, which are issued by the General Directorate of Commerce in the Ministry of Economy, Transportation, and Communications, require the endorsement of the central bank and are generally valid for 90 days; they are renewable. The provision of foreign exchange is guaranteed when the license has been previously certified by the central bank. Licenses are, in general, granted liberally for imports of medicines, capital goods, and other development-related equipment. The Ministry of Tourism, Industry, and Commerce establishes a list of products for which imports are subject to a global annual quota. This list includes mostly locally produced food items and beverages, (e.g., fish, bread, tomatoes, bananas, cereals, salt, beer, and soft drinks), with some items subject to seasonal quotas (e.g., potatoes, onions, and poultry).

Payments for Invisibles

All payments for invisibles require prior authorization. Any person traveling abroad may take out foreign currency equivalent to C.V. Esc 100,000. Nationals of Cape Verde traveling abroad as tourists are required to buy round-trip tickets in advance.

Cape Verdean nationals studying abroad are allowed up to a maximum of C.V. Esc 100,000 on leaving the country; students who do not hold scholarships are, in addition, entitled to a monthly allowance that varies according to the country of destination. Persons traveling abroad on business may take an amount of foreign currency that varies according to the country of destination and the duration of each trip. Persons traveling abroad for medical treatment may take out an amount of foreign currency that varies according to medical needs. Applications for these allowances must be accompanied by medical certification before the trip, and medical bills must be presented on return to Cape Verde.

Transfers by foreign technical assistance personnel working in Cape Verde are authorized within the limits specified in the individual contracts. These contracts, as well as other contracts involving foreign exchange expenditures, are subject to prior screening by the central bank. Requests by other foreigners are examined on a case-by-case basis. The exportation of domestic currency by travelers is prohibited. Foreign travelers may bring in any amount of foreign currency but may re-export only up to the amount of currency they declared upon entry.

Exports and Export Proceeds

All exports exceeding C.V. Esc 2,500 are subject to licensing and to approval by the central bank.

Export proceeds must be repatriated within three months of the date of issuance of the license, but this period may be extended.

Proceeds from Invisibles

Receipts from invisibles must be surrendered to a commercial bank. The importation of domestic currency is prohibited.

Capital

Any private capital transaction must be approved in advance by the central bank, but legally imported capital may be re-exported without limitation. The exportation of resident-owned capital is not normally permitted. Foreign direct investments are allowed to be repatriated (within 30 days of submission of applications to the Bank of Cape Verde).

Gold

Imports, exports, or re-exports of gold in either coins or bars require prior licensing by the monetary authorities.

Changes During 1994

No significant changes occurred in the exchange and trade system.

CENTRAL AFRICAN REPUBLIC

(Position as of December 31, 1994)

Exchange Arrangement

The currency of the Central African Republic is the CFA Franc,[1] which is pegged to the French franc, the intervention currency, at the fixed rate of CFAF 1 per F 0.01. Exchange transactions in French francs between the BEAC and commercial banks take place at the rate of CFAF 100 per F 1, free of commission. Buying and selling rates for certain other foreign currencies are also officially posted, with quotations based on the fixed rate for the French franc and the rates in the Paris exchange market for the currencies concerned. A commission of 0.25 percent is levied on all capital transfers to countries that are not members of the BEAC, except those made for the account of the Treasury and for the expenses of students. There are no taxes or subsidies on purchases or sales of foreign exchange.

With the exception of measures relating to gold, the exchange control measures of the Central African Republic do not apply to (1) France (and its overseas departments and territories) and Monaco; and (2) all other countries whose bank of issue is linked with the French Treasury by an Operations Account (Benin, Burkina Faso, Cameroon, Chad, Comoros, Congo, Côte d'Ivoire, Equatorial Guinea, Gabon, Mali, Niger, Senegal, and Togo). All payments to these countries may, therefore, be made freely. All other countries are considered foreign countries.

Administration of Control

All draft legislation, directives, correspondence, and contracts having a direct or indirect bearing on the finances of the state require the prior approval of the Minister of Finance, who has delegated approval authority to the Director of the Budget. The Autonomous Amortization Fund (CAADE) of the Ministry of Finance supervises borrowing abroad. The Office of Foreign Financial Relations of the same ministry supervises lending abroad; the issuing, advertising, or offering for sale of foreign securities in the Central African Republic; and inward and outward direct investment. Exchange control is administered by the Minister of Finance, who has delegated some approval authority to the BEAC,[2] to authorized banks, and to the Postal Administration. All exchange transactions relating to foreign countries must be effected through authorized banks. Export declarations are to be made through the Directorate of Foreign Trade of the Ministry of Commerce and Industry, except those for gold, which are to be made through the BEAC.

Arrears are maintained with respect to external payments.

Prescription of Currency

Since the Central African Republic is an Operations Account country, settlements with France (as defined above), Monaco, and the Operations Account countries are made in CFA francs, French francs, or the currency of any other institute of issue that maintains an Operations Account with the French Treasury. Settlements with all other countries are usually made in the currencies of those countries or in French francs through foreign accounts in francs.

Nonresident Accounts

The regulations pertaining to nonresident accounts are based on regulations applied in France. The principal nonresident accounts are foreign accounts in francs. As the BEAC has suspended the repurchase of BEAC banknotes circulating outside the territories of the CFA franc zone, BEAC banknotes received by the foreign correspondents of authorized banks and mailed to the BEAC agency in Bangui by the Bank of France or the Central Bank of West African States (BCEAO) may not be credited to foreign accounts in francs.

Imports and Import Payments

No imports from any country are subject to licensing requirements or quotas. Imports of firearms are prohibited irrespective of origin. Import declarations are required for all imports, and all import transactions relating to foreign countries must be domiciled with an authorized bank. The import li-

---

[1]The CFA franc circulating in the Central African Republic is issued by the Bank of Central African States (BEAC) and is also legal tender in Cameroon, Chad, Congo, Equatorial Guinea, and Gabon.

[2]The authority delegated to the BEAC relates to (1) control over the external position of the banks, (2) the granting of exceptional travel allocations in excess of the basic allowances, and (3) control over the repatriation of net export proceeds.

cense entitles importers to purchase the necessary exchange, provided that the shipping documents are submitted to the authorized bank.

Payments for Invisibles

Payments for invisibles to France (as defined above), Monaco, and the Operations Account countries are permitted freely; those to other countries are subject to approval. Approval authority for many types of payment has been delegated to authorized banks. Payments for invisibles related to trade are permitted freely when the basic trade transaction has been approved or does not require authorization. Transfers of income accruing to nonresidents in the form of profits, dividends, and royalties are also permitted freely when the basic transaction has been approved.

Residents traveling for tourism or business purposes to countries in the franc zone are allowed to take out BEAC banknotes up to a limit of CFAF 2 million; amounts in excess of this limit may be taken out in the form of means of payment other than banknotes. The allowances for travel to countries outside the franc zone are subject to the following regulations: (1) for tourist travel, CFAF 100,000 a day, with a maximum of CFAF 2 million a trip; (2) for business travel, CFAF 250,000 a day, with a maximum of CFAF 5 million a trip; (3) allowances in excess of these limits are subject to the authorization of the Ministry of Finance or, by delegation, the BEAC; and (4) the use of credit cards, which must be issued by resident financial intermediaries and approved by the Ministry of Finance, is limited to the ceilings indicated above for tourism and business travel. Returning resident travelers are required to declare all means of payment in their possession upon arrival at customs and surrender within eight days all means of payment exceeding the equivalent of CFAF 25,000. All resident travelers, regardless of destination, must declare in writing all means of payment at their disposal at the time of departure. The re-exportation by nonresident travelers of means of payment other than banknotes registered in their name and issued abroad is not restricted; however, documentation is required that such means of payment have been purchased with funds drawn from a foreign account in CFA francs or with other foreign exchange. The re-exportation of foreign banknotes is allowed up to the equivalent of CFAF 250,000; the re-exportation of foreign banknotes above these ceilings requires documentation demonstrating either the importation of foreign banknotes or their purchase against other means of payment registered in the name of the trav-

eler or through the use of nonresident deposits held in local banks.

Exports and Export Proceeds

All exports require a declaration. Proceeds from exports to foreign countries must be collected and repatriated within one month of the due date, which must not be later than 90 days after the arrival of the goods at their destination, unless special authorization is obtained. Export proceeds received in currencies other than French francs or those of an Operations Account country must be surrendered. All export transactions must be domiciled with an authorized bank.

Proceeds from Invisibles

Proceeds from transactions in invisibles with France (as defined above), Monaco, and the Operations Account countries may be retained. All amounts due from residents of other countries in respect of services, and all income earned in those countries from foreign assets, must be collected within one month of the due date. If payment is received in foreign currency, it must be surrendered within one month of the date of receipt. Resident and nonresident travelers may bring in any amount of banknotes and coins issued by the BEAC, the Bank of France, or any other bank of issue maintaining an Operations Account with the French Treasury, as well as any amount of foreign banknotes and coins (except gold coins) of countries outside the Operations Account Area.

Capital

Capital movements between the Central African Republic and France (as defined above), Monaco, and the Operations Account countries are free of exchange control; capital transfers to all other countries require exchange control approval and are restricted, but capital receipts from such countries are permitted freely. All foreign borrowing by the Government or its public and semipublic enterprises, as well as all foreign borrowing with a government guarantee, requires the prior approval of the Director of the Budget.

Special controls (in addition to any exchange control requirements that may apply) are maintained over borrowing and lending abroad; over inward and outward direct investment; and over the issuing, advertising, or offering for sale of foreign securities in the Central African Republic. These controls relate to the transactions themselves, not to payments or receipts. With the exception of those controls over the sale or introduction of foreign securities in the Central African Republic, the measures do not apply to France (as defined above), Monaco, and the Operations Account countries.

Direct investments abroad[3] require the prior approval of the Ministry of Finance, unless they take the form of a capital increase resulting from the reinvestment of undistributed profits. The full or partial liquidation of such investments also requires prior approval from the Ministry of Finance, unless the operation involves the relinquishing of a participation that had previously been approved as constituting a direct investment abroad. Foreign direct investments in the Central African Republic[4] must be declared to the Minister of Finance, unless they take the form of a capital increase resulting from the reinvestment of undistributed profits; the Minister has a period of two months from receipt of the declaration during which he may request postponement. The full or partial liquidation of direct investments in the Central African Republic must also be declared to the Minister, unless the operation involves the relinquishing of a participation that had previously been approved as constituting a direct investment in the Central African Republic. All direct investments, whether Central African Republic investments abroad or foreign investments in the Central African Republic, that are made or liquidated must be reported to the Minister within 20 days of each operation. (Direct investments are defined as those that imply control of a company or an enterprise. Mere participation is not considered direct investment, provided that it does not exceed 20 percent of the capital of a company whose shares are quoted on a stock exchange.)

The issuing, advertising, or offering for sale of foreign securities in the Central African Republic requires prior authorization from the Minister of Finance. Exempt from authorization, however, are operations in connection with (1) loans backed by a guarantee from the Government, and (2) shares similar to securities, when issuing, advertising, or offering them for sale in the Central African Republic has previously been authorized.

Borrowing abroad by natural or juridical persons, whether public or private, whose normal residence or registered office is in the Central African Repub-

lic, or by branches or subsidiaries in the Central African Republic of juridical persons whose registered office is abroad, requires prior authorization from the Minister of Finance. The following are, however, exempt from this authorization: (1) loans constituting a direct investment abroad for which prior approval has been obtained, as indicated above; (2) loans directly connected with the rendering of services abroad by the persons or firms mentioned above, or with the financing of commercial transactions either between the Central African Republic and countries abroad or between foreign countries in which those persons or firms take part; (3) loans contracted by registered banks; and (4) loans other than those mentioned above, when the total amount of loans outstanding does not exceed CFAF 50 million for any one borrower. Loans referred to under (4) and each repayment must be reported to the Office of Foreign Financial Relations within 20 days of the operation, unless the total outstanding amount of all loans contracted abroad by the borrower is less than CFAF 500,000.

Lending abroad by natural or juridical persons, whether public or private, whose normal residence or registered office is in the Central African Republic, or by branches or subsidiaries in the Central African Republic of juridical persons whose registered office is abroad, requires prior authorization from the Minister of Finance. The following are, however, exempt from this authorization: (1) loans granted by registered banks, and (2) other loans when the total amount of loans outstanding does not exceed CFAF 50 million for any one lender. The contracting of loans that are exempt from authorization, and each repayment, must be reported to the Office of Foreign Financial Relations within 20 days of the operation, except when the amount of the loan granted abroad by the lender is less than CFAF 500,000.

Under Law No. 62/355 of February 19, 1963 (as amended by Ordinance No. 69/47 of September 2, 1969) and Decision No. 18/65 of December 14, 1965, of the Central African Customs and Economic Union, industrial, tourist, agricultural, and mining enterprises (both foreign and domestic) established in the Central African Republic are granted, under certain conditions, a reduction in duties and taxes on the importation of specified equipment. In addition, certain enterprises are exempt from direct taxes on specified income.

The law also provides for three categories of preferential treatment (A, B, and C) that allow fiscal and other privileges to be accorded to firms investing either in new enterprises or in the expansion of existing ones in most sectors of the economy, except the

---

[3]Including those made through foreign companies that are directly or indirectly controlled by persons in the Central African Republic and those made by branches or subsidiaries abroad of companies in the Central African Republic.

[4]Including those made by companies in the Central African Republic that are directly or indirectly under foreign control and those made by branches or subsidiaries of foreign companies in the Central African Republic.

commercial sector. Requests for approval of preferential treatment must be submitted to the Minister of Industry, who is Chairman of the Investment Commission that considers the application. If the Commission gives a positive decision, the proposed authorization is submitted to the Council of Ministers. Preferential treatments A and C are granted by decree from the Council of Ministers. Preferential treatment B is granted by an Act of the Board of Directors of the Equatorial Customs Union upon the recommendation of the Council of Ministers.

Gold

Residents are free to hold, acquire, and dispose of gold in any form in the Central African Republic. Imports and exports of gold from or to any other country require a license, which is seldom granted; in practice, imports and exports are made by an authorized purchasing office. Exempt from prior authorization are (1) imports and exports by or on behalf of the Treasury, and (2) imports and exports of manufactured articles containing a small quantity of gold (such as gold-filled or gold-plated articles). Both licensed and exempt imports of gold are subject to customs declaration. Certain companies have been officially appointed as Offices for the Purchase, Import, and Export of Gold and Raw Diamonds.

Changes During 1994

Exchange Arrangement

January 12. The CFA franc was devalued to CFAF 100 per F 1 from CFAF 50 per F 1.

Administration of Control

May 13. The Ministry of Finance issued a regulation that brought exchange regulations of the Central African Republic in line with those adopted by the other BEAC countries (following the suspension of the repurchase of CFA banknotes in circulation outside the BEAC zone).

CHAD

(Position as of December 31, 1994)

Exchange Arrangement

The currency of Chad is the CFA Franc,[1] which is pegged to the French franc, the intervention currency, at the fixed rate of CFAF 1 per F 0.01. The official buying and selling rate is CFAF 100 per F 1. Exchange transactions in French francs between the BEAC and commercial banks take place at the same rate. Buying and selling rates for certain other foreign currencies are also officially posted, with quotations based on the fixed rate for the French franc and the rates in the Paris exchange market for the currencies concerned. A commission of 0.25 percent is levied on all capital transfers abroad by the banks for their own account, except those made for the account of the Treasury, for students' bursaries, and to the member countries of the BEAC. There are no taxes or subsidies on the purchase or sale of foreign exchange.

With the exception of those relating to gold, Chad's exchange control measures do not apply to (1) France (and its overseas departments and territories) and Monaco; and (2) all other countries whose bank of issue is linked with the French Treasury by an Operations Account (Benin, Burkina Faso, Cameroon, the Central African Republic, Comoros, Congo, Côte d'Ivoire, Equatorial Guinea, Gabon, Mali, Niger, Senegal, and Togo). Hence, all payments to these countries may be made freely. However, they must be declared and made only through authorized banks, using bank checks. Payments to all other countries are subject to exchange control.

Forward cover for imports is permitted only for specified commodities and requires the prior approval of the Office of the Minister of Economy and Commerce.

Administration of Control

Exchange control is administered by the Minister of Finance, who has delegated approval authority in part to the External Finance and Exchange Control Subdirectorate, which issues instructions to the authorized banks. All exchange transactions relating to countries outside the Operations Account Area must be made through authorized banks. Import and export licenses are issued by the Ministry of Commerce and Industrial Promotion. The Ministry of Finance supervises public and private sector borrowing and lending abroad, the issuing, advertising, or offering for sale of foreign securities in Chad, and inward and outward direct investment. It also issues import and export authorizations for gold.

Arrears are maintained with respect to debt-service payments on public debt.

Prescription of Currency

Since Chad is an Operations Account country, settlements with France (as defined above), Monaco, and other Operations Account countries are made in CFA francs, French francs, or the currency of any other institute of issue that maintains an Operations Account with the French Treasury. Settlements with all other countries are usually made through correspondent banks in France in any of the currencies of those countries or in French francs through foreign accounts in francs.

Nonresident Accounts

The regulations pertaining to nonresident accounts are based on regulations applied in France. The repurchase of banknotes issued by the BEAC and in circulation outside the BEAC area is suspended; BEAC banknotes received by the foreign correspondents of authorized banks and mailed to the BEAC agency in Chad by the Bank of France or the Central Bank of West African States (BCEAO) may not be credited to foreign accounts in francs.

Imports and Import Payments

Imports of wheat, wheat flour, and sugar from all sources require licenses. All other imports from countries in the French Franc Area and the original member states of the EU (other than France) may be made freely. All imports from non-EU countries outside the Operations Account Area are subject to licensing in accordance with an annual import program. This program and the amount of foreign exchange required to implement it are determined by the Ministry of Commerce and Industrial Promotion on the basis of proposals drawn up by the Committee on Imports.

---

[1]The CFA franc in circulation in Chad is issued by the Bank of Central African States (BEAC) and is legal tender also in Cameroon, the Central African Republic, Congo, Equatorial Guinea, and Gabon.

The import program contains global quotas for imports from non-EU countries outside the Operations Account Area and a special quota for imports of cotton textiles from countries judged to have abnormal competitive advantages. In addition, the program contains global quotas for imports of wheat, wheat flour, and sugar from EU countries, countries in the Operations Account Area, and other countries. Specified goods from certain neighboring countries not belonging to the Operations Account Area, up to a value of CFAF 3 million a year, may be imported through compensation transactions by an importer. The issuance of import licenses for sugar and a specified brand of cigarettes has been suspended until further notice.

All import transactions valued at CFAF 100,000 or more and relating to foreign countries must be domiciled with an authorized bank. Import licenses entitle importers to purchase the necessary exchange, provided that shipping documents are submitted to the authorized bank.

Payments for Invisibles

Payments for invisibles to France (as defined above), Monaco, and the Operations Account countries are permitted freely. Only a simple declaration is required for transfers to countries outside the BEAC area by residents not exceeding CFAF 500,000; for transfers of more than CFAF 500,000, prior authorization must be obtained from the competent authorities. For many types of payment, approval authority has been delegated to authorized banks. Authorized banks are required to execute promptly all duly documented transfer orders, and in any case to dispatch cable transfers within 24 hours of receipt of the relevant request. Payments for invisibles related to trade are permitted freely if the basic trade transaction has been approved or does not require authorization. Transfers of bona fide income accruing to nonresidents in the form of profits, dividends, and royalties are also permitted freely. Some current payments, however, may be subject to delay. On a temporary basis, nonresidents, except diplomatic missions and their staff, international organizations and their staff, agencies with equivalent status and their staff, as well as employees and self-employed members of the professions (professionally active in Operations Account Area countries for less than a year) are not permitted to send transfers to countries that are not franc zone members without prior authorization from the competent authorities. They may, however, receive transfers from abroad.

Insurance on all imports to Chad with values exceeding CFA 500,000 on f.o.b. terms must be arranged with local insurance companies by the importer.

The exportation (and importation) of banknotes issued by the BEAC to areas outside the BEAC area is prohibited.

Travelers—civil servants on missions, students, persons on pilgrimage, etc.—must use the following payments instruments: foreign exchange, traveler's checks; bank drafts, bank and postal transfers, etc. Residents visiting other franc zone countries may obtain an unlimited allocation in French francs. This allocation can be provided in banknotes, traveler's checks, bank drafts, bank or postal transfers, etc. For travel to countries outside the franc zone, the exchange allocation shall depend on the type of travel (as indicated below) and is subject to prior authorization from the relevant administrative authorities. This allocation can be made in banknotes, traveler's checks, bank drafts, or postal transfers. Residents traveling outside the franc zone for tourism may obtain an exchange allocation equivalent to CFAF 100,000 a day up to a maximum of CFAF 2 million a trip a person over 10 years of age; for children under 10, the allocation is reduced by one-half. Residents traveling to countries outside the franc zone for tourism may obtain an exchange allocation equivalent to CFAF 250,000 a day, up to a maximum of CFAF 5 million a trip. Students or trainees leaving for the first time or returning to their normal place of study in countries outside the franc zone may obtain an exchange allocation equivalent to a three-month scholarship plus expenses for supplies. However, a student, whether or not the holder of a scholarship, may obtain an exchange allocation not exceeding the equivalent of CFAF 1 million. Civil servants and government employees traveling on official business to countries outside the franc zone may obtain an exchange allocation equivalent to the allowances stipulated for such travel. However, civil servants and government employees may obtain an exchange allocation on the same basis as tourists only if their mission costs are less than a daily allocation of CFAF 100,000, up to a limit of CFAF 2 million. Residents traveling to countries outside the franc zone for medical treatment may obtain an exchange allocation equivalent to CFAF 100,000 a day up to a limit of CFAF 2.5 million. Residents traveling to countries outside the franc zone for reasons other than those listed above (sporting events, participation in expositions, organization of fairs, participation in seminars or international meetings in a personal capacity, pilgrimages, etc.) shall be granted exchange allocations on the same basis as those traveling for tourism. Resident and nonresident travelers may import into BEAC area countries an unlimited amount of coins and banknotes other than those denominated in CFA francs.

Exports and Export Proceeds

All exports to non-EU countries outside the French Franc Area require licenses. Specified exports to certain neighboring countries, including Nigeria and Sudan, may be made through compensation transactions. Exports of cotton are the monopoly of COTONTCHAD.

Export transactions relating to foreign countries must be domiciled with an authorized bank when their value exceeds CFAF 50,000. Export proceeds received in currencies other than those of France or an Operations Account country must be surrendered. Export proceeds normally must be received within 180 days of the arrival of the commodities at their destination. The proceeds must be collected and, if received in a foreign currency, surrendered within two months of the due date.

Proceeds from Invisibles

Proceeds from transactions in invisibles with France (as defined above), Monaco, and Operations Account countries may be retained. All amounts due from residents of other countries in respect of services, and all income earned in those countries from foreign assets, must be collected and, if received in foreign currency, surrendered within two months of the due date.

Nonresidents traveling from one BEAC member country to another may take with them an unlimited amount of franc zone banknotes and coins. Nonresident travelers may take out foreign exchange or other foreign means of payment up to the amount they declared on entry into the BEAC area. If they have made no declaration on entry into one of the BEAC countries, they may take out only up to the equivalent of CFAF 250,000.

Capital

Capital movements between Chad and France (as defined above), Monaco, and the Operations Account countries are free of exchange control; capital transfers to all other countries require exchange control approval and are restricted, but capital receipts from such countries are permitted freely. All foreign securities, foreign currencies, and titles embodying claims on foreign countries or nonresidents held by residents or nonresidents in Chad must be deposited with authorized banks in Chad.

Special controls in addition to any exchange control requirements that may be applicable or suspended are maintained over borrowing and lending abroad; over inward and outward direct investment; and over the issuing, advertising, or offering for sale of foreign securities in Chad. These controls relate only to the transactions themselves, not to payments or receipts. With the exception of those controls over the sale or introduction of foreign securities in Chad, the measures do not apply to France (as defined above), Monaco, and the Operations Account countries.

Direct investments abroad[2] require the prior approval of the Minister of Finance, irrespective of the method of financing; the full or partial liquidation of such investments also requires the prior approval of the Minister. Foreign direct investments in Chad[3] require the prior approval of the Minister of Finance, unless they take the form of a mixed-economy enterprise; the full or partial liquidation of direct investments in Chad must also be declared to the Minister. Both the making and the liquidation of direct investments, whether Chadian investments abroad or foreign investments in Chad, must be reported to the Minister within 30 days of each operation. (Direct investments are defined as investments implying control of a company or enterprise.)

The issuing, advertising, or offering for sale of foreign securities in Chad requires prior authorization from the Minister of Finance. Exempt from authorization, however, are operations in connection with (1) loans backed by a guarantee from the Chadian Government, and (2) shares similar to securities, when issuing, advertising, or offering them for sale in Chad has already been authorized.

Borrowing abroad by natural or juridical persons, whether public or private, residing in Chad, or by branches or subsidiaries in Chad of juridical persons whose registered office is abroad, requires prior authorization from the Minister of Finance. The following are, however, exempt from this authorization: (1) loans constituting a direct investment abroad for which prior approval has been obtained, as indicated above; (2) loans directly connected with the rendering of services abroad by the persons or firms mentioned above, or with the financing of commercial transactions either between Chad and countries abroad or between foreign

---

[2]Including those made through foreign companies that are directly or indirectly controlled by persons in Chad and those made by overseas branches or subsidiaries of companies in Chad.

[3]Including those made by companies in Chad directly or indirectly under foreign control and those made by branches or subsidiaries of foreign companies in Chad.

countries in which these persons or firms take part; and (3) loans other than those mentioned above when the total amount of the loan outstanding does not exceed CFAF 10 million for any one borrower, the interest rate is no higher than 7 percent, and the maturity is two years or less. The contracting of loans referred to under (3) that are free of authorization and each repayment must be declared to the Minister of Finance within 30 days of the operation.

Lending abroad by natural or juridical persons, whether public or private, residing in Chad, or by branches or subsidiaries in Chad of juridical persons whose registered office is abroad, requires prior authorization from the Minister of Finance. The following are, however, exempt from this authorization: (1) loans directly connected with the rendering of services abroad by the persons or firms mentioned above, or with the financing of commercial transactions either between Chad and countries abroad or between foreign countries in which these persons or firms take part; and (2) other loans when the total amount of these loans outstanding does not exceed CFAF 5 million for any one lender. The making of loans referred to under (2) that are free of authorization and each repayment must be declared to the Minister of Finance within 30 days of the operation. Commercial banks must maintain a specified minimum amount of their assets in Chad.

Under the Investment Code published on December 9, 1987, any domestic or foreign enterprise established in Chad is granted, under certain conditions, reduced duties and taxes on specified imports and exemption from direct taxes on specified income. The code provides for four categories of enterprises that may be eligible to receive various forms of preferential treatment (including certain tax privileges). Requests for preferential treatment must be submitted to the Minister of Finance, who, after examining the documents, transmits them to the Investment Commission. With the recommendation of this commission, the project is submitted to the Council of Ministers for approval.

Gold

Chad has issued gold coins with face values of CFAF 1,000, CFAF 3,000, CFAF 5,000, CFAF 10,000, and CFAF 20,000, which are legal tender. Residents who are not producers of gold may not hold unworked gold without specific authorization. Imports and exports of gold, whether unworked or refined, require prior authorization from both the Ministry of Finance and the Directorate of Geological and Mining Research, as well as a visa from the External Finance Department. Exempt from this requirement are (1) imports and exports by or on behalf of the monetary authorities, and (2) imports and exports of manufactured articles containing a small quantity of gold (such as gold-filled or gold-plated articles). Unworked gold may be exported only to France. Both licensed and exempt imports of gold are subject to customs declaration.

Changes During 1994

Exchange Arrangement

January 12. The CFA franc was devalued to CFAF 100 per F 1 from CFAF 50 per F 1.

CHILE

(Position as of December 31, 1994)

Exchange Arrangement

The currency of Chile is the Chilean Peso (Ch$). Its external (reference) value is pegged to a fixed basket of currencies consisting of 0.45 U.S. dollar, 0.4691 deutsche mark, and 24.6825 Japanese yen; the weight of each currency in the basket is based on its relative importance in Chile's international transactions. The external value of the basket is adjusted daily on the basis of the exchange rate relationships between the currencies included in the basket and the differential between the domestic and the foreign rates of inflation. The Central Bank of Chile conducts foreign exchange transactions with the official exchange market entities within margins of 10 percent around the reference rate. On December 31, 1994, the reference rate was Ch$419.62 per US$1 and the interbank rate was Ch$404.09 per US$1. The official foreign exchange market consists of commercial banks, exchange houses, and other entities licensed by the Central Bank. Fifty percent of proceeds from exports of goods and services; debt-service payments; remittances of dividends and profits; and authorized capital transactions, including loan receipts, must be transacted through this market. In addition, there is an informal exchange market through which all transactions not required to be channeled through the official foreign exchange market are allowed to take place. In both markets, economic agents are free to negotiate exchange rates.

The banks are authorized to sell their excess foreign exchange holdings to other banks. Foreign exchange may be bought for the repayment of capital or interest abroad due within 90 days if these debts are properly registered at the Central Bank. The Central Bank provides an exchange subsidy on the following service payments on some debts contracted before August 6, 1982 (the original amount of the debt was about $8 billion):[1] (1) payments to Chilean banks or financial companies whose debt is indexed to the official exchange rate; and (2) payments abroad on debt obligations registered with the Central Bank. The subsidy is paid by means of notes indexed to inflation with a minimum maturity of six years and an interest rate of 3 percent. On December 31, 1994, the subsidized rate was Ch$40.55 above the official reference rate. As of the end of 1994, only those debtors whose obligations were equal to or less than US$50,000 on June 30, 1985 have had access to this subsidized rate. However, the actual amount for which this exchange rate was being applied at the end of 1994 was nil, due to the bankruptcy of many of the affected debtors and to the fact that the official reference rate was lower than the preferential rate.

Administration of Control

The Central Bank is responsible for implementing exchange control policy. The Chilean Copper Commission is responsible for supervising copper exports and all imports of the copper industry in accordance with general rules enacted by the Central Bank.

Prescription of Currency

Settlements with Argentina, Bolivia, Brazil, Colombia, the Dominican Republic, Ecuador, Mexico, Paraguay, Peru, Uruguay, and Venezuela are made through accounts maintained with each other by the Central Bank of Chile and the central banks of each of the countries concerned within the framework of the multilateral clearing system of the Latin American Integration Association (LAIA).

Imports and Import Payments

Most imports are free of controls, with the exception of used motor vehicles. Most imports require a document (*Informe de Importación*) issued by the Central Bank, which must be obtained and processed through the intermediary local commercial bank. Payment for visible trade transactions, through the official foreign exchange market, is not permitted unless an *Informe de Importación* has been issued.

Importers meeting the documentary requirements are granted access to the official foreign exchange market, regardless of the terms of the obligation involved, at least 30 days after the obligation's expiration date as it appears in the *Informe de Importación*. Imports are subject to a uniform tariff rate of 11 percent. A few items are exempt from the general tariff regime, including items on which tariffs have been negotiated with LAIA countries and under a number of bilateral trade agreements.

---

[1]This exchange subsidy was being phased out with the repayment of the covered debt and the fact that the differential between the official reference rate and the preferential rate became negative during the fourth quarter of 1994.

Imports of wheat, maize, edible oil, and sugar are subject to a special regime involving price margins within which the after-duty price must remain. In addition, tariff duties or surcharges are applied, on a temporary basis, to imports of certain products that are subsidized in the country of origin or dumped in Chile.

Payments for Invisibles

Specified allowances are granted for certain transactions; others must take place through the informal exchange market. Authorization is provided upon presentation of the appropriate documents. The limit for tourist travel (in addition to the fares) is US$3,000 a trip for travel to Latin American and Caribbean countries and US$5,000 a trip to other countries. Higher amounts for travel other than for purposes of tourism may be authorized by the Central Bank upon presentation of adequate justification. Travelers may also purchase additional foreign currency in the informal exchange market.

Residents may purchase from commercial banks foreign exchange up to US$3,000 a month for study abroad, subscriptions to magazines and books, registrations for seminars, social security payments, medical treatment payments, or remittances of rents earned by real estate owners living abroad; for all these transactions, the appropriate documents must be presented. Remittances of earnings by foreign workers must be channeled through the informal exchange market. Remittances of profits and dividends earned from foreign direct investments require the prior approval of the Central Bank.

There are no special provisions for exports of domestic banknotes.

Insurance activities within the country are limited to Chilean companies or to authorized foreign companies.

Exports and Export Proceeds

All products may be freely exported. All foreign exchange proceeds from exports must be surrendered through commercial banks, which are required to inform the Central Bank. Commercial banks are authorized to purchase all spot foreign exchange proceeds from exporters. Exporters are allowed to retain, and freely dispose of, up to 50 percent of export proceeds, with a cumulative limit of US$50 million during a 12-month period. Windfall receipts from copper exports of CODELCO (the state copper mines) must be deposited in a special foreign currency account at the Central Bank, and withdrawals from this account are permitted only under certain circumstances.

Export proceeds subject to surrender requirements must be repatriated within 270 days of shipment and surrendered within 11 days. However, export proceeds may be surrendered within 90 days of repatriation if they are held as foreign exchange deposits with domestic banks. Repatriation periods may be extended for certain products.

Exporters of a limited number of products (approximately 6 percent of the country's annual exports) have the option of taking a tax reimbursement (within 120 days of surrendering the proceeds) in lieu of benefits under the existing import duty drawback scheme; alternatively, exporters of these products may avail themselves of the provisions of Law No. 19.024, under which they may obtain refunds of the duties paid on imported inputs. Eligible products were defined initially as those whose average annual export values in 1990 were equal to or less than US$5 million. The list of eligible products is reviewed annually in the light of their export value during the previous year. Annual export values are also subject to adjustment each year.

Proceeds from Invisibles

In general, foreign exchange proceeds from invisibles must be surrendered only when required by a legal provision. Royalties and copyright fees, commissions, proceeds from insurance, and other benefits related to foreign trade are subject to the same surrender requirement. The proceeds from family remittances, other commissions, or the surplus foreign exchange from travel allocations are not required to be surrendered.

There are no special provisions for imports of domestic banknotes.

Capital

All new foreign borrowing or refinancing of existing credits by commercial banks requires prior registration at, or approval from, the Central Bank; exceptions are lines of credit of up to one-year maturity with foreign correspondents. Short-term loans are subject to a limit determined mainly by a bank's capital and reserves. However, the Central Bank must still be notified of foreign borrowings that do not require its approval. All foreign borrowings, except for credits that are provided directly to Chilean exporters by foreign importers or by foreign suppliers to Chilean importers, are subject to a reserve requirement of 30 percent; this requirement may be satisfied by lodging a deposit in U.S. dollars at the Central Bank without interest or by entering into a special repurchase agreement with the Central Bank that effectively imposes a cost equivalent to the interest forgone. The length of the period during which the reserve requirement must be held in the Central Bank is one year for loans and bonds. Credit lines and deposits must also satisfy the 30 percent reserve requirement, which is based on the average monthly outstanding balance. Credits granted by foreign commercial banks to Chilean commercial banks as part of restructuring packages are exempt from the reserve requirement. Foreign capital may enter Chile under one of the following arrangements, depending on the purpose and type of the investment:

(1) Title I, Chapter XIV of the Compendium of Rules on International Exchange stipulates that capital brought into the country in the form of foreign borrowing (*créditos externos*) must be sold through authorized banks. Although there is no minimum term on the maturity of foreign borrowing, the 30 percent reserve requirement against external credits entering under Chapter XIV must be retained for one year. Repatriation is allowed only in accordance with the amortization schedule established at the time of registration. Accelerated payments or extensions of payment are subject to special authorization. Since June 1990, under Chapter XXVI of Title I, which refers to American Depository Receipts (ADRs), individuals and legal entities that are domiciled and resident abroad and that meet certain conditions have been permitted to remit abroad proceeds from the sale of stocks of registered corporations domiciled in Chile that were purchased with funds abroad through the official exchange market. The remittance of dividends and profits accruing from such stocks is also allowed through the official exchange market.

(2) Chapter XIV of Title I of the Compendium of Rules authorizes the Central Bank to make exemptions to the general rules concerning the inflow and outflow of capital or credits. Chilean enterprises and banks were authorized under Chapter XIV Regulations on May 13, 1992 to issue bonds in foreign markets. As of April 15, 1994, nonfinancial enterprises with a credit rating from an international rating company that is equal to or better than that assigned to Chile can issue bonds with a minimum value of US$25 million. Issues of bonds by banks are subject to prior authorization by the Central Bank. In accordance with Chapter XXVI regulations, Chilean enterprises and banks are also authorized to issue ADRs. Requirements as of September 15, 1994 are that (a) the issue be equal to at least US$25 million; and (b) the company be rated at least BBB+ by two international rating agencies.

(3) Decree-Law No. 600 of July 7, 1974 (amended by Decree-Law No. 1748 of March 18, 1977), the Foreign Investment Statute, establishes a special regime for long-term capital investment. Authorization to make a foreign exchange investment in Chile is granted by the Foreign Investment Committee through a contract that stipulates that capital transfers to Chile will not normally exceed eight years for mining and three years for other projects. Investments of less than US$5 million may be approved by the Executive Vice President of the Committee, with a few exceptions. There are no general limitations on profit remittances, but specific agreements in this regard may be included in the above-mentioned investment contract. Since March 1993, capital may be repatriated after one year unless specified otherwise in the investment contract. Foreign investors may opt for one of two income tax systems. Both systems are based on the regular Chilean corporate income tax of 15 percent on profit repatriation. Under the first system, a fixed rate of 42 percent (which includes the corporate income tax of 15 percent) is guaranteed over a period of 10 years. Alternatively, they may select a tax system that is similar to that which is applied to domestic investors. This system applies a 35 percent rate on profits before tax and deducts from it the 15 percent corporate income tax. The first system results in an effective rate of 38 percent on gross profits (before tax) and the second system in an effective rate of 35 percent on gross profits. Any foreign credits involved must be on financial terms authorized by the Central Bank. Foreign capital that entered Chile before the promulgation of Decree-Law No. 600 and that is not subject to that law continues to be subject to the regulations prevailing on the date of entry. Contract awards in the oil sector are decided by the Government under presidential decree; rights and responsibilities under such a decree may be vested in the Empresa Nacional de Petróleo (ENAP) by the Ministry of Mines.

(4) Chapters XVIII and XIX of the Chilean Compendium of Rules on International Exchange, introduced in May 1985 and amended several times since, regulate the purchase abroad and repatriation of selected Chilean foreign debt instruments at a discount. Eligible instruments are defined as external debt payable in foreign currency outside Chile with a maturity of more than one year when the debtor is either the Treasury, the Central Bank, a public sector entity, the Development Corporation (CORFO), a financial institution, or a private sector resident having a guarantee from a financial institution. Chapter XIX governs the use of Chilean debt instruments by foreign residents for direct invest-

ment in Chile with remittance rights. Upon approval from the Central Bank, the foreign currency obligation is exchanged into a domestic currency obligation, the proceeds of which must be used for direct investment purposes, with the intermediation of a financial institution; special regulations apply to the repatriation of such capital as well as to dividend payments.

Under Chapter XIX, foreign investors may sell their investments to domestic investors after paying a fee to the Central Bank. The last operation of debt conversion under these schemes took place in 1991. Chapter XVIII specifies the regulations for the conversion into peso assets (without remittance rights) of debt purchased abroad by residents and nonresidents at a discount with foreign exchange not obtained in the official market and of private sector external debt not guaranteed by the Government. Transactions under Chapter XVIII are also channeled through financial institutions, subject to an overall quota assigned on the basis of an auction system.

(5) Chapter XXVII of Title I of the Chilean Compendium of Rules on International Exchange, introduced in August 1990, stipulates that foreign capital investment funds may have access to the official exchange market for repatriation abroad of imported capital, profits earned on such capital, and payments of expenses involved in foreign investment activities under certain conditions.

Foreign currency deposits in banks are also subject to a reserve requirement of 30 percent, based on the average monthly balance. Banks may sell foreign exchange using their term deposits in foreign exchange.

Gold

Chile has issued three gold coins, which are not legal tender. Monetary gold may be traded only by authorized houses, but ordinary transactions in gold between private individuals may be freely undertaken. Imports and exports of gold are unrestricted, subject to compliance with the normal formalities for import and export transactions, including registration with the Central Bank.

Changes During 1994

Exports and Export Proceeds

April 15. The proportion of export proceeds exempted from surrender requirements was increased to 15 percent from 10 percent. The maximum

amount exempted was increased to US$10 million from US$5 million per exporter in any 12-month period. The period during which foreign exchange must be repatriated was extended to 180 days from 150 days.

September 9. The proportion of export proceeds exempted from surrender requirements was increased to 25 percent from 15 percent. The maximum amount exempted was increased to US$15 million from US$10 million per exporter in any 12-month period. The period during which foreign exchange must be repatriated was extended to 210 days from 180 days.

November 30. The proportion of export proceeds exempted from surrender requirements was increased to 50 percent from 25 percent. The maximum amount exempted was increased to US$50 million from US$15 million per exporter in any 12-month period. The period during which foreign exchange must be repatriated was extended to 270 days from 210 days.

Capital

April 15. The requirement that nonfinancial enterprises be rated A by the National Risk Classification Commission in order to be eligible to issue bonds in foreign markets or to issue American Depository Receipts (ADRs) was replaced with the requirement that they be rated BBB+. The minimum amount for each ADR issue or band issue was lowered to US$25 million from US$50 million for these issuers. The maximum amount that pension funds, insurance companies, and mutual funds are allowed to invest abroad was raised to 4 percent from 3 percent of their portfolio.

September 9. The issuance of ADRs but not of bonds by banks was simplified: the minimum amount for each issue was lowered to US$25 million from US$50 million, and the requirement that the issuing bank be rated A by the National Risk Classification Commission was replaced by the requirement that it be rated BBB+ by two international rating agencies.

September 29. Rules regulating investments by banks and financial institutions in offshore financial institutions were established.

November 30. The ceiling on foreign exchange positions held by commercial banks was eliminated, and all reserve requirements on foreign borrowing were required to be held solely in U.S. dollars.

PEOPLE'S REPUBLIC OF CHINA

(Position as of March 31, 1995)

Exchange Arrangement

The currency of the People's Republic of China is the Renminbi, the external value of which is determined in the interbank market.[1] At the start of each trading day, the People's Bank of China (PBC) announces a reference rate based on the weighted average of the buying and selling rates against the U.S. dollar during the previous day's trading. Daily movement of the exchange rate of the renminbi against the U.S. dollar is limited to 0.3 percent on either side of the reference rate. The PBC publishes the middle rates of the renminbi against 21 convertible currencies, except the U.S. dollar, on the basis of the exchange rate of the currencies concerned in the international markets.[2] Based on the middle rate published by the PBC, the designated banks then quote their buying and selling rates to their customers within a range of 0.25 percent. On December 31, 1994, the middle market rate of the renmimbi against the U.S. dollar was Y 8.4462 per US$1.

Administration of Control

The PBC exercises central bank functions and control over foreign exchange; the State Administration of Exchange Control (SAEC), as a government institution under the leadership of the PBC, is responsible for implementing exchange regulations and for administering the foreign exchange market in accordance with state policy. There are a number of SAEC sub-bureaus in the provinces, main municipalities, autonomous regions, and special economic zones. The Bank of China (BOC) is China's principal foreign exchange bank. Other banks and financial institutions, including affiliates of nonresident banks, may handle designated transactions with the approval of the SAEC. Currently, more than two hundred institutions are authorized to handle foreign exchange transactions. Individuals may hold foreign exchange but generally may not deal in it or conduct arbitrage operations. Financial institutions may hold foreign exchange.

Prescription of Currency

As of the end of 1994, an operative bilateral payments agreement was maintained with Cuba.[3] Unless there are specific regulations, the currencies used in transactions are determined by the terms of the respective contracts.

Nonresident and Foreign Currency Accounts

Nonresidents[4] remaining in China for a short time may open nonresident accounts with the BOC and other authorized banks and financial institutions. Foreign-funded enterprises (FFEs), including joint ventures, may also open foreign exchange current accounts and use them to make payments abroad. In addition, the PBC has specified other categories of foreign exchange for which domestic establishments can open foreign exchange accounts with designated banks by presenting the certificates of permit issued by the SAEC. Branches of foreign banks and other financial institutions may grant loans in foreign exchange and accept foreign currency deposits from FFEs and enterprises approved by the SAEC.

Individuals may open resident foreign currency savings accounts with authorized banks and may withdraw foreign currency from, or deposit it to, such accounts without restriction.

Imports and Exports

Primary responsibility for formulating foreign trade policies and ensuring the implementation of regulations and policy measures rests with the Ministry of Foreign Trade and Economic Cooperation (MOFTEC), which also issues the licenses required for restricted imports and a large number of exports.[5]

---

[1]On April 1, 1994, the China Foreign Exchange Trading System (CFETS) in Shanghai—a nationally integrated electronic system for interbank foreign exchange trading—became operational. At present, 22 foreign exchange trading centers in major cities—accounting for the bulk of all foreign exchange transactions—are electronically linked to the CFETS. To trade in the system, financial institutions must become members of the CFETS. Designated domestic financial institutions are allowed to buy and sell foreign exchange on their own account. Other financial institutions, including branches of foreign banks, may trade foreign exchange as brokers on behalf of their customers.

[2]This practice was discontinued effective April 1, 1995.

[3]An inoperative bilateral payments agreement is maintained with Mongolia.

[4]Nonresidents include Chinese working overseas and residents of foreign countries and of the Hong Kong and Macao regions. Diplomatic representatives are also included.

[5]MOFTEC itself issues licenses for some restricted imports into Beijing; for the rest, it delegates its authority to its special commission offices at major ports and to its regional counterparts, the Commission on Foreign Economic Relations and Trade.

MOFTEC does not engage in direct foreign trade transactions and is no longer involved in the daily management of trading corporations. Foreign trade is conducted by foreign trade corporations (FTCs) and other entities licensed by MOFTEC to conduct foreign trade. At the end of 1994, about 4,000 FTCs were in operation. In addition, some 60,000 FFEs are permitted to conduct international trade directly.

All enterprises other than registered FTCs must obtain approval from the local foreign trade bureau in accordance with MOFTEC authorization, as well as a license from the local bureau for industry and commerce, to engage in foreign trade. All foreign exchange earnings from exports must be repatriated and must be sold to designated banks, except those of FFEs and those approved by the SAEC. FFEs are allowed to retain all their foreign exchange and to sell or purchase foreign exchange in the swap centers. In principle, beginning in 1995, the SAEC has been conducting annual examinations for FFEs. The FFEs passing the annual examinations need no further approval from the SAEC to conduct foreign exchange transactions. The purpose of approval is to ensure that export and contractual obligations are met. In practice, SAEC approval for purchase transactions was quite liberal in 1994.

Authorized local banks provide foreign exchange for imports when import contracts and commercial documentation are presented. Import licenses, when required, are examined by the banks. Residents may not pay for imports with local currency, except in border trade.

Imports into China are classified into two categories—restricted imports and unrestricted imports.[6] The importation of products on the restricted list is controlled through licensing requirements or quotas. The importation of the following products is subject to canalization (i.e., restricted to designated FTCs): wheat, chemical fertilizer, crude oil, oil products, rubber, steel, timber, plywood, polyester synthetic fibers, tobacco and its products, cotton, and wool.

Imports of all secondhand garments, poisons, narcotic drugs, diseased animals, and plants are prohibited. In addition, the importation and exportation of weapons, ammunition and explosives, radio receivers and transmitters, Chinese currency exceeding Y 6,000, manuscripts, printed and recorded materials, and films that are deemed to be detrimental to Chinese political, economic, cultural, and moral interests are prohibited. All imports and exports require prior inspection before they can be released by customs at the port of entry or exit. Exports of specified machine tools require a license from the State Administration for the Inspection of Import and Export Commodities as a means of quality control. Controls in the form of registration for surveillance purposes are exercised on the importation of machinery and electric equipment to monitor the equilibrium of supply and demand.

The customs regulations in force are the Customs Law of China and the Regulations on Import and Export Tariff of China. The tariff rates for imports fall into two categories: general and preferential. General rates apply to imports originating in the countries or regions with which China has not concluded trade treaties or agreements with reciprocal favorable tariff clauses; preferential rates apply to imports originating in the countries with which China has concluded such treaties and agreements. The duties are calculated on the basis of the transaction value of imported goods. At the end of 1994, the average unweighted tariff rate was 36.4 percent.

Imports into Tibet are subject to a separate system of customs duties established by the State Council. The tariff applies to goods imported for use in Tibet on a nondiscriminatory basis and irrespective of their origin. It does not apply to imports into Tibet by mail or brought in as part of the luggage carried by travelers, which are subject to the regular Chinese tariff.

Domestic enterprises are liable to a product tax and a value-added tax on imports of certain products into China; FFEs are liable to a consolidated industrial and commercial tax. Since January 1, 1994, a uniform value-added tax has been applied to both domestic and imported products; the relevant provisions are contained in Provisional Regulations of the People's Republic of China on Value-Added Tax (December 13, 1993), and Provisional Regulations of the People's Republic of China on Consumption Tax (December 13, 1993).

Before 1991, special economic zones were set up in Shantou, Shenzhen, Xiamen, Zhuhai, and Hainan. A special development area was established in Pudong (Shanghai), and economic and technological development zones were established in 14 designated coastal cities. In 1992, approval was granted for the establishment of a large number of similar zones in selected inland cities and border regions that have recently been declared open to foreign trade and investment. Foreigners, Chinese working overseas, and Chinese from Hong Kong, Macao, and Taiwan Province of China are permitted to invest in and open businesses in these zones and areas either through wholly owned ventures or joint ventures with Chinese investors.

---

[6]At the end of 1994, 49 items were on the restricted list.

Equipment and machinery or parts and components thereof, and other means of production imported by and intended to be used in the production of the enterprises in the zones are exempt from import duties.

A number of restrictions are imposed on exports, primarily raw materials and food products. At the end of 1994, 114 product items were subject to export-licensing requirements or quotas, and 47 product items were subject to export duties. A portion of output of goods not produced in adequate quantities but for which a strong demand exists in the foreign market is set aside for export. Exports of certain products, such as valuable cultural relics, rare books, and animals, seeds, plants, precious metals, and artifacts made from precious metals are prohibited.

Export quotas for certain products are allocated, on an experimental basis, through a public bidding system.[7] Successful bidders are required to guarantee maximum export value by offering higher benchmark export prices. During 1994, 24 items subject to export quotas were distributed under the bidding system.

Purchases of foreign exchange other than by foreign-funded enterprises for trade (and trade-related) transactions do not require the approval of the SAEC.

Foreign exchange for trade may be purchased from designated banks, provided that the importer has a valid import contract and a notice of payment from a foreign financial institution; for imports subject to licensing, quotas, or registration procedures, presentation of the certificates concerned is also required.

Payments for and Proceeds from Invisibles

Foreign exchange may be purchased to pay for trade-related services upon presentation of contracts or payment notices. The remittance of profits and dividends earned on foreign direct investment is not restricted after applicable taxes have been paid.

After-tax profits of foreign funded enterprises may be remitted in accordance with foreign exchange regulations; such remittances should be paid through the foreign exchange account of the joint venture. If the outstanding balance of such an account is not sufficient, FFEs may buy foreign exchange from foreign exchange adjustment centers.

Foreign exchange needed for nontrade and noncommercial payments by budgeted organizations, institutions, and social bodies may be purchased from the BOC, upon presenting the Application for Nontrade Payments, at the exchange rate of the day of purchase and within the limits specified by the SAEC. Off-budget domestic establishments may purchase foreign exchange for nontrade and noncommercial payments from designated banks by presenting the Exchange Sale Instruction issued by the SAEC.

Chinese residents wishing to spend money on travel abroad or remit money abroad may apply to the designated banks. In cases of serious illness, death, or injury affecting Chinese residents' parents, spouses, or children outside China, the residents may apply for foreign exchange up to a specified limit on presentation of documentary verification. In general, if permission is granted to travel abroad, Chinese residents are allowed to take a reasonable amount of their own foreign exchange to cover expenses for transport and subsistence. There is no tax on travel. Chinese residents who retire and emigrate are normally permitted to receive their pensions abroad, but transfers of proceeds from the sale of their assets in China are limited.

Income from royalties, dividends, interest, and rentals earned by foreign businesses without establishments in China is subject to a 20 percent withholding tax; a preferential rate of 10 percent is applied to foreign and overseas Chinese partners in joint ventures set up in the special economic zones and the economic and technological development areas in the 14 open coastal cities and the newly opened inland and border cities.

Enterprises, except for FFEs, must sell their foreign exchange earnings from invisible transactions to an authorized bank. Foreign exchange remitted from abroad or from Hong Kong and Macao to Chinese residents may be retained and used to open a savings account at an authorized bank or sold for renminbi at the rate quoted by the banks. Similarly, foreign exchange owned by immigrants or returning Chinese before they become residents may be retained.

The following must be repatriated and may not be deposited abroad: all foreign exchange earned by Chinese residents working abroad, in Hong Kong, or in Macao; or earned from publication fees, copyright fees, awards, subsidies, honoraria, or other premiums. Individuals may retain or deposit exchange receipts with designated banks.

---

[7]Three types of bidding are conducted under the system: (1) *"negotiated"* bidding is applied to products whose exportation is to be balanced by the state; (2) *"invitation"* bidding is applied to raw materials produced in geographically concentrated areas; and (3) *"oriented"* bidding is applied to products that are manufactured in geographically concentrated areas and whose export channels are limited. Only one type of bidding is conducted for a product in any calendar year.

Foreign staff members and employees of FFEs, as well as those from Hong Kong and Macao,[8] may remit their salaries and other income earned in China after paying taxes and deducting their living expenses in China and after receiving approval from the relevant local authorities.

Capital

Foreign borrowing is classified as either "plan" or "nonplan" borrowing.[9] Plan borrowing includes (1) borrowing by the government sector (through the PBC, the Ministry of Finance, the Ministry of Agriculture, and MOFTEC and enterprises under the MOFTEC's control) from foreign governments or international organizations and bilateral sources; (2) external borrowings of Chinese financial institutions; and (3) external borrowings of authorized Chinese enterprises. Nonplan borrowing includes (1) borrowing of FFEs; (2) branches of foreign banks operating in China; and (3) short-term trade credits.

Within these limits, the SPC coordinates foreign borrowing for projects included in the annual and five-year plans. Under this procedure, the project-executing agencies (the Ministry of Finance, MOFTEC, foreign trade corporations, and provincial governments) propose projects to the SPC. The proposals indicate the total amount of foreign exchange needed, how much of it will be earned and how much will be borrowed from abroad, and the kinds of imports for which the loans are intended. The SPC reviews these plans and, in cooperation with the SAEC, the Ministry of Finance, and MOFTEC, recommends to the State Council the overall number of projects and their associated financing. Loans for vital projects or projects that have a rapid rate of return are given priority approval.

Within these guidelines, loans from international financial institutions and foreign governments require the clearance of the SPC and the approval of the State Council. Loans from the World Bank are generally the responsibility of the Ministry of Finance; borrowing from the International Monetary Fund (IMF) and the Asian Development Bank (ADB) are the responsibility of the PBC; and intergovernmental loans are the responsibility of MOFTEC. Local governments and enterprises usually borrow through the BOC (or with its guarantee) or through specialized agencies, such as international trust and investment companies, rather than borrowing directly abroad themselves. The SPC sets an annual limit on such borrowing. Resident organizations issuing securities for foreign exchange must be approved by the PBC.

All medium- and long-term commercial borrowing abroad (including bond issues) under the plan requires prior approval from the SAEC on a case-by-case basis and may be conducted through authorized Chinese financial institutions. Borrowing quotas are allocated under the annual plan. The China International Trust and Investment Corporation (CITIC) has been permitted, on an experimental basis, to borrow abroad without first obtaining approval for each loan from the SAEC, as long as its outstanding debt is within the limits set by the State Council. Chinese financial institutions are permitted an annual ceiling by the SAEC for the balance outstanding on short-term loans.

All foreign direct investment projects are, in principle, subject to the approval of MOFTEC. However, a number of provincial and local authorities have been granted the authority to approve foreign direct investment projects up to specified amounts. The policy with respect to foreign capital is designed both to make up for insufficient domestic capital and to facilitate the introduction of modern technology and management.

Joint-venture enterprises and wholly foreign-owned companies are required to balance their foreign exchange receipts and payments, and foreign borrowing must be reported to, and filed with, the SAEC.[10] Most foreign exchange earned by joint ventures and other enterprises involving nonresident capital must be deposited with an authorized bank; outward transfers of capital generally require SAEC approval. Enterprises involved in the exploitation of offshore petroleum reserves may also hold foreign exchange abroad or in Hong Kong or Macao. When a joint venture ceases operation, the net claims belonging to the foreign investor may be remitted with SAEC approval. Alternatively, the foreign investor may apply for repayment of paid-in capital.

---

[8] Including those employed by enterprises that have been established with capital provided by Chinese residing abroad.

[9] The SAEC is the sole agency for monitoring and collecting statistics for China's external borrowing. It permits the BOC and other financial and nonfinancial institutions responsible for undertaking commercial borrowing to contract short-term loans up to specified limits without prior approval. All bond issues, however, are subject to prior approval from the SAEC. In August 1987, comprehensive regulations were issued requiring that all foreign borrowing be registered with the SAEC. Borrowers who do not comply will not be permitted to transfer foreign exchange abroad to service their external debt obligations and will be subject to other penalties.

---

[10] To help individual enterprises balance their foreign receipts and payments, enterprises with a surplus of foreign exchange may sell it to enterprises lacking sufficient foreign exchange through the foreign exchange adjustment centers.

The profits of joint ventures in special economic zones, the 14 coastal cities, the newly opened inland and border cities, and those exploiting petroleum, natural gas, and other specified resources are subject to tax at the rate of 15 percent. A joint venture scheduled to operate for ten years or more may be exempted from income tax in the first one or two profit-making years and allowed reductions of 50 percent for the following three years. Joint ventures in low-profit operations, such as farming and forestry, or located in areas considered to be economically underdeveloped may, upon the approval of the Ministry of Finance, be allowed a further 15–30 percent reduction in income tax for another ten years. A participant in a joint venture that reinvests its share of profit in China for a period of not less than five years may obtain a refund of 40 percent of the tax paid on the reinvested profit.

Foreign companies, enterprises, and other economic organizations with establishments in China that are engaged in independent business operations, cooperative production, or joint business operations with Chinese enterprises are subject to tax only on their net income from sources in China. Under the Income Tax Law of the Peoples' Republic of China for Enterprises with Foreign Investment and Foreign Enterprises (July 1, 1991), a standard income tax rate of 33 percent is levied on all foreign investment enterprises and foreign enterprises; it consists of a 30 percent state income tax and a 3 percent local tax. Certain exemptions and reductions from income tax are available in the special economic zones and other special open investment areas. Correspondingly, foreign state banks located in countries where income from interest on the deposits and loans of China's state banks is exempt from income tax are also exempt from this Chinese tax. Foreign business without establishments in China are subject to a reduced tax of 10 percent (half the usual rate) on interest income or leasing fees (less than the value of equipment) earned under credit, trade, and leasing agreements made with Chinese companies and enterprises from 1983 to 1985 but only for the duration of the agreements. For fees collected by foreign businessmen for the use of special technology provided in such fields as agriculture, animal husbandry, research, energy, communications, transport, environmental protection, and the development of important techniques, income tax may, with the approval of the tax authorities, be levied at the reduced rate of 10 percent or waived for advanced technology provided on favorable terms.

Foreign investment by Chinese enterprises is subject to approval; profits earned thereby must be sold to designated banks, except for a portion that may be retained abroad as a working balance.

Gold

The PBC buys and sells gold and has central control over dealings in gold and silver. Sales of gold and silver are restricted to pharmaceutical, industrial, and other approved uses. Private persons may hold gold but may not trade or deal in it. The amount of gold, gold products, silver, and silver products that may be imported is unlimited but must be declared on entry. When exporting gold or silver, the exporter must present an import document from customs or a PBC export permit. Nonresidents may buy gold and silver and gold and silver products at special stores but must present the invoice when exporting them.

Changes During 1994

Exchange Arrangement

January 1. The official exchange rate and the swap market rate were unified at the prevailing swap market rate. Issuance of export retention quotas ceased except those for outstanding contracts. Enterprises were allowed to use their outstanding retention quotas to purchase foreign exchange at the official exchange rate prevailing on December 31, 1993. In addition, for undistributed quotas for which foreign exchange was sold before December 31, 1993, the distribution and deposit of quotas into relevant accounts were required to be completed before the end of January 1994. The redemption of outstanding retention quotas was terminated at the end of 1994.

January 1. Foreign Exchange Certificates (FECs) ceased to be issued. The existing FECs were withdrawn from circulation by the end of 1994 at the official exchange rate prevailing at the end of December 1993, and outstanding FECs were to be converted into foreign exchange only through the end of June 1995.

April 1. The China Foreign Exchange Trade System (CFETS) in Shanghai (an integrated electronic system for interbank foreign exchange trading) came into operation. Twenty-two cities were linked to this system by the end of 1994.

Imports and Exports

January 1. The foreign exchange retention system was abolished; enterprises were allowed to continue to use outstanding retention quotas to purchase foreign exchange at the official exchange rate prevailing at the end of 1993. The priority import list was abolished. Foreign exchange for trade transactions could be purchased from designated banks, provided that the importer has a valid import contract and a notice of payment from a foreign financial institution; for imports subject to licensing, quotas, or registration procedures, these documents would also be required.

January 1. The mandatory import plan was abolished. The approval procedures for domestic enterprises engaged in foreign trade were liberalized.

February 1. A public bidding system for allocation of export quotas was introduced. Three types of bidding would be conducted under the system: (1) *"negotiated"* bidding applied to products whose exportation is to be balanced by the state; (2) *"invitation"* bidding applied to raw materials produced in geographically concentrated areas; and (3) *"oriented"* bidding applied to products manufactured in geographically concentrated areas and whose export channels are limited. Only one type of bidding would be conducted for a product in any calendar year. Successful bidders would be required to guarantee maximum profits by higher benchmark prices.

May 1. Import-licensing requirements and quota controls on 195 items were eliminated.

September 1. Import-licensing requirements and quota controls on 125 items were eliminated.

Payments for and Proceeds from Invisibles

April 1. The requirement to obtain approval from the SAEC for the purchase of foreign exchange for trade and trade-related transactions (for domestic enterprises) and the priority list governing purchases of foreign exchange were abolished.

COLOMBIA

(Position as of December 31, 1994)

Exchange Arrangement

The currency of Colombia is the Colombian Peso. All foreign exchange operations take place at a market-determined exchange rate. The Superintendency of Banks calculates a representative market exchange rate based on market rates.[1] The Banco de la República conducts foreign exchange transactions only with the Ministry of Finance and authorized financial intermediaries and does not conduct foreign exchange transactions directly with the nonbank private sector. The Banco de la República announces the upper and lower limits of a 14 percentage point band ten days in advance for indicative purposes. The Banco de la República quotes buying and selling rates for certain other currencies[2] daily on the basis of the buying and selling rates for the U.S. dollar in markets abroad. On December 31, 1994, the representative market exchange rate was Col$831.27 per US$1.

Other effective exchange rates result from (1) tax credit certificates for nontraditional exports (*certificados de reembolso tributarios* or CERTs) granted at three different percentage rates; (2) an 8 percent surtax on remittances of earnings on existing non-oil foreign investments (to be reduced to 7 percent by 1996), a 15 percent surtax on remittances of earnings on existing foreign investments in the oil sector (to be reduced to 12 percent in 1996), and a 12 percent surtax on remittances of earnings from foreign investments made after 1993; and (3) a 10 percent withholding tax on foreign exchange receipts from personal services and other transfers. The Government purchases foreign exchange for all public debt payments and other expenditures included in the national budget under the same conditions as other authorized intermediaries.[3]

Residents are permitted to buy forward cover against exchange rate risks in respect of foreign exchange debts in convertible currencies registered at the Banco de la República on international markets. Residents may also deal in over-the-counter forward swaps and options in U.S. dollars.

Administration of Control

All imports require registration at the Colombian Institute of Foreign Trade (INCOMEX). The Customs and Taxes Direction (DIAN), within the Ministry of Finance, enforces ex post control and supervision over trade transactions and is responsible for applying penalties for any violation of the exchange regulations. The authorized foreign exchange intermediaries are commercial banks, financial corporations, Financiera Energética Nacional (FEN) and Banco de Comercio Exterior de Colombia (BANCOLDEX), and savings and loan corporations. Commercial banks are required to hold a net foreign exchange position equivalent to at least 40 percent of their foreign exchange liabilities (outstanding at the end of June 1991). There are no regulations governing the net foreign exchange positions of exchange houses; they may sell their excess foreign holdings to authorized financial intermediaries because they do not have access to the Banco de la República.

The Foreign Trade Council (FTC), which includes representatives of the Ministry of Finance, INCOMEX, other public entities, and two officers of the FTC, determines overall import and export policy. INCOMEX, through its Import Board, controls those imports that are subject to prior licensing, and administers Plan Vallejo, which is a special import-export arrangement concerning a rebate of taxes paid on imported inputs used in the production of exported goods. INCOMEX, together with the Committee on Commercial Practices, administers antidumping cases. The National Council for Economic and Social Policy (CONPES) issues directives to the

---

[1]The representative market exchange rate is calculated as the weighted average of buying and selling rates, effected by foreign exchange market intermediaries, excluding teller transactions (Resolution No. 21 of September 3, 1993).

[2]Austrian schillings, Belgian francs, Canadian dollars, Danish kroner, deutsche mark, French francs, Italian lire, Japanese yen, Netherlands guilders, pounds sterling, Spanish pesetas, Swedish kronor, and Swiss francs.

[3]The Banco de la República stands ready to sell foreign exchange warrants (*títulos canjeables por certificados de cambio*) to public enterprises in the electric sector and to the National Federation of Coffee Growers (Federación Nacional de Cafeteros) in accordance with the terms of Resolution No. 16/1991 of the

Banco de la República. These warrants, expressed in U.S. dollars, have a maturity of 12 months and, within their period of validity, may be sold to the Banco de la República for pesos at the reference market buying rate on the date of repurchase. Warrants bear interest at the rate equal to that of the external loan but never higher than the average 30-day rate on primary certificates of deposit at the close of operations in the New York market for the day before the certificate is issued less 1 percentage point if held by public sector recipients of external loans. Warrants held longer than 12 months may be resold to the Banco de la República at the reference market rate on the last day of the twelfth month.

Banco de la República and the National Planning Department concerning foreign direct investment in Colombia. The Banco de la República keeps an accounting record both of foreign investment in Colombia and of debts abroad and controls the movement of foreign capital as well as the transfer of profits, dividends, and commissions.

Prescription of Currency

Payments and receipts are normally effected in U.S. dollars, but residents and financial intermediaries are allowed to carry out operations in any currency. Settlements for commercial transactions with countries with which Colombia has reciprocal credit agreements may be made through special accounts in accordance with the provisions of such agreements. Settlements between Colombia and Argentina, Bolivia, Brazil, Chile, the Dominican Republic, Ecuador, Mexico, Paraguay, Peru, Uruguay, and Venezuela may be made through accounts maintained within the framework of the multilateral clearing system of the Latin American Integration Association (LAIA). There are also reciprocal credit agreements with the People's Republic of China, Hungary, and the Russian Federation.

Nonresident Accounts

Residents may maintain foreign accounts, registered at the Banco de la República (compensation accounts), to pay for imports, to invest abroad in financial assets, or to carry out any other foreign exchange operations. Proceeds from services (except interest and profits) and transfers may be used to maintain foreign accounts abroad; these accounts do not have to be registered at the Banco de la República. Credit institutions are authorized to receive short-term deposits in foreign currency from nonresident individuals or firms; these deposits are freely available to the holders. Banks must report transactions through these accounts to the Banco de la República.

Imports and Import Payments

Importers may obtain foreign exchange from the exchange market with exchange certificates purchased in the market or may purchase foreign exchange directly from the exchange market. In addition, they may use the proceeds from deposits held abroad. Foreign enterprises in the oil, coal, and natural gas sectors and firms in the free trade areas are not permitted to purchase foreign exchange from financial intermediaries. Import payments must be made within four months of the due date

of payment indicated in the import registration form; otherwise, they are treated as debt (as discussed below).

Imports are subject to one of the following two regimes: (1) freely importable goods, requiring registration only with INCOMEX;[4] and (2) goods subject to prior approval and requiring an import license. Most imports are in the free-import regime, where there is a global free list applicable to all countries, a national list applicable only to member countries of the LAIA, and special lists applicable only to member countries of the LAIA and members of the Andean Pact. Imports subject to a prior licensing requirement consist of medicines and chemical products (30 tariff positions) and weapons and munitions (39 tariff positions).

A distinction is drawn between reimbursable and nonreimbursable imports. Reimbursable imports involve purchases of official foreign exchange from a financial intermediary, including imports of machinery and equipment financed by international credit institutions. Nonreimbursable imports consist mainly of aid imports under grants and commodities constituting part of a direct investment.

Import registrations are granted automatically. However, import registrations by some public sector agencies are screened by INCOMEX to determine whether local substitutes are available. Both import licenses and registrations are valid for 6 months, except those for agricultural and livestock products, which are valid for 3 months, and those for capital goods, which are valid for 12 months. Import licenses may be extended for only one period. The charge for import registration is Col$12,800. Imports of crude oil and petroleum products are effected by Empresa Colombiana de Petroleo (ECOPETROL).

Payments for Invisibles

Foreign exchange for payments for invisibles may be obtained through foreign exchange intermediaries or exchange houses.

Exports and Export Proceeds

Export licenses are not required. All exchange proceeds from exports of goods that are repatriated must be surrendered to authorized financial intermediaries within six months or must be maintained in foreign accounts registered at the Banco de la República. However, exporters are permitted to re-

---

[4]Imports or shipments with an f.o.b. value of less than US$500 are classified as minor imports and do not have to be registered with INCOMEX. All other imports are subject to registration.

tain their export proceeds abroad, in compensation accounts, to settle import payments, to invest in financial assets, to pay back debt, or to effect any other payment operation. In addition, foreign enterprises in the oil, coal, and natural gas sectors and firms in free trade areas are not required to surrender their foreign exchange. On surrendering their export proceeds in the foreign exchange market, exporters of products other than coffee, petroleum and petroleum products, and exports effected through special arrangements (such as barter and compensation) may receive tax credit certificates in an amount corresponding to a specified percentage of the f.o.b. value surrendered. Three rates—2.5 percent, 4 percent, and 5 percent—are applied, depending on the product and the country of destination; the rates are calculated on domestic value added. These certificates, which are freely negotiable and are quoted on the stock exchange, are accepted at par by tax offices for the payment of income tax, customs duties, and certain other taxes.

Exports of coffee are subject to the following regulations: (1) a minimum surrender price is fixed on the basis of the international market prices; (2) exporters pay a coffee contribution, which is determined by the difference between the export value of coffee surrendered and its estimated cost, taking into account the domestic buying price for coffee intended for export; (3) exporters pay a 6.4 percent tax on surrendered export proceeds, of which 2.7 percent is earmarked for the National Federation of Coffee Growers and 3.7 percent for the National Coffee Fund; (4) exporters must either surrender without payment (in the form of untreated coffee) a certain proportion of the volume of excelso coffee that they wish to export or pay the National Federation of Coffee Growers the peso equivalent if the National Coffee Committee (composed of the Ministers of Finance and Agriculture and the Managing Director of the Federation) so decides (as of the end of 1991, this provision was not in operation); and (5) the National Coffee Committee establishes a domestic buying price based on international prices, for coffee intended for re-export, expressed in pesos for each load of 125 kilograms.

Foreign exchange proceeds earned by the public sector may be surrendered to financial intermediaries or to the Banco de la República.

Proceeds from Invisibles

Exchange proceeds from services and transfers are not required to be surrendered through the foreign exchange market but may be sold to exchange houses or to financial intermediaries or used through foreign accounts. There is no restriction on the amount of foreign exchange travelers may bring into the country.

Capital

All inward and outward capital transfers are effected at market rates.

All foreign investments and foreign loans, direct lines of foreign credit obtained by nonbank residents,[5] and the transfer of capital previously imported (except loans previously registered under Decree No. 2322 of September 2, 1965) must be registered with the Banco de la República. Foreign direct investments in Colombia are governed by Law No. 9 of 1991 (January 17, 1991) and CONPES Resolution No. 49, 51–57 of 1991. These regulations are in accordance with the provisions of Decision Nos. 291 and 292 of the Cartagena Agreement, which govern foreign investments within the member countries of the Andean Pact. Foreign investment is freely allowed up to 100 percent of ownership in any sector of the economy except in defense and waste disposal. Special regimes remain in effect in the financial, petroleum, and mining sectors. While foreign capital participation in the financial sector is permitted up to 100 percent, the purchase of 10 percent or more of the shares of a Colombian financial institution requires the prior approval of the Superintendent of Banks. CONPES can legislate special conditions affecting foreign investment in specific sectors of the economy and overrule the above-mentioned provisions (CONPES Resolution No. 49, 51–57 of October 1991). Member countries of the Andean Pact are treated as Colombian investors for purposes of fulfilling the Colombian ownership requirement, provided that profit and capital remittances remain within the country of origin and shares are not sold outside the area.

Registration of capital with the Banco de la República entitles the investor to export profits and to repatriate capital under specified conditions. Limitations on annual transfers of profits abroad were abolished in October 1991. Colombian investment abroad should also be registered at the Banco de la República.

Short-term foreign borrowing to finance any activity is permitted. Foreign loans with maturities ranging from 30 days to 5 years are subject to a nonremunerated deposit requirement ranging from 43 percent to 140 percent of the loan, respectively.

---

[5]Loans by financial entities for the importation of goods also require registration. Public sector loans are subject to an interest rate ceiling of 2.5 percent over the New York prime rate or the London interbank offered rate (LIBOR).

The deposits are held for a period corresponding to the loan maturities. Exempted from the deposit requirement are credits for imports of capital goods; short-term loans granted by BANCOLDEX to Colombian exporters;[6] credit card balances; loans destined for Colombian investments abroad; and green coffee, coal, and oil preshipment financing.[7] The limit on contractual interest rates of 2.5 percent over LIBOR or the U.S. prime rate remains in effect for the public sector, and there is a limit of 20 percent a year in U.S. dollar terms for the private sector. Foreign loans for government entities in excess of specified amounts require prior authorization from the Ministry of Finance and the National Planning Department. For loans to the Government, or guaranteed by the Government, the following are also required: prior authorization from the National Council for Economic and Social Policy and from the Banco de la República; prior consultation with the Interparliamentary Committee on Public Credit; and ex post approval from the President of the Republic. Such loans are also subject to the executive decree that authorizes the initiation of negotiations.

Foreign investments in the form of placement of shares in a fund established to make investments in the stock exchange and in debt papers issued by the financial sector are permitted with the approval of the National Planning Board. Such investments must be maintained in Colombia for at least 18 months.

Contracts involving royalties, commissions, trademarks, or patents should be registered with INCOMEX for statistical purposes only.

---

[6]BANCOLDEX is entitled to lend up to US$450 million under this regime.

[7]Up to a total of US$100 million for green coffee and up to US$200 for coal and oil. These loans should be registered with the Banco de la República in order to avoid exceeding the limits.

Colombian residents are authorized to maintain assets and earned income abroad.

Gold

Under Law No. 9 of January 17, 1991, Colombian residents are allowed to purchase, sell, hold, import, and export gold.

The Banco de la República makes domestic sales of gold for industrial use directly at a price equivalent to the average quotation in the gold market in London during the previous day; this price is converted into pesos at the representative market exchange rate.

The Banco de la República from time to time issues commemorative gold coins, which are legal tender. Residents and nonresidents may freely buy such coins.

Changes During 1994

Exchange Arrangement

January 21. The system of exchange certificates was abolished. The Banco de la República stopped issuing exchange certificates.

Imports and Import Payments

August 16. The maximum payment period for imports was reduced to four months from six months.

Capital

August 12. New deposit requirements on foreign borrowing, varying with each additional month of maturity, were introduced as follows: 140 percent for loans with maturities of up to 30 days; 127 percent for those with maturites of 6 months; 112 percent for those with maturities of 12 months; 100 percent for those with maturities of 18 months; 69 percent for those with maturities of 3 years; and 43 percent for those with maturities of 5 years.

COMOROS

(Position as of December 31, 1994)

Exchange Arrangement

The currency of the Comoros is the Comorian Franc, which is pegged to the French franc, the intervention currency, at the fixed rate of CF 1 per F 0.0133. The current buying and selling rates for the French franc are CF 75 per F 1. Exchange rates for other currencies are officially quoted on the basis of the fixed rate of the Comorian franc for the French franc and the Paris exchange market rates for other currencies. There are no taxes or subsidies on purchases or sales of foreign exchange.

With the exception of those relating to gold, the exchange control measures of the Comoros do not apply to (1) France (and its overseas departments and territories) and Monaco; and (2) all other countries whose bank of issue is linked with the French Treasury by an Operations Account (Benin, Burkina Faso, Cameroon, Central African Republic, Chad, Congo, Côte d'Ivoire, Equatorial Guinea, Gabon, Mali, Niger, Senegal, and Togo). Hence, all payments to these countries may be made freely. All other countries are considered foreign countries. Forward cover against exchange rate risk is authorized by the Central Bank of the Comoros and is provided to traders by the commercial bank (the only authorized dealer) for up to three months.

Administration of Control

Exchange control is administered by the Central Bank of the Comoros. The Ministry of Finance and Budget supervises borrowing and lending abroad, inward direct investment, and all outward investment. Part of the approval authority in respect of exchange control has been delegated to the commercial bank and the Postal Administration. All exchange transactions relating to foreign countries must be made through the authorized bank or the Postal Administration. Import and export licenses are issued by the Directorate-General of Economic Affairs in the Ministry of Economy and Trade.

Arrears are maintained with respect to external payments.

Prescription of Currency

The Central Bank of the Comoros maintains an Operations Account with the French Treasury; settlements with France (as defined above), Monaco, and the Operations Account countries are made in Comorian francs, French francs, or the currency of any other Operations Account country. Settlements with all other countries are usually made through correspondent banks in France in any of the currencies of those countries or in French francs through foreign accounts in francs.

Imports and Import Payments

The importation of certain goods is prohibited from all countries. The importation of other goods, except those originating from member countries of the European Union, Monaco, and the Operations Account countries, is subject to individual licensing. All import transactions must be domiciled with the (single) authorized bank if the value is CF 500,000 or more.

Payments for Invisibles

Payments for invisibles to France (as defined above), Monaco, and the Operations Account countries are permitted freely. Payments for invisibles related to authorized imports are not restricted. Invisible payments to other countries are subject to approval, which is granted when supporting documents can be produced. These regulations apply to allowances for education, family maintenance, and medical treatment, as well as to remittances by foreign workers of savings from their earnings.

Residents traveling to France (as defined above), Monaco, and the other Operations Account countries may take out the equivalent of CF 500,000 in banknotes and any amount in other means of payment. Residents traveling to countries other than France (as defined above), Monaco, and the other Operations Account countries may take out any means of payment up to the equivalent of CF 250,000 a person a trip. Any amount in excess of these limits is subject to the prior approval of the Central Bank, which is granted if supporting documentation is provided.

Nonresident travelers may export the equivalent of CF 500,000 in banknotes and any means of payment issued abroad in their name without providing documentary justification. Other cases are authorized pursuant to the Exchange Regulations when supporting documents can be produced.

Repatriation of dividends and other earnings from nonresidents' direct investment is authorized and guaranteed under the Investment Code.

Exports and Export Proceeds

With a few exceptions, exports to any destination are free of licensing requirements. Proceeds from exports to foreign countries must be repatriated within 30 days of the expiration of the commercial contract and sold immediately to the authorized bank. All export transactions must be domiciled with the authorized bank if the value is CF 500,000 or more.

Proceeds from Invisibles

Proceeds from transactions in invisibles with France (as defined above), Monaco, and the Operations Account countries may be retained. All amounts due from residents of other countries in respect of services and all income earned in those countries from foreign assets must be repatriated and, if received in foreign currency, surrendered to the authorized bank within one month of the due date or date of receipt. Resident and nonresident travelers may bring in any amount of domestic and foreign banknotes and coins.

Capital

Capital movements between the Comoros and France (as defined above), Monaco, and the Operations Account countries are, in principle, free of exchange control; capital transfers to all other countries require exchange control approval, but capital receipts from such countries are normally permitted freely.

Special controls (in addition to any applicable exchange control requirements) are maintained over borrowing abroad, inward direct investment, and all outward investment; these controls relate to approval of the underlying transactions, not to payments or receipts.

Gold

Imports and exports of monetary gold require prior authorization. Imports and exports of articles containing gold are subject to declaration, but transfers of personal jewelry within the limit of 500 grams a person are exempt from such declaration.

Changes During 1994

Exchange Arrangement

January 12. The Comorian franc was devalued to CF 75 per F 1 from CF 50 per F 1.

REPUBLIC OF CONGO

(Position as of December 31, 1994)

Exchange Arrangement

The currency of the Republic of Congo is the CFA Franc,[1] which is pegged to the French franc, the intervention currency, at the fixed rate of CFAF 1 per F 0.01. The official buying and selling rate is CFAF 100 per F 1. Exchange transactions in French francs between the BEAC and commercial banks take place at the same rate. Buying and selling rates for certain other foreign currencies are also officially posted, with quotations based on the fixed rate for the French franc and the rates in the Paris exchange market for the currencies concerned.

Payments to all countries are subject to a commission of 0.75 percent, with a minimum charge of CFAF 75; exempt from this commission are payments of the state, the Postal Administration, the BEAC, salaries of Congolese diplomats abroad, expenditures of official missions abroad, scholarships of persons studying or training abroad, and debt-service payments due from companies that have entered into an agreement with the Congo. Foreign exchange purchased by the Diamond Purchase Office is subject to a commission of 0.5 percent, with a minimum charge of CFAF 100. An additional commission of 0.25 percent is levied on all payments to countries that are not members of the BEAC. There are no taxes or subsidies on purchases or sales of foreign exchange.

Administration of Control

Payments to the following countries, although subject to declaration, are unrestricted: (1) France (and its overseas departments and territories) and Monaco; and (2) all other countries whose bank of issue is linked with the French Treasury by an Operations Account (Benin, Burkina Faso, Cameroon, Central African Republic, Chad, Comoros, Côte d'Ivoire, Equatorial Guinea, Gabon, Mali, Niger, Senegal, and Togo). Settlements and investment transactions with all foreign countries, however, are subject to control. (Foreign countries are defined as all countries other than the Congo.)

The General Directorate of Credit and Financial Relations in the Ministry of Finance and the Budget

---

[1]The CFA franc circulating in the Congo is issued by the Bank of Central African States (BEAC) and is legal tender also in Cameroon, the Central African Republic, Chad, Equatorial Guinea, and Gabon.

supervises borrowing and lending abroad. Exchange control is administered by the Minister of Finance and the Budget, who has delegated approval authority to the General Directorate. All exchange transactions must be effected through authorized banks or the Postal Administration. Import and export licenses are issued by the Foreign Trade Directorate in the Ministry of Commerce. The system of import licenses has been replaced by a system of ex post declarations for all but 13 products (Decree No. 88/414, May 28, 1988).

Arrears are maintained with respect to external payments.

Prescription of Currency

Because the Congo is an Operations Account country, settlements with France (as defined above), Monaco, and the Operations Account countries are made in CFA francs, French francs, or the currency of any other institute of issue that maintains an Operations Account with the French Treasury. Settlements with all other countries are usually made in any of the currencies of those countries or in French francs through foreign accounts in francs.

Nonresident Accounts

The regulations pertaining to nonresident accounts are based on those applied in France. As the BEAC has suspended the repurchase of BEAC banknotes circulating outside the territories of the issuing zone, BEAC banknotes received by foreign correspondents of authorized banks mailed to the BEAC agency in Brazaville may not be credited to foreign accounts in francs.

Imports and Import Payments

The imports regime is, in principle, liberal; only certain items require import licenses. An annual import program classifies imports by zones: (1) the countries of the Central African Customs and Economic Union (UDEAC); (2) France; (3) other Operations Account countries; (4) European Union (EU) countries other than France; and (5) all remaining countries. Thirteen product items under this program require licenses, and others are subject to ex post declaration. The quotas for non-EU countries may be used to import goods originating in any non-Operations Account country.

All import transactions relating to countries other than France (as defined above), Monaco, and the Operations Account countries must be domiciled with an authorized bank. Licenses for imports from countries other than France (as defined above), Monaco, and the Operations Account countries must be domiciled with an authorized bank and require a visa from the Foreign Trade Directorate and the General Directorate of Credit and Financial Relations. The approved import license entitles importers to purchase the necessary exchange, provided that the shipping documents are submitted to an authorized bank.

In April 1994, a new tariff structure was introduced in the context of the UDEAC tax and customs reform with a view to rationalizing protection rates by narrowing dispersion while eliminating quantitative restrictions. The common duty rate of the UDEAC member countries for basic necessities was reduced to 5 percent, to 10 percent for raw materials and capital goods, to 20 percent for intermediate and miscellaneous goods, and to 30 percent for products requiring special protection. Customs duties on imports from UDEAC member countries were set at preferential rates equivalent to 20 percent of the corresponding common external tariff rate.

All imports must be insured with the state insurance company, Société d'assurances et de réassurances du Congo (SARC). To implement this measure, the Congolese Customs Service releases imports only after an insurance certificate issued by the SARC has been produced.

Payments for Invisibles

Payments for invisibles to France (as defined above), Monaco, and the Operations Account countries are permitted freely, provided that they have been declared and are made through an authorized intermediary; those to other foreign countries are subject to approval. Payments for invisibles related to trade are permitted freely when the basic trade transaction has been approved or does not require authorization. Transfers of income accruing to nonresidents in the form of profits, dividends, and royalties are permitted with the authorization of the General Directorate of Credit and Financial Relations.

Residents traveling for tourist or business purposes to countries in the franc zone are allowed to take out an unlimited amount in banknotes or other payment instruments in French francs. The allowances for travel to countries outside the franc zone are subject to the following regulations: (1) for tourist travel, CFAF 100,000 a day, with a maximum of CFAF 2 million a trip; (2) for business travel, CFAF 250,000 a day, with a maximum of CFAF 5 mil-

lion a trip; (3) for official travel, the equivalent of expenses paid and CFAF 100,000 a day, with a maximum of CFAF 2 million a trip; and (4) for medical expenses abroad, CFAF 100,000 a day, with a maximum of CFAF 2.5 million a trip. Allowances in excess of these limits are subject to the authorization of the Ministry of Finance. The use of credit cards, which must be issued by resident financial intermediaries and approved by the Ministry of Finance, is limited to the ceilings indicated above for tourist and business travel. Returning resident travelers are required to declare all means of payment in their possession upon arrival at customs and surrender within eight days all means of payment exceeding the equivalent of CFAF 25,000. All resident travelers, regardless of destination, must declare in writing all means of payment at their disposal at the time of departure. The re-exportation by nonresident travelers of means of payments other than banknotes issued abroad and registered in the name of the nonresident traveler is not restricted, subject to documentation that they had been purchased with funds drawn from a foreign account in CFA francs or with other foreign exchange. The re-exportation of foreign banknotes is allowed up to the equivalent of CFAF 250,000; the re-exportation of foreign banknotes above these ceilings requires documentation demonstrating either the importation of foreign banknotes or their purchase against other means of payment registered in the name of the traveler or through the use of nonresident deposits lodged in local banks.

The transfer of the entire net salary of a foreigner working in the Congo is permitted upon presentation of the appropriate pay voucher, provided that the transfer takes place within three months of the pay period. Transfers by residents of amounts smaller than CFAF 500,000 to nonmember countries of the franc zone are subject to simple declaration, and those exceeding CFAF 500,000 require prior authorization. Transfers to nonmember countries by nonresidents living in the Congo for less than one year are subject to authorization. Members of diplomatic missions, employees of international organizations, employees of companies operating in the Congo, and government employees, as well as members of liberal professions, are exempt from this regulation.

Exports and Export Proceeds

In principle, all exports require an exchange commitment, but most exports to France (as defined above), Monaco, and the Operations Account countries may be made freely; among the exceptions are commodities exported by the National Marketing Office for Agricultural Products (Office du café et du cacao and Office des cultures vivrières) and by the Congolese Marketing Office for Timber (Office congolais du bois).

Proceeds from exports to foreign countries must be collected and repatriated, generally within 180 days of arrival of the commodities at their destination. Export proceeds must be surrendered within a month of the due date. All export transactions relating to countries other than France (as defined above), Monaco, and the Operations Account countries must be domiciled with an authorized bank.

Proceeds from Invisibles

All amounts due from residents of foreign countries in respect of services and all income earned in those countries from foreign assets must be collected when due and surrendered within a month of the due date. Resident and nonresident travelers may bring in any amount of banknotes and coins issued by the Bank of France, or any other bank of issue maintaining an Operations Account with the French Treasury, as well as any amount of foreign banknotes and coins (except gold coins).

Capital

Capital movements between the Congo and France (as defined above), Monaco, and the Operations Account countries are free, although ex post declarations are required. Such movements to countries that are not members of the BEAC are subject to a commission of 0.25 percent in addition to the 0.75 percent commission. Most international capital transactions are subject to prior authorization. Capital transfers abroad require exchange control approval and are restricted, but capital receipts from abroad are generally permitted freely. All foreign securities, foreign currency, and titles embodying claims on foreign countries or nonresidents that are held in the Congo by residents or nonresidents must be deposited with authorized banks in the Congo.

Special controls (in addition to any exchange control requirements that may apply) are maintained over borrowing and lending abroad, over inward and outward direct investment, and over the issuing, advertising, and offering for sale of foreign securities in the Congo; these controls relate to the transactions themselves, not to payments or receipts.

Direct investments abroad[2] require the prior approval of the Minister of Finance and the Budget;

the full or partial liquidation of such investments also requires the prior approval of the minister. Foreign direct investments in the Congo[3] require the prior approval of the Minister of Finance and the Budget, unless they involve the creation of a mixed-economy enterprise. The full or partial liquidation of direct investments in the Congo must be declared to the minister. Both the making and the liquidation of direct investments, whether Congolese investments abroad or foreign investments in the Congo, must be reported to the minister within 20 days. (Direct investments are defined as investments implying control of a company or enterprise.)

The issuing, advertising, or offering for sale of foreign securities in the Congo requires prior authorization from the Minister of Finance and the Budget. Exempt from authorization, however, are operations in connection with (1) borrowing backed by a guarantee from the Congolese Government, and (2) shares similar to securities whose issuing, advertising, or offering for sale in the Congo has already been authorized.

Borrowing by residents from nonresidents requires prior authorization from the Minister of Finance and the Budget. However, loans contracted by registered banks and small loans, where the total amount outstanding does not exceed CFAF 10 million for any one borrower, the interest is no higher than 5 percent, and the term is at least two years, are exempt from this requirement. The contracting of loans that are free of authorization, and each repayment, must be reported to the General Directorate of Credit and Financial Relations within 20 days of the operation.

Lending by residents to nonresidents is subject to exchange control, and all lending in CFA francs to nonresidents is prohibited unless special authorization is obtained from the Minister of Finance and the Budget. The following are, however, exempt from this authorization: (1) loans in foreign currency granted by registered banks, and (2) other loans when the total amount outstanding of these loans does not exceed the equivalent of CFAF 5 million for any one lender. The making of loans that are free of authorization, and each repayment, must be reported to the General Directorate of Credit and Financial Relations within 20 days.

Under the Investment Code of April 26, 1973, a number of privileges may be granted to approved

---

[2] Including those made through foreign companies that are directly or indirectly controlled by persons in the Congo and those made by overseas branches or subsidiaries of companies in the Congo.

[3] Including those involving the transfer, between nonresidents, of funds in the form of participation in the capital of a Congolese company.

foreign investments. The code provides for four categories of preferential treatment.

Gold

By virtue of Decree No. 66/236 of July 29, 1966, as amended by Decree No. 66/265 of August 29, 1966, residents are free to hold gold in the form of coins, art objects, or jewelry; however, to hold gold in any other form or to import or export gold in any form, from or to any other country, the prior authorization of the Minister of Finance and the Budget is required. Exempt from the latter requirement are (1) imports and exports by or on behalf of the Treasury or the BEAC, and (2) imports and exports of manufactured articles containing a small quantity of gold (such as gold-filled or gold-plated articles). Both licensed and exempt imports of gold are subject to customs declaration. There are no official exports of gold.

Changes During 1994

Exchange Arrangement

January 12. The CFA franc was devalued to CFAF 100 per F 1 from CFAF 50 per F 1.

Imports and Import Payments

April 1. A new tariff structure was introduced in the context of the UDEAC tax and customs reform with a view to rationalizing protection rates by narrowing dispersion while eliminating quantitative restrictions. The common duty rate adopted by the UDEAC member countries for imported basic necessities was reduced to 5 percent, to 10 percent for raw materials and capital goods, to 20 percent for intermediate and miscellaneous goods, and to 30 percent for products requiring special protection. Customs duties on imports from UDEAC member countries were set at preferential rates equivalent to 20 percent of the corresponding common external tariff rate.

COSTA RICA

(Position as of December 31, 1994)

Exchange Arrangement

The currency of Costa Rica is the Costa Rican Colón, the external value of which is determined freely by commercial banks and other financial institutions in the interbank market.[1] A tax of ₡ 0.68 per US$1 applies to all foreign exchange transactions in the official market. The difference between buying and selling rates of authorized banks and financial institutions may not exceed 0.7 percent. The Government and public sector institutions conduct foreign exchange transactions directly with the Central Bank. These operations are carried out at the official reference exchange rate, which is calculated at the close of each business day as the weighted average of the exchange rates used in the market during the day. On December 31, 1994, the buying and selling bank rates were ₡ 164.51 and ₡ 165.63, respectively, per US$1.

There are no arrangements for forward cover against exchange rate risks operating in the official or the commercial banking sector.

Costa Rica formally accepted the obligations of Article VIII, Sections 2, 3, and 4 of the Fund Agreement, as from February 1, 1965.

Administration of Control

Exchange regulations are issued by the Central Bank. The only institutions authorized to deal in foreign exchange are the Central Bank, the state commercial banks, private banks, and other nonbank financial institutions authorized by the Central Bank.

Arrears of the nonfinancial public sector are maintained with respect to external payments.

Prescription of Currency

Nearly all payments for exchange transactions are made in U.S. dollars. Trade payments to Central America may be made in U.S. dollars or in local currencies.

Imports and Import Payments

A limited number of imports are subject to licensing requirements. All payments for imports may be made freely. Imports made on a barter basis require a barter license (*licencia de trueque*), issued by the Ministry of Economy and Commerce.

Customs tariff rates on most goods range from zero to 20 percent. In addition to any applicable customs tariff, the following taxes are levied on imports: (1) a tax of 1 percent on import value; (2) a sales tax of 10 percent, from which certain essential items are exempt; and (3) a selective consumption tax at rates varying from zero to 75 percent, depending on the essential quality of the item.

Payments for Invisibles

Payments for invisibles are not restricted. Withholding taxes of 15 percent are levied on remittances of dividends. The 5 percent withholding tax is levied on dividends distributed by stock companies whose shares were acquired at an officially acknowledged stock exchange. Remittances of interest abroad are subject to a 15 percent withholding tax, except for remittances to foreign banks or to their financial entities recognized by the Central Bank as institutions normally engaged in international transactions, including payments to foreign suppliers for commodity imports. Interest on loans from foreign institutions recognized by the Central Bank as first-rate institutions is not taxed if the funds are used by resident firms for industrial or agricultural/livestock activities. Interest on government borrowing abroad is exempt.

Exports and Export Proceeds

Sixty percent of export proceeds from all exports may be retained by exporters, and the remainder must be sold to any financial institution authorized to operate in the interbank market. In turn, a financial institution must transfer to the Central Bank 25 percent of total purchases of foreign exchange related to exports. The exchange rate applicable to this transfer is the buying exchange rate of the institution plus ₡ 0.10 per US$1. Exporters of nontraditional products to markets outside Central America are entitled to receive freely negotiable tax credit certificates (CATs) at the following rates based on the f.o.b. value: 15 percent for exports to the United

---

[1] Foreign exchange trading occurs in the organized MONED electronic foreign exchange market among authorized traders and in which the Central Bank carries out its intervention operations. Foreign exchange trading also takes place directly between authorized institutions outside the MONED.

States, Puerto Rico, and Europe; and 20 percent for exports to Canada.[2]

Most export licenses have been eliminated. However, licenses are required for goods, such as armaments, munitions, scrap iron, and scrap of nonferrous base metals (from the Ministry of Economy and Commerce); sugar (from the Agricultural Industrial Board for Sugarcane); beans, rice, root of ipecacuanha, onions, cotton, meat, and purebred cattle (from the National Council of Production); airplanes (from the Civil Aviation Board and the Ministry of Economy and Commerce); Indian art objects made of gold, stone, or clay (from the National Museum); tobacco (from the Tobacco Defense Board); textiles; flowers, lumber, certain livestock, and animals and plants of forest origin (from the Ministry of Agriculture and Livestock); and coffee (from the Coffee Institute); in addition, when there is a lien on coffee in favor of a bank, that bank's approval is required before the Central Bank grants an export license.

Exchange proceeds from exports of coffee, bananas, sugar, beef, and bovine cattle must be surrendered within 30 days of shipment; those from exports of other perishable agricultural items, within 60 days of shipment; those from exports of industrial products (excluding those indicated next) and other agricultural products, within 120 days of shipment; those from exports of durable and semi-durable industrial consumer products, within 180 days of shipment; and those from exports of capital goods, within 360 days of shipment. There are no taxes on nontraditional exports to countries outside the Central American area and Panama; taxes are levied on traditional exports and, in some cases, are graduated in line with international prices.

Proceeds from Invisibles

Proceeds from invisibles are free from controls or restrictions, but receipts from invisibles may be exchanged into colones only at the Central Bank or other authorized institutions.

Capital

There are no restrictions on capital transfers, and capital transactions between residents and nonresidents are permitted. An annual limit of 6.25 percent of the face value of the debt converted is imposed on dividend remittances associated with debt/equity conversions.

The National Budget Authority[3] is in charge of authorizing the negotiation of new external credits contemplated by the Central Government, decentralized agencies, and state enterprises. Foreign and domestic capital transferred from abroad may be deposited as time deposits in U.S. dollars with agent banks in the form of specified foreign currencies or invested in certificates of deposit denominated in colones; such funds, when they mature, are repaid in the currency in which the deposits were made.

Gold

The Central Bank may purchase, sell, or hold gold coins or bars as part of the monetary reserves in accordance with regulations established by its Board. Natural and juridical persons may buy or sell, subject to approval from the Ministry of Energy and Natural Resources, at home or abroad, domestically produced gold (except national archaeological treasures, pursuant to Law No. 6703 of December 18, 1981), provided there is no infraction of international agreements. Licenses from the Central Bank are required for exports of gold. Gold may also be held in any form in Costa Rica. The Central Bank may sell unrefined gold to artistic or professional users or to enterprises that export jewelry.

Changes During 1994

Exchange Arrangement

April 13. The Central Bank announced that the spread between the buying and selling rates of authorized banks and financial institutions cannot exceed 0.7 percent.

Administration of Control

December 19. The assembly approved a comprehensive trade agreement with Mexico that would become effective January 1, 1995. The trade agreement covers trade in foods and services, investment, intellectual property rights, and disputed settlement and envisages free trade of over 90 percent of goods within five years and of almost all goods within ten years.

---

[2]CATs ceased to be issued to new exporters after December 31, 1992. Existing exporters continue to benefit from the CATs consistent with their specific contractual arrangements.

[3]Composed of the Minister of Finance, the Minister of Planning, and the President of the Central Bank.

Exports and Export Proceeds

April 13. The surrender requirement for proceeds from exports was reduced 40 percent, and the requirement was extended to all exports.

August 4. All financial institutions authorized to operate in the interbank market were required to transfer to the Central Bank 25 percent of their purchases of foreign exchange related to exports.

CÔTE D'IVOIRE

(Position as of December 31, 1994)

Exchange Arrangement

The currency of Côte d'Ivoire is the CFA Franc,[1] which is pegged to the French franc, the intervention currency, at the fixed rate of CFAF 1 per F 0.01. The official buying and selling rate is CFAF 100 per F 1. Exchange rates for other currencies are derived from the rates in the Paris exchange market for the currencies concerned and the fixed rate between the French franc and the CFA franc. The BCEAO levies no commission on transfers to or from countries outside the West African Monetary Union (WAMU).[2] Banks and the postal system levy a commission on transfers to all countries outside the WAMU; commissions must be surrendered to the Treasury. There are no taxes or subsidies on purchases or sales of foreign exchange.

With the exception of measures relating to gold and the repatriation of export proceeds, the exchange control measures of Côte d'Ivoire do not apply to (1) France (and its overseas departments and territories) and Monaco; and (2) all other countries whose bank of issue is linked with the French Treasury by an Operations Account (Benin, Burkina Faso, Cameroon, Central African Republic, Chad, Comoros, Congo, Equatorial Guinea, Gabon, Mali, Niger, Senegal, and Togo). Hence, all payments to these countries may be made freely. All other countries are considered foreign countries.

Spot foreign exchange cover is limited to imports effected by means of documentary credits; the transaction must be domiciled with an authorized intermediary, and goods must be shipped within eight days of the exchange operation. Forward exchange cover for eligible imports must not extend beyond one month for certain specified goods and three months for goods designated essential commodities; no renewal of cover is possible. Forward cover against exchange rate risk is permitted, with prior authorization from the Directorate of the Treasury, Monetary and Banking Affairs in the Ministry of Economy, Finance, and Planning, only for payments for imports of goods and only for the currency stipulated in the commercial contract. There are no official schemes for currency swaps or guaranteed exchange rates for debt servicing.

Administration of Control

Exchange control is administered by the Directorate of the Treasury, Monetary and Banking Affairs in the Ministry of Economy, Finance, and Planning. The BCEAO is authorized to collect any information necessary to compile balance of payments statistics, either directly or through the banks, other financial institutions, the Postal Administration, and notaries public. All exchange transactions relating to foreign countries must be effected through authorized banks or the Postal Administration. Import licenses for a short list of controlled products (Decree No. 93–313 of March 11, 1993) are issued by the Directorate of External Trade Promotion in the Ministry of Commerce.

Arrears are maintained with respect to the external debt-servicing obligations of the central Government.

Prescription of Currency

Because Côte d'Ivoire is an Operations Account country, settlements with France (as defined above), Monaco, and the Operations Account countries are made in CFA francs, French francs, or the currency of any other Operations Account country. Current payments to or from The Gambia, Ghana, Guinea, Guinea-Bissau, Liberia, Mauritania, Nigeria, and Sierra Leone are normally made through the West African Clearing House. Settlements with all other countries are effected through correspondent banks in France, in any of the currencies of those countries, or in French francs through foreign accounts in francs.

Nonresident Accounts

The regulations pertaining to nonresident accounts are based on regulations applied in France. Because the BCEAO has suspended the repurchase of BCEAO banknotes circulating outside the territories of the CFA franc zone, foreign accounts in francs may not be credited or debited with BCEAO banknotes or show an overdraft position without prior authorization.

---

[1] The CFA franc is issued by the Central Bank of West African States (BCEAO) and is the common currency in Benin, Burkina Faso, Côte d'Ivoire, Mali, Niger, Senegal, and Togo.

[2] Transfers between member countries of the WAMU are subject to the flat commission of CFAF 100 levied on settlements between agencies of the BCEAO.

Imports and Import Payments

Under the current regulations, all imports are classified into three categories, as follows: (1) goods requiring prior authorization or the approval of ministries; (2) goods subject to quantitative or other restrictions requiring licenses issued by the Directorate of External Trade Promotions; and (3) freely importable goods.

Quantitative or other limits for goods in the second category are set each year by the Minister of Industry and Commerce, in light of market conditions, local production, and following consultation with the Competitiveness Committee. With certain specific exceptions (e.g., diplomatic imports and used vehicles), all unrestricted imports with an f.o.b. value exceeding CFAF 3 million are subject to a preshipment inspection to verify their price, quantity, and quality; for values between CFAF 1.5 million and CFAF 3 million, imports may be subject to random inspection. For all imports (except those with prior authorization) whose f.o.b. value exceeds CFAF 500,000, an import information declaration for statistical purposes is also required.

A maximum tariff rate of 35 percent has been in effect since January 1994. A statistical tax of 2.5 percent of the c.i.f. value is levied on all imports. Imports from member countries of the West African Economic Community (WAEC) and the Economic Community of West African States (ECOWAS) are exempt from the surcharges.

All import operations valued at more than CFAF 500,000 conducted with foreign countries must be domiciled with an authorized bank; transactions of lower value must also be domiciled with an authorized bank if a financial transaction is to be undertaken before customs clearance. The import licenses or import attestations entitle importers to purchase the necessary foreign exchange, but not earlier than eight days before shipment if a documentary credit is opened, and only on the due date of payment if the commodities have already been imported. Since June 15, 1981, foreign exchange for import payments must be purchased either on the settlement date specified in the commercial contract or when the required downpayment is made.

Payments for Invisibles

Payments for invisibles to France (as defined above), Monaco, and the Operations Account countries are permitted freely; those to other countries must be approved. Payments for invisibles related to trade are permitted freely when the basic trade transaction has been approved or does not require authorization. Transfers of income accruing to nonresidents in the form of profits, dividends, and royalties are also permitted freely when the underlying transaction has been approved.

Residents traveling for tourism or business purposes to countries in the franc zone that are not members of the WAMU are allowed to take out banknotes other than the CFA banknotes up to the equivalent of CFAF 2 million; amounts in excess of this limit may be taken out in the form of means of payment other than banknotes. The allowances for travel to countries outside the franc zone are subject to the following regulations: (1) for tourist travel, CFAF 500,000 without limit on the number of trips or differentiation by the age of the traveler; (2) for business travel, CFAF 75,000 a day for up to one month, corresponding to a maximum of CFAF 2.25 million (business travel allowances may be combined with tourist allowances); (3) allowances in excess of these limits are subject to the authorization of the Ministry of Economy and Finance; and (4) credit cards, which must be issued by resident financial intermediaries and authorized by the respective ministers of finance, may be used up to the ceilings indicated above for tourist and business travel. Returning resident travelers are required to declare all means of payment in their possession upon arrival at customs and surrender within eight days all means of payment exceeding the equivalent of CFAF 25,000. All resident travelers, when traveling to countries that are not members of the WAMU, must declare in writing all means of payment at their disposal at the time of departure. Nonresident travelers may freely re-export means of payment, other than banknotes issued abroad and registered in their name, subject to documentation that they used funds drawn from a foreign account in CFA francs or other foreign exchange to purchase the means of payment. The re-exportation of foreign banknotes is allowed up to the equivalent of CFAF 250,000; the re-exportation of foreign banknotes above these ceilings requires documentation demonstrating either their importation or their purchase against other means of payment registered in the name of the traveler or through the use of nonresident deposits lodged in local banks.

Exports and Export Proceeds

All exports are free of restrictions, with the exception of certain metals, including precious metals and gems, the exportation of which requires prior authorization. Exports of ivory (above a minimum weight) and certain types of tropical wood are prohibited. Exports require a customs declaration but not a license. Exports of lumber are subject to quantitative quotas allocated through auction. Exports of cocoa and coffee are subject to a specific unitary export tax and can be effected only by exporters authorized by the Price Stabilization Fund.

Payment for exports to foreign countries, including those in the Operations Account Area, must be made within 120 days of the arrival of the goods at their destination. Regardless of the currency of settlement and of the country of destination, export receipts must be collected and repatriated through authorized intermediary banks within one month of the due date. Regardless of destination, all export transactions valued at more than CFAF 1 million must be domiciled with an authorized bank.

Proceeds from Invisibles

Proceeds from transactions in invisibles with France (as defined above), Monaco, and the Operations Account countries may be retained. All amounts due from residents of other countries for services, and all income earned in those countries from foreign assets, must be collected and surrendered within two months of the due date or the date of receipt. Resident and nonresident travelers may import any amount of banknotes and coins issued by the BCEAO, the Bank of France, or any bank of issue maintaining an Operations Account with the French Treasury, as well as any amount of foreign banknotes and coins (except gold coins) of countries outside the Operations Account Area. Residents bringing in foreign banknotes or other foreign means of payment must surrender any amount in excess of CFAF 5,000 to an authorized bank within eight days and must make a declaration to customs upon entry.

Capital

Capital movements between Côte d'Ivoire and France (as defined above), Monaco, and the Operations Account countries are free of exchange control; capital transfers to all other countries require exchange control approval, but capital receipts from such countries are permitted freely.

Special controls, in addition to any exchange control requirements that may apply, are maintained over borrowing abroad by the private sector, foreign inward direct investment, all outward direct investment in foreign countries, and over the issuing, advertising, or offering for sale of foreign securities in Côte d'Ivoire. Such operations, as well as issues by Côte d'Ivoire companies, require prior authorization from the Ministry of Economy, Finance, and Planning. Exempt from authorization, however, are operations in connection with (1) loans

backed by a guarantee from the Government of Côte d'Ivoire, and (2) foreign shares similar to securities whose issuing, advertising, or offering for sale in Côte d'Ivoire has already been authorized. With the exception of controls relating to foreign securities, these measures do not apply to relations with France (as defined above), Monaco, member countries of the WAMU, and the Operations Account countries. Special controls are also maintained over the soliciting of funds for deposit with foreign private persons and foreign firms and institutions, and over publicity aimed at placing funds abroad or at subscribing to real estate and building operations abroad; these special controls also apply to France (as defined above), Monaco, and the Operations Account countries.

All investments abroad by residents of Côte d'Ivoire require prior authorization from the Minister of Economy, Finance, and Planning.[3] Foreign direct investments in Côte d'Ivoire must be authorized in advance by the Minister of Economy, Finance, and Planning.[4] Effective June 15, 1981, at least 75 percent of investments abroad by residents of Côte d'Ivoire must be financed by borrowing abroad. The liquidation of direct and other investments in Côte d'Ivoire or abroad must also be reported in advance to the Minister. Both the making and the liquidation of investments, whether Ivoirien investments abroad or foreign investments in Côte d'Ivoire, must be reported to the Minister within 20 days of each operation. (Direct investments are defined as those that imply control of a company or an enterprise. Mere participation is not considered as direct investment, provided that it does not exceed 20 percent of the capital of a company whose shares are quoted on a stock exchange.)

Borrowing by residents from nonresidents must be authorized in advance by the Minister of Economy, Finance, and Planning. The following are, however, exempt from this authorization: (1) loans taken up by industrial firms to finance transactions abroad, to finance imports into or exports from Côte d'Ivoire, or loans approved by international trading houses to finance international trade transactions; (2) loans contracted by authorized banks; and (3) loans other than those mentioned above whose total outstanding amount, including the new borrowing, does not exceed CFAF 50 million for

---

[3]Including those made through foreign companies that are directly or indirectly controlled by persons resident in Côte d'Ivoire and those made by branches or subsidiaries abroad of companies resident in Côte d'Ivoire.

[4]Including those made in Côte d'Ivoire by companies that are directly or indirectly under foreign control and those made by branches or subsidiaries of foreign companies in Côte d'Ivoire.

any one borrower and whose annual interest rate does not exceed the normal market rate. The repayment of loans constituting a direct investment is subject to the formalities prescribed for the liquidation of direct investments. The repayment of other loansrequires authorization only if the loan itself was subject to prior approval. Lending abroad is subject to exchange control authorization.

Under the investment code introduced in 1984, special incentives are provided for foreign and domestic investments in certain priority sectors and priority geographical areas. The incentives include exemption from customs duties and tariffs on all imported capital equipment and spare parts for investment projects, provided that no equivalent item is produced in Côte d'Ivoire. In addition, all such investments are exempt for a specified period, depending on the investment sector or area, from corporate profit taxes, patent contributions, and capital assets taxes. In general, the exemption covers 100 percent of applicable tax up to the fourth-to-last year of the exemption period and is reduced progressively to 75 percent of the tax in the third-to-last year, 50 percent in the second-to-last year, and 25 percent in the last year. Imports of raw materials for which no equivalents are produced locally are not exempt from import duties and taxes.

Gold

Residents are free to hold, acquire, and dispose of gold in any form in Côte d'Ivoire. Imports and exports of gold to or from any other country require prior authorization from the Minister of Economy, Finance, and Planning; authorization is rarely granted. Exempt from this requirement are (1) imports and exports by the Treasury or the BCEAO, (2) imports and exports of manufactured articles containing a small quantity of gold (such as gold-filled or gold-plated articles), and (3) imports and exports by travelers of gold articles up to a weight of 250 grams. Both licensed and exempt imports and exports of gold are subject to customs declaration.

Changes During 1994

Exchange Arrangement

January 12. The CFA franc was devalued to CFAF 100 per F 1 from CFAF 50 per F 1.

Imports and Import Payments

January 19. The revision of the tariff regime that began in October 1992 was completed. The new regime consists of a single customs duty rate of 5 percent and six fiscal duties ranging from 5 percent to 30 percent. A few specific rates were retained on some products.

January 21. The minimum value of imports requiring preshipment inspection was raised to CFAF 3 million.

August 1. Imports of luxury rice were liberalized.

December 29. Twelve groups of products subject to prior authorization or approval were liberalized.

Exports and Export Proceeds

January 15. The export premium on locally manufactured products and agricultural products (excluding unprocessed coffee, cocoa, cotton, and pineapples) was eliminated.

January 25. The single export tax on cocoa and coffee was introduced.

September 23. (1) The period during which proceeds from exports must be received was shortened to 120 days from 180 days, and (2) the value of export transactions to which the domiciliation requirement applies was raised to CFAF 1 million.

CROATIA

(Position as of December 31, 1994)

Exchange Arrangement

The currency of Croatia is the Kuna, the external value of which is determined in the interbank market. The exchange rates in the interbank market are determined by authorized banks that transact with each other at freely negotiated rates. The National Bank of Croatia may set intervention exchange rates at which it will transact with banks outside the interbank market for purposes of smoothing undue fluctuations in the exchange rate. On December 31, 1994, the average interbank market rate for the U.S. dollar was HRK 5.6287 per US$1.

There are no taxes or subsidies on purchases or sales of foreign exchange.

Croatia formally accepted the obligations of Article VIII, Sections 2, 3, and 4 of the Fund Agreement, as from May 29, 1995.

Administration of Control

Foreign exchange transactions are governed by the Law on the Foreign Exchange System, Foreign Exchange Operations, and Gold Transactions, which was enacted on October 7, 1993. The National Bank formulates and administers exchange rate policy and may issue foreign exchange regulations under this law. A foreign trade law (coordinated with domestic trade legislation) is under preparation. Companies wishing to engage in foreign trade must register with the commercial courts. The representative offices of foreign companies must be registered with the Ministry of Economy.

Foreign exchange transactions must be conducted through authorized banks; currently 39 commercial banks in Croatia are licensed to conduct foreign exchange transactions. Restricted licenses are given to banks that may open accounts for resident natural persons and may buy and sell banknotes and checks (currently 13 banks).

Arrears are maintained with respect to external payments.

Prescription of Currency

Settlements between residents and nonresidents may be effected in any convertible currency.

Resident and Nonresident Accounts

Resident natural and juridical persons may, in principle, open and operate foreign exchange accounts only in Croatia. However, the National Bank has the authority to allow resident juridical persons to keep foreign exchange in accounts with foreign banks in order to cover the costs of business operations and meet the requirement of regular foreign trade activities abroad. The law also makes specific provisions for resident juridical persons engaged in capital project construction abroad to maintain accounts with foreign banks, subject to a license issued by the National Bank.

Nonresidents may open foreign exchange accounts with fully licensed banks in Croatia. These accounts may be credited freely with foreign exchange and debited for payments abroad for conversion into domestic currency; reconversion of domestic currency into a foreign currency is permitted. Juridical persons may not credit these accounts with foreign banknotes up to the limit of $20,000 without special permission from the National Bank.

Nonresident natural and juridical persons may open accounts in domestic currency with the proceeds from sales of goods and services or with foreign exchange transferred from abroad. They may purchase foreign exchange with funds held in these accounts without restriction.

Imports and Import Payments

Imports from the Federal Republic of Yugoslavia (Serbia/Montenegro) are prohibited in accordance with UN Security Council resolutions. Pending the introduction of a new import regime, the product classification of the import regime of the former Socialist Federal Republic of Yugoslavia is maintained, with a free list (LB), a list of items subject to quotas, and a list of items subject to ad hoc licensing (D).

Items on the free list (just under 6,000 out of a total of about 6,600) comprise about 90 percent of the value of imports. Of the restricted items, only about 2 percent of imports are subject to licensing and about 2 percent to quotas. The Ministry of Economy, in consultation with the Chamber of Commerce, administers the quotas and licensing. List D includes items whose importation is controlled by international agreement for noneconomic reasons (such as, arms, gold, illegal drugs and narcotics, and artistic and historic work). The importation of these items is allowed on a case-by-case basis and for specific purposes.

Imports are subject to a customs tariffs of up to 18 percent (compared with up to 25 percent in the former Socialist Federal Republic of Yugoslavia) plus a tax of up to 10 percent, and a customs administration fee of 1 percent. The exemption for duty-free imports by travelers is $100. Goods imported by travelers and postal shipments up to the value of $500 are subject to a simplified customs procedure with a unified tariff rate of 8 percent. For imports exceeding that value, the regular import tariffs and taxes are applied. Returning citizens may bring into the country household effects duty-free up to the equivalent of $45,000 for household effects and $100,000 for private business purposes. Under certain conditions, goods imported by nonresidents for investment purposes are exempt from import duties. Also, raw materials and intermediate products used in the production of exports are exempt from all import duties and taxes, except the 1 percent customs fee, provided that the value added of the export product is at least 30 percent of the value of the imported items and that export proceeds are received in convertible currency.

Payments for authorized imports by juridical persons are not restricted.

Advance payments for imports are not permitted, except where down payments are required by suppliers in accordance with customary international practices.

Payments for Invisibles

Payments for invisibles related to authorized imports by juridical persons may be made freely. Payments of leasing fees are permitted provided that temporary imports have been registered with the Customs Office. Natural persons may also purchase foreign exchange in the interbank market for the payment of goods and services abroad and for deposit in a foreign exchange account for the purpose of future payments. Resident juridical persons (including tradesmen, natural persons engaging in independent activities) may purchase foreign exchange only for authorized payments abroad, except to make payments for activities related to scientific, humanitarian, cultural, or sport events. Payments of royalties, insurance, and legal obligations and contracting of life and casualty insurance policies with foreign companies are also permitted.

Resident natural persons may take out of the country foreign currency equivalent to DM 1,000. An additional amount equivalent up to DM 2,000 may be taken out, provided that it is withdrawn from foreign currency accounts or purchased from banks for travel expenses. In both cases the Na-

tional Bank may allow higher amounts to be taken out on a case-by-case basis. The exportation of Croatian currency by both residents and nonresidents is limited to HRK 2,000 a person.

Exports and Export Proceeds

Exports to the Federal Republic of Yugoslavia (Serbia/Montenegro) are prohibited in accordance with UN Security Council resolutions. In principle, exports are free of restrictions except for certain products for which permits must be obtained (list D products: e.g., weapons, drugs, and art objects); several basic foodstuffs to ensure adequate domestic supplies; and high-quality wood.

Export proceeds must be collected and repatriated in full to Croatia within 60 days of the date of exportation; this period may be extended with the permission of the National Bank. If payment terms in excess of 60 days have been agreed with foreign importers, the credit arrangement must be registered with the National Bank.

Proceeds from Invisibles

Proceeds from services are, in principle, subject to the same regulations as those applying to merchandise exports. The importation of Croatian currency by both residents and nonresidents is limited to HRK 2,000 a person.

Capital

Resident juridical persons, including commercial banks, may borrow abroad. They are required to register the loans contracted, including commercial credits, with the National Bank. Financial credits may be extended to nonresidents by resident juridical persons, including tradesmen and natural persons engaging in independent activities, only if these credits are financed from profits or credit obtained from abroad. Natural persons are permitted to obtain loans from nonresidents in domestic or foreign currency. The foreign exchange positions of commercial banks are subject to a limit.

Foreign direct investment by nonresidents may take the form of joint ventures or full ownership and must be registered with the commercial courts. Repatriation of capital and transfers abroad of profits are not restricted. In principle, domestic and foreign investment is treated equally, but in practice nonresident investors enjoy certain benefits. If the foreign equity capital participation exceeds 20 percent, inputs used in the project are exempt from import duties. Earnings in the first year of operation are exempt from the profit tax, and 50 percent and

25 percent of earnings in the second and third years, respectively, are exempt from the profit tax. Foreign direct investment abroad by residents must be registered with the Ministry of Economy. Such investment must generally be undertaken through loans abroad or through reinvestment of profits. Inward portfolio investment is not restricted, but outward portfolio investment is restricted.

Nonresident natural persons may acquire real estate in Croatia through inheritance as long as their country of residence extends reciprocal treatment to residents of Croatia. Nonresident natural persons not engaged in economic activities in Croatia may purchase real estate only under the same conditions. Nonresident natural or juridical persons engaged in economic activities in Croatia may also purchase real estate under these conditions and may sell it to resident or nonresident juridical persons. In principle, residents may acquire real estate abroad on the basis of reciprocity of treatment, but in practice, they are not permitted to purchase foreign exchange in the exchange market for this purpose; the use of balances in foreign exchange accounts for this purpose is also prohibited.

Gold

The exportation or importation of gold, except unprocessed gold by producers of gold and gold coins or by authorized commercial banks, is subject to the approval of the National Bank.

Changes During 1994

Exchange Arrangement

May 30. The kuna replaced the Croatian dinar as the national currency at the ratio of 1 kuna for 1,000 Croatian dinars.

October 7. Foreign exchange repurchase agreements were introduced by the National Bank of Croatia. Although these are offered to commercial banks at the initiative of the National Bank for monetary management purposes, they can be used by commercial banks to manage forward exchange risks.

Prescription of Currency

June 30. Croatia canceled unilaterally the bilateral payments agreement with Slovenia.

Changes During 1995

Exchange Arrangement

May 29. Croatia formally accepted the obligations of Article VIII, Sections 2, 3, and 4 of the Fund Agreement.

CYPRUS

(Position as of December 31, 1994)

Exchange Arrangement

The currency of Cyprus is the Cyprus Pound, the external value of which is pegged to a basket based on the European Currency Unit (ECU) at ECU 1.7086 per £C 1, within margins of ±2.25 percent around the ECU central rate. On December 31, 1994, the official buying and selling rates for the U.S. dollar, the intervention currency, were £C 0.4759 and £C 0.4778, respectively, per US$1. The Central Bank of Cyprus also quotes daily buying and selling rates for the ECU, deutsche mark, the Greek drachma, and the pound sterling. These rates are subject to change throughout the day. It also quotes indicative rates for other foreign currencies[1] on the basis of market rates in international money market centers. Subject to certain limitations, including a limit on spreads between the buying and selling rates, authorized dealers (banks) are free to determine and quote their own buying and selling rates. There are no taxes or subsidies on purchases or sales of foreign exchange.

Authorized dealers are allowed to trade in the forward market at rates that may be freely negotiated with their customers. For U.S. dollars and pounds sterling, however, forward rates may not differ by more than the premiums or discounts that are applied by the Central Bank for cover for a similar period. Authorized dealers are allowed to purchase forward cover from the Central Bank at prevailing rates or to conduct forward operations between two foreign currencies for cover in one of the two currencies. The Central Bank offers authorized dealers facilities for forward purchases of U.S. dollars and pounds sterling for exports for periods of up to 24 months. Cover for imports is normally provided for up to 6 months. When justified (for example, payments for imports of raw materials for exports or capital goods), rates are quoted for up to 15 months. Forward contracts must be based on genuine commercial commitments. Forward cover may also be provided for up to 12 months to residents for specific financial commitments.

Cyprus formally accepted the obligations of Article VIII, Sections 2, 3, and 4 of the Fund Agreement, as from January 9, 1991.

Administration of Control

Exchange controls are administered by the Central Bank in cooperation with authorized dealers. Authority to approve applications for the allocation of foreign exchange for a number of purposes has been delegated to authorized dealers.

Prescription of Currency

Payments may be made by crediting Cyprus pounds to an external account, or in any foreign currency;[2] the proceeds of exports to all countries may be received in Cyprus pounds from an external account, or in any foreign currency.

Resident and Nonresident Accounts

Residents of countries outside Cyprus may open and maintain with authorized dealers nonresident accounts in Cyprus pounds, designated external accounts, or foreign currency accounts. These accounts may be credited freely with payments from nonresidents of Cyprus (such as transfers from other external accounts or foreign currency accounts), proceeds from sales of any foreign currency by nonresidents (including declared bank notes), and the entire proceeds, including capital appreciation, from the sale of an investment made by a nonresident in Cyprus with the approval of the Central Bank and with authorized payments in Cyprus pounds. External accounts and foreign currency accounts may be debited for payments to residents and nonresidents, for remittances abroad, for transfers to other external accounts or foreign currency accounts, and for payments in cash (Cyprus pounds) in Cyprus. Companies registered or incorporated in Cyprus that are accorded nonresident status (generally designated as offshore companies) by the Central Bank as well as their nonresident employees may maintain external accounts and foreign currency accounts in Cyprus or abroad, as well as local disbursement accounts for meeting their payments in Cyprus. Resident per-

---

[1]Australian dollars, Austrian schillings, Belgian francs, Canadian dollars, Danish kroner, Finnish markkaa, French francs, Italian lire, Japanese yen, Netherlands guilders, Norwegian kroner, Portuguese escudos, Spanish pesetas, Swedish kronor, and Swiss francs.

[2]Foreign currencies are all currencies other than the Cyprus pound.

sons and firms dealing with transit trade or engaged in manufacturer-exporter activities or in the hotel business may open and maintain foreign currency accounts subject to certain requirements. Residents dealing with transit trade may deposit up to 95 percent of sale proceeds in these accounts and use balances to pay for the value of traded goods. Residents engaged in manufacturer-exporter activities may deposit up to 50 percent of export proceeds in these accounts and use balances to pay for imports of raw materials used in production. Both transit traders and manufacturers-exporters are, however, required to convert into Cyprus pounds at the end of each year any balances in excess of the amount that is necessary for payments of the value of traded goods of raw materials during the following three months. Resident hoteliers may deposit in foreign currency accounts part of their receipts in foreign currency and use balances to make installment payments on foreign currency loans. Cypriot repatriates may keep in foreign currency, in external accounts in Cyprus or in accounts abroad, all of their foreign currency holdings and earnings accruing from properties they own abroad.

Blocked accounts are maintained in the name of nonresidents for funds that may not immediately and in their entirety be transferred outside Cyprus under the existing exchange control regulations. Blocked funds may either be held as deposits or be invested in government securities or government-guaranteed securities. Income earned on blocked funds is freely transferable to the nonresident beneficiary or may be credited to an external account or foreign currency account. In addition to income, up to £C 10,000[3] in principal may be released annually from blocked funds for transfer outside Cyprus. Funds can also be released from blocked accounts to meet reasonable expenses in Cyprus of the account holder and his or her family, including educational expenses, donations to charitable institutions in Cyprus, payments for the acquisition of immovable property in Cyprus, and any other amounts authorized by the Central Bank.

Imports and Import Payments

Most imports are free of licensing requirements. An import license is required for certain commodities such as fresh fruits, fresh vegetables, fresh meat, and other goods produced or manufactured locally.

The Minister of Commerce and Industry may amend the list of commodities subject to licensing as deemed necessary to regulate the importation of goods for the encouragement of local production and manufacture and for the improvement of the balance of payments. Exchange is allocated freely and without restriction through authorized dealers to pay for imports, provided that documentary evidence of shipment or actual importation of goods is available.

Advance payments before shipment require the prior approval of the Central Bank, except for imports whose value does not exceed £C 20,000. Authorized dealers are allowed to sell to departing residents of Cyprus foreign exchange up to £C 20,000 for purchases and for the importation of goods into Cyprus; foreign exchange in excess of this limit may be sold to departing residents with the approval of the Central Bank. An import surcharge of 3.8 percent (2.5 percent for imports from European Union countries) ad valorem is levied on all imports, except food, pharmaceuticals, and goods imported by the Government.

Payments for Invisibles

Payments for invisibles abroad require the approval of the Central Bank, but approval authority for certain types of payments has been delegated to authorized dealers. Profits, dividends, and interest from approved foreign investments may be transferred abroad without limitation, after payment of any due charges and taxes. Insurance premiums owed to foreign insurance companies may be remitted after all contingencies have been deducted. Nonresidents who are temporarily employed in Cyprus by resident firms or individuals and are paid in local currency may transfer abroad their remuneration less local living expenses and taxes.

Allowances are granted to residents for study abroad at colleges, universities, or other institutions of higher education, and certain lower-level institutions of learning.[4] Exchange allowances are based on the cost of living, which is reviewed yearly, and cover the full amount of tuition fees plus living expenses for the student. The current annual allowance for living expenses for studies in Western European countries, excluding Greece, is £C 5,000; for Greece, £C 3,300; for Canada and the United States, £C 6,600; for Australia, £C 4,000; and for all other countries, £C 3,300. There is no limit on the remittance of foreign exchange for payment of tuition fees.

---

[3]On January 1, 1995, this amount was increased to £C 50,000.

[4]The amount that can be transferred without reference to the Central Bank is £C 400 a month.

Authorized dealers are allowed, without any reference to the Central Bank, to sell to resident travelers foreign exchange up to £C 750 a person a trip for tourist travel; the Central Bank approves applications for allocations of additional foreign exchange without limitation to cover genuine travel expenses. The allowance for business travel is not fixed but depends on the length of stay abroad. Authorized dealers are empowered to provide up to £C 150 a day with a maximum of £C 1,500 a trip; additional amounts may be granted with the approval of the Central Bank on proof of need.

Company credit cards valid abroad are issued to resident businessmen and professionals traveling abroad on business. These international credit cards entitle the holders to charge their expenses for hotels, restaurants, unlimited transportation and international telephone calls, cash withdrawals of up to £C 100 a trip, and any other expense up to £C 300 a trip, as well as payments abroad or from Cyprus up to £C 300 per case for certain additional purposes such as subscriptions to professional bodies or societies and fees for enrollment in educational seminars or conferences. If resident travelers hold an international credit card, authorized dealers are allowed to provide an allowance of up to £C 80 a day with a maximum of £C 800 a trip for business travel. Additional amounts for business travel may be provided with the approval of the Central Bank. In addition, enterprises may use international credit cards for payments of up to £C 300 for mail orders of books or other items. Authorized dealers are also allowed to issue personal credit cards, valid abroad, to certain categories of residents. Foreign exchange for medical expenses abroad is granted without limit, and authorized dealers are empowered to provide allowances of up to £C 3,000 without reference to the Central Bank.

On leaving Cyprus, travelers may take out with them up to £C 50 in Cyprus currency notes. There is no limit on the amount of foreign currency notes that departing residents may take out of the country as part of any of their foreign exchange allowances. Nonresident travelers may take out any amount of foreign currency notes they declared on arrival less expenses incurred in Cyprus. Nonresidents entering Cyprus should declare any foreign exchange that they plan to use to purchase goods to export, to purchase properties, or to deposit with authorized dealers. Nonresidents may export up to $1,000 in foreign currency notes that they imported, even if these notes were not declared on arrival. In addition, authorized dealers may convert up to £C 100 into foreign currency for departing nonresidents and are permitted to issue to departing nonresidents, as well

as to departing resident employees of offshore companies, any amount of foreign currency notes against external funds.

Exports and Export Proceeds

All exports whose value exceeds £C 1,000 are subject to exchange control monitoring to ensure the repatriation of the sale proceeds. Export proceeds must be surrendered to authorized dealers without delay. Exports of potatoes and carrots are carried out by the respective marketing boards, and exports of wheat, barley, and maize are carried out by the Cyprus Grain Commission.

Proceeds from Invisibles

Receipts from invisibles must be sold to an authorized dealer. Persons entering Cyprus may bring in any amount in foreign currency notes and up to £C 50 in Cyprus currency notes.

Capital

Transfers abroad of a capital nature require authorization from the Central Bank. Direct investment abroad by residents is permitted, provided that the proposed investments will promote exports of goods and services or will benefit the Cypriot economy. Outward portfolio investment by residents is not permitted, except for insurance companies (up to 20 percent of their reserves); Cypriot repatriates who hold foreign currency or external accounts; and resident employees of multinational enterprises who participate in the employee stock purchase plan offered to them by their employer.

Investments in Cyprus by nonresidents require the prior approval of the Central Bank, which, in considering applications, gives due regard to the purpose of the investment, the extent of possible foreign exchange savings or earnings, the introduction of know-how, and, in general, the benefits accruing to the national economy. Foreigners may own up to 100 percent of the capital of enterprises engaged in the manufacture of goods exclusively for export. Foreign participation of up to 49 percent is allowed for manufacture of new products, certain tourist activities, and other industrial projects. Inward investment is particularly welcome in projects that upgrade the tourist product (such as marinas, golf courses, and theme parks). In sectors of specific treatment, such as banking and finance, applications are examined on a case-by-case basis. Foreign direct investment is discouraged in saturated sectors such as trading, real estate development, travel agencies, restaurants, and local transportation. Foreign participation in inward portfolio investment in listed company securities is permitted up to a limit of 30 percent generally and 40 percent in investment companies and mutual funds. Foreigners are allowed to purchase government securities in domestic currency. Annual profits and proceeds from the liquidation of approved foreign investments, including capital gains, may be repatriated in full at any time after payment of taxes.

Commercial credits from abroad with a maturity of less than 200 days and commercial credit from Cyprus with a maturity of less than 180 days may be negotiated freely. With the permission of the Council of Ministers, nonresident aliens may acquire immovable property in Cyprus for use as a residence or holiday home; they must, however, purchase such property with foreign exchange. The sales proceeds of such property are transferable abroad up to the original purchase price of the property; the remaining balance is transferable at an annual rate of £C 10,000, plus interest. The same treatment is accorded to nonresident Cypriots purchasing a holiday home in Cyprus.

Residents of Cyprus (Cypriots or foreign nationals) who take up residence outside Cyprus may immediately transfer abroad up to £C 20,000 per household; any excess amount is deposited in a blocked account and released at the rate of £C 10,000 a year.[5] The transfer abroad of funds from estates and intestacies and from the sale of real estate, other than that referred to in the preceding paragraph, is limited to £C 10,000, with any excess amount to be credited to a blocked account and also released at the rate of £C 10,000 a year. Interest earned on a blocked account can be freely transferred abroad.

Transactions in foreign securities owned by residents require prior permission from the Central Bank. In principle, all securities held abroad by residents are subject to registration.

Gold

Residents may hold and acquire gold coins in Cyprus for numismatic purposes. Residents other than the monetary authorities, authorized dealers in gold, and industrial users are not allowed to hold or acquire gold in any form, other than jewelry, at home or abroad. Authorized dealers in gold are permitted to import gold only for the purpose of disposing of it to industrial users. The exportation of gold requires the permission of the exchange control authorities.

Changes During 1994

Payments for Invisibles

April 4. The use of international credit cards was expanded so as to cover additional payments for telephone calls abroad without limit and payments abroad up to £C 300 for each occurrence for the following additional purposes: examination fees and application fees to educational institutions abroad, subscriptions to professional bodies or societies, fees for enrollment in educational seminars or conferences, and hotel reservation fees.

---

[5]This amount will increase to £C 50,000 as from January 1, 1995.

CZECH REPUBLIC

(Position as of December 31, 1994)

Exchange Arrangement

The currency of the Czech Republic is the Czech Koruna. Its external value is determined on the basis of a basket consisting of the deutsche mark (65 percent) and the U.S. dollar (35 percent). This exchange rate applies to all transactions except those with the Slovak Republic. On December 31, 1994, the buying and selling rates in terms of the U.S. dollar were Kč 27.91 and Kč 28.19, respectively, per US$1. A floating exchange rate applies to tourist transactions with the Slovak Republic.

The Czech National Bank (CNB) quotes daily buying and selling rates for 22 convertible currencies,[1] European currency units (ECUs), and SDRs. The market value of the koruna, which is determined at daily fixing sessions attended by the CNB and participants in the domestic interbank foreign exchange market, is allowed to fluctuate within a margin of ±0.5 percent around its theoretical level, based on exchange rates in the international market. The exchange rates for other currencies are based on the cross rates of these currencies against the U.S. dollar. The exchange rates set at the daily fixing sessions are used as the official exchange rates at which customers can choose to trade the next day. Forward foreign exchange transactions are permitted.

Administration of Control

The Ministry of Finance and the CNB are responsible for the administration of exchange controls and regulations in accordance with the Foreign Exchange Act. In general, the Ministry of Finance exercises authority over governmental credits and over budgetary and subsidized organizations, civic associations, churches, religious societies, foundations, and other legal persons not engaged in business activities and over the nonbusiness activities of natural persons. The CNB exercises authority over the activities of all registered enterprises and entrepreneurs.

---

[1]Australian dollars, Austrian schillings, Belgian francs, Canadian dollars, Danish kroner, deutsche mark, Finnish markkaa, French francs, Greek drachmas, Irish pounds, Italian lire, Japanese yen, Luxembourg francs, Netherlands guilders, New Zealand dollars, Norwegian kroner, Portuguese escudos, pounds sterling, Spanish pesetas, Swedish kronor, Swiss francs, and U.S. dollars.

Prescription of Currency

Payments to and receipts from countries are effected in convertible currencies, with the exception of payments to and receipts from the Slovak Republic. Since February 1993, all commercial transactions with the Slovak Republic, excluding transactions relating to re-exports and payments from foreign exchange accounts, have been required to be effected through a clearing account maintained by the central banks of the two countries. Transactions are converted from the currency of the contract into clearing ECUs at a rate that may differ by up to 5 percent from the market cross rate against the ECU, as set by the central banks. As of December 31, 1994, the exchange rate of the Czech koruna against the clearing ECU was the same as the market cross rate. If the balances on the account outstanding at the end of each month exceed clearing ECU 130 million, the excess balances are settled in a convertible currency by the fifteenth of the following month. Payments by juridical persons and entrepreneurs in connection with obligations incurred before February 8, 1993 are effected through another set of clearing accounts denominated in clearing koruny at the exchange rate of 1 clearing koruna per Kč 1 or Sk 1 (Slovak koruna). Their exchange rate to the clearing ECU equals the exchange rate of the Czech koruna to the ECU that was in effect on February 8, 1993. These accounts are settled every month.

Resident and Nonresident Accounts

Resident Accounts. Without revealing the source of foreign exchange, resident natural persons may open interest-bearing foreign exchange accounts at any resident commercial bank authorized to deal in foreign exchange. Balances on these accounts may be used by the account holder without restriction. Resident enterprises that had outstanding foreign exchange accounts on December 31, 1990 and entrepreneurs that had outstanding foreign exchange accounts are also allowed to maintain these accounts. However, enterprises opening such accounts after December 31, 1990 must obtain a permit exempting them from the 100 percent surrender requirement and allowing them to use balances on these accounts freely to finance their activities. These permits are granted liberally.

Nonresident Accounts. Nonresidents (natural and juridical persons) may maintain two types of interest-bearing accounts:

(1) *Domestic currency accounts*, which may be opened with commercial banks in koruny. Balances on these accounts may be used freely to make payments in the Czech Republic. All transfers abroad from these accounts, except for those relating to bilateral agreements on support and protection of investments and those relating to inheritance and alimony, require a permit from the CNB or the Ministry of Finance.

(2) *Foreign currency accounts*, in which foreign exchange may be deposited freely and from which payments may be made, in the Czech Republic or abroad, without restriction.

Imports and Exports

Imports and exports may be undertaken by any registered enterprise or entrepreneur. Import licenses are required for a few strategic items, such as uranic ore, its concentrates, coal, poisons, military materials, firearms and ammunition, and narcotics. In addition, an automatic licensing system accompanied by levies applies to some agricultural products, mineral fuel and oils, iron and steel and their products, and some chemical products. All imports, including those by individuals, are subject to an ad valorem customs duty ranging up to 80 percent and to a value-added tax (VAT) of 5 percent or 23 percent.[2] Imports from the Slovak Republic are exempt from customs duties. Imports from developing countries are granted preferential treatment under the Generalized System of Preferences (GSP). Under the GSP, 43 "least developed" countries benefit from a duty exemption, and 80 developing countries are granted a 75 percent reduction from the applicable customs duties; tropical products are granted reductions of 85–100 percent.

Resident individuals are required to repatriate foreign exchange acquired abroad and to sell to a bank or deposit in a private foreign exchange account foreign exchange (including gold and gold bullion but not gold coins) exceeding the equivalent of Kč 5,000. Resident enterprises and entrepreneurs are normally required to repatriate, without delay, foreign exchange receipts from exports and sell them to commercial banks or keep them in foreign exchange accounts.

A limited number of products require export licenses for purposes of health control (including livestock and plants), facilitating voluntary restraints on products on which partner countries have imposed import quotas (such as textiles and steel products), or preserving for the internal market natural resources or imported raw materials (such as energy, metallurgical materials, wood, foodstuffs, pharmaceutical products, and construction materials). For the two latter groups of products, neither quantitative nor value limits are in force.

Payments for and Proceeds from Invisibles

Czech resident individuals may withdraw an unlimited amount of foreign exchange from their foreign currency accounts to make invisible payments. In addition, residents are entitled to buy foreign exchange to travel abroad, up to the equivalent of Kč 12,000. Transfers of alimony may be made to a citizen of a country that is a party to an international agreement on enforcement of alimonies or that does not restrict such transfers to the Czech Republic. Transfers of inherited assets abroad are allowed to all countries on a reciprocal basis. A special permit is required in most instances for remittances relating to family maintenance, education, and medical treatment.

Foreign investors may freely transfer abroad their dividends, profits, capital gains, and interest earnings. Transfers of payments connected with debenture bonds denominated in koruny that are payable within one year are permitted with the approval of the CNB.

Repatriation of wage savings by nonresident workers must be authorized by the CNB unless stipulated differently by an intergovernmental agreement. With certain exceptions related to tourism, exports and imports of koruna banknotes exceeding Kč 5,000 and their transfer abroad are permitted only with a foreign exchange license issued by the CNB. Licenses are not required for the importation or exportation of foreign exchange assets, including foreign currencies, by nonresidents.

Capital

Resident enterprises and entrepreneurs may freely obtain suppliers' credits. Financial credits may be obtained from foreign banks with the approval of the CNB, and foreign direct investments abroad must be approved by the CNB, the Ministry of Finance, and the Ministry of Industry and Trade. There is no limit on equity participation by nonresidents. In the event of liquidation of the enterprise, foreign investors are allowed to repatriate freely the

---

[2]The incidence of customs tariffs was 5 percent in 1994 (measured as a weighted average).

full value of their capital participation and capital gains in the original currency after payment of taxes.

Gold

Within 30 days of acquisition, residents are required to sell gold to commercial banks that are authorized to conduct foreign exchange transactions. Nonresidents may export gold coins without a license, provided that they submit a certificate confirming that the coins are of no historical value, and they may export gold that they have imported into the country. To export gold bullion, exporters must obtain a foreign exchange license.

Changes During 1994

Prescription of Currency

March 3. The exchange rate of the Czech koruna against the clearing ECU was adjusted from 3 percent above the market cross rate to parity with the market cross rate.

Resident and Nonresident Accounts

February 24. Procedures for enterprises to obtain permits to keep foreign currency accounts were simplified and partially liberalized.

Payments for and Proceeds from Invisibles

January 1. The maximum allowance for foreign travel was raised to the equivalent of Kč 12,000 a year.

September 1. The limit on the amount of the domestic currency that can be imported or exported was increased to Kč 5,000.

Capital

September 1. (1) purchases of foreign securities by residents were partially liberalized; (2) the rules for acquiring properties abroad were simplified; and (3) exports and imports of securities denominated in koruny were permitted without restriction.

DENMARK

(Position as of December 31, 1994)

Exchange Arrangement

The currency of Denmark is the Danish Krone. Denmark participates with Austria, Belgium, France, Germany, Ireland, Luxembourg, the Netherlands, Portugal, and Spain in the exchange rate and intervention mechanism (ERM) of the European Monetary System (EMS).[1] In accordance with this agreement, Denmark maintains the spot exchange rates between the Danish krone and the currencies of the other participants within margins of 15 percent above or below the cross rates based on the central rates expressed in European currency units (ECUs).[2]

The agreement implies that the Danmarks Nationalbank (the central bank) stands ready to buy or sell the currencies of the other countries participating in the EMS in unlimited amounts at specified intervention rates. On December 31, 1994, these rates were as follows:

Specified Intervention Rates per:	Danish Kroner	
	Upper limit	Lower limit
100 Austrian schillings	62.95610	46.69100
100 Belgian or Luxembourg francs	21.47470	15.92660
100 Deutsche mark	442.96800	328.46100
100 French francs	132.06600	97.94300
1 Irish pound	10.67920	7.92014
100 Netherlands guilders	393.10500	291.54400
100 Portuguese escudos[3]	4.47770	3.32090
100 Spanish pesetas[4]	5.59850	4.15190

The participants in the EMS do not maintain the exchange rates for other currencies within fixed limits. Danmarks Nationalbank, however, does intervene in other situations for the purpose of smoothing out fluctuations in exchange rates and has an obligation to intervene on the Danish for-eign exchange market only at the intervention rates agreed within the EMS. Middle rates (average of buying and selling rates) for 21 foreign currencies, the SDR, and the ECU[5] are officially fixed daily and reflect the rates prevailing at the time of the fixing. On December 30, 1994, the official rate for the U.S. dollar was Dkr 6.0830 per US$1.

All remaining foreign exchange regulations were lifted with effect from October 1, 1988. Residents may hold positions in foreign currencies without limitation with respect to the amounts, currencies, or instruments involved.

There are no restrictions on foreign exchange dealing. The Executive Order on Foreign Exchange Regulations, issued by the Ministry of Business and Industry with effect from July 23, 1994, stipulates that payments of more than Dkr 60,000 between residents and nonresidents must be reported to Danmarks Nationalbank for statistical purposes.

For tax control purposes, residents (with certain exceptions) must deposit foreign securities and Danish bonds issued abroad either with a Danish or a foreign bank or with the issuer. Residents who are holding accounts with foreign banking institutions, have deposited securities abroad, or have entered into contracts with foreign life insurance companies are required to provide the Danish tax authorities with relevant information concerning these transactions.

Denmark formally accepted the obligations of Article VIII, Sections 2, 3, and 4 of the Fund Agreement, as from May 1, 1967.

Exchange Control Territory

The Danish Monetary Area comprises Denmark, Greenland, and the Faeroe Islands. The Faeroe Islands are still subject to the regulations in force before July 23, 1994.

Administration of Control

No exchange control requirements are imposed on capital receipts or payments by residents or nonresidents. Reporting requirements for statistical

---

[1] Austria became a member of the European Union on January 1, 1995 and joined the ERM of the EMS on January 9, 1995.

[2] Effective August 2, 1993, the intervention thresholds of the currencies participating in the ERM of the EMS, except those of the deutsche mark and the Netherlands guilder, were widened from ±2.25 percent to ±15 percent around the bilateral exchange rates; the fluctuation band of the deutsche mark and the Netherlands guilder remained at ±2.25 percent.

[3] Effective March 6, 1995, the upper and lower limits were changed to 4.32100 and 3.20400.

[4] Effective March 6, 1995, the upper and lower limits were changed to 5.20640 and 3.86140.

[5] Australian dollars, Austrian schillings, Belgian francs, Canadian dollars, deutsche mark, Greek drachmas, Finnish markkaa, French francs, Icelandic krónur, Irish pounds, Italian lire, Japanese yen, Netherlands guilders, New Zealand dollars, Norwegian kroner, Portuguese escudos, pounds sterling, Spanish pesetas, Swedish kronor, Swiss francs, and U.S. dollars.

purposes are administered by Danmarks National-bank and by the foreign exchange dealers, whereas reporting requirements for tax purposes on depositing foreign securities and on accounts abroad are part of the tax legislation and are administered by the tax authorities and the foreign exchange dealers. Foreign exchange dealers are commercial banks, savings banks, and stockbrokerage companies or other financial institutions, as defined in the Executive Order, provided that they settle payments between residents and nonresidents on a commercial basis through accounts held in or on behalf of foreign banking institutions (correspondent banks). Danmarks Nationalbank has drawn up a list of foreign exchange dealers.

Licenses for imports and exports, when required, are issued by the Ministry of Industry or the Ministry of Agriculture and Fisheries.

In accordance with the Fund's Executive Board Decision No. 144–(52/51) adopted on August 14, 1952, Denmark notified the Fund on July 27, 1992, that certain restrictions had been imposed on the making of payments and transfers for current international transactions in respect of the Federal Republic of Yugoslavia (Serbia/Montenegro).

Prescription of Currency

There are no prescription of currency requirements.

Imports and Import Payments

Imports of most products, except for textiles, are free of licensing from all sources. For textiles, a common European Union (EU) system of export-import licenses has been established for almost all countries exporting low-priced textiles. A few items require a license when originating in Japan, the Republic of Korea, or any other country outside the EU that is not a state trading country. A larger number of items require a license when originating in or purchased from Albania, Bulgaria, China, the Czech Republic, Hungary, the Democratic People's Republic of Korea, Mongolia, Poland, Romania, the Slovak Republic, the Baltic countries, Russia, and the other countries of the former Soviet Union, and Viet Nam.

No exchange control requirements are imposed on payments for imports.

Exports and Export Proceeds

Except for certain items subject to strategic controls, licenses for exports are required only for the waste and scrap of certain metals.

No exchange control requirements are imposed on receipts from exports.

Payments for and Proceeds from Invisibles

No exchange control requirements are imposed on payments for or receipts from invisibles.

Capital

There are no restrictions on inward or outward capital transfers. The general rules on exchange control issued by the Ministry of Business and Industry are based on Articles 23a - 73a of the EU Treaty on Capital Movements and on the Organization for Economic Cooperation and Development Capital Code; no distinction is made in these rules between residents of member countries of the EU and those of the rest of the world.

Gold

Residents may freely buy, hold, and sell gold in bars or coins in Denmark; they may also import gold in bars or coins. Imports of gold in bars or coins, unless made by or on behalf of the monetary authorities, are subject to a value-added tax at the rate of 25 percent; domestic transactions in gold are also taxed at the rate of 25 percent. There is no customs duty on imports of gold in bars or coins.

Changes During 1994

Administration of Control

July 23. By executive order, reporting requirements for tax purposes on depositing foreign securities and on accounts abroad were made part of the tax legislation and would be administered by the tax authorities and by foreign exchange dealers instead of by Danmarks Nationalbank.

Imports and Import Payments

(See Appendix for a summary of trade measures introduced and eliminated on an EU-wide basis during 1994, page 554.)

DJIBOUTI

(Position as of December 31, 1994)

Exchange Arrangement

The currency of Djibouti is the Djibouti Franc, the external value of which is pegged to the U.S. dollar, the intervention currency, at DF 177.721 per US$1. Buying and selling rates for currencies other than the U.S. dollar are set by local banks on the basis of the cross rates for the U.S. dollar in international markets. The posted rates are subject to commission charges of 0.5–6 percent set by the commercial banks, depending on the currency concerned. A fixed commission of about DF 3,000 is charged on transfers in foreign currencies. There are no taxes or subsidies on purchases or sales of foreign exchange. Commercial enterprises are free to negotiate forward exchange contracts for commercial and financial transactions through local banks or banks abroad. All transactions are negotiated at free market rates. There are no arrangements for forward cover against exchange rate risk operating in the official or the commercial banking sector.

Djibouti formally accepted the obligations of Article VIII, Sections 2, 3, and 4 of the Fund Agreement as from September 19, 1980 .

Administration of Control

There is no exchange control, except that all settlements with Israel are prohibited. The Djibouti franc is issued in notes and coins by the National Bank of Djibouti, which issues and redeems the currency against U.S. dollars.

Prescription of Currency

There are no prescription of currency requirements.

Imports and Import Payments

Djibouti has a free trade zone in the port of Djibouti, but the territory as a whole does not constitute a free zone. Formally, customs duties are not charged on imports, but, in practice, fiscal duties are levied by means of the general consumption tax, at the rate of 33 percent. Certain commodities, including alcoholic beverages, noncarbonated mineral water, petroleum products, khat, and tobacco, are subject to a surtax at various rates. Additional taxes are levied on imported milk products and fruit juice.

Exports and Export Proceeds

There are virtually no restrictions. Export proceeds may be retained.

Payments for and Proceeds from Invisibles

No restrictions are imposed on payments for or proceeds from invisibles. A tax of 10 percent applies to fees and salaries paid to individuals and legal entities who, for professional purposes, are not permanent residents of Djibouti.

Capital

There are no restrictions on inward or outward capital transfers. Under the Investment Code of February 13, 1984, enterprises established or expanded to undertake certain specific economic activities are eligible for various tax exemptions. Under the regime of "franc enterprises," firms engaged in manufacturing and service activities that use high technology and are export oriented are exempted from the profit tax during the first ten years of operation and from the export tax in respect of goods and services that are exported.

Changes During 1994

Capital

October 1. For purposes of promoting industries in the private sector, a law establishing the regime of "franc enterprises" was enacted. Firms operating under this regime must be engaged in manufacturing or service activities using high technology and must be export oriented. They would be exempted from the profit tax during the first ten years of operation and from the export tax in respect of goods and services that are exported. The law established a National Commission on Investment with responsibility for administering simplified procedures for approving investment applications and resolving labor disputes.

DOMINICA

(Position as of December 31, 1994)

Exchange Arrangement

The currency of Dominica is the Eastern Caribbean Dollar,[1] which is issued by the Eastern Caribbean Central Bank (ECCB). The Eastern Caribbean dollar is pegged to the U.S. dollar, the intervention currency, at EC$2.70 per US$1. On December 31, 1994, the buying and selling rates for the U.S. dollar were EC$2.69 and EC$2.71, respectively, per US$1. The ECCB also quotes daily rates for the Canadian dollar and the pound sterling.

There are no arrangements for forward cover against exchange rate risk operating in the official or the commercial banking sector.

Dominica informed the Fund on December 13, 1979 that it formally accepted the obligations of Article VIII, Sections 2, 3, and 4 of the Fund Agreement.

Administration of Control

Exchange control is administered by the Ministry of Finance and applies to all countries outside the ECCB area. The Ministry of Finance has delegated to commercial banks certain of its powers to approve sales of foreign currencies within specified limits. The Ministry of Trade administers import and export arrangements and controls.

Prescription of Currency

Settlements with residents of territories participating in the ECCB Agreement must be made in Eastern Caribbean dollars; those with member countries of the Caribbean Common Market (CARICOM)[2] must be made in the currency of the CARICOM country concerned. Settlements with residents of other countries may be made in any foreign currency that is acceptable to the country where the settlement is being made.[3]

Foreign Currency Accounts

Foreign currency accounts may be operated only with the permission of the Ministry of Finance; permission is normally confined to major exporters and foreign nationals not ordinarily resident in Dominica. The accounts can only be credited with foreign currencies obtained outside Dominica. Payments from these accounts do not require approval.

Imports and Import Payments

All imports from Iraq are prohibited, and all imports originating from the member countries of the former Council for Mutual Economic Assistance, that is, Albania, Cambodia, China, and the Democratic People's Republic of Korea, require a license. Imports of specified goods originating outside the Organization of Eastern Caribbean States (OECS)[4] and CARICOM require a license. The Common External Tariff of CARICOM states is applied to all imports.

Payments for authorized imports are permitted upon presentation to a commercial bank of documentary evidence of purchase. Advance payments for imports require prior approval from the Ministry of Finance.

Payments for Invisibles

All settlements overseas require exchange control approval. However, commercial banks have been delegated authority to sell foreign currency to local residents, as specified below (1) for incidentals, EC$100, subject to a limit of EC$500 a person a year; (2) for each trip outside the area served by the ECCB, EC$3,000, subject to a maximum of two trips in any 12-month period, and upon presentation of travel documents; (3) for bona fide business travelers, EC$1,000 for each day outside Dominica, provided the total does not exceed EC$30,000 in any 12-month period, and upon presentation of travel documents; (4) for overseas travel for medical treatment, EC$1,000 a day up to a maximum of EC$30,000 in any 12-month period, subject to the presentation of travel documents and a medical certificate stating that the journey is necessary; (5) for educational expenses, including accommodation, up to EC$15,000 a student in each academic year; and (6) for dependents residing abroad, EC$2,400 in any 12-month period (EC$3,600 for minor or incapacitated dependents).

---

[1]The Eastern Caribbean dollar is also the currency of Anguilla, Antigua and Barbuda, Grenada, Montserrat, St. Kitts and Nevis, St. Lucia, and St. Vincent and the Grenadines.

[2]The CARICOM countries are Antigua and Barbuda, The Bahamas, Barbados, Belize, Dominica, Grenada, Guyana, Jamaica, Montserrat, St. Kitts and Nevis, St. Lucia, St. Vincent and the Grenadines, and Trinidad and Tobago.

[3]Foreign currencies comprise all currencies other than the Eastern Caribbean dollar.

[4]The member countries are Antigua and Barbuda, Dominica, Grenada, Montserrat, St. Kitts and Nevis, St. Lucia, and St. Vincent and the Grenadines.

Amounts in excess of specified limits may be obtained with approval from the Ministry of Finance. Specific approval from the Ministry of Finance must also be obtained for outward remittances of cash gifts up to EC$1,000 a year to each recipient. Earnings of foreign workers and profits and dividends from foreign direct investment may be remitted after settlement of all tax or other public liabilities.

The exportation of Eastern Caribbean banknotes and coins (other than numismatic coins) by residents and nonresidents traveling to destinations outside the ECCB area is limited to amounts prescribed by the Central Bank.

Exports and Export Proceeds

Exports to Iraq are prohibited, and specific licenses are required for the exportation of certain goods to any destination. The conversion of export proceeds to an ECCB currency account is mandatory, unless the exporter has a foreign currency account into which the proceeds may be paid. Bananas exported by the Dominica Banana Marketing Corporation are subject to a levy of 1 percent if the export price is between 55 cents and 60 cents a pound; if the export price exceeds 60 cents a pound, an additional levy equivalent to 25 percent of the excess is imposed.

Proceeds from Invisibles

Foreign currency proceeds from transactions in invisibles must be sold to a bank or paid into a foreign currency account. There is no restriction on the importation of foreign banknotes and coins.

Capital

All outward transfers of capital or profits require exchange control approval. The purchase by residents of foreign currency securities and of real estate located abroad is not normally permitted. Capital transfers, such as inheritances, to nonresidents require approval, which is normally granted, subject to the payment of any taxes due. Emigrants leaving Dominica to take up residence outside the ECCB area may transfer up to EC$30,000 a family from their assets, subject to income tax clearance.

Direct investment in Dominica by nonresidents may be made with exchange control approval. The remittance of earnings on, and liquidation proceeds from, such investment is permitted, subject to the discharge of any related liabilities. The approval of the Ministry of Finance is required for nonresidents to borrow in Dominica.

Gold

Residents are permitted to acquire and hold gold coins for numismatic purposes only. Small quantities of gold may be imported for industrial purposes only with the approval of the Ministry of Finance.

Changes During 1994

No significant changes occurred in the exchange and trade system.

DOMINICAN REPUBLIC

(Position as of December 31, 1994)

Exchange Arrangement

The currency of the Dominican Republic is the Dominican Peso, the external value of which is determined in the interbank market. Since September 1994, the official exchange rate has been set weekly on the basis of the average of the previous week's exchange rates in the interbank market, in which the rates are determined by supply and demand. On December 31, the official exchange rate was RD$12.87 per US$1.

A commission equivalent to 3 percent of the f.o.b. value of imports has not been collected since June 1994 as its gradual elimination is provided for in Law No. 11–12 on tax reform by the Central Bank for the servicing of external debt.[1] A commission of 1.5 percent is charged on sales of foreign exchange in both the bank market and the official market. There are no arrangements for forward cover against exchange rate risk operating in the official or the commercial banking sector.

The Dominican Republic formally accepted the obligations of Article VIII, Sections 2, 3, and 4 of the Fund Agreement, as from August 1, 1953.

Administration of Control

Exchange control policy is determined by the Monetary Board and is administered by the Central Bank. Thirteen commercial banks (including the state-owned Reserve Bank) are operating in the foreign exchange market.

Arrears are maintained with respect to external payments.

Prescription of Currency

Settlements with Bolivia, Brazil, Chile, Colombia, Ecuador, Mexico, Peru, and Uruguay may be made through special accounts established under reciprocal credit agreements within the framework of the Latin American Integration Association (LAIA). Settlements under the reciprocal credit agreement with Argentina and Venezuela have been suspended. All payments must be invoiced in U.S. dollars; otherwise, no obligations are imposed on importers, exporters, or other residents regarding

the currency to be used for payments to or from nonresidents. Service payments on the external public debt are executed in the same currency in which the loan is denominated.

Imports and Import Payments

Payments for imports of coal for the use of the electric company and priority imports for public enterprises are transacted through the Central Bank at the official exchange rate. Imports on a document-against-payments basis must be denominated in U.S. dollars; for these imports, certification of the use of foreign currency is required for customs clearance. All other imports are transacted through the free interbank market and are subject only to verification of appropriate documentation.

Most tariff rates range from 5 percent to 35 percent, and certain luxury imported goods are subject to an excise tax ranging from 5 percent to 80 percent.

Payments for Invisibles

All invisible payments may be made freely through commercial banks, subject to documentation requirements. Annual profit remittances cannot exceed the equivalent of 25 percent of the net value of original and additional investment plus reinvestment minus repatriation, duly registered with the Central Bank.

Nonresident tourists may freely convert pesos to dollars upon departure.

Exports and Export Proceeds

Certain exports are prohibited, including some food products and animal species, unprocessed wood (for environmental protection purposes), and blood (for public health reasons). For purposes of exchange surrender, declared export prices must equal or exceed the minimum export prices established by the Central Bank for certain exports. Firms operating in the industrial free zones and dealing in ferro-nickel exports are exempt from the surrender requirement; firms operating in the industrial free zones are not subject to export price restrictions.

The issuance of tax credit certificates (*certificados de abono tributario*), provided for by Law No. 69, was abolished by Law No.11–92. Law No. 69 still regu-

---

[1]Imports of food, fertilizer, petroleum and its derivatives, medicine, newsprint paper and equipment, and agricultural products are exempt from this commission.

lates the system of temporary admission for imports, under which duties are waived for any imports used in the manufacture of nontraditional products to be exported within a year.

The system of refunding a portion of import duties paid on raw materials and on inputs for nontraditional exports was abolished by Law No. 11–92 on tax reform or Law No. 14–93 on customs codes, respectively. The 100 percent refund of import duties in the industrial free trade zones was deleted from Law No. 299 and included in Law No. 8–90. (Exporters of nontraditional products eligible under the temporary system of Law No. 69 are also exempt from taxes.) Exporters may not extend credit with a maturity of more than 30 days from the date of shipment to foreign buyers without authorization from the Central Bank.

Proceeds from Invisibles

Foreign exchange proceeds from all invisibles may be sold in the interbank market. Certain other receipts from invisibles (including international telephone calls, international credit card transactions, jet fuel, foreign embassies, alimonies, donations, and real estate) must be surrendered to the Central Bank.

Capital

There are no restrictions on the inward movement of capital by either residents or nonresidents. However, foreign direct investment is regulated by Law No. 861 of July 19, 1978, which created the Directorate of Foreign Investment to approve direct investment requests. Such investments must be registered with the Central Bank.

External debt can be contracted directly by the central Government, subject to congressional authorization. According to Decree No. 101 of August 20, 1982 and Law No. 749 of January 6, 1978, new loans by other public entities require authorization from the President of the Republic for their subsequent registration by the Monetary Board. According to a set of criteria established by the Monetary Board on December 13, 1976, priority is given to the approval of new loans associated with exports, import substitution, and social projects, such as housing and education. Total financial charges on foreign loans are not allowed to exceed the principal international interest rate by more than a certain margin. There are also minimum maturity requirements according to the type of financing.

The Central Bank provides foreign exchange for the servicing of public external debt at the official exchange rate; the servicing of private external debt that is not guaranteed by the Government is effected through the interbank market.

Gold

Residents may purchase, hold, and sell gold coins for numismatic purposes. With this exception, residents other than the monetary authorities and authorized industrial users are not allowed to hold or acquire gold in any form other than jewelry in the Dominican Republic or abroad. Imports and exports of gold in any form other than jewelry constituting the personal effects of a traveler require licenses issued by the Central Bank; such licenses are not normally granted except for imports and exports by or on behalf of the monetary authorities and industrial users.

Changes During 1994

Exchange Arrangement

September 7. The Monetary Board announced that the official exchange rate would be set weekly on the basis of the average of the previous week's exchange rates in the interbank market; previously, the official exchange rate was set on a daily basis to reflect the previous day's exchange rates in the interbank market.

Proceeds from Invisibles

September 7. The proceeds originating from international credit card transactions were subject to the surrender requirements.

ECUADOR

(Position as of December 31, 1994)

Exchange Arrangement

The currency of Ecuador is the Ecuadoran Sucre. There are two exchange rates: (1) the free market rate; and (2) the central bank official exchange rate. The selling rate of the Central Bank of Ecuador is established weekly at a level equal to the average selling rate in the free market of the previous week. The buying rate of the Central Bank is set 2 percent lower than its selling rate. The Central Bank's buying rate for the export proceeds of the state petroleum company (PETROECUADOR) is set S/. 180 lower than the selling rate. The Central Bank's selling rate is applied to all external payments of the public sector.

All legally permitted foreign exchange transactions, other than those conducted through the Central Bank, may be conducted in the free market. On December 31, 1994, the buying and selling rates in the free market were S/. 2,268 and S/. 2,270, respectively. The Central Bank is authorized to intervene in the free market.

Banks and other financial institutions authorized to conduct foreign exchange transactions are permitted to conduct forward swaps and options and transactions in other financial derivative instruments, subject to the supervision and control of the Superintendency of Banks.

External credits contracted by the private sector must be registered at the Central Bank within 45 days of disbursement. Private sector credit arrangements that are not registered within the 45-day period are subject to a service charge equivalent to 0.25 percent of the credit amount.

Ecuador formally accepted the obligations of Article VIII, Sections 2, 3, and 4 of the Fund Agreement, with effect from August 31, 1970.

Administration of Control

Public sector foreign exchange transactions are carried out exclusively through the Central Bank. Private sector foreign exchange transactions related to the exploration for, and production, transportation, and commercialization of, oil and its derivatives may be carried out through the free market or through the Central Bank. Foreign exchange transactions of the private sector may be effected through banks and exchange houses authorized by the Monetary Board. Exports must be registered with the Central Bank to guarantee repatriation of any foreign exchange proceeds from the transaction. Import licenses granted by the Central Bank are required.

Prescription of Currency

Some settlements with Cuba and Hungary take place through bilateral accounts. Payments between Ecuador and Argentina, Bolivia, Brazil, Chile, Colombia, the Dominican Republic, Mexico, Paraguay, Peru, Uruguay, or Venezuela may be made within the framework of the multilateral clearing system of the Latin American Integration Association (LAIA). Exchange proceeds from other countries must be received in convertible currencies. Whenever possible, import payments must be made in the currency stipulated in the import license.

Imports and Import Payments

Permitted imports are divided into two categories. List I comprises priority goods (the "Special" Group), essential goods (Group A, consisting of capital goods, inputs for agriculture and industry, and consumer goods with no local substitutes), and semiessential goods (Group B, consisting of products with some local equivalent, except luxury goods). List II covers luxury goods. Imports of all goods not included on these two lists are prohibited, primarily to protect industry, the environment, and health. Imports of antiques and certain items related to health and national security are also prohibited. Certain imports require prior authorization from government ministries or agencies.

Prior import licenses are required for all permitted imports except books, newspapers, periodicals, printed music, medicines, and spare parts for machinery and automotive vehicles valued at $5,000 f.o.b. or less. In addition, PETROECUADOR may, without a license, import supplies, materials, and equipment during emergencies. Import licenses are issued free of charge irrespective of the origin of goods, provided that 80 percent of the import tax has been paid, prior ministerial authorization (when needed) has been obtained, and insurance has been arranged in Ecuador. Certain agricultural crops, milled flour, and cooking oil are granted special protection through the licensing process. All private sector imports are subject to the 10 percent value-added tax. There is a temporary import admission regime for inputs used in export production.

For certain agricultural imports, standard import tariffs were supplemented in 1993 by a system of corrective tariffs adopted with the announced intention of reducing the variation, over time, of the cost of such imports. The system incorporates upper and lower benchmark prices for each product. For imports priced below the lower benchmark, the supplementary corrective tariff is applied so as to raise import costs to the lower benchmark level. For imports priced above the upper benchmark, a rebate is available on the standard import tariff, so as to minimize the excess relative to the benchmark.

For automobiles, official reference prices are published for purposes of calculating tariffs. The reference prices establish a minimum f.o.b. value and when importers declare a higher value, tariffs are calculated on the basis of the higher value. Under the current import tariff regime, most goods are subject to the rates of 5 percent, 10 percent, 15 percent, or 20 percent, with the exception of automobiles, which are subject to a tariff of 40 percent.

Prepayments for imports by the private sector are permitted.

Payments for Invisibles

All public sector payments for invisibles, including interest on public debt, are transacted at the central bank rate. Other payments for current invisibles must be settled in the free market. There are no limitations on the amount of domestic and foreign banknotes that travelers may take out. The remittance abroad of dividends and profits is not restricted.

Residents and nonresidents traveling abroad by air must pay a tax of $25 for each exit visa. Airline tickets for foreign travel are taxed at 10 percent, and tickets for travel by ship are taxed at the rate of 8 percent for departure from Ecuador and 4 percent for the return trip.

Exports and Export Proceeds

All exports require licenses. A list of agricultural exports and a list of exports subject to quotas ("exportable surplus") are reviewed by the relevant ministries. All goods not on these lists may be exported freely. All export proceeds must be surrendered to authorized financial entities no later than (1) 90 days from the date of shipment for bananas and plantains, shrimp, unprocessed coffee and cocoa, fish and other unprocessed seafood, and other perishable and primary products; and (2) 180 days from the date of shipment for all other products.

When exporters and foreign buyers agree on sight terms of payment, foreign exchange proceeds must be surrendered within 15 days of the date of shipment. Those who disregard the above surrender requirements are subject to penalty, and the Central Bank is authorized to carry out the inspections it considers necessary to verify the proper surrender of export proceeds. Authorized financial entities may purchase foreign exchange in anticipation of future exports within a maximum period of 180 days before the projected date of the export settlement.

The surrender requirement does not apply to exports effected under authorized barter transactions. However, barter transactions require the prior approval of the Ministry of Industry, Commerce, Integration, and Fisheries; they must be registered with the Central Bank and are subject to specific limitations. The surrender requirement does not apply to exports to countries with which Ecuador has bilateral payments agreements. In such cases, exporters are required to provide official documentation from the recipient country establishing the applicable forms of payment. Exporters may deduct up to 15 percent from their surrender requirement to cover the actual cost of consular fees and commissions paid abroad. Exporters of marine products are permitted to retain up to 30 percent of the f.o.b. value of their shipments to cover the actual cost of leasing foreign ships. Minimum reference prices are established for exports of bananas, coffee, fish products, cocoa, and semifinished products of cocoa to help ensure that exchange proceeds are fully surrendered. Payment of foreign exchange for petroleum exports is made on the basis of the sale prices stated in the sales contracts and must be surrendered within 30 days of the date of shipment. All crude oil exports are subject to a tax of S/. 5 a barrel; in addition, a tax of $0.05 a barrel is paid on crude oil exported through the pipeline.

Proceeds from Invisibles

All receipts from invisibles must be sold in the free market, except for interest income on exchange reserves of the central bank and all invisible receipts of the public sector, which are transacted at the central bank rate. Travelers may bring in any amount of foreign or domestic banknotes.

Capital

Capital may freely enter or leave the country through the free market. Loan disbursements to the public sector must be transacted at the central bank rate. Unless specifically stated, new foreign direct investments do not require prior authorization. Both domestic and foreign enterprises are subject to a 25 percent income tax rate.

Repatriation of capital and remittances of profits on foreign investments are handled through the free exchange market if investments were made through this market. Transfers of all other gains are subject to a tax rate of 33 percent.

All foreign loans granted to or guaranteed by the Government or official entities, whether or not they involve the disbursement of foreign exchange, are subject to prior approval from the Monetary Board. Suppliers' credits of up to one year's maturity are exempt from this requirement. A request for such approval must be submitted by the Minister of Finance to the Monetary Board, accompanied by detailed information on the loan contract and the investment projects it is intended to finance. In examining the request, the Monetary Board considers the effects that the loan and the related investment may have on the balance of payments and on monetary aggregates. For public sector entities, the projects to be financed must be included in the General Development Plan or receive a favorable ruling from the National Council for Development (CONADE). New external credits with a maturity of over one year that are contracted by the private sector, either directly or through the domestic financial system, must be registered with the Central Bank.

Gold

The private sector is authorized to buy and sell gold in the international and domestic markets.

Changes During 1994

Exchange Arrangement

November 1. (1) The spread between the Central Bank's buying and selling rates applied to purchases of foreign exchange from the private sector was set at a 2 percent spread instead of S/. 250 per US$1. During the period from November 2 through December 31, 1994, the Central Bank reduced the spread between the buying and selling rates applied to export transactions by PETROECUADOR from S/. 250 per US$1 to S/. 180 per US$1; (2) the maximum period of 180 days for conducting forward foreign exchange operations was eliminated.

Administration of Control

November 1. Hydrocarbon transactions between foreign companies and PETROECUADOR were permitted to be carried out through the Central Bank's exchange market or through the free exchange market.

Imports and Import Payments

August 16. Prepayments for private sector imports were allowed to be made without prior authorization from the Monetary Board and were permitted to be negotiated freely.

Capital

January 25. The commission of 0.25 percent applied to public sector foreign loan disbursements was abolished.

EGYPT

(Position as of December 31, 1994)

Exchange Arrangement

The currency of Egypt is the Egyptian Pound, the external value of which is determined in a free market. The U.S. dollar is used as the intervention currency. Nonbank foreign exchange dealers are permitted to operate in the free market. They may buy and sell domestic and foreign means of payment (banknotes, coins, and traveler's checks) on their own accounts. These transactions, however, must be conducted through the accounts maintained by dealers with authorized banks in Egypt. In addition, authorized nonbank dealers may broker any foreign exchange operation and transaction except transfers to and from the country, on the accounts of their bank or nonbank customers. On December 29, 1994, the exchange rate in the free market was LE 3.4 per US$1.

A special exchange rate of LE 1.30 per US$1 is applied to transactions effected under the bilateral payments agreement with Sudan. In addition, a separate rate of LE 0.3913 per US$1 is used for the liquidation of balances related to past bilateral payments agreements.

Authorized commercial banks are permitted to conduct forward foreign exchange transactions for their own accounts. No prior approval by the Central Bank of Egypt is required, and the banks are free to determine the rates applied for forward transactions.

Administration of Control

Banks are authorized to execute foreign exchange transactions, within the framework of a general authorization, without obtaining specific exchange control approval. The Ministry of Economy and Foreign Trade formulates external trade policy. The monopoly of the public sector over the exportation and importation of certain products has been abolished. Port Said City has held the status of a free zone since 1977.

Arrears are maintained with respect to external payments.

Prescription of Currency

Payments may be made in any convertible currency. Settlements with Sudan, the only country with which Egypt maintains an operative bilateral payments agreement, are made in accordance with the terms of the agreement. Payments not covered by the agreement may be made in any convertible currency. Certain settlements with countries with which indemnity agreements concerning compensation for nationalized property are in force are made through special accounts in Egyptian pounds with the Central Bank. Suez Canal dues are expressed in SDRs and are paid by debiting free accounts in foreign currency.

Nonresident Accounts

In addition to the special accounts related to Egypt's bilateral payments agreements, the indemnity agreements concluded with certain countries, there are four types of accounts: free accounts, "D" accounts, special capital accounts, and capital and operations accounts.

Free accounts in foreign currency may be opened in the name of any entity. These accounts may be credited with transfers of convertible currencies from abroad and transfers from other similar accounts, foreign banknotes, foreign currency equivalents from funds transferred from previously existing free accounts in Egyptian pounds, and interest earned on these accounts. These accounts may be debited for transfers abroad, transfers to other similar accounts, withdrawals in foreign banknotes by the owner or others, and for payments in Egypt.

"D" accounts may be opened in the name of residents of Sudan. These accounts are largely historical. They are usually credited with transfers under the respective payments agreement. Balances are used to make local payments allowed under the bilateral agreement, including for imports from Egypt. Currently, outstanding balances on these accounts are minimal.

Special capital accounts may be credited with proceeds from sales of real estate owned by foreigners residing abroad. Authorized banks may transfer funds abroad from these accounts up to the amount in foreign exchange previously transferred and surrendered for Egyptian pounds at the time of the acquisition of the property, plus 5 percent of the value of the property for each year following the first five years of ownership until the property is sold; the remainder may be paid and/or transferred in five equal installments.

Capital and operations accounts may be opened by companies covered by Law No. 230 of July 1989. These accounts may be credited with transfers from abroad, advance payments and long-term rents in foreign exchange, loans, funds purchased from the free market, and funds purchased from the free accounts to meet the project requirement; they may be debited for payments by the account holder (e.g., imports, profit remittances, interest, other invisibles, and financing of local expenditures).

Imports and Import Payments

The Ministry of Economy and Foreign Trade formulates long-term export and import policies and prepares indicative annual export and import plans. Both public and private entities are allowed to trade with all countries with which Egypt maintains a bilateral payments agreement.

All imports financed by the Central Bank are effected at the free market rate, with the exception of imports under the bilateral payments agreement, which are effected at a more appreciated rate.

Import payments in foreign exchange by the private sector are effected through the commercial banks or through importers' own foreign exchange resources. All products may be freely imported, with the exception of a few items, such as inputs for industrial production, which may be incorporated with the approval of the Ministry of Industry.

For customs purposes, products are classified into eight groups, on which tariff rates range from 5 percent to 70 percent (with several exceptions). In 1994, the unweighted statutory average rate was 28 percent, excluding alcoholic beverages, and 34 percent, including alcoholic beverages. Surcharges at the rates of 2 percent and 5 percent are levied on most imports.

Payments for Invisibles

Commercial banks and other agencies authorized to deal in foreign exchange may sell without restriction foreign currencies for payments for invisibles to the Government, public authorities, the public and private sectors, and companies established under the domestic investment regime, in accordance with the provisions of the Investment Law.

Travelers may not take out more than LE 1,000 in domestic banknotes but are permitted to take out foreign banknotes and other instruments of payment in foreign currency without limitation.

Exports and Export Proceeds

Apart from a limited number of products required for the national economy that may be restricted, exports may be effected without license. Exports of cotton, rice, and petroleum are no longer a public sector monopoly. There are no repatriation requirements.

Proceeds from exports by the private and public sectors to the bilateral payments agreement country (i.e., Sudan) are obtained in Egyptian pounds, in accordance with the provisions of the relevant agreement.

Proceeds from Invisibles

Foreign exchange earned abroad may be held abroad or retained indefinitely in free accounts.

Persons arriving in Egypt from abroad may import up to LE 1,000 in Egyptian banknotes and are permitted to bring in, and to use locally, unlimited amounts of foreign exchange.

Capital

Proceeds of sales of Egyptian and foreign securities registered at the stock market in Egypt may be transferred through the free market for foreign exchange. The same treatment is applied to the transfer of income earned from Egyptian securities and profits owed to foreigners from investments in projects established in Egypt.

Payments for real estate that foreigners are allowed to own must be made in convertible currencies. Proceeds from sales of property owned in Egypt by foreigners or their heirs must be deposited in a special capital account in the name of the foreign seller at an authorized bank. The authorized bank may transfer funds abroad from the account, but the transfer must be limited to the amount of foreign exchange units previously transferred and surrendered for Egyptian pounds at the time of the acquisition of the property, plus 5 percent of the value of the property for each year following the first five years of ownership until the property was sold; the remainder may be paid and/or transferred in five equal annual installments.

The ratio of foreign currency liabilities to foreign currency assets of authorized commercial banks is subject to a maximum limit of 105 percent, and the open foreign exchange position for a single currency and for all currencies combined is subject to limits of 10 percent and 20 percent, respectively, of their capital. Nonbank foreign exchange dealers may maintain foreign exchange working balances of up to $225,000 for the first LE 1 million of paid-up capital and up to $295,000 for each LE 1 million after the first LE 1 million of paid-up capital.

Gold

Banks are not authorized to deal or speculate (for their own or their customers' account) in precious metals.

Changes During 1994

Administration of Control

June 3. A foreign exchange law came into effect.

Prescription of Currency

November 30. An account containing unsettled payment orders related to the bilateral payments agreement with the Russian Federation was closed.

Imports and Import Payments

February 1. The maximum tariff rate was reduced to 70 percent from 80 percent, and the rates above 30 percent were reduced by 10 percentage points. In addition, the tariff rates on some capital goods were reduced to 10 percent or 5 percent.

February 14. Import surcharges at the rates of 2 percent and 5 percent were imposed on most imports.

June 9. The requirement that an importer must furnish documentation establishing that importing actually took place was abolished.

Payments for Invisibles

August 4. The limit on the amount of domestic banknotes that travelers may take out of the country was raised to LE 1,000 from LE 100.

Exports and Export Proceeds

June 9. The repatriation requirements for proceeds from exports were eliminated.

Proceeds from Invisibles

August 4. The limit on the amount of domestic banknotes that travelers may bring into the country was raised to LE 1,000 from LE 100.

Capital

June 3. A number of restrictions on the purchase of assets were eliminated. In addition, the regulation governing the transfers of proceeds from sales of real estate by nonresidents was modified.

July 12. Nonbank foreign exchange dealers may maintain foreign exchange working balances of up to $225,000 for the first LE 1 million of paid-up capital and up to $295,000 for each LE 1 million after the first LE 1 million of paid-up capital.

EL SALVADOR

(Position as of December 31, 1994)

Exchange Arrangement

The currency of El Salvador is the Salvadoran Colón, the external value of which is set by commercial banks and exchange houses at a rate determined by supply and demand conditions. The Central Reserve Bank establishes the daily exchange rates, which are applied to its transactions with the public sector, and the calculation of tax obligations. This exchange rate is the simple average of the exchange rates set by commercial banks and exchange houses of the previous working day. In addition, the Central Reserve Bank may purchase or sell foreign exchange to commercial banks and exchange houses at the rate prevailing in the market at the time of the transaction.

On December 31, 1994, the Central Reserve Bank's buying and selling exchange rates were ₡8.71 and, ₡8.71 respectively, per US$1; the average buying and selling exchange rates of commercial banks were ₡8.71 and ₡8.78, respectively, per US$1, and the average buying and selling rates of exchange houses were ₡8.71 and ₡8.79, respectively, per US$1.

There are no arrangements for forward cover against exchange rate risk operating in the official, commercial banking, or exchange house sector.

On November 6, 1946, El Salvador notified the Fund that it was prepared to formally accept the obligations of Article VIII, Sections 2, 3, and 4 of the Fund Agreement.

Administration of Control

Exchange regulations are administered by the Central Reserve Bank in accordance with its organic law. All private sector imports and payments for invisibles are delegated to the commercial banks and exchange houses.

Exports of a number of products require permits issued by the Centro de Trámites de Exportación (CENTREX). The Salvadoran Coffee Council issues permits freely to private sector traders to conduct external or domestic trade in coffee.

Prescription of Currency

There are no prescription of currency requirements. Settlements are usually made in U.S. dollars or other convertible currencies.

Foreign Currency Deposit Accounts

Both residents and nonresidents may maintain deposit accounts in foreign currencies with authorized banks. Balances on these accounts may be sold to the commercial banks or used to make payments abroad without restriction. Transfers of funds between these accounts are also not restricted. The commercial banks are required to submit periodic reports to the Central Reserve Bank on the use of such accounts. The reserve requirement on foreign currency deposits is 50 percent compared with 30 percent on checking deposits and 20 percent on savings deposits in national currency.

Imports and Import Payments

Import permits are issued by the Ministry of Economy and are required for only a few items, including gasoline, kerosene, fuel oil, asphalt, propane and butane gas, cloth and jute sacks, sugar, and molasses.

The commercial banks and exchange houses are authorized to make payments for private imports. Payments for public sector imports and settlements of official lines of credit are made by the commercial banks and the Central Reserve Bank after deposits have been made in local currency to cover the full value of credit.

Import tariffs range from 5 percent to 20 percent although some products, such as automobiles, alcoholic drinks, textiles, and luxury items, are subject to an import tariff of 30 percent.

Payments for Invisibles

Payments for invisibles of a personal nature (e.g., medical treatment and study and travel abroad) are free of restrictions, and the authority to grant foreign exchange for expenses relating to foreign travel and study abroad is delegated to the commercial banks and exchange houses.

Exports and Export Proceeds

CENTREX issues certificates of origin and health when foreign importers require them. All exports, irrespective of value, must be registered. Export permits are issued by the Ministry of Economy and are required for diesel fuel and liquefied petroleum gas.

Proceeds from exports of goods must be surrendered to the commercial banks; proceeds from exports outside of Central America amounting to less than $25,000 may be surrendered to exchange houses.

Exporters of nontraditional products to markets outside Central America receive a drawback of taxes paid in cash on imported raw materials equivalent to 6 percent of the f.o.b. value of their exports.

Since December 1992, proceeds from exports of coffee have been subject to an income tax, which replaced the export tax.

Proceeds from Invisibles

All exchange receipts from invisibles must be surrendered to commercial banks or exchange houses.

Capital

Foreign direct investments and inflows of capital with a maturity of more than one year must be registered with the Ministry of Economy but are not restricted. Outward remittance of interest and amortization on external loans may be made without restriction.

Act No. 279 of March 27, 1969 sets certain minimum capital requirements for businesses owned by foreign residents and those having foreign resident shareholders. This act defines foreign residents as persons residing in El Salvador who are not citizens of one of the five member countries of the Central American Common Market (CACM).[1]

Gold

Gold coins in the denomination of ₡2,500 have been issued as legal tender. Residents and nonresidents may hold and acquire gold coins for numismatic purposes. Gold coins in denominations of ₡25, ₡50, ₡100, and ₡200 have been issued as legal tender but do not circulate. These coins are not available for sale and exist only for numismatic purposes in the Central Reserve Bank collection. The importation and exportation of gold in any form are not restricted.

Changes During 1994

Exports and Export Proceeds

May 1. The 50 percent surrender requirement on proceeds from coffee exports was eliminated.

December 19. The Foreign Exchange Electronic Negotiation System (SINED) was introduced to improve the competitiveness and transparency of the foreign exchange market. Commercial banks, exchange houses, and the Central Reserve Bank participate in this system and conduct foreign exchange transactions at the rates determined by supply and demand conditions.

---

[1]Member countries of the CACM are Costa Rica, El Salvador, Guatemala, Honduras, and Nicaragua.

EQUATORIAL GUINEA

(Position as of December 31, 1994)

Exchange Arrangement

The currency of Equatorial Guinea is the CFA Franc,[1] which is pegged to the French franc, the intervention currency, at the fixed rate of CFAF 1 per F 0.01. The official buying and selling rate is CFAF 100 per F 1. Exchange transactions in French francs between the BEAC and commercial banks take place at the same rate. Buying and selling rates for certain other foreign currencies are also officially posted, with quotations based on the fixed rate for the French franc and the rates in the Paris exchange market for the currencies concerned. A commission of 0.5 percent is levied on transfers to countries that are not members of the BEAC, except transfers in respect of central and local government operations, payments for imports covered by a duly issued license domiciled with a bank, scheduled repayments on loans properly obtained abroad, travel allowances paid by the Government and its agencies for official missions, and payments of reinsurance premiums. There are no taxes or subsidies on purchases or sales of foreign exchange.

With the exception of those relating to gold, Equatorial Guinea's exchange control measures generally do not apply to (1) France (and its overseas departments and territories) and Monaco; and (2) all other countries whose bank of issue is linked with the French Treasury by an Operations Account (Benin, Burkina Faso, Cameroon, Central African Republic, Chad, Comoros, Congo, Côte d'Ivoire, Gabon, Mali, Niger, Senegal, and Togo). Hence, all payments to these countries may be made freely, but all financial transfers of more than CFAF 500,000 to countries of the Operations Account Area must be declared to the authorities for statistical purposes. All other countries are considered foreign countries. There are no arrangements for forward cover against exchange rate risk operating in the official or the commercial banking sector.

Administration of Control

Exchange control is administered by the Directorate General of Exchange Control (ONCC) of the Ministry of Finance. Exchange transactions relating to all countries must be effected through authorized intermediaries—that is, authorized banks. Import and export licenses are issued by the Ministry of Commerce and Industry. Arrears are maintained with respect to external payments.

Prescription of Currency

Because Equatorial Guinea is an Operations Account country, settlements with France (as defined above), Monaco, and the Operations Account countries are made in CFA francs, French francs, or the currency of any other institute of issue that maintains an Operations Account with the French Treasury. Settlements with all other countries are usually made through correspondent banks in France in any of the currencies of those countries or in French francs through foreign accounts in francs.

Nonresident Accounts

The regulations pertaining to nonresident accounts are based on regulations applied in France. The principal nonresident accounts are foreign accounts in francs. As the BEAC suspended the repurchase of BEAC banknotes circulating outside the territories of the CFA franc zone, BEAC banknotes received by the foreign correspondents of authorized banks and mailed to the BEAC agency in Equatorial Guinea by the Bank of France or the Central Bank of West African States (BCEAO) may not be credited to foreign accounts in francs.

Imports and Import Payments

Imports valued at more than CFAF 50,000 are subject to license, but licenses are issued freely.

All import transactions whose value exceeds CFAF 50,000 must be domiciled with an authorized bank. Import transactions by residents involving goods for use outside Equatorial Guinea must be domiciled with a bank in the country of final destination. Settlements for imports effected under an import license benefit from the authorization of uninterrupted transfer given to the authorized banks by the Ministry of Finance.

In April 1994, a new tariff structure was introduced in the context of the tax and customs reform of the Central African Customs and Economic Union (UDEAC). For UDEAC member countries, the common duty rate for basic necessities was re-

---

[1]The CFA franc circulating in Equatorial Guinea is issued by the Bank of Central African States (BEAC) and is legal tender also in Cameroon, the Central African Republic, Chad, the Congo, and Gabon.

duced to 5 percent, for raw materials and capital goods to 10 percent, for intermediate and miscellaneous goods to 20 percent, and for consumer goods to 30 percent.

Payments for Invisibles

Payments in excess of CFAF 500,000 for invisibles to France (as defined above), Monaco, and the Operations Account countries require prior declaration but are permitted freely; those to other countries are subject to the approval of the Ministry of Finance. Payments for invisibles related to trade are permitted freely when the basic trade transaction has been approved or does not require authorization. Transfers of income accruing to nonresidents in the form of profits, dividends, and royalties are also permitted freely when the basic transaction has been approved.

Residents traveling for tourism or business purposes to countries in the franc zone are allowed to take out BEAC banknotes up to a limit of CFAF 2 million; amounts in excess of this limit may be taken out in the form of means of payment other than banknotes. The allowances for travel to countries outside the franc zone are subject to the following regulations: (1) for tourist travel, CFAF 100,000 a day, with a maximum of CFAF 2 million a trip; (2) for business travel, CFAF 250,000 a day, with a maximum of CFAF 5 million a trip; (3) allowances in excess of these limits are subject to the authorization of the Ministry of Finance or, by delegation, the BEAC; and (4) the use of credit cards, which must be issued by resident financial intermediaries and approved by the Ministry of Finance, is limited to the ceilings indicated above for tourist and business travel. Returning resident travelers are required to declare all means of payment in their possession upon arrival at customs and to surrender within eight days all means of payment exceeding the equivalent of CFAF 25,000. All resident travelers, regardless of destination, must declare in writing all means of payment at their disposal at the time of departure. The re-exportation by nonresident travelers of means of payments other than banknotes issued abroad and registered in the name of the nonresident traveler is not restricted, subject to documentation that they had been purchased with funds drawn from a foreign account in CFA francs or with other foreign exchange. The re-exportation of foreign banknotes is allowed up to the equivalent of CFAF 250,000; the re-exportation of foreign banknotes above these ceilings requires documentation demonstrating either the importation of foreign banknotes or their purchase against other means of payment registered in the name of the traveler or through the use of nonresident deposits lodged in local banks.

The transfer of rent from real property owned in Equatorial Guinea by foreign nationals is permitted up to 50 percent of the income declared for taxation purposes, net of tax. Remittances for current repair and management of real property abroad are limited to the equivalent of CFAF 200,000 every two years. The transfer abroad of the salaries of expatriates working in Equatorial Guinea is permitted upon presentation of the appropriate pay voucher as well as justification of expenses, provided that the transfer takes place within three months of the pay period concerned. Except in the case of expatriates working in Equatorial Guinea on a temporary basis, payments of insurance premiums of up to CFAF 50,000 to foreign countries are permitted; larger amounts may be authorized by the ONCC.

Exports and Export Proceeds

Export transactions valued at CFAF 50,000 or more must be domiciled with an authorized bank. Exports to all countries are subject to domiciliation requirements for the appropriate documents. Proceeds from exports to all countries must be repatriated within 30 days of the payment date stipulated in the sales contract. Payments for exports must be made within 30 days of the arrival date of the merchandise at its destination.

Proceeds from Invisibles

Proceeds from transactions in invisibles with France (as defined above), Monaco, and the Operations Account countries may be retained. All amounts due from residents of other countries in respect of services, and all income earned in those countries from foreign assets, must be collected within a month of the due date and surrendered within a month of collection if received in foreign currency. Resident and nonresident travelers may bring in any amount of banknotes and coins issued by the BEAC, the Bank of France, or a bank of issue maintaining an Operations Account with the French Treasury, as well as any amount of foreign banknotes and coins (except gold coins) of countries outside the Operations Account Area.

Capital

Capital movements between Equatorial Guinea and France (as defined above), Monaco, and the Operations Account countries are free of exchange control. Capital transfers to all other countries require exchange control approval and are restricted, but capital receipts from such countries are freely permitted.[2]

Under the investment code of April 30, 1992 (as modified June 6, 1994), a number of privileges may be granted to approved foreign investments. These privileges include exemption from import- and export-licensing requirements and free transfer abroad of debt payments and net profits.

Gold

Residents are free to hold, acquire, and dispose of gold jewelry in Equatorial Guinea. They must have the approval of the Directorate of Mines to hold gold in any other form. Approval is not normally given because there are no industrial users in Equatorial Guinea. Newly mined gold must be declared to the Directorate of Mines, which authorizes either its exportation or its sale in the domestic market. Exports are allowed only to France. Imports and ex-

---

[2]Regulations on capital transactions, such as the sale of foreign securities in Equatorial Guinea or direct investments, have been prepared and are pending approval. The authorities are also in the process of drafting legislation aimed at stimulating foreign investment in the agricultural, forestry, construction, public works, mining, and industrial equipment maintenance sectors.

ports of gold require prior authorization from the Directorate of Mines and the Minister of Finance; authorization is seldom granted for imports. Exempt from this requirement are (1) imports and exports by or on behalf of the monetary authorities, and (2) imports and exports of manufactured articles containing a small quantity of gold (such as gold-filled or gold-plated articles). Both licensed and exempt imports of gold are subject to customs declaration.

Changes During 1994

Exchange Arrangement

January 12. The CFA franc was devalued to CFAF 100 per F 1 from CFAF 50 per F 1.

Imports and Import Payments

April 6. A new tariff structure was introduced in the context of the UDEAC tax and customs reform. The common duty rate adopted by the UDEAC member countries for imported basic necessities was reduced to 5 percent, to 10 percent for raw materials and capital goods, to 20 percent for intermediate and miscellaneous goods, and to 30 percent for consumer goods.

ERITREA[1]

(Position as of December 31, 1994)

Exchange Arrangement

The provisional legal tender of Eritrea is the Ethiopian Birr, which is issued by the National Bank of Ethiopia and is pegged to the U.S. dollar at the rate of Br 5.95 per US$1. The official exchange rate applies only to transactions between Eritrea and Ethiopia that are associated with refinery services. The Bank of Eritrea applies the marginal auction rate determined in the fortnightly auctions conducted by the National Bank of Ethiopia to all aid-funded imports and most service transactions. The marginal rate established in an auction is effective for the two-week period following the auction. There is also a more depreciated preferential exchange rate that is used for the remaining external transactions, including the conversion of foreign exchange remittances by Eritreans living abroad, export proceeds, and most imports. The preferential exchange rate is fixed by the authorities, but it is close to the rate quoted in the parallel market.

The Bank of Eritrea undertakes transactions with authorized dealers, which in turn carry out transactions with the public on its behalf. There is also a limited number of unofficial, but sanctioned, dealers that buy and sell foreign exchange at the preferential rate. Exchange rates for currencies other than the U.S. dollar[2] are communicated daily by the Bank of Eritrea to the authorized dealers on the basis of same day early morning cross quotations in the London market against the U.S. dollar. For all foreign currency transactions, except transactions involving foreign currency notes, the Bank of Eritrea prescribes a commission of 0.5 percent for purchases of foreign exchange and 1.5 percent for sales of foreign exchange. The authorized dealers are permitted, but not obliged, to levy a service charge for their own account of up to 0.25 percent buying and 0.75 percent selling and, for currencies other than the U.S. dollar, to include a margin charge that is applied by the correspondents abroad.

There are no taxes or subsidies on purchases or sales of foreign exchange. There is no forward cover provided in foreign exchange by the Bank of Eritrea or the authorized dealers.

Administration of Control

The Bank of Eritrea, during the transitional period, is working to ensure that all foreign exchange transactions are effected through the authorized dealers who are licensed in accordance with the Monetary and Banking Proclamation No. 32/1993. Under this proclamation, the Bank of Eritrea may from time to time issue regulations, directives, and instructions on foreign exchange matters. Comprehensive foreign exchange regulations, as well as a new Central Bank Act, have been prepared and submitted for the Government's approval.

The Exchange Control Department of the Bank of Eritrea issues permits only for those imports that require foreign exchange from the banking system. The Ministry of Trade and Industry issues licenses for importers, exporters, and commercial agents, and has authority to regulate foreign investments (Investment Proclamation No. 59/1994); it vets and licenses technology transfer agreements, as well as investment projects (including joint ventures) that are eligible to take advantage of the tax, foreign exchange, and other concessions of the Investment Proclamation. The Asmara Chamber of Commerce issues certificates of origin for exports.

Prescription of Currency

Settlements may be made in currencies quoted by the Bank of Eritrea or in any other convertible currency it deems acceptable. All transactions with Ethiopia, except for those related to the imports of spare parts for the refinery in Assab, are settled in the Ethiopian birr.

Under the agreement of friendship and cooperation, signed by the Presidents of Eritrea and Ethiopia in September 1993, these two countries undertook to cooperate closely and develop common policies concerning a wide range of issues, including matters pertaining to their exchange and trade systems. A joint ministerial commission is entrusted to ensure that implementation of the provisions of the agreement, notably its Article 9, which calls for mutual consultation on the use of the Ethiopian birr and the exploration of the possibilities of adopting a common currency by both countries. In May 1994, a communiqué was issued to further un-

---

[1]Eritrea became a member of the IMF on July 6, 1994.

[2]At present, Belgian francs, Canadian dollars, deutsche mark, Netherlands guilders, French francs, Italian lire, Japanese yen, pounds sterling, and Swiss francs. The Bank of Eritrea intends to start quoting rates for the Danish krone, the Norwegian krone, and the Swedish krona in the near future.

derscore the need for harmonization and coordination, but no detailed agreement has yet been concluded.

An agreement that governs trade between Eritrea and Ethiopia has not yet been concluded. Both Governments are committed to encourage bilateral trade on a free-market basis, to exempt such trade from customs duties, and to harmonize their customs tariffs, as well as the rules and formalities of trade between both countries, in order to facilitate the exchange, storage, and shipment of goods and transfer of payments. Payments are generally made in the Ethiopian birr, although the Government of Ethiopia has required payments in foreign currencies for Eritrea's purchases of Ethiopia's exports, as well as for goods that are in short supply in Ethiopia. Under an intergovernmental agreement between Eritrea and Ethiopia, Eritrea pays Ethiopia in birr for its domestic requirements of petroleum products. The refinery in Assab is reimbursed in birr for the costs of refining the derivative products consumed by Ethiopia, except that the portion corresponding to the depreciation of equipment is paid for in foreign exchange.

As stipulated under an intergovernmental transit and port services agreement as well as a customs arrangement (amended annually), the port of Assab is a free port for Ethiopia, with its own Ethiopian customs branch office, and goods shipped to or from Ethiopia remain exempt from the Eritrean customs duties and related charges. Procedures for the clearing of goods and the exchange of documentation are to be coordinated, and the port and shipping charges are paid in Ethiopian birr.

Resident and Nonresident Accounts

With the approval of the Bank of Eritrea, nonresidents may open accounts denominated in U.S. dollars or in Ethiopian birr with the Commercial Bank of Eritrea. These accounts may be credited with foreign currencies, apart from exceptional cases that are subject to approval by the Bank of Eritrea. The Bank of Eritrea has also authorized the maintenance of interest-bearing accounts denominated in U.S. dollars for Eritreans residing abroad since November 1, 1993. Members of the diplomatic community, welfare organizations, nongovernmental organizations, and their personnel may maintain nonresident accounts denominated in birr. Joint ventures and other business firms that invest their capital wholly or partly in foreign exchange may also maintain nonresident accounts in birr.

Residents are not allowed to maintain foreign currency accounts, with the exception of investors who, in accordance with the regulations of the Bank of Eritrea, may maintain foreign currency accounts in Eritrea, and any individuals earning foreign exchange in connection with foreign trade. Nonbank residents may not open accounts abroad, except where they are specifically authorized by the Bank of Eritrea.

Imports and Import Payments

All importers must possess a valid trade license issued by the Ministry of Trade and Industry. These licenses must be renewed each year at a fee of Br 200.[3] Import payments made through the banking system require permits that are issued by the Bank of Eritrea upon presentation of pro forma invoices providing information as to type, quantity, unit price, and freight cost (where applicable). A commission of 2 percent is collected on imports that do not require official foreign exchange and are not aid funded. The Bank of Eritrea ensures full collection of *franco valuta* commissions by requesting the display of a payment document to the Customs Office at the time of the import declaration. Imports of cars and other motor vehicles require prior permission from the Ministry of Transport to ensure their suitability for existing infrastructure and other similar considerations. There are no priority and negative lists for imports, except that a public enterprise producing tobacco and matches holds a monopoly over the import of these products. Most imports requiring official foreign exchange are effected under letters of credit or on a cash-against-documents basis. Suppliers' credits must be registered by the Bank of Eritrea.

Payments for Invisibles

Payments for invisibles may be made to all countries with a foreign exchange permit, which is issued free of charge by the Bank of Eritrea. The travel allowance for business trips is $50 a person a day for up to 20 days and is limited to no more than two trips a year. In bona fide cases, these limits may be exceeded with the approval of the Bank of Eritrea. Also, exporters may freely use their retention accounts for this purpose. For personal travel, the allowance is $100 a person (adult or minor) for up to two trips a year. Medical expenses of up to $2,000 for treatment abroad are allowed upon the recommendation of the Medical Board of the Ministry of Health. This limit may be exceeded in exceptional circumstances. Residents may remit premiums on

---

[3]The annual license fee for commercial agents of foreign companies is Br 500.

life insurance policies that were taken out before May 1991.

Upon the approval of the new foreign exchange regulations, foreign investors may freely remit net profits and dividends accrued from investment and fees and royalties in respect of any technology transfer agreements. Foreign employees may remit up to 40 percent of their net earnings each month, and up to 60 percent of their cumulative earnings upon completion of their term of service in Eritrea.

Exports and Export Proceeds

Exporters must be licensed by the Ministry of Trade and Industry. The annual licensing fee is Br 300 for producers and Br 500 for the commercial agents of foreign companies. All exports require documentation by the Bank of Eritrea, which examines the sales contracts as to type of product, quantity, and unit price. Certain commodities may require clearance from specific government bodies (e.g., the Eritrean Institute of Standards). In particular, livestock and cereals require the permission of the Ministry of Agriculture, and marine products require the permission of the Ministry of Marine Resources. Exports of hides and skins have been suspended since mid-1993 in an attempt to improve the supply to domestic tanneries and processors.

Exports may be made under a letter of credit or on an advance payments basis; in some cases, exports can be permitted on a consignment basis. All export proceeds must be repatriated to an authorized bank within 90 days of shipment; where justified, this deadline can be extended by another 90 days. Exporters may retain up to 100 percent of the sales proceeds.

Proceeds from Invisibles

Except for temporary visitors to Eritrea, all foreign exchange receipts from current invisibles by residents must be surrendered to authorized dealers. However, residents earning foreign exchange from foreign trade, such as consultants and engineers working temporarily abroad for foreign companies, may on request be permitted by the Bank of Eritrea to hold foreign exchange in Eritrea in interest-bearing U.S. dollar accounts provided for nonresident Eritreans, or in accounts abroad. Travelers are not required to declare their foreign exchange holdings at the point of entry into Eritrea and are not allowed to reconvert their balances back into foreign currency upon departure.

Capital

Foreign exchange proceeds representing capital inflows must be surrendered to the Bank of Eritrea, except for funds deposited in authorized nonresident accounts. Capital inflows must be registered with the Bank of Eritrea in order to ensure the smooth transfer of profits, dividends and interest, amortization of principal, and proceeds of the sale of shares to residents or from the liquidation of investments.

Direct foreign investments (including joint ventures) in Eritrea are governed by the provisions of the Investment Proclamation No. 59/1994 (which repealed Proclamation No. 18/1991). Foreign direct investment is permitted in all sectors, except that domestic retail and wholesale trade, and import and commission agencies are open to foreign investors only when Eritrea has a bilateral agreement of reciprocity with the country of the investor; the latter condition may be waived by the Government. Approved investments and their subsequent expansion enjoy exemption from customs duties and sales tax for capital goods and spare parts associated with the investment. There are no exemptions from income tax. Under the foreign exchange regulations submitted to the Government, foreign investors may freely remit proceeds received from liquidation of investment and/or expansion, and payments received from the sale or transfer of shares. Petroleum contractors and subcontractors may freely transfer abroad funds accruing from petroleum operations and pay subcontractors and expatriate staff abroad.

Foreign borrowing by residents in Eritrea has to be registered with the Bank of Eritrea. Authorized banks are permitted to purchase and hold foreign banknotes up to the equivalent of $500,000. Amounts exceeding this limit must be surrendered to the Bank of Eritrea or deposited in the correspondent accounts abroad. With the approval of the Bank of Eritrea, authorized banks may borrow abroad or overdraw their correspondent accounts abroad. They may acquire securities under similar conditions.

Gold

Residents may own gold jewelry without restrictions. Beyond this, ownership or possession of gold or other precious metals or ores requires the authorization of the Ministry of Energy, Mines and Water Resources.

ESTONIA

(Position as of December 31, 1994)

Exchange Arrangement

The currency of Estonia is the Kroon. Since the introduction of a currency board system, the convertibility of the kroon has been guaranteed by the Bank of Estonia (BOE); the BOE exchanges kroon banknotes and reserve deposits of commercial banks with the BOE into deutsche mark and vice versa at the exchange rate of EEK 8 per DM1. The kroon is fully convertible for all current international transactions and for virtually all international capital transactions.

Transactions in convertible currencies are freely handled by the commercial banks, and commercial banks are free to quote their own exchange rates.

Estonia formally accepted the obligations of Article VIII, Sections 2, 3, and 4 of the Fund Agreement, as from August 15, 1994.

Administration of Control

The authority to issue and enforce foreign exchange regulations is based on the Central Bank Law. Import and export controls are administered by the Ministry of Finance.

Prescription of Currency

Settlements with the Baltic countries, Russia, and the other countries of the former Soviet Union can be effected through a system of correspondent accounts maintained by the BOE with the respective central banks. Balances accrued in these accounts may be used freely by their holders, to purchase either goods or services in the country concerned. In operating these accounts, the Bank of Estonia acts as an intermediary only and does not convert any balances to krooni. Kroon balances held by central banks of the Baltic countries, Russia, and the other countries of the former Soviet Union on their correspondent accounts are fully convertible without delay. These agreements also allow for separate decentralized payments arrangements between commercial banks in the respective states and do not provide for swing credits or overdraft facilities. In addition, Estonian exporters and importers may effect payments without undue delays. Settlements with countries with which Estonia maintains bilateral payments agreements are effected in accordance with the terms of the agreements.[1]

Commercial banks in Estonia are permitted and encouraged to open their own correspondent accounts with counterpart commercial banks in the Baltic countries, Russia, and other countries of the former Soviet Union to effect payments associated with trade with those countries.

Estonia maintains outstanding balances on inoperative correspondent accounts with a number of countries of the former Soviet Union.

Resident and Nonresident Accounts

Enterprises must obtain a license to open and operate foreign exchange accounts with foreign banks abroad; licenses, whose sole purpose is to enforce the monthly reporting requirements, are granted freely. Enterprises need not obtain licenses to open and operate foreign currency accounts in domestic banks.

Imports and Exports

Imports are not subject to licensing requirements or quantitative restrictions. Import tariffs of 16 percent are levied on fur and fur goods and of 10 percent on automobiles, bicycles, launches, and yachts.[2] In addition, imports are subject to a 0.5 percent ad valorem fee to cover the cost of administrative processing and are subject to an 18 percent value-added tax, which is also levied on domestically produced goods. Alcoholic beverages and tobacco products are subject to excise taxes levied, at point of entry by the customs authority, at the following rates: wine, 20 percent; vodka, 100 percent; and raw tobacco and cigarettes, 40 percent.

Quantitative restrictions on exports have been completely eliminated with the removal on October 18, 1994 of the remaining quotas on gravel, specialized clay, and quartz sand. Export duties apply only to items of cultural value at a rate of up to 100 percent. The exportation of metals is subject to state monopoly; private exports of metal are subject to licenses. In addition, all exports are subject to an ad valorem fee of 0.5 percent to cover the cost of administrative processing.

---

[1]At the end of 1993, Estonia maintained bilateral payments agreements with Azerbaijan, Belarus, Kazakhstan, the Kyrgyz Republic, Latvia, Lithuania, Moldova, the Russian Federation, Turkmenistan, Ukraine, and Uzbekistan.

[2]These tariffs are planned to be replaced by domestic excise taxes in 1995.

Enterprises are not required to repatriate export proceeds.

Payments for and Proceeds from Invisibles

There are no regulations governing payments for or proceeds from invisibles.

The importation and exportation of domestic banknotes are not restricted.

Capital

Inward and outward capital transfers are not controlled or restricted.

Gold

International and domestic trade in gold is subject to the licensing requirement administered by the Ministry of Finance.

Changes During 1994

Exchange Arrangement

August 15. Estonia formally accepted the obligations of Article VIII, Sections 2, 3, and 4 of the Fund Agreement.

Resident and Nonresident Accounts

March 23. Individuals were permitted to open foreign exchange accounts with domestic banks.

Imports and Exports

January 1. The ban on exports of oil shale was abolished.

October 18. The remaining export quotas on gravel, clay, and quartz sand were eliminated.

ETHIOPIA

(Position as of December 31, 1994)

Exchange Arrangement

The currency of Ethiopia is the Ethiopian Birr. The exchange rate system consists of two rates: the official rate and the auction rate. The official exchange rate is pegged to the U.S. dollar and is adjusted occasionally on the basis of the marginal rates derived from the auctions. It is applied to imports of petroleum products, fertilizers, pharmaceutical goods, Ethiopia's contributions to international organizations, and external debt-service payments. On December 31, 1994, the official exchange rate was Br 5.95 per US$1. Buying and selling rates for certain other currencies are set daily by the National Bank of Ethiopia (the central bank) on the basis of both the auction rate and the official exchange rate for the U.S. dollar and the previous day's closing rate of the currency against the U.S. dollar in London. The auction rate is determined in a biweekly auction (Dutch type), with successful bidders receiving an allocation of foreign exchange based on the exchange rate contained in their bids.

The marginal exchange rate from the auction ("secondary market exchange rate") serves as the exchange rate until the next auction for all current and capital transactions outside the auction, except for transactions to which the official exchange rate applies. It is applied to all foreign exchange inflows and to foreign exchange provided by the National Bank outside the auction market for limited expenses, including tuition fees, medical treatment abroad, business travel, and personal remittances by expatriate workers. On December 31, 1994, the marginal exchange rate was Br 6.25 per US$1.

All licensed importers are allowed to submit bids to the auction if foreign exchange is to be used to import goods that are not included on a negative list. Applicants must deposit 100 percent of the birr equivalent in advance. Authorized dealers must observe a prescribed commission of 0.50 percent on buying and 1.50 percent on selling, the proceeds of which accrue to the National Bank. Dealers are authorized to levy service charges of up to 0.25 percent on buying and 0.75 percent on selling for their own accounts. For currencies other than the U.S. dollar, dealers are authorized to include the margin charges applied by the correspondents abroad. In practice, the authorized charges are usually levied. The commission and service charges are also ap-

plied by the National Bank in its dealings with the Government and certain public sector entities.

There are no taxes or subsidies on purchases or sales of foreign exchange. There are no arrangements for forward cover against exchange rate risk operating in the official or the commercial banking sector.

Administration of Control

All foreign exchange transactions must be carried out through an authorized dealer under the control of the National Bank. The Exchange Controller of the National Bank issues exchange licenses for all exports and payments abroad and issues permits for all shipments. The Minister of Trade formulates external trade policy. Arrears are maintained with respect to external payments.

Prescription of Currency

Outgoing payments are normally made in convertible foreign exchange appropriate to the country of the recipient or in U.S. dollars. Settlements with Eritrea, except those relating to imports of spare parts for the refinery in Assab, Eritrea, are made in birr. The net proceeds of exports must be surrendered in a freely convertible foreign currency or in any other acceptable foreign currency.

Nonresident Accounts

Nonresidents may open accounts either in birr or in foreign currencies at authorized banks upon approval of the Exchange Control Department of the National Bank. Deposits to these accounts must be made only in foreign exchange. Balances on nonresident foreign currency accounts may be freely transferred abroad, and transfers between nonresident accounts do not require prior approval. Members of the diplomatic community must use transferable or nontransferable birr accounts for payment of local expenses. Joint ventures are permitted to open foreign currency accounts or transferable or nontransferable birr accounts to purchase raw materials, equipment, and spare parts not available in the local market. As soon as the goods are received, documentary evidence of the entry of the goods purchased with such funds must be submitted to the Exchange Control Department of the National Bank. In general, these accounts may be replenished only after the documents have been presented.

Blocked accounts of nonresidents maintained with authorized banks are used to retain funds in excess of Br 20,000 arising from disinvestments in Ethiopia (see the section on Capital, below). Resident Ethiopian nationals are not allowed to maintain a bank account abroad.

Imports and Import Payments

Payments abroad for imports require exchange licenses, which can be obtained when a valid importer's license is presented. Applications for exchange licenses must be accompanied by information on costs and payment terms and by evidence that adequate insurance has been arranged with the Ethiopian Insurance Corporation, particularly for goods imported under letters of credit. Foreign exchange is not made available for imports included in a negative list. Most goods on this negative list may, however, be imported under the *franco valuta* arrangement (i.e., imports are financed with foreign exchange from external sources) without a license. Imports of cars and other vehicles require prior authorization from the Minister of Transport and Communications, and authorization is readily granted without restriction if the imports are financed with foreign exchange balances held abroad. Exchange licenses are granted in the currency appropriate to the country of origin or in any convertible currency that may be requested. Payments by letter of credit, mail transfer, telegraphic transfer, or cash against documents at sight are all normally acceptable, but the National Bank must be consulted regarding imports on a cash-against-documents basis.

Certain imports (about 100 items, mostly consumer goods) may not be financed on an acceptance basis, and virtually no imports take place on this basis. Importation on suppliers' credits requires prior approval of the terms and conditions of the credit, and such imports are limited to raw and intermediate materials, pharmaceuticals, and machinery and transport equipment.

All imports are subject to a general (ad valorem) sales tax.

Payments for Invisibles

Payments for invisibles require exchange licenses. Invisibles connected with trade transactions are treated on the same basis as the goods to which they relate. Foreign employees may remit monthly up to 30 percent of their net earnings but only for the first three years of their contract if employed by the private sector; they may remit a maximum of between 40 percent and 50 percent of total net earnings during the period of service and upon final departure. Other expatriate employees may on final departure take out the same maximum amount, but not more than Br 20,000 in any one year. Foreign nationals who are not entitled to remittance facilities may, however, remit up to 30 percent of their net earnings for the education of their children.

Persons traveling abroad for business purposes related to importing or exporting are granted foreign exchange up to $120 a day for a maximum period of 20 days in any one calendar year; for other business travel, the limits for tourism are applied. For tourism purposes, persons 18 years of age and over are allowed up to $50 a trip with a maximum of two trips a year. For government travel, the schedule of rates varies by country and city based on cost of living. Students are allowed foreign exchange up to the equivalent of Br 1,200 to study abroad. With approval of the Ministry of Education, Ethiopian nationals with dependents pursuing higher studies at accredited institutions abroad are allowed to remit funds to meet school fees and reasonable expenses. Residents may remit premiums on insurance policies taken out before April 1962. Subject to certain limits and verification by a medical board and the Ministry of Health, residents may obtain a foreign exchange allocation of up to Br 30,000 for medical treatment and travel abroad. After providing for payment of local taxes, foreign companies may remit dividends on their invested and reinvested capital in any currency. Travelers may take with them a maximum of Br 10 in Ethiopian banknotes.

Exports and Export Proceeds

Exports of most cereals to any destination other than Djibouti are prohibited. All commodity exports require permits from the Exchange Controller and some require, in addition, the approval of specified public bodies. When applying for a permit, an exporter must specify the goods to be exported, their destination, and their value. For exports on a c.i.f. basis, exporters must obtain full insurance from the Ethiopian Insurance Corporation. The granting of a permit by the Exchange Controller enables the goods to pass through customs. The licensing system is used to ensure that foreign exchange receipts are surrendered to the National Bank, generally within three months, and that export proceeds are received in an appropriate currency (see the section on Prescription of Currency, above). Exports of raw hides and skins are regulated or prohibited until the needs of local factories are met. The exportation of coffee is subject to a coffee export duty at the rate of Br 15 a quintal, a coffee export cess at the rate of Br 5 a quintal, and a coffee surtax.

Proceeds from Invisibles

Foreign exchange receipts from invisibles must be surrendered. Travelers may bring in Br 10 in Ethiopian currency and must declare any foreign exchange in their possession entering Ethiopia. Except for short-term visitors, travelers must have authorization to re-export foreign exchange. Reconversion of birr must be supported by documentary evidence of prior exchange of foreign currency.

Capital

Controls over capital movements are designed to restrict outflows, prevent an unwarranted accumulation of external debt, and keep the authorities informed of the country's external debt position.

All receipts of capital in the form of foreign exchange must be surrendered. Authorization of the Exchange Controller is required for repatriation of capital, and registration of capital inflows with the exchange control authorities establishes the evidence of inflows that is required for authorization. All recognized and registered foreign investments may be terminated on presentation of documents regarding liquidation and on payment of all taxes and other liabilities. Subject to appropriate documentation, foreign businessmen with nonregistered investments may transfer their capital abroad on liquidation and final departure from Ethiopia but may not transfer more than Br 20,000 in any one calendar year; funds in excess of this amount must be deposited in a blocked account with an authorized bank. This regulation does not apply to joint ventures established under Council of State Special Decree No. 11/1989 (of July 5, 1989) and investments made under Proclamation No. 15/1992 (of May 25, 1992). Transfers by emigrants who have operated their own businesses are restricted to Br 20,000 in any one calendar year.

Foreign investors are permitted to hold a majority share in a joint venture, except in certain sectors: precious metals, public utilities, telecommunications, banking and insurance, transport, and trade in selected products deemed essential to the economy by law. All applications for joint ventures must be approved by the Investment Office; a minimum of 25 percent of share capital must be paid before registration. Exemptions from income taxes are granted for up to five years for new projects and for up to three years for major extensions to existing projects. Imports of investment goods and spare parts for such ventures are also eligible for exemption from customs duties and other specified import levies. Proceeds from the liquidation of a joint venture (as well as dividends received from the activities of a joint venture and payments received from the sale or transfer of shares) may be remitted abroad in convertible currency without restriction. A joint venture may also transfer abroad in convertible currency payments in respect of debt contracted and fees or royalties in respect of technology transfer agreements.

Borrowing abroad requires approval from the Exchange Control Department and is restricted. Authorized banks may freely place their funds abroad except on fixed-term deposit but may not acquire securities denominated in foreign currency without the permission of the National Bank. In addition, they need prior approval from the National Bank to overdraw their accounts with foreign correspondents, borrow funds abroad, or accept deposits in foreign currency.

Gold

The ownership of personal jewelry of which gold or platinum forms a part is permitted. Unless specifically authorized by the Minister of Mines and Energy, the possession or custody of 50 ounces or more of raw or refined gold or platinum, or of gold or platinum in the form of nuggets, ores, or bullion, is not permitted. Newly mined gold is sold by the Ethiopian Mineral Resources Development Corporation to the National Bank. Imports and exports of gold in any form other than jewelry require exchange licenses issued by the National Bank. Such licenses are not normally granted except for imports and exports by or on behalf of the monetary authorities.

Changes During 1994

Exchange Arrangement

April 1. The official exchange rate was adjusted to reach 85 percent of the average of the marginal auction rates of the preceding month.

May 16. The official exchange rate was adjusted to reach 90 percent of the average of the marginal auction rates of the preceding month.

November 7. The official exchange rate was adjusted to reach 95 percent of the average of the marginal auction rates of the preceding month.

Imports and Import Payments

September 26. The negative list of imports to which auction exchange rates apply was shortened, with textiles, perfumes, beverages, tobacco products, television and radio receivers, and used materials remaining the principal items on this list.

Payments for Invisibles

April 19. The regulations related to availability of foreign exchange for business and government travel were modified.

FIJI

(Position as of December 31, 1994)

Exchange Arrangement

The currency of Fiji is the Fiji Dollar, the external value of which is determined on the basis of the fixed relationship between the Fiji dollar and a weighted basket consisting of the Australian dollar, the Japanese yen, the New Zealand dollar, the pound sterling, and the U.S. dollar. The weights in the formula are reviewed annually; the most recent revision was made in April 1993. The exchange rate of the Fiji dollar in terms of the U.S. dollar, the intervention currency, is fixed daily by the Reserve Bank of Fiji on the basis of quotations for the U.S. dollar and other currencies included in the basket. On December 31, 1994, the midpoint exchange rate for the Fiji dollar in terms of the U.S. dollar was F$1.409 per US$1. The Reserve Bank provides official quotations only for the U.S. dollar. There are no taxes or subsidies on purchases or sales of foreign exchange. Forward exchange facilities are provided by authorized dealers for trade transactions for forward periods of up to six months for exports and nine months for imports.

Fiji formally accepted the obligations of Article VIII, Sections 2, 3, and 4 of the Fund Agreement, as from August 4, 1972.

Administration of Control

Exchange control is administered by the Reserve Bank acting as agent of the Government; the Reserve Bank delegates to authorized dealers the authority to approve normal import payments, and other current payments and transfers up to specified limits or full amounts in some cases.

Prescription of Currency

Transactions with all countries are subject to exchange control. Settlements with residents of any country may be made in Fiji dollars through an external account or in any foreign currency.[1]

Resident and Nonresident Accounts

A nonresident may open and operate an external account in Fiji dollars or a foreign currency account with an authorized dealer without specific approval from the Reserve Bank.[2] These accounts may be credited freely with the account holder's salary (net of tax), with interest payable on the account, with payments from other external accounts, with the proceeds of sales of foreign currency or foreign coins by the account holder, and with Fiji banknotes that the account holder brought into Fiji or acquired by debit to an external account or by the sale of foreign currency in the country during a temporary visit. External accounts may also be credited with payments by residents for which either general or specific authority has been given. External accounts may be debited for payments to residents of Fiji, transfers to other external accounts, payments in cash in Fiji, and purchases of foreign exchange.

Exporters may retain up to 10 percent of proceeds from exports in foreign currency accounts and use the proceeds for import payments (see section on Exports and Export Proceeds, below).

Imports and Import Payments

Imports of most goods are under open general license; imports of bulk butter and lubrication oil products in any form require a specific license. The Ministry of Trade and Commerce is responsible for issuing import licenses, with the exception of those for gold, timber, and butter. Import licenses for gold are issued by the Ministry of Finance and Economic Planning, for timber by the Ministry of Forestry, and for butter by the Ministry of Primary Industries and Cooperatives. Export licenses are issued by various government departments and monitored by the Comptroller of Customs. A wide range of consumer goods are imported by national cooperative societies under a joint arrangement with six other Pacific island countries. The importation of a few commodities from all sources is prohibited for security, health, or public policy reasons.

Payments for authorized imports are permitted upon application and submission of documentary evidence to authorized dealers, who may allow payments for goods that have been imported under either a specific import license or an open general license. Authorized banks may approve advance

---

[1]Under Fiji's exchange control regulations, foreign currencies are all currencies other than the Fiji dollar.

[2]A nonresident is a person or firm whose country of normal domicile or established residence is a country other than Fiji. For individuals, a resident of Fiji is a person who either has lived, or intends to continue living, in Fiji for at least three years.

payments for imports of up to F$50,000 an application without specific approval from the Reserve Bank, if such payments are required by the supplier.

Payments for Invisibles

Payments for invisibles are permitted under a delegated authority to authorized dealers up to specific limits, as follows: (1) family maintenance expenses, F$4,000 a year; (2) subscription payments for clubs, societies, and trade organizations, F$5,000 an application; (3) travel allowances, F$6,000 an applicant a trip; (4) payments of royalties, commissions, patents, brokerage, and copyrights, F$10,000 an application; (5) gift remittances, F$500 a donor a year; and (6) professional fees, F$10,000 a year a beneficiary. The use of credit cards for travel-related expenses is not restricted, except for a F$2,000 limit on its use for shopping on each trip; in addition, F$400 a month may be withdrawn in cash. Emigrants are allowed to transfer, after one year abroad, the full amount of the current year's dividends or profits earned on assets left in Fiji.

Prior approval from the Reserve Bank is not required to make the following payments if they are accompanied by supporting documentary proof: (1) for medical treatment and for educational expenses, up to F$10,000, in addition to tuition fees, direct to the institution; (2) wage payments by shipping companies to foreign crew members, up to F$20,000; (3) advertising fees, up to F$10,000; (4) payments of charges for movie film rental and news services; and (5) proceeds from the maturity of life insurance, up to F$15,000 an applicant, subject to completion of emigration procedures with the Reserve Bank. Amounts exceeding the established limits may be granted with the approval of the Reserve Bank upon presentation of documents certifying that the payments are bona fide.

Nonresident-owned companies must obtain permission from the Reserve Bank to transfer dividends abroad. Under the present policy, remittance of the current year's profits and two years' retained earnings that have not previously been remitted is allowed. The remittance abroad of rent accruing on properties owned by emigrants is permitted as part of the transfers of F$25,000 an emigrant is allowed to make every six months (see section on Capital, below).

Exports and Export Proceeds

Specific licenses are required only for exports of sugar, wheat bran, copra meal, certain lumber, certain animals, and a few other items. Irrespective of export-licensing requirements, however, exporters are required to produce an export permit for commercial consignment of all goods with an f.o.b. value of more than F$1,000; this permit is required for exchange control purposes. Exporters are required to collect the proceeds from exports within six months of the date of shipment of the goods from Fiji and may not, without specific permission, grant more than six months' credit to a nonresident buyer. At least 90 percent of the value of 1993 export proceeds must be offered for sale to an authorized dealer; up to 10 percent of 1993 export proceeds may be kept in foreign currency accounts maintained with an authorized dealer or a foreign bank abroad with approval from the Reserve Bank; the rate of retention from each export receipt is not subject to control. Payments are admissible for imports of raw materials, professional and management fees, loan repayments, and remittances of profits and dividends.

Proceeds from Invisibles

All receipts from invisibles must be surrendered to authorized dealers. Travelers may bring in freely Fijian and foreign currency banknotes, but must declare them to customs or immigration officials on arrival in order to export the unused balance on departure. Residents are required to sell their foreign currency holdings to an authorized dealer within one month of their return.

Receipts of interest, dividends, and amortization must be surrendered semiannually unless approval for reinvestment abroad has been granted by the Reserve Bank.

Capital

Repatriation of capital funds sources from, or withdrawal of foreign investment in, Fiji requires specific permission from the Reserve Bank, which is readily granted with evidence that the investment funds originated offshore. Foreign investment in Fiji is normally expected to be financed from a nonresident source. Such foreign investment may be given "approved status," which guarantees the right to repatriate dividends and capital. Special tax incentives and concessions are granted for investments that qualify under Fiji's Tax Free Factory Zone status, and an investment allowance similar to that for hotels is provided for large-outlay investment projects that support the tourist industry.

Nonresident-owned companies are permitted to repatriate in full the proceeds from sales of assets and capital gains on investments of up to F$5 million a year.

The transfer of inheritances and dowries owed to nonresidents is permitted, as is the transfer of the proceeds from the sale of a house owned by a nonresident. The transfer of funds by emigrants on departure is limited to F$125,000 for a family and F$75,000 for a single person; thereafter, the emigrant is allowed an automatic transfer of F$25,000 every six months commencing six months after emigration until the amount cleared by the Inland Revenue Department has been fully transferred; emigrants intending to leave Fiji within 12 months are allowed to transfer up to F$100,000 a family and up to F$50,000 a single person. Nonresidents departing Fiji permanently may remit up to F$250,000 on departure and thereafter up to F$50,000 every six months. Overseas investments and other forms of capital transfers abroad have been temporarily suspended. The purchase of personal property abroad is not permitted.

Authorized dealers may lend up to F$100,000 to a newly established company or a branch of a company in Fiji (other than a bank) that is controlled directly or indirectly by persons who reside outside Fiji and up to F$30,000 to individual nonresident customers; individual nonresident borrowers must repay their loans before leaving Fiji. Any amounts in excess of these limits require prior approval from the Reserve Bank. The banks may not lend foreign currency to any resident of Fiji without the specific permission of the Reserve Bank. Residents must obtain prior permission from the Reserve Bank to borrow foreign currency in Fiji or abroad.

Individuals are allowed to invest up to a maximum of F$5,000 a family a year offshore for a total of up to F$10 million as follows: F$5 million in foreign currency and F$5 million in securities to acquire foreign currency securities. Nonbank financial institutions are allowed to invest offshore up to F$15 million on approval. Local companies are allowed to remit up to F$300,000 to set up sales office or subsidiaries abroad. The proceeds from the sale or realization of such investment must be sold to authorized dealers. Authorized dealers must obtain permission from the Reserve Bank to borrow abroad.

Gold

Residents may freely purchase, hold, and sell gold coins, but not gold bullion, in Fiji. The exportation of gold coins, except numismatic coins and collectors' pieces, requires specific permission from the Reserve Bank. The importation of gold, other than gold coins, from all sources requires a specific import license issued by the Ministry of Finance and Economic Planning; these are restricted to authorized gold dealers. Gold coins and gold bullion are exempt from fiscal duty but are subject to 10 percent value-added tax (VAT). Gold jewelry is also exempt from fiscal duty but subject to a 10 percent VAT and is not under licensing control. Samples of gold and gold jewelry sent by foreign manufacturers require import licenses if their value exceeds F$200.

Exports of gold jewelry are free of export duty but require licenses if their value exceeds F$1,000. Exports of gold bullion are subject to an export duty of 3 percent. All newly mined gold is refined in Australia and sold at free market prices.

Changes During 1994

Exchange Arrangement

January 1. Transactions eligible for the forward exchange contracts concluded by authorized dealers were extended to include payments for dividends and services.

November 11. Provision of forward cover facility to the commercial banks by the Reserve Bank of Fiji was suspended.

Resident and Nonresident Accounts

January 1. The limit on deposits that expatriates are permitted to make in their external accounts was increased to F$20,000 a family from the sale of assets upon departure from Fiji.

Imports and Import Payments

January 1. The limit on advance payments for imports that commercial banks are authorized to make was raised to F$50,000 from F$10,000.

Payments for Invisibles

January 1. The limit on travel allowances that commercial banks are authorized to provide was increased to F$6,000 from F$4,000 an applicant a trip.

January 1. The limit on the use of credit cards for shopping was increased to F$2,000 from F$1,000 for each trip.

January 1. In addition to tuition fees for education, commercial banks were authorized to provide up to F$10,000 a year for students' living allowances.

January 1. The limit on subscription payments that commercial banks are authorized to provide was raised to F$5,000 from F$1,000 a subscription.

January 1. Commercial banks were authorized to pay up to F$15,000 an applicant in proceeds from life insurance that has reached maturity.

January 1. Commercial banks were authorized to pay the full amount due on re-insurance and premium payments.

January 1. Commercial banks were authorized to pay up to F$10,000 a year a beneficiary for professional fees.

January 1. The limit on profit remittances by companies was increased to F$5 million from F$1 million a year. The limit on local companies' remittances to set up sales offices or subsidiaries abroad was increased to F$300,000 from F$200,000.

Capital

January 1. Commercial banks were permitted to lend up to F$100,000 to new and existing companies controlled by nonresidents.

January 1. Nonbank institutions were allowed to invest up to a maximum of F$15 million offshore.

January 1. Individuals were allowed to invest offshore F$5,000 a family up to a total of F$10 million in foreign currency deposits and securities.

FINLAND

(Position as of December 31, 1994)

Exchange Arrangement

The currency of Finland is the Finnish Markka, the external value of which is determined on the basis of underlying supply and demand conditions in the exchange market. The Finnish authorities do not maintain margins in respect of foreign exchange transactions. On December 31, 1994, the middle rate for the U.S. dollar was Fmk 4.7432 per US$1. There are no taxes or subsidies on purchases or sales of foreign exchange.

Authorized banks may deal among themselves, with residents, and with nonresident banks in U.S. dollars and other convertible currencies. Forward premiums and discounts quoted by authorized banks reflect interest rate differentials in the countries of the currencies concerned. The Suomen Pankki (Bank of Finland) does not provide forward cover for commercial banks.

Finland formally accepted the obligations of Article VIII, Sections 2, 3, and 4 of the Fund Agreement, as from September 25, 1979.

Administration of Control

There are no exchange controls. Import and export licensing are administered mainly by a special unit in the Ministry of Trade and Industry. This unit is headed by a board composed of government officials, including a representative of the Suomen Pankki.

In accordance with the Fund's Executive Board Decision No. 144-(52/51) adopted on August 14, 1952, Finland notified the Fund on July 6, 1992 that, in compliance with UN Security Council Resolution No. 757 (1992), certain restrictions had been imposed on the making of payments and transfers for current international transactions in respect of the Federal Republic of Yugoslavia (Serbia/Montenegro).

Prescription of Currency

Settlements with all countries may be made in any convertible currency or through convertible accounts.

Nonresident Accounts

Nonresident accounts may be held in an authorized bank in any convertible currency, including Finnish markkaa. These accounts may be freely credited and debited.

Imports and Import Payments

Most goods may be imported without a license. However, an import license is required for certain agricultural products including those imported under bilateral trade agreements, foodstuffs, fish, fodder, and cut flowers. A monitoring license is required for imports of certain steel products. In addition, all imports from the Democratic People's Republic of Korea and all textile imports and imports of certain plastic products from Taiwan Province of China require a license.

Payments for Invisibles

Payments for invisible transactions are not restricted.

Exports and Export Proceeds

Proceeds from exports are not subject to exchange control. Export licenses are required only for exports of metal ships to be scrapped and goods related to international export control regimes. Sales of arms are strictly controlled.

Proceeds from Invisibles

Receipts from current invisibles are not subject to controls. The funds may be held in a domestic foreign currency account in Finland. The importation of domestic and foreign banknotes and coins is unrestricted.

Capital

Capital transactions, except the acquisition of real estate by foreigners in Finland, are allowed without restriction. Permits are required if the property is to be used for a vacation dwelling. Restrictions on foreign ownership in Finnish companies have been lifted, but a monitoring system concerning the acquisition of the largest companies by foreigners has been put in place. The system is intended to provide the Government an opportunity to intervene if important national interests are considered to be in jeopardy.

The international banking activities of authorized Finnish banks are free from regulation and subject only to certain supervisory reporting requirements.

Gold

Residents may freely hold, buy, and sell gold in any form in Finland.

Changes During 1994

Imports and Import Payments

(See Appendix for a summary of trade measures introduced and eliminated on an EU-wide basis during 1994, page 554.)

Exports and Export Proceeds

July 1. The export levy on corn was suspended until the end of 1994.

FRANCE

(Position as of December 31, 1994)

Exchange Arrangement

The currency of France is the Franc. France participates with Austria, Belgium, Denmark, Germany, Ireland, Luxembourg, the Netherlands, Portugal, and Spain in the exchange rate and intervention mechanism (ERM) of the European Monetary System (EMS).[1] In accordance with this agreement, France maintains the spot exchange rates between the franc and the currencies of the other participants within margins of 15 percent above and below the cross rates based on the central rates expressed in European currency units (ECUs).[2]

The agreement implies that the Bank of France (the central bank) stands ready to buy or sell the currencies of the other participating states in unlimited amounts at specified intervention rates. On December 31, 1994, these rates were as follows:

Specified Intervention Rates per:	Francs	
	Upper limit	Lower limit
100 Austrian schillings	65.35450	41.05330
100 Belgian or Luxembourg francs	18.88000	14.00500
100 Danish kroner	102.10000	75.72000
100 Deutsche mark	389.48000	288.81000
1 Irish pound	9.38950	6.96400
100 Netherlands guilders	345.65000	256.35000
100 Portuguese escudos[3]	3.93700	2.91990
100 Spanish pesetas[4]	4.92250	3.65050

The participants in the EMS do not maintain the exchange rates for other currencies within fixed limits. However, to ensure a proper functioning of the system, they intervene in concert to smooth out fluctuations in exchange rates, the intervention currencies being each other's, the ECU, and the U.S. dollar. Indicative rates for 21 currencies are published daily by the central bank on the basis of market rates.[5] On December 31, 1994, the rate was F 5.3350 per US$1. There are no taxes or subsidies on purchases or sales of foreign exchange.

Fixed conversion rates in terms of the franc apply to the CFP franc, which is the currency of the overseas territories of French Polynesia, New Caledonia, and Wallis and Futuna Islands, and to the two CFA francs, which are the currencies of two groups of African countries that are linked to the French Treasury through an Operations Account.[6] These fixed parities are CFPF 1 per F 0.055 and CFAF 1 per F 0.01, respectively.

Registered banks in France and Monaco, which may also act on behalf of banks established abroad or in Operations Account countries, are permitted to deal spot or forward in the exchange market in France. Registered banks may also deal spot and forward with their correspondents in foreign markets in all currencies. Nonbank residents may purchase foreign exchange forward in respect of specified transactions. All residents, including nonenterprise individuals, may purchase or sell foreign exchange forward without restriction. Forward sales of foreign currency are not restricted, whether or not they are for hedging purposes.

France formally accepted the obligations of Article VIII, Sections 2, 3, and 4 of the Fund Agreement, as from February 15, 1961.

Administration of Control

All exchange control regulations have been phased out on the basis of Decree No. 89–938 of December 29, 1989.

The Directorate of the Treasury of the Ministry of the Economy is the coordinating agency for financial relations with foreign countries. It is responsible for all matters relating to inward and outward direct investment and has certain powers over mat-

---

[1]Austria became a member of the European Union on January 1, 1995 and joined the ERM of the EMS on January 9, 1995.

[2]Effective August 2, 1993, the intervention thresholds of the currencies participating in the ERM of the EMS, except those of the deutsche mark and the Netherlands guilder, were widened from ± 2.25 percent to ± 15 percent around the bilateral central exchange rates; the fluctuational band of the deutsche mark and the Netherlands guilder remained unchanged at ± 2.25 percent.

[3]Effective March 6, 1995, the upper and lower limits were changed to 3.79920 and 2.51770.

[4]Effective March 6, 1995, the upper and lower limits were changed to 4.57780 and 3.38510.

[5]Austrian schillings, Belgian francs, Canadian dollars, Danish kroner, deutsche mark, Djibouti francs, ECUs, Finnish markkaa, Greek drachmas, Irish pounds, Italian lire, Japanese yen, Netherlands guilders, Norwegian kroner, Portuguese escudos, pounds sterling, Spanish pesetas, Swedish kronor, Swiss francs, U.S. dollars, and new zaïres.

[6]Benin, Burkina Faso, Côte d'Ivoire, Mali, Niger, Senegal, and Togo (franc de la Communauté financière Africaine, issued by the BCEAO); and Cameroon, Central African Republic, Chad, Congo, Equatorial Guinea, and Gabon (franc de la Coopération financière Afrique centrale, issued by the BEAC).

ters relating to insurance, reinsurance, annuities, and the like. The execution of all transfers has been delegated to registered banks and stockbrokers and to the Postal Administration. The Directorate General of Customs and Indirect Taxes establishes import and export procedures and controls within the framework of commercial policy directives given by the Directorate of Foreign Economic Relations (DREE). Technical visas required for certain imports and exports are issued by the appropriate ministry or by the Directorate General of Customs and Indirect Taxes. The Ministry of Industry has certain responsibilities in respect of licensing contracts and technical assistance contracts.

Prescription of Currency

Settlements with the Operations Account countries may be made in francs or the currency issued by any institute of issue that maintains an Operations Account with the French Treasury.[7] Settlements with all other countries may be made in any of the currencies of those countries or through nonresident foreign accounts in francs. Importers and exporters are free to invoice in any currency.

Resident and Nonresident Accounts

All residents, including individuals and enterprises not engaged in international trade, are permitted to hold ECU-denominated accounts in France, accounts denominated in foreign currency in France or abroad, and accounts denominated in French francs abroad.

Nonresident accounts in francs may be freely opened by registered banks for nonresidents, including French nationals (other than officials) who are residing abroad. Since March 1989, all restrictions on overdrafts and advances on nonresident-held franc accounts have been lifted.

Emigrants of foreign or French nationality may take out all of their assets upon departure. In addition, nonresidents may hold foreign currency accounts with French and foreign-owned banks.

Imports and Import Payments

Imports of goods that originate in other countries and that are subject to quantitative restrictions require individual licenses. Some imports from non-EU countries are subject to minimum prices; these require an administrative visa and sometimes, ex-

ceptionally, an import license. Certain imports require certificates of origin.

For import control purposes, countries other than those that are accorded privileged treatment are divided into three groups according to the extent of import liberalization: (1) the former Organization for European Economic Cooperation (OEEC) countries, their dependent territories and certain former dependent territories, Canada, Egypt, Ethiopia, Fiji, Finland, Israel, Jordan, Lebanon, Liberia, Sudan, Syrian Arab Republic, United States, and Western Samoa; (2) some specified countries;[8] and (3) China, Democratic People's Republic of Korea, and Mongolia. Goods covered by the import liberalization arrangements applicable to one country may be imported freely from another country, provided that the country of origin and the country of shipment both benefit from the same degree of liberalization.

Imports of practically all industrial products from countries in group (1) are free of quantitative restrictions, but restrictions are applied to a number of agricultural and electronic products; there is relatively little difference between the lists of goods that may be imported freely from different countries in this group. Imports of certain industrial products from countries in group (2) are restricted, and restrictions are applied to these and to certain additional industrial products from group (3) countries. For some commodities, global quotas are allocated annually (for petroleum and petroleum products) or semiannually and apply to all countries (other than those that have bilaterally negotiated quotas or receive privileged treatment). Imports from all countries of certain agricultural items and certain raw materials are free of quantitative restrictions.

Imports from non-EU countries of most products covered by the Common Agricultural Policy (CAP) of the EU are subject to variable import levies that have replaced all previous barriers to imports; common EU regulations are also applied to imports from non-EU countries of most other agricultural and livestock products.

Liberalized imports are not subject to trade controls but do require a customs document, which constitutes the customs declaration. For some liberalized imports, an administrative visa issued by the

----

[7]Comprising the institutes of issue of the Operations Account countries and the Overseas Institute of Issue (for New Caledonia, French Polynesia, Mayotte, and Wallis and Futuna Islands).

[8]The Islamic State of Afghanistan, Argentina, Australia, Bhutan, Bolivia, Brazil, Chile, Colombia, Costa Rica, Cuba, Dominican Republic, Ecuador, El Salvador, Guatemala, Haiti, Honduras, India, Indonesia, Islamic Republic of Iran, Iraq, Republic of Korea, Libyan Arab Jamahiriya, Mexico, Myanmar, Nepal, New Zealand, Nicaragua, Pakistan, Panama, Paraguay, Peru, Philippines, Saudi Arabia, South Africa, Sri Lanka, Thailand, Uruguay, Venezuela, and Republic of Yemen.

Central Customs Administration or by the appropriate ministry is required on an import declaration. Imports of the products of the European Coal and Steel Community (ECSC) require such administrative visas when originating in non-ECSC countries.

Other imports generally require individual import licenses. These are granted up to quotas determined on an individual commodity basis or for a group of commodities and apply to specified countries or areas in accordance with trade agreements or an import plan drawn up for a definite period. Imports of some products must pass through designated customs offices. Documents accompanying goods passing through customs must be written in or translated into French.

Quantitative import restrictions consist of EU-wide restrictions and national restrictions. The former include bilaterally agreed restrictions on textile imports under the Multifiber Arrangement (MFA) and voluntary export restraints on a number of agricultural and industrial products negotiated at the EU level. EU-wide restrictions are enforced through import licensing subject to prior authorization. National restrictions on imports from third countries that are in free circulation within the EU are enforced through temporary import restrictions authorized by the EU Commission under Article 115 of the EEC Treaty. In cases where the restrictions are not officially recognized by the EU (e.g., industry-to-industry understandings that do not directly involve member governments), import restrictions are enforced through national import licensing or standards and certification procedures. Automatic licensing is granted for imports that are under surveillance at either the EU or the national level.

Payments for imports from foreign countries may be made by credit to a foreign account in francs, with foreign currency purchased in the French exchange market, or by debiting a foreign currency account in France or abroad. All residents and international trading houses may freely open accounts in foreign currencies in France with registered banks or abroad (also in French francs) without limit on the credit balance. Payments may be made by transfer through a registered bank, by credit card, by check, by compensation of debts or claims, or by banknotes. The amounts that may be transferred through postal channels are not subject to limitation, but, in practice, the Postal Administration does not make import payments valued at over F 250,000. Registered banks may, without special authorization, permit advance payments to be made that are provided for in the commercial contract. There is no restriction on the use of suppliers' credits.

Payments for Invisibles

Payments to foreign countries by residents for current invisibles have to be reported for statistical purposes but are not restricted as to amount. Registered banks are permitted to approve applications for payments for all categories of current invisibles without limitation. Remittances abroad for family support and donations to nonresidents are freely permitted.

Irrespective of the exchange control regulations, certain transactions between persons or firms in France and abroad are subject to restriction; these include certain transactions relating to insurance, reinsurance, and road and river transport.

There are no limits on expenditures for travel abroad. There is no restriction on the amount of foreign or domestic banknotes resident and nonresident travelers may take out, but amounts exceeding F 50,000 or its equivalent must be declared to customs upon departure.

Exports and Export Proceeds

Certain goods on a prohibited list may be exported only under a special license. Some other exports also require individual licenses, but if their total value does not exceed F 10,000 (F 100,000 for art objects or collectors' items), they may be permitted without any formality, subject to certain exceptions.

Exporters are allowed to cover forward for an unlimited period and may hold foreign currency accounts at home and abroad without limit on the credit balance. Registered banks may freely extend foreign currency advances to exporters; such advances and their repayment may be settled by the receipts of the corresponding exports.

Certain goods purchased in France by persons not normally residing in France are considered exports, even when paid for in francs, and are exempt from taxes.

Proceeds from Invisibles

All proceeds from transactions in invisibles may be retained. With minor exceptions for certain types of transactions, services performed for nonresidents do not require licenses.

Resident and nonresident travelers may bring in any amount of banknotes and coins (except gold coins) in francs, CFA francs, CFP francs, or any foreign currency; amounts of F 50,000 or more, however, must be declared to customs upon arrival. At the request of Algeria, Morocco, and Tunisia, banknotes issued by those countries may not be exchanged.

Capital

Capital movements between France and Monaco and the Operations Account countries are free of exchange control; purchases of French and foreign securities abroad and the corresponding outward transfers of resident-owned capital are free; capital receipts from foreign countries are permitted freely. Residents' capital assets abroad are not subject to repatriation. The transfer abroad of nonresident-owned funds, including the sales proceeds of capital assets, is not restricted.

French and foreign securities held in France by nonresidents may be exported, provided that they have been deposited with a registered bank in a foreign dossier (*dossier étranger de valeurs mobilières*); French securities held under a foreign dossier may also be sold in France, and the sale proceeds may be transferred abroad. Foreign securities held in France by nonresidents must be deposited with a registered bank; French securities held in France by nonresidents need not be deposited but may not be dealt with or exported unless they have been deposited. Foreign securities held in France by residents must be deposited with a qualified bank or broker. Residents may hold French and foreign securities abroad under the control of a French registered bank or broker.

Subject to compliance with the special regulations concerning inward and outward direct investment, residents may purchase abroad, through registered banks abroad, French and foreign securities that are not quoted on a recognized stock exchange. French and foreign securities may be held or sold abroad but may also be imported and then either held or sold on a French stock exchange. Correspondingly, nonresidents holding French or foreign securities abroad (whether acquired before November 24, 1968 or later) may import them into France through a registered bank and hold them in a foreign dossier or sell them on a French stock exchange.

The exchange control regulations include control over inward direct investments in existing French firms. The basis for control over foreign direct investments is Decree No. 89–938 of December 29, 1989, as amended by Decree No. 92–134 of February 1992, which applies to financial relations with all countries except Monaco and those belonging to the Operations Account Area.

Direct investments are defined as investments leading to control of a company or enterprise. Any participation leading foreign investors to hold more than one-third of the capital is considered direct investment. In the case of firms whose shares are quoted on the stock exchange, the threshold is re-duced to 20 percent of the capital and applies to each individual foreign participation but not to the total of foreign participation. To determine whether a company is under foreign control, the Ministry of Economy and Finance may also take into account any special relationships resulting from stock options, loans, patents and licenses, and commercial contracts.

EU or non-EU investments in new firms are not subject to a prior declaration to the Ministry of Economy. Foreign direct investments in existing French firms generally require prior declaration to the Ministry of Economy. The following foreign investments, however, do not require increases in capital of subsidiaries in which foreign ownership or voting rights exceed 66.66 percent: loans and transactions involving less than F 10 million in craft trades; retail trade; hotels; restaurants; various commercial services; quarries and gravel pits; and acquisitions of agricultural lands, except vineyards and wine-making properties. Juridical and natural persons may freely invest in any project that is at least 50 percent owned by juridical and natural persons residing in the EU, but the completion of the project must be reported to the Ministry of Economy. Investments of EU groups having permanent recognition of EU status are not subject to any prior declaration and are required only to report to the Ministry of Economy within 20 days of completion. The Minister of Economy may issue a finding within one month to prohibit the EU investment if public health, order, security, or national security is considered to be in danger. Non-EU investments of less than F 50 million, if the turnover of the acquired firm is less than F 500 million, are not restricted but must be reported to the Ministry of Economy before completion. The Minister of Economy may issue a finding within 30 days, at the maximum, to prohibit the investment if public health, order, security, or national security is considered to be in danger.

The Minister of the Economy is allowed a one month period, at the maximum, during which a non-EU investment can be suspended if the investment involves more than F 50 million or if the turnover of the acquired firm is more than F 500 million.

The liquidation proceeds of foreign direct investment in France may be freely transferred abroad; the liquidation must be reported to the Ministry within 20 days of its occurrence. Foreign direct investments by residents are not restricted, but if such investments exceed F 5 million, they must be reported to the Bank of France within 20 days. The liquidation of direct investments abroad is free from any prior application, provided that the corresponding funds, if they exceed F 5 million, are reported to the Bank of France.

Foreign issues on the French capital market, except issues originating in EU countries, are subject to prior authorization from the Ministry of Economy and Finance. Exempt from authorization, however, are operations in connection with (1) loans backed by a guarantee from the French Government, and (2) shares similar to securities that are already officially quoted on a stock exchange in France.

Borrowing abroad in French francs or foreign currencies by natural or juridical persons, whether public or private persons, whose normal residence or registered office is in France or by branches or subsidiaries in France of juridical persons whose registered office is abroad, is unrestricted. Application of the controls over direct investment and borrowing is delegated to the Bank of France insofar as these activities relate to French firms engaged primarily in real estate business. Lending in French francs to nonresidents is not restricted. Registered banks are free to lend foreign currency to residents. Nonresidents may freely purchase French short-term securities, including treasury bills, *bons de caisse*, and private drafts.

Gold

Residents are free to hold, acquire regularly, and dispose of gold in any form in France. They may continue to hold abroad any gold they held there before November 25, 1968. There is a free gold market for bars and coins in Paris, to which residents and nonresidents have free access and in which normally no official intervention takes place.

Imports and exports of "monetary" gold (defined as gold having a fineness or a weight that is recognized in the gold market) into or from the territory of continental France are now governed by the regulations applying to ordinary goods. Movements of industrial gold are subject to a simple declaration, as are imports and exports of manufactured articles containing a minor quantity of gold, such as gold-filled and gold-plated articles. Collectors' items of gold and gold antiques are subject to specific regulations.

Most gold coins are traded on the Paris stock exchange. In domestic trading, purchases of bars and coins are not subject to a value-added tax. Imports of monetary gold, except gold imported by the Bank of France, are subject to customs duty and value-added tax. Domestic transactions in gold and gold coins are subject to a capital gains tax.

Changes During 1994

No significant changes occured in the exchange and trade system during 1994.

(See Appendix for a summary of trade measures introduced and eliminated on an EU-wide basis during 1994, page 554.)

GABON

(Position as of December 31, 1994)

Exchange Arrangement

The currency of Gabon is the CFA Franc,[1] which is pegged to the French franc, the intervention currency, at the fixed rate of CFAF 1 per F 0.01. The official buying and selling rate is CFAF 100 per F 1. Exchange transactions in French francs between the BEAC and commercial banks take place at the same rate. Buying and selling rates for certain foreign currencies are also officially posted, with quotations based on the fixed rate for the French franc and the rate for the currency concerned in the Paris exchange market, and include a commission. Commissions are levied at the rate of 0.25 percent on transfers made by the banks for their own accounts and on all private capital transfers to countries that are not members of the BEAC, except those made for the account of the Treasury, national accounting offices, national and international public agencies, and private entities granted exemption by the Ministry of Finance, Budget, and Participations because of the nature of their activities. There are no taxes or subsidies on purchases or sales of foreign exchange. There are no arrangements for forward cover against exchange rate risk operating in the official or the commercial banking sector.

With the exception of those relating to gold, Gabon's exchange control measures do not apply to (1) France (and its overseas departments and territories) and Monaco; and (2) all other countries whose bank of issue is linked with the French Treasury by an Operations Account (Benin, Burkina Faso, Cameroon, Central African Republic, Chad, Comoros, Congo, Côte d'Ivoire, Equatorial Guinea, Mali, Niger, Senegal, and Togo). Hence, all payments to these countries may be made freely. All other countries are considered foreign countries.

Administration of Control

The Directorate of Financial Institutions of the Ministry of Finance, Budget, and Participations supervises borrowing and lending abroad. Exchange control is administered by the Minister of Finance,

Budget, and Participations, who has partly delegated approval authority for current payments to the authorized banks and that with respect to the external position of the banks to the BEAC. All exchange transactions relating to foreign countries must be effected through authorized intermediaries—that is, the Postal Administration and authorized banks. Import and export authorizations, where necessary, are issued by the Directorate of External Trade of the Ministry of Commerce and Industry.

Prescription of Currency

Since Gabon is an Operations Account country, settlements with France (as defined above), Monaco, and the Operations Account countries are made in CFA francs, French francs, or the currency of any other institute of issue that maintains an Operations Account with the French Treasury. Settlements with all other countries are usually made through correspondent banks in France in any of the currencies of those countries or in French francs through foreign accounts in francs.

Nonresident Accounts

The regulations pertaining to nonresident accounts are based on regulations applied in France. Because the BEAC has suspended the repurchase of BEAC banknotes circulating outside the territories of its member countries, BEAC banknotes received by foreign correspondents' authorized banks and mailed to the BEAC agency in Libreville may not be credited to foreign accounts in francs.

Imports and Import Payments

Imports from member countries of the Central African Customs and Economic Union (UDEAC) are free of formalities, with the exception of refined vegetable oil, which requires prior approval. All imports whose value exceeds CFAF 500,000 from countries outside the UDEAC are subject to authorization. Quantitative restrictions are maintained only on imports of sugar, vegetable oil, soap, mineral water, and cement. For perishables and spare parts, an anticipatory authorization is given to simplify administrative procedures. Imports from countries outside the UDEAC that are similar to, and compete with, domestic products are subject to

---

[1]The CFA franc circulating in Gabon is issued by the Bank of Central African States (BEAC) and is legal tender also in Cameroon, the Central African Republic, Chad, the Congo, and Equatorial Guinea.

licensing, but, with a few exceptions[2] that are established by ministerial order, import authorizations are granted liberally. Some imports are prohibited for security and health reasons. All imports of commercial goods must be insured through authorized insurance companies in Gabon.

Effective January 30, 1994, a new tariff structure was introduced in the context of the UDEAC tax and customs reform. The common duty rates of the UDEAC member countries were reduced to 5 percent for basic necessities, to 10 percent for raw materials and capital goods, to 20 percent for intermediate goods, and to 30 percent for consumer goods.

Quantitative restrictions on the importation of edible oils, bottled water, soap, and cement were lifted with effect from July 5. Quantitative restrictions on the importation of sugar remain in effect.

All import transactions relating to foreign countries must be domiciled with an authorized bank. Authorizations duly endorsed by the Ministry of Foreign Trade and the Ministry of Finance, Budget, and Participations (Directorate of Financial Institutions) entitle importers to purchase the necessary foreign exchange, provided that the shipping documents are submitted to the authorized bank.

Payments for Invisibles

Payments for invisibles to France (as defined above), Monaco, and the Operations Account countries are permitted freely; those to other countries are subject to approval, which is granted when the appropriate documents are submitted. For many types of payment, the approval authority has been delegated to authorized banks. Payments for invisibles related to trade are permitted freely when the basic trade transaction has been approved or does not require authorization. Transfers of income, in the form of profits, dividends, and royalties, accruing to nonresidents are also permitted freely when the basic transaction has been approved.

Residents traveling for tourism or business purposes to countries in the franc zone are allowed to take out BEAC banknotes up to a limit of CFAF 2 million; amounts in excess of this limit may be taken out in the form of means of payments other than banknotes. Allowances for travel to countries outside the franc zone are subject to the following regulations: (1) for tourist travel, CFAF 100,000 a day, with a maximum of CFAF 2 million a trip; (2) for business travel, CFAF 250,000 a day, with a

maximum of CFAF 5 million a trip; (3) allowances in excess of these limits are subject to the authorization of the Ministry of Finance or, by delegation, the BEAC; and (4) the use of credit cards, which must be issued by resident financial intermediaries and approved by the Ministry of Finance, is limited to the ceilings indicated above for tourism and business travel. Bona fide requests for travel allowances in excess of the existing limits have been granted. Returning resident travelers are required to declare all means of payment in their possession upon arrival at customs and surrender within eight days all means of payment exceeding the equivalent of CFAF 25,000. All resident travelers, regardless of destination, must declare in writing all means of payment at their disposal at the time of departure. The re-exportation by nonresident travelers of means of payment other than banknotes issued abroad and registered in the name of the nonresident traveler is not restricted, subject to documentation that they were purchased with funds drawn from a foreign account in CFA francs or with other foreign exchange. The re-exportation of foreign banknotes is allowed up to the equivalent of CFAF 250,000; the re-exportation of foreign banknotes above these ceilings requires documentation demonstrating either the importation of foreign banknotes or their purchase against other means of payment registered in the name of the traveler or through the use of nonresident deposits lodged in local banks.

Exports and Export Proceeds

Exports require authorization, irrespective of destination. Export transactions relating to foreign countries must be domiciled with an authorized bank. Export proceeds received in currencies other than those of France or an Operations Account country must be surrendered. Export proceeds normally must be received within 150 days of the arrival of the commodities at their destination. The proceeds must be collected and, if received in a foreign currency, surrendered within one month of the due date. All export taxes, other than those on mining and forestry products, have been eliminated; the taxes on mining and forest products are 0.5 percent and 5–11 percent, respectively.

Proceeds from Invisibles

Proceeds from transactions in invisibles with France (as defined above), Monaco, and the Operations Account countries may be retained. All amounts due from residents of other countries in respect of services and all income earned in those

---

[2]Currently totaling about thirty items, including cement, ham, mineral water, plastic goods, sugar, batteries, and refined vegetable oil.

countries from foreign assets must be collected and, if received in foreign currency, surrendered within a month of the due date. Resident and nonresident travelers may bring in any amount of banknotes and coins issued by the BEAC, the Bank of France, or any other bank of issue maintaining an Operations Account with the French Treasury, as well as any amount of foreign banknotes and coins (except gold coins) of countries outside the Operations Account Area.

Capital

Capital movements between Gabon and France (as defined above), Monaco, and the Operations Account countries are free of exchange control. Capital transfers to all other countries exceeding CFAF 500,000 are restricted and require the approval of the Directorate of Financial Institutions, but capital receipts from these countries are permitted freely. All foreign securities, foreign currency, and titles embodying claims on foreign countries or nonresidents that are held in Gabon by residents or nonresidents must be deposited with authorized banks in Gabon.

Special controls in addition to any exchange control requirements that may apply are maintained over borrowing and lending abroad, over inward and outward direct investment, and over the issuing, advertising, or offering for sale of foreign securities in Gabon; these controls apply to the transactions themselves, not to payments or receipts. With the exception of controls over the sale or introduction of foreign securities in Gabon, the control measures do not apply to France (as defined above), Monaco, and the Operations Account countries.

Direct investments abroad[3] must be declared to the Ministry of Finance, Budget, and Participations unless they take the form of a capital increase resulting from reinvestment of undistributed profits; the full or partial liquidation of investments must also be declared to the Ministry unless the operation involves the relinquishing of a shareholding that had previously been approved as constituting a direct investment abroad. Foreign direct investments in Gabon [4] must be declared to the Ministry unless they take the form of a capital increase re-

sulting from the reinvestment of undistributed profits; within two months of receipt of the declaration, the Ministry may request the postponement of the project. The full or partial liquidation of direct investments in Gabon must also be declared to the Ministry unless the operation involves the relinquishing of a shareholding that had previously been approved as constituting a direct investment in Gabon. Both the making and the liquidation of direct investments, whether Gabonese investments abroad or foreign investments in Gabon, must be reported to the ministry within 20 days of the operation. (Direct investments are defined as those that imply control of a company or enterprise.)

The issuing, advertising, or offering for sale of foreign securities in Gabon requires prior authorization from the Ministry of Finance, Budget, and Participations. Exempt from authorization, however, are operations in connection with (1) loans backed by a guarantee from the Gabonese Government; and (2) shares similar to securities whose issuing, advertising, or offering for sale in Gabon has previously been authorized.

Borrowing abroad by natural or juridical persons, whether public or private, whose normal residence or registered office is in Gabon, or by branches or subsidiaries in Gabon of juridical persons whose registered office is abroad, requires prior authorization from the Ministry of Finance, Budget, and Participations. The following are, however, exempt from this authorization: (1) loans constituting a direct investment abroad for which prior approval has been obtained, as indicated above; (2) loans directly connected with the rendering of services abroad by the persons or firms mentioned above, or with the financing of commercial transactions either between Gabon and countries abroad or between foreign countries in which these persons or firms take part; (3) loans contracted by registered banks; and (4) loans other than those mentioned above, when the total amount outstanding does not exceed CFAF 50 million for any one borrower. However, the contracting of loans referred to under (4) that are free of authorization and each repayment must be declared to the Directorate of Financial Institutions within 20 days of the operation unless the total outstanding amount of all loans contracted abroad by the borrower is CFAF 5 million or less.

Lending abroad by natural or juridical persons, whether public or private, whose normal residence or registered office is in Gabon, or by branches or subsidiaries in Gabon of juridical persons whose registered office is abroad, requires prior authorization from the Ministry of Finance, Budget, and

---

[3]Including those made through foreign companies that are directly or indirectly controlled by persons in Gabon and those that are made by branches or subsidiaries abroad of companies in Gabon.

[4]Including those made by companies in Gabon that are directly or indirectly under foreign control and those made by branches or subsidiaries in Gabon of foreign companies.

Participations. The following are, however, exempt from this authorization: (1) loans granted by registered banks; and (2) other loans, when the total amount outstanding does not exceed CFAF 50 million for any one lender. However, loans that are free of authorization and each repayment must be declared to the Directorate of Financial Institutions within 20 days of the operation except when the total outstanding amount of all loans granted abroad by the lender does not exceed CFAF 5 million.

Under the Investment Code of July 6, 1989, any enterprise to be established in Gabon, whether domestic or foreign, is granted, under certain conditions, reduced duties and taxes on specified income. In addition to fiscal privileges, the code provides for four categories of preferential treatment. Eligible companies may receive protection against foreign competition and may be given priority in the allocation of imports, public credit, and government contracts. Foreign companies investing in Gabon must offer shares for purchase by Gabonese nationals for an amount equivalent to at least 10 percent of the companies' capital. Non-Gabonese firms or individuals are not permitted to own land in Gabon.

Gold

Residents are free to hold, acquire, and dispose of gold in any form in Gabon. Imports and exports of gold require the authorization of the Ministry of Finance, Budget, and Participations. Exempt from this requirement are (1) imports and exports by or on be-half of the monetary authorities, and (2) imports and exports of manufactured articles containing a small quantity of gold (such as gold-filled or gold-plated articles). The exportation of gold is the monopoly of the Société gabonaise de recherches et d'exploitation minières. However, imports of gold exempted from licensing and authorization requirements are subject to customs declaration.

Changes During 1994

Exchange Arrangement

January 12. The CFA franc was devalued to CFAF 100 per F 1 from CFAF 50 per F 1.

Imports and Import Payments

January 30. A new tariff structure was introduced in the context of the UDEAC tax and customs reform. The common duty rates of the UDEAC member countries were reduced to 5 percent for basic necessities, to 10 percent for raw materials and capital goods, to 20 percent for intermediate goods, and to 30 percent for consumer goods.

July 5. Quantitative restrictions on the importation of edible oils, bottled water, soap, and cement were lifted and replaced by a temporary surtax of 30 percent.

Exports and Export Proceeds

July 5. All export taxes, other than those on mining and forestry products, were eliminated.

THE GAMBIA

(Position as of December 31, 1994)

Exchange Arrangement

The currency of The Gambia is the Gambian Dalasi. Commercial banks and foreign exchange bureaus are free to transact among themselves, with the Central Bank of The Gambia (CBG), or with customers at exchange rates agreed on by the parties to these transactions. The CBG conducts a foreign exchange market review session on the last working day of each week with the participation of the commercial banks and foreign exchange bureaus. During this session, the average market rate during the week is announced as the rate for customs valuation purposes for the following week. On December 31, 1994, the midpoint exchange rate of the dalasi in the interbank market was D 9.5785 per US$1. There are no arrangements for forward cover against exchange rate risk operating in the official or the commercial banking sector. There are no taxes or subsidies on purchases or sales of foreign exchange.

The Gambia formally accepted the obligations of Article VIII, Sections 2, 3, and 4 of the Fund Agreement as from January 21, 1993.

Administration of Control

The Exchange Control Act was repealed in November 1992, and no exchange controls are in force.

Prescription of Currency

Settlements with other countries may be made and received from nonresident sources in dalasis or in any convertible currency. Settlements with the Central Bank of West African States (BCEAO) (Benin, Burkina Faso, Côte d'Ivoire, Niger, Senegal, and Togo), and also Ghana, Guinea, Guinea-Bissau, Liberia, Mali, Mauritania, Nigeria, and Sierra Leone are normally made through the West African Clearing House.

External Accounts

Accounts denominated in dalasis held by residents of other countries are designated external accounts. Such accounts may be opened without reference to the CBG when commercial banks are satisfied that the account holder's source of funds is from abroad in convertible foreign currency. Designated external accounts may be credited with payments from residents of other countries, with transfers from other external accounts, and with the proceeds of sales through the banking system of other convertible currencies. They may be debited for payments to residents of other countries, for transfers to other external accounts, and for purchases of other convertible currencies.

Imports and Import Payments

The importation of certain specified goods is prohibited from all sources for social, health, or security reasons. All other imports are freely permitted under open general licenses.

All merchandise imports are subject to a national sales tax of 10 percent of the c.i.f. value; imports by the Government, diplomatic missions, and charitable organizations are exempt from this tax.

Payments for Invisibles

There are no restrictions on payments for invisibles. Visitors to The Gambia are not required to declare foreign currency in their possession.

Exports and Export Proceeds

The exportation of forestry products is subject to prior authorization from the Forestry Department. The exportation of all other goods can take place without individual licenses.

Proceeds from Invisibles

There is no restriction on the importation of foreign currency notes or Gambian banknotes.

Capital

Inward transfers for purposes of direct equity investment are not restricted but must be reported to the CBG for statistical purposes. Prior approval from the CBG is not required for residents to accept loans in foreign currency from any source.

Commercial banks may provide overdraft facilities to members of diplomatic and international missions in The Gambia. Since the repeal of the Exchange Control Act in November 1992, loans and advances by commercial banks to nonresidents no longer require authorization from the CBG. Foreign exchange working balances held by the commercial banks and exchange bureaus are subject to limits set by the CBG; amounts held in excess of these limits must be offered for sale in the interbank market or offered to the CBG. These limits must be observed on a weekly basis and transactions must be reported daily to the CBG. In addition, The Gambia Telecommunication Company (GamTel), which is a parastatal organization, is temporarily permitted to maintain limited working balances in foreign exchange. The limits must be observed on a monthly basis, and the amounts held must be reported within the same period to the CBG. Any amount in excess of the limit must be surrendered to a commercial bank in The Gambia.

Gold

The importation of gold coins and bullion requires the approval of the CBG.

Changes During 1994

No significant changes occurred in the exchange and trade system.

GEORGIA

(Position as of December 31, 1994)

Exchange Arrangement

The currency of the Republic of Georgia is the Georgian Coupon (GEK),[1] the external value of which is determined in fixing sessions that are held at the Tbilisi Interbank Currency Exchange, in which the National Bank of Georgia (NBG) and the major commercial banks participate.[2] The official exchange rates for the U.S. dollar and the Russian ruble are determined in these sessions. The official rates are determined for convertible currencies on the basis of the cross rates for the U.S. dollar and the currencies concerned in the international market. For the currencies of the Baltic countries, rates are determined on the basis of the official cross rates for the Russian ruble as published by the Central Bank of Russia. The official exchange rates are used for budget and tax accounting purposes, as well as for all payments between the Government and enterprises and other legal entities. At the end of December 1994, the official exchange rate quoted by the NBG for the U.S. dollar was GEK 1.28 million per US$1. For all commercial transactions, the exchange rates of the coupon are negotiated freely between the banks and foreign exchange bureaus that are licensed by the NBG and their customers.

Foreign exchange bureaus are permitted to buy and sell foreign currency notes. There are no taxes or subsidies on purchases or sales of foreign exchange. There are no arrangements for forward cover against exchange rate risk operating in the official or the commercial banking sector.

Administration of Control

The NBG is responsible for administering exchange control regulations, which are formulated in collaboration with the Ministry of Finance. Decree No. 259 of March 5, 1992, First-Stage of Liberalization of Foreign Exchange Activity, established the legal basis for the conduct of foreign economic activities in Georgia. The main provisions of this decree (1) allow all enterprises to engage directly in foreign trade, (2) allow all residents to acquire and hold foreign currency and engage in foreign transactions with a licensed foreign exchange dealer, and (3) authorize banks to open foreign exchange accounts for all residents. Trade with countries other than the Baltic countries, Russia, and the other countries of the former Soviet Union is controlled by the State Committee on Foreign Economic Relations (SCFER) (Decree No. 265 of March 31, 1993 on Quotas and Licensing of Merchandise Trade).

The NBG has the authority to issue general foreign exchange licenses to banks that will permit them to engage in foreign exchange transactions with residents and nonresidents and to open correspondent accounts with banks outside Georgia. The NBG also has the authority to issue internal licenses to banks that will permit them to engage in the same range of foreign exchange transactions as general license holders, except that holders of internal licenses may not open correspondent accounts with banks abroad. All transfers of foreign exchange by holders of internal licenses must be carried out through correspondent accounts held either with the NBG or with a bank that holds a general license. As of the end of December 1994, 35 banks held general licenses, while 88 banks held internal licenses. The NBG also has the authority to issue licenses for the establishment of exchange bureaus to engage in cash transactions of all kinds.

Prescription of Currency

Settlements with the Baltic countries, Russia, and the other countries of the former Soviet Union are made in some cases through a system of correspondent accounts and in others, in convertible currency. Settlements with countries (including the Baltic countries, Russia, and the other countries of the former Soviet Union) with which Georgia maintains bilateral payments agreements are effected in accordance with the terms of the agreements. Settlements with other countries may be made in any convertible currency.

Resident and Nonresident Accounts

Resident individuals and enterprises are permitted to open and operate foreign exchange accounts at authorized banks. There are no restrictions on the use of these accounts, and the balances may be used for all authorized transactions. The opening of for-

---

[1]On April 5, 1993, the National Bank of Georgia began to issue coupons to circulate along with the Russian ruble; on August 3, 1993, the Georgian coupon was declared sole legal tender.

[2]The frequency of the auction was increased from once to twice a week from mid-September 1994.

eign exchange accounts abroad is subject to authorization by the Ministry of Finance and the NBG. Nonresidents may maintain foreign exchange and local currency accounts with banks in Georgia.

Imports and Exports

There are no quantitative restrictions on imports, and licenses are not required, except for weapons, narcotics, industrial equipment, pharmaceuticals, and agricultural pesticides; licenses are issued by the SCFER. A customs duty of 12 percent is levied on all imports, except food items (excluding tobacco and alcoholic beverages) and imports under barter operations, irrespective of the currency denomination of the contract. A customs duty of 20 percent is levied on all imports under barter operations but not on imports under government agreements. All imports are subject to a general customs processing fee of 0.2 percent. Foreign exchange to pay for imports may be purchased freely from authorized banks at market rates.

There is no legal prohibition on exports, but licenses are required for items such as food and raw materials. Exports of arms, narcotics, precious metals, and some raw materials are subject, in practice, to prohibitions. Exports of some raw materials may be limited to the quantities available after allocation for domestic consumption has been made or export commitments under bilateral agreements have been met. The licensing of exports is administered by the SCFER, which takes into account whether exports would create shortages of goods in the domestic market and whether quotas under bilateral agreements have been, or will be, fulfilled. All exports are subject to a general customs processing fee of 0.2 percent.

Exporters are required to surrender to the NBG 32 percent of proceeds in convertible currencies.

Payments for and Proceeds from Invisibles

Residents may freely purchase foreign exchange to make payments for invisible transactions or use foreign exchange balances in their foreign exchange accounts with authorized banks without restriction. Proceeds from invisibles are subject to the same reg-

ulations and procedures as those applicable to proceeds from exports.

The importation of foreign currency notes is unrestricted, but amounts must be declared on arrival.

The exportation of foreign currency notes by nonresidents is permitted up to a limit equal to the amount originally imported. The exportation of foreign currency notes by residents is limited to $500, or its equivalent, without supporting documentation from a commercial bank that the notes were legally obtained and to $4,000 with such documentation. Nominal remittances remain unrestricted.

Capital

Inward and outward capital operations are not restricted but are subject to registration requirements for monitoring purposes.

Gold

A license is required to conduct both international and domestic trade in gold.

Changes During 1994

Exchange Arrangement

April 1. Transactions in the Tbilisi Interbank Currency Exchange were permitted only in cash.

September 19. The official and interbank exchange rates were unified, as noncash as well as cash transactions were permitted on the Tbilisi Interbank Currency Exchange.

Resident and Nonresident Accounts

September 1. Restrictions on the withdrawal of foreign currency and coupon currency from bank accounts were lifted.

Payments for and Proceeds from Invisibles

October 19. A limit was introduced on the amount of foreign currency notes that residents would be permitted to carry abroad. The limit would be $500 without supporting documentation from a commercial bank that notes were legally obtained and $4,000 with such documentation.

GERMANY

(Position as of December 31, 1994)

Exchange Arrangement

The currency of Germany is the Deutsche Mark. Germany participates with Austria, Belgium, Denmark, France, Ireland, Luxembourg, the Netherlands, Portugal, and Spain in the exchange rate and intervention mechanism (ERM) of the European Monetary System (EMS).[1]

The arrangements imply that the Deutsche Bundesbank (the central bank) stands ready to buy or sell the currencies of the other participating states in unlimited amounts at specified intervention rates.[2] On December 31, 1994, these rates were as follows:

Specified Intervention Rates per:	Deutsche Mark	
	Upper limit	Lower limit
100 Austrian schillings	16.5050	12.2410
100 Belgian or		
Luxembourg francs	5.6300	4.1750
100 Danish kroner	30.4450	22.5750
100 French francs	34.6250	25.6750
1 Irish pound	2.8000	2.0760
100 Netherlands guilders	90.7708	86.7800
100 Portuguese escudos[3]	1.1740	0.8710
100 Spanish pesetas[4]	1.4680	1.0880

In principle, interventions within the EMS are made in participating currencies but may also take place in third currencies, such as the U.S. dollar. Participants in the EMS do not maintain exchange rates for other currencies within fixed limits but do intervene from time to time to smooth out erratic fluctuations in exchange rates.

Official middle, buying, and selling rates are quoted for 17 foreign currencies on the foreign exchange market of Frankfurt am Main.[5] On Decem-

ber 31, 1994, the official middle rate for the U.S. dollar was DM 1.5488 per US$1. There are no taxes or subsidies on purchases or sales of foreign exchange. Residents and nonresidents may freely negotiate forward exchange contracts for both commercial and financial transactions in all leading convertible currencies in the domestic exchange market and at major international foreign exchange markets. There are no officially fixed rates in the forward exchange market, and all transactions are negotiated at free market rates.

Germany formally accepted the obligations of Article VIII, Sections 2, 3, and 4 of the Fund Agreement, as from February 15, 1961.

Administration of Control

The administration of control in respect of imports and exports of goods and services is operated by the Federal Ministry of Economics; the Federal Ministry of Finance; the Federal Ministry of Transportation; the Federal Office for Economics; the Federal Office for Export Control; the Federal Ministry for Food, Agriculture, and Forestry; the Federal Office for Food and Forestry; the Federal Office for Agricultural Marketing Organization; and the Ministries of Economics of the Laender. All banks in Germany are permitted to carry out foreign exchange transactions.

In accordance with the Fund's Executive Board Decision No. 144–(52/51) adopted on August 14, 1952, Germany notified the Fund on November 5, 1992 that, in compliance with UN Security Council Resolution No. 757 (1992), certain restrictions had been imposed on the making of payments and transfers for current international transactions in respect of the Federal Republic of Yugoslavia (Serbia/Montenegro). Furthermore, in compliance with UN resolutions, restrictions have been imposed on the making of payments and transfers for current international transactions in respect of Iraq and the Libyan Arab Jamahiriya.

Imports and Import Payments

The import list comprises 10,370 statistical positions. Their treatment is as follows:

---

[1]Austria became a member of the European Union (EU) on January 1, 1995 and joined the ERM of the EMS on January 9, 1995.

[2]Effective August 2, 1993, the intervention thresholds of the currencies participating in the ERM of the EMS, except those of the deutsche mark and the Netherlands guilder, were widened to ±15 percent from ±2.25 percent around the bilateral exchange rates; the fluctuation band of the deutsche mark and the Netherlands guilder remained unchanged at ±2.25 percent.

[3]Effective March 6, 1995, the upper and lower limits were changed to 1.1328 and 0.8401.

[4]Effective March 6, 1995, the upper and lower limits were changed to 1.3650 and 1.0123.

[5]Austrian schillings, Belgian and Luxembourg francs, Canadian dollars, Danish kroner, Finnish markkaa, French francs, Irish pounds, Italian lire, Japanese yen, Netherlands guilders

Norwegian kroner, Portuguese escudos, pounds sterling, Spanish pesetas, Swedish kronor, Swiss francs, and U.S. dollars.

The importation of 1,363 textile items (under the arrangements regarding international trade in textiles) and of certain steel items is governed by bilateral agreements and regulations of the EU with various supplier countries. Imports of pit coal from countries that are not members of the EU and the European Free Trade Association (EFTA) are permitted within the framework of an annual global quota. Imports of brown coal are subject to import licensing from countries on country List C[6] except Bulgaria, the Czech Republic, Poland, Romania, and the Slovak Republic. The importation of certain nontextile goods from China is subject to an annual global quota of the EU. The Common Agricultural Policy of the EU covers 2,054 statistical items; most of these are subject to variable import levies, which have in large part replaced previous barriers to imports. A new recording system for imports of goods and services from other EU member countries was put in place with the completion of the single European market on January 1, 1993.

Payments for imports are unrestricted. Commodity futures may be dealt in freely, and most transit trade transactions may be carried out freely.

Payments for Invisibles

All payments for invisibles may be made freely without individual license. German and foreign notes and coins and other means of payment may be exported freely.

The following transactions—but not the related payments—between residents and nonresidents are subject to restriction: the chartering of foreign ships from residents of specified countries and the conclusion of related sea freight contracts; the use of foreign boats in certain inland waterway traffic; and transactions with specified countries (which do not grant reciprocal treatment) for hull and marine liability insurance and aviation insurance, except passenger accident insurance.

Exports and Export Proceeds

With few exceptions (for strategic goods), export transactions may be carried out freely. For statistical purposes, an export notification is required for all goods. Certain exports (mostly strategic goods) are subject to individual or general licensing. The customs authorities exercise control over export declarations. Foreign exchange proceeds from exports do

not have to be declared or surrendered and may be used for all payments.

Proceeds from Invisibles

With few exceptions, services performed for nonresidents do not require a license. However, licenses are required for transactions related to specific sea services and for technical assistance involving the delivery to residents of non-OECD countries of construction drawings, materials, and instructions for manufacture, if such assistance is for the production of goods whose exportation requires a license (strategic goods). There are no restrictions on the receipt of payments for services rendered to nonresidents. German and foreign notes and coins and other means of payment may be imported freely.

Capital

Residents and nonresidents may export capital freely without a license. Foreign and international bond issues on the German capital market do not require official approval. All resident banks, including legally independent foreign-owned banks, may lead-manage issues of bonds denominated in deutsche mark. Domestic and foreign securities of all types may be imported and exported freely.

Following the changes in regulations beginning March 12, 1981, no restrictions are applied to the sale of German money market papers and fixed-interest securities by residents to nonresidents. Nonresidents' direct investments in Germany, purchases of real estate in Germany for investment or personal use, and purchases of German or foreign equities do not require approval. There are no limitations on the disposal of legacies located in Germany and inherited by nonresidents or on legacies located abroad and inherited by residents. Residents are not required to repatriate or surrender their foreign exchange earnings or holdings.

Banks are subject to minimum reserve requirements on the level of their foreign liabilities with maturities of less than four years. The minimum reserve ratios on foreign liabilities, which are, in principle, the same as those applied to domestic liabilities, were reduced effective March 1, 1993 and effective March 1, 1994 and are now 5 percent on sight deposits and 2 percent on savings and time deposits. Book liabilities to nonresidents in foreign currency are exempt from reserve requirements to the extent of the book claims on nonresidents in foreign currency with maturities of less than four years. Banks are free to pay interest on domestic or foreign currency balances held by nonresidents.

---

[6]Countries on List C are Albania, the former member countries of the Council for Mutual Economic Assistance (CMEA) except China, Hungary, the Democratic People's Republic of Korea, and Viet Nam. All other countries are on List A or B.

Gold

Residents may freely hold gold in any form and may negotiate with residents or nonresidents, both at home or abroad. There is a free gold market in Frankfurt am Main. Imports and exports of gold in any form by residents and nonresidents are unrestricted and free of license; a customs declaration, however, is required.

Imports of gold bullion and coins, unworked gold, and gold alloys, while free of customs duty, are subject to value-added tax at the rate of 15 percent. In the case of imports of gold coins on which the assessment basis exceeds 250 percent of the fine gold value, the value-added tax is levied at a rate of 7 percent. Imports of monetary gold by the Bundesbank are exempt from value-added tax and customs duty. Domestic transactions in gold are subject to value-added tax at the same rate as imports, but under certain conditions no value-added tax is levied on transactions in gold bullion carried out on gold exchanges between brokers admitted to these exchanges. Commercial imports and exports of articles containing gold are subject to the general foreign trade regulations and in all cases are liberalized.

Changes During 1994

Imports and Import Payments

(See Appendix for a summary of trade measures introduced on an EU-wide basis during 1994, page 554.)

Capital

January 1. In accordance with the coming into force of Stage 2 of the Maastricht Treaty on the EMU, the system of "cash advances" by the Bundesbank to the central and regional authorities was abolished.

March 1. The minimum reserve requirements for sight deposits were reduced to 5 percent from between 6.6 percent and 12.1 percent, and domestic and foreign liabilities were subjected to the same rate.

GHANA

(Position as of December 31, 1994)

Exchange Arrangement

The currency of Ghana is the Ghanaian Cedi, whose exchange rate is determined in the interbank market. The average exchange rate in this market is used for official valuation purposes but is not always applied by authorized banks in their transactions with each other or with their customers. Rates are quoted by authorized dealers for certain other currencies,[1] with daily quotations based on the buying and selling rates for the U.S. dollar in markets abroad. Rates for certain nonconvertible currencies of the West African region, including the Nigerian naira, are also quoted daily but are applied only to transactions under the West African Clearing House arrangement. The other quoted nonconvertible currencies are the Gambian dalasi, the Guinean franc, the Sierra Leonean leone, the Guinea-Bissau peso, and the Mauritanian ouguiya. Authorized banks may exchange Ghanaian currency for any foreign currency. On December 31, 1994, the exchange rate in the interbank market was ₵1,050 per US$1.

Since February 1, 1988, any person, bank, or institution licensed by the Bank of Ghana is allowed to operate a foreign exchange bureau. Foreign exchange bureaus may purchase traveler's checks only in pounds sterling and U.S. dollars and may purchase and sell currency notes only in Canadian dollars, deutsche mark, French (and CFA) francs, Japanese yen, pounds sterling, Swiss francs, and U.S. dollars. In practice, however, traveler's checks in other foreign currencies and other foreign currency notes are also transacted in this market. Sellers of foreign exchange to the bureaus are not required to identify their sources. Each foreign exchange bureau is free to quote buying and selling rates. All bona fide imports and approved services may be funded through the bureaus. With effect from May 17, 1991, all authorized foreign exchange dealers (which include some nonbank foreign exchange bureaus) have been subject to limits on their net open positions in foreign exchange; holdings of foreign exchange in excess of these limits must be sold to other dealers or to the Bank of Ghana.

International organizations, embassies, and similar institutions are not permitted to transfer funds into Ghana through any foreign exchange bureau or to carry out foreign exchange transactions under the foreign exchange bureau scheme. There are no arrangements for forward exchange transactions, currency swaps, or guaranteed exchange rates for external debt-service payments.

Ghana formally accepted the obligations of Article VIII, Sections 2, 3, and 4 of the Fund Agreement, as from February 2, 1994.

Administration of Control

The Controller of Imports and Exports of the Ministry of Trade is empowered to prohibit or regulate all imports. The Foreign Transactions Examinations Office (FTEO) of the Bank of Ghana records and confirms foreign capital inflows and administers foreign exchange for official payments and travel. All foreign exchange transactions by the private sector are approved and transacted by authorized banks without reference to the Bank of Ghana.

Prescription of Currency

Settlements between residents of Ghana and residents of other countries may be made in permitted currencies. However, settlements related to transactions covered by bilateral payments agreements are made through clearing accounts maintained by the Bank of Ghana and the central or state banks of the countries concerned.[2] Furthermore, proceeds from exports to countries with which Ghana does not have bilateral payments agreements must be received in the currency of the importing country (if that currency is quoted by the Bank of Ghana) or be debited for authorized inward payments to residents of Ghana, for transfers to other official accounts related to the same country, and for transfers to the related clearing account at the Bank of Ghana.

Nonresident Accounts

Nonresident account status is granted to embassies, legations, consulates, and offices of high com-

---

[1]Australian dollars, Austrian schillings, Belgian francs, Canadian dollars, CFA francs, Danish kroner, French francs, deutsche mark, Italian lire, Japanese yen, Netherlands guilders, New Zealand dollars, Norwegian kroner, pounds sterling, Spanish pesetas, Swedish kronor, and Swiss francs.

[2]Ghana maintains bilateral payments agreements with Bulgaria, China, Cuba, the Czech Republic, Poland, Romania, and the Slovak Republic. These agreements are inoperative, and the clearing balances are being settled.

missioners in Ghana and to the non-Ghanaian members of their staffs. It is also available to international institutions and foreign-registered companies operating in Ghana and to nonresident Ghanaians. The opening of these accounts must be approved by the Bank of Ghana. The accounts may be credited with authorized outward payments, with transfers from other foreign accounts, and with the proceeds from sales of convertible currency. They may be debited for inward payments, for transfers to other foreign accounts, and for purchases of external currencies.

Nonresident accounts maintained under the provisions of bilateral payments agreements are called official accounts or territorial accounts. They may be credited with authorized outward payments by residents; with transfers from foreign accounts; with payments received through the Bank of Ghana for settlements with bilateral payments agreement countries; and with proceeds from sales of external currencies, other than restricted currencies. They may be debited for authorized inward payments to residents of Ghana, for transfers to other official accounts related to the same country, and for transfers to the related clearing account at the Bank of Ghana.

Funds not placed at the free disposal of nonresidents—for example, certain types of capital proceeds—may be deposited in blocked accounts, which may be debited for authorized payments, including for purchases of approved securities.

Imports and Import Payments

All imports have been liberalized, except for those prohibited for reasons of health and security and those prohibited by Ghanaian laws. Effective January 14, 1989, all import-licensing requirements were abolished; importers are now required to file an Import Declaration Form, which is not subject to approval, through the authorized banks for statistical purposes only. Certain imports are channeled through a bulk purchasing agent, the Ghana National Procurement Agency, while public sector imports must go through the Ghana Supply Commission.

Most imports are effected with confirmed letters of credit established through authorized Ghanaian banks on a sight basis. For all imports other than pharmaceutical products and canned, bottled, and other prepacked food products valued at more than $3,000 (f.o.b.), authorized banks are not allowed to make payments against letters of credit or bank drafts unless the import documents include a clean report of findings issued by international agencies with respect to the goods and unless they verify the

price, quality, and quantity in the country of origin or shipment.

Payments for Invisibles

All payments for invisibles are approved and effected by authorized banks, provided that applications are supported by appropriate documentary evidence.

Transfers of normal bank charges payable to overseas banks for import payments are generally authorized. Commission payments on imports are permitted up to a limit of 3 percent of f.o.b. value. Freight charges may be paid to the local shipping agents; the transfer of funds to cover such charges is normally permitted, provided that the application is properly documented. Residents traveling abroad are permitted to carry a maximum of $3,000 or its equivalent in other foreign currencies. In addition, resident travelers are permitted to carry a maximum of $5,000 or its equivalent in other foreign currencies for direct purchases abroad. However, all bona fide applications in excess of the specified limits are approved. Authorized dealer banks are permitted to remit profits and foreign investments without prior approval from the Bank of Ghana. The exportation of Ghanaian banknotes is permitted up to ₵5,000.

Exports and Export Proceeds

Exports of narcotics and carrots are prohibited, as are goods prohibited by Ghanaian laws. With the exception of cocoa, which is exported through the Cocoa Board, exports of agricultural commodities have been liberalized. Diamonds are exported through the Precious Metal Marketing Corporation and Ghana Consolidated Diamond Company. Exports of cocoa are subject to an export tax that is calculated as the difference between export proceeds, on the one hand, and payments to farmers together with the Cocoa Board's operational costs, on the other, if the proceeds exceed the payments.

With the exceptions noted below, exporters are required to collect and repatriate in full the proceeds from their exports within 60 days of shipment; proceeds from exports of nontraditional products may be sold in a foreign exchange bureau upon receipt. Exporters are generally allowed to retain up to 35 percent of their export proceeds in foreign exchange accounts. However, the retention ratio is 60 percent for the Ashanti Gold Mining Company, 20 percent for log exporters, and 2 percent for the Cocoa Board. The retention scheme does not apply to exports of residual oil and electricity. However, receipts from the exportation of electricity do not have to be surrendered to the Bank of Ghana. Retained earnings may be held in accounts abroad for financing essential imports or credited to the exporters' foreign exchange accounts with banks located in Ghana. Provided that payments from the foreign exchange accounts of exporters are supported by relevant documents, retained export earnings may be sold at the foreign exchange bureaus or be used to import goods through a bank, to purchase airline tickets, or for foreign travel, for medical services, or educational expenses abroad, or for any other approved invisible payments.

Proceeds from Invisibles

All receipts from invisibles must be sold to authorized dealers. Foreign currency notes may be imported freely. Repurchases of foreign exchange acquired for the purpose of foreign travel are subject to a processing fee of 0.5 percent.

Capital

Foreign investors in Ghana require the prior approval of the Ghana Investment Center if they are to benefit from the facilities available under the Investment Code of 1981, under which approved investors are guaranteed, in principle, the right to transfer profits and, in the event of sale or liquidation, capital proceeds. Tax holidays and initial capital allowances are also available for approved investments. The code stipulates that the assets of foreign investors may not be expropriated. Disputes over the amount of compensation are settled in accordance with the established procedure for conciliation—for example, through arbitration by the International Center for Settlements of Investment Disputes or the United Nations Commission on International Trade and Law. Certain areas of economic activity are not open to foreigners. The proceeds from sales of foreign ownership to Ghanaian nationals are permitted to be transferred by authorized dealer banks.

Under a supplementary investment code issued in July 1985, incentives are provided to promote foreign investments that promise to be net foreign exchange earners. The main features of the 1981 and 1985 codes, which offer incentives and guarantees to encourage foreign investments in areas other than petroleum and mining (already covered by a minerals code), are as follows: (1) exemption from customs duties on imports of plant, machinery, and equipment; (2) more favorable depreciation or capital allowances; (3) permission to operate an external account in which at least 25 percent of the investing company's foreign exchange earnings may be retained for procuring machinery and equipment, spare parts, and raw materials, for servicing of debt, and for transfers of dividends and profits; (4) guarantee for the remittance of foreign capital in the event of sale or liquidation; and (5) protection against expropriation. The minimum qualifying amount of investment capital is $10,000 for joint ventures with a Ghanaian partner and $100,000 for enterprises that are wholly foreign owned.

All outgoing capital movements must be approved by the Bank of Ghana; applications for such transfers must be supported by documentary evidence and are considered on their merits. Transfers to beneficiaries under wills and intestacies are approved provided that all local indebtedness has been settled. Requests for the transfer of funds representing personal assets of foreign residents in Ghana who emigrate are considered individually on their merits. Applications must be supported by appropriate documentation showing that the savings are genuine and that no illegal transfer of capital is involved. Loan and overdraft facilities to resident companies do not require approval.

Residents who are private persons are not normally granted foreign exchange for the acquisition of securities or personal real estate abroad. Nonresidents may deal in securities listed on the Ghana Stock Exchange and they may hold up to 10 percent of such security listings. Total holdings of all external residents in a company may not exceed 14 percent. For portfolio investments, residents must obtain approval to switch holdings of securities issued by nonresidents. Private sector and commercial bank borrowing require the approval of the Bank of Ghana, as do private import credits for machinery and equipment valued at $100,000 or more. Foreign borrowing by Ghanaian nationals is subject to certain government guidelines. Lending to nonresidents is prohibited, except for export credits, which require exchange control approval and are normally limited to 60 days.

Under a system of external accounts for debt-service payments introduced in 1980 to enable export-oriented industries to receive external aid, the industries are allowed to operate foreign exchange accounts (in addition to their regular retention accounts) with funds earmarked from export earnings for the purpose of debt-service payments. The opening of such accounts requires the approval of the Committee on Suppliers' Credits and the Bank of Ghana; the latter also monitors receipts and payments out of these accounts. Accounts have also been established for the diamond sector and for the fishing and timber companies financed with suppliers' credits.

Gold

Domestic transactions in gold, as well as imports and exports, may be authorized by the State Gold Mining Corporation in collaboration with the Bank of Ghana, and certain domestic sales may be carried out by permit under the Gold Mining Products Protection Ordinance. Ghanaian residents may not buy or borrow any gold from, or sell or lend any gold to, any person other than an authorized dealer. Imports of gold other than those by or on behalf of the monetary authorities are not normally licensed. The import duty on gold, including bullion and partly worked gold, is levied at a uniform rate of 30 percent. The gold mines export their output in semi-refined form.

Changes During 1994

Exchange Arrangement

February 2. Ghana formally accepted the obligations of Article VIII, Sections 2, 3, and 4 of the Articles of Agreement.

GREECE

(Position as of December 31, 1994)

Exchange Arrangement

The currency of Greece is the Greek Drachma. The Greek authorities operate a managed float for the drachma. Exchange rates for the U.S. dollar, the main intervention currency, and other currencies[1] are determined during the daily fixing session, in which the Bank of Greece and the authorized commercial banks participate. In the domestic spot exchange market, the commercial banks quote their own rates. On December 30, 1994, buying and selling rates in the interbank market were Dr 248.472 and Dr 249.968, respectively, per US$1. The commercial banks may levy a commission on all foreign exchange transactions on the domestic spot and forward exchange market.

Credit institutions in Greece may also freely conduct forward foreign exchange transactions, including currency swaps and options. The Bank of Greece provides credit institutions forward foreign exchange transactions including currency swaps and options.

Greece is a member of the European Monetary System (EMS). The drachma is included in the ECU basket, but Greece does not participate in the exchange rate mechanism of the EMS.

Greece formally accepted the obligations of Article VIII, Sections 2, 3, and 4 of the Fund Agreement, as from July 22, 1992.

Administration of Control

Foreign exchange regulations are administered by the Bank of Greece. Commercial banks are authorized to carry out all the necessary formalities for the settlement of imports and exports.

Natural and legal persons must inform the central bank for statistical purposes of transactions of sums greater than ECU 2,000 if a domestic banking institution is not involved.

The commercial banks are also authorized to undertake transactions in foreign exchange for invisibles and capital transactions within the framework of existing regulations.

---

[1]Australian dollars, Austrian schillings, Belgian francs, Canadian dollars, Cyprus pounds, Danish kroner, deutsche mark, European currency units (ECUs), French francs, Irish pounds, Italian lire, Japanese yen, Netherlands guilders, Norwegian kroner, Portuguese escudos, pounds sterling, Spanish pesetas, Swedish kronor, and Swiss francs.

Prescription of Currency

Settlements with all countries may be made in any convertible foreign currency or through nonresident deposit accounts in drachmas.

Accounts in Foreign Currency and Nonresident Accounts in Drachmas

Accounts in foreign currency. These accounts may be maintained in Greece by nonresident persons and entities, foreigners of Greek origin residing abroad, Greek nationals residing and working abroad (including seamen), Greek residents, and nonprofit private legal entities with a head office in Greece. These accounts may be credited with foreign exchange brought into Greece and with foreign banknotes brought into Greece and declared upon entry. Principal and interest on these accounts are freely transferable abroad. Savings and time deposits may be opened for up to 12 months. Greek residents may also open these accounts with undeclared foreign banknotes; principal and interest on these accounts may be withdrawn in drachmas and in foreign exchange but may not be transferred abroad. The Bank of Greece sets a maximum limit on interest on these accounts, except for the rate on residents' deposits, which is fixed by the Bank of Greece, and the rate on nonresidents' deposits in certain currencies, which is negotiable. Greek residents may also maintain accounts in foreign currency with foreign financial institutions abroad, provided that their original maturity is at least one year. In August 1994 the currency market was deregulated. Foreign exchange loan facilities of credit institutions are authorized to all natural and legal persons residing in Greece. Deposits in foreign exchange are now permitted for money originating from foreign exchange loan facilities.

Nonresident accounts in drachmas. Nonresidents may open sight and time deposits in convertible drachmas. These accounts may be credited with (1) drachma proceeds from foreign exchange; (2) transfers of drachmas from other similar accounts of the same or other depositors, as long as the proceeds do not originate from restricted short-term transactions; and (3) drachmas derived from liberalized transactions. Interest rates on these deposits are freely negotiable. Credit institutions operating in Greece are allowed to invest these deposits in the drachma market.

Blocked accounts. Claims of non-European Union (EU) residents denominated in drachmas and deposited in blocked accounts can be withdrawn and transferred abroad without the approval of the Bank of Greece, with effect from July 1, 1993.

Imports and Import Payments

Imports from the member countries of the EU are not subject to approval or clearance procedures. Approval for imports from non-EU member countries is granted automatically by the commercial banks, either before or after the goods are shipped and the required amount of foreign exchange is made available. Imports of certain products from the former Yugoslav Republic of Macedonia are prohibited. Special import licenses are required for textiles and iron and steel products that come from low-cost countries; these products are under surveillance according to EU quotas. Special regulations govern imports of certain items such as medicines, narcotics, and motion picture films.

Import payments are not subject to official regulations; in almost all cases, they are effected on the basis of agreements between the contracting parties.

Payments for Invisibles

Authorized banks are permitted to provide foreign exchange for all invisible payments. Payments of interest, profits, and dividends are governed by the regulations that are applied to capital transfers to Greece (see section on Capital, below). Remittances for family maintenance and earnings by foreign workers are permitted, subject to documentary requirements regarding proof of need and source of income. Monthly foreign exchange allowance for studies and for trips abroad is ECU 2,000 a person. Foreign banks operating in Greece are permitted to repatriate their profits, irrespective of the nature of their operations.

Nonresidents leaving Greece within a year of their arrival may take out foreign banknotes up to the equivalent of $1,000, as well as traveler's checks and other means of payment in their name, irrespective of amount; they may also take out Dr 20,000 in Greek banknotes. Larger amounts in foreign banknotes can be taken out no later than December 31 of the calendar year following the year in which the nonresident entered Greece, provided that they were declared upon entry into Greece.

Exports and Export Proceeds

Exports of certain products to the former Yugoslav Republic of Macedonia are prohibited.

Export proceeds must be surrendered within 180 days of the date of shipment of the goods. In special cases, the authorities may extend this time limit by approving time settlement of the value of exports. Export goods are not subject to the value-added tax. Exporters are allowed to maintain balances in foreign currency accounts equivalent to 20 percent of proceeds from exports in the previous calendar year with banks operating in Greece. Exporters may use these balances to repay external obligations, including suppliers' credits, and conduct authorized capital transactions.

Proceeds from Invisibles

Foreign exchange earnings representing payments for services must be surrendered within 90 days of the date of issue of the relevant invoice; 10 percent of these earnings of the previous calendar year may also be deposited in foreign currency accounts with banks operating in Greece. Earnings from ocean-going shipping are exempt from the surrender requirements, but shipowners must cover their disbursements and expenses in Greece by converting foreign exchange into drachmas.

Greek residents may bring in any amount of foreign exchange but must declare it upon entry, if they wish to take it out on their next departure, not later than December 31 of the calendar year following the year in which they entered Greece; they may also bring in a maximum of Dr 40,000 in banknotes.

Nonresident travelers may import any amount of foreign currency and need not declare it, provided they do not intend to take out amounts in excess of the equivalent of $1,000. Traveler's checks and other means of payment in a traveler's name are not subject to a limit. The amount of Greek banknotes a nonresident may bring into Greece is limited to Dr 100,000.

Capital

Greek natural and juridical persons are allowed to borrow foreign exchange from banks, foreign juridical persons, or individuals residing abroad, without prior approval from the Bank of Greece. Authorized credit institutions operating in Greece may conduct any transaction in foreign exchange, including currency and interest rate swaps and transactions in derivatives with resident and nonresidents, and they may extend loans in any form and currency to nonresidents on freely negotiated terms.

The following direct investments by residents of non-EU member countries are restricted: (1) investment in border regions; (2) investment in maritime transport; (3) acquisition of mining rights; and

(4) participation in new or existing enterprises if these are engaged in radio and television broadcasting or air transport.

Direct investments are governed by Legislative Decree No. 2687/1953, Presidential Decrees Nos. 207/1987 and 96/1993, Acts of the Governor of the Bank of Greece Nos. 825/1986 and 2227/1993.

Gold

Residents may freely purchase new gold sovereigns from the Bank of Greece through licensed stockbrokers at a price set by the Bank of Greece. These gold coins may be resold only to the Bank of Greece or to the Athens Stock Exchange. Holders of gold coins acquired in the free market that existed before December 22, 1965 may sell them without any formality to the Bank of Greece or to an authorized bank at the official price. Imports of gold against payment in foreign exchange require a special license; licenses are normally issued to importers for distribution to jewelers and dentists. Gold bars and gold coins may be imported for other than commercial purposes when no payment in foreign exchange is involved. Exports of gold other than by the Bank of Greece are not approved, except when gold bars or coins are brought in by travelers and declared upon entry, in which case they may be re-exported after being approved by the Bank of Greece.

Changes During 1994

Exchange Arrangement

May 16. Authorized credit institutions operating in Greece were allowed to conduct any transaction in foreign exchange, including currency and interest rate swaps and transactions in derivatives with residents and nonresidents. Ceilings on the foreign exchange exposure of credit institutions were removed, but these positions would continue to be monitored, where appropriate, in the context of prudential supervision.

Administration of Control

April 1. Bank of Greece announced to the press abolition of the obligation on the part of banks to check the authenticities of transactions and abolition of the compulsory importation and conversion into drachmas of foreign exchange within a specified period. Natural and legal persons would, however, have to inform the central bank for statistical purposes of transactions of sums greater than ECU 2,000, if a domestic banking institution is not involved.

Accounts in Foreign Currency and Nonresident Accounts in Drachmas

November 1. Funds originating from foreign exchange borrowing were allowed to be deposited into these accounts.

Imports and Import Payments

February 1. Imports of certain products from the former Yugoslav Republic of Macedonia were prohibited.

(See Appendix for a summary of trade measures introduced and eliminated on an EU-wide basis during 1994, page 554.)

Payments for Invisibles

March 1. Monthly foreign exchange allowance for studies and for trips abroad was raised to ECU 2,000.

Exports and Export Proceeds

February 10. Exports of certain products to the former Yugoslav Republic of Macedonia were prohibited.

Capital

May 16. (1) Remaining exchange controls on short-term capital movements (mainly loans and deposits with an original maturity of less than one year) and some forward and swap contracts (for less than three months) were abolished; and (2) authorized credit institutions were also allowed to extend loans in any form and currency for nonresidents on freely negotiated terms.

GRENADA

(Position as of December 31, 1994)

Exchange Arrangement

The currency of Grenada is the Eastern Caribbean Dollar,[1] which is issued by the Eastern Caribbean Central Bank (ECCB). The Eastern Caribbean dollar is pegged to the U.S. dollar, the intervention currency, at EC$2.70 per US$1. On December 31, 1994, the buying and selling rates for the U.S. dollar quoted by the ECCB in its transactions with commercial banks were EC$2.69 and EC$2.71, respectively, per US$1. The ECCB also quotes daily rates for the Canadian dollar and the pound sterling. There are no arrangements for forward cover against exchange rate risk operating in the official or the commercial banking sector.

Grenada formally accepted the obligations of Article VIII, Sections 2, 3, and 4 of the Fund Agreement, as from January 24, 1994.

Administration of Control

Exchange control, which is administered by the Ministry of Finance, applies to all countries. The Ministry delegates to authorized dealers the authority to approve some import payments and certain other outward payments. The Trade Division of the Ministry of Finance administers trade control.

Prescription of Currency

Settlements with residents of member countries of the Caribbean Common Market (CARICOM)[2] may be made either through external accounts in Eastern Caribbean dollars, in the currency of the CARICOM country concerned, or in U.S. dollars. Settlements with residents of the former Sterling Area countries, other than CARICOM countries, may be made in pounds sterling, in any other former Sterling Area currency, or in Eastern Caribbean dollars to and from external accounts. Settlements with residents of countries outside the former Sterling Area may be made in any foreign currency[3] or through an external account in Eastern Caribbean dollars.

Resident and Nonresident Accounts

Authorized dealers may open external accounts for nonresidents and residents without permission from the Ministry of Finance. Nonresidents may also maintain these accounts in Eastern Caribbean dollars. Foreign currency accounts may be freely debited but may be credited only with foreign exchange earned or received from outside the Eastern Caribbean area.

Foreign Currency Accounts

Residents and nonresidents are permitted to open foreign currency accounts without referring to the Ministry of Finance. Such accounts may be freely debited but can be credited only with foreign exchange earned or received from outside the ECCB area.

Imports and Import Payments

Most goods may be freely imported, but there are certain goods whose importation is prohibited or that are subject to quantitative restrictions and require a license. Prohibited goods are identified within various laws that pertain to trade, agriculture, national security, and health and include whole chickens, chicken eggs, live breeding poultry, war toys, animal skins, and various drugs deemed to be dangerous. Restricted items are divided between restricted items from non-CARICOM sources and restricted items from the CARICOM area. Restricted items from non-CARICOM sources include milk, sugar, rice, a variety of tropical fruits and vegetables, carbonated beverages, arms and ammunition, industrial gas, paints, and miscellaneous items associated with furniture, clothing, and the construction industry. Items from the CARICOM area that require licenses include curry products, beer, cigarettes, industrial gas, furniture, exotic birds, solar water heaters, and various tropical fruits and vegetables.

Payments for documented imports are free of restrictions. Payments for restricted imports and any goods (and services) in excess of the limits of authorized dealers require permission from the Ministry of Finance.

Imports of capital equipment are exempt from import duties, as are imports by domestic associations involved in the production of major crops, provided that such imports are intended for quality improvements in the growing or packaging of ba-

---

[1]The Eastern Caribbean dollar is also the currency of Anguilla, Antigua and Barbuda, Dominica, Montserrat, St. Kitts and Nevis, St. Lucia, and St. Vincent and the Grenadines.

[2]The CARICOM countries are Antigua and Barbuda, The Bahamas, Barbados, Belize, Dominica, Grenada, Guyana, Jamaica, Montserrat, St. Kitts and Nevis, St. Lucia, St. Vincent and the Grenadines, and Trinidad and Tobago.

[3]Foreign currencies include all currencies other than the Eastern Caribbean dollar.

nanas, nutmeg, and maize. Imports of fuel by the Grenada Electric Company are exempt from customs duty as are the fuel imports of a substantial number of enterprises in the manufacturing and hotel industries. Imports that are not exempt from customs duties are subject to a value-added tax of either 15 percent, 20 percent, or 55 percent. All imports are subject to a customs service charge of 2.5 percent, and all non-CARICOM goods are subject to the common external tariff of 35 percent.

Payments for Invisibles

Authority has been delegated to authorized dealers to provide basic allocations of foreign exchange for payments for invisibles, including up to EC$10,000 a person a year for travel abroad, up to EC$15,000 a person a year for business travel, and EC$10,000 for payment of medical expenses. Payments for subscriptions to magazines and periodicals, and life insurance premiums on policies contracted before June 1975 are also effected through authorized dealers. Applications for additional amounts, or for purposes for which there is no basic allocation, are approved by the Ministry of Finance provided that no unauthorized transfer of capital is involved. Nonresident travelers may export, with the approval of the Ministry of Finance, any foreign currency they previously brought into Grenada.

Exports and Export Proceeds

Specific licenses are required for the exportation of certain goods to any destination. There exists a short list of items that require a license prior to exportation from Grenada. These include exotic birds, coral, mineral products, and live sheep and goats. There are no formal regulations to ensure that export proceeds are surrendered within a certain period after the date of shipment, but export proceeds must be repatriated.

Proceeds from Invisibles

The collection of foreign currency proceeds from invisibles is mandatory. Travelers may freely bring in notes and coins in Eastern Caribbean currency or in any foreign currency.

Capital

All outward capital transfers require exchange control approval. Residents may not purchase foreign currency securities or real estate abroad for private purposes. Certificates of title to foreign currency securities held by residents must be lodged with an authorized depository in Grenada, and earnings on these securities must be repatriated.

Personal capital transfers, such as inheritances to nonresidents, require exchange control approval, which is normally granted subject to the payment of estate and succession duties. The transfer of funds by emigrants is allowed. The Ministry of Finance considers transfer applications from foreign nationals who have resided in Grenada and are proceeding to take up permanent residence abroad on a case-by-case basis.

With exchange control approval, nonresidents may invest directly in Grenada. The remittance of earnings on, and the liquidation of proceeds from, such investment is permitted, provided that all related liabilities have been discharged and that the original investment was registered with the Ministry of Finance. Nonresidents may use foreign currency to acquire real estate in Grenada for private purposes; local currency financing is not ordinarily permitted. The repatriation of proceeds from the realization of investments requires the approval of the Ministry of Finance.

The approval of the Ministry of Finance is required for residents to borrow abroad or for nonresidents to borrow in Grenada. Authorized dealers may freely assume short-term liability positions in foreign currencies to finance approved transfers for both trade and nontrade transactions. They may also freely accept deposits from nonresidents. Any borrowing abroad by authorized dealers to finance their domestic operations requires the approval of the Ministry of Finance. Effective March 15, 1991, all restrictions on transfers of Eastern Caribbean dollars from Grenada to countries served by the Eastern Caribbean Central Bank were eliminated.

Gold

Residents other than the monetary authorities, authorized dealers, and industrial users are not permitted to hold or acquire gold in any form other than jewelry or coins for numismatic purposes. Imports of gold are permitted for industrial purposes only and are subject to customs duties and charges. The Ministry of Finance issues licenses to import gold. The exportation of gold is not normally permitted.

Changes During 1994

Exchange Arrangement

January 1. The 2.5 percent exchange tax was eliminated.

January 24. Grenada formally accepted the obligations of Article VIII, Sections 2, 3, and 4 of the Fund Agreement.

GUATEMALA

(Position as of December 31, 1994)

Exchange Arrangement

The currency of Guatemala is the Guatemalan Quetzal. Since March 14, 1994, exchange rates have been determined in the interbank market according to market forces. Financial institutions authorized to operate in the exchange market are commercial banks, finance companies, and exchange houses. Foreign exchange proceeds are not required to be surrendered to the central bank, but must be sold to any authorized financial institution at market-determined rates. The Bank of Guatemala intervenes in the exchange market only to moderate undue fluctuations, to purchase foreign exchange on behalf of the public sector, and to service its own external debt. All foreign exchange transactions of the public sector must take place through the Bank of Guatemala at a reference rate that is equivalent to the weighted average of the buying and selling rates in the interbank market during the previous day. Banks and finance companies may maintain a net foreign exchange position of up to 25 percent of the value of their capital and reserves; for the exchange houses, this limit is set at 100 percent. Foreign exchange exceeding these limits at the end of each day must be deposited at the Bank of Guatemala.

On December 31, 1994, the buying and selling rates in the bank market were Q 5.63181 and Q 5.66524, respectively, per US$1. Buying and selling rates for currencies other than the U.S. dollar are freely quoted, mainly on the basis of their rates in the New York market.

The Bank of Guatemala does not issue exchange rate guarantees. There are no arrangements for forward cover against exchange rate risk operating in the official or the commercial banking sector.

On January 27, 1947, Guatemala formally accepted the obligations of Article VIII, Sections 2, 3, and 4 of the Fund Agreement.

Administration of Control

The Foreign Exchange Department of the Bank of Guatemala is in charge of administering the Transitional Law on the Foreign Exchange Regime. Foreign exchange transactions of the public sector are carried out exclusively through the Bank of Guatemala; those of the private sector are made through banks and foreign exchange houses authorized by the Monetary Board. Exports of goods must be registered in the Foreign Exchange Department to guarantee repatriation of the corresponding foreign exchange proceeds.

Arrears are maintained with respect to certain external payments.

Prescription of Currency

In practice, most transactions in foreign exchange are denominated in U.S. dollars, domestic currency, or other means of payment, in accordance with special payments agreements.

Imports and Import Payments

Guatemala is a member of the Central American Common Market (CACM). Import tariff rates on goods from outside the region range from 5 percent to 20 percent, in accordance with Guatemala's agreement with other Central American countries on a common external tariff, and virtually all goods traded among Central American countries are exempted from tariffs. The average tariff was about 8.5 percent in 1994. At present, between 2 percent and 3 percent of imported items, such as vehicles and beverages, are subject to tariffs that were established freely by each member country of the CACM. The agreement provides temporary exceptions for textiles, clothing, and footwear. By December 31, 1994, the tariffs on textiles and footwear were reduced to 20 percent from 30 percent; the tariff on tires was reduced to 15 percent from 30 percent; and the tariff on clothing was reduced to 25 percent from 30 percent. A number of exceptions and special tariff regimes remain, for example books are subject to a tariff of 0.5 percent; some products traded within the CACM, such as coffee, sugar, oil, wheat, and alcohol, are subject to tariffs of between 5 percent and 20 percent; some agricultural products (yellow maize, rice, and sorghum) are subject to a band of prices with variable tariffs (between 5 percent and 45 percent);[1] and imports of chicken up to a monthly quota of 300 tons are subject to a tariff at the rate of 20 percent, and imports exceeding this quota are subject to a tariff of 45 percent.

Imports of most goods are unrestricted and require neither registration nor a license. Import licenses issued by the Ministry of Economy are

---

[1]Changes to the maximum and minimum prices for the band and the corresponding tariff table are determined at the beginning of each agricultural season.

required for imports of coffee beans and coffee plants, lead, poultry, milk, eggs, sugar, wheat flour, and cottonseed; these licenses are issued freely.

Exports and Export Proceeds

Certain exports are subject to licenses issued by the Ministry of Economy. A few other items, including gold (unless the Bank of Guatemala issues a special export license) and silver, may not be exported in any form. Exports of wheat flour, ethyl alcohol, roasted coffee, and tobacco and cigarettes to Central American countries are temporarily restricted.

Exporters must obtain an export permit issued by the Foreign Exchange Department before the Guatemalan customs can authorize shipment of the merchandise. The granting of export permits is contingent upon agreement to sell export proceeds to the Bank of Guatemala or an authorized bank within 90 days of the date of issuance (this period may be extended to 180 days).

In the case of exports to Central America, there are arrangements among the central banks to settle payments in their own national currencies or U.S. dollars or through barter. If the economic agents decide to settle their payments in U.S. dollars, the export revenues must be sold to the Bank of Guatemala.

Payments for and Proceeds from Invisibles

Invisible transactions relating to travel outside the country, school fees, study expenses, international credit card payments, and certain others are permitted without restriction.

Capital

All capital transactions may take place without restriction. Nonresident (and resident) investors are exempted from a 12.5 percent tax on interest paid on foreign borrowing if the funds are channeled through the domestic banking system. Foreign direct investment in the petroleum sector is governed by special legislation.

Gold

The Bank of Guatemala may buy and sell gold coins and bullion either directly or through authorized banks and is entitled to buy gold holdings surrendered by any resident. The banks sell gold to domestic artistic or industrial users in accordance with the directives of the Monetary Board. The exportation of gold is prohibited except when the Bank of Guatemala issues a special export license. Gold is imported only by the Bank of Guatemala.

Changes during 1994

Exchange Arrangement

March 14. The system of exchange auctions administered by the central bank was abolished and replaced by an interbank market in which authorized financial institutions participate.

March 14. Financial institutions were required to deposit net holdings of foreign exchange (defined as holdings minus obligations in foreign currency with a maturity of less than 30 days) in excess of the operational limit (25 percent of capital and reserves) with the Bank of Guatemala.

Imports and Import Payments

December 31. The tariff rate on textiles and footwear was reduced to 20 percent from 30 percent; the tariff rate on tires was reduced to 15 percent from 30 percent; and the tariff rate on clothing was reduced to 25 percent from 30 percent.

GUINEA

(Position as of December 31, 1994)

Exchange Arrangement

The currency of Guinea is the Guinean Franc. Its external value is determined by the supply and demand for foreign exchange between the authorized foreign exchange dealers and their clients or among the dealers themselves. The Central Bank of Guinea, a net recipient of nonproject aid funds and mining company receipts, also participates in the interbank market, as it remains a net supplier of foreign exchange. The exchange rate of the Guinean franc against the CFA franc results from the relationship between this currency and the French franc. The exchange rates for other currencies are determined on the basis of the rate of these currencies against the French franc in the international market. On December 31, 1994, the official exchange rate for the Guinean franc vis-à-vis the U.S. dollar was GF 981.02 per US$1. Foreign exchange bureaus are in operation, and exchange rates in the market are determined by supply and demand conditions. There are no arrangements for forward cover against exchange rate risk operating in the official or the commercial banking sector.

Administration of Control

Exchange control authority is vested in the Central Bank of Guinea, which has delegated to the commercial banks authority to (1) approve import forms (*descriptifs d'importation*) and import application forms (*demandes descriptives d'importation*) for amounts of up to $200,000; (2) allocate foreign exchange to travelers holding foreign airline tickets (travelers holding tickets issued by Compagnie Nationale Air Guinée must apply to the Central Bank for their travel allowances); and (3) manage foreign currency accounts opened in the name of nonresidents. All settlements with foreign countries, including payments for imports, require approval from the Exchange Department of the Central Bank.

Arrears are maintained with respect to external payments.

Prescription of Currency

Settlements on account of transactions covered by bilateral payments agreements are made in currencies prescribed by, and through accounts established under, the provisions of the agreements.[1]

---

[1]Guinea maintains bilateral payments agreements with China, Cuba, and Viet Nam; all agreements are inoperative.

Settlements with the Central Bank of West African States (BCEAO) (Benin, Burkina Faso, Côte d'Ivoire, Mali, Niger, Senegal, and Togo) and The Gambia, Ghana, Guinea-Bissau, Liberia, Mauritania, Nigeria, and Sierra Leone are normally made through the West African Clearing House. Settlements with other countries are made in designated convertible currencies quoted by the Central Bank. All current transactions effected in Guinea must be settled in Guinean francs.

Resident Foreign Currency Accounts

Guinean residents may maintain and operate deposit accounts in foreign currency at the domestic commercial banks. Exporters may hold up to 25 percent of their revenue in foreign currency in local bank accounts. For gold exporters, this proportion can be as high as 50 percent.

Nonresident Accounts

There are two types of nonresident accounts: nonresident transferable accounts in foreign currencies, which may be opened freely, subject to notification of the Central Bank by commercial banks; and nonresident accounts in Guinean francs, which may also be opened freely.

Accounts in Convertible Guinean Francs

Accounts in convertible Guinean francs may be opened by residents and nonresidents. They are to be credited with deposits in foreign exchange, irrespective of its origin. The accounts may be debited freely and converted by commercial banks into foreign currencies without prior authorization from the Central Bank. Interest rates on these are negotiated between the account holder and the bank.

Imports and Import Payments

All products except armaments, ammunition, and narcotics may be freely imported into Guinea.

All imports of less than $200,000 require authorization, which is granted by the commercial banks on behalf of the Central Bank. Authorization is given for two types of imports: (1) imports for which importers have access to foreign exchange provided at rates determined during weekly fixing sessions; and (2) imports financed with importers' own foreign exchange resources (*autorisation sans achat de devises*).

To obtain authorization, importers are required to fill out either an import form (for imports valued at $5,000 or less f.o.b.) or an import application request form (for imports valued at more than $5,000 f.o.b.), on which they must provide information on products to be imported, including price, quantity, quality, and financing terms.

For imports with access to the auction market, authorization is given only after price, quality, and terms of financing (for import credits) are verified. Requests for foreign exchange must be submitted through commercial banks at the weekly fixing sessions.

Certain imports are effected outside the auction system. This category comprises goods for which foreign exchange is derived from sources other than the official foreign exchange resources of Guinea and mainly covers imports by three "mixed-economy" companies (the Friguia Company; the Guinea Bauxite Company; and AREDOR, the diamond company) and foreign embassies.

All products are subject to a 12 percent turnover tax, customs duties (DFE) of 8 percent, and customs charges (DDE) of 7 percent, with the following exceptions: animals, flour, sugar, pharmaceutical products, and fertilizers are subject to a 6 percent DFE and 2 percent DDE; and imports for the food industry, cement, and agricultural machinery are subject to an 8 percent DFE and a 2 percent DDE. In addition, a surtax of 20 percent or 30 percent is imposed on all luxury goods, and a surtax of 30–60 percent is levied on nonalcoholic beverages, certain wines, and spirits. Imports of the three mixed enterprises in the mining sector are regulated by special agreements and are subject to a 5.6 percent levy.

Payments for Invisibles

All payments for invisibles may be made freely.

The Investment Law of 1985 (as amended in 1987) guarantees that profits earned from approved foreign investments may be transferred abroad and that certified dividends and royalties may be transferred in full. It also provides for certain tax incentives. The transfer abroad of salaries by expatriate workers is authorized up to a limit of 50 percent of base earnings and only for those contracts approved by the Ministry of Labor. The exportation of Guinean currency is limited to GF 5,000 a person a trip.

Exports and Export Proceeds

All private sector exports require domiciliation with a commercial bank and submission of an export description to help prevent shortages of goods needed for domestic consumption and to identify capital outflows. Exports of the mining sector are exempt from this requirement.

The exportation of wild animals (dead or alive), meats, articles of historic or ethnographic interest, jewelry, articles made of precious metals, and plants and seeds requires special authorization from designated agencies. Planters may be granted special authorization to export a specific quantity of pineapples, bananas, or citrus fruits.

Private traders may be permitted to retain a part of their export proceeds to finance authorized imports. Gold exporters and vendors are required to surrender their export proceeds but may retain 25 percent to 50 percent of proceeds in foreign exchange deposits with commercial banks. This amount may be increased depending on the volume and type of products, especially with respect to gold and diamonds. The mixed-economy companies are allowed to retain all of their export proceeds abroad and may use the balances to pay for their imports and operating requirements and to service their external debt.

Proceeds from Invisibles

In principle, residents must surrender exchange proceeds accruing from invisibles if they do not hold foreign currency accounts. The importation of foreign banknotes and traveler's checks is permitted freely, subject to declaration on entry; residents, however, must surrender both to commercial banks within 15 days of their return. Certain residents, by virtue of their occupation, are authorized to deposit their foreign exchange proceeds in foreign currency or convertible Guinean franc accounts. The Central Bank of Guinea levies a fee of 0.25 percent of proceeds in foreign banknotes transferred through commercial banks. The importation of Guinean currency is limited to GF 5,000 a traveler a trip.

Capital

All capital transfers through the official exchange market require authorization. Outward capital transfers by Guinean nationals through the official market are prohibited.

The Investment Law of 1985 provides guarantees against the nationalization of foreign investments in the industrial and mining sectors. It also provides for preferential tax and customs treatment applicable to foreign investments and for the transfer of profits, interest, amortization, and liquidation proceeds of such investments. Small and medium-size enterprises in which at least GF 50 million is invested over a 3-year period may receive import tax reductions and exemptions from other taxes for a period of 8–10 years. Exemptions for up to 15 years may be granted on long-term investments of particular importance to the economy. The minimum foreign investment in Guinean enterprises is GF 10 million. Guinean nationals must have controlling interests in enterprises requiring foreign investment of GF 10 million to GF 50 million.

Gold

The Central Bank purchases gold in Guinean francs at international prices; at the seller's request, the Central Bank may purchase 50 percent of output in foreign currency. Since the monetary reform of 1986, Guinea has issued fine silver commemorative coins of GF 10,000, which are legal tender. Transactions in nonmonetary gold are not subject to restriction. Only the exportation of gold is subject to prior authorization by the Central Bank.

Changes During 1994

Payments for Invisibles

July 1. All restrictions on payments and transfers for current international transactions were eliminated.

GUINEA-BISSAU

(Position as of December 31, 1994)

Exchange Arrangement

The currency of Guinea-Bissau is the Guinea-Bissau Peso. The Central Bank of Guinea-Bissau sets official buying and selling exchange rates for its transactions and for those of government agencies. The official buying rate against the U.S. dollar, which serves as the intervention currency, is adjusted, as necessary, and maintained within a 2 percent average of the freely determined rates quoted by the two commercial banks and an exchange bureau and the parallel market rate. The spread between the buying and selling rates of the official and commercial rates is subject to a maximum of 2 percent. The Central Bank occasionally intervenes in the market through sales of foreign currencies to the commercial banks.

On December 31, 1994, the official buying and selling rates for the U.S. dollar were PG 15,369 and PG 15,677, respectively, per US$1.

There are no taxes or subsidies on purchases or sales of foreign currency in Guinea-Bissau. There are no arrangements for forward cover against exchange rate risk in the banking or commercial sector.

Administration of Control

The Central Bank exercises control over foreign exchange transactions involving the use of foreign exchange belonging to or administered by it. Foreign exchange transactions effected by commercial banks with resources derived from sources other than those of the Central Bank are, in general, not controlled by the Central Bank. Residents are permitted to sell foreign exchange in their possession without revealing its sources. Arrears are maintained with respect to external payments.

Prescription of Currency

Settlements with foreign countries are normally made in foreign currency, although certain external obligations have been settled with goods on a few occasions in the past. Guinea-Bissau participates in the West African Clearing House, which includes member countries of the Central Bank of West African States (Benin, Burkina Faso, Côte d'Ivoire, Mali, Niger, Senegal, and Togo) as well as The Gambia, Ghana, Guinea, Liberia, Mauritania, Nigeria, and Sierra Leone.

Nonresident Foreign Currency Accounts

Nonresidents may open demand and time accounts in foreign currency with commercial banks and may use balances on these accounts without restriction, except that they must give prior notice for withdrawals above certain pre-established limits. Residents may also maintain these accounts (1) if they are authorized to engage in foreign currency transactions; or (2) if they receive income in foreign currency under contracts with nonresidents. Banks may pay interest up to 4 percent a year on demand accounts in foreign currency, whereas interest rates on time deposits may be negotiated freely.

Imports and Import Payments

All imports, regardless of whether they involve use of official or free market foreign exchange, require a prior import license (*Boletim de Registo Prévio de Importação*) issued by the Ministry of Commerce and Tourism. Since official availability of foreign exchange in the country is not considered when licenses are issued, import licenses are not a foreign exchange allocation instrument, and their possession does not guarantee the importers access to the official exchange market. Except for a short negative list, licenses are issued automatically after verification of invoice prices for goods to be imported.

Importers are free to arrange for payment through the banking system with their own foreign exchange or foreign exchange purchased on the parallel market. However, payments for imports with foreign exchange purchased from, or administered by, the Central Bank require authorization from the Central Bank, which is granted on the basis of the priority of the products involved and the availability of foreign exchange.

On December 31, 1991, the state monopoly on imports of petroleum and petroleum products was abolished.

Payments for Invisibles

Payments for invisibles by the public sector at the official exchange rate are effected through the Central Bank.

Payments for invisibles by the private sector take place at the freely determined exchange rate and may be made without restriction. These payments may take place through commercial banks and the foreign exchange house.

Foreign travelers may take out on departure any unspent foreign exchange that they declared upon entry.

Exports and Export Proceeds

All exports require a prior export license (*Boletim de Registo Prévio de Exportação*). Only exporters registered with the Ministry of Commerce and Tourism may obtain these licenses, which are granted automatically in most cases. As in the case of imports, prior licenses are intended primarily for statistical purposes, although they are also used to check the prices of exports. There are no products whose exportation is reserved solely for the public sector.

In general, all exports are subject to a customs services tax of 6 percent (5 percent for cashew nuts). In addition, exports of cashew nuts are subject to a special tax, whose rate has been reduced over the years and is currently 13 percent. Agricultural exports are also subject to a rural property tax (*Contribuição Predial Rústica*), at the rate of 2 percent on processed products and 1 percent on unprocessed products.

Special arrangements apply to exports to member countries of the Economic Community of West African States (ECOWAS), to which Guinea-Bissau belongs; for example, exports to these countries are exempt from the 6 percent customs services tax.

Exporters are required to surrender 40 percent of proceeds to the Central Bank and the remainder to the commercial banks.

Proceeds from Invisibles

Under the foreign exchange regulations that came into effect in 1991, neither residents nor nonresidents are required to sell to the Central Bank foreign exchange they receive from abroad, and they are free to sell foreign exchange in their possession on the free exchange market.

Capital

Foreign direct investments are governed by the Investment Code of 1985, which was amended most recently by Decree-Law No. 4/91, promulgated on September 30, 1991. Under the Investment Code, a number of incentives to foreign direct investment have been established, and foreign and domestic investments have been subject to the same terms with respect to access to domestic credit. The Investment Code provides protection against nationalization of investment and expropriation of assets, and recognizes the right of foreign investors to transfer foreign currency abroad in respect of profits (net of taxes), to sell or liquidate investments, to service loans obtained for project financing, and to make payments for imported supplies and technical assistance.

Gold

Exports and imports of gold are prohibited unless expressly authorized by the appropriate government authorities. The Central Bank may engage in gold purchases and sale transactions with the public.

Changes During 1994

Imports and Import Payments

June 30. The port service charge on imports was raised to 15 percent; it was raised again to 20 percent on December 15.

Exports and Export Proceeds

March 1. The special tax on exports of cashew nuts was reduced to 13 percent from 18 percent.

June 1. Minimum quantity shipping requirements for agricultural exports were abolished.

GUYANA

(Position as of December 31, 1994)

Exchange Arrangement

The currency of Guyana is the Guyana Dollar, the external value of which is determined freely by market forces in the cambio market. The Bank of Guyana conducts certain transactions on the basis of the cambio rate by averaging quotations of the three largest dealers in the cambio market on the date the transaction takes place. In accordance with the bilateral agreements with the central banks of the Caribbean Community and Common Market (CARICOM), the Bank of Guyana quotes weekly rates for certain CARICOM currencies.[1] On December 31, 1994, the average buying and selling rates in the cambio market were G$141.31 and G$143.9, respectively, per US$1. The Bank of Guyana quotes rates for pounds sterling and Canadian dollars on the basis of the U.S. dollar-pound sterling and the U.S. dollar-Canadian dollar cross rates quoted by the Bank of England. The Bank of Guyana charges commissions at different rates on purchases and sales of officially quoted currencies.

Transactions effected through the Bank of Guyana are limited, on the receipts side, to exports of sugar, bauxite, and gold and, on the payments side, mainly to imports of fuel and to official debt-service payments. All other transactions are effected in the cambio market. There are no taxes or subsidies on the purchases or sales of foreign exchange.

The only arrangement for forward cover against exchange rate risk operates in the official sector in respect of exchange rate guarantees that are provided to certain deposits in blocked accounts. (See section on Resident and Nonresident Accounts, below.)

Guyana formally accepted the obligations of Article VIII, Sections 2, 3, and 4 of the Fund Agreement, as from December 27, 1966.

Administration of Control

Exchange control authority is vested in the Minister of Finance, who has entrusted this authority to the Bank of Guyana. The Ministry of Trade, Tourism, and Industry is responsible for issuing import and export licenses.

With the establishment of the cambio market under the Dealers in Foreign Currency (Licensing) Act of March 13, 1990, the Bank of Guyana, under the Exchange Control Act, suspended exchange control notices that related to (1) basic travel allowances; (2) correspondence courses; (3) subscriptions to clubs and societies, including entrance fees; (4) payments for periodicals, magazines, etc.; and (5) emigration. Also, until further notice, dealers are no longer authorized to accept deposits into the external payments deposit scheme for payment of imports from countries outside CARICOM.

Under the Dealers in Foreign Currency (Licensing) Act, with the payment of a fee of G$250,000, individuals, partnerships, and companies may be licensed for a period of one year (renewable) to engage in foreign currency dealings; these dealers are required to submit weekly returns of the transactions they conduct to the Bank of Guyana.

Prescription of Currency

Settlements with residents of foreign countries may be made in any foreign currency or through an external account in Guyana dollars.[2]

Resident and Nonresident Accounts

There are two categories of accounts for persons who are not residents of Guyana: external accounts, blocked accounts, and nonresident foreign exchange accounts.

External accounts may be opened, with exchange control approval, for persons who reside outside Guyana. They may be credited freely with all authorized payments by residents of Guyana to nonresidents and with transfers from other external accounts; other credits require approval. They may be debited freely for payments for any purpose to residents of any country, for transfers to other external accounts, and for withdrawals by the account holder while he or she is in Guyana; other debits require approval.

Blocked accounts may, in principle, be credited with funds that are not placed at the free disposal of nonresidents (for example, certain capital pro-

---

[1]For the operations of the CARICOM Bilateral Settlement Arrangements, the Bank of Guyana sets rates for the CARICOM currencies every Friday on the basis of the average rates of the commercial banks and the five largest nonbank cambio dealers in the week ending the preceding Wednesday. The currencies to which this rate applies are the Barbados dollar, the Eastern Caribbean dollar, and the Belize dollar.

[2]Foreign currencies comprise all currencies other than the Guyana dollar.

ceeds); these accounts may be debited for certain authorized payments, including purchases of approved securities. Since mid-1978, blocked accounts have been used to hold domestic currency deposits equivalent in value to pending applications for foreign exchange. Such deposits carry a market-related interest rate. The Bank of Guyana provides a partial exchange rate guarantee at the rates of G$3.25–G$3.75 per US$1 for deposits made before the devaluation of January 1984; at G$5.0 per US$1 for deposits made between January 1984 (after devaluation) and the end of January 1987; at G$10 per US$1 for deposits made between January 1987 and the end of March 1989; and no exchange rate guarantee for deposits made after March 1989.

Nonresident Foreign Currency Accounts may be opened by commercial banks without the prior approval of the central bank for citizens of Guyana residing permanently abroad, citizens of other countries temporarily residing in Guyana; nonresidents attached to diplomatic missions or international organizations; branches of companies incorporated outside of Guyana; and companies incorporated in Guyana but controlled by nonresidents abroad. These accounts may be credited with noncash instruments of convertible foreign currencies transferred through the banking system and transfers from external accounts. They may be debited freely for any payments at the discretion of the account holder.

Exporters are allowed to maintain and operate foreign exchange accounts. These accounts are approved on merit but are generally granted to bona fide exporters who require imported inputs for production and/or have external loan obligations. These accounts may be credited with all or a portion of retained export proceeds and proceeds of foreign currency loans. They may be debited freely for any payments at the discretion of the account holder.

Imports and Import Payments

Imports of certain products are also restricted, subject to import-licensing controls, from all non-CARICOM sources. These restrictions are currently applicable to four categories of food, that is, unprocessed meat, poultry, fruit, and processed fruit items. There are no licensing requirements for permissible imports, except for petroleum products and some twenty items affecting national security, health, public safety, and the environment.

Intra-CARICOM trade is free of import duties, quotas, and import-licensing arrangements. The Common External Tariff (CET) of CARICOM is applied to imports from outside CARICOM. Guyana is a party to an agreement among CARICOM member states to implement a phased reduction in the CET rate structure from a band of 30 percent to 5–20 percent by January 1, 1998.[3]

There are no import quotas. Import payments effected by commercial banks on behalf of the Bank of Guyana require the Bank's prior approval. Before the introduction of the cambio market, all applications for official foreign exchange were required to be accompanied by a domestic currency deposit of equivalent value, to be held in blocked accounts with commercial banks. Commercial banks are required to maintain a 100 percent reserve requirement against these deposits at the Bank of Guyana.

In general, import transactions effected through the cambio exchange market are permitted without restriction; most imports of consumer goods take place on this basis.

Payments for Invisibles

Payments for invisibles to all countries may be freely effected through the cambio market. Foreign exchange for tourist travel and education may be purchased in the cambio market without restriction. Resident and nonresident travelers are subject to an exit tax of G$1,500 on departure.

There are no restrictions on the amount of foreign or local currency that may be taken out for foreign travel.

Exports and Export Proceeds

Sugar may be exported only by the Guyana Sugar Corporation (GUYSUCO), and bauxite and alumina only by Linmine, Bermine, and Aroaima Bauxite Company. Certain other exports are also channeled through official agencies. Rice may be exported by the Guyana Rice Export Board and the private sector. Most exports do not require export licenses, but transactions are monitored by the Bank of Guyana and the Customs and Excise Department to ensure that all proceeds of exports are repatriated and offered for sale to a licensed dealer. Exchange control forms have to be completed for all exports whose value exceeds G$20,000.

A foreign exchange retention scheme permits some exporters to retain a certain percentage of export proceeds. The retention ratio is 40 percent for sugar, and gold and 100 percent for all other exports. Retained foreign exchange may be used freely in the cambio market.

---

[3]As a first step, the maximum tariff rate was lowered to 30 percent on January 14, 1994.

Proceeds from Invisibles

Proceeds from invisibles are not subject to surrender requirements and may be retained or sold in the cambio market without restriction. Travelers may freely bring in any amount in foreign or domestic currency notes; travelers entering the country with foreign currency in excess of the equivalent of $10,000 must declare the amount.

Capital

Private investment, both foreign and domestic, is governed by the Guyana Investment Policy of 1988. Foreign-based companies and their subsidiaries may borrow in Guyana only with the express approval of the Bank of Guyana. There are no restrictions on repatriation of capital. Residents and nonresidents have unlimited access to the cambio market for repatriation of funds.

Borrowing from nonresidents requires exchange control approval.

Gold

Residents may hold and acquire gold coins in Guyana for numismatic purposes, and also jewelry. Residents other than the monetary authorities, authorized dealers, producers of gold, and authorized industrial users are not allowed to hold or acquire gold in any form, at home or abroad, without special permission. Imports and exports of gold in any form by or on behalf of the monetary authorities, authorized dealers, producers of gold, and industrial users require permits issued by the Guyana Geology and Mines Commission.

Changes During 1994

Resident and Nonresident Accounts

June 6. Exporters were permitted to maintain and operate foreign exchange accounts.

June 30. Nonresidents were permitted to maintain and operate foreign exchange accounts.

Imports and Import Payments

January 13. Customs Amendment Act No. 2 of 1994 was passed in the National Assembly and approved by the President on January 28.

February 1. The first-stage reduction in the new CARICOM Common External Tariff (CET) to a maximum of 30 percent became effective.

Exports and Export Proceeds

May 31. The foreign exchange retention ratio for sugar exports was raised to 30 percent from 20 percent.

June 10. The foreign exchange retention ratio for gold exports through the Gold Board was raised to 30 percent from 20 percent.

November 14. The foreign exchange retention ratio for sugar exports and for gold exports through the Gold Board was raised to 40 percent from 30 percent, and bauxite producers were authorized to transact freely in the cambio market.

HAITI

(Position as of December 31, 1994)

Exchange Arrangement

The currency of Haiti is the Haitian Gourde, and its external value is determined on the basis of demand and supply conditions in the exchange market. The U.S. dollar circulates freely and is generally accepted in Haiti. Commercial banks quote buying and selling rates for certain other currencies, based on the buying and selling rates of the U.S. dollar in exchange markets abroad. Commercial banks are required to limit the spread between their buying and selling rates to no more than 3 percent.

There are no arrangements for forward 'cover against exchange rate risk operating in the official or the commercial banking sector.

Haiti formally accepted the obligations of Article VIII, Sections 2, 3, and 4 of the Fund Agreement, as from December 22, 1953.

Administration of Control

The Bank of the Republic of Haiti (the central bank) administers the foreign exchange system. Article 52 of the decree-law of September 28, 1991 provides for a penalty, payable to the tax authorities, equal to 20 percent on any commercial foreign exchange transaction not conducted through a bank established in Haiti.

Prescription of Currency

There are no obligations prescribing the method or currency for payments to or from nonresidents. Arrears are maintained with respect to external payments.

Resident Accounts

Commercial banks may open accounts in foreign exchange in favor of residents; in accordance with Article 2 of the decree of January 18, 1990, these accounts may be credited with export proceeds,with transfers from abroad received by exchange houses, or with receipts from maritime agencies and nongovernmental organizations.

Imports and Import Payments

Seven products (rice, millet, chicken, beans, maize, sugar, and pork) are subject to licensing requirements with quantitative restrictions. Customs tariffs are levied at the following rates: gasoline,

25 percent; maize, rice, and flour, 50 percent; sugar, 15 percent; and rice and cement, 3 percent. Equipment, raw materials, most inputs, and pharmaceutical products are exempt from tariffs. Customs tariffs and the value-added tax applicable to most imports are calculated on the basis of the gourde equivalent of the c.i.f. value of the imported good, calculated at the market exchange rate. For tax and tariff purposes, equipment and inputs for the agricultural and industrial sectors are valued at a more favorable exchange rate. All imports, except for inputs used by certain export industries, are subject to a consular fee of 3 percent, which is payable in Haiti.

Exports and Export Proceeds

Exports of agricultural products require prior authorization from the Ministry of Commerce and Industry. Authorization is usually granted freely but may be withheld when domestic supplies are low. In accordance with the decree of July 7, 1989, a percentage (currently 40 percent) of all export proceeds must be surrendered to the central bank through the commercial banks at the reference rate.[1] Exporters are required to negotiate documentary drafts with local commercial banks to ensure the repatriation of their export proceeds. The customs administration does not grant export approval unless those drafts are cleared by the central bank. Exchange houses are required to surrender all foreign exchange transfers to the authorized foreign exchange dealers.[2]

Payments for and Proceeds from Invisibles

Payments for invisibles are not restricted. Residents traveling abroad must pay a tax of G 275 on tickets. All travelers must pay an airport tax. The tax for Haitian residents is G 125 and for nonresidents, $25. Diplomats and staff members of international organizations accredited in Haiti are exempt from both taxes. Proceeds from invisibles are not required to be surrendered. There are no limits on the

---

[1]The reference rate is the weighted average of the exchange rates quoted by all commercial banks, money brokers, and cambios during the preceding day.

[2]As of December 31, 1991, only the surrender requirement applicable to export proceeds was being enforced.

importation or exportation of foreign or domestic banknotes.

Capital

Capital transactions in gourdes are restricted; in practice, however, these restrictions are not implemented. Foreign investment in Haiti is regulated by a decree of October 30, 1982 and requires prior government approval. Permission is normally not granted to nonresidents to invest in handicraft industries. Under a decree of April 6, 1973, private banks operating in Haiti are required to keep a minimum of 85 percent of their liabilities in the form of domestic assets for local customers.

Gold

Residents may hold and acquire gold coins in Haiti for numismatic purposes. With this exception, residents other than the monetary authorities and authorized industrial users are not allowed to hold or acquire gold in any form other than jewelry, at home or abroad. The central bank has the exclusive right to purchase gold domestically and to export gold in the form of coins, mineral dust, or bars.

Gold in any form, other than jewelry carried as personal effects by travelers, may be imported and exported only by the central bank; exports of gold require, in addition, prior authorization from the Ministry of Commerce and Industry and the Ministry of Finance and Economic Affairs, as well as an endorsement from the Ministry of Commerce and Industry, before customs clearance. However, commercial imports of articles containing a small amount of gold, such as gold watches, are freely permitted and do not require an import license or other authorization. Several gold coins have been issued, which are legal tender but do not circulate.

Changes During 1994

Imports and Import Payments

April 10. The customs tariffs on the following products were changed from the range of zero to 57.8 percent to the range of zero to 25.0 percent with the following rates: gasoline, 25 percent; sugar, 15 percent; and rice and cement, 3 percent. Equipment, raw materials, and most inputs are exempt. The value of imported goods would be valued at the market exchange rate.

HONDURAS

(Position as of December 31, 1994)

Exchange Arrangement

The currency of Honduras is the Honduran Lempira. The interbank foreign exchange system was suspended temporarily, and a foreign exchange auction system was introduced on July 17, 1994. Under this system, banks and exchange houses are required to sell all their daily foreign exchange purchases to the Central Bank of Honduras, which auctions at least 60 percent of its purchases. Buyers (banks, exchange houses, or private individuals) bid a price that cannot differ from a base price set by the authorities by more than 1 percent in either direction. The maximum bid in an auction is US$200,000. The base price is modified each time the reference exchange rate (the weighted average of successful bids) differs in the same direction from the base prices for 15 consecutive auctions. Auctions are held once each working day. At the end of 1994, the base price was L 9.29 per US$1 and the reference rate was L 9.40 per US$1. Banks and exchange houses sell foreign exchange to the public at the auction price plus a commission of less than 1.5 percent. Debt conversions are conducted at the rate of L 2 per US$1. Purchases and sales of the currencies of other Central American countries are effected on the basis of quotations in lempiras, taking into account the value of those currencies in terms of U.S. dollars in the interbank markets of the countries concerned. There are no taxes or subsidies on purchases or sales of foreign exchange. There are no arrangements for forward cover against exchange rate risk operating in the official or the commercial banking sector.

Honduras formally accepted the obligations of Article VIII, Sections 2, 3, and 4 of the Fund Agreement, as from July 1, 1950.

Administration of Control

The Central Bank of Honduras administers exchange control regulations. Exporters are required to present a declaration to the External Financing Department of the Central Bank (DERFE), which maintains an import registry for statistical purposes only. Foreign investment regulations are administered by the Secretary of Economy and Trade. Arrears are maintained with respect to external payments.

Prescription of Currency

There are no regulations prescribing the method of payment to or from nonresidents. Trade transactions with the rest of Central America may be carried out in local currencies, barter and compensation mechanisms, or U.S. dollar proceeds from exports to the rest of the Central American countries.

Foreign currency accounts may be maintained with domestic banks without restriction. Banks are required to hold these deposits in (1) foreign currency notes in their vaults, (2) special accounts at correspondent banks abroad, (3) investments in high-liquidity foreign instruments, or (4) advance export- or import-financing instruments.

Imports and Import Payments

Registration is required for all imports valued at more than $5,000. Imports of arms and similar items require a license issued by the Ministry of Defense.

Imports are financed either through the banking system or through exchange houses, with foreign exchange purchased in the free market or with credits obtained abroad (except for financing obtained through export advances or government credit agreements with external institutions).

Imports are subject to customs duties, ranging from zero to 20 percent.[1] In addition, certain consumer goods are subject to a customs surcharge of 10 percent of the c.i.f. import value.[2] The duty-free zone in Puerto Cortés, industrial processing zones, and firms registered under the regime of temporary imports (a drawback regime) are exempt from customs duties.

Exports and Export Proceeds

Exports are required to be registered only for statistical purposes. All foreign exchange proceeds must be surrendered to authorized banks or exchange houses. Exporters are allowed to retain up to 30 percent of their foreign exchange proceeds to finance their own imports, as well as to pay for their authorized foreign exchange obligations. Proceeds from exports of coffee and bananas must be surrendered within 25 days; the surrender period for other exports ranges from 30 days to 120 days. The commercial banks and exchange houses are re-

---

[1]Over 1,600 products from other Central American countries are exempt from customs duties, except for an import surcharge of 5 percent.

[2]The surcharge was eliminated on January 1, 1995.

quired to sell to the Central Bank all their foreign exchange purchases. Exports of coffee are supervised by the Honduran Coffee Institute.

Bananas are subject to an export tax at the rate of $0.50 for each 40-pound box, but production from newly planted areas is exempt from the tax, and production from rehabilitated areas is subject to a tax at the rate of $0.25 a box. Sugar is subject to an export tax if its export price exceeds a specified level. Coffee exports whose f.o.b. value is more than $80 a quintal (100 kilograms) are subject to a 5 percent export tax (and a 10 percent income tax) on the difference between the export price and price of $80 a quintal.

Payments for and Proceeds from Invisibles

All buyers of foreign exchange are required to fill out a form stating the purpose for which the funds will be used. There are no limits on the amount purchased. There are no restrictions on the importation of foreign banknotes by travelers. Proceeds from invisibles are not required to be repatriated.

Capital

There are no restrictions on activities involving the receipt of foreign exchange and its transfer abroad for investment in mutual funds, housing developments, real estate, or similar activities. Foreign mutual funds and similar financial institutions must have permission to collect funds in Honduras for deposit or investment abroad. The approval of Congress is required for all public sector foreign borrowing. Private sector external debt contracts must be registered with the Central Bank for statistical purposes only.

Purchases of capital shares in existing domestic firms and foreign direct investments are permitted in all sectors without restriction, with the exception of defense-related industries, hazardous industries, and small-scale industry and commerce. Investments in hazardous industries require prior approval. All foreign investments must be registered with the Secretary of Economy and Trade, and repatriation of registered capital and transfers of dividends and profits earned on such capital are not restricted. Investment insurance may be arranged in Honduras or abroad without restriction.

Gold

Residents may hold and acquire gold coins in Honduras for numismatic purposes. With this exception, residents other than the monetary authorities and authorized industrial users are not allowed to hold or acquire gold in any form other than jewelry, at home or abroad. Imports and exports of gold in any form other than jewelry require licenses issued by the Central Bank; such licenses are not normally granted except for imports and exports by or on behalf of the monetary authorities, industrial users, and producers of gold. All locally produced gold is exported in the form of ore for refining. Commercial imports and exports of jewelry and other articles containing gold require licenses issued by the Ministry of Economy; for most articles, licenses are granted freely. Exports of gold are subject to a tax of 5 percent.

Changes During 1994

Exchange Arrangement

July 17. The interbank foreign exchange system was suspended temporarily, and a foreign exchange auction system was introduced. Under the auction system, banks and exchange houses are required to sell all their daily foreign exchange purchases to the Central Bank, which auctions at least 60 percent of the foreign exchange it has purchased at a "base price" that it has set. The base price is changed each time the reference exchange rate (the weighted average of successful bids) differs in the same direction from the base prices for 15 consecutive auctions. The bid (buying) price in the auctions cannot be different from the base price by more than 1 percent, and the maximum bid in an auction cannot exceed $200,000.

Changes During 1995

Imports and Import Payments

January 1. The 10 percent customs surcharge was eliminated.

HONG KONG[1]

(Position as of December 31, 1994)

Exchange Arrangement

The currency of Hong Kong is the Hong Kong Dollar. The authorities do not maintain margins in respect of exchange transactions. Since October 17, 1983, the Hong Kong dollar has been linked to the U.S. dollar, the intervention currency, at the rate of HK$7.80 per US$1. Under this linked exchange rate arrangement, the three note-issuing banks must deliver to the Exchange Fund an amount in U.S. dollars that is equivalent to the local currency issued at the linked exchange rate as backing for their Hong Kong dollar note issues. The Exchange Fund, in turn, issues to each rate-issuing bank non-interest-bearing certificates of indebtedness denominated in Hong Kong dollars. Conversely, the note-issuing banks may redeem U.S. dollars from the Exchange Fund by delivering certificates of indebtedness and withdrawing local banknotes from circulation at the same linked exchange rate. The amount of indebtedness of the Government represented by the certificates of indebtedness will be reduced accordingly. Other banks may acquire local currency notes from the note-issuing banks against Hong Kong dollar deposits at parity. For other transactions, the exchange rate of the Hong Kong dollar is set in the exchange market at freely negotiated rates. However, the possibility of interest rate arbitrage and currency arbitrage, together with the capability of the Hong Kong Monetary Authority to intervene in the market, tends to keep the market rate in line with the linked rate. On December 31, 1994, the middle rate in the interbank foreign exchange market for the U.S. dollar was HK$7.738 per US$1. There are no taxes or subsidies on purchases or sales of foreign exchange. The forward exchange markets are operated on private sector initiatives, and the Government has no official role.

Administration of Control

There are no exchange controls. Import and export licensing is carried out mainly by the Director-General of Trade.

Prescription of Currency

No prescription of currency requirements are in force. Settlements between residents of Hong Kong and nonresidents may be made and received freely in Hong Kong dollars or any other currency.

Nonresident Accounts

No distinction is made between resident and nonresident accounts.

Imports and Import Payments

Imports are free of restrictions, except for those restrictions maintained for reasons of health, safety, environmental protection, or security. All imports are free of duties, although an excise tax for revenue and health purposes is levied on imported and domestically produced cigarettes and other tobacco products, alcoholic liquors, methyl alcohol, and some hydrocarbon oils. With a few exceptions, a trade declaration must be lodged with the Customs and Excise Department within 14 days of importation or exportation in respect of each consignment of goods imported into or exported from Hong Kong. Payments for permitted imports may be made freely, at any time and in any currency.

Exports and Export Proceeds

Export licenses and certificates of origin are required for certain textile products to enable Hong Kong to fulfill its international obligations under the Multifiber Arrangement and under a number of bilateral textile agreements. Other restrictions are maintained for reasons of health, environmental protection, safety, or security. Export proceeds may be collected at any time and in any currency and need not be repatriated or surrendered.

Payments for and Proceeds from Invisibles

There are no limitations on payments for or receipts from invisibles. Income from foreign sources, capital gains, distribution from trusts, and dividends are not taxed in Hong Kong; interest income from domestic sources received by licensed banks and corporations carrying on business in Hong Kong is subject to a profit tax. Interest earned on bank deposits by individuals is exempt from the profit tax. Resident and nonresident travelers may

---

[1]Hong Kong is a nonmetropolitan territory in respect of which the United Kingdom has accepted the Fund's Articles of Agreement.

freely bring in and take out any amount in domestic or foreign banknotes, traveler's checks, and other means of payment.

Capital

No exchange control requirements are imposed on capital receipts or payments by residents or non-residents. A license or an authorization is required for companies, whether incorporated in Hong Kong or elsewhere, to conduct banking or insurance and securities dealings. Otherwise, all overseas companies are required only to register with the Companies Registry within one month of establishing a place of business in Hong Kong.

Gold

There are free and unrestricted markets for gold and gold futures that are open to residents and non-residents. Imports and exports of gold in any form (including finished jewelry) are freely permitted and do not require licenses. Residents may hold gold in any form and amount in Hong Kong or abroad. Commemorative gold coins of HK$1,000 are legal tender but do not circulate.

Changes During 1994

No significant changes occurred in the exchange and trade system.

HUNGARY

(Position as of December 31, 1994)

Exchange Arrangement

The currency of Hungary is the Hungarian Forint. The exchange rate of the forint is determined on the basis of a currency basket comprising the European currency unit (ECU)[1] (70 percent) and the U.S. dollar (30 percent). The value of the forint in terms of the basket is adjusted at irregular intervals, principally in light of the difference between the domestic and foreign rates of inflation.

The official exchange rate is fixed at about noon every day against the basket and is calculated for 20 convertible currencies and the ECU within margins of ±2.5 percent, but licensed banks are free to determine their own margins within this band. The National Bank of Hungary (NBH) intervenes at the market rate to keep it within the margin of the peg. The official spot buying and selling rates in U.S. dollars on December 31, 1994 were Ft 107.223 and Ft 107.757, respectively, per US$1. Banks are free to set the exchange rates for currency notes and traveler's checks.

As a transitional measure, transferable and clearing rubles continue to be used (1) for the settlement of certain outstanding financial claims related to contracts concluded before the end of 1990, and (2) for other settlements that are to be phased out. For outstanding claims, official exchange rates are quoted for the transferable and clearing ruble. At the end of December 1994, the middle rate for the forint against 1 transferable or clearing ruble was Ft 27.5. The NBH does not quote the exchange rate of the forint for currencies of countries belonging to the former Council for Mutual Economic Assistance (CMEA) and many other countries; for cash transactions in those currencies the exchange rates are freely determined by the commercial banks and exchange offices.

Agreements between Hungary and the Slovak Republic permit their national currencies to be converted into each other's currency through their respective banking systems for the purpose of tourist travel between the two countries at exchange rates freely determined by the commercial banks and exchange offices; they also stipulate limits on the importation of banknotes by travelers. Another agreement, concluded at the end of September 1991, extends the arrangement to payments through interbank settlements for a list of noncommercial transactions. Interbank settlements between the two countries in Hungarian forint and Slovak crowns have been actually made in low volume, through only one Hungarian and one Slovak commercial bank. The Czech Republic abandoned the same agreements with Hungary in the first half of 1993. As far as cash transactions are concerned, a free exchange market exists for the Slovak crown, with trading handled by about thirty organizations; for the Czech koruna, trading is handled by four or five organizations; and for the currencies of Bulgaria, Poland, Romania, the Baltic countries, Russia, and the other countries of the former Soviet Union, most trading is handled by one organization.

The commercial banks may engage in forward transactions with terms ranging from seven days to one year, and forward exchange rates may be negotiated freely between the banks and their customers. The commercial banks may also enter into foreign currency swaps with the NBH.

Administration of Control

Authority for enforcement of foreign exchange regulations is vested in the Minister of Finance, who exercises related functions through the NBH, except for those functions reserved for the Minister himself or delegated to other institutions. The NBH may entrust other agencies, such as banking institutions and travel agencies, with the performance of specified tasks.

All economic organizations and private persons in Hungary are entitled to carry out foreign trade activity, provided that foreign trade was part of their business activities when incorporated, in convertible currencies and Hungarian forint after registering with the NBH (the Ministry of International Economic Relations before January 1, 1992).

In accordance with the Fund's Executive Board Decision No. 144-(52/51) adopted on August 14, 1952, Hungary notified the Fund on July 22, 1992 that, in compliance with UN Security Council Resolution No. 757 (1992), it had imposed certain restrictions on the making of payments and transfers for

---

[1]Australian dollars, Austrian schillings, Belgian francs, Canadian dollars, Danish kroner, deutsche mark, Finnish markkaa, French francs, Irish pounds, Italian lire, Japanese yen, Kuwaiti dinars, Netherlands guilders, Norwegian kroner, Portuguese escudos, pounds sterling, Spanish pesetas, Swedish kronor, Swiss francs, and U.S. dollars. Exchange rates are also quoted for banknotes and traveler's checks in Greek drachmas.

current international transactions in respect of the Federal Republic of Yugoslavia (Serbia/Montenegro). Restrictions on the provision of financial services to the Federal Republic of Yugoslavia (Serbia/Montenegro) were also imposed on May 6, 1993, in accordance with UN Resolution No. 820.

Prescription of Currency

Payments to and from countries with which Hungary has bilateral payments agreements are made in the currencies and in accordance with the procedures set forth in those agreements. If there are no specific agreements, or if trade takes place outside the scope of the agreements, settlement is normally made in a convertible currency officially quoted in Hungary or in Hungarian forint. At the end of 1994, bilateral agreements were maintained with Albania, Bulgaria, Cambodia, the Lao People's Democratic Republic, Poland, Romania, the Russian Federation, and Viet Nam for the settlement of outstanding transferable or clearing ruble balances with shipments of goods; at the end of 1994, agreements were concluded with Cuba, the Democratic People's Republic of Korea, and Mongolia.

Hungary's only remaining operative bilateral payments agreements are with Brazil and Ecuador. Under these agreements, outstanding balances are settled every 90 days.

With respect to outstanding balances under inoperative bilateral payments agreements, most of which are with former CMEA members and other socialist countries, agreements for settlement have been reached in most cases. Hungary was a net debtor only to the former German Democratic Republic and has agreed on a schedule of payments to settle the outstanding balance in convertible currency by the end of 1995. The Russian Federation, the largest net debtor to Hungary, has agreed to settle the amount owed by the end of 1997 through the delivery of goods and services or debt-equity swaps.

Resident and Nonresident Accounts

Nonresident natural and juridical persons as well as resident natural persons may freely maintain convertible currency accounts at authorized commercial banks. Resident juridical persons may open convertible currency accounts only with funds originating from specific sources, such as capital paid in convertible currency by the foreign owners of joint-venture companies or donations paid in convertible currency for foundations, churches and social organizations, and budgetary institutions. The accounts carry interest, payable in the currency of deposit, and have a guarantee of repayment up to a maximum of the equivalent of Ft 1 million but no exchange rate guarantee in case of conversion. The interest rates on deposits are determined by the commercial banks. No authorization is required to open such accounts or to draw on them.

Imports and Exports

Beginning in December 1990, a general authorization was granted to all entities to import and export items without specific license except for those on a negative list. A global quota is reported to the World Trade Organization (WTO) on imports of consumer goods that are subject to license by the Ministry of Industry and Commerce and settled in convertible currencies. A license is required for imports that are for the account of the settlement of the outstanding balances in transferable or clearing rubles.

Importers have an automatic right to purchase foreign exchange through the banking system for all bona fide imports. When applying for foreign exchange, importers have to complete a declaration, stating the use of foreign exchange. The NBH conducts a random check of banks and enterprises for compliance with the regulations.

Commercial banks may enter into deferred payment arrangements on behalf of their clients without restriction for a period of up to one year; arrangements exceeding three months must be reported to the NBH by the client. These arrangements need not be secured by bank obligations. For deferred payments of over one year, permission from the NBH is required.

Export proceeds must be received in officially quoted convertible currencies or in Hungarian forint. In the former case, such proceeds must be surrendered against Hungarian forint to a licensed bank within eight days of receipt of the foreign exchange. Certain exemptions are granted, subject to specific approval by the NBH. Export earnings must be repatriated immediately following the shipment of goods. Enterprises engaged in foreign trade are required to provide the NBH with semiannual reports showing claims outstanding in connection with their export activities. The collection of export contracts exceeding Ft 4 million must be guaranteed by either letter of credit, bank guarantee, or bank collection. Export proceeds received in forint by nonresidents may be deposited in foreign trade accounts with licensed banks, and nonresidents are allowed to convert balances in such accounts into foreign exchange for transfer abroad.

Noncommercial goods imported by returning Hungarian travelers are subject to a general import duty of 15 percent based on the actual invoice price with a duty-free allowance of Ft 8,000. Residents, if they are employees of a domestic agency and if they are stationed abroad for more than one year may import, free of customs duty, goods up to a value equivalent to 40 percent of their earnings.

Certain exports are prohibited for sanitary, security, and other noneconomic reasons. An export subsidy may be provided for exports of agricultural products and processed foods settled in convertible currencies or Hungarian forint. The value-added tax paid on goods that are exported is refunded. The refund and the subsidy are calculated on the basis of the customs invoice value.

Hungary has negotiated new trade agreements with former CMEA countries based on free market principles and providing for settlements in convertible currencies at world market prices, with no official overdraft, credit, or clearing facilities. As of December 1992, new trade agreements were in effect with Albania, Armenia, Belarus, Bulgaria, the Czech Republic, Estonia, Georgia, Lithuania, Moldova, Poland, Romania, the Russian Federation, the Slovak Republic, Ukraine, Uzbekistan, and Viet Nam. At the end of 1993, new trade agreements were in effect with the People's Republic of China, Croatia, Kazakhstan, and Latvia. The Trade Protocol of the Association Agreement between Hungary and the European Union entered into force on March 1, 1992 with the help of the Interim Agreement. The Visegrad agreements of the Central European Free Trade Area (CEFTA) with Poland, the Czech Republic, and the Slovak Republic entered into effect in March 1993, and the trade agreement with five European Free Trade Association (EFTA) countries (Austria, Liechtenstein, Norway, Sweden, and Switzerland) entered into effect in October 1993.

Payments for and Proceeds from Invisibles

Payments for invisibles related to merchandise transactions, including transportation and advertising, are freely granted. Other transactions require general or individual authorization, irrespective of their amount, mostly from the NBH and, in some special cases, from the Ministry of Finance or another responsible authority. Foreign exchange for related payments is made available automatically once the underlying transactions have been authorized.

Budgetary or social institutions may obtain general authorizations for transactions up to specified amounts in connection with their own activities. General authorization up to specified amounts or a certain proportion of turnover is given to enterprises engaging in foreign economic activities for the purpose of defraying expenses other than those

directly related to trade. Such authorizations relate to expenses for travel and other expenses, such as the maintenance of foreign representation and related personnel expenses. Compliance with the conditions of the general authorizations is reviewed on an ex post basis by the NBH or the Ministry of Industry and Commerce.

There are no restrictions on purchase of foreign exchange for business travel purposes.

Until June 1992, foreign exchange allowances for travel were granted to passport holders in convertible currencies, subject to an annual limit of $50 a year. For passport holders over 14 years of age, the allowance was available annually or up to the total amount of unused previous annual allowances. In addition, a bonus of $50 or $100 would have been available in 1992 and 1993 if the allowances had not been used in 1990 or 1991, respectively. Those travelers who used more than one-half of the total allowance available for the three-year period 1988 to 1990 could not receive further allowances in 1991 to 1992. Since April 1, 1994, exchange allowances for tourist travel have been increased by the equivalent of $800 a passport holder over 14 years of age and to $300 for those under 14. Unused amounts of the annual $800 and $300 cannot be carried over to subsequent years. Package tours may be freely purchased in forint.

No minimum spending or conversion requirement applies to nonresident travelers to Hungary, but to cover their anticipated expenditures while in Hungary, they must have a certain amount of money at their disposal, which is checked at the borders. Nonresidents may take out of the country foreign exchange assets and economic assets, in addition to their personal effects, without a license from the foreign exchange authority, provided that they have filled out a "Certified Declaration on Brought-In Assets" on arrival. Foreign travelers may take out of the country without restriction all of the articles purchased in Hungary with forint converted from convertible currency; conversion into forint must, however, be verified with presentation of records.

Since August 1, 1992, residents may, without a license from the foreign exchange authority, bring into or take out of the country domestic currency in an amount not exceeding Ft 10,000 a person (in denominations not exceeding Ft 1,000); the corresponding limit for nonresidents was also set at Ft 10,000 effective May 1, 1994. Coins made of precious metal may not be taken out of the country at all.

No foreign exchange is made available for study abroad. Students' living expenses and tuition fees while abroad must be covered by scholarships or financial support from nonresidents or from convertible currency accounts of the person in question (see section on Resident and Nonresident Accounts, above). Transfers abroad by nonresident workers in Hungary, other than those employed in joint ventures, are allowed on a case-by-case basis. Nonresident employees of joint ventures may transfer abroad up to 50 percent of their taxed income.

Capital

Under the new Central Banking Law approved by the Parliament on December 1, 1991, financial institutions must report all foreign borrowing to the NBH. Foreign borrowing of other legal entities is subject to the approval of the NBH. Granting credits to foreigners by the Hungarian financial institutions is in most cases limited to credits with maturities of up to six months. Commercial credits in connection with foreign trade activities between nonfinancial legal entities with maturities of over one year need authorization.

Foreign investment in the form of joint ventures with Hungarian enterprises may be established without approval, but in the case of banks and insurance companies, foreign participation exceeding 10 percent of equity requires government approval. Joint ventures may also be established in duty-free zones. In both cases, the joint venture is considered a Hungarian legal entity, but those in duty-free zones are exempted from several regulations. Machines and equipment, technical know-how, and patents may qualify as foreign investment. Joint ventures are granted a 60 percent allowance on the profit tax in the first five years of operation and 40 percent thereafter until the end of the tenth year, provided the equity capital exceeds Ft 50 million, the foreign partner's ownership exceeds 30 percent, and more than one-half of proceeds come from production of goods; this compares with a generally applied profit tax rate of 40 percent. The reinvestment of profits is encouraged by a reduction in the profit tax. Joint ventures in preferred fields of activities are granted 100 percent of profit tax allowance for five years and pay 60 percent thereafter until the end of the tenth year. The right to these incentives could be obtained until December 31, 1993. The inputs imported by joint ventures are exempt from customs duties. Guarantee is given for the transfer of the foreign investors' share of profits or, if the joint venture is liquidated, of the invested capital and capital gains. In addition, a guarantee may be obtained from the NBH to cover losses on invested assets as a result of state measures or from Hungarian banking institutions to cover the fulfillment of obligations of the Hungarian partner.

Foreign investment by resident economic organizations, either by establishing subsidiaries or affiliates or by acquiring an interest in a foreign enterprise, is subject to the approval of the Ministry of Industry and Commerce. In addition, approval is required from the Minister of Finance in his capacity as the foreign exchange authority.

Except for gifts with a market value of up to Ft 3,000, the transfer of economic assets abroad by residents is subject to licensing administered by the NBH. Gifts (movable property that is in Hungary) from nonresidents to residents in excess of Ft 100,000 a person and from Hungarian residents to nonresidents in excess of Ft 20,000 a person are also subject to licensing. Nonresidents are generally not allowed to acquire real estate, or other immovable property in Hungary, except through inheritance. Joint ventures can own real estate necessary for their activities without authorization.

Outward capital transfers by resident natural persons are not generally approved. For certain established categories, such as inheritances, transfers may be authorized on the basis of agreements and reciprocity with other countries, subject to the approval of the NBH.

Emigrants are allowed to take out of the country assets valued up to Ft 500,000, and gold and jewelry considered to be personal effects. Other assets of emigrants, as well as the assets of nonresidents, are held either in the care of a person designated by the nonresident owner or, in the case of financial assets, in a nonresident forint account or deposit. In the case of emigrants, the licenses for transfers of assets are granted by the NBH.

Gold

All trade in gold and gold objects is subject to the authority of the NBH, in concurrence with the responsible authority if for industrial or artistic use. All ingots and gold coins must be offered to the NBH for sale. Except for transactions with enterprises specifically authorized to transact in gold, all transactions in gold are subject to licensing administered by the NBH.

Changes During 1994

Exchange Arrangement

January 1. The margins for official spot buying and selling rates were widened from ±0.3 percent to ±0.5 percent. A minimum amount for transactions with the NBH was raised from the equivalent of $1 million to $2 million.

January 3. The exchange rate was depreciated by 1.0 percent.

February 16. The exchange rate was depreciated by 2.6 percent.

May 13. The exchange rate was depreciated by 1.0 percent.

May 16. The currency composition of the basket to which the forint is pegged was changed from the deutsche mark and the U.S. dollar (with equal weights) to the ECU (70 percent) and the U.S. dollar (30 percent).

June 10. The exchange rate was depreciated by 1.2 percent.

August 5. The margins for official spot buying and selling rates were widened from ±0.5 percent to ±1.25 percent.

August 5. The exchange rate was depreciated by 8.0 percent.

October 11. The exchange rate was depreciated by 1.1 percent.

November 29. The exchange rate was depreciated by 1.0 percent.

December 23. The margin for official spot intervention rates was widened from ±1.25 percent to ±2.25 percent.

Resident and Nonresident Accounts

June 1. Nonresidents were allowed to convert balances in foreign trade forint accounts into foreign exchange for transfer abroad.

Payments for and Proceeds from Invisibles

April 1. The annual allowance for tourists who travel abroad was increased from $300 to $800 a person for adults (from $150 to $300 for children under 14 years of age). The limit on the number of trips that may be taken abroad was eliminated. The availability of foreign exchange to travel agents would not be limited.

May 1. (1) The restriction on purchases of foreign exchange for business travel purposes was eliminated; (2) the limit on the amount of package tours that may be purchased in forint was abolished; (3) the limit on the amount of domestic currency rates a nonresident may take out of Hungary was increased to Ft 10,000; and (4) the limits on the value of gifts a nonresident may give to a Hungarian resident and that a Hungarian resident may give to a nonresident without a license were increased to Ft 10,000 and Ft 20,000, respectively.

ICELAND

(Position as of January 31, 1995)

Exchange Arrangement

The currency of Iceland is the Icelandic Króna. The external value of the króna is pegged to a basket of currencies consisting of European currency unit (ECU), Japanese yen, and U.S. dollar. The official exchange rate is determined in the interbank market in a daily fixing meeting. The participants in the market are the Central Bank of Iceland and four commercial banks. The Central Bank intervenes in the exchange market to keep the exchange rate within a margin of ±2.25 percent around the central rate. On December 31, 1994, the buying and selling rates were ISK 68.21 and ISK 68.39, respectively, per US$1, the principal trading currency in Iceland. Banks and other foreign exchange dealers are free to set their own commercial exchange rates and to decide the spread between buying and selling rates. A special tax of 15 percent is levied on any fees the exchange dealers charge for selling or transferring foreign exchange abroad.[1]

Iceland formally accepted the obligations of Article VIII, Sections 2, 3, and 4 of the Fund Agreement, as from September 19, 1983.

Administration of Control

The Ministry of Industry and Commerce has ultimate responsibility for matters concerning imports and, in consultation with the Central Bank, on foreign exchange regulations. Export controls are administered by the Ministry of Foreign Affairs and Foreign Trade. All foreign exchange transactions, including capital transactions, are free of restrictions unless explicitly prohibited by provisions of the Exchange Act No. 87/1992 or the Foreign Exchange Regulation that came into effect on January 1, 1995.

Currently, the exchange control functions of the Central Bank include authorizing foreign exchange dealers to operate on a commercial basis, carrying out reporting requirements for statistical purposes, and regulating foreign direct investments. The administrative control of foreign trade in goods, such as tax duties and documentation, is carried out by the customs authorities.

In accordance with the Fund's Executive Board Decision No. 144-(52/51) adopted on August 14, 1952, Iceland notified the Fund on July 31, 1992 that, in compliance with UN Security Council Resolution No. 757 (1992), certain restrictions had been imposed on the making of payments and transfers for current international transactions in respect of the Federal Republic of Yugoslavia (Serbia/Montenegro).

Prescription of Currency

There are no prescription of currency requirements.

Nonresident Accounts

There are no restrictions on nonresident accounts with respect to the amounts, currencies, or instruments involved. All accounts in domestic banks must be identified by name and identification number, and the banks must report to the Central Bank the monthly position of nonresident accounts.

Imports and Import Payments

Most goods can be imported freely without a license. The main exemptions are live animals and certain agricultural products. Certain imports, including fertilizers, tobacco, and alcoholic beverages, can only be imported under state trading arrangements. Some fresh vegetables, including potatoes, and flowers are subject to periodic import control. For imports that require a license, a fee of 1 percent is assessed on the króna value of the import license when it is issued.

Automobiles are subject to a special import tax ranging between zero and 32 percent, depending on the weight of the vehicle and its engine capacity. Buses, heavy trucks, ambulances, and public service vehicles are exempt. Certain goods, whether imported or domestic, are subject to a special excise tax of 24 percent or 30 percent ad valorem. A specific import tax applies to wines and spirits, with the amount of tax depending on the alcohol content and volume.

No exchange control requirements are imposed on payments for imports.

Exports and Export Proceeds

Exports of fisheries and agricultural products require licenses issued by the Ministry of Foreign Affairs and Foreign Trade.

No exchange controls are imposed on receipts from exports.

---

[1]This tax is expected to be abolished on January 1, 1996.

Payments for and Proceeds from Invisibles

No exchange controls are imposed on payments for or proceeds from invisibles.

Capital

The general rules are that both inward and outward capital transfers are free of restrictions if not prohibited by provisions of exchange regulations or other special legislation. Foreign governments, local authorities, and other public authorities are prohibited from issuing debt instruments in Iceland unless permitted to do so by the Central Bank.

Foreign direct investments in Iceland are regulated, in accordance with special legislation No. 34/1991, as follows: (1) nonresidents are free to make investments in Iceland, subject to the conditions laid down in general legislation governing foreign investment or sector-specific legislation; (2) only resident Icelandic citizens or domestically registered companies wholly owned by resident Icelandic citizens may fish within the Icelandic fishing limit or operate primary fish processing; (3) only Icelandic state and local authorities, resident Icelandic citizens, and domestically registered Icelandic companies wholly owned by resident Icelandic citizens may acquire the right to harness waterfalls and geothermal energy. The restrictions apply to power production and distribution companies; (4) investment by nonresidents in domestic airlines is restricted to 49 percent; (5) investment by nonresidents in domestic incorporated commercial banks is restricted to 25 percent, but foreign commercial banks are allowed to open branches in Iceland; and (6) total investment by single nonresidents, or by financially linked nonresidents, in excess of ISK 300 million a year is subject to authorization by the Minister of Commerce. This financial limit is subject to change in the price index. Total investment by nonresidents in any sector must not exceed 25 percent, but the Minister of Commerce may grant an exemption to that limit.

In some sectors of the economy, sectoral legislation stipulates that either some or all of the founders or managing directors of a company must be residents. The legislation on joint-stock companies stipulates that the majority of founders must be residents before the company is established. The managing director and a majority of the members of the board of directors of a company must be residents. Citizens of the European Economic Area are exempted from this restriction, and the Minister of Commerce may grant exceptions to this requirement.

The ownership and uses of real estate in Iceland are governed by the provision of Act No. 19/1966 with amendments in 1991 and 1993. The conditions to own real estate in Iceland are (1) individuals must be Icelandic citizens; (2) in the case of unlimited companies, all owners must be Icelandic citizens; and (3) joint-stock companies must be registered in Iceland, at least 80 percent must be owned by Icelandic citizens, and all of the members of the board of directors must be Icelandic citizens. Icelandic citizens must control the majority of the voting power at annual meetings. The same conditions apply if the real estate is to be leased for more than three years or if the lease agreement cannot be terminated with less than one year's notice. However, a company that is granted an operating license in Iceland may acquire real estate for its own use as long as the license does not carry with it the right to exploit natural resources. Citizens of the European Union and other foreign citizens that have been domiciled in Iceland for at least five years are exempted from these restrictions. The Minister of Justice may grant others exemption from these requirements.

Short-term foreign borrowing and lending by residents to nonresidents, other than trade credits, are permitted up to a limit of ISK 5 million.

Gold

A commemorative gold coin with a face value of ISK 100 is legal tender but does not circulate. Residents may hold and acquire gold in Iceland and abroad.

Changes During 1994

Capital

January 1. All financial restrictions on investments in long-term foreign securities by residents were removed. Investments in inward and outward short-term securities were permitted. subject to a limit of ISK 1 million for resident individuals and of ISK 175 million for resident mutual funds. The limit on investments in short-term domestic securities by nonresidents was set at ISK 75 million. Short-term foreign borrowing and lending by residents to nonresidents other than trade credits were permitted up to a limit of ISK 5 million. The ceiling on deposits of residents with foreign institutions was removed.

Changes During 1995

Administration of Control

January 1. A new exchange regulation came into effect. This regulation confirmed the liberalization of foreign exchange transactions as was gradually set out in Exchange Act No. 87/1992. The surrender requirement for foreign exchange receipts by residents was abolished. All financial limits on short-term capital movements were removed. The requirement that securities must be purchased through intermediary authorized dealers was abolished, and restrictions on forward contracts and other financial derivatives were abolished. The only remaining restrictions on capital movements concern the issuing of debt instruments by foreign governments in Iceland. Foreign direct investments by nonresidents in some business sectors are restricted by Act No. 34/1991, and purchases or rights to use real estate in Iceland are governed by the provisions of Act No. 19/1966.

INDIA

(Position as of December 31, 1994)

Exchange Arrangement

The currency of India is the Indian Rupee, the exchange value of which is determined on the basis of underlying demand and supply conditions in the interbank market. The Reserve Bank of India purchases spot U.S. dollars from any authorized person at its designated offices or branches at the rate determined on the basis of the market exchange rate. It does not normally purchase spot deutsche mark, Japanese yen, or pounds sterling, and it does not purchase or sell forward any currency. The Reserve Bank is obligated to sell spot U.S. dollars on the basis of the market exchange rate only for debt-service payment purposes on behalf of the Government of India.

The Reserve Bank does not sell forward any currency to authorized dealers but may enter into swap transactions, under which it buys spot U.S. dollars and sells forward for two to six months. Purchases and sales of U.S. dollars are made by the Reserve Bank in multiples of $5,000, with a minimum of $25,000.

Exchange rates against other currencies are derived from the cross rate of the U.S. dollar with the Indian rupee. The Reserve Bank stands ready to purchase and sell spot and sell forward currencies of the member countries of the Asian Clearing Union (ACU)[1] at rates determined on the basis of the Reserve Bank's reference rate for the rupee in terms of the U.S. dollar, which is calculated with reference to the rates prevailing in the interbank market around noon and the SDR-U.S. dollar rate published by the IMF.

Authorized dealers may maintain balances and positions in "permitted currencies," that is, foreign currencies that are freely convertible (currencies that the authorities of the countries concerned permit to be converted into major currencies and for which a fairly active market exists for dealings against other major currencies). Authorized dealers are also permitted to maintain abroad balances and positions in European currency units (ECUs). Authorized dealers are permitted to deal spot or forward in any permitted currency; however, there are restrictions on authorized dealers' net foreign exchange exposure in respect of their borrowing and lending activities abroad. Forward purchases or sales of foreign currencies against rupees with banks abroad are prohibited. On December 31, 1994, the indicative market rate (average of the buying and selling rates) for telegraphic transfers in the New York market was Rs 31.41 per US$1; on December 30, 1994, the Reserve Bank's spot buying rate for the U.S. dollar was Rs 31.37 per US$1.

The Export Credit Guarantee Corporation of India, Ltd. (ECGC) provides protection against exchange fluctuation in respect of deferred receivables from the date of a bid up to 15 years after the award of a contract; exchange cover is offered in Australian dollars, deutsche mark, French francs, Japanese yen, pounds sterling, Swiss francs, U.A.E. dirhams, and U.S. dollars. For payments specified in other convertible currencies, cover is provided at the discretion of the ECGC.

Administration of Control

India formally accepted the obligations of Article VIII, Sections 2, 3, and 4 of the Fund Agreement, as from August 15, 1994.

Exchange control is administered by the Reserve Bank in accordance with the general policy laid down by the Government in consultation with the Reserve Bank. Much of the routine work of exchange control is delegated to authorized dealers. Import and export licenses, where necessary, are issued by the Director General of Foreign Trade (DGFT).

Prescription of Currency

For prescription of currency purposes, countries are divided into two groups: member countries of the ACU (except Nepal) and the external group (all other countries). Payments to countries other than the member countries of the ACU may be made in Indian rupees to the accounts of a resident of any of these countries or in any permitted currency.[2]

---

[1]Bangladesh, Islamic Republic of Iran, Myanmar, Pakistan, and Sri Lanka; Nepal is a member of the ACU, but the Reserve Bank does not deal in Nepalese rupees.

[2]All remittances by nationals of China to any country outside India and all remittances to China by any person residing in India, whether for personal or trade purposes, were prohibited with effect from November 3, 1962. Since the resumption of trade between India and China, remittances arising out of trade transactions are permitted in comformity with exchange control regulations. Restrictions on non-trade-related transactions with China have been abolished. Authorized dealers are permitted to open rupee accounts on their books in the names of their branches or correspondents in China or Pakistan without prior

Receipts from countries other than the member countries of the ACU may be obtained in Indian rupees from accounts maintained with an authorized dealer or in banks situated in any of the countries in the external group or in any permitted currency.

Receipts from the external group of countries may be obtained in rupees from the accounts of banks situated in any country in the group; the accounts must be maintained with an authorized dealer or in any permitted currency. However, special rules may apply in respect of exports under lines of credit extended by the Government of India to the governments of certain foreign countries. All payments on account of eligible current international transactions between India and other members of the ACU except Nepal are required to be settled through the ACU arrangement, as are transactions effected on a deferred basis with the ACU countries.

Resident and Nonresident Accounts

The accounts of Indians and of Bhutanese and Nepalese nationals residing in Bhutan and Nepal, as well as the accounts of offices and branches of Indian, Bhutanese, and Nepalese firms, companies, or other organizations in Bhutan and Nepal, are treated as resident accounts.[3] Accounts related to all other foreign countries are treated as nonresident accounts. Accounts of banks in the external group of countries may be credited with payments for imports, interest, dividends, and other authorized purposes with authorized transfers from the nonresident accounts of persons and firms (including banks), and with proceeds from sales of permitted currencies. They may be debited for payments of exports and for other payments to residents of India. These accounts may also be debited for transfers to nonresident accounts of persons and firms (including banks) and transfers to nonresident external rupee (NRER) accounts. The balances in the accounts of banks may be converted into any permitted currency. All other entries on bank accounts require prior approval from the Reserve Bank.

Ordinary nonresident rupee accounts of individuals or firms may be credited with (1) the proceeds of remittances received in any permitted currency from abroad through normal banking channels, balances sold by the account holder in any permitted currency during his or her visit to India, or balances transferred from rupee accounts of nonresident banks, and (2) legitimate dues paid in rupees by the account holder in India. For credits exceeding Rs 10,000, the authorized dealers are required to ascertain the bona fide nature of the transaction before crediting the account. Authorized dealers may debit the ordinary nonresident rupee accounts for all local disbursements, including investments in India that are covered by the general or special permission of the Reserve Bank, other than for payments toward investments in India.

Nonresident external rupee accounts may be opened by authorized dealers in India for persons of Indian nationality or origin who reside outside India or for overseas companies and partnership firms of which at least 60 percent is owned by nonresidents of Indian nationality or origin. In addition to authorized dealers holding licenses under the 1973 Foreign Exchange Regulation Act, some state cooperative banks and certain urban cooperative banks and scheduled commercial banks not holding such licenses have also been permitted by the Reserve Bank to open and maintain nonresident rupee accounts subject to certain conditions. Such accounts may also be opened for eligible persons during temporary visits to India against the tender of foreign currency traveler's checks, notes, or coins. They may be credited with new funds remitted through banking channels from the country of residence of the account holder or from any country other than the members of the ACU. They may also be credited with the proceeds of foreign currency traveler's checks, personal checks, and drafts in the name of the account holder, as well as foreign currency notes and coins tendered by the account holder while in India and also with income on authorized investments. The transfer of funds from other NRER accounts or foreign currency nonresident accounts is also allowed for bona fide personal purposes if the transferrers and transferees are residents of countries other than those in the ACU. The accounts may be debited for disbursement in India and for transfers abroad. Debiting is also permitted for any other transaction if covered under general or special permission granted by the Reserve Bank.

Balances may also be used to purchase foreign currency, rupee traveler's checks, or traveler's letters of credit for the use of the account holder, his or her family and dependents, and, in the case of corporate entities, for the use of directors and employees. Investments in the shares of Indian companies

---

reference to the Reserve Bank but must obtain approval before opening such accounts in the names of branches of Pakistan banks operating outside Pakistan. Authorized dealers may effect remittances to Pakistan on behalf of private importers as in the case of imports from other countries; they may also effect certain types of personal remittances in accordance with regulations applicable to such remittances; remittances for other purposes require prior approval from the Reserve Bank.

[3]However, residents of Nepal obtain their foreign exchange requirements from the Nepal Rastra Bank.

or in partnership firms and the like or in immovable property may be made with the specific or general approval of the Reserve Bank. Interest on deposits in nonresident external accounts in any bank in India is exempt from the personal income tax although juridical persons are not entitled to this exemption. Interest earnings are transferable. The balances held in such accounts by natural and juridical persons are exempt from the wealth tax; gifts to close relatives in India from the balances in these accounts are exempt from the gift tax.

Foreign currency nonresident (FCNR) accounts denominated in deutsche mark, Japanese yen, pounds sterling, or U.S. dollars may be held in the form of term deposits by persons of Indian nationality and by overseas companies specified above. These accounts may be credited with amounts received through normal banking channels, including interest. Balances may be repatriated at any time without reference to the Reserve Bank. Balances may also be used for the purposes for which debits to NRER accounts are allowed. Effective May 15, 1993, a new FCNR (Banks) Scheme was introduced, and the previous FCNR (A) scheme was abolished, effective August 14, 1994; however, the exchange rate guarantees (issued by the RBI) on existing deposits under the scheme will remain in effect until the deposits mature. The FCNR (B) operates in the same manner as the existing FCNR accounts, except that the issuing bank (not the RBI) provides the exchange rate guarantee on deposit balances.

Nonresident (Nonrepatriable) rupee deposit accounts may be opened by nonresident Indian nationals, overseas corporate bodies predominately owned by nonresident Indian nationals, and foreign citizens of non-Indian origin (except Pakistani and Bangladeshi nationals). These accounts may be opened with funds in freely convertible foreign exchange remitted from abroad or funds transferred from existing NRER or FCNR accounts. The funds in these accounts may not be repatriated abroad at any time. With effect from October 1, 1994, accruing interest has been permitted to be transferred abroad.

Foreign currency ordinary (nonrepatriable) deposit accounts may be maintained by nonresidents.[4] These accounts may be denominated in U.S. dollars and credited with funds received from abroad in freely convertible foreign exchange or transferred from existing NRER or FCNR accounts. On maturity of deposits, the rupee value of the principal and ac-

crued interest may be credited to the ordinary nonresident rupee accounts of the depositor.

Imports and Import Payments

Imports from Fiji, Iraq, and the Federal Republic of Yugoslavia (Serbia/Montenegro) are prohibited.

The current export and import policy, which came into effect on April 1, 1992 and—with its subsequent amendments—is valid for five years, contains the policy governing imports. Capital goods, raw materials, components, spare parts, accessories, instruments, and other goods are freely importable without any restriction by any person, whether the actual user or not, unless such imports are regulated by the negative list of imports.

The negative list of imports consists of prohibited items, restricted items, and canalized items. The prohibited items are tallow, fat, and/or oils that are rendered, unrendered, or otherwise of any animal origin, animal rennet, wild animals (including their parts and products), and ivory. All consumer goods (including consumer durables) except those specifically permitted are restricted and their importation is permitted only against a license. Also the importation of certain specified precious, semiprecious, and other stones; safety, security, and related items; seeds, plants, and animals; insecticides and pesticides; drugs and pharmaceuticals; chemicals and allied items relating to the small-scale sector; and certain other items is restricted. The importation of restricted items is allowed selectively against a license or in accordance with general schemes laid down through public notices for import based on the merit of the application. A large number of consumer goods, including all edible oils (excluding coconut oil, palm kernel oil, RED palm oil and ABD palm stearin) sugar, cameras, roasted or decaffeinated coffee (in bulk packaging), paper and paper products of various types, sports goods, and wood and wood products of various types, are freely importable. The importation of restricted items has been liberalized by permitting a large number of specified restricted items (including certain consumer goods) to be imported against freely transferable special import licenses that are granted to export houses, trading houses, star trading houses, super star trading houses, and exporters and manufacturers who have acquired prescribed quality certification. Certain specified types of petroleum products, fertilizers, edible and nonedible oils, seeds and cereals are canalized for import through the state trading enterprises, i.e., Indian Oil Corporation Ltd., Minerals and Metals Trading Corporation of India Ltd., State Trading Corporation of

---

[4]With effect from August 20, 1994, commercial banks have been prohibited from accepting new deposits, and, with effect from October 1, 1994, interest accruing on existing balances has been permitted to be transferred abroad.

India Ltd., and the Food Corporation of India. Gold and silver may be imported with transferable special import licenses. However, the importation of gold up to 5 kilograms is allowed as part of the baggage of passengers of Indian origin or passengers holding a valid passport issued under the Passports Act of 1967 coming to India after staying abroad for a period of not less than six months and subject to payment of customs duty in convertible currency.

Import licenses are issued with a validity of 12 months; in the case of capital goods imports, they are valid for 24 months. Advance licenses are granted for duty-free imports of raw materials, intermediates, components, consumables, parts, accessories, packing materials, and computer software required for direct use in the product to be exported. When a valid import license is held, the required foreign exchange is released by an authorized bank on presentation of the exchange control copy of the license and the shipping documents. License holders may make payments by opening letters of credit or by remitting against sight drafts. The contracting of suppliers' credits exceeding 180 days and other long-term import credits is subject to prior approval. Payments for imports may not generally be made before shipping documents are submitted, except for goods with import values of up to 15 percent with a maximum of up to $5,000. Advance payments in excess of $5,000 (up to 15 percent in the case of capital goods) may be made by authorized dealers against guarantees from a bank of international repute outside India. However, in special cases—for example, imports of machinery and capital goods for which deposits have to be made with overseas manufacturers—the Reserve Bank grants special authorization for advance payment for a part of the value of the import.

In addition to any applicable import duty, imports are subject to an auxiliary duty of up to 50 percent ad valorem. Among the exemptions are food grains, raw cotton, and books.

Payments for Invisibles

Authority has been delegated to authorized dealers to approve payments for invisibles and remittances up to specified limits. These limits are indicative, and all bona fide requests for amounts exceeding these limits are approved by the Reserve Bank. Authority has also been delegated to authorized banks to approve remittances for certain purposes, without any limits, subject to certain guidelines. Restrictions on the transfer abroad of current income (net of taxes) earned on investments by nonresident Indians and overseas corporations predominantly owned by nonresident Indians and other current income, such as pensions, are to be eliminated in a phased manner during the financial years 1994/95 to 1996/97. Earnings that have accumulated during the period up to March 31, 1994, however, will remain nontransferable. Under the statement of industrial policy announced in July 1991, transfers abroad of dividends by nonresident investors in consumer goods industries must be balanced by export earnings for a period of seven years from the date of commencement of commercial production.

Premiums on insurance policies issued in foreign currency to foreign nationals who do not reside permanently in India may be paid only in foreign currency; payment in rupees may be made only on annuities issued against payment from recognized superannuation or pension funds; Indian residents are prohibited from taking out life insurance policies in foreign currencies.

Branches of foreign banks are not allowed to transfer abroad any profits arising from the sale of nonbanking assets. Profit remittances by branches of foreign firms, companies, and banks require the prior approval of the Reserve Bank. Remittances of profits, dividends, and interest to beneficiaries whose permanent residence is outside of India are allowed, subject to certain conditions and provided that all current tax and other liabilities in India have been cleared.

Foreign nationals temporarily residing in India on account of their employment are permitted to make reasonable remittances to their own countries to pay insurance premiums, to support their families, and for other expenses. Authorized dealers may allow such remittances by foreign nationals, other than those from China, Pakistan, and South Africa, up to 75 percent of net income, provided that they hold valid employment visas.

Resident Indian nationals may travel abroad freely without exchange formalities. Effective March 1, 1994, exchange facilities have been available to resident Indian nationals under the Basic Travel Quota Scheme. Under this scheme, foreign exchange up to $2,000 a person may be released by authorized dealers for one or more trips abroad, except visits to Bhutan and Nepal; in the determination of eligibility under this scheme, all foreign travel other than that covered under the Basic Travel Quota is disregarded.

The exportation of Indian currency notes and coins, except to Bhutan and Nepal, is, in general, prohibited. The exportation to Nepal of Indian currency notes in denominations higher than Rs 100 is also prohibited. However, resident Indians may take with them Indian currency notes not exceeding Rs 1,000 a person at any one time to countries other than Nepal when going abroad on a temporary visit. Exchange bureaus and authorized money changers are permitted to sell foreign currency notes and coins up to the equivalent of Rs 100 to travelers going to Bangladesh and up to $50 or its equivalent to those going to other countries except Bhutan and Nepal. Nonresidents may take out the foreign currency that they brought in (and declared on entry if it exceeded $10,000), less the amounts sold to authorized dealers and authorized money changers in India. Unspent rupee amounts may be reconverted into foreign currency and taken out. Students going to foreign universities with full bursaries receive a foreign exchange allowance of up to $1,500 a person for settling in and for purchasing initial equipment. There is also an allowance of $500 to cover the initial expenses of persons traveling abroad for employment purposes and a travel allowance of $500 for medical checkups and consultations abroad.

Exports and Export Proceeds

Exports to Fiji, Iraq, and the Federal Republic of Yugoslavia (Serbia/Montenegro) are prohibited. Border trade (that is, frontier trade) between India and the Tibet region of China is allowed. Goods may be exported without a license, provided that they are not prohibited, restricted through licensing, or canalized. Restricted products[5] may not be exported unless covered by a valid license issued by the licensing authority concerned.

Some exports are prohibited,[6] and hides, skins, and leather are subject to export duties; other items, including stone boulders and wheat, are subject to minimum export prices as may be set if required.[7] A substantial number of exports, mainly new manufactures (such as engineering goods, chemicals, plastic goods, leather goods, sporting goods, marine products, processed food and agricultural products, handicrafts, textiles, and jute and coir products), receive import duty drawbacks, a refund of the central excise duty, and exemptions. Bona fide foreign tourists may, with the approval of customs, take out of India articles purchased with foreign exchange or with rupees acquired against foreign exchange without a value limit.

Exchange control is exercised over the proceeds from exports to countries other than Bhutan and Nepal. Exporters must declare that the full export proceeds will be received and dealt with in accordance with the prescription of currency regulations. Foreign exchange earnings, including the proceeds of exports, must be offered for sale against rupees to an authorized dealer. Exporters and other recipients of foreign exchange are permitted to retain up to 20 percent of receipts in foreign currency accounts with banks in India. In the case of 100 percent export-oriented units, units in export processing zones, and units in hardware/software technology parts, up to 50 percent of foreign exchange receipts may be retained. Export proceeds must be repatriated by the due date of receipt or within six months of shipment, whichever is earlier, and surrendered to authorized dealers, as required, unless specifically permitted by general or special permission from the Reserve Bank to retain them either with authorized dealers in India or with banks abroad. In respect of exports made to Indian-owned warehouses abroad established with the permission of the Reserve Bank, a maximum period of 15 months is allowed for realization of export proceeds. Exporters are required to obtain permission from the Reserve Bank through authorized dealers in the event that the export value is not realized within the prescribed period. The Reserve Bank also administers a scheme under which engineering goods (capital goods and consumer durables) may be exported under deferred credit arrangements, so that the full export value is paid in installments over more than six months.

The status of exporters is based on their average gross and average net export earnings in the preceding three years, as follows (figures in parentheses indicate minimum average gross and minimum average net export earnings, respectively: export houses (Rs 100 million and Rs 60 million); trading houses (Rs 500 million and 300 million); star trading houses (Rs 2.5 billion and Rs 1.25 billion); and super star trading houses (Rs 7.5 billion and Rs 4 billion). Exporters are also granted a certificate of export, trading, star trading, or super star trading house status (1) if their gross export earnings during the preceding year were Rs 150 million, Rs 750

---

[5]The exportation of certain products, including some mineral ores and concentrates, is permitted subject to licensing.

[6]These include all forms of wildlife, including their parts and products; exotic birds; all items of plants included in Appendix I of the convention on International Trade in Endangered Species; beef; human skeletons; tallow, fats and/or oils of any animal origin excluding fish oil; and wood and wood products in the form of logs, timber, stumps, roots, bark, chips, powder, flakes, dust, pulp, and charcoal. With effect from April 1, 1993, wild orchids, chemicals included in Schedule I of the Chemical Weapons Convention of the United Nations, sandalwood excluding some fully finished products, and red sanders wood in any form were included on the prohibited list of exports.

[7]Exports of footwear and roasted and salted peanuts are permitted on a decontrolled basis.

million, Rs 3 billion, or Rs 10 billion, respectively; (2) if their net foreign exchange earnings during the preceding licensing year were Rs 120 million, Rs 600 million, Rs 1,500 million, or Rs 6,000 million, respectively, or (3) if their net export earnings during the preceding licensing year were Rs 150 million, Rs 750 million, Rs 3 billion, or Rs 10 million, respectively.

Proceeds from Invisibles

Proceeds from invisibles must be repatriated and sold in the interbank market. The importation of Indian currency notes and coins is prohibited. However, any person may bring into India Indian currency notes (other than notes of denominations larger than Rs 100) from Nepal. Indian travelers may bring in up to Rs 1,000 a person in Indian currency notes from other countries if they previously took out this amount when leaving India to travel abroad on a temporary visit. Foreign currency notes may be brought into India without limit, provided that the total amount brought in is declared to the customs authorities upon arrival if the value of foreign notes, coins, and traveler's checks exceeds $10,000 or its equivalent. Foreign currency notes may be sold to any authorized dealer in foreign exchange or to any authorized money changer.

Capital

There are no restrictions on receipts of inward remittances from any country through authorized dealers in India; the subsequent use of such funds in India is, however, subject to approval in most cases. Foreign investments, once admitted, are eligible for the same treatment that Indian enterprises receive.

Banks in India may borrow freely from their branches and correspondents abroad, subject to the maximum of $500,000 or its equivalent for meeting requirements of normal exchange business. They may obtain loans or overdrafts from their overseas branches or correspondents in excess of this limit solely for the purpose of replenishing their rupee resources in India without prior approval from the Reserve Bank; repayment of such borrowings requires prior approval from the Reserve Bank or may be accorded only when the debtor bank has no outstanding borrowings in India from the Reserve Bank or any other bank or financial institution and is clear of all money market borrowings for a period of at least four weeks before the repayment.

Persons residing in India may not borrow any foreign exchange from persons residing inside or outside India without prior permission from the Reserve Bank. The contracting of all foreign currency loans and credits secured from nonresident persons and companies (including banks) as well as repayment of such loans and credits and payments of interest and other charges on such loans require prior permission from the Reserve Bank. The procedure prescribed for raising foreign currency loans by Indian entities envisages that borrowing proposals, except when loans are for less than one year, must be cleared by the Ministry of Finance before they may be approved by the Reserve Bank.

Nonresidents, noncitizens, and nonbank companies not incorporated under Indian law must have permission from the Reserve Bank to initiate, expand, or continue any business activity in India and to hold or acquire shares of any company carrying on a trading, commercial, or industrial activity in India.[8]

---

[8] Persons of Indian nationality or origin who reside abroad may invest freely in any public or private limited company engaged in any activity except agricultural or plantation activities and real estate business (excluding real estate development, that is, construction of houses, etc.), or in any partnership or proprietary concern engaged in any activity other than real estate business and agricultural or plantation activity, provided that funds for investment are either remitted from abroad through normal banking channels or are drawn from their nonresident accounts, that an undertaking is given that repatriation of the capital invested or the profits and dividends arising therefrom will not be requested, and that overall limits on holdings of shares and convertible debentures bought through the stock exchange by nonresident Indians (see below) are adhered to. Overseas companies, societies, and partnership firms that are owned to the extent of at least 60 percent by nonresidents of Indian nationality or origin and overseas trusts in which at least 60 percent of the beneficial interest is irrevocably held by nonresident Indians are also allowed to invest in any public or private limited companies in accordance with the above provisions. Nonresident Indians and overseas companies as defined above may use funds derived from fresh remittances or held in their nonresident (external) or foreign currency (nonresident) accounts to (1) make portfolio investments, with repatriation benefits, up to 1 percent of the capital, provided that their holdings of shares and convertible debentures held on either a repatriable or a nonrepatriable basis do not exceed (a) 5 percent of the paid-up capital of the company concerned or (b) 5 percent of the total paid-up value of each series of convertible debentures issued by the company concerned. However, if a company so resolves through a General Body Resolution, then purchases of shares or debentures of such a company could be made up to 24 percent as against 5 percent mentioned at (b) above; (2) invest freely in National Savings Certificates with full repatriation benefits; (3) invest up to 40 percent of the new equity capital issued by a company setting up industrial manufacturing projects, hospitals (including diagnostic centers), hotels of at least three-star category, and shipping, software, and oil exploration services with repatriation rights for capital and income, subject to deduction of applicable Indian taxes; (4) invest up to 100 percent of new investments, including expansion of existing industrial undertakings in specified priority industries listed in Annex III to the Statement on New Industrial Policy with free repatriation of such investment; and (5) investment in companies engaged in real estate development (e.g., construction of houses, etc.) up to 100 percent of new investments may have to be locked-in for a period of three years for disinvestment. After three years, remittances of disinvestment will be allowed up to

Foreign Direct Investment in India. Before the announcement of the new industrial policy on July 24, 1991, foreign investment in India was being permitted provided that it was accompanied by a technology transfer. Foreign direct investments were permitted in industries that required sophisticated technology, industries that were experiencing critical production gaps, or industries that could expand their exports. Generally, an equity participation of up to 40 percent was permitted. If the required foreign technology was highly sophisticated or the project was predominantly export oriented, a larger foreign equity participation was permitted. The policy relating to foreign investment in free trade zones and export-oriented industrial units was relatively more liberal, and foreign equity up to 100 percent was permitted. Approval for these investments was granted by the Secretariat for Industrial Approvals (SIA) in the Ministry of Industry or, for firms in the free trade zones, by the Ministry of Commerce.

On July 24, 1991, a new industrial policy was announced under which industrial licensing, foreign direct investments, foreign technology agreements, and public sector policy were liberalized. In the area of foreign direct investment, the requirement that such investments must involve transfer of technology was abolished, and the Reserve Bank was authorized to grant automatic approval for investments up to 51 percent of the paid-up capital of the Indian companies that are engaged in manufacturing activities in the 35 priority manufacturing sectors. Applications for investments in areas that do not fall within the authority of the Reserve Bank but that are covered by the foreign investment policy are approved by the Foreign Investment Promotion Board (FIPB). Such investments may be approved up to 100 percent of capital on a case-by-case basis. The SIA in the Ministry of Industry is the relevant agency for all issues related to foreign direct investment, including approvals.

Foreign institutional investors (FIIs) including institutions (e.g., pension funds, mutual funds, investment trusts, asset management companies, nominee companies, and incorporated or institutional portfolio managers) are permitted to make investments in all securities traded on the primary and secondary markets, including equity and other securities and instruments of companies listed on the stock exchange in India. FIIs are required to register initially with the Securities and Exchange Board of India (SEBI) and with the Reserve Bank. The authorization from the Reserve Bank enables FIIs to (1) open accounts denominated in foreign currency; (2) open nonresident rupee accounts for the purposes of operating securities investments; (3) transfer balances between foreign currency accounts and the rupee account; and (4) transfer abroad repatriate capital, capital gains, dividends, and interest income. Portfolio investments in primary or secondary markets are subject to a ceiling of 5 percent of the issued share capital for individual FIIs holding and 24 percent of issued share capital for the total holdings of all registered FIIs in any one company, with the exception of (1) foreign investments under financial collaboration, which are permitted up to 51 percent, and (2) investments through offshore single and regional funds, global depository receipts, and convertibles in the euromarket.

Investment in Trading Companies. Trading companies must be registered with the Ministry of Commerce and must obtain a certificate of their status as either export, trading, star trading, or super star trading house before applying to the Reserve Bank of India for remittance or dividends. Foreign direct investment is permitted in trading companies. The Reserve Bank is responsible for permitting foreign investment of up to 51 percent of the paid-up capital of such Indian companies. A higher percentage is considered for approval by the FIPB and even 100 percent foreign equity may be approved, provided that the funding company is primarily engaged in exports.

Increase in Foreign Equity in Existing Companies. Foreign equity shares in the existing joint-venture companies may raise the ratio to 51 percent of their capital through expansion of their capital base or through preferential allocation of shares to the foreign investor. Firms in certain manufacturing industries and tourist industries (hotels, restaurants, and beach resorts) may increase the equity ratio immediately. Others may increase the equity ratio as part of expansion, provided the expansion is in specified manufacturing or tourist industries. In both cases, the Reserve Bank grants automatic approval.

---

the original investment in foreign exchange. In case of overseas corporate bodies, profits will be allowed to be repatriated up to 16 percent. Income from the investment will also be allowed to be repatriated after deduction of applicable domestic taxes. Nonresident Indians and overseas companies as defined above may also place funds with public limited companies in India as deposits, with full repatriation benefits, provided that (1) the deposits are made for three years, (2) the deposits are made in conformity with the prevailing rules and within the limits prescribed for acceptance of deposits by such companies, and (3) the funds are made available by the depositors through remittances from abroad or through payments from their nonresident (external) or foreign currency (nonresident) accounts. Special tax concessions apply to investments by nonresident Indians.

Prior approval from the Reserve Bank is required for all transfers of shares of Indian companies by nonresidents or foreign nationals to residents. However, sales and transfers of shares of Indian companies through stock exchanges in India by nonresidents of Indian nationality or origin in favor of Indian citizens or persons of Indian origin and Indian companies do not require the Reserve Bank's clearance when the proceeds of such shares sold by the transferrer are credited to his or her ordinary nonresident rupee account with a bank authorized to deal in foreign exchange in India without a right of repatriation outside India. The transfer of shares by nonresidents in favor of nonresidents, residents, or non-FERA companies does not require clearance from the Reserve Bank, provided that the shares are purchased by the nonresidents under the portfolio investment scheme on a repatriation basis and are sold on stock exchanges through the same authorized dealer. In such cases, the sale proceeds may be credited to NRE or FCNR accounts after deduction of tax or may be remitted abroad.

The following capital transactions by residents require approval from the Reserve Bank: (1) holding, acquiring, transferring, or disposing of immovable property outside India (unless acquired while a nonresident of India); (2) exportation of Indian securities and transfers of Indian securities to nonresidents; (3) guaranteeing of obligations of a nonresident or of a resident in favor of a nonresident; and (4) association with, or participation in, the capital of any business concern outside India.

Capital invested in approved projects by residents of other countries, including capital appreciation on the original investment, may be generally repatriated at any time. However, approval must be obtained from the Reserve Bank before effecting a sale that involves repatriation of assets. The proceeds from liquidated foreign investments not eligible for repatriation are kept in a nonresident account.

Indian nationals are granted foreign exchange facilities up to $500 a person or $1,000 a family for emigration purposes. In cases of exceptional hardship, foreign exchange may be released up to a reasonable amount in one lump sum; the remainder of the emigrant's assets and income is kept in a nonresident account, and no further remittances, including pensions, if any, are normally allowed. However, Indian nationals who left the country permanently before the introduction of exchange controls in India (that is, July 1947, against the former Sterling Area countries, and September 1939 against other countries) are permitted to transfer abroad capital assets up to the equivalent of Rs 1 million in one lump sum, and the remaining balance in annual installments not exceeding Rs 500,000. Foreign nationals who are temporarily residing in India (other than nationals of Pakistan) and foreign diplomatic persons are permitted at the time of their retirement to transfer to their own countries the proceeds from the sale of their investments, subject to a limit of Rs 1 million for each family at the time of retirement, and the remainder in annual installments not exceeding Rs 500,000; in addition, they may transfer all their current remittable assets in India.

There are no restrictions on the importation into India of Indian or foreign securities. The acquisition, sale, transfer, exportation, or other disposal of foreign securities requires approval. Residents (other than foreign nationals temporarily but not permanently residing in India and their foreign-born wives also not permanently residing in India) who are natural persons are not normally permitted to purchase securities or personal real estate outside India. Foreign-born widows of Indian nationals are permitted to transfer initially a sum of Rs 1 million when they leave India permanently; thereafter, they are allowed to remit up to Rs 500,000 a year out of capital and income. Transfers abroad of legacies, inheritances, and bequests by persons who were never residents of India are subject to the same limits.

Indian nationals and persons of Indian origin holding foreign passports, residing abroad, and wishing to return to India are not required to surrender, on their arrival, foreign currency assets they acquired lawfully while residing outside India, provided they stayed abroad continuously for at least one year.

Under the Resident Foreign Currency Account Scheme, Indian nationals (returning permanently to India from abroad) are permitted, within three months of their arrival, to open and operate without restriction resident foreign currency accounts in any permitted currency with authorized dealers in India; all foreign exchange transferred from abroad may be credited to these accounts.

Gold

The Gold Control Act of 1968 was repealed on June 6, 1990 by the Gold Control Repeal Act of 1990, which eliminated restrictions on internal trade in gold. However, gold mines continue to sell gold to industrial users through the distribution network of the State Bank of India as well as through market sales. Forward trading in gold or silver is prohibited; exports of silver bullion, sheets, and plates are banned, and exports of silver products are subject to quota restrictions.

The importation and exportation of gold in any form by residents are regulated by the import policy in force. Authorities require special authorization from the Reserve Bank. Exporters of gold and silver jewelry may import their essential inputs such as gold, silver mountings, findings, rough gems, precious and semiprecious synthetic stones and unprocessed pearls, etc., with import licenses granted by the licensing authority. Under this scheme, the foreign buyer may supply, in advance, gold or silver, free of charge, for manufacture and ultimate export of gold or silver jewelry and articles thereof.

Under the Gold Jewelry and Articles Export Promotion and Replenishment Scheme, exporters of gold jewelry and articles are entitled for replenishment of gold, through the designated branches of the State Bank of India or any other agency nominated by the Ministry of Commerce at a price indicated in the certificate issued by the State Bank of India after purchase of gold. The Scheme is limited to exports that are supported by an irrevocable letter of credit, payment of cash on a delivery basis, or advance payment in foreign exchange. Exports of gold jewelry may also be allowed on a collection basis (documents against acceptance). The exporter has the option to obtain gold from the State Bank of India in advance. On presentation of required documents, the appropriate release order and gem replenishment license may be issued by the licensing authority, provided that the exporters satisfy value-added and other requirements under the Scheme. Special permission for imports of gold and silver is granted only in exceptional cases where either no foreign exchange transaction is involved or the metals are needed for a particular purpose. Special permission is also granted when the gold or silver is imported for processing and re-exportation, provided that payments for the importation will not be required, the entire quantity of metal imported will be re-exported in the form of jewelry, and the value added will be repatriated to India in foreign exchange through an authorized dealer.

Exports of gold in any form other than jewelry produced in India for exportation with a gold value not exceeding 10 percent of total value and jewelry constituting the personal effects of a traveler, subject to certain monetary limits, are prohibited unless effected by or on behalf of the monetary authorities. The net exportation of gold from India is not permitted.

Changes During 1994

Exchange Arrangement

August 15. India formally accepted the obligations of Article VIII, Sections 2, 3, and 4 of the Articles of Agreement.

Resident and Nonresident Accounts

August 14. Exchange rate guarantees provided on deposits under the Foreign Currency Nonresident Account Scheme were abolished (guarantees on existing deposits, however, will remain in effect until these deposits mature).

August 19. The authorities announced that, with effect from October 1, 1994, interest accruing under the Nonresident (Nonrepatriable) Rupee Deposit Scheme would be allowed to be transferred abroad.

August 19. Commercial banks were prohibited from accepting new deposits under the Foreign Currency (Ordinary) Nonrepatriable Deposit Scheme. With effect from October 1, 1994, interest accruing on existing balances would be permitted to be transferred abroad.

Payments for Invisibles

August 14. (1) The authorities announced that the limits on foreign exchange allowances for certain payments and transfers for current international transactions that commercial banks are authorized to provide are indicative, and that all bona fide requests for amounts exceeding these limits, as well as those for foreign exchange for which there are no specific limits, would be approved by the Reserve Bank of India without delay. (2) The present restrictions on transfers abroad of income (net of tax) earned on investment by nonresident Indian nationals would be liberalized as follows: (a) with immediate effect, $1,000 earned during the financial year 1994/95 plus one-third of the amount in excess of $1,000 would be allowed to be transferred; (b) during the financial year 1995/96, $1,000 earned during the year plus two-thirds of the amount in excess of $1,000 will be allowed to be transferred; and (c) beginning in the financial year 1996/97, the full amount of income earned during the year would be allowed to be transferred. Earnings that have been accumulated during the period up to the financial year 1994/95, however, would remain nontransferable.

INDONESIA

(Position as of December 31, 1994)

Exchange Arrangement

The currency of Indonesia is the Indonesian Rupiah. Its exchange value is determined by Bank Indonesia under a system of managed float, under which Bank Indonesia announces daily buying and selling rates that are computed on the basis of a basket of weighted currencies with a spread of plus or minus Rp 15. The U.S. dollar is the intervention currency. On December 31, 1994, the buying and selling rates for spot transactions were Rp 2,185 and Rp 2,215, respectively, per US$1. Exchange rates for certain other currencies[1] are determined by reference to the cross rates of the U.S. dollar and the currencies concerned in international markets. There are no taxes or subsidies on purchases or sales of foreign exchange.

Exchange rates announced by Bank Indonesia apply only to certain transactions undertaken at certain times of the day. For all other transactions, banks are free to set their own rates. Purchases and sales of foreign currency bills by Bank Indonesia are conducted from 8:00 a.m. to 11:45 a.m. on the basis of buying and selling rates announced at 3:00 p.m. of the previous business day. Spot and forward transactions, however, are conducted at rates fixed bilaterally between Bank Indonesia and the bank concerned. In addition, from 3:00 p.m. to 4:00 p.m. on Monday through Friday, Bank Indonesia fixes a rate for spot transactions with banks; such transactions are normally conducted to enable the banks to adjust their net open positions. At other times, spot and forward transactions are conducted at rates fixed bilaterally between Bank Indonesia and the banks concerned. Foreign exchange transactions are restricted to the authorized foreign exchange banks, nonbank financial institutions, and licensed money changers. Bank Indonesia trades unlimited amounts of foreign exchange or rupiah with authorized traders at its intervention rates for the day.

Two types of swap facilities are operated by Bank Indonesia: liquidity swaps on the initiative of Bank Indonesia and investment swaps with a maturity of more than two years operated on the initiative of banks.

The commercial banks' weekly net foreign exchange open positions are limited to 25 percent of capital. Separate limits apply to total exposures and off-balance-sheet exposures. A bank whose net open position exceeds the limit is subject to a penalty.

Indonesia formally accepted the obligations of Article VIII, Sections 2, 3, and 4 of the Fund Agreement, as from May 7, 1988.

Administration of Control

Administration of the exchange and trade system is entrusted to Bank Indonesia, the Ministry of Trade, the Ministry of Finance, foreign exchange banks, and the customs authorities. Policies on foreign exchange market operations are established by Bank Indonesia.

Prescription of Currency

Payments and receipts must be effected through the authorized foreign exchange banks and are normally effected in convertible currencies. Indonesia maintains no operative bilateral payments agreements.

Nonresident Accounts

There are no restrictions on the opening by residents or foreign nationals of accounts in Indonesia in rupiah or foreign currencies with authorized foreign exchange banks. However, if holders of accounts in foreign exchange wish to withdraw funds, they must send a letter to the bank; no checks may be drawn on foreign currency accounts.

Imports and Import Payments

There is a registry of authorized importers. Only Indonesian nationals may be authorized as importers, although foreign investors are permitted to import the items required for their own projects. Although all imports into Indonesia are subject to licensing requirements, most are classified under the nonresident license (also called General Importer License).

---

[1]Those commonly used in Indonesia's international transactions: Australian dollars, Austrian schillings, Belgian francs, Brunei dollars, Canadian dollars, Danish kroner, deutsche mark, French francs, Hong Kong dollars, Italian lire, Japanese yen, Malaysian ringgit, Netherlands guilders, New Zealand dollars, Norwegian kroner, Philippine pesos, pounds sterling, Singapore dollars, Swedish kronor, Swiss francs, and Thai baht.

Imports from Israel and the countries against which the UN has imposed a trade embargo are prohibited, as are imports from all sources of most secondhand goods and of certain products. In addition, secondhand engines and their parts and other capital goods may be imported by industrial firms for their own use or for the reconditioning of their industry, in accordance with the guidelines of the Ministries of Trade and of Industry. Certain categories of agricultural imports, including different categories of food, beverages, and fruits, may be imported only by registered importers designated by the Minister of Trade. The procurement policies of companies approved for the importation of fruit, alcoholic beverages, and chickens are evaluated annually by the Government, although explicit quantitative restrictions are not placed on these products.

Since mid-1985, import controls on several product categories (e.g., certain chemicals, steel, foods and beverages, textiles, and agricultural products) have been progressively removed. Controls remain on about 12 percent of total imports. Imports of certain goods remain restricted to approved importers, most of which are state enterprises. For example, Pertamina has a monopoly on the importation of lubricating oil and lubricating fats, and PT Dahana, on the importation of ammunition and explosive gelatin. The Board of Logistics (BULOG) has the sole right to import rice, fertilizer, and sugar, but its monopoly on maize imports was revoked in September 1989 and that on soybean meal in June 1991. The monopoly rights of approved importers (sole agents) also remain in effect for the importation of certain heavy equipment and motor vehicles, although this right may be transferred to general importers. The importation of trucks is subject to restriction. Certain products are granted preferential duties within the framework of the Association of South East Asian Nations (ASEAN).

Imports into Indonesia are subject to preshipment inspection in the exporting country by agencies designated by the Government of Indonesia; inspection expenses are borne by the Indonesian Government. Following inspection, the PT Surveyor Indonesia in Jakarta is required to issue on behalf of its agency in the exporting country a survey report (LPS) specifying the type, quality, quantity, and estimated cost of the goods, the applicable tariff code, freight charges, import duties, and value-added taxes; the LPS must be sent by the agency in Jakarta directly to the bank that has opened letters of credit or, for imports not covered by letters of credit, to the bank designated by the importer. After paying taxes and duties based on the price fixed by the agency, the importer presents all import documents to customs for release of the shipment. The Directorate General of Customs and Excise does not examine goods that have an LPS, except those that are valued at less than $5,000 or are suspected to be illegally imported. Imports for foreign capital investment and domestic capital investment must have an LPS. Cement-asbestos sheets, dry batteries, steel slabs, low-voltage electric cord, and electric light bulbs are subject to quality control.

Exports and Export Proceeds

Exports to Israel and the countries against which the UN has imposed a trade embargo are prohibited, as are exports to all countries of certain categories of unprocessed or low-quality rubber, brass, and copper scrap (except from Irian Jaya), iron scrap, steel scrap, and antiques of cultural value. Exporters are required to possess trade permits, which are issued by the Ministry of Trade. Certain producer-exporters of rubber, plywood, and animal feed may issue certificates of quality for their products. Quality controls are also maintained on certain products, including fish, manioc (cassava), shrimp, coffee, tea, pepper, spices, vegetable oil, and cocoa beans. Exports of certain domestically produced commodities must have prior authorization from the Ministry of Trade in order to maintain supplies to meet domestic demand and to encourage domestic processing of certain raw materials.[2] Concern about domestic price stability sometimes leads to suspension of exports of various items in this category. In 1990, producer-exporters of cement and clinkers were allowed to export these products with the approval of the Ministry of Trade, as shortages developed on the domestic market. Several categories of gold and silver may be exported only by exporters who possess certification from PT Aneka Tambang and authorization from the Ministry of Trade.

Most other products are freely exported by registered private firms and state trading firms. However, manioc (cassava) may be exported only by approved exporters. As of November 1, 1989, pepper is exempt from certain previous export restrictions and may henceforth be exported by all companies possessing a trade permit. Exports of

---

[2]Items affected by such controls include clove seeds, logs, fertilizer, cement, construction reinforcements of iron, automobile tires, paper, asphalt, stearin, cattle, salt, wheat flour, maize, soybeans, rice, copra, olein, raw rattan, meat, and all goods produced from subsidized raw materials.

nutmeg and mace, cassiavera, tengkowang seeds, coffee, and vegetables from North Sumatra have been liberalized since May 1990. Textiles and textile products subject to import quotas in the consuming countries may be exported only by approved textile exporters, who may transfer their allocated quotas to other approved exporters through the Commodity Exchange Board.

All exports of rattan, leather, wood, and wood products must be examined before shipment. Exports of sawn timber and wood products require approval from the joint marketing body and may be made only by approved exporters. A minimum price of $250 a cubic meter applies to exports of sawn and processed timber, and export taxes ranging from $250 to $4,800 a cubic meter are imposed on these products. In 1992, bans on log exports were replaced with export taxes. Although export taxes on raw logs range from $500 to $4,800 a cubic meter, certain processed woods, such as finger-jointed walls, panels, and molding, are not taxed. Certain other products are subject to export taxes, which range from 5 percent to 30 percent (the tax rate on leather products is 20 percent, and the tax rates on rattan are $14–$15 a kilogram).

For all goods subject to the export tax and the export surcharge, payment is due when the exports are registered with foreign exchange banks. If the export tax and export surcharge are not yet settled at the time of registration, exporters are required to submit promissory notes for their value. Promissory notes may be settled in three ways. Exports without a letter of credit should be settled with the foreign exchange bank not later than 30 days from the date of export registration. Exports using consignment and usance letters of credit should be settled not later than 90 days from the date of export registration. Exports with sight letters of credit conditions must be settled not later than 30 days from the date the exports are registered with the foreign exchange bank. There are no restrictions on the type of financial arrangement exporters may use. There are no surrender or repatriation requirements for export proceeds. In the calculation of export taxes on the principal commodities, other than petroleum and gas, sale prices must not be lower than the "indicative" prices determined periodically by the Minister of Trade.

To enable producer-exporters to obtain their imported inputs at international prices, exporters and suppliers of inputs for exporters are permitted to bypass the import-licensing system and import tariffs or, if they cannot bypass the system, to reclaim

import duties; the costs imposed by non-tariff barriers, however, cannot be rebated.[3]

Certain commodities produced in border regions may be exported to Malaysia and the Philippines in exchange for certain goods. In this "border-crossing" trade with Malaysia, the value of import or export transactions must not exceed M$600 (Malaysian ringgit) for a single trip or M$3,000 a month, whether transported overland or by sea. For the Philippines, the value of imports or exports must not exceed the rupiah or peso equivalent of US$150 for a single trip if transported by seagoing vessels or US$1,500 if transported by smaller boats.

Since January 1982, the Indonesian Government may require all foreign firms bidding for government-sponsored construction or procurement projects whose import component is valued at more than Rp 500 million to agree to fulfill a counterpurchase obligation. Bidders for projects that include counterpurchase requirements must submit with their bids a letter in which they agree to purchase and export the equivalent of the contract's f.o.b. value in selected Indonesian products during the life of the contract.[4] Goods that may be used to meet the counterpurchase requirement include agricultural products and manufactured and other products, excluding petroleum, natural gas, and items subject to export quotas. The foreign supplier may fulfill the counterpurchase requirement either directly or through a third party, possibly from another country that is acceptable to the Indonesian Government. Such an arrangement must meet the condition of "additionality"; that is, the counterpurchases by the third party have to be in addition to regular exports from Indonesia. Indonesian products other than oil and natural gas purchased

---

[3]Under this scheme, exporters are classified as producer-exporters (firms that export at least 65 percent of their total production) or as exporter-producers (firms that export 85 percent of their production and producers of textiles in general). Producer-exporters may bring into the country their imports free of licensing restrictions and import duties, but with ex post documentation. If exporter-producers can demonstrate that their output was, or will be, exported or that their output was an input in an exported output, then they can also receive the same permission to import their inputs as producer-exporters. The scheme also allows indirect exporters to reclaim import duties through a duty drawback facility.

[4]The following are exempt from these requirements: (1) sources of import financing derived from soft loans and loans from the World Bank, the Islamic Development Bank, and the Asian Development Bank; (2) domestic components contained in the contract with the foreign suppliers, such as components of services, goods, and taxes or duties; (3) services that are used by various government agencies related to specific expertise, such as foreign accountants, lawyers, surveyors, consultants' services, purchases of technology (patents), etc.; and (4) purchases or imports under the joint-venture system between state companies and foreign companies.

under countertrade arrangements must be shipped regularly and in stages during the validity of the contract on the government procurement, and these shipment obligations must be completed at the end of such a purchasing contract. If, when the project is completed or the purchase is implemented (government import) the exportation from Indonesia has not yet been completed, a penalty amounting to 50 percent of the export value will be imposed on the responsible party (to date this provision has not been implemented).

Payments for and Proceeds from Invisibles

These are neither restricted nor subject to control. Proceeds from invisibles need not be surrendered. Travelers may take out and bring in any amount in foreign banknotes but only Rp 50,000 in Indonesian notes and coins, other than gold and silver commemorative coins (see section on Gold, below).

Capital

Incentives for foreign direct investments include an exemption or relief from import duties on capital goods, raw materials, auxiliary goods, and spare parts; an annual depreciation allowance of 25 percent for fiscal purposes on virtually all machinery and other productive capital goods; and deferral of value-added tax on imports of capital goods.

All foreign enterprises are eligible to receive preferential customs duty treatment for imports of required raw materials for the first two years of production activity. Raw materials may be imported with no time limit. In addition, an enterprise exporting more than 65 percent of its production is free to hire foreign experts as needed to maintain its export commitments. Managers of representative offices of a foreign company are granted multiple exit and re-entry permits for six months and are exempt from the Rp 25,000 departure tax.

Full foreign ownership in foreign direct investments is allowed in certain sectors if the investments meet certain criteria. Pursuant to Government Regulation No. 20/1944 (July 29, 1994), foreign investors may reinvest profits in the shares of other foreign firms. Investors are granted the right to repatriate capital, to transfer profits (after settlement of taxes and financial obligations in Indonesia), and to make transfers relating to expenses connected with the employment of foreign nationals in Indonesia and relating to depreciation allowances. The law provides that no transfer permit shall be issued for capital repatriation as long as investment benefits from

tax relief are being received; at present, however, foreign payments do not require a transfer permit.

Foreign ownership of direct investment must begin to be divested by the eleventh year of production. For large investments (above $50 million), divestment of 51 percent must be completed within 20 years. For smaller investments, the divestment requirement is less stringent.

There are no limitations on the remittance to Indonesia of capital in the form of foreign exchange or commodities. Both residents and nonresidents may hold foreign currency deposits with foreign exchange banks. However, foreign exchange banks are subject to Bank Indonesia directives with respect to borrowing abroad, the acceptance of deposits from nonresidents, and the issuance of certificates of deposit to nonresidents. A reserve requirement of 2 percent is applicable to the foreign currency liabilities of foreign exchange banks; no reserve requirements are applicable to the foreign borrowings of nonbank financial institutions or private companies. As of November 1991, banks' short-term foreign exchange liabilities may not exceed 30 percent of their own capital, and they are required to allocate at least 80 percent of all foreign exchange credits to export-oriented businesses that earn foreign exchange. A Commercial Offshore Loan Team (consisting of the State Secretary, the ministers of all economic portfolios, and the Governor of Bank Indonesia) established in September 1991, supervises all foreign commercial loan transactions. The prior approval of the team is required before any public enterprise, commercial bank, or public sector body may accept a loan from abroad. These limits do not apply to private enterprises.

Indonesian citizens and residents of foreign nationality may freely transfer, negotiate, import, and export securities denominated in rupiah or in foreign currency.

The exploration and development of petroleum resources are governed principally by the Petroleum Law of 1960.

Gold

Indonesia has issued two commemorative gold coins, which are legal tender. Residents may freely purchase, hold, and sell gold and gold coins in Indonesia. Travelers may freely take out up to Rp 65,000 a person in Indonesian commemorative gold and silver coins issued in August 1970 and up to Rp 130,000 a person in gold and silver coins issued in October 1974; amounts in excess of these limits require the prior approval of Bank Indonesia.

Gold may be imported freely. Imports are subject to an additional levy of Rp 25 per US$1.

Changes During 1994

Exchange Arrangement

September 6. Bank Indonesia ceased to announce an indicative exchange rate in the morning. Instead it began announcing buying and selling rates at 3:00 p.m., computed on the basis of a basket of weighted currencies with a spread of plus or minus Rp 15. (Prior to that date, the spread was plus or minus Rp 10.) In addition, the limits on banks' open positions were liberalized whereby banks were required to meet a net open position of 25 percent of capital instead of 20 percent, and the open position requirement would no longer apply to individual currencies.

Imports and Import Payments

June 27. The Government announced import deregulation measures, including reductions in capital imports on 739 tariff codes, the liberalization of nontariff barriers on 27 product lines, and the lifting of surcharges from 108 import items. At the same time, import duties were increased on 38 tariff codes related to alcoholic products. In addition, any remaining nontariff protection of domestic industry, such as import restrictions and regulations, were to be gradually replaced by tariff protection.

ISLAMIC REPUBLIC OF IRAN

(Position as of December 31, 1994)

Exchange Arrangement

The currency of the Islamic Republic of Iran is the Iranian Rial. The exchange rate system consists of the following rates: (1) the official rate, which is fixed at Rls 1,750 per US$1, applies mainly to the imports of essential goods; (2) the official export rate, which is fixed at Rls 2,345 per US$1, is applied mainly to imports of raw materials and spare parts (the supply of foreign exchange at the first two rates comes from the Government's oil export proceeds); (3) the authorized dealers' market rate, which is determined by supply (mainly tourist receipts) and demand (mainly for nonessential services and transfers, such as the travel allowance) (on December 31, 1994, this rate was Rls 2,680 per US$1); and (4) the free market exchange rate, which results largely from direct transactions between importers and exporters, with little intermediation from the banks and no intervention from Bank Markazi. On December 31, 1994, this rate varied between Rls 3,000 and Rls 3,100 per US$1.

There are no taxes or subsidies on purchases or sales of foreign exchange. There are no arrangements for forward cover against exchange rate risk operating in the banking system.

Administration of Control

Exchange control authority is vested in Bank Markazi. All foreign exchange transactions, other than those permitted through the free exchange market, must take place through the banking system. Imports and exports are governed by regulations issued periodically by the Ministry of Commerce after approval from the Council of Ministers.

Prescription of Currency

Settlements of current transactions with the member countries of the Asian Clearing Union (ACU) (Bangladesh, India, the Islamic Republic of Iran, Myanmar, Nepal, Pakistan, and Sri Lanka) are required to be effected in Asian monetary units (AMUs); settlements with these countries are made every two months through conversion of AMUs.

All bilateral payment arrangements have been terminated and the outstanding credit balances are in the process of being settled.

Nonresident Accounts

Foreign nationals may maintain rial accounts and foreign currency accounts with authorized banks. The balances of the rial accounts may be used only in the Islamic Republic of Iran.

Imports and Import Payments

All imports into the Islamic Republic of Iran are required to be authorized by the Ministry of Commerce before being registered with authorized banks, except for special military goods, pharmaceuticals, and souvenirs and gifts brought in by incoming travelers. Imports from Israel and the Federal Republic of Yugoslavia (Serbia/Montenegro) are prohibited.

The import policy is re-examined periodically at the end of each Iranian calendar year (March 20), and new regulations effective for the following year are published by the Ministry of Commerce. The regulations distinguish between "authorized," "conditional," and "prohibited" goods. The importation of authorized goods is unrestricted. Conditional goods are those goods whose importation is temporarily prohibited by the Government or is contingent on the fulfillment of certain requirements. Imports of prohibited goods are not allowed. Advance payments for imports of up to the full value are allowed, depending on the goods.

Most imports are subject to the commercial benefit tax, which is either specific or ad valorem and is imposed in addition to applicable customs duties. The monopoly taxes, if any, are included in the commercial benefit tax; the rate of the commercial benefit tax for each year is specified in the Export-Import Regulations. The commercial benefit tax must be paid to customs before clearance of goods. Clearance through customs is authorized upon presentation of shipping documents endorsed by an authorized bank and of a permit issued by the Ministry of Commerce (this permit may be issued at the same time that letters of credit are opened and it need not be reissued). Certain goods, such as pharmaceuticals and imports by the Ministry of Post, Telegraph, and Telephone, must be accompanied by a special permit when they are cleared through customs. Payments for imports made with foreign currency must be accompanied by evidence that the currency was obtained from an Iranian bank before the goods may be released from customs. In the transportation of imported goods for which import letters of credit have been opened, priority must be accorded to Iranian transportation carriers (air, land, or sea). The ceiling on the amount of goods that an incoming traveler is permitted to import is governed by the export-import regulations.

Payments for Invisibles

The transfer of premiums for reinsurance at the official rate can be made by the Central Insurance Company of Iran, Iran Insurance Company, Asia Insurance Company, and Alborz Insurance Company through their respective foreign exchange accounts. Insurance companies owned by Iranian residents may issue insurance contracts denominated in foreign currency for imports of goods; only Iran Insurance Company may issue war-risk insurance in foreign currency. The transfer of income in rials earned from ticket sales by foreign airline companies located in Iran may be allowed at the official exchange rate with the permission of Bank Markazi.

Persons requiring medical treatment abroad may obtain foreign exchange at the official exchange rate up to the amount specified by the High Medical Council of the Ministry of Health. Foreign exchange allowances at the official exchange rate are granted to students in nonmedical fields with the approval of the Ministry of Culture and Higher Education, and to those in the medical field, with the approval of the Ministry of Health, Treatment, and Medical Education. The amount of allowances varies according to the cost of living in the country of study, up to a maximum of $1,470 a month; an additional 60 percent of the basic allowance for a spouse and 30 percent for each child is authorized. In certain cases when this allowance is not sufficient to cover tuition, additional amounts to cover university fees and expenses may be allowed.

The transfer of profits and dividends earned on foreign direct investment can be made freely at the official exchange rate. Foreign nationals working in the Islamic Republic of Iran whose services are considered essential are allowed to remit up to 30 percent of their net salaries at the official exchange rate with the prior approval of Bank Markazi.

Iranian nationals traveling abroad may export up to $1,000 for each individual passport; a maximum of $500 a person may be exported if a person travels with a group passport. Iranian nationals leaving the country must pay an exit fee of Rls 70,000 for each trip. Travelers leaving the Islamic Republic of Iran may take out with them up to Rls 200,000 in Iranian banknotes, but they may import any amount of Iranian banknotes through foreign branches of Iranian banks.

Foreign exchange from accounts denominated in foreign currency originating abroad may be transferred by natural persons without limitation.

Exports and Export Proceeds

Exports of all products must be made in accordance with relevant regulations. Exports to Israel, and the Federal Republic of Yugoslavia (Serbia/Montenegro) are prohibited. Exports of non-oil products are not subject to limitation; the only requirement is that authorization be obtained for statistical purposes from the Ministry of Commerce. Exporters of non-oil products may sell foreign exchange proceeds to commercial banks at the export rate.

Proceeds from Invisibles

Iranian nationals may retain their foreign exchange earnings in foreign currency accounts with the authorized banks. There is no limit on the amount of foreign exchange travelers may bring into the country. The sale of foreign exchange to the banking system at the official exchange rate by both resident and nonresident juridical and natural persons is permitted.

Capital

Foreign direct investment is supervised by the Organization for Investment and Economic and Technical Assistance of the Ministry of Economic Affairs and Finance, if the investment was originally brought into the country in accordance with the law concerning the attraction and protection of foreign capital investments in Iran. Repatriation of capital may be effected with the approval of this agency and Bank Markazi, and in accordance with the above-mentioned law.

Gold

No Iranian gold coin is legal tender. Residents may freely and without license purchase, hold, and sell gold, platinum, and silver in the domestic market. Authority to export or import gold for monetary purposes is reserved for Bank Markazi. The exportation of finished articles made of gold, platinum, and silver may be effected in accordance with the relevant regulations. The exportation of gold, platinum, and silver in the form of ingots, coins, or semifinished products is prohibited except by Bank Markazi. Natural and juridical persons, including authorized banks, may import gold, platinum, and silver bullion for commercial purposes in accordance with the relevant regulations. Travelers may bring in jewelry up to a value equivalent to Rls 5 million, and take out the entire value, provided that it is recorded on their passport; the importation of personal jewelry with a value exceeding this amount requires approval from Bank Markazi. The exportation of Iranian gold coins for numis-matic purposes requires prior approval from Bank Markazi.

Changes During 1994

Exchange Arrangement

May 4. An "export rate" was introduced.

IRAQ

(Position as of December 31, 1994)

Exchange Arrangement

The currency of Iraq is the Iraqi Dinar, which is pegged to the U.S. dollar, the intervention currency, at ID 1 per US$3.2169. The official buying and selling rates on December 31, 1994 were US$3.224933 and US$3.208889, respectively, per ID 1. Buying and selling rates for certain other currencies[1] are also officially quoted, with daily quotations based on the buying and selling rates for the U.S. dollar in markets abroad. The Central Bank of Iraq undertakes transactions in the listed currencies only with authorized dealers. There are no taxes or subsidies on purchases or sales of foreign exchange. There are no arrangements for forward cover against exchange rate risk in the official or the commercial banking sector.

Administration of Control

Exchange control authority is vested in the Board of Administration of the Central Bank. Certain approval authority has been delegated to the Department of Foreign Exchange and Banking Supervision of the Central Bank and to licensed dealers. Foreign exchange transactions must take place through a licensed dealer unless otherwise authorized by the governor. Branches of the Rafidain Bank and the Rasheed Bank are licensed dealers. The Ministry of Trade formulates import policy and the annual program.

Prescription of Currency

Settlements with foreign countries normally must be made in any of the listed currencies or in Iraqi dinars from a nonresident account, provided that the funds in the account were obtained originally through credits in any one of the listed currencies. Payments to and receipts from Israel are prohibited.

Resident and Nonresident Accounts

Residents and nonresidents of Iraqi and Arab nationality are allowed to open foreign currency accounts at the commercial banks and to use the balances in these accounts without restriction, provided the accounts have been credited with foreign banknotes. Nonresident accounts are divided into ordinary nonresident accounts, which arise from transactions in respect of current payments, and special nonresident accounts, which arise from transactions in respect of capital transfers.

Imports and Import Payments

Imports of commodities are normally handled by the public sector. All private imports are subject to licenses, except imports of materials constituting basic elements for development projects benefiting from the Law for Major Development Projects, No. 157 of 1973 (for old contracts) or from the Law for Major Development Projects, No. 60 of 1985 (for new projects).

Under Resolution No. 767 of October 1, 1987, foreign companies implementing development projects in Iraq are exempt from all import duties and domestic taxes accruing from the implementation of these projects, including income taxes due on the earnings of their non-Iraqi workers. These exemptions apply to new projects that are contracted after the effective date of Resolution No. 767. The Law for Major Development Projects, No. 60 of 1985 has ceased to be effective, except that its provisions continue to apply to projects that were contracted before Resolution No. 767 took effect. In principle, licenses are issued in accordance with an annual import program. Imports of all goods from Israel are prohibited. Imports of some commodities on a protected list are, in principle, prohibited from all sources.

To finance the Export Subsidy Fund, a tax of 0.5 percent is levied on imports of capital goods, and a tax of 0.75 percent is levied on imports of consumer goods. All imports subject to import duty are also subject to a customs surcharge according to the available list of classified goods.

The Rafidain Bank or the Rasheed Bank makes exchange available upon presentation of the exchange control copy of the import license except in some instances, when reference must be made to the Central Bank. Imports financed by foreign exchange obtained by nonresident Iraqis are given special import licenses.

Payments for Invisibles

All payments for invisibles require permission. Exchange is usually granted for educational and

---

[1]Austrian schillings, Belgian francs, Canadian dollars, Danish kroner, deutsche mark, French francs, Italian lire, Japanese yen, Netherlands guilders, Norwegian kroner, pounds sterling, Swedish kronor, and Swiss francs.

medical expenses abroad, freight on exports effected on a c. & f. basis, insurance premiums, royalties, and the like. Exchange is not granted to merchants to purchase insurance abroad for their imports or exports. The Rafidain Bank and the Rasheed Bank are permitted to transfer salaries of teachers who are Arab nationals and employed by the Ministry of Higher Education and of scientific researchers and medical doctors in accordance with the terms of their contracts. Certain nonresident private sector workers who have contracts with public institutions in Iraq are permitted to transfer the amounts provided for in those contracts; those not employed under contracts may transfer abroad a monthly amount of ID 10 for each person who is not insured and ID 20 for each person who is insured and is working in the private sector. Skilled noncontractual workers employed in the nationalized sector by the Government are entitled to ID 40 a person a month. Persons under 16 years and over 55 years of age, however, are not allowed to transfer their earnings abroad.

The basic allowance for travel to Arab and socialist countries, Cyprus, Greece, and Turkey is ID 300 a trip for each person 18 years of age or over (ID 50 for persons under 18 years); the basic allowance for other countries is ID 500 a trip for each person 18 years of age or over (ID 250 for persons under 18 years). Students abroad are allocated a fixed amount in Iraqi dinars to be transferred to the country of their residence, except for certain countries (such as India, socialist countries, and North Africa), where students are paid a fixed amount in U.S. dollars.

Travelers may take out ID 5 in Iraqi currency notes, which is considered part of the basic travel allowance, and the balance in traveler's checks. Residents on pilgrimage to Saudi Arabia are permitted to transfer the equivalent of ID 250 for personal expenses in addition to all other traveling expenses paid to the local travel agent. Half of this allowance is permitted for persons under 18 years. Exchange allowances for pilgrimages are unrelated to other traveling allowances during the year.

Exports and Export Proceeds

All exports to Israel and exports of certain goods to all other countries are prohibited. The Ministry of Trade may prohibit the exportation of any commodity when supply falls short of domestic demand. All exports are licensed freely through the General Company for Exhibitions and Trading Services. Exporters of 13 goods manufactured by firms in the public sector must undertake to repatriate 60 percent of their foreign exchange proceeds through the Rafidain Bank or the Rasheed Bank and to surrender them within two months of shipment. Other exporters may retain their export proceeds in foreign exchange accounts with the commercial banks for three years and use them to pay for licensed imports.

An export subsidy fund was established in 1969 for the purpose of promoting non-oil exports by providing financial incentives to eligible exporters. The scheme is intended to introduce Iraqi goods abroad, whether from the private or socialist sector, and to improve their competitive position. The financial subsidies are granted upon presentation of the necessary documents.

Proceeds from Invisibles

Foreign exchange receipts in excess of ID 100 from invisibles must be surrendered to a licensed dealer within three months. Travelers may bring in foreign exchange, including currency notes (other than Israeli currency) in unlimited amounts, provided that they declare the funds on an exchange control form; amounts not intended to be taken out of the country are exempt from declaration. The importation of Iraqi banknotes by travelers is limited to ID 1,000.

Capital

Nonresidents may import capital freely, except from Israel, but must deposit it with the Rafidain Bank or the Rasheed Bank. Deposits may be converted into local currency at the official rate, and repatriation to the country of origin is permitted. Under Resolution No. 1646 of the Revolutionary Command Council, enacted in November 1980, no foreign (defined as non-Arab) participation is allowed in the capital of private sector companies, but citizens of Arab states may participate with Iraqis in projects in the industrial, agricultural services, and tourism sectors. All transfers of capital abroad by residents, whether Iraqis or foreigners, require exchange control approval. Iraqi nationals, foreigners, and nonresidents may transfer foreign exchange to Iraq and deposit it with a licensed dealer in accounts bearing interest rates comparable to international rates. Balances on these accounts with interest are freely transferable abroad in foreign currencies, provided that the funds have been deposited with licensed dealers within three months of transfer. Iraqi nationals residing abroad (or their legal representatives) may withdraw from their nonresident accounts up to ID 100,000 a year in three installments to cover personal expenses inside their country of residence.

Arab investors are allowed to transfer capital in a convertible currency through a licensed bank or physical assets that will be used in the enterprises they are planning to establish, provided that used machinery and equipment have at least one-half of their productive life left. Investments by Arab nationals are encouraged by Arab Investment Law No. 46 of 1988. The law permits (1) Iraqi investors to participate in enterprises in which their capital participation does not exceed 49 percent, provided that their contribution and profits will be paid in Iraqi dinars and the minimum capital of the enterprise is ID 0.5 million; (2) Arab investors to transfer annually up to 100 percent of profits to be distributed to them, provided that the profit does not exceed 20 percent of their paid-in capital; and (3) Arab nationals to bring capital into Iraq in Iraqi currency for industrial and agricultural investment purposes

in accordance with certain regulations; such inflows are treated as working capital.

Gold

Under Resolution No. 801 (dated October 10, 1987), Iraqi residents, nonresidents, or foreigners may bring into Iraq, free of customs duty, worked and unworked gold, regardless of its weight, provided that they declare it upon importation. Iraqi residents may take out with them worked gold not exceeding 5 grams a person, subject to declaration; such gold may be brought back on their return to the country. Nonresident Iraqis are allowed to take out with them worked gold that they brought with them for personal use when they entered Iraq.

Changes During 1994

No significant changes occurred in the exchange and trade system.

IRELAND

(Position as of December 31, 1994)

Exchange Arrangement

The currency of Ireland is the Irish Pound. Ireland participates with Austria, Belgium, Denmark, France, Germany, Luxembourg, the Netherlands, Portugal, and Spain in the exchange rate and intervention mechanism of the European Monetary System (EMS).[1] In accordance with this agreement, Ireland maintains spot exchange rates between the Irish pound and the currencies of the other participants within margins of 15 percent above or below the cross rates based on the central rates expressed in European currency units.[2]

The agreement commits the Central Bank of Ireland to buy or sell the currencies of the other participating states in unlimited amounts at specified intervention rates. On January 9, 1995, these rates were as follows:

Specified Intervention Rates per:	Irish Pounds	
	Upper limit	Lower limit
100 Austrian schilling	6.34544	5.07635
100 Belgian or Luxembourg francs	2.33503	1.73176
100 Danish kroner	12.62610	9.36403
100 Deutsche mark	48.16960	35.71430
100 French francs	14.35990	10.65000
100 Netherlands guilders	42.74390	31.70070
100 Portuguese escudos[3]	4.86881	3.61092
100 Spanish pesetas[4]	6.08731	4.51462

The participants in the EMS do not maintain exchange rates for other currencies within fixed limits. On December 31, 1994, the official midpoint closing rate for the U.S. dollar was $1.4066 per £Ir 1. There are no taxes or subsidies on purchases or sales of foreign exchange.

Ireland formally accepted the obligations of Article VIII, Sections 2, 3, and 4 of the Fund Agreement, as from February 15, 1961.

Administration of Control

No exchange controls are in effect in Ireland.

Import licenses, when necessary, are issued by the Department of Tourism and Trade for industrial goods and by the Department of Agriculture, Food, and Forestry for agricultural goods; import licenses are also issued in some cases by the Department of Health or the Department of Justice. Import and export controls are administered by the Revenue Commissioners.

In accordance with the Fund's Executive Board Decision No. 144–(52–51) adopted on August 14, 1952, Ireland notified the IMF on July 21, 1992 that, in compliance with UN Security Council Resolution No. 757 (1992), certain restrictions had been imposed on the making of payments and transfers for current international transactions in respect of the Federal Republic of Yugoslavia (Serbia/Montenegro).

Ireland introduced restrictions in respect of Haiti on November 30, 1993 in accordance with UN Security Control Resolution No. 841 of 1993. Restrictions were also introduced in respect of Libya on December 23, 1993 in accordance with UN Security Council Resolution No. 883 of 1993.

Prescription of Currency

There are no prescription of currency requirements.

Nonresident Accounts

Nonresidents may maintain deposits in Irish pounds without restriction.

Imports and Import Payments

Imports of certain goods (including textiles, steel, footwear, and ceramic products) originating in certain non-European Union (EU) countries are subject to either quantitative restrictions or surveillance measures.

Imports from non-EU countries of products covered by the Common Agricultural Policy of the EU may be subject to various charges, such as levies and monetary compensatory amounts under that

---

[1]Austria became a member of the European Union on January 1, 1995 and joined the ERM of the EMS on January 9, 1995.

[2]Effective August 2, 1993, the intervention thresholds of the currencies participating in the ERM of the EMS, except those of the deutsche mark and the Netherlands guilder, were widened from ±2.25 percent (in the case of Portugal and Spain, 6 percent) to ±15 percent around the bilateral central exchange rates; the fluctuation band of the deutsche mark and the Netherlands guilder remained unchanged at ±2.25 percent.

[3]Effective March 6, 1995, the upper and lower limits were changed to 4.69841 and 3.48453.

[4]Effective March 6, 1995, the upper and lower limits were changed to 6.86120 and 4.19850.

policy and to duties under the common customs tariff.

For reasons of national policy, imports of certain goods (for example, specified drugs, explosives, and firearms and ammunition) are prohibited without special licenses.

Exports and Export Proceeds

Export proceeds are not regulated.

Payments for and Proceeds from Invisibles

There are no restrictions on payments for and proceeds from invisibles. Travelers may import or export any amount of domestic and foreign banknotes or any other means of payment.

Capital

There are no exchange controls or restrictions on inward or outward capital transfers by residents or nonresidents.

Gold

Residents may freely hold, buy, borrow, sell, or lend gold coins in Ireland.

Changes During 1994

No significant changes occurred in the exchange and trade system.

(See Appendix for a summary of trade measures introduced and eliminated on an EU-wide basis during 1994, page 554.)

ISRAEL

(Position as of December 31, 1994)

Exchange Arrangement

The currency of Israel is the New Sheqel (plural New Sheqalim). Its exchange rate is defined in relation to a currency basket consisting of the deutsche mark, the French franc, the Japanese yen, the pound sterling, and the U.S. dollar. The market exchange rate fluctuates within a range of 5 percent above and below the midpoint rate in response to market forces and intervention policy. Since December 17, 1991, both the midpoint and the band have been adjusted gradually at a daily rate ("slope" of the band) that reflects the annual difference between the domestic inflation target and the projected inflation in the main trading partners. The current slope of the band, set as of July 26, 1993, is 6 percent on an annual basis. On December 31, 1994, the exchange rate of the new sheqel in terms of the U.S. dollar was NIS 3.018 per US$1.

Forward exchange transactions between foreign currencies are permitted. Transactions in futures and options, including traded contracts, on foreign currencies, foreign interest rates, commodities, and securities prices by both resident companies and individuals are allowed. However, a juridical person may enter into such contracts only to cover commercial risks arising from permitted transactions; transactions in commodities may be entered into only in order to cover risks; and transactions, other than in traded contracts, must be concluded against an authorized dealer bank, or, through it, against a foreign bank or broker.

Israel formally accepted the obligations of Article VIII, Sections 2, 3, and 4 of the Fund Agreement, as from September 21, 1993.

Administration of Control

Exchange control is the responsibility of the Controller of Foreign Exchange; it is administered by the Bank of Israel, in cooperation with other government agencies and is carried out through authorized banks that are permitted to deal in foreign exchange; other institutions (e.g., securities brokers and foreign exchange dealers) possess, or may obtain, a limited license to deal in foreign exchange.

Prescription of Currency

Payments and receipts must be effected in the currency and manner prescribed by the exchange control authorities.

Nonresident Accounts

Nonresidents' funds are held either in foreign currency accounts or in local currency accounts. The opening of nonresident foreign currency accounts does not require prior approval. Account holders may freely effect transfers from their foreign currency account and may also convert funds held in the account into local currency at the market exchange rate.

There are no restrictions on the opening of convertible local currency accounts by nonresidents; funds in these accounts may be used in permitted transactions, including transfers between nonresidents. The sales proceeds of real estate and other investments may be transferred abroad in their entirety if the original investment was made through an authorized dealer with foreign currency or through a local currency nonresident account.

Resident Accounts in Foreign Currency

There are two main types of foreign currency accounts that Israeli residents may hold:

(1) *Foreign currency deposit accounts (PAMAH).* Export proceeds and unilateral transfers directly received from abroad, as well as unused travel allowances, may be deposited in these accounts. The liquidity requirements are 6 percent for a current account and 3 percent for a time deposit account with a maturity of up to one year, and zero for a time deposit account with a maturity exceeding one year. *Resident restitution deposit accounts* may be maintained under PAMAH. These accounts may be held only by recipients of restitution payments or certain disability pensions. The liquidity requirement for these accounts was 45 percent on December 31, 1994 (it has been gradually and automatically reduced at a fixed monthly rate since November 1991, when the rate was 90 percent). Funds deposited in these accounts are tax free and may be used up to a limit of $1,800 for additional travel allowances.

(2) *Exempt resident deposit accounts.* Certain residents (mostly immigrants) may deposit funds brought from abroad in these accounts. Certain regulations stipulate the types of funds that may be deposited in these accounts. Balances on these accounts may be freely transferred abroad.

In addition, a resident may open a deposit account linked to a foreign currency (PATZAM) with a maturity period of not less than one month.

Imports and Import Payments

With the exception of agricultural products, imports are free of quantitative restrictions. A special regime applies to imports from countries that restrict or prohibit imports from Israel.

Banks automatically grant foreign exchange to pay for authorized imports when the relevant documents (import documents, bills of lading, and letters of credit) are presented. Foreign exchange is also provided automatically for repayment of suppliers' credits. Importers are allowed to use foreign currency proceeds of loans obtained abroad directly for import payments without first depositing the funds with an authorized Israeli bank. Advance payments for imports of goods to be supplied within one year are allowed.

A value-added tax of 17 percent is levied on almost all imported and domestically produced goods, other than fresh fruits and vegetables.

Payments for Invisibles

Foreign exchange for payments abroad on account of invisibles, including tourism expenses, is provided automatically upon proof of the nature of the transaction. The indicative limit on foreign travel allowances in cash, traveler's checks, and cash withdrawals on credit cards while overseas was raised to $7,000 a person a trip, with effect from November 1, 1994. Additionally, the quantitative restrictions on the use of credit cards for purchasing tourist services overseas was removed. With these changes, the requirement for pre-departure approval for the use of credit cards while overseas will effectively be abolished. Residents may make support or gift remittances abroad of up to $2,000 a year. The exchange allowance for students studying at institutions of higher education abroad is $1,000 a month in addition to tuition expenses. Foreign exchange in excess of the above-mentioned amounts is provided on submission of documentary proof of need. Residents going abroad for medical treatment who require hospitalization are permitted to pay up to the equivalent of $30,000 in advance. While abroad, they are permitted to pay the remainder of their expenses. Additional payments may be authorized on request. Residents, while in Israel, are permitted to make credit card payments abroad of up to $1,500 a year.

Resident travelers may take out Israeli banknotes not exceeding the equivalent of $200 a person a trip.

Nonresident travelers leaving Israel are permitted to take out Israeli banknotes up to the equivalent of $100, and to repurchase, through an authorized dealer at the port of departure, foreign currency up to the equivalent of $500. Nonresidents may purchase foreign currency on presentation of documents showing previous conversion of foreign currency into Israeli currency, with a limit for each visit of $5,000 for a person over 18 years and of $2,000 for a person under 18 years (a temporary leave of less than two weeks during the visit does not affect the person's right). Commercial banks are authorized to sell abroad unlimited amounts of Israeli currency. Requests for any additional amount will be approved upon submission of the necessary documents.

Remittances of earnings by foreign workers are not restricted. Remittances of profits and dividends from foreign direct investment are permitted after local taxes are paid.

Exports and Export Proceeds

Most exports do not require licenses. Export proceeds in foreign currencies must be received within 12 months of the date of export; they may be held in a PAMAH account or sold to authorized banks. However, exporters may retain in a bank account abroad an amount equivalent to the maximum of either 10 percent of their capital or 5 percent of their turnover in the preceding year and use the funds to pay for imports and to make other authorized payments abroad. For inputs directly imported by an exporter, there is a system of rebates of customs duties, wharf charges, and other related charges.

Proceeds from Invisibles

Exchange proceeds from invisibles may, in general, be kept in foreign exchange in PAMAH accounts or sold to authorized banks. Any resident is free to accept specified convertible currencies from tourists in payment for customary tourist services and commodities other than securities and real estate.

For 30 years after entering Israel, new immigrants are exempt from the requirement to surrender their foreign exchange to authorized banks, and they may hold these foreign currencies freely with authorized banks in Israel or with banks abroad. There is no limit on the amount of Israeli banknotes or foreign currency that may be brought in by travelers.

Capital

Nonresidents are permitted to purchase real estate, traded securities, and units of mutual trust funds in Israel. To repatriate the principal on these investments, nonresidents must prove to an authorized bank that these were purchased through a nonresident account. Direct loans from nonresidents to Israeli residents are not restricted. Foreign exchange brought into Israel for the purpose of investment in the form of equity capital or shareholders' loans may be granted preferential tax treatment in accordance with the Law for the Encouragement of Capital Investment.

Institutional investors (provident pension and insurance funds) are permitted to invest up to 2 percent of their total assets in recognized foreign securities. Income and profits earned by institutional investors from these investments, as well as those earned on exchange rate-indexed deposit and credit, including capital gains, are taxed at the rate of 35 percent.

Active incorporated Israeli companies are permitted to undertake direct investment abroad (e.g., in subsidiaries and real estate) without any quantitative limit on the size of the investment and to hold foreign securities and deposits (exporters only) abroad, provided that the investment does not amount to more than 10 percent of their equity or 5 percent of their sales turnover, whichever is larger.

Nonresidents holding Israeli securities or real estate are allowed to deposit income from these assets in their foreign currency accounts. Proceeds from sales of these assets are allowed to be deposited in their nonresident accounts, provided that the investment was carried out through a nonresident account. Emigrants are permitted to transfer abroad up to the equivalent of $20,000 a year of their assets kept in Israel up to the end of the second year of stay abroad; during the second to the seventh year of stay abroad, they may transfer up to the equivalent of $50,000 a year.

Direct loans in any form from Israeli residents to nonresidents are subject to licensing. Domestic banks are permitted to lend to nonresidents; if collateral is required, it has to be in the form of assets convertible into foreign currency. Individual residents may buy foreign securities traded abroad, provided that the securities are held in a safekeeping deposit with an authorized dealer. Israeli mutual trust funds are permitted to invest abroad up to 10 percent of their portfolio of financial assets (up to 50 percent in the case of funds specializing in foreign currency investments).

Resident exporters and airline and shipping companies may maintain foreign bank accounts. New immigrants may retain their foreign assets for 30 years; otherwise, residents are not normally permitted to retain abroad real estate, money, securities, or income from these assets.

Proceeds accruing from the repatriation or liquidation of foreign assets must be surrendered.

Gold

Residents are allowed to import and export gold, subject to the same regulations as those applied to merchandise trade, and to transact in gold bullion and coins. Gold certificates are treated as foreign securities.

Changes During 1994

Payments for Invisibles

November 1. The indicative limit on foreign travel allowances in cash, traveler's checks, and cash withdrawals on credit cards while overseas was raised to $7,000 from $3,000 a person a trip. The quantitative restrictions on the use of credit cards for purchasing tourist services overseas was removed. As a result the requirement for predeparture approval for the use of credit cards while overseas was effectively abolished.

Capital

August 16. (1) Institutional investors (provident pension and insurance funds) were permitted to invest up to 2 percent of their total assets in recognized foreign securities. Income and profits earned by institutional investors from these investments, as well as those earned on exchange-rate indexed deposit and credit, including capital gains, were taxed at the rate of 35 percent. (2) Active incorporated Israeli companies were permitted to undertake direct investment abroad (e.g., in subsidiaries and real estate) without any quantitative limit on the size of the investment and to hold foreign securities and deposits abroad, provided that the investment does not amount to more than 10 percent of their equity or 5 percent of their sales turnover, whichever is larger.

October 1. Foreign currency regulations were amended to allow foreign residents holding Israeli securities or real estate, legally acquired, to deposit income from these assets in foreign currency accounts. Proceeds from sales of these assets would be allowed to be deposited in their nonresident accounts, provided that the investment was carried out through a nonresident account.

ITALY

(Position as of December 31, 1994)

Exchange Arrangement

The currency of Italy is the Italian Lira.[1] The Italian authorities generally do not intervene in the exchange market, and spot and forward exchange rates are determined on the basis of demand and supply conditions. Rates for 20 foreign currencies[2] are monitored every working day by the Bank of Italy exclusively for informational purposes. On December 31, 1994, the rate for the U.S. dollar was Lit 1,624 per US$1. There are no taxes or subsidies on purchases or sales of foreign exchange.

Authorized banks are allowed to engage in spot and forward exchange transactions in any currency, and premiums and discounts in the forward exchange market are normally left to the interplay of market forces. Residents may carry out spot and forward foreign exchange operations and transact currency options either with authorized banks or with foreign counterparts.

Italy formally accepted the obligations of Article VIII, Sections 2, 3, and 4 of the Fund Agreement, as from February 15, 1961.

Administration of Control

Residents are allowed to conduct foreign exchange transactions freely, with settlements to be effected either through authorized intermediaries (the Bank of Italy, authorized banks, and the Postal Administration) or directly, that is, by drawing on external accounts or by offsetting debts and credits vis-à-vis other residents or nonresidents. In the case of material delivery of means of payment in Italy or abroad, Italian residents are allowed to take with them into or out of the country Italian or foreign banknotes and bearer securities of any denomination up to the equivalent of Lit 20 million. For fiscal and anti-money-laundering purposes, transfers exceeding this amount must be carried out through authorized intermediaries. Residents are allowed to enter and leave the country carrying securities de-

nominated in lire or in foreign currencies worth Lit 20 million, provided that they are not bearer securities and that they are declared to customs. Nonresidents may take up to Lit 20 million in banknotes and securities of any denomination into and out of Italy without formalities. If they bring in banknotes and securities in an amount in excess of Lit 20 million, they must declare the excess amount to customs on a special form upon entering Italy. Nonresidents may re-export larger sums but only up to the amount in excess of Lit 20 million that they have imported and declared. No limit applies to exports of other securities; nonresidents need only submit the above-mentioned form to customs. The limitations described above do not apply to transfers effected by banks when they act as senders or beneficiaries. However, banks are also obliged to declare their transfers by filling out a special customs form.

Operators and authorized intermediaries must, for statistical purposes, transmit data to the Italian Foreign Exchange Office (Ufficio Italiano dei Cambi (UIC)) on their foreign transactions that exceed the equivalent of Lit 20 million by filling out a foreign exchange statistical return (*Comunicazione valutaria statistica*).

In accordance with the Fund's Executive Board Decision No. 144–(52/51) adopted on August 14, 1952, Italy notified the Fund on August 28, 1992 that, in compliance with UN Security Council Resolution No. 757 (1992), certain restrictions had been imposed on the making of payments and transfers for current international transactions in respect of the Federal Republic of Yugoslavia (Serbia/Montenegro).[3]

Prescription of Currency

Settlements with foreign countries are normally made in quoted currencies or in lire on foreign accounts.

Italy maintains clearing accounts with Croatia and Slovenia. The accounts are used for trade in cross-border areas. The balances in these accounts may be used only to finance trade between certain districts of Croatia and Slovenia and the Italian province of Trieste. The balances are not transfer-

---

[1] With effect from September 17, 1992, Italy withdrew from the exchange rate and intervention mechanism of the European Monetary System.

[2] Australian dollars, Austrian schillings, Belgian francs, Canadian dollars, Danish kroner, deutsche mark, ECUs, Finnish markkaa, French francs, Greek drachmas, Irish pounds, Japanese yen, Netherlands guilders, Norwegian kroner, Portuguese escudos, pounds sterling, Spanish pesetas, Swedish kronor, Swiss francs, and U.S. dollars.

[3] Similar restrictions were applied against Haiti, Libya, and the movement UNITA in Angola toward the end of 1993.

able. There is no automatic mechanism through which outstanding balances are settled within 90 days. Only Italy is allowed to maintain a debit balance on these accounts.

Nonresident Accounts

Nonresidents may maintain accounts with authorized banks in lire and in foreign exchange, which may be freely debited and credited upon their request.

Imports and Import Payments

Imports are governed by Decree No. 313 of July 14, 1990 and Decree No. 68 of October 30, 1990, both of which entered into effect on November 20, 1990. The import regulations vary with the country of origin. Countries are grouped into three major areas: Zone A, which is subdivided into subzones A/1 (EU countries), A/2 (overseas countries and territories, member countries of the European Free Trade Association (EFTA), and other countries associated with the EU), and A/3 (third countries); Zone B, which comprises most of the Eastern European countries, China, the Democratic People's Republic of Korea, and Viet Nam; and Zone C (Japan). The import control procedures distinguish between goods that may be imported without quantitative restrictions and those that require a special license. Import liberalization is virtually complete for subzones A/1 and A/2, and very few quantitative restrictions remain for subzone A/3 and for some countries of Zones B and C. Imports from non-EU countries of most products covered by the Common Agricultural Policy (CAP) of the EU are subject to variable import levies, which have replaced all previous barriers to imports. Common EU regulations are also applied to imports of most other agricultural and livestock products from non-EU countries. Payments for imports are not regulated, without prejudice to the general rules cited in the section on Administration of Control.

Payments for Invisibles

Payments for invisibles may be made freely, without prejudice to the general rules cited in the section on Administration and Control. Domestic and foreign banknotes up to Lit 20 million or its equivalent exported across the border by residents are free of restrictions. Exports exceeding this amount must be made through authorized intermediaries for recording and fiscal monitoring purposes and according to the regulations on money laundering.

Exports and Export Proceeds

Since the inception of the Single European Market, exports have been regulated by a ministerial decree of October 19, 1992. The decree liberalized exports to non-EU countries, with the exception of high-technology products included in the ministerial decrees of June 24, 1993 and of oil and gas extracted from the seabed, which are subject to ministerial authorization. Receipts from exports are subject to the general rules cited in the section on Administration of Control.

Proceeds from Invisibles

There are no limitations on receipts from invisibles, without prejudice to the general rules cited in the section on Administration of Control.

Capital

Foreign investments of any kind in Italy, including both direct and portfolio investment and the purchase of real estate, are not restricted, and no restrictions are applied to their repatriation. Residents and nonresidents are subject to the general regulations described in the section on Administration of Control.

Gold

Purchases and sales of gold abroad are legally reserved for the monetary authorities. Residents may purchase and import unrefined gold under ministerial license for industrial purposes. Loans for the importation of gold are freely assumable. The exportation of unrefined gold is subject to licensing by the Ministry of Foreign Trade. The importation and exportation of gold coins, including coins that are legal tender in a foreign country, are unrestricted. Imports of unrefined gold are not subject to the value-added tax, whereas imports of gold coins are subject to a value-added tax at 19 percent.

Changes During 1994

No significant changes occurred in the exchange and trade system.

(See Appendix for summary of trade measures introduced and eliminated on an EU-wide basis during 1994, page 554.)

JAMAICA

(Position as of December 31, 1994)

Exchange Arrangement

The currency of Jamaica is the Jamaica Dollar. The Jamaican authorities do not maintain margins in respect of exchange transactions, and the spot and forward exchange rates are determined by demand and supply conditions in the interbank market. On December 31, 1994, the average spot buying and selling rates for the U.S. dollar were J$33.0239 and J$33.3619, respectively, per US$1. There are no taxes or subsidies on purchases or sales of foreign exchange.

The foreign exchange market is operated by the commercial banks, other authorized dealers, and the Bank of Jamaica. The commercial banks buy and sell for their own account. Foreign exchange bureaus function as points of collection, and they are required to sell to the Bank of Jamaica a prescribed minimum amount of foreign exchange that they have purchased. Excess foreign exchange may be sold without restrictions to the commercial banks, other authorized dealers, and the general public. Proceeds from official loans, divestment of government assets, and taxes on the bauxite sector payable in foreign currency are sold directly to the Bank of Jamaica. While there is no restriction on transactions in any currency, the principal foreign currencies accepted in the exchange market are the Canadian dollar, the pound sterling, and the U.S. dollar (trade in other currencies is optional and negotiable between participating banks).

While the Bank of Jamaica is primarily responsible for payments of obligations on government imports of goods and services and official debt, the public entities are free to conduct their own foreign exchange transactions. Since the amounts sold directly to the Bank of Jamaica from the sources indicated above are insufficient to meet the payments it must make, the Bank of Jamaica purchases its additional requirement from the foreign exchange market at the prevailing rate.

All private sector payments are transacted through the commercial banking system, other authorized dealers, and foreign exchange bureaus. The commercial banks also handle most service payments.

On November 1, 1990, the Bank of Jamaica, in consultation with the other central banks in the Caribbean Common Market (CARICOM), suspended clearing arrangements within the framework of CARICOM. The Bank of Jamaica no longer intervenes in CARICOM private sector commercial transactions; settlements for such transactions are effected by the commercial banking sector in convertible currencies.

Jamaica formally accepted the obligations of Article VIII, Sections 2, 3, and 4 of the Fund Agreement, as from February 22, 1963.

Administration of Control

The Exchange Control Act, previously administered by the Bank of Jamaica on behalf of the Minister of Finance, was repealed on August 17, 1992. The provision regarding prohibition of trading in foreign exchange, except by and through an authorized dealer, was incorporated in the Bank of Jamaica Act. The Minister of Finance, however, retains the authority to issue directions to specified classes of persons regarding the acquisition of foreign assets.

Prescription of Currency

Payments to all countries may be made by crediting Jamaica dollars to an external account or a foreign currency account.[1] Receipts from all countries must be received by debit of an external account or in any foreign currency.

Foreign Currency Accounts

Authorized dealers are allowed to open foreign currency accounts for residents and nonresidents. Funds on these accounts may be transferred freely between residents and nonresidents. External accounts may be credited with payments by residents of Jamaica, with transfers from other external accounts, and with the proceeds from the sale to an authorized dealer of gold or foreign currencies. They may be debited for payments to residents of Jamaica, for transfers to other external accounts, and for the purchase of foreign currencies. Authorized dealers are allowed to hold, for residents and nonresidents, "A" Accounts in foreign currency and "B" Accounts in Jamaica dollars, both of which are exempt from tax on interest earned on all deposits, provided that (1) in the case of A Accounts operated by nonresidents, no new accounts have been operating and no new deposits have been made in

---

[1]All currencies other than the Jamaica dollar are considered foreign currencies. All foreign currencies have been designated as specified currencies.

existing accounts after September 22, 1991 and (2), in the case of B Accounts operated by residents as of September 22, 1991, deposits are held as certificates of deposit with at least one year maturity.

Before September 25, 1991, accounts that were credited mainly by proceeds of sales of properties owned by emigrants and not placed at the free disposal of nonresidents of Jamaica (including capital gains from the sale of undeveloped land and proceeds from the sale of emigrants' real estate and financial assets) were designated as blocked accounts. Following the liberalization of the foreign exchange market, no new accounts were opened after September 25, 1991. A timetable was established for the phasing out of existing accounts, and effective April 1, 1992, all remaining balances in blocked accounts became freely convertible.

Imports and Import Payments

Import licenses are required for pharmaceutical products and items that endanger public health or security; otherwise, goods may be imported freely without a license. Import licenses, when required, are issued by the Trade Administrator, who is responsible to the Minister of Industry and Commerce. Since June 1991, imports of motor vehicles have not required a license, but a permit is required for government statistical purposes. Payments for imports may be made by commercial banks without reference to the Bank of Jamaica.

Imports are subject to customs tariffs in compliance with the Common External Tariff (CET) Arrangement of CARICOM. The member countries of CARICOM have agreed (in October 1992) on a phased reduction in the level and dispersion of the regional CET over the next five years. As a result, the range of import tariff rates in Jamaica was changed to 5–30 percent from 0–45 percent, effective April 1, 1993, to 0–30 percent effective April 1, 1994,[2] and will eventually be reduced to 0–20 percent by the end of 1996. Some agricultural products will remain subject to a stamp duty at a rate of up to 95 percent, and these will be reduced over a three-year period to be consistent with the CET.

Exports and Export Proceeds

Most goods may be exported without restriction. However, specific licenses are required for the exportation of certain agricultural products, ammunition, explosives, firearms, antique furniture, motor vehicles, mineral and metal ores, paintings, jewelry, and petroleum products.

All proceeds from exports may be used in transactions in the foreign exchange market without restriction.

Payments for and Proceeds from Invisibles

Commercial banks and other authorized dealers provide foreign exchange for most service transactions, including business and other travel, insurance, commissions, private interest payments, medical expenses, foreign exchange refunds, cash gifts, pensions, and miscellaneous payments, such as registration and subscription fees. All interest and dividends payable to nonresident investors are repatriable without restriction.

All proceeds from invisibles may be used in transactions in the foreign exchange market without restriction.

Capital

As of September 25, 1991, all capital flows (both inflows and outflows) became free of restrictions, except transfers abroad of balances on blocked accounts of emigrants, which were allowed from April 1, 1992.

Commercial banks and licensed deposit-taking institutions are liable to be required to match their Jamaica dollar liabilities to their clients with Jamaica dollar assets.

In July 1987, a debt-equity program was introduced for the conversion of certain foreign commercial bank debts to Jamaica into equity investments in approved public and private sector entities. Under this program, profit repatriation was prohibited for three years. Capital repatriation was also prohibited for three years for investments in priority sectors and for seven years for investments in other qualified sectors.[3]

Gold

Commemorative gold coins in denominations of J$20, J$100, and J$250 are legal tender but do not circulate. There are no restrictions on the purchase, sale, or holding of gold for numismatic or industrial purposes.

Changes During 1994

Exchange Arrangement

April 1. An exchange bureau system was established. Operators of bureaus would be allowed to purchase foreign currency notes and traveler's

---

[2] Zero to 25 percent effective April 1, 1995.

[3] The program is scheduled to be discontinued after March 31, 1995.

checks in unlimited amounts. Drafts and money orders may be purchased up to a maximum of US$100,000 or its equivalent in other currencies in any one transaction. Foreign exchange may be sold by bureau operators in banknotes or traveler's checks, but a minimum amount of 20 percent and a maximum of 45 percent of gross foreign currency purchases must be sold to the Bank of Jamaica.

JAPAN

(Position as of December 31, 1994)

Exchange Arrangement

The currency of Japan is the Japanese Yen. The authorities of Japan do not maintain margins in respect of exchange transactions, and exchange rates are determined on the basis of underlying demand and supply conditions in the exchange markets. However, the authorities intervene when necessary in order to counter disorderly conditions in the markets. The principal intervention currency is the U.S. dollar. The closing interbank rate for the U.S. dollar in the New York market on December 31, 1994 was ¥111.85 per US$1. Authorized banks may freely carry out spot and forward exchange transactions with their customers, with nonresident banks, and among themselves. Forward exchange contracts may be negotiated against foreign currencies quoted on the Tokyo exchange market and in other major international foreign exchange markets. There are no officially set rates in the forward market, and forward exchange transactions are based on free market rates. There are no taxes or subsidies on purchases or sales of foreign exchange.

Japan formally accepted the obligations of Article VIII, Sections 2, 3, and 4 of the Fund Agreement, as from April 1, 1964.

Administration of Control

The exchange and trade control system is operated mainly by the Ministry of Finance, the Ministry of International Trade and Industry (MITI), and the Bank of Japan acting as the Government's agent. Most of the authority for verifying normal payments is, however, delegated to authorized banks, referred to as foreign exchange banks. Import- and export-reporting requirements are handled by the MITI. With effect from January 1, 1992, inward direct investments have to be reported to the Minister of Finance and other appropriate ministers after such investments take place, in accordance with the amendment of the law enacted in April 1991. Outward direct investments require prior notice to the Ministry of Finance.

Prescription of Currency

Payments to all countries may be made in any currency, including yen, and receipts may also be obtained in any currency.

Nonresident Accounts

Nonresident accounts in yen may be opened by any nonresident with any authorized bank in Japan. There are no restrictions on credits to or payments from these accounts, and balances may be converted freely into any foreign currency. Payment of interest on balances in such accounts may be restricted when it is deemed necessary to prevent drastic fluctuations in the exchange rate of the yen.

Imports and Import Payments

Imports may be made freely, with the exception of specifically restricted items or items from designated countries. The Import Restriction System covers 77 items (four-digit Harmonized Commodity Description and Coding System (HS) base), which are subject to import restrictions falling under the state trading, national security, public health, and moral protection provisions of the GATT. For the restricted items, once importers obtain authorization from the MITI, they receive an import quota certificate that entitles them to receive an import license from an authorized foreign exchange bank automatically upon application. For the importation of certain other goods from certain countries or shipping areas, individual authorization must be obtained from the MITI. Imports from Croatia and Bosnia and Herzegovina, the Federal Republic of Yugoslavia (Serbia/Montenegro), Iraq, and the Libyan Arab Jamahiriya require permission from the MITI. For transactions that involve payments from Japan to residents of Bosnia and Herzegovina, Serbia/Montenegro, Iraq, and the Libyan Arab Jamahiriya or by residents of these countries to foreign countries through Japan, permission from the Minister of Finance is required. Intermediary trade of petroleum and its products destined for Angola require permission from the MITI. All other payments for invisibles from Japan to residents of the Federal Republic of Yugoslavia (Serbia/Montenegro), Iraq, and Libya require permission from the MITI.

Import settlements effected under the special methods (i.e., those effected by means of open accounts or those involving payments made more than two years before import declaration or after more than two years of shipment) require authorization from the MITI.

Payments for Invisibles

Payments for invisibles may be made without limit. Gifts and donations (except by government institutions) to nonresidents (except relatives abroad) that are valued at more than ¥5 million are referred to the Bank of Japan, which approves the payment after verifying its authenticity. However, remittances to relatives abroad may be made without limit. Other current payments for invisibles, such as the purchase of foreign currencies in connection with travel abroad, may be made without limit. The exportation of domestic banknotes exceeding ¥5 million requires ministerial approval. Intermediating businesses involving Croatia and Bosnia and Herzegovina, the Federal Republic of Yugoslavia (Serbia/Montenegro), and Iraq require permission from the MITI.

Exports and Export Proceeds

Export restraint may be exercised by virtue of the Export and Import Transactions Law and the Export Trade Control Order issued under the Foreign Exchange and Foreign Trade Control Law. Export restraint may be applied either globally or to certain destinations, and it may cover export volume, export prices, or other conditions. At the end of 1993, voluntary restraints were applied to exports of certain textile items to the United States and the European Union (EU), to exports of passenger cars to the United States, and to exports of forklift trucks to the EU. In addition, exports of some other products, including passenger cars, light commercial vehicles, and videocassette recorders to the EU, were subject to monitoring by the Government.

At the end of 1993, 27 export cartels were operating under the provisions of the Export and Import Transactions Law. In addition, 228 items were subject to a license under the Foreign Exchange and Foreign Trade Control Law to control their exportation to specified destinations either because of short supply in the domestic market (e.g., nickel) or to forestall the imposition of import restrictions by other countries (e.g., certain textiles). Exports under processing contracts and exports for which settlements are effected under the special methods described above require authorization from the MITI. Exports of specified raw materials for foreign processing and reimportation require individual licenses. Exports to Croatia and Bosnia and Herzegovina, the Federal Republic of Yugoslavia (Serbia/Montenegro), Iraq, and the Libyan Arab Jamahiriya require permission from the MITI.

Proceeds from Invisibles

Receipts from invisibles may generally be accepted without a license. Residents as well as nonresidents may freely bring in any amount in Japanese or foreign currency. Intermediating business related to trade between the Federal Republic of Yugoslavia (Serbia/Montenegro) or Iraq and other countries and exports of services to the Federal Republic of Yugoslavia (Serbia/Montenegro) or Iraq require permission from the MITI.

Capital

Capital transactions are, in principle, free unless certain procedures are specifically required. Such procedures may take the form of requiring (1) prior approval; (2) prior notice with a waiting period, during which the Minister of Finance or the MITI may request or order that the transaction be suspended or that its particulars be modified on the basis of prescribed criteria; or (3) prior notice without a waiting period. Acquisition of securities for portfolios may be made freely through designated securities firms, and foreign exchange banks and designated institutional investors may freely acquire securities for portfolio investments. However, acquisition of such securities through securities firms other than the designated ones and borrowings by residents require prior notice without a waiting period. Under emergency conditions, however, most capital transactions that are not subject to prior approval in normal conditions may be made subject to prior approval. Emergency conditions are defined as situations in which a capital transaction might (1) make the maintenance of equilibrium in Japan's balance of payments difficult; (2) result in drastic fluctuations in the exchange rate; or (3) result in an international flow of funds large enough to affect Japan's money or capital market adversely.

A distinction is made between direct investments in Japan and other capital transactions. Besides majority equity ownership of enterprises or establishment of branch operations, investments that come under the direct investment regulations include (1) any acquisition of shares in unlisted companies; (2) acquisition by a foreign investor of the shares of a listed company (including individual companies for which the stock price in over-the-counter transactions is made public by the Securities Dealers Association) that reach 10 percent or more when added to those owned by related persons; and (3) acquisition of loans of more than one-year maturity or securities privately placed in Japan, under certain circumstances. Any change of business objectives of a company with one-third or more foreign ownership is also subject to the direct investment provisions. Requests or orders for suspension or modification of specific aspects of the transaction may be made if the minister or ministers concerned consider the transaction to have adverse implications for national security, public order, public safety, the activities of Japanese enterprises in related lines of activities, the general performance of the economy, or the maintenance of mutual equality of treatment of direct investment with other countries. In April 1991, an amendment to the law governing foreign direct investment was introduced. Under the revised law, foreign investors are required to report only after undertaking investment unless national security interest is involved, except for four areas reserved under the Capital Movements Code of Liberalization of the OECD (agriculture, forestry and fishery, mining and petroleum, and leather and leather products); this exception became effective on January 1, 1992.

Outward investments by residents in the form of loans, issue of bonds abroad by residents, issue of bonds in Japan by nonresidents, and direct investment abroad are subject to prior notice with a 20-day waiting period. Transactions requiring prior notice with a 20-day waiting period may be subject to suspension or modification by the Minister of Finance if, in the Minister's opinion, the transaction might adversely affect (1) international financial markets or Japan's international credit standing; (2) domestic and financial capital markets; (3) business activities of a sector of Japanese industries or the smooth performance of the national economy; and (4) implementation of Japan's international agreements, international peace and security, or the maintenance of public order. The Minister of Finance may shorten the waiting period when the transaction under consideration is deemed without adverse consequences. Other transactions by nonresidents may generally be carried out freely. Overseas deposits by residents, borrowing and lending in foreign currency between residents other than those carried out by an authorized bank in Japan, and issuance of yen-denominated bonds abroad by nonresidents may require prior approval. Other external transactions by residents may normally be carried out freely. Issuance of securities or bonds by residents abroad and of foreign-currency-denominated securities or bonds by residents in Japan requires prior notice to the Minister of Finance.

Foreign loans by banks are legally subject to prior notice with a waiting period but, in most cases, may be made upon notification. The banks are free to lend yen on a long-term basis overseas to borrow-

ers of their choice and may accept foreign currency deposits from residents and nonresidents and make foreign currency loans to residents. Foreign currency or yen deposits of nonresidents and residents are subject to minimum reserve requirements adjusted from time to time by the Bank of Japan. Foreign banks are licensed to operate in Japan, subject to Japanese banking regulations; they may obtain resources from inward remittances of foreign currency as well as from money markets in Japan.

Financial institutions apply the following prudential guidelines to capital transactions: (1) a limit on the holding by insurance companies of securities issued by nonresidents equivalent to 30 percent of total assets; (2) the same ratio applied to purchases of foreign-currency-denominated assets; (3) a limit on the holdings by the Post Office Insurance Fund of bonds equivalent to 20 percent of the reserve funds issued by nonresidents; (4) a ceiling on foreign-currency-denominated assets purchased by pension funds equivalent to 30 percent of pension trust assets (for the new money deposited from April 1, 1990, effective December 27, 1991, the ceiling was relaxed to 50 percent on the basis of each institutional account, and the ceiling for foreign-affiliated companies was raised to 70 percent); (5) a ceiling on the investment by credit cooperatives in foreign-currency-denominated bonds, excluding corporate bonds issued by nonresidents equivalent to 30 percent of their net worth; and (6) a ceiling of 5 percent of assets for investment in foreign-currency-denominated securities by the loan trust accounts of trust banks.

Both residents and nonresidents may maintain foreign currency deposits with authorized banks in Japan and may freely transfer any amount in any foreign currency. Overseas deposits by residents up to the equivalent of ¥100 million are not restricted. Qualified Japanese enterprises in insurance, transportation, and securities are permitted to maintain overseas deposits under blanket licensing.

Gold

Residents, including domestic producers of gold, may freely hold gold and purchase and sell it in domestic transactions. The importation and exportation of gold bullion are free from licensing. External futures in gold may be freely traded by designated companies.

Changes During 1994

No significant changes occurred in the exchange and trade system.

JORDAN

(Position as of April 30, 1995)

Exchange Arrangement

The currency of Jordan is the Jordan Dinar. Its exchange rate is determined on the basis of its relationship to the basket of five currencies that constitute the SDR, with the weights determined by the currencies' relative importance to Jordan's international transactions. On April 30, 1995, the official buying and selling rates quoted by the Bank of Jordan (the central bank) for the U.S. dollar were JD 0.693 and JD 0.695, respectively, per US$1. Buying and selling rates for other foreign currencies[1] are fixed on the basis of the cross rates between the U.S. dollar and the currencies concerned in international financial markets.

A fee of 0.10 percent is levied on exchange permits approved by the central bank for sales of exchange for imports, except imports of government departments and certain other approved institutions. Authorized banks are permitted to enter into forward contracts in major currencies against the Jordan dinar for commercial transactions, provided that they cover such operations abroad. For corporations or projects considered to be of vital national interest, the central bank may offer a forward exchange facility in respect of forward exchange cover provided by Jordanian banks. There are no taxes or subsidies on purchases or sales of foreign exchange.

Jordan formally accepted the obligations of Article VIII, Sections 2, 3, and 4 of the Fund Agreements, as from February 20, 1995.

Administration of Control

Exchange control is administered by the Foreign Exchange Control Department of the central bank, which also issues exchange permits; the central bank has delegated to authorized banks the issuance of exchange permits for import payments and, within permitted annual limits, for personal invisible payments. Import policy is determined by the Ministry of Industry and Trade in cooperation with the Ministries of Finance, Supply, and Agriculture.

Arrears are maintained with respect to certain external payments.

Prescription of Currency

No prescription of currency requirements are in force. Jordan's bilateral trade and payments agreement with the Republic of Yemen is inactive.

Nonresident Accounts

Subject to the prior approval of the central bank, authorized banks may open nonresident accounts in domestic and foreign currency. Withdrawals and transfers from foreign currency accounts are free of restrictions. Balances on these accounts may be withdrawn freely in convertible currency and may be used for any purpose. Interest rates are determined in line with rates prevailing in international markets.

Resident Foreign Currency Accounts

Accounts denominated in a foreign currency may be opened at the central bank or at any other licensed bank or financial institution by governmental and semigovernmental entities, as well as by the specialized credit institutions and domestic corporations of vital national interest, including public shareholding companies, provided that outstanding balances (including interest earnings) in each account do not exceed JD 1 million. This ceiling may be raised in certain cases.

Jordanian nationals residing in Jordan may maintain foreign currency deposits with licensed banks in Jordan, provided that the total balance of the deposits that any one person holds does not exceed the equivalent of JD 500,000. Balances in these accounts can be utilized for making current payments abroad consistent with regulations governing import and invisible payments. Jordanians who have worked abroad for more than six months and have decided to return may continue to keep accounts in foreign currencies without limit for up to five years, after which the deposits in excess of the equivalent of JD 500,000 must be converted into Jordan dinars. Licensed banks and financial companies may extend credit facilities in Jordan dinars to residents and nonresidents against their foreign currency deposits. Extending credit facilities to residents against their foreign currency deposits requires the prior approval of the central bank. The amounts of credit facilities extended to nonresidents against their foreign currency deposits should not exceed 5 percent of total credit granted by a bank or a financial company. Fur-

---

[1]Belgian francs, deutsche mark, French francs, Italian lire, Japanese yen, Netherlands guilders, pounds sterling, Swedish kronor, and Swiss francs.

thermore, the balance of the foreign currency deposit used as collateral against the extended credit facilities should not, at any time, be less than the outstanding balance of credit facilities.

Imports and Import Payments

The draft law lifting the ban on imports from Israel has been submitted to Parliament. Other imports, unless mentioned in Article 3 of the Import and Export System,[2] require import licenses if their c. & f. value exceeds JD 2,000. A fee of 5 percent of the c. & f. value is charged when the import license is issued.

Imports requiring a license also require an exchange permit, which is granted automatically when an import license has been obtained; the importer holding an exchange permit may either open a letter of credit or pay against documents. A fee of 0.10 percent is levied on exchange permits for imports except those made by government departments and certain approved institutions and individual permits of less than JD 300. The use of suppliers' credits is subject to prior approval from the central bank, which is normally given for essential imports only.

Imports into Free Zones

Payments for imports into free zones and for transit trade are subject to the prior approval of the central bank. In principle, however, it is the importer's responsibility to provide foreign currency to finance such transactions. Banks are authorized to set the percentage of advance import deposits they collect from customers against these imports at their discretion.

Payments for Invisibles

Payments for invisibles related to authorized imports are not restricted.

Residents are permitted to transfer foreign means of payment equivalent to JD 35,000 a year to meet current payments for invisibles (travel, education, medication, pilgrimage, residence abroad, family assistance, and others) without obtaining the prior approval of the central bank and without presenting any document to justify these payments. They may transfer amounts in excess of JD 35,000 when justified by supporting documents. In comparison, transfers from nonresident accounts are free of re-

striction. The authorized amount for subscriptions to newsletters, magazines, and specific bulletins is the equivalent of JD 1,000. The policy on payments for invisibles is, in general, liberal and nondiscriminatory. In practice, the central bank does not restrict remittances of income accruing to nonresidents or of savings of foreign nationals returning to their own countries.

A fee of 0.10 percent is levied on exchange permits for invisible payments, except those of government departments and certain approved institutions, permits financed from nonresident accounts in foreign currency credited from sources outside Jordan, and permits with a value of less than JD 300. Remittances may be made by postal order for imports not to exceed JD 10 a person a month to any person residing abroad.

Premiums for life insurance policies issued by insurance companies operating in the Kingdom in favor of nonresidents or Jordanians working abroad must be collected in foreign currency from abroad or from nonresident accounts.

In addition to any exchange allowances for travel, residents and nonresidents traveling abroad may take out up to JD 5,000 in Jordanian banknotes and coins. Nonresidents working in Jordan who do not have nonresident accounts may transfer up to JD 400 a month, up to a maximum of JD 5, 000 a year. Furthermore, all travelers may take out checks, traveler's checks, or letters of credit issued by authorized banks in Jordan, in accordance with exchange permits authorized by the central bank. Tourists and other nonresidents may also take out foreign currency notes and coins and any other foreign means of payment that they had or that they had previously brought in and declared to the customs authorities at the time of entry.

Exports and Export Proceeds

The draft law lifting the ban on exports to Israel has been submitted to Parliament. There are no requirements affecting export proceeds.

Proceeds from Invisibles

Travelers entering Jordan may bring in any amount of Jordanian and foreign notes and coins.[3] Individuals who, for exchange control purposes, are considered residents of Jordan may retain only the equivalent of JD 500,000 a person in foreign currency in the Kingdom, as stipulated in the Foreign

---

[2]These include imports made on behalf of His Majesty the King, imports by government departments and certain approved institutions, and goods in transit.

[3]Approval is not granted for the crediting of such Jordanian currency to a nonresident account or for the remittance abroad of the equivalent in foreign currency.

Exchange Control Regulations. They must sell the excess amount to licensed banks, financial companies, or authorized dealers.

Capital

Inward transfers of capital are not restricted, but outward transfers by residents require approval and are not normally permitted. However, the central bank may grant permission to banks, insurance companies, contractors, and industrial, agricultural, trading, and tourist firms, to transfer funds abroad for specified investment or operating purposes. The transfer of funds for purposes of investment in Arab countries is permitted only if mutual treatment or bilateral agreements exist between Jordan and the country, and it is the investor's responsibility to provide foreign exchange to finance such investments. Current income resulting from nonresident investments in Jordan may be transferred abroad. Under the Law Regulating Arab and Foreign Investments, capital, profits, and dividends from foreign investments may be remitted. The Foreign Companies Registration Law No. 58 (1985) provides various benefits to foreign companies establishing branches in Jordan for purposes of conducting business outside the country; such branches may also be granted nonresident status for exchange control purposes. Nonresidents may use convertible currencies to purchase Premium Development Bonds denominated in Jordan dinars. Proceeds from redemption at maturity, including interest, are transferable in any convertible currency.

Gold

The central bank has issued ten gold coins, which, although legal tender, do not circulate and are available only to nonresidents and domestic numismatists. Residents may purchase, hold, and sell gold coins in Jordan for numismatic or investment purposes. Imports of gold in any form are permitted without the prior approval of the central bank, while imports of gold to be used in crafts and then re-exported are subject to the prior approval of the central bank. Exports of gold, other than gold that has been crafted and whose value has thus increased, require the prior approval of the central bank.

Changes During 1994

Nonresident Accounts

January 25. Licensed banks and financial companies were authorized to open accounts in foreign currencies for nonresidents without any conditions.

In addition, withdrawals and transfers from non-resident accounts were permitted freely.

Imports and Import Payments

January 25. Applications for exchange permits that include advance payments were required to be supported with either one of the following two guarantees (instead of the first one only) to ensure the repatriation of foreign currency transferred through the same bank that issued the exchange permit: (1) An external banking guarantee of an amount equal to the advance payment; or (2) a local guarantee of an amount equal to 20 percent of the advance payment in favor of the central bank.

Payments for Invisibles

January 25. Any resident is permitted to transfer foreign means of payment equivalent to JD 35,000 a year, instead of JD 20,000 a year, to meet current payments for invisibles (travel, education, medication, pilgrimage, residence abroad, family assistance, and others) without obtaining the prior approval of the central bank and without presenting any document to justify these payments. Transfers by residents in excess of the JD 35,000 for invisibles are also permitted when justified by supporting documents.

Exports and Export Proceeds

January 25. The regulation under which export proceeds were to be repatriated within a specified period was abolished.

Changes During 1995

Exchange Arrangement

February 20. Jordan formally accepted the obligations of Article VIII, Sections 2, 3, and 4 of the Fund Agreement.

Imports and Import Payments

January 25. Applications for exchange permits that include advance payments were required to be supported with a letter of undertaking of an amount equal to the advance payment in favor of the central bank. No banking guarantee is required for exchange permits covered either from foreign currency deposits or incoming confirmed letters of credit or from external guarantees.

Payments for Invisibles

April 4. Nonresidents working in Jordan who do not have nonresident accounts were permitted to transfer up to JD 400 a year instead of JD 100 a month, up to a maximum of JD 5,000, instead of JD 1,200 a year.

KAZAKHSTAN

(Position as of January 31, 1995)

Exchange Arrangement

The currency of the Republic of Kazakhstan is the Tenge.[1] Exchange rates of the tenge against the U.S. dollar and other foreign currencies are determined at twice-weekly auctions held by the Kazakhstan Interbank Currency Exchange (KICE), which includes 21 commercial banks and the National Bank of Kazakhstan (NBK).[2] These rates are also used for all official transactions. Banks may participate in auctions on their own account or on behalf of their clients. In between auctions, banks and enterprises are permitted to engage in spot and cash transactions at freely negotiated rates. The policy of the Government is to limit intervention in the auction only to smooth out sharp fluctuations in the exchange rate and to let supply and demand conditions determine the rates at the auctions. Purchasers of foreign exchange are subject to a commission of 0.3 percent payable at the auction and a 1 percent commission payable to the authorized bank. Residents planning to sell or purchase foreign currency at the auction (via authorized banks) are required to present documents establishing compliance with prevailing foreign exchange regulations. Foreign exchange purchased at the auction and not used within two months must be reauctioned. Only spot transactions are permitted at the auctions. The spread between the buying and selling rates is not allowed to exceed 10 percent. At the end of December 1994, the average exchange rate of the tenge against the U.S. dollar was T 54.26 per US$1.

Administration of Control

Parliament approved a foreign exchange law in April 1993 that established the principle of convertibility for current international transactions. The Ministry of Economy prepares the overall quotas for delivery outside Kazakhstan on the basis of territorial and specific commodity level material balances and has the power to establish export quotas for sales of export goods through auctions. The Ministry of Foreign Economic Relations is the authority that grants licenses for export or import. The Cabinet of Ministers may decide to limit the export or import of goods not subject to quotas and licenses, depending on the economic situation. In addition, the heads of local governments may set up regimes of quotas and licenses for consumer goods other than food.

Prescription of Currency

Kazakhstan does not maintain bilateral payments arrangements with any country outside of the former Soviet Union. Settlements with the Baltic countries, Russia, and the other countries of the former Soviet Union are made through a system of correspondent accounts of the NBK and commercial banks. Residents of Kazakhstan may make and receive international payments and transfers in any convertible currency as well as in Russian rubles. In general, foreign currency may not be used for the settlement of domestic transactions between residents.[3] It is prohibited to use foreign exchange cash in retail trade and services on Kazak territory. Transactions between residents and nonresidents involving the sale or purchase of foreign currency are limited to those conducted through authorized banks.

Resident and Nonresident Accounts

Resident individuals and enterprises may maintain convertible foreign exchange accounts at authorized banks. These accounts, which bear interest, may be credited with retained export earnings and foreign exchange transferred from abroad, and balances in these accounts may be freely used for any purpose. Residents may also maintain convertible currency accounts abroad with permission from the NBK.

Nonresidents may hold accounts in Kazakhstan in domestic or foreign currencies; only one account is permitted. Withdrawals from these accounts, including transfers abroad, are not restricted.

---

[1]The tenge was issued on November 15, 1993 as the national currency and became sole legal tender in Kazakhstan as of November 18, 1993.

[2]The exchange operates in U.S. dollars, deutsche mark, Russian rubles, Kyrgyz soms, Uzbek sum, and Ukrainian karbovanets. Daily official rates for 32 other currencies are set on the basis of the tenge-dollar rates in the auction and the cross rates in international markets.

[3]Exemptions are permitted for payments to residents providing freight, insurance, or other intermediary services in respect of foreign-currency-denominated trade; payments to residents supplying inputs required for the production of exports sold for foreign currencies; payments for selected domestic telecommunications services; payments to banks and other financial institutions in respect of liabilities incurred in foreign currencies; and where otherwise specially authorized by the NBK.

Imports and Exports

Trade with the Baltic countries, the Russian Federation, and the other countries of the former Soviet Union under trade agreements is conducted through acquisitions and shipments by financially independent state trading organizations, Kazcontract (formerly the Ministry of Material Resources), and sectoral trading organizations (including Kazrisheprom, Kazpisheprom, Kazhleboprodukt, Kazgazifikatsia, Leginvest, and Stroymaterialy). Trade with other countries is also effected under a system of intergovernmental trade agreements, quotas, and licenses. Overall export quotas are prepared by the Ministry of Economy on the basis of balances of specific products in various territories. There are no import quotas.

All export and import licenses are granted by the Ministry of Foreign Economic Relations, and the exportation or importation of goods not subject to quotas and licenses may be restricted by the Cabinet of Ministers, depending on the domestic economic situation.

For both exports and imports, general or specific licenses may be granted. A general license is given for the period necessary to complete the export or import operations, but in any case not for a period exceeding one year. Operations under a general license may take place with more than one contract but must be of the same general nature. Specific licenses are provided for an individual export or import transaction and are valid for one calendar year. The number of commodity groups subject to export licenses was reduced from 55 at the end of 1993 to 50 by late January 1994 and to 32 by the end of December 1994. The number of commodity groups subject to import licenses was reduced to 11 as of the end of December 1994.

By a decree of the Cabinet of Ministers of March 10, 1993, the export quotas for a list of items considered consistent with state needs was established. The items are energy products, metals, chemicals and petrochemicals, equipment for building machinery, construction materials, consumer goods, and food items. These quotas are assigned to various ministries and ultimately to individual exporting enterprises.

The list of overall export quotas for 1994 was set in a decree of the Cabinet of Ministers of November 16, 1993.[4] These export quotas cover a shorter list of goods "of national importance" and are in addition to the export quotas set for interstate trade; they were assigned to various ministries by the Ministry of Economics, and these ministries have prepared quota assignments for exporting enterprises and submitted them to the Ministry of Foreign Economic Relations, which in turn assigned specific quantities of products to individual trading companies. Unused quotas cannot be carried over to the next year unless supporting documents indicate that they are for the export of goods produced in the previous year.

Under a presidential decree of July 30, 1993, certain products of "importance to the state" are required to be exported and re-exported exclusively through state foreign trade organizations, and the quotas for these products are compulsory for the enterprises producing these goods. All export proceeds except for those of joint ventures are subject to the surrender requirement at the rate of 50 percent. Auction rates at the KICE are applied to the surrendered foreign exchange.

Payments for and Proceeds from Invisibles

Purchases by residents of foreign exchange for tourist purposes are limited to $500 a person; there are no limits on withdrawals from convertible currency accounts for the same purposes. Purchases of foreign exchange for business travel abroad are, in principle, subject to limits, which are based on country-specific norms for accommodation and subsistence expenses but are not officially enforced. In practice, banks are free to grant exemptions to these limits. Foreign exchange may be purchased without limit for purposes of study abroad if the appropriate documents are produced. Remittances for family maintenance purposes are subject to certain limits.

Payments for invisibles that residents are permitted to make are officially tolerated for nonresidents. Nonresident workers in Kazakhstan are free to make transfers abroad. The remittance of dividends and profits is subject to approval.

Proceeds from invisibles earned by enterprises are subject to the same surrender requirement as that which is applied to merchandise exports. Proceeds from invisibles earned by private individuals are not subject to surrender requirements.

There are no restrictions on the amount of domestic currency that residents and nonresidents may bring into or take out of the country.

Capital

Capital transactions between residents and nonresidents require approval from the NBK. Foreign

---

[4]Included in the export quota list for 1994 are oil, coal, various fuels, copper, zinc, lead, bauxite, ferrous metals, tin, raw leather, cotton fiber, pure wool, sturgeon caviar, and cereals.

direct investments in the defense sector are prohibited. Neither residents nor nonresidents are permitted to own land. Foreign investors are entitled to tax holidays and exemption from licensing and quota restrictions and can freely repatriate their profits.

Gold

All transactions in gold must be effected through the NBK, which buys gold products in the country at world market prices.

Changes During 1994

Administration of Control

January 1. The Republican Hard Currency Fund was abolished. All foreign exchange transactions would be effected through the budget, and all transactions in convertible currencies would be made through the NBK.

Imports and Exports

January 1. A decree imposing full compulsory surrender at a uniform rate of 50 percent came into effect; joint ventures would be exempted from the surrender requirement. Auction rates at the KICE would be applied to surrendered foreign exchange. Foreign exchange taxes on export proceeds were abolished.

February 1. The number of goods subject to export quotas was reduced to 25 from 34.

April 1. The number of goods subject to export and import quotas was reduced, respectively, to 7 and 11.

KENYA

(Position as of December 31, 1994)

Exchange Arrangement

The currency of Kenya is the Kenya Shilling. On October 18, 1993, the market and the official exchange rates were unified. The market rate is determined on the basis of underlying supply and demand conditions in the interbank market. The official exchange rate is set at the previous day's average market rate. The principal intervention currency is the U.S. dollar. The official exchange rate applies only to government and government-guaranteed external debt-service payments and to government imports for which there is a specific budget allocation. On December 31, 1994, the exchange rate was K Sh 44.84 per US$1.

The operation of foreign exchange bearer certificates (FEBCs) has been phased out.

Under an export foreign exchange retention scheme, exporters are allowed to retain 100 percent of foreign exchange proceeds in foreign exchange accounts with banks in Kenya and may use the retained proceeds to finance business-related current expenses and debt-service payments or sell them to banks at a market-determined exchange rate. Banks, in turn, are permitted to sell foreign exchange they purchase in the retention market to any client at market-determined exchange rates for the same purposes, to purchase foreign exchange in the retention market for their own accounts, to offer forward exchange contracts to exporters and importers at market-determined rates without restriction on the amount or period covered, or to sell foreign exchange they purchase in the retention market to another bank.

Commercial banks are authorized to enter into forward exchange contracts with their customers at market-determined exchange rates in currencies of their choice; there are no limits on the amount or period of cover. There are no official schemes for currency swaps or exchange rate guarantee schemes for external debt servicing, except for the Exchange Risk Assumption Fund, which covers the foreign exchange losses associated with exchange rate fluctuations occurring after July 1, 1989, for three development finance institutions.

Kenya formally accepted the obligations of Article VIII, Sections 2, 3, and 4 of the Fund Agreement, as from June 30, 1994.

Administration of Control

The Minister for Finance has delegated the administration of exchange control to the Central Bank. Authority is delegated to the authorized banks to approve certain payments for imports, payments for certain current invisibles, and some capital payments.

Import controls are administered by the Director of Internal Trade in the Ministry of Commerce. Import and foreign exchange allocation licenses were abolished in May 1993, except for a short negative list of goods prohibited for health, security, or environmental reasons. The responsibility for issuing import licenses, when required, rests with the Director. The Director issues special licenses for the exportation of restricted goods, including certain agricultural products and goods whose exportation is restricted based on security and environmental reasons.

Arrears are maintained with respect to external payments.

Prescription of Currency

Payments to residents of other countries may be made in Kenya shillings to the credit of an external account in Kenya or in any foreign currency. Receipts may be obtained in Kenya shillings from an external account in Kenya or in any marketable foreign currency.

Resident and Nonresident Accounts

Kenyan residents who have foreign exchange earnings (including earnings from services) are allowed to open foreign currency accounts with local banks. Use of funds in these accounts is limited in the same manner as use of export retention accounts. Export retention accounts may be converted into foreign currency accounts. Foreigners with work permits in Kenya may open foreign currency accounts with Kenyan banks and may credit their local earnings to these accounts; use of funds in these accounts is not restricted. Accounts in foreign currency held by residents of other countries with authorized banks in Kenya are designated foreign currency accounts. They may be freely credited with authorized payments by residents of Kenya, with transfers from other foreign currency accounts, with the proceeds from sales of any currency and gold by nonresidents to authorized dealers, and with retained foreign exchange earnings. Foreign currency accounts may be freely debited for payments to residents and nonresidents. Payment of interim dividends to nonresident shareholders may be remitted without limit, provided that the application is supported by adequate documentation. Commercial banks may, without reference to the Central Bank, remit pension contributions to nonresidents.

Nontransferable funds of nonresidents relating to investments made prior to February 28, 1994, are credited to blocked accounts. Remittances from blocked accounts are permitted freely, except for those relating to investments made prior to February 28, 1994. Remittances of funds in blocked accounts relating to investments made prior to February 28, 1994, may be made by commercial banks up to $10,000 a year without referral to the Central Bank; amounts exceeding this limit must be referred to the Central Bank.

Nonresidents may also operate undesignated nonresident accounts alongside foreign currency accounts denominated in Kenya shillings. These accounts may be credited freely with proceeds of drawings from foreign currency accounts for local use. Funds in these accounts are not transferable to foreign currency accounts. Enterprises operating in export processing zones (EPZs) are permitted to hold foreign currency accounts abroad or with authorized banks in Kenya and may use the balances on these amounts to pay business-related expenses (including imports, debt service, and dividends). They are not required to surrender foreign exchange earnings to the Central Bank.

Imports and Import Payments

Import and foreign exchange allocation licenses are not required except for a few items that, for health, security, and environmental reasons, are included on a negative list.

Customs tariffs are applied as the sole form of protection of domestic industry. There are seven customs tariff nomenclatures, with rates varying from zero to 75 percent. Exporters of horticultural goods and agro-based products are exempt from import duties and value-added tax on imported inputs.

Authorized banks are permitted to provide foreign exchange against the following documents: a copy of the import declaration, a final invoice, an original clean report of findings from a nominated inspection agency, and a copy of the customs entry. Prior exchange control approval must be obtained for imports of machinery and equipment, which are regarded as contributions toward equity capital or

are on a loan basis. Advance payments for imports may be made through commercial banks without prior approval from the Central Bank.

All imports with an f.o.b. value of more than K Sh 100,000 are subject to preshipment inspection for quality, quantity, and price, and require a clean report of findings. Authorized banks in Kenya may not issue shipping guarantees for the clearance of imports until they receive the report. All goods purchased by importers in Kenya must be insured with companies licensed to conduct insurance business in Kenya.

Payments for Invisibles

All payments for invisibles may be made without restriction. Foreign workers may transfer abroad any amount of their earnings upon verification of income and payment of taxes.

The exportation of domestic banknotes exceeding K Sh 100,000 requires approval from the Central Bank and must be declared to customs.

Exports and Export Proceeds

Most goods may be exported without special licenses. Exports of certain foodstuffs and agricultural products require special licenses and may be restricted to ensure adequate supplies in the domestic market. Exports of tea, coffee, minerals, precious stones, and other essential strategic materials are also subject to special licensing. Coffee, tea, and horticultural produce may be exported only if a sales contract is registered with the Coffee Board, Tea Board, and Horticultural Crops Development Authority, respectively. Export proceeds in foreign currencies must be repatriated to Kenya in an approved manner within three months of the date of exportation but need not be surrendered.

Proceeds from Invisibles

All receipts from invisibles may be kept in retention accounts. Travelers may freely bring in and take out foreign currency notes, except those of countries with restrictions on the exportation of currencies; however, foreign currency notes in excess of the equivalent of $5,000 must be declared at the point of entry or departure. The importation of domestic banknotes is limited to K Sh 100,000; amounts exceeding this limit require prior approval from the Central Bank.

Capital

Capital transfers to all countries are regulated. With the exception of expatriate employees who have opted to remit savings from their salaries, an emigrant is allowed to transfer up to K Sh 600,000 a family unit from his declared assets as a settling-in allowance to the new country of residence. Of this sum, K Sh 200,000 is made available for immediate remittance, and the remainder will be authorized for remittance in not more than five annual installments, not exceeding the equivalent of K Sh 80,000 each year. The initial settling-in allowance of K Sh 200,000 lapses if it is not remitted within the first two years of the emigrant's departure from Kenya. All remaining funds must be credited to a blocked account; they may then be invested in approved securities, and redemption proceeds become transferable, provided that redemption does not take place earlier than five years from the date of purchase.

The investment of foreign funds in Kenya is generally not restricted, but to ensure eventual repatriation it is necessary to obtain from the treasury a "certificate of approved enterprise" for the investment. Foreign and domestic investment in specified types of production require approval. Foreign investors may repatriate the value of the original equity investment denominated in the currency in which it was initially made and the value of any profits that were reinvested and denominated in the currency of the original investment. Borrowing by foreign-controlled companies on the domestic market is not restricted.

Outward investments: Residents may invest freely up to $500,000 without referring to the Central Bank. Investments above $500,000 should be referred to the Central Bank, which will approve all bona fide transactions without undue delay.

Inward investments: At end-December 1994, transactions were limited and controlled by the Exchange Control Act. Residents may invest freely up to $500,000 without referring to the Central Bank.

Offshore borrowing by residents is allowed without limit, provided that (1) interest does not exceed LIBOR plus 2 percentage points, and (2) such borrowing is not guaranteed by the government. Applications for borrowing on other terms must be referred to the Central Bank.

Gold

Residents may hold and acquire gold coins in Kenya for numismatic purposes. With this exception, residents other than the monetary authorities and authorized industrial and professional users are not allowed to hold or acquire gold in any form other than jewelry, at home or abroad. Exports of gold in any form other than jewelry constituting the personal effects of a traveler require exchange control approval. Import licenses for gold bullion (ingots, bars, or sheets) are issued restrictively and only to goldsmiths.

Changes During 1994

Exchange Arrangement

June 30. Kenya formally accepted the obligations of Article VIII, Sections 2, 3, and 4 of the Fund Agreement.

Resident and Nonresident Accounts

February 21. Remittances from blocked accounts were liberalized, except those relating to investments made prior to February 28, 1994. Remittances of funds in blocked accounts relating to investments made prior to February 28, 1994, may be made by commercial banks up to $100,000; applications for remittances in excess of $100,000 must be referred to the Central Bank of Kenya.

February 21. Kenyan residents who have foreign exchange earnings (including earnings from services) were allowed to open foreign currency accounts with local banks. Use of funds in these accounts would be limited in the same manner as use of export retention accounts. Export retention accounts may be converted into foreign currency accounts. Foreigners with work permits in Kenya may open foreign currency accounts with Kenyan banks and may credit their local earnings to these accounts; use of funds in the accounts would not be restricted.

Payments for Invisibles

February 21. Restrictions on remittances by foreigners of monthly earnings were removed, subject to verification of income and payment of tax.

February 21. Persons leaving Kenya were allowed to export Kenyan banknotes up to K Sh 100,000; exportation of amounts in excess of K Sh 100,000 would require approval from the Central Bank.

Exports and Export Proceeds

February 21. The export retention ratio was increased to 100 percent of export earnings for all exporters. The requirement to repatriate export proceeds within three months remained in effect.

Capital

February 21. Borrowing by foreign-controlled companies on the domestic market was fully liberalized.

February 21. Offshore borrowing by residents was allowed without limit, provided that (1) interest does not exceed LIBOR plus 2 percentage points, and (2) such borrowing is not guaranteed by the government. Applications for borrowings on other terms must be referred to the Central Bank.

KIRIBATI

(Position as of December 31, 1994)

Exchange Arrangement

The official currency of Kiribati is the Australian Dollar; a small number of Kiribati coins are also in circulation. There is no central monetary institution, and the authorities do not buy or sell foreign exchange. The Bank of Kiribati (the only commercial bank) quotes daily rates for 15 currencies[1] on the basis of their respective values against the Australian dollar. There are no taxes or subsidies on purchases or sales of foreign exchange. There are no arrangements for forward cover against exchange rate risk operating in the official or the commercial banking sector.

Kiribati formally accepted the obligations of Article VIII, Sections 2, 3, and 4 of the Fund Agreement, as from August 22, 1986.

Prescription of Currency

Both outward and inward payments may be settled in Australian currency or in any foreign currency.[2] Purchases and sales of foreign currencies in exchange for Australian dollars must be undertaken with the Bank of Kiribati, the only authorized foreign exchange dealer.

Imports and Import Payments

Import licenses are normally not required. The importation of a limited range of goods is prohibited for health, safety, or environmental reasons. Tariffs apply to most private imports and range up to 75 percent.

Exports and Export Proceeds

There are no surrender requirements for export proceeds. There are no taxes or quantitative restrictions on exports, but copra can be exported only through the Kiribati Copra Cooperative Society.

Payments for and Proceeds from Invisibles

There are no restrictions on payments for or receipts from invisibles.

Capital

The authorities maintain a liberal attitude toward foreign direct investment and encourage export-promoting or import-substituting investments. All applications for foreign investment must be made to the Foreign Investment Commission, which approves applications of total foreign capital contribution up to $A 250,000. Applications with a higher capital contribution are approved by the Cabinet. Under the Foreign Investment Promotion Act, investors may be granted duty-free imports of capital goods and raw materials. Investments in pioneer industries are eligible for a tax holiday of up to six years. Repatriation of profits and capital is normally unrestricted.

Changes During 1994

No significant changes occurred in the exchange and trade system.

---

[1]Canadian dollars, deutsche mark, Fiji dollars, Hong Kong dollars, Japanese yen, New Zealand dollars, Papua New Guinea kina, pounds sterling, Singapore dollars, Solomon Islands dollars, Swiss francs, U.S. dollars, Tongan pa'anga, Vanuatu vatu, and Western Samoa tala.

[2]Foreign currencies are defined as all currencies other than the Australian dollar.

KOREA

(Position as of December 31, 1994)

Exchange Arrangement

The currency of Korea is the Korean Won. Since the introduction of a market average rate (MAR) system on March 2, 1990, the Korean won-U.S. dollar rate has been determined on the basis of the weighted average of interbank rates for Korean won-U.S. dollar spot transactions of the previous day. During each business day, the Korean won-U.S. dollar exchange rate in the interbank market is allowed to fluctuate within fixed margins of ±1.5 percent against the MAR of the previous day. The exchange rates of the won against currencies other than the U.S. dollar are determined in relation to the exchange rate of the U.S. dollar against these currencies in the international market. On December 31, 1994, the middle rate for the U.S. dollar was W 788.70. The buying and selling rates offered to customers are set freely by foreign exchange banks. There are no taxes or subsidies on purchases or sales of foreign exchange.

Foreign exchange banks may conduct forward transactions, futures transactions, swaps, and options between foreign currencies, as well as between the Korean won and foreign currencies. There are no specific restrictions on the terms of forward contracts in respect of interbank transactions. However, the terms of forward contracts between foreign exchange banks and nonbank customers must be based on a bona fide transaction, and the contract amount must not exceed the expected receipt or payment of the transaction. Forward transactions involving foreign currencies or those involving domestic currency in amounts not exceeding $10 million are exempt from the "underlying documentation" requirement. There are no ceilings on foreign exchange deposits payable in Korean won, which are exempt from this requirement.

Korea formally accepted the obligations of Article VIII, Sections 2, 3, and 4 of the Fund Agreement, as from November 1, 1988.

Administration of Control

The Ministry of Economy and Finance initiates policy with respect to prescription of currency and method of settlement, foreign exchange operations, payments for nonmerchandise transactions, and capital transactions and transfers. The Bank of Korea, as the Government's agent, executes most of the above functions; it also regulates operations in the exchange market and is authorized to intervene in it. The Bank of Korea has been delegated authority to control payments related to invisibles and certain capital transactions. Foreign exchange banks, as well as the branch offices of foreign banks in Korea, are authorized to engage in commercial international banking and in all foreign exchange dealings, with the exception of those specifically prohibited.

Prescription of Currency

All settlements between Korea and other countries may be made in convertible currencies. The proceeds of exports must be obtained in prescribed currencies.[1] Residents are permitted to carry out current transactions denominated in Korean won, provided that settlements will be made in designated foreign currencies; for transactions up to $300, the settlements of exports and imports in Korean won are permitted. There are no limits for reinsurance transactions.

Nonresident and Resident Accounts

Nonresidents, including Korean workers abroad, may maintain foreign currency deposit accounts with foreign exchange banks. Remittances from such accounts and withdrawals in the form of currency notes upon departure from Korea may, in general, be made freely. The approval of the bank where the account is held is not required for remittances abroad or transfers to other foreign currency accounts, for purchases and withdrawals of foreign means of payment, or for payments relating to approved transactions. Nonresidents are allowed to hold free won accounts.

All residents are allowed to open foreign currency deposit accounts. Holders of these accounts may change the foreign currency composition of the accounts as they wish.

Imports and Import Payments

All imports require licenses; for most imports (see below), licenses are issued upon application.

---

[1]In addition to the currencies of the member countries of the IMF that have accepted the obligations of Article VIII of the Articles of Agreement, this includes the European Currency Unit (ECU) and the currencies of China and Hong Kong.

Imports are divided into two categories: automatic approval items and restricted items. All commodities may be imported freely (i.e., applications for import licenses are automatically approved) unless they are on the restricted list. As of December 1994, 150 of the 10,417 basic items on the Harmonized System were classified as restricted. Imports of raw materials for the production of exports are normally approved automatically, irrespective of their classification. Import licenses are granted only to registered traders, who are required to have exported and/or imported a minimum value of $500,000 in any one of the last two calendar years. The commercial terms of payment on which imports may be contracted are regulated. Safeguards against excessive imports are provided under the Foreign Trade Act of 1987.

A seven-member Trade Commission established under this act determines whether imports have harmed domestic industries, and, if its finding is affirmative, it recommends the form of import relief to be provided, including quotas and quality standards.

Payments for Invisibles

All payments for invisibles require an individual license. Those connected with foreign trade, along with certain other items such as banking charges, insurance premiums, communication fees, and periodicals, are licensed automatically. Korean companies are authorized to obtain foreign exchange to meet the expenses of their overseas branches.

Residents traveling abroad may, in general, purchase foreign exchange up to the equivalent of $5,000 a trip as the basic travel allowance; additional foreign exchange may also be purchased for specified expenses, including transportation costs. The monthly allowance for residents staying abroad for over 60 days is $3,000 (the allowance for Korean nationals working as overseas correspondents of mass media is $10,000). For those staying abroad for over one year, an additional $20,000 is allowed at the time of departure. Credit card holders are allowed to charge on an unlimited basis all expenses directly associated with their travel during business and official trips to foreign countries. The basic monthly allowance for individual students living abroad is $2,000; students with a family receive an additional allowance of $500 for a spouse and each child.

Korean residents are allowed to remit up to $5,000 a transaction to their parents and children abroad for living expenses and to their relatives abroad for a wedding gift or funeral donation. In addition, residents may remit up to $10,000 a year without approval, provided that the reason for the remittance is confirmed by a foreign exchange bank. The Governor of the Bank of Korea approves any bona fide exchange application for additional amounts.

Korean currency notes in excess of W 2 million and foreign currency notes in excess of the equivalent of $10,000 may not be exported without special permission. Upon leaving the country, nonresidents may acquire foreign exchange up to the amount for which they have proof of conversion. Foreigners employed by Korean and expatriate firms in Korea may remit their salaries, except for basic living expenses, and retirement allowances to their home countries.

Exports and Export Proceeds

Certain exports on the restricted list require individual licenses. All other products may be exported freely under an automatic approval procedure. Resident business firms may retain up to 30 percent of the aggregate value of their imports and exports in foreign exchange abroad, with a maximum of $300 million.

Proceeds from Invisibles

Proceeds derived from invisibles must be either sold to a foreign exchange bank for won or deposited in foreign exchange accounts in the banks. Korean residents are permitted to hold foreign currencies freely, but, once they are converted into won, a limit applies to reconversion. Nonresidents must register the foreign exchange they bring into Korea if the amount exceeds the equivalent of $10,000. The importation by travelers of Korean currency in excess of W 2 million is restricted.

The proceeds received by construction companies from construction activity abroad must be deposited in foreign currency accounts, and a foreign exchange bank must approve the conversion of these funds after ascertaining the bona fide nature of the transactions; approval is virtually automatic.

Capital

Overseas investments and loans by residents to nonresidents generally require approval. Overseas direct investments of less than $10 million by Korean residents are subject to notification; investments exceeding $10 million require approval from both the Bank of Korea and the Deliberation Committee for Overseas Investment. There are no restrictions on foreign borrowing for overseas investment and related operations. A Korean business incorporated abroad is allowed to retain profits for the purpose of expanding its overseas investment business or improving its financial status. Overseas portfolio investments of institutional investors are not restricted. Also, companies whose export and import value exceeds $10 million are awarded institutional investor status. Loans by resident banks to nonresidents of less than $2 million are permitted freely; loans ranging from $2 million require export notification and loans exceeding $20 million require prior notification. Loans by Korean residents to nonresidents and loans to residents of countries with which Korea does not have diplomatic relations require prior approval from the Ministry of Economy and Finance. Issuance of stocks and bonds abroad is subject only to the notification requirement. The value of overseas issuance of stocks or equity-linked bonds is limited to 15 percent of firms' total equity. Firms are prohibited from issuing won-denominated bonds abroad.

The foreign exchange allowance for emigrants varies with family size. Additional allowances for emigrant investment abroad are subject to the approval of the Governor of the Bank of Korea. Foreign exchange banks may grant authorization for such remittances.

The overbought and oversold positions of foreign exchange banks are limited to 10 percent and 20 percent, respectively, of their capital base; the portion used to hedge capital or operational funds is exempt from this limit.

Regulations governing foreign investment in Korea and the contracting of loans to residents by nonresidents are as follows:

Foreign Investment

Direct investments are allowed in all industries, except those specified on a "negative" list. In December 1994, the negative list consisted of 108 out of a total of 1,148 industries, resulting in a liberalization ratio of 90.6 percent. In the manufacturing sector, the negative list consisted of 10 out of 585 industries, resulting in a liberalization ratio of 98.3 percent. In the nonmanufacturing sector, the negative list consists of 98 out of 563 industries, resulting in a liberalization of 82.6 percent.

In general, foreign-financed companies are no longer required to set up partnerships with local firms. There are no restrictions on the maximum value of foreign investment. Tax privileges may be granted to foreign-financed projects that are accompanied by advanced technology. Tax privileges have been continuously reduced, and post-invest-

ment controls have also been relaxed to treat foreign and local companies equally.

All foreign direct investments, except those in industries on the negative list, are subject to a notification requirement. A foreign firm is permitted to engage in business within three hours of submitting this notification, unless the notification is not accepted for reasons of national security, protection of the environment, or violation of antitrust or fair trade laws. The notification system has gradually been expanded since the beginning of January 1993. Foreign direct investments in equity-linked bonds are allowed, including nonguaranteed convertible bonds issued by small and medium-size enterprises (SMEs), up to an aggregate of 30 percent, and individual bonds up to 5 percent of the amount of money listed (for each company). The conversion of bonds to equity is limited to 15 percent of foreign ownership (the total limit to foreign ownership is 2 percent). The purchase of government and public bonds, with interest rates comparable to international rates, is allowed in the primary market. Acquisition of land by foreign-financed companies in the manufacturing sector is subject only to a notification requirement. For companies in nonmanufacturing sectors, approval from local authorities must be sought, and approval is normally granted within 60 days. Remittances abroad of dividends and legitimate profits accrued from stocks or shares owned by a foreign investor are freely permitted. The repatriation of foreign capital is also freely permitted. Foreign ownership of firms listed on the Korean Stock Market may not exceed 12 percent of a firm's equity, and individual foreign investors may not hold more than 3 percent of a firm's equity.

Direct investments abroad of up to $300,000 by residents are approved by foreign exchange banks. Direct overseas stock investments by residents up to W 100 million (W 300 million for general juridical persons) are allowed.

Loans

Authorization is required for all foreign borrowing by firms other than banks. Foreign borrowing by these firms of more than $1 million and with a maturity of more than three years is governed by the Foreign Capital Inducement Act. In practice, firms are not allowed to borrow from abroad. However, firms do have access to limited foreign currency loans extended by domestic foreign exchange banks, but this type of lending is permitted only for certain purposes, such as to import capital goods and for research and development activities. Short-term foreign currency borrowing from domestic banks with a maturity of less than one year is not permitted.

Foreign-financed companies are, in principle, subject to the same regulations governing foreign borrowing as other enterprises. However, borrowing by high-technology foreign-financed manufacturing companies is allowed up to 100 percent of the foreign-invested capital; also, maturity is limited to three years or less, and limitations are imposed on the use of funds.

Foreign borrowing repayable within three years is governed by the Foreign Exchange Act. The maximum maturity period permitted for deferred payments is 150 days for imports of consumer goods and of raw materials for export production.

Foreign exchange banks must report to the Minister of Finance and Economy all borrowing exceeding $10 million with a maturity of over one year. Their oversold foreign exchange position may not exceed 30 percent of the average outstanding amount of foreign exchange bought in the previous month or $20 million, whichever is greater. (For spot transactions only, the corresponding limit is 5 percent or $5 million, whichever is greater.) Banks may instead choose to submit to an oversold limit of 10 percent of their equity capital base.

Subject to certain ceilings, branches of foreign banks may enter into foreign currency swap transactions with the Bank of Korea at a fixed yield of 0.3 percent to secure funds for their domestic currency lending.

Gold

Residents may freely buy, hold, or sell gold in any form in Korea. Imports of gold in any form other than gold coins in circulation do not require any approval or license. This means that certain commemorative coins that are legal tender but not in circulation may be freely imported. Exports of gold in any form, other than finished and processed products whose primary component is gold, require the approval of the Bank of Korea. Domestically produced gold may be disposed of in the free market.

Changes During 1994

Exchange Arrangement

November 1. The fluctuation limit of the won against the U.S. dollar was widened from ±1 percent to ±1.5 percent around the weighted average of the previous day's interbank rate for spot transactions.

Capital

January 15. (1) The overseas borrowing limit for high-technology foreign-financed manufacturing companies was raised to 75 percent from 50 percent of the foreign-invested capital; (2) the deferred payment period on imports of raw material for exports was liberalized, from 30 days to 60 days for countries in the region (for instance, Japan and Taiwan Province of China); and (3) general manufacturing industries were included in the types of foreign-financed companies that are eligible for short-term overseas borrowing.

February 25. (1) Overseas stock investments of institutional investors were liberalized (these include securities companies and investment trust and insurance companies); (2) companies whose total export and import value exceeds $10 million were given institutional investor status (investment limit was raised to $300 million, or 30 percent of the total export and import value, whichever is greater); (3) the limit on the amount of investments foreign exchange banks are authorized to approve was raised to $300,000; (4) the ceiling on the amount resident corporations operating abroad and their overseas branches may borrow from nonresident financial institutions located abroad was abolished; and (5) the limit on the amount of foreign exchange resident business firms may retain abroad was increased to the equivalent of 30 percent of their total import and export value, with the maximum increased to $300 million from $100 million.

February 28. The list of restricted overseas foreign investment by residents was shortened to 14 categories from 17.

March 2. Foreign firms were allowed to engage in business operation within three hours of submitting notification (previously this time requirement was 20–30 days).

April 2. Rules governing land acquisition were liberalized.

June 1. (1) The deferred payment period for imports was further liberalized for imports of consumer goods, from 90 days to 60 days, and for imports of raw material for exports, to 150 days from 120 days; the upper limit on import and export transactions that can be settled in Korean won was raised to $300,000 from $100,000; (2) residents were permitted to hold foreign exchange freely without limit (once converted into won, foreign exchange can be converted back to foreign currencies only within the limits determined by foreign exchange sales of the past three months); and (3) residents were allowed to retain foreign exchange proceeds from exports without surrendering them to a foreign exchange bank or depositing them in foreign currency accounts in banks.

July 1. Direct overseas stock investments by residents up to a limit of W 100 million (W 300 million for general juridical persons) were allowed, and foreign direct investments in equity-linked bonds were allowed, including nonguaranteed convertible bonds issued by listed small and medium-size enterprises, up to an aggregate of 30 percent and individual bonds up to 5 percent of the amount of money listed (for each company). Also, the purchase of government and public bonds, with interest rates comparable to international interest rates, was allowed in the primary market.

September 12. Floating rate notes were permitted to be issued in the domestic market.

December 1. (1) The ceiling on portfolio investment in stocks of Korean firms by nonresidents was raised to 12 percent from 10 percent of a firm's equity; and (2) the overseas borrowing limit for high-technology foreign-financed companies was raised to 100 percent from 75 percent of the foreign-invested capital.

KUWAIT

(Position as of December 31, 1994)

Exchange Arrangement

The currency of Kuwait is the Kuwaiti Dinar. The exchange value of the Kuwaiti dinar is determined on the basis of a fixed but adjustable relationship between the Kuwaiti dinar and a weighted basket of currencies, with the weights reflecting the relative importance of these currencies in Kuwait's trade and financial relations. The Central Bank of Kuwait sets the rate for the U.S. dollar on the basis of the latest available market quotations for that currency in relation to the other currencies included in the basket. On December 31, 1994, the Central Bank's buying and selling rates for the U.S. dollar were KD 0.30017 and KD 0.30070, respectively, per US$1. There are no taxes or subsidies on purchases or sales of foreign exchange. The most common arrangement in the official and the commercial banking sectors for handling cover against exchange rate risk is through dealings in the international forward exchange markets. The forward market for Kuwaiti dinar trading, however, has been suspended since the war with Iraq.

On April 5, 1963, Kuwait formally accepted the obligations of Article VIII, Sections 2, 3, and 4 of the Fund's Articles of Agreement.

Administration of Control

There is no exchange control, and residents and nonresidents may freely purchase and sell foreign currencies in Kuwait. Dealings in the currency of Israel are prohibited.[1] General and individual import licenses are issued by the Ministry of Commerce and Industry. The Ministry of Commerce and Industry and the Customs and Ports Administration mantain limited control over exports.

Prescription of Currency

There are no prescription of currency requirements. Trade and economic agreements are maintained with China, Cyprus, Egypt, Hungary, Italy, Jordan, Morocco, Thailand, and Turkey.

Nonresident Accounts

Nonresidents may freely open accounts in Kuwaiti dinars and foreign currencies. The use of such accounts is not restricted.

Imports and Import Payments

Import licenses are required for all commercial imports other than fresh fruits and vegetables; licenses, except for wheat and flour, are issued freely to registered Kuwaiti merchants and companies. Registered importers handling a variety of commodities may obtain a general license valid for one year. Other importers must obtain specific licenses for individual commodities, which are also valid for one year. Imports of industrial equipment, machinery, and their spare parts require industrial licenses, valid for one-time use. Licenses are issued to registered and licensed industrial establishments with the approval of the Industrial Development Commission at the Ministry of Commerce and Industry. Private imports of personal objects may be permitted under individual or specific licenses. The importation of certain items (mainly oxygen, certain steel and asbestos pipes, pork and foodstuffs containing pork, alcoholic beverages, used vehicles over five years old, portable telephones, chewing tobacco, and gas cylinders) is prohibited.

Commercial imports are limited to registered importers. To be registered, the importer must be either a Kuwaiti citizen, a firm in which all partners are Kuwaiti nationals, or a shareholding or limited liability company in which Kuwaiti nationals own at least 51 percent of the stock. Imports from any permitted source may be paid freely.

In concert with the other member states of the Gulf Cooperation Council (GCC) (Bahrain, Oman, Qatar, Saudi Arabia, and the United Arab Emirates), Kuwait adopted a uniform tariff structure on September 1, 1983. In line with the GCC Ministerial Council Resolution adopted on May 18–19, 1983, a minimum tariff of 4 percent was fixed on imports from non-GCC states; tariffs on imports from other GCC countries that have a local value-added component of at least 40 percent were abolished.

Imports of foodstuffs as well as some industrial establishments' imports of machinery and equipment,

---

[1] In addition, all imports from and all exports to Israel are prohibited; payments may not be made to or received from Israel for any type of transaction.

spare parts, and raw materials are exempt from import duties. In accordance with a GCC resolution (of 1985), Kuwait has implemented a system of preferential tariffs allowing industries catering to at least 40 percent of the local market to apply for tariff protection. Tariff rates differ, depending on the domestic value-added content of the products in question. If the domestically produced goods contain at least 20 percent, 30 percent, or 40 percent of domestic value added, protective duties of 15 percent, 20 percent, and 25 percent, respectively, may be applied to competing imports. The degree of protection given by the formula is reduced by 5 percent in the case of consumer goods. The maximum duty that may be imposed on products that compete with locally manufactured goods is 100 percent. As a general rule, protection is accorded to a firm only if the value added is more than 40 percent. In 1985, tariffs of between 15 percent and 25 percent were applied to such products as gypsum, portland cement, fiberglass, paper products, biscuits, glass bottles, and linens.

During 1986, customs tariffs continued to be used for the protection of domestically produced goods; in this context, the list of items receiving similar tariff protection was expanded to include paint, building materials, reinforced glass products, commercial refrigeration units, central air-conditioning units with a capacity of 20–25 tons, electric and telephone cables, and synthetic sponges. In 1987, the tariffs on steel and iron that had been removed in 1986 were reinstated. During 1989, tariffs were imposed on imports of air filters for automobiles (25 percent) and on wooden nails (15 percent); tariff protection on a number of other items was extended. Imports of portable telephones, chewing tobacco, and gas cylinders were prohibited for health or safety reasons. In line with a resolution of the November 1986 session of the GCC, Kuwait adopted a priority system for government procurement of goods and services, which provides for preference to be accorded to Kuwaiti-produced goods up to a price margin of 5 percent over goods produced in the other GCC states, and 10 percent over goods produced outside the GCC. Similarly, goods produced in the other GCC states are accorded a 5 percent price margin over goods produced outside the GCC.

On March 14, 1991, the tariff rate was reduced to zero for a transitional period of six months to encourage imports of goods into Kuwait for postwar reconstruction. On December 29, 1991, this exemption was extended through March 1992. In July 1992,

import duties were reinstated at the rate of 4 percent, except for capital goods and raw materials.

Exports and Export Proceeds

Exports of live sheep and poultry and of certain other items (such as sugar, fats, rice, meat, eggs, milk, cheese, butter, olive oil, fresh fruits, vegetables in any form, beans, lentils, chickpeas, jams, and cement) may be prohibited in time of emergency or shortage in Kuwait. These items may be exported in limited quantities only under a special license issued by the Ministry of Commerce and Industry. Exports of arms and ammunition require licenses but licenses are not required for other exports or re-exports. No requirements are attached to receipts from exports or re-exports; the proceeds need not be repatriated or surrendered and they may be disposed of freely, regardless of the currency involved.

Payments for and Proceeds from Invisibles

All payments for current invisibles may be made freely. Travelers may bring in or take out any amount in Kuwaiti or foreign banknotes.

Capital

There are no exchange controls or restrictions on the transfer into Kuwait of resident or nonresident capital in any currency. Government agreement is necessary for the participation of nonresident capital in resident corporations in Kuwait; new Kuwaiti companies must be at least 51 percent owned by nationals. Beginning in 1983, the participation of nationals of GCC countries in companies established in Kuwait may reach up to 75 percent of the capital. In January 1985, the Ministry of Commerce and Industry resolved, in line with a GCC resolution, to eliminate restrictions on participation in retail trade enterprises by non-Kuwaiti GCC nationals, effective March 1987. However, import-licensing requirements were to remain in effect for non-Kuwaiti GCC nationals.

No restrictions are imposed on outward capital transfers by residents or nonresidents. Dealings in domestic or foreign stocks on the Kuwait Stock Exchange are subject to the approval of the Exchange Committee. Besides the approved domestic stocks, trading is permitted in certain stocks of companies of the GCC countries. The listing on the Exchange of bonds denominated in Kuwaiti dinars is also subject to the approval of the Exchange Committee. Dealings in stocks are restricted to Kuwaiti citizens, but foreigners are permitted to buy and sell bonds in the Exchange.

Gold

Monetary authorities and merchants registered with the Ministry of Commerce and Industry may import and export gold in any form, provided that such gold is not less than 18-karat fine; gold jewelry may not be imported or sold unless it is properly hallmarked. Kuwaiti nationals may freely, and without license, purchase, hold, and sell gold in any form, at home or abroad. Other residents may, on arrival or departure, carry their holdings of gold in any form, without restriction or license. Jewelry and precious metals in any form, manufactured or unmanufactured, are subject to an import duty of 4 percent.

Changes During 1994

No significant changes occurred in the exchange and trade system.

KYRGYZ REPUBLIC

(Position as of December 31, 1994)

Exchange Arrangement

The currency of the Kyrgyz Republic is the Som.[1] The National Bank of the Kyrgyz Republic (NBK) publishes daily the exchange rate of the som in terms of the U.S. dollar and the Russian ruble; this rate is calculated from the transaction rates in the Bishkek interbank foreign currency market. On December 31, 1994, the exchange rate of the som in terms of the U.S. dollar quoted by the NBK was Som 10.65 per US$1. In addition to the NBK, the commercial banks are authorized to conduct foreign exchange transactions. Authorized banks are allowed to quote their own buying and selling rates. Purchases and sales of foreign exchange are permitted without restriction.

There are no taxes or subsidies on purchases or sales of foreign exchange. There are no arrangements for forward cover against exchange rate risk operating in the official or the commercial banking sector.

The Kyrgyz Republic formally accepted the obligations of Article VIII, Sections 2, 3, and 4 of the Fund Agreement as from March 29, 1995.

Administration of Control

The new central bank law, approved by Parliament in December 1992, established the NBK's responsibility for managing the country's gold and foreign exchange reserves. A decree signed by the president on May 5, 1993 (which became effective on May 15) established the full convertibility of the som with no restrictions on buying, selling, or holding foreign currencies. The NBK is also responsible for issuing foreign exchange licenses to commercial banks.

Foreign trade is regulated by the Ministry of Trade and Material Resources, which issues import and export licenses when required. Licenses for foreign investment and registration of foreign investors are granted by the State Commission for Foreign Investments and Economic Aid (Goskominvest), in coordination with the Ministry of Economics and Finance.

Prescription of Currency

There are no prescription of currency requirements, and settlements may be made in any convertible currency.[2]

Resident and Nonresident Accounts

Residents are allowed to maintain foreign exchange accounts at authorized banks and abroad. Nonresidents may hold accounts in domestic or foreign currencies. There are no specific restrictions on the operations of these accounts, including transfers abroad of balances held in the accounts.

Imports and Exports

Except for some items, which may not be imported for reasons of national interest, imports are permitted free of restriction. The prohibited items include armaments, explosive materials, nuclear materials and equipment, poisons, narcotics, works of art, and antiques. Imports are subject to customs duties ranging up to 30 percent. The rates exceeding 10 percent are imposed on the following products: bed linen, TV sets, and vehicles (10 percent); beer (15 percent); tobacco (20 percent); and alcoholic beverages (30 percent).

In early 1994, the Kyrgyz trade system was substantially liberalized. All remaining import- and export-licensing requirements have been lifted, with the exception of a list of eight restricted items: weapons, explosives, nuclear materials, poisons, drugs, works of arts and antiques, precious rare earth materials, and rare animal and vegetable matter used in pharmaceutical production.

There is no requirement to repatriate foreign exchange.

Payments for and Proceeds from Invisibles

Residents are allowed to purchase any amount of foreign exchange for travel abroad or any other reason. The importation and exportation of Russian ruble notes and other foreign banknotes are freely allowed.

There are no restrictions on remittances of dividends and profits by foreign investors. Profits

---

[1]The som was issued on May 10, 1993, and the conversion (from the Russian ruble to the som) was completed by May 15, 1993.

[2]The countries with which the Kyrgyz Republic has bilateral trade agreements are the Baltic countries, China, Pakistan, Russia, the other countries of the former Soviet Union, and Turkey.

earned on direct foreign investments are taxed at a rate of 30 percent (the same tax rate is applied to profits earned by domestic enterprises).

Capital

There are no restrictions on foreign borrowing by residents or enterprises. Legislation on foreign direct investment is being drawn up.

Gold

All gold produced in the Kyrgyz Republic is sold at market prices, either in the domestic market or abroad, but the NBK has priority in purchasing it at the market price.

Changes During 1994

Exchange Arrangement

January 10. Exchange bureaus were allowed to participate in the interbank market.

Imports and Exports

February 5. Most import- and export-licensing requirements were abolished.

May 16. Export taxes were abolished on all but nine items; export taxes were further reduced to four on February 14, 1995.

May 28. An import tariff at the rate of 10 percent was introduced on all imports that are not financed with external aid or not originating in the Baltic countries, Russia, and the other countries of the former Soviet Union.

Changes During 1995

Exchange Arrangement

March 29. The Kyrgyz Republic formally accepted the obligations of Article VIII, Sections 2, 3, and 4 of the Fund Agreement.

LAO PEOPLE'S DEMOCRATIC REPUBLIC

(Position as of December 31, 1994)

Exchange Arrangement

The currency of the Lao People's Democratic Republic is the Kip (KN). The exchange rates are set by the Bank of the Lao People's Democratic Republic (the central bank). On December 31, 1994, the official exchange rates for the U.S. dollar quoted by the central bank for buying and selling remained unchanged at KN 718 and KN 720, respectively, per US$1; these rates are used for all transactions between the central bank and the commercial banks. Buying and selling rates for certain other currencies[1] are also officially quoted, based on the cross rates for these currencies in relation to the U.S. dollar. Commercial banks and foreign exchange bureaus are permitted to buy and sell foreign exchange at freely determined rates, provided that the spread between the buying and selling rate remains less than 2 percent. Foreign exchange may be sold by the bureaus for payment for services. There are no arrangements for forward cover against exchange rate risk. There are no taxes or subsidies on purchases or sales of foreign exchange.

Administration of Control

The state-owned Lao Bank for Foreign Trade (BCEL) handles most authorized foreign exchange transactions related to foreign trade and services. All other official transactions are handled by the central bank, which also administers exchange controls. The Ministry of Commerce and Tourism grants import and export authorization to state trading companies, mixed companies (joint ventures between domestic enterprises and foreign investors), cooperatives, and other public and private enterprises.

Prescription of Currency

No prescription of currency requirements are imposed on receipts or payments but, in principle, the central bank provides and accepts only deutsche mark, French francs, Japanese yen, pounds sterling, Swiss francs, Thai baht, and U.S. dollars. Bilateral trading arrangements are maintained with China, Thailand, a number of countries of the former Soviet Union, and Viet Nam.

Resident and Nonresident Accounts

Resident Accounts. Resident individuals and juridical persons may open foreign exchange accounts with an authorized commercial bank. These accounts may be credited with (1) proceeds from exports of goods and services; (2) transfers from abroad that do not result from exports of goods and services; (3) transfers or payments from foreign currency accounts opened with commercial banks within the Lao PDR; and (4) foreign banknotes and coins. These accounts, which are interest bearing, may be debited for conversion into kip for domestic expenditure, or foreign exchange balances may be used for authorized external payments and transfers.

Nonresident Accounts. Nonresidents may open foreign currency accounts and convertible kip accounts. Their foreign currency accounts may be credited with (1) remittances from abroad; (2) transfers from other nonresident and resident foreign currency accounts in the Lao PDR; and (3) foreign currency brought into the country by the account holder and duly declared upon arrival. Nonresidents are not allowed to accept, for deposit to their accounts, foreign currency proceeds from exports of goods and services of residents without the approval of the central bank. These accounts, which bear interest, may be debited for (1) conversion into kip; (2) transfers into residents' and nonresidents' foreign currency accounts maintained with an authorized commercial bank; (3) payments in kip to accounts of residents or nonresidents; and (4) payments and transfers abroad.

Nonresidents may open convertible kip accounts, which may be credited with (1) sales of foreign currencies, and (2) transfers from other convertible kip accounts of holders of the same category. Nonresidents are not permitted to deposit kip belonging to residents to their convertible kip accounts. These accounts may be debited for (1) payments in kip, and (2) conversion into foreign currency at the prevailing buying rate of the commercial bank concerned.

Imports and Import Payments

Imports may be made by any registered export-import business. These consist of state trading companies, joint-venture trade companies, and private trade companies. These companies are categorized as enterprises producing mainly either for export, for

---

[1]Deutsche mark, French francs, Japanese yen, pounds sterling, Swiss francs, and Thai baht.

import substitution only, for general multi-commodity, for export-import, or for export promotion. Imports are classified into the following nine categories: food and food products; textile garments and daily supplies; office supplies, school instruments, sports equipment, and cultural instruments; machines and equipment for agriculture, animal husbandry, fishing, and production of handicrafts; luxury goods; materials for construction and electrical products and instruments; vehicles and spare parts; medicine, medical equipment, and chemical products for manufacturing; and fuel. Enterprises that are producing import substitutes are allowed to import products only from the last four categories.

Import licenses, which are issued by the Ministry of Commerce and Tourism and provincial government authorities, are required only for a selected number of goods and are not linked to the ability to export. The goods requiring import licenses are rice, fuel, cement, reinforced wires, motorcycles and motor vehicles, and petroleum products. These goods are also subject to individual enterprise quota restrictions. Imports of gold and silver are subject to authorization from the central bank.

Margin deposits are required against letters of credit, and the rates are freely determined by the BCEL and other commercial banks and do not involve any government intervention.

Payments for Invisibles

Payments for invisibles are not restricted.

Exports and Export Proceeds

Any registered export or import business is permitted to engage in export activities. Any export licenses, which are issued by the Ministry of Commerce and Tourism and provincial government authorities, are required only for coffee, timber, wood products, rattan, and livestock. These goods are also subject to individual enterprise quota restrictions; at present, restrictive quotas are applied only to timber. The public sector no longer has the monopoly on the exportation of timber, which is now open to the private sector. The exportation of timber was banned from April 1991 to June 1992. All goods may now be freely exported by the private sector. Export shipment of gold and silver requires authorization from the central bank.

Export earnings are not subject to the surrender requirement, and they may be kept in foreign exchange deposits with a commercial bank (to pay for authorized imports of goods and services, and to make cash withdrawals in kip).

Proceeds from Invisibles

Proceeds from invisibles are, in practice, treated in the same way as foreign exchange earnings accruing from merchandise exports.

Capital

Outward capital transfers by residents are not permitted. Under the Foreign Investment Law of 1988 and March 1994, inward foreign capital transfers, profit remittances, and the repatriation of foreign investment capital are not restricted.

Gold

Residents may buy and sell gold within the country but may not take it abroad for commercial purposes unless authorized by the central bank.

Changes During 1994

Imports and Import Payments

January 5. The number of tariff bands was reduced to 6 from 11, the maximum tariff rate was lowered to 40 percent from 100 percent, and the minimum rate was raised to 5 percent from 3 percent. The rates above 40 percent were retained on three categories of goods on a temporary basis.

LATVIA

(Position as of December 31, 1994)

Exchange Arrangement

The currency of Latvia is the Lats.[1] The Bank of Latvia's policy is to ensure orderly conditions in the exchange market and limit short-term fluctuations in the exchange rate of the lats against convertible currencies. The Bank of Latvia reviews domestic and international exchange markets on a daily basis and announces buying and selling rates for the lats against a basket of currencies. The Bank of Latvia stands ready to transact with commercial banks at these rates. The exchange rates for the lats against convertible currencies other than the U.S. dollar are quoted on the basis of the cross rates between the U.S. dollar and the currencies concerned in the international market. A margin of 2 percent is applied in the quotations of the buying and selling rates for the above currencies. Banks and other authorized exchange dealers also trade in these currencies, and their buying and selling rates may deviate from time to time from the quoted rates. Since November 1, 1993, the Bank of Latvia also quotes daily the midpoint of the buying and selling rates of the lats against convertible currencies. These rates are used for various accounting purposes, including customs duties, taxation, and other valuations; they are valid through the next day and are communicated to all commercial banks. On December 31, 1994, the official exchange rate of the lats was Ls 0.548 per US$1. The use of convertible currencies for domestic settlements is also permitted.

The Bank of Latvia also quotes weekly the accounting rates of the lats for the currencies of the Baltic countries, Russia, and the other countries of the former Soviet Union that participate in the system of correspondent accounts.

Latvia has accepted the obligation of Article VIII, Sections 2, 3, and 4 of the Fund Agreement, as of June 10, 1994.

Administration of Control

Government decisions adopted by the Cabinet of Ministers and approved by Parliament prevail in foreign exchange and trade matters, but the authority to issue regulations governing foreign exchange transactions has been delegated to the Bank of Latvia. All foreign exchange transactions must be effected through authorized banks and enterprises licensed by the Bank of Latvia.

Prescription of Currency

Settlements with the Baltic countries, the Russian Federation, and the other countries of the former Soviet Union can be made through any means, including a system of correspondent accounts. Settlements with countries with which the Bank of Latvia maintains agreements on mutual settlement of accounts are effected in accordance with the terms of these agreements.[2] At the end of 1994, Latvia also maintained trade and economic cooperation agreements providing for most-favored-nation (MFN) status with a number of countries.[3]

Resident and Nonresident Accounts

Resident natural persons and enterprises are allowed to hold foreign currencies in cash or in domestic or foreign bank accounts and to use these funds for domestic payments. Nonresident natural persons are permitted to hold bank accounts in Latvia denominated in either foreign or domestic currency.

Imports and Exports

There are virtually no licensing requirements for imports except on imports of sugar, cereals, tobacco and tobacco products, alcoholic beverages, and nonferrous and ferrous metals. For national health and safety reasons, licenses are also required for pyrotechnic products, arms and ammunition, combat vehicles, and prepared explosives. A new tariff law became effective on December 1, 1994. It replaced

---

[1]Effective July 20, 1992, the Latvian ruble replaced the Russian ruble as legal tender in Latvia, and in March 1993, the lats began to be issued as permanent currency at the conversion rate of Latvian ruble 200 per Ls 1. At this conversion rate, the exchange rate of the lats for the U.S. dollar was Ls 1 per US$1.5. The Latvian lats became the sole legal tender effective October 18, 1993.

[2]At the end of 1994, Latvia maintained bilateral payments agreements with Azerbaijan, Belarus, Estonia, Georgia, Kazakhstan, the Kyrgyz Republic, Lithuania, Moldova, the Russian Federation, Turkmenistan, Ukraine, and Uzbekistan.

[3]Armenia, Azerbaijan, Belarus, Canada, Cuba, the European Union, Hungary, Iceland, India, Moldova, Poland, the Russian Federation, Turkmenistan, Ukraine, the United States, and Uzbekistan. Similar agreements were signed in 1992 with the Czech Republic and the Slovak Republic. Latvia had free trade agreements with the other Baltic countries, the European Union, Finland, Norway, Sweden, and Switzerland.

most specific tariffs with ad valorem rates and established basic tariff rates of 20 percent (15 percent for countries with MFN status) for nonagricultural final goods. Excluding agricultural tariffs, in 1994, 67 percent of Latvia's imports were assessed with MFN duties of 15 percent or less. An additional 23 percent of Latvia's imports were assessed with lower duties under the free trade agreements, and only 10 percent of Latvia's imports were assessed basic rate tariffs of 20 percent or less. A high ad valorem tariff rate of 55 percent applies to six agricultural commodities. Most raw materials and spare parts are assessed an import duty of 1 percent (0.5 percent when originating in countries with which MFN relations are maintained). A number of final goods are also exempt from import tariffs, and certain goods such as fruit, nuts, coffee, and tea, were subject to reduced tariffs of 1 percent (0.5 percent when originating in countries with which MFN relations are maintained). Specific tariff rates are levied on seeds, animal feed, certain grains, flour, bread, sugar, certain confectionery products containing chocolate, alcohol, cigarettes, and cars. The Free Trade Agreement between Latvia and the EU covers substantially all goods traded with the EU. According to this agreement, free trade areas will be gradually established within a maximum of four years starting from January 1, 1995.

Upon entering the territory of Latvia, natural persons are entitled to deliver across the border of the Republic of Latvia without any customs payments, all kinds of goods and articles intended for purposes other than commerce, whose importation is not forbidden or limited by law, and whose customs value does not exceed Ls 300. A total customs value of foodstuffs not exceeding Ls 15 a person is exempted from taxes.

Persons over 18 are exempt from taxes on alcoholic drinks up to 1 liter or one measured unit in original packing not exceeding 3 liters, and on a maximum of either 200 cigarettes, 20 cigars, or 200 grams of tobacco.

The importation of certain goods, such as firearms, is prohibited.

There are no export quotas. Export duties are levied on waste and scrap metals, certain categories of round logs, certain mineral products, works of art, antiques, and certain books.

Export proceeds are not subject to repatriation or surrender requirements.

Payments for and Proceeds from Invisibles

No exchange control or restrictions are imposed on payments for or proceeds from invisibles.

Capital

There are no exchange control regulations governing capital transactions.

Gold

At present, there are no regulations governing international trade in gold. A license is required to deal in gold in the domestic market.

Changes During 1994

Exchange Arrangement

June 10. Latvia accepted the obligations of Article VIII, Sections 2, 3, and 4 of the Fund Agreement.

Imports and Import Payments

December 1. A new tariff law came into effect that replaced most tariffs with ad valorem rates.

LEBANON

(Position as of December 31, 1994)

Exchange Arrangement

The currency of Lebanon is the Lebanese Pound. The authorities do not maintain margins in respect of foreign exchange transactions, and exchange rates are determined on the basis of demand and supply conditions in the exchange market. However, the authorities may announce buying or selling rates for certain currencies and intervene when necessary in order to maintain orderly conditions in the foreign exchange market. On December 30, 1994, the rate for the U.S. dollar was LL 1,670 per US$1. There are no taxes or subsidies on purchases or sales of foreign exchange. The duties and taxes on imported goods and services invoiced or expressed in foreign currencies are calculated at a conversion rate of LL 800 per US$1. Banks are allowed to engage in spot transactions in any currency (except in Israeli new sheqalim). They are prohibited from engaging in forward transactions (against the Lebanese pound) unless the transactions are related to foreign trade.

Lebanon formally accepted the obligations of Article VIII, Sections 2, 3, and 4 of the Fund Agreement, as from July 1, 1993.

Prescription of Currency

No restrictions are imposed on exchange payments abroad or receipts in Lebanon.

Imports and Import Payments

Imports of a few goods (mainly arms and ammunition, narcotics, and similar products) are either prohibited or reserved for the Government. All imports from Israel are prohibited. Imports prohibited year-round include citrus fruits, apples, and liquid milk; imports prohibited during a certain period of the year include squash, eggplant, green beans, watermelons, peas, peaches, apricots, potatoes, onions, cucumbers, tomatoes, garlic, jew's mallow, okra, muskmelons, pears, almonds, grapes, green peppers, pomegranates, and green plums. Imports of certain other agricultural products and all seeds require a license. Import licenses are also required for certain finished goods, sanitary ceramic wares, insulated electric and telephone wires, and copper cables. All other commodities may be imported without a license. Foreign exchange to pay for imports may be obtained freely.

Banks are obliged to ensure that importers possess a valid import license, if required, before issuing letters of credit. Importers must place with their banks a prior deposit (in the same currency as that in which letters of credit are opened) in an amount equivalent to 15 percent of the value of import letters of credit; the banks are not required to deposit such amounts with the Bank of Lebanon.

A municipality tax of 3.5 percent is levied on the value of all goods imported, except those originating in an Arab country (if imported overland). A stamp tax is levied on all imports, except gold and banknotes, at the rate of LL 3 per LL 1,000 of the value of the goods. The tariff regime is based on the Brussels Tariff Nomenclature. Ad valorem duty rates on most products range up to 75 percent, with the exception of bananas to which 100 percent is applied, and duties are applied on a most-favored-nation basis, except for certain imports from member countries of the EU and Arab countries, which are accorded a preferential rate. A few products are subject to a specific duty. A surcharge of 10 percent of the applicable import duty is levied on certain textiles and garments. Surcharges are also levied on motor vehicles, imitation jewelry, watches, and alcoholic beverages. The tax on motor vehicles is levied at the following rates: 35 percent on the first LL 10 million and 60 percent on the remaining value. The surcharge, called the reconstruction tax, is levied at the rate of 1 percent on vehicles holding more than nine passengers and 3 percent on vehicles holding fewer than nine passengers. The following rates of surcharge apply to alcoholic beverages: beer, 30 percent of the value; champagne, 60 percent of the value; wine and arak, 20 percent of the value; and whiskey, 30 percent of the value. An additional construction tax of 11 percent is levied on champagne, wine, and vermouths; a municipality tax and an internal tax ranging from LL 250 to LL 2,000 a liter are also imposed on beer, champagne, wine, liqueurs, and whiskey. A tax of 60 percent is imposed on other beverages.

Payments for Invisibles

There are no restrictions on payments for invisibles. Foreign exchange may be obtained in the free market.

Exports and Export Proceeds

Exports of certain goods (mainly arms and ammunition, narcotics, and similar products) to any destination and all exports to Israel are prohibited. Exports of wheat and wheat derivatives to any country and all exports to the Democratic People's Republic of Korea require a license. Foreign exchange receipts from exports may be retained, used, or sold in the free market.

Proceeds from Invisibles

Foreign exchange receipts from invisibles may be retained, used, or sold in the free market.

Capital

There are no limitations on capital payments or receipts. Foreign exchange may be obtained or sold in the free market. Banks are prohibited from extending to nonresidents loans in Lebanese pounds and loans secured by guarantees from nonresident banks unless the transactions are for commercial or investment purposes in Lebanon. Banks are prohibited from receiving deposits or opening accounts in Lebanese pounds for nonresident banks and financial institutions. Bank credit in Lebanese pounds to residents for the purchase of foreign exchange for purposes other than foreign trade transactions is subject to a special reserve requirement; the required reserve amounts to 40 percent of Lebanese pound loans that give rise directly to foreign currency deposits, and 15 percent of foreign currency deposits directly arising from Lebanese pound loans to depositors. Banks are authorized (since December 1993) to maintain a trading position in foreign currency amounting to up to 5 percent (short or long) of the core capital of banks and a fixed position in foreign currency (long) amounting to 65 percent of core capital in Lebanese pounds. The amounts of investments in foreign currencies in nonresident banks and financial institutions are included in net foreign currency positions. Investments in nonresident banks and other foreign institutions are exempt from the net foreign currency positions. Under a "free zone" banking facility, commercial banks are exempt from reserve requirements and fees for deposit insurance in respect of foreign currency deposits by nonresidents. Beginning in 1994, income from all accounts with banks have been exempt from the income tax. Also, nonresidents are exempt from the 10 percent tax on interest earnings from foreign currency deposits.

Under the National Investment Insurance Scheme, new foreign investments are insured against losses arising from noncivil risks, including war. Compensation is paid on losses that are more than 10 percent of the insured value.

Gold

Residents may freely hold gold in any form at home or abroad and may freely negotiate gold in any form with residents and nonresidents, at home or abroad. The importation and exportation of gold in any form are freely permitted and do not require a license but must be officially recorded. The importation, exportation, and domestic sale of foreign gold coins must be covered by a certificate, issued by the Office for the Protection of the Consumer, that indicates the gold content and weight.

Changes During 1994

No significant changes occurred in the exchange and trade system.

LESOTHO

(Position as of December 31, 1994)

Exchange Arrangement

The currency of Lesotho is the Loti (plural Maloti), which is pegged to the South African rand at M 1 per R 1. Under the Common Monetary Area (CMA) Agreement, the rand is also legal tender in Lesotho. The principal intervention currency is the U.S. dollar. On December 31, 1994, the buying and selling rates for the U.S. dollar were M 3.4000 and M 3.4013, respectively, per US$1. Authorized dealers are permitted to conduct forward exchange operations through their correspondent banks abroad at rates quoted by the latter. Forward exchange cover is not, however, common in Lesotho. There are no taxes or subsidies on purchases or sales of foreign exchange.

By virtue of its membership in the CMA, Lesotho also maintains the financial rand system of South Africa. Under the financial rand system, local sales proceeds of CMA securities and other investments owned by non-CMA residents cannot be transferred in foreign currency but must be retained in the form of financial rand balances. These balances are transferable among nonresidents at a freely determined exchange rate and may be used to purchase securities (quoted and unquoted) and to finance investments in new firms and certain properties. There are no forward cover arrangements for exchange transactions in the financial rand market.

Exchange Control Territory

Lesotho forms part of the CMA, which is an exchange control territory comprising Lesotho, Namibia, South Africa, and Swaziland. The amended Trilateral Monetary Agreement among Lesotho, South Africa, and Swaziland became effective on April 1, 1986 (and was amended in 1989). Namibia, which was an indirect party to the agreement by virtue of its relationship with South Africa, officially became a party following its independence in March 1990. Payments within the CMA are unrestricted and unrecorded except for statistical and customs purposes. In its relations with countries outside the CMA, Lesotho applies exchange controls that are largely similar to those applied by South Africa and Swaziland.

Administration of Control

The Central Bank of Lesotho controls external currency transactions and delegates to commercial banks the authority to approve certain types of current payments up to established limits. Permits are issued by the Department of Customs and Excise on the recommendation of the Department of Trade and Industry. Licenses for financial institutions accepting deposits and insurance companies, brokers, and agents are issued by the Central Bank.

Prescription of Currency

There are no regulations prescribing the currencies that can be used in particular transactions.

Imports and Import Payments

Lesotho is a member of the Southern African Customs Union (SACU) with Botswana, Namibia, South Africa, and Swaziland. Imports originating in any country of the SACU are unrestricted; those from countries outside the SACU are usually licensed in conformity with the import regulations of the SACU; Lesotho reserves the right to restrict certain imports. Import permits are valid for all countries and entitle the holder to buy the foreign exchange required to make payments for imports from outside the SACU.

Exports and Export Proceeds

Certain exports are subject to licensing for revenue purposes; this requirement, in practice, is restricted to the exportation of diamonds. Most exports are shipped without license to or through South Africa. Unless otherwise permitted, all export proceeds must be remitted to Lesotho and surrendered within six months of the date of the export transaction.

Payments for and Proceeds from Invisibles

Payments to nonresidents for current transactions, although subject to control, are not normally restricted. Authorized dealers are permitted to approve some types of current payments up to established limits. The basic annual exchange allowance for tourist travel to neighboring countries outside the CMA area—Malawi, Mozambique, Zambia, and Zimbabwe—is M 6,000 for an adult and M 3,000 for a child; the corresponding annual allowance for tourist travel to other countries outside the CMA region is M 23,000 and M 11,500, respectively. For business travel to neighboring countries outside the CMA region, the basic annual allowance is M 12,000 a person at rates not exceeding M 900 a day; the corresponding limits for business travel to other countries are M 34,000 and M 1,800, respectively. Larger allowances may be obtained for travel for business and medical treatment. The education allowance is M 3,500 a student a month. Payments of professional fees of up to a maximum of M 10,000 are allowed, and M 50,000 is allowed for charges related to repairs or adjustments to goods temporarily exported. Lesotho residents may also effect payment of fees owed for technical services brought into Lesotho within an overall limit of M 50,000. Lesotho residents may enter into contracts with visiting artists, entertainers, and sportspersons, provided the commitment does not exceed M 75,000. Guarantees by Lesotho residents up to a limit of M 25,000 in respect of overdraft facilities for residents of Botswana, Malawi, Zambia, and Zimbabwe for domestic, farming, and business purposes may also be approved. Emigrant allowances may be transferred through the financial rand market, up to M 200,000 a family or up to M 100,000 a person. The maximum amount of earnings on blocked assets that emigrants are allowed to transfer through normal banking channels is M 300,000 a year.

Capital

Inward capital transfers should be properly documented to facilitate the subsequent repatriation of interest, dividends, profits, and other income. No person may either borrow foreign currency, register shares in the name of a nonresident, or act as a nominee for a nonresident without prior approval.

Applications for outward transfers of capital are considered on their merits. The rulings on applications for inward and outward capital transfers may depend on whether the applicant is a temporary resident foreign national, a nonresident, or a resident. Certain tax incentives for inward direct investment are provided to manufacturers approved by the Pioneer Industries Board under the Pioneer Industries Encouragement Act of 1969. Funds in blocked maloti accounts may be invested in quoted securities and other such investments approved by the Central Bank. The free transfer of income from an emigrant's blocked assets is limited to an annual maximum of M 300,000 a family unit. The transfer by nonresidents of dividends and profits from investments held in Lesotho is not restricted, provided these funds were not obtained through excessive use of local borrowing facilities. An emigrant family or an individual may export one automobile only, with a maximum value of M 75,000, provided that the automobile was purchased at least one year before emigration.

The limit on settling-in allowances that immigrants are permitted to transfer through the financial rand mechanism is M 500,000 for a family and M 250,000 for an unmarried person, of which M 20,000 may be in cash; the remainder may be used to acquire residential properties and a motor vehicle.

Gold

Residents may freely purchase, hold, and sell any gold coins that are legal tender.

Changes During 1994

No significant changes occurred in the exchange and trade system.

LIBERIA[1]

(Position as of December 31, 1994)

Exchange Arrangement

The currency of Liberia is the Liberian Dollar, which is pegged to the U.S. dollar at Lib$1 per US$1. There is no official intervention currency. The currency of the United States is legal tender in Liberia and circulates along with Liberian currency.[2] The official exchange rate is limited to settlement of tax obligations and data reporting, while the parallel exchange rate (about Lib$50 per US$1) applies to most transactions, including government spending. There are no taxes or subsidies on purchases or sales of foreign exchange. There are no arrangements for forward cover against exchange rate risk operating in the official or the commercial banking sector.

Administration of Control

Export- and import-licensing regulations are administered by the Ministry of Commerce and Industry. Arrears are maintained with respect to external payments.

Prescription of Currency

Some exporters must pay withholding taxes and corporate income taxes in U.S. dollars. Hotels are required to receive payments from foreign guests in foreign exchange. Settlements with the Central Bank of West African States (for Benin, Burkina Faso, Côte d'Ivoire, Niger, Senegal, and Togo) and The Gambia, Ghana, Guinea, Guinea-Bissau, Mali, Mauritania, Nigeria, and Sierra Leone are normally made through the West African Clearing House.

Imports and Import Payments

There is no general system of import control, but the importation of some items is subject to licensing and quantitative restrictions. Licensing requirements are liberally enforced. These items include safety matches, electrode welding rods, and liquefied petroleum gas. Imports of arms, ammunition, and explosives require prior licenses. In addition, imports of certain goods (for example, narcotics, other than for medicinal purposes) are prohibited. The Liberian National Petroleum Company (LNPC) no longer has the exclusive right to import petroleum products; all eligible importers that obtain an Import Declaration Form from the Ministry of Commerce and Industry may import them. Licenses to import inexpensive, widely consumed varieties of rice are issued to private distributors by the Ministry of Commerce and Industry. The importation of more expensive rice is not subject to official controls. The nominal tariff rate on imports is about 31 percent on average.

Preshipment inspection of imports is required to ascertain the country of origin, the quality, the quantity, and the value of all goods to be shipped to Liberia. Both final and intermediate goods are subject to inspection, except for imports with an f.o.b. value of less than $3,000.

Exports and Export Proceeds

Export licenses are at present required for elephant tusks and ivory; wild animals; cement; agricultural products other than rubber, flour, and sugar; and certain other items, such as arms, ammunition, and explosives. Licenses are generally issued freely and serve mainly to enforce the 25 percent surrender of export proceeds and taxation or, for agricultural products, to assure certification of quality and origin. In August 1988, a regulation requiring that wood products for exportation have a local processing content of at least 5 percent was enacted. The required local content was raised to 10 percent in 1990. Exporters are required to surrender 25 percent of export proceeds to the National Bank of Liberia through the commercial banks; this requirement is not strictly enforced. The Government and the National Bank of Liberia receive priority for the purchase of this foreign exchange. That portion of the foreign exchange surrender that is not purchased by the public sector is

---

[1]As of December 31, 1994, the IMF had not received from the Liberian authorities the information needed for a description of the exchange and trade system.

[2]There are two Liberian dollar notes, Liberty notes and J.J. Roberts notes. Although officially at par, the Roberts notes are traded at premium against Liberty notes. Liberty notes are prohibited from circulation in certain regions. U.S. dollar notes, which used to form the major portion of the currency in circulation, have almost totally disappeared. Full convertibility between the Liberian dollar and the U.S. dollar at par does not, de facto, exist. The U.S. dollar attracts a substantial premium in large parallel market transactions, and commercial banks charge abnormally high commissions for their sales of offshore funds. Foreign exchange dealers other than banks are permitted to buy and sell currencies other than the U.S. dollar at market-determined exchange rates.

then made available to commercial banks at par. An export tax at the rate of 15 percent a troy ounce is levied on diamonds.

Payments for and Proceeds from Invisibles

There are no governmental limitations on payments for or receipts from invisibles.

Capital

No exchange control requirements are imposed on capital receipts or payments by residents or nonresidents. Under the Investment Incentive Code of 1966 (as amended in 1973), enterprises undertaking new investment projects may be granted a five-year 90 percent duty exemption on imports of raw materials and machinery, total tax exemption on reinvested profits, a 50 percent exemption on distributable profits, and a protective tariff on competing imported products. The five-year incentive may be renewed for two additional years in certain circumstances. Most mining, logging, and rubber enterprises, however, operate under special redundant agreements that provide for tax concessions for a period ranging up to 70 years.

Gold

Imports and exports of gold in any form are subject to licenses issued by the Ministry of Land, Mines, and Energy; import licenses are issued freely, but export licenses are granted restrictively.

SOCIALIST PEOPLE'S LIBYAN ARAB JAMAHIRIYA

(Position as of December 31, 1994)

Exchange Arrangement

The currency of the Socialist People's Libyan Arab Jamahiriya (Libya) is the Libyan Dinar, which is pegged to the SDR at the rate of LD 1.00 per SDR 2.80. Margins not exceeding 47 percent are allowed around this fixed relationship, and the dinar has been depreciated to the maximum extent permitted within those margins to LD 1.00 per SDR 1.905. Buying and selling rates of the Libyan dinar in terms of 16 currencies[1] are based on their exchange rates against the SDR, as communicated by the IMF. The middle rate for the U.S. dollar, the intervention currency, on December 31, 1994 was LD 0.360 per US$1.

Commercial banks may not deal among themselves in foreign currencies but only through their foreign correspondents. Neither authorized banks nor importers or exporters are allowed to enter into forward commitments in foreign currencies. Since 1985, fees have been levied on outward foreign exchange transfers for the purpose of financing the Great Man-Made River Project. These fees have resulted in a deviation of more than 2 percent between the official exchange rate and the effective rate applied to these transfers. There are no other taxes or subsidies on purchases or sales of foreign exchange.

Administration of Control

Exchange control is administered by the Central Bank of Libya, which has delegated some of its powers to authorized banks. Policy relating to imports and exports is determined by the General People's Congress and executed by the Secretariat of Planning and Finance.

Prescription of Currency

All settlements with Israel are prohibited. Settlements with other countries are made in convertible currencies. A bilateral trade and payments agreement is maintained with Malta; outstanding balances are settled in convertible currencies.

---

[1]Austrian schillings, Belgian francs, Canadian dollars, Danish kroner, deutsche mark, French francs, Italian lire, Japanese yen, Netherlands guilders, Norwegian kroner, pounds sterling, Saudi Arabian riyals, Swedish kronor, Swiss francs, Tunisian dinars, and U.S. dollars.

Nonresident and Resident Accounts

Nonresidents (as defined by the Central Bank) who are gainfully employed in the country are permitted under the exchange control regulations to open and maintain nonresident accounts in Libyan dinars with any authorized bank. Such nonresidents may credit their legitimate earnings to their nonresident accounts. All other credits to nonresident accounts require the prior approval of the Central Bank. (For debits of such accounts, see section on Payments for Invisibles, below.)

Funds brought in by nonresident contractors undertaking contracts in their own names must be kept with an authorized bank. Payments received by contractors in respect of their contracts may also be credited to these accounts. Remittances from these accounts are subject to the prior approval of the Central Bank after submission of the prescribed evidence, but, in general, remittance is permitted up to the net-of-tax amount specified in the contract.

Nonresident-owned capital that is not permitted to be transferred abroad is credited to blocked accounts. With the approval of the Central Bank, funds in blocked accounts (with certain exceptions) may be used for expenditures in Libya, up to LD 500 a year, to cover the cost of visits by the owner of the funds or a close relative; for payment of legal fees and taxes; for remittances to the owner of the funds in his country of permanent residence (up to LD 1,000 in a calendar year); and for remittances in cases of hardship. When the funds have been in a blocked account for five years, they qualify, upon payment of due taxes, for remittance in full to the owner in his country of permanent residence. The blocked accounts of persons (with certain exceptions) who have left the country permanently are being released in installments; balances credited before March 31, 1966 have been released. With authorization of the Central Bank, individual residents are allowed to keep foreign currencies in domestic bank accounts and to transfer balances abroad without restriction.

Imports and Import Payments

All imports from Israel are prohibited. Imports undertaken by state-owned enterprises do not require licenses if they are authorized within the annual commodity budget. Importers are required to deal directly with producers abroad and not through intermediaries. However, imports not included in the annual commodity budget are subject to licensing. Resident firms undertaking development projects may import needed items that are not included in the annual commodity budget and not available locally, and foreign exchange to pay for these imports is provided by the Government; similar imports by nonresidents, however, must be financed with foreign exchange resources from abroad.

There is a prohibited import list, consisting mainly of consumer and luxury goods.[2] Only government agencies may act as commercial agents, including import agents, for foreign companies. A state-owned company controlled by the Central Bank has a monopoly over the importation of gold and precious metals. Under Decision No. 248 of January 1989, import trade by private companies and partnerships has been permitted. With the exception of strategic goods [3] retained by public corporations, all other goods may be imported by either public or private entities within the provisions of the annual commodity budget.

With certain exceptions, all exchange permits require central bank approval. Exchange permits required for imports are readily granted by the authorized banks following central bank approval, provided that a firm contract exists and an import license has been obtained from the Secretariat of Planning and Finance and, if imports are to be financed under letters of credit, that a marine insurance policy from a local insurance company is submitted before the letter of credit is established. However, an authorized bank may not open a letter of credit without an advance import deposit equal to at least 20 percent of the value of the import. Importers must present to the bank granting the exchange permit, within two months of customs clearance, a customs declaration confirming clearance and stating the valuation. The approval of the Exchange Control Department of the Central Bank is required for all payments by residents.

Imports are subject to customs duties and customs surcharges, the latter consisting of 10 percent of the applicable customs duty. All products originating in Arab countries are exempted from customs duties, provided that their domestic value added is at least 40 percent. Private individuals are allowed to import goods on the commodity budget

list up to a maximum value of LD 3,000 per year from Arab countries.

Payments for Invisibles

Payments for invisibles related to authorized imports are not restricted.

Nonresidents employed by the state, by state-owned enterprises, and by foreign companies may remit up to 50 percent of their net salaries each month if their contracts do not specify that lodging, board, or both will be made available free of charge by the employer, or up to 75 percent of their net salaries if their contracts specify that, in accordance with applicable Libyan laws and regulations, the employer will provide both lodging and board free of charge at work sites in remote areas. Staff of UN agencies, embassies, consulates, and medical institutions are exempt from these regulations. Banks may issue traveler's checks and foreign currency notes to nonresident workers and technicians within the limits mentioned.

Residents leaving for personal travel abroad, including tourist travel, may take out foreign exchange in the form of foreign currency notes, traveler's checks, and letters of credit not exceeding a total value of LD 300 (LD 150 for children between the ages of 10 and 18) in a calendar year as a basic travel allowance; the exchange may be obtained from any authorized bank in Libya. Additional amounts may be granted in special circumstances. Pilgrims to Saudi Arabia are entitled to a special quota. Temporary residents may take out any traveler's checks or foreign currency notes that they had previously brought in and declared to customs. Travelers leaving Libya may not take out Libyan currency.

All other payments for invisibles, as well as payments in excess of the approval authority delegated to the banks, require the prior approval of the Central Bank. Applications are considered on their merits.

Exports and Export Proceeds

Export licenses are required for raw wool, hides and skins, and agricultural products. Export proceeds must be received through an authorized bank within six months of shipment. Exports of nonmonetary gold (other than for processing abroad), scrap metals, eggs, chicken, fish, olive oil, paint, tires, steel, and tractors are prohibited; exports or reexports of wheat, wheat flour, crushed wheat, barley, rice, tea, sugar, tomato paste, and macaroni, which are subsidized commodities, are also prohibited. Exports of domestically produced vegetable

---

[2]These include mineral water, fruit juices, instant tea, certain types of coffee, green vegetables, poultry, preserved meats and vegetables, alcoholic beverages, peanuts, oriental rugs, soaps, envelopes, crystal chandeliers, toy guns, luxury cars, and furs.

[3]These are nine essential food items, medicine, insecticides, petroleum products, tobacco, and gold.

oils are permitted. All exports to Israel are prohibited. The Export Promotion Council established under Decision No. 523 of September 1988 helps exporters to enter foreign markets by providing information on demand conditions abroad and on potential exports. Also, as an incentive to export, exporters are allowed to retain up to 40 percent of foreign exchange earnings in a special account that may be used to finance imports of raw materials, spare parts, and machinery needed for export production. Exporters do not need an export license for these exports but must register with the council and supply, on a regular basis, the relevant documentation on their exports.

Proceeds from Invisibles

All foreign exchange receipts must be surrendered. Traveler's checks or foreign currency notes may be encashed only at an authorized bank, an exchange office, or a hotel licensed by the Central Bank.

Travelers entering the country may bring with them traveler's checks, letters of credit, securities, coupons, and other negotiable instruments in unlimited amounts, which they must declare to customs. Foreign exchange converted into Libyan dinars by visiting tourists may be reconverted upon departure, with the exception of a minimum local expenditure of $50 for each day spent in the country.

Capital

Under the provisions of Foreign Capital Investment Law No. 37 of July 31, 1968, foreign capital invested in projects deemed to contribute to the economic development of the country, as well as profits thereon, may be transferred freely to the country of origin, provided that the paid-up capital is not less than LD 200,000 and that at least 51 percent of the shares are held by foreign nationals. Salaries of foreign staff employed on such projects may be transferred (as described in the section on Payments for Invisibles, above). Central bank approval is required and customarily granted freely for all such transfers. Foreign participation in industrial ventures set up after March 20, 1970 is permitted on a minority basis but only if it leads to increased production in excess of local require-

ments, introduction of the latest technology, and cooperation with foreign firms in exporting the surplus production. Insurance companies and foreign shareholdings in banks have been nationalized.

Only Libyans may own real estate in Libya. Nonresident-owned capital that is not permitted to be transferred abroad is credited to blocked accounts (see section on Nonresident Accounts, above). Residents must obtain the prior approval of the Central Bank to borrow funds abroad. As a rule, residents must have prior permission from the Committee of the People's Bureau for Foreign Affairs and International Economic Cooperation to purchase real estate abroad or to invest abroad in securities. The investment of national capital abroad is governed by Law No. 25 of April 20, 1973.

Gold

Residents may freely purchase, hold, and sell gold in any form other than bars. The Central Bank imports processed and unprocessed gold and precious metals; it also sells gold bars to domestic goldsmiths for manufacture at prices announced from time to time. The gold is processed before it may be sold to the public. Unworked gold is subject to an import duty of 15 percent.

Changes During 1994

Exchange Arrangement

November 1. The margin within which the exchange rate is allowed to fluctuate against the SDR was widened to 47 percent from 25 percent.

Payments for Invisibles

January 1. Allowances for transfers by nonresidents employed by the state, state-owned enterprises, and foreign companies were reduced to 75 percent from 90 percent of net salaries for those with contracts specifying free provision of lodging and board, and to 50 percent from 60 percent for all others.

Exports and Export Proceeds

June 1. A ban on certain exports was imposed, including eggs, chicken, fish, olive oil, paint, tires, steel, and tractors.

LITHUANIA

(Position as of December 31, 1994)

Exchange Arrangement

The currency of Lithuania is the Litas (plural: Litai). The external value of the litas has been pegged to the U.S. dollar at Llt 4 per US$1 since April 1, 1994 when the currency board arrangement was established. Authorized banks quote exchange rates for other convertible currencies on the basis of their cross-rate relationships for the currencies concerned on international markets. Authorized banks also quote buying and selling rates for the Russian ruble at varying rates. The Bank of Lithuania also calculates an accounting rate, which is used to value balance sheet items. Accounting rates for convertible currencies and for the currencies of the Baltic countries, Russia, and the other countries of the former Soviet Union are calculated daily.[1]

There are no limits on the net open positions of authorized banks. There are no taxes or subsidies on purchases or sales of foreign exchange. There are no arrangements for forward cover against exchange rate risk operating in the official or the commercial banking sector.

Lithuania formally accepted the obligations of Article VIII, Sections 2, 3, and 4 of the Fund Agreement, as from May 3, 1994.

Administration of Control

Parliament has the legislative authority in foreign exchange and trade matters; it has adopted a banking law delegating to the Bank of Lithuania the authority to issue regulations governing foreign exchange transactions.

All foreign exchange transactions must be effected through authorized banks licensed by the Bank of Lithuania. To date, 20 banks have been authorized to deal in foreign exchange. Authorized banks are allowed to transact among themselves, as well as with residents and nonresidents of Lithuania, and they are divided into four categories, depending on the types of transactions they are permitted to conduct. The simplest type of license limits the operations to buying and selling foreign exchange (cash and traveler's checks). At present, eight banks have been granted a general license that allows them to offer a full range of banking services (including issuing letters of credit) in foreign exchange operations, and they are permitted to open correspondent accounts with banks abroad.

Prescription of Currency

There are no prescription of currency requirements, and settlements may be made in any convertible currency.[2]

Resident and Nonresident Accounts

Resident natural and juridical persons may open foreign exchange accounts at authorized banks, and these accounts may be credited and debited without restriction. Nonresident individuals and representative offices of foreign enterprises and diplomatic missions may open foreign exchange accounts at the authorized banks, and these accounts may be credited and debited without restriction.

Imports and Import Payments

There are no quantitative restrictions or licensing requirements on imports, except for health and national security reasons. Imports subject to bilateral trade agreements are allocated by the Ministry of Trade and Industry. For most imports, a 10 percent tariff rate applies. Higher tariff rates are levied only on specific products (such as live animals, agricultural products, alcohol and tobacco, and a few manufacturing goods), some exceeding 30 percent.

A tax at the uniform rate of 0.01 percent is imposed on imports (and exports) for the sole purpose of collecting statistical information on trade.

Payments for Invisibles

Payments for all invisibles may be made without restriction.

---

[1]The accounting rates for the convertible currencies are identical to the middle rates on Tuesdays and at the end of each month, whereas the accounting rates for the currencies of the Baltic states, Russia, and the other countries of the former Soviet Union are calculated by the Bank of Lithuania using the cross rates for the U.S. dollar quoted by the respective central banks.

[2]Correspondent accounts exist between the Bank of Lithuania and the central banks of the Baltic countries, Russia, and the other countries of the former Soviet Union. These accounts need not be used for payments originating after October 1992. Ruble-denominated correspondent accounts maintained with the central banks of the Baltic countries, Russia, and the other countries of the former Soviet Union have been closed and are in the process of being settled.

Exports and Export Proceeds

Proceeds from exports are not required to be repatriated to Lithuania. Exports are not subject to licensing requirements. Export duties are levied on certain raw materials and selected products.

Proceeds from Invisibles

Proceeds from invisibles are not subject to any control or restriction.

Capital

Authorized banks may borrow abroad or extend loans in foreign currencies to residents and nonresidents without restriction. Resident firms may borrow foreign exchange from authorized banks or borrow directly from banks abroad with the approval of the Bank of Lithuania.

Foreign direct investment is regulated by the Law of Foreign Investments promulgated in December 1990 and amended in February and June 1992. The law permits the state to sell shares to nonresidents, guarantees nondiscriminatory national treatment to foreign investors, and protects investments against nationalization and expropriation. The purchase of state-owned enterprises is subject to authorization from the Central Privatization Committee. One of the main conditions in this process is that the company must remain involved in the same type of business for at least one year under the new ownership. While firms with 100 percent foreign capital ownership are allowed to operate in Lithuania, the Government reserves the right to establish limits on foreign investment in Lithuanian enterprises. Foreign investors are prohibited from operating in the defense industry, public utilities, and energy exploration. In joint ventures in the transportation and communication sectors, the domestic partner is required to hold the majority of the shares. Wholly owned ventures in the alcoholic beverage or to-bacco industries are prohibited. Enterprises with foreign investment must be insured by Lithuanian insurance companies, even if the company retains other insurance services outside Lithuania.

The ownership of land by nonresidents in Lithuania is prohibited, but lease contracts with limits to 2 hectares of land in Vilnius and 10 hectares outside the capital are permitted for up to 99 years and may be renewed thereafter.

The Law of Foreign Investments also guarantees the free repatriation of all after-tax profits as well as the invested capital, with no limitation on timing or amount. It also provides for important tax incentives. If the foreign investment was made before the end of 1993, the profit tax is reduced by 70 percent, that is, to 8.7 percent from 29 percent for five years. For another three years, the profit tax is reduced by 50 percent. If the investment is made between January 1994 and December 1995, profits will be taxed at a rate reduced by 50 percent for six years. For joint ventures, these reductions are proportional to the foreign capital invested.

Gold

Residents may freely hold, buy, or sell gold in any form in Lithuania.

Changes During 1994

Exchange Arrangement

April 1. A currency board was established, and the external value of the litas was set at Llt 4 per US$1.

May 3. Lithuania accepted the obligations of Article VIII, Sections 2, 3, and 4 of the Articles of Agreement.

Administration of Control

April 1. The Baltic Free Trade Agreement came into force.

FORMER YUGOSLAV REPUBLIC OF MACEDONIA[1]

(Position as of December 31, 1994)

Exchange Arrangement

The currency of the former Yugoslav Republic of Macedonia is the Denar, the external value of which is determined freely in the exchange market. Buying and selling rates for transactions between authorized banks and enterprises have to be reported to the National Bank of Macedonia, which calculates an average daily rate. Based on this rate and cross rates on the international market, the National Bank publishes rates for 22 currencies. On December 31, 1994, the midpoint exchange rate for the U.S. dollar published by the National Bank was Mden 40.5962 per US$1. The National Bank deals at the published midpoint rates ± a margin of 0.3 percent. At the end of each week, the average of the daily published rates is established for customs valuation purposes for the following week. There is no tax on the purchase or sale of foreign exchange, and banks are free to set commissions for their services. Forward foreign exchange contracts for trade transactions are permitted.

The exchange market operates at two levels—wholesale and retail. The wholesale level includes enterprises, commercial banks, and the National Bank, all of which may buy and sell foreign exchange in this market. The Government also participates in this market through the National Bank. The retail level of the foreign exchange market consists of foreign exchange bureaus, which are owned and operated by banks, enterprises, or natural persons. Foreign exchange bureaus may hold overnight foreign exchange positions equivalent to 100 percent of the preceding day's foreign exchange purchases. Natural persons may purchase foreign currency from these bureaus without limit, subject to availability.

Administration of Control

The Parliament has the authority to legislate laws governing foreign exchange and trade transactions. Certain changes in the trade regime may be made through government regulations.

According to the Foreign Exchange Act and the National Bank Act, the National Bank is authorized to control foreign exchange operations of banks and other financial institutions. The Ministry of Finance is authorized to control foreign exchange and trade operations and the credit relations of enterprises abroad, as well as other forms of business activities abroad, encompassing all enterprises that operate internationally. Certain foreign exchange control activities have been delegated to the participants in the foreign exchange market and the customs office. The Ministry of Foreign Relations administers the Foreign Trade Act and the Foreign Investments Act.

Medium- and long-term loans must be registered with the National Bank as stipulated by the Foreign Credit Relations Act. This obligation does not apply to short-term loans, which are permitted without restriction, except those related to imports, with a maturity exceeding 6 months. Short-term loans related to commercial banks' credit lines with a maturity exceeding 90 days should also be registered.

Prescription of Currency

Residents of the former Yugoslav Republic of Macedonia may receive payments and transfers in any convertible currency.

Resident and Nonresident Accounts

Nonresidents may open foreign exchange accounts with authorized banks in the former Yugoslav Republic of Macedonia. These accounts may be credited freely with foreign exchange and debited for payments abroad or for conversion into denars.

Resident natural persons may open foreign exchange accounts in the former Yugoslav Republic of Macedonia. Foreign exchange balances predating September 1, 1990 have de facto been frozen, but these deposits may be used to purchase community-owned apartments, community-owned business premises, or shares in enterprises as part of the privatization process. In special cases (weddings, funerals, payments of health care costs), depositors are allowed to make withdrawals from their frozen deposits up to the equivalent of 1,000 deutsch mark. Withdrawals in foreign currency may used to make payments abroad on presentation of appropriate documentation for medical treatment (including purchases of medicine), education, and airfares (airfares have been temporarily restricted for budgetary reasons). Resident natural persons may not maintain foreign exchange accounts abroad or hold other financial assets abroad. In spe-

---

[1]The former Yugoslav Republic of Macedonia succeeded to the membership of the former Socialist Federal Republic of Yugoslavia in the IMF on December 14, 1992.

cific cases (such as enterprises with foreign operations), enterprises may hold foreign exchange accounts abroad with the approval of the National Bank.

Imports and Import Payments

Payments for authorized imports are not restricted. Imports from the Federal Republic of Yugoslavia (Serbia/Montenegro) are prohibited, in accordance with UN Security Council Resolutions Nos. 757, 787, and 820. In addition, transit trade through the Federal Republic of Yugoslavia is banned under UN Security Council Resolutions Nos. 787 and 820. Since January 1, 1994, a new trade regime has been in effect. Under the new regime, goods in almost 98 percent of import categories are importable without quota restrictions. Goods in approximately 2 percent of import categories are subject to quota restrictions that are designed to protect domestic production; these products include certain chemical and steel products; buses; and, for three months of the year, certain seasonal food products. Customs duties are levied on imported goods; the rates of customs duties range from zero to 17 percent, with imports of crude oil and essential items subject to duty at a low rate (1 percent on crude oil), 5 percent on raw materials and equipment, 10 percent on oil derivatives, and about 12–15 percent on consumer products. Imports of certain goods, such as weapons and medicine, are subject to licensing requirements for security or public health reasons. In 1994, the effective average rate of duty was about 9.5 percent. Since September 30, 1994, importers have been allowed to purchase foreign exchange to pay letters of credit on imports 180 days in advance to the maturity date.

Payments for Invisibles

Resident juridical persons may purchase foreign exchange freely to make payments for invisibles on presentation of documentation showing the nature of the services bought abroad or transfers made, such as invoices and health declarations.

Exports and Export Proceeds

Exports to the Federal Republic of Yugoslavia are prohibited under UN Security Council Resolutions Nos. 713, 757, 787, and 820. In addition, transit trade through the Federal Republic of Yugoslavia is prohibited under UN Security Council Resolutions Nos. 787 and 820. Under the trade regime in force since January 1, 1994, the exportation of certain products (sugar, flour, wheat, and soya) remains temporarily restricted to protect domestic supply. The exportation of a small number of items is banned for security, public health, or cultural reasons (for example, arms, drugs, historic artifacts).

Exporters must sell their proceeds to importers within 4 business days, or use the proceeds for payments abroad, or deposit them in banks for a period of up to 90 days, after which they must sell their proceeds in the foreign exchange market.

Proceeds from Invisibles

Proceeds from invisibles are subject to the same regulations as those applicable to merchandise exports.

Capital

Resident natural persons are not allowed to engage in borrowing or lending operations with nonresidents. Contracting of commercial credits by juridical persons is free of restrictions. Outward direct investment requires approval from and registration with the Ministry of Foreign Affairs. Banks may take foreign exchange positions subject to individual limits.

Foreign direct investment in the former Yugoslav Republic of Macedonia is allowed except in a few sectors (such as arms production). Nonresidents are allowed to invest in existing firms, establish their own firms, or establish joint ventures. Imports of raw materials, spare parts, and equipment not produced domestically by joint-venture firms are exempt from customs duties if the foreign share in the investment is at least 20 percent. Foreign investors are exempt from the company income tax during the first three years of operation. All foreign investment registered with the Ministry of Foreign Relations is protected from nationalization. There are no restrictions on the transfer abroad of profits and dividends, provided that all financial obligations within the country have been met. There are no regulations governing inward portfolio investment. Outward portfolio investment by resident natural and juridical persons is not permitted.

Gold

The importation and exportation of gold require approval of the National Bank.

Changes During 1994

No significant changes occured in the exchange and trade system.

MADAGASCAR

(Position as of December 31, 1994)

Exchange Arrangement

The currency of Madagascar is the Malagasy franc (FMG), the external value of which is determined freely in the official interbank market. The French franc is the only currency quoted on this market, and the exchange rates of other countries are determined on the basis of cross-rate relationships of the currencies concerned in the Paris exchange market. Exporters' surrender requirement has been transferred from the Central Bank of Madagascar (CBM) to the market; thus, the CBM is a normal dealer, participating in the market on the same basis as the five commercial banks. The five banks are permitted to maintain an exchange position up to the limits set up by the prudential regulation (40 percent of their respective capital base). There are limited arrangements for forward cover against exchange rate risk. On December 31, 1994, the midpoint rate for the French franc quoted on the market was FMG 720.00 per F 1.

Administration of Control

All countries other than Madagascar are considered foreign countries, and financial relations with all foreign countries are subject to exchange control. Exchange control is administered by the Exchange Operations Monitoring Unit of the General Directorate of the Treasury, which also supervises borrowing and lending abroad by residents; the issue, sale, or introduction of foreign securities in Madagascar; all outward investments; and inward direct investment. Some approval authority for exchange control has been delegated to authorized intermediaries, and all exchange transactions relating to foreign countries must be effected through such intermediaries. All economic agents are allowed to import. Private operators and state trading companies are authorized to export all products to any market at prices freely negotiated by exporters and importers, with the exception of vanilla, for which a minimum export price of $60 a kilogram is administratively set.

Prescription of Currency

Payments and receipts may be effected through authorized intermediaries in any currency. A bilateral payments agreement with Mauritius has been inoperative for some time.

Resident and Nonresident Accounts

Accounts in Foreign Currency. Since May 1994, residents and nonresidents have been freely permitted to open accounts in foreign currency with local commercial banks. Only transfers from abroad or from another foreign currency account, foreign banknotes, or traveler's and bank checks may be deposited in such accounts without justification. These accounts may be freely debited either for conversion into Malagasy francs through a sale on the interbank market or by transfer to a foreign account in Madagascar or abroad. Conversion into foreign banknotes is allowed only within the limits stipulated under the applicable foreign exchange control regulation.

Nonresidents are also authorized to open nonresident accounts in Malagasy francs. Such accounts may be debited and credited only for transactions between nonresidents and for explicitly authorized transactions between residents and nonresidents. When Malagasy francs accruing to a nonresident are not eligible for credit to a foreign account, they must be credited to a special blocked account, the balance of which may be used by the holder for personal expenses in Madagascar, subject to a limit of FMG 20,000 a day for the account holder and FMG 10,000 a day for each accompanying family member. Any other operation requires prior approval from the Ministry of Finance. Transactions between enterprises in the free trade zone and residents are conducted through the enterprises' foreign accounts in Malagasy francs. These enterprises are also permitted to maintain foreign exchange accounts with local banks.

Imports and Import Payments

Under the Liberalized Imports System (SILI), all economic agents listed in the trade register who are in good standing legally and with the tax administration may import and receive the total amount of foreign currency requested at the prevailing exchange rate. A short list of imports is subject to administrative control, primarily for reasons of security and health. Import licenses are not required for imports financed with foreign exchange already owned by the importers and deposited in their foreign currency accounts, and all administrative formalities are handled by the banks through which the import transactions are effected.

298

No restrictions of any kind apply to the opening of credit or the means of financing imports; importers may use their own resources, borrow from the banking system, or avail themselves of external loans, including suppliers' credits, to finance imports. The temporary requirement under the SILI that importers set aside provisions in local currency covering the full amount of their imports was abolished on May 10, 1988, and each commercial bank is free to decide on the desirability of requiring such a provision on the basis of its financial evaluation of importers. Most imports require a documentary credit, under which a local bank will agree to open a credit line for an importer on condition that the export is confirmed by the exporter's corresponding bank. Local banks attach varying conditions to granting loans to their customers, with some banks requiring a deposit in foreign currency equivalent to 100 percent of the import cost (dépôt en devises). Importers are allowed to buy the necessary foreign exchange for their imports up to 120 days before settlement, although such amounts may be used only for the imports stipulated in the documentary credit. In accordance with the provisions of Decree No. 92.424 (April 3, 1992) on the Regulations of Merchandise Imports and Exports, all import prohibitions have been lifted, except for a few that remain restricted for health and security reasons.

On January 1, 1988, the authorities introduced the first stage of a comprehensive tariff reform that replaced quantitative import restrictions with a simplified system of 16 rates (multiples of 5), with the minimum rate set at 5 percent and the maximum at 70 percent. A temporary surcharge of 30 percent was levied on certain products to facilitate the transition. All imports except those for which exemptions were granted in accordance with international treaties were made subject to a minimum rate of 5 percent on a collection basis. In the second stage of the reform, which took effect on January 1, 1989, the tariffs tended to be harmonized at the four-digit level; and the minimum tariff rate was raised to 10 percent, except on certain products (fertilizers, pesticides, pharmaceutical products and inputs, and optical glass). In addition, the Government reduced certain tariffs and the temporary surcharge, which was lowered from 30 percent to 10 percent and suspended entirely for meats and edible organs. On January 1, 1990, the 10 percent temporary surcharge was eliminated, and the maximum tariff rate of 70 percent was applied to products previously subject to the surcharge. In 1991, the maximum tariff rate was reduced to 60 percent for all categories of merchandise. The Finance Law of 1991 lowered the maximum tariff rate further to

50 percent for a large number of products. The third stage of the reform, completed in 1992, concerned mainly the classification of imported goods into five categories, which are taxed at rates of 10 percent to 50 percent. The Financial Law of 1994 (II) further lowered the maximum tariff rate to 30 percent. Since the introduction of a floating exchange arrangement, there has been no difference between the exchange rate applied to finance and to tax imports and exports.

Payments for Invisibles

All payments for invisibles require prior approval from the Ministry of Finance, which has delegated approval authority to the General Directorate of the Treasury and to authorized intermediaries, either up to specified limits or for any amount that is properly documented. Payments for invisibles related to authorized imports are not restricted, except for agency fees (commissions de représentations), whose settlement is subject to the submission of a contract previously approved by the Minister of Finance (Treasury General Directorate).

Residents traveling as tourists may purchase foreign exchange up to an annual limit equivalent to F 6,000 a person a trip, irrespective of the number of trips taken (F 3,000 for children under 15 years). The foreign exchange allowance for business travel is the equivalent of F 25,000 a person, irrespective of the number of trips made. Applications for additional foreign exchange must be submitted to the Ministry of Finance and may be approved for bona fide business trips and medical treatment abroad, but not for tourism. Allocations for different types of travel may not be combined without the prior approval of the General Directorate of the Treasury.

Limits are set for educational expenses and certain other current invisibles. The transfer of dividends and profits to nonresident shareholders who are natural or juridical persons has been fully liberalized under the terms of the Investment Code and the Industrial Free Trade Zone. Foreigners working in Madagascar may transfer savings from wages and salaries upon presentation of the work contract and employment permit, provided that the transfer takes place within three months of the pay period. The amounts allowed are up to 35 percent of net salary for bachelors and persons whose families reside in Madagascar; up to 60 percent for those whose families live outside Madagascar; and 100 percent for both categories during leave spent outside Madagascar. Remittances for medical treatment abroad are permitted when properly documented.

Resident and nonresident travelers to foreign countries may take out up to FMG 25,000 in Malagasy banknotes. There is no longer a requirement to fill a declaration of foreign means of payment upon entry into Madagascar, unless the amount brought in is more than F 50,000.

Exports and Export Proceeds

All exporters listed in the trade register who are in good standing and have no outstanding tax obligations may freely export their products (except vanilla) without restriction at prices negotiated directly between exporters and importers. Furthermore, the Government's quality control or certification requirement for exportable goods has been abolished for a number of products and is now limited to only four: vanilla, coffee, seafood, and meat. Certificates of quality on exports of cloves have also been abolished. Mining products are covered by a special arrangement under the mining law. Quality control itself is limited to a quality or sanitary inspection certificate from the relevant government agency or, at the option of the exporter, from an internationally recognized specialized private company. For vanilla and coffee, the control is effected at the level of stocks and not at the time of embarkation. For seafood and meat, the certificate of origin and quality standard must be included in the documents for embarkation in the absence of an arrangement directly agreed upon by the importer and exporter in conformity with international agreements.

Since the 1990/91 crop year, all coffee producers have been permitted to negotiate and execute export contracts freely. The list of exports prohibited or subject to prior approval, including mineral products, flora, and fauna, was reduced by Decree No. 92.424 (April 3, 1992). Vanilla continues to be the only export subject to taxation. Effective September 1, 1994, a single export tax was introduced at the rate of 35 percent.

Export proceeds must be repatriated within 90 days of the date of shipment unless an exemption is granted by the Ministry of Finance. Exporters are required to sell the proceeds from their exports on the interbank market; however, they are allowed to deposit in their foreign exchange account 20 percent of the proceeds if the repatriation occurs within the first 30 days, 15 percent if the repatriation occurs within 60 days, and 10 percent if the repatriation occurs within between 60 days and 90 days of the shipment. In addition, most exports over FMG 1 million are subject to a domiciliation requirement, under which the exporter must present to a certified intermediary (a local bank) a valid commercial contract and a written commitment to repatriate the foreign exchange proceeds. Export proceeds of enterprises operating in the free trade zone must be repatriated within 190 days of the date of shipment. Some large enterprises are granted exceptions from the surrender requirements on a case-by-case basis and are permitted to retain all their earnings.

Proceeds from Invisibles

All amounts due from residents of other countries in respect of services, and all income or proceeds accruing in those countries or from nonresidents, must be repatriated within one month of the due date. Resident and nonresident travelers may bring in any amount of foreign currency as means of payment and up to FMG 25,000 in Malagasy banknotes.

Capital

Capital movements between Madagascar and foreign countries and between residents and nonresidents are subject to prior authorization from the Ministry of Finance. Special controls are maintained over borrowing abroad; inward direct investment and all outward investment; and the issuing, advertising, or offering for sale of foreign securities in Madagascar.

Foreign direct investments in Madagascar, including those made by companies in Madagascar that are directly or indirectly under foreign control and those made by branches or subsidiaries of foreign companies in Madagascar, as well as corresponding transfers, require prior approval from the Ministry of Finance. Foreign direct investments abroad by Malagasy nationals, including those made through foreign companies directly or indirectly controlled by persons resident in Madagascar and those made by branches or subsidiaries abroad of companies located in Madagascar, are subject to prior authorization from the Ministry of Finance. The total or partial liquidation of such investments must be declared to the Ministry of Finance. Both the making and the liquidation of direct investments, whether Malagasy investments abroad or foreign investments in Madagascar, must be reported to the minister within 20 days of each transaction. Participation that does not exceed 20 percent of the capital of a company is not considered direct investment. Proceeds from the liquidation of foreign investment may be repatriated with the prior authorization of the Ministry of Finance.

The issuing, advertising, or offering for sale of foreign securities in Madagascar requires prior authorization from the Ministry of Finance. Exempt from authorization are operations in connection with shares similar to securities whose issuing or offering for sale in Madagascar has previously been authorized. Borrowing abroad by natural or juridical persons, whether public or private, requires prior authorization from the Ministry of Finance, although loans contracted by authorized banks or credit institutions with special legal status are exempt. Enterprises in the free trade zone are permitted to contract and service foreign loans freely, and interest and amortization payments on foreign loans contracted directly by these companies are not restricted. Lending abroad is subject to authorization by the Ministry of Finance.

In accordance with the Investment Code of December 29, 1989 (Law No. 89026), enterprises benefiting from preferential treatment under the code are exempted from import taxes exceeding 10 percent on materials used in the production process. Enterprises operating in the industrial free trade zone established on December 29, 1989 may import these materials free of duty and tax.

Gold

Approved collectors acting in their own name and on their own account may purchase gold within the country from holders of valid gold-mining titles or from authorized holders of gold-washing rights. The price of gold may be set freely by buyers and sellers. Imports and exports of gold require prior authorization from the Ministry of Commerce after review by the Directorate of Energy and Mines. Exempt from this requirement are (1) imports and exports by or on behalf of the CBM, and (2) imports and exports of manufactured articles containing a minor quantity of gold (such as gold-filled or gold-plated articles). Travelers are authorized to export 50 grams or 250 carats of gold jewelry or gold articles a person and 50 grams or 250 carats of numismatic items a person. Imports of gold, whether licensed or exempt from license, are subject to customs declaration. Holders of a valid gold-mining title or a gold-washing permit or rights are free to sell the gold recovered to any approved collector. However, Malagasy authorities, represented by the CBM or its agents, have first rights to purchase gold produced in the country.

Changes During 1994

Exchange Arrangement

May 9. The interbank exchange market began to operate.

May 5. The requirement to surrender foreign exchange proceeds to the CBM was abolished.

Resident and Nonresident Accounts

May 5. Both residents and nonresidents were freely permitted to open foreign currency accounts.

Imports and Import Payments

March 1. The maximum tariff on imports was reduced to 30 percent from 50 percent.

May 5. Most of the import prohibitions introduced earlier in the year were eliminated.

Exports and Export Proceeds

September 1. Vanilla exports were subject to a single tax rate of 35 percent.

MALAWI

(Position as of December 31, 1994)

Exchange Arrangement

The currency of Malawi is the Malawi Kwacha, the external rate of which is determined on the basis of supply and demand conditions in the exchange market. Authorized dealer banks may buy and sell foreign currencies at freely determined market exchange rates. Foreign exchange bureaus are authorized to conduct spot transactions with the general public on the basis of exchange rates negotiated with their clients, and foreign exchange brokers are authorized to match orders from buyers and sellers of foreign exchange on an agency basis.[1] The Reserve Bank of Malawi (RBM) operates a trading desk for buying and selling foreign exchange in the market. At the end of December 1994, the RBM's buying and selling rates for the U.S. dollar were MK 15.2221 and MK 15.3751, respectively, per US$1. The exchange rates for the Canadian dollar, the deutsche mark, the French franc, the Japanese yen, the pound sterling, the South African rand, the Swiss franc, and the Zimbabwe dollar are determined on the basis of the cross rates of the U.S. dollar for the currencies concerned. There are no taxes or subsidies on purchases or sales of foreign exchange. There are no arrangements for forward cover against exchange rate risk operating in the official or the commercial banking sector.

Administration of Control

Exchange control is administered by the RBM under the authority delegated to it by the Minister of Finance. Import policy is formulated by the Ministry of Commerce and Industry (MCI), which is also responsible for issuing import and export licenses. Commercial banks, foreign exchange bureaus, and brokers are authorized dealers in foreign exchange.

Prescription of Currency

Payments to nonresidents may be made in Malawi kwacha to the credit of a nonresident account maintained by the recipient or in any convertible foreign currency[2] traded in Malawi. Payments from residents of other countries may be received in Malawi kwacha from a nonresident account or in any convertible foreign currency.

Resident and Nonresident Accounts

Accounts in Malawi kwacha held by residents of other countries are designated nonresident accounts. These accounts may be credited with the proceeds of sales of any convertible foreign currency, with authorized payments in Malawi kwacha to foreign countries by Malawian residents, and with transfers from other nonresident accounts. Balances on these accounts may be used to make payments to residents of Malawi for any purpose and may be transferred freely to other nonresident accounts; these accounts may also be debited for payments to account holders temporarily residing in Malawi.

Blocked accounts in Malawi kwacha are held with authorized dealer banks (ADBs) by nonresidents. Debits and credits to such accounts do not require the prior authorization of the exchange control authorities. Normally, authorization is given for the balances of blocked accounts to be invested in an approved manner. On application to the ADBs, account holders may normally transfer the interest on blocked account balances to their country of residence.

Residents receiving foreign exchange regularly from abroad, including exporters, may maintain foreign currency accounts with ADBs for a period of 30 to 90 days, and balances in the accounts may be used to make authorized payments or transfers without restriction.

Imports and Import Payments

Most imports are subject to the open general license system. However, for a number of items,[3] specific import licenses are required from the MCI. Goods originating in Commonwealth countries or in non-Commonwealth countries that are members of the General Agreement on Tariffs and Trade may be imported under an open general license. Specific import licenses are usually issued within a week of application and are normally valid for six months.

---

[1]Foreign exchange brokering has been temporarily suspended since the end of November 1994.

[2]Under Malawi's exchange control regulations, all currencies other than the Malawi kwacha are considered foreign currencies.

[3]Certain agricultural and food products, new (military-type) and used clothing, gold, fertilizers, flick knives, explosives, arms and ammunition, wild animals, live fish, and copyright articles.

Commercial banks are authorized to provide foreign exchange, without referring to the RBM, for payment of all applications to import goods and services.

When imports arrive in the country and payment is due, the importer must submit applications for foreign exchange. Such applications must be accompanied by relevant importation and customs documents. Depending on means of payment (for example, letters of credit), commercial banks may require counterpart deposits. This is a matter of banking practice and is not required by official regulations.

Prepayment for imports is not allowed. Importers are free to choose any method of payment, and imports may be paid for in Malawi currency to an appropriate local nonresident account or in any convertible currency.

Customs tariffs on nongovernment imports are ad valorem and range from zero to 45 percent of the c.i.f. value, with a weighted average of about 21 percent. The only exception is textiles for which the tariff rate is 70 percent.[4] Government imports are exempt from customs tariffs. Imports are also subject to a surtax, which is applied on the c.i.f. value, including customs tariffs.[5] The surtax rates range from zero to 20 percent for most imported items.

Payments for Invisibles

Commercial banks are authorized to provide foreign exchange, without reference to the exchange control authorities, for all current invisible payments, but certain invisible payments, such as private travel, business travel, and medical treatment, are subject to limits. The basic exchange allowances for each trip abroad are $3,000 for private travel (holiday); $5,000 for business travel; and $4,000 for medical purposes. Foreign exchange in excess of the limits in the case of medical treatment will be granted upon verification of expenses. There is no limit on the frequency of trips that may be taken. Travelers may take out, in addition to their basic travel allowance, up to MK 200.

Foreign nationals employed in Malawi on contracts and holding a temporary employment permit are allowed to remit, subject to ADBs' approval, up to two-thirds of their current net earnings to their country of normal residence or any country of their choice.

Exports and Export Proceeds

Certain products[6] are subject to export licensing, mainly to ensure the adequacy of domestic supplies. Export proceeds can be held in foreign currency accounts. Holders of foreign currency accounts are free to sell foreign exchange within 30 days. After 30 days, 90 percent of the foreign exchange has to be converted into kwacha at the RBM rate. However, the holders can keep the funds for 90 days if funds are required to make approved foreign payments. Specific duties or cesses are levied on exports of hides and skins and tobacco.[7] Under a duty drawback scheme, customs tariffs paid on imports of certain inputs used for manufactured exports are rebated.

Proceeds from Invisibles

Receipts from invisibles may be retained in full and held in foreign-currency-denominated accounts with ADBs. There is no limit on the amount of foreign currency notes and coins that travelers may import, but they may not bring in more than MK 200 in Malawi currency notes and coins.

Capital

Inward transfers of nondebt-creating capital are not restricted. The taking up of loans from abroad by residents requires prior exchange control approval, which is normally granted provided that the terms of repayment, including the servicing costs, are acceptable. Outward transfers of capital are controlled mainly for residents. Nonresidents are permitted to repatriate their investments when they have satisfied the authorities that the original investment was made with funds brought into the country. Apart from the need to obtain the ADBs' approval, there are no restrictions on the transfer abroad of dividends and profits of foreign-owned companies, provided that no recourse is being made to local borrowing to finance the transfer.

Residents may not purchase any foreign securities without specific exchange control approval. In general, residents are not permitted to transfer capital abroad, and, with certain exceptions, they are required to offer for sale to an authorized dealer any foreign exchange that accrues to them.

All applications for emigrants' allowances must be submitted to ADBs for approval. Upon departure,

---

[4]The effective maximum tariff for most tariff lines is 40 percent, as almost all trading partners qualify for preferential tariffs under various international conventions.

[5]The surtax is levied on both imported and domestically produced manufactured goods.

[6]Implements of war, petroleum products, nickel, atomic energy materials, and certain agricultural and animal products.

[7]The cess is also levied, with some exemptions, on tobacco sold locally and on hides and skins at the rate of 2 percent of export value.

emigrants are allowed to exchange the equivalent of up to the amount approved. The balance, if any, of emigrants' funds is blocked, but on the first anniversary of their departure date from Malawi, a sum equal to the original emigration allowance may be transferred to the new country of residence.

Gold

Residents may purchase, hold, and sell gold coins in Malawi for numismatic purposes. With this exception, residents other than the monetary authorities and authorized industrial users are not allowed to hold or acquire gold at home or abroad in any form other than jewelry. Imports of gold in any form other than jewelry require licenses issued by the Minister of Commerce and Industry in consultation with the Ministry of Finance; such licenses are not normally granted except for imports by or on behalf of the monetary authorities and industrial users.

Changes During 1994

Exchange Arrangement

February 7. A new exchange arrangement based on an interbank market was introduced. The exchange rate would be determined on the basis of supply and demand conditions in the exchange market. Authorized dealer banks would be permitted to buy and sell foreign currency at freely determined market exchange rates. Foreign exchange bureaus would be authorized to conduct spot transactions with the general public on the basis of exchange rates negotiated with their clients, and foreign exchange brokers would be authorized to match orders from buyers and sellers of foreign exchange on an agency basis. The RBM would hold a monthly fixing session at which offers to buy and sell foreign exchange from authorized participants would be matched to arrive at a clearing exchange rate. Authorized participants at the fixing would be authorized dealer banks, foreign exchange brokers, foreign exchange bureaus (selling only), the RBM,

companies registered under the Companies Act, and licensed enterprises meeting operational requirements of the fixing sessions.

November 1. Exposure limits on foreign exchange holdings by the authorized dealers were introduced.

November 30. Foreign exchange brokers' licenses were suspended.

Resident and Nonresident Accounts

February 7. Residents earning foreign exchange on a regular basis were allowed to maintain foreign currency accounts with authorized banks and use the balances for authorized payments and transfers.

October 20. Authorized dealer banks were required to convert 90 percent of foreign currency accounts.

Imports and Import Payments

February 7. The negative list for imports was abolished.

Payments for Invisibles

February 7. The limits on travel allowance were increased, and the limit on the number of trips permitted was eliminated.

Exports and Export Proceeds

February 7. The surrender requirement was abolished, except for the proceeds from exports of tea, tobacco, and sugar; 10 percent of the proceeds from these commodities would be required to be sold to the RBM.

November 1. Holders of foreign currency accounts were free to sell their foreign exchange balances in the market within 30 days. After 30 days, the holders have to convert 90 percent of the funds to Malawi kwacha at prevailing RBM rates. If the holders can present evidence of an approved and confirmed import order the funds can be held for 90 days.

November 1. The 10 percent surrender requirement for the proceeds from exports of tea, tobacco, and sugar was abolished.

MALAYSIA

(Position as of December 31, 1994)

Exchange Arrangement

The currency of Malaysia is the Ringgit. Its external value is determined by supply and demand conditions in the foreign exchange market. The Central Bank of Malaysia intervenes only to maintain orderly market conditions and to avoid excessive fluctuations in the value of the ringgit. The external value of the currency is monitored against a basket of currencies weighted in terms of Malaysia's major trading partners and the currencies of settlement. The commercial banks are free to determine and quote exchange rates, whether spot or forward, to all customers for all currencies other than those of Israel and the Federal Republic of Yugoslavia (Serbia/Montenegro). On December 31, 1994, the middle rate for the U.S. dollar was RM 2.5578 per US$1. There are no taxes or subsidies on purchases or sales of foreign exchange.

Forward exchange contracts may be effected for both commercial and financial transactions. Forward cover for the commercial banks is usually provided for up to six months at market rates for both purchases and sales.

Malaysia formally accepted the obligations of Article VIII, Sections 2, 3, and 4 of the Fund Agreement, as from November 11, 1968.

Administration of Control

The Central Bank administers exchange control throughout Malaysia on behalf of the Malaysian Government, the Governor of the Bank being the Controller of Foreign Exchange. There are no restrictions on payments or transfers for current international transactions. Residents are required only to complete a statistical form for any payment, irrespective of its purpose, that exceeds RM 50,000 or its equivalent in foreign currency. The authority for import control rests with the Royal Customs and Excise Department of the Federal Ministry of Finance. Import licensing throughout Malaysia is administered daily by the Ministry of International Trade and Industry together with other specified authorities, such as the Ministry of Primary Industries, the Malaysian Timber Board, and the Veterinary Department, on behalf of the Royal Customs and Excise Department.

In accordance with the Fund's Executive Board Decision No. 144-(52/51) adopted on August 14, 1952, Malaysia notified the Fund on June 23, 1993 that in compliance with UN Security Council Resolution No. 757 (1992), certain restrictions had been imposed on the making of payments and transfers for current international transactions in respect of the Federal Republic of Yugoslavia (Serbia/Montenegro).

Prescription of Currency

All payments to countries other than Israel and the Federal Republic of Yugoslavia (Serbia/Montenegro) may be made either in ringgit or in any currency other than those of Israel and the Federal Republic of Yugoslavia (Serbia/Montenegro). Special rules apply to settlements with these two countries.

Nonresident Accounts

Ringgit accounts of nonresidents of Malaysia are designated external accounts. There are no restrictions on debits to external accounts. Credits to these accounts are freely permitted, subject only to the completion of statistical forms for amounts exceeding RM 50,000 if such payments are made by residents. Proceeds from the sale of any foreign currency may be credited to external accounts, and the balances may be transferred to any other resident or nonresident account or converted into any currency, except those of Israel and the Federal Republic of Yugoslavia (Serbia/Montenegro). Accounts of residents of these two countries are designated as Israeli accounts and Federal Republic of Yugoslavia (Serbia/Montenegro) accounts, respectively. All debits and credits to such accounts require prior approval.

Imports and Import Payments

Tariffs and import controls for the various parts of Malaysia have been fully standardized. Import licenses are required for certain goods as specified in Customs (Prohibition of Imports) Order No. 1988, for reasons of health, security, or public policy; various conditions must be satisfied before import licenses for such goods are issued. Certain other imports are subject to quantitative restrictions, which are reviewed periodically, to protect local industries temporarily when required. Imports from Israel are prohibited.

Imports of motor vehicles are subject to a quota and require an import license that details the quantitative restrictions. The movement of live animals between Peninsular Malaysia, Sabah, and Sarawak is subject to a permit issued by the Veterinary Department. Imports of the meat, bones, hides, hooves, horns, and offal of any animal or any portion of an animal from all countries require an import license. Imports of primates require an import license, subject to approval from the Department of Wildlife and National Parks. Payments for permitted imports are freely allowed. Raw materials and machinery for the manufacturing sector are eligible for preferential duty treatment as follows: (1) for the production of goods for the domestic market, raw materials that are not manufactured locally are subject to a reduced rate of customs duty of 3 percent; (2) manufacturers for the domestic market may be further exempted from this duty if they comply with specific requirements regarding equity participation, management, and employment structure; (3) all raw materials for the production of taxable goods may be acquired free of duty, subject to conditions as specified in the Sales Tax Act of 1972; (4) for companies that manufacture products for the export market, full exemption from customs duty is granted when local raw materials are not available or are not competitive in price or quality; (5) all customs duties and sales taxes on imported machinery and equipment that are unavailable locally and are directly used in the manufacturing process can be considered for exemption; and (6) manufacturers may claim customs duties and sales tax drawbacks on imported raw materials or components that are incorporated into finished products and exported within 12 months of the date of import.

Payments for Invisibles

Payments for invisibles to all countries other than Israel and the Federal Republic of Yugoslavia (Serbia/Montenegro) may be made without restriction. There is no restriction on the amount of foreign exchange available for travel abroad. Remittances to nonresidents of dividends, royalties, and profits on all bona fide investments are permitted, subject only to the completion of exchange control forms for amounts in excess of RM 50,000. There is no restriction on the exportation of currency notes in the immediate possession of a traveler. The exportation of Ringgit currency by any other means requires prior approval from the Controller of Foreign Exchange.

Exports and Export Proceeds

Exports to Israel and the Federal Republic of Yugoslavia (Serbia/Montenegro) are prohibited. Exports of logs from Peninsular Malaysia and Sabah are restricted.

The customs areas and export control systems among the three territories of Malaysia are standardized. Exchange control forms must be completed for exports valued at more than RM 100,000 f.o.b. a shipment. Proceeds from exports must be received and repatriated according to the payment schedule specified in the commercial contract, but no longer than six months after the date of exportation. This regulation does not apply to commercial samples or goods exported for repair or exchange and reimported into Malaysia. Exporters are allowed to retain a portion of their export proceeds in foreign currency accounts with authorized banks in Malaysia up to RM 5 million.[1] Exports of rubber from Peninsular Malaysia require a certificate issued by the Malaysian Rubber Exchange and Licensing Board. Exports of roofing tiles, bricks, minerals, rice and paddy in any form, milk and specified milk products, textiles, and all other goods as specified in the second schedule of Customs (Prohibition of Exports) Order No. 1988 of the 1967 Customs Act are subject to permits.

Export incentives are provided to companies that export Malaysian products. The primary incentives include a double deduction of expenses incurred in overseas promotion, export credit refinancing, and duty drawbacks.

Proceeds from Invisibles

The exchange control authorities do not regulate the timeliness of exchange receipts from invisibles. No limitation is imposed on the importation of currency notes by a traveler. The importation of domestic banknotes by other than authorized banks, or by any other means, requires prior approval from the Controller of Foreign Exchange.

Capital

The following inward investments, covered by the guidelines issued on February 20, 1974 (regarding the acquisition of assets, mergers, and takeovers), require prior approval from the Foreign Investment Committee (FIC): (1) proposed acquisition of any substantial fixed assets by foreign inter-

---

[1]Seven banks—designated as "first-tier banks"—are permitted to offer foreign currency accounts. All other domestic banks must continue to obtain permission from the Controller of Foreign Exchange before offering currency accounts to residents.

ests; (2) proposed acquisition of assets or interests, mergers, and takeovers of companies and businesses in Malaysia by any means that will cause ownership or control to pass to foreign interests; (3) proposed acquisition of 15 percent or more of the voting power (equity interests) by any foreign interest or associated group or by a foreign interest in the aggregate of 30 percent or more of the voting power of a Malaysian company or business; (4) control of Malaysian companies and businesses through any form of joint-venture agreement, management agreement, or technical assistance or other arrangement; (5) merger or takeover of any company or business in Malaysia; and (6) any other proposed acquisition of assets or interests exceeding RM 5 million in value.

Incorporation of a Malaysian company by a foreign entity does not require the approval of the FIC. However, increases in the paid-up capital of a Malaysian company that involve any foreign entity require the approval of the FIC under the following conditions: (1) the total of the foreign entity's new investment exceeds RM 5 million; (2) the total of the foreign entity's new investment exceeds 15 percent of the voting power in the relevant company; (3) as a result of the increase in paid-up capital, any foreign entity increases its voting power to more than 15 percent in the relevant company; (4) the total of the new investment by several foreign entities increases their joint voting power to 30 percent or more of the voting power in the relevant company; (5) as a result of the increase in paid-up capital, the aggregate holding of several foreign entities increases to 30 percent or more of the voting power in the relevant company; and (6) an increase in the paid-up capital of any Malaysian company to more than RM 5 million on incorporation, the holding of foreign entities constitutes more than 15 percent of the voting power, or the joint holding of several foreign entities constitutes 30 percent or more of the voting power of the company concerned.

Foreign investors are permitted to hold equity of up to 100 percent if they export 80 percent or more of their production. For projects exporting between 51 percent and 79 percent of their production, foreign equity ownership of up to 79 percent is permitted, depending on such factors as the level of technology, spin-off effects, size of the investment, location, value added, and the use of local raw materials and components. For projects exporting between 20 percent and 50 percent of their production, foreign equity ownership of between 30 percent and 51 percent is allowed. For projects exporting less than 20 percent of their production, foreign equity is allowed up to a maximum of 30 percent. For the purpose of equity determination, export sales are defined as excluding sales to free zones and licensed manufacturing warehouses so as to promote greater links between multinational corporations and domestic industries.

Notwithstanding the above, for projects producing high-technology products or priority products for the domestic market, foreign equity ownership of up to 100 percent may be allowed. These equity guidelines do not apply to new projects in certain sectors where foreign equity ownership of up to 60 percent is allowed for domestic sales (including sales to free zones and licensed manufacturing warehouses) for the following sectors: press-working and stamping industry, plastic components for the electrical and electronic industry, plastic compounds and masterbatch, electroplating, heat treatment activities, fabrication of furniture components such as nylon chair bases and arms, foundry products, connectors, transformers and coils, hot stamping, spray painting and silk screen printing services, and polished granite and marble slabs and tiles.

For projects involving extracting, mining, and processing mineral ores, a majority foreign equity participation of up to 100 percent is permitted. To determine the percentage for these projects, various criteria (e.g., level of investment, technology, and activities involved; availability of Malaysian expertise in the area of exploration, mining, and processing of the minerals concerned; degree of integration; and level of value added involved) are taken into consideration. For new hotel and tourist projects, foreign equity ownership of up to 100 percent is allowed for five years from the date the operation begins, after which such ownership must be reduced to 51 percent.

Permission of the Controller of Foreign Exchange is not required for direct and portfolio investments by Malaysian residents in countries other than Israel and the Federal Republic of Yugoslavia (Serbia/Montenegro), provided that the resident concerned has not obtained any domestic credit and that payments are made in foreign currency. If investors have any domestic credit, they must obtain prior approval from the Controller of Foreign Exchange for their investment abroad. Commercial banks are not encouraged to give loans to finance investments abroad that are considered unlikely to lead to long-term benefits for the economy; such funds should be used to finance the expansion of productive capacity in Malaysia. Commercial banks are permitted to have a short or a long open foreign exchange position, ranging from RM 10 million to

RM 150 million, based on the limit approved by the Controller of Foreign Exchange.

The proceeds of investments may be repatriated freely on resale, subject to the completion of a statistical form for amounts above RM 50,000. Nonresident-controlled companies in Malaysia are permitted to borrow up to RM 10 million, including immovable property loans, without exchange control approval, provided that at least 60 percent of total credit facilities from banking institutions in Malaysia are from Malaysian-owned financial institutions. Nonresidents who have valid work permits are allowed to borrow freely from domestic financial institutions to finance up to 60 percent of the purchase price of residential property for their own accommodation.

Residents are allowed to borrow in foreign currencies from nonresidents as well as from commercial banks and merchant banks in Malaysia up to the aggregate of RM 5 million, including financial guarantees, from nonresident financial institutions. For aggregate amounts exceeding RM 5 million, however, approval must be obtained from the Controller of Foreign Exchange, stating the main terms and conditions of the loan and the purpose for which the loan proceeds will be used. Approval is readily granted if the loan is to be used for productive investment within the country and the resident borrower is judged to be able to generate sufficient foreign exchange to service the loan. Offshore guarantees for loans, whether denominated in ringgit or foreign currency, obtained from licensed offshore banks do not require permission if the amount is less than the equivalent of RM 1 million, but these must be reported to the Controller of Foreign Exchange. Foreign borrowing in ringgit of any amount requires prior approval, which is not usually granted. Service payments on approved foreign loans may be effected by commercial banks, provided that payments are made in accordance with the approved terms and conditions of the loans. Commercial banks and merchant banks in Malaysia may lend in foreign currency to residents and accept deposits in foreign currency from nonresidents. As an incentive, interest paid to nonresidents by the commercial banks is exempted from the 20 percent withholding tax.

Intercompany accounts, which exclude proceeds from the exportation of Malaysian goods and proceeds from loans extended to Malaysian companies, may be maintained with any company outside Malaysia, provided that monthly returns are submitted to the Controller of Foreign Exchange. In addition, companies located in free trade zones or those licensed as manufacturing warehouses may, with prior permission from the Controller of Foreign Exchange, offset their export proceeds through intercompany accounts against payables to overseas companies for the supply of raw materials and components.

Gold

Residents of Malaysia are free to deal (purchase, sell, import, export, borrow, etc.) in gold in any state or form with any person, except residents of Israel, and the Federal Republic of Yugoslavia (Serbia/Montenegro).

Changes During 1994

Nonresident Accounts

February 1. The limit up to which the filing of a statistical form is not required for payments to nonresidents was raised to RM 50,000 from RM 10,000.

Exports and Export Proceeds

December 1. (1) The limit up to which the completion of an exchange control form for export is not required was raised to RM 100,000 from RM 20,000 a shipment to any country, including exports that are permitted by the relevant government authorities to Israel and the Federal Republic of Yugoslavia (Serbia/Montenegro); and (2) exporters were allowed to retain a portion of their export proceeds in foreign currency accounts maintained with designated banks in Malaysia.

Capital

January 24. Residents were prohibited to sell the following Malaysian securities to nonresidents: (1) banker's acceptances; (2) negotiable instruments of deposit; (3) Bank Negara bills; (4) Malaysian government treasury bills; (5) Malaysian government securities (including Islamic securities) with a remaining maturity of one year or less; and (6) Cagamas bonds and notes (whether or not sold or traded on a discount basis) with a remaining maturity of one year or less.

February 7. (1) Residents were prohibited to sell to nonresidents all forms of private debt securities (including commercial papers, but excluding securities convertible into ordinary shares) with a remaining maturity of one year or less; and (2) the restriction on the sale of Malaysian securities to nonresidents was extended to both the initial issue of the relevant security and the subsequent secondary market trade.

August 12. (1) The restriction on the sale of Malaysian securities, imposed on January 24, 1994 and February 7, 1994, was lifted; and (2) residents were permitted to sell to nonresidents any Malaysian securities.

December 1. (1) Nonresident-controlled companies were allowed to obtain credit facilities, including immovable property loans, up to RM 10 million without specific approval, provided that at least 60 percent of their total credit facilities from banking institutions were obtained from Malaysian-owned banking institutions; (2) nonresidents with valid work permits were allowed to obtain domestic borrowing to finance up to 60 percent of the purchase price of residential property for their own accommodation; and (3) residents were allowed to borrow in foreign currency up to a total of the equivalent of RM 5 million from nonresidents as well as from commercial banks and merchant banks in Malaysia.

MALDIVES

(Position as of December 31, 1994)

Exchange Arrangement

The currency of Maldives is the Maldivian Rufiyaa. Since March 1, 1987, the Maldives Monetary Authority (MMA) has followed a floating exchange rate policy under which the exchange rate has been determined by demand and supply conditions in the market, although the MMA may intervene in the market when deemed appropriate. The midpoint exchange rate of the rufiyaa in terms of the U.S. dollar on December 31, 1994, was Rf 11.77 per US$1. The MMA charges commercial banks a flat 1 percent for remitting foreign banknotes abroad, and there is a daily limit of US$5,000 in a bank's access to foreign currency notes from the MMA. The MMA carries out transactions freely with the private sector through the operations of the Government Exchange Counter. The MMA periodically sets daily limits for each individual's or enterprise's access to foreign exchange through the Counter, based on the availability of official reserves. As of January 1994, the limits were US$300 a person for cash, and US$2,000 a person or enterprise for checks. There are no arrangements for forward cover against exchange rate risk.

Administration of Control

There is no exchange control legislation. Trade regulations are administered by the Ministry of Trade and Industries, which also issues import and export licenses.

Prescription of Currency

There are no restrictions on maintaining bank accounts or holding cash in foreign currency. Foreign currency must be converted to rufiyaa through a bank or a licensed money changer who is authorized by the MMA to exchange foreign currencies.

Nonresident Accounts

No distinction is made between accounts held by residents and those held by nonresidents; there are no restrictions on keeping foreign currency balances.

Imports and Import Payments

Imports from Iraq, Israel, and the Federal Republic of Yugoslavia (Serbia/Montenegro) are prohibited. Import operations may be conducted only after being registered and licensed at the Ministry of Trade and Industries. Staple commodities (such as rice, wheat, flour, and sugar) are imported mainly by the State Trading Organization. All goods may be imported under an open general license (OGL) system. Licenses are issued on application. Ad valorem import duties are calculated on the c.i.f. or c. & f. value of imports, as appropriate. The following are exempt from duties: staple commodities (rice, flour, and sugar) imported mainly by the State Trading Organization, which also holds the exclusive right to procure certain categories of imports for the Government; essential medicines specified by the Ministry of Health and Welfare; textbooks specified by the Ministry of Education; and certain products imported for personal use. Duty rates on daily necessities and essentials range from 5 percent to 20 percent; on items essential for the development of domestic industries, from 10 percent to 20 percent; on items that will enhance the economic welfare of the country, from 25 percent to 35 percent; and on items considered to be luxuries and to impede the development of domestic industries, from 35 percent to 200 percent.

Payments for Invisibles

There are no restrictions on payments for invisibles. Travelers may take out any amount in domestic or foreign currency without restriction.

Exports and Export Proceeds

Export licenses are issued by the Ministry of Trade and Industries. The private sector may export most items, with the exception of fresh and frozen tuna. Locals and foreigners are encouraged to fish in the exclusive economic zone (EEZ) outside a 75-mile zone from the shoreline, which is reserved for traditional fishing. They must pay the Government a royalty on fish they catch in the EEZ. Exports of fish and fish products (except ambergris) caught by local residents are exempt from duties. Exports of fish caught by foreigners and joint-venture parties are subject to an export duty; re-exports are exempt from the duty.

Proceeds from Invisibles

Private sector receipts from current invisibles need not be surrendered and may be disposed of freely through the foreign exchange market. Travelers may bring in any amount of foreign currency without restriction.

Capital

Residents and nonresidents may freely import and export capital through the foreign exchange market, and residents do not require permission to maintain foreign currency accounts at home or abroad. Inward direct investment requires approval. All foreign investors are required to provide at least 75 percent of their capital investment in the form of either cash or capital goods financed from outside Maldives. Transfers of profits are permitted freely. Exemption from duties and taxes other than the tourism tax may be granted for a period as specified by the Government.

Gold

Transactions in gold are not subject to regulation. Residents may freely hold and negotiate gold in any form, at home or abroad, and the importation and exportation of gold are not restricted.

Changes During 1994

Exchange Arrangement

January 10. Daily limits on MMA sales of foreign exchange through the Government Exchange Counter were reduced to $300 from $500 a person for cash, and to $2,000 from $5,000–$15,000 a person or enterprise for checks.

MALI

(Position as of December 31, 1994)

Exchange Arrangement

The currency of Mali is the CFA Franc,[1] which is pegged to the French franc, the intervention currency, at the fixed rate of CFAF 1 per F 0.01. The official buying and selling rate is CFAF 100 per F 1. Exchange rates for all other currencies that are officially quoted on the Paris exchange market are based on the fixed rate for the French franc and the Paris exchange market rate for the currencies concerned. The banks levy a commission of 2.5 per mil on transfers to or from nonmember countries of the West African Monetary Union (WAMU), all of which must be transferred to the Treasury. There are no taxes or subsidies on purchases or sales of foreign exchange. Foreign exchange transfers are subject to a stamp tax.

Residents may obtain forward exchange rate cover for payments of imports or exports of goods on specified lists. Forward exchange rate cover must be denominated in the currency prescribed in the contract and is subject to prior authorization by the Minister of Finance. Forward exchange contracts for imports must be for a forward period of up to one month and cannot be renewed. For certain products, the duration of forward exchange rate cover may be extended to three months but cannot be renewed. For exports, the duration of forward exchange contracts may not exceed 120 days after the arrival of the goods at their destination.

With the exception of measures relating to the repatriation of export proceeds, Mali's exchange controls do not apply to (1) France (and its overseas departments and territories) and Monaco, and (2) all other countries whose bank of issue is linked with the French Treasury by an Operations Account (Benin, Burkina Faso, Cameroon, Central African Republic, Chad, Comoros, Congo, Côte d'Ivoire, Equatorial Guinea, Gabon, Niger, Senegal, and Togo). Hence, all payments to these countries may be made freely. All other countries are considered foreign countries.

Administration of Control

The Minister of Finance and Trade has sole authority in exchange control matters but has delegated certain exchange control powers to the BCEAO and to authorized banks. Imports and exports are subject to registration with the Directorate-General of Economic Affairs in the Ministry of Finance and Trade. Arrears are maintained with respect to external payments.

Prescription of Currency

Because Mali has an Operations Account with the French Treasury, settlements with France (as defined above), Monaco, and the countries linked to the French Treasury by an Operations Account are made in CFA francs, French francs, or the currency of any other member of the Operations Account Area. Settlements with all other countries with which no payments agreement is in force are usually made through correspondent banks in France in any of the currencies of those countries or in French francs through foreign accounts in francs. Settlements with The Gambia, Ghana, Guinea, Guinea-Bissau, Liberia, Mauritania, Nigeria, and Sierra Leone are normally made through the West African Clearing House.

Nonresident Accounts

Nonresident accounts may not be credited with CFA banknotes, French banknotes, or banknotes issued by any other institute of issue maintaining an Operations Account with the French Treasury. As the BCEAO has suspended the repurchase of BCEAO banknotes circulating outside the territories of the CFA franc zone, nonresident accounts may not be credited or debited with BCEAO banknotes without prior authorization.

Imports and Import Payments

Effective June 15, 1989, all import-licensing requirements and quotas were abolished. All imports, except those from Israel, which are prohibited, are required only to be registered, and permits are issued automatically.

A new, revised tariff regime took effect on February 26, 1991. Under this regime, products are classified into seven categories and subject to the same rate; under the previous system, about 4,000 categories were subject to different rates. With the exception of petroleum products, tariff rates are ad valorem and based on the c.i.f. value; under the

---

[1]The CFA franc is issued by the Central Bank of West African States (BCEAO) and is the common currency in Benin, Burkina Faso, Côte d'Ivoire, Mali, Niger, Senegal, and Togo.

old regime, a number of taxes were levied on the basis of administrative values (*valeurs mercuriales*). Petroleum products are subject to a variable levy, based on administrative values established with reference to prices charged by refineries in Dakar and Abidjan. Imports are subject to additional taxes ranging from 7.5 percent to 55 percent. (These additional taxes were temporarily suspended on January 28, 1994.)

Payments for Invisibles

Payments for invisibles to France (as defined above), Monaco, and the countries linked to the French Treasury by an Operations Account are permitted freely; those to other countries are subject to approval. Payments for invisibles related to trade are permitted freely when the basic trade transaccion has been approved or does not require authorization. Transfers of income accruing to nonresidents in the form of profits, dividends, and royalties are subject to approval.

Residents traveling to non-BCEAO countries in the franc zone are allowed to take out the equivalent of CFAF 2 million in banknotes, and they may take out amounts exceeding this limit in other means of payment. The allowances for travel to countries outside the franc zone are subject to the following regulations: (1) for tourist travel, the equivalent of CFAF 500,000 without limit on the number of trips or differentiation by the age of the traveler; (2) for business travel, the equivalent of CFAF 75,000 a day for up to one month, corresponding to a maximum of CFAF 2.25 million (business travel allowances may be combined with tourism allowances); (3) allowances in excess of these limits must be authorized by the respective ministries of finance or, by delegation, the BCEAO; and (4) credit cards, which must be issued by resident financial intermediaries and authorized by the respective ministers of finance, may be used up to the ceilings indicated above for tourist and business travel. Residents traveling to non-BCEAO countries are not allowed to take out BCEAO banknotes. Upon arrival at customs, returning resident travelers are required to declare all means of payment in their possession and must surrender within eight days all means of payment exceeding the equivalent of CFAF 25,000. All resident travelers to non-BCEAO countries must declare in writing, at the time of departure, all means of payment at their disposal. Nonresident travelers may re-export means of payment, other than banknotes, issued abroad and registered in their name. The re-exportation of foreign banknotes is allowed up to

the equivalent of CFAF 250,000; the re-exportation of foreign banknotes above these ceilings and other means of payment issued in Mali requires documentation demonstrating either the importation of foreign banknotes or their purchase against other means of payment registered in the name of the traveler or through the use of nonresident deposits lodged in local banks.

The transfer of the entire salary of a foreigner working in Mali is permitted upon presentation of the appropriate pay voucher, provided that the transfer takes place within three months of the pay period or that there is a reciprocity agreement with the foreigner's country of nationality. Remittances abroad for family maintenance, education allowances, and medical treatment, and transfers of profits or dividends from foreign direct investment may be made freely by authorized intermediaries when the appropriate documentation is presented.

Exports and Export Proceeds

Exports to foreign countries must be recorded with an authorized bank, and all export proceeds, including those originating in France and other countries linked to the French Treasury by an Operations Account, must be repatriated through the BCEAO and surrendered within 30 days of the payment due date or within 120 days of shipment if no payment date is specified in the sales contract. All exports require only a certificate of registration.

Proceeds from Invisibles

Proceeds from transactions in invisibles with France (as defined above), Monaco, and the countries linked to the French Treasury by an Operations Account may be retained. All amounts due from residents of other countries for services and all income earned in those countries from foreign assets must be collected and surrendered. Resident and nonresident travelers may bring in any amount of banknotes and coins issued by the BCEAO, the Bank of France, or a bank of issue maintaining an Operations Account with the French Treasury, as well as any amount of foreign banknotes and coins (except gold coins) of countries outside the Operations Account Area. However, they must declare the amounts they bring in.

Capital

Capital movements between Mali and France (as defined above), Monaco, and the countries linked to the French Treasury by an Operations Account are free of restrictions; capital transfers to all other countries require authorization from the Ministry of Finance and Commerce and are restricted, but capital receipts from these countries are permitted freely.

Special controls (in addition to any exchange control requirements that may apply) are maintained over borrowing abroad. The special control measures also do not apply to relations with France (as defined above) and the countries linked to the French Treasury by an Operations Account.

A new investment code was adopted on January 1, 1991, which simplified procedures for foreign and domestic investors to obtain preferential treatment with respect to domestic taxes for investments that meet specific criteria on employment creation, domestic content of production, location, and value of investment.

Gold

Travelers may export gold jewelry and personal belongings, other than gold coins and ingots, up to a maximum weight of 500 grams. Commercial imports and exports of gold do not require authorization from the Ministry of Finance and Commerce but are subject to all foreign trade regulations, including bank domiciliation, customs declaration, and the obligation to repatriate export proceeds.

Changes During 1994

Exchange Arrangement

January 12. The CFA franc was devalued to CFAF 100 per F 1 from CFAF 50 per F 1.

MALTA

(Position as of March 31, 1995)

Exchange Arrangement

The currency of Malta is the Maltese Lira, the external value of which is determined on the basis of a weighted basket consisting of the pound sterling, the U.S. dollar, and the European currency unit (ECU). The Central Bank of Malta computes the daily exchange rate between the Maltese lira and the U.S. dollar (the intervention currency) on the basis of the latest available market quotations for the U.S. dollar and other currency components of the basket; the ECU component is computed in a similar way on the basis of its own currency composition. The Central Bank also quotes daily rates for various other currencies,[1] taking as a basis the rates of the lira against the U.S. dollar and the cross rates of these currencies against the U.S. dollar, as quoted in the international market. Revised quotations for all major currencies are published by the Central Bank on an hourly basis. The Central Bank applies a spread of 0.125 percent to the middle rate to determine the buying and selling rates for transactions with the credit institutions. There is no limit on the spread between the buying and selling rates the credit institutions may quote. On December 30, 1994, the middle rate for the Maltese lira in terms of the U.S. dollar was US$2.7166 per Lm 1.

There are no taxes or subsidies on purchases or sales of foreign exchange, except for a subsidy in the form of a guaranteed exchange rate for the pound sterling provided temporarily by the Central Bank to tour operators from the United Kingdom and Ireland. This rate is being gradually phased out, and will cease to apply from the middle of 1997.

Malta formally accepted the obligations of Article VIII, Sections 2, 3, and 4 of the Fund Agreement, as from November 30, 1994.

Credit institutions are permitted to provide their customers with forward cover for certain specified transactions in a number of major currencies.[2] Forward rates are published by the Central Bank. Since September 1994, forward rates have been based on differences between domestic and foreign interest rates. Any forward contract concluded between a credit institution and a customer must be accompanied by a similar contract between that credit institution and the Central Bank. The forward facilities offered by the Central Bank to credit institutions are intended to provide cover for firm contractual commitments involving transactions in goods and services. However, in certain cases, the Central Bank may also permit credit institutions to offer forward facilities for other current account transactions. The Central Bank assumes all the exchange rate risk entailed in its forward contracts with credit institutions and also provides forward foreign exchange directly to government departments and public sector enterprises for imports of goods and services.

Administration of Control

The Central Bank of Malta, as agent for the Minister of Finance, administers exchange controls; the Director of Imports and Internal Trade in the Ministry of Finance administers trade controls. Approval authority for the allocation of foreign exchange for certain purposes has been delegated to the credit institutions. They may also give or renew guarantees and indemnities in connection with payments made under delegated authority. In the case of nonresidents, the credit institutions must hold full cash cover in external Maltese liri, foreign currency, or foreign securities for the duration of the guarantee or indemnity.

Authority to approve foreign exchange payments solely for travel purposes has also been delegated to a limited number of foreign exchange bureaus. The Central Bank is responsible for issuing licenses to operators of such agencies.

Prescription of Currency

Authorized payments to all countries may be made by crediting Maltese liri to an external account or in any foreign currency, while the proceeds of exports to all countries may be received in any foreign currency.[3]

A bilateral trade and payments agreement is maintained with the Libyan Arab Jamahiriya,[4] with

---

[1]The Central Bank quotes daily rates for 30 other currencies in addition to the U.S. dollar, among which are the Belgian franc, deutsche mark, French franc, Italian lira, Japanese yen, Netherlands guilder, pound sterling, Swiss franc, and the ECU.

[2]Belgian francs, deutsche marks, French francs, Italian lira, Japanese yen, Netherlands guilders, pounds sterling, Swiss francs, U.S. dollars, and ECUs.

[3]Foreign currencies are defined as all currencies other than the Maltese lira.

[4]Since January 1, 1995, transactions under the agreement have been settled within 90 days.

outstanding balances being settled in convertible currencies.

Nonresident Accounts

Nonresidents may hold foreign currencies or Maltese liri in external accounts with the authorized banks.[5] These accounts may be credited freely with authorized payments from residents to nonresidents with transfers from other external accounts belonging to nonresidents, with proceeds from sales of gold or foreign currency (including banknotes), and with interest due on balances in the accounts. External accounts may be debited freely for payments to residents, for transfers to other external accounts, for payments in cash in Malta, and for purchases of any foreign currency (including banknotes).

Subject to exchange control permission, companies controlled by nonresidents may maintain foreign currency accounts in Malta and abroad.

Imports and Import Payments

Licenses are required for the importation of items that need clearance for health, safety, security, and environmental reasons, as well as for particularly sensitive items, such as lace and gold and silver filigree. Other products may be imported without restriction under open general licenses (OGL). The importation of barley, maize, hard and soft wheat, boneless beef, fresh fish, and certain petroleum products is undertaken only by a state-owned enterprise.

Payments for all authorized imports may be made freely, provided that currency regulations are complied with and that supporting documents, including the customs entry form for imports over Lm 20,000 and related import license, where applicable, are submitted to the intermediary bank. As a form of exchange cover, export-oriented companies may retain foreign exchange earnings for a maximum period of four months to make payments for imports that are connected to their exporting business; on the same basis, import payments may also be offset against export proceeds.

Payments for Invisibles

Payments for invisibles require the approval of the exchange control authorities if the amounts involved exceed the limits delegated to the authorized banks. These limitations are indicative and are intended to prevent illegal capital outflows. In the case of leisure and business travel, there are no restrictions on payments for accommodation and transportation purchased in Malta or abroad with credit cards or Euro-checks. There are, however, limitations on the amount of foreign currency (cash and traveler's checks) residents may take abroad. In any calendar year, each person is entitled to an annual travel allowance equivalent to Lm 2,500. Business travelers are granted an exchange allocation equivalent to Lm 200 a person a day. Amounts in excess of the above limits may be granted upon submission of documentary proof of need. The allowance for educational expenses is unlimited. Remittances for cash gifts and family maintenance may be made up to an annual maximum of Lm 250 a person and Lm 2,000 a person, respectively, directly through credit institutions. Remittances above these limits require exchange control approval.

The transfer of profits, dividends, and interest from approved foreign investments is permitted without limit, but is subsequent to verification by the Central Bank.

The Insurance Business Act of 1981 requires that life insurance be contracted only in Maltese currency with duly licensed insurance companies.

Nonresident travelers may export foreign currency up to the amount they brought in and declared to customs on entry; they may export up to Lm 25 a person in Maltese notes and coins.

Exports and Export Proceeds

With the exception of works of art and certain essential goods, all products may be exported freely. However, certain textile products for export to countries in the European Union (EU) require licenses for administrative purposes. Export proceeds must be received within six months of shipment. Exporters may retain export proceeds in foreign currency deposit accounts with authorized banks for up to four months to make import payments connected with their exporting business.

Export trade is supported by the Government in a variety of ways. Manufactured exports and tourism benefit from extensive investment and training incentives provided by the Government. The Malta Export Trade Corporation acts as a technical unit and support agency for the development and promotion of trade (mainly exports) in both manufactured goods and selected services. Malta is the beneficiary of trade concessions granted by its main trade partners. The Association Agreement with the EU signed in 1970 guarantees that manufactured products (excluding processed foodstuffs) originat-

---

[5]Nonresidents are defined as persons who are not residents. Residents are defined as persons who are living in Malta and either have lived in Malta for at least three years or intend to continue living in Malta for at least three years.

ing in Malta may enter the EU duty free, subject to the rules of origin. Exports also benefit from the Generalized System of Preference treatment granted by Australia, Canada, Japan, New Zealand, the United States, the European Free Trade Association, and a number of other countries.

Proceeds from Invisibles

Receipts from invisibles must be offered for sale to an authorized bank. Travelers may bring in any amount in foreign currency notes. Without the authorization of the Minister of Finance, only Lm 50 in notes and coins that are or have been legal tender in Malta may be imported.

Capital

Applications for direct investment in Malta by nonresidents must be approved in advance by the Ministry of Finance. Due regard is given to the purpose of the investment and the potential benefits accruing to the local economy. The remittance of liquidation proceeds from such investments requires approval from the Central Bank; such approval is always granted, contingent on compliance with certain formalities, such as the submission of documentary evidence of the original investment. Exchange control approval is required for residents to issue or transfer securities to nonresidents and vice versa; approval, however, is not required for purchases by nonresidents of financial instruments listed on the Malta Stock Exchange.

Under the Immovable Property (Acquisition by Nonresidents) Act of 1974, administered by the Ministry of Finance, nonresidents may acquire immovable property in Malta only for their own use, with the permission of the Minister, on the condition that the cost of property to be acquired is not less than Lm 15,000.[6]

All transfers abroad of a capital nature by residents require approval from the Central Bank, unless they fall under the authority delegated to credit institutions. Applications for direct investment overseas are considered on their own merits. Portfolio investment abroad by residents is permitted by the Central Bank under certain conditions: the

resident must be over 18 and must not invest more than Lm 2,500 a year.

Capital receipts repatriated by residents must be either surrendered to a credit institution for conversion into domestic currency or held in the form of an interest-earning foreign currency account with a credit institution. Residents are permitted to hold foreign currency in the form of cash up to a maximum limit equivalent to Lm 1,000.

Although applications by residents to purchase real estate abroad are not usually permitted, the Central Bank considers each case on its own merits. Residents are, however, allowed to switch financial investments already held overseas into real estate assets situated outside Malta.

Foreign nationals who have been residing in Malta and are taking up residence abroad are allowed to transfer all of their assets to their new country of residence. Emigrating Maltese nationals may transfer all assets abroad without limit. Credit institutions, other than those licensed to borrow and lend only outside Malta (that is, offshore banks), may hold foreign assets in their portfolio up to a limit specified by the Central Bank; this limit is exclusive of foreign assets held to back foreign currency liabilities. Credit institutions may extend loans in foreign currencies to residents up to an amount equivalent to a proportion of their foreign currency liabilities.

Gold

Malta has issued 23 denominations of gold coins, which are legal tender. Residents are allowed to hold coins and acquire jewelry but must obtain permission from the Central Bank to purchase and sell any gold coins that are not legal tender. The importation of gold coins is controlled to ensure that such coins are used for genuine numismatic purposes. A specific import license is required for the importation of gold coins, gold bullion, and manufactured and semimanufactured articles of gold; imports of filigree work of gold and silver are restricted. Subject to exchange control permission, authorized importers may import gold bullion solely for the use of jewelers and other industrial users. The exportation of gold by residents other than the monetary authorities also requires exchange control permission. Gold bullion and gold coins are free of import duty.

Changes During 1994

Exchange Arrangement

November 30. Malta formally accepted the obligations of Article VIII, Sections 2, 3, and 4 of the Articles of Agreement.

---

[6]For the purposes of this act, the term nonresident includes individuals who are not residing in Malta but excludes Maltese citizens living abroad and foreign spouses of citizens of Malta; as well as any association of persons, or any entity, whether corporate or not, if (1) it is registered outside Malta; (2) it has its principal place of residence or business outside Malta; (3) 25 percent or more of its shares or other capital is owned by a nonresident person; or (4) it is in any manner, whether directly or indirectly, controlled by one or more nonresident persons.

Imports and Import Payments

March 3. Used motor cars were exempted from import-licensing control.

April 18. Imports of evaporated milk were removed from state monopoly.

Payments for Invisibles

January 1. Approval authority for the transfer of funds abroad to other family members was delegated to credit institutions for amounts not exceeding Lm 2,000 a year.

January 1. The requirement of an auditor's certificate for the transfer of profits and dividends to nonresidents was eliminated.

Exports and Export Proceeds

January 1. The period during which export proceeds are allowed to be retained in foreign currency accounts with local commercial banks was extended to four months.

Capital

January 1. The maximum annual amount that a resident over 18 years of age can invest in foreign currency was raised from Lm 1,000 to Lm 2,500 annually.

January 1. The maximum amount of foreign currency that a resident may keep in his or her possession was raised to Lm 1,000 from Lm 50.

January 1. Proceeds from life insurance policies or from compensation awards for disability and similar cases became fully eligible for investment overseas without exchange control approval.

Changes During 1995

Exchange Arrangement

March 20. The Central Bank began quoting the exchange rates for the Maltese lira. Deals with credit institutions may be made in deutsche mark, pounds sterling, and U.S. dollars, in amounts of not less than Lm 150,000; the interbank market would be al-

lowed to handle transactions in smaller amounts. The Central Bank, in addition, ceased to cover forward deals of credit institutions.

Imports and Import Payments

January 16. Imports of boneless beef were removed from state monopoly.

Payments for Invisibles

January 1. The travel allowance to which residents are entitled was increased to Lm 2,500 for every trip, irrespective of the purpose of the trip.

January 1. The maximum annual amount of funds each resident may transfer abroad to other family members or as a cash gift under the authority delegated to credit institutions was raised to Lm 2,500.

January 1. Authority to approve the payment of dividends to nonresidents was delegated to credit institutions.

Capital

January 1. Resident individuals and companies were allowed to invest directly up to Lm 50,000 a year in overseas firms.

January 1. The maximum annual amount of foreign currency that residents over 18 years of age are allowed to invest was raised to Lm 5,000 from Lm 2,000. Resident companies were allowed to invest up to Lm 5,000 a year in foreign currency.

January 1. Loans of up to Lm 5,000 between residents and nonresidents were allowed to be made through credit institutions. Resident companies were allowed to obtain loans in excess of Lm 5,000 from foreign sources, provided that they are in a position to produce updated audited accounts. However, in cases where such borrowing is for a period of less than three years' maturity, approval authority from the Central Bank would be required.

Gold

January 1. Gold bullion and gold coins were subject to a value-added tax.

REPUBLIC OF THE MARSHALL ISLANDS

(Position as of December 31, 1994)

Exchange Arrangement

The currency of the Republic of the Marshall Islands is the U.S. Dollar.[1] There is no central monetary institution and there are no exchange control regulations. The authorities do not buy or sell foreign exchange. Foreign exchange transactions are handled by three commercial banks, which are authorized foreign exchange dealers. These commercial banks buy and sell foreign exchange at the rates quoted in the international markets. Forward transactions may be conducted through these commercial banks without restriction. There are no taxes or subsidies on purchases or sales of foreign exchange.

The Republic of the Marshall Islands formally accepted the obligations of Article VIII, Sections 2, 3, and 4 of the Fund Agreement, as from May 21, 1992.

Administration of Control

There are no exchange control regulations.

Prescription of Currency

Both outward and inward payments may be settled in U.S. currency or in any other convertible currency.

Imports and Import Payments

Imports are not subject to import-licensing requirements, but importers must obtain a business license. Imports of certain products are prohibited for environmental, health, safety, or social reasons.

Specific and ad valorem duties are levied under the Import Duties Act of 1989. Specific duties are levied at the following rates: cigarettes, 50 cents a pack (of 20); carbonated nonalcoholic beverages, 25 cents a can or bottle (of 12 fluid ounces); beer and malt beverages, 50 cents a can or bottle (of 12 fluid ounces); spirits and distilled alcoholic beverages,

---

[1] The Marshall Islands must consult the United States if it decides to issue its own currency.

$25 a U.S. gallon; wines, $15 a U.S. gallon; gasoline, 25 cents a U.S. gallon; propane, 3 cents a pound; jet fuel, 15 cents a U.S. gallon; and kerosene, 5 cents a U.S. gallon. Ad valorem duties range from 5 percent to 75 percent. With the exception of food items, medicines, building materials, and heavy machinery, which carry a rate of 5 percent, most other products are subject to a duty at the rate of 10 percent.

Exports and Export Proceeds

There are no surrender requirements for export proceeds. Exports are not subject to licensing requirements, and there are no taxes or quantitative restrictions on exports. The purchasing, processing, and exportation of copra and copra by-products are solely conducted by the government-owned Tobolar Copra Processing Plant, Inc.

Payments for and Proceeds from Invisibles

There are no restrictions on payments for or receipts from invisibles.

Capital

Foreign investors are required to submit applications to the Cabinet and obtain a license in order to engage in business or to acquire an interest in a business in the Marshall Islands. The Cabinet has the authority to formulate policies regarding incentives and priorities for foreign direct investment.

All other inward and outward capital transfers are unrestricted with the exception that commercial banks cannot transfer abroad more than 25 percent of deposits received from Marshallese citizens, including domestic corporations and the authorities. This provision does not prevent a depositor from transferring any deposits abroad.

Changes During 1994

No significant changes occurred in the exchange and trade system.

MAURITANIA

(Position as of December 31, 1994)

Exchange Arrangement

The currency of Mauritania is the Mauritanian Ouguiya. The exchange rate for the ouguiya is determined on the basis of a basket of currencies comprising the Belgian franc, the deutsche mark, the French franc, the Italian lira, the Spanish peseta, and the U.S. dollar. The relative weights assigned to these currencies are based on the currencies' relative importance in Mauritania's total exchange transactions and are revised from time to time. The opening spot rates of the currencies in the basket against the U.S. dollar on the international foreign exchange market, as published by Reuters, are used to determine the ouguiya's daily exchange rate against the U.S. dollar. Daily exchange rates for 16 other currencies,[1] including those used in the basket, are obtained from the daily reference rate for the U.S. dollar and the cross rates for these currencies as published by Reuters. On December 31, 1994, the midpoint exchange rate of the ouguiya in terms of the U.S. dollar was UM 128.37 per US$1.

Commissions of 0.75 percent are applied to purchases and sales through commercial bank accounts. The Central Bank of Mauritania sells foreign currency notes and traveler's checks only for official travel and for other purposes judged to be exceptional; commissions of 1.75 percent are applied to purchases and sales involving traveler's checks and foreign currencies. There are no taxes or subsidies on purchases or sales of foreign exchange.

The commercial banks are free to set their exchange rates for foreign currency notes and traveler's checks, which they may buy on a no-questions-asked basis.

The average exchange rate is applied to foreign clearing transactions of the Postal Administration. This exchange rate is also applied to remittances by Mauritanian workers residing abroad. There are no arrangements for forward cover against exchange rate risk operating in the official or the commercial banking sector.

Administration of Control

Exchange control authority is vested in the Central Bank, the Ministry of Economy and Finance, and the Ministry of Commerce. The Central Bank has delegated to authorized banks the power to conduct transactions through convertible ouguiya accounts that it has approved and to sell foreign currency notes and traveler's checks to meet bona fide invisible payments up to specified limits. The Central Bank is authorized to obtain any information necessary to compile balance of payments statistics. All exchange transactions relating to foreign countries must be effected through authorized banks or, in some cases, through the Postal Administration. All imports require exchange control approval from the Central Bank. Special regimes apply to the imports of government entities and state enterprises. A tax of 3 percent is levied on international trade to finance the collection of statistics.

Arrears are maintained with respect to external payments.

Prescription of Currency

All settlements with Israel are prohibited. Settlements with other countries usually take place in convertible currencies.

Nonresident Accounts

There are two kinds of nonresident accounts: convertible ouguiya accounts and convertible foreign currency accounts. Convertible ouguiya accounts may be credited only with (1) transfers from other convertible ouguiya accounts, (2) 15 percent of the repatriated proceeds from fish exports through the Mauritanian Fish Marketing Company, and (3) 25 percent of the repatriated proceeds from exports by qualifying enterprises. These accounts may be debited in foreign currency only for expenses relating to exporters' production activities. Convertible foreign currency accounts may be credited only with proceeds from the sale of foreign currency and transfers from other convertible foreign currency accounts; they may be debited for any payment without approval from the Central Bank, but payments and withdrawals from these accounts may not be made in foreign banknotes without the prior approval of the Central Bank.

---

[1]Austrian schillings, Belgian francs, Canadian dollars, CFA francs, Danish kroner, deutsche mark, French francs, Italian lire, Japanese yen, Moroccan dirhams, Netherlands guilders, Norwegian kroner, pounds sterling, Spanish pesetas, Swedish kronor, and Swiss francs.

Imports and Import Payments

Imports from Israel are prohibited, and imports of a few goods are prohibited for reasons of health or public policy. Only holders of importer-exporter cards or holders of special authorizations from the Ministry of Commerce are permitted to engage in import transactions. Importer-exporter cards must be renewed every year. Debtors in arrears with the banking system cannot have their cards renewed. Prepayment of the minimum turnover tax (TCA) in the amount of UM 300,000 is necessary to obtain the card. Imports of all goods must receive foreign exchange approval from the Central Bank.

Import transactions must be domiciled with an authorized bank, except for imports directly financed from abroad. Import permits are auctioned monthly by the Central Bank. Only holders of importer-exporter cards, public enterprises, and other special enterprises can participate in the auctions. Permits are valid for one month. After buying the permit at an auction, the importer is entitled to purchase the necessary foreign exchange but not earlier than ten days before shipment of goods by a foreign supplier if a documentary credit is opened, or eight days before the payment is due if the goods have already arrived. Advance payments for imports require the prior approval of the Central Bank. The Central Bank authorizes only the payment of import bills quoting c. & f. prices, and all imports must be insured with the Mauritanian State Insurance and Reinsurance Company. There are special arrangements for imports in border areas.

There is a general customs duty rate of 15 percent, and a reduced rate of 5 percent applies to selected goods. Certain capital goods and various consumer goods, such as tea, salt, and medicines, are exempt. All imports from the West African Economic Community (WAEC) that are not subject to the regional cooperation tax are also exempt, as are some imports from Algeria, Morocco, Tunisia, and the European Union (EU). In addition to the customs duty, import taxes are levied at rates ranging from 5 percent to 166 percent (with various exemptions); a turnover tax is levied at a minimum rate of 10 percent and a maximum rate of 20 percent (with various exemptions); and a regional cooperation tax is levied on certain industrial products imported from WAEC countries in lieu of import duties that are levied on other imports.

Payments for Invisibles

Payments to Israel are prohibited. There are no limits on the acquisition and transfer of foreign exchange through the free market in banknotes and traveler's checks for travel, medical treatment, and study abroad. However, requests exceeding UM 15,000 a day for a trip abroad must be submitted to the Central Bank. Other payments for invisibles must be approved by the Central Bank. Foreigners working in Mauritania may transfer savings from their salaries up to varying percentages, according to marital status. At the end of their stay in Mauritania, they may transfer all their assets abroad. Travelers are not allowed to take out domestic banknotes.

Exports and Export Proceeds

All exports to Israel are prohibited. Only holders of importer-exporter cards and holders of special authorization from the Ministry of Commerce are permitted to engage in export transactions. Export transactions to all countries in excess of UM 20,000 must be domiciled with an authorized bank. Exporters must submit to the Central Bank for approval Certificates for Export, on which they specify the quantity, value, and destination of the goods to be exported, and they must undertake to repatriate and surrender foreign exchange proceeds. Export proceeds must be surrendered no later than the due date of the receipt, which normally must not be longer than 60 days after the date of shipment. Exports of iron ore are the monopoly of the National Industrial and Mining Company, and a special exemption applies to the repatriation of its export proceeds. Exports of demersal fish are the monopoly of the Mauritanian Fish Marketing Company. Exporters are allowed to retain 20 percent of their proceeds in foreign exchange accounts maintained at domestic banks.

A tax is levied on exports of fish and crustaceans, at rates ranging from 8 percent to 20 percent for specialized fisheries and at a rate of 5 percent for shrimp and lobster.

Proceeds from Invisibles

All amounts due from nonresidents for services and all income earned abroad from foreign assets must be collected; 90 percent of proceeds must be surrendered within four months of the due date of the payment; the remaining 10 percent may be retained in foreign currency accounts at domestic banks. The importation of domestic banknotes by travelers is prohibited.

Authorized banks may buy foreign currency notes and traveler's checks on a no-questions-asked basis. Only authorized banks may hold foreign exchange notes and traveler's checks. Resident and nonresident Mauritanians can freely import foreign exchange notes and traveler's checks, but they must exchange them at an authorized bank within 15 days of arrival. Nonresident non-Mauritanians must declare imported foreign currency notes and traveler's checks in excess of $2,000; they can re-export the declared amount deducted by the equivalent of UM 10,000 for each day of their stay.

Capital

Transfers of capital between Mauritania and Israel are prohibited. Capital movements between Mauritania and all foreign countries are subject to exchange control; capital transfers to all countries require exchange control approval and are restricted, but capital receipts are normally permitted freely, although the subsequent investment of the funds in Mauritania may require approval, as indicated below.

Residents must have prior authorization from the Central Bank to invest abroad. Foreign direct investments in Mauritania[2] and Mauritanian direct investments abroad[3] must be declared to the Central Bank before they are made. The Central Bank has the right to request the postponement of the projects within 15 days of receipt of the declaration. The full or partial liquidation of inward or outward investments must also be declared. Both the making and the liquidation of investments, whether Mauritanian investments abroad or foreign invest-

ments in Mauritania, must be reported to the Central Bank within 20 days of each operation. Direct investments are defined as investments implying control of a company or enterprise. Mere participation is not considered as direct investment, provided that it does not exceed 20 percent of the capital of a company whose shares are quoted on a stock exchange.

The issuing, advertising, or offering for sale of foreign securities in Mauritania requires prior authorization from the Central Bank, as does borrowing by residents from nonresidents.

The Investment Code of January 23, 1989 provides for various benefits for private investments in Mauritania and stipulates that profits and dividends accruing from these investments can be transferred freely.

Gold

Residents are free to hold, acquire, and dispose of gold in any form in Mauritania. All imports and exports of gold require prior authorization from the Central Bank. Exempt from this requirement are imports and exports by the Central Bank and manufactured articles containing a minor quantity of gold (such as gold-filled or gold-plated articles).

Changes During 1994

Exports and Export Proceeds

October 30. The proportion of export proceeds that an exporter may retain in foreign currency amounts with domestic banks was raised to 10 percent from 5 percent for services and to 20 percent from 10 percent for goods.

---

[2]Including those made by companies in Mauritania that are directly or indirectly under foreign control and those made by branches or subsidiaries of foreign companies in Mauritania.

[3]Including those made through foreign companies that are directly or indirectly controlled by persons in Mauritania and those made by branches or subsidiaries abroad of companies in Mauritania.

MAURITIUS

(Position as of December 31, 1994)

Exchange Arrangement

The currency of Mauritius is the Mauritian Rupee, the external value of which is determined by supply and demand in the interbank exchange market. On December 31, 1994, the buying and selling rates were Mau Rs 17.997 and Mau Rs 18.221, respectively, per US$1. A duty of 5 percent applies, under certain conditions, to purchases of gold coins.

Companies operating in the export processing zone (EPZ) and other Mauritian exporters and traders dealing in priority imports are authorized to engage in forward cover transactions in foreign exchange markets abroad through their banks in Mauritius. Companies operating in the EPZ and the service zone and certain other companies are authorized to maintain, with local commercial banks, accounts denominated in foreign currencies.

Mauritius formally accepted the obligations of Article VIII, Sections 2, 3, and 4 of the Fund Agreement, as from September 29, 1993.

Administration of Control

Exchange control is administered by the Bank of Mauritius under powers delegated by the Financial Secretary. The Bank of Mauritius issues foreign exchange dealing licenses, and commercial banks, as agents of the Bank of Mauritius, are authorized to approve and effect payments for current transactions. The Ministry of Trade and Shipping is responsible for issuing import permits where necessary.

Prescription of Currency

Payments to nonresidents may be made in Mauritian rupees from a nonresident account or in any convertible foreign currency. Similarly, payments from nonresidents may be received in Mauritian rupees from a nonresident account or in any convertible foreign currency. Mauritius maintains a bilateral payments agreement with Madagascar.

Resident and Nonresident Accounts

External accounts may be opened by residents and firms of other countries and may be credited with (1) authorized payments by residents of Mauritius, (2) transfers from other external accounts, and (3) the proceeds of sales to authorized dealers of any convertible foreign currency by nonresidents. These accounts may be debited for (1) payments to residents of Mauritius, (2) transfers to other external accounts, and (3) the cost of purchase of any convertible foreign currency or gold. The Nonresident (External Account) Scheme reintroduced on September 25, 1985 is intended to provide Mauritians abroad with incentives to transfer their savings to Mauritius and to open savings or fixed-deposit accounts with commercial banks in Mauritius in rupees and term deposit accounts (for a minimum of one year) in foreign currencies. Interest on such deposits is exempted from income tax. As long as they are abroad, holders of such accounts are free at any time to transfer the balances of their accounts, together with interest. As of August 16, 1993, the Bank of Mauritius no longer provides exchange rate guarantees for balances in nonresident accounts with respect to new deposits.

Blocked accounts are used to credit funds owned by persons and firms residing outside Mauritius and realized from investments not made with funds transferred from abroad, as well as funds representing emigrants' assets in excess of Mau Rs 500,000. Such accounts may be credited with payments made by residents of Mauritius and specifically authorized for credit to a blocked account; these accounts may also be debited for certain specified transactions. Funds from blocked accounts may be invested in Mauritius. Upon the realization of such investments, however, the proceeds are once more directed to a blocked account.

Imports and Import Payments

Importers must be licensed under the Licenses Ordinance. Under the Supply (Control of Imports) Regulations of 1991, controlled goods, as specified in the first schedule, require import permits from the Ministry of Trade and Shipping. Certain imports are subject to customs surcharges, and a duty of 17 percent based on the c.i.f. value is levied on most imports. Commercial banks are authorized to approve and transfer funds for import payments without limit.

Payments for Invisibles

Payments for invisibles related to imports and purchases of foreign exchange for travel are permitted without restriction. Residents may hold international credit cards and use them to pay for travel expenses abroad.

Resident and nonresident travelers may take out Mau Rs 350 in domestic currency. Nonresident travelers may take out any foreign currency they declared upon entry.

Exports and Export Proceeds

Exports of (1) articles made wholly or partially of gold, platinum, or silver; (2) diamonds, precious and semiprecious stones, pearls, and articles mounted with these; and (3) works of art are prohibited unless permission is obtained from the Bank of Mauritius. Exports of certain foodstuffs, including fruits, are controlled. The Mauritius Sugar Syndicate is the sole exporter of sugar. No tax is levied on the first 3,000 tons of sugar exports, but a uniform tax of 18.75 percent is levied on exports above that amount. Exporters are allowed to operate foreign exchange accounts at the commercial banks. All export proceeds must be repatriated within six months of shipment and offered for sale to an authorized dealer or credited to a foreign currency account to meet payments for imports.

Exports to Canada and the United States of knit shirts and sweaters of cotton, wool, and man-made fibers are effected under bilateral export restraint agreements.

Proceeds from Invisibles

Receipts from invisibles must be repatriated and offered for sale to an authorized dealer. There is no limitation on the amount of foreign currency notes and coins that may be imported, but travelers may not import more than Mau Rs 700 in domestic currency notes and coins.

Capital

Inward transfers of capital are not restricted. Outward transfers of capital are subject to certain restrictions. Foreign investors are allowed to repatriate their capital, without paying a tax and without prior approval from the Bank of Mauritius, if the investments are made with funds transferred from abroad, including capital gains. Proceeds from the sale or liquidation of investments not made through transfers of funds from abroad must be credited to blocked accounts. The blocked funds may, however, be released either for transfer abroad against payment of the 5 percent duty or for investment in Mauritius without payment of the duty.

Legislation permitting the establishment of offshore banking facilities came into force on January 1, 1989.

Emigrants to any country may take out, at the official rate of exchange and free of duty, the equivalent of Mau Rs 500,000 a family from their Mauritian assets upon redesignation as nonresidents, which occurs upon departure. The balance of an emigrant's funds must be credited to a blocked account; any releases that may be approved for transfer abroad are subject to a 5 percent duty.

Gold

Residents other than the monetary authorities are permitted to hold gold for numismatic purposes (gold coins of Mau Rs 100, Mau Rs 250, Mau Rs 500, and Mau Rs 1,000, and such commemorative gold coins as Mau Rs 200 and Mau Rs 1,000) or as personal jewelry and ornaments. The importation and exportation of monetary gold are prohibited, except when made by the monetary authorities. Imports of gold for industrial purposes are subject to a specific import permit. Exports of articles made wholly or partially of gold, other than jewelry constituting the personal effects of a traveler, are prohibited. Payments for private imports of gold coins and gold bullion are subject to a 5 percent duty. Imports of certain jewelry are subject to temporary customs surcharges.

Changes During 1994

Exchange Arrangement

July 1. The Bank of Mauritius stopped quoting exchange rates. The external value of the Mauritian Rupee began to be determined by supply and demand in the Port Louis interbank exchange market.

July 1. Foreign exchange dealing licenses began to be issued. Foreign exchange dealers were permitted to provide forward cover without restriction.

July 1. Commercial banks were no longer required to seek approval from the Bank of Mauritius to carry out international transactions.

July 1. The capital transfer tax of 5 percent was abolished.

MEXICO

(Position as of December 31, 1994)

Exchange Arrangement

The currency of Mexico is the New Mexican Peso[1], the external value of which is determined in the interbank market on the basis of supply and demand conditions. On December 31, 1994, the exchange rate was Mex$5.325 per US$1. No limitations apply on access to ownership or transfer of foreign exchange. Forward cover is available from commercial banks.

On November 12, 1946, Mexico formally accepted the obligations of Article VIII, Sections 2, 3, and 4 of the Fund Agreement.

Administration of Control

The licensing of imports and exports is handled mostly by the Secretariat of Commerce and Industrial Promotion (SECOFI). Foreign exchange policies are established by the Secretariat of Finance and Public Credit (SHCP) and the Bank of Mexico.

Prescription of Currency

In accordance with payments agreements with the central banks of Argentina, Bolivia, Brazil, Chile, Colombia, the Dominican Republic, Ecuador, Paraguay, Peru, Uruguay, and Venezuela, payments to these countries may be made through the Bank of Mexico and the central bank of the country concerned within the framework of the multilateral clearing system of the Latin American Integration Association (LAIA). Similar payments arrangements exist with the central banks of Costa Rica, El Salvador, Malaysia, and Nicaragua.

Resident and Nonresident Accounts

Mexican banks are prohibited from receiving domestic currency deposits from foreign financial institutions abroad or from non-Mexican exchange houses, except in cases (1) where such funds represent the counterpart of foreign currency sold to the Mexican bank where the account is held; (2) where the funds represent the counterpart of foreign currency sold to other Mexican banks; (3) where the funds represent the redemption, sale, or interest payments of securities held in custody in the Mexican bank in which the account is held, only if the securities were bought with the proceeds from any of the transactions defined in (1) or (2); and (4) where authorized on a case-by-case basis by the Manager of Provisions to the Financial System in the Bank of Mexico. Commercial banks are permitted to open checking accounts denominated in U.S. dollars in Mexico only for (1) residents in the northern border area of Mexico, (2) firms operating in Mexico in any part of the country, and (3) official representatives of foreign governments and international organizations and foreigners working in these institutions. Commercial banks are permitted to open, in any part of the country, time deposits denominated in U.S. dollars and payable only abroad for firms established in Mexico.

Imports and Import Payments

Import licenses from SECOFI are required for only 149 of the 10,065 items on which Mexico's general import tariff is levied, except for temporary imports of raw materials and intermediate goods for export industries. On average, import licenses cover the applicant's import needs for nine months and may be extended for three months. Import needs are estimated at 20 percent above the amount of previous actual imports but may be increased when justified. New licenses are issued only if the applicant can demonstrate that at least 70 percent of earlier licenses have been effectively used. For some commodities, "open-ended" import licenses may be granted, allowing imports to be effected during a period of six months to one year, subject to an overall limit. Depending on the importer's performance, the license may be renewed repeatedly.

All imports must be accompanied by an exporter's declaration of shipment. Since July 1, 1988, the import tariff structure has been based on the harmonized product description and coding system of the General Agreement on Tariffs and Trade (GATT). Imports from the member countries of the LAIA and other Latin American countries are subject to preferential tariffs. A free trade zone regime is granted until August 31, 1995 for certain regions[2] in the country, including the newly established border zone with Guatemala. This regime allows im-

---

[1]On January 1, 1993, a new currency, the new Mexican peso, equivalent to 1,000 (old) Mexican pesos, was introduced.

[2]These regions are the free trade zones of Baja California, Baja California Sur, Quintana Roo, and the partial free trade zone of Sonora.

ports into these regions without customs tariffs as long as the imported goods are not similar to those produced domestically in the same regions.

Payments for Invisibles

Payments for invisibles may be made freely. The contracting of personal insurance policies abroad is not restricted, but casualty insurance policies intended to cover events that will take place in Mexico may be contracted only with Mexican companies, including subsidiaries of foreign insurance companies established in Mexico. Reinsurance may be contracted with foreign reinsurance companies.

Exports and Export Proceeds

Most exports do not require licenses. Exports of a few specified items are prohibited. Under the Program for Integral Promotion of Exports (PROFIEX), a drawback system of import duty payments by exporters and their domestic suppliers is in operation.

Proceeds from Invisibles

There are no restrictions on the use of proceeds from invisibles.

Capital

Foreign direct investments are normally allowed up to 100 percent of equity without prior authorization, with certain exceptions. (1) Investments in the following sectors are reserved for the state: oil and other hydrocarbons; basic petrochemicals; electricity; generation of nuclear energy; radioactive minerals; communication via satellite; telegraphs; radiotelegraphy; postal service; railroads; issuance of paper money; minting of coins; control and supervision of ports; and airports and heliports. (2) Investments in the following sectors are reserved exclusively for Mexican nationals or Mexican corporations with a foreign exclusion clause: retail trade of gasoline and distribution of liquified petroleum gas; radio and television broadcasting, with the exception of cable television; road transport (excluding courier and packaged goods transport services); credit unions and development banks; and certain professional and technical services. However, foreign investors wishing to invest in these activities may, through the Neutral Investment Mechanism, acquire shares in companies engaged in these sectors. (3) Investments in the following sectors require prior authorization: acquisition of more than 49 percent of the equity in a Mexican corporation if the total value of assets exceeds US$25 million; maritime transport and certain port services; administration of air terminals; cellular

telephones; construction activities, including the construction of pipelines for oil and its derivatives; oil and gas drilling; legal services; private education; credit information; security rating institutions; and insurance agents. In order to obtain prior authorization, investors must submit their proposals to the National Commission of Foreign Investment. Approval is automatic if a formal response is not made within 45 working days of the date of application. In reaching its decision, the Commission takes into account the impact of investments on employment and training of workers, the technological contribution, compliance with environmental provisions in relevant laws, and the contribution to the economy. (4) Ceilings on foreign ownership are applied to the following sectors: financial institutions; air transportation; manufacturing of explosives and firearms; printing and publication of domestic newspapers; agricultural land; cable television and basic telephone services; video text and packet-switching services; and transportation by air and land, and certain activities related to maritime transport. Mexican banks are authorized to grant loans in foreign currency for export activities.

Upon registration with the Ministry of Foreign Relations, Mexican companies with foreign participation may be allowed to own land for nonresidential purposes in restricted border (within 100 kilometers) and seacoast (within 50 kilometers) areas. The acquisition of land rights by foreigners for residential purposes in restricted areas must be effected through a renewable 50-year trust held by a Mexican bank and requires prior authorization from the Ministry of Foreign Relations.

There are no restrictions on portfolio investments.

Gold

Gold may be freely bought or sold in Mexico at the prevailing exchange rate.

Changes During 1994

Exchange Arrangement

December 20. The upper limit of the exchange rate band was raised to Mex$3.99 per US$1, representing a devaluation of 15 percent.

December 22. The peso was allowed to float, and the exchange regime based on the crawling peg was abandoned.

Imports and Import Payments

September 22. SECOFI imposed punitive import tariffs of 279 percent on bicycle tires and inner tubes, 181 percent on brass padlocks, and 149 percent on bicycles shipped from China.

October 27. An import tariff of 28 percent was imposed on fish flour from Chile.

Exports and Export Proceeds

February 2. Powdered milk was exempted from the licensing requirement.

FEDERATED STATES OF MICRONESIA

(Position as of December 31, 1994)

Exchange Arrangement

The currency of the Federated States of Micronesia is the U.S. Dollar.[1] There is no central monetary institution. A statutory banking board, established in 1980, regulates the financial system. Foreign exchange transactions are handled by three commercial banks, which buy and sell foreign exchange at the rates quoted in international markets. Forward transactions may be conducted through commercial banks without restriction. There are no taxes or subsidies on purchases or sales of foreign exchange.

Administration of Control

There are no exchange control regulations.[2]

Prescription of Currency

Both outward and inward payments may be settled in U.S. currency or in any other convertible currency.

Imports and Import Payments

Imports are not subject to any import-licensing requirements, but importers must obtain a business license. Imports of certain products are prohibited for environmental, health, safety, or social reasons.

Import duties are levied on an ad valorem or specific basis, as follows: cigarettes, carbonated nonalcoholic beverages, drink mixes, drink preparations, coffee, tea, beer and malt beverages, and wines, 25 percent; spirits and distilled alcoholic beverages, $10 a U.S. gallon; and gasoline and diesel fuel, 5 cents a U.S. gallon. Ad valorem duties are 3 percent on foodstuffs, 100 percent on laundry bar soap, and 4 percent on all other products.

Exports and Export Proceeds

There are no surrender requirements for export proceeds. Exports are not subject to licensing requirements, but exporters must obtain an export business license. There are no taxes or quantitative restrictions on exports. The purchasing and exportation of copra are conducted solely by the Coconut Development Authority. Commercial export documents are verified by the customs authorities.

Payments for and Proceeds from Invisibles

There are no restrictions on payments for or receipts from invisibles.

Capital

Foreign investors are regulated by federal and state authorities. They must obtain an application from the federal Government and submit it for review and action to the Foreign Investment Board of the state in which the business will be located. They must obtain a license from the federal Government to engage in business or to acquire an interest in a business in the Federated States of Micronesia. If a foreign investor wishes to conduct business in more than one state, an application for each state must be obtained from the federal Government and submitted to the Federal Investment Board of the state in which the business will be located and operated. Priorities for foreign investment are reviewed by the federal and state authorities from time to time. Although no special financial incentives are offered to foreign investors, a number of incentives are available under certain U.S. laws (e.g., duty-free access to the U.S. market for some products). Foreign investment in the real estate and construction sectors is prohibited in accordance with laws prohibiting land ownership by foreigners.[3] Foreign investors normally obtain long-term leases (usually up to 25 years with an option to renew for another 25 years) for land acquired for their business.[4] There are no restrictions on the repatriation of profit or capital.

Changes During 1994

No significant changes occurred in the exchange and trade system.

---

[1]The Federated States of Micronesia must consult with the United States if it decides to issue its own currency.

[2]The Compact Agreement with the United States exempts the importation, use, possession, and exportation of U.S. currency by U.S. armed forces and U.S. contractors or personnel from any form of regulation, restriction, or control by the Federated States of Micronesia.

[3]Article XII, Section 4 of the Constitution of the Federated States of Micronesia prohibits a noncitizen, or a corporation not wholly owned by citizens, from acquiring title to land or waters in the country.

[4]Article XII, Section 5 of the Constitution prohibits "agreements for the use of land for an indefinite period."

MOLDOVA

(Position as of February 28, 1995)

Exchange Arrangement

The currency of the Republic of Moldova is the Moldovan Leu (plural: Lei).[1] The exchange rate system consists of the official exchange rate against the U.S. dollar for noncash transactions, which is established in the fixing sessions at the Chisinau Interbank Foreign Currency Exchange (CIFCE), and the exchange rate for cash transactions, which is freely determined in the exchange market operated by exchange bureaus and other authorized dealers. The official exchange rate applies to foreign exchange transactions carried out by the National Bank of Moldova (NBM), including official external debt-service payments, and is used for accounting and tax valuation purposes. CIFCE fixing sessions are conducted three times a week at the NBM. Since February 1995, sessions have been conducted daily. Enterprises engaging in importing activities may purchase foreign exchange through authorized banks. On December 31, 1994, the average official exchange rate was MDL 4.27 per US$1.

There are no taxes or subsidies on purchases or sales of foreign exchange. There are no arrangements for forward cover against exchange rate risk operating in the banking sector.

Moldova formally accepted the obligations of Article VIII, Section 2, 3, and 4 of the Fund Agreement as from June 30, 1995.

Administration of Control

Foreign exchange transactions are governed by the Regulations on Currency Control in the Republic of Moldova, which came into effect on January 17, 1994. The NBM has the ultimate authority in the area of foreign exchange arrangements and is responsible for managing the country's foreign exchange reserves, regulating the currency market, and granting licenses to engage in foreign currency transactions. Institutions eligible to deal in foreign exchange are authorized banks and foreign exchange bureaus that are authorized to purchase from and sell to residents and nonresidents foreign banknotes and traveler's checks in any currency that is recognized by the NBM. Authorized banks and foreign exchange bureaus may set their own buying and selling rates for the foreign exchange transactions of natural persons, subject to a maximum margin of 10 percent between the buying and selling rates.

Prescription of Currency

Certain settlements with the Baltic countries, Russia, and the other countries of the former Soviet Union, and Romania are made through a system of correspondent accounts, in the national currencies of the parties as well as in hard currencies. The majority of settlements with these countries are effected through commercial banks. With other countries the settlements are made in hard currencies.

Resident and Nonresident Accounts

Resident natural and juridical persons may open currency accounts, which they may use at their own discretion at authorized banks. Since November 15, 1994, the surrender requirement of hard currency on the residents' accounts was abolished. The source of foreign exchange is not subject to investigation. All foreign currency earnings of residents must be deposited in their accounts at authorized banks in the Republic of Moldova. The opening of current and other accounts by Moldova residents in foreign banks abroad requires approval from the NBM. Account holders may not use foreign exchange balances in their accounts to settle domestic transactions.

Nonresidents with foreign currency deposits at authorized banks in Moldova may freely transfer the balances abroad or sell them on the foreign exchange market through authorized banks.

Nonresident entities with accounts in Moldovan lei received as a result of current international operation with residents of the Republic of Moldova, may convert MDL into any other currency and repatriate it.

Imports and Exports

A few products (medicine, medical equipment, chemicals, and industrial waste) are subject to licenses for the purpose of protecting the consumer and ensuring compliance with domestic standards. Imports from the countries of the former Soviet Union are not subject to any taxes, except for a license fee of 0.1 percent of the value of the goods, which is converted into

---

[1]The national currency, the Moldovan leu, was introduced on November 29, 1993 at the conversion rate of 1,000 Moldovan rubles to 1 leu.

the national currency on the date of payment at the rate established by the National Bank, and a customs fee of 0.25 percent of the value of the goods. Imports from other countries are subject to import tariffs, customs fees, and license fees. In September 1993, Moldova introduced a new tariff regime (amended in March 1994), under which most tariff rates range up to 50 percent. Energy, medicine, medical equipment, raw materials, cereals, and baby food are exempt from tariffs. The tariff rate for chemical products, cotton, and minerals is 3 percent; rates exceeding 30 percent are levied on alcoholic beverages (100 percent), cigarettes (70 percent), vehicles (50 percent), and TV receivers (50 percent). Exports of a number of goods (e.g., those subject to administrative prices, goods considered to be important for national security, medicines, and goods of cultural value) are subject to licenses.

Proceeds from exports must be repatriated within 60 days from the day stipulated for the receipt of payment, but not later than 180 days from the issuance of the custom declaration or the day a bill, statement, or protocol confirming that services have been rendered or work has been done. However, the NBM can extend the period for a valid reason. Proceeds from exports may be retained by exporters.

There are no taxes on exports except for a customs fee of 0.25 percent of the value of the shipment.

The customs tariff approved by the Parliament of the Republic of Moldova envisages successive reductions in the rates during 1995, so that they will not exceed 20 percent by December 31, 1995.

Payments for and Proceeds from Invisibles

Residents may freely purchase foreign exchange in the exchange market. For travel abroad, residents may purchase foreign exchange up to $1,000 in the exchange market for each trip and take it abroad without additional authorization. Payments by resident individuals in excess of $500 are subject to approval on a case-by-case basis under Moldovan law.

All proceeds from invisibles, except the earnings of workers residing abroad, must be repatriated.

Capital

All capital transactions and credits obtained from nonresidents require specific approval from the NBM. Loan agreements with nonresidents are required to be registered with the NBM.

Gold

A license is required to conduct international trade in gold. Regulations governing domestic trade in gold are established by the Ministry of Finance.

Changes During 1994

Exchange Arrangement

January 17. A new legal framework for regulating foreign exchange transactions and allowing residents to purchase foreign exchange for most current international transactions came into effect.

Imports and Exports

November 15. The surrender requirement on proceeds from exports was abolished.

Changes During 1995

Exchange Arrangement

June 30. Moldova formally accepted the obligations of Article VIII, Section 2, 3, and 4 of the Fund Agreement.

MONGOLIA

(Position as of December 31, 1994)

Exchange Arrangement

The currency of Mongolia is the Tugrik (100 Mongo per 1 Tugrik). The exchange rate is determined by demand and supply conditions in the interbank exchange market. The central bank may intervene in the market to moderate undue fluctuations in the exchange rate. The central bank rate is set by the Bank of Mongolia as the midpoint of the previous day's average buying and selling rates established by transactions among market participants. The central bank rate is applied to the public sector's transactions in imports and services, including debt-service payments, and to trade and service transactions conducted under bilateral payments arrangements. All other transactions, including sales of retained foreign exchange by public sector enterprises, take place at the free market rate. On December 31, 1994, the average (middle) rate in the interbank exchange market was Tug 415.5 per US$1.

Exchange rates for other convertible currencies are calculated on the basis of the cross rates of the U.S. dollar against the currencies concerned in international markets.

Administration of Control

International transactions are governed by the Foreign Exchange Law of June 1, 1994. The Foreign Exchange Law provides the framework for a liberal exchange system where the exchange rate is set by the central bank, based on market rates, and the public is free to maintain accounts in foreign exchange with authorized banks and perform current and capital international transactions.

In accordance with the Fund's Executive Board Decision No. 144–(52/51), adopted on August 14, 1952, Mongolia notified the Fund on November 4, 1994 that restrictions had been imposed on certain transactions with the Federal Republic of Yugoslavia (Serbia/Montenegro).

Prescription of Currency

Trade with all countries is conducted at world prices in convertible currencies. Trade with certain former members of the Council for Mutual Economic Assistance (CMEA) is conducted on an ad hoc basis under bilateral arrangements concluded before 1991. While some of the outstanding balances under the clearing arrangements of the former International Bank for Economic Cooperation (IBEC) have been settled, others are still under negotiation. Under the inoperative bilateral trade arrangement, there are also outstanding balances with China, the Islamic State of Afghanistan, and the Federal Republic of Yugoslavia (Serbia/Montenegro). Mongolia maintains a bilateral clearing agreement with the Democratic People's Republic of Korea.

Resident Accounts

Resident Foreign Exchange Accounts. Resident persons and enterprises may maintain foreign exchange accounts at authorized banks. They may credit these accounts with retained export earnings and foreign exchange transferred from abroad and may use the balances on the accounts for any purpose without restriction.

Imports and Exports

Imports and exports are free of quantitative restrictions, except for the ban on the export of raw cashmere and for bona fide environmental, health, and security reasons. Imports of drugs, materials that encourage or depict violence or pornography, and items that could cause environmental damage are banned. Trade in the following items requires a special permit: historical artifacts, precious metals, weapons, radioactive materials, ferrous and nonferrous metals, and goods and services requiring licenses under international contracts and agreements.

Exporters are allowed to retain all of their foreign exchange earnings. Exporters may use their foreign exchange earnings for any purpose, including sale in the foreign exchange market or deposit in a foreign exchange account.

Imports are subject to a uniform 15 percent customs duty. Machinery and equipment imported by joint ventures and equipment used by disabled people are exempt from the customs duty.

Payments for and Proceeds from Invisibles

Foreign exchange for payments for invisibles is not provided at the official exchange rate but may be purchased without restriction on the interbank exchange market. Remittances of dividends and profits from investments in convertible currencies are permitted under the Law on Foreign Investment of May 1990 (see below). Proceeds from invisibles may be sold in the interbank exchange market without restriction. The importation and exportation of domestic banknotes are prohibited. There is no limit on the amount of foreign currency notes residents or nonresidents may import or export.

Capital

Foreign direct investment has been liberalized, and foreign investment by private corporations is now being encouraged. The Law on Foreign Investment of July 1993 has codified the procedures for establishing foreign firms in Mongolia and provides certain guarantees and privileges to foreign investors. Among its provisions are that these firms will not be nationalized and that foreign investors will have the right to dispose of their assets. Transfers of profits abroad are not restricted. The maximum rate of profit tax is 40 percent, and foreign investors are exempt from the tax for various periods (from three to ten years), depending on the sector and export performance. In addition, the law stipulates that entities with foreign participation may export at world prices or other agreed prices, and they may import or export directly or in cooperation with foreign trade enterprises. The law particularly encourages investment in export promotion, projects using advanced technology, and the exploitation of natural resources.

Changes During 1994

Exchange Arrangement

June 1. A new foreign exchange law was adopted, retaining the interbank market system but empowering the Bank of Mongolia to intervene more directly.

Administration of Control

June 1. A new foreign exchange law came into effect.

Prescription of Currency

April 1. The bilateral payments agreements with China and the Russian Federation became inoperative.

Imports and Exports

April 1. A ban was introduced on exports for raw cashmere.

June 1. The exemptions from customs duties for selected chemicals, wood products, industrial construction equipment, and motor vehicles imported for personal use were removed.

July 1. The list of goods subject to import duty rates of less than the uniform 15 percent was narrowed to 21 categories from 31. The uniform rate would now apply to seeds, flour, yeast, chemicals, sawed wood, timber, sacks, spare parts of audio and video equipment, electrical consumer goods, and spare parts for transport vehicles.

August 1. The export-licensing requirements for meat, wheat, and live animals (except for breeding) were abolished.

MOROCCO

(Position as of February 28, 1995)

Exchange Arrangement

The currency of Morocco is the Moroccan Dirham. Bank Al-Maghrib fixes a daily rate for the French franc on the basis of variations in the value of the currencies of Morocco's principal trading partners, weighted in accordance with the geographic distribution of Morocco's foreign trade and the pattern of currencies of settlement. Rates for most other currencies quoted in Morocco[1] are established on the basis of the daily dirham-French franc rate and the cross rates for those currencies in relation to the French franc in the Paris exchange market. On December 31, 1994, the exchange rate for the French franc was DH 1.67626 per F 1, and the exchange rate for the U.S. dollar was DH 8.9596 per US$1.

All sales and purchases of foreign currency are centralized in Bank Al-Maghrib, but authorized banks are permitted to offset purchases and sales on behalf of private customers in each separate currency. Each day, authorized banks must purchase from or sell to Bank Al-Maghrib the balances of their purchases and sales in each currency; transactions are effected at rates fixed by Bank Al-Maghrib. Clearing operations between banks are not permitted; thus, no foreign exchange market exists in Morocco. Bank Al-Maghrib also establishes buying and selling rates for transactions by travelers in banknotes, traveler's checks, and letters of credit denominated in convertible currencies (those listed in footnote 1 and French francs, but excluding Algerian dinars, Libyan dinars, Mauritanian ouguiya, and Tunisian dinars) and specified other currencies;[2] the authorized banks sell to Bank Al-Maghrib their excess holdings of banknotes and replenish them at Bank Al-Maghrib when necessary.

A forward foreign exchange cover facility is available for exports and imports of items benefiting from special customs arrangements. Forward contracts for the purchase or sale of foreign exchange that have been concluded between banks and their customers result in reverse contracts between the banks and Bank Al-Maghrib. They may be concluded in any foreign currency quoted by Bank Al-Maghrib for maturity periods ranging from a minimum of 1 month to a maximum of 12 months; the guaranteed exchange rate corresponds to the spot exchange rate, against the payment of a commission of 2 percent a year, of which a share amounting to 0.25 percent is retained by authorized banks; provisions are made for extending contract terms, revising contracts in part, or canceling them in whole or in part. Arbitrage operations may be executed freely in favor of nonresident customers.

Morocco formally accepted the obligations of Article VIII, Sections 2, 3, and 4 of the Fund Agreement, as from January 21, 1993.

Administration of Control

Exchange control is administered by the Exchange Office, an agency under the Ministry of Finance. This office has delegated the execution of the main exchange control measures to authorized banks.

Import and export licenses, when required, are issued by the Ministry of Foreign Trade. Imports not involving payment do not require authorization.

Part of the Port of Tangier is designated a free trade zone and is exempt from taxation and from trade, customs, and exchange controls.

Prescription of Currency

Payments between Morocco and the rest of the world may be made in any currency quoted by Bank Al-Maghrib (see footnote 1) or through foreign accounts in convertible dirhams or foreign currency accounts opened in Moroccan banks.

Resident and Nonresident Accounts

The following accounts may be opened and operated by nonresidents.

Foreign currency accounts in the name of foreign nationals may be maintained by natural or juridical persons of foreign nationality, who are either residents or nonresidents. These accounts may be freely credited with transfers from abroad with foreign banknotes, checks, traveler's checks, or any other means of payment denominated in foreign currency and with foreign currency withdrawn from Bank Al-Maghrib, following general or special

---

[1] Algerian dinars, Austrian schillings, Belgian francs, Canadian dollars, Danish kroner, deutsche mark, European currency units (ECUs), Finnish markkaa, Italian lire, Japanese yen, Kuwaiti dinars, Libyan dinars, Mauritanian ouguiya, Netherlands guilders, Norwegian kroner, Portuguese escudos, pounds sterling, Saudi Arabian riyals, Spanish pesetas, Swedish kronor, Swiss francs, Tunisian dinars, U.A.E. dirhams, and U.S. dollars.

[2] Gibraltar pounds.

authorization from the Exchange Office. They may be freely debited for transfers abroad in favor of the account holder or to a foreign third party, for the surrender of foreign currency to Bank Al-Maghrib and for the payment of checks denominated in foreign currency.

Foreign currency accounts in the name of Moroccan residents living abroad may be opened by individuals of Moroccan nationality residing abroad on condition that the initial deposit equals or exceeds the foreign currency equivalent of DH 100,000. These accounts may be credited freely with transfers from abroad, checks or any other means of payment denominated in foreign currency, foreign currency withdrawn from Bank Al-Maghrib following general or special authorization from the Exchange Office, the return on investments effected on the basis of these accounts, and transfers from another foreign currency account or from an account in convertible dirhams. They may be freely debited for transfers abroad, transfers to another account in foreign currency or in convertible dirhams, foreign currency subscriptions for notes issued by the Moroccan Treasury, and for surrender of foreign currency to Bank Al-Maghrib.

Foreign currency accounts of exporters may be opened freely by Moroccan exporters of goods and services who are already holders of convertible accounts for export promotion. Those who do not hold such an account must have the prior consent of the Exchange Office. These accounts may be freely credited with 10 percent of foreign exchange receipts in the case of exporters of goods and 5 percent in the case of exporters of services. The recording of foreign currency amounts corresponding to these rates must be effected simultaneously with the surrender to Bank Al-Maghrib of the remaining 90 percent or 95 percent as appropriate. These accounts may also be credited freely with the return on invested funds lodged therein and with transfers from another foreign currency account of the same holder. They may be debited for professional expenses covered by exchange regulations, investment with authorized intermediary banks, subscriptions for notes issued by the Moroccan Treasury, for credit of another foreign currency account or a convertible dirham account for exporters (CCPEX) opened in the name of the same holder, and for surrender of foreign currency to Bank Al-Maghrib.

Foreign accounts in convertible dirhams may be opened by natural or juridical persons of foreign nationality, who may be residents or nonresidents. These accounts may be credited freely with generally or specifically authorized transfers in favor of the account holder and with dirhams obtained from the sale to Bank Al-Maghrib of foreign exchange, including banknotes. They may be debited freely for payments in Morocco and for purchases of foreign exchange from Bank Al-Maghrib. Transfers between foreign accounts in convertible dirhams may be made freely, and there are no restrictions on the interest rate payable. Holders of these accounts may obtain international credit cards to settle their bills in Morocco and abroad.

Convertible dirham accounts may be freely opened in the name of nonresident Moroccans residing abroad. Overdrafts are not allowed, and there are no restrictions on the interest rate payable. These accounts may be credited freely with (1) dirhams from the sale of convertible currencies, including banknotes, to Bank Al-Maghrib; (2) transfers authorized by the Exchange Office; (3) payments of interest accrued on these accounts; (4) transfers from foreign accounts in convertible dirhams; and (5) transfers from term deposits in convertible dirham accounts. They may be debited freely for (1) the purchase of foreign exchange from Bank Al-Maghrib; (2) dirham payments in Morocco; (3) transfers to foreign accounts in convertible dirhams; and (4) transfers to term deposits in convertible dirham accounts. These accounts may also be debited freely, either for the benefit of the account holder or for other nonresidents, for the purchase of foreign banknotes, traveler's checks, or other foreign-currency-denominated means of payment.

Convertible dirham accounts for exporters may be opened by exporters of goods or services with Moroccan banks. These accounts may be credited with the equivalent of 20 percent of the foreign currency repatriated and surrendered to Bank Al-Maghrib in the case of exporters of goods or 10 percent in the case of exporters of services. Balances on these accounts may be used to finance expenditure contracted abroad and linked to the professional activity of those concerned. Fishing companies may credit to these accounts up to 100 percent of the foreign currency repatriated. Exporters have the choice of maintaining either foreign currency accounts or convertible dirham accounts for exporters. They may also hold both accounts simultaneously, provided that the overall percentage of export earnings to be credited to both accounts does not exceed 20 percent of foreign exchange earnings in the case of exporters of goods and 10 percent in the case of exporters of services, with a maximum of 10 percent to be credited to the foreign currency accounts in the case of exporters of goods and 5 percent in the case of exporters of services.

Convertible term accounts are designed to attract funds from nonresident foreigners who are not entitled to guaranteed transfers. These funds may be transferred henceforth within a maximum period of five years. The holders of such accounts may use the available funds, without prior authorization from the Exchange Office, to fund investments in Morocco, buy treasury bonds, purchase Moroccan marketable securities, settle expenses incurred in Morocco and, in the case of foreign corporations, provide their Moroccan subsidiaries with current account advances. They may also freely transfer the balances to resident or nonresident foreigners or to Moroccan nationals residing abroad. The beneficiaries of the proceeds of these accounts may use them to cover expenses incurred by foreign companies shooting films in Morocco; to purchase secondary residences under certain conditions; and to finance up to 50 percent of an investor's participation in investments in Morocco (the remainder must be financed with funds transferred from abroad). Funds invested with the proceeds of convertible term accounts may be transferred abroad without restriction in the event of liquidation or transfer, except for certain categories that are subject to a three-year waiting period.

Imports and Import Payments

Imports are not subject to restriction unless goods are included in the list requiring import licenses. After the elimination of 460 product items in March 1992, the negative list includes petroleum products, sugar, edible oil, cereals and products derived from these, as well as arms, explosives, and certain vehicles.[3] In addition, imports of products that affect public security, morale, and health may be prohibited. Except for goods imported by air, insurance policies for imports must be taken out with insurance companies in Morocco. However, for a limited group of goods, insurance policies may be underwritten abroad; this group includes externally funded imports, if the financing terms include foreign insurance, capital goods and equipment under turnkey contracts, or duly authorized investment programs, crude and diesel oil, gas, cattle, and wood.

For all imports, the importer must subscribe to a security—a certificate of import commitment—that must be lodged with an authorized bank, which may make payments related to goods and incidental costs upon submission of the required documents. Special procedures are applicable to specified imports financed with foreign aid or loans. Imports used for the production of export goods may be financed directly from the proceeds of foreign exchange claims of the same exporter within the framework of special lines of credit that Moroccan commercial banks are authorized to contract with their foreign correspondents. Moroccan commercial banks may make advance payments abroad for imports of capital goods up to 25 percent of the f.o.b. value of the goods.

Customs duties are levied on an ad valorem basis, with a maximum tariff rate of 35 percent, except for a limited number of agricultural goods, for which the maximum rate is 45 percent, and a minimum tariff rate of 5 percent on consumer goods not produced in Morocco. In addition to regular customs tariffs, fiscal levies of 10 percent, 12.5 percent, or 15 percent ad valorem are levied, according to the category of goods. Imports used to manufacture goods for export production activities are exempt from customs duties and other import restrictions under the temporary admission scheme. Preferential customs tariff treatments are also granted for imports of capital goods to enterprises in the tourist and shipping sectors and other industrial enterprises qualifying under the provisions of Morocco's Industrial Investment Code. Imports of a relatively small number of items representing about 8 percent of industrial production are subject to minimum import prices (reference prices) for antidumping or safeguarding purposes.

Payments for Invisibles

Authorized banks are permitted to make payments and settle expenses incidental to commercial transactions covered by the relevant import or export documents without authorization from the Exchange Office. Moroccan enterprises are permitted to settle in dirhams the expenses incurred by their foreign managers and nonresident foreigners working for or on behalf of these enterprises.

Foreigners residing in Morocco and employed in either the private or public sector or engaged in professions in industry, commerce, and agriculture may transfer up to 50 percent of their income, whether or not their spouses reside in Morocco. Retired persons and foreign spouses of Moroccans have the same entitlement; they may also freely contribute to their retirement or social security funds in their country of origin.

Commercial banks are authorized to provide Moroccan residents with a travel allowance in foreign

---

[3]Imports of sugar, cereals (and products derived from cereals), and edible oil are planned to be liberalized during the second half of 1995.

exchange equivalent to a maximum of DH 5,000 a person a year for travel purposes without Exchange Office approval. This allowance may be increased by DH 1,500 for a minor child on the passport of the beneficiary parent and accompanying said parent at the time of travel abroad. The same allocation may also be granted to Moroccan residents living abroad upon their return to their country of residence at the end of their stay in Morocco, provided they have not benefited from the 15 percent allocation on remittances effected 12 months previously up to a limit of DH 20,000. Residents of foreign nationality who wish to travel abroad may be granted foreign exchange equivalent to all of their savings from income. A foreign exchange allocation equivalent to a maximum of DH 2,000 a month may be granted to foreign nationals residing in Morocco to cover the cost of higher education for a child studying abroad. Business travel by exporters of goods and services may be financed without restriction by debiting convertible export promotion accounts or foreign currency accounts maintained with Moroccan banks. In the case of business travel allowances for others, annual foreign exchange allowances are approved by the Exchange Office on the basis of need, with a daily maximum limit of DH 2,000. These banks have been empowered to provide advance allowances of up to DH 40,000 to small and medium-size enterprises and of up to DH 20,000 a year for business travel by individuals not belonging to either of these categories. In all cases, business travel allowances may be added to allowances for tourist travel. Commercial banks are authorized to sell foreign exchange to persons traveling abroad for medical treatment up to the equivalent of DH 20,000 and to make transfers on their behalf for treatment abroad in favor of hospitals and medical institutions concerned. They are also authorized to transfer retirement pensions provided by public and private agencies in favor of persons residing abroad permanently.

Deep-sea fishing companies may maintain convertible dirham or foreign currency accounts with Moroccan banks. Convertible dirham accounts may be credited with the full dirham equivalent of foreign exchange earnings, and foreign currency accounts may be credited with 25 percent of foreign exchange earnings. The operating expenses of these companies, including travel expenses of employees, may be financed from these accounts. Foreign airlines operating in Morocco may transfer, without prior authorization from the Exchange Office, any surplus revenue from the proceeds of ticket sales, excess baggage, and air freight. Transfers with respect to sea and road transportation may be made directly to authorized banks.

Moroccan film distribution companies may transfer to foreign film producers or distributors user fees and other additional expenses related to the showing of these films in Morocco.

Commercial banks are authorized to sell foreign exchange to individuals studying abroad without prior Exchange Office authorization as follows: (1) an annual installation allowance equivalent to DH 10,000 and the same amount for a person accompanying a minor student leaving Morocco for the first time; (2) school fees to foreign academic institutions, upon submission of documentary evidence and without limit; and (3) a monthly llowance for living expenses amounting to the equivalent of DH 6,000 a month for nonscholarship holders and DH 4,000 for scholarship holders. In addition to these facilities, banks are authorized to effect the transfer of rent and corresponding charges in favor of the foreign landlord once the student or his or her legal guardian has submitted a properly drawn-up lease and a certificate of residence or any other equivalent document. Applications for additional amounts must be referred to the Exchange Office for approval, which is granted on proof of need.

Transfers relating to remittances for family maintenance are approved upon presentation of documentary evidence.

Visitors to Morocco are permitted to repurchase foreign exchange against presentation of exchange certificate(s) up to the amount remaining from the original conversion of foreign exchange into dirhams.

The exportation of domestic banknotes is prohibited.

Exports and Export Proceeds

Almost all goods may be exported freely. Only flour, charcoal, certain animals, plants, and archaeological items are subject to authorization. However, for phosphates, the Cherifien Phosphate Office (OCP) has the export monopoly. Mineral products are subject to an ad valorem export tax of 0.5 percent, except for hydrocarbons, for which the tax is 5 percent, and phosphates, for which a tax on phosphate exploration equivalent to DH 34 for each ton of gross phosphates has been levied since 1992. A 1 percent quality control tax is levied on exports of foodstuffs.

All exporters must sign a guarantee to repatriate and surrender foreign exchange proceeds. The foreign exchange must be surrendered within one month of the date of payment by foreign buyers specified in the commercial contract; in principle, this date must not be more than 150 days from the date of arrival of the merchandise. This deadline may be extended if warranted by business conditions and approved by the Exchange Office. Export proceeds collected abroad may be used directly abroad to finance imports of goods and raw materials of goods for export.

Proceeds from Invisibles

Residents of Moroccan nationality, including individuals and corporations, must repatriate foreign exchange receipts accruing from all their noncommercial claims and surrender them to an authorized bank. Other residents must surrender noncommercial receipts only if the receipts result from their activities in Morocco. Moroccans working abroad must surrender within one month all foreign exchange in their possession, but on departure from Morocco, they may export without restriction foreign banknotes obtained by debiting their accounts in convertible dirhams. If they do not have such an account, they may take out 15 percent of foreign exchange repatriated and surrendered 12 months before to Moroccan banks up to a limit of DH 20,000. If these facilities are not available, Moroccan residents living abroad may take advantage of the same DH 5,000 tourist allocation that applies to residents. Nonresident travelers may freely bring in foreign banknotes, traveler's checks, and other means of payment denominated in foreign currency. Resident travelers may also bring in foreign banknotes in any amount, as well as any other means of payment in foreign exchange but must surrender them within 30 days of their return to Morocco. The importation of domestic banknotes is prohibited.

Capital

The industrial investment code, which came into force in February 1983, provides for full foreign ownership of Moroccan companies in certain sectors and eases the repatriation of capital; it also grants fiscal and other incentives for foreign investment. In addition, an investment code introduced for the tourist sector in August 1983 offers tax and other incentives to domestic and foreign investors and provides for full repatriation of tourist-related after-tax profits, without any time restriction.

All types of investment are permitted without prior authorization from the Exchange Office, including (1) participation in the equity capital of a company being established; (2) subscription to the capital increase of an existing company; (3) purchases of Moroccan securities; (4) contributions to partnerships; (5) purchases of real property; (6) self-financing construction projects; (7) establishment or purchase of a sole proprietorship; and (8) operations to increase capital through the capitalization of reserves, carryovers, or reserve provisions that have become available or through the consolidation of partnership current accounts. Operations involving transfers of investment ownership between foreigners do not require the authorization of the Exchange Office.

As of September 1992, a convertibility regime was introduced in favor of foreign investment, which includes investment by foreign corporations, resident or nonresident foreign individuals, and Moroccans residing abroad. Such investment must be financed in foreign exchange or by a similar method: capitalization of reserves and profits, contributions in kind, consolidation of trade claims, or use of assets in convertible term accounts. Under this convertibility regime, exchange regulations permit the investors in question to invest freely in Morocco, remit the income thus generated directly to the banking system with no restriction on amounts or time, and repatriate the proceeds of the liquidation or sale of such investment, including any profits, also without prior authorization.

The holders of convertible term accounts may freely use funds in these accounts for the following purposes: for financing investment operations in Morocco in all sectors of economic activity, regardless of the kind of investment; for purchasing treasury bonds under the existing laws; for current account advances from foreign corporations to their subsidiaries in Morocco and any other placements the account holder may make; for acquiring transferable securities quoted on the Casablanca Stock Exchange; for settling living expenses and any other expenses in dirhams in Morocco incurred by account holders or their spouses, direct ancestors, and direct descendants (in the case of individuals) or by duly designated agents (in the case of corporations) with no limits on the amount; and for paying duties and taxes due in Morocco by account holders. Furthermore, the original holders of convertible term accounts may freely transfer funds from their accounts to resident or nonresident foreigners or to nonresident Moroccan nationals. The above-mentioned purchasers may use the funds (1) to cover all dirham expenses incurred in Morocco by foreign film production companies for shooting films in Morocco; (2) to purchase secondary residences (provided they are located in a tourist development area for the buyers' personal use); (3) to finance up to

50 percent of capital increases of subsidiaries of foreign corporations established in Morocco, provided that the rest is financed with foreign exchange transferred from abroad; and (4) to partially finance investment operations in Morocco in all sectors, regardless of the form of investment (in this case, financing of investment with debiting of convertible term account is allowed to cover only up to 50 percent of the investment, provided that the remaining 50 percent is financed with foreign exchange transferred from abroad).

External financing operations by Moroccan enterprises in respect of external credit facilities, purchaser or supplier credits, export financing credits, advances on partnership current accounts, and refinancing operations have been liberalized. Authority has been delegated to the banks to remit maturities due under these financing operations in principal, interest, and any applicable charges.

Transfers of capital by foreigners leaving the country permanently are limited to DH 25,000 for each year spent in Morocco.

Moroccan nationals residing in the country and corporations established in Morocco may invest abroad with the authorization of the Exchange Office. However, they are required to remit the income generated by their investments and, as appropriate, the proceeds from liquidation of their investments.

Gold

Commemorative gold coins with a face value of DH 250 and DH 500 have been issued and are legal tender. Residents may purchase, hold, and sell gold coins in Morocco for numismatic or investment purposes. Ten different types of foreign gold coins are traded on the Casablanca Stock Exchange, which does not, however, deal in gold bars. Imports of gold are subject to authorization from the Directorate of Customs and Indirect Taxes Administration. Each year, the Ministry of Finance fixes a quota for the importation of gold ingots. The quota is then allocated among jewelers and industrial users of precious metals. Exports of gold are prohibited.

Changes During 1994

Imports and Import Payments

May 10. Importers were allowed to change the bank with which their import documents are domiciled if an import transaction is finally settled by means other than a documentary credit or any other commitment of said bank in connection with the import transaction in question.

July 19. Goods imported free of customs duty under the commercial or tariff agreements as well as stationary diesel engines intended for agriculture and new tour buses were allowed to be imported pursuant to an import commitment (*engagement d'importation*) signed directly with authorized banks.

July 27. A list of goods subject to quantitative import restrictions was published.

November 16. The tariffs on 500 consumer goods not produced in Morocco were reduced to 5 percent.

Exports and Export Proceeds

February 24. Nonresident foreigners exporting goods of Moroccan origin valued at DH 50,000 or less and bought with dirhams during visits to Morocco were exempted from the requirement to sign export documentation.

July 25. A list of goods subject to quantitative export restrictions was published.

October 7. Formalities relating to certain exports by individuals or legal persons not included in the registry of commerce, as well as certain exports on consignment, and exports involving no payment and on a noncommercial basis were liberalized.

Changes During 1995

Imports and Import Payments

February 7. The following timetable was announced for liberalization of exports of unrefined sugar (January 1, 1995), refined sugar and products derived therefrom (February 1, 1995), oilseeds (March 1, 1995), cereals and products derived therefrom (April 1, 1995), unrefined oils and filterpress cake (May 1, 1995), and refined oils and products derived therefrom (June 1, 1995).

MOZAMBIQUE

(Position as of December 31, 1994)

Exchange Arrangement

The currency of Mozambique is the Metical (plural Meticais), the external value of which is determined by supply and demand conditions in the exchange market. On December 31, 1994, the average exchange rate of the metical of the central bank in terms of the U.S. dollar was Mt 6,497.00 per US$1, and the average exchange rate of the metical in the secondary market in terms of the U.S. dollar was Mt 6,618.00 per US$1.

There are no taxes or subsidies on purchases or sales of foreign exchange. There are no arrangements for forward cover against exchange rate risk operating in the official or the commercial banking sector.

Administration of Control

The National Planning Commission prepares annually, in consultation with the Ministries of Finance, Commerce, and Cooperation, as well as with the Bank of Mozambique (BM), a global foreign exchange budget for the following year as part of the Government's Economic and Social Program. Imports and exports are authorized through licenses issued for statistical purposes by the Ministry of Commerce. Invisible transactions are controlled by the Ministry of Finance. All five commercial banks—the Banco Commercial de Mozambique (BCM), Banco Popular de Desenvolvimento (BPD), Banco Standard Totta de Moçambique (BSTM), Banco de Fomento e Exterior (BFE), and Banco Portugues do Atlântico (BPA)—are licensed to operate in the foreign exchange market. Thirteen financial institutions—SOCIEF, SAFRIQUE, LUSOGLOBO, PROINVEST, AFZAL, CAMBIOS, ALKIS, MACROLPULOS, EXCHANGE HOUSE, LUNAT, MIAMI TRAVEL AND TOURS, MOCAMBIOS, and NATAIR—are licensed to operate in the secondary exchange market.

Prescription of Currency

Mozambique maintains a bilateral clearing agreement with Tanzania, but transactions under it have been suspended. It also maintains bilateral payments arrangements with Malawi, Swaziland, and Zimbabwe, but these relate to the use of national currencies for border trade. There are no other prescription of currency requirements.

Nonresident Accounts

Foreigners residing in Mozambique may open accounts denominated in foreign exchange at the BCM, the BPD, the BSTM, the BFE, and the BPA. They may also open domestic currency accounts in the same banks, but transfers of such funds abroad require proof that the amounts originated in foreign currency. Persons or businesses residing abroad may open nonresident bank accounts for specific purposes based on their legitimate interests in Mozambique; credits and debits to these accounts must comply with the regulations established by the relevant authorities. Withdrawals may be made for payments of taxes, certain types of debt (fees and obligations to the Government, government agencies, credit institutions, and insurance companies, provided that such debts are properly verified); family maintenance and expenses incurred by the account holders while visiting the country; and other payments for which authorization is obtained from the Ministry of Finance.

Imports and Import Payments

All imports exceeding the equivalent of $500 are subject to licensing by the Ministry of Commerce; licenses are provided routinely. The license specifies, among other things, the place of embarkation or disembarkation of the goods, the amount and currency of payment, and the source of financing. A negative product list exists for imports financed by donors' funds. In order to ensure that donors' requirements are met, the Office for the Coordination of Import Programs reviews import requests. Tied import support funds are allocated by the BM to the commercial banks. Individuals may import goods up to the equivalent of $500 without an import license if the goods are financed with their own foreign exchange resources and tied-aid funds are not involved. Preshipment inspection is required for all imports in excess of $5,000.

Payments for Invisibles

Payments for invisibles are processed by the five commercial banks upon presentation of authorization granted by the Ministry of Finance. Payments for invisibles related to authorized imports are not restricted. Individuals are permitted to buy foreign exchange up to certain limits to pay expenses associated with travel remittances for education and for medical treatment. An annual ceiling equivalent to $4,000 is applied to most travelers. Remittances for education abroad are subject to a monthly ceiling equivalent to $500, and remittances for health-related expenses abroad are subject to an annual ceiling of $4,000. Each ministry is subject to a ceiling on foreign exchange for official business and educational travel expenses. Foreign experts working in Mozambique may remit abroad all or part of their salaries, depending on the terms of their employment contracts. Nonresidents may export foreign banknotes up to the amount they declared on entry. Exports and re-imports of domestic currency are prohibited. An airport fee equivalent to $10–$20 in foreign currency is levied by the airport authorities on international departures, depending on the destination.

Remittances of profit and dividends from foreign direct investment may be made in accordance with the specific project authorization.

Exports and Export Proceeds

All exports are subject to a license. All export proceeds must be collected through the five commercial banks and may be sold in the secondary exchange market. In mid-1994, exports of cashew nuts were banned. On December 31, 1994, the export duty of 0.5 percent was suspended for a period of five years.

Proceeds from Invisibles

Commercial banks and other financial institutions may hold a limited amount of foreign exchange. Certain Mozambican nationals working abroad under officially arranged contracts (specifically, miners in the Republic of South Africa) are obliged to remit 60 percent of their earnings through the BM and convert them into meticais.

Capital

The Government and the BM are authorized to borrow abroad. Public and private enterprises are also allowed to borrow abroad, provided that loans are guaranteed by the BM. All foreign borrowing must be registered with the BM. The Foreign Direct Investment Law, approved on June 8, 1995, aims to encourage foreign investments owned fully by foreign interests or jointly with Mozambican enterprises. The law guarantees investors the right to repatriate capital and transfer abroad a portion of profits. The incentives for foreign investments include tax and customs exemptions for specified periods and for access to domestic credit. Foreign investment proposals are processed by the Foreign Investment Promotion Office.

Gold

The marketing and exportation of gold are regulated by Decree No. 11/81 of July 25, 1981. The BM is responsible for enforcing this decree. The importation of gold and other precious metals is governed by special regulations.

Changes During 1994

Exports and Export Proceeds

July 1. The exportation of unprocessed cashew nuts was banned.

September 1. Export procedures, including export authorization *(registo de venda)*, were simplified, and a uniform export duty rate of 0.5 percent was introduced. (On December 31, 1994, this duty was suspended for five years.)

Capital

June 8. A new investment law was introduced.

MYANMAR

(Position as of December 31, 1994)

Exchange Arrangement

The currency of Myanmar is the Myanmar Kyat, which is officially pegged to the SDR at K 8.50847 per SDR 1. Myanmar applies margins of 2 percent to spot exchange transactions, based on the fixed kyat-SDR rate. The buying and selling rates of the kyat for the deutsche mark, the French franc, the Japanese yen, the pound sterling, the Swiss franc, and the U.S. dollar, quoted by the Myanma Foreign Trade Bank, are determined on the basis of the daily calculations of the value of these currencies against the SDR, as are rates for the currencies of some member countries of the Asian Clearing Union (ACU) (i.e., the Bangladesh taka, the Indian rupee, the Iranian rial, the Nepalese rupee, the Pakistan rupee, and the Sri Lanka rupee). On December 31, 1994, the buying and selling rates for the U.S. dollar were K 5.8445 and K 5.9614, respectively, per US$1. The buying and selling rates for the Belgian franc, the Italian lira, the Hong Kong dollar, the Malaysian ringgit, the Netherlands guilder, and the Singapore dollar are determined daily on the basis of the appropriate cross rates in the Singapore market, and the buying and selling rates for other currencies are based on the appropriate cross rates published in the *Asian Wall Street Journal* or the *London Financial Times*.

Since February 1993, foreign exchange certificates (FECs) have been issued by the Central Bank of Myanmar through authorized dealers and licensed FEC changers. An unofficial parallel market for foreign exchange also exists. The rates in this market have been relatively stable for the past two years. FECs are widely used and serve the needs of not only visitors coming to Myanmar but also investors in Myanmar.

There are no taxes or subsidies on purchases or sales of foreign exchange. There are no arrangements for forward cover against exchange rate risk operating in the official or the commercial banking sector. Bilateral trade arrangements have been negotiated with neighboring countries; these arrangements do not provide for the extension of credit.

Administration of Control

Exchange control is administered by the Central Bank in accordance with instructions from the Ministry of Finance and Revenue. A Foreign Exchange Control Board headed by the Deputy Prime Minister allocates foreign exchange for the public sector.

Arrears are maintained with respect to external payments for the debt service of the central Government.

Prescription of Currency

Settlements with member countries of the ACU are made in the currency of the member country through the ACU mechanisms. Payments to other countries may be made in any foreign currency or by crediting kyats to an external account in Myanmar. Receipts must be collected in convertible currencies or to the debit of an external account in Myanmar.

Resident and Nonresident Accounts

Accounts in kyats held by nonresidents are designated nonresident accounts; all debits and credits require prior authorization. Foreign currency accounts of foreign diplomatic missions and international organizations and their home-based personnel may be kept with the Myanma Foreign Trade Bank or the Myanma Investment and Commercial Bank. Other foreign residents may open foreign currency accounts with any bank authorized to deal in foreign exchange. Transfers of funds between these accounts are permitted. Both residents and nonresidents are allowed to purchase FECs with foreign exchange earned from legal sources and may open foreign currency accounts subject to a 10 percent bank charge.

In addition to the use of FECs, the following regulations apply to the operation of foreign currency accounts by residents:

Foreign currency accounts of national firms. Private exporters who are registered with the Ministry of Trade may retain 100 percent of their merchandise export proceeds. Also for border trade, exporters are allowed to retain 100 percent of their earnings. However, 5 percent and 10 percent of proceeds from exports of goods and services and receipts from remittances must be paid as commercial tax and income tax, respectively. Exporters may open foreign currency accounts with their earnings at either the Myanma Foreign Trade Bank, the Myanma Investment and Commercial Bank, or private domestic banks, which are permitted to conduct foreign exchange business. Account holders are allowed to import under import licenses issued by the Ministry of Trade on the basis of letters of credit or on a collection basis.

Foreign currency accounts of national individuals. The following individuals are allowed to open foreign currency accounts: (1) Myanmar nationals returning from abroad after completing their assignments; (2) Myanmar nationals working abroad with foreign firms under official permits; (3) Myanmar seamen working with foreign shipping lines under existing regulations; (4) Myanmar nationals working with the United Nations and its affiliated organizations; (5) service personnel of the Ministry of Foreign Affairs performing their duties with Myanmar embassies abroad; (6) Myanmar nationals receiving pensions in foreign currency after serving with foreign governments or international organizations; (7) Myanmar nationals receiving foreign exchange for services rendered to foreign individuals, foreign organizations and firms, or foreign governments; (8) Myanmar nationals receiving their pay in foreign currency abroad for services rendered as agents to foreign firms; (9) Myanmar nationals receiving rentals in foreign currency for their tangible and intangible assets; (10) Myanmar nationals receiving foreign currency from an inheritance; (11) Myanmar nationals receiving foreign currency in compensation from a foreign firm or insurance company for the death or disability of a family member while serving with a foreign firm; (12) Myanmar nationals receiving foreign currency in the form of gifts from relatives or friends living abroad; and (13) Myanmar nationals holding the equivalent of at least $100 in FECs.

A foreign currency account may be opened in U.S. dollars only. With prior approval, account holders may use funds from their accounts to purchase air tickets for family visits abroad and to make payments for personal imports, for examination fees for their children, and for medical treatment abroad. Transfers of balances between accounts are permitted.

Foreign currency accounts of joint ventures and foreign participants. Under the Union of Myanmar Foreign Investment Law enacted on November 30, 1988, economic organizations formed with permits issued by the Union of Myanmar Investment Commission (MIC) and foreigners employed by these economic organizations are required to open both a foreign currency account and a kyat account. The following may be transferred abroad through a bank with the approval of the Central Bank: (1) foreign currency belonging to the person who brought in foreign capital for investment in Myanmar in accordance with regulations stipulated by

the MIC; (2) net profits remaining after all taxes and prescribed funds have been deducted from the annual profits received by the person who brought in foreign capital; and (3) balances of salary and lawful income earned by the foreign person for services performed in the state and remaining after payment of taxes and deduction of living expenses incurred by him or her and family members.

Imports and Import Payments

Import trade may be conducted with any country without restriction, except with countries under UN embargo or with which Myanmar has severed diplomatic relations. There are currently 22 bands of import tariffs, ranging from zero to 500 percent. Import tariffs are assessed on the basis of the official exchange rate. Agricultural implements, raw materials, and other essential imports are taxed at very low rates, while the highest rate is applied to luxury items. There is a long list of exemptions from customs duties, and the Ministry of Finance and Revenue is empowered to grant exemptions on a case-by-case basis.

Certain items, such as opium and other narcotics, playing cards, and gold and silver bullion, may not be imported from any source.

An import program for the public sector is prepared annually as part of the foreign exchange budget drawn up jointly by the Ministry of National Planning and Economic Development and the Ministry of Finance and Revenue. Some public sector imports are made outside the foreign exchange budget with revolving funds. All imports involving use of official foreign exchange are handled by the public sector through the ministries. With a few exceptions, private sector imports require import licenses for each transaction and are largely financed from the importer's foreign currency account. Import licenses may be obtained for priority items (List A), nonpriority items (List B), and "neutral" items. An importer wishing to import items on List B or neutral items is generally required to import goods on List A at a value equivalent to 50 percent and 25 percent, respectively, of the values of goods on List B and of neutral items. On a case-by-case basis, joint ventures with private interest may be granted open general licenses and are exempt from these requirements. Private importers must register at the Ministry of Trade as importers and renew their licenses annually. State economic enterprises may import goods for their own use and for resale with open general licenses, whereas government departments may import only for their own use. Imports by government departments are exempted from prescribed fees but those by the private sector are not. Most imports are effected on an f.o.b. basis, and shipments are made on vessels owned or chartered by the Myanmar Five-Star Shipping Line whenever possible.

All payments for imports not originating from border trade are made through the Myanma Foreign Trade Bank, the Myanma Investment and Commercial Bank, and private domestic banks permitted to conduct foreign exchange business. State economic enterprises obtain foreign exchange directly from the Myanma Foreign Trade Bank, within the approved foreign exchange budget, after receiving endorsement from the respective ministries.

Border imports require permits. Payments for border imports may be effected directly from the proceeds from border exports. Exporters of agricultural, forestry, and fisheries products are encouraged to import up to the equivalent of 25 percent of the export value of selected items that will contribute to the production in these sectors (Ministry of Trade Press Communiqué No. 5/91, dated July 12, 1991).

Myanmar nationals who have opened foreign currency accounts are allowed to make unlimited payments for personal imports with the funds from their accounts. Myanmar nationals working abroad under official permits who have not yet opened foreign currency accounts may make payments on their personal imports out of their accumulated savings of legitimate funds. Myanmar nationals and other travelers may bring in a reasonable amount of personal and other classified goods when they enter the country.

Payments for Invisibles

All payments for invisibles outside the public sector are subject to approval and are considered on a case-by-case basis. Payments for membership fees and tuition abroad and payments for subscriptions to certain foreign periodicals require prior permission from the Central Bank. Family remittances are permitted only for foreign technicians employed under contract by the Government; the limit is one-half of the net salary if the spouse is living abroad and one-third of the net salary if the spouse is living in Myanmar. Outward remittances of insurance premium payments other than for Myanma Insurance are not permitted. The remittance of pension payments to retired government employees is permitted only if the persons concerned have been nonnationals throughout their term of service and are now residing in their native countries. Personal

money order remittances to neighboring countries through post offices are not permitted.

Residents who have been granted an official permit to travel abroad are allowed to exchange $50 from the state's foreign exchange with their own domestic currency and also the equivalent of K 100 in the currency of the country of destination or, if that currency is not available, in U.S. dollar notes.

Nonresidents leaving Myanmar within six months of arriving may take out any balance of foreign currency they brought in with them and may also reconvert the remaining balance of the kyats obtained through conversion of foreign currency, including FECs. The exportation of Myanmar currency is prohibited.

Exports and Export Proceeds

Export trade may be conducted with any country without restriction, except those under UN embargo or with which Myanmar has severed diplomatic relations. Export taxes are levied on a small number of goods at both ad valorem and specific rates: an ad valorem duty rate of 5 percent is levied on oil cakes, pulses and cereals, and raw hides and skins; a specific duty rate of 10 kyats a metric ton is levied on all varieties of rice.

In practice, state agencies responsible for production may export any product in excess of what is needed for domestic consumption. Special permits are required for exports of antiques. The state economic enterprises have a monopoly on the exportation of rice, teak, petroleum and natural gas, pearls, jade, and precious stones and metals. The exportation of these products and other controlled items by foreign or domestic firms in the private sector may be permitted. Rice is exported by the Myanma Agricultural Produce Trading through the Myanma Export-Import Services; private traders and cooperatives are also permitted to export a number of beans and pulses, rattan, flour, and cut flowers under valid export permits issued by the Ministry of Trade. Border trade of certain products, including rice, teak, rubber, petroleum, hides, leather, some beans and pulses, maize, cotton, and groundnuts, is not permitted.

Export proceeds must be obtained in accordance with existing foreign exchange management regulations. An export-retention scheme is in operation, under which 100 percent of foreign exchange proceeds from merchandise exports and 90 percent of proceeds from most invisible exports may be retained by exporters. When exports are made on an f.o.b. basis, buyers are free to choose the carrier, but exports made on a c.i.f. basis must be shipped by the Myanmar Five-Star Shipping Line or on vessels chartered or nominated by it.

Proceeds from Invisibles

Ten percent of exchange receipts from invisibles must be paid as income tax unless the exchange control authorities grant a special waiver. Travelers may bring in foreign currency up to $2,000 or its equivalent without any declaration. Tourists arriving in Myanmar are required to purchase foreign exchange certificates equivalent to a minimum value of $300, but amounts in excess of this minimum may be reconverted into foreign exchange at departure. The importation of Myanmar currency is prohibited.

Myanmar nationals working abroad with permission from the Government are required to pay an income tax at the rate of 10 percent of their gross earnings in foreign exchange. Myanmar seamen serving abroad and Myanmar nationals working abroad under their own arrangements must pay as income tax 10 percent of their gross earnings. Myanmar nationals working abroad in UN organizations are not required to pay income tax. Myanmar nationals working abroad in private organizations are required to transfer to Myanmar as tax 10 percent of their gross earnings in foreign exchange through embassies in their country of residence.

Capital

Under the Union of Myanmar Foreign Investment Law enacted on November 30, 1988, by the Union of Myanmar State Law and Order Restoration Council, the Foreign Investment Commission is empowered to accept proposals for investment in Myanmar from foreigners for full ownership and under joint venture, with the share of foreign capital representing at least 35 percent of the total capital. To facilitate and promote foreign investment, the commission may grant exemption from customs duties and other internal taxes on machinery and equipment imported during construction of the project, spare parts used in business, and raw materials imported for the first three years of commercial production, as well as exemption from the income tax for a period of up to three consecutive years, including the year when production of goods and services began, or for longer than three years, depending upon the profitability of the enterprise. Furthermore, accelerated depreciation allowances may be granted.

The Government guarantees that an economic enterprise formed under a permit will not be nationalized during the term of the contract or during an extended term. In accordance with existing rules and regulations, repatriation of profits is allowed through banks after payment of taxes and prescribed funds.

Gold

Residents may hold and trade in gold jewelry, gold coins, and unworked gold in Myanmar. Imports and exports of gold are not allowed for the private sector. Jewelry for personal wear may be brought into Myanmar, subject to customs declaration at the port of arrival. Personal jewelry of prescribed value is permitted to be taken out, subject to the condition that the jewelry will be brought back to the country. No conditions are attached, however, to the taking out of personal jewelry that was declared to customs when it was brought into Myanmar.

Changes During 1994

Exchange Arrangement

April 1. The minimum amount of FECs that tourists are required to purchase was raised from the equivalent of $200 to the equivalent of $300.

NAMIBIA

(Position as of December 31, 1994)

Exchange Arrangement

The currency of Namibia is the Namibia Dollar. The Namibia dollar is pegged at par to the South African rand, which is also legal tender. The exchange rates of the Namibia dollar against other currencies are determined on the basis of cross rates of the South African rand against the currencies concerned in international markets. On December 31, 1994, the exchange rate of the Namibia dollar against the U.S. dollar was N$1 per US$0.2821.

Authorized dealers are permitted to conduct spot and forward exchange operations, including forward cover, with residents in any foreign currency in respect of authorized trade and nontrade transactions. Forward exchange contracts may cover the entire period of the outstanding commitments and accruals. Forward cover is also provided to nonresidents subject to certain limitations. Forward cover is provided in U.S. dollars only and is available to authorized dealers for maturities not exceeding 12 months at a time in the form of swap transactions involving Namibia dollars (South African rand) and U.S. dollars with a margin based on an interest rate differential between the two currencies. Special forward cover at preferential rates is provided in respect of import financing. Gold mining companies and houses may sell forward anticipated receipts of their future gold sales. There are no taxes or subsidies on purchases or sales of foreign exchange.

Under the financial rand system of the Common Monetary Area (CMA)—a single exchange control territory comprising Lesotho, Namibia, South Africa, and Swaziland—local sales and redemption proceeds of CMA securities and other investments owned by non-CMA residents, capital remittances by emigrants and immigrants, and approved outward capital transfers by residents are not allowed to be transferred in foreign currency but must be retained in the form of financial rand balances. These balances are transferable among nonresidents at a freely determined exchange rate, and the exchange rate for the financial rand is usually discounted from the commercial rand rate. These balances may be used to purchase securities (quoted and unquoted) and to finance investments in new firms and certain properties.

Exchange Control Territory

Namibia is part of the CMA. No restrictions are applied to payments within the CMA. In its relations with countries outside the CMA, Namibia applies exchange controls that are almost identical to those applied by the other CMA members.

Administration of Control

The Bank of Namibia, on behalf of the Ministry of Finance, controls all external currency transactions. Import and export permits, where required, are issued by the Ministry of Trade and Industry. The authorized dealers automatically provide foreign exchange for imports from outside the Southern African Customs Union (SACU)[1] upon presentation of the necessary documents. Advance payments for imports require the approval of the Bank of Namibia.

Prescription of Currency

All countries outside the CMA constitute the nonresident area. The rand is legal tender in Namibia and Lesotho but not in Swaziland.

Nonresident Accounts

Accounts of nonresidents[2] are divided into nonresident accounts, financial rand accounts, and emigrant blocked accounts. The regulations that apply to these accounts in South Africa also apply in Namibia.

Imports and Import Payments

There are no restrictions on imports originating in any country of the SACU. Imports from countries outside the SACU are usually licensed in conformity with South Africa's import regulations. For purposes of import permit issuance, Schedule IA of the Import Control Regulations of South Africa is currently enforced. These permits are valid for one year, are expressed in value terms, and are valid for imports from any country outside the SACU. At present, about 90 percent of imports require a permit. Namibia has the right to restrict certain im-

---

[1]The members of the SACU are Botswana, Lesotho, Namibia, South Africa, and Swaziland.

[2]A nonresident is a person (that is, a natural person or legal entity) whose normal place of residence, domicile, or registration is outside the CMA.

ports (through customs duties or quantitative restrictions) from countries outside the SACU, and, under certain conditions, from countries within the SACU. A wide range of imports from countries outside the SACU is subject to a general sales tax of 11 percent (as are locally produced goods) and to surcharges ranging from 7.5 percent on certain foodstuffs to 40 percent on nonessential luxury goods.

Payments for Invisibles

Authorized dealers are empowered to approve trade-related invisible payments without limitation and other invisible payments up to established limits, as follows: (1) annual allowances for tourist travel of N$19,000 for an adult and N$9,500 for a child under 12 years (basic annual allowances for travel to the neighboring countries—Angola, Botswana, Malawi, Mozambique, Zaïre, Zambia, and Zimbabwe—are N$6,000 for an adult and N$3,000 for a child under 12 years); and (2) business travel allowances of not more than N$1,800 a day, with a maximum of N$28,000 in a calendar year (to the neighboring countries mentioned above, allowances may not exceed N$900 a day and N$12,000 a year). Residents leaving Namibia for destinations outside the CMA are allowed to take the full applicable allowance in any form. The exchange control authorities may grant a larger amount if petitioned. There are no prescribed limits on remittances for education and family maintenance, and reasonable amounts are granted on a case-by-case basis.

Exports and Export Proceeds

Most exports are permitted without a license. All export proceeds are normally required to be remitted to Namibia and surrendered within six months of shipment or within seven days of the date of accrual. In order to enforce the repatriation requirement, exporters are required to cover forward their export proceeds within seven days of shipment.

Proceeds from Invisibles

Proceeds from invisibles must be surrendered within seven days of the date of accrual unless exemption is obtained. Upon entry from countries outside the CMA, residents and nonresidents may bring in a total of N$500 in Namibian banknotes or R 500 in South African banknotes. There are no limitations on the importation of domestic currency from Lesotho and Swaziland.

Capital

All capital transfers to and from destinations outside the CMA in the form of loans are subject to specific approval from the Bank of Namibia. Approval is generally given for borrowing abroad with a maturity of at least six months by domestic entrepreneurs, except for speculation or consumer credit. Authorized dealers are generally permitted to raise funds abroad in their own names for the financing of Namibia's foreign trade and for other approved purposes. Inward transfers of capital from non-CMA countries for equity investment are freely permitted, whereas applications by residents to retain funds in, or transfer them to, countries outside the CMA for bona fide long-term investments in specific development projects or for the expansion of existing projects owned or controlled by residents are considered on their own merits.

Proceeds from the sale of quoted or unquoted CMA securities, real estate, and other equity investments by nonresidents are transferable only through the medium of financial rand. Nonresidents are not allowed to purchase farms and residential properties with financial rand. Families emigrating to destinations outside the CMA are granted the normal travel (tourist) allowance and are permitted to remit up to N$200,000 (N$100,000 for single persons) through the medium of financial rand. Any balance exceeding this limit must be credited to an emigrant blocked account; the balance, including earned income, may be transferred under prescribed conditions. At the time of their arrival, immigrants are required to furnish the exchange control authorities with a complete return of their foreign assets and liabilities. Any foreign assets they transfer to the CMA may, through the same channel, be retransferred abroad within the first five years of their arrival.

Gold

Residents are permitted to purchase, hold, and sell gold coins within the CMA for numismatic and investment purposes only. All exports and imports of gold require the prior approval of the monetary authorities.

Changes During 1994

No significant changes occurred in the exchange and trade system.

NEPAL

(Position as of December 31, 1994)

Exchange Arrangement

The currency of Nepal is the Nepalese Rupee. The official exchange rate is determined, in practice, by linking it closely to the Indian rupee (NRs 1.6 per Rs 1 at the end of 1994), with cross rates against other currencies determined by commercial banks on the basis of demand and supply. On December 31, 1994, the buying and selling rates for the U.S. dollar, the intervention currency, were NRs 49.64 and NRs 50.12, respectively, per US$1.[1] Buying and selling rates are quoted daily for certain other currencies,[2] with quotations based on the buying and selling rates for the U.S. dollar in markets abroad. Convertibility between the Indian rupee and the Nepalese rupee is unrestricted in Nepal, and the Indian rupee may be used to effect all bona fide transactions. Purchases of Indian currency in excess of Rs 10,000 must be documented, and the purpose must be specified. Forward exchange cover for trade transactions is available and is provided only by authorized banks.

Nepal formally accepted the obligations of Article VIII, Sections 2, 3, and 4 of the Fund Agreement, as from May 30, 1994.

Administration of Control

Payments in convertible currencies may be made without permission, subject to the procedures prescribed by the Nepal Rastra Bank (NRB). All exchange transactions must be settled through authorized dealers (the Himalayan Bank, Nepal Bank Ltd., Nepal Arab Bank, Nepal Grindlay's Bank, Nepal Indosuez Bank, Nepal SBI Bank, and the Rastriya Banijya Bank). Nonbank authorized dealers are licensed to accept foreign currencies only for their services to foreign nationals.

Prescription of Currency

All current transactions with member countries of the Asian Clearing Union (ACU) other than India (i.e., Bangladesh, the Islamic Republic of Iran, Myan-mar, Pakistan, and Sri Lanka) must be effected through the ACU. Payments for selected imports from India may be settled in U.S. dollars; other imports and proceeds from exports to India must be settled in Indian rupees. Proceeds from exports to other countries must be received in convertible currencies.

Foreign Currency Accounts

Commercial banks may accept deposits denominated in Australian dollars, Canadian dollars, deutsche mark, French francs, Japanese yen, Netherlands guilders, pounds sterling, Singapore dollars, Swiss francs, and U.S. dollars and are free to determine the rate of interest paid on deposits. Eligibility for opening such accounts is limited, however, to (1) Nepalese citizens earning foreign exchange from working abroad (except in Bhutan and India) for more than three months; (2) international organizations and foreign nationals; (3) Bhutanese and Indian citizens residing in countries other than Bhutan and India; and (4) exporters who are allowed to deposit up to 100 percent of export earnings in a foreign exchange account to cover trade-related expenses. Current accounts may be opened with a minimum of $500 (or the equivalent in another currency), and time deposits with a minimum of $3,000 (or the equivalent). Nonresidents may withdraw their deposits at any time and convert them into any convertible currency at the authorized banks.

Nonresident Accounts

Foreign diplomats, foreign nationals working in projects financed with foreign-donated funds under bilateral or multilateral agreements with the Government, and nonresidents may freely open foreign currency accounts with Nepalese banks. Accounts may be maintained in all specified convertible currencies, and balances on these accounts may be freely transferred abroad. Nonresidents who receive or bring into Nepal foreign currencies, which they convert into Nepalese rupees and deposit with a Nepalese bank, may reconvert them for transfer out of the country, subject to the prior approval of the NRB.

Imports and Import Payments

Most private sector imports are allowed under open general licenses (OGL). However, imports of certain items, such as arms, ammunition, wireless

---

[1] The exchange rate system was unified in February 1993.

[2] Australian dollars, Canadian dollars, deutsche mark, French francs, Indian rupees, Japanese yen, Netherlands guilders, pounds sterling, Singapore dollars, and Swiss francs. In addition, buying rates are quoted for Austrian schillings, Belgian francs, Danish kroner, Hong Kong dollars, Italian lire, Saudi Arabian riyals, and Swedish kronor.

transmitters, precious metals, and jewelry (except under baggage rules), require special permission from the Government.

Silver is mostly imported by the NRB and sold to silver jewelers and handicraft-exporting industries through the commercial banks. However, since March 1994, imports of silver up to 150 kilograms have been allowed for those who have stayed abroad more than one month and have an official source of foreign exchange earnings.

Nepalese citizens returning from abroad who have spent at least 15 nights out of the country are allowed to bring in goods worth NRs 1,000, free of customs duties and sales taxes. Those who have official sources of foreign exchange earnings and have stayed abroad for more than one month are allowed additional imports with proper documentation.

Payments for Invisibles

Payments for invisibles are not restricted, provided that applications for foreign exchange are supported by documentary proof of need and the amounts are reasonable. Nepalese and Indian currencies may not be exported to countries other than India, and they may be taken to India only by Nepalese and Indian nationals. Foreign banknotes, other than Indian banknotes, may not be taken out by residents without permission. Nonresidents may take out the unchanged amount of any foreign banknotes they bring in; however, nonresidents other than Indian nationals may not take out Nepalese or Indian banknotes. Since April 1993, Nepalese travelers and migrant workers are allowed to take out of the country the equivalent of $1,500 a year.

Exports and Export Proceeds

Proceeds from exports must be repatriated within 180 days of receipt but are not required to be surrendered. Exports valued at more than $1,000 to countries other than India are allowed only against irrevocable letters of credit or advance payments by foreign banks. Exports of items having archaeological and religious importance and certain other exports, including old coins, narcotics, and explosive materials, are prohibited. The re-exportation to India of non-Nepalese goods and the re-exportation to any destination of goods imported from India are prohibited.

The export volume of ready-made garments to the United States is restricted by a quota that increases annually by 6 percent. Import duties paid by exporters on goods from bonded warehouses are refunded. When exporters purchase imports from the bonded warehouses, the duty payable is deposited in an escrow bank account and is released when the garments made from these imports are exported and the documentation required to verify the use of imports is provided.

Foreign tourists leaving Nepal may take out as souvenirs, without permission, Nepalese goods whose value does not exceed the value of the foreign currency they exchanged in Nepal.

Commercial banks may grant pre-export credit of up to 70 percent of the f.o.b. value of products specified by the Government to all individuals and institutions holding irrevocable letters of credit opened or endorsed by foreign banks acceptable to the Nepalese banks. Such credit may be provided for a maximum of three months; this period may be extended without penalty under special circumstances beyond the control of the exporter.

Proceeds from Invisibles

Nepalese and Indian currencies may be brought in only from India and only by Nepalese and Indian nationals. Nonresidents other than Indian nationals are not allowed to bring in Nepalese or Indian banknotes. Residents and nonresidents may freely bring in other foreign banknotes but must declare them if the amount exceeds the equivalent of $2,000.

Capital

Repatriation of capital requires prior approval from the NRB; approval is automatically granted, provided capital transfers have been cleared by the Industrial Promotion Board. Nepalese citizens, whether they reside in Nepal or not, are prohibited from making any type of investment in foreign countries, except investment specifically exempted by government notice; the exemptions include the purchase and sale of insurance policies abroad, and investments abroad by any banking or financial institution incorporated in Nepal.

All foreign direct investment in Nepal requires prior approval in the form of a guarantee from the Industrial Promotion Board. Foreign investors who have obtained an investment guarantee are eligible to make remittances abroad for the following items: all or part of the sales proceeds of investment, dividends, interest, or principal repayment; amounts arising from the transfer of technology; and compensations on acquired assets. The Industrial Enterprises Act contains provisions regarding local equity requirements for foreign investment in enterprises. Foreign investment is not permitted in cottage, small-scale, or defense-related industries unless substantial transfers of technology are involved.

Foreign investors can hold 100 percent equity in large- and medium-scale industries. Small-scale industries are defined as those with fixed assets valued at up to NRs 10 million; for medium-scale industries, the asset value limit is NRs 50 million, and those with fixed assets in excess of NRs 50 million are considered large-scale industries.

Gold

Residents may freely purchase, hold, and sell gold in any form in Nepal. Since March 1993, imports of gold up to 10 kilograms have been allowed for those who have stayed abroad for more than one month and have an official source of foreign earnings.

Changes During 1994

Exchange Arrangement

May 30. Nepal formally accepted the obligations of Article VIII, Sections 2, 3, and 4 of the Fund Agreement.

NETHERLANDS

(Position as of December 31, 1994)

Exchange Arrangement

The currency of the Netherlands is the Netherlands Guilder. The Netherlands participates with Austria, Belgium, Denmark, France, Germany, Ireland, Luxembourg, Portugal, and Spain in the exchange rate and intervention mechanism (ERM) of the European Monetary System (EMS).[1] In accordance with this agreement, the Netherlands maintains the spot exchange rates between the Netherlands guilder and the currencies of the other participants within margins of 15 percent above and below the cross rates based on the central rates expressed in European currency units (ECUs). Under the special bilateral agreement, the spot exchange rate of the Netherlands guilder and the deutsche mark is maintained within a fluctuation band of ±2.25 percent.

The agreement implies that the Netherlands Bank stands ready to buy or sell the currencies of the other participating states in unlimited amounts at specified intervention rates. On December 31, 1994, the rates were as follows:

Specified Intervention Rates per:	Netherlands Guilders	
	Upper limit	Lower limit
100 Austrian schillings	18.59630	13.79180
100 Belgian or Luxembourg francs	6.34340	4.70454
100 Danish kroner	34.30020	25.43850
100 Deutsche mark	115.23500	110.16750
100 French francs	39.00910	28.93810
1 Irish pound	3.15450	2.33952
100 Portuguese escudos[2]	1.32266	0.98094
100 Spanish pesetas[3]	1.65368	1.22644

The participants in the EMS do not maintain exchange rates for other currencies within fixed limits. On occasion, they can intervene in concert to smooth out fluctuations in exchange rates, the intervention currencies being mainly each other's, the ECU, and the U.S. dollar.

Banks quote buying and selling rates for all major foreign currencies. On December 30, 1994, the middle rate for the U.S. dollar was f. 1.7351 per US$1. There are no taxes or subsidies on purchases or sales of foreign exchange.

Residents and nonresidents are freely permitted to buy and sell convertible and nonconvertible currencies, both spot and forward, at negotiated rates. Forward exchange contracts are not limited as to delivery period, nor is an underlying trade transaction required. Residents and nonresidents are free to hold Netherlands guilder and foreign currency accounts in the Netherlands and abroad.

The Kingdom of the Netherlands formally accepted the obligations of Article VIII, Sections 2, 3, and 4 of the Fund Agreement, as from February 15, 1961.

Administration of Control

There are no exchange controls, except for the reporting requirements (in accordance with the External Financial Relations Act of 1994). Import and export licensing, including transit trade,[4] is handled by the Central Import-Export Agency and the delegated offices, under directives from the Directorate-General for Foreign Economic Relations of the Ministry of Economic Affairs. Residents are generally required to supply information on their payments to and receipts from nonresidents to the Netherlands Bank either through credit institutions or other providers of financial services who act as intermediaries, or directly in cases where residents do not use the services of the financial institutions within the scope of the regulations based on the External Financial Relations Act of 1994 (see section on Capital, below). To facilitate the compilation of the balance of payments, residents are required to indicate on reporting forms, for all payments to and receipts from nonresidents exceeding f. 25,000 or its equivalent in foreign currencies, the nature of the underlying transaction as well as the currency and amount paid or received. Separate regulations govern the reporting of settlements where no transfer of money is involved.

Residents are free to open and maintain bank accounts abroad and to maintain current accounts abroad for the purpose of settlements. Such accounts must be declared to the Netherlands Bank,

---

[1]Austria became a member of the European Union on January 1, 1995, and joined the ERM of the EMS on January 9, 1995.

[2]Effective March 6, 1995, the upper and lower limits were changed to 1.27637 and 0.84661, respectively.

[3]Effective March 6, 1995, the upper and lower limits were changed to 1.63793 and 1.14050, respectively.

[4]The only transit trade transactions still subject to specific license are purchases and sales of strategic goods.

and entries in them must be reported to the Bank in accordance with relevant regulations.

In compliance with the relevant UN Security Council resolutions, certain restrictions are imposed on financial transactions with Iraq, the Libyan Arab Jamahiriya, the Federal Republic of Yugoslavia (Serbia/Montenegro), and areas of the Republic of Bosnia and Herzegovina under the control of Bosnian Serb forces.

Prescription of Currency

In effecting payments to nonresidents or collecting receipts from them, residents may use guilders or any foreign currency. Payments in any foreign currency between residents may be made freely. There are no bilateral payments agreements in force. Nonresidents are free to open and maintain nonresident accounts with authorized banks in the Netherlands in guilders or in any foreign currency, and to effect payments to, or collect receipts from, residents. All payments or receipts are freely permitted, as are transfers of balances to and from other nonresident accounts.

Imports and Import Payments

Imports from Iraq, the Federal Republic of Yugoslavia (Serbia/Montenegro), and areas of the Republic of Bosnia and Herzegovina under the control of Bosnian Serb forces are prohibited.

Import licenses are required for imports originating in Hong Kong, Japan, and state trading countries,[5] as well as for the importation of goods of unknown origin. In addition, import licenses are required for a limited number of products, mainly those of the agricultural, steel, and textile sectors. Except for imports of textiles originating in the Far East and in state trading countries, most imports that require an import license are free from quantitative restriction. Most imports from Eastern European countries have been formally liberalized.

Imports from non-European Union (EU) countries of most products covered by the Common Agricultural Policy of the EU are subject to import levies that have replaced all previous barriers to imports; common EU regulations are also applied to imports of most other agricultural and livestock products from non-EU countries.

Payments for imports may be made freely, provided that the method of payment conforms to the relevant exchange control regulations (i.e., transfers are properly reported).

Payments for Invisibles

Payments abroad for invisibles are permitted freely. Residents may take out any amount in foreign and domestic banknotes and coins or documents of value. Payments for interest, dividends, and contractual amortization due to nonresidents are permitted freely.

Nonresidents may export all unused documents of value for travel purposes, as well as foreign and Netherlands banknotes and coins that they have imported or obtained in the Netherlands by drawing on their accounts or by exchanging other currencies.

Exports and Export Proceeds

Exports to Iraq, the Federal Republic of Yugoslavia (Serbia/Montenegro), and areas of the Republic of Bosnia and Herzegovina under the control of Bosnian Serb forces are prohibited. Certain exports to the Libyan Arab Jamahiriya are also prohibited.

Export licenses are required for only a few commodities, mostly of a strategic character, for some agricultural products, and for iron and steel scrap and related products.

Residents may freely grant credit in respect of nonprohibited exports. There is no repatriation surrender requirement for export proceeds.

Proceeds from Invisibles

There are no requirements attached to receipts by residents from current invisibles. Nonresidents may bring into the Netherlands for travel purposes any amount of foreign banknotes and documents of value; these may be used for traveling expenses in the Netherlands, as well as for purchases for which payment in cash is customary in the trade concerned.

Capital

Inward and outward capital transfers by residents and nonresidents are not restricted, except that they are subject to reporting requirements based on the External Financial Relations Act of 1994.

External capital transactions are unrestricted. For direct investment in the form of capital participation (inward and outward), no license is required. Neither short-term lending (for less than two years) nor long-term lending to nonresidents (whether affiliated companies or others) requires a license. Since

---

[5]State trading countries are defined for this purpose as consisting of China, the Democratic People's Republic of Korea, and Viet Nam.

May 20, 1994, the existing regime requiring that lead managers of issues of bearer paper denominated in guilders must be registered in credit institutions in the Netherlands and that issues of such paper must be reported at least one working day before announcement in the market has been abolished.

Transactions between residents and nonresidents in all stocks and bonds listed on the Amsterdam Stock Exchange take place at official market exchange rates and are unrestricted. Residents may freely purchase officially listed securities abroad. Placement with residents of unlisted foreign debentures denominated in guilders (such as foreign Euroguilder notes) and transactions in unlisted stocks are free of license. Nonresidents may have their securities, domestic or foreign, exported to them; securities held in the Netherlands are not subject to deposit.

Nonresidents may freely purchase real estate in the Netherlands for personal use or investment, and residents may freely purchase real estate abroad. Extension of payment and mortgage borrowing from nonresidents is free of license.

Gifts and donations to nonresidents are free. Emigrants may export any amount in foreign and domestic currency. They acquire nonresident status upon leaving the Netherlands and may have their total assets in the Netherlands remitted to them upon departure. Nonresidents inheriting from estates in the Netherlands may have the proceeds transferred to them freely.

There are no restrictions on commercial banks' spot external positions for foreign exchange control reasons. However, for prudential reasons, limits are imposed on banks' total position in foreign currency and precious metals. Banks are required to report to the Netherlands Bank their position in each foreign currency and precious metal (spot, forward, and option positions) at the end of each month.

Authorized banks may freely extend foreign currency and guilder loans to nonresidents. The banks' freedom to accept deposits from nonresidents and to borrow abroad is unrestricted.

All capital transfers by residents must be reported to the Netherlands Bank. Total amounts of security transactions must be reported periodically by securities brokers and authorized banks or, if transactions take place through a foreign bank account, by the resident parties concerned.

Gold

Neither the Netherlands Bank nor any government agency imports or markets gold for industrial use. Banks and nonbank residents may freely purchase, hold, and sell gold (fine gold, gold coins, and gold alloys) in the Netherlands or abroad. Imports and exports of gold do not require exchange licenses or import and export licenses. There is a free gold market in Amsterdam. Except for transactions of the Netherlands Bank, transfers of gold in bars and other elementary forms are subject to a value-added tax of 6 percent, as are domestic sales of gold coins. All other gold transactions are taxed at the standard value-added tax rate of 17.5 percent. Commercial imports of gold jewelry and of articles containing minor quantities of gold, such as watches, require import licenses only when they originate in Hong Kong, Japan, or state trading countries.

Changes During 1994

No significant changes occurred in the exchange and trade system.

(See Appendix for a summary of trade measures introduced and eliminated on an EU-wide basis during 1994, page 554.)

NETHERLANDS ANTILLES

(Position as of December 31, 1994)

Exchange Arrangement

The currency of the Netherlands Antilles is the Netherlands Antillean Guilder, which is pegged to the U.S. dollar, the intervention currency, at NA f 1.7900 per US$1. The official buying rates for the U.S. dollar on December 31, 1994 were NA f 1.77 per US$1 for banknotes and NA f 1.78 per US$1 for drafts, checks, and transfers. The official selling rate was NA f 1.80 per US$1. Official buying and selling rates for certain other currencies[1] are set daily on the basis of rates for the U.S. dollar abroad. A foreign exchange tax of 1.3 percent is levied on payments made by residents to nonresidents.[2] Purchases of foreign exchange by resident companies with nonresident status for exchange control purposes are exempt from the exchange tax. There are no arrangements for forward cover against exchange rate risk in the official or the commercial banking sector.

Administration of Control

The central bank issues exchange licenses, where required. The Department of Finance issues import licenses, where required. The central bank permits the commercial banks to provide foreign exchange for almost all current transactions without prior approval.

Prescription of Currency

Payments may be made in any currency except the legal tender of the Netherlands Antilles. Receipts may be accepted in any convertible currency except the legal tender of the Netherlands Antilles. All payments made by residents to nonresidents and receipts through authorized banks, as well as through banks abroad, must be reported to the central bank for the compilation of the balance of payments.

Nonresident Accounts

Nonresidents may freely open nonresident accounts in any foreign currency. Nonresidents are permitted to hold nonresident accounts with authorized banks (positive balances) in Netherlands Antillean guilders. Balances in such accounts may not exceed NA f. 200,000 without the approval of the central bank.

Imports and Import Payments

Payments for imports may be made freely. Imports whose delivery dates exceed payment dates by more than 12 months must be reported to the central bank. The importation of 42 items for which there are locally produced substitutes is subject to tariffs ranging from 25 percent to 90 percent. Certain commodities are subject to import surcharges in Bonaire and Curaçao.

Payments for Invisibles

All types of current invisible payments and remittances may be made freely. A license is required if the delivery and payment dates are more than one year apart; the central bank must receive notification.

Nonresidents may take with them on departure any foreign currency that they brought in. The exportation of Netherlands Antillean banknotes is prohibited, except for traveling purposes. Transfers of profits and dividends are allowed by the central bank upon application.

Exports and Export Proceeds

Exports require no licenses. Export proceeds must be repatriated but need not be surrendered. If export proceeds are not received within 12 months of shipment, the delay must be reported to the central bank.

Proceeds from Invisibles

Residents are not required to surrender invisible proceeds. Travelers may bring in with them any amount of checks, traveler's checks, or banknotes denominated in foreign currency.

Capital

Foreign investments and transfers of loans to residents in the Netherlands Antilles require licenses, which are normally granted.

---

[1]Aruban florins, Canadian dollars, deutsche mark, European Currency Units, French francs, Italian lire, Japanese yen, Netherlands guilders, pounds sterling, Suriname guilders, and Swiss francs. All currencies other than the Netherlands Antillean guilder are considered foreign currencies.

[2]Payments by certain entities, for example international companies and pension funds, are exempted from the foreign exchange tax.

Outward flows of resident-owned capital are subject to control. Investments by residents in real estate abroad, as well as capital loans to nonresidents, require a license. Investment and disinvestment by nonresidents in real estate in the Netherlands Antilles do not require a license. Investment by residents in officially listed foreign securities (and in mutual funds whose shares are officially quoted) is permitted free of license up to NA f. 100,000 a year. Reinvestment of proceeds from the sale of securities is also allowed.

Residents are allowed to hold foreign bank accounts without a special license. Transfers from a local bank account to these foreign accounts are allowed up to NA f. 10,000 a quarter.

Authorized banks' overall position with nonresidents is subject to limits set by the central bank and must always be positive and in currencies considered "freely usable," as defined under Article XXX(f) of the Fund's Articles of Agreement, and/or in Netherlands guilders.

Gold

Residents may hold and acquire gold coins in the Netherlands Antilles. Authorized banks may freely negotiate gold coins among themselves and with other residents. Imports and exports of gold do not require a special license.

Changes During 1994

No significant changes occurred in the exchange and trade system.

NEW ZEALAND

(Position as of December 31, 1994)

Exchange Arrangement

The currency of New Zealand is the New Zealand Dollar, the external value of which is determined by demand and supply conditions in the exchange market. The Reserve Bank of New Zealand, however, retains discretionary power to intervene in the foreign exchange market and may signal its desired exchange rate range. Foreign exchange dealers are free to adjust exchange rate quotations in response to market conditions throughout each business day. On December 31, 1994, the closing buying and selling rates for the U.S. dollar were US$ 0.6415 and US$ 0.6420, respectively, per $NZ1. There are no taxes or subsidies on purchases or sales of foreign exchange.

Financial institutions are permitted to conclude with their customers forward exchange contracts to buy or sell foreign currencies at market-determined rates in exchange for New Zealand dollars, irrespective of the source of the funds.

On August 5, 1982, New Zealand formally accepted the obligations of Article VIII, Sections 2, 3, and 4 of the Fund Agreement.

Administration of Control

Receipts and remittances of foreign exchange are free from control. Since February 1990, when exchange controls were abolished, no authorization has been required to deal in foreign exchange. The Reserve Bank of New Zealand, however, requires registered banks to report foreign exposure levels for prudential supervision purposes. The only remaining requirements are for purposes of statistical information to assist Statistics of New Zealand.

Prohibitions and restrictions are imposed on the trade of certain products, principally for reasons of human, plant, and animal health. Most of the restrictions are conditional.

The Overseas Investment Commission administers the regulations governing foreign direct investment in New Zealand.

In accordance with the Fund's Executive Board Decision No. 144–(52/51) adopted on August 14, 1952, New Zealand notified the Fund on September 6, 1990 that, in compliance with UN Security Council Resolution No. 661 (1990), certain restrictions had been imposed on the making of payments and transfers for current international transactions in respect of Iraq, and similarly on September 30, 1992, in respect of the Federal Republic of Yugoslavia (Serbia/Montenegro) in compliance with UN Security Council Resolution No. 757 (1992).

Prescription of Currency

Payments to and from residents of countries other than New Zealand may be made or received in any foreign currency,[1] as may payments to and from New Zealand currency accounts held with banks in New Zealand by banks not domiciled in New Zealand.

Nonresident Accounts

Nonresidents may maintain and operate accounts without formality and may repatriate funds without restriction. Overseas banks' accounts in New Zealand may be used to settle transactions with other countries.

Imports and Import Payments

Most tariffs on industrial products were reduced by approximately one-half over the period July 1, 1988 to July 1, 1992. The majority of the tariffs will be reduced by a further one-third between July 1, 1993 and July 1, 1996. The only tariffs over 20 percent apply to motor vehicles, tires and other motor vehicle components, and certain products (including textiles, clothing, footwear, and carpets). Most tariffs are ad valorem, but specific tariffs apply to some products (e.g., clothing) if they produce more revenue. Import prohibitions and restrictions affect some seventy products or classes of products, primarily plants, animals, and products considered dangerous to human health or not in the public interest.

Under the terms of the Australia-New Zealand Closer Economic Relations and Trade Agreement (ANZCERTA) and the South Pacific Regional Trade and Economic Cooperation Agreement (SPARTECA),[2]

---

[1] Foreign currencies are defined as all currencies other than New Zealand currency.

[2] The islands under this arrangement constitute the South Pacific Forum (in addition to Australia and New Zealand): Cook Islands, Fiji, Kiribati, Nauru, Niue, Papua New Guinea, Solomon Islands, Tonga, Tuvalu, Vanuatu, and Western Samoa.

imports of qualifying goods enter duty-free from Australia and the SPARTECA countries. In addition, under the ANZCERTA, antidumping remedies have been replaced by domestic laws regulating trade practices.

Less comprehensive preferential trade arrangements affect specified imports from Canada, Malaysia, and the United Kingdom.

Eligible imports from developing countries that have not graduated beyond a specified threshold are accorded tariff preferences under the Generalized System of Preferences (GSP). Certain product areas are excluded from the coverage of the GSP (e.g., clothing, footwear, and motor vehicles). In most cases, these preferential rates are 80 percent of the normal tariff rates; in no case is the margin of preference less for developing countries.

In addition, duty-free access is granted to most imports from 36 countries classified by the United Nations as "least developed."

Special safeguard mechanisms apply under the GSP: a developing country with a per capita GNP equal to or greater than 70 percent of New Zealand's loses its preferential status under the criterion of "country graduation," and a developing country loses its preference with respect to specific tariff items when minimum market share exceeds a minimum value under the criterion of "product graduation."

Payments for Invisibles

Payments for invisibles are unrestricted, except for transactions involving nationals of Iraq and the Federal Republic of Yugoslavia (Serbia/Montenegro), although there is a reporting requirement for statistical purposes.

ANZCERTA also provides a framework for the liberalization of trade in services between Australia and New Zealand subject to the foreign investment policies of both countries. It provides for free trade in services based on national treatment. All services are covered except for those on a negative list prepared by each government; the list includes certain aspects of telecommunications, aviation, coastal shipping, and postal services; Australia's list also includes radio and television broadcasting and insurance, banking, and consultancy services.

Exports and Export Proceeds

Export earnings (including foreign currency earned for performing services in New Zealand for foreign nationals) need not be returned through the banking system. Certain items classified as strategic goods may be exported only when specific requirements have been met and an export permit has been issued.

Many of New Zealand's exports are currently restricted by quotas and other quantitative restrictions imposed by its principal trading partners. For example, exports of lamb and butter to the European Union and exports of beef and dairy products to the United States are subject to either quotas or voluntary export restraints.

Proceeds from Invisibles

Remuneration for services provided (or to be provided) in New Zealand, by New Zealand residents, (including corporate bodies ordinarily resident in New Zealand), and on behalf of overseas residents as well as interest and dividends earned overseas from portfolio investment, do not have to be repatriated. ANZCERTA provides for liberalization of trade in services rendered by New Zealand residents in Australia, subject to certain conditions (as noted in the section on Payments for Invisibles, above).

The disposal overseas by New Zealand residents of foreign income from other invisibles, such as interest and dividends, is permitted. Travelers may bring into the country unlimited amounts of foreign and domestic bank notes and coins.

Capital

In general, consent is not required in respect of capital receipts, although overseas entities seeking to establish themselves in New Zealand must, in some cases, obtain the approval of the Overseas Investment Commission (OIC). Nonresident persons or companies wishing to make a direct investment in a New Zealand company by purchasing or exchanging shares are required to obtain the consent of the OIC in respect of any proposed offer for such shares whenever the investment would confer on the offerer the beneficial entitlement of 25 percent or more of the voting power at any general meeting. However, if the consideration and gross assets of the offeree company are less than $NZ 10 million, the company is exempt from this requirement. The $NZ 10 million level also triggers the need for OIC approval when a foreign entity wishes to acquire the assets of a New Zealand company or establish a New Zealand subsidiary or branch. More restrictive rules apply in the commercial fishing and rural land sectors deemed to be sensitive. The $NZ 10 million trigger level does not apply to investments in these sectors.

Gold

Residents may hold and acquire gold coins in New Zealand without restriction. There are no restrictions or licensing requirements on the importation and exportation of gold.

Changes During 1994

No significant changes occurred in the exchange and trade system.

NICARAGUA

(Position as of December 31, 1994)

Exchange Arrangement

The currency of Nicaragua is the Córdoba. The exchange rate system consists of two rates: the official rate, which is pegged to the U.S. dollar, is devalued daily at an annual rate of 12 percent; and the free exchange rate, which is determined through transactions of private exchange houses. In addition, there is an unrecognized parallel market. Most export receipts, official receipts and payments, import payments, and direct investments are transacted in the official market, while the remaining transactions take place in the free market. On December 31, 1994, the buying and selling rates in the official market were C$7.11 and C$7.18, respectively, per US$1, and the buying and selling rates in the free market were C$7.25 and C$7.35 per US$1. There are no arrangements for forward cover against exchange rate risk operating in the official or the commercial banking sector. Foreign-currency-denominated accounts and córdoba accounts with exchange guarantee (maintenance of value) contracts may be opened with commercial banks. Banks may also make loans denominated in foreign currency or in local currency with exchange guarantees. The Central Bank of Nicaragua charges a commission of 1 percent on sales of foreign exchange.

Nicaragua formally accepted the obligations of Article VIII, Sections 2, 3, and 4 of the Fund Agreement, as from July 30, 1964.

Administration of Control

The exchange control system is administered by the Central Bank, which has sole authority to buy and sell foreign exchange but has authorized commercial banks and exchange houses to make foreign exchange transactions. The Central Bank approves all foreign exchange transactions on the basis of priority criteria that are established in accordance with sources of foreign exchange. The Central Bank is also responsible for issuing export authorizations. Some transactions not eligible for official foreign exchange may be effected through an authorized foreign currency deposit account or with currencies acquired from exchange houses.

Importers using their own foreign currency accounts are not required to go through the exchange approval process, nor are they expected to reveal the sources of their funds.

Arrears are maintained with respect to external payments.

Prescription of Currency

There is no prescription of currency, but the Central Bank has the power to prohibit an export if the currency stipulated for payment is not readily convertible into U.S. dollars in international markets.

Imports and Import Payments

All importers effecting payments through the official market are required to be registered with the Ministry of Economic Affairs and Development. This requirement is waived for individuals who import only occasionally for their own needs. Importer registration certificates are valid for five years.

For individual imports, other than those financed from an individual's own foreign currency deposit account or with foreign exchange from the exchange house market, a specific license is required from the Ministry of Economic Affairs and Development, and registration is required at the Central Bank. In principle, general import licenses are valid for five years. Payments for imports from outside the Central American region must be settled in the official foreign exchange market (Central Bank and commercial banks). Some import payments are made with sight drafts, but most are made through letters of credit.

In addition to customs duties, certain imports, irrespective of origin, are subject to a specific consumption tax and to a customs fee. In addition, most commodities, whether imported or domestically produced, are subject to a 15 percent general sales tax.

Payments for Invisibles

Payments for invisibles related to authorized imports are effected in the official markets. Payments for other invisibles, such as travel, educational expenses, family maintenance, and medical expenses, take place through the free market.

Exports and Export Proceeds

All exports except gold are free, requiring only registration (Registro Unico de Exportación) with the Central Bank. Exports of gold remain under the control of the Central Bank. Export registration certificates are valid for 30 days. An export license is required for the exportation of traditional products.

Foreign exchange proceeds from traditional exports must be received within 45 days of shipment and surrendered to an authorized bank within 2 workings days. Exporters who fail to surrender their proceeds will lose their export authorization. They may retain the proceeds from nontraditional exports to countries outside the Central American area in special accounts at a commercial bank and use the funds for import payment purposes. Exporters may use the proceeds from exports of bananas, coconuts and coconut by-products, and copra through the ports of the region of El Cabo and the Department of Zelaya to pay for imports consumed in these areas. They may retain all proceeds from exports from the free zone and 75 percent of proceeds from exports of seafood products to countries outside the Central American area in special accounts with a commercial bank. Funds in these accounts may be used only for import payments; these exporters do not have access to the official foreign exchange market.

Proceeds from Invisibles

Proceeds from invisibles may be retained or sold in the free market. There is no limit on the amount of foreign exchange persons arriving in Nicaragua from abroad may bring in and use locally.

Capital

All capital transactions require authorization from the Central Bank. For servicing private external debt, authorization depends on the availability of foreign exchange.

Gold

The Nicaraguan Mining Institute manages the country's gold production. The Central Bank is in charge of selling gold at prices prevailing in international gold markets and may sell gold to domestic, industrial, and other users. Commemorative gold coins were issued in 1967, 1975, and 1980. Natural and juridical persons may trade gold coins for numismatic purposes only.

Changes During 1994

Exchange Arrangement

May 1. The Central Bank introduced a commission of 1 percent on sales of foreign exchange.

Imports and Import Payments

May 2. The selective consumption tax (ISC) and the tax on luxury consumption (IBS) were abolished and replaced by a temporary tariff (applying to 750 import items) and a specific consumption tax (applying to all products previously subject to the ISC and the IBS).

NIGER

(Position as of January 31, 1995)

Exchange Arrangement

The currency of Niger is the CFA Franc,[1] which is pegged to the French franc, the intervention currency, at the fixed rate of CFAF 1 per F 0.01. The official buying and selling rates are CFAF 100 per F 1. Exchange rates for other currencies are derived from the rate for the currency concerned in the Paris exchange market and the fixed rate between the French franc and the CFA franc. The BCEAO does not levy a commission on transfers to or from countries outside the West African Monetary Union (WAMU). Transfers by banks to countries outside the WAMU are subject to an exchange commission of 2.5 percent of the amount of the transfer. All revenue from commissions charged by the banks on transfers to countries outside the WAMU is transferred to the Treasury. There are no taxes or subsidies on purchases or sales of foreign exchange.

With the exception of measures relating to gold transactions, the domiciliation of exports, and the repatriation of export proceeds, Niger's exchange controls do not apply to (1) France (and its overseas departments and territories) and Monaco; and (2) all other countries whose bank of issue is linked with the French Treasury by an Operations Account (Benin, Burkina Faso, Cameroon, Central African Republic, Chad, Comoros, Congo, Côte d'Ivoire, Equatorial Guinea, Gabon, Mali, Senegal, and Togo). Hence, all payments to these countries may be made freely. All other countries are considered foreign countries.

The contracting of forward exchange cover requires prior authorization from the Financial Relations Directorate of the Ministry of Finance and Planning. Such cover may be provided for payments for permitted imports and for the currency stipulated in the commercial contract. The maturity period must not exceed one or three months, depending on the nature of the goods involved, and is not renewable. There is no official scheme for currency swaps or guaranteed exchange rates for external debt servicing.

Arrears are maintained with respect to external payments.

Administration of Control

Exchange control is administered by the Financial Relations Directorate. The BCEAO is authorized to collect, either directly or through the banks, financial institutions, Postal Administration, and notaries public, any information necessary to compile balance of payments statistics. All exchange transactions relating to foreign countries must be made through the BCEAO, Postal Administration, or authorized banks.

Prescription of Currency

Since Niger has an Operations Account with the French Treasury, settlements with France (as defined above), Monaco, and the countries linked with the French Treasury by Operations Accounts are made in CFA francs, French francs, or the currency of any Operations Account country. Current payments to or from The Gambia, Ghana, Guinea, Guinea-Bissau, Liberia, Mauritania, Nigeria, and Sierra Leone are normally made through the West African Clearing House. Settlements with all other countries are usually effected either in foreign currencies through correspondent banks in France or in French francs through foreign accounts in francs.

Nonresident Accounts

Nonresident accounts are subject to strict regulations, which stipulate authorized debit and credit operations. These accounts may not be credited with banknotes of the BCEAO, the Bank of France, or any other bank of issue with an Operations Account with the French Treasury.

Imports and Import Payments

All import restrictions and prohibitions, including temporary measures affecting imports of certain products, and all remaining licensing requirements for imports, including imports on transit, were abolished by the end of August 1994. A customs tariff regime, introduced in September 1994, consists of three categories of products with ad valorem rates of 5 percent, 10 percent, and 30 percent.

All import monopolies and quasi monopolies (de facto monopolies and exclusive trading contracts), with the exception of imports of petroleum products, were abolished during the second half of 1985. In particular, since October 1, 1985, the Société na-

---

[1]The CFA franc is issued by the Central Bank of West African States (BCEAO) and is the common currency in Benin, Burkina Faso, Côte d'Ivoire, Mali, Niger, Senegal, and Togo.

tionale de commerce et de production du Niger (COPRONIGER) no longer maintains a monopoly on the importation of specified commodities, including salt, cigarettes, green tea, and certain textiles. All import transactions with foreign countries with a c.i.f. value exceeding CFAF 25,000 at the border must be domiciled with an authorized bank. Foreign exchange may not be purchased before the payment due date if the goods have already been imported, or until eight days before the shipment date if the goods are covered by documentary credit.

Payments for Invisibles

Payments for invisibles to France (as defined above), Monaco, and countries linked with the French Treasury by an Operations Account are permitted freely; those to other countries are subject to the approval of the External Relations Directorate, which, for certain transactions, has delegated its powers to authorized banks. Payments for invisibles related to trade are permitted freely when the basic trade transaction has been approved or does not require authorization. Transfers of income accruing to nonresidents in the form of profits, dividends, and royalties are also permitted freely when the basic transaction has been approved. Foreigners working in Niger may transfer savings from their salaries with the prior approval of the External Relations Directorate, but these transfers are normally limited to 50 percent of net pay. Larger transfers are permitted, however, if supported by appropriate documentary evidence.

Residents traveling for tourist or business purposes to countries in the franc zone that are not members of the WAMU are allowed to take out the equivalent of up to CFAF 2 million in banknotes other than CFA franc banknotes; amounts in excess of this limit may be taken out in means of payment other than banknotes. The allowances for travel to countries outside the franc zone are subject to the following regulations: (1) for tourist travel, the equivalent of CFAF 500,000 without limit on the number of trips or differentiation by the age of the traveler; (2) for business travel, the equivalent of CFAF 75,000 a day for up to one month, corresponding to a maximum of CFAF 2.25 million (business travel allowances may be combined with tourist allowances); (3) allowances in excess of these limits are subject to the authorization of the Ministry of Finance or, by delegation, the BCEAO; and (4) credit cards, which must be issued by resident financial intermediaries and specifically authorized by the Minister of Finance, may be used

up to the ceilings indicated above for tourist and business travel. Returning resident travelers are required to declare all means of payment in their possession upon arrival at customs and surrender within eight days all means of payment exceeding the equivalent of CFAF 25,000. All resident travelers proceeding to countries that are not members of the WAMU must declare in writing all means of payment at their disposal at the time of departure. The re-exportation by nonresident travelers of means of payments other than banknotes issued abroad and registered in the name of the nonresident traveler is not restricted, subject to documentation that these means of payment were purchased with funds drawn from a foreign account in CFA francs or with other foreign exchange. The re-exportation of foreign banknotes is allowed up to the equivalent of CFAF 250,000; the re-exportation of foreign banknotes above these ceilings requires documentation demonstrating either the importation of foreign banknotes or their purchase against other means of payment registered in the name of the traveler or through the use of nonresident deposits lodged in local banks.

Exports and Export Proceeds

Exports of certain products (livestock, leather and skins, onions, rice, and sugar) are subject to submission of a statistic registration certificate (FES) for statistical compilation and monitoring purposes. Exports to France (as defined above) and the Operations Account countries may be made freely. Exports of domestic products and imported commodities to other countries require an exchange commitment. In principle, the due date of payment for exports to foreign countries must not be later than 180 days after the goods arrive at their destination. Proceeds from exports, regardless of the buying country, must be collected and surrendered through an authorized intermediary bank within one month of the due date. All exports exceeding a value of CFAF 500,000 must be domiciled with an authorized bank.

Proceeds from Invisibles

Proceeds from transactions in invisibles with France (as defined above), Monaco, and the other countries linked with the French Treasury by Operations Accounts may be retained. All amounts due from residents of other countries in respect of services and all income earned in those countries from foreign assets must be collected and surrendered within two months of the due date or date of receipt. Resident and nonresident travelers may import any amount of banknotes and coins issued by the BCEAO, the Bank of France, or a bank of issue maintaining an Operations Account with the French Treasury, as well as any amount of foreign banknotes and coins (except gold coins). Residents must surrender within eight days of entry any foreign currency in excess of the equivalent of CFAF 25,000.

Capital

Capital transactions between Niger and France (as defined above), Monaco, and the other countries linked with the French Treasury by Operations Accounts are free of exchange control; capital transfers to all other countries require approval from the exchange control authority and are restricted, but capital receipts from such countries are permitted freely.

Special controls (additional to any exchange control requirements that may apply) are maintained over borrowing abroad, inward and outward investment, and the issuance, advertising, or offering for sale of foreign securities in Niger. Such operations require prior authorization from the Minister of Finance. Exempt from authorization, however, are operations in connection with (1) loans backed by a guarantee from the Nigerien Government, and (2) shares that are identical with, or may be substituted for, securities whose issuance or sale in Niger has previously been authorized. With the exception of controls over foreign securities, these measures do not apply to relations with France (as defined above), Monaco, member countries of the WAMU, and other countries linked with the French Treasury by Operations Accounts. Special controls are also maintained over the soliciting of funds for deposit with foreign private persons and foreign firms and institutions and over publicity aimed at placing funds abroad or at subscribing to real estate development operations abroad; these special controls also apply to France (as defined above), Monaco, and countries linked with the French Treasury by Operations Accounts. All the special provisions described in this paragraph apply only to transactions and not to associated payments or collections.

All investments abroad by residents of Niger require prior authorization from the Minister of Finance;[2] 75 percent of the value must be financed from borrowing abroad. Foreign direct investments in Niger must be declared to the Minister of Finance

before they are made.[3] The Minister has a period of two months from receipt of the declaration to request postponement of the project. The full or partial liquidation of either type of investment also requires prior declaration to the Minister. Both the making and the liquidation of Nigerien investments abroad or foreign investments in Niger must be reported to the Minister of Finance and the BCEAO within 20 days of each operation. (Direct investments are those implying control of a company or an enterprise; mere participation is not considered direct investment, provided that it does not exceed 20 percent of the capital of a company whose shares are quoted on a stock exchange.) Lending abroad is also subject to prior authorization from the Minister of Finance.

Borrowing by residents from nonresidents requires prior authorization from the Minister of Finance. The following are, however, exempt from this authorization: (1) loans constituting a direct investment, which are subject to prior declaration, as indicated above; (2) loans contracted by authorized banks; and (3) loans other than those mentioned above, when the total outstanding amount of these loans, including the new borrowing, does not exceed CFAF 2 million for any one borrower, the annual interest rate does not exceed the normal market rate, and the proceeds are immediately sold on the exchange market or debited to a foreign account in francs. The repayment of a foreign loan constituting a direct investment is subject to the same formalities as the liquidation of a direct investment; the repayment of other loans requires authorization only if the loans were subject to prior authorization.

Foreign investments in Niger may be granted certain guarantees and facilities under the Investment Code of July 31, 1988 and its amendments. The facilities granted under the previous Investment Code have been maintained. In addition, the new Investment Code provides for regular or privileged treatment. Regular treatment provides assurances, for both new and existing enterprises, with respect to indemnities in the event of expropriation and concerning nondiscrimination between Nigerien nationals and foreign nationals; tax exemptions may be granted for new investments. Privileged treatment is reserved for enterprises deemed to be of special importance to national economic development and falling within specified categories of industrial activities. Such treatment

---

[2]Including those made through foreign companies directly or indirectly controlled by persons in Niger and those made by branches or subsidiaries abroad of companies in Niger.

[3]Including those made by companies in Niger that are directly or indirectly under foreign control and those made by branches or subsidiaries of foreign companies in Niger.

may be accorded under two different regimes—the approval regime and the agreement regime.

Gold

Residents are free to hold, acquire, and dispose of gold in any form in Niger. Imports and exports of gold from or to any other country require prior authorization from the Minister of Finance. Exempt from this requirement are (1) imports and exports by or on behalf of the Treasury or the BCEAO; (2) imports and exports of manufactured articles containing a minor quantity of gold (such as gold-filled or gold-plated articles); and (3) articles of gold up to a combined weight of 500 grams when carried by a traveler. Both licensed and exempt imports of gold are subject to customs declaration.

Changes During 1994

Exchange Arrangement

January 12. The CFA franc was devalued to CFAF 100 per F 1 from CFAF 50 per F 1.

Imports and Import Payments

August 10. All import licensing requirements and import restrictions were abolished.

September 1. A customs tariff regime, consisting of three product categories with ad valorem rates of 5 percent, 10 percent, and 30 percent, was introduced.

NIGERIA

(Position as of December 31, 1994)

Exchange Arrangement

The currency of Nigeria is the Nigerian Naira, the external value of which is pegged to the U.S. dollar, the intervention currency, at the rate of ₦21.9 per US$1. Foreign exchange is sold directly by Central Bank of Nigeria fortnightly to end users through designated banks, which act as agents of the Central Bank.[1] The banks are allowed to collect only the normal charges and prescribed commissions. The Central Bank determines the allocation of foreign exchange on the basis of an allocation formula in which 50 percent of the foreign exchange resources go to manufacturing imports, 10 percent to agricultural imports, 20 percent to finished goods, and 10 percent to service payments. Foreign exchange bureaus are allowed to transact in foreign exchange banknotes at a rate 10 percent lower than the official exchange rate.

Administration of Control

The Federal Ministry of Finance is responsible for basic exchange control policy and, in principle, for approving applications for transfers of capital abroad; for remittances of profits and dividends; for granting "approved status" to nonresident investments in Nigeria; and for approving any dealings in foreign securities. The Central Bank is the principal administrator of foreign exchange regulations. All licensed commercial banks and merchant banks have been appointed as authorized dealers by the Ministry of Finance and are empowered to deal in foreign currencies and to approve applications in accordance with the guidelines issued by the Central Bank. Any application that does not fall within the scope of the authority of these authorized dealers must be submitted to the Ministry of Finance for the transactions mentioned above. Hotels and rest houses are allowed to receive payments of hotel bills and incidental expenses in foreign currency from travelers to Nigeria.

The Federal Ministry of Trade administers trade regulations.

Prescription of Currency

Authorized payments may be made in naira or in any foreign currency to an external account in Nigeria. Settlements with the central banks of the member states of the Economic Community of West African States (Benin, Burkina Faso, Côte d'Ivoire, The Gambia, Ghana, Guinea, Guinea-Bissau, Liberia, Mali, Mauritania, Niger, Senegal, Sierra Leone, and Togo) are normally made through the West African Clearing House in West African Units of Account.

Resident and Nonresident Accounts

There are three categories of resident and nonresident accounts: external accounts, nonresident accounts, and blocked accounts. External accounts are maintained for diplomatic representatives of all countries and international organizations. They may be credited with authorized payments by residents of Nigeria to residents of foreign countries, with payments from other external accounts, and with proceeds from sales of foreign currencies. They may be debited for payments to residents of Nigeria, for payments to other external accounts, and for purchases of foreign currencies. Funds derived from local sources may be deposited in nonresident accounts. Such accounts may be credited with proceeds from services rendered locally, provided that the operation of such accounts has been reported to and approval has been obtained from the Central Bank before any foreign transfers are effected. Blocked accounts are accounts to which funds that are blocked by directives given under Section 27 of the Exchange Control Act are credited.

Imports and Import Payments

Import licenses are not required. The importation of the following products is prohibited: poultry, eggs, vegetables, processed wood, fresh or preserved fruit, fruit juices, mosquito repellant oils, textile fabrics, plastic domestic articles, beer, rice and rice products, mineral water, soft drinks, and all sparkling wine.

All imports valued at the equivalent of $1,000 (c. & f.) or more, except those specifically exempted by the government, are subject to preshipment inspection to ensure that all imports into Nigeria are of the correct quality and quantity according to the contracts and that only the normal price of that

---

[1]The frequency of allocation sessions was, however, effectively reduced to once every three weeks toward the end of the year.

product in the country of supply is paid as well as the correct import duty.[2] Unless a "Clean Report of Findings" on the goods to be imported has been issued, foreign exchange settlement for imports may not be effected.

Payment for imports covered by confirmed letters of credit is made by the overseas correspondents on behalf of Nigerian banks, on presentation of the specified documents to the overseas correspondents. However, such payment is made on the understanding that the goods paid for will arrive in Nigeria and that all shipping documents relating to the imported goods are lodged by importers with the authorized dealer as agents of the Nigerian Government within 21 days of negotiation of the specified documents. Bills of entry (for imports covered by confirmed letters of credit) must be submitted to the authorized dealer within 90 days of negotiation and payment by overseas correspondent banks. For all other means of payment, the full set of documents, evidencing the receipt of the goods in Nigeria, must be submitted to the authorized dealer.

Payments for Invisibles

Persons needing foreign exchange to make invisible payments must submit applications to the Central Bank through designated banks. Basic allowances are provided for some payments. As with imports, verification is on an ex post basis—that is, depending on the payments arrangements, based on documentation obtained after the purchase of foreign exchange. The basic allowance for tourist travel is the equivalent of $500 a year, and for business travel, the equivalent of $5,000 a trip for an enterprise.

Payments for international air tickets may be made in naira by residents. Hotels are allowed to accept settlement of hotel bills and incidental expenses in foreign currency from travelers to Nigeria, who are required to settle their bills and incidental expenses in foreign currency. However, when there is documentary evidence that an adequate amount of foreign currency has been exchanged into local currency at any licensed bank or *bureau de change*, payment in local currency must be accepted in settlement of hotel bills by foreign visitors to Nigeria. Remittances abroad by expatriate residents of up to 75 percent of net salary after tax

are considered by authorized dealers subject to documentation requirements. Final balance applications involving the transfer of accumulated savings are considered subject to the approved guidelines and confirmation by the Central Bank that the expatriate concerned had not previously been granted his final balance entitlement. The exportation of domestic currency in excess of ₦100 is prohibited.

Exports and Export Proceeds

The exportation of African antiques, works of art, and objects used in African ceremonies is prohibited, except under prescribed conditions. Exports of timber (processed and unprocessed), raw hides and skins, raw palm kernel, cassava, maize, rice, yam, and all imported food items are prohibited. Exports of unrefined gold and petroleum products require an export license. Exports of petroleum are handled by the Nigerian National Petroleum Corporation and are subject to special arrangements.

All proceeds from exports by both private and public sectors are required to be surrendered to the Central Bank.

Proceeds from Invisibles

All proceeds from invisibles must be received through the Central Bank or designated banks and surrendered to the Central Bank. The importation of domestic currency in excess of ₦100 is prohibited.

Capital

Applications for capital transfers abroad are approved by the Federal Ministry of Finance and Economic Development subject to satisfactory documentation. Except for the purpose of financing imports or exports, permission is required from the Ministry of Finance for any individual, firm, company, or branch resident in Nigeria to borrow abroad. In addition, official agencies and state-controlled corporations require the prior approval of the Ministry of Finance for any foreign borrowing. The contracting of suppliers' credits abroad by state-controlled corporations or agencies is also subject to approval from the Ministry of Finance. The permission of the Ministry of Finance is required for borrowing in Nigeria (1) by any nonresident individual or company, and (2) by any company registered in Nigeria (other than a bank) that is controlled directly or indirectly from outside Nigeria. However, to enable entities mentioned under (2) to meet temporary shortages of funds, licensed banks in Nigeria may grant loans or overdrafts for periods not exceeding 14 days, or

---

[2]The following items are exempt from the inspection requirement: gold; precious stones; works of art; explosives and pyrotechnic products; ammunition; implements of war; live animals; scrap metals; household and personal effects, including used motor vehicles; parcel post or samples; and petroleum and refined petroleum products.

may increase the amount of any advance or overdraft by the amount of loan interest or bank charges payable thereon. General permission is also given for any loan, bank overdraft, or other credit facility to be arranged to finance Nigerian imports or exports of goods.

Residents of Nigeria may not deal in foreign currency securities or buy from or sell to nonresidents of Nigeria any security payable in naira without the permission of the Ministry of Finance. The capital proceeds of securities registered in Nigeria and owned by nonresidents may be collected and negotiated through authorized dealers, provided that the prior permission of the Ministry of Finance is obtained.

Exchange for the transfer of certain assets by emigrants or expatriates is granted on final departure from the country, but the transfer of the proceeds of assets realized in order to comply with the Nigerian Enterprises Promotion Decrees of 1972 and 1977 may take place upon receipt.

Ceilings for foreign capital participation in the equity capital of enterprises in various sectors of the economy have been set by the Indigenization Decree of 1972, as amended in February 1974, July 1976, January 1977, and January 1989. Nonresidents intending to make direct investments in Nigeria may apply to the Ministry of Finance for approved status, the granting of which means that sympathetic consideration will be given to future requests to repatriate the capital and related profits and dividends. Remittable dividends may be reinvested without the requirement that matching capital must be imported. However, the granting of approved status for such investment is subject to the approval of the Federal Ministry of Finance. The granting of approved status is not applicable to the purchase of shares on the stock exchange in Nigeria unless this forms an integral part of the approved investment project. Furthermore, this status is not normally granted when internally generated funds from profits, dividends, rents, bank credit, or locally raised loans are invested in local enterprises. Foreign-owned companies and banks operating in Nigeria must be incorporated in Nigeria.

To facilitate the inflow of direct capital investment, the Industrial Development and Coordinating Committee deals with all matters relating to approval for direct capital investment, subject to the provisions of the Nigerian Enterprises Promotion Decree, 1977. Applications for the remittance of profits, dividends, etc., in respect of capital investment made through authorized foreign exchange dealers, are considered by the Federal Ministry of Finance and approved subject to documentation requirements. Funds so approved are repatriated through the Foreign Exchange Market (FEM).

In July 1988, the Central Bank of Nigeria published guidelines for an external debt-conversion program for Nigeria and established a Debt Conversion Program (DCP) to be supervised by a Debt Conversion Committee (DCC) appointed by the Federal Government. The DCC and DCP regulate the purchase of selected Nigerian foreign debt instruments at a discount and the disposition of the naira proceeds of conversions of such debt. Eligible instruments were initially defined as uninsured trade debt denominated in promissory notes. When the rescheduling agreement with commercial banks was completed in early 1989, additional instruments representing debt to commercial banks were made eligible for the debt-conversion provisions. All legitimate holders of promissory notes or other debt instruments are eligible to apply to the DCC for debt conversion, provided that the foreign exchange used to acquire the instruments originated from abroad and not from foreign exchange purchases in Nigeria.

Eligible uses for the naira proceeds from debt conversion are (1) conversion to cash for the purpose of making a gift or grant to Nigerian entities; (2) conversion for expansion or recapitalization of investments in privatized enterprises; and (3) conversion for investment in completely new projects. The DCC evaluates each application and determines eligibility for participation in an auction to be conducted by the Central Bank. The amounts and timing of the auction are determined by the DCC.

Restrictions on remittances of redemption proceeds and incomes arising therefrom are the following: (1) interest income, profits/dividends, patent license fees, and other invisibles connected with approved projects under the DCP may not be repatriated for a minimum period of five years from the date of release of redemption proceeds for actual investment or five years after such profits or dividends are made or paid, whichever is later; (2) any capital proceeds arising from subsequent disposal of the investment made under the program may not be repatriated for a minimum period of ten years after effective investment of the proceeds; (3) repatriation of capital after ten years may not exceed 20 percent a year.

Gold

With the permission of the Federal Ministry of Finance, residents may hold and acquire gold coins in Nigeria for numismatic purposes. Residents other than the monetary authorities, producers of gold, and authorized industrial users are not allowed, without special permission, to hold or acquire gold in any form other than jewelry or coins, at home or abroad. The importation and exportation of gold in any form other than jewelry require specific licenses issued by the Federal Ministry of Finance; such licenses are not normally granted except for imports and exports by or on behalf of the monetary authorities, producers of gold, and industrial users. Furthermore, the importation of gold coins requires an import license. Imports of gold coins and gold and silver bullion are free of duty when made by the Central Bank; otherwise, such imports are subject to customs duty at 100 percent ad valorem.

Changes During 1994

Exchange Arrangement

January 26. Foreign exchange bureaus were prohibited from selling foreign exchange; they were allowed to purchase foreign exchange only from their clients as agents of the Central Bank at the official exchange rate and are required to surrender the proceeds to the Central Bank.

February 4. The Central Bank issued guidelines for the allocation of foreign exchange directly to end-users through the banks designated as their agents. Authorized dealers were prohibited from conducting foreign exchange transactions directly with their clients for their own account and were allowed to collect only the normal charges and prescribed commissions.

February 17. The Central Bank resumed foreign exchange sales.

September 16. Foreign exchange bureaus were allowed to buy and sell foreign exchange banknotes at a margin of 10 percent above the official rate.

Imports and Import Payments

February 4. Unutilized foreign exchange that was allocated to importers was required to be surrendered to the Central Bank within one month. All import payments exceeding $1,000 were required to be made under letters of credit supported by the Import Duty Report (IDR) and Clean Report of Findings (CRF) issued by the customs office.

Payments for Invisibles

February 4. End-users were required to apply for a foreign exchange allocation through designated banks. Payments for invisibles were allocated 10 percent of the total amount of the application once every two weeks.

Exports and Export Proceeds

February 4. All foreign exchange proceeds from exports by private and public sectors were required to be surrendered to the Central Bank.

Proceeds from Invisibles

February 4. All foreign exchange proceeds from services by private and public sectors were required to be surrendered to the Central Bank.

NORWAY

(Position as of December 31, 1994)

Exchange Arrangement

The currency of Norway is the Norwegian Krone. The Norwegian authorities do not maintain margins in respect of exchange transactions, and spot and forward exchange rates are determined on the basis of demand and supply conditions in the exchange market. However, the Bank of Norway may intervene from time to time to maintain stability in the market. The Bank of Norway quotes daily the exchange rate of the krone against 19 other currencies[1] and the European currency unit (ECU) for information purposes on the basis of the market rates. On December 31, 1994, the middle rate quoted against the U.S. dollar was Nkr 7.518 per US$1.

Residents (Norwegian companies and private individuals) may freely enter into forward and interest rate contracts with Norwegian foreign exchange banks and nonresidents. There are no taxes or subsidies on purchases or sales of foreign exchange.

Norway formally accepted the obligations of Article VIII, Sections 2, 3, and 4 of the Fund Agreement, as from May 11, 1967.

Administration of Control

Exchange control is administered by the Bank of Norway in cooperation with the Ministry of Finance and Customs. Import and export licenses, when required, are issued by the Ministry of Foreign Affairs and, in certain cases, by the Ministry of Agriculture or the Ministry of Fisheries.

In accordance with the Fund's Executive Board Decision No. 144–(52/51) adopted on August 14, 1952, Norway notified the Fund on July 21, 1992 that, in compliance with UN Security Council Resolution No. 757 (1992), certain restrictions had been imposed on the making of payments and transfers for current international transactions in respect of the Federal Republic of Yugoslavia (Serbia/Montenegro); these restrictions have been reinforced in accordance with UN Security Council Resolution No. 820 (1993). Restrictions have also been imposed on financial transactions with the Socialist People's Libyan Arab Jamahiriya (in accordance with UN

Security Council Resolution No. 748/92), with the Islamic Republic of Iran (in accordance with the UN Security Council Resolution No. 670/90), and with the areas of the Republic of Bosnia and Herzegovina that are controlled by the Bosnian Serbs (in accordance with UN Security Council Resolution No. 942/94). Restrictions were imposed on financial transactions with Haiti (in accordance with UN Security Council Resolutions No. 873/93, No. 841/93, and No. 917/94). These sanctions were subsequently lifted with UN Security Council Resolution No. 944/94.

Prescription of Currency

Settlements with all countries may be made in any convertible currency, including Norwegian kroner, in convertible krone accounts (see section on Resident and Nonresident Accounts, below).

Resident and Nonresident Accounts

Residents may also open foreign exchange accounts at domestic banks without restriction. The main type of nonresident account is the convertible krone account. Such accounts may be held by residents of all foreign countries. They may be credited with authorized payments from any country, with transfers from other convertible krone accounts, and with proceeds from the sale in Norway of convertible currencies. They may be debited for authorized payments from any country to residents of Norway, for transfers to other convertible krone accounts, and for purchases in Norway of any foreign currency. Authorized banks are also permitted to open foreign exchange accounts for nonresidents without restriction. Both convertible krone accounts and foreign exchange accounts must be reported to the Bank of Norway.[2]

Imports and Import Payments

Imports of industrial goods do not require an import license, but all imports from Iraq, from the Socialist People's Libyan Arab Jamahiriya, from the Federal Republic of Yugoslavia (Serbia/Montenegro), and from areas of the Republic of Bosnia and Herzegovina that are controlled by the Bosnian

---

[1]Austrian schillings, Belgian francs, Canadian dollars, Danish kroner, deutsche mark, Finnish markkaa, French francs, Greek drachmas, Icelandic króna, Irish pounds, Italian lire, Japanese yen, Netherlands guilders, Portuguese escudos, pounds sterling, Spanish pesetas, Swedish kronor, Swiss francs, and U.S. dollars.

[2]Residents may also open foreign exchange accounts at domestic banks without restriction.

Serbs are prohibited. Certain textiles and garments are subject to import licensing for surveillance purposes. Following Norway's accession to the previous Multifiber Arrangement (MFA) on July 1, 1984, the global quotas formerly in force under Article XIX of the General Agreement on Tariffs and Trade (GATT) have been phased out and replaced by bilateral agreements, which have been concluded with 19 textile suppliers. The agreements entered into under the current MFA are considerably more liberal than those that Norway had under the previous MFA. Norway has been able to maintain its policy of not introducing restraints on imports from developing countries. Besides textile products, footwear from Taiwan Province of China is subject to licensing requirements. With these exceptions, industrial goods may be imported freely upon presentation of the original invoice.

Imports of certain agricultural goods are restricted, irrespective of origin. A global quota list contains a few quotas for agricultural products for which imports are permitted up to fixed limits. These quotas apply to all countries, and, for some of these products, import restrictions are imposed only seasonally. New and secondhand ships and certain categories of fishing vessels may be imported freely. The importation of radio remittance equipment, such as radio controls, is subject to approval by the Directorate of Telecommunications in respect of frequency. The importation of a small number of goods is prohibited for health and similar reasons, and certain goods (some grains, alcoholic beverages, pharmaceutical products, and drugs) are imported by government monopolies.

Direct trade credits may be extended for import (and export) financing without a license from the Bank of Norway.

Payments for Invisibles

Payments for invisibles may be made freely. There are no restrictions on the types of payments a person (resident or nonresident) may take out of Norway, but banknotes exceeding the equivalent of Nkr 25,000 (both Norwegian and foreign) must be reported to the customs authorities.

Exports and Export Proceeds

Most goods may be exported freely to any country against a declaration or a license. Exports to Iraq and the Socialist People's Libyan Arab Jamahiriya are prohibited. Exports to the Federal Republic of Yugoslavia (Serbia/Montenegro) and areas of the Republic of Bosnia and Herzegovina that are controlled by the Bosnian Serbs are also prohibited,

with the exception of medical supplies and certain food items. Exports subject to regulation are listed and require export licenses. Exports to any country valued at not more than Nkr 2,000 are exempt from declaration or export license; for arms and ammunition, this limit is Nkr 500, and for fish and fish products, Nkr 1,000.

Export proceeds need not be repatriated to Norway.

Proceeds from Invisibles

There is no limit on the amount of foreign exchange a person (resident or nonresident) may bring into Norway, but banknotes exceeding the equivalent of Nkr 25,000 (both Norwegian and foreign) must be reported to the customs authorities.

Capital

Norwegian companies and private individuals are permitted to make direct investments abroad; direct investments in the form of shares that are not normally traded in a European Economic Area (EEA) country must, however, be made through Norwegian stockbrokers. Securities subject to the stockbroker requirement that are kept abroad must be deposited with a Norwegian bank or stockbroker. The stockbroker and deposit requirements will not apply if documentation of proof can be provided that the security is subject to regulatory and supervisory arrangements equivalent to EEA standards. Foreign exchange banks, exposure-regulated financial institutions, insurance companies, and stockbrokers dealing in foreign securities on their own account are exempt from the stockbroker and deposit requirements. Foreign exchange banks are also exempted when dealing on behalf of a resident. However, foreign exchange banks and financial institutions subject to exposure regulation must submit reports on their net foreign currency position to the Bank of Norway. Net positions of up to 10 percent of the financial institutions' equity and subordinated loan capital may be taken out in individual currencies, and the aggregate position must be kept within 20 percent of the financial institutions' equity and subordinated loan capital.

There is no limit on purchases by residents of foreign currency bonds, and residents are permitted to purchase foreign bonds and certificates. Purchases by residents of insurance services abroad, other than injury insurance, are prohibited if the insurance company is not registered in an EEA country. Nonresidents may purchase Norwegian bonds and certificates without restriction. There is no restriction on the importation into or exportation from Norway of securities.

Personal capital transfers, such as transfers relating to family loans, gifts, inheritances, legacies, dowries, emigrants' assets, savings of nonresident workers, and amounts in settlement of immigrants' debts, may be made freely.

Gold

Residents may freely purchase, hold, and sell gold in any form. No customs duties or other charges or fees are payable on imports or exports of gold bullion and gold coins not contained in jewelry. Domestic sales of gold bullion and gold coins are subject to the regular value-added tax at a rate of 22 percent, except gold coins produced after January 1, 1967.

Changes During 1994

Administration of Control

May 27. Sanctions against Haiti were introduced in accordance with UN Security Council Resolution No. 917/94.

October 16. The sanctions against Haiti were lifted in accordance with UN Security Council Resolution No. 944/94.

December 2. Sanctions were imposed on those areas of the Republic of Bosnia and Herzegovina that are controlled by the Bosnian Serbs, in accordance with UN Security Council Resolution No. 942/94.

Capital

January 14. As a result of the EEA agreement, the requirement that residents' investments in securities have to be made through domestic stockbrokers and deposited with a domestic stockbroker or bank, was modified. Also modified was the prohibition against purchases by residents of insurance services abroad.

April 29. Norwegian companies and branches of foreign companies established in accordance with rules laid down in the EEA agreement, that issue payment cards for use by residents abroad (or in Norway by nonresidents) were required to be registered with Norges Bank and report transactions to the Central Bank.

OMAN

(Position as of December 31, 1994)

Exchange Arrangement

The currency of Oman is the Rial Omani, which is pegged to the U.S. dollar, the intervention currency, at RO 1 per US$2.6008. The Central Bank of Oman maintains fixed buying and selling rates for the U.S. dollar; on December 31, 1994, the rates were RO 1 per US$2.6042 (buying) and RO 1 per US$2.5974 (selling). The commercial bank rates for other currencies are based on market rates in London. There are arrangements for forward cover against exchange rate risk operating in the official and commercial banking sectors. There are no taxes or subsidies on purchases or sales of foreign exchange.

Oman informed the Fund on June 19, 1974 that it formally accepted the obligations of Article VIII, Sections 2, 3, and 4 of the Fund Agreement.

Administration of Control

Exchange control authority is vested in the Central Bank, but there is no exchange control legislation in Oman.

In accordance with the Fund's Executive Board Decision No. 144-(52/51) adopted on August 14, 1952, Oman notified the Fund, on January 27, 1993, that certain restrictions had been imposed on the making of payments and transfers for current international transactions in respect of the Federal Republic of Yugoslavia (Serbia/Montenegro).

Prescription of Currency

All settlements with Israel and the Federal Republic of Yugoslavia (Serbia/Montenegro) are prohibited, as is the use of their currencies. No other prescription of currency requirements are in force.

Nonresident Accounts

No distinction is made between accounts held by residents and those held by nonresidents.

Imports and Import Payments

All imports from Israel and the Federal Republic of Yugoslavia (Serbia/Montenegro) are prohibited. Imports of a few commodities are prohibited for reasons of health, security, or public policy. Also, seasonal bans are imposed on the importation of fruits and vegetables that are grown locally. In addition, companies operating in Oman and trading in manufactured oil products are prohibited from importing specified products as long as domestic production is deemed adequate to satisfy local demand. Licenses are required for imports. Foreign exchange for payments abroad for authorized imports may be obtained freely.

The customs regime consists of five bands, and the rates range from 5 percent for most general goods to 100 percent on alcoholic beverages, pork, and limes. Customs duties are not levied on government imports.

Exports and Export Proceeds

All exports to Israel and the Federal Republic of Yugoslavia (Serbia/Montenegro) are prohibited, and exports or re-exports of live animals and foodstuffs may be prohibited in times of shortage in Oman. All other commodities may be exported freely. No requirements are attached to receipts from exports or re-exports; the proceeds need not be repatriated or surrendered, and they may be disposed of freely, regardless of the currency involved. Exports of Maria Theresa dollars are prohibited.

Payments for and Proceeds from Invisibles

Payments for and proceeds from invisibles are not restricted. Payments must not, however, be made to or received from Israel or the Federal Republic of Yugoslavia (Serbia/Montenegro). Travelers may bring in or take out any amount in domestic or foreign banknotes.

Capital

No exchange control requirements are imposed on capital receipts or on payments by residents or nonresidents, except that no payments may be made to or received from Israel or the Federal Republic of Yugoslavia (Serbia/Montenegro). Investment in business firms in Oman by foreign natural or juridical persons requires prior approval and is regulated by the Law for the Organization and Encouragement of Industry, which came into effect on January 15, 1979, and the Foreign Investment Law enacted in June 1983. Under the 1983 Foreign Investment Law, joint ventures are offered a five-year tax holiday, renewable for an additional five years under certain conditions.

The Oman Development Bank can provide medium- and long-term loans at preferential interest rates for project financing in the petroleum, agricultural, fishery, and mineral sectors; it can also give assistance in preinvestment research. The direction of foreign capital to large production or manufacturing projects is encouraged. In addition, the Government provides loans at subsidized interest rates for those projects with a majority Omani shareholding that are used for industrial production for exportation, industrial production using indigenous raw materials or labor, or the development of tourism.

Gold

The monetary authorities and authorized resident and nonresident banks may, without license, purchase, hold, and sell gold in any form at home or abroad. They may also import and export gold in any form without a license and without payment of customs duties or taxes. Transactions involving Israel and the Federal Republic of Yugoslavia (Serbia/Montenegro) are prohibited.

Changes During 1994

No significant changes occurred in the exchange and trade system.

PAKISTAN

(Position as of February 28, 1995)

Exchange Arrangement

The currency of Pakistan is the Pakistan Rupee, for which the U.S. dollar is the intervention currency. A managed floating exchange rate system is operated, under which the State Bank of Pakistan sets the rate at which it will purchase and sell U.S. dollars in transactions with authorized dealers. On December 31, 1994, the State Bank's spot buying and selling rates for transactions with authorized dealers were PRs 30.800 and PRs 30.954, respectively, per US$1. All foreign exchange transactions with the public must be conducted through authorized dealers and money changers and effected at rates authorized by the State Bank. In the calculation of spot exchange rates for other currencies, a margin of 0.2 percent is provided on the previous day's closing buying and selling rates for the currency concerned in the New York market.

Authorized dealers in Pakistan are permitted to cover their requirements of specified currencies in foreign exchange markets abroad. They may also cover their permitted transactions in specified currencies against U.S. dollars or Pakistan rupees, either spot or forward for a limited period, with their agents in the countries concerned. In addition, they offer forward cover in the currencies of the member countries of the Asian Clearing Union (ACU) for exports and imports effected under that arrangement. On June 22, 1994, the State Bank eliminated its foreign exchange risk cover for the private sector's direct borrowings inclusive of suppliers' credit, Pay-As-You-Earn (PAYE) loans, etc.

Forward exchange cover for private foreign currency deposits is provided by the State Bank, which charges an annual fee of 3 percent, 6 percent, 2.5 percent, and 4.75 percent, respectively, on deposits in deutsche mark, Japanese yen, pounds sterling, and U.S. dollars.

Residents and nonresidents may use foreign exchange to purchase foreign currency bearer certificates (FCBCs) with a maturity of up to five years denominated in deutsche mark, Japanese yen, pounds sterling, or U.S. dollars. FCBCs are available in various denominations (deutsche mark, from DM 100 to DM 100,000; Japanese yen, from ¥10,000 to ¥10 million; pounds sterling, from £100 to £50,000; and U.S. dollars, from $100 to $100,000). They may be freely brought into and taken out of the country, encashed at any time in Pakistan rupees or in foreign exchange at the exchange rate prevailing at the time of the encashment, and used by residents to undertake any current or international capital transactions. FCBCs yield rates of return related to market interest rates for each respective currency. Sales of bearer certificates denominated in U.S. dollars (DBCs) with a maturity of one year were discontinued on November 22, 1994. Anyone was allowed to purchase them without revealing the source of foreign exchange and may encash the principal and accrued returns either in foreign exchange or in Pakistan rupees at the official rate. At the end of December 1994, the return on these certificates was 0.25 percent above LIBOR. Foreign exchange bearer certificates (FEBCs) denominated in Pakistan rupees are available in denominations ranging from PRs 500 to PRs 100,000; their face value is 14.5 percent higher one year after issuance, 31 percent higher after two years, 52 percent higher after three years, 74 percent higher after four years, 99 percent higher after five years, and 131 percent higher after six years.

Pakistan formally accepted the obligations of Article VIII, Sections 2, 3, and 4 of the Fund Agreement, as from July 1, 1994.

Administration of Control

The State Bank has delegated authority to a number of banks and financial institutions to deal in all foreign currencies, to supervise surrender requirements, and to sell foreign exchange for certain purposes within limits prescribed by the State Bank. Certain foreign trade transactions are conducted through various state trading agencies, such as the Trading Corporation of Pakistan, Ltd. (TCP), the Cotton Export Corporation of Pakistan, Ltd. (CECP), and the Rice Export Corporation of Pakistan, Ltd. (RECP).

Prescription of Currency

Exchange receipts and payments abroad must be effected through an authorized foreign exchange dealer, in principle, in any convertible currency or in Pakistan rupees to or from nonresident rupee bank accounts. Certain settlements with specified countries are channeled through special accounts. Letters of credit for imports from all other countries must be established in foreign currency or in Pakistan rupees for credit to a nonresident bank account of the country of the beneficiary or of the country of origin or shipment of goods.

Payments to, and receipts from, member countries of the ACU (Bangladesh, India, Islamic Republic of Iran, Myanmar, Nepal, and Sri Lanka) in respect of current transactions are effected through the ACU in Asian Monetary Units (AMUs) or in the domestic currency of one of the member countries involved. No exchange control is exercised over transactions with the Islamic State of Afghanistan, and settlements are made in Pakistan rupees or in afghanis. Payments between Pakistan and Israel are not permitted.[1]

Resident and Nonresident Accounts

Resident foreign currency accounts. Residents of Pakistan are allowed to open and maintain foreign currency accounts (FCAs) with banks in Pakistan on the same basis as nonresidents. These accounts may be credited with remittances from abroad, traveler's checks, foreign currency notes, and proceeds from FEBCs and FCBCs, including DBCs. Sources of acquisition of foreign exchange are not required to be revealed. However, receipts from exports of goods and services; earnings from services of residents; earnings and profits of overseas offices or branches of Pakistani firms or companies and banks; and foreign exchange released from Pakistan for any specified purpose may not be credited to these accounts. Balances held in these accounts are freely transferable abroad, and there are no limits on amounts of withdrawal. These accounts may be permanently retained, and the rate of interest on term deposits (of three months and up to three years) is fixed by the State Bank with the approval of the Government. The rates are based on the Eurodollar deposit rate of Barclays Bank, London. The margins over the Eurodollar deposit rates range from 0.75 of 1 percent for three-month deposits to 1.625 percent for three-year deposits.

Nonresident accounts. The accounts of individuals, firms, or companies residing outside Pakistan are designated nonresident accounts.[2] Authorized banks are permitted to open nonresident accounts for nonbank nonresidents without the prior approval of the State Bank when the accounts are opened with funds received from abroad through banking channels or with rupee funds accepted for remittance abroad. Debits and credits to nonresi-

dent accounts for specified purposes may be made by authorized banks without the prior approval of the State Bank. Accounts of residents of India, other than the accounts of the Indian Embassy and its personnel, are blocked.

Pakistani nationals residing abroad and foreign nationals, whether residing abroad or in Pakistan, and firms, corporations, and charitable bodies owned by persons who are otherwise eligible to open FCAs may open FCAs with banks in Pakistan without the prior approval of the exchange control authorities. The accounts may be denominated in deutsche mark, French francs, Japanese yen, pounds sterling, and U.S. dollars; credit balances may be transferred abroad, and interest on such accounts is exempt from income tax. Deposit holders wishing to make payments in Pakistan must first convert the foreign exchange drawn from their accounts into Pakistan rupees. If Pakistani nationals holding such accounts return to Pakistan, they may retain the accounts permanently. Banks in Pakistan receiving such deposits must sell the foreign exchange to the State Bank. Authorized dealers under the FCA facility may accept term deposits in foreign currency from their overseas branches and foreign banks operating abroad, including financial institutions owned by them; such term deposits must be at least $5 million (or the equivalent in other currencies) for a maturity period of at least six months.

Imports and Import Payments

Annual Import Policy Orders (IPOs) outline the regulations that apply to imports. All items that do not appear on either the negative list or the list of items permitted to be imported subject to health and safety requirements may be freely imported. The negative list mainly consists of items banned for religious and health reasons, or to discourage consumption of luxury items, and goods banned in accordance with international agreements.[3]

The negative list of imports was shortened in July 1993 and again in July and December 1994. Some items on the negative list may be imported under certain circumstances, principally by export industries, public sector agencies, or under the personal baggage scheme. Import licensing was eliminated in July 1993. The 6 percent import license fee was abolished on June 5, 1994.

The import regime is subject to certain other supplementary qualifications, the most important of

---

[1]The restrictions on trade and payments with South Africa were lifted in July 1994.

[2]Different rules apply to the nonresident rupee accounts of individuals, firms, or companies, on the one hand, and to the nonresident rupee accounts of banks, on the other hand.

[3]Some of the currently prohibited imports fall outside these categories (i.e., some prohibited items are not produced in Pakistan and do not fit into the category of goods banned for religious, health, or luxury consumption reasons).

which are the following: (1) Imports from Israel are prohibited, as are imports of goods originating in Israel but shipped from other countries. Both the private and the public sectors may import 324 specified items or categories of goods directly from India. (2) Special provisions govern the importation by export industries of items importable on fulfillment of conditions and of items on the negative list.

Import payments may be made against irrevocable letters of credit, provided that the letters do not stipulate payment of any amount by way of interest in the case of usance bills and, further, that in the case of books, journals, magazines, and periodicals, they stipulate payment on a sight draft or usance bills basis.

Imports on a consignment basis are allowed by the State Bank of Pakistan. When the importers desire to import on a joint basis from any country either for the sake of their own convenience or economy, or because of the suppliers' inability to supply goods in small consignments, the importers may establish joint letters of credit. For imports under barters or any other special trading arrangement, the letters of credit may be opened within such a period as may be specified in the relevant public notice issued by the authorities. In case of imports under loans or credits, which require the contracts to be approved by the agencies of the Government of Pakistan, the importer shall open a letter of credit within 60 days of the date the contract is approved. In case of imports under suppliers' credit and the PAYE scheme, letters of credit may be opened only if the contract has been registered with the State Bank of Pakistan. Letters of credit are generally established for up to 12 months, with the following exceptions: (1) when machinery and millwork must be specifically fabricated and the period of manufacture is more than 12 months, letters of credit shall be established with a validity period of up to 24 months; (2) for all items other than machinery and millwork the period of 12 months may be extended for an additional 24 months on payment of an additional fee of 0.25 percent of the unused value of the letter of credit for each period of 6 months from the date of its expiry; (3) in the case of machinery, letters of credit may be extended for up to 24 months from the date of expiry of initial validity on additional payment of 0.25 percent of the unused value of the letter of credit for each 6-month period; and (4) if the letters of credit are opened against loans, credits, barters, or special trading arrangements whereby shipment could not take place owing to circumstances beyond the control of the importer, revalidation may be allowed within the validity of the loan, credit, barter, or special trading arrangement without additional payment.

Payment for Invisibles

Payments for invisibles are controlled by the State Bank and in many cases require its prior approval. Payments to Israel are not permitted.

Payments for invisibles connected with imports are generally given the same treatment as that accorded to the underlying trade transaction. Except with respect to certain aid shipments, transport insurance must be taken out with insurance companies in Pakistan. Commissions, brokerage, or other charges paid to foreign importers or agents by Pakistani exporters are generally limited to a maximum of 5 percent of the invoice value, except for cotton and cement, for which the maximum is 1 percent. The maximum percentage for sporting goods, surgical instruments, cutlery, leather goods, ready-made garments and other textile made-ups, carpets, and plastic manufactures is 7 percent; for engineering goods, it is 10 percent; and for books, journals, and magazines, it is 33⅓ percent.

The remittance of dividends declared on current profits is allowed freely to foreign shareholders if the investment was made on a repatriable basis. The remittance of profits by branches of foreign companies other than banks and those engaged in insurance, shipping, and the airline business is permitted without restriction provided that the required documents are submitted to the State Bank. The same regulation applies to head office expenses charged to a branch's profit-and-loss account and accepted for tax purposes by the Pakistani income tax authorities.

Since August 30, 1993, foreign exchange for private travel to countries other than the Islamic State of Afghanistan, Bangladesh, and India is granted at the rate of $50 a day for up to 42 days during a calendar year on submission of travel documents to the authorized dealers. Requests for foreign exchange in excess of these amounts are to be referred by the authorized dealers to the State Bank of Pakistan giving justification for the additional amount. Unspent foreign exchange, however, must be surrendered to an authorized dealer. The entitlement can be used in installments. Remittances for undergraduate and postgraduate studies abroad and correspondence courses are not restricted. Foreign exchange for business travel, medical treatment, education, and sponsored cultural trips may be granted on a case-by-case basis. Foreign exchange allowances for students' tuition fees and expenses as required by institutions may be obtained from authorized dealers without approval from the State

Bank. Allowances for professional training abroad are granted at $1,200 a month. Requests for foreign exchange in excess of $1,200 a month for professional training must be referred to the State Bank duly accompanied by cogent reasons and supporting documents. There are also specific allowances for pilgrims' travel to Saudi Arabia. Exporters of goods with annual export earnings of more than PRs 2.5 million and exporters of services with annual earnings of more than PRs 0.25 million are granted a renewable business travel allowance of $200 a day, up to $6,000 for each business trip. In addition, business travelers may settle credit card charges of up to $100 a day, subject to a maximum of $3,000 for a 30-day visit, with the encashment of FCBCs. The 5 percent advance tax on the value of foreign exchange purchased for travel was abolished on July 1, 1994. Foreigners may make family remittances to the extent of the difference between the net income of the applicant and his or her estimated expenses in Pakistan. In case the family of a resident Pakistani is temporarily living abroad for personal reasons, foreign exchange will be provided upon bona fide request.

Persons leaving Pakistan (foreigners and Pakistani nationals) may take out with them foreign currency without limit.

Exports and Export Proceeds

Exports of specified commodities[4] to any destination and all exports to Israel are prohibited. Exports of most other commodities are allowed freely. However, certain exports are subject to export quotas (e.g., maize, gram, split gram, and camels), quality controls (such as batteries, electric bulbs and appliances, and oil cakes), or minimum export prices (e.g., onyx blocks). The Cotton Export Corporation of Pakistan, Ltd. is responsible for the exportation of cotton, although the private sector has also been allowed into the export trade. Cotton is exported to India without involvement of any public sector agency; Basmati and other types of rice are exported through the Rice Exportation Corporation of Pakistan, Ltd., but private traders are also allowed. Cement and sugar, which may be exported by public and private sector entities, are subject to a quota.

Chemical fertilizers may also be exported by private sector units. Trade samples that may be exported without prior approval from the State Bank are limited to the equivalent of $2,000; the limit for leather garments is 50 pieces, without a value limit. There are no quantitative or value ceilings if samples are damaged. The State Bank requires a declaration from the exporter that payment will be received in accordance with the prescribed method and within the prescribed time except for goods manufactured in the export processing zones. The authorized dealer certifies the export form for shipment. Exporters are obliged to collect and surrender export proceeds within four months of shipment, although the State Bank may allow an extension of this period. Exporters may, however, with the prior approval of the State Bank, grant deferred payment terms. The surrender of afghanis accruing from exports to the Islamic State of Afghanistan is not required.

Under the Export Processing Unit (EPU) Scheme, selected industries, raw materials, intermediate goods used for the manufacturing of exports, imports of machinery, and components not manufactured locally are exempt from import duties and local taxes.[5] The export-output ratio required to qualify for the EPU scheme is 50 percent in the first two years and 60 percent in the third year and beyond.

In November 1994, a new Special Industrial Zone scheme was introduced for 12 designated underdeveloped areas with concessions for import duties and sales tax on imported plants and machinery, provided that letters of credit are opened before June 1996 and for income tax (time bound for 10 years) provided the projects commence operation by June 30, 1999. Projects whose cost is higher than $10 million and that employ more than 100 persons are exempted from 25 percent of customs duty on raw materials provided they commence operation before June 30, 1999, and letters of credit are opened before June 30, 1996.

Export financing at concessional rates is provided for all exports, with the exception of 24 specified items,[6] based on irrevocable letters of credit or firm

---

[4]Prohibited exports include ferrous and nonferrous metals (excluding iron and steel manufactured goods), unprocessed edible oils, certain grains, certain dairy products, certain live animals, beef and mutton, timber, certain hides and skins, pulses and beans, wet-blue leather made from cowhides and calfhides, charcoal, certain animal products, intoxicants, certain oil seeds, wooden crates, arms, ammunition, explosives, fissionable material, maps and charts, paper waste, unfinished hockey sticks and blades, human skeletons, certain imported goods, and antiques.

[5]The industries included are textiles and clothing (other than spinning), leather and leather manufactures, chemicals and pharmaceuticals, engineering and electronics, ceramics, furniture, sporting goods, surgical instruments, and cutlery.

[6]The exceptions are raw cotton; cotton yarn; fish other than frozen and preserved; mutton and beef; petroleum products; raw vegetable material; wool and animal hair; raw animal material; animal fodder; all grains including grain flour; stone, sand, and gravel; waste and scrap of all kinds; crude fertilizer; oilseeds, nuts, and kernels; jewelry exported under the Entrustment Scheme; live animals; hides and skins; wet-blue leather; inorganic elements, oxides, etc.; crude minerals; works of art and antiques; all metals; furs; and wood in rough or squared form.

export orders on a case-by-case basis under Part I of the Export Finance Scheme,[7] or, alternatively, based on the exporter's performance in the previous year on a revolving basis under Part II of the scheme. However, the State Bank is phasing out its outstanding stock of concessional loans to the export sector at the rate of 25 percent a year, so as to completely eliminate the outstanding amount by July 1, 1996. Under the new system, the State Bank refinancing in excess of the above limit is held in a blocked account (special deposit account) in favor of the lending bank. Interest is paid on the account at the average weighted treasury bill rate from the last auction. The amount refinanced by the State Bank totaled PRs 2.78 billion as of December 31, 1994; of this amount, PRs 18.5 billion was held in the special deposit account.

Rebates of 25 percent and 50 percent are available against the tax payable on income attributable to the sales proceeds from exports of semifinished goods and finished goods, respectively, that are manufactured in Pakistan. For value-added items, such as engineering products, garments, leather and leather products, textile products, and hand-knotted carpets and rugs, the rate of rebate is 75 percent; the rebate rate on engineering goods is 90 percent. Industrial units established under the PAYE scheme are permitted to use a maximum of 50 percent of the f.o.b. value of exports for payments of foreign exchange obligations in respect of royalties, technical fees, and incidental charges. Under the Open Bond Manufacturing Scheme, raw materials and intermediate goods imported or purchased locally and used for manufacturing for exports are exempt from import duties and local taxes. At present, the following industries are covered by this scheme: textiles and clothing (other than spinning), leather and leather manufactures, chemicals and pharmaceuticals, engineering and electronics, ceramics, furniture, sporting goods, and surgical instruments. The exportation of cows is subject to quota restrictions. Exporters who are members of export houses may retain up to 5 percent of their foreign exchange earnings for export promotion and related costs.

---

[7]Under specified conditions, authorized dealers may grant concessional financing, without the State Bank's approval, against an irrevocable letter of credit or a firm export order. Smaller projects set up in these zones enjoy complete exemption from import duties on plants, machinery, equipment, and raw materials for a period of ten years, provided they commence operation by June 30, 1999, and letters of credit are opened by June 30, 1996.

Proceeds from Invisibles

With the exception of afghanis, which may be retained, foreign exchange earned from invisibles must be surrendered within three months. Travelers may bring in PRs 500 a person in Pakistan currency notes from India; the limit for other sources is PRs 3,000 a person. There is no limit on the importation of other currency notes and coins, except coins that are legal tender in India; these coins may be imported only up to the value of Indian Rs 5 a person at a time.

Travel agents and tour agents are permitted to retain up to 5 percent of their foreign exchange earnings for marketing and related export promotion expenses.

Capital

Approval from the Government is required for the establishment of industries involving (1) arms and ammunition; (2) printing securities and currency and minting coins; (3) high explosives; (4) radioactive substances (investments in these areas by domestic investors are also subject to approval); and (5) agricultural land, forestry irrigation, real estate, insurance, and health.

Currently, the Foreign Private Investment (Promotion and Protection) Act of 1976 does not guarantee repatriation of capital for investments undertaken before September 1954. These investments are regulated by the terms and conditions governing each investment. Amendments to these provisions are under consideration.

Foreign nationals in Pakistan or abroad may register their investments in National Prize Bonds issued by the Government of Pakistan; the principal in such transactions may be repatriated at any time, but the prize funds are treated as savings for the purpose of exchange control regulations on outward transfers.

Transfers of capital abroad by resident nationals are, in general, not permitted; the purchase of foreign securities by Pakistani residents is permitted through FEBCs and must be reported to the State Bank. Detailed rules govern the transfer of capital by persons emigrating or retiring from Pakistan, depending upon the nationality of the person and the country to which the transfer is to be made. Foreign nationals temporarily residing in Pakistan are treated as nonresidents for purposes of transfers of securities. The issuance, sale, or transfer of Pakistani securities in favor of nonresident Pakistanis is permitted, provided that the securities are registered at the address in Pakistan of the purchaser and investment is made on the basis of nonrepatriation of capital and return. Pakistani securities held by non-resident foreign nationals may be transferred to other nonresident foreign nationals against payments abroad, subject to the same terms and conditions as those applicable to the transferor. General permission has also been granted to Pakistani nationals residing outside Pakistan and to foreign nationals residing in or outside Pakistan to make investments in units of the National Investment Trust, on a repatriable basis against payment in foreign exchange. Public limited companies whose shares are quoted on stock exchanges in Pakistan and private limited or unlisted public limited companies engaged in manufacturing are permitted to issue or transfer shares on a repatriable basis to a nonresident Pakistani national, a person with two nationalities (including Pakistani), a foreign national, or a company incorporated outside Pakistan (excluding branches in Pakistan of such companies and a company owned or controlled by a foreign government), provided that the issue price or purchase price in the case of a listed company is not less than the price as certified by a stock exchange broker and that, in the case of private limited or unlisted public limited companies, the value of shares is paid in foreign exchange either through a remittance of foreign currency from abroad or out of a foreign currency account maintained by the subscriber in Pakistan. Nonresidents are permitted to invest in corporate debt instruments on a repatriable basis against payment in foreign exchange.

Permission is not required for exports of share certificates by companies whose shares can be issued or transferred in favor of nonresidents covered by the general authority granted by the State Bank. Proceeds accruing from the liquidation of nonresident capital assets not covered by repatriation arrangements must be credited to nonresident accounts. Balances in blocked accounts may be invested in approved government securities payable in Pakistan rupees or placed as time deposits with banks.

Foreign banks functioning in Pakistan may underwrite share issues of companies incorporated in Pakistan, provided that the total value of shares in each issue does not exceed 30 percent of the capital offered to the general public for subscription or 30 percent of its own paid-up capital and reserve, whichever is less. The foreign banks may also underwrite public issues of participation term certificates, term finance certificates, and modaraba certificates, provided that when the terms and conditions of their issue grant the option to the holders to convert the securities into ordinary shares, only 30 percent of total capital may be offered to the general public.

Pakistani nationals residing abroad may invest in new public share offers in Pakistan by remitting foreign exchange or by debiting their foreign currency accounts in Pakistan; dividends, as well as the proceeds upon sale, may be transferred abroad, provided that tax, if applicable, is paid. Pakistani nationals require prior approval from the State Bank to sell movable or immovable assets held abroad, and liquidation proceeds must be repatriated to Pakistan through normal banking channels.

Gold

The exportation of gold is prohibited unless authorized by the State Bank; such permission is not usually granted. Pakistani nationals and foreign nationals coming from abroad are allowed to bring in unlimited quantities of gold in their personal baggage. Similarly, individual firms or companies who are residents of Pakistan are allowed to import up to 500 troy ounces at a time.

Changes During 1994

Exchange Arrangement

June 30. The foreign exchange forward cover operations for trade credit and foreign loans for working capital of foreign resident companies were abolished. The forward cover fee for foreign currency deposits surrendered by banks was raised to 4.5 percent from 4 percent (for dollar deposits).

July 1. Pakistan formally accepted the obligations of Article VIII, Sections 2, 3, and 4 of the Fund Agreement.

October 11. The annual forward cover fees for foreign currency deposits surrendered by banks were raised as follows: to 4.75 percent from 4 percent for U.S. dollar deposits; to 2.5 percent from 2.25 percent for pound sterling deposits (and to 3.5 percent on January 1, 1995); to 6 percent from 5.75 percent for Japanese yen deposits (and to 9 percent on January 1, 1995); and to 3 percent from 2.25 percent for deutsche mark deposits (and to 5.5 percent on January 1, 1995).

Imports and Import Payments

January 11. The restricted list was abolished, and the items on this list were transferred to a list of permitted items subject to fulfillment of certain conditions for importation.

February 8. The value ceiling applicable to the importation of machinery was abolished.

June 15. The 6 percent import license fee was abolished.

Payments for Invisibles

June 5. The 5 percent advance tax on purchase of foreign exchange for travel was abolished.

Exports and Export Proceeds

June 5. All export duties levied on raw cotton, cotton yarn, oil cakes, molasses, raw hides and skins, and onyx blocks were removed.

PANAMA

(Position as of December 31, 1994)

Exchange Arrangement

The currency of Panama is the Panamanian Balboa, which is pegged to the U.S. dollar at B 1 per US$1. The U.S. dollar is legal tender and circulates freely in Panama; locally issued currency is limited to coins, including several commemorative coins in small denominations. Commercial banks quote buying and selling rates for certain other currencies based on the buying and selling rates for the U.S. dollar in markets abroad. There are no taxes or subsidies on purchases or sales of foreign exchange. There are no arrangements for forward cover against exchange rate risk operating in the official or the commercial banking sector.

Panama formally accepted the obligations of Article VIII, Sections 2, 3, and 4 of the Fund Agreement, as from November 26, 1946.

Administration of Control

In general, import or export licenses are not required. Only a few products are banned or require special import permits. Individuals or companies engaged in import activities require a commercial or industry license, which is issued by the Ministry of Commerce and Industry (MICI). Specific export licenses are required for products that are subject to export taxes and for certain other goods; these licenses are issued by the Ministry of Finance and Treasury. The MICI, through the Panama Trade Development Institute, is responsible for determining all aspects of agreements on free trade and bilateral preferential treatment with countries in the region. Panama has bilateral trade agreements with Costa Rica, the Dominican Republic, El Salvador, Guatemala, Honduras, and Nicaragua. Under an agreement with Mexico, 70 products may be exported from Panama to Mexico. The Ministry of Agriculture and Livestock Development (MIDA) and the Agricultural Marketing Institute (IMA), through various product-specific commissions, determine the import quotas for certain agricultural commodities.

Arrears are maintained with respect to external payments.

Prescription of Currency

There are no prescription of currency requirements.

Imports and Import Payments

There are no quantitative restrictions on industrial products, but import quotas, established by the MIDA and the IMA, are maintained on some products in the agricultural sector and agro-industries, including timber, salt, fishmeal, milk, and sugar. Imports by the public sector are subject to special requirements. Payments abroad may be made freely.

The tariff schedule is based on the Customs Cooperation Council Nomenclature (CCCN). However, a harmonized commodity description and coding system for customs tariffs will be introduced on January 1, 1995. Most tariff rates are on an ad valorem basis and are assessed on the c.i.f. value of imports. The present range of tariffs for the main agricultural products is between 30 percent and 100 percent. For some products, the tax is specific and is calculated on the basis of their weight in kilos. In cases where both tax rates are stated, the applicable rate is the one that produces the higher tax revenue. If the tax is specific, an additional tax of 7.5 percent on the c.i.f. value of imports is charged, except for (1) specified pharmaceutical products and foodstuffs, for which the additional tax rates are 2.5 percent and 3.5 percent, respectively; and (2) books and certain agricultural inputs, which are duty free. Many local industries are protected by tariffs aimed at promoting local and export industries. Exemptions from import and customs duties on equipment, machinery, and spare parts apply mainly to export-oriented industries and to industries concentrating on the local market, provided that certain conditions are met. A tariff reform program involving reductions in tariff ceilings and conversion of specific tariffs to ad valorem rates was implemented in August 1991 and continued into 1994. All imports into the city of Colón, designated as the Colón Free Zone, and the newly established export-processing zones are exempt from duties.

Exports and Export Proceeds

Export taxes are levied on gold, silver, platinum, manganese, other minerals, unrefined sugar, bananas, coconuts, scrap metal, pearls, animal wax, nispero gum, ipecac root, and rubber. Exports of firearms and ammunition are prohibited. Certain nontraditional exports (with a minimum local cost-of-production content of 20 percent) are eligible for tax credit certificates equivalent to 20 percent of value added. The export-processing zones are exempt from all taxes (and as such receive no tax credit certificates). Proceeds from exports are not subject to exchange control.

Any product (including raw materials and machinery) may be imported into the Colón Free Zone and be stored, modified, processed, assembled, repacked, and re-exported without being subject to customs procedures.

Payments for and Proceeds from Invisibles

Payments for and proceeds from invisibles are not restricted. A travel tax of 4 percent is levied on air and sea tickets bought in Panama and on tickets purchased for travel starting in Panama.

Capital

Inward and outward capital transfers by residents and nonresidents are not subject to exchange control. Some foreign-controlled banks are authorized to conduct business only with nonresidents.

Gold

Panama has issued two commemorative gold coins with face values of B 100 and B 500, which are legal tender but do not circulate. Residents may freely hold gold in any form, at home or abroad, and may freely negotiate gold in any form with residents or nonresidents, at home and abroad. Imports and exports of gold in any form other than jewelry carried as personal effects by travelers require a license if made by residents other than the monetary authorities; import licenses are issued by the Ministry of Commerce and Industry, and export licenses by the Ministry of Finance and Treasury. Exports of unworked gold produced in Panama are subject to an export duty of 1 percent ad valorem, and exports of gold coins (other than U.S. coins, which are exempt) are subject to a duty of 0.5 percent.

Changes During 1994

Imports and Import Payments

August 3. Quotas and prior approval requirements for imports of wheat, barley, broad soybeans, flour, and other glutens were abolished.

PAPUA NEW GUINEA

(Position as of December 31, 1994)

Exchange Arrangement

The currency of Papua New Guinea is the Papua New Guinea Kina, the external value of which is determined freely in twice-daily auctions on the basis of bids and offers. The authorized dealer banks participate in the auctions, with the Bank of Papua New Guinea acting as broker. Trading with retail customers is effected outside the auctions at a margin over the closing rate obtained from the preceding auction. The closing rate also becomes the official exchange rate, which on December 31, 1994, was US$0.8485 per K 1. The commercial banks, the only authorized foreign exchange dealers, publish rates for all current transactions with their customers within a maximum spread between the buying and selling rates of 2 percent. There are no taxes or subsidies on purchases or sales of foreign exchange.

Exporters and importers are free to take out forward cover with the commercial banks at market-determined rates. Each commercial bank is subject to a prudential limit on its uncovered forward position. At its discretion, the Bank of Papua New Guinea may intervene in the forward foreign exchange market.

Papua New Guinea formally accepted the obligations of Article VIII, Sections 2, 3, and 4 of the Fund Agreement, as from December 4, 1975.

Administration of Control

Foreign exchange control is administered by the Bank of Papua New Guinea under the Central Banking (Foreign Exchange and Gold) Regulations, Chapter 138. Overall policy is determined by the Government with the advice of the Bank of Papua New Guinea and the Ministry of Finance. The Bank of Papua New Guinea has delegated considerable powers to the commercial banks operating in Papua New Guinea, which have been appointed authorized dealers in foreign exchange and gold. Export licensing is administered by the Department of Foreign Affairs and Trade.

In accordance with the Fund's Executive Board Decision No. 144–(52/51) adopted on August 14, 1952, Papua New Guinea notified the Fund on July 22, 1992 that, in compliance with UN Security Council Resolution No. 757 (1992), certain restrictions had been imposed on the making of payments and transfers for current international transactions in respect of the Federal Republic of Yugoslavia (Serbia/Montenegro).

Prescription of Currency

Contractual commitments to persons residing outside Papua New Guinea and expressed in a foreign currency must be paid in foreign currency.[1] Export proceeds may be received in any foreign currency.

Nonresident Accounts

Authorized foreign exchange dealers (at present, the five commercial banks) may open and maintain foreign currency accounts and foreign currency term deposits in Papua New Guinea for residents and nonresidents.

Imports and Import Payments

Imports of a limited number of goods are restricted for reasons of health and security, and imports of a number of items, including meat, sugar, and pork, are prohibited to protect domestic markets. The importation of most fresh fruits and vegetables is banned (except for apples, onions, and potatoes for processing). In the event of shortages on the domestic market, special import licenses are issued and imports are subject to a 50 percent tariff.

Authorized dealers may, without referring to the Bank of Papua New Guinea, approve applications for import transactions that are not subject to quotas or licensing requirements. The tariff regime consists of the following rates: (1) essential items, including food staples (rice, and canned fish and meat that is not produced domestically), and medical and educational supplies, duty free; (2) basic goods, including some consumer goods and raw materials, 11 percent; (3) intermediate goods, including goods with satisfactory domestic substitutes, 40 percent; and (4) luxury goods, including jewelry, cosmetics, poker machines, and nonessential food and beverage items, 55 percent (except for television sets, cameras, video recorders, and hi-fi equipment, for which the tariff rate is 10 percent).

Payments for Invisibles

Approval is readily granted for most payments for invisibles, provided that supporting documentation is produced. Authorized foreign exchange dealers may approve payments and transfers up to

---

[1]Foreign currencies are defined as all currencies other than the kina.

the equivalent of K 500,000 a year for any purpose for all adult individuals or corporations. Payments and transfers in excess of the equivalent of K 500,000, except payments for the servicing of foreign debt, must be referred to the Bank of Papua New Guinea for approval. Payments for the servicing of foreign debt may be approved without a fixed limit by authorized dealers. For payments or transfers exceeding the equivalent of K 50,000 a year, a certificate of tax payment is required.

Travelers may not take or send out of Papua New Guinea domestic currency in excess of K 200 in notes and K 5 in coins; however, domestic coins issued for numismatic purposes may be taken out freely. Overseas visitors are free to take out any currency they brought in and declared on arrival.

Exports and Export Proceeds

Residents of Papua New Guinea may export goods without exchange control formality on the condition that they comply with the terms of the general authority issued by the Bank of Papua New Guinea. The essential conditions of this authority are that payments for goods exported must be received within six months of the date of export and that the proceeds must be sold to the Bank of Papua New Guinea or an authorized dealer in Papua New Guinea. When exporters are not in a position to comply with the conditions of the general authority, they must apply to the Bank for specific authority. No authority is needed for certain categories of goods, including travelers' personal effects. Export licenses are required for certain goods (e.g., logs, pearls, fishery and marine products, woodchips, sandalwood, rattan, coffee, cocoa, and copra) under the Export (Valuation and Control) Act. Log export licenses are issued subject to minimum export price guidelines. There is no export license requirement on timber. Although exports of most unprocessed products are subject to export levies, these have been temporarily waived, except those on fishery and forestry products. Export taxes on logs range from 26 percent to 46 percent. Fish exports are subject to a tax of 10 percent.

Proceeds from Invisibles

Approval is required for the disposal of foreign currency proceeds, other than by sale to an authorized dealer in Papua New Guinea, or for its retention. Residents are not permitted to retain foreign exchange earnings from any source without the approval of the Bank of Papua New Guinea. Overseas visitors may bring in any amount of currency for travel expenses.

Capital

Outward transfers of foreign-owned capital are allowed, provided that tax clearance certificates are produced. Direct investments outside Papua New Guinea are subject to certain limitations. Authorized dealers may approve outward investments by resident individuals and corporations up to the equivalent of K 500,000 a year. Income from the investment must be returned to Papua New Guinea as received, and details of investments held and income received must be submitted annually to the Bank of Papua New Guinea. Prior clearance from the tax authorities is required for these transactions if the amount exceeds K 10,000 in any calendar year.

Permission is required for residents to enter into an agreement to borrow in foreign currencies. However, authorized foreign exchange dealers may approve offshore foreign currency borrowing by residents, other than businesses involved in mineral resources exploration, up to a maximum limit equivalent to K 5 million, provided that the term is for not less than three years and that interest rates and fees do not exceed the levels specified by the Bank of Papua New Guinea. Repayment of principal is subject to a six-month moratorium, commencing on the date of disbursements. A maximum debt-to-equity ratio of 5:1 applies to net outstanding borrowing of up to the equivalent of K 5 million; the maximum debt-to-equity ratio for net aggregate borrowing in excess of the equivalent of K 5 million is determined by the Bank of Papua New Guinea. In the case of a business involved in mineral resource exploration activities, inward investment is considered non-interest-bearing equity or loan funds (including preference shares) until the business is successful, at which point any excess above the minimum equity-to-debt ratio specified for that operation can be converted into an interest-bearing loan.

Authorized dealers may approve applications for inward direct investment and for inward portfolio investment, provided that the aggregate amount does not exceed K 500,000 a year. Applications for larger investments must be referred to the Bank of Papua New Guinea.

Gold

Dealings in gold in Papua New Guinea are not regulated. The exportation of gold is restricted to licensed gold exporters. For the large mines, the licenses are contained in their respective mining agreements. For exports of alluvial gold, specific export licenses are required from the central bank.

Changes During 1994

Exchange Arrangement

September 11. The kina was devalued by 12 percent against the basket of currencies to which it is pegged. In terms of the U.S. dollar, the rate changed from K 1.0563 per US$1 to K 0.9204 per US$1, representing a devaluation of 12.9 percent.

October 10. The exchange rate of the kina was allowed to float. Under the new arrangement, the exchange rate of the kina would be determined in twice-daily auctions organized by the Bank of Papua New Guinea in which the authorized dealer banks would participate, on the basis of bids and offers supplied to each auction session. During a period between two consecutive auctions, the banks would trade foreign currencies with their retail customers at a margin over the closing rate of the previous auction.

Imports and Import Payments

March 8. Three import duty rates were increased as follows: (1) the basic rate was increased by one percentage point to 11 percent; (2) the protective rate was increased to 33 percent from 30 percent; and (3) the luxury rate was increased to 55 percent from 50 percent.

November 9. The protective rate was raised to 40 percent from 33 percent.

Exports and Export Proceeds

March 8. The duties on logs were increased to a range of 26–46 percent.

PARAGUAY

(Position as of December 31, 1994)

Exchange Arrangement

The currency of Paraguay is the Paraguayan Guaraní. The authorities do not maintain margins in respect of foreign exchange transactions, and exchange rates are determined largely on the basis of demand and supply conditions in the exchange market. Although the Central Bank of Paraguay intervenes when necessary to smooth out undesirable fluctuations, it does not interfere with underlying market trends. The intervention currency is the U.S. dollar. Private transactions in respect of merchandise imports and exports, services, and capital are carried out through the authorized commercial banks; public transactions are carried out through the Central Bank or commercial banks. On December 31, 1994, the average rate prevailing in this market was ₲1,918.48 per US$1. Public debt-service payments and payments for services by the Government are channeled through the Central Bank at the rate prevailing on the day of the transaction. No commissions are assessed on these transactions if debtors have foreign exchange deposit accounts with the Central Bank.

The commercial banks may maintain a daily foreign exchange overbought position not exceeding 100 percent of their capital and reserves, or an oversold position of up to 50 percent of their capital and reserves. Exchange houses may maintain a daily overbought position of $250,000. Commercial banks are permitted to enter into forward transactions with respect to trade transactions on terms that may be negotiated freely with customers.

Paraguay formally accepted the obligations of Article VIII, Sections 2, 3, and 4 of the Fund Agreement, as from August 23, 1994.

Administration of Control

The Central Bank has the authority, under the Constitution, to determine foreign exchange policy in consultation with other agencies of the Government. In practice, decisions are taken by the Economic Cabinet on the advice of the Central Bank. The Central Bank is responsible for the execution of the decisions of the Economic Cabinet. The Central Bank supervises, through the Superintendency of Banks, foreign exchange transactions carried out by the banks and the exchange houses.

Prescription of Currency

Payments between Paraguay and Argentina, Bolivia, Brazil, Chile, Colombia, the Dominican Republic, Ecuador, Mexico, Peru, Uruguay, and Venezuela are made through accounts maintained with the Central Bank of Paraguay and the other central banks concerned, within the framework of the multilateral clearing arrangements of the Latin American Integration Association (LAIA). Clearing takes place every four months. There are no other prescription of currency requirements.

Imports and Import Payments

Imports of certain products that may be harmful to public health, national industries, or animal or plant health are prohibited; these restrictions, however, may be waived to ensure adequate domestic supplies. Imports of most petroleum and petroleum products are made through the National Petroleum Company, Petropar. Liquefied natural gas and aviation fuel may be imported by the private sector. All importers must be registered at the Central Bank.

The tariff regime is as follows: zero tax on inputs; 5 percent on capital goods; and 10 percent on consumer goods, except automobiles, on which a rate of 15 percent or 20 percent is applied. Taxes are payable at the time of delivery of documents for customs clearance.

The following are the principal items that are exempt from tariffs: imports for religious, charitable, cultural, or educational purposes; furniture acquired through inheritance; all imports exempted under international treaties; the accompanied baggage of international passengers or nationals returning to establish residence in Paraguay; books and periodicals; and imports under the investment law. Until the end of 1994, certain imports to be used by the tourist industry, especially those at the border cities of Ciudad del Este, Encarnación, and Pedro Juan Caballero, were taxed at the rate of 6 percent.

All trade barriers within the Southern Cone Common Market (MERCOSUR; comprising Paraguay, Argentina, Brazil, and Uruguay) were eliminated on December 31, 1994. Under the MERCOSUR Customs Union, which came into force on January 1, 1995, common external tariff rates ranging from zero to 20 percent were established with certain exceptions, such as those on computers, telecommunications, and capital goods, the tariff rates for which will converge according to schedule through the year 2006. There will also be a list of products on which tariffs will be paid in intra-zone trade, as described in the Customs Union harmonization list. When import payments are made under the LAIA Reciprocal Payments Agreement, the Central Bank levies a commission of 0.125 percent.

Payments for Invisibles

Payments for current invisibles are carried out through commercial banks or exchange houses without restriction. Travelers may take out any amount in foreign or domestic currency. A 2.5 percent value-added tax is levied on international air transport tickets issued in the country.

Exports and Export Proceeds

Exports of logs and unprocessed forest products, raw hides, and wild animals are prohibited. Certain other exports require prior authorization from the appropriate agency. All other exports are not restricted, except with regard to the technical standards imposed by the National Institute of Technology and Standardization, the Ministry of Industry and Commerce, the Ministry of Public Health, or the Ministry of Agriculture and Livestock, depending on the product exported.

All exporters are required to be registered at the Central Bank. The proceeds of exports must be collected within 120 days of completion of the banking formalities related to the shipping documents but may be retained by exporters.

Proceeds from Invisibles

There are no surrender requirements for proceeds from invisibles, except for royalties and remuneration from the binational entities, which are transferred in full to the Central Bank for the account of the Ministry of Finance. Similarly, administrative expenditure outlays of the binational entities are paid through the operating banks.

Capital

All capital transfers must be channeled through the commercial banks or exchange houses. Repatriation of earnings of foreign enterprises through the free exchange market is allowed, subject to a 5 percent levy, payment of income tax, and prior authorization from the Central Bank. The Government may grant exemptions from taxes, customs, and import surcharges on proposed investments that are duly registered and approved.

Gold

The Central Bank may prescribe the maximum amount of gold that residents may hold. This requirement does not apply to amounts held by the Central Bank or by institutions authorized to deal in foreign currencies. In practice, residents may freely purchase, hold, and sell gold in any form, in Paraguay or abroad, and exchange houses may freely deal in gold coins, gold bars, and gold leaf with residents and nonresidents. The exportation and importation of gold by nonbank residents and industrial users in any form other than jewelry require the prior authorization of the Central Bank. Payments for gold imports by industrial users must be made through commercial banks.

Changes During 1994

Exchange Arrangement

August 23. Paraguay formally accepted the obligations of Article VIII, Sections 2, 3, and 4 of the Fund Agreement.

Capital

July 29. The daily overbought and oversold foreign exchange positions of banks were set at 100 percent and 50 percent, respectively, of their capital and reserve base.

PERU

(Position as of December 31, 1994)

Exchange Arrangement

The currency of Peru is the Nuevo Sol, the external value of which is freely determined by participants in the exchange market on the basis of supply and demand conditions. On December 31, 1994, the average interbank transaction rate, as registered and published by the Superintendency of Banking, was S/. 2.19 per US$1. Exchange transactions may be conducted in any currency, including the U.S. dollar, and the cross rate relationships with currencies other than the U.S. dollar are determined on the basis of the rate for the U.S. dollar in the international market.

Since 1991, the exchange system has been free of controls on both current and capital transactions. Enterprises and natural persons may hold foreign exchange balances abroad and in domestic banks. There are arrangements for forward cover against exchange rate risk operating only in the commercial banking sector. Bank accounts in foreign currencies may be held with domestic banks.

As from February 15, 1961, Peru formally accepted the obligations of Article VIII, Sections 2, 3, and 4 of the Fund Agreement.

Administration of Control

Exchange houses are authorized to purchase foreign exchange and traveler's checks from residents and nonresidents and to sell foreign exchange for tourism abroad and for repurchases by nonresidents.

Borrowing abroad by the public sector, as well as borrowing abroad by the private sector with a government guarantee, is subject to prior approval by supreme decree, within the limits established by the Financing Requirement Law of the public sector.

Arrears are maintained with respect to external payments of unguaranteed suppliers' credits, of commercial banks, and of official loans obtained from Eastern European countries.

Prescription of Currency

Payments between Peru and Argentina, Bolivia, Brazil, Chile, Colombia, the Dominican Republic, Ecuador, Mexico, Paraguay, Uruguay, and Venezuela may be made through accounts maintained with each other by the Central Reserve Bank of Peru and the other central banks concerned, within the framework of the multilateral clearing system of the Latin American Integration Association (LAIA).

Imports and Import Payments

Imports of certain goods are prohibited from all sources for social, health, or security reasons. No other imports are restricted. Imports of raw materials and intermediate goods are exempt from import duties, provided that the appropriate ministry determines that such imports qualify under the Temporary Admission Regime. All monopolies on the importation of goods have been abolished, including the monopoly over the importation of milk powder and wheat by the National Enterprise for Input Marketing, and that over crude petroleum and petroleum derivatives by PETROPERU, a state-owned enterprise.

With some specified exemptions, imported goods are subject to a uniform value-added tax of 18 percent of the c.i.f. value of imports in addition to the import duty; exempted from the value-added tax are some agricultural products. The tariff regime consists of two basic rates: 25 percent (maximum) affecting 15 percent of products and 15 percent for the remainder, excluding imports subject to trade agreements. Agricultural products are subject to a variable import surcharge.

Advance payments for all imports are allowed without restriction. Legislation has been enacted requiring preinspection at the port of embarkation by international firms for imports exceeding $2,000 (f.o.b.).

Payments for Invisibles

Payments for almost all invisibles other than public debt service are not subject to payment authorization.

Remittances of net profits are permitted freely. Foreign investment by petroleum companies is subject to special contracts with the Peruvian Government.

Exports and Export Proceeds

Export prohibitions apply to 75 items, mainly rare wildlife (including wild animal skins and textiles made from them), plants, cottonseed cakes, natural rubber, and mineral ores. State enterprise monopolies over the exportation of mining and petroleum products were eliminated in 1991. Proceeds from exports are not subject to a repatriation requirement.

Proceeds from Invisibles

Proceeds from invisibles are not subject to surrender requirements.

Capital

Outward capital transfers, including amortization of private sector debts that are not guaranteed by the Government, are not restricted.

Short-term trade credits that have been subject to a refinancing agreement or assumed by the Government began to be rolled over beginning August 1, 1983. Other short-term trade credits may be repaid in accordance with bilateral agreements concluded before June 1992 or through renegotiation after that date with the approval of the External Debt Committee.

New foreign investments must be registered with the National Commission on Foreign Investment and Technology. Foreign companies incorporated in Peru may benefit from the duty-free program of the Cartagena Agreement under the same conditions as domestic enterprises.

Investments in the mining sector are governed by the General Mining Law, enacted in June 1992. The Government may grant tax incentives to mining concessionaires (initiating large-scale investment programs).

Under the Private Sector Investment Guarantee Regime, the Government guarantees nondiscriminatory treatment for foreign investors and private enterprises, protection of property rights, the development of any economic activity, free internal and external trade, and capital repatriation. In addition, investors may enter into contracts that guarantee tax stability, nondiscriminatory treatment, foreign currency availability, capital repatriation, free labor contracts, and export incentives.

Gold

The exportation and importation of gold are not restricted.

Changes During 1994

Administration of Control

May 6. Peru resumed its participation in the Andean Pact.

Imports and Import Payments

April 26. A revised general customs law was published.

Exports and Export Proceeds

February 11. The use of the Seguro de Crédito a la Exportación (SECREX) was modified.

PHILIPPINES

(Position as of December 31, 1994)

Exchange Arrangement

The currency of the Philippines is the Philippine Peso. The authorities of the Philippines do not maintain margins in respect of exchange transactions, and exchange rates are determined on the basis of demand and supply in the exchange market. However, the authorities intervene when necessary to maintain orderly conditions in the exchange market and in light of their other policy objectives in the medium term. On December 31, 1994, the reference exchange rate of the peso was ₱24.418 per US$1. The Central Bank of the Philippines, officially known as the Bangko Sentral ng Pilipinas, BSP, is not governed by the trading rules of the Bankers' Association of the Philippines in making its own purchases and sales of foreign exchange, except for transactions conducted at the trading center. Commercial banks trade in foreign exchange through the Philippine Dealing System (PDS) or by telephone.

Administration of Control

Exchange regulations are administered by the BSP on the basis of policy decisions adopted by the Monetary Board. Without prior approval, non-Philippine nationals not otherwise disqualified by law may engage in business in the Philippines or invest in a domestic enterprise up to 100 percent of their capital except in areas restricted by law. Nonresidents may purchase foreign exchange from authorized agent banks only up to the amount they have converted into pesos through the banking system or deposited in foreign currency accounts.

Pursuant to Circular No. 1353, dated September 1, 1992 (superseded by Circular No. 1389), foreign exchange may be freely sold and purchased outside the banking system. Foreign exchange received in the Philippines or acquired abroad may also be deposited in accounts denominated in foreign currency. However, in order that foreign loans and foreign investments can be serviced with foreign exchange purchased from the banking system, the investments must be registered with the BSP, and the loans must be approved, registered with, or reported to the BSP. All categories of banks (except offshore banking units) duly licensed by the Central Bank are considered authorized agent banks. Thrift banks may be authorized to offer foreign currency accounts, subject to prudential regulations.

Commercial banks are allowed to maintain open foreign exchange positions, subject to the limitation that long and short positions do not exceed 25 percent and 5 percent, respectively, of unimpaired capital. All forward transactions to purchase foreign exchange, including renewals thereof, from nonresidents require prior approval of the BSP.

Prescription of Currency

There are no prescription of currency requirements for outgoing payments, but all exchange proceeds from exports and invisibles must be obtained in prescribed currencies.[1] Payments may be made in pesos for exports to ASEAN countries, provided that the BSP is not asked to intervene in the clearing of any balances from this payment scheme. Authorized agent banks may accept notes denominated in the prescribed currencies for conversion into pesos.

Nonresident Accounts

Bank accounts denominated in pesos may be opened in the names of individual or corporate nonresidents without the prior approval of the BSP. Nonresident accounts may be credited only with the proceeds from inward remittances of foreign exchange or convertible foreign currencies and with peso income earned from the Philippines belonging to nonresidents. Nonresident accounts may be freely debited for peso withdrawals.

Both residents and nonresidents may maintain foreign currency deposit accounts with authorized agent banks in the Philippines (see section on Proceeds from Invisibles, below). Residents are allowed to maintain deposits abroad without restriction.

Imports and Import Payments

Generally, all merchandise imports are allowed without a license. However, the importation of certain products is regulated or restricted for reasons of public health and safety, national security,

---

[1]Australian dollars, Austrian schillings, Bahrain dinars, Belgian francs, Brunei dollars, Canadian dollars, deutsche mark, French francs, Hong Kong dollars, Indonesian rupiahs, Italian lire, Japanese yen, Kuwaiti dinars, Malaysian ringgit, Netherlands guilders, pounds sterling, Saudi Arabian riyals, Singapore dollars, Swiss francs, Thai baht, U.A.E. dirhams, U.S. dollars, and other such currencies that may be declared acceptable by the Central Bank.

international commitments, and development and protection of local industries.

Imports are classified into three categories: freely importable, regulated, and prohibited. Applications to import freely importable products may be processed by authorized agent banks without prior approval or clearance from any government agency. To import regulated products, a clearance of permit is required from the appropriate government agency (including the Central Bank). Prohibited products are those that may not be imported under existing laws. Import arrangements not involving payments using foreign exchange purchased from the banking system, such as self-funded/no-dollar imports and importations on consignment basis, are allowed without prior approval from the Central Bank. Under the Comprehensive Imports Supervision Scheme (CISS), preshipment inspection is required for imports valued at more than $500 from all countries. Imports declared in the shipping documents as off-quality, used, secondhand, scraps, off-grade, or a similar term indicating that the article is not brand new are subject to CISS inspection even if the value of the imports is less than $500.

Commercial banks may sell foreign exchange to service payments for imports under letters of credit (L/C), documents against acceptance (D/A), documents against payments (D/P), open account (O/A) arrangement, and direct remittance. Letters of credit must be opened on or before the date of shipment and are valid for one year. Only one letter of credit may be opened for each import transaction; amendments to such an arrangement need not be referred to the BSP for prior approval. Registration of D/A and O/A imports with the BSP is needed only if payments are to be made from the banking system for monitoring purposes; prior approval of the BSP, regardless of maturity, is not required. Import arrangements not involving payments using foreign exchange purchased from the banking system, such as self-funded/no-dollar imports and importation on consignment basis, are allowed without prior approval from the BSP.

Payments for Invisibles

Authorized banks may sell foreign exchange to residents for payments of any nontrade transactions against appropriate written applications without limit and without prior approval from the BSP, except for payments related to foreign loans or investments that require documentation showing central bank approval and/or registration.

Full and immediate repatriation of profits and dividends (net of taxes) accruing to nonresidents from all types of investment may be effected directly through commercial banks without prior approval from the BSP. However, service payments relating to foreign loans or foreign direct investments effected by purchases of foreign exchange through authorized agent banks are limited to those transactions whose original capital transfer has previously been registered with the BSP. Service payments related to option-to-purchase or transfer of ownership at a later date do not require prior BSP approval.

Remittances of profits dividends and earnings made in connection with the program for the conversion of external debt into equity investments are unrestricted.

Resident and nonresident travelers must have prior authorization from the BSP to take out more than ₱5,000 in domestic banknotes and coins or checks, money orders, and other bills of exchange drawn in pesos. When traveling abroad, citizens of the Philippines must pay a travel tax of ₱2,700 for first-class passage and ₱1,620 for economy-class passage. Reduced rates of ₱1,350 for first-class passengers and ₱810 for economy-class passengers are provided for groups of people traveling for recognized special purposes. Reduced rates of ₱400 for first-class passengers and ₱300 for economy-class passengers are provided for dependents of contract workers duly registered with the Philippine Overseas Employment Administration. Departing nonresidents are allowed to reconvert at airports or other ports of exit unspent pesos of up to a maximum of $200 or an equivalent amount in other foreign exchange (calculated at prevailing exchange rates) without proof of sales of foreign exchange to authorized agent banks.

Exports and Export Proceeds

Exports are allowed without restriction, except for those that are regulated or prohibited for reasons of national interest. Exports of selected seeds and shoots of native plants, endangered fish and wildlife (including selected marine species), and stalactites and stalagmites are prohibited.

All exports must be covered by export declarations. Authorized agent banks may issue and amend an export declaration before negotiation without prior approval from the BSP. Payments for exports may be made in prescribed currencies, under the following forms without prior BSP approval: L/C, D/P, D/A, O/A, cash against documents arrangements, consignment, export advance, and prepayment. Foreign currency deposit units and authorized agent banks may purchase export bills directly from exporters and indirect exporters.

Foreign exchange receipts or earnings of residents from exports may be sold for pesos to authorized banks or outside the banking system, retained, or deposited in foreign currency accounts, whether in the Philippines or abroad, and they may be used freely for any purpose. There are no export taxes.

Proceeds from Invisibles

There are no mandatory surrender requirements on proceeds from invisibles, which may be used without restriction. Travelers may freely bring in any amount of foreign currency and up to ₱5,000 in domestic banknotes and coins and checks, money orders, and other bills of exchange drawn in pesos.

Capital

Registration of inward investments with the BSP is required only if the foreign exchange needed to service the repatriation of capital and remittances of dividends and profits from these investments is to be funded through the banking system. When applications for registration of new inward foreign investments (in kind or in cash) are reviewed, no priority or preference is given to the category of industry in which the investment is made, as long as (1) there is inward remittance of foreign exchange for cash investments; or (2) in the case of investment in kind, there has been an actual transfer of assets to the Philippines. Full and immediate repatriation is guaranteed on all BSP-registered foreign investments without restriction.

Foreign companies are eligible to obtain loans in domestic currency from domestic sources, provided that they have a maximum debt-equity ratio of at most 60:40 in high-priority sectors, of 55:45 in medium-priority sectors, and of 50:50 in low-priority sectors. Investments in domestic commercial banks registered with the BSP may be repatriated without restriction.

Foreign direct investments may be either (1) foreign equity in Philippine firms or enterprises; (2) investment in government securities or securities listed on the stock exchange; or (3) investment in money instruments or bank deposits. Foreign direct investment may be in cash or in kind. Investments are permitted in connection with the Program for the Conversion of Philippine External Debt into Equity Investments. Under this program, most categories of external debt, including rescheduled debt, may be converted into equity investment.

Under the Foreign Investments Act of 1991, non-Philippine nationals not otherwise disqualified by law may, upon registration with the Securities and Exchange Commission, conduct business in the country or invest in domestic enterprises up to 100 percent of capital unless participation is prohibited or limited by existing law. However, enterprises seeking to apply for incentives, as well as foreign investors in export enterprises, must also register with the Board of Investments. Issues of securities abroad by residents under initial public offering are required to advise the BSP of receipt of proceeds within five days.

All industrial enterprises, whether owned by nationals or nonnationals, shall comply with the environmental standards set by the Government.

Outward investments by resident natural and juridical persons may be made freely, except those purchased from authorized agent banks that exceed $6 million an investor a year; such investments require prior BSP approval.

All public and certain private sector loans from foreign creditors, offshore banking units, and Foreign Currency Deposit Units (FCDUs) must be referred to the BSP for prior approval. These loans include (1) publicly guaranteed loans; (2) those covered by foreign exchange guarantees by local commercial banks; (3) those guaranteed by FCDUs and funded or collateralized by offshore loans or deposits; and (4) loans with a maturity of more than one year. Approval for public sector loans must be obtained before actual negotiations commence. Other private sector loans from the above-mentioned creditors require prior approval from and/or registration at the Central Bank only if they are to be serviced using foreign exchange purchased from the banking system. Non-guaranteed private sector short-term loans not exceeding 360 days generally do not require prior approval from the BSP and may be serviced with foreign exchange purchased from the banking system, but must be reported to the BSP. Refinancing of such loans would require prior BSP approval. Private sector loans from foreign currency deposit units (FCDUs) and offshore sources, irrespective of maturity, to be serviced with foreign exchange purchased outside the banking system do not require BSP approval.

Loans requiring prior BSP approval are normally expected to finance export-oriented projects and those registered with the Board of Investment, projects listed in the Investment Priorities Plan and the Medium-Term Public Investment Program, and projects that may be declared high priority under the country's socioeconomic development plan by the National Economic and Development Authority or Congress. Inward remittances of loan proceeds intended to finance only local requirements of projects may be sold to the banking system or deposited in FCDUs and/or offshore accounts. Proceeds intended to finance foreign costs may not be inwardly remitted and may be paid directly to the supplier or deposited in an offshore account.

Terms of loans to be obtained by the national Government and government corporations must be in accordance with the provisions of pertinent laws, although other loans may be made on terms similar to those prevailing in the international capital markets.

Nineteen foreign banks are operating offshore banking units in the Philippines. These units may engage in a wide range of foreign currency transactions with nonresidents and with other offshore banking units. They are permitted to lend to resident importers and exporters, provided that such loans do not have public guarantees, that the funds have been remitted from abroad and sold to the banking system, and that loans are authorized by the BSP. Offshore banking units may open and maintain deposit accounts in pesos exclusively with domestic agent banks to meet administrative and other operating expenses and to pay designated local beneficiaries of nonresident Philippine or multinational companies the equivalent of foreign exchange remittances channeled through the offshore banking units' correspondent banks abroad. Offshore banking units may also sell inward remittances of foreign exchange to the BSP.

Gold

Small-scale miners are required to sell all of their production to the BSP. All other forms or types of gold may, at the option of the owner or producer and with the consent of the BSP, be sold and delivered to the BSP. Producers are paid in Philippine pesos on the basis of the latest London fixing price and the prevailing Philippine peso–U.S. dollar exchange rate. The gold so acquired is deemed to be part of official international reserves. The BSP may sell gold grains, pellets, bars, and sheets to local jewelry manufacturers and other industrial users upon application, or to banks only for resale to jewelry manufacturers and industrial users, at the BSP's gold-selling price plus a service fee to cover costs, including the cost of conversion and packaging. The exportation of gold in any form, except that produced by small-scale miners, is permitted. There are no restrictions on the importation of any form of gold except coin blanks essentially of gold, gold coins, and coins without any indication of actual fineness of gold content.

Various denominations of gold coins have been issued by the BSP as follows: a 1 peso Paul VI coin (1970); a 1,000 piso Ang Bagong Lipunan coin (1975); a 1,500 piso IMF-IBRD coin (1976); the 1,500 piso Ang Bagong Lipunan coins (1977 and 1978); a 5,000 piso Ang Bagong Lipunan coin (1977); a 2,500 piso Douglas MacArthur centenary coin (1980); a 1,500 piso Pope John Paul II coin (1980 and 1981); a 1,500 piso Bataan-Corregidor coin (1982); a 2,500 piso Aquino-Reagan coin (1986); and a 10,000 piso Democracy Restored coin (1992). Transactions in legal tender gold coins are governed by the provisions of Central Bank Circular No. 960 (Sections 175 and 176), dated October 21, 1983.

Changes During 1994

Exchange Arrangement

July 28. All forward transactions to purchase foreign exchange from nonresidents (including offshore banking units), including renewals thereof, were required to be submitted for prior clearance to the BSP (Circular No. 36).

Administration of Control

June 9. All foreign exchange sales made through international ATMs and credit cards must be reported to the Foreign Exchange Department of the BSP within two days; the annual limit on such sales was set at $50,000 a person.

Imports and Import Payments

August 24. Restrictions limiting the use of documents against acceptance (O/A) and open account arrangement (O/A) to eligible firms were removed. D/A and O/A arrangements, however, must be registered with the BSP for monitoring purposes, but the BSP would no longer issue central bank release certificates. Any extension of maturities must be reported to the BSP 30 days before the effective date. The preapproval requirements by the BSP of D/A and O/A arrangements with maturities of more than 360 days were removed. Payments for export advances and prepayments would no longer be subject to a time limit of 30 days (Circular No. 40, Amendments to the Consolidated Foreign Exchange Rules and Regulations).

Capital

March 7. Banks were authorized to engage in direct purchases of export bills of resident exporters subject to the following conditions (Circular No. 16): (1) only export transactions covered by usance letters of credit would be allowed to be purchased by FCDUs (foreign currency deposit units); (2) the sale of export bills must be on a "without recourse" basis to the exporters; (3) export bills negotiated or purchased by the bank's regular unit and outstanding in its books may not be allowed to be purchased by its FCDU; and (4) all outstanding export bills purchased in the FCDU books, except those classified as bad or uncollectible accounts, must form part of the authorized asset cover against the FCDU's deposits and other foreign exchange liabilities.

June 21. Restrictions on repayment and repatriation of foreign investments funded by debt-to-equity conversion transactions were eliminated. Also repealed were the limitations on the remittance of dividends, profits, and earnings on such transactions (Circular No. 28).

June 30. Thrift banks were authorized to operate an FDCU subject to compliance with minimum net worth/combined capital accounts of ₱50 million and to meeting other requirements applicable to commercial banks. Thrift banks would need to meet profitability requirements for two years (rather than the one applied to commercial banks), although this criterion could be waived subject to certain conditions related to the experience of the FDCU operators and the level of net profits (Circular No. 30).

July 19. Limitations on short-term loans to private sector borrowers by FDCUs (as well as authorized agent banks) were liberalized to exempt loans to indirect exporters who are defined to include cottage and small and medium-size industries (producers/manufacturers) that have supply arrangements with direct exporters who are holders of an export letter of credit or a confirmed purchase order or sales contract from a foreign buyer. (This provision was added to the Consolidated Foreign Exchange Rules and Regulations in August 1994 under Section 4, Subsection 4a (Circular No. 31)). The ceiling on the annual amount of funds for investment that may originate from authorized agent banks was raised to $3 million from $1 million. The exclusion of export bills on a "without recourse" basis from FDCU purchases specified in Circular No. 16 (1994 series) was abolished.

August 24. (1) The Consolidated Foreign Exchange Rules and Regulations were amended (Circular No. 40). All short-term loans of private exporters and importers from offshore banking units and foreign banks with branches in the Philippines would be subject to the same provision as those applicable to private short-term loans issued under the Revolving Trade Credits and would not

require BSP approval. For both types of short-term loan, as well as those associated with relending programs of foreign creditors, refinancing by a medium- or long-term loan would require approval; a time limit of five days for notification of the BSP of a loan assignment was introduced; and new reporting requirements were specified. For relending programs of foreign creditors, approval of the operation was given for a one-year period but subject to semiannual review if commitment or use falls below 50 percent. Private sector loans with a maturity of more than one year that are not guaranteed by foreign governments or official export credit agencies would be exempted from BSP approval, as would those granted by foreign companies to local branches or subsidiaries that are used to finance eligible projects. All public sector loans require prior approval from the BSP.

With respect to financing schemes involving an option to purchase or a transfer of ownership at a later date, BSP approval is not required, thus eliminating the previous approval requirement for loans and the servicing of such loans in an original amount in excess of $1 million. Servicing of such loans without the approval of BSP would remain restricted to those loans previously registered with the BSP. New bank reporting requirements were introduced.

October 14. The entry of foreign banks to operate in the Philippines was liberalized (Circular No. 51). Such entry can be effected through a purchase of 60 percent of the voting stock of an existing domestic bank or of a new banking subsidiary incorporated in the Philippines or through the establishment of branches with full banking authority, subject to the licensing requirements of the BSP. For a foreign bank branch (new or already established), permanently assigned capital of the dollar equivalent of ₱210 million (converted at the exchange rate of ₱26.979 per US$1—the rate prevailing on June 5, 1994) must be remitted and converted into pesos, which will allow for the establishment of three branches. For each three additional branches to be opened, the U.S. dollar equivalent of ₱35 million must be remitted.

November 5. The Consolidated Foreign Exchange Rules and Regulations (Circular No. 53) were amended. The provision for unrestricted inward remittance of loan proceeds, where the loan is to be serviced using foreign exchange from the banking system, was amended to restrict inward remittance to only loan proceeds intended to fund local costs. Proceeds intended to fund foreign exchange costs would not be allowed to be remitted inward, but may be paid directly to suppliers or deposited in an offshore account. The requirements for registration of such loans with the BSP were tightened to require documentary proof on the disposition of loan proceeds.

The prepayment or acceleration of payments on medium- and long-term loans duly registered with the BSP that take place within two years of final maturity was exempted from prior approval by the BSP. The registry of foreign investments with the BSP was modified to allow the funds to be deposited in an FCDU (in addition to allowing them to be sold for pesos). The procedures for registry of foreign direct investment were amended accordingly.

November 11. The limit on short foreign exchange open position was reduced to 5 percent from 15 percent of unimpaired capital (Circular No. 54).

November 21. The regulations on foreign loans requiring BSP approval were amended (Circular No. 55). All loans, regardless of maturity, must finance only foreign exchange costs (previously this requirement applied to short-term loans, and medium- and long-term loans could also be used to finance local costs). Provisions were added to require issuers of securities under initial public offerings transacted outside the Philippines to advise the BSP through the Foreign Exchange Department of the receipt of proceeds of such sales within five days. The annual limitation on outward investment by Philippine residents on funds that originate in au-

thorized agent banks was raised to $6 million from $1 million. The requirement for prior approval by the BSP for amounts in excess of the limit was amended accordingly.

November 26. Local branches of foreign banks licensed to engage in commercial banking in the Philippines must exclude their permanently assigned capital pursuant to Section 68 of Republic Act No. 337, as amended, from their foreign exchange liabilities for purposes of computing their net foreign exchange position (Circular No. 56).

December 9. Effective December 1, 1994, an Exporters' Dollar Facility (EDF) was established at the BSP (Circular No. 57). Eligible banks were allowed to avail themselves of EDF for dollar-denominated loans to direct and indirect exporters (including technical, professional, and other services) up to a maximum of 100 percent of the face amount or the outstanding balance of the loan, with maturity set at 90 days for export-packing credits, and with a variable maturity, depending on the geographical location of the drawee bank for export bills; the maturity for service exporters would be 180 days. Repayment of the loan will be in dollars. Availments against the EDF would be charged against the bank's rediscount ceiling; for foreign banks, the rediscount ceiling will be 25 percent of "net-due-to" item plus assigned capital.

POLAND

(Position as of June 30, 1995)

Exchange Arrangement

The currency of Poland is the Zloty (100 Groszy per Zl 1), the external value (central rate) of which is pegged to a basket of five currencies.[1] The central rate is adjusted under a crawling peg policy. On November 30, 1994, the rate of depreciation was set at 1.4 percent a month, and on February 15, 1995, it was changed to 1.2 percent a month. Since May 16, 1995, the National Bank of Poland has allowed the external value of the zloty to fluctuate within margins of ±7 percent around the central rate. The exchange rates between the zloty and other convertible currencies are determined on the basis of the exchange rates between the U.S. dollar and the currencies concerned on international markets. The National Bank of Poland (NBP) quotes exchange rates for the European currency unit (ECU), the SDR, and the currencies of 28 countries considered market economies.[2] The spread between the buying and selling rates for notes and coins is set at 4 percent.[3] Rates for currencies other than the U.S. dollar are set daily and are based on the quoted rate for the U.S. dollar and the dollar rates for the relevant currencies in international markets.

The exchange rate on the foreign exchange bureau market, in which natural persons are allowed to transact freely provided that the transaction is not a commercial one, is determined by market forces and may differ from the official rate set by the NBP.[4] During 1994, the exchange rate on the for-eign exchange bureaus market remained closely in line with the official rate.

Poland formally accepted the obligations of Article VIII, sections 2, 3, and 4 of the Fund Agreement as from June 1, 1995

Administration of Control

The authority to make basic changes in the Foreign Exchange Law rests with Parliament.[5] Implementing regulations are promulgated by the Minister of Finance in the form of general foreign exchange permits or by the president of the NBP in the form of individual permits. General permits are issued for all residents and nonresidents and for specified groups. The procedures for issuing individual permits are established by the president of the NBP in cooperation with the Minister of Finance. The authority to enforce foreign exchange regulations rests with the Minister of Finance, who exercises related functions mainly through the president of the NBP. However, decisions concerning individual foreign exchange permits are subject to appeal to the Supreme Administrative Court.

Residents must repatriate foreign exchange within two months of receipt or within two months of returning to Poland.

Foreign exchange control is exercised by the Ministry of Finance, the NBP, the foreign exchange banks, customs offices, the border guard, and post offices.

Prescription of Currency

Outstanding balances under the (inoperative) bilateral payments agreements with Bangladesh, Brazil, China, Egypt, India, the Islamic Republic of Iran, Lebanon, and Turkey are being settled in accordance with the terms of the agreements. Balances outstanding under the arrangements of the International Bank for Economic Cooperation are still being settled in transferable rubles. Settlements with all other currencies may be made in any convertible currency.

Since January 1, 1991, almost all trade with the former member countries of the Council for Mutual Economic Assistance (CMEA) has been settled in convertible currencies; a limited amount of

---

[1]The basket consists of (figures in parentheses represent weights) the U.S. dollar (45 percent); the deutsche mark (35 percent); the pound sterling (10 percent); the French franc (5 percent); and the Swiss franc (5 percent). On January 1, 1995, new currency notes and coins began to circulate, replacing old currency at a conversion rate of 1 to 10,000. Old currency will remain in circulation until the end of 1996.

[2]Australian dollars, Austrian schillings, Belgian francs, Canadian dollars, Danish kroner, deutsche mark, Finnish markkaa, French francs, Greek drachmas, Indian rupees, Italian lire, Iranian rials, Irish pounds, Japanese yen, Kuwaiti dinars, Lebanese pounds, Libyan dinars, Luxembourg francs, Netherlands guilders, Norwegian kroner, Portuguese escudos, pounds sterling, Spanish pesetas, Swedish kronor, Swiss francs, Turkish liras, U.S. dollars, and Yugoslav dinars.

[3]Since January 13, 1992, banks in Poland have been given more freedom in determining the exchange rates to use in foreign exchange transactions. Specifically, they are permitted to set buying and selling rates within a margin of 2 percent around the middle rate set by the NBP. Banks' transactions with the NBP now take place at the buy/sell ratio set by the NBP, whereas previously they took place at the NBP's middle rate.

[4]Foreign exchange bureaus (*kantors*) must obtain licenses to operate.

---

[5]A new foreign exchange law was passed in December 1994 and came into effect on January 1, 1995.

trade, both under pre-existing contracts and in settlement of ruble balances outstanding at the end of 1990, continues to be transacted in transferable rubles.

Resident and Nonresident Accounts

Resident Accounts: Residents, both natural and juridical persons, may hold foreign exchange in the form of currency and securities. Residents who are natural persons may maintain currency accounts "A," and these accounts may be freely credited with convertible currency brought in or transferred from abroad and/or deposited without declaring the sources of funds. Account holders may use balances freely to effect transfers abroad, to buy goods and services, to finance tourist travel abroad by themselves or other persons, and to effect gifts to family members or other persons. Balances in these accounts cannot be used to effect settlements between individuals but can be sold in foreign exchange bureau markets. Withdrawals in zlotys, converted at the prevailing exchange rate, are freely permitted. Accounts maintained in deutsche mark, French francs, pounds sterling, Swiss francs, and U.S. dollars in demand deposits earn interest at an annual rate of 2.5–4 percent. Accounts maintained in these currencies in one-, two-, and three-year term deposits earn interest at an annual rate of 2.5 percent. Funds in A Accounts cannot be used for business activity. When leaving the country permanently, individuals are allowed under the general foreign exchange permit to transfer all funds from this account.

Foreign Exchange Accounts for Foreign Settlements (ROD): ROD Accounts are held by juridical persons. Although all foreign exchange receipts from exports, in principle, must be surrendered, juridical persons are allowed to retain foreign exchange accumulated in ROD Accounts before January 1, 1990.

Resident individuals and enterprises who demonstrate proof of need may hold foreign exchange accounts abroad with the permission of the NBP. Under the general foreign exchange permit, such an account may also be held by enterprises earning foreign exchange from performing specific contracts. Balances in these accounts may not exceed $100,000.

Nonresident Accounts: Nonresident natural and juridical persons are free to maintain both convertible currency and zloty accounts.

Nonresidents may maintain convertible currency accounts ("C" Accounts) at all foreign exchange banks. These accounts may be credited with funds brought in or transferred to Poland, with transfers from other C Accounts, and with convertible currency amounts legally acquired in Poland.[6] Deposits are freely transferable abroad, and may be used to make gifts to residents. The funds earn interest in foreign currency at the same rates as funds on the A Accounts. Nonresidents are free to open and hold zloty accounts, but depositors must declare the source of the zlotys; this declaration requirement is aimed at ensuring that payments into the accounts result from contracts or other operations that comply with the provisions of the foreign exchange law. Apart from zlotys legally earned in Poland, these accounts may also be credited with foreign exchange converted into zlotys at the official exchange rate. Permits for conversion back into foreign exchange or for foreign exchange transfers abroad are normally granted. These accounts do not pay interest; however, nonresidents may also deposit their earnings in savings accounts, on which interest is paid. Balances in zloty accounts may be transferred to nonresidents or residents with foreign exchange permits, except for gift payments to residents. Permits for transfers to nonresidents are granted only for transfers to family members. Permits for transfers to residents are granted without restriction.

Imports and Exports

Licenses are not required for imports from the convertible currency area, with the exception of imports of radioactive materials and military equipment, temporary imports of capital goods, transport equipment for leasing, and inputs subject to a quota system. Licenses are required for imports carried out within the framework of international agreements that stipulate bilateral settlements. The importation of certain mineral oils, tobacco products, and alcoholic beverages is subject to a quota. Imports of certain alcohol products, combine harvesters older than 4 years; passenger cars older than 10 years; trucks, vans, and utility cars older than 3 years; and cars with two-cycle engines are prohibited.

Export quotas cover only items subject to import restrictions by other countries. Export licenses are required for (1) goods subject to export quotas (raw hides and ferrous waste and scrap); (2) exports carried out within the framework of international agreements that stipulate bilateral settlements; and (3) temporary exports of capital goods and transport equipment for leasing. Nonresidents in Poland

---

[6]Since January 1, 1995, a foreign national entitled to transfer foreign currency has been allowed to hold "unrestricted foreign accounts"; funds in these accounts are freely transferable abroad.

(persons domiciled abroad but not foreign corporate entities operating in Poland) are required, temporarily, to apply for export permits. Exports of live geese and eggs, hide scraps, and nonferrous metals are prohibited.

All commercial imports, regardless of country of origin or provenance, are subject to an ad valorem import tariff based on the Harmonized Commodity Description and Coding System (HCDCS) and the combined nomenclature of the EC of 1991, with six basic rates: zero on equipment for the disabled, mineral resources, textiles, and cattle hides; 0–5 percent on other raw materials; 7–13 percent on basic parts of semifinished and finished goods; 17–29 percent on industrial goods; 25–40 percent on agricultural and textile products; and 29–43 percent on luxury goods. Imports from developing countries are granted preferential treatment under the General System of Preferences. Also, imports from 42 developing countries, tropical products from Chapters 6 to 24 of the HCDCS, and many goods from Chapters 32 and 94 of the HCDCS that are of interest to developing countries enter Poland duty free. For the remaining goods imported from non-European developing countries whose per capita GDP is lower than Poland's, duties are reduced to 30 percent of the most-favored-nation (MFN) rate. Some special regulations pertain to border trade with the Baltic countries, Russia, and the other countries of the former Soviet Union.

Imports are subject to a surcharge of Zl 50,000 and an additional turnover tax of 6 percent; alcoholic beverages, tobacco products, fuels, and automobiles are exempt from the turnover tax. Exports other than coal are free from turnover taxes. Duties and turnover taxes on imports for export production are refunded.

Exporters must declare all foreign currency receipts from exports, repatriate them within two months of receipt, and surrender them to the Polish foreign exchange banks within 14 days of receiving notice that foreign exchange has been deposited in their accounts in Poland.

Payments for and Proceeds from Invisibles

Payments for invisible expenses arising from merchandise transactions, including insurance and transportation costs, are permitted freely if related to trade transactions. All other invisible transactions are carried out under either a general or an individual permit. Foreign exchange for such payments is made available automatically once the transaction is authorized.

For official and business travel, separate allowances are established by the Ministry of Finance to reflect reasonable costs. Business travelers may take out of Poland up to the equivalent of $10,000 from the foreign currency accounts maintained by the enterprises that employ them for travel expenses or purchases of goods and services associated with their business activity.

Polish nationals departing Poland are permitted to take abroad up to $2,000 or the equivalent in convertible foreign currencies, checks, and traveler's checks that they purchased from foreign exchange banks to pay outstanding obligations to foreign nationals resulting from (1) the purchase of movable assets and proprietary interests, and (2) transportation and insurance services. Documentary proof of origin is necessary for amounts exceeding this limit. However, holders of A Accounts may take out of the country the balance of their accounts without limit. When leaving Poland, tourists from convertible currency area countries may reconvert zlotys up to the equivalent they brought into Poland, provided that the amount is not more than that originally converted into zlotys less the required conversion amounts. Residents must repatriate foreign exchange within two months of receipt or within two months of returning to Poland. Residents may, without approval, bring into or take out of the country domestic banknotes and coins in an amount not exceeding Zl 5 million a person. Foreign visitors must declare foreign exchange they bring into the country in order to take out the unspent amount and are not permitted to bring zlotys into the country or to take them out.

Business entities may use their ROD Accounts to pay wages and salaries to nonresident employees. They may also use their ROD Accounts, or foreign exchange purchased from foreign exchange banks, to pay outstanding obligations relating to (1) procurement costs, including costs of participation in exhibitions and fairs, and advertising costs; (2) fees for agent representational services; (3) costs of repairing and overhauling imported machinery and equipment; (4) costs associated with protecting intellectual property; and (5) costs related to auditing, consulting, and information services. Similarly, individuals may remit foreign exchange to pay for (1) participation in international organizations and international hotel networks abroad; (2) costs of court or arbitration proceedings up to the equivalent of $20,000 a case; (3) costs of obtaining legal counsel and trial representation in a given case up to $50,000 or the equivalent; (4) taxes, customs duties, or administrative fees payable abroad; and (5) study abroad. Amounts in excess of established limits may be remitted if supporting documents showing the bona fide nature of the transaction are provided.

Transfers abroad by nonresident workers in Poland, other than in the context of employment in joint ventures, are determined on the basis of agreements between domestic and foreign institutions or enterprises and through individual foreign exchange permits. Nonresident employees of joint ventures may transfer abroad up to 100 percent of their income. Residents may remit pensions and annuities in convertible foreign exchange at the official exchange rate to nonresidents who are entitled to such payments on the basis of a ruling from the social security administration.

Profits on direct investment by nonresidents, other than those from joint ventures, or the acquisition of shares in Polish companies, may be transferred abroad without restriction. If the investment yields a net surplus in convertible currency in any fiscal year, up to 50 percent of the surplus may be transferred abroad, provided that the transfer does not exceed 50 percent of net profits after taxes. The Minister of Finance may permit a transfer in excess of 50 percent of the surplus. On liquidation, the investor may transfer abroad the proceeds from the sale of the remaining assets sold in foreign currency.

Capital

Parliament annually sets an upper limit on the public sector's external indebtedness. Within this limit, foreign borrowing takes place on the basis of intergovernmental agreements and in various forms of bank and commercial credits. Under the provisions of the banking law, the NBP, Bank Handlowy, Bank PKO, S.A., and the Export Development Bank are empowered to borrow abroad, on short or long term, and to extend foreign credits. The Minister of Finance sets limits on the foreign borrowing of the banks, and the contracting of foreign loans is subject to approval.

Negotiable export documents are discountable by foreign banks. With a permit, exports of goods (other than fuels and raw materials) and services may be financed with a credit of up to the equivalent of $1 million, with repayment terms of up to 360 days. With a permit, imports with a value of up to the equivalent of $1 million may also be financed with a credit with repayment terms of up to three years.

A new foreign investment law (Law on Companies with Foreign Participation) came into effect on July 4, 1991, replacing the old Law on Economic Activity with Participation of Foreign Parties, which had governed all new foreign direct investments since December 23, 1988. Under the 1991 law, new businesses will need to register only with local courts, except for investments in the areas of seaports, airports, real estate transactions, defense, legal services, and wholesale trade in imported products, which will continue to require permits. Although the previous three-year tax holiday for new businesses was abolished, the taxation system was simplified, and imports of capital goods for new joint ventures are exempt from customs duties. Investors in certain priority sectors will also be eligible for tax concessions, as will investments exceeding ECU 2 million a year. The 10 percent ceiling on purchases in shares of privatization issues has been abolished, and a permit is not required unless such shares relate to the above-mentioned sectors. For joint ventures, as well as for investments in shares of Polish companies, all limits on the transfer of profits have been lifted, and invested capital may be repatriated once outstanding obligations to creditors are met. The transfer of profits or repatriation of capital from bonds is not restricted. The 1991 law does not stipulate a minimum amount of capital that foreign nationals must invest in Poland, thus eliminating the requirement of $50,000. Nevertheless, the minimum capital requirement set forth in the Polish commercial code for a limited liability company and a joint-stock company is still in effect.

Foreign investment by residents, either to establish subsidiaries or affiliates or to acquire an interest in a foreign enterprise, requires a foreign exchange permit.

All categories of capital transfers, including gifts, by resident natural persons require a foreign exchange permit. However, for certain categories, such as inheritances, transfers are authorized on the basis of agreements and reciprocity with other countries. Emigrants to other countries must obtain an individual permit from the NBP to take out their convertible currency deposits with domestic banks. Other financial assets may be deposited in a nonresident zloty account.

Except in the form of an inheritance, nonresidents may acquire real estate or other immovable property in Poland only with permission from the Ministry of Interior.

Gold

Resident individuals may hold gold in any form. Trading in gold, other than jewelry, is subject to permission from the foreign exchange authorities. Polish and foreign nationals may take abroad gold coins that bear value in foreign exchange. They may also bring into Poland coins made from precious metals that are legal tender in Poland. Only one enterprise, Jubiler, has general permission to buy and sell in gold in any form.

Changes During 1994

Exchange Arrangement

September 13. The monthly rate of depreciation of the zloty was reduced to 1.5 percent from 1.6 percent.

November 30. The monthly rate of depreciation of the zloty was reduced to 1.4 percent from 1.5 percent.

Administration of Control

December 2. A new Foreign Exchange Law was passed removing some exchange restriction on current international transactions. The new law took effect January 1, 1995.

Changes During 1995

Exchange Arrangement

January 1. New currency notes and coins were issued replacing old currency at a conversion rate of 1 to 10,000. Old currency would remain in circulation until the end of 1996.

May 16. The National Bank of Poland allowed the external value of the zloty to fluctuate within margins of ±7 percent around the central rate.

June 1. Poland formally accepted the obligations of Article VIII, Sections 2, 3, and 4 of the Fund Agreement.

Administration of Control

March 27. Amended general foreign exchange permits came into force.

Imports and Exports

January 1. The rate of import surcharge was reduced to 5 percent from 6 percent.

PORTUGAL

(Position as of March 31, 1995)

Exchange Arrangement

The currency of Portugal is the Portuguese Escudo. Portugal participates with Austria, Belgium, Denmark, France, Germany, Ireland, Luxembourg, the Netherlands, and Spain in the exchange rate and intervention mechanism (ERM) of the European Monetary System (EMS).[1] In accordance with this agreement, Portugal maintains the spot exchange rates between the Portuguese escudo and the currencies of the other participants within margins of 15 percent above and below the cross rates based on the central rates expressed in European currency units (ECUs).[2]

The agreement implies that the Banco de Portugal (the central bank) stands ready to buy or sell the currencies of the other participating states in unlimited amounts at specified intervention rates. On March 6, 1995, these rates were as follows:

Specified Intervention Rates per:	Portuguese Escudos	
	Upper limit	Lower limit
100 Austrian schillings	1,691.800	1,254.700
100 Belgian or Luxembourg francs	577.090	428.000
100 Danish kroner	3,120.500	2,314.300
100 Deutsche mark	11,903.300	8,827.700
100 French francs	3,549.000	2,832.100
1 Irish pound	286.983	212.838
100 Netherlands guilders	10,584.000	7,834.700
100 Spanish pesetas	139.920	103.770

The participants in the EMS do not maintain the exchange rates for other currencies within fixed limits. However, in order to ensure a proper functioning of the system, they intervene in concert to smooth out fluctuations in exchange rates, the intervention currencies being each other's, the ECU, and the U.S. dollar.

Official exchange rates for the U.S. dollar and other currencies[3] are based on information on the exchange rate of the Portuguese escudo in terms of the deutsche mark provided by the banking system and are announced daily by the Banco de Portugal. These rates are a reference for the banks' bid and offer rates, which are freely set. On December 31, 1994, the official rate for the U.S. dollar was Esc 159.093 per US$1. A tax of 0.9 percent is levied on all sales of foreign exchange except on interbank transactions.

Banks are allowed to engage in spot and forward exchange transactions in any currency among themselves and with residents and nonresidents at free market rates of exchange. Nonbank residents may also conduct spot or forward exchange operations with nonresident counterparts. The degree of foreign exchange risks that banks are authorized to take must fall within the limits established by the Banco de Portugal for their foreign exchange positions (calculated as the sum of the positions against escudos in each foreign currency).

Portugal formally accepted the obligations of Article VIII, Sections 2, 3, and 4 of the Fund Agreement, as from September 12, 1988.

Administration of Control

There are no exchange controls. Foreign trade policy is implemented by the Ministry of Commerce and Tourism. The Direcção-Geral do Comércio in this ministry is responsible for administering trade controls and for issuing import and export licenses, declarations, and certificates.

Prescription of Currency

There are no prescription of currency requirements. Settlements may be effected in any currency.

Resident and Nonresident Accounts

Residents and nonresidents are free to open and operate accounts in Portugal or abroad in either escudos or foreign currencies.

Imports and Import Payments

As a general rule, imports may be freely made into Portugal. For products under EU surveillance, import declarations, when required, are issued for

---

[1]Austria became a member of the European Union on January 1, 1995, and joined the ERM of the EMS on January 9, 1995.

[2]Effective August 2, 1993, the intervention thresholds of the currencies participating in the ERM of the EMS, except those of the deutsche mark and the Netherlands guilder, were widened from ±2.25 percent (in the case of Portugal and Spain, 6 percent) to ± 15 percent around the bilateral central exchange rates; the fluctuation band of the deutsche mark and the Netherlands guilder remained unchanged at ±2.25 percent.

[3]Australian dollars, Austrian schillings, Belgian francs, Canadian dollars, Danish kroner, deutsche mark, European currency units (ECUs), Finnish markkaa, French francs, Greek drachmas, Italian lire, Irish pounds, Japanese yen, Macao patacas, Netherlands guilders, Norwegian kroner, pounds sterling, South African rand, Spanish pesetas, Swedish kronor, and Swiss francs. The Macao pataca is pegged to the Hong Kong dollar at a parity rate of P 1.03 per HK$1.

statistical surveillance purposes and are granted automatically in four to five days. Imports of certain products are subject to an import license and are allowed under specific conditions or are prohibited for reasons of health, public order, and the prevention of commercial fraud. Imports subject to quantitative restrictions require an import license. The validity of import licenses is six months for customs clearance purposes.

For agricultural products covered by the common agricultural policy of the EU, the EU may require an import certificate.

A few industrial products, such as steel products and some textiles and clothing, are subject to import restrictions in the EU when they originate in certain third countries. A more extensive restricted list applying to China includes some textiles and a small number of finished products.

Exports and Export Proceeds

Exports are free of restrictions. Proceeds from exports are not subject to repatriation or surrender requirements.

Payments for and Proceeds from Invisibles

There are no restrictions on payments for and proceeds from invisibles. Travelers may import or export any amount of domestic and foreign banknotes or any other means of payment. The exportation or importation by residents or nonresidents of banknotes or coins and traveler's checks in excess of the equivalent of Esc 2.5 million must be declared to customs.

Capital

There are no exchange restrictions or controls on capital transactions, and no distinction is made between capital transactions with residents of EU member countries and residents of non-EU member countries. Foreign direct investments are permitted in all sectors except those that, under general law, are closed to private enterprise corporations. Foreign direct investment operations require prior declaration to the Investmentos Comércio e Turismo de Portugal (ICEP) and are considered approved if the ICEP does not reply within two months. Projects submitted by non-EU investors may be subject to review.

The establishment of a financial institution in Portugal in which a majority voting right is held by natural persons who are not nationals of an EU member country or by legal persons with their main office and central management in a non-EU

country is subject to previous authorization from the Minister of Finance, which may consider prudential requirements as well as other criteria. Similar regulations apply to the establishment in Portugal of branches of a financial institution located in a non-EU member country.

The establishment in a non-EU member country of branches of financial institutions by nonresidents is subject to prior authorization from the Banco de Portugal.

Gold

Residents may freely buy, hold, and sell gold in any form in Portugal. Residents and nonresidents may also import and export bullion, coins, and unworked gold, but a customs declaration is required for amounts exceeding Esc 2.5 million.

Changes During 1994

Administration of Control

January 22. The movements of any funds in Portugal that are controlled by public authorities or companies of Libya were prohibited (the Bank of Portugal's Notice No. 8/93).

Imports and Import Payments

(See Appendix for a summary of trade measures introduced on an EU-wide basis during 1994, page 554).

Capital

February 28. Foreign participation in the capital of wholly privatized companies was not allowed to exceed 25 percent, unless the legislation governing the privatization process of those companies sets a higher limit (Decree Law No. 65/94).

April 2. The withholding tax on the interest earned on government securities owned by nonresidents was eliminated (Decree Law No. 88/94).

August 2. Issue of securities by nonresidents in the domestic capital market was liberalized (Decree Law No. 204/94).

September 14. Issue of commercial papers in the domestic market was liberalized (Decree Law No. 231/94).

Changes During 1995

March 6. The upper and lower limits of the escudo for the currencies of participants in the ERM of the EMS were changed.

QATAR

(Position as of December 31, 1994)

Exchange Arrangement

The currency of Qatar is the Qatar Riyal, which is pegged to the SDR at QR 4.7619 per SDR 1. Qatar has established margins of 7.25 percent around this rate, but these margins were exceeded during March through December 1994. The Qatar Central Bank sets daily market rates for the U.S. dollar, the intervention currency. On December 31, 1994, the buying and selling rates for the Qatar riyal in terms of the U.S. dollar were QR 3.6415 and QR 3.6385, respectively, per US$1.

The exchange rates of commercial banks for transactions in U.S. dollars are based on the Qatar Central Bank's buying and selling rates. A spread of QR 0.0087 is applied to exchange transactions with the public. The buying and selling rates of commercial banks for other currencies are based on the Qatar Central Bank's rates for the U.S. dollar and on market rates for the currency concerned against the U.S. dollar. There are no taxes or subsidies on purchases or sales of foreign exchange. There are no arrangements for forward cover against exchange rate risk operating in the official banking sector. In the commercial banking sector, importers may purchase foreign exchange in the forward market.

Qatar formally accepted the obligations of Article VIII, Sections 2, 3, and 4 of the Fund Agreement, as from June 4, 1973.

Administration of Control

The Qatar Central Bank is the exchange control authority, but there is at present no exchange control legislation. Import licenses are issued by the Ministry of Finance, Economy, and Commerce. Financial transactions with the Federal Republic of Yugoslavia (Serbia/Montenegro) are prohibited.

Prescription of Currency

All settlements with Iraq and Israel are prohibited. No other prescription of currency requirements are in force.

Nonresident Accounts

No distinction is made between accounts held by residents and those held by nonresidents.

Imports and Import Payments

All imports from Iraq and Israel are prohibited, as are imports of pork and its derivatives. Imports of alcoholic beverages, firearms, ammunition, and certain drugs are subject to licensing for reasons of health or public policy. Otherwise, imports are not restricted. There are no restrictions on payments for permitted imports. Imports of general goods are subject to a customs tariff at the rate of 4 percent, which is the minimum rate applied by member countries of the Cooperation Council for the Arab States of the Gulf (GCC). The customs tariff on steel is 20 percent; on tobacco 104 percent; and on alcoholic beverages 100 percent. Imports of goods from other member countries of the GCC are not subject to a customs tariff.

Exports and Export Proceeds

All exports to Iraq and Israel are prohibited. Otherwise, all commodities may be exported freely. No requirements are attached to receipts from exports or re-exports; the proceeds need not be repatriated or surrendered, and they may be disposed of freely, regardless of the currency involved.

Payments for and Proceeds from Invisibles

Payments may not be made to or received from Iraq and Israel. Otherwise, there are no limitations on payments for and proceeds from invisibles.

Capital

No exchange control requirements are imposed on capital receipts or payments by residents or nonresidents, although payments may not be made to or received from Iraq and Israel. Noncitizens may engage in simple crafts as well as in commerce, industry, agriculture, and services jointly with Qatari partners, provided that the latter's share is not less than 51 percent. Noncitizens may also establish companies specializing in contracting business with Qatari partners, subject to the above conditions, if it is determined that there is a need to establish such companies or if there is a need for the experience and technology they provide.

Gold

The monetary authorities and all other residents and nonresidents (including private persons) may freely and without license purchase, hold, and sell gold in any form, at home or abroad. For trading purposes, the buying and selling of gold and precious metals require an import license and are subject to customs duty. Transactions involving Iraq and Israel are prohibited.

Changes During 1994

No significant changes occurred in the exchange and trade system.

ROMANIA

(Position as of December 31, 1994)

Exchange Arrangement

The currency of Romania is the Romanian Leu. The exchange rate against the U.S. dollar (the reference exchange rate) is determined in the interbank foreign exchange market. The National Bank of Romania (NBR) does not intervene in the exchange market except to smooth out fluctuations in exchange rates and to build up foreign exchange reserves. Only commercial banks authorized by the NBR can participate in the exchange market. Juridical persons other than authorized commercial banks may purchase or sell foreign exchange through authorized banks. All transactions between resident juridical persons and between juridical persons and natural persons must be made in the national currency. In certain circumstances, the NBR may authorize foreign exchange operations between juridical persons. On December 31, 1994, the exchange rate was Lei 1,767 per US$1. The NBR quotes rates for 23 other currencies,[1] based on the rates for these currencies against the U.S. dollar in the countries concerned, and for the European currency unit. Foreign exchange bureaus conduct transactions only in foreign currency banknotes and traveler's checks and only with natural persons. Since September 19, 1994, these bureaus have been allowed to set their exchange rates freely.

The transferable ruble, the currency used for commercial transactions with the member countries of the former Council for Mutual Economic Assistance (CMEA), has been abolished but continues to be used as a unit of account for the purpose of liquidating outstanding balances.

There are no arrangements for forward cover against exchange rate risk operating in the official or the commercial banking sector.

Administration of Control

Under the provision of the law setting up the NBR as the country's central bank, which came into force on May 3, 1991, the NBR issues rules and regulations related to control of foreign exchange transactions. The NBR authorizes all capital transfers, including those connected with inheritances, proceeds from the liquidation of capital assets owned by foreign natural persons, and pension payments abroad on the basis of visas issued by the Ministry of Economy and Finance.[2] Domestic commercial banks are authorized by the NBR to conduct foreign exchange transactions abroad for current international transactions and are permitted to have foreign banks as correspondents or to borrow directly abroad with NBR authorization.

Prescription of Currency

Payments to and from countries with which Romania has bilateral payments agreements are made only in the currency and in accordance with the procedures set forth in those agreements.[3] If no agreement exists, settlement is usually made in a convertible currency.

Resident and Nonresident Accounts

All juridical and natural persons may maintain foreign currency accounts with commercial banks authorized by the NBR to operate in Romania.

Resident juridical persons may open and maintain foreign exchange accounts abroad or other assets in foreign currency with the prior authorization of the NBR. Romanian natural persons and foreigners permanently domiciled in Romania and receiving foreign exchange income abroad may hold and use foreign means of payment in foreign exchange accounts held in financial and banking institutions abroad. Natural persons may also hold foreign exchange in the form of banknotes and coins or in accounts opened with commercial banks authorized to operate in Romania and, within the laws and conditions specified by foreign exchange regulations, may freely use such foreign exchange to effect international current payments and capital payments. The deposits may also be exchanged for lei

---

[1]Australian dollars, Austrian schillings, Belgian francs, Canadian dollars, Danish kroner, deutsche mark, Egyptian pounds, Finnish markkaa, French francs, Greek drachmas, Indian rupees, Irish pounds, Italian lire, Japanese yen, Luxembourg francs, Netherlands guilders, Norwegian kroner, Portuguese escudos, pounds sterling, Spanish pesetas, Swedish kronor, Swiss francs, and Turkish liras.

[2]Authorization is not required to operate nonresident deposits held by resident banks; loans and credits received by residents and guaranteed by the state; and deposits that resident banks place in their own name.

[3]At the end of 1994, Romania maintained bilateral payments agreements with Albania, Bangladesh, Brazil, China, Egypt, Ghana, Greece, India, the Islamic Republic of Iran, the Democratic People's Republic of Korea, Pakistan, and the former CMEA countries.

through the foreign exchange bureaus authorized to operate in Romania.

Imports and Exports

Import and export transactions were liberalized on May 1, 1992 and in general are not subject to licensing, except for a few consumer goods that are subject to quantitative restrictions, goods covered by international arrangements signed by Romania, and certain controlled strategic goods. Both the Ministry of Trade and Tourism and the Ministry of Finance may take measures to restrict imports for purposes of protecting the balance of payments, or for reasons of public health, national defense, and state security, in accordance with the provisions of the General Agreement on Tariffs and Trade (GATT).

Import tariff rates are ad valorem, and range from zero to 60 percent, with a simple average rate estimated to be about 19 percent. A differential import surcharge is levied on certain imported agricultural products.

Exports of some goods (including wheat, butter, a few hydrocarbon products, certain minerals, blood products, logs and wood products, and scrap metals) have been suspended. Certain goods (including timber, livestock, sunflower seeds, maize, certain mineral oils, chemical fertilizers, and copper alloys) are subject to export quotas.

Resident juridical persons must maintain foreign exchange export proceeds in accounts opened at domestic commercial banks or foreign commercial banks authorized to operate in Romania but are free to use the balances in these accounts.

Payments for and Proceeds from Invisibles

All juridical economic agents may effect foreign exchange transfers for payments for invisible (or any international current account) transactions through authorized commercial banks. Commercial banks must verify, based on supporting documents, that the requested transfer is for bona fide current account purposes.

Foreign exchange bureaus are permitted to sell foreign exchange to resident natural persons for the purpose of travel abroad up to the annual limit of $500.

Natural persons residing in Romania may take out of the country foreign exchange in the form of banknotes and coins up to a maximum amount equivalent to $5,000 a person a trip to effect current transactions (such as expenses for group or individual travel, medical treatments or purchases of medicines, participation in conferences, education,

purchases of consumer goods for personal use, and payments for services); no documentation is required for amounts of $1,000 or less. Natural persons must make all transfers exceeding $5,000 through banks. Transfers to banks abroad for current operations may also be made from the accounts of natural persons domiciled permanently in Romania and from the accounts of other Romanian juridical persons, except in special cases (as stipulated by law) requiring prior authorization from the NBR; such authorization is granted on a case-by-case basis. Banks may not limit the volume of bona fide current operations.

The maximum amount of foreign currency banknotes and coins that natural persons may bring into Romania is the equivalent of $10,000 a person a trip. Natural persons who are Romanian or foreign citizens staying in the country temporarily and who enter Romania in possession of more than the equivalent of $1,000 in foreign currency banknotes are required to declare the excess amount. Amounts not converted into lei may be taken out of the country. The maximum amount of domestic banknotes that can be brought into or taken out of Romania is Lei 100,000 a person a trip in denominations no larger than Lei 5,000.

Capital

All inward and outward transfers of foreign exchange and all capital transfers of foreign exchange must be authorized by the NBR. Capital transfers connected with inheritances, proceeds from the liquidation of capital assets owned by foreign natural persons, and pension payments abroad are authorized by the NBR on the basis of permits issued by the Ministry of Economy and Finance.

Under the investment law that came into effect on May 3, 1991, there are no limits on foreign equity participation in a commercial firm set up in Romania, and foreign investments may be made in all sectors of the economy, except where the environment or Romania's national security and defense interests must be protected.

Foreign investors can participate in the management of the investment operation or assign contractual rights and obligations to other Romanian or foreign investors. In addition, foreign investors can transfer abroad (1) the entire amount of their share of profits earned in convertible currencies; (2) with the authorization of the fiscal authorities and the NBR, part of their share of annual profits earned in lei and converted into convertible currency; (3) the total or partial proceeds in convertible currencies from sales of stocks, shares, bonds, and other securities, as well as from the liquidation of investments; and (4) the proceeds in lei from the liquidation of investments in freely convertible currencies. Imported machinery, equipment, installations, means of transport, and any other goods in kind constituted as participation of the foreign investor are exempt from custom duties. Foreign investors also benefit from certain tax advantages.

Gold

The NBR has sole authority to purchase or sell gold in any manner, at home or abroad. It, in turn, authorizes certain juridical persons to hold gold, to use it, and to engage in gold transactions. Natural persons may, without restriction, own gold jewelry and artistic and cultural objects for domestic and personal use.

Changes During 1994

Exchange Arrangement

April 11. The reference exchange rate was set at the level of the market clearing exchange rate.

August 1. Foreign exchange auctions were replaced by an interbank foreign exchange market.

September 19. Foreign exchange bureaus were permitted to buy and sell through the interbank exchange market.

Resident and Nonresident Accounts

October 14. Requirements for natural persons to report sources of funds deposited in foreign exchange accounts and uses of funds withdrawn from these accounts were eliminated.

Payments for and Proceeds from Invisibles

January 1. The maximum amount of foreign exchange a resident natural person can purchase from foreign exchange bureaus was set at $500 a year.

Imports and Exports

January 1. Export-licensing requirements for certain products were introduced.

March 16. A statistical monitoring regime for imports of 100 tariff lines was introduced.

June 27. Reference prices and a compensation tax system for certain agricultural food products were established.

July 27. Quotas for the second half of 1994 on the export of live animals to EU countries were established.

RUSSIAN FEDERATION

(Position as of December 31, 1994)

Exchange Arrangement

The currency of the Russian Federation is the Ruble. An official exchange rate is quoted by the Central Bank of Russia (CBR) based upon market exchange rates that are determined in daily auctions held at the Moscow Interbank Currency Exchange (MICEX).[1] Auction markets are also organized in other major cities, including St. Petersburg, Ekaterinburg, Vladivostok, Rostov, and Novosibirsk. There is a growing interbank exchange market outside of the currency exchanges. Currencies traded on the MICEX include Belarus rubles, deutsche mark, French francs, Kazakh tenge, pounds sterling, and Ukrainian karbovanets. Currencies traded on other exchanges also include Finnish markkaa and Japanese yen.

The U.S. dollar is the intervention currency of the CBR in the MICEX and on other exchanges where the CBR operates. The CBR participates in the MICEX as a net buyer and seller of the U.S. dollar to smooth out short-term fluctuations in the exchange rate; it occasionally trades in foreign exchange through direct dealing on the interbank market outside the auctions. There is no spread between the buying and selling rates of the CBR. The CBR exchange rate is announced twice a week and is equal to the midpoint of the closing rates at the Tuesday and Thursday MICEX auctions. It becomes effective on the following day and remains in effect until the Friday and Wednesday auctions, respectively. Exchange rates announced by the CBR are used for accounting and taxation purposes, and operations with the Ministry of Finance. The CBR quotes exchange rates of the ruble for the ECU and 26 convertible currencies on the basis of the MICEX ruble-U.S. dollar rate and the cross rate relationships between the U.S. dollar and the currencies concerned in the international market on the day preceding auctions. The CBR provides reference exchange rates for the currencies of the states of the former Soviet Union against the ruble, based on market exchange rates in the Russian Federation (auction rates of currency exchanges) or local markets; these reference rates are used for taxation and accounting purposes, and authorized commercial banks are free to quote the rates for these currencies in their transactions. The CBR also calculates the (former) Gosbank exchange rate of the ruble (the so-called official exchange rate; about Rub 0.6 per US$1) as a unit of account for the valuation of external claims of the countries of the former Soviet Union and related transactions.[2]

An interbank, mainly noncash, market operates outside the auctions among the major authorized banks, mainly in a given region; the regional segmentation stems from the length of settlement of the ruble leg of foreign exchange transactions between banks affiliated with different payment centers; this feature hampers effective arbitrage between regional markets and leads the CBR to operate in the regional exchanges in order to apply the same exchange rate throughout the country. Authorized banks may trade on behalf of their customers and on their own accounts in these markets, subject to exposure limits defined by the CBR.[3]

There are no taxes or subsidies on purchases or sales of foreign exchange.[4] There are no official arrangements for forward cover against exchange rate risk. A futures trading market has developed in Moscow and is regulated as part of the CBR exposure limits, and forward contracts are also sold by authorized banks.

---

[1]The MICEX is a joint stock company of resident foreign exchange banks and nonbank licensed organizations. The Central Bank of Russia is a shareholder and founder of the MICEX. The CBR issues three kinds of foreign exchange license: internal licenses, which allow a bank to deal in foreign exchange inside the Russian Federation, including establishing foreign exchange bureaus, and to open correspondent accounts in the banks of the former Soviet Union (e.g., Moscow Narodony); limited licenses, which allow banks to open up to six correspondent accounts in banks of their choice, in addition to correspondent accounts in former Soviet banks abroad and to deal in up to six currencies; and general licenses, which allow banks to carry out the full range of foreign exchange operations, including portfolio transactions. The MICEX receives a commission in U.S. dollars of 0.1 percent on net purchases of U.S. dollars and a commission in rubles of 0.1 percent on net purchases of rubles. The other currency exchanges of the Russian Federation are organized in a similar manner as the MICEX; the CBR is not necessarily a shareholder of these exchanges but may operate on them.

[2]The official rate was defined by the Soviet Gosbank in relation to a currency basket of six convertible currencies, and the value of that unit of account, therefore, fluctuates with the exchange rates of those currencies.

[3]End-of-day exposures must not exceed $100,000 for each Rub 1 billion of capital up to Rub 10 billion. Exposures of banks with a capital exceeding Rub 10 billion must obtain individual limits from the CBR.

[4]A local turnover tax of 0.1 percent has been imposed by the city of Moscow since March 1, 1994.

Administration of Control

The responsibility for regulating foreign trade and exchange transactions is shared by the CBR, the Ministry of Finance, the Ministry of Foreign Economic Relations, the Federal Service of Currency and Exchange Control, and the State Tax Service. The CBR is responsible for administering exchange control regulations, supervising and monitoring transactions of authorized banks, including accounting procedures for the revaluation of foreign currency items, and regulating banks' open foreign exchange positions. It has delegated to the authorized banks the responsibility for enforcing capital controls and repatriation and surrender requirements; the CBR, the Inspectorate of State Control, and the State Tax Service monitor the banks' enforcement. The Ministry of Finance supervises compliance with regulations concerning export quotas, licensing, and transactions in precious metals and unprocessed precious stones. The State Tax Service supervises the payment of taxes on income in foreign currencies.

The Law of the Russian Federation on Currency Regulations and Currency Controls stipulates that Parliament is responsible for overseeing the Government's foreign exchange reserves. The authority for changing the rules for the mandatory sale of foreign exchange from export earnings rests with the President of the Russian Federation.

In accordance with the Fund's Executive Board Decision No. 144–(52/51) adopted on August 14, 1952, the Russian Federation notified the IMF on April 1, 1993 that, in compliance with UN Security Council Resolution No. 757 (1992), certain restrictions had been imposed on the making of payments and transfers for current international transactions in respect of the Federal Republic of Yugoslavia (Serbia/Montenegro).

Arrears are maintained with respect to external debt-service payments.

Prescription of Currency

The Russian Federation's payment and settlement arrangements with other countries follow the principle that trade should be valued at world prices and settled in freely convertible currencies unless otherwise stated in intergovernmental agreements. Existing official payment arrangements fall into three categories (1) payment arrangements related to trade; (2) payment arrangements related to intergovernmental credits; and (3) payment arrangements related to foreign investment. Payment arrangements in credit and investment agreements may affect current account transactions in that pay-

ments may be effected in kind and at nonmarket exchange rates.

At present, the Russian Federation maintains bilateral payments agreements with Bulgaria, China, Cuba, the Czech Republic, Hungary, Mongolia, Poland, the Slovak Republic, and Slovenia. Agreements with the Islamic State of Afghanistan, Cuba, Egypt, India, and the Syrian Arab Republic specify clearing currencies for the settlement of merchandise trade according to indicative commodity lists and for the payment of technical assistance from the Russian Federation. Payments for technical assistance to Albania, Cambodia, China, India, the Democratic People's Republic of Korea, the Lao People's Democratic Republic, Mongolia, and Viet Nam are effected in convertible currency or by credit repayable in kind. Receipts in convertible currency from Albania and Mongolia are deposited in special accounts for payment for imports from these countries by the Russian Federation only. When specific agreements do not exist or trade takes place outside the framework of the agreements, settlements are effected in convertible currency. In particular, centralized exports by the Government (mostly fuel and other energy products) to the former CMEA member countries must be settled in convertible currencies, while the settlement of other exports is left to the contracting parties.

Settlements among the Baltic countries and the other countries of the former Soviet Union are made principally through correspondent accounts of authorized banks in rubles or in convertible currencies. Payments to the Russian Federation are also effected through the central banks of the Baltic countries and other countries of the former Soviet Union through a system of bilateral correspondent accounts; balances in these accounts may not be settled multilaterally. At the end of 1994, the CBR held a sizable surplus balance denominated in rubles with the central banks of these countries.[5]

Resident and Nonresident Accounts

Natural and juridical persons may open foreign currency accounts at authorized resident banks. Resident natural persons may maintain bank accounts abroad only while working abroad; otherwise, they must obtain permission from the CBR. Resident juridical persons, including branches of Russian banks, may not maintain accounts abroad

---

[5]Most of this balance was renegotiated on market terms following the demonetization of the pre-1993 rubles and after the CBR ceased to extend new credit to these central banks.

without special permission from the CBR. Resident banks may open correspondent accounts abroad in accordance with the procedures set out in the CBR's foreign exchange licenses. Since July 16, 1993, authorized Russian banks have been allowed to open correspondent accounts in the countries of the former Soviet Union without restriction, provided that they comply with the regulation on exposure limits.

Nonresidents may hold four types of accounts: "T" accounts, which are used for the servicing of export-import operations by their representative offices in the Russian Federation; correspondent ruble accounts for nonresident banks under the same regime applicable to "T" accounts; "I" accounts, which can be used for investment activities (including privatization operations); and nonresident accounts for physical persons. The use of balances in "T" accounts and correspondent ruble accounts is limited to domestic transactions; "I" accounts may be used for a wide range of investment activities. Nonresidents may sell or buy foreign exchange with funds in these latter accounts.

Imports and Exports

Imports are generally free of quotas and licenses. Licenses are required for imports of medicines, raw materials for the production of medicines and pesticides, and industrial waste. A customs duty ranging from 5 percent to 15 percent is levied on most goods; duties on some goods range up to 150 percent. The following products are exempt from customs duties: foodstuffs; medicines; inputs for production of medicine; medical supplies and equipment; printed materials; children's articles; accompanied baggage, except motor vehicles, up to $2,000; equipment for the oil and gas industries; and ships and boats. Imports from the CIS countries and "least developed" countries are also exempt, and the customs duties on imports from other developing countries are reduced by one-half. Customs duties are payable in rubles at the exchange rates of the CBR. Foreign-owned companies, banks, and organizations that are officially accredited in the Russian Federation may import unlimited office-related goods duty free.

Foreign exchange for imports may be obtained up to 180 days prior to delivery.

Exports are not subject to quotas, and licensing is limited to a small group of products. Exports of strategically important goods require registration of contracts with the MFER. In addition, exports of materials considered strategically important are effected through approved intermediaries (so-called

special exporters, consisting mainly of former state trading associations and industry associations).[6] A limited number of goods, mainly determined by the Ministry of Environment, may be exported only under a licensing regime. The export regimes apply to exports to all countries.

Export licenses are issued in accordance with application procedures established by the MFER and are required for a limited number of other products (e.g., military equipment and arms, gold, diamonds, other precious metals and stones, certain food products, wildlife, medicines, chemical raw materials for the production of medicines, and minerals).

Export duties are levied on about one hundred product groups. Specific duties are denominated in ECUs and range from ECU 1 to ECU 80,000 a ton. Ad valorem duties range up to 30 percent (15 percent and 20 percent for foods). Specific duties on goods exported under barter trade arrangements are 50 percent higher, as are specific duties on exports that are not subject to the 50 percent surrender requirement. The export duties are imposed on exports to all countries of the former Soviet Union except for goods delivered to meet state needs in accordance with intergovernmental agreements and that were sold by the state corporations (Roskontract and Rosagrokhim). Duties on goods exported to the Baltic countries and the other countries of the former Soviet Union may be paid in rubles, and on goods exported to other countries, in any of the currencies quoted by the CBR, using CBR exchange rates prevailing on the day the payment for the goods is received. A number of discretionary exemptions are granted on a case-by-case basis.[7] Export duties are payable when the goods cross the border, but payments may be postponed for up to 60 days if a bank guarantee for the subsequent payment is provided. Fifty percent of export earnings must be surrendered to the authorized banks. There are exceptions for exporters of oil and gas.

Payments for and Proceeds from Invisibles

Payments for invisibles are not restricted, and residents may purchase foreign exchange for all bona fide invisible transactions from authorized banks with proper documentation. There are no re-

---

[6]This requirement was eliminated on March 25, 1995.

[7]Oil- and gas-producing enterprises are exempt from export duties for the decentralized portion of their exports. This exemption does not apply to enterprises with foreign investments registered after January 1, 1992 that provide goods for centralized exports.

strictions on the amount of foreign banknotes a person may take out of the country, provided that a certificate from an authorized bank on the origin of the funds is presented to customs. The use of internationally accepted credit cards issued by domestic banks to customers who have foreign currency accounts is not restricted.

Residents and nonresidents traveling to areas where the ruble is sole legal tender are allowed to take out a maximum of Rub 500,000 in banknotes.

The transfer of income from investments by nonresidents is not restricted. Nonresidents may freely convert their income into foreign exchange. Proceeds from invisibles, except those from banking services, are subject to the surrender requirement.

Authorized banks holding general foreign exchange licenses are permitted to import and export foreign currency banknotes, treasury notes, coins in circulation, and securities without restriction, provided that they observe customs regulations.

Capital

Capital transfers of residents, with the exception of repayments of foreign loans, must be authorized by the CBR.

External borrowing by juridical persons is subject to control. Both resident and nonresident juridical persons have the right to import or transfer foreign exchange to the country without restriction, provided that they observe the regulations. Foreign borrowing by nonresident juridical persons is subject to a special license and authorization by the CBR and also by the Ministry of Finance when a state guarantee is involved. Borrowing by banks possessing a general foreign exchange license does not require a special license. Nonresident juridical persons may transfer abroad foreign currency assets up to the amount imported, provided that the foreign exchange is in their possession. Nonresidents may buy or sell foreign currency for investment purposes in exchange for rubles through "I" accounts without limit. Investment in Russian enterprises by nonresidents through joint ventures or through outright ownership is not restricted, except in some sectors like banking and exploration of natural resources (special license required) or land ownership (prohibited). Enterprises with foreign capital shares must register with the Ministry of Economy, and investments exceeding Rub 100 million require a permit from the Council of Ministers. Foreign direct investments are accorded the same rights and privileges with regard to property ownership and economic activities as those accorded to residents.[8] Foreign direct investments may be nationalized or expropriated only in exceptional cases, in accordance with legislation, and, in such cases the investor would be entitled to compensation.

Gold

Domestic trade in gold is not permitted, except that monetary gold intended to be part of the country's foreign exchange reserves is purchased by the CBR and the Government at world prices quoted on the London market converted at the market exchange rate. Exports of gold and swaps require authorization of each transaction by the Government, with the transaction made through authorized banks with special licenses. The license for each transaction is issued by the CBR. The Ministry of Finance has issued gold-backed certificates, which can also be bought by nonresidents.

Changes During 1994

Exchange Arrangement

January 1. A ban on the use of foreign currency banknotes in domestic retail operations was introduced.

January 28. The Rostov Foreign Currency Exchange began trading Ukrainian karbovanets.

February 4. A special 0.1 percent tax on foreign exchange transactions was introduced in the MICEX.

March 1. The MICEX started daily trading sessions in Ukrainian karbovanets and regular trading sessions in Kazakh tenge.

December 13. French francs began to be traded on the MICEX.

Imports and Exports

January 1. The duty-free limit for imports by individual travelers was lowered to $2,000 from $5,000.

January 1. The CBR tightened control over the repatriation of foreign exchange earnings of exporters.

February 2. Rules for conducting trade with the Baltic countries and other countries of the former Soviet Union were issued. Goods supplied to the Russian Federation by these countries are not subject to import duties, the VAT, or excises. Exports

---

[8]A presidential decree of September 27, 1993 introduced several provisions to protect foreign investment, including a "grandfather" clause that protects foreign investment for a three-year period from regulatory acts that would adversely affect their activities and a provision that any restrictions on activities of foreign investors can be introduced only by laws of the Russian Federation or by presidential decree.

from the Russian Federation to these countries (except individual strategic raw materials) were exempted from all taxes and levies. Bilateral trade with these countries conducted on a clearing basis was regulated by bilateral intergovernmental accords. Quotas and licenses for exports from the Russian Federation to these countries were preserved for 14 major goods and raw materials. When goods are exported from the Russian Federation to these countries, exporters must submit "transaction passports" for exports of major raw materials and, as of March 12, for all exports..

November 1. Foreign-owned companies, banks, and organizations that are officially accredited in the Russian Federation were authorized to import unlimited office-related goods duty free, provided they keep them for their own use and export them if and when their accreditation expires.

Payments for and Proceeds from Invisibles

January 17. Regulations on the procedure for registering exporters of strategic raw materials (special exporters) were published.

Capital

February 10. Nonresidents were allowed to purchase up to 10 percent of the issue of domestic treasury bills.

November 26. Foreign investors were exempted from customs duties on imports of machinery, equipment, and components under contracts signed before January 1, 1993, as well as similar goods financed by credits provided to the Russian Government by foreign countries and international organizations.

RWANDA

(Position as of March 31, 1995)

Exchange Arrangement

The currency of Rwanda is the Rwanda Franc, the external value of which is determined freely in the exchange market in which commercial banks and foreign exchange bureaus operate. The National Bank of Rwanda does not announce official exchange rates, but it calculates and publishes daily the average market exchange rate for reference purposes. At the end of March 31, 1995, the average exchange rate quoted by commercial banks and foreign exchange bureaus was RF 247.73 per US$1.

There are no taxes or subsidies on purchases or sales of foreign banknotes. Purchases of traveler's checks are subject to a commission of 2 per mil with a minimum of RF 200 and a maximum of RF 20,000. Other outward and inward transfers are subject to a commission of 3 per mil, with a minimum of RF 500 and a maximum of RF 20,000. There are no arrangements for forward cover against exchange risk.

Administration of Control

Control over foreign exchange transactions is vested in the National Bank; authority to carry out some of these transactions is delegated to authorized banks. Arrears are maintained with respect to external payments.

Prescription of Currency

To facilitate trade and other external transactions, the National Bank maintains agreements with the central banks of the Economic Community of the Great Lakes Countries (CEPGL), Burundi, and Zaïre. Under these arrangements, settlements are made through reciprocal accounts in convertible domestic currency; balances on such accounts are periodically transferable. Payments to and from other member countries of the Preferential Trade Area for Eastern and Southern African States (PTA) (Burundi, Comoros, Djibouti, Ethiopia, Kenya, Lesotho, Malawi, Mauritius, Somalia, Swaziland, Tanzania, Uganda, Zambia, and Zimbabwe) are made through the PTA's clearinghouse. Otherwise, payments for imports must be made in the currency quoted by the National Bank, which, in principle, is the currency of the country of origin. Payments from any country may be received in Belgian francs, deutsche mark, French francs, Italian lire, Japanese yen, Netherlands guilders, pounds sterling, Swiss francs, and U.S. dollars. Foreign payments, except in border trade, are generally made by bank transfer; the National Bank may, however, authorize other means of payment, such as checks or telegraphic transfers.

Imports and Import Payments

All imports of narcotics are prohibited. Imports of all other goods have been permitted under an open general license (OGL) system since July 1, 1992. Residents are free to purchase foreign exchange from commercial banks and foreign exchange bureaus and to make payments for imports. Certain categories of imports, such as explosives and weapons, require prior approval from the relevant authorities, regardless of origin and value. For reasons of health, the importation of human or veterinary medicines, disinfectants, insecticides, rodent poisons, fungicides, herbicides, and other toxic or potentially toxic chemicals is subject to approval of the pro forma invoices by the Ministry of Health.

The National Bank levies a validation fee of 1 percent of the f.o.b. value on imports that are subject to inspection by international agencies; the validation fee for fuel is 1 per mil. Before orders are placed, import declarations must be submitted to an authorized bank. The declarations enable importers to obtain the required foreign exchange from an authorized bank or a foreign exchange bureau. Since March 1990, the National Bank has also authorized imports of goods financed with foreign exchange outside official channels.

Imports whose f.o.b. value on the pro forma invoice is greater than $10,000 in the case of ordinary licenses, and RF 0.5 million are subject to inspection by international agencies for quality and quantity in the country of origin before shipment. Prices are verified at the same time. Import licenses must be presented when the goods are cleared through customs, and a copy of the customs clearance form must be sent to the National Bank. For imports of products originating in member countries of the CEPGL, import licenses are replaced by CEPGL import notices. The import tariff regime is governed by the tariff code of January 1, 1993.

Payments for Invisibles

Residents are free to purchase foreign exchange from commercial banks and foreign exchange bureaus and to make payments for invisibles.

Salaries and wages earned by foreign nationals employed in Rwanda under contract, net of taxes and employee's share of social security contributions, may be transferred. Transfers of the net earned income of self-employed foreign nationals, whether engaged in a profession or established as independent traders, are also made net of taxes and after deduction of local expenses. A fee of 0.4 percent is levied on transfers abroad.

Official travel requires a travel authorization issued by the Government or by an authorized agency. Fixed daily allowances are granted for travel. The frequency of business travel is not restricted, but business travel is restricted to licensed businessmen who may purchase foreign exchange up to the equivalent of $10,000 a trip. Other travel by residents requires valid documents justifying the reason for the trip (e.g., education and training abroad or medical treatment). Up to the equivalent of $4,000 is available for tourist travel. Travel by nonresidents is allowed according to the terms stipulated in their employment contracts. Remittances for payments for certain other invisibles may be authorized on an ad hoc basis.

Travelers may take out domestic banknotes up to the equivalent of $100 without declaration. Commercial banks are not permitted to export domestic banknotes.

Exports and Export Proceeds

All exports, except trade samples and personal and household effects of travelers are subject to prior declaration. Declarations for exports must be submitted to an authorized bank. Receipts from exports must be repatriated within seven business days of the date of receipt. Settlements among the member countries of the CEPGL and the PTA are effected through clearing arrangements maintained by the central banks of the countries concerned. Exporters may sell their foreign exchange earnings freely on the domestic foreign exchange market or retain them in accounts held with domestic banks. Ninety percent of earnings from exports of coffee and tea must be sold to commercial banks at the average market reference exchange rate quoted by the National Bank of Rwanda.

Proceeds from Invisibles

All receipts from invisibles may be sold freely to commercial banks or foreign exchange bureaus. Travelers from abroad may bring in up to the equivalent of $100 in domestic banknotes and any amount in foreign banknotes. Commercial banks are not permitted to import domestic banknotes. The law requiring that travelers declare foreign exchange on entering Rwanda was abolished on December 1, 1990.

Capital

All outward transfers of capital require the prior approval of the National Bank. Transfers of dividends to foreign shareholders are allowed. Repatriation guarantees may be given by the National Bank in respect of short-term capital inflows. There is no time limit for retransfer of these foreign currencies.

Gold

Trade in gold is restricted to dealers approved by the relevant ministry. Imports and exports of gold require an import or an export declaration.

Changes During 1994

Exchange Arrangement

March 6. Commercial banks and foreign exchange bureaus were permitted to set freely the exchange rate for the Rwanda franc against foreign currencies. The National Bank of Rwanda ceased to announce official exchange rates for the Rwanda franc. It would calculate and publish for reference purposes each day the average market exchange rate to be applied in transactions.

Imports and Import Payments

March 6. Rwandan residents were permitted to purchase foreign exchange freely from commercial banks and foreign exchange bureaus and to make payments abroad for all imports.

Payments for Invisibles

March 6. Rwandan residents were freely permitted to purchase foreign exchange and make payments for invisibles.

Exports and Export Proceeds

March 6. Exporters would be permitted to sell their foreign exchange earnings freely on the domestic foreign exchange market or to retain them in accounts held with domestic banks. Ninety percent of export earnings from coffee and tea, however, would have to be sold to the banking system at the average market reference exchange rate quoted by the National Bank of Rwanda.

Capital

March 6. Prudential limits on banks' open foreign exchange positions of 20 percent of capital were introduced for commercial banks.

ST. KITTS AND NEVIS

(Position as of December 31, 1994)

Exchange Arrangement

The currency of St. Kitts and Nevis is the Eastern Caribbean Dollar, [1] which is issued by the Eastern Caribbean Central Bank (ECCB) and is pegged to the U.S. dollar, the intervention currency, at EC$2.70 per US$1. On December 31, 1994, the buying and selling rates were EC$2.6882 and EC$2.2719, respectively, per US$1. The ECCB also quotes daily rates for the Canadian dollar and the pound sterling. There are no arrangements for forward cover against exchange rate risk operating in the official or the commercial banking sector.

St. Kitts and Nevis formally accepted the obligations of Article VIII, Sections 2, 3, and 4 of the Fund Agreement, as from December 3, 1984.

Administration of Control

Exchange control is administered by the Ministry of Finance and applies to all countries.

Prescription of Currency

Settlements with residents of ECCB countries must be effected in Eastern Caribbean dollars.

Foreign Currency Accounts

U.S. dollar currency accounts may be operated freely, but permission of the Ministry of Finance is required to operate other foreign currency accounts; such permission is normally confined to major exporters and foreign nationals not ordinarily residing in St. Kitts and Nevis. These accounts may be credited only with foreign currency earned or received from outside St. Kitts and Nevis and may be freely debited. A minimum balance of US$1,000 must be maintained at all times to operate a U.S. dollar currency account.

Imports and Import Payments

Most goods are imported under open general licenses. Individual licenses are required for imports that compete with local products unless they come from another member country of the Caribbean Common Market (CARICOM).[2] Payments for authorized imports payable in U.S. dollars are permitted on presentation of documentary evidence of purchase to a bank, but payments in currencies other than the U.S. dollar need the approval of the Ministry of Finance. The Common External Tariff (CET) is between zero and 30 percent.

Payments for Invisibles

All settlements overseas require exchange control approval, except where the currency involved is the U.S. dollar, in which case commercial banks are authorized to pay on presentation of documentary evidence. Where the currency involved is not the U.S. dollar, application must be made directly to the Ministry of Finance; authorization is normally granted for certain specific purposes and services.

Residents of St. Kitts and Nevis may purchase foreign exchange from authorized banks up to the equivalent of EC$1,500 a year for travel outside the ECCB area, subject to presentation of evidence of intention to travel for bona fide purposes. For business travel, allowances of foreign exchange may be made available up to EC$5,000 a year a company. These allocations can be increased in bona fide cases with the authorization of the Ministry of Finance. Residents traveling abroad for medical treatment are eligible for an allowance of EC$1,000, which may be raised without any limitation, provided that a medical certificate is presented. There is a 7.5 percent ad valorem tax on all travel tickets.

Education allowances are subject to approval by the Ministry of Finance. Residents may also make cash gifts to nonresidents not exceeding a total value of EC$250 a donor a year. Profits and dividends may be remitted in full, subject to confirmation of registration by the Commissioner of Inland Revenue for income tax purposes.

Exports and Export Proceeds

Specific licenses are required for the exportation of certain goods to any destination. Export proceeds must be deposited into an ECCB currency account or an approved U.S. dollar foreign cur-

---

[1]The Eastern Caribbean dollar is also the currency of Anguilla, Antigua and Barbuda, Dominica, Grenada, Montserrat, St. Lucia, and St. Vincent and the Grenadines.

[2]The CARICOM countries are Antigua and Barbuda, The Bahamas, Barbados, Belize, Dominica, Grenada, Guyana, Jamaica, Montserrat, St. Kitts and Nevis, St. Lucia, St. Vincent and the Grenadines, and Trinidad and Tobago.

rency account. Export duties are levied on a few products.

Proceeds from Invisibles

Foreign currency proceeds from transactions in invisibles must be sold to a bank or deposited into an approved U.S. dollar account if the proceeds are in U.S. dollars. Travelers to St. Kitts and Nevis may freely bring in notes and coins denominated in Eastern Caribbean dollars or in any foreign currency.

Capital

All outward capital transfers require exchange control approval. The purchase by residents of foreign currency securities and of real estate situated abroad for private purposes is not normally permitted. Personal capital transfers, such as inheritances, to nonresidents require approval, which is normally granted subject to payment of any taxes due. Emigrants leaving St. Kitts and Nevis to take up residence outside the area served by the ECCB may transfer their assets with the permission of the Ministry of Finance.

Direct investments in St. Kitts and Nevis by nonresidents do not require exchange control approval. The remittance of proceeds from earnings on, and liquidation of, such investments is permitted, subject to the discharge of any liabilities related to the investment. The approval of the Ministry of Finance is required for nonresidents to borrow in St. Kitts and Nevis.

Gold

There are no restrictions on the purchase, sale, and holding of gold for either numismatic or industrial purposes.

Changes During 1994

Exchange Arrangement

February 28. The 2 percent tax on gross sales of foreign exchange was eliminated.

ST. LUCIA

(Position as of December 31, 1994)

Exchange Arrangement

The currency of St. Lucia is the Eastern Caribbean Dollar,[1] which is issued by the Eastern Caribbean Central Bank (ECCB). The Eastern Caribbean dollar is pegged to the U.S. dollar, the intervention currency, at EC$2.70 per US$1. On December 31, 1994, the buying and selling rates for the U.S. dollar were EC$2.6994 and EC$2.7084, respectively, per US$1. The ECCB also quotes daily rates for the Canadian dollar and the pound sterling. There are no arrangements for forward cover against exchange rate risk operating in the official or the commercial banking sector.

St. Lucia formally accepted the obligations of Article VIII, Sections 2, 3, and 4 of the Fund Agreement, as from May 30, 1980.

Administration of Control

Exchange control is administered by the Ministry of Finance and Planning and applies to all currencies other than the Eastern Caribbean dollar. Export licensing is required for a range of primary products. Import and export licenses are issued by the Ministry of Trade; those for agricultural products are issued by the Ministry of Agriculture.

Prescription of Currency

Settlements with residents of member countries of the Caribbean Common Market (CARICOM)[2] must be made either in the currency of the CARICOM country concerned or in Eastern Caribbean dollars. Settlements with residents of other countries may be made either in any foreign currency[3] or in Eastern Caribbean dollars. When justified by the nature of the transaction, approval may be given to make payments for goods and services in a currency other than that of the country to which payment is to be made.

Nonresident (External) Accounts

External accounts may be opened for nonresident individuals or companies with the approval of the Ministry of Finance and are maintained in Eastern Caribbean dollars. These accounts may be credited only with foreign drafts or checks, but hotels may also deposit currency notes in them. Such accounts may be debited for payments to residents payable in Eastern Caribbean dollars and, after approval by the Ministry of Finance, for the cost of foreign exchange required for travel or business purposes. As funds in an external account are normally convertible into a foreign currency, deposits to and withdrawals from such an account require exchange control approval by the Ministry of Finance.

Foreign Currency Accounts

A foreign currency account is defined as an account denominated in a currency other than the Eastern Caribbean dollar. With the prior permission of the Ministry of Finance, residents or nonresidents may open foreign currency accounts with authorized dealers in St. Lucia. Such permission is granted in special cases where the applicant earns foreign exchange and has to make frequent payments abroad. A resident or nonresident (whether an individual, firm, company, association, or institution) wishing to open a foreign currency account must apply to the Ministry of Finance through an authorized dealer, stating the nature and estimated volume of receipts and payments in the desired foreign currency. All payments from a foreign currency account require the prior approval of the Ministry of Finance. Where permission is granted, the authorized dealer must submit to the Ministry of Finance a monthly statement of account, together with full details of payments and receipts, to ensure that the conditions for holding foreign currency are observed.

Imports and Import Payments

All goods, except certain agricultural and manufactured products, may be imported without a license. Certain other commodities require individual licenses unless they are imported from CARICOM countries. The importation of selected consumer items (e.g., rice, flour, and sugar) in bulk form is a state monopoly. Payments in foreign cur-

---

[1]The Eastern Caribbean dollar is also the currency of Anguilla, Antigua and Barbuda, Dominica, Grenada, Montserrat, St. Kitts and Nevis, and St. Vincent and the Grenadines.

[2]The CARICOM countries are Antigua and Barbuda, The Bahamas, Barbados, Belize, Dominica, Grenada, Guyana, Jamaica, Montserrat, St. Kitts and Nevis, St. Lucia, St. Vincent and the Grenadines, and Trinidad and Tobago.

[3]Foreign currencies comprise all currencies other than the Eastern Caribbean dollar.

rency for authorized imports are permitted upon application to a local bank and submission of certified customs entry. Advance payments for imports require prior approval from the Ministry of Finance.

Goods produced or manufactured in the CARICOM region may be imported duty free. Imports of live animals, milk, meat, fish, eggs, fertilizers, and most agricultural and industrial machinery are exempt from import duties. Other exempt items include most imports from CARICOM and the member countries of the Organization of Eastern Caribbean States (OECS); certain imports for use in industry, agriculture, fishing, and air and sea transport (under industrial incentive legislation); and items exempted under the Hotel Aid Ordinance and Fiscal Incentives Ordinance. St. Lucia implemented the first stage of the CARICOM Common External Tariff (CET) by lowering rates to a range between zero and 35 percent (except for imports by companies involved in local agricultural production) on July 1, 1993. A customs service charge of 2 percent of the c.i.f. value is levied on all imports except fertilizers, for which the rate is 0.20 percent. Certain imports are subject to a consumption tax that is based on the c.i.f. value plus import duty.

Payments for Invisibles

Residents may purchase foreign exchange from authorized banks up to the equivalent of EC$3,000 a year for travel; this limit may be exceeded only with permission from the Ministry of Finance. Persons traveling within the CARICOM area using CARICOM traveler's checks (which are denominated in Trinidad and Tobago currency) receive the basic allowance of EC$2,000 a year. A travel tax is levied on the sale of airline tickets at the rate of 2.5 percent of the price of the ticket for travel within the CARICOM area and 5 percent for travel elsewhere. The Eastern Caribbean dollar is freely transferable within the ECCB area. With the approval of the Ministry of Finance, profits may be remitted in full, subject to confirmation by the Comptroller of Inland Revenue that local tax liabilities have been discharged. However, in cases where profits are deemed to be high, the Ministry of Finance and Planning reserves the right to phase remittances over a reasonable period. Insurance premiums are taxed as follows: life insurance, 1.5 percent for residents and 3 percent for nonresident companies; general insurance, 3 percent for residents and 5 percent for nonresident companies.

Exports and Export Proceeds

Certain commodities may be exported to any destination without a license. Proceeds must, in principle, be surrendered. A duty at the rate of 2.5 percent of the f.o.b. value is levied on banana exports. A special fee of US$0.02 a barrel is applied on re-exports of petroleum.

Proceeds from Invisibles

Foreign currency proceeds from transactions in invisibles must, in principle, be surrendered. Travelers to St. Lucia may freely bring in notes and coins denominated in Eastern Caribbean dollars or in any foreign currency. Foreign currency coins are not normally exchanged by the banks.

Capital

All outward capital transfers require exchange control approval. Residents are not normally permitted to purchase foreign currency securities and real estate situated abroad for private purposes. Personal capital transfers, such as inheritances to nonresidents, require approval, which is normally granted, provided that local tax liabilities have been discharged. Nonresidents who purchase property are taxed at a higher rate than are residents.

Any resident who requires a loan from local sources must first have the approval of the Ministry of Finance. Applications for nonresident loans are submitted by the authorized dealer (or other financial intermediary) to the Ministry of Finance on behalf of the applicant.

Gold

There are no restrictions on imports of gold.

Changes During 1994

Exchange Arrangement

April 1. The 1 percent tax on sales of foreign exchange was eliminated.

ST. VINCENT AND THE GRENADINES

(Position as of December 31, 1994)

Exchange Arrangement

The currency of St. Vincent and the Grenadines is the Eastern Caribbean Dollar,[1] which is issued by the Eastern Caribbean Central Bank (ECCB). The Eastern Caribbean dollar is pegged to the U.S. dollar, the intervention currency, at EC$2.70 per US$1. On December 31, 1994, the buying and selling rates for the U.S. dollar were EC$2.6882 and EC$2.7169, respectively, per US$1. The ECCB also quotes daily rates for the Canadian dollar and the pound sterling. There are no arrangements for forward cover against exchange rate risk operating in the official or the commercial bank sector.

St. Vincent and the Grenadines formally accepted the obligations of Article VIII, Sections 2, 3, and 4 of the Fund Agreement, as from August 24, 1981.

Administration of Control

Exchange control is administered by the Ministry of Finance and applies to all countries outside the ECCB area. The Ministry delegates to authorized dealers the authority to approve some import payments and certain other payments.

Prescription of Currency

Settlements with residents of member countries of the Caribbean Common Market (CARICOM)[2] must be made either through external accounts in Eastern Caribbean dollars or in the currency of the CARICOM country concerned. Settlements with residents of other countries may be made in any foreign currency[3] or through an external account in Eastern Caribbean dollars.

Nonresident Accounts

External accounts may be opened for nonresidents with the authorization of the Ministry of Finance. They are maintained in Eastern Caribbean dollars and may be credited with inward remittances in foreign currency and with transfers from other external accounts. Except with the prior approval of the Ministry of Finance, remittances in Eastern Caribbean currency, foreign currency notes and coins, and payments by residents may not be credited to external accounts. These accounts may, however, be freely debited for payments abroad and to residents without the prior authorization of the Ministry of Finance. The operating banks must submit quarterly statements of the accounts to the Ministry of Finance.

Foreign Currency Accounts

Accounts denominated in foreign currencies may be opened by nonresidents with the authorization of the Ministry of Finance; these accounts may be credited only with funds in the form of remittances from overseas. Except with the prior permission of the Ministry of Finance, remittances in Eastern Caribbean currency, foreign currency notes and coins, and payments by residents may not be credited to a foreign currency account. These accounts may be debited for payments abroad without prior authorization from the Ministry of Finance. The operating banks must submit quarterly statements of the accounts to the Ministry of Finance.

Imports and Import Payments

Import items are divided into three categories: the largest category covers goods that may be freely imported; imports of some goods that compete with typical exports of other member countries of the CARICOM and the Organization of Eastern Caribbean States (OECS)[4] are subject to licenses; and imports of goods that compete with locally made products are prohibited in some cases.

Payments for authorized imports are permitted upon application and submission of documentary evidence and, where required, of the license. In 1993, import licenses covered about 8 percent of the total import value. Advance payments for imports require prior approval from the Ministry of Finance. The import tariff rates range from zero to 35 percent. In addition to customs duties, imports are subject to a consumption tax, which ranges from

---

[1]The Eastern Caribbean dollar is also the currency of Anguilla, Antigua and Barbuda, Dominica, Grenada, Montserrat, St. Kitts and Nevis, and St. Lucia.

[2]The CARICOM countries are Antigua and Barbuda, The Bahamas, Barbados, Belize, Dominica, Grenada, Guyana, Jamaica, Montserrat, St. Kitts and Nevis, St. Lucia, St. Vincent and the Grenadines, and Trinidad and Tobago.

[3]Foreign currencies include all currencies other than the Eastern Caribbean dollar.

[4]The OECS comprises Antigua and Barbuda, Dominica, Grenada, Montserrat, St. Kitts and Nevis, St. Lucia, and St. Vincent and the Grenadines.

5 percent to 50 percent and is levied on the tariff-inclusive value of imports. Goods imported from the member countries of the CARICOM are exempt from import tariffs and are subject only to the consumption tax. A customs service charge of 2 percent is imposed on the c.i.f. value of all imported goods with certain exceptions.

Payments for Invisibles

Payments for invisibles related to authorized imports are not restricted. Payments for travel, medical treatment, education, subscription and membership fees, and gifts are subject to limits. All other payments exceeding EC$100 must be approved by the Ministry of Finance, and approval is granted routinely. Residents may purchase foreign exchange from authorized banks up to the equivalent of EC$2,500 a year for travel outside the ECCB area; for business travel, additional allocations of foreign exchange may be made available up to EC$6,000 a year. These allocations may be increased with the authorization of the Ministry of Finance. Purchases of foreign currency to cover expenses for medical treatment abroad are authorized by the Ministry of Finance when a local medical practitioner presents a written statement of the need for the treatment. The amount approved is based on the actual cost of the treatment. A 5 percent tax is levied on the value of all tickets for travel originating in St. Vincent and the Grenadines, whether or not they are purchased in the country.

Students attending educational institutions overseas are permitted to purchase foreign exchange to cover the cost of tuition and living expenses. Documentary proof of acceptance and attendance at the institution is required. The amount of foreign currency that may otherwise be purchased without the approval of the Ministry of Finance is limited to the equivalent of EC$50 a trip.

Exports and Export Proceeds

Specific licenses are required for the exportation to any destination of some agricultural goods included in the CARICOM marketing protocol and in the CARICOM Oils and Fats Agreement. The licenses are issued by the Ministry of Trade, which, in some cases, has delegated its authority to the St. Vincent Central Marketing Corporation. Exports of goats, sheep, and lobsters are subject to licensing to prevent depletion of stocks. All export proceeds must be surrendered within six months. A 2 percent export duty is levied on bananas.

Proceeds from Invisibles

Foreign currency proceeds from transactions in invisibles must be surrendered. Travelers may freely bring in notes and coins denominated in Eastern Caribbean dollars or in any foreign currency.

Capital

All outward capital transfers require exchange control approval. Residents are normally not permitted to purchase foreign currency securities or real estate situated abroad for private purposes. On presenting documentary proof that they are taking up permanent residence in a foreign country, emigrants may apply to the Ministry of Finance to transfer funds abroad based on the value of assets held in St. Vincent and the Grenadines. The transfer of funds is normally limited to EC$100,000 a year as is the transfer of proceeds from sales of assets held by emigrants already residing in a foreign country.

Direct investment in St. Vincent and the Grenadines by nonresidents is not subject to exchange control. The remittance of earnings on, and liquidation of proceeds from, such investment is permitted, subject to the discharge of any liabilities related to the investment. The approval of the Ministry of Finance is required for nonresidents to borrow in St. Vincent and the Grenadines. Any borrowing abroad by authorized dealers to finance their domestic operations requires the approval of the Ministry of Finance.

Gold

Residents are permitted to acquire and hold gold coins for numismatic purposes only. Under license by the Ministry of Finance, imports of gold are permitted for industrial purposes only.

Changes During 1994

Imports and Import Payments

January 1. The banana industry was exempted from the 2 percent customs service charge.

Exports and Export Proceeds

January 1. The 3 percent export duty on bananas was reduced to 2 percent.

Capital

January 1. The annual limit on funds an emigrant is allowed to transfer abroad was increased to EC$100,000 from EC$20,000.

SAN MARINO

(Position as of December 31, 1994)

Exchange Arrangement

The currency of San Marino is the Italian Lira.[1] The central monetary institution is the Istituto di Credito Sammarinese. There are no taxes or subsidies on purchases or sales of foreign exchange. Forward transactions may be conducted through commercial banks without restriction at rates quoted in Italian markets.

San Marino formally accepted the obligations of Article VIII, Sections 2, 3, and 4 of the Fund Agreement, as from September 23, 1992.

Administration of Control

Under the terms of the Agreement on Financial and Exchange Relations of May 1991, the Central Bank of San Marino is a foreign exchange bank with the authority to grant foreign exchange dealer status to Sammarinese financial institutions; currently, Sammarinese banks may maintain accounts only with financial institutions in Italy. As a result, foreign exchange transactions of domestic banks are effectively limited to buying foreign exchange at rates similar to those quoted in Italy and to conducting third-country transactions through Italian correspondents.

Residents of San Marino are allowed to conduct foreign exchange transactions freely, with settlement effected through authorized Italian intermediaries (the Bank of Italy, the Italian Foreign Exchange Office, authorized banks, and the Postal Administration). Direct settlements (with residents drawing on their own external accounts) authorized under Italian Exchange Control Regulations in 1990 have not yet been utilized.

Prescription of Currency

Settlements with foreign countries are made in convertible currencies or in lire on foreign accounts.

San Marino does not maintain any bilateral payments arrangements.

Resident and Nonresident Accounts

Residents and nonresidents are free to maintain any type of deposit accounts; in practice, deposit accounts other than in lire are not offered by domestic banks.

Imports and Import Payments

Imports from Italy are not subject to restriction, whereas imports from third countries are subject to control by the relevant Italian regulations. No license, other than the general business license, is required to engage in trade transactions. Trade is free of regulation except that the importation of electricity, gas, and water is reserved for the public sector. Payments for imports are unrestricted.

Imports into Italy are currently governed by Decree No. 40 of December 22, 1972, as amended.

Customs duties on imports from non-European Union (EU) member countries are collected by the EU customs authorities on behalf of San Marino. A sales tax is levied on all imports at the time of entry. The structure of this tax corresponds closely to the Italian value-added tax, but the average effective rate is about 4 percent lower. Sales tax levied on imports is rebated when the goods are re-exported.

Payments for Invisibles

There are no restrictions on payments for invisibles.

Exports and Export Proceeds

Export proceeds are not subject to surrender requirements. There are no taxes or quantitative restrictions on exports.

Exports to Italy are not regulated, while exports to third countries are governed by relevant Italian regulations. Exports from Italy are currently governed by Decree No. 40 of December 22, 1972, as amended. Exports to any country of products listed in Decree No. 68 require export licenses; other exports do not require authorization.

Proceeds from Invisibles

Proceeds from invisibles are not regulated.

---

[1]The Monetary Agreement between San Marino and Italy, renewed on December 21, 1991, provides for San Marino to issue annually agreed amounts of San Marino lira coins equivalent in form to Italian coinage; these coins will be legal tender in both countries. The San Marino gold scudo is also issued but is legal tender only in San Marino. It is not generally used in transactions because its numismatic value exceeds its defined legal value (Lit 50,000 per 1 scudo).

Capital

All inward and outward capital transfers, with few exceptions, are not restricted. Foreign direct investments, irrespective of the extent of ownership, require government approval, which is based on conformity with long-term developmental and environmental policy considerations. The purchase and ownership of real property by nonnationals require approval from the Council of Twelve, and approval is granted on merit and on a case-by-case basis. There are no restrictions on the repatriation of profits or capital. Foreign investors are accorded equal treatment with national firms; that is, investment incentives that are available to domestic investors are equally available to foreign investors.

Gold

International trade in gold is governed by the Italy-San Marino Agreement on Financial and Exchange Relations.

Changes During 1994

No significant changes occurred in the exchange and trade system.

SÃO TOMÉ AND PRÍNCIPE

(Position as of December 31, 1994)

Exchange Arrangement

The currency of São Tomé and Príncipe is the São Tomé and Príncipe Dobra, the external value of which is determined in the interbank market on the basis of demand and supply conditions. On December 31, 1994, the exchange rate (middle rate) for the U.S. dollar, the intervention currency, was Db 1,185.31 per US$1. Rates for certain other currencies are determined on the basis of the exchange rates of the U.S. dollar for the currencies concerned.

Foreign exchange transactions are divided into three categories for the purpose of assessing charges on purchases and sales of foreign exchange—namely, import payments, transactions in foreign checks, and collection of export proceeds.

On import-related exchange transactions, the arrangements are as follows: when a letter of credit is opened, a charge of 1.125 percent of the import value is payable, with an additional commission of 0.5 percent to the Central Bank of São Tomé and Príncipe. A stamp duty of 0.35 percent is also payable, as well as a postage levy of Db 140. Any change in the letter of credit carries a further charge of Db 250.

On foreign checks for collection, a commission is applied in favor of the collecting foreign correspondent and varies from bank to bank. In addition, the International Bank of São Tomé and Príncipe charges a postage levy of Db 90 for each transaction, together with an endorsement stamp fee of Db 30. For collection of export proceeds, a commission of 0.25 percent is charged when the letter of credit is opened, and a fee of 0.125 percent is charged when the funds are received. A postage levy of Db 1,200 is also charged.

There are no arrangements for forward cover against exchange rate risk operating in the official or the commercial banking sector.

Administration of Control

All foreign exchange transactions are controlled by the Central Bank, which applies the exchange controls flexibly. All foreign exchange proceeds must be surrendered to the Central Bank, and all exchange payments must be made through the Central Bank, with the exception of 30 percent of earnings retained by producer-exporters for import payments. (See the section on Exports and Export Proceeds, below.)

Import and export licenses are automatically granted and recorded by the Directorate of External Commerce for statistical purposes.

Arrears are maintained with respect to external payments.

Prescription of Currency

The Central Bank may prescribe the currency in which foreign exchange transactions shall be made.

A bilateral payments agreement is maintained with Cape Verde. Transactions under this agreement have normally covered São Tomé and Príncipe's imports from Cape Verde, as well as receipts and payments for various services and transfers. This agreement provides for the central banks of the two countries to grant each other a reciprocal non-interest-bearing credit of $200,000; it also provides that, should this balance be depleted and a debit balance persist for more than six months, the imbalance would be settled through appropriate trade transactions.

Imports and Import Payments

All imports require prior licenses. All registered importers (including productive entities) are permitted to engage in import activity. Fuels and lubricants are imported by the public fuel enterprise, and medicines by the public pharmaceutical enterprise and the private pharmaceutical sector. Import licenses are automatically granted by the Directorate of External Commerce. However, the Chamber of Commerce, in collaboration with the Ministry of Commerce, designates eligible importers. Licenses are issued in accordance with Advance Import Registration Bulletins, which are valid for six months but may be extended if necessary. The license specifies the quantity and the c.i.f. and f.o.b. values of the product to be imported, together with the currency of settlement. However, legal importers may import products without a license if imports are to be settled with their own foreign exchange, and imports are registered for customs operations. When importers open letters of credit, the International Bank requires them to lodge a non-interest-bearing deposit in domestic currency equivalent to 40 percent of the value of the letters of credit; the remainder may be financed with a 120-day loan. Prepayment for imports is permitted only through the opening of letters of credit.

Payments for Invisibles

Payments for invisibles related to authorized imports are not restricted. Payments for other invisibles are approved within limits established by the Central Bank. These limits, which allow for additional amounts in justifiable cases, include those on (1) transfers for medical treatment abroad when local facilities are inadequate; (2) transfers of remittances to students; (3) transfers of savings from earnings under technical cooperation agreements with the Government; and (4) transfers for payment of fares, freight, and costs of communication with foreign countries. Purchases of foreign exchange by residents for purposes of tourism are limited, although air fares may be paid in domestic currency. Transfers of profits by foreign companies established in São Tomé and Príncipe before independence have been suspended. There are no limitations on remittances for subscriptions to periodicals and books or on the payments of interest on external debt.

Foreign exchange allowances for medical purposes are permitted up to the equivalent of Db 1 million. Payments for technical assistance and other services in the national interest are allowed. At the beginning of the school year, a student is granted permission to transfer up to the equivalent of Db 150,000 a month, or Db 425,000 a quarter, for expenses related to courses taken abroad; additional amounts must be approved by the Ministry of Education and Culture.

All payments related to invisibles are subject to a stamp tax of 0.5 percent.

Exports and Export Proceeds

All exports require an export license, as set out in Advance Export Registration Bulletins, which specify the quantity and c.i.f. or f.o.b. value of the export. All export proceeds must be repatriated and collected through the International Bank. However, producers of exported goods may retain 30 percent of export proceeds in accounts with banks, including those abroad (if they are correspondent banks of the Central Bank), and may use the balances to meet their import requirements.

Proceeds from Invisibles

Travelers may bring in any amount of foreign exchange.

Capital

Inward foreign investments are governed by the Investment Code, which was implemented on October 15, 1992. Foreign capital investments, excluding the extraction of hydrocarbons and other mining industries, are permitted on the same basis as domestic investment. Repatriation of profits is permitted up to 10 percent a year of the value of the investment. Transfers are permitted for repayment of financing under agreements with the Government and for the amortization of private sector investments in activities considered to be in the national interest. Personnel under technical assistance programs are allowed to transfer their savings in accordance with the terms of their contracts.

Gold

Exports and imports of gold require special authorization from the Central Bank.

Changes During 1994

Exchange Arrangement

December 2. The peg to the U.S. dollar was discontinued, and the external value of the dobra was allowed to be determined by market forces.

Imports and Import Payments

January 1. The annual import plan and the system of advance import registration vouchers were abolished.

SAUDI ARABIA

(Position as of December 31, 1994)

Exchange Arrangement

The currency of Saudi Arabia is the Saudi Arabian Riyal, which is pegged to the SDR at SRls 4.28255 per SDR 1. In principle, margins not exceeding 7.25 percent around the fixed relationship are allowed; these margins were suspended on July 22, 1981. The intervention currency is the U.S. dollar; its rate against the riyal is determined by the Saudi Arabian Monetary Agency. On December 31, 1994, the Monetary Agency's middle rate for the U.S. dollar was SRls 3.745 per US$1; the selling rate for U.S. dollars to banks was SRls 3.75 per US$1, and the buying rate from banks was SRls 3.74 per US$1. These rates, which have not changed since June 1, 1986, serve as the basis for exchange quotations in the market, the banks being permitted to charge up to 0.125 percent above and below the Monetary Agency's buying and selling rates. There are no taxes or subsidies on purchases or sales of foreign exchange. The commercial banking sector has an active forward market to cover exchange risks of up to 12 months.

Saudi Arabia formally accepted the obligations of Article VIII, Sections 2, 3, and 4 of the Fund Agreement, as from March 22, 1961.

Administration of Control

In accordance with the Fund's Executive Board Decision No. 144-(52/51) adopted on August 14, 1952, Saudi Arabia notified the Fund on September 5, 1990 that certain restrictions had been imposed on the making of payments and transfers for current international transactions in respect of Iraq and on September 15, 1992 that, in compliance with UN Security Council Resolution No. 757 (1992), certain restrictions had been imposed on the making of payments and transfers for current international transactions in respect of the Federal Republic of Yugoslavia (Serbia/Montenegro).

Prescription of Currency

The use of the currency of Israel is prohibited.[1] No other prescription of currency requirements are in force.

Imports and Import Payments

Import licenses are not required, and exchange for payments abroad is obtained freely. The importation of a few commodities is prohibited for reasons of religion, health, or national security. Most imports are subject to customs duties at rates ranging between zero and 12 percent; for a short list of imports, the rate is 20 percent, and for tobacco products, 30 percent. Imports from member states of the Cooperation Council for the Arab States of the Gulf (GCC) are exempt, provided that at least 40 percent of the value added in each case is effected in GCC countries and that at least 51 percent of the capital of the producing firm is owned by citizens of GCC member countries.

Exports and Export Proceeds

Export licenses are not required, and no control is exercised over export proceeds. Certain imported items that are subsidized by the Government may not be re-exported.

Payments for and Proceeds from Invisibles

Payments for and proceeds from invisibles are not restricted. Travelers may freely import and export Saudi Arabian banknotes and coins.

Capital

No exchange control requirements are imposed on capital receipts or payments by residents or nonresidents. The Monetary Agency has issued guidelines to its foreign correspondent banks requiring them to seek approval before floating loans denominated in riyals. Local banks are required to obtain the approval of the Monetary Agency before inviting foreign banks to participate in riyal-denominated syndicated transactions inside or outside Saudi Arabia. Prior approval from the Monetary Agency is also required for local banks to participate in either riyal-syndicated transactions arranged abroad or foreign currency-syndicated transactions arranged for nonresidents. The Foreign Capital Investment Law provides for certain benefits to be extended to approved foreign investments in Saudi Arabia. Approved foreign capital enjoys the same privileges as domestic capital under the 1962 Law for the Protection and Promotion of National Industry. Foreign capital invested in indus-

---

[1]In addition, all imports from and all exports to this country are prohibited; payments may neither be made to it nor received from it for any type of transaction, whether current or capital.

trial or agricultural projects with at least 25 percent Saudi Arabian participation is exempt from income and corporate tax for ten years after production has begun.

Gold

The monetary authorities and all other residents, including private persons, may freely and without license purchase, hold, and sell gold in any form, at home or abroad. They may also, without a license

and without paying any customs duty or tax, import and export gold in any form, except manufactured gold and jewelry, which are subject to a 12 percent customs duty; gold of 14 karats or less may not be imported.

Changes During 1994

Prescription of Currency

May 5. Restrictions on the use of South African currency were lifted.

SENEGAL

(Position as of December 31, 1994)

Exchange Arrangement

The currency of Senegal is the CFA Franc,[1] which is pegged to the French franc, the intervention currency, at the fixed rate of CFAF 1 per F 0.01. The official buying and selling rate is CFAF 100 per F 1. Exchange rates for other currencies are derived from the rate in the Paris exchange market for the currency concerned and the fixed rate between the French franc and the CFA franc. The BCEAO no longer levies a commission on transfers to and from countries outside the West African Monetary Union (WAMU).[2] Banks charge an exchange commission of 0.125–1.0 per mil on purchases and sales of foreign exchange, depending on the amount, other than those directly related to external transactions. In addition, they levy a commission of 2.5 per mil on transfers to all countries outside the WAMU, all of which must be surrendered to the treasury. There are no taxes or subsidies on purchases or sales of foreign exchange.

Forward cover against exchange rate risk is available to residents only for imports of a specified category of goods. All forward cover against exchange rate risk must be authorized by the Directorate of Money and Credit in the Ministry of Economy, Finance, and Planning. Forward cover may be provided only in the currency of settlement stipulated in the commercial contract. Maturities must correspond to the due date of foreign exchange settlement stipulated in the commercial contract and must not exceed one month. For some specified products, the maturity of forward cover may be extended one time for up to three months.

With the exception of measures relating to gold and the repatriation of export proceeds, the issuance, publicizing, and tendering of transferable securities and real property, and applications for investment abroad, Senegal's exchange controls do not apply to (1) France (and its overseas departments and territories) and Monaco; and (2) all other countries whose bank of issue is linked with the French Treasury by an Operations Account (Benin, Burkina Faso, Cameroon, Central African Republic, Chad, Comoros, Congo, Côte d'Ivoire, Equatorial Guinea, Gabon, Mali, Niger, and Togo). Hence, all payments to these countries may be made freely. All other countries are considered foreign countries.

Arrears are maintained with respect to external payments.

Administration of Control

Exchange control is administered by the Directorate of Money and Credit, which has delegated a part of the approval authority for exchange control to the BCEAO and to authorized banks. The BCEAO is authorized to collect, either directly or through the banks, other financial institutions, the Postal Administration, and notaries public, any information necessary to compile balance of payments statistics. All exchange transactions relating to foreign countries must be effected through authorized banks, the Postal Administration, or the BCEAO. The Ministry of Commerce and Handicrafts issues export authorizations and prior import authorizations for listed products.

Prescription of Currency

Because Senegal is an Operations Account country, settlements with France (as defined above), Monaco, and the Operations Account countries are made in CFA francs, French francs, or the currency of any other Operations Account country. Current transactions with The Gambia, Ghana, Guinea, Guinea-Bissau, Liberia, Mauritania, Nigeria, and Sierra Leone may be settled through the West African Clearing House arrangement. Settlements with all other countries are usually effected through correspondent banks in France, in any of the currencies of those countries or in French francs.

Nonresident Accounts

The regulations pertaining to nonresident accounts are based on those applied in France. The crediting to nonresident accounts of CFA banknotes, French banknotes, or banknotes issued by any other institute of issue that maintains an Operations Account with the French Treasury is not permitted. Nonresident accounts may not be credited with BCEAO banknotes, French franc notes, or banknotes issued by central banks that maintain an Operations Account with the French Treasury. Funds may be transferred freely between nonresident ac-

---

[1]The CFA franc is issued by the Central Bank of West African States (BCEAO) and is the common currency in Benin, Burkina Faso, Côte d'Ivoire, Mali, Niger, Senegal, and Togo.

[2]Transfers between member countries of the WAMU are free of commission.

427

counts. These accounts may not be overdrawn without prior authorization of the Minister of Finance.

Imports and Import Payments

Imports originating in or transshipped from Israel are prohibited. With respect to other countries, the principle of most-favored-nation treatment of all Senegal's commercial partners was established in 1981. Moreover, quantitative restrictions and prior authorization requirements for certain imports are being phased out. The requirement for prior authorization for imports of cereals, jewelry, newspapers and documentaries, kola nuts, jute bags, prerecorded tapes, and mineral and chemical fertilizers was abolished in June 1994. Quantitative restrictions may be applied for various reasons, such as agricultural policy, sanitation, or protection of certain products (cement, fertilizers, sugar, wheat flour, and tomatoes).

All import transactions relating to foreign countries must be domiciled with an authorized bank when their value exceeds CFAF 500,000 (delivered at the Senegalese border or c.i.f.). The exchange authorizations entitle importers to purchase the necessary exchange but not earlier than eight days before the goods are shipped to Senegal if a documentary credit is opened, or on the due date for settlement if the commodities have already been imported (if no documentary credit has been opened, on presentation of the bill of lading). Furthermore, payments for imports, with the exception of down payments, are permitted only after the proper documents for customs clearance are submitted. Advance payments for imports require authorization, and importers may not acquire foreign exchange until the contractual date of the payments.

All imports, except those in transit and those intended for the free zone of Dakar, are subject to a service fee of 6 percent or 12 percent, depending on their customs classification. All imports valued (f.o.b.) at more than CFAF 1.5 million are subject to inspection by international agencies with respect to quality, quantity, price, and tariff classification.

Payments for Invisibles

Payments for invisibles to France (as defined above), Monaco, and the Operations Account countries are permitted freely; those to other countries are subject to exchange approval. Payments for invisibles related to trade are permitted freely when the basic trade transaction has been approved or does not require authorization. Authorized intermediary banks are empowered to effect abroad payments of up to CFAF 20,000 on behalf of residents without requiring documents. Transfers of income accruing to nonresidents in the form of profits, dividends, and royalties are also permitted when a request for exchange authorization is submitted to the Ministry of Finance.

Limitations on allowances for travelers are administered in a nonrestrictive manner, and all bona fide requests in excess of the established limits are granted. Residents traveling for tourism or business purposes to countries in the franc zone that are not members of the WAMU are allowed to take out banknotes other than CFA franc notes up to the equivalent of CFAF 2 million; amounts in excess of this limit may be taken out in the form of means of payment other than banknotes. The allowances for travel to countries outside the franc zone are subject to the following regulations: (1) for tourist travel, CFAF 500,000 without limit on the number of trips or differentiation by the age of the traveler; (2) for business travel, CFAF 75,000 a day for up to one month, corresponding to a maximum of CFAF 2.25 million (business travel allowances may be combined with tourism allowances); (3) allowances in excess of these limits are subject to the authorization of the respective ministries of finance; and (4) credit cards, which must be issued by resident financial intermediaries and specifically authorized by the respective ministers of finance, may be used up to the ceilings indicated above for tourist and business travel. Upon arrival at customs, returning resident travelers are required to declare all means of payment in their possession and must surrender within eight days all means of payment exceeding the equivalent of CFAF 25,000. All residents traveling to countries that are not members of the WAMU must declare in writing all means of payment at their disposal at the time of departure. Nonresident travelers may re-export means of payment other than banknotes issued abroad and registered in their name. The re-exportation of foreign banknotes is allowed up to the equivalent of CFAF 250,000; the re-exportation of foreign banknotes above these ceilings and other means of payment issued in Senegal requires documentation demonstrating either the importation of foreign banknotes or their purchase against other means of payment registered in the name of the traveler or through the use of nonresident deposits lodged in local banks.

A foreigner working in Senegal may transfer his full net salary upon presenting the appropriate pay voucher, provided that the transfer takes place within three months of the pay period.

Exports and Export Proceeds

All exports to Israel are prohibited. With a few exceptions (e.g., gold, diamonds, fine pearls, precious and similar stones, plated or coated precious metals, articles made of these metals, and precious metal products), exports do not require prior authorization. The requirement for prior authorization for exports of cereals, groundnuts, fresh tomatoes, and jewelry was abolished in June 1994. Certain nontraditional exports are eligible for an export subsidy equivalent to 25 percent based on industrial value added at international prices. Proceeds from exports to foreign countries, including members of the WAMU and the Operations Account countries, must normally be collected within 120 days of the arrival of the goods at their destination and repatriated through BCEAO not later than one month after the due date. All export transactions exceeding CFAF 500,000 must be domiciled with an authorized intermediary bank.

Proceeds from Invisibles

Proceeds from transactions in invisibles with France (as defined above), Monaco, and the Operations Account countries may be retained. All amounts due from residents of other countries for services and all income earned in those countries from foreign assets must be collected and surrendered, if received in foreign currency, within one month of the due date or the date of receipt. Resident and nonresident travelers may bring in any amount of banknotes and coins issued by the BCEAO, the Bank of France, or any bank of issue maintaining an Operations Account with the French Treasury, as well as any amount of foreign banknotes and coins (except gold coins) of countries outside the Operations Account area. Residents bringing in foreign banknotes must declare them to customs upon entry and sell them to an authorized bank within eight days.

Capital

Capital movements between Senegal and France (as defined above), Monaco, and the Operations Account countries are free of exchange control; capital transfers to all other countries require the approval of the Ministry of Economy, Finance, and Planning, but capital receipts from such countries are permitted freely.

Controls are maintained over borrowing abroad, over inward direct investment and all outward investment, and over the issuing, advertising, or offering for sale of foreign securities in Senegal.

Such operations require the prior authorization of the Minister of Economy, Finance, and Planning. Exempt from authorization, however, are operations in connection with (1) loans backed by a guarantee from the Senegalese Government, and (2) shares that are identical with, or may be substituted for, securities whose issuance or offering for sale in Senegal has previously been authorized. With the exception of controls over foreign securities, these measures do not apply to France, Monaco, member countries of the WAMU, and the Operations Account countries. Special controls are maintained also over imports and exports of gold, over the soliciting of funds for deposit with foreign private persons and foreign firms and institutions, and over publicity aimed at placing funds abroad or at subscribing to real estate and building operations abroad; these special controls also apply to France, Monaco, and the Operations Account countries.

All investments abroad by residents of Senegal require prior authorization from the Minister of Economy, Finance, and Planning;[3] 75 percent of such investments must be financed with borrowing from abroad. Foreign direct investments in Senegal[4] must be declared to the Minister of Economy, Finance, and Planning before they are made. The Minister has two months from receiving the declaration to request postponement of the project. Both the making and the liquidating of direct and other investments, whether Senegalese investments abroad or foreign investments in Senegal, must be reported to the Minister of Economy, Finance, and Planning and the BCEAO within 20 days of each operation. Direct investments constitute investments implying control of a company or enterprise. Mere participation is not considered direct investment, provided that it does not exceed 20 percent of the capital of a company whose shares are quoted on a stock exchange. Lending abroad requires prior authorization from the Minister of Economy, Finance, and Planning.

Borrowing by residents from nonresidents requires prior authorization from the Minister of Economy, Finance, and Planning. The following are, however, exempt from this authorization: (1) loans constituting a direct investment, which are subject to prior declaration, as indicated above; and

---

[3]Including investments made through foreign companies that are directly or indirectly controlled by persons in Senegal and those made by overseas branches or subsidiaries of companies in Senegal.

[4]Including those made by companies in Senegal that are directly or indirectly under foreign control and those made by branches or subsidiaries of foreign companies in Senegal.

(2) loans contracted by authorized banks. The repayment of loans not constituting a direct investment requires the authorization of the Minister of Economy, Finance, and Planning if the loan itself was subject to such approval but is exempt because it did not require authorization.

The Investment Code provides various facilities and benefits for approved foreign investments in Senegal. Special facilities for export industries are established in the Dakar export processing zone.

Gold

Residents are free to hold, acquire, and dispose of gold in any form in Senegal. Imports and exports of gold (gold jewelry and gold materials) from or to any other country require prior authorization from the Minister of Economy, Finance, and Planning. Exempt from this requirement are (1) imports and exports by the Treasury or the BCEAO; (2) imports and exports of manufactured articles containing a minor quantity of gold (such as gold-filled or gold-plated articles); and (3) imports and exports by travelers of gold articles up to a combined weight of 200 grams. Brokers in precious metals require authorization from the Minister of Economy, Finance, and Planning to conduct their business. Imports of gold are subject to customs declaration. Purchases abroad of nonmonetary gold by brokers are subject to a 25 percent ad valorem tax. Commercial imports of gold jewelry require prior import authorization from the Minister of Commerce and Handicrafts; imports of ornaments require the prior approval of the Directorate of Handicrafts and the Directorate of Foreign Trade of the Ministry of Commerce and Handicrafts.

Changes During 1994

Exchange Arrangement

January 12. The CFA franc was devalued to CFAF 100 per F 1 from CFAF 50 per F 1.

Administration of Control

February 28. Ordinance Nos. 94–28 and 94–29, relating to financial relations with foreign entities and disputes pertaining to exchange control violations, respectively, were promulgated in order to standardize regulations within the WAMU.

Imports and Import Payments

January 10. The maximum import duty rate was reduced to 45 percent from 75 percent and a minimum duty of 5 percent was established. The duty on petroleum was reduced to 35 percent from 45 percent.

February 15. Ordinance No. 94–25 reduced the customs stamp tax applicable to all imported goods to a uniform rate of 5 percent.

June 1. Prior import authorization was abolished for the following products: cereals, gold jewelry and other jewelry, newspapers, kola nuts, jute bags, prerecorded tapes, and mineral and chemical fertilizers. The COSEC levy on imports used in the manufacture of goods for export was abolished.

September 1. Prior authorization for imports of tomato paste and polypropylene bags was abolished.

November 5. Prior authorization for imports of cement was abolished.

December 10. Restrictions on the import of vegetable oils were abolished.

Payments from Invisibles

June 10. The monopoly of the COSENAM in maritime transportation was abolished.

Exports and Export Proceeds

January 31. Following the devaluation of the CFA franc on January 12, 1994, Ordinance No. 94–19 eliminated export tax measures.

June 1. Prior authorization for exports of cereals, groundnuts, fresh tomatoes, and jewelry was abolished. The COSEC levy on exports was eliminated.

September 10. Prior authorization for exports of tomato concentrate was abolished.

SEYCHELLES

(Position as of December 31, 1994)

Exchange Arrangement

The currency of Seychelles is the Seychelles Rupee, which is pegged to the SDR at SR 7.2345 per SDR 1. Exchange rates for various currencies (including the pound sterling, the intervention currency) are quoted on the basis of their New York closing rates for the U.S. dollar on the previous day, using the U.S. dollar rate for the Seychelles rupee as derived from the fixed parity to the SDR. The Central Bank of the Seychelles circulates these rates daily to the commercial banks. On December 31, 1994, the buying and selling rates of the Central Bank for the pound sterling were SR 7.7377 and SR 7.8152, respectively, per £1. The Central Bank charges a commission of 0.125 percent on purchases and 0.875 percent on sales of pounds sterling, U.S. dollars, and French francs. The commercial banks are authorized to deal in pounds sterling and other currencies at rates based on the exchange rates circulated daily by the Central Bank for the respective currencies. Commercial banks are required to transfer 15 percent of their gross inflows of foreign exchange to the Central Bank.

There are no taxes or subsidies on purchases or sales of foreign exchange. There are no arrangements for forward cover against exchange rate risk in the official or the commercial banking sector.

Seychelles formally accepted the obligations of Article VIII, Sections 2, 3, and 4 of the Fund Agreement, as from January 3, 1978.

Administration of Control

Exchange controls are maintained in the form of administrative allocations of foreign exchange for the making of payments. The Ministry of Finance partially controls foreign trade and domestic marketing through a mechanism of import and price controls. Import controls are exercised over prescribed goods by the Trade and Commerce Division of the Ministry of Finance, while price controls are administered by the Consumer Relations Unit on behalf of the Ministry. Arrears are maintained with respect to external commercial payments.

Prescription of Currency

There are no prescription of currency requirements.

Imports and Import Payments

No restrictions are placed on payments for imports. Importers, other than individuals, are required to obtain import licenses from the Seychelles Licensing Authority. For prescribed goods, they must also apply for import permits from the Trade and Commerce Division of the Ministry of Finance. Certain prescribed goods (including sugar, flour, oil, margarine, rice, and animal feed) can be imported only by the Seychelles Marketing Board. Most imports are subject to a trade tax at rates ranging up to 600 percent, with the bulk of imported commodities falling in the range of 25 percent to 30 percent.

Payments for Invisibles

There are no restrictions on payments for invisibles, and no limits are imposed on the provision of travel exchange. Travelers may take or send out of Seychelles any amount of foreign currency and up to SR 100 in domestic currency.

Exports and Export Proceeds

Exports require permits issued by the Trade and Commerce Division of the Ministry of Finance. Residents may export goods without exchange control formality to any country. There are no regulations governing the repatriation of export proceeds.

Proceeds from Invisibles

Exchange receipts from invisibles may be disposed of freely. However, trading in foreign currencies by persons other than authorized dealers is prohibited (trading is defined as both buying and selling). Foreign currency may be accepted by businesses in payment for goods and services. Overseas visitors may bring in any amount of currency for travel expenditure.

Capital

Transfers of foreign-owned capital are allowed without restriction. Nonnationals are permitted to repatriate their surplus earnings without limitation.

Investment outside Seychelles by permanent residents and by companies and other organizations operating in Seychelles is not subject to any limitations. Foreign investment (whether portfolio, direct investment, additional investments in existing entities in the form of loans, or equity capital) is freely permitted, provided that such investments do not involve ownership of land.

Commercial banks in Seychelles are required to restrict credit to nonnationals primarily for working capital purposes and generally to an amount not in excess of overseas funds invested in Seychelles in enterprises in certain priority sectors, that is, agriculture and fishing, manufacturing, construction, and tourism. Additionally, penalty loan rates are imposed on credit secured by foreign assets.

Gold

Residents may freely purchase, hold, and sell gold in any form, but dealings in gold bullion are restricted to authorized dealers. Seychelles has issued the following commemorative gold coins, which are also legal tender: (1) two coins issued by the Currency Board (1976) in the denominations of SR 1,500 and SR 1,000; (2) a coin in the denomination of SR 20 to commemorate the fifth anniversary of the Central Bank in December 1983; (3) a coin in the denomination of SR 25 issued in April 1984 to mark the World Fisheries Conference of the Food and Agriculture Organization; (4) a coin in the denomination of SR 500 issued in February 1986 to commemorate the United Nations Decade for Women; (5) a coin in the denomination of SR 1,000 issued in June 1986 to mark the tenth anniversary of Seychelles' independence; (6) a coin in the denomination of SR 1,000 issued in June 1987 to commemorate the tenth anniversary of the fifth of June 1977 Liberation; (7) two coins in the denominations of SR 100 and SR 1,000 issued in December 1988 to mark the tenth anniversary of the Central Bank; (8) a coin in the denomination of SR 500 issued in April 1990 to mark EXPO '90 in Osaka, Japan; (9) a coin in the denomination of SR 1,000 issued in December 1993 to commemorate the fifteenth anniversary of the Central Bank; and (10) a series of coins with wildlife motifs issued in June 1994, including the magpie robin in the denominations of SR 250 and SR 50, and the milkweed butterfly in the denominations of SR 250, SR 150, and SR 50.

Changes During 1994

No significant changes occurred in the exchange and trade system.

SIERRA LEONE

(Position as of December 31, 1994)

Exchange Arrangement

The currency of Sierra Leone is the Sierra Leonean Leone. Exchange rates are freely determined on the basis of demand and supply conditions in the market. Commercial banks and licensed foreign exchange bureaus may buy and sell foreign exchange with customers and trade among themselves or with the Bank of Sierra Leone (the central bank) on a freely negotiable basis. The central bank determines the exchange rate to be used in official transactions, including for customs valuation purposes, which is based on the weighted-average rate of commercial bank and foreign exchange bureau transactions in the previous week. On December 31, 1994, the official buying and selling rates were Le 606.92 and Le 619.06, respectively, per US$1. There are no taxes or subsidies on purchases or sales of foreign exchange. There are no arrangements for forward cover against exchange rate risk operating in the official or the commercial banking and foreign exchange bureau sectors.

Administration of Control

Exchange control policy is formulated by the Department of Finance, in consultation with the central bank, but the day-to-day administration of exchange control is carried out by the central bank with the assistance of the commercial banks.

Arrears are maintained with respect to external payments.

Prescription of Currency

Foreign exchange transactions are subject to exchange control. Payments for imports from other countries may be made in leones to the credit of an external account in the currency of the exporting country, in pounds sterling, or in U.S. dollars. The West African Clearing House provides for settlements with the Central Bank of West African States (for Benin, Burkina Faso, Côte d'Ivoire, Mali, Niger, Senegal, and Togo) as well as with The Gambia, Ghana, Guinea, Guinea-Bissau, Liberia, Mali, Mauritania, and Nigeria. Receipts from exports to countries other than China may be obtained in leones from an external account in the currency of the importing country or in any specified currency.[1]

Resident and Nonresident Accounts

Residents and nonresidents in Sierra Leone are permitted to maintain foreign currency accounts denominated in any convertible currency with a commercial bank in Sierra Leone. These accounts, for which minimum balances vary from bank to bank, earn interest at a rate determined by the commercial banks. They may be credited with funds transferred from abroad, and balances on these accounts may be converted into leones to meet the account holder's local expenditures. Transfers abroad of balances in foreign currency accounts are permitted without prior approval from the Bank of Sierra Leone, provided that all requirements in respect of current account transactions are met.

Accounts in leones held with authorized banks in Sierra Leone on behalf of diplomatic missions, UN agencies, and their accredited staff are designated as external accounts. In addition, there are blocked accounts, the balances on which are blocked at a bank by order of the Secretary of State for Finance.

Imports and Import Payments

All goods may be imported freely without a license. Authority to approve transactions is delegated to the commercial banks. All applications for purchases of foreign exchange to pay for imported goods must be supported by shipping documents and submitted to a commercial bank in Sierra Leone. Goods to be financed with importers' own foreign exchange resources are permitted without letters of credit established with a local commercial bank.

All goods imported into Sierra Leone, except petroleum and goods specifically exempted by the Secretary of State for Finance, are subject to preshipment inspection and price verification by an international company appointed by the Government.

A sales tax of 20 percent of the landed value is levied on all imports except for capital goods and their spare parts, petroleum products, and baby food. All imports by unincorporated businesses are subject to a tax of 2 percent as advance payment of income taxes.

---

[1]Austrian schillings, Belgian francs, Canadian dollars, CFA francs, Danish kroner, deutsche mark, French francs, Italian lire, Japanese yen, Netherlands guilders, Norwegian kroner, Portuguese escudos, pounds sterling, Spanish pesetas, Swedish kronor, Swiss francs, and U.S. dollars.

Payments for Invisibles

Authority to provide foreign exchange for legitimate expenses is delegated to the commercial banks. Applications for basic travel allowances in excess of $5,000 a trip must be referred to the central bank for approval.

Commercial banks are authorized to approve school fees up to the full amount payable directly to the school upon presentation of bills by the schools concerned. They may also approve educational and maintenance expenses abroad of $10,000 a year and medical treatment expenses of up to $10,000. Applications for payments in excess of the amounts prescribed must be submitted to the Bank of Sierra Leone for approval. Applications for foreign exchange in excess of limits, including allowances for medical treatment abroad, are approved upon submission of documentary proof of need.

A maximum of 40 percent of an expatriate's gross salary may be remitted abroad for family maintenance purposes. At the end of their contract, foreigners are allowed to remit all of their savings.

Profits and dividends earned from foreign investment may be repatriated on submission of documentary evidence that capital was originally brought into the country.

Public sector employees on official business may take out foreign exchange from Sierra Leone up to the amount of the per diem allowance provided for that purpose. Nonresident travelers may take out any amount of foreign currency notes they declared on arrival. On leaving Sierra Leone, travelers may take out with them up to Le 50,000 in Sierra Leonean currency notes. A travel tax of 10 percent is levied on the price of tickets purchased locally and is payable when the ticket is purchased.

Exports and Export Proceeds

Licenses are required only for exports of gold and diamonds; these export licenses, valid for six months, are issued by the Department of Mines.

All exporters are required to complete export forms. Commercial exports must be endorsed by the exporter's commercial bank and the central bank. Exports of the following articles are prohibited: those containing more than 25 percent silver; those manufactured or produced more than 75 years before the date of exportation; those mounted or set with diamonds, precious stones, and pearls (excluding personal jewelry or ornaments up to a value not exceeding the leone equivalent of $1,000); postage stamps of philatelic interest; and works of art. Licensed exporters of diamonds are allowed to transact their business in U.S. dollars

and must pay an administrative fee of 1.0 percent and an income tax of 1.5 percent, which are based on the value of the diamonds exported and payable in U.S. dollars. Proceeds from exports of diamonds that were prefinanced are not subject to the repatriation requirement. Licensed exporters of gold must pay a 2.5 percent royalty on their exports.

All goods exported from Sierra Leone, except for those exempted by the Secretary of State for Finance, are subject to preshipment inspection and price verification, which is undertaken by an inspection company appointed by the Government. Exporters who are subject to inspection must pay an export inspection fee of 1 percent before clearing their goods through customs.

Proceeds from Invisibles

Receipts from invisibles can be offered for sale to authorized dealers. The importation of domestic banknotes is limited to Le 50,000 for each traveler.

Capital

Capital payments to nonresidents of Sierra Leone are subject to exchange control. Residents of Sierra Leone are required to obtain permission from the central bank to purchase foreign currency securities or real estate situated abroad. Investments by nonresidents, including profits, may be repatriated at any time, provided that exchange control approval of the investment was obtained at the outset.

The Sierra Leonean Exchange Control Act of 1954 imposes control on the issue and transfer of securities. The placing of an issue in Sierra Leone requires permission if either the person acquiring the securities or the person for whom he or she serves as nominee resides outside Sierra Leone. Permission must also be obtained before a security registered in Sierra Leone may be transferred to a nonresident. Capital in respect of securities registered in Sierra Leone may not be transferred abroad without permission. Where permission has been given for securities registered in Sierra Leone to be sold to persons residing abroad, the company is usually required to obtain bank certification of the funds brought into Sierra Leone. Income tax and customs duty concessions are granted to foreign and domestic companies undertaking industrial or agricultural activities that are needed for the development of the country. Noncitizens are prohibited from owning or controlling certain types of business under the Noncitizens Trade and Business Act of 1969.

Residents can hold foreign exchange in cash form, offer it for sale to an authorized dealer or a foreign exchange bureau, or deposit it in a foreign currency account. Exemption is granted for authorized dealers, diplomats, and holders of sterling assets held before June 24, 1972, for which exemption has been claimed and granted by the central bank. Exempted securities may be sold outside the former Sterling Area, and any income therefrom may be retained in the former Sterling Area or reinvested in other Sterling Area securities. Any certificate of securities purchased with the proceeds of the sale of securities exempted under this permission is exempt from deposit requirements. Any assets held outside the former Sterling Area by any foreign national temporarily residing in Sierra Leone are also exempt from surrender and deposit requirements, provided that exemption has been claimed and granted by an authorized dealer or by the central bank.

Gold

Residents may freely purchase, hold, and sell gold coins in Sierra Leone for numismatic purposes. Also, residents and nonresidents may freely purchase, hold, sell, or export certain Sierra Leonean commemorative gold coins. Residents are not allowed to hold gold in the form of bars or dust without a valid miner's or dealer's license. Imports of gold in any form other than jewelry constituting the personal effects of a traveler require individual import licenses, which are not normally granted.

Changes During 1994

Prescription of Currency

March 1. The bilateral payments agreement with China was terminated.

Imports and Import Payments

January 25. The sales tax levied uniformly on domestically manufactured and imported goods was raised to 20 percent from 17.5 percent.

Exports and Export Proceeds

January 1. The administrative fee on diamond exports was lowered to 1 percent from 1.5 percent.

Proceeds from Invisibles

April 1. The requirement that arriving nonresident travelers must convert a certain amount of foreign exchange to domestic currency was eliminated.

SINGAPORE

(Position as of December 31, 1994)

Exchange Arrangement

The currency of Singapore is the Singapore Dollar. Singapore follows a policy under which the Singapore dollar is permitted to float, and its exchange rate in terms of the U.S. dollar, the intervention currency, and all other currencies is freely determined in the foreign exchange market. However, the Monetary Authority of Singapore (MAS) monitors the external value of the Singapore dollar against a trade-weighted basket of currencies, with the objective of promoting noninflationary sustainable economic growth. The closing interbank buying and selling rates for the U.S. dollar on December 30, 1994 were S$1.4002 and S$1.4067, respectively, per US$1. Rates for other currencies are available throughout the working day and are based on the currencies' exchange rates against the U.S. dollar in international markets. Banks are free to deal in all currencies, with no restrictions on amount, maturity, or type of transaction.

Foreign currency futures are traded at the Singapore International Monetary Exchange. Banks can hedge their exchange rate risk through a forward foreign exchange transaction. There is an active short-term foreign exchange swap market among the banks in the domestic money market. Singapore and Brunei currency notes and coins are freely interchangeable, at par and without charge, in Singapore and Brunei. There are no taxes or subsidies on purchases or sales of foreign exchange.

Singapore formally accepted the obligations of Article VIII, Sections 2, 3, and 4 of the Fund Agreement, as from November 9, 1968.

Administration of Control

There are no formal exchange controls, but the MAS retains responsibility for exchange control matters. The Trade Development Board under the Ministry of Trade and Industry administers import- and export-licensing requirements for a very small number of products under its control. Financial assets owned by residents of Haiti, Iraq, Libya, and the Federal Republic of Yugoslavia (Serbia/Montenegro) are blocked.

Prescription of Currency

There are no prescription of currency requirements.

Nonresident Accounts

There is no distinction between accounts of residents and nonresidents of Singapore. Debits and credits to all accounts may be made freely.

Imports and Import Payments

Very few items imported into Singapore are dutiable. Customs duties are levied on imports of liquors, tobacco, petroleum, and motor cars. A few imports are controlled for health, safety, or security reasons. Singapore is a party to the Agreement on the Common Effective Preferential Tariff (CEPT) Scheme for the ASEAN Free Trade Area (AFTA). The CEPT Scheme came into operation on January 1, 1993.

Payments for Invisibles

All payments for invisibles may be made freely. There are no restrictions on the amount of foreign exchange that may be used for travel abroad. Remittances to nonresidents of dividends, interest, and profits may be made freely. Resident and nonresident travelers may take out any amount in foreign or Singapore banknotes.

Exports and Export Proceeds

Singapore observes the export prohibitions governed by the United Nations Security Council Resolutions. Certain exports originating in Singapore—for example, textiles and textile products—are subject to quantitative restrictions and other nontariff barriers in the importing countries, particularly the United States, Canada, Norway, and the members of the European Union. Export licenses are required for substances that deplete the ozone, timber, and rubber, but there is no restriction on export proceeds.

Proceeds from Invisibles

Exchange receipts from invisibles need not be surrendered and may be disposed of freely. Resident and nonresident travelers may bring in any amount in foreign banknotes and coins, including Singapore gold coins.

Capital

There are no restrictions on capital transfers. With the complete liberalization of exchange controls in

1978, Singapore residents, including corporations, are allowed to make payments in all currencies to any country outside Singapore without restriction. Residents may invest, borrow, and lend in foreign currencies without prior exchange control approval and may deal freely in spot and forward foreign exchange transactions in all currencies. However, banks, merchant banks, and finance and insurance companies must consult the Monetary Authority of Singapore if they intend to grant loans in Singapore dollars in excess of S$5 million to nonresidents; loans in excess of S$5 million to residents for use outside Singapore must also have the approval of the Monetary Authority of Singapore.

Banks in Singapore may freely accept deposits in foreign currencies. Financial institutions that have been approved to operate Asian monetary units (AMUs) in Singapore are able to offer better rates for foreign currency deposits placed with the Asian Currency Union because of the absence of minimum cash reserve and liquidity requirements. An AMU is a separate accounting unit of financial institutions that enjoy a concessional tax rate of 10 percent on their income from transacting with nonresidents in foreign currency; these institutions operate in the Asian dollar market. Transactions in Singapore dollars cannot be booked in AMUs.

There are no restrictions on either direct or portfolio investments in Singapore by nonresidents or abroad by residents.

Government approval is required for foreign investment in residential and other properties (including vacant land) that has been zoned or approved for industrial or commercial use. Foreigners may, however, freely purchase residential units in buildings of six or more stories and in approved condominium developments without such approval. Foreigners who make an economic contribution to Singapore will be given favorable consideration to purchase other residential properties for their own use and, in the case of foreign companies, to accommodate their senior personnel. The maximum limit on the proportion of foreign shareholding in local banks is 40 percent.

Gold

There is a free gold market in Singapore. Both resident and nonresident individuals and companies are permitted to import, hold, negotiate, and export gold freely; imports and exports require neither exchange control approval nor import or export licenses, and any person in Singapore can deal freely in gold. For imports, gold bars weighing 1 kilogram and above and 10-tola bars are exempt from the 3 percent goods and services tax (GST) if they are meant for re-exports. Movement of gold between two bonded warehouses in Singapore is also exempt from the GST.

Gold may also be traded in the local market and the spot or futures markets. In the spot market, most of the trading is done on a "loco-London" basis for delivery of 995 fine gold. Kilobars of 999.9 fineness are most commonly traded, while 10-tola bars are also becoming popular. Spot gold prices for settlement in Singapore are derived by adjusting the "loco-London" price with the location premium, which takes into account the cost of transportation and insurance. A gold futures contract is also available on the Singapore International Monetary Exchange.

Changes During 1994

No significant changes occurred in the exchange and trade system.

SLOVAK REPUBLIC

(Position as of December 31, 1994)

Exchange Arrangement

The currency of the Slovak Republic is the Slovak Koruna. The official exchange rate is pegged to a basket of two currencies and determined in fixing sessions conducted by the National Bank of Slovakia.[1] On December 31, 1994, the central rate was Sk 31.277 per US$1. There are no taxes or subsidies on purchases or sales of foreign exchange.

Administration of Control

The National Bank is responsible for the administration of exchange controls and regulations in coordination with the Ministry of Finance. In general, the Ministry of Finance has authority over governmental credits and over budgetary and subsidized organizations, civic associations, churches, foundations, and juridical persons who are not engaged in entrepreneurial activities. The National Bank has authority over the activities of all registered enterprises and entrepreneurs.

Prescription of Currency

Except for trade with the Czech Republic, settlements are effected in convertible currency. Since February 1993, commercial transactions with the Czech Republic must be effected through a clearing account maintained by the central banks of the two countries. Transactions are converted from the currency of the contract into clearing ECUs at a rate that may differ by up to 5 percent from the market cross rate against the ECU set by the central banks. If the balances on the account outstanding at the end of each month exceed clearing ECU 130 million, the excess amount is settled by the fifteenth of the following month. Payments by legal persons and enterprises in connection with obligations incurred before February 8, 1993 are effected through another set of clearing accounts denominated in clearing koruny converted to ECUs at the exchange rate of February 8, 1993. These accounts are settled every three months.

Resident and Nonresident Accounts

Resident Accounts

Slovak resident individuals (including unregistered entrepreneurs) may open interest-bearing for-eign exchange accounts at any resident commercial bank without revealing the source of foreign exchange. Balances on these accounts may be used by the account holder without restriction. Resident enterprises that had outstanding foreign exchange accounts on December 31, 1990 have been allowed to maintain such accounts; new foreign exchange accounts, however, may be opened by enterprises after December 31, 1990, with only a prior permit from the National Bank that exempts enterprises from the 100 percent surrender requirement. Balances on these accounts may be freely used to finance enterprises' activities.

Nonresident Accounts

Nonresidents (natural and juridical persons) may maintain two types of interest-bearing accounts:

(1) *Domestic currency accounts* may be opened with commercial banks in koruny. Balances on these accounts may be used freely to make payments in the Slovak Republic. All payments abroad from these accounts for invisibles, except transfers relating to inheritance and alimony, require a permit from the National Bank. These permits are granted only in exceptional cases.

(2) *Foreign currency accounts* may be opened by nonresidents. Foreign exchange may be deposited freely in these accounts, and payments may be made from these accounts, in the Slovak Republic or abroad, without restriction.

Imports and Exports

Imports and exports may be undertaken by any registered enterprise or private individual. Import licenses are required for a few strategic items, namely, crude oil, natural gas, firearms and ammunition, and narcotics. In addition, an automatic licensing system accompanied by variable levies applies to imports of 12 agricultural products and coal. All imports, except those from the Czech Republic, are subject to an ad valorem import tariff, ranging from zero to 15 percent, with a few exceptions. Imports from developing countries are granted preferential treatment under the Generalized System of Preferences (GSP). Under the GSP, 42 developing countries benefit from a duty exemption, and 80 others are granted a 75 percent reduction from the applicable customs duties; tropical products are granted an 85 percent reduction from

---

[1]The currencies are the deutsche mark (weight 60 percent) and the U.S. dollar (weight 40 percent).

the applicable customs duties. All consumer goods are also subject to a temporary import surcharge of 10 percent.

Advance payments for imports are restricted to 15 percent for imports exceeding Sk 1 million.

A resident individual is required to repatriate foreign exchange acquired abroad and to sell to a bank or deposit in a private foreign exchange account foreign exchange (including gold, with the exception of gold coins) exceeding the equivalent of Sk 5,000. Resident enterprises are normally required to repatriate, without delay, foreign exchange receipts from exports and sell them to commercial banks.

A limited number of products require export licenses for purposes of health control (including livestock and plants), to facilitate voluntary restraints on products on which partner countries have imposed import quotas (such as textiles and steel products), or to preserve natural resources or imported raw materials (such as energy, metallurgical materials, wood, foodstuffs, pharmaceutical products, and construction materials) for the domestic market. For the two latter groups of products, neither quantitative nor value limits are in force. Fees are applied to noncommercial exports of a few products (certain food items and selected types of porcelain and glassware) in excess of a certain value.

Payments for and Proceeds from Invisibles

Slovak residents may withdraw an unlimited amount of foreign exchange from their foreign currency accounts to make invisible payments. In addition, the annual limit on foreign exchange allowances for tourist travel abroad is the equivalent of Sk 16,000 (effective January 1, 1995). Official travel by employees of budgetary and subsidized organizations is subject to different allowances, depending on the country of destination. Transfers of alimony may be made to all countries. A special permit is required in most instances for remittances relating to family maintenance, education, and medical treatment.

Repatriation of wage savings in koruny by nonresident workers must be authorized by the National Bank. With certain exceptions related to tourism, the exportation and importation of koruna banknotes abroad are restricted. Licenses are not required for the importation or exportation of foreign exchange assets, including foreign currencies, by nonresidents.

Capital

Registered enterprises may freely obtain trade credits. Financial credits from abroad require a special permit from the National Bank. Foreign direct investments abroad are subject to approval from the National Bank; approval is normally granted if such investments are considered to facilitate exports from the Slovak Republic.

There is no limit on equity participation by nonresidents. Credits may be obtained from foreign banks with the approval of the National Bank. Foreign exchange equity participation of foreign investors can be deposited in a foreign exchange account with a resident commercial bank. Foreign investors may freely transfer abroad their dividends, profits, capital gains, and interest earnings. In the event of liquidation of the enterprise, they are allowed to repatriate freely the full value of their capital participation and capital gains in the original currency after payment of taxes.

Transfers of inherited assets abroad are allowed to all countries on a reciprocal basis.

Gold

Residents are required to sell gold (with the exception of gold coins) to financial institutions dealing in foreign exchange within 30 days of acquisition. Without a foreign exchange license, nonresidents may export inherited gold coins, provided that they submit a certificate confirming that the coins are of no historical value, and they may export gold that they have imported into the country. To export any other gold, nonresidents must have a foreign exchange license.

Changes During 1994

Exchange Arrangement

July 14. The basket against which the official exchange rate of the koruna was pegged changed from five currencies to two currencies (the deutsche mark, 60 percent, and the U.S. dollar, 40 percent).

Imports and Exports

March 1. A temporary surcharge at the rate of 10 percent was introduced on consumer goods.

Payments for and Proceeds from Invisibles

January 1. The annual limit on foreign exchange allowance for tourist travel abroad was increased to the equivalent of Sk 9,000.

Changes During 1995

Payments for and Proceeds from Invisibles

January 1. The annual limit on foreign exchange allowance for tourist travel abroad was increased to Sk 16,000 from Sk 9,000.

SLOVENIA

(Position as of December 31, 1994)

Exchange Arrangement

The currency of Slovenia is the Tolar, which was introduced on October 8, 1991 and replaced the Yugoslav dinar at parity. The external value of the tolar is determined in the exchange market by demand and supply conditions. The Bank of Slovenia (BOS) may also participate in the foreign exchange market and may buy and sell foreign exchange in transactions with the Government and commercial banks. Residents may conduct unlimited exchange transactions among themselves, and households may conduct foreign exchange transactions with banks or foreign exchange offices at freely negotiated rates. The BOS does not prescribe spreads between buying and selling rates for banks' transactions with the public, and banks are free to set their own commissions. On December 31, 1994, the official exchange rate in terms of the U.S. dollar was SIT 126.4 per US$1. The BOS publishes daily a moving two-month average exchange rate for customs valuation and accounting purposes. There is no forward market for foreign exchange, but forward foreign exchange transactions are not prohibited. There are no taxes or subsidies on purchases or sales of foreign exchange.

Administration of Control

Foreign exchange market operations are governed by the Law on Foreign Exchange Business (promulgated on June 25, 1991). The law introduced a free foreign exchange market operated by banks and exchange offices and stipulated the rules and regulations for foreign exchange transactions. The Law on Foreign Trade Transactions, approved by Parliament in February 1993, sets out the rules and regulations governing foreign trade activities. It came into force on March 27, 1993.

Prescription of Currency

Slovenia maintains a payments agreement with the former Yugoslav Republic of Macedonia, under which trade between the two countries may be settled through accounts in local currency or in foreign currencies.

Resident and Nonresident Accounts

Resident individuals and nonresidents are allowed to open and operate foreign currency accounts without restriction. Nonresidents may open local currency accounts with proceeds from the sale of foreign exchange or of goods and services to residents. Balances (including accrued interest) in these accounts may be converted into convertible currencies and repatriated. Transfers of inheritance are allowed under conditions of reciprocity. Domestic legal entities are, in principle, not allowed to maintain foreign currency accounts; exceptions are provided for in the Law on Foreign Exchange Business.

To accept foreign cash payments, as well as to pay with foreign cash, is restricted. Residents are required, in accordance with the Law on Foreign Exchange Business, to obtain permission from the BOS.

Imports and Import Payments

Licensing requirements in the form of permits, for the purpose of control only, have been retained for specific groups of goods (e.g., drugs, explosives, precious metals, and arms and ammunition) for security and public health reasons, in accordance with international conventions and codes. Slovenia maintains a system of import quotas applicable only to certain textile products. Under the system managed by the Chamber of Commerce, quotas are frequently revised and allocated to Slovenian importers. In general, the quotas are distributed among the applicants in the volume of production (for a producer) or turnover (for a trader).

Imports from the Federal Republic of Yugoslavia (Serbia/Montenegro) are prohibited, in accordance with the relevant UN resolution.

In the interim, the tariff regime under the Customs Tariff Law of the former Socialist Federal Republic of Yugoslavia is in force.[1] A new law on customs tariffs has been adopted but has not come into effect.

Payments for Invisibles

There are no restrictions on payments for invisibles, except that residents are not allowed to transfer abroad receipts from services (including interest), and earnings must be spent in Slovenia.

---

[1]The new law is expected to come into force at the beginning of 1996. Under the new law, the 1 percent customs clearance tax and the 1 percent equalization tax are expected to be eliminated.

Exports and Export Proceeds

In accordance with the sanctions of the United Nations against the Federal Republic of Yugoslavia (Serbia/Montenegro), exports from the FRY are prohibited. Except for certain items that are subject to licensing for security or health reasons in accordance with the international conventions and codes, exports are not restricted. Exports of textile products to the European Union (EU) are governed by the Agreement between the EU and the Republic of Slovenia on Trade in Textile Products, initialed on July 23, 1993; textile products originating in Slovenia are free from quantitative limits. The EU imposes tariff ceilings for only five categories of products. Export taxes are levied on the following products: unworked wood, 15 percent; worked wood, 10 percent; and scrap metal, 25 percent.

Exporters are free to agree on payment terms with foreign importers. However, if the collection of export proceeds is delayed by more than one year, the transactions must be registered with the Bank of Slovenia as credit arrangements. Once received, export proceeds must be repatriated. Exporters have two business days to sell their proceeds to importers at a freely negotiated exchange rate or to use the proceeds for payments abroad. After that term, they must sell their proceeds to an authorized bank.

Exporters are exempt from customs duties payable on raw materials and intermediate and semiprocessed goods used to produce export goods, provided that the value of exports is at least 30 percent higher than the value of imports if there is no domestic production of imported goods.

Proceeds from Invisibles

No exchange control requirements are imposed on proceeds from invisibles.

Capital

In accordance with the provisions of the Law on Foreign Credit Transactions, resident juridical persons may borrow abroad on commercial terms without restriction. The Government may, however, issue guarantees and borrow abroad only in accordance with specific laws passed by Parliament.

Resident juridical persons may maintain accounts abroad only in specific cases as provided for by law and with the permission of the BOS. Only banks licensed for foreign payments may maintain accounts abroad.

Resident companies may extend loans to nonresident persons only with profits obtained from abroad.

The Law on Foreign Investments of the former Socialist Federal Republic of Yugoslavia is still being applied in Slovenia. A new law is under consideration.

Deposit money banks are required to hold foreign exchange deposits abroad as cover against domestically held foreign exchange deposits of domestic and foreign individual persons. The required deposits range from 5 percent to 100 percent, depending on the maturity of domestically held deposits. They are also required to hold deposits abroad in an amount equal to 35 percent of their average monthly turnover of convertible payments over the preceding three months.

Short-term bank borrowing abroad is restricted.

Changes During 1994

Administration of Control

June 6. A free trade arrangement with the Slovak Republic came into effect.

August 20. A free trade arrangement with the Czech Republic came into effect.

Prescription of Currency

December 31. The bilateral payments agreement with Croatia was terminated.

Capital

July 6. Restrictions on the transferability of tolar balances held by certain nonresidents were eliminated.

September 5. Short-term bank borrowing was restricted.

SOLOMON ISLANDS

(Position as of December 31, 1994)

Exchange Arrangement

The currency of Solomon Islands is the Solomon Islands Dollar, which is issued by the Central Bank of Solomon Islands. The exchange rate for the Solomon Islands dollar is determined on the basis of its relationship to a trade-weighted basket of the currencies of Solomon Islands' four major trading partners. The Central Bank may make discretionary adjustments in the exchange value of the Solomon Islands dollar against the U.S. dollar each month within margins of 0.5 percent above or below the middle rate prevailing at the end of the previous month. The Central Bank provides the commercial banks with daily limits on the buying and selling rates for the U.S. dollar in transactions with the Central Bank and the public. On December 31, 1994, the buying and selling rates quoted by the banks in dealings with the public were US$0.3025 and US$0.3007, respectively, per SI$1.

The commercial banks in Solomon Islands are free to determine their exchange rates for all other foreign currencies. A tax of SI$3 is levied on sales of foreign exchange exceeding SI$3,000. A forward cover facility exists mainly for bona fide trade or trade-related transactions. Commercial banks may enter into forward contracts with permanent residents of Solomon Islands in any currency. However, the Central Bank will provide cover only in U.S. dollars for periods of one to six months. The Central Bank also provides the commercial banks with daily limits as a percentage of the forward buying and selling rates for the U.S. dollar for one to six months for their dealings with the Central Bank. Commercial banks are allowed to apply a margin of up to ten basis points above or below the Central Bank's forward rates in respect of their U.S. dollar forward contracts with the public.

Solomon Islands formally accepted the obligations of Article VIII, Sections 2, 3, and 4 of the Fund's Articles of Agreement on July 24, 1979.

Administration of Control

Exchange control is administered by the Central Bank through the Exchange Control (Foreign Exchange) Regulations, which came into force on March 1, 1977. The Central Bank delegates extensive powers to commercial banks, which have been appointed authorized dealers in foreign exchange and may approve certain types of applications for exchange control approval, up to specified limits.

All persons residing in Solomon Islands are regarded as permanent residents for exchange control purposes, unless they have been granted temporary resident status by an authorized dealer or the Central Bank. Applications for temporary resident status are normally approved for citizens of foreign countries who intend to reside in Solomon Islands for a period of less than four years or have already resided in Solomon Islands for over four years but can produce evidence of firm intention to resume permanent residence overseas in the near future. Ownership of real estate or a business indicates permanent resident status, regardless of the duration of residence in Solomon Islands. Temporary resident status does not release a person from the obligation to comply with all provisions of the exchange control regulations.

In accordance with the Fund's Executive Board Decision No. 144-(52/51) adopted on August 14, 1952, Solomon Islands notified the Fund, on October 14, 1992, that certain restrictions had been imposed on the making of payments and transfers for current international transactions in respect of the Federal Republic of Yugoslavia (Serbia/Montenegro).

Prescription of Currency

Contractual commitments in a foreign currency to persons resident outside Solomon Islands may be met only by payments in that currency. Export proceeds may be received in any foreign currency or in Solomon Islands dollars from an account of an overseas bank with a bank in Solomon Islands.

Nonresident Accounts

Nonresidents may open nonresident accounts in Solomon Islands dollars with authorized dealers, but approval from the Central Bank is required in order for these accounts to be credited from Solomon Islands sources. Balances on such accounts may be transferred abroad with the approval of the Central Bank or authorized dealers.

Imports and Import Payments

No restrictions are placed on payments for imports, provided evidence that they are properly due overseas is submitted. Authorized dealers are permitted to approve most transactions up to SI$25,000 without reference to the Central Bank. The rate of import levy is set at 8 percent.

Payments for Invisibles

Payments for invisibles related to authorized imports are not restricted. Approval is readily given for payments for services and remittances of dividends, profits, and other earnings accruing to overseas residents from companies in Solomon Islands, provided it can be shown they are properly due overseas. Permanent residents are permitted to purchase foreign exchange for payment of all types of invisibles if supporting documents are provided. Transfers by postal order to persons residing permanently outside Solomon Islands are permitted, provided the total amount transferred does not exceed SI$100 a week.

Approval is normally given for the purchase of foreign currency for travel. Applications for travel funds must be lodged with an authorized dealer, and applicants are required to present their passports and airline tickets. Travelers may not take out Solomon Islands currency notes and coins in excess of SI$250 without the approval of the Central Bank; approval is not normally given.

Exports and Export Proceeds

Residents may export goods other than round logs without exchange control formality, but they must comply with the terms of the General Authority issued by the Central Bank. The essential conditions of this General Authority require that payments for exported goods be received within three months of the date of exportation, that the export price be no lower than the price an exporter might reasonably be expected to receive for the goods for export to the destination involved at the date when those goods were sold or contracted to be sold under open market conditions, and that the proceeds be sold promptly to an authorized dealer. If exporters are not in a position to comply with the conditions of the General Authority, they must apply to the Central Bank for a Specific Authority. Authority is not needed for goods under SI$250 in value in any one consignment or for certain exempt categories of goods, including most personal effects of passengers.

Exports of round logs require Specific Authority from the Central Bank. The condition for issuance of a specific authority to export round logs is a market price certificate issued by the Ministry of Forestry, Conservation and Environment. Exports of logs are subject to an export duty of 27 percent if valued at US$75 or less (a cubic meter) and of 32 percent if valued at more than US$75 (a cubic meter).

Proceeds from Invisibles

Approval is required for the disposal of foreign currency proceeds other than by sale to an authorized dealer. Overseas residents visiting Solomon Islands may bring in any amount of currency for travel expenditures.

Capital

All outward transfers of capital require exchange control approval. All applications for transfers must be referred to the Central Bank. Approval is readily given for the withdrawal of nonresident-owned investment capital, repayment of loans contracted overseas, and the remittance of temporary residents' and emigrants' funds.

New investment abroad by permanent residents or by companies and other organizations operating in Solomon Islands is subject to certain limitations. Direct investment overseas is permitted when it is likely to be of benefit to Solomon Islands. For portfolio investments, approval from the Central Bank is needed before permanent residents may acquire or dispose of foreign securities. Approval is not normally given for the acquisition of overseas portfolio investments. Restrictions are not normally imposed on the disposal of foreign securities acquired before March 1, 1977.

Approval from the Central Bank is required for a resident to borrow funds from or to issue equity capital to a nonresident. The Solomon Islands branch of a company or firm incorporated overseas must have approval from the Central Bank before it may borrow funds from a nonresident, including the branch's overseas head office. If initial or increased foreign investment is concerned, the Foreign Investment Board must also give its approval.

Gold

Solomon Islanders alone are granted a license to pan for alluvial gold. Commercial banks and all other residents are required to obtain a permit issued by the Ministry of Natural Resources to mine, buy, or export gold. The Central Bank is authorized to buy, sell, and hold gold but has not yet undertaken any such transactions.

Changes During 1994

No significant changes occurred in the exchange and trade system.

SOMALIA[1]

(Position as of December 31, 1994)

Exchange Arrangement

The currency of Somalia is the Somali Shilling, which is pegged to a basket of currencies of Somalia's main trading partners. The official exchange rate is adjusted weekly to reflect changes in the cross rates of currencies in the basket and the relative rates of inflation in Somalia and its trading partners. The official exchange rate applies to imports of goods and services and debt-service payments of the Government. The exchange rate in the free market is negotiated freely between resident holders of foreign exchange accounts, that is, export/import accounts and external accounts. The Central Bank of Somalia carries out transactions in certain other currencies,[2] taking into account rates in exchange markets abroad. The official exchange market in Somalia comprises the Central Bank and the two commercial banks operating as the authorized dealers of the Central Bank in respect of transactions in foreign currencies.

There are no arrangements for forward cover against exchange risk operating in the official sector. The commercial banks also do not conduct forward exchange transactions on behalf of the public, although they are not prohibited from doing so.

Administration of Control

The Ministry of Industry and Commerce is the principal government agency charged with implementing and operating trade controls. The state-trading organization, the National Grain Agency, is responsible for importing and distributing certain commodities received under aid programs. Exchange controls are administered by the Central Bank.

Arrears are maintained with respect to external payments.

Prescription of Currency

Settlements with other countries must be made in Somali shillings or in specified currencies (the U.S. dollar and others listed in footnote 2); however, residents are not permitted to make settlements with Israel or South Africa.

Nonresident and Foreign Currency Accounts

Nonresident accounts in foreign currency and external accounts in U.S. dollars may be opened with the Central Bank by foreign embassies, international institutions, and nonresidents. External accounts in U.S. dollars may be opened by both residents and nonresidents with the commercial banks. These accounts may be credited with foreign exchange transferred from abroad and may be debited for any external payment. Residents may transfer funds to other external accounts. Funds in these accounts may be used for invisible payments under existing regulations as well as for merchandise import payments. All transactions between residents and nonresidents taking place through external accounts are effected at the official exchange rate.

Exporters of goods and services may deposit 40 percent of their foreign exchange proceeds from exports into export/import accounts. Funds in these accounts may be sold to importers holding export/import accounts and may be used only for merchandise import payments.

Imports and Import Payments

Imports of goods originating in or shipped from Israel and South Africa are prohibited. Imports of alcohol, tobacco and tobacco products, crude oil and petroleum products, medical and pharmaceutical products, explosives, precious metals and jewelry, and minerals are subject to prior approval. All other items, except those prohibited for reasons of public safety and social policy, may be imported freely. The National Petroleum Agency is responsible for importing all fuels and fuel products. Capable entrepreneurs in the private sector are permitted to import and distribute petroleum products provided that they have safe storage and distribution facilities.

All payments for private imports must be effected through letters of credit. Private importers may open letters of credit for imports at a commercial bank on the basis of foreign exchange made available for that purpose through a foreign currency account with the commercial bank; in such a case, the foreign exchange involved is kept in a suspense account until the time of settlement of the

---

[1]As of December 31, 1994, the IMF had not received from the Somali authorities the information needed for a description of the exchange and trade system.

[2]Deutsche mark, Djibouti francs, French francs, Italian lire, Kuwaiti dinars, pounds sterling, Saudi Arabian riyals, Swiss francs, and U.A.E. dirhams.

letter of credit. A noninterest-bearing cash advance deposit of 100 percent is required to open letters of credit for private sector imports; the deposit is retained until the letters of credit are settled.

Funds provided by the Italian Government under the Commodity Import Program are disbursed through a sale mechanism, under which importers submit requests for foreign exchange, accompanied by a 10 percent nonrefundable levy on the amount requested. Before June 1990, the official exchange rate applied to these transactions. If the requests for foreign exchange exceeded the available funds, foreign exchange was allocated proportionally among importers. Since then these funds have been sold through a Dutch auction mechanism (bidders purchasing foreign exchange at their bid price), with the official exchange rate serving as the floor price.

Payments for Invisibles

Payments to Israel are prohibited. To prevent unauthorized capital transfers, payments for current invisibles through external accounts, as well as through the commercial banks selling foreign exchange on their own account, are subject to licensing. Transfers of salaries, wages, gratuities, and allowances paid in Somalia to foreign personnel by enterprises registered under the Foreign Investment Law are allowed up to 50 percent. The Central Bank provides foreign exchange only for official travel expenses. Foreign exchange for private travel expenses may be purchased only from holders of external accounts with the approval of the Central Bank, subject to the following limits: (1) education allowances, $1,000 a year; (2) business and tourist travel, $200 a person a trip; and (3) medical treatment, $3,000 a year. The Central Bank may approve applications for larger amounts in exceptional cases. All foreign travelers are required to pay an airport departure tax of $20 or equivalent of $20 in any foreign currency, and Somali nationals are required to pay the tax equivalent to $10 in domestic currency.

Exports and Export Proceeds

Exports and re-exports to Israel are prohibited. Bananas are exported only by SOMALFRUIT (previously, the National Banana Board). The exportation of various types of ivory, hides and skins, and minerals is subject to prior approval; the state monopoly in exports of hides and skins was discontinued in 1990.

All export proceeds must be repatriated. Exporters of bananas and livestock may retain 40 percent of their foreign exchange receipts in export/import accounts and must surrender the remainder to the Central Bank or to authorized dealers. Exporters of nontraditional goods may retain 70 percent of their export earnings. For exports other than those made under letter-of-credit arrangements, an advance payment deposit of 100 percent of the value of exports is required. A tax of 25 percent is levied on exports of livestock, on the basis of minimum export prices used for purposes of duty collection.

Proceeds from Invisibles

Proceeds from invisibles must be repatriated and declared. Exporters of services may retain up to 40 percent of their foreign exchange receipts in external accounts; they must surrender the remainder to the Central Bank or to authorized dealers within five business days of their receipt.

Nonresidents may freely bring in with them any amount in foreign exchange and up to So. Sh. 1,000 in Somali banknotes and coins; they must make a currency declaration when entering the country. Nonresident Somalis and foreign national travelers without diplomatic status are required, upon their arrival in Somalia, to convert at least $100 or its equivalent to Somali shillings at the airport branch of the Commercial and Savings Bank on behalf of the Central Bank. Unspent foreign exchange may be taken out of the country without restriction. Resident travelers may bring in up to So. Sh. 1,000 in Somali banknotes and coins and are obliged, upon arrival, to declare any foreign exchange they bring in and to deposit it in external accounts or sell it to the commercial banks at the official exchange rate.

Capital

Capital transactions are subject to licensing unless they are authorized by the Foreign Investment Law of February 1960, as amended in January 1977 and May 1987. The amended Foreign Investment Law stipulates priorities for foreign investments in the agricultural, livestock raising, fishing, mining, tourism, and industrial and service sectors. Under this law, investments may be made, apart from the transfer of convertible currency, in the form of machinery, equipment, current production inputs, and intangibles (patent rights, trademarks, and studies and documentation prepared in connection with the intended investment). There are no outright and sectoral restrictions to foreign investment or phase-out provisions; nor does the law preclude the possibility of participating or acquiring stock in an existing Somali enterprise.

Proposed foreign investment is reviewed for approval in each case within a 60-day period by the

Foreign Investment Board, which has final authority over all matters concerning foreign investment. The Foreign Investment Board is assisted by the Foreign Investment Promotion Office, which provides advice and guidance to foreign investors on Somalia's legal, regulatory, and institutional framework, and assists at the incorporation and setting-up stages. The original foreign investment and any reinvested profit may be registered in convertible currency. There are no restrictions on reinvestment of profit. Profit is freely transferable, and profit not transferred, or portions of it, may be transferred in any subsequent year. Foreign investment (original investment plus any profit reinvested) may be freely repatriated five years from the date of the registration of the original investment. Repatriation may be effected in convertible currency or, at the investor's option, in the form of physical assets. The Foreign Investment Board may reduce the above-mentioned five-year period. Capital gains resulting from the sale of shares or liquidation of assets are freely transferable, after taxes are paid. The Foreign Investment Law restricts the possibility of expropriation to cases where public interest cannot be satisfied by other measures. In such cases, prompt and freely transferable compensation is payable in an amount that reflects the investment's fair market value as a going concern.

Investment disputes are settled in a manner to be agreed upon with the investor, or in the absence of such agreement, under the agreements in force between the investor's home country and Somalia or, in their absence, under the 1985 World Bank Convention for the Settlement of Investment Disputes. If no agreement is applicable, the law provides for resolution by a three-member arbitration board, whose chairman is to be appointed by agreement or, in its absence, by the President of Somalia's Supreme Court.

Gold

Residents may hold and acquire in Somalia, for numismatic purposes only, gold coins that are not legal tender in any country. With this exception, residents other than the monetary authorities and authorized industrial users are not allowed to hold or acquire gold in any form other than jewelry, at home or abroad. Imports and exports of gold in any form other than jewelry require the permission of the Central Bank; permission is not normally granted except for imports and exports by or on behalf of the monetary authorities and industrial users. Gold imported by jewelers must be melted down within one month to a fineness of not more than 22 karats. Imports of gold that originate in member countries of the European Union are exempt from customs duty; imports from elsewhere are subject to a 10 percent duty.

SOUTH AFRICA

(Position as of March 31, 1995)

Exchange Arrangement

The currency of South Africa is the South African Rand. The authorities of South Africa do not maintain margins in respect of exchange transactions but do intervene in the exchange market to affect rates quoted by the commercial banks. The principal intervention currency is the U.S. dollar. On March 31, 1995, the commercial banks' spot rates for the U.S. dollar in transactions with the public were R 3.5905 buying and R 3.5916 selling, respectively, per US$1.

Subject to certain limitations, authorized dealers are permitted to conduct forward exchange operations, including cover for transactions by nonresidents. Authorized dealers are permitted to provide forward exchange cover in any foreign currency to residents for any firm and ascertained foreign exchange commitments and accruals due to or by nonresidents arising from authorized trade and nontrade transactions. Forward exchange contracts may cover the entire period of the outstanding commitments or accruals. Subject to certain limitations, forward exchange cover may also be provided to nonresidents. The Reserve Bank of South Africa provides forward cover against U.S. dollars only; such cover is given to authorized dealers for maturities not exceeding 12 months in the form of rand-U.S. dollar swap transactions, with the margin based on an interest rate differential between the U.S. dollar and the rand. Forward cover for periods in excess of 12 months is available at market rates in certain freely transferable currencies for long-term offshore financing of capital goods imports and affected indebtedness that has been converted into long-term loans. Gold mining companies and houses may sell forward anticipated receipts of their future gold sales. There are no taxes or subsidies on purchases or sales of foreign exchange.

South Africa formally accepted the obligations of Article VIII, Sections 2, 3, and 4 of the Fund Agreement, as from September 15, 1973.

Administration of Control

Exchange licensing is the responsibility of the Treasury, which has delegated this authority to the Reserve Bank; in turn, the Reserve Bank has delegated many of its powers to the authorized dealers. Import and export permits, when required, are generally issued by the Director of Import and Export Control acting on behalf of the Ministers of Trade and Industry. Exchange for licensed imports is made available by authorized dealers upon proof of shipment or, when advance payment is proposed, upon presentation of other documentary evidence, which must include the prior approval of the Reserve Bank.[1]

Prescription of Currency

All countries outside the Common Monetary Area constitute the Nonresident Area. The rand is legal tender in Lesotho and Namibia but not in Swaziland.[2] Settlements by or to residents of the Common Monetary Area with the Nonresident Area may be made in rand to and from a nonresident account and in any foreign currency.[3]

Nonresident Accounts

The rand accounts of nonresidents[4] are divided into nonresident accounts and emigrant blocked accounts.

Nonresident accounts may be credited with all authorized payments by South African residents, with the proceeds of sales to authorized dealers in South Africa of foreign currency, and with payments from other nonresident accounts in South Africa. They may be debited for payments to Common Monetary Area residents for any purpose (other than loans); for payments to nonresidents for any purpose, by transfer to a local nonresident account or for remittance to any country outside the Common Monetary Area; for the cost of purchases of any foreign currency; and for payments to account holders residing in South Africa for short periods.

Emigrant blocked accounts are the accounts of emigrants from the Common Monetary Area and are subject to exchange control restrictions. Any cash or proceeds from any other South African asset held at

---

[1]Authorized dealers can permit, without the Reserve Bank's approval, advance payment of up to $33\frac{1}{3}$ percent of the ex factory cost of capital goods if suppliers require it.

[2]Lilangeni banknotes issued by Swaziland, Maloti banknotes issued by Lesotho, and Namibia dollar notes issued by Namibia are freely convertible into rand at par, but they are not legal tender in South Africa.

[3]Foreign currency, foreign exchange, exchange, and specified currency refer to any currency other than currency that is legal tender in the Republic of South Africa but not to the currencies of Lesotho, Namibia, and Swaziland.

[4]A nonresident is a natural or juridical person whose usual place of residence, domicile, or registration is outside the Common Monetary Area.

the time of departure and subsequently sold must be credited to this type of account. These funds may not be transferred from South Africa or to another emigrant blocked account in South Africa but may be retained on deposit with an authorized dealer, used within certain limits for the holder's living expenses while visiting South Africa, for other specified payments to residents, or for investment in any locally quoted securities (such securities may not, however, be exported and sold abroad).

Imports and Import Payments

Goods subject to import control are listed in Schedule IA of the Import Control Regulations published on December 23, 1988, as amended.

All importers requiring import permits for trade or manufacturing purposes must be registered with the Director of Import and Export Control. The permits are valid for imports from any country. Imports that do not require a permit include all goods from Botswana, Lesotho, Malawi, Namibia, Swaziland, and Zimbabwe that are grown, produced, or manufactured in these countries, with the exception of a limited range of agricultural products from Malawi and Zimbabwe.

Importers are automatically granted exchange to pay for current imports upon presenting to their bank the necessary consignment documents (proof of importation) and an import permit when required. Payments are not normally allowed before the date of shipment or dispatch, except with prior approval or special authorization from the Reserve Bank (see footnote 1). The system of import quotas, which affects most agricultural and a number of manufactured products, is being phased out and replaced with selective tariff measures. With certain exceptions, imports are subject to a value-added tax; locally produced goods are also subject to the tax. Import surcharges at the rate of 15 percent are levied on essential goods and at the rate of 40 percent on nonessential goods.

Payments for Invisibles

Authority is delegated to authorized dealers to approve certain current payments for invisibles without limitation and for others up to established limits. Applications for amounts in excess of these limits are considered on their merits by the Reserve Bank. Authorized dealers may, without consulting the Reserve Bank, approve current income payments, such as declared dividends, profits, and royalties, that accrue in South Africa, provided that (1) the Department of Trade and Industry and the Reserve Bank have approved the relevant royalty

agreement, and (2) the remittance of profits and dividends is based on normal trading profits generated after January 1, 1984 and does not involve local credit facilities. The Reserve Bank gives favorable consideration to such transfers when the use of local credit facilities is not regarded as excessive. Income earned from securities held by nonresidents is freely transferable to their country of residence, and limited amounts of exchange to pay for such items as membership fees and family maintenance are authorized.

There is an indicative limit on the travel allowance of R 23,000 a year for an adult (R 11,500 for a child under 12). Separately, there is an annual basic exchange allocation of R 6,000 for an adult (R 3,000 for a child under 12) for travel to neighboring countries (Angola, Botswana, Malawi, Mozambique, Zaïre, Zambia, and Zimbabwe). In addition to the tourist allowances, authorized dealers may grant allowances for overseas business trips at a rate not exceeding R 1,800 a day, up to R 30,000 in a calendar year. The separate applicable allowance for business trips to the neighboring countries listed above is R 12,000 a year, at a rate not exceeding R 900 a day. Exchange allowances in excess of the above limits may be provided with the approval of the Reserve Bank.

Residents and contract workers leaving South Africa for destinations outside the Common Monetary Area may take up to one-third of their allowance in foreign banknotes. The amount of South African Reserve Bank notes, however, may not exceed R 500, but this amount is not regarded as part of the basic travel allowance. Foreign visitors leaving South Africa may take with them up to R 500 in Reserve Bank notes and any amount of foreign notes brought into the country or obtained through the disposal of instruments of exchange brought into and converted in South Africa. These limitations on the exportation of Reserve Bank notes do not apply to contract workers returning to neighboring countries, who are permitted to take with them reasonable amounts in banknotes. There are no limitations on the exportation of domestic currency to Lesotho, Namibia, and Swaziland.

Exports and Export Proceeds

To be sold outside the Southern African Customs Union, exports of specified commodities considered to be in relatively short supply or controlled for strategic reasons require export permits.

Unless otherwise permitted, all export proceeds must be remitted to South Africa and surrendered within six months of the date of shipment or seven days of the date of accrual. To ensure that exchange control procedures are more effectively applied when export proceeds are repatriated, except exports made on a cash-on-delivery basis or those for which the full proceeds are received in advance, exporters are required to cover forward their export proceeds within seven days of shipment.

Authorized dealers may permit exporters to grant credit for up to 12 months, provided the credit is necessary in the particular trade or needed to protect an existing export market or capture a new one. Exporters benefit from an incentive scheme, under which they receive payments based on the f.o.b. value of exports, the local content of products, the extent of processing involved, and the movement in the real effective exchange rate in terms of a basket of currencies of South Africa's major trading partners since 1979.

Proceeds from Invisibles

Proceeds from invisibles must be surrendered within seven days of the date of accrual unless an exemption is obtained. Residents and nonresidents entering from countries outside the Common Monetary Area may bring in R 500 in South African Reserve Bank notes. There are no limitations on the importation of domestic currency from Lesotho, Namibia, and Swaziland.

Capital[5]

All inward loan transfers require specific approval,[6] although inward transfers for investment in equity capital are freely permitted. Foreign exchange accruing to residents from capital transfers and transactions must be surrendered. Outward transfers of capital by residents to destinations outside the Common Monetary Area require the approval of the Reserve Bank. Local borrowing by nonresident-owned or nonresident-controlled firms is subject to limitation. Transfers by residents for the purchase of South African (or other) shares on foreign stock exchanges are generally not permit-

ted. South African stockbrokers may engage in arbitrage transactions in securities, subject to certain conditions designed to prevent any net outflow of exchange.

Applications by South African residents to retain funds in, or transfer them to, countries outside the Common Monetary Area for bona fide long-term investment in specific development projects, or for the expansion of existing projects owned or controlled by South Africans, are considered by the Reserve Bank on their merits. Investments designed to foster exports and maintain or expand markets abroad are normally viewed favorably.

Immigrants are required to furnish the exchange control authorities with a complete statement of their foreign assets and liabilities at the time of their arrival. Any foreign assets transferred to South Africa may, through the same channel, be retransferred abroad within the first five years after arrival.

The proceeds of the sale of quoted or unquoted South African securities, real estate, and other equity investments by nonresidents of South Africa to residents must be credited to financial rand accounts and are accordingly transferable through this medium.

Emigrant families are entitled to the normal travel allowance and are permitted to transfer up to R 200,000 (R 100,000 for single persons). Any balance exceeding the permissible transferable amount must be credited to an emigrant blocked account. Up to R 350,000 per fiscal year of income earned by emigrants may be transferred through normal banking channels or credited to a nonresident account. A family or single person emigrating can export one motor vehicle with a maximum value of R 75,000, provided that the vehicle was purchased at least one year before emigration. Emigrants can export other household and personal effects up to a value of R 75,000, provided that such goods, other than clothing, have been in their possession for at least one year.

Favorable consideration is given to nonresident-owned branches and subsidiaries for the transfer of open or approved loan account balances;[7] current profits earned after January 1, 1984; and dividends declared on profits from trading generated after January 1, 1984, provided such remittances do not involve the excessive use of local credit facilities. The physical exportation from South Africa of nonresident-owned securities is permitted, except by emigrants.

---

[5]Securities are defined not only as quoted stocks, shares, debentures, and rights, but also as unquoted shares in public companies, shares in private companies, government, municipal, and public utility stocks, nonresident-owned mortgage bonds, or participations in mortgage bonds. "Scrip" and "share certificates" include any temporary or substitute documents of title, such as letters of allotment, option certificates, balance receipts, and any other receipts for scrip.

[6]Domestic entrepreneurs are generally given approval for borrowing abroad with a maturity of at least six months, except for speculation or consumer credit. Authorized dealers are generally permitted to raise funds abroad in their own names to finance South African foreign trade and for other approved purposes.

---

[7]Subject, however, to the 1994 Debt Arrangements, where applicable.

Gold

Residents of South Africa may purchase, hold, and sell gold coins in South Africa for numismatic purposes and investment. With this exception, residents of South Africa other than the monetary authorities, authorized dealers, registered gold producers, and authorized industrial and professional users are not allowed to purchase, hold, or sell gold in any form other than jewelry, at home or abroad. All exports of gold must be approved in advance by the Reserve Bank. Approval authority has been delegated to authorized dealers for exports of jewelry constituting the personal effects of a traveler, up to a value of R 40,000 (subject to a written declaration that the jewelry will be brought back to South Africa on the traveler's return); and for exports of gold jewelry by manufacturing jewelers (except those to Botswana, Malawi, Zambia, and Zimbabwe), subject to a written declaration that the articles are in fully manufactured form and that the gold content of each does not exceed 80 percent of the selling price to the ultimate consignee. Furthermore, after approval by the Reserve Bank, residents are allowed to export currency coins, including certain gold coins, for sale to numismatists. The gold mining industry must sell its output to the Reserve Bank, which has been nominated as agent for the Treasury, within one month of production. With effect from October 1987, the Reserve Bank pays the gold mines in U.S. dollars for their sales of produc-

tion. As a special concession, the industry may retain approximately one-third of its production for the minting of gold coins and kilo bars.

The mint strikes gold coins and the Krugerrand, which are legal tender, without a face value, and these are made available in limited numbers to the local market.

Changes During 1994

Payments for Invisibles

September 1. The indicative annual limit on allowances that authorized dealers may provide for traveling to countries, other than neighboring countries, was increased as follows: (1) the basic tourist allowance, to R 23,000 from R 20,000 for an adult and to R 11,500 from R 10,000 for a child; and (2) the limit on additional allowances for business travel, to R 34,000 from R 30,000.

August 31. The amount of foreign banknotes residents and contract workers are permitted to take out of South Africa was limited to up to one-third of the applicable travel allowance (previously, the full amount was permitted to be taken out).

Changes During 1995

Exchange Arrangement

March 13. The financial rand system was abolished.

SPAIN

(Position as of December 31, 1994)

Exchange Arrangement

The currency of Spain is the Spanish Peseta. Spain participates with Austria, Belgium, Denmark, France, Germany, Ireland, Luxembourg, the Netherlands, and Portugal in the exchange rate and intervention mechanism (ERM)[1] of the European Monetary System (EMS). In accordance with this agreement, Spain maintains the spot exchange rates between the Spanish peseta and the currencies of the other participants within margins of 15 percent above or below the cross rates based on the central rates expressed in European currency units (ECUs).[2]

The agreement implies that the Bank of Spain (the central bank) stands ready to buy or sell the currencies of the other participating states in unlimited amounts at specified intervention rates. On March 6, 1995, the maximum intervention rates[3] were as follows:

Specified Intervention Rates per:	Spanish Peseta	
	Upper limit	Lower limit
100 Austrian schillings	1,404.1000	1,041.3000
100 Belgian or Luxembourg francs	478.9440	365.2080
100 Danish kroner	2,589.8000	1,920.7000
100 deutsche mark	9,878.5000	7,326.0000
100 French francs	2,945.4000	2,184.4000
1 Irish pound	238.1750	176.6410
100 Netherlands guilders	8,767.3000	6,502.2000
100 Portuguese escudos	96.3670	71.4890

The participants in the EMS do not maintain the exchange rates for other currencies within fixed limits. However, in order to ensure a proper functioning of the system, they intervene in concert to smooth out fluctuations in exchange rates, the intervention currencies being each other's, the U.S. dollar, and the ECU.

Official rates for specified currencies[4] are quoted on the basis of market rates and are published daily. On December 31, 1994, the rate for the U.S. dollar was Ptas 114.62 per US$1.

Authorized banks are allowed to operate in foreign markets for spot and forward transactions. All future transactions involving an identifiable exchange·risk are eligible for forward cover. There are no limits on periods to be covered. There are no limits on forward or spot foreign currency positions of individual banks, except those stemming indirectly from prudential rules on maximum net foreign exchange exposure. Under existing regulations, consolidated net foreign exchange exposure must not exceed a percentage, determined by the Bank of Spain, of the consolidated own resources of each banking group.

Spain formally accepted the obligations of Article VIII, Sections 2, 3, and 4 of the Fund Agreement, as of July 15, 1986.

Exchange Control Territory

The Peninsular Territories of the Spanish State, the Canary Islands, the Balearic Islands, Ceuta, and Melilla constitute a single exchange control territory.

Administration of Control

The Ministry of Economy and Finance, through the Directorate-General of External Transactions, handles exchange control regulations, including prior verification and remaining administrative authorization corresponding to the exportation and importation of certain means of payment, foreign investment, investment abroad by Spanish residents, and domestic borrowing by foreigners. The Bank of Spain handles the foreign exchange market (both spot and forward), regulates and supervises commercial banks' activities, and is responsible for foreign exchange accounts and all nontrade foreign borrowing (both short-term and long-term) by domestic residents.

In accordance with the Fund's Executive Board Decision No. 144-(52/51) adopted on August 14,

---

[1]Austria became a member of the European Union on January 1, 1995 and joined the ERM of the EMS on January 9, 1995.

[2]Effective August 2, 1993, the intervention thresholds of the currencies participating in the ERM of the EMS, except those of the deutsche mark and the Netherlands guilder, were widened from ±2.25 percent (in the case of Portugal and Spain, 6 percent) to ±15 percent around the bilateral central exchange rates; the fluctuation band of the deutsche mark and the Netherlands guilder remained unchanged at ±2.25 percent.

[3]Effective intervention rates may vary within the limits of these maximum intervention rates, depending on daily fluctuations in the cross rates between currencies.

---

[4]Australian dollars, Austrian schillings, Belgian francs, Canadian dollars, Danish kroner, deutsche mark, European currency units (ECUs), Finnish markkaa, French francs, Greek drachmas, Irish pounds, Italian lire, Japanese yen, Netherlands guilders, Norwegian kroner, Portuguese escudos, pounds sterling, Swedish kronor, Swiss francs, and U.S. dollars.

1952, Spain notified the Fund on September 21, 1992 that, in compliance with UN Security Council Resolution No. 757 (1992), certain restrictions had been imposed on the making of payments and transfers for current international transactions in respect of the Federal Republic of Yugoslavia (Serbia and Montenegro).

Prescription of Currency

Settlements on account of merchandise transactions and invisibles may be made in pesetas or in any of the currencies specified in footnote 4 but are usually made in the currency of the country of origin or destination.

Resident and Nonresident Accounts

Nonresidents may open any kind of deposit account in pesetas or foreign currency in all financial institutions. Residents may open accounts in pesetas or foreign currency with any financial institution abroad. Nonresidents' accounts in Spain and residents' accounts abroad are subject to reporting requirements.

Imports and Import Payments

As a general rule, imports into Spain may be made freely. However, imports of certain goods (e.g., tractors, explosives, seed oil, and gold) must be authorized by the Directorate-General of Foreign Trade, irrespective of the country of origin, or when imported from specific geographical areas (with distinctions being made among the members of the European Union (EU), those of the European Free Trade Association (EFTA) and the Mediterranean and the ACP,[5] member countries of the World Trade Organization, and state trading countries).

Foreign exchange in the appropriate currency to pay for authorized imports is granted freely.

Payments for Invisibles

Payments for invisibles may be made freely through accounts in domestic and foreign financial institutions or other means of payment, including checks and transfers, subject to certain reporting requirements. The exportation of more than the equivalent of Ptas 1 million in banknotes, coins, and bearer checks must be declared and that of more than the equivalent of Ptas 5 million requires authorization. Nonresident holders of Spanish securities may freely transfer abroad accrued interest,

dividends, proceeds from the disposal of subscription rights, and the proceeds from the liquidation of such securities. Profits and dividends on direct investments and rents on nonresident-owned real estate are freely transferable abroad. A general license permits the reinsurance abroad of risks insured in Spain with Spanish firms or with foreign insurance companies operating in Spain. Unless special authorization is otherwise granted, insurance contracts abroad are restricted to cover exports and imports of goods and related operations.

Exports and Export Proceeds

As a general rule, exports may be made freely. However, exports of a limited number of goods (e.g., textiles, steel, and some copper by-products) require prior authorization from the Directorate-General of Foreign Trade irrespective of destination.

Proceeds from Invisibles

The importation of more than the equivalent of Ptas 1 million in banknotes, coins, and bearer checks must be declared only when they are intended for investment or banking purposes. All proceeds from invisibles may be used freely.

Capital

Foreign direct investments in Spain are defined in accordance with guidelines established by the Organization for Economic Cooperation and Development (OECD) that take into account whether effective control over the company has been obtained. Effective control is deemed to exist if the share of the investment is at least 10 percent of the company's capital or if the Directorate-General of External Transactions considers that an important or predominant source of influence exists. Foreign investments effected through participation in Spanish companies are permitted freely in most cases. Prior verification is required only when foreign participation exceeds 50 percent and at least one of the following conditions applies: (1) foreign participation exceeds Ptas 500 million, and (2) foreign investors are residents of tax haven countries. Special authorization is required for non-EU foreign investment in defense-related industries, telecommunications (over 25 percent of capital), television, radio, air transport, and gambling. Special authorization is also required for a foreign government's participation in Spanish companies (other than governments of EU countries) unless otherwise regulated by international treaties.

---

[5]African, Caribbean, and Pacific state signatories to the Lomé Convention with the EU.

The reinvestment of profits or proceeds from liquidation of existing investments is not restricted.

Nonresidents may freely purchase any kind of financial assets and contract all types of commercial credit without restriction but must report these transactions to the Bank of Spain. Verification is required before Spanish companies issue shares in foreign markets; otherwise, securities operations are permitted freely. Real estate investments require prior verification for amounts exceeding Ptas 500 million or if investors are residents of tax haven countries.

The proceeds from the liquidation of nonresident investments and capital are freely transferable abroad, provided that these investments have been duly registered at the Registry of Foreign Investment (Registro de Inversiones Extranjeras).

Direct investments abroad by residents are permitted freely, although the following exceptions require prior verification: (1) the amount of the investment exceeds Ptas 250 million, (2) the purpose of investment is to hold shares of other companies, and (3) investment is in a tax haven country. Residents may purchase freely securities issued by nonresidents (irrespective of the market of issuance) or by residents in a foreign market. Strict information requirements apply to investments in securities and foreign lending. Prior authorization is required for direct investments by residents in non-EU countries where ownership of Spanish real estate or Spanish companies is transferred as a result of the operation. Investments in real estate by residents abroad is permitted, but those that exceed Ptas 250 million require prior verification.

Gold

The acquisition of gold must be authorized by the Directorate-General of Foreign Trade. Imports of bullion are permitted if they are used as raw materials for manufactured goods. Imports of gold in manufactured form (e.g., coins, medals, and the like) may be subject to quantitative restrictions, depending on the country of origin. Purchases of gold, silver, and platinum ingots are subject to a value-added tax at the rate of 33 percent.

Changes During 1994

No significant changes occurred in the exchange and trade system.

(See Appendix for a summary of trade measures introduced and eliminated on an EU-wide basis during 1994, page 554.)

Changes During 1995

Exchange Arrangement

March 6. The upper and lower limits of the peseta for the currencies of the participants in the ERM of the EMS were changed.

SRI LANKA

(Position as of December 31, 1994)

Exchange Arrangement

The currency of Sri Lanka is the Sri Lanka Rupee. The Central Bank announces the daily spot buying and selling rates of the U.S. dollar, the intervention currency, against the Sri Lanka rupee for transactions with the commercial banks, within margins of 1 percent, and purchases and sells the U.S. dollar on a spot basis at the established rates. On December 31, 1994, the buying and selling rates for the U.S. dollar were SL Rs 49.73 and SL Rs 50.23, respectively, per US$1. There are no taxes or subsidies on purchases or sales of foreign exchange.

Forward sales are permitted to cover all transactions, with the exception of capital transfers and amortization of loans, up to a period not exceeding 360 days. The commercial banks provide a forward exchange market in which rates for current transactions are freely determined. They may cover such purchases by selling forward to their clients (that is, importers and shipping agents) or to other authorized dealers. Authorized dealers are permitted to quote forward rates for up to 360 days.

Sri Lanka formally accepted the obligations of Article VIII, Section 2, 3, and 4 of the Fund Agreement, as from March 15, 1994.

Administration of Control

Exchange control is administered by the Department of Exchange Control of the Central Bank as an agent of the Government. All remittances of foreign exchange in Sri Lanka must normally be made through commercial banks authorized to carry out operations in foreign currencies in accordance with the exchange control procedures prescribed by the Controller of Exchange. Remittances may also be made through post offices under permits issued by the Controller of Exchange.

The Board of Investments (BOI), formerly the Greater Colombo Economic Commission (GCEC), has taken over the approval functions of the Foreign Investment Advisory Committee, which has been abolished, and now handles all applications relating to foreign investments in Sri Lanka. Approval for foreign investment is granted on the basis of the types of activity and the proportion of foreign capital ownership; approval is automatically granted for foreign investment with equity capital ownership of up to 40 percent, except for a small number of activities reserved for citizens of Sri Lanka or regulated by a special law or a specific organization.

Prescription of Currency

Payments to and receipts from the member countries of the Asian Clearing Union (ACU) (i.e., Bangladesh, India, Islamic Republic of Iran, Myanmar, Nepal, and Pakistan) in respect of current transactions must be effected in Asian Currency Units or in the currency of the respective member of the Asian Clearing Union.

For settlements with all other countries, payments for imports may be made in any foreign currency or in Sri Lanka rupees. Other payments may be made either in the currency of the country to which the payment is due or by crediting Sri Lanka rupees to a nonresident rupee account. Proceeds from exports must be received either in designated foreign currencies,[1] in Sri Lanka rupees from a nonresident account a foreign bank maintains with an authorized dealer, or in any other nonresident account a person maintains with an authorized dealer, as approved by the Central Bank.

Resident and Nonresident Accounts

Nonresident accounts in Sri Lanka rupees may be held in any commercial bank in Sri Lanka by (1) nonnationals residing outside Sri Lanka; (2) firms and companies registered outside Sri Lanka; (3) Sri Lanka nationals residing outside Sri Lanka, who are classified for this purpose into two categories (those whose current or savings accounts are redesignated as nonresident accounts following their departure, and those whose accounts are opened after their departure); (4) emigrants; and (5) foreign banks.

The opening of these accounts for categories (1), (2), (3), and (4), the crediting of the initial and subsequent deposits arising from inward remittances, and debits for local disbursements or outward remittances may be effected without the prior approval of the Department of Exchange Control; however, local credits to these require prior approval. Accounts in category (4) are designated in the first instance as nonresident blocked accounts

---

[1] Australian dollars, Belgian francs, Canadian dollars, Danish kroner, deutsche mark, French francs, Hong Kong dollars, Japanese yen, Netherlands guilders, Norwegian kroner, pounds sterling, Swedish kronor, Swiss francs, and U.S. dollars.

only when instructions to that effect are received from the Department of Exchange Control. Local debits to such accounts may be effected without the prior approval of the Department of Exchange Control; however, local credits to them and debits for outward remittances require prior approval under certain circumstances. Under category (5), foreign banks may be permitted to open and operate non-resident accounts with a local commercial bank without the prior approval of the Department of Exchange Control.

Nonresident blocked accounts are used for holding funds, usually owned by nonresidents, repatriates, and emigrants, that have not been accepted for transfer abroad. Authorized dealers are permitted to debit these accounts for local disbursements and credit them on account of pensions, income tax refunds, and profits and dividends without prior approval. Funds in blocked accounts may be invested in any local enterprise without the prior approval of the Controller of Exchange. Subject to exchange control approval, proceeds from the liquidation of such investments can be credited to blocked accounts. Balances of nonresident foreign citizens and foreign companies in approved blocked accounts outstanding on March 25, 1991, excluding Sri Lankan citizens who have emigrated or acquired foreign citizenship and Indian and Pakistani expatriates, may be remitted abroad. Sri Lankans who have emigrated and acquired foreign citizenship, and Sri Lankan citizens who have acquired permanent resident status abroad and whose accounts have been blocked for more than five years as of June 30, 1992, are also permitted to remit their account balances abroad. In all other cases, remittances of up to a maximum of SL Rs 350,000 are allowed from these accounts without prior approval from the exchange control authorities. Remittance of interest accrued to blocked accounts is fully transferable after deduction of taxes. Also retained in blocked accounts is a proportion of local currency earnings derived from the exhibition of foreign-owned films; the owner may use such retained funds for certain specified purposes, including the making of films in Sri Lanka.

Sri Lanka nationals who are or have been employed abroad, and nonnationals of Sri Lankan origin who reside outside Sri Lanka, are allowed to maintain nonresident foreign currency (NRFC) accounts in Sri Lanka in designated foreign currencies.[2] Sri Lankans may also open such accounts within 90 days of their arrival in Sri Lanka with foreign exchange they brought in or received from abroad. Credits to the accounts are limited to the proceeds of remittances from abroad and foreign exchange earnings brought into the country by individuals at the time of arrival; in addition, interest payments in designated currencies may be credited to the accounts. These accounts may be freely debited without exchange control approval for payments abroad, with the exception of payments received for purchase consideration in respect of the sale of moveable or immoveable property in Sri Lanka, or for payments within Sri Lanka (converted to Sri Lanka rupees). Balances on NRFC accounts may be invested in enterprises approved by the BOI, with exemptions granted under Section 17 of the BOI Act. Dividends and profits earned and sales proceeds of such investments received in foreign currency may be credited to the NRFC accounts without the prior approval of the Controller of Exchange. Rupee loan facilities for third parties against NRFC balances are also permitted. Employment agencies that recruit Sri Lankan nationals for foreign employment are also allowed to maintain NRFC accounts, to which their commission earnings may be credited.

Commercial banks operating in Sri Lanka may establish foreign currency banking units. These units may accept time and demand deposits in any designated foreign currency from nonresidents, resident commercial banks, and any resident BOI enterprise. They may extend loans and advances in any designated foreign currency to any nonresident, any resident commercial bank, any resident enterprise having BOI status, any exporter for the purchase of imported inputs, and a few other specified organizations with approval from the Central Bank. In addition, the foreign currency banking units are allowed to accept time and demand deposits from and grant loans and advances to any other resident approved by the Central Bank. Foreign currency banking units are also authorized to operate savings accounts. However, accounts allowing the withdrawal of funds by checks are not permitted.

Sri Lankan residents may open and operate resident foreign currency (RFC) accounts with a minimum balance of $500 (or its equivalent) in designated currencies without prior approval or documentary evidence of receipt of such funds through customs declarations for up to $5,000. Exporters of goods and services who have increased their export earnings in foreign exchange over the previous year are permitted to open RFC accounts with up to 5 percent of their increased (annual) earnings.

---

[2]In Australian dollars, Canadian dollars, Danish kroner, deutsche mark, French francs, Japanese yen, pounds sterling, Singapore dollars, Swedish kronor, Swiss francs, and U.S. dollars.

Imports and Import Payments

Except for certain specified imports, no prior licensing is required. Imports that are subject to prior licensing include those controlled for security reasons; precious metals; alcohol; apparatus and equipment used in photographic and cinematographic laboratories; screens for projectors; multicolored photocopying apparatuses; articles of cement (whether reinforced or not); concrete cement blocks; encasements of industrial waste slugs, slag dress, ash and residues; other slag and ash, including kelp; fertilizers; drugs and pharmaceuticals; aircraft, including spare parts; certain motor cars; certain consumer goods; rice, flour, and wheat grain; and various inorganic chemicals and compounds.

The tariff regime, which was introduced as part of the measures of the 1992 budget (and revised in the 1994 budget), consists of four basic rate categories (45 percent, 35 percent, 20 percent, and 10 percent); exceptions are automobiles (50–100 percent), most textiles and garments (50 percent), cement clinker (5 percent), and certain portland cement in bulk (7.5 percent). Certain essential products are exempted from duties at the discretion of the Ministry of Finance: pharmaceuticals, rice, wheat, flour, and sugar. Specific tariffs are also levied on several items, including locally grown agricultural goods (e.g., chili peppers and potatoes), certain petroleum products, and alcoholic beverages and spirits.

Imports of specified items[3] known as "reserved items" are restricted to government or state corporations. Prior approval procedures apply to imports of certain capital goods: certain machinery imports relating to foreign investment require the approval of the BOI, and certain machinery imports relating to local investment require the prior approval of the Local Investment Advisory Committee. No prior approval is required if any single consignment does not exceed SL Rs 700,000.

Holders of balances in convertible rupee accounts, which were closed to new credits as of November 16, 1977, may use these funds to pay for certain imports, subject to licensing by the Controller of Imports and Exports.

Except for imports by export processing industries and other specified transactions, all other imports may be effected only against letters of credit on document-against-payment terms valid for shipment for 180 days. Letters of credit on document against acceptance terms may be opened in respect of imports for export-oriented industries and other high-priority areas for periods ranging from 120 days to 180 days. A stamp duty of 2 percent is levied on letters of credit for other imports (excluding inputs used in export industries) not fully covered by advance deposits. An authorized dealer may, without the prior approval of the Controller of Exchange, approve applications to remit foreign exchange or to credit nonresident accounts against applications for the opening of a letter of credit and against proof of a valid import license, when applicable. These requirements do not apply if the value of a consignment does not exceed $7,000 (c.i.f.), consists of raw materials and spare parts for industries, and is for the direct use of the importer. Imports valued at $5,000 (c.i.f.) or less are permitted on document against agreement (D/A) terms without letters of credit when import documents are channelled through commercial banks.

Payments for Invisibles

All payments for invisibles by residents may be made freely. Foreign technical personnel employed by approved enterprises may remit up to two-thirds of their monthly earnings if their employment contract does not exceed three years, and up to one-third if the employment contract exceeds three years. Foreign technical personnel employed in the free trade zone may remit up to 90 percent of their monthly earnings.

Commissions up to 5 percent of the f.o.b., c. & f., or c.i.f. value, as appropriate, are allowed on export orders secured through agents abroad; commissions exceeding 5 percent require specific approval. Remittances of premium for insurance on exports are not permitted, and such insurance must be obtained from a local state insurance corporation or a private insurer. Remittances of premium to foreign reinsurers for reinsurance are permitted. Holders of funds in convertible rupee accounts with credit balances outstanding as of November 15, 1977, may use these funds for travel expenditures and other current invisibles without the prior approval of the Controller of Exchange.

Profit remittances of nonresident partners of partnerships in Sri Lanka and remittances of dividends to nonresident shareholders of companies whose financial assets are in rupees may be effected through commercial banks without prior exchange control approval if they relate to the year of application and do not include undistributed profits of the previous years or reserves of the company.

For interim profits, the following documents should be furnished: (1) a certificate from the com-

---

[3]These include wheat, guns, and explosives, as well as certain chemicals and petroleum products.

pany's auditors confirming that the amount to be remitted represents profits for the period to which it relates; (2) a preliminary computation of the remittable profits; (3) a tax clearance (only in the case of a nonresident partner) in respect of the profits to be remitted; (4) a certificate confirming that the beneficiary resides abroad; and (5) a schedule indicating the names of the beneficiaries and the net amount owed to each. For final profits, the following documents must be submitted: an audited copy of the company's profit and loss account and the balance sheet for the year to which the remittance relates; a certificate from the auditors confirming that the remittance represents the final installment of the profits, declared in respect of the year under reference; a computation of the remittable profits; and the documents listed in (3), (4), and (5) above.

Remittances of interim dividends can be made, provided that the following documents are submitted: (1) certification from the company's auditors confirming that the amount to be remitted represents dividends only for the period to which it relates; (2) certification that the remittance constitutes an interim dividend based on the unaudited accounts for the period; (3) a certificate confirming that the beneficiary resides outside Sri Lanka; (4) a schedule indicating the names of the beneficiaries and the net amounts owed to them; and (5) documentary evidence from auditors confirming payment of dividend tax. The remittance of a final dividend requires the submission of an audited copy of the company's profit and loss account and the balance sheet for the year to which the remittance relates; a certificate from the auditors confirming that the remittance represents dividends only for the period to which it relates; and the documents listed in (3), (4), and (5) above.

Resident foreigners may maintain foreign currency accounts with domestic commercial banks in any of ten designated currencies[4] without prior exchange control approval. These accounts must be operated by the domestic unit of the bank and not by its Foreign Currency Banking Unit. The accounts may be current, savings, or deposit accounts, but withdrawal of funds by check is not permitted. Credits to these accounts are limited to inward remittances and to amounts in Sri Lanka rupees authorized by the Controller of Exchange for remittance abroad; debits are limited to outward remittances and to payments in foreign currency converted into Sri Lanka rupees.

Unspent rupee balances from foreign exchange sold by foreign passport holders may be reconverted into foreign currency notes and coins only at the exit point (Katunayake Airport/Colombo Port). Reconversion into drafts, telegraphic transfers, or traveler's checks can be made at all branches of the authorized dealers as well as at the exit point. For this purpose, the original encashment receipts or memos issued by the authorized dealers or money changers must be furnished. Sri Lankan and foreign passport holders may take out convertible foreign currency equivalent to $5,000 without declaration, irrespective of the number of trips they make. The amount of foreign currency notes that diplomats, other foreign missions, and their non-Sri Lankan staff traveling abroad can take with them is limited to 20 percent of their travel expenses. Residents may take out foreign currency notes and coins not exceeding £20 a person (£10 for a child under 12 years) of the exchange authorized for travel. All persons leaving Sri Lanka may take out domestic currency notes not exceeding SL Rs 1,000 a person.

Exports and Export Proceeds

Exports of the following products require a license: coral shanks and shells, betel leaves, minerals and mineral products, metal ores, timber, metal and metal scraps, old vehicles (manufactured before 1945), ivory and ivory products, and fertilizers.[5] Exports of betel leaves to Pakistan, Singapore, and the Middle East are handled by three individual firms. The State Gem Corporation exercises quality control over the exportation of gems; the private sector may export gems on a consignment basis with the prior approval of the exchange control authorities. The Corporation handles exports in the name of miners who wish to export their gems. Re-exports of nonmonetary gold, silver, diamonds, and platinum are allowed only in special circumstances.

Foreign exchange proceeds from exports are not required to be repatriated. Special arrangements apply to exports made under trade and payments agreements and to exports made to a member country of the ACU. Commercial banks are permitted to grant foreign currency loans from their foreign currency banking units to exporters for the financing of the importation of inputs required for the purpose of executing export orders. This facility is limited to 70 percent of the total value of the confirmed

---

[4]Deutsche mark, French francs, Hong Kong dollars, Japanese yen, Netherlands guilders, pounds sterling, Singapore dollars, Swedish kronor, Swiss francs, and U.S. dollars.

[5]Effective January 10, 1994, the licensing requirement was abolished except for timber, coral shanks and shells, ivory and ivory products, and old vehicles (manufactured before 1945).

export order. The period of repayment of these loans is eight months.

Companies engaged in indirect exports may obtain foreign currency loans for the importation of raw materials on the basis of back-to-back letters of credit opened in foreign currency for receipt of payment in foreign currency, including payments from BOI enterprises.

Proceeds from Invisibles

Foreign exchange proceeds from invisibles are not required to be surrendered. A traveler entering Sri Lanka must declare his/her foreign exchange holdings exceeding $5,000, including currency notes and coins. The amount of foreign funds that may be carried into Sri Lanka in the form of travel credit instruments is not restricted. Residents and nonresidents may bring in any amount of nonconvertible currencies after making a declaration to customs. A person entering Sri Lanka may bring in domestic currency notes not exceeding SL Rs 1,000.

Capital

Foreign direct investments are permitted in new projects with or without prior approval from the Controller of Exchange as approved by the BOI. Proceeds from the sale or liquidation of investments in these projects, along with the capital appreciation, may be remitted in full. Investments in shares by nonresidents, up to 100 percent of the equity capital of existing listed and unlisted public companies, are permitted, subject to certain exclusions and limitations, without prior approval from the Controller of Exchange through a share investment external rupee account maintained at a commercial bank. Proceeds from the sale of these shares may be repatriated automatically, net of any tax. Blocked funds held by nonresidents with the approval of the Controller of Exchange in commercial banks are also permitted for investment in approved projects. Sale proceeds of such investments must be credited to blocked accounts. Proceeds from the sale or liquidation of other foreign investments in Sri Lanka may be repatriated in full only with prior approval from the Minister of Finance.

Investments abroad by residents are not generally permitted unless there is evidence that they will promote the country's exports and generate reasonable profits. Resident-owned securities, on which principal, interest, or dividends are payable (either contractually, or at the option of the holder) in any foreign currency, must be declared to the Controller of Exchange, and the sale or transfer of such securities is allowed only with the permission of the Controller of Exchange. Companies incorporated abroad are permitted to invest in securities traded at the Colombo Stock Exchange, subject to the same terms and conditions as those applicable to such investments by approved country funds, approved regional funds, and nonresident individuals, including Sri Lankans residing abroad.

Authorized dealers may grant foreign exchange allocations to emigrants upon presentation of appropriate documentation. At the time of departure, emigrants may be granted foreign exchange to cover passage to the country of migration by normal direct route plus 20 percent of the passage fare to cover excess baggage expenses. Foreign exchange equivalent up to £500 an adult and £250 a child under 12 years of age can also be purchased at the time of departure. Personal effects up to SL Rs 30,000 an adult and SL Rs 15,000 a child under 12 years, plus jewelry up to SL Rs 100,000 for each married woman, SL Rs 60,000 for each unmarried woman, SL Rs 30,000 for each female emigrant under 12 years of age, and SL Rs 25,000 for each male emigrant can be exported. Emigrants have also been permitted to effect capital transfers of up to SL Rs 750,000 per individual, up to a maximum limit of SL Rs 1 million per family unit. The Department of Exchange Control may approve the transfer of pensions and interest income up to £100 a month, subject to submission of an income tax clearance certificate.

Expatriates leaving Sri Lanka for residence in the country of their permanent domicile are permitted to transfer in full assets representing their retirement funds and savings. Persons who have had small businesses in Sri Lanka are allowed to transfer the capital they originally brought into the country, plus a reasonable amount of savings, subject to certain limits. Special provisions, governed by an agreement between Sri Lanka and India, apply to Indian families returning to India.

Gold

Imports and exports of gold in any form require licenses issued by the Controller of Imports and Exports with the approval of the Controller of Exchange. Commercial banks may obtain a license from the Controller of Imports and Exports and import gold for sale to the public, subject to payment of duty and turnover tax. Commercial banks are also permitted to import gold on a consignment basis for duty-free sale to passengers at the Colombo International Airport, with a license issued by the Controller of Imports and Exports. Commercial imports of jewelry and other articles containing gold are restricted, except for imports of gold for the production of jewelry for exportation.

Changes During 1994

Exchange Arrangement

March 15. Sri Lanka formally accepted the obligations of Article VIII, Sections 2, 3, and 4 of the Fund Agreement.

Resident and Nonresident Accounts

June 1. Nonresident accounts in Sri Lanka rupees held by Sri Lanka nationals residing outside Sri Lanka and by emigrants were subjected to the same treatment as those held by nonnationals residing outside Sri Lanka. Remittances abroad from these accounts were no longer subject to the prior approval of the Controller of Exchange.

Exports and Export Proceeds

January 10. The licensing requirement was abolished except for timber, coral shanks and shells, ivory and ivory products, and vehicles manufactured before 1945.

Capital

June 1. The emigrant allowance for individuals was raised to SL Rs 750,000.

SUDAN

(Position as of December 31, 1994)

Exchange Arrangement

The currency of Sudan is the Sudanese Dinar,[1] the external value of which is determined in the interbank market. Commercial banks are authorized to quote on a daily basis buying and selling exchange rates—subject to a maximum spread of LSd 7—to be applied to all formal banking sector transactions, other than certain compulsory sales of foreign exchange to the Bank of Sudan. On December 31, 1994, the average commercial bank buying and selling rates for the U.S. dollar were LSd 41.2 and LSd 42.1, respectively per US$1. Sixty-five percent of foreign exchange surrendered to commercial banks is subject to compulsory sale to the Bank of Sudan: 40 percent at each bank's quoted selling rate, and 25 percent at the Bank of Sudan's reference exchange rate (or the bank's selling rate, whichever is lower). The Bank of Sudan's reference rate is determined daily as a weighted average of the buying rates of the commercial banks; owing to reporting lags, the reference exchange rate is based on interbank exchange rates in effect two business days earlier. The Bank of Sudan's selling rate for official exchange transactions is determined by applying a margin to the reference exchange rate of LSd 7.

In principle, commercial banks are authorized by the Bank of Sudan to sell foreign exchange to be transferred abroad for all purposes. In practice, rigidities in the market mean that commercial banks conduct informal rationing by making foreign exchange available according to the priorities established by each bank manager. In the case of payments for imports, commercial banks are authorized to sell foreign exchange to licensed traders, except for categories of goods that are on the negative list. Under a central bank regulation, the commercial banks are obligated to require 100 percent cash cover before agreeing to the sale of foreign exchange. When foreign exchange is made available by a commercial bank against a letter of credit, the amount is immediately deposited in a suspended account on behalf of the purchaser, while foreign exchange made available on the basis of cash against documents is transferred to the purchaser

immediately. Commercial banks do not bear any exchange risk for any foreign exchange transaction.

There are no arrangements for forward cover against exchange rate risk operating in the official or the commercial banking sector.

Administration of Control

Exchange control is administered by the Bank of Sudan with the assistance of the authorized banks and specialized banks acting as exchange houses. Commercial banks and specialized banks may effect payments from their foreign exchange accounts without verification by the Bank of Sudan in accordance with the guidelines specified by the Bank of Sudan. Authorized banks are prohibited from conducting foreign exchange transactions with any public body and from disposing of balances in foreign currency accounts held by such bodies in domestic banks without prior approval from the Bank of Sudan. Commercial banks are responsible for verifying that exports and imports under the trade protocol with Egypt are in accordance with licenses issued by the Ministry of Trade. The issuance of commercial certificates is the responsibility of the Ministry of Commerce, Cooperation, and Supply. The Bank of Sudan has the authority to request any information or details from authorized banks. All exporters and importers are required to register with the Ministry of Trade.

Arrears are maintained with respect to external payments.

Prescription of Currency

Payments to all countries—except Egypt, with which Sudan maintains a bilateral payments agreement—and all monetary areas (the "convertible area") may be made in foreign currency from any free foreign currency account or special foreign currency account, while receipts from the convertible area may be accepted in any convertible currency.

Resident and Nonresident Foreign Currency Accounts

Sudanese resident individuals and legal entities, with the exception of the Government, public institutions, and public sector enterprises, are allowed to keep foreign exchange in free accounts. Free accounts may be credited with any means of payment

---

[1]The Sudanese pound (LSd) also circulates and has a fixed relationship to the Sudanese dinar (Sd) of LSd 10 per Sd 1.

without restriction, other than a customs declaration for cash deposits. Withdrawals from free accounts may be used (1) to make transfers abroad; (2) to make transfers to other free accounts; (3) to purchase domestic currency; (4) to make payments in foreign exchange to domestic institutions authorized to sell goods and services for foreign exchange; (5) to finance imports; and (6) to finance overseas travel of up to $5,000 a person in banknotes and any additional amount in other means of payment, based on evidence of travel authorization and tickets.

The following are allowed to open special accounts with authorized banks in foreign and local currency: diplomatic, foreign, international, and regional missions and organizations; foreign charities and aid organizations; and foreign companies, foreign contractors, and the foreign personnel of these organizations. Special foreign exchange accounts may be credited with transfers from abroad. Special foreign currency accounts may be debited for transfers abroad, to finance foreign travel, to purchase local currency in order to finance local payments, to make foreign currency payments to local institutions authorized to sell goods and services for foreign currency, and to finance imports. Withdrawals can be made for the purpose of travel by the account holder or his or her family, and for local payments in Sudanese pounds, requiring conversion to Sudanese currency at the central bank window rate.

Airline companies are allowed to open foreign currency accounts without approval from the Bank of Sudan. These accounts may be credited with payments by their passengers, consignors, and agents, who are allowed to buy travel tickets in foreign currency.

Transfers between free and special foreign currency accounts are prohibited.

Imports and Import Payments

Imports from Israel are prohibited. Import licenses are not required, except for goods imported through bilateral and preferential trade arrangements. All applications for the importation of goods (except crude oil and petroleum products) not included on the negative list must be channeled through the commercial or specialized banks and must be accompanied by the following: (1) a pro forma invoice; (2) a valid commercial registration certificate (issued annually by the Ministry of Commerce) that verifies that the importer is a trader; (3) a valid tax clearance certificate; and (4) the written consent of the authorized bodies for certain categories of goods such as drugs, medical tools and equipment (Ministry of Health); veterinary medicines and equipment (Ministry of Agriculture and Veterinary Resources); food (Ministry of Health); seeds (Ministry of Agriculture); ammunition and explosives (Ministry of Interior); airport equipment (Civil Aviation Security); communications—telephone, facsimile, and telex—equipment (Security Telecommunication Corporation); insecticides and fertilizer (Ministry of Agriculture); inputs used by the chicken and dairy industries (Ministry of Agriculture and Veterinary Resources); irrigation pumps (Ministry of Irrigation); and agricultural sprayers (Ministry of Agriculture).

As from July 9, 1994, the negative list covered only sugar and automobiles, in addition to imports prohibited for reasons of religion, health, and national security.

In principle, commercial banks are authorized to sell foreign exchange to finance all imports (except those on the negative list) irrespective of their final use. Authorized banks are also allowed to provide import credit facilities for imports of specified capital goods by means of sight credit or documents against acceptance, provided that maturity is no less than two years and repayments do not begin until one year after the arrival of the goods.[2] Authorized banks are free to obtain from importers a deposit of any amount in foreign currency at least one month before the importers receive the shipping documents; the remaining foreign exchange may be provided when the shipping documents are received. Commercial banks are authorized to finance on credit imports of capital goods (provided that the credit agreement allows a grace period of at least one year) and of wheat and flour.

Commercial and specialized banks are required to furnish the Bank of Sudan with the following information every two weeks: applicant's name, goods to be imported and their value, terms of payment, approval number, and commercial registration number. Authorized banks, when filing import applications, are required to provide the Ministry of Commerce, Cooperation, and Supply with information on the type and quantity of commodities every two weeks.

Insurance for imports must normally be taken out with local companies. Imports financed at the commercial market rate, including those financed through the opening of letters of credit, could be

---

[2]These goods include agricultural equipment, such as tractors and harvesters; all means of transportation, excluding sedans; mining equipment; all kinds of industrial and service equipment; and road, irrigation, building, and construction equipment.

subject to an advance deposit of up to the full c.i.f. value.

Payments for Invisibles

Commercial banks are authorized to transfer up to 50 percent of net salaries of foreign consultants, provided that the following documents are submitted: evidence of work permit, certificate showing net basic salary, and certificate showing no tax obligation. On this basis, up to 50 percent of net salaries may be remitted abroad. Formal restrictions on other payments for invisibles apply only to the personal limit of $5,000 on withdrawals of banknotes for foreign travel; there is no limit on the amount that can be withdrawn as traveler's checks or bank checks. In practice, sales of foreign exchange for invisible payments differ among commercial and specialized banks owing to the informal rationing procedures established by each bank. Most commercial banks provide a nominal amount of foreign exchange for travel abroad after travel verification is obtained. When foreign exchange is in short supply, business travel is favored over vacation travel. For medical treatment abroad, a commensurate amount of foreign exchange is provided after the applicant has obtained certification from the medical committee.

Exports and Export Proceeds

All exports to Israel are prohibited, as is the exportation of hides and skins.[3] Export licenses are not required for any category of exports (except for exports under bilateral protocol arrangements and on account of barter trade). However, exporters must comply with administrative procedures designed to ensure full repatriation and surrender of foreign exchange export proceeds. Export contracts are subject to approval by the Ministry of Commerce. To prevent underinvoicing, the Board of Exported Commodities enforces a set of minimum export prices, which are updated on a periodic basis. In addition, the Ministry of Commerce would normally deny export permits for any commodities subject to export prohibition and to exporters not in compliance with repatriation and surrender requirements in earlier export activities.

All export proceeds, except those permitted to be retained under the Export Enhancement Scheme,

must be repatriated and sold to the domestic banking system within 45 days of the date of the bill of lading. Sixty-five percent of export proceeds must be on-sold to the Bank of Sudan: 40 percent at each bank's quoted selling rate, and 25 percent at the Bank of Sudan's reference exchange rate (or the bank's selling rate, whichever is lower).

Export taxes are levied on all categories of goods (except exports under bilateral protocol arrangements and under barter trade). The tax is collected by customs and deposited in its account at the Bank of Sudan. The applicable tax rates are 10 percent on cotton and gum arabic, and 5 percent on other exports.

Proceeds from Invisibles

Sudanese nationals working abroad are required to remit annually to domestic residents a minimum amount of foreign exchange, ranging from $300 (for ordinary workers, clerical and medical assistants, and soldiers) to $800–$5,000 (for professors, physicians, specialists in international organizations, and businessmen).[4] Exemptions are provided, however, for Sudanese nationals, other than employees of international organizations, working in a number of countries.

Travelers entering Sudan may bring in foreign currencies without restriction and may export any amount of Sudanese currency. Residents and non-residents entering Sudan must declare their holdings of foreign currency and re-export them within three months, after which foreign exchange must be surrendered to the banking system either for deposit in free foreign exchange accounts or for conversion into local currency. Commercial banks are prohibited from accepting foreign currencies without valid declaration forms.

Shipping agencies are permitted to accept foreign currency in payment for any services; however, they are required to sell all the foreign currency proceeds to authorized banks on the day following their receipt at the central bank exchange rate.

Sales of tickets and freight services in foreign currencies by airline companies in Sudan are restricted to (1) foreign tourists and businessmen; (2) foreigners working with diplomatic missions and organizations and international, regional, and national organizations; (3) foreigners employed by foreign relief, charitable, and religious organizations; and (4) foreigners working with foreign companies and branches of companies operating in the fields of

---

[3]The prohibition on exports of hides and skins is aimed at encouraging local processing. From January 16, 1994, the prohibition was extended to include reptile skins. On August 1, 1994, reptile skins were again exempted from this prohibition on exports, until January 18, 1995.

[4]These minimum remittances are in addition to a tax payable when obtaining a passport.

contracting, investment, and prospecting for petroleum and minerals. Airline companies are allowed to receive payments for tickets and freight services in foreign currency on condition that payments are made in the form of deposits to their foreign currency accounts. Sales in foreign exchange deposited in the foreign currency accounts must be remitted to the company's head office accompanied by a certificate issued by the Civil Aviation Authority.

Capital

Foreign direct investments are permitted in accordance with existing laws and regulations. Repatriation of share capital and amortization payments on loans to nonresidents is subject to certification from the Bank of Sudan regarding the original value of the foreign share in capital and loans. Repatriation of share capital and amortization payments on loans to nonresidents is subject to certification from the Investment Public Corporation.

Gold

Residents may purchase, hold, and sell gold coins in Sudan for numismatic purposes. Subject to certain conditions, residents may also purchase, hold, and sell domestically produced gold in Sudan. With these exceptions, residents other than the monetary authorities and authorized industrial users are not allowed to hold or acquire gold in any form other than jewelry, at home or abroad. Imports and exports of gold in any form other than jewelry require licenses issued by the Ministry of Commerce, Cooperation, and Supply; such licenses are not normally granted except for imports and exports by or on behalf of the monetary authorities and industrial users. Some newly mined gold is exported for processing, and the full value of the gold processed must be kept in an escrow account abroad in favor of the exporting company.

Changes During 1994

Exchange Arrangement

July 2. The dual exchange rate system was abolished and replaced by a unified official exchange rate to be determined in the interbank market. Commercial banks were authorized to quote on a daily basis buying and selling exchange rates—subject to a maximum spread of LSd 7—to be applied to all formal banking sector transactions other than certain compulsory sales of foreign exchange to the Bank of Sudan, which would take place at the Bank of Sudan's reference exchange rate. The reference rate would be determined daily as a weighted

average of the buying rates quoted by commercial banks during the preceding day. The Bank of Sudan's selling rate for official transactions would be determined by applying a margin of ± LSd 7 to the reference exchange rate.

Resident and Nonresident Foreign Currency Accounts

April 27. Regulations governing the operations of free foreign currency accounts and special foreign currency accounts were issued. Free accounts could henceforth be opened by all Sudanese resident individuals and legal entities, other than the Government, public institutions, and public sector enterprises. Such accounts could be freely credited with remittances from abroad, foreign exchange (where the depositor has a valid customs declaration), transfers from other free accounts, foreign currency banknotes purchased from the Sudanese banking system, and checks drawn on overseas accounts. Foreign exchange withdrawn from free accounts must be used within one month to make transfers abroad, to make transfers to other free accounts, to purchase domestic currency, to make payments in foreign exchange to domestic institutions authorized to sell goods and services for foreign exchange, to finance imports, and to finance overseas travel (of up to $5,000 in banknotes a person and any amount in other means of payment, based on evidence of travel authorization and tickets).

Special foreign currency accounts could be opened by diplomatic, foreign, and regional missions and organizations; foreign charities and aid organizations; and foreign companies, foreign contractors, and the foreign personnel of such organizations. Special foreign currency accounts may be credited with transfers from abroad. They may also be used to make transfers abroad to finance foreign travel, to purchase local currency in order to finance local payments, to make foreign currency payments to local institutions authorized to sell goods and services for foreign currency, and to finance imports.

The transfer of foreign exchange between free and special foreign currency accounts would be prohibited.

Imports and Import Payments

February 28. The following products were eliminated from the negative import list: household utensils, other than plastic utensils; textiles (except for certain coarse upholstery fabrics, polyester, and women's wear); watches and alarm clocks; cameras and photographic equipment; jewelry; chains, including key chains; picture frames; electric hair dryers; wallets; photo albums; umbrellas; pearls; bags, other than leather; fire-resistant safes; sickles; nail clippers; cooking grills; and diapers.

Imports of the following products were authorized to be effective through the Duty-Free Corporation: air-conditioning equipment; refrigerators, water coolers, and freezers; TVs and VCRs; tape recorders and radios; rugs and carpets; washing machines and water heaters; electric heaters; vacuum cleaners; electric irons; and stoves and ovens.

April 14. The following items were eliminated from the negative import list: reconditioned distributors for vehicles and agricultural machinery and shredded vegetable fiber for upholstery. Plain white calico and its derivatives were added to the negative import list.

April 27. The authorization to import products through the Duty-Free Corporation (established in February 1994) was broadened to cover women's saris and veils.

April 29. The prohibition on imports of Egyptian fava beans was lifted.

July 9. All items except the following were eliminated from the negative import list: alcoholic drinks and narcotics; gambling equipment; unlicensed weapons, ammunition, and explosives; sugar; and passenger saloon cars.

July 20. Sudanese individuals in the following categories were permitted to import automobiles for personal use: residents abroad returning to Sudan on a permanent basis; Sudanese deported from other countries; emigrant experts and advisors returning to official positions; students in higher education abroad returning to Sudan; and diplomats returning to Sudan.

September 21. The categories of Sudanese individuals authorized to import cars for personal use were widened to include Sudanese working abroad for Sudanese maritime lines, the Sudanese Airlines, overseas centers of Sudanese state-owned corporations, and workers in international organizations.

Exports and Export Proceeds

January 16. Reptile skins were included in the prohibition on exports of hides and skins.

March 30. The prohibition on exports of semiprocessed leather (imposed in May 1993) was lifted.

May 10. The exportation of scrap aluminum and scrap copper was prohibited.

July 1. The ban on exports of scrap aluminum and copper was eliminated.

August 1. Reptile skins were exempted until January 18, 1995 from the prohibition on exports of unprocessed hides and skins.

October 4. The prohibition on exports of maize was lifted. A minimum export price for maize was established as $100 for each ton bulk, and $120 a ton in sacks.

December 17. The proportion of export proceeds subject to compulsory sale at the Bank of Sudan's reference exchange rate was reduced to 65 percent from 80 percent.

December 17. The proportion of export proceeds subject to compulsory sale to the Bank of Sudan was reduced to 25 percent from 50 percent.

Proceeds from Invisibles

March 31. The system of income taxes payable by Sudanese workers abroad (adopted in January 1992) was replaced by a schedule of minimum annual transfers to Sudan, ranging from $300 for ordinary workers, clerical and medical assistants, and soldiers to $800–$5,000 for professors, physicians, specialists in international organizations, and businessmen.

SURINAME

(Position as of December 31, 1994)

Exchange Arrangement

The currency of Suriname is the Suriname Guilder. Exchange rates are freely determined on the basis of demand and supply conditions in the market. Commercial banks and licensed foreign exchange houses may trade foreign exchange with customers, among themselves, or with the Central Bank of Suriname on a freely negotiable basis. The Central Bank determines the exchange rate to be used in official transactions, which is based on the weighted-average rate of commercial bank transactions on the previous working day.

One percent is charged on purchases of foreign exchange, which is payable to the Central Bank. The commercial banks charge commissions of 2 percent on sales of foreign exchange and 9.25 percent on transfers. There are no arrangements for forward cover against exchange rate risk operating in the official or the commercial banking sector.

Suriname formally accepted the obligations of Article VIII, Sections 2, 3, and 4 of the Fund Agreement, as from June 29, 1978.

Administration of Control

All foreign exchange transactions are subject to licensing, as are transactions between residents and nonresidents in domestic currency and other domestic assets. Import licenses are granted by the Ministry of Trade and Industry.[1] In case of payment by letter of credit, the import license must also be approved by the Central Bank. The Central Bank is empowered to provide foreign exchange for import payments (subject to presentation of an import license, which serves as a general authorization for payment); the latter authority is exercised through the commercial banks, which have been appointed authorized banks by the Foreign Exchange Commission. External payments, other than for the importation of goods, require a license from the Foreign Exchange Commission. Except for limited amounts of foreign exchange for invisible payments not requiring an exchange license, the authorized banks are not permitted to sell foreign exchange un-

less the remitter submits an exchange license. Exports also require a license from the Ministry of Trade and Industry. Commercial banks may accept free of license those inward transfers of foreign exchange that do not result from borrowing abroad; the taking up of foreign loans must be approved by the Foreign Exchange Commission.

Arrears are maintained with respect to external payments.

Prescription of Currency

Settlements in Suriname guilders between Suriname and foreign countries are not permitted; they must, in general, be made in specified convertible currencies.[2]

Resident and Nonresident Accounts

Nonresidents, whether banks or nonbanks, may freely open accounts in U.S. dollars with domestic banks; no overdrafts are permitted. Nonresidents other than banks may freely open accounts in Suriname guilders with domestic banks; certain debits and credits are covered by a general license, and all others are subject to a specific license. These accounts must not be overdrawn and, except for certain specified purposes, debits must not exceed a total of Sf 3,000 a month. Authorized banks may open nonresident accounts in Suriname guilders in the name of nonresident banks; these accounts also must not be overdrawn. Authorized banks may open nonresident accounts on behalf of nonresidents drawing pensions from the Government or under company plans. A special permit is required to transfer pensions abroad. Nonresident accounts in guilders may not be credited with Suriname banknotes mailed from abroad; nonresident foreign currency accounts may not be credited with Surinamese tender.

Resident nonbanks are allowed to open foreign currency accounts with domestic and foreign banks and to hold foreign securities, provided that the funds have not been acquired from sales of real estate in Suriname or from exports. Balances in for-

---

[1]However, two specified mining companies do not need licenses for their own import requirements. Similar exemptions may be granted to foreign companies for their industrial activities in Suriname, provided that they pay for imports from their own foreign exchange holdings.

[2]Australian dollars, Austrian schillings, Barbados dollars, Belgian francs, Canadian dollars, Danish kroner, deutsche mark, Eastern Caribbean dollars, French francs, Guyana dollars, Italian lire, Japanese yen, Netherlands guilders, Norwegian kroner, Portuguese escudos, pounds sterling, Swedish kronor, Swiss francs, Trinidad and Tobago dollars, and U.S. dollars.

eign currency accounts and holdings of foreign assets may be used freely, except for travel; use of these accounts and foreign assets for travel is limited to Sf 1,500 a person a year.

Imports and Import Payments

Import licenses are required for all imports. Imports of some commodities are prohibited,[3] and imports of another group of commodities are subject to quotas under the Comprehensive Decree of May 11, 1982.[4]

The import license serves as a general authorization for payment. In case of payment by letter of credit, the import license must be approved by the Central Bank. Import licenses are valid for six months, within which period the goods must be landed and paid for. In addition to customs duties, a license fee of 1.5 percent is levied on the c.i.f. value of all imports. A statistical fee of 2.0 percent is levied on the c.i.f. value of imports of bauxite companies, and 0.5 of the c.i.f. value of other imports, including imports of gold.

Payments for Invisibles

Transactions involving outward remittances of foreign exchange are subject to licensing; application for a license must be submitted to the Foreign Exchange Commission at least one month before the intended date for effecting such a transaction. Authorized banks and the General Post Office have authority to provide foreign exchange up to Sf 150 a month for each item on account of certain services (bank charges, legal fees, membership dues, copy and patent rights, and so forth) as well as for advertising expenses and payments for books.

Travel allowances for residents are subject to licensing and are limited to the equivalent of Sf 1,500 a person a calendar year. The authorized bank must enter on the travel ticket the amount of foreign exchange sold and the date, and the purchase of exchange for travel is not permitted until three days before departure. Bona fide applications for larger amounts of exchange for travel purposes are approved on a case-by-case basis. Remittances for support of family members abroad require an individual license, which is granted only for full-time registered students of disciplines essential to, but not taught in, Suriname.

Payments due as interest on loans and as net income from other investments, and payments of moderate amounts for the amortization of loans or depreciation or direct investments, may be made if an application, supported by an auditor's report, is duly presented to the Foreign Exchange Commission for verification. These payments are temporarily suspended. Both resident and nonresident travelers may take out Sf 100 in Suriname currency. The exportation of foreign banknotes by traveling residents is limited to the amount of their travel allowance.

Exports and Export Proceeds

Exports require export licenses issued by the Ministry of Economic Affairs. Licenses are issued if the exports are covered by letters of credit opened by buyers abroad. Exporters of the bauxite, banana, and rice sectors must surrender foreign exchange proceeds to the Central Bank within 30 days. Other exporters must surrender their proceeds to authorized commercial banks, and are allowed to buy back up to 85 percent of the amount surrendered. The Ministry of Trade and Industry ascertains with the relevant government agency whether the export price as reported by the exporter is in accordance with world market prices. Export licenses for cattle, pigs, fresh beef and pork, and planting materials are granted only on the advice of the Director of Agriculture, Animal Husbandry, and Fisheries. The export of baboonwood is prohibited and that of rice is subject to special regulations. Certain export companies have received special permission from the Foreign Exchange Commission to maintain current accounts in foreign currency with their parent companies abroad and to use these for specified payments and receipts (including export proceeds). Exports of processed and semiprocessed wood are subject to a tax of 100 percent of the f.o.b. value. Exports of bauxite

---

[3]The prohibition applies to imports of pigs (excluding those for breeding); chicken, duck, turkey meat, pork, fish (excluding kwie kwie fish and smoked herring), shrimp, and crab (fresh, cooled, or frozen, salted, dried, or precooked); vegetables (excluding potatoes, onions, and garlic); edible roots and tubers; citrus fruits, bananas, plantains, and coconuts; green and roasted coffee (excluding decaffeinated); rice and rice products (excluding baby food); sugar (excluding cubes and tablets weighing 5 grams or less a cube or tablet), aromatized or colored sugar, or sugar syrup; noodles and macaroni; jam, jelly, and marmalade (excluding those for diabetics); peanut butter; syrups and concentrates for nonalcoholic beverages in packages of less than 5 kilograms (excluding those for diabetics); firewood and other nonprocessed wood, railroad ties, shingles, wooden structures for construction, wooden tiles and panels, wooden tools, handles, and coat hangers; men's and boys' shoes (excluding rubber and plastic boots and sport shoes); and sand, gravel, sidewalk tiles, and road bricks. Imports of some other items, such as explosives and narcotics, are prohibited for reasons of public policy or health.

[4]The commodities to which import quotas are applied include kwie kwie fish, milk powder, potatoes, onions, garlic, fruits and nuts (other than citrus fruits, bananas, plantains, and coconuts), decaffeinated coffee, peanuts, baby food, tomato paste, certain preserved vegetables, matches, furnishings, ready-made clothing, and furniture (excluding those for business establishments, such as offices, theaters, clinics, hotels, restaurants, and libraries).

are subject to a statistical fee of 2.0 percent of their f.o.b. value, and other exports are subject to a statistical fee of 0.5 percent of their f.o.b. value.

Proceeds from Invisibles

Foreign exchange receipts from invisibles must be surrendered to an authorized bank. Travelers may bring in unlimited foreign currency and up to Sf 100 in domestic currency. Travelers must declare all domestic and foreign currency in their possession on entry; resident travelers must exchange at an authorized bank any foreign currency in their possession. The amount that nonresidents may take out of the country in foreign currency must be smaller than the amount they brought in and declared on entry.

Capital

A decision of September 21, 1960 of the Foreign Exchange Commission provides for the transfer abroad of capital proceeds from the sale to residents, or the liquidation of, fully or partly foreign-owned companies or other forms of enterprise. The decision covers investments made by nonresidents with foreign capital after July 31, 1953. It also provides for the annual transfer of profits and for the transfer at any time of the foreign exchange (including loans) imported by the nonresident entrepreneur for the company's use. Profits must be transferred within three years; otherwise, they are considered to have become part of the firm's working capital and may be transferred only in annual installments of 20 percent. Transfers in accordance with these decisions have been temporarily suspended.

The Foreign Exchange Commission may, at its discretion, grant licenses for transfers abroad from the estate of a deceased person, up to a maximum of Sf 10,000. For estates valued at more than Sf 10,000, further annual transfers are permitted so as to spread them over a period of not more than ten years. The Commission may allow emigrants (heads of family) to transfer in foreign exchange the equivalent of Sf 5,000 in a lump sum, and subsequently, Sf 5,000 a year. The head of a repatriating family may be permitted to transfer the equivalent of Sf 10,000 plus 10 percent of his total taxable earnings in Suriname accrued during his period of residence. If his Surinamese assets exceed the sum thus calculated, the excess may be transferred at a rate of Sf 10,000 a year. Transfers abroad in excess of Sf 10,000 a year may be authorized under exceptional circumstances. Outward transfers for these purposes have been temporarily reduced.

Subject to certain requirements, residents may purchase or sell in specified countries[5] Surinamese corporate shares that have been designated as negotiable by the Foreign Exchange Commission. Transfers for investment abroad or for the purchase of other foreign securities or real estate by residents are not permitted, although exceptions may be made for direct investments abroad when it is considered that Surinamese interests will benefit. All borrowing from nonresidents by nonbank residents requires the prior approval of the Foreign Exchange Commission. The foreign transactions of authorized banks are restricted, in principle, to those undertaken for the account of their customers, and banks are required, in principle, to surrender to the Central Bank any excess of foreign currency purchased.

Authorized banks are permitted to place a part of their liquid funds abroad and to use the short-term credit lines extended by their foreign correspondent banks as a source of operating funds. The Central Bank, the authorized banks, and the correspondent banks have made an arrangement whereby the Central Bank guarantees the letters of credit issued by the authorized banks by pledging its balances up to a specified ceiling, while the authorized banks keep their balances abroad at a minimum level.[6] The authorized banks may place abroad in short-term U.S. dollar assets the amounts corresponding to balances in their nonresident U.S. dollar accounts.

Gold

Producers of gold may sell only to the authorized gold buyers (the Central Bank and Grassalco). Locally produced gold must be surrendered to the Foreign Exchange Commission by sale to the Central Bank. The authorized gold buyers are permitted, however, to sell nuggets at freely agreed prices for industrial and artistic purposes; dealings between residents in gold bars and other forms of unworked gold, with the exception of nuggets, are prohibited. As local production does not meet demand for industrial purposes, the Central Bank may import some gold.

Three kinds of gold coins—with face values of Sf 100, Sf 200, and Sf 250—are legal tender. Residents may hold and acquire gold coins in Suriname for numismatic and investment purposes; authorized

---

[5]Belgium, Canada, France, Germany, Italy, Luxembourg, Netherlands, Netherlands Antilles, United Kingdom, and United States.

[6]This arrangement applies to the nationally controlled Landbouw Bank, De Surinaamsche Bank, and Hakrinbank, but not to the Dutch-owned Algemene Bank Nederland.

banks may freely negotiate gold coins among themselves and with other residents. Residents other than the monetary authorities, producers of gold, and authorized industrial and dental users are not allowed without special permission to hold or acquire gold in any form other than nuggets, jewelry, or coins, at home or abroad. Imports and exports of gold in any form other than jewelry require exchange licenses issued by the Foreign Exchange Commission; licenses are not normally granted except for imports and exports of coins by authorized banks and for imports and exports by or on behalf of the monetary authorities, producers of gold, and industrial users. Residents arriving from abroad, however, may freely bring in gold, subject to declaration and provided that they surrender it to the Central Bank within 20 days. Nonresident travelers may also freely bring in gold, subject to declaration; they may re-export the declared amount freely.

Imports of gold coins are duty free and those of unworked gold are subject to a duty of Sf 1.00 a gram, irrespective of origin. The general tariff for gold ornaments is 60 percent ad valorem. Imports and exports of all forms of gold are subject to a statistical fee of 0.5 percent; in addition, imports are subject to a licensing fee of 1.5 percent.

Changes During 1994

Exchange Arrangement

January 1. The exchange rate applicable to foreign exchange surrendered by the two bauxite companies for payment of local expenses was changed to Sf 55 per US$1 from Sf 8 per US$1.

July 11. The multiple exchange rate system was unified.

Administration of Control

October 1. Import licensing requirements were liberalized.

SWAZILAND

(Position as of December 31, 1994)

Exchange Arrangement

The currency of Swaziland is the Lilangeni (plural Emalangeni), which is pegged to the South African rand at E 1 per R 1. Exchange rates for the U.S. dollar quoted by the Central Bank of Swaziland (CBS) are based on the exchange rate of the South African commercial rand against the U.S. dollar. On December 31, 1994, the closing buying and selling rates were E 3.5440 and E 3.5455, respectively, per US$1. Rates are also quoted for the Canadian dollar, the deutsche mark, the French franc, the Japanese yen, the pound sterling, and the Swiss franc, based on the London and New York market quotations for these currencies against the U.S. dollar, and for the European currency unit (ECU).

The CBS also quotes rates for the currencies of the member states of the Preferential Trade Area of Eastern and Southern African States (PTA), based on their relationship with the SDR as reported by the PTA clearinghouse. These currencies include the Kenya shilling, the Malawi kwacha, the Zambian kwacha, and the Zimbabwe dollar. There are no taxes or subsidies on purchases or sales of foreign exchange. The CBS permits authorized dealers to engage in forward exchange operations. Commercial banks are generally able to meet demands for forward sales of foreign currency against emalangeni. The forward exchange rates are market determined.

Swaziland formally accepted the obligations of Article VIII, Sections 2, 3, and 4 of the Fund Agreement, as from December 11, 1989.

Exchange Control Territory

Swaziland is part of the Common Monetary Area (CMA), a single exchange control territory comprising Lesotho, Namibia, South Africa, and Swaziland. No restrictions are applied to payments within the CMA, and, in principle, payments are not controlled. Residents of Swaziland have access to the Johannesburg market in accordance with the terms and conditions ruling in that market. In relations with countries outside the CMA, Swaziland applies exchange controls that are generally similar to those of South Africa but has not adopted the dual exchange rate system that was reintroduced in that country in September 1985. Financial rand may not be acquired by, or held for account of, any resident of Lesotho, South Africa, or Swaziland.

Administration of Control

The Central Bank of Swaziland, on behalf of the Ministry of Finance, controls all external currency transactions.

Imports and Import Payments

Swaziland is a member of the Southern African Customs Union (SACU) with Botswana, Lesotho, Namibia, and South Africa, and no import restrictions are imposed on goods originating in any country of the customs union. Imports from South Africa do not require licenses and include an unknown quantity of goods originating outside the customs union. Imports from countries outside the customs union are licensed in conformity with specific import regulations. Import licenses granted in Swaziland entitle the holder to buy the foreign exchange required to make the import payment. Ports of entry outside Swaziland may be used, but the Swazi authorities are responsible for controlling import licenses and payments procedures.

Exports and Export Proceeds

All exports are subject to licensing. For those goods that are shipped to any one member of the customs area, licenses are used mainly for tax levy purposes. For goods shipped to countries outside the customs area, licensing is administered to ensure that export proceeds are repatriated in the prescribed manner and within the stipulated period.

Payments for and Proceeds from Invisibles

Payments to nonresidents for current transactions, while subject to control, are not normally restricted. Authority to approve some types of current payments up to established limits is delegated to authorized dealers. The basic exchange allowances for tourist travel are E 23,000 for each adult, and E 11,500 for each child, a year. For business travel, the basic allowance is E 1,800 a person a day, not exceeding E 34,000 a year. Larger amounts are granted upon application supported by proof of bona fide need. Residents traveling to the member countries of the PTA must use traveler's checks denominated in the units of account of the PTA (UA-PTAs). To use credit cards outside the CMA, a resident cardholder must complete a letter of undertaking before departure.

Capital

All inward capital transfers require the prior approval of the CBS and must be properly documented in order to facilitate the subsequent repatriation of interest, dividends, profits, and other income. No person may borrow foreign currency or register shares in the name of a nonresident, or act as a nominee for a nonresident, without prior approval. In August 1987, an agreement was reached between the Reserve Bank of South Africa and the CBS to allow some nonresidents to invest in specific projects in Swaziland through the financial rand mechanism by acquiring shares in new companies and by purchasing shares in existing nonquoted companies through South African intermediaries. Priority is given to investments involving the establishment or expansion of manufacturing enterprises, subject to evidence of investment in fixed assets of most of the funds provided through financial rand.

Applications for most outward transfers of capital are considered on their merits. Blocked emalangeni may be invested in quoted securities and other such investments as may be approved by the CBS.

Changes During 1994

No significant changes occurred in the exchange and trade system.

SWEDEN

(Position as of December 31, 1994)

Exchange Arrangement

The currency of Sweden is the Swedish Krona. The Swedish authorities do not maintain margins in respect of exchange transactions, and spot and forward exchange rates are determined on the basis of demand and supply conditions in the exchange market. The Sveriges Riksbank, however, has the discretionary power to intervene in the exchange market. On December 31, 1994, the buying and selling rates for the U.S. dollar were Skr 7.4425 and Skr 7.4825, respectively, per US$1. There are no taxes or subsidies on purchases or sales of foreign exchange.

Authorized banks may buy from and sell to other authorized banks and residents any foreign currency on a spot or forward basis against another foreign currency or Swedish kronor. Authorized banks may also purchase (sell) foreign currencies, spot or forward, from (to) foreign banks and other nonresidents against any foreign currency or Swedish kronor credited (debited) to a krona account. Also, currency option contracts may be concluded freely with both residents and nonresidents.

For prudential purposes, limits are placed on the net foreign exchange positions (spot, forward, options) in individual foreign currencies and on the total net position in all foreign currencies. The limit for each foreign currency and for the total net position is equal to 10 percent of a bank's capital base. For a bank that is a recognized market maker, the limit is equal to 15 percent of its capital base. Banks may grant overdrafts to nonresidents and may incur foreign exchange net liabilities for which the same limits apply. This enables the banks to borrow foreign currency from nonresidents for on-lending to foreign banks or other nonresidents or to residents. Lending abroad in kronor is also freely permitted. Swedish banks may, while observing their limits on net foreign exchange holdings, borrow abroad freely in order to sell the proceeds against Swedish kronor in the market. A limit also exists on a bank's total net positions calculated as the sum of all liability positions. This limit is equal to 20 percent of the bank's capital base and to 30 percent for recognized market makers.

Sweden formally accepted the obligations of Article VIII, Sections 2, 3, and 4 of the Fund Agreement, as from February 15, 1961.

Administration of Control

All current and capital transactions are free from exchange control. When required, import and export licenses are issued by the National Board of Trade, except those for foodstuffs, which are issued by the National Agricultural Market Board.

In accordance with the Fund's Executive Board Decision No. 144-(52/51) adopted on August 14, 1952, Sweden notified the Fund on August 7, 1992 that, in compliance with UN Security Council Resolution No. 757 (1992), certain restrictions had been imposed on the making of payments and transfers for current international transactions in respect of the Federal Republic of Yugoslavia (Serbia/Montenegro). These restrictions were extended on September 23, 1994 to include areas of the Republic of Bosnia and Herzegovina under the control of Bosnian Serb forces. Certain restrictions were imposed on the Libyan Arab Jamahiriya and Angola, according to UN Security Council Resolution No. 748 (1992) of March 31, 1992, and UN Security Council Resolution No. 864 (1993) of September 15, 1993, respectively. Financial transactions with Iraq are prohibited in accordance with UN Security Council Resolution No. 661 (1990) and other relevant UN resolutions.

Prescription of Currency

Payments to and from foreign countries may be made in any foreign currency or in Swedish kronor through an external krona account (see section on Nonresident Accounts, below).

Nonresident Accounts

External krona accounts may be held by nonresidents domiciled abroad, including persons who have become nonresidents after emigrating. They may be used for payments and transfers and may be converted into any foreign currency.

Imports and Import Payments

With the exception of some agricultural and fishery products, practically all goods are free from quantitative restriction and import licensing when imported from countries other than Belarus, China, Hungary, Kazakhstan, the Democratic People's Republic of Korea, the Russian Federation, and Ukraine. However, most imports from these countries are liberalized. Imports of most iron and steel products from all countries, except from the members of the European Union (EU) and the European Free Trade Association (EFTA), are subject to import licensing for surveillance purposes. With a few exceptions, imports from Iraq, the Federal Republic of Yugoslavia (Serbia/Montenegro), and areas of the Republic of Bosnia and Herzegovina under the control of Bosnian Serb forces are prohibited.

Payments for imports may be made freely. Importers are also permitted to accept foreign suppliers' credits.

Payments for Invisibles

Payments for invisibles may be made by residents in favor of nonresidents without limit or restriction. Travelers may export any amount of domestic and foreign banknotes or any other means of payment.

While abroad, residents may open accounts, provided that the amounts are reported to the Swedish National Tax Board for tax control and to the Riksbank for statistical purposes.

Exports and Export Proceeds

Exports to the Democratic People's Republic of Korea are subject to export licensing. All other exports, with the exception of scrap metal to countries other than member countries of the EU and the EFTA, are free from license. With a few exceptions, exports to Iraq, the Federal Republic of Yugoslavia (Serbia/Montenegro), and areas of the Republic of Bosnia and Herzegovina under the control of Bosnian Serb forces are prohibited. Some exports to the Libyan Arab Jamahiriya and Angola are prohibited. Proceeds from exports of goods may be sold for kronor or kept in a foreign currency account in Sweden and used by the holder to make payments abroad.

Proceeds from Invisibles

Receipts from current invisibles are subject to the same treatment as those from exports (see section on Exports and Export Proceeds, above). Travelers may import any amount of domestic and foreign banknotes or any other means of payment.

Capital

All capital transactions are free from restriction. For tax control and statistical purposes, however, residents depositing funds in foreign bank accounts or transacting through such an account must report the amount to the Swedish National Tax Board and to the Riksbank. Transactions in securities may be carried out freely. Foreign securities held by individuals must be deposited with an authorized currency dealer who is a securities broker or a broker who has received special approval from the Riksbank or a similar foreign institution.

Gold

There are no special regulations on trading in gold.

Changes During 1994

Administration of Control

July 1. Certain areas in Bosnia and Herzegovina became subject to sanctions in September 1994. Some imports from the Czech Republic, Hungary, Poland, and the Slovak Republic were liberalized.

Imports and Import Payments

(See Appendix for a summary of trade measures introduced and eliminated on an EU-wide basis during 1994, page 554.)

SWITZERLAND

(Position as of December 31, 1994)

Exchange Arrangement

The currency of Switzerland is the Swiss Franc. The Swiss National Bank does not maintain margins in respect of exchange transactions; exchange rates are determined, in principle, on the basis of underlying demand and supply conditions in the exchange markets. However, the Swiss National Bank reserves the right to intervene if and when circumstances warrant. The principal intervention currency is the U.S. dollar. On December 31, 1994, the midpoint market rate for the Swiss franc in terms of the U.S. dollar was Sw F 1.3118 per US$1.

All settlements may be made at free market rates. Foreign banknotes are negotiated freely in Switzerland at rates determined by the interplay of supply and demand. Residents and nonresidents may freely negotiate foreign exchange contracts with banks in all currencies, in respect of both commercial and financial transactions. No officially fixed premiums and discount rates apply to forward exchange contracts, all of which are negotiated at free market rates. Under the Export Risk Guarantee System, export receipts, excluding exchange rate risks, may be insured by the Government under certain conditions.

Exchange Control Territory

For all purposes of importation and exportation, the Principality of Liechtenstein is included in the Swiss customs territory. For purposes of monetary policy measures, natural persons domiciled in Liechtenstein are considered by Switzerland as residents, as are juridical persons, including banks. However, this rule does not apply to the acquisition of Swiss real estate. Liechtenstein is considered a foreign country for purposes of banking supervision.

Administration of Control

Authority to impose measures for the control of imports, exports, and payments is vested in the Swiss Federal Council, acting on the advice of the Federal Department of Public Economy, the Federal Department of Foreign Affairs, or the Federal Department of Finance. The Swiss National Bank is the advisory and executive authority in matters of currency for both Switzerland and Liechtenstein. Capital export transactions of financial institutions, however, are subject to approval by the Swiss National Bank (see section on Capital, below).

In accordance with the Fund's Executive Board Decision No. 144–(52/51) adopted on August 14, 1952, Switzerland notified the Fund that, in accordance with the relevant UN Security Council resolutions, certain restrictions had been imposed on the making of payments and transfers for current international transactions in respect of Iraq, the Libyan Arab Jamahiriya, and the Federal Republic of Yugoslavia (Serbia/Montenegro). Restrictions have also been imposed on payments and transfers to Haiti, Iraq, and the Libyan Arab Jamahiriya.

Prescription of Currency

Settlements may be made or received in any currency.

Imports and Import Payments

With minor exceptions, imports into Switzerland may be made freely. The importation of alcohol is a state monopoly. The most important commodities subject to license, irrespective of their origin, are certain agricultural products. Import permits for goods under license are generally granted freely, within the global quotas established for certain agricultural products. Payments for imports from all countries may be made freely.

Payments for Invisibles

Payments for invisibles may be made freely. The exportation of Swiss and foreign banknotes is unrestricted.

Exports and Export Proceeds

The exportation (including the re-exportation) of some goods, including weapons, dual-use goods, and scrap metal, is controlled through individual licenses. This export-licensing system is operated in part with the assistance of appropriate semiofficial or private organizations. Export proceeds are freely disposable.

Proceeds from Invisibles

Proceeds from invisibles are freely disposable. The importation of Swiss and foreign banknotes is unrestricted.

Capital

Transfers of capital may be made without formality, except that foreign bond issues in Switzerland amounting to or exceeding Sw F 10 million each and with a maturity of 12 months or more require permission from the Swiss National Bank. In practice, this requirement is administered very liberally. Foreign institutions are allowed to participate in syndicated Swiss franc security issues, provided that the lead manager is domiciled in Switzerland. For direct bank participations or subscriptions by Swiss banks in issues and bank credits (exceeding Sw F 10 million and with a maturity of longer than 12 months) abroad, the Swiss National Bank grants a general permit. Each generally authorized capital export transaction must be reported to the Swiss National Bank. The physical importation and exportation of Swiss and foreign securities are unrestricted.

Selected banks and finance companies are required to report their positions (their own assets and liabilities in foreign currencies, spot and forward) in domestic and foreign currencies on a monthly basis.

Purchases of real estate in Switzerland by or on behalf of persons or firms of foreign nationality who are domiciled or residing abroad require approval by the canton in which the property is situated. The approval of the canton is subject to supervision and appeal by the federal Government.

Gold

Swiss gold coins are not legal tender. Residents may freely purchase, hold, and sell gold in any form, at home or abroad. There is a free gold market in Zurich. Imports and exports of gold in any form by residents and nonresidents are unrestricted and free of license. No customs duties or other charges are levied on exports of gold. Imports of gold bars and of certain gold coins are exempt from customs duty. Import and export licenses, which are issued freely, are required for commercial imports and exports of certain articles containing gold.

Changes During 1994

Capital

March 18. Parliament passed a law revising the banking law (the law came into force on February 1, 1995). The law abolished the former permit requirement for foreign bond issues exceeding Sw F 10 million each and with a maturity of 12 months or more and introduced instead a reporting requirement for foreign and domestic bond issues. In case of any turmoil on the capital markets, the federal Government may reintroduce the permit requirement. In addition, the reporting requirement for direct bank participation or subscriptions by Swiss banks in credits and issues of equities was abolished.

October 7. Parliament passed a law that would liberalize foreign ownership of real estate for such purposes as agriculture, industry, trade, banking, and insurance. (If it is approved by a referendum, the law would come into effect on June 25, 1995.)

SYRIAN ARAB REPUBLIC

(Position as of January 31, 1995)

Exchange Arrangement

The currency of the Syrian Arab Republic is the Syrian Pound, which is pegged to the U.S. dollar, the intervention currency. The exchange rate system consists of the following four rates: (1) the official rate of LS 11.20/11.25 per US$1 applies, on the receipts side, to government transactions, public sector exports of petroleum and some agricultural products; and, on the payments side, to government transactions, public sector imports of some agricultural products, and public sector invisibles payments; (2) the "rate in neighboring countries" of LS 42/43 per US$1 applies, on the receipts side, to all public and private capital inflows, receipts from tourists, 25 percent of export proceeds surrendered by the private sector, and that part of the 75 percent of export proceeds retained by private sector exporters that is not used to finance their own imports or others; and on the payments side, to travel allowances, tourism and medical expenses, some student allowances, remittances abroad and payments by the public sector approved by the Committee for Foreign Exchange, and as an accounting rate for some government transactions and for customs valuation of some imports; [1] (3) the promotion rate of LS 20/22 per US$1, which is used only for payments of allowances to students who started overseas study before January 1, 1991; and (4) the "government fee rate" (LS 42.95/43.00 per US$1) applies to a number of fees, including those on transit and port services, and as an accounting rate for some government transactions as well as for customs valuation of some imports.

In addition to the above rates, there is also a Beirut free market rate, which stood at LS 51.20 per US$1 on December 15, 1994. There is also an "export proceeds" market in which a market-determined rate applies to a number of newly permitted goods that may be imported only with foreign exchange earned through exports. Exporters who do not use all of their export earnings to import goods may sell their retained foreign exchange earnings to importers in this market; in December 1994, the exchange rate in this market stood at LS 57.00 per US$1.

Exchange rates between the Syrian pound and other major currencies are set on the basis of the exchange rate between the Syrian pound and the U.S. dollar in relation to the exchange rates of the currencies concerned in the international markets.

There are no arrangements for forward cover against exchange rate risk operating in the official or the commercial banking sector.

Administration of Control

Policy with regard to imports and exports is determined by the Ministry of Economy and Foreign Trade. Under an agreement between the Central Bank of Syria and the Administrative Committee of the Exchange Office, all transactions of the Exchange Office are carried out through the Central Bank. Import licenses are issued by the Ministry of Economy and Foreign Trade, and exchange licenses for invisibles and capital transactions by the Exchange Office. Only the Central Bank and the Commercial Bank of Syria may deal in foreign exchange. The Commercial Bank of Syria opens letters of credit and accepts bills for collection without prior approval, provided that certain conditions are fulfilled.

Arrears are maintained with respect to external payments.

Prescription of Currency

The Exchange Office is empowered to prescribe the currencies that can be obtained for exports. Proceeds from exports to all countries may be obtained in any convertible currency. Prescription of currency requirements are not applied to outgoing payments. All payments to, and receipts from, Israel are prohibited.

The Syrian Arab Republic maintains bilateral payments agreements with the Islamic Republic of Iran, the Russian Federation, and Sri Lanka; however, the agreements with the Russian Federation and Sri Lanka are inoperative, and payments for imports from the Islamic Republic of Iran may also be made in convertible currencies.

Nonresident and Foreign Currency Accounts

Nonresident accounts in Syrian pounds may be credited with the proceeds of foreign currencies

---

[1] In 1994, the "airline rate," which applies, on the receipts side, to purchases of airline tickets by nonresidents, and, on the payments side, to transfers abroad by airline companies, was adjusted to LS 42/43 per US$1 and was effectively merged with the "rate in neighboring countries."

sold to the authorized banks and with other receipts; they may be debited without prior approval to pay for Syrian exports to the country of the account holder and for expenses in the Syrian Arab Republic. Nonresidents (individuals and corporations) may open accounts in convertible foreign currencies at the Commercial Bank of Syria for the deposit of funds from abroad. Balances in such accounts may be sold to local banks, transferred abroad without restriction, or used to pay for authorized imports. Temporary nonresident accounts may be opened in the name of nonresidents temporarily residing in the Syrian Arab Republic. These accounts may not be used, however, for funds received in settlement currencies, through payment conventions, or by diplomatic and United Nations (UN) missions and their staffs. Diplomatic and UN missions and their staffs must exchange 50 percent of their transfers to the Syrian Arab Republic at the official rate and may keep the remaining 50 percent on deposit in foreign exchange with the Commercial Bank of Syria or convert it into Syrian pounds at the rate in neighboring countries. The debiting for expenditures in the Syrian Arab Republic and abroad is free.

Residents not involved in export activities and wishing to open foreign currency accounts are required to present written evidence that they have sources of income from abroad.

Imports and Import Payments

Imports of commodities originating in Israel are prohibited. Many basic commodities (including paper, salt, tobacco, wheat, iron and steel, and certain agricultural machinery) are imported only by state trading agencies or, for their own account, by certain private sector importers. Agencies having the sole authority to import may be required to import certain commodities to meet the raw material needs of the private sector. The list of items that the private sector is permitted to import includes certain agricultural goods, industrial goods, and raw materials.

Imports of goods not on the permitted list are prohibited, with certain exceptions. In principle, imports must come directly from the country of origin, without the intervention of any foreign firm. The Ministry of Economy and Foreign Trade has the authority, however, to permit certain goods to be imported from countries other than the country of origin. Imports from the Syrian free zones are allowed for certain industrial goods and for goods with a free-zone value added of at least 40 percent.

All imports valued at more than LS 2,000 (LS 500 for imports from Lebanon) require licensing.[2] The foreign exchange requirements of the state trading agencies are met from the annual foreign exchange budget; these agencies automatically receive import licenses upon submission of documentation of their import requirements. A fee ranging from LS 25 to LS 200 is charged upon issuing the import license. Additionally, an import surcharge of 2 percent is charged on all imports; government imports and imports of certain essential items (including raw materials, petroleum, and petroleum products) are exempted. Imports for customs duty purposes are valued at the official exchange rate (as of 1993, this excludes items subject to duty at the rate of 75 percent or higher). Following the reform of import duties and surcharges in 1989, import tariffs range from zero to 200 percent, and all the previous special levies on imports have been replaced by a unified import surcharge ranging from 6 percent to 35 percent.[3] Private importers are authorized to import products specified on the permitted list by opening letters of credit at the Commercial Bank of Syria. However, when foreign exchange is not made available, private sector imports must be financed with the importers' own resources through external credit arrangements, foreign currency deposits maintained in Syria by nonresidents, the importers' own foreign exchange deposited in the Commercial Bank of Syria under the export proceeds retention regulations, or foreign exchange purchased from other private or mixed sector enterprises through the intermediary of the Commercial Bank of Syria at the rate in neighboring countries. Imports of a number of goods are restricted to specific methods of financing. For example, a number of imports may be imported using only foreign exchange generated through exports.

A non-interest-bearing advance import deposit is required. These deposits, which are held for six months, range from 10 percent to 40 percent of the value of imports. For several categories of goods, an advance import deposit equal to 100 percent of the value of the import, plus a 3 percent fee, are required.

---

[2]In accordance with the Arab Common Market Agreement, certain imports from Jordan, Lebanon, and Saudi Arabia are exempted from the licensing requirement; in these cases, an authorization to import is granted upon written request.

[3]The simple and weighted average (using 1987 import values as weights) of basic tariffs are 19.9 percent and 10.4 percent, respectively. The simple and weighted average of all import duties (defined as the sum of the basic tariffs, unified surcharges, and the 2 percent import license fee) are 35 percent and 22.8 percent, respectively.

Payments for Invisibles

Most payments for invisibles must be made at the rate in neighboring countries.

Residents traveling abroad may take with them foreign exchange, up to a limit of $2,000 a trip to all countries except Jordan and Lebanon. Of this amount, up to the equivalent of LS 5,000 a trip may be purchased at the rate in neighboring countries for travel to Arab countries (except Jordan and Lebanon) and up to the equivalent of LS 7,500 a trip for travel to non-Arab countries. Travelers to Jordan and Lebanon are not eligible for a foreign exchange travel allowance but may take with them up to LS 5,000 a trip in Syrian banknotes. With this exception, Syrian banknotes may not be taken out of the country. For children 10 years old or younger, the allowances are 50 percent of these amounts. Workers on secondment to a foreign country may take with them the entire amount of the allocations on producing proof that they have transferred foreign exchange from abroad; otherwise they may take with them only foreign exchange equivalent to 25 percent of the above-mentioned allocations. For travel to countries with which payments agreements are maintained, 50 percent of the travel allocation must be handled through the clearing account concerned (30 percent for travel on official business). On departure, residents of Syrian nationality must pay an exit tax of LS 600 a person if traveling to Arab countries and LS 1,500 a person for other destinations. An airport stamp tax of LS 200 is added to this tax.

Fixed allocations are maintained for other transactions in invisibles. A maximum of 60 percent of the salaries received by foreign technicians and experts employed in Syria, and 50 percent of the salaries of personnel of foreign diplomatic and international missions in Syria may be transferred. All other transactions require prior approval from the Exchange Office, with the exception of embassies and international organizations; such entities may convert up to 50 percent of transfers at the rate in neighboring countries and the remaining 50 percent at the official exchange rate. Nonresidents leaving the country are not allowed to reconvert Syrian currency into foreign exchange. The allowance for education abroad is subject to prior authorization from the Ministry of Higher Education. The transfer of funds abroad for family maintenance is limited to LS 250 for each transfer and is effected upon presentation of proof of need. The allowance for medical treatment must be authorized by the Ministry of Health. Remittances of profits from investment must be authorized by the Exchange Of-fice upon documentation (for example, a certificate confirming payment of income tax). Profits from projects approved by the Higher Committee for Investment under the new investment law can be repatriated freely.

Exports and Export Proceeds

Exports of wheat, barley, cotton, cotton yarn, and their derivatives are made by the government organizations dealing in cereals and cotton.[4] Petroleum exports are handled by the Petroleum Marketing Office. Exports of certain other commodities are also reserved for government agencies, state trading agencies, or specified companies. Exports of a few goods to all countries and all exports to Israel are prohibited. Exports under bilateral payments agreements and of all goods of foreign origin require licensing; no repatriation commitment is required, with the exporter repatriating and surrendering the proceeds to the Commercial Bank of Syria within 45 days of the date of shipment to Lebanon, within 3 months of the date of export shipment to other Arab countries, and within 4 months of the date of export shipment to other countries.

Public sector enterprises may retain 100 percent of their export proceeds in special foreign currency accounts with the Commercial Bank of Syria to finance imports on the permitted list; the retained portion of foreign exchange earnings can be deposited at the Commercial Bank of Syria in special foreign currency accounts until import payments are made or foreign exchange is voluntarily sold to the Commercial Bank of Syria. In the case of fruits and vegetables, public and private sector exporters may convert 100 percent of the proceeds at the rate in neighboring countries.

The Commercial Bank of Syria may accept prepayments for exports of Syrian products by residents and nonresidents without referring to the Central Bank of Syria. Subsidies for exports of ginned cotton from the Fund for the Development of Exports of Industrial Products have been suspended. A tax ranging from 9 percent to 12 percent ad valorem is charged on the value of exports of agricultural origin, except fruits and vegetables (which are exempt) and cotton (for which the export tax is 12.5 percent of the value of the exports (f.o.b.), less the cost of transportation within the Syrian Arab Republic). Exports of other agricultural commodities are subject to an ad valorem agricultural tax of 7 percent.

---

[4]The General Organization for Cereals Trade and Production and the General Organization for Cotton Ginning and Marketing.

Proceeds from Invisibles

Proceeds from transactions by the public sector must be sold at the official rate and those from transactions by the private sector must be sold at the rate in neighboring countries. Nonresidents entering Syria are permitted to bring in unlimited foreign exchange and Syrian pounds without declaration, if the amount does not exceed $5,000. All Syrian nationals employed by Arab, foreign, or international organizations within Syria and paid in full or in part in foreign currencies are required to exchange all such earnings at the Commercial Bank of Syria at the official exchange rate.

With few exceptions, non-Syrians visiting Syria are required to settle their bills in foreign exchange. All Syrian employees working abroad are subject to an annual tax of $50–$700, depending on their profession, and are allowed import tax exemptions on luxury items (valued between $500 and $7,000) if the equivalent funds are surrendered at the rate in neighboring countries. Syrian government employees who are on leave and working abroad are required to repatriate and convert a minimum of 25 percent of each year's earnings received in foreign exchange at the rate in neighboring countries.

Capital

All capital transfers to and from Syria by the public and private sector take place at the rate in neighboring countries. Exports of capital and foreign borrowings require the approval of the Exchange Office, as does most borrowing abroad.

Syria provides special facilities for the investment of funds of immigrants and of nationals of Arab states, including a seven-year tax exemption from all taxes in the tourism and agricultural industries. Under Investment Law No. 10, projects with minimum fixed assets of LS 10 million approved by the Government benefit from a number of exemptions from exchange and trade regulations, including exemption from customs duties of imports of required machinery, equipment, and vehicles. Mixed companies with at least 25 percent public participation are exempted from all taxes for seven years and private companies are exempted for five years; exemption periods may be extended by an additional two years if the company exports at least 50 percent of its output. Investors are permitted to hold foreign exchange accounts with the Commercial Bank of Syria to finance convertible currency requirements. These accounts comprise all capital and loans secured in foreign currency and 75 percent of foreign currency exports. Funds from such accounts may be provided on demand and may be used for the com-

pensation of foreign staff. Investors are free to repatriate foreign exchange capital after five years from the date of investment. Capital may be repatriated after six months if the project suffers from events beyond the control of the investor. All profits may be transferred freely. Foreign staff are entitled to transfer abroad 60 percent of salaries and 100 percent of severance pay.

Syria has investment guarantee agreements with France, the Federal Republic of Germany, Switzerland, and the United States. Nonresidents and foreign nationals may acquire immovable property in Syria only after presenting evidence that they have converted into Syrian pounds the foreign exchange equivalent of the price of the property at an authorized local bank.

Gold

Residents may hold, acquire, and sell manufactured gold in the Syrian Arab Republic without restriction. Domestic transactions in manufactured gold take place at free market prices that are in line with free market prices abroad. Imports of gold are exempt from import licensing, but exports are subject to export licensing. Foreign exchange proceeds from exports by residents must be surrendered. Exports of gold previously imported by nonresidents out of their resources abroad are subject to a repatriation commitment covering the cost of manufacturing and the profit earned.

Changes During 1994

Exchange Arrangement

January 1. The rate in neighboring countries was applied to some products for customs valuation purposes. Hence, three rates were used for customs valuation: the official exchange rate, a rate of LS 23.00 per US$1, and the rate in neighboring countries.

January 31. A new government fee exchange rate of LS 22.95/23.00 per US$1 was established, which covers fees on some government services and is used as an accounting rate for some government transactions.

Administration of Control

August 21. Restrictions on trade with South Africa were abolished.

Change During 1995

Exchange Arrangement

January 2. The government fee exchange rate was changed to LS 42.95/43.00 per US$1.

TAJIKISTAN

(Position as of December 31, 1994)

Exchange Arrangement

The currency of Tajikistan is the Ruble.[1] The exchange rate system consists of three rates. There is no organized interbank foreign exchange market, but commercial banks are free to trade in foreign exchange, and the rates quoted by commercial banks are based on supply and demand conditions. The National Bank of the Republic of Tajikistan (NBT) quotes twice a week an official representative exchange rate for the ruble based on the midpoint of buying and selling rates for the Russian ruble against the U.S. dollar in the Moscow Interbank Currency Exchange (MICEX), as established by the Central Bank of the Russian Federation. This official rate is used for official debt-service payments and all transactions involving the State Foreign Currency Fund (the holder of the official foreign exchange reserves of Tajikistan), including the required surrender of foreign currency export receipts. An official accounting exchange rate of 1.7562 rubles per US$1 is used for the valuation of foreign exchange reserves.

The spread between buying and selling rates of the commercial banks is regulated by the NBT and may not exceed 10 percent. In December 1994, the average commercial bank exchange rate ranged from Rub 4,688 to Rub 5,360 per US$1.

Administration of Control

Regulations and procedures for foreign exchange and ruble transactions between residents and non-residents were temporarily established by the National Bank of the Republic of Tajikistan in March 1993. The Ministry of Finance has responsibility for handling financial relations between Tajikistan and foreign countries, and the Vneshekonombank is its agent and the depository of the Foreign Currency Fund. Arrears are maintained with respect to external payments.

Prescription of Currency

Residents of Tajikistan may make and receive payments and transfers in any convertible currency as well as in rubles, but major transactions are au-thorized and monitored by the National Bank of the Republic of Tajikistan. Commercial banks authorized by the National Bank of the Republic of Tajikistan may use their correspondent accounts for commercial transactions with the countries of the former Soviet Union. Most enterprises arrange commercial transactions on a barter basis.[2]

Resident and Nonresident Accounts

Residents (natural or juridical persons) may open foreign exchange accounts in banks abroad with authorization from the National Bank of the Republic of Tajikistan and foreign currency accounts with licensed banks in Tajikistan without coordinating with or notifying the National Bank of the Republic of Tajikistan; the source of foreign exchange need not be revealed. Foreign exchange held in these accounts may be transferred to residents' bank accounts abroad opened according to established procedure. There are no limits on the amount of foreign currency banknotes that residents may purchase with rubles from licensed foreign exchange dealers. They may place these amounts in a foreign exchange account or use them for transactions with nonresidents.

Nonresident individuals may open foreign exchange accounts with licensed domestic banks and may transfer balances on these accounts abroad or convert them into rubles. Foreign governments, institutions, and enterprises may open accounts in rubles with domestic banks with the authorization of the National Bank of the Republic of Tajikistan and may use the balances for domestic transactions.

Imports and Exports

Payments for imports may be made in accordance with normal commercial practices, but most trade is bartered. Foreign exchange may be purchased from commercial banks at market rates or drawn from a domestic foreign exchange account. Imports are largely free of restriction, including tariffs or quotas, with the exception of firearms and narcotics, the importation of which is prohibited.

All exports require licenses. All exports are subject to a system of state order and quota. Exports are sub-

---

[1]Since January 8, 1994, post-1993 Russian rubles have been in circulation only in cash form, and only the very small denominations of pre-1993 Russian rubles remain in circulation. All other pre-1993 Russian rubles remain frozen in bank accounts.

[2]Tajikistan maintains bilateral trade agreements with the Baltic countries, Russia, and the other countries of the former Soviet Union.

ject to tariffs, ranging from 5 percent to 1,000 percent of their ruble value; specific tariffs, ranging from $10 to $25,000, are levied on exports sold for convertible currency.

Seventy percent of the proceeds from Tajikistan's main exports (excluding cotton and aluminum) received in convertible currency must be surrendered to the Republican Foreign Exchange Fund for rubles at the MICEX exchange rate prevailing on the day the proceeds are paid to exporters' accounts; 100 percent of the proceeds from cotton and aluminum must be surrendered. All other exports are subject to the surrender requirement of 30 percent. Foreign exchange proceeds from exports must be transferred to authorized banks within 30 days of receipt.

The exportation of cotton is a government monopoly.

Payments for and Proceeds from Invisibles

Residents traveling abroad for tourism purposes are granted an allowance of $400 a person a year. Foreign exchange needed for public or private business or other travel (e.g., education) are also subject to limits, which vary according to destination. Minimum spending or conversion requirements for nonresident travelers do not exist. Nonresidents from outside the Baltic countries, Russia, and the other countries of the former Soviet Union must pay for transportation and hotel services in convertible currencies.

Capital

Inward and outward capital transactions require licenses issued by the National Bank of the Republic of Tajikistan. There are no limits on inward capital transactions. Foreign investors are required to register with the Ministry of Finance. There are no restrictions on the repatriation of foreign direct investment or profits. Profits may be reinvested in Tajikistan, held in banks in rubles or foreign currency, or transferred abroad.

Changes During 1994

Imports and Exports

February 1. The surrender requirement rate for monopoly products other than cotton and aluminum was reduced to 70 percent from 100 percent.

December 3. A presidential decree placing the cotton trade under the sole control of a government agency, with effect from January 1, 1995, was announced.

TANZANIA

(Position as of December 31, 1994)

Exchange Arrangement

The currency of Tanzania is the Tanzania Shilling, the external value of which is determined in the interbank market. The exchange rates for other currencies are determined on the basis of the cross rates of the U.S. dollar against the currencies concerned in international markets.[1] On December 30, 1994, the exchange rate in the interbank market was T Sh 528.74 per US$1. Certain transactions may be effected through foreign exchange bureaus that are authorized to buy and sell foreign exchange at freely negotiated rates.

The Bank of Tanzania (BOT) does not offer forward cover against exchange rate risk. However, authorized dealers may, at their discretion, enter into forward contracts for purchases and sales of foreign currencies with their customers in export and import transactions. There are no taxes or subsidies on purchases or sales of foreign exchange.

Administration of Control

The Minister of Finance has delegated authority to administer exchange control to the Bank of Tanzania. In October 1993, the Bank of Tanzania delegated authority to make payments abroad to the five authorized banks—the National Bank of Commerce, the Cooperative and Rural Development Bank, the People's Bank of Zanzibar, the Meridien Bank, and the Standard Chartered Bank, as well as to authorized foreign exchange bureaus; control over exchange operations in Zanzibar is exercised by the People's Bank of Zanzibar.

Zanzibar administers an independent system of foreign trade controls through its Board of Trade; all imports and the principal exports are effected by the state trading agencies (Bizanje and the Zanzibar State Trading Corporation).

Prescription of Currency

Settlements between residents of Tanzania and nonresidents must be made either in convertible currencies or in Tanzania shillings by debit or credit to a convertible nonresident account.

Nonresident Accounts

Nonresident accounts are those maintained by foreign nationals temporarily residing in Tanzania; by firms, companies, or other organizations registered or incorporated outside Tanzania; and by foreign diplomatic missions, the United Nations, or other international organizations and their officials in Tanzania. These accounts are divided into two broad categories: convertible and nonconvertible. Balances on convertible accounts are eligible for transfer from Tanzania without any further scrutiny by or approval from the Bank of Tanzania. The balances of nonconvertible accounts may be transferred from Tanzania after approval is obtained from the Bank of Tanzania. There are six subcategories of nonresident accounts: external, shipping/airline, special, ordinary, expatriate, and unspecified. Tanzanian nationals and foreign nationals who usually reside in Tanzania may maintain nonresident accounts in the form of a current, savings, or deposit account.

Imports and Import Payments

Certain imports to the mainland from any source may be prohibited for reasons of health or security. The import-licensing requirement was abolished during the last quarter of 1993. For informational purposes only, imports of goods with a value exceeding $2,000 require an import declaration form and a preshipment inspection document called a Clean Report of Finding.

Customs tariffs are levied on the c.i.f. value of imports, and the tariff schedule is ad valorem. The tariff regime comprises four bands of 5 percent, 20 percent, 30 percent, and 40 percent, with a minimum rate of 5 percent. Certain imports, including those for new investments, are exempt from tariffs. Specific duties are levied on alcoholic beverages, tobacco, and petroleum products. Statutory exemptions are granted for the diplomatic corps; religious, educational, and welfare institutions; aircraft engines; aviation fuel; scientific, educational, and religious films; printed matter; cable and telephone material; sewing machines; and timber used by mining companies. Discretionary full or partial ex-

---

[1]Australian dollars, Austrian schillings, Belgian francs, Canadian dollars, Comorian francs, Danish kroner, deutsche mark, Ethiopian birr, French francs, Indian rupees, Italian lire, Japanese yen, Kenya shillings, Lesotho maloti, Malawian kwacha, Mauritian rupees, Mozambican meticais, Netherlands guilders, Norwegian kroner, Pakistan rupees, pounds sterling, Rwanda francs, Somali shillings, Swaziland emalangeni, Swedish kronor, Swiss francs, Uganda shillings, Zambian kwacha, and Zimbabwe dollars.

emptions are allowed by the Minister of Finance if imports are considered to be in the public interest.

All imports with a value exceeding $500 are subject to compulsory preshipment inspection by international agencies for quantity, quality, and price; imports with a value greater than $20,000 must be financed with letters of credit unless specific approval is granted from the Bank of Tanzania. All merchandise imports to the mainland must be insured with the National Insurance Corporation of Tanzania, and premiums must be paid in Tanzania shillings. All imports to Zanzibar are made by Bizanje. Most imports, irrespective of their origin, are subject to a sales tax at rates ranging up to 30 percent of the c.i.f. value plus import duty. This tax is also assessed on sales of domestic products.

Payments for Invisibles

There are no limits on purchases of foreign exchange for travel, education, and other invisible payments and transfers. Commercial banks and foreign exchange bureaus have the authority to approve remittances abroad of up to one-third of the salary, throughout the period of employment, of foreigners temporarily working in Tanzania under contract and having a firm commitment to leave the country. Applications to remit more than one-third of a salary, or more than T Sh 6,000 a month, are considered on their merits by the Bank of Tanzania.

A traveler may take out of the country up to T Sh 1,000 in domestic currency. Nonresident travelers may take out foreign currency notes, traveler's checks, and letters of credit for any remaining amount of the foreign exchange brought in.

Exports and Export Proceeds

With effect from June 1, 1993, export licenses have been required for only a few items for health, sanitary, or national heritage reasons. All principal exports of Zanzibar are sold abroad by the Zanzibar State Trading Corporation.

Export proceeds must be repatriated within two months of the date of exportation, but they need not be surrendered. However, on application to the Bank of Tanzania, this period may be extended.

Proceeds from Invisibles

Receipts from invisibles must be sold to an authorized dealer. Travelers may freely bring in convertible foreign currency notes; a returning traveler may bring in Tanzania shilling notes and coins up to T Sh 1,000.

Capital

Capital transfers to all countries are subject to approval by commercial banks or the Investment Promotion Center. Gifts to nonresidents require the prior approval of the Commissioner of Customs.

Investment of foreign funds is not restricted in Tanzania, but, to ensure eventual repatriation, these investments must be recognized by the Investment Promotion Center, and a certificate of status as an approved enterprise under the National Investment Promotion Act of 1990 should be obtained from the Ministry of Finance. The act distinguishes three areas for foreign investments: (1) controlled areas, which are reserved for public investment or joint public and private enterprises; (2) reserved areas, which are reserved exclusively for investment by the public sector; and (3) areas that are reserved exclusively for Tanzanian citizens. Registered foreign investors are permitted to use up to 50 percent of their net foreign exchange earnings for debt servicing or remittances of profits and dividends.

All imports and exports of securities require approval. Approval is freely granted for the purchase of Tanzanian securities by nonresidents from residents, provided that payment is received in foreign exchange. Income from such securities is remittable, as are the proceeds from resale. Purchases of securities outside Tanzania by residents are not permitted.

All loans or overdrafts from residents to nonresidents or to foreign-controlled resident bodies require approval from the Bank of Tanzania.

Gold

Commemorative gold coins are legal tender but do not circulate within Tanzania. Residents may hold and acquire gold in any form at home or abroad. Import licenses are not required.

Changes During 1994

Exchange Arrangement

June 30. An interbank foreign exchange market replaced the foreign exchange auctions, and the official rate was based on the rate emerging from the trading sessions.

Administration of Control

December 30. Restrictions arising from bilateral payments arrangements with Burundi, Mozambique, and Zimbabwe were eliminated.

Imports and Import Payments

February 1. The negative list for imports was further shortened to cover products that would be prohibited from importation only for health reasons.

Payments for Invisibles

July 1. The limits on purchases of foreign exchange for travel, education, and other invisible payments and transfers were eliminated.

THAILAND

(Position as of December 31, 1994)

Exchange Arrangement

The currency of Thailand is the Thai Baht. The external value of the baht is determined on the basis of the relationship of the baht to a weighted basket of currencies of Thailand's major trading partners and on other considerations. The Exchange Equalization Fund announces the daily buying and selling rates for the U.S. dollar, the intervention currency, for transactions between itself and commercial banks; it also announces daily minimum buying and maximum selling rates that commercial banks must observe when dealing with the public in Brunei dollars, deutsche mark, Hong Kong dollars, Indonesian rupiah, Japanese yen, Malaysian ringgit, Philippine pesos, pounds sterling, Singapore dollars, and U.S. dollars.

On December 30, 1994, the middle official rate was B 25.09 per US$1. There are no taxes or subsidies on purchases or sales of foreign exchange. Forward exchange transactions are carried out between commercial banks and customers and among the commercial banks. All forward transactions must be related to underlying trade and financial transactions. The open foreign exchange positions of commercial banks are restricted by the Bank of Thailand. The forward premium in the baht-U.S. dollar rate is freely determined and usually reflects interest differentials between the two currencies.

Thailand formally accepted the obligations of Article VIII, Sections 2, 3, and 4 of the Fund Agreement, as from May 4, 1990.

Administration of Control

Exchange control is administered by the Bank of Thailand on behalf of the Ministry of Finance; the Bank of Thailand delegates responsibility to authorized banks (commercial banks) for approving most transactions. Apart from authorized banks, authorized companies and authorized persons are also allowed to deal in foreign exchange operations, although their activities are limited to the buying and selling of foreign banknotes and traveler's checks up to a set amount prescribed by the Bank of Thailand. Import and export licenses are issued by the Ministry of Commerce.

Prescription of Currency

There are no special requirements for currencies that can be used in settlements with foreign countries; most payments are made in U.S. dollars.

Nonresident Accounts

Accounts in foreign currencies are designated as foreign currency accounts. No restrictions are placed on the opening of foreign currency accounts as long as the funds originate abroad. Foreign currency borrowed by nonresidents from authorized banks may be freely deposited in these accounts. Balances on these accounts earn interest and may be transferred abroad without restriction.

Nonresidents may also open nonresident baht accounts. These accounts may be debited without restriction, and foreign currency arising from withdrawals from these accounts can be freely deposited in foreign currency accounts. Nonresident baht accounts may also be credited freely with payments for goods and services by residents and with funds transferred from other nonresident baht accounts. These accounts may also be freely credited with proceeds from the sale of foreign currency withdrawn from nonresidents' foreign currency accounts, as well as baht proceeds borrowed from authorized banks.

Imports and Import Payments

Most commodities may be imported freely, but import licenses are required for certain goods. Imports of some goods are prohibited for protective or social reasons. Importers of tea leaf, tea dust, and skimmed milk are required to purchase a proportionate quantity of the same type of goods produced in Thailand. A few agricultural goods are subject to temporary import surcharges.

Importers are required to complete foreign exchange transaction forms for transactions whose values exceed B 500,000 when submitting the import entry form at customs, except for certain goods, such as military equipment imported by the Ministry of Defense, donated goods, and samples. Payments for imports may be made through any authorized bank. Importers may freely purchase foreign currency or draw foreign exchange from their own foreign currency accounts for payments.

Payments for Invisibles

Remittances abroad of service fees, royalties, insurance premiums, educational expenses, and family maintenance are permitted without restriction. Remittances of dividends and profits on all bona fide investments may be made freely. Authorized banks are also permitted to sell up to $100,000 a person a year in foreign exchange for remittances to families and relatives living abroad and up to $1 million a person a year for remittances from the personal assets of Thai emigrants who have permanent residence permits abroad. Foreign exchange transaction forms must be completed for transactions involving amounts of more than $5,000. Authorized money changers are allowed to sell up to $2,000, or its equivalent, a person in foreign exchange.

Travelers may take out domestic currency up to B 50,000; those traveling to Viet Nam and the countries bordering Thailand are allowed to take out or remit a maximum of B 500,000. Authorized banks are permitted to sell foreign exchange in foreign banknotes for purposes of travel without any restriction. Nonresidents may take out foreign currency notes up to the amount brought into Thailand.

Exports and Export Proceeds

Certain categories of exports are subject to licensing and quantitative restrictions and, in a few cases, to prior approval, irrespective of destination.[1] All other products may be exported freely. Exporters are required to complete foreign exchange transaction forms for transactions involving more than B 500,000 when submitting the export entry form at customs. Export proceeds exceeding B 500,000 must be received within 180 days of shipment. Exporters are required to surrender foreign exchange proceeds to authorized banks or deposit them in foreign currency accounts with authorized banks in Thailand within 15 days of receipt, except that they are allowed to use foreign exchange proceeds to service external obligations without having to first surrender or deposit them in domestic banking accounts.

Proceeds from Invisibles

Foreign exchange earnings from invisibles must be surrendered to authorized banks or retained in foreign currency accounts with authorized banks in Thailand within 15 days of receipt. Travelers passing through Thailand, foreign embassies, and international organizations are exempted from this requirement. Authorized money changers are allowed to purchase foreign currency notes and coins or traveler's checks in foreign currencies, but the latter must be resold to authorized banks within 15 days of purchase. Travelers may bring in domestic or foreign bank notes and coins without restriction.

Capital

Capital investments in Thailand through equity participation or portfolio investments are permitted freely. Foreign investments in Thailand that receive promotional privileges from the Board of Investment under the Investment Promotion Act (B.E. 2520) are accorded various incentives and special benefits.

Foreign capital may be brought into the country and loans contracted without restriction, but proceeds must be surrendered to authorized banks or deposited in foreign currency accounts with authorized banks in Thailand within 15 days of receipt. Repatriation of investment funds, loan repayments, and interest payments may be made without restriction. Inflows and outflows of funds exceeding $5,000 or its equivalent are subject to completion of foreign exchange transaction forms. External borrowing by the public sector must be approved by the Foreign Debt Committee.

Authorized banks in Thailand may lend to nonresidents in foreign currency without restriction. Foreign currency loans may be extended to residents for outward remittance or domestic use. If loans are used domestically, resident borrowers are required to convert the foreign currency obtained into baht, which they are not allowed to deposit in foreign currency accounts.

Direct investments abroad by Thai residents or lending to companies abroad that have at least 25 percent equity participation by Thai residents is permitted up to $10 million a year without authorization from the Bank of Thailand. Portfolio investments and purchases of properties abroad by Thai residents require approval from the Bank of Thailand.

Gold

Residents may hold and negotiate domestically gold jewelry, gold coins, and unworked gold. Purchases or sales of gold on commodity futures exchanges are prohibited. Imports and exports of gold other than gold jewelry are prohibited unless a license has been obtained from the Ministry of Finance or the transaction is made on behalf of the monetary authorities. Foreign tourists may take out precious stones, gold or platinum ornaments, and other articles without restriction. Exports of gold bullion are prohibited. Exporters and importers of gold ornaments exceeding B 500,000 in value must complete foreign exchange transaction forms at customs when submitting import or export entry forms. Gold ornaments are not subject to export duty or taxes.

---

[1]These include sorghum, rice, canned tuna, all types of sugar, and certain types of coal, charcoal, and textile products.

Changes During 1994

Nonresident Accounts

February 2. Foreign currency borrowed by residents from the Bangkok International Banking Facility, foreign currency borrowed by nonresidents from authorized banks, and foreign currency arising from withdrawals from nonresident baht accounts may be freely deposited in foreign currency accounts. Nonresident baht accounts may be freely credited with baht resulting from the sale of foreign currency withdrawn from nonresidents' foreign currency accounts, as well as baht proceeds borrowed from authorized banks.

Payments for Invisibles

February 2. The limit on domestic currencies that persons traveling to Viet Nam and the countries bordering Thailand may remit or take out was increased to B 500,000 a person from B 250,000 a person.

Exports and Export Proceeds

February 2. Resident exporters were permitted to use foreign exchange originating from abroad to service external obligations without surrendering or depositing it in domestic banking accounts.

Capital

February 2. The ceiling on the amount authorized banks are permitted to lend to nonresidents in foreign currency was eliminated. The maximum amount of foreign direct investments or loans that domestic residents may provide to their affiliates without authorization from the Bank of Thailand was increased to $10 million a year from $5 million a year.

April 21. Finance and securities companies were required to hold a daily long and short foreign exchange position not exceeding 25 percent and 20 percent, respectively, of first-tier capital funds.

November 4. The average weekly net long and short foreign exchange position that authorized banks are required to hold were changed to 20 percent and 15 percent, respectively, of first-tier capital funds from 25 percent and 20 percent, or $5 million, whichever is larger.

TOGO

(Position as of December 31, 1994)

Exchange Arrangement

The currency of Togo is the CFA Franc,[1] which is pegged to the French franc, the intervention currency, at the fixed rate of CFAF 1 per F 0.01. The official buying and selling rates are CFAF 100 per F 1. Exchange rates for other currencies are derived from the rate for the currency concerned in the Paris exchange market and the fixed rate between the French franc and the CFA franc. Banks levy a proportional commission of 2.50 per mil with a maximum collection of CFAF 100 and a freely determined charge for each transaction. The proportional commission must be surrendered to the Treasury.[2] There are no taxes or subsidies on purchases or sales of foreign exchange. The contracting of forward exchange cover requires the prior authorization of the Minister of Economy and Finance, and permission may be granted only in respect of the importation of certain clearly specified goods. The maturity of exchange contracts can be no more than three months for goods deemed essential or strategic and one month for all other goods. There is no official currency swap scheme or guaranteed exchange rate for debt servicing.

With the exception of measures relating to gold; the repatriation of export proceeds; the issuing, advertising, or offering for sale of securities; capital assets; and the soliciting of funds for investments abroad, Togo's exchange controls do not apply to (1) France (and its overseas departments and territories) and Monaco; and (2) all other countries whose bank of issue is linked to the French Treasury by an Operations Account (Benin, Burkina Faso, Cameroon, Central African Republic, Chad, Comoros, Congo, Côte d'Ivoire, Equatorial Guinea, Gabon, Mali, Niger, and Senegal). Hence, all payments to these countries may be made freely. All other countries are considered foreign countries.

Administration of Control

Exchange control is administered by the Ministry of Economy and Finance, which also supervises borrowing abroad; the issuing, advertising, or offering for sale of foreign securities in Togo; inward direct investment and all outward investment; and the soliciting of funds in Togo for placement in foreign countries. The Foreign Exchange Legal Commission has been created to advise the Minister of Economy and Finance on requests to settle cases involving violations of foreign exchange regulations for amounts of CFAF 500,000 or more and on specific requests from violators of foreign exchange regulations. Some of the approval authority in respect of exchange control has been delegated to authorized intermediaries and the BCEAO. The BCEAO is authorized to collect, either directly through economic agents or through the banks, financial institutions, Postal and Telecommunications Office (Office des postes et télécommunications), and offices of government ministries, any information necessary to compile balance of payments statistics. The forwarding and receipt through the mail by authorized intermediaries of banknotes, other than those issued by the BCEAO, are subject to control by the BCEAO. The forwarding and receipt through the mail, by authorized intermediaries of banknotes issued by the BCEAO are prohibited. All exchange transactions relating to foreign countries must be effected through authorized banks, the Postal and Telecommunications Office, or the BCEAO. All required import licenses and virtually all required export licenses are issued by the Foreign Trade Division in the Ministry of Commerce and Transport, except those for gold, which are granted by the Ministry of Economy and Finance. Exports of locally manufactured products, cereals and other food crops, and imports of most products are not subject to licensing.

Prescription of Currency

Because Togo is an Operations Account country, settlements with France (as defined above), Monaco, and the Operations Account countries are made in CFA francs, French francs, or the currency of any other Operations Account country. Current payments involving The Gambia, Ghana, Guinea, Guinea-Bissau, Liberia, Mauritania, Nigeria, and Sierra Leone are normally effected through the West African Clearing House. Settlements with all other countries are usually effected through correspondent banks in France, in any of the currencies of

---

[1]The CFA franc is issued by the Central Bank of West African States (BCEAO) and is the common currency in Benin, Burkina Faso, Côte d'Ivoire, Mali, Niger, Senegal, and Togo.

[2]The commission on transfers between member countries of the BCEAO is freely fixed by the banks.

those countries, or in French francs through foreign accounts in francs.

Nonresident Accounts

Because the BCEAO has suspended the repurchase of BCEAO banknotes circulating outside the territories of the CFA franc zone, foreign accounts in francs may not be credited or debited with BCEAO banknotes without authorization.

Imports and Import Payments

All imports may be made freely, with the following exceptions, for which licenses are required: (1) cement, corrugated iron, concrete reinforcement, and wheat flour, imports of which are subject to the prior issuance of a license by the Ministry of Commerce and Transport; (2) pharmaceuticals, explosives, and firearms; and (3) imports of potatoes, which may be prohibited during the period when local production is adequate to meet local demand (between August and February).

The following taxes are imposed on all imports: (1) a statistical tax of 3 percent; (2) a fiscal import duty of 5 percent to 35 percent; (3) a general tax of 5 percent to 30 percent on businesses; and (4) a temporary tax of 15 percent on imports of locally produced goods. With the exception of the general business tax, which is assessed on the basis of the c.i.f. value of imports inclusive of fiscal import duties, all other taxes are levied on c.i.f. values.

All import transactions must be domiciled with an authorized bank when their value exceeds CFAF 500,000, with the exception of imports not involving payment or financing through the Postal and Telecommunications Office and certain imports of a private nature. Importers may purchase foreign exchange for import payments after establishing bank payment order accounts (*dossiers de domiciliation*) and submitting supporting documents, but not earlier than eight days before shipment if a documentary credit is opened, or on the due date of payment if the products have already been imported. Purchases of foreign exchange for down payments are subject to prior authorization from the Minister of Economy and Finance; such authorization may be granted only on the date payment is due and only for up to 30 percent for each transaction involving capital goods and up to 10 percent for other transactions. For all import operations exceeding CFAF 200,000, merchandise insurance must be taken out and domiciled with an approved insurance company in Togo. Inspection of the quality, quantity, and price of imports has been suspended.

Payments for Invisibles

Payments for invisibles to France (as defined above), Monaco, and the Operations Account countries are permitted freely; those to other countries are subject to approval. Payments for invisibles related to trade are permitted by a general authorization when the basic trade transaction has been approved or does not require authorization. Transfers of income accruing to nonresidents in the form of profits, dividends, and royalties are also generally permitted.

Residents traveling for tourism or business purposes to countries in the franc zone that are not members of the WAMU are allowed to take out up to the equivalent of CFAF 2 million in banknotes other than CFA banknotes; amounts in excess of this limit may be taken out in the form of other means of payment. The allowances for travel to countries outside the franc zone are subject to the following regulations: (1) for tourist travel, CFAF 500,000 without limit on the number of trips or differentiation by the age of the traveler; (2) for business travel, CFAF 75,000 a day for up to one month, corresponding to a maximum of CFAF 2.25 million (business travel allowances may be combined with tourist allowances); (3) allowances in excess of these limits must be authorized by the respective ministries of finance or, by delegation, the BCEAO; and (4) credit cards, which must be issued by resident financial intermediaries and authorized by the respective ministers of finance may be used up to the ceilings indicated above for tourist and business travel. Upon arrival at customs, returning resident travelers are required to declare all means of payment in their possession and must surrender within eight days all means of payment exceeding the equivalent of CFAF 25,000. All resident travelers, when traveling to countries that are not members of the WAMU, must declare in writing at the time of departure all means of payment at their disposal. Nonresident travelers may re-export means of payment other than banknotes issued abroad and registered in their name, subject to documentation that they had used funds drawn from a foreign account in CFA francs or with other foreign exchange to purchase these means of payment. The re-exportation of foreign banknotes is allowed up to the equivalent of CFAF 250,000; the re-exportation of foreign banknotes above these ceilings requires documentation demonstrating either the importation of foreign banknotes or their purchase against other means of payment registered in the name of the traveler or through the use of nonresident deposits lodged in local banks.

The transfer of the entire net salary of a foreign national working in Togo is permitted upon presentation of the appropriate pay voucher, residence permit, or work permit, provided that the transfer takes place within three months of the pay period.

Exports and Export Proceeds

Exports to all countries require licenses in certain cases. The Togolese Office of Phosphates has a monopoly over the exportation of phosphates, and the Office of Togolese Agricultural Products has a monopoly over the exportation of cocoa, coffee, and cotton fiber. Exports of cereals are permitted, but licenses are generally granted only in years when the Technical Committee for Cereal Exports determines that there is a food grain surplus. The Technical Committee meets twice a year—at the beginning of March to make forecasts of the exportable surplus and again before November 10 to establish the actual export ceilings. The due date for payment for exports to foreign countries, including the Operations Account Area, may not be later than 180 days after the arrival of the goods at their destination, and the proceeds must be surrendered within a month of the due date to authorized intermediaries; authorized diamond purchasing officers, however, may retain foreign currency proceeds in foreign currency accounts with authorized banks in Togo. All export transactions, including those with the Operations Account countries, must be domiciled with an authorized bank when their value exceeds CFAF 500,000. The domiciling bank is responsible for ensuring effective repatriation of such receipts through the BCEAO.

Proceeds from Invisibles

Proceeds from invisibles transactions with France (as defined above), Monaco, and the Operations Account countries may be retained. All amounts due from residents of other countries in respect of services, and all income earned in those countries from foreign assets, must be collected and surrendered within one month of the due date or the date of receipt. Resident and nonresident travelers may bring in any amount of banknotes and coins issued by the BCEAO, the Bank of France, or any institute of issue maintaining an Operations Account with the French Treasury, as well as any amount of foreign banknotes and coins (except gold coins) of countries outside the Operations Account Area. Residents bringing in foreign banknotes and foreign currency traveler's checks in excess of CFAF 25,000 must sell them to an authorized bank within eight days.

Capital

Capital movements between Togo and France (as defined above), Monaco, and the other countries of the Operations Account Area are free of exchange control; capital transfers to all other countries require exchange control approval from the Minister of Economy and Finance and are restricted, but capital receipts from such countries are permitted freely.

Special controls (in addition to any exchange control requirements that may be applicable) are maintained over borrowing abroad, inward direct investment, and all outward investment; the issuing, advertising, or offering for sale of foreign securities in Togo; and the soliciting of funds in Togo for placement abroad. Such operations require prior authorization from the Minister of Economy and Finance. Exempt from authorization, however, are operations in connection with (1) loans backed by a guarantee from the Togolese Government; and (2) shares that are identical to, or can be substituted for, securities whose issuing, advertising, or offering for sale in Togo has already been authorized. With the exception of controls relating to foreign securities and the soliciting of funds in Togo, these measures do not apply to relations with France (as defined above), Monaco, member countries of the West African Monetary Union, and the Operations Account countries.

All investments abroad by residents of Togo require prior authorization from the Minister of Economy and Finance,[3] and at least 75 percent of such investments must be financed by foreign borrowing. Foreign direct investments in Togo[4] must be reported to the Minister of Economy and Finance before they are made. The Minister may request postponement of the projects within two months of receiving the declaration. Total or partial liquidation of any inward direct investment or any outward investment also requires prior reporting to the Minister of Economy and Finance. Both the making and the liquidation of investments, whether Togolese investments abroad or foreign investments in Togo, must be reported to the Minister of Economy and Finance and to the BCEAO within 20 days of each operation. (Direct investments are investments implying control of a company or enterprise. Mere participation is not considered direct investment,

---

[3]Including investments made through foreign companies directly or indirectly controlled by persons in Togo and those made by branches or subsidiaries abroad of companies in Togo.

[4]Including those made by companies in Togo directly or indirectly under foreign control and those made by branches or subsidiaries of foreign companies in Togo.

provided that it does not exceed 20 percent of the capital of a company whose shares are quoted on a stock exchange.)

Borrowing by residents from nonresidents requires prior authorization from the Minister of Economy and Finance. The following are, however, exempt from this authorization: (1) loans constituting a direct investment, which are subject to prior declaration, as indicated above; (2) loans contracted by authorized banks; (3) loans taken up either by industrial firms to finance operations abroad or by approved international merchanting houses to finance imports or exports; and (4) in certain circumstances, any other loans, provided that the outstanding amount for any one borrower does not exceed CFAF 100 million. The repayment of any foreign borrowing requires the prior authorization of the Minister of Economy and Finance; exempt from this requirement are loans constituting a direct investment, loans taken up by authorized banks, and loans exempted by the Minister. Lending abroad is subject only to special authorization from the Directorate of Economy.

Under the provisions of the general tax legislation, certain fiscal benefits are accorded to specified new investment (foreign and domestic) in both new and existing enterprises. In addition, certain enterprises, in accordance with their importance to the economic development of Togo, may, for a specified number of years, be granted special privileges relating to the maintenance of existing taxes and exemption from import duties. Such privileges are negotiated by the Government and the investor.

The Investment Code adopted on October 31, 1989 aims at promoting local employment and small and medium-size Togolese enterprises and at developing local resources. To obtain the tax benefits under this code, firms must (1) provide an amount from equity equivalent to at least 25 percent of the amount net of taxes to finance new projects (excluding working capital), and (2) pay at least 60 percent of their wage bill to workers who are nationals of Togo. Tax benefits include primarily exemptions from the minimum *forfait* tax and corporate income taxes for five years for small and medium-size enterprises, seven years for enterprises that process domestic raw materials, and three years for other enterprises. The code guarantees the right of free transfer abroad of capital invested in Togo and of all investment income therefrom.

Gold

Residents are free to hold, acquire, and dispose of gold in any form in Togo. The importation and exportation of gold to or from any other country require prior authorization from the Minister of Economy and Finance. Exempt from this requirement are (1) imports and exports by or on behalf of the Treasury or the BCEAO; (2) imports and exports of manufactured articles containing a minor quantity of gold (such as gold-filled or gold-plated articles); and (3) imports and exports by travelers of gold objects up to a combined weight of 500 grams. Both licensed and exempt imports of gold are subject to customs declaration.

Changes During 1994

Exchange Arrangement

January 12. The CFA franc was devalued to CFAF 100 per F 1 from CFAF 50 per F 1.

TONGA

(Position as of December 31, 1994)

Exchange Arrangement

The currency of Tonga is the Pa'anga. Its external value is determined on the basis of a weighted basket of currencies, comprising the U.S. dollar, the Australian dollar, and the New Zealand dollar. These weights are related to the shares of the currencies in Tonga's international transactions. The National Reserve Bank of Tonga (the central bank) maintains buying and selling rates for the U.S. dollar, the intervention currency. The commercial banks quote daily rates for 16 currencies[1] on the basis of their values against the pa'anga. The spread between the commercial banks' buying and selling rates is approximately 2 percent. Sales of foreign exchange are at a premium of approximately 1.5 percent, and purchases are at a discount of approximately 0.5 percent. On December 30, 1994, the central bank's buying and selling rates for the U.S. dollar were T$1.256 and T$1.258, respectively, per US$1.[2] There are no taxes or subsidies on purchases or sales of foreign exchange. Commercial banks are allowed to provide forward exchange cover, but their gross foreign exchange liabilities must not exceed US$1 million.

Tonga formally accepted the obligations of Article VIII, Sections 2, 3, and 4 of the Fund Agreement, as from March 22, 1991.

Administration of Control

Tonga's trade and payments system is relatively free of controls. Foreign exchange transactions are regulated by the National Reserve Bank of Tonga and the Ministry of Finance.

Prescription of Currency

There are no regulations prescribing the currencies that can be used in particular transactions.

Imports and Import Payments

Licenses are required for all imports, although these are generally issued freely. Import quotas apply only to fresh eggs and are intended to protect domestic producers. The importation of certain items is restricted for cultural or environmental reasons or to protect the health and safety of residents. Tariffs, which range up to 35 percent and apply to most private sector imports, are aimed primarily at increasing revenues, but protective tariffs are levied on a few items, such as beer, paint, and wire fencing. Tariffs are levied at an ad valorem rate on the c.i.f. value of imports, except for a few items (petroleum, tobacco products, and alcoholic beverages), which are subject to either specific tariffs or ad valorem rates ranging up to 300 percent of the c.i.f. value, whichever is higher. The maximum tariff rate, which is levied on motor vehicles, is 45 percent. Goods imported by the reigning monarch, by the government and the public sector, and by diplomatic missions, goods imported under certain technical assistance agreements, and personal effects are exempt from tariffs. Imports are also subject to a 20 percent port and services tax, except for items under the Industrial Development Incentives (IDI) Act, which qualify for concessional rates, and imports of government and quasi-government organizations, which are exempt.

Exports and Export Proceeds

All export proceeds must be repatriated within 12 months, but this regulation is not enforced. Commercial banks must surrender all of their foreign exchange, apart from small working balances, to the central bank. Licenses are required for all exports, except for shipments weighing less than 10 kilograms. With the exception of squash, which is subject to an export quota,[3] the authorities maintain a liberal attitude toward granting those licenses. Effective January 1, 1992, the monopoly of the Commodities Board on exports of coconut and coconut derivatives, vanilla, and bananas was abolished.

Payments for and Proceeds from Invisibles

Commercial banks are authorized to provide foreign exchange for invisible payments up to T$1,000 a year. The Ministry of Finance may approve requests for larger amounts upon submission of satisfactory documentary evidence that the underlying

---

[1]Australian dollars, Canadian dollars, deutsche mark, Fiji dollars, French francs, Hong Kong dollars, Indian rupees, Italian lire, Japanese yen, Netherlands guilders, New Zealand dollars, pounds sterling, Singapore dollars, Swedish kronor, Swiss francs, and U.S. dollars.

[2]For transactions with the commercial banks. Buying and selling rates were T$1.253 and T$1.261, respectively, per US$1 for transactions with other organizations, including the Government.

[3]The export quota applies only to the October–December season and not to the small May crop.

transaction is a bona fide current international transaction. Such approvals are routinely granted without undue delay.

Shipping and airline agencies may remit income earned from activities in Tonga upon producing income statements relating to local business activities that have been submitted to their respective head offices.

Capital

The authorities maintain a liberal attitude toward foreign direct investment, although so far such investment remains small. Foreign investors are required to apply for licenses, with approval depending on the type of investment. Investors are permitted a wide range of activities, but activities that complement domestic production rather than compete with it are generally preferred, and selected sectors are reserved for Tongan nationals. Under the IDI Act, foreign investors involved in manufacturing are allowed duty-free imports of capital inputs, a maximum 15-year tax holiday, and, on a case-by-case basis, repatriation of profits and capital.

In principle, Tongan residents are not permitted to acquire financial assets abroad, although this restriction is not enforced. Direct investment abroad requires the approval of the Ministry of Finance.

Changes During 1994

Exports and Export Proceeds

July 1. The quota for squash exports during the October–December season was set at 17,000 metric tons.

TRINIDAD AND TOBAGO

(Position as of January 31, 1995)

Exchange Arrangement

The currency of Trinidad and Tobago is the Trinidad and Tobago Dollar. The exchange rate of the Trinidad and Tobago dollar is determined in the interbank market on the basis of supply and demand conditions. On December 31, 1994, the buying and selling rates were TT$5.82 and TT$5.93, respectively, per US$1. Banks are allowed to conduct foreign exchange transactions, both spot and forward, with the public without limitation. Commercial banks must notify the Central Bank of Trinidad and Tobago in advance of any planned significant adjustment to the exchange rate. At the end of each trading day, the Central Bank publishes a nominal rate for the Trinidad and Tobago dollar against each of the major currencies, based on a weighted average of the rates at which these currencies have been trading.

Trinidad and Tobago formally accepted the obligations of Article VIII, Sections 2, 3, and 4 of the Fund Agreement, as from December 13, 1993.

Administration of Control

The authority to administer exchange control is vested in the Central Bank, which acts under the authority of the Ministry of Finance.

Commercial banks can purchase foreign currency notes from the public, and the Central Bank in turn buys certain of these currencies from the commercial banks for repatriation to the respective monetary authorities under bilateral arrangements. The Central Bank does not repatriate Trinidad and Tobago currency.

Prescription of Currency

Settlements may be made in U.S. dollars or in specified currencies.[1] Authorized payments, including payments for imports, to all countries may be made in U.S. dollars or in one of the specified currencies. Payments from all countries with which trade is allowed must be received in U.S. dollars or in any of the specified currencies.

Foreign Currency Accounts

Foreign currency accounts denominated in foreign currency may be maintained at local banks by residents and nonresidents.

Imports and Import Payments

All goods, unless excepted for reasons of health and security, may be imported under open general license (OGL) arrangements. Imports of firearms, ammunition, and narcotics are either prohibited or rigidly controlled for security and health reasons. Imports of animal feed, flour, rice, petroleum, and edible oil are traded principally by state companies. All imports of food and drugs must satisfy prescribed standards. Imports of meat, live animals, plants, and mining materials are subject to specific regulations.

Duty-free licenses are granted to local concessionaire manufacturers for imports of certain inputs for manufacturing industries. Where goods are subject to import license, a general import license is used in addition to the duty-free license.

Imports from non-CARICOM countries[2] may be paid for in any currency in which goods are satisfactorily invoiced.

The customs duty rates on most goods range from 5 percent to 30 percent; the rate on agricultural produce is 40 percent. The duty rates on consumer goods, such as perfumes, cosmetics, jewelry, clothing, and cotton and silk fabrics, range from 25 percent to 30 percent; the rate on motor vehicles is 35 percent.

Some foodstuffs, fertilizers, and raw materials, and all goods originating from CARICOM countries are exempt from customs duties. Local enterprises producing import substitutes or export goods may be granted exemptions from customs duties by the Minister of Trade and Industry and the Tourism Industrial Development Company Limited (TIDCO).

Payments for Invisibles

Residents and nonresidents may take out of Trinidad and Tobago local currency notes up to the value of TT$20,000. For amounts exceeding TT$20,000,

---

[1]Austrian schillings, Belgian francs, Canadian dollars, Danish kroner, deutsche mark, French francs, Italian lire, Japanese yen, Myanmar kyats, Netherlands guilders, Norwegian kroner, Portuguese escudos, Spanish pesetas, Swedish kronor, Swiss francs, and pounds sterling.

[2]The CARICOM countries are Antigua and Barbuda, The Bahamas, Barbados, Belize, Dominica, Grenada, Guyana, Jamaica, Montserrat, St. Kitts and Nevis, St. Lucia, St. Vincent and the Grenadines, and Trinidad and Tobago.

there is no restriction but a customs declaration is required.

Exports and Export Proceeds

Exports of certain goods usually require an individual license. These include some foodstuffs, firearms and explosives, animals, gold, and petroleum and petroleum products produced in Trinidad and Tobago, as well as specified products not produced locally. Exports of all other commodities are permitted under OGL. In addition, general licenses may be issued at the discretion of the Ministry of Trade and Industry.

There are no requirements for the repatriation of export proceeds received in foreign currencies. In practice, the foreign-owned petroleum company operating in Trinidad and Tobago repatriates all foreign exchange after providing for the equivalent of its local currency needs.

Proceeds from Invisibles

Residents and nonresidents may bring into Trinidad and Tobago domestic currency notes up to the value of TT$20,000. For larger amounts, a customs declaration is required. Both resident and nonresident travelers may bring in foreign currency notes up to US$5,000 without declaration to the controller of customs.

Capital

Capital transfers abroad do not require prior approval.

The laws of Trinidad and Tobago do not discriminate between nationals and foreigners in the formation and operation of companies in the country. Foreign investors are required, however, to comply with the provisions of the Foreign Investment Act of 1990 in order to hold an interest in real estate or shares in local companies. Following passage of the Central Bank Amendment Act of 1993, exchange control restrictions were removed, and foreign investors are no longer required to obtain approval from the Central Bank to repatriate capital or capital gains. There are no limitations on borrowing by foreign investors on the local financial market.

The Government has enacted basic incentive legislation designed to attract domestic and foreign investment in manufacturing and in import-substitution industries. Since 1973, these policies have been effected within the framework of a CARICOM agreement on the harmonization of fiscal incentives. Certain concessions may be granted to approved enterprises, including temporary relief from import duties and taxes and other privileges outlined in the Investment Policy document issued by the Industrial Development Corporation.

A commercial bank, as an authorized dealer, is allowed to hold an "open" asset or liability position in foreign exchange. Cross-border trading of shares of companies listed on the respective stock exchanges is permitted among the residents of Barbados, Jamaica, and Trinidad and Tobago; residents and companies of the other two countries are designated as residents of Trinidad and Tobago for exchange control purposes in cross-border trading.

Gold

Gold is defined by the Exchange Control Act of 1970 as gold coins and bullion. The regulations stipulate that, except with specific exemptions and permissions granted by the Minister of Finance, (1) one party to every transaction in gold between residents must be an authorized bank, and (2) gold may not be taken or sent out of Trinidad and Tobago. When appropriate, however, residents are permitted to purchase, hold, or sell gold coins in Trinidad and Tobago for numismatic purposes.

Exports of gold are controlled by the Ministry of Trade and Industry. Imports of gold jewelry are subject to an open general license, but imports of other forms of gold are controlled by the Central Bank. Exports of gold in any form are subject to specific export licenses; licenses for gold other than jewelry are not usually granted except to the monetary authorities, who may need to get authorization from the Central Bank.

Changes During 1994

Imports and Import Payments

September 1. Certain agricultural items were removed from the negative list during the period May to September. These items included rice, flour, and vegetable oil.

Changes During 1995

Imports and Import Payments

January 1. The customs duties were reduced to the 5–30 percent range. The stamp duty was removed, and the import surcharge on all nonagricultural goods was removed.

TUNISIA

(Position as of December 31, 1994)

Exchange Arrangement

The currency of Tunisia is the Tunisian Dinar, the external value of which is determined in the interbank market in which commercial banks (including offshore banks acting on behalf of their resident customers) conduct transactions at freely negotiated rates. The spread between the buying and selling rates, however, may not exceed 0.25 percent. The Central Bank of Tunisia intervenes in the market by buying or selling dinars for foreign exchange. It publishes an indicative interbank exchange rate for foreign currencies and banknotes by the following day, at the latest. On December 31, 1994, the average interbank spot rates were D 0.18521 per F 1 and D 0.9912 per US$1, respectively[1].

Forward rates are published daily by the Central Bank. Forward cover may be requested for a minimum of the equivalent of D 10 million in foreign exchange. The forward rates published daily by the Central Bank of Tunisia are merely indicative when cover is requested for amounts equal to or more than the foreign currency equivalent of D 10 million. Different rates may be set for these requests; the authorized bank is notified thereof prior to the conclusion of the forward contract. Importers and exporters are authorized to obtain forward exchange cover from the authorized banks as of the date the contract is signed or the date on which the foreign commercial paper is domiciled, depending on the arrangements for the product concerned. Forward cover may be established for a maximum of 12 months for imports and a maximum of 9 months for exports. Persons who provide services are eligible for exchange cover for up to 12 months, to be provided within 30 days of the date on which the claim originated. Currencies quoted forward are Belgian francs, deutsche mark, French francs, Italian lire, Netherlands guilders, pounds sterling, and U.S. dollars. Swaps are permitted among foreign currency operators. Trading on 3-month, 6-month, and 1-year foreign currency options on French francs, deutsche mark, and U.S. dollars is available to resident borrowers of foreign exchange under standard contracts. The Central Bank extends exchange rate guarantees to certain officially guaranteed loans, with risk premiums based on domestic and international interest rates.

Tunisia formally accepted the obligations of Article VIII, Sections 2, 3, and 4 of the Fund Agreement, as from January 6, 1993.

Administration of Control

Exchange control is administered by the Central Bank, which delegates authority over payments for imports and most invisibles to the authorized banks. Foreign trade control is administered by the Ministry of Trade, which issues import and export authorization for products when required.

Prescription of Currency

Settlements between Tunisia and foreign countries may be made in any convertible currency (traded in the interbank market) or in convertible Tunisian dinars through foreign accounts. Settlements between Tunisia and Algeria, the Socialist People's Libyan Arab Jamahiriya, Mauritania, and Morocco may be effected through convertible accounts in the national currencies concerned at the respective central banks. Payments to Israel are prohibited.

Resident and Nonresident Accounts

Special accounts in foreign currency or convertible dinars may be opened by (1) natural persons of Tunisian nationality changing their normal residence to Tunisia from abroad and any other natural or juridical persons of Tunisian nationality for their nontransferable assets legitimately acquired abroad; (2) natural persons of foreign nationality residing in Tunisia; (3) foreign juridical persons for their establishments located in Tunisia; and (4) Tunisian diplomats and civil servants stationed abroad. No formalities are required for the opening of these accounts by foreigners; a declaration of holdings, however, is required for Tunisians. Funds legitimately acquired abroad, not from the exportation of goods or services from Tunisia, may be credited to these accounts. They may be debited for (1) foreign

---

[1]Currencies quoted spot for account holdings and banknotes are Austrian schillings, Belgian francs, Canadian dollars, Danish kroner, deutsche mark, European monetary units (ECUs), Finnish markkaa, French francs, Italian lire, Japanese yen, Kuwaiti dinars, Libyan dinars, Moroccan dirhams, Netherlands guilders, Norwegian kroner, pounds sterling, Saudi Arabian riyals, Spanish pesetas, Swedish kronor, Swiss francs, U.A.E. dirhams, and U.S. dollars. Currencies quoted spot for banknotes only are CFA francs, Luxembourg francs, and Qatar riyals. Algerian dinars are quoted spot only.

exchange surrendered to the Central Bank; (2) foreign exchange remitted to the account holder, his or her spouse, parents, and offspring to undertake foreign travel; (3) amounts credited to another special account in foreign currency or convertible dinars; and (4) any payments abroad (including those for the acquisition of movable or immovable tangible property located abroad, of ownership rights abroad, or of foreign claims and for payments for imports subject to applicable foreign trade formalities).

Foreign accounts in convertible dinars and convertible currencies may be opened freely by all nonresidents regardless of nationality. These accounts may be credited freely with (1) receipts in convertible foreign currencies or the dinar proceeds from sales of convertible currencies to the Central Bank; banknotes must be declared to customs; (2) convertible foreign currencies remitted to the account holder by a nonresident; (3) foreign currency purchased from the Central Bank by debit of a foreign account in convertible dinars; (4) authorized payments by residents in favor of the account holder; (5) interest on balances in these accounts and interest payable by the authorized intermediaries on foreign exchange deposits in the accounts whenever they can use the funds thus deposited at remunerative rates; (6) transfers from other foreign accounts; and (7) proceeds from the cashing of checks, traveler's checks, or drafts expressed in convertible currencies and made out by a nonresident to the order of the account holder. All other crediting requires prior authorization from the Central Bank, either direct or by delegation. These accounts may be debited freely for (1) payments of any kind in Tunisia (irrespective of the payer's country of residence); (2) transfers to other foreign accounts; (3) the purchase of any foreign currency from, or sales of any foreign exchange to, the Central Bank; and (4) transfers abroad or delivery of foreign currency to the account holder, to any other nonresident beneficiary, or to residents with the status of permanent representatives or salaried employees of the account holder.

Professional accounts in foreign currency may be opened by any natural person residing in Tunisia or by any Tunisian or foreign juridical person for their foreign currency assets in connection with their establishments located in Tunisia. These accounts are essentially designed to allow their holders to cover themselves against exchange risks. They may be credited with (1) up to 40 percent of the export receipts of their holders; (2) the interest generated by the amounts deposited in such accounts; and (3) transfers from another professional account of the

holder, either in the same foreign currency or another one. They may be debited for (1) payment of any current operation pertaining to the activity for which they were opened; and (2) any other transaction with general or specific authorization. Balances may also be placed on the foreign exchange market.

Professional accounts in convertible dinars may be opened by natural or juridical persons residing in Tunisia with resources in foreign exchange, subject to central bank authorization. These accounts may be credited and debited under the terms laid down by the Central Bank in the authorization to open such accounts.

Internal nonresident accounts may be opened freely by authorized intermediaries in the name of nonresident individuals of foreign nationality residing temporarily in Tunisia. These accounts may be credited without authorization from the Central Bank with the following: (1) amount of transfers of funds carried out in convertible currencies from a foreign country; (2) revenue of any kind accruing in Tunisia to the holder of the account (in particular, the nontransferable part of remuneration for services rendered by that person in Tunisia); (3) liquid assets from estates opened in Tunisia; (4) proceeds from the repayment of loans previously granted in dinars with funds from the account holder's internal nonresident account; and (5) transfers from another internal nonresident account opened in the name of the account holder. They may be debited for (1) support of the account holder and his or her family in Tunisia; (2) payment of costs of managing property in Tunisia; (3) lending to residents; and (4) transfers to another internal nonresident account opened in the name of the account holder.

Special dinar accounts may be freely opened by nonresident foreign enterprises holding contracts in Tunisia approved by the Central Bank. Such enterprises are authorized to open, for each contract, a single special account in dinars, in which they may deposit the portion of the contract price payable in dinars to cover their local expenses. Such accounts may also be credited with funds from a foreign account in convertible dinars, the dinar equivalent of foreign currency drawn on a foreign account in convertible foreign currency, the dinar equivalent of any transfer in convertible foreign currency from abroad, and interest accruing on funds deposited in the account. The account may be freely debited for the enterprise's contract-related expenses in Tunisia.

Any transfer operations from such accounts must be authorized by the Central Bank. Interest is paid at rates comparable to those applied to resident accounts in dinars.

Suspense accounts may be opened by all nonresidents regardless of nationality and may be used for crediting all proceeds accruing to nonresidents and awaiting utilization. These proceeds may, upon general or specific approval, be used in Tunisia for specific purposes, transferred abroad, or transferred to other nonresident accounts. Subject to certain conditions, suspense accounts may be debited, without the prior authorization of the Central Bank, for purchases of Tunisian securities, subscriptions to issues of short-term debentures or bonds, portfolio management expenses in respect of certain securities, payments to the Tunisian Government or public institutions, or payments of the expenses of managing securities deposited in a suspense file opened in the name of the account holder. They may also be debited for settlement of living expenses incurred in Tunisia by the account holder and his or her family up to D 100 a person a week, provided that the total withdrawals in any calendar year from one or more accounts do not exceed D 2,000 a family. In addition, a suspense account holder traveling in Tunisia between November 1 and March 31 of the next year may withdraw from the account an amount equal to the foreign exchange imported for the trip and surrendered to the Central Bank, an authorized intermediary, or a subagency, provided that total withdrawals for the living expenses of the account holder and his or her family do not exceed D 2,000 a year. Up to D 50 a person a month may be debited to assist the offspring or parents of the resident account holder. Individuals or juridical persons of French or Italian nationality holding suspense accounts may transfer all funds in their accounts regardless of the date of deposit. These accounts do not pay interest.

Capital accounts may be opened in the name of a nonresident natural person of foreign nationality or by a nonresident juridical person. The opening of these accounts by a nonresident of Tunisian nationality or his or her spouse must be authorized by the Central Bank. Foreign banks may hold global capital accounts for their nonresident customers. Subject to certain conditions, capital accounts may be credited, without the prior approval of the Central Bank, with the proceeds of the sale on the stock exchange, or of the contractual or advance redemption, of transferable Tunisian securities; the sales proceeds of real estate through an attorney at the Supreme Court (Cour de cassation), or rights to real estate situated in Tunisia; and with funds from another capital account. Irrespective of the account holder's country of residence, capital accounts may be freely debited for the living expenses in Tunisia of the account holder and his or her family, up to D 100 a person a week, provided that total withdrawals from one or more capital accounts in a calendar year do not exceed D 2,000 a family for trips to Tunisia between November 1 and March 31 of the subsequent year. In addition, a capital account holder traveling in Tunisia between November 1 and March 31 may withdraw from the account an amount equal to the foreign exchange imported for the trip and surrendered to the Central Bank, an authorized intermediary, or a subagency, provided that total withdrawals for the living expenses of the account holder and his or her family do not exceed D 2,000 a year.

Such accounts may also be debited, subject to certain conditions, for expenses connected with the management of Tunisian securities; for the maintenance, repair, and insurance of real estate and all taxes; and for transfer to the credit of another capital account. Balances on capital accounts are freely transferable between nonresidents of foreign nationality, with the exception of juridical persons governed by public law. Subject to certain conditions, they may also be debited to assist the account holder's parents and offspring residing in Tunisia, at a maximum rate of D 50 a person a month. These accounts do not pay interest and may not be overdrawn. Individuals and juridical persons of French or Italian nationality holding capital accounts may transfer all funds in their accounts regardless of the date of deposit.

Imports and Import Payments

All imports from Israel are prohibited. All imports are liberalized except those that have an impact on law and order, hygiene, health, morals, protection of flora and fauna, and cultural heritage. Some goods may only be imported temporarily, subject to an import authorization. The list of items not subject to import liberalization is set by decree. Some items, the list of which is drawn up by decree by the Minister of Trade, are subject to technical import controls. A countervailing import duty may be applied to any item that has been dumped or subsidized and that when used, is or could be detrimental to the national production of a similar product. The importation of liberalized products is effected by an import certificate upon presentation of a contract domiciled with an authorized intermediary. Goods not subject to liberalization are imported under cover of an import authorization issued by the Ministry of Trade.

Imports of raw materials, semifinished products, spare parts, and equipment, paid from sources outside Tunisia, may be effected without foreign trade formalities by enterprises for their own use up to a value of D 100,000. Furthermore, companies exclusively engaged in exporting goods or services and set up under the Investment Incentives Code promulgated by Law No. 93–120 of December 27, 1993 and companies established in a free trade zone under Law No. 92–81 of August 3, 1992 on free trade zones may import freely without foreign trade formalities any goods required for their production process, subject only to customs declaration.

Importers must receive a customs code number before they can obtain an import certificate. All import documents involving payments must be handled by an authorized intermediary. Foreign currency may be purchased from the Central Bank or a delegated commercial bank for all payments. Resident importers are authorized to buy forward foreign currencies required for future settlement of their merchandise imports, for a maximum term of 12 months, at rates established daily by the Central Bank. In addition to customs duties, imports are subject to the value-added tax and, in some cases, to the consumption tax. In some cases, imports destined for domestic investment projects are eligible for full or partial exemption from import duties.

Payments for Invisibles

Authorized banks are empowered to provide foreign exchange for tourist and business travel, study and educational expenses, expenses related to travel abroad for reasons of health, and salary transfers, up to prescribed limits. The annual limits for tourist travel allowances are D 500 for an adult and D 250 for a child under the age of 10. The annual settlement and the monthly educational expense allowances for a student are D 1,000 and D 600, respectively. Amounts exceeding these limits may be authorized by the Central Bank. Business travel allowances are granted for all exporters of goods and services, all enterprises, including liberal professions, who have declared their business turnover during the previous year to the tax authorities, and promoters of new projects. The allowance for exporters is 10 percent of export proceeds for the current year, with an annual limit of D 80,000. The annual limit on the allowance for business travel by importers ranges from D 5,000 to D 30,000, depending on turnover, and the annual limit on the allowance for business travel by other professions ranges from D 2,000 to D 20,000, depending on turnover declared to the tax authorities. The allowance for promoters of new projects is a maximum of D 5,000, and is granted only once for the duration of the project.

Contractually employed foreign nationals and foreign experts employed by the public sector may transfer up to 50 percent of their earnings; for technical assistants, limits on transfers are specified in their contracts.

Persons traveling abroad for health reasons may transfer up to D 750 a year for travel expenses. Additional amounts may be allowed for this purpose if the state of their health requires several trips abroad during the same year. Persons accompanying patients may transfer up to D 250 a trip in the case of medical or paramedical staff and D 500 in all other cases. Other payments for invisibles may be made freely.

Regardless of nationality, residents traveling abroad by air or sea, except to the countries of the Arab Maghreb Union, are subject to a travel tax of D 45 a trip. Nonresidents, diplomats, persons traveling under the Agence de coopération technique, emigrant workers, a man or woman residing in Tunisia whose spouse resides abroad, children living in Tunisia one or both of whose parents reside abroad, students, pilgrims to Mecca, and those traveling for medical reasons are exempt from the tax. The exportation of Tunisian dinar banknotes and coins is prohibited.

Exports and Export Proceeds

All exports to Israel are prohibited. All exports are liberalized, except those indicated in a list established by decree. Certain products, the list of which is established by edict of the Ministry of Trade, are subject to technical export control.

Liberalized items are exported upon presentation to customs of the final invoice. The exports must be domiciled within eight days of the date of shipment of the merchandise.

Goods not subject to liberalization are exported upon presentation of an authorization issued by the Minister of Trade. Companies exclusively engaged in exporting goods or services and set up under the Investment Incentives Code and companies established in a free economic zone may export freely without foreign trade formalities, subject only to customs declarations. As a general rule, all export proceeds must be repatriated within ten days of the payment due date. If no credit is extended, payment is due within 30 days of the date of shipment. Under certain conditions, approval from the Central Bank is not required for the extension of export credits of up to 180 days. Resident exporters may sell forward, for a maximum term of 9 months (12 months for providers of services), foreign currencies representing the proceeds from their merchandise exports through authorized intermediaries.

Resident exporters may credit up to 40 percent of their foreign exchange proceeds to their professional accounts (see section on Resident and Nonresident Accounts above). Balances in these accounts may be used for any foreign exchange transaction with specific or general authorization, such as payments of expenses needed for the enterprise's activities and servicing of external obligations. Nonresident companies exclusively engaged in exporting goods or services and covered by the Investment Incentives Code, nonresident international trading companies, and nonresident enterprises constituted in a free trade zone are not required to repatriate or surrender their export proceeds.

Proceeds from Invisibles

Residents must repatriate and surrender all amounts derived from services rendered to persons residing abroad and all other income or proceeds from invisibles received from foreign countries. However, the facilities associated with professional accounts in foreign exchange in convertible dinars apply to proceeds from services (see sections on Exports and Export Proceeds and Resident and Nonresident Accounts). Foreign banknotes and coins (except gold coins) may be brought in freely, but importation of Tunisian dinar banknotes and coins is prohibited.

Nonresident travelers wishing to re-export the foreign exchange equivalent of amounts exceeding D 1,000 must declare to customs the foreign currencies they are importing upon their entry into Tunisia. There is no ceiling on the reconversion of Tunisian banknotes by nonresident travelers. Foreign exchange from dinar reconversion may be re-exported upon presentation of a foreign exchange voucher or receipt if the amount to be re-exported is less than D 1,000 or if the foreign exchange used in the purchase of the dinars was received from abroad in the form of a check, draft, money order, or any other evidence of a claim or by debiting a foreign account in foreign currency or convertible dinars. The foreign exchange import declaration approved by customs is also required if the amount of foreign exchange from dinar reconversion exceeds the equivalent of D 1,000 derived from the surrender of foreign currencies physically imported from abroad.

Capital

All foreign direct investments carried out legitimately in Tunisia with foreign exchange transferred from abroad are guaranteed the right to repatriate the net proceeds from the sale or liquidation of the invested capital, even if the net proceeds exceed the initial value of foreign exchange invested.

Foreign direct investments in agriculture and fisheries, manufacturing, public works, tourism, handicrafts, transport, education and teaching, vocational training, the production of culture and related industries, youth coordination and child supervision, health, environmental conservation, real estate promotion, and other nonfinancial activities and services benefit from the incentives contained in the Investment Incentives Code, promulgated by Law No. 93–120 of December 27, 1993. Foreign direct investments in the financial and banking sector and those carried out in a free trade zone benefit from the incentives provided for in Law No. 85–108 of December 6, 1985 (on incentives for financial and banking establishments conducting business essentially with nonresidents), and in Law No. 92–81 of August 3, 1992 (on free trade zones), respectively. The investment incentives include tax and financial benefits, as well as facilities, with regard to laws and regulations governing foreign exchange and foreign trade that are essentially oriented toward export promotion.

Foreign nationals who have been residents of Tunisia and have left the country permanently are entitled to transfer the following: 50 percent of their assets (with a minimum of D 1,750 and a maximum of D 3,500) if they left Tunisia before August 20, 1970; [2] D 4,000 if they left between August 20, 1970 and December 31, 1973; D 5,000 if they left between January 1, 1974 and December 31, 1974; D 10,000 if they left after December 31, 1974; D 15,000 if they left Tunisia after December 31, 1978, are over 60 years of age, and are Tunisian nationals; and an unlimited amount if they are of French or Italian nationality, regardless of their date of departure from Tunisia.

To support their export activities, resident exporters may, depending on their turnover for the previous financial year, transfer abroad amounts ranging from D 20,000 to D 100,000 a calendar year to cover installation, maintenance, and operating costs of branches and subsidiaries or to finance equity participation, and D 10,000 to D 50,000 to cover installation, maintenance, and operating costs of liaison or representative offices.

Resident financial institutions, and other resident enterprises may freely contract foreign currency

---

[2] Such persons may transfer D 1,750 if the total value of their assets does not exceed D 3,500.

loans from nonresidents up to an annual limit of D 10 million and D 3 million, respectively.

All other transfers by residents, the contracting of foreign loans by residents, and the extension of loans to nonresidents require approval from the Central Bank, except for investment loans extended by resident banks for nonresident industrial enterprises with funds held abroad.

Gold

Five denominations of commemorative gold coins are legal tender but do not circulate. Residents may acquire and hold gold in any form in Tunisia. The Central Bank has a monopoly over the importation and exportation of monetary gold. Other imports of gold require joint authorization from the Central Bank and the Ministry of Trade. Only dentists, artisan jewelers, and cooperatives formed by artisans are eligible to purchase gold from the Central Bank. The exportation of gold is prohibited.

Changes During 1994

Exchange Arrangement

February 1. An interbank foreign exchange market system was introduced.

Administration of Control

January 31. Law No. 94–14 became effective, modifying and completing Law No. 92–81 on free trade zones.

Imports and Import Payments

January 1. Law No. 93–125 with the following main provisions came into effect: (1) the list of products subject to temporary complementary import duties was modified and duty rates introduced in 1993 were reduced by 10 percentage points; (2) the temporary surcharge on import duties and taxes was incorporated in the import duties; (3) import duties on certain products were modified; and (4) the service fee on imports was raised to 2 percent from 1.5 percent of the import duties and taxes paid.

March 7. Law No. 94–41 established freedom to export and import except for commodities to be specified by decree; Law No. 94–42 became effective, setting regulations for the activities of international trade enterprises.

August 29. Decrees governing the following were established: (1) the list of products excluded from the regime of free international trade; (2) the modalities for undertaking international trade activities; (3) the procedures for technical control of imports and exports; and (4) the conditions and modalities for determining unfair import practices. Import duties and the value-added tax for spare parts, accessories, and goods destined for agriculture and fishing sectors were reduced to 10 percent and suspended, respectively.

September 19. Raw materials and semifinished products used for the assembly of vehicles for international road transport were exempted from import duties and taxes. Import duties for raw materials, semifinished goods, and other inputs used in domestic transformation were reduced to 10 percent.

September 26. The value-added tax and import duties on equipment and inputs for equipment destined for energy saving and renewable energy activities were suspended and reduced to 10 percent (Decree No. 94–1998).

Capital

February 14. Law No. 93–120 (December 27, 1993), promulgating the Investment Incentives Code, was implemented.

February 28. Decrees listing the activities of sectors envisaged in Articles 1, 2, 3, and 27 of the Investment Incentive Code and activities of areas benefiting from the incentives provided in Article 43 of the Investment Incentives Code were announced.

March 10. A decree establishing investment incentives for new promoters was announced.

April 12. The minimum capital requirements for international trading companies were established.

TURKEY

(Position as of March 31, 1995)

Exchange Arrangement

The currency of Turkey is the Turkish Lira. Turkey follows a flexible exchange rate policy under which the exchange rate for the Turkish lira is determined on a daily basis. Commercial banks, special finance institutions, authorized institutions, post, telephone, and telegraphic offices (PTT), and precious metal intermediary institutions are free to set their exchange rates according to prevalent market conditions. The lowest and highest rates applied in these transactions are to be reported daily to the central bank. The daily rates for foreign exchange and foreign currency notes announced at 3:00 p.m. on each business day by the central bank are freely determined by taking into account the developments in the international and domestic markets. These exchange rates are mainly indicative. On March 31, 1995, the average buying and selling rates in the interbank market for the U.S. dollar were LT 41.830 and LT 41.925, respectively, per US$1.

The commercial banks can deal freely in forward transactions within the predetermined limits imposed by the central bank. Forward exchange rates are freely established between the banks and their customers in accordance with international practices. Banks enter into swap transactions with the central bank with terms of quarterly periods up to 12 months.

Turkey formally accepted the obligations of Article VIII, Sections 2, 3, and 4 of the Fund Agreement, as from March 22, 1990.

Administration of Control

Exchange and trade controls are the responsibility of the Prime Ministry, to which the Undersecretariat of the Treasury is attached. Administration of exchange controls has been delegated to the central bank, which regulates all matters related to foreign exchange operations. All commercial banks have been authorized by the Undersecretariat of the Treasury to engage in foreign exchange operations on their own account. Export registration is carried out by trade organizations, according to instructions from the Undersecretariat of Foreign Trade, who also issues export licenses for special cases but may delegate this authority to the relevant trade organizations.

In accordance with the Fund's Executive Board Decision No. 144–(52/51) adopted on August 14, 1952, Turkey notified the Fund on September 12, 1990 that certain restrictions were imposed on the making of payments and transfers for current international transactions to the Government of Iraq, and on August 5, 1992, that, in compliance with UN Security Council Resolution No. 757 (1992), certain restrictions had been imposed on the making of payments and transfers for current international transactions in respect of the Federal Republic of Yugoslavia (Serbia/Montenegro).

Prescription of Currency

Certain commercial transactions with the Baltic countries, the Czech Republic, Poland, the Russian Federation, the Slovak Republic, and the other countries of the former Soviet Union are made through special accounts denominated in U.S. dollars. Settlements with all other countries are made in convertible currencies.

Resident and Nonresident Accounts

Persons holding valid Turkish passports and having permission or the right to work or reside abroad may open interest-bearing foreign currency deposit accounts or "super" foreign currency accounts, depending on the amount deposited and the maturity, with the head office of the central bank in Ankara. These accounts may be maintained upon the return of these persons to Turkey.

Nonresidents may open accounts denominated in foreign exchange and Turkish liras with authorized commercial banks. The holders may dispose of such accounts at their discretion.

Imports and Import Payments

All goods are freely importable, except for those explicitly prohibited by law, such as narcotics, weapons, foreign coins made of metals other than gold, and ammunition. Imports of these goods are allowed only with a special permit from the authorities. Old, used and reconditioned, defective, substandard, soiled, or poor quality goods may be imported only with special permission from the Undersecretariat of the Treasury. But certain used goods that are not older than five years may be imported freely.

All commercial imports require import licenses; their length of validity is determined by the authorized parties and may be extended according to principles determined by the central bank. Import licenses are issued to registered importers, industrialists, state economic enterprises, and government departments. No special permit is required for any authorized person to apply to any bank for an import license. The import license permits the necessary foreign exchange payments to be made and permits goods to be cleared through customs. Payments for imports may be made against letters of credit, documents, or goods (i.e., upon customs clearance), or through acceptance credits or prepayments. Partial prepayments are authorized under certain conditions.

Import payments may be made through foreign exchange deposit accounts held with banks. Exporters and providers of services are freely allowed to use foreign exchange earned from exports of goods (excluding the portion subject to surrender requirements) and services for payment of their own imports.

Regulations governing imports made without allocations of foreign exchange from the banking system mainly affect imports of goods for personal or professional use by travelers domiciled in Turkey and temporary imports by Turkish workers employed abroad and maintaining foreign exchange accounts with the central bank.

Since January 1, 1993, various import taxes calculated on the basis of the c.i.f. value of goods were consolidated into customs duties. Certain goods are subject to various rates of levy, which are transferred to extrabudgetary funds ("funds list").

The import regime was liberalized in 1994 to bring it in line with Turkey's commitments for completing the customs union with the EU, its relationship with EFTA, and its obligations under the World Trade Organization. To this end, customs duties were revised with the objective of aligning them to the common customs tariff of the EU in 12 or 22 years. Under this framework, in addition to the 10 percent reduction in the customs duty realized in 1993, a further 10 percent reduction became effective on January 1, 1994.

Payments for Invisibles

Residents may freely make payments for invisible transactions relating to all services to nonresidents at home or abroad.

All residents traveling abroad may carry foreign currency notes up to the equivalent of $5,000 a person without proof of exchange allocation by com-mercial banks, and banks are permitted to sell foreign exchange to residents and nonresidents without restriction. Residents are allowed to use credit cards on a revolving basis up to a limit of $10,000 for travel and expenses abroad; balances exceeding $10,000 must be settled within 30 days. Turkish citizens traveling abroad are subject to a tax equivalent to $100, payable in Turkish liras, regardless of whether there are related purchases of foreign exchange; the tax is reduced by one-half for travelers 18 years or younger. Individuals engaged in border trade, as well as those traveling to Turkish republics with the permission of the governor of the province concerned must pay the equivalent of $25 in Turkish liras, and immigrants and refugees traveling abroad must pay the equivalent of $50 in Turkish liras. Exempt from payment of this tax are (1) all foreign nationals; (2) first-time pilgrims to Mecca; (3) Turkish workers employed abroad and their families; (4) crews of ships and planes and truck drivers; (5) those living in border areas, who may leave the country by administrative permit; (6) those going abroad for medical treatment and those accompanying them; (7) private students studying abroad and civil servants (and their families) sent abroad on permanent assignment; (8) spectators going abroad to watch Turkish teams participating in international competitions; (9) the personnel of institutions that are exempt from paying funds, who are appointed to work abroad; (10) travel, which is limited to once a year, by refugees or immigrants who have become Turkish citizens to their countries of origin; (11) academicians who are attending international congresses, symposiums, and seminars abroad; and (12) permanent residents working abroad independently.

Travelers are permitted to take out up to the equivalent of $5,000 in foreign currency notes and Turkish lira notes and coins. Nonresidents and Turkish citizens working abroad who are considered residents may take out foreign currency notes exceeding the equivalent of $5,000, provided that they have declared the amount upon their arrival; residents may take out foreign currency notes exceeding the equivalent of $5,000, provided that they produce proof of purchase from banks and special financial institutions.

Exports and Export Proceeds

Commercial exports are classified into the following categories: (1) free exports (i.e., exports not requiring any official permission); (2) free exports subject to registration, which covers exports of goods for which premiums are paid to the Support and Price Stabilization Fund; raw materials for textiles; all textiles and garments; raw and finished leather; leather garments and other leather products; semifinished steel and iron products; natural gas under agreement with the Baltic countries, the Russian Federation and the other countries of the former Soviet Union, products to which quantitative restrictions are applied, and raw vegetable oils (including olive oil) and oil seeds. The Free Export Declarations related to the goods that fall into this category must be registered by the professional institutions, the Undersecretariat of Foreign Trade, and/or the customs administration upon the application of the exporter; and (3) exports that require the permission of the Undersecretariat of Foreign Trade or the professional institutions authorized by the Undersecretariat. These include exports on credit, consignment and temporary exports, exports undertaken by the construction companies that are awarded construction and installation work abroad, or exports intended for use in international fairs and exhibitions.

All companies are allowed to conduct barter trade in accordance with established procedures.

Foreign exchange receipts from merchandise exports must be surrendered within 180 days of the date of shipment. If exchange receipts are surrendered within 90 days, exporters are entitled to retain 30 percent of proceeds, which they may deposit in foreign exchange accounts with commercial banks, keep abroad, or dispose of freely. Commercial banks, special financial institutions and the PTT are required to sell to the central bank 25 percent of all foreign exchange they obtain from exports and invisible transactions within a period agreed with the central bank.

A system of export incentives in the form of subsidized credits administered by the Turkish Eximbank is in operation. Under the Foreign Trade Companies Rediscount Credit Program (introduced in January 1990), exporters whose annual export turnover exceeds $50 million are eligible to receive credit either in Turkish liras, with the interest rate related to the rediscount rate of the central bank, or in foreign currency, with the interest rate linked to LIBOR. The Eximbank also maintains a program of preshipment credit designed to meet the financing needs of manufacturers and exporters. The credits under this program are extended for up to 120 days with fixed interest rate of between 25 percent and 50 percent of the f.o.b. value of the export commitment, depending on the maturity. In addition, the Eximbank provides buyers' credit facilities to support Turkish exports to certain countries, including Albania, Algeria, Bulgaria, the Czech Republic,

Hungary, Romania, the Slovak Republic, the Syrian Arab Republic, Tunisia, and some of the countries of the former Soviet Union; it provides insurance against commercial and political risks on commercial terms.

Premiums are paid from the Support and Price Stabilization Fund for selected export products; in 1993, 110 items were eligible for these premiums. Exporters of manufactured goods exceeding $250,000 in value are eligible to deduct 5 percent of the gross value of their exports from their taxable income. Exporters holding export encouragement certificates are permitted to import inputs free of customs duties or levies for extrabudgetary funds. To benefit from this facility, exporters must undertake to achieve a certain export turnover and must present documentary proof that they have used duty-free imports in the manufacture of exported goods. Normally, the value of duty-free imports may not exceed 40 percent of the export value.

The eligibility of exporters to deduct 5 percent of the gross value of the exports of manufactured goods worth at least $250,000 in the calculation of the corporate tax since January 1993 has been waived, and this facility was abolished on January 1, 1994.

Proceeds from Invisibles

Residents may accept foreign currency from nonresidents for transactions processed in Turkey. Foreign exchange earned by residents in exchange for services they have rendered to nonresidents or on behalf of them in Turkey or abroad (including contracting services), as well as foreign exchange corresponding to expenses incurred in the name, and on behalf of, nonresidents, may be disposed of freely.

Capital

Nonresident individuals and corporations wishing to invest in Turkey must import the required capital in kind or in the form of foreign exchange and must obtain a license from the Undersecretariat of the Treasury. In establishing partnerships or joint companies in the Turkish private sector, foreign investors must bring in a minimum of $50,000 of capital. Certain investments are allowed under the provisions of the Law for the Encouragement of Foreign Investments or the Petroleum Law. For commercial activities other than forming a company or opening a branch in accordance with the Capital and Petroleum Law, foreign investors must obtain the permission of the Undersecretariat of the Treasury. Profits and dividends and the proceeds from sales and liquidation of foreign capital may be transferred abroad and must be reported to the central bank.

Resident individuals or corporations may invest abroad and in the free trade zones in Turkey up to the equivalent of $5 million in cash or in kind. The exportation of capital in amounts exceeding the equivalent of $5 million requires the authorization of the ministry to which the Undersecretariat of the Treasury is attached. Nonresidents may transfer abroad proceeds from sales of real estate without restriction. Purchases and sales by nonresidents (including investments, partnerships, and mutual funds abroad) of all kinds of securities and other capital instruments through the banks and intermediary institutions authorized according to the capital legislation may be made freely. The transfer of the income from such securities and instruments as well as the proceeds from their sale may be effected freely through banks and special finance institutions. Purchases and sales by residents of the securities traded in foreign financial markets are also free, provided that the transactions are carried out by banks, special finance institutions, and intermediary institutions authorized according to the capital market legislation and that the transfer of their purchase value abroad is made through banks and special financial institutions. Residents may also issue, introduce, and sell securities and other capital market instruments in the financial markets abroad. Also the issuance, public introduction, and sales of securities and other capital market instruments in Turkey by nonresidents are unrestricted within the provisions of capital market legislation.

Commercial banks may open foreign exchange accounts for residents or nonresidents. Funds in such accounts may be freely disposed of by the holders, and interest rates and other conditions on the above accounts are freely negotiable between the parties. Commercial banks are free to conduct foreign exchange transactions according to their needs, within the margins of certain ratios set by the central bank.

Gold

Under a decree issued on December 21, 1994, exports and imports of precious metals, stones, and articles have been freed within the framework of the Foreign Trade Regime. However, only the central bank is currently authorized to import unprocessed gold. The central bank and the intermediary institutions that are the members of the Istanbul Gold Exchange may import unprocessed gold without being subject to the provisions of the Foreign Trade Regime. Until the opening of the Istanbul Gold Exchange, banks, authorized institutions, special financial institutions, and intermediary institutions dealing with precious metals that have fulfilled their foreign exchange liabilities with the central bank are permitted to purchase and sell gold within the Foreign Exchange and Foreign Currency Notes Markets established by the central bank. Travelers may bring into or take out of Turkey precious metals or stones in their possession with a value of up to $15,000. Exports or imports of metals or stones exceeding this value are subject to declaration.

Changes During 1994

Exchange Arrangement

April 15. The rate of surrender of foreign exchange receipts to the central bank by commercial banks, special financial institutions, the PTT, and precious metal intermediary institutions was raised to 25 percent from 20 percent.

December 21. Under a decree amending Decree No. 32 regarding the protection of the value of the Turkish currency, precious metal intermediary institutions were added to the institutions authorized to conduct foreign exchange operations.

Resident and Nonresident Accounts

July 15. Turkish nationals working or residing abroad are permitted to open interest-bearing foreign currency accounts or "super" foreign currency accounts, depending on the amount deposited and the maturity, in the head office in Ankara of the Turkish central bank. These accounts may be maintained upon the return of these persons to Turkey.

Changes During 1995

Resident and Nonresident Accounts

January 27. Communiqué No. 95–32/13 regarding gold deposit accounts and credits was put into effect. Under the Communiqué, banks were authorized to open bank deposits in the accounts of residents and nonresidents and to extend gold credits to natural persons and legal entities engaged in the jewelry business in accordance with the principles of banking legislation.

Capital

March 1. A communiqué regarding the standard ratio of foreign exchange net general position to the capital base was put into effect. The communiqué required the authorized banks to apply a maximum ratio of 50 percent of their net general position to their capital base.

March 11. The definition of foreign currency holdings, claims, and debts that are to be taken into account in calculating the foreign currency liquidity ratio, and foreign exchange position ratio was modified by a calculation of the liquidity ratio, and the foreign exchange ratio will also include gold holdings and liabilities relating to gold transactions.

TURKMENISTAN

(Position as of December 31, 1994)

Exchange Arrangement

The currency of Turkmenistan is the Manat.[1] The exchange rate system consists of a commercial exchange (official) rate that is fixed in terms of the U.S. dollar and an exchange rate for cash transactions between individuals and commercial banks. On December 31, 1994, the commercial exchange rate in terms of the U.S. dollar was Manat 75 per US$1, and the cash exchange rate was Manat 220 per US$1. Exchange rates for other currencies are determined on the basis of the cross rates of the U.S. dollar against the currencies concerned in the international market.

Administration of Control

Under existing laws, only the Central Bank of Turkmenistan (CBT), alone or together with the Ministry of Economy and Finance and the Tax Authority, depending on the type of operation involved, is empowered to issue exchange control regulations.

The Foreign Exchange Regulation Law, which came into effect November 1, 1993, provides for freedom to make payments and transfers for current international transactions and for nonresidents to export previously imported capital. This law gives the Government the priority right to acquire foreign exchange according to the exchange arrangements established by the CBT. The use of foreign exchange reserves is controlled by the President of Turkmenistan.

Arrears are maintained with respect to external payments.

Prescription of Currency

Settlement with some Baltic countries, the Russian Ferderation, and the other countries of the former Soviet Union are made through a system of correspondent accounts. Settlements with countries with which Turkmenistan has bilateral payments agreements are effected in accordance with the procedures set forth in these agreements. Transactions with other countries are made in convertible currencies.

External payments must be made through the authorized banks.

Foreign Exchange Accounts

Authorized banks that have received a general license from the CBT to deal in foreign exchange may open foreign exchange accounts for natural and juridical persons if they possess a certificate of registration issued by the Ministry of Foreign Economic Relations. Interest is payable on balances in these accounts in the currency of the account at a rate to be determined by the authorized bank.

Imports and Exports

Trade with some countries is conducted under trade agreements. All goods may be imported and exported without restriction except for those on the negative list. In addition to certain items (such as arms and narcotics, and antiquities) whose trade is prohibited for national security reasons, quantitative and price restrictions are imposed on exports of cotton and other raw materials to protect domestic supplies.

An advance import deposit is required to be lodged with commercial banks at the rate of 100 percent.

All exports require a special license. A fee is collected at the rate of 0.01 percent of the value of the licensed product that is sold in convertible currencies; the fee on exports to the Baltic countries, Russia, and the other countries of the former Soviet Union is 0.1 percent of the ruble value of the licensed product. In principle, all export proceeds of private enterprises must be surrendered in full at the commercial exchange rate through authorized banks within three working days of receipt. Private enterprises are allowed to retain 100 percent of their foreign exchange earnings under a special presidential decree. All government entities, except oil and gas producing enterprises, are required to surrender 50 percent of their foreign exchange earnings to the CBT.

Payments for and Proceeds from Invisibles

Residents must possess valid passports to purchase foreign exchange for travel abroad. The maximum amount of foreign exchange a person may purchase from authorized banks without approval

---

[1]The national currency, the manat, was introduced on November 1, 1993 at the conversion rate of Manat 1 to Russian ruble 500, and the official exchange rate was set at Manat 2 per US$1.

from the CBT is $500; additional amounts may be granted on proof of need. All other payments for invisibles require approval from the CBT.

Proceeds from invisibles are not regulated.

Capital

Both inward and outward capital transfers are subject to the approval of the CBT. The Law on Foreign Investments in Turkmenistan permits, in principle, foreign direct investments by juridical persons with foreign participation in all sectors. Investors are required to obtain authorization from the Ministry of Foreign Economic Relations.[2] Foreign investments are protected from nationalization. The law provides that, at the request of investors, for a period of ten years the law in force at the time of registration will be applied. After required tax payments have been made, profits may be reinvested in Turkmenistan, held in bank accounts in national or other currencies, or transferred abroad.

Gold

A license is required to engage in international trade in gold. Laws regulating trade in gold are in effect.

---

[2]If the amount of investment is more than $500,000, the approval of the Cabinet of Ministers of Turkmenistan is required.

Changes During 1994

Exchange Arrangement

January 20. A procedure allowing foreign exchange to be used temporarily as a means of payment in Turkmenistan was introduced.

December 10. A special exchange rate for cash transactions between individuals and authorized banks of Manat 220 per US$1 was introduced.

Imports and Exports

January 1. The tax on exports of goods and services was eliminated.

January 1. A new procedure by which state enterprises transfer part of their foreign exchange proceeds to the Government's foreign exchange fund was introduced.

December 14. A presidential decree was issued that required that all government entities, except oil and gas-producing enterprises, must sell 50 percent of their foreign exchange earnings to the CBT at the rate established by the CBT. Private enterprises may retain 100 percent of their foreign exchange earnings.

Payments for and Proceeds from Invisibles

December 10. Under a temporary regulation introduced by authorized banks, the maximum amount of foreign exchange a person may purchase from authorized banks without approval from the CBT was increased to $500.

UGANDA

(Position as of December 31, 1994)

Exchange Arrangement

The currency of Uganda is the Uganda Shilling, the external value of which is determined in the interbank foreign exchange market. Certain transactions may be effected in foreign exchange bureaus that are licensed to buy and sell foreign exchange at freely negotiated rates. On December 31, 1994, the buying and selling rates in the interbank foreign exchange market were U Sh 922.10 and U Sh 931.44, respectively, per US$1.

Authorized banks may deal forward with customers in pounds sterling, U.S. dollars, and certain other convertible currencies, provided that there is an underlying approved import or export contract. Authorized foreign exchange dealers may impose a service charge of not more than 1.0 percent.

There are no taxes or subsidies on purchases or sales of foreign exchange. There are no arrangements for forward cover against exchange rate risk operating in the official sector.

Uganda formally accepted the obligations of Article VIII, Sections 2, 3, and 4 of the Fund Agreement, as from April 5, 1994.

Administration of Control

The Bank of Uganda administers exchange controls on behalf of the Minister of Finance but has delegated a broad range of exchange control responsibilities to authorized banks and exchange bureaus. Import and export control regulations are administered by the Ministry of Commerce, which has powers to prohibit imports and exports.

Prescription of Currency

The Bank of Uganda settles accounts in U.S. dollars with the member countries of the Preferential Trade Area (PTA) for Eastern and Southern African States through the PTA clearinghouse. Authorized payments, including payments for imports by residents of Uganda to residents of foreign countries, may be made in Uganda shillings to the credit of an external account in Uganda or in any other currency that is appropriate to the country of residence of the payee. Uganda maintains bilateral clearing arrangements with Burundi, Rwanda, and Zaïre, but these are inoperative. Inoperative bilateral trade and payments agreements are also maintained with Algeria, Cuba, Egypt, the Democratic People's Republic of Korea, and the Libyan Arab Jamahiriya.

External Accounts

Accounts in foreign exchange held by persons with diplomatic status are designated external accounts. They may be credited with authorized payments by residents of Uganda and with transfers from other external accounts or any other external source. They may be debited freely for payments to nonresidents, for transfers to other external accounts in Uganda, and for purchases of foreign currencies from authorized dealers.

Convertible Currency Accounts

Private Ugandan residents who are exporters of goods who are earning commissions, consulting fees, rent, and other incomes in foreign exchange may operate foreign exchange accounts with commercial banks in Uganda. Payments made from these accounts are subject to the same regulations as those governing sales of foreign exchange in the foreign exchange bureaus.

Imports and Import Payments

Most imports are controlled through the import-licensing system. Foreign exchange sales to various ministries and departments must be backed by documents showing the approval of the Central Tender Board.

Importers are provided with a renewable certificate, which is valid for six months and which permits them to import a broad range of goods not on the negative list. The certificate does not prescribe the importation of a specific good. The importation of pornographic materials is prohibited. Imports of firearms, ammunition, beer, soda, and cigarettes require special permission. Private sector importers may purchase foreign exchange in the interbank market or in foreign exchange bureaus to pay for imports without restriction.

Payments for Invisibles

All payments for invisibles, except for debt-service payments, are financed through the interbank foreign exchange market. With the permission of the Director of Exchange Control of the Bank of Uganda, residents of Uganda may transfer abroad profits, fees, and savings. The following limits apply to foreign exchange that may be purchased in the interbank market or in the foreign exchange bureaus without referring to the Bank of Uganda: (1) travel, $4,000 a trip; (2) medical treatment, $20,000 a person to be transferred through a bank with supporting documents; and (3) education, $25,000 a person a year.

Dividends may be transferred through the interbank market without restriction and without reference to the Bank of Uganda.

Payments by the private nonbank sector for all other invisible transactions and for certain capital transfers are subject to a combined limit (see section on Capital, below).

Exports and Export Proceeds

All exports require certificates from the Ministry of Commerce and Trade, which are valid for six months and are renewable; they may be restricted to ensure sufficient supplies for consumption in Uganda. Exporters may retain proceeds from exports and sell them in the interbank foreign exchange market.

Proceeds from Invisibles

Proceeds from invisibles may be sold in the foreign exchange interbank market. Travelers may freely bring in foreign currency banknotes and traveler's checks.

Capital

Capital transfers to all countries require individual exchange control approval.

Principal payments on nonguaranteed overseas loans by resident companies or individuals are transferable. There are no restrictions on nonguaranteed overseas loans by resident companies or individuals. Foreign investment in Uganda is permitted with or without government participation. To secure a guarantee of repatriation, it is necessary to obtain "approved status" for the investment in terms of the Investment Code of 1991. In normal circumstances, approved status is given freely.

All imports and exports of securities require approval. Approval is freely granted for the purchase by nonresidents of Ugandan securities, provided that payment is received in an appropriate manner. The income from such securities is remittable, as are the proceeds on resale in most cases.

Gold

Residents may hold and acquire gold coins in Uganda for numismatic purposes. Only monetary authorities and licensed dealers are allowed to hold or acquire gold in Uganda in any form other than jewelry. Imports and exports of gold in any form other than jewelry constituting the personal effects of a traveler require licenses issued by the Ministry of Mines.

Changes During 1994

Exchange Arrangement

April 5. Uganda formally accepted the obligations of Article VIII, Sections 2, 3, and 4 of the Fund Agreement.

Capital

August 3. The requirement to obtain approval for loans and overdraft facilities to nonresident persons was abolished.

UKRAINE

(Position as of December 31, 1994)

Exchange Arrangement

The currency of the Republic of Ukraine is the Ukrainian Karbovanets. The official exchange rates of the karbovanets against the U.S. dollar, the deutsche mark, the Russian ruble, and the Belarussian ruble are determined through competitive bidding of commercial banks at the auction conducted by the National Bank of Ukraine (NBU) twice a week. The official rates for all other convertible currencies are determined daily on the basis of the cross rates of the U.S. dollar for the currencies concerned in the international market. The official rate applies to all external transactions. The NBU is the major provider of the U.S. dollar funds that it has purchased from exporters during the week at the previous auction rate. The NBU may also participate in the auctions and buy foreign exchange for its own reserves. Commercial banks may participate in the auctions without limitation provided they hold contracts for import payments; they may not participate in the auction on their own behalf. The exchange rate for cash transactions for individuals at commercial banks is freely determined and quoted on a daily basis by commercial banks; the spread between the selling and buying rates for such transactions, however, must not exceed 2.5 percent. On December 31, 1994, the official rate was Krb 104.200 per US$1.

There are no taxes or subsidies on purchases or sales of foreign exchange. There are no arrangements for forward cover against exchange rate risk operating in the official or the commercial banking sector.

Administration of Control

Exchange control is administered by the NBU. Commercial banks must be licensed by the NBU to engage in foreign exchange transactions. As of February 28, 1994, 38 commercial banks were licensed to engage in international transactions and to hold foreign exchange accounts abroad.

Arrears are maintained with respect to external payments.

Prescription of Currency

Settlements with the Baltic countries, the Russian Federation, and the other countries of the former Soviet Union are made through a system of correspondent accounts. Payments to and receipts from countries with which Ukraine has bilateral payments agreements are made in the currencies and in accordance with the procedures set forth in those agreements.[1] Trade with all other countries is settled in convertible currencies. Nonbarter trade with the countries of the former Soviet Union is settled in the currencies of these countries as stipulated in the agreements, with the exception of trade through commodity exchanges, which is transacted in convertible currencies.

Resident and Nonresident Accounts

Residents and nonresidents may open and operate foreign currency deposits under certain conditions. The opening and operation of accounts in domestic currency by nonresidents is restricted.

Imports and Exports

Licenses issued by the Ministry of Foreign Economic Relations are required for import transactions.[2] There are no quantitative restrictions on imports; nontariff barriers were limited to the standard rules that imported goods must meet national safety and environmental standards. The customs tariff regime contains three categories of duty rates. The first category (preferred duty rates) applies to goods entering from countries that belong, with Ukraine, to customs unions; those imported from developing countries (agricultural and industrial goods); and those imported under intergovernmental preferential agreements. The rate of duty for these goods, except for tobacco and alcohol products, is zero. The second category (concessional duty rates) applies to goods imported from countries that have entered into a most-favored-nation arrangement with Ukraine and to goods imported from developing countries that are not covered under the first category. The average rate in this category is 6 percent. The third category applies to goods imported from all other countries; the average rate in this category is 12 percent. A value-

---

[1] At the end of 1994, Ukraine maintained bilateral trade and payments agreements with Bulgaria, the Czech Republic, Hungary, the Islamic Republic of Iran, Mongolia, and the Slovak Republic.

[2] A license fee of 0.1 percent of the total amount exported or imported is levied on all importers.

added tax at the rate of 28 percent has been levied on all imported goods since January 1, 1994.

All export quotas and licenses, with few exceptions, were abolished as of November 1, 1994. Quotas and licenses apply to exports of grain, ferrous and nonferrous scrap, cast iron, coal, and goods subject to voluntary export restraint under international agreements. Exporters may obtain a quota in one of three ways: (1) by signing a state contract, under which the Government will purchase exportable goods for karbovanets at domestic market prices and use trading firms to sell them abroad for convertible currency; (2) by signing a state order to fulfill interstate barter agreements; or (3) by purchasing a license at the monthly auctions organized by the Ministry of Foreign Economic Relations and local commodity exchanges. About one-fifth of the total quota for some products is earmarked for sale at the auctions. Quotas are not transferable.

The exportation of manufactured goods is not subject to quotas. Regional authorities are authorized to export up to 5 percent of certain locally produced nonmanufactured goods outside the quota system.[3] Strategic raw materials falling under the special export regime may be exported only by firms that have been authorized by the Cabinet of Ministers. In 1994, the number of items under the special export regime was reduced from eight to three (coal, nonferrous metals, and mineral fertilizers). The exportation of goods and services produced by enterprises established with foreign capital investments is exempt from quota restrictions and licensing requirements as well as from export duties unless otherwise stipulated in domestic legislation or by international agreements.

Effective January 1, 1994, all export taxes were eliminated.

Firms must repatriate all of their foreign exchange proceeds from exports to domestic commercial bank accounts within 30 days of shipment, and sell, within 5 days of repatriation, 50 percent of the foreign currency export proceeds. Foreign exchange proceeds from exports by foreign firms are exempt from the surrender requirements. Forty percent of foreign exchange proceeds must be sold at the auctions, and the remaining 10 percent must be sold to the NBU at the official exchange rate.

Payments for and Proceeds from Invisibles

Exporters of services, such as the tourist industry, are also subject to the surrender requirement. Exemptions from these repatriation and surrender requirements are limited to the following: (1) a few enterprises engaging in international operations, such as the international airline company, are not required to repatriate their foreign exchange earnings; (2) individuals who provide services to nonresidents are not required to hold foreign exchange earnings in domestic foreign currency accounts or surrender them to the Government or the NBU; (3) exporters who need to service external debt obligations that have been approved by the NBU, if the maturity exceeds 90 days, may retain foreign exchange needed for external debt-service obligations before surrendering proceeds; and (4) intermediary firms in the foreign trade sector are required to surrender 50 percent of their profits in foreign exchange rather than 50 percent of revenues in foreign exchange.

Residents may purchase foreign exchange without limit. Residents may export foreign banknotes up to $400; they may export foreign banknotes up to $2,000 with the permission of authorized banks and up to $10,000 with the permission of the NBU.

The Law on Foreign Investment guarantees that foreign investors may, after paying taxes and fees, transfer abroad without restriction dividends, profits, and other foreign exchange assets obtained legally in connection with their investments.

Capital

The contracting of external loans with maturities exceeding 90 days must be approved by the NBU. The NBU does not guarantee any loan. Lending to foreign borrowers also requires permission from the NBU.

Foreign investments in Ukraine are governed by the Law on Foreign Economic Activity (of April 16, 1991), the Law on Income Tax for Companies and Organizations (of February 21, 1992), the Law on Foreign Investment (of March 3, 1992), and the Cabinet of Ministers Decree on Foreign Investment Regimes (of May 20, 1993).[4] Foreign investments in most types of business are permitted, although licenses are required in some cases. A license from the Ministry of Finance is required for investments in insurance and businesses engaged in intermediation activities. A license from the NBU is required for investments in the banking sector. In addition, concessions from the Council of Ministers are required for investments in the mining sector; such concessions

---

[3]These include pig iron, ferro-silicon, potassium chloride, silicon carbide, artificial corundum, and urea.

[4]The State Program for Attraction of Foreign Investment of December 17, 1993 came into force on March 1, 1994. The program provides foreign investors with investment incentives on tax, insurance, credit, and depreciation for 32 branches of the Ukrainian economy.

may be for a maximum of 49 years. Foreign investment in Ukraine must be made in convertible currency or in kind. The Russian ruble is not regarded as convertible currency for this purpose.

Tax relief is granted to enterprises established with foreign capital investments. The nature of the relief depends on the activity of the enterprise or organization, its turnover, and the proportion of foreign equity capital ownership. The basic profit tax rate is 18 percent, although special tax rates apply in certain sectors. For joint ventures whose foreign equity capital ownership is less than 20 percent, the basic tax rate is also 18 percent. Firms other than those engaged in trading and intermediating activities are exempt from the profit tax for five years from the first year in which profit is recorded; thereafter, the profit tax rate is reduced by 50 percent from the rates applicable to domestic enterprises. Moreover, they are granted a further five-year tax exemption from any new taxes imposed in the future. Trading firms are exempt from the profit tax for the first three years, and intermediating firms for the first two years, from the first year in which profit is recorded; thereafter, the profit tax rate is reduced by 30 percent from the applicable tax rate. In cases where the foreign equity capital ownership is 100 percent, taxable profits may be reduced by the amount of capital actually invested in Ukraine; additional relief may be granted for investments in priority sectors or in special economic zones.

Gold

The NBU grants permission to commercial banks to export and import gold and other monetary metals. Other residents are required to obtain a license from the Ministry of Finance to deal in precious metals and stones. Permission to export precious metals and precious stones is granted by the Cabinet of Ministers of Ukraine.

Changes During 1994

Exchange Arrangement

February 5. Weekly auctions of nonconvertible currencies (mostly the currencies of the countries of the former Soviet Union) began to be conducted.

February 25. The weekly auction for the U.S. dollar was resumed.

October 6. The Ukrainian Interbank Currency Exchange (UICEX) resumed its operations.

October 24. The Tender Committee, which previously allocated foreign exchange surrendered at the official rate, was abolished.

November 27. Foreign exchange auctions began to be conducted twice a week.

Imports and Exports

January 1. A value-added tax on imported goods was introduced at the rate of 28 percent.

January 1. The option of exporting outside the quotas if an export license was obtained on the Ukrainian Stock Exchange by paying an export duty in national currency equivalent to 5–30 percent of the price of the goods exported was discontinued. All export taxes were eliminated.

February 15. The Ministry of Foreign Economic Relations issued a decree authorizing regional authorities to export up to 5 percent of certain locally produced nonmanufactured goods outside the quota system.

March 1. Import quotas were introduced for an extensive list of goods.

May 3. All import quotas were eliminated.

November 1. All export quotas and licenses other than those on grain, ferrous, and nonferrous scrap, cast iron, coal, and goods subject to voluntary export restraint under international agreements were abolished.

UNITED ARAB EMIRATES[1]

(Position as of December 31, 1994)

Exchange Arrangement

The currency of the United Arab Emirates is the U.A.E. Dirham, which is pegged to the SDR at Dh 4.76190 per SDR 1. The United Arab Emirates has established margins of 7.25 percent around the official rate; since November 1980, the U.A.E. dirham has maintained an unchanged relationship with the U.S. dollar, the intervention currency. The United Arab Emirates Central Bank publishes buying and selling rates for the U.S. dollar only. On December 31, 1994, the official buying and selling rates were Dh 3.6730 and Dh 3.6990, respectively, per US$1. The Central Bank sets no limits on the amount of U.S. dollars that it is prepared to buy from or sell to any commercial bank. Commercial banks are free to enter into foreign exchange transactions, including forward contracts related to commercial and financial transactions, at rates of their own choosing; the rates quoted by commercial banks for currencies other than the U.S. dollar are determined on the basis of international quotations.

The Central Bank maintains a swap facility, which the commercial banks may use to purchase dirhams spot and sell dirhams forward for periods of one week, one month, and three months. For each bank, maximum limits of $20 million outstanding for one-month and three-month swaps and $10 million outstanding for one-week swaps are in effect. There is also a limit of $3 million a day on purchases by each bank for one-month and three-month swaps. Swap facilities are not available to banks having a short position in dirhams, except for the covering of forward transactions for commercial purposes. There are no taxes or subsidies on purchases or sales of foreign exchange.

The United Arab Emirates formally accepted the obligations of Article VIII, Sections 2, 3, and 4 of the Fund Agreement on February 13, 1974.

Administration of Control

There is neither exchange control legislation nor an exchange control authority in the United Arab Emirates, and there are no registration requirements for inward or outward transfers. There is no regime of export and import licensing.

Prescription of Currency

All settlements with Israel are prohibited. No other prescription of currency requirements are in force.

Nonresident Accounts

Distinction is drawn between accounts held by residents and those held by nonresidents. Nonresident accounts consist of those held with commercial banks on behalf of U.A.E. citizens working abroad; all foreigners working in the United Arab Emirates but who do not have residency; all embassies and diplomatic agencies in the country; all trade and financial companies, banks, and industrial companies incorporated outside the U.A.E. that have no local branches; and branches of local institutions in foreign countries.

Imports and Import Payments

Imports from Israel are prohibited, as are imports of products manufactured by foreign companies blacklisted by the Arab League. Imports of a few commodities are prohibited from all sources for health or security reasons, but virtually all other commodities may be freely imported without an individual import permit. However, only licensed parties can enter the import trade, and importers may import only the commodities specified in their license. There are no restrictions on the availability of foreign exchange for payments in respect of permitted imports. With the exception of specified items, imports into the United Arab Emirates are subject to a customs duty of 4 percent of the c.i.f. value. Imports originating from member countries of the Cooperation Council for the Arab States of the Gulf (GCC) are not subject to customs duty.

Exports and Export Proceeds

Exports and re-exports to Israel are prohibited. Virtually all commodities may be exported or re-exported freely and without an export license to any other destination.

Each Emirate establishes its own export regulations. The proceeds from exports need not be repatriated or surrendered and may be disposed of freely, regardless of the currency involved.

Payments for and Proceeds from Invisibles

All payments for current invisibles may be made freely, with the exception of payments to Israel,

---

[1]The seven federated states of the United Arab Emirates are Abu Dhabi, Dubai, Sharjah, Ajman, Umm al Qaiwain, Ras al Khaimah, and Fujairah.

which are prohibited. There are no requirements governing receipts. Travelers may take out and bring in any amount in foreign or domestic bank notes.

Capital

No exchange control requirements are imposed on capital receipts or payments by residents or nonresidents. Commercial banks operating in the United Arab Emirates are prohibited from engaging in nonbanking operations (as specified in Article 90 of the Central Bank Act of 1980) and from owning real estate except for the purpose of carrying on business and for accommodation. Under the United Arab Emirates Company Law (Law No. 8 of 1984), at least 51 percent of the equity of companies, other than branches of foreign companies, must be held by nationals of the United Arab Emirates. Nationals of the other member countries of the GCC are permitted to hold (1) up to 75 percent of the equity of companies in the industrial, agricultural, fisheries, and construction sectors, and in the consultancy areas (Law No. 2 of 1984); and (2) up to 100 percent of the equity of companies in the hotel industry. Furthermore, nationals of the other member countries

of the GCC are permitted to engage in wholesale and retail trade activities, except in the form of companies, in which case they are subject to the Company Law of 1984. Profits on foreign capital invested in the United Arab Emirates may be remitted freely. Banks operating in the United Arab Emirates are required to maintain special deposits with the Central Bank equal to 30 percent of their placements with, or lending to, nonresident banks in dirhams with a remaining life of one year or less. The profits of certain banks are subject to a fee levied by local authorities at an annual rate of 20 percent.

Gold

Residents and nonresidents may freely purchase, hold, and sell gold in any form, at home or abroad. They may also, without a permit, import and export gold in any form, but only licensed parties may import gold for trade purposes. Gold bullion is exempt from import duty, but jewelry is not.

Changes During 1994

No significant changes occurred in the exchange and trade system.

UNITED KINGDOM

(Position as of December 31, 1994)

Exchange Arrangement

The currency of the United Kingdom is the Pound Sterling. The U.K. authorities do not maintain margins in respect of exchange transactions, and spot and forward exchange rates are determined on the basis of demand and supply conditions in the exchange markets. However, the authorities may intervene at their discretion with a view to moderating undue fluctuations in the exchange rate.[1] On December 31, 1994, the closing buying and selling rates for the pound sterling against the U.S. dollar in foreign exchange markets in London as observed by the Bank of England were US$1.5650 and US$1.5640, respectively, per £1. Banks are allowed to engage in spot and forward exchange transactions in any currency, and they may deal among themselves and with residents and nonresidents in foreign notes and coins at free market exchange rates.

The United Kingdom formally accepted the obligations of Article VIII, Sections 2, 3, and 4 of the Fund Agreement, as from February 15, 1961.

Administration of Control

There are no exchange controls. The licensing of imports and exports is handled mostly by the Department of Trade and Industry, but other departments also issue licenses in specialized fields.

In accordance with the Fund's Executive Board Decision No. 144-(52/51) adopted on August 14, 1952, the United Kingdom notified the IMF on July 26, 1992 that, in compliance with UN Security Council Resolution No. 757 (1992), certain restrictions had been imposed on the making of payments and transfers for current international transactions in respect of the Federal Republic of Yugoslavia (Serbia/Montenegro).

The United Kingdom also notified the IMF on September 22, 1994 that, in compliance with UN Security Council Resolution No. 883 and 841 (1993), certain restrictions had been imposed on the making of payments and transfers for current international transactions in respect of the Libyan Arab Jamahiriya and Haiti. Restrictions against Iraq, as reported to the IMF on August 13, 1990, continue to be enforced.

Prescription of Currency

There are no prescription of currency requirements.

Imports and Import Payments

Most imports are admitted to the United Kingdom under an open general import license. The remaining restrictions concern textiles and clothing under the Multifiber Arrangement (MFA) and maintained under various European Union bilateral agreements with third countries that are not members of the MFA, certain steel products from the Russian Federation and Ukraine that are subject to the EU bilateral agreements, autonomous EU-wide restrictions on imports of certain steel products from Kazakhstan, EU-wide tariff quotas on certain products produced in the Czech Republic and the Slovak Republic, and EU-wide quotas on seven categories of goods originating in China. Imports of cars from Japan are also subject to restraint under a separate agreement (The Elements of Consensus) between the EU and the Japanese Government. Imports of cereals and cereal products, beef and veal, mutton and lamb, poultry meat, and dairy products, other than butter and cheese, are subject to minimum import prices enforced through autonomously imposed variable import levies. Imports of many other agricultural, horticultural, and livestock products are subject to EU regulations. A few articles may be imported under open individual licenses, that is, without limit as to quantity or value.

Exports and Export Proceeds

Most exports are free of export control, and there are no requirements affecting export proceeds.[2] Under the Tender to Contract Facility of the Export Credits Guarantee Department, exporters bidding for major capital projects in Canadian dollars, deutsche mark, Japanese yen, Swiss francs, or U.S. dollars, when the U.K. element of the contract is for the equivalent of at least £10 million, may obtain cover against exchange rate fluctuations between the sub-

---

[1]The United Kingdom suspended intervention obligations with respect to the exchange rate and intervention mechanism of the European Monetary systems (EMS) on September 16, 1992.

[2]Exports of certain products are controlled for reasons of national security, animal welfare, national heritage, and in accordance with international agreements.

mission of their bid and the awarding of the contract.

Payments for and Proceeds from Invisibles

There are no restrictions on payments for and proceeds from invisibles. Travelers may import or export any amount of domestic and foreign banknotes or any other means of payment.

Capital

There are no restrictions or exchange control requirements on capital transfers by residents or nonresidents. Residents and nonresidents may freely transfer assets to and from the United Kingdom.

Investments, whether direct or portfolio, may be freely made by nonresidents in the United Kingdom or by residents abroad. However, investments involving the takeover of existing U.K. companies that are considered a vital part of U.K. industry may be subject to the provisions of the Fair Trading Act of 1973. The Government also has the power, under the Industry Act of 1975, to prevent or undo undesirable foreign takeovers of important manufacturing undertakings.

There are no restrictions or formalities on transactions in sterling or foreign currency securities. Banks may freely accept foreign currency deposits and employ them in their foreign currency business or convert them to sterling, subject to prudential guidelines issued by the Bank of England concerning the limitation of risks arising from their foreign exchange exposure. Net spot liabilities in foreign currencies (that is, the net amount of foreign currency resources funding sterling assets) form part of a bank's eligible liabilities that are subject to a 0.35 percent non-interest-bearing deposit requirement with the Bank of England and may also be subject to calls for special deposits to be placed with the bank. There is currently no special deposit call.

Gold

Gold bullion and gold coins are not subject to control in the United Kingdom. Gold sovereigns and Britannias are legal tender but do not circulate. Gold coins have also been issued in Jersey and the Isle of Man and are legal tender there. Except under license granted by the Treasury, it is an offense to melt down or break up any metal coin that is for the time being current in the United Kingdom or that, having been current there, has at any time after May 16, 1969 ceased to be so. The exportation of gold in manufactured form over 50 years old and valued at £8,000 and over for each item or matching set of items also requires a license from the Department of Trade and Industry. There is a free gold market in London in which gold bars are freely traded.

Changes During 1994

No significant changes occurred in the exchange and trade system.

(See Appendix for a summary of trade measures introduced and eliminated on an EU-wide basis during 1994, page 554.)

UNITED STATES

(Position as of December 31, 1994)

Exchange Arrangement

The currency of the United States is the U.S. Dollar. The U.S. authorities do not maintain margins in respect of exchange transactions, and spot and forward exchange rates are determined on the basis of demand and supply conditions in the exchange markets. However, the authorities intervene when necessary to counter disorderly conditions in the exchange markets or when otherwise deemed appropriate. There are no taxes or subsidies on purchases or sales of foreign exchange.

The United States formally accepted the obligations of Article VIII, Sections 2, 3, and 4 of the Fund Agreement, as from December 10, 1946.

Administration of Control

The Department of the Treasury administers economic sanction programs involving direct or indirect financial or commercial transactions with Cuba, the Democratic People's Republic of Korea, Iraq, the Libyan Arab Jamahiriya, the Federal Republic of Yugoslavia (Serbia/Montenegro), the areas of Bosnia and Herzegovina controlled by Bosnian Serb forces and the UN-protected areas of Croatia as specified under, respectively, the Cuban Assets Control Regulations, the Foreign Assets Control Regulations, the Libyan Sanctions Regulations, the Iraqi Sanctions Regulations, and the Federal Republic of Yugoslavia (Serbia/Montenegro) Sanctions Regulations. It also has administrative responsibility for blocked accounts of the above countries, Cambodian accounts blocked in the name of the Exchange Support Fund for the Khmer Republic, and certain remaining blocked Vietnamese funds. The Department of the Treasury regulates the importation into the United States of goods or services originating from the Islamic Republic of Iran under the Iranian Transactions Regulations and restricts the sale or supply of arms and petroleum products, regardless of origin, to UNITA (otherwise known as Armed Forces for the Liberation of Angola) and to the territory of Angola under the UNITA (Angola) Sanctions Regulations.

The Customs Service of the Treasury Department administers import quotas; such quotas, however, are frequently established or allocated by other agencies. The Committee for the Implementation of Textile Agreements, chaired by the Department of Commerce and represented by other agencies, decides when to request consultation with exporting countries to limit imports on the basis of the guidelines of the Multifiber Arrangement (MFA) and bilateral restraint agreements. Import quotas on certain dairy products are administered by the Department of Agriculture through the issuance of import licenses. For items subject to export control—other than munitions items and items qualified below—the Department of Commerce is, in general, the responsible authority.

There are no restrictions on foreign payments, except those imposed under Treasury Department regulations on transactions involving the governments or nationals of Cuba, the Democratic People's Republic of Korea, the Government of Libya, and the governments of or entities located in or controlled from the Federal Republic of Yugoslavia (Serbia/Montenegro), as well as those on imports from, and certain assets of, the Islamic Republic of Iran and on prohibited exports to UNITA or to the territory of Angola. Transfers of funds are also prohibited to persons in Iraq and the Federal Republic of Yugoslavia (Serbia/Montenegro), or to or for the benefit of entities, wherever located, owned or controlled by entities in the Federal Republic of Yugoslavia (Serbia/Montenegro), pursuant to UN Security Council resolutions, or to or through Libyan financial institutions or to entities owned or controlled by the Government of Libya. Certain payments to Cuba and to the Democratic People's Republic of Korea related to authorized travel are permitted, as are certain payments in connection with travel to and in the United States by nationals of these countries.

In accordance with the Fund's Executive Board Decision No. 144-(52/51) adopted on August 14, 1952, the United States notified the Fund on June 26, 1992 that, in compliance with UN Security Council Resolution No. 757 (1992), certain restrictions had been imposed on the making of payments and transfers for current international transactions in respect of the Federal Republic of Yugoslavia (Serbia/Montenegro).

Imports and Import Payments

The importation of goods and services originating in Cuba, the Islamic Republic of Iran, Iraq, the Democratic People's Republic of Korea, the Libyan Arab Jamahiriya, and the Federal Republic of

Yugoslavia (Serbia/Montenegro), and those areas of Bosnia and Herzegovina controlled by the Bosnian Serb forces and the UN-protected areas of Croatia is prohibited unless specifically authorized.

Under authority of Section 22 of the Agricultural Adjustment Act of 1993, as amended, import quotas are in effect for certain agricultural products, including cotton of specified staple lengths, certain cotton waste and products, certain dairy products, peanuts, and certain products containing sugar. Import quotas, except those for peanuts, certain cotton products, butter, certain other dairy products, and certain products containing sugar, are on a country-of-origin basis. Quotas may be imposed on certain types of meat under conditions set forth in the Meat Import Act of 1979. Most dairy products that are subject to quotas are also subject to import licensing.

The United States is a party to the MFA negotiated within the framework of the General Agreement on Tariffs and Trade (GATT). It maintains bilateral textile agreements with 31 countries negotiated in accordance with the MFA's provisions, and 7 agreements with nonsignatories of the MFA. These agreements control trading partners' exports of textiles and apparel to the United States in specific product categories and provide for orderly expansion of trade while minimizing the disruption of the U.S. market for these products. Imports from both agreement and nonagreement countries are monitored along with domestic industry performance to determine whether market disruption exists or is threatened. When necessary, consultations with exporting countries are requested to establish limitations.

Free trade area agreements are in force with Canada, Israel, and Mexico.

The Generalized System of Preferences (GSP), which provided for duty-free treatment for approximately 4,400 items from 146 beneficiary developing countries, has been in operation since January 1976.[1] Under the program, a procedure referred to as "product graduation" allowed eligibility for duty-free treatment to be withdrawn for a particular product in which a beneficiary country became competitive as defined by statute. However, the President has the authority to waive such treatment. Cumulative treatment under the GSP scheme was extended to beneficiary members of the Andean Group, the Association of South East Asian Nations (ASEAN), and the Caribbean Common Market (CARICOM); cumulation allowed two or more member countries of an eligible association to contribute jointly to the requirement that at least 35 percent of the direct cost of producing a given product originate in the beneficiary country. Exempt from competitive needs limits is a category of countries designated as "least developed" beneficiaries; currently, 36 countries are thus designated.[2] Under the Caribbean Basin Economic Recovery Act, 24 countries and entities[3] were designated to receive preferential tariff treatment on specified imports.

Exports and Export Proceeds

Ammunition may be exported only under license issued by the Office of Defense Trade Controls in the Department of State. The Department of Commerce administers controls directly on exports of crime control and detection equipment, as well as on instruments and related technical data, to all countries except other members of the North Atlantic Treaty Organization (NATO), Australia, Japan, and New Zealand. The Department of Commerce administers controls directly on exports of other goods from the United States and on re-exports of goods of U.S. origin from any area.

With the exception of publications and other information materials, personal baggage, and similar items, all exports from the United States to Cuba, Iraq, the Democratic People's Republic of Korea, the Libyan Arab Jamahiriya, the Federal Republic of Yugoslavia (Serbia/Montenegro), those areas of Bosnia and Herzegovina controlled by the Bosnian Serb forces, and the UN-protected areas of Croatia are prohibited unless licensed by the Department of Commerce and/or the Treasury Department. The Treasury Department administers controls on exports from third countries to Cuba, and to the Democratic People's Republic of Korea, of goods of U.S. or foreign origin by U.S. nationals or by foreign firms that are owned or controlled by U.S. nationals, and on certain third-country exports by U.S. nationals to the Libyan Arab Jamahiriya. Third-

---

[1] It expired on July 4, 1993, but on August 11, Congress extended the GSP until September 30, 1999 and removed the countries of the former Soviet Union from the list of countries that were banned as GSP beneficiaries.

[2] Bangladesh, Benin, Bhutan, Botswana, Burkina Faso, Burundi, Cape Verde, Central African Republic, Chad, Comoros, Djibouti, Equatorial Guinea, The Gambia, Guinea, Guinea-Bissau, Haiti, Kiribati, Lesotho, Malawi, Maldives, Mali, Mozambique, Nepal, Niger, Rwanda, São Tomé and Príncipe, Sierra Leone, Somalia, Sudan, Tanzania, Togo, Tuvalu, Uganda, Vanuatu, Western Samoa, and Yemen Arab Republic.

[3] Antigua and Barbuda, Aruba, The Bahamas, Barbados, Belize, British Virgin Islands, Costa Rica, Dominica, Dominican Republic, El Salvador, Grenada, Guatemala, Guyana, Haiti, Honduras, Jamaica, Montserrat, Netherlands Antilles, Nicaragua, Panama, St. Kitts and Nevis, St. Lucia, St. Vincent and the Grenadines, and Trinidad and Tobago.

country exports by U.S. nationals to Iraq, the Federal Republic of Yugoslavia (Serbia/Montenegro), exports by U.S. nationals of arms and petroleum products, regardless of origin, to UNITA, or to the territory of Angola other than through certain designated points of entry, are also prohibited. Restrictions on exports of certain military equipment to South Africa remain in effect along with a munitions embargo. Exports to all other countries, except Canada, of designated strategic materials and equipment require validated licenses from the Department of Commerce.

Persons subject to U.S. jurisdiction require a Treasury Department license to participate in offshore transactions in strategic goods involving certain countries regardless of the origin of the goods. For many commodities being exported to countries other than the Islamic State of Afghanistan, former member countries of the Council for Mutual Economic Assistance (CMEA), Cuba, the Democratic People's Republic of Korea, the Lao People's Democratic Republic, the Libyan Arab Jamahiriya, Viet Nam, and the Federal Republic of Yugoslavia (Serbia/Montenegro), distribution licenses may be obtained from the Commerce Department to cover multiple shipments.

Under the Export Administration Act of 1979, amended in 1985, the President can suspend the exportation of nonagricultural goods for reasons of national security, foreign policy, or short supply in the domestic economy, although efforts are made to minimize the use of such authority. Export suspension of agricultural commodities may not be imposed for reasons of short supply, foreign policy, or national security unless a national emergency is declared. For agricultural commodities such as wheat, flour, corn, sorghum, rice, soybeans and soybean products, and cotton, exporting companies are required to participate in a reporting system designed to improve market information and allow for more orderly exporting. The proceeds of exports are not subject to exchange control.

Payments for and Proceeds from Invisibles

Payments and transfers abroad may be made freely, except for payments to or for the account of the governments or nationals of Cuba, and the Democratic People's Republic of Korea, or to or for the accounts of the governments and government-controlled entities worldwide of Iraq, the Libyan Arab Jamahiriya, the Federal Republic of Yugoslavia (Serbia/Montenegro), the military and civilian authorities in those areas of Bosnia and Herzegovina

controlled by Bosnian Serb forces, and certain payments relating to the Islamic Republic of Iran.[4]

Transfers of funds to persons in Iraq and in the Federal Republic of Yugoslavia (Serbia/Montenegro) are prohibited. Effective December 19, 1991, the Libyan Arab Jamahiriya was prohibited from clearing funds involving third countries through U.S. banks. Payments and transfers to entities located in or controlled from the Federal Republic of Yugoslavia (Serbia/Montenegro), or those areas of Bosnia and Herzegovina under the control of Bosnian Serb forces, are prohibited. Remittances of up to $1,000 to Cuba are allowed to aid a relative's emigration from Cuba to the United States. Receipts of funds from Cuba and the Democratic People's Republic of Korea are subject to blocking, as are payments involving a governmental interest from Iraq, the Libyan Arab Jamahiriya, and the Federal Republic of Yugoslavia (Serbia/Montenegro) and payments involving an interest of an entity or undertaking in or controlled from the Federal Republic of Yugoslavia (Serbia/Montenegro), or those areas of Bosnia and Herzegovina controlled by Bosnia Serb forces. Individuals leaving or entering the United States with more than $10,000 in domestic or foreign currency, traveler's checks, money orders, or bearer-form negotiable securities must declare these to customs at the point of exit or entry.

Capital

Incoming or outgoing capital payments by residents or nonresidents are not subject to exchange control. In addition, inward and outward direct or portfolio investment is generally free of any other form of approval requirement. Investments involving ownership interest in banks are subject to federal and state banking laws and regulations. However, as noted above, there are restrictions on certain transactions with, or involving, Cuba, Iraq, the Democratic People's Republic of Korea, the Libyan Arab Jamahiriya, the Federal Republic of Yugoslavia (Serbia/Montenegro), and those areas of Bosnia and Herzegovina controlled by Bosnian Serb forces.

The 1988 Omnibus Trade Act contained a provision authorizing the President to suspend or prohibit foreign acquisitions, mergers, and takeovers in the United States (the Exon-Florio Amendment) if he determines that the foreign investor might take

---

[4]Certain payments and transfers to the Government of the Islamic Republic of Iran, its instrumentalities, and controlled entities involving obligations contracted before January 19, 1981 are subject to restrictions, as are payments for goods or services imported from the Islamic Republic of Iran.

action that would threaten to impair national security and if existing laws, except the International Economic Emergency Preparedness Act and the Exon-Florio provision itself, are not, in the President's judgment, adequate or appropriate to protect national security.

The Johnson Act, 18 U.S.C. 955, prohibits, with certain exceptions, persons within the United States from dealing in financial obligations or extending loans to foreign governments that have defaulted on payments of their obligations to the U.S. Government. The act does not apply to those foreign governments that are members of both the IMF and the World Bank.

There is no restriction on the amount of cash or negotiable instruments that may be brought into or taken out of the United States; however, there are certain reporting requirements for travelers entering or leaving the United States when they are carrying more than $10,000 in cash or negotiable instruments (as well as corresponding reporting requirements for shipments of currency or bearer assets through the mails). In addition, ownership of U.S. agricultural land by foreign nationals or by U.S. corporations in which foreign owners have a significant interest (at least 10 percent) or substantial control must be reported to the U.S. Department of Agriculture. Certain states in the United States impose varying restrictions on foreign nationals' purchases of land within their borders.

The foreign currency positions of banks, whether overall or with respect to individual currencies, are not subject to quantitative limitations, but banks are subject to prudential oversight. U.S. agencies and branches of foreign banks, as well as domestic banks, may be subject to reserve requirements by the Federal Reserve system.

Beginning December 3, 1981, U.S.-chartered depository institutions, U.S. offices of Edge Act and Agreement Corporations,[5] and U.S. branches and agencies of foreign banks have been allowed to establish international banking facilities (IBFs) in the United States. IBFs may accept deposits only from foreign residents (including foreign offices of domestic banks), from other IBFs, or from the institution establishing the IBF. Such funds are exempt from reserve requirements under Regulation D. For nonbank foreign residents, the minimum maturity or notice requirement is two business days, and the minimum transaction amount is $100,000. Funds raised by an IBF may be used only to extend credit

to foreign residents (including foreign offices of domestic banks), to other IBFs, or to the entity establishing the IBF. Credit may be extended to nonbank foreign residents only if the proceeds are used to finance the operations of the borrower or its affiliates outside the United States. Advances from an IBF to its establishing entity in the United States are subject to Eurocurrency reserve requirements (currently set at zero percent) in the same manner as advances to the establishing entity from the entity's foreign branches. A number of individual states (but not the federal Government) have granted favorable tax treatment under state or local law to IBF operations. In addition, federal legislation was enacted to exempt deposits at IBFs from Federal Deposit Insurance Corporation insurance coverage and assessments. Effective December 31, 1988, U.S. banks have been permitted to accept foreign currency deposits.

Gold

U.S. citizens or residents may freely purchase, hold, and sell gold in any form, at home or abroad, except for certain gold transactions (e.g., imports or exports) involving Cuba, Iraq, the Democratic People's Republic of Korea, the Libyan Arab Jamahiriya, the Federal Republic of Yugoslavia (Serbia/Montenegro), and those areas of Bosnia and Herzegovina controlled by Bosnian Serb forces and the UN-protected areas of Croatia. Commercial banks may deal in gold bullion and gold coins, with the same exceptions. Treasury Department licensing for importers, exporters, producers, refiners, and processors of gold is not required, with the same country exceptions. Gold producers may sell their output in the free market, with the same country exceptions. Gold, but not counterfeit gold coins, may be freely imported, except from the countries mentioned above. U.S. gold coins are legal tender at their face value.

Commercial imports of gold jewelry are free of quantitative restrictions but are subject to import duty at a rate of approximately 12 percent. There is no duty on gold ore, bullion, or coins. All forms of gold must be declared at the point of entry into the United States.

Changes During 1994

Administration of Control

During 1994, the United States concluded trade agreements with a number of countries. The most significant were the following:

---

[5]These are defined as domestically chartered corporations authorized to engage in international banking and financial operations.

January 12. The Bilateral Investment Treaty between the United States and the Kyrgyz Republic came into force.

January 12. The Bilateral Investment Treaty between the United States and Kazakhstan came into force.

January 15. The Bilateral Investment Treaty between the United States and Romania came into force.

January 17. The United States and China concluded an agreement limiting textile and apparel exports from China to the United States.

February 4. The Bilateral Investment Treaty between the United States and Jamaica was concluded.

April 30. The United States identified 37 trading partners that deny adequate and effective protection of intellectual property rights.

June 2. The Bilateral Investment Treaty between the United States and Bulgaria came into force.

August 30. Additional restrictions on transfers to Cuba were imposed.

October 2. The Bilateral Investment Treaty between the United States and Mongolia was concluded.

October 16. Sanctions prohibiting direct or indirect financial and commercial transactions with Haiti were lifted.

October 25. Blocking and restrictions concerning the authorities in, entities in or owned or controlled from, and transfers to those areas of Bosnia and Herzegovina controlled by the Bosnian Serb forces were imposed.

November 25. Blocking of most assets of Cambodia was terminated.

December 16. The Bilateral Investment Treaty between the United States and Uzbekistan was signed.

Imports and Import Payments

February 16. Kazakhstan and Romania became eligible to benefit from the General System of Preferences (GSP).

March 4. Ukraine became eligible to benefit from the GSP.

July 1. Mauritania was suspended from the GSP.

August 11. Country-by-country allocations of sugar imports subject to the tariff-rate quota were announced.

August 18. Belarus and Uzbekistan became eligible to benefit from the GSP.

Exports and Export Proceeds

January 27. A successor agreement to the International Tropical Timber Agreement was concluded.

March 12. The United States and Japan reached an agreement on opening the Japanese market to cellular telephone systems.

March 31. Multilateral Export Controls were eliminated by the Coordinating Committee for Multilateral Export Controls (COCOM), relaxing various high-technology export restrictions to China, the Baltic countries, Russia, and the other countries of the former Soviet Union.

December 12. The United States and Japan reached agreement on expanding market access in Japan for exports of flat glasses from the United States.

URUGUAY

(Position as of December 31, 1994)

Exchange Arrangement

The currency of Uruguay is the Uruguayan Peso. The Central Bank of Uruguay intervenes to ensure that the exchange rate will remain within the higher and lower limits of the exchange rate band (currently 7 percent) and allows market rates to float freely within these limits. The Central Bank periodically announces its intervention buying and selling rates. On December 31, 1994, the buying and selling interbank rates for the U.S. dollar, the intervention currency, were Ur$5.601 and Ur$5.603, respectively, per US$1. Rates for other currencies are based on the cross-rate relationship between the U.S. dollar and the currencies concerned in the international market.

Purchases of foreign exchange by public sector institutions are subject to a tax of 2 percent. There are no arrangements for forward cover against exchange rate risk operating in the official or the commercial banking sector.

There are no limits on the amount of foreign exchange that the Central Bank may sell to or buy from the state-owned Bank of the Republic, the Mortgage Bank, the private commercial banks, and financial and exchange houses.

Uruguay formally accepted the obligations of Article VIII, Sections 2, 3, and 4 of the Fund Agreement, as from May 2, 1980.

Administration of Control

Exchange transactions are carried out through authorized banks, financial houses, exchange houses, and the Bank of the Republic. Any person or firm may conduct exchange transactions in the market, provided this does not become a customary business. Exchange houses also must be authorized by the Central Bank.

Prescription of Currency

Payments between Uruguay and the countries with which Uruguay has concluded reciprocal credit agreements may be made through accounts maintained with each other by the central banks, within the framework of the multilateral clearing system of the Latin American Integration Association (LAIA); these countries are Argentina, Bolivia, Brazil, Chile, Colombia, Dominican Republic, Ecuador, Mexico, Paraguay, Peru, and Venezuela. There are separate arrangements for trade in specified goods with Argentina, Brazil, and Mexico, among other countries. There is a similar arrangement with Cuba, but settlements are effected in a currency other than the U.S. dollar. All settlements of balances under the multilateral clearing system are made in U.S. dollars.

Imports and Import Payments

All imports are subject to registration. The registrations are generally valid for 180 days, and goods must be cleared through customs during this period.

The Treaty of Asunción, signed in 1991 by Argentina, Brazil, Paraguay, and Uruguay, created the Southern Cone Common Market (MERCOSUR). The parties agreed on a customs union that began to operate on January 1, 1995. The most important instrument of the customs union is the common external tariff (CET), which consists of the tariffs and a new nomenclature (the *Nomenclatura Arancelaria* MERCOSUR). There are 11 different tariff levels, ranging from zero to 20 percent. Regionally produced capital goods and telecommunications are subject to a tariff of 14 percent and 16 percent, respectively.

The parties to the MERCOSUR are allowed to exempt up to 300 goods from the CET until the year 2001 (in the case of Paraguay, the number is 399). The tariff rates on these exempted goods are to converge linearly and automatically to the CET by 2001. Uruguay and Paraguay are also allowed to converge in the same way to the CET in respect of capital goods and telecommunications equipment until the year 2006 (Argentina and Brazil will converge to CET in 2001 in the case of capital goods and in 2006 in the case of telecommunications equipment). Buses and trucks are subject to a tariff of 20 percent, to which Uruguay may converge by 2006. The CET for cars and sugar is still under negotiation.

Except for a precise number of items, which are included in the *Régimen de Adecuación*, there are no remaining import duties among MERCOSUR countries.

Duties on the imports of sugar, textiles, and apparel are computed on the basis of "minimum export prices" (*precios mínimos de exportación*), which, in addition, provide the basis for a sliding surcharge to be paid by the importer, representing the difference between the minimum export and the declared c.i.f. import price. Those minimum export prices are set by government decree but are established transitorily by a decision of the Ministry of Finance.

Automobile assembly plants are allowed to import finished cars at a preferential tariff if they export assembled automobiles or parts that are produced in Uruguay for a similar value. Imports of used cars are prohibited.

Payments for Invisibles

There are no limitations on payments for invisibles or the exportation of foreign or domestic banknotes.

Exports and Export Proceeds

From time to time, and for special reasons (for example, stock position, protection, or sanitary considerations), certain exports are prohibited or are subject to special requirements.

Exports of dry, salted, and pickled hides are subject to an export tax at the rate of 5 percent.

Access to the market conditions established by the bilateral trade agreements with Argentina (CAUCE) and Brazil (PEC), which allow Uruguay to export limited amounts of specific goods with preferential treatment, will be maintained until 2001, despite MERCOSUR.

Proceeds from Invisibles

There are no surrender requirements on the proceeds from invisibles, and there are no limitations on the importation of foreign or domestic banknotes.

Capital

Inward and outward private capital transfers by either residents or nonresidents may be made freely, with the exception of certain inward and outward transfers relating to investments registered under the Foreign Investment Law. (In practice, however, this exception is not enforced.) The amortization or liquidation proceeds of foreign capital registered under this law cannot normally be transferred abroad until three years after the date on which the investment was approved.

Gold

Residents and nonresidents may freely purchase, hold, and sell financial gold with a fineness of not less than 0.9 in Uruguay or abroad. Gold for industrial purposes is subject to the general policy that governs the exportation, importation, and trading of goods.

Changes During 1994

Imports and Import Payments

January 1. Tariff preferences for imports from member countries of MERCOSUR were increased to 82 percent from 75 percent.

January 31. Import valuation and identification were made the exclusive responsibility of the customs administration; the Bank of the Republic would retain the role of ex post comptroller of import transactions.

July 1. Tariff preferences for imports from the member countries of MERCOSUR were increased to 89 percent from 82 percent.

November 1. All import reference prices were eliminated.

Changes During 1995

Imports and Import Payments

January 1. Tariffs on imports from member countries of MERCOSUR were eliminated (except for a number of products), and the CET, ranging from zero to 20 percent (with 11 different positions), would apply to most products from non-MERCOSUR countries.

UZBEKISTAN

(Position as of December 31, 1994)

Exchange Arrangement

The currency of the Republic of Uzbekistan is the Sum. The official exchange rate is quoted by the Central Bank of Uzbekistan once a week[1] on the basis of the foreign exchange auctions at the Republican Currency Exchange. Exchange rates for currencies not traded at the auction are determined from cross rates in the international market. On December 31, 1994, the official rate quoted by the Central Bank was Sum 25 per US$1. Foreign exchange transactions are conducted by 13 authorized banks, which are required to quote buying and selling rates with a maximum spread of 1 percent for noncash foreign exchange transactions and 10 percent for cash foreign exchange transactions.

Since October 15, 1994, all domestic payments and settlements must be effected in sum. Authorized banks may maintain an overall open foreign exchange position of up to 10 percent of statutory capital.

Administration of Control

Control of foreign exchange transactions is vested in the Central Bank, the Ministry of Finance, and the State Tax Committee of the Republic of Uzbekistan.

Prescription of Currency

Settlements with those countries with which Uzbekistan maintains bilateral payments agreements are effected in accordance with the terms of the agreements.[2] Transactions with other countries are settled in convertible currencies.

Resident and Nonresident Accounts

Both resident and nonresident natural and juridical persons may open and operate convertible currency accounts without restriction.

Imports and Exports

Proceeds from exports in convertible currencies are subject to a 30 percent surrender requirement, and receipts in the currencies of the Baltic countries, the Russian Federation, and the other countries of the former Soviet Union are subject to a 15 percent surrender requirement.

The Ministry of Foreign Economic Relations (MFER) is responsible for negotiating trade agreements with nontraditional trading partners as well as those agreements denominated in hard currency with traditional trading partners, and for implementing foreign trade agreements and external trade policy through the issuance of licenses and export quotas.

The MFER must register and review all contracts and agreements by entities requiring licenses as well as those concluded on the basis of intergovernmental agreements and centralized deliveries. Since the November 17, 1994 decree of the Cabinet of Ministers, the MFER issues export licenses for 11 types of goods, in accordance with fixed quotas: cotton fiber and waste, energy products (oil, natural gas, electric power, nonferrous metals, and petroleum products), and others. There are also certain specific goods and services (such as medicines, weapons, precious metals, uranium and other radioactive substances, foreign motion pictures and videos, and research data) that require export and import licenses from the MFER. Quotas do not apply to these goods or services and licensing requirements are consistent with international procedures. A license is required for each shipment. Nine types of goods are prohibited for exportation from Uzbekistan.[3]

At present, Uzbekistan has three types of trade agreements. The first category includes agreements with countries other than the Baltic countries, the Russian Federarion, and other countries of the former Soviet Union, that focus only on defining trade regimes (tariffs, duties, etc.). In these agreements there are no indicative lists of goods, and trade is generally conducted in freely convertible currencies. The second category of trade agreements is based upon convertible currencies and a list of indicative goods that the country is selling. The delivery of such goods is not compulsory because governments do not agree to supply such goods. Commercial enterprises carry out such

---

[1]Since April 1, 1995, twice a week.

[2]Uzbekistan maintains bilateral payments agreements with Armenia, Belarus, China, Estonia, India, Indonesia, the Islamic Republic of Iran, Kazakhstan, the Kyrgyz Republic, Latvia, Lithuania, Malaysia, Moldova, the Russian Federation, Tajikistan, Turkmenistan, and Ukraine.

[3] Flour and cereals from state resources, livestock and poultry, meat, butter and dry milk, tea, sugar, ethylene alcohol, and antique items.

transactions through contracts. Agreements in this category are those with the Baltic countries, Belarus, Armenia, and until 1994, Eastern European countries (which are currently in the first category). In 1992, China, Indonesia, and Malaysia were also in this group. The third category includes agreements with the Baltic countries, the Russian Federation, and other countries of the former Soviet Union, in which there are indicative lists, as well as lists of commodities to be supplied on a mutual basis.[4] Under these trade agreements governments assume responsibility for mutually agreed supplies and are thus guarantors of the contracts, which are set in freely convertible currencies. Export duties ranging from 5 percent to 50 percent are levied on some 65 items. Art items are subject to a tax of 100 percent.

Payments for and Proceeds from Invisibles

Foreign exchange for payments for invisibles, including transportation, is made available automatically once the underlying merchandise transactions have been approved. Resident individuals are allowed to buy up to $300 in foreign exchange from authorized banks that stamp their passport to indicate the amount of the purchase. Foreign exchange in excess of this amount is not available. No documentation is required for exports of less than $500 in foreign exchange; for amounts in excess of $500, it is necessary to provide a certificate from authorized banks in Uzbekistan. There are no restrictions on bringing foreign currency into Uzbekistan.

Nonresidents are allowed to take freely convertible currency out of Uzbekistan.

Proceeds from invisibles are subject to the same surrender requirements as those applicable to proceeds from exports.

Capital

Enterprises may establish joint ventures as foreign direct investment with the approval of the Ministry of Finance (as of January 1, 1995, the Ministry of Justice). Foreign equity capital participation of up to 100 percent is allowed. Joint ventures are exempt from the profit tax during the first two years after registration; joint ventures with a foreign equity capital share exceeding 50 percent are exempted from the profit tax during the first five years. Joint ventures are allowed to export their

products and import inputs without licenses and to retain all of their foreign exchange earnings. Remittance of the foreign investors' share of profits is guaranteed, and the repatriation of capital is not restricted.

Gold

Trade in gold is prohibited (with the exception of jewelry and collectibles); however, transactions in gold may be conducted by the Ministry of Finance, the Central Bank, and the National Bank for Foreign Economic Activity with the approval of the Government. Joint ventures operating in the precious metals sector may export a portion of their output, corresponding to the share of profits of the foreign participant, without restriction.

Emigrants are allowed to take out of the country 100 grams of gold and 200 grams of silver in the form of jewelry or personal effects.

Changes During 1994

Exchange Arrangement

April 1. Authorized banks were permitted to carry out transactions in foreign banknotes.

April 15. The official exchange rate of the sum-coupon in terms of the U.S. dollar and other currencies would be determined in weekly trading sessions on the Uzbek Republican Currency Exchange.

July 1. The sum was introduced as the national currency, and its external value was set at Sum 7 per US$1.

Imports and Exports

January 1. The tax on foreign exchange proceeds was reduced to 15 percent from 35 percent, and the mandatory surrender requirement at the ratio of 15 percent and at the official exchange rate was introduced.

January 21. All import tariffs were eliminated until July 1, 1995.

April 15. The tax on foreign exchange proceeds was replaced with the surrender requirement, whereby 15 percent of proceeds are to be surrendered to the Central Bank and 15 percent of proceeds are to be surrendered to the Foreign Exchange Fund.

November 15. The full amount of proceeds in convertible currencies subject to the surrender requirement was required to be transferred to the Central Bank.

---

[4]Clearing arrangements are in effect with Kazakhstan, the Kyrgyz Republic, the Russian Federation, and Ukraine.

VANUATU

(Position as of December 31, 1994)

Exchange Arrangement

The currency of Vanuatu is the Vatu, the external value of which is determined on the basis of an undisclosed transactions-weighted (trade and tourism receipts) basket of currencies, consisting of a basket of currencies of its major trading partners. The Reserve Bank of Vanuatu buys and sells foreign exchange daily, and buying and selling rates of the vatu against the currencies in the basket are quoted twice a day within margins ranging between 0.25 percent and 0.30 percent around the middle rate. The Reserve Bank deals with the commercial banks only in U.S. dollars on a spot basis and buys and sells foreign exchange only in transactions with commercial banks for the Government's account or for commercial bank operations. On December 31, 1994, the buying and selling rates for the U.S. dollar (for telegraphic transfers) were VT 111.80 and VT 112.36, respectively, per US$1. There are no taxes or subsidies on purchases or sales of foreign exchange.

There are no arrangements for forward exchange rate cover facilities operating in the official sector. Commercial banks provide forward exchange rate cover facilities.

Vanuatu formally accepted the obligations of Article VIII, Sections 2, 3, and 4 of the Fund Agreement, as from December 1, 1982.

Prescription of Currency

There are no prescription of currency requirements.

Nonresident Accounts

No distinction is made between the accounts of residents and nonresidents. Debits and credits to all accounts may be made freely.

Imports and Import Payments

All items may be freely imported with the exception of the following: any goods that are controlled under internal legislation in the interest of national health and well-being, such as explosives and dangerous drugs. The importation of frozen chicken, chicken pieces, T-shirts bearing a Vanuatu motif, firearms and ammunition, animals and plants, transistor and telephone equipment, and television aerials is restricted through import-licensing arrangements. A similar restriction is applied to the importation of five basic products—rice, sugar, flour, canned fish, and tobacco products—under a scheme designed to provide funds for the Vanuatu Cooperative Federation. Currently, about two dozen importers pay a commission of 3 percent (4 percent in the case of tobacco products) to the cooperative for the right to import these five products.

Customs duties are levied mainly on an ad valorem basis on the c.i.f. value of imports. Certain goods, including spirits, wine, beer, tobacco products, and petroleum products, are subject to specific rates of import duty. Imported goods that compete with locally produced equivalents are generally subject to high duty rates. A customs service tax of 5 percent is applied to most imports, based on the duty-inclusive import value. Under a regional trade agreement that came into operation in September 1994, canned tuna from the Solomon Islands and tea from Papua New Guinea may be imported free of import duty.

Goods imported for a specified end use may be exempt from import duties. These include goods imported by or on behalf of the Government and funded by external aid, goods imported for sale to and exported by tourists, ships' stores (including fuels), goods imported for processing and re-exportation, and goods imported for investment projects.

Payments for Invisibles

There are no restrictions on payments for invisibles.

Exports and Export Proceeds

With a few exceptions, no restrictions are imposed on exports. The exportation of logs has been banned for environmental reasons since 1990 although exemptions have been granted in certain circumstances. Exports of trochus, green snails, bêches-de-mer, mother of pearl, aquarium fish, and crustaceans[1] are subject to authorization by the Minister of Agriculture, Fisheries, and Forestry. Exports of copra, cocoa, and kava are channeled through the Vanuatu Commodities Marketing Board (VCMB); however, exports of kava can be undertaken by individuals subject to authorization from the VCMB. Artifacts having a special value either as a result of ceremonial use or because they

---

[1]Including coconut crabs for conservation purposes.

are more than 10 years old are subject to authorization from the Cultural Center.

Most exports are subject to export duties, mainly on an ad valorem basis (f.o.b.); specific duties are levied on timber products and some other minor exports. There are no surrender requirements for export proceeds.

Proceeds from Invisibles

Exchange proceeds from invisibles need not be surrendered.

Capital

All inward and outward movements of capital are unrestricted.

Gold

There are no restrictions on gold transactions.

Changes During 1994

Imports and Import Payments

September 1. A new regional trade agreement came into operation that exempted from tariff canned tuna from the Solomon Islands and tea from Papua New Guinea.

Exports and Export Proceeds

February 1. The exportation of round logs and square flitches was prohibited.

VENEZUELA

(Position as of December 31, 1994)

Exchange Arrangement

The currency of Venezuela is the Venezuelan Bolívar, the external value of which is pegged to the U.S. dollar. On December 31, 1994, the official rate of the Central Bank of Venezuela was Bs 170 per US$1.

Resident commercial banks and exchange houses are designated as authorized foreign exchange dealers. Tourist establishments are allowed to offer their clients foreign exchange services in the form of purchases of foreign currency notes, coins, and traveler's checks.

Venezuela formally accepted the obligations of Article VIII, Sections 2, 3, and 4 of the Fund Agreement as of July 1, 1976.

Administration of Control

Under the system of exchange controls established on July 11, 1994, the newly created Exchange Administration Board and the associated Technical Administration Office are responsible for the administration of exchange transactions. These bodies were established initially by presidential decree, but the powers to designate an Exchange Administration Board were formalized subsequently in a new foreign exchange law, dated December 1, 1994, and signed into law in April 1995, under which the President of the Republic may establish exchange restrictions when warranted by the economic and financial conditions of the country. When required, export and import licenses are issued by the Ministry of Agriculture and Livestock, the Ministry of Development, the Ministry of Defense, or the Ministry of Foreign Relations, depending on the product.

The Superintendency of Foreign Investment (SIEX), attached to the Ministry of Finance, oversees the registration of foreign direct investments, contracts involving technology transfers, and the use of foreign patents and trademarks.

Arrears are maintained with respect to certain external payments.

Prescription of Currency

No prescription of currency requirements are in force. Payments between Venezuela and Argentina, Bolivia, Brazil, Chile, Colombia, Cuba, the Dominican Republic, Ecuador, Jamaica, Malaysia, Mexico, Peru, and Uruguay may be settled through accounts maintained with each other by the Central Bank of Venezuela and the central banks of the countries concerned.

Imports and Import Payments

Some imports, irrespective of country of origin, are subject to licensing requirements for environmental, health, or security reasons. The importation of military arms must be authorized by the Defense Ministry; the importation of nonmilitary weapons and ammunitions must be authorized by the Ministry of Domestic Affairs. At the end of 1994, some 54 tariff items, of which 17 were chemicals used in drug production and approximately 29 were agro-industrial products, were subject to Legal Regime No. 2 and required approval from the import office. Quantitative restrictions apply to a small number of agricultural imports. Applications for the purchase of foreign exchange for all imports must be approved by the Exchange Administration Board in accordance with official quarterly targets for net international reserves. Prior to consideration by the Exchange Administration Board, all requests must be processed and verified by the Technical Administration Office. Applications are approved as long as the importer complies with the required administrative procedures. However, delays are being experienced in processing import applications and in the selling of foreign exchange.

Most customs tariffs on manufactured goods are on an ad valorem basis; there are four basic rates of 5 percent, 10 percent, 15 percent, and 20 percent, except for motor vehicles, which are subject to a special regime under the Andean Pact. The common external tariff on motor vehicles is 35 percent for passenger cars; 15 percent for cargo and commercial vehicles (except for cargo vehicles under 4,500 kg., such as pickup trucks, for which the rate is 25 percent); and 3 percent for imported components and parts for vehicles assembled in the member countries. The importation of used vehicles is prohibited, with the exception of hearses, prison vans, and ambulances. The trade liberalization program initiated in 1989 is now virtually complete. Specific tariffs apply to agricultural products and to certain products included in Chapter 27 of the tariff code (e.g., mineral fuels, oil, mineral wax, distilled products, and bituminous substances).

In addition to customs tariffs, all imports are subject to a customs service charge of 1 percent. Storage charges apply to imports that remain in customs warehouses for more than 12 days. The industrial free zone of Paraguana and the Free Port of Margarita Island enjoy a special customs regime that includes exemptions from customs tariffs.

Colombia, Ecuador, and Venezuela extend duty-free access to each other's imports. Duty-free entry is also granted to certain goods originating from the member countries of the CARICOM region. Venezuela maintains a bilateral trade agreement with Chile, which aims at a gradual reduction of tariffs on each other's imports and at a coordination of the tariff structure with other trading partners. On December 29, 1994, the law approving the Trade Treaty of the Group of Three was passed and became effective on January 1, 1995.

Payments for Invisibles

All payments for invisibles must be authorized by the Exchange Administration Board. The annual limits on the purchase of foreign exchange for travel abroad are as follows: $1,000 a year for travel to Caribbean destinations; $3,000 for travel to the United States and Mexico; and $4,000 for travel to other destinations. Monthly remittances to students abroad, in addition to enrollment fees, are allocated according to level of study as follows: $700 for secondary school students; $1,000 for undergraduate students; $1,500 for single postgraduate students; and $2,500 for married postgraduate students. Remittances from senior citizens to individuals are limited to $200 a month, and remittances to pensioners and retirees of Venezuelan institutions are limited to $1,000 a month. Remittances of dividends resulting from investments associated with debt-to-equity conversions may not exceed 10 percent of the total investment for a three-year period from the date it was registered (see section on Capital, below).

Exports and Export Proceeds

There are no controls or restrictions on exports. Export proceeds are subject to surrender requirements and must be sold to the Central Bank through authorized foreign exchange dealers.[1] PDVSA exports are subject to a surcharge of 8 percent. Exporters may retain up to 10 percent of the foreign exchange to meet commitments abroad.

Exports of agricultural commodities, with the exception of those exported to Andean Pact member countries, are entitled to a fiscal credit at the rate of 10 percent of the f.o.b. value in the form of a negotiable bond that is issued by the Ministry of Finance. These bonds may be used for tax payments. Fiscal credits for manufactured exports have been replaced by a system of drawback of customs duties that are paid on imported inputs used in export production. Drawbacks take the form of tax reimbursement certificates issued by the Ministry of Finance.

PDVSA and Ferrominera Orinoco have monopolies over the exportation of hydrocarbons and iron ore, respectively. The law phasing out export tax values applicable to exports of hydrocarbons was promulgated on July 1, 1993. This law established the following percentage reductions in the tax rates: 16 percent in 1993, 8 percent in 1994, 4 percent in 1995, and elimination by the end of 1996.

Proceeds from Invisibles

Proceeds from invisibles are subject to surrender requirements. Travelers may freely import domestic and foreign currency, except that foreign coins other than gold coins may not be imported for commercial purposes.

Capital

Capital outflows not related to the amortization of external debt and the repatriation of capital by foreigners are prohibited. Foreign direct investments in the petroleum and iron ore sectors are subject to specific regulations.

Mass media, communications, newspapers in Spanish, and security services are reserved for national ownership. New investments do not require prior authorization from the SIEX but must be registered with the SIEX after the fact, and approval is automatically granted if the new investment is consistent with national legislation. Foreign investments in the financial sector are allowed (beginning in 1994) in accordance with a new banking law. Foreign enterprises may establish subsidiaries in Venezuela without prior authorization as long as they are consistent with the Commerce Code; the SIEX must, however, be notified within 60 working days about newly established subsidiaries. The reinvestment of profits does not require prior authorization and is not restricted. Sales of foreign exchange for the repatriation of capital are subject to the authorization of the Exchange Administration Board. Foreign investors are allowed to purchase corporate stocks in the Caracas Stock Exchange but must inform the SIEX of such purchases at the end of each calendar year.

---

[1]Prior to June 27, 1994, only the state petroleum company (PDVSA) and its Venezuelan affiliates were required to surrender their foreign exchange earnings, although they were allowed to maintain working balances of foreign exchange at a level pre-approved by the Board of the Central Bank of Venezuela. Foreign exchange proceeds of loan disbursements to the public sector were also required to be surrendered to the Central Bank.

Certain external public debt can be converted into equity. In accordance with Decree No. 2530 of September 28, 1992, as amended by Decree No. 99 of March 23, 1994, the Central Bank will purchase the debt instruments at a price fixed at 20 percent above the average price prevailing in the market for those instruments within the ten banking business days before the date of conversion. The eligible areas are infrastructure (ports, bridges, and railways); aqueducts and water treatment plants; terrestrial and fluvial transportation; wholesale markets for agricultural products (including construction, maintenance, and administration); educational institutions; funds for financing research and studies for Venezuelan students in Venezuela or overseas; and medical assistance centers. The maximum component of the investment to be covered by the conversion of the external public debt will be determined by the Ministry of Finance.

To effect a debt conversion, the Central Bank purchases the external debt with domestic currency (or public debt securities denominated in domestic currency), which is then deposited into a trust account opened by the investor with a fiduciary agent (normally a commercial bank) in Venezuela. The agent is responsible for ensuring the proper use of the trust account and releases the funds in step with the implementation of the investment project. (As part of the required documentation, investors must submit in advance a timetable for the investment and its domestic component to be financed through debt conversion.) To further ensure the proper use of the conversion proceeds, investors must deposit with a fiduciary agent a guarantee (equivalent to 5 percent of the total investment), which can be reduced in line with the implementation of the investment.

There are no restrictions on conversions of private external debt into private domestic debt or equity; these conversions may be effected freely through the interbank market.

Gold

Venezuelan gold coins are legal tender but do not circulate. Residents may hold, acquire, and sell gold coins in Venezuela for numismatic and investment purposes. Gold coins, medallions, and bars are freely negotiated among authorized dealers, exchange houses, and the public. Commercial banks may freely negotiate gold coins among themselves and other residents but do not normally deal in gold with the public. Imports and exports of monetary gold and imports of gold coins that are legal tender in Venezuela are reserved for the Central Bank.

The exportation of nonmonetary gold (other than jewelry for personal use) and gold coins eligible as legal tender in Venezuela or abroad are subject to prior authorization from the Central Bank. Under the terms of the agreement between the National Executive and the Central Bank, imports of nonmonetary gold may be regulated. The Central Bank may authorize private exporters to export gold bars, provided that the exported gold bars will be reimported after undergoing processing that is not available in the country and that the reimported gold is used as an input in domestic production.

Changes During 1994

Exchange Arrangement

April 28. The authorities of Venezuela accelerated the rate of depreciation of the crawling peg exchange rate, previously set at the average daily rate of depreciation of Bs 0.15, and allowed the bolívar to depreciate by about 5 percent during the ensuing week.

May 4. The Central Bank of Venezuela introduced a system of daily foreign exchange auctions for foreign exchange receipts from the oil sector, limiting the amount on which participants in the auction could bid and requiring that commercial banks resell foreign exchange acquired in the auctions at no more than Bs 0.20 above the auction rate. As a result of these measures, a dual exchange market emerged.

May 24. The Central Bank modified the auction system to eliminate the restrictions that had given rise to a dual market and began to sell foreign exchange at the highest offer price, while allowing the resale of U.S. dollars at the market-determined exchange rate.

June 27. The foreign exchange market was closed, and a comprehensive system of exchange controls covering all current and capital account transactions was introduced.

July 11. The exchange market reopened under a pegged exchange regime, and the exchange rate was set at Bs 170 per US$1.

Administration of Control

July 11. An Exchange Administration Board with the responsibility of managing foreign exchange controls was created.

December 1. A new Foreign Exchange Law was approved. The Foreign Exchange Law was subsequently returned to Congress for reconsideration after the President changed 22 of 30 articles. The law was finally signed into law in April 1995 but has not yet been published in the Official Gazette.

VIET NAM

(Position as of December 31, 1994)

Exchange Arrangement

The currency of Viet Nam is the Dong. All foreign exchange transactions take place either on the inter-bank market, which began operations on October 14, 1994, or transitionally on the foreign exchange trading floors of the auction markets located at the branches of the State Bank of Viet Nam (SBVN) in Hanoi and Ho Chi Minh City. Spot and forward transactions are permitted between the Vietnamese dong and six other currencies.[1] Trading must take place at exchange rates within ranges stipulated daily by the SBVN. Only the SBVN, state-owned banks, such as the Bank of Investment and Development, shareholding banks, joint-venture banks, and branches of foreign banks may participate in the exchange markets. Foreign exchange (only spot U.S. dollars) in the auction market is held twice a week in Hanoi (Tuesdays and Thursdays) and three times a week in Ho Chi Minh City (Mondays, Wednesdays, and Fridays). About 80 operators, consisting of foreign exchange banks, foreign trade organizations, and companies that produce gold are licensed for the Hanoi Center and about 100 are licensed for the Ho Chi Minh City Center.[2] The centers obtain bids for the purchase and sale of foreign exchange before each session. Economic entities that need foreign exchange for their import needs or debt-repayment obligations are allowed to submit their bids to the market seven days before the due date of payment. Banks are required to ensure that economic entities' applications for foreign exchange purchases conform with current foreign trade and exchange restrictions (such as the requirement to have an import license) and that they actually possess resources before engaging in a transaction. The final (closing) rate at each trade session is the fixing rate. Between the end of one session and the opening of the following session, all commercial banks are required to buy at the fixing rate and sell at a rate within a maximum margin of 0.5 percent of the fixing rate. On December 31, 1994, the average buying and selling rates in the interbank market were D 11,045 and D 11,056, respectively, per US$1.

Administration of Control

Exchange control is administered by the SBVN. Foreign trade is administered by the Ministry of Trade and Tourism, which supervises the operations carried out by the foreign trade organizations (FTOs) and firms with direct foreign trading rights. Import and export licenses, which are required for all trade transactions, are issued by the Ministry of Trade and Tourism. FTOs and firms engaged in international trade must submit annual plans for their imports and exports to the State Planning Committee; revisions of the plans may be requested every three months. Most grants in convertible currencies from bilateral official donors and international organizations are under the supervision of the Committee for Reception and Management of Aid, an agency attached to the Ministry of Finance. Foreign investment is monitored and coordinated by the State Committee for Cooperation and Investment.

Arrears are maintained with respect to external payments.

Prescription of Currency

Transactions with Cambodia are settled under a clearing arrangement in domestic currencies at a bilaterally agreed exchange rate of D 12 per 1 Cambodian riel. Bilateral payments agreements with Mali and the Syrian Arab Republic have been inoperative for several years. In 1993, Viet Nam also entered into a bilateral payments arrangement with Malaysia, but the implementing guidelines are yet to be issued.

Resident and Nonresident Accounts

Nonresidents are permitted to maintain nonresident accounts either in foreign currencies or in convertible dong; however, they may not open interest-yielding bank accounts in dong. Nonresidents can freely reconvert into foreign currency and transfer abroad unused balances in Vietnamese currency that have been acquired against foreign currency. Vietnamese citizens are allowed to sell foreign exchange in their possession to banks, or to deposit it into interest-bearing foreign currency bank ac-

---

[1]Including deutsche mark, French francs, Hong Kong dollars, Japanese yen, pounds sterling, and U.S. dollars.

[2]An annual participation fee of $200 is levied in dong; in addition, a commission of 0.01 percent is payable on each transaction in dong by purchasers of foreign exchange, with a maximum of $100. The trading floor has a management board composed of four state bank employees and three commercial bank employees; a representative of the SBVN serves as the chairman.

counts. Foreign currency deposited in a bank may be withdrawn for payments or transferred to other units or individuals. Savings accounts in foreign currency for households were introduced in May 1991. The minimum interest rate on these accounts is 3.2 percent for time deposits and 1.5 percent for sight deposits.

Imports and Exports

Manufacturing firms and local authorities are allowed to conduct trade; some export transactions and all import transactions require a license issued by the Ministry of Trade. Trade transactions are carried out by about 700 firms, including 140 FTOs, that produce exportable goods or purchase them from producers, but trade of certain products is regulated by quotas. About 200 producers have temporary or permanent trading rights, which allow them to export and import directly; about 160 foreign-owned or joint-venture firms trade directly with foreign partners. State-owned firms with an annual export turnover of more than $5 million may obtain permanent foreign direct trading rights, whereas those with an annual export turnover in the range of $2–5 million may obtain temporary foreign direct trading rights. Other firms may obtain direct export permits on the basis of shipments or trade with an FTO. Decree No. 114 entered into force in April 1992; it permits private commercial trading houses to engage in import and export activities.

During 1994, imports of the following products were prohibited: (1) weapons, ammunition and explosives, and military equipment; (2) drugs and toxic chemicals; (3) dangerous and unhealthy cultural products; (4) "reactionary and depraved" cultural products; (5) fireworks and children's toys that detrimentally influence personality, education, social order, and safety; (6) most used consumer goods; (7) most left-hand drive cars; and (8) materials and additives required for making cigarettes. All import quotas are formally approved by the Government. The State Planning Committee, in coordination with the Ministry of Trade, may impose ad hoc temporary quantity controls. During 1994, quantitative controls were placed on, among other items, fertilizers, electric appliances, and sugar.[3] The issuance of import licenses is on a shipment-by-shipment basis for all products. Import tariffs range up to a maximum of 200 percent, with some 29 rate schedules. Machinery and equipment as well as medicine are exempt from tariffs, while high tariffs of 50 percent and above are applied to garments and footwear, soft drinks, and cosmetics. Automobiles are subject to a tariff of 200 percent.

Local FTOs are permitted to export all commodities, and local firms may import the commodities that they need for production. The procurement of exportable goods is normally unrestricted, except for some sensitive goods (such as rice), for which a minimum export price prevails. Only exports of rice are subject to a quota. For rice, crude oil, products made of wool and rattan, and re-exported goods, export licenses must be obtained for each shipment. Under Decision No. 188 of the Council of Ministers, export earnings are subject to various surrender requirements, ranging up to 30 percent; however, this regulation is not strictly enforced. In practice, the authorities have tolerated full retention of foreign exchange receipts. All receipts must be repatriated within 30 days, except for special cases authorized by the Governor of the State Bank, such as for firms with marketing or representative activities abroad. Organizations and enterprises must deposit all foreign exchange proceeds in foreign exchange accounts at domestic commercial banks that are licensed to conduct foreign exchange business in Viet Nam. Limits on foreign exchange holdings in such accounts are set by the commercial banks using rules set by the SBVN. Deposits in excess of those limits must be sold to the commercial banks. While foreign exchange must normally be deposited in banks in Viet Nam, firms that are permitted to open branch offices abroad may be granted special permission to deposit these funds in foreign accounts.

Payments for and Proceeds from Invisibles

All transactions in invisibles require individual authorization from the Ministry of Finance. Foreign exchange is made available upon authorization of the transaction. Payments for invisibles related to authorized imports are not restricted. As of November 1, 1994, the foreign exchange allocation for travel abroad was raised to $5,000 for each trip, but travelers may use their own foreign exchange. Remittances of profits are subject to a tax of 5–10 percent. Receipts from transactions in invisibles must be surrendered to the SBVN.

Organizations and enterprises must deposit all foreign exchange proceeds from invisibles transactions in foreign exchange accounts at domestic commercial banks, according to the same rules and conditions that apply to export proceeds. While such funds must normally be deposited in banks

---

[3]Quotas will remain on these items in 1995, but the list of imports subject to quotas is expected to be reduced from 15 items in 1994 to 7 items in 1995.

within Viet Nam, firms in the aviation, shipping, postal, and insurance sectors, as well as commercial banks, finance companies, and other firms permitted to open branches abroad may be granted special permission to deposit these funds in foreign accounts.

Capital

Foreign direct investment is regulated by a foreign investment code approved by the National Assembly in 1987 and amended in December 1992. The code provides for three forms of foreign investment: (1) contracted business cooperation, such as product-sharing arrangements; (2) joint ventures between a foreign investor and a Vietnamese private enterprise or state economic organization; and (3) firms wholly owned by foreign investors. The permitted share of foreign capital is no less than 30 percent, and there is no maximum limit. Other provisions in the code include (1) a 50- to 70-year limit on the duration of the enterprise with foreign capital; (2) a tax of 5–10 percent on the remittance of profits abroad; and (3) profit taxes to be paid at rates of 15–25 percent, starting two years after the first profit-making year (foreign joint ventures in priority sectors are, however, exempt from the tax in their first two years of eligibility, and the tax rate is halved in the following two years). In 1992, the code was amended to allow domestic private firms to participate with foreign firms in investment projects. Provisions for repatriating profits were also amended to allow the use of domestic currency to purchase and export domestically produced goods and retain the proceeds from these exports abroad.

The authority to grant foreign investment licenses is entrusted to the State Committee for Cooperation and Investment for projects under $1 million; for projects over $1 million, the provincial authorities concerned are consulted. Since 1988, some 1,000 projects have been approved, with a total committed capital of about $11 billion. In principle, 100 percent of profits may be repatriated; however, in practice, the conversion of domestic currency profits into foreign currency for repatriation is governed by the prevailing foreign exchange regulations. Land cannot be owned by foreign investors but must be leased from the state.

Beginning in October 1988, Vietnamese organizations and citizens who need foreign currency for production and business purposes have been permitted, upon verification by competent agencies, to borrow foreign currency or obtain a bank guarantee for loans in foreign currency. If allowed to borrow directly from foreign countries under commercial credit, the borrower must report periodically to the SBVN the expenditures in foreign currency from funds deposited abroad, including loan repayments.

Gold

Gold may be brought into the country, provided that required customs declarations are made and a customs tariff is paid; nonresidents are entitled to export gold up to the amount they brought in. The price of gold for domestic transactions is set at auctions organized by the Viet Nam Gold and Silver Trading Company. The importation of gold by residents requires a license from the SBVN. The authority of the provincial council to issue gold import licenses was withdrawn in 1989.

Changes During 1994

Exchange Arrangement

October 14. The interbank foreign exchange market began operation, permitting spot and forward transactions in six currencies. Trading must take place within trading ranges stipulated by the SBVN.

Imports and Exports

January 19. Imports of most used consumer goods were prohibited.

July 1. Export licenses are required only for crude oil, rice, products made of wood and rattan, and re-exported goods.

September 5. Organizations and enterprises were required to deposit all foreign exchange proceeds earned at home and abroad in foreign exchange accounts at domestic commercial banks.

November 7. New inspection standards introduced on a range of exports and imports, including imports of petroleum, fertilizers, electronic goods, unassembled machines and equipment, steel and pharmaceuticals, and exports of crude oil, rice, rubber, coffee, peanuts, tea, knitwear, and garments.

Payments for and Proceeds from Invisibles

September 5. Organizations and enterprises must deposit all foreign exchange proceeds from invisibles in foreign exchange accounts at domestic commercial banks. However, firms in the aviation, shipping, postal and insurance sectors, as well as commercial banks, finance companies, and other firms permitted to open branches abroad, may be granted special permission to deposit these funds in foreign accounts. Commercial banks, finance companies, and other firms permitted to open branch offices abroad that already have licenses to hold foreign deposits abroad need not be relicensed.

November 1. Foreign exchange allocation for travel abroad is raised to $5,000 from $3,000.

WESTERN SAMOA

(Position as of December 31, 1994)

Exchange Arrangement

The currency of Western Samoa is the Western Samoa Tala. Its exchange rate is determined on the basis of a fixed relationship with a weighted basket of currencies of Western Samoa's main trading partners. The Central Bank of Samoa has the authority to make discretionary exchange rate adjustments against the currency basket within a margin of up to 2 percent. On December 31, 1994, the buying and selling rates of the tala in terms of the U.S. dollar, the intervention currency, were US$0.4117 and US$0.4027, respectively, per WS$1. Exchange rates for the tala against other currencies are established on the basis of their daily rates against the U.S. dollar. An exchange levy of 1 percent is charged on gross sales of foreign exchange. There are no arrangements for forward cover against exchange rate risk in the official or the commercial banking sector.

Western Samoa formally accepted the obligations of Article VIII, Sections 2, 3, and 4 of the Fund Agreement, as from October 6, 1994.

Administration of Control

Overall responsibility for the administration of exchange control rests with the Central Bank, which delegates part of its powers to authorized banks. In principle, all payments to nonresidents of Western Samoa require the Central Bank's approval. However, the Bank of Western Samoa and the Pacific Commercial Bank—the only authorized banks—are empowered to approve certain payments up to any amount and others up to specified amounts.

Prescription of Currency

There are no prescriptions on currencies that may be used for making or receiving payments to or from nonresidents of Western Samoa.

Nonresident Accounts

Nonresidents and residents who earn foreign exchange in the normal course of their business may open, with the approval of the Central Bank, external or foreign currency accounts with one of the two commercial banks. No other distinction is made between the accounts of residents and nonresidents of Western Samoa.

Imports and Import Payments

There are no import-licensing requirements. The importation of a few products is prohibited for reasons of security or health. Other products may be imported from any source without restriction, with the exception of used cars, the importation of which requires prior approval from the Central Bank, which does not, for safety reasons, grant approval for imports of cars more than five years old. Approvals for this item are, however, granted liberally. Imports with a c.i.f. value of more than WS$15,000 must be financed by a letter of credit. Imports with a c.i.f. value of between WS$5,000 and WS$15,000 must be settled with a sight draft. Imports with a c.i.f. value of less than WS$5,000 may be imported under open account, provided that payments are effected within 30 days of their arrival in Western Samoa.

Import duties are applied on an ad valorem basis and assessed on the c.i.f. value of imports. Most products are subject to a tariff of 35 percent. The tariff rates on machinery and agricultural inputs are generally levied at 20 percent or lower, while those on motor vehicles are levied at 50 percent. In addition, an import excise tax is levied on the value of a limited range of imports, inclusive of import duties. That tax is, for example, either 50 percent, 60 percent, or 70 percent on passenger cars, according to engine size. Approved enterprises producing goods for export may receive full or partial exemption from customs duties and excise tax paid on capital equipment, motor vehicles for business use, building materials, and raw materials and components.

Payments for Invisibles

Payments for certain invisibles may be approved by the authorized banks up to specified limits. Payments in excess of these limits, as well as payments for all other invisibles, require the prior approval of the Central Bank, which is granted when applications are supported by documentary proof that capital transactions are not involved. The Central Bank's approval process governing the remittance of invisible payments is concerned only with whether a transaction is bona fide. Residents and expatriates traveling overseas for private purposes are entitled to a foreign currency allowance equivalent to WS$200 a person a day, subject to a limit of WS$3,000 a person a trip; children under 15 years of age are entitled to 50 percent of the adult allowances. A daily allowance of WS$300 a person is allotted for business travel, with a limit of WS$4,500 a trip. The Central Bank grants supplementary allocations against evidence that foreign exchange is being used for approved purposes. As part of their foreign currency allowance, resident travelers may take out foreign banknotes equivalent to WS$1,000 a person a trip.

All requests from residents of Western Samoa to remit funds to residents studying abroad to cover their education expenses must be supported by documentary evidence confirming that the beneficiary is enrolled at an educational institution abroad. There is no specific limit for such remittances, but the amount requested must be supported by documentary evidence for costs (e.g., fees, accommodation, and meals) and must be in line with the prevailing costs in the countries of study. Residents of Western Samoa with dependents living abroad may remit, from personal resources, an amount not exceeding WS$2,000 a donor a year to support such dependents. The Central Bank considers requests in excess of this amount on merit. Although no limit is set on remittances to cover expenses for medical treatment abroad, documentary evidence must be provided to support requests for such remittances.

Expatriate workers with local contracts of one year and longer are considered residents and need central bank approval if they wish to repatriate funds in excess of 80 percent of their net earnings on a fortnightly or monthly basis. Earnings not repatriated during the contract may be repatriated at the end of the contract.

Travelers may not take out any domestic currency. A 15 percent withholding tax is levied on remittances of dividends at the source and on interest payments on overseas loans.

Exports and Export Proceeds

All exports require export licenses issued by the Customs Department. Exports may be prohibited by the Director of Agriculture on grounds of low quality, or by order of the head of state to alleviate domestic shortages.

Export proceeds from goods shipped to countries other than American Samoa must be surrendered to the authorized banks within three months of the date of shipment; export proceeds from goods shipped to American Samoa must be surrendered to the authorized bank within four weeks of the date of shipment. Certificates validated by an authorized bank are required for exports in excess of WS$250.

Proceeds from Invisibles

All foreign currencies earned by residents performing services for nonresidents must be surrendered to the authorized banks. Resident travelers must, on their return, sell to the banks all unused foreign currency brought in. Resident and nonresident travelers may bring in any amount in foreign banknotes but may not bring in any domestic banknotes.

Capital

All outward capital transfers by residents require the specific approval of the Central Bank, as does all borrowing abroad by residents, including banks. Inward capital remittances do not normally require approval. Authorized banks may approve transfers of gifts to relatives and dependents, either for special family occasions or for maintenance, up to WS$250 a person a year. Requests for larger amounts may be approved by the Central Bank on a case-by-case basis.

Foreign investment in specified activities in Western Samoa is encouraged. Under the Enterprises Incentive Act, persons engaged in approved enterprises are granted some relief from income tax and business license fees. Both the repatriation of capital and profit remittances on foreign capital must be approved by the Central Bank; such approval is granted when the appropriate documentation is supplied.

Gold

Residents may freely purchase, hold, and sell gold in any form. There are no restrictions on imports or exports of gold.

Changes During 1994

Exchange Arrangement

October 6. Western Samoa formally accepted the obligations of Article VIII, Sections 2, 3, and 4 of the Fund Agreement.

REPUBLIC OF YEMEN

(Position as of December 31, 1994)

Exchange Arrangement

The currency of the Republic of Yemen is the Yemeni Rial, which is pegged to the U.S. dollar, the intervention currency, at YRls 12.01 per US$1.[1] On December 31, 1994, the official buying and selling rates for the U.S. dollar were YRls 12.00 and YRls 12.02, respectively,[2] per US$1. Buying and selling rates for 12 other currencies[3] are fixed daily by the Central Bank of Yemen on the basis of rates for the U.S. dollar in markets abroad.

The official rate applies to oil exports, imports of wheat and flour, as well as to payments of interest and principal on public external debt, government receipts from nonresidents, official travel abroad, limited allocations of foreign exchange for students studying abroad or residents traveling abroad for medical treatment, the Government's transactions with Yemeni embassies, payments for hotel bills and airline tickets by non-Yemeni nationals, and payments to nonnationals working for the Government. A diplomatic accounting rate of YRls 5 per US$1 is used to convert the salaries and allowances of staff working in Yemeni embassies abroad to the local currency.[4] Foreign embassies, oil companies, and bilateral and multilateral assistance agencies are authorized to sell foreign exchange to the Central Bank at the incentive rate of YRls 25 per US$1. Part of expatriates' salaries paid by oil companies are required in principle to be converted at the incentive rate. The incentive rate also applies to imports financed under bilateral and multilateral assistance, and to imports of certain medicines. All other foreign exchange transactions take place in the parallel market. There are two rates in effect in the parallel market—the free market rate, which was YRls 103 per US$1 at the end of 1994, and the fixed rate of YRls 84 per US$1, which was set in mid-November 1994 by the oversight committee established under the 1992 Law on Money Changers. This committee, consisting of representatives of the commercial banks, money changers, the business community, and a central bank observer, is required to monitor conditions in the market and set the rate in accordance with market indicators. The money changers operate both inside Yemen and in neighboring countries (mainly in Saudi Arabia), where they acquire foreign exchange primarily from expatriate Yemeni workers, which they remit to their offices in Yemen, which credit the workers' accounts. The great majority of parallel market transactions take place at the free market rate, and most private sector foreign exchange transactions take place in the parallel market. Commercial banks are not permitted to operate in the parallel market.

There are no arrangements for forward cover against exchange rate risk operating in the official or the commercial banking sector.

Administration of Control

The Central Bank establishes a foreign exchange budget in parallel with a commodity budget prepared by the Ministry of Supply and Trade and the Ministry of Industry in consultation with the Central Bank. All but a few imports require a license issued by the Ministry of Supply and Trade. Licenses are sent directly to banks opening letters of credit. Commercial banks must provide an implementation guarantee in Yemeni rials equivalent to 2 percent of the value of the import. Transactions in invisibles are supervised by the Central Bank. Commercial banks operate in the official foreign exchange market only as agents for and on behalf of the Central Bank.

Prescription of Currency

With the exception of hotel bills and airline tickets of nonresidents, which must be paid in foreign currency at the official rate, there are no prescription of currency requirements.

Foreign Exchange Accounts

Commercial banks are permitted to open freely transferable foreign currency-denominated accounts for residents and nonresidents, provided that the funds in these accounts are derived from (1) foreign currency transfers from abroad; (2) foreign exchange

---

[1]The dinar of the former People's Democratic Republic of Yemen (YD) is also circulating as legal tender at the rate of YRls 26 per YD 1 but is gradually being withdrawn from circulation. The exchange rate was changed to YRls 50.04 per US$1, effective March 29, 1995.

[2]Effective March 29, 1995, the buying and selling rates were changed to YRls 50 and YRls 50.08, respectively, per US$1.

[3]Deutsche mark, French francs, Italian lire, Japanese yen, Jordan dinars, Kuwaiti dinars, Lebanese pounds, Netherlands guilders, pounds sterling, Saudi Arabian riyals, Swedish kronor, and Swiss francs.

[4]The difference between the diplomatic rate and the official rate is paid to the Central Bank by the Ministry of Finance.

receipts from exports; (3) income from services rendered abroad or to nonresidents; (4) transfers from other freely transferable foreign currency accounts; or (5) foreign currencies, traveler's checks, or bank checks that have been declared to customs. These accounts may be used to (1) finance licensed imports; (2) transfer foreign exchange abroad without prior approval from the Central Bank; (3) withdraw foreign currency in cash; (4) make transfers to another freely transferable or nontransferable foreign currency account; and (5) pay expenses and bank commissions.

Commercial banks are permitted to open nontransferable accounts denominated in foreign currency for residents and nonresidents. Funds deposited in these accounts may derive from (1) transfers from transferable or nontransferable foreign currency accounts; (2) foreign currency bills, traveler's checks, or bank checks, regardless of source; or (3) bank interest in the same foreign currency in which the account is denominated if it is the going rate on world money markets. These accounts may be used for (1) transfers to finance licensed imports; (2) local payments for a transaction in foreign exchange; (3) foreign transfers related to the operations of the account holder, subject to a maximum of $10,000 for each transfer, with transfers in excess of these limits requiring prior approval from the Central Bank; (4) payment of foreign currency bills or other foreign exchange instruments that a bank agrees to sell, debiting the account, in order to cover the expenses of the account holder or his designee, provided that such amounts do not exceed $10,000 for each transfer; and (5) expenses and bank commissions.

Imports and Import Payments

An annual foreign exchange budget is prepared by the Central Bank and is approved by the Supreme Council for Economic, Oil, and Investment Affairs. In conjunction with the foreign exchange budget, an import program is prepared annually by the Ministry of Supply and Trade and the Ministry of Industry. The priority categories are foodstuffs, petroleum products, medicines, and inputs for production.

Imports from Israel and imports of certain types of used machinery for resale are prohibited. Most other imports require licenses and must be processed through local commercial banks. Imports of capital equipment by foreign oil companies do not require a license. Also, all enterprises are permitted to import spare parts up to a maximum value of $5,000 for each unlicensed shipment to meet emergency requirements. The value of imports under this facility is not allowed to exceed $50,000 a year for each enterprise. Yemeni nationals returning from abroad who use their savings in foreign exchange to establish small enterprises or craft shops are allowed to import machinery and spare parts needed for their business activities up to a limit of $40,000 with the authorization of the Ministry of Supply and Trade. In addition, the importation of certain products requires the permission of certain government agencies, and imports of petroleum products are reserved for the Yemen Petroleum Company, a public corporation. With the exception of medical imports, insurance for all imports must be purchased locally.

All importers holding an import license for wheat or flour may obtain the necessary foreign exchange from the Central Bank. Imports of other commodities must be self-financed, and foreign exchange may be obtained from any source other than the Central Bank. The commercial banks are authorized to open letters of credit for the importation of most goods, provided that such imports are self-financed. The commercial banks are thus authorized to accept import licenses in respect of these imports (which have been issued by the Ministry of Supply and Trade) without approval from the Central Bank.

In addition to the applicable customs duty, imports are subject to a tax of 1 percent for reconstruction related to earthquake damage. Imports transported over land routes without a license are subject to a 100 percent surcharge and an advance payment of profits tax equal to 3 percent of their value. A conversion rate of YR1s 18 per US$1 is applied to all imports for the purpose of customs valuation.

Payments for Invisibles

There is no restriction on invisible payments, although amounts sold by the Central Bank at the official exchange rate are limited. The Central Bank sells foreign exchange to students studying abroad as well as to individuals seeking medical treatment abroad; the amount allowed for treatment depends on the patient's destination and may not exceed $2,500. Larger amounts are granted on presentation of an official medical report. There are no restrictions on outward remittances in foreign exchange by expatriate workers. Payments of hotel bills and airline tickets by non-Yemeni nationals must be made in foreign currencies. The exportation of Yemeni rial banknotes is prohibited.

Exports and Export Proceeds

Exports to Israel are prohibited. All exports must be registered for statistical purposes on forms issued by banks. Exporters of products other than petroleum may use 100 percent of their foreign exchange receipts to finance imports of either their own inputs or any other permitted goods, as long as they have an import license. Exporters do not have to repatriate or surrender their foreign exchange proceeds, which they may retain in free foreign currency accounts with domestic banks.

Proceeds from Invisibles

Proceeds from invisibles need not be repatriated. Travelers may freely bring in any amount in foreign banknotes. The importation of Yemeni rial banknotes is prohibited.

Capital

Inward and outward capital transfers are not restricted.

Foreign direct investment is subject to the provisions of the Investment Law administered by the Public Investment Authority. For approved and registered projects, this law guarantees freedom of investment, equal treatment of foreigners and nationals, the transfer abroad of net profits after taxes attributable to foreign capital, and the repatriation of registered capital on liquidation in the currency of investment. In practice, investors are free to transfer abroad any portion of their share of net profits after taxes and other provisions and to repatriate their capital. Nationalization and confiscation are prohibited, except in cases of urgent public necessity, and then only with compensation and permission to transfer foreign capital abroad. Direct investments are authorized by the Public Foreign Investment Authority for projects deemed to be economically viable and socially acceptable; a reasonable timetable for completion and other conditions must be specified. Certain tax and import duty exemptions and concessions are granted for five years to approved projects that meet specific economic criteria. The registration of direct foreign investments and the authentication of intended profit and capital repatriation are undertaken by the Public Investment Authority. Private capital transactions unrelated to direct investments may also be made without restriction. External public debt transactions are conducted through the Central Bank, which also maintains accounts of outstanding amounts and service payments due.

Gold

Residents are free to purchase, hold, and sell gold in any form in the Republic of Yemen.

Changes During 1994

Exchange Arrangement

June 7. Commercial banks were prohibited from operating in the foreign exchange market on behalf of customers.

November 15. A fixed parallel market exchange rate of YRls 84 per US$1 was set by the oversight committee of the Law on Monetary Changers.

Imports and Import Payments

May 1. Imports of low-quality rice are no longer financed by the Central Bank at the official rate.

ZAÏRE

(Position as of December 31, 1994)

Exchange Arrangement

The currency of Zaïre is the New Zaïre.[1] In principle, the external value of the new zaïre is determined on the basis of demand and supply conditions prevailing in the foreign exchange market, with the Bank of Zaïre (the central bank) quoting the rate that prevailed in the market during the previous day. In addition to the Bank of Zaïre, all commercial banks and financial institutions are permitted to participate in the foreign exchange market. At the end of each day, all participating commercial banks and financial institutions are required to determine the total value of purchase and sales transactions in Belgian francs, French francs, and U.S. dollars with customers and with other commercial banks and financial institutions. The banks must also determine the value in new zaïres of the transactions in each of the three currencies and report to the Bank of Zaïre the calculated average effective buying and selling rates of the three currencies as well as the highest and lowest rates quoted in these transactions. The Bank of Zaïre uses this information to arrive at the average effective exchange rate of the new zaïre against 23 other currencies and units, based on the rates provided by the IMF between the U.S. dollar and the currencies concerned.[2] These rates are then used as indicative rates at the opening of trading on the day of their publication and are applied to all government operations, including debt-service payments and the transactions of government-owned enterprises. On December 31, 1994, the rate published by the Bank of Zaïre was NZ 3,200 per US$1 and the interbank rate was NZ 3,145.55 per US$1.

Charges or commissions are not assessed on interbank market transactions. In their transactions with customers, commercial banks and financial institutions may charge an exchange commission not exceeding 1 percent. The spread between the buying and selling rates for foreign banknotes set by the commercial banks and financial institutions in the foreign exchange market must not exceed 5 per-cent. Forward transactions may be conducted in the foreign exchange market.

Administration of Control

The Bank of Zaïre has full regulatory authority over all foreign trade and payments, including discretionary power to authorize residents to hold and use foreign exchange abroad and within Zaïre. The Bank of Zaïre may delegate this authority to certain bank or nonbank intermediaries.

The Public Debt Management Office (OGEDEP), operating under the aegis of the Department of Finance, manages the medium- and long-term external and domestic public and publicly guaranteed debt, is responsible for its servicing, and advises the Executive Council on external debt policy, including terms and guarantees extended by the Government on loans contracted by public, semipublic, and private enterprises. In principle, no new external borrowing may be contracted or guaranteed by the Government without the prior advice of OGEDEP and the central bank.

Arrears are maintained with respect to external payments.

Prescription of Currency

Payments from nonresidents to residents must be made in one of the listed convertible currencies whose rates are published daily by the Bank of Zaïre (see footnote 1). Special authorization for the acceptance of any other currency may be given only in respect of currencies that can be exchanged freely without a discount. Residents must make payments to nonresidents in one of the listed convertible currencies or by crediting nonresident accounts in new zaïres or in foreign currency.

Settlements with the member countries of the Economic Community of the Great Lakes Countries (CEPGL), Burundi and Rwanda, and the member countries of the Economic Community of Central African States (CEEAC)[3] are made through convertible accounts established under arrangements concluded by the Bank of Zaïre with the central banks of the countries concerned. Balances on these convertible accounts at the end of settlement periods— each quarter for CEPGL countries and each month

---

[1]The new zaïre was introduced on October 22, 1993 at the conversion rate of NZ 1 to 3 million old zaïres.

[2]Austrian schillings, Belgian francs, Burundi francs, Canadian dollars, CFA francs, Danish kroner, deutsche mark, European currency units, French francs, Italian lire, Japanese yen, Kenya shillings, Netherlands guilders, Norwegian kroner, Portuguese escudos, pounds sterling, Rwanda francs, SDRs, South African rand, Spanish pesetas, Swedish kronor, and Swiss francs.

[3]Burundi, Cameroon, Central African Republic, Chad, Congo, Equatorial Guinea, Gabon, Rwanda, and São Tomé and Príncipe.

for the CEEAC countries—are transferable into the currency stipulated by the creditor. Virtually all settlements (other than for re-exports) with member countries of the CEEAC are effected through the Central African Clearing House (Chambre de compensation de l'Afrique centrale) through its account with the Bank of Zaïre.

Resident and Nonresident Accounts

There are four categories of nonresident accounts: nonresident foreign currency accounts (*comptes de non-résidents en devises*), nonresident convertible accounts (*comptes étrangers convertibles*), nonresident ordinary accounts (*comptes étrangers ordinaires*), and nonresident special accounts (*comptes étrangers indisponibles*). All nonresident accounts must be maintained as sight deposits and may not show a debit balance.

Nonresident foreign currency accounts, as well as nonresident convertible and special accounts, can be opened at any authorized commercial bank without the prior authorization of the Bank of Zaïre. The opening of nonresident ordinary accounts requires the prior authorization of the Bank of Zaïre. Such authorization is not required when accounts are opened for embassies and other diplomatic missions (including those representing international and official multilateral organizations) or for official civil and military cooperation programs.

Nonresident foreign currency accounts may be credited with foreign currency payments by residents or nonresidents in the following cases: (1) payments authorized by the Bank of Zaïre; (2) transfers of foreign currencies from nonresident convertible accounts; (3) proceeds from arbitrage transactions; (4) inward transfers in foreign currencies from nonresidents and from foreign exchange accounts held abroad; (5) payments in foreign currencies made by nonresidents; and (6) transfers in foreign currencies from other nonresident foreign currency accounts. Nonresident foreign currency accounts may be debited freely for the following purposes: (1) payments authorized by the Bank of Zaïre; (2) sales of foreign currency to any authorized bank against new zaïres; (3) arbitrage of foreign currencies against other foreign currencies authorized by the Bank of Zaïre; (4) outward transfers in foreign currencies; (5) transfers to other nonresident foreign currency accounts; (6) withdrawals of banknotes or traveler's checks by the holder of such accounts; and (7) banking commissions and fees.

Nonresident convertible accounts may be credited with (1) transfers of means of payment in foreign currency at banks or authorized financial institu-

tions; (2) transfers from other nonresident convertible accounts as well as from resident foreign currency accounts; and (3) payments by authorized commercial banks in connection with operations for which the Bank of Zaïre authorizes those banks either to credit nonresident convertible accounts or to deliver foreign currency as stipulated by the exchange regulation. These accounts may be freely debited for (1) payments to residents for operations other than exports of goods and services; (2) purchases in the foreign exchange market of foreign currencies or any other means of payment for travel expenses abroad; (3) transfers to other nonresident convertible accounts and purchases of banknotes or any other means of payment in new zaïres at any authorized commercial bank; and (4) banking commissions and fees.

Nonresident ordinary accounts may be credited with (1) sales of foreign exchange against new zaïres received as down payments or transferred from abroad; (2) transfers in new zaïres from nonresident convertible accounts; and (3) receipts in new zaïres from residents for services rendered in Zaïre, property rentals, transportation fares, consular and chancery fees, and other services as specified by the Bank of Zaïre at the time such accounts are opened. Nonresident ordinary accounts may be debited for (1) payments in new zaïres to residents for local purchases of goods and services, dues, taxes, and banking commissions and fees; (2) transfers to other nonresident ordinary accounts of the same holder; and (3) withdrawals of banknotes or any other means of payment in new zaïres. In addition, assets held in nonresident ordinary accounts are not transferable abroad, nor can they be transferred to nonresident convertible accounts.

Nonresident special accounts can be opened for nonresidents entitled to receive specified payments on account of (1) the sale of, or rental income from, real estate properties and other fixed capital located in Zaïre and owned by nonresidents; and (2) the sale of businesses and goodwill, as well as shares in agricultural, commercial, industrial, and service companies located in Zaïre and owned by nonresidents. In addition, all assets denominated in new zaïres and owned by non-Zaïrian residents permanently leaving Zaïre must be deposited in or transferred to a nonresident special account opened on behalf of or under the name of the respective persons. The same requirements apply to proceeds from the sale of real estate or the rental of fixed capital owned by non-Zaïrian residents who subsequently become nonresidents. Accounts under this category can be debited only for (1) travel expenses incurred by the holders of such accounts;

(2) transfers to religious organizations or any non-profit cultural, philanthropic, or social organizations; (3) banking commissions and fees; (4) local taxes payable to the central Government of Zaïre; (5) insurance and maintenance fees of fixed capital (including real estate properties); and (6) any other payment authorized by the Bank of Zaïre.

Resident foreign currency accounts. Residents are permitted to open foreign currency accounts at local commercial banks. These accounts may be credited with funds arising from capital transactions, receipts from exports of goods and services and prefinancing credits in respect of such exports within the limits established by the Bank of Zaïre. These accounts may be sight or term accounts, may bear interest, and may be denominated in any currency for which the Bank of Zaïre publishes exchange rates. Overdrafts on these accounts are not permitted. Deposits in these accounts may be used to meet virtually any foreign exchange obligation, including import payments, and funds may be transferred from one foreign exchange account to another opened in the name of the same holder, with the exception of accounts opened by artisanal diamond and gold marketing agencies. Existing regulatory and administrative provisions relating to imports apply to imports financed from these accounts. Anyone permitted to make import payments through this method (using Form I) may do so by debiting these accounts. Authorized banks may pay royalties, merchandise transport costs, services, and capital retransfer to nonresidents out of these accounts on the instruction of the account holders, who provide the supporting documents required under the exchange regulations. For account holders with the requisite supporting documentation, Form V is not required for withdrawals to cover travel or living expenses abroad, medical expenses incurred or that will be incurred abroad, educational or training expenses incurred or that will be incurred abroad, and tickets for international travel.

Imports and Import Payments

Certain imports, including arms, explosives and ammunition, narcotics, materials contrary to public morals, and certain alcoholic beverages, are prohibited or require special authorization from the Government. Most other imports are subject only to an import declaration at the authorized banks. In general, import declarations remain valid for 12 months; an importer wishing to extend the validity period must so indicate in the import documents accompanying the declaration. The validity may be extended for the first time by the authorized banks if shipment has begun; if shipment has not begun, ex-

tension of the validity period requires authorization from the Bank of Zaïre. Imports of goods intended for expansion of a capital base or for the importer's own use may be effected without a declaration to an authorized bank, provided that the value does not exceed SDR 1,000 for each tariff item and SDR 5,000 for each shipment and that the shipments are financed from the importer's own resources.

All goods shipped by sea to Zaïre must be transported on vessels belonging to shipowners that are bonded with the Office zaïrois de gestion des frets maritimes (OGEFREM) and whose freight charges have been negotiated with that office.

Payments for imports may be made either upon arrival or upon shipment (including payments up to 30 days from date of shipment). Banks may pay freight charges only upon presentation of invoices from the carriers or their agents. The mode of payment must be indicated on all import declaration forms. Authorized banks are allowed to pay transportation and insurance costs in foreign exchange only on imports for which they are directly involved in the financing on an f.o.b. basis. With a few exceptions, imports are subjected to a preshipment inspection. The amount, the invoice price, and the quality of imports must be verified and found acceptable by the foreign agents of the Zaïrian Control Office (OZAC); however, in special cases, verification may be effected upon arrival, subject to a waiver from the Bank of Zaïre. Verification certificates are not required for import values (f.o.b.) of SDR 1,000 or less for each tariff item, or of SDR 5,000 or less for each shipment.

Prior approval from the Bank of Zaïre is required for (1) imports in the form of foreign contributions to capital intended for resale; (2) imports financed by suppliers' credits or other interest-bearing foreign financing with a maturity of more than one year, except imports contracted or guaranteed by the government; (3) imports requiring a down payment in foreign currency before shipment; and (4) imports requiring special authorization from the government and imports of currency, coins, and articles imitating or bearing the monetary symbols of Zaïrian currency.

Prior approval from the Bank of Zaïre is no longer required for imports by air provided that: (1) such imports are of an emergency nature; (2) goods to be imported are fragile or perishable; or (3) the cost to the final destination in Zaïre is less than or equivalent to any other means of transport.

The customs tariff rates range from 15 percent to 50 percent, with a special rate of 5 percent for some equipment. The rate of the turnover tax ranges from zero to 20 percent.

Payments for Invisibles

All payments for invisibles must be made through an authorized bank. When the approval of the Bank of Zaïre is required, it must be requested by the authorized banks concerned. The Bank of Zaïre will not authorize the payment in foreign exchange of commissions in favor of shippers or purchasing agents.

Other payments relating to services performed by nonresidents are, in principle, permitted. However, outward remittances of salaries of expatriate employees are limited to the levels authorized during the preceding year. The transfer abroad of salaries of newly hired expatriates is limited to 50 percent of net salary, provided that the nontransferable amount is sufficient to meet local needs. Transfers pertaining to certain administrative expenses that firms incur abroad, payment of interest on private loans, and certain portions of insurance premiums are generally permitted. Transfers of net profits of firms with foreign participation are authorized. Transfers of rental income received by nonresidents and residents who are foreign nationals are suspended. Payments for commissions, brokerage charges and miscellaneous fees, and royalties may be authorized in some cases.

Tickets for travel abroad may be purchased in new zaïres or in foreign currency for trips originating in Zaïre. Zaïrian nationals traveling abroad may buy foreign exchange from banks or authorized financial institutions, including money changers. Residents who are foreign nationals and who are entitled to transfer part of their income abroad are not allowed to obtain foreign currency from authorized banks to pay for their tickets for international travel and their living expenses abroad involving private travel. For trips to Burundi and Rwanda, tourists and households residing in the border area are entitled to purchase the equivalent of SDR 100 in Burundi or Rwanda francs once a month.

The exportation of Zaïrian banknotes and coins by residents and nonresidents is permitted only up to the equivalent of $100. However, the exportation of Zaïrian banknotes and coins by travelers from Burundi and Rwanda is authorized within the limits of the agreements concluded between the members of the CEPGL.

Exports and Export Proceeds

Exporters must file an exchange document (declaration of foreign exchange commitment), which banks are normally authorized to validate, for all exports. These declarations must specify the type of merchandise to be exported, its price, and the currency in which payment is to be received. Declarations of foreign exchange commitment are normally valid for 90 days. Exports must be carried out and proceeds must be received and surrendered within this period, which must not exceed 45 days from the date of shipment, except for export earnings from artisanal gold and diamonds, which must be repatriated before the declaration of foreign exchange commitment is validated at a bank.

Exporters are authorized to retain the following in their resident foreign currency (RME) accounts at authorized banks: (1) 80 percent of their export-generated revenue from artisanal gold and diamonds, and 40 percent from all other goods, to the extent that repatriation occurs within the legally required period of 45 days from the date of shipment; and (2) 100 percent of funds received as prefinancing for products intended for exportation. The corresponding ratios are: 45 percent for Générale des carrières et des mines du Zaïre, 50 percent for Société de développement industriel et minier du Zaïre; and 20 percent for Société minière de Bakwanga. The Bank of Zaïre may authorize the holding abroad of a portion of earnings from exports.

The exportation, turnover, and statistical taxes on coffee exports have been suspended. Economic transactors may export coffee, subject to inspection and quality certificates issued respectively by the OZAC and the Zaïrian Office for Coffee (OZACAF). As in the case of other export products, coffee may be exported under prefinancing contracts.

Artisanal gold and diamonds may be exported only through authorized marketing agencies (comptoirs agréés).

The Bank of Zaïre purchases and exports gold on its own account, along with the authorized marketing agencies in the market. Industrial diamonds and gold may be exported directly by the mining companies involved.

Proceeds from Invisibles

Proceeds from invisibles must be repatriated and transferred through authorized banks. A declaration must be made for each transaction and checked by the bank. For some operations, proceeds may be credited to a resident foreign currency account.

An unlimited amount of banknotes and other means of payment in foreign currency may be brought into the country by resident and nonresident travelers. The importation of Zaïrian banknotes and coins is permitted only up to the equivalent of $100.

Capital

The repatriation of foreign capital brought in under the provisions of the Investment Code is permitted only at the time of liquidation, nationalization, or partial or total transfers of shares. Borrowed capital and equity contributions are authorized. Transfers abroad of such contributions made under the Investment Code are guaranteed. The Bank of Zaïre also guarantees transfers abroad of interest, dividends, and profits in respect of foreign capital.

Gold

Only Zaïrian nationals are allowed to purchase, transport, sell, or hold gold within Zaïre, outside the boundaries of areas covered by exclusive mining concessions. Foreign individuals or corporate persons and corporate persons under Zaïrian law may do so only on behalf of and for the account of authorized marketing agencies. Exports of gold and diamonds by authorized marketing agencies do not require prior authorization from the Bank of Zaïre.

Changes During 1994

Exports and Export Proceeds

April 1. The share of funds exporters are allowed to retain in their resident foreign currency accounts at authorized banks was changed as follows: artisanal gold and diamonds, 80 percent; and all other goods, 40 percent.

ZAMBIA

(Position as of December 31, 1994)

Exchange Arrangement

The currency of Zambia is the Zambian Kwacha. All foreign exchange transactions take place at market-determined exchange rates. The official exchange rate of the Bank of Zambia is set at the weighted-average buying exchange rate quoted by commercial banks; a 2 percent spread is maintained to arrive at the Bank of Zambia selling rate. Transactions effected at the Bank of Zambia official rate include purchases of the portion of the foreign exchange earnings of the Zambia Consolidated Copper Mines (ZCCM), all government transactions (including donor assistance and debt service), and sales of foreign exchange for imports under the OGL system.[1]

As a transition to a fully integrated foreign exchange interbank market, the Bank of Zambia also conducts three weekly interbank dealing sessions, during which it receives mostly bids from commercial banks for the purchase of foreign exchange. The Bank of Zambia then selects bids that it considers appropriate in terms of exchange rates and amounts involved. The weighted-average selling rate thereby established in this market is usually close to the weighted-average selling rate in the commercial bank market. This transitional foreign exchange market is intended to be replaced by a single interbank market in the near future.

The Bank of Zambia deals with the Government and authorized commercial banks in U.S. dollars, which is also its currency of intervention. However, banks are free to deal in the currencies of neighboring countries, on the basis of cross rates with the U.S. dollar prevailing in the major international foreign exchange markets. With the lifting of exchange controls, all fees and charges applied by commercial banks and foreign exchange bureaus for processing traveler's checks and other foreign exchange transactions are now determined competitively.

There are no arrangements for forward cover against exchange rate risk operating in the official or the commercial banking sector. Banks are allowed to maintain open foreign exchange positions. Foreign exchange bureaus are allowed to maintain an open foreign exchange position of up to $100,000 at the end of each business day.

Administration of Control

All exchange controls have been abolished, with effect from January 28, 1994. The only exceptions are that (1) the ZCCM must sell all or part of its foreign exchange earnings to the Bank of Zambia until a more integrated interbank market develops and foreign exchange earnings from nontraditional exports become increasingly significant; and (2) prior approval of the Bank of Zambia must be obtained for servicing of private debt incurred prior to January 28, 1994. The Ministry of Commerce is responsible for trade control.

Arrears are still maintained with respect to external payments.

Prescription of Currency

Authorized payments, including payments for imports, from residents of Zambia to residents of other countries may be made in any foreign currency. Payments from residents of other countries may be received in pounds sterling or in Zambian currency from an external account, or in any foreign currency freely exchangeable for U.S. dollars or pounds sterling.

External Accounts

Both residents and nonresidents are free to establish and maintain foreign currency accounts at commercial banks in Zambia and abroad.

Imports and Import Payments

Imports in general require a license, which is granted automatically by commercial banks. Imports may be effected under the OGL system, which operates on the basis of a negative list.[2] Imports covered by the OGL system do not require a license. Goods imported under the OGL system and valued at more than $1 million may be procured under simplified international bidding procedures. Personal and household effects, trade samples, diplomatic shipments, and vehicles

---

[1]As a result of the recent liberalization of the exchange and trade system, most imports are now mostly financed outside the OGL system.

[2]The negative list includes gold, silver, platinum, jewelry, weapons and ammunition, alcoholic beverages, tobacco, televisions, radios, videocassette recorders and camcorders, and passenger automobiles.

brought into Zambia temporarily may also be imported without a license.

Payments for imports for which foreign exchange is requested from the Bank of Zambia's OGL window must be made by irrevocable documentary letters of credit. For imports of goods valued at up to $50,000, importers must submit one invoice price quotation; for imports valued at between $50,000 and $500,000, importers are required to provide three separate invoice quotations, and, for those valued at more than $500,000, importers must provide evidence that they have attempted to obtain the most competitive price through international competitive bidding. All imports are subject to preshipment inspection by international agencies except when the f.o.b. value of each import consignment is less than $10,000. An increasing proportion of imports is settled with private funds or through the Bank of Zambia's bidding mechanism three times a week.

Imports are subject to a tariff with a minimum rate of 15 percent and a maximum rate of 50 percent (except for a few luxury goods). Some imports are exempt under the provisions of bilateral agreements, and nontraditional exporters and certain import-competing firms are exempt under the 1991 Investment Act. In addition, imported goods are subject to an "uplift factor" in computing domestic sales tax.

Payments for Invisibles

All payments for invisibles, except external debt-service payments, may be effected through banks and foreign exchange bureaus without the prior approval of the Bank of Zambia. Remittances of profits and dividends may be made without restriction after payment of all taxes.

Foreign nationals working on contract in Zambia may remit any amount, including "inducement allowances" and gratuities, without restriction. Payments to expatriates employed by the ZCCM and other exporters may be made from exporters' own foreign exchange holdings, or they may acquire foreign exchange from the free market to effect such payments.

Travelers may take out any amount in any currency without prior permission, although they are required to make a declaration if the amounts involved exceed the equivalent of $5,000.

Exports and Export Proceeds

All exports must be declared on the prescribed export declaration form for statistical purposes. Although export licenses are required for most goods, they are administered routinely by commercial banks under the authority delegated by the Ministry of Commerce and Industry. Exports of white maize and fertilizers may be subject to quantitative restrictions when domestic supplies are short; exports of ivory are prohibited. Forty percent of the foreign exchange earnings of the ZCCM must be surrendered to the Bank of Zambia. Exporters of nontraditional products are allowed to retain all of their foreign exchange earnings without restriction.

Proceeds from Invisibles

Receipts from invisibles may be retained in full. There is no limit on the amount of foreign exchange or domestic currency notes a traveler may bring in, but amounts exceeding the equivalent of $5,000 must be declared to customs.

Capital

All borrowings outside Zambia must be registered with the Bank of Zambia for statistical purposes. Outward transfers of capital are free of controls. Disinvestment and repatriation of capital are also unrestricted, subject to verification that no tax obligations are due. No restrictions apply to the sale of assets between foreigners and between Zambians and foreigners. Local borrowing by companies controlled either directly or indirectly from outside Zambia is now unrestricted. Nonresidents may participate in the treasury bill and government bond markets without restriction and are free to remit proceeds from the sales of these instruments after payment of applicable taxes.

Gold

Residents may hold and acquire gold coins in Zambia for numismatic and any other purpose. Imports and exports of gold in any form other than jewelry require exchange control approval.

Changes During 1994

Exchange Arrangement

January 5. The requirement that foreign exchange bureaus endorse passports in respect of the foreign currency sold to Zambian residents traveling abroad for the purchase of goods for import into Zambia, up to $4,000 ($2,000 for travel and $2,000 for imports of goods) was reinstituted.

Administration of Control

January 29. The Minister of Finance issued a directive suspending the Exchange Control Act with effect from January 28, 1994. The Exchange Control Act can be reinstated only by an act of Parliament.

Payments for Invisibles

January 29. The $2,000 monthly limit on remittances of inducement income by expatriate employees on existing contracts was withdrawn, but permission by the employer to transfer the inducement income abroad must include a letter confirming that appropriate provision has been made for the payment of applicable taxes.

January 29. The limits on emigration allowances for expatriates and prior authorization by the Bank of Zambia were eliminated; responsibility for checking documentation was delegated to commercial banks.

January 29. All restrictions on insurance, life assurance, and re-insurance transactions and related payments were abolished; remittances would be allowed against supporting vouchers or documentation without reference to the Bank of Zambia.

January 29. Airlines and their agents were permitted to transfer abroad payments for airline tickets paid in kwacha through commercial banks without reference to the Bank of Zambia, subject to appropriate documentation requirements.

January 29. Remittances of charter hire of foreign aircraft and vessels were permitted without reference to the Bank of Zambia. Earnings of visiting artists, entertainers, and golf players were permitted to be remitted without reference to the Bank of Zambia.

January 29. Clearing and forward charges payable by residents of Zambia to nonresident beneficiaries on imports into or exports from Zambia may be remitted by commercial banks upon presentation of supporting vouchers or bills.

January 29. The Zambia Consolidated Copper Mines (ZCCM) was allowed to make all types of payments without restriction. Zambia Airways was permitted to purchase foreign exchange for settlement of its external obligations without restriction.

March 9. Remittances of dividends by commercial banks were permitted freely, subject to supporting documentation (including the audited profit and loss accounts and balance sheet for the relevant year and tax payments).

May 5. Individuals taking out foreign exchange in excess of $5,000 were required to declare the amount to customs.

Capital

April 5. All previously blocked kwacha accounts were unblocked.

April 5. At the request of subsidiaries or associates in Zambia of companies of nonresident corporations, commercial banks were allowed, without reference to the Bank of Zambia, to transfer recurring contributions to pension funds administered outside Zambia.

April 5. Selected controls on foreign direct investment were abolished, and investment approved under the Investment Act, including the issuance of shares to nonresident investors, would be unrestricted. Nonresidents were allowed to participate in the treasury bill and government bond markets without restriction, and the proceeds from redemption would be permitted without reference to the Bank of Zambia after payment of applicable taxes.

ZIMBABWE

(Position as of February 28, 1995)

Exchange Arrangement

The currency of Zimbabwe is the Zimbabwe Dollar. The external value of the Zimbabwe dollar is determined on the basis of supply and demand conditions in the exchange market. The U.S. dollar is the intervention currency. The spread applied by the Reserve Bank of Zimbabwe (RBZ) between the buying and selling rates is 0.8 percent for all currencies. Authorized dealers (authorized commercial and merchant banks) may charge an additional 0.25 percent on either side of the quoted rates of major currencies. The authorized dealers base their rates for other currencies on current international market rates. On December 31, 1994, the exchange rate quoted by the RBZ was Z$8.3472 per US$1.

Forward exchange contracts are permitted only for trade transactions. There is no limit on the size of such contracts, but their period must be at least one year, depending on the currencies involved and the type of coverage. The RBZ does not offer forward foreign exchange contracts. Forward sales of foreign exchange take place at the spot preferential telex transfer rate plus a premium loading for six months, depending on the currencies involved and type of coverage. Authorized dealers are expected to quote to their customers the dealers' own telex transfer rates. Authorized dealers are subject to overnight net foreign currency exposure limits, but no other restrictions from the RBZ apply to interbank trading.

Zimbabwe formally accepted the obligations of Article VIII, Sections 2, 3, and 4 of the Fund Agreement, as from February 5, 1995.

Administration of Control

Exchange control is administered by the RBZ under powers delegated to it by the Minister of Finance, in keeping with the Exchange Control Act, Chapter 170, and the Exchange Control Regulations of 1977. Authorized dealers have been empowered to approve certain foreign exchange transactions in accordance with Exchange Control Instructions Issued to Authorized Dealers (July 1, 1981, as amended) and Exchange Control Circulars (issued periodically). Import and export controls may be administered in accordance with the Control of Goods (importation and exportation) (agriculture) Regulations of 1965, as amended; the Control of Goods (importation and exportation) (commerce) Regulations of 1974, as amended; the Control of Goods (exportation of minerals and metals) Order, 1979; the Control of Goods (open general import license) Notice of 1979; and the Control of Goods (open general export license) Notice, 1977.

Prescription of Currency

All payments by nonresidents to residents must be effected in denominated currencies,[1] with the exception of payments otherwise specified or effected through nonresident accounts. Under the Clearing House Agreement, which went into effect on February 1, 1984, within the Preferential Trade Area for Eastern and Southern African States (PTA), residents of member countries may use national currencies in day-to-day payments during a transaction period of two calendar months; the monetary authorities settle net balances at the end of this period in convertible currencies.

Resident and Nonresident Accounts

Nonresident accounts may be opened with the approval of the exchange control authorities by persons who have never been residents of Zimbabwe. Nonresident accounts may be credited with foreign currencies, with payments from other nonresident accounts, or with payments by residents that would be eligible for transfer outside Zimbabwe. Nonresident accounts may be debited for payments to residents, for payments to other nonresident accounts, or for payments abroad. Only former residents now residing outside Zimbabwe may maintain emigrants' accounts in Zimbabwe. Cash assets held in Zimbabwe in the names of emigrants must be blocked in these accounts, and all payments to and from these accounts are subject to various exchange restrictions.

Residents and nonresident individuals may open foreign currency accounts in one of the denominated currencies in local branches of authorized dealers. Funds in these accounts are traded at market-determined exchange rates. Funds withdrawn from these accounts and converted into local currency, however,

---

[1]Seventeen denominated currencies are freely convertible through authorized dealers: Austrian schillings, Belgian francs, Canadian dollars, Danish kroner, deutsche mark, French francs, Italian lire, Japanese yen, Netherlands guilders, Norwegian kroner, Portuguese escudos, pounds sterling, South African rand, Spanish pesetas, Swedish kronor, Swiss francs, and U.S. dollars.

may not be redeposited in the account, except in the case of the initial investment, and income or capital gains from investments in the stock exchange, unlisted companies, or money markets.

Imports and Import Payments

There are no import-licensing requirements. The negative list for imports includes, besides items restricted for health or security reasons, textiles and apparel, alcoholic beverages, canned beverages, nonmonetary gold, pearls, precious and semiprecious stones, and some jewelry items. Imports of certain goods (mostly agricultural and processed food products) require a special permit issued by the Ministry of Agriculture. Certain agricultural products (coffee, maize, sorghum, soybeans, and wheat) may be imported only by the Grain Marketing and Cotton Marketing Boards or by others with the permission of the Boards. No quotas are in force, but seasonal restrictions are applied to certain agricultural products.

Authorized dealers may approve applications to effect payments for authorized imports, provided the necessary documentation (including the details of import licenses or open general licenses) is submitted. Payments for imports into Zimbabwe from all countries may be made in Zimbabwean currency to a local nonresident account or in any foreign currency.

The customs duty regime consists mainly of ad valorem duties, which range up to a maximum of 35 percent of the c.i.f. value for most consumer goods (up to 60–75 percent for vehicles) with a surtax of 10 percent, and specific duties on a number of products. Generally, imports are subject to an additional tax (between 12.5 percent and 20 percent) equivalent to the sales taxes imposed at the same rates on goods sold domestically. Government imports and capital goods for statutory bodies are exempt from customs duties.

Payments for Invisibles

Foreign exchange to pay for invisibles related to imports and, within certain limits, for other purposes is provided by commercial banks under delegated authority. Applications for foreign exchange exceeding the limit established for commercial banks are approved by the RBZ, which deals with each case on its merits.

All dividends declared by foreign investors in the export sector after January 1, 1995 may be remitted to foreign shareholders without restriction after payment of applicable taxes. If direct foreign exchange allocation was used, the following rules apply: (1) a wholly foreign-owned company that meets the criteria to qualify as an export firm and funds its projects through a combination of foreign exchange, "switched blocked funds," or surplus funds is permitted to remit the declared dividends from net after-tax profits on a basis proportionate to the level of foreign exchange invested but limited to a maximum of 50 percent for five years from the beginning of operations, after which the company will qualify for 100 percent remittance of dividends (blocked and surplus funds are assets held by foreigners as a result of the limited remittance of dividends; switched blocked funds are blocked funds purchased by a foreigner from the original owner); (2) a wholly foreign-owned company with its own blocked funds is permitted to repatriate 100 percent of its declared dividends, provided it meets all its foreign exchange requirements from external sources; and (3) in the case of a new joint venture that meets the criteria to qualify as an export firm and has at least 30 percent local participation, the foreign partner is allowed to remit 100 percent of its share of declared dividends, provided that it meets its share of foreign exchange requirements from external sources. Outward remittances in respect of services are subject to a 20 percent tax; in cases that fall under double taxation agreements, the tax rate is 10 percent. Foreign companies established prior to September 1979 are permitted to remit 50 percent of net after-tax profits if exports comprise more than 25 percent of total sales.

The following regulations apply to investments in the mining sector: (1) a wholly foreign-owned company that funds its projects through foreign funds is allowed to repatriate 100 percent of its net after-tax profits, provided that it qualifies as an export-oriented project; (2) a wholly foreign-owned company that funds its projects through a combination of foreign funds and either its own blocked funds, switched blocked funds, or surplus funds (subject to a minimum matching formula of 50–50) is allowed to remit dividends of up to 50 percent in proportion to the matching ratio; and (3) the level of dividend remittance for joint ventures subject to the minimum 30 percent local participation criterion is also determined by the matching formula used by the foreign shareholder. After five years, the company can remit 100 percent of its dividends to the foreign shareholder.

The basic foreign exchange allowance for holiday travel is Z$5,000 a year. Children under 10 years are entitled to one-half this amount. The basic foreign exchange allowance for import-related business travel is Z$600 a day, up to a maximum of Z$6,000 a trip, with an overall annual maximum of Z$12,000;

for export-related business travel, the exchange allowance is Z$700 a day, up to a maximum of Z$8,000 a trip and Z$16,000 a year. Applications for holiday and business travel allowances exceeding the specified limits are subject to the approval of the RBZ and are granted in bona fide cases.

Foreign exchange is provided for education abroad beyond the secondary school level for certain diploma and degree courses. All applications for educational allowances must be submitted to the RBZ for approval. For medical treatment, foreign exchange is provided up to Z$200 a day each for the patient and any necessary accompanying companion for a maximum of 30 days. Applications for additional amounts must be submitted to the RBZ for approval. Remittances of up to Z$500 for subscriptions to learned or technical societies and Z$100 for other societies are allowed; the limit for an initial membership fee is Z$250. Remittances to close relatives permanently resident outside Zimbabwe, not exceeding Z$100 a month for each individual beneficiary and Z$200 a month for each family unit, are permitted with the approval of the Reserve Bank.

Applications for emigrant status must be submitted to the RBZ. Beginning March 27, 1984, the settling-in allowance that emigrants may remit abroad is limited to Z$1,000 a family unit. In exceptional and deserving cases, the exchange control authorities will consider applications exceeding this maximum. Since April 1, 1984, all those applying for emigrant status have been required to take steps to liquidate their assets within six months and to invest the total proceeds, less any settling-in allowance granted, in 4 percent, 12-year Zimbabwean government external bonds. If emigrants are unable to comply with the six-month limit, the matter may be referred to the RBZ. Transferable allowances at the time of emigration are as follows: (1) single persons under the age of 40 years, Z$500; (2) single persons aged 40–59 years, Z$1,000; (3) family units and single persons (under 60 years of age) with dependents, Z$1,000; (4) family units (husband over 60 years of age) and single persons over 60, Z$7,000; (5) persons over 80 years of age, Z$10,000; and (6) handicapped or disabled persons, Z$10,000. A further release of capital is authorized as an annual allowance on each anniversary of the emigrant's departure, as follows: persons over 65 years of age, Z$2,000; and persons over 70 years of age, Z$3,000.

Travelers leaving Zimbabwe may take out, as part of their travel allowance, not more than Z$250 in Zimbabwean currency, together with a maximum of the equivalent of Z$250 in foreign banknotes. Nonresident travelers may take out the traveler's checks they brought in, less the amount they sold to authorized dealers. Upon departure from Zimbabwe, nonresident travelers may reconvert unspent Zimbabwean currency into foreign currencies on presentation of exchange certificates.

Exports and Export Proceeds

Exporters must have licenses to export the following: (1) any ore, concentrate, or other manufactured product of chrome, copper, lithium, nickel, tin, or tungsten; (2) petroleum products; (3) jute and hessian bags; (4) road or rail tankers for carrying liquids or semiliquids; (5) bitumen, asphalt, and tar; (6) wild animals and wild animal products; (7) certain wood products; (8) ammonium nitrate; and (9) implements of war. Export-licensing requirements are imposed for reasons of health and social welfare, as well as to ensure an adequate domestic supply of essential products.

Export permits are required from the Ministry of Lands and Agriculture for some basic agricultural commodities, including maize, oilseeds, cheese, skimmed milk, seeds, potatoes, citrus fruits, apples, bananas, and tomatoes.

Goods may not be exported without permission unless the customs authorities are satisfied that payment has been made in an approved manner or will be made within three months of the date of shipment (or a longer period if permitted by the RBZ). Payments for exports must be received in one of the following ways: (1) in a denominated currency; (2) in Zimbabwean currency from a nonresident account; and (3) in the case of Malawi and Botswana, by checks drawn in Malawi kwacha or Botswana pula, respectively. Under the PTA arrangement, member countries may use national currencies in the settlement of payments during a transaction period of two months, with net balances at the end of this period to be settled in convertible currencies. Exports to some fifty countries are approved only upon advance payment of export proceeds or if payment is covered by an irrevocable letter of credit issued or confirmed before exportation by a reputable overseas bank. The retention rate was raised to 50 percent from 5 percent on April 1 and to 100 percent from 60 percent on July 2, 1995.

An export subsidy in the form of tax exemption at the rate of 9 percent of the f.o.b. value is granted on specified exports of manufactured products with a minimum domestic value added of 25 percent.

Proceeds from Invisibles

Receipts from invisibles must be sold to authorized banks within a reasonable period of time. Residents performing services abroad may also retain a portion of their earnings. Foreign currency and traveler's checks may be imported without restriction but must be sold or exchanged in Zimbabwe only through authorized dealers. A traveler may bring in Zimbabwean currency up to a maximum of Z$250.

Capital

Inward transfers of capital through normal banking channels are not restricted. The limit on foreign borrowing without prior approval of the External Loans Coordinating Committee is up to US$5 million.

Outward transfers of capital are controlled. However, all foreign investments, irrespective of their source, that have been undertaken through normal banking channels since September 1, 1979 may be considered for repatriation up to the value of capital invested less dividends transferred abroad. The balance may be transferred only through the established medium of six-year external government bonds bearing interest at the rate of 4 percent a year. Repatriation may be permitted without restriction if funds are used to acquire foreign exchange and if dividends were not remitted with such funds.

The repatriation of capital invested before September 1, 1979 is prohibited; however, shareholders are allowed, within limits, to apply to the RBZ for the remittance of such capital upon the sale of shares to local residents, and if such application is approved, the capital is invested in external government bonds bearing interest at the rate of 4 percent a year and carrying a maturity of 12 years (for individuals) or 20 years (for firms). Repatriation at accelerated rates that depend on discounted sales prices of net equity is allowed.

Former residents holding blocked assets and new emigrants are allowed to invest their funds in government external bonds with a maturity of 12 years and an annual interest rate of 4 percent. Remittance of a former resident's Zimbabwean pension is guaranteed under the constitution. All other outward transfers of capital are subject to approval by the RBZ, as are dealings in external securities.

Previously blocked funds, whether already converted into government bonds or not, can qualify as new venture capital if they are reinvested in Zimbabwe in an approved project and matched by an inflow of investment funds of up to 50 percent of the reinvested blocked funds, as determined by the RBZ. Blocked funds can be used by third parties, foreign as well as domestic, for investment on freely negotiated terms; as new venture capital, the total investment is eligible to be remitted as dividends

for up to 50 percent of after-tax profits. However, the "blocked" portion of the new investment, unlike new venture capital, must be reinvested in Zimbabwe for at least five years. Gold producers undertaking new expansion projects have been permitted access to offshore financing in the form of gold loans. Foreign investors are permitted to participate in the Zimbabwe Stock Exchange Market using currency received in Zimbabwe through normal banking channels. Purchase of shares by foreign investors is limited to 25 percent of the total equity of the company, with a limit of 5 percent for one investor. These limits are in addition to any existing foreign shareholdings in the companies. The initial investment plus any capital gains and dividend income may be remitted without restriction. Foreign investors may also invest up to a maximum of 15 percent of the assets brought to Zimbabwe in primary issues of bonds and stocks.

Locally owned companies (greater than 75 percent equity owned by residents) may buy blocked funds from the original owners for investment purposes by using funds from the export retention scheme, provided that they export at least 75 percent of their output.

Direct foreign investments up to US$40 million in the preferred areas (mining, agro-industry, manufacturing, tourism, and high-technology services) are approved by the Zimbabwe Investment Centre (ZIC). In the preferred areas, 100 percent foreign ownership is permitted; it is restricted to 25 percent in other areas.

Gold

The exportation of gold in unmanufactured form is controlled and licensed under the Control of Goods (exportation of minerals and metals) Order, 1979, which is administered by the Ministry of Mines. No person may export any precious metal or certain other specified metals and minerals without an export license; no such licenses for gold are issued. These controls do not, however, apply to the Reserve Bank. The importation of gold is controlled by the Gold Trade Act, which requires those intending to import gold into Zimbabwe to meet certain requirements.

No person, either as principal or agent, is entitled to deal in or possess gold unless that person is (1) the holder of a license or permit; (2) the holder or distributor of a registered mining location from which gold is being produced; or (3) the employee or agent of any of the persons mentioned in (1) and (2) above and authorized by an employer or principal to deal in or possess gold that is already in the lawful possession of such employer or principal. A mining commissioner may issue to any person a permit authorizing the acquisition, possession, or disposal of any gold, provided the quantity does not exceed 1 troy ounce. In all other cases, permission can be issued only by the Secretary for Mines. Three types of licenses may be issued under the terms of the Gold Trade Act: a gold dealing license, a gold recovery works license, and a gold assaying license. Barclays Bank of Zimbabwe, Ltd., is the only authorized dealer under the terms of the act. Each holder or distributor of a registered mining location is required to lodge with this bank all gold acquired each month by the tenth day of the following month. Any person intending to smelt gold or any article containing gold must first obtain a license issued by a district commissioner under the terms of the Secondhand Goods Act that authorizes the possession of smelting equipment.

Changes During 1994

Exchange Arrangement

January 1. The official exchange rate was devalued by 17 percent, and a dual exchange rate regime was introduced comprising a market-determined rate for the private sector and an official exchange rate for government transactions. Access to official foreign exchange was restricted to imports of petroleum, government imports of goods and services, imports from PTA countries, outstanding entitlements under the export retention scheme, existing forward exchange contracts, and legal commitments to provide foreign exchange at the official rate for some private sector debt service. The RBZ stopped offering forward foreign exchange contracts. Commercial banks started applying market rates for forward exchange contracts.

July 2. Exchange rates were unified at the level of the market-determined exchange rate.

Resident and Nonresident Accounts

January 1. Foreign currency accounts for the retention of export proceeds were introduced for corporations.

July 2. The 90-day limit on holding foreign exchange in foreign currency accounts was removed.

Imports and Import Payments

January 1. Import-licensing requirements were removed. The import surtax was reduced to 15 percent from 20 percent.

August 1. The import surtax was reduced to 10 percent from 15 percent. Capital goods were exempted from the customs duties. Customs duties on textiles were reduced to 5 percent from 10 percent, and on clothing to 15 percent from 20–35 percent.

Payments for Invisibles

January 1. The foreign exchange allowance for holiday travel was increased to Z$5,000 from Z$2,000.

Exports and Export Proceeds

January 1. The export retention rate was increased to 60 percent from 50 percent.

July 2. The export retention rate was increased to 100 percent.

Capital

January 1. The limit on foreign borrowing without prior approval of the External Loans Coordinating Committee was raised to US$5 million.

December 1. All dividends declared by foreign investors in the export sector after January 1, 1995 would be allowed to be remitted abroad after payment of applicable taxes.

Changes During 1995

Exchange Arrangement

February 5. Zimbabwe formally accepted the obligations of Article VIII, Sections 2, 3, and 4 of the Articles of Agreement.

Capital

February 1. A timetable for the liquidation, over a three-year period starting July 1, 1995, of blocked funds relating to profits and dividends earned on foreign investments made prior to May 1993 was established.

APPENDIX

European Union: Selected Trade Measures
Introduced and Eliminated on an EU-Wide Basis During 1994[1]

Antidumping Duties

1. Introduction

January 12. Provisional antidumping duty was imposed on imports of hematite pig iron originating in Brazil, Poland, the Russian Federation, and Ukraine (Commission Decision No. 67/94).

February 1. Definitive antidumping duty was imposed on imports of ethanolamine originating in the United States (Council Regulation No. 229/94).

February 17. Provisional antidumping duty was imposed on imports of large aluminum electrolytic capacitors originating in the Republic of Korea and Taiwan Province of China (Commission Regulation No. 371/94).

February 21. Definitive antidumping duty was imposed on imports of gas-fueled, non-refillable flint lighters originating in the People's Republic of China, Japan, the Republic of Korea, and Thailand (Council Regulation No. 398/94).

March 9. Provisional antidumping duty was imposed on imports of certain magnetic disks (3.5-inch microdisks) originating in Hong Kong and the Republic of Korea (Commission Regulation No. 534/94).

March 17. Definitive antidumping duty was imposed on imports of ferro-silicon originating in the People's Republic of China and South Africa (Council Regulation No. 621/94).

March 29. Definitive antidumping duty was imposed on isobutanol originating in the Russian Federation (Council Regulation No. 721/94).

April 12. Definitive antidumping duty was imposed on imports of silicon carbide originating in the People's Republic of China, Poland, the Russian Federation, and Ukraine (Council Regulation No. 821/94).

April 19. Definitive antidumping duty was imposed on imports of certain ball bearings originating in Japan (Council Regulation No. 872/94).

April 21. Provisional antidumping duty was imposed on imports of calcium metal originating in the People's Republic of China and the Russian Federation (Commission Regulation No. 892/94).

June 13. Definitive antidumping duty was imposed on imports of large aluminum electrolytic capacitors originating in the Republic of Korea and Taiwan Province of China (Council Regulation No. 1384/94).

June 20. Provisional antidumping duty was imposed on imports of artificial corundum originating in the People's Republic of China (Commission Regulation No. 1418/94).

July 15. Definitive antidumping duty was imposed on imports of hematite pig iron originating in Brazil, Poland, the Russian Federation, and Ukraine (Commission Decision No. 1751/94).

July 18. Provisional antidumping duty was imposed on imports of furfuraldehyde originating in the People's Republic of China (Commission Decision No. 1783/94).

July 22. Definitive quantitative limit on imports of certain textile products (Category 28) originating in Pakistan (Commission Regulation No. 1802/94).

July 25. Definitive antidumping duty was imposed on imports of cotton yarn originating in Brazil and Turkey (Council Regulation No. 1828/94).

September 9. Definitive antidumping duty was imposed on imports of certain magnetic disks (3.5-inch microdisks) originating in Hong Kong and the Republic of Korea (Council Regulation No. 2199/94).

September 14. Definitive antidumping duty was imposed on imports of ferro-silicon originating in Brazil (Council Regulation No. 2238/94).

September 21. Provisional antidumping duty was imposed on imports of tungsten ores and concentrates, tungstic oxide, tungstic acid, tungsten carbide, and fused tungsten carbide originating in the People's Republic of China (Commission Regulation No. 2286/94).

September 27. Provisional antidumping duty was imposed on imports of color television receivers originating in the People's Republic of China, the Republic of Korea, Malaysia, Singapore, and Thailand (Commission Regulation No. 2376/94).

October 19. Definitive antidumping duty was imposed on imports of artificial corundum originating in the People's Republic of China, the Russian Federation, and Ukraine (Council Regulation No. 2556/94).

October 19. Definitive antidumping duty was imposed on imports of calcium metal originating in the People's Republic of China and the Russian Federation (Council Regulation No. 2557/94).

November 17. Definitive antidumping duty was imposed on imports of potassium permanganate

[1]Source: Official Journals of the European Communities.

originating in the People's Republic of China (Council Regulation No. 2819/94).

December 12. Provisional antidumping duty was imposed on imports of urea ammonium nitrate solution originating in Bulgaria and Poland (Commission Decision No. 825/94).

December 19. Provisional antidumping duty was imposed on imports of ferro-silico-manganese originating in Brazil, the Russian Federation, South Africa, and Ukraine (Commission Regulation No. 3119/94).

December 22. Definitive antidumping duty was imposed on imports of urea ammonium nitrate solution originating in Bulgaria and Poland (Council Regulation No. 3319/94).

2. Extension

January 24. Provisional antidumping duty on imports of isobutanol originating in the Russian Federation was extended (Council Regulation No. 162/94).

February 7. Provisional antidumping duty on imports of television camera systems originating in Japan was extended (Council Regulation No. 301/94).

April 29. Provisional antidumping duty on imports of hematite pig iron originating in Brazil, Poland, the Russian Federation, and Ukraine was extended (Commission Decision No. 1022/94).

June 8. Provisional antidumping duty on imports of certain magnetic disks (3.5-inch microdisks) originating in Hong Kong and the Republic of Korea was extended (Council Regulation No. 1340/94).

July 18. Provisional antidumping duty on imports of calcium metal originating in the People's Republic of China and the Russian Federation was extended (Council Regulation No. 1777/94).

September 9. Provisional antidumping duty on imports of calcium metal originating in the People's Republic of China and the Russian Federation was extended (Council Regulation No. 2198/94).

October 24. Provisional antidumping duty on imports of urea ammonium nitrate solution originating in Bulgaria and Poland was extended (Council Regulation No. 2620/94).

November 17. Provisional antidumping duty on imports of furfuraldehyde originating in the People's Republic of China was extended (Council Regulation No. 2818/94).

3. Elimination

December 8. Antidumping duty on imports of certain polyester yarns originating in India was eliminated (Council Regulation No. 3009/94).

Countervailing Charges

1. Introduction

January 7. Countervailing charge was introduced on fresh clementines originating in Morocco (Commission Regulation No. 32/94).

February 24. Countervailing charge was introduced on artichokes originating in Egypt (Commission Regulation No. 404/94).

March 2. Countervailing charge was introduced on fresh lemons originating in Turkey (Commission Regulation No. 475/94).

March 8. Countervailing charge was introduced on fresh lemons originating in Turkey (Commission Regulation No. 514/94).

March 10. Countervailing charge was introduced on apples originating in Turkey (Commission Regulation No. 543/94).

March 14. Countervailing charge was introduced on artichokes originating in Egypt (Commission Regulation No. 559/94).

April 6. Countervailing charge was introduced on tomatoes originating in Morocco (Commission Regulation No. 769/94).

April 12. Countervailing charge was introduced on tomatoes originating in Turkey (Commission Regulation No. 815/94).

April 13. Countervailing charge was introduced on tomatoes originating in Morocco (Commission Regulation No. 831/94).

May 16. Countervailing charge was introduced on tomatoes originating in Morocco (Commission Regulation No. 1119/94).

May 24. Countervailing charge was introduced on tomatoes originating in Morocco (Commission Regulation No. 1175/94).

August 1. Countervailing charge was introduced on certain varieties of plums originating in Hungary (Commission Regulation No. 1985/94).

August 10. Countervailing charge was introduced on certain varieties of plums originating in Romania (Commission Regulation No. 2036/94).

August 10. Countervailing charge was introduced on certain varieties of plums originating in Hungary (Commission Regulation No. 2037/94).

August 22. Countervailing charge was introduced on certain varieties of plums originating in Romania (Commission Regulation No. 2084/94).

September 5. Countervailing charge was introduced on certain varieties of plums originating in Hungary (Commission Regulation No. 2173/94).

September 5. Countervailing charge was introduced on certain varieties of plums originating in Romania (Commission Regulation No. 2174/94).

September 6. Countervailing charge was introduced on certain varieties of plums originating in Turkey (Commission Regulation No. 2180/94).

September 8. Countervailing charge was introduced on certain varieties of plums originating in Hungary (Commission Regulation No. 2196/94).

September 19. Countervailing charge was introduced on certain varieties of plums originating in Hungary (Commission Regulation No. 2259/94).

September 19. Countervailing charge was introduced on certain varieties of plums originating in Hungary (Commission Regulation No. 2260/94).

September 19. Definitive countervailing charge was imposed on imports of ball bearings with a maximum external diameter not exceeding 30 mm. originating in Thailand (Council Regulation No. 2271/94).

September 20. Countervailing charge was introduced on certain varieties of plums originating in Turkey (Commission Regulation No. 2269/94).

September 21. Countervailing charge was introduced on certain varieties of plums originating in Romania (Commission Regulation No. 2275/94).

October 27. Countervailing charge was introduced on fresh lemons originating in Argentina (Commission Regulation No. 2617/94).

November 8. Countervailing charge introduced on fresh lemons originating in Argentina was amended (Commission Regulation No. 2721/94).

November 15. Countervailing charge was introduced on fresh lemons originating in Uruguay (Commission Regulation No. 2775/94).

November 28. Countervailing charge was introduced on fresh lemons originating in Turkey (Commission Regulation No. 2886/94).

2. Elimination

January 14. Countervailing charge on fresh clementines originating in Morocco was eliminated (Commission Regulation No. 72/94).

March 15. Countervailing charge on fresh lemons originating in Turkey was eliminated (Commission Regulation No. 571/94).

April 21. Countervailing charge on tomatoes originating in Morocco was eliminated (Commission Regulation No. 887/94).

April 25. Countervailing charge on tomatoes originating in Turkey was eliminated (Commission Regulation No. 910/94).

June 1. Countervailing charge on tomatoes originating in Morocco was eliminated (Commission Regulation No. 1271/94).

June 15. Countervailing charge on tomatoes originating in Turkey was eliminated (Commission Regulation No. 1364/94).

November 24. Countervailing charge on fresh lemons originating in Uruguay was eliminated (Commission Regulation No. 2850/94).

December 2. Countervailing charge on fresh lemons originating in Turkey was eliminated (Commission Regulation No. 2948/94).

Quantitative Restrictions

Introduction

March 2. Provisional quantitative limit was established on imports of certain textile products originating in the People's Republic of China (Commission Regulation No. 469/94).

March 30. Provisional quantitative limit was established on imports of certain textile products originating in the People's Republic of China (Commission Regulation No. 747/94).

April 12. Provisional quantitative limit was established on imports of certain textile products originating in Indonesia (Commission Regulation No. 811/94).

May 18. Provisional quantitative limit was established on imports of certain textile products originating in Pakistan (Commission Regulation No. 1134/94).

May 18. Provisional quantitative limit was established on imports of certain textile products originating in the People's Republic of China (Commission Regulation No. 1135/94).

May 18. Provisional quantitative limit was established on imports of certain textile products originating in the People's Republic of China (Commission Regulation No. 1136/94).

June 2. Provisional quantitative limit was established on imports of fresh sour cherries originating in Bosnia and Herzegovina, Croatia, Slovenia, and the former Yugoslav Republic of Macedonia (Commission Regulation No. 1281/94).

July 5. Provisional quantitative limit was established on imports of certain textile products originating in Indonesia (Commission Regulation No. 1629/94).

July 18. Provisional quantitative limit was established on imports of textile products originating in the People's Republic of China (Commission Regulation No. 1756/94).

November 14. Provisional quantitative limit was established on imports of certain textile products originating in the People's Republic of China (Council Regulation No. 2797/94).

Customs Duties

Reintroduction

March 15. Customs duties on certain textile products originating in Indonesia, to which the preferential tariff arrangements applied, were reintroduced (Commission Regulation No. 581/94).

March 15. Customs duties on certain industrial products originating in the People's Republic of China, Indonesia, Lithuania, Malaysia, Singapore, and Thailand, to which the preferential tariff arrangements applied, were reintroduced (Commission Regulation No. 582/94).

April 21. Customs duties on certain industrial products originating in Brazil, the People's Republic of China, India, Indonesia, Lithuania, Mexico, and Pakistan, to which the preferential tariff arrangements applied, were reintroduced (Commission Regulation No. 893/94).

April 21. Customs duties on certain textile products originating in the People's Republic of China, India, and Indonesia, to which the preferential tariff arrangements applied, were reintroduced (Commission Regulation No. 894/94).

May 18. Customs duties applicable to certain products falling within CN Code 4820 50 00 originating in the Republic of Korea, to which the preferential tariff arrangements applied, were reintroduced (Commission Regulation No. 1143/94).

May 18. Customs duties on certain industrial products originating in the People's Republic of China and Estonia, to which the preferential tariff arrangements applied, were reintroduced (Commission Regulation No. 1144/94).

May 27. Customs duties applicable to products falling within CN Code 2817 00 00 originating in the People's Republic of China, to which the preferential tariff arrangements applied, were reintroduced (Commission Regulation No. 1221/94).

June 9. Customs duties on certain industrial products originating in Argentina, India, Malaysia, Pakistan, and Thailand, to which the preferential tariff arrangements applied, were reintroduced (Commission Regulation No. 1341/94).

June 23. Customs duties applicable to products falling within CN Code 2929 90 00 originating in Brazil, to which the preferential tariff arrangements applied, were reintroduced (Commission Regulation No. 1458/94).

June 30. Customs duties applicable to certain textile products originating in Brazil, the People's Republic of China, India, Indonesia, Pakistan, and Thailand, to which the preferential tariff arrange-ments applied, were reintroduced (Commission Regulation No. 1604/94).

July 26. Customs duties applicable to products of the combined nomenclature Codes 3102 40 10 and 3102 40 90, originating in the Czech Republic and the Slovak Republic, to which the preferential tariff arrangements applied, were reintroduced (Commission Regulation No. 1830/94).

August 19. Customs duties applicable to certain industrial products originating in the People's Republic of China, Indonesia, and Malaysia, to which the preferential tariff arrangements applied, were reintroduced (Commission Regulation No. 2086/94).

September 7. Customs duties applicable to certain industrial products originating in the People's Republic of China, to which the preferential tariff arrangements applied, were reintroduced (Commission Regulation No. 2192/94).

September 13. Customs duties applicable to certain industrial products originating in India, and Thailand, to which the preferential tariff arrangements applied, were reintroduced (Commission Regulation No. 2226/94).

September 13. Customs duties applicable to certain textile products originating in Belarus, the People's Republic of China, India, Indonesia, Pakistan, and Thailand, to which the preferential tariff arrangements applied, were reintroduced (Commission Regulation No. 2227/94).

September 29. Customs duties applicable to certain textile products originating in the People's Republic of China, India, Indonesia, Pakistan, and Thailand, to which the preferential tariff arrangements applied, were reintroduced (Commission Regulation No. 2378/94).

September 30. Customs duties applicable to products falling within CN Code 3102 80 00 originating in Poland, to which the preferential tariff arrangements applied, were reintroduced (Commission Regulation No. 2380/94).

October 6. Customs duties applicable to certain textile products originating in India, Indonesia, and Pakistan, to which the preferential tariff arrangements applied, were reintroduced (Commission Regulation No. 2436/94).

October 20. Customs duties applicable to certain industrial products originating in Brazil, the People's Republic of China, Indonesia, Singapore, and Thailand, to which the preferential tariff arrangements applied, were reintroduced (Commission Regulation No. 2558/94).

October 20. Customs duties applicable to certain industrial products originating in Indonesia and Malaysia, to which the preferential tariff arrangements applied, were reintroduced (Commission Regulation No. 2559/94).

October 20. Customs duties applicable to certain textile products originating in India, to which the preferential tariff arrangements applied, were reintroduced (Commission Regulation No. 2560/94).

October 31. Customs duties applicable to products falling within CN Code 3102 40, originating in Poland, to which the preferential tariff arrangements applied, were reintroduced (Commission Regulation No. 2657/94).

November 8. Customs duties applicable to products falling within CN Code 8509 originating in the People's Republic of China, to which the preferential tariff arrangements applied, were reintroduced (Commission Regulation No. 2731/94).

November 8. Customs duties applicable to certain industrial products originating in Malaysia, Singapore, and Thailand, to which the preferential tariff arrangements applied, were reintroduced (Commission Regulation No. 2732/94).

November 14. Customs duties applicable to products falling within CN Code 8544 originating in the People's Republic of China, to which the preferential tariff arrangements applied, were reintroduced (Commission Regulation No. 2774/94).

November 14. Customs duties applicable to certain industrial products originating in Indonesia, the People's Republic of China, Indonesia, and Thailand, to which the preferential tariff arrangements applied, were reintroduced (Commission Regulation No. 2773/94).

November 21. Customs duties applicable to certain textile products originating in India, Indonesia, Pakistan, the Republic of Korea, and Thailand, to which the preferential tariff arrangements applied, were reintroduced (Commission Regulation No. 2821/94).

November 21. Customs duties applicable to certain industrial products originating in Brazil and Pakistan, to which the preferential tariff arrangements applied, were reintroduced (Commission Regulation No. 2822/94).

November 21. Customs duties applicable to certain textile products originating in India and Indonesia, to which the preferential tariff arrangements applied, were reintroduced (Commission Regulation No. 2823/94).

November 23. Customs duties applicable to products falling within CN Code 4820 50 00 originating in the Republic of Korea, to which the preferential tariff arrangements applied, were reintroduced (Commission Regulation No. 2846/94).

November 23. Customs duties applicable to certain textile products originating in India, Indonesia, Pakistan, Malaysia, the Philippines, and Thailand, to which

the preferential tariff arrangements applied, were reintroduced (Commission Regulation No. 2847/94).

November 25. Customs duties applicable to certain textile products originating in Indonesia, the Philippines, and Thailand, to which the preferential tariff arrangements applied, were reintroduced (Commission Regulation No. 2895/94).

December 1. Customs duties applicable to certain industrial products originating in the People's Republic of China, Indonesia, and Thailand, to which the preferential tariff arrangements applied, were reintroduced (Commission Regulation No. 2936/94).

December 1. Customs duties applicable to certain textile products originating in India, Malaysia, the Philippines, and Thailand, to which the preferential tariff arrangements applied, were reintroduced (Commission Regulation No. 2937/94).

December 13. Customs duties applicable to products of CN Codes ex 7304, ex 7305, and ex 7306 originating in Bosnia and Herzegovina, Croatia, Slovenia, and the former Yugoslav Republic of Macedonia, to which the preferential tariff arrangements applied, were reintroduced (Commission Regulation No. 3028/94).

December 19. Customs duties applicable to certain textile products originating in Brazil, the People's Republic of China, Lithuania, Malaysia, and Mexico, to which the preferential tariff arrangements applied, were reintroduced (Commission Regulation No. 3120/94).

December 19. Customs duties applicable to certain textile products originating in the People's Republic of China, India, Iran, and Pakistan, to which the preferential tariff arrangements applied, were reintroduced (Commission Regulation No. 3121/94).

December 21. Customs duties applicable to products falling within CN Code 3102 30, originating in Poland, to which the preferential tariff arrangements applied, were reintroduced (Commission Regulation No. 3150/94).

Preferential Customs Duties

1. Re-establishment

January 6. Preferential customs duty on imports of small-flowered roses originating in Israel was re-established (Commission Regulation No. 19/94).

March 21. Preferential customs duty on imports of single-flower (standard) carnations originating in Israel was re-established (Commission Regulation No. 632/94).

April 22. Preferential customs duty on imports of single-flower (standard) carnations originating in Israel was re-established (Commission Regulation No. 902/94).

May 6. Preferential customs duty on imports of small-flowered roses originating in Israel was re-established (Commission Regulation No. 1068/94).

May 30. Preferential customs duty on imports of multiflorous (spray) carnations originating in Israel was re-established (Commission Regulation No. 1233/94).

June 2. Preferential customs duty on imports of small-flowered roses originating in Israel was re-established (Commission Regulation No. 1284/94).

September 9. Preferential customs duty on imports of single-flower (standard) carnations originating in Israel was re-established (Commission Regulation No. 2208/94).

October 21. Preferential customs duty on imports of multiflorous (spray) carnations originating in Israel was re-established (Commission Regulation No. 2571/94).

2. Suspension

January 6. Preferential customs duty on imports of small-flowered roses originating in Israel was suspended and common customs tariff duty was re-established (Commission Regulation No. 6/94).

February 21. Preferential customs duty on imports of small-flowered roses originating in Israel was suspended and common customs tariff duty was re-established (Commission Regulation No. 383/94).

March 14. Preferential customs duty on imports of uniflorous (standard) carnations originating in Israel was suspended and common customs tariff duty was re-established (Commission Regulation No. 563/94).

April 12. Preferential customs duty on imports of uniflorous (standard) carnations originating in Israel was suspended and common customs tariff duty was re-established (Commission Regulation No. 814/94).

May 16. Preferential customs duty on imports of uniflorous (standard) carnations originating in Israel was suspended and common customs tariff duty was re-established (Commission Regulation No. 1120/94).

May 16. Preferential customs duty on imports of small-flowered roses originating in Israel was suspended and common customs tariff duty was re-established (Commission Regulation No. 1121/94).

June 20. Preferential customs duty on imports of small-flowered roses originating in Israel was suspended and common customs tariff duty was re-established (Commission Regulation No. 1410/94).

June 23. Preferential customs duty on imports of uniflorous (standard) carnations originating in Israel was suspended and common customs tariff duty was re-established (Commission Regulation No. 1451/94).

June 24. Preferential customs duty on imports of multiflorous (spray) carnations originating in Israel was suspended and common customs tariff duty was re-established (Commission Regulation No. 1464/94).

September 30. Preferential customs duty on imports of small-flowered roses originating in Israel was suspended and common customs tariff duty was re-established (Commission Regulation No. 2390/94).

November 8. Preferential customs duty on imports of uniflorous (spray) carnations originating in Israel was suspended and common customs tariff duty was re-established (Commission Regulation No. 2717/94).

November 8. Preferential customs duty on imports of multiflorous (spray) carnations originating in Israel was suspended and common customs tariff duty was re-established (Commission Regulation No. 2718/94).

November 8. Preferential customs duty on imports of large-flowered roses originating in Israel was suspended and common customs tariff duty was re-established (Commission Regulation No. 2719/94).

November 8. Preferential customs duty on imports of small-flowered roses originating in Israel was suspended and common customs tariff duty was re-established (Commission Regulation No. 2720/94).

Community Tariff Quotas

Introduction

January 24. Community tariff quota for high-quality fresh, chilled, or frozen meat of bovine animals falling within CN Codes 0201 and 0202 and for products falling within CN 0206 10 95 and 0206 26 91 was established (Council Regulation No. 129/94).

January 24. Community tariff quota for frozen meat of bovine animals falling within CN Codes 0202 and products falling within CN 0206 29 91 was established (Council Regulation No. 130/94).

January 24. Community tariff quota for frozen buffalo meat falling within CN Code 0202 30 90 was established (Council Regulation No. 131/94).

January 24. Community tariff quota for frozen thin skirt of bovine animals falling within CN Code 0206 29 91 was established (Council Regulation No. 132/94).

January 24. Community tariff quota for table cherries originating in Switzerland was established (Council Regulation No. 218/94).

January 24. Community tariff quota for certain fish and fishery products originating in the Faroe Islands was established (Council Regulation No. 261/94).

January 24. Community tariff quota for certain agricultural and industrial products originating in the Czech Republic, Hungary, Poland, and the Slovak Republic was established (Council Regulation No. 262/94).

February 7. Community tariff quota for certain agricultural products originating in Algeria, Egypt, Morocco, and Tunisia was established (Council Regulation No. 297/94).

February 7. Community tariff quota for certain agricultural products originating in Cyprus was established (Council Regulation No. 298/94).

February 7. Community tariff quota for certain agricultural products originating in Israel was established (Council Regulation No. 300/94).

February 7. Community tariff quota for certain agricultural products originating in Bulgaria, and Romania was established (Council Regulation No. 314/94).

February 7. Community tariff quota for certain agricultural and industrial products originating in the Czech Republic, Hungary, Poland, and the Slovak Republic was established (Council Regulation No. 342/94).

February 14. Community tariff quota for certain petroleum products refined in Turkey was established (Council Regulation No. 354/94).

February 14. Community tariff quota for certain agricultural and fishery products originating in Austria, Norway, and Sweden was established (Council Regulation No. 369/94).

March 21. Community tariff quota for certain products originating in Bosnia and Herzegovina, Croatia, the former Yugoslav Republic of Macedonia, and Slovenia was established (Council Regulation No. 652/94).

March 21. Community tariff quota for products originating in Armenia, Azerbaijan, Belarus, Bosnia and Herzegovina, Bulgaria, Croatia, the Czech Republic, Estonia, Georgia, Hungary, Kazakhstan, the Kyrgyz Republic, Latvia, Lithuania, the former Yugoslav Republic of Macedonia, Moldova, Poland, Romania, the Russian Federation, the Slovak Republic, Slovenia, Tajikistan, Turkmenistan, Ukraine, and Uzbekistan was established (Council Regulation No. 665/94).

March 21. Community tariff quota for certain products originating in Bosnia and Herzegovina, Croatia, the former Yugoslav Republic of Macedonia, and Slovenia was established (Council Regulation No. 653/94).

March 28. Community tariff quota for certain textile products originating in certain third countries that participated in 1994 trade fairs organized in the European Community was established (Council Regulation No. 689/94).

March 29. Community tariff quota for certain high-quality beef, pork, poultry, wheat, meslin, bran, sharps, and other residues was established (Council Regulation No. 774/94).

June 13. Community tariff quota for frozen hake fillets and for the processing required by certain textile products under Community outward processing arrangements was established (Council Regulation No. 1385/94).

June 22. Community tariff quota for poultry and certain other agricultural products was established (Council Regulation No. 1431/94).

June 22. Community tariff quota for pork and certain other agricultural products was established (Council Regulation No. 1432/94).

July 18. Community tariff quota for certain agricultural products originating in Bulgaria, the Czech Republic, Hungary, Poland, Romania, and the Slovak Republic was established (Council Regulation No. 1798/94).

July 18. Community tariff quota for certain alpine and mountain breeds of bulls, cows, and heifers, other than those intended for slaughter, was established (Council Regulation No. 1800/94).

July 18. Community tariff quota for rum, tafia, and arrack originating in the overseas countries and territories (OCT) associated with the European Union was established (Council Regulation No. 1827/94).

July 25. Community tariff quota for certain products originating in Algeria, Cyprus, Egypt, Israel (and the occupied territories), Jordan, Malta, Morocco, Tunisia, and Turkey was established (Council Regulation No. 1981/94).

July 27. Community tariff quota determined in the GATT for certain agricultural and industrial products was established (Council Regulation No. 1988/94).

July 27. Community tariff quota for rum, tafia, and arrack originating in the African, Caribbean, and Pacific (ACP) countries was established (Council Regulation No. 1989/94).

October 24. Community tariff quota for certain agricultural and industrial products originating in the Czech Republic, Hungary, Poland, and the Slovak Republic was established (Council Regulation No. 2622/94).

November 14. Community tariff quota for certain agricultural products originating in the African, Caribbean, and Pacific countries was established (Council Regulation No. 2763/94).

November 23. Community tariff quota for certain agricultural and industrial products (first series 1995) was established (Council Regulation No. 2878/94).

November 25. Community tariff quota for certain agricultural and industrial products (first series 1994) was established (Council Regulation No. 2893/94).

December 21. Community tariff quota for certain agricultural products originating in the African, Caribbean, and Pacific countries was established (Council Regulation No. 3144/94).

December 22. Community tariff quota for certain products originating in Bosnia and Herzegovina, Croatia, and the former Yugoslav Republic of Macedonia was established (Council Regulation No. 3356/94).

Import Surveillance

Introduction

January 28. Community surveillance was introduced on imports of iron and steel products, covered by the ECSC Treaty, that originate in third countries (Council Regulation No. 176/94).

September 13. Temporary arrangement for retrospective Community surveillance in respect of Atlantic salmon imports was introduced (Council Regulation No. 2218/94).

September 16. Retrospective Community surveillance on imports of certain steel cables originating in nonmember countries was introduced (Council Regulation No. 2248/94).

December 22. Community surveillance on imports originating in Bosnia and Herzegovina, Croatia, and the former Yugoslav Republic of Macedonia was introduced (Council Regulation No. 3357/94).

	Afghanistan, Islamic State of	Albania	Algeria	Angola	Antigua and Barbuda	Argentina	Armenia	Aruba	Australia	Austria	Azerbaijan	Bahamas, The	Bahrain	Bangladesh	Barbados	Belarus	Belgium and Luxembourg	Belize	Benin	Bhutan	Bolivia	Botswana	Brazil	Bulgaria	Burkina Faso
A. Acceptance of Article Status																									
1. Article VIII status	—	—	—	—	●	●	—	●	●	●	—	●	●	●	●	—	●	●	—	—	●	—	—	—	—
2. Article XIV status	●	●	●	●	—	—	●	—	—	—	●	—	—	—	—	●	—	—	●	●	—	●	●	●	●
B. Exchange Arrangement[3]																									
1. Exchange rate determined on the basis of:																									
(a) A peg to:																									
(i) the U.S. dollar	—	—	—	—	●	●	—	●	—	—	—	●	—	—	●	—	—	●	—	—	—	—	—	—	—
(ii) the pound sterling	—	—	—	—	—	—	—	—	—	—	—	—	—	—	—	—	—	—	—	—	—	—	—	—	—
(iii) the French franc	—	—	—	—	—	—	—	—	—	—	—	—	—	—	—	—	—	—	●	—	—	—	—	—	●
(iv) other currencies[4]	—	—	—	—	—	—	—	—	—	—	—	—	—	—	—	—	—	—	—	●	—	—	—	—	—
(v) a composite of currencies	—	—	—	—	—	—	—	—	—	—	—	—	—	●	—	—	—	—	—	—	—	●	—	—	—
(b) Limited flexibility with respect to:																									
(i) single currency	—	—	—	—	—	—	—	—	—	—	—	—	●	—	—	—	—	—	—	—	—	—	—	—	—
(ii) cooperative arrangement	—	—	—	—	—	—	—	—	—	●	—	—	—	—	—	—	●	—	—	—	—	—	—	—	—
(c) More flexible arrangements:																									
(i) adjusted according to a set of indicators	—	—	—	—	—	—	—	—	—	—	—	—	—	—	—	—	—	—	—	—	—	—	—	—	—
(ii) other managed floating	—	—	●	●	—	—	—	—	—	—	—	—	—	—	—	●	—	—	—	—	—	—	●	—	—
(iii) independently floating	●	●	—	—	—	—	●	—	●	—	●	—	—	—	—	—	—	—	—	—	●	—	—	●	—
2. Separate exchange rate(s) for some or all capital transactions and/or some or all invisibles	●	—	—	—	—	●	—	—	—	—	—	●	●	—	—	—	—	—	—	—	●	—	●	●	—
3. More than one rate for imports	●	—	●	—	—	●	—	—	—	—	●	—	—	—	—	—	—	—	—	—	●	—	●	●	—
4. More than one rate for exports	●	—	●	—	—	●	—	—	—	—	●	—	—	—	—	—	—	—	—	—	●	—	●	●	—
5. Import rate(s) different from export rate(s)	●	—	●	—	—	●	—	—	—	—	●	—	—	—	—	—	—	—	—	—	●	—	●	●	—
C. Payments Arrears	—	●	—	●	●	—	—	—	—	—	—	●	—	—	—	—	—	—	●	—	—	—	—	●	●
D. Bilateral Payments Arrangements																									
1. With members	●	●	●	—	—	●	—	—	—	●	—	—	●	—	●	—	●	—	●	—	—	—	—	●	●
2. With nonmembers	—	●	—	—	—	—	—	—	—	—	—	—	—	●	—	—	—	—	—	—	—	—	—	●	—
E. Payments Restrictions																									
1. Restrictions on payments for current transactions[5]	●	●	●	●	—	—	●	—	—	—	●	—	—	—	—	—	—	—	—	●	●	—	●	●	—
2. Restrictions on payments for capital transactions[5, 6]	●	●	●	●	—	—	●	●	—	—	●	●	—	●	●	●	—	●	●	●	●	—	●	●	●
F. Cost-Related Import Restrictions																									
1. Import surcharges	—	—	—	—	●	—	—	—	—	—	—	—	—	—	—	—	—	—	—	—	●	—	—	●	●
2. Advance import deposits	●	—	—	—	—	—	—	—	—	—	—	—	—	—	—	—	—	—	—	—	—	—	—	—	—
G. Surrender or Repatriation Requirement for Export Proceeds	●	●	●	●	—	—	●	—	—	●	●	●	—	●	●	●	—	●	●	—	●	●	●	●	●

For key and footnotes, see page 568.

	Burundi	Cambodia	Cameroon	Canada	Cape Verde	Central African Republic	Chad	Chile	China	Colombia	Comoros	Congo	Costa Rica	Côte d'Ivoire	Croatia	Cyprus	Czech Republic	Denmark	Djibouti	Dominica	Dominican Republic	Ecuador	Egypt	El Salvador	Equatorial Guinea	Eritrea	Estonia	Ethiopia	Fiji	Finland	France	Gabon	Gambia, The	Georgia	Germany	Ghana
	—	—	—	•	—	—	—	•	—	—	—	—	•	—	•	•	—	•	•	•	•	•	—	•	—	—	•	—	•	•	•	—	—	•	•	•
	•	•	•	—	•	•	•	•	—	•	•	•	•	—	•	—	—	•	—	—	—	—	•	—	•	•	—	•	—	—	—	•	—	•	—	—
	—	—	—	—	—	—	—	—	—	—	—	—	—	—	—	—	—	—	•	•	—	—	—	—	—	—	—	—	—	—	—	—	—	—	—	—
	—	—	—	—	—	—	—	—	—	—	—	—	—	—	—	—	—	—	—	—	—	—	—	—	—	—	—	—	—	—	—	—	—	—	—	—
	—	—	•	—	—	•	•	—	—	—	•	•	—	•	—	—	—	—	—	—	—	—	—	•	—	—	—	—	—	—	—	—	•	—	—	—
	—	—	—	—	—	—	—	—	—	—	—	—	—	—	—	—	—	—	—	—	—	—	—	—	—	—	•	—	—	—	—	—	—	—	—	—
	•	—	—	—	•	—	—	—	—	—	—	—	—	—	•	•	—	—	—	—	—	—	—	—	—	—	—	—	•	—	—	—	—	—	—	—
	—	—	—	—	—	—	—	—	—	—	—	—	—	—	—	—	—	—	—	—	—	—	—	—	—	—	—	—	—	—	—	—	—	—	—	—
	—	—	—	—	—	—	—	—	—	—	—	—	—	—	—	—	—	•	—	—	—	—	—	—	—	—	—	—	—	•	—	—	—	—	•	—
	—	—	—	—	—	—	—	•	—	—	—	—	—	—	—	—	—	—	—	—	—	•	—	—	—	—	—	—	—	—	—	—	—	—	—	—
	—	•	—	—	—	—	—	•	•	—	—	—	—	—	—	—	—	—	—	—	•	—	•	—	•	—	—	—	—	—	—	•	—	—	—	—
	—	—	—	•	—	—	—	—	—	—	•	—	—	—	—	—	—	—	—	—	—	—	—	—	—	—	•	—	•	—	—	—	•	—	—	•
	—	—	—	—	—	—	—	•	—	—	•	—	—	—	—	—	—	—	—	•	—	•	—	—	—	—	•	—	—	—	—	—	•	—	—	•
	—	—	—	—	—	—	—	—	—	•	—	—	—	—	—	—	—	—	—	•	—	•	—	—	—	—	•	—	—	—	—	—	•	—	—	•
	—	—	—	—	—	—	—	—	—	•	—	—	—	—	—	—	—	—	—	•	—	•	—	—	—	—	•	—	—	—	—	—	•	—	—	•
	—	—	—	—	—	—	—	—	—	•	—	—	—	—	—	—	—	—	—	•	—	•	—	—	—	—	•	—	—	—	—	—	•	—	—	•
	—	—	•	—	•	•	•	—	—	—	•	•	•	•	•	—	—	—	—	—	•	—	•	—	•	—	—	•	—	—	—	—	—	—	—	—
	—	—	—	—	•	—	—	•	—	•	—	—	•	—	•	—	—	—	—	•	—	•	—	•	—	—	•	—	—	—	—	—	—	•	—	•
	—	—	—	—	—	—	—	•	—	—	—	—	—	—	—	—	—	—	—	—	—	•	—	—	—	—	—	—	—	—	—	—	—	—	—	•
	•	•	—	—	•	—	—	•	•	•	•	•	—	—	•	—	•	—	—	•	•	•	—	•	•	—	•	•	•	—	•	—	—	•	•	•
	•	•	•	—	•	•	•	•	•	•	•	•	•	•	•	•	—	—	•	—	•	•	•	•	•	•	—	•	•	—	—	•	•	—	•	•
	—	—	•	—	—	—	—	•	—	—	—	•	•	—	•	•	—	—	—	•	—	•	—	—	—	—	—	—	—	—	—	—	•	—	•	—
	—	—	—	—	—	—	—	—	—	—	—	—	—	—	—	—	—	—	—	—	—	—	—	—	—	—	—	—	—	—	—	—	—	—	—	—
	•	•	•	—	•	•	•	•	•	•	•	•	•	•	•	•	—	—	•	•	•	•	—	•	•	—	•	•	—	—	•	—	•	—	—	•

	Greece	Grenada	Guatemala	Guinea	Guinea-Bissau	Guyana	Haiti	Honduras	Hong Kong	Hungary	Iceland	India	Indonesia	Iran, Islamic Rep. of	Iraq	Ireland	Israel	Italy	Jamaica	Japan	Jordan	Kazakhstan	Kenya	Kiribati	Korea
A. Acceptance of Article Status																									
1. Article VIII status	●	●	●	—	—	●	●	●	●	—	●	●	●	—	—	●	●	●	●	●	●	—	●	●	●
2. Article XIV status	—	—	—	●	●	—	—	—	—	●	—	—	—	●	●	—	—	—	—	—	—	●	—	—	—
B. Exchange Arrangement[3]																									
1. Exchange rate determined on the basis of:																									
(a) A peg to:																									
(i) the U.S. dollar	—	●	—	—	—	—	—	—	—	—	—	—	—	—	●	—	—	—	—	—	—	—	—	—	—
(ii) the pound sterling	—	—	—	—	—	—	—	—	—	—	—	—	—	—	—	—	—	—	—	—	—	—	—	—	—
(iii) the French franc	—	—	—	—	—	—	—	—	—	—	—	—	—	—	—	—	—	—	—	—	—	—	—	—	—
(iv) other currencies[4]	—	—	—	—	—	—	—	—	—	—	—	—	—	—	—	—	—	—	—	—	—	—	—	●	—
(v) a composite of currencies	—	—	—	—	—	—	—	—	—	●	●	—	—	—	—	—	—	—	—	—	●	—	—	—	—
(b) Limited flexibility with respect to:																									
(i) single currency	—	—	—	—	—	—	—	—	—	—	—	—	—	—	—	—	—	—	—	—	—	—	—	—	—
(ii) cooperative arrangement	—	—	—	—	—	—	—	—	—	—	—	—	—	—	—	●	—	—	—	—	—	—	—	—	—
(c) More flexible arrangements:																									
(i) adjusted according to a set of indicators	—	—	—	—	—	—	—	—	—	—	—	—	—	—	—	—	—	—	—	—	—	—	—	—	—
(ii) other managed floating	●	—	—	—	—	—	●	●	●	—	—	●	—	●	—	—	●	—	—	—	—	—	—	—	●
(iii) independently floating	—	—	●	●	●	●	—	—	—	—	—	—	●	—	—	—	—	●	●	●	—	●	●	—	—
2. Separate exchange rate(s) for some or all capital transactions and/or some or all invisibles	—	—	—	●	●	—	—	—	—	—	—	—	—	●	—	—	—	—	—	—	—	●	●	—	—
3. More than one rate for imports	—	—	—	—	●	●	—	—	—	—	—	—	—	●	—	—	—	—	—	—	—	●	●	—	—
4. More than one rate for exports	—	—	—	—	●	●	—	—	—	—	—	—	—	●	—	—	—	—	—	—	—	●	●	—	—
5. Import rate(s) different from export rate(s)	—	—	—	—	●	●	—	—	—	—	—	—	—	●	—	—	—	—	—	—	—	●	●	—	—
C. Payments Arrears	—	—	●	●	●	—	●	●	—	—	—	—	—	—	—	—	—	—	●	—	●	—	●	—	—
D. Bilateral Payments Arrangements																									
1. With members	—	—	—	●	—	—	—	—	—	●	—	●	—	●	—	—	—	—	—	—	●	●	—	—	—
2. With nonmembers	—	—	—	●	—	—	—	—	—	—	—	—	—	●	—	—	—	—	—	—	—	●	—	—	—
E. Payments Restrictions																									
1. Restrictions on payments for current transactions[5]	—	—	—	●	●	—	—	—	—	●	—	●	—	●	●	—	—	—	●	—	●	●	●	—	—
2. Restrictions on payments for capital transactions[5,6]	●	●	—	●	●	●	●	●	—	—	●	●	●	●	●	●	—	●	—	●	●	●	●	—	●
F. Cost-Related Import Restrictions																									
1. Import surcharges	●	●	—	●	—	—	—	—	—	●	●	●	—	—	—	—	—	●	—	●	—	—	—	—	—
2. Advance import deposits	—	—	—	—	—	—	—	—	—	—	—	—	●	—	—	—	—	—	—	—	—	—	—	—	—
G. Surrender or Repatriation Requirement for Export Proceeds	●	●	●	●	●	●	●	●	—	●	—	●	●	●	●	—	●	—	●	—	●	●	●	—	●

For key and footnotes, see page 568.

Trade Systems in Member Countries[1] *(continued)*
country page)[2]

Kuwait	Kyrgyz Republic	Lao People's Dem. Rep.	Latvia	Lebanon	Lesotho	Liberia	Libyan Arab Jamahiriya	Lithuania	Macedonia, former Yugoslav Republic of	Madagascar	Malawi	Malaysia	Maldives	Mali	Malta	Marshall Islands	Mauritania	Mauritius	Mexico	Micronesia, Fed. States of	Moldova	Mongolia	Morocco	Mozambique	Myanmar	Namibia	Nepal	Netherlands	Netherlands Antilles	New Zealand	Nicaragua	Niger	Nigeria
●	●	—	●	●	—	—	—	●		—	—	●	—	—	●	●	—	●	●	●	●	—	●	—	—	—	●	●	●	●	●	—	—
—	—	●	—	—	●	●	●	—	●	●	●	—	●	●	—	—	●	—	—	—	—	●	—	●	●	●	—	—	—	—	—	●	●
—	—	—	—	—	—	●	—	●	—	—	—	—	—	—	—	●	—	—	—	●	—	—	—	—	—	—	●	—	—	—	—	—	●
—	—	—	—	—	—	—	—	—	—	—	—	—	—	—	—	—	—	—	—	—	—	—	—	—	—	—	—	—	—	—	—	—	—
—	—	—	—	—	—	—	—	—	—	—	—	—	—	●	—	—	—	—	—	—	—	—	—	—	—	—	—	—	—	—	—	●	—
—	—	—	—	—	●	—	—	—	—	—	—	—	—	—	—	—	—	—	—	—	—	—	—	—	—	●	—	—	—	—	—	—	—
●	—	—	—	—	—	—	●	—	—	—	—	—	—	—	—	●	—	●	—	—	—	—	●	—	●	—	●	—	—	—	—	—	—
—	—	—	—	—	—	—	—	—	—	—	—	—	—	—	—	—	—	—	—	—	—	—	—	—	—	—	—	—	—	—	—	—	—
—	—	—	—	—	—	—	—	—	—	—	—	—	—	—	—	—	—	—	—	—	—	—	—	—	—	—	—	—	●	—	—	—	—
—	—	—	—	—	—	—	—	—	—	—	—	—	—	—	—	—	—	—	—	—	—	—	—	—	—	—	—	—	—	—	●	—	—
—	—	●	—	—	—	—	—	—	●	—	—	●	●	—	—	—	—	●	—	—	—	—	—	—	—	—	—	—	—	—	—	—	—
—	●	—	●	●	—	—	—	—	—	●	●	—	—	—	—	—	—	—	●	—	●	—	●	●	—	—	—	—	—	●	—	—	—
—	—	●	—	●	—	—	—	—	—	—	—	—	—	—	—	—	—	—	—	—	—	—	—	●	—	—	—	—	—	—	—	—	●
—	—	●	—	—	—	—	—	—	—	—	—	—	—	—	—	—	—	—	—	—	—	—	—	—	—	—	—	—	—	—	—	—	●
—	—	●	—	—	—	—	—	—	—	—	—	—	—	—	—	—	—	—	—	—	—	—	—	—	—	—	—	—	—	—	—	—	—
—	—	●	—	—	—	—	—	—	—	—	—	—	—	—	—	—	—	—	—	—	—	—	—	—	—	—	—	—	—	—	—	—	—
—	—	—	—	—	—	●	—	—	—	—	—	—	—	●	—	—	●	—	—	—	—	—	—	—	●	—	—	—	—	—	●	●	—
—	●	●	●	●	—	—	●	●	—	●	—	●	—	●	●	—	—	●	●	—	●	●	●	●	—	—	—	—	—	—	—	—	—
—	—	—	—	—	—	—	—	●	—	—	—	—	—	—	—	—	—	—	—	—	—	●	—	—	—	—	—	—	—	—	—	—	—
—	—	●	—	—	—	—	●	—	●	●	●	—	—	—	—	—	—	●	—	—	●	—	●	●	—	●	●	—	—	—	—	—	●
—	●	●	—	—	●	●	●	—	—	●	●	●	●	●	—	—	●	●	●	—	●	—	●	●	●	●	—	●	—	—	●	●	●
—	—	●	—	—	●	●	●	—	—	—	—	—	—	—	—	—	—	●	●	—	—	—	—	—	—	●	—	—	—	—	●	—	—
—	—	●	—	—	—	●	—	—	—	—	—	—	—	—	—	—	—	—	—	—	—	—	—	—	—	—	—	—	—	—	—	—	—
—	—	●	—	—	●	●	●	—	●	●	●	●	●	●	●	—	●	●	—	—	●	●	●	●	●	●	●	—	●	—	●	●	●

	Norway	Oman	Pakistan	Panama	Papua New Guinea	Paraguay	Peru	Philippines	Poland	Portugal	Qatar	Romania	Russian Federation	Rwanda	St. Kitts and Nevis	St. Lucia	St. Vincent and Grenadines	San Marino	São Tomé and Príncipe	Saudi Arabia	Senegal	Seychelles	Sierra Leone	Singapore	Slovak Republic
A. Acceptance of Article Status																									
1. Article VIII status	●	●	●	●	●	●	●	—	●	●	●	—	—	—	●	●	●	●	—	●	—	●	—	●	—
2. Article XIV status	—	—	—	—	—	—	—	●	—	—	—	●	●	●	—	—	—	—	●	—	●	—	●	—	●
B. Exchange Arrangement[3]																									
1. Exchange rate determined on the basis of:																									
(a) A peg to:																									
(i) the U.S. dollar	—	●	—	●	—	—	—	—	—	—	—	—	—	—	●	●	●	—	—	—	—	—	—	—	—
(ii) the pound sterling	—	—	—	—	—	—	—	—	—	—	—	—	—	—	—	—	—	—	—	—	—	—	—	—	—
(iii) the French franc	—	—	—	—	—	—	—	—	—	—	—	—	—	—	—	—	—	—	—	—	●	—	—	—	—
(iv) other currencies[4]	—	—	—	—	—	—	—	—	—	—	—	—	—	—	—	—	—	●	—	—	—	—	—	—	—
(v) a composite of currencies	—	—	—	—	—	—	—	—	—	—	—	—	—	—	—	—	—	—	—	—	—	●	—	—	●
(b) Limited flexibility with respect to:																									
(i) single currency	—	—	—	—	—	—	—	—	—	—	●	—	—	—	—	—	—	—	—	●	—	—	—	—	—
(ii) cooperative arrangement	—	—	—	—	—	—	—	—	—	●	—	—	—	—	—	—	—	—	—	—	—	—	—	—	—
(c) More flexible arrangements:																									
(i) adjusted according to a set of indicators	—	—	—	—	—	—	—	—	—	—	—	—	—	—	—	—	—	—	—	—	—	—	—	—	—
(ii) other managed floating	—	—	●	—	—	—	—	—	●	—	—	—	—	—	—	—	—	—	—	—	—	—	—	●	—
(iii) independently floating	●	—	—	—	●	●	●	●	—	—	—	●	●	—	—	—	—	—	●	—	—	—	●	—	—
2. Separate exchange rate(s) for some or all capital transactions and/or some or all invisibles	—	—	—	—	—	—	—	—	●	—	—	●	—	—	—	—	—	—	—	—	—	—	—	—	—
3. More than one rate for imports	—	—	—	—	—	—	—	—	●	—	—	●	—	—	—	—	—	—	—	—	—	—	—	—	—
4. More than one rate for exports	—	—	—	—	—	—	—	—	●	—	—	●	—	—	—	—	—	—	—	—	—	—	—	—	—
5. Import rate(s) different from export rate(s)	—	—	—	—	—	—	—	—	●	—	—	●	—	—	—	—	—	—	—	—	—	—	—	—	—
C. Payments Arrears	—	—	—	●	—	●	●	—	—	—	—	—	—	●	—	—	—	—	●	—	—	●	●	●	—
D. Bilateral Payments Arrangements																									
1. With members	—	—	—	—	—	—	—	—	●	—	—	●	●	●	—	—	—	—	●	—	—	—	—	●	●
2. With nonmembers	—	—	—	—	—	—	—	—	—	—	—	●	●	—	—	—	—	—	—	—	—	—	—	—	●
E. Payments Restrictions																									
1. Restrictions on payments for current transactions[5]	—	—	●	—	—	—	—	●	—	—	—	●	—	—	—	—	—	—	●	—	—	—	●	●	—
2. Restrictions on payments for capital transactions[5,6]	●	—	●	—	●	●	—	●	—	—	—	●	●	—	●	●	●	—	●	●	—	●	●	●	●
F. Cost-Related Import Restrictions																									
1. Import surcharges	—	—	●	●	—	●	—	●	—	—	—	●	—	—	—	—	—	—	●	—	—	—	—	—	—
2. Advance import deposits	—	—	—	—	—	—	—	—	—	—	—	—	—	—	—	—	—	—	●	—	—	—	—	—	—
G. Surrender or Repatriation Requirement for Export Proceeds	—	—	●	—	●	●	—	—	●	—	—	●	—	●	●	●	●	—	●	—	●	●	●	—	●

For key and footnotes, see page 568.

Trade Systems in Member Countries[1] *(concluded)*
country page)[2]

Slovenia	Solomon Islands	Somalia	South Africa	Spain	Sri Lanka	Sudan	Suriname	Swaziland	Sweden	Switzerland	Syrian Arab Republic	Tajikistan	Tanzania	Thailand	Togo	Tonga	Trinidad and Tobago	Tunisia	Turkey	Turkmenistan	Uganda	Ukraine	United Arab Emirates	United Kingdom	United States	Uruguay	Uzbekistan	Vanuatu	Venezuela	Viet Nam	Western Samoa	Yemen, Republic of	Zaïre	Zambia	Zimbabwe
—	●	—	●	●	●	—	●	●	●	●	—	—	—	●	—	●	●	●	●	—	●	—	●	●	●	●	—	●	●	—	●	—	—	—	●
●	—	●	—	—	—	●	—	—	—	—	●	●	●	—	●	—	—	—	—	●	—	●	—	—	—	—	●	—	—	●	—	●	●	●	—
—	—	—	—	—	—	—	—	—	—	—	●	—	—	—	—	—	—	—	—	●	—	—	—	—	—	—	—	—	●	—	—	●	—	—	—
—	—	—	—	—	—	—	—	—	—	—	—	—	—	—	—	—	—	—	—	—	—	—	—	—	—	—	—	—	—	—	—	—	—	—	—
—	—	—	—	—	—	—	—	—	—	—	—	—	—	—	●	—	—	—	—	—	—	—	—	—	—	—	—	—	—	—	—	—	—	—	—
—	—	—	—	—	—	—	—	●	—	—	—	●	—	—	—	—	—	—	—	—	—	—	—	—	—	—	—	—	—	—	—	—	—	—	—
—	●	—	—	—	—	—	—	—	—	—	—	—	—	●	—	●	—	—	—	—	—	—	—	—	—	—	—	●	—	—	●	—	—	—	—
—	—	—	—	—	—	—	—	—	—	—	—	—	—	—	—	—	—	—	—	—	—	—	●	—	—	—	—	—	—	—	—	—	—	—	—
—	—	—	—	●	—	—	—	—	—	—	—	—	—	—	—	—	—	—	—	—	—	—	—	—	—	—	—	—	—	—	—	—	—	—	—
—	—	—	—	—	—	—	—	—	—	—	—	—	—	—	—	—	—	—	—	—	—	—	—	—	—	—	—	—	—	—	—	—	—	—	—
●	—	—	—	●	●	—	—	—	—	—	—	—	—	—	●	●	—	—	—	—	—	—	—	—	—	—	●	—	—	●	—	—	—	—	—
—	—	●	●	—	—	—	—	●	●	●	—	—	—	●	—	—	—	●	—	—	●	●	—	—	—	—	●	—	—	—	—	●	●	●	●
—	—	●	—	—	●	●	—	—	—	—	●	●	—	—	—	—	—	—	—	—	●	—	●	—	—	—	—	—	—	—	—	●	—	●	—
—	—	●	—	—	—	●	—	—	—	—	●	—	—	—	—	—	—	—	—	—	●	—	●	—	—	—	—	—	—	—	—	●	—	●	—
—	—	●	—	—	—	●	—	—	—	—	●	—	—	—	—	—	—	—	—	—	●	—	●	—	—	—	—	—	—	—	—	●	—	●	—
—	—	●	—	—	—	●	—	—	—	—	●	—	—	—	—	—	—	—	—	—	●	—	●	—	—	—	—	—	—	—	—	●	—	●	—
—	—	●	—	—	—	●	●	—	—	—	●	●	●	—	—	—	—	—	—	—	●	—	●	—	—	—	—	●	●	—	—	—	●	●	—
●	—	—	—	—	●	●	—	—	—	—	●	●	—	—	—	—	—	—	—	●	●	—	—	—	—	—	●	●	—	●	—	—	●	—	—
—	—	—	—	—	—	—	—	—	—	—	—	—	—	—	—	—	—	—	—	—	●	—	—	—	—	—	—	—	●	—	—	—	—	—	—
●	—	●	—	—	●	●	—	●	—	—	●	●	—	—	—	—	—	—	—	●	●	●	—	—	—	●	●	—	●	●	—	●	●	—	—
●	●	●	●	—	●	●	●	●	—	—	●	●	—	●	●	●	●	●	—	—	●	●	—	—	—	●	●	—	●	●	●	●	●	●	●
—	—	●	—	—	—	●	—	—	—	—	●	—	—	●	—	—	—	—	—	—	—	—	—	—	—	●	—	●	●	—	—	●	—	—	●
—	—	●	—	—	—	●	—	—	—	—	—	—	—	—	—	—	—	—	—	●	●	—	—	—	—	—	—	—	—	—	—	●	—	—	—
●	●	●	●	—	—	●	●	●	—	—	●	●	—	●	●	●	—	●	●	●	—	—	—	●	●	—	●	●	—	●	●	●	●	●	●

567

Summary Features
of Exchange and Trade Systems
in Member Countries

Key and Footnotes

• indicates that the specified practice is a feature of the exchange and trade system.

– indicates that the specified practice is not a feature of the system.

▫ indicates that the composite is the SDR.

[1] The listing includes the nonmetropolitan territory of Hong Kong, for which the United Kingdom has accepted the Fund's Articles of Agreement, and Aruba and the Netherlands Antilles, for which the Kingdom of the Netherlands has accepted the Fund's Articles of Agreement. Exchange practices indicated in individual countries do not necessarily apply to all external transactions.

[2] Usually December 31, 1994.

[3] It should be noted that existence of a separate rate does not necessarily imply a multiple currency practice under Fund jurisdiction. Exchange arrangements involving transactions at a unitary rate with one group of countries and at another unitary rate with a second group of countries are considered, from the viewpoint of the overall economy, to involve two separate rates for similar transactions.

[4] Australian dollar, deutsche mark, Indian rupee, Italian lira, South African rand, or Russian ruble.

[5] Restrictions (i.e., official actions directly affecting the availability or cost of exchange, or involving undue delay) on payments to member countries, other than restrictions evidenced by external payments arrears and restrictions imposed for security reasons under Executive Board Decision No. 144-(52/51) adopted August 14, 1952.

[6] Resident-owned funds.

Definitions of Acronyms

Note: This list does not include acronyms of purely national institutions mentioned in the country chapters

ACU	Asian Clearing Union
AFTA	ASEAN free trade area (see ASEAN, below)
AMU	Asian monetary unit
ANZCERTA	Australia-New Zealand Closer Economic Relations and Trade Agreement
ASEAN	Association of South East Asian Nations
BCEAO	Central Bank of West African States (Banque centrale des Etats de l'Afrique de l'Ouest)
BEAC	Bank of Central African States (Banque des Etats de l'Afrique Centrale)
BLEU	Belgian-Luxembourg Economic Union
CACM	Central American Common Market
CAP	Common agricultural policy (of the EU)
CARICOM	Caribbean Common Market
CEEAC	Economic Community of Central African States
CEFTA	Central European free trade area
CEPGL	Economic Community of the Great Lakes Countries
CEPT	Common effective preferential tariff of the ASEAN free trade area
CET	Common external tariff (of CARICOM)
CFA	Communauté financière africaine
CIS	Commonwealth of Independent States
CMA	Common monetary area
CMEA	Council for Mutual Economic Assistance (dissolved)
COCOM	Coordinating Committee for Multilateral Export Controls
ECCB	Eastern Caribbean Central Bank
ECLAC	Economic Commission for Latin America and the Caribbean
ECOWAS	Economic Community of West African States (Cedeao)
ECSC	European Coal and Steel Community
ECU	European currency unit
EEA	European economic area
EFTA	European Free Trade Association
EMS	European monetary system
ERM	Exchange rate mechanism (of the EMS)
EU	European Union (formerly European Community)
GATT	General Agreement on Tariffs and Trade
GCC	Gulf Cooperation Council (Cooperation Council for the Arab States of the Gulf)
GSP	Generalized system of preferences
HCDCS	Harmonized commodity description and coding system
LAIA	Latin American Integration Association
LIBOR	London interbank offered rate
MERCOSUR	Southern Cone Common Market
MFA	Multifiber Arrangement
MFN	Most favored nation
MTN	Multilateral trade negotiations (the Uruguay Round)
NAFTA	North American Free Trade Agreement
NATO	North Atlantic Treaty Organization
OECD	Organization for Economic Cooperation and Development
OECS	Organization of Eastern Caribbean States
OGL	Open general license
PTA	Preferential trade area for Eastern and Southern African states
SACU	Southern African Customs Union
SPARTECA	South Pacific Regional Trade and Economic Cooperation Agreement
UAPTA	Unit of account of the PTA

Definitions of Acronyms

UDEAC	Central African Customs and Economic Union
WAEC	West African Economic Community (CEAO) (dissolved)
WAEMU	West African Economic and Monetary Union
WAMU	West African Monetary Union
WTO	World Trade Organization (supercedes GATT)

EXCHANGE ARRANGEMENTS
AND
EXCHANGE RESTRICTIONS

ANNUAL REPORT 1996

© 1996 International Monetary Fund

Editors: Gail Berre
         Martha Bonilla

Design and composition: IMF Graphics Section

Library of Congress Cataloging-in-Publication Data

International Monetary Fund.
   Annual report on exchange arrangements and exchange restrictions.
1979—

Continues: International Monetary Fund. Annual report on exchange
restrictions, 1950–1978
   1. Foreign exchange — Law and legislation — Periodicals. 2. Foreign
exchange — Control — Periodicals. I. Title.
K4440.A13 I57 [date] 341.7'51 79-644506
ISSN 0250-7366
ISBN 1-55775-588-4

Price: US$76.00
(US$38.00 to full-time university faculty members and students)

Please send orders to:
International Monetary Fund, Publication Services
700 19th Street, N.W., Washington, D.C. 20431, U.S.A.
Tel.: (202) 623-7430   Telefax: (202) 623-7201
Internet: publications@imf.org

recycled paper

Letter of Transmittal to Members
and Governors of the Fund

August 9, 1996

Dear Sir:

I have the honor to transmit to you a copy of the International Monetary Fund's *Annual Report on Exchange Arrangements and Exchange Restrictions, 1996*, which has been prepared in accordance with the provisions of Article XIV, Section 3 of the Articles of Agreement.

On behalf of the Executive Board, I should like to express our appreciation of the cooperation of the countries in the preparation of the Report.

Sincerely yours,

Michel Camdessus
*Chairman of the Executive Board
and Managing Director*

CONTENTS

	Page
Preface	ix
Introduction	1

	Page			Page
Afghanistan, Islamic State of*		Côte d'Ivoire	130
Albania	3	Croatia	134
Algeria	5	Cyprus	137
Angola	9	Czech Republic	142
Antigua and Barbuda	12	Denmark	144
Argentina	14	Djibouti	146
Armenia	17	Dominica	147
Aruba	20	Dominican Republic	149
Australia	22	Ecuador	151
Austria	26	Egypt	154
Azerbaijan	28	El Salvador	157
Bahamas, The	31	Equatorial Guinea	159
Bahrain	35	Eritrea	162
Bangladesh	37	Estonia	165
Barbados	43	Ethiopia	167
Belarus	47	Fiji	171
Belgium and Luxembourg	52	Finland	174
Belize	54	France	176
Benin	56	Gabon	181
Bhutan	60	Gambia, The	185
Bolivia	61	Georgia	187
Bosnia and Herzegovina	63	Germany	189
Botswana	66	Ghana	192
Brazil	69	Greece	196
Brunei Darussalam	76	Grenada	199
Bulgaria	78	Guatemala	201
Burkina Faso	81	Guinea	203
Burundi	85	Guinea-Bissau	206
Cambodia	88	Guyana	208
Cameroon	90	Haiti	211
Canada	94	Honduras	213
Cape Verde	97	Hong Kong	215
Central African Republic	99	Hungary	217
Chad	103	Iceland	221
Chile	107	India	224
China	112	Indonesia	234
Colombia	117	Iran, Islamic Republic of	238
Comoros	122	Iraq*	
Congo, Republic of	124	Ireland	241
Costa Rica	128	Israel	243

*The IMF has not received from the authorities of Afghanistan, Iraq, and Somalia the information required for a description of the exchange and trade system as of December 31, 1995.

	Page		Page
Italy	247	Paraguay	377
Jamaica	249	Peru	380
Japan	251	Philippines	382
Jordan	255	Poland	388
Kazakstan	258	Portugal	393
Kenya	261	Qatar	395
Kiribati	264	Romania	397
Korea	265	Russian Federation	400
Kuwait	270	Rwanda	404
Kyrgyz Republic	272	St. Kitts and Nevis	406
Lao People's Democratic Republic	274	St. Lucia	408
Latvia	276	St. Vincent and the Grenadines	410
Lebanon	278	San Marino	412
Lesotho	280	São Tomé and Príncipe	414
Liberia	282	Saudi Arabia	416
Libyan Arab Jamahiriya	284	Senegal	418
Lithuania	287	Seychelles	422
Macedonia, former Yugoslav Republic of	290	Sierra Leone	424
Madagascar	292	Singapore	427
Malawi	296	Slovak Republic	429
Malaysia	299	Slovenia	432
Maldives	303	Solomon Islands	434
Mali	305	Somalia*	
Malta	308	South Africa	436
Marshall Islands	312	Spain	440
Mauritania	313	Sri Lanka	443
Mauritius	316	Sudan	448
Mexico	318	Suriname	452
Micronesia, Federated States of	321	Swaziland	456
Moldova	323	Sweden	458
Mongolia	325	Switzerland	460
Morocco	327	Syrian Arab Republic	462
Mozambique	333	Tajikistan	467
Myanmar	335	Tanzania	470
Namibia	339	Thailand	473
Nepal	342	Togo	476
Netherlands	345	Tonga	480
Netherlands Antilles	348	Trinidad and Tobago	482
New Zealand	350	Tunisia	484
Nicaragua	353	Turkey	490
Niger	355	Turkmenistan	495
Nigeria	358	Uganda	497
Norway	362	Ukraine	499
Oman	364	United Arab Emirates	502
Pakistan	366	United Kingdom	504
Panama	372	United States	506
Papua New Guinea	374	Uruguay	511

*The IMF has not received from the authorities of Afghanistan, Iraq, and Somalia the information required for a description of the exchange and trade system as of December 31, 1995.

CONTENTS

Uzbekistan 513
Vanuatu. 516
Venezuela 518
Vietnam. 522
Western Samoa. 525
Yemen, Republic of 527
Zaïre. 530
Zambia. 535

Zimbabwe 537
Appendix. EU: Selected Trade Measures
   Introduced and Eliminated on an EU-Wide
   Basis During 1995. 542
Summary Features of Exchange and
   Trade Systems in Member Countries. 546
Definition of Acronyms 553

Note: The term "country," as used in this publication, does not in all cases refer to a territorial entity that is a state as understood by international law and practice; the term also covers some territorial entities that are not states but for which statistical data are maintained and provided internationally on a separate and independent basis..

PREFACE

The *Annual Report on Exchange Arrangements and Exchange Restrictions* has been published annually by the IMF since 1950. It draws on information available to the IMF from a number of sources, including that provided in the course of official visits to member countries, and it has been prepared in close consultation with national authorities.

The project is coordinated in the Exchange Regime and Market Operations Division of the Monetary and Exchange Affairs Department. It draws on the specialized contributions of staff of that Department (for specific countries), with assistance from staff members of the IMF's seven Area Departments, together with staff of other Departments.

INTRODUCTION

The Report provides a detailed description of the exchange and trade systems of individual member countries, including the nonmetropolitan territory of Hong Kong, for which the United Kingdom has accepted the IMF's Articles of Agreement, and Aruba and the Netherlands Antilles, for which the Kingdom of the Netherlands has accepted the IMF's Articles of Agreement.

In general, the description relates to the exchange and trade systems as of the end of 1995, but in appropriate cases reference is made to significant developments that took place in early 1996.

A standardized approach has been followed, under which the description of each system is broken down into similar headings, and the coverage for each country includes a final section that lists chronologically the more significant changes during 1995 and in early 1996.

The description of the exchange and trade system is not necessarily confined to those aspects involving exchange restrictions or exchange controls. As in previous Reports, questions of definition and jurisdiction have not been raised, and an attempt has been made to describe exchange and trade systems in their entirety, except for the tariff structure and, in most cases, direct taxes on imports and exports. Thus, the coverage extends to such features as import licensing, advance import deposit requirements, import surcharges, travel taxes, export licensing, and export incentive schemes. Similarly, the section *Changes During 1995* (and 1996) includes references to certain developments that may have a direct impact on international transactions, such as major revisions of import tariffs or developments in regional cooperation, but are not necessarily reflected in the body of the country descriptions.

The description given in the section *Exchange Arrangement* is in line with the notification of exchange arrangements that member countries have furnished to the IMF under Article IV, Section 2(*a*). The structure of exchange markets is described, and the official exchange rate is given. The rates quoted are those effective on December 31, 1995, unless stated otherwise.

Under *Administration of Control*, some indication is given of the authorities responsible for policy and administration of the controls and of the extent to which their powers are delegated for working purposes.

The section on *Prescription of Currency* describes the requirements affecting the selection of the currency and method of settlement for transactions with other countries. When a country has concluded payments agreements with other countries, the terms of these agreements often lead to prescription of the currency for specified categories of payments to and from the countries concerned. The countries with which bilateral payments agreements are in force are listed either in the text or in a footnote.

Under *Resident/Nonresident Accounts*, and, in some instances, *External Accounts* or *Foreign Currency Accounts*, a description is given of the manner in which the country treats accounts, if any, maintained in its currency by account holders who are residents or not regarded as residents of that country, and the facilities and limitations attached to such accounts. When there is more than one type of resident/nonresident account, the nature and operation of the various types are also described.

In the section on *Imports and Import Payments*, import-licensing requirements are described briefly, and details are given of other requirements imposed on payments for imports and of any advance deposit requirements. The term "open general license" indicates arrangements whereby certain imports or other international transactions are exempt from the restrictive application of licensing requirements, in contrast to an "individual license," which may be given either freely or restrictively according to administrative decisions.

Under *Payments for Invisibles*, the procedures for permitting payments abroad for current transactions in invisibles are described briefly, together with any limitations on the exportation of foreign and domestic banknotes. For some countries that do not impose limitations on payments for invisibles, this section is combined with the section on *Proceeds from Invisibles* (see below).

Export-licensing requirements and procedures are described under *Exports and Export Proceeds*, with an outline of the requirements that may be imposed on the handling of proceeds from exports. The expression "exchange receipts must be surrendered" indicates that the recipient is required by the regulations to sell any foreign exchange proceeds in return for local currency, sometimes at a specified exchange rate, to the central bank, commercial banks, or exchange dealers authorized for this purpose. In some countries, there is a requirement

1

that such exchange or part thereof be sold in a free market.

Under *Proceeds from Invisibles*, any regulations governing exchange derived from transactions in invisibles are given, and any limitations on the importation of foreign and domestic banknotes are described.

In the section on *Capital*, the special arrangements or limitations attached to international capital movements are described. When regulations on foreign capital also cover the income thereon, they are usually dealt with in this section rather than in the sections on *Payments for Invisibles* and *Proceeds from Invisibles*.

The section on *Gold* gives a summary of the principal regulations that govern the holding, negotiation, importation, and exportation of gold coins and gold in other forms.

ALBANIA

(Position as of December 31, 1995)

Exchange Arrangement

The currency of Albania is the Lek. The exchange rate of the lek is determined on the basis of demand and supply conditions in the domestic market. Exchange rates for other currencies are determined on the basis of the cross rate relationship between the U.S. dollar and the currencies concerned in the international market. The Bank of Albania calculates and announces the daily average exchange rates for the U.S. dollar and other major currencies. No margins are set between buying and selling rates for the official exchange rate. Government transactions are conducted at market rates. However, the commercial banks charge commissions ranging from 0.5 percent to 1.5 percent, depending on the amount, for cashing traveler's checks. The commercial banks are free to determine the margins on purchases and sales of foreign banknotes, but they do not charge commissions. On December 31, 1995, the official (middle) rate for the U.S. dollar was lek 94.24 per $1. There are no taxes or subsidies on purchases or sales of foreign exchange. There are no arrangements for forward exchange cover against exchange rate risk operating in the official or the commercial banking sector.

Administration of Control

The foreign exchange market is governed by regulations issued on May 1, 1994 by the Bank of Albania, under the authority of Decree No. 127 of March 25, 1994 of the Council of Ministers. The Bank of Albania is vested with the powers to administer exchange controls.

All commercial banks are authorized to conduct foreign exchange transactions and hold accounts abroad. The Bank of Albania may (1) authorize banks and other dealers to conduct foreign exchange operations; (2) define the limits of their activities; and (3) supervise foreign exchange operations to prevent any participant from dominating the market. It charges licensed banks and foreign exchange bureaus and dealers with ensuring that their operations comply with foreign exchange regulations. There is a reporting requirement by banks and exchange bureaus for transactions above $15,000, or its equivalent.

Arrears are maintained with respect to external payments.

Prescription of Currency

All merchandise trade is conducted in convertible currencies. All transactions under bilateral payments agreements were suspended in 1992, and the settlement of clearing accounts is pending the outcome of negotiations.[1] Resident individuals are not permitted to open accounts with banks and financial institutions abroad without the prior written approval of the Bank of Albania.

Resident and Nonresident Accounts

Resident and nonresident natural and juridical persons are permitted to hold accounts in domestic and foreign currencies with commercial banks. Residents and nonresidents may freely receive payments and make payments abroad for current transactions. Authorized banks must maintain 90 percent cover on the foreign deposits placed with them, of which 10 percent represents the reserve requirement. Commercial banks may conduct foreign exchange transactions and hold accounts abroad. There are no restrictions on withdrawals of foreign exchange from foreign exchange accounts by residents or nonresidents. Interest rates paid on foreign currency accounts are determined by banks.

Imports and Exports

All state and private enterprises, individuals, and juridical persons are free to engage in foreign trade activities. The lists of products subject to import licenses are issued by the Ministry of Industry and Trade. Licenses are required to import hazardous materials and arms.

Exports of unprocessed wood, metal scrap, and copper are prohibited. There are no export licensing requirements. There are no surrender requirements, but all private and public companies or individuals operating in the export sector are required to repatriate their foreign exchange receipts to Albania. They

---

[1]At the end of 1995, Albania maintained bilateral payments agreements in nonconvertible currencies with Bulgaria, Cuba, the Czech Republic, Hungary, the Democratic People's Republic of Korea, Poland, Romania, the Slovak Republic, and Vietnam. Albania also maintained bilateral payments agreements in convertible currencies with Algeria, Bulgaria, China, Cuba, the Czech Republic, Egypt, Greece, the Democratic People's Republic of Korea, Romania, the Slovak Republic, Turkey, Vietnam, and Federal Republic of Yugoslavia (Serbia/Montenegro).

are free to retain these proceeds in or outside the banking system or to convert them into leks.

There are three customs duty rates ranging from 7 percent to 40 percent that are applied to both private and public sector imports. In addition, a surcharge of 5 percent, based on the c.i.f. value, is levied on all imports except wheat, flour, and investment goods.

Payments for and Proceeds from Invisibles

Payments for current invisible transactions are free of restrictions. There is no restriction on transfers of dividends and profits. Proceeds from invisibles are subject to the same repatriation requirements as those from merchandise exports.

Capital

With certain exceptions, capital transfers are subject to the prior written approval of the Bank of Albania. The following capital transfers may be made freely: (1) inward capital transfers by residents or nonresidents; (2) outward transfers representing recorded capital inflows; (3) transfers of proceeds or withdrawal of nonresident deposits; (4) transfers undertaken in accordance with the Law No. 7764 on foreign investment of November 1993, providing for the free repatriation of capital liquidation proceeds; and (5) transfers of the proceeds of the liquidation of Albanian assets by emigrants on departure from Albania. Foreign direct investment into Albania is free of registration or preapproval requirements for most sectors. All requests for establishing joint ventures with government entities involving over $50,000 in foreign capital must be approved by the Council of Ministers. Similar requests from financial institutions are approved by the Bank of Albania. Profits of joint ventures may be subject to tax rates of up to 50 percent, depending on the activity of the enterprise; profits are not subject to any tax during the first two years of operation for long-term (at least ten-year) investment projects. Enterprises are eligible for reduced tax rates when they reinvest profits in Albania.

Gold

There are no restrictions on gold holdings. Precious metal exports are prohibited by the Council of Ministers Decree No. 135 of March 29, 1994.

Changes During 1995

Imports and Exports

January 9. The remaining four export licensing requirements were abolished and export bans were introduced on unprocessed wood, metal scrap, and copper.

May 18. Parliament adopted a new customs tariff law, which came into effect on July 1. The law included a simplification of import tariffs from four to three rate categories, 7 percent, 25 percent, and 40 percent, in conjunction with the elimination of major import tariff exemptions (for investment machinery and equipment, medical equipment, and agricultural machinery). A surcharge of 5 percent, based on the c.i.f. value on all imports, except wheat, flour, and investment goods, was abolished.

October 19. Customs tariffs for wheat, maize, and flour were temporarily suspended (until June 16, 1996); the tariff rate for these items was 7 percent.

October 31. The customs tariff rate for electric heaters was raised to 100 percent from 25 percent, and kerosene heaters were zero rated.

November 30. The tariff rate on meat was reduced to 25 percent from 40 percent.

ALGERIA

(Position as of January 31, 1996)

Exchange Arrangement

The currency of Algeria is the Algerian Dinar. During 1995, daily buying and selling rates for the U.S. dollar, the intervention currency, and other specified currencies[1] were established by the Bank of Algeria in fixing sessions with the participation of commercial banks. Effective January 2, 1996, the Bank of Algeria (the central bank) established an interbank foreign exchange market. No margin limits are imposed on buying and selling exchange rates in the interbank foreign exchange market. However, a margin of DA 0.017 has been established between the buying and selling rates of the Bank of Algeria for the dinar against the U.S. dollar. On December 31, 1995, the buying and selling rates for the U.S. dollar by the Bank of Algeria were DA 32.1655 and DA 32.1825, respectively, per $1.

Official exchange reserves are centralized in the Bank of Algeria. With the establishment of an interbank foreign exchange market, the authorized banks were allowed to keep open foreign currency positions.

Residents may obtain from the commercial banks forward cover against exchange rate risk in the form of forward contracts to buy or sell foreign exchange. No forward cover is provided by the Bank of Algeria.

Administration of Control

The Bank of Algeria has general jurisdiction over exchange control. It formulates exchange legislation and regulations and is responsible for their application by the authorized banks. Authority for a number of exchange control procedures has been delegated to five commercial banks and the Postal Administration.

Prescription of Currency

Settlements with countries with which no payment agreements are in force are made in convertible currencies.[2] Payments under foreign supply

---

[1]Austrian schillings, Belgian francs, Canadian dollars, Danish kroner, deutsche mark, Finnish markkaa, French francs, Italian lire, Japanese yen, Netherlands guilders, Norwegian kroner, pounds sterling, Spanish pesetas, Swedish kronor, and Swiss francs.

[2]Specified noncommercial settlements with Morocco and Tunisia are channeled through a dirham account at the Bank of Morocco and an account in Tunisian dinars at the Bank of Tunisia.

contracts (*contrats de fourniture*) can be made in either the currency in use at the headquarters of the supplier or that of the country of origin of the merchandise, except that transactions with Morocco can be effected in U.S. dollars through special clearing accounts maintained at the central banks of the respective countries. Foreign holders of servicing contracts are required to open local nonresident accounts to which payments are made by the Algerian contracting party; such accounts must be closed within six months of the end of the contract; beyond this date, these accounts may not be used for purposes unrelated to the contracts.

Nonresident Accounts

Most nonresident accounts are foreign accounts in convertible dinars or internal nonresident accounts. There are four types of accounts, as follows:

Individual suspense accounts may be opened without authorization and may be credited with payments from any country. Balances in such accounts opened before January 1, 1975, by nonresident natural persons of foreign nationality have been released for transfer abroad.

Foreign accounts in foreign currency may be opened, under Regulation No. 91/02, by juridical and natural persons of foreign nationality. These accounts may be denominated in the convertible currency of the holder's choice. Such accounts may be credited with (1) banknotes and other means of payment denominated in foreign currency, and (2) other dinar-denominated funds that meet all the requirements for transfer abroad. They may be debited without restriction to make transfers abroad, to export foreign banknotes, and to make dinar payments in Algeria. These accounts pay interest and may not show a net debit position.

Final departure accounts may be opened, without prior authorization, in the name of any natural person residing in Algeria, not of Algerian nationality, who intends to leave Algeria to return to his or her country of origin. These accounts may be credited freely with (1) an amount equivalent to the holdings on October 20, 1963, of the person concerned; (2) the proceeds from sales of real estate by the account holder, provided that the funds are paid directly by a ministerial officer; (3) the proceeds of the sale of securities through a bank; and (4) any other payments, up to DA 2,000. These accounts may be debited without prior approval for certain payments in Algeria on behalf of the account holder. Outward transfers require individual approval.

Foreign currency accounts may be opened by natural and juridical Algerian nationals residing in Algeria or by nonresident Algerian nationals who have resided for more than six months in a foreign country. Such accounts may be freely credited with (1) book transfers of convertible currencies from abroad using either postal or banking facilities, (2) imported convertible foreign currencies that were declared at the time of the account holder's entry into the country, and (3) domestic bank-to-bank book transfers between accounts held by individuals. The accounts may be freely debited for book transfers abroad but only through the banking system; they may also be debited for purchases of dinars, for book transfers in dinars, and for purchases of convertible foreign currencies to be physically exported by the account holder. The interest rate payable on deposits in these accounts is fixed quarterly by the Bank of Algeria. Since 1990, economic entities have also been able to open foreign currency accounts for receiving and making foreign currency transfers, including the retained proportion of their export proceeds. They may transfer funds in these accounts to other foreign currency accounts or use them to make payments in Algeria or to make foreign payments for goods and services pertaining to their businesses.

Imports and Import Payments

Imports from Israel are prohibited. A small number of imports are prohibited, regardless of origin, for religious, cultural, or safety reasons.

All import licenses have been abolished. Any juridical or natural person licensed under the Commercial Register (including concessionaires and wholesalers) may import goods without prior authorization. All these imports are subject to obligatory domiciliation at an authorized intermediary bank, which an importer must establish by submitting a commercial contract or pro forma invoice. Import payments may be made freely but only through the domiciled bank, which effects payments in foreign exchange and debits the importer's account with corresponding amounts in dinars valued at the official exchange rate. Before import payments are effected, domiciled banks may require from the importer a deposit in dinars up to the full value of the imports. Importers maintaining foreign currency accounts at authorized intermediary banks may use them to pay for imports. Payments for imports of gold, other precious metals, and precious stones must be made from foreign currency accounts.

External borrowing by importers for import financing purposes must be arranged through the authorized intermediary banks. External borrowing may not exceed the import value. In April 1995, the requirement that commercial credits to finance imports of capital goods valued at more than $500,000 have at least a three-year maturity was eliminated.

Except as otherwise indicated by the Bank of Algeria, down payments for import payments may not exceed 15 percent of the total value of imports. Imports must be insured by Algerian insurers. When a public agency, public enterprise, or ministry is effecting expenditures for imports deemed to be urgent or exceptional, the bank may effect payments before exchange and trade control formalities have been completed.

Payments for Invisibles

The Bank of Algeria must approve all payments for invisibles to all countries. When supporting documents are presented, however, approval may be granted by authorized banks, or sometimes by the Postal Administration, either freely or up to specified limits for certain payments, such as (1) those relating to approved trade transactions and maritime contracts, (2) business or official travel expenses, (3) transfers of salaries and wages, (4) educational expenses, and (5) advertising expenses. For payments for which the approval authority has not been delegated, the central bank or the Ministry of Economy must authorize the granting of exchange.

Residents of other countries working in Algeria under technical cooperation programs for public enterprises and agencies or for certain mixed companies may transfer abroad a percentage of their net salaries.

Foreign exchange allocations for tourism abroad by Algerian residents were suspended in October 1986. Residents requiring medical treatment abroad are entitled to a foreign exchange allowance of up to DA 100,000 a year upon presentation to the Bank of Algeria of documentation verifying the bona fide nature of the transaction. Emigrant Algerian workers who take their vacations in Algeria may, when returning abroad, re-export foreign exchange that was freely imported and duly declared on their arrival in Algeria. In June 1995, the Bank of Algeria delegated to the Postal Administration authority to provide foreign exchange for educational expenses abroad by residents, up to DA 5,000 a month in each school year.

Pilgrims traveling to Saudi Arabia receive an allowance in Saudi Arabian riyals; the amount is fixed for each pilgrimage and may be furnished in the form of checks that may be cashed on arrival for those traveling by air or by sea. Resident travelers may take out Algerian dinar banknotes up to DA 200 a person. Foreign nonresident travelers may also re-export any foreign currency they declared upon entry. Travel tickets that are bought by nonresidents for travel abroad must be paid for with imported foreign exchange.

Exports and Export Proceeds

All exports to Israel are prohibited. Certain exports are prohibited for social or cultural reasons regardless of destination. All proceeds from exports of crude and refined hydrocarbons, by-products from gas, and mineral products must be surrendered. Exporters of other products may retain 50 percent of their export earnings in a foreign currency account. Since December 1995, proceeds from exports of nonhydrocarbons, and nonminerals may be surrendered to commercial banks and other authorized participants in the interbank foreign exchange market. Entities may use these funds for imports or other payments pertaining to their business or they may transfer the funds to another foreign currency account. Exports other than hydrocarbons benefit from certain incentive measures granted by the Government, including exemption from the tax on industrial and commercial profits and the flat rate levy on the wage bill.

Sales on consignment must be authorized by the Ministry of Economy and must always be registered before customs clearance. Export proceeds must be repatriated within 120 days of collection. Those petroleum companies that hold mineral rights must repatriate to Algeria the proceeds from their exports of hydrocarbons, calculated on the basis of a contractual price for each barrel, which is fixed by agreement with the companies concerned. The petroleum company that holds mineral rights, however, has different repatriation requirements.

Proceeds from Invisibles

Proceeds from invisibles must be repatriated, and 50 percent of the proceeds must be surrendered. There are no restrictions on the importation of foreign banknotes, coins (except gold coins), checks, and letters of credit, but nonresidents, including those of Algerian nationality, must declare such holdings when they enter Algeria. Resident travelers may reimport Algerian dinar banknotes up to DA 200 a

person. Nonresident travelers are not permitted to bring in Algerian banknotes.

Capital

Residents are obliged to repatriate and surrender capital assets (or the sales proceeds thereof) held or acquired outside Algeria. Capital transfers to any destination abroad are subject to individual license.

Foreign direct investment is freely permitted, except in certain specified sectors, provided that it conforms to the laws and regulations governing regulated activities and that prior declaration is made to the authorities. The Law of Money and Credit of April 14, 1990, and Legislative Decree No. 93-12 on Investment Promotion provide guarantees on foreign direct investments in accordance with international codes that have been ratified by Algeria. Repatriation in respect of the sale or liquidation proceeds from invested foreign capital is guaranteed. The law also stipulates that profit remittances on such investments will be permitted, provided that documentation requirements on tax payments are met. Tax facilities may be granted, and investments of more than DA 5 million may be given exclusive rights in a specified geographic area and may be accorded tariff protection. Remittances of profits and retransfers of capital are permitted only in respect of investments approved under the code. Legislative Decree No. 93-12 provides for various tax and other incentives for foreign investment for periods of up to five years.

Algerian banks offer three-year interest-free bonds in dinars, which entitle the subscriber to exchange 20 percent of the placement value annually into a convertible currency at the official exchange rate.

Gold

Residents may purchase, hold, and sell gold coins in Algeria for numismatic purposes. Under Ordinance No. 70-6 of January 16, 1970, unworked gold for industrial and professional use is distributed by the Agence nationale pour la distribution et la transformation de l'or et des autres métaux précieux (AGENOR). This agency is also authorized to purchase in Algeria, and to hold, process, and distribute any other precious metal, and, within the exchange control regulations, to import and export any precious metal, including gold. Gold for use by dentists and goldsmiths is imported by AGENOR. Gold and other precious metals are included on the list of items importable by concessionaires.

Changes During 1995

Exchange Arrangement

December 23. The Bank of Algeria established an interbank market and authorized commercial banks to maintain open foreign exchange positions and offer forward cover to residents. In addition, the surrender of nonhydrocarbon and nonmineral export proceeds to commercial banks and other authorized participants in the interbank foreign exchange market was allowed (earlier, foreign exchange surrender was exclusively to the Bank of Algeria).

December 26. Regulations on spot and forward foreign exchange positions of the participants in the interbank foreign exchange market were issued.

Imports and Import Payments

April 22. The minimum requirement of three years for the maturity of commercial credits to finance imports of capital goods was eliminated.

Payments for Invisibles

June 14. The Bank of Algeria delegated to the Postal Administration the authority to provide foreign exchange for educational expenses abroad to Algerian residents up to DA 5,000 a month for each school year. In addition, the Bank of Algeria authorized the provision of foreign exchange for medical expenses overseas by Algerian residents up to DA 100,000 a year upon presentation of documentation to the Bank of Algeria to verify the bona fide nature of the transaction.

Changes During 1996

Exchange Arrangement

January 2. The Bank of Algeria established an interbank foreign exchange market.

ANGOLA

(Position as of December 31, 1995)

Exchange Arrangement

The currency of Angola is the Adjusted Kwanza. The official exchange rate against the U.S. dollar is fixed by the Government, and foreign exchange is sold to commercial banks based on allocations determined by administrative priorities that are set at fixing sessions held from time to time.[1] Exchange rates for 17 other currencies[2] are established using the weekly average cross rates of the currencies concerned on the Brussels, Frankfurt, London, New York, Paris, and Zurich markets.

The primary official rate is used for transactions between the National Bank of Angola (the central bank) and the commercial banks. The commercial banks are authorized to engage in transactions at market-determined exchange rates when buying and selling foreign exchange outside the fixing sessions. The National Bank applies a spread of 2 percent to its buying and selling exchange rates, and commercial banks apply a spread of 6.1 percent to their buying and selling rates. Foreign exchange dealers licensed by the National Bank to operate in foreign exchange are also authorized to operate at market-determined exchange rates. On December 31, 1995, the average official exchange rate for the U.S. dollar was KZR 5,692 per $1.

There are no taxes or subsidies on purchases or sales of foreign exchange. There are no arrangements for forward cover against exchange rate risk operating in the official or the commercial banking sector.

Administration of Control

The Organic Law of the National Bank and the Financial Institutions Law, promulgated on April 20, 1991, established the National Bank and the commercial banks as the financial institutions that are legally authorized to conduct exchange transactions with foreign parties. The National Bank has delegated authority to banks to license and execute permitted invisible foreign exchange transactions.

All imports and exports are subject to licensing by the Ministry of Commerce. The National Bank has issued guidelines and delegated authority to commercial banks to license invisible and capital foreign exchange transactions carried out by their clients. With the exception of government transactions and those in the oil sector, all foreign exchange transactions must be carried out by the commercial banks and the foreign exchange dealers.

Arrears are maintained with respect to external payments.

Prescription of Currency

The National Bank prescribes the currency to be used for import and export transactions, which is that of the country of origin of imports and the country of destination of exports, or the U.S. dollar. Bilateral settlement arrangements, which do not entail bilateral payment mechanisms, are maintained with Brazil, Portugal, and Spain.

Resident and Nonresident Accounts

Residents and nonresidents (natural persons or enterprises) may maintain foreign exchange accounts without prior authorization from the National Bank. Checkbooks may not be issued against personal accounts. These accounts may be credited with retained export earnings, foreign currency transferred from abroad, cash, traveler's checks, foreign payment orders, and interest accrued; they may be debited with sales against domestic currency or the issue of any instrument normally accepted on the international financial market in settlement of imports of goods and invisibles or capital payments. Transfers between these accounts are prohibited. The opening of foreign exchange accounts by nonresidents is subject to authorization by the National Bank. These accounts may be credited with foreign exchange transferred from abroad or with the proceeds from the account holder's activities in Angola; they may be debited with the sale of foreign exchange or the repatriation of all or part of the existing deposit.

Imports and Import Payments

All imports are subject to licensing based on a positive list. The issue of import licenses for transactions

---

[1] Frequently the amount of foreign exchange sold to a particular commercial bank or during a particular period of time covers only the transactions on the National Bank's priority list; as a result, other transactions have to take place outside the fixing sessions at a more depreciated rate.

[2] Austrian schillings, Belgian francs, Canadian dollars, Danish kroner, deutsche mark, ECUs, Finnish markkaa, French francs, Italian lire, Japanese yen, Netherlands guilders, Norwegian kroner, Portuguese escudos, pounds sterling, Spanish pesetas, Swedish kronor, and Swiss francs.

to be carried out with foreign exchange purchased from the banking system is subject to the availability of foreign exchange; the corresponding positive list assigns priority to particular transactions, which are periodically announced by the National Bank. Import licenses are also required for statistical purposes even if foreign exchange is not purchased from the banking system. These licenses are issued upon application.

Licenses are granted only to registered enterprises of proven technical, commercial, and financial capacity, and are issued only for imports of goods for which the enterprise is registered. To obtain a license, enterprises must present bids from three foreign suppliers to the sectoral ministries and the Ministry of Commerce. The approved offer may be considered for an import license application, which, in turn, must be approved by the Ministry of Commerce. Import licenses specify the importer, supplier, intermediary, product (Brussels Nomenclature Classification, volume, and unit price), shipping and insurance companies, cost, and method and currency of payment. Import licenses are valid for 180 days after issue and may be extended once for an additional 180 days. A license fee of 0.1 percent of the import value is levied.

Payments for Invisibles

Service contracts with nonresidents are subject to licensing. Preferential treatment is given to domestic air and sea transportation companies, and imports not insured domestically are approved only in exceptional cases. Remittances of dividends and profits from foreign investments are permitted under the Foreign Investment Law. Foreign investors are guaranteed the right to remit dividends, provided the investment in the resident company exceeds $250,000, and, in these cases, an authorization from the Ministry of Finance is required only as a formality.

Individuals are permitted to buy foreign exchange up to certain limits to pay expenses associated with travel, education allowances, and medical treatment.

Resident nationals who wish to travel abroad may, upon presentation of their passport and airline tickets, purchase foreign exchange from financial institutions as follows: (1) children up to the age of 16 years, up to $500 a person a trip to neighboring countries and up to $1,000 a trip to other countries; and (2) individuals over 16 years, up to $1,500 a person a trip to neighboring countries and up to $3,000 a trip to other countries. Companies may purchase foreign exchange from financial institutions to cover their employees' travel expenses abroad for trips of up to 30 days, for business, service, or training, with the following daily limits: (1) president or equivalent, $350; (2) vice president or equivalent, $300; and (3) department director or equivalent, $200. If a person returns to Angola earlier than planned, the remaining foreign exchange must be resold to a financial institution. For medical treatment abroad, up to $5,000 is provided through the National Health Board on a case-by-case basis at the official rate. Education travel expenses are normally expected to be covered by scholarships, but an additional foreign exchange amount may be granted. A maximum monthly allowance of $2,500 is granted to residents who spend up to 90 days abroad for educational, scientific, or cultural purposes. Up to the equivalent of $1,500 a month may be granted to Angolans or foreigners residing abroad who are direct ascendants or descendants of, and financially dependent on, residents in Angola, provided that (1) they are minor descendants under 18 years or, if of legal age, demonstrate that they are students or are incapable of working; or (2) they are ascendants over 60 years or, if younger, demonstrate they are incapable of working.

The exportation of domestic currency is prohibited. When leaving Angola, nonresidents visiting the country for purposes of tourism or business are permitted, upon presentation of the corresponding sales vouchers, to repurchase up to 50 percent of the foreign exchange they sold to institutions accredited to deal in foreign exchange.

Exports and Export Proceeds

With the exception of exports of foreign oil companies, all exports of goods are subject to licensing. Exports of certain goods are prohibited.[3] Re-exports of goods other than capital goods and personal belongings are also prohibited. Exports of products that are in short domestic supply are restricted. With the exception of foreign oil companies, all export proceeds must be surrendered to the National Bank or the commercial bank through which the exports were transacted. The National Bank may authorize exporters of goods and services to retain a certain proportion of foreign exchange earnings to be deposited in accounts to be held at local banks. Proceeds from exports must be collected and surrendered within 30 days of shipment.

---

[3]Arms and ammunition, ethnological collections, ships, ostrich products, cattle, and ivory products. Special export regimes apply to aircraft, animals and animal products, historical objects, minerals and mineral products, toxic substances, cotton, rice, pork, coffee, cereals, wood and wood products, tobacco, and petroleum.

Proceeds from Invisibles

Service contracts with nonresidents must be approved by the National Bank. The sectoral ministries supervise the execution of contracts. All proceeds must be surrendered to the National Bank within 30 days of receipt unless authorized by the National Bank to retain a portion of the proceeds.

There are no limits on the amount of foreign banknotes or traveler's checks in foreign exchange that a person may bring into the country, but any amount exceeding the equivalent of $10,000 must be declared upon arrival. Residents are permitted to leave the country with more than $5,000 in foreign exchange only if they present exchange purchase documents; nonresidents must present such documents when the amount exceeds $10,000. The importation of domestic currency is prohibited.

Capital

All capital transfers are subject to licensing by the National Bank, which has delegated certain authority to the commercial banks. The Foreign Investment Law of 1994 (Law No. 15/94 of September 23, 1994) prohibits investment in strategic sectors.[4] Direct investments in the oil sector are encouraged. Resident foreign companies must obtain prior authorization from the Ministry of Finance to borrow abroad. Dividends and capital may be repatriated upon liquidation with the prior approval of the Ministry of Finance. Transfers of personal capital, such as inheritances, dowries, savings from wages and salaries, and proceeds from sales of personal property, are permitted only on a case-by-case basis.

Gold

The importation and exportation of gold are a monopoly of the National Bank. Residents are permitted to hold gold only in the form of jewelry.

Changes During 1995

Exchange Arrangement

No significant changes occurred in the exchange and trade system.

---

[4]Defense, law and order, education, health, utilities, communications, and transportation infrastructure.

ANTIGUA AND BARBUDA

(Position as of December 31, 1995)

Exchange Arrangement

The currency of Antigua and Barbuda is the Eastern Caribbean Dollar,[1] which is issued by the Eastern Caribbean Central Bank (ECCB). The Eastern Caribbean dollar is pegged to the U.S. dollar, the intervention currency, at EC$2.70 per US$1. On December 31, 1995, the buying and selling rates for the U.S. dollar quoted by the ECCB in its transactions with commercial banks were EC$2.6949 and EC$2.7084, respectively, per US$1. The ECCB also quotes daily rates for the Canadian dollar and the pound sterling. There are no arrangements for forward cover against exchange risks operating in the official or the commercial banking sector.

Antigua and Barbuda accepted the obligations of Article VIII, Sections 2, 3, and 4 of the Fund Agreement on November 22, 1983.

Administration of Control

Exchange control applies to all currencies and is administered by the Ministry of Finance. Export licenses are required for a range of products, particularly those subject to export duties. Import licenses are issued by the Collector of Customs in the Ministry of Finance and by the Ministry of Trade, Industry, and Commerce, depending on the type of commodity.

Arrears are maintained with respect to external payments.

Prescription of Currency

Settlements with residents of member countries of the Caribbean Common Market (CARICOM)[2] must be made either in the currency of the CARICOM country concerned or in Eastern Caribbean dollars. Settlements with residents of other countries may be made in any foreign currency or in Eastern Caribbean dollars.

Nonresident Accounts

External accounts may be opened for nonresidents with the approval of the Ministry of Finance and may be maintained in any currency. With the approval of the Ministry of Finance, such accounts may also be opened by resident individuals or firms, especially in tourism-oriented industries or export trade, whose receipts are primarily in foreign currency and whose inputs are mainly imported or financed in foreign currency. External accounts can be credited with receipts from sales of merchandise (whether from export-oriented or local production) or from remittances. Commercial banks are required to report external accounts operations to the Ministry of Finance on a monthly basis.

Imports and Import Payments

Most goods may be freely imported under open general licenses granted by the Ministry of Trade, Industry, and Commerce. Certain other commodities require individual licenses, unless imported from CARICOM countries. Antigua and Barbuda follows the CARICOM rules of origin adopted in June 1981. Payments for authorized imports are permitted upon application and submission of documentary evidence.

Imports exempt from import duties include basic foods and agricultural imports. All other exemptions for machinery, equipment, and raw materials are granted on a case-by-case basis, generally under the Fiscal Incentives Act of 1975 and the Hotel Incentives Act.

On January 1, 1995, Antigua and Barbuda implemented the first stage of CARICOM's common external tariff; tariff rates were lowered to a range of zero to 35 percent for nearly all items, entailing a decrease in the average tariff rate. Tariff rates on a number of items, including milk and poultry meat, were reduced to zero.

Payments for Invisibles

Payments for invisibles related to authorized imports are not restricted. Upon presentation of supporting documents, and with the authorization of the Ministry of Finance, residents may purchase foreign exchange, including CARICOM traveler's checks (which are denominated in Trinidad and Tobago currency), for each trip outside the area served by

---

[1]The Eastern Caribbean dollar is also the currency of Anguilla, Dominica, Grenada, Montserrat, St. Kitts and Nevis, St. Lucia, and St. Vincent and the Grenadines.

[2]The CARICOM countries are Antigua and Barbuda, The Bahamas, Barbados, Belize, Dominica, Grenada, Guyana, Jamaica, Montserrat, St. Kitts and Nevis, St. Lucia, St. Vincent and the Grenadines, and Trinidad and Tobago. Exports to Jamaica are settled in U.S. dollars.

the Central Bank. Foreign exchange allowances for education, family maintenance, medical treatment, and remittances of earnings by foreign workers are approved on a case-by-case basis. Profits on foreign direct investment may be remitted in full, subject to confirmation by the Inland Revenue Department that the enterprise is registered for corporate income tax purposes. There are no limits on the amount of local currency that may be taken out of the country.

Exports and Export Proceeds

No export licenses are required for certain commodities to any destination. Surrender of export proceeds is not required, and re-exports are not subject to any tax if transactions take place within the bonded area.

Proceeds from Invisibles

Travelers to Antigua and Barbuda may freely bring in notes and coins denominated in Eastern Caribbean dollars or in any foreign currency. Foreign currency coins are not normally exchanged. Checks and drafts in U.S. and Canadian currency can be tendered up to US$1,000 without restriction; for amounts over US$1,000, approval from the Ministry of Finance must be obtained. Levy exemptions for transfers, especially for charitable purposes, are usually granted.

Capital

There are no legislated restrictions on capital movements. Foreign investment is granted the same incentives as domestic investment under the Fiscal Incentives Law and the Hotel Incentives Act. Large transfers abroad for investment purposes can be phased out over time by the Financial Secretary.

Gold

There are no restrictions on the importation of gold.

Changes During 1995

Imports and Import Payments

January 1. Antigua and Barbuda implemented the first stage of CARICOM's common external tariff in 1995; tariff rates were lowered to a range of zero to 35 percent for nearly all items, entailing a decrease in the average tariff rate.

January 1. Tariffs rates on a number of items, including milk and poultry meat, were reduced to zero.

ARGENTINA

(Position as of December 31, 1995)

Exchange Arrangement

The currency of Argentina is the Peso, the external value of which is pegged to the U.S. dollar. On December 31, 1995, the middle rate of the peso in terms of the U.S. dollar was Arg$1 per US$1. Exchange rates of other currencies are based on the buying and selling rates for the U.S. dollar in markets abroad. Swap transactions and forward exchange operations are permitted in any currency, and the rates may be freely negotiated. Deposits denominated in pesos and maintained by the financial institutions at the Central Bank of the Republic of Argentina to meet cash reserve requirements are automatically converted into U.S. dollars. As of November 1, 1995, reserve requirements have been replaced by minimum cash requirements, which may include earning assets *(activos retribuibles)*.

Argentina accepted the obligations of Article VIII, Sections 2, 3, and 4 of the Fund Agreement on May 14, 1968.

Administration of Control

All exchange transactions are carried out through entities authorized expressly for this purpose, with no restrictions on the purchase or sale of foreign exchange at market prices. These authorized entities include banks, exchange agencies, exchange houses, exchange offices, and financial companies; each type of institution is subject to separate regulations. Credit funds and mortgage savings and loan companies may also effect certain foreign exchange transactions, on the condition that they meet certain additional capital requirements.

Prescription of Currency

Within the framework of the multilateral clearing system of the Latin American Integration Association (LAIA), payments between Argentina and Brazil, Chile, Colombia, Ecuador, Mexico, Paraguay, Peru, Uruguay, and Venezuela are settled voluntarily through payments agreements and a reciprocal credit mechanism. All payments between Argentina and Bolivia and the Dominican Republic must be effected through the accounts specified in the agreements. Argentina has also signed similar agreements with Bulgaria, Cuba, Hungary, Malaysia, and Russia, whereby payments between Argentina and these countries are settled on a voluntary basis through the accounts maintained by the Central Bank of Argentina and the central banks concerned, with the exception of Bolivia and Cuba, where settlement through the accounts specified in the agreements is obligatory. Transactions with other countries must be settled in freely convertible currencies.

Resident and Nonresident Accounts

Authorized banks may open accounts in pesos or foreign exchange in the name of residents or nonresidents who have met certain identification requirements that are aimed at, among other things, preventing money laundering. Accounts in foreign exchange must be denominated in convertible currencies and may be credited only with cash or with remittances from abroad in the following currencies: U.S. dollars for current accounts, savings, and fixed-term deposits; and deutsche mark and other currencies that the Central Bank explicitly authorizes at the request of financial institutions for deposits in savings and fixed-term accounts. Both resident and nonresident holders of demand or time foreign currency accounts may use their credit balances freely in Argentina or abroad. Transfers between accounts may be made freely. Use of checking accounts denominated in U.S. dollars is allowed for domestic transactions.[1]

Imports and Import Payments

Import payments may be effected in convertible currencies, and they may be freely settled by authorized financial entities.

The Treaty of Asunción, signed in 1991, became effective in January 1995. It established the Southern Cone Common Market (Mercosur) between Argentina, Brazil, Paraguay, and Uruguay and implemented a 47 percent reduction in tariffs on goods traded among Mercosur countries, retroactive to June 30, 1991. Thereafter, tariffs were reduced at a rate

---

[1] Since January 12, 1995, the minimum cash requirements for deposits and other obligations in pesos must be covered in U.S. dollars. Financial institutions accepting savings and fixed-term deposits in foreign currencies must limit them to no more than six times the liabilities included in the computation of capital, and the resulting lending capacity must be applied mainly to financing productive activities and external trade. Any funds not used for these purposes may be placed in alternative investments expressly allowed by law and by the Central Bank (government securities, sight placements in the New York branch of the Banco de la Nación Argentina, etc.).

of 7 percent every six months until they were completed at the end of 1994; the tariff positions exempted from these reductions were also eliminated during this period. At the end of 1994, a substantial portion of intra-MERCOSUR trade was conducted at a zero tariff rate and the nontariff barriers listed in the Schedule of the 1991 Asunción Treaty were also removed.

Since January 1, 1995, Argentina and the MERCOSUR countries have been applying a common external tariff (CET) to imports from the rest of the world that encompasses all products, with certain exceptions (Argentina has 300 exceptions) that are subject to a transitional regime until the years 2001 and 2006. CET rates currently range from zero to 20 percent. At the end of the transitional period in 2001, the CET will be 14 percent for capital goods; in 2006, the maximum CET will be 16 percent for computer and telecommunications equipment.

Argentina applies a special regime to automobile and sugar imports with the authorization of MERCOSUR, pending agreement on a common regime for these sectors. Quantitative restrictions are applied to the automobile sector and to some paper, and iron and steel products. Other restrictions are in force solely for security, hygiene, and public health reasons.

A statistical tax of 3 percent is applied to imports from all countries, except those from MERCOSUR. This tax is waived for capital goods, fuel, and sensitive goods from the paper, computer, and telecommunications sectors.

Payments for Invisibles

Neither payments for invisibles nor the exportation of domestic and foreign banknotes are restricted.

Exports and Export Proceeds

Export proceeds are not required to be repatriated.

Until the end of 1994, export rebates equal to the import duties applied to the products concerned (Decree No. 1239/92). On January 1, 1995, export rebate rates were changed when MERCOSUR became effective (Decree No. 2275/94). Subsequently, the applicable rates were reduced by 25 percent (Resolution ME&OSP No. 310/95 of March 20, 1995).

Other export promotion measures involving rebates are the regime for exporting turnkey plants, under which exports of industrial plants and engineering operations sold under turnkey contracts benefit from the highest effective rebate rate (15 percent outside the zone and 10 percent within the zone); and the regime for Puerto Patagónicos, under which exports through the ports and customs posts located on the Colorado River received an additional rebate ranging from 7 percent to 12 percent until the end of 1994. Since January 1, 1995, these rates are being reduced by 1 percent a year.

The drawback regime allows exporters to recover import duties, the statistical tax, and the value-added tax (VAT) that are levied on inputs used in the processing of products for export. To be eligible for drawback, the exporter must be a direct importer of inputs. Since March 10, 1995, the drawback regime has been adapted to the new MERCOSUR terms, distinguishing between the treatment of exports to member countries of MERCOSUR and those to nonmember countries (Resolution ME&OSP No. 288/95).

The temporary admission regime permits the importation, free of consumer and statistical taxes, of merchandise for industrial processing, provided that such goods are exported in their new form within 180 days, which may be extended for a further 180 days. To be eligible for the temporary admission regime, the exporter must be the direct user of the merchandise subject to temporary importation. Temporary admission is an alternative to the drawback system, and both cannot be used simultaneously.

Quantitative restrictions on exports are maintained only on arms, protected animal species, and products subject to international agreements.

The financing system for promoted exports has been suspended by Communication "A" 1807 of March 8, 1991, except with respect to those products that were in the process of exportation at that time. Under Communication "A" 1994 of August 31, 1992, this system was transferred to the Banco de Inversión y Comercio Exterior (Investment and Foreign Trade Bank).

Proceeds from Invisibles

Proceeds from invisible transactions of the private sector need not be repatriated. The importation of domestic and foreign banknotes is not subject to exchange control.

Capital

Beneficiaries of loans in foreign currencies are not required to convert them into domestic currency in the exchange market. Foreign borrowing by the public sector is regulated by Law No. 24.156 of October 29, 1992.

Decree Law No. 1853 of September 1993 governs foreign investment, combining in one law the liberalization measures contained in the Economic Emergency and State Reform Acts of 1989 and the Foreign Investment Law of 1993. This law allows foreign companies to invest in Argentina, without prior government approval, on an equal footing with domestic firms, thus effectively applying national treatment to foreign investors. Foreign investors are entitled to the same rights and subject to the same obligations as domestic investors and may enter into any area of economic activity on their own, because no law or regulation forces them to be associated with local partners.

There are no approvals or procedures required to effect foreign investment; irrespective of the amount or areas of economic activities concerned, this principle applies even in cases where a foreign investment results in full foreign ownership of a domestic company.

In the banking and insurance sectors, where special statutes require all operators to apply for licenses, foreign and domestic investors are guaranteed access to such licenses on an equal footing. The principle of nondiscrimination applied to banking laws is extended to eliminate the traditional reciprocity requirement when considering a foreign bank application to do business in Argentina, which effectively gives foreign banks full legal equality with their domestic counterparts.

Foreign investors are entitled to repatriate their capital and transfer abroad their realized earnings at any time without any approval or authorization. Foreign investors may repatriate the full amount of their invested capital at any time, irrespective of the duration of investment. Their access to the foreign exchange market is also unrestricted. These rights to assist foreign investors have been further established under international law by means of over 30 investment promotion and protection agreements, including all countries where foreign investment usually originates, such as Canada, France, Germany, Italy, Spain, Sweden, Switzerland, the United Kingdom, and the United States. Argentina is a member of the Multilateral Investment Guarantee Agency and the International Center for the Settlement of Investment Disputes and maintains a valid and active agreement with the Overseas Private Investment Corporation.

Gold

Residents may hold gold coins and gold in any other form in Argentina or abroad. Financial institutions, exchange houses, and exchange agencies may buy or sell gold in the form of coins or good delivery bars among themselves and may buy such gold from their clients as well as other precious metals whose market value is based on the daily list prices of major transactions. The importation of gold coins and good delivery bars is not restricted. Gold exports must be paid for in convertible currencies. Imports of gold by industrial users are subject to a statistical duty of 0.6 percent, and those by other users are also subject to a sales tax. Institutions may carry out arbitrage operations with their clients in gold coins or good delivery gold against foreign banknotes. Authorized institutions may export gold to entities abroad.

Changes During 1995

Imports and Import Payments

January 1. The Treaty of Asunción (1991), establishing the Southern Core Common Market (Mercosur) became effective. Tariffs on imports from the member countries of Mercosur were eliminated (except for a number of products), and a common external tariff (CET) ranging from zero to 20 percent (with 11 different positions) would be applied to most products from non-Mercosur countries.

March 1. The statistical tax of 3 percent was reimposed on all imports, with the exception of capital goods, fuel, and goods produced in the paper, computer, and telecommunications sectors. All goods imported from the member countries of Mercosur were also exempted.

Exports and Export Proceeds

January 1. When Mercosur became effective, export rebates were changed.

March 20. Export rebates were reduced by 25 percent.

ARMENIA

(Position as of April 30, 1996)

Exchange Arrangement

The currency of the Republic of Armenia is the Dram; the exchange rate vis-à-vis the U.S. dollar is determined on the basis of foreign exchange auctions held five times a week in the Yerevan Stock Exchange and twice a week in the Gjumry Stock Exchange. Banks and financial dealers holding licenses from the Central Bank of Armenia may participate in the auctions. Anyone may buy and sell at the auction through banks. Foreign exchange transactions may also be made through the interbank market. On April 30, 1996, the average auction rate for the U.S. dollar was dram 405 per $1, and the average exchange rate at the exchange offices was dram 407 per $1.

The Central Bank quotes official rates in terms of U.S. dollars daily on the basis of the weighted average rate at foreign exchange auctions on the previous trading day (Central Bank Decree No. 189, issued on December 1, 1995). This rate is used for accounting valuation of all foreign exchange transactions of all economic agents. Exchange rates for other major currencies are calculated either on the basis of quotations on the Yerevan Stock Exchange, when applicable, or solely on the basis of quotations for the U.S. dollar in major international interbank markets against the currencies concerned.

Enterprises or any other physical or juridical persons (including state enterprises) are free to buy and sell foreign exchange without restriction through authorized banks and licensed cash bureaus.

Forward transactions, futures, and options in foreign exchange transactions are permitted.

Administration of Control

Central Bank Decision No. 33 of May 17, 1994, sets out the principles and procedures for foreign exchange and currency transactions between residents and nonresidents. The Central Bank has overall responsibility for regulating financial relations between Armenia and other countries in close collaboration with the Ministry of Finance. The Ministry of Finance has the authority over trade transactions, including customs tariff policies.

Banks are granted two types of foreign exchange licenses. A general license gives a bank authority to conduct any type of foreign exchange transaction, including those with nonresidents abroad and including gold transactions that require an additional license. Banks with a full license may offer a full range of currency transactions, including gold. A second, more restricted form of license allows banks operating in Armenia to buy and sell foreign exchange only on behalf of their clients.

Prescription of Currency

Settlements with other states are made through correspondent accounts maintained by the commercial banks, which may be opened freely without notifying the Central Bank. The settlements can also be effected through the correspondent accounts of the Central Bank. Settlements with countries with which Armenia maintains bilateral payments agreements are effected in accordance with the terms of the agreements.[1] Settlements with all other countries may be made in any currency.

Resident and Nonresident Accounts

Under Central Bank Resolution No. 179 of October 20, 1995, and Resolution No. 8 of January 1, 1996, resident and natural and juridical persons may open, maintain, and use accounts in banks abroad with prior notification to the Central Bank. They may also open, maintain, and use foreign currency accounts at licensed banks in Armenia. There are no limits on the amount of foreign currency banknotes that can be purchased with drams from banks or cash bureaus, and banknotes can be deposited in a foreign exchange account or used for transactions with nonresidents. Resident enterprises may maintain and use foreign exchange accounts in banks abroad with the authorization of the Central Bank. The opening and use of domestic foreign exchange accounts are not restricted, except that residents may not transfer these balances to other residents in order to make payments for goods and services, because this would contravene the dram's status as sole legal tender in Armenia.

Nonresident natural and juridical persons may freely open and use foreign exchange accounts with licensed domestic banks. According to Central Bank Resolution No. 124 of July 28, 1995, such persons are also free to make withdrawals to effect current transactions. Balances in these accounts may be trans-

---

[1]At the end of 1995, Armenia maintained bilateral payments agreements with Russia and Turkmenistan and bilateral clearing agreements with the Baltic countries and the other countries of the former Soviet Union, but all have become largely inoperative.

ferred abroad or sold to the licensed domestic banks for drams. Central Bank Resolution No. 177 of October 20, 1995, permits nonresident juridical persons to open accounts in drams and use them for domestic transactions. Foreign governments and international institutions may freely open dram accounts with banks in Armenia without prior authorization from the Central Bank.

Imports and Exports

Imports of a number of products are restricted for public health, national security, and environmental reasons. A license from the Ministry of Agriculture and the Ministry of Health, granted on a case-by-case basis, is required to import medicinal preparations and chemical agents for plant protection (pesticides). Imports of weapons, military equipment and parts, and explosives require special authorization from the Government. The Agreement on the Creation of a Free Trade Zone, signed in April 1994, establishes the legal framework for the signing of free trade agreements between Armenia and other countries of the former Commonwealth of Independent States (CIS). To date, bilateral free trade agreements have been signed with the Kyrgyz Republic, Moldova, Russia, Tajikistan, Turkmenistan, and Ukraine. Currently, only the one with Russia has been ratified. Products imported from countries of the former CIS are exempt from customs tariffs. The customs tariffs range from zero to 10 percent. There are no tariffs on exports.

In accordance with Government Decision No. 17 of January 17, 1995, export licenses are required for three product groups: medicines, wild animals and plants, and textile products exported to the European Union. In addition, special government permission is required for the export of nuclear technology, nuclear waste and related non-nuclear products, and technology with direct military applications. Minimum threshold prices for the export of ferrous and nonferrous metals and the re-export of foreign-produced goods made thereof remain in force. In accordance with Government Decree No. 615 of December 10, 1994, all restrictions on barter trade have been removed. Proceeds from exports must be repatriated within 30 days of receipt, and, as of April 1, 1995, are not subject to the surrender requirement. Expenses, commissions, and taxes paid abroad relating to exports may be deducted from export proceeds prior to repatriation.

Payment for and Proceeds from Invisibles

Resident persons and enterprises may freely purchase foreign exchange or use foreign exchange balances in their foreign exchange accounts with domestic banks to conduct invisible transactions. There are no limits on foreign exchange allowances for travel.

Proceeds from cultural activities performed abroad are exempt from the repatriation requirements. Proceeds from other invisibles are subject to the same regulations as those applicable to proceeds from merchandise exports.

The importation of foreign currency banknotes is not restricted. The exportation of foreign currency banknotes is also not restricted, but a declaration must be made for amounts exceeding the equivalent of $500.

Capital

Foreign investors, including joint ventures, are not required to obtain authorization from the Ministry of Finance. A foreign investment law passed on July 31, 1994, reflecting current international practices, is liberal in its treatment of foreign direct investment. Other inward and outward capital transfers require approval from the Ministry of Finance.

Gold

A license is required to conduct trade in gold. There are no specific regulations governing domestic trade in gold. Regulations on purchases, sales, and holdings of gold and precious metals by banks have been prepared by the Central Bank, and they are expected to come into force in 1996.

Changes During 1995

Exchange Arrangement

July 28. Interbank foreign exchange transactions were permitted.

December 1. The official exchange rate was determined on a daily basis instead of three times weekly (Decision No. 189).

Resident and Nonresident Accounts

July 28. Nonresidents were allowed to open accounts at Armenian banks without restrictions (Decision No. 214).

Imports and Exports

January 1. The rate of surrender requirement for export receipts was reduced to 30 percent from 50 percent.

January 10. The number of categories for which export licenses are required was reduced to three product groups from nine product groups.

January 27. The number of tariff rates was reduced to five, with zero rates for most imports (Government Decree No. 39).

April 1. The surrender requirement for export receipts was eliminated.

Changes During 1996

Resident and Nonresident Accounts

January 1. Resolution No. 8 regulating foreign exchange accounts held by residents abroad and in Armenia was issued.

ARUBA[1]

(Position as of December 31, 1995)

Exchange Arrangement

The currency of Aruba is the Aruban Florin, which is pegged to the U.S. dollar at Af. 1.7900 per US$1. The Centrale Bank van Aruba, the Central Bank, deals with local commercial banks within margins of 0.002795 percent on either side of parity. On December 31, 1995, the official buying and selling rates were Af. 0.98 and Af. 1.002, respectively, per NA f. 1.00. Official buying and selling rates for other currencies[2] are set daily on the basis of U.S. dollar rates on the international exchange market. A foreign exchange commission of 1.3 percent is levied on all payments made by residents to nonresidents, except when settled in Netherlands Antillean guilders. Purchases of foreign exchange by resident companies with nonresident status for foreign exchange control purposes are exempted from the commission.

There are no taxes or subsidies on purchases or sales of foreign exchange. No arrangements for forward cover against exchange rate risk are operating in the official or the commercial banking sector.

Administration of Control

Foreign exchange controls are administered by the Central Bank. Import licenses, when required, are issued by the Department of Economic Affairs, Commerce, and Industry.

Prescription of Currency

Payments to and receipts from nonresidents may be made in any convertible currency. For purposes of the compilation of the balance of payments, all payments made by residents to nonresidents, as well as receipts through local banks and banks abroad must be reported to the Central Bank.

Nonresident Accounts

Nonresidents may freely open accounts in any foreign currency and are also permitted to hold accounts in Aruban florins up to Af. 200,000.

Resident Foreign Bank Accounts

Residents are obligated to report in writing to the Central Bank the opening of accounts with nonresidents, including foreign bank accounts.

Imports and Import Payments

Imports, other than eggs, are not subject to any quantitative restrictions. The restriction on the importation of eggs, however, is administered liberally, depending on the domestic supply situation. Payments for imports may be made freely.

Payments for Invisibles

The majority of payments for invisibles exceeding Af. 50,000 a quarter require a license from the Central Bank. Allowances for education remittances for family maintenance and allowances for medical treatment are granted liberally. Residents may buy foreign exchange for travel purposes, up to a maximum amount equivalent to Af. 400 for each day of travel, Af. 8,000 a trip, or Af. 15,000 each calendar year, without a special permit, and up to a maximum amount equivalent to Af. 2,500 without presenting travel documents. Transfers of profits and dividends require a license from the Central Bank. The exportation of Aruban banknotes is prohibited, and that of foreign currencies requires a license.

Exports and Export Proceeds

Exports do not require a license. Unless specifically exempted, export proceeds must be converted into local currency within eight working days and credited to a foreign currency account with a local bank or with a foreign bank with the approval of the Central Bank.

Proceeds from Invisibles

The regulations governing export proceeds also apply to proceeds from invisibles. Nonresidents may bring in any amount of checks, traveler's checks, or banknotes denominated in foreign currency.

Capital

The following transactions require a license from the Central Bank: (1) purchases from and sales to nonresidents of domestic and officially listed securi-

---

[1]On January 1, 1986, the Island of Aruba, which was formerly a part of the Netherlands Antilles, became a separate nonmetropolitan territory within the Kingdom of the Netherlands.

[2]Canadian dollars, deutsche mark, European currency units, French francs, Italian lire, Japanese yen, Netherlands guilders, Netherlands Antillean guilders, pounds sterling, and Swiss francs.

ties (a resident natural person must obtain a license if values exceed Af. 200,000 per year); (2) purchases from and sales to nonresidents of domestic and foreign real estate, or resident natural persons must obtain a license if the amount of the transaction exceeds Af. 200,000 per year; (3) proceeds from the liquidation of direct foreign investments; (4) loans received from, and extended to, nonresidents; and

(5) other short- and long-term investments by residents abroad, or by nonresidents in Aruba or by resident natural persons if the amount of the transaction exceeds Af. 200,000 a year.

Changes During 1995

No significant changes occurred in the exchange and trade system.

AUSTRALIA

(Position as of December 31, 1995)

Exchange Arrangement

The currency of Australia is the Australian Dollar.[1] The Australian authorities do not maintain margins in respect of exchange transactions; spot and forward exchange rates are determined on the basis of demand and supply conditions in the foreign exchange market, but the Reserve Bank of Australia retains discretionary power to intervene in the foreign exchange market. There is no official exchange rate for the Australian dollar. The Reserve Bank of Australia publishes an indicative rate for the Australian dollar based on market observation at 4 p.m. daily. On December 31, 1995, the indicative rate in terms of the U.S. dollar was $A 1.3423 per US$1. There are no taxes or subsidies on purchases or sales of foreign exchange.

Authorized foreign exchange dealers may deal among themselves, with their customers, and with overseas counterparties at mutually negotiated rates for both spot and forward transactions in any currency, in respect of trade- and non-trade-related transactions. The Reserve Bank sets a limit for each dealer's net open overnight foreign exchange exposure.

Australia accepted the obligations of Article VIII, Sections 2, 3, and 4 of the Fund Agreement on July 1, 1965.

Administration of Control

The only restrictions on external payments and transfers are those introduced to give effect to UN Security Council Resolutions imposing sanctions against Iraq and Libya.

Prescription of Currency

Both outward and inward payments may be settled in Australian currency or in any foreign currency,[2] but purchases and sales of foreign currency by persons in Australia must be undertaken with an authorized foreign exchange dealer.

Nonresident Accounts

Nonresidents may establish and operate accounts without formality and may repatriate funds without restriction. Accounts may be denominated in foreign currency, but purchases and sales of foreign currency in Australia must be handled through authorized dealers. Special requirements apply to interest-bearing investments by foreign government monetary authorities (see section on Capital, below).

Imports and Import Payments

There are no import-licensing requirements or quotas on imports other than the tariff quota, which applies to certain cheeses and curd. Australia is not a signatory of the Multifiber Arrangement. For some products, imports are allowed only if written authorization is obtained from the relevant authorities or if certain regulations are complied with. Among the goods subject to control are narcotic, psychotropic, and therapeutic substances, firearms and certain weapons, particular chemicals, certain primary commodities, some glazed ceramic ware, and various dangerous goods. These controls are maintained mainly to meet health and safety requirements; to meet certain requirements for labeling, packaging, or technical specifications; and to satisfy certain obligations arising from Australia's membership in international commodity agreements.

Australia is implementing a tariff reduction program under which most tariffs are to be reduced to a maximum level of 5 percent by July 1996. Tariffs are to be reduced on passenger automobiles from 35 percent to 15 percent, and in the textile, footwear, and clothing sectors, to a maximum of 25 percent by the year 2000. Tariff quotas in the textile, clothing, and footwear sectors were eliminated in March 1993. Most specific duty rates were converted to ad valorem rates in July 1993.

Australia's antidumping and countervailing legislation, primarily the revised Custom Tariff (Antidumping) Act of 1988, was amended in accordance with World Trade Organization rules and reflected in Uruguay Round changes to the GATT texts on antidumping and countervailing measures and came into effect on January 1, 1995. The amendments included (1) a requirement for a set level of support by Australian industry before an investigation can be initiated; (2) the inclusion of prescribed methodologies to establish dumping margins; and (3) a requirement that investigations will be terminated promptly where it is established that the margins of dumping (or level of subsidization) are de

---

[1]The Australian dollar also circulates in several other countries, including Kiribati, Nauru, and Tuvalu.

[2]Foreign currencies are defined as all currencies other than the Australian dollar.

minimis or there are negligible volumes of dumped (or subsidized) imports. A provision to allow for a combination of company-specific and residual rates of duty applying to exporters from subject countries was also introduced. The legislation also provided detailed guidelines on what constitutes a counter-vailable subsidy, giving preferential treatment to developing countries in the consideration of coun-tervailing duties. Specific criteria are listed for mak-ing a determination regarding the existence of threat of material injury. The legislation now requires greater levels of evidence from interested parties and notification by authorities. The Anti-dumping Authority and Australian customs share responsibility for implementing the Government's antidumping policies.

Under the terms of the Australia-New Zealand Closer Economic Relations and Trade Agreement (ANZCERTA), trade in goods across the Tasman became free from July 1, 1990 (five years ahead of schedule). The provision for antidumping actions against imports of New Zealand origin ceased after July 1, 1990, and domestic trade practices legisla-tion was amended at the same time to provide redress for unfair competition from New Zealand. However, provision for countervailing action to be taken on goods from New Zealand still exists.

The South Pacific Regional Trade and Economic Cooperation Agreement (SPARTECA) provides for duty-free and unrestricted access to Australian and New Zealand markets on a nonreciprocal basis for most of the products exported by the member coun-tries. In the case of Papua New Guinea, although it obtains trade concessions from New Zealand under SPARTECA, its trade and commercial relations with Australia are covered by the Agreement on Trade and Commercial Relations between Australia and Papua New Guinea.[3]

Developing countries obtain tariff preferences on their exports to Australia under the Australian Sys-tem of Tariff Preference for Developing Countries. Since 1986, a uniform preferential margin of 5 percentage points on dutiable goods has applied to all developing countries; if the general tariff rate is below 5 percent, imports from developing coun-tries enter duty free. From July 1, 1993, the develop-ing countries preferences have been phased out for Hong Kong, the Republic of Korea, and Taiwan Province of China, and margins applicable to cer-

tain industries, including textiles, clothing and foot-wear, chemicals, vegetable and fruit preparations, tuna, and sugar have been removed for all but the least-developed countries and the South Pacific Island Territories. The preferential rates for these specified industries will be frozen until the General Tariff rate falls to the preference rate; the General Tariff rate will then apply. Both the 1991 and 1993 decisions came into effect on July 1, 1993.

Payments for Invisibles

Payments for invisibles are unrestricted, except for certain transactions involving Iraq and Libya. There is no restriction on the amount of Australian or foreign currency that can be taken out of Australia, so long as the foreign currency was pur-chased from an authorized dealer. Travelers who are not residents of Australia may also take out any foreign currency that they brought into Australia.

Persons leaving Australia with cash (banknotes and coins) in any currency totaling $A 5,000 or more must complete a report for the Australian Transac-tion Reports and Analysis Center (AUSTRAC); the report forms are available at ports or airports from the Australian customs authorities.

The ANZCERTA also provides, through a protocol, for a progressive liberalization of the trade in ser-vices between Australia and New Zealand, subject to the foreign investment policies of both countries. In addition, certain service activities are excluded from the agreement. Among Australia's exclusions are the areas of telecommunications, airport ser-vices and aviation, coastal shipping, limits on for-eign ownership of broadcasting and television, and postal services.

Exports and Export Proceeds

The export regime is designed to encourage the relatively unrestricted exportation of Australian products. Bounties are paid to producers of a limited number of products, some of which may be exported. Export prohibitions and restrictions in effect are designed to ensure quality control over specified goods; administer trade embargoes and meet obligations under international arrangements; restrict the exportation of certain defense goods; reg-ulate the exportation of goods that involve high technology and have dual civilian and military applications;[4] and maintain adequate measures of control over designated cultural property, resources,

---

[3]The areas covered by this agreement are those constituting the South Pacific Forum (in addition to Australia and New Zealand)—Cook Islands, Fiji, Kiribati, Nauru, Niue, Papua New Guinea, Solomon Islands, Tonga, Tuvalu, Vanuatu, and Western Samoa.

[4]Australia became a participant in the Coordinating Commit-tee for Multilateral Export Controls (COCOM), effective May 1989.

and flora and fauna. There are no formalities regulating the disposal of export proceeds.

The Government also exercises export controls to secure national conservation objectives and to respond to specific market distortions abroad that have an impact on the export prices of certain products. Remaining controls on primary products apply mainly to food and agricultural products.

The Government monitors trade in the bauxite, alumina, coal, and iron ore sectors and retains authority to withhold export approval for shipments at prices not in line with market conditions. Export controls apply to uranium to ensure compliance with the Government's nonproliferation policy obligations. Restrictions also apply to the exportation of certain other nuclear and related materials.

Licenses are required for the exportation of unprocessed wood, including wood chips. Licensing requirements are intended to ensure compliance with the Government's policy regarding environmental protection, elimination of market distortions, and promotion of further processing in Australia.

The Australian Dairy Corporation administers export control powers in relation to prescribed dairy products under the provisions of the Dairy Produce Act. All exporters of controlled dairy products must be licensed. This system allows the control of exports to markets where quantitative restrictions apply and ensures that export prices do not fall below minimum prices agreed to under the General Agreement on Tariffs and Trade (GATT) for these products. Exports of red meat and livestock can be made only by persons or firms licensed by the Australian Meat and Livestock Corporation (AMLC). The AMLC has the power to engage in export trading in its own right and may introduce arrangements to control Australian exports to that market to observe quantitative restrictions in any particular market. Other Commonwealth statutory marketing authorities that have export control powers are the Australian Horticultural Corporation, the Australian Honey Board, the Australian Wheat Board, and the Australian Wine and Brandy Corporation. The Australian Wheat Board's powers make it the sole exporter of Australian wheat.

Proceeds from Invisibles

Earnings from invisibles in foreign currencies may be retained or sold for Australian dollars. Travelers may bring in any amount in Australian or foreign currency, subject to completion of an AUSTRAC report for cash amounts (notes and coins) totaling $A 5,000 or more. (See section on Payments for Invisibles, above.)

Capital

The vast majority of transactions involving transfers of interest-bearing capital from Australia and nonresident investments in Australia may be undertaken without formality. The only exceptions are a ban on the issue of bearer bonds and foreign governments, their agencies, and international organizations. When borrowing in the Australian capital market, these entities must advise the Treasury or Reserve Bank of the details of each borrowing after its completion for information purposes only. Although there are no limits on the interest-bearing investments of international organizations or of foreign central banks and other monetary authorities, the Reserve Bank may determine an amount up to which the investment of foreign government monetary institutions (which also undertake commercial investments) will be regarded as having been undertaken for official foreign reserve management purposes. All investing agencies are expected to be stable holders of Australian dollar assets and to keep the Reserve Bank informed of their Australian dollar portfolios. Interest-bearing investments of a foreign government's official foreign reserves are exempt from taxation consistent with the principle of sovereign immunity. Income derived by a foreign government from the conduct of commercial operations is not exempt from Australian taxation.

Under Australia's foreign investment policy, proposals by foreign investors for the acquisition or investment of more than $A 50 million are subject to full examination. These include (1) acquisitions of substantial interests in existing Australian businesses; and (2) proposals for the establishment of new businesses. Proposals for investments in the following areas are subject to examination irrespective of size: (1) investment in the media; (2) direct investment by foreign governments or their agencies; and (3) acquisition of residential real estate (unless exempt under the regulations). Foreign investors may acquire residential real estate within a designated integrated tourist resort (ITR) without obtaining approval under the foreign investment guidelines.

In most industry sectors, the Government normally approves proposals to establish new businesses involving total investments of $A 10 million or more and those to acquire existing businesses with total assets valued at $A 5 million or more ($A 3 million or more if more than half of the assets of the business are attributable to rural land) unless judged to be contrary to the national interest.

Certain restrictions apply to proposed acquisitions of real estate, but approval is normally granted to (1) acquisitions of real estate for development; (2) purchases of vacant residential land (on condition that continuous development occurs within 12 months) and home units and townhouses that are "off the plan" or under construction (on condition that no more than half of the units in any one development are sold to foreign interests); and (3) acquisitions of developed nonresidential commercial real estate valued at over $A 5 million (acquisitions of developed nonresidential commercial real estate valued at less than $A 5 million do not require approval).

In applying the policy, the authorities make every effort to avoid unnecessary interference in normal commercial processes and recognize the special characteristics and circumstances that may arise in individual cases. The policy is nondiscriminatory as to the country of origin of investors, and the Foreign Investment Review Board, which acts as an independent advisor to the Government on foreign investment matters, stands ready to assist and advise foreign investors in formulating their proposals.

Since February 1992, foreign banks have had the option of being authorized under the Banking Act to operate as wholesale banks in the form of a branch (previously, foreign banks could be authorized only as incorporated subsidiaries). All foreign corporations seeking authorization to conduct banking business in Australia must satisfy the Reserve Bank of their willingness and capacity to adhere to high standards of prudential management. Foreign bank branches are not required to maintain endowed capital in Australia and, consequently, the Reserve Bank does not impose any capital-based large exposure limits on these branches.

Gold

Australia has no restrictions applying to owning, buying, selling, importing, or exporting gold and gold coins. If the exportation or importation of coins (together with any notes) totals $A 5,000 or more, it must be reported to AUSTRAC.

Changes During 1995

No significant changes occurred in the exchange and trade system.

AUSTRIA

(Position as of December 31, 1995)

Exchange Arrangement

The currency of Austria is the Austrian Schilling. Austria participates with Belgium, Denmark, France, Germany, Ireland, Luxembourg, the Netherlands, Portugal, and Spain in the exchange rate mechanism (ERM) of the European Monetary System (EMS).[1] In accordance with this agreement, Austria maintains the spot exchange rates between the schilling and the currencies of the other participants within margins of 15 percent above and below the cross rates, based on the central rates expressed in European currency units (ECUs)[2] and continues to keep the schilling's external value constant against the deutsche mark.

The arrangements imply that the Oesterreichische Nationalbank (the central bank) stands ready to buy or sell the currencies of the other participating states in unlimited amounts at specified intervention rates. On December 31, 1995, these rates were as follows:

Specified Intervention Rates Per:	Austrian Schilling	
	Upper limit	Lower limit
100 Belgian or Luxembourg francs	39.6089	29.3757
100 Danish kroner	214.1740	158.8410
100 Deutsche mark	816.9270	605.8770
100 French francs	243.5860	180.6540
1 Irish pound	19.6971	14.6082
100 Netherlands guilders	725.0650	537.7400
100 Portuguese escudos	7.9700	5.9108
100 Spanish pesetas	9.60338	7.1220

The participants in the EMS do not maintain the exchange rates for other currencies within fixed limits. However, to ensure a proper functioning of the system, they intervene in concert with the other EMS members to smooth out fluctuations in exchange rates, the intervention currencies being each other's and the U.S. dollar.

Forward transactions are permitted. Forward premiums and discounts are left to the interplay of market forces, and the Oesterreichische Nationalbank does not intervene in the forward market or provide cover for the forward positions of commercial banks. On December 28, 1995, the buying and selling rates for the U.S. dollar were S 10.038 and S 10.183, respectively, per $1. There are no exchange taxes or subsidies.

Austria accepted the obligations of Article VIII, Sections 2, 3, and 4 of the Fund Agreement on August 1, 1962.

Administration of Control

Most exchange transactions are effected through Austrian banks authorized by the central bank. Certain restrictions on payments and transfers for current international transactions to the Government of Iraq are still in force.

In accordance with the Fund's Executive Board Decision No. 144-(52/51), adopted on August 14, 1952, Austria notified the Fund on July 7, 1992, that, in compliance with UN Security Council Resolution No. 757 (1992), certain restrictions had been imposed on the making of payments and transfers for current international transactions in respect of the Federal Republic of Yugoslavia (Serbia/Montenegro).[3] Restrictions are imposed on certain current payments and transfers to Libya in accordance with UN Security Council Resolution No. 883 (1993).

Export and import licenses required under the Foreign Trade Act of 1995 and its amendments must be issued by the Federal Ministry for Economic Affairs for industrial products and by the Federal Ministry of Agriculture and Forestry for agricultural products.[4]

Prescription of Currency

Settlements with all countries may be made either in foreign currencies or through free schilling accounts.

---

[1]Austria became a member of the European Union on January 1, 1995, and joined the ERM of the EMS on January 9, 1995.

[2]Effective August 2, 1993, the intervention thresholds of the currencies participating in the ERM of the EMS, except those of the deutsche mark and the Netherlands guilder, were widened to ±15 percent from ±2.25 percent around the bilateral central exchange rates; the fluctuation band of the deutsche mark and the Netherlands guilder remained unchanged at ± 2.25 percent.

[3]These sanctions were suspended on December 22, 1995, in accordance with UN Security Council Resolution No. 1022 (1995). As Austria is a member of the European Union (EU), the Regulation No. 241/94 of the EU Council regarding the further discontinuation of the economic and financial relations between the EU and the areas of Bosnia and Herzegovina, under the control of Bosnian Serb forces, has been in force since January 1, 1995.

[4]Licenses are issued with due consideration for the provisions of relevant EU-trade agreements and the fulfillment of quotas established in accordance with such agreements and the need of the Austrian economy.

Nonresident Accounts

There is only one category of nonresident account in schillings, namely, free schilling accounts. These accounts may be freely opened by Austrian banks on behalf of nonresidents and are not subject to restrictions. Balances may be freely converted into any foreign currency. Transfers between these accounts are free.

Nonresidents may also maintain nonresident accounts in foreign currencies. These are subject to the same conditions as free schilling accounts.

Imports and Import Payments

As a member of the European Union, Austria applies the Common Import Regimes. Payments for imports are not restricted.

Payments for Invisibles

Residents are permitted to conclude transactions with nonresidents involving payments for invisibles without restriction.

Residents traveling abroad for purposes of tourism may purchase foreign exchange from authorized banks or obtain short-term advances from nonresidents without limitation.

Exports and Export Proceeds

Licenses for exports regulated under the Foreign Trade Law must be obtained from the relevant ministry or, at the time of clearance, from the customs authorities. For most exports, licenses are not required. Export licenses are issued with due consideration for the provisions of relevant EU trade agreements and the fulfillment of quotas established in accordance with such agreements, and the needs of the Austrian economy.

Proceeds from Invisibles

Proceeds from invisibles may be deposited without restriction. Persons entering Austria may import Austrian or foreign banknotes and coins without limit.

Capital

The acquisition by nonresidents of Austrian securities and shares and participation by nonresidents in Austrian companies are unrestricted. The acquisition of real estate is subject to approval by local authorities. Nonresidents are permitted to issue bonds on the domestic market.

Foreign banks are permitted to establish branches in Austria. In the auditing and legal profession, the transport sector, and the electric power generation sector, there are certain restrictions for investments by nonresidents and Austrian residents who are not nationals of one of the countries of the European Economic Area.

Residents and nonresidents may export capital freely without a license. Nonresidents direct investments in Austria and the purchases of Austrian or foreign equities do not require approval.

The transfer of funds owned by emigrants and payments due to nonresidents on account of dowries, inheritances, and settlements under certain agreements between heirs are permitted. Residents may also grant loans to nonresidents, as well as to foreign banks and financial institutions.

Residents are allowed to acquire participation rights in foreign companies, associations, and other enterprises; earnings accrued from such investment may be freely used. Residents are permitted to acquire real estate abroad and to purchase from nonresidents securities denominated in Austrian and foreign currencies without restriction. Residents are also permitted to open bank accounts and issue bonds abroad.

Gold

Residents may freely hold gold in any form and may trade with residents and nonresidents both at home and abroad. Imports and exports of gold in any form by residents and nonresidents are unrestricted and free of license.

Changes During 1995

Exchange Arrangement

January 9. Austria joined the exchange rate mechanism of the EMS.

Administration of Control

January 1. Austria became a member of the European Union.

Imports and Import Payments

January 1. Austria became a member of the World Trade Organization (WTO).

(See Appendix for a summary of trade measures introduced and eliminated on an EU-wide basis during 1995.)

AZERBAIJAN

(Position as of December 31, 1995)

Exchange Arrangement

The currency of the Republic of Azerbaijan is the Manat. The external value of the manat for noncash operations is determined in auctions held three times a week at the Baku Interbank Currency Exchange (BICEX). Participation in the auctions is restricted to the commercial banks that are licensed to deal in foreign exchange bidding on behalf of their customers.[1] Since April 17, 1995, the Azerbaijan National Bank has been quoting an official exchange rate against the U.S. dollar every Wednesday, which is equal to the Wednesday auction rate. The official rate is used for all official foreign exchange transactions and valuation of foreign assets.

Authorized banks are free to set buying and selling rates for cash transactions. These rates are published weekly by the International Bank. On December 31, 1995, the official exchange rate for the U.S. dollar was manat 4,440 per $1, and the December monthly average buying and selling rates for cash transactions were manat 4,502, and manat 4,556, respectively, per $1. No commission is assessed on purchases of foreign exchange by the International Bank, but a commission of 2–3 percent is added for sales of foreign exchange.

All residents of the Azerbaijan Republic (legal entities and enterprises and organizations that do not enjoy a right of legal entity) must sell 30 percent of their foreign exchange earnings through the BICEX auctions.

There are no taxes or subsidies on purchases or sales of foreign exchange. There are no arrangements for forward cover against exchange rate risk provided by the official or the commercial banking sectors. The sum of the long and short positions of authorized commercial banks in convertible currencies must not exceed 15 percent of their capital; the ratio for the currencies of the Baltic countries, Russia, and the other countries of the former Soviet Union is 5 percent.

Administration of Control

Foreign exchange transactions are regulated by the National Bank Law, which gives the National Bank responsibility for regulating the exchange rate of the manat, conducting foreign currency operations, and administering gold and convertible currency reserve holdings. The National Bank also has overall responsibility for issuing licenses to deal in foreign exchange; for regulating foreign exchange operations, including implementing and monitoring compliance with the law; and for establishing prudential rules governing foreign exchange operations.

Foreign trade is regulated under the Foreign Economic Activity Law by the Ministry of Foreign Economic Relations. The Customs Service Law regulates the organization and operation of customs. Enterprises engaged in foreign trade must register with the Ministry of Justice.

Foreign private investment in joint ventures must be registered with the Ministry of Foreign Economic Relations and the Ministry of Finance. Investment abroad by both Azerbaijani nationals and companies is regulated by a state decree that limits the opening of foreign exchange accounts in foreign countries. A license must be obtained from the National Bank as well as permission from the Cabinet of Ministers to open such accounts.

Prescription of Currency

Residents may, once a transaction is approved, make and receive payments and transfers in any convertible currency. Settlements with the Baltic countries, Russia, and the other countries of the former Soviet Union are effected through correspondent accounts of the commercial banks in these states or through correspondent accounts of the respective central banks. Azerbaijan maintains a bilateral payments arrangement with the Islamic Republic of Iran.

Resident and Nonresident Accounts

Resident persons or enterprises may open and use foreign exchange bank accounts at banks abroad subject to authorization by the National Bank. Residents may freely open and use foreign currency accounts maintained at licensed banks in Azerbaijan. No declaration of the origin of foreign

---

[1]The convertible currencies commercial banks are authorized to deal in are Australian dollars, Austrian schillings, Belgian francs, Canadian dollars, deutsche mark, Finnish markkaa, French francs, Italian lire, Japanese yen, Netherlands guilders, Norwegian kroner, pounds sterling, Swedish kronor, Swiss francs, Turkish liras, and U.S. dollars. An official exchange rate against the ECU is also posted.

exchange is required for individuals. Individuals may transfer foreign exchange held in these accounts freely up to $5,000 and, upon authorization, larger amounts may be transferred to the holder's bank account abroad or may be freely converted into domestic currency. Enterprises are obliged to repatriate the foreign exchange held in accounts abroad (except the amount used for paying for imports) and to sell 30 percent of foreign exchange earnings through the BICEX.

Nonresident persons and enterprises are free to open foreign exchange accounts with licensed domestic banks. Foreign exchange in these accounts may be transferred abroad or sold to the banks for manat. Nonresident enterprises may also open and operate accounts in manat and use them for domestic transactions in accordance with instructions issued by the National Bank. Foreign governments and international institutions may open and operate manat accounts with specific authorization from the National Bank.

Imports and Exports

Payments for imports from the Baltic countries, Russia, and the other countries of the former Soviet Union may be made in any mutually agreed currency, including banknotes, or through the system of correspondent accounts operated by the National Bank and the commercial banks. Payments for imports from the rest of the world are made in accordance with normal commercial practices. There are no restrictions on the use of foreign exchange for import payments from enterprises' own accounts.

There are no licensing requirements for imports except for reasons of health, environmental protection, or security. Bilateral trade agreements exist with Turkmenistan, Ukraine, and the Islamic Republic of Iran; however, these agreements are fulfilled by procurement through market mechanisms.

Duties are levied on imports in accordance with Resolution No. 252 of June 27, 1994, of the Cabinet of Ministers. Duty rates vary by product but not by origin. A customs fee of 0.15 percent is levied on imports from all sources.

Resident persons and enterprises are required to repatriate proceeds from exports within three months and transfer them to a licensed bank in Azerbaijan within ten days of receipt unless specifically exempted by the Government. Expenses, commissions, and taxes paid abroad relating to economic activities may be deducted from the proceeds prior to transfer to a licensed bank, which in turn should be instructed by the exporter to sell 30 percent of export proceeds at the BICEX auction.

As of November 1, 1995, there are no licensing requirements for exports, including those of strategic goods. However, export contracts for strategic goods remain subject to review by the Ministry of Foreign Economic Relations with respect to the contract price and payment terms in order to prevent underinvoicing. Some export bans exist, mainly on defense equipment.

Export duties were imposed in March 1995 on strategic goods whose domestic prices remained significantly below world market levels, notably oil products and cotton; as a result, 70 percent of the difference between the domestic and the export price was taxed away. This tax was removed for petroleum products in November 1995, when domestic prices were raised to world market levels.

A customs fee of 0.15 percent is levied on exports to all destinations.

Payments for and Proceeds from Invisibles

There are no restrictions on the availability of foreign exchange for invisibles payments by resident individuals, but documentation is required.

The exportation of foreign banknotes is regulated by the National Bank and the Ministry of Finance, in conformity with customs regulations.

Proceeds from invisibles must be repatriated within three months and transferred to a licensed bank within ten days of receipt. The importation of foreign banknotes is regulated by the National Bank and the Ministry of Finance in conformity with customs regulations.

Capital

Inward private capital transfers are not restricted, and borrowing abroad by the Government is subject to an annual ceiling determined by Parliament. Foreign exchange transactions of private investors are protected by the Protection of Foreign Investment Law adopted on January 15, 1992. Under this law, the treatment of foreign investment cannot be less favorable than that extended to domestic investment, and foreign investment may receive preferential treatment.

Foreign investment is protected from nationalization and expropriation unless state interests or force majeure is involved. If nationalization or expropriation occurs, adequate compensation is paid. Profits may be reinvested in local currency, held in Azerbaijan, or converted into foreign currency and transferred without restriction. Foreign investors are granted certain privileges: enterprises or joint ventures with foreign equity capital ownership of more than 30 percent are entitled to a two-year holiday on profit taxes; imports and exports of goods and services may be undertaken without licenses; and exporters of manufactured goods are allowed to retain 100 percent of their foreign exchange earnings.

Gold

A license is required to conduct international trade in gold. There are no regulations governing domestic trade in gold.

Changes During 1995

Exchange Arrangement

April 17. The National Bank began to quote an official exchange rate against the U.S. dollar every Wednesday, which is equal to the Wednesday auction rate. The official rate is to be used for all official foreign exchange transactions, and valuation of foreign assets.

Imports and Exports

March 13. Regulations governing surrender requirements were replaced with a full repatriation requirement. All residents of Azerbaijan (legal entities and enterprises, and organizations that do not enjoy a right of legal entity) were required to sell 30 percent of their foreign exchange earnings through BICEX auctions.

November 1. Export quotas and licensing requirements were abolished. Export contracts for strategic goods remain subject to review by the Ministry of Foreign Economic Relations with respect to the contract price and payment terms in order to prevent underinvoicing.

THE BAHAMAS

(Position as of December 31, 1995)

Exchange Arrangement

The currency of The Bahamas is the Bahamian Dollar, which is pegged to the U.S. dollar, the intervention currency, at B$1 per US$1. The U.S. dollar circulates concurrently with the Bahamian dollar. The official buying and selling rates for the U.S. dollar are B$1.0025 and B$1.0040, respectively, per US$1. Buying and selling rates for the pound sterling are also officially quoted, with the buying rate based on the rate in the New York market; the selling rate is 0.5 percent above the buying rate. The Central Bank of The Bahamas deals only with commercial banks. For transactions with the public, commercial banks are authorized to charge a commission of 0.50 percent buying and 0.75 percent selling per US$1, and 0.50 percent buying or selling per £1. A stamp tax of 1.5 percent is applied to all outward remittances.

There is also a market in which investment currency[1] may be negotiated between residents through the Central Bank at freely determined rates, usually attracting a premium above the official market rate.

Commercial banks may provide forward cover for residents of The Bahamas when the resident is due to receive or must pay foreign currency under a contractual commitment. Commercial banks may not, however, sell foreign currency spot to be held on account in cover of future requirements without the Central Bank's permission. Authorized dealers may deal in foreign currency forward with nonresidents without prior approval from the Central Bank. Commercial banks may deal forward among themselves at market rates and must ensure when carrying out all forward cover arrangements that their open spot or forward position does not exceed the equivalent of B$500,000 long or short. There are no forward cover arrangements in the official sector.

The Bahamas accepted the obligations of Article VIII, Sections 2, 3, and 4 of the Fund Agreement on December 5, 1973.

Administration of Control

Exchange control is administered by the Central Bank, which delegates to authorized dealers[2] the authority to approve allocations of foreign exchange for certain current payments, including payments for imports up to B$100,000; approval authority for cash gifts is not delegated, except in the Family Islands.[3] Import and export licenses are not required except for crawfish, conch, arms and ammunition, and, in certain cases, industrial gold. The Department of Agriculture and Fisheries issues export licenses for crawfish and conch, and the police department issues import and export licenses for arms and ammunition.

Prescription of Currency

The exchange control system of The Bahamas makes no distinction between foreign territories. Settlements with residents of foreign countries may be made in any foreign currency[4] or in Bahamian dollars through an external account.

Nonresident Accounts

Authorized banks may freely open external accounts denominated in Bahamian dollars for winter residents and for persons with residency permits who are not gainfully employed in The Bahamas. With the prior approval of the Central Bank, authorized banks may also open external accounts in Bahamian dollars for nonresident companies that have local expenses in The Bahamas and for nonresident investors. External accounts in Bahamian dollars are normally funded entirely from foreign currency originating outside The Bahamas, but income on registered investments may also be credited to these accounts with the approval of the Central Bank. Balances may be converted freely into foreign currency and transferred abroad.[5]

The accounts of residents emigrating from The Bahamas and who are redesignated upon departure

---

[1]Foreign currency that the Central Bank permits to be retained and used or disposed of as investment currency. Such permission may exist for foreign currency accruing to residents of The Bahamas from the sale or redemption of foreign currency securities; the sale, liquidation, redemption, or realization of property; or direct investments outside The Bahamas. The use of investment currency is prescribed for the purchase of foreign currency securities from nonresidents and the making of direct investments outside The Bahamas. In 1995, total purchases amounted to B$203,898, and total sales to B$268,533.

[2]Nine commercial banks are appointed authorized dealers.

[3]In June 1988, the Central Bank established a branch of its Exchange Control Department in Grand Bahama to serve the foreign exchange needs of residents in that area.

[4]Foreign currencies comprise all currencies other than the Bahamian dollar.

[5]Foreign nationals who have been granted temporary resident status are treated in some respects as nonresidents but are not permitted to hold external accounts in Bahamian dollars

as nonresidents are blocked for amounts in excess of B$25,000 for a period of four years. Balances on blocked accounts are transferable through the official exchange market after that time or through the Investment Currency Market at any time; they may also be invested with the approval of the Central Bank in certain resident-held assets or they may be spent locally for any other purpose.

Imports and Import Payments

The importation of certain commodities is prohibited or controlled for social, humanitarian, or health reasons. All other goods may be imported without a license. Prior approval from the Central Bank is required to make payments for imports exceeding B$100,000, irrespective of origin;[6] this approval is normally given automatically upon submission of pro forma invoices or other relevant documents proving the existence of a purchase contract. Import duties vary from zero to 200 percent, depending on the type of goods; the tariff rate on most goods is 42 percent, and the average tariff rate is 35 percent. Stamp duties on imports vary from 2 percent to 27 percent. For all imports of agricultural products, a permit must be obtained from the Ministry of Agriculture. Customs entries are subject to a stamp tax at a rate of 7 percent.

Payments for Invisibles

There are no restrictions on current payments. Authorized dealers may make payments to nonresidents on behalf of residents for certain services and other invisibles, such as commissions, royalties, education, freight, ships' disbursements, and insurance premiums within specified limits. On application to the Central Bank, residents are entitled to a foreign exchange allowance for tourist travel equivalent to B$1,000 a person above the age of 18 years and B$500 a person up to the age of 18 years a trip; B$10,000 a person a year for business or professional travel; B$3,000 for educational travel; and B$1,000 for travel for medical reasons. The allowance for tourist travel excludes the cost of fares and travel services, which are normally obtained against payment in Bahamian dollars to a travel agent in The Bahamas. Applications for foreign exchange in excess of the official amounts must be referred to the Central Bank, which approves bona fide applications. Foreign exchange obtained for travel may not be retained abroad or used abroad for purposes other than travel; any unused balance must be surrendered within a week

of issue or, if the traveler is still abroad, within one week of return to The Bahamas.

Subject to adequate documentary evidence, an education allowance is granted without a limit. Temporary residents may, with the approval of the Central Bank, remit up to 50 percent of their wages and salaries, but if commitments outside The Bahamas are more than 50 percent of wages and salaries, additional amounts may be remitted. Temporary residents may also repatriate all of their accumulated savings resulting from their employment in The Bahamas.

A traveler may export Bahamian banknotes not exceeding B$70 in value; Bahamian travelers may not export the banknotes of any other country, except with specific approval from the Central Bank.

Exports and Export Proceeds

Export licenses are not required except for crawfish, conch, and arms and ammunition. The proceeds of exports must be offered for sale to an authorized dealer as soon as the goods have reached their destination or within six months of shipment; alternatively, export proceeds may be used in any manner acceptable to the Central Bank.

Proceeds from Invisibles

Residents are obliged to collect without delay all amounts due to them from nonresidents and to offer the foreign currency proceeds for sale to an authorized dealer without delay. There are no restrictions on the importation of foreign banknotes. The importation of domestic banknotes is subject to the approval of the Central Bank.

Capital

All capital transfers to countries outside The Bahamas require exchange control approval, and outflows of resident-owned capital are restricted. Inward transfers by nonresidents, which are encouraged, are required to go through the manual exchange control approval process, although the subsequent use of the funds in The Bahamas may require authorization. The permission of the Central Bank is required for any action whereby nonresidents acquire control of or participate in an incorporated company controlled by residents. Resident individuals and companies require the specific permission of the Central Bank to maintain foreign currency bank accounts locally or abroad.[7]

---

[6]Except in the Family Islands, where this authority is delegated to clearing bank branches.

[7]Banks and trusts established in The Bahamas are exempt from certain exchange control regulations, particularly with regard to their offshore operations.

The use of official exchange for direct investment abroad is limited to B$100,000 or 30 percent of the total cost of the investment (whichever is greater) for investments from which the additional benefits expected to accrue to the balance of payments from export receipts, profits, or other earnings within 18 months of the investment will at least equal the total amount of investment and will continue thereafter. Investments abroad that do not meet the above criteria may be financed by foreign currency borrowed on suitable terms subject to individual approval from the Central Bank, by foreign currency purchased in the investment currency market, or by the retained profits of foreign subsidiary companies. Permission is not given for investments that are likely to have adverse effects on the balance of payments.

In principle, inward investment by nonresidents is unrestricted. However, the consent of the Central Bank is required for the issue or transfer of shares in a Bahamian company to a nonresident and for the transfer of control of a Bahamian company to a nonresident. Foreigners intending to purchase land for commercial purposes or property larger than five acres must obtain a permit from the Investments Board, under the provisions of the International Persons Landholding Act of 1993. If such an application is approved, payment for the purchase may be made either in Bahamian dollars from an external source or in foreign currency. Nonresidents wishing to purchase property for residential purposes may do so without prior approval but are required to obtain a certificate of registration from the Foreign Investment Board on completion of the transaction.

For all investments with approved status, permission is given upon application for the transfer of profits and dividends representing earned trading profits and investment income. In the event of a sale or liquidation, nonresident investors are permitted to repatriate the proceeds, including any capital appreciation, through the official foreign exchange market.

Residents require the specific approval of the Central Bank to buy property outside The Bahamas; such purchases, if for personal use, may be made only with investment currency, and approval is limited to one property a family. Incidental expenses connected with the purchase of property for personal use may normally be met with investment currency. Expenditures necessary for the maintenance of the property or arising directly from its ownership may, with permission, be met with foreign currency bought at the current market rate in the official foreign exchange market.

The transfer of legacies and inheritances to nonresident beneficiaries under the wills or intestacies of persons who were Bahamian residents at the time of their death is permitted.

Residents may make cash gifts to nonresidents not exceeding a total of B$1,000 a donor a year. This amount may be exceeded, with permission, in special circumstances.

Foreign nationals domiciled in The Bahamas, who have been designated residents for exchange control purposes, may be eligible for a measure of exemption from certain exchange control obligations, notably with respect to the mandatory deposit of foreign currency securities and the surrender of certain other foreign capital assets.

Nonresident buyers of Bahamian dollar-denominated securities must fund the acquisition of such securities from foreign currency sources. Interest, dividends, and capital payments on such securities may not be remitted outside The Bahamas unless the holdings have been properly acquired by nonresidents. Bahamian residents are not permitted to purchase foreign currency securities with official exchange, export proceeds, or other current earnings; payment must be made with investment currency. All purchases, sales, and swaps of foreign currency securities by Bahamian residents require permission from the Central Bank and are normally transacted through authorized agents.[8] These institutions are free to act on behalf of nonresidents in relation to such transactions without any further approval from the Central Bank.

All foreign securities purchased by residents of The Bahamas must be held by or to the order of an authorized agent. Securities of other former Sterling Area countries are considered foreign currency securities. Sale proceeds from such resident-held foreign currency securities, if registered at the Central Bank by December 31, 1972, are eligible for sale in the investment currency market. Unregistered securities may be offered for sale at the official rate of exchange.

Residents emigrating from The Bahamas and who are redesignated upon departure as nonresidents may transfer, at the current market rate in the official foreign exchange market, up to B$25,000 of their Bahamian dollar assets to the new country of residence and may also take their household and personal effects with them; assets exceeding B$25,000 are deposited in blocked accounts (see Nonresident Accounts, above). Once a person is redesignated a

---

[8]Thirteen banks and trust companies are authorized to deal in Bahamian and foreign currency securities and to receive securities as deposits.

nonresident, income accruing from assets remaining in The Bahamas is remittable at the current market rate in the official foreign exchange market.

Residents other than authorized banks must obtain permission to borrow foreign currency from nonresidents, and authorized dealers are subject to exchange control direction of their foreign currency loans to residents. Residents must also obtain permission to pay interest on, and to repay the principal of, foreign currency loans by conversion of Bahamian dollars. When permission is granted for residents to accept foreign currency loans, it is conditional upon the currency being offered for sale without delay to an authorized dealer unless the funds are required to meet payments to nonresidents for which permission has been specifically given.

A resident company wholly owned by nonresidents is not allowed to raise fixed capital in Bahamian dollars although approval may be granted to obtain working capital in local currency. If the company is partly owned by residents, the amount of local currency borrowing for fixed capital purposes is determined in relation to the resident interest in the equity of the company. Banks and other lenders resident in The Bahamas must have permission to extend loans in domestic currency to any corporate body (other than a bank) that is also resident in The Bahamas but is controlled by any means, whether directly or indirectly, by nonresidents. However, companies set up by nonresidents primarily to import and distribute products manufactured outside The Bahamas are not allowed to borrow Bahamian dollars from residents for either fixed or working capital. Instead, they must provide all their financing in foreign currency, and foreign currency loans are normally permitted on application.

Gold

Residents of The Bahamas, other than authorized dealers, are not permitted to hold or deal in gold bullion. However, residents who are known users of gold for industrial purposes may, with the approval of the Central Bank, meet their current industrial requirements. Authorized dealers are not required to obtain licenses for bullion or coins, and no import duty is imposed on these items. Commercial imports of gold jewelry do not require a license and are duty free, but they are subject to a 10 percent stamp tax. There is no restriction on residents' acquisition or retention of gold coins. The Bahamas has issued commemorative coins in denominations of B$10, B$20, B$50, B$100, B$150, B$200, B$250, B$1,000, and B$2,500 in gold, and B$10 and B$25 in silver; these are legal tender but do not circulate.

Changes During 1995

No significant changes occurred in the exchange and trade system.

BAHRAIN

(Position as of December 31, 1995)

Exchange Arrangement

The currency of Bahrain is the Bahrain Dinar, which is pegged to the SDR at the rate of BD 0.46190 per SDR 1. The exchange rate for the Bahrain dinar in terms of the SDR may be set within margins of ±7.25 percent of this fixed relationship. In practice, however, the Bahrain dinar has maintained a stable relationship with the U.S. dollar, the intervention currency; the exchange rate has remained unchanged at BD 1 per $2.6596 since December 1980. The middle rate of the Bahrain dinar for the U.S. dollar is quoted by the Bahrain Monetary Agency.

The Bahrain Monetary Agency does not deal with the public. It provides daily recommended rates to banks dealing with the public for amounts up to BD 1,000 in U.S. dollars, pounds sterling, and deutsche mark, based on the latest available U.S. dollar rates against those currencies. On December 31, 1995, the Bahrain Monetary Agency's buying and selling rates for the U.S. dollar were BD 0.375 and BD 0.377, respectively, per $1. In their dealings with the public, commercial banks are required to use the Bahrain Monetary Agency's rates for U.S. dollars, pounds sterling, and deutsche mark, but they are authorized to charge an exchange commission of 2 per mil (special rates of commission apply for transactions up to BD 1,000). The banks' rates for other currencies are based on the Bahrain Monetary Agency's U.S. dollar rates and the New York market rates against the U.S. dollar.

There are no taxes or subsidies on purchases or sales of foreign exchange. There are no arrangements for forward cover against exchange rate risk operating in the official sector. The Bahrain Monetary Agency monitors the forward exchange transactions of commercial banks through the open position of the banks' monthly returns.

Bahrain accepted the obligations of Article VIII, Sections 2, 3, and 4 of the Fund Agreement on March 20, 1973.

Administration of Control

The Bahrain Monetary Agency is the exchange control authority, but there is no exchange control legislation in Bahrain. No import or export licenses are required (except for arms, ammunition, and alcoholic beverages). However, importers and exporters must be registered with the commercial registry maintained by the Ministry of Commerce and must be members of the Bahrain Chamber of Commerce and Industry.

Prescription of Currency

All settlements with Israel are prohibited. Otherwise, no requirements are imposed on exchange payments or receipts.

Nonresident Accounts

A distinction is made between accounts held by residents and those held by nonresidents. Offshore banking units are not normally permitted to hold resident accounts.

Imports and Import Payments

All imports from Israel are prohibited. Imports of a few commodities are prohibited from all sources for reasons of health, public policy, or security. Imports of cultured pearls are prohibited. In practice, rice is imported mainly by the Bahrain Import-Export Company.

The rates of customs tariffs range between 5 percent and 10 percent on most commodities but the rate is 20 percent on vehicles, 50 percent on tobacco, and 125 percent on alcoholic beverages. Mandatory government procurements give preference to goods produced in Bahrain and member countries of the Cooperation Council for the Arab States of the Gulf (GCC), provided that the quality and prices of these goods are within specified margins of the prices of imported substitutes (10 percent for goods produced in Bahrain and 5 percent for goods produced in member countries of the GCC). Foreign exchange for payments of permitted imports may be obtained freely.

Exports and Export Proceeds

All exports to Israel are prohibited. Otherwise, all products may be exported freely. No requirements are attached to receipts from exports or re-exports; the proceeds need not be repatriated or surrendered, and they may be disposed of freely, regardless of the currency involved.

Payments for and Proceeds from Invisibles

Payments for and proceeds from invisibles are not restricted, except that payments must not be made to or received from Israel. Travelers may bring in or take out of Bahrain any amount in domestic or foreign banknotes.

Capital

No exchange control requirements are imposed on capital receipts or payments by residents or nonresidents, but payments may not be made to or received from Israel. Profits from foreign investments in Bahrain may be transferred abroad freely, except that, under Article 72 of the Monetary Agency Law, the banks are subject to special rules regarding the payment of dividends and the remittance of profits. Licensed offshore banking units may freely engage in transactions with nonresidents, although transactions with residents are not normally permitted. The stock exchange began operations on January 2, 1989, and trading on the floor of the exchange began on June 17, 1989.

Gold

Residents may freely purchase, hold, and sell gold in any form, at home or abroad. Imports and exports of gold in any form are freely permitted and do not require a license. Imports of gold jewelry are subject to a 10 percent customs duty, but gold ingots are exempt. Brokers doing business in gold and other commodities must obtain approval from the Bahrain Monetary Agency before they can register with the Ministry of Commerce and Agriculture. Such businesses are subject to a minimum deposit requirement equivalent, in the case of gold, to BD 3,000 or 10 percent of the contract value, whichever is higher.

Changes During 1995

No significant changes occurred in the exchange and trade system.

BANGLADESH

(Position as of January 31, 1996)

Exchange Arrangement

The currency of Bangladesh is the Bangladesh Taka. Bangladesh Bank, the central bank, determines its buying and selling rates for the U.S. dollar (the intervention currency) vis-à-vis authorized dealers with reference to a weighted basket consisting of the currencies of the country's major trading partners. On December 31, 1995, the (spot) middle rate of the taka in terms of the U.S. dollar was Tk 40.75 per $1, and the spot buying and selling rates for authorized dealers were Tk 40.65 and Tk 40.85, respectively, per $1. Bangladesh Bank deals with authorized dealers only in U.S. dollars and the currencies of the member countries of the Asian Clearing Union (ACU).[1] Authorized banks are free to set their own buying and selling rates for the U.S. dollar and the rates for other currencies based on cross rates in international markets. The interbank market has expanded substantially during 1995, with most transactions other than official foreign aid and official debt-service payments being transacted in this market. Bangladesh Bank places prudential limits on each authorized dealer's open exchange position, taking into account the dealer's past foreign exchange operations approximated by the volume of letters of credit business and the quality of the dealer's management.

Forward contracts are available from authorized banks, covering periods of up to six months for export proceeds and import payments and covering up to three months for remittances of surplus collection of foreign shipping companies and airlines. For the currencies of ACU member countries, the authorized banks may, in turn, take forward cover from Bangladesh Bank against transactions entered into through forward contracts with their customers.[2] Bangladesh Bank does not transact in the forward market, nor does it regulate transactions beyond the normal requirements of prudential supervision.

Authorized banks are permitted to retain working balances with their foreign correspondents. Currency swaps and forward exchange transactions are permitted when they are against underlying approved commercial transactions.

Bangladesh accepted the obligations of Article VIII, Sections 2, 3, and 4 of the Fund Agreement on April 11, 1994.

Administration of Control

Exchange control is administered by Bangladesh Bank in accordance with general policy formulated in consultation with the Ministry of Finance. The commercial banks and specialized financial institutions are issued licenses as authorized dealers (authorized banks) in foreign exchange. The Chief Controller of Imports and Exports of the Ministry of Commerce is responsible for registering exporters and importers and for issuing the Import Policy Order (IPO). Registered importers can make their imports in terms of the IPO against letters of credit. Letters of credit authorization forms are issued by authorized dealers and do not require a separate import license. Certain trade transactions are conducted through state-owned agencies, including the Trading Corporation of Bangladesh (TCB).

Settlements with Iraq and the Federal Republic of Yugoslavia (Serbia/Montenegro) are prohibited pursuant to UN Security Council Resolution No. 757 (1992).

Prescription of Currency

Settlements normally take place in convertible currencies, and in some cases, through nonresident taka accounts. Settlements with ACU member countries are required to be effected through the ACU in terms of the Asian monetary unit (AMU).[3] Bangladesh has commodity exchange agreements with Bulgaria, the Czech Republic, and Hungary. Settlements for trade under these agreements are effected through special nonconvertible U.S. dollar accounts, and Bangladesh is committed to settling promptly any outstanding liability on these accounts. Payments for imports may be made to the country of origin of the goods or to any other country (with the exception of those countries from which importation is prohibited). They may be made (1) in taka for credit in Bangladesh to a nonresident bank account of the country concerned; (2) in the currency of the country concerned; or (3) in any freely convertible currency. Export proceeds must be received in freely

---

[1]Members of the Asian Clearing Union are Bangladesh, India, the Islamic Republic of Iran, Myanmar, Nepal, Pakistan, and Sri Lanka.

[2]Effective January 1, 1996, Bangladesh Bank ceased to deal in the currencies of ACU member countries.

[3]The AMU is equivalent in value to the SDR and is used for recording transactions through the ACU.

convertible foreign exchange or in taka from a non-resident taka account.

Resident and Nonresident Accounts

Nonresident accounts of individuals, firms, or companies are regarded for exchange control purposes as accounts related to the country in which the account holder is a permanent resident.[4] Nonresident foreign currency accounts may be opened by authorized dealers without prior approval from Bangladesh Bank for Bangladesh nationals and foreign nationals who reside abroad and for foreign firms operating abroad. Specified debits and credits to these accounts may be made in the account holder's absence by authorized dealers without prior approval from Bangladesh Bank. Certain other debits and credits may be made without prior approval from Bangladesh Bank but are subject to ex post reporting.

Convertible taka accounts. All diplomatic missions operating in Bangladesh, their diplomatic officers, home-based members of the mission staffs, international nonprofit organizations (including charitable organizations functioning in Bangladesh and their respective personnel), foreign oil companies engaged in oil exploration in Bangladesh and their expatriate employees, UN organizations and other international organizations, foreign contractors and consultants engaged in specific projects, and foreign nationals residing in Bangladesh (regardless of their status) are allowed to maintain convertible taka accounts. These accounts may be credited freely with the proceeds of inward remittances in convertible foreign exchange and may be debited freely at any time for local disbursements in taka, as well as for remittances abroad in convertible currencies. Transfers between convertible taka accounts are freely permitted. Foreign missions and embassies, their expatriate personnel, foreign airline and shipping companies, and international nonprofit organizations in Bangladesh may open interest-bearing accounts, but the interest earned can be disbursed only in local currency.

Foreign currency accounts of Bangladesh nationals working abroad. Bangladesh nationals and persons of Bangladesh origin who are working abroad are permitted to open foreign currency accounts denominated in deutsche mark, Japanese yen, pounds sterling, or U.S. dollars. These accounts may be credited with (1) remittances in convertible currencies received from abroad through normal banking and

postal channels; (2) proceeds of convertible currencies (banknotes, traveler's checks, drafts, etc.) brought into Bangladesh by the account holders, provided that amounts exceeding $5,000 have been declared to customs upon arrival in Bangladesh; (3) transfers from other foreign currency accounts opened under the former Wage Earners' Scheme (WES); and (4) transfers from nonresident foreign currency deposit accounts. The accounts may be debited without restriction, subject to reporting to Bangladesh Bank.

Nonresident foreign currency deposit accounts. Bangladesh nationals residing abroad; foreign nationals, companies, and firms registered or incorporated abroad; banks and other financial institutions, including institutional investors; officers and staff of Bangladesh missions and government institutions; autonomous bodies; and commercial banks may open interest-bearing nonresident foreign currency deposit accounts denominated in deutsche mark, Japanese yen, pounds sterling, or U.S. dollars. These accounts, whose terms range from one month to one year, may be credited in initial minimum amounts of $1,000 or £500 ($25,000 for foreigners), equivalent, with remittances in convertible currencies and transfers from existing foreign currency deposit accounts maintained by Bangladesh nationals abroad. The balance, including interest earned, may be transferred in foreign exchange by the account holder to any country or to any foreign currency deposit account maintained by Bangladesh nationals abroad. The balances in the accounts, which are freely convertible into taka, must be reported monthly by banks to Bangladesh Bank.

Nonresident Bangladesh who do not open or maintain a foreign currency deposit account while abroad may open a nonresident foreign currency deposit with foreign exchange brought in from abroad within six months of the date of their return to take up permanent residence in Bangladesh.

Resident foreign currency deposit (RFCD) accounts. Resident Bangladesh, at the time of their return from travel abroad, may bring in any amount of foreign currency with a declaration and up to $5,000 or the equivalent without a declaration and may maintain an RFCD account with the foreign exchange brought in. However, proceeds of exports of goods and services from Bangladesh or commissions arising from business deals in Bangladesh are not allowed to be credited to such accounts. Balances in these accounts are freely transferable abroad and may be used for travel in the usual manner. These accounts may be opened in deutsche mark, Japanese yen, pounds sterling, or U.S. dollars. Exporters and local joint-venture firms executing projects financed by a for-

---

[4]The accounts of the United Nations and its agencies are treated as resident accounts.

eign donor or international agency may open foreign currency accounts. Foreign currency accounts may also be opened in the names of diplomatic missions in Bangladesh, their expatriates, and diplomatic bonded warehouses (duty-free shops).

Imports and Import Payments

Imports are financed either from Bangladesh's own resources or from foreign aid, loans, and barter arrangements. Imports are guided by a two-year IPO announced by the Government. The controlled list contains 110 items in about 1,400 categories at the four-digit level of the Harmonized System Codes. The importation of these items is restricted or prohibited either for public safety, religious, environmental, and social reasons, or because similar items are produced locally. Up to 26 items are restricted purely for trade purposes (7 of which are banned and 19 are restricted). Items not specified in the control list of the IPO are freely importable, provided that the importer has a valid import registration certificate. The maximum tariff rate is 50 percent.

All importers (including all government departments with the exception of the Ministry of Defense) are required to obtain letter of credit authorization forms (LCAFs) for all imports. Under the authority of the IPO issued by the Chief Controller, importers are allowed to effect imports against LCAFs issued by authorized dealer banks without an import license. Single-country LCAFs are issued for imports under bilateral trade or payments agreements and for imports under tied-aid programs. LCAFs are otherwise valid worldwide, except that imports from Israel and imports transported on flag vessels of Israel are prohibited. Goods must be shipped within 17 months of the date of issuance of LCAFs in the case of machinery and spare parts and 9 months in the case of all other items.

Payment against imports is generally permissible only under cover of irrevocable letters of credit. Recognized export-oriented units operating under the bonded warehouse system may effect imports of up to four months' requirement of their raw and packing materials by establishing letters of credit without reference to any export letters of credit. They may also effect such imports by opening back-to-back letters of credit (either on a sight basis under the Export Development Fund, or up to 180 days usance basis) against export letters of credit received by them. Public sector importers may import on a cash-against-documents basis, subject to authorization from Bangladesh Bank.

Imports of specified raw materials and packing materials by industrial consumers are governed by an entitlement system, based on the requirements for various industries during each import program period established by the Board of Investment. Firms in the industrial sector are given an entitlement to import specified raw materials and packing materials, and letter of credit authorization forms are issued on the basis of the entitlement. The entitlement system does not apply to raw materials and packing materials that are freely importable but does apply to items appearing on the controlled list. Separately, industrial consumers may be issued with LCAFs for parts and accessories of machinery. Goods imported against LCAFs issued to industrial consumers must be used in the industry concerned and must not be sold or transferred without prior approval.

Authorized dealers may establish letters of credit on an f.o.b. basis without the approval of Bangladesh Bank, subject to the following conditions: (1) cost of goods, cost of freight, and insurance will be accommodated within the amount recorded in the LCAF issued in favor of the importer; (2) cost of freight will be paid locally out of the LCAF value in local currency; and (3) other directives of the IPO will be duly complied with. Foreign exchange for authorized imports is provided automatically by authorized dealers when payments are due. Advance payments for imports require approval from Bangladesh Bank, which is normally given only for specialized or capital goods.

In September 1995, Bangladesh Bank required nationalized commercial banks (NCBs) and domestic private banks to impose a minimum deposit requirement of 25 percent on opening letters of credit for "commercial" imports. In October 1995, the minimum requirement ratios were changed to 50 percent for consumer durable goods, 30 percent for other consumer goods, 15 percent for raw materials, and 10 percent for capital goods. These requirements are, however, not applied to foreign banks, and importers are allowed, without any restrictions, to open letters of credit through these banks. Although there are no penalties for noncompliance, these requirements are generally adhered to by both NCBs and domestic private banks. The deposits are remunerated at market interest rates.

Payments for Invisibles

Payments for invisibles connected with authorized trade transactions are generally not restricted. Applications for foreign exchange for family maintenance and education abroad are accepted upon verification of their bona fide nature. For medical treatment, up to $10,000 can be obtained without prior approval; for larger amounts, the total amount required is granted, subject to the approval of Bangladesh Bank. The indicative allowance for personal travel by resident Bangladesh nationals to countries other than Bhutan, India, Maldives, Myanmar, Nepal, Pakistan, and Sri Lanka is $3,000 a year; the allowance for air travel to these seven countries is $1,000 a person a year. Larger amounts are available upon verification by Bangladesh Bank of the bona fide nature of the request. Foreign currency for education is made available up to the cost of tuition and living expenses, as estimated by the educational institution concerned. Foreign exchange is available for the costs of dependents abroad, after production of a certificate from the Bangladesh embassy in the country concerned, up to a reasonable level assessed by the embassy in light of prevailing prices. For new exporters, the indicative limit for business travel is $6,000, while established exporters are permitted to utilize balances held under the export retention scheme (7.5 percent of exports of ready-made garments and 40 percent of other export proceeds). Manufacturers producing for domestic market and importers are granted, respectively, business travel allowances equivalent to (1) 1 percent of turnover as declared in tax returns, and (2) 1 percent of the value of imports. In both cases, the allowance is subject to an annual ceiling of $5,000. Foreign nationals working in Bangladesh may freely remit up to 50 percent of net salary in terms of service contracts approved by the Government; the entire amount of their leave salaries and savings can also be remitted freely. No prior permission is required for the remittance of royalties and technical fees of up to 6 percent of sales; training and consultancy fees of up to 1 percent of sales; and fees for undergraduate, postgraduate, and some professional courses.

Nonresident travelers may take out the foreign currency and traveler's checks they brought in and declared on entry or up to $5,000 or the equivalent brought in without declaration. They may also, without obtaining the approval of Bangladesh Bank, reconvert taka notes up to Tk 6,000 into convertible foreign currencies at the time of their departure. Resident travelers may take out foreign currency and traveler's checks up to the amount of any travel allowance they are granted, and also up to $5,000 they brought in without declaration while returning from a previous visit abroad. A Bangladesh or a foreign national may take out Tk 500 in domestic currency; otherwise, the exportation of Bangladesh currency notes and coins is prohibited.

Authorized dealers are allowed to remit dividends to nonresident shareholders without the prior approval of Bangladesh Bank on receipt of applications from the companies concerned; applications must be supported by an audited balance sheet and profit-and-loss account, a board resolution declaring dividends out of profit derived from the normal business activities of the company, and an auditor's certificate that tax liabilities are covered. Authorized dealers may remit profits of foreign firms, banks, insurance companies, and other financial institutions operating in Bangladesh to their head office on receipt of applications supported by documentation. These remittances are, however, subject to ex post checking by Bangladesh Bank.

Exports and Export Proceeds

Exports to Israel are prohibited. Exports of about 20 product categories are banned or restricted. Some of these, such as arms, are restricted for nontraded reasons, while others are restricted to ensure the supply of the domestic market. Export licenses are required for all banned or restricted items. Quotas are imposed on garment exports as a result of the Multifiber Arrangement restrictions. Quotas are allocated by the Export Promotion Bureau on the basis of the previous year's performance. The Export Promotion Bureau monitors quota use to be able to reallocate unfilled quotas.

Proceeds from exports must be received within four months of shipment unless otherwise allowed by Bangladesh Bank. Exporters are permitted to retain 7.5 percent of the proceeds of exports of ready-made garments and 40 percent of the proceeds of other exports; they may use retained earnings for bona fide business purposes, such as business travel abroad, participation in trade fairs and seminars, and imports of raw materials, spare parts, and capital goods. They may also be used to set up offices abroad without prior permission from Bangladesh Bank.

Joint ventures, other than in the garment industry, located in export processing zones (EPZs) are allowed to retain 80 percent of their export earnings in a foreign currency deposit account and place the remaining 20 percent in a bank account in domestic currency.

Proceeds from Invisibles

Exporters of services are permitted to retain 5 percent of the proceeds and use retained earnings for bona fide business purposes. Bangladesh nationals working abroad may retain their earnings in foreign currency accounts or in nonresident foreign currency deposit accounts. Unless specifically exempted by Bangladesh Bank, all Bangladesh nationals who reside in Bangladesh must surrender any foreign exchange coming into their possession, whether held in Bangladesh or abroad, to an authorized dealer within one month of the date of acquisition. However, returning residents may keep, in a resident foreign currency account opened in their name, foreign exchange brought in at the time of return from abroad, provided that the amount does not represent proceeds of exports from Bangladesh or commissions earned from business activities in Bangladesh. Residents may retain on hand up to $5,000 brought in without declaration.

Foreign nationals residing in Bangladesh continuously for more than six months are required to surrender within one month of the date of acquisition any foreign exchange representing their earnings in respect of business conducted in Bangladesh or services rendered while in Bangladesh. Foreign exchange held abroad or in Bangladesh by foreign diplomats and by foreign nationals employed in embassies and missions of foreign countries in Bangladesh is, however, exempt from this requirement.

The importation of Bangladesh currency notes and coins exceeding Tk 500 is prohibited. Foreign currency traveler's checks and foreign currency notes may be brought in up to $5,000 without declaration and up to any amount without limit, provided the amount brought in is declared to customs upon arrival in Bangladesh.

Capital

All outward transfers of capital require approval, which is not normally granted for resident-owned capital. Inward capital transfers other than portfolio investment and direct investment in the industrial sector also require approval. Movable and immovable assets, including foreign exchange, owned in any country other than Bangladesh must be declared to Bangladesh Bank by resident Bangladesh nationals. However, Bangladesh residents may continue to maintain foreign currency accounts opened during their stay abroad. There is no restriction on the importation of securities into Bangladesh. The issuing and transfer of shares and securities in favor of nonresidents against foreign investment or inward remittance are allowed without the prior permission of Bangladesh Bank. The transfer of Bangladesh shares and securities from one nonresident holder to another nonresident holder also does not require prior approval from Bangladesh Bank. Nonresident persons and institutions, including nonresident Bangladesh, may buy Bangladesh shares and securities through stock exchanges in Bangladesh against freely convertible foreign currency remitted from abroad through the banking channels. Proceeds from sales including capital gains and dividends earned on the shares or securities bought in this manner may be remitted abroad in freely convertible currency.

Authorized dealers may obtain short-term loans and overdrafts from overseas branches and correspondents for a period not exceeding seven days at a time. Private sector industrial units in Bangladesh may borrow funds from abroad without the approval of the Board of Investment if the interest rate does not exceed 4 percent above the LIBOR, the repayment period is not less than seven years, and the down payment is not more than 10 percent; industrial units in the export promotion zones, including foreign-owned and joint ventures, may obtain short-term foreign loans without prior approval. Local currency loans to enterprises controlled by foreigners or residents do not require Bangladesh Bank's approval. Lending by authorized dealers in local currency against overseas or collateral outside Bangladesh requires approval from Bangladesh Bank. Authorized dealers may grant, without reference to Bangladesh Bank and according to banking practice, loans without a specific limit in domestic currency to foreign-owned manufacturing companies located in Bangladesh. Authorized dealers may also approve loans, overdrafts, or credit facilities against goods intended for exportation from Bangladesh to companies controlled by persons residing outside Bangladesh. Authorized dealers must obtain approval before making any loans in foreign currencies to residents or nonresidents, whether secured or unsecured.

When their work in Bangladesh is finished, expatriate workers may transfer their savings abroad, provided that their salaries and benefits were initially certified by the Board of Investment.

Foreign private investment is governed by the Foreign Private Investment (Promotion and Protection) Act of 1980 and is permitted in collaboration with both the Government and private entrepreneurs. The act provides for the protection and equitable treatment of foreign private investment, indemnification, protection against expropriation and nationalization, and guarantee for repatriation of investment. With the exception of a few reserved sectors, private foreign investment is freely allowed.

There is no ceiling on private investment. Tax holidays are granted for periods of up to nine years, depending on the location. There is no upper limit on the foreign equity portion of an industrial investment, and there is no prior approval requirement for investments, which should, however, be registered with the Investment Board. Nonresidents must also obtain the permission of Bangladesh Bank to continue to operate or to establish an office or branch in Bangladesh for the purpose of trading or for commercial activities. Dividends on foreign capital may be remitted freely after payment of taxes.

Gold

The importation and exportation of gold and silver are prohibited without special permission. However, adult female passengers are free to bring in or take out any amount of gold jewelry without prior approval from Bangladesh Bank. Exports of gold jewelry and imports of gold and silver for exports/ manufacturer of jewelry are also allowed under the Jewelry Export Scheme. There are no restrictions on the internal sale, purchase, or possession of gold or silver ornaments (including coins) and jewelry, but there is a prohibition on the holding of gold and silver in all other forms except by licensed industrialists or dentists.

Changes During 1995

Resident and Nonresident Accounts

August 1. Persons/firms eligible to maintain foreign currency accounts with authorized dealers were permitted to maintain these accounts in deutsche mark, Japanese yen, pounds sterling, and U.S. dollars.

Imports and Import Payments

July 1. The maximum import tariff was reduced to 50 percent from 60 percent.

Payments for Invisibles

July 1. (1) The annual travel allowance for private travel was increased to $1,000 from $500 for visits to SAARC member countries and Myanmar (in case of overland visits, to $500 from $250); and to $3,000 from $2,500 for visits to other countries; (2) manufacturers producing for domestic market and importers were granted, respectively, business travel allow-ance equivalent to (1) 1 percent of turnover as declared to tax authorities and (2) 1 percent of the value of imports settled. In both cases, the allowance is subject to an annual ceiling of $5,000.

Exports and Export Proceeds

June 30. Joint venture (type B) and wholly locally owned (type C) units (other than garment units) in EPZs were allowed to retain in foreign currency accounts up to 80 percent of export receipts, instead of 70 percent.

October 1. The export earnings retention ratio was increased to 7.5 percent from 5 percent for exports of ready-made garments, and to 40 percent from 25 percent for other exports.

Capital

September 1. Bangladesh Bank required nationalized commercial banks (NCBs) and domestic private banks to impose a minimum deposit requirement of 25 percent on opening letters of credit for "commercial" imports. In October 1995, the minimum requirement ratios were changed to 50 percent for consumer durable goods, 30 percent for other consumer goods, 15 percent for raw materials, and 10 percent for capital goods. These requirements were not applied to foreign banks, and importers would be allowed, without any restrictions, to open letters of credit through these banks. Although there were no penalties for noncompliance, the requirements were generally adhered to by both NCBs and domestic private banks. The deposits would be remunerated at market interest rates.

October 1. Bangladesh Bank ceased to prescribe overall foreign currency holding limits for ADs but would continue to prescribe and monitor their open exchange position limits.

Changes During 1996

Exchange Arrangement

January 1. Bangladesh Bank ceased to deal in the currencies of ACU member countries.

BARBADOS

(Position as of December 31, 1995)

Exchange Arrangement

The currency of Barbados is the Barbados Dollar, which is pegged to the U.S. dollar, the intervention currency, at BDS$2 per US$1. On December 31, 1995, the official buying and selling rates for the U.S. dollar were BDS$1.9975 and BDS$2.0350, respectively, per US$1. Buying and selling rates for the Canadian dollar, the deutsche mark, and the pound sterling are also officially quoted on the basis of their cross rate relationships to the U.S. dollar. The quoted rates include commission charges of 0.125 percent buying and 1.75 percent selling against the U.S. dollar, and 0.1875 percent buying and 1.8125 percent selling against the Canadian dollar, the deutsche mark, and the pound sterling.

Under clearing arrangements with regional monetary authorities, the Central Bank of Barbados currently sells currencies of only three Caribbean Common Market (Caricom) countries;[1] these are the Guyana dollar, the Eastern Caribbean dollar, and the Belize dollar. The Trinidad and Tobago dollar and the Jamaica dollar float against the U.S. dollar, and the Central Bank fixes daily selling rates based on rates supplied by the monetary authorities of these countries. These rates are applicable only to government transactions. All selling rates fixed by the Central Bank in respect of Caricom currencies include a commission of 0.125 percent. The Central Bank purchases Eastern Caribbean dollar notes only. The rate applied mutually for the purchase of currency notes is the parity rate between each pair of currencies determined on the basis of the U.S. dollar rate. The Central Bank regulates the commission that the commercial banks may charge their customers for Caricom currencies. Purchases of foreign exchange for private sector remittances abroad (except for remittances for payment of imports, travel allowances, education, and nontrade payments up to BDS$500, and certain other items) are subject to a levy collected in the approval process by the Central Bank at the rate of 1 percent of the value of the transaction.

The Central Bank periodically obtains forward cover in the international foreign exchange market to cover or hedge its own or the central Government's exchange risks associated with foreign exchange loans that are not denominated in U.S. dollars. Commercial banks are allowed to obtain forward cover in the international markets. The Central Bank and commercial banks enter into swap transactions in U.S. dollars, while commercial banks may freely switch between nonregional currencies.

Barbados accepted the obligations of Article VIII, Sections 2, 3, and 4 of the Fund Agreement on November 3, 1993.

Administration of Control

Exchange control applies to all countries and is administered by the Central Bank, which delegates to authorized dealers the authority to approve normal import payments and the allocation of foreign exchange for certain other current payments and for cash gifts. Security considerations do not influence decisions on payments restrictions. The exchange control system stipulates that foreign exchange should normally be surrendered to an authorized dealer. Trade controls are administered by the Ministry of Industry, Commerce, and Business Development.

Prescription of Currency

Settlements with residents of countries outside the Caricom area may be made in any foreign currency,[2] or through an external account in Barbados dollars. Settlements with residents of Caricom countries, other than Jamaica and Trinidad and Tobago, must be made either through external accounts (in Barbados dollars) or in the currency of the Caricom country concerned, except that commercial banks may issue U.S. dollar traveler's checks to Barbadian residents traveling to other Caricom countries, within the approved limits for travel allowances. With effect from September 21, 1991, and April 13, 1993, the Bank of Jamaica and the Central Bank of Trinidad and Tobago abolished exchange control in Jamaica and Trinidad and Tobago, respectively; as a result, settlements with residents of Jamaica and Trinidad and Tobago are made in U.S. dollars.

---

[1]The Caricom countries are Antigua and Barbuda, The Bahamas, Barbados, Belize, Dominica, Grenada, Guyana, Jamaica, Montserrat, St. Kitts and Nevis, St. Lucia, St. Vincent and the Grenadines, and Trinidad and Tobago.

[2]Foreign currencies comprise all currencies other than the Barbados dollar.

Resident and Nonresident Accounts

Authorized dealers may, in most instances, maintain foreign currency accounts in the names of residents of Barbados and of other countries. Such accounts are opened on the basis of anticipated frequency of receipts and payments in foreign currency. Certain receipts and payments may be credited and debited to foreign currency accounts under conditions established at the time the account is opened. Other credits and debits require individual approval. However, where authority has not been delegated to authorized dealers, the permission of the Central Bank is required.

Authorized dealers may open external accounts for nonresidents without consulting the Central Bank. These accounts, maintained in Barbados dollars, may be credited with proceeds from the sale of foreign currencies, with transfers from other external accounts, with bank interest (payable on external accounts or blocked accounts), and with payments by residents for which the Central Bank has given general or specific permission. They may be debited for payments to residents of Barbados, for the cost of foreign exchange required for travel or business purposes, and for any other payment covered by delegated authority to authorized dealers. Other debits and any overdrafts require individual approval.

The Exchange Control Act of 1967 (as amended) empowers the Central Bank to require certain payments in favor of nonresidents that are ineligible for transfer to be credited to blocked accounts. Balances in blocked accounts may not be withdrawn without approval, other than for the purchase of approved securities.

Imports and Import Payments

Certain imports require individual licenses.[3] However, not all goods that are subject to import licensing are subject to quantitative restrictions or import surcharges. Some items on the import-licensing list may be freely imported throughout the year, while others are subject to temporary restrictions (particularly

---

[3]On August 17, 1995, the following items were deleted from the list of items requiring import licenses: orange juice concentrate, other orange juice, grapefruit juice concentrate, and other grapefruit juice; organic surface active agents, surface active preparations, washing preparations, and cleaning preparations, whether or not containing soap; transport-type passenger motor vehicles, cars, and other motor vehicles, including station wagons and racing cars, principally designed for the transport of persons (not for public transport); chassis with or without engines for the assembly of coaches and buses; and yachts and other vessels for pleasure or sport. On November 16, 1995, uncooked pasta, unstuffed or otherwise prepared, was added to the list of items requiring import licenses.

agricultural products, which tend to be subject to seasonal restrictions). Individual licenses are also required for imports of commodities that are subject to the provisions of the Oils and Fats Agreement between the governments of Barbados, Dominica, Grenada, Guyana, St. Lucia, St. Vincent and the Grenadines, and Trinidad and Tobago, whether the goods are being imported from CARICOM countries or from elsewhere. Special licensing arrangements have been made for the regulation of trade between Barbados and other CARICOM countries in 22 agricultural commodities.

The customs duty rates on most goods range from 5 percent to 30 percent, the same range as the Common External Tariff (CET) of the CARICOM region. The maximum tariff was lowered to 30 percent on April 1, 1995. Import surcharges in the form of stamp duties, consumption taxes, and luxury taxes amount to a total of up to 203 percent.

Payments for authorized imports, including derivatives of crude oil other than reformate, are permitted upon application and submission of documentary evidence (invoices and customs warrants) to authorized dealers; payments for imports of crude oil and its derivatives are subject to the prior approval of the Central Bank. Authorized dealers may release foreign currency up to the equivalent of BDS$100,000 (c.i.f.) for advance payments for imports into Barbados. Other advance payments require the prior approval of the Central Bank.

Payments for Invisibles

Payments for invisibles require exchange control approval. Payments for all commercial transactions are permitted freely when the application is supported by appropriate documentary evidence.

Authority has been delegated to authorized dealers to provide basic allocations of foreign exchange for certain personal and sundry payments. These include foreign travel (for which up to BDS$5,000 a person a calendar year may be allocated for private travel inside or outside the CARICOM area); and BDS$500 a day for business travel, up to BDS$40,000 a person a calendar year, expenses for education abroad (BDS$40,000 a person a year), remittances of cash gifts not exceeding BDS$1,000 a donor a year, subscriptions to newspapers and magazines (BDS$50,000 a person a year), remittances for medical purposes up to BDS$50,000 a year, income tax refunds, official payments, and life insurance premiums. Authority has also been delegated to authorized dealers to provide foreign exchange in respect to other current transactions such as profits, dividends, and interest up to BDS$100,000 a transaction, royalties and management fees not exceeding BDS$250,000 a transaction, other current payments including services, up to BDS$250,000 a transaction, and other insurance payments and premiums, excluding investment, pension, and surplus funds, as long as the amount is approved for payment by the Supervisor of Insurance. Applications for additional amounts or for purposes for which there is no basic allocation are approved by the authorities, provided that no unauthorized transfer of capital appears to be involved. The cost of transportation to any destination may be settled in domestic currency and is not deducted from the travel allocation.

Any person traveling to a destination outside Barbados may take out foreign currency notes and coins up to the value of BDS$500 and Barbados notes up to BDS$200. Nonresident visitors may freely export any foreign currency they previously brought in.

Exports and Export Proceeds

Specific licenses are required for the exportation of certain goods to any country, including rice, cane sugar, rum, molasses, and certain other food products, sewing machines, portland cement, and petroleum products. All other goods may be exported without license. The collection of export proceeds is supervised by the Central Bank to ensure that foreign exchange proceeds are surrendered to authorized dealers within six months of the date of shipment. Exports of sugar to the United Kingdom and the United States are subject to bilateral export quotas, as are exports of rum to the European Union.

Proceeds from Invisibles

Foreign currency proceeds from invisibles must be sold to authorized dealers. Travelers to Barbados may freely bring in notes and coins denominated in Barbados dollars or in any foreign currency. Residents returning to Barbados are required to sell their holdings of foreign currencies to an authorized dealer.

Capital

All outward capital transfers, including direct investments by residents and the purchase by residents of foreign currency securities and real estate abroad, require exchange control approval. Certificates of title to foreign currency securities held by residents must be lodged with an authorized depository in Barbados, and earnings on these securities must be repatriated and surrendered to an authorized dealer.

Personal capital transfers, such as inheritances due to nonresidents, require exchange control approval. Transfers in respect of inheritances are restricted to BDS$30,000 a year for each nonresident beneficiary. Dowries in the form of settlements and cash gifts may be transferred to nonresidents under delegated authority, normally up to BDS$1,000 a donor a year. Emigrating Barbadian nationals are granted settling-in allowances from their declared assets at the rate of BDS$30,000 a family unit a year. The Central Bank also considers applications from foreign nationals who have resided in Barbados and are proceeding to take up permanent residence abroad, provided that they declare the assets they hold in Barbados.

Direct investment by nonresidents may be made with exchange control approval. The remittance of earnings on, and liquidation of proceeds from, such investment is permitted, provided that evidence documenting the validity of the remittance is submitted, all liabilities related to the investment have been discharged, and the original investment was registered with the Central Bank.

The issuance and transfer to nonresidents of securities registered in Barbados require exchange control approval, which is freely given provided that an adequate amount of foreign currency is brought in for their purchase. Proceeds from the realization of these securities may be remitted when it is established that the original investment was financed from foreign currency sources. Nonresidents may acquire real estate in Barbados for private purposes with funds from foreign currency sources; local currency financing is not ordinarily permitted. Proceeds from the realization of such investments equivalent to the amount of foreign currency brought in may be repatriated freely. Capital sums realized in excess of this amount may be repatriated freely on the basis of a calculated rate of return on the original foreign investment, as follows: for the last five years, at 8 percent a year; for the five years immediately preceding the last five years, at 5 percent; and for any period preceding the last ten years, at 4 percent. Amounts in excess of the sum so derived are restricted to the remittance of BDS$30,000 a year.

The approval of the Central Bank is required for residents to borrow abroad or for nonresidents to borrow in Barbados. Authorized dealers may assume short-term liability positions in foreign currencies for the financing of approved transfers in respect of both trade and nontrade transactions. They may also freely accept deposits from nonresidents. Any borrowing abroad by authorized dealers to finance their domestic operations requires the approval of the Central Bank.

A 6 percent tax is levied on portfolio investments of pension funds with foreign companies that are not registered with the Barbados Supervisor of Insurance.

Gold

Gold coins with face values of BDS$50, BDS$100, BDS$150, BDS$200, and BDS$500 are legal tender and are in limited circulation. Residents who are private persons are permitted to acquire and hold gold coins for numismatic purposes only. Otherwise, any gold acquired in Barbados must be surrendered to an authorized dealer, unless exchange control approval is obtained for its retention. Residents other than monetary authorities, authorized dealers, and industrial users are not permitted to hold or acquire gold in any form other than jewelry or coins for numismatic purposes. The importation of gold by residents is permitted for industrial purposes and is subject to customs duties and charges. Licenses to import gold are issued by the Ministry of Industry, Commerce, and Business Development; no license is required to export gold, but exchange control permission is required.

Changes During 1995

Administration of Control

March 1. Authorized dealers were allowed to release foreign exchange for (1) advertising, legal fees, commissions, subscriptions, and film processing not exceeding BDS$50,000 a nonresident beneficiary; (2) dividends, profits, and interest not exceeding BDS$100,000 a transaction; (3) personal loan repayments not exceeding BDS$20,000 a year; (4) advance payments for imports into Barbados up to BDS$100,000 c.i.f., against specified documentary evidence; (5) education not exceeding BDS$40,000 a person an academic year; and (6) management fees and royalties not exceeding BDS$250,000 a transaction.

Authorized dealers may open and maintain foreign currency accounts for companies operating in Barbados earning a minimum of BDS$100,000 annually in foreign exchange; open and maintain foreign currency accounts in the names of nonresidents of Barbados; and open and maintain foreign currency accounts for residents of Barbados earning at least BDS$50,000 annually in foreign exchange.

Imports and Import Payments

April 1. The maximum import tariff was lowered to 30 percent.

August 7. The following items were deleted from the list of items requiring import licenses: orange juice concentrate, other orange juice, grapefruit juice concentrate, and other grapefruit juice; organic surface active agents, surface active preparations, washing preparations, and cleaning preparations, whether or not containing soap; transport-type passenger motor vehicles, cars and other motor vehicles, including station wagons and racing cars, principally designed for the transport of persons (not for public transport); chassis with or without engines for the assembly of coaches and buses; and yachts and other vessels for pleasure or sport.

November 16. Uncooked pasta, unstuffed or otherwise prepared, was added to the list of items requiring import licenses.

BELARUS

(Position as of December 31, 1995)

Exchange Arrangement

The currency of Belarus is the Rubel. On August 20, 1994, the rubel become the unit of account replacing the Belarussian ruble, which was formally recognized as the sole legal tender on May 18, 1994.[1] The conversion took place at the rate of 10 Belarussian rubles per 1 rubel. Restrictions on conversion of noncash rubles into cash (and vice versa) were abolished on December 31, 1995. This has eliminated the differentiation that existed between cash and noncash rubels against foreign currencies. The exchange rates of the rubel against the U.S. dollar, the deutsche mark, the Russian ruble, and the Ukrainian karbovanets are established in daily auctions[2] at the Minsk Interbank Currency Exchange, with the participation of the commercial banks licensed to conduct foreign currency operations and the National Bank of Belarus. The authorities regularly intervene in the auctions. On December 31, 1995, the exchange rate for the U.S. dollar was Rbl 11,500 per $1.

Banks can buy foreign currencies at the auction only for confirmed import orders.[3] Authorized banks are also free to trade foreign currencies on the interbank market, although this market was effectively closed in November 1995, when a low maximum trading amount was set. There is no formal forward market in foreign currency.

Repatriation of profits in convertible currencies is subject to a 15 percent tax payable in a convertible currency.

Administration of Control

The Parliament is responsible for legislating exchange control regulations and the National Bank is responsible for administering them. The authority to amend exchange control regulations rests with the Parliament, which determines general principles and adopts laws on foreign exchange regulations and control. Foreign exchange regulations are based on provisional regulations issued by the Parliament in March 1992 and subsequently amended on occasion. The National Bank manages the Government's official currency reserves, except for a small amount of government deposits, which are controlled by the Cabinet of Ministers through the Ministry of Finance. Local governments control the local foreign exchange funds. Foreign exchange for official import payments is administratively allocated through state and local government foreign exchange funds.

Only banks may obtain licenses to engage in foreign exchange transactions. Enterprises may obtain permission to open foreign exchange offices, sell goods, and render services for freely convertible currency within Belarus. About half of the commercial banks operating in Belarus hold a general license that enables them to open correspondent accounts outside the country; banks holding a domestic license can conduct foreign exchange operations through general licensed banks. A small number of banks are not allowed to conduct foreign exchange operations.

Prescription of Currency

Payments to countries with which Belarus has bilateral payments agreements are effected in the currencies specified in these agreements and in accordance with their regulations.[4] Payments in the currencies of the Baltic countries, Russia, and the other countries of the former Soviet Union are made in accordance with the rules specified in an agreement signed on October 21, 1994. The agreement with these countries provides for settlement through bilateral clearing accounts held with central banks or authorized commercial banks. Recently, about 10 percent of such settlements have taken place through central bank correspondent accounts, with the balance being settled through commercial bank correspondent accounts. Since January 1, 1995, no trade, other than certain trade with Russia, goes through official correspondent accounts. Settlement may take place in convertible currencies, national currencies, or Russian rubles.

Bilateral clearing accounts have been established with the Baltic countries, Russia, and the other countries of the former Soviet Union. However, there were only two intergovernmental clearing agreements in 1995: the "Roscontract" agreement with

---

[1] Prior to August 20, 1994, the Russian ruble also served as legal tender in Belarus.

[2] Prospective buyers are obliged to pay the countervalue in domestic currency into a special account before the auction takes place.

[3] In November 1995, a list of imports, for which priority is given for purchases of foreign exchange in the auctions, was adopted.

[4] At the end of 1995, Belarus maintained bilateral trade and/or payments agreements with Bulgaria, China, Cuba, Czech Republic, Finland, Hungary, the Democratic People's Republic of Korea, Mongolia, Poland, Slovak Republic, Slovenia, and Vietnam.

Russia, which specified the intergovernmental exchange of crude oil from Russia for strategic products from Belarus, and a clearing agreement with Uzbekistan calling for the exchange of cotton from Uzbekistan for strategic goods from Belarus on a balanced basis.

Foreign trade payments outside the Baltic countries, Russia, and the other countries of the former Soviet Union are made in convertible currency. A significant, albeit declining, share of trade is conducted within the framework of barter agreements. An attempt is being made to balance the trade with a cash-trading partner, but if an imbalance emerges, it is settled with deliveries of goods or in convertible currency. Since September 9, 1992, barter trade of certain goods has required approval from the Commission of the Council of Ministers on the Issuance of Authorization to Engage in Commodity-Exchange Operations.

Payments in foreign currency for goods and services (including wage payments) in connection with transactions among residents are prohibited.

Resident and Nonresident Accounts

Without declaring the sources of their foreign exchange, residents may open foreign currency accounts at commercial banks in Belarus that are authorized to deal in foreign exchange. Residents may maintain bank accounts abroad only with the permission of the National Bank. Foreign exchange earnings by resident juridical persons must be repatriated within 60 days of the date the exports leave the country, and these funds must transit accounts of authorized banks in Belarus, unless the Ministry of Foreign Economic Relations approves a delay in this repatriation.[5]

Nonresident juridical persons may maintain foreign exchange accounts with authorized banks in Belarus. The sources of the funds can be receipts from abroad; proceeds from the sale of goods and services in the territory of Belarus, including sales to residents; debt-service payments; interest earned on balances in the accounts; funds from other foreign exchange accounts of nonresidents in Belarus; and earnings from investments in the Baltic countries, Russia, and the other countries of the former Soviet Union. These accounts may be debited for purchases of goods and services and for investments in the Baltic countries, Russia, and the other countries of the former Soviet Union, as well as for payments to resi-

dents and nonresidents. Funds from these accounts may be freely repatriated or exchanged for rubels at the market exchange rate through authorized banks.

Nonresident juridical persons can also open two types of accounts in rubels at authorized commercial banks. These are designated as "L" accounts and "N" accounts. L accounts can be credited with the rubel counterpart of foreign exchange sold to the National Bank or authorized banks, dividends from foreign-owned enterprises or joint ventures, returns on securities, and sales of such securities within Belarus. Funds from these accounts may be used freely in the territory of the Republic of Belarus and may be converted into foreign currency at the market exchange rate. N accounts can be funded by proceeds from the sale of goods produced in Belarus or from the sale of goods directly imported from abroad. Balances in these accounts may be used only for business travel expenses; to purchase inputs used for the production of goods for export from Belarus; to purchase foreign exchange at the market exchange rate at auctions (up to the limit of nonresidents' initial investment plus proceeds from sales of their output in Belarus); for payment of wages; and for investment purposes as determined by the Government with the permission of the Ministry of Foreign Economic Relations.[6]

Imports and Exports

Trade with the Baltic countries, Russia, and the other countries of the former Soviet Union is conducted primarily through intergovernmental agreements or interenterprise deals.

The bilateral trade agreements Belarus maintains with other countries include appendices that list the goods to be delivered by each party.[7] In some cases these lists include volume and/or prices. Increasingly, these lists are used only as indicators. The guarantee of the delivery of goods under these agreements was previously in the form of state orders. However, state orders have been reduced and, for most products, constitute less than 30 percent of total bilateral trade under the agreements (except for oil and certain chemical products, where state orders may exceed 50 percent of the total).[8]

---

[5]The period allowed for repatriation of export proceeds is 180 days for barter transactions and 30 days for service transactions. With the approval of the National Bank, the transit account may be held in a bank abroad.

[6]Restrictions on the conversion of funds held in nonresident accounts were reintroduced in November 1995.

[7]Belarus has long-term bilateral trade agreements with Kazakstan, Kyrgyz Republic, Ukraine, and Uzbekistan. Annual protocols are signed under these agreements each year. Belarus regularly signs annual agreements with Latvia, Lithuania, Moldova, Russia, and Tajikistan. Negotiations are under way on a protocol for a bilateral trade agreement with Armenia.

[8]Enterprises that fill state orders have priority access to products imported under trade agreements.

Therefore, trade under these agreements is increasingly conducted directly by the enterprises with the assistance of such organizations as Belkontract. Defense-related goods are excluded from trade agreements.

Bilateral trade agreements are used primarily for two reasons. First, goods traded under such agreements are generally subject to zero or reduced tax rates; second, for key goods from some countries, access to these goods is possible only via a quota that is issued by that country's government as part of a bilateral trade agreement.

Trade in these products exceeding the volume specified in the appendices and in products not included in the appendices of the trade agreements is mainly conducted through interenterprise deals. Settlement difficulties, primarily due to lack of foreign exchange on the part of one or both enterprises, have caused most such deals to be conducted on a barter basis.

As a result of the customs union agreement between Belarus and Russia signed January 6, 1995, and the Protocol on Free Trade between Belarus and Russia signed on January 5, 1995, there are now no customs barriers on trade between the two countries, and the countries have adopted a common trade policy toward other countries.

Since May 1, 1995, export earnings in Russian rubles are exempt from surrender requirements. All export proceeds must be deposited in a "transit" account in a bank in Belarus within 60 days of shipping, unless special permission for a longer period of repatriation has been approved by the Ministry of Foreign Economic Relations; the period is 180 days for goods exported under a barter or clearing contract and 30 days for service exports.

Surrender requirements on foreign exchange proceeds in convertible currencies were eliminated as of July 1, 1995. Prior to the elimination of the surrender requirements, these proceeds were sold in the interbank currency auction. Export proceeds in convertible currencies are subject to the same repatriation requirements as those exports to countries of the Baltic countries, Russia, and the other countries of the former Soviet Union.

Residents do not need a license or approval from the National Bank to conduct foreign exchange operations related to trade, except for (1) down payments for imports or services exceeding $10,000 or the equivalent that represent more than 30 percent of the value of the goods or services imported; (2) payments for imports more than 60 days in advance of receipt of the goods in Belarus, which requires the advance permission of the Ministry of Foreign Economic Relations;[9] and (3) interest pay-

ments to nonresidents on returned down payments when an original contract is not fulfilled. Foreign exchange purchased for imports has to be used within a period of 30 days from the date of purchase.

Export bans exist for some medicinal herbs, arts and antique collections, certain wild animals, goods imported into Belarus on a humanitarian basis, and certain types of leather. The list of items under export quotas and licensing requirements includes only crude oil and some refined oil products, mineral fertilizers, and certain types of nonprocessed timber. Belarus had abolished all export taxes on December 2, 1994. However, under the customs union agreement with Russia, Belarus adopted Russian export taxes by Decree 218 of the Cabinet of Ministers, approved April 19, 1995.[10]

A new import tariff structure was similarly introduced by the Cabinet of Ministers Decree 219, approved on April 19, 1995, whereby Belarus adopted Russian import duties. As a result of changes in Russian customs duties, Belarus adopted a new amended Decree 340 of June 29, 1995. These duties were implemented in three phases (on May 1, June 10, and August 20, 1995). Import duty rates for goods subject to minimum rates (plants, seeds, individual foodstuffs, raw materials, ores, petroleum, and spare parts) range from 1 percent to 5 percent, while import duty rates for goods subject to maximum rates (weapons, ammunition, precious metal products, carpets, and motor vehicles) range from 40 percent to 100 percent. There are numerous exceptions. Regular import duty rates apply to countries that have been accorded most-favored-nation treatment. Import duty rates are doubled if goods are imported from a country that has not been accorded most-favored-nation treatment. These are halved or reduced to zero for developing countries covered by Russia's provisional system of preferences. The importing of radioactive or toxic wastes, as well as publications or videos that are against state morals, health, or security are prohibited, while import licenses are required for the importing of certain pesticides, herbicides, and industrial wastes.

Payments for and Proceeds from Invisibles

Resident individuals are permitted to purchase up to $500 a year at the market exchange rate for tourist travel; larger amounts may be taken out with cus-

---

[9]For goods imported under barter or clearing arrangements, the period is 180 days, while for service imports, the period is 30 days.
[10]A wide range of exported goods, including pharmaceuticals, fish, meat, weapons, crude petroleum, natural gas, gasoline, and fertilizers, are subject to ad valorem or specific rates.

toms declaration proof that they were brought into Belarus or with a certificate from an authorized bank that they were exchanged legally. However, persons with international credit cards who use such cards for tourist travel expenses can purchase foreign exchange to settle the obligations on those cards. There are no restrictions on the purchase of foreign exchange for bona fide expenses related to business travel or invisible transactions such as education, medical treatment, family maintenance, repatriation of salaries and wages, payment of insurance premiums, and profit remittances.

Post-1992 Russian banknotes up to Rub 500 may be taken abroad or brought into the country when traveling to the Baltic countries, Russia, and the other countries of the former Soviet Union; a similar policy applies to the importation and exportation of rubel banknotes, for which the limit is Rbl 100,000 for travel to the Baltic countries, Russia, and the other countries of the former Soviet Union. Residents of the Baltic countries, Russia, and the other countries of the former Soviet Union may pay for air and train tickets as well as hotel expenses in Russian rubles; nonresidents may be required to pay for these expenses in a convertible currency.

Capital

The properties owned by foreign investors in Belarus are protected from expropriation.[11] Foreign investors are guaranteed full freedom to repatriate their initial investment capital and profits earned in Belarus. Foreign investment must be registered at the Ministry of Foreign Economic Relations and, in the case of financial institutions, also at the National Bank. At the time of registration, the enterprise obtains a license to engage in activities in a particular area of specialization and may not pursue other activities. The proportion of equity capital share by nonresidents in direct investments is not restricted, except in the financial sector where it cannot exceed 49 percent. Nonresidents may participate in foreign exchange auctions through authorized banks. As of March 29, 1995, the importing of securities issued by non-Belarussian companies is prohibited, except with the approval of the Ministry of Finance.

Enterprises with more than 30 percent foreign capital ownership are permitted to export their products and import inputs necessary for their production without restriction. These enterprises are exempted from income tax for the three years fol-

---

[11]The law on Foreign Investment of the Supreme Soviet (dated November 14, 1991) guarantees that terms offered to foreign investors would remain unchanged for at least five years.

lowing the first year the enterprise reports a profit. If the enterprise is deemed to be essential for the economy of Belarus by the Cabinet of Ministers, the income tax rate may be reduced by 50 percent for an additional three-year period.

External borrowing by residents must be registered with the Ministry of Finance, and the opening of bank accounts abroad requires approval from the National Bank.

Gold

A license is required for the exportation of gold, which is on the short list of products (together with arms, radioactive materials, and narcotics) under the strictest licensing requirements.

Changes During 1995

Exchange Arrangement

January 1. The restrictions on the conversion of noncash rubels into cash rubels were removed, and the foreign exchange market, which had been segmented into cash and noncash transactions, was unified.

July 1. Banks were authorized to trade both U.S. dollars and Russian rubles on the interbank market in addition to the auction market (Resolution No. 543, National Bank of Belarus, adopted in June).

November 1. A list of imports, for which priority is given for purchases of foreign exchange in the auctions, was adopted.

November 13. A low maximum trading amount was set for operations in the interbank market that effectively closed it down.

Resident and Nonresident Accounts

August 2. The limitation on the convertibility of interest earned on so-called rubel "N" accounts was removed (National Bank letter No. 629 to banks).

November 13. Restrictions on the conversion of funds held in nonresident accounts were reintroduced.

Imports and Exports

January 6. The customs union agreement between Belarus and Russia was signed.

April 19. Belarus adopted Russian export taxes (Decree No. 218 of the Cabinet of Ministers) and decided to adopt Russian import duties in three phases: on May 1, June 10, and August 1, 1995 (Decree No. 219 of the Cabinet of Ministers).

May 1. Surrender requirements for export earnings in Russian rubles were eliminated.

May 1. Repatriation requirements were tightened. All export proceeds were required to be deposited in a "transit" account in a bank in Belarus or, with special permission of the National Bank, abroad (Presidential Decree No. 52).

May 15. Surrender requirements for export proceeds in U.S. dollars and other hard currencies were reduced to 30 percent.

May 26. The customs union between Russia and Belarus came into effect. All export taxes on trade, as well as other barriers between the two countries, were eliminated. Belarus adopted new schedules for export and import tariffs to conform with those in effect in Russia.

June 27. The lists of minimum and maximum export and import prices were abolished (Resolution No. 334 of the Cabinet of Ministers).

June 29. The schedule for import duties was amended as a result of changes in Russian customs duties (Decree No. 340 of the Cabinet of Ministers).

July 1. Surrender requirements for export proceeds in U.S. dollars and other hard currencies were eliminated.

November 13. The period within which foreign exchange purchased for imports must be used was reduced to 30 days from 45 days.

Capital

March 29. Imports of securities issued by non-Belarussian companies were subject to the approval of the Ministry of Finance.

BELGIUM AND LUXEMBOURG

(Position as of December 31, 1995)

Exchange Arrangement

The currency of Belgium is the Belgian Franc, and the currency of Luxembourg is the Luxembourg Franc. Belgium and Luxembourg are linked in a monetary association, and the Luxembourg franc is at par with the Belgian franc. Belgium and Luxembourg participate with Austria, Denmark, France, Germany, Ireland, the Netherlands, Portugal, and Spain in the exchange rate and intervention mechanism (ERM) of the European Monetary System (EMS).[1] In accordance with this agreement, Belgium and Luxembourg maintain spot exchange rates between their currencies and the currencies of the other participants within margins of 15 percent above or below the cross rates derived from the central rates expressed in European currency units (ECUs).[2]

The agreement implies that the National Bank of Belgium stands ready to buy or sell the currencies of the other participating states in unlimited amounts at specified intervention rates. On December 31, 1995, these rates were as follows:

Specified Intervention Rates Per:	Belgian Francs or Luxembourg Francs	
	Upper limit	Lower limit
100 Austrian schilling	340.4200	252.4700
100 Danish kroner	627.8800	465.6650
100 Deutsche mark	2,395.2000	1,776.2000
100 French francs	714.0300	529.6600
1 Irish pound	57.7445	42.8260
100 Netherlands guilders	2,125.6000	1,576.4500
100 Portuguese escudos[3]	23.3645	17.3285
100 Spanish pesetas[4]	28.1525	20.8795

The participants in the EMS do not maintain the exchange rates for other currencies within fixed lim-

its. However, to ensure a proper functioning of the system, they intervene in concert to smooth out fluctuations in exchange rates, the intervention currencies being each other's and the U.S. dollar.

There are no taxes or subsidies on purchases or sales of foreign exchange. On December 29, 1995, the indicative middle rate for the U.S. dollar was BF 29.445 per $1.

Banks are allowed to engage in spot and forward exchange transactions in any currency, and they may deal among themselves and with residents and nonresidents in foreign notes and coins.

Belgium and Luxembourg accepted the obligations of Article VIII, Sections 2, 3, and 4 of the Fund Agreement on February 15, 1961.

Administration of Control

In general, there are no exchange controls. In accordance with the Fund's Executive Board Decision No. 144-(52/51) adopted in August 14, 1952, Belgium notified the Fund that, in compliance with UN Security Council Resolution No. 757 (1992), certain restrictions had been imposed on the making of payments and transfers for current international transactions in respect of the Federal Republic of Yugoslavia (Serbia/Montenegro). Belgium also imposed restrictions against Iraq and Libya.

The Belgian-Luxembourg Administrative Commission has the authority to license trade transactions; it determines import and export policy but has delegated authority to issue import and export licenses to the licensing offices of the Belgian-Luxembourg Economic Union (BLEU), one of which is located in each country. Bank supervision in Belgium is exercised by the Banking and Finance Commission and in Luxembourg, by the Luxembourg Monetary Institute (LMI).

For purposes of compiling balance of payments statistics, residents are required to transmit to the Belgian-Luxembourg Exchange Institute (BLEI) the following information on all of their professional transactions with foreign countries: amount, currency, economic nature, and country of residence of the foreign party in the transaction. For foreign payments executed or received through a bank in Belgium or Luxembourg, residents provide this information to the BLEI through their banks; for all other professional foreign transactions, residents report to the BLEI directly on a monthly basis.

---

[1] The United Kingdom withdrew from the exchange rate and intervention mechanism of the EMS on September 16, 1992, and Italy withdrew on September 17, 1992.

[2] Effective August 2, 1993, the intervention thresholds of the currencies participating in the ERM of the EMS, except those of the deutsche mark and the Netherlands guilder, were widened from ±2.25 percent to ±15 percent around the bilateral central exchange rates; the fluctuation band of the deutsche mark and the Netherlands guilder remained unchanged at ±2.25 percent.

[3] Prior to March 6, 1995, the upper and lower limits were 24.2120 and 17.9570, respectively.

[4] Prior to March 6, 1995, the upper and lower limits were 30.2715 and 22.4510, respectively.

Prescription of Currency

No prescription of currency requirements are in force.

Imports and Import Payments

Payments for imports may be made freely. Individual licenses are required for (1) certain specified imports from all countries,[5] including many textile and steel products, certain agricultural products and foodstuffs, diamonds, weapons, and products other than textiles from China. All other commodities are free of license requirements. Many commodities subject to individual licensing are also admitted without quantitative restriction. Along with other EU countries, the BLEU applies quotas on a number of textile products from non-EU countries in the framework of the Multifiber Arrangement (MFA) quota on a number of steel products from Russia, Ukraine, and Kazakstan, and quotas on a number of products from China (toys, shoes, ceramics, porcelain, and glassware) and also applies a system of minimum import prices to foreign steel products.

Imports from non-EU countries of most products covered by the Common Agricultural Policy (CAP) of the EU are subject to import levies, which have replaced all previous barriers to imports. Common EU regulations are also applied to imports of most other agricultural and livestock products from non-EU countries.

Payments for Invisibles

All payments for invisibles may be made freely. Domestic and foreign banknotes and coins and other means of payment may be exported freely.

Exports and Export Proceeds

Export licenses are required only for a few products, mostly of a strategic character, and for diamonds, and some iron and steel products.

Foreign exchange proceeds from exports do not have to be surrendered and may be used for all payments.

---

[5]Most imports do not require an import license when imported from the member countries of the European Union (EU).

Proceeds from Invisibles

There are no restrictions on the receipt of payments for services rendered to nonresidents. Domestic and foreign notes and coins and other means of payment may be imported freely.

Capital

Residents and nonresidents may export capital freely. Investments, whether direct or portfolio, may be freely made in the BLEU by nonresidents or abroad by residents. There are no restrictions on transactions in Belgian or Luxembourg francs or foreign currency securities, which may be exported or imported without formality. Banks may freely accept foreign currency deposits from residents or nonresidents.

The prior approval of the Ministry of Finance is required for issues of securities on the Belgian capital market by nonresidents and for public bids by nonresidents for the purchase or exchange of shares issued by Belgian companies except if the foreign company or individual involved is a resident of an EU country.

Bonds denominated in Belgian or Luxembourg francs may be issued freely on the Luxembourg capital market. After they are issued, they are reported to the Luxembourg Monetary Institute, mainly for statistical purposes.

Gold

Residents may freely purchase, hold, and sell gold coins and bars, at home or abroad. Imports and exports of gold in these forms by residents and nonresidents are unrestricted and free of license. Settlements of gold may be made freely. Imports and transactions in monetary gold are subject to a 1 percent value-added tax in Belgium.

Changes During 1995

No significant changes occurred in the exchange and trade system.

(See Appendix for a summary of trade measures introduced and eliminated on an EU-wide basis during 1995.)

BELIZE

(Position as of December 31, 1995)

Exchange Arrangement

The currency of Belize is the Belize Dollar, which is pegged to the U.S. dollar, the intervention currency, at a rate of BZ$1 per US$0.50. The buying and selling rates for transactions between the Central Bank of Belize and the commercial banks are BZ$1.9937 and BZ$2.0063, respectively, per US$1. On December 31, 1995, the buying and selling rates in transactions between the banks and members of the public were BZ$1.9825 and BZ$2.0175, respectively, per US$1. The Central Bank quotes daily rates for the Canadian dollar, the pound sterling, and a number of currencies of member countries of CARICOM.[1] A stamp duty of 1.25 percent is levied on all conversions from the Belize dollar to a foreign currency.

Belize accepted the obligations of Article VIII, Sections 2, 3, and 4 of the Fund Agreement on June 14, 1983.

Administration of Control

The Central Bank is responsible for administering exchange control, which applies to all countries. Authority covering a wide range of operations is delegated to the commercial banks in their capacity as authorized dealers. Only in exceptional cases or in applications involving substantial amounts is reference made directly to the Central Bank. However, all applications for foreign exchange processed by authorized dealers are regularly forwarded to the Central Bank for audit and record keeping. The Ministry of Commerce and Industry administers trade controls.

Prescription of Currency

The only prescription of currency requirement relates to a specified list of currencies[2] in which authorized intermediaries are permitted to deal with the public. Payments to a CARICOM member country must be made in the currency of that country.

Nonresident Accounts

Banks must have permission from the Central Bank to open external or foreign currency accounts. The Central Bank may also stipulate that sums to be credited or paid to foreign residents be credited to a blocked account.

Imports and Import Payments

Payments for imports require authorization from the Central Bank; in most cases such authorization is delegated to the commercial banks. However, in June 1995, the Central Bank began to ration its sales of foreign exchange to commercial banks on an ad hoc basis, except for a few essential import items such as fuel and pharmaceuticals. For reasons of health, standardization, and protection of domestic industries, import licenses from the Ministry of Commerce and Industry are required for a number of goods–mostly food and agricultural products, and certain household and construction products; such licenses are liberally administered. There are no quota limits or other quantitative restrictions for balance of payments reasons. Most imports are subject to a stamp duty of 14 percent of the c.i.f. value. Imports by most of the public sector and certain nonprofit entities, imports of an emergency or humanitarian nature, and goods for re-export are exempt from import duties; goods originating from the CARICOM area are also exempt. In November 1995, specific taxes on imports of beer, tobacco products, and fuel were raised.[3]

Payments for Invisibles

Authorized dealers have the power to provide foreign exchange for such payments within certain limits. The following limits are applied to purchases of foreign exchange: (1) nonbusiness travel by resi-

---

[1] The CARICOM countries are Antigua and Barbuda, The Bahamas, Barbados, Belize, Dominica, Grenada, Guyana, Jamaica, Montserrat, St. Kitts and Nevis, St. Lucia, St. Vincent and the Grenadines, and Trinidad and Tobago. The Central Bank quotes exchange rates for Barbados dollars, Eastern Caribbean dollars, Guyana dollars, and Trinidad and Tobago dollars.

[2] Barbados dollars, Canadian dollars, Eastern Carribean dollars, Guyana dollars, pounds sterling, Trinidad and Tobago dollars, and U.S. dollars.

[3] The surcharge (revenue replacement duty) on imported beer was raised to BZ$22.81 per imperial gallon from BZ$19.06; the import duty on cigars, cheroots, and cigarillos was raised to BZ$26.67 per lb. from BZ$16.67; the import duty on other cigars and tobacco products was raised to BZ$20.00 per lb. from BZ$12.50; the import duty on snuff was raised to BZ$24.80 per lb. from BZ$15.50 per lb.; and the surcharge (revenue replacement duty) on fuel imports was raised by 25 cents per imperial gallon.

dents, up to BZ$5,000 a person a calendar year; (2) business travel by residents, BZ$500 a day a person, up to a maximum of BZ$20,000 a year; (3) business or nonbusiness travel by nonresidents, BZ$500 a person a year, unless payment is made from an external account or from proceeds of foreign currency; and (4) gifts, BZ$100 a donor. Requests in excess of these amounts are referred to the Central Bank, which grants all bona fide requests. Since June 1995, the Central Bank has also rationed its sale of foreign exchange for invisible payments to commercial banks on an ad hoc basis except for a few essential items such as insurance. Foreign exchange is provided for payment of correspondence courses by the authorized dealers when applications are properly documented.

Exports of foreign and domestic banknotes and currency are subject to limits as follows: each traveler may carry domestic banknotes up to BZ$100 and the equivalent of BZ$400 in foreign currency, except that a visitor may take out such notes up to the amount imported. Amounts beyond these limits require the approval of the Central Bank, which is liberally granted when justified.

Exports and Export Proceeds

Export licenses are required for most export products. Export proceeds must be surrendered to authorized dealers not later than six months after the date of shipment, unless directed otherwise by the Central Bank. A small number of items[4] are subject to an ad valorem export duty of 5 percent. Reexports and transshipments are subject to a 3 percent customs administration fee. Since mid-1995, the Central Bank has resorted to direct purchases of sugar export proceeds bypassing the traditional practice of purchasing from commercial banks.

---

[4] Lobster, shrimp, conch, fish, turtles, mahogany, and wild animals. For sugar, the export duty is 2 percent.

Proceeds from Invisibles

Foreign currency proceeds from invisibles must be sold to an authorized dealer. Travelers to Belize are free to bring in notes and coins denominated in Belize dollars up to BZ$100 a person, but imports of foreign currency are not restricted. Resident travelers are required to sell their excess holdings of foreign currencies to an authorized dealer upon returning to Belize.

Capital

All capital transfers require the approval of the Central Bank, but control is liberally administered. Foreign direct investment is encouraged, and investors benefit from a number of fiscal incentives.

Gold

Residents may not hold gold except with specific authorization from the Central Bank. Gold may be neither imported nor exported without the approval of the Central Bank.

Changes During 1995

Imports and Import Payments

November 7. Parliament raised the import taxes, as follows: (1) the surcharge (revenue replacement duty) on imported beer was raised to BZ$22.81 per imperial gallon from BZ$19.06; (2) the import duty on cigars, cheroots, and cigarillos was raised to BZ$26.67 per pound from BZ$16.67; (3) the import duty on cigarettes was raised to BZ$34.40 per pound from BZ$21.50; (4) the import duty on other cigars and tobacco products was raised to BZ$20.00 per pound from BZ$12.50; (5) the import duty on snuff was raised to BZ$24.80 per pound from BZ$15.50; and (6) the surcharge (revenue replacement duty) on fuel imports was raised by 25 cents per imperial gallon.

BENIN

(Position as of June 30, 1996)

Exchange Arrangement

The currency of Benin is the CFA Franc,[1] which is pegged to the French franc, the intervention currency, at the fixed rate of CFAF 1 per F 0.01. The official buying and selling rate is CFAF 100 per F 1. Exchange rates for other currencies are derived from the rate for the currency concerned in the Paris exchange market and the fixed rate between the French franc and the CFA franc. They include a bank commission of 2.5 per mil on transfers to all countries outside the West African Monetary Union (WAEMU), which must be surrendered in its entirety to the Treasury. There are no taxes or subsidies on purchases or sales of foreign exchange. Forward exchange contracts may be arranged with the prior authorization of the Minister of Finance. The maturity period cannot be extended.

With the exception of those relating to gold, the repatriation of export proceeds, the issuing, advertising, offering for sale of securities and capital assets, and the soliciting of funds for investment abroad, the exchange control measures do not apply to (1) France (and its overseas departments and territories) and Monaco; and (2) all other countries whose bank of issue is linked with the French Treasury by an Operations Account (Burkina Faso, Cameroon, Central African Republic, Chad, Comoros, the Congo, Côte d'Ivoire, Equatorial Guinea, Gabon, Mali, Niger, Senegal, and Togo). Hence, all payments to these countries may be made freely. All other countries are considered foreign countries. For certain controls relating to capital flows, the countries specified in this paragraph are also regarded as foreign countries.

Benin accepted the obligations of Article VIII, Sections 2, 3, and 4 of the Fund Agreement on June 1, 1996.

Administration of Control

Exchange control is administered by the Directorate of Monetary and Banking Affairs in the Ministry of Finance, in conjunction with the Directorate of External Commerce in the Ministry of Commerce and Tourism. The Ministry of Finance, however, in collaboration with the BCEAO, draws up the exchange control regulations. The BCEAO is authorized to collect, either directly or through banks, financial institutions, and the Postal Administration, any information necessary to compile balance of payments statistics. All exchange transactions relating to foreign countries must be carried out by authorized intermediaries. Import licenses for goods from the African, Caribbean, and Pacific (ACP) State signatories to the Lomé Convention and from member countries of European Union (EU) and Operations Account countries have been abolished. Upon the recommendation of the Directorate of Monetary and Financial Affairs of the Ministry of Finance, exports of diamonds or other precious or semiprecious stones and precious metals require authorization from the Directorate of External Commerce.

Prescription of Currency

Because Benin is linked to the French Treasury through an Operations Account, settlements with France (as defined above), Monaco, and other countries linked to the French Treasury through an Operations Account are made in CFA francs, French francs, or the currency of any other Operations Account country. Current payments to or from The Gambia, Ghana, Guinea, Guinea-Bissau, Liberia, Mauritania, Nigeria, and Sierra Leone are normally made through the West African Clearing House. Settlements with all other countries are usually effected through correspondent banks in France, in any of the currencies of those countries or in French francs through foreign accounts in francs.

Nonresident Accounts

Because the BCEAO has suspended the repurchase of banknotes circulating outside the territories of the CFA franc zone, nonresident accounts may not be credited or debited with BCEAO banknotes. These accounts may not be overdrawn without the prior authorization of the Ministry of Finance. Transfers of funds between nonresident accounts are not restricted.

Imports and Import Payments

Certain imports, such as narcotics, are prohibited from all sources. Certain agencies have an import monopoly over specified commodities.

Imports of goods from all origins and sources are freely imported. Before shipment, goods from all

---

[1]The CFA franc is issued by the Central Bank of West African States (BCEAO) and is the common currency in Benin, Burkina Faso, Côte d'Ivoire, Mali, Niger, Senegal, and Togo.

sources are subject to inspection for quality and price.

All imports valued at more than CFAF 500,000 must be domiciled with an authorized intermediary bank. Importers may not purchase foreign exchange to pay for imports earlier than eight days before suppliers ship the goods if a documentary credit is opened, and only on the due date of payment if the goods have already been imported.

Customs duties consist of five bands (i.e., zero, 5 percent, 10 percent, 15 percent, and 20 percent). A statistical tax of 3 percent is levied on the c.i.f. value of imports.

Payments for Invisibles

Payments for invisibles to France (as defined above), Monaco, and countries linked to the French Treasury through an Operations Account are permitted freely; those to other countries are subject to the approval of the Directorate of Monetary and Financial Affairs of the Ministry of Finance, but for many types of invisibles, the approval authority has been delegated to authorized intermediary banks. Authorized banks and the Postal Administration have been empowered to make payments abroad freely on behalf of residents, up to CFAF 50,000 a transfer. Payments for invisibles related to trade are permitted freely when the basic trade transaction has been approved or does not require authorization. Transfers of income accruing to nonresidents in the form of profits, dividends, and royalties are subject to prior authorization.

Residents traveling for tourism or business purposes to countries in the franc zone other than WAEMU member countries are allowed to take out the equivalent of CFAF 2 million in banknotes other than the CFA franc; amounts in excess of this limit may be taken out in the form of means of payment other than banknotes. The allowances for travel to countries outside the franc zone are subject to the following regulations: (1) for tourist travel, CFAF 500,000 without limit on the number of trips or differentiation by the age of the traveler; (2) for business travel, CFAF 75,000 a day for up to one month, corresponding to a maximum of CFAF 2.25 million (business travel allowances may be combined with tourist allowances); (3) allowances in excess of these limits are subject to the authorization of the respective ministries of finance; and (4) credit cards, which must be issued by resident financial intermediaries specifically approved by the Ministry of Finance, may be used up to the ceilings indicated above for tourist and business travel. Returning resident travelers are required to declare all means of payment in their possession upon arrival at customs and surrender within eight days all means of payment exceeding the equivalent of CFAF 25,000. Upon departure, all residents traveling to countries that are not members of the WAEMU must declare in writing all means of payment in their possession. Nonresident travelers may re-export all means of payment other than banknotes issued abroad and registered in their name, subject to documentation that they had used funds drawn from a foreign account in CFA francs or other foreign exchange to purchase these means of payment. The re-exportation of foreign banknotes is allowed up to the equivalent of CFAF 250,000; the re-exportation of foreign banknotes above these ceilings requires documentation demonstrating either the importation of the foreign banknotes or their purchase against other means of payment registered in the name of the traveler or through the use of nonresident deposits lodged in local banks.

Upon presentation of an appropriate pay voucher, a residence permit, and documents indicating family situation, foreigners working in Benin may transfer up to 50 percent of their net salary abroad if they live with their family in Benin, or up to 80 percent if their family is living abroad.

Exports and Export Proceeds

Exports to all foreign countries, including those in the Operations Account area, must be domiciled with an authorized intermediary bank when valued at more than CFAF 500,000. Exports are permitted on the basis of a simple authorization from the Directorate of Foreign Trade. Exports of diamonds, gold, and all other precious metals, however, are subject to prior authorization from the Ministry of Finance, with the exception of articles with a small gold content, travelers' personal effects weighing less than 500 grams, and coins (fewer than ten pieces, irrespective of their face value and denomination). Prior authorization for exports of these three product categories is granted by the Directorate of Monetary and Financial Affairs of the Ministry of Finance. Receipts from exports must be repatriated to Benin, through the BCEAO, at the initiative of the authorized bank within 30 days of the contractual due date, and must be sold to authorized banks within 180 days of the arrival of the shipment at its destination.

Proceeds from Invisibles

Proceeds from transactions in invisibles with France (as defined above), Monaco, and countries maintaining Operations Accounts with the French Treasury may be retained. All amounts due from residents of other countries in respect of services and all income earned in those countries from foreign assets must be collected and surrendered. Resident and nonresident travelers may bring in any amount of banknotes and coins issued by the BCEAO, the Bank of France, or a bank of issue maintaining an Operations Account with the French Treasury, as well as any amount of foreign banknotes and coins (except gold coins) of countries outside the Operations Account area.[2] Resident travelers bringing in foreign banknotes and foreign currency traveler's checks exceeding the equivalent of CFAF 25,000 must declare them to customs upon entry and sell them to an authorized intermediary bank within eight days of their return to Benin.

Capital

Capital movements between Benin and France (as defined above), Monaco, and countries linked to the French Treasury through an Operations Account are free of exchange control; most capital transfers to all other countries require prior approval from the Minister of Finance and are restricted, but capital receipts from such countries are permitted freely.

Special controls, in addition to any exchange control requirements that may be applicable, are maintained over borrowing abroad; over inward foreign direct investment and all outward investment in foreign countries; and over the issuing, advertising, or offering for sale of foreign securities in Benin. Such operations require prior authorization from the Minister of Finance. Exempt from authorization, however, are operations in connection with (1) loans backed by a guarantee from the Beninese Government, and (2) shares that are similar to, or may be substituted for, securities whose issuance or sale in Benin has already been authorized. With the exception of controls over foreign securities, these measures do not apply to France (as defined above), Monaco, member countries of the WAEMU, and the countries linked to the French Treasury through an Operations Account. Special controls are also maintained over imports and exports of gold, over the soliciting of funds for deposit or investment with foreign private persons and foreign firms and institutions, and over publicity aimed at placing funds abroad or at subscribing to real estate and building operations abroad; these special controls also apply to France (as defined above), Monaco, and countries maintaining Operations Accounts.

All investments abroad by residents of Benin require prior authorization from the Minister of Finance; at least 75 percent of the investments must be financed from foreign borrowing.[3] Foreign direct investments in Benin[4] must be declared to the Minister before they are made. The Minister may request postponement of the operations within a period of two months. The full or partial liquidation of either type of investment also requires declaration. Both the making and the liquidation of investments, whether these are Beninese investments abroad or foreign investments in Benin, must be reported to the Minister and to the BCEAO within 20 days of each operation. Direct investments are defined as those that imply control of a company or enterprise. Investment that does not exceed 20 percent of the capital of a company whose shares are quoted on a stock exchange is not considered direct investment.

Borrowing by residents from nonresidents requires prior authorization from the Minister of Finance. The following are, however, exempt from this authorization: (1) loans constituting a direct investment, which are subject to prior declaration as indicated above; (2) loans taken up by industrial firms to finance operations abroad, by international trade and export-import firms (approved by the Minister of Finance) to finance transit trade, or by any type of firm to finance imports and exports; (3) loans contracted by authorized intermediary banks; and (4) subject to certain conditions, loans other than those mentioned above when the total amount outstanding of these loans, including the new borrowing, does not exceed CFAF 50 million for any one borrower. The repayment of loans not constituting a direct investment requires the special authorization of the Minister of Finance, if the loan itself was subject to such approval, but is exempt if the loan was exempt from special authorization. Lending abroad is subject to prior authorization from the Minister of Finance.

The Investment Code (Law No. 90-002 of May 9, 1990) stipulates that preferential status may be granted to foreign and domestic investments in industry, mining, fisheries, agriculture, and tourism that are deemed to contribute to national development. Fiscal benefits are extended to approved investors under two regimes: the preferential and the special regimes. The preferential regime consists of three categories: A, B, and C. Category A applies

---

[2]Effective August 1, 1993, the repurchase of CFAF notes of the BCEAO in circulation outside member countries of the WAEMU was suspended.

[3]Including those made through foreign companies that are directly or indirectly controlled by persons in Benin and those made by branches or subsidiaries abroad of companies in Benin.

[4]Including those made by companies in Benin that are directly or indirectly under foreign control and those made by branches or subsidiaries of foreign companies in Benin.

to small and medium-size enterprises; category B, to large enterprises; and category C, to very large enterprises.

Enterprises falling under category A must have investments valued at between CFAF 20 million and CFAF 500 million and employ at least five permanent Beninese workers. These enterprises are exempt from customs duties and levies on equipment and materials during the investment period (excluding the local roads and statistical taxes), as well as from income tax for five to nine years, depending on the geographic location of their investment in Benin. Enterprises qualifying for category B must undertake investments valued at more than CFAF 500 million (but less than CFAF 3 billion) and employ at least 20 Beninese workers. These enterprises are exempt from virtually all border taxes on imports of equipment and materials for the period the investment is being undertaken, and, for the duration of the investment, they are exempt from export taxes and from taxes on profits. Enterprises qualifying for category C benefits must undertake investments in excess of CFAF 3 billion. They enjoy the same tax and duty privileges as category B enterprises. In addition, enterprises in this category are guaranteed stability of tax status for the duration of the agreement.

Enterprises qualifying under the special regime are those with investments valued at between CFAF 5 million and CFAF 20 million that provide services in health, education, or public works. They benefit from a 75 percent reduction in the applicable border taxes (excluding the local roads and statistical taxes) on imported equipment and materials related to their operations. The modalities of implementing this legislation are set out in Decree No. 91-2 of January 4, 1991.

Gold

Authorization from the Directorate of External Commerce, issued after a favorable ruling by the Directorate of Monetary and Financial Affairs of the Ministry of Finance, is required to hold, sell, import, export, or deal in raw diamonds and precious and semiprecious materials. In practice, residents are free to hold, acquire, and dispose of gold in any form in Benin. Imports and exports of gold from or to any other country require prior authorization from the Ministry of Finance, which is seldom granted. Exempt from this requirement are (1) imports and exports by or on behalf of the Treasury or the BCEAO; (2) imports and exports of manufactured articles containing a minor quantity of gold (such as gold-filled or gold-plated articles); and (3) imports and exports by travelers of gold articles up to a maximum weight to be determined by an Order of the Minister. Both licensed and exempt imports of gold are subject to customs declaration.

Changes During 1995

Imports and Import Payments

June 22. Imports of goods from all origins and from all sources were liberalized.

Exports and Export Proceeds

May 19. Exports of food crops were temporarily suspended during the summer of 1995. The suspension was lifted on September 15.

Changes During 1996

Exchange Arrangement

June 1. Benin accepted the obligations of Article VIII, Sections 2, 3, and 4 of the Fund Agreement.

BHUTAN

(Position as of December 31, 1995)

Exchange Arrangement

The currency of Bhutan is the Ngultrum, the external value of which is pegged to the Indian rupee. Indian rupees also circulate in Bhutan at a rate of Nu 1 per Re 1. The rates for currencies other than Indian rupees are determined on the basis of the prevailing quotations by the Reserve Bank of India for those currencies. If no large transactions are involved, exchange rates for other currencies may be determined on the basis of the most recent quotations by the Reserve Bank of India. No other exchange rates apply to international transactions, and there are no subsidies or taxes on exchange transactions. On December 29, 1995, the buying and selling rates of the ngultrum for the U.S. dollar (cash) were Nu 34.45 and Nu 35.65, respectively, per $1, the buying and selling rates of the ngultrum for the U.S. dollar (traveler's checks) were Nu 34.60 and Nu 35.45, respectively, per $1. There are no arrangements for forward cover against exchange rate risk operating in the official or the commercial banking sector.

Administration of Control

The Ministry of Finance controls external transactions and provides foreign exchange for most current and capital transactions. The Ministry of Finance has delegated to the Royal Monetary Authority the authority to release foreign exchange (other than Indian rupees) for current transactions. The Royal Monetary Authority is charged with implementing the surrender requirements for proceeds from merchandise exports and approving the use of foreign exchange for imports.

Prescription of Currency

There are no regulations prescribing the use of specific currencies in external receipts and payments.

Imports and Import Payments

Except for imports of large capital goods, for which clearance by the Ministry of Finance is required, there are no restrictions on payments or transfers relating to any current account transaction with India. Clearance by the Ministry of Finance is required for the importation of capital and intermediate goods from third countries. The release of foreign exchange is managed separately by the Royal Monetary Authority upon recommendation by the Ministry of Finance. The Royal Monetary Authority does not provide foreign exchange to importers of consumer goods; the latter must make their own arrangements to obtain the foreign exchange before an import license is issued.

Customs duties are levied on imports other than those from India.

Exports and Export Proceeds

There are no export taxes. Exports to countries other than India receive a rebate at one of four rates ranging from 5 percent to 20 percent of the c.i.f. value, with the lowest rate applying to unprocessed primary products and the highest rate applying to processed products. Exports of antiques of Bhutanese origin require government approval. Proceeds of exports in currencies other than the Indian rupee must be surrendered to the Royal Monetary Authority either directly or through the Bank of Bhutan within 90 days.

Payments for and Proceeds from Invisibles

Most invisible payments, other than those made in Indian rupees, must be approved by the Royal Monetary Authority. All receipts from invisible transactions in currencies other than the Indian rupee must be surrendered to the Royal Monetary Authority.

Capital

All capital transactions must be approved by the Ministry of Finance.

Gold

There are no specific regulations on transactions in gold.

Changes During 1995

No significant changes occurred in the exchange and the trade system.

BOLIVIA

(Position as of December 31, 1995)

Exchange Arrangement

The currency of Bolivia is the Boliviano. The official selling exchange rate is the weighted average of public sales of foreign exchange performed by the Central Bank of Bolivia. This official exchange rate applies to all foreign exchange operations in Bolivia. The auctions are conducted by the Committee for Exchange and Reserves (Comité de Cambio y Reservas) in the Central Bank. Before each auction, the Committee decides on the amount of foreign exchange to be auctioned and a floor price below which the Central Bank will not accept any bids. This floor price is the official exchange rate and is based on the exchange rates of the deutsche mark, Japanese yen, pound sterling, and U.S. dollar. The Central Bank is required to offer in all auctions unitary lots of $5,000 or multiples of this amount; the minimum allowable bid is $5,000. Successful bidders are charged the exchange rate specified in their bid. In general, the spreads between the maximum and minimum bids have been less than 2 percent. On December 31, 1995, the official buying and selling rates were Bs 4.93 and Bs 4.94, respectively, per $1.

Sales of foreign exchange by the Central Bank to the public are subject to a commission of Bs 0.01 per $1 over its buying rate. Except for the requirement to surrender the net proceeds from the exportation of goods and services, all banks, exchange houses, companies, and individuals may buy and sell foreign exchange freely. Successful bids channeled through the banking system are voided if the banking institution submitting the bid is not complying with the obligation of transferring funds from its accounts at the Commercial Bank of Bolivia to a special account at the Central Bank (*cuenta "provisión bolsini"*) that is for the sole purpose of buying foreign exchange. Banks are allowed to hold foreign exchange positions up to the value of the net worth minus fixed assets. All public sector institutions, including public enterprises, must purchase foreign exchange for imports of goods and services through the Central Bank auction market.

There is a parallel but tolerated exchange market, in which the buying and selling exchange rates on December 31, 1995, were Bs 4.93 and Bs 4.95, respectively, per $1. There are no arrangements for forward cover against exchange rate risk operating in the official or the commercial banking sector.

Bolivia accepted the obligations of Article VIII, Sections 2, 3, and 4 of the Fund Agreement on June 5, 1967.

Administration of Control

The Central Bank is in charge of operating the auction market for foreign exchange. It is also the enforcing agency for export surrender requirements as well as for other exchange control regulations. The Ministry of Finance, together with the Central Bank, is in charge of approving public sector purchases of foreign exchange for debt-service payments.

Prescription of Currency

There are no prescription of currency requirements. Settlements are usually made in U.S. dollars or other convertible currencies. Payments between Bolivia and Argentina, Brazil, Chile, Colombia, Ecuador, Mexico, Paraguay, Peru, Uruguay, and Venezuela may be made through accounts maintained with each other by the Central Bank of Bolivia and the central bank of the country concerned, within the framework of the multilateral clearing system of the Latin American Integration Association (LAIA).

Imports and Import Payments

All goods may be freely imported, with the exception of those controlled for reasons of public health or national security.

Bolivia has a general uniform tariff of 10 percent. A tariff rate of 5 percent is applied to capital goods, and a rate of 2 percent is applied to imports of books and printed material. Donations of food, including wheat, are exempt from the import tariff.

Payments for Invisibles

There are no restrictions on payments for invisibles. Profit remittances abroad are subject to a 12.5 percent tax (which is computed as equivalent to the 25 percent income tax times the presumed net profit of 50 percent of the amount remitted). Residents traveling by air to neighboring countries are required to pay a travel tax of Bs 100; the tax on travel to other foreign destinations is Bs 150. Public sector purchases of foreign exchange for debt service must be approved by the Ministry of Finance and the Central Bank. The Investment Law does not restrict remittance of profits abroad.

Exports and Export Proceeds

All goods may be freely exported. All proceeds from exports of the public and private sectors must be sold to the Central Bank at the official exchange rate within 15 days of receipt, with the exception of reasonable amounts deducted for foreign exchange expenditures undertaken to effect the export transaction. Exports other than hydrocarbons are subject to an inspection fee of 1.55 percent for nontraditional products and 1.6 percent for traditional products; these fees are paid by the Government and not by the exporters. A system of tax rebates reimburses exporters for indirect taxes and import duty paid on inputs of exported goods and services, including the duty component of depreciation of capital goods used. Exporters of small items whose value in Bolivia's annual exports is less than $3 million receive tax rebates of 2 percent or 4 percent of the f.o.b. export value under a simplified procedure, and other exporters receive tax and import duty rebates based on annually determined coefficients that reflect their documented cost structure.

Proceeds from Invisibles

Banks, exchange houses, hotels, and travel agencies may retain the proceeds from their foreign exchange purchases from invisible transactions, including those from tourism. They are required, however, to report daily their purchases on account of these transactions.

Capital

Foreign exchange for outward capital transfers by residents or nonresidents can be purchased only from the commercial banks or from the Central Bank. Inward capital transfers may be made freely, but government receipts of transfers and grants and all proceeds of borrowings from foreign public sector agencies must be surrendered to the Central Bank. All foreign credits, including suppliers' credits, to government agencies and autonomous entities, and credits to the private sector with official guarantees are subject to prior authorization by the Ministry of Finance and to control by the Central Bank. Financial institutions in Bolivia may make loans in the form of credits denominated in foreign currency for imports of capital goods and inputs for the external sector with resources from international financial institutions, foreign government agencies, or external lines of credit. Under Supreme Decree No. 21060 of August 29, 1985, banks are authorized to conduct foreign trade operations, such as letters of credit, bonds and guarantees, advances and acceptances, loans for required financing with their correspondents abroad, and other operations generally accepted in international banking, in favor of the country's exporters and importers.

Banks are allowed to hold foreign exchange positions up to the value of their net worth minus fixed assets.

Foreign investments in Bolivia, except those involving petroleum and mining, are governed by the provisions of the Investment Law of September 1990 (Law No. 1182 on Investment), which treats domestic and foreign investors equally. The law is administered by the Secretariat of Industry and Commerce. Investments in petroleum and mining are governed by the Hydrocarbons Law and the Mining Law.

Gold

Under Supreme Decree No. 21060 of August 29, 1985, gold may be traded freely, subject to a tax of 3 percent on the gross value of sale of gold bullion (Supreme Decree No. 23394, February 3, 1993).

Changes During 1995

Imports and Import Payments

November 6. The import tariffs on wheat flour, sugar, and maize were suspended for 180 days (Supreme Decree No. 24519).

BOSNIA AND HERZEGOVINA[1]

(Position as of December 31, 1995)

Exchange Arrangement

The currency of Bosnia and Herzegovina is the Bosnian Dinar, which has been pegged to the deutsche mark at BDin 100 per DM 1 since its introduction in July 1994. The Bosnian dinar is issued by the National Bank of Bosnia and Herzegovina and is legal tender in the Bosnian-majority area of Bosnia. It is not legal tender in the Croat- or Serbian-majority areas of Bosnia and Herzegovina; these two areas use the Croatian kuna and the Yugoslav dinar, respectively. The Bosnian- and Croatian-majority areas form the Federation while the Serbian-majority area is known as the Republika Srpska. The deutsche mark is widely used in all three areas. Until December 9, 1995, the National Bank of Bosnia and Herzegovina also used a "stimulation exchange rate" to help build foreign reserves, which at the time of its elimination was BDin 105 per DM 1.

The National Bank of Bosnia and Herzegovina, which operates as a de facto currency board, communicates exchange rates to the commercial banks at least once a day. If there are significant changes in the rate during the day (that is, to the second decimal place), revised rates are communicated. Banks must charge the same rates for all transactions. In the Republika Srpska, the National Bank of Republika Srpska receives from the National Bank of the Former Republic of Yugoslavia at the close of each business day a list of buying and selling exchange rates for the major currencies. These rates are forwarded to the commercial banks and applied to the next day's transactions. Banks must charge the same rates for all transactions. There is no bank in the Croatian-majority area that acts as a central bank. The National Bank of Bosnia and Herzegovina is responsible for some central banking functions in the Croatian-majority area but not for the use of Croatian kuna.

In both the Bosnian- and Serbian-majority areas, commercial banks are free to buy and sell foreign exchange in the interbank market without restrictions but must report all transactions to the National Bank of Bosnia and Herzegovina on a regular basis and to the National Bank of Republika Srpska, on a daily basis.

---

[1]On December 20, 1995, Bosnia and Herzegovina became a member of the Fund by succeeding to the membership of the former Socialist Republic of Yugoslavia.

Administration of Control

The National Bank of Bosnia and Herzegovina administers foreign exchange control regulations in the Federation with limited delegation to commercial banks. The National Bank of Republika Srpska oversees foreign exchange regulations in the Republika Srpska, although the commercial banks are responsible for implementing controls; the banks provide the National Bank of Republika Srpska with the documentation for all foreign exchange transactions on a regular basis.

Resident and Nonresident Accounts

There are no restrictions on the holding of foreign exchange by individuals or enterprises in the Bosnian-majority area, although there is a limit of DM 2,000 on the amount of cash that an individual is permitted to carry across international borders at any one time. There is no limit on the frequency of border crossings with less than DM 2,000. Individuals and exporters can hold foreign exchange in accounts with commercial banks and do not need to supply evidence of the source of these funds. There are no restrictions on withdrawals from these accounts for domestic transactions. There are restrictions on withdrawals for the purpose of making foreign transactions. Foreign exchange held in these accounts need not be surrendered to the National Bank of Bosnia and Herzegovina, but if a bank purchases any of the foreign exchange held in these accounts, 45 percent of that amount must be surrendered to the National Bank of Bosnia and Herzegovina. There are no regulations on banks' foreign exchange open positions.

Individuals and exporters in the Republika Srpska can hold foreign exchange in accounts with commercial banks and do not need to supply evidence of the source of these funds. There are no restrictions on withdrawals from these accounts for domestic transactions, however, there are restrictions on withdrawals for the purpose of making payments abroad. The limit on cash taken across international borders is DM 1,000 a trip, but there is no limit on the frequency of border crossings with less than DM 1,000. No foreign currency exposure limits apply to commercial banks that accept foreign currency deposits, but the banks must provide a guarantee and insure the accounts with an insurance company.

Imports and Exports

All importers in the Federation must be registered with a local court and with the Ministry of Foreign Trade. An importer can purchase foreign exchange for importing goods and services without drawing on foreign exchange held in bank accounts. Foreign exchange is rationed, with priority given to raw materials and essentials such as drugs; a list is maintained with goods and services listed in descending order of priority. Also, the Ministry of Foreign Trade classifies goods into three regimes: free; subject to quotas (for the protection of local industry); and banned (for health, environmental, or military reasons).

In the Republika Srpska, an importer must use all foreign exchange held in bank accounts before being entitled to purchase any further foreign exchange from a commercial bank or from the National Bank of Republika Srpska. Commercial banks ration foreign exchange, with priority given to raw materials and goods that meet basic human needs. Restrictions are imposed on the importation of goods for which domestic production is significant.

Fifteen percent of proceeds from exports of goods and services in the Bosnian-majority area must be surrendered to the National Bank of Bosnia and Herzegovina within 48 hours of repatriation in exchange for Bosnian dinars at the official exchange rate. Exports by companies that deal abroad are subject to a surrender requirement of 5 percent. There are no quantitative restrictions on exports from the Federation but exporters must be registered with the Ministry of Foreign Trade and a local court. There are no taxes or subsidies on exports and no monopolies granted for any exports.

In the Republika Srpska, 20 percent of the proceeds from exports of goods and services must be surrendered to the National Bank of Republika Srpska immediately upon repatriation. There are no quantitative restrictions on exports, but the exporter must be registered with the National Bank of Republika Srpska and with a local court. The Ministry of Foreign Trade also imposes some controls on the re-exportation of some imports.

Payments for and Proceeds from Invisibles

The National Bank of Bosnia and Herzegovina makes foreign exchange available as a priority for the importation of business-related services. However, debt-service payments were removed from the priority list in April 1992. Foreign exchange for individual travel abroad is limited to DM 2,000 a trip for the total cost of the trip (including airfare). However, there is no limit on payments for travel made before departure and effected through the commercial banks. Also, there is no limit on the frequency of trips in any period. Special authorization is required for larger amounts. Payments abroad for medical care are on the priority list but require documentation from the Ministry of Health and from the Ministry of Finance. The importation of other services by individuals requires approval by the commercial banks, in consultation with the National Bank of Bosnia and Herzegovina.

Payments of pensions from Germany resumed in December 1995 following an agreement in which the National Bank of Bosnia and Herzegovina provides documentation to Germany that the pensions have been paid by the commercial banks under its jurisdiction.

In the Republika Srpska, the purchase of foreign exchange for business-related services is unrestricted upon provision of the appropriate documentation to the commercial banks. The purchase of foreign exchange for individual travel abroad is limited to DM 1,000 a trip for the total cost of the trip (including airfare). There is no limit on the number of trips, but special authorization is required for larger amounts. Payments abroad for medical care require documentation from the Ministry of Health and a pro forma invoice from the service provider. The purchase of foreign exchange by individuals for the importation of other services requires approval from the commercial banks, in consultation with the National Bank of Republika Srpska.

Pension receipts from Germany have fallen to low levels as a result of sanctions and emigration.

Capital

There are no restrictions on direct foreign investments in the Federation, provided all other regulations in force are complied with. Full repatriation of after-tax profits and capital are permitted. Foreign investors are exempt from taxation of initial imports and of raw materials imported in the first year of operation. Loans from abroad involving a government guarantee must be approved by Parliament on the advice of the National Bank of Bosnia and Herzegovina and the Ministry of Finance. Neither of these institutions has been delegated the authority to contract or guarantee loans, but the National Bank of Bosnia and Herzegovina can borrow abroad for up to one year. A special law would be required for each state loan or guarantee.

Direct and portfolio investments abroad by Bosnian-majority area residents requires permission from the National Bank of Bosnia and Herzegovina.

The Republika Srpska also imposes no restrictions on direct investment from abroad and allows full repatriation of after-tax profits and capital after all domestic financial claims have been settled. Loans from abroad involving a guarantee from commercial banks require permission from the National Bank of Republika Srpska to ensure that the debt-servicing requirements are consistent with the future availability of foreign exchange.

A special license is required from the Government, based on advice from the National Bank of Republika Srpska and the Ministry of Foreign Trade, in order for Republika Srpska residents to undertake direct and portfolio investment abroad. Capital transfers abroad of inheritances and pensions are permitted, subject to documentation requirements. Other capital transfers abroad require special permission from the National Bank of Republika Srpska.

BOTSWANA

(Position as of December 31, 1995)

Exchange Arrangement

The currency of Botswana is the Botswana Pula. Its external value in terms of the U.S. dollar, the intervention currency, is determined with reference to a weighted basket of currencies comprising the SDR and currencies of the country's major trading partners. On December 31, 1995, the closing middle rate for the U.S. dollar was P 2.8217 per $1; on the same date, the rate for the SDR was P 4.1876 per SDR 1. Buying and selling rates for certain other dealing currencies[1] are quoted on the basis of their rates against the U.S. dollar in international markets. For information only, middle rates are quoted for certain other currencies.[2] There are no taxes or subsidies on purchases or sales of foreign exchange.

External loans undertaken by parastatals before October 1, 1990 have been protected from exchange rate movements under a foreign exchange risk-sharing scheme. At the end of 1995, the scheme applied to 16 outstanding loans. Under the scheme, risks associated with exchange rate fluctuations up to 4 percent are fully borne by the borrower, while the next 6 percent and the following 5 percent of fluctuations are shared between the borrower and the Government on a 50:50 and 25:75 basis, respectively. Risks associated with exchange rate fluctuations in excess of 15 percent are fully borne by the Government. The scheme is symmetrical in that the borrower and the Government share any gains from an appreciation in the external value of the pula on the same basis. Forward exchange cover is also offered by the commercial banks. Forward cover may be given in respect of the foreign currency proceeds derived from the exportation of goods for up to six months.

Botswana accepted the obligations of Article VIII, Sections 2, 3, and 4 of the Fund Articles of Agreement on November 17, 1995.

Administration of Control

Exchange control is applicable to transactions with all countries. The Minister of Finance and Development Planning has delegated most of the administration of exchange controls to the Bank of Botswana, the central bank. The latter, in turn, has delegated considerable powers to banks appointed as authorized dealers. Since January 1, 1994, remittances for payments of imports of goods and services have been handled by the commercial banks without reference to the central bank.

Prescription of Currency

Payments to or from residents of foreign countries must normally be made or received in a foreign currency or through a nonresident-held pula account in Botswana.

Resident and Nonresident Accounts

Companies operating in Botswana are permitted to open foreign currency accounts with commercial banks in deutsche mark, pounds sterling, South African rand, and U.S. dollars.

Commercial banks are authorized to open foreign currency accounts for permanent and temporary residents and nonresidents. The accounts are to facilitate foreign receipts and payments for approved transactions, without having to convert foreign currency receipts into pula and vice versa, and to protect against changes in exchange rates. The restriction on specified foreign currencies was removed, and commercial banks were allowed to open foreign currency accounts in any currency at their discretion.

Imports and Import Payments

Botswana is a member of the Southern African Customs Union (SACU) with Lesotho, Namibia, South Africa, and Swaziland, and there are generally no import restrictions on goods moving among the five countries. The arrangement provides for the free movement of goods and the right of transit among members, as well as a common external tariff. Certain imported goods, including firearms, ammunition, fresh meat, and some agricultural and horticultural products, require permits regardless of the country of supply. There are no restrictions on payments for authorized imports. Goods of domestic origin may move freely between Botswana and Zimbabwe by virtue of a customs agreement of 1956, provided they meet certain local value-added requirements and are not intended for re-export.

---

[1] Deutsche mark, pounds sterling, and South African rand.

[2] Australian dollars, Canadian dollars, Danish kroner, French francs, Japanese yen, Netherlands guilders, Norwegian kroner, Swedish kronor, Swiss francs, European currency units, and SDRs.

Import shipments exceeding P 5,000 require documentation before foreign exchange is released.

Applications for forward purchases of foreign currency to cover payment for imports when the contract covers a period exceeding six months must be referred to the central bank.

Exports and Export Proceeds

Certain exports are subject to licensing, mainly for revenue reasons. Proceeds from exports must be received in a foreign currency or from a nonresident pula account within six months of the date of exportation. Retention of export proceeds for up to one year to finance certain transactions may be permitted by the central bank on a case-by-case basis. The value of goods that can be given as gifts to nonresidents is limited to P 3,000 per year. A few items, such as precious and semiprecious stones, require permits before they can be exported.

Payments for and Proceeds from Invisibles

Payments to nonresidents for current transactions, although subject to control, are not restricted. Authority to approve a range of current payments within limits is delegated to commercial banks; any remittances in excess of those limits must be referred to the central bank for prior approval. Once the bona fide nature of applications has been established and all other requirements have been fulfilled by the applicant, remittances are approved. On January 1, 1995, annual consolidated personal foreign payment allowances (including for travel, subscriptions, and other payments) were set at the equivalent of P 100,000 per calendar year for an adult and P 50,000 for a child under the age of 18 years. On the same date, a consolidated business allowance to cover business travel, royalties, franchises, management fees, etc., was set at P 1 million per year. Permanent residents may use credit cards in Botswana for settlement of both pula and foreign currency liabilities; airline tickets may be purchased directly from travel agents or remitted from abroad, and they are not counted as part of the annual travel allowance. The amount of unused foreign currency for travel that a resident may retain for future travel use is the equivalent of P 2,000 in currency or traveler's checks; any excess amount must be surrendered within six months of the date of return.

A temporary resident employed on a contractual basis may remit abroad annually, without reference to the central bank, P 25,000 or 65 percent of total eligible earnings, whichever is greater; the limit applicable to a self-employed temporary resident is P 50,000 or 65 percent of eligible earnings, whichever is greater. The period during which temporary residents are allowed to remit their earnings abroad is a block of 36 months, or the period of employment, whichever is shorter. Separately, travelers residing in Botswana may take out domestic banknotes and/or foreign currency in amounts of P 5,000 a trip, and may freely bring in any amount of domestic banknotes and coins. Visitors may take out any foreign currency that they brought in with them.

The central bank may authorize residents to maintain foreign currency accounts with banks abroad in cases where there is a proven commercial need for such a facility.

Capital

Pension and life insurance funds may invest up to one-half of their funds abroad, subject to the requirement of 12 month's advance notice to the central bank of the intention to repatriate funds. Businesses and individuals may invest abroad up to P 1 million and P 100,000, respectively. However, companies must be commercially active for at least two years and must be registered with the Department of Taxes. Foreign inward direct investment in new or existing businesses is generally encouraged but must be financed with funds from external sources. On disinvestment by a nonresident, the central bank allows immediate repatriation of proceeds up to a maximum of P 50 million. The excess may be required to be repatriated in installments over a period not exceeding three years. Authorized dealers may approve remittances of dividends/ profits without referring to the central bank. Remittances of interim dividends are permitted only for companies listed in the Botswana Stock Exchange. Inward portfolio investment is also permitted in shares issued by companies quoted on the Botswana Stock Exchange, provided the funds for financing the acquisitions originate with a nonresident source. Nonresident-controlled companies incorporated in Botswana may make similar investments (referred to as internal portfolio investments), which need not be financed with funds from external sources. In the case of both inward and internal portfolio investments, a shareholder or his nominee may not acquire an interest in excess of 5 percent of the company's paid-up stock. Total portfolio holdings by nonresidents, including nonresident-controlled companies, may not exceed 49 percent of the "free stock" of a local company, that is, total stock issued and paid up less stock held by nonresident direct investors.

Nonresident-controlled companies may also invest with domestic currency funds in any securities issued by the central bank. Nonresident-controlled companies (including branches of foreign companies) are permitted to borrow locally from all sources up to P 500,000; borrowing in excess of that amount may be approved by the central bank, provided that the resulting debt-equity ratio does not exceed 4:1. Borrowed funds may be used for working capital purposes or for acquisition of new fixed assets (e.g., plant, machinery, equipment, and buildings); these funds may not be used to acquire financial assets. Equity is defined as paid-up capital, reserves, and retained earnings. The 4:1 limit may be exceeded by nonresident-controlled manufacturing companies, if there is evidence that the project will provide a specialist skill to Botswana or will create significant employment. Any external borrowing by a local business must have at least a three-month grace period.

Permanent residents are eligible for an emigration allowance of up to P 150,000 in addition to household and personal effects whose value does not exceed P 75,000. Applications for remittances in excess of these amounts are dealt with by the central bank. Such remittances are normally authorized if the amount is not too large; if the amount is excessive, remittances may be permitted in installments over three years.

Nonresident-controlled companies are allowed to invest domestically generated funds in pula as well as those from external sources in any securities issued by the central bank.

Departing temporary residents are entitled to a basic remittable terminal allowance of up to P 25,000. Double taxation agreements exist between Botswana and South Africa, Sweden, and the United Kingdom.

Changes During 1995

Exchange Arrangement

November 17. Botswana accepted the obligations of Article VIII, Sections 2, 3, and 4 of the Fund Articles of Agreement.

Resident and Nonresident Accounts

January 1. Companies operating in Botswana were permitted to open foreign currency accounts with commercial banks in deutsche mark, pounds sterling, South African rand, and U.S. dollars.

July 31. Commercial banks were authorized to open foreign currency accounts for individual permanent and temporary residents, nonresident individuals, and incorporated entities. The accounts are to facilitate foreign receipts and payments for approved transactions, without having to convert foreign currency receipts into pula and vice versa, and to protect against changes in exchange rates. The restriction on specified foreign currencies was removed and commercial banks were allowed to open foreign currency accounts in any currency at their discretion.

Payments for and Proceeds from Invisibles

January 1. An annual consolidated allowance to meet personal foreign payments—travel, subscriptions, and other payments—was set at an indicative limit of P 100,000 an adult and P 50,000 a child under 18 years of age.

January 1. An annual consolidated business allowance was set at an indicative limit of P 1 million to cover business travel, royalties, management fees, and other payments (excluding imports).

Capital

January 1. Individuals and businesses were permitted to make direct or portfolio investments abroad up to P 100,000 and P 1 million, respectively. However, a qualifying company must have been operational for the previous two years and registered with the Department of Taxes.

BRAZIL

(Position as of February 29, 1996)

Exchange Arrangement

The currency of Brazil is the Real (R$), the external value of which is determined by demand and supply in the interbank exchange market, although the Central Bank of Brazil has set an adjustable band for the external value of the real of R$0.97–R$1.06 per U.S. dollar as of January 30, 1996. The previous band of R$0.91–R$0.99 per U.S. dollar was established on June 22, 1995. Transactions in the exchange market are carried out by banks, brokers, and tourist agencies authorized to deal in foreign exchange; the tourist agencies and brokers deal only in banknotes and traveler's checks. The exchange rates are freely negotiated between the authorized institutions and their clients in all operations. On December 31, 1995, the buying and selling rates in the interbank exchange market were R$0.973 and R$0.977, respectively, per US$1. Rates for other currencies are based on the U.S. dollar rates in Brazil and the rates for the currencies concerned in the international market.

A financial transactions tax (*imposto sobre operações de crédito, câmbio e seguro, e sobre operações relativas a títulos e valores mobiliarios* (IOF)) of up to 25 percent is levied on exchange operations effected for the payment of imports of services.

Limits for the short position of banks are determined according to the size of the bank's total net assets indicated in the financial statements of June and December. No limit is imposed on the long position, but authorized banks must deposit overnight at the Central Bank the amounts needed to eliminate overbought positions that exceed the equivalent of US$5 million in the free exchange market. The limit for the long position in the exchange market of floating rates is fixed at US$1 million. The banks are permitted to buy and sell foreign exchange to each other without restriction; such transactions may be carried out either on a spot basis by cable or on a forward basis and must be settled within 2 working days for spot transactions or within 180 days for forward transactions. Banks may pay their clients a premium, corresponding to the expected variation of the domestic currency in relation to the currency subject of negotiation, by reason of forward operations. In addition, when an exchange contract for forward settlement is concluded, banks can provide short-term financing to exporters by providing domestic currency in advance, before or after the shipment of goods.

Administration of Control

The National Monetary Council is responsible for formulating overall foreign exchange policy. In accordance with the guidelines established by the council, exchange controls regulations affecting foreign capital, and the management of international reserves are under the jurisdiction of the Central Bank. The Ministry of Planning enforces limits on foreign borrowing by the public sector.

The foreign trade policy is formulated by the Ministry of Industry, Trade, and Tourism, implemented by the Secretariat of Foreign Trade (SECEX) and carried out by the Technical Department of Commercial Interchange (DTIC).

The Technical Department of Tariffs (DTT) of the Ministry of Industry, Trade, and Tourism is responsible for formulating guidelines for tariff policy. The DTT also decides on changes in customs duties under the provisions of existing legislation. The Ministry of Finance coordinates public sector import policy.

Prescription of Currency

In principle, prescription of currency is related to the country of origin of imports or the country of final destination of exports, unless otherwise prescribed or authorized. Settlements with bilateral payments agreement countries are made in "agreement dollars" through the relevant agreement account. A bilateral account is maintained with Hungary, but settlements are made in third-country currencies every 90 days, and interest rates payable on balances are based on those in the international capital market. Payments between Brazil and Argentina, Bolivia, Chile, Colombia, the Dominican Republic, Ecuador, Mexico, Paraguay, Peru, Uruguay, and Venezuela can be made through special central bank accounts within the framework of the multilateral clearing system of the Latin American Integration Association (LAIA). Settlements with countries with which Brazil has no payments agreements and no special payments arrangements are made in U.S. dollars.

Imports and Import Payments

All importers must be registered with the SECEX, and goods may be imported only by registered firms or persons. Imports are grouped into the following three categories: (1) imports that do not require prior administrative documentation, including samples without commercial value and certain educational materials; (2) imports that require an import certificate issued by the DTIC; and (3) prohibited imports (agrochemical products not authorized under Brazilian regulations, and certain drugs that are not licensed for reasons of security, health, morality, or industrial policy). Importers are permitted to purchase foreign exchange in the exchange market within 180 days of the settlement date.

There is also a limit on the direct importation and purchase on the domestic market of consumer goods by the public sector (the Government, autonomous agencies, and public enterprises).[1]

Most imports require prior approval from the DTIC, which is usually given promptly to registered importers of nonprohibited items.[2] The DTIC is authorized to levy a processing fee of up to 0.9 percent on the value of import certificates; as a rule, certificates are valid for 60 days, except for imports of capital goods. The DTIC issues clearance certificates for certain groups of commodities to special bonded warehouse importers. Import certificates for a number of specified imports may be obtained after the commodities have been landed but before they clear customs.

The importation of certain products requires the approval of the Ministry of Science and Technology. For some products, eligibility for exemption from import duties may be precluded by the existence of satisfactory domestic equivalents (*similares nacionais*).

Goods imported into the Manaus and Tabatinga free zones are subject to an annual quota. Foreign goods up to the equivalent of US$600 imported into the Manaus free trade zone can be transferred to other parts of Brazil (as a passenger's baggage) free of import taxes.

The SECEX may approve applications for payment for imports of any goods at terms of up to 720 days from the date of shipment without prior authorization from the Central Bank. External financing at terms in excess of 720 days for imports must be authorized by the Central Bank, which will evaluate them in the light of foreign debt policy. Payment of the amount financed at maturities over

360 days and accrued interest may be made only upon presentation of a certificate of authorization and a payment schedule issued by the Department of Foreign Capital (FIRCE) of the Central Bank. On January 11, 1995, the time to settle anticipatory settlements for critical imports was set at 60 days.

Exchange contracts may be settled within 180 days. The drafts, or letters of credit, relative to such contracts must be settled on maturity against the presentation of the appropriate documents by the importer. Official education and research institutions and the Ministry of Health may settle exchange contracts within 360 days following the same rules. Exchange contracts for imports financed under letters of credit must be closed on the date of settlement or two working days before the maturity date of the letters of credit.

Payments for Invisibles

Payments for current invisibles not covered by current regulations require approval from the Central Bank's Exchange Department (DECAM) or the FIRCE; remittances are authorized freely, subject to the presentation of supporting documents as evidence that a bona fide current transaction is involved.

There is no limit on the purchase of foreign exchange for Brazilian residents traveling abroad. Remittances abroad of income from foreign direct investments and reinvestment and remittances in respect of royalties and technical assistance are governed by Decree No. 55762 of February 17, 1965, which contains the regulations implementing the Foreign Investment Law No. 4131 of September 1962. Remittances are allowed only when the foreign capital concerned, including reinvestment, and the contracts for patents and trademarks and for technical, scientific, and administrative assistance are registered with the FIRCE in accordance with the established rules (see section on Capital, below). The registration of contracts or deeds for technical assistance or the use of patents or trademarks is subject to approval by the National Institute of Industrial Property. Remittances of interest on loans and credits and of related amortization payments are permitted freely in accordance with the terms stipulated in the respective contract and recorded in the certificate of registration. The private sector and both the financial and nonfinancial public sector are allowed access to foreign exchange for the purpose of servicing their debts, including those owed to nonresident banks.

Profit remittances are exempt from withholding for income tax purposes according to the Law No. 9249 of December 26, 1995.

---

[1]Under instructions issued by the Economic Development Council, federal ministries and subordinate agencies and public enterprises are required to submit, for approval by the president, an annual investment program specifying their expected import requirements.

[2]Selected imports are exempt from the prior approval requirement, including imports to the free trade zone of Manaus, wheat and petroleum imports, imports under the drawback scheme, and imports of goods included in trade agreements negotiated with LAIA member countries.

Amounts due as royalties for patents or for the use of trademarks, as well as for technical, scientific, and administrative assistance and the like, may be deducted from income tax liability to determine the taxable income, up to the limit of 5 percent of gross receipts in the first five years of the company's operation; amounts exceeding this limit are considered profits. The percentages are the same as those established in Brazil's tax laws for determining the maximum permissible deductions for such expenses.

Outward transfers other than capital may be made directly through authorized banks upon presentation by the remitters of the appropriate documentation. Outward transfers not included in public regulations need prior authorization from the Central Bank.

Purchasers of foreign exchange for a number of current invisibles are subject to the financial transaction tax of 25 percent. The financial transaction tax applicable to purchases of foreign exchange for payments of contracts involving transfers of technology that are registered with the National Institute of Industrial Property was reduced to zero in 1994.

Travelers may take out domestic and foreign banknotes without restriction but must declare to customs any amount over US$10,000 or the equivalent in other currencies. Foreign tourists leaving Brazil may buy foreign currency up to 50 percent percent of the amount exchanged into domestic currency during the visit.

Exports and Export Proceeds

Exports requiring the prior approval of the SECEX include those effected through bilateral accounts, exports without exchange cover, exports on consignment, re-exports, commodities for which minimum export prices are fixed by the SECEX, and exports requiring prior authorization from government agencies. Exports of hides of wild animals in any form are prohibited.

This Integrated Foreign Trade System (*Sistema Integrado de Comércio Exterior*—SISCOMEX) introduced by Decree No. 660, dated September 25, 1992, and implemented on January 4, 1993, integrates the activities related to registration, monitoring, and control of foreign trade operations in a single computerized flow of information. The SISCOMEX comprises two subsystems; the exports subsystem eliminated, for more than 90 percent of Brazilian exports, all paperwork (forms, licenses, and certificates), allowing exporters, carriers, banks, and brokers to register the various stages of an export process directly through the interlinked computers

of the SECEX, customs, and the Central Bank. The import subsystem is being developed.

On January 11, 1995, advances on foreign exchange contracts were reinstated for operations with terms exceeding 360 days. On January 11, 1995, the time for anticipatory settlements was extended from 90 days to 180 days for exporters exporting more than US$10 million per year and from 150 days to 180 days for small exporters. For products considered essential for the supply of the domestic market (fuel, mineral oils, chemical products, plastics, wood pastes, paper, cotton, linen and synthetic thread, flat steel, and aluminum) the maximum period was extended from 30 days to 60 days; the period was extended to 180 days in November 1995.

Proceeds from Invisibles

Exchange proceeds from current invisibles must be sold to the authorized banks at the prevailing market rate. Travelers may freely bring in domestic and foreign currency notes but must declare to customs any values over US$10,000 or the equivalent in other currencies.

Capital

Brazilian banks are permitted to sell foreign exchange to Brazilian investors in MERCOSUR countries in the exchange market.

Capital inflows in the form of financial loans under National Monetary Council Resolution No. 63, as amended, or under the provision of Law No. 4131 on foreign investment, require prior approval from the Central Bank. Prior approval from the Central Bank is required for borrowing by the private or public sector when the foreign funds originate from official financial institutions abroad; when the transaction is to be guaranteed by the national Treasury or, on its behalf, by any official credit institution; and for other foreign borrowing by the public sector. In addition, prior approval from the Central Bank is required for borrowing by the private sector when the funds originate abroad. Proceeds of foreign borrowing converted into domestic currency are subject to a financial transaction tax with rates that range from 5 percent for loans with maturities under three years to zero percent for loans with maturities over six years. Otherwise, inward transfers are unrestricted and free of control, although subsequent use of the proceeds for the acquisition of certain domestic assets may be restricted.

There is a separate regime for inward portfolio investment. Portfolio investment by foreign investors in fixed-income instruments is restricted to two classes of fixed-income funds: the Fixed-Income

Funds that are subject to a transaction tax of 7 percent and the Privatization Funds that are subject to a transaction tax of 5 percent. For the purposes of the repatriation and remittance of income, however, inward transfers of foreign capital and the reinvestment of profits on foreign capital must be registered with the FIRCE. Foreign capital is defined for this purpose as (1) goods, machinery, and equipment used to produce goods or render services that have entered the country without an initial corresponding expenditure of foreign exchange; and (2) financial and monetary resources brought into the country for investment in economic pursuits, provided that, in either case, the owner is a person or firm residing or domiciled abroad or with headquarters abroad.

Foreign capital other than capital invested in Brazilian securities is classified, for purposes of registration, as direct investment or loan and includes reinvested profits from foreign capital. Direct investment is defined as the foreign capital that constitutes part of the corporate capital and participates directly in the risk inherent in an economic undertaking. Foreign capital that is not part of the corporate capital of any enterprise is considered to be a loan, except portfolio investments. Any loan obtained to purchase capital goods abroad is considered import financing, whether financed by the manufacturer (suppliers' credit) or by a third party.

Foreign investments in the Brazilian capital market may be made through one of the five alternatives established under National Monetary Council Resolution 1289, Annexes I–V, dated March 20, 1987. Annex I is for investment companies that are open to natural persons and companies, and residents domiciled or headquartered abroad. Such companies take the form of authorized capital corporations whose objective is to invest in diversified securities portfolios. They are managed by investment banks, brokerage firms, or securities and exchange dealers. Through Annex II, or investment funds, natural persons and companies, and residents domiciled or headquartered abroad, as well as funds or other foreign collective investment entities, can invest in a securities portfolio established as an open fund without legal representation. Annex III is for diversified stock portfolios managed by an investment bank, a brokerage firm, or a securities and exchange dealer, headquartered in Brazil and owned jointly with a foreign institution. Annex IV is for funds and other collective investment entities established abroad including pension funds, portfolios belonging to financial institutions and insurance companies, and mutual investment funds that may acquire portfolios of bonds and

other securities in Brazil once the constitutions and administrations of these entities have been approved by the Central Bank and the Securities and Exchange Commission. Through Annex V, or depository receipts, it is possible to purchase abroad certificates representing stocks of a domestic public company (open capital). These papers represent the securitizations of the stocks of an issuing company. Portfolio investment in fixed-income instruments may be made through the purchase of quotas of the Investment Fund, Foreign Capital. Portfolio investments are exempt from the capital gains tax, but earning resulting from variable income assets are subject to a 10 percent income tax and earning resulting from fixed-income assets are subject to a 15 percent income tax. Invested capital may be repatriated freely. The issuance of debentures that can be converted into stocks in domestic enterprises is permitted. Externally financed nonprofit organizations are permitted to undertake debt-for-nature swaps.

Investments made in the form of goods are subject to approval and registration at the Central Bank and SECEX. To register loans made in a foreign currency, the interest rate must correspond to that prevailing in the loan's original market; the amortization schedule must not be disproportionately heavy in the early stages of repayment.

Reinvestment is defined as the profits of companies established in Brazil and accruing to persons or companies residing abroad when they have been reinvested in the same companies that produced them or in another sector of the Brazilian economy. The registration of reinvested profits is made simultaneously in Brazilian currency and the currency of the country to which the profits could have been remitted. The conversion is calculated at the average exchange rate prevailing on the date the profits are reinvested.

Special regulations govern borrowing abroad. Under National Monetary Council Resolution No. 63 (as amended), private, commercial, investment, and development banks and the Banco Nacional de Desenvolvimento Económico e Social may be authorized to take up foreign currency credits abroad for domestic relending in order to finance working capital. Safeguards against excessive use of such credits include limitations on the foreign obligations that each bank may assume (related to the terms of the credit and the size of the bank) and the provision that the ultimate borrower must agree to bear the exchange risk. Financial and nonfinancial institutions are authorized to obtain resources from abroad by issuing commercial papers, notes, and bonds, including securities, that can be converted into stocks. Brazilian banks located abroad are allowed to issue medium- and long-term certificates of deposit, and exporters are allowed to issue medium-term debt instruments secured with future export receipts. Financial institutions of the National System of Rural Credit are allowed to contract foreign resources with a minimum maturity of 180 days for the financing in the agricultural sector (Resolution No. 2148). Financial institutions are allowed to contract resources with a minimum maturity of 720 days for the financing of the construction and acquisition of new real estate ventures (Resolution No. 2170), all other financial loans in foreign currency are governed by the general provisions of Law No. 4131 on foreign investment. Loans contracted under this law also require prior authorization from the Central Bank, but the Central Bank does not undertake to provide specific exchange cover for them. Loans contracted under Resolution No. 63 and Law No. 4131 must have a minimum term of 36 months, except for relending operations to the agricultural sector, which may have a minimum term of 6 months. Exemptions to amount and maturity requirements are established in Resolutions Nos. 2148 and 2170, as mentioned above. There are requirements established from time to time by the Central Bank, which permits the total of loans outstanding to rise only to the extent that the servicing commitments on Brazil's total external indebtedness do not depart from the guidelines set by the National Monetary Council. However, provided that the full amount of the foreign exchange remains committed to Brazil for the minimum specified maturity, loans to the final borrower in Brazil, as well as loans to banks under Resolution No. 63, may be made on terms shorter than the final maturity of the debt abroad, and these funds may subsequently be relent to the same or to a second borrower.

Remittances of proceeds from sales of property and inheritance are permitted

Gold

There are two separate markets for gold transactions: the financial market, where over 50 percent of transactions occur and which is regulated by the Central Bank; and commercial markets. The first domestic negotiation of newly mined gold on the financial market is subject to a 1 percent financial transactions tax. Rules regarding gold transactions for industrial purposes are defined separately by the federal states, which also establish different rates for the commercial tax levied on them. The Central Bank and authorized institutions are empowered to buy and sell gold on the domestic

and international markets (Law No. 4595 of December 31, 1964, and Law No. 7766 of May 11, 1989). Purchases of gold are made at current domestic and international prices; the international price is considered a target price. Imports of gold are subject to the issuance of an import certificate by the SECEX. Exports of gold are subject to the same procedures as those that are applied through the SECEX in respect of other products.

Changes During 1995

Exchange Arrangement

March 6. A new exchange rate system based on bands was introduced. The band was set at R$0.86–R$0.90 per U.S. dollar until May 2, when it would be changed to R$0.86–R$0.98 per U.S. dollar.

March 10. The exchange rate band was changed to R$0.88–R$0.93 per U.S. dollar for an undetermined period of time. The Central Bank specified that it would intervene in the foreign exchange market using electronic auctions.

June 22. The exchange rate band was changed to R$0.91–R$0.99 per U.S. dollar.

Imports and Import Payments

April 20. The anticipated payment for imports was limited to 20 percent of the value of the merchandise, except in some specific cases (Circular No. 2561).

Exports and Export Proceeds

January 11. The reserve requirement of 15 percent on Advances for Export Contracts (ACC) was eliminated (Circular No. 2534).

January 11. The anticipated payment for export operations was reinstated with a minimum term of 360 days (Circular No. 2538).

January 11. The maximum period for ACCs was lengthened from 90 days to 180 days for large exporters and from 150 days to 180 days for small exporters (Circular No. 2539). For products considered essential to internal supply, the maximum period was increased from 30 days to 60 days.

April 27. Anticipated payments for exports by foreign individuals, corporations, or financial institutions were authorized.

November 22. The period for the contracting of foreign exchange prior to shipment of merchandise considered essential for domestic supply was increased from 60 days to 180 days (Circular No. 2639).

December 20. Exports of goods and services may be financed with the resources of the Export Financing Program (PROEX) through a discount of export credit securities and if there is a financing contract between the Brazilian government and foreign public sector entities (Resolution No. 2224). The channeling of PROEX resources into establishing of any credit lines for foreign public or private entities was prohibited.

Capital

March 9. The minimum period for the renewal and extension of foreign credit operations through floating rate notes, fixed rate notes, floating rate certificates of deposits, fixed rate certificates of deposits, private and public bonds, notes, and commercial paper was lowered from 36 months to 6 months (Circulars Nos. 2547 and 2559, and Carta-Circular No. 2533).

March 9. The limits of the long position of banks and dealers in the fluctuating foreign exchange market were lowered from US$10 million to US$1 million, and from US$1 million to US$0.5 million, respectively (Circular No. 2548). The long position of banks in the commercial foreign exchange market was lowered from US$50 million to US$5 million (Circular No. 2549).

March 9. The IOF was reduced from 7 percent to zero percent on foreign loans, from 9 percent to 5 percent on investments in fixed-income funds, and from 1 percent to zero percent on investment in stocks (Portaria No. 95 of the Ministry of Finance).

March 9. The minimum average term for contracting financial loans was lowered from 36 months to 24 months (Circular No. 2546).

March 9. The minimum term for relending operations related to Resolution No. 63 was lowered from 540 days to 90 days (Circular No. 2545).

March 9. The permission granted for anticipated payment of financial loans and import financing was revoked (Resolution No. 2147).

March 16. Financial institutions of the National System of Rural Credit were allowed to contract foreign resources with a minimum maturity of 180 days for the financing of investment, marketing, and other expenses in the agricultural sector (Resolutions Nos. 2148 and 2151). The resources were exempted from the minimum period of three years for credit operations and fixed at 180 days, and from the financial taxation of 5 percent.

April 27. The limits on the short position of banks in the fluctuating and commercial foreign exchange markets were increased by 50 percent (Circulars Nos. 2565 and 2566).

June 30. Financial institutions were allowed to contract resources with a minimum maturity of 720 days for the financing of the construction and acquisition of new real estate ventures (Resolution No. 2170).

August 11. The tax on financial transactions (IOF) for interbank operations in the floating foreign exchange markets among financial institutions abroad and in Brazil was extended (Decree No. 1591). The IOF rate for these operations was set at 7 percent, and the IOF rates were raised for financial loans from zero to 5 percent, and for investments in fixed income funds, from 5 percent to 7 percent (Directive No. 202 of the Ministry of Finance).

August 11. Foreign investors were prohibited from channeling resources into operations in the futures and option markets.

August 15. The IOF rate for foreign resources for the agricultural sector was set at zero.

September 15. Differentiated IOF rates for financial loans with different maturities were established (Directive No. 228 of the Ministry of Finance).

September 28. The conversion of federal public sector entities' foreign debt into investments, in the framework of the National Privatization Program, was regulated. The initial discount of 25 percent was reduced to zero (Resolution No. 2203 and Circular No. 2623).

October 12. Resources originating from the liquidation of ACCs must be used to pay the credit lines provided by foreign financial institutions for such purposes to financial institutions in Brazil that came under bankruptcy, extrajudicial liquidation, or intervention (Provisional Measure No. 1113).

Changes During 1996

Exchange Arrangement

January 30. The exchange rate band was set at R$0.97–R$1.06 per US$1.

Capital

January 1. Profits and dividends remitted abroad were exempted from income tax, while the tax rate applied to profits on direct investments were reduced from 25 percent to 15 percent. The maximum rate applicable to interests remitted abroad was also reduced from 25 percent to 15 percent. Profits from investments listed in Annexes I to IV of the Resolution No. 1289/87 were subject to a 10 percent income tax if they originated in variable income assets and to a 15 percent tax if they originated in fixed-income assets.

February 8. The resources obtained abroad under the terms of Resolution No. 63 may be invested in interbank on-lending operations and leasing operations, and in acquiring credit rights tied to exchange rate floating (Circular No. 2660).

February 8. The minimum average term for contracting, renewing, or extending foreign loans was increased from 24 months to 36 months, except for loans under the Resolution No. 2148 (Rural Credit System, minimum of 180 days), the Resolution No. 2170 (Real Estate, minimum of 720 days), and for loans carried out by financial institutions under the Special Temporary Administration (RAET, minimum of 24 months) (Circular No. 2661).

February 8. The IOF rate for foreign investments in Privatization Funds was extended (Decree No. 1815). The IOF rate for these investments was set at 5 percent (Directive No. 28).

February 8. The IOF rate for foreign investments in Real Estate Investment Funds and Mutual Investment Funds in Emergent Enterprises, over sale, redemption, or transferring value, for applications in quotas of the fund, was set at 10 percent when the fund has not been constituted or has not begun to work regularly, 5 percent when the fund has been constituted and is working regularly, and up to one year after its constitution, and zero after one year of the fund's constitution (Decree No. 1814).

February 8. Foreign investors cited in Appendices I–IV to Resolution No. 1289 were prohibited from acquiring Agrarian Debt Securities (TDAO), National Development Fund Obligations (OFND), and debentures issued by Siderurgia Brasileira S.A. (SIDERBRAS) (Resolution No. 2246).

February 8. Foreign investors were allowed to buy quotas of Real Estate Investment Funds, constituted with authorization from the Securities and Exchange Commission—CVM (Resolution No. 2248).

February 8. Foreign investors were allowed to buy quotas of Mutual Investment Funds in Emergent Enterprises constituted with authorization from the Securities and Exchange Commission—CVM (Resolution No. 2247).

March 1. The resources obtained abroad under the terms of Resolution No. 63 may be invested in national currency deposits in the Central Bank, without remuneration (Circular No. 2670).

April 18. The operations carried out by the states, Federal District, the municipalities, and their respective semi-autonomous agencies were restricted according to several criteria (Resolution No. 2271).

BRUNEI DARUSSALAM[1]

(Position as of December 31, 1995)

Exchange Arrangement

The currency of Brunei Darussalam is the Brunei Dollar (Ringgit in Malaysia). It is issued by the Brunei Currency Board, only against payment in Singapore dollars and at par. Under the terms of a 1967 Currency Interchangeability Agreement between the Brunei Currency Board and the Board of Commissioners of Currency of Singapore, the Singapore dollar is customary tender in Brunei Darussalam and the Brunei dollar is customary tender in Singapore. The Brunei Currency Board and Board of Commissioners of Currency of Singapore have undertaken to accept each other's currency and exchange it, at par and without charge, into their own, and have instructed their banks to do the same with their customers. Any excess in currency is regularly repatriated with the issuing institution bearing the costs, and settlements are made in the other country's currency. The Brunei Currency Board only deals in Singapore dollars and does not quote rates for other currencies. Banks, however, are free to deal in all currencies, with no restrictions on amount, maturity, or type of transaction.

The Brunei Association of Banks fixes daily buying and selling rates for telegraphic transfers and sight drafts in terms of 17 other currencies on the basis of these currencies' interbank quotations in relation to the Singapore dollar.[2] Banks in Brunei Darussalam must apply these rates for transactions with the general public in amounts up to B$100,000. Exchange rates for amounts exceeding B$100,000 are set competitively by each bank on the basis of the current interbank quotations for the Singapore dollar in the Singapore market.

There is no forward market for foreign exchange in Brunei Darussalam. However, as a result of the Currency Interchangeability Agreement with Singapore, foreign exchange risk can be hedged in terms of Singapore dollars by resorting to facilities available in that country, including foreign currency futures and options traded on the Singapore International Monetary Exchange (SIMEX), over-the-counter forward transactions arranged by banks in

Singapore, and short-term foreign exchange swap market operated among the banks in the Singapore money market.

There are no taxes or subsidies on purchases or sales of foreign exchange.

Brunei Darussalam accepted the obligations of Article VIII, Sections 2, 3, and 4 of the Fund Agreement on October 10, 1995.

Administration of Control

There are no formal exchange controls, but under the 1956 Exchange Control Act (as amended most recently in 1984), the Ministry of Finance retains responsibility for exchange control matters. The Ministry of Finance also licenses and supervises commercial banks, including foreign-owned banks incorporated in Brunei Darussalam and branches of foreign banks operating in Brunei Darussalam.

The Economic Development Board in the Ministry of Finance is responsible for elaborating and administering programs to encourage foreign investment. It may issue certificates granting tax relief for certain approved projects and may enter into joint-venture agreements with foreign investors. It may also purchase, hold, and lease land for industrial purposes. A one-stop agency in the Ministry of Industry and Primary Resources facilitates inward investment. The Registrar of Companies controls the functioning within Brunei Darussalam of enterprises incorporated locally or registered as the branch of a foreign limited company. The Tourism Promotion Committee in the Ministry of Industry and Primary Resources works to encourage tourism.

Prescription of Currency

There are no prescription of currency requirements. Settlements with residents of Singapore and the Eastern Malaysian states of Sabah and Sarawak are normally effected in the currencies of the countries involved or in third currencies, as agreed between the parties concerned.

Resident and Nonresident Accounts

There is no distinction between accounts of residents and nonresidents of Brunei Darussalam, and accounts may be maintained in both domestic and foreign currencies. Debits and credits to all accounts may be made freely.

---

[1]Brunei Darussalam became a member of the IMF on October 10, 1995.

[2]The currencies are the Australian dollar, Canadian dollar, deutsche mark, French franc, Hong Kong dollar, Indian rupee, Indonesian rupiah, Japanese yen, Malaysian ringgit, Netherlands guilder, New Zealand dollar, Philippine peso, pound sterling, Saudi riyal, Swiss franc, Thai baht, and the U.S. dollar.

Imports and Import Payments

There are no restrictions on the origin of imports. A few imports are banned or restricted for nature conservation, health, safety, security, or religious reasons. Restricted items may be imported only with the permission of the relevant ministry. Except for cigarettes and alcoholic beverages, all imports are subject to ad valorem tariff rates ranging from zero to 200 percent. Some 70 percent of items (including basic foodstuffs, and construction and educational materials) are zero rated. Rates of 5 percent, 15 percent, and 20 percent apply to most other items. Fireworks are subject to a 30 percent duty while automobiles are subject to duties of 40 percent to 200 percent, depending on engine size. Brunei Darussalam is a party to the Agreement on the Common Effective Preferential Tariff (CEPT) Scheme for the ASEAN Free Trade Area (AFTA). The CEPT Scheme came into operation in Brunei Darussalam on June 1, 1994, and under its terms, Brunei Darussalam will lower its tariff rates on imports from other ASEAN countries to zero by 2003, with the exception of about 120 tariff lines that are permanently excluded under the terms of the CEPT Scheme.

Payments for Invisibles

All payments for invisibles may be made freely. There are no restrictions on the amount of foreign exchange that may be used for travel abroad. Remittances to nonresidents of dividends, interest, and profits may be made freely, but interest payments to nonresidents are subject to a 20 percent withholding tax. Interest on loans exceeding B$200,000 that are used for the purchase of productive equipment (so-called approved foreign loans) may be exempt from the tax, subject to submission of the loan documentation. Resident and nonresident travelers may take out any amount in foreign or Brunei banknotes.

Exports and Export Proceeds

There are no restrictions on the destination of exports. Certain exports originating in Brunei Darussalam—for example, textiles and textile products—are subject to quantitative restrictions and other nontariff barriers in the importing countries, particularly Canada, Norway, the United States, and the members of the European Union. The Muara Export Zone, a free trade area, serves as an entry point for goods destined for the East ASEAN Growth Area (EAGA).

Export licenses are required for alcoholic beverages, cigarettes, diesel, gasoline, kerosene, rice, salt, and sugar. There are no export taxes.

Export proceeds need not be repatriated or surrendered.

Proceeds from Invisibles

Proceeds from invisibles need not be repatriated or surrendered and may be disposed of freely. Resident and nonresident travelers may bring in any amount in foreign banknotes and coins, including Brunei gold coins.

Capital

There are no restrictions on inward or outward capital transfers. Nonresidents are free to repatriate capital or profits or to borrow from banks in Brunei Darussalam. Banks may accept deposits and make loans in foreign currency.

There are no sectoral restrictions on inward foreign direct investment. Activities relating to national food security and those based on local resources require some degree of local participation. Industries producing for the local market that are not related to national food security and industries that solely export may be fully foreign owned. Joint ventures are particularly encouraged in export-oriented industries and activities supporting such industries. At least one-half of the directors of a company must be either Brunei citizens or residents of Brunei Darussalam.

The Industrial Incentives Act provides exemption from income tax and import duties to companies granted pioneer status, as well as established companies planning expansion. There is a double taxation agreement with the United Kingdom. Under the terms of the agreement, tax credits are available only for resident companies.[3]

Only Brunei citizens are allowed to own land. However, foreign investors may lease land on a long-term basis, including on-sites set aside for industry, agriculture, agroforestry, and aquaculture.

Gold

Only banks licensed to operate in Brunei Darussalam and gold dealers and jewelers specifically authorized by the Ministry of Finance may buy and sell gold bars. Gold bars are not subject to import duty, but a 10 percent import duty is levied on the importation of gold jewelry.

---

[3]A company, whether incorporated in Brunei Darussalam or overseas, is considered a resident of Brunei Darussalam for tax purposes if the control and management of its activities are exercised in Brunei Darussalam. This is, inter alia, considered to be the case if its directors' meetings are held in Brunei Darussalam.

BULGARIA

(Position as of December 31, 1995)

Exchange Arrangement

The currency of Bulgaria is the Lev (plural Leva). The Bulgarian National Bank quotes daily the exchange rate of the lev in terms of the U.S. dollar based on the weighted average of transactions in the interbank exchange market during the previous trading day. This rate is called the central exchange rate. Exchange rates for other currencies are determined by their cross rate relationships with the U.S. dollar in the international exchange market. On December 31, 1995, the exchange rate quoted by the Bulgarian National Bank in terms of the U.S. dollar was leva 70.7 per $1. Exchange bureaus are allowed to conduct foreign exchange transactions in cash only. There are no taxes or subsidies on purchases or sales of foreign exchange. There are no arrangements for forward cover against exchange rate risk operating in the official or the commercial banking sector.

Administration of Control

Exchange controls are administered by the Ministry of Finance and the Bulgarian National Bank. The Bulgarian National Bank is responsible for implementing the exchange rate policy. Twenty commercial banks, 2 branches of foreign banks, and 1 financial institution conduct foreign exchange transactions. Another 13 banks are authorized to open bank accounts for settlement of payments abroad.

Prescription of Currency

Payments to and from countries with which Bulgaria maintains bilateral agreements are made in the currencies and in accordance with the procedures set forth in those agreements.[1] Transactions generally are settled through clearing accounts. Balances in these accounts (annual and multiyear) generally are to be settled in goods during the six months after the agreement has been terminated; thereafter, they are settled in convertible currencies.

---

[1]At the end of 1995, Bulgaria maintained bilateral clearing and barter agreements with the Islamic State of Afghanistan, Bangladesh, Cambodia, China, Ethiopia, Ghana, Guinea, Guyana, India, the Islamic Republic of Iran, the Lao People's Democratic Republic, Mozambique, Nicaragua, Pakistan, Romania, Syria, and Tanzania. Bulgaria has outstanding transferable ruble accounts with Germany, Hungary, Mongolia, Poland, Romania, and Russia. Only one intergovernmental arrangement with Bangladesh is still actively being used to settle trade.

Resident and Nonresident Accounts

Residents may maintain foreign currency deposit accounts in Bulgaria, which may be credited without restriction, and from which transfers abroad may be made with permission from the Ministry of Finance and the Bulgarian National Bank (pursuant to the provisions of Decree No. 15 of the Council of Ministers of 1991). Balances on these accounts earn interest at international market rates. Nonresidents may maintain accounts in foreign currencies and leva without authorization, limitation, or restriction for purposes of making transactions in Bulgaria. The crediting and debiting of foreign currency accounts are not subject to any regulations, and transfers abroad from these accounts are free of restriction.

Imports and Exports

Imports of some sensitive goods are subject to registration at the Ministry of Trade. Imports of ice cream are subject to a quota; the removal of this quota is under consideration. Imports of certain goods are restricted for health and security reasons. Import tariff rates range from 5 percent to 55 percent. Tariffs are calculated on the transaction values (actual invoice price paid) in foreign currency and converted to leva. The import surcharge (which was 3 percent when introduced in August 1993, then reduced to 2 percent on January 1, 1994, and then to 1 percent on January 1, 1995) was eliminated at the end of 1995. The surcharge was waived for the importation of certain energy products, pharmaceuticals, and facilities for environmental protection. Under Government Decree No. 241 (January 1, 1994), certain goods in these categories are exempt from customs duty or are subject to ceilings for duty-free imports or reduced-duty imports.

Proceeds from exports must be repatriated within one month but do not have to be surrendered; they may be retained in foreign currencies or sold in the interbank exchange market. Under Government Decree No. 241, export taxes are levied on certain types of timber, hides, wool, sunflower oil, grain, and some copper products. The export tax is quoted in U.S. dollars but paid in leva. Exports and imports of tobacco products, coal, petroleum, livestock and meat, dairy products, certain grains, textiles, ferrous metals and alloys, and imports of flat glass are required to be registered. The only export quotas still in place relate to certain wheat exports and metal scrap. Wheat quotas were introduced in 1994 in conjunction with a narrowing of the coverage of the temporary export bans, which currently include only certain types of grains and metal scrap.

Special licenses are required for transactions under barter and clearing arrangements, for exports proceeds to be received in leva; exports under government credits and exports subject to quotas and voluntary export restraint agreements; imports and exports of military hardware and related technologies; endangered flora and fauna; radioactive and hazardous materials; crafts and antiques; pharmaceuticals; herbicides; pesticides; flour; unbottled alcohol; intellectual property; jewelry; and rare and precious metals. Licenses are normally granted within two working days. Exports of ferrous and nonferrous scrap metal, female livestock, and grains were prohibited until the end of 1994. The exportation of goods received as humanitarian aid and of human blood and plasma is prohibited.

Bulgaria has resumed its efforts to accede to the World Trade Organization (WTO) (it applied for accession to the GATT in 1986). Toward ensuring compatibility of its trade regime with the requirements of WTO and its member countries, Bulgaria has taken measures that include the passage of legislation on intellectual property and the granting of tariff concessions.

Payments for and Proceeds from Invisibles

Foreign exchange allowances for business travel are granted without restriction. Allowances for tourist travel and certain other invisible payments are limited to the leva equivalent of up to $2,000 a person a year for people without foreign currency deposits. Resident holders of foreign exchange deposits may use balances on these deposit accounts without restriction.

Commercial banks may sell foreign exchange freely to resident individuals or resident legal persons if proper documentation certifies that foreign exchange is needed for (1) authorized imports of goods and services; (2) transportation and other expenses related to the conveyance of goods and passengers carried out by nonresidents; (3) interest and amortization with respect to credits approved by the Bulgarian National Bank; (4) business travel in compliance with the established procedures; (5) insurance fees; (6) banking commissions; (7) education and training; (8) health care; (9) diplomatic, consular, and other government agencies of Bulgaria abroad; (10) commercial representative offices of Bulgarian traders abroad; (11) commissions, advertising fees, and other expenses related to economic activities (including

fairs and exhibitions); (12) membership fees in international organizations; and (13) participation in international contests and festivals.

Nonresidents may purchase foreign currency from Bulgarian commercial banks to transfer abroad (1) investment income received in leva; (2) compensation received following nationalization of investment enterprises; (3) proceeds from liquidation of investment; (4) proceeds from sales of investment enterprises received in leva; and (5) amounts received in leva under judicial settlement of guaranteed claims. Transfers abroad in compliance with the above cases may be effected upon presentation of documents that certify that outstanding liabilities have been paid. Remittances of earnings by foreign workers and remittances for family maintenance are not explicitly mentioned in Decree No. 15 (of February 8, 1991), which governs foreign exchange control, but they have been treated implicitly as transfers abroad that are not related to merchandise imports. The following transfers abroad require prior permission from the Bulgarian National Bank in consultation with the Ministry of Finance as stipulated by the Decree No. 15: (1) indirect investments; (2) official credits extended to and received from abroad; (3) investments abroad; and (4) free transfers in foreign currency when they are not connected with imports of goods and services.

Proceeds from invisibles must be repatriated within one month but do not have to be surrendered and may be retained in foreign currencies or sold in the interbank exchange market.

Residents and nonresidents may take out or bring in Bulgarian banknotes and coins up to leva 10,000; permission from the Bulgarian National Bank is required to import or export amounts exceeding this limit. Residents may take out foreign currency notes up to the equivalent of $1,000 without restriction. There is no limit on foreign currency notes nonresidents may bring into the country but the amount must be declared, and they may take out unspent foreign currency notes upon departure.

Capital

Licensed banks may borrow abroad without the authorization of the Bulgarian National Bank. The forex-licensed commercial banks, however, may borrow abroad only if they do not request a guarantee from the Government of Bulgaria and if their borrowing complies with the prudential regulations set up by the Bulgarian National Bank. They may also extend foreign currency and lev loans to residents and nonresidents.

Foreign direct investments in Bulgaria are governed by the Law on the Economic Activity of Foreign Persons and Protection of Foreign Investments (State Gazette No. 8/1992). Foreign direct investments must be registered with the Ministry of Finance and require authorization only if they are undertaken in sectors that are considered sensitive. Foreign direct investments are guaranteed against expropriation, except for nationalization through legal process. Foreign firms are granted the same status as domestic firms; they may, under certain conditions, benefit from preferential treatment, including reduced taxation and access to judicial appeal outside the system of state arbitration. In general, fully owned foreign firms are subject to a profit tax of 40 percent, and joint ventures are subject to a profit tax of 30 percent; all other firms with foreign participation are subject to the same profit tax as domestic firms (40 percent). Repatriation of liquidated capital and after-tax profits is not restricted, and transfers of profits in domestic currency do not require a special authorization.

Gold

The Ministry of Finance controls the acquisition, possession, processing, and disposal of gold, silver, and platinum. The Bulgarian National Bank is the only institution entitled to purchase, sell, hold, import, or export gold for monetary and nonmonetary purposes. All domestic transactions for industrial purposes must be conducted at current prices through the Bulgarian National Bank. Commercial banks are not authorized to deal or speculate (on their own or on their customers' behalf) in precious metals, with the exception that the Bulgarian Foreign Trade Bank is licensed to deal in precious metals. Resident individuals may hold gold but may not trade or deal in it. The amount of gold and jewelry products that they may import is limited. Nonresidents are permitted to bring in and take out their jewelry but may not trade. Nonresidents must have permission from the Ministry of Finance, the Bulgarian National Bank, and the Ministry of Industry and Commerce to buy gold, silver, and platinum products.

Changes During 1995

Imports and Exports

January 1. The import surcharge was reduced from 2 percent to 1 percent. The exportation of the following products was banned: goods received as humanitarian aid, blood products, natural mud for medical purposes, and unmanufactured and nonfermented tobacco. Temporary export bans on the following products were established: barley for the brewing industry (until October 30, 1995); maize (until October 30, 1995); ferrous waste and scrap; nonferrous waste and scrap; ingots and billets of copper; potassium iodate, potassium iodide, and iodized salt.

December 1. The import surcharge was eliminated.

BURKINA FASO

(Position as of June 30, 1996)

Exchange Arrangement

The currency of Burkina Faso is the CFA Franc,[1] the external value of which is pegged to the French franc, the intervention currency, at the fixed rate of CFAF 1 per F 0.01. The official buying and selling rate is CFAF 100 per F 1. Exchange rates for other currencies are derived from the rate in the Paris exchange market and the fixed rate between the French franc and the CFA franc. Banks levy a commission of 2.5 per mil on transfers to all countries outside the West African Economic and Monetary Union (WAEMU), all of which must be surrendered to the Treasury.[2] There are no taxes or subsidies on purchases or sales of foreign exchange.[3]

In the official and commercial banking sectors, forward exchange cover may be arranged only by residents for settlements with respect to imports of goods on certain lists. All contracts for forward exchange cover must be denominated in the currency of payment stipulated in the contract and are subject to prior authorization by the Minister of Finance. Nonrenewable forward exchange contracts may be concluded for one month. For certain products, the maturity period of forward exchange cover may be renewed once for three months.

With the exception of measures relating to gold, the repatriation of export proceeds, the issuing, advertising, or offering for sale of securities and capital assets, and the soliciting of funds for investments abroad, exchange controls do not apply to (1) France (and its overseas departments and territories) and Monaco; and (2) all countries whose bank of issue is linked with the French Treasury by an Operations Account (Benin, Cameroon, Central African Republic, Chad, Comoros, Congo, Côte d'Ivoire, Equatorial Guinea, Gabon, Mali, Niger, Senegal, and Togo). All payments to these countries may be made freely. All other countries are considered foreign countries.

Burkina Faso accepted the obligations of Article VIII, Sections 2, 3, and 4 of the Fund Agreement on June 1, 1996.

Administration of Control

Exchange control is administered by the Directorate of the Treasury in the Ministry of Finance. The approval authority for exchange control (except for imports and exports of gold, forward exchange cover, and the opening of external accounts in foreign currency) has been delegated to the BCEAO and, within limits specified in the exchange control regulations, to its authorized intermediaries. The BCEAO is also authorized to collect, either directly or through banks, financial institutions, the Postal Administration, or judicial agents, any information necessary to compile balance of payments statistics. All exchange transactions relating to foreign countries must be effected through authorized banks, the Postal Administration, or the BCEAO. Import and export licenses are issued by the Directorate-General of Foreign Trade in the Ministry of Industry, Commerce, and Mines. Import certificates for liberalized commodities and export attestations are made out by the importer or exporter. Settlements with a country outside the Operations Account area must be formally approved by the customs administration.

Arrears are maintained with respect to external payments.

Prescription of Currency

Because Burkina Faso is an Operations Account country, settlements with France (as defined above), Monaco, and other Operations Account countries are made in CFA francs, French francs, or the currencies of Operations Account countries. Current transactions with The Gambia, Ghana, Guinea, Guinea-Bissau, Liberia, Mauritania, Nigeria, and Sierra Leone are settled through the West African Clearing House. Certain settlements are channeled through special accounts.[4] Settlements with all other countries are usually effected either through correspondent banks in France or the country concerned in the currencies of those countries, or through foreign accounts in francs in French francs or other currencies of the Operations Account area.

---

[1]The CFA franc is issued by the Central Bank of West African States (BCEAO) and is the common currency in Benin, Burkina Faso, Côte d'Ivoire, Mali, Niger, Senegal, and Togo.

[2]Banks are free to determine and collect a commission on transfers between member countries of the WAEMU.

[3]Banks may levy a commission of 2 percent on the exchange of CFAF banknotes for French franc notes.

[4]A bilateral agreement maintained with Ghana is inoperative.

Nonresident Accounts

The crediting to nonresident accounts of BCEAO banknotes, French banknotes, or banknotes issued by any other institute of issue that maintains an Operations Account with the French Treasury is prohibited. These accounts may not be overdrawn without prior authorization.

Imports and Import Payments

Imports of goods originating in or shipped from other countries for commercial purposes under any customs regulations may be made freely; prior acquisition of an official import document is necessary for imports exceeding a value of CFAF 250,000. A special import license (*authorization spéciale d'importation*) is required for imports of sugar, rice, explosives, arms, munitions, and military equipment.

A technical import visa (*certificat de conformité*) is required for the following products: sugar, selected pharmaceutical products (tables R06, R6, R20), insecticides, printed fabric and bleached and tinted threads, wheat and cereal flour, tomato paste, tires and inner tubes for motorcycles, and mats and bags of polyethylene and polypropylene. Imports of certain other products, a list of which is established by decree, may be exempted from the import document requirement. The Minister of Industry, Commerce, and Mines may, on the basis of criteria established by the Ministry, waive the prescribed formalities for imports from countries with which Burkina Faso has concluded a customs union or free trade area agreement. Imports, with a few exceptions, are subject to customs duties of 5 percent; the rates on cereals range from 4 percent to 26 percent, plus a statistical tax of 4 percent.

All imports from outside the Economic Community of West African States (ECOWAS) are subject to a solidarity communal levy of 1 percent, and imports of certain goods that are also locally produced are subject to a protection tax ranging from 10 percent to 30 percent.

Imports of the following products are prohibited: oil-carrying tank trucks, used coaches and buses, moped inner tubes, bicycle tires and inner tubes, wheat flour from countries other than those of the West African Economic Community (WAEC), ivory, and fishing nets with a mesh not greater than 3 square centimeters.

All import transactions with a value of more than CFAF 500,000 that are effected with foreign countries must be domiciled with an authorized bank. Import licenses or prior import authorizations entitle importers to purchase the necessary exchange not earlier than eight days before shipment if a documentary credit is opened, on the due date for payment if the commodities have already been imported, or at the time of the payment on account if such a payment must be made before importation.

Payments for Invisibles

Payments for invisibles to France (as defined above), Monaco, and other Operations Account countries are permitted freely. Those to other countries are subject to exchange control approval, which, for many invisibles has been delegated to authorized intermediaries. Authorized intermediary banks and the Postal Administration are empowered to make payments of up to CFAF 50,000 a transfer to foreign countries on behalf of residents without requiring justification. Payments for invisibles related to trade are permitted freely when the basic trade transaction has been approved or does not require authorization. Transfers of income accruing to nonresidents in the form of profits, dividends, and royalties are also permitted.

Residents traveling for tourism or business purposes to countries in the franc zone that are not members of the WAEMU are allowed to take out banknotes other than CFAF banknotes up to the equivalent of CFAF 2 million; amounts in excess of this limit may be taken out in the form of other means of payment. The allowances for travel to countries outside the franc zone are subject to the following regulations: (1) for tourist travel, CFAF 500,000 without limit on the number of trips or differentiation by the age of the traveler; (2) for business travel, CFAF 75,000 a day within the limit of one month, corresponding to a maximum of CFAF 2.25 million (business travel allowances may be cumulated with tourist allowances); (3) allowances in excess of these limits are subject to the authorization of the respective ministries of finance or, by delegation, the BCEAO; and (4) the use of credit cards, which must be issued by resident financial intermediaries and specifically authorized by the respective ministries of finance, is limited to the ceilings indicated above for tourist and business travel. Returning resident travelers are required to declare all means of payment in their possession upon arrival at customs and to surrender within eight days all means of payment exceeding the equivalent of CFAF 25,000. All resident travelers, when traveling to countries that are not members of the WAEMU, must declare in writing all means of payment at their disposal at the time of departure. The re-exportation by nonresident travelers of means of payment other than banknotes issued abroad and registered in the name of the nonresident traveler is not restricted, subject to documentation that such means of payment had been purchased with funds drawn from a foreign account in CFA francs or with other foreign exchange. The re-exportation of foreign banknotes is allowed up to the equivalent of CFAF 250,000; the re-exportation of foreign banknotes above these ceilings requires documentation demonstrating either the importation of foreign banknotes or their purchase against other means of payment registered in the name of the traveler or through the use of nonresident deposits held in local banks.

Exports and Export Proceeds

Exports and re-exports from Burkina Faso may be made freely. However, for the purpose of monitoring, exports or re-exports of certain products may require prior official authorization from the relevant services of the Ministry of Industry, Commerce, and Mines, except in the case of certain goods, a list of which is established by decree. In accordance with criteria defined by the Minister of Industry, Commerce, and Mines, exports of ivory are subject to special regulations (*authorization spéciale d'exportation*). Exports to Ghana are also subject to special regulations. Export proceeds must be surrendered within one month of the date on which the payment falls due (the due date stipulated in the commercial contract must not, in principle, be more than 180 days after the goods arrive at their destination). All export transactions of more than CFAF 500,000 relating to foreign countries, including countries in the Operations Account area, must be domiciled with an authorized bank. The exporter must sign a foreign exchange commitment and submit an export attestation form. Most exports are subject to a customs stamp tax of 6 percent and a statistical duty of 3 percent.

Proceeds from Invisibles

Proceeds from transactions in invisibles with France (as defined above), Monaco, and the Operations Account countries may be retained. All amounts due from residents of other countries in respect of services and all income earned in those countries from foreign assets must be collected and surrendered within two months of the due date. Resident and nonresident travelers may bring in any amount of banknotes and coins issued by the BCEAO, the Bank of France, or any bank of issue maintaining an Operations Account with the French Treasury, as well as any amount of foreign banknotes and coins (except gold coins) of countries outside the Operations Account area. Resident travelers

must declare to customs any foreign means of payment in excess of CFAF 25,000 that they bring in and must surrender these to an authorized bank within eight days of their return.

Capital

Capital movements between Burkina Faso and France (as defined above), Monaco, and the Operations Account countries are free of exchange control; capital transfers to all other countries require exchange control approval and are restricted, but capital receipts from such countries are permitted freely.

Special controls in addition to any exchange control requirements that may be applicable are maintained over borrowing abroad, over inward direct investment and all outward investment, and over the issuing, advertising, or offering for sale of foreign securities in Burkina Faso. Such operations require prior authorization from the Minister of Finance. Exempt from authorization, however, are operations in connection with (1) loans backed by a guarantee from the Burkinabé Government; and (2) shares that are similar to, or may be substituted for, securities whose issue, advertising, or sale in Burkina Faso has already been authorized. With the exception of controls over foreign securities, these measures do not apply to France (as defined above), Monaco, member countries of the WAEMU, and the Operations Account countries. Special controls are also maintained over imports and exports of gold, over the soliciting of funds for deposit with foreign firms, institutions, and private individuals, as well as over publicity aimed at placing funds abroad or at subscribing to real estate and building operations abroad. These special controls also apply to France, Monaco, and the Operations Account countries. All special provisions described in this paragraph apply only to transactions and not to the associated payments or collections.

All investments abroad by residents of Burkina Faso require prior authorization from the Minister of Finance[5] and, unless the Minister specifically exempts them, 75 percent of such investments must be financed from borrowing abroad. Foreign direct investments in Burkina Faso[6] must be declared to the Minister of Finance before they are made. The

---

[5]Including those made through foreign companies that are directly or indirectly controlled by persons residing in Burkina Faso and those made by branches or subsidiaries abroad of companies having their headquarters in Burkina Faso.

[6]Including those made by companies operating in Burkina Faso that are directly or indirectly under foreign control and those made by branches or subsidiaries in Burkina Faso of foreign companies.

Minister has a period of two months from receipt of the declaration to request postponement of the project. The full or partial liquidation of either type of investment also requires prior declaration to the Minister. Both the making and the liquidation of investments, whether Burkinabé investments abroad or foreign investments in Burkina Faso, must be reported to the Minister of Finance. Direct investments constitute investments implying control of a company or enterprise. Mere participation is not considered direct investment, provided that it does not exceed 20 percent of the capital of a company whose shares are quoted on a stock exchange. Foreign firms operating in Burkina Faso in vital or priority sectors are required to have Burkinabé participation in their capital of at least 51 percent and of at least 35 percent in all other sectors. The sale to residents of Burkina Faso of securities of foreign companies operating in Burkina Faso requires prior authorization from the Minister of Finance, who establishes the sale value.

Borrowing by residents from nonresidents also requires prior authorization from the Minister of Finance. The following are, however, exempt from this authorization: (1) loans constituting a direct investment, which are subject to prior declaration, as indicated above; (2) loans taken up by industrial firms to finance operations abroad, by any type of firm to finance imports into or exports from Burkina Faso, or by international trading houses approved by the Minister of Finance to finance international merchant transactions; (3) loans contracted by authorized banks; and (4) loans other than those mentioned above, when the total amount of these loans outstanding—including the new borrowing—does not exceed CFAF 100 million for any one borrower, the annual interest rate does not exceed the normal market rate, and the proceeds are immediately surrendered by the sale of foreign currency on the exchange market or debited to a foreign account in francs. The repayment of loans not constituting a direct investment requires the special authorization of the Minister of Finance if the loan itself is subject to such approval but is exempt if the loan is exempt from special authorization. Lending abroad is subject only to exchange control authorization by the BCEAO acting on behalf of the Minister of Finance.

The Investment Code provides preferential treatment for foreign investment in Burkina Faso, except for enterprises whose capital stock belongs entirely to foreigners. Three preferential categories (A, B, and C) are established, in accordance with which special guarantees and tax and customs incentives may be granted for up to eight years to any enterprise that undertakes to create or considerably expand activities likely to contribute to the country's economic and social development. Enterprises that the Government deems to be of a priority nature may also be given privileged treatment.

Gold

Residents are free to hold, acquire, and dispose of gold in any form in Burkina Faso. Imports and exports of gold from or to any other country require prior authorization from the Minister of Finance. Exempt from this requirement are (1) imports and exports by or on behalf of the Treasury or the BCEAO; (2) imports and exports of manufactured articles containing a minor quantity of gold (such as gold-filled or gold-plated articles); and (3) imports and exports by travelers of gold objects up to a combined weight of 500 grams. Both licensed and exempt imports of gold are subject to customs declaration.

The Comptoir burkinabé des métaux précieux has a monopoly on exports of gold from Burkina Faso.

Changes During 1995

No significant changes occurred in the exchange and trade system.

Changes During 1996

Exchange Arrangement

June 1. Burkina Faso accepted the obligations of Article VIII, Sections 2, 3, and 4 of the Fund Agreement.

BURUNDI

(Position as of December 31, 1995)

Exchange Arrangement

The currency of Burundi is the Burundi Franc, the external value of which is pegged to a basket of currencies that reflects the pattern of Burundi's international trade. On December 31, 1995, the official buying and selling rates for the U.S. dollar were FBu 275.94 and FBu 279.9, respectively, per $1. Exchange rates for 18 currencies[1] and for 2 units of account, European currency units (ECUs) and units of account of the Common Market for Eastern and Southern Africa, are quoted by the Bank of the Republic of Burundi, the central bank, on the basis of the Burundi franc-U.S. dollar rate and the transaction value of these currencies and units in terms of the U.S. dollar. Commercial banks are authorized to buy and sell foreign exchange on their own account and on behalf of their customers at rates within maximum margins of 1 percent on either side of the middle rate established by the Bank of Burundi. Commercial banks are allowed to borrow foreign exchange to hedge against exchange rate risks. Exporters of coffee are also allowed to borrow foreign exchange through their banks or from their customers for purposes of crop financing and hedging against exchange risks.

Administration of Control

Control over foreign exchange transactions and foreign trade is vested in the Bank of Burundi. Authority to carry out some transactions is delegated to six authorized banks.

Prescription of Currency

Settlements relating to trade with Rwanda and Zaïre in products specified in the commercial agreements between these countries are effected through SDR accounts maintained with the Bank of Burundi and authorized banks of each signatory country. With these exceptions, outgoing payments may be made and receipts may be obtained in any convertible currency.

Nonresident (Foreign Currency Convertible Burundi Franc) Accounts

Accounts in convertible Burundi francs may be maintained by (1) natural persons of foreign nationality (such as staff of diplomatic missions) who are temporarily established in Burundi, (2) juridical persons of foreign nationality with special status (such as diplomatic missions and international organizations), and (3) any other natural or juridical persons authorized by the Bank of Burundi. These accounts may be credited freely with any convertible currency, and they may be debited freely for withdrawals of Burundi francs or for conversion into foreign exchange. Up to FBu 20,000 in foreign currency may be withdrawn in banknotes upon presentation of travel documents (a passport and an airline ticket) for an unlimited number of trips. Withdrawals of banknotes in excess of this amount are subject to the prior authorization of the Bank of Burundi. These accounts may bear interest freely and must not be overdrawn.

Certain nonresidents whose main activities are outside of Burundi may maintain accounts in foreign currencies with an authorized bank. These accounts may be maintained by (1) natural and juridical persons of foreign nationality who reside abroad, (2) enterprises authorized to operate in the free trade zone, (3) exporters of nontraditional products who are authorized to retain 30 percent of their export proceeds, (4) Burundi nationals resident abroad, and (5) any other natural or juridical persons authorized by the Bank of Burundi.

These accounts may be credited freely with any convertible currency received from abroad. They may be debited freely for (1) conversion into Burundi francs for payments in Burundi; and (2) payments abroad for travel and representation or for the purchase of foreign goods, except for banknotes. These accounts must not be overdrawn; however, they may bear interest freely. The related bank charges and commissions must be settled in foreign exchange; and (3) as in the case of accounts in convertible Burundi francs, up to FBu 20,000 may be withdrawn in banknotes upon presentation of travel documents. Withdrawals in excess of this amount are subject to the prior authorization of the Bank of Burundi. If no deposits are made to the foreign account within three months of its opening, the account must be closed.

---

[1] Austrian schillings, Belgian francs, Canadian dollars, Danish kroner, deutsche mark, French francs, Italian lire, Japanese yen, Kenya shillings, Netherlands guilders, Norwegian kroner, pounds sterling, Rwanda francs, Swedish kronor, Swiss francs, Tanzania shillings, Uganda shillings, and U.S. dollars.

Imports and Import Payments

Imports are fully liberalized, except for a limited number of goods the importation of which is restricted mainly for health or security reasons. All goods imported into Burundi must be insured by approved Burundi insurers, and premiums must be paid in Burundi francs. All consignments of imports exceeding FBu 1 million in value (f.o.b.) may be subject to preshipment inspection with regard to quality and price by an international supervising and oversight organization on behalf of the Burundi authorities.

In principle, foreign exchange is made available either at the time the goods are shipped, on the basis of the shipping documents, or after the goods are imported. All imports are subject to a service tax of 4 percent ad valorem in addition to any applicable customs duties and fiscal duties.

Payments for Invisibles

All payments for invisibles require approval. Shipping insurance on coffee exports normally must be taken out in Burundi francs with a Burundi insurer. Upon presentation of evidence of payment of taxes, foreign nationals residing and working in Burundi are permitted to transfer abroad up to 70 percent of their net annual income (80 percent in the case of foreign nationals working for companies that export at least 50 percent of their production). Private joint-stock companies may freely and immediately transfer 100 percent of the return on foreign capital and of the share allocated to foreign directors after payment of taxes. Airlines are authorized to transfer abroad 100 percent of their earnings after deduction of local expenses.

Persons leaving Burundi permanently are authorized to transfer abroad their holdings of Burundi francs that consist of unremitted savings or the sale proceeds of their personal effects. Transfer of rental income is permitted (after payment of taxes and a deduction of 20 percent for maintenance expenses).

Residents may apply for foreign exchange needed for foreign travel. The foreign exchange allowance for business travel is $200 a person a day or its equivalent ($250 for exporters), subject to a maximum limit of 15 days a trip; there is no limit on the number of trips a person may make. Limits on foreign exchange allowances for business or other travel may be exceeded on a bona fide basis. All travelers may take out up to FBu 5,000 in Burundi banknotes.

Exports and Export Proceeds

All exports are free. Export proceeds must be collected within 30 days of the date of export declara-

tion at customs for shipment by air or within 90 days for all other shipments. Exporters operating in the free trade area are not required to surrender their export proceeds to an authorized bank. Deadlines for the collection of proceeds from exports of nontraditional products are set by individual banks. All proceeds from traditional exports must be surrendered to an authorized bank. Exporters of nontraditional products may retain up to 30 percent of proceeds. Exports of mineral products, coffee, and hides are subject to export duties as are exports of all goods that do not qualify for export promotion. Duties paid on raw materials at the time of importation may be refunded, provided that the manufactured products are exported and the proceeds collected. In the case of fully paid exports of nontraditional primary products, the refund will cover 10 percent of the value of such payments.

Proceeds from Invisibles

Exchange receipts from invisibles must be surrendered to authorized banks. Travelers may bring in any amount of foreign currency quoted by the central bank and traveler's checks, as well as a maximum of FBu 5,000 in Burundi banknotes.

Nonresidents staying in a hotel or guest house in Burundi must pay their hotel bills by selling convertible currencies or by using a credit card. Payment in Burundi francs is, however, acceptable in the case of guests for whom a resident company or individual has assumed responsibility with prior authorization from the Bank of Burundi and in the case of nationals of Rwanda and Zaïre who produce declarations of means of payment issued under the auspices of the Economic Community of the Great Lakes Countries (CEPGL).

Capital

Under the Investment Code introduced on January 14, 1987, new investments that fulfill specified conditions as to amount and economic importance may be granted priority status to which specified privileges are attached, mainly in the form of exemptions from import duties and from taxes on income from the investment. Import duties and taxes may be reduced or suspended for goods and equipment needed for starting a particular project and, during a period of five years, for other merchandise needed for the manufacturing process or for the upkeep of the original investment. Taxes on profits and real estate may likewise be reduced or suspended for up to eight years. Enterprises accorded priority status may be granted a reduction or suspension of export taxes and import taxes on equipment and raw materials for renewable periods of five years. In addition to these privileges, companies undertaking investments that are considered to be of prime importance to Burundi's economic development may be granted, under a separate agreement, a guarantee that direct taxes on their activities will not be increased for ten years. An investment commission under the Ministry of Development Planning and Reconstruction is responsible for examining requests for priority status and granting the necessary authorization. In addition, Burundi guarantees each foreign investor the right to move into the country; foreign investors are also assured an allocation of foreign exchange for the purchase of raw materials abroad as well as for the repayment of loans taken out under the investment agreement.

Capital transfers by residents and transfers of foreign capital on which a repatriation guarantee has been granted require individual authorization. The guarantee is furnished for foreign exchange imported by resident enterprises to provide working capital in foreign exchange; it applies to any of the currencies quoted by the central bank. The retransfer may take place as soon as the funds to be transferred are available and with no time limitation. The guarantee provides for the transfer of the amount received from abroad. The repatriation of invested capital in the event of sale or shutdown of the business is also guaranteed.

Gold

All natural or juridical persons holding gold mining permits issued by the ministers responsible for mining and customs may open purchasing houses for gold mined by artisans in Burundi. Gold produced by artisans may be sold only to approved houses. Exports of gold must be declared in Burundi francs at the average daily rates communicated by the Bank of Burundi. Gold exports are authorized jointly by the mining and customs departments.

Changes During 1995

Payments for Invisibles

December 26. The limit on transfers of rental income was removed.

December 28. Limits on foreign exchange allowances for travel abroad were liberalized. In addition, these limits may be exceeded in bona fide cases.

CAMBODIA

(Position as of December 31, 1995)

Exchange Arrangement

The currency of Cambodia is the Cambodian Riel. The exchange rate system comprises two rates: the official rate and the market rate. Since September 1994, adjustments to the official exchange rate are made daily by the National Bank of Cambodia so as to limit the spread between the official and parallel market rates to less than 1 percent. The official exchange rate applies mainly to external transactions conducted by the Government and state-owned enterprises. On December 31, 1995, the official exchange rate for the U.S. dollar was CR 2526 per $1, and the market rate was CR 2560 per $1.

The National Bank is responsible for quoting daily official rates, at which the Foreign Trade Bank of Cambodia and the Phnom Penh Municipal Bank (two state-owned commercial banks) buy and sell foreign exchange. Other commercial banks are free to buy and sell foreign exchange at their own rates. Exchange transactions take place at the rate prevailing in the market. Foreign exchange dealers are permitted to buy only banknotes and traveler's checks and are required by law to conduct their transactions at the official rate. In practice, however, these transactions take place at the market rate. There are no taxes or subsidies on purchases or sales of foreign exchange.

There are no arrangements for forward cover against exchange rate risk operating in the official or the commercial banking sector.

Administration of Control

The exchange control regime is defined by the 1991 Law on the Management of Foreign Exchange, Precious Metals, and Stones. This law vests responsibility for the management of foreign exchange (as well as precious metals and stones) with the Ministry of Economy and Finance and the National Bank. The National Bank is authorized to license commercial banks and other agents to engage in foreign exchange transactions and to regulate current and capital transactions. State-owned enterprises must be authorized by the Ministry of Economy and Finance to engage in export/import trade or in any other businesses generating foreign exchange and are required to repatriate foreign exchange earnings. Registered trading companies are not required to have a license to engage in foreign trade activities.

New foreign exchange legislation that eliminates the foreign exchange restrictions contained in the 1991 law is expected to be presented to the National Assembly during 1996.

Prescription of Currency

There are no prescription of currency requirements. Cambodia does not maintain operative bilateral payments agreements.

Resident and Nonresident Accounts

Residents and nonresidents are permitted to maintain foreign currency accounts with commercial banks. Although there are no limits on the balances of these accounts, under the 1991 law, the funds may not be used to settle domestic obligations but must be converted into domestic currency. In practice, however, all transactions can be settled in foreign currency.

Imports and Import Payments

Trade policy is formulated by the Ministry of Commerce in consultation with the Ministry of Economy and Finance.

Imports undertaken by registered trading companies require no license, and there are no quantitative restrictions on imports, although imports of certain products are subject to control or are prohibited for reasons of national security, health, environmental well-being, or public morality.

Effective September 1, 1995, preshipment import inspection for certain goods is required to improve customs duty collection. The coverage of the requirements will be gradually widened.

An excise tax of 10 percent applies to selected imports.

Payments for Invisibles

Payments for invisibles related to trade are not restricted but are regulated by the Investment Law of the Kingdom of Cambodia of August 1994. The repatriation of profits is permitted in accordance with the relevant laws and regulations issued by the National Bank.

Under the 1991 law, an exchange allowance for travel in the equivalent of $3,000 a person is granted at the official rate for Cambodians going abroad for all types of travel, irrespective of the length of stay; amounts in excess of this limit must be approved by the National Bank. In practice, however, there are no limits on the use of foreign exchange for travel abroad. There are no officially established limits on other invisible payments.

Exports and Export Proceeds

Exports of most products by registered trading companies may be undertaken without a license. Exports of a limited list of goods by both state-owned and private sector entities must be licensed by the Ministry of Commerce. Exports licenses are required for sawed timber logs and rice. Exports of rice, gems, and sawed timber are subject to a quota. There are also export restrictions on gold, silver, and antiquities. All proceeds from exports by state-owned enterprises must be repatriated and sold to or deposited with the Foreign Trade Bank of Cambodia (FTBC); private sector entities must repatriate and hold export proceeds in accounts with resident commercial banks.

An excise tax of 10 percent of the estimated market value applies to exports of timber and other selected exports. An ad-valorem tax of 10 percent applies on exports of rubber.

Proceeds from Invisibles

Proceeds from invisibles received by private sector entities are not subject to the repatriation or surrender requirement. Proceeds from invisibles earned by state-owned enterprises are subject to the same regulations as those governing proceeds from merchandise exports.

Capital

Borrowing abroad by public sector agencies is permitted only with the approval of the Ministry of Economy and Finance. Foreign investors are required to submit investment applications to the Cambodia Investment Board at the Council for Development of Cambodia for review and approval under the Investment Law. The Investment Law eliminated foreign exchange restrictions applying to investors in Cambodia.

Changes During 1995

Exchange Arrangement

March 25. New banknotes were issued, with denominations ranging up to CR 100,000.

Imports and Import Payments

September 1. Certain imports were subject to pre-shipment inspection.

CAMEROON

(Position as of June 30, 1996)

Exchange Arrangement

The currency of Cameroon is the CFA Franc,[1] which is pegged to the French franc, the intervention currency, at the fixed rate of CFAF 1 per F 0.01. The official buying and selling rate is CFAF 100 per F 1. Exchange transactions in French francs between the BEAC and commercial banks take place at the same rate. Buying and selling rates for certain other foreign currencies are also officially posted, with quotations based on the fixed rate for the French franc and the rates in the Paris exchange market for the currencies concerned. A commission of 0.25 percent is levied on transfers to countries that are not members of the BEAC, except transfers in respect of central and local government operations, payments for imports covered by a duly issued license domiciled with a bank, scheduled repayments on loans properly obtained abroad, travel allowances and official representation expenses paid by the Government and its agencies for official missions, and payments of reinsurance premiums. There are no taxes or subsidies on purchases or sales of foreign exchange.

With the exception of those relating to gold, Cameroon's exchange control measures generally do not apply to France (and its overseas departments and territories) and Monaco; and all other countries whose bank of issue is linked with the French Treasury by an Operations Account (Benin, Burkina Faso, Central African Republic, Chad, Comoros, the Congo, Côte d'Ivoire, Equatorial Guinea, Gabon, Mali, Niger, Senegal, and Togo). Hence, all payments to these countries may be made freely, but all financial transfers in excess of CFAF 500,000 to the Operations Account countries must be declared to the authorities for statistical purposes.

Forward exchange cover requires the prior authorization of the exchange control authorities. It must be denominated in the currency of settlement prescribed in the contract, and the maturity period must not be less than three months or more than nine months. Settlements must be effected within eight days of the maturity date of the forward contract.

Cameroon accepted the obligations of Article VIII, Sections 2, 3, and 4 of the Fund Agreement on June 1, 1996.

---

[1] The CFA franc circulating in Cameroon is issued by the Bank of Central African States (BEAC) and is also legal tender in the Central African Republic, Chad, the Congo, Equatorial Guinea, and Gabon.

Administration of Control

Exchange control is administered by the Directorate of Economic Controls and External Finance of the Ministry of Finance. Exchange transactions relating to all countries must be effected through authorized intermediaries—that is, the Postal Administration and authorized banks. Import licenses for goods other than gold are issued by the Ministry of Commerce and Industry, and those for gold by the Ministry of Mines, Water, and Energy. Export licenses are issued by the Ministry of Finance.

Prescription of Currency

As Cameroon has an Operations Account with the French Treasury, settlements with France (as defined above), Monaco, and the Operations Account countries are made in CFA francs, French francs, or the currency of any other Operations Account country. Settlements with all other countries are usually made through correspondent banks in France in any of the currencies of those countries or in French francs through foreign accounts in francs.

Resident and Nonresident Accounts

The regulations pertaining to nonresident accounts are based on those applied in France. As the BEAC has suspended the repurchase of BEAC banknotes circulating outside the territories of its zone of issue, BEAC banknotes received by the foreign correspondents of authorized banks and mailed to the BEAC agency in Yaoundé may not be credited to foreign accounts in francs. Nonresidents are allowed to maintain bank accounts in convertible francs. These accounts, held mainly by diplomatic missions, international institutions, and their nonresident employees, may be credited only with (1) proceeds of spot or forward sales of foreign currencies transferred from abroad by account owners; (2) transfers from other nonresident convertible franc accounts; and (3) payments by residents in accordance with exchange regulations. These accounts may be debited only for (1) purchases of foreign currencies; (2) transfers to other nonresident convertible franc accounts; and (3) payments to residents in accordance with exchange regulations. Nonresidents may not maintain accounts in CFA francs abroad or accounts in foreign currency in Cameroon. Residents are not permitted to maintain accounts abroad or accounts in foreign currency in Cameroon.

Imports and Import Payments

Certain imports are prohibited for ecological, health, or safety reasons. Surcharges apply to imports of maize meal and cement.

All import transactions valued at more than CFAF 500,000 must be domiciled with an authorized bank if the goods are not considered in transit. Transactions involving goods in transit must be domiciled with a foreign bank. Advance import deposits are permitted if underlying contracts stipulate them.

Since January 1994, import tariff rates range from 5 percent to 30 percent and duties on products imported from the member countries of the Central African Customs and Economic Union (UDEAC) are 20 percent of the corresponding rate applicable to imports from other countries. In September 1994, a 30 percent temporary import surcharge was introduced on maize meal, and in November 1994, a 20 percent temporary import surcharge was introduced on trailers, plastic bags, iron reinforcing bars, and cement. In July 1995, these import surcharges were phased out for trailers, iron reinforcing bars, and plastic bags. They were maintained on maize meal and were lowered on cement to 10 percent from 20 percent.

Payments for Invisibles

Payments in excess of CFAF 500,000 for invisibles to France (as defined above), Monaco, and the Operations Account countries require prior declaration and are subject to presentation of relevant invoices. Payments for invisibles related to trade follow the same regime as basic trade transactions, as do transfers of income accruing to nonresidents in the form of profits, dividends, and royalties.

Residents traveling for tourism or business purposes to countries other than France (as defined above), Monaco, and the Operations Account countries may be granted foreign exchange allowances subject to the following regulations: (1) for tourist travel, CFAF 100,000 a day, with a maximum of CFAF 2 million a trip; (2) for business travel, CFAF 250,000 a day, with a maximum of CFAF 5 million a trip; (3) allowances in excess of these limits are subject to the authorization of the Ministry of Finance or, by delegation, the BEAC; and (4) the use of credit cards, which must be issued by resident financial intermediaries and approved by the Ministry of Finance is limited to the ceilings indicated above for tourism and business travel. However,

these regulations are administered liberally and bona fide requests for allowances in excess of these limits are normally granted. Returning resident travelers are required to declare all means of payment in their possession upon arrival at customs and to surrender within eight days all means of payment exceeding the equivalent of CFAF 25,000. All resident travelers, regardless of destination, must declare in writing all means of payment at their disposal at the time of departure. The re-exportation by nonresident travelers of means of payment, other than banknotes, issued abroad and registered in the name of the nonresident traveler is not restricted, subject to documentation that they were purchased with funds drawn from an account in CFA francs or with other foreign exchange. The re-exportation of foreign banknotes is allowed up to the equivalent of CFAF 250,000; re-exportation above this ceiling requires documentation showing either the importation of foreign banknotes or their purchase against other means of payment registered in the name of the traveler or through the use of deposits lodged in local banks.

The transfer of rent from real property owned in Cameroon by foreign nationals is limited, in principle, to up to 50 percent of the income declared for taxation purposes, net of repair costs and tax payments. Remittances for current repair and management of real property abroad are normally limited to the equivalent of CFAF 200,000 every two or three years. The transfer of up to 50 percent of the salary of a foreigner working in Cameroon, depending on the number of dependents abroad, is permitted upon presentation of the appropriate pay voucher, provided that the transfer takes place within one month of the pay period concerned. Except in the case of foreigners working in Cameroon temporarily who have been insured previously, residents and nonresidents are not allowed to contract insurance abroad when the same services are available in Cameroon.

However, payments of premiums for authorized contracts are not restricted.

Exports and Export Proceeds

Export transactions valued at CFAF 500,000 or more must be domiciled with an authorized bank. Exports to all countries are subject to domiciliation requirements for the appropriate documents. Proceeds from exports to all countries must be repatriated within 30 days of the payment date stipulated in the sales contract, and proceeds received in currencies other than those of France or an Operations Account country must be surrendered within a month of collection.

Proceeds from Invisibles

All receipts from services and all income earned abroad must be collected within a month of the due date, and foreign currency receipts must be surrendered within a month of collection. Resident and nonresident travelers may bring into Cameroon any amount of banknotes and coins issued by the Bank of France, or a bank of issue maintaining an Operations Account with the French Treasury, as well as any amount of foreign banknotes and coins (except gold coins) of countries outside the Operations Account area.

Capital

Capital transactions between Cameroon and France (as defined above), Monaco, and the Operations Account countries are free of exchange control. Outward capital transfers to all other countries require exchange control approval and are restricted. Inward capital transfers are free of restrictions, except for foreign direct investments and borrowing, which are subject to registration and authorization. Provided they have met their tax obligations, emigrants to countries outside the Operations Account area may transfer abroad their full savings.

Direct investments abroad[2] require the prior approval of the Ministry of Finance, unless they take the form of a capital increase resulting from the reinvestment of undistributed profits or do not exceed 20 percent of the fair market value of the company being purchased. The full or partial liquidation of such investments requires only a report to the Minister of Finance, unless the operation involves the relinquishing of a participation that had previously been approved as constituting a direct investment abroad. Foreign direct investments in Cameroon[3] require prior declaration to the Minister of Finance, unless they take the form of a capital increase resulting from reinvestment of undistributed profits; the Minister has a period of two months from receipt of the declaration during which he may request postponement. The full or partial liquidation of direct investments in Cameroon requires only a report to the Minister of Finance, unless the operation involves the relinquishing of a participation that had previously been approved as constituting a direct investment in Cameroon. Both the making and the liquidation of direct

investments, whether Cameroonian investments abroad or foreign investments in Cameroon, must be reported to the Minister of Finance within 20 days of each operation. (Direct investments are defined as investments implying control of a company or enterprise. Mere participation is not considered direct investment, provided that it does not exceed 20 percent of the capital of a company whose shares are quoted on a stock exchange.)

The issuing, advertising, or offering for sale of foreign securities in Cameroon requires prior authorization from the Minister of Finance and must subsequently be reported to him. Exempt from authorization, however, and subject only to a report after the fact, are operations in connection with (1) loans backed by a guarantee from the Cameroonian Government and (2) shares similar to securities, when their issuing, advertising, or offering for sale in Cameroon has already been authorized. All foreign securities and titles embodying claims on nonresidents must be deposited with an authorized intermediary and are classified as foreign, whether they belong to residents or nonresidents.

Borrowing abroad by natural and juridical persons, whether public or private, whose normal residence or registered office is in Cameroon, or by branches or subsidiaries in Cameroon of juridical persons whose registered office is abroad, requires prior authorization from the Minister of Finance and must subsequently be reported to him. The following are, however, exempt from this authorization and require only a report: (1) loans directly connected with the rendering of services abroad by the persons or firms mentioned above, or with the financing of commercial transactions either between Cameroon and countries abroad or between foreign countries, in which these persons or firms take part; and (2) loans contracted by registered banks and credit institutions.

Lending abroad by natural and juridical persons, whether public or private, whose normal residence or registered office is in Cameroon, or by branches or subsidiaries in Cameroon of juridical persons whose registered office is abroad, requires prior authorization from the Minister of Finance and must subsequently be reported to him. The following are, however, exempt from prior authorization and require only a report: (1) loans constituting a direct investment abroad for which prior approval has been obtained, as indicated above; (2) loans directly connected with the rendering of services abroad by the persons or firms mentioned above, or with the financing of commercial transactions either between Cameroon and countries abroad or between foreign countries, in which these persons or firms take part;

---

[2]Including those made through foreign companies that are directly or indirectly controlled by persons in Cameroon and those made by branches or subsidiaries abroad of companies in Cameroon.

[3]Including those made by companies in Cameroon that are directly or indirectly under foreign control and those made by branches or subsidiaries of foreign companies in Cameroon.

and (3) loans not exceeding CFAF 500,000, provided the maturity does not exceed two years and the rate of interest does not exceed 6 percent a year.

Under the Investment Code of November 1990, generalized fiscal benefits are provided to encourage exports and the development of natural resources, and further benefits are provided to enterprises qualifying for inclusion in one of the five regimes described below. The generalized fiscal benefits include an exemption from export duties and taxes on insurance and transportation for exports and a deduction of 5 percent of the value of exports from the exporter's taxable income. In addition, firms are exempted under certain conditions from all duties and purchase taxes on raw materials or intermediate inputs produced in Cameroon or the UDEAC region. The new code grants fiscal benefits to domestic and foreign firms undertaking new projects in the raw material processing, mining, forestry, agriculture, fishing, food, construction, equipment maintenance, industrial research, and tourism sectors. These benefits are provided as follows: (1) The basic regime applies to firms whose investment is labor intensive (defined as one job for each CFAF 10 million investment), export-oriented firms, and firms that use domestic natural resources. During a three-year installation phase, firms under this regime are entitled to a reduced tax rate of 15 percent, including their fiscal and customs duties, internal turnover tax, and all other import taxes relating to imported inputs; in addition, these firms are entitled to certain fiscal exemptions. During a five-year exploitation phase, certain tax exemptions are maintained. (2) The small and medium-size enterprise regime applies to firms that are labor intensive (defined as one job for each CFAF 5 million investment), whose investment is of modest size (less than CFAF 1.5 billion), and whose level of Cameroonian participation is at least 35 percent of capital. The benefits under this regime are the same as those under the basic regime, except that during the exploitation phase of seven years, firms may deduct from taxable income 25 percent of salaries paid to Cameroonian nationals. (3) The strategic regime applies to enterprises declared strategic by the Cameroonian authorities and fulfilling certain other conditions. This regime provides the same benefits as those under the basic regime during the installation phase, which is five years, and the same benefits as those available under the small and medium-size enterprise regime during the exploitation phase, which is twelve years. (4) The free trade zone regime is available to enterprises devoted exclusively to exporting; terms are fixed by individual agreements. (5) Firms that expand by more than 20 percent or that satisfy certain other conditions are eligible for benefits under the reinvestment regime. For three years, firms are subject to a reduced tax rate of 15 percent, which includes their fiscal and customs duties, internal turnover tax, and all other import taxes relating to imported inputs; in addition, these firms are entitled to certain fiscal exemptions.

Law No. 90/19 of August 10, 1990 provides that Cameroonian interests should hold at least one-third of the share capital of each banking institution. This law also requires banks with foreign majority participation to submit to the monetary authorities information on all current transactions abroad and to obtain prior approval for any changes in the structure of their equity holdings. Foreign managers must be approved by the monetary authorities and reside in Cameroon.

Gold

Residents are free to hold, acquire, and dispose of gold jewelry in Cameroon. They require the approval of the Ministry of Mines, Water, and Energy to hold gold in any other form. Such approval is normally given only to industrial users, including jewelers. Newly mined gold must be declared to the Ministry of Mines, Water, and Energy, which authorizes either its exportation or its sale to domestic industrial users; exports are made only to France. Imports and exports of gold require prior authorization from the Ministry of Mines, Water, and Energy and the Minister of Finance, although such authorization is seldom granted for imports. Exempt from this requirement are (1) imports and exports by or on behalf of the monetary authorities, and (2) imports and exports of manufactured articles containing a small quantity of gold (such as gold-filled or gold-plated articles). Both licensed and exempt imports of gold are subject to customs declaration.

Changes During 1995

Imports and Import Payments

July 1. Import surcharges introduced in late 1994 were eliminated on iron reinforcing bars, plastic bags, and trailers; the surcharge on maize meal was maintained at the rate of 30 percent, and the rate on cement was lowered to 10 percent from 20 percent.

July 1. The import of crude oil was liberalized.

Changes During 1996

Exchange Arrangement

June 1. Cameroon accepted the obligations of Article VIII, Sections 2, 3, and 4 of the Fund Agreement.

CANADA

(Position as of December 31, 1995)

Exchange Arrangement

The currency of Canada is the Canadian Dollar. The Canadian authorities do not maintain margins in respect of exchange transactions, and exchange rates are determined on the basis of demand and supply in the exchange market; however, the authorities intervene from time to time to maintain orderly conditions in that market. The principal intervention currency is the U.S. dollar. The closing exchange rate (midpoint) for the U.S. dollar on December 31, 1995 was Can$1.3640 per US$1. Forward exchange rates are similarly determined in the market, and it is not the practice of the authorities to intervene. There are no taxes or subsidies on purchases or sales of foreign exchange.

Canada accepted the obligations of Article VIII, Sections 2, 3, and 4 of the Fund Agreement on March 25, 1952.

Administration of Control

There are no exchange controls. The licensing of imports and exports, when required, is handled mostly by the Department of Foreign Affairs and International Trade, but other departments also issue licenses in specialized fields.

In accordance with the Fund's Executive Board Decision No. 144-(52/51) adopted on August 14, 1952, Canada notified the Fund on July 23, 1992 that in compliance with UN Security Council Resolution No. 757 (1992), certain restrictions had been imposed on the making of payments and transfers for current international transactions in respect of the Federal Republic of Yugoslavia (Serbia/Montenegro). Canada has also imposed restrictions on financial transactions with Bosnia and Herzegovina in accordance with UN Resolution No. 942.

Prescription of Currency

No prescription of currency requirements are in force.

Imports and Import Payments

Import permits are required for only a few agricultural items, certain textile products and clothing, certain endangered species of fauna and flora, natural gas, and material and equipment for the production or use of atomic energy. In 1995, permits were required for the importation of controlled substances classified as dangerous drugs and certain military armaments. In addition, Health Canada does not permit the importation of drugs not registered with it. Import permits are required for carbon and specialty steel products for monitoring purposes only. Commercial imports of used motor vehicles (less than 15 years old) have been generally prohibited. However, the prohibition on imports of used vehicles from the United States was phased out over a five-year period that began in 1989, and the prohibition on imports of used vehicles from Mexico will be phased out by January 1, 2019. Imports of some clothing and certain textile products, usually in the form of bilateral restraint agreements (Memoranda of Understanding) concluded under the Multifiber Arrangement negotiated within the framework of the General Agreement on Tariffs and Trade (GATT), are also subject to quantitative restrictions. In accordance with the provisions of the Uruguay Round Agreement on textiles and clothing, Canada's system of import controls on textiles and clothing is being liberalized in stages over a ten-year period beginning January 1, 1995. As a result of the commitments made under the Uruguay Round Agreement, Canada replaced agricultural import restrictions and prohibitions with tariff rate quotas for most products on January 1, 1995, and for certain dairy and grain products on August 1, 1995. Under the new system, a quantity of imports (the current or minimum access commitment called for in the Uruguay Round negotiating modalities, or the level of access required by the provisions of the Canada-U.S. Free Trade Agreement) enters at a low tariff, while additional imports are subject to a higher tariff rate.

Exports and Export Proceeds

To support their export sales, exporters may have access to financing and insurance services provided by the Export Development Corporation.

The surrender of proceeds from exports is not required and exchange receipts are freely disposable. The principal legal instrument governing export controls is the Export and Import Permits Act, which controls trade through the Export Control List and Area Control List. The Export Control List identifies all goods that are controlled in order to implement intergovernmental arrangements, maintain supplies, or ensure security. It includes all items identified in the International Munitions List, the International Industrial List, and the International Atomic Energy List. In addition, controls are maintained for supply reasons and for purposes of promoting further processing in Canada (such as logs, roe herring, and (for nonproliferation purposes) chemical, biological, and nuclear weapons and their delivery systems.

The Area Control List includes a limited number of countries to which all exports are controlled. At present, Angola and the Libyan Arab Jamahiriya are on the Area Control List.

Permits are required for the exportation of listed goods to all countries except, in most cases, the United States, as well as for all goods destined to countries on the Area Control List.

Payments for and Proceeds from Invisibles

No exchange control requirements are imposed on exchange payments for or exchange receipts from invisibles.

Capital

No exchange control requirements are imposed on capital receipts or payments by residents or nonresidents. Specific restrictions exist on inward direct investments in the broadcasting, telecommunication, transportation, fishery, and energy sectors. As a result of the Uruguay Round Agreement, Canada has eliminated the few remaining restrictions in the financial services sector. Specifically, the 10 percent individual and 25 percent collective limitations on the foreign ownership of Canadian-controlled, federally regulated financial institutions, and the 12 percent asset ceiling on the size of the foreign bank sector in Canada were eliminated. This became effective on December 14, 1994, when amendments to the Bank Act, the Trust and Loan Companies Act, the Insurance Companies Act, the Cooperative Insurance Companies Act, and the Investment Companies Act received Royal Assent as part of the World Trade Organization Agreement Implementation Act. These restrictions had already been lifted in the North American Free Trade Agreement (NAFTA). In addition, under the provisions of the Investment Canada Act, new foreign investments are in general subject to notification requirements but not to review requirements. As a result of the NAFTA, only direct acquisitions of businesses with assets exceeding Can$168 million are subject to review beginning in 1996. Indirect acquisitions are no longer subject to review. These provisions were multilateralized as part of Canada's implementation of the Uruguay Round results. Investments subject to review are required only to pass a test proving

that they will yield a net benefit to Canada. In addition, acquisitions below these threshholds and investments to establish new businesses in culturally sensitive sectors may be reviewed. There are no controls on outward direct investment or on inward or outward portfolio investment.

Gold

Residents may freely purchase, hold, and sell gold in any form, at home or abroad. Gold of U.S. origin requires a permit when re-exported to all countries except the United States. Commercial imports of articles containing minor quantities of gold, such as watches, are unrestricted and free of license. Legal tender gold coins with a face value of Can$100 have been issued annually since 1976, and Can$50 "bullion" coins containing 1 ounce of gold have also been issued since 1979. In 1982, Can$5 and Can$10 coins containing $\frac{1}{10}$ and $\frac{1}{4}$ of an ounce of gold, respectively, were issued; in 1986, a coin containing $\frac{1}{2}$ of an ounce of gold with a face value of Can$50 was issued.

Changes During 1995

Administration of Control

June 7. Formal negotiations on Chile's accession to NAFTA were initiated in Toronto. (Pending passage by the U.S. Congress of fast-track negotiating authority, Canada and Chile began negotiations on an interim bilateral trade accord in January 1996, consistent with the ultimate aim of NAFTA accession.)

July 24. Under the auspices of the World Trade Organization (WTO), Canada agreed to be part of the interim agreement on financial services reached on July 26, 1995. Canada is a full participant in the OECD-based negotiations of a Multilateral Agreement on Investment (MAI), formally launched in September 1995.

Imports and Import Payments

January 1. Most agricultural import restrictions were replaced with tariff rate quotas.

February 9. Final antidumping duties were imposed on golden delicious and red delicious apples.

June 13. A number of tariff changes and related Customs Tariff amendments were introduced and subsequently approved as part of Bill C-102 on December 5, 1995. These included reductions in tariffs on a wide range of manufacturing inputs (classified under some 1,500 tariff lines). Tourist exemption levels were increased.

July 5. Countervailing duties were revoked on refill paper.

August 1. Remaining agricultural import restrictions were replaced with tariff rate quotas.

October 20. Final antidumping duties were imposed on caps, lids, and jars.

November 6. Final antidumping and/or countervailing duties were imposed on imports of refined sugar.

December 21. Further reductions in preferential rates under Canada's generalized system of preferences scheme, effective January 1, 1996, were announced.

CAPE VERDE

(Position as of December 31, 1995)

Exchange Arrangement

The currency of Cape Verde is the Cape Verde Escudo, which is pegged to a weighted basket of currencies issued by the nine countries (other than the United States) that are the most important suppliers of imports and sources of emigrant remittances. The composition of the basket is revised annually; weights are determined using a formula giving a two-thirds weight to imports and a one-third weight to remittances. The exchange rate of the Cape Verde escudo is expressed in terms of the U.S. dollar, the intervention currency, and fixed daily on the basis of quotations for the U.S. dollar and the other currencies included in the basket. On December 31, 1995, the buying and selling rates for the U.S. dollar were C.V. Esc 74.46 and C.V. Esc 77.86, respectively, per $1.

Most dealings in foreign exchange with the general public are conducted by the two commercial banks, Banco Comercial do Atlantico (BCA) and Caija Económica de Cabo Verde (CECV), which are allowed net foreign exchange positions of up to the equivalent of $1.5 million and $1 million, respectively.[1] In addition to the two commercial banks, hotels and tourist agencies are authorized to buy foreign exchange from the public. There are no taxes or subsidies on purchases or sales of foreign exchange. There are no arrangements for forward cover against exchange rate risk operating in the official or the commercial banking sector.

Administration of Control

All foreign exchange transactions are under the control of the Bank of Cape Verde, the central bank. Certain categories of imports, exports, and re-exports exceeding specified limits are subject to Bank of Cape Verde licensing.

Arrears are maintained with respect to external payments.

There are payments restrictions for security reasons in effect.

Prescription of Currency

Export proceeds and proceeds from invisibles must be repatriated in convertible currencies. Cape Verde maintains inoperative bilateral payments agreements with Angola and São Tomé and Príncipe, under which Cape Verde is a net creditor.

Nonresident Accounts

Nonresidents may open demand deposit accounts in local currency. These accounts may be credited only with the proceeds from the sale, or surrender of receipts, of convertible currencies and may be debited for payment of any obligations in Cape Verde. Outward transfers of balances from such accounts may be made freely. Embassies and foreign officials of embassies are required to open special accounts in foreign currency and in local currency; such accounts must be replenished exclusively with foreign exchange. Foreign enterprises may maintain accounts in foreign currency.

Special Accounts (Emigrants)

Three types of special interest-bearing deposit accounts are available for emigrants: (1) foreign exchange deposit accounts, (2) savings-credit deposit accounts, and (3) special accounts in Cape Verde escudos. These accounts may be credited only with convertible foreign currencies, and holders of savings-credit deposit accounts are allowed to benefit from loans on special terms for financing small-scale projects. Interest on all three types of accounts may be freely remitted abroad.

Imports and Import Payments

Imports with a value of less than C.V. Esc 100,000 are exempt from the licensing requirement. Imports of goods exceeding C.V. Esc 100,000 and not involving payments from the country's foreign exchange resources are subject to the preregistration requirement. The importation of maize, rice, sugar, and cooking oil is a government monopoly.

Licenses, which are issued by the General Directorate of Commerce in the Ministry of Economy, Transportation, and Communications, require the endorsement of the Bank of Cape Verde and are generally valid for 90 days; they are renewable. The provision of foreign exchange is guaranteed when the license has been previously certified by the Bank of Cape Verde. Licenses are, in general, granted liberally for imports of medicines, capital goods, and other development-related equipment. The Ministry of Tourism, Industry, and Commerce establishes a

---

[1]Two Portuguese banks that recently obtained licenses are not authorized to conduct foreign exchange transactions.

list of products for which imports are subject to a global annual quota. This list includes mostly locally produced food items and beverages, (e.g., fish, bread, tomatoes, bananas, cereals, salt, beer, and soft drinks), with some items subject to seasonal quotas (e.g., potatoes, onions, and poultry).

Payments for Invisibles

Any persons traveling abroad may take out foreign currency equivalent to C.V. Esc 100,000. Nationals of Cape Verde traveling abroad as tourists are required to buy round-trip tickets in advance. Cape Verdean nationals studying abroad are allowed a maximum of C.V. Esc 100,000 on leaving the country; students who do not hold scholarships are, in addition, entitled to a monthly allowance that varies according to the country of destination. Persons traveling abroad on business may take an amount of foreign currency that varies according to the country of destination and the duration of each trip. Persons traveling abroad for medical treatment may take out an amount of foreign currency that varies according to medical needs. Applications for these allowances must be accompanied by medical certification before the trip, and medical bills must be presented on return to Cape Verde.

Transfers by foreign technical assistance personnel working in Cape Verde are authorized within the limits specified in the individual contracts. These contracts, as well as other contracts involving foreign exchange expenditures, are subject to prior screening by the Bank of Cape Verde. Requests by other foreigners are examined on a case-by-case basis. The exportation of domestic currency by travelers is prohibited. Foreign travelers may bring in any amount of foreign currency but may re-export only up to the amount of currency they declared upon entry.

Exports and Export Proceeds

No licenses are required for exports. Proceeds from exports and invisibles must be sold to the commercial banks. Export proceeds must be repatriated within three months, but this period may be extended. Law 92/IV/93, concerning export incentives, and Law Decree 2/94, concerning capital operations, considerably reduce the effectiveness of this requirement.

Proceeds from Invisibles

Receipts from invisibles must be surrendered to a commercial bank. The importation of domestic currency is prohibited.

Capital

Any private capital transaction must be approved in advance by the Bank of Cape Verde, but legally imported capital, including foreign direct investment, may be re-exported without limitation. The exportation of resident-owned capital is not normally permitted.

Gold

Imports, exports, or re-exports of gold in either coins or bars require prior licensing by the Bank of Cape Verde.

Changes During 1995

No significant changes occurred in the exchange and trade system.

CENTRAL AFRICAN REPUBLIC

(Position as of June 30, 1996)

Exchange Arrangement

The currency of the Central African Republic is the CFA Franc,[1] which is pegged to the French franc, the intervention currency, at the fixed rate of CFAF 1 per F 0.01. Exchange transactions in French francs between the Bank of Central African States (BEAC) and commercial banks take place at the rate of CFAF 100 per F 1, free of commission. Buying and selling rates for certain other foreign currencies are also officially posted, with quotations based on the fixed rate for the French franc and the rates in the Paris exchange market for the currencies concerned. A commission of 0.25 percent is levied on all capital transfers to countries that are not members of the BEAC, except those made for the account of the Treasury and for the expenses of students. There are no taxes or subsidies on purchases or sales of foreign exchange.

With the exception of those relating to gold, the exchange control measures of the Central African Republic do not apply to (1) France (and its overseas departments and territories) and Monaco; and (2) all other countries whose bank of issue is linked with the French Treasury by an Operations Account (Benin, Burkina Faso, Cameroon, Chad, Comoros, the Congo, Côte d'Ivoire, Equatorial Guinea, Gabon, Mali, Niger, Senegal, and Togo). Hence, all payments to these countries may be made freely. All other countries are considered foreign countries.

The Central African Republic accepted the obligations of Article VIII, Sections 2, 3, and 4 of the Fund Agreement on June 1, 1996.

Administration of Control

All draft legislation, directives, correspondence, and contracts having a direct or indirect bearing on the finances of the state require the prior approval of the Minister of Finance, who has delegated approval authority to the Director of the Budget. The Autonomous Amortization Fund (CAADE) of the Ministry of Finance supervises borrowing abroad. The Office of Foreign Financial Relations of the same ministry supervises lending abroad; the issuing, advertising, or offering for sale of foreign securities in the Central African Republic; and inward and outward direct investment. Exchange control is administered by the Minister of Finance, who has delegated some approval authority to the BEAC,[2] to authorized banks, and to the Postal Administration. All exchange transactions relating to foreign countries must be effected through authorized banks. Export declarations are to be made through the Directorate of Foreign Trade of the Ministry of Commerce and Industry, except those for gold, which are to be made through the BEAC.

Arrears are maintained with respect to external payments.

Prescription of Currency

Since the Central African Republic is an Operations Account country, settlements with France (as defined above), Monaco, and other Operations Account countries are made in CFA francs, French francs, or the currency of any other institute of issue that maintains an Operations Account with the French Treasury. Settlements with all other countries are usually made in the currencies of those countries or in French francs through foreign accounts in francs.

Nonresident Accounts

The regulations pertaining to nonresident accounts are based on regulations applied in France. The principal nonresident accounts are foreign accounts in francs. As the BEAC has suspended the repurchase of these banknotes circulating outside the territories of the CFA franc zone, these banknotes received by the foreign correspondents of authorized banks and mailed to the BEAC agency in Bangui by the Bank of France or the Central Bank of West African States (BCEAO) may not be credited to foreign accounts in francs.

Imports and Import Payments

Imports from all countries are free of licensing requirements or quotas. Imports of firearms are prohibited irrespective of origin. Import declarations are required for all imports, and all import transactions relating to foreign countries must be domiciled

---

[1] The CFA franc circulating in the Central African Republic is issued by the Bank of Central African States (BEAC) and is also legal tender in Cameroon, Chad, Congo, Equatorial Guinea, and Gabon.

[2] The authority delegated to the BEAC relates to (1) control over the external position of the banks, (2) the granting of exceptional travel allocations in excess of the basic allowances, and (3) control over the repatriation of net export proceeds.

with an authorized bank. The import license entitles importers to purchase the necessary exchange, provided that the shipping documents are submitted to the authorized bank.

Payments for Invisibles

Payments for invisibles to France (as defined above), Monaco, and the Operations Account countries are permitted freely; those to other countries are subject to approval. Approval authority for many types of payment has been delegated to authorized banks. Payments for invisibles related to trade are permitted freely when the basic trade transaction has been approved or does not require authorization. Transfers of income accruing to nonresidents in the form of profits, dividends, and royalties are also permitted freely when the basic transaction has been approved.

Residents traveling for tourism or business purposes to countries in the franc zone are allowed to take out BEAC banknotes up to a limit of CFAF 2 million; amounts in excess of this limit may be taken out in the form of means of payment other than banknotes. The allowances for travel to countries outside the franc zone are subject to the following regulations: (1) for tourist travel, CFAF 100,000 a day, with a maximum of CFAF 2 million a trip; (2) for business travel, CFAF 250,000 a day, with a maximum of CFAF 5 million a trip; (3) allowances in excess of these limits are subject to the authorization of the Ministry of Finance or, by delegation, the BEAC; and (4) the use of credit cards, which must be issued by resident financial intermediaries and approved by the Ministry of Finance, is limited to the ceilings indicated above for tourism and business travel. However, these regulations are administered liberally and bona fide requests for allowances in excess of these limits are normally granted. Returning resident travelers are required to declare all means of payment in their possession upon arrival at customs and surrender within eight days all means of payment exceeding the equivalent of CFAF 25,000. All resident travelers, regardless of destination, must declare in writing all means of payment at their disposal at the time of departure. The re-exportation by nonresident travelers of means of payment other than banknotes registered in their name and issued abroad is not restricted; however, documentation is required that such means of payment have been purchased with funds drawn from a foreign account in CFA francs or with other foreign exchange. The re-exportation of foreign banknotes is allowed up to the equivalent of CFAF 250,000; the re-exportation of foreign banknotes above these ceilings requires documentation

demonstrating either the importation of foreign banknotes or their purchase against other means of payment registered in the name of the traveler or through the use of nonresident deposits held in local banks.

Exports and Export Proceeds

All exports require a declaration. Proceeds from exports to foreign countries must be collected and repatriated within one month of the due date, which must not be later than 90 days after the arrival of the goods at their destination, unless special authorization is obtained. Export proceeds received in currencies other than French francs or those of an Operations Account country must be surrendered. All export transactions must be domiciled with an authorized bank.

Proceeds from Invisibles

Proceeds from transactions in invisibles with France (as defined above), Monaco, and the Operations Account countries may be retained. All amounts due from residents of other countries in respect of services, and all income earned in those countries from foreign assets, must be collected within one month of the due date. If payment is received in foreign currency, it must be surrendered within one month of the date of receipt. Resident and nonresident travelers may bring in any amount of banknotes and coins issued by the BEAC, the Bank of France, or any other bank of issue maintaining an Operations Account with the French Treasury, as well as any amount of foreign banknotes and coins (except gold coins) of countries outside the Operations Account Area.

Capital

Capital movements between the Central African Republic and France (as defined above), Monaco, and the Operations Account countries are free of exchange control; capital transfers to all other countries require exchange control approval and are restricted, but capital receipts from such countries are permitted freely. All foreign borrowing by the Government or its public and semipublic enterprises, as well as all foreign borrowing with a government guarantee, requires the prior approval of the Director of the Budget.

Special controls (in addition to any exchange control requirements that may apply) are maintained over borrowing and lending abroad; over inward and outward direct investment; and over the issuing, advertising, or offering for sale of foreign securities in the Central African Republic. These controls relate to the transactions themselves, not to payments or receipts. With the exception of those controls over the sale or introduction of foreign securities in the Central African Republic, the measures do not apply to France (as defined above), Monaco, and the Operations Account countries.

Direct investments abroad[3] require the prior approval of the Ministry of Finance, unless they take the form of a capital increase resulting from the reinvestment of undistributed profits. The full or partial liquidation of such investments also requires prior approval from the Ministry of Finance, unless the operation involves the relinquishing of a participation that had previously been approved as constituting a direct investment abroad. Foreign direct investments in the Central African Republic[4] must be declared to the Minister of Finance, unless they take the form of a capital increase resulting from the reinvestment of undistributed profits; the Minister has a period of two months from receipt of the declaration during which he may request postponement. The full or partial liquidation of direct investments in the Central African Republic must also be declared to the Minister, unless the operation involves the relinquishing of a participation that had previously been approved as constituting a direct investment in the Central African Republic. All direct investments, whether Central African Republic investments abroad or foreign investments in the Central African Republic, that are made or liquidated must be reported to the Minister within 20 days of each operation. (Direct investments are defined as those that imply control of a company or an enterprise. Mere participation is not considered direct investment, provided that it does not exceed 20 percent of the capital of a company whose shares are quoted on a stock exchange.)

The issuing, advertising, or offering for sale of foreign securities in the Central African Republic requires prior authorization from the Minister of Finance. Exempt from authorization, however, are operations in connection with (1) loans backed by a guarantee from the Government, and (2) shares similar to securities, when issuing, advertising, or offering them for sale in the Central African Republic has previously been authorized.

---

[3]Including those made through foreign companies that are directly or indirectly controlled by persons in the Central African Republic and those made by branches or subsidiaries abroad of companies in the Central African Republic.

[4]Including those made by companies in the Central African Republic that are directly or indirectly under foreign control and those made by branches or subsidiaries of foreign companies in the Central African Republic.

Borrowing abroad by natural or juridical persons, whether public or private, whose normal residence or registered office is in the Central African Republic, or by branches or subsidiaries in the Central African Republic of juridical persons whose registered office is abroad, requires prior authorization from the Minister of Finance. The following are, however, exempt from this authorization: (1) loans constituting a direct investment abroad for which prior approval has been obtained, as indicated above; (2) loans directly connected with the rendering of services abroad by the persons or firms mentioned above, or with the financing of commercial transactions either between the Central African Republic and countries abroad or between foreign countries in which those persons or firms take part; (3) loans contracted by registered banks; and (4) loans other than those mentioned above when the total amount of loans outstanding does not exceed CFAF 50 million for any one borrower. Loans referred to under (4) and each repayment must be reported to the Office of Foreign Financial Relations within 20 days of the operation, unless the total outstanding amount of all loans contracted abroad by the borrower is less than CFAF 500,000.

Lending abroad by natural or juridical persons, whether public or private, whose normal residence or registered office is in the Central African Republic, or by branches or subsidiaries in the Central African Republic of juridical persons whose registered office is abroad, requires prior authorization from the Minister of Finance. The following are, however, exempt from this authorization: (1) loans granted by registered banks, and (2) other loans when the total amount of loans outstanding does not exceed CFAF 50 million for any one lender. The contracting of loans that are exempt from authorization, and each repayment, must be reported to the Office of Foreign Financial Relations within 20 days of the operation, except when the amount of the loan granted abroad by the lender is less than CFAF 500,000.

Under Law No. 62/355 of February 19, 1963 (as amended by Ordinance No. 69/47 of September 2, 1969) and Decision No. 18/65 of December 14, 1965, of the Central African Customs and Economic Union, industrial, tourist, agricultural, and mining enterprises (both foreign and domestic) established in the Central African Republic are granted, under certain conditions, a reduction in duties and taxes on the importation of specified equipment. In addition, certain enterprises are exempt from direct taxes on specified income.

The law also provides for three categories of preferential treatment (A, B, and C) that allow fiscal and other privileges to be accorded to firms investing either in new enterprises or in the expansion of existing ones in most sectors of the economy, except the commercial sector. Requests for approval of preferential treatment must be submitted to the Minister of Industry, who is Chairman of the Investment Commission that considers the application. If the Commission gives a positive decision, the proposed authorization is submitted to the Council of Ministers. Preferential treatments A and C are granted by decree from the Council of Ministers. Preferential treatment B is granted by an act of the Board of Directors of the Equatorial Customs Union upon the recommendation of the Council of Ministers.

Gold

Residents are free to hold, acquire, and dispose of gold in any form in the Central African Republic. Imports and exports of gold require a license, which is seldom granted; in practice, imports and exports are made by an authorized purchasing office.

Exempt from prior authorization are (1) imports and exports by or on behalf of the Treasury, and (2) imports and exports of manufactured articles containing a small quantity of gold (such as gold-filled or gold-plated articles). Both licensed and exempt imports of gold are subject to customs declaration. Certain companies have been officially appointed as Offices for the Purchase, Import, and Export of Gold and Raw Diamonds.

Changes During 1995

No significant changes occurred in the exchange and trade system.

Changes During 1996

Exchange Arrangement

June 1. The Central African Republic accepted the obligations of Article VIII, Sections 2, 3, and 4 of the Fund Agreement.

CHAD

(Position as of June 30, 1996)

Exchange Arrangement

The currency of Chad is the CFA Franc issued by the Bank of Central African States (BEAC),[1] which is pegged to the French franc, the intervention currency, at the fixed rate of CFAF 1 per F 0.01. The official buying and selling rate is CFAF 100 per F 1. Exchange transactions in French francs between the BEAC and commercial banks take place at the same rate. Buying and selling rates for certain other foreign currencies are also officially posted, with quotations based on the fixed rate for the French franc and the rates in the Paris exchange market for the currencies concerned. All transfers and exchange operations are subject to a commission levied by the Treasury. The commission rate amounts to 0.25 percent in the franc zone and 0.5 percent outside the franc zone. There are no taxes or subsidies on the purchase or sale of foreign exchange.

Chad's exchange control measures, with the exception of those relating to gold, do not apply to (1) France (and its overseas departments and territories) and Monaco; and (2) all other countries whose bank of issue is linked with the French Treasury by an Operations Account (Benin, Burkina Faso, Cameroon, the Central African Republic, Comoros, Congo, Côte d'Ivoire, Equatorial Guinea, Gabon, Mali, Niger, Senegal, and Togo). Hence, all payments to these countries may be made freely. However, they must be declared and made only through authorized banks, using bank checks. Payments to all other countries are subject to exchange control.

Forward cover for imports is permitted only for specified commodities and requires the prior approval of the Office of the Minister of Economy and Commerce.

Chad accepted the obligations of Article VIII, Sections 2, 3, and 4 of the Fund Agreement on June 1, 1996.

Administration of Control

Exchange control is administered by the Minister of Finance, who has delegated approval authority in part to the External Finance and Exchange Control Subdirectorate, which issues instructions to the authorized banks. All exchange transactions relating to countries outside the Operations Account area

must be made through authorized banks. The Ministry of Finance supervises public and private sector borrowing and lending abroad, the issuing, advertising, or offering for sale of foreign securities in Chad, and inward and outward direct investment. It also issues import and export authorizations for gold.

Arrears are maintained with respect to debt-service payments on public debt.

Prescription of Currency

Since Chad is an Operations Account country, settlements with France (as defined above), Monaco, and other Operations Account countries are made in CFA francs, French francs, or the currency of any other institute of issue that maintains an Operations Account with the French Treasury. Settlements with all other countries are usually made through correspondent banks in France in any of the currencies of those countries or in French francs through foreign accounts in francs.

Nonresident Accounts

The regulations pertaining to nonresident accounts are based on regulations applied in France. The repurchase of banknotes issued by the BEAC and in circulation outside the BEAC area is suspended; BEAC banknotes received by the foreign correspondents of authorized banks and mailed to the BEAC agency in Chad by the Bank of France or the Central Bank of West African States (BCEAO) may not be credited to foreign accounts in francs.

Imports and Import Payments

All import transactions valued at CFAF 100,000 or more and relating to foreign countries must be domiciled with an authorized bank.

A special import authorization by the Ministry of Commerce and Industrial Promotion is required for imports of sulphur and other explosives. The import of sugar is the monopoly of the SONASUT.

Payments for Invisibles

Payments for invisibles to France (as defined above), Monaco, and the Operations Account countries are permitted freely. Only a simple declaration is required for transfers not exceeding CFAF 500,000 to countries outside the BEAC area by residents; for transfers of more than CFAF 500,000, prior authori-

---

[1]The CFA is legal tender also in Cameroon, the Central African Republic, Congo, Equatorial Guinea, and Gabon.

zation must be obtained from the competent authorities. For many types of payment, approval authority has been delegated to authorized banks. Authorized banks are required to execute promptly all duly documented transfer orders, and in any case to dispatch cable transfers within 48 hours of receipt of the relevant request. Payments for invisibles related to trade are permitted freely if the basic trade transaction has been approved or does not require authorization. Transfers of bona fide income accruing to nonresidents in the form of profits, dividends, and royalties are also permitted freely. Some current payments, however, may be subject to delay. On a temporary basis, nonresidents, except diplomatic missions and their staff, international organizations and their staff, agencies with equivalent status and their staff, as well as employees and self-employed members of the professions (professionally active in Operations Account area countries for less than a year) are not permitted to send transfers to countries that are not franc zone members without prior authorization from the competent authorities. They may, however, receive transfers from abroad.

Insurance on all imports to Chad with values exceeding CFA 500,000 on f.o.b. terms must be arranged with local insurance companies by the importer.

The exportation (and importation) of banknotes issued by the BEAC to areas outside the BEAC area is prohibited.

Travelers—civil servants on missions, students, persons on pilgrimage, etc.—must use the following payments instruments: foreign exchange, traveler's checks; bank drafts, bank and postal transfers, etc. Residents visiting other franc zone countries may obtain an unlimited allocation in French francs. This allocation can be provided in banknotes, traveler's checks, bank drafts, and bank or postal transfers. For travel to countries outside the franc zone, the exchange allocation depends on the type of travel (as indicated below) and is subject to prior authorization from the relevant administrative authorities. This allocation can be made in banknotes, traveler's checks, bank drafts, or postal transfers. Residents traveling outside the franc zone for tourism may obtain an exchange allocation equivalent to CFAF 200,000 a day up to a maximum of CFAF 4 million a trip for a person over 10 years of age; for children under 10, the allocation is reduced by one-half. Residents traveling to countries outside the franc zone for business may obtain an exchange allocation equivalent to CFAF 500,000 a day, up to a maximum of CFAF 10 million a trip. Students or trainees leaving for the first time or returning to their normal place of study in countries outside the franc zone may obtain an exchange allocation equivalent to a three-month scholarship plus expenses for supplies. However, a student, whether or not the holder of a scholarship, may obtain an exchange allocation up to the equivalent of CFAF 2 million. Civil servants and government employees traveling on official business to countries outside the franc zone may obtain an exchange allocation equivalent to the allowances stipulated for such travel. However, such civil servants and government employees may obtain an exchange allocation on the same basis as tourists only if their mission costs are less than a daily allocation of CFAF 200,000, up to a limit of CFAF 4 million. Residents traveling to countries outside the franc zone for medical treatment may obtain an exchange allocation equivalent to CFAF 250,000 a day up to a limit of CFAF 5 million. Residents traveling to countries outside the franc zone for reasons other than those listed above (sporting events, participation in expositions, organization of fairs, participation in seminars or international meetings in a personal capacity, pilgrimages, etc.) shall be granted exchange allocations on the same basis as those traveling for tourism. However, these regulations are administered liberally and bona fide requests for allowances in excess of these limits are normally granted. Resident and nonresident travelers may import into BEAC area countries an unlimited amount of coins and banknotes other than those denominated in CFA francs.

Exports and Export Proceeds

Export transactions relating to foreign countries must be domiciled with an authorized bank when their value exceeds CFAF 50,000. Export proceeds received in currencies other than those of France or an Operations Account country must be surrendered. Export proceeds normally must be received within 180 days of the arrival of the commodities at their destination. The proceeds must be collected and, if received in a foreign currency, surrendered within two months of the due date.

Specified exports to certain neighboring countries, including Nigeria and Sudan, may be made through compensation transactions. Exports of cotton are the monopoly of COTONTCHAD.

Proceeds from Invisibles

Proceeds from transactions in invisibles with France (as defined above), Monaco, and Operations Account countries may be retained. All amounts due from residents of other countries in respect of services, and all income earned in those countries from foreign assets, must be collected and, if received in foreign currency, surrendered within one month of the due date.

Nonresidents traveling from one BEAC member country to another may take with them an unlimited amount of franc zone banknotes and coins. Nonresident travelers may take out foreign exchange or other foreign means of payment up to the amount they declared on entry into the BEAC area. If they have made no declaration on entry into one of the BEAC countries, they may take out only up to the equivalent of CFAF 500,000.

Capital

Capital movements between Chad and France (as defined above), Monaco, and the Operations Account countries are free of exchange control; capital transfers to all other countries require exchange control approval and are restricted, but capital receipts from such countries are permitted freely. All foreign securities, foreign currencies, and titles embodying claims on foreign countries or nonresidents held by residents or nonresidents in Chad must be deposited with authorized banks in Chad.

Special controls in addition to any exchange control requirements that may be applicable or suspended are maintained over borrowing and lending abroad; over inward and outward direct investment; and over the issuing, advertising, or offering for sale of foreign securities in Chad. These controls relate only to the transactions themselves, not to payments or receipts. With the exception of those controls over the sale or introduction of foreign securities in Chad, the measures do not apply to France (as defined above), Monaco, and the Operations Account countries.

Direct investments abroad[2] require the prior approval of the Minister of Finance, irrespective of the method of financing; the full or partial liquidation of such investments also requires the prior approval of the Minister. Foreign direct investments in Chad [3] require the prior approval of the Minister of Finance, unless they take the form of a mixed-economy enterprise; the full or partial liquidation of direct investments in Chad must also be declared to the Minister. Both the making and the liquidation of direct investments, whether Chadian investments abroad or foreign investments in Chad, must be reported to the Minister within 30 days of each oper-

ation. (Direct investments are defined as investments implying control of a company or enterprise.)

The issuing, advertising, or offering for sale of foreign securities in Chad requires prior authorization from the Minister of Finance. Exempt from authorization, however, are operations in connection with (1) loans backed by a guarantee from the Chadian Government, and (2) shares similar to securities, when issuing, advertising, or offering them for sale in Chad has already been authorized.

Borrowing abroad by natural or juridical persons, whether public or private, residing in Chad, or by branches or subsidiaries in Chad of juridical persons whose registered office is abroad, requires prior authorization from the Minister of Finance. The following are, however, exempt from this authorization: (1) loans constituting a direct investment abroad for which prior approval has been obtained, as indicated above; (2) loans directly connected with the rendering of services abroad by the persons or firms mentioned above, or with the financing of commercial transactions either between Chad and countries abroad or between foreign countries in which these persons or firms take part; and (3) loans other than those mentioned above when the total amount of the loan outstanding does not exceed CFAF 10 million for any one borrower, the interest rate is no higher than 7 percent, and the maturity is two years or less. The contracting of loans referred to under (3) that are free of authorization and each repayment must be declared to the Minister of Finance within 30 days of the operation.

Lending abroad by natural or juridical persons, whether public or private, residing in Chad, or by branches or subsidiaries in Chad of juridical persons whose registered office is abroad, requires prior authorization from the Minister of Finance. The following are, however, exempt from this authorization: (1) loans directly connected with the rendering of services abroad by the persons or firms mentioned above, or with the financing of commercial transactions either between Chad and countries abroad or between foreign countries in which these persons or firms take part; and (2) other loans when the total amount of these loans outstanding does not exceed CFAF 5 million for any one lender. The making of loans referred to under (2) are free of authorization but each repayment must be declared to the Minister of Finance within 30 days of the operation. Commercial banks must maintain a specified minimum amount of their assets in Chad.

Under the Investment Code published on December 9, 1987, any domestic or foreign enterprise established in Chad is granted, under certain conditions, reduced duties and taxes on specified imports and

---

[2]Including those made through foreign companies that are directly or indirectly controlled by persons in Chad and those made by overseas branches or subsidiaries of companies in Chad.

[3]Including those made by companies in Chad directly or indirectly under foreign control and those made by branches or subsidiaries of foreign companies in Chad.

exemption from direct taxes on specified income. The code provides for four categories of enterprises that may be eligible to receive various forms of preferential treatment (including certain tax privileges). Requests for preferential treatment must be submitted to the Minister of Finance, who, after examining the documents, transmits them to the Investment Commission. With the recommendation of this commission, the project is submitted to the Council of Ministers for approval.

Gold

Chad has issued gold coins with face values of CFAF 1,000, CFAF 3,000, CFAF 5,000, CFAF 10,000, and CFAF 20,000, which are legal tender. Residents who are not producers of gold may not hold unworked gold without specific authorization. Imports and exports of gold, whether unworked or refined, require prior authorization from both the Ministry of Finance and the Directorate of Geological and Mining Research, as well as a visa from the External Finance Department. Exempt from this requirement are (1) imports and exports by or on behalf of the monetary authorities, and (2) imports and exports of manufactured articles containing a small quantity of gold (such as gold-filled or gold-plated articles). Unworked gold may be exported only to France. Both licensed and exempt imports of gold are subject to customs declaration.

Changes During 1995

Imports and Import Payments

June 29. Import and export licenses were abolished.

October 25. Imports of sulphur and explosives were subject to a special authorization.

Payments for Invisibles

August 21. Authorized banks were required to execute within 48 hours (formerly 24 hours) all duly documented transfer orders.

August 21. The allocation for residents traveling outside the CFA franc zone for tourism was increased to CFAF 200,000 a day from CFAF 100,000, to a maximum of CFAF 4 million a trip a person from CFAF 2 million. The limit for business trips was increased to CFAF 500,000 a day from CFAF 250,000, to a maximum of a CFAF 10 million a trip a person from CFAF 5 million. The allocation for students was increased to CFAF 2 million from CFAF 1 million. The allocation for civil servants and government employees could be the same as others if their mission costs are less than a daily allocation of CFAF 200,000, up to a limit of CFAF 4 million. The allocation for residents traveling outside the CFA franc zone for medical treatment was increased to CFAF 250,000 a day from CFAF 100,000, up to a maximum of CFAF 5 million from CFAF 2.5 million.

Proceeds from Invisibles

August 21. The maximum amount of foreign exchange or other foreign means of payment that nonresidents can take out without declaration at entry was increased to CFAF 500,000 from CFAF 250,000.

Changes During 1996

Exchange Arrangement

June 1. Chad accepted the obligations of Article VIII, Sections 2, 3, and 4 of the Fund Agreement.

CHILE

(Position as of April 30, 1996)

Exchange Arrangement

The currency of Chile is the Chilean Peso (Ch$). Its external (reference) value is based on a fixed basket of currencies consisting of 0.45 U.S. dollar, 0.4691 deutsche mark, and 24.6825 Japanese yen; the weight of each currency in the basket is based on its relative importance in Chile's international transactions. The external value of the basket is adjusted daily on the basis of the exchange rate relationships between the currencies included in the basket and the differential between the domestic and the foreign rates of inflation, adjusted for an estimate of the appreciation trend of Chile's exchange rate. The Central Bank of Chile conducts foreign exchange transactions with the official exchange market entities within margins of 10 percent around the reference rate. On December 31, 1995, the reference rate was Ch$434.02 per US$1 and the interbank rate was Ch$413.50 per US$1. The official foreign exchange market consists of commercial banks, authorized exchange houses, and other entities licensed by the Central Bank. Debt-service payments; remittances of dividends and profits; and authorized capital transactions, including loan receipts, must be transacted through this market. In addition, there is an informal exchange market through which all transactions not required to be channeled through the official foreign exchange market are allowed to take place. In both markets, economic agents are free to negotiate exchange rates.

The banks are authorized to sell their excess foreign exchange holdings to other banks or to the Central Bank. Foreign exchange may be bought for the repayment of capital or interest abroad in due time if these debts are properly registered at the Central Bank. Pension funds and insurance companies may purchase foreign exchange through the official market to make investments abroad, subject to individual limits on such investments. Mutual funds must purchase foreign exchange for foreign investments through the informal market for foreign exchange.

Chile accepted the obligations of Article VIII, Sections 2, 3, and 4 of the Fund Agreement on July 27, 1977.

Administration of Control

The Central Bank is responsible for implementing exchange control policy. The Chilean Copper Commission is responsible for supervising copper exports and all imports of the copper industry in accordance with general rules enacted by the Central Bank.

Prescription of Currency

Settlements with Argentina, Bolivia, Brazil, Colombia, the Dominican Republic, Ecuador, Malaysia, Mexico, Paraguay, Peru, Uruguay, and Venezuela are made through accounts maintained with each other by the Central Bank of Chile and the central banks of each of the countries concerned within the framework of the multilateral clearing system of the Latin American Integration Association (LAIA).

Imports and Import Payments

Most imports are free of controls, with the exception of used motor vehicles. Most imports require a document (*Informe de Importación*) issued by the Central Bank, which must be obtained and processed through the intermediary of a local commercial bank. Payment for visible trade transactions through the official foreign exchange market is not permitted unless an *Informe de Importación* has been issued.

Importers meeting the documentary requirements are granted access to the official foreign exchange market, regardless of the terms of the obligation involved, at least 30 days after the obligation's expiration date as it appears in the *Informe de Importación*. Imports are subject to a uniform tariff rate of 11 percent. A few items are exempt from the general tariff regime, including items on which tariffs have been negotiated with LAIA countries and under a number of bilateral trade agreements. Imports of wheat, maize, edible oil, and sugar are subject to a special regime involving price margins within which the after-duty price must remain. In addition, tariff duties or surcharges are applied on a temporary basis to imports of certain products that are subsidized in the country of origin or dumped in Chile.

Payments for Invisibles

From April 17, 1996, foreign exchange houses were allowed to sell up to US$15,000, or its equivalent in other foreign currencies, a calendar month, to any person for travel expenses; payments to international organizations; payments for studies abroad; social security payments; payments of real estate rents; subscriptions to magazines; purchase of books and other publications; medical treatment expenses; and other nonspecified expenses upon presentation of a sworn declaration indicating the amount and use of the foreign exchange requested.

There are no special provisions for exports of domestic banknotes.

Insurance activities within the country are limited to Chilean companies or to authorized foreign companies.

Exports and Export Proceeds

All products may be freely exported. Foreign exchange proceeds from exports are not subject to a surrender requirement, although export transactions must be reported to the Central Bank. Commercial banks are authorized to purchase all spot foreign exchange proceeds from exporters. Windfall receipts from copper exports of CODELCO (the state copper company) must be deposited in a special foreign currency account at the Central Bank, and withdrawals from this account are permitted only under certain circumstances.

Exporters of a limited number of products (approximately 6 percent of the country's annual exports) have the option of taking a tax reimbursement (within 120 days of repatriating the proceeds) in lieu of benefits under the existing import duty drawback scheme. Alternatively, exporters of these products may avail themselves of the provisions of Law No. 19.024, under which they may obtain refunds of the duties paid on imported inputs. Eligible products were defined initially as those whose average annual export values in 1990 were equal to or less than US$5 million. The list of eligible products is reviewed annually in the light of their export value during the previous year. Annual export values are also subject to adjustment each year.

Proceeds from Invisibles

In general, foreign exchange proceeds from invisibles must be surrendered only when required by a legal provision. Royalties and copyright fees, commissions, proceeds from insurance, and other benefits related to foreign trade are subject to the same surrender requirement. The proceeds from family remittances, other commissions, or the surplus foreign exchange from travel allocations are not required to be surrendered.

There are no special provisions for imports of domestic banknotes.

Capital

All new foreign borrowing or refinancing of existing credits by commercial banks requires prior regis-

tration at, or approval from, the Central Bank; exceptions are lines of credit of up to one-year maturity with foreign correspondents. Short-term loans are subject to a limit determined mainly by a bank's capital and reserves. However, the Central Bank must still be notified of foreign borrowing that does not require its approval. All foreign investment is subject to a minimum one-year withholding period. All foreign borrowing, except for credits that are provided directly to Chilean exporters by foreign importers or by foreign suppliers to Chilean importers, and foreign financial investment (including sales of existing equity in Chilean companies by Chilean residents to nonresidents) are subject to a reserve requirement of 30 percent; this requirement may be satisfied by lodging a deposit in U.S. dollars at the Central Bank without interest or by entering into a special repurchase agreement for promissory notes with the Central Bank that effectively imposes a cost equivalent to the forgone interest. Banks and other financial institutions may reduce this reserve requirement through financial investments in foreign exchange up to the maximum limit of such investments. The length of the period during which the reserve requirement must be held in the Central Bank is one year for loans and bonds. Credit lines and foreign exchange deposits are also subject to the 30 percent reserve requirement, which is based on the average monthly outstanding balance. Foreign capital may enter Chile under one of the following arrangements, depending on the purpose and type of investment:

(1) Title I, Chapter XIV of the Compendium of Rules on International Exchange stipulates that capital brought into the country in the form of foreign borrowing (*créditos externos*) must be sold through authorized banks. Although there is no minimum term on the maturity of foreign borrowing, the 30 percent reserve requirement against external credits entering under Chapter XIV must be retained for one year. Repatriation is allowed only in accordance with the amortization schedule established at the time of registration. Accelerated payments or extensions of payment are subject to special authorization. Since June 1990, under Chapter XXVI of Title I, which refers to American depository receipts (ADRs), individuals and legal entities that are domiciled and resident abroad and that meet certain conditions have been permitted to remit abroad proceeds from the sale of stocks of registered corporations domiciled in Chile that were purchased with funds abroad through the official exchange market. The remittance of dividends and profits accruing from such stocks is also allowed through the official exchange market.

(2) Chapter XIV of Title I of the Compendium of Rules authorizes the Central Bank to make exemptions to the general rules concerning the inflow and outflow of capital or credits. Chilean enterprises and banks were authorized under Chapter XIV Regulations on May 13, 1992, to issue bonds in foreign markets. Nonfinancial enterprises with a credit rating from an international rating company that is equal to or better than that assigned to Chile can issue bonds with a minimum value of US$25 million. Issues of bonds by banks are subject to prior authorization by the Central Bank. In accordance with Chapters XXVI regulations, Chilean enterprises and banks are also authorized to issue ADRs. Since November 1995, the first issue should be for a minimum of US$25 million; the second issue should be for a minimum of US$10 million. The issuing company must be rated by two international rating agencies at least BBB+ in the case of banks and BBB for other companies.

(3) Decree-Law No. 600 of July 7, 1974 (amended by Decree-Law No. 1748 of March 18, 1977), the Foreign Investment Statute, establishes a special regime for long-term capital investment. Authorization to make a foreign exchange investment in Chile is granted by the Foreign Investment Committee through a contract that stipulates that capital transfers to Chile will not normally exceed eight years for mining and three years for other projects. The deadline may be extended up to twelve years for mining and up to eight years for other investments exceeding US$50 million. Investments of less than US$5 million may be approved by the Executive Vice President of the Committee, with a few exceptions. There are no general limitations on profit remittances, but specific agreements in this regard may be included in the above-mentioned investment contract. Capital may be repatriated after one year unless specified otherwise in the investment contract. Foreign investors may opt for one of two income tax systems. Both systems are based on the regular Chilean corporate income tax of 15 percent on profit repatriation. Under the first system, a fixed rate of 42 percent (which includes the corporate income tax of 15 percent) is guaranteed over a period of 10 years (up to 20 years for investments in excess of US$50 million). Alternatively, foreign investors may select a tax system that is similar to that which is applied to domestic investors. This system applies a 35 percent rate on profits before tax and deducts from it the 15 percent corporate income tax. The first system results in an effective rate of 38 percent on gross profits (before tax) and the second system in an effective rate of 35 percent on gross profits. Any foreign credits involved must be on

financial terms authorized by the Central Bank. Foreign capital that entered Chile before the promulgation of Decree-Law No. 600 and that is not subject to that law continues to be subject to the regulations prevailing on the date of entry. Contract awards in the oil sector are decided by the Government under presidential decree; rights and responsibilities under such a decree may be vested in the Empresa Nacional de Petróleo (ENAP) by the Ministry of Mines.

(4) Chapter XXVI of the Compendium of Foreign Exchange Regulations permits Chilean corporations with a minimum specified international credit rating which are listed on foreign exchanges to issue shares or share-backed instruments (a minimum of US$25 million or its equivalent if it is a first issue, and US$10 million or its equivalent for second issues) for purchase abroad, provided at least 90 percent of the initial issue is purchased by foreign investors. To be eligible, banks and other financial institutions must be rated at least BBB+; other corporations must be rated at least BBB. The issue must be underwritten by a foreign bank with a minimum capital of at least US$1 billion and five years' operating experience at the time of reaching an agreement with the Central Bank. Under this chapter, individuals and legal entities that are domiciled and resident abroad and that meet certain conditions are also permitted to remit abroad proceeds from the sale of stocks of registered corporations domiciled in Chile that were purchased with funds abroad through the official exchange market. The remittance of dividends and profits accruing from such stocks is also allowed through the official exchange market.

(5) Law No. 18.657 permits foreign capital investment funds to invest in shares in Chilean corporations, instruments guaranteed by the banking system, letters of credit, bonds, and other securities approved by the Securities Commission, provided such funds meet certain portfolio diversification requirements and have a minimum paid-up capital of not less than 6,000 UF (a value reference unit). Repatriation of capital from sales of such instruments is allowed only after five years. No restrictions apply to profit remittances by these funds. These funds have access to the official foreign exchange market for repatriation of capital, profits earned on such capital, and payments of expenses involved in foreign investment activities under certain conditions.

(6) Chilean corporations are permitted to invest abroad through a number of channels. Under Title I of Chapter XII of the Compendium of Rules on International Exchange, Chilean banks may invest up to 25 percent of their capital and reserves abroad, of which 20 percent may be in equity of foreign finan-

cial institutions, with approval from the Central Bank and the Office of the Superintendent of Banks and Financial Institutions. Up to 30 percent of the total amount permitted may be invested in financial instruments with a minimum rating of BB–. Pension funds may make foreign investments for amounts equivalent to up to 9 percent of their assets; up to 4.5 percent can be invested in equity instruments. Life insurance companies may invest up to 10 percent of their assets in foreign financial instruments and up to 3 percent in urban nonresidential real estate. General insurance companies may invest up to 15 percent in foreign financial instruments and up to 3 percent in urban nonresidential real estate. Mutual funds may invest up to 30 percent of their assets in foreign investments. Except for mutual funds, foreign investments must meet certain minimum risk criteria. Insurance companies must also meet certain portfolio diversification criteria. Except for mutual funds, foreign exchange for these transactions may be purchased through the official market for foreign exchange.

Gold

Chile has issued three gold coins, which are not legal tender. Monetary gold may be traded only by authorized houses, but ordinary transactions in gold between private individuals may be freely undertaken. Imports and exports of gold are unrestricted, subject to compliance with the normal formalities for import and export transactions, including registration with the Central Bank.

Changes During 1995

Exchange Arrangement

March 16. The Central Bank (1) defined norms and requirements for exchange houses and brokerage companies through which pension funds can carry out domestic and foreign financial transactions (these exchange houses and brokerage companies constitute the "formal secondary market"); (2) specified that mutual funds will not be granted access to the formal exchange market to carry out exchange operations related to their investments abroad.

Exports and Export Proceeds

April 18. The Central Bank extended until April 19, 1996, the general exchange restrictions contained in the Compendium of Foreign Exchange Regulations, and established that as of June 16, 1995, exporters would no longer be required to surrender export proceeds to the Central Bank, although they would still be required to inform the Central Bank of these operations for statistical purposes.

Capital

January 5. The Central Bank specified that the maximum amount of financial investment that banks and financial institutions can deduct from the foreign exchange position used to calculate their reserve requirement is equal to the maximum limit on such investments.

January 12. The Central Bank established the following ceilings on investment abroad: (1) for pension funds, the ceiling was raised to 6 percent from 3 percent of their total assets; (2) for life insurance companies, 10 percent of their assets in foreign financial instruments and up to 3 percent in urban nonresidential real estate; (3) for general insurance companies, 15 percent of their assets in foreign financial instruments and up to 3 percent in urban nonresidential real estate; (4) for mutual funds, 30 percent of their total assets, without reference to any minimum rating requirement or any specific number of countries. Pension funds and insurance companies are granted access to the formal exchange market to carry out these operations.

As a transitory provision, the Superintendency of Banks and Financial Institutions would determine the time period during which banks will be required to adjust the ratio between their foreign investments and their total assets to the ceiling established by the Central Bank.

March 2. The Central Bank authorized exchange houses operating in the formal exchange market to carry out exchange operations related to investment abroad by pension funds, insurance companies, and mutual funds.

May 17. The limit on foreign investment by pension funds was increased to 9 percent from 6 percent of the total value of the fund, and investment in variable income securities up to 4.5 percent of the value of the fund was allowed.

July 3. The coverage of the existing 20 percent reserve requirement on foreign liabilities was broadened to include investment flows that do not constitute an increase in the capital stock but only a transaction of assets from residents to nonresidents. Investment through the DL600 (the Foreign Investment Statute) and through Foreign Capital Investment Funds (FICEs) would be specifically excluded from the application of the reserve requirement. The Central Bank eased the ceiling on foreign investment by banks and financial institutions by allowing 30 percent of the 25 percent ceiling of capital and reserves to be invested in instruments with a minimum rating of BB–, but the remaining 70 percent must be invested in BBB– or less risky securities, below the minimum A– requirement in place earlier. The credit rating of the securities in which pension funds can invest was lowered from A– to BBB–. For the stock investments of insurance companies, instead of considering the country risk of the issuing country, a minimum BBB– credit rating requirement for the country where the stocks are traded was established.

August 7. Chapters XVIII and XIX of the Compendium on Foreign Exchange Regulations, which governed the purchase of selected Chilean foreign debt instruments abroad and restricted related profit and capital remittances, were eliminated, thus lifting restrictions on the remittances of profits and the three-year holding for capital entered under these regulations.

September 20. The Central Bank reduced to 5 days from 65 days the period in which banks can sell or purchase foreign exchange in connection with American depository receipts (ADR) transactions.

November 10. The Central Bank introduced an estimate of differentials in productivity growth between Chile and its trading partners as a new factor in the determination of the official reference exchange rate. This new factor will allow for a gradual yearly appreciation of 2 percent in real terms.

November 22. Corporations with ADRs in foreign stock exchanges were allowed to make new issues of ADRs with a minimum of US$10 million or its equivalent in other currencies.

Changes During 1996

Payments for Invisibles

April 17. Foreign exchange houses were allowed to sell up to US$15,000, or its equivalent in other foreign currencies, a calendar month, to any person for travel expenses; payments to international organizations; and payments for studies abroad.

PEOPLE'S REPUBLIC OF CHINA

(Position as of April 30, 1996)

Exchange Arrangement

The currency of the People's Republic of China is the Renminbi, the external value of which is determined in the interbank market.[1] At the start of each trading day, the People's Bank of China announces a reference rate based on the weighted average of the buying and selling rates against the U.S. dollar during the previous day's trading. Daily movement of the exchange rate of the renminbi against the U.S. dollar is limited to 0.3 percent on either side of the reference rate. Based on the middle rate published by the PBC, the designated banks quote their buying and selling rates to their customers within a range of 0.25 percent. On December 31, 1995, the middle market rate of the renminbi against the U.S. dollar was Y 8.3179 per $1.

There are no forward exchange market arrangements operating in the official or commercial banking sectors.

Administration of Control

The People's Bank of China exercises central bank functions and control over foreign exchange; the State Administration of Exchange Control (SAEC), as a government institution under the leadership of the People's Bank of China, is responsible for implementing exchange regulations and for administering the foreign exchange market in accordance with state policy. There are a number of SAEC sub-bureaus in the provinces, main municipalities, autonomous regions, and special economic zones. The Bank of China is China's principal foreign exchange bank. Other banks and financial institutions, including affiliates of nonresident banks, may handle designated transactions with the approval of the SAEC. Currently, more than 2,500 institutions are authorized to handle foreign exchange transactions. Individuals may hold foreign exchange but generally may not deal in it or conduct arbitrage

operations. Financial institutions may hold foreign exchange.

Prescription of Currency

As of the end of 1995, an operative bilateral payments agreement was maintained with Cuba.[2] Unless there are specific regulations, the currencies used in transactions are determined by the terms of the respective contracts.

Nonresident and Foreign Currency Accounts

Nonresidents[3] remaining in China for a short time may open nonresident accounts with the Bank of China and other authorized banks and financial institutions. Foreign-funded enterprises (FFEs), including joint ventures, may also open foreign exchange current accounts and use them to make payments abroad. In addition, the People's Bank of China has specified other categories of foreign exchange accounts that domestic enterprises may maintain with designated banks by presenting the certificates of permit issued by the SAEC. Branches of foreign banks and other financial institutions may grant loans in foreign exchange and domestic banks may accept foreign currency deposits from FFEs and domestic enterprises approved by the SAEC.

Individuals may open resident foreign currency savings accounts with designated banks and may withdraw foreign currency from, or deposit it to, such accounts without restriction.

Imports and Exports

Primary responsibility for formulating foreign trade policies and ensuring the implementation of regulations and policy measures rests with the Ministry of Foreign Trade and Economic Cooperation (MOFTEC), which also issues the licenses required for restricted imports and a large number of exports.[4]

---

[1]Since April 1, 1994, the China Foreign Exchange Trading System (CFETS), a nationally integrated electronic system for interbank foreign exchange trading, has been operating in Shanghai. At present, 22 foreign exchange trading centers in major cities—accounting for the bulk of all foreign exchange transactions—are electronically linked to the CFETS. To trade in the system, financial institutions must become members of the CFETS. Designated domestic financial institutions are allowed to buy and sell foreign exchange on their own account. Other financial institutions, including branches of foreign banks, may trade foreign exchange as brokers on behalf of their customers.

[2]Inoperative bilateral payments agreements are maintained with the Democratic People's Republic of Korea, Mongolia, the Russian Federation, and Vietnam.

[3]Nonresidents include Chinese working overseas and residents of foreign countries and of the Hong Kong and Macao regions. Diplomatic representatives are also included.

[4]MOFTEC itself issues licenses for some restricted imports into Beijing; for the rest, it delegates its authority to its special commission offices at major ports and to its regional counterpart, the Commission on Foreign Economic Relations and Trade.

MOFTEC does not engage in direct foreign trade transactions and is not involved in the daily management of trading corporations. Foreign trade is conducted by foreign trade corporations (FTCs) and other entities licensed by MOFTEC to conduct foreign trade. At the end of 1995, 4,228 FTCs were in operation. In addition, FFEs are permitted to conduct international trade directly.

All enterprises other than registered FTCs must obtain approval from the local foreign trade bureau in accordance with MOFTEC authorization, as well as a license from the local bureau for industry and commerce, to engage in foreign trade.

All foreign exchange earnings from exports must be repatriated and sold to designated banks, except those of FFEs and those approved by the SAEC. FFEs are allowed to retain all of their foreign exchange and to sell or purchase foreign exchange in the swap centers. Since the beginning of 1995, FFEs that have passed an annual audit by the SAEC have not been required to obtain approval for each foreign exchange transaction in the swap centers; FFEs that have failed the audit are required to obtain approval for each transaction. The purpose of annual auditing is to ensure that export and contractual obligations are met. In 1995, SAEC approval was liberally granted. Since April 1996, FFEs are allowed to participate, directly or indirectly through a bank, in the interbank foreign exchange market.

Authorized local banks provide foreign exchange for imports when import contracts and commercial documentation are presented. Import licenses, when required, are examined by the banks. Residents may not pay for imports with local currency except in border trade.

Imports into China are classified into two categories—restricted imports and unrestricted imports.[5] The importation of products on the restricted list is controlled through licensing requirements or quotas. The importation of the following products is subject to canalization (i.e., restricted to designated FTCs): wheat, chemical fertilizers, crude oil and oil products, rubber, steel, timber, plywood, polyester fibers, tobacco and its products, cotton, and wool.

Imports of all secondhand garments, poisons, narcotic drugs, diseased animals, and plants are prohibited. In addition, the importation and exportation of weapons, ammunition and explosives, radio receivers and transmitters, Chinese currency exceeding Y 6,000, manuscripts, printed and recorded materials, and films that are deemed to be detrimental to Chinese political, economic, cultural, and moral interests are prohibited. All imports and exports require prior inspection before they can be released by customs at the port of entry or exit. Exports of specified machine tools require a license from the State Administration for the Inspection of Import and Export Commodities for purposes of quality control. Controls in the form of registration for surveillance purposes are exercised on the importation of machinery and electric equipment in order to monitor the supply and demand situation.

The customs regime is regulated by the Customs Law of China and the Regulations on Import and Export Tariffs of China. The tariff rates for imports fall into two categories: general and preferential. General rates apply to imports originating in the countries or regions with which China has not concluded trade treaties or agreements with reciprocal favorable tariff clauses; preferential rates apply to imports originating in the countries with which China has concluded such treaties and agreements. The duties are calculated on the basis of the transaction value of imported goods. At the end of 1995, the average unweighted tariff rate was 35.7 percent.

Imports into Tibet are subject to a separate system of customs duties established by the State Council. The tariff applies to goods imported for use in Tibet on a nondiscriminatory basis and irrespective of origin; it does not apply to imports into Tibet by mail or in the luggage of travelers, which are subject to the regular Chinese tariff.

A uniform value-added tax is applied to both domestic and imported products; the relevant provisions are contained in Provisional Regulations of the People's Republic of China on Value-Added Tax (December 13, 1993), and Provisional Regulations of the People's Republic of China on Consumption Tax (December 13, 1993).

Before 1991, special economic zones were set up in Shantou, Shenzhen, Xiamen, Zhuhai, and Hainan. A special development area was established in Pudong (Shanghai), and economic and technological development zones were established in 14 designated coastal cities. In 1992, approval was granted for the establishment of a large number of similar zones in selected inland cities and border regions that have recently been declared open to foreign trade and investment. Foreigners, Chinese working overseas, and Chinese from Hong Kong, Macao, and Taiwan Province of China are permitted to invest in and open businesses in these zones and areas either through wholly owned ventures or joint ventures with Chinese investors. Equipment and machinery or parts and components thereof, and other means of production imported by and intended to be used

---

[5]At the end of 1995, 354 tariff lines were on the restricted list.

in the production of the enterprises in the zones are exempt from import duties.

A number of restrictions are imposed on exports, primarily raw materials and food products. At the end of 1995, product items were subject to export-licensing requirements or quotas, and 47 product items were subject to export duties. A portion of the output of goods not produced in adequate quantities but for which a strong demand exists in the foreign market is set aside for export. Exports of certain products, such as valuable cultural relics, rare books, and animals, seeds, plants, precious metals, and artifacts made from precious metals are prohibited.

Export quotas for certain products are allocated, on an experimental basis, through a public bidding system that allows free competition among enterprises leading to higher export prices, greater returns for exports, and higher efficiency of foreign trade enterprises.[6] During 1995, 24 product items subject to export quotas were distributed under the bidding system.

Purchases of foreign exchange, other than by FFEs, for trade (and trade-related) transactions do not require the approval of the SAEC.

Foreign exchange for trade may be purchased from designated banks, provided that the importer has a valid import contract and a notice of payment from a foreign financial institution; for imports subject to licensing, quotas, or registration procedures, presentation of the certificates concerned is also required.

Payments for and Proceeds from Invisibles

Foreign exchange may be purchased to pay for trade-related services upon presentation of contracts or payment notices.

The remittance of profits and dividends earned on foreign direct investment is not restricted after applicable taxes have been paid.

After-tax profits of foreign-funded enterprises may be remitted in accordance with foreign exchange regulations; such remittances must be paid through the foreign exchange account of the joint venture. If the outstanding balance of such an account is not sufficient, FFEs may buy foreign exchange from swap centers or in the interbank market. Income from interest, royalties, and rent earned by foreign businesses without establishments in China is subject to a 10 percent withholding tax in the special economic zones, in the economic and technological development areas of the 14 open coastal cities, and in the newly opened inland and border cities; and a 20 percent tax applies to all other regions.

Foreign exchange needed for nontrade and noncommercial payments by budgeted organizations, institutions, and social bodies may be purchased from the Bank of China, upon presenting the Application for Nontrade Payments, at the exchange rate of the day of purchase and within the limits specified by the SAEC. Off-budget domestic establishments may purchase foreign exchange for nontrade and noncommercial payments from designated banks by presenting the Exchange Sale Instruction issued by the SAEC.

Chinese residents wishing to travel abroad or remit funds abroad may apply to the designated banks. In cases of serious illness, death, or injury affecting Chinese residents' parents, spouses, or children outside China, the residents may apply for foreign exchange up to a specified limit on presentation of documentary verification. In general, if permission is granted to travel abroad, Chinese residents are allowed to take a reasonable amount of their own foreign exchange to cover expenses for transport and subsistence. There is no tax on travel. Chinese residents who retire and emigrate are normally permitted to receive their pensions abroad, but transfers of proceeds from the sale of their assets in China are limited.

All enterprises, except FFEs, must sell their foreign exchange earnings from invisible transactions to an authorized bank. Foreign exchange remitted from abroad or from Hong Kong and Macao to Chinese residents may be retained and used to open a savings account at a designated bank or sold for renminbi at the rate quoted by the banks. Similarly, foreign exchange owned by immigrants or returning Chinese before they become residents may be retained.

All foreign exchange earned by Chinese residents working abroad, including Hong Kong and Macao, and foreign exchange earned from publication fees, copyright fees, awards, subsidies, honoraria, or other premiums must be repatriated. Individuals may retain or deposit exchange receipts with designated banks.

Foreign members and employees of FFEs, as well as those from Hong Kong and Macao,[7] may remit

---

[6]Three types of bidding are conducted under the system: (1) *negotiated* bidding is applied to products whose exportation is to be balanced by the state; (2) *invitation* bidding is applied to raw materials produced in geographically concentrated areas; and (3) *oriented* bidding is applied to products that are manufactured in geographically concentrated areas and whose export channels are limited. Only one type of bidding is conducted for a product in any calendar year.

[7]Including those employed by enterprises that have been established with capital provided by Chinese residing abroad.

their salaries and other income earned in China after paying taxes and deducting their living expenses in China and after receiving approval from the relevant local authorities.

Capital

Foreign borrowing is classified as either "plan" or "nonplan" borrowing.[8] Plan borrowing includes (1) borrowing by the government sector (through the People's Bank of China, the Ministry of Finance, the Ministry of Agriculture, and MOFTEC or enterprises under the MOFTEC's control) from foreign governments or international organizations and bilateral sources; (2) external borrowing by Chinese financial institutions; (3) external borrowing by authorized Chinese enterprises; and (4) short-term trade credits over three months. Nonplan borrowing includes (1) borrowing by FFEs; and (2) borrowing from branches of foreign banks or jointly invested banks operating in China.

Within these limits, the State Planning Commission (SPC) coordinates foreign borrowing for projects included in the annual and five-year plans. Under this procedure, the project-executing agencies (the Ministry of Finance, MOFTEC, foreign trade corporations, and provincial governments) propose projects to the SPC. The proposals indicate the total amount of foreign exchange needed, projected foreign exchange earnings, projected foreign borrowing, and the types of imports for which the loans are intended. The SPC reviews these plans and, in cooperation with the SAEC, the Ministry of Finance, and MOFTEC, recommends to the State Council the overall number of projects and their associated financing. Loans for vital projects or projects that have a rapid rate of return are given priority approval.

Within these guidelines, loans from international financial institutions and foreign governments require the clearance of the SPC and the approval of the State Council. Loans from the World Bank are generally the responsibility of the Ministry of Finance; borrowing from the International Monetary Fund (IMF) and the Asian Development Bank (ADB) is the responsibility of the People's Bank of

China; and intergovernmental loans are the responsibility of MOFTEC. Local governments and enterprises usually borrow through the Bank of China (or with its guarantee) or through specialized agencies, such as international trust and investment companies, rather than borrowing directly abroad themselves. The SPC sets an annual limit on such borrowing. Resident organizations issuing securities for foreign exchange must be approved by the People's Bank of China.

All medium- and long-term commercial borrowing abroad (including bond issues) under the plan requires prior approval from the SAEC on a case-by-case basis and must be conducted through authorized Chinese financial institutions. Borrowing quotas are allocated under the annual plan. The China International Trust and Investment Corporation (CITIC) has been permitted, on an experimental basis, to borrow abroad without first obtaining approval for each loan from the SAEC, as long as its outstanding debt is within the limits set by the State Council. Chinese financial institutions are permitted an annual ceiling by the SAEC on the outstanding balance of short-term loans.

All foreign direct investment projects are, in principle, subject to the approval of MOFTEC. However, a number of provincial and local authorities have been granted the authority to approve foreign direct investment projects up to specified amounts. The policy with respect to foreign capital is designed both to make up for insufficient domestic capital and to facilitate the introduction of modern technology and management.

Joint-venture enterprises and wholly foreign-owned companies are required to balance their foreign exchange receipts and payments, and foreign borrowing must be reported to, and filed with, the SAEC.[9] Most foreign exchange earned by joint ventures and other enterprises involving nonresident capital must be deposited with an authorized bank; outward transfers of capital generally require SAEC approval. Enterprises involved in the exploitation of offshore petroleum reserves may also hold foreign exchange abroad or in Hong Kong or Macao. When a joint venture ceases operation, the net claims belonging to the foreign investor may be remitted with SAEC approval. Alternatively, the foreign investor may apply for repayment of paid-in capital.

---

[8]The SAEC is the sole agency for monitoring and collecting statistics for China's external borrowing. It permits the Bank of China and other financial and nonfinancial institutions responsible for undertaking commercial borrowing to contract short-term loans up to specified limits without prior approval. All bond issues, however, are subject to prior approval from the SAEC. All foreign borrowing must be registered with the SAEC. Borrowers who do not comply are not permitted to transfer foreign exchange abroad to service their external debt obligations and are subject to other penalties.

---

[9]To help individual enterprises balance their foreign receipts and payments, enterprises with a surplus of foreign exchange may sell it to enterprises lacking sufficient foreign exchange through the foreign exchange adjustment centers, or in the interbank market.

The profits of joint ventures in special economic zones, the 14 coastal cities, the newly opened inland and border cities, and of those exploiting petroleum, natural gas, and other specified resources are subject to tax at the rate of 15 percent. A joint venture scheduled to operate for ten years or more may be exempted from income tax in the first one or two profit-making years and allowed reductions of 50 percent for the following three years. Joint ventures in low-profit operations, such as farming and forestry, or located in areas considered to be economically underdeveloped may, upon the approval of the Ministry of Finance, be allowed a further 15–30 percent reduction in income tax for another ten years. A participant in a joint venture that reinvests its share of profit in China for a period of not less than five years may obtain a refund of 40 percent of the tax paid on the reinvested profit.

Foreign companies, enterprises, and other economic organizations with establishments in China that are engaged in independent business operations, cooperative production, or joint business operations with Chinese enterprises are subject to tax only on their net income from sources in China. Under the Income Tax Law of the People's Republic of China for Enterprises with Foreign Investment and Foreign Enterprises (July 1, 1991), a standard income tax rate of 33 percent is levied on all foreign investment enterprises and foreign enterprises; it consists of a 30 percent state income tax and a 3 percent local tax. Certain exemptions and reductions from income tax are available in the special economic zones and other special open investment areas. Correspondingly, foreign state banks located in countries where income from interest on the deposits and loans of China's state banks is exempt from income tax are also exempt from this Chinese tax. Foreign business without establishments in China are subject to a reduced tax of 10 percent (half the usual rate) on interest income or leasing fees (less than the value of equipment) earned under credit, trade, and leasing agreements made with Chinese companies and enterprises from 1983 to 1985 but only for the duration of the agreements. For fees collected by foreign businessmen for the use of special technology provided in such fields as agriculture, animal husbandry, research, energy, communications, transport, environmental protection, and the development of important techniques,

income tax may, with the approval of the tax authorities, be levied at the reduced rate of 10 percent or waived for advanced technology provided on favorable terms.

Foreign investment by Chinese enterprises is subject to approval; profits earned thereby must be sold to designated banks, except for a portion that may be retained abroad as a working balance.

Gold

The People's Bank of China buys and sells gold and has central control over dealings in gold and silver. Sales of gold and silver are restricted to pharmaceutical, industrial, and other approved uses. Private persons may hold gold but may not trade or deal in it. The amount of gold, gold products, silver, and silver products that may be imported is unlimited but must be declared on entry. When exporting gold or silver, the exporter must present an import document from customs or a People's Bank of China export permit. Nonresidents may buy gold and silver and gold and silver products at special stores but must present the invoice when exporting them.

Changes During 1995

Imports and Exports

January 13. FFEs that have passed an annual audit by the SAEC are no longer required to obtain approval for each foreign exchange transaction in the swap centers. FFEs that have failed the audit are required to obtain approval for each transaction.

June 30. Import restrictions on 367 tariff lines were abolished. The main liberalized product items included crude oil, grain, chemical fiber fabrics, and some electronic goods.

July 1. Import tariff rates on a number of manufactured goods were reduced, including video tapes (from 100 percent to 50 percent) and vehicles (from 180 percent to 100 percent).

Changes During 1996

Administration of Control

April 1. The SAEC issued new foreign exchange control regulations.

COLOMBIA

(Position as of June 30, 1996)

Exchange Arrangement

The currency of Colombia is the Colombian Peso. All foreign exchange operations take place at a market-determined exchange rate. The Superintendency of Banks calculates a representative market exchange rate based on market rates.[1] The Banco de la República, the central bank, conducts foreign exchange transactions only with the Ministry of Finance and authorized financial intermediaries and does not conduct foreign exchange transactions directly with the nonbank private sector. The Banco de la República announces the upper and lower limits of a 14 percentage point band ten days in advance for indicative purposes. It also quotes buying and selling rates for certain other currencies[2] daily on the basis of the buying and selling rates for the U.S. dollar in markets abroad. On December 31, 1995, the buying and selling rates of the Banco de la República were Col$884.70 and Col$1,017.88, respectively, per US$1. The representative market exchange rate was Col$987.65 per US$1.

Other effective exchange rates result from (1) tax credit certificates for nontraditional exports (*certificados de reembolso tributarios* or CERTs) granted at three different percentage rates; (2) an 8 percent surtax on remittances of earnings on existing non-oil foreign investments (to be reduced to 7 percent by 1996); a 15 percent surtax on remittances of earnings on existing foreign investments in the oil sector (to be reduced to 12 percent in 1996), and a 12 percent surtax on remittances of earnings from foreign investments made after 1993; and (3) a 3 percent withholding tax on foreign exchange receipts from personal services and other transfers (the rate was 10 percent during 1995). The Government purchases foreign exchange for all public debt payments and other expenditures included in the national budget under the same conditions as other authorized intermediaries.[3]

Residents are permitted to buy forward cover against exchange rate risks in respect of foreign exchange debts in convertible currencies registered at the Banco de la República on international markets. Residents may also deal in over-the-counter forward swaps and options in U.S. dollars.

Administration of Control

All imports require registration at the Colombian Institute of Foreign Trade (INCOMEX). The Customs and Taxes Directorate (DIAN), within the Ministry of Finance, enforces ex post control and supervision over trade transactions and is responsible for applying penalties for any violation of the exchange regulations relating to trade. The Superintendency of Trade and Industry and the Superintendency of Banks are also responsible for the enforcement of exchange regulations. The authorized foreign exchange intermediaries are commercial banks, financial corporations, Financiera Energética Nacional (FEN), Banco de Comercio Exterior de Colombia (BANCOLDEX), and savings and loans corporations. Exchange houses (*casas de cambio*) are authorized to carry out a range of foreign exchange activities. Financial intermediaries are allowed to hold a net foreign exchange position equivalent to no more than 20 percent of their net worth. There are no regulations governing the net foreign exchange positions of exchange houses; they may sell their excess foreign holdings to authorized financial intermediaries, because they do not have access to the Banco de la República.

The Foreign Trade Council (FTC), which includes representatives of the Ministry of Finance, INCOMEX, other public entities, and two of its own officers, determines overall import and export policy. INCOMEX, through its Import Board, controls those imports that are subject to prior licensing, and administers Plan

---

[1]The representative market exchange rate is calculated as the weighted average of buying and selling rates, effected by foreign exchange market intermediaries, excluding teller transactions (Resolution No. 21 of September 3, 1993).

[2]Austrian schillings, Belgian francs, Canadian dollars, Danish kroner, deutsche mark, French francs, Italian lire, Japanese yen, Netherlands guilders, pounds sterling, Spanish pesetas, Swedish kronor, and Swiss francs.

[3]The Banco de la República stands ready to sell foreign exchange warrants (*títulos canjeables por certificados de cambio*) to public enterprises in the electricity sector and to the National Fed-

eration of Coffee Growers (Federación Nacional de Cafeteros) in accordance with the terms of Resolution 16/1991 of the Banco de la República. These warrants, expressed in U.S. dollars, have a maturity of 12 months, and, within their period of validity, may be sold to the Banco de la República for pesos at the reference market buying rate on the date of repurchase. Warrants bear interest at the rate equal to that of external loans, but never higher than the average 30-day rate on primary certificates of deposit at the close of operations in the New York market for the day before the certificate is issued, less 1 percentage point if held by public sector recipients of external loans. Warrants held longer than 12 months may be resold to the Banco de la República at the reference market rate on the last day of the twelfth month.

Vallejo, which is a special import-export arrangement concerning a rebate of taxes paid on imported inputs used in the production of exported goods. INCOMEX, together with the Committee on Commercial Practices, administers antidumping cases. The Government regulates the foreign direct investments through legislative and executive decrees, in consultation with the National Council for Economic and Social Policy (CONPES). The Banco de la República keeps a record both of foreign investment in Colombia and of debts abroad, and controls the movement of foreign capital as well as the transfer of profits, dividends, and commissions.

Prescription of Currency

Payments and receipts are normally effected in U.S. dollars, but residents and financial intermediaries are allowed to carry out operations in any currency. Settlements for commercial transactions with countries with which Colombia has reciprocal credit agreements may be made through special accounts in accordance with the provisions of such agreements. Settlements between Colombia and Argentina, Bolivia, Brazil, Chile, the Dominican Republic, Ecuador, Mexico, Paraguay, Peru, Uruguay, and Venezuela may be made through accounts maintained within the framework of the multilateral clearing system of the Latin American Integration Association (LAIA). There are also reciprocal credit agreements with China.

Nonresident Accounts

Residents may maintain foreign exchange accounts (compensation accounts) registered at the Banco de la República to pay for imports, to invest abroad in financial assets, or to carry out any other foreign exchange operations. Proceeds from services (except interest and profits) and transfers may be used to maintain foreign accounts abroad; these accounts do not have to be registered at the Banco de la República. Foreign exchange intermediaries may receive deposits in domestic currency from nonresident individuals and juridical persons. The deposits need not be registered at the Banco de la República; they may only be used in trade-related transactions. Banks must report transactions through these accounts to the Banco de la República.

Imports and Import Payments

Importers may purchase foreign exchange directly from the exchange market. In addition, they may use the proceeds from deposits held abroad. Foreign enterprises in the oil, coal, and natural gas sectors and firms in the free-trade areas are not permitted to purchase foreign exchange from financial intermediaries. Import payments must be made within six months of the due date of the bill of lading.

Imports are subject to one of the following two regimes: (1) freely importable goods requiring registration only with INCOMEX;[4] and (2) goods subject to prior approval and requiring an import license. Most imports are in the free-import regime, where there is a global free list applicable to all countries, a national list applicable only to member countries of the LAIA, and special lists applicable only to member countries of the LAIA and members of the Andean Pact. With certain exceptions, imports are subject to the common external tariff of the Andean Pact. Imports subject to a prior licensing requirement consist of medicines and chemical products (30 tariff positions) and weapons and munitions (39 tariff positions).

Import registrations are granted automatically. However, import registrations by some public sector agencies are screened by INCOMEX to determine whether local substitutes are available. Both import licenses and registrations are valid for 6 months, except those for agricultural and livestock products, which are valid for 3 months, and those for capital goods, which are valid for 12 months; import licenses may be extended only once for the same period. The charge for import registration is Col$12,800. Imports of crude oil and petroleum products are effected by Empresa Colombiana de Petroleo (ECOPETROL).

Payments for Invisibles

Foreign exchange for payments for invisibles may be obtained through foreign exchange intermediaries or exchange houses.

Exports and Export Proceeds

Export licenses are not required. All exchange proceeds from exports of goods that are repatriated must be surrendered to authorized financial intermediaries within six months or must be maintained in foreign accounts registered at the Banco de la República. However, exporters are permitted to retain their export proceeds abroad or in compensation accounts, to invest in financial assets, or to effect any other payment operations. In addition, firms with foreign capital engaged in exploration and production of oil and natural gas are not required to surrender their foreign exchange. These firms, how-

---

[4]Imports or shipments with an f.o.b. value of less than US$500 are classified as minor imports and do not have to be registered with INCOMEX. All other imports are subject to registration.

ever, may not purchase foreign exchange in the exchange market for any purpose, and must sell foreign exchange in the exchange market for domestic currency to pay for expenses in Colombia. Firms that do not wish to take advantage of this special arrangement must inform the Banco de la República, and all of their exchange operations will be subject to the provisions of regular exchange regulations for an irrevocable period of ten years.

On surrendering their export proceeds in the foreign exchange market, exporters of products other than coffee, petroleum, and petroleum products may receive tax credit certificates in an amount corresponding to a specified percentage of the f.o.b. value surrendered. Three rates—2.5 percent, 4 percent, and 5 percent—are applied, depending on the product and the country of destination; the rates are calculated on domestic value added. These certificates, which are freely negotiable and are quoted on the stock exchange, are accepted at par by tax offices for the payment of income tax, customs duties, and certain other taxes. For a specified list of exports, the applicable rate of the certificate was raised by 3 percentage points during the period May–December 1995.

Exports of coffee are subject to the following regulations: (1) a minimum surrender price is the sales price shown on the export declaration; (2) exporters pay a coffee contribution on the basis of international market prices; (3) the National Coffee Committee (composed of the Ministers of Finance and Agriculture and the Managing Director of the Federation) may establish a physical coffee contribution on the basis of international market prices; and (4) the National Coffee Committee establishes a domestic buying price based on international prices for export-type coffee expressed in pesos per cargo of 125 kilograms.

Foreign exchange proceeds earned by the public sector may be surrendered to financial intermediaries or to the Banco de la República.

Proceeds from Invisibles

Exchange proceeds from services and transfers are not required to be surrendered through the foreign exchange market but may be sold to exchange houses or to financial intermediaries or used through foreign accounts. There is no restriction on the amount of foreign exchange travelers may bring into the country.

Capital

All inward and outward capital transfers are effected at market rates.

All foreign investments and foreign loans, direct lines of foreign credit obtained by nonbank residents,[5] and the transfer of capital previously imported must be registered with the Banco de la República. Foreign direct investments in Colombia are governed by Law No. 9 of 1991 (January 17, 1991) and the CONPES Resolution No. 49, 51–57 of 1991. These regulations are in accordance with the provisions of Decisions Nos. 291 and 292 of the Cartagena Agreement, which govern foreign investments within the member countries of the Andean Pact. Foreign investment is freely allowed up to 100 percent of ownership in any sector of the economy, except in defense and waste disposal. Special regimes remain in effect in the financial, petroleum, and mining sectors. While foreign capital participation in the financial sector is permitted up to 100 percent, except in the areas of defense, disposal of foreign nuclear or chemical waste, and real estate, the purchase of 10 percent or more of the shares of a Colombian financial institution requires the prior approval of the Superintendent of Banks. CONPES can legislate special conditions affecting foreign investment in specific sectors of the economy and overrule the above-mentioned provisions (Resolution No. 51, of 1991, CONPES).

Registration of capital with the Banco de la República entitles the investor to export profits and to repatriate capital under specified conditions. Annual transfers of profits abroad and repatriation of capital is not restricted, but they may be temporarily restricted if international reserve holdings of the Banco de la República fall below the equivalent of three months of imports. Colombian investment abroad should also be registered with the Banco de la República.

Short-term foreign borrowing to finance any activity is permitted. Foreign loans with maturities ranging from one day to five years were subject to a nonremunerated deposit requirement of 140 percent and 43 percent of the loan, respectively, up to March 15, 1996. On that date, this maturity range was changed from one day to three years. The deposits are held for a period corresponding to the loan maturities. Exempted from the deposit requirement are credits for imports of capital goods; short-term loans granted by BANCOLDEX to Colombian exporters up to a maximum of 12 months;[6] credit card balances; loans destined for Colombian invest-

---

[5]Loans by financial entities for the importation of goods also require registration. Public sector loans are subject to an interest rate ceiling of 2.5 percent over the New York prime rate or the London interbank offered rate (LIBOR).

[6]BANCOLDEX is entitled to lend up to US$550 million under this regime.

ments abroad; and green coffee, coal, and oil pre-shipment financing.[7] The limit on contractual interest rates of 2.5 percent over LIBOR or the U.S. prime rate remains in effect for the public sector. Foreign loans for government entities in excess of specified amounts require prior authorization from the Superintendency of Values. For loans to the Government, or those guaranteed by the Government, the following are also required: prior authorization from CONPES and from the Banco de la República, prior consultation with the Interparliamentary Committee on Public Credit, and ex post approval from the President of the Republic. Such loans are also subject to the executive decree that authorizes the initiation of negotiations.

Foreign investments in the form of placement of shares in a fund established to make investments in the stock exchange and in debt papers issued by the financial sector are permitted with the approval of the National Planning Department.

Contracts involving royalties, commissions, trademarks, or patents should be registered with INCOMEX for statistical purposes only.

Colombian residents are authorized to maintain assets and earned income abroad.

Gold

Under Law No. 9 of January 17, 1991, Colombian residents are allowed to purchase, sell, hold, import, and export gold.

The Banco de la República sells gold for domestic industrial use directly at a price equivalent to the average quotation in the London gold market of the previous day; this price is converted into pesos at the representative market exchange rate.

The Banco de la República from time to time issues commemorative gold coins that are legal tender. Residents and nonresidents may freely buy such coins.

Changes During 1995

Exchange Arrangement

January 26. Exchange houses were authorized to participate in the official foreign exchange market for selected types of transactions, subject to licensing by the Superintendency of Banks.

Nonresident Accounts

September 29. Nonresidents were permitted to hold domestic currency deposits in domestic financial institutions. No registration with the Banco de la

República was required. Financial institutions were also required to include transactions in domestic currency deposit accounts in the quarterly report on transactions in foreign currency accounts submitted to the Banco de la República and the Superintendency of Banks.

Imports and Import Payments

February 1. The common external tariff of the countries of the Andean Pact, of which Colombia is a signatory, was introduced.

March 17. Items of the tariff code defined as capital goods imports, whose delayed payment is exempt from the deposit requirement, were specified.

August 18. The maximum time limit for payment of imports not subject to the deposit requirement was increased to six months from four months.

Exports and Export Proceeds

April 21. BANCOLDEX was authorized to increase the total amount of loans to exporters that may be exempted from the deposit requirement to a maximum of US$500 million from US$350 million. The maximum maturity was increased to one year from six months.

June 16. The exemption from the deposit requirement for prefinancing of coffee exports was limited to prefinancing contracted as of December 1994; previously, the exemption applied to prefinancing contracted as of January 1994. Private coffee exporters were also permitted to use up to US$50 million of prefinancing authorized for the National Coffee Federation

September 23. The amount of authorized export prefinancing by BANCOLDEX not subject to the deposit requirement was increased to US$550 million from US$500 million.

Capital

January 20. The range of external debt prepayments subject to a deposit requirement was widened.

February 10. The deposit requirement to change the external holder of a credit in cases of spinoffs, mergers, liquidations, or concordats of enterprises was eliminated.

September 7. A limit on the net foreign exchange position of financial intermediaries equal to 45 percent of net worth was established; (the limit was to be reduced to 30 percent as of January 1, 1996) and a schedule was set up for phasing out the minimum required net foreign exchange position of 40 percent of the June 1991 level of liabilities by January 1, 1996.

November 10. The minimum required net foreign exchange position of banks and other financial institutions was eliminated.

---

[7]Up to a total of US$100 million for green coffee and up to US$200 million for coal and oil. These loans should be registered with the Banco de la República.

Changes During 1996

Exchange Arrangement

January 1. The withholding tax on foreign exchange receipts was reduced to 3 percent from 10 percent.

Administration of Control

January 1. Financial intermediaries were allowed to hold a net foreign exchange position equivalent to no more than 20 percent of their net worth (compared with 45 percent earlier).

COMOROS

(Position as of December 31, 1995)

Exchange Arrangement

The currency of the Comoros is the Comorian Franc, which is pegged to the French franc, the intervention currency, at the fixed rate of CF 1 per F 0.0133. The current buying and selling rates for the French franc are CF 75 per F 1. Exchange rates for other currencies are officially quoted on the basis of the fixed rate of the Comorian franc for the French franc and the Paris exchange market rates for other currencies. There are no taxes or subsidies on purchases or sales of foreign exchange.

With the exception of those relating to gold, the exchange control measures of the Comoros do not apply to (1) France (and its overseas departments and territories) and Monaco; and (2) all other countries whose bank of issue is linked with the French Treasury by an Operations Account (Benin, Burkina Faso, Cameroon, Central African Republic, Chad, the Congo, Côte d'Ivoire, Equatorial Guinea, Gabon, Mali, Niger, Senegal, and Togo). Hence, all payments to these countries may be made freely. All other countries are considered foreign countries. Forward cover against exchange rate risk is authorized by the Central Bank of the Comoros and is provided to traders by the commercial bank (the only authorized dealer) for up to three months.

Administration of Control

Exchange control is administered by the Central Bank. The Ministry of Finance and Budget supervises borrowing and lending abroad, inward direct investment, and all outward investment. Part of the approval authority in respect of exchange control has been delegated to the commercial bank and the Postal Administration. All exchange transactions relating to foreign countries must be made through the authorized bank or the Postal Administration. Import and export licenses are issued by the Directorate-General of Economic Affairs in the Ministry of Economy and Trade.

Arrears are maintained with respect to external payments.

Prescription of Currency

The Central Bank maintains an Operations Account with the French Treasury; settlements with France (as defined above), Monaco, and the Operations Account countries are made in Comorian francs, French francs, or the currency of any other Operations Account country. Settlements with all other countries are usually made through correspondent banks in France in any of the currencies of those countries or in French francs through foreign accounts in francs.

Imports and Import Payments

The importation of certain goods is prohibited from all countries. The importation of other goods, except those originating from member countries of the European Union, Monaco, and the Operations Account countries, is subject to individual licensing. All import transactions must be domiciled with the authorized bank if the value is CF 500,000 or more.

Payments for Invisibles

Payments for invisibles to France (as defined above), Monaco, and the Operations Account countries are permitted freely. Payments for invisibles related to authorized imports are not restricted. Invisibles payments to other countries are subject to approval, which is granted when supporting documents can be produced. These regulations apply to allowances for education, family maintenance, and medical treatment, as well as to remittances by foreign workers of savings from their earnings.

Residents traveling to France (as defined above), Monaco, and the other Operations Account countries may take out the equivalent of CF 500,000 in banknotes and any amount in other means of payment. Residents traveling to countries other than France (as defined above), Monaco, and the other Operations Account countries may take out any means of payment up to the equivalent of CF 250,000 a person a trip. Any amount in excess of these limits is subject to the prior approval of the Central Bank, which is granted if supporting documentation is provided.

Nonresident travelers may export the equivalent of CF 500,000 in banknotes and any means of payment issued abroad in their name without providing documentary justification. Other cases are authorized pursuant to the Exchange Regulations when supporting documents can be produced.

Repatriation of dividends and other earnings from nonresidents' direct investment is authorized and guaranteed under the Investment Code.

Exports and Export Proceeds

With a few exceptions, exports to any destination are free of licensing requirements. Proceeds from exports to foreign countries must be repatriated within 30 days of the expiration of the commercial contract and sold immediately to the authorized bank. All export transactions must be domiciled with the authorized bank if the value is CF 500,000 or more.

Proceeds from Invisibles

Proceeds from transactions in invisibles with France (as defined above), Monaco, and the Operations Account countries may be retained. All amounts due from residents of other countries in respect of services and all income earned in those countries from foreign assets must be repatriated and, if received in foreign currency, surrendered to the authorized bank within one month of the due date or date of receipt. Resident and nonresident travelers may bring in any amount of domestic and foreign banknotes and coins.

Capital

Capital flows between the Comoros and France (as defined above), Monaco, and Operations Account countries are, in principle, free of exchange control; capital transfers to all other countries require exchange control approval, but capital receipts from such countries are normally permitted freely.

Special controls (in addition to any applicable exchange control requirements) are maintained over borrowing abroad, inward direct investment, and all outward investment; these controls relate to approval of the underlying transactions, not to payments or receipts.

Gold

Imports and exports of monetary gold require prior authorization. Imports and exports of articles containing gold are subject to declaration, but transfers of personal jewelry within the limit of 500 grams a person are exempt from such declaration.

Changes During 1995

No significant changes occurred in the exchange and trade system.

REPUBLIC OF CONGO

(Position as of June 30, 1996)

Exchange Arrangement

The currency of the Republic of Congo is the CFA Franc,[1] which is pegged to the French franc, the intervention currency, at the fixed rate of CFAF 1 per F 0.01. The official buying and selling rate is CFAF 100 per F 1. Exchange transactions in French francs between the BEAC and commercial banks take place at the same rate. Buying and selling rates for certain other foreign currencies are also officially posted, with quotations based on the fixed rate for the French franc and the rates in the Paris exchange market for the currencies concerned.

Payments to all countries are subject to a commission of 0.75 percent, with a minimum charge of CFAF 75; exempt from this commission are payments of the state, the Postal Administration, the BEAC, salaries of Congolese diplomats abroad, expenditures of official missions abroad, scholarships of persons studying or training abroad, and debt-service payments due from companies that have entered into an agreement with the Congo. Foreign exchange purchased by the Diamond Purchase Office is subject to a commission of 0.5 percent, with a minimum charge of CFAF 100. An additional commission of 0.25 percent is levied on all payments to countries that are not members of the BEAC. There are no taxes or subsidies on purchases or sales of foreign exchange.

The Congo accepted the obligations of Article VIII, Sections 2, 3, and 4 of the Fund Agreement on June 1, 1996.

Administration of Control

Payments to the following countries, although subject to declaration, are unrestricted: (1) France (and its overseas departments and territories) and Monaco; and (2) all other countries whose bank of issue is linked with the French Treasury by an Operations Account (Benin, Burkina Faso, Cameroon, Central African Republic, Chad, Comoros, Côte d'Ivoire, Equatorial Guinea, Gabon, Mali, Niger, Senegal, and Togo). Settlements and investment transactions with all foreign countries, however, are

subject to control. (Foreign countries are defined as all countries other than the Congo.)

The General Directorate of Credit and Financial Relations in the Ministry of Finance and the Budget supervises borrowing and lending abroad. Exchange control is administered by the Minister of Finance and the Budget who has delegated approval authority to the General Directorate. All exchange transactions must be effected through authorized banks or the Postal Administration. Import and export licenses are issued by the Foreign Trade Directorate in the Ministry of Commerce. The system of import licenses has been replaced by a system of ex post declarations for all but 13 products (Decree No. 88/414, May 28, 1988).

Arrears are maintained with respect to external payments.

Prescription of Currency

Because the Congo is an Operations Account country, settlements with France (as defined above), Monaco, and the Operations Account countries are made in CFA francs, French francs, or the currency of any other institute of issue that maintains an Operations Account with the French Treasury. Settlements with all other countries are usually made in any of the currencies of those countries or in French francs through foreign accounts in francs.

Nonresident Accounts

The regulations pertaining to nonresident accounts are based on those applied in France. As the BEAC has suspended the repurchase of BEAC banknotes circulating outside the territories of the issuing zone, such banknotes received by foreign correspondents of authorized banks and mailed to the BEAC agency in Brazzaville may not be credited to foreign accounts in francs.

Imports and Import Payments

The imports regime is, in principle, liberal; only certain items require import licenses. An annual import program classifies imports by zones: (1) the countries of the Central African Customs and Economic Union (UDEAC); (2) France; (3) other Operations Account countries; (4) European Union (EU) countries other than France; and (5) all remaining countries. Thirteen product items under this pro-

---

[1]The CFA franc circulating in the Congo is issued by the Bank of Central African States (BEAC) and is legal tender also in Cameroon, the Central African Republic, Chad, Equatorial Guinea, and Gabon.

gram require licenses, and others are subject to ex post declaration. The quotas for non-EU countries may be used to import goods originating in any non-Operations Account country.

All import transactions relating to countries other than France (as defined above), Monaco, and the Operations Account countries must be domiciled with an authorized bank. Licenses for imports from countries other than France (as defined above), Monaco, and the Operations Account countries must be domiciled with an authorized bank and require a visa from the Foreign Trade Directorate and the General Directorate of Credit and Financial Relations. The approved import license entitles importers to purchase the necessary exchange, provided that the shipping documents are submitted to an authorized bank.

In April 1994, a new tariff structure was introduced in the context of the UDEAC tax and customs reform with a view to rationalizing protection rates by narrowing dispersion while eliminating quantitative restrictions. The common duty rate of the UDEAC member countries was reduced to 5 percent for basic necessities, to 10 percent for raw materials and capital goods, to 20 percent for intermediate and miscellaneous goods, and to 30 percent for products requiring special protection. Customs duties on imports from UDEAC member countries were set at preferential rates equivalent to 20 percent of the corresponding common external tariff rate.

All imports may be insured with any insurance company.

Payments for Invisibles

Payments for invisibles to France (as defined above), Monaco, and the Operations Account countries are permitted freely, provided that they have been declared and are made through an authorized intermediary; those to other foreign countries are subject to approval. Payments for invisibles related to trade are permitted freely when the basic trade transaction has been approved or does not require authorization. Transfers of income accruing to nonresidents in the form of profits, dividends, and royalties are permitted with the authorization of the General Directorate of Credit and Financial Relations.

Residents traveling for tourist or business purposes to countries in the franc zone are allowed to take out an unlimited amount in banknotes or other payment instruments in French francs. The allowances for travel to countries outside the franc zone are subject to the following regulations: (1) for tourist travel, CFAF 100,000 a day, with a maximum of

CFAF 2.5 million a trip; (2) for business travel, CFAF 250,000 a day, with a maximum of CFAF 5 million a trip; (3) for official travel, the equivalent of expenses paid and CFAF 100,000 a day, with a maximum of CFAF 2 million a trip; and (4) for medical expenses abroad, CFAF 100,000 a day, with a maximum of CFAF 2.5 million a trip. Allowances in excess of these limits are subject to the authorization of the Ministry of Economy and Finance. The use of credit cards, which must be issued by resident financial intermediaries and approved by the Ministry of Economy and Finance, is limited to the ceilings indicated above for tourist and business travel. However, these regulations are administered liberally and bona fide requests for allowances in excess of these limits are normally granted. Returning resident travelers are required to declare all means of payment in their possession upon arrival at customs and to surrender within eight days all means of payment exceeding the equivalent of CFAF 25,000. All resident travelers, regardless of destination, must declare in writing all means of payment at their disposal at the time of departure. The re-exportation by nonresident travelers of means of payments other than banknotes issued abroad and registered in the name of the nonresident traveler is not restricted, subject to documentation that they had been purchased with funds drawn from a foreign account in CFA francs or with other foreign exchange. The re-exportation of foreign banknotes is allowed up to the equivalent of CFAF 250,000; the re-exportation of foreign banknotes above these ceilings requires documentation demonstrating either the importation of foreign banknotes or their purchase against other means of payment registered in the name of the traveler or through the use of nonresident deposits lodged in local banks.

The transfer of the entire net salary of a foreigner working in the Congo is permitted upon presentation of the appropriate pay voucher, provided that the transfer takes place within three months of the pay period. Transfers by residents of amounts smaller than CFAF 500,000 to nonmember countries of the franc zone are subject to simple declaration, and those exceeding CFAF 500,000 require prior authorization. Transfers to nonmember countries by nonresidents living in the Congo for less than one year are subject to authorization. Members of diplomatic missions, employees of international organizations, employees of companies operating in the Congo, government employees, and members of liberal professions are exempt from this regulation.

Exports and Export Proceeds

In principle, all exports require an exchange commitment, but most exports to France (as defined above), Monaco, and the Operations Account countries may be made freely; among the exceptions are commodities exported by the National Marketing Office for Agricultural Products (Office du café et du cacao and Office des cultures vivrières) and by the Congolese Marketing Office for Timber (Office congolais du bois).

Proceeds from exports to foreign countries must be collected and repatriated, generally within 180 days of arrival of the commodities at their destination. Export proceeds must be surrendered within eight days of the due date. All export transactions relating to countries other than France (as defined above), Monaco, and the Operations Account countries must be domiciled with an authorized bank.

Proceeds from Invisibles

All amounts due from residents of foreign countries in respect of services and all income earned in those countries from foreign assets must be collected when due and surrendered within a month of the due date. Resident and nonresident travelers may bring in any amount of banknotes and coins issued by the Bank of France, or any other bank of issue maintaining an Operations Account with the French Treasury, as well as any amount of foreign banknotes and coins (except gold coins).

Capital

Capital movements between the Congo and France (as defined above), Monaco, and the Operations Account countries are free, although ex post declarations are required. Such movements to countries that are not members of the BEAC are subject to a commission of 0.25 percent in addition to the 0.75 percent commission. Most international capital transactions are subject to prior authorization. Capital transfers abroad require exchange control approval and are restricted, but capital receipts from abroad are generally permitted freely. All foreign securities, foreign currency, and titles embodying claims on foreign countries or nonresidents that are held in the Congo by residents or nonresidents must be deposited with authorized banks in the Congo.

Special controls (in addition to any exchange control requirements that may apply) are maintained over borrowing and lending abroad, over inward and outward direct investment, and over the issuing, advertising, and offering for sale of foreign securities in the Congo; these controls relate to the transactions themselves, not to payments or receipts.

Direct investments abroad[2] require the prior approval of the Minister of Economy and Finance; the full or partial liquidation of such investments also requires the prior approval of the Minister. Foreign direct investments in the Congo[3] require the prior approval of the Minister of Economy and Finance, unless they involve the creation of a mixed-economy enterprise. The full or partial liquidation of direct investments in the Congo must be declared to the Minister. Both the making and the liquidation of direct investments, whether Congolese investments abroad or foreign investments in the Congo, must be reported to the Minister within 20 days. (Direct investments are defined as investments implying control of a company or enterprise.)

The issuing, advertising, or offering for sale of foreign securities in the Congo requires prior authorization from the Minister of Economy and Finance. Exempt from authorization, however, are operations in connection with (1) borrowing backed by a guarantee from the Congolese Government; and (2) shares similar to securities whose issuing, advertising, or offering for sale in the Congo has already been authorized.

Borrowing by residents from nonresidents requires prior authorization from the Minister of Economy and Finance. However, loans contracted by registered banks and small loans, where the total amount outstanding does not exceed CFAF 10 million for any one borrower, the interest is no higher than 5 percent, and the term is at least two years, are exempt from this requirement. The contracting of loans that are free of authorization, and each repayment, must be reported to the General Directorate of Credit and Financial Relations within 20 days of the operation.

Lending by residents to nonresidents is subject to exchange control, and all lending in CFA francs to nonresidents is prohibited unless special authorization is obtained from the Minister of Economy and Finance. The following are, however, exempt from this authorization: (1) loans in foreign currency granted by registered banks, and (2) other loans whose total amount outstanding does not exceed the equivalent of CFAF 5 million for any one lender. The making of loans that are free of authorization, and each repayment, must be reported to the General

---

[2]Including those made through foreign companies that are directly or indirectly controlled by persons in the Congo and those made by overseas branches or subsidiaries of companies in the Congo.

[3]Including those involving the transfer between nonresidents of funds in the form of participation in the capital of a Congolese company.

Directorate of Credit and Financial Relations within 20 days.

Under the Investment Code of April 10, 1992, a number of privileges may be granted to approved foreign investments. The code provides for four categories of preferential treatment.

Gold

By virtue of Decree No. 66/236 of July 29, 1966, as amended by Decree No. 66/265 of August 29, 1966, residents are free to hold gold in the form of coins, art objects, or jewelry; however, to hold gold in any other form or to import or export gold in any form, from or to any other country, the prior authorization of the Minister of Economy and Finance is required. Exempt from the latter requirement are (1) imports and exports by or on behalf of the Treasury or the BEAC, and (2) imports and exports of manufactured articles containing a small quantity of gold (such as gold-filled or gold-plated articles). Both licensed and exempt imports of gold are subject to customs declaration. There are no official exports of gold.

Changes During 1995

No significant changes occurred in the exchange and trade system.

Changes During 1996

Exchange Arrangement

June 1. Congo accepted the obligations of Article VIII, Sections 2, 3, and 4 of the Fund Agreement.

COSTA RICA

(Position as of December 31, 1995)

Exchange Arrangement

The currency of Costa Rica is the Costa Rican Colón, the external value of which is determined by commercial banks and other financial institutions in the interbank market.[1] A tax of 15 percent calculated on the average daily spread between buying and selling rates applies to all foreign exchange transactions in the interbank market. The Government and public sector institutions conduct foreign exchange transactions with the State Commercial Banks and the Central Bank. These operations are carried out at the official reference exchange rate, which is calculated at the close of each business day as the weighted average of the exchange rates used in the market during the day. On December 31, 1995, the buying and selling bank rates for the U.S. dollar were C 194.43 and C 195.37, respectively, per $1.

There are no arrangements for forward cover against exchange rate risks operating in the official or the commercial banking sector.

Costa Rica accepted the obligations of Article VIII, Sections 2, 3, and 4 of the Fund Agreement on February 1, 1965.

Administration of Control

Exchange regulations are issued by the Central Bank. Institutions authorized to deal in foreign exchange are the Central Bank, the state commercial banks, private banks, and other nonbank financial institutions authorized by the Central Bank and under the purview of the Superintendency of Banks and Financial Institutions (SUGEF).

Arrears are maintained with respect to external payments obligations of the nonfinancial public sector.

Prescription of Currency

Nearly all payments for exchange transactions are made in U.S. dollars. Trade payments to Central America may be made in U.S. dollars or in local currencies.

Imports and Import Payments

All payments for imports may be made freely. Imports made on a barter basis require a barter license (*licencia de trueque*), issued by the Ministry of Economy and Commerce.

Customs tariff rates on most goods range from 5 percent to 20 percent. In addition to any applicable customs tariff, the following taxes are levied on imports: (1) a sales tax of 15 percent, from which certain essential items are exempt; and (2) a selective consumption tax at rates varying from zero to 75 percent, depending on the essential nature of the item.

Payments for Invisibles

Payments for invisibles are not restricted. Withholding taxes of 15 percent are levied on remittances of dividends and profits. Remittances of interest abroad are subject to a 15 percent withholding tax, except for remittances to foreign banks or to their financial entities recognized by the Central Bank as institutions normally engaged in international transactions, including payments to foreign suppliers for commodity imports. Interest on government borrowing abroad is exempt.

Exports and Export Proceeds

Export proceeds are not subject to surrender requirements. However, proceeds from exports must be repatriated within 90 days before the end of each fiscal year. Exporters of nontraditional products to markets outside Central America are entitled to receive freely negotiable tax credit certificates (CATs) at the following rates based on the f.o.b. value: 15 percent for exports to the United States, Puerto Rico, and Europe; and 20 percent for exports to Canada.[2]

Licenses are required for exports of goods such as armaments, munitions, scrap iron, and scrap of nonferrous base metals (from the Ministry of Economy and Commerce); sugar (from the Agricultural Industrial Board for Sugarcane); beans, rice, ipecacuanha root, onions, cotton, meat, and purebred cattle (from the National Council of Production); airplanes (from

---

[1]Foreign exchange trading occurs in the organized electronic foreign exchange market (MONED) among authorized traders and in which the Central Bank carries out its intervention operations. Foreign exchange trading also takes place directly between authorized institutions outside the MONED.

[2]CATs ceased to be issued to new exporters after December 31, 1992. Existing exporters continue to benefit from the CATs consistent with their specific contractual arrangements.

the Civil Aviation Board and the Ministry of Economy and Commerce); Indian art objects made of gold, stone, or clay (from the National Museum); tobacco (from the Tobacco Defense Board); textiles; flowers, lumber, certain livestock, and animals and plants of forest origin (from the Ministry of Agriculture and Livestock); and coffee (from the Coffee Institute); in addition, when there is a lien on coffee in favor of a bank, that bank's approval is required before the Central Bank grants an export license.

There are no taxes on nontraditional exports to countries outside the Central American area and Panama; taxes are levied on traditional exports and, in some cases, are graduated in line with international prices.

Proceeds from Invisibles

Proceeds from invisibles are free from controls or restrictions but must be repatriated within 90 days of the end of each fiscal year.

Capital

There are no restrictions on capital transfers, and capital transactions between residents and nonresidents are permitted.

The National Budget Authority[3] is in charge of authorizing the negotiation of new external credits contemplated by the central Government, decentralized agencies, and state enterprises.

Gold

The Central Bank may purchase, sell, or hold gold coins or bars as part of the monetary reserves in accordance with regulations established by its

Board. Natural and juridical persons may buy or sell, at home or abroad, domestically produced gold (except national archaeological treasures, pursuant to Law No. 6703 of December 18, 1981), provided there is no infraction of international agreements. Licenses from the Central Bank are required for exports of gold. Gold may also be held in any form in Costa Rica. The Central Bank may sell unrefined gold to artistic or professional users or to enterprises that export jewelry.

Changes During 1995

Exchange Arrangement

May 30. The Central Bank announced that the spread between the buying and selling rates of authorized banks and financial institutions cannot exceed 0.56 percent.

November 28. Spreads between the buying and selling rates can be freely set by authorized banks and financial institutions. A tax of 15 percent calculated on the average daily spread between the buying and selling rates is applied to all foreign trade transactions in the interbank market. All other taxes (transfers to some public enterprises) collected through the exchange system were eliminated.

Exports and Export Proceeds

May 24. The surrender requirement rate for proceeds from exports was reduced to 20 percent. All commercial banks and financial institutions authorized to operate in the interbank market were required to transfer to the Central Bank 34 percent of their purchases of foreign exchange.

November 28. Surrender and transfer requirements were eliminated. Exchange proceeds from goods (and services exports and tourism) must be repatriated within 90 days of the end of each fiscal year.

---

[3]Composed of the Minister of Finance, the Minister of Planning, and the President of the Central Bank.

CÔTE D'IVOIRE

(Position as of June 30, 1996)

Exchange Arrangement

The currency of Côte d'Ivoire is the CFA Franc,[1] which is pegged to the French franc, the intervention currency, at the fixed rate of CFAF 1 per F 0.01. The official buying and selling rate is CFAF 100 per F 1. Exchange rates for other currencies are derived from the rates in the Paris exchange market for the currencies concerned and the fixed rate between the French franc and the CFA franc. The BCEAO levies no commission on transfers to or from countries outside the West African Economic and Monetary Union (WAEMU).[2] Banks and the postal system levy a commission on transfers to all countries outside the WAEMU; commissions must be surrendered to the Treasury. There are no taxes or subsidies on purchases or sales of foreign exchange.

With the exception of measures relating to gold and the repatriation of export proceeds, the exchange control measures of Côte d'Ivoire do not apply to (1) France (and its overseas departments and territories) and Monaco; and (2) all other countries whose bank of issue is linked with the French Treasury by an Operations Account (Benin, Burkina Faso, Cameroon, Central African Republic, Chad, Comoros, Congo, Equatorial Guinea, Gabon, Mali, Niger, Senegal, and Togo). Hence, all payments to these countries may be made freely. All other countries are considered foreign countries and subject to the exchange control measures listed hereafter.

Spot foreign exchange cover is limited to imports effected by means of documentary credits; the transaction must be domiciled with an authorized intermediary, and goods must be shipped within eight days of the exchange operation. Forward exchange cover for eligible imports must not extend beyond one month for certain specified goods and three months for goods designated essential commodities; no renewal of cover is possible. Forward cover against exchange rate risk is permitted, with prior authorization from the Directorate of the Treasury, Monetary and Banking Affairs in the Ministry of Economy, Finance, and Planning, only for payments for imports of goods and only for the currency stipu-lated in the commercial contract. There are no official schemes for currency swaps or guaranteed exchange rates for debt servicing.

Côte d'Ivoire accepted the obligations of Article VIII, Sections 2, 3, and 4 of the Fund Agreement on June 1, 1996.

Administration of Control

Exchange control is administered by the Directorate of the Treasury, Monetary and Banking Affairs in the Ministry of Economy, Finance, and Planning. The BCEAO is authorized to collect any information necessary to compile balance of payments statistics, either directly or through the banks, other financial institutions, the Postal Administration, and notaries public. All exchange transactions relating to foreign countries must be effected through authorized banks or the Postal Administration. Import licenses for a short list of controlled products (Decree No. 93-313 of March 11, 1993) are issued by the Directorate of External Trade Promotion in the Ministry of Commerce. At the end of 1995, a total of 25 products were subject to import licenses.

Arrears are maintained with respect to the external debt-servicing obligations of the central Government.

Prescription of Currency

Because Côte d'Ivoire is an Operations Account country, settlements with France (as defined above), Monaco, and the Operations Account countries are made in CFA francs, French francs, or the currency of any other Operations Account country. Current payments to or from The Gambia, Ghana, Guinea, Guinea-Bissau, Liberia, Mauritania, Nigeria, and Sierra Leone are normally made through the West African Clearing House. Settlements with all other countries are effected through correspondent banks in France, in any of the currencies of those countries, or in French francs through foreign accounts in francs.

Nonresident Accounts

Because the BCEAO has suspended the repurchase of BCEAO banknotes circulating outside the territories of the CFA franc zone, foreign accounts in francs may not be credited or debited with BCEAO

---

[1]The CFA franc is issued by the Central Bank of West African States (BCEAO) and is the common currency in Benin, Burkina Faso, Côte d'Ivoire, Mali, Niger, Senegal, and Togo.

[2]Transfers between member countries of the WAEMU are subject to the flat commission of CFAF 100 levied on settlements between agencies of the BCEAO.

banknotes. In addition, they may not show an overdraft position without prior authorization.

Imports and Import Payments

Under the current regulations, all imports are classified into the following three categories: (1) goods requiring prior authorization or the approval of ministries; (2) goods subject to quantitative or other restrictions requiring licenses issued by the Directorate of External Trade Promotions; and (3) freely importable goods.

Quantitative or other limits for goods in the second category are set each year by the Minister of Industry and Commerce in light of market conditions and local production, and following consultation with the Competitiveness Committee. With certain specific exceptions (e.g., diplomatic imports and used vehicles), all unrestricted imports with an f.o.b. value exceeding CFAF 3 million are subject to a preshipment inspection to verify their price, quantity, and quality; for values between CFAF 1.5 million and CFAF 3 million, imports may be subject to random inspection. For all imports (except those with prior authorization) whose f.o.b. value exceeds CFAF 500,000, an import information declaration for statistical purposes is also required.

A maximum tariff rate of 35 percent has been in effect since January 1994. A statistical tax of 2.5 percent of the c.i.f. value is levied on all imports. Imports from member countries of the West African Economic Community (WAEC) and the Economic Community of West African States (ECOWAS) are exempt from the surcharges.

All import operations valued at more than CFAF 500,000 conducted with foreign countries must be domiciled with an authorized bank; transactions of lower value must also be domiciled with an authorized bank if a financial transaction is to be undertaken before customs clearance. The import licenses or import attestations entitle importers to purchase the necessary foreign exchange, but not earlier than eight days before shipment if a documentary credit is opened, and only on the due date of payment if the commodities have already been imported. Since June 15, 1981, foreign exchange for import payments must be purchased either on the settlement date specified in the commercial contract or when the required down payment is made.

Payments for Invisibles

Payments for invisibles to France (as defined above), Monaco, and the Operations Account countries are permitted freely; those to other countries must be approved. Payments for invisibles related to

trade are permitted freely when the basic trade transaction has been approved or does not require authorization. Transfers of income accruing to nonresidents in the form of profits, dividends, and royalties are also permitted freely when the underlying transaction has been approved.

Residents traveling for tourism or business purposes to countries in the franc zone that are not members of the WAEMU are allowed to take out banknotes other than the CFA banknotes up to the equivalent of CFAF 2 million; amounts in excess of this limit may be taken out in the form of means of payment other than banknotes. The allowances for travel to countries outside the franc zone are subject to the following regulations: (1) for tourist travel, CFAF 500,000 without limit on the number of trips or differentiation by the age of the traveler; (2) for business travel, CFAF 75,000 a day for up to one month, corresponding to a maximum of CFAF 2.25 million (business travel allowances may be combined with tourist allowances); (3) allowances in excess of these limits are subject to the authorization of the Ministry of Economy and Finance; and (4) credit cards, which must be issued by resident financial intermediaries and authorized by the respective ministers of finance, may be used up to the ceilings indicated above for tourist and business travel. Returning resident travelers are required to declare all means of payment in their possession upon arrival at customs and surrender within eight days all means of payment exceeding the equivalent of CFAF 25,000. All resident travelers, when traveling to countries that are not members of the WAEMU, must declare in writing all means of payment at their disposal at the time of departure. Nonresident travelers may freely re-export means of payment, other than banknotes issued abroad and registered in their name, subject to documentation that they used funds drawn from a foreign account in CFA francs or other foreign exchange to purchase the means of payment. The re-exportation of foreign banknotes is allowed up to the equivalent of CFAF 250,000; the re-exportation of foreign banknotes above these ceilings requires documentation demonstrating either their importation or their purchase against other means of payment registered in the name of the traveler or through the use of nonresident deposits lodged in local banks.

Exports and Export Proceeds

All exports are free of restrictions, with the exception of certain metals, including precious metals and gems, the exportation of which requires prior authorization, and the export of timber, which is prohibited except for a small quota pending a review of environmental and taxation issues. Exports of ivory (above a minimum weight) and certain types of tropical wood are prohibited. Exports require a customs declaration but not a license. Exports of lumber are subject to quantitative quotas allocated through auction. Exports of cocoa and coffee are subject to a specific unitary export tax and can be effected only by exporters authorized by the Price Stabilization Fund.

Proceeds from exports to foreign countries, including those in the Operations Account area, must be received within 120 days of the arrival of the goods at their destination. Regardless of the currency of settlement and of the country of destination, export receipts must be collected and repatriated through authorized intermediary banks within one month of the due date. Regardless of destination, all export transactions valued at more than CFAF 1 million must be domiciled with an authorized bank.

Proceeds from Invisibles

Proceeds from transactions in invisibles with France (as defined above), Monaco, and the Operations Account countries may be retained. All amounts due from residents of other countries for services, and all income earned in those countries from foreign assets, must be collected and surrendered within two months of the due date or the date of receipt. Resident and nonresident travelers may import any amount of banknotes and coins issued by the BCEAO, the Bank of France, or any bank of issue maintaining an Operations Account with the French Treasury, as well as any amount of foreign banknotes and coins (except gold coins) of countries outside the Operations Account area. Residents bringing in foreign banknotes or other foreign means of payment must surrender any amount in excess of CFAF 5,000 to an authorized bank within eight days and must make a declaration to customs upon entry.

Capital

Capital movements between Côte d'Ivoire and France (as defined above), Monaco, and the Operations Account countries are free of exchange control; capital transfers to all other countries require exchange control approval, but capital receipts from such countries are permitted freely.

Special controls, in addition to any exchange control requirements that may apply, are maintained over borrowing abroad by the private sector; over foreign inward direct investment; over all outward

direct investment in foreign countries; and over the issuing, advertising, or offering for sale of foreign securities in Côte d'Ivoire. Such operations, as well as issues by Ivoirien companies, require prior authorization from the Ministry of Economy, Finance, and Planning. Exempt from authorization, however, are operations in connection with (1) loans backed by a guarantee from the Government of Côte d'Ivoire; and (2) foreign shares similar to securities whose issuing, advertising, or offering for sale in Côte d'Ivoire has already been authorized. With the exception of controls relating to foreign securities, these measures do not apply to relations with France (as defined above), Monaco, member countries of the WAEMU, and the Operations Account countries. Special controls are also maintained over the soliciting of funds for deposit with foreign natural persons and foreign firms and institutions, and over publicity aimed at placing funds abroad or at subscribing to real estate and building operations abroad; these special controls also apply to France (as defined above), Monaco, and the Operations Account countries.

All investments abroad by residents of Côte d'Ivoire require prior authorization from the Minister of Economy, Finance, and Planning.[3] Foreign direct investments in Côte d'Ivoire must be authorized in advance by the Minister of Economy, Finance, and Planning.[4] As from June 15, 1981, at least 75 percent of investments abroad by residents of Côte d'Ivoire had to be financed by borrowing abroad. The liquidation of direct and other investments in Côte d'Ivoire or abroad must also be reported in advance to the Minister. Both the making and the liquidation of investments, whether Ivoirien investments abroad or foreign investments in Côte d'Ivoire, must be reported to the Minister within 20 days of each operation. (Direct investments are defined as those that imply control of a company or an enterprise. Mere participation is not considered as direct investment, provided that it does not exceed 20 percent of the capital of a company whose shares are quoted on a stock exchange.) In addition, the BCEAO subjects commercial banks' foreign exchange positions to discretionary controls for prudential reasons. These restrictions apply to all correspondent accounts, including those located in France, Monaco, and the Operation Account countries.

---

[3]Including those made through foreign companies that are directly or indirectly controlled by persons resident in Côte d'Ivoire and those made by branches or subsidiaries abroad of companies resident in Côte d'Ivoire.

[4]Including those made in Côte d'Ivoire by companies that are directly or indirectly under foreign control and those made by branches or subsidiaries of foreign companies in Côte d'Ivoire.

Borrowing by residents from nonresidents must be authorized in advance by the Minister of Economy, Finance, and Planning. The following are, however, exempt from this authorization: (1) loans taken up by industrial firms to finance transactions abroad, to finance imports into or exports from Côte d'Ivoire, or loans approved by international trading houses to finance international trade transactions; (2) loans contracted by authorized banks; and (3) loans other than those mentioned above whose total outstanding amount, including the new borrowing, does not exceed CFAF 50 million for any one borrower and whose annual interest rate does not exceed the normal market rate. The repayment of loans constituting a direct investment is subject to the formalities prescribed for the liquidation of direct investments. The repayment of other loans requires authorization only if the loan itself was subject to prior approval. Lending abroad is subject to exchange control authorization.

Under the investment code introduced in 1984, special incentives are provided for foreign and domestic investments in certain priority sectors and priority geographical areas. The incentives include exemption from customs duties and tariffs on all imported capital equipment and spare parts for investment projects, provided that no equivalent item is produced in Côte d'Ivoire. In addition, all such investments are exempt for a specified period, depending on the investment sector or area, from corporate profit taxes, patent contributions, and capital assets taxes. In general, the exemption covers 100 percent of applicable tax up to the fourth-to-last year of the exemption period and is reduced progressively to 75 percent of the tax in the third-to-last year, 50 percent in the second-to-last year, and 25 percent in the last year. Imports of raw materials for which no equivalents are produced

locally are not exempt from import duties and taxes.

Gold

Residents are free to hold, acquire, and dispose of gold in any form in Côte d'Ivoire. Imports and exports of gold to or from any other country require prior authorization from the Minister of Economy, Finance, and Planning; authorization is rarely granted. Exempt from this requirement are (1) imports and exports by the Treasury or the BCEAO, (2) imports and exports of manufactured articles containing a small quantity of gold (such as gold-filled or gold-plated articles), and (3) imports and exports by travelers of gold articles up to a weight of 250 grams. Both licensed and exempt imports and exports of gold are subject to customs declaration.

Changes During 1995

Imports and Import Payments

March 1. Quantitative restrictions on imports of coffee, tobacco, used sacks, and cloth made of synthetic or artificial fibers were eliminated.

Exports and Export Proceeds

September 6. Exports of timber were prohibited by a decree pending the review of environmental and taxation issues.

Changes During 1996

Exchange Arrangement

June 1. Côte d'Ivoire accepted the obligations of Article VIII, Section 2, 3, and 4 of the Fund Agreement.

CROATIA

(Position as of February 29, 1996)

Exchange Arrangement

The currency of Croatia is the Kuna, the external value of which is determined in the interbank market. The exchange rates in the interbank market are determined by authorized banks that transact with each other at freely negotiated rates. The National Bank of Croatia may set intervention exchange rates, which it applies in transactions with banks outside the interbank market for purposes of smoothing undue fluctuations in the exchange rate. On December 31, 1995, the average interbank market rate for the U.S. dollar was HRK 5,3161 per $1.

There are no taxes or subsidies on purchases or sales of foreign exchange.

Croatia accepted the obligations of Article VIII, Sections 2, 3, and 4 of the Fund Agreement on May 29, 1995.

Administration of Control

Foreign exchange transactions are governed by the Law on the Foreign Exchange System, Foreign Exchange Operations, and Gold Transactions, which was enacted on October 7, 1993. The National Bank formulates and administers exchange rate policy and may issue foreign exchange regulations under this law. A Trade Law, coordinated with domestic trade and foreign trade legislation, was passed on January 31, 1996, and came into force on February 17, 1996. Companies wishing to engage in foreign trade must register with the commercial courts. The representative offices of foreign companies must be registered with the Ministry of Economy.

Foreign exchange transactions must be conducted through authorized banks; currently 48 commercial banks in Croatia are licensed to conduct foreign exchange transactions. Restricted licenses are given to those banks that are authorized to open accounts for resident natural persons and may buy and sell banknotes and checks (currently nine banks).

Arrears are maintained with respect to external payments.

Prescription of Currency

Settlements between residents and nonresidents may be effected in any convertible currency.

Resident and Nonresident Accounts

Resident natural and juridical persons may, in principle, open and operate foreign exchange accounts only in Croatia. However, the National Bank has the authority to allow resident juridical persons to keep foreign exchange in accounts with foreign banks in order to cover the costs of business operations and meet the requirement of regular foreign trade activities abroad. The law also makes specific provisions for resident juridical persons engaged in capital project construction abroad to maintain accounts with foreign banks, subject to a license issued by the National Bank.

Nonresidents may open foreign exchange accounts with fully licensed banks in Croatia. These accounts may be credited freely with foreign exchange and debited for payments abroad for conversion into domestic currency; reconversion of domestic currency into a foreign currency is permitted. With special permission from the National Bank, juridical persons may credit these accounts with foreign banknotes up to the limit of $20,000.

Nonresident natural and juridical persons may open accounts in domestic currency with the proceeds from sales of goods and services or with foreign exchange transferred from abroad. They may purchase foreign exchange with funds held in these accounts without restriction.

Imports and Import Payments

Imports from the Federal Republic of Yugoslavia (Serbia/Montenegro) are prohibited in accordance with UN Security Council Resolutions. Pending the introduction of a new import regime, the product classification of the 1994 import regime is maintained, with a free list (LB), a list of items subject to quotas and a list of items subject to ad hoc licensing (D).

Items on the free list account for about 96 percent of the total tariff items. Of the restricted items, only about 2 percent of imports are subject to licensing and about 1 percent to quotas. The Ministry of Economy, in consultation with the Chamber of Commerce, administers the quotas. List D includes items whose importation is controlled by international agreement for noneconomic reasons (such as arms, gold, illegal drugs and narcotics, and artistic and historic work). The importation of these items is allowed on a case-by-case basis and for specific purposes.

Imports are subject to a customs tariffs of up to 18 percent (compared with up to 25 percent in the former Socialist Federal Republic of Yugoslavia) plus a tax of up to 10 percent, and a customs administration fee of 1 percent. The exemption for duty-free imports by travelers is the equivalent of $100. Goods imported by travelers and postal shipments up to a value of $500 are subject to a simplified customs procedure with a unified tariff rate of 8 percent. For imports exceeding that value, the regular import tariffs and taxes are applied. Returning citizens may bring into the country household effects duty free in an amount that is relative to the period spent abroad without restrictions, subject to the approval of the Ministry of Finance on a case-by-case basis. Under certain conditions, goods imported by nonresidents for investment purposes are exempt from import duties. Also, raw materials and intermediate products used in the production of exports are exempt from all import duties and taxes, except the 1 percent customs fee, provided that the value added of the export product is at least 30 percent of the value of the imported items and that export proceeds are received in convertible currency. Payments for authorized imports by juridical persons are not restricted.

Advance payments for imports are permitted, where down payments are required by suppliers in accordance with customary international practices.

Payments for Invisibles

Payments for invisibles related to authorized imports by juridical persons may be made freely. Payments of leasing fees are permitted provided that temporary imports have been registered with the Customs Office. Natural persons may also purchase foreign exchange in the interbank market for the payment of goods and services abroad and for deposit in a foreign exchange account for the purpose of future payments. Resident juridical persons (including tradesmen, natural persons engaging in independent activities) may purchase foreign exchange only for authorized payments abroad, except to make payments for activities related to scientific, humanitarian, cultural, or sports events. Payments of royalties, insurance, and legal obligations and contracting of life and casualty insurance policies with foreign companies are also permitted.

Resident natural persons may take out of the country foreign currency equivalent to DM 1,000. An additional amount equivalent up to DM 2,000 may be taken out, provided that it is withdrawn from for-

eign currency accounts or purchased from banks for travel expenses. In both cases, the National Bank may allow higher amounts to be taken out on a case-by-case basis. The exportation of Croatian currency by both residents and nonresidents is limited to HRK 2,000 a person.

Exports and Export Proceeds

Exports to the Federal Republic of Yugoslavia (Serbia/Montenegro) are prohibited in accordance with UN Security Council Resolutions. In principle, exports are free of restrictions except for certain products for which permits must be obtained (list D products: e.g., weapons, drugs, and art objects); several basic foodstuffs to ensure adequate domestic supplies; and high-quality wood.

Export proceeds must be collected and repatriated in full to Croatia within 90 days of the date of exportation; this period may be extended with the permission of the National Bank. If payment terms in excess of 90 days have been agreed with foreign importers, the credit arrangement must be registered with the National Bank.

Proceeds from Invisibles

Proceeds from services are, in principle, subject to the same regulations as those applying to merchandise exports. The importation of Croatian currency by both residents and nonresidents is limited to HRK 2,000 a person.

Capital

Resident juridical persons, including commercial banks, may borrow abroad. They are required to register the loans contracted, including commercial credits, with the National Bank. Financial credits may be extended to nonresidents by resident juridical persons, including tradesmen and natural persons engaging in independent activities, only if these credits are financed from profits or credit obtained from abroad. Natural persons are permitted to obtain loans from nonresidents in domestic or foreign currency. The foreign exchange positions of commercial banks are limited to 30 percent of the bank's capital.

Foreign direct investment by nonresidents may take the form of joint ventures or full ownership and must be registered with the commercial courts. Repatriation of capital and transfers abroad of profits are not restricted. In principle, domestic and foreign investment is treated equally (e.g., "national treatment"). If the foreign equity capital participation exceeds 20 percent, inputs used in the project are exempt from import duties. The profit tax rate is uniform at 25 percent. Foreign direct investment abroad by residents must be registered with the Ministry of Economy within a 30-day period commencing from signature of the contract. Such investment must generally be undertaken through loans abroad or through reinvestment of profits. Inward portfolio investment is not restricted, except in central bank short-term securities in the primary market. In general, outward portfolio investment is restricted.

Nonresident natural persons may acquire real estate in Croatia through inheritance as long as their country of residence extends reciprocal treatment to residents of Croatia. Nonresident natural persons not engaged in economic activities in Croatia may purchase real estate only under the same conditions. Nonresident natural or juridical persons engaged in economic activities in Croatia may also purchase real estate under these conditions and may sell it to resident or nonresident juridical persons. In principle, residents may acquire real estate abroad on the basis of reciprocity of treatment, but in practice, they are not permitted to purchase foreign exchange in the exchange market for this purpose; the use of balances in foreign exchange accounts for this purpose is also prohibited.

Gold

The National Bank may export gold and gold coins without any restrictions. Unprocessed gold may be exported with the approval of the National Bank.

Gold coins may be exported by authorized commercial banks, with the approval of the National Bank.

Importation of gold is subject to the approval of the Ministry of Economy.

Changes During 1995

Exchange Arrangement

May 29. Croatia accepted the obligations of Article VIII, Sections 2, 3, and 4 of the Fund Agreement.

Changes During 1996

Imports and Import Payments

February 17. The Trade Law became effective.

Capital

January 1. The Law on Insurance and Sale of Securities came into force.

January 3. The Law on Investment Funds came into force.

CYPRUS

(Position as of March 31, 1996)

Exchange Arrangement

The currency of Cyprus is the Cyprus Pound, the external value of which is pegged to a basket based on the European Currency Unit (ECU) at ECU 1.7086 per £C 1, within margins of ±2.25 percent around the ECU central rate. On December 29, 1995, the official buying and selling rates for the U.S. dollar, the intervention currency, were £C 0.4549 and £C 0.4567, respectively, per $1. The Central Bank of Cyprus also quotes daily buying and selling rates for the ECU, the deutsche mark, the Greek drachma, and the pound sterling. These rates are subject to change throughout the day. It also quotes indicative rates for other foreign currencies[1] on the basis of market rates in international money market centers. Subject to certain limitations, including a limit on spreads between the buying and selling rates, authorized dealers (banks) are free to determine and quote their own buying and selling rates. There are no taxes or subsidies on purchases or sales of foreign exchange.

Authorized dealers are allowed to trade in the forward market at rates that may be freely negotiated with their customers. For U.S. dollars and pounds sterling, however, forward margins may not differ by more than the premiums or discounts that are applied by the Central Bank for cover for a similar period. Authorized dealers are allowed to purchase forward cover from the Central Bank at prevailing rates or to conduct forward operations between two foreign currencies for cover in one of the two currencies. The Central Bank offers authorized dealers facilities for forward purchases of U.S. dollars and pounds sterling for exports for up to 24 months. Cover for imports is normally provided for up to 6 months. When justified (for example, payments for imports of raw materials or capital goods), rates are quoted for up to 15 months. Forward contracts must be based on genuine commercial commitments. Forward cover may also be provided for up to 12 months to residents for specific financial commitments, and for up to 15 months for incoming tourism.

---

[1] Australian dollars, Austrian schillings, Belgian francs, Canadian dollars, Danish kroner, Finnish markkaa, French francs, Italian lire, Japanese yen, Netherlands guilders, Norwegian kroner, Portuguese escudos, Spanish pesetas, Swedish kronor, and Swiss francs.

Cyprus accepted the obligations of Article VIII, Sections 2, 3, and 4 of the Fund Agreement on January 9, 1991.

Administration of Control

Exchange controls are administered by the Central Bank in cooperation with authorized dealers. Authority to approve applications for the allocation of foreign exchange for a number of purposes has been delegated to authorized dealers. Economic sanctions pursuant to United Nations Security Council resolutions are administered by the Central Bank and relevant government departments. Such sanctions are in effect against Iraq, Libya, and the UNITA organization in Angola. There are also certain restrictions still in effect in relation to the Federal Republic of Yugoslavia (Serbia/Montenegro), in accordance with the UN Security Council resolution 1022 (1995), and an embargo on deliveries of weapons and military equipment to the constituent republics of the former Socialist Federal Republic of Yugoslavia, in accordance with the UN Security Council resolution 1021 (1995). Under Executive Board Decision No. 144-(52/51), the Central Bank had notified the Fund on October 7, 1993, of restrictions imposed previously against the Federal Republic of Yugoslavia (Serbia/Montenegro) pursuant to earlier UN Security Council resolutions.

Prescription of Currency

Payments may be made by crediting Cyprus pounds to an external account, or in any foreign currency (i.e., other than the Cyprus pound); the proceeds of exports to all countries may be received in Cyprus pounds from an external account, or in any foreign currency.

Resident and Nonresident Accounts

Nonresidents may open and maintain with authorized dealers nonresident accounts in Cyprus pounds, designated external accounts, or foreign currency accounts. These accounts may be credited freely with payments from nonresidents of Cyprus (such as transfers from other external accounts or foreign currency accounts), proceeds from sales of any foreign currency by nonresidents (including declared banknotes), and the entire proceeds, including capital appreciation, from the sale of an investment made by a nonresident in Cyprus with the approval of the Central Bank and with authorized payments in Cyprus pounds. External accounts and foreign currency accounts may be debited for payments to residents and nonresidents, for remittances abroad, for transfers to other external accounts or foreign currency accounts, and for payments in cash (Cyprus pounds) in Cyprus. Authorized dealers are allowed to grant medium- and long-term foreign currency loans to nonresidents of up to 20 percent of their deposit liabilities in foreign currencies. In addition, they are allowed to grant short-term loans and credits to offshore companies of up to 10 percent of their deposit liabilities in foreign currencies.

Companies registered or incorporated in Cyprus that are accorded nonresident status (generally designated as offshore companies) by the Central Bank as well as their nonresident employees may maintain external accounts and foreign currency accounts in Cyprus or abroad, as well as local disbursement accounts for meeting their payments in Cyprus. Resident persons and firms dealing with transit trade or engaged in manufacturer-exporter activities or in the hotel business may open and maintain foreign currency accounts subject to certain requirements. Residents dealing with transit trade may deposit up to 95 percent of sale proceeds in these accounts and use balances to pay for the value of traded goods. Residents engaged in manufacturer-exporter activities may deposit up to 50 percent of export proceeds in these accounts and use balances to pay for imports of raw materials used in production. Both transit traders and manufacturers-exporters are, however, required at the end of each year to convert into Cyprus pounds any balances in excess of the amount that is necessary for payments of the value of traded goods or raw materials during the following three months. Resident hoteliers may deposit in foreign currency amounts that they need to make imminent installment payments on foreign currency loans.

Cypriot repatriates may keep in foreign currency, or external accounts with banks in Cyprus, or in accounts with banks abroad, all of their foreign currency holdings and earnings accruing from properties they own abroad. Resident persons temporarily working abroad may maintain their foreign currency earnings in foreign currency or external accounts with banks in Cyprus, or in accounts with banks abroad.

Other residents apart from those referred to in the preceding two paragraphs may hold foreign currency accounts with prior approval of the Central Bank, on a case-by-case basis.

Blocked accounts are maintained in the name of nonresidents for funds that may not immediately and in their entirety be transferred outside Cyprus under the existing exchange control regulations. Blocked funds may either be held as deposits or be invested in government securities or government-guaranteed securities. Income earned on blocked funds is freely transferable to the nonresident beneficiary or may be credited to an external account or foreign currency account. In addition to income, up to £C 50,000 in principal may be released annually from blocked funds for transfer outside Cyprus. Funds can also be released from blocked accounts to meet reasonable expenses in Cyprus of the account holder and his or her family, including educational expenses, donations to charitable institutions in Cyprus, payments for the acquisition of immovable property in Cyprus, and any other amounts authorized by the Central Bank.

Imports and Import Payments

Nearly all imports are free of licensing requirements. An import license is required for certain commodities prescribed by the Minister of Commerce, Industry, and Tourism. The list of commodities currently subject to import licensing includes fresh beef, cheese, and certain chemicals.

Exchange is allocated freely and without restriction through authorized dealers to pay for imports, provided that documentary evidence of shipment or actual importation of goods is available.

Remittances for advance payments before shipment require the prior approval of the Central Bank if they exceed £C 50,000. Authorized dealers are allowed to sell to departing residents of Cyprus foreign exchange up to £C 20,000 for purchases and for the importation of goods into Cyprus; foreign exchange in excess of this limit may be sold to departing residents with the approval of the Central Bank. For advance import payments exceeding £C 20,000, 10 percent of the amount must be deposited with the Central Bank as a guarantee, unless the foreign purchaser provides a bank guarantee for the return of the advance payment in case the shipment is not carried out.

Payments for Invisibles

Payments for invisibles abroad require the approval of the Central Bank, but approval authority for certain types of payments has been delegated to authorized dealers. Profits, dividends, and interest from approved foreign investments may be transferred abroad without limitation, after payment of any due charges and taxes. Insurance premiums owed to foreign insurance companies may be remitted after all contingencies have been deducted. Nonresidents who are temporarily employed in Cyprus by resident firms or individuals and are paid in local currency may deposit with authorized dealers up to £C 500 of their monthly remuneration in external or foreign currency accounts, the balance of which may be freely transferred abroad without reference to the Central Bank; deposits or transfers of greater amounts need the specific approval of the Central Bank.

Allowances are granted to residents for study abroad at colleges, universities, or other institutions of higher education, and certain lower-level institutions of learning. Exchange allowances are based on the cost of living, which is reviewed yearly. The current annual allowance for living expenses for studies in Western European countries, excluding Greece, is £C 5,500; for Greece, £C 3,600; for Canada and the United States, £C 6,600; for Australia, £C 4,000; and for all other countries, £C 3,600. There is no limit on the remittance of foreign exchange for payment of tuition fees.

Authorized dealers are allowed, without any reference to the Central Bank, to sell to resident travelers foreign exchange up to £C 1,000 a person a trip for tourist travel; the Central Bank approves applications for allocations of additional foreign exchange without limitation to cover genuine travel expenses. The allowance for business travel is not fixed but depends on the length of stay abroad. Authorized dealers may provide up to £C 150 a day with a maximum of £C 1,500 a trip, or £C 80 a day with a maximum of £C 800 a trip if the traveler holds an international business card (see below); additional amounts may be granted with the approval of the Central Bank on proof of need. Authorized dealers may also sell to departing residents foreign exchange up to £C 5,000 for medical expenses abroad; unlimited additional amounts are provided with the approval of the Central Bank.

Authorized dealers may issue personal cards valid abroad to any resident, except for residents studying abroad or temporarily living abroad for any reason. These cards, which are designated as international personal cards, may be used abroad for payments to hotels and restaurants, payments for transportation expenses, payments to doctors, clinics, or hospitals, and unlimited international telephone calls, as well as payments abroad or from Cyprus up to £C 300 for each transaction for the following purposes: student examination fees, subscription to professional bodies or societies, fees for enrollment in professional or educational seminars or conferences, and hotel reservation fees.

Authorized dealers may also issue company cards valid abroad (designated as international business cards) to resident businesspeople and professionals who are involved in international trade of goods or services and travel abroad on business. Moreover, authorized dealers may issue special personal cards valid abroad (designated as special international personal cards) to certain categories of residents, such as public officials and university professors. Holders of special international personal cards and holders of international business cards are entitled to charge the following, in addition to the expenses allowed for holders of international personal cards: cash withdrawals up to £C 100 a trip and any other expenses up to £C 300 a trip, as well as mail orders of books (in the case of special international personal cards) or books and equipment for the company (in the case of international business cards) up to £C 1,000.

Authorized dealers may approve, without reference to the Central Bank, applications by resident travel agents to pay foreign travel agents and hotels up to £C 10,000 a trip. The Central Bank approves applications for higher amounts to cover genuine expenses without limitation. Authorized dealers may carry out, without prior reference to the Central Bank, payments of fares and freights by order of resident airlines, agents of foreign airlines, shipping agents, or other resident transport companies in favor of foreign airlines, shipping or other transport companies; if the payment exceeds £C 5,000, documentary evidence must be subsequently submitted to the Central Bank.

On leaving Cyprus, resident travelers may take out up to £C 100 in Cypriot banknotes. There is no limit on the amount of foreign banknotes that departing residents may take out of the country as part of any of their foreign exchange allowances. Nonresident travelers may take out any amount of Cypriot or foreign banknotes they declared on arrival (see text under Proceeds from Invisibles). Nonresidents may also export up to $1,000 in Cypriot or foreign banknotes that they imported, even if these notes were not declared on arrival. In addition, nonresident travelers may take out up to £C 100 in Cypriot banknotes. Furthermore, authorized dealers may convert up to £C 100 into foreign currency for departing nonresidents and are permitted to issue to departing nonresidents, as well as to departing resident employees of offshore companies, any amount of foreign banknotes against external funds.

Exports and Export Proceeds

All exports whose value exceeds £C 1,000 are subject to exchange control monitoring to ensure the repatriation of the sale proceeds. Export proceeds must be surrendered to authorized dealers without delay. Exports of potatoes and carrots are carried out by the respective marketing boards, and exports of wheat, barley, and maize are carried out by the Cyprus Grain Commission.

Proceeds from Invisibles

Receipts from invisibles must be sold to an authorized dealer. Persons entering Cyprus may bring in any amount of Cypriot or foreign banknotes. Nonresidents entering Cyprus should declare to customs any Cypriot or foreign banknotes that they plan to re-export, or to deposit with authorized dealers, or to use to purchase immovable property or goods to export.

Capital

Capital transfers abroad require authorization from the Central Bank. Direct investment abroad by residents is permitted, provided that the proposed investments will promote exports of goods and services or will benefit the Cypriot economy. Outward portfolio investment is permitted only for the following residents: insurance companies (up to 20 percent of their trust fund); Cypriot repatriates and residents temporarily working abroad who hold foreign currency or external accounts; resident employees of multinational enterprises who participate in the employee stock purchase plan offered to them by their employer; and investment companies that have been admitted to the official stock exchange of Cyprus (which started to operate on March 29, 1996). These investment companies are allowed to invest abroad up to 20 percent of their capital.

Investments in Cyprus by nonresidents require the prior approval of the Central Bank, which, in considering applications, gives due regard to the purpose of the investment, the extent of possible foreign exchange savings or earnings, the introduction of know-how, and, in general, the benefits accruing to the national economy. Foreigners may own up to 100 percent of the capital of enterprises engaged in the manufacture of goods exclusively for export. Foreign participation of up to 49 percent is allowed for manufacture of new products, certain tourist activities, and other industrial projects. Inward investment is particularly welcome in projects that upgrade the tourist product (such as marinas, golf courses, and theme parks). In sectors of specific treatment, such as banking and finance, applications are examined on a case-by-case basis. Foreign direct investment is discouraged in saturated sectors, such as trading, real estate development, travel agencies, restaurants, and local transportation. Foreign participation in inward portfolio investment in listed company securities is permitted up to a limit of 30 percent generally and 40 percent in investment companies and mutual funds. Foreigners are allowed to purchase government securities in domestic currency. Annual profits and proceeds from the liquidation of approved foreign investments, including capital gains, may be repatriated in full at any time after payment of taxes.[2]

Commercial credits from abroad with a maturity of less than 200 days and commercial credit from Cyprus with a maturity of less than 180 days may be negotiated freely. With the permission of the Council of Ministers, nonresident aliens may acquire immovable property in Cyprus for use as a residence or holiday home, or as office or factory in the case of an authorized direct investment. They must, however, purchase such property with foreign exchange. The sales proceeds of such property are transferable abroad up to the original purchase price of the property; the remaining balance is transferable at an annual rate of £C 50,000, plus interest. The same treatment is accorded to nonresident Cypriots purchasing a holiday home in Cyprus.

Residents of Cyprus (Cypriots or foreign nationals) who take up residence outside Cyprus may immediately transfer abroad up to £C 50,000 for each household; any excess amount is deposited in a blocked account and released at the rate of £C 50,000 a year. The transfer abroad of funds from estates and intestacies and from the sale of real estate, other than that referred to in the preceding paragraph, is limited to £C 50,000, with any excess amount to be credited to a blocked account and also released at the rate of £C 50,000 a year. Interest earned on a blocked account can be freely transferred abroad.

Transactions in foreign securities owned by residents require prior permission from the Central Bank. In principle, all securities held abroad by residents are subject to registration.

---

[2]The Central Bank and the Government are currently reviewing their policy as regards nonresident investments in Cyprus, with the aim of implementing a far more liberal policy.

Gold

Residents may hold and acquire gold coins in Cyprus for numismatic collection purposes. Residents other than monetary authorities, authorized dealers in gold, and industrial users are not allowed to hold or acquire gold bullion at home or abroad. Authorized dealers in gold are permitted to import gold bullion only for the purpose of disposing of it to industrial users. The exportation of gold coins or bullion requires the permission of the Central Bank.

Changes During 1995

Payments for Invisibles

March 1. The amount of foreign exchange that authorized dealers may sell to departing residents, for tourist travel abroad, without reference to the Central Bank was increased from £C 750 to £C 1,000 a person a trip.

April 6. The Central Bank empowered authorized dealers to carry out, without subsequent reference to the Central Bank, payments of fares and freights by order of resident airlines, agents of foreign airlines, shipping agents, or other resident transport companies in favor of foreign airlines, shipping or other transport companies up to £C 5,000.

May 26. Nonresident travelers were allowed to export any amount of Cypriot banknotes they imported and declared to customs on arrival. Nonresident travelers were allowed to take out up to the equivalent of $1,000 in Cypriot or foreign banknotes that they imported, even if they did not declare them on arrival. In addition, both resident and nonresident travelers were allowed to take out up to £C 100 in Cypriot banknotes; previously, the amount of Cypriot banknotes that a resident or nonresident traveler could export was limited to £C 50. Furthermore, authorized dealers were allowed to send any amount of Cypriot banknotes to foreign banks without reference to the Central Bank.

June 13. Authorized dealers were allowed to approve, without reference to the Central Bank, applications by resident travel agents to pay foreign travel agents and hotel for expenses up to £C 10,000 a trip.

July 1. The amount of foreign exchange that authorized dealers may sell to departing residents for medical expenses abroad without reference to the Central Bank was increased from £C 3,000 to £C 5,000.

The Central Bank empowered authorized dealers to issue personal cards valid abroad to any resident, except for residents studying abroad or temporarily living abroad for any reason. These cards, which are designated as international personal cards, may be used abroad for payments to hotels and restaurants, payments for transportation expenses, payments to doctors, clinics or hospitals, and international phone calls, without limit, as well as payments abroad or from Cyprus up to £C 300 for each transaction for the following purposes: examination fees, subscriptions to professional bodies or societies, fees for enrollment in professional or educational seminars or conferences, and hotel reservation fees.

July 10. The amount that may be paid through special international personal cards or international business cards for mail orders of books or equipment was increased from £C 300 to £C 1,000.

November 20. The amount that residents may remit through authorized dealers to nonresidents (e.g., relations) as financial assistance or gift, without reference to the Central Bank, was increased from £C 100 to £C 200 every six months. Prior approval of the Central Bank is required for higher amounts.

Proceeds from Invisibles

May 26. Restrictions on the import of Cypriot banknotes were abolished.

Changes During 1996

Imports and Import Payments

January 1. Most quantitative import restrictions were abolished; specifically, the number of commodities for which an import license is required was drastically reduced.

Capital

March 29. Investment companies admitted to the official stock exchange of Cyprus were allowed to invest abroad up to 20 percent of their capital.

CZECH REPUBLIC

(Position as of December 31, 1995)

Exchange Arrangement

The currency of the Czech Republic is the Czech Koruna. Its external value is determined on the basis of a basket consisting of the deutsche mark (approximately 65 percent) and the U.S. dollar (approximately 35 percent). The Czech National Bank quotes daily official exchange rates of the koruna against two currencies, the deutsche mark and the U.S. dollar. The National Bank may also intervene in the foreign exchange market according to rules specified in its relevant official announcements. On December 31, 1995, the middle rate of the koruna in terms of the U.S. dollar was Kč 26.602.

The National Bank announces daily foreign exchange rates for 21 other convertible currencies,[1] including the Slovak koruna, European currency units (ECUs), and SDRs. Up to February 28, 1996, the foreign exchange rate of the Czech koruna, quoted by the National Bank was allowed to fluctuate within band limits of ±0.5 percent around the theoretical central rate; since then, the band has been ±7.5 percent. Forward foreign exchange transactions are permitted.

The Czech Republic accepted the obligations of Article VIII, Sections 2, 3, and 4 of the Fund Agreement on October 1, 1995.

Administration of Control

The Ministry of Finance and the National Bank are responsible for the administration of exchange controls and regulations in accordance with the Foreign Exchange Act. In general, the Ministry of Finance exercises authority, governmental credits (central and local authorities), budgetary organizations, and state funds. The National Bank exercises authority over all other agents.

Prescription of Currency

There are no prescription of currency requirements in effect.

Resident and Nonresident Accounts

There are no distinctions between resident and nonresident accounts.

Imports and Exports

Imports and exports may be undertaken by any registered enterprise or entrepreneur. Import licenses are required for a few strategic items, such as uranic ore, its concentrates, coal, poisons, military materials, firearms and ammunition, and narcotics. In addition, an automatic licensing system accompanied by levies applies to some agricultural products, mineral fuel and oils, iron and steel and their products, and some chemical products. All imports, including those by individuals, are subject to an ad valorem customs duty (industrial products up to a rate of 45 percent, agricultural products up to 232.7 percent) and to a value-added tax (VAT) of 5 percent or 22 percent.[2] Imports from the Slovak Republic are exempt from customs duties under a customs union. Imports from developing countries are granted preferential treatment under the Generalized System of Preferences (GSP). Under the GSP, 74 "least developed" countries benefit from a duty exemption, and 104 developing countries are granted a 50–100 percent reduction from the applicable customs duties; tropical products are granted reductions of 100 percent.

Residents are required to repatriate domestic and foreign currency acquired abroad.

A limited number of products require export licenses for purposes of health control (including livestock and plants), facilitating voluntary restraints on products on which partner countries have imposed import quotas (such as textiles and steel products), or preserving for the internal market natural resources or imported raw materials (such as energy, metallurgical materials, wood, foodstuffs, pharmaceutical products, and construction materials). For the two latter groups of products, neither quantitative nor value limits are in force.

Payments for and Proceeds from Invisibles

There are no restrictions, other than the general repatriation requirement, on invisible transactions.

---

[1] Australian dollars, Austrian schillings, Belgian francs, Canadian dollars, Danish kroner, deutsche mark, Finnish markkaa, French francs, Greek drachmas, Irish pounds, Italian lire, Japanese yen, Luxembourg francs, Netherlands guilders, New Zealand dollars, Norwegian kroner, Portuguese escudos, pounds sterling, Slovak koruny, Spanish pesetas, Swedish kronor, Swiss francs, and U.S. dollars.

[2] The incidence of customs tariffs was 4.8 percent in 1995 (measured as a weighted average).

Capital

Portfolio investment by residents abroad may be, with some exceptions, executed only through authorized domestic agents or with prior approval. Prior approval is required when residents extend to nonresidents credits or guarantee an obligation of nonresident guarantees. The extension of credits and guarantees by nonresidents to residents is unrestricted.

Gold

Gold bullion may generally be traded only with authorized agents (banks). Export and import of gold bullion and/or more than 10 gold coins must be reported.

Changes During 1995

Exchange Arrangement

April 24. The National Bank introduced a fee of 0.25 percent on its foreign exchange transactions with banks.

October 1. The Czech Republic accepted the obligations of Article VIII, Sections, 2, 3, and 4 of the Fund Agreement.

October 1. The new Foreign Exchange Law (No. 219/1995) came into effect.

Prescription of Currency

September 30. The bilateral clearing arrangement with the Slovak Republic was terminated by mutual agreement.

Capital

June 22. The National Bank announced that effective August 3, 1995, borrowing abroad by banks would be curtailed by limiting open positions of the National Bank vis-à-vis nonresidents.

DENMARK

(Position as of December 31, 1995)

Exchange Arrangement

The currency of Denmark is the Danish Krone. Denmark participates with Austria, Belgium, France, Germany, Ireland, Luxembourg, the Netherlands, Portugal, and Spain in the exchange rate and intervention mechanism (ERM) of the European Monetary System (EMS).[1] In accordance with this agreement, Denmark maintains the spot exchange rates between the Danish krone and the currencies of the other participants within margins of 15 percent above or below the cross rates based on the central rates expressed in European currency units (ECUs).[2]

The agreement implies that the Danmarks Nationalbank, the central bank, stands ready to buy or sell the currencies of the other countries participating in the EMS in unlimited amounts at specified intervention rates. On December 31, 1995, these rates were as follows:

Specified Intervention Rates Per:	Danish Kroner	
	Upper limit	Lower limit
100 Austrian schillings	62.95610	46.69100
100 Belgian or Luxembourg francs	21.47470	15.92660
100 Deutsche mark	442.96800	328.46100
100 French francs	132.06600	97.94300
1 Irish pound	10.67920	7.92014
100 Netherlands guilders	393.10500	291.54400
100 Portuguese escudos	4.32100	3.20400
100 Spanish pesetas	5.20640	3.86140

The participants in the EMS do not maintain the exchange rates for other currencies within fixed limits. The National Bank, however, does intervene in other situations for the purpose of smoothing out fluctuations in exchange rates and has an obligation to intervene on the Danish foreign exchange market only at the intervention rates agreed within the EMS. Middle rates (average of buying and selling rates)

for 21 foreign currencies,[3] the SDR, and the ECU are officially fixed daily and reflect the rates prevailing at the time of the fixing. On December 31, 1995, the official rate for the U.S. dollar was DKr 5.546 per $1.

All remaining foreign exchange regulations were lifted with effect from October 1, 1988. Residents may hold positions in foreign currencies without limitation with respect to the amounts, currencies, or instruments involved.

There are no restrictions on foreign exchange dealing. The Executive Order on Foreign Exchange Regulations, issued by the Ministry of Business and Industry with effect from July 23, 1994, stipulates that payments of more than DKr 60,000 between residents and nonresidents must be reported to the National Bank for statistical purposes.

For tax control purposes, residents (with certain exceptions) must deposit foreign securities and Danish bonds issued abroad either with a Danish or a foreign bank or with the issuer. Residents who are holding accounts with foreign banking institutions, who have deposited securities abroad, or who have entered into contracts with foreign life insurance companies are required to provide the Danish tax authorities with relevant information concerning these transactions.

Denmark accepted the obligations of Article VIII, Sections 2, 3, and 4 of the Fund Agreement on May 1, 1967.

Exchange Control Territory

The Danish Monetary Area comprises Denmark, Greenland, and the Faeroe Islands. The Faeroe Islands are still subject to the regulations in force before July 23, 1994.

Administration of Control

No exchange control requirements are imposed on capital receipts or payments by residents or nonresidents. Reporting requirements for statistical purposes are administered by the National Bank and by the foreign exchange dealers, whereas reporting requirements for tax purposes on depositing foreign

---

[1]Austria became a member of the European Union on January 1, 1995, and joined the ERM of the EMS on January 9, 1995.

[2]Effective August 2, 1993, the intervention thresholds of the currencies participating in the ERM of the EMS, except those of the deutsche mark and the Netherlands guilder, were widened from ± 2.25 percent to ± 15 percent around the bilateral exchange rates; the fluctuation band of the deutsche mark and the Netherlands guilder remained unchanged at ± 2.25 percent.

[3]Australian dollars, Austrian schillings, Belgian francs, Canadian dollars, deutsche mark, Greek drachmas, Finnish markkaa, French francs, Icelandic krónur, Irish pounds, Italian lire, Japanese yen, Netherlands guilders, New Zealand dollars, Norwegian kroner, Portuguese escudos, pounds sterling, Spanish pesetas, Swedish kronor, Swiss francs, and U.S. dollars.

securities and on accounts abroad are part of the tax legislation and are administered by the tax authorities and the foreign exchange dealers. Foreign exchange dealers are commercial banks, savings banks, and stockbrokerage companies or other financial institutions, as defined in the Executive Order, provided that they settle payments between residents and nonresidents on a commercial basis through accounts held in or on behalf of foreign banking institutions (correspondent banks). The National Bank has drawn up a list of foreign exchange dealers.

Licenses for imports and exports, when required, are issued by the Ministry of Industry or the Ministry of Agriculture and Fisheries.

In accordance with the Fund's Executive Board Decision No. 144-(52/51) adopted on August 14, 1952, Denmark notified the Fund on September 10, 1990, and on July 27, 1992, that certain restrictions had been imposed on the making of payments and transfers for current international transactions in respect of Iraq and the Federal Republic of Yugoslavia (Serbia/Montenegro), respectively.

Prescription of Currency

There are no prescription of currency requirements.

Imports and Import Payments

Imports of most products, except for textiles, are free of licensing from all sources. For textiles, a common European Union (EU) system of export-import licenses has been established for almost all countries exporting low-priced textiles. A few items require a license when originating in Japan, the Republic of Korea, or any other country outside the EU that is not a state trading country. A larger number of items require a license when originating in or purchased from Albania, Bulgaria, China, the Czech Republic, Hungary, the Democratic People's Republic of Korea, Mongolia, Poland, Romania, the Slovak Republic, the Baltic countries, Russia, the other countries of the former Soviet Union, and Vietnam.

No exchange control requirements are imposed on payments for imports.

Exports and Export Proceeds

Except for certain items subject to strategic controls, licenses for exports are required only for the waste and scrap of certain metals.

No exchange control requirements are imposed on receipts from exports.

Payments for and Proceeds from Invisibles

No exchange control requirements are imposed on payments for or receipts from invisibles.

Capital

There are no restrictions on inward or outward capital transfers. The general rules on exchange control issued by the Ministry of Business and Industry are based on Articles 23a through 73a of the EU Treaty on Capital Movements and on the Organization for Economic Cooperation and Development Capital Code; no distinction is made in these rules between residents of member countries of the EU and those of the rest of the world.

Gold

Residents may freely buy, hold, and sell gold in bars or coins in Denmark; they may also import gold in bars or coins. Imports of gold in bars or coins, unless made by or on behalf of the monetary authorities, are subject to a value-added tax at the rate of 25 percent; domestic transactions in gold are also taxed at the rate of 25 percent. There is no customs duty on imports of gold in bars or coins.

Changes During 1995

No significant changes occurred in the exchange and trade system.

(See Appendix for a summary of trade measures introduced and eliminated on an EU-wide basis during 1995.)

DJIBOUTI

(Position as of December 31, 1995)

Exchange Arrangement

The currency of Djibouti is the Djibouti franc, the external value of which is pegged to the U.S. dollar, the intervention currency, at DF 177.721 per $1. Buying and selling rates for currencies other than the U.S. dollar are set by local banks on the basis of the cross rates for the U.S. dollar in international markets. The posted rates are subject to commission charges of 0.5–6 percent set by the commercial banks, depending on the currency concerned. A fixed commission of about DF 3,000 is charged on transfers in foreign currencies. There are no taxes or subsidies on purchases or sales of foreign exchange. Commercial enterprises are free to negotiate forward exchange contracts for commercial and financial transactions through local banks or banks abroad. All transactions are negotiated at free market rates. There are no arrangements for forward cover against exchange rate risk operating in the official or the commercial banking sector.

Djibouti accepted the obligations of Article VIII, Sections 2, 3, and 4 of the Fund Agreement, on September 19, 1980.

Administration of Control

There is no exchange control. The Djibouti franc is issued in notes and coins by the National Bank of Djibouti, which issues and redeems the currency against U.S. dollars.

Prescription of Currency

There are no prescription of currency requirements.

Imports and Import Payments

Djibouti has a free trade zone in the port of Djibouti, but the territory as a whole does not constitute a free zone. However, a 1994 law authorizes the establishment of industrial export processing enterprises (*enterprises franches industrielles*) anywhere in the country. Formally, customs duties are not charged on imports, but, in practice, fiscal duties are levied by means of the general consumption tax at the rate of 33 percent. Certain commodities, including alcoholic beverages, noncarbonated mineral water, petroleum products, khat, and tobacco, are subject to a surtax at various rates. Additional taxes are levied on imported milk products and fruit juice.

Exports and Export Proceeds

There are virtually no restrictions. Export proceeds may be retained.

Payments for and Proceeds from Invisibles

No restrictions are imposed on payments for or proceeds from invisibles. A tax of 10 percent applies to fees and salaries paid to individuals and legal entities who, for professional purposes, are not permanent residents of Djibouti.

Capital

There are no restrictions on inward or outward capital transfers. Under the Investment Code of February 13, 1984, enterprises established or expanded to undertake certain specific economic activities are eligible for various tax exemptions. Under an arrangement governing export processing enterprises, export-oriented manufacturing and services are exempt from the profit tax during the first ten years of operation, and their exports of goods and services are exempt from the export tax.

Changes During 1995

No significant changes occurred in the exchange and trade system.

DOMINICA

(Position as of December 31, 1995)

Exchange Arrangement

The currency of Dominica is the Eastern Caribbean Dollar,[1] which is issued by the Eastern Caribbean Central Bank (ECCB). The Eastern Caribbean dollar is pegged to the U.S. dollar, the intervention currency, at EC$2.70 per US$1. On December 31, 1995, the buying and selling rates for the U.S. dollar were EC$2.69 and EC$2.71, respectively, per US$1. The ECCB also quotes daily rates for the Canadian dollar and the pound sterling.

There are no arrangements for forward cover against exchange rate risk operating in the official or the commercial banking sector.

Dominica accepted the obligations of Article VIII, Sections 2, 3, and 4 of the Fund Agreement on December 13, 1979.

Administration of Control

Exchange control is administered by the Ministry of Finance and applies to all countries outside the ECCB area. The Ministry of Finance has delegated to commercial banks certain powers to approve sales of foreign currencies within specified limits. The Ministry of Trade administers import and export arrangements and controls.

Prescription of Currency

Settlements with residents of territories participating in the ECCB Agreement must be made in Eastern Caribbean dollars; those with member countries of the Caribbean Common Market (CARICOM)[2] must be made in the currency of the country concerned. Settlements with residents of other countries may be made in any foreign currency that is acceptable to the country where the settlement is being made.[3]

Foreign Currency Accounts

Foreign currency accounts may be operated only with the permission of the Ministry of Finance; per-mission is normally confined to major exporters and foreign nationals not ordinarily resident in Dominica. The accounts can only be credited with foreign currencies obtained outside Dominica. Payments from these accounts do not require approval.

Imports and Import Payments

All imports from Iraq are prohibited, and all imports originating from the member countries of the former Council for Mutual Economic Assistance (Albania, Cambodia, China, and the Democratic People's Republic of Korea) require a license. Imports of specified goods originating outside the Organization of Eastern Caribbean States (OECS),[4] Belize, and CARICOM require a license. Imports of a subset of these goods from the more developed countries of CARICOM (Barbados, Jamaica, Guyana, and Trinidad and Tobago) also require a license. In addition, there are certain quantitative restrictions on imports of beverages, flour, and margarine; quotas are allocated to traditional importers based on their historical market shares. The Common External Tariff (CET) of CARICOM countries is applied to all imports.

Payments for authorized imports are permitted upon presentation to a commercial bank of evidence of purchase. Advance payments for imports require prior approval from the Ministry of Finance.

Payments for Invisibles

All settlements overseas require exchange control approval. However, commercial banks have been delegated authority to sell foreign currency to local residents, as specified below: (1) for incidentals, EC$100, subject to a limit of EC$500 a person a year; (2) for each trip outside the area served by the ECCB, EC$3,000, subject to a maximum of two trips in any 12-month period and upon presentation of travel documents; (3) for bona fide business travelers, EC$1,000 for each day outside Dominica, provided the total does not exceed EC$30,000 in any 12-month period and upon presentation of travel documents; (4) for overseas travel for medical treatment, EC$1,000 a day up to a maximum of EC$30,000 in any 12-month period, subject to the presentation of travel documents and a medical certificate stating that the jour-

---

[1] The Eastern Caribbean dollar is also the currency of Anguilla, Antigua and Barbuda, Grenada, Montserrat, St. Kitts and Nevis, St. Lucia, and St. Vincent and the Grenadines.

[2] The CARICOM countries are Antigua and Barbuda, The Bahamas, Barbados, Belize, Dominica, Grenada, Guyana, Jamaica, Montserrat, St. Kitts and Nevis, St. Lucia, St. Vincent and the Grenadines, and Trinidad and Tobago.

[3] Foreign currencies comprise all currencies other than the Eastern Caribbean dollar.

[4] The member countries are Antigua and Barbuda, Dominica, Grenada, Montserrat, St. Kitts and Nevis, St. Lucia, and St. Vincent and the Grenadines.

ney is necessary; (5) for educational expenses, including accommodation, up to EC$15,000 a student in each academic year; and (6) for dependents residing abroad, EC$2,400 in any 12-month period (EC$3,600 for minor or incapacitated dependents).

Amounts in excess of specified limits may be obtained with approval from the Ministry of Finance. Specific approval from the Ministry of Finance must also be obtained for outward remittances of cash gifts up to EC$1,000 a year to each recipient. Earnings of foreign workers and profits and dividends from foreign direct investment may be remitted after settlement of all tax or other public liabilities.

The exportation of Eastern Caribbean banknotes and coins (other than numismatic coins) by residents and nonresidents traveling to destinations outside the ECCB area is limited to amounts prescribed by the ECCB.

Exports and Export Proceeds

Exports to Iraq are prohibited, and specific licenses are required for the exportation of certain goods to any destination. The conversion of export proceeds to an ECCB currency account is mandatory, unless the exporter has a foreign currency account into which the proceeds may be paid. Bananas exported by the Dominica Banana Marketing Corporation are subject to a levy of 1 percent if the export price is between 55 cents and 60 cents a pound; if the export price exceeds 60 cents a pound, an additional levy equivalent to 25 percent of the excess is imposed.

Proceeds from Invisibles

Foreign currency proceeds from transactions in invisibles must be sold to a bank or paid into a for-

eign currency account. There is no restriction on the importation of foreign banknotes and coins.

Capital

All outward transfers of capital or profits require exchange control approval. The purchase by residents of foreign currency securities and of real estate located abroad is not normally permitted. Capital transfers, such as inheritances, to nonresidents require approval, which is normally granted, subject to the payment of any taxes due. Emigrants leaving Dominica to take up residence outside the ECCB area may transfer up to EC$30,000 a family from their assets, subject to income tax clearance.

Direct investment in Dominica by nonresidents may be made with exchange control approval. The remittance of earnings on, and liquidation proceeds from, such investment is permitted, subject to the discharge of any related liabilities. The approval of the Ministry of Finance is required for nonresidents to borrow in Dominica.

Gold

Residents are permitted to acquire and hold gold coins for numismatic purposes only. Small quantities of gold may be imported for industrial purposes only with the approval of the Ministry of Finance.

Changes During 1995

Imports and Import Payments

October 1. The CET was reduced by 5 percentage points on selected items.

DOMINICAN REPUBLIC

(Position as of December 31, 1995)

Exchange Arrangement

The currency of the Dominican Republic is the Dominican Peso, the external value of which is determined in the interbank market. The official exchange rate, based on a September 1994 resolution[1] is set weekly on the basis of the average of the previous week's exchange rates in the interbank market, in which the rates are determined by supply and demand. However, since December 1994, the official exchange rate has been pegged to the U.S. dollar at RD$12.87. On December 31, 1995, the official exchange rate was RD$12.87 per US$1.

The commission equivalent to 3 percent of the f.o.b. value of imports was eliminated in June 1995 as provided for in Law No. 11-12 on tax reform by the Central Bank for the servicing of external debt. A commission of 1.5 percent is charged on sales of foreign exchange in both the bank market and the official market. There are no arrangements for forward cover against exchange rate risk operating in the official or the commercial banking sector.

The Dominican Republic accepted the obligations of Article VIII, Sections 2, 3, and 4 of the Fund Agreement, as from August 1, 1953.

Administration of Control

Exchange control policy is determined by the Monetary Board and is administered by the Central Bank. Thirteen commercial banks (including the state-owned Reserve Bank) are operating in the foreign exchange market.

Arrears are maintained with respect to external payments.

Prescription of Currency

Settlements with Bolivia, Brazil, Chile, Colombia, Ecuador, Mexico, Peru, and Uruguay may be made through special accounts established under reciprocal credit agreements within the framework of the Latin American Integration Association (LAIA). Settlements under the reciprocal credit agreement with Argentina and Venezuela have been suspended. All payments must be invoiced in U.S. dollars; otherwise, no obligations are imposed on importers, exporters, or other residents regarding the currency to be used for payments to or from nonresidents.

Service payments on the external public debt are executed in the same currency in which the loan is denominated.

Imports and Import Payments

Payments for the oil bill are transacted through the Central Bank at the official exchange rate. Imports on a document-against-payments basis must be denominated in U.S. dollars; for these imports, certification of the use of foreign currency is required for customs clearance. All other imports are transacted through the free interbank market and are subject only to verification of appropriate documentation.

Most tariff rates range from 5 percent to 35 percent, and certain luxury imported goods are subject to an excise tax ranging from 5 percent to 80 percent.

Payments for Invisibles

All invisible payments may be made freely through commercial banks, subject to documentation requirements. The new Foreign Investment Law eliminated restrictions on profit remittances. Investors should submit to the Central Bank for its approval a timetable for the gradual remittance of the profits withheld under the terms of the former Foreign Investment Law. The timetable should not be less than five years.

Nonresident tourists may freely convert pesos to dollars upon departure.

Exports and Export Proceeds

Certain exports are prohibited, including some food products and animal species, unprocessed wood (for environmental protection purposes), and blood (for public health reasons). Firms operating in the industrial free zones and dealing in ferro-nickel exports are exempt from the surrender requirement; firms operating in the industrial free zones are not subject to export price restrictions.

The issuance of tax credit certificates (*certificados de abono tributario*), provided for by Law No. 69, was abolished by Law No.11-92. Law No. 69 still regulates the system of temporary admission for imports, under which duties are waived for any imports used in the manufacture of nontraditional products to be exported within a year.

---

[1]Monetary Board Resolution No. 3 (September 7, 1994).

The 100 percent refund of import duties in the industrial free trade zones was deleted from Law No. 299 and included in Law No. 8–90. (Exporters of nontraditional products eligible under the temporary system of Law No. 69 are also exempt from taxes.) Exporters may not extend credit with a maturity of more than 30 days from the date of shipment to foreign buyers without authorization from the Central Bank.

Proceeds from Invisibles

Foreign exchange proceeds from invisibles may be sold in the interbank market with certain exceptions (including international telephone calls, international credit card transactions, jet fuel, foreign embassies, alimonies, donations, and real estate), which must be surrendered to the Central Bank.

Capital

There are no restrictions on the inward movement of capital by either residents or nonresidents. Such investments must be registered with the Central Bank.

External debt can be contracted directly by the central Government, subject to congressional authorization. According to Decree No. 101 of August 20, 1982, and Law No. 749 of January 6, 1978, new loans by other public entities require authorization from the President of the Republic for their subsequent registration by the Monetary Board. Total financial charges on foreign loans are not allowed to exceed the principal international interest rate by more than a certain margin.

The Central Bank provides foreign exchange for the servicing of public external debt at the official exchange rate; the servicing of private external debt that is not guaranteed by the Government is effected through the interbank market.

Gold

Residents may purchase, hold, and sell gold coins for numismatic purposes. With this exception, residents other than the monetary authorities and authorized industrial users are not allowed to hold or acquire gold in any form other than jewelry in the Dominican Republic or abroad. Imports and exports of gold in any form other than jewelry constituting the personal effects of a traveler require licenses issued by the Central Bank; such licenses are not normally granted except for imports and exports by or on behalf of the monetary authorities and industrial users.

Changes During 1995

Payments for Invisibles

January 2. Persons traveling abroad cannot take out foreign currency in traveler's checks or cash for an amount exceeding US$10,000 (Executive Decree No. 7-12).

Exports and Export Proceeds

September 14. Minimum prices for agricultural exports were eliminated (Monetary Board Resolution No. 19).

Capital

January 13. Commercial banks must sell any excess of foreign exchange after 48 hours of the purchase to the Central Bank at the official rate (Monetary Board Resolution No. 28).

July 20. Payments of interest on dollar accounts in commercial banks can be made in U.S. dollars (Monetary Board Resolution No. 3).

November 26. The Foreign Investment Law (No. 1695) was passed.

ECUADOR

(Position as of December 31, 1995)

Exchange Arrangement

The currency of Ecuador is the Ecuadoran Sucre. There are two exchange rates, (1) the free market rate, and (2) the central bank official exchange rate. The market rate of the sucre against the U.S. dollar fluctuates freely within a band that is preannounced by the Central Bank of Ecuador, having a width of 5 percent on each side of its midpoint; the midpoint depreciates at an annual rate of 16.5 percent. The selling rate of the Central Bank of Ecuador is established weekly at a level equal to the average selling rate in the free market of the previous week. The buying rate of the Central Bank is set 2 percent lower than its selling rate. The Central Bank's selling rate is applied to all external payments of the public sector; on December 29, 1995, the official buying and selling rates were S/. 2,864 and S/. 2,922, respectively, per $1.

All legally permitted foreign exchange transactions, other than those conducted through the Central Bank, may be conducted in the free market. On December 29, 1995, the buying and selling rates in the free market were S/. 2,922 and S/. 2,925, respectively, per $1. The Central Bank is authorized to intervene in the free market.

Banks and other financial institutions authorized to conduct foreign exchange transactions are permitted to conduct forward swaps and options and transactions in other financial derivative instruments, subject to the supervision and control of the Superintendency of Banks.

Ecuador accepted the obligations of Article VIII, Sections 2, 3, and 4 of the Fund Agreement on August 31, 1970.

Administration of Control

Public sector foreign exchange transactions are carried out exclusively through the Central Bank. Private sector foreign exchange transactions related to the exploration for, and production, transportation, and commercialization of, oil and its derivatives may be carried out through the free market or through the Central Bank. Foreign exchange transactions of the private sector may be effected through banks and exchange houses authorized by the Monetary Board. Exports must be registered with the Central Bank to guarantee repatriation of any foreign exchange proceeds from the transaction, and

for statistical reasons. Import licenses granted by the Central Bank are required.

Arrears are maintained with respect to public and publicly guaranteed debt service payments to official and private creditors.

Prescription of Currency

Some settlements with Cuba and Hungary take place through bilateral accounts. Payments between Ecuador and Argentina, Bolivia, Brazil, Chile, Colombia, the Dominican Republic, Mexico, Paraguay, Peru, Uruguay, or Venezuela may be made within the framework of the multilateral clearing system of the Latin American Integration Association (LAIA). Exchange proceeds from other countries must be received in convertible currencies. Whenever possible, import payments must be made in the currency stipulated in the import license.

Imports and Import Payments

Imports of all goods except for a small group of goods prohibited, primarily to protect the environment and health, are permitted. Imports of antiques and certain items related to health and national security are also prohibited. Certain imports require prior authorization from government ministries or agencies for ecological, health, and national security reasons. In August 1995, Ecuador joined the World Trade Organization (WTO) and, in this context, has begun a review of its trade regulations to conform them to WTO norms.

Prior import licenses are required for all permitted imports. In addition, PETROECUADOR may, without a license, import supplies, materials, and equipment during emergencies. All private sector imports are subject to the 10 percent value-added tax. There is a temporary import admission regime for inputs used in export production.

For certain agricultural imports, standard import tariffs were supplemented in 1993 by a system of corrective tariffs adopted with the announced intention of reducing the variation, over time, of the cost of such imports. The system incorporates upper and lower benchmark prices for each product. For imports priced below the lower benchmark, the supplementary corrective tariff is applied so as to raise import costs to the lower benchmark level. For imports priced above the upper benchmark, a rebate is available on the standard import tariff, so as to minimize the excess relative to the benchmark. Under provisions of the WTO, Ecuador has agreed to eliminate price bands of imports of 130 farm products over a seven-year period.

For automobiles, official reference prices are published for purposes of calculating tariffs. The reference prices establish a minimum f.o.b. value and when importers declare a higher value, tariffs are calculated on the basis of the higher value. Under the current import tariff regime, most goods are subject to the rates of 5 percent, 10 percent, 15 percent, 20 percent, or 35 percent, with the exception of automobiles, which are subject to a tariff of 40 percent.

Prepayments for imports by the private sector are permitted.

Payments for Invisibles

All public sector payments for invisibles, including interest on public debt, are transacted at the central bank rate. Other payments for current invisibles must be settled in the free market. There are no limitations on the amount of domestic or foreign banknotes that travelers may take out. The remittance abroad of dividends and profits is not restricted.

Residents and nonresidents traveling abroad by air must pay a tax of $25 a person. Airline tickets for foreign travel are taxed at 10 percent, and tickets for travel by ship are taxed at the rate of 8 percent for departure from Ecuador and 4 percent for the return trip.

Exports and Export Proceeds

Exports do not require licenses but must be registered for statistical purposes. All export proceeds must be surrendered to authorized financial entities. Those who disregard the above surrender requirements cannot proceed with a new export operation until they comply with the requirement on the previous export. The Central Bank is authorized to carry out the inspections it considers necessary to verify the proper surrender of export proceeds. Authorized financial entities may purchase foreign exchange in anticipation of future exports.

The surrender requirement does not apply to exports effected under authorized barter transactions. However, barter transactions require the prior approval of the Ministry of Industry, Commerce, Integration, and Fisheries; they must be registered with the Central Bank and are subject to specific limitations. The surrender requirement does not apply to exports to countries with which Ecuador has bilateral payments agreements. In such cases, exporters are required to provide official documentation from the recipient country establishing the applicable

forms of payment. Exporters may deduct up to 15 percent from their surrender requirement to cover the actual cost of consular fees and commissions paid abroad. Exporters of marine products are permitted to retain up to 30 percent of the f.o.b. value of their shipments to cover the actual cost of leasing foreign ships. Minimum reference prices are established for exports of bananas, coffee, fish products, cocoa, and semifinished products of cocoa to help ensure that exchange proceeds are fully surrendered. Payment of foreign exchange for petroleum exports is made on the basis of the sale prices stated in the sales contracts and must be surrendered within 30 days of the date of shipment. All crude oil exports are subject to a tax of S/. 5 a barrel; in addition, a tax of $1.02 a barrel is paid on crude oil exported through the pipeline.

Proceeds from Invisibles

All receipts from invisibles must be sold in the free market, except for interest income on exchange reserves of the Central Bank and all invisible receipts of the public sector, which are transacted at the central bank rate. Travelers may bring in any amount of foreign or domestic banknotes.

Capital

Capital may freely enter or leave the country through the free market. Loan disbursements to the public sector must be transacted at the central bank rate. Unless specifically stated, new foreign direct investments do not require prior authorization. Both domestic and foreign enterprises are subject to a 25 percent income tax rate.

Repatriation of capital and remittances of profits on foreign investments are handled through the free exchange market if investments were made through this market. Transfers of all other gains are subject to a tax rate of 33 percent.

All foreign loans granted to or guaranteed by the Government or official entities, whether or not they involve the disbursement of foreign exchange, are subject to prior approval from the Monetary Board. A request for such approval must be submitted by the Minister of Finance and Public Credit to the Monetary Board, accompanied by detailed information on the loan contract and the investment projects it is intended to finance. In examining the request, the Monetary Board considers the effects that the loan and the related investment may have on the balance of payments and on monetary aggregates. For public sector entities, the projects to be financed must be included in the General Development Plan or receive a favorable ruling from the Planning Office (CONADE).

New external credits with a maturity of over one year that are contracted by the private sector, either directly or through the domestic financial system, must be registered with the Central Bank.

External credits contracted by the private sector must be registered at the Central Bank within 45 days of disbursement. Private sector credit arrangements not registered within the 45-day period are subject to a service charge equivalent to 0.25 percent of the credit amount.

Gold

The private sector is authorized to buy and sell gold in the international and domestic markets.

Changes During 1995

Exchange Arrangement

February 16. The midpoint of the preannounced exchange rate band was depreciated by about 3 percent.

June 30. The more appreciated central bank rate applied to the export proceeds of the state petroleum company was eliminated.

October 27. The exchange rate band was widened to 5 percent on each side of the midpoint (from about 2 percent); its midpoint was depreciated by 3.1 percent; and the annual pace of depreciation was accelerated to 16.5 percent (from 12 percent).

EGYPT

(Position as of December 31, 1995)

Exchange Arrangement

The currency of Egypt is the Egyptian Pound, the external value of which is determined in the free market. The U.S. dollar is used as the intervention currency. Nonbank foreign exchange dealers are permitted to operate in the free market. They may buy and sell domestic and foreign means of payment (banknotes, coins, and traveler's checks) on their own accounts. These transactions, however, must be conducted through the accounts maintained by dealers with authorized banks in Egypt. In addition, authorized nonbank dealers may broker any foreign exchange operation and transaction except transfers to and from the country, on the accounts of their bank or nonbank customers. On December 31, 1995, the exchange rate for the U.S. dollar in the free market was LE 3.4 per $1.

A special exchange rate of LE 1.30 per $1 is applied to transactions effected under the bilateral payments agreement with Sudan. In addition, a separate rate of LE 0.3913 per $1 is used for the liquidation of balances related to past bilateral payments agreements.

Authorized commercial banks are permitted to conduct forward foreign exchange transactions for their own accounts. No prior approval by the Central Bank of Egypt is required, and the banks are free to determine the rates applied for forward transactions.

Administration of Control

Banks are authorized to execute foreign exchange transactions, within the framework of a general authorization, without obtaining specific exchange control approval. The Ministry of Trade and Supply formulates external trade policy. The monopoly of the public sector over the exportation and importation of certain products has been abolished. Port Said City has held free zone status since 1977.

Pursuant to UN Security Council Resolution No. 883 of November 8, 1993, certain restrictions have been imposed on financial transactions in respect of the Libyan Arab Jamahiriya.

Arrears are maintained with respect to external payments.

Prescription of Currency

Payments may be made in any convertible currency. Settlements with Sudan, the only country with which Egypt maintains an operative bilateral payments agreement, are made in accordance with the terms of the agreement. Payments not covered by the agreement may be made in any convertible currency. Certain settlements with countries with which indemnity agreements concerning compensation for nationalized property are in force are made through special accounts in Egyptian pounds with the Central Bank. Suez Canal dues are expressed in SDRs and are paid by debiting free accounts in foreign currency.

Nonresident Accounts

In addition to the "D" accounts and the special accounts related to Egypt's bilateral payments agreement with Sudan, as well as the indemnity agreements concluded with certain countries, there are three types of accounts: free accounts, special capital accounts, and capital and operations accounts.

D accounts may be opened in the name of residents of Sudan. These accounts are largely historical. They are usually credited with transfers under the respective payments agreement. Balances are used to make local payments allowed under the bilateral agreement, including payments for imports from Egypt. Currently, outstanding balances on these accounts are minimal.

Free accounts in foreign currency may be opened in the name of any entity. These accounts may be credited with transfers of convertible currencies from abroad and transfers from other similar accounts, foreign banknotes (convertible currencies), foreign currency equivalents from funds transferred from and interest earned on these accounts. These accounts may be debited for transfers abroad, transfers to other similar accounts, withdrawals in foreign banknotes by the owner or others, and for payments in Egypt.

Special capital accounts may be credited with proceeds from sales of real estate owned by foreigners residing abroad. Authorized banks may transfer funds abroad from these accounts up to the amount in foreign exchange previously transferred and surrendered for Egyptian pounds at the time of the acquisition of the property, plus 5 percent of the value of the property for each year following the first five years of ownership until the property is sold; the remainder, as well as the balances of special accounts that were credited by the sale values of real estate previously purchased with transfers of convertible foreign exchange from abroad, may be paid in five equal annual installments with a minimum of LE 100. However, if the account balance is not exhausted after five years, this balance may be treated as a balance of a current account in Egyptian pounds.

Capital and operations accounts may be opened by companies covered by Law No. 230 of July 1989. These accounts may be credited with transfers from abroad, advance payments and long-term rents in foreign exchange, loans, funds purchased from the free market, and funds purchased from the free accounts to meet the project requirement; they may be debited for payments by the account holder (e.g., imports, profit remittances, interest, other invisibles, and financing of local expenditures).

Imports and Import Payments

The Ministry of Trade and Supply formulates long-term export and import policies and prepares indicative annual export and import plans. Both public and private entities are allowed to trade with all countries in convertible currencies, with the exception of Sudan, with which Egypt maintains a bilateral payments agreement.

All imports financed by the Central Bank are effected at the free market rate, with the exception of imports under the bilateral payments agreement with Sudan, which are effected at a more appreciated rate.

Import payments in foreign exchange by the private sector are effected through the commercial banks or through importers' own foreign exchange resources. All products may be freely imported, with the exception of textiles, which may be imported as inputs for production with the approval of the Ministry of Industry.

For customs purposes, products are classified into eight categories on which tariff rates range from 5 percent to 70 percent (with several exceptions). Surcharges ranging from 2 percent to 5 percent are levied on most imports.

Payments for Invisibles

Commercial banks and other agencies authorized to deal in foreign exchange may sell without restriction foreign currencies for payments for invisibles to the Government, public authorities, the public and private sectors, and companies established under the domestic investment regime, in accordance with the provisions of the Investment Law.

Travelers may not take out more than LE 1,000 in domestic banknotes but are permitted to take out foreign banknotes and other instruments of payment in foreign currency without limitation.

Exports and Export Proceeds

Apart from a limited number of products required for the national economy that may be restricted (e.g., hides and scrap metal) all goods may be exported without a license. Exports of cotton, rice, and petroleum are no longer a public sector monopoly. There are no requirements for repatriation of export proceeds.

Proceeds from exports by the private and public sectors under the bilateral payments agreement with Sudan are obtained in Egyptian pounds in accordance with the provisions of the relevant agreement.

Proceeds from Invisibles

Foreign exchange earned abroad may be held abroad or retained indefinitely in free accounts.

Persons arriving in Egypt from abroad may import up to LE 1,000 in Egyptian banknotes and are permitted to bring in, and to use locally, unlimited amounts of foreign exchange.

Capital

Proceeds of sales of Egyptian and foreign securities registered at the stock market in Egypt may be transferred through the free market for foreign exchange. The same treatment is applied to the transfer of income earned from Egyptian securities and profits owed to foreigners from investments in projects established in Egypt.

Payments for real estate that foreigners are allowed to own must be made in convertible currencies. Proceeds from sales of property owned in Egypt by foreigners or their heirs must be deposited in a special capital account in the name of the foreign seller at an authorized bank. The authorized bank may transfer funds abroad from the account, but the transfer must be limited to the amount of foreign exchange units previously transferred and surrendered for Egyptian pounds at the time of the acquisition of the property, plus 5 percent of the value of the property for each year following the first five years of ownership until the property was sold. (See section on special capital accounts under Nonresident Accounts, above.)

The ratio of foreign currency liabilities to foreign currency assets of authorized commercial banks is subject to a maximum limit of 105 percent, and the open foreign exchange position for a single currency and for all currencies combined is subject to limits of 10 percent and 20 percent, respectively, of their capital. Nonbank foreign exchange dealers may maintain foreign exchange working balances of up to $225,000 for the first LE 1 million of paid-up capital and up to $295,000 for each LE 1 million exceeding the first LE 1 million of paid-up capital.

Gold

Banks are not authorized to deal or speculate, either for their own or their customers' account, in precious metals.

Changes During 1995

No significant changes occurred in the exchange and trade system.

EL SALVADOR

(Position as of December 31, 1995)

Exchange Arrangement

The currency of El Salvador is the Salvadoran Colón. Since January 1, 1994, the Central Reserve Bank has intervened in the foreign exchange market to maintain the exchange rate at C 8.75 per $1. The Central Reserve Bank establishes the daily exchange rates, which are applied to its transactions with the public sector, and the calculation of tax obligations. This exchange rate is the simple average of the exchange rates set by commercial banks and exchange houses on the previous working day. On December 31, 1995, the buying and selling exchange rates of the Central Reserve Bank, the commercial banks, and the exchange houses were C 8.72 and C 8.79, respectively, per $1.

There are no arrangements for forward cover against exchange rate risk operating in the official, commercial banking, or exchange house sector.

El Salvador accepted the obligations of Article VIII, Sections 2, 3, and 4 of the Fund Agreement on November 6, 1946.

Administration of Control

Exchange regulations are administered by the Central Reserve Bank in accordance with its organic law. All private sector imports and payments for invisibles are delegated to the commercial banks and exchange houses.

Exports of a number of products require permits issued by the Centro de Trámites de Exportación (CENTREX). The Salvadoran Coffee Council issues permits freely to private sector traders to conduct external or domestic trade in coffee.

Prescription of Currency

There are no prescription of currency requirements. Settlements are usually made in U.S. dollars or other convertible currencies.

Foreign Currency Deposit Accounts

Both residents and nonresidents may maintain deposit accounts in foreign currencies with authorized banks. Balances on these accounts may be sold to the commercial banks or used to make payments abroad without restriction. Transfers of funds between these accounts are also not restricted. The commercial banks are required to submit periodic reports to the Central Reserve Bank on the use of such accounts. Reserve requirements on foreign currency deposits are the same as those for domestic currency deposits (30 percent on checking deposits and 20 percent on savings deposits).

Imports and Import Payments

Import permits are issued by the Ministry of Economy and are required for only a few items, including gasoline, kerosene, fuel oil, asphalt, propane and butane gas, cloth and jute sacks, sugar, and molasses.

The commercial banks and exchange houses are authorized to make payments for private imports. Payments for public sector imports and settlements of official lines of credit are made by the commercial banks and the Central Reserve Bank after deposits have been made in local currency to cover the full value of credit.

Import tariffs range from 5 percent to 20 percent although some products, such as automobiles, alcoholic drinks, textiles, and luxury items, are subject to an import tariff of 30 percent. Capital goods are subject to a 1 percent import tariff.

Payments for Invisibles

Payments for invisibles of a personal nature (e.g., medical treatment and study and travel abroad) are free of restrictions, and the authority to grant foreign exchange for expenses relating to foreign travel and study abroad is delegated to the commercial banks and exchange houses.

Exports and Export Proceeds

CENTREX issues certificates of origin and of plants and animal health as required by foreign importers, and extends textile visas for the categories with U.S. quotas. All exports must be registered, with the exception of exports amounting to less than $5,000, unless the product specifications call for such certification. Export permits issued by the Ministry of Economy are required for diesel fuel, liquefied petroleum gas, gray cement, and raw sugarcane for the U.S. preferential quota.

Proceeds from exports of goods may be surrendered to the commercial banks; proceeds from exports outside of Central America amounting to less than $25,000 may be surrendered to exchange houses.

Exporters of nontraditional products to markets outside Central America receive a drawback of taxes paid in cash on imported raw materials equivalent to 6 percent of the f.o.b. value of their exports.

Since December 1992, proceeds from exports of coffee have been subject to an income tax, which replaced the export tax.

Proceeds from Invisibles

All exchange receipts from invisibles must be surrendered to commercial banks or exchange houses.

Capital

Foreign direct investments and inflows of capital with a maturity of more than one year must be registered with the Ministry of Economy but are not restricted. External borrowing by financial institutions is subject to a reserve requirement of 10 percent. The net foreign asset position of commercial banks is limited to 20 percent of capital. Outward remittance of interest and amortization on external loans may be made without restriction.

Act No. 279 of March 27, 1996, sets certain minimum capital requirements for businesses owned by foreign residents and those having foreign resident shareholders. This act defines foreign residents as persons residing in El Salvador who are not citizens of one of the five member countries of the Central American Common Market (CACM).

Gold

Gold coins in the denomination of C 2,500 have been issued as legal tender. Residents and nonresidents may hold and acquire gold coins for numismatic purposes. Gold coins in denominations of C 25, C 50, C 100, and C 200 have been issued as legal tender but do not circulate. These coins are not available for sale and exist only for numismatic purposes in the Central Reserve Bank collection. The importation and exportation of gold in any form are not restricted.

Changes During 1995

Foreign Currency Deposit Accounts

April 29. Reserve requirements on domestic and foreign currency deposits were unified.

Imports and Import Payments

April 1. Import tariffs on capital goods were lowered to 1 percent from 5 percent.

Capital

May 20. The net foreign asset position of commercial banks was increased to 20 percent from 10 percent of their capital.

September 30. The reserve requirement on financial system external borrowing, eliminated in March 1995, was reimposed at 10 percent.

EQUATORIAL GUINEA

(Position as of June 30, 1996)

Exchange Arrangement

The currency of Equatorial Guinea is the CFA Franc,[1] which is pegged to the French franc, the intervention currency, at the fixed rate of CFAF 1 per F 0.01. The official buying and selling rate is CFAF 100 per F 1. Exchange transactions in French francs between the BEAC and commercial banks take place at the same rate. Buying and selling rates for certain other foreign currencies are also officially posted, with quotations based on the fixed rate for the French franc and the rates in the Paris exchange market for the currencies concerned. A commission of 0.5 percent is levied on transfers to countries that are not members of the BEAC, except for transfers in respect of central and local government operations, payments for imports covered by a duly issued license domiciled with a bank, scheduled repayments on loans properly obtained abroad, travel allowances paid by the Government and its agencies for official missions, and payments of insurance premiums. There are no taxes or subsidies on purchases or sales of foreign exchange.

With the exception of those relating to gold, Equatorial Guinea's exchange control measures generally do not apply to France (and its overseas departments and territories), Monaco, and all other countries whose bank of issue is linked with the French Treasury by an Operations Account (Benin, Burkina Faso, Cameroon, Central African Republic, Chad, Comoros, Congo, Côte d'Ivoire, Gabon, Mali, Niger, Senegal, and Togo). All payments to these countries may be made freely, but financial transfers of more than CFAF 500,000 to countries of the Operations Account area must be declared to the authorities for statistical purposes. All other countries are considered foreign countries. There are no arrangements for forward cover against exchange rate risk operating in the official or the commercial banking sector.

Equatorial Guinea accepted the obligations of Article VIII, Sections 2, 3, and 4 of the Fund Agreement on June 1, 1996.

Administration of Control

Exchange control is administered by the Directorate General of Exchange Control (ONCC) of the

---

[1]The CFA franc circulating in Equatorial Guinea is issued by the Bank of Central African States (BEAC) and is legal tender also in Cameroon, the Central African Republic, Chad, the Congo, and Gabon.

Ministry of Finance. Exchange transactions relating to all countries must be effected through authorized banks. Import and export licenses are issued by the Ministry of Commerce and Industry.

Arrears are maintained with respect to external payments.

Prescription of Currency

Because Equatorial Guinea is an Operations Account country, settlements with France (as defined above), Monaco, and the Operations Account countries are made in CFA francs, French francs, or the currency of any other institute of issue that maintains an Operations Account with the French Treasury. Settlements with all other countries are usually made through correspondent banks in France in any of the currencies of those countries or in French francs through foreign accounts in francs.

Nonresident Accounts

The regulations pertaining to nonresident accounts are based on regulations applied in France. The principal nonresident accounts are foreign accounts in francs. Because the BEAC suspended the repurchase of BEAC banknotes circulating outside the territories of the CFA franc zone, BEAC banknotes received by the foreign correspondents of authorized banks and mailed to the BEAC agency in Equatorial Guinea by the Bank of France or the Central Bank of West African States (BCEAO) may not be credited to foreign accounts in francs.

Imports and Import Payments

Imports valued at more than CFAF 50,000 are subject to licensing, but licenses are issued freely.

All import transactions whose value exceeds CFAF 50,000 must be domiciled with an authorized bank. Import transactions by residents involving goods for use outside Equatorial Guinea must be domiciled with a bank in the country of final destination. Settlements for imports effected under an import license benefit from the authorization of uninterrupted transfer given to the authorized banks by the Ministry of Finance.

In April 1994, a new tariff structure was introduced in the context of the tax and customs reform of the Central African Customs and Economic Union (UDEAC). For UDEAC member countries, the common duty rate for basic necessities was reduced to 5 percent; for raw materials and capital goods, 10 percent; for intermediate and miscellaneous goods, 20 percent; and for consumer goods, 30 percent.

Payments for Invisibles

Payments in excess of CFAF 500,000 for invisibles to France (as defined above), Monaco, and the Operations Account countries require prior declaration but are permitted freely; those to other countries are subject to the approval of the Ministry of Finance. Payments for invisibles related to trade are permitted freely when the basic trade transaction has been approved or does not require authorization. Transfers of income accruing to nonresidents in the form of profits, dividends, and royalties are also permitted freely when the basic transaction has been approved.

Residents traveling for tourism or business purposes to countries in the franc zone are allowed to take out BEAC banknotes up to a limit of CFAF 2 million; amounts in excess of this limit may be taken out in the form of means of payment other than banknotes. The allowances for travel to countries outside the franc zone are subject to the following regulations: (1) for tourist travel, CFAF 100,000 a day, with a maximum of CFAF 2 million a trip; (2) for business travel, CFAF 250,000 a day, with a maximum of CFAF 5 million a trip; (3) allowances in excess of these limits are subject to the authorization of the Ministry of Finance or, by delegation, the BEAC; and (4) the use of credit cards, which must be issued by resident financial intermediaries and approved by the Ministry of Finance, is limited to the ceilings indicated above for tourist and business travel. However, these regulations are administered liberally, and bona fide requests for allowances in excess of these limits are normally granted. Returning resident travelers are required to declare all means of payment in their possession upon arrival at customs and to surrender within eight days all means of payment exceeding the equivalent of CFAF 25,000. All resident travelers, regardless of destination, must declare in writing all means of payment at their disposal at the time of departure. The re-exportation by nonresident travelers of means of payments other than banknotes issued abroad and registered in the name of the nonresident traveler is not restricted, subject to documentation that they had been purchased with funds drawn from a foreign account in CFA francs or with other foreign exchange. The re-exportation of foreign banknotes is allowed up to the equivalent of CFAF 250,000; the re-exportation of foreign banknotes above these ceilings requires documentation demonstrating either the importation of foreign banknotes or their purchase against other means of payment registered in the name of the traveler or through the use of nonresident deposits lodged in local banks.

The transfer of rent from real property owned in Equatorial Guinea by foreign nationals is permitted up to 50 percent of the income declared for taxation purposes, net of tax. Remittances for current repair and management of real property abroad are limited to the equivalent of CFAF 200,000 every two years. The transfer abroad of the salaries of expatriates working in Equatorial Guinea is permitted upon presentation of the appropriate pay voucher as well as justification of expenses, provided that the transfer takes place within three months of the pay period concerned. Except in the case of expatriates working in Equatorial Guinea on a temporary basis, payments of insurance premiums of up to CFAF 50,000 to foreign countries are permitted; larger amounts may be authorized by the ONCC.

Exports and Export Proceeds

Export transactions valued at CFAF 50,000 or more must be domiciled with an authorized bank. Exports to all countries are subject to domiciliation requirements for the appropriate documents. Proceeds from exports to all countries must be repatriated within 30 days of the payment date stipulated in the sales contract. Payments for exports must be made within 30 days of the arrival date of the merchandise at its destination.

Proceeds from Invisibles

Proceeds from transactions in invisibles with France (as defined above), Monaco, and the Operations Account countries may be retained. All amounts due from residents of other countries in respect of services and all income earned in those countries from foreign assets must be collected within a month of the due date and surrendered within a month of collection if received in foreign currency. Resident and nonresident travelers may bring in any amount of banknotes and coins issued by the BEAC, the Bank of France, or a bank of issue maintaining an Operations Account with the French Treasury, as well as any amount of foreign banknotes and coins (except gold coins) of countries outside the Operations Account area.

Capital

Capital movements between Equatorial Guinea and France (as defined above), Monaco, and the

Operations Account countries are free of exchange control. Capital transfers to all other countries require exchange control approval and are restricted, but capital receipts from such countries are freely permitted.[2]

Under the investment code of April 30, 1992 (as modified June 6, 1994), a number of privileges may be granted to approved foreign investments. These privileges include exemption from import- and export-licensing requirements and free transfer abroad of debt payments and net profits.

Gold

Residents are free to hold, acquire, and dispose of gold jewelry in Equatorial Guinea. They must have the approval of the Directorate of Mines to hold gold in any other form. Approval is not normally given because there are no industrial users in Equatorial Guinea. Newly mined gold must be declared to the

---

[2]Regulations on capital transactions, such as the sale of foreign securities in Equatorial Guinea or direct investments, have been prepared and are pending approval. The authorities are also in the process of drafting legislation aimed at stimulating foreign investment in the agricultural, forestry, construction, public works, mining, and industrial equipment maintenance sectors.

Directorate of Mines, which authorizes either its exportation or its sale in the domestic market. Exports are allowed only to France. Imports and exports of gold require prior authorization from the Directorate of Mines and the Minister of Finance; authorization is seldom granted for imports. Exempt from this requirement are (1) imports and exports by or on behalf of the monetary authorities, and (2) imports and exports of manufactured articles containing a small quantity of gold (such as gold-filled or gold-plated articles). Both licensed and exempt imports of gold are subject to customs declaration.

Changes During 1995

No significant changes occurred in the exchange and trade system.

Changes During 1996

Exchange Arrangement

June 1. Equatorial Guinea accepted the obligations of Article VIII, Sections 2, 3, and 4 of the Fund Agreement.

ERITREA

(Position as of March 31, 1996)

Exchange Arrangement

The provisional legal tender of Eritrea is the Ethiopian Birr, which is issued by the National Bank of Ethiopia. Prior to July 30, 1995, an official rate, the marginal auction rate (determined in the fortnightly auction conducted by the National Bank), and a preferential exchange rate existed in Ethiopia. Effective July 30, 1995, the official and marginal auction exchange rates were unified. This rate was Br 6.32 per U.S. dollar at the end of March 1996. The preferential exchange rate on that date was Br 7.20 per $1. The marginal auction rate applies to most transactions between Eritrea and Ethiopia, to government imports, and to all aid-funded imports. The preferential exchange rate is used for most private imports, all exports, and the conversion of foreign exchange remittances by Eritreans living abroad. The preferential exchange rate is fixed by the authorities for purchases of foreign exchange at Br 7.05 per $1, and for sales of foreign exchange at Br 7.20 per $1. There is also a parallel market rate, which stood at about Br 7.5 per $1 at the end of 1995.

The National Bank undertakes transactions with authorized dealers, which in turn carry out transactions with the public on its behalf. There is also a limited number of unofficial but sanctioned dealers that buy and sell foreign exchange at the preferential rate. Exchange rates for currencies other than the U.S. dollar[1] are communicated daily by the National Bank to the authorized dealers on the basis of same day early morning cross quotations in the London market against the U.S. dollar. For all foreign currency transactions, except transactions involving foreign currency notes, the National Bank prescribes a commission of 0.5 percent for purchases of foreign exchange and 1.5 percent for sales of foreign exchange. The authorized dealers are permitted, but not obliged, to levy a service charge for their own account of up to 0.25 percent buying and 0.75 percent selling and, for currencies other than the U.S. dollar, to include a margin charge that is applied by the correspondents abroad.

There are no taxes or subsidies on purchases or sales of foreign exchange. There is no forward cover

provided in foreign exchange by the National Bank or the authorized dealers.

Administration of Control

The National Bank is working to ensure that all foreign exchange transactions are effected through the authorized dealers who are licensed in accordance with the Monetary and Banking Proclamation No. 32/1993. Under this Proclamation, the National Bank may from time to time issue regulations, directives, and instructions on foreign exchange matters. Comprehensive foreign exchange regulations, as well as a new Central Bank Act, have been prepared and submitted for the Government's approval.

The Exchange Control Department of the National Bank issues permits only for those imports that require foreign exchange from the banking system. The National Licensing Office issues licenses for importers, exporters, and commercial agents, and the Ministry of Trade and Industry has authority to regulate foreign investments (Investment Proclamation No. 59/1994); it vets and licenses technology transfer agreements, as well as investment projects (including joint ventures) that are eligible to take advantage of the tax, foreign exchange, and other concessions of the Investment Proclamation. The Asmara Chamber of Commerce issues certificates of origin for exports.

Prescription of Currency

Settlements may be made in currencies quoted by the National Bank or in any other convertible currency it deems acceptable. All transactions with Ethiopia, except for those related to the imports of spare parts for the refinery in Assab, are settled in Ethiopian birr.

Under the agreement of friendship and cooperation signed by the Presidents of Eritrea and Ethiopia in September 1993, these two countries undertook to cooperate closely and develop common policies concerning a wide range of issues, including matters pertaining to their exchange and trade systems. A joint ministerial commission is entrusted to ensure that implementation of the provisions of the agreement, notably its Article 9, which calls for mutual consultation on the use of the Ethiopian birr and the exploration of the possibilities of adopting a common currency by both countries.

---

[1]At present, Austrian schillings, Belgian francs, Canadian dollars, Danish kroner, deutsche mark, French francs, Italian lire, Japanese yen, Netherlands guilders, Norwegian kroner, pounds sterling, Swedish kronor, and Swiss francs.

An agreement to establish a free trade area (FTA) between Eritrea and Ethiopia was signed on April 4, 1995.

Payments are generally made in Ethiopian birr, although the Government of Ethiopia has required payments in foreign currencies for Eritrea's purchases of Ethiopia's exports, as well as for goods that are in short supply in Ethiopia. Under an intergovernmental agreement between Eritrea and Ethiopia, Eritrea pays Ethiopia in birr for its domestic requirements of petroleum products. The refinery in Assab is reimbursed in birr for the costs of refining the derivative products consumed by Ethiopia, except that the portion corresponding to the depreciation of equipment is paid for in foreign exchange.

As stipulated under an intergovernmental transit and port services agreement as well as a customs arrangement (amended annually), the port of Assab is a free port for Ethiopia, with its own Ethiopian customs branch office, and goods shipped to or from Ethiopia remain exempt from the Eritrean customs duties and related charges. Procedures for the clearing of goods and the exchange of documentation are to be coordinated, and the port and shipping charges are paid in Ethiopian birr.

Resident and Nonresident Accounts

All residents are allowed to maintain foreign currency accounts. Nonbank residents may not open accounts abroad, unless they are specifically authorized by the National Bank.

With the approval of the National Bank, nonresidents may open accounts denominated in U.S. dollars or in Ethiopian birr with the Commercial Bank of Eritrea.

Imports and Import Payments

All importers must possess a valid trade license issued by the National Licensing Office. These licenses must be renewed each year at a fee of Br 200–Br 500. Import payments made through the banking system require permits that are issued by the National Bank upon presentation of pro forma invoices providing information as to type, quantity, unit price, and freight cost (where applicable). A commission of 2 percent is collected on imports that do not require official foreign exchange and are not aid funded. The National Bank ensures full collection of franco valuta commissions by requesting the display of a payment document to the Customs Office at the time of the import declaration. Imports of cars and other motor vehicles require prior permission from the Ministry of Transport to ensure their suitability for existing infrastructure and other similar considerations. There are no priority and negative lists for imports, except that a public enterprise producing tobacco and matches holds a monopoly over the import of these products. Most imports requiring official foreign exchange are effected under letters of credit or on a cash-against-documents basis. Suppliers' credits must be registered with the National Bank.

There is a negative list for imports that must be financed through the banking system; however, goods included on this list may still be imported through the franco valuta system. As of March 30, 1996, the National Bank has not provided foreign exchange for the import of goods in the following categories: perfumes and cosmetics; hair wigs and dyes; toys and games; plastic shopping bags; jewelry and other ornaments; dishes and similar kitchen equipment, except for hotels; ready-made clothing; biscuits and confectionery items; fresh fruits, fruit juices, and vegetables, except for hotels and duty-free shops; live animals, except for breeding purposes; fresh or tinned meat, eggs, and fish; liquor and soft drinks, except for hotels and duty-free shops; salt; articles of decoration and Christmas trees; postcards, holiday or other greeting cards, and collectors' postage stamps; ivory; and smoking articles. Effective November 11, 1995, importers have no longer been required to submit customs declarations to the National Bank for discharging purposes.

Payments for Invisibles

Payments for invisibles may be made to all countries with a foreign exchange permit, which is issued free of charge by the National Bank. The travel allowance for business trips abroad, except to Ethiopia, is $250 a person a day for up to 30 days. In bona fide cases, these limits may be exceeded with the approval of the National Bank. Exporters may freely use balances in their retention accounts for business travel purposes. For personal travel, the allowance is $100 a person (adult or minor) for up to two trips a year. The allowance for medical treatment abroad, other than Ethiopia, is up to $10,000 on recommendation of the Medical Board of the Ministry of Health. Residents may remit premiums on life insurance policies that were taken out before May 1991. Generally, the National Bank grants approval for purchase of foreign exchange exceeding limits. Effective November 11, 1995, the requirement to submit bills of settlement by authorized dealers of foreign exchange (e.g., hotels and duty-free shops) has been suspended, and the National Bank notified the general public that all Eritrean nationals could purchase air travel tickets in local or foreign currency.

In accordance with the Investment Code (Proclamation No. 59/1994), foreign investors may freely remit net profits and dividends accrued from investments, fees, and royalties in respect of any technology transfer agreements. Foreign employees may remit up to 40 percent of their net earnings each month, and up to 60 percent of their cumulative earnings upon completion of their term of service in Eritrea.

Exports and Export Proceeds

Exporters must be licensed by the National Licensing Office. The annual licensing fee is Br 300 for producers and Br 500 for the commercial agents of foreign companies. All exports require documentation by the National Bank, which examines the sales contracts as to type of product, quantity, and unit price. Certain products may require clearance from specific government bodies (e.g., the Eritrean Institute of Standards). In particular, livestock and cereals require the permission of the Ministry of Agriculture, and marine products require the permission of the Ministry of Marine Resources. Exports of unprocessed hides and skins have been suspended since mid-1993 in an attempt to improve the supply to domestic tanneries and processors.

Exports may be made under a letter of credit or on an advance payments basis; in some cases, exports may be permitted on a consignment basis. All export proceeds must be repatriated to an authorized bank within 90 days of shipment; where justified, this deadline can be extended by another 90 days. Exporters may retain up to 100 percent of the sales proceeds.

Proceeds from Invisibles

Foreign exchange receipts from current invisibles by residents must be surrendered to authorized dealers. Travelers are not required to declare their foreign exchange holdings at the point of entry into Eritrea and are not allowed to reconvert their balances back into foreign currency upon departure.

Capital

Foreign exchange proceeds representing capital inflows must be registered at the National Bank to ensure the smooth transfer of dividends and interest, amortization of principal, and proceeds of the sale of shares to residents or from the liquidation of investments.

Direct foreign investments (including joint ventures) in Eritrea are governed by the provisions of the Investment Proclamation No. 59/1994. Foreign direct investment is permitted in all sectors, except that domestic retail and wholesale trade, and import and commission agencies are open to foreign investors only when Eritrea has a bilateral agreement of reciprocity with the country of the investor; the latter condition may be waived by the Government. Approved investments and their subsequent expansion enjoy exemption from customs duties and sales tax for capital goods and spare parts associated with the investment. There are no exemptions from income tax. Under the foreign exchange regulations submitted to the Government, foreign investors may freely remit proceeds received from liquidation of investment and/or expansion, and payments received from the sale or transfer of shares. Petroleum contractors and subcontractors may freely transfer abroad funds accruing from petroleum operations to pay subcontractors and expatriate staff abroad.

Foreign borrowing by residents in Eritrea must be registered with the National Bank. Authorized banks are permitted to purchase and hold foreign banknotes up to the equivalent of $500,000. Amounts exceeding this limit must be surrendered to the National Bank or deposited in the correspondent accounts abroad. With the approval of the National Bank, authorized banks may borrow abroad or overdraw their correspondent accounts abroad. They may acquire securities under similar conditions.

Gold

Residents may own gold jewelry without restrictions. Ownership or possession of gold or other precious metals or ores requires the authorization of the Ministry of Energy, Mines, and Water Resources.

Changes During 1995

Exchange Arrangement

July 25. The official and marginal auction exchange rates were unified, and the marginal auction rate of Ethiopia (determined in the fortnightly foreign exchange auctions conducted by the National Bank of Ethiopia) was to be considered the official exchange rate of Eritrea.

Prescription of Currency

April 4. An agreement to establish a free trade area (FTA) between Eritrea and Ethiopia was signed.

Changes During 1996

Imports and Import Payments

March 30. The National Bank ceased to provide foreign exchange for the import of certain goods.

ESTONIA

(Position as of December 31, 1995)

Exchange Arrangement

The currency of Estonia is the Kroon. Since the introduction of a currency board system, the convertibility of the kroon has been guaranteed by the Bank of Estonia; the Bank of Estonia exchanges kroon banknotes and reserve deposits of commercial banks with the Bank of Estonia into deutsche mark and vice versa at the exchange rate of EEK 8 per DM1. The kroon is fully convertible for all current international transactions and for virtually all international capital transactions.

Transactions in convertible currencies are freely handled by the commercial banks, and commercial banks are free to quote their own exchange rates.

Estonia accepted the obligations of Article VIII, Sections 2, 3, and 4 of the Fund Agreement on August 15, 1994.

Administration of Control

The authority to issue and enforce foreign exchange regulations is based on the Central Bank Law. Import and export controls are administered by the Ministry of Finance.

Prescription of Currency

Settlements with the Baltic countries, Russia, and other countries of the former Soviet Union can be effected through a system of correspondent accounts maintained by the Bank of Estonia with the respective central banks. Balances accrued in these accounts may in most cases be used freely by their holders, to purchase either goods or services in the country concerned. In operating these accounts, the Bank of Estonia acts as an intermediary only and does not convert any balances to krooni. Kroon balances held by central banks of the Baltic countries, Russia, and other countries of the former Soviet Union on their correspondent accounts are fully convertible without delay. These agreements also allow for separate decentralized payments arrangements between commercial banks in the respective states and do not provide for swing credits or overdraft facilities. In addition, Estonian exporters and importers may effect payments without undue delays. Settlements with countries with which Estonia maintains bilateral payments agreements are effected in accordance with the terms of the agreements.[1]

Commercial banks in Estonia are permitted and encouraged to open their own correspondent accounts with counterpart commercial banks in the Baltic countries, Russia, and other countries of the former Soviet Union to effect payments associated with trade with those countries.

Estonia maintains outstanding balances on inoperative correspondent accounts with a number of countries of the former Soviet Union.

Resident and Nonresident Accounts

No licenses are needed to open and operate these accounts.

Imports and Exports

Imports are not subject to quantitative restrictions. Licenses are required for the following: metals, spirits, tobacco and tobacco goods, drugs, cars, weapons, ammunition and explosives, fuel and motor oil, and lottery tickets. Custom duties are levied on fur, fur goods, launches, yachts, and water- or motorskis. In addition, imports are subject to state duty and an 18 percent value-added tax, which is also levied on domestically produced goods. With the exception of beer, imported alcoholic beverages and tobacco products are subject to the same excise taxes levied on domestic products.[2]

Exports are not subject to quantitative restrictions. Licenses are required for the following: metals, spirits, tobacco and tobacco goods, drugs, cars, weapons, ammunition and explosives, fuel and motor oil, and lottery tickets. Customs duties are levied on items of cultural value. In addition, exports are subject to state duty for customs clearance.

Enterprises are not required to repatriate export proceeds. There are no surrender requirements.

Payments for and Proceeds from Invisibles

There are no regulations governing payments for or proceeds from invisibles.

---

[1]At the beginning of 1996, Estonia maintained bilateral payments agreements with Belarus, Kazakstan, Latvia, Lithuania, Russia, and Ukraine.

[2]The import duty on beer is planned to be replaced by the domestic excise on beer in 1996.

The importation and exportation of domestic banknotes are not restricted.

Capital

Inward and outward capital transfers are not controlled or restricted.

Gold

International and domestic trade in gold is subject to the licensing requirement administered by the Ministry of Finance.

Changes During 1995

Imports and Exports

January 1. Free trade agreement with the European Union (EU) came into effect.

April 1. The import tariffs levied on fur, fur good, automobiles, bicycles, launches, and yachts were replaced with excises applicable for both domestic and imported products.

The ad valorem import and export processing fee of 0.5 percent was replaced by a specific fee in line with the World Trade Organization (WTO) principles.

December 31. Imported alcoholic beverages, except beer, and tobacco products were subject to the same excises as domestic products.

Capital

March 1. New prudential ratios for banks, set at international acceptable levels, became effective.

ETHIOPIA

(Position as of December 31, 1995)

Exchange Arrangement

The currency of Ethiopia is the Ethiopian Birr. Since May 1, 1993, the National Bank of Ethiopia has made foreign exchange available to licensed importers through a biweekly auction. Until May 15, 1995, the exchange system consisted of two rates: the official rate and the auction rate. The official exchange rate was pegged to the U.S. dollar and adjusted occasionally on the basis of the marginal rates derived from the auctions. On May 15, 1995, the two rates were unified in practice, with the official rate set at the average of the auctions rates during the preceding month. On July 25, 1995, the official and auction rates were unified de jure, with the official rate set equal to the marginal rate arising from the auction. The biweekly auctions are of the Dutch type, under which a preannounced quantity of foreign exchange is allocated among importers beginning with the highest price bid. Successful bids are completed at the respective bid prices, and the marginal exchange rate is determined by the lowest successful bid.

All licensed importers are allowed to submit bids to the auction if foreign exchange is to be used to import goods that are not included on a negative list. Authorized dealers must observe a prescribed commission of 0.50 percent on buying and 1.50 percent on selling, the proceeds of which accrue to the National Bank. Dealers are authorized to levy service charges of up to 0.25 percent on buying and 0.75 percent on selling for their own accounts. For currencies other than the U.S. dollar, dealers are authorized to include the margin charges applied by the correspondents abroad. In practice, the authorized charges are usually levied. The commission and service charges are also applied by the National Bank in its dealings with the Government and certain public sector entities.

There are no taxes or subsidies on purchases or sales of foreign exchange. There are no arrangements for forward cover against exchange rate risk operating in the official or the commercial banking sector.

Administration of Control

All foreign exchange transactions must be carried out through an authorized dealer under the control of the National Bank. The purchase of foreign exchange for imports of petroleum products, pharmaceuticals, and fertilizers takes place outside the auction, with foreign exchange obtained directly from the National Bank at the official rate. Imports financed with suppliers' credits require prior approval and are limited to raw and intermediate materials, pharmaceuticals, machinery, and transport equipment. The Exchange Controller of the National Bank issues exchange licenses for all exports and payments abroad and issues permits for all shipments. The Minister of Trade formulates external trade policy.

Arrears are maintained with respect to external payments.

Prescription of Currency

Outgoing payments are normally made in convertible foreign exchange appropriate to the country of the recipient or in U.S. dollars. Settlements with Eritrea, except those relating to imports of spare parts for the refinery in Assab, Eritrea, are made in birr. The net proceeds of exports must be surrendered in a freely convertible foreign currency or in any other acceptable foreign currency.

Nonresident Accounts

Nonresidents may open accounts either in birr or in foreign currencies at authorized banks upon approval of the Exchange Control Department of the National Bank. Deposits to these accounts must be made only in foreign exchange. Balances on nonresident foreign currency accounts may be freely transferred abroad, and transfers between nonresident accounts do not require prior approval. Members of the diplomatic community must use transferable or nontransferable birr accounts for payment of local expenses. Joint ventures are permitted to open foreign currency accounts or transferable or nontransferable birr accounts to purchase raw materials, equipment, and spare parts not available in the local market. As soon as the goods are received, documentary evidence of the entry of the goods purchased with such funds must be submitted to the Exchange Control Department of the National Bank. In general, these accounts may be replenished only after the documents have been presented.

Blocked accounts of nonresidents maintained with authorized banks are used to retain funds in excess of Br 20,000 arising from disinvestments in Ethiopia (see the section on Capital, below). Resident Ethiopian nationals are not allowed to maintain bank accounts abroad.

Imports and Import Payments

Unless importers have their own sources of foreign exchange (franco valuta imports) or obtain foreign exchange directly from the National Bank, they must participate in the foreign exchange auction. As of December 1995, the requirement that importers participating in the auction deposit 100 percent covers in an account with the National Bank was reduced to 25 percent. These deposits are not remunerated; if the importer is successful at the auction, the National Bank will open a letter of credit for the importer. Once the imports have arrived, foreign exchange is released by the National Bank against the import documents. The process may take up to six months, during which time the importer's deposit is held with the National Bank.

Payments abroad for imports require exchange licenses, which can be obtained when a valid importer's license is presented. Applications for exchange licenses must be accompanied by information on costs and payment terms and by evidence that adequate insurance has been arranged with the Ethiopian Insurance Corporation, particularly for goods imported under letters of credit. Foreign exchange is not made available for imports included in a negative list. Most goods on this negative list may, however, be imported under the franco valuta arrangement (i.e., imports are financed with foreign exchange from external sources) without a license. Imports of cars and other vehicles require prior authorization from the Minister of Transport and Communications, and authorization is readily granted without restriction if the imports are financed with foreign exchange balances held abroad. Exchange licenses are granted in the currency appropriate to the country of origin or in any convertible currency that may be requested. Payments by letter of credit, mail transfer, telegraphic transfer, or cash against documents at sight are all normally acceptable, but the National Bank must be consulted regarding imports on a cash-against-documents basis.

Certain imports (about 100 items, mostly consumer goods) may not be financed on an acceptance basis, and virtually no imports take place on this basis.

All imports are subject to a general (ad valorem) sales tax.

Payments for Invisibles

Payments for invisibles require exchange licenses. Invisibles connected with trade transactions are treated on the same basis as the goods to which they relate. Foreign employees may remit monthly up to 40 percent of their net earnings but only for the first three years of their contract if employed by the private sector; they may remit a maximum of between 40 percent and 50 percent of total net earnings during the period of service and upon final departure. Other expatriate employees may take out the same maximum amount on final departure, but not more than Br 20,000 in any one year. Foreign nationals who are not entitled to remittance facilities may, however, remit up to 30 percent of their net earnings for the education of their children.

Persons traveling abroad for business purposes related to importing or exporting are granted foreign exchange up to $250 a day for a maximum period of 30 days in any one calendar year. For other business travel, the limits for tourism are applied. For tourism purposes, persons 18 years of age and over are allowed up to $300 a year. For government travel, the schedule of rates varies by country and city based on cost of living. Foreign exchange is not generally available to pay for education abroad. Residents sent abroad for training are allowed foreign exchange up to the equivalent of Br 1,200 a year. Residents may remit premiums on insurance policies taken out before April 1962. The limit on foreign exchange for medical treatment abroad was increased from $5,000 to $10,000, and subsequently eliminated on July 10, 1995. After providing for payment of local taxes, foreign companies may remit dividends on their invested and reinvested capital in any currency. Travelers may take with them a maximum of Br 10 in Ethiopian banknotes.

Exports and Export Proceeds

Exports of most cereals to any destination other than Djibouti are prohibited. All commodity exports require permits from the Exchange Controller and some require, in addition, the approval of specified public bodies. When applying for a permit, an exporter must specify the goods to be exported, their destination, and their value. For exports on a c.i.f. basis, exporters must obtain full insurance from the Ethiopian Insurance Corporation. The granting of a permit by the Exchange Controller enables the goods to pass through customs. The licensing system is used to ensure that foreign exchange receipts are surrendered to the National Bank, generally within three months, and that export proceeds are received in an appropriate currency (see the section on Prescription of Currency, above). Exports of raw hides and skins are regulated or prohibited until the needs of local factories are met. The exportation of coffee is subject to a coffee export duty at the rate of

Br 15 a quintal, a coffee export cess at the rate of Br 5 a quintal, and a coffee surtax.

Proceeds from Invisibles

Foreign exchange receipts from invisibles must be surrendered. Travelers may bring in Br 10 in Ethiopian currency and must declare any foreign exchange in their possession entering Ethiopia. Except for short-term visitors, travelers must have authorization to re-export foreign exchange. Reconversion of birr must be supported by documentary evidence of prior exchange of foreign currency.

Capital

All receipts of capital in the form of foreign exchange must be surrendered. Authorization of the Exchange Controller is required for repatriation of capital, and registration of capital inflows with the exchange control authorities establishes the evidence of inflows that is required for authorization. All recognized and registered foreign investments may be terminated on presentation of documents regarding liquidation and on payment of all taxes and other liabilities. Subject to appropriate documentation, foreign businessmen with nonregistered investments may transfer their capital abroad on liquidation and final departure from Ethiopia but may not transfer more than Br 20,000 in any one calendar year; funds in excess of this amount must be deposited in a blocked account with an authorized bank. This regulation does not apply to joint ventures established under Council of State Special Decree No. 11/1989 (of July 5, 1989) and investments made under Proclamation No. 15/1992 (of May 25, 1992). Transfers by emigrants who have operated their own businesses are restricted to Br 20,000 in any one calendar year.

Foreign investors are permitted to hold a majority share in a joint venture, except in the following sectors: precious metals, public utilities, telecommunications, banking and insurance, transport, and trade in selected products deemed essential to the economy by law. All applications for joint ventures must be approved by the Investment Office; a minimum of 25 percent of share capital must be paid before registration. Exemptions from income taxes are granted for up to five years for new projects and for up to three years for major extensions to existing projects. Imports of investment goods and spare parts for such ventures are also eligible for exemption from customs duties and other specified import levies. Proceeds from the liquidation of a joint venture (as well as dividends received from the activities of a joint venture and payments received from the sale or transfer of shares) may be remitted abroad in convertible currency without restriction. A joint venture may also transfer abroad in convertible currency payments for debts, fees, or royalties in respect of technology transfer agreements.

Borrowing abroad requires approval from the Exchange Control Department and is restricted. Authorized banks may freely place their funds abroad except on fixed-term deposit but may not acquire securities denominated in foreign currency without the permission of the National Bank. In addition, they need prior approval from the National Bank to overdraw their accounts with foreign correspondents, borrow funds abroad, or accept deposits in foreign currency.

Gold

Ownership of gold or platinum personal jewelry is permitted. Unless authorized by the Minister of Mines and Energy, the possession or custody of 50 ounces or more of raw refined gold or platinum, or in the form of nuggets, ore, or bullion, is not permitted. Newly mined gold is sold by the Ethiopian Mineral Resources Development Corporation to the National Bank. Imports and exports of gold in any form other than jewelry require exchange licenses issued by the National Bank. Such licenses are not normally granted except for imports and exports by or on behalf of the monetary authorities.

Changes During 1995

Exchange Arrangement

July 25. The official and marginal auction exchange rates were unified.

Imports and Import Payments

February 3. The negative list of imports excluded from the foreign exchange auction was narrowed to used goods and imports restricted for reasons of health and security.

Payments for Invisibles

February 3. The share of net earnings that foreign employees may remit abroad monthly was increased from 30 percent to 40 percent.

February 3. The daily allowance of foreign exchange for business travelers was increased from $120 to $250, while the maximum period of days was raised from 20 to 30, and the requirement for an equivalent birr deposit was lifted. For tourism purposes, the allowance was raised to $300 a year from $50 a trip with a maximum of two trips a year.

February 3. The limit for the provision of foreign exchange for medical treatment abroad was increased to $10,000 from $5,000.

July 10. The limit for the provision of foreign exchange for medical treatment abroad was eliminated.

FIJI

(Position as of January 31, 1996)

Exchange Arrangement

The currency of Fiji is the Fiji Dollar, the external value of which is determined on the basis of the fixed relationship between the Fiji dollar and a weighted basket consisting of the Australian dollar, the Japanese yen, the New Zealand dollar, the pound sterling, and the U.S. dollar. The weights in the formula were reviewed annually, but the most recent revision was made in April 1993. The exchange rate of the Fiji dollar in terms of the U.S. dollar, the intervention currency, is fixed daily by the Reserve Bank of Fiji on the basis of quotations for the U.S. dollar and other currencies included in the basket. On December 31, 1995, the midpoint exchange rate for the Fiji dollar in terms of the U.S. dollar was F$1.4294 per US$1. The Reserve Bank provides official quotations only for the U.S. dollar. There are no taxes or subsidies on purchases or sales of foreign exchange. Forward exchange facilities are provided by authorized dealers for trade transactions for periods of up to six months for exports and nine months for imports.

Fiji accepted the obligations of Article VIII, Sections 2, 3, and 4 of the Fund Agreement on August 4, 1972.

Administration of Control

Exchange control is administered by the Reserve Bank acting as agent of the Government; the Reserve Bank delegates to authorized dealers the authority to approve normal import payments and other current payments and transfers up to specified limits or full amounts in some cases.

Prescription of Currency

Transactions with all countries are subject to exchange control. Settlements with residents of any country may be made in Fiji dollars through an external account or in any foreign currency.[1]

Resident and Nonresident Accounts

A nonresident[2] may open and operate an external account in Fiji dollars or a foreign currency account with an authorized dealer without specific approval from the Reserve Bank. These accounts may be credited freely with the account holders' salaries (net of tax), with interest payable on the account, with payments from other external accounts, with the proceeds of sales of foreign currency or foreign coins by the account holder, and with Fiji banknotes that the account holder brought into Fiji or acquired by debit to an external account or by the sale of foreign currency in the country during a temporary visit. External accounts may also be credited with payments by residents for which either general or specific authority has been given. External accounts may be debited for payments to residents of Fiji, transfers to other external accounts, payments in cash in Fiji, and purchases of foreign exchange. On January 1, 1996, residents (individuals) were allowed to open foreign currency accounts with domestic banks.

Exporters may retain up to 20 percent of proceeds from exports in foreign currency accounts and use the proceeds for import payments (see section on Exports and Export Proceeds, below).

Imports and Import Payments

Imports of most goods are under open general license; imports of bulk butter and lubrication oil products in any form require a specific license. The Ministry of Trade and Commerce is responsible for issuing import licenses, with the exception of those for gold, timber, and butter. Import licenses for gold are issued by the Ministry of Finance and Economic Planning, for timber, by the Ministry of Forestry, and for butter, by the Ministry of Primary Industries and Cooperatives. Export licenses are issued by various government departments and monitored by the Comptroller of Customs. A wide range of consumer goods are imported by national cooperative societies under a joint arrangement with six other Pacific island countries. The importation of a few commodities from all sources is prohibited for security, health, or public policy reasons.

Payments for authorized imports are permitted upon application and submission of documentary evidence to authorized dealers, who may allow payments for goods that have been imported under either a specific import license or an open general license. Authorized banks may approve advance payments for imports of up to F$50,000 an application without specific approval from the Reserve Bank, if such payments are required by the supplier.

---

[1]Under Fiji's exchange control regulations, foreign currencies are all currencies other than the Fiji dollar.

[2]A nonresident is a person or firm whose country of normal domicile or established residence is a country other than Fiji. For individuals, a resident of Fiji is a person who either has lived or intends to continue living in Fiji for at least three years.

Payments for Invisibles

Payments for invisibles are permitted under a delegated authority to authorized dealers up to specific limits, as follows: (1) family maintenance expenses, F$4,000 a year; (2) subscription payments for clubs, societies, and trade organizations, F$5,000 an application; (3) travel allowances, F$6,000 an applicant a trip; (4) payments of royalties, commissions, patents, brokerage, and copyrights, F$10,000 an application; (5) gift remittances, F$1,000 a donor a year; and (6) professional fees, F$10,000 a year a beneficiary. The use of credit cards for travel-related expenses is not restricted, except for a F$2,000 limit on its use for shopping on each trip; in addition, F$400 a month may be withdrawn in cash. Emigrants are allowed to transfer, after one year abroad, the full amount of the current year's dividends or profits earned on assets left in Fiji.

Prior approval from the Reserve Bank is not required to make the following payments if they are accompanied by supporting documentary proof: (1) for medical treatment and for educational expenses, up to F$15,000, in addition to tuition fees, direct to the institution; (2) wage payments by shipping companies to foreign crew members, up to F$20,000; (3) advertising fees, up to F$10,000; (4) payments of charges for movie film rental and news services; (5) subscriptions to clubs, societies, and trade organizations, up to F$100,000; and (6) proceeds from the maturity of life insurance, up to F$15,000 an applicant, subject to completion of emigration procedures with the Reserve Bank. Amounts exceeding the established limits may be granted with the approval of the Reserve Bank upon presentation of documents certifying that the payments are bona fide.

Nonresident-owned companies must obtain permission from the Reserve Bank to transfer dividends abroad. Under the present policy, remittance of the current year's profits and three years' retained earnings that have not previously been remitted is allowed. The remittance abroad of rent accruing on properties owned by emigrants is permitted as part of the transfers of F$25,000 that each emigrant is allowed to make every six months (see section on Capital, below).

Exports and Export Proceeds

Specific licenses are required for exports of sugar, wheat bran, copra meal, certain kinds of lumber, certain animals, and a few other items. Irrespective of export-licensing requirements, however, exporters are required to produce an export permit for commercial consignment of all goods with an f.o.b. value of more than F$1,000; this permit is required for exchange control purposes. Exporters are required to collect the proceeds from exports within six months of the date of shipment of the goods from Fiji and may not, without specific permission, grant more than six months' credit to a nonresident buyer. Exporters may retain, with prior approval of the Reserve Bank, up to 20 percent of the 1993 export proceeds in foreign currency accounts maintained with an authorized dealer or a foreign bank abroad; the rate of retention from each export receipt is not subject to control. Payments are admissible for imports of raw materials, professional and management fees, loan repayments, and remittances of profits and dividends.

Proceeds from Invisibles

All receipts from invisibles must be surrendered to authorized dealers. Travelers may bring in freely Fijian and foreign currency banknotes, but must declare them to customs or immigration officials on arrival in order to export the unused balance on departure. Residents are required to sell their foreign currency holdings to an authorized dealer within one month of their return.

Receipts of interest, dividends, and amortization must be surrendered semiannually unless approval for reinvestment abroad has been granted by the Reserve Bank.

Capital

Repatriation of capital funds sources from, or withdrawal of foreign investment in, Fiji requires specific permission from the Reserve Bank, which is readily granted with evidence that the investment funds originated offshore. Foreign investment in Fiji is normally expected to be financed from a nonresident source. Such foreign investment may be given "approved status," which guarantees the right to repatriate dividends and capital. Special tax incentives and concessions are granted for investments that qualify under Fiji's Tax Free Factory/Zone status, and an investment allowance similar to that for hotels is provided for large-outlay investment projects that support the tourist industry.

Nonresident-owned companies are permitted to repatriate in full the proceeds from sales of assets and capital gains on investments of up to F$10 million a year. The transfer of inheritances and dowries owed to nonresidents is permitted, as is the transfer of the proceeds from the sale of a house owned by a nonresident. The transfer of funds by emigrants on departure is limited to F$200,000 for a family and F$100,000 for a single person; thereafter, the emigrant is allowed an automatic transfer of

F$25,000 every six months commencing six months after emigration until the amount cleared by the Inland Revenue Department has been fully transferred; emigrants intending to leave Fiji within 12 months are allowed to transfer up to F$100,000 a family and up to F$50,000 a single person. Nonresidents departing Fiji permanently may remit up to F$250,000 on departure and thereafter up to F$50,000 every six months. Overseas investments and other forms of capital transfers abroad have been temporarily suspended. The purchase of personal property abroad is not permitted.

Authorized dealers may lend up to F$100,000 to a newly established company or a branch of a company in Fiji (other than a bank) that is controlled directly or indirectly by persons who reside outside Fiji and up to F$30,000 to individual nonresident customers; individual nonresident borrowers must repay their loans before leaving Fiji. Any amounts in excess of these limits require prior approval from the Reserve Bank. The banks may not lend foreign currency to any resident of Fiji without the specific permission of the Reserve Bank. Residents must obtain prior permission from the Reserve Bank to borrow foreign currency in Fiji or abroad.

Individuals are allowed to invest up to a maximum of F$5,000 a family a year offshore for a total of up to F$10 million, as follows: F$5 million in foreign currency and F$5 million in securities to acquire foreign currency securities. Nonbank financial institutions are allowed to invest offshore up to F$20 million on approval. Local companies are allowed to remit up to F$300,000 to set up sales office or subsidiaries abroad. The proceeds from the sale or realization of such investment must be sold to authorized dealers. Authorized dealers must obtain permission from the Reserve Bank to borrow abroad.

Gold

Residents may freely purchase, hold, and sell gold coins, but not gold bullion, in Fiji. The exportation of gold coins, except numismatic coins and collectors' pieces, requires specific permission from the Reserve Bank. The importation of gold, other than gold coins, from all sources requires a specific import license issued by the Ministry of Finance and Economic Planning; these are restricted to authorized gold dealers. Gold coins and gold bullion are exempt from fiscal duty but are subject to 10 percent value-added tax (VAT). Gold jewelry is also exempt

from fiscal duty but subject to a 10 percent VAT and is not under licensing control. Samples of gold and gold jewelry sent by foreign manufacturers require import licenses if their value exceeds F$200.

Exports of gold jewelry are free of export duty but require licenses if their value exceeds F$1,000. Exports of gold bullion are subject to an export duty of 3 percent. All newly mined gold is refined in Australia and sold at free market prices.

Changes During 1995

No significant changes occurred in the exchange and trade system.

Changes During 1996

Resident and Nonresident Accounts

January 1. Residents (individuals) were allowed to open foreign currency accounts with domestic banks.

Payments for Invisibles

January 1. The limit on remittances of company profits was increased to operating profits earned during the current year plus retained earnings during the previous three years if not previously remitted (previously, two years); the limit for capital profits was increased to US$10 million a year from US$5 million a year.

January 1. Allowances for education expenses were increased to F$15,000 from F$10,000; for gift payments, to F$1,000 from F$500; and for subscriptions to clubs, societies, and trade organizations, to F$100,000 from F$50,000.

Exports and Export Proceeds

January 1. With prior approval of the Reserve Bank, exporters were allowed to retain up to 20 percent, previously 10 percent, of their total annual export earnings in a foreign currency account to meet import payments and other liabilities.

Capital

January 1. Nonbank financial institutions were allowed to invest up to US$20 million offshore in 1996.

January 1. Emigration allowances were increased to F$200,000 from F$125,000 for a family, and to F$100,000 from F$75,000 for a single person and, in both cases, to F$25,000 every six months thereafter.

FINLAND

(Position as of December 31, 1995)

Exchange Arrangement

The currency of Finland is the Finnish Markka, the external value of which is determined on the basis of supply and demand conditions in the exchange market. Finland became a member of the European Union (EU) without entry into the exchange rate mechanism (ERM). Necessary adjustments have been implemented under the European Economic Area (EEA) agreement.

The Finnish authorities do not maintain margins in respect of foreign exchange transactions. On December 29, 1995, the middle rate for the U.S. dollar was Fmk 4.3435 per $1. There are no taxes or subsidies on purchases or sales of foreign exchange.

Authorized banks may deal among themselves, with residents, and with nonresident banks in U.S. dollars and other convertible currencies. Forward premiums and discounts quoted by authorized banks reflect interest rate differentials in the countries of the currencies concerned. The Suomen Pankki (Bank of Finland) does not provide forward cover for commercial banks.

Finland accepted the obligations of Article VIII, Sections 2, 3, and 4 of the Fund Agreement on September 25, 1979.

Administration of Control

There are no exchange controls. Export licensing is administered by the Ministry of Trade and Industry. The import licensing authority is the National Board of Customs; import licenses for firearms, etc., are issued by the Ministry of Internal Affairs. Export licensing for agricultural products relating to GATT export ceilings is administered by the Intervention Unit of the Ministry of Agriculture and Forestry.

In accordance with the Fund's Executive Board Decision No. 144-(52/51) adopted on August 14, 1952, Finland notified the Fund on July 20, 1995, of exchange restrictions pursuant to UN Security Council Resolution on Libya, and of changes in exchange restrictions pursuant to UN Security Council Resolution on Iraq and the Federal Republic of Yugoslavia (Serbia/Montenegro)[1] as well as on certain areas in Bosnia and Herzegovina, Libya, and Iraq.

[1]These restrictions were suspended in December 1995 pursuant to a UN Security Council Resolution.

Prescription of Currency

Settlements with all countries may be made in any convertible currency or through convertible accounts.

Nonresident Accounts

Nonresident accounts may be held in an authorized bank in any convertible currency, including Finnish markkaa. These accounts may be freely credited and debited.

Imports and Import Payments

Most goods may be imported without a license. However, an import license is required for certain agricultural products, certain steel and textile products, and certain industrial products originating from China.

Payments for Invisibles

Payments for invisible transactions are not restricted.

Exports and Export Proceeds

Proceeds from exports are not subject to exchange control. Export licenses are required only for exports of goods related to international export control regimes. Sales of arms are strictly controlled.

Proceeds from Invisibles

Receipts from current invisibles are not subject to controls. The funds may be held in a domestic foreign currency account in Finland. The importation of domestic and foreign banknotes and coins is unrestricted.

Capital

Capital transactions, except the acquisition of real estate by foreigners in Finland, are allowed without restriction. Permits are required if the property is to be used for a vacation dwelling. There are no restrictions on foreign ownership in Finnish companies, but a monitoring system concerning the acquisition of the largest companies by foreigners is in place; this monitoring system does not apply to OECD country residents as of

January 1, 1996. The system is intended to provide the Government with an opportunity to intervene if important national interests are considered to be in jeopardy.

The international banking activities of authorized Finnish banks are free from regulation and subject only to certain supervisory reporting requirements.

Gold

Residents may freely hold, buy, and sell gold in any form in Finland.

Changes During 1995

Exchange Arrangement

January 1. Finland became a member of the EU without entry into the exchange rate mechanism (ERM). Necessary adjustments have been implemented under the EEA agreement. At the same time, membership in the European Free Trade Association (EFTA) was terminated.

March 1. Exchange rate losses resulting from foreign-currency-denominated credits raised for private professional purposes are deductible in taxation according to the Income Tax Act.

FRANCE

(Position as of December 31, 1995)

Exchange Arrangement

The currency of France is the Franc. France participates with Austria, Belgium, Denmark, Germany, Ireland, Luxembourg, the Netherlands, Portugal, and Spain in the exchange rate and intervention mechanism (ERM) of the European Monetary System (EMS). In accordance with this agreement, France maintains the spot exchange rates between the franc and the currencies of the other participants within margins of 15 percent above and below the cross rates based on the central rates expressed in European currency units (ECUs).[1]

The agreement implies that the Bank of France, the central bank, stands ready to buy or sell the currencies of the other participating states in unlimited amounts at specified intervention rates. On December 31, 1995, these rates were as follows:

Specified Intervention Rates Per:	Francs	
	Upper limit	Lower limit
100 Austrian schillings	65.35450	41.05330
100 Belgian or Luxembourg francs	18.88000	14.00500
100 Danish kroner	102.10000	75.72000
100 Deutsche mark	389.48000	288.81000
1 Irish pound	9.38950	6.96400
100 Netherlands guilders	345.65000	256.35000
100 Portuguese escudos	3.79920	2.51770
100 Spanish pesetas	4.57780	3.38510

The participants in the EMS do not maintain the exchange rates for other currencies within fixed limits. However, to ensure a proper functioning of the system, they intervene in concert to smooth out fluctuations in exchange rates, the intervention currencies being each other's, the ECU, and the U.S. dollar. Indicative rates for 21 currencies are published daily by the central bank on the basis of market rates.[2] On December 31, 1995, the rate for the U.S. dollar was F 4.9000 per $1. There are no taxes or subsidies on purchases or sales of foreign exchange.

Fixed conversion rates in terms of the franc apply to the CFP franc, which is the currency of the overseas territories of French Polynesia, New Caledonia, and Wallis and Futuna Islands, and to the two CFA francs, which are the currencies of two groups of African countries that are linked to the French Treasury through an Operations Account.[3] These fixed parities are CFPF 1 per F 0.055 and CFAF 1 per F 0.01, respectively.

Registered banks in France and Monaco, which may also act on behalf of banks established abroad or in Operations Account countries, are permitted to deal spot or forward in the exchange market in France. Registered banks may also deal spot and forward with their correspondents in foreign markets in all currencies. Nonbank residents may purchase foreign exchange forward in respect of specified transactions. All residents, including nonenterprise individuals, may purchase or sell foreign exchange forward without restriction. Forward sales of foreign currency are not restricted, whether or not they are for hedging purposes.

France accepted the obligations of Article VIII, Sections 2, 3, and 4 of the Fund Agreement on February 15, 1961.

Administration of Control

All exchange control regulations have been phased out on the basis of Decree No. 89–938 of December 29, 1989.

The Directorate of the Treasury of the Ministry of the Economy is the coordinating agency for financial relations with foreign countries. It is responsible for all matters relating to inward and outward direct investment and has certain powers over matters relating to insurance, reinsurance, annuities, and the like. The execution of all transfers has been delegated to registered banks and stockbrokers and to the Postal Administration. The Directorate General of Customs and Indirect Taxes establishes import and export procedures and controls within the

---

[1]Effective August 2, 1993, the intervention thresholds of the currencies participating in the ERM of the EMS, except those of the deutsche mark and the Netherlands guilder, were widened from ±2.25 percent to ±15 percent around the bilateral central exchange rates; the fluctuational band of the deutsche mark and the Netherlands guilder remained unchanged at ±2.25 percent.

[2]Austrian schillings, Belgian francs, Canadian dollars, Danish kroner, deutsche mark, Djibouti francs, ECUs, Finnish markkaa, Greek drachmas, Irish pounds, Italian lire, Japanese yen, Netherlands guilders, Norwegian kroner, Portuguese escudos, pounds sterling, Spanish pesetas, Swedish kronor, Swiss francs, U.S. dollars, and Zaïrian new zaïres.

[3]Benin, Burkina Faso, Côte d'Ivoire, Mali, Niger, Senegal, and Togo (*franc de la Communauté financière africaine*, issued by the BCEAO); and Cameroon, Central African Republic, Chad, Congo, Equatorial Guinea, and Gabon (franc de la Coopération financière en Afrique centrale, issued by the BEAC).

framework of commercial policy directives given by the Directorate of Foreign Economic Relations (DREE). Technical visas required for certain imports and exports are issued by the appropriate ministry or by the Directorate General of Customs and Indirect Taxes. The Ministry of Industry has certain responsibilities in respect of licensing contracts and technical assistance contracts.

Prescription of Currency

Settlements with the Operations Account countries may be made in francs or in the currency issued by any institute of issue that maintains an Operations Account with the French Treasury.[4] Settlements with all other countries may be made in any of the currencies of those countries or through nonresident foreign accounts in francs. Importers and exporters are free to invoice in any currency.

Resident and Nonresident Accounts

All residents, including individuals and enterprises not engaged in international trade, are permitted to hold ECU-denominated accounts in France, accounts denominated in foreign currency in France or abroad, and accounts denominated in French francs abroad.

Nonresident accounts in francs may be freely opened by registered banks for nonresidents, including French nationals (other than officials) who are residing abroad. Since March 1989, all restrictions on overdrafts and advances on nonresident-held franc accounts have been lifted.

Emigrants of foreign or French nationality may take out all of their assets upon departure. In addition, nonresidents may hold foreign currency accounts with French and foreign-owned banks.

Imports and Import Payments

Imports of goods that originate outside the European Union (EU) and that are subject to quantitative restrictions require individual licenses. Some imports from non-EU countries are subject to minimum prices; these require an administrative visa and sometimes, exceptionally, an import license. Certain imports require certificates of origin.

For import control purposes, countries other than those that are accorded privileged treatment are divided into three groups according to the extent of import liberalization (1) the former Organization for European Economic Cooperation (OEEC) countries, their dependent territories and certain former dependent territories, Canada, Egypt, Ethiopia, Fiji, Finland, Israel, Jordan, Lebanon, Liberia, Sudan, Syrian Arab Republic, United States, and Western Samoa; (2) some specified countries;[5] and (3) China, Democratic People's Republic of Korea, and Mongolia. Goods covered by the import liberalization arrangements applicable to one country may be imported freely from another country, provided that the country of origin and the country of shipment both benefit from the same degree of liberalization.

Imports of practically all industrial products from countries in group (1) are free of quantitative restrictions, but restrictions are applied to a number of agricultural and electronic products; there is relatively little difference between the lists of goods that may be imported freely from different countries in this group. Imports of certain industrial products from countries in group (2) are restricted, and restrictions are applied to these and to certain additional industrial products from group (3) countries. For some commodities, global quotas are allocated annually (for petroleum and petroleum products) or semiannually and apply to all countries (other than those that have bilaterally negotiated quotas or receive privileged treatment). Imports from all countries of certain agricultural items and certain raw materials are free of quantitative restrictions.

Imports from non-EU countries of most products covered by the Common Agricultural Policy (CAP) of the EU are subject to variable import levies that have replaced all previous barriers to imports; common EU regulations are also applied to imports from non-EU countries of most other agricultural and livestock products.

Liberalized imports are not subject to trade controls but do require a customs document, which constitutes the customs declaration. For some liberalized imports, an administrative visa issued by the Central Customs Administration or by the appropriate ministry is required on an import declaration. Imports of the products of the European Coal and Steel Community (ECSC) require such administrative visas when originating in non-ECSC countries.

---

[4]Comprising the institutes of issue of the Operations Account countries and the Overseas Institute of Issue (for New Caledonia, French Polynesia, Mayotte, and Wallis and Futuna Islands).

[5]The Islamic State of Afghanistan, Argentina, Australia, Bhutan, Bolivia, Brazil, Chile, Colombia, Costa Rica, Cuba, Dominican Republic, Ecuador, El Salvador, Guatemala, Haiti, Honduras, India, Indonesia, Islamic Republic of Iran, Iraq, Republic of Korea, Libyan Arab Jamahiriya, Mexico, Myanmar, Nepal, New Zealand, Nicaragua, Pakistan, Panama, Paraguay, Peru, Philippines, Saudi Arabia, South Africa, Sri Lanka, Thailand, Uruguay, Venezuela, and Republic of Yemen.

Other imports generally require individual import licenses. These are granted up to quotas determined on an individual commodity basis or for a group of commodities and apply to specified countries or areas in accordance with trade agreements or an import plan drawn up for a definite period. Imports of some products must pass through designated customs offices. Documents accompanying goods passing through customs must be written in or translated into French.

Quantitative import restrictions consist of EU-wide restrictions and national restrictions. The former include bilaterally agreed restrictions on textile imports under the Multifiber Arrangement (MFA) and voluntary export restraints on a number of agricultural and industrial products negotiated at the EU level. EU-wide restrictions are enforced through import licensing subject to prior authorization. National restrictions on imports from third countries that are in free circulation within the EU are enforced through temporary import restrictions authorized by the EU Commission under Article 115 of the EEC Treaty. In cases where the restrictions are not officially recognized by the EU (e.g., industry-to-industry understandings that do not directly involve member governments), import restrictions are enforced through national import licensing or standards and certification procedures. Automatic licensing is granted for imports that are under surveillance at either the EU or the national level.

Payments for imports from foreign countries may be made by credit to a foreign account in francs, with foreign currency purchased in the French exchange market, or by debiting a foreign currency account in France or abroad. All residents and international trading houses may freely open accounts in foreign currencies in France with registered banks or abroad (also in French francs) without limit on the credit balance. Payments may be made by transfer through a registered bank, by credit card, by check, by compensation of debts or claims, or by banknotes. The amounts that may be transferred through postal channels are not subject to limitation, but, in practice, the Postal Administration does not make import payments valued at over F 250,000. Registered banks may, without special authorization, permit advance payments to be made that are provided for in the commercial contract. There is no restriction on the use of suppliers' credits.

Payments for Invisibles

Payments to foreign countries by residents for current invisibles have to be reported for statistical purposes but are not restricted as to amount. Registered banks are permitted to approve applications for payments for all categories of current invisibles without limitation. Remittances abroad for family support and donations to nonresidents are freely permitted.

Irrespective of the exchange control regulations, certain transactions between persons or firms in France and abroad are subject to restriction; these include certain transactions relating to insurance, reinsurance, and road and river transport.

There are no limits on expenditures for travel abroad. There is no restriction on the amount of foreign or domestic banknotes resident and nonresident travelers may take out, but amounts exceeding F 50,000 or its equivalent must be declared to customs upon departure.

Exports and Export Proceeds

Certain goods on a prohibited list may be exported only under a special license. Some other exports also require individual licenses, but if their total value does not exceed F 10,000 (F 100,000 for art objects or collectors' items), they may be permitted without any formality, subject to certain exceptions.

Exporters are allowed to cover forward for an unlimited period and may hold foreign currency accounts at home and abroad without limit on the credit balance. Registered banks may freely extend foreign currency advances to exporters; such advances and their repayment may be settled by the receipts of the corresponding exports.

Certain goods purchased in France by persons not normally residing in France are considered exports, even when paid for in francs, and are exempt from taxes.

Proceeds from Invisibles

All proceeds from transactions in invisibles may be retained. With minor exceptions for certain types of transactions, services performed for nonresidents do not require licenses.

Resident and nonresident travelers may bring in any amount of banknotes and coins (except gold coins) in francs, CFA francs, CFP francs, or any foreign currency; amounts of F 50,000 or more, however, must be declared to customs upon arrival. At the request of Algeria, Morocco, and Tunisia, banknotes issued by those countries may not be exchanged.

Capital

Capital movements between France and Monaco and the Operations Account countries are free of exchange control; purchases of French and foreign securities abroad and the corresponding outward transfers of resident-owned capital are free; capital receipts from foreign countries are permitted freely. Residents' capital assets abroad are not subject to repatriation. The transfer abroad of nonresident-owned funds, including the sales proceeds of capital assets, is not restricted.

French and foreign securities held in France by nonresidents may be exported, provided that they have been deposited with a registered bank in a foreign dossier (*dossier étranger de valeurs mobilières*); French securities held under a foreign dossier may also be sold in France, and the sale proceeds may be transferred abroad. Foreign securities held in France by nonresidents must be deposited with a registered bank; French securities held in France by nonresidents need not be deposited but may not be dealt with or exported unless they have been deposited. Foreign securities held in France by residents must be deposited with a qualified bank or broker. Residents may hold French and foreign securities abroad under the control of a French registered bank or broker.

Subject to compliance with the special regulations concerning inward and outward direct investment, residents may purchase abroad, through registered banks abroad, French and foreign securities that are not quoted on a recognized stock exchange. French and foreign securities may be held or sold abroad but may also be imported and then either held or sold on a French stock exchange. Correspondingly, nonresidents holding French or foreign securities abroad (whether acquired before November 24, 1968, or later) may import them into France through a registered bank and hold them in a foreign dossier or sell them on a French stock exchange.

The exchange control regulations include control over inward direct investments in existing French firms. The basis for control over foreign direct investments is Decree No. 89–938 of December 29, 1989, as amended by Decree No. 92–134 of February 1992, which applies to financial relations with all countries except Monaco and those belonging to the Operations Account area.

Direct investments are defined as investments leading to control of a company or enterprise. Any participation where foreign investors hold more than one-third of the capital is considered direct investment. In the case of firms whose shares are quoted on the stock exchange, the threshold is reduced to 20 percent of the capital and applies to each individual foreign participation but not to the total of foreign participation. To determine whether a company is under foreign control, the Ministry of

Economy and Finance may also take into account any special relationships resulting from stock options, loans, patents and licenses, and commercial contracts.

EU or non-EU investments in new firms are not subject to a prior declaration to the Ministry of Economy. Foreign direct investments in existing French firms generally require prior declaration to the Ministry of Economy. The following foreign investments, however, do not require increases in capital of subsidiaries in which foreign ownership or voting rights exceed 66.66 percent: loans and transactions involving less than F 10 million in craft trades; retail trade; hotels; restaurants; various commercial services; quarries and gravel pits; and acquisitions of agricultural lands except vineyards and wine-making properties. Juridical and natural persons may freely invest in any project that is at least 50 percent owned by juridical and natural persons residing in the EU, but the completion of the project must be reported to the Ministry of Economy. Investments of EU groups having permanent recognition of EU status are not subject to any prior declaration and are required only to report to the Ministry of Economy within 20 days of completion. The Minister of Economy may issue a finding within one month to prohibit the EU investment if public health, order, security, or national security is considered to be in danger. Non-EU investments of less than F 50 million, if the turnover of the acquired firm is less than F 500 million, are not restricted but must be reported to the Ministry of Economy before completion. The Minister of Economy may issue a finding within 30 days, at maximum, to prohibit the investment if public health, order, security, or national security is considered to be in danger.

The Minister of Economy is allowed a one-month period, at maximum, during which a non-EU investment can be suspended if the investment involves more than F 50 million or if the turnover of the acquired firm is more than F 500 million.

The liquidation proceeds of foreign direct investment in France may be freely transferred abroad; the liquidation must be reported to the Ministry within 20 days of its occurrence. Foreign direct investments by residents are not restricted, but if such investments exceed F 5 million, they must be reported to the Bank of France within 20 days. The liquidation of direct investments abroad is free from any prior application, provided that the corresponding funds, if they exceed F 5 million, are reported to the Bank of France.

Foreign issues on the French capital market, except issues originating in EU countries, are subject to prior authorization from the Ministry of Economy and Finance. Exempt from authorization, however, are operations in connection with (1) loans backed by a guarantee from the French Government, and (2) shares similar to securities that are already officially quoted on a stock exchange in France.

Borrowing abroad in French francs or foreign currencies by natural or juridical persons, whether public or private persons, whose normal residence or registered office is in France or by branches or subsidiaries in France of juridical persons whose registered office is abroad, is unrestricted. Application of the controls over direct investment and borrowing is delegated to the Bank of France insofar as these activities relate to French firms engaged primarily in real estate business. Lending in French francs to nonresidents is not restricted. Registered banks are free to lend foreign currency to residents. Nonresidents may freely purchase French short-term securities, including treasury bills, *bons de caisse*, and private drafts.

Gold

Residents are free to hold, acquire regularly, and dispose of gold in any form in France. They may continue to hold abroad any gold they held there before November 25, 1968. There is a free gold market for bars and coins in Paris, to which residents and nonresidents have free access and in which normally no official intervention takes place.

Imports and exports of "monetary" gold (defined as gold having a fineness or a weight that is recognized in the gold market) into or from the territory of continental France are now governed by the regulations applying to ordinary goods. Movements of industrial gold are subject to a simple declaration, as are imports and exports of manufactured articles containing a minor quantity of gold, such as gold-filled and gold-plated articles. Collectors' items of gold and gold antiques are subject to specific regulations.

Most gold coins are traded on the Paris stock exchange. In domestic trading, purchases of bars and coins are not subject to a value-added tax. Imports of monetary gold, except gold imported by the Bank of France, are subject to customs duty and value-added tax. Domestic transactions in gold and gold coins are subject to a capital gains tax.

Changes During 1995

No significant changes occurred in the exchange and trade system.

(See Appendix for a summary of trade measures introduced and eliminated on an EU-wide basis during 1995.)

GABON

(Position as of June 30, 1996)

Exchange Arrangement

The currency of Gabon is the CFA Franc,[1] which is pegged to the French franc, the intervention currency, at the fixed rate of CFAF 1 per F 0.01. The official buying and selling rate is CFAF 100 per F 1. Exchange transactions in French francs between the BEAC and commercial banks take place at the same rate. Buying and selling rates for certain foreign currencies are also officially posted, with quotations based on the fixed rate for the French franc and the rate for the currency concerned in the Paris exchange market, and include a commission. Commissions are levied at the rate of 0.25 percent on transfers made by the banks for their own accounts and on all private capital transfers to countries that are not members of the BEAC, except those made for the account of the Treasury, national accounting offices, national and international public agencies, and private entities granted exemption by the Ministry of Finance, Economy, Budget, and Participations because of the nature of their activities. There are no taxes or subsidies on purchases or sales of foreign exchange. There are no arrangements for forward cover against exchange rate risk operating in the official or the commercial banking sector.

With the exception of those relating to gold, Gabon's exchange control measures do not apply to (1) France (and its overseas departments and territories) and Monaco; and (2) all other countries whose bank of issue is linked with the French Treasury by an Operations Account (Benin, Burkina Faso, Cameroon, Central African Republic, Chad, Comoros, Congo, Côte d'Ivoire, Equatorial Guinea, Mali, Niger, Senegal, and Togo). Hence, all payments to these countries may be made freely. All other countries are considered foreign countries.

Gabon accepted the obligations of Article VIII, Sections 2, 3, and 4 of Fund Agreement on June 1, 1996.

Administration of Control

The Directorate of Financial Institutions of the Ministry of Finance, Economy, Budget, and Participations supervises borrowing and lending abroad. Exchange control is administered by the Minister of Finance, Economy, Budget, and Participations, who has partly delegated approval authority for current payments to the authorized banks and that with respect to the external position of the banks to the BEAC. All exchange transactions relating to foreign countries must be effected through authorized intermediaries—that is, the Postal Administration and authorized banks. Import and export authorizations, where necessary, are issued by the Directorate of External Trade of the Ministry of Commerce and Industry.

Prescription of Currency

Since Gabon is an Operations Account country, settlements with France (as defined above), Monaco, and the Operations Account countries are made in CFA francs, French francs, or the currency of any other institute of issue that maintains an Operations Account with the French Treasury. Settlements with all other countries are usually made through correspondent banks in France in any of the currencies of those countries or in French francs through foreign accounts in francs.

Nonresident Accounts

The regulations pertaining to nonresident accounts are based on regulations applied in France. Because the BEAC has suspended the repurchase of BEAC banknotes circulating outside the territories of its member countries, BEAC banknotes received by foreign correspondents' authorized banks and mailed to the BEAC agency in Libreville may not be credited to foreign accounts in francs.

Imports and Import Payments

Imports from member countries of the Central African Customs and Economic Union (UDEAC) are free of formalities, with the exception of refined vegetable oil, which requires prior approval. All imports whose value exceeds CFAF 500,000 from countries outside the UDEAC are subject to authorization. Quantitative restrictions are maintained only on imports of sugar. For perishables and spare parts, an anticipatory authorization is given to simplify administrative procedures. Imports from countries outside the UDEAC that are similar to, and compete with, domestic products are subject to licensing, but, with a few exceptions that are established by minis-

---

[1]The CFA franc circulating in Gabon is issued by the Bank of Central African States (BEAC) and is legal tender also in Cameroon, the Central African Republic, Chad, the Congo, and Equatorial Guinea.

terial order,[2] import authorizations are granted liberally. Some imports are prohibited for security and health reasons. All imports of commercial goods must be insured through authorized insurance companies in Gabon.

Effective January 30, 1994, a new tariff structure was introduced in the context of the UDEAC tax and customs reform. The common duty rates of the UDEAC member countries were reduced to 5 percent for basic necessities, to 10 percent for raw materials and capital goods, to 20 percent for intermediate goods, and to 30 percent for consumer goods.

There are quantitative restrictions on the importation of sugar, but those on the importation of edible oils, bottled water, soap, and cement were lifted on July 5, 1994.

All import transactions relating to foreign countries must be domiciled with an authorized bank. Authorizations duly endorsed by the Ministry of Foreign Trade and the Ministry of Finance, Economy, Budget, and Participations (Directorate of Financial Institutions) entitle importers to purchase the necessary foreign exchange, provided that the shipping documents are submitted to the authorized bank.

Payments for Invisibles

Payments for invisibles to France (as defined above), Monaco, and the Operations Account countries are permitted freely; those to other countries are subject to approval, which is granted when the appropriate documents are submitted. For many types of payment, the approval authority has been delegated to authorized banks. Payments for invisibles related to trade are permitted freely when the basic trade transaction has been approved or does not require authorization. Transfers of income in the form of profits, dividends, and royalties accruing to nonresidents are also permitted freely when the basic transaction has been approved.

Residents traveling for tourism or business purposes to countries in the franc zone are allowed to take out BEAC banknotes up to a limit of CFAF 2 million; amounts in excess of this limit may be taken out in the form of means of payments other than banknotes. Allowances for travel to countries outside the franc zone are subject to the following regulations: (1) for tourist travel, CFAF 100,000 a day, with a maximum of CFAF 2 million a trip; (2) for business travel, CFAF 250,000 a day, with a maximum of CFAF 5 million a trip; (3) allowances in

excess of these limits are subject to the authorization of the Ministry of Finance, Economy, Budget, and Participations or, by delegation, the BEAC; and (4) the use of credit cards, which must be issued by resident financial intermediaries and approved by the Ministry of Finance, Economy, Budget, and Participations is limited to the ceilings indicated above for tourism and business travel. Bona fide requests for travel allowances in excess of the existing limits have been granted. Returning resident travelers are required to declare all means of payment in their possession upon arrival at customs and surrender within eight days all means of payment exceeding the equivalent of CFAF 25,000. All resident travelers, regardless of destination, must declare in writing all means of payment at their disposal at the time of departure. The re-exportation by nonresident travelers of means of payment other than banknotes issued abroad and registered in the name of the nonresident traveler is not restricted, subject to documentation that they were purchased with funds drawn from a foreign account in CFA francs or with other foreign exchange. The re-exportation of foreign banknotes is allowed up to the equivalent of CFAF 250,000; the re-exportation of foreign banknotes above these ceilings requires documentation demonstrating either the importation of foreign banknotes or their purchase against other means of payment registered in the name of the traveler or through the use of nonresident deposits lodged in local banks.

Exports and Export Proceeds

Exports require authorization, irrespective of destination. Export transactions relating to foreign countries must be domiciled with an authorized bank. Export proceeds received in currencies other than those of France or an Operations Account country must be surrendered. Export proceeds normally must be received within 150 days of the arrival of the commodities at their destination. The proceeds must be collected and, if received in a foreign currency, surrendered within one month of the due date. All export taxes, other than those on mining and forestry products, have been eliminated; the taxes on mining and forest products are 0.5 percent and 5 percent to 11 percent, respectively.

Proceeds from Invisibles

Proceeds from transactions in invisibles with France (as defined above), Monaco, and the Operations Account countries may be retained. All amounts due from residents of other countries in respect of services and all income earned in those countries

---

[2]Currently totaling about 30 items, including cement, ham, mineral water, plastic goods, sugar, batteries, and refined vegetable oil.

from foreign assets must be collected and, if received in foreign currency, surrendered within a month of the due date. Resident and nonresident travelers may bring in any amount of banknotes and coins issued by the BEAC, the Bank of France, or any other bank of issue maintaining an Operations Account with the French Treasury, as well as any amount of foreign banknotes and coins (except gold coins) of countries outside the Operations Account area.

Capital

Capital movements between Gabon and France (as defined above), Monaco, and the Operations Account countries are free of exchange control. Capital transfers to all other countries exceeding CFAF 500,000 are restricted and require the approval of the Directorate of Financial Institutions, but capital receipts from these countries are permitted freely. All foreign securities, foreign currency, and titles embodying claims on foreign countries or nonresidents that are held in Gabon by residents or nonresidents must be deposited with authorized banks in Gabon.

Special controls in addition to any exchange control requirements that may apply are maintained over borrowing and lending abroad, over inward and outward direct investment, and over the issuing, advertising, or offering for sale of foreign securities in Gabon; these controls apply to the transactions themselves, not to payments or receipts. With the exception of controls over the sale or introduction of foreign securities in Gabon, the control measures do not apply to France (as defined above), Monaco, and the Operations Account countries.

Direct investments abroad[3] must be declared to the Ministry of Finance, Economy, Budget, and Participations unless they take the form of a capital increase resulting from reinvestment of undistributed profits; the full or partial liquidation of investments must also be declared to the Ministry unless the operation involves the relinquishing of a shareholding that had previously been approved as constituting a direct investment abroad. Foreign direct investments in Gabon[4] must be declared to the Ministry unless they take the form of a capital increase resulting from the reinvestment of undistributed profits. Within two months of receipt of the declaration, the Ministry may request the postponement of the project. The full or partial liquidation of direct

investments in Gabon must also be declared to the Ministry unless the operation involves the relinquishing of a shareholding that had previously been approved as constituting a direct investment in Gabon. Both the making and the liquidation of direct investments, whether Gabonese investments abroad or foreign investments in Gabon, must be reported to the Ministry within 20 days of the operation. (Direct investments are defined as those that imply control of a company or enterprise.)

The issuing, advertising, or offering for sale of foreign securities in Gabon requires prior authorization from the Ministry of Finance, Economy, Budget, and Participations. Exempt from authorization, however, are operations in connection with (1) loans backed by a guarantee from the Gabonese Government; and (2) shares similar to securities whose issuing, advertising, or offering for sale in Gabon has previously been authorized.

Borrowing abroad by natural or juridical persons, whether public or private, whose normal residence or registered office is in Gabon, or by branches or subsidiaries in Gabon of juridical persons whose registered office is abroad, requires prior authorization from the Ministry of Finance, Economy, Budget, and Participations. The following are, however, exempt from this authorization: (1) loans constituting a direct investment abroad for which prior approval has been obtained, as indicated above; (2) loans directly connected with the rendering of services abroad by the persons or firms mentioned above, or with the financing of commercial transactions either between Gabon and countries abroad or between foreign countries in which these persons or firms take part; (3) loans contracted by registered banks; and (4) loans other than those mentioned above whose total outstanding amount does not exceed CFAF 50 million for any one borrower. However, the contracting of loans referred to under (4) that are free of authorization and each repayment must be declared to the Directorate of Financial Institutions within 20 days of the operation unless the total outstanding amount of all loans contracted abroad by the borrower is CFAF 5 million or less.

Lending abroad by natural or juridical persons, whether public or private, whose normal residence or registered office is in Gabon, or by branches or subsidiaries in Gabon of juridical persons whose registered office is abroad, requires prior authorization from the Ministry of Finance, Economy, Budget, and Participations. The following are, however, exempt from this authorization: (1) loans granted by registered banks; and (2) other loans whose total outstanding amount does not exceed CFAF 50 million for any one lender. However, loans that are free

---

[3]Including those made through foreign companies that are directly or indirectly controlled by persons in Gabon and those made by branches or subsidiaries abroad of companies in Gabon.

[4]Including those made by companies in Gabon that are directly or indirectly under foreign control and those made by branches or subsidiaries in Gabon of foreign companies.

of authorization and each repayment must be declared to the Directorate of Financial Institutions within 20 days of the operation except when the total outstanding amount of all loans granted abroad by the lender does not exceed CFAF 5 million.

Under the Investment Code of July 6, 1989, any enterprise established in Gabon, domestic or foreign, is granted, under certain conditions, reduced duties and taxes on specified income. In addition to fiscal privileges, the code provides for four categories of preferential treatment. Eligible companies may receive protection against foreign competition and may be given priority in the allocation of imports, public credit, and government contracts. Foreign companies investing in Gabon must offer shares for purchase by Gabonese nationals for an amount equivalent to at least 10 percent of the companies' capital. Non-Gabonese firms or individuals are not permitted to own land in Gabon.

Gold

Residents are free to hold, acquire, and dispose of gold in any form in Gabon. Imports and exports of gold require the authorization of the Ministry of Finance, Economy, Budget, and Participations. Exempt from this requirement are (1) imports and exports by or on behalf of the monetary authorities, and (2) imports and exports of manufactured articles containing a small quantity of gold (such as gold-filled or gold-plated articles). The exportation of gold is the monopoly of the Société gabonaise de recherches et d'exploitation minières. However, imports of gold exempted from licensing and authorization requirements are subject to customs declaration.

Changes During 1995

No significant changes occurred in the exchange and trade system.

Changes During 1996

June 1. Gabon accepted the obligations of Article VIII, Sections 2, 3, and 4 of the Fund Agreement.

THE GAMBIA

(Position as of December 31, 1995)

Exchange Arrangement

The currency of The Gambia is the Gambian Dalasi. Commercial banks and foreign exchange bureaus are free to transact among themselves, with the Central Bank of The Gambia or with customers at exchange rates agreed on by the parties to these transactions. The Central Bank conducts a foreign exchange market review session on the last working day of each week with the participation of the commercial banks and foreign exchange bureaus. During this session, the average market rate during the week is announced as the rate for customs valuation purposes for the following week. On December 31, 1995, the midpoint exchange rate of the dalasi in the interbank market was D 9.6492 per $1. There are no arrangements for forward cover against exchange rate risk operating in the official or the commercial banking sector. There are no taxes or subsidies on purchases or sales of foreign exchange.

The Gambia accepted the obligations of Article VIII, Sections 2, 3, and 4 of the Fund Agreement on January 21, 1993.

Administration of Control

The Exchange Control Act was repealed in November 1992, and no exchange controls are in force.

Prescription of Currency

Settlements with other countries may be made and received from nonresident sources in dalasis or in any convertible currency. Settlements with the Central Bank of West African States (BCEAO) (Benin, Burkina Faso, Côte d'Ivoire, Niger, Senegal, and Togo), and also Ghana, Guinea, Guinea-Bissau, Liberia, Mali, Mauritania, Nigeria, and Sierra Leone are normally made through the West African Monetary Agency.

External Accounts

Accounts denominated in dalasis held by residents of other countries are designated external accounts. Such accounts may be opened without reference to the Central Bank when commercial banks are satisfied that the account holder's source of funds is from abroad in convertible foreign currency. Designated external accounts may be credited with payments from residents of other countries, with transfers from other external accounts, and with the proceeds of sales through the banking system of other convertible currencies. They may be debited for payments to residents of other countries, for transfers to other external accounts, and for purchases of other convertible currencies.

Imports and Import Payments

The importation of certain specified goods is prohibited from all sources for social, health, or security reasons. All other imports are freely permitted under open general licenses.

All merchandise imports are subject to a national sales tax of 10 percent of the c.i.f. value; imports by the Government, diplomatic missions, and charitable organizations are exempt from this tax.

Payments for Invisibles

There are no restrictions on payments for invisibles. Visitors to The Gambia are not required to declare foreign currency in their possession.

Exports and Export Proceeds

The exportation of forestry products is subject to prior authorization from the Forestry Department. The exportation of all other goods can take place without individual licenses.

Proceeds from Invisibles

There is no restriction on the importation of foreign currency notes or Gambian banknotes.

Capital

Inward transfers for purposes of direct equity investment are not restricted but must be reported to the Central Bank for statistical purposes. Prior approval from the Central Bank is not required for residents or nonresidents to accept loans in foreign currency from any source.

Commercial banks may provide overdraft facilities to members of diplomatic and international missions in The Gambia. Loans and advances by commercial banks to nonresidents do not require authorization from the Central Bank, however, it continues to set limits on foreign exchange working balances held by the commercial banks and exchange bureaus; amounts held in excess of these limits must be offered for sale in the interbank market or offered to the Central Bank. These limits must be observed on a weekly basis and transactions must be reported daily to the Central Bank. In addition, The Gambia Telecommunication Company (GamTel), which is a parastatal organization, is temporarily permitted to maintain limited working balances in foreign exchange. The limits must be observed on a monthly basis, and the amounts held must be reported within the same period to the Central Bank. Any amount in excess of the limit must be surrendered to a commercial bank in The Gambia.

Gold

The importation of gold coins and bullion requires the approval of the Central Bank.

Changes During 1995

No significant changes occurred in the exchange and trade system.

GEORGIA

(Position as of January 31, 1996)

Exchange Arrangement

The currency of Georgia is the Lari, the external value of which is determined in daily fixing sessions held at the Tbilisi Interbank Currency Exchange (TICEX) in which the National Bank of Georgia and the major commercial banks participate. The official exchange rate for the U.S. dollar is determined in these sessions. The official rates for other currencies are determined on the basis of the cross rates for the U.S. dollar and the currencies concerned in the international market. The official exchange rates are used for budget and tax accounting purposes, as well as for all payments between the Government and enterprises and other legal entities. On December 31, 1995, the official exchange rate quoted by the National Bank for the U.S. dollar was lari 1.23, per $1. For all commercial transactions, the exchange rate of the lari is negotiated freely between the banks and foreign exchange bureaus that are licensed by the National Bank and their customers.

Foreign exchange bureaus are permitted to buy and sell foreign currency notes. There are no taxes or subsidies on purchases or sales of foreign exchange. There are no arrangements for forward cover against exchange rate risk operating in the official or the commercial banking sector.

Administration of Control

The National Bank of Georgia law, which came into effect in 1995, provides the bank with exchange control authority. Decree No. 259 of March 5, 1992, the First Stage of Liberalization of Foreign Exchange Activity, established the legal basis for the conduct of foreign economic activities in Georgia. The main provisions of this decree (1) allow all enterprises to engage directly in foreign trade, (2) allow all residents to acquire and hold foreign currency and engage in foreign transactions with a licensed foreign exchange dealer, and (3) authorize banks to open foreign exchange accounts for all residents. Trade with countries other than the Baltic countries, Russia, and the other countries of the former Soviet Union is controlled by the State Committee on Foreign Economic Relations (SCFER) (Decree No. 265 of March 31, 1993, on Quotas and Licensing of Merchandise Trade).

The National Bank has the authority to issue general foreign exchange licenses to banks that will permit them to engage in foreign exchange transactions with residents and nonresidents and to open correspondent accounts with banks outside Georgia. The National Bank also has the authority to issue internal licenses to banks that will permit them to engage in the same range of foreign exchange transactions as general license holders, except that holders of internal licenses may not open correspondent accounts with banks abroad. All transfers of foreign exchange by holders of internal licenses must be carried out through correspondent accounts held either with the National Bank or with a bank that holds a general license. As of the end of December 1995, 43 banks held general licenses, while 35 banks held internal licenses. The National Bank also has the authority to issue licenses for the establishment of exchange bureaus to authorized banks in Georgia.

Prescription of Currency

Settlements with the Baltic countries, Russia, and the other countries of the former Soviet Union and certain other countries are made in some cases through a system of correspondent accounts and in other cases in convertible currency. Settlements with other countries may be made in any convertible currency.

Resident and Nonresident Accounts

Resident individuals and enterprises are permitted to open and operate foreign exchange accounts at authorized banks. There are no restrictions on the use of these accounts, and the balances may be used for all authorized transactions. The opening of foreign exchange accounts abroad by resident natural persons is not restricted. The requirement for resident legal persons to obtain authorization of the Ministry of Finance and the National Bank is waived. Nonresidents may maintain foreign exchange and local currency accounts with banks in Georgia.

Imports and Exports

There are no quantitative restrictions on imports, and licenses are not required, except for weapons, narcotics, industrial equipment, pharmaceuticals, and agricultural pesticides; licenses are issued by the SCFER. A customs duty of 12 percent is levied on all imports, except food items (excluding tobacco and alcoholic beverages) and imports under barter operations, irrespective of the currency denomination of the contract. A customs duty of 20 percent is levied on all imports under barter operations but not on imports under government agreements. All imports are subject to a general customs processing fee of 0.2 percent. Foreign exchange to pay for imports may be purchased freely from authorized banks at market rates.

There is no legal prohibition on exports, but licenses are required for items such as food and raw materials. Exports of arms, narcotics, precious metals, and some raw materials are subject, in practice, to prohibitions. The licensing of exports is administered by the SCFER, which takes into account whether exports would create shortages of goods in the domestic market. All exports are subject to a general customs processing fee of 0.2 percent.

Payments for and Proceeds from Invisibles

Residents may freely purchase foreign exchange to make payments for invisible transactions or use foreign exchange balances in their foreign exchange accounts with authorized banks without restriction. Proceeds from invisibles are subject to the same regulations and procedures as those applicable to proceeds from exports.

The importation of foreign currency notes is unrestricted, but amounts must be declared on arrival. The exportation of foreign currency notes by nonresidents is permitted up to a limit equal to the amount originally imported. Residents may export up to the equivalent of $500 without restriction. Amounts in excess of $500 are subject to a "special fee" ranging from 2 percent for amounts up to the equivalent of $10,000 to 3 percent for amounts above $10,000.

Capital

Inward and outward capital operations are not restricted but are subject to registration requirements for monitoring purposes.

Gold

A license is required to conduct both international and domestic trade in gold.

Changes During 1995

Exchange Arrangement

September 25. A new national currency, the lari, was introduced, with 100 tetri equal to 1 lari.

Administration of Control

July 1. The National Bank law provided the bank with exchange control authority.

Changes During 1996

Exchange Arrangement

January 1. The frequency of auctions in the TICEX was increased to daily from three times weekly.

Imports and Exports

January 1. The previous requirement for exporters to surrender 32 percent of proceeds in convertible currencies to the National Bank was eliminated.

GERMANY

(Position as of December 31, 1995)

Exchange Arrangement

The currency of Germany is the Deutsche Mark. Germany participates with Austria, Belgium, Denmark, France, Ireland, Luxembourg, the Netherlands, Portugal, and Spain in the exchange rate and intervention mechanism (ERM) of the European Monetary System (EMS).[1]

The arrangements imply that the Deutsche Bundesbank (the central bank) stands ready to buy or sell the currencies of the other participating states in unlimited amounts at specified intervention rates.[2] On December 31, 1995, these rates were as follows:

Specified Intervention	Deutsche Mark	
Rates Per:	Upper limit	Lower limit
100 Austrian schillings	16.5050	12.2410
100 Belgian or Luxembourg francs	5.6300	4.1750
100 Danish kroner	30.4450	22.5750
100 French francs	34.6250	25.6750
1 Irish pound	2.8000	2.0760
100 Netherlands guilders	90.7708	86.7800
100 Portuguese escudos	1.1328	0.8401
100 Spanish pesetas	1.3650	1.0123

In principle interventions within the EMS are made in participating currencies but may also take place in third currencies, such as the U.S. dollar. Participants in the EMS do not maintain exchange rates for other currencies within fixed limits but do intervene from time to time to smooth out erratic fluctuations in exchange rates.

Official middle buying and selling rates are quoted for 17 foreign currencies on the foreign exchange market of Frankfurt am Main.[3] On December 31, 1995, the official middle rate for the U.S. dollar was DM 1.4335 per $1. There are no taxes or subsidies on purchases or sales of foreign exchange. Residents and nonresidents may freely negotiate forward exchange contracts for both commercial and financial transactions in all leading convertible currencies in the domestic exchange market and at major international foreign exchange markets. There are no officially fixed rates in the forward exchange market, and all transactions are negotiated at free market rates.

Germany accepted the obligations of Article VIII, Sections 2, 3, and 4 of the Fund Agreement on February 15, 1961.

Administration of Control

The administration of control in respect of imports and exports of goods and services is operated by the Federal Ministry of Economics; the Federal Ministry of Finance; the Federal Ministry of Transportation; the Federal Office for Economics; the Federal Office for Export Control; the Federal Ministry for Food, Agriculture, and Forestry; the Federal Office for Food and Forestry; the Federal Office for Agricultural Marketing Organization; and the Ministries of Economics of the Laender. All banks in Germany are permitted to carry out foreign exchange transactions.

In accordance with the Fund's Executive Board Decision No. 144-(52/51) adopted on August 14, 1952, Germany notified the Fund on November 5, 1992 that, in compliance with UN Security Council Resolution No. 757 (1992), certain restrictions had been imposed on the making of payments and transfers for current international transactions in respect of the Federal Republic of Yugoslavia (Serbia/Montenegro). Furthermore, in compliance with UN resolutions, restrictions have been imposed on the making of payments and transfers for current international transactions in respect of Iraq and the Libyan Arab Jamahiriya.

Imports and Import Payments

The import list comprises 10,370 statistical positions. Their treatment is as follows: The importation of 1,363 textile items (under the arrangements regarding international trade in textiles) and of certain steel items is governed by bilateral agreements and regulations of the European Union (EU) with various supplier countries. Imports of pit coal from countries that are not members of the EU and the

---

[1] Austria became a member of the European Union (EU) on January 1, 1995 and joined the ERM of the EMS on January 9, 1995.

[2] Effective August 2, 1993, the intervention thresholds of the currencies participating in the ERM of the EMS, except those of the deutsche mark and the Netherlands guilder, were widened to ±15 percent from ±2.25 percent (and ±6 percent respectively) around the bilateral exchange rates; the fluctuation band of the deutsche mark and the Netherlands guilder remained unchanged at ±2.25 percent.

[3] Austrian schillings, Belgian and Luxembourg francs, Canadian dollars, Danish kroner, Finnish markka, French francs, Irish pounds, Italian lire, Japanese yen, Netherlands guilders, Norwegian kroner, Portuguese escudos, pounds sterling, Spanish pesetas, Swedish kronor, Swiss francs, and U.S. dollars.

European Free Trade Association (EFTA) are permitted within the framework of an annual global quota. Imports of brown coal are subject to import licensing from countries on country List C[4] except Bulgaria, the Czech Republic, Poland, Romania, and the Slovak Republic. The importation of certain nontextile goods from China is subject to an annual global quota of the EU. The Common Agricultural Policy of the EU covers 2,054 statistical items; most of these are subject to variable import levies, which have in large part replaced previous barriers to imports. A new recording system for imports of goods and services from other EU member countries was put in place with the completion of the single European market on January 1, 1993.

Payments for imports are unrestricted. Commodity futures may be dealt in freely, and most transit trade transactions may be carried out freely.

Payments for Invisibles

All payments for invisibles may be made freely without individual license. German and foreign notes and coins and other means of payment may be exported freely.

The following transactions—but not the related payments—between residents and nonresidents are subject to restriction: the chartering of foreign ships from residents of specified countries and the conclusion of related sea freight contracts; the use of foreign boats in certain inland waterway traffic; and transactions with specified countries (which do not grant reciprocal treatment) for hull and marine liability insurance and aviation insurance, except passenger accident insurance.

Exports and Export Proceeds

With few exceptions (for strategic goods), export transactions may be carried out freely. For statistical purposes, an export notification is required for all goods. Certain exports (mostly strategic goods) are subject to individual or general licensing. The customs authorities exercise control over export declarations. Foreign exchange proceeds from exports do not have to be declared or surrendered and may be used for all payments.

Proceeds from Invisibles

With few exceptions, services performed for nonresidents do not require a license. However, licenses

are required for transactions related to specific sea services and for technical assistance involving the delivery to residents of non-OECD countries of construction drawings, materials, and instructions for manufacture, if such assistance is for the production of goods whose exportation requires a license (strategic goods). There are no restrictions on the receipt of payments for services rendered to nonresidents. German and foreign notes and coins and other means of payment may be imported freely.

Capital

Residents and nonresidents may export capital freely without a license. Foreign and international bond issues on the German capital market do not require official approval. All resident banks, including legally independent foreign-owned banks, may lead or manage issues of bonds denominated in deutsche mark. Domestic and foreign securities of all types may be imported and exported freely.

No restrictions are applied to the sale of German money market papers and fixed-interest securities by residents to nonresidents. Nonresidents' direct investments in Germany, purchases of real estate in Germany for investment or personal use, and purchases of German or foreign equities do not require approval. There are no limitations on the disposal of legacies located in Germany and inherited by nonresidents or on legacies located abroad and inherited by residents. Residents are not required to repatriate or surrender their foreign exchange earnings or holdings.

Banks are subject to minimum reserve requirements on the level of their foreign liabilities with maturities of less than four years of 2 percent on sight deposits and 1.5 percent on savings and time deposits; these requirements are, in principle, the same as those applied to domestic liabilities. Book liabilities to nonresidents in foreign currency are exempt from reserve requirements to the extent of the book claims on nonresidents in foreign currency with maturities of less than four years. Banks are free to pay interest on domestic or foreign currency balances held by nonresidents.

Gold

Residents may freely hold gold in any form and may negotiate with residents or nonresidents, both at home or abroad. There is a free gold market in Frankfurt am Main. Imports and exports of gold in any form by residents and nonresidents are unrestricted and free of license; a customs declaration, however, is required.

---

[4]Countries on List C are Albania, the former member countries of the Council for Mutual Economic Assistance (CMEA) except China, Hungary, the Democratic People's Republic of Korea, and Vietnam. All other countries are on List A or B.

Imports of gold bullion and coins, unworked gold, and gold alloys, while free of customs duty, are subject to value-added tax at the rate of 15 percent. In the case of imports of gold coins on which the assessment basis exceeds 250 percent of the fine gold value, the value-added tax is levied at a rate of 7 percent. Imports of monetary gold by the Bundesbank are exempt from value-added tax and customs duty. Domestic transactions in gold are subject to value-added tax at the same rate as imports, but under certain conditions no value-added tax is levied on transactions in gold bullion carried out on gold exchanges between brokers admitted to these exchanges. Commercial imports and exports of articles containing gold are subject to the general foreign trade regulations and in all cases are liberalized.

Changes During 1995

Capital

August 1. The minimum reserve ratios on sight and savings deposits were reduced to 2 percent and 1.5 percent, respectively. Cash holdings were excluded from the assets eligible for meeting the reserve requirement.

(See Appendix for a summary of trade measures introduced and eliminated on an EU-wide basis during 1995.)

GHANA

(Position as of December 31, 1995)

Exchange Arrangement

The currency of Ghana is the Ghanaian Cedi, whose exchange rate is determined in the interbank market. The average exchange rate in this market is used for official valuation purposes but is not always applied by authorized banks in their transactions with each other or with their customers. Rates are quoted by authorized dealers for certain other currencies[1] with daily quotations based on the buying and selling rates for the U.S. dollar in markets abroad. Rates for certain nonconvertible currencies of the West African region, including the Nigerian naira, are also quoted daily but are applied only to transactions under the West African Clearing House arrangement. The other quoted nonconvertible currencies are the Gambian dalasi, the Guinean franc, the Sierra Leonean leone, the Guinea-Bissau peso, and the Mauritanian ouguiya. Authorized banks may exchange Ghanaian currency for any foreign currency. On December 31, 1995, the exchange rate in the interbank market was ₵ 1,446.14 per $1.

Any person, bank, or institution licensed by the Bank of Ghana is allowed to operate a foreign exchange bureau. Foreign exchange bureaus may purchase traveler's checks only in pounds sterling and U.S. dollars and may purchase and sell currency notes only in Canadian dollars, deutsche mark, French (and CFA) francs, Japanese yen, pounds sterling, Swiss francs, and U.S. dollars. In practice, however, traveler's checks in other foreign currencies and other foreign currency notes are also transacted in this market. Sellers of foreign exchange to the bureaus are not required to identify their sources. Each foreign exchange bureau is free to quote buying and selling rates. All bona fide imports and approved services may be funded through the bureaus. All authorized foreign exchange dealers (which include some nonbank foreign exchange bureaus) are subject to limits on their net open positions in foreign exchange; holdings of foreign exchange in excess of these limits must be sold to other dealers or to the Bank of Ghana.

International organizations, embassies, and similar institutions are not permitted to transfer funds into Ghana through any foreign exchange bureau or to carry out foreign exchange transactions under the foreign exchange bureau scheme. There are no arrangements for forward exchange transactions, currency swaps, or guaranteed exchange rates for external debt-service payments.

Ghana accepted the obligations of Article VIII, Sections 2, 3, and 4 of the Fund Agreement on February 2, 1994.

Administration of Control

The Controller of Imports and Exports of the Ministry of Trade is empowered to prohibit or regulate all imports. The Foreign Transactions Examinations Office (FTEO) of the Bank of Ghana records and confirms foreign capital inflows and administers foreign exchange for official payments and travel. All foreign exchange transactions by the private sector are approved and transacted by authorized banks without reference to the Bank of Ghana.

Prescription of Currency

Settlements between residents of Ghana and residents of other countries may be made in permitted currencies. However, settlements related to transactions covered by bilateral payments agreements are made through clearing accounts maintained by the Bank of Ghana and the central or state banks of the countries concerned. Ghana maintains bilateral payments agreements with Bulgaria, China, Cuba, the Czech Republic, Poland, Romania, and the Slovak Republic. These agreements are inoperative, and the clearing balances are being settled. Proceeds from exports to countries with which Ghana does not have bilateral payments agreements must be received in the currency of the importing country (if that currency is quoted by the Bank of Ghana) or be debited for authorized inward payments to residents of Ghana, for transfers to other official accounts related to the same country, and for transfers to the related clearing account at the Bank of Ghana.

Nonresident Accounts

Nonresident account status is granted to embassies, legations, consulates, and offices of high commissioners in Ghana and to the non-Ghanaian members of their staffs. It is also available to interna-

---

[1] Australian dollars, Austrian schillings, Belgian francs, Canadian dollars, CFA francs, Danish kroner, French francs, deutsche mark, Italian lire, Japanese yen, Netherlands guilders, New Zealand dollars, Norwegian kroner, pounds sterling, Spanish pesetas, Swedish kronor, and Swiss francs.

tional institutions and foreign-registered companies operating in Ghana and to nonresident Ghanaians. The opening of these accounts must be approved by the Bank of Ghana. The accounts may be credited with authorized outward payments, with transfers from other foreign accounts, and with the proceeds from sales of convertible currency. They may be debited for inward payments, for transfers to other foreign accounts, and for purchases of external currencies.

Nonresident accounts maintained under the provisions of bilateral payments agreements are called official accounts or territorial accounts. They may be credited with authorized outward payments by residents; with transfers from foreign accounts; with payments received through the Bank of Ghana for settlements with bilateral payments agreement countries; and with proceeds from sales of external currencies, other than restricted currencies. They may be debited for authorized inward payments to residents of Ghana, for transfers to other official accounts related to the same country, and for transfers to the related clearing account at the Bank of Ghana.

Funds not placed at the free disposal of nonresidents—for example, certain types of capital proceeds—may be deposited in blocked accounts, which may be debited for authorized payments, including for purchases of approved securities.

Imports and Import Payments

Imports, except for those prohibited for reasons of health and security and those prohibited by Ghanaian laws, are not subject to all import-licensing requirements, but importers are required to file an Import Declaration Form, which is not subject to approval, through the authorized banks for statistical purposes. Certain imports are channeled through a bulk purchasing agent, the Ghana National Procurement Agency, while public sector imports must go through the Ghana Supply Commission.

Most imports are effected with confirmed letters of credit established through authorized Ghanaian banks on a sight basis. For all imports other than pharmaceutical products and canned, bottled, and other prepacked food products valued at more than $3,000 (f.o.b.), authorized banks are not allowed to make payments against letters of credit or bank drafts unless the import documents include a clean report of findings issued by international agencies with respect to the goods and unless they verify the price, quality, and quantity in the country of origin or shipment.

Payments for Invisibles

All payments for invisibles are approved and effected by authorized banks, provided that applications are supported by appropriate documentary evidence.

Transfers of normal bank charges payable to overseas banks for import payments are generally authorized. Commission payments on imports are permitted up to a limit of 3 percent of f.o.b. value. Freight charges may be paid to the local shipping agents; the transfer of funds to cover such charges is normally permitted, provided that the application is properly documented. Residents traveling abroad are permitted to carry a maximum of $3,000 or its equivalent in other foreign currencies. In addition, resident travelers are permitted to carry a maximum of $5,000 or its equivalent in other foreign currencies, in bank drafts or traveler's checks for direct purchases abroad. However, all bona fide applications in excess of the specified limits are approved. Authorized dealer banks are permitted to remit profits and foreign investments without prior approval from the Bank of Ghana. The exportation of Ghanaian banknotes is permitted up to 5,000.

Exports and Export Proceeds

Exports of narcotics and carrots are prohibited, as are goods prohibited by Ghanaian laws. With the exception of cocoa, which is exported through the Cocoa Board, exports of agricultural commodities have been liberalized. Diamonds are exported through the Precious Minerals Marketing Corporation and the Ghana Consolidated Diamond Company. Exports of cocoa are subject to an export tax that is calculated as the difference between export proceeds, on the one hand, and payments to farmers together with the Cocoa Board's operational costs, on the other, if the proceeds exceed the payments.

With the exceptions noted below, exporters are required to collect and repatriate in full the proceeds from their exports within 60 days of shipment; proceeds from exports of nontraditional products may be sold in a foreign exchange bureau upon receipt. Exporters are generally allowed to retain up to 35 percent of their export proceeds in foreign exchange accounts. However, the retention ratio is 60 percent for the Ashanti Gold Mining Company, 20 percent for log exporters, and 2 percent for the Cocoa Board. The retention scheme does not apply to exports of residual oil and electricity. However, receipts from the exportation of electricity do not have to be surrendered to the Bank of Ghana. Retained earnings may be held in accounts abroad for financing essential imports or credited to the exporters' foreign exchange accounts with banks located in Ghana. Provided that payments from the foreign exchange accounts of exporters are supported by relevant documents, retained export earnings may be sold at the foreign exchange bureaus or be used to import goods through a bank, to purchase airline tickets, or for foreign travel, for medical services, or educational expenses abroad, or for any other approved invisibles payments.

Proceeds from Invisibles

All receipts from invisibles must be sold to authorized dealers. Foreign currency notes may be imported freely. Repurchases of foreign exchange acquired for the purpose of foreign travel are subject to a processing fee of 0.5 percent.

Capital

Foreign investments in Ghana require the prior approval of the Ghana Investment Center if they are to benefit from the facilities available under the Investment Code of 1981, under which approved investments are guaranteed, in principle, the right to transfer profits and, in the event of sale or liquidation, capital proceeds. Tax holidays and initial capital allowances are also available for such investments. The code stipulates that the assets of foreign investors may not be expropriated. Disputes over the amount of compensation are settled in accordance with the established procedure for conciliation—for example, through arbitration by the International Center for Settlements of Investment Disputes or the United Nations Commission on International Trade and Law. Certain areas of economic activity are not open to foreigners. The proceeds from sales of foreign ownership to Ghanaian nationals are permitted to be transferred by authorized dealer banks.

Under a supplementary investment code issued in July 1985, incentives are provided to promote foreign investments that promise to be net foreign exchange earners. The main features of the 1981 and 1985 codes, which offer incentives and guarantees to encourage foreign investments in areas other than petroleum and mining (already covered by a minerals code), are as follows: (1) exemption from customs duties on imports of plant machinery and equipment; (2) more favorable depreciation or capital allowances; (3) permission to operate an external account in which at least 25 percent of the investing company's foreign exchange earnings may be retained for procuring machinery and equipment, spare parts, and raw materials; for servicing of debt; and for transfers of dividends and profits;

(4) guarantee for the remittance of foreign capital in the event of sale or liquidation; and (5) protection against expropriation. The minimum qualifying amount of investment capital is $60,000 for joint ventures with a Ghanaian partner and $100,000 for enterprises that are wholly foreign owned.

Under the Ghana Investment Promotion Center Act of 1994 (Act 478), the minimum qualifying amount of investment by a non-Ghanaian are as follows: (1) $10,000 or its equivalent in capital goods by way of equity participation in a joint-venture enterprise with a Ghanaian partner; (2) $450,000 or its equivalent in capital goods by way of equity where the enterprise is wholly owned by a non-Ghanaian; and (3) $300,000 or its equivalent in goods by way of equity capital where the enterprise shall employ at least 10 Ghanaians in the trading enterprise, involving the purchasing and selling of goods, which is either wholly or partly owned by a non-Ghanaian. All outgoing capital movements must be approved by the Bank of Ghana; applications for such transfers must be supported by documentary evidence and are considered on their merits. Transfers to beneficiaries under wills and intestacies are approved provided that all local indebtedness has been settled. Requests for the transfer of funds representing personal assets of foreign residents in Ghana who emigrate are considered individually on their merits. Applications must be supported by appropriate documentation showing that the savings are genuine and that no illegal transfer of capital is involved. Loan and overdraft facilities to resident companies do not require approval.

Resident individuals are not normally granted foreign exchange for the acquisition of securities or personal real estate abroad. Nonresidents may deal in securities listed on the Ghana Stock Exchange and they may hold up to 10 percent of such security listings. Total holdings of all external residents in a company may not exceed 14 percent. For portfolio investments, residents must obtain approval to switch holdings of securities issued by nonresidents. Private sector and commercial bank borrowing requires the approval of the Bank of Ghana, as do private import credits for machinery and equipment valued at $100,000 or more. Foreign borrowing by Ghanaian nationals is subject to certain government guidelines. Lending to nonresidents is prohibited, except for export credits, which require exchange control approval and are normally limited to 60 days.

Under a system of external accounts for debt-service payments introduced in 1980 to enable export-oriented industries to receive external aid, the industries are allowed to operate foreign exchange accounts (in addition to their regular retention accounts) with funds earmarked from export earnings for the purpose of debt-service payments. The opening of such accounts requires the approval of the Committee on Suppliers' Credits and the Bank of Ghana; the latter also monitors receipts and payments out of these accounts. Accounts have also been established for the diamond sector and for the fishing and timber companies financed with suppliers' credits.

Gold

Domestic transactions in gold, as well as imports and exports, may be authorized by the State Gold Mining Corporation in collaboration with the Bank of Ghana, and certain domestic sales may be carried out by permit under the Gold Mining Products Protection Ordinance. Ghanaian residents may not buy or borrow any gold from, or sell or lend any gold to, any person other than an authorized dealer. Imports of gold other than those by or on behalf of the monetary authorities are not normally licensed. The import duty on gold, including bullion and partly worked gold, is levied at a uniform rate of 30 percent. The gold mines export their output in semirefined form.

Changes During 1995

No significant changes occurred in the exchange and trade system.

GREECE

(Position as of December 31, 1995)

Exchange Arrangement

The currency of Greece is the Greek Drachma. Exchange rates for the U.S. dollar, the main intervention currency, and other currencies[1] are determined during a daily fixing session, in which the Bank of Greece and the authorized commercial banks participate. In the domestic spot exchange market, the commercial banks quote their own rates. On December 31, 1995, buying and selling rates in the interbank market for the U.S. dollar were Dr 236.329 and Dr 237.751, respectively, per $1. The commercial banks may levy a commission on all foreign exchange transactions on the domestic spot and forward exchange market.

Credit institutions in Greece may also freely conduct forward foreign exchange transactions, including currency swaps and options. The Bank of Greece provides credit institutions forward foreign exchange transactions including currency swaps and options.

Greece is a member of the European Monetary System (EMS). The drachma is included in the ECU basket, but Greece does not participate in the exchange rate mechanism of the EMS.

Greece accepted the obligations of Article VIII, Sections 2, 3, and 4 of the Fund Agreement on July 22, 1992.

Administration of Control

Foreign exchange regulations are administered by the Bank of Greece. Commercial banks are authorized to carry out all the necessary formalities for the settlement of imports and exports.

For statistical purposes, natural and legal persons must inform the Bank of Greece of transactions of sums greater than ECU 2,000 if a domestic banking institution is not involved.

The commercial banks are also authorized to undertake transactions in foreign exchange for invisibles and capital transactions within the framework of existing regulations.

Prescription of Currency

Settlements with all countries may be made in any convertible foreign currency or through nonresident deposit accounts in drachmas.

Accounts in Foreign Currency and Nonresident Accounts in Drachmas

Accounts in foreign currency. These accounts may be maintained in Greece by nonresident persons and entities, foreigners of Greek origin residing abroad, Greek nationals residing and working abroad (including seamen), Greek residents, and nonprofit private legal entities with a head office in Greece. These accounts may be credited with foreign exchange brought into Greece and with foreign banknotes brought into Greece and declared upon entry. Principal and interest on these accounts are freely transferable abroad. Savings and time deposits may be opened for up to 12 months. Greek residents may also open these accounts with undeclared foreign banknotes; principal and interest on these accounts may be withdrawn in drachmas and in foreign exchange but may not be transferred abroad. The Bank of Greece sets a maximum interest limit on these accounts, except for the rate on residents' deposits, which is fixed by the Bank of Greece, and the rate on nonresidents' deposits in certain currencies, which is negotiable. Greek residents may also maintain accounts in foreign currency with foreign financial institutions abroad, provided that their original maturity is at least one year. Foreign exchange loan facilities of credit institutions are authorized to all natural and legal persons residing in Greece. Deposits in foreign exchange are now permitted for money originating from foreign exchange loan facilities.

Nonresident accounts in drachmas. Nonresidents may open sight and time deposits in convertible drachmas. These accounts may be credited with (1) drachma proceeds from foreign exchange; (2) transfers of drachmas from other similar accounts of the same or other depositors, as long as the proceeds do not originate from restricted short-term transactions; and (3) drachmas derived from liberalized transactions. Interest rates on these deposits are freely negotiable. Credit institutions operating in Greece are allowed to invest these deposits in the drachma market.

---

[1] Australian dollars, Austrian schillings, Belgian francs, Canadian dollars, Cyprus pounds, Danish kroner, deutsche mark, European currency units (ECUs), French francs, Irish pounds, Italian lire, Japanese yen, Netherlands guilders, Norwegian kroner, Portuguese escudos, pounds sterling, Spanish pesetas, Swedish kronor, and Swiss francs.

Blocked accounts. Claims of non-European Union (EU) residents denominated in drachmas and deposited in blocked accounts can be withdrawn and transferred abroad without the approval of the Bank of Greece.

Imports and Import Payments

Imports from the member countries of the EU are not subject to approval or clearance procedures. Approval for imports from non-EU member countries is granted automatically by the commercial banks, either before or after the goods are shipped and the required amount of foreign exchange is made available. Imports of certain products from the former Yugoslav Republic of Macedonia are prohibited. Special import licenses are required for textiles and iron and steel products that come from low-cost countries; these products are under surveillance according to EU quotas. Special regulations govern imports of certain items such as medicines, narcotics, and motion picture films.

Import payments are not subject to official regulations; in almost all cases, they are effected on the basis of agreements between the contracting parties.

Payments for Invisibles

Authorized banks are permitted to provide foreign exchange for all invisible payments. Payments of interest, profits, and dividends are governed by the regulations that are applied to capital transfers to Greece (see section on Capital, below). Remittances for family maintenance and earnings by foreign workers are permitted, subject to documentary requirements regarding proof of need and source of income. The monthly foreign exchange allowance for studies and for trips abroad is ECU 2,000 a person. Foreign banks operating in Greece are permitted to repatriate their profits, irrespective of the nature of their operations.

Nonresidents leaving Greece within a year of their arrival may take out foreign banknotes up to the equivalent of $1,000, as well as traveler's checks and other means of payment in their name, irrespective of amount; they may also take out Dr 20,000 in Greek banknotes. Larger amounts in foreign banknotes can be taken out no later than December 31 of the calendar year following the year in which the nonresident entered Greece, provided that the banknotes are declared upon entry into Greece.

Exports and Export Proceeds

Exports of certain products to the former Yugoslav Republic of Macedonia are prohibited.

Export proceeds must be surrendered within 180 days of the date of shipment of the goods. In special cases, the authorities may extend this time limit by approving time settlement of the value of exports. Export goods are not subject to the value-added tax. Exporters are allowed to maintain balances in foreign currency accounts equivalent to 20 percent of proceeds from exports in the previous calendar year with banks operating in Greece. Exporters may use these balances to repay external obligations, including suppliers' credits, and to conduct authorized capital transactions.

Proceeds from Invisibles

Foreign exchange earnings representing payments for services must be surrendered within 90 days of the date of issue of the relevant invoice; 10 percent of these earnings from the previous calendar year may also be deposited in foreign currency accounts with banks operating in Greece. Earnings from ocean-going shipping operations are exempt from the surrender requirements, but shipowners must cover their disbursements and expenses in Greece by converting foreign exchange into drachmas.

Greek residents may bring in any amount of foreign exchange but must declare it upon entry, if they wish to take it out on their next departure, not later than December 31 of the calendar year following the year in which they entered Greece; they may also bring in a maximum of Dr 40,000 in banknotes.

Nonresident travelers may import any amount of foreign currency and need not declare it, provided they do not intend to take out amounts in excess of the equivalent of $1,000. Traveler's checks and other means of payment in a traveler's name are not subject to a limit. The amount of Greek banknotes that a nonresident may bring into Greece is limited to Dr 100,000.

Capital

Greek natural and juridical persons are allowed to borrow foreign exchange from banks, foreign juridical persons, or individuals residing abroad without prior approval from the Bank of Greece. Authorized credit institutions operating in Greece may conduct any transaction in foreign exchange, including currency and interest rate swaps and transactions in derivatives with residents and nonresidents, and they may extend loans in any form and currency to nonresidents on freely negotiated terms.

The following direct investments by residents of non-EU member countries are restricted: (1) investment in border regions; (2) investment in maritime transport; (3) acquisition of mining rights; and

(4) participation in new or existing enterprises if these are engaged in radio and television broadcasting or air transport.

Direct investments are governed by Legislative Decree No. 2687/1953, Presidential Decrees Nos. 207/1987 and 96/1993, Acts of the Governor of the Bank of Greece Nos. 825/1986 and 2227/1993.

Gold

Residents may freely purchase new gold sovereigns from the Bank of Greece at the price it has set through licensed stockbrokers. These gold coins may be resold only to the Bank of Greece or to the Athens Stock Exchange. Holders of gold coins acquired in the free market that existed before December 22, 1965, may sell them without any formality to the Bank of Greece or to an authorized bank at the official price. Imports of gold against payment in foreign exchange require a special license; licenses are normally issued to importers for distribution to jewelers and dentists. Gold bars and gold coins may be imported for other than commercial purposes when no payment in foreign exchange is involved. Exports of gold other than by the Bank of Greece are not authorized, except when gold bars or coins are brought in by travelers and declared upon entry, in which case they may be re-exported after being approved by the Bank of Greece.

Changes During 1995

Exchange Arrangement

February 10. The authorities announced a targeted rate of depreciation against the ECU of 3 percent by the end of 1995.

Imports and Import Payments

(See Appendix for a summary of trade measures introduced and eliminated on an EU-wide basis during 1995.)

Capital

May 16. Manufacturing firms were permitted to extend loans in foreign exchange to exporters and to hold deposits in foreign exchange with earned foreign exchange income.

GRENADA

(Position as of February 1, 1996)

Exchange Arrangement

The currency of Grenada is the Eastern Caribbean Dollar,[1] which is issued by the Eastern Caribbean Central Bank (ECCB). The Eastern Caribbean dollar is pegged to the U.S. dollar, the intervention currency, at EC$2.70 per US$1. On December 31, 1995, the buying and selling rates for the U.S. dollar quoted by the ECCB in its transactions with commercial banks were EC$2.7169 and EC$2.682, respectively, per US$1. The ECCB also quotes daily rates for the Canadian dollar and the pound sterling. There are no arrangements for forward cover against exchange rate risk operating in the official or the commercial banking sector.

Grenada accepted the obligations of Article VIII, Sections 2, 3, and 4 of the Fund Agreement on January 24, 1994.

Administration of Control

Exchange control, which is administered by the Ministry of Finance, applies to all countries. The Ministry delegates to authorized dealers the authority to approve some import payments and certain other outward payments. The Trade Division of the Ministry of Finance administers trade control.

Prescription of Currency

Settlements with residents of member countries of the Caribbean Common Market (CARICOM)[2] may be made either through external accounts in Eastern Caribbean dollars, in the currency of the CARICOM country concerned, or in U.S. dollars. Settlements with residents of the former Sterling Area countries, other than CARICOM countries, may be made in pounds sterling, in any other former Sterling Area currency, or in Eastern Caribbean dollars to and from external accounts. Settlements with residents of other countries may be made in any foreign currency[3] or through an external account in Eastern Caribbean dollars.

---

[1]The Eastern Caribbean dollar is also the currency of Anguilla, Antigua and Barbuda, Dominica, Montserrat, St. Kitts and Nevis, St. Lucia, and St. Vincent and the Grenadines.

[2]The CARICOM countries are Antigua and Barbuda, The Bahamas, Barbados, Belize, Dominica, Grenada, Guyana, Jamaica, Montserrat, St. Kitts and Nevis, St. Lucia, St. Vincent and the Grenadines, and Trinidad and Tobago.

[3]Foreign currencies include all currencies other than the Eastern Caribbean dollar.

Resident and Nonresident Accounts

Authorized dealers may open external accounts for nonresidents and residents without permission from the Ministry of Finance. Nonresidents may also maintain these accounts in Eastern Caribbean dollars. Foreign currency accounts may be freely debited but may be credited only with foreign exchange earned or received from outside the Eastern Caribbean area.

Foreign Currency Accounts

Residents and nonresidents are permitted to open foreign currency accounts without referring to the Ministry of Finance. Such accounts may be freely debited but can be credited only with foreign exchange earned or received from outside the ECCB area.

Imports and Import Payments

Most goods may be freely imported, but there are certain goods whose importation is prohibited or that are subject to quantitative restrictions and require a license. Prohibited goods are identified within various laws that pertain to trade, agriculture, national security, and health and include whole chickens, chicken eggs, live breeding poultry, war toys, animal skins, and various drugs deemed to be dangerous. Restricted items from non-CARICOM sources include milk, sugar, rice, a variety of tropical fruits and vegetables, carbonated beverages, arms and ammunition, industrial gas, paints, and miscellaneous items associated with furniture, clothing, and the construction industry. Items from the CARICOM area that require licenses include curry products, beer, cigarettes, industrial gas, furniture, exotic birds, solar water heaters, and various tropical fruits and vegetables.

Payments for documented imports are free of restrictions. Payments for restricted imports and any goods (and services) in excess of the limits of authorized dealers require permission from the Ministry of Finance.

Imports of capital equipment are exempt from import duties, as are imports by domestic associations involved in the production of major crops, provided that such imports are intended for quality improvements in the growing or packaging of bananas, nutmeg, and maize. Imports of fuel by the

Grenada Electric Company are exempt from customs duty as are the fuel imports of a substantial number of enterprises in the manufacturing and hotel industries. Imports that are not exempt from customs duties are subject to a consumption tax of either 15 percent, 20 percent, or 55 percent. All imports are subject to a customs service charge of 50 percent, and all non-CARICOM goods are subject to the common external tariff of 30–35 percent.

Payments for Invisibles

Authority has been delegated to authorized dealers to provide allocations of foreign exchange for payments for invisibles, of up to EC$100,000 a person a year. Applications for additional amounts are approved by the Ministry of Finance provided that no unauthorized transfer of capital is involved. Nonresident travelers may export, with the approval of the Ministry of Finance, any foreign currency they previously brought into Grenada.

Exports and Export Proceeds

Specific licenses are required for the exportation of certain goods to any destination. There exists a short list of items that require a license prior to exportation from Grenada. These include exotic birds, coral, mineral products, and live sheep and goats. There are no formal regulations to ensure that export proceeds are surrendered within a certain period after the date of shipment, but export proceeds must be repatriated.

Proceeds from Invisibles

The collection of foreign currency proceeds from invisibles is mandatory. Travelers may freely bring in notes and coins in Eastern Caribbean currency or in any foreign currency.

Capital

All outward capital transfers require exchange control approval. Residents may not purchase foreign currency securities or real estate abroad for private purposes. Certificates of title to foreign currency securities held by residents must be lodged with an authorized depository in Grenada, and earnings on these securities must be repatriated.

Personal capital transfers, such as inheritances to nonresidents, require exchange control approval, which is normally granted subject to the payment of estate and succession duties. The transfer of funds by emigrants is allowed. The Ministry of Finance considers transfer applications from foreign nationals who have resided in Grenada and are proceeding to take up permanent residence abroad on a case-by-case basis.

With exchange control approval, nonresidents may invest directly in Grenada. The remittance of earnings on, and the liquidation of proceeds from, such investment is permitted, provided that all related liabilities have been discharged and that the original investment was registered with the Ministry of Finance. Nonresidents may use foreign currency to acquire real estate in Grenada for private purposes; local currency financing is not ordinarily permitted. The repatriation of proceeds from the realization of investments requires the approval of the Ministry of Finance.

The approval of the Ministry of Finance is required for residents to borrow abroad or for nonresidents to borrow in Grenada. Authorized dealers may freely assume short-term liability positions in foreign currencies to finance approved transfers for both trade and nontrade transactions. They may also freely accept deposits from nonresidents. Any borrowing abroad by authorized dealers to finance their domestic operations requires the approval of the Ministry of Finance. Effective March 15, 1991, all restrictions on transfers of Eastern Caribbean dollars from Grenada to countries served by the ECCB were eliminated.

Gold

Residents other than monetary authorities, authorized dealers, and industrial users are not permitted to hold or acquire gold in any form other than jewelry or coins for numismatic purposes. Imports of gold are permitted for industrial purposes only and are subject to customs duties and charges. The Ministry of Finance issues licenses to import gold. The exportation of gold is not normally permitted.

Changes During 1995

No significant changes occurred in the exchange and trade system.

Changes During 1996

Payment for Invisibles

February 1. The limit on foreign exchange a person may purchase from authorized dealers without obtaining exchange control approval was increased to EC$100,000 from EC$10,000.

GUATEMALA

(Position as of December 31, 1995)

Exchange Arrangement

The currency of Guatemala is the Guatemalan Quetzal. Since March 14, 1994, exchange rates have been determined in the interbank market according to market forces. Participants in the interbank market are the Bank of Guatemala, banks, foreign exchange houses, and any other institution authorized by the Monetary Board. The Bank of Guatemala intervenes in the exchange market only to moderate undue fluctuations, to purchase foreign exchange on behalf of the public sector, and to service its own external debt. All foreign exchange transactions of the public sector must take place through the Bank of Guatemala at a reference rate that is equivalent to the weighted average of the buying and selling rates in the interbank market during the day before the previous business day.

On December 31, 1995, the buying and selling rates for the U.S. dollar in the bank market were Q 5.99034 and Q 6.01834, respectively, per $1. Buying and selling rates for currencies other than the U.S. dollar are freely quoted, mainly on the basis of their rates in the New York market.

The Bank of Guatemala does not issue exchange rate guarantees. There are no arrangements for forward cover against exchange rate risk operating in the official or the commercial banking sector.

Banks and finance companies may maintain a net foreign exchange position of up to 25 percent of the value of their paid-up capital and reserves; for the foreign exchange houses, this limit is set at 100 percent. Foreign exchange exceeding these limits at the end of each day must be negotiated in the interbank market or sold to the Bank of Guatemala.

Guatemala accepted the obligations of Article VIII, Sections 2, 3, and 4 of the Fund Agreement on January 27, 1947.

Administration of Control

The Foreign Exchange and International Department (FEID) of the Bank of Guatemala is in charge of administering the Foreign Exchange Regime. Foreign exchange transactions of the public sector are carried out exclusively through the Bank of Guatemala; those of the private sector are made through any authorized participant in the interbank market other than the Bank of Guatemala. Exports of goods must be registered in the FEID to guarantee repatriation of the corresponding foreign exchange proceeds.

Arrears are maintained with respect to certain external payments.

Prescription of Currency

In practice, most transactions in foreign exchange are denominated in U.S. dollars, domestic currency, or other means of payment, in accordance with special payments agreements.

Imports and Import Payments

Guatemala is a member of the Central American Common Market (CACM). Import tariff rates on goods from outside the region range from 1 percent to 20 percent, in accordance with Guatemala's agreement with other Central American countries on a common external tariff, and virtually all goods traded among Central American countries are exempted from tariffs. The average weighted tariff was about 7.5 percent in 1994 and 8.0 percent in 1995. At present, about 3 percent of imported items, such as vehicles and beverages, are subject to tariffs that were established freely by each member country of the CACM. The agreement provides temporary exceptions for textiles, clothing, and footwear. On December 31, 1995, the tariffs on textiles and footwear were 20 percent, on tires 15 percent, and on clothing 25 percent. A number of exceptions and special tariff regimes remain; for example, books are subject to a tariff of 0.5 percent; some products traded within the CACM, such as coffee, sugar, oil, wheat, and alcohol, are subject to tariffs of 5 percent to 20 percent; some agricultural products (yellow maize, rice, and sorghum) are subject to a band of prices with variable tariffs (between 5 percent and 45 percent);[1] and imports of chicken are subject to tariffs of 20 percent up to a monthly quota of 300 tons and of 45 percent for imports exceeding this quota.

Imports of most goods are unrestricted and require neither registration nor a license.

Exports and Export Proceeds

Foreign exchange proceeds are not required to be surrendered to the Bank of Guatemala, but must be sold to any authorized participant in the interbank

---

[1]Changes to the maximum and minimum prices for the band and the corresponding tariff table are determined at the beginning of each agricultural season.

market, other than the Bank of Guatemala. Certain exports are subject to licenses issued by the Ministry of Economy. A few other items, including gold (unless the Bank of Guatemala issues a special export license) and silver, may not be exported in any form.

Exporters must obtain an export license issued by the FEID before the Guatemalan customs can authorize shipment of the merchandise. The granting of export licenses is contingent upon agreement to sell export proceeds to any authorized participant in the interbank market, other than the Bank of Guatemala within 90 days of the date of issuance (this period may be extended to 180 days).

In the case of exports to Central America, there are arrangements among the central banks to settle payments in their own national currencies or in U.S. dollars, or through barter. If the economic agents decide to settle their payments in U.S. dollars, the export revenues must be sold to any authorized participant in the interbank market, other than the Bank of Guatemala.

Payments for and Proceeds from Invisibles

Invisible transactions relating to travel outside the country, school fees, study expenses, international credit card payments, and certain others are permitted without restriction. Proceeds from invisibles must be sold to any authorized participant in the interbank market, other than the Bank of Guatemala.

Capital

All capital transactions may take place without restriction. Nonresident (and resident) investors are exempted from a 20 percent tax on interest paid on foreign borrowing if the funds are channeled through the domestic banking system. Foreign direct investment in the petroleum sector is regulated by special legislation.

Gold

The Bank of Guatemala may buy and sell gold coins and bullion either directly or through authorized banks and is entitled to buy gold holdings surrendered by any resident. The Bank of Guatemala sells gold to domestic artistic or industrial users in accordance with the guidelines issued by the Monetary Board with the Government's approval. Exports of gold are prohibited except when the Bank of Guatemala issues a special export license. Gold is imported only by the Bank of Guatemala.

Changes During 1995

Imports and Import Payments

November 15. The Central American tariff rate on imports of capital goods was reduced to 1 percent.

GUINEA

(Position as of December 31, 1995)

Exchange Arrangement

The currency of Guinea is the Guinean Franc. Its external value is determined by the supply and demand for foreign exchange between the authorized foreign exchange dealers and their clients or among the dealers themselves. The Central Bank of Guinea, a net recipient of nonproject aid funds and mining company receipts, also participates in the interbank market because it remains a net supplier of foreign exchange. The exchange rate of the Guinean franc against the CFA franc results from the relationship between this currency and the French franc. The exchange rates for other currencies are determined on the basis of the rate of these currencies against U.S. dollar in the international market. On December 31, 1995, the official exchange rate for the Guinean franc vis-à-vis the U.S. dollar was GF 997.9843 per $1. Foreign exchange bureaus are in operation, and exchange rates in the market are determined by supply and demand conditions. There are no arrangements for forward cover against exchange rate risk operating in the official or the commercial banking sector.

Guinea's payments and transfers for current international transactions were fully liberalized in July 1994 when the remaining exchange restrictions relating to foreign travel and certain income transfers were eliminated.

Guinea accepted the obligations of Article VIII, Sections 2, 3, and 4 of the Fund Agreement on November 17, 1995.

Administration of Control

Exchange control authority is vested in the Central Bank, which has delegated to the commercial banks authority to (1) approve import forms (*descriptifs d'importation*) and import application forms (*demandes descriptives d'importation*); (2) allocate foreign exchange to travelers holding foreign airline tickets; and (3) manage foreign currency accounts opened in the name of nonresidents and residents. All settlements with foreign countries, including payments for imports, may be effected by the commercial banks.

Arrears are maintained with respect to external payments.

Prescription of Currency

Settlements on account of transactions covered by bilateral payments agreements are made in currencies prescribed by, and through accounts established under, the provisions of the agreements. Guinea maintains bilateral payments agreements with Bulgaria, China, Czech Republic, Egypt, Romania, and Slovak Republic; all agreements are inoperative. Settlements with the Central Bank of West African States (BCEAO) (Benin, Burkina Faso, Côte d'Ivoire, Mali, Niger, Senegal, and Togo) as well as The Gambia, Ghana, Guinea-Bissau, Liberia, Mauritania, Nigeria, and Sierra Leone are normally made through the West African Clearing House. Settlements with other countries are made in designated convertible currencies quoted by the Central Bank. All current transactions effected in Guinea must be settled in Guinean francs.

Resident and Nonresident Accounts

Guinean residents may maintain and operate deposit accounts in foreign currency at the domestic commercial banks. Exporters may hold all of their foreign exchange receipts in local bank accounts.

Nonresidents may maintain accounts in Guinean francs and, subject to notification of the Central Bank by commercial banks, nonresident transferable accounts in foreign currencies.

Accounts in convertible Guinean francs may be opened by residents and nonresidents. They are to be credited with deposits in foreign exchange, irrespective of its origin. The accounts may be debited freely and converted by commercial banks into foreign currencies without prior authorization from the Central Bank. Interest rates on these accounts are negotiated between the account holder and the bank.

Imports and Import Payments

All products except armaments, ammunition, and narcotics may be freely imported into Guinea.

All imports of less than $200,000 require authorization, which is granted by the commercial banks on behalf of the Central Bank.

To obtain authorization, importers are required to fill out either an import form (for imports valued at $5,000 or less f.o.b.) or an import application request form (for imports valued at more than $5,000 f.o.b.), on which they must provide information concerning the products to be imported, including price, quantity, quality, and financing terms.

For imports financed with foreign exchange obtained from the interbank foreign exchange market, where rates are determined freely by demand and supply, authorization is given only after price, quality, and terms of financing (for import credits) are verified. Requests for foreign exchange must be submitted through commercial banks at the daily fixing sessions.

Imports financed with importers' own foreign exchange resources (*autorisation sans achat de devises*) comprise goods for which foreign exchange is derived from sources other than the official foreign exchange resources of Guinea and mainly covers imports by two "mixed-economy" companies the Friguia Company and the Guinea Bauxite Company, and foreign embassies.

All imports are subject to a 13 percent turnover tax, custom duties (DFE) of 8 percent, and customs charges (DDE) of 7 percent, with the following exceptions: animals, flour, sugar, pharmaceutical products, and fertilizers are subject to a 6 percent DFE and a 2 percent DDE; and imports for the food industry, cement, and agricultural machinery are subject to an 8 percent DFE and a 2 percent DDE. In addition, a surtax of 20 percent or 30 percent is imposed on all luxury goods, and a surtax of 30 percent to 60 percent is levied on nonalcoholic beverages, certain wines, and spirits. Imports of the three mixed enterprises in the mining sector are regulated by special agreements and are subject to a 5.6 percent levy.

Payments for Invisibles

All payments for invisibles may be made freely.

The Investment Law of 1985 (as amended in 1987 and 1995) guarantees that profits earned from approved foreign investments may be transferred abroad and that certified dividends and royalties may be transferred in full. It also provides for certain tax incentives. The transfer abroad of salaries by expatriate workers is authorized up to a limit of 50 percent of base earnings and only for those contracts approved by the Ministry of Labor. The exportation of Guinean currency is limited to GF 5,000 a person a trip.

Exports and Export Proceeds

All private sector exports require domiciliation with a commercial bank and submission of an export description to help prevent shortages of goods needed for domestic consumption and to identify capital outflows. Exports of the mining sector are exempt from this requirement.

The exportation of wild animals (dead or alive), meats, articles of historic or ethnographic interest, jewelry, articles made of precious metals, and plants and seeds require special authorization from designated agencies. Planters may be granted special authorization to export a specific quantity of pineapples, bananas, or citrus fruits.

Private traders may retain all of their export proceeds to finance authorized imports. Gold exporters and vendors are required to surrender their export proceeds but may retain 25 percent to 50 percent of proceeds in foreign exchange deposits with commercial banks. This amount may be increased depending on the volume and type of products, especially with respect to gold and diamonds. The mixed-economy companies are allowed to retain all of their export proceeds abroad and may use the balances to pay for their imports and operating requirements and to service their external debt.

Proceeds from Invisibles

Residents are not required to surrender exchange proceeds accruing from invisibles. The importation of foreign banknotes and traveler's checks is permitted freely, subject to declaration on entry; residents, however, must surrender both to commercial banks within 15 days of their return. Residents are authorized to deposit their foreign exchange proceeds in foreign currency or convertible Guinean franc accounts. The Central Bank levies a fee of 0.5 percent of proceeds in foreign banknotes transferred through commercial banks. The importation of Guinean currency is limited to GF 5,000 a traveler a trip.

Capital

All capital transfers through the official exchange market require authorization from the Central Bank. Outward capital transfers by Guinean nationals through the official market are prohibited.

The Investment Law of 1985 (as amended in 1987 and 1995) provides guarantees against the nationalization of foreign investments in the industrial and mining sectors. It also provides for preferential tax and customs treatment applicable to foreign investments and for the transfer of profits, interest, amortization, and liquidation proceeds of such investments. Small and medium-size enterprises with assets of GF 15–200 million are granted import tax reductions and exempted from the minimum corporate tax for a period of 8–10 years. Exemptions for up to 15 years may be granted on long-term investments of particular importance to the economy. The minimum foreign investment in Guinean enterprises is GF 10 million.

Guinean nationals must have controlling interests in enterprises requiring foreign investment of GF 10 million to GF 50 million.

Gold

The Central Bank purchases gold in Guinean francs at international prices; at the seller's request, the Central Bank may purchase 50 percent of output in foreign currency. Since the monetary reform of 1986, Guinea has issued fine silver commemorative coins of GF 10,000, which are legal tender. Transactions in nonmonetary gold are not subject to restriction. Only the exportation of gold is subject to prior authorization by the Central Bank.

Changes During 1995

Exchange Arrangement

November 17. Guinea accepted the obligations of Article VIII, Sections 2, 3, and 4 of the Fund Agreement.

Imports and Import Payments

January 1. All imports were subject to a turnover tax of 13 percent to be applied to the value of the imports, inclusive of the import tariff.

GUINEA-BISSAU

(Position as of December 31, 1995)

Exchange Arrangement

The currency of Guinea-Bissau is the Guinea-Bissau Peso. The Central Bank of Guinea-Bissau sets official buying and selling exchange rates for its transactions and for those of government agencies. The official buying rate against the U.S. dollar, which serves as the intervention currency, is adjusted as necessary and maintained within a 2 percent average of the freely determined rates quoted by the two commercial banks, exchange bureaus, and the parallel market rate. The spread between the buying and selling rates of the official and commercial rates is subject to a maximum of 2 percent. The Central Bank regularly intervenes in the market through sales of foreign currencies to the commercial banks and legally established exchange bureaus.

On December 31, 1995, the official buying and selling rates for the U.S. dollar were PG 21,927 and PG 22,365, respectively, per $1.

There are no taxes or subsidies on purchases or sales of foreign currency in Guinea-Bissau. There are no arrangements for forward cover against exchange rate risk in the banking or commercial sector.

Administration of Control

The Central Bank exercises control over foreign exchange transactions involving the use of foreign exchange belonging to or administered by it. Foreign exchange transactions effected by commercial banks with resources derived from sources other than those of the Central Bank are, in general, not controlled by the Central Bank. Residents are permitted to sell foreign exchange in their possession without revealing its sources.

Arrears are maintained with respect to external payments.

Prescription of Currency

Settlements with foreign countries are normally made in foreign currencies, although certain external obligations have been settled with goods on a few occasions in the past. Guinea-Bissau participates in the West African Clearing House, which includes member countries of the Central Bank of West African States (Benin, Burkina Faso, Côte d'Ivoire, Mali, Niger, Senegal, and Togo) as well as The Gambia, Ghana, Guinea, Liberia, Mauritania, Nigeria, and Sierra Leone.

Nonresident Foreign Currency Accounts

Nonresidents may open demand and time accounts in foreign currency with commercial banks and may use balances in these accounts without restriction, except that they must give prior notice for withdrawals above certain pre-established limits. Residents may also maintain these accounts (1) if they are authorized to engage in foreign currency transactions; or (2) if they receive income in foreign currency under contracts with nonresidents. Banks may pay interest up to 4 percent a year on demand accounts in foreign currency, whereas interest rates on time deposits may be negotiated freely.

Imports and Import Payments

All imports, regardless of whether they involve use of official or free market foreign exchange, require a prior import license (*Boletim de Registo Prévio de Importação*) issued by the Ministry of Commerce and Tourism. Since official availability of foreign exchange in the country is not considered when licenses are issued, import licenses are not a foreign exchange allocation instrument, and their possession does not guarantee the importers access to the official exchange market. Except for a short negative list, licenses are issued automatically after verification of invoice prices for goods to be imported.

Importers are free to arrange for payment through the banking system with their own foreign exchange or foreign exchange purchased on the free market. However, payments for imports with foreign exchange purchased from, or administered by, the Central Bank require its authorization, which is granted on the basis of the priority of the products involved and the availability of foreign exchange.

Under the general regime, imports are subject to a customs service tax of 6 percent to 10 percent and, since June 1995, to a surcharge of 3 percent.

Payments for Invisibles

Payments for invisibles by the public sector at the official exchange rate are effected through the Central Bank. Payments for invisibles by the private sector take place at the freely determined exchange rate and may be made without restriction. These payments may take place through commercial banks and the foreign exchange bureaus. Residents are allowed up to the equivalent of $5,000 for travel expenses but may be granted foreign exchange in excess of that amount with special authorization from the Central Bank.

Foreign travelers may take out on departure any unspent foreign exchange that they declared upon entry.

Exports and Export Proceeds

All exports require a prior export license (*Boletim de Registo Prévio de Exportação*). Only exporters registered with the Ministry of Commerce and Tourism may obtain these licenses, which are granted automatically in most cases. As in the case of imports, prior licenses are intended primarily for statistical purposes, although they are also used to check the prices of exports.

In general, all exports are subject to a customs service tax of 5 percent. In addition, exports of cashew nuts are subject to a special tax, whose rate has been reduced over the years and is currently 13 percent. Agricultural exports are also subject to a rural property tax (*Contribuição Predial Rústica*), at the rate of 2 percent on processed products and 1 percent on unprocessed products.

Special arrangements apply to exports to member countries of the Economic Community of West African States (Ecowas), to which Guinea-Bissau belongs; for example, exports to these countries are exempt from the 6 percent customs service tax.

All export proceeds must be surrendered to the national banking system; the intermediary bank purchases for its own account 70 percent of the proceeds at a rate freely agreed with the exporter and purchases the remaining 30 percent on the account of the Central Bank at the official buying rate in the exchange table issued by the Central Bank effective on the date of settlement of the export transactions (Circulars Nos. 4/92, 1/94, and 1/96).

Proceeds from Invisibles

There is no surrender requirement on foreign exchange received from abroad, which can be sold freely in the exchange market.

Capital

Foreign direct investments are governed by the Investment Code of 1985, which was amended most recently by Decree-Law No. 4/91, promulgated on September 30, 1991. Foreign and domestic investments are subject to the same terms with respect to access to domestic credit. The Investment Code provides incentives to foreign direct investment and protection against nationalization of investment and expropriation of assets, and recognizes the right of foreign investors to transfer foreign currency abroad in respect of profits (net of taxes), to sell or liquidate investments, to service loans obtained for project financing, and to make payments for imported supplies and technical assistance.

Gold

Exports and imports of gold are prohibited unless expressly authorized by the appropriate government authorities. The Central Bank may engage in gold purchases and sales transactions with the public.

Changes During 1995

Imports and Import Payments

June 30. A 3 percent tariff surcharge on the customs value of imports was implemented (exemptions were granted to certain entities).

Exports and Export Proceeds

July 31. The portion of export proceeds that must be surrendered at the official exchange rate was reduced to 30 percent from 40 percent.

GUYANA

(Position as of December 31, 1995)

Exchange Arrangement

The currency of Guyana is the Guyana Dollar, the external value of which is determined freely by market forces in the cambio market. The Bank of Guyana conducts certain transactions on the basis of the cambio rate by averaging quotations of the three largest dealers in the cambio market on the date the transaction takes place. In accordance with the bilateral agreements with the central banks of the Caribbean Community and Common Market (CARICOM), the Bank of Guyana quotes weekly rates for certain CARICOM currencies.[1] On December 31, 1995, the average buying and selling rates in the cambio market were G$137.57 and G$141.66, respectively, per US$1. The Bank of Guyana quotes rates for pounds sterling and Canadian dollars on the basis of the U.S. dollar-pound sterling and the U.S. dollar-Canadian dollar cross rates quoted by the Bank of England. The Bank of Guyana charges commissions at different rates on purchases and sales of officially quoted currencies.

Transactions effected through the Bank of Guyana are limited, on the receipts side, to exports of sugar, and gold, and, on the payments side, mainly to imports of fuel, and official debt-service payments. All other transactions are effected in the cambio market. There are no taxes or subsidies on the purchases or sales of foreign exchange.

The only arrangement for forward cover against exchange rate risk operates in the official sector in respect of exchange rate guarantees that are provided to certain deposits in blocked accounts. (See section on Resident and Nonresident Accounts, below.)

Guyana accepted the obligations of Article VIII, Sections 2, 3, and 4 of the Fund Agreement on December 27, 1966.

Administration of Control

Exchange control authority is vested in the Minister of Finance, who has entrusted this authority to the Bank of Guyana. The Ministry of Trade, Tourism, and Industry is responsible for issuing import and export licenses.

With the establishment of the cambio market under the Dealers in Foreign Currency (Licensing) Act (on March 13, 1990), the Bank of Guyana, under the Exchange Control Act, suspended exchange control notices that related to (1) basic travel allowances; (2) correspondence courses; (3) subscriptions to clubs and societies, including entrance fees; (4) payments for periodicals, magazines, etc.; and (5) emigration. Also, until further notice, dealers are no longer authorized to accept deposits into the external payments deposit scheme.

Under the Dealers in Foreign Currency (Licensing) Act, with the payment of a fee of G$250,000, individuals, partnerships, and companies may be licensed for one year (renewable) to engage in foreign currency dealings; these dealers are required to submit weekly returns of the transactions they conduct to the Bank of Guyana.

Prescription of Currency

Settlements with residents of foreign countries may be made in any foreign currency or through an external account in Guyana dollars.[2]

Resident and Nonresident Accounts

There are three categories of accounts for persons who are not residents of Guyana: external accounts, blocked accounts, and nonresident foreign exchange accounts.

External accounts may be opened, with exchange control approval, for persons who temporarily reside in Guyana and who enjoy diplomatic privileges and immunities. They may be credited freely with all authorized payments by residents of Guyana to nonresidents and with transfers from other external accounts; other credits require approval. They may be debited freely for payments for any purpose to residents of any country, for transfers to other external accounts, and for withdrawals by the account holder while he or she is in Guyana.

Blocked accounts may, in principle, be credited with funds that are not placed at the free disposal of nonresidents (for example, certain capital pro-

---

[1]For the operations of the CARICOM Bilateral Settlement Arrangements, the Bank of Guyana sets rates for the CARICOM currencies every Friday on the basis of the average rates of the commercial banks and the five largest nonbank cambio dealers in the week ending the preceding Wednesday. The currencies to which this rate applies are the Barbados dollar, the Eastern Caribbean dollar, and the Belize dollar.

[2]Foreign currencies comprise all currencies other than the Guyana dollar.

ceeds); these accounts may be debited for certain authorized payments, including purchases of approved securities. Since mid-1978, blocked accounts have been used to hold domestic currency deposits equivalent in value to pending applications for foreign exchange. Such deposits carry a market-related interest rate. The Bank of Guyana provides a partial exchange rate guarantee at the rates of G$3.25–G$3.75 per US$1 for deposits made before the devaluation of January 1984; at G$5 per US$1 for deposits made between January 1984 (after devaluation) and the end of January 1987; at G$10 per US$1 for deposits made between January 1987 and the end of March 1989; and no exchange rate guarantee for deposits made after March 1989.

Nonresident foreign currency accounts may be opened by commercial banks without the prior approval of the central bank for citizens of Guyana residing permanently abroad; citizens of other countries temporarily residing in Guyana; nonresidents attached to diplomatic missions or international organizations; branches of companies incorporated outside of Guyana; and companies incorporated in Guyana but controlled by nonresidents abroad. These accounts may be credited with noncash instruments of convertible foreign currencies transferred through the banking system and transfers from external accounts. They may be debited freely for any payments at the discretion of the account holder.

Exporters are allowed to maintain and operate foreign exchange accounts. These accounts are approved on merit but are generally granted to bona fide exporters who require imported inputs for production and/or have external loan obligations. These accounts may be credited with all or a portion of retained export proceeds and proceeds of foreign currency loans. They may be debited freely for any payments at the discretion of the account holder.

Imports and Import Payments

Imports of unprocessed meat, poultry, fruit, and processed fruit items, are restricted, subject to import-licensing controls, from all non-CARICOM sources. There are no licensing requirements for permissible imports, except for petroleum products and some 20 items affecting national security, health, public safety, and the environment.

Intra-CARICOM trade is free of import duties, quotas, and import-licensing arrangements. The Common External Tariff (CET) of the CARICOM is applied to imports from outside the CARICOM. Guyana, in compliance with an agreement among the CARICOM members, is implementing a phased reduction in the CET rate structure from a band of 30 percent to

one ranging between 30 percent and 5 percent to one ranging from 5 percent to 20 percent by January 1, 1998. The maximum tariff rate was lowered from 30 percent to 25 percent at the beginning of September 1995.

There are no import quotas. Import payments effected by commercial banks on behalf of the Bank of Guyana require the Bank's prior approval. Before the introduction of the cambio market, all applications for official foreign exchange were required to be accompanied by a domestic currency deposit of equivalent value, to be held in blocked accounts with commercial banks. Commercial banks are required to maintain a 100 percent reserve requirement against these deposits at the Bank of Guyana.

In general, import transactions effected through the cambio exchange market are permitted without restriction; most imports of consumer goods take place on this basis.

Payments for Invisibles

Payments for invisibles to all countries may be freely effected through the cambio market. Foreign exchange for tourist travel and education may be purchased in the cambio market without restriction. Resident and nonresident travelers are subject to an exit tax of G$1,500 on departure.

There are no restrictions on the amount of foreign or local currency that may be taken out for foreign travel.

Exports and Export Proceeds

Sugar may be exported only by the Guyana Sugar Corporation, and bauxite and alumina only by Linmine, Bermine, and Aroaima Bauxite Company. Certain other exports are also channeled through official agencies. Rice may be exported by the Guyana Rice Development Board and the private sector. Most exports do not require export licenses, but transactions are monitored by the Bank of Guyana and the Customs and Excise Department to ensure that all proceeds of exports are repatriated and offered for sale to a licensed dealer. Exchange control forms have to be completed for all exports whose value exceeds G$20,000.

A foreign exchange retention scheme permits some exporters to retain a certain percentage of export proceeds. The retention ratio is 70 percent for sugar and gold exported through the Guyana Gold Board and 100 percent for all other exports. Retained foreign exchange may be used freely in the cambio market.

Proceeds from Invisibles

Proceeds from invisibles are not subject to surrender requirements and may be retained or sold in the cambio market without restriction. Travelers may freely bring in any amount in foreign or domestic currency notes; travelers entering the country with foreign currency in excess of the equivalent of G$10,000 must declare the amount.

Capital

Private investment, both foreign and domestic, is governed by the Guyana Investment Policy of 1988. Foreign-based companies and their subsidiaries may borrow in Guyana only with the express approval of the Bank of Guyana. There are no restrictions on repatriation of capital. Residents and nonresidents have unlimited access to the cambio market for repatriation of funds.

Borrowing from nonresidents requires exchange control approval.

Gold

Residents other than monetary authorities, authorized dealers, producers of gold, and authorized industrial users are not allowed to hold or acquire gold in any form (except gold coins held for numis-matic purposes and jewelry), at home or abroad, without special permission. Imports and exports of gold in any form by or on behalf of monetary authorities, authorized dealers, producers of gold, and industrial users require permits issued by the Guyana Gold Board.

Changes During 1995

Resident and Nonresident Accounts

May 26. The Capital Issues (Control) Act of 1995 was passed in the National Assembly, substantially repealing the Capital Issues (Control) Act of 1973.

Imports and Import Payments

September 1. The second stage reduction in the new CARICOM CET to a maximum of 25 percent became effective.

Exports and Export Proceeds

April 18. The foreign exchange retention ratio for sugar and gold exports through the Guyana Gold Board was raised from 40 percent to 50 percent.

December 31. The retention ratio for proceeds from sugar exports and from gold export through the Guyana Gold Board was raised from 50 percent to 70 percent.

HAITI

(Position as of December 31, 1995)

Exchange Arrangement

The currency of Haiti is the Haitian Gourde, and its external value is determined on the basis of demand and supply in the exchange market. The U.S. dollar circulates freely and is generally accepted in Haiti; since April 1995, the Bank of the Republic of Haiti, the central bank, has been operating a dollar clearinghouse. Commercial banks quote buying and selling rates for certain other currencies, based on the buying and selling rates of the U.S. dollar in exchange markets abroad.

On December 31, 1995, the buying and selling rates were 16.41 and 16.61, respectively, per $1.

There are no arrangements for forward cover against exchange rate risk operating in the official or the commercial banking sector.

Haiti accepted the obligations of Article VIII, Sections 2, 3, and 4 of the Fund Agreement on December 22, 1953.

Administration of Control

The Bank of the Republic of Haiti administers the foreign exchange system. Article 52 of the decree-law of September 28, 1991 provides for a penalty, payable to the tax authorities, equal to 20 percent on any commercial foreign exchange transaction not conducted through a bank established in Haiti.

Prescription of Currency

There are no obligations prescribing the method or currency for payments to or from nonresidents.

Resident Accounts

Commercial banks may open accounts in foreign exchange in favor of residents; in accordance with Article 2 of the Decree of January 18, 1990, these accounts may be credited with export proceeds, with transfers from abroad received by exchange houses, or with receipts from maritime agencies and non-governmental organizations.

Imports and Import Payments

The tariff regime includes four tariffs rates (zero, 5 percent, 10 percent, and 15 percent). Four products have special rates: gasoline (25 percent), and cement, rice, and sugar (3 percent). Customs tariffs and the value-added tax applicable to most imports are calculated on the basis of the gourde equivalent of the c.i.f. value of the imported good, valued at the market exchange rate. The domestic turnover tax (TCA) is based, legally, on the c.i.f. value plus import duties. All imports, except for inputs used by certain export industries, are subject to a consular fee of 3 percent, which is payable in Haiti. Also, a 1 percent administrative fee is levied on all imports.

Exports and Export Proceeds

There is no surrender requirement. Exports of agricultural products require prior authorization from the Ministry of Commerce and Industry. Authorization is usually granted freely but may be withheld when domestic supplies are low. Exporters are required to negotiate documentary drafts with local commercial banks to ensure the repatriation of their export proceeds. The customs administration does not grant export approval unless those drafts are cleared by the Bank of the Republic of Haiti.

Payments for and Proceeds from Invisibles

Payments for invisibles are not restricted. Residents traveling abroad must pay a tax of G 275 on tickets. All travelers pay an airport tax. The tax for Haitian residents is G 125 and for nonresidents, $25 or G 30. Diplomats and staff members of international organizations accredited in Haiti are exempt from both taxes. Proceeds from invisibles are not required to be surrendered. There are no limits on the importation or exportation of foreign or domestic banknotes.

Capital

Capital transactions in gourdes are restricted; in practice, however, these restrictions are not implemented. Foreign investment in Haiti is regulated by the Decree of October 30, 1982, and requires prior government approval. Permission is normally not granted for nonresidents to invest in handicraft industries. Private banks operating in Haiti are required to keep a minimum of 85 percent of their liabilities in the form of domestic assets for local customers. This requirement is not enforced.

Gold

Residents may hold and acquire gold coins in Haiti for numismatic purposes. With this exception, residents other than the monetary authorities and authorized industrial users are not allowed to hold or acquire gold in any form other than jewelry, at home or abroad. The Bank of the Republic of Haiti has the exclusive right to purchase gold domestically and to export gold in the form of coins, mineral dust, or bars. Gold in any form, other than jewelry carried as personal effects by travelers, may be imported and exported only by the central bank; exports of gold require, in addition, prior authorization from the Ministry of Commerce and Industry and the Ministry of Finance and Economic Affairs, as well as an endorsement from the Ministry of Commerce and Industry, before customs clearance. However, commercial imports of articles containing a small amount of gold, such as gold watches, are freely permitted and do not require an import license or other authorization. Several gold coins have been issued, which are legal tender but do not circulate.

Changes During 1995

Exchange Arrangement

April 1. The Bank of the Republic of Haiti began to operate a dollar clearinghouse.

Administration of Control

May 30. External payments arrears were eliminated.

Imports and Import Payments

April 1. The maximum import tariff was lowered to 15 percent from 57 percent (excluding tariff on gasoline set at 25 percent). The tariff regime was simplified to four tariff rates ranging from zero to 15 percent. The value of imports would be determined at the market exchange rate.

June 30. A 1 percent administrative surcharge was applied to all imports.

Exports and Export Proceeds

March 31. The surrender requirement was eliminated.

HONDURAS

(Position as of April 30, 1996)

Exchange Arrangement

The currency of Honduras is the Honduran Lempira. The interbank foreign exchange system was suspended temporarily on July 17, 1994, and a foreign exchange auction system was introduced. Under this system, banks and exchange houses are required to sell all their daily foreign exchange purchases to the Central Bank of Honduras, which auctions at least 60 percent of its purchases. Buyers (banks, exchange houses, or private individuals) bid a price that cannot differ from a base price set by the authorities by more than 1 percent in either direction. The maximum bid in an auction is $200,000. The base exchange rate is adjusted every Monday on the basis of the average of the rates realized during the previous week's auctions. Auction rates cannot deviate from the base rate by more than 0.5 percent in either direction. Auctions are held once each working day. Effective April 19, 1996, natural and juridical persons were allowed to participate in the auction through a foreign exchange dealer, directly or indirectly. The base rate would be modified after every five auctions according to changes in the differential between domestic and international inflation and in the exchange rates of the currencies of trading partners of Honduras with respect to the U.S. dollar. At the end of 1995, the base price vis-à-vis the U.S. dollar was L 9.18 per $1 and the reference rate was L 9.28 per $1. Banks and exchange houses sell foreign exchange to the public at the auction price plus a commission of less than 1.5 percent. Debt conversions are conducted at the rate of L 2 per $1. Purchases and sales of the currencies of other Central American countries are effected on the basis of quotations in lempiras, taking into account the value of those currencies in terms of U.S. dollars in the interbank markets of the countries concerned. There are no takes or subsidies on purchases or sales of foreign exchange. There are no arrangements for forward cover against exchange rate risk operating in the official or the commercial banking sector.

Honduras accepted the obligations of Article VIII, Sections 2, 3, and 4 of the Fund Agreement on July 1, 1950.

Administration of Control

The Central Bank administers exchange control regulations. Exporters are required to present a declaration to the External Financing Department of the Central Bank (DERFE), which maintains an import registry for statistical purposes only. Foreign investment regulations are administered by the Secretary of Economy and Trade. Arrears are maintained with respect to external payments.

Prescription of Currency

There are no regulations prescribing the method of payment to or from nonresidents. Trade transactions with the rest of Central America may be carried out in local currencies, barter and compensation mechanisms, or U.S. dollar proceeds from exports to the rest of the Central American countries.

Resident and Nonresident Accounts

Foreign currency accounts may be maintained with domestic banks without restriction. Banks are required to hold these deposits in (1) foreign currency notes in their vaults, (2) special accounts at correspondent banks abroad, (3) investments in high-liquidity foreign instruments, or (4) advance export- or import-financing instruments.

Imports and Import Payments

Registration is required for all imports valued at more than $5,000. Imports of arms and similar items require a license issued by the Ministry of Defense.

The financing of imports is channeled either through the banking system or through exchange houses, with foreign exchange purchased in the free market or with credits obtained abroad (except for financing obtained through export advances or government credit agreements with external institutions).

Imports are subject to customs duties, ranging from zero to 20 percent.[1] The duty-free zone in Puerto Cortés, industrial processing zones, and firms registered under the regime of temporary imports (a drawback regime) are exempt from customs duties.

Exports and Export Proceeds

Exports are required to be registered only for statistical purposes. All foreign exchange proceeds, except those from trade with other Central American

---

[1] Over 1,600 products from other Central American countries are exempt from customs duties, except for an import surcharge of 1.5 percent.

countries, must be surrendered to authorized banks or exchange houses. Exporters are allowed to retain up to 30 percent of their foreign exchange proceeds to finance their own imports, as well as to pay for their authorized foreign exchange obligations. Proceeds from exports of coffee and bananas must be surrendered within 25 days; the surrender period for other exports ranges from 30 days to 120 days. The commercial banks and exchange houses are required to sell to the Central Bank all their foreign exchange purchases. Exports of coffee are supervised by the Honduran Coffee Institute.

Bananas are subject to an export tax at the rate of $0.50 for a 40-pound box, but production from newly planted areas is exempt from the tax, and production from rehabilitated areas is subject to a tax at the rate of $0.25 a box. Sugar is subject to an export tax if its export price exceeds a specified level. Coffee exports of which the f.o.b. value is more than $80 a quintal (100 kilograms) are subject to a 10 percent income tax on the obtained above export price and price of $80 a quintal.

Payments for and Proceeds from Invisibles

All buyers of foreign exchange are required to fill out a form stating the purpose for which the funds will be used. There are no limits on the amount purchased. There are no restrictions on the importation of foreign banknotes by travelers. Proceeds from invisibles are not required to be repatriated.

Capital

There are no restrictions on activities involving the receipt of foreign exchange and its transfer abroad for investment in mutual funds, housing developments, real estate, or similar activities. Foreign mutual funds and similar financial institutions must have permission to collect funds in Honduras for deposit or investment abroad. The approval of Congress is required for all public sector foreign borrowing. Private sector external debt contracts must be registered with the Central Bank for statistical purposes only.

Purchases of capital shares in existing domestic firms and foreign direct investments are permitted in all sectors without restriction, with the exception of defense-related industries, hazardous industries, and small-scale industry and commerce. Investments in hazardous industries require prior approval. All foreign investments must be registered with the Secretary of Economy and Trade, and repatriation of registered capital and transfers of dividends and profits earned on such capital are not

restricted. Investment insurance may be arranged in Honduras or abroad without restriction.

Gold

Residents may hold and acquire gold coins in Honduras for numismatic purposes. With this exception, residents other than the monetary authorities and authorized industrial users are not allowed to hold or acquire gold in any form other than jewelry at home or abroad. Imports and exports of gold in any form other than jewelry require licenses issued by the Central Bank; such licenses are not normally granted except for imports and exports by or on behalf of the monetary authorities, industrial users, and producers of gold. All locally produced gold is exported in the form of ore for refining. Commercial imports and exports of jewelry and other articles containing gold require licenses issued by the Ministry of Economy; for most articles, licenses are granted freely. Exports of gold are subject to a tax of 5 percent.

Changes During 1995

Exchange Arrangement

October 24. The method of adjusting the exchange rate was changed: the frequency of adjustments was increased to once a week (previously the base rate was adjusted only after the average auction rate stayed at the upper limit of a band of 1 percent, in each direction, of the existing basic rate for 15 consecutive days), and the band within which the auction rate can move was narrowed to 1 percent, that is, 0.5 percent in each direction.

Imports and Import Payments

January 1. The 10 percent customs surcharge was eliminated, and the 5 percent customs service surcharge was lowered to 3 percent.

Changes During 1996

Exchange Arrangement

April 19. Natural and juridical persons were allowed to participate in the auction through a foreign exchange dealer, directly or indirectly. The base rate would be modified after every five auctions according to changes in the differential between domestic and international inflation and in the exchange rates of the currencies of trading partners of Honduras with respect to the U.S. dollar.

Imports and Import Payments

January 1. The customs service surcharge was lowered to 1.5 percent.

HONG KONG[1]

(Position as of December 31, 1995)

Exchange Arrangement

The currency of Hong Kong is the Hong Kong Dollar. The authorities do not maintain margins in respect of exchange transactions. Since October 17, 1983, the Hong Kong dollar has been linked to the U.S. dollar, the intervention currency, at the rate of HK$7.80 per US$1. Under this linked exchange rate arrangement, the three note-issuing banks must deliver to the Exchange Fund an amount in U.S. dollars that is equivalent to the local currency issued at the linked exchange rate as backing for their Hong Kong dollar note issues. The Exchange Fund, in turn, issues to each note-issuing bank non-interest-bearing certificates of indebtedness denominated in Hong Kong dollars. Conversely, the note-issuing banks may redeem U.S. dollars from the Exchange Fund by delivering certificates of indebtedness and withdrawing local banknotes from circulation at the same linked exchange rate. The amount of indebtedness of the Exchange Fund represented by the certificates of indebtedness will be reduced accordingly. Other banks may acquire local currency notes from the note-issuing banks against Hong Kong dollar deposits for Hong Kong dollar value. The exchange rate of the Hong Kong dollar is set in the exchange market at freely negotiated rates for all transactions except those that are conducted for the note-issuing purposes between the Exchange Fund and the note-issuing banks. On December 30, 1995, the middle rate in the interbank foreign exchange market for the U.S. dollar was HK$7.732 per US$1. There are no taxes or subsidies on purchases or sales of foreign exchange. The forward exchange markets are operated on private sector initiatives, and the Government has no official role.

Administration of Control

There are no exchange controls. Import and export licensing is carried out mainly by the Director-General of Trade.

Prescription of Currency

No prescription of currency requirements are in force. Settlements between residents of Hong Kong and nonresidents may be made and received freely in Hong Kong dollars or any other currency.

Nonresident Accounts

No distinction is made between resident and nonresident accounts.

Imports and Import Payments

There are no restrictions on imports, except for those maintained for reasons of health, safety, environmental protection, or security. All imports are free of duties, although an excise tax for revenue and health purposes is levied on imported and domestically produced cigarettes and other tobacco products, liquors, methyl alcohol, and some hydrocarbon oils. With a few exceptions, a trade declaration must be lodged with the Customs and Excise Department within 14 days of importation or exportation in respect of each consignment of goods imported into or exported from Hong Kong. Payments for permitted imports may be made freely, at any time and in any currency.

Exports and Export Proceeds

Export licenses and certificates of origin are required for certain textile products to enable Hong Kong to fulfill its international obligations under the World Trade Organization (WTO) Agreement on Textiles and Clothing. Other export restrictions are maintained for reasons of health, environmental protection, safety, or security. Export proceeds may be collected at any time and in any currency, and need not be repatriated or surrendered.

Payments for and Proceeds from Invisibles

There are no limitations on payments for or receipts from invisibles. Income from foreign sources, capital gains, distribution from trusts, and dividends are not taxed in Hong Kong; interest income from domestic sources received by licensed banks and corporations carrying on business in Hong Kong is subject to a profit tax. Interest earned on bank deposits by individuals is exempt from the salary tax. Resident and nonresident travelers may

---

[1] Hong Kong is a nonmetropolitan territory in respect of which the United Kingdom has accepted the Fund's Articles of Agreement.

freely bring in and take out any amount in domestic or foreign banknotes, traveler's checks, and other means of payment.

Capital

No exchange control requirements are imposed on capital receipts or payments by residents or non-residents. A license or an authorization is required for companies, whether incorporated in Hong Kong or elsewhere, to conduct banking, insurance, securities, and futures dealings. Otherwise, all overseas companies are required only to register with the Companies Registry within one month of establishing a place of business in Hong Kong.

Gold

Free and unrestricted markets for gold and gold futures are open to residents and nonresidents. Imports and exports of gold in any form (including finished jewelry) are freely permitted and do not require licenses. Residents may hold gold in any form and amount in Hong Kong or abroad. Commemorative gold coins of HK$1,000 are legal tender but do not circulate.

Changes During 1995

No significant changes occurred in the exchange and trade system.

HUNGARY

(Position as of January 31, 1996)

Exchange Arrangement

The currency of Hungary is the Hungarian Forint. Since March 13, 1995, the exchange rate of the forint is adjusted in accordance with a preannounced rate of crawl; the rate of devaluation, which takes place against a currency basket comprising the European currency unit (ECU) (70 percent) and the U.S. dollar (30 percent), was 1.9 percent a month between March 13 and June 30, 1995, and was reduced to 1.3 percent during the second half of 1995. Prior to March 13, 1995, the peg was adjusted periodically, mainly to accommodate differences between the domestic and foreign inflation rates.

The official exchange rate is fixed at about noon every day against the basket and is calculated for 20 convertible currencies and the ECU,[1] within margins of ± 2.25 percent, but licensed banks are free to determine their own margins within this band. The National Bank of Hungary intervenes at the market rate to keep it within the margin of the peg. The official spot buying and selling rates for the U.S. dollar on December 31, 1995, were Ft 139.1 and Ft 139.8, respectively, per $1. Banks are free to set the exchange rates for currency notes and traveler's checks.

As a transitional measure, transferable and clearing rubles continue to be used (1) for the settlement of certain outstanding financial claims related to contracts concluded before the end of 1990, and (2) for other settlements that are to be phased out. For outstanding claims, official exchange rates are quoted for the transferable and clearing ruble. At the end of December 1995, the middle rate for the forint against one transferable or clearing ruble was Ft 27.50. The National Bank of Hungary does not quote the exchange rate of the forint for currencies of countries belonging to the former Council for Mutual Economic Assistance (CMEA) and many other countries; for cash transactions in those currencies, the exchange rates are freely determined by the commercial banks and exchange offices.

Agreements between Hungary and the Slovak Republic permit their national currencies to be converted into each other's currency through their respective banking systems for the purpose of tourist travel and the settlement of certain noncommercial transactions between the two countries at exchange rates freely determined by the commercial banks and exchange offices; they also stipulate limits on the importation of banknotes by travelers. Interbank settlements between the two countries in Hungarian forint and Slovak koruny have been small and are effected through only one Hungarian commercial bank and one Slovak commercial bank. The Czech Republic abandoned similar agreements with Hungary in the first half of 1993. As far as cash transactions are concerned, a free exchange market exists for the Slovak koruna, with trading handled by about 30 organizations; for the Czech koruna, trading is handled by four or five organizations; and for the currencies of Poland, the Baltic countries, Russia, and the other countries of the former Soviet Union, most trading is handled by one organization.

The commercial banks may engage in forward transactions with terms ranging from seven days to one year, and forward exchange rates may be negotiated freely between the banks and their customers. The commercial banks may also enter into foreign currency swaps with the National Bank.

Hungary accepted the obligations of Article VIII, Sections 2, 3, and 4 of the Fund Agreement on January 1, 1996.

Administration of Control

Authority for enforcement of foreign exchange regulations is vested in the National Bank.

All economic organizations and private persons in Hungary are entitled to carry out foreign trade activity in convertible currencies and Hungarian forint provided that foreign trade was part of their business activities when incorporated.

Hungary continues to maintain payments restrictions against Iraq, in accordance with UN Security Council Resolution No. 661.

Prescription of Currency

Payments to and from countries with which Hungary has bilateral payments agreements are made in the currencies and in accordance with the procedures set forth in those agreements. If there are no specific

---

[1] Australian dollars, Austrian schillings, Belgian francs, Canadian dollars, Danish kroner, deutsche mark, Finnish markkaa, French francs, Irish pounds, Italian lire, Japanese yen, Kuwaiti dinars, Netherlands guilders, Norwegian kroner, Portuguese escudos, pounds sterling, Spanish pesetas, Swedish kronor, Swiss francs, and U.S. dollars. In addition to the above, exchange rates are quoted for banknotes and traveler's checks in Greek drachmas.

agreements, or if trade takes place outside the scope of the agreements, settlement is normally made in forint or in a convertible currency officially quoted in Hungary. At the end of 1995, inoperative bilateral agreements were maintained with Albania, Bulgaria, Cambodia, Lao People's Democratic Republic, Poland, Romania, Russia, and Vietnam for the settlement of outstanding transferable or clearing ruble balances in connection with shipments of goods.

Hungary's only remaining operative bilateral payments agreements are with Brazil and Ecuador. Under these agreements, outstanding balances are settled every 90 days.

With respect to outstanding balances under inoperative bilateral payments agreements, settlements have been reached in most cases. Hungary was a net debtor only to the former German Democratic Republic and settled the outstanding balance in convertible currency at the end of 1995. Russia, the largest net debtor to Hungary, has agreed to settle the amount owed by the end of 1997 through the delivery of goods and services or debt-equity swaps.

Resident and Nonresident Accounts

Nonresident natural and juridical persons, as well as resident natural persons, may freely maintain convertible currency accounts at authorized commercial banks. Resident juridical persons may open convertible currency accounts only with funds originating from specific sources, such as export receipts; foreign borrowing; capital paid in convertible currency by the foreign owners of joint-venture companies; donations paid in convertible currency for foundations, churches, and social organizations; and budgetary institutions. The accounts carry interest that is payable in the currency of deposit and have a guarantee of repayment up to a maximum of the equivalent of Ft 1 million with no exchange rate guarantee in case of conversion. The interest rates on deposits are determined by the commercial banks. No authorization is required to open such accounts or to draw on them.

Nonresidents may open convertible joint accounts that may be credited with lawfully acquired forints; proceeds from the conversion of convertible currency or forints acquired illegally can be placed in a nonconvertible forint account, which does not bear interest.

Imports and Exports

Beginning in December 1990, a general authorization was granted to all entities to import and export goods without a specific license except for those items on a negative list. A global quota is reported to the World Trade Organization (WTO) on imports of certain consumer goods that are subject to license by the Ministry of Industry and Commerce and settled in convertible currencies. A license is required for imports that are destined for the settlement of outstanding balances in transferable or clearing rubles.

Importers have the right to purchase foreign exchange through the banking system for all bona fide imports. When applying for foreign exchange, importers have to complete a declaration stating the use of the foreign exchange. The National Bank conducts a random check of banks and enterprises for compliance with the regulations.

Commercial banks and enterprises may enter into deferred payment arrangements on behalf of their clients without restriction; arrangements exceeding three months must be reported to the National Bank by the client. These arrangements need not be secured by bank obligations.

Export proceeds must be received in officially quoted convertible currencies, in Hungarian forint, or in a nonconvertible currency. In all cases, such proceeds must be repatriated to Hungary within eight days of receipt of the foreign exchange. Certain exemptions are granted, subject to specific approval by the National Bank. Since April 1, 1995, foreign exchange receipts may be deposited in a foreign exchange account at a domestic bank but can only be used for all liberalized transactions. Enterprises engaged in foreign trade are required to provide the National Bank with annual reports showing claims outstanding in connection with their export activities. Export proceeds received in forint by nonresidents may be deposited in convertible forint accounts with licensed banks, and nonresidents are allowed to convert balances in such accounts into foreign exchange for transfer abroad.

Goods for personal use brought in by returning Hungarian travelers are subject to a general import duty of 15 percent, based on the actual invoice price with a duty-free allowance of Ft 8,000. Residents, if they are employees of a domestic agency and if they are stationed abroad for more than one year, may import, free of customs duty, goods for personal use up to a value equivalent to 40 percent of their earnings. A temporary 8 percent import surcharge was introduced on March 20, 1995.

Certain exports are prohibited for health, security, and other noneconomic reasons. An export subsidy may be provided for exports of agricultural products and processed foods settled in convertible currencies or forint. The value-added tax paid on goods that are exported is refunded. The refund and the subsidy are calculated on the basis of the customs invoice value.

New trade agreements with former CMEA countries, based on free market principles and providing for settlements in convertible currencies at world market prices with no official overdraft, credit, or clearing facilities, are in effect since December 1992, with Albania, Armenia, Belarus, Bulgaria, the Czech Republic, Estonia, Georgia, Lithuania, Moldova, Poland, Romania, Russia, the Slovak Republic, Ukraine, Uzbekistan, and Vietnam. Such agreements are in effect with China, Croatia, Kazakstan, and Latvia since end-1993. The Trade Protocol of the Association Agreement between Hungary and the European Union entered into force on March 1, 1992, with the help of the Interim Agreement. The Association Agreement entered into force in its entirety at the beginning of 1994. The Visegrad agreements of the Central European Free Trade Area (CEFTA) with Poland, the Czech Republic, and the Slovak Republic entered into effect in March 1993, and the trade agreement with five European Free Trade Association (EFTA) countries (Austria, Liechtenstein, Norway, Sweden, and Switzerland) entered into effect in October 1993. Hungary concluded a free trade agreement with Slovenia with effect from January 1, 1996.

Payments for and Proceeds from Invisibles

The foreign exchange law of November 7, 1995, abolished restrictions on all payments and transfers for current international transactions.

Capital

Under the National Bank Law, approved by the Parliament on December 1, 1991, financial institutions must report all foreign borrowing to the National Bank. Foreign borrowing of other legal entities with a maturity of less than one year is subject to the approval of the National Bank. The granting of credits to foreigners by Hungarian financial institutions is, in most cases, limited to credits with maturities of up to one year. Commercial credits with maturities of over one year made in connection with foreign trade activities between nonfinancial legal entities need authorization.

Foreign investment in the form of joint ventures with Hungarian enterprises may be established without approval, but in the case of banks, foreign participation exceeding 10 percent of equity requires government approval. Joint ventures may also be established in duty-free zones. In both cases, the joint venture is considered as a Hungarian legal entity, but those in duty-free zones are exempted from several regulations. Machines and equipment, technical know-how, and patents may qualify as foreign investment. Guarantee is given by law for the transfer of the foreign investors' share of profits or, if the joint venture is liquidated, of the invested capital and capital gains. In addition, a guarantee may be obtained from Hungarian banking institutions to cover the fulfillment of obligations of the Hungarian partner.

Foreign investment by resident economic organizations, either by establishing subsidiaries or affiliates or by acquiring an interest in a foreign enterprise, is free if the equity share is more than 10 percent.

Portfolio investment inflows must be registered, and permission, in most cases granted by the National Bank, is not automatic. In September 1994, foreigners were permitted to buy one-year discount Treasury bills and, under the foreign exchange law, they were allowed to buy most Hungarian securities with maturities longer than one year without obtaining permission from the National Bank, effective January 1, 1996.

Except for gifts with a market value of up to Ft 100,000, the transfer of economic assets abroad by residents is subject to licensing administered by the National Bank. Gifts (movable property that is in Hungary, except securities and other such instruments) from nonresidents to residents and vice versa, in excess of Ft 100,000 a person can be freely given and accepted. Nonresidents are not generally allowed to acquire real estate or other immovable property in Hungary, except through inheritance, and authorization is granted by the county municipalities. Joint ventures can own the real estate necessary for their activities without authorization.

Outward capital transfers by resident natural persons are generally free, except for security transactions, which are subject to the same restrictions as enterprises.

Emigrants to OECD countries can freely take with them all their assets; emigrants to other countries can take assets up to Ft 1 million.

Gold

All trade in monetary gold is subject to the authority of the National Bank. All ingots and gold coins must be repatriated. Except for transactions with enterprises specifically authorized to transact in gold, all transactions in monetary gold are subject to licensing administered by the National Bank.

Changes During 1995

Exchange Arrangement

March 13. The exchange rate was devalued by 8.3 percent and from that date, the exchange rate peg has been adjusted in accordance with a preannounced rate of crawl; prior to that date, the exchange rate was adjusted at irregular intervals.

November 7. A new foreign exchange law was passed by Parliament to take effect as of January 1, 1996.

Imports and Exports

January 1. Food items and underwear were eliminated from the global import quota list.

March 20. A temporary 8 percent import surcharge was introduced. (Authorities intend to remove the import surcharge in mid-1997.)

April 1. Exporters were granted an exception to the general rule that requires conversion into forint of export proceeds. Under this rule, exporters are allowed to deposit export receipts in domestic banks.

Changes During 1996

Exchange Arrangement

January 1. Hungary accepted the obligations of Article VIII, Sections 2, 3, and 4 of the Fund Agreement.

Capital

January 1. Under the new foreign exchange law, some capital account restrictions were eliminated; foreigners were allowed to buy most Hungarian securities with maturities longer than one year without obtaining permission from the National Bank, and outward equity investment was permitted, provided that an equity share of over 10 percent is acquired.

ICELAND

(Position as of December 31, 1995)

Exchange Arrangement

The currency of Iceland is the Icelandic Króna. The external value of the króna is pegged to a basket of 16 currencies.[1] The official exchange rate is determined in the interbank market in a daily fixing meeting. The participants in the market are the Central Bank of Iceland and four commercial banks, including the Savings Bank Association. The Central Bank intervenes in the exchange market to keep the exchange rate within a margin of ±6 percent around the central rate. On December 31, 1995, the buying and selling rates were ISK 65.14 and ISK 65.22, respectively, per US$1, the principal trading currency in Iceland. Banks and other foreign exchange dealers are free to set their own commercial exchange rates and to decide the spread between buying and selling rates. There is no organized forward market and no forward exchange rate is quoted for the Icelandic króna by either the Central Bank or the private sector. However, forward cover may be freely obtained in other currencies.

Iceland accepted the obligations of Article VIII, Sections 2, 3, and 4 of the Fund Agreement on September 19, 1983.

Administration of Control

The Ministry of Industry and Commerce has ultimate responsibility for matters concerning imports and, in consultation with the Central Bank, on foreign exchange regulations. Export controls are administered by the Ministry of Foreign Affairs and Foreign Trade. All foreign exchange transactions, including capital transactions, are free of restrictions unless explicitly prohibited by provisions of the Exchange Act No. 87/1992 or the Foreign Exchange Regulation that came into effect on January 1, 1995.

Currently, the exchange control functions of the Central Bank include authorizing foreign exchange dealers to operate on a commercial basis, carrying out reporting requirements for statistical purposes, and implementing the regulation on foreign direct investments. The administrative control of foreign trade in goods, such as tax duties and documentation, is carried out by the customs authorities.

In accordance with the Fund's Executive Board Decision No. 144–(52/51) adopted on August 14, 1952, Iceland notified the Fund on July 31, 1992 that, in compliance with UN Security Council Resolution No. 757 (1992), certain restrictions had been imposed on the making of payments and transfers for current international transactions in respect of the Federal Republic of Yugoslavia (Serbia/Montenegro). On December 1, 1995, Iceland notified the Fund that exchange restrictions against Libya had been imposed in accordance with UN Security Council Resolution No. 883 (1993).

Prescription of Currency

There are no prescription of currency requirements.

Nonresident Accounts

There are no restrictions on nonresident accounts with respect to the amounts, currencies, or instruments involved. All accounts in domestic banks must be identified by name and identification number, and the banks must report to the Central Bank the monthly position of nonresident accounts.

Imports and Import Payments

Imports of goods are free of restriction, except by provision in other legislation or international agreements. Such a restriction would not apply to foreign embassies except for health reasons.

Most goods can be imported freely without a license. The main exemptions are live animals and certain agricultural products. Certain imports, including fertilizers, tobacco, and alcoholic beverages, can only be imported under state trading arrangements. Some fresh vegetables, including potatoes, and flowers are subject to periodic import control. For imports that require a license, a fee of 1 percent is assessed on the króna value of the import license when it is issued.

Automobiles are subject to a special import tax ranging between zero and 32 percent, depending on the weight of the vehicle and its engine capacity. Buses, heavy trucks, ambulances, and public service vehicles are exempt. Certain goods, whether imported or domestic, are subject to a special excise

---

[1] These currencies are the Belgian franc, Canadian dollar, Danish krone, deutsche mark, Finnish markka, French franc, Italian lira, Japanese yen, Netherlands guilder, Norwegian krone, Portuguese escudo, the pound sterling, Spanish peseta, Swedish krona, Swiss franc, and U.S. dollar.

tax of 24 percent or 30 percent ad valorem. On September 1, 1995, restrictions on alcoholic beverages were lifted; their retail sales, however, remain under a state trading arrangement. A specific import tax applies to wines and spirits, with the amount of tax depending on the alcohol content and volume.

No exchange control requirements are imposed on payments for imports.

Exports and Export Proceeds

Exports of fish and agricultural products require licenses issued by the Ministry of Foreign Affairs and Foreign Trade.

No exchange controls are imposed on receipts from exports.

Payments for and Proceeds from Invisibles

No exchange controls are imposed on payments for or proceeds from invisibles.

Capital

Both inward and outward capital transfers are generally free of restrictions if not prohibited by provisions of exchange regulations or other special legislation. Foreign governments, local authorities, and other public authorities are prohibited from issuing debt instruments in Iceland unless permitted by the Central Bank.

Foreign direct investments in Iceland are regulated, in accordance with special legislation No. 34/1991, as follows: (1) nonresidents are free to make investments in Iceland, subject to the conditions laid down in general legislation governing foreign investment or sector-specific legislation; (2) only resident Icelandic citizens or domestically registered companies wholly owned by resident Icelandic citizens may fish within the Icelandic fishing limit or operate primary fish processing facilities; (3) only Icelandic state and local authorities, resident Icelandic citizens, and domestically registered Icelandic companies wholly owned by resident Icelandic citizens may acquire the right to harness waterfalls and geothermal energy; the restrictions apply to power production and distribution companies; (4) investment by nonresidents in domestic airlines is restricted to 49 percent; (5) investment by nonresidents in domestic incorporated commercial banks is restricted to 25 percent, but foreign commercial banks are allowed to open branches in Iceland; and (6) total investment by single nonresidents, or by financially linked nonresidents, in excess of ISK 250 million per year is subject to

authorization by the Minister of Commerce. This financial limit is subject to change in the price index.

In some sectors of the economy, sectoral legislation stipulates that either some or all of the founders or managing directors of a company must be residents. The legislation on joint-stock companies stipulates that the majority of founders must be residents before the company is established. The managing director and a majority of the members of the board of directors of a company must be residents. Citizens of the European Economic Area are exempted from this restriction, and the Minister of Commerce may grant exceptions to this requirement.

The ownership and uses of real estate in Iceland are governed by the provision of Act No. 19/1966 with amendments in 1991 and 1993. The conditions to own real estate in Iceland are (1) individuals must be Icelandic citizens; (2) in the case of unlimited companies, all owners must be Icelandic citizens; and (3) joint-stock companies must be registered in Iceland, at least 80 percent must be owned by Icelandic citizens, and all of the members of the board of directors must be Icelandic citizens. Icelandic citizens must control the majority of the voting power at annual meetings. The same conditions apply if the real estate is to be leased for more than three years or if the lease agreement cannot be terminated with less than one year's notice. However, a company that is granted an operating license in Iceland may acquire real estate for its own use as long as the license does not carry with it the right to exploit natural resources. Citizens of the European Economic Area and other foreign citizens that have been domiciled in Iceland for at least five years are exempted from these restrictions. The Minister of Justice may grant others exemption from these requirements.

Short-term foreign borrowing and lending by residents to nonresidents are permitted without limits.

Gold

A commemorative gold coin with a face value of ISK 100 is legal tender but does not circulate. Residents may hold and acquire gold in Iceland and abroad.

Changes During 1995

Exchange Arrangement

September 6. The official basket of currencies against which the exchange rate of the króna is determined was changed from one composed by the ECU, the U.S. dollar, and the Japanese yen to one composed of 16 currencies. Additionally, the authorities widened the band for the fluctuation of the currency around the central exchange rate from ±2.25 percent to ±6.0 percent.

Administration of Control

January 1. The surrender requirement for foreign exchange receipts by residents was abolished. All financial limits on short-term capital movements were removed. The requirement that securities must be purchased through intermediary authorized dealers was abolished, and restrictions on forward contracts and other financial derivatives were abolished.

December 1. Iceland notified the Fund that exchange restrictions against Libya had been imposed in accordance with UN Security Council Resolution No. 883 (1993).

Imports and Import Payments

July 1. A license fee of 1 percent for imports that require a license was abolished.

September 1. Imports of alcoholic beverages became free of restrictions but their retail sale remains under a state trading arrangement.

Capital

January 1. Limits on short-term financial transactions were removed.

INDIA

(Position as of December 31, 1995)

Exchange Arrangement

The currency of India is the Indian Rupee, the exchange value of which is determined by demand and supply in the interbank market. The Reserve Bank of India purchases spot U.S. dollars from authorized persons at the central office at a rate determined on the basis of the market exchange rate. It does not normally purchase spot deutsche mark, Japanese yen, or pounds sterling. The Reserve Bank has on occasion purchased or sold forward U.S. dollars. The Reserve Bank may enter into swap transactions, under which it buys spot U.S. dollars and sells forward for up to six months. The Reserve Bank is obligated to sell spot U.S. dollars on the basis of the market exchange rate only for debt service payment purposes on behalf of the Government of India. Since July 6, 1995, debt service payments of the Government are being increasingly effected through the exchange market. On December 29, 1995, the indicative market rate for the U.S. dollar (average of the buying and selling rates) as announced by the Foreign Exchange Dealers Association of India (FEDAI) was Re 25.75 per $1; on December 30, 1995, the Reserve Bank's reference rate for the U.S. dollar was Re 35.18 per $1.[1]

Exchange rates against other currencies are derived from the cross rate of the U.S. dollar with the Indian rupee. The Reserve Bank stands ready to purchase and sell spot and to sell forward currencies of the member countries of the Asian Clearing Union (ACU)[2] at rates determined on the basis of the Reserve Bank's reference rate for the rupee in terms of the U.S. dollar, which is calculated with reference to the rates prevailing in the interbank market around noon and the SDR–U.S. dollar rate published by the International Monetary Fund (IMF).[3]

Authorized dealers may maintain balances and positions in "permitted currencies," that is, foreign currencies that are freely convertible (currencies that the authorities of the countries concerned permit to be converted into major currencies and for which a fairly active market exists for dealings against other major currencies). Authorized dealers are also permitted to maintain balances and positions in European currency units (ECUs) abroad. Authorized dealers are permitted to deal spot or forward in any permitted currency; however, there are restrictions on authorized dealers' net foreign exchange exposure and on their borrowing and lending activities abroad. Forward purchases or sales of foreign currencies against rupees with banks abroad are prohibited.

The Export Credit Guarantee Corporation of India, Ltd. (ECGC) provides protection against exchange fluctuation in connection with deferred receivables from the date of a bid up to 15 years after the award of a contract; exchange cover is offered in Australian dollars, deutsche mark, French francs, Japanese yen, pounds sterling, Swiss francs, U.A.E. dirhams, and U.S. dollars. For payments specified in other convertible currencies, cover is provided at the discretion of the ECGC.

India accepted the obligations of Article VIII, Sections 2, 3, and 4 of the Fund Agreement, as from August 20, 1994.

Administration of Control

Exchange control is administered by the Reserve Bank in accordance with the general policy laid down by the Government in consultation with the Reserve Bank. Much of the routine work of exchange control is delegated to authorized dealers. Import and export licenses, where necessary, are issued by the Director General of Foreign Trade.

Prescription of Currency

For prescription of currency purposes, countries are divided into two groups: member countries of the ACU (except Nepal) and the external group (all other countries). Payments to countries other than those of the ACU may be made in Indian rupees to the accounts of a resident of any of these countries or in any permitted currency. Receipts from countries other than member countries of the ACU may be obtained in Indian rupees from accounts maintained with an authorized dealer or in banks situated in any of the countries in the external group or in any permitted currency.

---

[1]The reference rate is the rate announced by the Reserve Bank of India at 12 noon, based on quotations from five major banks.

[2]Bangladesh, Islamic Republic of Iran, Myanmar, Pakistan, and Sri Lanka; Nepal is a member of the ACU, but the Reserve Bank does not deal in Nepalese rupees.

[3]In accordance with the amendments in the ACU Agreement and the Procedure Rules of September 1, 1995, trade among ACU countries (except between India and Nepal) has been settled in U.S. dollars or any other convertible currency since January 1, 1996.

All remittances by nationals of China to any country outside of India and all remittances to China by any person residing in India, whether for personal or trade purposes, were prohibited as of November 3, 1962. Since the resumption of trade between India and China, remittances arising out of trade transactions are permitted in conformity with exchange control regulations. Restrictions on non-trade-related transactions with China have been abolished. Authorized dealers are permitted to open rupee accounts in the names of their branches or correspondents in Pakistan without prior notification to the Reserve Bank but must obtain approval before opening such accounts in the names of branches of Pakistan banks operating outside Pakistan. Authorized dealers may effect remittances to Pakistan on behalf of private importers, as in the case of imports from other countries; they may also effect certain types of personal remittances in accordance with regulations applicable to such remittances; remittances for other purposes require prior approval from the Reserve Bank.

Receipts from the external group of countries may be obtained in rupees from the accounts of banks situated in any country in the group; the accounts must be maintained with an authorized dealer or in any permitted currency. However, special rules may apply to exports under lines of credit extended by the Government of India to the governments of certain foreign countries. All payments on account of eligible current international transactions between India and other members of the ACU except Nepal are required to be settled through the ACU arrangement, as are transactions effected on a deferred basis with ACU countries. However, settlement of payments for imports of sugar, fertilizer, and pulses from any of the ACU countries may be made outside the ACU mechanism in any permitted currency. Payments relating to current transactions financed with loans from international institutions are also effected outside the ACU mechanism. Indian exporters are also permitted to accept payment in free foreign exchange for their exports to ACU countries, provided such payment is voluntarily offered by the importer in the ACU country.

Resident and Nonresident Accounts

The rupee accounts of Indians and of Bhutanese and Nepalese nationals residing in Bhutan and Nepal, as well as the accounts of offices and branches of Indian, Bhutanese, and Nepalese firms, companies, or other organizations in Bhutan and Nepal, are treated as resident accounts. However, residents of Nepal may obtain their foreign exchange requirements from the Nepal Rastra Bank; accounts related to all other foreign countries are treated as nonresident accounts. Accounts of banks in the external group of countries may be credited with payments for imports, interest, dividends, and other authorized purposes with authorized transfers from the nonresident accounts of persons and firms (including banks), and with proceeds from sales of permitted currencies. They may be debited for payments of exports and for other payments to residents of India. These accounts may also be debited for transfers to nonresident accounts of persons and firms (including banks) and transfers to nonresident external rupee (NRER) accounts. The balances in the accounts of banks may be converted into any permitted currency. All other entries on bank accounts require prior approval from the Reserve Bank.

Ordinary nonresident rupee accounts of individuals or firms may be credited with (1) the proceeds of remittances received in any permitted currency from abroad through normal banking channels, balances sold by the account holder in any permitted currency during his or her visit to India, or balances transferred from rupee accounts of nonresident banks; and (2) legitimate dues paid in rupees by the account holder in India. For credits exceeding Re 10,000, authorized dealers are required to ascertain the bona fide nature of the transaction before crediting the account. Authorized dealers may debit the ordinary nonresident rupee accounts for all local disbursements, including investments in India that are covered by the general or special permission of the Reserve Bank.

Nonresident external rupee accounts may be opened by authorized dealers in India for persons of Indian nationality or origin who reside outside of India, or for overseas companies and partnership firms of which at least 60 percent is owned by nonresidents of Indian nationality or origin. In addition to authorized dealers holding licenses under the 1973 Foreign Exchange Regulation Act, some state cooperative banks, certain urban cooperative banks, and certain commercial banks not holding such licenses have also been permitted by the Reserve Bank to open and maintain nonresident rupee accounts, subject to certain conditions. Such accounts may also be opened for eligible persons during temporary visits to India against the tender of foreign currency traveler's checks, notes, or coins. They may be credited with new funds remitted through banking channels from the country of residence of the account holder or from any country. They may also be credited with foreign currency traveler's checks, personal checks, and drafts in the name of the account holder, with foreign currency notes and coins tendered by the account holder while in India, and with income on authorized investments. The transfer of funds from other NRER accounts or foreign currency nonresident (FCNR) accounts is also allowed for bona fide personal purposes. The accounts may be debited for disbursement in India and for transfers abroad. Debiting is also permitted for any other transaction if covered under general or special permission granted by the Reserve Bank.

Balances may also be used to purchase foreign currency, rupee traveler's checks, or traveler's letters of credit for the use of the account holder; his or her family and dependents; and, in the case of corporate entities, for the use of directors and employees. Investments in the shares of Indian companies or in partnership firms and the like or in immovable property may be made with the specific or general approval of the Reserve Bank. Interest on deposits in nonresident external accounts in any bank in India is exempt from the personal income tax, although juridical persons are not entitled to this exemption. Interest earnings are transferable. The balances held in such accounts by natural and juridical persons are exempt from the wealth tax; gifts to close relatives in India from the balances in these accounts are exempt from the gift tax.

Foreign currency nonresident accounts denominated in deutsche mark, Japanese yen, pounds sterling, or U.S. dollars may be held in the form of term deposits by persons of Indian nationality or origin and by overseas companies specified above. These accounts may be credited with amounts received through normal banking channels, including interest. Balances may be repatriated at any time without notification to the Reserve Bank. Balances may also be used for the same purposes as those allowed for debits to NRER accounts. Effective May 15, 1993, a new FCNR (Banks) Scheme was introduced, and the previous FCNR A Scheme was abolished, effective August 15, 1994; however, the exchange rate guarantees issued by the Reserve Bank on existing deposits under the scheme remain in effect until the deposits mature. The FCNR B Scheme operates in the same manner as the previously existing accounts, except that the issuing bank (not the Reserve Bank) provides the exchange rate guarantee on deposit balances.

Nonresident (nonrepatriable) rupee deposit accounts may be opened by nonresident Indian nationals, overseas corporate bodies predominantly owned by nonresident Indian nationals, and foreign citizens of non-Indian origin (except Pakistani and Bangladeshi nationals). These accounts may be opened with funds in freely convertible foreign exchange remitted from abroad or funds transferred from existing NRER or FCNR accounts. The funds in these accounts may not be repatriated abroad at any time. Since October 1994, accruing interest has been permitted to be transferred abroad.

Foreign currency ordinary (nonrepatriable) deposit accounts may be maintained by nonresidents.[4] These accounts may be denominated in U.S. dollars and credited with funds received from abroad in freely convertible foreign exchange or transferred from existing NRER or FCNR accounts. On maturity of deposits, the rupee value of the principal and accrued interest may be credited to the ordinary nonresident rupee accounts of the depositor.

Imports and Import Payments

Imports from Fiji and Iraq are prohibited.

Capital goods, raw materials, components, spare parts, accessories, instruments, and other goods are freely importable without restriction by anyone, whether the actual user or not, unless such imports are regulated by the negative list of imports.

The negative list of imports consists of prohibited items, restricted items, and canalized items. The prohibited items are tallow, fat and/or oils that are rendered, unrendered, or otherwise of animal origin; animal rennet; wild animals (including their parts and products); and ivory.

All consumer goods (including consumer durables), except those specifically permitted, are restricted, and their importation is permitted only with a license. Also the importation of certain specified precious, semiprecious, and other stones; safety, security, and related items; seeds, plants, and animals; insecticides and pesticides; drugs and pharmaceuticals; chemicals and allied items relating to the small-scale sector; and certain other items is restricted. The importation of restricted items is allowed selectively with a license or in accordance with general schemes laid down through public notices for import based on the merit of the application. A large number of consumer goods, including all edible oils (excluding coconut oil, palm kernel oil, RED palm oil, and RBO palm stearin); sugar; cameras; roasted or decaffeinated coffee; paper and paper products of various types; sporting goods; and wood and wood products of various types, are freely importable. The importation of

---

[4]With effect from August 20, 1994, commercial banks have been prohibited from accepting new deposits and, with effect from October 1, 1994, interest accruing on existing balances has been permitted to be transferred abroad.

restricted items has been liberalized by permitting a large number of specified restricted items (including certain consumer goods) to be imported with freely transferable special import licenses that are granted to export houses, trading houses, star trading houses, super star trading houses, exporters of electronic and telecommunications equipment, deemed exporters, and exporters and manufacturers who have acquired prescribed quality certification. Certain specified types of petroleum products, fertilizers, edible and nonedible oils, and seeds and cereals are canalized for import through the state trading enterprises, i.e., Indian Oil Corporation Ltd., Minerals and Metals Trading Corporation of India Ltd., State Trading Corporation of India Ltd., and the Food Corporation of India. Gold and silver may be imported with transferable special import licenses. However, the importation of gold up to five kilograms is allowed as part of the baggage of passengers of Indian origin or passengers holding a valid passport issued under the Passports Act of 1967, who come to India after staying abroad for a period of not less than six months, and is subject to payment of customs duty in convertible currency.

Import licenses are issued with a validity of 12 months; in the case of capital goods imports, they are valid for 24 months. Advance licenses are granted for duty-free imports of raw materials, intermediates, components, consumables, parts, accessories, packing materials, and computer software required for direct use in the product to be exported. When a valid import license is held, the required foreign exchange is released by an authorized bank on presentation of the exchange control copy of the license and the shipping documents. License holders may make payments by opening letters of credit or by remitting against sight drafts. The contracting of suppliers' credits exceeding 180 days and other long-term import credits is subject to prior approval. Payments for imports may not generally be made before shipping documents are submitted, except for goods with import values of up to 15 percent with a maximum of $5,000. Advance payments in excess of $5,000 (up to 15 percent in the case of capital goods) may be made by authorized dealers against guarantees from a bank of international repute outside India. However, in special cases—for example, imports of machinery and capital goods for which deposits have to be made with overseas manufacturers—the Reserve Bank grants special authorization for advance payment for a portion of the value of the import.

In addition to any applicable import duty, imports are subject to an auxiliary duty of up to 50 percent ad valorem. Among the exemptions are food grains, raw cotton, and books.

Payments for Invisibles

Authority has been delegated to authorized dealers to approve payments for invisibles and remittances up to specified limits. These limits are indicative, and the dealers have been authorized to approve all bona fide requests for amounts exceeding these limits for purposes including business travel, participation in overseas conferences or seminars, studies or study tours abroad, medical treatment and checkups, and specialized apprenticeship training. Authority has also been delegated to authorized banks to approve remittances for certain purposes, without limit, subject to certain guidelines. Restrictions on the transfer abroad of current income (net of taxes) earned on investments by nonresident Indians and overseas corporations predominantly owned by nonresident Indians, and of other current income, such as pensions, are to be phased out during the financial years 1994/95 to 1996/97. Earnings that have accumulated during the period up to March 31, 1994, however, will remain nontransferable. Under the statement of industrial policy announced in July 1991, transfers abroad of dividends from consumer goods industries by nonresident investors must be balanced by export earnings for a period of seven years from the date of commencement of commercial production.

Premiums on insurance policies issued in foreign currency to foreign nationals who do not reside permanently in India may be paid only in foreign currency; payment in rupees may be made only on annuities issued against payment from recognized superannuation or pension funds; Indian residents are prohibited from taking out life insurance policies in foreign currencies.

Branches of foreign banks are not allowed to transfer abroad any profits arising from the sale of nonbanking assets. Profit remittances by branches of foreign firms, companies, and banks require the prior approval of the Reserve Bank. Remittances of profits, dividends, and interest to beneficiaries whose permanent residence is outside of India are allowed, subject to certain conditions and provided that all current tax and other liabilities in India have been cleared.

Foreign nationals temporarily residing in India on account of their employment are permitted to make reasonable remittances to their own countries to pay insurance premiums, to support their families, and for other expenses. Authorized dealers may allow such remittances by foreign nationals, other than those from Pakistan, up to 75 percent of net income, provided that they hold valid employment visas.

Resident Indian nationals may travel abroad freely without exchange formalities. Effective March 1, 1994, exchange facilities have been available to resident Indian nationals under the Basic Travel Quota Scheme. Under this scheme, foreign exchange up to $2,000 a person a year may be released by authorized dealers for one or more trips abroad, except for visits to Bhutan and Nepal; in the determination of eligibility under this scheme, all foreign travel other than that covered under the Basic Travel Quota is disregarded.

The indicative limits for various categories of business travel were raised in 1995 as follows: (1) The per diem for senior executives under the Special Scale was raised to $500, and for the others under the General Scale to $350. (2) Indian firms participating in trade fairs and exhibitions abroad can obtain foreign exchange up to $20,000 or its equivalent, as compared to Re 200,000 previously. This is also applicable to private printers and publishers wishing to participate in overseas book fairs and exhibitions. (3) The limit for remittances by Indian shipping companies toward fees for solicitors and adjusters was raised to $10,000 from $5,000. (4) The limit for remittances to foreign data service vendors for the use of international data bases was increased to $10,000.

The exportation of Indian currency notes and coins, except to Bhutan and Nepal, is, in general, prohibited. The exportation to Nepal of Indian currency notes in denominations higher than Re 100 is also prohibited. However, resident Indians may take with them Indian currency notes not exceeding Re 1,000 a person at any one time to countries other than Nepal when going abroad on a temporary visit. Authorized dealers, exchange bureaus, and authorized money changers are permitted to sell foreign currency notes and coins up to the equivalent of Re 100 to travelers going to Bangladesh and up to $50 or its equivalent to those going to other countries, except Bhutan and Nepal. Nonresidents may take out the foreign currency that they brought in (and declared on entry if it exceeded $2,500), less the amounts sold to authorized dealers and authorized money changers in India. Unspent rupee amounts may be reconverted into foreign currency and taken out. Students going to foreign universities with full scholarships receive a foreign exchange allowance of up to $1,500 a person for settling in and for purchasing initial equipment. There is also an allowance of $500 to cover the initial expenses of persons traveling abroad for employment purposes, and a travel allowance of $500 for medical checkups and consultations abroad.

Exports and Export Proceeds

Exports to Fiji and Iraq are prohibited. Border trade between India and the Tibet region of China, and between India and Myanmar is allowed. Goods may be exported without a license, provided that they are not prohibited, restricted through licensing, or canalized. Restricted products through licensing include some mineral ores and concentrates, and chemicals including those specified in the UN Chemical Weapons Convention and Montreal Protocol on ozone-depleting substances. Some exports are prohibited. These include all forms of wildlife, including their parts and products; exotic birds; all items of plants included in Appendices I and II of the Convention on International Trade in Endangered Species; beef; human skeletons; tallow, fats, and oils of any animal origin, including fish oil; wood and wood products in the form of logs, timber, stumps, roots, bark, chips, powder, flakes, dust, pulp, and charcoal; wild orchids; chemicals included in Schedule I of the UN Chemical Weapons Convention; sandalwood, excluding some fully finished products; and certain specified categories of red sanders wood. Other items, including stone boulders and wheat, are subject to minimum export prices. Exports of footwear, and roasted and salted peanuts are permitted on a decontrolled basis. A substantial number of exports, mainly new manufactures such as engineering goods, chemicals, plastic goods, leather goods, sporting goods, marine products, processed food and agricultural products, handicrafts, textiles, and jute and coil products, receive import duty drawbacks, a refund of the central excise duty, and exemptions. Bona fide foreign tourists may, with the approval of Customs, take out of India articles purchased with foreign exchange or with rupees acquired against foreign exchange with no limit on value.

Exchange control is exercised over the proceeds of exports to countries other than Bhutan and Nepal. Exporters must declare that full export proceeds will be received and dealt with in accordance with the prescription of currency regulations. Foreign exchange earnings, including the proceeds of exports, must be offered for sale against rupees to an authorized dealer. Exporters and other recipients of foreign exchange are permitted to retain up to 25 percent of receipts in foreign currency accounts with banks in India. In the case of 100 percent export-oriented units, units in export-processing zones, and units in hardware and software technology, up to 50 percent of foreign exchange receipts may be retained. Export proceeds must be repatriated by the due date of receipt or within six months of shipment, whichever is earlier, and surrendered to authorized dealers as required, unless specifically permitted by general or special permission from the Reserve Bank to retain them either with authorized dealers in India or with banks abroad. Concerning exports made to Indian-owned warehouses abroad established with the permission of the Reserve Bank, a maximum period of 15 months is allowed for realization of export proceeds. Exporters are required to obtain permission from the Reserve Bank through authorized dealers in the event that the export value is not realized within the prescribed period. The Reserve Bank also administers a scheme under which engineering goods (capital goods and consumer durables) may be exported under deferred credit arrangements, so that the full export value is paid in installments over more than six months.

The status of exporters is based on their average gross and average net export earnings in the preceding three years as follows: export houses, Re 100 million and Re 60 million, respectively; trading houses, Re 500 million and Re 300 million, respectively; star trading houses, Re 2.5 billion and Re 1.25 billion, respectively; and super star trading houses, Re 7.5 billion and Re 4 billion, respectively. Exporters are also granted a certificate of export, trading, star trading, or super star trading house status (1) if their gross export earnings during the preceding year were Re 150 million, Re 750 million, Re 3 billion, or Re 10 billion, respectively; (2) if their net foreign exchange earnings during the preceding licensing year were Re 120 million, Re 600 million, Re 1,500 million, or Re 6,000 million, respectively.

Proceeds from Invisibles

Proceeds from invisibles must be repatriated and sold in the interbank market. The importation of Indian currency notes and coins is prohibited. However, any person may bring into India Indian currency notes (other than notes of denominations larger than Re 100) from Nepal. Indian travelers may bring in up to Re 1,000 a person in Indian currency notes from other countries if they previously took out this amount when leaving India to travel abroad on a temporary visit. Foreign currency notes may be brought into India without limit, provided that the total amount brought in is declared to the customs authorities upon arrival if the value of foreign notes, coins, and traveler's checks exceeds $10,000 or its equivalent and/or the aggregate value of foreign currency notes brought in at any one time exceeds $2,500 or its equivalent. Foreign currency notes may be sold to any authorized dealer in foreign exchange or to any authorized money changer.

Capital

There are no restrictions on receipts of inward remittances from any country through authorized dealers in India; the subsequent use of such funds in India is, however, subject to approval in most cases. Foreign investments, once admitted, are eligible for the same treatment that Indian enterprises receive.

Banks in India may borrow freely from their branches and correspondents abroad, subject to a maximum of $500,000 or its equivalent for meeting requirements of normal exchange business. They may obtain loans or overdrafts from their overseas branches or correspondents in excess of this limit solely for the purpose of replenishing their rupee resources in India without prior approval from the Reserve Bank; repayment of such borrowings requires prior approval from the Reserve Bank or may be allowed only when the debtor bank has no outstanding borrowings in India from the Reserve Bank or any other bank or financial institution, and is clear of all money market borrowings for a period of at least four weeks before the repayment.

Persons residing in India may not borrow any foreign exchange from other persons residing inside or outside of India without prior permission from the Reserve Bank. The contracting of all foreign currency loans and credits secured from nonresident persons and companies (including banks), as well as repayment of such loans and credits and payments of interest and other charges on such loans, requires prior permission from the Reserve Bank. The procedure prescribed for raising foreign currency loans by Indian entities envisages that borrowing proposals, except when loans are for less than one year, must be cleared by the Ministry of Finance before they are approved by the Reserve Bank.

Nonresidents, noncitizens, and nonbank companies not incorporated under Indian law must have permission from the Reserve Bank to initiate, expand, or continue any business activity in India and to hold or acquire shares of any company carrying on a trading, commercial, or industrial activity in India. Persons of Indian nationality or origin who reside abroad may invest freely in any public or private limited company engaged in any activity except agricultural or plantation activities and real estate business (excluding real estate development, that is, construction of houses, etc.), or in any partnership or proprietary concern engaged in any activity other than real estate business and agricultural or plantation activity, provided that (1) funds for investment are either remitted from abroad through normal banking channels or are drawn from their nonresident accounts; (2) that repatriation of the capital invested or the profits and dividends arising therefrom will not be requested; and (3) that overall limits on holdings of shares and convertible debentures bought through the stock exchange by nonresident Indians (see below) are adhered to.

Overseas companies, societies, and partnership firms of which at least 60 percent is owned by nonresidents of Indian nationality or origin, and overseas trusts in which at least 60 percent of the beneficial interest is irrevocably held by nonresident Indians, are also allowed to invest in any public or private limited companies in accordance with the above provisions.

Nonresident Indians and overseas companies, as defined above, may use funds derived from fresh remittances or held in their nonresident (external) or foreign currency (nonresident) accounts to (1) make portfolio investments with repatriation benefits up to 1 percent of the capital, provided that their total holdings of shares and convertible debentures held on either a repatriable or nonrepatriable basis by all nonresident investors do not exceed (a) 5 percent of the paid-up capital of the company concerned, or (b) 5 percent of the total paid-up value of each series of convertible debentures issued by the company concerned. However, if a company so resolves through a general body resolution, then purchases of shares or debentures of such a company could be made up to 24 percent as against 5 percent mentioned at (b) above; (2) invest freely in national savings certificates with full repatriation benefits; (3) invest up to 40 percent of the new equity capital issued by a company setting up industrial manufacturing projects, hospitals (including diagnostic centers), hotels of at least three-star category, and shipping, software, and oil exploration services with repatriation rights for capital and income, subject to deduction of applicable Indian taxes; and (4) invest up to 100 percent of new investments, including expansion of existing industrial undertakings in specified priority industries listed in Annex III to the Statement on New Industrial Policy with free repatriation of such investment.

Investments in companies engaged in real estate development (e.g., construction of houses) up to 100 percent of new investments may have to be locked in for a period of three years for disinvestment. After three years, remittances of disinvestment will be allowed up to the original investment in foreign exchange. In case of overseas corporate bodies, profits will be allowed to be repatriated up to

16 percent. Income from the investment will also be allowed to be repatriated after deduction of applicable domestic taxes.

Nonresident Indians and overseas companies, as defined above, may also place funds with public limited companies in India as deposits, with full repatriation benefits, provided that (1) the deposits are made for three years; (2) the deposits are made in conformity with the prevailing rules and within the limits prescribed for acceptance of deposits by such companies; and (3) the funds are made available by the depositors through remittances from abroad or through payments from their nonresident (external) or foreign currency (nonresident) accounts. Special tax concessions apply to investments by nonresident Indians.

The Reserve Bank may grant automatic approval for foreign direct investments up to 51 percent of the paid-up capital of the Indian companies that are engaged in manufacturing activities in the 35 priority manufacturing sectors. Applications for investments in areas that do not fall within the authority of the Reserve Bank but that are covered by the foreign investment policy are approved by the Foreign Investment Promotion Board (FIPB). Such investments may be approved up to 100 percent of capital on a case-by-case basis. The Ministry of Industry is the relevant agency for all issues related to foreign direct investment, including approvals.

Foreign institutional investors (FIIs) (e.g., pension funds, mutual funds, investment trusts, asset management companies, nominee companies, and incorporated or institutional portfolio managers) are permitted to make investments in all securities traded on the primary and secondary markets, including equity and other securities and instruments of companies listed on the stock exchange in India. FIIs are required to register initially with the Securities and Exchange Board of India (SEBI) and with the Reserve Bank. Authorization from the Reserve Bank enables FIIs to (1) open accounts denominated in foreign currency; (2) open nonresident rupee accounts for the purposes of operating securities investments; (3) transfer balances between foreign currency accounts and the rupee account; and (4) transfer abroad capital, capital gains, dividends, and interest income. There is no restriction on the value of investments by FIIs in the primary and secondary markets, but investment in debt instruments may not exceed 30 percent of total investment. Portfolio investments in primary or secondary markets are subject to a ceiling of 5 percent of the issued share capital for individual FII holdings and 24 percent of issued share capital for the total holdings of all registered FII in any one company, with the exception of (1) foreign investments under financial collaboration, which are permitted up to 51 percent; and (2) investments through offshore single and regional funds, global depository receipts, and convertibles in the Euromarket.

Investment in trading companies. Trading companies must be registered with the Ministry of Commerce and must obtain a certificate of their status as either export, trading, star trading, or super star trading house before applying to the Reserve Bank for remittances or dividends. Foreign direct investment is permitted in trading companies. The Reserve Bank has the authority to permit foreign investment of up to 51 percent of the paid-up capital of such Indian companies. A higher percentage is considered for approval by the FIPB, and even 100 percent foreign equity may be approved, provided that the funding company is primarily engaged in exports.

Increase in foreign equity in existing companies. Existing joint-venture companies may raise the ratio of foreign equity shares to 51 percent of their capital through expansion of their capital base or through preferential allocation of shares to the foreign investor. Firms in certain manufacturing industries and tourist industries (hotels, restaurants, and beach resorts) may increase the equity ratio immediately. Others may increase the equity ratio as part of expansion, provided the expansion is in specified manufacturing or tourist industries. In both cases, the Reserve Bank grants automatic approval.

The Reserve Bank issued revised guidelines to determine the issue price of shares issued to nonresidents by existing Indian companies through preferential allotments, in order to bring them in line with those issued by the Government and the SEBI. Accordingly, every preferential allotment of shares by listed companies to foreign investors should be at the market price.[5]

Prior approval from the Reserve Bank is required for all transfers of shares of Indian companies by nonresidents or foreign nationals to residents. However, sales and transfers of shares of Indian companies through stock exchanges in India by non-residents of Indian nationality or origin in favor of Indian citizens or persons of Indian origin and Indian companies do not require the Reserve Bank's clearance when the proceeds of such shares sold by

the transferer are credited to his or her ordinary nonresident rupee account with a bank authorized to deal in foreign exchange in India without a right of repatriation outside India. The transfer of shares by nonresidents in favor of nonresidents, residents, or non-Foreign Exchange Regulation Act companies does not require clearance from the Reserve Bank, provided that the shares are purchased by the nonresidents under the portfolio investment scheme on a repatriation basis and are sold on stock exchanges through the same authorized dealer. In such cases, the sale proceeds may be credited to NRER or FCNR accounts after deduction of tax or may be remitted abroad.

Nonresident Indians and overseas corporate bodies are allowed to (1) invest in the schemes of all domestic public sector and private sector mutual funds and also invest through secondary markets on a repatriation basis after complying with certain conditions; and (2) invest in bonds issued by public sector undertakings in India on a repatriation basis after complying with necessary stipulations. Nonresident Indians in Nepal are permitted to invest in India, but funds must be remitted in free foreign exchange through banking channels. The repatriation of such investment would, however, be subject to the existing terms and conditions.

The following capital transactions by residents require approval from the Reserve Bank: (1) holding, acquiring, transferring, or disposing of immovable property outside India (unless acquired while a nonresident of India); (2) exportation of Indian securities and transfers of Indian securities to nonresidents; (3) guaranteeing of obligations of a nonresident or of a resident in favor of a nonresident; and (4) association with, or participation in, the capital of any business concern outside India.

Capital invested in approved projects by residents of other countries, including capital appreciation on the original investment, may be generally repatriated at any time. However, approval must be obtained from the Reserve Bank before effecting a sale that involves repatriation of assets. The proceeds from liquidated foreign investments not eligible for repatriation are kept in a nonresident account.

Indian nationals are granted foreign exchange facilities up to $500 a person or $1,000 a family for emigration purposes. In cases of exceptional hardship, foreign exchange may be released up to a reasonable amount in one lump sum; the remainder of the emigrant's assets and income is kept in a nonresident account, and no further remittances, including pensions, if any, are normally allowed. However, Indian nationals who left the country permanently

---

[5]As per the revised guidelines, the valuation of such shares, effective 30 days prior to the shareholders' general meeting, is required to be at least the higher of the average of weekly highs and lows of the closing share prices for the preceding six months quoted on a stock exchange for the preceding fortnight or the average of weekly highs and lows of the closing prices on a stock exchange on which the highest trading volume in respect of the shares of the company have been recorded.

before the introduction of exchange controls in India (that is, July 1947 against the former Sterling Area countries, and September 1939 against other countries) are permitted to transfer abroad capital assets up to the equivalent of Re 1 million in one lump sum, and the remaining balance in annual installments not exceeding Re 500,000. Foreign nationals who are temporarily residing in India (other than nationals of Pakistan) and foreign diplomatic persons are permitted at the time of their retirement to transfer to their own countries the proceeds from the sale of their investments, subject to a limit of Re 1 million for each family at the time of retirement, and the remainder in annual installments not exceeding Re 500,000; in addition, they may transfer all their current remittable assets in India.

There are no restrictions on the importation into India of Indian or foreign securities. The acquisition, sale, transfer, exportation, or other disposal of foreign securities requires approval. Natural persons who are residents (other than foreign nationals temporarily but not permanently residing in India and their foreign-born wives also not permanently residing in India) are not normally permitted to purchase securities or personal real estate outside India. Foreign-born widows of Indian nationals are permitted to transfer initially a sum of Re 1 million when they leave India permanently; thereafter, they are allowed to remit up to Re 500,000 a year out of capital and income. Transfers abroad of legacies, inheritances, and bequests by persons who were never residents of India are subject to the same limits.

Indian nationals, legal heirs, resident donees, and persons of Indian origin holding foreign passports, who reside abroad and wish to return to India, are not required to surrender on their arrival foreign currency assets they acquired lawfully while residing outside India, provided they stayed abroad continuously for at least one year.

Under the Resident Foreign Currency Account Scheme, Indian nationals (returning permanently to India from abroad) are permitted, within three months of their arrival, to open and operate without restriction resident foreign currency accounts in any permitted currency with authorized dealers in India; all foreign exchange transferred from abroad may be credited to these accounts.

Gold

The Gold Control Repeal Act of 1990 eliminated restrictions on internal trade in gold. However, gold mines continue to sell gold to industrial users through the distribution network of the State Bank of India as well as through market sales. Forward trading in gold or silver is prohibited; exports of silver bullion, sheets, and plates are banned, and exports of silver products are subject to quota restrictions.

The importation and exportation of gold in any form by residents are regulated by the import policy in force. Exporters of gold and silver jewelry may import their essential inputs such as gold, silver mountings, findings, rough gems, precious and semiprecious synthetic stones, and unprocessed pearls with import licenses granted by the licensing authority. Under this scheme, the foreign buyer may supply in advance gold or silver free of charge for the manufacture and ultimate export of gold or silver jewelry and articles thereof.

Under the Gold Jewelry and Articles Export Promotion and Replenishment Scheme, exporters of gold jewelry and articles are entitled to replenish gold through the designated branches of the State Bank of India or any other agency nominated by the Ministry of Commerce at a price indicated in the certificate issued by the State Bank of India after purchase of gold. The Scheme is limited to exports that are supported by an irrevocable letter of credit, payment of cash on a delivery basis, or advance payment in foreign exchange. Exports of gold jewelry may also be allowed on a collection basis (documents against acceptance). The exporter has the option to obtain gold from the State Bank of India in advance. On presentation of required documents, the appropriate release order and gem replenishment license may be issued by the licensing authority, provided that the exporters satisfy value-added and other requirements under the Scheme. Special permission for imports of gold and silver is granted only in exceptional cases where either no foreign exchange transaction is involved or the metals are needed for a particular purpose. Special permission is also granted when the gold or silver is imported for processing and re-exportation, provided that payments for the importation will not be required, the entire quantity of metal imported will be re-exported in the form of jewelry, and the value added will be repatriated to India in foreign exchange through an authorized dealer.

Exports of gold in any form, other than jewelry produced in India for exportation, with a gold value not exceeding 10 percent of total value and jewelry constituting the personal effects of a traveler, subject to certain monetary limits, are prohibited unless effected by or on behalf of the monetary authorities. The net exportation of gold from India is not permitted.

Changes During 1995

Prescription of Currency

December 4. Settlement of payments for imports of sugar, fertilizer, and pulses from any of the ACU countries were allowed to be made outside the ACU mechanism in any permitted currency. Indian exporters were also permitted to accept payment in free foreign exchange for their exports to ACU countries, provided such payment is voluntarily offered by the importer in the ACU country.

Payments for Invisibles

June 30. The indicative limits for various categories of business travel were raised as follows: (1) The per diem for senior executives under the Special Scale was raised to $500 and for others under the General Scale to $350. (2) Indian firms participating in trade fairs and exhibitions abroad could now obtain foreign exchange up to $20,000 or its equivalent, as compared to Re 200,000 previously. This is also applicable to private printers and publishers wishing to participate in overseas book fairs and exhibitions. (3) The limit for remittances by Indian shipping companies toward fees for solicitors and adjusters was raised to $10,000 from $5,000. (4) The limit for remittances to foreign data service vendors for the use of international data bases was increased to $10,000.

July 5. Authorized dealers were allowed to provide foreign exchange to their customers without prior approval of the Reserve Bank, beyond the specified indicative limits for purposes including business travel, participation in overseas conferences and seminars, studies and study tours abroad, medical treatment and checkups, and specialized apprenticeship training, provided that they were satisfied about the bona fide character of the application.

November 11. Family units of resident Indian nationals may remit through authorized dealers up to $5,000 a calendar year to their close relatives residing abroad for their maintenance expenses.

Proceeds from Invisibles

June 22. Incoming travelers were required to declare foreign currency notes brought in at any one time when the aggregate amount exceeds $2,500.

June 22. Resident donees and legal heirs were included in the definition of "returning Indians" and, therefore, will not be required to surrender their foreign currency assets.

Capital

June 16. The Reserve Bank issued revised guidelines to determine the issue price of shares issued to nonresidents by existing Indian companies through preferential allotments, in order to bring them in line with those issued by the Government and the SEBI. Accordingly, every preferential allotment of shares by listed companies to foreign investors should be at the market price. The shares allotted on a preferential basis are not transferable in any manner for a period of five years from the date of their allotment.

November 11. Nonresident Indians and overseas corporate bodies were allowed to (1) invest in the schemes of all domestic public sector and private sector mutual funds and also invest through secondary markets on a repatriation basis after complying with certain conditions; (2) invest in bonds issued by public sector undertakings in India with repatriation of both the principal and interest; and (3) purchase shares of Indian public sector enterprises on a repatriation basis after complying with necessary stipulations. Nonresident Indians in Nepal were permitted to invest in India with funds remitted in free foreign exchange through banking channels. The repatriation of such investments would, however, be subject to the existing terms and conditions.

INDONESIA

(Position as of December 31, 1995)

Exchange Arrangement

The currency of Indonesia is the Indonesian Rupiah. Its exchange value is determined by Bank Indonesia under a system of managed float, under which the bank announces daily buying and selling rates that are computed on the basis of a basket of weighted currencies with a spread of ±Rp 22. The U.S. dollar is the intervention currency. On December 31, 1995, the buying and selling rates for spot transactions were Rp 2.293 and Rp 2.323, respectively, per $1. Exchange rates for certain other currencies[1] are determined by reference to the cross rates of the U.S. dollar and the currencies concerned in international markets. There are no taxes or subsidies on purchases or sales of foreign exchange.

Exchange rates announced by Bank Indonesia apply only to certain transactions undertaken at certain times of the day. For all other transactions, banks are free to set their own rates. Purchases and sales of foreign currency bills by Bank Indonesia are conducted from 8:00 a.m. to 11:45 a.m. on the basis of buying and selling rates announced at 3:00 p.m. of the previous business day. Spot and forward transactions, however, are conducted at rates fixed bilaterally between Bank Indonesia and the bank concerned. In addition, from 3:00 p.m. to 4:00 p.m. on Monday through Friday, Bank Indonesia fixes a rate for spot transactions with banks; such transactions are normally conducted to enable the banks to adjust their net open positions. At other times, spot and forward transactions are conducted at rates fixed bilaterally between Bank Indonesia and the banks concerned. Foreign exchange transactions are restricted to the authorized foreign exchange banks, nonbank financial institutions, and licensed money changers. Bank Indonesia trades unlimited amounts of foreign exchange or rupiah with authorized traders at its intervention rates for the day.

Bank Indonesia does not accept investment swaps with a maturity of more than two years offered at the initiative of banks, and only provides liquidity swaps on its initiative.

The commercial banks' weekly net foreign exchange open positions are limited to 25 percent of capital. Separate limits apply to total exposures and off-balance sheet exposures. A bank whose net open position exceeds the limit is subject to a penalty.

Indonesia accepted the obligations of Article VIII, Sections 2, 3, and 4 of the Fund Agreement on May 7, 1988.

Administration of Control

Administration of the exchange and trade system is entrusted to Bank Indonesia, the Ministry of Trade, the Ministry of Finance, foreign exchange banks, and the customs authorities. Policies on foreign exchange market operations are enacted by Bank Indonesia.

Prescription of Currency

Payments and receipts must be effected through the authorized foreign exchange banks and are normally effected in convertible currencies. Indonesia maintains no operative bilateral payments agreements.

Nonresident Accounts

There are no restrictions on the opening by residents or foreign nationals of accounts in Indonesia in rupiah or foreign currencies with authorized foreign exchange banks. However, if holders of accounts in foreign exchange wish to withdraw funds, they must send a letter to the bank; no checks may be drawn on foreign currency accounts.

Imports and Import Payments

There is a registry of authorized importers. Only Indonesian nationals may be authorized as importers, although foreign investors are permitted to import the items required for their own projects. Although all imports into Indonesia are subject to licensing requirements, most are classified under the nonresident license (also called General Importer License).

Imports from Israel and the countries against which the United Nations (UN) has imposed a trade embargo are prohibited, as are imports from all sources of most secondhand goods and of certain products. In addition, secondhand engines and their parts and other capital goods may be imported by industrial firms for their own use or for the recondi-

---

[1]Those commonly used in Indonesia's international transactions: Australian dollars, Austrian schillings, Belgian francs, Brunei dollars, Canadian dollars, Danish kroner, deutsche mark, French francs, Hong Kong dollars, Italian lire, Japanese yen, Malaysian ringgit, Netherlands guilders, New Zealand dollars, Norwegian kroner, Philippine pesos, pounds sterling, Singapore dollars, Swedish kronor, Swiss francs, and Thai baht.

tioning of their industry, in accordance with the guidelines of the Ministries of Trade and of Industry. Certain categories of agricultural imports, including foodstuffs, beverages, and fruits may be imported only by registered importers designated by the Minister of Trade. The procurement policies of companies approved for the importation of fruit, alcoholic beverages, and chickens are evaluated annually by the Government, although explicit quantitative restrictions are not placed on these products.

Import controls remain on about 12 percent of total imports. Imports of certain goods remain restricted to approved importers, most of which are state enterprises. For example, Pertamina has a monopoly on the importation of lubricating oil and lubricating fats, and PT Dahana, on the importation of ammunition and explosive gelatin. The Board of Logistics (BULOG) has the sole right to import rice, fertilizer, and sugar. The monopoly rights of approved importers (sole agents) also remain in effect for the importation of certain heavy equipment and motor vehicles, although this right may be transferred to general importers. The importation of trucks is subject to restriction. Certain products are granted preferential duties within the framework of the Association of South East Asian Nations (ASEAN).

Imports into Indonesia are subject to preshipment inspection in the exporting country by agencies designated by the Government of Indonesia; inspection expenses are borne by the Indonesian Government. Following inspection, the PT Surveyor Indonesia in Jakarta is required to issue on behalf of its agency in the exporting country a survey report (LPS) specifying the type, quality, quantity, and estimated cost of the goods, the applicable tariff code, freight charges, import duties, and value-added taxes; the LPS must be sent by the agency in Jakarta directly to the bank that has opened letters of credit or, for imports not covered by letters of credit, to the bank designated by the importer. After paying duties based on the price fixed by the agency and taxes, the importer presents all import documents to customs for release of the shipment. The Directorate General of Customs and Excise does not examine goods that have an LPS, except those that are valued at less than $5,000 or are suspected to be illegally imported. Imports for foreign capital investment and domestic capital investment must have an LPS. Cement-asbestos sheets, dry batteries, steel slabs, low-voltage electric cord, and electric light bulbs are subject to quality control.

Exports and Export Proceeds

Exports to Israel, and the countries against which the UN has imposed a trade embargo, are prohib-

ited, as are exports to all countries of certain categories of unprocessed or low-quality rubber, brass and copper scrap (except from Irian Jaya), iron scrap, steel scrap, and antiques of cultural value. Exporters are required to possess trade permits, which are issued by the Ministry of Trade. Certain producer-exporters of rubber, plywood, and animal feed may issue certificates of quality for their products. Quality controls are also maintained on certain products, including fish, manioc (cassava), shrimp, coffee, tea, pepper, spices, vegetable oil, and cocoa beans. Exports of certain domestically produced commodities must have prior authorization from the Ministry of Trade in order to maintain supplies to meet domestic demand and to encourage domestic processing of certain raw materials.[2] Concern about domestic price stability sometimes leads to suspension of exports of various items in this category. In 1990, producer-exporters of cement and clinkers were allowed to export these products with the approval of the Ministry of Trade, as shortages developed on the domestic market. Several categories of gold and silver may be exported only by exporters who possess certification from PT Aneka Tambang and authorization from the Ministry of Trade.

Most other products are freely exported by registered private firms and state trading firms. However, manioc (cassava) may be exported only by approved exporters. Textiles and textile products subject to import quotas in the consuming countries may be exported only by approved textile exporters, who may transfer their allocated quotas to other approved exporters through the Commodity Exchange Board.

All exports of rattan, leather, wood, and wood products must be examined before shipment. Exports of sawn timber and wood products require approval from the joint marketing body and may be made only by approved exporters. A minimum price of $250 a cubic meter applies to exports of sawn and processed timber, and export taxes ranging from $250 to $4,800 a cubic meter are imposed on these products. Exports of logs are subject to export taxes ranging from $500 to $4,800 a cubic meter; certain processed woods, such as finger-jointed walls, panels, and molding, are not taxed. Certain other products are subject to export taxes, which range from 5 percent to 30 percent (the tax rate on leather prod-

---

[2] Items affected by such controls include clove seeds, logs, fertilizer, cement, construction reinforcements of iron, automobile tires, paper, asphalt, stearin, cattle, salt, wheat flour, maize, soybeans, rice, copra, olein, raw rattan, meat, and all goods produced from subsidized raw materials.

ucts is 20 percent, and the tax rates on rattan are $14–$15 a kilogram).

For all goods subject to the export tax and the export surcharge, payment is due when the exports are registered with foreign exchange banks. If the export tax and export surcharge are not yet settled at the time of registration, exporters are required to submit promissory notes for their value. Promissory notes may be settled in three ways. Exports without a letter of credit should be settled with the foreign exchange bank not later than 30 days from the date of export registration. Exports using consignment and usance letters of credit should be settled not later than 90 days from the date of export registration. Exports with sight letters of credit must be settled not later than 30 days from the date the exports are registered with the foreign exchange bank. There are no restrictions on the type of financial arrangements exporters may use. There are no surrender or repatriation requirements for export proceeds. In the calculation of export taxes on the principal commodities, other than petroleum and gas, sale prices must not be lower than the "indicative" prices determined periodically by the Minister of Trade.

To enable producer-exporters to obtain their imported inputs at international prices, exporters and suppliers of inputs for exporters are permitted to bypass the import-licensing system and import tariffs or, if they cannot bypass the system, to reclaim import duties; the costs imposed by non-tariff barriers, however, cannot be rebated.[3]

Certain commodities produced in border regions may be exported to Malaysia and the Philippines in exchange for certain goods. In this "border-crossing" trade with Malaysia, the value of import or export transactions must not exceed Rp 600 a single trip or Rp 3,000 a month, whether transported by land or by sea. For the Philippines, the value of imports or exports must not exceed the rupiah or peso equivalent of $150 a single trip if transported by seagoing vessels or $1,500 if transported by smaller boats.

The Indonesian Government may require all foreign firms bidding for government-sponsored construction or procurement projects, whose import component is valued at more than Rp 500 million, to agree to fulfill a counterpurchase obligation. Bidders for projects that include counterpurchase requirements must submit with their bids a letter in which they agree to purchase and export the equivalent of the contract's f.o.b. value in selected Indonesian products (agricultural products, and manufactured and other products, excluding petroleum, natural gas, and items subject to export quotas) during the life of the contract.[4] The foreign supplier may fulfill the counterpurchase requirement either directly or through a third party, possibly from another country that is acceptable to the Indonesian Government. Such an arrangement must meet the condition of "additionality"; that is, the counterpurchases by the third party have to be in addition to regular exports from Indonesia. Indonesian products purchased under countertrade arrangements must be shipped regularly and in stages during the validity of the contract on the government procurement, and these shipment obligations must be completed at the end of such a purchasing contract. If, when the project is completed or the purchase is implemented (government import) the exportation from Indonesia has not yet been completed, a penalty amounting to 50 percent of the export value will be imposed on the responsible party (to date this provision has not been implemented).

Payments for and Proceeds from Invisibles

These are neither restricted nor subject to control. Proceeds from invisibles need not be surrendered. Travelers may take out and bring in any amount in foreign banknotes, but only Rp 50,000 in Indonesian notes and coins, other than gold and silver commemorative coins (see section on Gold, below).

Capital

Incentives for foreign direct investments include an exemption or relief from import duties on capital goods, raw materials, auxiliary goods, and spare parts; an annual depreciation allowance of 25 percent for fiscal purposes on virtually all machinery

---

[3]Under this scheme, exporters are classified as producer-exporters (firms that export at least 65 percent of their total production) or as exporter-producers (firms that export 85 percent of their production and producers of textiles in general). Producer-exporters may bring into the country their imports free of licensing restrictions and import duties, but with ex post documentation. If exporter-producers can demonstrate that their output was, or will be, exported or that their output was an input in an exported output, then they can also receive the same permission to import their inputs as producer-exporters. The scheme also allows indirect exporters to reclaim import duties through a duty drawback facility.

[4]The following are exempt from these requirements: (1) sources of import financing derived from soft loans and loans from the World Bank, the Islamic Development Bank, and the Asian Development Bank; (2) domestic components contained in the contract with the foreign suppliers, such as components of services, goods, and taxes or duties; (3) services that are used by various government agencies related to specific expertise, such as foreign accountants, lawyers, surveyors, consultants' services, purchases of technology (patents), etc.; and (4) purchases or imports under the joint-venture system between state companies and foreign companies.

and other productive capital goods; and deferral of value-added tax on imports of capital goods.

All foreign enterprises are eligible to receive preferential customs duty treatment for imports of required raw materials for the first two years of production activity. Raw materials may be imported with no time limit. In addition, an enterprise exporting more than 65 percent of its production is free to hire foreign experts as needed to maintain its export commitments. Managers of representative offices of a foreign company are granted multiple exit and re-entry permits for six months and are exempt from the Rp 25,000 departure tax.

Full foreign ownership in foreign direct investments is allowed in certain sectors if the investments meet certain criteria. Pursuant to Government Regulation No. 20/1994 (July 29, 1994), foreign investors may reinvest profits in the shares of other foreign firms. Investors are granted the right to repatriate capital, to transfer profits (after settlement of taxes and financial obligations in Indonesia), and to make transfers relating to expenses connected with the employment of foreign nationals in Indonesia and relating to depreciation allowances. The law provides that no transfer permit shall be issued for capital repatriation as long as investment benefits from tax relief are being received; at present, however, foreign payments do not require a transfer permit.

Foreign ownership of direct investment must begin to be divested by the eleventh year of production. For investments above $50 million, divestment of 51 percent must be completed within 20 years. For smaller investments, the divestment requirement is less stringent.

There are no limitations on the remittance to Indonesia of capital in the form of foreign exchange or commodities. Both residents and nonresidents may hold foreign currency deposits with foreign exchange banks. However, foreign exchange banks are subject to Bank Indonesia directives with respect to borrowing abroad, the acceptance of deposits from nonresidents, and the issuance of certificates of deposit to nonresidents. A reserve requirement of 2 percent is applicable to the foreign currency liabilities of foreign exchange banks; no reserve require-

ments are applicable to the foreign borrowings of nonbank financial institutions or private companies. Banks' short-term foreign exchange liabilities may not exceed 30 percent of their own capital, and they are required to allocate at least 80 percent of all foreign exchange credits to export-oriented businesses that earn foreign exchange. A Commercial Offshore Loan Team (consisting of the State Secretary, the ministers of all economic portfolios, and the Governor of Bank Indonesia) established in September 1991, supervises all foreign commercial loan transactions. The prior approval of the team is required before any public enterprise, commercial bank, or public sector body may accept a loan from abroad. These limits do not apply to private enterprises.

Indonesian citizens and residents of foreign nationality may freely transfer, negotiate, import, and export securities denominated in rupiah or in foreign currency.

The exploration and development of petroleum resources are governed principally by the Petroleum Law of 1960.

Gold

Indonesia has issued two commemorative gold coins, which are legal tender. Residents may freely purchase, hold, and sell gold and gold coins in Indonesia. Travelers may freely take out up to Rp 65,000 a person in Indonesian commemorative gold and silver coins issued in August 1970, and up to Rp 130,000 a person in gold and silver coins issued in October 1974; amounts in excess of these limits require the prior approval of Bank Indonesia. Gold may be imported freely. Imports are subject to an additional levy of Rp 25 per $1.

Changes During 1995

Exchange Arrangement

June 30. Bank Indonesia began announcing buying and selling rates computed on the basis of a basket of weighted currencies with a spread of ±Rp 22. (Prior to that date, the spread was ±Rp 15.)

July 17. Bank Indonesia terminated the provision of investment swaps.

ISLAMIC REPUBLIC OF IRAN

(Position as of December 31, 1995)

Exchange Arrangement

The currency of the Islamic Republic of Iran is the Iranian Rial. The exchange rate system consists of two rates for the U.S. dollar: (1) the official rate, which is fixed at Rls 1,750 per $1, applies mainly to the imports of essential goods; and (2) the export rate, which is fixed at Rls 3,000 per $1, applies to all other transactions.

There are no taxes or subsidies on purchases or sales of foreign exchange. There are no arrangements for forward cover against exchange rate risk operating in the banking system.

Administration of Control

Exchange control authority is vested in Bank Markazi. All foreign exchange transactions must take place through the banking system. Imports and exports are governed by regulations issued periodically by the Ministry of Commerce after approval from the Council of Ministers.

Prescription of Currency

Settlements of current transactions with the member countries of the Asian Clearing Union (ACU)—Bangladesh, India, the Islamic Republic of Iran, Myanmar, Nepal, Pakistan, and Sri Lanka—are required to be effected in Asian monetary units (AMUs); settlements with these countries are made every two months through conversion of AMUs.

All bilateral payment arrangements have been terminated and the outstanding credit balances are in the process of being settled.

Nonresident Accounts

Foreign nationals may maintain rial accounts and foreign currency accounts with authorized banks. The balances of rial accounts may be used only in the Islamic Republic of Iran. Foreign currency accounts bear interest at LIBOR plus 1 percent.

Imports and Import Payments

All imports into the Islamic Republic of Iran must be authorized by the Ministry of Commerce before being registered with authorized banks, except for special military goods, pharmaceuticals, and souvenirs and gifts brought in by incoming travelers.

Imports from Israel and the Federal Republic of Yugoslavia (Serbia/Montenegro) are prohibited.

The import policy is re-examined periodically at the end of each Iranian calendar year (March 20), and new regulations effective for the following year are published by the Ministry of Commerce. The regulations distinguish between "authorized," "conditional," and "prohibited" goods. The importation of authorized goods is unrestricted. Conditional goods are those goods whose importation is temporarily prohibited by the Government or is contingent on the fulfillment of certain requirements. Imports of prohibited goods are not allowed. Advance payments for imports of up to the full value are allowed, depending on the goods.

Most imports are subject to the commercial benefit tax, which is ad valorem, and is imposed in addition to applicable customs duties. The rate of the commercial benefit tax for each year is specified in the Export-Import Regulations. The commercial benefit tax must be paid to customs before clearance of goods. Clearance through customs is authorized upon presentation of shipping documents endorsed by an authorized bank and of a permit issued by the Ministry of Commerce (this permit may be issued at the same time that letters of credit are opened and it need not be reissued). Certain goods, such as pharmaceuticals and imports by the Ministry of Post, Telegraph, and Telephone, must be accompanied by a special permit when they are cleared through customs. Payments for imports made with foreign currency must be accompanied by evidence that the currency was obtained from an Iranian bank before the goods may be released from customs. In the transportation of imported goods for which import letters of credit have been opened, priority must be accorded to Iranian transportation carriers (air, land, or sea). The ceiling on the amount of goods that an incoming traveler is permitted to import is governed by the Export-Import Regulations.

Payments for Invisibles

The transfer of premiums for reinsurance at the official rate can be made by the Central Insurance Company of Iran, Iran Insurance Company, Asia Insurance Company, and Alborz Insurance Company through their respective foreign exchange accounts. Insurance companies owned by Iranian residents may issue insurance contracts denominated in foreign currency for imports of goods; only Iran Insurance Company may issue war-risk insurance in foreign currency. The transfer of income in rials earned from ticket sales by foreign airline companies located in Iran may be allowed at the official exchange rate by Bank Markazi.

Persons requiring medical treatment abroad may obtain foreign exchange at the official exchange rate up to the amount specified by the Ministry of Health. Foreign exchange allowances at the official exchange rate are granted to students under scholarships in nonmedical fields with the approval of the Ministry of Culture and Higher Education, and to those in the medical field, with the approval of the Ministry of Health, Treatment, and Medical Education. Students without scholarships are allocated foreign exchange at the export rate upon evidence of acceptance by an institution and receipt of tuition invoice. The amount of allowances varies according to the cost of living in the country of study, up to a maximum of $1,470 a month; an additional 60 percent of the basic allowance for a spouse and 30 percent for each child is authorized. In certain cases when this allowance is not sufficient to cover tuition, additional amounts to cover university fees and expenses may be allowed.

The transfer of profits and dividends earned on foreign direct investment can be made freely at the official exchange rate.

Foreign nationals working in the Islamic Republic of Iran whose services are considered essential are allowed to remit up to 30 percent of their net salaries at the official exchange rate with the prior approval of Bank Markazi.

Allowances for Iranian nationals traveling abroad are up to $1,000 for each individual passport and a maximum of $500 a person traveling if a person travels with a group passport.

Foreign exchange from accounts denominated in foreign currency originating abroad may be transferred by natural persons without limitation.

Exports and Export Proceeds

Exports to Israel and the Federal Republic of Yugoslavia (Serbia/Montenegro) are prohibited. Exports of non-oil products are not subject to limitation; the only requirement is that authorization be obtained for statistical purposes from the Ministry of Commerce. Exporters of non-oil products are subjected to 100 percent repatriation and surrender requirements, with the exception of carpets, for which 70 percent repatriation is required. Oil export proceeds are subject to a 50 percent repatriation and surrender requirement.

Proceeds from Invisibles

Repatriation and surrender requirements do not apply to service receipts and private transfers. There is no limit on the amount of foreign exchange travelers may bring into the country. The sale of foreign exchange to the banking system at the official exchange rate by both resident and nonresident juridical and natural persons is permitted.

Capital

Foreign direct investment is supervised by the Organization for Investment and Economic and Technical Assistance of the Ministry of Economic Affairs and Finance, if the investment was originally brought into the country in accordance with the Law Concerning the Attraction and Protection of Foreign Capital Investments in Iran. Repatriation of capital is guaranteed with the approval of this agency and Bank Markazi, and in accordance with the abovementioned law. In the case of portfolio investment, nonresidents can invest in instruments traded at the Tehran Stock Exchange, but this form of investment does not qualify for protection under the investment law.

Gold

No Iranian gold coin is legal tender. Residents may freely and without license purchase, hold, and sell gold, platinum, and silver in the domestic market. Authority to export or import gold for monetary purposes is reserved for Bank Markazi. The exportation of finished articles made of gold, platinum, and silver may be effected in accordance with the relevant regulations. The exportation of gold, platinum, and silver in the form of ingots, coins, or semifinished products is prohibited, except by Bank Markazi. Natural and juridical persons, including authorized banks, may import gold, platinum, and silver bullion for commercial purposes in accordance with the relevant regulations. Travelers may bring in jewelry up to a value equivalent to Rls 5 million, and take out the entire value, provided that it is recorded on their passport; the importation of personal jewelry with a value exceeding Rls 5 million requires approval from Bank Markazi. The exportation of Iranian gold coins for numismatic purposes requires prior approval from Bank Markazi.

Changes During 1995

Exchange Arrangement

January 3. A 50 percent repatriation and surrender requirement was imposed on proceeds from non-oil exports.

May 20. The export exchange rate was depreciated to Rls 3,000 from Rls 2,354 per $1.

Exports and Export Proceeds

May 20. The repatriation and surrender requirements at the export rate for proceeds from exports of non-oil goods were raised to 100 percent.

August 6. The repatriation and surrender requirements for proceeds from carpet exports were lowered to 70 percent.

IRELAND

(Position as of December 31, 1995)

Exchange Arrangement

The currency of Ireland is the Irish Pound. Ireland participates with Austria, Belgium, Denmark, France, Germany, Luxembourg, the Netherlands, Portugal, and Spain in the Exchange Rate Mechanism (ERM) of the European Monetary System (EMS). In accordance with this mechanism, Ireland maintains spot exchange rates between the Irish pound and the currencies of the other participants within margins of 15 percent above or below the cross rates based on the central rates expressed in European currency units.[1]

The agreement commits the Central Bank of Ireland to buy or sell the currencies of the other participating states in unlimited amounts at specified intervention rates. On December 31, 1995, these rates were as follows:

Specified Intervention Rates Per:	Irish Pounds	
	Upper limit	Lower limit
100 Austrian schillings	6.85	5.08
100 Belgian or Luxembourg francs	2.34	1.73
100 Danish kroner	12.63	9.36
100 Deutsche mark	48.16	35.72
100 French francs	14.36	10.65
100 Netherlands guilders	42.74	31.70
100 Portuguese escudos	0.47	0.35
100 Spanish pesetas	0.57	0.42

The participants in the EMS do not maintain exchange rates within fixed limits with any other currencies. On December 31, 1995 the official midpoint closing rate for the U.S. dollar was $1.60 per Irish pound. There are no taxes or subsidies on purchases or sales of foreign exchange.

Ireland accepted the obligations of Article VIII, Sections 2, 3, and 4 of the Fund Agreement, on February 15, 1961.

Administration of Control

No exchange controls are in effect in Ireland.

Import licenses, when necessary, are issued by the Department of Tourism and Trade for industrial goods and by the Department of Agriculture, Food, and Forestry for agricultural goods; import licenses are also issued in some cases by the Department of Health or the Department of Justice. Import and export controls are administered by the revenue commissioners.

In accordance with the IMF's Executive Board Decision No. 144-(52–51) adopted on August 14, 1952, Ireland notified the IMF on July 21, 1992 that, in compliance with UN Security Council Resolution No. 757 of 1992, certain restrictions had been imposed on the making of financial transfers for current international transactions in respect of the Federal Republic of Yugoslavia (Serbia/Montenegro). Ireland has suspended restrictions in relation to the Federal Republic of Yugoslavia (Serbia/Montenegro) in accordance with UN Security Council Resolution No. 1022 of November 22, 1995.

Ireland revoked restrictions in respect of Haiti on December 21, 1994, in accordance with UN Security Council Resolution No. 944 of 1994. Restrictions were also introduced in respect of Iraq on August 10, 1990 in accordance with UN Security Council Resolution No. 661 of 1990, and also in respect of the Libyan Arab Jamahiriya on December 23, 1993, in accordance with UN Security Council Resolution No. 883 of 1993.

Prescription of Currency

There are no prescription of currency requirements.

Nonresident Accounts

Nonresidents may maintain deposits in Irish pounds without restriction.

Imports and Import Payments

Imports of certain goods (including textiles, steel, footwear, and ceramic products) originating in certain non-European Union (EU) countries are subject to either quantitative restrictions or surveillance measures.

Imports from non-EU countries of products covered by the Common Agricultural Policy of the EU may be subject to various charges and tariffs under that policy and to duties under the common customs tariff.

---

[1]Effective August 2, 1993, the intervention thresholds of the currencies participating in the ERM of the EMS were widened from ±2.25 percent (in the case of Portugal and Spain, 6 percent) to ±15 percent around the bilateral central exchange rates; the fluctuation band of the deutsche mark and the Netherlands guilder remained unchanged at ±2.25 percent.

For reasons of national policy, imports of certain goods (for example, specified drugs, explosives, and firearms and ammunition) are prohibited without special licenses.

Exports and Export Proceeds

Export proceeds are not regulated.

The Department of Tourism and Trade is responsible for administering export control policy. Export controls are implemented on the basis of (1) the Control of Exports Act of 1983 and the orders contained thereunder; (2) EU Regulation No. 3381/94 and Council Decision 94/942/CFSP, regarding the control of exports of dual-use goods to both EU and non-EU countries that may require export licenses; and (3) UN/EU trade sanctions in force. Trade sanctions are currently in force against Angola, Burma, China, Iraq, Liberia, Libya, Nigeria, Somalia, Sudan, and Syria. Trade sanctions have been suspended in relation to the Federal Republic of Yugoslavia (Serbia/Montenegro) in accordance with UN Security Council Resolution No. 1022 of 1995.

Payments for and Proceeds from Invisibles

There are no restrictions on payments for and proceeds from invisibles. Travelers may import or export any amount of domestic and foreign banknotes or any other means of payment.

Capital

There are no exchange controls or restrictions on inward or outward capital transfers by residents or nonresidents.

Gold

Residents may freely hold, buy, borrow, sell, or lend gold coins in Ireland.

Changes During 1995

No significant changes occurred in the exchange and trade system.

(See Appendix for a summary of trade measures introduced and eliminated on an EU-wide basis during 1995.)

ISRAEL

(Position as of December 31, 1995)

Exchange Arrangement

The currency of Israel is the New Sheqel (plural New Sheqalim). Its exchange rate is defined in relation to a currency basket consisting of the deutsche mark, the French franc, the Japanese yen, the pound sterling, and the U.S. dollar. The market exchange rate fluctuates within a band of ±7 percent around the midpoint rate in response to market forces and intervention policy. Since December 17, 1991, both the midpoint and the band have been adjusted gradually at a daily rate ("slope" of the band) that reflects the annual difference between the domestic inflation target and the projected inflation in the main trading partners. The slope of the band has been 6 percent on an annual basis since July 26, 1993. On December 29, 1995, the exchange rate of the new sheqel in terms of the U.S. dollar was NIS 3.135 per $1.

Forward exchange transactions between foreign currencies are permitted. Transactions in futures and options, including traded contracts, on foreign currencies, foreign interest rates, commodities, and securities prices by both resident companies and individuals are allowed. However, resident firms may only enter into such contracts in order to cover commercial risks arising from permitted transactions; transactions in commodities may only be entered into to cover risks; and transactions, other than in traded contracts, must be carried out against an authorized dealer bank or, through it, against a foreign bank or broker. Forward exchange transactions between the new sheqel and foreign currencies are permitted only for up to one month and under the condition that underlying transactions are authorized up to the maturity of the forward contract. There is, however, a market for derivatives (forwards, swaps, options) of assets linked to, but not payable in, foreign currency. These assets and derivatives are close substitutes for foreign currency, but there is still some segmentation between the markets.

Israel accepted the obligations of Article VIII, Sections 2, 3, and 4 of the Fund Agreement on September 21, 1993.

Administration of Control

Exchange control is the responsibility of the Controller of Foreign Exchange; it is administered by the Bank of Israel, in cooperation with other government agencies, and is carried out through banks that are authorized to deal in foreign exchange; other institutions (e.g., securities brokers and foreign exchange dealers) possess, or may obtain, a limited license to deal in foreign exchange.

Prescription of Currency

Payments and receipts must be effected in the currency and manner prescribed by the exchange control authorities.

Nonresident Accounts

Nonresidents' funds are held either in foreign currency accounts or in local currency accounts. The opening of nonresident foreign currency accounts does not require prior approval. Account holders may freely effect transfers from their foreign currency account and may also convert funds held in the account into local currency at the market exchange rate.

There are no restrictions on the opening of convertible local currency accounts by nonresidents; funds in these accounts may be used in permitted transactions, including transfers between nonresidents. The sales proceeds of real estate and other investments may be transferred abroad in their entirety if the original investment was made through an authorized dealer with foreign currency or through a local currency nonresident account.

Resident Accounts in Foreign Currency

There are two main types of accounts:

(1) *Foreign currency deposit accounts (PAMAH).* Export proceeds and unilateral transfers directly received from abroad, as well as unused travel allowances, may be deposited in these accounts. The liquidity requirements are 6 percent for a current account of up to six days and 3 percent for a time deposit account with a maturity of up to one year, and zero for a time deposit account with a maturity exceeding one year. *Resident restitution deposit accounts* may be maintained under PAMAH. These accounts may be held only by recipients of restitution payments or certain disability pensions. The liquidity requirement for these accounts was 25.5 percent on December 31, 1995 (it has been gradually and automatically reduced at a fixed monthly rate since November 1991, when the rate was 90 percent with the objective of reaching the rate for

PAMAH). Funds deposited in these accounts are tax free and may be used up to a limit of $1,800 for additional travel allowances.

(2) *Exempt resident deposit accounts.* Certain residents (mostly immigrants) may deposit funds brought from abroad in these accounts. Certain regulations stipulate the types of funds that may be deposited in these accounts. Balances of these accounts may be freely transferred abroad.

In addition, a resident may open a deposit account linked to a foreign currency (PATZAM) with a maturity period of not less than one month.

Imports and Import Payments

With the exception of agricultural products, imports are free of quantitative restrictions. A special regime applies to imports from countries that restrict or prohibit imports from Israel.

Banks automatically grant foreign exchange to pay for authorized imports when the relevant documents (import documents, bills of lading, and letters of credit) are presented. Foreign exchange is also provided automatically for repayment of suppliers' credits. Importers are allowed to use foreign currency proceeds of loans obtained abroad directly for import payments without first depositing the funds with an authorized Israeli bank. Advance payments for imports of goods to be supplied within one year are allowed.

A value-added tax of 17 percent is levied on almost all imported and domestically produced goods, other than fresh fruits and vegetables.

Payments for Invisibles

Foreign exchange for payments abroad on account of invisibles, including tourism expenses, is provided automatically upon proof of the nature of the transaction. The limit on foreign travel allowances in cash, traveler's checks, and cash withdrawals on credit cards while overseas is $7,000 a person a trip; additional cash allowances are granted if needed. There are no quantitative restrictions on the use of credit cards for purchasing tourist services. Residents may make support or gift remittances abroad of up to $2,000 a year. The exchange allowance for students studying at institutions of higher education abroad is $1,000 a month in addition to tuition expenses. Foreign exchange in excess of the above-mentioned amounts may be provided on submission of documentary proof of need. A resident going abroad for medical treatment who requires hospitalization is permitted to pay up to the equivalent of $30,000 in advance. While abroad, he or she is permitted to pay the remainder of expenses on submis-

sion of receipts. Residents, while in Israel, are permitted to make credit card payments abroad, of up to $5,500 a year.

Resident travelers may take out Israeli banknotes not exceeding the equivalent of $200 a person a trip. Nonresident travelers leaving Israel are permitted to take out Israeli banknotes up to the equivalent of $100, and to repurchase, through an authorized dealer at the port of departure, foreign currency up to the equivalent of $500. Nonresidents may purchase foreign currency on presentation of documents showing previous conversion of foreign currency into Israeli currency, with a limit for each visit of $5,000 for a person over 18 years and of $2,000 for a person under 18 years (a temporary leave of less than two weeks during the visit does not affect the person's right).

Remittances of earnings by foreign workers are not restricted. Remittances of profits and dividends from foreign direct investment are permitted.

Exports and Export Proceeds

Most exports do not require licenses. Exports of oil and certain defense equipment require licensing. Export proceeds in foreign currencies must be received within 12 months of the date of export; they may be held in a PAMAH account or sold to authorized banks. However, exporters may retain in a bank account abroad up to 10 percent of export proceeds received over the previous 12 months and use the funds to pay for imports and other authorized payments abroad. In cases where the exporter is a firm with limited liabilities, the amount allowed to be deposited in a bank account abroad is also part of the overall limit on the portfolio investment abroad of the firm. For inputs directly imported by an exporter, there is a system of rebates of customs duties, wharf charges, and other related charges.

Proceeds from Invisibles

Exchange proceeds from invisibles may, in general, be kept in foreign exchange in PAMAH accounts or sold to authorized banks. Residents are free to accept specified convertible currencies from tourists in payment for customary tourist services and commodities other than securities and real estate.

For 30 years after entering Israel, immigrants are exempt from the requirement to surrender their foreign exchange to authorized banks, and they may hold these foreign currencies freely with authorized banks in Israel or with banks abroad. There is no limit on the amount of Israeli banknotes or foreign currency that may be brought in by travelers.

Capital

Nonresidents are permitted to purchase real estate, traded securities, and units of mutual trust funds in Israel. To repatriate the principal on these investments, nonresidents must prove to an authorized bank that these were purchased through a nonresident account or from foreign currency transferred from abroad. Direct loans from nonresidents to Israeli residents are not restricted. Foreign exchange brought into Israel for the purpose of investment in the form of equity capital or shareholders' loans may be granted preferential tax treatment in accordance with the Law for the Encouragement of Capital Investment.

Provident funds are permitted to invest up to 2 percent of their total assets in recognized foreign securities. Income and profits earned in foreign currency by institutional investors from these investments, including capital gains, are taxed at the rate of 35 percent.

Active incorporated Israeli companies are permitted to undertake direct investment abroad (e.g., in subsidiaries and real estate) without any quantitative limit on the size of the investment and to hold foreign securities and deposits (exporters only) abroad, provided that the investment does not amount to more than 10 percent of their equity or 5 percent of their sales turnover, whichever is larger.

Nonresidents holding Israeli securities or real estate are allowed to deposit income from these assets in their foreign currency accounts. Proceeds from sales of these assets are allowed to be deposited in their nonresident accounts, provided that the investment was carried out through a nonresident account or from foreign currency transferred from abroad. Emigrants are permitted to transfer abroad up to the equivalent of $20,000 a year of their assets kept in Israel from the third year of stay abroad up to the sixth year. As from the seventh year of stay abroad (or if they are over 60 years of age), they may transfer up to the equivalent of $50,000 a year.

Direct loans in any form from Israeli residents to nonresidents are generally subject to licensing. Domestic banks are permitted to lend to nonresidents; if collateral is required, it has to be in the form of assets convertible into foreign currency. Individual residents may buy foreign securities traded abroad, provided that the securities are held in a safekeeping deposit with an authorized dealer. Israeli mutual trust funds are permitted to invest abroad up to 10 percent of their portfolio of financial assets (up to 50 percent in the case of funds specializing in foreign currency investments).

Resident exporters and airline and shipping companies may maintain foreign bank accounts. New immigrants may retain their foreign assets for 30 years; otherwise, residents are not normally permitted to retain abroad real estate, money, securities, or income from these assets.

Proceeds accruing from the repatriation or liquidation of foreign assets must be surrendered.

Gold

Residents are allowed to import and export gold, subject to the same regulations as those applied to merchandise trade, and to transact in gold bullion and coins. Gold certificates are treated as foreign securities.

Changes During 1995

Exchange Arrangement

June 1. The exchange rate band was widened from ±5 to ±7 percent of the central parity rate.

June 5. The composition of the currency basket was adjusted on the basis of the difference between the composition of trade and the composition of the basket in 1994. It was also announced that each year, the final trade figures for the preceding year would be reviewed. If the review indicates that a change of 2 percentage points or more is required in the weight of any of the currencies comprising the basket, all the components of the basket will automatically be adjusted on April 30 of that year.

August 1. Authorized dealer banks were permitted to undertake swap transactions of domestic currencies for foreign currencies with the Bank of Israel.

Resident Accounts in Foreign Currency

April 1. The period during which foreign currency may be held in a resident transfer deposit (PAMAH) was extended from 14 to 30 days.

Imports and Import Payments

July 1. The requirements regarding the various documents that had to be submitted to the authorized dealer bank when making payments for imports were harmonized, so that for each transaction only three documents have to be submitted (a bill of lading or import list, the supplier's invoice, and the importer's statement).

July 2. Payment of up to $3,000 for imports was allowed to be made upon presentation of a notice published by the supplier in a newspaper or an advertising prospectus, and payment was allowed to be made for crates remaining abroad within the framework of importing services.

Payments for Invisibles

July 1. Upon leaving Israel, a nonresident was allowed to purchase foreign currency of up to $500 at any border crossing point and not only at an airport or seaport, as was formerly the case.

July 1. The currency control regulations governing transactions between a resident and a nonresident, and between a resident traveling abroad were extended to transactions between a resident in the Taba and Southern Sinai region and a resident traveling to Egypt or Southern Sinai via the Taba border crossing. As a result, a resident traveling to that region may buy the foreign currency travel allowance (currently $7,000), and all transactions with that region may be executed in foreign currency, as is the case with transactions abroad.

Exports and Export Proceeds

June 1. Port fees were applied to both exports and imports so as to eliminate an existing implicit export subsidy.

Capital

February 1. Provident funds were permitted to invest in approved and/or recognized foreign securities and undertake forward and other future transactions permitted to an individual resident, provided their total investments of this kind did not exceed 2 percent of their assets. (Until the change, the provident funds were allowed to invest only in approved foreign securities.)

April 1. (1) In addition to their investment in approved foreign securities and deposits abroad of exporters, Israeli firms were permitted to invest in recognized foreign securities provided this consti-

tuted no more than 10 percent of their equity or 5 percent of their sales turnover, whichever was highest; (2) Active Israeli firms were permitted to establish or buy firms abroad and invest capital in them as an equity holder's loan or as a guarantee; (3) Active Israeli firms were also permitted to purchase real estate abroad. In this respect, an active firm is defined as one whose audited accounts show that it has been in business for at least one year and one whose turnover for value-added tax purposes in the previous 12 months was not less than NIS 1.5 million (indexed to the December 1994 CPI); and (4) Permits for investment abroad (both direct and financial) by Israeli firms are subject to the conditions determined by the Controller of Foreign Exchange, including the following reporting requirements: (a) a company whose financial investment abroad exceeds $0.5 million must make a monthly report of its securities and deposits abroad; and (b) a company whose direct investment abroad exceeds $0.5 million must make an annual report of its direct investments abroad.

July 1. A resident who has received a foreign security of any kind (even if it is neither recognized nor approved) as a gift from a nonresident is allowed to retain it, provided it is placed in a custody deposit on his or her name with an authorized dealer bank. This has brought the regulations concerning securities received as a gift into line with those concerning securities received as a bequest.

July 1. The maximum amount a resident can transfer abroad as an alimony payment was increased. A resident may now purchase foreign currency and transfer it abroad to pay alimony in accordance with the amount stipulated in the court's decision, or four times the amount permitted under the alimony legislation, whichever is lower.

ITALY

(Position as of December 31, 1995)

Exchange Arrangement

The currency of Italy is the Italian Lira.[1] The Italian authorities generally do not intervene in the exchange market, and spot and forward exchange rates are determined on the basis of demand and supply conditions. Rates for 20 foreign currencies[2] are monitored every working day by the Bank of Italy exclusively for informational purposes. On December 29, 1995, the rate for the U.S dollar was Lit 1,584.72 per $1. There are no taxes or subsidies on purchases or sales of foreign exchange.

Authorized banks are allowed to engage in spot and forward exchange transactions in any currency, and premiums and discounts in the forward exchange market are normally left to the interplay of market forces. Residents may carry out spot and forward foreign exchange operations and transact currency options either with authorized banks or with foreign counterparts.

Italy accepted the obligations of Article VIII, Sections 2, 3, and 4 of the Fund Agreement, on February 15, 1961.

Administration of Control

Residents are allowed to conduct foreign exchange transactions freely, with settlements to be effected either through authorized intermediaries (the Bank of Italy, authorized banks, and the Postal Administration) or directly, by drawing on external accounts or by offsetting debts and credits vis-à-vis other residents or nonresidents. In the case of material delivery of means of payment in Italy or abroad, Italian residents are allowed to take with them into or out of the country Italian or foreign banknotes and bearer securities of any denomination up to the equivalent of Lit 20 million. For fiscal and anti-money-laundering purposes, transfers exceeding this amount must be carried out through authorized intermediaries. Residents are allowed to enter and leave the country carrying securities denomi-

nated in lire or in foreign currencies worth Lit 20 million, provided that they are not bearer securities and that they are declared to customs. Nonresidents may take up to Lit 20 million in banknotes and securities of any denomination into and out of Italy without formalities. If they bring in banknotes and securities in an amount in excess of Lit 20 million, they must declare the excess amount to customs on a special form upon entering Italy. Nonresidents may re-export larger sums but only up to the amount in excess of Lit 20 million that they have imported and declared. No limit applies to exports of nonbearer securities; nonresidents need only submit the above-mentioned form to customs. The limitations described above do not apply to transfers effected by banks when they act as senders or beneficiaries. However, banks are also obliged to declare their transfers by filling out a special customs form.

Operators and authorized intermediaries must, for statistical purposes, transmit data to the Italian Foreign Exchange Office (Ufficio Italiano dei Cambi (UIC)) on their foreign transactions that exceed the equivalent of Lit 20 million by filling out a foreign exchange statistical return (*Comunicazione valutaria statistica*).

In accordance with the Fund's Executive Board Decision No. 144–(52/51), adopted on August 14, 1952, Italy notified the Fund on August 28, 1992 that, in compliance with UN Security Council Resolution No. 757 (1992), certain restrictions had been imposed on the making of payments and transfers for current international transactions in respect of the Federal Republic of Yugoslavia (Serbia/Montenegro). The above restrictions have been suspended in accordance with UN Security Council Resolution Nos. 1021 and 1022 of November 22, 1995. Similar restrictions are in force against Iraq, Libya, and the movement UNITA in Angola.

Prescription of Currency

Settlements with foreign countries are normally made in quoted currencies or in lire on foreign accounts.

Italy maintains clearing accounts with Croatia and Slovenia. The accounts are used for trade in cross-border areas. The balances in these accounts may be used only to finance trade between certain districts of Croatia and Slovenia and the Italian provinces of Trieste and Gorizia. The balances are

---

[1] With effect from September 17, 1992, Italy suspended its exchange rate intervention obligations of the European Monetary System (EMS).

[2] Australian dollars, Austrian schillings, Belgian francs, Canadian dollars, Danish kroner, deutsche mark, ECUs, Finnish markkaa, French francs, Greek drachmas, Irish pounds, Japanese yen, Netherlands guilders, Norwegian kroner, Portuguese escudos, pounds sterling, Spanish pesetas, Swedish kronor, Swiss francs, and U.S. dollars.

not transferable. There is no automatic mechanism through which outstanding balances are settled within 90 days. Only Italy is allowed to maintain a debit balance on these accounts.

Nonresident Accounts

Nonresidents may maintain accounts with authorized banks in lire and in foreign exchange, which may be freely debited and credited upon their request.

Imports and Import Payments

Imports are governed by European Union (EU) regulations according to which imports of most products, except for textiles and some products originating from China, are free of licensing and quantitative restrictions. Imports from non-EU countries of most products covered by the Common Agricultural Policy (CAP) of the EU are subject to variable import levies, which have replaced all previous barriers to imports. Common EU regulations are also applied to imports of most other agricultural and livestock products from non-EU countries. Payments for imports are not regulated, without prejudice to the general rules cited in the section on Administration of Control.

Payments for Invisibles

Payments for invisibles may be made freely, without prejudice to the general rules cited in the section on Administration and Control. Domestic and foreign banknotes up to Lit 20 million or its equivalent exported across the border by residents are free of restrictions. Exports exceeding this amount must be made through authorized intermediaries for recording and fiscal monitoring purposes and according to the regulations on money laundering.

Exports and Export Proceeds

Exports to non-EU countries are free, with the exception of high-technology products included in EU Regulation 3381/94 and of oil extracted from the seabed, both of which are subject to ministerial authorization.

Proceeds from Invisibles

There are no limitations on receipts from invisibles, without prejudice to the general rules cited in the section on Administration of Control.

Capital

Foreign investments of any kind in Italy, including both direct and portfolio investment and the purchase of real estate, are not restricted, and no restrictions are applied to their repatriation. Residents and nonresidents are subject to the general regulations described in the section on Administration of Control.

Gold

Purchases and sales of gold abroad are legally reserved for the monetary authorities. Residents may purchase and import unrefined gold under ministerial license for industrial purposes. Loans for the importation of gold are freely assumable. The exportation of unrefined gold is subject to licensing by the Ministry of Foreign Trade. The importation and exportation of gold coins, including coins that are legal tender in a foreign country, are unrestricted. Imports of unrefined gold are not subject to the value-added tax, whereas imports of gold coins are subject to a value-added tax at 19 percent.

Changes During 1995

Administration of Control

April 7. The embargo against Haiti, in accordance with UN Security Council Resolution No. 944, was removed.

November 22. The embargo against Serbia/Montenegro was suspended, in accordance with UN Security Council Resolution Nos. 1021 and 1022.

(See Appendix for summary of trade measures introduced and eliminated on an EU-wide basis during 1995.)

JAMAICA

(Position as of December 31, 1995)

Exchange Arrangement

The currency of Jamaica is the Jamaica Dollar. The Jamaican authorities do not maintain margins in respect of exchange transactions, and the spot and forward exchange rates are determined by demand and supply in the interbank market. On December 31, 1995, the average spot buying and selling rates for the U.S. dollar were J$39.4 and J$39.8, respectively, per US$1. There are no taxes or subsidies on purchases or sales of foreign exchange.

The foreign exchange market is operated by the commercial banks, other authorized dealers, and the Bank of Jamaica. The commercial banks buy and sell for their own account. Foreign exchange bureaus and cambios function as points of collection, and they are required to sell to the Bank of Jamaica a prescribed minimum amount of foreign exchange that they have purchased. Excess foreign exchange may be sold without restrictions to the commercial banks, other authorized dealers, and the general public. Proceeds from official loans, divestment of government assets, and taxes on the bauxite sector payable in foreign currency are sold directly to the Bank of Jamaica. While there is no restriction on transactions in any currency, the principal foreign currencies accepted in the exchange market are the Canadian dollar, the pound sterling, and the U.S. dollar (trade in other currencies is optional and negotiable between participating banks).

While the Bank of Jamaica is primarily responsible for payments of obligations on government imports of goods and services and official debt, the public entities are free to conduct their own foreign exchange transactions. Since the amounts sold directly to the Bank of Jamaica from the sources indicated above are insufficient to meet the payments it must make, the Bank of Jamaica purchases its additional requirement from the foreign exchange market at the prevailing rate.

All private sector payments are transacted through the commercial banking system, other authorized dealers, and foreign exchange bureaus. The commercial banks also handle most service payments.

On November 1, 1990, the Bank of Jamaica, in consultation with the other central banks in the Caribbean Common Market (CARICOM), suspended clearing arrangements within the framework of CARICOM. The Bank of Jamaica no longer intervenes in CARICOM private sector commercial transactions; settlements for such transactions are effected by the commercial banking sector in convertible currencies.

Jamaica accepted the obligations of Article VIII, Sections 2, 3, and 4 of the Fund Agreement on February 22, 1963.

Administration of Control

The Exchange Control Act, previously administered by the Bank of Jamaica on behalf of the Minister of Finance, was repealed on August 17, 1992. The provision regarding prohibition of trading in foreign exchange, except by and through an authorized dealer, was incorporated in the Bank of Jamaica Act. The Minister of Finance, however, retains the authority to issue directions to specified classes of persons regarding the acquisition of foreign assets.

Prescription of Currency

Payments to all countries may be made by crediting Jamaica dollars to an external account or a foreign currency account.[1] Receipts from all countries must be received by debit of an external account or in any foreign currency.

Foreign Currency Accounts

Authorized dealers are allowed to open foreign currency accounts for residents and nonresidents. Funds on these accounts may be transferred freely between residents and nonresidents. External accounts may be credited with payments by residents of Jamaica, with transfers from other external accounts, and with the proceeds from the sale to an authorized dealer of gold or foreign currencies. They may be debited for payments to residents of Jamaica, for transfers to other external accounts, and for the purchase of foreign currencies. Authorized dealers are allowed to hold, for residents and nonresidents, "A" accounts in foreign currency and "B" accounts in Jamaica dollars, both of which are exempt from tax on interest earned on all deposits, provided that (1) in the case of A accounts operated by nonresidents, no new accounts have been operating and no new deposits have been made in existing accounts

---

[1]All currencies other than the Jamaica dollar are considered foreign currencies. All foreign currencies have been designated as specified currencies.

after September 22, 1991; and (2) in the case of B accounts operated by residents as of September 22, 1991, deposits are held as certificates of deposits with at least a one-year maturity.

Imports and Import Payments

Import licenses are required for pharmaceutical products and items that endanger public health or security; otherwise, goods may be imported freely without a license. Import licenses, when required, are issued by the Trade Administrator, who is responsible to the Minister of Industry and Commerce. Imports of motor vehicles do not require a license, but a permit is required for government statistical purposes. Payments for imports may be made by commercial banks without reference to the Bank of Jamaica.

Imports are subject to customs tariffs in compliance with the Common External Tariff (CET) Arrangement of CARICOM. The member countries of CARICOM agreed in October 1992 on a phased reduction in the level and dispersion of the regional CET over the next five years. As a result, the range of import tariff rates in Jamaica was changed from zero to 45 percent to 5 to 30 percent, effective April 1, 1993; to zero to 30 percent effective April 1, 1994; to zero to 25 percent effective April 1, 1995; and will eventually be reduced to zero to 20 percent by the end of 1996. Some agricultural products will remain subject to a stamp duty at a rate of up to 95 percent, and these will be reduced over a three-year period to be consistent with the CET.

Exports and Export Proceeds

Most goods may be exported without restriction. However, specific licenses are required for the exportation of certain agricultural products, ammunition, explosives, firearms, antique furniture, motor vehicles, mineral and metal ores, paintings, jewelry, and petroleum products.

All proceeds from exports may be used in transactions in the foreign exchange market without restriction.

Payments for and Proceeds from Invisibles

Commercial banks and other authorized dealers provide foreign exchange for most service transactions, including business and other travel, insurance, commissions, private interest payments, medical expenses, foreign exchange refunds, cash gifts, pensions, and miscellaneous payments, such as registration and subscription fees. All interest and dividends payable to nonresident investors are repatriable without restriction.

Proceeds from invisibles may be used in foreign exchange market transactions without restriction.

Capital

All capital flows (both inflows and outflows) are free of restrictions.

Commercial banks and licensed deposit-taking institutions may be required to match their Jamaica dollar liabilities to their clients with Jamaica dollar assets.

In July 1987, a debt-equity program was introduced for the conversion of certain foreign commercial bank debts to Jamaica into equity investments in approved public and private sector entities. Under this program, profit repatriation was prohibited for three years. Capital repatriation was also prohibited for three years for investments in priority sectors and for seven years for investments in other qualified sectors. This program ended on March 31, 1995.

Gold

Commemorative gold coins in denominations of J$20, J$100, and J$250 are legal tender but do not circulate. No restrictions exist on the purchase, sale, or holding of gold for numismatic or industrial purposes.

Changes During 1995

Capital

March 31. The debt-equity program to convert certain commercial bank debts to Jamaica into equity investment, in place since July 1987, ended.

JAPAN

(Position as of December 31, 1995)

Exchange Arrangement

The currency of Japan is the Japanese Yen. The authorities of Japan do not maintain margins in respect of exchange transactions, and exchange rates are determined on the basis of demand and supply in the exchange markets. However, the authorities intervene when necessary in order to counter disorderly conditions in the markets. The principal intervention currency is the U.S. dollar. The closing interbank rate for the U.S. dollar in the Tokyo market on December 29, 1995 was ¥102.905 per $1. Authorized banks may freely carry out spot and forward exchange transactions with their customers, with nonresident banks, and among themselves. Forward exchange contracts may be negotiated against foreign currencies quoted on the Tokyo exchange market and in other major international foreign exchange markets. There are no officially set rates in the forward market, and forward exchange transactions are based on free market rates. There are no taxes or subsidies on purchases or sales of foreign exchange.

Japan accepted the obligations of Article VIII, Sections 2, 3, and 4 of the Fund Agreement on April 1, 1964.

Administration of Control

The exchange and trade control system is operated mainly by the Ministry of Finance, the Ministry of International Trade and Industry (MITI), and the Bank of Japan acting as the Government's agent. Most of the authority for verifying normal payments is, however, delegated to authorized banks, referred to as foreign exchange banks. Import- and export-reporting requirements are handled by the MITI. Inward direct investments have to be reported to the Minister of Finance and other appropriate ministers after such investments take place. Outward direct investments require prior notice to the Ministry of Finance.

Prescription of Currency

Payments to all countries may be made in any currency, including yen, and receipts may also be obtained in any currency.

Nonresident Accounts

Nonresident accounts in yen may be opened by nonresidents with any authorized bank in Japan. There are no restrictions on credits to or payments from these accounts, and balances may be converted freely into any foreign currency. Payment of interest on balances in such accounts may be restricted when it is deemed necessary to prevent drastic fluctuations in the exchange rate of the yen.

Imports and Import Payments

Imports may be made freely, with the exception of specifically restricted items or items from designated countries. The Import Restriction System covers 77 items (four-digit Harmonized Commodity Description and Coding System (HS) base), which are subject to import restrictions falling under the state trading, national security, public health, and moral protection provisions of the GATT. For the restricted items, once importers obtain authorization from the MITI, they receive an import quota certificate that entitles them to receive an import license from an authorized foreign exchange bank automatically upon application. For the importation of certain other goods from certain countries or shipping areas, individual authorization must be obtained from the MITI. Imports from Croatia, Bosnia and Herzegovina, the Federal Republic of Yugoslavia (Serbia/Montenegro), Iraq, and the Libyan Arab Jamahiriya require permission from the MITI. For transactions that involve payments from Japan to residents of Bosnia and Herzegovina, the Federal Republic of Yugoslavia (Serbia/Montenegro), Iraq, and the Libyan Arab Jamahiriya or by residents of these countries to foreign countries through Japan, permission from the Minister of Finance is required. Intermediary trade of petroleum and its products destined for Angola require permission from the MITI.

Import settlements effected under the special methods (i.e., those effected by means of open accounts or those involving payments made more than two years before import declaration or after more than two years of shipment) require authorization from the MITI.

Payments for Invisibles

Payments for invisibles may be made without limit. Gifts and donations (except by government institutions) to nonresidents (except relatives abroad) that are valued at more than ¥5 million are referred to the Bank of Japan, which approves the payment after verifying its authenticity. However, remittances to relatives abroad may be made without limit. Other current payments for invisibles, such as the purchase of foreign currencies in connection with travel abroad, may be made without limit. The exportation of domestic banknotes exceeding ¥5 million requires ministerial approval. Intermediating businesses involving Croatia, Bosnia and Herzegovina, the Federal Republic of Yugoslavia (Serbia/Montenegro), and Iraq require permission from the MITI.

Exports and Export Proceeds

Export restraint may be exercised by virtue of the Export and Import Transactions Law and the Export Trade Control Order issued under the Foreign Exchange and Foreign Trade Control Law. Export restraint may be applied either globally or to certain destinations, and it may cover export volume, export prices, or other conditions. Voluntary restraints are applied to exports of certain textile items to the United States and the European Union (EU), to exports of passenger cars to the United States, and to exports of forklift trucks to the EU. In addition, exports of some other products, including passenger cars, light commercial vehicles, and videocassette recorders to the EU, were subject to monitoring by The Government.

Twenty-seven export cartels were operating under the provisions of the Export and Import Transactions Law. In addition, 228 items were subject to a license under the Foreign Exchange and Foreign Trade Control Law to control their exportation to specified destinations either because of short supply in the domestic market (e.g., nickel) or to forestall the imposition of import restrictions by other countries (e.g., certain textiles). Exports under processing contracts and exports for which settlements are effected under the special methods described above require authorization from the MITI. Exports of specified raw materials for foreign processing and reimportation require individual licenses. Exports to Croatia, Bosnia and Herzegovina, the Federal Republic of Yugoslavia (Serbia/Montenegro), Iraq, and the Libyan Arab Jamahiriya require permission from the MITI.

Proceeds from Invisibles

Receipts from invisibles may generally be accepted without a license. Residents as well as nonresidents may freely bring in any amount in Japanese or foreign currency. Intermediating business related to trade between the Federal Republic of Yugoslavia (Serbia/Montenegro) or Iraq and other countries and exports of services to these two countries require permission from the MITI.

Capital

Capital transactions are, in principle, free unless certain procedures are specifically required. Such procedures may take the form of requiring (1) prior approval; (2) prior notice with a waiting period, during which the Minister of Finance or the MITI may request or order that the transaction be suspended or that its particulars be modified on the basis of prescribed criteria; or (3) prior notice without a waiting period. Acquisition of securities for portfolios may be made freely through designated securities firms, and foreign exchange banks and designated institutional investors may freely acquire securities for portfolio investments. However, acquisition of such securities through securities firms other than the designated ones and borrowings by residents require prior notice without a waiting period. Under emergency conditions, however, most capital transactions that are not subject to prior approval in normal conditions may be made subject to prior approval. Emergency conditions are defined as situations in which a capital transaction might (1) make the maintenance of equilibrium in Japan's balance of payments difficult; (2) result in drastic fluctuations in the exchange rate; or (3) result in an international flow of funds large enough to affect Japan's money or capital market adversely.

A distinction is made between direct investments in Japan and other capital transactions. Besides majority equity ownership of enterprises or establishment of branch operations, investments that come under the direct investment regulations include (1) any acquisition of shares in unlisted companies; (2) acquisition by a foreign investor of the shares of a listed company (including individual companies for which the stock price in over-the-counter transactions is made public by the Securities Dealers Association) that reach 10 percent or more when added to those owned by related persons; and (3) acquisition of loans of more than one-year maturity or securities privately placed in Japan, under certain circumstances. Any change of business objectives of a company with one-third or more foreign ownership is also subject to the direct investment provisions. Requests or orders for suspension or modification of specific aspects of the transaction may be made if the minister or ministers concerned consider the transaction to have adverse implications for national security, public order, public safety, the activities of Japanese enterprises in related lines of activities, the general performance of the economy, or the maintenance of mutual equality of treatment of direct investment with other countries. In April 1991, an amendment to the law governing foreign direct investment was introduced. Under the revised law, foreign investors are required to report only after undertaking investment unless concerns mentioned above, such as national security interest, arise.

Outward investments by residents in the form of loans, issue of bonds abroad by residents, issue of bonds in Japan by nonresidents, and direct investment abroad are subject to prior notice with a 20-day waiting period. Transactions requiring prior notice with a 20-day waiting period may be subject to suspension or modification by the Minister of Finance if, in the Minister's opinion, the transaction might adversely affect (1) international financial markets or Japan's international credit standing; (2) domestic and financial capital markets; (3) business activities of a sector of Japanese industries or the smooth performance of the national economy; and (4) implementation of Japan's international agreements, international peace and security, or the maintenance of public order. The Minister of Finance may shorten the waiting period when the transaction under consideration is deemed without adverse consequences. Other transactions by nonresidents may generally be carried out freely. Overseas deposits by residents, borrowing and lending in foreign currency between residents other than those carried out by an authorized bank in Japan, and issuance of yen-denominated bonds abroad by nonresidents may require prior approval. Other external transactions by residents may normally be carried out freely. Issuance of securities or bonds by residents abroad and of foreign-currency-denominated securities or bonds by residents in Japan requires prior notice to the Minister of Finance.

Foreign loans by banks are legally subject to prior notice with a waiting period but, in most cases, may be made upon notification. The banks are free to lend yen on a long-term basis overseas to borrowers of their choice and may accept foreign currency deposits from residents and nonresidents and make foreign currency loans to residents. Foreign currency or yen deposits of nonresidents and residents are subject to minimum reserve requirements adjusted from time to time by the Bank of Japan. Foreign banks are licensed to operate in Japan, subject to Japanese banking regulations; they may obtain resources from inward remittances of foreign currency as well as from money markets in Japan.

Financial institutions apply the following prudential guidelines to capital transactions: (1) a limit on the holding by insurance companies of securities issued by nonresidents equivalent to 30 percent of total assets; (2) the same ratio applied to purchases of foreign-currency-denominated assets; (3) a limit on the holdings by the Post Office Insurance Fund of bonds equivalent to 20 percent of the reserve funds issued by nonresidents; (4) a ceiling on foreign-currency- denominated assets purchased by pension funds equivalent to 30 percent of pension trust assets (for the new money deposited from April 1, 1990, effective December 27, 1991, the ceiling was relaxed to 50 percent on the basis of each institutional account, and the ceiling for foreign-affiliated companies was raised to 70 percent); (5) a ceiling on the investment by credit cooperatives in foreign-currency-denominated bonds, excluding corporate bonds issued by nonresidents equivalent to 30 percent of their net worth; and (6) a ceiling of 5 percent of assets for investment in foreign-currency-denominated securities by the loan trust accounts of trust banks.

Both residents and nonresidents may maintain foreign currency deposits with authorized banks in Japan and may freely transfer any amount in any foreign currency. Overseas deposits by residents up to the equivalent of ¥ 200 million are not restricted. Qualified Japanese enterprises in insurance, transportation, and securities are permitted to maintain overseas deposits under blanket licensing.

In August 1995, the Ministry of Finance announced the following measures to promote overseas investments and loans by institutional investors: (1) Foreign-currency-denominated external loans by insurance companies are to be liberalized. (2) Restrictions on yen-denominated external loans by insurance companies (so-called 50 percent rule) are to be removed. (3) The offshore seasoning period on Euroyen bonds issued by nonresidents is to be removed immediately and completely. (4) The following accounting methods with respect to foreign bonds owned by institutional investors are to be allowed: (a) with regard to the evaluation of U.S. Treasury Bonds where only cost method has been permitted, companies are allowed to adopt either the market method or the cost method, which makes the treatment equal to that for the Japanese Government Bonds; (b) with regard to the evaluation of listed bonds, the adoption of different methods (i.e., either the cost method or the market method) is to be permitted for yen-denominated bonds and foreign-currency-denominated bonds, respectively. This measure is expected to facilitate the adoption of the cost method for nonresident-issued Euroyen bonds; (c) the Ministry of Finance confirmed that the application of the so-called 15 percent rule is within each company's discretion, that is, each company can decide whether or not to count the valuation loss in foreign-currency-denominated bonds when foreign exchange rates move significantly. And (5) the regulation on foreign exchange positions imposed on authorized foreign exchange banks is to be eased to promote their yen assets to be invested into foreign-currency-denominated bonds.

Gold

Residents, including domestic producers of gold, may freely hold gold and purchase and sell it in domestic transactions. The importation and exportation of gold bullion are free from licensing. External futures in gold may be freely traded by designated companies.

Changes During 1995

Capital

August 2. The Ministry of Finance annouced measures to promote overseas investments and loans by institutional investors.

JORDAN

(Position as of December 31, 1995)

Exchange Arrangement

The currency of Jordan is the Jordan Dinar. Its exchange rate is determined on the basis of its relationship to the basket of five currencies that constitute the SDR, with the weights determined by the currencies' relative importance to Jordan's international transactions. On December 31, 1995, the official buying and selling rates quoted by the Bank of Jordan, the central bank, for the U.S. dollar were JD 1.4103 and JD 1.4505, respectively, per $1. Buying and selling rates for other foreign currencies[1] are fixed on the basis of the cross rates between the U.S. dollar and the currencies concerned in international financial markets.

A fee of 0.10 percent is levied on exchange permits approved by the central bank for sales of exchange for imports, except imports of government departments and certain other approved institutions. Authorized banks are permitted to enter into forward contracts in major currencies against the Jordan dinar for commercial transactions, provided that they cover such operations abroad. For corporations or projects considered to be of vital national interest, the central bank may offer a forward exchange facility in respect of forward exchange cover provided by Jordanian banks. There are no taxes or subsidies on purchases or sales of foreign exchange.

Jordan accepted the obligations of Article VIII, Sections 2, 3, and 4 of the Fund Agreement on February 20, 1995.

Administration of Control

Exchange control is administered by the Foreign Exchange Control Department of the central bank, which also issues exchange permits; the central bank has delegated to authorized banks the issuance of exchange permits for import payments and, within permitted annual limits, for personal invisible payments. Import policy is determined by the Ministry of Industry and Trade in cooperation with the Ministries of Finance, Supply, and Agriculture.

Arrears are maintained with respect to certain external payments.

Prescription of Currency

No prescription of currency requirements is in force. Jordan's bilateral trade and payments agreement with the Republic of Yemen is inactive.

Nonresident Accounts

Subject to the prior approval of the central bank, authorized banks may open nonresident accounts in domestic and foreign currency. Withdrawals and transfers from foreign currency accounts are free of restrictions. Balances on these accounts may be withdrawn freely in convertible currency and may be used for any purpose. Interest rates are determined in line with rates prevailing in international markets.

Resident Foreign Currency Accounts

Accounts denominated in a foreign currency may be opened at the central bank or at any other licensed bank or financial institution by governmental and semigovernmental entities, as well as by the specialized credit institutions and domestic corporations of vital national interest, including public shareholding companies, provided that outstanding balances (including interest earnings) in each account do not exceed JD 1 million. This ceiling may be raised in certain cases.

Jordanian nationals residing in Jordan may maintain foreign currency deposits with licensed banks in Jordan, provided that the total balance of the deposits that any one person holds does not exceed the equivalent of JD 500,000. Balances in these accounts can be utilized for making current payments abroad consistent with regulations governing import and invisible payments. Jordanians who have worked abroad for more than six months and have decided to return may continue to keep accounts in foreign currencies without limit for up to five years, after which the deposits in excess of the equivalent of JD 500,000 must be converted into Jordan dinars. Licensed banks and financial companies may extend credit facilities in Jordan dinars to residents and nonresidents against their foreign currency deposits. Extending credit facilities to residents against their foreign currency deposits requires the prior approval of the central bank. The amounts of credit facilities extended to nonresidents against their foreign currency deposits should not exceed 5 percent of total credit granted by a bank or a financial company. Fur-

---

[1]Belgian francs, deutsche mark, French francs, Italian lire, Japanese yen, Netherlands guilders, pounds sterling, Swedish kronor, and Swiss francs.

thermore, the balance of the foreign currency deposit used as collateral against the extended credit facilities should not, at any time, be less than the outstanding balance of credit facilities.

Imports and Import Payments

The draft law lifting the ban on imports from Israel has been submitted to Parliament. Other imports, unless mentioned in Article 3 of the Import and Export System,[2] require import licenses if their c. & f. value exceeds JD 2,000. Licenses are freely granted, except for five products that are reserved to state monopoly. A fee of 5 percent of the c. & f. value is charged when the import license is issued.

Imports requiring a license also require an exchange permit, which is granted automatically when an import license has been obtained; the importer holding an exchange permit may either open a letter of credit or pay against documents. A fee of 0.10 percent is levied on exchange permits for imports except those made by government departments and certain approved institutions and individual permits of less than JD 300. The use of suppliers' credits is subject to prior approval from the central bank, which is normally given for essential imports only.

Imports into Free Zones

Payments for imports into free zones and for transit trade are subject to the prior approval of the central bank. In principle, however, it is the importer's responsibility to provide foreign currency to finance such transactions. Banks are authorized to set the percentage of advance import deposits they collect from customers against these imports at their discretion.

Payments for Invisibles

Payments for invisibles related to authorized imports are not restricted.

Residents are permitted to transfer foreign means of payment equivalent to JD 35,000 a year to meet current payments for invisibles (travel, education, medication, pilgrimage, residence abroad, family assistance, and others) without obtaining the prior approval of the central bank and without presenting any document to justify these payments. They may transfer amounts in excess of JD 35,000 when justi-

fied by supporting documents. In comparison, transfers from nonresident accounts are free of restriction. The authorized amount for subscriptions to newsletters, magazines, and specific bulletins is the equivalent of JD 1,000. The policy on payments for invisibles is, in general, liberal and nondiscriminatory. In practice, the central bank does not restrict remittances of income accruing to nonresidents or of savings of foreign nationals returning to their own countries.

A fee of 0.10 percent is levied on exchange permits for invisible payments, except those of government departments and certain approved institutions, permits financed from nonresident accounts in foreign currency credited from sources outside Jordan, and permits with a value of less than JD 300. Remittances may be made by postal order for imports not to exceed JD 10 a person a month to any person residing abroad.

Premiums for life insurance policies issued by insurance companies operating in the Kingdom in favor of nonresidents or Jordanians working abroad must be collected in foreign currency from abroad or from nonresident accounts.

In addition to any exchange allowances for travel, residents and nonresidents traveling abroad may take out up to JD 5,000 in Jordanian banknotes and coins. Nonresidents working in Jordan who do not have nonresident accounts may transfer up to JD 400 a month, up to a maximum of JD 5,000 a year. Furthermore, all travelers may take out checks, traveler's checks, or letters of credit issued by authorized banks in Jordan, in accordance with exchange permits authorized by the central bank. Tourists and other nonresidents may also take out foreign currency notes and coins and any other foreign means of payment that they had or that they had previously brought in and declared to the customs authorities at the time of entry.

Exports and Export Proceeds

The draft law lifting the ban on exports to Israel has been submitted to Parliament. There are no requirements affecting export proceeds.

Proceeds from Invisibles

Travelers entering Jordan may bring in any amount of Jordanian and foreign banknotes and coins.[3] Individuals who, for exchange control purposes, are considered residents of Jordan may retain

---

[2]These include imports made on behalf of His Majesty the King, imports by government departments and certain approved institutions, and goods in transit.

[3]Approval is not granted for the crediting of such Jordanian currency to a nonresident account or for the remittance abroad of the equivalent in foreign currency.

only the equivalent of JD 500,000 a person in foreign currency in the Kingdom, as stipulated in the Foreign Exchange Control Regulations. They must sell the excess amount to licensed banks, financial companies, or authorized dealers.

Capital

Inward transfers of capital are not restricted, but outward transfers by residents require approval and are not normally permitted. However, the central bank may grant permission to banks, insurance companies, contractors, and industrial, agricultural, trading, and tourism firms, to transfer funds abroad for specified investment or operating purpose. Commercial banks are permitted to invest abroad up to 50 percent of their foreign exchange holdings. The transfer of funds for purposes of investment in Arab countries is permitted only if mutual treatment or bilateral agreements exist between Jordan and the country, and it is the investor's responsibility to provide foreign exchange to finance such investments. Current income resulting from nonresident investments in Jordan may be transferred abroad. Under the Law Regulating Arab and Foreign Investments, capital, profits, and dividends from foreign investments may be remitted. The Foreign Companies Registration Law No. 58 (1985) provides various benefits to foreign companies establishing branches in Jordan for purposes of conducting business outside the country; such branches may also be granted nonresident status for exchange control purposes. Nonresidents may use convertible currencies to purchase Premium Development Bonds denominated in Jordan dinars. Proceeds from redemption at maturity, including interest, are transferable in any convertible currency.

Gold

The central bank has issued ten gold coins, which, although legal tender, do not circulate and are available only to nonresidents and domestic numisma-

tists. Residents may purchase, hold, and sell gold coins in Jordan for numismatic or investment purposes. Imports of gold in any form are permitted without the prior approval of the central bank, while imports of gold to be used in crafts and then reexported are subject to the prior approval of the central bank. Exports of gold, other than gold that has been crafted and whose value has thus increased, require the prior approval of the central bank.

Changes During 1995

Exchange Arrangement

February 20. Jordan accepted the obligations of Article VIII, Section 2, 3, and 4 of the Fund Agreement.

Imports and Import Payments

January 25. Applications for exchange permits that include advance payments were required to be supported with a letter of undertaking indicating an amount equal to the advance payment in favor of the central bank. No banking guarantee is required for exchange permits covered either from foreign currency deposits or incoming confirmed letters of credit or from external guarantees.

Payments for Invisibles

April 4. Nonresidents working in Jordan who do not have nonresident accounts were permitted to transfer up to JD 400 a month instead of JD 100 a month, up to a maximum of JD 5,000 a year, instead of up to a maximum of JD 1,200 a year.

May 31. The remaining quantitative restrictions were eliminated, with the exception of those on essential products subject to state monopoly.

Capital

August 31. Commercial banks were permitted to invest abroad up to 50 percent of their foreign currency holdings.

KAZAKSTAN

(Position as of December 31, 1995)

Exchange Arrangement

The currency of the Republic of Kazakstan is the Tenge. Exchange rates of the tenge against the U.S. dollar and other foreign currencies are determined at auctions that are held three times a week in the Kazakstan Interbank Currency Exchange (KICE). Banks may participate in auctions on their own account or on behalf of their clients. In between auctions, banks and enterprises are permitted to engage in spot and cash transactions at freely negotiated rates. The official exchange rate is determined on the basis of the auction rates, and is announced each Friday by the National Bank of Kazakstan.[1] Purchasers of foreign exchange are subject to a commission fixed by the Board of the KICE, currently at 0.02 percent. Residents planning to sell or purchase foreign currency at the auction (via authorized banks) are required to present documents establishing compliance with prevailing foreign exchange regulations. There are more than 2,000 licensed exchange bureaus in Kazakstan. At the end of December 1995, the end-period exchange rate of the tenge against the U.S. dollar was T 66.4 per $1.

Administration of Control

The foreign exchange of April 1993 establishes the principle of convertibility for current international transactions. The Ministry of Foreign Economic Relations is the authority that grants licenses for export or import. The Cabinet of Ministers may decide to limit the export or import of goods not subject to licenses, depending on the economic situation. In addition, the heads of local governments may set up regimes of quotas and licenses for consumer goods other than food.

The National Bank, together with the Ministry of Finance, is responsible for the supervision of transactions in foreign currencies.

Prescription of Currency

Settlements with the Baltic countries, Russia, and the other countries of the former Soviet Union are made through a system of correspondent accounts of the National Bank and commercial banks. Residents of Kazakstan may make and receive international payments and transfers in any convertible currency as well as in Russian rubles. In general, foreign currency may not be used for the settlement of domestic transactions between residents.[2] It is prohibited to use foreign exchange cash in retail trade and services on Kazak territory. Transactions between residents and nonresidents involving the sale or purchase of foreign currency are limited to those conducted through authorized banks.

Resident and Nonresident Accounts

Resident individuals and enterprises may maintain convertible foreign exchange accounts at authorized banks. These accounts, which bear interest, may be credited with retained export earnings and foreign exchange transferred from abroad, and balances in these accounts may be freely used for any purpose. Residents may also maintain convertible currency accounts abroad with permission from the National Bank.

Nonresidents may hold accounts in Kazakstan in domestic or foreign currencies; only one account is permitted. Withdrawals from these accounts, including transfers abroad, are not restricted for "I" accounts, which are for investment activities, while funds in "T" accounts, used for export and import operations with residents, cannot be freely converted and transferred abroad. There are also restrictions on the making of pre- and post-delivery import payments.

Imports and Exports

Trade with the Baltic countries, Russia, and the other countries of the former Soviet Union under trade agreements is conducted through acquisitions and shipments by financially independent state trading organizations, whose monopoly rights were canceled in early 1995, and other trading organizations. Trade with other countries is also effected under a system of intergovernmental trade agree-

---

[1]Official rates for more than 30 other currencies are set on the basis of the tenge-dollar rates in the auction and the cross rates in international markets.

[2]Exemptions are permitted for payments to residents providing freight, insurance, or other intermediary services in respect of foreign-currency-denominated trade; payments to residents supplying inputs required for the production of exports sold for foreign currencies; payments for selected domestic telecommunications services; payments to banks and other financial institutions in respect of liabilities incurred in foreign currencies; and where otherwise specially authorized by the National Bank.

ments, quotas, and licenses. Overall export quotas are prepared by the Ministry of Economy on the basis of balances of specific products in various territories. There are no import quotas.

In early 1995, export quotas and export and import licenses were eliminated except for a short negative list for national security, health, and safety reasons.

The number of commodity groups subject to export licenses, which stood at 55 at the end of 1993, was reduced to 50 by January 1994, to 32 by the end of December 1994, and to 9 by February 1995. The number of commodity groups subject to import licenses was reduced to 11 as of end-December 1994.

Export duty rates vary from zero to 25 percent for 27 major product groups, including military equipment. Import duty rates for most products fall in the range of 5 percent to 30 percent, with a 50 percent rate for pearls, gems, and precious and semiprecious stones, and the maximum duty rate of 100 percent for alcoholic drinks, weapons, and ammunition.

Payments for and Proceeds from Invisibles

Purchases by residents of foreign exchange for tourist purposes are limited to $500 a person; there are no limits on withdrawals from convertible currency accounts for the same purposes. Purchases of foreign exchange for business travel abroad are, in principle, subject to limits, which are based on country-specific norms for accommodation and subsistence expenses but are not officially enforced. In practice, banks are free to grant exemptions to these limits. Foreign exchange may be purchased without limit for purposes of study abroad if the appropriate documents are produced. Remittances for family maintenance purposes are subject to certain limits.

Payments for invisibles that residents are permitted to make are officially tolerated for nonresidents. Nonresident workers in Kazakstan are free to make transfers abroad. The remittance of dividends and profits is subject to approval.

There are no restrictions on the amount of domestic currency that residents and nonresidents may bring into or take out of the country.

Capital

Capital transactions between residents and nonresidents require approval from the National Bank. Foreign direct investments in the defense sector are prohibited. Both residents and nonresidents are permitted to own land, but nonresidents cannot own agricultural land. Foreign investors are entitled to tax holidays and can freely repatriate their profits via their I accounts.

Gold

All transactions in gold must be effected through the primary market that is to be established, where the National Bank and the Ministry of Finance will have the first right to participate at world market prices with adjustments for insurance and freight. Until the primary market is established, the National Bank buys gold in the country at world market prices.

Changes During 1995

Administration of Control

August 31. The National Bank continued to be in charge of the supervision of foreign exchange transactions, but the Cabinet of Ministers issued a decree stipulating that the Ministry of Finance is to establish a new agency that shall be responsible for enforcing foreign exchange supervision and at the same time take into account the National Bank's supervisory functions.

Imports and Exports

January 5. Belarus, Kazakstan, and Russia agreed to form a customs union. The first stage, which was completed in March, involved the elimination of tariffs between the three countries. The second stage, which involved common external tariffs, was largely completed in October/November.

February 2. Export quotas and export and import licenses were eliminated, except for a short negative list for national security, health, and safety reasons. Export licenses would be required for 9 items and import licenses for 11 items. The monopoly rights of 14 state trading organizations were abolished.

August 2. Surrender requirements were abolished. Repatriation requirements would remain, unless a special license is issued. The authority to reintroduce surrender requirements, previously exercised by the President, was vested with the National Bank.

Capital

December 26. Private ownership of land was legalized, but nonresidents were not authorized to own agricultural land.

Gold

July 20. A presidential decree was promulgated whereby foreign investors were allowed to refine precious metals, including gold and precious stones, and to export raw materials, if the refined products are sold in the primary market that is to be established in Kazakstan. Domestic producers would refine precious metals in Kazakstan and sell them in the primary market. In addition to the National Bank, the Ministry of Finance and commercial banks to be licensed by the National Bank would be allowed to participate in the primary market for gold, but the National Bank and the Ministry of Finance would have the first right to buy and sell. Gold not sold on the primary market could be sold on the secondary market, including international markets.

KENYA

(Position as of July 31, 1996)

Exchange Arrangement

The currency of Kenya is the Kenya Shilling, the external value of which is determined on the basis of supply and demand in the interbank market. The official exchange rate is set at the previous day's average market rate. The principal intervention currency is the U.S. dollar. The official exchange rate applies only to government and government-guaranteed external debt-service payments and to government imports for which there is a specific budget allocation. On December 31, 1995, the exchange rate was K Sh 55.94 per $1.

Banks are permitted to sell foreign exchange they purchase in the interbank market to any client at market-determined exchange rates, to purchase foreign exchange in the interbank market for their own accounts, to offer forward exchange contracts to exporters and importers at market-determined rates without restriction on the amount or period covered, or to sell foreign exchange they purchase in the interbank market to another bank. Foreign exchange bureaus were authorized to deal in cash and buy foreign traveler's checks on January 5, 1995.

Commercial banks are authorized to enter into forward exchange contracts with their customers at market-determined exchange rates in currencies of their choice; there are no limits on the amount or period of cover. There are no official schemes for currency swaps or exchange rate guarantee schemes for external debt servicing, except for the Exchange Risk Assumption Fund (ERAF), which covers the foreign exchange losses associated with exchange rate fluctuations occurring after July 1, 1989, for three development finance institutions. ERAF ceased to take on new commitments effective June 1994.

Kenya accepted the obligations of Article VIII, Sections 2, 3, and 4 of the Fund Agreement on June 30, 1994.

Administration of Control

On December 29, 1995, the Exchange Control Act was repealed. The Central Bank Act was amended on the same date, giving it powers to license and regulate foreign exchange transactions.

There are no import controls. Import and foreign exchange allocation licenses were abolished in May 1993, except for a short negative list of goods prohibited for health, security, or environmental reasons. The responsibility for issuing import licenses, when required, rests with the Director of Internal Trade in the Ministry of Commerce and Industry. The Director also issues special licenses for the exportation of restricted goods, including certain agricultural products and goods whose exportation is restricted based on security and environmental reasons.

Arrears are maintained with respect to external payments.

Prescription of Currency

Payments to residents of other countries may be made in Kenya shillings to the credit of an external account in Kenya or in any foreign currency. Receipts may be obtained in Kenya shillings from an external account in Kenya or in any marketable foreign currency.

Resident and Nonresident Accounts

Kenyan residents who have foreign exchange earnings (including earnings from services) are allowed to open foreign currency accounts with local banks. There is no limit on the balances in these accounts. Foreigners with work permits in Kenya may open foreign currency accounts with Kenyan banks and may credit their local earnings to these accounts; use of funds in these accounts is not restricted. Accounts in foreign currency held by residents of other countries with authorized banks in Kenya are designated foreign currency accounts. They may be freely credited with authorized payments by residents of Kenya, with transfers from other foreign currency accounts, with the proceeds from sales of any currency and gold by nonresidents to authorized dealers, and with foreign exchange earnings. Foreign currency accounts may be freely debited for payments to residents and nonresidents.

Enterprises operating in export processing zones (EPZs) are permitted to hold foreign currency accounts abroad or with authorized banks in Kenya and may use the balances on these amounts to pay business-related expenses (including imports, debt service, and dividends).

Imports and Import Payments

Import and foreign exchange allocation licenses are not required except for a few items that, for health, security, and environmental reasons, are included on a negative list.

Customs tariffs are applied as the sole form of protection of domestic industry. As of June 1995, there were six customs tariff nomenclatures, with rates varying from zero to 40 percent; and as of June 1996, the tariff bands were reduced to five, with the rates ranging from zero to 35 percent. Exporters of horticultural goods and agro-based products are exempt from import duties and value-added tax on imported inputs.

Authorized banks are permitted to provide foreign exchange against the following documents: a copy of the import declaration, a final invoice, an original clean report of findings from a nominated inspection agency, and a copy of the customs entry.

Advance payments for imports may be made through commercial banks without prior approval from the Central Bank of Kenya.

All imports with an f.o.b. value of more than $1,000 are subject to preshipment inspection for quality, quantity, and price (previously $500), and require a clean report of findings from July 1996. Authorized banks in Kenya may not issue shipping guarantees for the clearance of imports until they receive the report. All goods purchased by importers in Kenya must be insured with companies licensed to conduct insurance business in Kenya.

Payments for Invisibles

All payments and transfers for invisibles transactions may be made without restrictions, provided that the application is supported by adequate documentation. Commercial banks may, without reference to the Central Bank, remit pension contributions to nonresidents. Payments of interim dividends to nonresident shareholders are not limited, provided that the application is supported by adequate documentation. Foreign workers may transfer abroad any amount of their earnings upon verification of income and payment of taxes. As of June 17, 1996, the exportation of domestic banknotes exceeding K Sh 300,000 must be declared to customs at the point of exit for statistical purposes only.

Exports and Export Proceeds

Most goods may be exported without licenses. Exports of certain foodstuffs and agricultural products require special licenses and may be restricted to ensure adequate supplies in the domestic market. Exports of tea, coffee, minerals, precious stones, and other essential strategic materials are also subject to special licensing. Coffee, tea, and horticultural produce may be exported only if a sales contract is registered with the Coffee Board, Tea Board, and Horticultural Crops Development Authority, respectively.

Proceeds from Invisibles

All receipts from invisibles may be kept in foreign currency accounts. Travelers may freely bring in and take out foreign currency notes, except those of countries with restrictions on the exportation of currencies. As of June 19, 1996, the importation of foreign currency banknotes exceeding $5,000 must be declared at the point of entry to customs officials for statistical purposes only.

Capital

All inward and outward capital transfers may be made freely. Borrowing by foreign-controlled companies on the domestic market is not restricted. Restrictions on investment by foreigners in shares and government securities were removed on January 4, 1995. The Capital Market Authority Act was amended to allow participation by foreign companies in portfolio investment of up to 40 percent of share capital of listed companies, and by individual portfolio investors up to 5 percent of shares of listed companies.

Offshore borrowing by residents is allowed without limit.

Gold

Residents may hold and acquire gold bullion (ingots, bars, or sheets) without restrictions.

Changes During 1995

Administration of Control

January 5. Foreign exchange bureaus were authorized to deal in cash and foreign traveler's checks.

December 29. The Exchange Control Act was repealed.

December 29. The Central Bank of Kenya Act was amended, giving it powers to license and regulate foreign exchange transactions.

Resident and Nonresident Accounts

February 21. Remittances from blocked accounts were liberalized, except those relating to investments made prior to February 28, 1994. Remittances of funds in blocked accounts relating to investments made prior to February 28, 1994, may be made by commercial banks up to $100,000; applications for remittances in excess of $100,000 must be referred to the Central Bank.

February 21. Kenyan residents who have foreign exchange earnings (including earnings from services) were allowed to open foreign currency accounts with local banks. Use of funds in these accounts would be limited in the same manner as use of export retention accounts. Export retention accounts may be converted into foreign currency accounts. Foreigners with work permits in Kenya may open foreign currency accounts with Kenyan banks and may credit their local earnings to these accounts; use of funds in the accounts would not be restricted.

Payments for Invisibles

February 21. Restrictions on remittances by foreigners of monthly earnings were removed, subject to verification of income and payment of tax.

February 21. Persons leaving Kenya were allowed to export up to K Sh 100,000 in banknotes; exportation of amounts exceeding K Sh 100,000 must be declared to customs.

Exports and Export Proceeds

February 21. The export retention ratio was increased to 100 percent of export earnings for all exporters.

Capital

January 4. Restrictions on investment by foreigners in shares and government securities were removed. The Capital Market Authority Act was amended to allow foreign equity participation of up to 40 percent of share capital of listed companies, while individuals are allowed to own up to 5 percent of shares of companies listed in the stock exchange.

February 21. Borrowing by foreign-controlled companies on the domestic market was fully liberalized.

February 21. Offshore borrowing by residents was allowed without limit, provided that (1) interest does not exceed LIBOR plus 2 percentage points, and (2) such borrowing is not guaranteed by the Government. Applications for borrowing on other terms must be referred to the Central Bank of Kenya.

Changes During 1996

Imports and Import Payments

July 1. The minimum value of imports subject to preshipments inspection was raised to an f.o.b. value of $1,000 from $500.

Proceeds from Invisibles

June 19. Exportation and importation of local and foreign currency notes exceeding $500 (K Sh 300,000) were required to be declared to customs for statistical purposes.

KIRIBATI

(Position as of December 31, 1995)

Exchange Arrangement

The official currency of Kiribati is the Australian Dollar; a small number of Kiribati coins are also in circulation. There is no central monetary institution, and the authorities do not buy or sell foreign exchange. The Bank of Kiribati (the only commercial bank) quotes daily rates for 15 currencies[1] on the basis of their respective values against the Australian dollar. There are no taxes or subsidies on purchases or sales of foreign exchange. There are no arrangements for forward cover against exchange rate risk operating in the official or the commercial banking sector.

Kiribati accepted the obligations of Article VIII, Sections 2, 3, and 4 of the Fund Agreement on August 22, 1986.

There are no payments restrictions for security reasons in effect.

Prescription of Currency

Both outward and inward payments may be settled in Australian currency or in any foreign currency.[2] Purchases and sales of foreign currencies in exchange for Australian dollars must be undertaken with the Bank of Kiribati, the only authorized foreign exchange dealer.

Imports and Import Payments

Import licenses are normally not required. The importation of a limited range of goods is prohibited for health, safety, or environmental reasons. Tariffs apply to most private imports and range up to 80 percent. Specific duties exist on a small range of goods, including rice, flour, petroleum products, alcoholic beverages, and tobacco products.

Exports and Export Proceeds

There are no surrender requirements for export proceeds. There are no taxes or quantitative restrictions on exports, but copra can be exported only through the Kiribati Copra Cooperative Society.

Payments for and Proceeds from Invisibles

There are no restrictions on payments for or receipts from invisibles.

Capital

The authorities maintain a liberal attitude toward foreign direct investment and encourage export-promoting or import-substituting investments. All applications for foreign investment must be made to the Foreign Investment Commission, which approves applications of total foreign capital contributions up to $A 250,000. Applications with a higher capital contribution are approved by the Cabinet. Under the Foreign Investment Promotion Act, investors may be granted duty-free imports of capital goods and raw materials. Investments in pioneer industries are eligible for a tax holiday of up to six years. Repatriation of profits and capital is normally unrestricted.

Changes During 1995

Exports and Export Proceeds

January 31. The 15 percent ad valorem tax on exports of scrap iron and aluminum cans was abolished.

---

[1]Canadian dollars, deutsche mark, Fiji dollars, Hong Kong dollars, Japanese yen, New Zealand dollars, Papua New Guinea kina, pounds sterling, Singapore dollars, Solomon Islands dollars, Swiss francs, Tongan pa'anga, U.S. dollars, Vanuatu vatu, and Western Samoa tala.

[2]Foreign currencies are defined as all currencies other than the Australian dollar.

KOREA

(Position as of June 30, 1996)

Exchange Arrangement

The currency of Korea is the Korean Won. Under the market average rate system (introduced on March 2, 1990), the Korean won-U.S. dollar rate has been determined on the basis of the weighted average of interbank rates for Korean won-U.S. dollar spot transactions of the previous day. During each business day, the Korean won-U.S. dollar exchange rate in the interbank market is currently allowed to fluctuate within margins of ±2.25 percent against the market average rate of the previous day. The exchange rates of the won against currencies other than the U.S. dollar are determined in relation to the exchange rate of the U.S. dollar against these currencies in the international market. On December 31, 1995, the basic rate for the U.S. dollar was W 774.70 per $1. Foreign exchange banks set freely the buying and selling rates they offer to customers. There are no taxes or subsidies on purchases or sales of foreign exchange.

Foreign exchange banks may conduct forward transactions, futures transactions, swaps, and options between foreign currencies, as well as between the Korean won and foreign currencies. There are no specific restrictions on the terms of forward contracts in respect of interbank transactions. However, the terms of forward contracts between foreign exchange banks and nonbank customers must be based on a bona fide transaction, with the exception of those subject to specific restrictions.

Korea accepted the obligations of Article VIII, Sections 2, 3, and 4 of the Fund Agreement on November 1, 1988.

Administration of Control

The Ministry of Finance and Economy initiates policy with respect to method of settlement, foreign exchange operations, payments for nonmerchandise transactions, and capital transactions and transfers. The Bank of Korea, as the Government's agent, executes most of the above functions; it also regulates operations in the exchange market and is authorized to intervene in it. The Bank of Korea has been delegated authority to control payments related to invisibles and certain capital transactions. Foreign exchange banks, as well as the branch offices of foreign banks in Korea, are authorized to engage in commercial international banking and in all foreign exchange dealings.

Prescription of Currency

All settlements between Korea and other countries may be made in any convertible currency except in won. Residents are permitted to carry out current transactions denominated in Korean won without restrictions, provided that settlements will be made in foreign currencies; for this purpose, nonresidents are allowed to maintain free won accounts (see section on Resident and Nonresident Accounts, below).

Resident and Nonresident Accounts

All residents are allowed to open foreign currency deposit accounts. Holders of these accounts may change the foreign currency composition of the accounts without restriction.

Nonresidents, including Korean workers abroad, may maintain foreign currency deposit accounts with foreign exchange banks. Remittances from such accounts and withdrawals in foreign currency may be made freely. The approval of the bank where the account is held is not required for remittances abroad or transfers to other foreign currency accounts, for purchases and withdrawals of foreign means of payment, or for payments relating to approved transactions. Nonresidents are allowed to hold free won accounts through which they may convert the funds in won into foreign currency and transfer them abroad.

Imports and Import Payments

All imports require licenses; for most imports (see below), licenses are issued upon application. Imports are divided into two categories: automatic approval items and restricted items. All commodities may be imported freely (i.e., applications for import licenses are automatically approved) unless they are on the restricted list. As of July 1, 1996, 81 of the 10,859 basic items on the Harmonized System were classified as restricted. Imports of raw materials for the production of exports are normally approved automatically, irrespective of their classification. Import licenses are granted only to registered traders, who are required to have exported and/or imported a minimum value of $500,000 in any one of the last two calendar years. The commercial terms of payment on which imports may be contracted are regulated. Safeguards against excessive imports are provided under the Foreign Trade Act of 1987. A seven-member Trade Commission established under this act determines whether imports have harmed domestic industries, and, if its finding is affirmative, it recommends the form of import relief to be provided, including quotas and quality standards.

Payments for Invisibles

Most payments for invisibles require a simple notification to foreign exchange banks. Payments of less than the equivalent of $5,000 do not require any documentation. Those connected with foreign trade, along with certain other items such as banking charges, insurance premiums, communication fees, and periodicals, are allowed with simple notification to foreign exchange banks. Korean companies are authorized to obtain foreign exchange to meet the expenses of their overseas branches.

Residents traveling abroad may, in general, purchase foreign exchange up to the equivalent of $10,000 a trip as the basic travel allowance; additional foreign exchange may also be purchased for specified expenses, including transportation costs. The monthly allowance for residents staying abroad for over 30 days is $10,000. For those staying abroad for over one year, a remittance of $50,000, inclusive of basic travel allowance, is allowed anytime within two months of departure. The basic monthly allowance for individual students living abroad under the age of 20 years is $3,000; students with a dependent family are granted an additional allowance of $500 for a spouse and each child. Resident travelers are allowed to pay for travel expenses with credit cards. Korean residents are allowed to remit up to $5,000 a transaction to their parents and children abroad for living expenses and to their relatives abroad for a wedding gift or funeral donation without any underlying documentation.

Korean currency notes in excess of W 8 million may not be exported without special permission from the Bank of Korea. When leaving the country, nonresidents may purchase foreign exchange up to the amount for which they have proof of conversion. Foreigners working in Korea may remit their salaries abroad.

Exports and Export Proceeds

Export earnings exceeding $50,000 must be repatriated to Korea within six months except in special cases. General trading companies licensed under the Foreign Trade Act and enterprises that had exported more than $5 million in the previous year, however, are permitted to retain up to 50 percent of the export value in deposits abroad, up to a maximum of $500 million.

Proceeds from Invisibles

Korean residents are permitted to hold foreign currency earned from invisible transactions, but once converted into won, a limit applies to reconversion. Residents and nonresidents must register domestic and foreign exchange they bring into Korea at customs if the amount exceeds the equivalent of $10,000. The importation by travelers of Korean currency in excess of W 2 million is restricted.

The proceeds received by construction companies from construction activity abroad must be deposited in foreign currency accounts at the domestic foreign exchange banks, and profits may be converted into won following the completion of each project. Domestic firms engaged in international construction and service businesses may deposit abroad up to 30 percent of the balance of their overseas contracts or $3 million, whichever is greater.

Capital

Overseas investments and loans by residents to nonresidents generally require notification or approval from the relevant authorities. Overseas direct investments of equal to or less than $10 million by Korean residents are subject to validation by foreign exchange banks. Investments exceeding $10 million must be reported to the Bank of Korea. Investments exceeding $50 million require approval from the Bank of Korea after the deliberation of the Overseas Capital Projects Deliberation Committee.

There are no restrictions on foreign borrowing for overseas investment and related operations. A Korean business incorporated abroad is allowed to retain profits for the purpose of expanding its overseas investment businesses or improving its financial status.

Overseas portfolio investments by residents are permitted. Foreign currency loans by resident banks to nonresidents of less than $2 million are permitted freely; loans ranging from $2 million to $20 million require ex post notification to the Ministry of Finance and Economy, and loans exceeding $20 million require prior notification to the Ministry of Finance and Economy. Institutional investors are free to grant foreign currency loans to nonresidents with prior notification to the Bank of Korea. General trading companies and corporations are allowed to grant foreign currency loans to nonresidents with prior notification to the Bank of Korea up to $10 million and $300,000, respectively. Loans by residents to nonresidents require prior approval from the Ministry of Finance and Economy. Foreign exchange banks and institutional investors are allowed to extend won currency loans to nonresidents up to W 100 million a borrower. Subject to prior notification to the Ministry of Finance and Economy, issuance of stocks and bonds abroad by residents is allowed, provided that the use of the proceeds is restricted. Domestic firms are prohibited from issuing won-denominated bonds abroad.

The foreign exchange allowance for emigrants varies with family size. The head of household may transfer abroad up to $400,000, and other family members may transfer up to $200,000 a person. Additional allowances for emigrants abroad are subject to the approval of the Bank of Korea.

The overbought and oversold position of foreign exchange banks is limited to 15 percent and 10 percent, respectively, of their capital base; the portion used to hedge capital or operational funds is exempt from this limit.

Institutional investors are permitted to hold deposits abroad for asset diversification purposes without quantitative ceiling. General corporations and individuals are permitted to hold deposits abroad of up to $3 million and $50,000 a year, respectively.

Regulations governing foreign investment in Korea and the contracting of loans to residents by nonresidents are as follows:

Foreign Investment

Direct investments are allowed in all industries, except those specified on a "negative" list. In December 1995, the negative list consisted of 195 industries out of 1,148 industries listed in the Korean standard industrial classification, resulting in a liberalization ratio of 90.7 percent. In the manufacturing sector, the negative list consisted of 25 industries out of 585 industries, resulting in a liberalization ratio of 98.3 percent. In the nonmanufacturing sector, the negative list consisted of 170 industries out of 563 industries, resulting in a liberalization of 82.7 percent.

In general, foreign-financed companies are no longer required to set up partnerships with local firms. There are no restrictions on the maximum value of foreign investment. Tax privileges may be granted to foreign-financed projects that are accompanied by advanced technology. Tax privileges have been continuously reduced, and post-investment controls have also been relaxed to treat foreign and local companies equally.

All foreign direct investments, except those in industries on the negative list, are subject to a notification requirement. A notification is deemed accepted by foreign exchange banks unless otherwise notified. The notification system has gradually been expanded since the beginning of January 1993. Foreign direct investments in equity-linked bonds are allowed, including nonguaranteed convertible bonds issued by small- and medium-sized enterprises, up to an aggregate of 30 percent, and individual bonds, up to 5 percent of the amount of money listed for each company. The conversion of bonds to equity is limited to 18 percent. The purchase of government and public bonds, with interest rates comparable to international rates, is allowed in the primary market. Remittances abroad of dividends and legitimate profits accrued from stocks or shares owned by a foreign investor are freely permitted. The repatriation of foreign capital is also freely permitted. Aggregate ceilings for foreign investment in firms listed on the Korean Stock Market may not exceed 18 percent of the firm's equity, and individual foreign investors may not hold more than 4 percent of a firm's equity.

Acquisition of land by foreign-financed companies in the manufacturing sector is only subject to the notification requirement. For companies in non-manufacturing sectors, approval from local authorities is generally required, and approval is normally granted within 60 days.

Loans

Authorization is required for all foreign borrowing by firms other than banks. Foreign borrowing by these firms of more than $1 million and with a maturity of more than three years is governed by the Foreign Capital Inducement Act. Within a limit, selected Korean enterprises (foreign-invested enterprises with high technology, firms engaged in certain types of "social overhead capital projects," and small- and medium-sized enterprises) are allowed to borrow from abroad for the financing of the imports of capital goods. Firms have access to limited foreign currency loans extended by domestic foreign exchange banks, but this type of lending is only permitted for certain purposes, such as the import of capital goods, and research and development activities.

Foreign-financed companies are, in principle, subject to the same regulations governing foreign borrowing as other enterprises. However, the borrowing by high-technology foreign-financed manufacturing companies is allowed up to 100 percent of the foreign-invested capital; also, maturity is limited to three years or less, and limitations are imposed on the use of funds.

Foreign borrowing repayable within three years is governed by the Foreign Exchange Act. The maximum maturity period permitted for deferred payments is 180 days for imports of raw materials for export production.

Foreign exchange banks must report to the Ministry of Finance and Economy all borrowing exceeding $10 million with a maturity of over one year. Their oversold foreign exchange position may not exceed 10 percent of the average outstanding amount of foreign exchange bought in the previous month or $20 million, whichever is greater. (For spot transactions only, the corresponding limit is 5 percent or $5 million, whichever is greater.) Subject to certain ceilings, branches of foreign banks may enter into foreign currency swap transactions with the Bank of Korea at a fixed yield of 0.3 percent to secure funds for their domestic currency lending.

Gold

Residents may freely buy, hold, or sell gold in any form in Korea. Residents are allowed to import and export gold other than gold coins, subject to the same regulations as those applied to merchandise trade (in accordance with the Foreign Trade Act). Domestically produced gold may be disposed of in the free market.

Changes During 1995

Exchange Arrangement

December 1. The margins within which the exchange rate for Korean won-U.S. dollars in the interbank market would be allowed to fluctuate daily were widened from ±1.5 percent to ±2.25 percent.

Resident and Nonresident Accounts

February 13. Residents were allowed to hold foreign exchange without registering with the banks.

Imports and Import Payments

December 1. The deferred import payments period was extended as follows. For large enterprises: (a) re-exports to the general area, to 180 days from 150 days, and re-exports to the regional area, to 90 days from 60 days, and (b) domestic consumption purposes to 90 days from 60 days in cases where the importing area is general, and to 60 days from 30 days in cases where the importing area is regional. For small- and medium-sized enterprises: (a) re-exports to the regional area, to 120 days from 90 days, and (b) domestic consumption purposes, to 120 days from 90 days in cases where the importing area is general, and to 90 days from 60 days in cases where the importing area is regional.

Payments for Invisibles

February 13. The limit on the amount of domestic banknotes permitted to be exported was raised to W 3 million from W 2 million.

February 13. Documentation requirements for payments and transfers abroad of less than $5,000 were eliminated.

February 13. (1) Basic travel allowances were raised to $10,000 from $5,000; (2) monthly travel allowances were raised to $10,000 from $3,000; and (3) resettlement expenses were raised to $50,000 from $20,000.

Proceeds from Invisibles

February 13. The limit on the amount of domestic banknotes permitted to be imported was raised to W 3 million from W 2 million.

Capital

February 13. The following measures were introduced: (1) limits on investments in securities abroad by pension funds and short-term financial companies were abolished. The limit for enterprises was increased to W 1 billion from W 300 million, and that for individuals, to W 500 million from W 100 million; (2) overseas deposits (for the purpose of asset diversification) were allowed up to under $100 million for institutional investors, and up to $1 million for other firms. For individuals, overseas deposits of up to $30,000 a year were allowed; (3) institutional investors were allowed to extend credit to nonresidents up to $10 million, and to others, up to $300,000. The foreign exchange concentration system was suspended, and residents were allowed to hold foreign currency without registering at banks; (4) the exemption from overseas credits collection requirement was raised to $30,000 from $20,000; (5) the types of firms allowed to hold deposits overseas were expanded from companies whose annual trading exceeds $10 million to those whose trade exceeds $5 million. The limit on the amount of foreign currency that could be held abroad by construction companies was raised to 20 percent of the balance of the construction contract from 10 percent; and (6) the scope of items eligible to be deposited in, or withdrawn from, free won accounts was expanded from trade transactions amounting up to $300,000 for each transaction to all current transactions amounting to a maximum of $300,000 for each transaction.

May 1. International financial institutions (for example, the Asian Development Bank) were permitted to issue won-denominated bonds in the domestic financial market.

May 3. Foreign enterprises with high technology, firms engaged in certain types of "social overhead capital projects," and small- and medium-sized enterprises were allowed to borrow abroad for the financing of imports of capital goods.

October 10. The restricted areas for overseas direct investment were reduced to 3 areas from 14 areas; restricted areas are leasing and selling real estate, and construction and operation of golf courses. The application procedure for outward direct foreign investment was simplified significantly.

November 15. The negative list of foreign direct investment was shortened, raising the liberalization ratio to 95.1 percent, as from January 1, 1996.

December 1. The limit on advances large enterprises are permitted to grant was extended to 10 percent from 5 percent of the firm's export volume in the previous year.

Changes During 1996

Prescription of Currency

June 1. The prescription of currency requirements applicable to foreign currencies were abolished.

Resident and Nonresident Accounts

June 1. Foreigners residing in Korea longer than five years would be treated as residents for foreign exchange control purposes.

Capital

January 1. The following measures were introduced: (1) regulations governing the foreign exchange positions of banks were modified, whereby the basis of the calculation was related to the volume of transactions or capital, whichever is greater. The ratios with respect to capital were set as follows: (a) overall overbought position, 15 percent of capital; (b) overall oversold position, 10 percent of capital; and (c) spot oversold position, 3 percent of capital or $5 million; (2) overseas deposits for asset diversification purposes were liberalized. For individuals and juridical persons, the ceilings were incrementally raised to $3 million and $50,000 a year, respectively; (3) the ceiling of $10 million on foreign currency loans an institutional investor may extend to nonresidents was abolished, while the ceilings for general trading companies and other firms were set at $10 million and $300,000, respectively; (4) the remaining underlying documentation requirement was abolished for forward exchange and financial futures transactions. However, the principle that a transaction should be based upon real demand (real-demand principle) would continue to be applied; (5) within the scope of nonresidents' real demand, derivative transactions between foreign and domestic currencies were allowed; (6) the opening of a free-won account by a nonresident in overseas branches/ subsidiaries of a foreign exchange bank was allowed; (7) the ceiling for current transactions ($300,000) that were allowed to be deposited in and withdrawn from the free-won account was eliminated. In addition, won currency funds deposited in the free-won account were allowed to be withdrawn to invest in domestic stocks; (8) resident foreign exchange banks and institutional investors were allowed to extend loans on domestic currency to nonresidents up to W 100 million a borrower; (9) procedures for remittance of funds to be used for operating overseas branches of domestic firms were liberalized; (10) export credits in the form of deferred receipts were liberalized; (11) the exemption from overseas credit collection requirements was raised to $50,000 from $30,000; (12) the limit on the amount of foreign currency that may be held abroad by construction companies was raised to 30 percent of the balance of the construction contract or $3 million, whichever is greater; from 20 percent or $2 million, whichever is greater; and (13) the head of an emigrating family was allowed to transfer up to $400,000 (previously $200,000), and other family members were allowed to transfer up to $200,000 a person (previously $100,000).

KUWAIT

(Position as of December 31, 1995)

Exchange Arrangement

The currency of Kuwait is the Kuwaiti Dinar. The exchange value of the Kuwaiti dinar is determined on the basis of its fixed but adjustable relationship with a disclosed weighted basket of currencies, the weights reflecting the relative importance of these currencies in Kuwait's trade and financial relations. The Central Bank of Kuwait sets the rate for the U.S. dollar on the basis of the latest available market quotations for that currency in relation to the other currencies included in the basket. On December 31, 1995, the Central Bank's buying and selling rates for the U.S. dollar were KD 0.29888 and KD 0.29898 respectively, per \$1. There are no taxes or subsidies on purchases or sales of foreign exchange. The most common arrangement in the official and the commercial banking sectors for handling cover against exchange rate risk is through dealings in the international forward exchange markets. The forward market for Kuwaiti dinar trading, however, has been suspended since the war with Iraq.

Kuwait accepted the obligations of Article VIII, Sections 2, 3, and 4 of the Fund Agreement on April 5, 1963.

Administration of Control

There is no exchange control, and residents and nonresidents may freely purchase and sell foreign currencies in Kuwait. Dealings in the currency of Israel are prohibited. In addition, all imports from and all exports to Israel are prohibited; payments may not be made to or received from Israel for any type of transaction.

Prescription of Currency

There are no prescription of currency requirements. Trade and economic agreements are maintained with China, Cyprus, Egypt, Hungary, Italy, Jordan, Morocco, Thailand, and Turkey.

Nonresident Accounts

Nonresidents may freely open accounts in Kuwaiti dinars and foreign currencies. The use of such accounts is not restricted.

Imports and Import Payments

General and individual import licenses are issued by the Ministry of Commerce and Industry. Import licenses are required for all commercial imports other than fresh fruits and vegetables; licenses, except for wheat and flour, are issued freely to registered Kuwaiti merchants and companies. Registered importers handling a variety of commodities may obtain a general license valid for one year. Other importers must obtain specific licenses for individual commodities, which are also valid for one year. Imports of industrial equipment, machinery, and their spare parts require industrial licenses valid for one-time use only. Licenses are issued to registered and licensed industrial establishments with the approval of the Industrial Development Commission at the Ministry of Commerce and Industry. Private imports of personal objects may be permitted under individual or specific licenses. The importation of certain items (mainly oxygen, certain steel and asbestos pipes, pork and foodstuffs containing pork, alcoholic beverages, used vehicles over five years old, portable telephones, chewing tobacco, and gas cylinders) is prohibited.

Commercial imports are limited to registered importers. To be registered, the importer must be either a Kuwaiti citizen, a firm in which all partners are Kuwaiti nationals, or a shareholding or limited liability company in which Kuwaiti nationals own at least 51 percent of the stock. Imports from any permitted source may be paid freely.

In concert with the other members of the Cooperation Council for the Arab States of the Gulf (GCC) (Bahrain, Oman, Qatar, Saudi Arabia, and United Arab Emirates), Kuwait adopted a uniform tariff structure on September 1, 1983. A minimum tariff of 4 percent was set on imports from non-GCC countries; tariffs on imports from other GCC countries that have a local value-added component of at least 40 percent were abolished. On March 14, 1991, the tariff rate was reduced to zero for a transitional period of six months to encourage imports of goods into Kuwait for postwar reconstruction. In July 1992, import duties were reinstated at the rate of 4 percent, except for capital goods and raw materials.

Imports of foodstuffs, as well as some imports of machinery and equipment, spare parts, and raw materials are exempt from import duties, Kuwait has a system of preferential tariffs for industries catering to at least 40 percent of the local market allowing them to apply for tariff protection. Tariff rates differ, depending on the domestic value-added content of the products in question. If the domestically produced goods contain at least 20 percent, 30 percent, or 40 percent of domestic value added, protective duties of 15 percent, 20 percent, and 25 percent, respectively, may be applied to competing imports. The degree of protection given by the formula is reduced by 5 percent in the case of consumer goods. The maximum duty imposed on products that compete with locally manufactured goods is 100 percent. As a general rule, protection is accorded to a firm only if the value added is more than 40 percent. The list of protected items includes paint, building materials, reinforced glass products, commercial refrigeration units, central air-conditioning units with a capacity of 20–25 tons, electric and telephone cables, synthetic sponges, steel and iron, air filters for automobiles (25 percent), and wooden nails (15 percent). Imports of portable telephones, chewing tobacco, and gas cylinders are prohibited for health or safety reasons.

Kuwait has adopted a priority system for government procurement of goods and services, which provides for preference to be accorded to Kuwaiti-produced goods up to a price margin of 5 percent over goods produced in the other GCC countries, and 10 percent over goods produced outside the GCC. Similarly, goods produced in the other GCC countries are accorded a 5 percent price margin over goods produced outside the GCC.

Exports and Export Proceeds

A limited control over exports is administered by the Ministry of Commerce and Industry and by the Customs and Ports Administration. Exports of live sheep and poultry and of certain other items (such as sugar, fats, rice, meat, eggs, milk, cheese, butter, olive oil, fresh fruits, vegetables in any form, beans, lentils, chickpeas, jams, and cement) may be prohibited in time of emergency or shortage in Kuwait. These items may be exported in limited quantities only under a special license issued by the Ministry of Commerce and Industry. Exports of arms and ammunition require licenses.

No requirements are attached to receipts from exports or re-exports; the proceeds need not be repatriated or surrendered, and they may be disposed of freely, regardless of the currency involved.

Payments for and Proceeds from Invisibles

All payments for current invisibles may be made freely. Travelers may bring in or take out any amount in Kuwaiti or foreign banknotes.

Capital

There are no exchange controls or restrictions on the transfer into Kuwait of resident or nonresident capital in any currency. Government agreement is necessary for the participation of nonresident capital in resident corporations in Kuwait; foreign participation in new Kuwaiti companies must be less than 49 percent. The participation of GCC nationals in companies established in Kuwait may reach up to 75 percent of the capital, and there are no restrictions on participation in retail trade enterprises by non-Kuwaiti GCC nationals. However, import-licensing requirements remain in effect for non-Kuwaiti GCC nationals.

No restrictions are imposed on capital exports by residents or nonresidents. Listings of domestic or foreign stocks on the Kuwait Stock Exchange are subject to the approval of the Exchange Committee. Besides the approved domestic stocks, trading is permitted in certain stocks of companies of the GCC countries. The listing of Kuwaiti dinar-denominated bonds on the Exchange is also subject to the approval of the Exchange Committee. Trading in stocks is restricted to Kuwaiti citizens, but foreigners are permitted to buy and sell bonds on the Exchange.

Gold

The monetary authorities and merchants registered with the Ministry of Commerce and Industry may import and export gold in any form, provided that such gold is not less than 18-karat fine; gold jewelry may not be imported or sold unless it is properly hallmarked. Kuwaiti nationals may freely, and without license, purchase, hold, and sell gold in any form, at home or abroad. Other residents may, on arrival or departure, carry their holdings of gold in any form, without restriction or license. Jewelry and precious metals in any form, manufactured or unmanufactured, are subject to an import duty of 4 percent.

Changes During 1995

No significant changes occurred in the exchange and trade system.

KYRGYZ REPUBLIC

(Position as of December 31, 1995)

Exchange Arrangement

The currency of the Kyrgyz Republic is the Som.[1] The U.S. dollar rate is determined on the basis of auctions that are held twice a week at the National Bank of the Kyrgyz Republic in which licensed commercial banks and foreign exchange bureaus participate. The National Bank publishes daily the exchange rate of the som in terms of the U.S. dollar and 38 other currencies. Exchange rates for other currencies are determined on the basis of cross rates. On December 31, 1995, the exchange rate of the som in terms of the U.S. dollar quoted by the National Bank was som 11.15 per $1. In addition to the National Bank, the commercial banks are authorized to conduct foreign exchange transactions. Authorized banks are allowed to quote their own buying and selling rates. Purchases and sales of foreign exchange are permitted without restriction.

There are no taxes or subsidies on purchases or sales of foreign exchange. There are no arrangements for forward cover against exchange rate risk operating in the official or the commercial banking sector.

The Kyrgyz Republic accepted the obligations of Article VIII, Sections 2, 3, and 4 of the Fund Agreement on March 29, 1995.

Administration of Control

The Central Bank Law, approved by Parliament in December 1992, established the National Bank's responsibility for managing the country's gold and foreign exchange reserves. Effective May 15, 1993, the full convertibility of the som was established, with no restrictions on buying, selling, or holding foreign currencies. The National Bank is also responsible for issuing foreign exchange licenses to commercial banks.

Foreign trade is regulated by the Ministry of Trade and Material Resources, which issues import and export licenses when required. Licenses for foreign investment and registration of foreign investors are granted by the State Commission for Foreign Investments and Economic Aid (GOSKOMINVEST), in coordination with the Ministry of Economy and the Ministry of Finance.

Prescription of Currency

There are no prescription of currency requirements, and settlements may be made in any currency, including nonconvertible currencies (e.g., Russian ruble and Kazak Tenge). The Kyrgyz Republic has bilateral trade agreements with the Baltic countries, China, Pakistan, Russia, the other countries of the former Soviet Union, and Turkey.

Resident and Nonresident Accounts

Residents are allowed to maintain foreign exchange accounts at authorized banks and abroad. These accounts must be registered with the National Bank and account information can be transmitted to the tax authorities. Nonresidents may hold accounts in domestic or foreign currencies. There are no specific restrictions on the operations of these accounts, including transfers abroad of balances held in the accounts.

Imports and Exports

Except for some items that may not be imported for reasons of national interest, imports are permitted free of restriction. The prohibited items include armaments, explosive materials, nuclear materials and equipment, poisons, narcotics, works of art, and antiques.

In early 1994, the trade system was substantially liberalized. There are no import- and export-licensing requirements, with the exception of eight items restricted for reasons of national interest: weapons, explosives, nuclear materials, poisons, drugs, works of arts and antiques, precious rare earth materials, and rare animal and vegetable matter used in pharmaceutical products. Imports from the Baltic countries, Russia, and the other countries of the former Soviet Union are imported duty-free while those coming from all other countries are subject to a flat customs duty of 10 percent. Excises are assessed on a small number of imported items (rates are set in specific terms), including cigarettes, furniture, gasoline, beer, alcoholic beverages, and certain electronic consumer goods.

There is no requirement to repatriate foreign exchange. A 20 percent export tax is assessed on exports of animal hides and silk cocoons; those taxes are scheduled to be removed in 1996.

---

[1] The som was issued on May 10, 1993, and the conversion from the Russian ruble to the som was completed by May 15, 1993.

Payments for and Proceeds from Invisibles

Residents are allowed to purchase any amount of foreign exchange for travel abroad or for any other payments or transfers in connection with current transactions. There are no restrictions on remittances of dividends and profits by foreign investors. The importation and exportation of Russian ruble notes and other foreign banknotes are freely allowed.

Capital

There are no restrictions on foreign borrowing by residents or enterprises. Legislation on foreign direct investment is in place, which protects the basic rights of foreign investors and provides incentives for new investment.

Gold

All gold produced in the Kyrgyz Republic is sold at market prices either in the domestic market or abroad, but the National Bank has the right of first refusal in purchasing it at that price.

Changes During 1995

Exchange Arrangement

March 29. The Kyrgyz Republic accepted the obligations of Article VIII, Sections 2, 3, and 4 of the Fund Agreement.

Imports and Exports

February 28. The number of export taxes was reduced to two from four (20 percent on animal hides and silk cocoons). The remaining two taxes are scheduled to be removed in early 1996.

LAO PEOPLE'S DEMOCRATIC REPUBLIC

(Position as of December 31, 1995)

Exchange Arrangement

The currency of the Lao People's Democratic Republic is the Kip (KN). The Thai baht and the U.S. dollar also circulate and are used widely for payments. In mid-September 1995, a floating exchange rate system was introduced by which the exchange rate is determined in the interbank market. On December 31, 1995, the average buying and selling market exchange rates for the U.S. dollar quoted by the central bank were KN 718 and KN 720, respectively, per $1. Buying and selling rates for certain other currencies[1] are also officially quoted, based on the cross rates for these currencies in relation to the U.S. dollar. Commercial banks and foreign exchange bureaus are permitted to buy and sell foreign exchange at freely determined rates, provided that the spread between the buying and selling rate remains less than 2 percent. Foreign exchange may be sold by the bureaus for payment for services. There are no arrangements for forward cover against exchange rate risk. There are no taxes or subsidies on purchases or sales of foreign exchange.

Administration of Control

Official transactions are handled by the central bank. The Ministry of Commerce and Tourism grants import and export authorization to state trading companies, mixed companies (joint ventures between domestic enterprises and foreign investors), cooperatives, and other public and private enterprises.

Prescription of Currency

No prescription of currency requirements are imposed on receipts or payments but, in principle, the central bank provides and accepts only deutsche mark, French francs, Japanese yen, pounds sterling, Swiss francs, Thai baht, and U.S. dollars. Bilateral trading arrangements are maintained with China, Thailand, a number of countries from the former Soviet Union, and Vietnam.

Resident and Nonresident Accounts

Resident accounts. Resident individuals and juridical persons may open foreign exchange accounts with an authorized commercial bank. Foreign exchange accounts may be credited with (1) proceeds from exports of goods and services; (2) transfers from abroad that do not result from exports of goods and services; (3) transfers or payments from foreign currency accounts opened with commercial banks within the Lao People's Democratic Republic; and (4) foreign banknotes and coins. These accounts, which are interest bearing, may be debited for conversion into kip for domestic expenditure, or foreign exchange balances may be used for authorized external payments and transfers.

Nonresident accounts. Nonresidents may open foreign currency accounts and convertible kip accounts. Their foreign currency accounts may be credited with (1) remittances from abroad; (2) transfers from other nonresident and resident foreign currency accounts in the Lao People's Democratic Republic; and (3) foreign currency brought into the country by the account holder and duly declared upon arrival. Nonresidents are not allowed to accept, for deposit to their accounts, foreign currency proceeds from exports of goods and services of residents without the approval of the central bank. These accounts, which bear interest, may be debited for (1) conversion into kip; (2) transfers into residents' and nonresidents' foreign currency accounts maintained with an authorized commercial bank; (3) payments in kip to accounts of residents or nonresidents; and (4) payments and transfers abroad.

Nonresidents may open accounts, which may be credited with (1) sales of foreign currencies, and (2) transfers from other convertible kip accounts of holders of the same category. Nonresidents are not permitted to deposit into their convertible kip accounts kip belonging to residents. These accounts may be debited for (1) payments in kip, and (2) conversion into foreign currency at the prevailing buying rate of the commercial bank concerned.

All foreign currency deposits are subject to reserve requirements after some level, as kip deposits are. Reserves on kip deposits are to be held in kip.

Imports and Import Payments

Imports may be made by any registered export-import business. These consist of state trading companies, joint-venture trading companies, and private trading companies. These companies are catego-

[1]Deutsche mark, French francs, Japanese yen, pounds sterling, Swiss francs, and Thai baht.

rized as enterprises producing mainly for export, for import substitution only, for general multicommodity, for export-import, or for export promotion. Imports are classified into the following nine categories: food and food products; textile garments and daily supplies; office supplies, educational instruments, sports equipment, and cultural instruments; machines and equipment used in agriculture, animal husbandry, fishing, and the production of handicrafts; luxury goods; materials for construction and electrical equipment; vehicles and spare parts; medicine, medical equipment, and chemical products for manufacturing; and fuels. Enterprises that are producing import substitutes are allowed to import products only from the last four categories.

Import licenses, which are issued by the Ministry of Commerce and Tourism and provincial government authorities, are required only for a selected number of goods and are not linked to the ability to export. The goods requiring import licenses are rice, fuel, cement, reinforced wires, motorcycles and motor vehicles, and petroleum products. These goods are also subject to individual enterprise quota restrictions. Imports of gold and silver are subject to authorization from the central bank.

Margin deposits are required against letters of credit, and the rates are freely determined by the state-owned Lao Bank for Foreign Trade (BCEL) and other commercial banks and do not involve any government intervention.

Payments for Invisibles

Payments for invisibles are not restricted.

Exports and Export Proceeds

Any registered export or import business is permitted to engage in export activities. Export licenses, which are issued by the Ministry of Commerce and Tourism and provincial government authorities, are required only for coffee, timber, wood products, rattan, and livestock. These goods are also subject to individual enterprise quota restrictions; at present, restrictive quotas are applied only to timber. The public sector no longer has the monopoly on the exportation of timber, which is now open to the private sector. The exportation of timber was banned from April 1991 to June 1992. All goods may now be freely exported by the private sector. Export shipments of gold and silver require authorization from the central bank.

Export earnings are not subject to the surrender requirement, and they may be kept in foreign exchange deposits with a commercial bank (to pay for authorized imports of goods and services, and to make cash withdrawals in kip).

Proceeds from Invisibles

Proceeds from invisibles are, in practice, treated in the same way as foreign exchange earnings accruing from merchandise exports.

Capital

Outward capital transfers by residents are not permitted. Under the Foreign Investment Law of 1988 and March 1994, inward foreign capital transfers, profit remittances, and the repatriation of foreign investment capital are not restricted.

Gold

Residents may buy and sell gold within the country but may not take it abroad for commercial purposes unless authorized by the central bank.

Changes During 1995

Exchange Arrangement

August 31. A transitional exchange system where the leading commercial bank set an exchange rate close to the parallel market rate was introduced.

September 31. A floating exchange rate system was adopted. The "official exchange rate" was abolished, thereby eliminating all exchange restrictions and the multiple currency practice. Subsequently, the rate used for the purchase and sale of foreign exchange by the Bank of Lao and for tax accounting purposes was based on the average of the rates set by commercial banks. The previous guidelines on the allocation of foreign exchange were abolished.

Resident and Nonresident Accounts

June 30. Reserve requirements (including those applying to foreign currency deposits) were increased to 12 percent.

LATVIA

(Position as of December 31, 1995)

Exchange Arrangement

The currency of Latvia is the Lats.[1] The Bank of Latvia's policy is to ensure orderly conditions in the exchange market and to limit short-term fluctuations in the exchange rate of the lats against convertible currencies. The Bank of Latvia reviews domestic and international exchange markets on a daily basis and announces buying and selling rates for the lats against a basket of currencies; since February 1994, the lats has maintained a fixed exchange rate vis-à-vis the SDR. The Bank of Latvia stands ready to transact with commercial banks at these rates. The exchange rates for the lats against convertible currencies other than the U.S. dollar are quoted on the basis of the cross rates between the U.S. dollar and the currencies concerned in the international market. A margin of 2 percent is applied in the quotations of the buying and selling rates for the above currencies. Banks and other authorized exchange dealers also trade in these currencies, and their buying and selling rates may deviate from time to time from the quoted rates. The Bank of Latvia also quotes daily the midpoint of the buying and selling rates of the lats against convertible currencies. These rates are used for various accounting purposes, including customs duties, taxation, and other valuations; they are valid through the next day and are communicated to all commercial banks. On December 31, 1995, the official exchange rate of the lats was LVL 0.537 per $1. The use of convertible currencies for domestic settlements is also permitted.

The Bank of Latvia also quotes weekly the accounting rates of the lats for the currencies of Russia, and the other countries of the former Soviet Union that participate in the system of correspondent accounts.

Latvia accepted the obligation of Article VIII, Sections 2, 3, and 4 of the Fund Agreement on June 10, 1994.

Administration of Control

Government decisions adopted by the Cabinet of Ministers and approved by Parliament prevail in foreign exchange and trade matters, but the authority to issue regulations governing foreign exchange transactions has been delegated to the Bank of Latvia. All foreign exchange transactions must be effected through authorized banks and enterprises licensed by the Bank of Latvia.

Prescription of Currency

Settlements with the Baltic countries, Russia, and the other countries of the former Soviet Union can be made through any means, including a system of correspondent accounts. Settlements with countries with which the Bank of Latvia maintains agreements on mutual settlement of accounts are effected in accordance with the terms of these agreements.[2] At the end of 1995, Latvia also maintained trade and economic cooperation agreements providing for most-favored-nation (MFN) status with a number of countries.[3]

Resident and Nonresident Accounts

Resident natural persons and enterprises are allowed to hold foreign currencies in cash or in domestic or foreign bank accounts and to use these funds for domestic payments. Nonresident natural persons are permitted to hold bank accounts in Latvia denominated in either foreign or domestic currency.

Imports and Exports

There are virtually no licensing requirements for imports except on imports of sugar, cereals, tobacco and tobacco products, alcoholic beverages, and nonferrous and ferrous metals. For national health and safety reasons, licenses are also required for

---

[1] Effective July 20, 1992, the Latvian ruble replaced the Russian ruble as legal tender in Latvia, and in March 1993, the lats began to be issued as permanent currency at the conversion rate of Latvian ruble 200 per LVL 1. At this conversion rate, the exchange rate of the lats for the U.S. dollar was LVL 1 per $1.5. The Latvian lats became the sole legal tender effective October 18, 1993.

[2] At the end of 1995, Latvia maintained bilateral payments agreements with Azerbaijan, Belarus, Estonia, Georgia, Kazakstan, the Kyrgyz Republic, Lithuania, Moldova, Russia, Turkmenistan, Ukraine, and Uzbekistan.

[3] Armenia, Azerbaijan, Belarus, Canada, Cuba, the European Union, Hungary, Iceland, India, Moldova, Poland, Russia, Turkmenistan, Ukraine, United States, and Uzbekistan. Similar agreements were signed in 1992 with the Czech Republic and the Slovak Republic. Latvia had free trade agreements with the other Baltic countries, the European Union, Finland, Norway, Sweden, and Switzerland.

pyrotechnic products, arms and ammunition, combat vehicles, and prepared explosives.

A new tariff law became effective on December 1, 1994. It replaced most specific tariffs with ad valorem rates and established basic import tariff rates of 20 percent (15 percent for countries with MFN status). Excluding agricultural tariffs, in 1995, 39 percent of Latvia's imports were assessed with MFN duties of 15 percent or less. An additional 57 percent of Latvia's imports were assessed with lower duties under the free trade agreements, and only 4 percent of Latvia's imports were assessed basic rate tariffs of 20 percent or less. An ad valorem tariff rate of 55 percent applies to six agricultural commodities. Most raw materials and spare parts are assessed an import duty of 1 percent (0.5 percent when originating in countries with which MFN relations are maintained). A number of final goods are also exempt from import tariffs, and certain goods such as fruit, nuts, coffee, and tea are subject to reduced tariffs of 1 percent (0.5 percent when originating in countries with which MFN relations are maintained). Specific tariff rates are levied on seeds, animal feed, certain grains, flour, bread, sugar, certain confectionery products including chocolate, alcohol, cigarettes, and cars. The Free Trade Agreement between Latvia and the EU covers substantially all goods traded with the EU. According to this agreement, free trade areas will be gradually established within a maximum of four years starting from January 1, 1995.

Upon entering the territory of Latvia, natural persons are entitled to deliver across the border of the Republic of Latvia without any customs payments all kinds of goods and articles intended for purposes other than commerce, whose importation is not forbidden or limited by law, and whose customs value does not exceed LVL 300. A total customs value of foodstuffs not exceeding LVL 15 per person is exempted from taxes.

Persons over 18 are exempt from taxes on alcoholic drinks up to 1 liter or one measured unit in original packing not exceeding 3 liters, and on a maximum of either 200 cigarettes, 20 cigars, or 200 grams of tobacco.

There are no export quotas. Export duties are levied on waste and scrap metals, certain categories of round logs, certain mineral products, works of art, antiques, and certain books.

Export proceeds are not subject to repatriation or surrender requirements.

Payments for and Proceeds from Invisibles

No exchange control or restrictions are imposed on payments for or proceeds from invisibles.

Capital

There are no exchange control regulations governing capital transactions.

Gold

There are no regulations governing international trade in gold. A license is required to deal in gold in the domestic market.

Changes During 1995

No significant changes occurred in the exchange and trade system.

LEBANON

(Position as of December 31, 1995)

Exchange Arrangement

The currency of Lebanon is the Lebanese Pound. The authorities do not maintain margins in respect of foreign exchange transactions, and exchange rates are determined on the basis of demand and supply in the exchange market. However, the authorities may announce buying or selling rates for certain currencies and intervene when necessary in order to maintain orderly conditions in the foreign exchange market. On December 30, 1995, the rate for the U.S. dollar was LL 1,596 per $1.

There are no taxes or subsidies on purchases or sales of foreign exchange. Banks are allowed to engage in spot transactions in any currency except in Israeli new sheqalim. They are prohibited from engaging in forward transactions against the Lebanese pound unless such transactions are related to foreign trade.

Lebanon accepted the obligations of Article VIII, Sections 2, 3, and 4 of the Fund Agreement on July 1, 1993.

Prescription of Currency

No restrictions are imposed on exchange payments abroad or receipts in Lebanon.

Imports and Import Payments

Imports of a few goods (mainly arms and ammunition, narcotics, and similar products) are either prohibited or reserved for the Government. All imports from Israel are prohibited. Imports prohibited year-round include citrus fruits, apples, and liquid milk; imports prohibited during a specified period of the year include squash, eggplant, green beans, watermelons, peas, apricots, potatoes, onions, cucumbers, tomatoes, garlic, jew's mallow, okra, muskmelons, pear peaches, green almonds, grapes, green peppers, pomegranates, and green plums. Imports of certain other agricultural products and all seeds require a license. Import licenses are also required for certain finished goods, insulated electric and telephone wires, and copper cables. Foreign exchange to pay for imports may be obtained freely without a license.

Banks are obliged to ensure that importers possess a valid import license, if required, before issuing letters of credit. Importers must place with their banks a prior deposit in the same currency as that in which letters of credit are opened in an amount equivalent to 15 percent of the value of import letters of credit; the banks are not required to deposit such amounts with the Bank of Lebanon.

The tariff regime is based on the Brussels Tariff Nomenclature. Ad valorem duty rates on most products range from zero to 20 percent and are applied on a most-favored-nation basis, except for certain imports from Arab countries, which are accorded a preferential rate. The tax on motor vehicles is levied at the following rates: 20 percent of the first LL 25 million and 35 percent on the remaining value. The following rates apply to alcoholic beverages: beer, 35 percent of the value; champagne, wine, and vermouths, 80 percent of the value; and arak, 50 percent of the value.

Payments for Invisibles

There are no restrictions on payments for invisibles. Foreign exchange may be obtained in the free market.

Exports and Export Proceeds

Exports of certain goods (mainly arms and ammunition, narcotics, and similar products) to any destination and all exports to Israel are prohibited. Exports of wheat and wheat derivatives to any country and all exports to the Democratic People's Republic of Korea require a license. Foreign exchange receipts from exports may be retained, used, or sold in the free market.

Proceeds from Invisibles

Foreign exchange receipts from invisibles may be retained, used, or sold in the free market.

Capital

There are no limitations on capital payments or receipts. Foreign exchange may be obtained or sold in the free market. Banks are prohibited from receiving deposits, extending credits or opening accounts in Lebanese pounds for nonresident banks and financial institutions. However, this restriction does not apply to guarantees issued by nonresident banks and financial institutions as collateral to loans in Lebanese pounds provided that such loans are for

278

commercial or investment activities in Lebanon. Banks are authorized to maintain a trading position in foreign currency amounting to up to 5 percent (short or long) of the core capital of banks and a fixed position in foreign currency (long) amounting to 60 percent of core capital in Lebanese pounds. Under a "free zone" banking facility, commercial banks are exempt from fees for deposit insurance in respect of foreign currency deposits by nonresidents. Income from all accounts with banks has been exempt from the income tax.

Under the National Investment Insurance Scheme, new foreign investments are insured against losses arising from noncivil risks, including war. Compensation is paid on losses that are more than 10 percent of the insured value.

Gold

Residents may freely hold gold in any form at home or abroad and may freely negotiate gold in any form with residents and nonresidents, at home or abroad. The importation and exportation of gold in any form does not require a license, but must be officially recorded. The importation, exportation, and domestic sale of foreign gold coins must be covered by a certificate, issued by the Office for the Protection of the Consumer, that indicates the gold content and weight.

Changes During 1995

No significant changes occurred in the exchange and trade system.

LESOTHO

(Position as of December 31, 1995)

Exchange Arrangement

The currency of Lesotho is the Loti (plural Maloti), which is pegged to the South African rand at M 1 per R 1. Under the Common Monetary Area (CMA) Agreement, the rand is also legal tender in Lesotho. The principal intervention currency is the U.S. dollar. On December 31, 1995, the buying and selling rates for the U.S. dollar were M 3.6470 and M 3.6480, respectively, per $1. Authorized dealers are permitted to conduct forward exchange operations through their correspondent banks abroad at rates quoted by the latter. Forward exchange cover is not, however, common in Lesotho. There are no taxes or subsidies on purchases or sales of foreign exchange. The financial rand system of South Africa was abolished in March 1995 and was accompanied by a similar action by Lesotho.

Exchange Control Territory

Lesotho forms part of the CMA, which is an exchange control territory comprising Lesotho, Namibia, South Africa, and Swaziland. The amended Trilateral Monetary Agreement among Lesotho, South Africa, and Swaziland became effective on April 1, 1986, and was amended in 1989. Namibia, which was an indirect party to the agreement by virtue of its relationship with South Africa, officially became a party following its independence in March 1990. Payments within the CMA are unrestricted and unrecorded except for statistical and customs purposes. In its relations with countries outside the CMA, Lesotho applies exchange controls that are largely similar to those applied by South Africa and Swaziland.

Administration of Control

The Central Bank of Lesotho controls external currency transactions and delegates to commercial banks the authority to approve certain types of current payments up to established limits. Permits are issued by the Department of Customs and Excise on the recommendation of the Department of Trade and Industry. Licenses for financial institutions accepting deposits and insurance companies, brokers, and agents are issued by the Central Bank.

Prescription of Currency

There are no regulations prescribing the currencies that can be used in particular transactions.

Imports and Import Payments

Lesotho is a member of the Southern African Customs Union (SACU) with Botswana, Namibia, South Africa, and Swaziland. All imports, except certain food imports originating in any country of the SACU, are unrestricted; those from countries outside the SACU are usually licensed in conformity with the import regulations of the SACU; Lesotho reserves the right to restrict certain imports. Import permits are valid for all countries and entitle the holder to buy the foreign exchange required to make payments for imports from outside the SACU.

Exports and Export Proceeds

Certain exports are subject to licensing for revenue purposes; this requirement, in practice, is restricted to the exportation of diamonds. Most exports are shipped without license to or through South Africa. Unless otherwise permitted, all export proceeds must be remitted to Lesotho and surrendered within six months of the date of the export transaction.

Payments for and Proceeds from Invisibles

Payments to nonresidents for current transactions, although subject to control, are not normally restricted. Authorized dealers are permitted to approve some types of current payments up to established limits. The basic annual exchange allowance for tourist travel to neighboring countries outside the CMA area—Malawi, Mozambique, Zambia, and Zimbabwe—is M 6,000 an adult and M 3,000 a child; the corresponding annual allowance for tourist travel to other countries outside the CMA region is M 25,000 and M 12,500, respectively. For business travel to neighboring countries outside the CMA region, the basic annual allowance is M 12,000 a person at rates not exceeding M 900 a day; the corresponding limits for business travel to other countries are M 38,000 and M 2,000, respectively. Larger allowances may be obtained for travel for business and medical treatment.

The education allowance is M 4,000 a student a month or M 8,000 a month for a student accompanied by a spouse who is not studying. Payments of professional fees of up to a maximum of M 10,000 are allowed, and M 50,000 is allowed for charges related to repairs or adjustments to goods temporarily exported. Lesotho residents may also effect payment of fees owed for technical services brought into Lesotho within an overall limit of M 50,000. Lesotho residents may enter into contracts with visiting artists, entertainers, and sportspersons, provided the commitment does not exceed M 75,000. Guarantees by Lesotho residents up to a limit of M 25,000 in respect of overdraft facilities for residents of Botswana, Malawi, Zambia, and Zimbabwe for domestic, farming, and business purposes may also be approved. Emigrant allowances may be transferred up to M 200,000 a family or up to M 100,000 a person. The maximum amount of earnings on blocked assets that emigrants are allowed to transfer through normal banking channels is M 300,000 a year.

Capital

Inward capital transfers should be properly documented to facilitate the subsequent repatriation of interest, dividends, profits, and other income. No person may borrow foreign currency, register shares in the name of a nonresident, or act as a nominee for a nonresident without prior approval.

Applications for outward transfers of capital are considered on their merits. The rulings on applications for inward and outward capital transfers may depend on whether the applicant is a temporary resident foreign national, a nonresident, or a resident. Certain tax incentives for inward direct investment are provided to manufacturers approved by the Pio-

neer Industries Board under the Pioneer Industries Encouragement Act of 1969. Funds in blocked maloti accounts may be invested in quoted securities and other such investments approved by the Central Bank. The free transfer of income from an emigrant's blocked assets is limited to an annual maximum of M 300,000 a family unit. The transfer by nonresidents of dividends and profits from investments held in Lesotho is not restricted, provided these funds were not obtained through excessive use of local borrowing facilities. An emigrant family or an individual may export one automobile only, with a maximum value of M 75,000, provided that the automobile was purchased at least one year before emigration.

The limit on settling-in allowances that immigrants are permitted to transfer is M 500,000 for a family and M 250,000 for a single person, of which M 20,000 may be in cash; the remainder may be used to acquire residential properties and a motor vehicle.

Gold

Residents may freely purchase, hold, and sell any gold coins that are legal tender.

Changes During 1995

Exchange Arrangement

March 13. The financial rand system was abolished in South Africa and Lesotho.

LIBERIA

(Position as of December 31, 1995)

Exchange Arrangement

The currency of Liberia is the Liberian Dollar, which is pegged to the U.S. dollar at Lib$1 per US$1. There is no official intervention currency. The currency of the United States is legal tender in Liberia and circulates along with Liberian currency. There are two Liberian dollar notes—Liberty notes introduced in 1992 and J.J. Roberts notes issued from 1988 to 1992 —which continue to circulate in parts of the territory. U.S. dollar notes, which previously formed the major portion of the currency in circulation, have almost totally disappeared. Full convertibility between the Liberian dollar and the U.S. dollar at par does not exist. The U.S. dollar attracts a substantial premium in large parallel market transactions, and commercial banks charge abnormally high commissions for their sales of offshore funds. Foreign exchange dealers other than banks are permitted to buy and sell currencies other than the U.S. dollar at market-determined exchange rates. The official exchange rate is limited to the settlement of tax obligations and data reporting, while the parallel exchange rate (about Lib$50 per US$1 for the Liberty notes in 1995, with J.J. Roberts notes trading at a premium over the Liberty notes) applies to most transactions, including government spending.

There are no taxes or subsidies on purchases or sales of foreign exchange. There are no arrangements for forward cover against exchange rate risk operating in the official or the commercial banking sector.

Administration of Control

Export- and import-licensing regulations are administered by the Ministry of Commerce and Industry. Arrears are maintained with respect to external payments.

Prescription of Currency

Some exporters must pay withholding taxes and corporate income taxes in U.S. dollars. Hotels are required to receive payments from foreign guests in foreign exchange. Settlements with the Central Bank of West African States (Benin, Burkina Faso, Côte d'Ivoire, Niger, Senegal, and Togo) and The Gambia, Ghana, Guinea, Guinea-Bissau, Mali, Mauritania, Nigeria, and Sierra Leone are normally made through the West African Clearing House.

Imports and Import Payments

There is no general system of import control, but the importation of some items is subject to licensing and quantitative restrictions. Licensing requirements are liberally enforced. These items include safety matches, electrode welding rods, and liquefied petroleum gas. Imports of arms, ammunition, and explosives require prior licenses. In addition, imports of certain goods (for example, narcotics, other than for medicinal purposes) are prohibited. The Liberian National Petroleum Company (LNPC) no longer has the exclusive right to import petroleum products; all eligible importers that obtain an import declaration form from the Ministry of Commerce and Industry may import them. Licenses to import inexpensive, widely consumed varieties of rice are issued to private distributors by the Ministry of Commerce and Industry. The importation of more expensive rice is not subject to official controls. The nominal tariff rate on imports is about 31 percent on average.

Preshipment inspection of imports is required to ascertain the country of origin, the quality, the quantity, and the value of all goods to be shipped to Liberia. Both final and intermediate goods are subject to inspection, except for imports with an f.o.b. value of less than US$3,000.

Exports and Export Proceeds

Export licenses are at present required for elephant tusks and ivory; wild animals; cement; agricultural products other than rubber, flour, and sugar; and certain other items, such as arms, ammunition, and explosives. Licenses are generally issued freely and serve mainly to enforce the 25 percent surrender of export proceeds and taxation or, for agricultural products, to assure certification of quality and origin. Wood products for exportation must have a local processing content of at least 10 percent. Exporters are required to surrender 25 percent of export proceeds to the National Bank of Liberia through the commercial banks. The Government and the National Bank receive priority for the purchase of such foreign exchange. The portion of foreign exchange surrendered that is not purchased by the public sector is made available to commercial banks at par. An export tax at the rate of 15 percent a troy ounce is levied on diamonds.

Payments for and Proceeds from Invisibles

There are no governmental limitations on payments for or receipts from invisibles.

Capital

No exchange control requirements are imposed on capital receipts or payments by residents or nonresidents. Under the Investment Incentive Code of 1966 (as amended in 1973), enterprises undertaking new investment projects may be granted a five-year 90 percent duty exemption on imports of raw materials and machinery, total tax exemption on reinvested profits, a 50 percent exemption on distributable profits, and a protective tariff on competing imported products. The five-year incentive may be renewed for two additional years in certain circumstances. Most mining, logging, and rubber enterprises, however, operate under special redundant agreements that provide for tax concessions for a period ranging up to 70 years.

Gold

Imports and exports of gold in any form are subject to licenses issued by the Ministry of Land, Mines, and Energy; import licenses are issued freely, but export licenses are granted restrictively.

Changes During 1995

No significant changes occurred in the exchange and trade system.

SOCIALIST PEOPLE'S LIBYAN ARAB JAMAHIRIYA

(Position as of December 31, 1995)

Exchange Arrangement

The currency of the Socialist People's Libyan Arab Jamahiriya (Libya) is the Libyan Dinar, which is pegged to the SDR at the rate of LD 1 per SDR 2.80. Margins not exceeding 47 percent are allowed around this fixed relationship, and the dinar has been depreciated to the maximum extent permitted within those margins to LD 1 per SDR 1.905. Buying and selling rates of the Libyan dinar in terms of 16 currencies[1] are based on their exchange rates against the SDR, as communicated by the International Monetary Fund (IMF). The middle rate for the U.S. dollar, the intervention currency, on December 31, 1995 was LD 0.353 per $1.

Commercial banks may not deal among themselves in foreign currencies but only through their foreign correspondents. Neither authorized banks nor importers or exporters are allowed to enter into forward commitments in foreign currencies. Since 1985, fees have been levied on outward foreign exchange transfers for the purpose of financing the Great Man-Made River Project. These fees have resulted in a deviation of more than 2 percent between the official exchange rate and the effective rate applied to these transfers. There are no other taxes or subsidies on purchases or sales of foreign exchange.

Administration of Control

Exchange control is administered by the Central Bank of Libya, which has delegated some of its powers to authorized banks. Policy relating to imports and exports is determined by the General People's Congress and executed by the Secretariat of Planning, the Economy, and Trade.

Prescription of Currency

All settlements with Israel are prohibited. Settlements with other countries are made in convertible currencies. A bilateral trade and payments agreement is maintained with Malta; outstanding balances are settled in convertible currencies annually.

---

[1] Austrian schillings, Belgian francs, Canadian dollars, Danish kroner, deutsche mark, French francs, Italian lire, Japanese yen, Netherlands guilders, Norwegian kroner, pounds sterling, Saudi Arabian riyals, Swedish kronor, Swiss francs, Tunisian dinars, and U.S. dollars.

Resident and Nonresident Accounts

Nonresidents (as defined by the Central Bank) who are gainfully employed in the country are permitted under the exchange control regulations to open and maintain nonresident accounts in Libyan dinars with any authorized bank. Such nonresidents may credit their legitimate earnings to their nonresident accounts. All other credits to nonresident accounts require the prior approval of the Central Bank. (For debits of such accounts, see section on Payments for Invisibles, below.)

Funds brought in by nonresident contractors undertaking contracts in their own names must be kept with an authorized bank. Payments received by contractors in respect of their contracts may also be credited to these accounts. Remittances from these accounts are subject to the prior approval of the Central Bank after submission of the prescribed evidence, but, in general, remittances are permitted up to the net-of-tax amount specified in the contract.

Nonresident-owned capital that is not permitted to be transferred abroad is credited to blocked accounts. With the approval of the Central Bank, funds in blocked accounts (with certain exceptions) may be used for expenditures in Libya, up to LD 500 a year, to cover the cost of visits by the owner of the funds or a close relative; for payment of legal fees and taxes; for remittances to the owner of the funds in his or her country of permanent residence (up to LD 1,000 each calendar year); and for remittances in cases of hardship. When the funds have been in a blocked account for five years, they qualify, upon payment of due taxes, for remittance in full to the owner in his or her country of permanent residence. The blocked accounts of persons (with certain exceptions) who have left the country permanently are being released in installments; balances credited before March 31, 1966, have been released. With the authorization of the Central Bank, individual residents are allowed to keep foreign currencies in domestic bank accounts and to transfer balances abroad without restriction.

Imports and Import Payments

All imports from Israel are prohibited. Imports undertaken by state-owned enterprises do not require licenses if they are authorized within the annual commodity budget. Importers are required to deal directly with producers abroad and not through intermediaries. However, imports not included in the annual commodity budget are subject to licensing. Resident firms undertaking development projects may import needed items that are not included in the annual commodity budget and not available locally, and foreign exchange to pay for these imports is provided by the Government; similar imports by nonresidents, however, must be financed with foreign exchange resources from abroad.

There is a prohibited import list, consisting mainly of consumer and luxury goods.[2] Only government agencies may act as commercial agents, including import agents, for foreign companies. A state-owned company controlled by the Central Bank has a monopoly over the importation of gold and precious metals. Under Decision No. 248 of January 1989, import trade by private companies and partnerships has been permitted. With the exception of strategic goods, (i.e., nine essential food items, medicine, insecticides, petroleum products, tobacco, and gold), retained by public corporations, all other goods may be imported by either public or private entities within the provisions of the annual commodity budget.

With certain exceptions, all exchange permits require central bank approval. Exchange permits required for imports are readily granted by the authorized banks following central bank approval, provided that a firm contract exists and an import license has been obtained from the Secretariat of Planning, the Economy, and Trade and, if imports are to be financed under letters of credit, that a marine insurance policy from a local insurance company is submitted before the letter of credit is established. However, an authorized bank may not open a letter of credit without an advance import deposit equal to at least 20 percent of the value of the import. Importers must present to the bank granting the exchange permit, within two months of customs clearance, a customs declaration confirming clearance and stating the valuation. The approval of the Exchange Control Department of the Central Bank is required for all payments by residents.

Imports are subject to customs duties and customs surcharges, the latter consisting of 10 percent of the applicable customs duty. All products originating in Arab countries are exempted from customs duties, provided that their domestic value added is at least 40 percent. Private individuals are allowed to import

goods on the commodity budget list up to a maximum value of LD 3,000 a year from Arab countries.

Payments for Invisibles

Payments for invisibles related to authorized imports are not restricted.

Nonresidents employed by the state, by state-owned enterprises, and by foreign companies may remit up to 50 percent of their net salaries each month if their contracts do not specify that lodging, board, or both will be made available free of charge by the employer, or up to 75 percent of their net salaries if their contracts specify that, in accordance with applicable Libyan laws and regulations, the employer will provide both lodging and board free of charge at worksites in remote areas. Staff of UN agencies, embassies, consulates, and medical institutions are exempt from these regulations. Banks may issue traveler's checks and foreign currency notes to nonresident workers and technicians within the limits mentioned.

In 1992, the granting of travel allowances was suspended. Previously, residents leaving for personal travel abroad, including tourist travel, could take out foreign exchange in the form of foreign currency notes, traveler's checks, and letters of credit not exceeding a total value of LD 300 (LD 150 for children between the ages of 10 and 18 years) in a calendar year as a basic travel allowance; the exchange could be obtained from any authorized bank in Libya. Additional amounts were granted in special circumstances. Pilgrims to Saudi Arabia were entitled to a special quota. Temporary residents may take out any traveler's checks or foreign currency notes that they had previously brought in and declared to customs. Travelers leaving Libya may not take out Libyan currency.

All other payments for invisibles, as well as payments in excess of the approval authority delegated to the banks, require the prior approval of the Central Bank. Applications are considered on their merits.

Exports and Export Proceeds

Export licenses are required for raw wool, hides and skins, and agricultural products. Export proceeds must be received through an authorized bank within six months of shipment. Exports of nonmonetary gold (other than for processing abroad), scrap metals, eggs, chicken, fish, olive oil, paint, tires, steel, and tractors are prohibited; exports or re-exports of wheat, wheat flour, crushed wheat, barley, rice, tea, sugar, tomato paste, and macaroni, which are subsidized commodities, are also prohibited. Exports of

---

[2]These include mineral water, fruit juices, instant tea, certain types of coffee, green vegetables, poultry, preserved meats and vegetables, alcoholic beverages, peanuts, oriental rugs, soaps, envelopes, crystal chandeliers, toy guns, luxury cars, and furs.

domestically produced vegetable oils are permitted. All exports to Israel are prohibited. The Export Promotion Council helps exporters to enter foreign markets by providing information on demand conditions abroad and on potential exports. Also, exporters are allowed to retain up to 40 percent of foreign exchange earnings in a special account that may be used to finance imports of raw materials, spare parts, and machinery needed for export production. In general, exporters do not need export licenses but must register with the Council and supply, on a regular basis, the relevant documentation on their exports.

Proceeds from Invisibles

All foreign exchange receipts must be surrendered. Traveler's checks or foreign currency notes may be cashed only at an authorized bank, an exchange office, or a hotel licensed by the Central Bank.

Travelers entering the country may bring in traveler's checks, letters of credit, securities, coupons, and other negotiable instruments in unlimited amounts, which they must declare to customs. Foreign exchange converted into Libyan dinars by visiting tourists may be reconverted upon departure, with the exception of a minimum local expenditure of $50 for each day spent in the country.

Capital

Under the provisions of Foreign Capital Investment Law No. 37 of July 31, 1968, foreign capital invested in projects deemed to contribute to the economic development of the country, as well as profits thereon, may be transferred freely to the country of origin, provided that the paid-up capital is not less than LD 200,000 and that at least 51 percent of the shares are held by foreign nationals. Salaries of foreign staff employed on such projects may be transferred (as described in the section on Payments for Invisibles, above). Central Bank approval is required and customarily granted freely for all such transfers. Foreign participation in industrial ventures set up after March 20, 1970, is permitted on a minority basis but only if it leads to increased production in excess of local requirements, introduction of the latest technology, and cooperation with foreign firms in exporting the surplus production. Insurance companies and foreign shareholdings in banks have been nationalized.

Only Libyans may own real estate in Libya. Nonresident-owned capital that is not permitted to be transferred abroad is credited to blocked accounts (see section on Resident and Nonresident Accounts, above). Residents must obtain the prior approval of the Central Bank to borrow funds abroad. As a rule, residents must have prior permission from the Committee of the People's Bureau for Foreign Affairs and International Economic Cooperation to purchase real estate abroad or to invest abroad in securities. The investment of national capital abroad is governed by Law No. 25 of April 20, 1973.

Gold

Residents may freely purchase, hold, and sell gold in any form other than bars. The Central Bank imports processed and unprocessed gold and precious metals; it also sells gold bars to domestic goldsmiths for manufacture at prices announced from time to time. The gold must be processed before it is sold to the public. Unworked gold is subject to an import duty of 15 percent.

Changes During 1995

No significant changes occurred in the exchange and trade system.

LITHUANIA

(Position as of December 31, 1995)

Exchange Arrangement

The currency of Lithuania is the Litas (plural Litai). The external value of the litas has been pegged to the U.S. dollar at Llt 4 per $1 since April 1, 1994, when the currency board arrangement was established. Authorized banks quote exchange rates for other convertible currencies on the basis of their cross rate relationships for the currencies concerned on international markets. Authorized banks also quote buying and selling rates for the Russian ruble at varying rates. The Bank of Lithuania also calculates an accounting rate, which is used to value balance sheet items. Accounting rates for convertible currencies and for the currencies of the Baltic countries, Russia, and other countries of the former Soviet Union are calculated daily.[1]

There are no limits on the net open positions of authorized banks. There are no taxes or subsidies on purchases or sales of foreign exchange. There are no arrangements for forward cover against exchange rate risk operating in the official or the commercial banking sector.

Lithuania accepted the obligations of Article VIII, Sections 2, 3, and 4 of the Fund Agreement on May 3, 1994.

Administration of Control

Parliament has the legislative authority in foreign exchange and trade matters; it has adopted a banking law delegating to the Bank of Lithuania the authority to issue regulations governing foreign exchange transactions.

All foreign exchange transactions must be effected through authorized banks licensed by the Bank of Lithuania. To date, 20 banks have been authorized to deal in foreign exchange. Authorized banks are allowed to transact among themselves, as well as with residents and nonresidents of Lithuania, and they are divided into four categories, depending on the types of transactions they are permitted to conduct. The simplest type of license limits the operations to buying and selling foreign exchange (cash and traveler's checks). At present, eight banks have

been granted a general license that allows them to offer a full range of banking services (including issuing letters of credit) in foreign exchange operations, and they are permitted to open correspondent accounts with banks abroad.

Prescription of Currency

There are no prescription of currency requirements, and settlements may be made in any convertible currency.[2]

Resident and Nonresident Accounts

Resident natural and juridical persons may open foreign exchange accounts at authorized banks, and these accounts may be credited and debited without restriction. Nonresident individuals and representative offices of foreign enterprises and diplomatic missions may open foreign exchange accounts at the authorized banks, and these accounts may be credited and debited without restriction.

Imports and Import Payments

There are no quantitative restrictions or licensing requirements on imports, except for health and national security reasons. Imports subject to bilateral trade agreements are allocated by the Ministry of Trade and Industry. A 10 percent tariff rate is applied to most imports. Higher tariff rates are levied only on specific products (such as live animals, agricultural products, alcohol and tobacco, and a few manufacturing goods), some exceeding 30 percent. Average import tariffs are presently very low by international standards. The majority of agricultural products (and other items such as alcohol) are subject to zero tariff rates but tariffs on certain such items remain quite high, and the tariff structure continues to be highly dispersed.

A tax at the uniform rate of 0.01 percent is imposed on imports (and exports) for the sole purpose of collecting statistical information on trade.

---

[1]The accounting rates for the convertible currencies are identical to the middle rates on Tuesdays and at the end of each month, whereas the accounting rates for the currencies of the Baltic states, Russia, and the other countries of the former Soviet Union are calculated by the Bank of Lithuania by using the cross rates for the U.S. dollar quoted by the respective central banks.

[2]Correspondent accounts exist between the Bank of Lithuania and the central banks of the Baltic countries, Russia, and the other countries of the former Soviet Union. These accounts need not be used for payments originating after October 1992. Ruble-denominated correspondent accounts maintained with the central banks of the Baltic countries, Russia, and the other countries of the former Soviet Union have been closed and are in the process of being settled.

There is a three-tier import tariff structure with different rates for each of the following country categories: (1) "conventional" rates apply to countries granted most-favored-nation (MFN) status by Lithuania, and to neighboring countries if trade with them is viewed as a foreign policy priority;[3] (2) "preferential" rates apply to countries with which Lithuania has a foreign trade agreement (FTA), as specified in the relevant FTA;[4] (3) "autonomous" rates apply to all other countries. On February 28, 1995, the Government specified the above three rates for many products; the autonomous rates are generally 5 to 10 percentage points higher than the conventional rates. Also, on that date, the Government subjected specific items to ad valorem tariffs; in the case of alcohol, sugar, tobacco, and used cars, these tariffs are mixed with specific duties. While the ad valorem equivalents of these specific duties are modest and are designed to limit underinvoicing, the Government intends to move away from specific tariffs over time, while strengthening customs valuation procedures.

Virtually all quantitative import restrictions have been replaced with tariffs, but imports of certain agricultural goods and alcoholic beverages are subject to reduced duty rates up to a certain level.[5] Other quantitative import restrictions are used to control trade in strategic goods and technology; to protect Lithuania's cultural heritage; and to prevent illegal trade in copper and other nonferrous metals, alloys, and scrap. Finally, alcoholic beverages and tobacco can be imported only by traders registered with the Government, although import quantities are unrestricted. Lithuania does not presently levy antidumping or countervailing duties.

Payments for Invisibles

Payments for all invisibles may be made without restriction.

Exports and Export Proceeds

Quantitative export restrictions have been almost eliminated. Proceeds from exports are not required to be repatriated to Lithuania. Exports are not sub-

ject to licensing requirements. Export duties are levied on certain raw materials and selected products.

Export tariffs were eliminated on November 1, 1994. At the same time, however, the Government extended a "temporary prohibition" on exports of six product groups until May 1, 1995, which was extended to May 1, 1996.[6] This prohibition serves to protect a small number of domestic processors of primary products. The export bans are not binding for countries that have signed an FTA with Lithuania. In the case of wood products, banned exports account for only 20 percent of total exports, because wood is mostly exported to Finland, Switzerland, and Germany, all of whom have FTAs with Lithuania. Regulations governing trade in strategic goods and technology, cultural objects, nonferrous scrap, and waste apply to exports as well as imports.

Proceeds from Invisibles

Proceeds from invisibles are not subject to any control or restriction.

Capital

Authorized banks may borrow abroad or extend loans in foreign currencies to residents and nonresidents without restriction. Resident firms may borrow foreign exchange from authorized banks or borrow directly from banks abroad with the approval of the Bank of Lithuania.

Foreign direct investment is regulated by the Law of Foreign Investments promulgated in December 1990 and amended in February and June 1992. The law permits the State to sell shares to nonresidents, guarantees nondiscriminatory national treatment to foreign investors, and protects investments against nationalization and expropriation. The purchase of state-owned enterprises is subject to authorization from the Central Privatization Committee. One of the main conditions in this process is that the company must remain involved in the same type of business for at least one year under the new ownership. While firms with 100 percent foreign capital ownership are allowed to operate in Lithuania, the Government reserves the right to establish limits on foreign investment in Lithuanian enterprises. Foreign investors are prohibited from operating in the defense industry, public utilities, and energy explo-

---

[3]The conventional rate applies to imports from Australia, Belarus, Bulgaria, Canada, China, Cuba, the Czech Republic, Hungary, Iceland, India, Kazakstan, Korea, Poland, Romania, Russia, Slovenia, Tajikistan, Turkey, Ukraine, and the United States.

[4]Lithuania presently has foreign trade agreements with Estonia, the EU, Latvia, Liechtenstein, Norway, and Switzerland.

[5]These include unbottled alcoholic beverages and raw materials for their production, raw sugar and half-finished products for sugar factories, technical ethyl alcohol, purebred birds' eggs for incubation, live purebred animals, live purebred poultry, cereals and combined fodder, and nonstandard clear glass bottles.

[6]The following products are subject to temporary export prohibitions: red clover seeds, feathers and down used for stuffing, raw hides and skins, unprocessed pine and birch timber with thin end diameter not less than 20 cm., unprocessed oak and ash timber, and glands and other organs used for pharmaceutical products and organotherapeutical uses without quotas issued by the Ministry of Health Care.

ration. In joint ventures in the transportation and communication sectors, the domestic partner is required to hold the majority of the shares. Wholly owned ventures in the alcoholic beverage or tobacco industries are prohibited. Enterprises with foreign investment must be insured by Lithuanian insurance companies, even if the company retains other insurance services outside Lithuania.

The ownership of land by nonresidents in Lithuania is prohibited, but lease contracts with limits to 2 hectares of land in Vilnius and 10 hectares outside the capital are permitted for up to 99 years and may be renewed thereafter.

The Law of Foreign Investments also guarantees the free repatriation of all after-tax profits as well as the invested capital, with no limitation on timing or amount. It also provides for important tax incentives. If the foreign investment was made before the end of 1993, the profit tax is reduced by 70 percent (to within a range of 8.7 percent to 29 percent) for five years. For another three years, the profit tax is reduced by 50 percent. For investments made between January 1994 and December 1995, profits will be taxed at a rate reduced by 50 percent for six years. For joint ventures, these reductions are proportional to the foreign capital invested.

Gold

Residents may freely hold, buy, or sell gold in any form in Lithuania.

Changes During 1995

Imports and Import Payments

January 18. Russia was granted most-favored-nation status.

Exports and Export Proceeds

May 1. A temporary prohibition on exports of five product groups, in place since November 1994, was extended until May 1, 1996. This prohibition serves to protect a small number of domestic processors of primary products.

FORMER YUGOSLAV REPUBLIC OF MACEDONIA[1]

(Position as of December 31, 1995)

Exchange Arrangement

The currency of the former Yugoslav Republic of Macedonia is the Denar, the external value of which is determined freely in the exchange market. Buying and selling rates for transactions between authorized banks and enterprises have to be reported to the National Bank of Macedonia, which calculates an average daily rate. Based on this rate and cross rates on the international market, the National Bank of Macedonia publishes rates for 22 currencies. On December 31, 1995, the midpoint exchange rate for the U.S. dollar published by the National Bank of Macedonia was MKD 37.9796 per $1. The National Bank of Macedonia deals at the published midpoint rates plus or minus a margin of 0.3 percent. At the end of each week, the average of the daily published rates is established for customs valuation purposes for the following week. There is no tax on the purchase or sale of foreign exchange, and banks are free to set commissions for their services. Forward foreign exchange contracts for trade transactions are permitted.

The exchange market operates at two levels—wholesale and retail. The wholesale level includes enterprises, commercial banks, and the National Bank of Macedonia, all of which may buy and sell foreign exchange in this market. The Government also participates in this market through the National Bank of Macedonia, which maintains the value of the denar against the deutsche mark at a level that meets their balance of payments objectives. The retail level of the foreign exchange market consists of foreign exchange bureaus, which are owned and operated by banks, enterprises, or natural persons. Foreign exchange bureaus may hold overnight foreign exchange positions equivalent to 100 percent of the preceding day's foreign exchange purchases. Natural persons may purchase foreign currency from these bureaus without limit, subject to availability.

Administration of Control

The Parliament has the authority to legislate laws governing foreign exchange and trade transactions. Certain changes in the trade regime may be made through government regulations.

According to the Foreign Exchange Act and the National Bank of Macedonia Act, the National Bank of Macedonia is authorized to control foreign exchange operations of banks and other financial institutions. The Ministry of Finance is authorized to control foreign exchange and trade operations and the credit relations of enterprises abroad, as well as other forms of business activities abroad, encompassing all enterprises that operate internationally. Certain foreign exchange control activities have been delegated to the participants in the foreign exchange market and the customs office. The Ministry of Foreign Relations administers the Foreign Trade Act and the Foreign Investments Act.

Medium- and long-term loans must be registered with the National Bank of Macedonia as stipulated by the Foreign Credit Relations Act. This obligation does not apply to short-term loans, which are permitted without restriction, except those related to imports, with a maturity exceeding six months. Short-term loans related to commercial banks' credit lines with a maturity exceeding 90 days should also be registered.

Prescription of Currency

Residents may receive payments and transfers in any convertible currency.

Resident and Nonresident Accounts

Nonresidents may open foreign exchange accounts with authorized banks; these accounts may be credited freely with foreign exchange and debited for payments abroad or for conversion into denars.

Resident natural persons may open foreign exchange accounts. Foreign exchange balances predating September 1, 1990 are freely disposable, that is, they can be withdrawn in foreign currency or converted into denars. Withdrawals in foreign currency may be used to make payments abroad on presentation of appropriate documentation for medical treatment (including purchases of medicine), education, and airfares (airfares have been temporarily restricted for budgetary reasons). Resident natural persons may not maintain foreign exchange accounts abroad or hold other financial assets abroad. In specific cases (such as enterprises with foreign operations), enterprises may hold foreign exchange accounts abroad with the approval of the National Bank of Macedonia.

---

[1]The former Yugoslav Republic of Macedonia succeeded to the membership of the former Socialist Federal Republic of Yugoslavia in the IMF on December 14, 1992.

Imports and Import Payments

Payments for authorized imports are not restricted. Imports and transit trade from the Federal Republic of Yugoslavia (Serbia/Montenegro) were prohibited, in accordance with UN Security Council Resolutions Nos. 757, 787, and 820. Since November 22, 1995, the UN Security Council has suspended indefinitely these resolutions according to Resolution No. 1022. Goods in almost 98 percent of import categories are importable without quota restrictions. Goods subject to quota restrictions include certain chemical and steel products; buses; and, for three months of the year, certain seasonal food products. Customs duties range from zero to 25 percent: imports of crude oil and essential items are subject to low rates (1 percent on crude oil); raw materials and equipment, to 5 percent; oil derivatives to 10 percent; and consumer products to rates ranging from 12 percent to 25 percent.

Imports of certain goods, such as weapons and medicine, are subject to licensing requirements for security or public health reasons. Two sets of import taxes of 7.5 percent each apply to most imports. There is also a 1 percent documentation fee. In 1995, the effective average rate of duty was about 10.1 percent. Importers are allowed to purchase foreign exchange to pay letters of credit on imports 180 days in advance of the maturity date. On November 30, 1995, the former Yugoslav Republic of Macedonia began to apply the same customs regime toward the Federal Republic of Yugoslavia as it imposes on third party countries.

Payments for Invisibles

Resident juridical persons may purchase foreign exchange freely to make payments for invisibles on presentation of documentation showing the nature of the services bought abroad or transfers made, such as invoices and health declarations.

Exports and Export Proceeds

Exports to and transit trade through the Federal Republic of Yugoslavia were prohibited under UN Security Council Resolutions Nos. 713, 757, 787, and 820, until No. 1022 suspended indefinitely these resolutions on November 22, 1995. The exportation of sugar, flour, wheat, and soya remains temporarily restricted to protect domestic supply. The exportation of a small number of items (including arms, drugs, and historic artifacts) is banned for security, public health, or cultural reasons.

All export proceeds from transactions that are not based on commodity credits have to be transferred by the exporters into the country within 90 days from the day the export was made. Exporters must sell their proceeds on the foreign exchange market within four business days of transferring them into the country, use the proceeds for payments abroad, or deposit them in banks for a period of up to 90 days, after which they must sell the proceeds in the foreign exchange market.

Proceeds from Invisibles

Proceeds from invisibles are subject to the same regulations as those applicable to merchandise exports.

Capital

Resident natural persons are not allowed to engage in borrowing or lending operations with nonresidents. Contracting of commercial credits by juridical persons is free of restrictions. Outward direct investment requires approval from and registration with the Ministry of Foreign Affairs. Banks may take foreign exchange positions subject to individual limits.

Foreign direct investment in the former Yugoslav Republic of Macedonia is allowed except in a few sectors (such as arms production). Nonresidents are allowed to invest in existing firms, establish their own firms, or establish joint ventures. Imports of raw materials, spare parts, and equipment not produced domestically by joint-venture firms are exempt from customs duties if the foreign share in the investment is at least 20 percent. Foreign investors are exempt from the company income tax during the first three years of operation. All foreign investment registered with the Ministry of Foreign Relations is protected from nationalization. There are no restrictions on the transfer abroad of profits and dividends, provided that all financial obligations within the country have been met. There are no regulations governing inward portfolio investment. Outward portfolio investment by resident natural and juridical persons is not permitted.

Gold

The importation and exportation of gold requires approval of the National Bank of Macedonia.

Changes During 1995

Administration of Control

November 22. Sanctions against the Federal Republic of Yugoslavia (Serbia/Montenegro) were suspended indefinitely in accordance with UN Resolution No. 1022.

MADAGASCAR

(Position as of December 31, 1995)

Exchange Arrangement

The currency of Madagascar is the Malagasy Franc (FMG), the external value of which is determined freely in the official interbank market. The French franc is the only currency quoted on this market, and the exchange rates of other countries are determined on the basis of cross-rate relationships of the currencies concerned in the Paris exchange market. Exporters' surrender requirement has been transferred from the Central Bank of Madagascar to the market; thus, the Central Bank is a normal dealer, participating in the market on the same basis as the five commercial banks. The five banks are permitted to maintain an exchange position up to the limits set up by the prudential regulation (40 percent of their respective capital base). There are limited arrangements for forward cover against exchange rate risk. On December 31, 1995, the midpoint rate for the French franc quoted on the market was FMG 697 per F 1, or FMG 3,423 per $1.[1]

Administration of Control

All countries other than Madagascar are considered foreign countries, and financial relations with all foreign countries are subject to exchange control. Exchange control is administered by the Exchange Operations Monitoring Unit of the General Directorate of the Treasury, which also supervises borrowing and lending abroad by residents; the issue, sale, or introduction of foreign securities in Madagascar; all outward investments; and inward direct investment. Some approval authority for exchange control has been delegated to authorized intermediaries, and all exchange transactions relating to foreign countries must be effected through such intermediaries. All economic agents are allowed to import. Private operators and state trading companies are authorized to export all products to any market at prices freely negotiated by exporters and importers.

Madagascar maintains arrears on certain external payments.

Prescription of Currency

Payments and receipts may be effected through authorized intermediaries in any currency. A bilat-

eral payments agreement with Mauritius has been inoperative for some time.

Resident and Nonresident Accounts

Since May 1994, residents and nonresidents have been freely permitted to open accounts in foreign currency with local commercial banks. Initially, only transfers from abroad or from another foreign currency account, foreign banknotes, or traveler's and bank checks may be deposited in such accounts without justification. Since June 1995, however, banknotes are permitted to be deposited on these accounts. These accounts may be freely debited either for conversion into Malagasy francs through a sale on the interbank market or by transfer to a foreign account in Madagascar or abroad. Conversion into foreign banknotes is allowed only within the limits stipulated under the applicable foreign exchange control regulation.

Nonresidents are also authorized to open nonresident accounts in Malagasy francs. Such accounts may be debited and credited only for transactions between nonresidents and for explicitly authorized transactions between residents and nonresidents. When Malagasy francs accruing to a nonresident are not eligible for credit to a foreign account, they must be credited to a special blocked account, the balance of which may be used by the holder for personal expenses in Madagascar, subject to a limit of FMG 20,000 a day for the account holder and FMG 10,000 a day for each accompanying family member. Any other operation requires prior approval from the Ministry of Finance. Transactions between enterprises in the free trade zone and residents are conducted through the enterprises' foreign accounts in Malagasy francs. These enterprises are also permitted to maintain foreign exchange accounts with local banks.

Imports and Import Payments

Under the Liberalized Imports System (SILI), all economic agents listed in the trade register who are in good standing legally and with the tax administration may import and receive the total amount of foreign currency requested at the prevailing exchange rate. A short list of imports is subject to administrative control, primarily for reasons of security and health. Import licenses are not required for imports financed with foreign exchange already

---

[1]This quotation was a low point in a very volatile market (on January 20, 1996, the rate was FMG 830 per F 1).

owned by the importers and deposited in their foreign currency accounts, and all administrative formalities are handled by the banks through which the import transactions are effected.

No restrictions of any kind apply to the opening of credit or the means of financing imports; importers may use their own resources, borrow from the banking system, or avail themselves of external loans, including suppliers' credits, to finance imports. Most imports require a documentary credit, under which a local bank will agree to open a credit line for an importer on condition that the export is confirmed by the exporter's corresponding bank. Local banks attach varying conditions to granting loans to their customers, with some banks requiring a deposit in foreign currency equivalent to 100 percent of the import cost (*dépôt en devises*). Importers are allowed to buy the necessary foreign exchange for their imports up to 120 days before settlement, although such amounts may be used only for the imports stipulated in the documentary credit. On April 3, 1992 (Decree No. 92.424 on the Regulations of Merchandise Imports and Exports), all import prohibitions were lifted, except for a few for health and security reasons. Import tariffs range from 10 percent to 30 percent. Imports are also subject to customs duties ranging from zero to 20 percent; some imports, mostly luxury goods, are subject to excise import taxes ranging from 10 percent to 120 percent.[2] Since the introduction of a floating exchange arrangement in 1994, there has been no difference between the exchange rate applied to finance and to tax imports and exports.

Payments for Invisibles

All payments for invisibles require prior approval from the Ministry of Finance, which has delegated approval authority to the General Directorate of the Treasury and to authorized intermediaries, either up to specified limits or for any amount that is properly documented. Payments for invisibles related to authorized imports are not restricted, except for agency fees (*commissions de représentations*), whose settlement is subject to the submission of a contract previously approved by the Minister of Finance (Treasury General Directorate).

Residents traveling as tourists may purchase foreign exchange up to an annual limit equivalent to F 6,000 a person a trip, irrespective of the number of trips taken (F 3,000 for children under 15 years). The foreign exchange allowance for business travel is the equivalent of F 25,000 a trip. Applications for additional foreign exchange must be submitted to the Ministry of Finance and may be approved for bona fide business trips and medical treatment abroad, but not for tourism. Allocations for different types of travel may not be combined without the prior approval of the General Directorate of the Treasury.

Limits are set for educational expenses (F 6,000 for the first month, and F 3,000 for the following months) and certain other current invisibles (an overall limit of F 6,000 a month). The transfer of dividends and profits to nonresident shareholders who are natural or juridical persons was liberalized under the terms of the Investment Code and the Industrial Free Trade Zone. Foreigners working in Madagascar may transfer savings from wages and salaries upon presentation of the work contract and employment permit, provided that the transfer takes place within three months of the pay period. The amounts allowed are up to 35 percent of net salary for bachelors and persons whose families reside in Madagascar; up to 60 percent for those whose families live outside Madagascar; and 100 percent for both categories during leave spent outside Madagascar. Remittances for medical treatment abroad are permitted when properly documented.

Resident and nonresident travelers may take abroad up to FMG 25,000 in Malagasy banknotes. There is no longer a requirement to fill a declaration of foreign means of payment upon entry into Madagascar, unless the amount brought in is more than F 50,000.

Exports and Export Proceeds

All exporters listed in the trade register who are in good standing and have no outstanding tax obligations may freely export their products (except vanilla) without restriction at prices negotiated directly between exporters and importers. The Government's quality control or certification requirement for exportable goods is limited to four products: vanilla, coffee, seafood, and meat. Mining products are covered by a special arrangement under the mining law. Quality control is limited to a quality or sanitary inspection certificate from the relevant government agency or, at the option of the exporter, from an internationally recognized specialized private company. For vanilla and coffee, the control is effected at the level of stocks and not at the time of embarkation. For seafood and meat, the certificate of origin and quality standard must be included in the documents for embarkation in the absence of an arrangement directly agreed upon by

---

[2]The sum of the import tariff and the customs duty does not exceed 30 percent.

the importer and exporter in conformity with international agreements.

Since the 1990/91 crop year, all coffee producers have been permitted to negotiate and execute export contracts freely. The list of exports prohibited or subject to prior approval, including mineral products, flora, and fauna, was reduced by Decree No. 92.424 (April 3, 1992). Vanilla continues to be the only export subject to taxation. On September 1, 1994, a single export tax was introduced at the rate of 35 percent, which was substituted in 1995 by a specific tax equivalent to about $21 a kilogram.

Export proceeds must be repatriated within 90 days of the date of shipment. Since June 1995, all exemptions to these rules were abolished. Exporters are required to sell the proceeds from their exports on the interbank market; however, they are allowed to deposit in their foreign exchange account 20 percent of the proceeds if the repatriation occurs within the first 30 days, 15 percent if the repatriation occurs within 60 days, and 10 percent if the repatriation occurs within 60 to 90 days of the shipment. In addition, most exports over FMG 1 million are subject to a domiciliation requirement, under which the exporter must present to a certified intermediary (a local bank) a valid commercial contract and a written commitment to repatriate the foreign exchange proceeds. Export proceeds of enterprises operating in the free trade zone must be repatriated within 90 days of the date of shipment.

Proceeds from Invisibles

All amounts due from residents of other countries in respect of services, and all income or proceeds accruing in those countries or from nonresidents, must be repatriated within one month of the due date. Resident and nonresident travelers may bring in any amount of foreign currency as means of payment and up to FMG 25,000 in Malagasy banknotes.

Capital

Capital movements between Madagascar and foreign countries and between residents and nonresidents are subject to prior authorization from the Ministry of Finance. Special controls are maintained over borrowing abroad; inward direct investment and all outward investment; and the issuing, advertising, or offering for sale of foreign securities in Madagascar.

Foreign direct investments in Madagascar, including those made by companies in Madagascar that are directly or indirectly under foreign control and those made by branches or subsidiaries of foreign companies in Madagascar, as well as corresponding

transfers, require prior approval from the Ministry of Finance. Foreign direct investments abroad by Malagasy nationals, including those made through foreign companies directly or indirectly controlled by persons resident in Madagascar and those made by branches or subsidiaries abroad of companies located in Madagascar, are subject to prior authorization from the Ministry of Finance. The total or partial liquidation of such investments must be declared to the Ministry of Finance. Both the making and the liquidation of direct investments, whether Malagasy investments abroad or foreign investments in Madagascar, must be reported to the Minister of Finance within 20 days of each transaction. Participation that does not exceed 20 percent of the capital of a company is not considered direct investment. Proceeds from the liquidation of foreign investment may be repatriated with the prior authorization of the Ministry of Finance.

The issuing, advertising, or offering for sale of foreign securities in Madagascar requires prior authorization from the Ministry of Finance. Exempt from authorization are operations in connection with shares similar to securities whose issuing or offering for sale in Madagascar has previously been authorized. Borrowings abroad by natural or juridical persons, whether public or private, require prior authorization from the Ministry of Finance, although loans contracted by authorized banks or credit institutions with special legal status are exempt. Enterprises in the free trade zone are permitted to contract and service foreign loans freely, and interest and amortization payments on foreign loans contracted directly by these companies are not restricted. Lending abroad is subject to authorization by the Ministry of Finance.

In accordance with the Investment Code of December 29, 1989 (Law No. 89026), enterprises benefiting from preferential treatment under the code are exempted from import taxes exceeding 10 percent on materials used in the production process. Enterprises operating in the industrial free trade zone established on December 29, 1989 may import these materials free of duty and tax.

Gold

Approved collectors acting in their own name and on their own account may purchase gold within the country from holders of valid gold-mining titles or from authorized holders of gold-washing rights. The price of gold may be set freely by buyers and sellers. Imports and exports of gold require prior authorization from the Ministry of Commerce after review by the Directorate of Energy and Mines and by the Ministry of Mining. Exempt from this requirement are (1) imports and exports by or on behalf of the Central Bank, and (2) imports and exports of manufactured articles containing a minor quantity of gold (such as gold-filled or gold-plated articles). Travelers are authorized to export 50 grams or 250 carats of gold jewelry or gold articles a person and 50 grams or 250 carats of numismatic items a person. Imports of gold, whether licensed or exempt from license, are subject to customs declaration. Holders of a valid gold-mining title or a gold-washing permit or rights are free to sell the gold recovered to any approved collector. However, Malagasy authorities, represented by the Central Bank or its agents, have first rights to purchase gold produced in the country. All gold exports have to be processed through the Gold Board, which was established in late 1995.

Changes During 1995

Imports and Import Payments

June 30. The value-added tax surcharge on imports was substituted by an excise tax ranging from 10 percent to 120 percent.

MALAWI

(Position as of December 31, 1995)

Exchange Arrangement

The currency of Malawi is the Malawi Kwacha, the external value of which is determined on the basis of supply and demand in the exchange market. Authorized dealer banks (ADB) may buy and sell foreign currencies at freely determined market exchange rates. Foreign exchange bureaus are authorized to conduct spot transactions with the general public on the basis of exchange rates negotiated with their clients, and foreign exchange brokers are authorized to match orders from buyers and sellers of foreign exchange on an agency basis.[1] The Reserve Bank of Malawi operates a trading desk for buying and selling foreign exchange in the market. On December 31, 1995, the Reserve Bank's buying and selling rates for the U.S. dollar were MK 15.2262 and MK 15.3792, respectively, per $1. The exchange rates for the Canadian dollar, the deutsche mark, the French franc, the Japanese yen, the pound sterling, the South African rand, the Swiss franc, and the Zimbabwe dollar are determined on the basis of the cross rates of the U.S. dollar for the currencies concerned on the international market. There are no taxes or subsidies on purchases or sales of foreign exchange. ADBs are free to make arrangements for forward cover against exchange risk operating in the official or the commercial banking sector.

Malawi accepted the obligations of Article VIII, Sections 2, 3, and 4 of the Fund Agreement on December 7, 1995.

Administration of Control

Exchange control is administered by the Reserve Bank under the authority delegated to it by the Minister of Finance. Import policy is formulated by the Ministry of Commerce and Industry (MCI), which is also responsible for issuing import and export licenses. All import and export licenses have been eliminated, with the exception of maize and the negative list of goods for security reasons. Commercial banks, foreign exchange bureaus, and brokers are authorized dealers in foreign exchange.

There are no payment restrictions in effect, except those imposed for security reasons.

Prescription of Currency

Payments to nonresidents may be made in Malawi kwacha to the credit of a nonresident account maintained by the recipient or in any convertible foreign currency[2] traded in Malawi. Payments from residents of other countries may be received in Malawi kwacha from a nonresident account or in any convertible foreign currency.

Resident and Nonresident Accounts

Accounts in Malawi kwacha held by residents of other countries are designated nonresident accounts. These accounts may be credited with the proceeds of sales of any convertible foreign currency, with authorized payments in Malawi kwacha to foreign countries by Malawian residents, and with transfers from other nonresident accounts. Balances on these accounts may be used to make payments to residents of Malawi for any purpose and may be transferred freely to other nonresident accounts; these accounts may also be debited for payments to account holders temporarily residing in Malawi.

Blocked accounts in Malawi kwacha are held with authorized dealer banks by nonresidents. Debits and credits to such accounts do not require the prior authorization of the exchange control authorities. Normally, authorization is given for the balances of blocked accounts to be invested in an approved manner. On application to the ADBs, account holders may normally transfer the interest on blocked account balances to their country of residence.

Residents receiving foreign exchange regularly from abroad, including exporters, may maintain foreign currency accounts with ADBs and use balances in the accounts to make authorized payments and transfers without restriction.

Imports and Import Payments

Most imports are subject to the open general license system. However, for certain agricultural and food products, new (military-type) and used clothing, gold, fertilizers, flick knives, explosives, arms and ammunition, wild animals, live fish, and copyright articles, specific import licenses are required from the MCI. Goods originating in Commonwealth

---

[1]Foreign exchange brokering has been temporarily suspended since the end of November 1994.

[2]Under Malawi's exchange control regulations, all currencies other than the Malawi kwacha are considered foreign currencies.

countries or in non-Commonwealth countries that are members of the General Agreement on Tariffs and Trade (GATT) may be imported under an open general license. Specific import licenses are usually issued within a week of application and are normally valid for six months.

Commercial banks are authorized to provide foreign exchange, without referring to the Reserve Bank, for payment of all applications to import goods and services.

When imports arrive in the country and payment is due, the importer must submit applications for foreign exchange. Such applications must be accompanied by relevant importation and customs documents. Depending on means of payment (for example, letters of credit), commercial banks may require counterpart deposits. This is a matter of banking practice and is not required by official regulations.

Prepayment for imports is not allowed. Importers are free to choose any method of payment, and imports may be paid for in Malawi currency to an appropriate local nonresident account or in any convertible currency.

Customs tariffs on nongovernment imports are ad valorem and range from zero to 45 percent of the c.i.f. value, with a weighted average of about 21 percent; the tariff on textiles is 35 percent. The effective maximum tariff for most tariff lines is 40 percent, as almost all trading partners qualify for preferential tariffs under various international conventions. Government imports are exempt from customs tariffs. Imports are also subject to a surtax, which is applied on the c.i.f. value, including customs tariffs.[3] The surtax rates range from zero to 20 percent for most imported items.

Payments for Invisibles

Commercial banks are authorized to provide foreign exchange, without reference to the exchange control authorities, for all current invisible payments, but certain invisible payments, such as private travel, business travel, and medical treatment are subject to indicative limits. The basic exchange allowance for each trip abroad is $3,000 for private travel (holiday); $5,000 for business travel; and $4,000 for medical purposes. Foreign exchange in excess of these limits are granted upon proof of need. There is no limit on the frequency of trips that may be taken. Travelers may take out, in addition to their basic travel allowance, up to MK 200 in domestic currency.

In December 1995, the Reserve Bank announced an indicative limit of 10 percent on the commission payable on merchandise trade transactions.

Foreign nationals employed in Malawi on contracts and holding a temporary employment permit are allowed to remit, subject to ADBs' approval, up to two-thirds of their current net earnings to their country of normal residence or any country of their choice.

Exports and Export Proceeds

Exports of implements of war, petroleum products, nickel, atomic energy materials, and certain agricultural and animal products are subject to export licensing, mainly to ensure the adequacy of domestic supplies. Export proceeds can be held in foreign currency accounts. ADBs are required to convert 60 percent of foreign exchange received from exports immediately upon receipt using the ruling buying exchange rate. The kwacha proceeds are credited to the customer's account. The remaining 40 percent may be credited to the exporter's foreign currency account. There are no longer any restrictions on the time period over which such balances may be held. This 60 percent conversion is also applied to U.S. dollar proceeds from the tobacco and tea auctions. In the case of tobacco proceeds, the conversion is 100 percent until the seller has fully repaid his overdraft with his bankers. The exporter or recipient of the U.S. dollar proceeds from the auction may freely sell his foreign exchange to any authorized foreign exchange dealer.

Specific duties or cesses are levied on exports of hides and skins, and tobacco.[4] Under a duty drawback scheme, customs tariffs paid on imports of certain inputs used for manufactured exports are rebated.

Proceeds from Invisibles

Receipts from invisibles may be retained in full and held in foreign-currency-denominated accounts with ADBs. There is no limit on the amount of foreign currency notes and coins that travelers may import, but they may not bring in more than MK 200 in Malawi currency notes and coins.

Capital

Inward transfers of nondebt-creating capital are not restricted. The taking up of loans from abroad by residents requires prior exchange control approval, which is normally granted provided that

---

[3]The surtax is levied on both imported and domestically produced manufactured goods.

[4]The cess is also levied, with some exemptions, on tobacco sold locally and on hides and skins at the rate of 2 percent of export value.

the terms of repayment, including the servicing costs, are acceptable. Outward transfers of capital are controlled mainly for residents. Nonresidents are permitted to repatriate their investments when they have satisfied the authorities that the original investment was made with funds brought into the country. Apart from the need to obtain the ADBs' approval, there are no restrictions on the transfer abroad of dividends and profits of foreign-owned companies, provided that no recourse is being made to local borrowing to finance the transfer.

Residents may not purchase any foreign securities without specific exchange control approval. In general, residents are not permitted to transfer capital abroad, and, with certain exceptions, they are required to offer for sale to an authorized dealer any foreign exchange that accrues to them.

All applications for emigrants' allowances must be submitted to ADBs for approval. Upon departure, emigrants are allowed to exchange the equivalent of up to the amount approved. The balance, if any, of emigrants' funds is blocked, but on the first anniversary of their departure date from Malawi, a sum equal to the original emigration allowance may be transferred to the new country of residence.

Gold

Residents may purchase, hold, and sell gold coins in Malawi for numismatic purposes. With this exception, residents other than the monetary authorities and authorized industrial users are not allowed to hold or acquire gold at home or abroad in any form other than jewelry. Imports of gold in any form other than jewelry require licenses issued by the Minister of Commerce and Industry in consultation with the Ministry of Finance; such licenses are not normally granted except for imports by or on behalf of the monetary authorities and industrial users.

Changes During 1995

Exchange Arrangement

December 7. Malawi accepted the obligations of Article VIII, Sections 2, 3, and 4 of the Fund Agreement.

Payments for Invisibles

April 12. The Reserve Bank changed the foreign exchange conversion/retention requirements.

MALAYSIA

(Position as of December 31, 1995)

Exchange Arrangement

The currency of Malaysia is the Ringgit. Its external value is determined by supply and demand in the foreign exchange market. Bank Negara Malaysia, the central bank, intervenes only to maintain orderly market conditions and to avoid excessive fluctuations in the value of the ringgit. The external value of the currency is monitored against a basket of currencies weighted in terms of Malaysia's major trading partners and the currencies of settlement. The commercial banks are free to determine and quote exchange rates, whether spot or forward, to all customers for all currencies other than those of Israel and the Federal Republic of Yugoslavia (Serbia/Montenegro). On December 31, 1995, the middle rate for the U.S. dollar was RM 2.5405 per $1. There are no taxes or subsidies on purchases or sales of foreign exchange.

Forward exchange contracts may be effected freely for commercial transactions; prior approval is required for financial transactions. For commercial transactions, forward cover for imports is provided for up to 12 months from the intended date of import, while for export purposes the forward cover would be up to six months from the export date.

Malaysia accepted the obligations of Article VIII, Sections 2, 3, and 4 of the Fund Agreement on November 11, 1968.

Administration of Control

Bank Negara Malaysia administers exchange control throughout Malaysia on behalf of the Malaysian Government, the Governor of the Bank being the Controller of Foreign Exchange. There are no restrictions on payments or transfers for current international transactions. Residents are required to complete a form for any payment, irrespective of its purpose, that exceeds RM 100,000 or its equivalent in foreign currency, only for statistical purposes.

In accordance with the Fund's Executive Board Decision No. 144-(52/51) adopted on August 14, 1952, Malaysia notified the Fund on June 23, 1993 that in compliance with UN Security Council Resolution No. 757 (1992), certain restrictions had been imposed on the making of payments and transfers for current international transactions in respect of the Federal Republic of Yugoslavia (Serbia/Montenegro).

Prescription of Currency

All payments to countries other than Israel and the Federal Republic of Yugoslavia (Serbia/Montenegro) may be made either in ringgit or in any currency other than those of Israel and the Federal Republic of Yugoslavia (Serbia/Montenegro). Special rules apply to settlements with these two countries.

Nonresident Accounts

Ringgit accounts of nonresidents of Malaysia are designated external accounts. There are no restrictions on debits to external accounts. Credits to these accounts are freely permitted, subject only to the completion of statistical forms for amounts exceeding RM 100,000 if such payments are made by residents. Proceeds from the sale of any foreign currency may be credited to external accounts, and the balances may be transferred to any other resident or nonresident account or converted into any currency, except those of Israel and the Federal Republic of Yugoslavia (Serbia/Montenegro). Accounts of residents of these two countries are designated as Israeli accounts and Federal Republic of Yugoslavia (Serbia/Montenegro) accounts, respectively. All debits and credits to such accounts require prior approval.

Imports and Import Payments

Tariffs and import controls for the various parts of Malaysia have been fully standardized. In 1995 import duties on more than 2,600 items, particularly on food and household items and raw materials, were reduced or abolished. In 1996, import duties on more than 1,500 raw materials, and components, and equipment were reduced or abolished. As part of its Uruguay Round commitments, Malaysia has agreed to reduce and bind tariffs on 7,200 items, representing 65 percent of all tariff lines, and to phase out nontariff barriers.

Import licenses are required for certain goods as specified in Customs (Prohibition of Imports) Order No. 1988, for reasons of health, security, or public policy; various conditions must be satisfied before import licenses for such goods are issued. Certain other imports are subject to nonautomatic licensing, which is reviewed periodically to protect local infant and strategic industries temporarily. Imports from

Israel are subject to licensing and imports from Haiti are prohibited.

Imports of finished motor vehicles are subject to nonautomatic import licensing, which is administered by the Ministry of International Trade and Industry. The movement of live animals between Peninsular Malaysia, Sabah, and Sarawak is subject to a permit issued by the Veterinary Department. Imports of the meat, bones, hides, hooves, horns, and offal of any animal or any portion of an animal from all countries require an import license. Imports of primates, whether dead or alive, require an import license, subject to approval from the Department of Wildlife and National Parks. Payments for permitted imports are freely allowed. Raw materials and machinery for the manufacturing sector are eligible for preferential duty treatment as follows: (1) for the production of goods for the domestic market, most of the raw materials that are not available locally are not subject to customs duty; (2) manufacturers for the domestic market may be further exempted from this duty if they comply with specific requirements regarding equity participation, management, and employment structure; (3) manufacturers are exempted from sales tax on all raw materials for the production of taxable goods that may be acquired free of duty, subject to conditions as specified in the Sales Tax Act of 1972; (4) for companies that manufacture products for the export market, full exemption from customs duty is granted when local raw materials are not available or are not competitive in price or quality; (5) all customs duties and sales taxes on imported machinery and equipment that are unavailable locally and are directly used in the manufacturing process can be considered for exemption; and (6) manufacturers may claim customs duties and sales tax drawbacks on imported raw materials or components that are incorporated into finished products and exported within 12 months of the date of import.

Payments for Invisibles

Payments for invisibles to all countries other than Israel and the Federal Republic of Yugoslavia (Serbia/Montenegro) may be made without restriction. There is no restriction on the amount of foreign exchange available for travel abroad. Remittances to nonresidents of dividends, royalties, and profits on all bona fide investments are permitted, subject only to the completion of statistical forms for amounts of RM 100,000 or more. There is no restriction on the exportation of currency notes in the immediate possession of a traveler. The exportation of ringgit by

any other means requires prior approval from the Controller of Foreign Exchange.

Exports and Export Proceeds

Exports to Israel and the Federal Republic of Yugoslavia (Serbia/Montenegro) require import licensing from the Ministry of International Trade and Industry. Exports of logs are restricted and need licensing from the Malaysian Timber Industries Board (MITB). Exports of petroleum and petroleum products, arms and related materials, military vehicles and equipment, and police equipment to Haiti are prohibited.

The customs areas and export control systems among the three territories of Malaysia are standardized. Exchange control forms must be completed for exports valued at more than RM 100,000 f.o.b. a shipment. Proceeds from exports must be received and repatriated according to the payment schedule specified in the commercial contract, but no longer than six months after the date of exportation. This regulation does not apply to commercial samples or goods exported for repair or exchange and reimported into Malaysia. Exporters are allowed to retain a portion of their export proceeds in foreign currency accounts with authorized banks in Malaysia up to $5 million.[1] Exports of rubber from Peninsular Malaysia require a certificate issued by the Malaysian Rubber Exchange and Licensing Board. Exports of roofing tiles, bricks, minerals, rice and paddy in any form, milk and specified milk products, textiles, and all other goods as specified in the second schedule of Customs (Prohibition of Exports) Order No. 1988 of the 1967 Customs Act are subject to permits.

Export incentives are provided to companies that export Malaysian products. The primary incentives include a double deduction of expenses incurred in overseas promotion, export credit refinancing, and duty drawbacks.

Proceeds from Invisibles

The exchange control authorities do not regulate the timeliness of exchange receipts from invisibles. No limitation is imposed on the importation of currency notes by a traveler. The importation of domestic banknotes by other than authorized banks, or by any other means, requires prior approval from the Controller of Foreign Exchange.

---

[1]Ten banks designated as "first-tier banks" are permitted to offer foreign currency accounts. All other domestic banks must continue to obtain permission from the Controller of Foreign Exchange before offering currency accounts to residents.

Capital

The following inward investments, covered by the guidelines issued on February 20, 1974 (regarding the acquisition of assets, mergers, and takeovers), require prior approval from the Foreign Investment Committee (FIC): (1) proposed acquisition of any substantial fixed assets by foreign interests; (2) proposed acquisition of assets or interests, mergers, and takeovers of companies and businesses in Malaysia by any means that will cause ownership or control to pass to foreign interests; (3) proposed acquisition of 15 percent or more of the voting power (equity interests) by any foreign interest or associated group or by a foreign interest in the aggregate of 30 percent or more of the voting power of a Malaysian company or business; (4) control of Malaysian companies and businesses through any form of joint-venture agreement, management agreement, or technical assistance or other arrangement; (5) merger or takeover of any company or business in Malaysia; and (6) any other proposed acquisition of assets or interests exceeding RM 5 million in value.

Incorporation of a Malaysian company by a foreign entity does not require the approval of the FIC. However, increases in the paid-up capital of a Malaysian company that involve any foreign entity require the approval of the FIC under the following circumstances: (1) the total value of the foreign entity's new subscription exceeds RM 5 million; (2) the total of the foreign entity's new subscription exceeds 15 percent of the voting power in the relevant company; (3) as a result of the increase in paid-up capital, any foreign entity increases its voting power to more than 15 percent in the relevant company; (4) the total of the new subscription by several foreign entities increases their joint voting power to 30 percent or more of the voting power in the relevant company; (5) as a result of the increase in paid-up capital, the aggregate holding of several foreign entities increases to 30 percent or more of the voting power in the relevant company; and (6) an increase in the paid-up capital of any Malaysian company to more than RM 5 million on incorporation, the holding of foreign entities constitutes more than 15 percent of the voting power, or the joint holding of several foreign entities constitutes 30 percent or more of the voting power of the company concerned.

Foreign investors are permitted to hold equity of up to 100 percent if they export 80 percent or more of their production. For projects exporting between 51 percent and 79 percent of their production, foreign equity ownership of up to 79 percent is permitted, depending on such factors as the level of technology, spin-off effects, size of the investment, location, value added, and the use of local raw materials and components. For projects exporting between 20 percent and 50 percent of their production, foreign equity ownership of between 30 percent and 51 percent is allowed, depending on factors similar to those mentioned earlier. For projects exporting less than 20 percent of their production, foreign equity is allowed up to a maximum of 30 percent. For the purpose of equity determination, export sales are defined as excluding sales to free zones and licensed manufacturing warehouses; the objective of this redefinition is to promote greater links between multinational corporations and domestic industries.

Notwithstanding the above, projects producing high-technology products or priority products for the domestic market, as determined by the Government from time to time, may be allowed foreign equity ownership of up to 100 percent. These equity guidelines do not apply to new projects in certain sectors where foreign equity ownership of up to 60 percent is allowed for domestic sales (including sales to free zones and licensed manufacturing warehouses) for the following sectors: press working and stamping industry; plastic injections, moulded components, and parts for the electrical, electronic, and telecommunications industry; plastic compounds and masterbatch, electroplating, and heat treatment activities; fabrication of furniture components such as nylon chair bases and arms; manufacture of foundry products, connectors, transformers, and coils; hot stamping; spray painting and silk screen printing services; and polished granite, marble slab, and tile production.

For projects involving extracting, mining, and processing mineral ores, a majority foreign equity participation of up to 100 percent is permitted. To determine the percentage for these projects, various criteria (e.g., levels of investment technology and risk involved; availability of Malaysian expertise in the areas of exploration, mining, and processing of the minerals concerned; degree of integration; and level of value added involved) are taken into consideration. For new hotel and tourist projects, foreign equity ownership of up to 100 percent is allowed for five years from the date the operation begins, after which such ownership must be reduced to 51 percent; for "budget hotels," a local equity ownership of 70 percent is required, 5 percent is imposed.

Permission of the Controller of Foreign Exchange is not required for direct and portfolio investments by Malaysian residents in countries other than Israel and the Federal Republic of Yugoslavia (Serbia/ Montenegro), provided that the resident concerned has not obtained any domestic credit and that payments are made in foreign currency. If investors have any domestic credit, they must obtain prior approval from the Controller of Foreign Exchange for their investment abroad. However, a corporate resident who has obtained a domestic credit facility is allowed to remit funds up to the equivalent of RM 10 million a calendar year for investment abroad. Commercial banks are not encouraged to give loans to finance investments abroad that are considered unlikely to lead to long-term benefits for the economy; such funds should be used to finance the expansion of productive capacity in Malaysia. Commercial banks and Tier-1 merchant banks are permitted to have either a short or a long open foreign exchange position ranging from RM 10 million to RM 500 million, based on the limit approved by the Controller of Foreign Exchange. Ceilings on banks' net external liability positions were removed in January 1995.

Investment proceeds may be repatriated freely on resale, subject to the completion of a statistical form, for amounts of RM 100,000 or more. Nonresident-controlled companies in Malaysia are permitted to borrow up to RM 10 million, including immovable property loans, without exchange control approval, irrespective of the amount of the loan; at least 60 percent of total credit facilities from banking institutions in Malaysia must be from Malaysian-owned financial institutions. Nonresidents who have valid work permits are allowed to borrow freely from domestic financial institutions to finance up to 60 percent of the purchase price of residential property for their own accommodation.

Residents are allowed to borrow in foreign currencies from nonresidents as well as from commercial banks and merchant banks in Malaysia up to the aggregate of the equivalent of RM 5 million, including financial guarantees, from nonresident financial institutions. For aggregate amounts exceeding RM 5 million, however, approval must be obtained from the Controller of Foreign Exchange, stating the main terms and conditions of the loan and the purpose for which the loan proceeds will be used. Approval is readily granted if the loan is to be used for productive investment within the country and the resident

borrower is judged to be able to generate sufficient foreign exchange to service the loan. Offshore guarantees for loans, whether denominated in ringgit or foreign currency, obtained from licensed offshore banks do not require authorization. Foreign borrowing in ringgit of any amount requires prior approval, which is not usually granted. Service payments on approved foreign loans may be effected by commercial banks, provided that payments are made in accordance with the approved terms and conditions of the loans. Commercial banks and merchant banks in Malaysia may lend in foreign currency to residents and accept deposits in foreign currency from nonresidents. As an incentive, interest paid to nonresidents by the commercial banks is exempted from the 15 percent withholding tax.

Intercompany accounts, which exclude proceeds from the exportation of Malaysian goods and proceeds from loans extended to Malaysian companies, may be maintained with any company outside Malaysia, provided that monthly returns are submitted to the Controller of Foreign Exchange. Prior permission from the Controller of Foreign Exchange is required for exporters to offset their export proceeds through intercompany accounts against payments to overseas companies for the supply of raw materials and components.

Gold

Residents of Malaysia are free to deal (purchase, sell, import, export, borrow, etc.) in gold in any state or form with any person, except residents of Israel and the Federal Republic of Yugoslavia (Serbia/Montenegro).

Changes During 1995

Capital

January 20. Ceilings on the net external liability positions of banks, imposed since January 24, 1994, were removed.

June 27. Corporate residents with a domestic credit facility were allowed to remit funds up to the equivalent of RM 10 million for overseas investment purposes each calendar year.

MALDIVES

(Position as of December 31, 1995)

Exchange Arrangement

The currency of Maldives is the Maldivian Rufiyaa. Since March 1, 1987, the Maldives Monetary Authority has followed a floating exchange rate policy under which the exchange rate has been determined by demand and supply conditions in the market, although the Monetary Authority may intervene in the market when deemed appropriate. The midpoint exchange rate of the rufiyaa in terms of the U.S. dollar on December 31, 1995 was Rf 11.77 per $1. The Monetary Authority charges commercial banks a flat 1 percent for remitting foreign banknotes abroad and there is a daily limit of $5,000 in a bank's access to foreign currency notes from the Monetary Authority. The Monetary Authority carries out transactions freely with the private sector through the operations of the Government Exchange Counter. The Monetary Authority periodically sets daily limits for each individual's or enterprise's access to foreign exchange through the Counter, based on the availability of official reserves. As of January 1994, the limits were $300 a person for cash, and $2,000 a person or enterprise for checks. There are no arrangements for forward cover against exchange rate risk.

Administration of Control

There is no exchange control legislation. Trade regulations are administered by the Ministry of Trade and Industries, which also issues import and export licenses.

Prescription of Currency

There are no restrictions on maintaining bank accounts or holding cash in foreign currency. Foreign currency must be converted to rufiyaa through a bank or a licensed money changer who is authorized by the Monetary Authority to exchange foreign currencies.

Nonresident Accounts

No distinction is made between accounts held by residents and those held by nonresidents; there are no restrictions on maintaining foreign currency balances. Residents do not require permission to maintain foreign currency accounts at home or abroad.

Imports and Import Payments

Imports from Iraq and the Federal Republic of Yugoslavia (Serbia/Montenegro) are prohibited. Import operations may be conducted only after being registered and licensed at the Ministry of Trade and Industries. All goods may be imported under an open general license system. Licenses are issued on application. Ad valorem import duties are calculated on the c.i.f. or c. & f. value of imports, as appropriate. Staple commodities (rice, flour, and sugar) are imported mainly by the State Trading Organization.

Duties are levied on all merchandise items other than rice, flour, and sugar.

Payments for Invisibles

There are no restrictions on payments for invisibles. Travelers may take out any amount in domestic or foreign currency without restriction.

Exports and Export Proceeds

Export licenses are issued by the Ministry of Trade and Industries. The private sector may export most items, with the exception of fresh and frozen tuna. Locals and foreigners are encouraged to fish in the exclusive economic zone (EEZ) outside of the 75-mile zone from the shoreline, which is reserved for traditional fishing. They must pay the Government a royalty on fish they catch in the EEZ. Exports of fish and fish products (except ambergris) are exempt from duties. Re-exports are exempt from duty.

Proceeds from Invisibles

Private sector receipts from current invisibles need not be surrendered and may be disposed of freely through the foreign exchange market. Travelers may bring in any amount of foreign currency without restriction.

Capital

Residents and nonresidents may freely import and export capital through the foreign exchange market. Inward direct investment requires approval. All foreign investors are required to provide at least 75 percent of their capital investment in the form of either cash or capital goods financed from outside Maldives. Transfers of profits are permitted freely.

Exemption from duties and taxes, other than the tourism tax, may be granted for a period as specified by the Government.

Gold

Transactions in gold are not subject to regulation. Residents may freely hold and negotiate gold in any form, at home or abroad, and the importation and exportation of gold are not restricted.

Changes During 1995

No significant changes occurred in the exchange and trade system.

MALI

(Position as of June 30, 1996)

Exchange Arrangement

The currency of Mali is the CFA Franc,[1] which is pegged to the French franc, the intervention currency, at the fixed rate of CFAF 1 per F 0.01. The official buying and selling rate is CFAF 100 per F 1. Exchange rates for all other currencies that are officially quoted on the Paris exchange market are based on the fixed rate for the French franc and the Paris exchange market rate for the currencies concerned. The banks levy a commission of 2.5 per mil on transfers to or from nonmember countries of the West African Economic and Monetary Union (WAEMU),[2] all of which must be transferred to the Treasury. There are no taxes or subsidies on purchases or sales of foreign exchange. Foreign exchange transfers are subject to a stamp tax.

Residents may obtain forward exchange rate cover for payments of imports or exports of goods on specified lists. Forward exchange rate cover must be denominated in the currency prescribed in the contract and is subject to prior authorization by the Minister of Finance and Commerce. Forward exchange contracts for imports must be for a forward period of up to one month and cannot be renewed. For certain products, the duration of forward exchange rate cover may be extended to three months but cannot be renewed. For exports, the duration of forward exchange contracts may not exceed 120 days after the arrival of the goods at their destination.

Mali accepted the obligations of Article VIII, Sections 2, 3, and 4 of the Fund Agreement on June 1, 1996.

Administration of Control

The Minister of Finance and Commerce has sole authority in exchange control matters, but has delegated certain exchange control powers to the BCEAO and to authorized banks. Imports and exports are subject to registration with the National Directorate of Economic Affairs in the Ministry of Finance and Commerce.

Prescription of Currency

Because Mali has an Operations Account with the French Treasury, settlements with France (as defined above), Monaco, and the countries linked to the French Treasury by an Operations Account are made in CFA francs, French francs, or the currency of any other member of the Operations Account Area. Settlements with all other countries with which no payments agreement is in force are usually made through correspondent banks in France in any of the currencies of those countries or in French francs through foreign accounts in francs. Settlements with The Gambia, Ghana, Guinea, Guinea-Bissau, Liberia, Mauritania, Nigeria, and Sierra Leone are normally made through the West African Clearing House.

Nonresident Accounts

Nonresident accounts may not be credited with CFA banknotes, French banknotes, or banknotes issued by any other institute of issue maintaining an Operations Account with the French Treasury. As the BCEAO has suspended the repurchase of BCEAO banknotes circulating outside the territories of the CFA franc zone, nonresident accounts may not be credited or debited with BCEAO banknotes without prior authorization.

Imports and Import Payments

There are no import-licensing requirements; imports are required only to be registered, and permits are issued automatically. Imports from Israel are prohibited.

A variety of tariffs are applied to imports, including a customs duty, a fiscal duty, and a customs services fee; certain goods are exempted from some of these taxes.

With the exception of petroleum products, tariff rates are ad valorem and based on the c.i.f. value. Petroleum products are subject to a variable levy, based on administrative values established with reference to prices charged by refineries in Dakar and Abidjan. Imports are subject to additional taxes ranging from 7.5 percent to 55 percent. (These additional taxes were temporarily suspended on January 28, 1994.)

Payments for Invisibles

Since August 1993 when the WAEMU monetary authorities suspended the repurchase of banknotes

---

[1]The CFA franc is issued by the Central Bank of West African States (BCEAO) and is the common currency in Benin, Burkina Faso, Côte d'Ivoire, Mali, Niger, Senegal, and Togo.

[2]The WAEMU replaced the West African Monetary Union (WAMU) on January 10, 1994. The WAEMU treaty was ratified and became effective on August 1, 1994.

issued by the BCEAO and exported outside the territories of the WAEMU countries, payments for invisibles to France and the BCEAO countries have been subject to the same restrictions as payments to other countries. Payments for invisibles related to trade are permitted freely when the basic trade transaction has been approved or does not require authorization. Transfers of income accruing to nonresidents in the form of profits, dividends, and royalties are subject to approval.

Residents traveling to non-BCEAO countries in the franc zone are allowed to take out the equivalent of CFAF 2 million in banknotes, and they may take out amounts exceeding this limit in other means of payment. The allowances for travel to countries outside the franc zone are subject to the following regulations: (1) for tourist travel, the equivalent of CFAF 500,000 without limit on the number of trips or differentiation by the age of the traveler; (2) for business travel, the equivalent of CFAF 75,000 a day for up to one month, corresponding to a maximum of CFAF 2.25 million (business travel allowances may be combined with tourism allowances); (3) allowances in excess of these limits must be authorized by the respective ministries of finance or, by delegation, the BCEAO; and (4) credit cards, which must be issued by resident financial intermediaries and authorized by the respective ministers of finance, may be used up to the ceilings indicated above for tourist and business travel. Residents traveling to non-BCEAO countries are not allowed to take out BCEAO banknotes. Upon arrival at customs, returning resident travelers are required to declare all means of payment in their possession and must surrender within eight days all means of payment exceeding the equivalent of CFAF 25,000. All resident travelers to non-BCEAO countries must declare in writing, at the time of departure, all means of payment at their disposal. Nonresident travelers may re-export means of payment, other than banknotes, issued abroad and registered in their name. The re-exportation of foreign banknotes is allowed up to the equivalent of CFAF 250,000; the re-exportation of foreign banknotes above these ceilings and other means of payment issued in Mali requires documentation demonstrating either the importation of foreign banknotes or their purchase against other means of payment registered in the name of the traveler or through the use of nonresident deposits lodged in local banks.

The transfer of the entire salary of a foreigner working in Mali is permitted upon presentation of the appropriate pay voucher, provided that the transfer takes place within three months of the pay period or that there is a reciprocity agreement with the foreigner's country of nationality. Remittances abroad for family maintenance, education allowances, and medical treatment, and transfers of profits or dividends from foreign direct investment may be made freely by authorized intermediaries when the appropriate documentation is presented.

Exports and Export Proceeds

Exports to foreign countries must be recorded with an authorized bank, and all export proceeds, including those originating in France and other countries linked to the French Treasury by an Operations Account, must be repatriated through the BCEAO and surrendered within 30 days of the payment due date or within 120 days of shipment if no payment date is specified in the sales contract. All exports require only a certificate of registration.

Proceeds from Invisibles

Proceeds from transactions in invisibles with France (as defined above), Monaco, and the countries linked to the French Treasury by an Operations Account may be retained. All amounts due from residents of other countries for services and all income earned in those countries from foreign assets must be collected and surrendered. Resident and nonresident travelers may bring in any amount of banknotes and coins issued by the BCEAO, the Bank of France, or a bank of issue maintaining an Operations Account with the French Treasury, as well as any amount of foreign banknotes and coins (except gold coins) of countries outside the Operations Account Area. However, they must declare the amounts they bring in.

Capital

Capital movements between Mali and France (as defined above), Monaco, and the countries linked to the French Treasury by an Operations Account are free of restrictions; capital transfers to all other countries require authorization from the Ministry of Finance and Commerce and are restricted, but capital receipts from these countries are permitted freely.

Special controls (in addition to any exchange control requirements that may apply) are maintained over borrowing abroad. The special control measures also do not apply to relations with France (as defined above) and the countries linked to the French Treasury by an Operations Account.

The investment code adopted on January 1, 1991, simplified procedures for foreign and domestic investors to obtain preferential treatment with respect to domestic taxes for investments that meet specific criteria on employment creation, domestic content of production, location, and value of investment.

Gold

Travelers may export gold jewelry and personal belongings, other than gold coins and ingots, up to a maximum weight of 500 grams. Commercial imports and exports of gold do not require authorization from the Ministry of Finance and Commerce, but are subject to all foreign trade regulations, including bank domiciliation, customs declaration, and the obligation to repatriate export proceeds.

Changes During 1995

No significant changes occurred in the exchange and trade system.

Changes During 1996

Exchange Arrangement

June 1. Mali accepted the obligations of Article VIII, Sections 2, 3, and 4 of the Fund Agreement.

MALTA

(Position as of April 30, 1996)

Exchange Arrangement

The currency of Malta is the Maltese Lira, the external value of which is determined on the basis of a weighted basket consisting of the pound sterling, the U.S. dollar, and the European currency unit (ECU). The Central Bank of Malta computes the daily exchange rate between the Maltese lira and the U.S. dollar on the basis of the latest available market quotations for the U.S. dollar in terms of the other currency components of the basket, with the ECU component being computed in terms of its own currency composition. The Central Bank also quotes daily rates for various other currencies,[1] taking as a basis the rates of the lira against the U.S. dollar and the cross rates of these currencies against the U.S. dollar, as quoted in the international market. Unless market conditions indicate otherwise, a spread of 0.125 percent is applied to the middle rate to compute the buying and selling rates for transactions between the Central Bank and the credit institutions (authorized banks). These transactions may be conducted in deutsche mark, pounds sterling, or U.S. dollars in amounts of less than Lm 50,000. Transactions in smaller amounts are handled through the interbank market. There is no limit on the spread between the buying and selling rates the credit institutions may quote. Authorized banks may also establish rates for currencies not quoted by the Central Bank based on the latest market rates as reported by Reuters. These rates are treated as provisional for large amounts and are quoted on request. The closing middle rate for the Maltese lira in terms of the U.S. dollar on December 29, 1995 was $2.8377 per Lm 1.

There are no taxes or subsidies on purchases or sales of foreign exchange, except for a subsidy in the form of a guaranteed exchange rate for the pound sterling against the Maltese lira which is offered to United Kingdom tour operators during the winter seasons (November–May). This arrangement is being gradually phased out, and will be terminated in May 1997.

Malta accepted the obligations of Article VIII, Sections 2, 3, and 4 of the Fund Agreement, on November 30, 1994.

Authorized banks are permitted to provide their customers with forward cover in respect of firm contractual commitments involving current account transactions. The Central Bank provides forward cover directly to government departments and public sector bodies in respect of such transactions. Forward rates are based on interest rate differentials.

Administration of Control

The Central Bank, as agent for the Minister of Finance, administers exchange controls; the Director of Imports and Internal Trade in the Ministry of Finance administers trade controls. The Central Bank has delegated most of its powers to approve exchange transactions to the authorized banks. They may also give or renew guarantees and indemnities in connection with payments by residents. In the case of nonresidents, the authorized banks must hold full cash cover in external Maltese liri, foreign currency, or foreign securities for the duration of the guarantee or indemnity.

Authority to approve foreign exchange payments solely for travel purposes has also been delegated to a limited number of foreign exchange bureaus, which hold licenses on financial institutions.

Prescription of Currency

Authorized payments to all countries may be made by crediting Maltese liri to an external account or in any foreign currency, while the proceeds of exports to all countries may be received in any foreign currency.[2]

Commercial transactions between Malta and the Libyan Arab Jamahiriya may be settled under a banking arrangement that is administered by the central banks of the respective countries. Transactions fall due within 90 days and are settled in convertible currencies.

Nonresident Accounts

Nonresidents may hold foreign currency or Maltese lira accounts with the authorized banks. These accounts may be credited freely with authorized payments from residents and with funds originating abroad. Nonresident accounts may be debited freely for payments to residents and for payments over-

---

[1]The Central Bank quotes daily rates for 30 other currencies in addition to the U.S. dollar, among which are Belgian francs, deutsche mark, French francs, Italian lire, Japanese yen, Netherlands guilders, pounds sterling, Swiss francs, and ECUs.

[2]Foreign currencies are defined as all currencies other than the Maltese lira.

seas. In effecting such operations, credit and financial institutions are subject to the requirement of the Prevention of Money Laundering Act of 1994, and other regulations in force pursuant to this Act.

Subject to exchange control permission, companies controlled by nonresidents may maintain foreign currency accounts in Malta and abroad. International trading companies[3] are exempted from the requirement to obtain approval for opening foreign currency accounts and for effecting foreign exchange payments.

Imports and Import Payments

Licenses are required for the importation of items that need clearance for health, safety, security, and environmental reasons, as well as for particularly sensitive items, such as handmade lace and gold and silver filigree. Imports of fresh and foreign fish are also controlled to safeguard the local fisheries industry. All other products may be freely imported under open general licenses (OGLs). The importation of barley, maize, hard and soft wheat, fresh fish, and certain petroleum products is undertaken only by state-owned enterprises.

Payments for all authorized imports may be made freely, provided that currency regulations are complied with and that supporting documents, including the customs entry form for imports over Lm 20,000 and related import license, where applicable, are submitted to the intermediary bank. As a form of exchange cover, export-oriented companies may retain foreign exchange earnings for a maximum period of four months to make payments for imports that are connected to their exporting business. On the same basis, import payments may also be offset against export proceeds.

Payments for Invisibles

Payments for invisibles may be made freely although, in some cases, they are subject to limits on the amounts remitted. These limits are intended to prevent funds from being remitted for capital transfer purposes. In the case of leisure and business travel, there are no restrictions on payments for accommodation and transportation expenses as long as they are paid for in Malta or abroad with credit cards. Furthermore, each person is entitled to a travel allowance equivalent to Lm 2,500 a trip. Amounts in excess of the above limit may be granted upon submission of documentary proof of need.

Nonresident travelers may export foreign currency up to the amount they brought in and declared to customs on entry; they may export up to Lm 25 a person in Maltese notes and coins.

The allowance for educational expenses is not restricted.[4] The maximum annual amount of funds each resident may transfer abroad to other family members or as a cash gift is Lm 2,500. Remittances above these limits require exchange control approval, which is usually granted upon the submission of documentary evidence. There are no restrictions on the remittance of profits and dividends by companies in Malta to nonresident shareholders provided supporting documents are presented to the authorized bank.

Exports and Export Proceeds

With the exception of works of art and certain essential goods, all products may be exported freely. However, certain textile products for export to countries in the European Union (EU) require licenses for administrative purposes. Export proceeds must be received within six months of shipment and surrendered to the authorized banks. However, exporters may retain export proceeds in foreign currency deposit accounts with authorized banks for up to four months to make import payments connected with their exporting business.

Proceeds from Invisibles

Foreign currency receipts from invisibles must be offered for sale to an authorized bank or deposited in a foreign currency account under the same conditions as those stipulated for exporters described above. Travelers may bring in any amount in foreign currency notes subject to the requirement of the money-laundering legislation. The importation of Maltese banknotes and coins in excess of Lm 50 is not permitted.

Capital

Applications for direct investment in Malta by nonresidents must be approved in advance by the Ministry of Finance. However, such authorization is withheld only in exceptional cases. Direct investment is usually prohibited where this involves such business activities as real estate and wholesale and retail trade (particularly importation of consumer goods for resale). Applications for direct investment in other activities may also be refused if the sectors

---

[3]These are companies owned entirely by nonresident shareholders (except for one share, which could be held by a Maltese resident) and engaging solely in activities outside Malta.

[4]For purposes of exchange allocations for travel and study, residents are defined as persons who are living in Malta and have either lived in Malta for at least three years or intend to continue living in Malta for at least three years.

involved are considered sensitive from a local economy perspective. The remittance of proceeds from the liquidation of such investments is also subject to approval by the Central Bank. This is usually granted once certain formalities, such as the submission of documentary evidence of the original investment are completed. In the case of residents, both individuals and companies are allowed to remit up to Lm 50,000 a year for direct investment purposes.

The Immovable Property (Acquisition by Nonresidents) Act of 1974, administered by the Ministry of Finance, prohibits the acquisition of immovable property in Malta by nonresidents[5] (with the exception of certain special cases related mainly to economic development). However, nonresidents are allowed to acquire immovable property in Malta with the permission of the Minister of Finance, provided that (1) the property is for residential use by the nonresident; (2) the value is not under Lm 15,000; and (3) funds for acquisition originate from overseas. Foreign nationals (residents of Malta) who decide to take up residence abroad are permitted to transfer all their assets held in Malta to their new country of residence.

Applications by residents to purchase real estate abroad require the approval of the Central Bank, which considers each case on its own merits. Residents are, however, allowed to purchase real estate overseas using funds already held in portfolio investments abroad. Emigrating Maltese nationals may transfer all their assets abroad without limit.

In the case of portfolio investment, where residents are concerned, both individuals and companies are permitted to invest up to a maximum of Lm 5,000 a year. Requests for portfolio investment above the Lm 5,000 limit require exchange control approval. Residents are permitted to take up life insurance policies only with licensed insurance companies in Maltese currency.

Investment funds repatriated by residents may either be surrendered to an authorized bank for conversion into domestic currency or held in foreign currency accounts with authorized banks. Insurance payments to residents received from nonresident sources are eligible for investment overseas. Residents are permitted to hold foreign currency in the form of cash up to a maximum limit equivalent to Lm 1,000.

Nonresidents must obtain approval from the Central Bank to purchase or acquire from residents securities that are not listed on the Malta Stock Exchange. Such approval is not required for portfolio investment undertaken by nonresidents in the form of bank deposits, government treasury bills, and securities listed on the Malta Stock Exchange. Loans of up to Lm 5,000 may be contracted between residents and nonresidents without approval, subject to the presentation of certain documentation to the remitting bank for verification purposes. Residents are also allowed to obtain loans in excess of Lm 5,000 from foreign sources, provided that the loan is for a period of over three years and related documentation is submitted for registration purposes. Borrowing in excess of Lm 5,000 for a period of less than three years' maturity is subject to Central Bank approval.

Authorized banks, other than those involved solely in offshore financial activities, as well as certain financial institutions, are permitted to hold a foreign asset portfolio up to a limit stipulated by the Central Bank. This limit is exclusive of other foreign assets held to back foreign currency liabilities. Authorized banks are allowed to borrow from overseas, provided that they cover their foreign exchange exposure. They are also permitted to extend loans in foreign currency to residents and nonresidents subject to the limits stipulated by the Central Bank with regard to foreign asset portfolio holdings.

Collective investment schemes are allowed to invest abroad, without exchange control approval, all funds originating from overseas or from resident sources, as long as the latter do not exceed the yearly portfolio investment allowance.

Gold

Malta has issued 23 denominations of gold coins, which are legal tender. Residents are allowed to hold coins and acquire jewelry but must obtain permission from the Central Bank to purchase and sell any gold coins that are not legal tender. The importation of gold coins is controlled to ensure that such coins are used for genuine numismatic purposes. A specific import license is required for the importation of gold coins, gold bullion, and manufactured and semimanufactured articles of gold; imports of filigree work of gold and silver are restricted. Subject to exchange control permission, authorized importers may import gold bullion solely for the use of jewelers and other industrial users. The exportation of gold by residents other than the monetary authorities also requires exchange control permission. Gold bullion and gold coins are subject to the value-added tax.

---

[5]For the purposes of this act, the term nonresident includes individuals who are not residing in Malta but excludes Maltese citizens living abroad and foreign spouses of citizens of Malta; and any association of persons, or any entity, whether corporate or not, if (1) it is registered outside Malta; (2) it has its principal place of residence or business outside Malta; (3) 25 percent or more of its shares or other capital is owned by a nonresident person; or (4) it is in any manner, whether directly or indirectly, controlled by one or more nonresident persons.

Changes During 1995

No significant changes occurred in the exchange and trade system.

Changes During 1996

Capital

January 1. The annual limit on direct investment that resident individuals and companies are allowed to undertake overseas was raised to Lm 150,000 from Lm 50,000.

March 29. Residents were allowed to contract in foreign currency life insurance policies with nonresidents who are lawfully engaged in the business of life insurance in Malta. Both the initial subscription and the annual premiums are, however, not to exceed the portfolio investment limit of Lm 5,000 a year that is currently granted to residents over 18 years of age.

REPUBLIC OF THE MARSHALL ISLANDS

(Position as of December 31, 1995)

Exchange Arrangement

The currency of the Republic of the Marshall Islands is the U.S. Dollar.[1] There is no central monetary institution. The authorities do not buy or sell foreign exchange; foreign exchange transactions are handled by three commercial banks, which are authorized foreign exchange dealers and are regulated by a statutory banking board. These commercial banks buy and sell foreign exchange at the rates quoted in the international markets. Forward transactions may be conducted through these commercial banks without restriction. There are no taxes or subsidies on purchases or sales of foreign exchange.

The Republic of the Marshall Islands accepted the obligations of Article VIII, Sections 2, 3, and 4 of the Fund Agreement on May 21, 1992.

Administration of Control

There are no exchange control regulations.

Prescription of Currency

Both outward and inward payments may be settled in U.S. currency or in any other convertible currency.

Imports and Import Payments

Imports are not subject to import licensing requirements, but importers must obtain a business license. Imports of certain products are prohibited for environmental, health, safety, or social reasons.

Specific and ad valorem duties are levied under the Import Duties Act of 1989. Specific duties are levied at the following rates: cigarettes, 50 cents a pack (of 20); carbonated nonalcoholic beverages, 25 cents a can or bottle (of 12 fluid ounces); beer and malt beverages, 50 cents a can or bottle (of 12 fluid ounces); spirits and distilled alcoholic beverages, $25 a U.S. gallon; wines, $15 a U.S. gallon; gasoline, 25 cents a U.S. gallon; propane, 3 cents a pound; jet fuel, 15 cents a U.S. gallon; and kerosene, 5 cents a U.S. gallon. Ad valorem duties range from 5 percent to 75 percent. With the exception of food items, medicines, building materials, and heavy machinery, which carry a rate of 5 percent, most other products are subject to a duty of 10 percent.

Exports and Export Proceeds

There are no surrender requirements for export proceeds. Exports are not subject to licensing requirements, and there are no taxes or quantitative restrictions on exports. The purchasing, processing, and exportation of copra and copra by-products are conducted solely by the government-owned Tobolar Copra Processing Plant, Inc.

Payments for and Proceeds from Invisibles

There are no restrictions on payments for or proceeds from invisibles.

Capital

Foreign investors are required to submit applications to the Cabinet and obtain a license in order to engage in business or to acquire an interest in a business in the Marshall Islands. The Cabinet has the authority to formulate policies regarding incentives and priorities for foreign direct investment. Although no special financial incentives are offered to foreign investors, a number of incentives are available under certain U.S. laws (for example, duty-free access to the U.S. market for most products). Foreigners are prohibited from owning land, but foreign investors can obtain long-term leases (the maximum period is 50 years, with an option to renew) for land acquired for their business.

All other inward and outward capital transfers are unrestricted, with the exception that commercial banks cannot transfer abroad more than 25 percent of deposits received from Marshallese citizens, including domestic corporations and the authorities. This provision does not prevent a depositor from transferring any deposits abroad.

Changes During 1995

No significant changes occurred in the exchange and trade system.

---

[1]The Marshall Islands must consult the United States if it decides to issue its own currency.

312

MAURITANIA

(Position as of February 29, 1996)

Exchange Arrangement

The currency of Mauritania is the Mauritanian Ouguiya. The exchange rate for the ouguiya is market determined; the average market rate of the day is used for all official transactions. Daily exchange rates for 16 other currencies,[1] including those used in the basket, are obtained from the daily reference rate for the U.S. dollar and the cross rates for these currencies as published by Reuters. On December 31, 1995, the midpoint exchange rate of the ouguiya in terms of the U.S. dollar was UM 137.11 per $1.

The Central Bank of Mauritania sells foreign currency notes and traveler's checks only for official travel and for other purposes judged to be exceptional; commissions of 1.75 percent are applied to purchases and sales by the Central Bank involving traveler's checks and foreign currencies. There are no taxes or subsidies on purchases or sales of foreign exchange, but authorized banks and exchange bureaus are free to set their commissions for foreign currency transactions. The commercial banks are free to set their exchange rates for foreign currency notes and traveler's checks, which they may buy on a no-questions-asked basis.

Only intermediary banks and foreign exchange bureaus licensed by the Central Bank are authorized to buy and sell foreign exchange at freely determined exchange rates. The source of foreign exchange need not be declared, and foreign exchange may be purchased anonymously. Hotels, shipping companies, travel agencies, and others alike may buy banknotes and traveler's checks in foreign currencies under the control of a licensed intermediary bank, but these entities are not authorized to sell such means of payments to the public and must surrender any foreign exchange they have purchased to the bank that granted them the "delegated" authorization.

The average exchange rate is applied to foreign clearing transactions of the Postal Administration. This exchange rate is also applied to remittances through the Postal Administration by Mauritanian workers residing abroad.

There are no arrangements for forward cover against exchange rate risk operating in the official or the commercial banking sector.

Administration of Control

Exchange control authority is vested in the Central Bank, the Ministry of Economy and Finance, and the Ministry of Commerce. The Central Bank has delegated this power to authorized banks and exchange bureaus. The Central Bank is authorized to obtain any information necessary to compile balance of payments statistics. All exchange transactions relating to foreign countries must be effected through authorized banks and exchange bureaus or, in some cases, through the Postal Administration. All imports require exchange control approval from the Central Bank. Special regimes apply to the imports of government entities and state enterprises. A tax of 3 percent is levied on international trade to finance the collection of statistics.

Arrears are maintained with respect to external payments.

Prescription of Currency

All settlements with Israel are prohibited. Settlements with other countries usually take place in convertible currencies.

Nonresident Accounts

Licensed intermediary banks may freely open foreign currency accounts for resident individuals and legal entities *(comptes d'escale)*. Accounts denominated in foreign currencies or convertible ouguiya may be credited with transfers from abroad or from another foreign account, proceeds from the encashment of checks drawn on a foreign bank or on another foreign account to open in a Mauritanian bank the order of the account holder, transfers issued by a licensed intermediary bank by order of a resident in payment of transactions authorized by the exchange control regulations, and proceeds from the surrender of foreign exchange on account on the foreign exchange market (banknotes, whether foreign or issued by the Central Bank, however, may not be deposited). These accounts may be debited for foreign exchange surrendered on the foreign exchange market, funds made available abroad, withdrawals of traveler's checks denominated in a foreign cur-

---

[1]Austrian schillings, Belgian francs, Canadian dollars, CFA francs, Danish kroner, deutsche mark, French francs, Italian lire, Japanese yen, Moroccan dirhams, Netherlands guilders, Norwegian kroner, pounds sterling, Spanish pesetas, Swedish kronor, and Swiss francs.

rency by the holder, transfers in favor of another foreign account or a resident, checks issued by the holder of the account in favor of another nonresident or of a resident, and withdrawals of banknotes issued by the Central Bank. Transit accounts may be opened freely by resident consignees on their books under the names of shipping companies.

Resident Accounts

Licensed banks and foreign exchange bureaus may freely open accounts with banks abroad to accommodate foreign exchange market transactions. Other residents may not open accounts abroad. Exporters holding an import-export permit may open foreign exchange accounts in Mauritanian banks to deposit retained balances of proceeds from export earnings in foreign exchange.

Imports and Import Payments

Imports of a few goods are prohibited for reasons of health or public policy. Goods imported by the holders of import-export permits are exempted from authorization and domiciliation requirement; the importer is required only to establish an import certificate endorsed by the Central Bank. Imports by nonholders of import-export permits are subject to the approval of the Ministry of Commerce, and import transactions must be domiciled with an authorized bank. Import-export permits must be renewed every year. All residents who pay the turnover tax (TCA) of at least UM 300,000 and who import or export on a regular basis (except debtors in arrears with the banking system) may obtain an import-export permit.

Upon presentation of the import certificate approved by the Central Bank, the importer may purchase the foreign exchange from an authorized bank or an exchange bureau. Advance payments for imports require the prior approval of the Central Bank. There are special arrangements for imports in border areas.

There is a general customs duty rate of 15 percent, and a reduced rate of 5 percent applies to selected goods. Certain capital goods and various consumer goods, such as tea, salt, and medicines, are exempt. All imports from the West African Economic Community (WAEC) that are not subject to the regional cooperation tax are also exempt, as are some imports from Algeria, Morocco, Tunisia, and the European Union (EU). In addition to the customs duty, import taxes are levied at rates ranging from 5 percent to 166 percent (with various exemptions); a minimum turnover tax is levied at a minimum rate of 10 percent and a maximum rate of 20 percent (with various exemptions); and a regional cooperation tax is levied on certain industrial products imported from WAEC countries in lieu of import duties that are levied on other imports.

Payments for Invisibles

There are no limits on the acquisition and transfer of foreign exchange through the foreign exchange market for all current transactions, subject to the presentation of documentary evidence of the authenticity and legitimacy of the transactions. For travel purposes, residents may freely purchase banknotes and traveler's checks denominated in foreign currencies, upon presentation of their passport and a travel ticket. Amounts exceeding UM 15,000 a day for the trip abroad are subject to the Central Bank's approval. The signing of a contract for services rendered by nonresidents to residents is subject to the Central Bank's endorsement; foreign exchange necessary to pay for their services may be acquired upon presentation of the endorsed contract and a bill of costs.

Exports and Export Proceeds

Exports of goods by holders of import-export permits are exempted from authorization, and the exporter is required only to establish an export certificate that must be endorsed by the Central Bank. Exports by nonholders of import-export permits are subject to the approval of the Ministry of Commerce. Export transactions to all countries exceeding UM 20,000 must be domiciled with an authorized bank. Export certificates submitted to the Central Bank for approval must specify the quantity, value, and destination of the goods to be exported, and they must undertake to repatriate and surrender foreign exchange proceeds. Export proceeds must be repatriated no later than the due date of the receipt. Exports of iron ore are the monopoly of the National Industrial and Mining Company, and a special exemption applies to the repatriation of its export proceeds. Exports of demersal fish are the monopoly of the Mauritanian Fish Marketing Company.

Exporters who hold import-export permits are allowed to retain 30 percent of their proceeds in foreign exchange accounts maintained at domestic banks (for up to 30 days). The Central Bank buys 40 percent of exporter proceeds directly from the export at the average market exchange rate, while the remaining 30 percent must be sold in the exchange market. Within the 30-day period, the foreign exchange must be used either to pay for imports of the account holder or for his or her other current account transactions, or surrendered in exchange for ouguiya to banks or foreign exchange bureaus.

A tax is levied on exports of fish and crustaceans, at rates ranging from 8 percent to 20 percent for specialized catches and at a rate of 5 percent for shrimp and crayfish.

Proceeds from Invisibles

Authorized banks and foreign exchange bureaus may buy foreign currency banknotes and traveler's checks on a no-questions-asked basis. Services routinely rendered abroad by residents must be domiciled at a licensed intermediary bank. Proceeds from such services must be repatriated within four months and surrendered in exchange for ouguiya in the same manner as proceeds from the export of goods.

Exports of banknotes and coins issued by the Central Bank are not permitted. Residents are authorized to export foreign exchange obtained legally but must present to customs their passport and ticket annotated by the bank or foreign exchange bureau that issued foreign exchange to them. Nonresidents of foreign nationality may freely bring in foreign currencies (subject to customs clearance for amounts exceeding $2,000) and export payment instruments denominated in foreign currencies in amounts up to those declared upon entry, less amounts surrendered in exchange for ouguiya in the minimum sum of UM 10,000 a day. Prior to their departure, these nonresidents may repurchase foreign exchange from banks or foreign exchange bureaus if they have surrendered foreign exchange during their stay in amounts exceeding UM 10,000. Nonresident holders of foreign accounts denominated in a foreign currency or in convertible ouguiya on the books of licensed intermediary banks may export any traveler's checks denominated in foreign currencies that have been purchased by debit to the aforementioned accounts.

Capital

Capital movements between Mauritania and all foreign countries are subject to exchange control; capital transfers to all countries require Central Bank approval and are restricted, but capital receipts are normally permitted freely, although the subsequent investment of the funds in Mauritania may require approval, as indicated below.

Residents must have prior authorization from the Central Bank to invest abroad. Foreign direct investments in Mauritania[2] and Mauritanian direct investments abroad[3] must be declared to the Central Bank before they are made.

The Investment Code of January 23, 1989, provides for various benefits for private investments in Mauritania and stipulates that profits and dividends accruing from these investments can be transferred freely.

Gold

Residents are free to hold, acquire, and dispose of gold in any form in Mauritania. All imports and exports of gold require prior authorization from the Central Bank. Exempt from this requirement are imports and exports by the Central Bank and manufactured articles containing a minor quantity of gold (such as gold-filled or gold-plated articles).

Changes During 1995

Exchange Arrangement

December 31. The official and the free market exchange rates were unified, and official transactions would be effected at the average exchange rate in the free market.

Imports and Import Payments

December 31. The system of auctioning import authorizations was abolished. Imports must be financed with foreign exchange purchased in the free market.

Changes During 1996

Exports and Export Proceeds

February 1. The rate of export proceeds required to be surrendered to the Central Bank was reduced from 40 percent to 30 percent.

---

[2]Including those made by companies in Mauritania that are directly or indirectly under foreign control and those made by branches or subsidiaries of foreign companies in Mauritania.

[3]Including those made through foreign companies that are directly or indirectly controlled by persons in Mauritania and those made by branches or subsidiaries abroad of companies in Mauritania.

MAURITIUS

(Position as of December 31, 1995)

Exchange Arrangement

The currency of Mauritius is the Mauritian Rupee, the external value of which is determined by supply and demand in the interbank exchange market. Daily opening rates for all banks' small transactions are determined by the Bank of Mauritius. On December 31, 1995, the buying and selling rates were Mau Rs 18.213 and Mau Rs 18.440, respectively, per $1.

Companies operating in the export processing zone (EPZ) and other Mauritian exporters and traders dealing in priority imports are authorized to engage in forward cover transactions in foreign exchange markets abroad through their banks in Mauritius. Companies operating in the EPZ and the service zone and certain other companies are authorized to maintain, with local commercial banks, accounts denominated in foreign currencies.

Commercial banks operate as authorized dealers. Offshore banks are allowed to lend to both residents and nonresidents in foreign currencies; however, lending to residents is subject to approval from the Bank of Mauritius.

Mauritius accepted the obligations of Article VIII, Sections 2, 3, and 4 of the Fund of Agreement on September 29, 1993.

Administration of Control

Exchange control is administered by the Bank of Mauritius under powers delegated by the Financial Secretary. The Bank of Mauritius issues foreign exchange dealing licenses; and commercial banks, as agents of the Bank of Mauritius, are authorized to approve and effect payments for current transactions. The Ministry of Trade and Shipping is responsible for issuing import permits where necessary.

Prescription of Currency

The Exchange Control Act has been suspended since July 27, 1994. Consequently, there are no prescription of currency requirements. Payments to nonresidents may be made in Mauritian rupees or in any convertible foreign currency. Similarly, payments from nonresidents may be received in Mauritian rupees or in any convertible foreign currency. Mauritius maintains a bilateral payments agreement with Madagascar.

Resident and Nonresident Accounts

There is no distinction between accounts of residents and nonresidents in Mauritius. Residents may maintain accounts denominated in foreign currencies abroad or with local commercial banks.

External accounts may be opened by residents and firms of other countries and may be credited with (1) authorized payments by residents of Mauritius, (2) transfers from other external accounts, and (3) the proceeds of sales to authorized dealers of any convertible foreign currency by nonresidents. These accounts may be debited for (1) payments to residents of Mauritius, (2) transfers to other external accounts, and (3) the cost of purchase of any convertible foreign currency or gold. The Nonresident (External Account) Scheme, reintroduced on September 25, 1985, allows Mauritians abroad to open savings or fixed-deposit accounts with commercial banks in Mauritius in rupees and term deposit accounts in foreign currencies. Interest on such deposits is exempted from income tax. As long as they are abroad, holders of such accounts are free at any time to transfer the balances of their accounts, together with interest. As of August 16, 1993, the Bank of Mauritius no longer provides exchange rate guarantees for balances in nonresident accounts with respect to new deposits.

Imports and Import Payments

Importers must be licensed under the Licenses Ordinance. Under the Supply (Control of Imports) Regulations of 1991, controlled goods, as specified in the first schedule, require import permits from the Ministry of Trade and Shipping. Customs duty, fiscal duty, and import levy are now merged into one single basic import duty. Certain items, namely vehicles, petroleum products, alcoholic drinks, and cigarettes are subject to excise duties. Commercial banks are authorized to approve and transfer funds for import payments without restriction.

Payments for Invisibles

Payments for invisibles related to imports and purchases of foreign exchange for travel are permitted without restriction. Residents may hold international credit cards and use them to pay for travel expenses abroad.

There are no restrictions on the amount of currency notes and coins that may be taken out of the country.

Exports and Export Proceeds

Exports of articles made wholly or partially of gold, platinum, or silver; diamonds, precious and semiprecious stones, pearls, and articles mounted with these; and works of art are prohibited unless permission is obtained from the Bank of Mauritius. Exports of certain foodstuffs, including fruits, are controlled. The Mauritius Sugar Syndicate is the sole exporter of sugar, and all export proceeds must be surrendered to the Bank of Mauritius. No tax is levied on sugar exports. Exporters are allowed to operate foreign exchange accounts at the commercial banks. All export proceeds must be repatriated within six months of shipment and offered for sale to an authorized dealer or credited to a foreign currency account to meet payments for imports.

Exports to Canada and the United States of knit shirts and cotton, wool, and man-made fiber sweaters are effected under bilateral export restraint agreements.

Proceeds from Invisibles

Receipts from invisibles must be repatriated and offered for sale to an authorized dealer. There is no limitation on the amount of foreign currency notes and coins that may be imported, but travelers may not import more than Mau Rs 700 in domestic currency notes and coins.

Capital

There are no restrictions on capital transfers into or out of Mauritius. However, noncitizens buying property in Mauritius must obtain the permission from the Minister of Internal Affairs under the Noncitizens Act (Property Restriction). Foreign investors are allowed to repatriate their capital, without paying a tax and without prior approval from the Bank of Mauritius.

Offshore banking facilities may be established since January 1, 1989.

Emigrants to any country may take out, at the official rate of exchange and free of duty, the equivalent of Mau Rs 500,000 a family from their Mauritian assets upon redesignation as nonresidents, which occurs upon departure. The balance of an emigrant's funds must be credited to a blocked account; any releases that may be approved for transfer abroad are subject to a 5 percent duty.

Gold

Residents other than the monetary authorities are permitted to hold gold for numismatic purposes (gold coins of Mau Rs 100, Mau Rs 500, and Mau Rs 1,000, and such commemorative gold coins as Mau Rs 200 and Mau Rs 1,000) or as personal jewelry and ornaments. Exports and imports of monetary gold are prohibited, except when made by the monetary authorities. The Bank of Mauritius is the sole importer of pure gold for sale to jewelers and industrialists.

Changes During 1995

No significant changes occurred in the exchange and trade system.

MEXICO

(Position as of December 31, 1995)

Exchange Arrangement

The currency of Mexico is the Mexican Peso;[1] its external value is determined in the interbank market on the basis of supply and demand. On December 29, 1995, the exchange rate for the U.S. dollar was Mex$7.6425 per US$1. No limitations apply on access to ownership or transfer of foreign exchange. Forward and futures are available from authorized banks.

In April 1995, the Chicago Mercantile Exchange started trading futures contracts on the peso.

Mexico accepted the obligations of Article VIII, Sections 2, 3, and 4 of the Fund Agreement on November 12, 1946.

Administration of Control

Effective November 11, 1991, all controls on exchange transactions were abolished. The licensing of imports and exports is handled mostly by the Secretariat of Commerce and Industrial Promotion (Sec-ofi). Foreign exchange policies are established by the Secretariat of Finance and Public Credit (SHCP) and the Bank of Mexico.

Prescription of Currency

In accordance with payments agreements with the central banks of Argentina, Bolivia, Brazil, Chile, Colombia, the Dominican Republic, Ecuador, Paraguay, Peru, Uruguay, and Venezuela, payments to these countries may be made through the Bank of Mexico and the central banks of the countries concerned within the framework of the multilateral clearing system of the Latin American Integration Association (LAIA). Similar payment arrangements exist with the central banks of Costa Rica, El Salvador, Guatemala, Honduras, Malaysia, and Nicaragua.

Resident and Nonresident Accounts

Mexican banks are prohibited from receiving domestic currency deposits from foreign financial institutions abroad or from non-Mexican exchange houses, except in cases where (1) such funds represent the counterpart of foreign currency sold to the Mexican bank where the account is held; (2) the funds represent the counterpart of foreign currency sold to other Mexican banks; (3) the funds represent the redemption, sale, or interest payments of securities held in custody in the Mexican bank in which the account is held, only if the securities were bought with the proceeds from any of the transactions defined in (1) or (2); (4) the funds represent the counterpart of a peso futures contract concluded in a market recognized by the Bank of Mexico; and (5) when the transaction is authorized on a case-by-case basis by the Management of the Financial System Regulations. Commercial banks are permitted to open checking accounts denominated in U.S. dollars payable in Mexico only for (1) residents in the northern border area of Mexico; (2) firms domiciled in any part of the country; and (3) official representatives of foreign governments and international organizations, and foreigners working in these institutions. Commercial banks are permitted to open in any part of the country time deposits denominated in U.S. dollars and payable only abroad for firms established in Mexico.

Imports and Import Payments

Import licenses from Secofi are required for only 149 of the 10,065 items on which Mexico's general import tariff is levied, except for temporary imports of raw materials and intermediate goods for export industries. On average, import licenses cover the applicant's import needs for nine months and may be extended for three months. Import needs are estimated at 20 percent above the amount of previous actual imports but may be increased when justified. New licenses are issued only if the applicant can demonstrate that at least 70 percent of earlier licenses have been effectively used. For some commodities, "open-ended" import licenses may be granted, allowing imports to be effected during a period of six months to one year, subject to an overall limit. Depending on the importer's performance, the license may be renewed repeatedly.

All imports must be accompanied by an exporter's declaration of shipment. The import tariff structure is based on the harmonized product description and coding system of the General Agreement on Tariffs and Trade (GATT). Imports from member countries of the LAIA and other Latin American countries are subject to preferential tariffs. A free-trade zone regime was in place until August 31, 1995 for certain

---

[1]The Mexican new peso, equivalent to 1,000 old Mexican pesos, was introduced on January 1, 1993. On January 1, 1996, the name of the currency was changed to Mexican peso.

regions of the country,[2] including the newly established border zone with Guatemala. This regime allowed imports into these regions without customs tariffs as long as the imported goods were not similar to those produced domestically in the same regions. Since February 1992, Mexico has maintained bilateral free trade agreements with Bolivia and Chile, and since January 1995, with Costa Rica.

Since January 1994, the North American Free Trade Agreement (NAFTA) between Canada, Mexico, and the United States entered into effect. Since January 1995, Mexico has maintained a trilateral free trade agreement with Colombia and Venezuela. In 1994, SECOFI imposed an import tariff of 279 percent on bicycle tires and inner tubes, 181 percent on brass padlocks, and 144 percent on bicycles shipped from China. In October 1994, an import tariff of 28 percent was imposed on fish flour from Chile. In May 1995, a 35 percent import duty was imposed on clothing, footwear, and leather products in an effort to promote the domestic industry. In June 1995, a provisional 29.3 percent anti-dumping duty was imposed on steel imports from the Baltic countries, Russia, and the other countries of the former Soviet Union. In August 1995, the following anti-dumping duties were imposed: 57.7 percent on corrugated rod from Brazil and 23.6 percent on doorknobs from the People's Republic of China; and in October 1995, an 82.4 percent duty was imposed on seamless tubes and pipes from the United States.

Payments for Invisibles

Payments for invisibles may be made freely. The contracting of personal insurance policies abroad is not restricted, but casualty insurance policies intended to cover events that might take place in Mexico may be contracted only with Mexican companies, including subsidiaries of foreign insurance companies established in Mexico. Reinsurance may be contracted with foreign reinsurance companies.

Exports and Export Proceeds

Most exports do not require licenses. Powdered milk was exempted from the licensing requirement in February 1995. Exports of a few specified items related to endangered species, drugs, and archaeological pieces are prohibited. Under the Program for Integral Promotion of Exports (PROFIEX), a drawback system of import duty payments by exporters and their domestic suppliers is in operation.

---

[2]These regions are the free-trade zones of Baja California, Baja California Sur, Quintana Roo, and the partial free-trade zone of Sonora.

Proceeds from Invisibles

There are no restrictions on the use of proceeds from invisibles.

Capital

Foreign direct investments are normally allowed up to 100 percent of equity without prior authorization, with certain exceptions: (1) Investments in the following sectors are reserved for the state: oil and other hydrocarbons; basic petrochemicals; electricity; nuclear energy generation; radioactive minerals; communication via satellite; telegraph; radiotelegraphy; postal service; railroads; issue of paper money; minting of coins; and the control and supervision of ports, airports, and heliports. (2) Investments in the following sectors are reserved exclusively for Mexican nationals or Mexican corporations with a foreign exclusion clause: retail trade of gasoline and distribution of liquified petroleum gas; radio and television broadcasting, with the exception of cable television; road transport (excluding courier and packaged goods transport services); credit unions and development banks; and certain professional and technical services. However, foreign investors wishing to invest in these activities may acquire shares in companies engaged in these sectors through the Neutral Investment Mechanism. (3) Investments in the following sectors require prior authorization: acquisition of more than 49 percent of the equity in a Mexican corporation if the total value of assets exceeds $25 million; maritime transport and certain port services; administration of air terminals; cellular telephones; construction activities, including the construction of pipelines for oil and its derivatives; oil and gas drilling; legal services; private education; credit information; securities rating institutions; and insurance agents. In order to obtain prior authorization, investors must submit their proposals to the National Commission of Foreign Investment. Approval is automatic if a formal response is not made within 45 working days of the date of application. In reaching its decision, the Commission takes into account the impact of investments on employment and training of workers, the technological contribution, compliance with environmental provisions in relevant laws, and the contribution to the economy. (4) Ceilings on foreign ownership are applied to the following sectors: financial institutions; air transportation; manufacturing of explosives and firearms; printing and publication of domestic newspapers; agricultural land; cable television and basic telephone services; video text and packet-switching services; and transportation by air and land, and certain activities related to maritime transport.

Upon registration with the Ministry of Foreign Relations, Mexican companies with foreign participation may be allowed to own land for nonresidential purposes in restricted border areas (within 100 kilometers) and seacoast areas (within 50 kilometers). The acquisition of land rights by foreigners for residential purposes in restricted areas must be effected through a renewable 50-year trust held by a Mexican bank and requires prior authorization from the Secretariat of Foreign Relations.

There are no restrictions on portfolio investments. The liabilities of commercial banks denominated in foreign currencies must not exceed the larger amount of either (1) 10 percent plus an additional 4 percent of their liabilities in domestic currency, or (2) 1.6 times their net capital. Commercial banks must balance their positions subject to exchange rate risk on a daily basis. Short and long positions are acceptable as long as they do not exceed 15 percent of banks' net capital.

Commercial banks must invest the resources from their liabilities in foreign currencies (1) in certain foreign currencies and highly liquid foreign-currency-denominated assets, (2) in foreign currency loans to finance exports of merchandise and capital goods made in Mexico, or (3) in foreign currency loans granted to enterprises earning foreign currency revenues sufficient to cover their exchange risk.

Gold

Gold may be freely bought and sold in Mexico at the prevailing exchange rate.

Changes During 1995

Exchange Arrangement

March 17. An over-the-counter market in forward and options in foreign exchange was introduced.

April 25. The Chicago Mercantile Exchange started trading futures contracts in pesos.

Imports and Import Payments

May 30. An import duty of 35 percent was imposed on clothing, footwear, and leather products.

June 12. A provisional anti-dumping duty of 29.3 percent was imposed on imports of steel from the Baltic countries, Russia, and other countries of the former Soviet Union.

August 11. An anti-dumping duty of 57.7 percent was imposed on corrugated rod from Brazil.

August 14. An anti-dumping duty of 23.6 percent was imposed on imports of doorknobs from China.

August 31. The free-trade zone regime for Baja California, Baja California Sur, Quintana Roo, and the partial free-trade zone of Sonora were abolished.

October 11. An anti-dumping duty of 82.4 percent was imposed on imports of seamless tubes and pipes from the United States.

FEDERATED STATES OF MICRONESIA

(Position as of December 31, 1995)

Exchange Arrangement

The currency of the Federated States of Micronesia is the U.S. Dollar.[1] There is no central monetary institution. A statutory banking board, established in 1980, regulates the financial system. Foreign exchange transactions are handled by three commercial banks, which buy and sell foreign exchange at the rates quoted in international markets. Forward transactions may be conducted through commercial banks without restriction. There are no taxes or subsidies on purchases or sales of foreign exchange.

Micronesia accepted the obligations of Article VIII, Sections 2, 3, and 4 of the Fund Agreement on June 24, 1993.

Administration of Control

There are no exchange control regulations.[2]

Prescription of Currency

Both outward and inward payments may be settled in U.S. currency or in any other convertible currency.

Imports and Import Payments

Imports are not subject to any import-licensing requirements, but importers must obtain a business license. Imports of certain products are prohibited for environmental, health, safety, or social reasons.

Import duties are levied on an ad valorem or specific basis, as follows: cigarettes, carbonated nonalcoholic beverages, drink mixes, drink preparations, coffee, tea, beer and malt beverages, and wines, 25 percent; spirits and distilled alcoholic beverages, US$10 a U.S. gallon; and gasoline and diesel fuel, US$0.05 a U.S. gallon. Ad valorem duties are 3 percent on foodstuffs, 100 percent on laundry bar soap, and 4 percent on all other products.

Exports and Export Proceeds

There are no surrender requirements for export proceeds. Exports are not subject to licensing requirements, but exporters must obtain an export business license. There are no taxes or quantitative restrictions on exports. The purchasing and exportation of copra are conducted solely by the Coconut Development Authority. Commercial export documents are verified by the customs authorities.

Payments for and Proceeds from Invisibles

There are no restrictions on payments for or receipts from invisibles.

Capital

Foreign investors are regulated by federal and state authorities. They must obtain an application from the Federal Government and submit it for review and action to the Foreign Investment Board of the state in which the business will be located. They must obtain a license from the Federal Government to engage in business or to acquire an interest in a business in the Federated States of Micronesia. If a foreign investor wishes to conduct business in more than one state, an application for each state must be obtained from the Federal Government and submitted to the Federal Investment Board of the state in which the business will be located and operated. Priorities for foreign investment are reviewed by the federal and state authorities from time to time. Although no special financial incentives are offered to foreign investors, a number of incentives are available under certain U.S. laws (e.g., duty-free access to the U.S. market for some products). Foreign investment in the real estate and construction sectors is prohibited in accordance with laws prohibiting land ownership by foreigners.[3] Foreign investors normally obtain long-term leases (usually up to 25 years with an option to renew for another 25 years) for land acquired for their business.[4] There are no restrictions on the repatriation of profit or capital.

---

[1]The Federated States of Micronesia must consult with the United States if it decides to issue its own currency.

[2]The Compact Agreement with the United States exempts the importation, use, possession, and exportation of U.S. currency by U.S. armed forces and U.S. contractors or personnel from any form of regulation, restriction, or control by the Federated States of Micronesia.

[3]Article XII, Section 4 of the Constitution of the Federated States of Micronesia prohibits a noncitizen, or a corporation not wholly owned by citizens, from acquiring title to land or waters in the country.

[4]Article XII, Section 5 of the Constitution prohibits "agreements for the use of land for an indefinite period."

Banks are prohibited from lending more than the equivalent of 50 percent of their deposits to nonresidents.

Changes During 1995

No significant changes occurred in the exchange and trade system.

MOLDOVA

(Position as of December 31, 1995)

Exchange Arrangement

The currency of the Republic of Moldova is the Moldovan Leu (plural Lei). The official exchange rate against the U.S. dollar is established in the fixing sessions at the Chisinau Interbank Foreign Currency Exchange (CIFCE). The official exchange rate applies to foreign exchange transactions carried out by the National Bank of Moldova, including official external debt service payments, and is used for accounting and tax valuation purposes. Since February 1995, CIFCE fixing sessions have been conducted daily. Institutions eligible to deal in foreign exchange are authorized banks and foreign exchange bureaus. The latter are authorized to purchase from and sell to residents and nonresidents foreign banknotes and traveler's checks in any currency. Authorized banks and foreign exchange bureaus may set their own buying and selling rates in their foreign exchange transactions. Enterprises engaging in importing activities may purchase foreign exchange through authorized banks. On December 31, 1995, the official exchange rate was MDL 4.50 per $1.

There are no taxes or subsidies on purchases or sales of foreign exchange. There are no arrangements for forward cover against exchange rate risk operating in the banking sector.

Moldova accepted the obligations of Article VIII, Sections 2, 3, and 4 of the Fund Agreement on June 30, 1995.

Administration of Control

Foreign exchange transactions are governed by the Regulations on Currency Control in the Republic of Moldova, which came into effect on January 17, 1994. The National Bank has the ultimate authority in the area of foreign exchange arrangements and is responsible for managing the country's foreign exchange reserves, regulating the currency market, and granting licenses to engage in foreign currency transactions.

Prescription of Currency

Settlements are made in convertible currencies and effected through commercial banks. The system of correspondent accounts in central banks that was used for certain settlements with the Baltic countries, Russia, and the other countries of the former Soviet Union is now inoperative.

Resident and Nonresident Accounts

Resident natural and juridical persons may open currency accounts, which they may use at their own discretion at authorized banks. Since November 15, 1994, the surrender requirement of convertible currencies on residents' accounts was abolished. The source of foreign exchange is not subject to investigation. All foreign currency earnings of residents must be deposited in their accounts at authorized banks in Moldova. The opening of current and other accounts by Moldova residents in foreign banks abroad requires approval from the National Bank. Account holders may not use foreign exchange balances in their accounts to settle domestic transactions.

Nonresidents with foreign currency deposits at authorized banks in Moldova may freely transfer the balances abroad or sell them on the foreign exchange market through authorized banks.

Nonresident entities with accounts in Moldovan lei received from current international operation with residents of Moldova may convert lei balances into any other currency and repatriate them.

Imports and Exports

A few products (medicine, medical equipment, chemicals, and industrial waste) are subject to import licenses for the purpose of protecting the consumer and ensuring compliance with domestic standards. Imports are subject to import tariffs and customs fees. The maximum tariff rate will be reduced to 20 percent, with a limited number of exceptions. The maximum rate is applied to consumer electronics, cars, tobacco products, alcoholic beverages, cocoa products, jewelry, and luxury furniture. Energy, medicine, medical equipment, raw materials, cereals, and baby food are exempt from tariffs. Exports of certain goods are subject to licenses in accordance with the regulations issued in August 21, 1995.

Proceeds from exports must be repatriated within 60 days from the day stipulated for the receipt of payment, but not later than 180 days from the issuance of the custom declaration or the day a bill, statement, or protocol confirming that services have been rendered or work done has been made. However, the National Bank can extend the period for a valid reason. Proceeds from exports may be retained by exporters.

There are no taxes on exports to countries other than the Baltic countries, Russia, and the other countries of the former Soviet Union, except for a customs fee of 0.25 percent of the value of the shipment.[1] Exports to the Baltic countries, Russia, and the other countries of the former Soviet Union are subject to excise taxes and VAT, as these taxes are assessed on the basis of the origin principle within the Baltic countries, Russia, and the other countries of the former Soviet Union.

Payments for and Proceeds from Invisibles

Residents may freely purchase foreign exchange in the exchange market. For travel abroad, residents may purchase foreign exchange up to $5,000 in the exchange market for each trip and take it abroad without additional authorization. Payments by resident individuals in excess of $1,000 are subject to approval on a case-by-case basis under Moldovan law.

---

[1]Excise taxes on exports to countries other than the Baltic countries, Russia, and the other countries of the former Soviet Union of unbottled wine and unprocessed tobacco were introduced in the 1996 budget law. They are expected to be eliminated by July 1, 1996.

All proceeds from invisibles, except the earnings of workers residing abroad, must be repatriated.

Capital

All capital transactions and credits obtained from nonresidents require specific approval from the National Bank. Loan agreements with nonresidents are required to be registered with the National Bank.

Gold

A license is required to conduct international trade in gold. Regulations governing domestic trade in gold are established by the Ministry of Finance.

Changes During 1995

Exchange Arrangement

June 30. Moldova accepted the obligations of Article VIII, Sections 2, 3, and 4 of the Fund Agreement.

Imports and Exports

August 21. A licensing requirement was introduced for exports of a range of goods.

MONGOLIA

(Position as of February 29, 1996)

Exchange Arrangement

The currency of Mongolia is the Tugrik (100 Möngö per 1 Tugrik). The exchange rate is determined by demand and supply in the interbank exchange market. The Bank of Mongolia, the central bank, may intervene in the market to moderate undue fluctuations in the exchange rate. The central bank rate is set as the midpoint of the previous day's average buying and selling rates established by transactions among market participants. The central bank rate is applied to the public sector's transactions in imports and services, including debt-service payments, and to trade and service transactions conducted under bilateral payments arrangements. All other transactions, including sales of retained foreign exchange by public sector enterprises, take place at the free market rate. On December 31, 1995, the average (middle) rate in the interbank exchange market was Tug 476.1 per $1.

Exchange rates for other convertible currencies are calculated on the basis of the cross rates of the U.S. dollar against the currencies concerned in international markets.

Mongolia accepted the obligations of Article VIII, Sections 2, 3, and 4 of the Fund Agreement on February 1, 1996.

Administration of Control

International transactions are governed by the Foreign Exchange Law of June 1, 1994. The Foreign Exchange Law provides the framework for a liberal exchange system where the exchange rate is set by the Bank of Mongolia, based on market rates, and the public is free to maintain accounts in foreign exchange with authorized banks and perform current and international capital transactions.

In accordance with the Fund's Executive Board Decision No. 144–(52/51), adopted on August 14, 1952, Mongolia notified the Fund on November 4, 1994, that restrictions had been imposed on certain transactions with the Federal Republic of Yugoslavia (Serbia/Montenegro).

Prescription of Currency

Trade with all countries is conducted at world prices in convertible currencies. Trade with certain members of the former Council for Mutual Economic Assistance (CMEA) is conducted on an ad hoc basis under bilateral arrangements concluded before 1991. While some of the outstanding balances under the clearing arrangements of the former International Bank for Economic Cooperation (IBEC) have been settled, others are still under negotiation. Under the inoperative bilateral trade arrangement, there are also outstanding balances with China, the Islamic State of Afghanistan, and the Federal Republic of Yugoslavia (Serbia/Montenegro). Mongolia maintains a bilateral clearing agreement with the Democratic People's Republic of Korea.

Resident Accounts

Resident foreign exchange accounts. Resident persons and enterprises may maintain foreign exchange accounts at authorized banks. They may credit these accounts with retained export earnings and foreign exchange transferred from abroad and may use the balances on the accounts for any purpose without restriction.

Imports and Exports

Imports and exports are free of quantitative restrictions, except for the ban on the export of raw cashmere and for bona fide environmental, health, and security reasons. Imports of drugs, materials that encourage or depict violence or pornography, and items that could cause environmental damage are banned. Trade in the following items requires a special permit: historical artifacts, precious metals, weapons, radioactive materials, ferrous and nonferrous metals, and goods and services requiring licenses under international contracts and agreements.

Exporters are allowed to retain all of their foreign exchange earnings. Exporters may use their foreign exchange earnings for any purpose, including sale in the foreign exchange market or deposit in a foreign exchange account.

Imports are subject to a uniform 15 percent customs duty. Machinery and equipment imported by joint ventures and equipment used by disabled people are exempt from the customs duty.

Payments for and Proceeds from Invisibles

Foreign exchange for payments for invisibles is not provided at the official exchange rate but may be purchased without restriction on the interbank exchange market. Remittances of dividends and profits from investments in convertible currencies are permitted under the Law on Foreign Investment of May 1990 (see section on Capital, below). Proceeds from invisibles may be sold in the interbank exchange market without restriction. The importation and exportation of domestic banknotes are prohibited. There is no limit on the amount of foreign currency notes residents or nonresidents may import or export.

Capital

Foreign direct investment by private corporations is encouraged. The Law on Foreign Investment of July 1993 has codified the procedures for establishing foreign firms in Mongolia and provides certain guarantees and privileges to foreign investors. Among its provisions are that these firms will not be nationalized and that foreign investors will have the right to dispose of their assets. Transfers of profits abroad are not restricted. The maximum rate of profit tax is 40 percent, and foreign investors are exempt from the tax for various periods (from three to ten years), depending on the sector and export performance. In addition, the law stipulates that entities with foreign participation may export at world prices or other agreed prices, and they may import or export directly or in cooperation with foreign trade enterprises. The law particularly encourages investment in export promotion, projects using advanced technology, and the exploitation of natural resources.

Changes During 1995

Exchange Arrangement

May 31. The Bank of Mongolia reduced the maximum permissible spread between commercial banks' buying and selling rates to 3 percent from 5 percent.

Changes During 1996

Exchange Arrangement

February 1. Mongolia accepted the obligations of Article VIII, Sections 2, 3, and 4 of the Fund Agreement.

MOROCCO

(Position as of December 31, 1995)

Exchange Arrangement

The currency of Morocco is the Moroccan Dirham. Bank Al-Maghrib fixes a daily rate for the French franc on the basis of variations in the value of the currencies of Morocco's principal trading partners, weighted in accordance with the geographic distribution of Morocco's foreign trade and the pattern of currencies of settlement. Rates for most other currencies quoted in Morocco[1] are established on the basis of the daily dirham-French franc rate and the cross rates for those currencies in relation to the French franc in the Paris exchange market. On December 29, 1995, the exchange rate for the French franc was DH 1.73028. The exchange rate for the U.S. dollar was DH 8.4689 per $1.

All sales and purchases of foreign currency are centralized in Bank Al-Maghrib, but authorized banks are permitted to offset purchases and sales on behalf of private customers in each separate currency. Each day, authorized banks must purchase from or sell to Bank Al-Maghrib the balances of their purchases and sales in each currency; transactions are effected at rates fixed by Bank Al-Maghrib. Clearing operations between banks are not permitted; thus, no foreign exchange market exists in Morocco. Bank Al-Maghrib also establishes buying and selling rates for transactions by travelers in banknotes, traveler's checks, and letters of credit denominated in convertible currencies (those listed in footnote 1 and French francs, but excluding Algerian dinars, Libyan dinars, Mauritanian ouguiya, Tunisian dinars, and Gibraltar pounds). The authorized banks sell their excess holdings of banknotes to Bank Al-Maghrib, where they also replenish them when necessary.

A forward foreign exchange cover facility is available for exports and imports of items benefiting from special customs arrangements. Forward contracts for the purchase or sale of foreign exchange that have been concluded between banks and their customers result in reverse contracts between the banks and Bank Al-Maghrib. They may be con-

cluded in any foreign currency quoted by Bank Al-Maghrib for maturity periods ranging from a minimum of 1 month to a maximum of 12 months. The guaranteed exchange rate corresponds to the spot exchange rate, against the payment of a commission of 2 percent per year, of which a share amounting to 0.25 percent is retained by authorized banks. Provisions are made for extending contract terms, revising contracts in part, or canceling them in whole or in part. Arbitrage operations may be executed freely in favor of nonresident customers.

Morocco accepted the obligations of Article VIII, Sections 2, 3, and 4 of the Fund Agreement on January 21, 1993.

Administration of Control

Exchange control is administered by the Exchange Office, an agency under the Ministry of Finance and Foreign Investment. This office has delegated the execution of the main exchange control measures to authorized banks.

Import and export licenses, when required, are issued by the Ministry of Foreign Trade. Imports not involving payment do not require authorization.

Part of the Port of Tangier is designated a free trade zone. The zone and offshore banks located there are exempt from customs, exchange, and foreign trade controls.

During 1995, payments restrictions for security reasons were imposed against Iraq and the Federal Republic of Yugoslavia (Serbia/Montenegro) pursuant to UN resolutions; these were never communicated to the Board.

Prescription of Currency

Payments between Morocco and the rest of the world may be made in any currency quoted by Bank Al-Maghrib (see footnote 1) or through foreign accounts in convertible dirhams or foreign currency accounts opened in Moroccan banks.

Resident and Nonresident Accounts

The following accounts may be opened and operated by nonresidents.

Foreign currency accounts in the name of foreign nationals may be maintained by natural or juridical persons of foreign nationality, who are either residents or nonresidents. These accounts may be freely

---

[1] Algerian dinars, Austrian schillings, Belgian francs, Canadian dollars, Danish kroner, deutsche mark, European currency units (ECUs), Finnish markkaa, Gibraltar pounds, Italian lire, Japanese yen, Kuwaiti dinars, Libyan dinars, Mauritanian ouguiya, Netherlands guilders, Norwegian kroner, Portuguese escudos, pounds sterling, Saudi Arabian riyals, Spanish pesetas, Swedish kronor, Swiss francs, Tunisian dinars, U.A.E. dirhams, and U.S. dollars.

credited with transfers from abroad with foreign banknotes, checks, traveler's checks, or any other means of payment denominated in foreign currency and with foreign currency withdrawn from Bank Al-Maghrib, following general or special authorization from the Exchange Office. They may be freely debited for transfers abroad in favor of the account holder or to a foreign third party, for the surrender of foreign currency to Bank Al-Maghrib and for the payment of checks denominated in foreign currency.

Foreign currency accounts in the name of Moroccan residents living abroad may be opened by individuals of Moroccan nationality residing abroad. These accounts may be credited freely with transfers from abroad, checks or any other means of payment denominated in foreign currency, foreign currency withdrawn from Bank Al-Maghrib following general or special authorization from the Exchange Office, the return on investments effected on the basis of these accounts, and transfers from another foreign currency account or from an account in convertible dirhams. They may be freely debited for transfers abroad, transfers to another account in foreign currency or in convertible dirhams, foreign currency subscriptions for notes issued by the Moroccan Treasury, and for surrender of foreign currency to Bank Al-Maghrib.

Foreign currency accounts of exporters may be opened freely by Moroccan exporters of goods and services who are already holders of convertible accounts for export promotion. Those who do not hold such an account must have the prior consent of the Exchange Office. These accounts may be freely credited with 20 percent of foreign exchange receipts. The recording of foreign currency amounts corresponding to these rates must be effected simultaneously with the surrender to Bank Al-Maghrib of the remaining 80 percent. These accounts may also be credited freely with the return on invested funds lodged therein and with transfers from another foreign currency account of the same holder. They may be debited for professional expenses covered by exchange regulations, investment with authorized intermediary banks, subscriptions for notes issued by the Moroccan Treasury, for credit of another foreign currency account or a convertible dirham account for exporters (CCPEX) opened in the name of the same holder, and for surrender of foreign currency to Bank Al-Maghrib.

Foreign accounts in convertible dirhams may be opened by natural or juridical persons of foreign nationality who may be residents or nonresidents. These accounts may be credited freely with generally or specifically authorized transfers in favor of the account holder and with dirhams obtained from the sale to Bank Al-Maghrib of foreign exchange, including banknotes. They may be debited freely for payments in Morocco and for purchases of foreign exchange from Bank Al-Maghrib. Transfers between foreign accounts in convertible dirhams may be made freely, and there are no restrictions on the interest rate payable. Holders of these accounts may obtain international credit cards to settle their bills in Morocco and abroad.

Convertible dirham accounts may be freely opened in the name of nonresident Moroccans residing abroad. Overdrafts are not allowed, and there are no restrictions on the interest rate payable. These accounts may be credited freely with (1) dirhams from the sale of convertible currencies, including banknotes, to Bank Al-Maghrib; (2) transfers authorized by the Exchange Office; (3) payments of interest accrued on these accounts; (4) transfers from foreign accounts in convertible dirhams; and (5) transfers from term deposits in convertible dirham accounts. They may be debited freely for (1) the purchase of foreign exchange from Bank Al-Maghrib; (2) dirham payments in Morocco; (3) transfers to foreign accounts in convertible dirhams; and (4) transfers to term deposits in convertible dirham accounts. These accounts may also be debited freely, either for the benefit of the account holder or for other nonresidents, and for the purchase of foreign banknotes, traveler's checks, or other foreign currency-denominated means of payment.

Convertible dirham accounts for exporters may be opened by exporters of goods or services with Moroccan banks. These accounts may be credited with the equivalent of 20 percent of the foreign currency repatriated and surrendered to Bank Al-Maghrib in the case of exporters of goods or 10 percent in the case of exporters of services. Balances on these accounts may be used to finance expenditure contracted abroad and linked to the professional activity of those concerned. Fishing companies may credit to these accounts up to 100 percent of the foreign currency repatriated. Exporters have the choice of maintaining either foreign currency accounts or convertible dirham accounts. They may also hold both accounts simultaneously, provided that the overall percentage of export earnings to be credited to both accounts does not exceed 20 percent of foreign exchange earnings.

Convertible term accounts are designed to attract funds from nonresident foreigners who are not entitled to guaranteed transfers. These funds may be transferred henceforth within a maximum period of five years. The holders of such accounts may use the available funds, without prior authorization from the Exchange Office, to fund investments in Morocco, buy treasury bonds, purchase Moroccan marketable securities, settle expenses incurred in Morocco and, in the case of foreign corporations, provide their Moroccan subsidiaries with current account advances. They may also freely transfer the balances to resident or nonresident foreigners or to Moroccan nationals residing abroad. The beneficiaries of the proceeds of these accounts may use them to cover expenses incurred by foreign companies shooting films in Morocco; to purchase secondary residences under certain conditions; and to finance up to 50 percent of an investor's participation in investments in Morocco (the remainder must be financed with funds transferred from abroad). Funds invested with the proceeds of convertible term accounts may be transferred abroad without restriction in the event of liquidation or transfer, except for certain categories that are subject to a three-year waiting period.

Imports and Import Payments

Imports are not subject to restriction unless goods that require import licenses are included in the list. The list includes sugar, edible oil, cereals and products derived from these, arms, explosives, and certain vehicles.[2] Imports of petroleum products were liberalized in early 1995. In addition, imports of products that affect public security, morale, and health may be prohibited. Except for goods imported by air, insurance policies for imports must be taken out with insurance companies in Morocco. However, for a limited group of goods, insurance policies may be underwritten abroad; this group includes externally funded imports, if the financing terms include foreign insurance; capital goods and equipment under turnkey contracts or duly authorized investment programs; crude and diesel oil; gas; cattle; and wood.

For all imports, the importer must subscribe to a security—an import license—that must be lodged with an authorized bank, which may make payments related to goods and incidental costs upon submission of the required documents. Special procedures are applicable to specified imports financed with foreign aid or loans. Imports used for the production of export goods may be financed directly from the proceeds of foreign exchange claims of the same exporter within the framework of special lines of credit that Moroccan commercial banks are autho-

rized to contract with their foreign correspondents. Moroccan commercial banks may make advance payments abroad for imports of capital goods up to 25 percent of the f.o.b. value of the goods.

Customs duties are levied on an ad valorem basis, their maximum and minimum rates are 35 percent and 2.5 percent, respectively, except for a limited number of agricultural goods. Consumer goods not produced in Morocco are subject to a 5 percent levy. In addition to regular customs duties, fiscal levies of 10 percent, 12.5 percent, or 15 percent ad valorem are levied, according to the category of goods. Imports used to manufacture goods for export are exempt from customs duties and other import restrictions under the temporary admission scheme. Preferential customs tariff treatments are also granted for imports of capital goods to enterprises in the tourist and shipping sectors and other industrial enterprises qualifying under the provisions of Morocco's Industrial Investment Code. Imports of a relatively small number of items representing about 8 percent of industrial production are subject to minimum import prices (reference prices) for antidumping or safeguarding purposes.

Payments for Invisibles

Authorized banks are permitted to make payments and settle expenses incidental to commercial transactions covered by the relevant import or export documents without authorization from the Exchange Office. Moroccan enterprises are permitted to settle in dirhams the expenses incurred by their foreign managers and nonresident foreigners working for or on behalf of these enterprises.

Foreigners residing in Morocco and employed in either the private or public sector or engaged in professions in industry, commerce, and agriculture may transfer up to 50 percent of their income, whether or not their spouses reside in Morocco. Retired persons and foreign spouses of Moroccans have the same entitlement; they may also freely contribute to their retirement or social security funds in their country of origin.

Commercial banks are authorized to provide Moroccan residents with a travel allowance in foreign exchange equivalent to a maximum of DH 5,000 a person a year without Exchange Office approval. This allowance may be increased by DH 1,500 for a minor child on the passport of the beneficiary parent and accompanying said parent at the time of travel abroad. The same allocation may also be granted to Moroccan residents living abroad upon their return to their country of residence at the end of their stay in Morocco, provided they have not

---

[2]Quantitative restrictions on imports of sugar, cereals (and products derived from cereals), and edible oil are planned to be replaced by tariffs in early 1996.

benefited from the 15 percent allocation on remittances effected 12 months previously up to a limit of DH 20,000. Residents of foreign nationality who wish to travel abroad may be granted foreign exchange equivalent to all of their savings from income. Business travel by exporters of goods and services may be financed without restriction by debiting convertible export promotion accounts or foreign currency accounts maintained with Moroccan banks. In the case of business travel allowances for others, annual foreign exchange allowances are approved by the Exchange Office on the basis of need, with a daily maximum limit of DH 2,000. These banks have been empowered to provide advance allowances of up to DH 40,000 to small and medium-size enterprises and of up to DH 20,000 a year for business travel by individuals not belonging to either of these categories. In all cases, business travel allowances may be added to allowances for tourist travel.

A foreign exchange allocation equivalent to a maximum of DH 2,000 a month may be granted to foreign nationals residing in Morocco to cover the cost of higher education for a child studying abroad. Commercial banks are authorized to sell foreign exchange to persons traveling abroad for medical treatment up to the equivalent of DH 20,000 and to make transfers on their behalf for treatment abroad in favor of hospitals and medical institutions concerned. They are also authorized to transfer retirement pensions provided by public and private agencies in favor of persons residing abroad permanently.

Deep-sea fishing companies may maintain convertible dirham or foreign currency accounts with Moroccan banks. Convertible dirham accounts may be credited with the full dirham equivalent of foreign exchange earnings, and foreign currency accounts may be credited with 25 percent of foreign exchange earnings. The operating expenses of these companies, including travel expenses of employees, may be financed from these accounts. Foreign airlines operating in Morocco may transfer, without prior authorization from the Exchange Office, any surplus revenue from the proceeds of ticket sales, excess baggage, and air freight. Transfers with respect to sea and road transportation may be made directly to authorized banks.

Moroccan film distribution companies may transfer to foreign film producers or distributors user fees and other additional expenses related to the showing of these films in Morocco.

Commercial banks are authorized to sell foreign exchange to individuals studying abroad without prior Exchange Office authorization as follows:

(1) an annual installation allowance equivalent to DH 10,000 and the same amount for a person accompanying a minor student leaving Morocco for the first time; (2) school fees to foreign academic institutions, upon submission of documentary evidence and without limit; and (3) a monthly allowance for living expenses amounting to the equivalent of DH 6,000 a month for nonscholarship holders and DH 4,000 for scholarship holders. In addition to these facilities, banks are authorized to effect the transfer of rent and corresponding charges in favor of the foreign landlord once the student or his or her legal guardian has submitted a properly drawn-up lease and a certificate of residence or any other equivalent document. Applications for additional amounts must be referred to the Exchange Office for approval, which is granted on proof of need.

Transfers relating to remittances for family maintenance are approved upon presentation of documentary evidence.

Visitors to Morocco are permitted to repurchase foreign exchange against presentation of exchange certificate(s) up to the amount remaining from the original conversion of foreign exchange into dirhams.

The exportation of domestic banknotes is prohibited.

Exports and Export Proceeds

Goods may be exported freely, with the exception of flour, charcoal, certain animals, plants, and archaeological items, which are subject to authorization. However, for phosphates, the Cherifien Phosphate Office (OCP) has an export monopoly. Mineral products are subject to an ad valorem export tax of 0.5 percent, except for hydrocarbons, for which the tax is 5 percent, and phosphates, for which a tax on phosphate exploration equivalent to DH 34 per ton of gross phosphates has been levied since 1992. A 1 percent quality control tax is levied on exports of foodstuffs.

All exporters must sign a guarantee to repatriate and surrender foreign exchange proceeds. The foreign exchange must be surrendered within one month of the date of payment by foreign buyers specified in the commercial contract; in principle, this date must not be more than 150 days from the date of arrival of the merchandise. This deadline may be extended if warranted by business conditions and approved by the Exchange Office. Export proceeds collected abroad may be used directly abroad to finance imports of goods and raw materials of goods for export.

Proceeds from Invisibles

Residents of Moroccan nationality, including individuals and corporations, must repatriate foreign exchange receipts accruing from all their noncommercial claims and surrender them to an authorized bank. Other residents must surrender noncommercial receipts only if the receipts result from their activities in Morocco. Moroccans working abroad must surrender within one month all foreign exchange in their possession, but on departure from Morocco, they may export without restriction foreign banknotes obtained by debiting their accounts in convertible dirhams. If they do not have such an account, they may take out 15 percent of foreign exchange repatriated and surrendered 12 months before to Moroccan banks up to a limit of DH 20,000. If these facilities are not available, Moroccan residents living abroad may take advantage of the same DH 5,000 tourist allocation that applies to residents. Nonresident travelers may freely bring in foreign banknotes, traveler's checks, and other means of payment denominated in foreign currency. Resident travelers may also bring in foreign banknotes in any amount, as well as any other means of payment in foreign exchange but must surrender them within 30 days of their return to Morocco. The importation of domestic banknotes is prohibited.

Capital

The industrial investment code of February 1983 provides for full foreign ownership of Moroccan companies in certain sectors and eases the repatriation of capital; it also grants fiscal and other incentives for foreign investment. In addition, an investment code introduced for the tourist sector in August 1983 offers tax and other incentives to domestic and foreign investors and provides for full repatriation of tourist-related after-tax profits, without any time restriction.

All types of investment are permitted without prior authorization from the Exchange Office, including (1) participation in the equity capital of a company being established; (2) subscription to the capital increase of an existing company; (3) purchases of Moroccan securities; (4) contributions to partnerships; (5) purchases of real property; (6) self-financing construction projects; (7) establishment or purchase of a sole proprietorship; and (8) operations to increase capital through the capitalization of reserves, carryovers, or reserve provisions that have become available or through the consolidation of partnership current accounts. Operations involving transfers of investment ownership between foreigners do not require the authorization of the Exchange Office.

In September 1992, foreign corporations, resident or nonresident foreign individuals, and Moroccans residing abroad were permitted to invest freely in Morocco; to remit the income thus generated directly to the banking system with no restriction on amounts or time; and to repatriate the proceeds of the liquidation or sale of such investment, including any profits, also without prior authorization. Such investment must be financed in foreign exchange or by a similar method such as capitalization of reserves and profits, contributions in kind, consolidation of trade claims, or use of assets in convertible term accounts.

The holders of convertible term accounts may freely use funds in these accounts for the following purposes: financing investment operations in Morocco in all sectors of economic activity, regardless of the kind of investment; purchasing treasury bonds under the existing laws; effecting current account advances from foreign corporations to their subsidiaries in Morocco and any other placements the account holder may make; acquiring transferable securities quoted on the Casablanca Stock Exchange; settling living expenses and any other expenses in dirhams in Morocco incurred by account holders or their spouses, direct ancestors, and direct descendants (in the case of individuals) or by duly designated agents (in the case of corporations) with no limits on the amount; and paying duties and taxes due in Morocco by account holders. Furthermore, the original holders of convertible term accounts may freely transfer funds from their accounts to resident or nonresident foreigners or to nonresident Moroccan nationals. The above-mentioned purchasers may use the funds (1) to cover all dirham expenses incurred in Morocco by foreign film production companies for shooting films in Morocco; (2) to purchase secondary residences (provided they are located in a tourist development area for the buyers' personal use); (3) to finance up to 50 percent of capital increases of subsidiaries of foreign corporations established in Morocco, provided that the rest is financed with foreign exchange transferred from abroad; and (4) to partially finance investment operations in Morocco in all sectors, regardless of the form of investment (in this case, financing of investment with debiting of convertible term account is allowed to cover only up to 50 percent of the investment, provided that the remaining 50 percent is financed with foreign exchange transferred from abroad).

External financing operations by Moroccan enterprises in respect of external credit facilities, purchaser or supplier credits, export financing credits, advances on partnership current accounts, and refinancing operations have been liberalized. Authority has been delegated to the banks to remit maturities due under these financing operations in principal, interest, and any applicable charges.

Transfers of capital by foreigners leaving the country permanently are limited to DH 25,000 for each year spent in Morocco.

Moroccan nationals residing in the country and corporations established in Morocco may invest abroad with the authorization of the Exchange Office. However, they are required to remit the income generated by their investments and, as appropriate, the proceeds from liquidation of their investments.

Gold

Commemorative gold coins with a face value of DH 250 and DH 500 have been issued and are legal tender. Residents may purchase, hold, and sell gold coins in Morocco for numismatic or investment purposes. Ten different types of foreign gold coins are traded on the Casablanca Stock Exchange, which does not, however, deal in gold bars. Imports of gold are subject to authorization from the Directorate of Customs and Indirect Taxes Administration. Each year, the Ministry of Finance fixes a quota for the importation of gold ingots. The quota is then allocated among jewelers and industrial users of precious metals. Exports of gold are prohibited.

Changes During 1995

Resident and Nonresident Accounts

July 12. The requirement of a minimum initial deposit for the opening of a foreign currency account by Moroccan residents living abroad was eliminated.

Imports and Import Payments

January 1. Licensing requirements for imports of petroleum products were eliminated, and price controls on such products were replaced by a revised taxation of imports of petroleum products, effectively linking retail prices to world market prices. (These reforms followed the privatization of the distribution sector during 1994.)

July 12. The amount of foreign exchange receipts that could be retained by exporters of goods or services was raised to 20 percent of receipts.

MOZAMBIQUE

(Position as of December 31, 1995)

Exchange Arrangement

The currency of Mozambique is the Metical (plural Meticais), the external value of which is determined by supply and demand in the exchange market. On December 31, 1995, the average central bank exchange rate of the metical in terms of the U.S. dollar was Mt 10,776.00 per $1, and the average exchange rate of the metical in the secondary market in terms of the U.S. dollar was Mt 10,890.00 per $1.

There are no taxes or subsidies on purchases or sales of foreign exchange. There are no arrangements for forward cover against exchange rate risk operating in the official or the commercial banking sector.

Administration of Control

Foreign exchange policy and control are under the administration of the Bank of Mozambique. Imports and exports are authorized through licenses issued for statistical purposes by the Ministry of Commerce.

Prescription of Currency

Mozambique does not maintain any prescription of currency requirements. All bilateral payment agreements were eliminated in 1995.

Nonresident Accounts

Foreigners residing in Mozambique may open accounts denominated in foreign exchange at authorized banks. Nonresidents may open domestic currency accounts to meet local expenses, provided that the funds come either from the conversion of foreign currency or from employment and technical assistance contracts approved by appropriate institutions. Outward transfers of funds from these accounts are prohibited.

Imports and Import Payments

All imports exceeding the equivalent of $500 are subject to licensing by the Ministry of Commerce; licenses are provided routinely. The license specifies, among other things, the place of embarkation or disembarkation of the goods, the amount and currency of payment, and the source of financing. A negative product list exists for imports financed by donors' funds. In order to ensure that donors' requirements are met, the Office for the Coordination of Import Programs reviews import requests. Tied import support funds are allocated by the Bank of Mozambique to the commercial banks. Individuals may import goods up to the equivalent of $500 without an import license if the goods are financed with their own foreign exchange resources and tied-aid funds are not involved. Preshipment inspection is required for all imports in excess of $2,500, with the exception of usual items such as perishable commodities and imports for personal needs of diplomats.

Payments for Invisibles

Commercial banks are authorized to sell foreign exchange up to $5,000 to individuals for the payment of expenses associated with travel, study, or medical treatment abroad, as well as for film rental, expenses for fairs and exhibitions, contributions to international organizations, and subscriptions to publications. Operations exceeding this amount, or for other purposes, are subject to licensing by the Bank of Mozambique. Each ministry is subject to a ceiling on foreign exchange for official business and educational travel expenses. Foreign experts working in Mozambique may remit abroad all or part of their salaries, depending on the terms of their employment contracts. Nonresidents may export foreign banknotes up to the amount they declared on entry. Exports and re-imports of domestic currency are prohibited. An airport fee equivalent to $10–$20 in foreign currency is levied by the airport authorities on international departures, depending on the destination.

Remittances of profit and dividends from foreign direct investment may be made in accordance with the specific project authorization.

Exports and Export Proceeds

All exports are subject to a license. All export proceeds must be collected through the commercial banks and may be sold in the secondary exchange market. Since March 1, 1995, the surrender requirement has been reduced to 35 percent of the proceeds. Surrender requirements do not apply to free trade zones. Companies that export more than 85 percent of their production qualify for the status of free trade zone. On December 31, 1994, the general export duty of 0.5 percent was suspended for a period of five years. In 1995, the ban on exports of raw cashew nuts was suspended and an export duty of 20 percent was imposed on these exports.

Proceeds from Invisibles

Commercial banks and other financial institutions may hold a limited amount of foreign exchange. Certain Mozambican nationals working abroad under officially arranged contracts are obliged to remit 60 percent of their earnings through the Bank of Mozambique and to convert them into meticais.

Capital

The Government and the Bank of Mozambique are authorized to borrow abroad. Public and private enterprises need approval from the Bank of Mozambique to borrow abroad if loans are guaranteed by the Government or domestic banks. Such borrowing is not allowed if maturity, including the grace period, is 12 years or less. All foreign borrowing must be registered with the Bank of Mozambique. The Foreign Direct Investment Law, approved on June 8, 1994, aims at encouraging foreign investments owned fully by foreign interests or jointly with Mozambican enterprises. The law guarantees investors the right to repatriate capital and transfer abroad a portion of profits. The incentives for foreign investments include tax and customs exemptions for specified periods and for access to domestic credit. Foreign investment proposals are processed by the Foreign Investment Promotion Office.

Gold

The marketing and exportation of gold are regulated by Decree No. 11/81 of July 25, 1981. The Bank of Mozambique is responsible for enforcing this decree. The importation of gold and other precious metals is governed by special regulations.

Changes During 1995

Nonresident Accounts

March 2. Nonresidents were allowed to open domestic currency accounts to meet local expenses, provided that the funds come either from the conversion of foreign currency or from employment and technical assistance contracts approved by appropriate institutions. Outward transfers of funds from these accounts are prohibited.

Payments for Invisibles

February 28. Commercial banks were authorized to sell foreign exchange up to $5,000 to individuals for the payment of expenses associated with travel, study, or medical treatment abroad, as well as for film rental, expenses for fairs and exhibitions, contributions to international organizations, and subscriptions to publications. Operations exceeding this amount, or for other purposes, are subject to licensing by the Bank of Mozambique.

Exports and Export Proceeds

March 1. The surrender requirement was reduced to 35 percent of the proceeds. Surrender requirements do not apply to free trade zones. Companies that export more than 85 percent of their production qualify for the status of free trade zone.

June 1. The ban on exports of raw cashew nuts was suspended and an export duty of 20 percent was imposed on these exports.

MYANMAR

(Position as of December 31, 1995)

Exchange Arrangement

The currency of Myanmar is the Myanmar Kyat, which is officially pegged to the SDR at K 8.50847 per SDR 1. Myanmar applies margins of 2 percent to spot exchange transactions, based on the fixed kyat-SDR rate. The buying and selling rates of the kyat for the deutsche mark, the French franc, the Japanese yen, the pound sterling, the Swiss franc, and the U.S. dollar, quoted by the Myanma Foreign Trade Bank, are determined on the basis of the daily calculations of the value of these currencies against the SDR, as are rates for the currencies of some member countries of the Asian Clearing Union (ACU) (i.e., the Bangladesh taka, the Indian rupee, the Iranian rial, the Nepalese rupee, the Pakistan rupee, and the Sri Lanka rupee). On December 31, 1995, the buying and selling rates for the U.S. dollar were K 5.8445 and K 5.9614, respectively, per $1. The buying and selling rates for the Belgian franc, the Italian lira, the Hong Kong dollar, the Malaysian ringgit, the Netherlands guilder, and the Singapore dollar are determined daily on the basis of the appropriate cross rates in the Singapore market, and the buying and selling rates for other currencies are based on the appropriate cross rates published in the *Asian Wall Street Journal* or the *London Financial Times*.

Foreign exchange certificates (FECs) are issued by the Central Bank of Myanmar through authorized dealers and licensed FEC changers. Authorized dealers may buy FECs from the Central Bank at a discount of 5 percent. FECs are widely used and serve the needs of both visitors and investors in Myanmar. FECs may also be purchased or sold for kyats at a market-determined rate at a new exchange center in Yangon. Holders of FECs may convert them into foreign exchange at a licensed foreign exchange bank; for private individuals, banks collect a 10 percent service charge for these transactions.

An unofficial parallel market for foreign exchange exists. The rates in this market (about K 125 per $1) have been relatively stable in recent months. Holders of FECs may convert them into foreign exchange at a licensed foreign exchange bank; for private individuals, banks collect a 10 percent service charge for these transactions.

There are no taxes or subsidies on purchases or sales of foreign exchange. There are no arrangements for forward cover against exchange rate risk operating in the official or the commercial banking sector.

Administration of Control

Exchange control is administered by the Central Bank in accordance with instructions from the Ministry of Finance and Revenue. A Foreign Exchange Control Board headed by the Deputy Prime Minister allocates foreign exchange for the public sector.

Arrears are maintained with respect to external payments for the debt service of the central Government.

Prescription of Currency

Settlements with member countries of the ACU are made in the currency of the member country through the ACU mechanisms. Payments to other countries may be made in any foreign currency or by crediting kyats to an external account in Myanmar. Receipts must be collected in convertible currencies or to the debit of an external account in Myanmar.

Resident and Nonresident Accounts

Accounts in kyats held by nonresidents are designated nonresident accounts; all debits and credits require prior authorization. Foreign currency accounts of foreign diplomatic missions and international organizations and their home-based personnel may be kept with the Myanma Foreign Trade Bank or the Myanma Investment and Commercial Bank. Other foreign residents may open foreign currency accounts with any bank authorized to deal in foreign exchange. Transfers of funds between these accounts are permitted. Both residents and nonresidents are allowed to purchase FECs with foreign exchange earned from legal sources and may open foreign currency accounts subject to a 10 percent bank charge.

In addition to the use of FECs, the following regulations apply to the operation of foreign currency accounts by residents:

Foreign currency accounts of national firms. Private exporters who are registered with the Ministry of Trade may retain 100 percent of their merchandise export proceeds. Also for border trade, exporters are allowed to retain 100 percent of their earnings. However, 5 percent and 10 percent of proceeds from exports of goods and services and receipts from remittances must be paid as commercial tax and income tax, respectively. Exporters may open foreign currency accounts with their earnings at either the Myanma Foreign Trade Bank, the Myanma Investment and Commercial Bank, or private domestic banks, which are permitted to conduct foreign exchange business. Account holders are allowed to import under import licenses issued by the Ministry of Trade on the basis of letters of credit or on a collection basis.

Foreign currency accounts of national individuals. Foreign currency accounts may be opened in U.S. dollars only by Myanmar nationals who are: (1) returning from abroad after completing their assignments; (2) working abroad with foreign firms under official permits; (3) seamen working with foreign shipping lines under existing regulations; (4) working with the United Nations and its affiliated organizations; (5) service personnel of the Ministry of Foreign Affairs performing their duties with Myanmar embassies abroad; (6) receiving pensions in foreign currency after serving with foreign governments or international organizations; (7) receiving foreign exchange for services rendered to foreign individuals, foreign organizations and firms, or foreign governments; (8) receiving their pay in foreign currency abroad for services rendered as agents to foreign firms; (9) receiving rentals in foreign currency for their tangible and intangible assets; (10) receiving foreign currency from an inheritance; (11) receiving foreign currency in compensation from a foreign firm or insurance company for the death or disability of a family member while serving with a foreign firm; (12) receiving foreign currency in the form of gifts from relatives or friends living abroad; and (13) holding the equivalent of at least $100 in FECs.

With prior approval, account holders may use funds from their accounts to purchase air tickets for family visits abroad and to make payments for personal imports, for examination fees for their children, and for medical treatment abroad. Transfers of balances between accounts are permitted, with prior authorization.

Foreign currency accounts of joint ventures and foreign participants. Under the Union of Myanmar Foreign Investment Law enacted on November 30, 1988, economic organizations formed with permits issued by the Union of Myanmar Investment Commission (MIC) and foreigners employed by these economic organizations are required to open both a foreign currency account and a kyat account. The following may be transferred abroad through a bank with the approval of the Central Bank: (1) foreign currency belonging to the person who brought in foreign capital for investment in Myanmar in accordance with regulations stipulated by the MIC; (2) net profits remaining after all taxes and prescribed funds have been deducted from the annual profits received by the person who brought in foreign capital; and (3) balances of salary and lawful income earned by the foreign person for services performed in the state and remaining after payment of taxes and deduction of living expenses incurred by him or her and family members.

Imports and Import Payments

Import trade may be conducted with any country without restriction, except with countries under UN embargo or with which Myanmar has severed diplomatic relations. There are currently 22 bands of import tariffs, ranging from zero to 500 percent. Import tariffs are assessed on the basis of the official exchange rate. Agricultural implements, raw materials, and other essential imports are taxed at very low rates, while the highest rate is applied to luxury items. There is a long list of exemptions from customs duties, and the Ministry of Finance and Revenue is empowered to grant exemptions on a case-by-case basis.

Certain items, such as opium and other narcotics, playing cards, and gold and silver bullion, may not be imported from any source.

An import program for the public sector is prepared annually as part of the foreign exchange budget drawn up jointly by the Ministry of National Planning and Economic Development and the Ministry of Finance and Revenue. Some public sector imports are made outside the foreign exchange budget with revolving funds. All imports involving use of official foreign exchange are handled by the public sector through the ministries. With a few exceptions, private sector imports require import licenses for each transaction and are largely financed from the importer's foreign currency account. Import licenses may be obtained for priority items (List A), nonpriority items (List B), and "ordinary" items. An importer wishing to import items on List B or ordinary items is generally required to import goods on List A at a value equivalent to 50 percent and 25 percent, respectively, of the values of goods on List B and of ordinary items. On a case-by-case basis, joint ventures with private interest may be granted open general licenses and are exempt from these requirements. Private importers must register at the Ministry of Trade as importers and renew their licenses annually. State economic enterprises may import goods for their own use and for resale with open general licenses, whereas government departments may import only for their own use. Imports by government departments are exempted from prescribed fees but those by the private sector are not. Most imports are effected on an f.o.b. basis, and shipments are made on vessels owned or chartered by the Myanmar Five-Star Shipping Line whenever possible.

All payments for imports not originating from border trade are made through the Myanma Foreign Trade Bank, the Myanma Investment and Commercial Bank, and private domestic banks permitted to conduct foreign exchange business. State economic enterprises obtain foreign exchange directly from the Myanma Foreign Trade Bank, within the approved foreign exchange budget, after receiving endorsement from the respective ministries.

Border imports require permits. Payments for border imports may be effected directly from the proceeds from border exports. Exporters of agricultural, forestry, and fisheries products are encouraged to import up to the equivalent of 25 percent of the export value of selected items that will contribute to the production in these sectors (Ministry of Trade Press Communiqué No. 5/91, dated July 12, 1991).

Myanmar nationals who have opened foreign currency accounts are allowed to make unlimited payments for personal imports with the funds from their accounts. Myanmar nationals working abroad under official permits who have not yet opened foreign currency accounts may make payments on their personal imports out of their accumulated savings of legitimate funds. Myanmar nationals and other travelers may bring in a reasonable amount of personal and other classified goods when they enter the country.

Payments for Invisibles

All payments for invisibles outside the public sector are subject to approval and are considered on a case-by-case basis. Payments for membership fees and tuition abroad and payments for subscriptions to certain foreign periodicals require prior permission from the Central Bank. Family remittances are permitted only for foreign technicians employed under contract by the Government; the limit is one-half of the net salary if the spouse is living abroad and one-third of the net salary if the spouse is living in Myanmar. Outward remittances of insurance premium payments other than for Myanma Insurance are not permitted. The remittance of pension payments to retired government employees is permitted only if the persons concerned have been nonnationals throughout their term of service and are now residing in their native countries. Personal money

order remittances to neighboring countries through post offices are not permitted.

Residents who have been granted an official permit to travel abroad are allowed to exchange $50 from the state's foreign exchange with their own domestic currency and also the equivalent of K 100 in the currency of the country of destination or, if that currency is not available, in U.S. dollar notes.

Nonresidents leaving Myanmar within six months of arriving may take out any balance of foreign currency they brought in with them and may also reconvert the remaining balance of the kyats obtained through conversion of foreign currency, including FECs purchased in excess of the minimum required purchase of $300. The exportation of Myanmar currency is prohibited.

Exports and Export Proceeds

Export trade may be conducted with any country without restriction, except those under UN embargo or with which Myanmar has severed diplomatic relations. Export taxes are levied on a small number of goods at both ad valorem and specific rates: an ad valorem duty rate of 5 percent is levied on oil cakes, pulses and cereals, and raw hides and skins; a specific duty rate of 10 kyats per metric ton is levied on all varieties of rice.

In practice, state agencies responsible for production may export any product in excess of what is needed for domestic consumption. Special permits are required for exports of antiques. The state economic enterprises have a monopoly on the exportation of rice, teak, petroleum and natural gas, pearls, jade, and precious stones and metals. The exportation of these products and other controlled items by foreign or domestic firms in the private sector may be permitted. Rice is exported by the Myanma Agricultural Produce Trading through the Myanma Export-Import Services; private traders and cooperatives are also permitted to export a number of beans and pulses, rattan, flour, and cut flowers under valid export permits issued by the Ministry of Trade. Border trade of certain products, including rice, teak, rubber, petroleum, hides, leather, some beans and pulses, maize, cotton, and groundnuts, is not permitted.

Export proceeds must be obtained in accordance with existing foreign exchange management regulations. An export-retention scheme is in operation, under which 100 percent of foreign exchange proceeds from merchandise exports and 90 percent of proceeds from most invisible exports may be retained by exporters. When exports are made on an f.o.b. basis, buyers are free to choose the carrier, but exports made on a c.i.f. basis must be shipped by the Myanmar Five-Star Shipping Line or on vessels chartered or nominated by it.

Proceeds from Invisibles

Ten percent of exchange receipts from invisibles must be paid as income tax unless the exchange control authorities grant a special waiver. Travelers may bring in foreign currency up to $2,000 or its equivalent without any declaration. Tourists arriving in Myanmar are required to purchase foreign exchange certificates equivalent to a minimum value of $300, but amounts in excess of this minimum may be reconverted into foreign exchange at departure. The importation of Myanmar currency is prohibited.

Myanmar nationals working abroad with permission from the Government are required to pay an income tax at the rate of 10 percent of their gross earnings in foreign exchange. Myanmar seamen serving abroad and Myanmar nationals working abroad under their own arrangements must pay as income tax 10 percent of their gross earnings. Myanmar nationals working abroad in UN organizations are not required to pay income tax. Myanmar nationals working abroad in private organizations are required to transfer to Myanmar as tax 10 percent of their gross earnings in foreign exchange through embassies in their country of residence.

Capital

Under the Union of Myanmar Foreign Investment Law of 1988, the Myanmar Investment Commission is empowered to accept proposals for investment in Myanmar from foreigners for full ownership and under joint venture, with the share of foreign capital representing at least 35 percent of the total capital. To facilitate and promote foreign investment, the commission may grant exemption from customs duties and other internal taxes on machinery and equipment imported during construction of the project, spare parts used in business, and raw materials imported for the first three years of commercial production, as well as exemption from the income tax for a period of up to three consecutive years, including the year when production of goods and services began, or for longer than three years, depending upon the profitability of the enterprise. Furthermore, accelerated depreciation allowances may be granted. Types of economic activity and the sectors open to foreign investment are specified in a detailed positive list.

The Government guarantees that an economic enterprise formed under a permit will not be nationalized during the term of the contract or during an extended term. In accordance with existing rules and regulations, repatriation of profits is allowed through banks after payment of taxes and prescribed funds.

Gold

Residents may hold and trade in gold jewelry, gold coins, and unworked gold in Myanmar. Imports and exports of gold are not allowed for the private sector. Jewelry for personal wear may be brought into Myanmar, subject to customs declaration at the port of arrival. Personal jewelry of prescribed value is permitted to be taken out, subject to the condition that the jewelry will be brought back to the country. No conditions are attached, however, to the taking out of personal jewelry that was declared to customs when it was brought into Myanmar.

Changes During 1995

Exchange Arrangement

December 8. Ten agencies were authorized to trade FECs in exchange for local currency at a new exchange center in Yangon at a market-determined rate.

NAMIBIA

(Position as of December 31, 1995)

Exchange Arrangement

The currency of Namibia is the Namibia Dollar. The Namibia dollar is pegged at par to the South African rand, which is also legal tender. The exchange rates of the Namibia dollar against other currencies are determined on the basis of cross rates of the South African rand against the currencies concerned in international markets. On December 31, 1995, the exchange rate of the Namibia dollar against the U.S. dollar was N$1 per US$0.2742.

Authorized dealers are permitted to conduct spot and forward exchange operations, including forward cover, with residents in any foreign currency in respect of authorized trade and nontrade transactions. Forward exchange contracts may cover the entire period of the outstanding commitments and accruals. Forward cover is also provided to nonresidents, subject to certain limitations. Forward cover is provided in U.S. dollars only and is available to authorized dealers for maturities not exceeding 12 months at a time in the form of swap transactions involving Namibia dollars (South African rand) and U.S. dollars with a margin based on an interest rate differential between the two currencies. Special forward cover at preferential rates is provided in respect of import financing. Gold mining companies and houses may sell forward anticipated receipts of their future gold sales. There are no taxes or subsidies on purchases or sales of foreign exchange.

The financial rand system of the Common Monetary Area (CMA)[1] was abolished, effective March 13, 1995. All CMA financial rand balances have been designated as either "nonresident" accounts in cases where account holders are living outside the CMA or "resident" accounts in cases where balances belong to immigrants. Balances on resident accounts are freely transferable within the CMA, whereas those on nonresident accounts are freely transferable from the CMA.

Exchange Control Territory

Namibia is part of the CMA within which no restrictions are applied to payments. In its relations with countries outside the CMA, Namibia applies exchange controls that are almost identical to those applied by the other CMA members.

Administration of Control

The Bank of Namibia, on behalf of the Ministry of Finance, controls all external currency transactions. Import and export permits, where required, are issued by the Ministry of Trade and Industry. The authorized dealers automatically provide foreign exchange for imports from outside the Southern African Customs Union (SACU)[2] upon presentation of necessary documents. Advance payments for imports require the approval of the Bank of Namibia.

Prescription of Currency

All countries outside the CMA constitute the nonresident area. The rand is legal tender in Namibia and Lesotho but not in Swaziland.

Nonresident Accounts

The rand accounts of nonresidents[3] are divided into nonresident accounts and emigrant blocked accounts. The regulations that apply to these accounts in South Africa also apply in Namibia.

Imports and Import Payments

There are no restrictions on imports originating in any country of the SACU. Imports from countries outside the SACU are usually licensed in conformity with South Africa's import regulations. For purposes of import permit issuance, Schedule IA of the Import Control Regulations of South Africa is currently enforced. These permits are valid for one year, are expressed in value terms, and are valid for imports from any country outside the SACU. At present, about 90 percent of imports require a permit. Namibia has the right to restrict certain imports (through customs duties or quantitative restrictions) from countries outside the SACU, and, under certain conditions, from countries within the SACU. A wide range of imports from countries outside the SACU are subject to a general sales tax of 11 percent (as are locally produced goods) and to surcharges ranging

---

[1]The members of the CMA are Lesotho, Namibia, South Africa, and Swaziland.

[2]The members of the SACU are Botswana, Lesotho, Namibia, South Africa, and Swaziland.

[3]A nonresident is a person (a natural person or a legal entity) whose normal place of residence, domicile, or registration is outside the CMA.

from 7.5 percent on certain foodstuffs to 40 percent on nonessential luxury goods.

Payments for Invisibles

Authorized dealers are empowered to approve trade-related invisible payments without limitation and other invisible payments up to established limits, as follows: (1) annual allowances for tourist travel of N$25,000 for an adult and N$12,500 for a child under 12 years. Basic annual allowances for travel to the neighboring countries of Angola, Botswana, Malawi, Mozambique, Zaïre, Zambia, and Zimbabwe are N$6,000 for an adult and N$3,000 for a child under 12 years; and (2) business travel allowances of not more than N$2,000 a day, with a maximum of N$38,000 a calendar year. To the neighboring countries mentioned above, allowances may not exceed N$900 a day and N$12,000 a year. Residents leaving Namibia for destinations outside the CMA are allowed to take no more than 50 percent of the foreign exchange allowance in the form of foreign banknotes; larger amounts may be granted on presentation of documentary proof of need. There are no prescribed limits on remittances for education and family maintenance, and reasonable amounts are granted on a case-by-case basis.

Exports and Export Proceeds

Most exports are permitted without a license. Permits are required for the exportation of goods in short supply to non-SACU countries. All export proceeds are normally required to be remitted to Namibia and surrendered within six months of shipment or within seven days of the date of accrual.

Proceeds from Invisibles

Proceeds from invisibles must be surrendered within seven days of the date of accrual unless exemption is obtained. Upon entry from countries outside the CMA, residents and nonresidents may bring in a total of N$500 in Namibian banknotes or R 500 in South African banknotes. There are no limitations on the importation of domestic currency from Lesotho and Swaziland.

Capital

All capital transfers to and from destinations outside the CMA in the form of loans are subject to specific approval from the Bank of Namibia. Approval is generally given for borrowing abroad with a maturity of at least six months by domestic entrepreneurs, except for speculative borrowings or consumer credit. Authorized dealers are generally permitted to raise funds abroad in their own names for the financing of Namibia's foreign trade and for other approved purposes. Inward transfers of capital from non-CMA countries for equity investment are freely permitted, whereas applications by residents to retain funds in, or transfer them to, countries outside the CMA for bona fide long-term investments in specific development projects or for the expansion of existing projects owned or controlled by residents are considered on their own merits.

Proceeds from the sale of quoted or unquoted CMA securities, real estate, and other equity investments by nonresidents are freely transferable. Families emigrating to destinations outside the CMA are granted the normal travel (tourist) allowance and are permitted to remit up to N$200,000 (N$100,000 for a single person). Any balance exceeding this limit must be credited to an emigrant blocked account; the balance, including earned income, may be transferred under prescribed conditions. At the time of their arrival, immigrants are required to furnish the exchange control authorities with a complete return of their foreign assets and liabilities. Any foreign assets they transfer to the CMA may, through the same channel, be retransferred abroad within the first five years of their arrival.

Gold

Residents are permitted to purchase, hold, and sell gold coins within the CMA for numismatic and investment purposes only. All exports and imports of gold require the prior approval of the monetary authorities.

Changes During 1995

Exchange Arrangement

March 13. The financial rand system ceased to operate in Namibia following its abolition by South Africa. Foreign investors were free to repatriate the sale proceeds of their investment through normal banking channels.

Payments for Invisibles

June 26. The period prior to departure within which prospective travelers may obtain foreign exchange allowances was extended to 28 days. In addition, the proportion of foreign banknotes available for holiday or business travel was increased to 50 percent.

October 9. The requirement that all exports on credit be covered by compulsory forward cover was revoked.

December 21. Limits were raised on other miscellaneous transactions, such as directors' fees and members' fees to emigrants and nonresidents, membership or affiliation fees, subscriptions, etc.

Capital

August 3. Institutional investors, such as pension funds, insurance companies, and unit trusts were allowed to invest a portion of their assets abroad. Proposals could be submitted to the Exchange Control Authorities allowing such institutions to obtain foreign investment by way of swap arrangements. Such arrangements would allow the exchange for foreign assets with foreign investors of part of their existing assets.

October 19. The requirement of an auditor's certificate for specified companies to transfer dividends to emigrants was abolished.

November 1. The requirement of an auditor's certificate for specified companies to transfer dividends to nonresidents was abolished.

NEPAL

(Position as of December 31, 1995)

Exchange Arrangement

The currency of Nepal is the Nepalese Rupee. The official exchange rate is determined by linking it closely to the Indian rupee (NRe 1.6 per Re 1 at the end of 1995), with cross rates against other currencies determined by commercial banks on the basis of demand and supply. On December 31, 1995, the buying and selling rates for the U.S. dollar, the intervention currency, were NRs 55.75 and NRs 56.25, respectively, per $1. Buying and selling rates are quoted daily for certain other currencies,[1] with quotations based on the buying and selling rates for the U.S. dollar in markets abroad. Convertibility between the Indian rupee and the Nepalese rupee is unrestricted in Nepal, and the Indian rupee may be used to effect all bona fide transactions. Purchases of Indian currency in excess of Rs 10,000 must be documented, and the purpose must be specified. It is possible to obtain forward exchange cover for trade transactions which is provided only by authorized banks.

Nepal accepted the obligations of Article VIII, Sections 2, 3, and 4 of the Fund Agreement on May 30, 1994.

Administration of Control

Payments in convertible currencies may be made without permission, subject to the procedures prescribed by the Nepal Rastra Bank. All exchange transactions must be settled through authorized dealers. Nonbank authorized dealers are licensed to accept foreign currencies only for their services to foreign nationals.

Prescription of Currency

All current transactions with member countries of the Asian Clearing Union (ACU) other than India (i.e., Bangladesh, the Islamic Republic of Iran, Myanmar, Pakistan, and Sri Lanka) must be effected through the ACU. Payments for selected imports from India may be settled in U.S. dollars; other imports and proceeds from exports to India must be settled in Indian rupees. Proceeds from exports to other countries must be received in convertible currencies.

Foreign Currency Accounts

Commercial banks may accept deposits denominated in Australian dollars, Canadian dollars, deutsche mark, French francs, Japanese yen, Netherlands guilders, pounds sterling, Singapore dollars, Swiss francs, and U.S. dollars, and are free to determine the rate of interest paid on deposits. Eligibility for opening such accounts is limited to (1) Nepalese citizens earning foreign exchange from working abroad (except in Bhutan and India) for more than three months; (2) international organizations and foreign nationals; (3) Bhutanese and Indian citizens residing in countries other than Bhutan and India; and (4) exporters who are allowed to deposit up to 100 percent of export earnings in a foreign exchange account to cover trade-related expenses. Current accounts may be opened with a minimum equivalent to $500, and time deposits with a minimum equivalent to $3,000. Nonresidents are permitted to withdraw their deposits at any time and convert them into any convertible currency at the authorized banks.

Nonresident Accounts

Foreign diplomats, foreign nationals working in projects financed with foreign-donated funds under bilateral or multilateral agreements with the Government, and nonresidents may freely open foreign currency accounts with Nepalese banks. Accounts may be maintained in all specified convertible currencies, and balances on these accounts may be freely transferred abroad. Nonresidents who receive or bring into Nepal foreign currencies, which they convert into Nepalese rupees and deposit with a Nepalese bank, may reconvert them for transfer out of the country, subject to the prior approval of the Nepal Rastra Bank.

Imports and Import Payments

Most private sector imports are allowed under open general licenses (OGLs). However, imports of certain items, such as arms, ammunition, wireless transmitters, precious metals, and jewelry (except under baggage rules), require special permission from the Government.

---

[1]Australian dollars, Canadian dollars, deutsche mark, French francs, Indian rupees, Japanese yen, Netherlands guilders, pounds sterling, Singapore dollars, and Swiss francs. In addition, buying rates are quoted for Austrian schillings, Belgian francs, Danish kroner, Hong Kong dollars, Italian lire, Saudi Arabian riyals, and Swedish kronor.

Silver was mostly imported by the Nepal Rastra Bank and sold to silver jewelers and handicraft-exporting industries through the commercial banks. However, since March 1994, imports of silver up to 150 kilograms have been allowed for those who have stayed abroad more than one month and have an official source of foreign exchange earnings.

Nepalese citizens returning from abroad who have spent at least 15 nights out of the country are allowed to bring in goods worth NRs 1,000, free of customs duties and sales taxes. Those who have official sources of foreign exchange earnings and have stayed abroad for more than one month are allowed additional imports with proper documentation.

Payments for Invisibles

Payments for invisibles are not restricted, provided that applications for foreign exchange are supported by documentary proof of need and the amounts are reasonable. Nepalese and Indian currencies may not be exported to countries other than India, and they may be taken to India only by Nepalese and Indian nationals. Foreign banknotes, other than Indian banknotes, may not be taken out by residents without permission. Nonresidents may take out the unchanged amount of any foreign banknotes they bring in; however, nonresidents other than Indian nationals may not take out Nepalese or Indian banknotes. Nepalese travelers and migrant workers are allowed to take out of the country the equivalent of $1,500 a year.

Exports and Export Proceeds

Proceeds from exports must be repatriated within 180 days of receipt, but are not required to be surrendered. Exports valued at more than $1,000 to countries other than India are allowed only against irrevocable letters of credit or advance payments by foreign banks. Exports of items having archaeological and religious importance and certain other exports, including old coins, narcotics, and explosive materials, are prohibited. The re-exportation to India of non-Nepalese goods and the re-exportation to any destination of goods imported from India are prohibited.

The export volume of ready-made garments to the United States is restricted by a quota that increases annually by 6 percent. Import duties paid by exporters on goods from bonded warehouses are refunded. When exporters purchase imports from the bonded warehouses, the duty payable is deposited in an escrow bank account and is released when the garments made from these imports are exported and

the documentation required to verify the use of imports is provided.

Foreign tourists leaving Nepal may take out as souvenirs, without permission, Nepalese goods whose value does not exceed the value of the foreign currency they exchanged in Nepal.

Commercial banks may grant pre-export credits of up to 70 percent of the f.o.b. value of products specified by the Government to all individuals and institutions holding irrevocable letters of credit opened or endorsed by foreign banks that are acceptable to the Nepalese banks. Such credits may be provided for a maximum of three months; this period may be extended without penalty under special circumstances that are beyond the control of the exporter.

Proceeds from Invisibles

Nepalese and Indian currencies may be brought in only from India and only by Nepalese and Indian nationals. Nonresidents other than Indian nationals are not allowed to bring in Nepalese or Indian banknotes. Residents and nonresidents may freely bring in other foreign banknotes but must declare them if the amount exceeds the equivalent of $2,000.

Capital

Repatriation of capital requires prior approval from the Nepal Rastra Bank; approval is automatically granted, provided capital transfers have been cleared by the Industrial Promotion Board. Nepalese citizens, whether they reside in Nepal or not, are prohibited from making any type of investment in foreign countries, except investments specifically exempted by government notice; the exemptions include the purchase and sale of insurance policies abroad, and investments abroad by any banking or financial institution incorporated in Nepal.

All foreign direct investment in Nepal requires prior approval in the form of a guarantee from the Industrial Promotion Board (projects of more than NRs 500 million) and the Department of Industry (projects of less than NRs 500 million). Foreign investors who have obtained an investment guarantee are eligible to make remittances abroad for all or part of the sales proceeds of investments, dividends, interest, or principal repayment; amounts arising from the transfer of technology; and compensation on acquired assets. The Industrial Enterprises Act contains provisions regarding local equity requirements for foreign investment in enterprises. Foreign investment is not permitted in cottage, small-scale, or defense-related industries unless substantial transfers of technology are involved. Foreign investors can hold 100 percent equity in large- and medium-scale industries. Small-scale industries are defined as those with fixed assets valued at up to NRs 10 million; for medium-scale industries, the asset value limit is NRs 50 million, and those with fixed assets in excess of NRs 50 million are considered large-scale industries.

Gold

Residents may freely purchase, hold, and sell gold in any form in Nepal. Imports of gold up to 10 kilograms are allowed for those who have stayed abroad for more than one month and have an official source of foreign earnings.

Changes During 1995

Capital

December 1. The Foreign Investment and Transfer of Technology Act of 1992 was amended. The main amendment is the lifting of the minimum size restriction, except for a negative list of activities. This negative list includes (1) personalized services such as barber and beauty parlor service; (2) retail businesses; and (3) areas of cultural or national interest such as handicrafts, cottage industries, trekking, and travel. In addition, the minimum size of foreign investment required to obtain a residential visa was lowered from $1 million to $10,000. Finally, the withholding tax of 15 percent levied on income generated by management and consultancy fees, and copyrights has now been removed, bringing Nepal in line with practices in neighboring countries.

NETHERLANDS

(Position as of December 31, 1995)

Exchange Arrangement

The currency of the Netherlands is the Netherlands Guilder. The Netherlands participates with Austria, Belgium, Denmark, France, Germany, Ireland, Luxembourg, Portugal, and Spain in the exchange rate and intervention mechanism (ERM) of the European Monetary System (EMS).[1] In accordance with this agreement, the Netherlands maintains the spot exchange rates between the Netherlands guilder and the currencies of the other participants within margins of 15 percent above and below the cross rates based on the central rates expressed in European currency units (ECUs). Under the special bilateral agreement, the spot exchange rate of the Netherlands guilder and the deutsche mark is maintained within a fluctuation band of ±2.25 percent.

The agreement implies that the Netherlands Bank stands ready to buy or sell the currencies of the other participating states in unlimited amounts at specified intervention rates. On December 31, 1995, the rates were as follows:

Specified Intervention Rates Per:	Netherlands Guilders	
	Upper limit	Lower limit
100 Austrian schillings	18.58630	13.79180
100 Belgian or Luxembourg francs	6.34340	4.70454
100 Danish kroner	34.30020	25.43850
100 Deutsche mark	115.23500	110.16750
100 French francs	39.00910	28.93810
1 Irish pound	3.15450	2.33950
100 Portuguese escudos	1.27640	0.94660
100 Spanish pesetas	1.53790	1.14060

The participants in the EMS do not maintain exchange rates for other currencies within fixed limits. On occasion, they can intervene in concert to smooth out fluctuations in exchange rates, the intervention currencies being mainly each other's, the ECU, the Japanese yen, the Swiss franc, and the U.S. dollar.

Banks quote buying and selling rates for all major foreign currencies. On December 31, 1995, the middle rate for the U.S. dollar was f. 1.6044 per $1. There are no taxes or subsidies on purchases or sales of foreign exchange.

Residents and nonresidents are freely permitted to buy and sell convertible and nonconvertible currencies, both spot and forward, at negotiated rates. Forward exchange contracts are not limited as to delivery period, nor is an underlying trade transaction required. Residents and nonresidents are free to hold Netherlands guilder and foreign currency accounts in the Netherlands and abroad.

The Kingdom of the Netherlands accepted the obligations of Article VIII, Sections 2, 3, and 4 of the Fund Agreement on February 15, 1961.

Administration of Control

There are no exchange controls, except for the reporting requirements (in accordance with the External Financial Relations Act of 1994). Import and export licensing, including transit trade,[2] is handled by the Central Import-Export Agency and the delegated offices, under directives from the Directorate-General for Foreign Economic Relations of the Ministry of Economic Affairs. Residents are generally required to supply information on their payments to and receipts from nonresidents to the Netherlands Bank either through credit institutions or other providers of financial services who act as intermediaries, or directly in cases where residents do not use the services of the financial institutions within the scope of the regulations based on the External Financial Relations Act of 1994 (see section on Capital, below). To facilitate the compilation of the balance of payments, residents are required to indicate on reporting forms, all payments to and receipts from nonresidents exceeding f. 25,000 or its equivalent in foreign currencies, the nature of the underlying transaction, as well as the currency and amount paid or received. Separate regulations govern the reporting of settlements where no transfer of money is involved.

Residents are free to open and maintain bank accounts abroad and to maintain current accounts abroad for the purpose of settlements. Such accounts must be declared to the Netherlands Bank, and deposits into them must be reported to the bank in accordance with relevant regulations.

---

[1]Austria became a member of the European Union on January 1, 1995, and joined the ERM of the EMS on January 9, 1995.

[2]The only transit trade transactions still subject to specific license are purchases and sales of strategic goods.

In compliance with the relevant UN Security Council resolutions, certain restrictions are imposed on financial transactions with Iraq, the Libyan Arab Jamahiriya, and areas of Bosnia and Herzegovina that are under the control of Bosnian Serb forces.

Prescription of Currency

In effecting payments to nonresidents or collecting receipts from them, residents may use guilders or any foreign currency. Payments in any foreign currency between residents may be made freely. There are no bilateral payments agreements in force. Nonresidents are free to open and maintain nonresident accounts with authorized banks in the Netherlands in guilders or in any foreign currency and to effect payments to, or collect receipts from, residents. All payments or receipts are freely permitted, as are transfers of balances to and from other nonresident accounts.

Imports and Import Payments

Imports from Angola, Iraq, and areas of Bosnia and Herzegovina under the control of Bosnian Serb forces are prohibited.

Import licenses are required for imports originating in Hong Kong, Japan, and state trading countries, (i.e., the People's Republic of China, the Democratic People's Republic of Korea, and Vietnam) as well as for the importation of goods of unknown origin. In addition, import licenses are required for a limited number of products, mainly those of the agricultural, steel, and textile sectors. Except for imports of textiles originating in the Far East and in state trading countries, most imports that require an import license are free from quantitative restriction. Most imports from Eastern European countries have been formally liberalized.

Imports from non-European Union (EU) countries of most products covered by the Common Agricultural Policy of the EU are subject to import levies that have replaced all previous barriers to imports; common EU regulations are also applied to imports of most other agricultural and livestock products from non-EU countries.

Payments for imports may be made freely, provided that the method of payment conforms to the relevant exchange control regulations (i.e., transfers are properly reported).

Payments for Invisibles

Payments abroad for invisibles are permitted freely. Residents may take out any amount in foreign and domestic banknotes and coins or documents of value. Payments for interest, dividends, and contractual amortization due to nonresidents are permitted freely.

Nonresidents may export all unused documents of value for travel purposes, as well as foreign and Netherlands banknotes and coins that they have imported or obtained in the Netherlands by drawing on their accounts or by exchanging other currencies.

Exports and Export Proceeds

Exports to Angola, Iraq, and areas of Bosnia and Herzegovina under the control of Bosnian Serb forces are prohibited. Certain exports to the Libyan Arab Jamahiriya are also prohibited.

Export licenses are required for only a few commodities, mostly of a strategic character; for some agricultural products; and for iron and steel scrap and related products.

Residents may freely grant credit in respect of nonprohibited exports. There is no repatriation or surrender requirement for export proceeds.

Proceeds from Invisibles

There are no requirements attached to receipts by residents from current invisibles. Nonresidents may bring into the Netherlands for travel purposes any amount of foreign banknotes and documents of value; these may be used for travel expenses in the Netherlands.

Capital

Inward and outward capital transfers by residents and nonresidents are not restricted, except that they are subject to reporting requirements based on the External Financial Relations Act of 1994.

External capital transactions are unrestricted. For direct investment in the form of capital participation (inward and outward), no license is required. Neither short-term lending (for less than two years) nor long-term lending to nonresidents (whether affiliated companies or others) requires a license.

Transactions between residents and nonresidents in all stocks and bonds listed on the Amsterdam Stock Exchange take place at official market exchange rates and are unrestricted. Residents may freely purchase officially listed securities abroad. Placement with residents of unlisted foreign debentures denominated in guilders (such as foreign Euroguilder notes) and transactions in unlisted stocks are free of license. Nonresidents may have their securities, domestic or foreign, exported to them; securities held in the Netherlands are not subject to deposit.

Nonresidents may freely purchase real estate in the Netherlands for personal use or investment, and residents may freely purchase real estate abroad. Extension of payment and mortgage borrowing from nonresidents is free of license.

Gifts and donations to nonresidents are free. Emigrants may export any amount in foreign and domestic currency. They acquire nonresident status upon leaving the Netherlands and may have their total assets in the Netherlands remitted to them upon departure. Nonresidents inheriting from estates in the Netherlands may have the proceeds transferred to them freely.

There are no restrictions on commercial banks' spot external positions for foreign exchange control reasons. However, for prudential reasons, limits are imposed on banks' total position in foreign currency and precious metals. Banks are required to report to the Netherlands Bank their position in each foreign currency and precious metal (spot, forward, and option positions) at the end of each month. Authorized banks may freely extend foreign currency and guilder loans to nonresidents. The banks' freedom to accept deposits from nonresidents and to borrow abroad is unrestricted.

All capital transfers by residents must be reported to the Netherlands Bank in accordance with the External Financial Act of 1994. Total amounts of security transactions must be reported periodically by securities brokers and authorized banks or, if transactions take place through a foreign bank account, by the resident parties concerned.

Gold

Neither the Netherlands Bank nor any government agency imports or markets gold for industrial use. Banks and nonbank residents may freely purchase, hold, and sell gold (fine gold, gold coins, and gold alloys) in the Netherlands or abroad. Imports and exports of gold do not require exchange licenses or import and export licenses. There is a free gold market in Amsterdam. Except for transactions of the Netherlands Bank, transfers of gold in bars and other elementary forms are subject to a value-added tax of 6 percent, as are domestic sales of gold coins. All other gold transactions are taxed at the standard value-added tax rate of 17.5 percent. Commercial imports of gold jewelry and of articles containing minor quantities of gold, such as watches, require import licenses only when they originate in Hong Kong, Japan, or state trading countries.

Changes During 1995

No significant changes occurred in the exchange and trade system.

(See Appendix for a summary of trade measures introduced and eliminated on an EU-wide basis during 1995.)

NETHERLANDS ANTILLES[1]

(Position as of December 31, 1995)

Exchange Arrangement

The currency of the Netherlands Antilles is the Netherlands Antillean Guilder, which is pegged to the U.S. dollar, the intervention currency, at NA f. 1.7900 per $1. The official buying rates for the U.S. dollar on December 31, 1995 were NA f. 1.77 per $1 for banknotes and NA f. 1.78 per $1 for drafts, checks, and transfers. The official selling rate was NA f. 1.80 per $1. Official buying and selling rates for certain other currencies[2] are set daily on the basis of rates for the U.S. dollar abroad. A foreign exchange tax of 1.3 percent is levied on payments made by residents to nonresidents, with international companies and pension funds exempted. Purchases of foreign exchange by resident companies with nonresident status for exchange control purposes are exempt from the exchange tax. There are no arrangements for forward cover against exchange rate risk in the official or the commercial banking sector.

Administration of Control

The central bank issues exchange licenses, where required. The Department of Finance issues import licenses, where required. The central bank permits the commercial banks to provide foreign exchange for almost all current transactions without prior approval.

Prescription of Currency

Payments may be made in any currency except the legal tender of the Netherlands Antilles. Receipts may be accepted in any convertible currency except the legal tender of the Netherlands Antilles. All payments made by residents to nonresidents and receipts through authorized banks, as well as through banks abroad, must be reported to the central bank for the compilation of the balance of payments.

Nonresident Accounts

Nonresidents may freely open nonresident accounts in any foreign currency. Nonresidents are permitted to hold nonresident accounts with authorized banks (positive balances) in Netherlands Antillean guilders. Balances in such accounts may not exceed NA f. 200,000 without the approval of the central bank.

Imports and Import Payments

Payments for imports may be made freely. Imports whose delivery dates exceed their payment dates by more than 12 months must be reported to the central bank. The importation of 42 items for which there are locally produced substitutes is subject to tariffs ranging from 25 percent to 90 percent. Certain commodities are subject to import surcharges in Bonaire and Curaçao.

Payments for Invisibles

All types of current invisible payments and remittances may be made freely. A license is required if the delivery and payment dates are more than one year apart; the central bank must receive notification.

Nonresidents may take with them on departure any foreign currency that they brought in. The exportation of Netherlands Antillean banknotes is prohibited, except for traveling purposes. Transfers of profits and dividends are allowed by the central bank upon application.

Exports and Export Proceeds

Exports require no licenses. Export proceeds must be repatriated but need not be surrendered. If export proceeds are not received within 12 months of shipment, the delay must be reported to the central bank.

Proceeds from Invisibles

Residents are not required to surrender invisible proceeds. Travelers may bring in with them any amount of checks, traveler's checks, or banknotes denominated in foreign currency.

Capital

Foreign investments and transfers of loans to residents in the Netherlands Antilles require licenses, which are normally granted.

---

[1]The Netherlands Antilles is a nonmetropolitan territory, in respect of which the Kingdom of the Netherlands has accepted the Fund's Articles of Agreement. On January 1, 1986, the island of Aruba, formerly a part of the Netherlands Antilles, became a separate nonmetropolitan territory within the Kingdom of the Netherlands.

[2]Aruban florins, Canadian dollars, deutsche mark, European currency units, French francs, Italian lire, Japanese yen, Netherlands guilders, pounds sterling, Suriname guilders, and Swiss francs. All currencies other than the Netherlands Antillean guilder are considered foreign currencies.

Outward flows of resident-owned capital are subject to control. Investments by residents in real estate abroad, as well as capital loans to nonresidents, require a license. Investment and disinvestment by nonresidents in real estate in the Netherlands Antilles do not require a license. Investment by residents in officially listed foreign securities (and in mutual funds whose shares are officially quoted) is permitted free of license up to NA f. 100,000 per year. Reinvestment of proceeds from the sale of securities is also allowed.

Resident individuals are allowed to hold foreign bank accounts without a special license. Transfers from a local bank account to these foreign accounts are allowed up to NA f. 10,000 per quarter.

Authorized banks' overall position with nonresidents is subject to limits set by the central bank and must always be positive and in currencies considered "freely usable," as defined under Article XXX (f) of the Fund's Articles of Agreement, and/or in Netherlands guilders.

Gold

Residents may hold and acquire gold coins in the Netherlands Antilles. Authorized banks may freely negotiate gold coins among themselves and with other residents. Imports and exports of gold do not require a special license.

Changes During 1995

No significant changes occurred in the exchange and trade system.

NEW ZEALAND

(Position as of January 31, 1996)

Exchange Arrangement

The currency of New Zealand is the New Zealand Dollar, the external value of which is determined by demand and supply conditions in the exchange market. The Reserve Bank of New Zealand, however, retains discretionary power to intervene in the foreign exchange market and may signal its desired exchange rate range. Foreign exchange dealers are free to adjust exchange rate quotations in response to market conditions throughout each business day. On December 31, 1995, the closing buying and selling rates for the U.S. dollar were US$ 0.6515 and US$ 0.6520, respectively, per $NZ1. There are no taxes or subsidies on purchases or sales of foreign exchange.

Financial institutions are permitted to conclude with their customers forward exchange contracts to buy or sell foreign currencies at market-determined rates in exchange for New Zealand dollars, irrespective of the source of the funds.

New Zealand accepted the obligations of Article VIII, Sections 2, 3, and 4 of the Fund Agreement on August 5, 1982.

Administration of Control

Receipts and remittances of foreign exchange are free from control since February 1990. The Reserve Bank of New Zealand, however, requires registered banks to publicly disclose, on a quarterly basis, foreign exposure levels for prudential supervision purposes. The only remaining requirements are for purposes of statistical information to assist Statistics of New Zealand.

Prohibitions and restrictions are imposed on the trade of certain products, principally for reasons of human/plant/animal health considerations. Most of the restrictions are conditional.

The Overseas Investment Commission administers the regulations governing foreign direct investment in New Zealand.

In accordance with the Fund's Executive Board Decision No. 144-(52/51) adopted on August 14, 1952, New Zealand notified the Fund on September 6, 1990 that, in compliance with UN Security Council Resolution No. 661 (1990), certain restrictions had been imposed on the making of payments and transfers for current international transactions in respect of Iraq, and similarly on September 30, 1992, in respect of the Federal Republic of Yugo-slavia (Serbia/Montenegro) in compliance with UN Security Council Resolution No. 757 (1992). Since December 3, 1993, and December 9, 1994, certain restrictions on the making of payments and transfers for current international transactions pursuant to the UN Security Council resolutions have been imposed with respect to the Libyan Arab Jamahiriya and Bosnia and Herzegovina, respectively.

Prescription of Currency

Payments to and from residents of countries other than New Zealand may be made or received in any foreign currency,[1] as may payments to and from New Zealand currency accounts held with banks in New Zealand by banks not domiciled in New Zealand.

Nonresident Accounts

Nonresidents may maintain and operate accounts without formality and may repatriate funds without restrictions. Overseas banks' accounts in New Zealand may be used to settle transactions with other countries.

Imports and Import Payments

Most tariffs on industrial products have been reduced by approximately one-half over the period since July 1988. The only tariffs over 20 percent apply to motor vehicles, tires and other motor vehicle components, and certain other products (including textiles, and clothing), footwear, and carpets. Most tariffs are ad valorem, but specific tariffs apply to some products (e.g., clothing). Import prohibitions and restrictions affect some 70 products or classes of products, primarily plants, animals, and products considered dangerous to human health or not in the public interest.

Under the terms of the Australia-New Zealand Closer Economic Relations and Trade Agreement (ANZCERTA) and the South Pacific Regional Trade and Economic Cooperation Agreement (SPARTECA),[2] imports of qualifying goods enter duty-free from Australia and the SPARTECA countries. In addition,

---

[1]Foreign currencies are defined as all currencies other than New Zealand currency.

[2]The islands under this arrangement constitute the South Pacific Forum (in addition to Australia and New Zealand), Cook Islands, Fiji, Kiribati, Nauru, Niue, Papua New Guinea, Solomon Islands, Tonga, Tuvalu, Vanuatu, and Western Samoa.

under the ANZCERTA, antidumping remedies have been replaced by domestic laws regulating trade practices.

Less comprehensive preferential trade arrangements affect specified imports from Canada, Malaysia, and the United Kingdom.

Eligible imports from developing countries that have not graduated beyond a specified threshold are accorded tariff preferences under the Generalized System of Preferences (GSP), except imports of clothing, footwear, and motor vehicles. In most cases, these preferential rates are 80 percent of the normal tariff rates; in no case is the margin of preference less for developing countries. A developing country with a per capita GNP equal to or greater than 70 percent of New Zealand's loses its preferential status under the criterion of "country graduation," and a developing country loses its preference with respect to specific tariff items when minimum market share exceeds a minimum value under the criterion of "product graduation."

In addition, duty-free access is granted to most imports from 36 countries classified by the United Nations as "least developed."

Payments for Invisibles

Payments for invisibles are unrestricted, except for transactions involving nationals of Iraq and the Federal Republic of Yugoslavia (Serbia/Montenegro), although there is a reporting requirement for statistical purposes.

The ANZCERTA also provides a framework for the liberalization of trade in services between Australia and New Zealand subject to the foreign investment policies of both countries. It provides for free trade in services based on national treatment. All services are covered except for those on a negative list prepared by each government; the list includes certain aspects of telecommunications, aviation, coastal shipping, and postal services; Australia's list also includes radio and television broadcasting, insurance, and banking.

Exports and Export Proceeds

Export earnings (including foreign currency earned for performing services in New Zealand for foreign nationals) need not be returned through the banking system. Certain items classified as strategic goods may be exported only when specific requirements have been met and an export permit has been issued.

Many of New Zealand's exports are currently restricted by quotas and other quantitative restrictions imposed by its principal trading partners. For example, exports of lamb and butter to the European Union and exports of beef and dairy products to the United States are subject to either quotas or voluntary export restraints.

Proceeds from Invisibles

Remuneration for services provided (or to be provided) in New Zealand, by New Zealand residents (including corporate bodies ordinarily resident in New Zealand), and on behalf of overseas residents as well as interest and dividends earned overseas from portfolio investment, do not have to be repatriated. The ANZCERTA provides for liberalization of trade in services rendered by New Zealand residents in Australia, subject to certain conditions (as noted in the section on Payments for Invisibles, above).

The disposal overseas by New Zealand residents of foreign income from other invisibles, such as interest and dividends, is permitted. Travelers may bring into the country unlimited amounts of foreign and domestic banknotes and coins.

Capital

In general, approval is not required in respect of capital receipts, although overseas entities seeking to establish themselves in New Zealand must, in some cases, obtain the approval of the Overseas Investment Commission (OIC). Nonresident persons who are not New Zealand citizens or companies wishing to make a direct investment in a New Zealand company by purchasing or exchanging shares are required to obtain the consent of the OIC in respect of any proposed offer for such shares whenever the investment would confer on the offerer the beneficial entitlement of 25 percent or more of the voting power at any general meeting. However, if the consideration and gross assets of the offeree company are less than $NZ 10 million, the company is exempt from this requirement. The $NZ 10 million level also triggers the need for OIC approval when a foreign entity wishes to acquire the assets of a New Zealand company or establish a New Zealand subsidiary or branch. More restrictive rules apply to any land purchase involving offshore islands, or worth more than $10 million and other specific land purchases involving offshore islands, reserves, conservation land, historic areas, foreshore, and lakes. The consent of the OIC is required for such purchases regardless of the value involved.

Gold

Residents may hold and acquire gold coins in New Zealand without restriction. There are no restrictions or licensing requirements on the importation and exportation of gold.

Changes During 1995

No significant changes occurred in the exchange and trade system.

Changes During 1996

Capital

January 16. The provision of the Overseas Investment Amendment Act, 1995 came into effect.

NICARAGUA

(Position as of January 31, 1996)

Exchange Arrangement

The currency of Nicaragua is the Córdoba. The Central Bank unified the exchange market effective January 1, 1996, thereby allowing the central Government and financial institutions to freely undertake purchases or sales of foreign exchange with the Central Bank, and permitting financial institutions and exchange houses to carry out transactions for foreign exchange with the private sector. Up until December 31, 1995, the exchange rate system consisted of two rates: an official rate, which is pegged to the U.S. dollar, is devalued daily at an annual rate of 12 percent; and a free exchange rate, which is determined by transactions of commercial banks and exchange houses. In addition, there was an unrecognized parallel market. Official receipts and payments were transacted in the official market, while the remaining transactions took place in the free market. On December 31, 1995, the buying and selling rates in the official market were C$7.9561 and C$8.0400, respectively per US$1, and the buying and selling rates in the free market were C$7.9980 and C$8.1243, respectively, per US$1. The Central Bank continues to set the exchange rate on its foreign exchange transactions.

There are no arrangements for forward cover against exchange rate risk operating in the official or the commercial banking sector. Foreign-currency-denominated accounts and córdoba accounts with exchange guarantee (maintenance of value) contracts may be opened with commercial banks. Banks may also make loans denominated in foreign currency or in local currency with exchange guarantees. The Central Bank of Nicaragua charges a commission of 1 percent on sales of foreign exchange.

Exporters benefiting from tax incentives must deposit their proceeds at an account at commercial banks. Foreign investors must surrender foreign exchange from new investments or additions to capital to the Central Bank through commercial banks.

Nicaragua accepted the obligations of Article VIII, Sections 2, 3, and 4 of the Fund Agreement on July 30, 1964.

Administration of Control

The exchange control system is administered by the Central Bank, which has authorized commercial banks and exchange houses to make foreign exchange transactions. Some transactions not eligible for official foreign exchange may be effected through an authorized foreign currency deposit account or with currencies acquired from exchange houses.

Arrears are maintained with respect to external payments.

Prescription of Currency

There is no prescription of currency.

Imports and Import Payments

All importers must submit an "import declaration" form either to commercial banks or to Customs in case they are using their own resources. Some import payments are made with sight drafts, but almost all are made through letters of credit.

Imports are subject to a temporary import tariff (applied to a list of 742 items), a stamp tax, both of which are applied to all goods independent of their origin, and to the Central American Common Tariff.

Payments for Invisibles

Payments for invisibles related to imports are effected in the free market.

Payments for other invisibles, such as travel, educational expenses, family maintenance, and medical expenses, take place through the free market.

Exports and Export Proceeds

All exports are free, requiring only registration (Registro Unico de Exportación) with the Central Bank. Export licenses are not required for the exportation of traditional or nontraditional products. Exporters benefiting from tax incentives must deposit their foreign exchange proceeds in an account at commercial banks, but may mobilize it freely afterward.

Proceeds from Invisibles

Proceeds from invisibles may be retained or sold in the free market. There is no limit on the amount of foreign exchange persons arriving in Nicaragua from abroad may bring in and use locally.

Capital

Capital transactions are not restricted.

Gold

The Nicaraguan Mining Institute manages the country's gold production. The Central Bank reserves the right to purchase up to 25 percent of gold production of private mines, at prices prevailing in international prices. However, the mines may export gold freely if the Central Bank does not purchase this amount during a certain period. Commemorative gold coins were issued in 1967, 1975, and 1980. Natural and juridical persons may trade gold coins for numismatic purposes only.

Changes During 1995

Exchange Arrangement

February 28. Restrictions on the making of payments through the official market were lifted for education expenses.

May 23. Restrictions on the making of payments through the official market were lifted for health and travel expenses.

Imports and Import Payments

June 28. The Central American Common Tariff for imports of capital goods was lowered to 1 percent from 5 percent.

July 1. The maximum tariff rate was reduced to 37 percent, by reducing the maximum temporary tariff to 12 percent.

Changes During 1996

Exchange Arrangement

January 1. The Monetary Board of the Central Bank unified the exchange market, thereby eliminating the compulsory sale of foreign exchange by exporters to the Central Bank, allowing the central Government and financial institutions to freely undertake purchase or sale of foreign exchange with the Central Bank, and permitting financial institutions and exchange houses to carry out foreign exchange transactions with the private sector. The Central Bank would continue to set the exchange rate for its foreign exchange transactions.

NIGER

(Position as of June 30, 1996)

Exchange Arrangement

The currency of Niger is the CFA Franc,[1] which is pegged to the French franc, the intervention currency, at the fixed rate of CFAF 1 per F 0.01. The official buying and selling rates are CFAF 100 per F 1. Exchange rates for other currencies are derived from the rate for the currency concerned in the Paris exchange market and the fixed rate between the French franc and the CFA franc. Transfers by banks to countries outside the West African Economic and Monetary Union (WAEMU)[2] are subject to an exchange commission of 2.5 per thousand of the amount of the transfer plus a lump sum commission freely determined by the banks. All revenue from commissions charged by the banks on transfers to countries outside the WAEMU is transferred to the Treasury. There are no taxes or subsidies on purchases or sales of foreign exchange.

With the exception of measures relating to gold transactions, the domiciliation of exports, and the repatriation of export proceeds, Niger's exchange controls do not apply to France (and its overseas departments and territories); Monaco; and all other countries whose bank of issue is linked with the French Treasury by an Operations Account (the West African States and Burkina Faso, Cameroon, Central African Republic, Chad, Comoros, Congo, Equatorial Guinea, and Gabon). Hence, all payments to these countries may be made freely. All other countries are considered foreign countries.

The contracting of forward exchange cover requires prior authorization from the Financial Relations Directorate of the Ministry of Finance and Planning. Such cover may be provided for payments for permitted imports and for the currency stipulated in the commercial contract. The maturity period must not exceed one or three months, depending on the nature of the goods involved, and is not renewable. There is no official scheme for currency swaps or guaranteed exchange rates for external debt servicing.

Arrears are maintained with respect to external payments.

---

[1]The CFA franc is issued by the Central Bank of West African States (BCEAO) and is the common currency in Benin, Burkina Faso, Côte d'Ivoire, Mali, Niger, Senegal, and Togo.

[2]The treaty creating the WAEMU came into effect on August 1, 1994. It coexists presently with the treaty instituting the West African Monetary Union (WAMU).

Niger accepted the obligations of Article VIII, Sections 2, 3, and 4 of the Fund Agreement on June 1, 1996.

Administration of Control

Exchange control is administered by the Financial Relations Directorate. The BCEAO is authorized to collect, either directly or through the banks, financial institutions, the Postal Administration, and notaries public, any information necessary to compile balance of payments statistics. All exchange transactions relating to foreign countries must be made through the BCEAO, the Postal Administration, and authorized banks.

Prescription of Currency

Since Niger has an Operations Account with the French Treasury, settlements with France (as defined above), Monaco, and the countries linked with the French Treasury by Operations Accounts are made in CFA francs, French francs, or the currency of any Operations Account country. Current payments to or from The Gambia, Ghana, Guinea, Guinea-Bissau, Liberia, Mauritania, Nigeria, and Sierra Leone are normally made through the West African Clearing House. Settlements with all other countries are usually effected either in foreign currencies through correspondent banks in France or in French francs through foreign accounts in francs.

Nonresident Accounts

Nonresident accounts are subject to strict regulations, which stipulate authorized debit and credit operations. These accounts may not be credited with banknotes of the BCEAO, the Bank of France, or any other bank of issue with an Operations Account with the French Treasury.

Imports and Import Payments

There are no import restrictions or prohibitions, including temporary measures affecting imports of certain products, or licensing requirements for imports including imports in transit. A customs tariff regime, introduced in October 1994, consists of three categories of products with ad valorem rates of 5 percent, 10 percent, and 30 percent.

All transactions with foreign countries on imports with a c.i.f. value exceeding CFAF 25,000 at the border must be domiciled with an authorized bank.

Foreign exchange may not be purchased before the payment due date if the goods have already been imported, or until eight days before the shipment date if the goods are covered by documentary credit.

Payments for Invisibles

Payments for invisibles to France (as defined above), Monaco, and countries linked with the French Treasury by an Operations Account are permitted freely; those to other countries are subject to the approval of the Monetary and Financial Relations Directorate (External Finance Unit), which for certain transactions has delegated its powers to authorized banks. Payments for invisibles related to trade are permitted freely. Transfers of income accruing to nonresidents in the form of profits, dividends, and royalties are also permitted freely once the basic transaction has been approved. Foreigners working in Niger may transfer abroad savings from their salaries with the prior approval of the Monetary and Financial Relations Directorate, but these transfers are normally limited to 70 percent of net pay. Larger transfers are permitted, however, if supported by appropriate documentary evidence.

Residents traveling for tourist or business purposes to countries in the franc zone that are not members of the WAEMU are allowed to take out the equivalent of up to CFAF 2 million in banknotes other than CFA franc banknotes; amounts in excess of this limit may be taken out in means of payment other than banknotes. The allowances for travel to countries outside the franc zone are subject to the following regulations: (1) for tourist travel, the equivalent of CFAF 500,000 without limit on the number of trips or differentiation by the age of the traveler; (2) for business travel, the equivalent of CFAF 75,000 a day for up to one month, corresponding to a maximum of CFAF 2.25 million (business travel allowances may be combined with tourist allowances); (3) allowances in excess of these limits are subject to the authorization of the Ministry of Finance or, by delegation, the BCEAO; and (4) credit cards, which must be issued by resident financial intermediaries and specifically authorized by the Minister of Finance, may be used up to the ceilings indicated above for tourist and business travel. Returning resident travelers are required to declare all means of payment in their possession upon arrival at customs and surrender within eight days all means of payment exceeding the equivalent of CFAF 25,000. All resident travelers proceeding to countries that are not members of the WAEMU must declare in writing all means of payment at their disposal at the time of departure. The re-exportation by nonresident travelers of means of payment other than banknotes issued abroad and registered in the name of the nonresident traveler is not restricted, subject to documentation that these means of payment were purchased with funds drawn from a foreign account in CFA francs or with other foreign exchange. The re-exportation of foreign banknotes is allowed up to the equivalent of CFAF 250,000; the re-exportation of foreign banknotes above these ceilings requires documentation demonstrating either the importation of foreign banknotes or their purchase against other means of payment registered in the name of the traveler, or through the use of nonresident deposits held in local banks.

Exports and Export Proceeds

Exports of certain products (livestock, leather and skins, onions, rice, and sugar) are subject to submission of a statistic registration certificate (FES) for statistical compilation and monitoring purposes. Exports to France (as defined above) and the Operations Account countries may be made freely. Exports of domestic products and imported commodities to other countries require an exchange commitment. In principle, the due date of payment for exports to foreign countries must not be later than 180 days after the goods arrive at their destination. Proceeds from exports must be repatriated and surrendered through an authorized intermediary bank within 15 days of the date of receipt, or at the latest within 15 days of the date on which the payment is due. All exports exceeding a value of CFAF 500,000 must be domiciled with an authorized bank.

Proceeds from Invisibles

Proceeds from transactions in invisibles with France (as defined above), Monaco, and the other countries linked with the French Treasury by Operations Accounts may be retained. All amounts due from residents of other countries for services and all income earned in those countries from foreign assets must be collected and surrendered within two months of the due date or date of receipt. Resident and nonresident travelers may import any amount of banknotes and coins issued by the BCEAO, the Bank of France, or a bank of issue maintaining an Operations Account with the French Treasury, as well as any amount of foreign banknotes and coins (except gold coins). Residents must surrender within eight days of entry any foreign currency in excess of the equivalent of CFAF 25,000.

Capital

Capital transactions between Niger and France (as defined above), Monaco, and the other countries linked with the French Treasury by Operations Accounts are free of exchange control; capital transfers to all other countries require approval from the exchange control authority and are restricted, but capital receipts from such countries are permitted freely.

Special controls (additional to any exchange control requirements that may apply) are maintained over borrowing abroad; inward and outward investment; and the issuing, advertising, or offering for sale of foreign securities in Niger. Such operations require prior authorization from the Minister of Finance, except in the case of operations in connection with loans backed by a guarantee from the Nigerien Government, and with shares that are identical to, or may be substituted for, securities whose issue or sale in Niger has previously been authorized. With the exception of controls over foreign securities, these measures do not apply to relations with France (as defined above), Monaco, member countries of the WAEMU, and other countries linked with the French Treasury by Operations Accounts. Special controls are also maintained over the soliciting of funds for deposit with foreign private persons and foreign firms and institutions and over publicity aimed at placing funds abroad or at subscribing to real estate development operations abroad. These special controls also apply to France (as defined above), Monaco, and countries linked with the French Treasury by Operations Accounts. All the special provisions described in this paragraph apply only to transactions and not to associated payments or collections.

All investments abroad by residents of Niger require prior authorization from the Minister of Finance;[3] 75 percent of the value must be financed from borrowing abroad. Foreign direct investments in Niger[4] must be declared to the Minister of Finance before they are made. Direct investments are those implying control of a company or an enterprise; however, the acquisition of an interest in a company not exceeding 20 percent of its capital is not considered direct investment. The Minister has a period of two months from receipt of the declaration in which to request postponement of the project. The full or partial liquidation of either type of investment also requires prior declaration to the Minister. Both the making and the liquidation of Nigerien investments abroad or foreign investments in Niger must be

reported to the Minister of Finance and the BCEAO within 20 days of each operation. Lending abroad is also subject to prior authorization from the Minister of Finance.

Borrowing by residents from nonresidents requires prior declaration to the Minister of Finance when the outstanding amount for any one borrower exceeds CFAF 30 million. The repayment of a foreign loan constituting a direct investment is subject to the same formalities as the liquidation of a direct investment; the repayment of other loans requires authorization only if the loans were subject to prior authorization.

Foreign investments in Niger may be granted certain guarantees and facilities under the Investment Code of July 31, 1988, and its amendments. The facilities granted under the previous Investment Code have been maintained. In addition, the new Investment Code provides for regular or privileged treatment. Regular treatment provides assurances, for both new and existing enterprises, with respect to indemnities in the event of expropriation and concerning nondiscrimination between Nigerien nationals and foreign nationals; tax exemptions may be granted for new investments. Privileged treatment is reserved for enterprises deemed to be of special importance to national economic development and falling within specified categories of industrial activities. Such treatment may be accorded under two different regimes—the approval regime and the agreement regime.

Gold

Residents are free to hold, acquire, and dispose of gold in any form in Niger. Imports and exports of gold from or to any other country require prior authorization from the Minister of Finance. Exempt from this requirement are (1) imports and exports by or on behalf of the Treasury or the BCEAO; (2) imports and exports of manufactured articles containing a minor quantity of gold (such as gold-filled or gold-plated articles); and (3) articles of gold up to a combined weight of 500 grams when carried by a traveler. Both licensed and exempt imports of gold are subject to customs declaration.

Changes During 1995

No significant changes occurred in the exchange and trade system.

Changes During 1996

Exchange Arrangement

June 1. Niger accepted the obligations of Article VIII, Sections 2, 3, and 4 of the Fund Agreement.

---

[3]Including those made through foreign companies directly or indirectly controlled by persons in Niger and those made by branches or subsidiaries abroad of companies in Niger.

[4]Including those made by companies in Niger that are directly or indirectly under foreign control and those made by branches or subsidiaries of foreign companies in Niger.

NIGERIA

(Position as of December 31, 1995)

Exchange Arrangement

The currency of Nigeria is the Nigerian Naira. The official exchange rate is pegged to the U.S. dollar, the intervention currency, at the rate of ₦22 per $1, and it is applied to official government transactions. All other transactions take place at market-determined exchange rates in an Autonomous Foreign Exchange Market (AFEM), which was established by the Foreign Exchange Decree of January 1995. Foreign exchange bureaus (Bureaux de Change) are allowed to transact in foreign currency banknotes and to buy foreign currency traveler's checks at the autonomous foreign exchange market rates, subject to a margin of 2 percent. Also, they are allowed to sell foreign currency notes only up to a maximum of $2,500 for each transaction.

Administration of Control

The Federal Ministry of Finance is responsible for basic exchange control policy and, in principle, for approving applications for transfers of capital abroad; for remittances of profits and dividends; for granting "approved status" to nonresident investments in Nigeria; and for approving any dealings in foreign securities. The Central Bank of Nigeria is the principal administrator of foreign exchange regulations. All licensed commercial banks and merchant banks have been appointed as authorized dealers by the Ministry of Finance, and are authorized to deal in foreign currencies and to approve applications in accordance with the guidelines issued by the Central Bank of Nigeria. Any application that does not fall within the scope of the authority of these authorized dealers must be submitted to the Ministry of Finance for the transactions mentioned above. Hotels and rest houses are allowed to receive payments for hotel bills and incidental expenses in foreign currency from travelers to Nigeria.

The Federal Ministry of Trade administers trade regulations.

Prescription of Currency

Authorized payments may be made in naira or in any foreign currency to an external account in Nigeria. Settlements with the central banks of the member states of the Economic Community of West African States (Benin, Burkina Faso, Côte d'Ivoire, The Gambia, Ghana, Guinea, Guinea-Bissau, Liberia, Mali, Mauritania, Niger, Senegal, Sierra Leone, and Togo) are normally made through the West African Clearing House in West African Units of Account.

Resident and Nonresident Accounts

There are three categories of accounts: external accounts, nonresident accounts, and domiciliary accounts. External accounts are maintained for diplomatic representatives of all countries and international organizations. They may be credited with authorized payments by residents of Nigeria to residents of foreign countries, with payments from other external accounts, and with proceeds from sales of foreign currencies. They may be debited for payments to residents of Nigeria, for payments to other external accounts, and for purchases of foreign currencies. Funds derived from local sources may be deposited in nonresident accounts. Such accounts may be credited with proceeds from services rendered locally, provided that the operation of such accounts has been reported to and approval has been obtained from the Central Bank of Nigeria before any foreign transfers are effected. Any person may open, maintain, and operate a domiciliary account designated in foreign currency with an authorized dealer, which may be funded by residents derived from external sources but not with foreign exchange purchases in the AFEM. An exporter of goods, including petroleum products, may retain foreign currency corresponding to the entire export proceeds into the foreign currency domiciliary account.

Imports and Import Payments

Import licenses are not required. The importation of the following products is prohibited: poultry, eggs, vegetables, processed wood, mosquito repellant oils, textile fabrics, plastic domestic articles, beer, rice and rice products, mineral water, soft drinks, and all sparkling wine.

All containerized imports irrespective of their value and uncontainerized imports valued at the equivalent of $1,000 (c.i.f.) or more are subject to pre-shipment inspection to ensure that all imports into Nigeria are of the correct quality and quantity according to the contracts, and that only the normal price of that product in the country of supply is paid as well as the correct import duty. Unless a "Clean

Report of Findings" on the goods to be imported has been issued, foreign exchange settlement for imports may not be effected.

Payment for imports covered by confirmed letters of credit is made by the overseas correspondents on behalf of Nigerian banks, on presentation of the specified documents to the overseas correspondents. However, such payment is made on the understanding that the goods paid for will arrive in Nigeria and that all shipping documents relating to the imported goods are lodged by importers with the authorized dealer as agents of the Nigerian Government within 21 days of negotiation of the specified documents. Bills of entry (for imports covered by confirmed letters of credit) must be submitted to the authorized dealer within 90 days of negotiation and payment by overseas correspondent banks. For all other means of payment, the full set of documents, evidencing the receipt of the goods in Nigeria, must be submitted to the authorized dealer.

Payments for Invisibles

Persons needing foreign exchange to make invisible payments must submit applications to the Central Bank of Nigeria through designated banks. Basic allowances are provided for some payments. As with imports, verification is on an ex post basis—that is, depending on the payments arrangements, based on documentation obtained after the purchase of foreign exchange. The basic allowance for tourist travel is the equivalent of $500 a year, and for business travel, the equivalent of $5,000 a trip for an enterprise.

Payments for international air tickets may be made in naira by residents. Hotels are allowed to accept settlement of hotel bills and incidental expenses in foreign currency from travelers to Nigeria, who are required to settle their bills and incidental expenses in foreign currency. However, when there is documentary evidence that an adequate amount of foreign currency has been exchanged into local currency at any licensed bank or foreign bureaus of exchange, payment in local currency must be accepted in settlement of hotel bills by foreign visitors to Nigeria. Remittances abroad by expatriate residents of up to 75 percent of net salary after tax are considered by authorized dealers subject to documentation requirements. Final balance applications involving the transfer of accumulated savings are considered subject to the approved guidelines and confirmation by the Central Bank of Nigeria that the expatriate concerned had not previously been granted his final balance entitlement. The

exportation of domestic currency in excess of ₦1,000 is prohibited.

Exports and Export Proceeds

The exportation of African antiques, works of art, and objects used in African ceremonies is prohibited, except under prescribed conditions. Exports of timber (processed and unprocessed), raw hides and skins, raw palm kernel, cassava, maize, rice, yams, and all imported food items are prohibited. Exports of unrefined gold and petroleum products require an export license. Exports of petroleum are handled by the Nigerian National Petroleum Corporation and are subject to special arrangements.

Exporters are permitted to sell their export proceeds to authorized dealer banks at autonomous foreign exchange market rates.

Proceeds from Invisibles

All proceeds from invisibles must be received through the Central Bank of Nigeria or designated banks and surrendered to the Central Bank of Nigeria. The importation of domestic currency in excess of ₦1,000, is prohibited.

Capital

Applications for capital transfers abroad are approved by the Federal Ministry of Finance and Economic Development subject to satisfactory documentation. Except for the purpose of financing imports or exports, permission is required from the Ministry of Finance for any individual, firm, company, or branch resident in Nigeria to borrow abroad. In addition, official agencies and state-controlled corporations require the prior approval of the Ministry of Finance for any foreign borrowing. The contracting of suppliers' credits abroad by state-controlled corporations or agencies is also subject to approval from the Ministry of Finance. The permission of the Ministry of Finance is required for borrowing in Nigeria (1) by any nonresident individual or company, and (2) by any company registered in Nigeria (other than a bank) that is controlled directly or indirectly from outside Nigeria. However, to enable entities mentioned under (2) to meet temporary shortages of funds, licensed banks in Nigeria may grant loans or overdrafts for periods not exceeding 14 days, or may increase the amount of any advance or overdraft by the amount of loan interest or bank charges payable thereon. General permission is also given for any loan, bank overdraft, or other credit facility to be arranged to finance Nigerian imports or exports of goods.

Residents of Nigeria may not deal in foreign currency securities or buy from or sell to nonresidents of Nigeria any security payable in naira without the permission of the Ministry of Finance. The capital proceeds of securities registered in Nigeria and owned by nonresidents may be collected and negotiated through authorized dealers, provided that the prior permission of the Ministry of Finance is obtained.

Exchange for the transfer of certain assets by emigrants or expatriates is granted on final departure from the country, but the transfer of the proceeds of assets realized in order to comply with the Nigerian Enterprises Promotion Decrees of 1972 and 1977 may take place upon receipt.

Ceilings for foreign capital participation in the equity capital of enterprises in various sectors of the economy have been set by the Indigenization Decree of 1972, as amended in February 1974, July 1976, January 1977, and January 1989. Nonresidents intending to make direct investments in Nigeria may apply to the Ministry of Finance for approved status, the granting of which means that sympathetic consideration will be given to future requests to repatriate the capital and related profits and dividends. Remittable dividends may be reinvested without the requirement that matching capital must be imported. However, the granting of approved status for such investment is subject to the approval of the Federal Ministry of Finance. The granting of approved status is not applicable to the purchase of shares on the stock exchange in Nigeria unless this forms an integral part of the approved investment project. Furthermore, this status is not normally granted when internally generated funds from profits, dividends, rents, bank credit, or locally raised loans are invested in local enterprises. Foreign-owned companies and banks operating in Nigeria must be incorporated in Nigeria.

The Nigerian Investment Promotion Commission deals with all matters relating to approval and the prescription of applicable incentives for direct capital investment in priority areas, subject to the provisions of the Nigerian Investment Promotion Commission Decree of 1995. Applications for the remittance of profits, dividends, etc., in respect of capital investment made through authorized foreign exchange dealers are considered by the Federal Ministry of Finance and approved subject to documentation requirements. Funds so approved are repatriated through the AFEM. A foreign investor in an enterprise to which the Nigerian Investment Promotion Commission Decree applies are guaranteed unconditional transferability of funds through an authorized foreign exchange dealer.

In July 1988, the Central Bank of Nigeria published guidelines for an external debt-conversion program for Nigeria and established a Debt Conversion Program (DCP) to be supervised by a Debt Conversion Committee (DCC) appointed by the Federal Government. The DCC and DCP regulate the purchase of selected Nigerian foreign debt instruments at a discount and the disposition of the naira proceeds of conversions of such debt. Eligible instruments were initially defined as uninsured trade debt denominated in promissory notes. When the rescheduling agreement with commercial banks was completed in early 1989, additional instruments representing debt to commercial banks were made eligible for the debt-conversion provisions. All legitimate holders of promissory notes/debt instruments are eligible to apply to the DCC for debt conversion, provided that the foreign exchange used to acquire the instruments originated from abroad and not from foreign exchange purchases in Nigeria.

Eligible uses for the naira proceeds from debt conversion are (1) cash gifts/grants to Nigerian entities; (2) expansion or recapitalization of investments in privatized enterprises; and (3) investment in new projects. The DCC evaluates each application and determines eligibility for participation in an auction conducted by the Central Bank of Nigeria. The amounts and timing of the auction are determined by the DCC.

Restrictions on remittances of redemption proceeds and incomes arising therefrom are the following: (1) interest income, profits/dividends, patent license fees, and other invisibles connected with approved projects under the DCP may not be repatriated for a minimum period of five years from the date of release of redemption proceeds for actual investment or five years after such profits/dividends are made or paid, whichever is later; (2) any capital proceeds arising from subsequent disposal of the investment made under the program may not be repatriated for a minimum period of ten years after effective investment of the proceeds; repatriation of capital after ten years may not exceed 20 percent a year.

Gold

With the permission of the Federal Ministry of Finance, residents may hold and acquire gold coins in Nigeria for numismatic purposes. Residents other than the monetary authorities, producers of gold, and authorized industrial users are not allowed, without special permission, to hold or acquire gold in any form other than jewelry or coins, at home or abroad. The importation and exportation of gold in any form other than jewelry require specific licenses issued by the Federal Ministry of Finance; such licenses are not normally granted except for imports and exports by or on behalf of the monetary authorities, producers of gold, and industrial users. Furthermore, the importation of gold coins requires an import license. Imports of gold coins and gold and silver bullion are free of duty when made by the Central Bank of Nigeria; otherwise, such imports are subject to customs duty at 100 percent ad valorem.

Changes During 1995

Exchange Arrangement

January 16. An Autonomous Foreign Exchange Market (AFEM), in which transactions in any convertible foreign currency can be freely conducted, was established.

January 16. Foreign exchange bureaus (Bureaux de Change) were allowed to transact foreign currency banknotes, coins, and traveler's checks at the autonomous foreign exchange market rates, subject to a margin of 2 percent.

Resident and Nonresident Accounts

January 1. The system of blocked accounts was abolished with the repeal of the 1962 Exchange Control Act.

Imports and Import Payments

January 16. All containerized imports, irrespective of their value, those which are not containerized, and imports valued at the equivalent of $1,000 (c.i.f.) or more were subject to preshipment inspection.

Exports and Export Proceeds

January 16. Exporters were allowed to sell their export proceeds to authorized banks at freely negotiated rates.

Proceeds from Invisibles

January 16. The amount of naira banknotes residents are allowed to keep to settle local expenses on their return to Nigeria was increased to ₦1,000 from ₦500.

NORWAY

(Position as of December 31, 1995)

Exchange Arrangement

The currency of Norway is the Norwegian Krone. The Norwegian authorities do not maintain margins in respect of exchange transactions, and spot and forward exchange rates are determined on the basis of demand and supply conditions in the exchange market. However, the Bank of Norway may intervene from time to time to maintain stability in the market. The Bank of Norway quotes daily the exchange rate of the krone against 23 other currencies[1] and the European currency unit (ECU) for information purposes on the basis of the market rates. On December 31, 1995, the middle rate quoted against the U.S. dollar was Nkr 6.319 per $1.

Residents (Norwegian companies and private individuals) may freely enter into forward and interest rate contracts with Norwegian foreign exchange banks and nonresidents. There are no taxes or subsidies on purchases or sales of foreign exchange.

Norway accepted the obligations of Article VIII, Sections 2, 3, and 4 of the Fund Agreement on May 11, 1967.

Administration of Control

Exchange control is administered by the Bank of Norway in cooperation with the Ministry of Finance and Customs. Import and export licenses, when required, are issued by the Ministry of Foreign Affairs and, in certain cases, by the Ministry of Agriculture or the Ministry of Fisheries.

In accordance with the Fund's Executive Board Decision No. 144-(52/51) adopted on August 14, 1952, Norway notified the Fund on July 21, 1992 that, in compliance with UN Security Council Resolution No. 757 (1992), certain restrictions had been imposed on the making of payments and transfers for current international transactions in respect of the Federal Republic of Yugoslavia (Serbia/Montenegro); these restrictions have been abolished in accordance with UN Security Council Resolution No. 1022 (1995). Restrictions have also been imposed on financial transactions with the Socialist People's Libyan Arab Jamahiriya (in accordance with UN Security Council Resolutions No. 661/90 and No. 670/90), and with the areas of the Republic of Bosnia and Herzegovina that are controlled by the Bosnian Serbs (in accordance with UN Security Council Resolution No. 942/94). Restrictions were imposed on financial transactions with Haiti (in accordance with UN Security Council Resolutions Nos. 873/93, 841/93, and 917/94). These sanctions were subsequently lifted with UN Security Council Resolution No. 944/94.

Prescription of Currency

Settlements with all countries may be made in any convertible currency, including Norwegian kroner, in convertible krone accounts (see section on Resident and Nonresident Accounts, below).

Resident and Nonresident Accounts

Residents may open foreign exchange accounts at domestic banks without restriction. The main type of nonresident account is the convertible krone account. Such accounts may be held by residents of all foreign countries. They may be credited with authorized payments from any country, with transfers from other convertible krone accounts, and with proceeds from the sale of convertible currencies in Norway. They may be debited for authorized payments from any country to residents of Norway, for transfers to other convertible krone accounts, and for purchases of any foreign currency in Norway. Authorized banks are also permitted to open foreign exchange accounts for nonresidents without restriction. Both convertible krone accounts and foreign exchange accounts must be reported to the Bank of Norway.

Imports and Import Payments

All imports from Iraq, from the Socialist People's Libyan Arab Jamahiriya, and from areas of the Republic of Bosnia and Herzegovina that are controlled by the Bosnian Serbs are prohibited. Industrial goods may be imported freely upon presentation of the original invoice, with the exception of textiles and certain footwear. Certain textiles and garments are subject to import licensing for surveillance purposes. Following Norway's accession to the previous Multifiber Arrangement (MFA) on July 1, 1984, the global quotas formerly in force under Article XIX of the General Agreement on Tariffs and Trade (GATT)

---

[1] Australian dollars, Austrian schillings, Belgian francs, Canadian dollars, Danish kroner, deutsche mark, Finnish markkaa, French francs, Greek drachmas, Hong Kong dollars, Icelandic krónur, Irish pounds, Italian lire, Japanese yen, Netherlands guilders, New Zealand dollars, Portuguese escudos, pounds sterling, Singapore dollars, Spanish pesetas, Swedish kronor, Swiss francs, and U.S. dollars.

have been phased out and replaced by bilateral agreements, which have been concluded with 19 textile suppliers. The agreements entered into under the current MFA are considerably more liberal than those that Norway had under the previous MFA. Norway has been liberalizing imports from developing countries. Besides textile products, footwear from Taiwan Province of China is subject to licensing requirements.

New and secondhand ships and certain categories of fishing vessels may be imported freely. The importation of radio remittance equipment, such as radio controls, is subject to approval by the Directorate of Telecommunications in respect of frequency. The importation of a small number of goods is prohibited for health and similar reasons.

Direct trade credits may be extended for import (and export) financing without a license from the Bank of Norway.

Payments for Invisibles

Payments for invisibles may be made freely. There are no restrictions on the types of payments a person (resident or nonresident) may take out of Norway, but banknotes exceeding the equivalent of Nkr 25,000 (both Norwegian and foreign) must be reported to the customs authorities.

Exports and Export Proceeds

Most goods may be exported freely to any country against a declaration or a license. Exports to Iraq and the Socialist People's Libyan Arab Jamahiriya are prohibited. Exports to the areas of the Republic of Bosnia and Herzegovina that are controlled by the Bosnian Serbs are also prohibited, with the exception of medical supplies and certain food items. Exports subject to regulation are listed and require export licenses. Exports to any country valued at up to Nkr 2,000 are exempt from declaration or export license; for arms and ammunition, this limit is Nkr 500, and for fish and fish products, Nkr 1,000.

Export proceeds need not be repatriated to Norway.

Proceeds from Invisibles

There is no limit on the amount of foreign exchange a person (resident or nonresident) may bring into Norway, but banknotes exceeding the equivalent of Nkr 25,000 (both Norwegian and foreign) must be reported to the customs authorities.

Capital

Norwegian companies and private individuals are permitted to make direct investments abroad; direct investments in the form of shares that are not normally traded in a country belonging to the Organization for Economic Cooperation and Development (OECD) must, however, be made through Norwegian stockbrokers. Securities subject to the stockbroker requirement that are kept abroad must be deposited with a Norwegian bank or stockbroker. The stockbroker and deposit requirements will not apply if documentation of proof can be provided that the security is subject to regulatory and supervisory arrangements equivalent to OECD standards. Foreign exchange banks, exposure-regulated financial institutions, insurance companies, and stockbrokers dealing in foreign securities on their own account are exempt from the stockbroker and deposit requirements. Foreign exchange banks are also exempted when dealing on behalf of a resident. However, foreign exchange banks and financial institutions subject to exposure regulation must submit reports on their net foreign currency position to the Bank of Norway. Net positions of up to 10 percent of the financial institutions' equity and subordinated loan capital may be taken out in individual currencies, and the aggregate position must be kept within 20 percent of the financial institutions' equity and subordinated loan capital.

There is no limit on purchases by residents of foreign currency bonds, and residents are permitted to purchase foreign bonds and certificates. Purchases by residents of insurance services abroad, other than injury insurance, are prohibited if the insurance company is not registered in a European Economic Area (EEA) country. Nonresidents may purchase Norwegian bonds and certificates without restriction. There is no restriction on the importation into or exportation from Norway of securities.

Personal capital transfers, such as transfers relating to family loans, gifts, inheritances, legacies, dowries, emigrants' assets, savings of nonresident workers, and amounts in settlement of immigrants' debts, may be made freely.

Gold

Residents may freely purchase, hold, and sell gold in any form. No customs duties or other charges or fees are payable on imports or exports of gold bullion and gold coins not contained in jewelry. Domestic sales of gold bullion and gold coins are subject to the regular value-added tax at a rate of 23 percent, except gold coins produced after January 1, 1967.

Changes During 1995

No significant changes occurred in the exchange and trade system.

OMAN

(Position as of December 31, 1995)

Exchange Arrangement

The currency of Oman is the Rial Omani, which is pegged to the U.S. dollar, the intervention currency, at RO 1 per $2.6008. The Central Bank of Oman maintains fixed buying and selling rates for the U.S. dollar; on December 31, 1995, the rates were RO 1 per $2.6042 (buying) and RO 1 per $2.5974 (selling). The commercial bank rates for other currencies are based on market rates in London. There are arrangements for forward cover against exchange rate risk operating in the official and commercial banking sectors. There are no taxes or subsidies on purchases or sales of foreign exchange.

Oman accepted the obligations of Article VIII, Sections 2, 3, and 4 of the Fund Agreement on June 19, 1974.

Administration of Control

Exchange control authority is vested in the Central Bank, but there is no exchange control legislation in Oman.

In accordance with the Fund's Executive Board Decision No. 144-(52/51) adopted on August 14, 1952, Oman notified the Fund, on January 27, 1993, that certain restrictions had been imposed on the making of payments and transfers for current international transactions in respect of the Federal Republic of Yugoslavia (Serbia/Montenegro).

Prescription of Currency

All settlements with Israel and the Federal Republic of Yugoslavia (Serbia/Montenegro) are prohibited, as is the use of their currencies. No other prescription of currency requirements are in force.

Nonresident Accounts

No distinction is made between accounts held by residents and those held by nonresidents.

Imports and Import Payments

All imports from Israel and the Federal Republic of Yugoslavia (Serbia/Montenegro) are prohibited. Imports of a few commodities are prohibited for reasons of health, security, or public policy. Also, seasonal bans are imposed on the importation of fruits and vegetables that are grown locally. In addition, companies operating in Oman and trading in manufactured oil products are prohibited from importing specified products as long as domestic production is deemed adequate to satisfy local demand. Licenses are required for imports. Foreign exchange for payments abroad for authorized imports may be obtained freely.

The customs regime consists of five bands, and the rates range from 5 percent for most general goods to 100 percent on alcoholic beverages, pork, and limes. Customs duties are not levied on government imports.

Exports and Export Proceeds

All exports to Israel and the Federal Republic of Yugoslavia (Serbia/Montenegro) are prohibited, and exports or re-exports of live animals and foodstuffs may be prohibited in times of shortage in Oman. All other commodities may be exported freely. No requirements are attached to receipts from exports or re-exports; the proceeds need not be repatriated or surrendered, and they may be disposed of freely, regardless of the currency involved. Exports of Maria Theresa dollars are prohibited.

Payments for and Proceeds from Invisibles

Payments for and proceeds from invisibles are not restricted. Payments must not, however, be made to or received from Israel or the Federal Republic of Yugoslavia (Serbia/Montenegro). Travelers may bring in or take out any amount in domestic or foreign banknotes.

Capital

No exchange control requirements are imposed on capital receipts or on payments by residents or nonresidents, except that no payments may be made to or received from Israel or the Federal Republic of Yugoslavia (Serbia/Montenegro). Investment in business firms in Oman by foreign natural or juridical persons requires prior approval and is regulated by the Law for the Organization and Encouragement of Industry of 1979, and the Foreign Investment Law of 1983. Under the latter, joint ventures are offered a five-year tax holiday, renewable for an additional five years under certain conditions.

The Oman Development Bank can provide medium- and long-term loans at preferential interest rates for project financing in the petroleum, agricultural, fishery, and mineral sectors; it can also give assistance in preinvestment research. The direction of foreign capital to large production or manufacturing projects is encouraged. In addition, the Government provides loans at subsidized interest rates for those projects with a majority Omani shareholding that are used for industrial production for exportation, industrial production using indigenous raw materials or labor, or the development of tourism.

Gold

The monetary authorities and authorized resident and nonresident banks may, without license, purchase, hold, and sell gold in any form at home or abroad. They may also import and export gold in any form without a license and without payment of customs duties or taxes. Transactions involving Israel, South Africa, or the Republic of Yugoslavia (Serbia/Montenegro) are prohibited.

Changes During 1995

No significant changes occurred in the exchange and trade system.

PAKISTAN

(Position as of December 31, 1995)

Exchange Arrangement

The currency of Pakistan is the Pakistani Rupee, for which the U.S. dollar is the intervention currency. A managed floating exchange rate system is operated, under which the State Bank of Pakistan sets the rate at which it will purchase and sell U.S. dollars in transactions with authorized dealers. On December 31, 1995, the State Bank's spot buying and selling rates for transactions with authorized dealers were PRs 34.250 and PRs 34.421, respectively, per $1. All foreign exchange transactions with the public must be conducted through authorized dealers and effected at rates authorized by the State Bank. In the calculation of spot exchange rates for other currencies, a margin of 0.2 percent is provided on the previous day's closing buying and selling rates for the currency concerned in the New York market.

Authorized dealers in Pakistan are permitted to cover their requirements of specified currencies in foreign exchange markets abroad. They may also cover their permitted transactions in specified currencies against U.S. dollars or Pakistani rupees, either spot or forward for a limited period, with their agents in the countries concerned. In addition, they offer forward cover in the currencies of the member countries of the Asian Clearing Union (ACU) for exports and imports effected under that arrangement.

Forward exchange cover for private foreign currency deposits is provided by the State Bank, which charges an annual fee of 6.3 percent, 9.7 percent, 3.9 percent, and 4.75 percent, respectively, on deposits in deutsche mark, Japanese yen, pounds sterling, and U.S. dollars.

Residents and nonresidents may use foreign exchange to purchase foreign currency bearer certificates (FCBCs) with a maturity of up to five years. FCBCs denominated in deutsche mark, Japanese yen, pounds sterling, or U.S. dollars are available in various denominations (deutsche mark, from DM 100 to DM 100,000; Japanese yen, from ¥10,000 to ¥10 million; pounds sterling, from £100 to £50,000; and U.S. dollars, from $100 to $100,000). They may be purchased by anyone without revealing the source of foreign exchange, freely brought into and taken out of the country, or cashed at any time in Pakistani rupees at the exchange rate prevailing at the time of the encashment or redeemed in original currency, they may be used by residents to undertake any current or international capital transactions. FCBCs yield rates of return related to market interest rates for each respective currency. Foreign exchange bearer certificates (FEBCs) denominated in Pakistani rupees are available in denominations ranging from PRs 500 to PRs 100,000; their face value is 14.5 percent higher one year after issue, 31 percent higher after two years, 52 percent higher after three years, 74 percent higher after four years, 99 percent higher after five years, and 131 percent higher after six years. These certificates may be cashed any time after issue; in Pakistani rupees, at any office of issue located in Pakistan; or in foreign currency, at any office of issue located abroad or at any office of issue located in Pakistan that is authorized to deal in foreign currency.

Pakistan accepted the obligations of Article VIII, Sections 2, 3, and 4 of the Fund Agreement on July 1, 1994.

Administration of Control

The State Bank has delegated authority to a number of banks and financial institutions to deal in all foreign currencies, to supervise surrender requirements, and to sell foreign exchange for certain purposes within limits prescribed by the State Bank. Certain foreign trade transactions are conducted through various state trading agencies, such as the Trading Corporation of Pakistan, Ltd. (TCP), the Cotton Export Corporation of Pakistan, Ltd. (CECP), and the Rice Export Corporation of Pakistan, Ltd. (RECP).

Prescription of Currency

Exchange receipts and payments abroad must be effected through an authorized foreign exchange dealer, in principle, in any convertible currency or in Pakistani rupees to or from nonresident rupee bank accounts. Certain settlements with specified countries are channeled through special accounts. Letters of credit for imports from all other countries may be established in foreign currency or in Pakistani rupees for credit to a nonresident bank account in the country of the beneficiary or in the country of origin or shipment of goods.

Payments to, and receipts from, member countries of the ACU (Bangladesh, India, Islamic Republic of Iran, Myanmar, Nepal, and Sri Lanka) in respect of current transactions are effected through the ACU in Asian monetary units (AMUs) or in the domestic currency of one of the member countries involved. No exchange control is exercised over transactions with the Islamic State of Afghanistan, and settlements are made in Pakistani rupees or in afghanis. Payments between Pakistan and Israel are not permitted.

Resident and Nonresident Accounts

Resident foreign currency accounts. Residents of Pakistan are allowed to open and maintain foreign currency accounts (FCAs) with banks in Pakistan on the same basis as nonresidents. These accounts may be credited with remittances from abroad, traveler's checks, foreign currency notes, proceeds from FEBCs, FCBCs, and dollar bearer certificates (DBCs). Sources of acquisition of foreign exchange are not required to be revealed. However, receipts from exports of goods and services; earnings from services of residents; earnings and profits of overseas offices or branches of Pakistani firms, companies, and banks; and foreign exchange released from Pakistan for any specified purpose may not be credited to these accounts. Balances held in these accounts are freely transferable abroad, and there are no limits on amounts of withdrawal. These accounts may be permanently retained, and the rate of interest on term deposits (of three months and up to three years) is fixed by the State Bank with the approval of the Government. The rates are based on the Eurodollar deposit rate of Barclays Bank, London. The margins over the Eurodollar deposit rates range from 0.75 percent for three-month deposits to 1.625 percent for three-year deposits.

Nonresident accounts. The accounts of individuals, firms, or companies residing outside Pakistan are designated nonresident accounts.[1] Authorized banks are permitted to open nonresident accounts for nonbank nonresidents without the prior approval of the State Bank when the accounts are opened with funds received from abroad through banking channels or with rupee funds accepted for remittance abroad. Debits and credits to nonresident accounts for specified purposes may be made by authorized banks without the prior approval of the State Bank. Accounts of residents of India, other than the accounts of the Indian Embassy and its personnel, are blocked.

Pakistani nationals residing abroad and foreign nationals, whether residing abroad or in Pakistan, and firms, companies, and charitable organizations owned by persons who are otherwise eligible to open FCAs may open FCAs with banks in Pakistan without the prior approval of the exchange control authorities. The accounts may be denominated in deutsche mark, French francs, Japanese yen, pounds sterling, and U.S. dollars; credit balances may be transferred abroad, and interest on such accounts is exempt from income tax. Deposit holders wishing to make payments in Pakistan must first convert the foreign exchange drawn from their accounts into Pakistani rupees. If Pakistani nationals holding such accounts return to Pakistan, they may retain the accounts permanently. Banks in Pakistan receiving such deposits must sell the foreign exchange to the State Bank. Authorized dealers under the FCA facility may accept term deposits in foreign currency from their overseas branches and foreign banks operating abroad, including financial institutions owned by them; such term deposits must be at least $5 million (or the equivalent in other currencies) for a maturity period of at least six months. The rates of interest paid on these deposits may not exceed 0.5 percent above LIBOR.

Imports and Import Payments

Annual Import Policy Orders (IPOs) outline the regulations that apply to imports. All items that do not appear on either the negative list or the list of items permitted to be imported subject to health and safety requirements may be freely imported without licenses. The negative list mainly consists of items banned for religious and health reasons, or to discourage consumption of luxury items, and goods banned in accordance with international agreements.[2] Some items on the negative list may be imported under certain circumstances, principally by export industries, public sector agencies, or under the personal baggage scheme. There exists a "procedural list," consisting of 17 items, and the importation of these items is subject to a certificate.

Imports from Israel are prohibited, as are imports of goods originating in Israel but shipped from other countries. Both the private and the public sectors may import 580 specified items or categories of goods directly from India. Special provisions govern the importation by export industries of items

---

[1]Different rules apply to the nonresident rupee accounts of individuals, firms, or companies, on the one hand, and to the nonresident rupee accounts of banks, on the other hand.

[2]Some of the currently prohibited imports fall outside these categories (i.e., some prohibited items are not produced in Pakistan and do not fit into the category of goods banned for religious, health, or luxury consumption reasons).

importable on fulfillment of conditions and of items on the negative list.

Import payments may be made against irrevocable letters of credit, provided that the letters do not stipulate payment of any amount by way of interest in the case of usance bills and, further, that in the case of books, journals, magazines, and periodicals, they stipulate payment on a sight draft or usance bill basis. Since July 1995, exporters are allowed to obtain short-term foreign currency loans from abroad based on the value of the export contract or letter of credit; both principal and interest have to be repaid from the export proceeds.

Imports can also be made on a consignment basis. When the importers desire to import on a joint basis from any country either for the sake of their own convenience or economy, or because of the suppliers' inability to supply goods in small consignments, the importers may establish joint letters of credit. For imports under any special trading arrangement, the letters of credit may be opened within such a period as may be specified in the relevant public notice issued by the authorities. In case of imports under loans or credits, which require the contracts to be approved by the agencies of the Government, the importer shall open a letter of credit within 60 days of the date the contract is approved. In case of imports under suppliers' credit and the PAYE scheme, letters of credit may be opened only if the contract has been registered with the State Bank. Letters of credit are generally established for up to 12 months, with the following exceptions: (1) when machinery and millwork must be specifically fabricated and the period of manufacture is more than 12 months, letters of credit shall be established with a validity period of up to 24 months; (2) for all items other than machinery and millwork, the period of 12 months may be extended for an additional 24 months on payment of an additional fee of 0.25 percent of the unused value of the letter of credit for each period of 6 months from the date of its expiry; (3) in the case of machinery, letters of credit may be extended for up to 36 months from the date of expiry of initial validity period of 12 months, or 24 months as the case may be, on additional payment of 0.25 percent of the unused value of the letter of credit for each 6-month period; and (4) if the letters of credit are opened against loans, credits, barters, or special trading arrangements whereby shipment could not take place owing to circumstances beyond the control of the importer, revalidation may be allowed within the validity of the loan, credit, barter, or special trading arrangement without additional payment.

Insurance on transportation must be taken out with insurance companies registered in Pakistan.

Payment for Invisibles

Payments for invisibles are controlled by the State Bank and in many cases require its prior approval. Payments to Israel are not permitted.

Payments for invisibles related to imports are generally given the same treatment as that accorded to the underlying trade transaction. Except with respect to certain aid shipments, transport insurance must be taken out with insurance companies in Pakistan. Commissions, brokerage, or other charges paid to foreign importers or agents by Pakistani exporters are generally limited to a maximum of 5 percent of the invoice value, except for cotton for which the maximum is 1 percent. The maximum percentage for sporting goods, surgical instruments, cutlery, leather goods, ready-made garments and other ready-made textile items, carpets, and plastic goods is 7 percent; for engineering goods it is 10 percent; and for books, journals, and magazines it is 33⅓ percent.

The remittance of dividends declared on current profits is allowed freely to foreign shareholders if the investment was made on a repatriable basis. The remittance of profits by branches of foreign companies other than banks and those engaged in insurance, shipping, and the airline business is permitted without restriction provided that the required documents are submitted to the State Bank. The same regulation applies to head office expenses charged to a branch's profit-and-loss account and accepted for tax purposes by the Pakistani income tax authorities.

Since August 30, 1993, foreign exchange for private travel to countries other than the Islamic State of Afghanistan, Bangladesh, and India is granted at the rate of $50 a day for up to 42 days during a calendar year on submission of travel documents to the authorized dealers. Requests for foreign exchange in excess of these amounts are to be referred by the authorized dealers to the State Bank giving justification for the additional amount. Unspent foreign exchange, however, must be surrendered to an authorized dealer. The entitlement can be used in installments. Remittances for undergraduate and postgraduate studies abroad and correspondence courses are not restricted. Foreign exchange for business travel, medical treatment, education, and sponsored cultural trips may be granted on a case-by-case basis. Foreign exchange allowances for students' tuition fees and expenses as required by institutions may be obtained from authorized dealers without approval from the State Bank. Allowances for professional training abroad are granted at

$1,200 a month. Requests for foreign exchange in excess of $1,200 a month for professional training must be referred to the State Bank duly accompanied by cogent reasons and supporting documents. There are also specific allowances for pilgrims' travel to Saudi Arabia. Exporters of goods with annual export earnings of more than PRs 2.5 million and exporters of services with annual earnings of more than PRs 0.25 million are granted a renewable business travel allowance of $200 a day, up to $6,000 a business trip. In addition, business travelers may settle credit card charges of up to $100 a day, subject to a maximum of $3,000 for a 30-day visit, with the encasement of FCBCs. Foreigners may make family remittances to the extent of the difference between the net income of the applicant and his or her estimated expenses in Pakistan. In case the family of a resident Pakistani is temporarily living abroad for genuine personal reasons, foreign exchange will be provided upon bona fide request.

Persons leaving Pakistan (foreigners and Pakistani nationals) may take out with them foreign currency without limit.

Exports and Export Proceeds

Exports of specified commodities[3] to any destination and all exports to Israel are prohibited. Exports of most other commodities are allowed freely. However, certain exports are subject to export quotas (e.g., maize, gram, split gram, and camels), quality controls (such as batteries, electric bulbs and appliances, and oil cakes), or minimum export prices (e.g., onyx blocks). The Cotton Export Corporation of Pakistan, Ltd., is responsible for the exportation of cotton, although the private sector has also been allowed into the export trade. Cotton is exported to India without involvement of any public sector agency; basmati and other types of rice are exported through the Rice Exportation Corporation of Pakistan, Ltd., but private traders are also allowed to export rice. Cement, which may be exported by public and private sector entities, is subject to a quota. Chemical fertilizers may also be exported by private sector units. Trade samples that may be exported without prior approval from the State Bank are limited to the equivalent of $2,000 a firm a year; the

limit for leather garments is 50 pieces, without a value limit. There are no quantitative or value ceilings if samples are damaged. The State Bank requires a declaration from the exporter that payment will be received in accordance with the prescribed method and within the prescribed time except for goods manufactured in the export processing zones. The authorized dealer certifies the export form for shipment. Exporters are obliged to collect and surrender export proceeds within four months of shipment, although the State Bank may allow an extension of this period. Exporters may, however, with the prior approval of the State Bank, grant deferred payment terms. The surrender of afghanis accruing from exports to the Islamic State of Afghanistan is not required.

Under the Export Processing Unit (EPU) Scheme, selected industries, raw materials, intermediate goods used for the manufacturing of exports, imports of machinery, and components not manufactured locally are exempt from import duties and local taxes.[4] The export-output ratio required to qualify for the EPU Scheme is 50 percent in the first two years and 60 percent in the third year and beyond.

Export financing at concessional rates is provided for all exports, with the exception of 24 specified items,[5] based on irrevocable letters of credit or firm export orders on a case-by-case basis under Part I of the Export Finance Scheme or, alternatively, based on the exporter's performance in the previous year on a revolving basis under Part II of the scheme. However, the State Bank is phasing out its outstanding stock of concessional loans to the export sector at the rate of 25 percent a year, so as to eliminate the outstanding amount by July 1, 1996. Under the new system, state bank refinancing in excess of the above limit is held in a blocked account (special deposit account) in favor of the lending bank. Interest at a rate of 3 percent above the rate applicable to the loan is paid on the account, providing de facto a 3 percent interest subsidy to the exporter. The amount refi-

---

[3]Prohibited exports include ferrous and nonferrous metals (excluding iron and steel manufactured goods), unprocessed edible oils, certain grains, certain dairy products, certain live animals, certain beef and mutton, timber, certain hides and skins, pulses and beans, wet-blue leather made from cowhides and calfhides, charcoal, certain animal products, intoxicants, certain oil seeds, wooden crates, arms, ammunition, explosives, fissionable material, maps and charts, paper waste, unfinished hockey sticks and blades, human skeletons, certain imported goods, and antiques.

[4]The industries included are those producing textiles and clothing (other than spinning), leather and leather manufactures, chemicals and pharmaceuticals, engineering and electronics equipment, ceramics, furniture, sporting goods, surgical instruments, and cutlery.

[5]The following are exceptions: raw cotton; cotton yarn; fish other than that which is frozen or preserved; mutton and beef; petroleum products; raw vegetable material; wool and animal hair; raw animal material; animal fodder; all grains including grain flour; stone, sand, and gravel; waste and scrap of all kinds; crude fertilizer; oilseeds, nuts, and kernels; jewelry exported under the Entrustment Scheme; live animals; hides and skins; wet-blue leather; inorganic elements, oxides, etc.; crude minerals; works of art and antiques; all metals; furs; and wood in rough or squared form.

nanced by the State Bank totaled PRs 48.7 billion as of December 31, 1995; of this amount, PRs 27.5 billion was outstanding against the special deposit account.

Rebates of 25 percent and 50 percent are available against the tax payable on income attributable to the sales proceeds from exports of semifinished goods and finished goods, respectively, that are manufactured in Pakistan. For value-added items, such as engineering equipment, garments, leather and leather products, textile products, and hand-knotted carpets and rugs, the rate of rebate is 75 percent; the rebate rate on engineering goods is 90 percent. Industrial units established under the PAYE scheme are permitted to use a maximum of 50 percent of the f.o.b. value of exports for payments of foreign exchange obligations in respect of their debt liability, and other foreign exchange payments on account of royalty, technical fees, and incidental charges. Under the Open Bond Manufacturing Scheme, raw materials and intermediate goods imported or purchased locally and used for manufacturing for exports are exempt from import duties and local taxes. At present, the following industries are covered by this scheme: textiles and clothing (other than spinning), leather and leather manufactures, chemical and pharmaceutical, engineering and electronics, ceramics, furniture, sporting goods, and surgical instruments.

Proceeds from Invisibles

With the exception of afghanis, which may be retained, foreign exchange earned from invisibles must be surrendered within three months. Travelers may bring in PRs 500 a person in Pakistani currency notes from India; the limit for other sources is PRs 3,000 a person. There is no limit on the importation of other currency notes and coins, except coins that are legal tender in India; these coins may be imported only up to the value of Indian Rs 5 a person at a time.

Travel and tour agents are permitted to retain up to 5 percent of their foreign exchange earnings for marketing and related export promotion expenses.

Capital

Approval from the Government is required for the establishment of industries involving (1) arms and ammunition; (2) printing securities and currency and minting coins; (3) high explosives; (4) radioactive substances (investments in these areas by domestic investors are also subject to approval); and (5) agricultural land, forestry irrigation, real estate, insurance, and health.

Currently, the Foreign Private Investment (Promotion and Protection) Act of 1976 does not guarantee repatriation of capital for investments undertaken before September 1954. These investments are regulated by the terms and conditions governing each investment.

Public limited companies whose shares are quoted on stock exchanges in Pakistan and private limited or unlisted public limited companies engaged in manufacturing are permitted to issue or transfer and export shares on a repatriable basis against payment in foreign exchange to the following nonresidents: (1) a Pakistani national residing abroad, (2) a person holding two nationalities including Pakistani nationality, (3) a foreign national, (4) a company incorporated outside Pakistan (excluding branches in Pakistan of such companies), and (5) a company owned or controlled by a foreign government.

The above nonresidents are allowed to trade freely in the shares quoted on the stock exchanges in Pakistan as well as the government securities (federal investment bonds and Treasury bills) through special convertible rupee accounts with banks in Pakistan. Such accounts are to be fed by remittances from abroad or by transfer from a foreign currency account of the nonresident in Pakistan.

Foreign nationals can make investments in government securities and in the units of national investment trusts on a repatriable basis against payment in foreign exchange. Pakistani nationals residing abroad are also allowed to invest in units of national investment trust on a repatriable basis against payment in foreign exchange.

Nonresidents, as defined in (1) to (5), above, are permitted to invest in registered corporate debt instruments on a repatriable basis against payment in foreign exchange.

Foreign nationals in or outside Pakistan may register their investments made in foreign exchange in national prize bonds issued by the Government; the principal of such transactions may be repatriated at any time, but the prize bonds are treated as savings for the purpose of foreign exchange regulations on outward transfers.

Nonresidents, including foreign-controlled companies incorporated in Pakistan, can make investments in Pakistani securities of all types, excluding shares of companies not quoted on stock exchanges, against payment in Pakistani rupees on a nonrepatriable basis of capital and dividends/profits.

Foreign banks functioning in Pakistan may underwrite share issues of companies incorporated in Pakistan to the extent of 30 percent of the capital offered to the general public for subscription or 30 percent of its own paid-up capital and reserve, whichever is less. The foreign banks may also underwrite public issues of participation term certificates, term finance certificates, and modaraba certificates provided that when the terms and conditions of their issue grant holders the option to convert the securities into ordinary shares, the restriction of 30 percent, as mentioned above, would apply.

Proceeds accruing from the liquidation of nonresident capital assets not covered by repatriation arrangements must be credited to nonresident accounts. Balances in blocked accounts may be invested in approved government securities payable in Pakistani rupees or placed as time deposits with banks.

Resident Pakistani nationals require prior approval from the State Bank to sell movable or immovable assets held abroad, and liquidation proceeds must be repatriated to Pakistan through normal banking channels.

Gold

The exportation of gold is prohibited unless authorized by the State Bank; such permission is not usually granted. Pakistani nationals and foreign nationals coming from abroad are allowed to bring in unlimited quantities of gold in their personal baggage. Similarly, individual firms or companies who are residents of Pakistan are allowed to import up to 500 troy ounces at a time.

Changes During 1995

Resident and Nonresident Accounts

March 31. Resident individuals and firms were allowed to make investments in foreign companies through FEBCs, subject to the condition that earnings would be repatriated.

Exports and Export Proceeds

July 31. Exporters were allowed to obtain short-term foreign currency loans from abroad based on the value of the export contract; both principal and interest would have to be serviced from the export proceeds.

PANAMA

(Position as of December 31, 1995)

Exchange Arrangement

The currency of Panama is the Panamanian Balboa, which is pegged to the U.S. dollar at B 1 per $1. The U.S. dollar is legal tender and circulates freely in Panama; locally issued currency is limited to coins, including several commemorative coins in small denominations. Commercial banks quote buying and selling rates for certain other currencies based on the buying and selling rates for the U.S. dollar in markets abroad. There are no taxes or subsidies on purchases or sales of foreign exchange. There are no arrangements for forward cover against exchange rate risk operating in the official or the commercial banking sector.

Panama accepted the obligations of Article VIII, Sections 2, 3, and 4 of the Fund Agreement on November 26, 1946.

Administration of Control

In general, import or export licenses are not required. Only a few products are banned or require special import permits. Individuals or companies engaged in import activities require a commercial or industrial license, which is issued by the Ministry of Commerce and Industry (MICI). Specific export licenses are required for products that are subject to export taxes and for certain other goods; these licenses are issued by the Ministry of Finance and Treasury. The MICI, through the Panama Trade Development Institute, is responsible for determining all aspects of agreements on free trade and bilateral preferential treatment with countries in the region. Panama has bilateral trade agreements with Costa Rica, the Dominican Republic, El Salvador, Guatemala, Honduras, and Nicaragua. Under an agreement with Mexico, 70 products may be exported to Mexico at preferential conditions. The Ministry of Agriculture and Livestock Development (MIDA) and the Agricultural Marketing Institute (IMA), through various product-specific commissions, determine the import quotas for certain agricultural commodities.

Arrears are maintained with respect to external payments. However, in May 1995, Panama reached agreement-in-principle with its creditor banks and suppliers on a debt and debt-service reduction operation of $3.5 billion. This agreement was to be concluded in the spring of 1996. In December 1995, agreement was reached to refinance enterprise debt in arrears.

Prescription of Currency

There are no prescription of currency requirements.

Imports and Import Payments

There are no quantitative restrictions on industrial products, but import quotas established by the MIDA and the IMA are maintained on some products in the agricultural sector and agro-industries, including timber, salt, fishmeal, milk, and sugar. Imports by the public sector are subject to special requirements. Payments abroad may be made freely.

A harmonized commodity description and coding system for customs tariffs was introduced on January 1, 1995. Most tariff rates are on an ad valorem basis and are assessed on the c.i.f. value of imports. For some products, the tax is specific and is calculated on the basis of weight (per kilogram). In cases where both tax rates are stated, the applicable rate is the one that produces the higher tax revenue. If the tax is specific, an additional tax of 7.5 percent on the c.i.f. value of imports is charged, except for (1) specified pharmaceutical products and foodstuffs, for which the additional tax rates are 2.5 percent and 3.5 percent, respectively; (2) books and certain agricultural inputs, which are duty free; and (3) specified raw materials for manufacturing, for which the tax is 5 percent. Many local industries are protected by tariffs aimed at promoting local and export industries. A tariff reform program involving reductions in tariff ceilings and conversion of specific tariffs to ad valorem rates was implemented in August 1991 and continued into 1994. Effective January 1, 1996, tariffs on the main agricultural products, except corn and soybeans[1] were reduced; the present range of tariffs for the main agricultural products is between 15 percent and 80 percent. In addition, tariffs on raw materials for the manufacturing sector were reduced to a uniform rate of 3 percent from a wide range of tariffs. All imports into the city of Colón designated as the Colón free zone and the newly established export-processing zones are exempt from duties.

---

[1]Tariffs on soybeans were increased to 50 percent from 40 percent, and tariffs on corn were increased to 70 percent from 40 percent.

Exports and Export Proceeds

Export taxes are levied on gold, silver, platinum, manganese, other minerals, unrefined sugar, coconuts, scrap metals, pearls, animal wax, nispero gum, ipecac root, and rubber. Exports of firearms and ammunition are prohibited. Certain nontraditional exports (with a minimum local cost-of-production content of 20 percent) are eligible for tax credit certificates equivalent to 20 percent of value added. The export-processing zones are exempt from all taxes (and as such receive no tax credit certificates). Proceeds from exports are not subject to exchange control.

Any product (including raw materials and machinery) may be imported into the Colón free zone, and stored, modified, processed, assembled, repacked and re-exported without being subject to customs procedures.

Payments for and Proceeds from Invisibles

Payments for and proceeds from invisibles are not restricted. A travel tax of 4 percent is levied on air and sea tickets bought in Panama or on tickets purchased for travel starting in Panama.

Capital

Inward and outward capital transfers by residents and nonresidents are not subject to exchange control. Some foreign-controlled banks are authorized to conduct business only with nonresidents.

Gold

Panama has issued two commemorative gold coins with face values of B 100 and B 500, which are legal tender but do not circulate. Residents may freely hold gold in any form, at home or abroad, and may freely negotiate gold in any form with residents or nonresidents at home and abroad. Imports and exports of gold in any form, other than jewelry carried as personal effects by travelers, require a license if made by residents other than the monetary authorities; import licenses are issued by the Ministry of Commerce and Industry, and export licenses are issued by the Ministry of Finance and Treasury. Exports of unworked gold produced in Panama are subject to an export duty of 1 percent ad valorem, and exports of gold coins (other than U.S. coins, which are exempt) are subject to a duty of 0.5 percent.

Changes During 1995

Imports and Import Payments

January 1. A harmonized commodity description and coding system for custom tariffs was introduced.

November 1. Import tariffs on raw materials for manufacturing were reduced to a uniform rate of 3 percent; previously there was a wide range of tariffs on these goods.

December 20. Import tariffs on the main agricultural products, except those on corn and soybeans, were reduced effective January 1, 1996. Tariffs on corn and soybeans were to be increased to 70 percent and 50 percent, respectively, effective April 1, 1996.

PAPUA NEW GUINEA

(Position as of December 31, 1995)

Exchange Arrangement

The currency of Papua New Guinea is the Papua New Guinea Kina, the external value of which is determined freely in the interbank market where the authorized dealer banks participate with the Bank of Papua New Guinea, which acts as broker. The closing rate in the interbank market becomes the official exchange rate, which on December 31, 1995, for the U.S. dollar was K 1 per $0.7490. The commercial banks, the only authorized foreign exchange dealers, publish rates for all current transactions with their customers within a maximum spread between the buying and selling rates of 2 percent. There are no taxes or subsidies on purchases or sales of foreign exchange.

Exporters and importers are free to take out forward cover with the commercial banks at market-determined rates. Each commercial bank is subject to a prudential limit on its uncovered forward position. At its discretion, the Bank of Papua New Guinea may intervene in the forward foreign exchange market.

Papua New Guinea accepted the obligations of Article VIII, Sections 2, 3, and 4 of the Fund Agreement on December 4, 1975.

Administration of Control

Foreign exchange control is administered by the Bank of Papua New Guinea under the Central Banking Act (Foreign Exchange and Gold Regulations, Chapter 138). Overall policy is determined by the Government in consultation with the Bank of Papua New Guinea. The Bank of Papua New Guinea has delegated considerable powers to the commercial banks operating in Papua New Guinea, which have been appointed authorized dealers in foreign exchange. Export licensing is administered by the Department of Foreign Affairs and Trade.

In accordance with the Fund's Executive Board Decision No. 144-(52/51) adopted on August 14, 1952, Papua New Guinea notified the Fund on July 22, 1992 that, in compliance with UN Security Council Resolution No. 757 (1992), certain restrictions had been imposed on the making of payments and transfers for current international transactions in respect of the Federal Republic of Yugoslavia (Serbia/Montenegro).

Prescription of Currency

Contractual commitments to persons residing outside Papua New Guinea and expressed in a foreign currency must be paid in foreign currency.[1] Export proceeds may be received in any foreign currency.

Foreign Currency Accounts

Authorized foreign exchange dealers (at present, the six commercial banks) may open and maintain foreign currency accounts and foreign currency term deposits in Papua New Guinea for residents and nonresidents. For resident business entities, the account holders are required to obtain the approval from the Bank of Papua New Guinea, except for term deposits that are placed for a minimum of 90 days.

Imports and Import Payments

Imports of a limited number of goods are restricted for reasons of health and security, and imports of a number of items, including sugar, poultry, and pork, are prohibited to protect domestic markets. The importation of most fresh fruits and vegetables is banned (except for apples, onions, and potatoes for processing). In the event of shortages on the domestic market, special import licenses are issued and imports are subject to a 50 percent tariff.

Authorized dealers may, without referring to the Bank of Papua New Guinea, approve applications for import transactions that are not subject to quotas or licensing requirements. The tariff regime consists of the following rates: (1) essential items, including food staples (rice and meat that are not produced domestically), and medical and educational supplies, duty free; (2) basic goods, including some consumer goods and raw materials, 8 percent or 11 percent; (3) intermediate goods, including goods with satisfactory domestic substitutes, 40 percent; (4) luxury goods, including jewelry, cosmetics, poker machines, and nonessential food and beverage items, 55 percent (except for electrical ovens, television sets, cameras, video recorders, and hi-fi equipment, for which the tariff rate is 10 percent); and (5) selected goods produced locally (tinned mackerel, citrus fruits), 15 percent or 100 percent.

---

[1]Foreign currencies are defined as all currencies other than the kina.

Payments for Invisibles

Approval is readily granted for most payments for invisibles, provided that supporting documentation is produced. Authorized foreign exchange dealers may approve payments and transfers up to the equivalent of K 500,000 a year for any purpose for all adult individuals or corporations. Payments and transfers in excess of the equivalent of K 500,000, except trade-related payments or payments for the servicing of foreign debt, must be referred to the Bank of Papua New Guinea for approval. Payments for the servicing of foreign debt may be approved without a fixed limit by authorized dealers. For payments or transfers exceeding K 50,000 a year, a certificate of tax payment is required.

Travelers wishing to take or send out Papua New Guinea domestic currency in excess of K 200 in notes and K 5 in coin must obtain the approval of the Bank of Papua New Guinea. Domestic coins issued for numismatic purposes may be taken out freely. Overseas visitors are free to take out any currency they brought in and declared on arrival.

Exports and Export Proceeds

Residents of Papua New Guinea may export goods without exchange control formalities on the condition that they comply with the terms of the general authority issued by the Bank of Papua New Guinea. The essential conditions of this authority are that payments for goods exported must be received within six months of the date of export and that the proceeds must be sold to authorized dealers in Papua New Guinea. When exporters are not in a position to comply with the conditions of the general authority, they must apply to the Bank of Papua New Guinea for specific authorization. No authorization is needed for certain categories of goods, including travelers' personal effects. Export licenses are required for certain goods (e.g., logs, pearls, fishery and marine products, woodchips, sandalwood, rattan, coffee, cocoa, and copra) under the Export (Valuation and Control) Act. Log export licenses are issued subject to minimum export price guidelines; there is no export license requirement on timber. Although exports of most unprocessed products are subject to export levies, these have been temporarily waived, except for fishery and forestry products. Export taxes on logs range from 15 percent to 70 percent. Fish exports are subject to a 10 percent tax.

Proceeds from Invisibles

Approval is required for the disposal of foreign currency proceeds, other than by sale to an authorized dealer in Papua New Guinea, or for its retention. Residents are not permitted to retain foreign exchange earnings from any source without the approval of the Bank of Papua New Guinea. Overseas visitors may bring in any amount of currency for travel expenses.

Capital

Outward transfers of foreign-owned capital are allowed, provided that tax clearance certificates are produced. Direct investments outside Papua New Guinea are subject to certain limitations. Authorized dealers may approve outward investments by resident individuals and corporations up to the equivalent of K 500,000 a year; investments in excess of the equivalent K 500,000 require the approval of the Bank of Papua New Guinea. Income from the investment must be returned to Papua New Guinea as received. Prior clearance from the tax authorities is required for these transactions if the amount exceeds K 50,000 in any calendar year.

Permission is required for residents to enter into an agreement to borrow in foreign currencies. However, authorized foreign exchange dealers may approve offshore foreign currency borrowing by residents, other than businesses involved in the forestry sector or mineral resources exploration, without limit, provided that the term is for not less than one year and that interest rates and fees do not exceed the levels specified by the Bank of Papua New Guinea. Repayment of principal is subject to a six-month moratorium, commencing on the date of disbursements. A maximum debt-to-equity ratio of 5:1 applies to net outstanding borrowing. In the case of a business involved in mineral resource exploration activities, inward investment is considered non-interest-bearing equity or loan funds (including preference shares) until the business is successful, at which point any excess above the minimum debt-to-equity ratio specified for that operation can be converted into an interest-bearing loan.

There are no restrictions on direct investment and for inward portfolio investment.

Gold

Dealings in gold in Papua New Guinea are not regulated. The exportation of gold is restricted to licensed gold exporters. For the large mines, the licenses are contained in their respective mining agreements. For exports of alluvial gold, specific export licenses are required from the Bank of Papua New Guinea.

Changes During 1995

Exchange Arrangement

August 14. The screen-based foreign exchange market was introduced, replacing the twice-daily "open-outcry" auctions, which were introduced as a transitional arrangement after the transition to the float in October 1994.

Foreign Currency Accounts

August 14. The authority to open residents' foreign exchange accounts was returned to the Bank of Papua New Guinea, following the discovery of some commercial banks' failure to comply with the regulations regarding the reporting of transactions in those accounts.

PARAGUAY

(Position as of December 31, 1995)

Exchange Arrangement

The currency of Paraguay is the Paraguayan Guaraní. The authorities do not maintain margins in respect of foreign exchange transactions, and exchange rates are determined largely on the basis of demand and supply in the exchange market. The Central Bank of Paraguay, however, intervenes in the market to smooth out any sharp fluctuations in the exchange rate of the guaraní due to seasonal changes in demand or supply conditions as well as to speculative capital flows. The intervention currency is the U.S. dollar. Private transactions in respect of merchandise imports and exports, services, and capital are carried out through the authorized commercial banks; public transactions are carried out through the Central Bank of Paraguay or commercial banks. On December 31, 1995, the average rate prevailing in the interbank market for the U.S. Dollar was ₲ 1.987 per $1. Public debt-service payments and payments for services by the Government are channeled through the Central Bank of Paraguay at the rate prevailing on the day of the transaction. No commissions are assessed on these transactions if debtors have foreign exchange deposit accounts with the Central Bank of Paraguay.

The commercial banks may maintain a daily foreign exchange overbought position not exceeding 100 percent of their capital and reserves, or an oversold position of up to 50 percent of their capital reserves. Exchange houses may maintain a daily overbought position of $250,000. Commercial banks are permitted to enter into forward transactions with respect to trade transactions and on terms that may be negotiated freely with customers.

Paraguay accepted the obligations of Article VIII, Sections 2, 3, and 4 of the Fund Agreement on August 23, 1994.

Administration of Control

The Central Bank of Paraguay has the authority, under the Constitution, to determine foreign exchange policy in consultation with other agencies of the Government. In practice, decisions are taken by the Economic Cabinet on the advice of the Central Bank of Paraguay, who is responsible for the execution of the decisions of the Economic Cabinet. The Central Bank of Paraguay supervises, through the Superintendency of Banks, foreign exchange trans-

actions carried out by the banks and the exchange houses.

Prescription of Currency

Payments between Paraguay and Argentina, Bolivia, Brazil, Chile, Colombia, the Dominican Republic, Ecuador, Mexico, Peru, Uruguay, and Venezuela are made through accounts maintained with the Central Bank of Paraguay and the other central banks concerned, within the framework of the multilateral clearing arrangements of the Latin American Integration Association (LAIA). Clearing takes place every four months. There are no other prescription of currency requirements.

Imports and Import Payments

Imports of certain products that may be harmful to public health, national security, or animal or plant health are prohibited; these restrictions, however, may be waived to ensure adequate domestic supplies. All importers must be registered at the Central Bank of Paraguay.

All trade barriers within the Southern Cone Common Market (Mercosur; comprising Paraguay, Argentina, Brazil, and Uruguay) were eliminated on December 31, 1994. Under the Mercosur, which came into force on January 1, 1995, common external tariff (CET) rates were established with certain exceptions. There are 11 different tariff levels, ranging from zero to 20 percent. The implementation of the Mercosur pact has increased Paraguay's import duties, although the main effects have been delayed due to extensive exceptions for imports of capital, telecommunications, and automotive goods. Paraguay was allowed to exempt 399 other items from the CET, consisting mostly of production inputs and goods destined for the tourist industry and the re-export market. These exemptions are to be phased out by 2006 by gradually raising tariff rates—to 14 percent on most capital goods and to 20 percent for telecommunications. Typical rates on exemptions from the CET are raw materials and intermediate goods, zero percent; capital goods, 5 percent; items for tourism, 6 percent; consumer goods, 10 percent; vehicles whose c.i.f. value exceeds $10,000, 15 percent; and vehicles whose c.i.f. value exceeds $20,000, 20 percent. Similarly, Paraguay was allowed 427 exceptions to the free trade agreement on intra-Mercosur trade that has enabled it to maintain protective tariffs ranging from 6 percent to 30 percent on some domestically produced manufactures and agricultural products. The exceptions to the free trade agreement are to be phased out by 2001. When import payments are made under the LAIA Reciprocal Payments Agreement, the Central Bank of Paraguay levies a commission of 0.125 percent.

Payments for Invisibles

Payments for current invisibles are carried out through commercial banks or exchange houses without restriction. Travelers may take out any amount in foreign or domestic currency. A 2.5 percent value-added tax is levied on international air transport tickets issued in the country.

Exports and Export Proceeds

Exports of logs and unprocessed forest products, rawhides, and wild animals are prohibited. Certain other exports require prior authorization from the appropriate agency. All other exports are not restricted, except with regard to the technical standards imposed by the National Institute of Technology and Standardization, the Ministry of Industry and Commerce, the Ministry of Public Health, or the Ministry of Agriculture and Livestock, depending on the product exported.

All exporters are required to be registered at the Central Bank of Paraguay. The proceeds of exports must be collected within 120 days after completion of the banking formalities related to the shipping documents, but may be retained by exporters.

Proceeds from Invisibles

There are no surrender requirements for proceeds from invisibles, except for royalties and remuneration from the binational entities, which are transferred in full to the Central Bank of Paraguay, for the account of the Ministry of Finance. Similarly, administrative expenditure outlays of the binational entities are paid through the operating banks.

Capital

All capital transfers must be channeled through the commercial banks or exchange bureaus, and records on transactions exceeding the equivalent of $10,000 should be kept for five years by these institutions to facilitate Central Bank of Paraguay control on money laundering. Also, for statistical purposes, banks and exchange bureaus should report all international movements of foreign banknotes and coins to the Superintendency of Banks. Repatriation of earnings of foreign enterprises through the free

exchange market is allowed—subject to a 5 percent levy, payment of income tax, and prior authorization of the Central Bank of Paraguay. The Government may grant exemptions from taxes, customs, and import surcharges on proposed investments that are duly registered and approved.

Gold

The Central Bank of Paraguay may prescribe the maximum amount of gold that residents may hold. This requirement does not apply to amounts held by the Central Bank of Paraguay or by institutions authorized to deal in foreign currencies. In practice, residents may freely purchase, hold, and sell gold in any form, in Paraguay or abroad, and exchange houses may freely deal in gold coins, gold bars, and gold leaf with residents and nonresidents. The exportation and importation of gold by nonbank residents and industrial users in any form other than jewelry require the prior authorization of the Central Bank of Paraguay. Payments for gold imports by industrial users must be made through commercial banks.

Changes During 1995

Exchange Arrangement

February 17. All records on foreign exchange transactions through banks and exchange bureaus in excess of $10,000 should be kept for five years to facilitate the equivalent of Central Bank of Paraguay control on money laundering.

Imports and Import Payments

January 1. The Southern Cone Common Market (MERCOSUR) took effect, imposing a common external tariff (CET) ranging from zero to 20 percent on imports from non-MERCOSUR countries and a zero tariff on intra-MERCOSUR trade. Paraguay is allowed exemptions from the CET for capital goods, telecommunications products, automotive products, and 399 other selected items, consisting mostly of inputs to production and goods destined to the tourist industry. There are also 427 exceptions to the agreement for duty-free intra-MERCOSUR trade. All quantitative restrictions on imports and exports were eliminated.

Capital

June 29. The Central Bank of Paraguay law was approved. The law defines the scope of foreign exchange transactions and the Central Bank of Paraguay exchange policy.

October 25. The requirement that banks and exchange bureaus report international movements of foreign banknotes and coins (currency, amount, and geographic origin or destiny of the transfer) was extended to include reporting to the Superintendency of Banks for statistical purposes.

PERU

(Position as of December 31, 1995)

Exchange Arrangement

The currency of Peru is the Nuevo Sol, the external value of which is freely determined by participants in the exchange market on the basis of supply and demand conditions. On December 31, 1995, the average interbank transaction rate, as registered and published by the Superintendency of Banking, was S/. 2.311, per $1. Exchange transactions may be conducted in any currency, including the U.S. dollar, and the cross rate relationships with currencies other than the U.S. dollar are determined on the basis of the rate for the U.S. dollar in the international market.

Since 1991, the exchange system has been free of controls on both current and capital transactions. Enterprises and natural persons may hold foreign exchange balances abroad and in domestic banks. There are arrangements for forward cover against exchange rate risk operating only in the commercial banking sector. Bank accounts in foreign currencies may be held with domestic banks.

Peru accepted the obligations of Article VIII, Sections 2, 3, and 4 of the Fund Agreement on February 15, 1961.

Administration of Control

Exchange houses are authorized to purchase foreign exchange and traveler's checks from residents and nonresidents and to sell foreign exchange for tourism abroad and for repurchases by nonresidents.

Borrowing abroad by the public sector, as well as borrowing abroad by the private sector with a government guarantee, is subject to prior approval by supreme decree, within the limits established by the Financing Requirement Law of the public sector.

Arrears are maintained with respect to external payments on nonguaranteed credits of suppliers, commercial banks, and official loans obtained from Eastern European countries.

Prescription of Currency

Payments between Peru and Argentina, Bolivia, Brazil, Chile, Colombia, the Dominican Republic, Ecuador, Malaysia, Mexico, Paraguay, Uruguay, and Venezuela may be made through accounts maintained with each other by the Central Reserve Bank of Peru and the other central banks concerned, within the framework of the multilateral clearing system of the Latin American Integration Association (LAIA).

Imports and Import Payments

Imports of certain goods are prohibited from all sources for social, health, or security reasons. No other imports are restricted. Imports of raw materials and intermediate goods are exempt from import duties, provided that the appropriate ministry determines that such imports qualify under the Temporary Admission Regime. All monopolies on the importation of goods have been abolished, including the monopoly over the importation of milk powder and wheat by the National Enterprise for Input Marketing, and that over crude petroleum and petroleum derivatives by Petroperu, a state-owned enterprise.

With some specified exemptions, imported goods are subject to a uniform value-added tax of 18 percent of the c.i.f. value of imports in addition to the import duty; exempted from the value-added tax are some agricultural products. The tariff regime consists of two basic rates: 25 percent (maximum) affecting 15 percent of products and 15 percent for the remainder, excluding imports subject to trade agreements. Agricultural products are subject to a variable import surcharge.

Advance payments for all imports are allowed without restriction. Legislation has been enacted requiring preinspection at the port of embarkation by international firms for imports exceeding $2,000 (f.o.b.).

Payments for Invisibles

Payments for almost all invisibles other than public debt service are not subject to payment authorization.

Remittances of net profits are permitted freely. Foreign investment by petroleum companies is subject to special contracts with the Peruvian Government.

Exports and Export Proceeds

Export prohibitions apply to 75 items, mainly rare wildlife (including wild animal skins and textiles made from them), plants, cottonseed cakes, natural rubber, and mineral ores. State enterprise monopolies over the exportation of mining and petroleum products were eliminated in 1991. Proceeds from exports are not subject to a repatriation requirement. A list of items excluded from the drawback to exports was abolished (R.M. No. 137-95-EF) on September 3, 1995.

Proceeds from Invisibles

Proceeds from invisibles are not subject to surrender requirements.

Capital

Outward capital transfers, including amortization of private sector debts that are not guaranteed by the Government, are not restricted.

Short-term trade credits that have been subject to a refinancing agreement or assumed by the Government began to be rolled over beginning August 1, 1983. Other short-term trade credits may be repaid in accordance with bilateral agreements concluded before June 1992 or through renegotiation after that date with the approval of the External Debt Committee. Short-term trade and working capital credits began to be rolled over beginning March 8, 1983.

New foreign investments must be registered with the National Commission on Foreign Investment and Technology. Foreign companies incorporated in Peru may benefit from the duty-free program of the Cartagena Agreement under the same conditions as domestic enterprises.

Investments in the mining sector are governed by the General Mining Law, enacted in June 1992. The Government may grant tax incentives to mining concessionaires (initiating large-scale investment programs).

Under the Private Sector Investment Guarantee Regime, the Government guarantees nondiscriminatory treatment for foreign investors and private enterprises, protection of property rights, the development of any economic activity, free internal and external trade, and capital repatriation. In addition, investors may enter into contracts that guarantee tax stability, nondiscriminatory treatment, foreign currency availability, capital repatriation, free labor contracts, and export incentives.

Gold

The exportation and importation of gold are not restricted.

Changes During 1995

Exports and Export Proceeds

June 23. A drawback of 5 percent on the f.o.b. value of exports is to be restituted to the exporter or export good's producer when (1) the c.i.f. value of the imported intermediate goods used to produce the exported good is less than 50 percent of the f.o.b. value of the latter; and (2) the f.o.b. value of the correspondent item was not more than $10 million in 1994 (Decreto Supremo No. 104-95-EF).

September 3. A list of items excluded from the drawback to exports was published (R.M. No. 137-95-EF).

PHILIPPINES

(Position as of December 31, 1995)

Exchange Arrangement

The currency of the Philippines is the Philippine Peso. The authorities of the Philippines do not maintain margins in respect of exchange transactions, and exchange rates are determined on the basis of demand and supply in the exchange market. However, the authorities intervene when necessary to maintain orderly conditions in the exchange market and in light of their other policy objectives in the medium term. On December 31, 1995, the reference exchange rate for the U.S. dollar was ₱26.214 per $1. The Central Bank of the Philippines, officially known as the Bangko Sentral ng Pilipinas, is not governed by the trading rules of the Bankers' Association of the Philippines in making its own purchases and sales of foreign exchange, except for transactions conducted at the trading center. Commercial banks trade in foreign exchange through the Philippine Dealing System (PDS) or by telephone. All forward transactions to purchase foreign exchange, including renewals thereof, from nonresidents require prior approval of the Central Bank. There is a forward exchange cover scheme for oil import payments, although the cover period has been phased down to 90 days from 180 days by the end of 1995.

The Philippines accepted the obligations of Article VIII, Sections 2, 3, and 4 of the Fund Agreement on September 8, 1995.

Administration of Control

Exchange regulations are administered by the Central Bank on the basis of policy decisions adopted by the Monetary Board. Without prior approval, non-Philippine nationals not otherwise disqualified by law may engage in business in the Philippines or invest in a domestic enterprise up to 100 percent of their capital except in areas restricted by law. Nonresidents may purchase foreign exchange from authorized agent banks only up to the amount they have converted into pesos through the banking system or deposited in foreign currency accounts.

Foreign exchange may be freely sold and purchased outside the banking system. Foreign exchange received in the Philippines or acquired abroad may be deposited in accounts denominated in foreign currency. However, in order that foreign loans and foreign investments can be serviced with foreign exchange purchased from the banking system, the investments must be registered with the Central Bank, and the loans must be approved, registered with, or reported to the Central Bank. All categories of banks (except offshore banking units) duly licensed by the Central Bank are considered authorized agent banks. Thrift banks may be authorized to offer foreign currency accounts, subject to prudential regulations.

The entry of foreign banks to operate in the Philippines has been liberalized. Their entry can be effected through a purchase of 60 percent of the voting stock of an existing domestic bank or of a new banking subsidiary incorporated in the Philippines or through the establishment of branches with full banking authority, subject to the licensing requirements of the Central Bank; 14 foreign banks were operating at the end of 1995.

Prescription of Currency

There are no prescription of currency requirements for outgoing payments, but all exchange proceeds from exports and invisibles must be obtained in prescribed currencies.[1] Payments may be made in pesos for exports to member countries of the Association of South East Asian Nations (ASEAN), provided that the Central Bank is not asked to intervene in the clearing of any balances from this payment scheme. Authorized agent banks may accept notes denominated in the prescribed currencies for conversion into pesos.

Resident and Nonresident Accounts

Bank accounts denominated in pesos may be opened in the names of individual or corporate nonresidents without the prior approval of the Central Bank. Nonresident accounts may be credited only with the proceeds from inward remittances of foreign exchange or convertible foreign currencies and with peso income earned from the Philippines belonging to nonresidents. Nonresident accounts may be freely debited for withdrawals in pesos.

---

[1] Australian dollars, Austrian schillings, Bahrain dinars, Belgian francs, Brunei dollars, Canadian dollars, deutsche mark, French francs, Hong Kong dollars, Indonesian rupiahs, Italian lire, Japanese yen, Kuwaiti dinars, Malaysian ringgit, Netherlands guilders, pounds sterling, Saudi Arabian riyals, Singapore dollars, Swiss francs, Thai baht, U.A.E. dirhams, U.S. dollars, and other such currencies that may be declared acceptable by the Central Bank.

Both residents and nonresidents may maintain foreign currency deposit accounts with authorized agent banks in the Philippines (see section on Proceeds from Invisibles, below). Residents are allowed to maintain deposits abroad without restriction.

Imports and Import Payments

Generally, all merchandise imports are allowed without a license. However, the importation of certain products is regulated or restricted for reasons of public health and safety, national security, international commitments, and development and protection of local industries.

Goods are classified into three categories: freely importable, regulated, and prohibited. Applications to import freely importable products may be processed by authorized agent banks without prior approval or clearance from any government agency. To import regulated products, a clearance of permit is required from the appropriate government agency (including the Central Bank). Prohibited products are those that may not be imported under existing laws. Under the Comprehensive Imports Supervision Scheme (CISS), preshipment inspection is required for imports valued at more than $500 from all countries. Imports declared in the shipping documents as off-quality, used, secondhand, scraps, off-grade, or a similar term indicating that the article is not brand new are subject to CISS inspection even if the value of the imports is less than $500. Certain exemptions are specifically provided if shipment is duty exempt or when inspection is deemed impractical.

Commercial banks may sell foreign exchange to service payments for imports under letters of credit (LCs), documents against acceptance (DAs), documents against payments (DPs), open account (OAs) arrangement, and direct remittance. LCs must be opened on or before the date of shipment with a validity period of up to one year. Only one LC may be opened for each import transaction; amendments to such an arrangement need not be referred to the Central Bank for prior approval, except when the amendment extends the total validity of the LC beyond one year. Imports under DA and OA arrangements must be registered with the Central Bank for monitoring purposes; prior approval of the Central Bank, regardless of maturity, is not required as long as these are importations of freely importable goods not guaranteed by foreign governments/official credit agencies. Any extension of maturities must be reported to the Central Bank 30 days before the effective date. Import arrangements not involving payments using foreign exchange purchased from the banking system, such as self-funded or no-dollar imports and importation on consignment basis, are allowed without prior approval from the Central Bank.

The tariff structure has four standard tariff bands: 3 percent, 10 percent, 20 percent, and 30 percent. Tariff rates on products in the higher bands will be phased down gradually, so that by the year 2003, virtually all products will be subject to a 3 percent band for raw materials or 10 percent for finished products. Tariff rates on imported capital goods are 3 percent and 10 percent, the former rate applying to goods not produced domestically. Exemptions to the tariff structure are as follows: (1) the applicable standard rate may be increased up to twice its value for final products of basic industries registered with "pioneer" status at the Board of Investment (BOI); (2) tariffs of up to double the standard rate (or up to negotiated bindings, in the case of agricultural products being liberalized under the World Trade Organization (WTO) agreement) may be imposed on products for which quantitative restrictions are being removed; and (3) imported capital goods may be duty exempt for firms registered with the BOI prior to January 1, 1995, or if subject to the provisions of two existing laws: RA 7369 and RA 7844, the Export Development Act. Some 300 capital goods (as specified under a 1992 law, RA 7369), as well as imports of machinery, equipment, and accompanying spare parts used in the manufacture of export products have zero duties. The BOI no longer offers tax and duty exemptions on imports of capital equipment and spare parts; instead, newly registering firms are able only to obtain duty reductions, to the minimum rate of 3 percent, on their eligible imports. Tariff rates for the textile and garments sector are 3 percent for inputs and 30 percent for final products. Legislation to remove quantitative restrictions on corn, wheat, and certain other agricultural products, with the exception of rice, has been presented to Congress.

Payments for Invisibles

Authorized banks may sell foreign exchange to residents for payments of any nontrade transaction against appropriate written applications without limit and without prior approval from the Central Bank, provided that (1) for sales of foreign exchange exceeding $25,000, banks must require a written application and supporting documents from the buyer of the foreign exchange; and (2) for sales of foreign exchange not exceeding $25,000, no written application or supporting documents will be required from the buyer, but the buyer must disclose to the bank concerned the specific purpose for the purchase. For payments related to foreign loans or investments, banks must require documentation showing central bank approval and/or registration for the loan or investment. Unregistered loans and investments can be serviced also through transactions in the nonbank market.

Full and immediate repatriation of profits and dividends (net of taxes) accruing to nonresidents from all types of investment may be effected directly through commercial banks without prior approval from the Central Bank. However, service payments relating to foreign loans or foreign direct investments effected by purchases of foreign exchange through authorized agent banks are limited to those transactions whose original capital transfer has previously been registered with the Central Bank. Service payments related to option-to-purchase or transfer of ownership at a later date do not require prior central bank approval.

Remittances of profits, dividends, and earnings made in connection with the program for the conversion of external debt into equity investments are unrestricted.

Resident and nonresident travelers must have prior authorization from the Central Bank to take out more than ₱10,000 in domestic banknotes and coins or checks, money orders, and other bills of exchange drawn in pesos. When traveling abroad, citizens of the Philippines must pay a travel tax of ₱2,700 for first-class passage and ₱1,620 for economy-class passage. Reduced rates of ₱1,350 for first-class passengers and ₱810 for economy-class passengers are provided for groups of people traveling for recognized special purposes. Reduced rates of ₱400 for first-class passengers and ₱300 for economy-class passengers are provided for dependents of contract workers duly registered with the Philippine Overseas Employment Administration. Departing nonresidents are allowed to reconvert at airports or other ports of exit unspent pesos of up to a maximum of $200 or an equivalent amount in other foreign exchange (calculated at prevailing exchange rates) without proof of sales of foreign exchange by authorized agent banks.

Exports and Export Proceeds

Exports are allowed without restriction, except for those that are regulated or prohibited for reasons of national interest. Exports of selected seeds and shoots of native plants, endangered fish and wildlife (including selected marine species), and stalactites and stalagmites are prohibited.

All exports must be covered by export declarations duly prepared by the exporter. Authorized agent banks may issue and amend an export declaration before negotiation without prior approval from the Central Bank. Payments for exports may be made in prescribed currencies, under the following forms without prior central bank approval: LC, DP, DA, and OA; cash against documents arrangements; consignment; export advance; and prepayment. Payments for export advances and prepayments are no longer subject to a time limit of 30 days. Foreign currency deposit units and authorized agent banks may purchase export bills directly from exporters and indirect exporters, subject to certain conditions (Circular No. 16 of March 7, 1994).

There are no surrender requirements. Foreign exchange receipts or earnings of residents from exports may be sold for pesos to authorized banks or outside the banking system, retained, or deposited in foreign currency accounts, whether in the Philippines or abroad, and they may be used freely for any purpose. There are no export taxes.

Proceeds from Invisibles

There are no mandatory surrender requirements on proceeds from invisibles, which may be used without restriction. Travelers may freely bring in any amount of foreign currency. The importation of domestic banknotes, coins, checks, money orders, and other bills of exchange drawn in pesos exceeding ₱10,000 requires prior authorization from the Central Bank.

Capital

Registration of inward investments with the Central Bank is required only if the foreign exchange needed to service the repatriation of capital and remittances of dividends and profits from these investments is to be funded through the banking system. When applications for central bank registration of new inward foreign investments (in kind or in cash) are reviewed, no priority or preference is given to the category of industry in which the investment is made, as long as they are funded by (1) inward remittance of foreign exchange for cash investments which may be either converted into pesos or deposited in foreign currency deposit accounts in local banks of the domestic investor firm, or (2) in the case of investment in kind, there has been an actual transfer of assets to the Philippines. Full and immediate repatriation is guaranteed on all central bank-registered foreign investments without restriction.

Foreign companies are eligible to obtain loans in domestic currency from banks or nonbank financial institutions, provided that they have a maximum debt-equity ratio of 70:30 in high-priority sectors (i.e., firms registered under RA 5786 or RA 6135, Philippine Export Zone Authority registered firms, Central Bank or central bank-certified firms, and firms engaged in vital industries under Circular 870); a maximum ratio of 65:35 (i.e., firms engaged in other manufacturing activities); and a maximum ratio of 60:40 in low-priority sectors (i.e., firms engaged in nonmanufacturing activities). Investments in domestic commercial banks registered with the Central Bank may be repatriated without restriction.

Foreign direct investments may be (1) foreign equity in Philippine firms or enterprises; (2) investment in government securities or securities listed on the stock exchange; or (3) investment in money instruments or bank deposits. Foreign direct equity investment may be in cash or in kind. Investments are permitted in connection with the Program for the Conversion of Philippine External Debt into Equity Investments. Under this program, most categories of external debt, including rescheduled debt, may be converted into equity investment. In 1993, however, investments permitted under the Debt-to-Equity Conversion Program of the Central Bank were suspended, except the debt swap for high social impact projects.

In 1994, the Government liberalized, under RA 7721, the entry and scope of operations of foreign banks to operate in the Philippines subject to prior approval by the Central Bank Monetary Board. Investments in domestic commercial banks and in local branches of foreign banks made prior to the enactment of RA 7721 as well as investments of foreign banks established under RA 7721 and registered with the Central Bank may be repatriated without restriction, subject to submission of certain documentary requirements, including clearance from the appropriate central bank supervision and examination departments.

Under the Foreign Investments Act of 1991, non-Philippine nationals not otherwise disqualified by law may, upon registration with the Securities and Exchange Commission, conduct business in the country or invest in domestic enterprises up to 100 percent of capital unless participation is prohibited or limited by existing law. However, enterprises seeking to apply for incentives, as well as foreign investors in export enterprises, must also register with the Board of Investments. Issues of securities abroad by residents under initial public offering are required to advise the Central Bank of receipt of proceeds within five days.

Outward investments by resident natural and juridical persons may be made freely, except those purchased from authorized agent banks that exceed $6 million an investor a year; such investments require prior central bank approval and registration.

All public sector loans from foreign creditors, offshore banking units, and foreign currency deposit units (FCDUs), except short-term FCDU loans, must be referred to the Central Bank for prior approval even before actual negotiations commence.

Loans of the private sector, irrespective of maturity, creditor, and the source of foreign exchange for servicing thereof, if guaranteed by government corporations and/or government financial institutions or local commercial banks or granted by FCDUs and specifically or directly funded from, or collateralized by, offshore loans or deposits, likewise require prior central bank approval or registration. Refinancing of such loans would require prior central bank approval. Otherwise, private sector loans from FCDUs and offshore sources, irrespective of maturity, to be serviced with foreign exchange not purchased from the banking system do not require central bank approval or registration. Private sector short-term loans for trade purposes granted by FCDUs or under a central bank-approved or a noted foreign creditors' lending program but not guaranteed by a government corporation, government financial institution, or local bank, and not refinanced by medium- and long-term foreign debt do not require prior approval from the Central Bank. These may be serviced with foreign exchange purchased from the banking system but must be reported to the Central Bank for registration purposes.

The prepayment or acceleration of payments on medium- and long-term loans duly registered with the Central Bank that takes place within two years of final maturity is exempt from prior approval by the Central Bank.

Loans requiring prior central bank approval are normally expected to finance export-oriented projects and those registered with the Board of Investment, projects listed in the Investment Priorities Plan and the Medium-Term Public Investment Program, and projects that may be declared high priority under the country's socioeconomic development plan by the National Economic and Development Authority or Congress. Inward remittances of loan proceeds intended to finance only local requirements of projects may be sold to the banking system or deposited in FCDUs and/or offshore accounts. Proceeds intended to finance foreign costs must not be inwardly remitted and may be either paid directly to the supplier or beneficiary concerned, or deposited in an offshore account.

Terms of loans to be obtained by the National Government must be in accordance with the provisions of pertinent laws, while terms of other loans must be the same as those prevailing in the international capital markets.

Commercial banks are allowed to maintain open foreign exchange positions, subject to the limitation that long and short positions do not exceed 20 percent and 10 percent, respectively, of unimpaired capital. Local branches of foreign banks licensed to engage in commercial banking in the Philippines must exclude their permanently assigned capital from their foreign exchange liabilities for purposes of computing their net foreign exchange position. All foreign exchange sales made through international ATMs and credit cards must be reported to the Foreign Exchange Department of the Central Bank within two days; the annual limit on such sales was set at $50,000 a person.

Foreign banks may operate in the Philippines through a purchase of 60 percent of the voting stock of an existing domestic bank or of a new banking subsidiary incorporated in the Philippines or through the establishment of branches with full banking authority, subject to the licensing requirements of the Central Bank. At the end of 1995, 14 foreign banks had branches operating in the Philippines; 1 foreign bank had acquired 60 percent of the voting stock of an existing domestic bank; and 18 foreign banks were operating offshore units. Foreign banks with offshore units in the Philippines may engage in a wide range of foreign currency transactions with nonresidents and with other offshore banking units. They are permitted to lend to resident importers and exporters, provided that such loans do not have public guarantees, that the funds have been remitted from abroad and sold to the banking system, and that loans are authorized by the Central Bank. Offshore banking units may open and maintain deposit accounts in pesos exclusively with domestic agent banks to meet administrative and other operating expenses and to pay designated local beneficiaries of nonresident Philippine or multinational companies the equivalent of foreign exchange remittances channeled through the offshore banking units' correspondent banks abroad. Offshore banking units may also sell inward remittances of foreign exchange to the Central Bank.

Gold

Small-scale miners are required to sell all of their production to the Central Bank. All other forms or types of gold may be bought, and without specific approval, sold and delivered to the Central Bank. Producers selling gold to the Central Bank are paid in Philippine pesos on the basis of the latest London fixing price and the prevailing Philippine peso-U.S. dollar exchange rate. The gold so acquired is deemed to be part of official international reserves. The Central Bank may sell gold grains, pellets, bars, and sheets to local jewelry manufacturers and other industrial users upon application, or to banks only for resale to jewelry manufacturers and industrial users, at the Central Bank's selling price for gold plus a service fee to cover costs, including the cost of conversion and packaging. The exportation of gold in any form, except that produced by small-scale miners, is permitted. There are no restrictions on the importation of any form of gold except coin blanks essentially of gold, gold coins, and coins without any indication of actual fineness of gold content.

Various denominations of gold coins have been issued by the Central Bank as follows: a 1 Peso Paul VI coin (1970); a 1,000 Piso Ang Bagong Lipunan coin (1975); a 1,500 Piso IMF-IBRD coin (1976); the 1,500 Piso Ang Bagong Lipunan coins (1977 and 1978); a 5,000 Piso Ang Bagong Lipunan coin (1977); a 2,500 Piso Douglas MacArthur Centenary coin (1980); a 1,500 Piso Pope John Paul II coin (1980 and 1981); a 1,500 Piso Bataan-Corregidor coin (1982); a 2,500 Piso Aquino-Reagan coin (1986); a 10,000 Democracy Restored coin (1992); and 5,000 and 2,000 Piso Pope's Visit coins (1995). Transactions in legal tender gold coins are governed by the provisions of Central Bank Circular No. 960 (Sections 175 and 176), dated October 21, 1983.

Changes During 1995

Exchange Arrangement

March 1. The period of the forward exchange cover scheme for oil import payments was reduced to 90 days from 180 days.

September 8. The Philippines accepted the obligations of Article VIII, Sections 2, 3, and 4 of the Fund Agreement.

Imports and Import Payments

January 1. Tariff rates on some 300 capital goods (as specified under a 1992 law, RA 7369), as well as on imports of machinery, equipment, and accompanying spare parts used in the manufacture of export products, were reduced to zero.

February 24. New expanding or modernizing enterprises that have been registered with the Board of Investments on or before December 31, 1994, would be exempted from 100 percent of national internal revenue taxes and customs duties on importations of machinery, equipment, and accompanying spare parts within the prescribed period under the law of registration or until December 31, 1997, whichever comes first. Those enterprises located outside the National Capital Region (NCR) may avail themselves of the aforementioned incentives until December 31, 1999. Enterprises registering after December 31, 1994, would be subject to the provisions of RA 7716 and to a 3 percent customs duty until December 31, 1997.

April 24. Works of art, current newspapers, periodicals, individually owned motor vehicles, and parcel post would be exempt from the requirement of inspection under the Global Comprehensive Import Supervision Scheme.

May 12. All imports of fresh, frozen, or chilled foodstuffs, fruits, and live animals shipped beginning May 27, 1995 (based on bill of lading or airway bill date) would be subject to the Societe Generale de Surveillance (SGS) preshipment inspection requirement.

Payments for Invisibles

July 1. The last round of tariff reductions under the Tariff Reform Program (TRP) of 1991 was introduced. As a result, the maximum tariff rate was reduced from 80 percent to 50 percent, and the number of principal tariff rates for goods other than those liberalized in the context of the Import Liberalization Program was halved from 12 percent to 6 percent (3 percent, 5 percent, 10 percent, 20 percent, 30 percent, and 50 percent). The average nominal tariff rate declined to 19 percent from almost 28 percent at the beginning of the TRP.

July 5. All imports from or exports to China would no longer require Philippine International Trading Corporation (PITC) clearance.

July 22. A new tariff reduction program for industrial products, excluding capital goods and textile and garments sector products, was formulated for the period 1995–2000. The new tariff structure has only four standard tariff bands: 3 percent, 10 percent, 20 percent, and 30 percent. The average nominal tariff rate on industrial goods declined to 16 percent.

August 29. Authorized agent banks (AABs) were to sell foreign exchange to residents for any non-trade purpose, without prior central bank approval, provided that (1) for sales of foreign exchange exceeding $25,000, the AAB would require a written application and supporting documents from the purchaser of the foreign exchange; and (2) for sales of foreign exchange not exceeding $25,000, no written application or supporting documents would be required from the purchaser who would only disclose to the AAB concerned the specific purpose for

the purchase, and the AAB would report the sale to the Central Bank under the appropriate report form.

October 19. Motor vehicles, parts, and components that require prior clearance from the Department of Trade and Industry or the Board of Investments were deleted from the list of regulated imports.

December 11. The importation (and exportation) and electronic transfers of legal tender Philippine notes and coins, checks, money orders, and other bills of exchange drawn in pesos against banks operating in the Philippines in an amount exceeding ₱10,000 were prohibited without authorization by the Central Bank.

Exports and Export Proceeds

June 6. The requirement that foreign exchange earnings from export transactions negotiated through offshore banking units be surrendered to domestic banks was abolished.

Capital

February 23. The maximum allowed overbought foreign exchange position of commercial banks was reduced to 20 percent from 25 percent of unimpaired capital, and the maximum oversold position was raised to 10 percent from 5 percent (Central Bank Circular 63).

April 12. Banks were allowed to avail themselves of the Exporters Dollar Facility (EDF) against the eligible dollar-denominated loans of their exporters-borrowers (both direct and indirect), including service exporters who are engaged in rendering technical, professional, and other services.

June 6. Offshore banking units (OBUs) were allowed to service importations through LC, DA, OA, and DP of resident borrowers, provided that such importations would be funded by a central bank-authorized OBU foreign currency loan to the resident-borrower involved, and provided further that DA and OA imports channeled through and serviced by OBUs would be subject to the registration and reporting requirements for DA and OA imports.

October 31. The definition of "foreign firms" was amended to refer to (1) partnerships with more than 40 percent of their capital owned by non-Filipino citizens, and (2) corporations with more than 40 percent of their total subscribed capital stock owned by non-Filipino citizens. In determining capital stock ownership by non-Filipino citizens, the equity of multilateral financial institutions would be excluded.

POLAND

(Position as of December 31, 1995)

Exchange Arrangement

The currency of Poland is the Zloty, the external value (central rate) of which is pegged to a basket of five currencies.[1] The central rate is adjusted under a crawling peg policy at a preannounced rate. Since May 16, 1995, the National Bank of Poland has allowed the external value of the zloty (i.e., the market rate) to fluctuate within margins of ±7 percent around the central rate. The exchange rates between the zloty and other convertible currencies are determined on the basis of the exchange rates between the U.S. dollar and the currencies concerned on international markets. The National Bank quotes exchange rates for the European currency unit (ECU), the SDR, and the currencies of 28 countries considered market-oriented economies.[2] Rates for currencies other than the U.S. dollar are set daily and are based on the quoted rate for the U.S. dollar and the dollar rates for the relevant currencies in international markets. Transactions between the National Bank and commercial banks are conducted in the interbank market. Banks are permitted to set buying and selling rates within a margin of 2 percent around the market rate, and their transactions with the National Bank take place at the market rate.

The exchange rate on the foreign exchange bureau market, in which natural persons are allowed to transact freely, provided that the transaction is not a commercial one, is determined by market forces. On December 31, 1995, the official rate for the U.S. dollar was Zl 2.4680 per $1.[3]

There are no formal forward exchange market arrangements, but a forward market exists for the stock market. However, large commercial banks provide forward contracts if requested.

Poland accepted the obligations of Article VIII, Sections 2, 3, and 4 of the Fund Agreement on June 1, 1995.

Administration of Control

The authority to make basic changes in the Foreign Exchange Law rests with Parliament.[4] Regulations are promulgated by the Minister of Finance in the form of general foreign exchange permits or by the president of the National Bank in the form of individual permits. General permits are issued for all residents and nonresidents and for specified groups. The procedures for issuing individual permits are established by the president of the National Bank in cooperation with the Minister of Finance. The authority to enforce foreign exchange regulations rests with the Minister of Finance, who exercises related functions mainly through the president of the National Bank. However, decisions concerning individual foreign exchange permits are subject to appeal to the Supreme Administrative Court.

Foreign exchange control is exercised by the Ministry of Finance, the National Bank, the foreign exchange banks, customs offices, the border guard, and post offices.

In accordance with the Fund's Executive Board Decision No. 144-(52/51), adopted on August 14, 1952, Poland notified the IMF that in compliance with UN Security Council Resolutions it had imposed certain restrictions on the making of payments and transfers for current international transactions in respect of Iraq and the Federal Republic of Yugoslavia (Serbia/Montenegro).

Prescription of Currency

Outstanding balances under the (inoperative) bilateral payments agreements with Bangladesh, Brazil, China, Egypt, India, the Islamic Republic of Iran, Lebanon, and Turkey are being settled in accordance with the terms of the agreements. Balances outstanding under the arrangements of the International Bank for Economic Cooperation are still being settled in transferable rubles. Settlements with all

---

[1]The basket consists of (figures in parentheses represent weights) the U.S. dollar (45 percent); the deutsche mark (35 percent); the pound sterling (10 percent); the French franc (5 percent); and the Swiss franc (5 percent). On January 1, 1995, new currency notes and coins began to circulate, replacing old currency at a conversion rate of 1 to 10,000. Old currency will remain in circulation until the end of 1996.

[2]Australian dollars, Austrian schillings, Belgian francs, Canadian dollars, Danish kroner, deutsche mark, Finnish markkaa, French francs, Greek drachmas, Indian rupees, Italian lire, Iranian rials, Irish pounds, Japanese yen, Kuwaiti dinars, Lebanese pounds, Libyan dinars, Luxembourg francs, Netherlands guilders, Norwegian kroner, Portuguese escudos, pounds sterling, Spanish pesetas, Swedish kronor, Swiss francs, Turkish liras, U.S. dollars, and Yugoslav dinars.

[3]Foreign exchange bureaus (*kantors*) must obtain licenses to operate. They are permitted to purchase foreign exchange from the interbank market without restriction.

[4]A new foreign exchange law was passed in December 1994 and came into effect on January 1, 1995.

other currencies may be made in any convertible currency.

Since January 1, 1991, nearly all trade with the member countries of the former Council for Mutual Economic Assistance (CMEA) has been settled in convertible currencies; a limited amount of trade, both under pre-existing contracts and in settlement of ruble balances outstanding at the end of 1990, continue to be transacted in transferable rubles.

Resident and Nonresident Accounts

Resident Accounts: Residents, both natural and juridical persons, may hold foreign exchange in the form of currency and securities. Residents who are natural persons may maintain currency accounts ("A" accounts), and these accounts may be freely credited with convertible currency brought in or transferred from abroad and/or deposited without declaring the sources of funds. Account holders may use balances freely to effect transfers abroad, to buy goods and services, to finance tourist travel abroad by themselves or other persons, and to effect gifts to family members or other persons. Balances in these accounts cannot be used to effect settlements between individuals but can be sold in foreign exchange bureau markets. Withdrawals in zlotys, converted at the prevailing exchange rate, are freely permitted. Accounts maintained in deutsche mark, French francs, pounds sterling, Swiss francs, and U.S. dollars in demand deposits earn interest at an annual rate of 2.5 percent to 4 percent; accounts maintained in these currencies in one-, two-, and three-year term deposits earn interest at an annual rate of 2.5 percent. Funds in A accounts cannot be used for business activities. When leaving the country permanently, individuals are allowed, under the general foreign exchange permit, to transfer all funds from this account.

Foreign Exchange Accounts for Foreign Settlements (ROD): ROD accounts are held by juridical persons. Until December 9, 1995, all foreign exchange receipts from exports, were in principle required to be surrendered, except that juridical persons were allowed to retain foreign exchange accumulated in ROD Accounts before January 1, 1990. On December 10, 1995, amendments to the Foreign Exchange Law came into effect allowing companies with international operations to maintain Polish accounts in a foreign currency and abolishing the surrender requirement.

Resident individuals and enterprises who demonstrate proof of need may hold foreign exchange accounts abroad with the permission of the National Bank. Under the general foreign exchange permit, such an account may also be held by enterprises earning foreign exchange from performing specific contracts. Balances in these accounts may not exceed $100,000.

Nonresident Accounts: Nonresident natural and juridical persons are free to maintain both convertible currency and zloty accounts. Nonresidents may maintain convertible currency accounts ("C" accounts) at all foreign exchange banks. These accounts may be credited with funds brought in or transferred to Poland, with transfers from other C accounts, and with convertible currency amounts legally acquired in Poland.[5] Deposits are freely transferable abroad, and may be used to make gifts to residents. The funds earn interest in foreign currency at the same rates as funds in the A accounts.

Depositors in zloty accounts must declare the source of the zlotys; this declaration requirement is aimed at ensuring that payments into the accounts result from contracts or other operations that comply with the provisions of the foreign exchange law. Apart from zlotys legally earned in Poland, these accounts may also be credited with zloty balances converted from foreign exchange at the official exchange rate. Permits for conversion back into foreign exchange or for foreign exchange transfers abroad are normally granted. These accounts do not pay interest; however, nonresidents may also deposit their earnings in savings accounts, on which interest is paid. Balances in zloty accounts may be transferred to nonresidents or residents with foreign exchange permits, except for gift payments to residents. Permits for transfers to nonresidents are granted only for transfers to family members. Permits for transfers to residents are granted without restriction.

Imports and Exports

Licenses are not required for imports from the convertible currency area, with the exception of imports of radioactive materials and military equipment; dairy products; alcoholic beverages, other than beer; and coal. Licenses are required for imports carried out within the framework of international agreements that stipulate bilateral settlements. The importation of certain mineral oils, tobacco products, and alcoholic beverages is subject to a quota. The importation of the following products is prohibited: certain alcohol products; passenger cars older than ten years; trucks, vans, and utility

---

[5]Since January 1, 1995, a foreign national entitled to transfer foreign currency has been allowed to hold "unrestricted foreign accounts"; funds in these accounts are freely transferable abroad.

cars older than six years; and cars with two-cycle engines.

Export quotas cover items subject to import restrictions by other countries and ferrous waste and scrap; export licenses are required for (1) goods subject to export quotas, (2) exports carried out within the framework of international agreements that stipulate bilateral settlements, and (3) temporary exports of capital goods and transport equipment for leasing. Nonresidents in Poland (persons domiciled abroad but not foreign corporate entities operating in Poland) are required, temporarily, to apply for export permits. Exports of protein feed and oats and, on a temporary basis, some alcoholic products, dairy products, some mineral oils, and natural gas are prohibited.

All commercial imports, regardless of country of origin or provenance, are subject to an ad valorem import tariff based on the Harmonized Commodity Description and Coding System (HCDCS) and the combined nomenclature of the European Community (EC) of 1991, with six basic rates: zero on equipment for the disabled, mineral resources, textiles, and cattle hides; zero to 5 percent on other raw materials; 7 percent to 13 percent on basic parts of semifinished and finished goods; 17 percent to 29 percent on industrial goods; 25 percent to 40 percent on agricultural and textile products; and 29 percent to 43 percent on luxury goods. Imports from developing countries are granted preferential treatment under the General System of Preferences. Also, imports from 42 developing countries, tropical products from Chapters 6 to 24 of the HCDCS, and many goods from Chapters 32 and 94 of the HCDCS that are of interest to developing countries enter Poland duty free. For the remaining goods imported from non-European developing countries whose per capita GDP is lower than Poland's, duties are reduced to 30 percent of the most-favored-nation (MFN) rate. Some special regulations pertain to border trade with the Baltic countries, Russia, and the other countries of the former Soviet Union.

Imports are subject to a surcharge of Zl 50,000 and an additional turnover tax of 6 percent; alcoholic beverages, tobacco products, fuels, and automobiles are exempt from the turnover tax. Duties and turnover taxes on imports for export production are refunded. Exports other than coal are free from turnover taxes.

Until recently, exporters were required to declare all foreign currency receipts from exports, to repatriate them within two months of receipt, and to surrender them to the Polish foreign exchange banks within 14 days of receiving notice that foreign exchange has been deposited in their accounts in Poland. Effective December 10, 1995, the surrender requirement was abolished for companies engaged in international operations.

Payments for and Proceeds from Invisibles

Payments for invisible expenses arising from merchandise transactions, including insurance and transportation costs, are permitted freely if related to trade transactions. All other invisible transactions are carried out under either a general or an individual permit. Foreign exchange for such payments is made available automatically once the transaction is authorized.

For official and business travel, separate allowances are established by the Ministry of Finance to reflect reasonable costs. Business travelers may take out of Poland up to the equivalent of $10,000 from the foreign currency accounts maintained by the enterprises that employ them for travel expenses or purchases of goods and services associated with their business activity. Additional amounts may be taken out upon proof of need.

Polish nationals leaving Poland are permitted to take abroad up to $2,000 or the equivalent in convertible foreign currencies, checks, and traveler's checks that they have purchased from foreign exchange banks to pay outstanding obligations to foreign nationals resulting from (1) the purchase of movable assets and proprietary interests, and (2) transportation and insurance services. Documentary proof of origin is necessary for amounts exceeding this limit. However, holders of A accounts may take out of the country the balance on their accounts without limit. When leaving Poland, tourists from convertible currency area countries may reconvert zlotys up to the equivalent they brought into Poland, provided that the amount is not more than that originally converted into zlotys.

Residents must repatriate foreign exchange within two months of receipt or within two months of returning to Poland. Residents may, without approval, bring into or take out of the country domestic banknotes and coins in an amount not to exceed Zl 5 million a person. Foreign visitors must declare foreign exchange they bring into the country in order to take out the unspent amount and are not permitted to bring zlotys into the country or to take them out.

Business entities may use their ROD accounts to pay wages and salaries to nonresident employees. They may also use their ROD accounts, or foreign exchange purchased from foreign exchange banks, to pay outstanding obligations relating to (1) procurement costs, including costs of participation in exhibitions and fairs, and advertising costs; (2) fees for agents' representational services; (3) costs of repairing and overhauling imported machinery and equipment; (4) costs associated with protecting intellectual property; and (5) costs related to auditing, consulting, and information services. Similarly, individuals may remit foreign exchange to pay for (1) participation in international organizations and international hotel networks abroad; (2) costs of court or arbitration proceedings up to the equivalent of $20,000 a case; (3) costs of obtaining legal counsel and trial representation in a given case up to $50,000 or the equivalent; (4) taxes, customs duties, or administrative fees payable abroad; and (5) study abroad. Amounts in excess of established limits can be remitted if supporting documents showing the bona fide nature of the transaction are provided.

Transfers abroad by nonresident workers in Poland, other than in the context of employment in joint ventures, are determined on the basis of agreements between domestic and foreign institutions or enterprises and through individual foreign exchange permits. Nonresident employees of joint ventures may transfer abroad up to 100 percent of their income. Residents may remit pensions and annuities in convertible foreign exchange at the official exchange rate to nonresidents who are entitled to such payments on the basis of a ruling from the social security administration.

Profits on direct investment by nonresidents, other than those from joint ventures, or the acquisition of shares in Polish companies, may be transferred abroad without restriction. If the investment yields a net surplus in convertible currency in any fiscal year, up to 50 percent of the surplus may be transferred abroad, provided that the transfer does not exceed 50 percent of net profits after taxes. The Minister of Finance may permit a transfer in excess of 50 percent of the surplus. On liquidation, the investor may transfer abroad the proceeds from the sale of the remaining assets sold in foreign currency.

Capital

Parliament annually sets an upper limit on the public sector's external indebtedness. Within this limit, foreign borrowing takes place on the basis of intergovernmental agreements and in various forms of bank and commercial credits. Under the provisions of the banking law, the National Bank, Bank Handlowy, Bank PKO, S.A., and the Export Development Bank are empowered to borrow abroad, on short or long term, and to extend foreign credits. The Minister of Finance sets limits on the foreign borrowing of the banks, and the contracting of foreign loans is subject to approval.

A foreign investment law, Law on Companies with Foreign Participation, came into effect on July 4, 1991, replacing the Law on Economic Activity with Participation of Foreign Parties, which had governed all new foreign direct investments since December 23, 1988. Under the 1991 law, new businesses need to register only with local courts, except for investments in the areas of seaports, airports, real estate transactions, defense, legal services, and wholesale trade in imported products, all of which continue to require permits. Imports of capital goods for new joint ventures are exempt from customs duties. Investors in certain priority sectors and investments exceeding ECU 2 million a year are also eligible for tax concessions. The 10 percent ceiling on purchases of shares of privatization issues has been abolished, and a permit is not required unless such shares relate to the above-mentioned sectors. The transfer of profits from joint ventures and from investments in shares of Polish companies is not restricted, and invested capital may be repatriated once outstanding obligations to creditors are discharged. The transfer of profits or repatriation of capital from bonds is not restricted. Although the 1991 law does not stipulate a minimum amount of capital that foreign nationals must invest in Poland, the minimum capital requirement set forth in the Polish commercial code for a limited liability company and a joint-stock company is in effect and is applied to foreign investment.

Foreign investment by residents, either to establish subsidiaries or affiliates or to acquire an interest in a foreign enterprise, requires a foreign exchange permit.

All categories of capital transfers, including gifts, by resident natural persons require a foreign exchange permit. Emigrants to other countries must obtain an individual permit from the National Bank to take out their convertible currency deposits with domestic banks. Other financial assets may be deposited in a nonresident zloty account.

Negotiable export documents may be discounted by foreign banks. With a permit, exports of goods (other than fuels and raw materials) and services may be financed by a credit of up to the equivalent of $1 million with repayment terms of up to 360 days. With a permit, imports with a value of up to the equivalent of $1 million may also be financed by a credit with repayment terms of up to three years.

Except in the form of an inheritance, nonresidents may acquire real estate or other immovable property in Poland only with permission from the Ministry of the Interior.

Gold

Resident individuals may hold gold in any form. Trading in gold, other than jewelry, is subject to permission from the foreign exchange authorities. Polish and foreign nationals may take abroad gold coins that bear value in foreign exchange. They may also bring into Poland coins made from precious metals that are legal tender in Poland. Only one enterprise, Jubiler, has general permission to buy and sell in gold in any form.

Changes During 1995

Exchange Arrangement

January 1. New currency notes and coins were issued replacing old currency at a conversion rate of 1 to 10,000. Old currency would remain in circulation until the end of 1996.

May 16. The National Bank allowed the external value of the zloty to fluctuate within margins of ±7 percent around the central rate. Foreign exchange bureaus were permitted to purchase foreign exchange from the interbank market without restriction.

June 1. Poland accepted the obligations of Article VIII, Sections 2, 3, and 4 of the Fund Agreement.

Administration of Control

January 1. A new Foreign Exchange Law removing remaining exchange restrictions on current international transactions came into effect.

March 27. Amended general foreign exchange permits came into force.

Imports and Exports

January 1. The rate of the import surcharge was reduced to 5 percent from 6 percent.

PORTUGAL

(Position as of December 31, 1995)

Exchange Arrangement

The currency of Portugal is the Portuguese Escudo. Portugal participates with Austria, Belgium, Denmark, France, Germany, Ireland, Luxembourg, the Netherlands, and Spain in the exchange rate and intervention mechanism (ERM) of the European Monetary System (EMS).[1] In accordance with this agreement, Portugal maintains the spot exchange rates between the Portuguese escudo and the currencies of the other participants within margins of 15 percent above and below the cross rates based on the central rates expressed in European currency units (ECUs).[2] The agreement implies that the Banco de Portugal (the central bank) stands ready to buy or sell the currencies of the other participating states in unlimited amounts at specified intervention rates. On December 31, 1995, these rates were as follows:

Specified Intervention Rates Per:	Portuguese Escudos	
	Upper limit	Lower limit
100 Austrian schillings	1,691.800	1,254.700
100 Belgian or Luxembourg francs	577.090	428.000
100 Danish kroner	3,120.500	2,314.300
100 Deutsche mark	11,903.300	8,827.700
100 French francs	3,549.000	2,632.100
1 Irish pound	286.983	212.838
100 Netherlands guilders	10,564.000	7,834.700
100 Spanish pesetas	139.920	103.770

The participants in the EMS do not maintain the exchange rates for other currencies within fixed limits. However, in order to ensure a proper functioning of the system, they intervene in concert to smooth out fluctuations in exchange rates, the intervention currencies being each other's, the ECU, and the U.S. dollar.

Official exchange rates for the U.S. dollar and other currencies[3] are based on information on the exchange rate of the Portuguese escudo in terms of the deutsche mark provided by the banking system and are announced daily by the Banco de Portugal. These rates are a reference for the banks' bid and offer rates, which are freely set. On December 31, 1995, the indicative rate for the U.S. dollar was Esc 149.413 per $1.

Banks are allowed to engage in spot and forward exchange transactions in any currency among themselves and with residents and nonresidents at free market rates of exchange. Nonbank residents may also conduct spot or forward exchange operations with nonresident counterparts. The degree of foreign exchange risks that banks are authorized to take must fall within the limits established by the Banco de Portugal for their foreign exchange positions (calculated as the sum of the positions against escudos in each foreign currency).

Portugal accepted the obligations of Article VIII, Sections 2, 3, and 4 of the Fund Agreement on September 12, 1988.

Administration of Control

There are no exchange controls. Foreign trade policy is implemented by the Ministry of Economy. The Direcção-Geral do Comércio in this ministry is responsible for administering trade controls and for issuing import and export licenses, surveillance documents, and certificates.

In accordance with the Fund's Executive Board Decision No. 144-(52/51) adopted on August 14, 1952, Portugal notified the IMF on September 12, 1990, that certain restrictions were imposed on the making of payments and transfers for current international transactions to residents or nationals of Iraq. Portugal also notified the IMF, in compliance with UN Security Council Resolution No. 883 (1993), that the movements of any funds in Portugal that are controlled by public authorities or Libyan companies are prohibited.

---

[1]Austria became a member of the European Union on January 1, 1995, and joined the ERM of the EMS on January 9, 1995.

[2]Effective August 2, 1993, the intervention thresholds of the currencies participating in the ERM of the EMS, except those of the deutsche mark and the Netherlands guilder, were widened from ±2.25 percent (in the case of Portugal and Spain, 6 percent) to ±15 percent around the bilateral central exchange rates; the fluctuation band of the deutsche mark and the Netherlands guilder remained unchanged at ±2.25 percent.

[3]Australian dollars, Austrian schillings, Belgian francs, Canadian dollars, Danish kroner, deutsche mark, European currency units (ECUs), Finnish markkaa, French francs, Greek drachmas, Italian lire, Irish pounds, Japanese yen, Macao patacas, Netherlands guilders, Norwegian kroner, pounds sterling, South African rand, Spanish pesetas, Swedish kronor, and Swiss francs. The Macao pataca is pegged to the Hong Kong dollar at a parity rate of P 1.03 per HK$1.

Prescription of Currency

There are no prescription of currency requirements. Settlements may be effected in any currency.

Resident and Nonresident Accounts

Residents and nonresidents are free to open and operate accounts in Portugal or abroad in either escudos or foreign currencies.

Imports and Import Payments

As a general rule, imports are free of restrictions. For products under European Union (EU) surveillance, the appropriate import documents, when required, are issued for statistical surveillance purposes and are granted automatically in four to five days. Imports of certain products are subject to an import license and are allowed under specific conditions or are prohibited for reasons of health, public order, and the prevention of commercial fraud. Imports subject to quantitative restrictions require an import license. Generally, the validity of import licenses is six months for customs clearance purposes.

For agricultural products covered by the common agricultural policy of the EU, the EU may require an import certificate.

A few industrial products, such as steel products and some textiles and clothing, are subject to import restrictions in the EU when they originate in certain third countries. A more extensive restricted list applying to China includes some textiles and a small number of finished products.

Exports and Export Proceeds

Exports are free of restrictions. Proceeds from exports are not subject to repatriation or surrender requirements.

Payments for and Proceeds from Invisibles

There are no restrictions on payments for and proceeds from invisibles. Travelers may import or export any amount of domestic and foreign banknotes or any other means of payment. The exportation or importation by residents or nonresidents of banknotes or coins and traveler's checks in excess of the equivalent of Esc 2.5 million must be declared to customs.

Capital

There are no exchange restrictions or controls on capital transactions, and no distinction is made between capital transactions with residents of EU member countries and residents of non-EU member countries. According to Decree Law No. 321/95 of November 28, 1995, foreign direct investments are permitted in all sectors except those that, under general law, are closed to private enterprise corporations. Foreign direct investment operations are submitted to a register that should be fulfilled within 30 days after the operations have been made. The projects with special interest to the Portuguese economy are covered by a separate and contractual regime.

The establishment of a financial institution in Portugal in which a majority voting right is held by natural persons who are not nationals of a European Economic Area (EEA) member country or by legal persons with their main office and central management in a non-EEA country is subject to previous authorization from the Minister of Finance, which may consider prudential requirements as well as other criteria. Similar regulations apply to the establishment in Portugal of branches of a financial institution located in a non-EEA member country.

The establishment in a non-EEA member country of branches of financial institutions by residents is subject to prior authorization from the Banco de Portugal.

Gold

Residents may freely buy, hold, and sell gold in any form in Portugal. Residents and nonresidents may also import and export bullion, coins, and unworked gold, but a customs declaration is required for amounts exceeding Esc 2.5 million.

Changes During 1995

Exchange Arrangement

March 6. The authorities realigned the central parity of the escudo by 3.5 percent, and the upper and lower limits of the escudo for the currencies of participants in the ERM of the EMS were changed accordingly.

Imports and Import Payments

(See Appendix for a summary of trade measures introduced and eliminated on an EU-wide basis during 1995.)

Capital

November 28. Liberalization of foreign direct investment (Decree-Law No. 321/95).

QATAR

(Position as of December 31, 1995)

Exchange Arrangement

The currency of Qatar is the Qatar Riyal, which is pegged to the SDR at QR 4.7619 per SDR 1. Qatar has established margins of 7.25 percent around this rate. The Qatar Central Bank sets daily market rates for the U.S. dollar, the intervention currency. On December 31, 1995, the buying and selling rates for the Qatar riyal in terms of the U.S. dollar were QR 3.6415 and QR 3.6385, respectively, per $1.

The exchange rates of commercial banks for transactions in U.S. dollars are based on the Central Bank's buying and selling rates. A spread of QR 0.0087 is applied to exchange transactions with the public. The buying and selling rates of commercial banks for other currencies are based on the Central Bank's rates for the U.S. dollar and on market rates for the currency concerned against the U.S. dollar. There are no taxes or subsidies on purchases or sales of foreign exchange. There are no arrangements for forward cover against exchange rate risk operating in the official banking sector. In the commercial banking sector, importers may purchase foreign exchange in the forward market.

Qatar accepted the obligations of Article VIII, Sections 2, 3, and 4 of the Fund Agreement, on June 4, 1973.

Administration of Control

The Central Bank is the exchange control authority, but there is at present no exchange control legislation. Import licenses are issued by the Ministry of Finance, Economy, and Commerce. Financial transactions with the Federal Republic of Yugoslavia (Serbia/Montenegro) are prohibited.

Prescription of Currency

All settlements with Iraq and Israel are prohibited. No other prescription of currency requirements are in force.

Nonresident Accounts

No distinction is made between accounts held by residents and those held by nonresidents.

Imports and Import Payments

All imports from Iraq and Israel are prohibited, as are imports of pork and its derivatives. Imports of alcoholic beverages, firearms, ammunition, and certain drugs are subject to licensing for reasons of health or public policy. Otherwise, imports are not restricted. There are no restrictions on payments for permitted imports. Imports of general goods are subject to a customs tariff at the rate of 4 percent, which is the minimum rate applied by member countries of the Cooperation Council for the Arab States of the Gulf (GCC). The customs tariff on steel is 20 percent; on tobacco, 104 percent; and on alcoholic beverages, 100 percent. Imports of goods from other member countries of the GCC are not subject to a customs tariff.

Exports and Export Proceeds

All exports to Iraq and Israel are prohibited. Otherwise, all commodities may be exported freely. No requirements are attached to receipts from exports or re-exports; the proceeds need not be repatriated or surrendered, and they may be disposed of freely, regardless of the currency involved.

Payments for and Proceeds from Invisibles

Payments may not be made to or received from Iraq and Israel. Otherwise, there are no limitations on payments for and proceeds from invisibles in effect.

Capital

No exchange controls are imposed on capital receipts or payments by residents or nonresidents, although payments may not be made to or received from Iraq and Israel. Noncitizens may engage in simple crafts as well as in commerce, industry, agriculture, and services jointly with Qatari partners, provided that the latter's share is not less than 51 percent. Noncitizens may also establish companies specializing in contracting business with Qatari partners, subject to the above conditions, if it is determined that there is a need to establish such companies or if there is a need for the experience and technology they provide.

Gold

The monetary authorities and all other residents and nonresidents (including private persons) may freely and without license purchase, hold, and sell gold in any form, at home or abroad. For trading purposes, the buying and selling of gold and precious metals require an import license and are subject to customs duty. Transactions involving Iraq and Israel are prohibited.

Changes During 1995

No significant changes occurred in the exchange and trade system.

ROMANIA

(Position as of December 31, 1995)

Exchange Arrangement

The currency of Romania is the Romanian Leu. The exchange rate against the U.S. dollar (the reference exchange rate) is determined in the interbank foreign exchange market. The National Bank of Romania is not committed to intervene in the exchange market except to smooth out fluctuations in exchange rates and to build up foreign exchange reserves. Only commercial banks authorized by the National Bank can participate in the exchange market. Juridical persons other than authorized commercial banks may purchase or sell foreign exchange through authorized banks, and individuals may purchase foreign currency at foreign exchange bureaus. All transactions between resident juridical persons and between juridical persons and natural persons must be made in the national currency. In certain circumstances, the National Bank may authorize foreign exchange operations between individuals and juridical persons. The authorization of the National Bank of Romania is not necessary for the forex transfers between residents resulting from foreign trade contracts. On December 31, 1995, the exchange rate for the U.S. dollar was lei 2,578 per $1. The National Bank quotes rates for 23 other currencies,[1] based on the rates for these currencies against the U.S. dollar in the countries concerned, as well as for the European currency unit and the SDR. Foreign exchange bureaus conduct transactions only in foreign currency banknotes, traveler's checks, and credit cards, and only with natural persons. Since September 19, 1994, these bureaus have been allowed to set their exchange rates freely.

The transferable ruble, the currency used for commercial transactions with the member countries of the former Council for Mutual Economic Assistance (CMEA), was abolished but continues to be used as a unit of account for the purpose of liquidating outstanding balances.

Forward exchange transactions to cover against exchange rate risks relating to current international transactions are permitted.

Administration of Control

The National Bank issues rules and regulations related to control of foreign exchange transactions according to the law that set up the National Bank as the country's central bank, on May 3, 1991. The National Bank authorizes all capital transfers, including those connected with inheritances, proceeds from the liquidation of capital assets owned by foreign natural persons, and pension payments abroad on the basis of visas issued by the Ministry of Economy and Finance.[2] Domestic commercial banks are authorized by the National Bank to conduct foreign exchange transactions abroad for current international transactions and are permitted to have foreign banks as correspondents or to borrow directly abroad with national bank authorization.

Prescription of Currency

Payments to and from countries with which Romania has bilateral payments agreements are made only in the currency and in accordance with the procedures set forth in those agreements.[3] If no agreement exists, settlement is usually made in a convertible currency.

Resident and Nonresident Accounts

All juridical and natural persons may maintain foreign currency accounts with commercial banks authorized by the National Bank to operate in Romania.

Resident juridical persons may open and maintain foreign exchange accounts abroad or other assets in foreign currency with the prior authorization of the National Bank. Romanian natural persons and foreigners permanently domiciled in Romania and receiving foreign exchange income abroad may hold and use foreign means of payment in foreign exchange accounts held in financial and banking institutions abroad. Natural persons may also hold foreign exchange in the form of banknotes and coins or in accounts opened with commercial banks authorized to operate in Romania and, within the laws and conditions specified by foreign exchange

---

[1]Australian dollars, Austrian schillings, Belgian francs, Canadian dollars, Danish kroner, deutsche mark, Egyptian pounds, Finnish markkaa, French francs, Greek drachmas, Indian rupees, Irish pounds, Italian lire, Japanese yen, Luxembourg francs, Netherlands guilders, Norwegian kroner, Portuguese escudos, pounds sterling, Spanish pesetas, Swedish kronor, Swiss francs, and Turkish liras.

[2]Authorization is not required to operate nonresident deposits held by resident banks; loans and credits received by residents and guaranteed by the state; and deposits that resident banks place in their own name.

[3]At the end of 1995, Romania maintained bilateral payments agreements with Albania, China, and Ghana.

regulations, may freely use such foreign exchange to effect current international payments. The deposits may also be exchanged for lei through the foreign exchange bureaus authorized to operate in Romania.

Imports and Exports

Import and export transactions were liberalized on May 1, 1992, and in general are not subject to licensing. There are no quantitative import restrictions. Exports of certain products (including timber, livestock, sunflower seeds, maize, certain mineral oils, chemical fertilizers, and copper alloys) are subject to a quota. Both the Ministry of Commerce and the Ministry of Finance may take measures to restrict imports for purposes of protecting the balance of payments, or for reasons of public health, national defense, and state security, in accordance with the provisions of the World Trade Organization.

Import tariff rates are ad valorem, and range from zero to 343 percent, with a simple average rate of about 19 percent. A differential import surcharge is levied on certain agricultural products.

Resident juridical persons are required to repatriate export proceeds but are allowed to keep them in accounts opened at domestic commercial banks or foreign commercial banks authorized to operate in Romania, and are free to use the balances in these accounts.

Payments for and Proceeds from Invisibles

Resident juridical persons may effect foreign exchange transfers for payments for invisibles (or any international current account) transactions through authorized commercial banks. Commercial banks must verify, based on supporting documents, that the requested transfer is for bona fide current account purposes.

Foreign exchange bureaus are permitted to sell foreign exchange to resident natural persons for the purpose of travel abroad up to the annual limit of $500 a person. Foreign exchange bureaus are permitted to sell to resident natural persons more than $500 in special situations such as trips abroad for medical treatments, participation in conferences, and educational purposes.

Natural persons residing in Romania may take out of the country foreign exchange in the form of banknotes and coins up to a maximum amount equivalent to $5,000 a person a trip to effect current transactions (such as expenses for group or individual travel, medical treatments or purchases of medicines, participation in conferences, education, purchases of consumer goods for personal use, and payments for services); no documentation is required for amounts of $1,000 or less. Amounts above $1,000 up to $5,000 must be documented. Natural persons must make all transfers exceeding $5,000 through banks. Resident natural persons representing juridical persons engaging in international transport or tourism activities may take cash out of the country up to the equivalent of $10,000. Transfers to banks abroad for current operations may also be made from the foreign exchange accounts of natural persons domiciled permanently in Romania and from the accounts of other Romanian juridical persons, except in special cases (as stipulated by law) requiring prior authorization from the National Bank; such authorization is granted on a case-by-case basis. Banks may not limit the volume of bona fide current operations.

The maximum amount of foreign currency banknotes and coins that natural persons may bring into Romania is the equivalent of $10,000 a person a trip. Cash amounts larger than $10,000 must be deposited with Customs at the Romanian border. In the case of nonresident natural persons, amounts not converted into lei may be taken out of the country. The maximum amount of domestic banknotes that can be brought into or taken out of Romania is lei 100,000 a person a trip in denominations no larger than lei 5,000.

Capital

All outward transfers of foreign currency must be authorized by the National Bank. The restriction on capital outflow concerns direct investments abroad, including the purchase of real estate, portfolio investment in international financial markets, bank accounts abroad, credits granted by residents abroad, and repayment of external credits received by Romanian residents.

Under the investment law that came into effect on April 3, 1991, there are no limits on foreign equity participation in a commercial firm set up in Romania, and foreign investments may be made in all sectors of the economy, except for security and defense reasons.

Foreign investors may participate in the management of the investment operation or assign contractual rights and obligations to other Romanian or foreign investors. In addition, foreign investors can transfer abroad (1) the entire amount of their share of profits earned in convertible currencies or in lei; (2) the total or partial proceeds in convertible currencies from sales of stocks, shares, bonds, and other securities, as well as from the liquidation of investments; and (3) the proceeds in lei from the liquidation of investments in freely convertible currencies.

Imported machinery, equipment, installations, means of transport, and any other goods in kind constituted as participation of the foreign investor are exempt from custom duties. Foreign investors also benefit from certain tax advantages.

Gold

The National Bank has sole authority to purchase or sell gold in any manner, at home or abroad. It, in turn, authorizes certain juridical persons to hold gold, to use it, and to engage in gold transactions. Natural persons may, without restriction, own gold jewelry and artistic and cultural objects for domestic and personal use.

Changes During 1995

Exchange Arrangement

May 31. Foreign exchange operations between residents and nonresidents settled in cash, and between residents settled in cash and through banking accounts must be authorized by the National Bank.

May 31. Foreign exchange bureaus were required to have assets of at least lei 200 million, constituted until January 31, 1996.

December 31. Foreign exchange bureaus were permitted to sell to resident natural persons more than $500 under certain conditions. The authorization of the National Bank is not necessary for foreign exchange transfers between residents that result from foreign trade contracts.

Administration of Control

June 30. Foreign banks were granted licenses to operate as foreign exchange dealers.

Resident and Nonresident Accounts

September 30. Enterprises were permitted to maintain foreign exchange accounts at more than one bank.

RUSSIAN FEDERATION

(Position as of June 30, 1996)

Exchange Arrangement

The currency of the Russian Federation is the Ruble. An official exchange rate is quoted by the Central Bank of Russia based on market exchange rates prevailing in daily auctions held at the Moscow Interbank Currency Exchange (MICEX)[1] where the rate for the U.S. dollar is determined within a band of Rub 4,300 to Rub 4,900 per $1. The band was changed to Rub 5,150 from Rub 4,550 on January 1, 1996, and is to be maintained until July 1, 1996. Auction markets are also organized in other major cities, including St. Petersburg, Ekaterinburg, Vladivostok, Rostov, and Novosibirsk. There is a growing interbank exchange market outside of the currency exchanges. Currencies traded on the MICEX include Belarus rubles, deutsche mark, French francs, Kazak tenge, pounds sterling, and Ukrainian karbovanets. Currencies traded on other exchanges also include Finnish markkaa and Japanese yen.

The Central Bank is a shareholder and founder of the MICEX. The Central Bank issues three kinds of foreign exchange licenses: (1) internal licenses, which allow a bank to deal in foreign exchange bureaus and to open correspondent accounts in the banks of the Baltic countries and the other countries of the former Soviet Union (e.g., Moscow narodnoy); (2) limited licenses, which allow banks to open up to six correspondent accounts in banks of their choice, in addition to correspondent accounts in former Soviet Union banks abroad and to deal in up to six currencies; and (3) general licenses, which allow banks to carry out the full range of foreign exchange operations, including portfolio transactions.

The U.S. dollar is the intervention currency of the Central Bank in the MICEX and on other exchanges where the Central Bank operates. The Central Bank participates in the MICEX as a net buyer and seller of the U.S. dollar to smooth out short-term fluctuations in the exchange rate; it occasionally trades in foreign exchange through direct dealing on the interbank market outside the auctions. There is no spread between the central bank buying and selling rates. The central bank exchange rate is announced twice a week; it becomes effective on the following day and remains in effect until the Friday and Wednesday auctions. Exchange rates announced by the Central Bank are used for accounting and taxation purposes and for operations with the Ministry of Finance. The Central Bank quotes exchange rates of the ruble for the ECU and 26 convertible currencies on the basis of the MICEX ruble-U.S. dollar rate and the cross-rate relationships between the U.S. dollar and the currencies concerned in the international market on the day preceding auctions. The Central Bank provides reference exchange rates for the currencies of the Baltic countries and the other countries of the former Soviet Union against the ruble, based on market exchange rates in Russia (auction rates of currency exchanges) or local markets. These reference rates are used for taxation and accounting purposes, and authorized commercial banks are free to quote the rates for these currencies in their transactions. The Central Bank also calculates the (former) Soviet Gosbank exchange rate of the ruble, the so-called official exchange rate (about Rub 0.6 per $1), as a unit of account for the valuation of external claims of the Baltic countries and other countries of the former Soviet Union and related transactions.[2]

An interbank, mainly noncash, market operates outside the auctions among the major authorized banks, mainly within regions; the regional segmentation stems from the length of settlement of the ruble leg of foreign exchange transactions between banks affiliated with different payment centers; this feature hampers effective arbitrage between regional markets and leads the Central Bank to operate in the regional exchanges in order to apply the same exchange rate throughout the country. Authorized banks may trade on behalf of their customers and on their own accounts in these markets, subject to exposure limits defined by the Central Bank.[3]

There are no taxes or subsidies on purchases or sales of foreign exchange.[4] There are no official

---

[1]The MICEX is a joint stock company of resident foreign exchange banks and nonbank licensed organizations. The MICEX receives a commission in U.S. dollars of 0.1 percent on net purchases of U.S. dollars and a commission in rubles of 0.1 percent on net purchases of rubles. The other currency exchanges of Russia are organized in a similar manner as the MICEX; the Central Bank is not necessarily a shareholder of these exchanges but may operate on them.

[2]The official rate was defined by the Soviet Gosbank in relation to a currency basket of six convertible currencies; the value of that unit of account, therefore, fluctuates with the exchange rates of those currencies.

[3]End-of-day exposures must not exceed $100,000 for each Rub 1 billion of capital up to Rub 10 billion. The Central Bank determines the exposure of banks with a capital exceeding Rub 10 billion.

arrangements for forward cover against exchange rate risk. A futures trading market has developed in Moscow and is regulated as part of the central bank exposure limits, and forward contracts are also sold by authorized banks.[5]

Russia accepted the obligations of Article VIII, Sections 2, 3, and 4 of the Fund Agreement on June 1, 1996.

Administration of Control

The responsibility for regulating foreign trade and exchange transactions is shared by the Central Bank, the Ministry of Finance, the Ministry of Foreign Economic Relations (MFER), the Federal Service of Currency and Exchange Control, and the State Tax Service. The Central Bank is responsible for administering exchange control regulations; supervising and monitoring transactions of authorized banks, including accounting procedures for the revaluation of foreign currency items; and regulating banks' open foreign exchange positions. It has delegated to the authorized banks the responsibility for enforcing repatriation and surrender requirements, and to the state foreign exchange control authorities and the State Tax Service for monitoring compliance of authorized banks with relevant regulations. The Ministry of Finance supervises compliance with regulations concerning export quotas, licensing, and transactions in precious metals and unprocessed precious stones. The State Tax Service supervises the payment of taxes on income in foreign currencies.

The Law of the Russian Federation on Currency Regulations and Currency Controls stipulates that Parliament is responsible for overseeing the Government's foreign exchange reserves. The authority for changing the rules for the mandatory sale of foreign exchange from export earnings rests with the President of Russia.

In accordance with the Fund's Executive Board Decision No. 144-(52/51), adopted on August 14, 1952, Russia notified the IMF on April 1, 1993, that, in compliance with UN Security Council Resolution No. 757 of 1992, certain restrictions had been imposed on the making of payments and transfers for current international transactions in respect of the Federal Republic of Yugoslavia (Serbia/Montenegro).

Arrears are maintained with respect to external debt-service payments.

Prescription of Currency

At present, Russia maintains inoperative bilateral payments agreements with the Islamic State of Afghanistan, Bulgaria, China, Cuba, the Czech Republic, Egypt, Hungary, India, Mongolia, Poland, the Slovak Republic, Slovenia, and the Syrian Arab Republic in which clearing currencies for the settlement of merchandise trade are specified; balances under some of these agreements are in the process of reconciliation, and the settlement of balances is expected to take place following reconciliation. There is also an arrangement with India providing for the settlement of India's debt obligations to Russia.

Settlements with the Baltic countries and the other countries of the former Soviet Union are no longer made through correspondent accounts; all outstanding balances on these accounts have been transformed into intergovernmental debts.

Resident and Nonresident Accounts

Natural and juridical persons may open foreign currency accounts at authorized resident banks. Nonresidents must register with the tax authorities before opening an account. There are no restrictions on the crediting or debiting of these accounts maintained by nonresidents. Balances on foreign currency accounts of residents may only be used for purposes of effecting current foreign exchange transactions. Residents may use balances in their current foreign exchange accounts for all types of current transactions; the use of foreign exchange proceeds for capital transactions, with the exception of individual transactions specified in Instruction No. 39, dated April 24, 1996, on "Changes in the Procedure of Conducting Several Types of Foreign Exchange Transactions in the Russian Federation," requires a central bank license. Resident natural persons may maintain bank accounts abroad only during their stay outside Russia for the purpose of education, employment, medical treatment, or tourism. Upon their return to Russia, bank accounts abroad must be closed, and balances must be credited to the accounts held in authorized banks operating in the territory of Russia. Resident juridical persons, including branches of Russian banks, may not maintain accounts abroad without special permission from the Central Bank. Resident banks may open correspondent accounts abroad in accordance with the procedures set out in the Central Bank's foreign

---

[4]A local turnover tax of 0.1 percent has been imposed by the city of Moscow since March 1, 1994.

[5]The open position limits are set in absolute amounts and differ according to bank capital as follows: (1) for capital up to Rub 1 billion, the limit is $100,000, while the limit/capital ratio may not be less than 33 percent; (2) for capital of Rub 1–5 billion, the limit is $500,000, while the limit/capital ratio is in the range of 33 percent to 165 percent; (3) for capital of Rub 5–10 billion, the limit is $1 million, while the limit/capital ratio is in the range of 33 percent to 66 percent; and (4) for banks with capital above Rub 10 billion, the Central Bank determines individual limits.

exchange licenses. Authorized Russian banks are allowed to open correspondent accounts in the Baltic countries and the other countries of the former Soviet Union without restriction, provided that they comply with the regulation on exposure limits.

Nonresidents may maintain four types of ruble accounts: (1) "T" accounts, which may be credited with proceeds from current international transactions (including proceeds from sales of goods and services to residents of Russia and interest earnings on the account itself, and debited for the servicing of export-import operations by their representative offices in Russia); (2) correspondent ruble accounts for nonresident banks under the same regime applicable to T accounts; (3) "I" accounts, which can be used for investment activities (including privatization operations); and (4) nonresident accounts for natural persons. The transfer abroad of balances in T accounts and correspondent ruble accounts accumulated after June 1, 1996, is not restricted; the use of balances accumulated up to May 31, 1996, is limited to domestic transactions. I accounts may be used for a wide range of investment activities, including profit and dividend transfers. Balances maintained in I accounts may be transferred abroad without restriction after payment of applicable taxes. Nonresident natural and juridical persons may purchase foreign exchange only with ruble balances held in I accounts.

Imports and Exports

Imports are generally free of quotas and licenses. Licenses are required for imports of medicines, raw materials for the production of medicines and pesticides, and industrial waste. A customs duty ranging from 5 percent to 15 percent is levied on most goods; duties on some goods range up to 150 percent. The following products are exempt from customs duties: foodstuffs; medicines; inputs for the production of medicines; medical supplies and equipment; printed materials; children's articles; accompanied baggage, except motor vehicles, up to the value of $2,000; equipment for the oil and gas industries; and ships and boats. Imports from the countries of the former Commonwealth of Independent States and "least developed" countries are also exempt, and the customs duties on imports from other developing countries are reduced by one-half. Customs duties are payable in rubles at central bank exchange rates. Foreign-owned companies, banks, and organizations that are officially accredited in Russia may import unlimited office-related goods duty free.

Foreign exchange transactions, associated deferred payments for exports of goods from Russia for a period exceeding 180 days, and deferrals granted to residents for making advance payments against deliveries of imported goods exceeding 180 days require the permission of the Central Bank.

Exports are not subject to quotas, and licensing is limited to a small group of products. Exports of strategically important goods require registration of contracts with the MFER. A limited number of goods, mainly determined by the Ministry of Environment, may be exported only under a licensing regime. The export regimes apply to exports to all countries.

Export licenses are issued in accordance with application procedures established by the MFER and are required for a limited number of other products (e.g., military equipment and arms, gold, diamonds, other precious metals and stones, certain food products, wildlife, medicines, chemical raw materials for the production of medicines, and minerals).

Residents must sell 50 percent of their export earnings through the authorized banks.

Export duties are levied on about 100 product groups. Specific duties are denominated in ECUs and range from ECU 1 to ECU 80,000 a ton. Ad valorem duties range up to 30 percent (15 percent and 20 percent for foods). Specific duties on goods exported under barter trade arrangements are 50 percent higher, as are specific duties on exports that are not subject to the 50 percent surrender requirement. The export duties are imposed on exports to the Baltic countries and the other countries of the former Soviet Union, except for goods delivered to meet state needs in accordance with intergovernmental agreements and that were sold by the state corporations (Roskontract and Rosagrokhim). Duties on goods exported to the Baltic countries and the other countries of the former Soviet Union may be paid in rubles, and on goods exported to other countries, in any of the currencies quoted by the Central Bank, which applies its exchange rates prevailing on the day the payment for the goods is received. A number of discretionary exemptions are granted on a case-by-case basis.[6] Export duties are payable when the goods cross the border, but payments may be postponed for up to 60 days if a bank guarantee for the subsequent payment is provided.

Payments for and Proceeds from Invisibles

Payments for invisibles are not restricted, and residents may purchase foreign exchange for all bona

---

[6]Oil- and gas-producing enterprises are exempt from export duties for the decentralized portion of their exports. This exemption does not apply to enterprises with foreign investments registered after January 1, 1992, that provide goods for centralized exports.

fide invisible transactions from authorized banks with proper documentation. There are no restrictions on the amount of foreign banknotes a person may take out of the country, provided that a certificate from an authorized bank on the origin of the funds is presented to customs. The use of internationally accepted credit cards issued by domestic banks to customers who have foreign currency accounts is not restricted.

Residents and nonresidents traveling to areas where the ruble is sole legal tender are allowed to take out a maximum of Rub 500,000 in banknotes.

The transfer of income from investments by nonresidents is not restricted. Nonresidents may freely convert funds held in their I accounts into foreign exchange. Proceeds from invisibles, except those from banking services, are subject to the surrender requirement. Payments to nonresidents for work and services within 180 days of completion are not restricted; under the existing regulations, payments after 180 days are treated as capital transfers and require a license from the Central Bank.

Authorized banks holding general foreign exchange licenses are permitted to import and export foreign currency banknotes, treasury notes, coins in circulation, and securities without restriction, provided that they observe customs regulations.

Capital

Capital transfers of residents, with the exception of repayments of foreign loans, must be authorized by the Central Bank.

External borrowing by juridical persons is subject to control. Both resident and nonresident juridical persons have the right to import or transfer foreign exchange without restriction, provided that they observe the regulations.

Capital transfers by residents abroad, including repayments of loans with maturities exceeding 180 days from the date of transaction, requires approval from the Central Bank. Transactions not requiring approval are listed in Instruction No. 39 of April 24, 1996, on "Changes in the Procedure of Conducting Several Types of Foreign Exchange Transactions in the Russian Federation." Receipts of foreign exchange credits by resident juridical persons from nonresidents are subject to central bank approval when their maturities exceed 180 days.

Borrowing by banks possessing a general foreign exchange license does not require a special license. Nonresident juridical persons may transfer abroad foreign currency assets up to the amount imported, provided that the foreign exchange is in their possession. Nonresidents may buy or sell foreign currency

for investment purposes in exchange for rubles through I accounts without limit. Investment in Russian enterprises by nonresidents through joint ventures or through outright ownership is not restricted, except in some sectors like banking and exploration of natural resources (special license required) or land ownership (prohibited). Enterprises with foreign capital shares must register with the Ministry of Economy, and investments exceeding Rub 100 million require a permit from the Council of Ministers. Foreign direct investments are accorded the same rights and privileges with regard to property ownership and economic activities as those accorded to residents.[7] Foreign direct investments may be nationalized or expropriated only in exceptional cases in accordance with legislation, and, in such cases, the investor is entitled to compensation.

Gold

Domestic trade in gold is not permitted, except that monetary gold intended to be part of the country's foreign exchange reserves is purchased by the Central Bank and the Government at world prices quoted on the London market converted at the market exchange rate. Transactions in precious metals (gold and silver bullion) require authorization; transactions must be made through authorized banks possessing special licenses issued by the Central Bank. The Ministry of Finance has issued gold-backed certificates, which can also be bought by nonresidents.

Changes During 1995

Exchange Arrangement

July 6. A band of Rub 4,300 to Rub 4,900 per $1 was introduced for the official exchange rate.

Changes During 1996

Exchange Arrangement

January 1. The band for the official exchange rate was adjusted to between Rub 4,550 and Rub 5,150; this band would be maintained until July 1, 1996.

June 1. Russia formally accepted the obligations of Article VIII, Sections 2, 3, and 4 of the Fund Agreement.

---

[7]A presidential decree of September 27, 1993, introduced several provisions to protect foreign investment, including a "grandfather" clause that protects foreign investment for a three-year period from regulatory acts that would adversely affect their activities and a provision that any restrictions on activities of foreign investors can be introduced only by laws of Russia or by presidential decree.

RWANDA

(Position as of December 31, 1995)

Exchange Arrangement

The currency of Rwanda is the Rwanda Franc, the external value of which is determined freely in the exchange market in which commercial banks and foreign exchange bureaus operate. The National Bank of Rwanda does not announce official exchange rates, but it calculates and publishes daily the average market exchange rate for reference purposes. On December 31, 1995, the average exchange rate for the U.S. dollar quoted by commercial banks and foreign exchange bureaus was RF 299.81 per $1.

There are no taxes or subsidies on purchases or sales of foreign banknotes. However, banks may apply four commissions to these operations. Outward and inward transfers are subject to a commission of 4 per mil, with a minimum of RF 500 and a maximum of RF 20,000. There are no arrangements for forward cover against exchange risk.

Administration of Control

Control over foreign exchange transactions is vested in the National Bank; authority to carry out some of these transactions is delegated to authorized banks. Arrears are maintained with respect to external payments.

Prescription of Currency

To facilitate trade and other external transactions, the National Bank maintains agreements with the central banks of the Economic Community of the Great Lakes Countries (CEPGL), Burundi, and Zaïre. Under these arrangements, settlements are made through reciprocal accounts opened with central banks and denominated in SDRs; balances on these accounts are periodically transferable. Payments to and from other member countries of the Preferential trade area for Eastern and Southern African states (PTA) (Burundi, Comoros, Djibouti, Ethiopia, Kenya, Lesotho, Malawi, Mauritius, Somalia, Swaziland, Tanzania, Uganda, Zambia, and Zimbabwe) are made through the PTA's clearinghouse. For other countries, payments for imports must be made in the currency quoted by the National Bank, which, in principle, is the currency of the country of origin. Payments from any country may be received in Belgian francs, deutsche mark, French francs, Italian lire, Japanese yen, Netherlands guilders, pounds sterling, Swiss francs, and U.S. dollars. Foreign payments are generally made by bank transfer checks, or telegraphic transfer. In addition, certain payments relating to border trade may be made in banknotes.

Foreign Exchange Accounts

Both residents and nonresidents may maintain foreign exchange accounts with authorized banks.

Imports and Import Payments

All imports, except those of narcotics, which are prohibited, are permitted under an open general license (OGL) system. Residents are free to purchase foreign exchange from commercial banks and foreign exchange bureaus and make payments for imports. Certain categories of imports, such as explosives and weapons, require prior approval from the relevant authorities, regardless of origin and value. For reasons of health, the importation of human or veterinary medicines, disinfectants, insecticides, rodent poisons, fungicides, herbicides, and other toxic or potentially toxic chemicals is subject to approval of the pro forma invoices by the Ministry of Health.

Before placing orders, importers must submit import declarations to an authorized bank. These declarations allow importers to obtain the required foreign exchange from an authorized bank or a foreign exchange bureau. Imports not involving the purchase of foreign exchange are also authorized. Imports with f.o.b. values equal to or exceeding $10,000 must be inspected by an international agency with regard to the quality, quantity, price, and customs tariff of the goods before goods are shipped to Rwanda.

A file processing charge equal to 1 percent of the f.o.b. value of goods is charged on import declarations for coverage of fees for the inspection agency. Fuel is subject to a file processing charge of 1 per mil.

Import declarations must be submitted upon clearance through customs, and one copy of the certificate of entry for home use must be addressed to the National Bank. For imports originating from CEPGL member countries, import declarations may be replaced by CEPGL import notices. The import tariff regime is governed by the tariff code promulgated on February 15, 1995.

Payments for Invisibles

Residents are free to purchase foreign exchange from commercial banks and foreign exchange bureaus and make payments for invisibles.

Salaries and wages earned by foreign nationals employed in Rwanda under contract, net of taxes and employee's share of social security contributions, may be transferred abroad. The net earned income of self-employed foreign nationals, whether engaged in a profession or established as independent traders, may also be transferred abroad after payment of taxes and deduction of local expenses. A fee of 0.4 percent is levied on transfers abroad.

Official travel requires a travel authorization issued by the Government. Daily allowances are granted for such travel. Foreign exchange for business travel purposes are limited to the equivalent of $10,000 a trip, but there is no restriction on the number of trips that may be taken.

Unless otherwise provided by the National Bank, purchases of foreign exchange for travel for education and training are authorized up to the limit of $25,000 a year, on presentation of supporting documents; for medical treatment, unless otherwise provided by the National Bank, residents are authorized to purchase up to $20,000, with proper supporting documents. A maximum of $4,000 is made available for other travel. Allocations for travel by nonresidents are authorized as stipulated in the pertinent labor agreements.

Remittances for payments for certain other invisibles may be authorized on an ad hoc basis.

The exportation of Rwanda franc banknotes exceeding the equivalent of $100 must be declared to customs.

Exports and Export Proceeds

All exports, except trade samples, personal and household effects of travelers, are subject to prior declaration to the authorized banks. Receipts from exports must be repatriated within seven business days of the date of receipt.

Settlements among member countries of the CEPGL and the PTA are effected through clearing arrangements maintained by the central banks of the countries concerned. Exporters may sell their foreign exchange earnings freely on the domestic foreign exchange market or retain them in accounts held with domestic banks. Ninety percent of earnings from exports of coffee and tea must be sold to commercial banks at a freely negotiated exchange rate.

Proceeds from Invisibles

All receipts from invisibles may be sold freely to commercial banks or foreign exchange bureaus. Travelers from abroad may bring in up to the equivalent of $100 in domestic banknotes and any amount in foreign banknotes.

Capital

All outward transfers of capital require the prior approval of the National Bank. Direct investments and portfolio investments by residents abroad require prior approval from the National Bank. Direct investments by nonresidents are allowed. Repatriation of such investments are pursuant to the investment code and must be registered by authorized banks.

Gold

Trade in gold is restricted to dealers approved by the relevant ministry. Imports and exports of gold require an import or an export declaration.

Changes During 1995

Exchange Arrangement

March 6. The system of a free exchange market was introduced. Foreign exchange bureaus were allowed to operate. The National Bank would compute and publish daily the average market exchange rate.

Administration of Control

March 6. A new foreign exchange regulation liberalizing controls came into effect.

Foreign Exchange Accounts

March 6. Residents and nonresidents were allowed to maintain foreign exchange accounts.

Imports and Import Payments

February 15. The Ministry of Finance published the new customs tariff schedule. The maximum entry tax was reduced from 100 percent to 60 percent.

Payments for Invisibles

March 6. (1) The foreign exchange allowance for business travel purposes was increased to $10,000 a trip; and (2) foreign exchange purchases for travel for education and training or medical care were permitted up to limits of $25,000 and $20,000 a year, respectively.

Exports and Export Proceeds

March 6. Exporters were no longer required to sell their foreign exchange proceeds to the National Bank of Rwanda, and they were permitted to sell their proceeds in the foreign exchange market or keep them in foreign exchange accounts opened with commercial banks, with the exception of 90 percent of proceeds from exports of coffee and tea, which must be sold in the foreign exchange market at a freely negotiated rate.

ST. KITTS AND NEVIS

(Position as of December 31, 1995)

Exchange Arrangement

The currency of St. Kitts and Nevis is the Eastern Caribbean Dollar,[1] which is issued by the Eastern Caribbean Central Bank (ECCB) and is pegged to the U.S. dollar, the intervention currency, at EC$2.70 per US$1. On December 31, 1995, the buying and selling rates were EC$2.6949 and EC$2.7084, respectively, per US$1. The ECCB also quotes daily rates for the Canadian dollar and the pound sterling. There are no arrangements for forward cover against exchange rate risk operating in the official or the commercial banking sector.

St. Kitts and Nevis accepted the obligations of Article VIII, Sections 2, 3, and 4 of the Fund Agreement on December 3, 1984.

Administration of Control

Exchange control is administered by the Ministry of Finance and applies to all countries.

Prescription of Currency

Settlements with residents of countries served by the ECCB must be effected in Eastern Caribbean dollars.

Foreign Currency Accounts

U.S. dollar currency accounts may be operated freely, but permission of the Ministry of Finance is required to operate other foreign currency accounts; such permission is normally confined to major exporters and foreign nationals not ordinarily residing in St. Kitts and Nevis. These accounts may be credited only with foreign currency earned or received from outside St. Kitts and Nevis and may be freely debited. A minimum balance of US$1,000 must be maintained at all times to operate a U.S. dollar currency account.

Imports and Import Payments

Most goods are imported under open general licenses. Individual licenses are required for imports that compete with local products unless they come from another member country of the Caribbean Common Market (CARICOM).[2] Payments for authorized imports payable in U.S. dollars are permitted on presentation of documentary evidence of purchase to a bank, but payments in currencies other than the U.S. dollar need the approval of the Ministry of Finance. The common external tariff (CET) is between zero and 30 percent.

Payments for Invisibles

All settlements overseas require exchange control approval, except where the currency involved is the U.S. dollar, in which case commercial banks are authorized to pay on presentation of documentary evidence. Where the currency involved is not the U.S. dollar, application must be made directly to the Ministry of Finance; authorization is normally granted for certain specific purposes and services.

Residents of St. Kitts and Nevis may purchase foreign exchange from authorized banks up to the equivalent of EC$1,500 a year for travel outside the area served by the ECCB, subject to presentation of evidence of intention to travel for bona fide purposes. For business travel, allowances of foreign exchange may be made available up to EC$5,000 a company a year. These allocations can be increased in bona fide cases with the authorization of the Ministry of Finance. Residents traveling abroad for medical treatment are eligible for an allowance of EC$1,000, which may be raised without any limitation, provided that a medical certificate is presented. There is a 7.5 percent ad valorem tax on all travel tickets.

Education allowances are subject to approval by the Ministry of Finance. Residents may also make cash gifts to nonresidents not exceeding a total value of EC$250 a donor a year. Profits and dividends may be remitted in full, subject to confirmation of registration by the Commissioner of Inland Revenue for income tax purposes.

Exports and Export Proceeds

Specific licenses are required for the exportation of certain goods to any destination. Export proceeds must be deposited into an ECCB currency account or

---

[1]The Eastern Caribbean dollar is also the currency of Anguilla, Antigua and Barbuda, Dominica, Grenada, Montserrat, St. Lucia, and St. Vincent and the Grenadines.

[2]The CARICOM countries are Antigua and Barbuda, The Bahamas, Barbados, Belize, Dominica, Grenada, Guyana, Jamaica, Montserrat, St. Kitts and Nevis, St. Lucia, St. Vincent and the Grenadines, and Trinidad and Tobago.

an approved U.S. dollar foreign currency account. Export duties are levied on a few products.

Proceeds from Invisibles

Foreign currency proceeds from transactions in invisibles must be sold to a bank or deposited into an approved U.S. dollar account if the proceeds are in U.S. dollars. Travelers to St. Kitts and Nevis may freely bring in notes and coins denominated in Eastern Caribbean dollars or in any foreign currency.

Capital

All outward capital transfers require exchange control approval. The purchase by residents of foreign currency securities and of real estate situated abroad for private purposes is not normally permitted. Personal capital transfers, such as inheritances, to nonresidents require approval, which is normally granted subject to payment of any taxes due. Emigrants leaving St. Kitts and Nevis to take up residence outside the area served by the ECCB may transfer their assets with the permission of the Ministry of Finance.

Direct investments in St. Kitts and Nevis by nonresidents do not require exchange control approval. The remittance of proceeds from earnings on, and liquidation of, such investments is permitted, subject to the discharge of any liabilities related to the investment. The approval of the Ministry of Finance is required for nonresidents to borrow in St. Kitts and Nevis.

Gold

There are no restrictions on the purchase, sale, and holding of gold for either numismatic or industrial purposes.

Changes During 1995

No significant changes occurred in the exchange and trade system.

ST. LUCIA

(Position as of December 31, 1995)

Exchange Arrangement

The currency of St. Lucia is the Eastern Caribbean Dollar,[1] which is issued by the Eastern Caribbean Central Bank. The Eastern Caribbean dollar is pegged to the U.S. dollar, the intervention currency, at EC$2.70 per US$1. On December 31, 1995, the buying and selling rates for the U.S. dollar were EC$2.6882 and EC$2.7169, respectively, per US$1. The Eastern Caribbean Central Bank also quotes daily rates for the Canadian dollar and the pound sterling. There are no arrangements for forward cover against exchange rate risk operating in the official or the commercial banking sector.

St. Lucia accepted the obligations of Article VIII, Sections 2, 3, and 4 of the Fund Agreement on May 30, 1980.

Administration of Control

Exchange control is administered by the Ministry of Finance and Planning and applies to all currencies other than the Eastern Caribbean dollar. Export licensing is required for a range of primary products. Import and export licenses are issued by the Ministry of Trade; those for agricultural products are issued by the Ministry of Agriculture.

Prescription of Currency

Settlements with residents of member countries of the Caribbean Common Market (CARICOM)[2] must be made either in the currency of the CARICOM country concerned or in Eastern Caribbean dollars. Settlements with residents of other countries may be made either in any foreign currency[3] or in Eastern Caribbean dollars. When justified by the nature of the transaction, approval may be given to make payments for goods and services in a currency other than that of the country to which payment is to be made.

Nonresident (External) Accounts

External accounts may be opened for nonresident individuals or companies with the approval of the Ministry of Finance and Planning and are maintained in Eastern Caribbean dollars. These accounts may be credited only with foreign drafts or checks, but hotels may also deposit currency notes in them. Such accounts may be debited for payments to residents payable in Eastern Caribbean dollars and, after approval by the Ministry of Finance and Planning, for the cost of foreign exchange required for travel or business purposes. As funds in an external account are normally convertible into a foreign currency, deposits to and withdrawals from such an account require exchange control approval by the Ministry of Finance and Planning.

Foreign Currency Accounts

A foreign currency account is defined as an account denominated in a currency other than the Eastern Caribbean dollar. With the prior permission of the Ministry of Finance and Planning, residents or nonresidents may open foreign currency accounts with authorized dealers in St. Lucia. Such permission is granted in special cases where the applicant earns foreign exchange and has to make frequent payments abroad. A resident or nonresident (whether an individual, firm, company, association, or institution) wishing to open a foreign currency account must apply to the Ministry of Finance and Planning through an authorized dealer, stating the nature and estimated volume of receipts and payments in the desired foreign currency. All payments from a foreign currency account require the prior approval of the Ministry of Finance and Planning. Where permission is granted, the authorized dealer must submit to the Ministry of Finance and Planning a monthly statement of account, together with full details of payments and receipts, to ensure that the conditions for holding foreign currency are observed.

Imports and Import Payments

All goods, except certain agricultural and manufactured products, may be imported without a license. Certain other commodities require individual licenses, unless they are imported from CARICOM countries. The importation of selected consumer

---

[1]The Eastern Caribbean dollar is also the currency of Anguilla, Antigua and Barbuda, Dominica, Grenada, Montserrat, St. Kitts and Nevis, and St. Vincent and the Grenadines.

[2]The CARICOM countries are Antigua and Barbuda, The Bahamas, Barbados, Belize, Dominica, Grenada, Guyana, Jamaica, Montserrat, St. Kitts and Nevis, St. Lucia, St. Vincent and the Grenadines, and Trinidad and Tobago.

[3]Foreign currencies comprise all currencies other than the Eastern Caribbean dollar.

items (e.g., rice, flour, and sugar) in bulk form is a state monopoly. Payments in foreign currency for authorized imports are permitted upon application to a local bank and submission of certified customs entry. Advance payments for imports require prior approval from the Ministry of Finance and Planning.

Goods produced or manufactured in the CARICOM region may be imported duty free. Imports of live animals, milk, meat, fish, eggs, fertilizers, and most agricultural and industrial machinery are exempt from import duties. Other exempt items include most imports from CARICOM and the member countries of the Organization of Eastern Caribbean States (OECS), certain imports for use in industry, agriculture, fishing, air and sea transport (under industrial incentive legislation), and items exempted under the Hotel Aid Ordinance and Fiscal Incentives Ordinance. St. Lucia implemented the first stage of the CARICOM Common External Tariff (CET) by lowering rates to a range between zero and 35 percent (except for imports of companies involved in local agricultural production) on July 1, 1993. A customs service charge of 2 percent of the c.i.f. value is levied on all imports except fertilizers, for which the rate is 0.20 percent. Certain imports are subject to a consumption tax that is based on the c.i.f. value plus import duty.

Payments for Invisibles

Residents may purchase foreign exchange from authorized banks up to the equivalent of EC$3,000 a year for travel; this limit may be exceeded only with permission from the Ministry of Finance and Planning. Persons traveling within the CARICOM area using CARICOM traveler's checks (which are denominated in Trinidad and Tobago currency) receive the basic allowance of EC$2,000 a year. A travel tax is levied on the sale of airline tickets at the rate of 2.5 percent of the price of the ticket for travel within the CARICOM area and 5 percent for travel elsewhere. The Eastern Caribbean dollar is freely transferable within the Eastern Caribbean Central Bank area. With the approval of the Ministry of Finance and Planning, profits may be remitted in full, subject to confirmation by the Comptroller of Inland Revenue that local tax liabilities have been discharged. However, in cases where profits are deemed to be high, the Ministry of Finance and Planning reserves the right to phase remittances over a reasonable period. Insurance premiums are taxed as follows: life insurance, 1.5 percent for residents and 3 percent for nonresident companies; general insurance, 3 percent for residents and 5 percent for nonresident companies.

Exports and Export Proceeds

Certain commodities may be exported to any destination without a license. Proceeds must, in principle, be surrendered. A duty at the rate of 2.5 percent of the f.o.b. value is levied on banana exports. A special fee of US$0.02 a barrel is applied on re-exports of petroleum.

Proceeds from Invisibles

Foreign currency proceeds from transactions in invisibles must, in principle, be surrendered. Travelers to St. Lucia may freely bring in notes and coins denominated in Eastern Caribbean dollars or in any foreign currency. Foreign currency coins are not normally exchanged by the banks.

Capital

All outward capital transfers require exchange control approval. Residents are not normally permitted to purchase foreign currency securities and real estate situated abroad for private purposes. Personal capital transfers, such as inheritances to nonresidents, require approval, which is normally granted, provided that local tax liabilities have been discharged. Nonresidents who purchase property are taxed at a higher rate than are residents.

Any resident who requires a loan from local sources must first have the approval of the Ministry of Finance and Planning. Applications for nonresident loans are submitted by the authorized dealer (or other financial intermediary) to the Ministry of Finance and Planning on behalf of the applicant.

Gold

There are no restrictions on imports or exports of gold.

Changes During 1995

No significant changes occurred in the exchange and trade system.

ST. VINCENT AND THE GRENADINES

(Position as of December 31, 1995)

Exchange Arrangement

The currency of St. Vincent and the Grenadines is the Eastern Caribbean Dollar,[1] which is issued by the Eastern Caribbean Central Bank. The Eastern Caribbean dollar is pegged to the U.S. dollar, the intervention currency, at EC$2.70 per US$1. On December 31, 1995, the buying and selling rates for the U.S. dollar were EC$2.6882 and EC$2.7169, respectively, per US$1. The Central Bank also quotes daily rates for the Canadian dollar and the pound sterling. There are no arrangements for forward cover against exchange rate risk operating in the official or the commercial bank sector.

St. Vincent and the Grenadines accepted the obligations of Article VIII, Sections 2, 3, and 4 of the Fund Agreement on August 24, 1981.

Administration of Control

Exchange control is administered by the Ministry of Finance and applies to all countries outside the central bank area. The Ministry of Finance delegates to authorized dealers the authority to approve some import payments and certain other payments.

Prescription of Currency

Settlements with residents of member countries of the Caribbean Common Market (CARICOM)[2] can be done in any currency. Settlements with residents of other countries may be made in any foreign currency[3] or through an external account in Eastern Caribbean dollars.

Nonresident Accounts

External accounts may be opened for nonresidents with the authorization of the Ministry of Finance. They are maintained in Eastern Caribbean dollars and may be credited with inward remittances in foreign currency and with transfers from other external accounts. Except with the prior approval of the Ministry of Finance, remittances in Eastern Caribbean currency, foreign currency notes and coins, and payments by residents may not be credited to external accounts. These accounts may, however, be freely debited for payments abroad and to residents without the prior authorization of the Ministry of Finance. The operating banks must submit quarterly statements of the accounts to the Ministry of Finance.

Foreign Currency Accounts

Accounts denominated in foreign currencies may be opened by nonresidents with the authorization of the Ministry of Finance; these accounts may be credited only with funds in the form of remittances from overseas. Except with the prior permission of the Ministry of Finance, remittances in Eastern Caribbean currency, foreign currency notes and coins, and payments by residents may not be credited to a foreign currency account. These accounts may be debited for payments abroad without prior authorization from the Ministry of Finance. The operating banks must submit quarterly statements of the accounts to the Ministry of Finance.

Imports and Import Payments

Import items are divided into three categories: the largest category covers goods that may be freely imported; imports of some goods that compete with typical exports of other member countries of the CARICOM and the Organization of Eastern Caribbean States (OECS)[4] are subject to licenses; and imports of goods that compete with locally made products are prohibited in some cases.

Payments for authorized imports are permitted upon application and submission of documentary evidence and, where required, of the license. In 1993, import licenses covered about 8 percent of the total import value. Advance payments for imports require prior approval from the Ministry of Finance. The import tariff rates range from zero to 35 percent. In addition to customs duties, imports are subject to a consumption tax, which ranges from 5 percent to 50 percent and is levied on the tariff-inclusive value of imports. Goods imported from the member coun-

---

[1]The Eastern Caribbean dollar is also the currency of Anguilla, Antigua and Barbuda, Dominica, Grenada, Montserrat, St. Kitts and Nevis, and St. Lucia.

[2]The CARICOM countries are Antigua and Barbuda, The Bahamas, Barbados, Belize, Dominica, Grenada, Guyana, Jamaica, Montserrat, St. Kitts and Nevis, St. Lucia, St. Vincent and the Grenadines, and Trinidad and Tobago.

[3]Foreign currencies include all currencies other than the Eastern Caribbean dollar.

[4]The OECS comprises Antigua and Barbuda, Dominica, Grenada, Montserrat, St. Kitts and Nevis, St. Lucia, and St. Vincent and the Grenadines.

tries of the CARICOM are exempt from import tariffs and are subject only to the consumption tax. A customs service charge of 2 percent is imposed on the c.i.f. value of all imported goods with certain exceptions.

Payments for Invisibles

Payments for invisibles related to authorized imports are not restricted. Payments for travel, medical treatment, education, subscriptions and membership fees, and gifts are subject to limits. All other payments exceeding EC$100 must be approved by the Ministry of Finance, and approval is granted routinely. Residents may purchase foreign exchange from authorized banks up to the equivalent of EC$2,500 a year for travel outside the central bank area; for business travel, additional allocations of foreign exchange may be made available up to EC$6,000 a year. These allocations may be increased with the authorization of the Ministry of Finance. Purchases of foreign currency to cover expenses for medical treatment abroad are authorized by the Ministry of Finance when a local medical practitioner presents a written statement of the need for the treatment. The amount approved is based on the actual cost of the treatment. A 5 percent tax is levied on the value of all tickets for travel originating in St. Vincent and the Grenadines, whether or not they are purchased in the country.

Students attending educational institutions overseas are permitted to purchase foreign exchange to cover the cost of tuition and living expenses. Documentary proof of acceptance and attendance at the institution is required. The amount of foreign currency that may otherwise be purchased without the approval of the Ministry of Finance is limited to the equivalent of EC$50 a trip.

Exports and Export Proceeds

Specific licenses are required for the exportation to any destination of some agricultural goods included in the CARICOM marketing protocol and in the CARICOM Oils and Fats Agreement. The licenses are issued by the Ministry of Trade, which, in some cases, has delegated its authority to the St. Vincent Central Marketing Corporation. Exports of goats, sheep, and lobsters are subject to licensing to prevent depletion of stocks. All export proceeds must be surrendered within six months. A 2 percent export duty is levied on bananas.

Proceeds from Invisibles

Foreign currency proceeds from transactions in invisibles must be surrendered. Travelers may freely bring in notes and coins denominated in Eastern Caribbean dollars or in any foreign currency.

Capital

All outward capital transfers require exchange control approval. Residents are normally not permitted to purchase foreign currency securities or real estate situated abroad for private purposes. On presenting documentary proof that they are taking up permanent residence in a foreign country, emigrants may apply to the Ministry of Finance to transfer funds abroad based on the value of assets held in St. Vincent and the Grenadines. The transfer of funds is normally limited to EC$100,000 a year as is the transfer of proceeds from sales of assets held by emigrants already residing in a foreign country.

Direct investment in St. Vincent and the Grenadines by nonresidents is not subject to exchange control. The remittance of earnings on, and liquidation of proceeds from, such investment is permitted, subject to the discharge of any liabilities related to the investment. The approval of the Ministry of Finance is required for nonresidents to borrow in St. Vincent and the Grenadines. Any borrowing abroad by authorized dealers to finance their domestic operations requires the approval of the Ministry of Finance.

Gold

Residents are permitted to acquire and hold gold coins for numismatic purposes only. Under license by the Ministry of Finance, imports of gold are permitted for industrial purposes only.

Changes During 1995

Prescription of Currency

December 31. Settlements with residents of member countries of the Caribbean Common Market can be effected in any currency.

SAN MARINO

(Position as of December 31, 1995)

Exchange Arrangement

The currency of San Marino is the Italian Lira.[1] The central monetary institution is the Istituto di Credito Sammarinese. There are no taxes or subsidies on purchases or sales of foreign exchange. Forward transactions may be conducted through commercial banks without restriction at rates quoted in Italian markets.

San Marino accepted the obligations of Article VIII, Sections 2, 3, and 4 of the Fund Agreement on September 23, 1992.

Administration of Control

Under the terms of the Agreement on Financial and Exchange Relations of May 1991, the Central Bank of San Marino is a foreign exchange bank with the authority to grant foreign exchange dealer status to Sammarinese financial institutions; currently, Sammarinese banks may maintain accounts only with financial institutions in Italy. As a result, foreign exchange transactions of domestic banks are effectively limited to buying foreign exchange at rates similar to those quoted in Italy and to conducting third-country transactions through Italian correspondents.

Residents of San Marino are allowed to conduct foreign exchange transactions freely, with settlement effected through authorized Italian intermediaries (the Bank of Italy, the Italian Foreign Exchange Office, authorized banks, and the Postal Administration). Direct settlements (with residents drawing on their own external accounts) authorized under Italian Exchange Control Regulations in 1990 have not yet been utilized.

Prescription of Currency

Settlements with foreign countries are made in convertible currencies or in lire on foreign accounts.

Resident and Nonresident Accounts

Residents and nonresidents are free to maintain any type of deposit accounts; in practice, deposit accounts other than in lire are not offered by domestic banks.

Imports and Import Payments

Imports from Italy are not subject to restriction, whereas imports from third countries are subject to control under the relevant Italian regulations. No license, other than the general business license, is required to engage in trade transactions. Trade is free of regulation except that the importation of electricity, gas, and water is reserved for the public sector. Payments for imports are unrestricted.

Imports into Italy are currently governed by Decree No. 40 of December 22, 1972, as amended.

Customs duties on imports from non-European Union (EU) member countries are collected by the EU customs authorities on behalf of San Marino. A sales tax is levied on all imports at the time of entry. The structure of this tax corresponds closely to the Italian value-added tax, but the average effective rate is about 4 percent lower. Sales tax levied on imports are rebated when the goods are re-exported.

Payments for Invisibles

There are no restrictions on payments for invisibles.

Exports and Export Proceeds

Export proceeds are not subject to surrender requirements. There are no taxes or quantitative restrictions on exports.

Exports to Italy are not regulated, while exports to third countries are governed by relevant Italian regulations. Exports from Italy are currently governed by Decree No. 40 of December 22, 1972, as amended. Exports to any country of products listed in Decree No. 68 require export licenses; other exports do not require authorization.

Proceeds from Invisibles

Proceeds from invisibles are not regulated.

Capital

Inward and outward capital transfers, with few exceptions, are not restricted. Foreign direct invest-

---

[1]The Monetary Agreement between San Marino and Italy, renewed on December 21, 1991, provides for San Marino to issue annually agreed amounts of San Marino lira coins equivalent in form to Italian coinage; these coins will be legal tender in both countries. The San Marino gold scudo is also issued but is legal tender only in San Marino. It is not generally used in transactions because its numismatic value exceeds its defined legal value (Lit 50,000 per 1 scudo).

ments, irrespective of the extent of ownership, require government approval, which is based on conformity with long-term developmental and environmental policy considerations. The purchase and ownership of real property by nonnationals require approval from the Council of Twelve, and approval is granted on merit and on a case-by-case basis. There are no restrictions on the repatriation of profits or capital. Foreign investors are accorded equal treatment with national firms; that is, investment incentives that are available to domestic investors are equally available to foreign investors.

Gold

International trade in gold is governed by the Italy-San Marino Agreement on Financial and Exchange Relations.

Changes During 1995

No significant changes occurred in the exchange and trade system.

SÃO TOMÉ AND PRÍNCIPE

(Position as of December 31, 1995)

Exchange Arrangement

The currency of São Tomé and Príncipe is the São Tomé and Príncipe Dobra. The official exchange rate is determined daily as an average of exchange rates in the exchange bureau, the parallel market, and a commercial bank. On December 31, 1995, the exchange rate (middle rate) for the U.S. dollar, the intervention currency, was Db 1,756.88 per $1. Rates for certain other currencies are determined on the basis of the exchange rates of the U.S. dollar for the currencies concerned.

Foreign exchange transactions are divided into three categories for the purpose of assessing charges on purchases and sales of foreign exchange, namely import payments, transactions in foreign checks, and collection of export proceeds.

On import-related exchange transactions, the arrangements are as follows: when a letter of credit is opened, a charge of 1.125 percent of the import value, with a minimum of $25 and a maximum of $300, is payable with an additional commission of 0.5 percent to the Central Bank of São Tomé and Príncipe. A stamp duty of 0.25 percent is also payable as well as a postage levy of $2.

On foreign checks for collection, a commission is applied in favor of the collecting foreign correspondent and varies from bank to bank and with the type of currency. In addition, the International Bank of São Tomé and Príncipe charges a postage levy of $2 for each transaction. For collection of export proceeds, a commission of 0.125 percent that is charged, with a minimum of $25 and a maximum of $300, when the letter of credit is opened, and a fee of 0.125 percent is charged when the funds are received. A postage levy of $7.50 is also charged.

There are no arrangements for forward cover against exchange rate risk operating in the official or the commercial banking sector.

Administration of Control

All foreign exchange transactions are controlled by the Central Bank, which applies the exchange controls flexibly. All foreign exchange proceeds must be surrendered to the Central Bank, and all exchange payments must be made through the Central Bank, with the exception of 30 percent of earnings retained by producer-exporters for import payments. (See the section on Exports and Export Proceeds, below.)

Import and export licenses are automatically granted and recorded by the Directorate of External Commerce for statistical purposes.

Arrears are maintained with respect to external payments.

Prescription of Currency

The Central Bank may prescribe the currency in which foreign exchange transactions are made.

A bilateral payment agreement with Cape Verde was terminated, and the corresponding debt to Cape Verde, which amounted to $1.65 million, was rescheduled on July 21, 1995, through an agreement between the Central Bank of Cape Verde and the Central Bank of São Tomé and Príncipe. The debt will be reimbursed in 20 equal semestrial installments.

Imports and Import Payments

All registered importers (including productive entities) are permitted to engage in import activity. Fuels and lubricants are imported by the public fuel enterprise, and medicines by the public pharmaceutical enterprise and the private pharmaceutical sector. Import licenses are automatically granted by the Directorate of External Commerce. When importers open letters of credit, the International Bank requires them to lodge a deposit[1] in domestic currency in the equivalent of zero to 100 percent of the value of the letters of credit, depending on the creditworthiness of the operator. Prepayment for imports is permitted only through the opening of letters of credit or through anticipated transfer when agreed upon by the Central Bank.

Payments for Invisibles

Payments for invisibles related to authorized imports are not restricted. Payments for other invisibles are approved within limits established by the Central Bank. These limits, which allow for additional amounts in justifiable cases, include those on (1) transfers for medical treatment abroad when local facilities are inadequate; (2) transfers of remittances to students; (3) transfers of savings from earnings under technical cooperation agreements with

---

[1]Currently, the International Bank of São Tomé and Príncipe does not remunerate these deposits, but it also chooses not to remunerate any other type of deposits.

the Government; and (4) transfers for payment of fares, freight, and costs of communication with foreign countries. Purchases of foreign exchange by residents for purposes of tourism are limited, although airfares may be paid in domestic currency. Transfers of profits by foreign companies established in São Tomé and Príncipe before independence have been suspended. There are no limitations on remittances for subscriptions to periodicals and books or on the payments of interest on external debt.

Foreign exchange allowances for medical purposes are flexible. Payments for technical assistance and other services in the national interest are allowed. At the beginning of the school year, a student is granted permission to transfer funds for expenses related to courses taken abroad; the amount of the transfer must first be approved by the Ministry of Education and Culture.

All payments related to invisibles are subject to a stamp tax of 0.5 percent. An additional charge of $2 is imposed on invisible operations.

Exports and Export Proceeds

All exports require an export license, as set out in Advance Export Registration Bulletins, which specify the quantity and the c.i.f. or f.o.b. value of the export. All export proceeds must be repatriated and collected through the International Bank. However, producers of exported goods may retain 30 percent of export proceeds in accounts with banks, including those abroad (if they are correspondent banks of the Central Bank), and may use the balances to meet their import requirements.

Proceeds from Invisibles

Travelers may bring in any amount of foreign exchange.

Capital

Inward foreign investments are governed by the Investment Code, implemented on October 15, 1992. Foreign capital investments, excluding the extraction of hydrocarbons and other mining industries, are permitted on the same basis as domestic investment. Repatriation of profits is permitted up to 15 percent a year of the value of the investment. Transfers are permitted for repayment of financing under agreements with the Government and for the amortization of private sector investments in activities considered to be in the national interest. Personnel under technical assistance programs are allowed to transfer their savings in accordance with the terms of their contracts.

Gold

Exports and imports of gold require special authorization from the Central Bank.

Changes During 1995

Imports and Import Proceeds

January 1. The authorities eliminated the annual import program, as well as the registration requirement for importers.

SAUDI ARABIA

(Position as of December 31, 1995)

Exchange Arrangement

The currency of Saudi Arabia is the Saudi Arabian Riyal, which is pegged to the SDR at SRls 4.28255 per SDR 1. In principle, margins not exceeding 7.25 percent around the fixed relationship are allowed; these margins were suspended on July 22, 1981. The intervention currency is the U.S. dollar; its rate against the riyal is determined by the Saudi Arabian Monetary Agency. Since June 1, 1986, the Monetary Agency's middle rate for the U.S. dollar has been SRls 3.745 per $1; the selling rate for U.S. dollars to banks has been SRls 3.75 per $1, and the buying rate from banks has been SRls 3.74 per $1. These rates serve as the basis for exchange quotations in the market, the banks being permitted to charge up to 0.125 percent above and below the Saudi Arabian Monetary Agency's buying and selling rates for commercial transactions. There are no taxes or subsidies on purchases or sales of foreign exchange. The commercial banking sector has an active forward market to cover exchange risks of up to 12 months.

Saudi Arabia accepted the obligations of Article VIII, Sections 2, 3, and 4 of the Fund Agreement on March 22, 1961.

Administration of Control

In accordance with the Fund's Executive Board Decision No. 144-(52/51) adopted on August 14, 1952, Saudi Arabia notified the Fund on September 5, 1990 that certain restrictions had been imposed on the making of payments and transfers for current international transactions in respect of Iraq and on September 15, 1992 that, in compliance with UN Security Council Resolution No. 757 (1992), certain restrictions had been imposed on the making of payments and transfers for current international transactions in respect of the Federal Republic of Yugoslavia (Serbia/Montenegro).

Prescription of Currency

The use of the currency of Israel is prohibited.[1] No other prescription of currency requirements are in force.

Imports and Import Payments

Import licenses are not required, and exchange for payments abroad is obtained freely. The importation of a few commodities is prohibited for reasons of religion, health, or national security. Most imports are subject to customs duties at rates ranging between zero and 12 percent; for a short list of imports, the rate is 20 percent, and for tobacco products, 30 percent. Imports from member states of the Cooperation Council for the Arab States of the Gulf (GCC) are exempt, provided that at least 40 percent of the value added in each case is effected in GCC countries and that at least 51 percent of the capital of the producing firm is owned by citizens of GCC member countries.

Exports and Export Proceeds

Export licenses are not required, and no control is exercised over export proceeds. Certain imported items that are subsidized by the Government may not be re-exported.

Payments for and Proceeds from Invisibles

Payments for and proceeds from invisibles are not restricted. Travelers may freely import and export Saudi Arabian banknotes and coins.

Capital

No exchange control requirements are imposed on capital receipts or payments by residents or nonresidents. The Saudi Arabian Monetary Agency requires local banks to obtain its approval before they invite foreign banks to participate in riyal-denominated syndicated transactions inside or outside Saudi Arabia. Prior approval from the Agency is also required for Saudi banks to participate in riyal-syndicated transactions arranged abroad. Similarly, the Agency's approval is required for lending to nonresidents that originates in Saudi Arabia. The Foreign Capital Investment Law provides for certain benefits to be extended to approved foreign investments in Saudi Arabia. Approved foreign capital enjoys the same privileges as domestic capital under the 1962 Law for the Protection and Promotion of National Industry. Foreign capital invested in industrial or agricultural projects with at least 25 percent Saudi

---

[1] In addition, all imports from and all exports to this country are prohibited; payments may neither be made to it nor received from it for any type of transaction, whether current or capital.

Arabian participation is exempt from income and corporate tax for ten years after production has begun.

Inward portfolio investment in shares of listed Saudi companies is restricted to Saudi nationals. Inward investment in domestic collective investment schemes that invest in shares of Saudi companies is also restricted to Saudi nationals.

The Saudi Arabian Monetary Agency's approval is required by Saudi banks before acquiring shares in a company established outside the Kingdom.

For interbank deposits originating from foreign banks, only riyal deposits are subject to the Agency's reserve requirements.

Gold

The monetary authorities and all other residents, including private persons, may freely and without license purchase, hold, and sell gold in any form, at home or abroad. They may also, without a license and without paying any customs duty or tax, import and export gold in any form, except manufactured gold and jewelry, which are subject to a 12 percent customs duty; gold of 14 karats or less may not be imported.

Changes During 1995

No significant changes occurred in the exchange and trade system.

SENEGAL

(Position as of June 30, 1996)

Exchange Arrangement

The currency of Senegal is the CFA Franc,[1] which is pegged to the French franc, the intervention currency, at the fixed rate of CFAF 1 per F 0.01. The official buying and selling rate is CFAF 100 per F 1. Exchange rates for other currencies are derived from the rate in the Paris exchange market for the currency concerned and the fixed rate between the French franc and the CFA franc. Authorized banks charge an exchange commission of 2 percent on purchases and sales of French francs and an exchange commission of 0.125 to 1.0 per mil on purchases and sales of foreign exchange other than those directly related to external transactions. In addition, the banks levy a commission of 2.5 per mil on transfers to all countries outside the West African Economic and Monetary Union (WAEMU),[2] all of which must be surrendered to the Treasury. There are no taxes or subsidies on purchases or sales of foreign exchange.

Forward cover against exchange rate risk is available to residents only for imports of a specified category of goods. All forward cover against exchange rate risk must be authorized by the Ministry of Economy, Finance, and Planning. Forward cover may be provided only in the currency of settlement stipulated in the commercial contract. Maturities must correspond to the due date of foreign exchange settlement stipulated in the commercial contract and must not exceed one month. For some specified products, the maturity of forward cover may be extended one time for up to three months.

With the exception of measures relating to gold; the repatriation of export proceeds; the issuing, publicizing, and tendering of transferable securities and real property; and applications for investment abroad, Senegal's exchange controls do not apply to France (and its overseas departments and territories) and Monaco. Nor do they apply to all other countries whose bank of issue is linked with the French Treasury by an Operations Account (Benin, Burkina Faso, Cameroon, Central African Republic, Chad, Comoros, Congo, Côte d'Ivoire, Equatorial Guinea, Gabon, Mali, Niger, and Togo). Hence, all payments to these countries may be made freely. All other countries are considered foreign countries.

Senegal accepted the obligations of Article VIII, Sections 2, 3, and 4 of the Fund Agreement on June 1, 1996.

Administration of Control

Exchange control is administered by the Ministry of Economy, Finance, and Planning, which has delegated a part of the approval authority for exchange control to the BCEAO and to authorized banks. The Directorate of Money and Credit examines the requests for exchange authorization. Customs officers monitor outflows of foreign exchange and confirm imports and exports of goods. All exchange transactions relating to foreign countries must be effected through authorized banks, the Postal Administration, or the BCEAO. The BCEAO exercises exchange controls ex post.

Prescription of Currency

Settlements with France (as defined above), Monaco, and the Operations Account countries are made in CFA francs, French francs, or the currency of any other Operations Account country. Current transactions with The Gambia, Ghana, Guinea, Guinea-Bissau, Liberia, Mauritania, Nigeria, and Sierra Leone may be settled through the West African Clearing House. Settlements with all other countries are usually effected through correspondent banks in France in the currencies of those countries or in French francs.

Nonresident Accounts

Nonresident accounts are subject to specific regulations indicating the credit and debit operations that are allowed. These accounts may not be credited with BCEAO banknotes, French franc notes, or banknotes issued by central banks that maintain an Operations Account with the French Treasury. They may not be overdrawn without prior authorization of the Minister of Economy, Finance, and Planning. Funds may be transferred freely between nonresident accounts.

Imports and Import Payments

The principle of most-favored-nation treatment applies to all Senegal's commercial partners. Quanti-

---

[1]The CFA franc is issued by the Central Bank of West African States (BCEAO) and is the common currency in Benin, Burkina Faso, Côte d'Ivoire, Mali, Niger, Senegal, and Togo.

[2]The treaty creating the WAEMU came into effect on August 1, 1994. It coexists presently with the treaty instituting the West African Monetary Union (WAMU).

tative restrictions and prior authorization requirements for certain imports are being phased out. At present, only unwrought gold, used vehicles, and secondhand clothing are subject to import authorization. Quantitative restrictions may be applied for products affecting public health and security.

All import transactions relating to foreign countries must be domiciled with an authorized bank when their value exceeds CFAF 500,000 (f.o.b.). The exchange authorizations entitle importers to purchase the necessary exchange but not earlier than eight days before the goods are shipped to Senegal if a documentary credit is opened, or on the due date of settlement if the commodities have already been imported (if no documentary credit has been opened, on presentation of the bill of lading). Furthermore, payments for imports, with the exception of down payments, are permitted only after the proper documents for customs clearance are submitted. Advance payments for imports require authorization, and importers may not acquire foreign exchange until the contractual date of the payments.

All imports, valued at more than CFAF 1.5 million (f.o.b.) are subject to inspection by international agencies with respect to quality, quantity, price, and tariff classification. Import duties range between 5 percent and 45 percent (including a service fee of 5 percent stamp duty).

Payments for Invisibles

Payments for invisibles to France (as defined above), Monaco, and the Operations Account countries are permitted freely; those to other countries are subject to exchange approval. Payments for invisibles related to trade are permitted freely when the basic trade transaction has been approved or does not require authorization. Authorized banks are empowered to effect payments abroad of up to CFAF 20,000 on behalf of residents without requiring documents. Transfers of income accruing to nonresidents in the form of profits, dividends, and royalties are also permitted when a request for exchange authorization is submitted to the Ministry of Economy, Finance, and Planning.

Limitations on allowances for travelers are administered in a nonrestrictive manner, and all bona fide requests in excess of the established limits are granted. Residents traveling for tourism or business purposes to countries in the franc zone that are not members of the WAEMU are allowed to take out banknotes other than CFA franc notes up to the equivalent of CFAF 2 million; amounts in excess of this limit may be taken out in the form of means of payment other than banknotes. The allowances for travel to countries outside the franc zone are subject to the following regulations: (1) for tourist travel, the equivalent of CFAF 500,000 without limit on the number of trips or differentiation by the age of the traveler; (2) for business travel, CFAF 75,000 a day for up to one month, corresponding to a maximum of CFAF 2.25 million (business travel allowances may be combined with tourism allowances); (3) allowances in excess of these limits are subject to the authorization of the Ministry of Economy, Finance, and Planning; and (4) credit cards, which must be issued by resident financial intermediaries and specifically authorized by the Ministry of Economy, Finance, and Planning may be used up to the ceilings indicated above for tourist and business travel. Upon arrival at customs, returning resident travelers are required to declare all means of payment in their possession exceeding the equivalent of CFAF 25,000. All residents traveling to countries that are not members of the WAEMU must declare in writing all means of payment at their disposal at the time of departure. Nonresident travelers may re-export means of payment other than banknotes issued abroad and registered in their name. The re-exportation of foreign banknotes is allowed up to the equivalent of CFAF 250,000; the re-exportation of foreign banknotes above these ceilings and other means of payment issued in Senegal requires documentation demonstrating either the importation of foreign banknotes or their purchase against other means of payment registered in the name of the traveler or through the use of nonresident deposits held in local banks.

A foreigner working in Senegal may transfer his full net salary upon presenting the appropriate pay voucher, provided that the transfer takes place within three months of the pay period.

Exports and Export Proceeds

With a few exceptions (e.g., precious metals, sugar, and groundnut oil) exports do not require prior authorization. Proceeds from exports to foreign countries, including members of the WAEMU and the Operations Account countries, must normally be collected within 120 days of the arrival of the goods at their destination and repatriated through BCEAO not later than one month after the due date. All export transactions exceeding CFAF 500,000 must be domiciled with an authorized bank.

Proceeds from Invisibles

Proceeds from transactions in invisibles with France (as defined above), Monaco, and the Operations Account countries may be retained. All amounts due from residents of other countries for services and all income earned in those countries from foreign assets must be collected and surrendered, if received in foreign currency, within one month of the due date or the date of receipt. Resident and nonresident travelers may bring in any amount of banknotes and coins issued by the BCEAO, the Bank of France, or any bank of issue maintaining an Operations Account with the French Treasury, as well as any amount of foreign banknotes and coins (except gold coins) of countries outside the Operations Account area. Residents bringing in foreign banknotes must declare them to customs upon entry and sell them to an authorized bank within eight days.

Capital

Capital movements between Senegal and France (as defined above), Monaco, and the Operations Account countries are free of exchange control; capital transfers to all other countries require the approval of the Ministry of Economy, Finance, and Planning, but capital receipts from such countries are permitted freely.

Controls are maintained over borrowing abroad, over all inward and outward direct investment and over the issuing, advertising, or offering for sale of foreign securities in Senegal. Such operations require the prior authorization from or prior notification to the Minister of Economy, Finance, and Planning. Exempt from prior authorization are operations in connection with (1) loans backed by a guarantee from the Senegalese Government, and (2) shares that are identical with, or may be substituted for, securities whose issue or offering for sale in Senegal has been previously authorized. With the exception of controls over foreign securities, these measures do not apply to France, Monaco, member countries of the WAEMU, and the Operations Account countries. Special controls are maintained also over imports and exports of gold, over the soliciting of funds for deposit with foreign private persons and foreign firms and institutions, and over publicity aimed at placing funds abroad or at subscribing to real estate and building operations abroad; these special controls also apply to France, Monaco, and the Operations Account countries.

All investments abroad by residents of Senegal[3] require prior authorization from the Ministry of Economy, Finance, and Planning; 75 percent of such investments must be financed with borrowing from abroad. Foreign direct investments in Senegal[4] must be reported to the Minister of Economy, Finance, and Planning before they are made. The Ministry has two months after receiving the notification to request postponement of the project. Both the making and the liquidating of direct and other investments, whether Senegalese investments abroad or foreign investments in Senegal, must be reported to the Ministry of Economy, Finance, and Planning and the BCEAO within 20 days of each operation. Direct investments constitute investments implying control of a company or enterprise. Mere participation is not considered direct investment, provided that it does not exceed 20 percent of the capital of a company whose shares are quoted on a stock exchange. Lending abroad requires prior authorization from the Ministry of Economy, Finance, and Planning.

Borrowing by residents from nonresidents requires prior authorization from the Ministry of Economy, Finance, and Planning, except in the cases of loans constituting a direct investment, which are subject to prior declaration, as indicated above, and loans contracted by authorized banks. The repayment of loans not constituting a direct investment requires the authorization of the Ministry of Economy, Finance, and Planning if the loan itself was subject to such approval.

The Investment Code provides various facilities and benefits for approved foreign investments in Senegal. Special facilities for export industries are established in the Dakar export processing zone.

Gold

Residents are free to hold, acquire, and dispose of gold in any form in Senegal. Imports and exports of gold (gold jewelry and gold materials) from or to any other country require prior authorization from the Minister of Economy, Finance, and Planning. Exempt from this requirement are (1) imports and exports by the Treasury or the BCEAO; (2) imports and exports of manufactured articles containing a minor quantity of gold (such as gold-filled or gold-plated articles); and (3) imports and exports by travelers of gold articles up to a combined weight of 200 grams. Purchases abroad of nonmonetary gold by brokers are subject to customs duties and taxes in effect.

---

[3]Including investments made through foreign companies that are directly or indirectly controlled by persons in Senegal and those made by overseas branches or subsidiaries of companies in Senegal.

[4]Including those made by companies in Senegal that are directly or indirectly under foreign control and those made by branches or subsidiaries of foreign companies in Senegal.

Changes During 1995

No significant changes occurred in the exchange and trade system.

Changes During 1996

Exchange Arrangement

June 1. Senegal accepted the obligations of Article VIII, Sections 2, 3, and 4 of the Fund Agreement.

SEYCHELLES

(Position as of December 31, 1995)

Exchange Arrangement

The currency of Seychelles is the Seychelles Rupee, which is pegged to the SDR at SDR 1 = SR 7.2345. Exchange rates for various currencies are quoted on the basis of their New York closing rates for the U.S. dollar on the previous day, using the U.S. dollar rate for the Seychelles rupee, as derived from the fixed parity to the SDR. The Central Bank of Seychelles circulates these rates daily to the commercial banks. The Central Bank charges a commission of 0.125 percent on purchases and 0.875 percent on sales of pounds sterling, U.S. dollars, and French francs.

The commercial banks are authorized to deal in pounds sterling and other currencies at rates based on the exchange rates circulated daily by the Central Bank for the respective currencies. Other authorized dealers include casinos, guesthouses, hotels, restaurants, self-catering establishments, tour operators, travel agents, shipping agents, and ship chandlers. These specific authorized dealers are restricted to buying only in the course of their licensed activity. They must sell all their foreign currency proceeds to the five commercial banks.

With effect from July 3, 1995, all other transactions in foreign exchange are prohibited, including one-way foreign exchange transactions that were previously, by implication, allowed. Moreover, with effect from the same date, all nonresident, non-Seychellois persons are prohibited from funding accounts in Seychelles rupees. Thus, it is necessary that all accounts owned by such persons are funded initially and on an ongoing basis in foreign currency.

Commercial banks are the only authorized sellers of foreign exchange. They allocate 64.8 percent of their foreign exchange inflows to a pipeline scheme for foreign exchange payments, which was introduced in April 1994. Under this scheme, commercial banks invite customers to deposit the rupee equivalent of their foreign exchange requirements in a special account. Since July 1995, the pipeline is divided into seven categories, depending on the type of payment. A certain percentage of foreign exchange inflows is allocated to each category. The system operates on a first-come, first-served basis for each category at banks.

The remaining 16.2 percent of foreign exchange inflows are used at the discretion of the commercial banks.

There are no taxes or subsidies on purchases or sales of foreign exchange. There are no arrangements for forward cover against exchange rate risk in the official or the commercial banking sector.

Seychelles accepted the obligations of Article VIII, Sections 2, 3, and 4 of the Fund Agreement on January 3, 1978.

Administration of Control

Exchange controls are maintained in the form of administrative allocation of foreign exchange for the making of certain payments. This applies to the 64.8 percent of foreign exchange inflows allocated to the seven pipeline categories and the 19 percent surrender requirements.

A team, consisting of Central Bank and Ministry of Finance representatives, has been created to administer and police the enforcement of the prohibition for those other than authorized dealers to undertake foreign exchange transactions.

The Ministry of Finance partially controls foreign trade and domestic marketing through a mechanism of import and price controls. Import controls are exercised over goods by the Trade and Commerce Division of the Ministry of Finance, while price controls are administered by the Consumer Relations Unit on behalf of the Ministry.

Prescription of Currency

There are no prescription of currency requirements.

Imports and Import Payments

No legal restrictions are placed on payments for imports. However, a shortage of foreign exchange has led to arrears with respect to commercial payments that constitute a de facto restriction on import payments.

Importers other than individuals are required to obtain import licenses from the Seychelles Licensing Authority, in accordance with objective criteria. In addition, for each shipment of commodities, an importer must apply for a permit to the Trade and Commerce Division of the Ministry of Finance. Granting of permits is at the discretion of this division. A permit is normally not granted for cars older than three years and for some nonessential commodities, for example, ornamental vases and chewing gum. In addition, certain goods can only be imported by the Seychelles Marketing Board.

Most imports are subject to a trade tax at rates ranging up to 600 percent, with the bulk of imported commodities falling in the range of 5 percent to 30 percent.

Payments for Invisibles

There are no legal restrictions on payments for invisibles, and no legal limits are imposed on the provision of travel exchange. Travelers may take or send out of Seychelles any amount of foreign currency and up to SR 100 of domestic currency.

Exports and Export Proceeds

Residents may export goods to any country, but a permit is required for each shipment of commodities. These permits are granted on a routine basis by the Trade and Commerce Division of the Ministry of Finance. Exporters are required to surrender 19 percent of foreign exchange receipts for purchases of essential imports by the Seychelles Marketing Board, loan repayments, and requirements by a utility company. Foreign currency may be accepted by businesses in payment for goods.

Proceeds from Invisibles

Exchange receipts from invisibles, with the exception of dividend remittances and transfers of management fees, may be disposed of freely. A prohibition on these items has been in place since July 3, 1995. Foreign currency may be accepted by businesses in payment for services. Overseas visitors may bring in any amount of currency for travel expenditure.

Capital

Since July 3, 1995, payment in respect of transfers of proceeds of sale of assets should be withheld. There are no other restrictions on capital transfers.

Investment outside Seychelles by permanent residents and by companies and other organizations operating in Seychelles is not subject to any limitations. Foreign investment is freely permitted, provided that such investment does not involve ownership of land.

Commercial banks in Seychelles are required to restrict credit to non-nationals primarily for working capital purposes and generally to an amount that does not exceed overseas funds invested in Seychelles in enterprises in certain priority sectors, that is, agriculture and fishing, manufacturing, construc-

tion, and tourism. Additionally, penalty loan rates are imposed on credit secured by foreign assets.

Gold

Residents may freely purchase, hold, and sell gold in any form, except for dealings in gold bullion, which are restricted to authorized dealers. Seychelles has issued the following commemorative gold coins, which are also legal tender: (1) two coins issued by the Currency Board in the denominations of SR 1,500 and SR 1,000; (2) a coin in the denomination of SR 20 to commemorate the fifth anniversary of the Central Bank in December 1983; (3) a coin in the denomination of SR 25 issued in April 1984 to mark the World Fisheries Conference of the Food and Agriculture Organization; (4) a coin in the denomination of SR 500 issued in February 1986 to commemorate the United Nations Decade for Women; (5) a coin in the denomination of SR 1,000 issued in June 1986 to mark the tenth anniversary of Seychelles' independence; (6) a coin in the denomination of SR 1,000 issued in June 1987 to commemorate the tenth anniversary of the June 5, 1977 Liberation; (7) two coins in the denominations of SR 100 and SR 1,000 issued in December 1988 to mark the tenth anniversary of the Central Bank; (8) a coin in the denomination of SR 500 issued in April 1990 to mark EXPO '90 in Osaka, Japan; (9) a coin in the denomination of SR 1,000 issued in December 1993 to commemorate the fifteenth anniversary of the Central Bank; (10) a series of coins with wildlife motifs issued in June 1994, including the magpie robin in denominations of SR 250 and SR 50, and the milkweed butterfly in the denominations of SR 250, SR 50, and SR 50; and (11) a gold coin issued in 1995 with the theme "Olympic Games 1996 — Surfing" in the denomination of SR 100.

Changes During 1995

Exchange Arrangement

July 3. Transactions in foreign exchange by commercial banks other than those for which they are licensed were prohibited, including one-way foreign exchange transactions that were previously, by implication, allowed. Moreover, with effect on the same date, nonresident persons were prohibited from funding accounts in Seychelles rupees.

July 3. The surrender requirement for exporters was increased to 19 percent from 15 percent of foreign exchange inflows, for purchases of essential imports by the Seychelles Marketing Board, loan repayments, and requirements by a utility company.

SIERRA LEONE

(Position as of December 31, 1995)

Exchange Arrangement

The currency of Sierra Leone is the Sierra Leonean Leone. Exchange rates are freely determined on the basis of demand and supply in the market. Commercial banks and licensed foreign exchange bureaus may buy and sell foreign exchange with customers and trade among themselves or with the Bank of Sierra Leone, the central bank, on a freely negotiable basis.

Foreign exchange bureaus are limited to spot transactions and are not allowed to sell traveler's checks. The central bank determines the exchange rate to be used in official transactions, including customs valuation purposes, which is based on the weighted-average rate of commercial bank and foreign exchange bureau transactions in the previous week. On December 31, 1995, the official buying and selling rates were Le 932.11 and Le 950.76, respectively, per US$1. There are no taxes or subsidies on purchases or sales of foreign exchange. There are no arrangements for forward cover against exchange rate risk operating in the official or the commercial banking and foreign exchange bureau sectors.

Sierra Leone accepted the obligations of Article VIII, Sections 2, 3, and 4 of the Fund Agreement on December 14, 1995.

Administration of Control

Exchange control policy is formulated by the Department of Finance, in consultation with the central bank, but the day-to-day administration of exchange control is carried out by the central bank with the assistance of the commercial banks.

Commercial arrears are maintained with respect to external payments.[1]

Prescription of Currency

Foreign exchange transactions are subject to exchange control. Payments for imports from other countries may be made in leones to the credit of an external account in the currency of the exporting country, in pounds sterling, or in U.S. dollars. Receipts from exports to countries other than China may be obtained in leones from an external account in the currency of the importing country or in any specified currency.[2] The West African Economic and Monetary Union (WAEMU) provides for settlements with the Central Bank of West African States (for Benin, Burkina Faso, Côte d'Ivoire, Niger, Senegal, and Togo) as well as with The Gambia, Ghana, Guinea, Guinea-Bissau, Liberia, Mali, Mauritania, and Nigeria.

Resident and Nonresident Accounts

Residents and nonresidents in Sierra Leone are permitted to maintain foreign currency accounts denominated in any convertible currency with a commercial bank in Sierra Leone. These accounts, for which minimum balances vary from bank to bank, earn interest at a rate determined by the commercial banks. They may be credited with funds transferred from abroad, and balances on these accounts may be converted into leones to meet the account holder's local expenditures. Transfers abroad of balances in foreign currency accounts for payment of current international transactions are permitted without prior approval from the central bank, subject to fulfilling the regulations governing the transaction.

Accounts in leones held with authorized banks in Sierra Leone on behalf of diplomatic missions, UN agencies, and their accredited staff are designated as external accounts.

Imports and Import Payments

All goods may be imported freely without a license. Authority to approve transactions is delegated to the commercial banks. All applications for purchases of foreign exchange to pay for imported goods must be supported by the following documents: a completed exchange control form A1, original tax pro forma invoice or final invoice, original bill of lading or airway bill, and tax clearance certificate, all of which should be submitted to a commercial bank (authorized dealer) in Sierra Leone. Goods to be financed with importers' own external foreign exchange resources do not require letters of credit

---

[1]The clearing of these arrears is being addressed under the second phase of the debt reduction program that is expected to be executed before the end of 1996.

[2]Austrian schillings, Belgian francs, Canadian dollars, CFA francs, Danish kroner, deutsche mark, French francs, Italian lire, Japanese yen, Netherlands guilders, Norwegian kroner, Portuguese escudos, pounds sterling, Spanish pesetas, Swedish kronor, Swiss francs, and U.S. dollars.

established with a local commercial bank (authorized dealer).

All goods imported into Sierra Leone, except petroleum and goods specifically exempted by the Secretary of State for Finance, are subject to preshipment inspection and price verification by an international company appointed by the Government.

A sales tax of 20 percent of the landed value is levied on all imports except for capital goods and their spare parts, petroleum products, and baby food. All imports by unincorporated businesses are subject to a tax of 2 percent as advance payment of income taxes.

Payments for Invisibles

Authority to provide foreign exchange for legitimate expenses is delegated to the commercial banks. In general, commercial banks are authorized to make payments for invisibles such as school fees, medical treatment abroad, interest on external loans, subscriptions, insurance premiums, and administrative expenses provided payments are made directly to the institution providing the service and appropriate documentary evidence is submitted, including a tax clearance certificate. Applications for basic travel allowances in excess of $5,000 a trip must be supported by traveling documents. Banks may also approve educational and maintenance expenses abroad of up to $10,000 a year. Authorized dealers, however, are free to remit expenses to bona fide students and dependents above the indicative limit without restrictions.

An expatriate's salary may be remitted abroad on submission of a valid work permit, the remuneration package agreement, and a tax clearance certificate. Remittances are limited to the remuneration package.

Commercial banks (authorized dealers) can transfer abroad profits earned by nonresidents from an authorized business or transaction in Sierra Leone without restrictions or reference to the central bank. Such profits include dividend income or net ordinary income and other investment income (royalty, rents, etc.). The request must be supported by documents evidencing profit payments and income tax deductions taken at the source, or a tax clearance certificate.

Travelers can take foreign exchange out of Sierra Leone up to $5,000 without restriction. Residents should declare on departure foreign exchange in excess of $5,000 with supporting documents. Nonresidents can take foreign exchange out of Sierra Leone up to the amount they brought in. Incoming nonresidents are, therefore, advised to disclose amounts of foreign currency brought into Sierra Leone if they anticipate taking out amounts in excess of the permitted allowance, disclosure is, however, optional. On leaving Sierra Leone, travelers may take out with them up to Le 50,000 in Sierra Leonean currency notes. A travel tax of 10 percent is levied on the price of tickets purchased locally and is payable when the ticket is purchased.

Exports and Export Proceeds

Licenses are required for exports of gold, diamonds, and other mineral products; these export licenses, valid for one year or six months, are issued by the Department of Mines.

All exporters are required to complete export forms that must be endorsed by the exporter's commercial bank. Exports of the following articles are prohibited: those containing more than 25 percent silver; those manufactured or produced more than 75 years before the date of exportation; those mounted or set with diamonds, precious stones, and pearls (excluding personal jewelry or ornaments up to a value not exceeding the leone equivalent of $1,000); postage stamps of philatelic interest; and works of art. Exporters are obligated to repatriate export proceeds within 90 days of the date of export (approval of the central bank is required for an extension beyond 90 days), but they are not required to surrender them to any government body. Licensed exporters of diamonds are allowed to transact their business in U.S. dollars and must pay an administrative fee of 1.0 percent and an income tax of 1.5 percent, which are based on the value of the diamonds exported and payable in U.S. dollars. Proceeds from exports of diamonds that were refinanced are not subject to the repatriation requirement. Licensed exporters of gold must pay a 2.5 percent royalty on their exports.

All goods exported from Sierra Leone and endorsed by a commercial bank, except those exempted by the Secretary of State for Finance, are subject to preshipment inspection and price verification, which is undertaken by an inspection company appointed by the Government. Exporters who are subject to inspection must pay an export inspection fee of 1 percent before clearing their goods through customs.

Proceeds from Invisibles

Receipts from invisibles may be offered for sale to authorized dealers or deposited in a foreign currency account. The importation of domestic banknotes is limited to Le 50,000 a traveler.

Capital

Capital payments to nonresidents of Sierra Leone are subject to exchange control. Residents of Sierra Leone are required to obtain permission from the central bank to purchase foreign currency securities or real estate situated abroad. Investments by non-residents, including profits, may be repatriated at any time, provided that exchange control approval of the investment was obtained at the outset. In addition, outward remittance of interest and amortization on external loans may be made upon submission of the appropriate documentary evidence including the loan agreement and a tax clearance certificate. The prior approval of the central bank is required in order to contract an external loan.

Issuance and transfers of securities are subject to exchange control by the central bank. The placing of an issue in Sierra Leone requires permission if either the person acquiring the securities or the person for whom he or she serves as nominee resides outside Sierra Leone. Permission must also be obtained before a security registered in Sierra Leone may be transferred to a nonresident. Capital in respect of securities registered in Sierra Leone may not be transferred abroad without permission; for permission to be given, the company is usually required to obtain bank certification of the funds brought into Sierra Leone. Income tax and customs duty concessions are granted to foreign and domestic companies undertaking industrial or agricultural activities that are needed for the development of the country. Non-citizens are prohibited from owning or controlling certain types of business, under the Noncitizen Trade and Business Act of 1969.

Gold

Residents may freely purchase, hold, and sell gold coins in Sierra Leone for numismatic purposes. Also, residents and nonresidents may freely purchase, hold, sell, or export certain Sierra Leonean commemorative gold coins. Residents are not allowed to hold gold in the form of bars or dust without a valid miner's or dealer's license. Imports of gold in any form, other than jewelry constituting the personal effects of a traveler, require individual import licenses.

Changes During 1995

Exchange Arrangement

December 14. Sierra Leone accepted the obligations of Article VIII, Sections 2, 3, and 4 of the Fund Agreement.

Payments for Invisibles

December 21. Commercial banks were allowed to provide foreign exchange in excess of applicable limits without the approval of the central bank.

SINGAPORE

(Position as of December 31, 1995)

Exchange Arrangement

The currency of Singapore is the Singapore Dollar. Singapore follows a policy under which the Singapore dollar is permitted to float, and its exchange rate in terms of the U.S. dollar, the intervention currency, and all other currencies is freely determined in the foreign exchange market. However, the Monetary Authority of Singapore monitors the external value of the Singapore dollar against a trade-weighted basket of currencies, with the objective of promoting noninflationary sustainable economic growth. The closing interbank buying and selling rates for the U.S. dollar on December 30, 1995 were S$1.4150 and S$1.4153, respectively, per US$1. Rates for other currencies are available throughout the working day and are based on the currencies' exchange rates against the U.S. dollar in international markets. Banks are free to deal in all currencies, with no restrictions on amount, maturity, or type of transaction.

Foreign currency futures are traded at the Singapore International Monetary Exchange. Banks can hedge their exchange rate risk through a forward foreign exchange transaction. There is an active short-term foreign exchange swap market among the banks in the domestic money market. Singapore and Brunei currency notes and coins are freely interchangeable, at par and without charge, in Singapore and Brunei. There are no taxes or subsidies on purchases or sales of foreign exchange.

Singapore accepted the obligations of Article VIII, Sections 2, 3, and 4 of the Fund Agreement on November 9, 1968.

Administration of Control

There are no formal exchange controls, but the Monetary Authority of Singapore retains responsibility for exchange control matters. The Trade Development Board under the Ministry of Trade and Industry administers import- and export-licensing requirements for a very small number of products under its control. Financial assets owned by residents of Iraq and the Libyan Arab Jamahiriya are blocked.

Prescription of Currency

There are no prescription of currency requirements.

Nonresident Accounts

There is no distinction between accounts of residents and nonresidents of Singapore. Debits and credits to all accounts may be made freely.

Imports and Import Payments

Very few items imported into Singapore are dutiable. Customs duties are levied on imports of liquor, tobacco, petroleum, and motorcars. A few imports are controlled for health, safety, or security reasons. Singapore is a party to the Agreement on the Common Effective Preferential Tariff (CEPT) Scheme for the ASEAN Free Trade Area (AFTA). The CEPT Scheme came into operation on January 1, 1993.

Import licenses are required for rice, irrespective of the country of origin. Singapore observes the import prohibitions governed by the United Nations Security Council Resolutions.

Payments for Invisibles

All payments for invisibles may be made freely. There are no restrictions on the amount of foreign exchange that may be used for travel abroad. Remittances to nonresidents of dividends, interest, and profits may be made freely. Resident and nonresident travelers may take out any amount in foreign or Singapore banknotes.

Exports and Export Proceeds

Singapore observes the export prohibitions governed by the United Nations Security Council Resolutions. Certain exports originating in Singapore—for example, textiles and textile products—are subject to quantitative restrictions and other nontariff barriers in the importing countries, particularly the United States, Canada, Norway, and the members of the European Union. Export licenses are required for substances that deplete the ozone, timber, and rubber, but there is no restriction on export proceeds.

Proceeds from Invisibles

Exchange receipts from invisibles need not be surrendered and may be disposed of freely. Resident and nonresident travelers may bring in any amount in foreign banknotes and coins, including Singapore gold coins.

Capital

There are no restrictions on capital transfers. Singapore residents, including corporations, are allowed to make payments in all currencies to any country outside Singapore without restriction. Residents may invest, borrow, and lend in foreign currencies without prior exchange control approval and may deal freely in spot and forward foreign exchange transactions in all currencies. However, banks, merchant banks, and finance and insurance companies must consult the Monetary Authority of Singapore if they intend to grant loans in Singapore dollars in excess of S$5 million to nonresidents; loans in excess of S$5 million to residents for use outside Singapore must also have the approval of the Monetary Authority of Singapore. Non-Singapore citizens (excluding permanent residents of Singapore) and non-Singapore companies are not granted Singapore dollar loans for the purchase of residential properties in Singapore. Permanent residents of Singapore, however, may be granted one Singapore dollar loan to purchase a residential property in Singapore for owner occupation.

Banks in Singapore may freely accept deposits in foreign currencies. Financial institutions that have been approved to deal in Asian currency units (ACUs) in Singapore are able to offer better rates for foreign currency deposits placed with ACUs because of the absence of minimum cash reserve and liquidity requirements. The ACU is a separate accounting unit of financial institutions that enjoy a concessional tax rate of 10 percent on their income from transacting with nonresidents in foreign currency; these institutions operate in the Asian dollar market. Transactions in Singapore dollars cannot be booked in ACUs.

There are no restrictions on either direct or portfolio investments in Singapore by nonresidents or abroad by residents.

Government approval is required for foreign investment in residential and other properties (including vacant land) that has been zoned or approved for industrial or commercial use. Foreigners may, however, freely purchase residential units in buildings of six or more stories and in approved condominium developments. Foreigners who make an economic contribution to Singapore will be given favorable consideration to purchase other residential properties for their own use and, in the case of foreign companies, to accommodate their senior personnel. The maximum limit on the proportion of foreign shareholding in local banks is 40 percent.

Gold

There is a free gold market in Singapore. Both resident and nonresident individuals and companies are permitted to import, hold, negotiate, and export gold freely; imports and exports require neither exchange control approval nor import or export licenses, and any person in Singapore can deal freely in gold. For imports, gold bars weighing 1 kilogram and above and 10-tola bars are exempt from the 3 percent goods and services tax (GST) if they are meant for re-exports. Movement of gold between two bonded warehouses in Singapore is also exempt from the GST.

Gold may also be traded in the local market and the spot or futures markets. In the spot market, most of the trading is done on a "loco-London" basis for delivery of 995 fine gold. Kilobars of 999.9 fineness are most commonly traded, while 10-tola bars are also becoming popular. Spot gold prices for settlement in Singapore are derived by adjusting the "loco-London" price with the location premium, which takes into account the cost of transportation and insurance. A gold futures contract is also available on the Singapore International Monetary Exchange.

Changes During 1995

No significant changes occurred in the exchange and trade system.

SLOVAK REPUBLIC

(Position as of December 31, 1995)

Exchange Arrangement

The currency of the Slovak Republic is the Slovak Koruna. The external value of the koruna is pegged to a basket of two currencies within margins of ±1.5 percent and the official exchange rate is determined in fixing sessions conducted by the National Bank of Slovakia.[1] On December 29, 1995, the middle rate for the U.S. dollar was Sk 29.6 per $1. There are no taxes or subsidies on purchases or sales of foreign exchange.

The Slovak Republic accepted the obligations of Article VIII, Sections 2, 3, and 4 of the Fund Agreement on October 1, 1995.

Administration of Control

The National Bank is responsible for the administration of exchange controls and regulations in coordination with the Ministry of Finance. In general, the Ministry of Finance has authority over governmental credits and over budgetary and subsidized organizations, civic associations, churches, foundations, and juridical persons who are not engaged in entrepreneurial activities. The National Bank has authority over the activities of all registered enterprises and entrepreneurs.

Prescription of Currency

Settlements are effected in convertible currency. From February 1993 through September 1995, commercial transactions with the Czech Republic had to be effected through a clearing account maintained by the central banks of the two countries. Transactions were converted from the currency of the contract into clearing ECUs at a rate that could differ by up to 5 percent from the market cross rate against the ECU set by the central banks. If the outstanding balance on the account at the end of any month exceeded clearing ECU 130 million, the excess amount was settled by the middle of the following month. Payments by legal persons and enterprises in connection with obligations incurred before February 8, 1993, were effected through another set of clearing accounts denominated in clearing koruny converted to ECUs at the exchange rate of

February 8, 1993. These accounts were settled every three months.

On September 30, 1995, the bilateral clearing arrangement with the Czech Republic was terminated, and the outstanding balance remaining in the clearing account under the arrangement was expected to be settled by April 1, 1996.

Resident and Nonresident Accounts

Resident Accounts. Slovak resident individuals (including unregistered entrepreneurs) may open interest-bearing foreign exchange accounts at any resident commercial bank without revealing the source of foreign exchange. Balances in these accounts may be used by the account holder without restriction. Resident enterprises that had outstanding foreign exchange accounts on December 31, 1990, have been allowed to maintain such accounts; new foreign exchange accounts, however, may be opened by enterprises after December 31, 1990, with only a prior permit from the National Bank that exempts enterprises from the 100 percent surrender requirement. Balances on these accounts may be freely used to finance enterprises' activities.

Nonresident Accounts. Nonresidents (natural and juridical persons) may maintain two types of interest-bearing accounts: (1) *Domestic currency accounts* may be opened with commercial banks in koruny. Balances on these accounts may be used freely to make payments in the Slovak Republic. All payments abroad from these accounts for invisibles, except transfers relating to inheritance and alimony, require a permit from the National Bank. These permits are granted only in exceptional cases; (2) *Foreign currency accounts* may be opened by nonresidents. Foreign exchange may be deposited freely in these accounts, and payments may be made from these accounts in the Slovak Republic or abroad without restriction.

Imports and Exports

Imports and exports may be undertaken by any registered enterprise or private individual. Import licenses are required for a few strategic items, namely, crude oil, natural gas, firearms and ammunition, and narcotics. In addition, an automatic licensing system accompanied by variable levies applies to imports of 12 agricultural products and coal. All imports, except those from the Czech

---

[1]The currencies are the deutsche mark (weight 60 percent) and the U.S. dollar (weight 40 percent). The margin around the central rate was widened to ±3 percent on January 1, 1995.

Republic, are subject to an ad valorem import tariff, ranging from zero to 15 percent, with a few exceptions. Imports from developing countries are granted preferential treatment under the Generalized System of Preferences (GSP). Under the GSP, 42 developing countries benefit from a duty exemption, and 80 others are granted a 75 percent reduction from the applicable customs duties; tropical products are granted an 85 percent reduction from the applicable customs duties. All consumer goods are also subject to a temporary import surcharge of 10 percent.

A resident individual is required to repatriate foreign exchange acquired abroad and to sell to a bank or deposit in a private foreign exchange account foreign exchange, including gold (with the exception of gold coins) exceeding the equivalent of Sk 5,000. Resident enterprises are normally required to repatriate without delay foreign exchange receipts from exports and sell them to commercial banks.

A limited number of products require export licenses for purposes of health control (including livestock and plants), to facilitate voluntary restraints on products on which partner countries have imposed import quotas (such as textiles and steel products), or to preserve natural resources or imported raw materials (such as energy, metallurgical materials, wood, foodstuffs, pharmaceutical products, and construction materials) for the domestic market. For the two latter groups of products, neither quantitative nor value limits are in force. Fees are applied to noncommercial exports of a few products (certain food items and selected types of porcelain and glassware) in excess of a certain value.

Payments for and Proceeds from Invisibles

Slovak residents may withdraw an unlimited amount of foreign exchange from their foreign currency accounts to make invisible payments. In addition, the annual limit on foreign exchange allowances for tourist travel abroad is Sk 60,000 (about $2,000). Official travel by employees of budgetary and subsidized organizations is subject to different allowances, depending on the country of destination. Transfers of alimony may be made to all countries. A special permit is required in most instances for remittances relating to family maintenance, education, and medical treatment.

Repatriation of wage savings in koruny by nonresident workers must be authorized by the National Bank. With certain exceptions related to tourism, the exportation and importation of koruna banknotes abroad are restricted. Licenses are not required for the importation or exportation of foreign exchange assets, including foreign currencies, by nonresidents.

Capital

Registered enterprises may freely obtain trade credits. Financial credits from abroad require a special permit from the National Bank. Foreign direct investments abroad are subject to approval from the National Bank; approval is normally granted if such investments are considered to facilitate exports from the Slovak Republic.

There is no limit on equity participation by nonresidents. Credits may be obtained from foreign banks with the approval of the National Bank. Foreign exchange equity participation of foreign investors can be deposited in a foreign exchange account with a resident commercial bank. Foreign investors may freely transfer abroad their dividends, profits, capital gains, and interest earnings. In the event of liquidation of the enterprise, they are allowed to repatriate freely the full value of their capital participation and capital gains in the original currency after payment of taxes.

Transfers of inherited assets abroad are allowed to all countries on a reciprocal basis.

Gold

Residents are required to sell gold (with the exception of gold coins) to financial institutions dealing in foreign exchange within 30 days of acquisition. Without a foreign exchange license, nonresidents may export inherited gold coins, provided that they submit a certificate confirming that the coins are of no historical value, and they may export gold that they have imported into the country. To export any other gold, nonresidents must have a foreign exchange license.

Changes During 1995

Exchange Arrangement

October 1. The Slovak Republic accepted the obligations of Article VIII, Sections 2, 3, and 4 of the Fund Agreement. A new foreign exchange law came into effect allowing the Slovak koruna to become fully convertible for current international transactions.

Prescription of Currency

May 19. The Slovak koruna was revalued by 4 percent under the bilateral payments agreement with the Czech Republic, thereby erasing most of the

5 percent devaluation against the Czech koruna in December 1993.

September 5. The Slovak koruna was revalued by a further 1 percent under the bilateral payments agreement with the Czech Republic.

September 30. The bilateral payments agreement with the Czech Republic was terminated; the balance remaining in the clearing account under the arrangement was to be settled no later than April 1, 1996.

Payments for and Proceeds from Invisibles

January 1. The annual limit on foreign exchange allowance for tourist travel was increased to Sk 16,000 a person from Sk 9,000.

July 1. The annual limit on foreign exchange for tourist travel was increased to the equivalent of Sk 30,000 a person.

October 1. The annual limit on foreign exchange for tourist travel was increased to the equivalent of Sk 60,000 a person.

SLOVENIA

(Position as of January 31, 1996)

Exchange Arrangement

The currency of Slovenia is the Tolar, the external value of which is determined in the exchange market by demand and supply. The Bank of Slovenia may also participate in the foreign exchange market and may buy and sell foreign exchange in transactions with the Government and commercial banks. Residents may conduct unlimited exchange transactions among themselves, and households may conduct foreign exchange transactions with banks or foreign exchange offices at freely negotiated rates. The Bank of Slovenia does not prescribe spreads between buying and selling rates for banks' transactions with the public, and banks are free to set their own commissions. On December 31, 1995, the official exchange rate in terms of the U.S. dollar was SIT 125.99 per $1. The Bank of Slovenia publishes daily a moving two-month average exchange rate for customs valuation and accounting purposes. There is no forward market for foreign exchange, but forward foreign exchange transactions are not prohibited. There are no taxes or subsidies on purchases or sales of foreign exchange.

Slovenia accepted the obligations of Article VIII, Sections 2, 3, and 4 of the Fund Agreement on September 1, 1995.

Administration of Control

Foreign exchange market operations are governed by the Law on Foreign Exchange Business promulgated on June 25, 1991, which introduced a free foreign exchange market operated by banks and exchange offices. The Law on Foreign Trade Transactions, effective March 27, 1993, sets out the rules and regulations governing foreign trade activities.

Prescription of Currency

Slovenia maintains a payments agreement with the former Yugoslav Republic of Macedonia, under which trade between the two countries may be settled through accounts in local currency or in foreign currencies.

Resident and Nonresident Accounts

Resident individuals and nonresidents are allowed to open and operate foreign currency accounts without restriction. Nonresidents may open local currency accounts with proceeds from the sale of foreign exchange or of goods and services to residents. Balances (including accrued interest) in these accounts may be converted into convertible currencies and repatriated. Transfers of inheritance are allowed under conditions of reciprocity. Domestic legal entities are, in principle, not allowed to maintain foreign currency accounts; exceptions are provided for in the Law on Foreign Exchange Business.

To accept foreign cash payments, as well as to pay with foreign cash, is restricted. Residents are required, in accordance with the Law on Foreign Exchange Business, to obtain permission from the Bank of Slovenia.

Imports and Import Payments

Licensing requirements in the form of permits, for the purpose of control only, have been retained for specific groups of goods (e.g., drugs, explosives, precious metals, and arms and ammunition) for security and public health reasons, in accordance with international conventions and codes. Slovenia maintains a system of import quotas applicable only to certain textile products. Under the system managed by the Chamber of Commerce, quotas are frequently revised and allocated to Slovenian importers. In general, the quotas are distributed among the applicants based on the volume of production (for a producer) or turnover (for a trader).

Imports from the Federal Republic of Yugoslavia (Serbia/Montenegro) and from areas in Bosnia and Herzegovina that are controlled by Bosnian Serbs are prohibited in accordance with UN Resolution No. 942.

A new Law on Customs and Tariffs came into effect on January 1, 1996. The Law covers more than 12,000 items, with tariff rates ranging form zero to 27 percent; the tariff rate for certain agricultural products is 70 percent.

Payments for Invisibles

There are no restrictions on payments for invisibles, except that residents are not allowed to transfer abroad receipts from services (including interest), and earnings must be spent in Slovenia.

Exports and Export Proceeds

In accordance with the sanctions of the United Nations against the Federal Republic of Yugoslavia

(Serbia/Montenegro), exports from this country are prohibited. Except for certain items that are subject to licensing for security or health reasons in accordance with the international conventions and codes, exports are not restricted. Exports of textile products to the European Union (EU) are governed by the Agreement between the EU and the Republic of Slovenia on Trade in Textile Products, initialed on July 23, 1993; textile products originating in Slovenia are free from quantitative limits. The EU imposes tariff ceilings for only five categories of products. Export taxes are levied on the following products: unworked wood, 15 percent; worked wood, 10 percent; and scrap metal, 25 percent.

Exporters are free to agree on payment terms with foreign importers. However, if the collection of export proceeds is delayed by more than one year, the transactions must be registered with the Bank of Slovenia as credit arrangements. Once received, export proceeds must be repatriated. Exporters have two business days to sell their proceeds to importers at a freely negotiated exchange rate or to use the proceeds for payments abroad. After that time, they must sell their proceeds to an authorized bank.

Exporters are exempt from customs duties payable on raw materials and intermediate and semiprocessed goods used to produce export goods, provided that the value of exports is at least 30 percent higher than the value of imports if there is no domestic production of imported goods.

Proceeds from Invisibles

No exchange control requirements are imposed on proceeds from invisibles.

Capital

In accordance with the provisions of the Law on Foreign Credit Transactions, resident juridical persons may borrow abroad on commercial terms without restriction. The Government may, however, issue guarantees and borrow abroad only in accordance with specific laws passed by Parliament. Borrowing abroad and postponement of payments for imports for a period exceeding one year must be reported to the Bank of Slovenia.

Short-term bank borrowing abroad was restricted in February 1995, when the Bank of Slovenia required borrowers to deposit 40 percent of foreign exchange loans with a maturity of less than five years (not used immediately to import) into an unremunerated tolar bank account.

Resident juridical persons may maintain accounts abroad only in specific cases as provided for by law and with the permission of the Bank of Slovenia. Only banks licensed for foreign payments may maintain accounts abroad.

Resident companies may extend loans to nonresident persons only with profits obtained from abroad.

The Law on Foreign Investments of the former Socialist Federal Republic of Yugoslavia is still being applied in Slovenia. A new law is under consideration.

Deposit money banks are required to hold foreign exchange deposits abroad as cover against domestically held foreign exchange deposits of domestic and foreign individual persons. The required deposits range from 5 percent to 100 percent, depending on the maturity of domestically held deposits. They are also required to hold deposits abroad in an amount equal to 35 percent of their average monthly turnover of convertible payments over the preceding three months.

Changes During 1995

Exchange Arrangement

September 1. Slovenia accepted the obligations of Article VIII, Sections 2, 3, and 4 of the Fund Agreement.

Capital

February 10. Forty percent of external borrowing with maturities of less than five years and not immediately utilized for import financing was required to be deposited to an unremunerated tolar bank account.

Changes During 1996

Imports and Import Payments

January 1. The Law on Customs and Tariffs, covering more than 12,000 items with tariff rates ranging up to 24 percent, came into effect.

SOLOMON ISLANDS

(Position as of December 31, 1995)

Exchange Arrangement

The currency of the Solomon Islands is the Solomon Islands Dollar, which is issued by the Central Bank of the Solomon Islands. The exchange rate for the Solomon Islands dollar is determined on the basis of its relationship to a trade-weighted basket of the currencies of the Solomon Islands' four major trading partners. The Central Bank may make discretionary adjustments in the exchange value of the Solomon Islands dollar against the U.S. dollar each month within margins of 0.5 percent above or below the middle rate prevailing at the end of the previous month. The Central Bank provides the commercial banks with daily limits on the buying and selling rates for the U.S. dollar in transactions with the Central Bank and the public. On December 31, 1995, the buying and selling rates quoted by the banks in dealings with the public were US$0.2879 and US$0.2851, respectively, per SI$1.

The commercial banks in the Solomon Islands are free to determine their exchange rates for all other foreign currencies. A tax of SI$3 is levied on sales of foreign exchange exceeding SI$3,000. The forward cover facility, which previously existed mainly for bona fide trade or trade-related transactions, was discontinued on November 12, 1995.

The Solomon Islands accepted the obligations of Article VIII, Sections 2, 3, and 4 of the Fund's Articles of Agreement on July 24, 1979.

Administration of Control

Exchange control is administered by the Central Bank through the Exchange Control (Foreign Exchange) Regulations, which came into force on March 1, 1977. The Central Bank delegates extensive powers to commercial banks, which have been appointed authorized dealers in foreign exchange and may approve certain types of exchange applications, up to specified limits.

All persons residing in the Solomon Islands are regarded as permanent residents for exchange control purposes, unless they have been granted temporary resident status by an authorized dealer or the Central Bank. Applications for temporary resident status are normally approved for citizens of foreign countries who intend to reside in the Solomon Islands for a period of less than four years or have already resided in the Solomon Islands for over four years but can produce evidence of firm intention to resume permanent residence overseas in the near future. Ownership of real estate or a business indicates permanent resident status, regardless of the duration of residence in the Solomon Islands. Temporary resident status does not release a person from the obligation to comply with all provisions of the exchange control regulations.

In accordance with the Fund's Executive Board Decision No. 144-(52/51) adopted on August 14, 1952, the Solomon Islands notified the Fund, on October 14, 1992, that certain restrictions had been imposed on the making of payments and transfers for current international transactions in respect of the Federal Republic of Yugoslavia (Serbia/Montenegro).

Prescription of Currency

Contractual commitments in a foreign currency to persons residing outside the Solomon Islands may be met only by payments in that currency. Export proceeds may be received in any foreign currency or in Solomon Islands dollars from an account of an overseas bank with a bank in the Solomon Islands.

Nonresident Accounts

Nonresidents may open nonresident accounts in Solomon Islands dollars with authorized dealers, but approval from the Central Bank is required in order for these accounts to be credited from the Solomon Islands sources. Balances on such accounts may be transferred abroad with the approval of the Central Bank or authorized dealers.

Imports and Import Payments

No restrictions are placed on payments for imports, provided evidence that they are properly due overseas is submitted. Authorized dealers are permitted to approve most transactions up to SI$25,000 without reference to the Central Bank. The rate of import levy is set at 8 percent.

Payments for Invisibles

Payments for invisibles related to authorized imports are not restricted. Approval is readily given for payments for services and remittances of dividends, profits, and other earnings accruing to overseas residents from companies in the Solomon Islands, provided it can be shown they are properly due overseas. Permanent residents are permitted to purchase foreign exchange for payment of all types of invisibles if supporting documents are provided. Transfers by postal order to persons residing permanently outside the Solomon Islands are permitted, provided the total amount transferred does not exceed SI$100 a week.

Approval is normally given for the purchase of foreign currency for travel. Applications for travel funds must be lodged with an authorized dealer, and applicants are required to present their passports and airline tickets. Travelers may not take out Solomon Islands currency notes and coins in excess of SI$250 without the approval of the Central Bank; approval is not normally given.

Exports and Export Proceeds

Residents may export goods other than round logs without exchange control formality, but they must comply with the terms of the General Authority issued by the Central Bank. The essential conditions of this General Authority require that payments for exported goods be received within three months of the date of exportation, that the export price be no lower than the price an exporter might reasonably be expected to receive for the goods for export to the destination involved at the date when those goods were sold or contracted to be sold under open market conditions, and that the proceeds be sold promptly to an authorized dealer. If exporters are not in a position to comply with the conditions of the General Authority, they must apply to the Central Bank for a Specific Authority. Authority is not needed for goods under SI$250 in value in any one consignment or for certain exempt categories of goods, including most personal effects of passengers.

Exports of round logs require Specific Authority from the Central Bank. The condition for issuance of a specific authority to export round logs is a market price certificate issued by the Ministry of Forestry, Conservation and Environment. Exports of logs are subject to an export duty of 27 percent if valued at US$75 or less (per cubic meter) and of 32 percent if valued at more than US$75 (per cubic meter).

Proceeds from Invisibles

Approval is required for the disposal of foreign currency proceeds other than by sale to an authorized dealer. Overseas residents visiting the Solomon Islands may bring in any amount of currency for travel expenditures.

Capital

All outward transfers of capital require exchange control approval. All applications for transfers must be referred to the Central Bank. Approval is readily given for the withdrawal of nonresident-owned investment capital, repayment of loans contracted overseas, and the remittance of temporary residents' and emigrants' funds.

New investment abroad by permanent residents or by companies and other organizations operating in the Solomon Islands is subject to certain limitations. Direct investment overseas is permitted when it is likely to be of benefit to the Solomon Islands. For portfolio investments, approval from the Central Bank is needed before permanent residents may acquire or dispose of foreign securities. Approval is not normally given for the acquisition of overseas portfolio investments. Restrictions are not normally imposed on the disposal of foreign securities acquired before March 1, 1977.

Approval from the Central Bank is required for a resident to borrow funds from or to issue equity capital to a nonresident. The Solomon Islands branch of a company or firm incorporated overseas must have approval from the Central Bank before it may borrow funds from a nonresident, including the branch's overseas head office. If initial or increased foreign investment is concerned, the Foreign Investment Board must also give its approval.

Gold

Solomon Islanders alone are granted a license to pan for alluvial gold. Commercial banks and all other residents are required to obtain a permit issued by the Ministry of Natural Resources to mine, buy, or export gold. The Central Bank is authorized to buy, sell, and hold gold but has not yet undertaken any such transactions.

Changes During 1995

No significant changes occurred in the exchange and trade system.

SOUTH AFRICA

(Position as of December 31, 1995)

Exchange Arrangement

The currency of South Africa is the South African Rand. The authorities of South Africa do not maintain margins in respect of exchange transactions but intervene in the exchange market to affect rates quoted by the commercial banks. The principal intervention currency is the U.S. dollar. On December 31, 1995, commercial banks' spot rates for the U.S. dollar in transactions with the public were R 3.6483 buying and R 3.6496 selling, respectively, per $1.

Subject to certain limitations, authorized dealers are permitted to conduct forward exchange operations, including cover for transactions by nonresidents. Authorized dealers are permitted to provide forward exchange cover in any foreign currency to residents for any firm and ascertained foreign exchange commitments and accruals due to or by nonresidents arising from authorized trade and nontrade transactions. Forward exchange contracts may cover the entire period of the outstanding commitments or accruals. Subject to certain limitations, forward exchange cover may also be provided to nonresidents. The South African Reserve Bank provides forward cover against U.S. dollars only; such cover is given to authorized dealers for maturities not exceeding 12 months in the form of rand-U.S. dollar swap transactions, with the margin based on an interest rate differential between the U.S. dollar and the rand. Forward cover for periods in excess of 12 months is available for certain forward transactions at market rates in certain freely transferable currencies for long-term loans. Gold mining companies and houses may sell forward anticipated receipts of their future gold sales. There are no taxes or subsidies on purchases or sales of foreign exchange.

South Africa accepted the obligations of Article VIII, Sections 2, 3, and 4 of the Fund Agreement on September 15, 1973.

Administration of Control

Exchange licensing is the responsibility of the Treasury, which has delegated this authority to the Reserve Bank; in turn, the Reserve Bank has delegated many of its powers to the authorized dealers. Import and export permits, when required, are generally issued by the Director of Import and Export Control acting on behalf of the Ministers of Trade and Industry. Exchange for licensed imports is made available by authorized dealers upon proof of shipment or, when advance payment is proposed, upon presentation of other documentary evidence, which must include the prior approval of the Reserve Bank.[1]

Prescription of Currency

All countries outside the Common Monetary Area (CMA) constitute the nonresident area. The rand is legal tender in Lesotho and Namibia but not in Swaziland.[2] Settlements by or to residents of the CMA with countries in the nonresident area may be made in rand to and from a nonresident account and in any foreign currency.[3]

Nonresident Accounts

The rand accounts of nonresidents[4] are divided into nonresident accounts, and emigrant blocked accounts.

Nonresident accounts may be credited with all authorized payments made by South African residents with the proceeds of sales of foreign currency to authorized dealers in South Africa and with payments from other nonresident accounts in South Africa. They may be debited for payments to CMA residents for any purpose (other than loans); for payments to nonresidents for any purpose, by transfer to a local nonresident account or for remittance to any country outside the CMA; for the cost of purchases of any foreign currency; and for payments to account holders residing in South Africa for short periods.

Emigrant blocked accounts are the accounts of emigrants from the CMA and are subject to exchange control restrictions. Cash or proceeds from any other South African assets held at the time of departure

---

[1] Authorized dealers can permit, without the Reserve Bank's approval, advance payment of up to 33⅓ percent of the ex factory cost of capital goods if suppliers require it.

[2] Lilangeni banknotes issued by Swaziland, maloti banknotes issued by Lesotho, and Namibian dollar notes issued by Namibia are freely convertible into rand at par, but they are not legal tender in South Africa.

[3] Foreign currency, foreign exchange, exchange, and specified currency refer to any currency other than currency that is legal tender in the Republic of South Africa, but not to the currencies of Lesotho, Namibia, and Swaziland.

[4] A nonresident is a natural or juridical person whose usual place of residence, domicile, or registration is outside the CMA.

and subsequently sold must be credited to this type of account. These funds may not be transferred out of South Africa or to another emigrant blocked account in South Africa but must either be retained on deposit with an authorized dealer, used within certain limits for the holder's living expenses while visiting South Africa, used to make other specified payments to residents, or invested in any locally quoted securities (such securities may not, however, be exported and sold abroad).

Imports and Import Payments

Goods subject to import control are listed in Schedule IA of the Import Control Regulations published on December 23, 1988, as amended.

All importers requiring import permits for trade or manufacturing purposes must be registered with the Subdirectorate of Import and Export Control. The permits are valid for imports from any country. Imports that do not require a permit include all goods from Botswana, Lesotho, Malawi, Namibia, Swaziland, and Zimbabwe that are grown, produced, or manufactured in these countries, with the exception of a limited range of agricultural products from Malawi and Zimbabwe.

Importers are automatically granted exchange to pay for current imports upon presenting to their bank the necessary consignment documents (proof of importation) and an import permit when required. Payments are not normally allowed before the date of shipment or dispatch, except with prior approval or special authorization from the Reserve Bank (see footnote 1). The system of import quotas, which affected most agricultural goods and a number of manufactured products, has, to a large extent, been phased out and replaced with selective tariff measures. With certain exceptions, imports are subject to a value-added tax; locally produced goods are also subject to the tax. Import surcharges have been abolished.

Payments for Invisibles

Authority is delegated to authorized dealers to approve certain current payments for invisibles without limitation and for others up to established limits. Applications for amounts in excess of these limits are considered on their merits by the Reserve Bank. Authorized dealers may, without consulting the Reserve Bank, approve current income payments, such as declared dividends, profits, and royalties, that accrue in South Africa, provided that (1) the Department of Trade and Industry and the Reserve Bank have approved the relevant royalty agreement, and (2) the remittance of profits and div-

idends had not involved excessive use of local credit facilities. The Reserve Bank gives favorable consideration to such transfers when the use of local credit facilities is not regarded as excessive. Income earned from securities held by nonresidents is freely transferable to their country of residence, and limited amounts of exchange to pay for such items as membership fees and family maintenance are authorized.

There is an indicative limit on the travel allowance of R 25,000 a year for an adult (R 12,500 for a child under 12). Separately, there is an annual basic exchange allocation of R 6,000 for an adult (R 3,000 for a child under 12) for travel to neighboring countries (Angola, Botswana, Malawi, Mozambique, Zaïre, Zambia, and Zimbabwe). In addition to the tourist allowances, authorized dealers may grant allowances for overseas business trips at a rate not exceeding R 2,000 a day, up to R 38,000 in a calendar year. The separate applicable allowance for business trips to the neighboring countries listed above is R 12,000 a year, at a rate not exceeding R 900 a day. Exchange allowances in excess of the above limits may be provided with the approval of the Reserve Bank.

Residents and contract workers leaving South Africa for destinations outside the CMA may take out up to 50 percent of their allowance in foreign banknotes. The amount of reserve banknotes, however, may not exceed R 500, but this amount is not regarded as part of the basic travel allowance. Foreign visitors leaving South Africa may take with them up to R 500 in reserve banknotes and any amount of foreign notes brought into the country or obtained through the disposal of instruments of exchange brought into and converted in South Africa. These limitations on the exportation of reserve banknotes do not apply to contract workers returning to neighboring countries, who are permitted to take with them reasonable amounts in banknotes. There are no limitations on the exportation of domestic currency to Lesotho, Namibia, and Swaziland.

Exports and Export Proceeds

A limited number of products considered to be in relatively short supply or controlled for strategic reasons that are exported to countries outside the Southern African Customs Union (SACU) require export permits.

Unless otherwise permitted, all export proceeds must be remitted to South Africa and surrendered within six months of the date of shipment or seven days of the date of accrual. Except for exports made on a cash-on-delivery basis or those for which the full proceeds are received in advance, exporters are permitted to cover forward their export proceeds within seven days of shipment.

Authorized dealers may permit exporters to grant credit for up to 12 months, provided the credit is necessary in the particular trade or needed to protect an existing export market or capture a new one. Exporters benefit from certain incentive schemes under which they receive payments based on, inter alia, the f.o.b. value of exports, the local content of products, and the extent of processing involved. The main scheme, the General Export Incentive Scheme, is expected to be terminated by the end of 1997.

Proceeds from Invisibles

Proceeds from invisibles must be surrendered within seven days of the date of accrual unless an exemption is obtained. Residents and nonresidents entering from countries outside the CMA may bring in R 500 in reserve banknotes. There are no limitations on the importation of domestic currency from Lesotho, Namibia, and Swaziland.

Capital[5]

All inward loan transfers require specific approval,[6] although inward transfers for investment in equity capital are freely permitted. Foreign exchange accruing to residents from capital transfers and transactions must be surrendered. Outward transfers of capital by residents to destinations outside the CMA require the approval of the Reserve Bank. Local borrowing by nonresident-owned or nonresident-controlled firms is subject to limitation. Transfers by residents for the purchase of South African (or other) shares on foreign stock exchanges are generally not permitted. South African stockbrokers may engage in arbitrage transactions in securities, subject to certain conditions designed to prevent any net outflow of exchange.

Applications by South African residents to retain funds in, or transfer them to, countries outside the CMA for bona fide long-term investment in specific

development projects, or for the expansion of existing projects owned or controlled by South Africans, are considered by the Reserve Bank on their merits. Investments designed to foster exports and maintain or expand markets abroad are normally viewed favorably.

Immigrants are required to furnish the exchange control authorities with a complete statement of their foreign assets and liabilities at the time of their arrival. Any foreign assets transferred to South Africa may be retransferred abroad through the same channel within the first five years after arrival.

The proceeds from the sales of any South African assets accrued by nonresidents are freely transferable abroad.

Emigrant families are entitled to the normal travel allowance and are permitted to transfer up to R 200,000 (R 100,000 for single persons). Any balance exceeding the permissible transferable amount must be credited to an emigrant blocked account. Income earned by emigrants may be transferred through normal banking channels or credited to a nonresident account. A family or single person emigrating can export one motor vehicle with a maximum value of R 75,000, provided that the vehicle was purchased at least one year before emigration. Emigrants can export other household and personal effects up to a value of R 75,000, provided that such goods, other than clothing, have been in their possession for at least one year.

Favorable consideration is given to nonresident-owned branches and subsidiaries for the transfer of open or approved loan account balances;[7] profits and dividends declared on profits are freely transferable, provided that such remittances do not involve the excessive use of local credit facilities. The physical exportation from South Africa of nonresident-owned securities is permitted, except by emigrants.

Gold

Residents of South Africa may purchase, hold, and sell gold coins in South Africa for numismatic purposes and investment. With this exception, residents of South Africa other than the monetary authorities, authorized dealers, registered gold producers, and authorized industrial and professional users are not allowed to purchase, hold, or sell gold in any form other than jewelry, at home or abroad. All exports of gold must be approved in advance by the Reserve Bank. Approval authority has been delegated to authorized dealers for exports of jewelry constitut-

---

[5] Securities are defined not only as quoted stocks, shares, debentures, and rights, but also as unquoted shares in public companies, shares in private companies, government bonds, municipal bonds, public utility stocks, nonresident-owned mortgage bonds, or participations in mortgage bonds. "Scrip" and "share certificates" include any temporary or substitute documents of title, such as letters of allotment, option certificates, balance receipts, and any other receipts for scrip.

[6] Domestic entrepreneurs are generally given approval for borrowing abroad with a maturity of at least three months, except for speculation or consumer credit. Authorized dealers are generally permitted to raise funds abroad in their own names to finance South African foreign trade and for other approved purposes.

---

[7] Subject, however, to the 1994 Debt Arrangements, where applicable.

ing the personal effects of a traveler, up to a value of R 40,000 (subject to a written declaration that the jewelry will be brought back to South Africa on the traveler's return); and for exports of gold jewelry by manufacturing jewelers, subject to a written declaration that the articles are in final manufactured form and that the gold content of each does not exceed 80 percent of the selling price to the ultimate consignee. Furthermore, after approval by the Reserve Bank, residents are allowed to export currency coins, including certain gold coins, for sale to numismatists. The gold mining industry must sell its output to the Reserve Bank, which has been nominated as agent for the Treasury, within one month of production. With effect from October 1987, the Reserve Bank pays the gold mines in U.S. dollars for their sales of production. As a special concession, the industry may retain approximately one-third of its production for the minting of gold coins and kilo bars.

The mint strikes gold coins and the krugerrand, which are legal tender, without a face value, and these are made available in limited numbers to the local market.

Changes During 1995

Exchange Arrangement

March 13. The financial rand system was abolished.

Imports and Import Payments

October 1. Import surcharges were abolished.

SPAIN

(Position as of December 31, 1995)

Exchange Arrangement

The currency of Spain is the Spanish Peseta. Spain participates with Austria, Belgium, Denmark, France, Germany, Ireland, Luxembourg, the Netherlands, and Portugal in the exchange rate and intervention mechanism (ERM) of the European Monetary System (EMS).[1] In accordance with this agreement, Spain maintains the spot exchange rates between the Spanish peseta and the currencies of the other participants within margins of 15 percent above or below the cross rates based on the central rates expressed in European currency units (ECUs).[2]

The agreement implies that the Bank of Spain, the central bank, stands ready to buy or sell the currencies of the other participating states in unlimited amounts at specified intervention rates. On December 31, 1995, these rates were as follows:

Specified Intervention Rates Per:	Spanish Peseta	
	Upper limit	Lower limit
100 Austrian schillings	1,404.1000	1,041.3000
100 Belgian or Luxembourg francs	478.9440	365.2080
100 Danish kroner	2,589.8000	1,920.7000
100 Deutsche mark	9,878.5000	7,326.0000
100 French francs	2,945.4000	2,184.4000
1 Irish pound	238.1750	176.6410
100 Netherlands guilders	8,767.3000	6,502.2000
100 Portuguese escudos	96.3670	71.4690

The participants in the EMS do not maintain the exchange rates for other currencies within fixed limits. However, to ensure a proper functioning of the system, they intervene in concert to smooth out fluctuations in exchange rates, the intervention currencies being each other's, the U.S. dollar, and the ECU.

Official rates for specified currencies[3] are quoted on the basis of market rates and are published daily.

On December 29, 1995, the exchange rate for the U.S. dollar was Ptas 121.41 per $1.

Authorized banks are allowed to operate in foreign markets for spot and forward transactions. All future transactions involving an identifiable exchange risk are eligible for forward cover. There are no limits on periods to be covered. There are no limits on forward or spot foreign currency positions of individual banks, except those stemming indirectly from prudential rules on maximum net foreign exchange exposure. Under existing regulations, consolidated net foreign exchange exposure must not exceed a percentage, determined by the Bank of Spain, of the consolidated resources of each banking group.

Spain accepted the obligations of Article VIII, Sections 2, 3, and 4 of the Fund Agreement on July 15, 1986.

Exchange Control Territory

The Peninsular Territories of the Spanish State, the Canary Islands, the Balearic Islands, Ceuta, and Melilla constitute a single exchange control territory.

Administration of Control

The Ministry of Economy and Finance, through the Directorate-General of External Transactions, handles exchange control regulations, including prior verification and remaining administrative authorization corresponding to the exportation of certain means of payment, foreign investment, and investment abroad by Spanish residents. The Bank of Spain handles the foreign exchange market (both spot and forward); regulates and supervises commercial banks' activities; and is responsible for reporting requirements concerning nonresident accounts in domestic banks, resident accounts in foreign banks, and borrowing (both nontrade short-term and long-term) between residents and nonresidents.

In accordance with the Fund's Executive Board Decision No. 144-(52/51) adopted on August 14, 1952, Spain notified the Fund on September 21, 1992, that, in compliance with UN Security Council Resolution No. 757 of 1992, certain restrictions had been

---

[1]Effective August 2, 1993, the intervention thresholds of the currencies participating in the ERM of the EMS, except those of the deutsche mark and the Netherlands guilder, were widened from ±2.25 percent (in the case of Portugal and Spain, 6 percent) to ±15 percent around the bilateral central exchange rates; the fluctuation band of the deutsche mark and the Netherlands guilder remained unchanged at ±2.25 percent.

[2]Effective intervention rates may vary within the limits of these maximum intervention rates, depending on daily fluctuations in the cross rates between currencies.

[3]Australian dollars, Austrian schillings, Belgian francs, Canadian dollars, Danish kroner, deutsche mark, European currency

units (ECUs), Finnish markkaa, French francs, Greek drachmas, Irish pounds, Italian lire, Japanese yen, Luxembourg francs, Netherlands guilders, New Zealand dollars, Norwegian kroner, Portuguese escudos, pounds sterling, Swedish kronor, Swiss francs, and U.S. dollars.

imposed on the making of payments and transfers for current international transactions with the Federal Republic of Yugoslavia (Serbia/Montenegro).

Prescription of Currency

Settlements on account of merchandise transactions and invisibles may be made in pesetas or in any other currency.

Resident and Nonresident Accounts

Nonresidents may open any kind of deposit account in pesetas or foreign currency in all financial institutions. Residents may open accounts in pesetas or foreign currency with any financial institution abroad. Nonresidents' accounts in Spain and residents' accounts abroad are subject to reporting requirements.

Imports and Import Payments

As a general rule, imports into Spain may be made freely. However, imports of certain goods (e.g., tractors, explosives, seed oil, and gold) must be authorized by the Directorate-General of Foreign Trade, irrespective of the country of origin, or when imported from specific geographical areas (with distinctions being made among the members of the European Union (EU), those of the European Free Trade Association (EFTA), the Mediterranean and the ACP,[4] member countries of the World Trade Organization (WTO), and state trading countries).

Foreign exchange in the appropriate currency to pay for authorized imports is granted freely.

Payments for Invisibles

Payments for invisibles may be made freely through accounts in domestic and foreign financial institutions or other means of payment, including checks and transfers, subject to certain reporting requirements. The exportation of more than the equivalent of Ptas 1 million in banknotes, coins, and bearer checks must be declared and that of more than the equivalent of Ptas 5 million requires authorization. Nonresident holders of Spanish securities may freely transfer abroad accrued interest, dividends, proceeds from the disposal of subscription rights, and the proceeds from the liquidation of such securities. Profits and dividends on direct investments and rents on nonresident-owned real estate are freely transferable abroad. A general license permits the reinsurance abroad of risks insured in Spain

with Spanish firms or with foreign insurance companies operating in Spain. Unless special authorization is otherwise granted, insurance contracts abroad are restricted to cover exports and imports of goods and related operations.

Exports and Export Proceeds

As a general rule, exports may be made freely. However, exports of a limited number of goods (e.g., textiles, steel, and some copper by-products) require prior authorization from the Directorate-General of Foreign Trade, irrespective of destination.

Proceeds from Invisibles

The importation of more than the equivalent of Ptas 1 million in banknotes, coins, and bearer checks must be declared only when they are intended for investment or banking purposes. All proceeds from invisibles may be used freely.

Capital

Foreign direct investments in Spain are defined in accordance with guidelines established by the Organization for Economic Cooperation and Development (OECD) that take into account whether effective control over the company has been obtained. Effective control is deemed to exist if the share of the investment is at least 10 percent of the company's capital or if the Directorate-General of External Transactions considers that an important or predominant source of influence exists. Foreign investments effected through participation in Spanish companies are permitted freely in most cases. Prior verification is required only when foreign participation exceeds 50 percent and at least one of the following conditions applies: (1) foreign participation exceeds Ptas 500 million; and (2) foreign investors are residents of tax haven countries. Special authorization is required for non-EU foreign investment in defense-related industries, telecommunications (over 25 percent of capital), television, radio, air transport, and gambling. Special authorization is also required for a foreign government's participation in Spanish companies (other than governments of EU countries) unless otherwise regulated by international treaties.

The reinvestment of profits or proceeds from liquidation of existing investments is not restricted.

Nonresidents may freely purchase any kind of financial assets and contract all types of commercial credit without restriction, but these transactions must be reported to the Bank of Spain. Verification is required before Spanish companies issue shares in

---

[4]African, Caribbean, and Pacific state signatories to the Lomé Convention with the EU.

foreign markets; otherwise, securities operations are permitted freely. Real estate investments require prior verification for amounts exceeding Ptas 500 million or if investors are residents of tax haven countries.

The proceeds from the liquidation of nonresident investments and capital are freely transferable abroad.

Direct investments abroad by residents are permitted freely, although the following exceptions require prior verification: (1) the amount of the investment exceeds Ptas 250 million, (2) the purpose of investment is to hold shares of other companies, and (3) investment is in a tax haven country. Residents may purchase freely securities issued by nonresidents (irrespective of the market of issuance) or by residents in a foreign market. Strict information requirements apply to investments in securities and foreign lending. Prior authorization is required for direct investments by residents in non-EU countries where ownership of Spanish real estate or Spanish companies is transferred as a result of the operation. Investments in real estate by residents abroad is permitted, but those that exceed Ptas 250 million require prior verification.

Gold

The acquisition of gold must be authorized by the Directorate-General of Foreign Trade. Imports of bullion are permitted if they are used as raw materials for manufactured goods. Imports of gold in manufactured form (e.g., coins, medals, and the like) may be subject to quantitative restrictions, depending on the country of origin. Purchases of gold, silver, and platinum ingots are subject to a value-added tax at the rate of 33 percent.

Changes During 1995

Exchange Arrangement

March 6. The upper and lower limits of the peseta for the currencies of participants in the ERM of the EMS were changed.

Imports and Import Payments

(See Appendix for a summary of trade measures introduced and eliminated on an EU-wide basis during 1995.)

SRI LANKA

(Position as of December 31, 1995)

Exchange Arrangement

The currency of Sri Lanka is the Sri Lanka Rupee. The Central Bank of Sri Lanka announces the daily spot buying and selling rates of the U.S. dollar, the intervention currency, against the Sri Lanka rupee for transactions with the commercial banks, within margins of 2 percent, and purchases and sells the U.S. dollar on a spot basis at the established rates. On December 31, 1995, the buying and selling rates for the U.S. dollar were SL Re 53.5268 and SL Re 54.6082, respectively, per $1. There are no taxes or subsidies on purchases or sales of foreign exchange.

Forward sales are permitted to cover all transactions, with the exception of capital transfers and amortization of loans, up to a period not exceeding 360 days. The commercial banks provide a forward exchange market in which rates for current transactions are freely determined. They may cover such purchases by selling forward to their clients (that is, importers and shipping agents) or to other authorized dealers. Authorized dealers are permitted to quote forward rates for up to 360 days.

Sri Lanka accepted the obligations of Article VIII, Sections 2, 3, and 4 of the Fund Agreement on March 15, 1994.

Administration of Control

Exchange control is administered by the Department of Exchange Control of the Central Bank as an agent of the Government. All remittances of foreign exchange in Sri Lanka must normally be made through commercial banks authorized to carry out operations in foreign currencies in accordance with the exchange control procedures prescribed by the Controller of Exchange. Remittances may also be made through post offices under permits issued by the Controller of Exchange. The Board of Investments (BOI) handles all applications relating to foreign investments in Sri Lanka.

Prescription of Currency

Payments to and receipts from the member countries of the Asian Clearing Union (ACU) (Bangladesh, India, Islamic Republic of Iran, Myanmar, Nepal, and Pakistan) in connection with current transactions must be effected in Asian currency units or in the currency of the respective member of the Asian Clearing Union.[1]

For settlements with all other countries, payments for imports may be made in any foreign currency or in Sri Lanka rupees, provided that the supplier maintains a nonresident account in Sri Lanka. Other payments may be made either in the currency of the country to which the payment is due or by crediting Sri Lanka rupees to a nonresident rupee account with the prior approval from the Exchange Control Department of the Central Bank. Proceeds from exports must be received either in designated foreign currencies,[2] in Sri Lanka rupees from a nonresident account maintained by a foreign bank with an authorized dealer, or in any other nonresident account maintained by an individual person with an authorized dealer, as approved by the Central Bank.

Resident and Nonresident Accounts

Nonresident accounts in Sri Lanka rupees may be held in any commercial bank in Sri Lanka by (1) foreign nationals residing outside Sri Lanka; (2) firms and companies registered outside Sri Lanka; (3) Sri Lanka nationals residing outside Sri Lanka, who are classified for this purpose into two categories, those whose current or savings accounts are redesignated as nonresident accounts following their departure, and those whose accounts are opened after their departure; (4) emigrants; and (5) foreign banks.

The opening of these accounts for categories (1), (2), (3), and (4); the crediting of the initial and subsequent deposits arising from inward remittances; and their debiting for local disbursements or outward remittances may be effected without the prior approval of the Department of Exchange Control. However, local credits to these accounts require prior approval. Accounts in category (4) are designated as nonresident blocked accounts only when instructions to that effect are received from the Department of Exchange Control. Local debits to such accounts may be effected without the prior approval of the Department of Exchange Control; however, local

---

[1]Following a decision taken by the Board of Directors of the Asian Clearing Union (ACU) in 1995, which came into effect on January 1, 1996, all transactions among member countries may be made in U.S. dollars.

[2]Australian dollars, Belgian francs, Canadian dollars, Danish kroner, deutsche mark, French francs, Hong Kong dollars, Japanese yen, Netherlands guilders, Norwegian kroner, pounds sterling, Swedish kronor, Swiss francs, and U.S. dollars.

credits to them and debits for outward remittances require prior approval under certain circumstances. Under category (5), foreign banks may be permitted to open and operate nonresident accounts with a local commercial bank without the prior approval of the Department of Exchange Control.

Nonresident blocked accounts are used for holding funds, usually owned by nonresidents, repatriates, and emigrants that have not been accepted for transfer abroad. Authorized dealers are permitted to debit these accounts for local disbursements and credit them with the proceeds from pensions, income tax refunds, and profits and dividends without prior approval. Funds in blocked accounts may be invested in any local enterprise without the prior approval of the Controller of Exchange. Subject to exchange control approval, proceeds from the liquidation of such investments can be credited to blocked accounts. Balances of nonresident foreign citizens and foreign companies in approved blocked accounts outstanding on March 25, 1991, excluding Sri Lanka citizens who have emigrated or acquired foreign citizenship, and Indian and Pakistani expatriates, may be remitted abroad. Sri Lankans who have emigrated and acquired foreign citizenship, and Sri Lanka citizens who have acquired permanent resident status abroad and whose accounts have been blocked for more than five years as of June 30, 1992, are also permitted to remit their account balances abroad. In all other cases, remittances of up to a maximum of SL Re 350,000 are allowed from these accounts without prior approval from the exchange control authorities. Remittance of interest accrued to blocked accounts is fully transferable after deduction of taxes. Also retained in blocked accounts is a proportion of local currency earnings derived from the showing of foreign-owned films; the owner may use such retained funds for certain specified purposes, including the making of films in Sri Lanka.

Sri Lanka nationals who are, or have been, employed abroad and foreign nationals of Sri Lanka origin who reside outside Sri Lanka are allowed to maintain nonresident foreign currency (NRFC) accounts in Sri Lanka in designated foreign currencies.[3] Sri Lankans may also open such accounts within 90 days of their arrival in Sri Lanka with foreign exchange they brought in or received from abroad. Credits to these accounts are limited to the proceeds of remittances from employment abroad

and foreign exchange earnings brought into the country by individuals at the time of arrival. In addition, interest payments in designated currencies may be credited to the accounts. These accounts may be freely debited without exchange control approval for payments abroad, with the exception of payments received as purchase consideration for the sale of moveable or immoveable property in Sri Lanka, or for payments within Sri Lanka (converted to Sri Lanka rupees). Balances on NRFC accounts may be invested in enterprises approved by the Board of Investments granted under Section 17 of the BOI Act. Dividends and profits earned and sales proceeds of such investments received in foreign currency may be credited to the NRFC accounts without the prior approval of the Controller of Exchange. Rupee loan facilities for members of the family of the account holder against NRFC balances are also permitted. Employment agencies that recruit Sri Lanka nationals for foreign employment are also allowed to maintain NRFC accounts, to which their commission earnings may be credited.

Commercial banks operating in Sri Lanka may establish foreign currency banking units (FCBUs). These units may accept time and demand deposits in any designated foreign currency from nonresidents, resident commercial banks, and any resident BOI enterprise permitted to have FCBU accounts. They may extend loans and advances in any designated foreign currency to any nonresident, any resident commercial bank, any resident enterprise having BOI status, any exporter for the purchase of imported inputs, and a few other specified organizations with approval from the Central Bank. Foreign currency banking units are also allowed to accept time and demand deposits from, and grant loans and advances to, any other resident approved by the Central Bank. Foreign currency banking units are also authorized to operate savings accounts. However, accounts allowing the withdrawal of funds by checks are not permitted.

Sri Lanka residents may open and operate resident foreign currency (RFC) accounts with a minimum balance equivalent to $10,000 in designated currencies without prior approval or documentary evidence of receipt of such funds through customs declarations for up to $5,000.

Imports and Import Payments

No prior licensing is required for imports, with the exception of imports requiring a license mostly for reasons of public health, public morals, environmental protection, and national security. The import licensing requirement for four items, namely, wheat,

---

[3]In Australian dollars, Canadian dollars, Danish kroner, deutsche mark, French francs, Hong Kong dollars, Japanese yen, Netherlands guilders, pounds sterling, Singapore dollars, Swedish kronor, Swiss francs, and U.S. dollars.

muslin, and wheat and muslin flour, was maintained in terms of a past contract. Certain agricultural items, namely, potatoes, onions, and chilies remained under licensing protection.

The four-band import tariff structure with rates of 45 percent, 35 percent, 20 percent, and 10 percent, which came into effect in November 1993, was replaced in February 1995 with a three-band system with rates of 35 percent, 20 percent, and 10 percent. However, a few categories of products, i.e., tobacco, liquor, crude oil, and some categories of motor vehicles, remained outside the new system. With the 1995 budget, the tariff structure was further simplified, with the elimination of several ad hoc duties, waivers, and exemptions. Duty waivers were considerably reduced during the latter half of 1995 by limiting them to well-defined purposes.

Imports of specified items known as "reserved items," which include wheat, guns, explosives, and certain chemicals and petroleum products are restricted to government or state corporations. Certain machinery imports relating to foreign investment require the approval of the BOI, and certain machinery imports relating to foreign investment require the prior approval of the Local Investment Advisory Committee. No prior approval is required for any single consignment not exceeding SL Re 700,000.

Holders of balances in convertible rupee accounts, which were closed to new credits as of November 16, 1977, may use these funds to pay for certain imports, subject to licensing by the Controller of Imports and Exports. However, on March 8, 1994, authorized dealers were informed that balances, if any, in the convertible rupee accounts should be treated as balances in ordinary rupee accounts.

Except for imports by export-processing industries and other specified transactions, all other imports may be effected only against sight documents or against payment-term letters of credit valid for shipment for 180 days. Letters of credit on document against acceptance (DA) terms may be opened for imports of export-oriented industries and other high-priority areas for periods ranging from 120 days to 180 days. A stamp duty of 2 percent is levied on letters of credit for other imports (excluding inputs used in export industries) not fully covered by advance deposits. An authorized dealer may, without the prior approval of the Controller of Exchange, approve applications to remit foreign exchange or to credit nonresident accounts against applications for the opening of a letter of credit and against proof of a valid import license, when applicable. These requirements do not apply if the value of a consignment does not exceed $3,000 (c.i.f.), con-

sists of raw materials and spare parts for industries, and is for the direct use of the importer. Imports valued at $7,500 (c.i.f.) or less are permitted on document against payments (DP) and on DA terms without letters of credit when import documents are channeled through commercial banks.

Payments for Invisibles

All payments for invisibles by residents may be made freely. Foreign technical personnel employed by approved enterprises may remit their entire savings after payment of local taxes and levies.

Reasonable amounts earned as commissions are allowed on export orders secured through agents abroad, provided that export proceeds have been repatriated to Sri Lanka. Remittances of premiums for insurance on exports are not permitted, and such insurance must be obtained from a local state insurance corporation or a private insurer. Remittances of premiums to foreign reinsurers for reinsurance are permitted.

Profit remittances of nonresident partners of partnerships in Sri Lanka and remittances of dividends to nonresident shareholders of companies whose financial assets are in rupees may be effected through commercial banks without prior exchange control approval if they relate to the year of application and do not include undistributed profits of the previous years or reserves of the company. For remittances of interim profits, the following documents must be furnished: (1) a certificate from the company's auditors confirming that the amount to be remitted represents profits for the period to which it relates; (2) a preliminary computation of the remittable profits; (3) a tax clearance (only in the case of a nonresident partner) for the profits to be remitted; (4) a certificate confirming that the beneficiary resides abroad; and (5) a schedule indicating the names of the beneficiaries and the net amount owed to each. For remittances of final profits, the following documents must be submitted: (1) an audited copy of the company's profits and loss account and the balance sheet for the year to which the remittance relates; (2) a certificate from the auditors confirming that the remittance represents the final installment of the profits, declared in respect of the year under reference; (3) a computation of the remittable profits; and (4) the documents listed in (3), (4), and (5), above, in connection with remittances of interim profits.

Remittances of interim dividends can be made, provided that the following documents are submitted: (1) certification from the company's auditors confirming that the amount to be remitted represents dividends only for the period to which it relates; (2) certification that the remittance constitutes an interim dividend based on the unaudited accounts for the period; (3) a certificate confirming that the beneficiary resides outside Sri Lanka; (4) a schedule indicating the names of the beneficiaries and the net amounts owed to them; and (5) documentary evidence from auditors confirming payment of dividend tax. The remittance of a final dividend requires the submission of an audited copy of the company's profit and loss account and the balance sheet for the year to which the remittance relates; a certificate from the auditors confirming that the remittance represents dividends only for the period to which it relates; and the documents listed in (3), (4), and (5) above.

Resident foreigners may maintain foreign currency accounts with domestic commercial banks in any of 10 designated currencies[4] without prior exchange control approval. These accounts must be operated by the domestic unit of the bank and not by its foreign currency banking unit. The accounts may be current, savings, or deposit accounts, but withdrawal of funds by check is not permitted. Credits to these accounts are limited to inward remittances and to amounts in Sri Lanka rupees authorized by the Controller of Exchange for remittance abroad; debits are limited to outward remittances and to payments after converting into Sri Lanka rupees.

Unspent rupee balances from foreign exchange sold by foreign passport holders may be reconverted into foreign currency notes and coins only at the exit point (Katunayake Airport or Colombo Port). Reconversion into drafts, telegraphic transfers, or traveler's checks can be made at all branches of the authorized dealers as well as at the exit points. For this purpose, the original encashment receipts or memos issued by the authorized dealers or money changers must be furnished. Sri Lankans and foreign passport holders may take out convertible foreign currency equivalent to $10,000 without declaration, irrespective of the number of trips they make. The amount of foreign currency notes that diplomats, other foreign missions, and their non-Sri Lanka staff traveling abroad can take with them is limited to 20 percent of their travel expenses. A person leaving Sri Lanka may take out domestic currency notes not exceeding SL Re 1,000.

Exports and Export Proceeds

Exports of the following products require a license: coral shanks and shells, timber, ivory and ivory products, wood and articles of wood, and passenger motor vehicles registered in Sri Lanka for reasons of protecting the environment and preservation of antiques. The State Gem Corporation exercises quality control over the exportation of gems; the private sector may export gems on a consignment basis with the prior approval of the exchange control authorities. The Corporation handles exports in the name of miners who wish to export their gems. Re-exports of nonmonetary gold, silver, diamonds, and platinum are allowed only in special circumstances.

Foreign exchange proceeds from exports are not required to be repatriated. Special arrangements apply to exports made under trade and payments agreements and to exports made to a member country of the ACU. Commercial banks are permitted to grant foreign currency loans from their foreign currency banking units to exporters for the financing of the importation of inputs required for the purpose of executing export orders. This facility is limited to 70 percent of the total value of the confirmed export order. The period of repayment of these loans is eight months.

Companies engaged in indirect exports may obtain foreign currency loans for the importation of raw materials on the basis of back-to-back letters of credit opened in foreign currency for receipt of payment in foreign currency, including payments from BOI enterprises.

Proceeds from Invisibles

Foreign exchange proceeds from invisibles are not required to be surrendered. A traveler entering Sri Lanka must declare his or her foreign exchange holdings exceeding $10,000, including currency notes and coins. The amount of foreign funds that may be carried into Sri Lanka in the form of travel credit instruments is not restricted. Residents and nonresidents may bring in any amount of nonconvertible currencies after making a declaration to customs. A Sri Lanka national entering Sri Lanka may bring in domestic currency notes not exceeding SL Re 1,000.

Capital

Approval for foreign investment is granted on the basis of the types of activity and the proportion of foreign capital ownership; approval is automatically granted for foreign investment with equity capital ownership of up to 40 percent, except for certain activities restricted by special law or specific organizations.

Foreign direct investments are permitted in new projects with or without prior approval from the

---

[4]Deutsche mark, French francs, Hong Kong dollars, Japanese yen, Netherlands guilders, pounds sterling, Singapore dollars, Swedish kronor, Swiss francs, and U.S. dollars.

Controller of Exchange in terms of Government Notification No. 721/9, dated June 29, 1992. Proceeds from the sale or liquidation of investments in these projects, along with the capital appreciation, may be remitted in full. Investments in shares by nonresidents, up to 100 percent of the equity capital of existing listed and unlisted public companies, are permitted, subject to certain exclusions and limitations, without prior approval from the Controller of Exchange through a share investment external rupee account maintained at a commercial bank. Proceeds from the sale of these shares may be repatriated automatically, net of any tax. Blocked funds held by nonresidents, with the approval of the Controller of Exchange, in commercial banks are also permitted for investment in approved projects. Sale proceeds of such investments must be credited to blocked accounts. Proceeds from the sale or liquidation of other foreign investments in Sri Lanka may be repatriated in full only with prior approval from the Minister of Finance.

Investments abroad by residents are not generally permitted unless there is evidence that they will promote the country's exports and generate reasonable profits. Resident-owned securities, on which principal, interest, or dividends are payable (either contractually, or at the option of the holder) in any foreign currency, must be declared to the Controller of Exchange, and the sale or transfer of such securities is allowed only with the permission of the Controller of Exchange. Companies incorporated abroad are permitted to invest in securities traded at the Colombo Stock Exchange, subject to the same terms and conditions as those applicable to such investments by approved country funds, approved regional funds, and nonresident individuals, including Sri Lankans residing abroad.

Authorized dealers may grant foreign exchange allocations to emigrants upon presentation of appropriate documentation. At the time of departure, emigrants may be granted foreign exchange to cover passage to the country of migration by normal direct route plus 20 percent of the passage fare to cover excess baggage expenses. Foreign exchange equivalent to a maximum of $2,000 an adult and $1,000 a child under 12 years of age can also be purchased at the time of departure. Personal effects of reasonable amounts plus jewelry up to SL Re 150,000 for each married woman, SL Re 60,000 for each unmarried woman, SL Re 30,000 for each girl under 12 years of age, and SL Re 37,500 for each man can be exported. Emigrants have also been permitted to effect capital transfers of up to SL Re 750,000 an individual, up to a maximum limit of SL Re 1 million a family unit. The transfer abroad of pensions in full and interest income are permitted without exchange control approval, subject to submission of an income tax clearance certificate.

Expatriates leaving Sri Lanka for residence in the country of their permanent domicile are permitted to transfer in full assets representing their retirement funds and savings. Persons who have had small businesses in Sri Lanka are allowed to transfer the capital they originally brought into the country, plus a reasonable amount of savings, subject to certain limits. Special provisions, governed by an agreement between Sri Lanka and India, apply to Indian families returning to India.

Gold

Exports of gold bullion require licenses issued by the Controller of Imports and Exports with the approval of the Controller of Exchange. Imports of gold by Sri Lankans are subject to payment of import duty, the turnover tax, and the defense levy. Commercial banks are permitted to import gold on a consignment basis for duty free sale to passengers at the Colombo International Airport, under a license issued by the Controller of Imports and Exports. Commercial imports of jewelry and other articles containing gold are permitted on payment of import duty, the turnover tax, and the defense levy. Imports of gold for the production of jewelry for exportation is permitted without payment of duties and taxes.

Changes During 1995

Exchange Arrangement

March 20. The Central Bank increased the spread between the intervention points for transactions in the interbank market from one to two percentage points.

Resident and Nonresident Accounts

December 29. The Central Bank approved the Italian lira as a designated currency for purposes of nonresident foreign currency accounts.

Imports and Import Payments

February 8. The maximum standard tariff rate was reduced to 35 percent from 45 percent by moving virtually all items into the 35 percent band from the 45 percent band. At the same time, various tariff rates were changed, most notably the rate on textiles and clothing, and carpets and other textile floor coverings was reduced to 35 percent from 50 percent.

SUDAN

(Position as of December 31, 1995)

Exchange Arrangement

The currency of Sudan is the Sudanese Dinar,[1] the external value of which is determined in the market of foreign exchange dealers. Both commercial banks and licensed foreign exchange bureaus are authorized to freely quote buying and selling exchange rates to be applied to all transactions, other than certain compulsory sales of foreign exchange by commercial banks to the Bank of Sudan. The spread between commercial banks' buying and selling rates was changed from LSd 7 per U.S. dollar to 1.5 percent of each bank's buying price. On December 31, 1995, the average buying and selling rates for the U.S. dollar were LSd 829 and LSd 841, respectively, per $1. Fifty percent of foreign exchange surrendered to commercial banks is subject to compulsory sale to the Bank of Sudan at each bank's quoted selling rate plus LSd 3. The Bank of Sudan's reference rate was eliminated in September 1995 and the official exchange rate is determined as the weighted average rate of all dealers in the market.

Foreign exchange dealers are authorized by the Bank of Sudan to sell foreign exchange to be transferred abroad for all purposes. Under a central bank regulation, the commercial banks are obligated to require 100 percent cash cover before agreeing to the sale of foreign exchange. When foreign exchange is made available by a commercial bank against a letter of credit, the amount is immediately deposited in a suspended account on behalf of the purchaser, while foreign exchange made available on the basis of cash against documents is transferred to the purchaser immediately. Since October 1993, commercial banks have been free to transact on their own account and with holders of foreign-currency-denominated accounts ("account to account" transfers). Commercial banks do not bear any exchange risk for any foreign exchange transaction. In May 1995, the Bank of Sudan issued comprehensive regulations for licensed nonbank foreign exchange dealers; these dealers are registered as joint-stock companies whose activities are limited to conducting foreign exchange transactions in the spot market. Foreign exchange bureaus began to operate in September 1995 and numbered 21 by mid-November 1995.

There are no arrangements for forward cover against exchange rate risk operating in the official or the commercial banking sector.

Administration of Control

Exchange control is administered by the Bank of Sudan with the assistance of the authorized dealers, that is, commercial and specialized banks as well as nonbanks acting as exchange houses. Commercial banks and specialized banks may effect payments from their foreign exchange accounts without verification by the Bank of Sudan in accordance with the guidelines specified by the Bank of Sudan. Authorized banks are prohibited from conducting foreign exchange transactions with same public bodies and from disposing of balances in foreign currency accounts held by them; other public bodies including research centers are allowed to transact in foreign exchange freely through their accounts held with domestic banks. Commercial banks are responsible for verifying that exports and imports under the trade protocol with Egypt are in accordance with licenses issued by the Ministry of Trade, although this agreement is essentially dormant. The issuance of commercial certificates is the responsibility of the Ministry of Commerce, Cooperation, and Supply. The Bank of Sudan has the authority to request any information or details from authorized banks. All exporters and importers are required to register with the Ministry of Trade.

Arrears are maintained with respect to external payments.

Prescription of Currency

Payments to all countries—except Egypt, with which Sudan maintains a bilateral payments agreement—and all monetary areas (the "convertible area") may be made in foreign currency from any free foreign currency account or special foreign currency account, while receipts from the convertible area may be accepted in any convertible currency.

Resident and Nonresident Foreign Currency Accounts

Sudanese resident individuals and legal entities, with the exception of the Government, public institutions, and public sector enterprises are allowed to keep foreign exchange in free accounts. Free

---

[1]The Sudanese pound (LSd) also circulates and has a fixed relationship to the Sudanese dinar (Sd) of LSd 10 per Sd 1.

accounts may be credited with any means of payment without restriction, other than a customs declaration for cash deposits. Withdrawals from free accounts may be used (1) to make transfers abroad; (2) to make transfers to other free accounts; (3) to purchase domestic currency; (4) to make payments in foreign exchange to domestic institutions authorized to sell goods and services for foreign exchange; (5) to finance imports; and (6) to withdraw funds when presenting "a personal withdrawal form" stating the purpose of the transaction, such as payments to domestic institutions authorized to sell goods and services for foreign exchange, travel expenses, selling to authorized foreign exchange dealers, recrediting the remaining amount to the same account during the one-month period from the date of issue while the form remains valid.

The following are allowed to open special accounts with authorized banks in foreign and local currency: diplomatic, foreign, international, and regional missions and organizations; foreign charities and aid organizations; foreign companies, foreign contractors, and the foreign personnel of these organizations. Special foreign exchange accounts may be credited with transfers from abroad. Special foreign currency accounts may be debited for transfers abroad, to finance foreign travel, to purchase local currency in order to finance local payments, to make foreign currency payments to local institutions authorized to sell goods and services for foreign currency, and to finance imports. Withdrawals can be made for the purpose of travel by the account holder or his or her family, and local payments in Sudanese pounds, requiring conversion to Sudanese currency at the commercial bank rate.

Airline companies are allowed to open foreign currency accounts without approval from the Bank of Sudan. These accounts may be credited with payments by their passengers, consignors, and agents, who are allowed to buy travel tickets in foreign currency.

Imports and Import Payments

Imports from Israel are prohibited. Import licenses are not required, except for goods imported through bilateral and preferential trade arrangements. All applications for the importation of goods (except crude oil and petroleum products) not included on the negative list must be accompanied by the following: (1) a pro forma invoice; (2) a valid commercial registration certificate (issued annually by the Ministry of Commerce) that verifies that the importer is a trader; (3) a valid tax clearance certificate; and (4) the written consent of the authorized

bodies for certain categories of goods such as drugs, medical tools, and equipment (Ministry of Health); veterinary medicines and equipment (Ministry of Agriculture and Veterinary Resources); food (Ministry of Health); seeds (Ministry of Agriculture); ammunition and explosives (Ministry of Interior); airport equipment (Civil Aviation Security); communications—telephone, facsimile, and telex—equipment (Security Telecommunication Corporation); insecticides and fertilizer (Ministry of Agriculture); inputs used by the chicken and dairy industries (Ministry of Agriculture and Veterinary Resources); irrigation pumps (Ministry of Irrigation); and agricultural sprayers (Ministry of Agriculture).

Since January 3, 1995, the negative list covers imports prohibited for reasons of religion, public health, and national security.

Foreign exchange dealers are authorized to sell foreign exchange to finance all imports (except those on the negative list) irrespective of their final use. Authorized banks are also allowed to provide import credit facilities for imports of specified capital goods by means of sight credit or documents against acceptance, provided that maturity is no less than two years and repayments do not begin until one year after the arrival of the goods.[2] Authorized banks are free to obtain from importers a deposit of any amount in foreign currency at least one month before the importers receive the shipping documents; the remaining foreign exchange may be provided when the shipping documents are received. Commercial banks are authorized to finance imports of capital goods (provided that the credit agreement allows a grace period of at least one year) and of wheat and flour.

Insurance for imports must normally be taken out with local companies. Imports financed at the commercial bank rate, including those financed through the opening of letters of credit, could be subject to an advance deposit of up to the full c.i.f. value.

Payments for Invisibles

Commercial banks are authorized to transfer up to 50 percent of net salaries of foreign consultants, provided that the following documents are submitted: evidence of work permit, certificate showing net basic salary, and certificate showing no tax obligation. On this basis, up to 50 percent of net salaries may be remitted abroad. There are no restrictions on other invisible payments, but a limit of $5,000

---

[2]These goods include agricultural equipment, such as tractors and harvesters; all means of transportation, excluding sedans; mining equipment; all kinds of industrial and service equipment; and road, irrigation, building, and construction equipment.

applies to banknotes that can be taken out of the country.

Exports and Export Proceeds

All exports to Israel are prohibited, as is the exportation of hides, skins, charcoal, and firewood.[3] Export licenses are not required for any category of exports (except for exports under bilateral protocol arrangements and on account of barter trade). However, exporters must comply with administrative procedures designed to ensure full repatriation and surrender of foreign exchange export proceeds, with exceptions rated below export contracts subject to approval by the Ministry of Commerce. To prevent underinvoicing, the Board of Exported Commodities enforces a set of minimum export prices, which are updated periorically. In addition, the Ministry of Commerce would normally deny export permits for any commodities subject to export prohibition and to exporters not in compliance with repatriation and surrender requirements in earlier export activities.

Most export proceeds must be repatriated and sold to the domestic banking system within 45 days of the date of the bill of lading. Exporters of winter cotton, cattle and meat, sunflower seeds, fruits and vegetables, and manufactured goods are allowed to retain 50 percent of their export proceeds in foreign currency. Fifty percent of all proceeds surrendered to the account of the Bank of Sudan opened with the commercial banks is bought by the Bank of Sudan at the commercial bank rate.

Export taxes are levied on all categories of goods (except exports under bilateral protocol arrangements and under barter trade). The tax is collected by customs and deposited in its account at the Bank of Sudan. The applicable tax rates are 10 percent on cotton and gum arabic, and 5 percent on other exports.

Proceeds from Invisibles

Sudanese nationals working abroad are required to remit annually to domestic residents a minimum amount of foreign exchange, ranging from $300 (for ordinary workers, clerical and medical assistants, and soldiers) to $800–$5,000 (for professors, physicians, specialists in international organizations, and businessmen).[4] Exemptions are provided, however,

for Sudanese nationals, other than employees of international organizations, working in a number of countries.

Travelers entering Sudan may bring in foreign currencies without restriction and may export any amount of Sudanese currency. Residents and nonresidents entering Sudan must declare their holdings of foreign currency and within three months either deposit the foreign exchange in a foreign currency account, sell it to an authorized dealer against local currency, or retransfer it abroad. Commercial banks are prohibited from accepting foreign currencies without valid declaration forms.

Shipping agencies are permitted to accept foreign currency in payment for any services; however, they are required to sell all the foreign currency proceeds to authorized banks on the day following their receipt.

Sales of tickets and freight services in foreign currencies by airline companies in Sudan are restricted to (1) foreign tourists and businessmen; (2) foreigners working with diplomatic missions and organizations and international, regional, and national organizations; (3) foreigners employed by foreign relief, charitable, and religious organizations; and (4) foreigners working with foreign companies and branches of companies operating in the fields of contracting, investment, and prospecting for petroleum and minerals. Airline companies are allowed to receive payments for tickets and freight services in foreign currency on condition that payments are made in the form of deposits to their foreign currency accounts. Sales in foreign exchange deposited in the foreign currency accounts must be remitted to the company's head office accompanied by a certificate issued by the Civil Aviation Authority.

Capital

Foreign direct investments are permitted in accordance with existing laws and regulations.

Repatriation of share capital and amortization payments on loans to nonresidents is subject to certification from the Bank of Sudan regarding the original value of the foreign share in capital and loans. Repatriation of share capital and amortization payments on loans to nonresidents is subject to certification from the Investment Public Corporation regarding the original value of the foreign share in capital and loans.

Gold

Residents may purchase, hold, and sell gold coins in Sudan for numismatic purposes. Subject to certain conditions, residents may also purchase, hold, and

---

[3]The prohibition on exports of hides and skins is aimed at encouraging local processing. From January 16, 1994, the prohibition was extended to include reptile skins. On August 1, 1994, reptile skins were again exempted from this prohibition on exports, until January 18, 1995.

[4]These minimum remittances are in addition to a tax payable when obtaining a passport.

sell domestically produced gold in Sudan. With these exceptions, residents other than the monetary authorities and authorized industrial users are not allowed to hold or acquire gold in any form other than jewelry, at home or abroad. Imports and exports of gold in any form other than jewelry require licenses issued by the Ministry of Commerce, Cooperation, and Supply; such licenses are not normally granted except for imports and exports by or on behalf of the monetary authorities and industrial users. Some newly mined gold is exported for processing, and the full value of the gold processed must be kept in an escrow account that is operated in accordance with the corresponding agreement between the Government and the exporting company.

Changes During 1995

Exchange Arrangement

March 20. The spread between commercial banks' buying and selling rates was changed from LSd 7 per U.S. dollar to 1.5 percent of each bank's buying price.

March 21. The commercial banks' surrender requirement to the Bank of Sudan was reduced from 65 percent to 50 percent; however, the Bank of Sudan continued to purchase 20 percent of the banks' foreign exchange proceeds at its reference rate. The commercial banks were required to report the use of the 50 percent allocated to them, indicating the type of commodity imported, the name of the importer, etc.

May 17. The Bank of Sudan issued comprehensive regulations for nonbank foreign exchange dealers.

August 5. The Bank of Sudan declared that receipts from the purchase and sale of foreign currency from "currency exchange companies" could be used for several purposes in addition to opening an unrestricted account in the name of the receipt holder.

September 27. All foreign exchange proceeds of commercial banks started to be sold to the Bank of Sudan at the corresponding commercial banks' selling rate plus LSd 3.

September 27. Commercial banks were authorized to transact foreign exchange for their own account with holders of foreign currency accounts. (This effectively legalized the former parallel market.)

September 27. All authorized dealers, banks and nonbanks, were allowed to set their buying and selling exchange rates freely without any specific margin limits.

Imports and Import Payments

January 3. Passenger cars and sugar were eliminated from the negative import list.

Exports and Export Proceeds

May 17. Exporters of cattle, meat, winter cotton, sunflower seeds, vegetables and fruits, and industrial goods were allowed to retain 50 percent of their foreign exchange proceeds in foreign currency. The rest must be sold to commercial banks, with half of this amount to be surrendered to the Bank of Sudan.

September 27. Exporters were permitted to sell to any commercial bank that portion of export proceeds not subject to the surrender requirement.

SURINAME

(Position as of December 31, 1995)

Exchange Arrangement

The currency of Suriname is the Suriname Guilder. Exchange rates are freely determined on the basis of demand and supply in the market. Commercial banks and licensed foreign exchange houses may trade foreign exchange with customers, among themselves, or with the Central Bank of Suriname on a freely negotiable basis. The Central Bank also trades foreign exchange with the Government but not with importers. The Central Bank determines the exchange rate to be used in official transactions, which is based on the weighted-average rate of commercial bank transactions over the last five days. Official transactions include payments on the Government's external debt and imports, transfers of funds to embassies abroad, and payments to international organizations. On December 31, 1995, the exchange rate was Sf 407 per US$1.

Commercial banks charge commissions of 2 percent on sales of foreign exchange and 9.25 percent on transfers. There are no arrangements for forward cover against exchange rate risk operating in the official or the commercial banking sector.

Suriname accepted the obligations of Article VIII, Sections 2, 3, and 4 of the Fund Agreement on June 29, 1978.

Administration of Control

All foreign exchange transactions are subject to licensing, as are transactions between residents and nonresidents in domestic currency and other domestic assets. Import licenses are granted by the Ministry of Trade and Industry.[1] In case of payment by letter of credit, the import license must also be approved by the Central Bank. The Central Bank is empowered to provide foreign exchange for import payments (subject to presentation of an import license that serves as a general authorization for payment); the latter authority is exercised through the commercial banks, which have been appointed authorized banks by the Foreign Exchange Commission (FEC). External payments, other than for the importation of goods, require a license from the FEC.

Except for limited amounts of foreign exchange for invisible payments not requiring an exchange license, the authorized banks are not permitted to sell foreign exchange unless the remitter submits an exchange license. Exports also require a license from the Ministry of Trade and Industry. Commercial banks may accept free of license those inward transfers of foreign exchange that do not result from borrowing abroad; foreign loans must be approved by the FEC.

Arrears are maintained with respect to external payments.

Prescription of Currency

Settlements in Suriname guilders between Suriname and foreign countries are not permitted; they must, in general, be made in specified convertible currencies.[2]

Resident and Nonresident Accounts

Nonresidents, whether banks or nonbanks, may freely open accounts in U.S. dollars with domestic banks; no overdrafts are permitted. Nonresidents other than banks may freely open accounts in Suriname guilders with domestic banks; certain debits and credits are covered by a general license, and all others are subject to a specific license. These accounts must not be overdrawn and, except for certain specified purposes, debits must not exceed a total of Sf 3,000 a month. Authorized banks may open nonresident accounts in Suriname guilders in the name of nonresident banks; these accounts must not be overdrawn. Authorized banks may open nonresident accounts on behalf of nonresidents drawing pensions from the Government or under company plans. A special permit is required to transfer pensions abroad. Nonresident accounts in guilders may not be credited with Suriname banknotes mailed from abroad; nonresident foreign currency accounts may not be credited with Surinamese tender.

Resident nonbanks are allowed to open foreign currency accounts with domestic and foreign banks and to hold foreign securities, provided that the

---

[1]However, two specified mining companies do not need licenses for their own import requirements. Similar exemptions may be granted to foreign companies for their industrial activities in Suriname, provided that they pay for imports from their own foreign exchange resources.

[2]Australian dollars, Austrian schillings, Barbados dollars, Belgian francs, Canadian dollars, Danish kroner, deutsche mark, Eastern Caribbean dollars, French francs, Guyana dollars, Italian lire, Japanese yen, Netherlands guilders, Norwegian kroner, Portuguese escudos, pounds sterling, Swedish kronor, Swiss francs, Trinidad and Tobago dollars, and U.S. dollars.

funds have not been acquired from sales of real estate in Suriname or from exports. Balances in foreign currency accounts and holdings of foreign assets may be used freely, except for travel; use of these accounts and foreign assets for travel is limited to Sf 1,500 a person a year.

Imports and Import Payments

Import licenses are required for all imports. Imports of some commodities are prohibited,[3] and imports subject to quotas include kwie kwie fish; milk powder; potatoes; onions; garlic; fruits and nuts (other than citrus, bananas, plantains, and coconuts); decaffeinated coffee; peanuts; baby food; tomato paste; certain preserved vegetables; matches; furnishings; ready-made clothing; and furniture (excluding those for business establishments, such as offices, theaters, clinics, hotels, restaurants, and libraries).

The import license serves as a general authorization for payment. In case of payment by letter of credit, the import license must be approved by the Central Bank. Import licenses are valid for six ·months, within which period the goods must be landed and paid for. In addition to customs duties, a license fee of 1.5 percent is levied on the c.i.f. value of all imports. A statistical fee of 2.0 percent is levied on the c.i.f. value of imports of bauxite companies, and 0.5 of the c.i.f. value of other imports, including imports of gold.

Payments for Invisibles

Transactions involving outward remittances of foreign exchange are subject to licensing; application for a license must be submitted to the FEC at least one month before the intended date for effecting such a transaction. Authorized banks and the General Post Office have authority to provide foreign exchange up to Sf 150 a month for each item in connection with certain services (bank charges, legal fees, membership dues, copy and patent rights, and so forth) as well as for advertising expenses and payment for books. The requirement of a license for remittances for the support of family members abroad was eliminated in June 1993.

Travel allowances for residents are subject to licensing and are limited to the equivalent of $1,500 a person a calendar year.

Payments due as interest on loans and as net income from other investments, and payments of moderate amounts for the amortization of loans or depreciation or direct investments, may be made if an application, supported by an auditor's report, is duly presented to the FEC for verification. These payments, however, have been suspended. Both resident and nonresident travelers may take out Sf 100. The exportating of foreign banknotes by traveling residents is limited to the amount of their travel allowance.

Exports and Export Proceeds

Exports require export licenses issued by the Ministry of Trade and Industry. Licenses are issued if the exports are covered by letters of credit opened by buyers abroad. Exporters of bauxite and bananas must surrender foreign exchange proceeds to the Central Bank at the official exchange rate.[4] Other exporters must surrender their proceeds to authorized commercial banks and are allowed to buy back up to 85 percent of the amount surrendered. The Ministry of Trade and Industry ascertains with the relevant government agency whether the export price as reported by the exporter is in accordance with world market prices. Export licenses for cattle, pigs, fresh beef and pork, and planting materials are granted only on the advice of the Director of Agriculture, Animal Husbandry, and Fisheries. The export of baboonwood is prohibited and that of rice is subject to special regulations. Certain export companies have received special permission from the FEC to maintain current accounts in foreign currency with their parent companies abroad and to use these for specified payments and receipts (including export proceeds). Exports of processed and semiprocessed wood are subject to a tax of 100 percent of the f.o.b. value. Exports of bauxite are subject to a statistical fee of 2.0 percent of their f.o.b. value, and other

---

[3]The prohibition applies to imports of pigs (excluding those for breeding); chicken, duck, turkey, and pork meat; fish (excluding kwie kwie fish and smoked herring), shrimp, and crab (fresh, cooled, frozen, salted, dried, or precooked); vegetables (excluding potatoes, onions, and garlic); edible roots and tubers; citrus fruits; bananas; plantains; coconuts; green and roasted coffee (excluding decaffeinated); rice and rice products (excluding baby food); sugar (excluding cubes and tablets weighing 5 grams or less a cube or tablet), aromatized or colored sugar or sugar syrup; noodles and macaroni; jam, jelly, and marmalade (excluding those for diabetics); peanut butter; syrups and concentrates for nonalcoholic beverages in packages of less than 5 kilograms (excluding those for diabetics); firewood and other nonprocessed wood, railroad ties, shingles, wooden structures for construction, wooden tiles and panels, wooden tools, handles, and coat hangers; men's and boys' shoes (excluding rubber and plastic boots and sport shoes); and sand, gravel, sidewalk tiles, and road bricks. Imports of some other items, such as explosives and narcotics, are prohibited for reasons of public policy or health.

[4]Bauxite companies are not subject to export surrender requirements but must sell foreign exchange to the Central Bank to pay for their local expenditures.

exports are subject to a statistical fee of 0.5 percent of their f.o.b. value.

Proceeds from Invisibles

Foreign exchange receipts from invisibles must be surrendered to an authorized bank. Travelers may bring in unlimited foreign currency and up to Sf 100 in domestic currency. Travelers must declare all domestic and foreign currency in their possession on entry. The amount that nonresidents may take out of the country in foreign currency must be smaller than the amount they brought in and declared on entry.

Capital

The transfer abroad of capital proceeds from the sale to residents, or the liquidation of, fully or partly foreign-owned companies or other forms of enterprise, and the transfer of profits and foreign exchange (including loans) imported by a nonresident entrepreneur for the company's use are temporarily suspended. This decision covers investments made by nonresidents with foreign capital after July 31, 1953.

The FEC may, at its discretion, grant licenses for transfers abroad from the estate of a deceased person, up to a maximum of Sf 10,000. For estates valued at more than Sf 10,000, further annual transfers are permitted so as to spread them over a period of not more than ten years. The Commission may allow emigrants (heads of family) to transfer in foreign exchange the equivalent of Sf 5,000 in a lump sum, and subsequently Sf 5,000 a year. The head of a repatriating family may be permitted to transfer the equivalent of Sf 10,000 plus 10 percent of his or her total taxable earnings in Suriname accrued during the period of residence. If his or her Surinamese assets exceed the sum thus calculated, the excess may be transferred at a rate of Sf 10,000 a year. Transfers abroad in excess of Sf 10,000 a year may be authorized under exceptional circumstances. Outward transfers for these purposes have been temporarily reduced.

Subject to certain requirements, residents may purchase or sell in specified countries[5] Surinamese corporate shares that have been designated as negotiable by the FEC. Transfers for investment abroad or for the purchase of other foreign securities or real estate by residents are not permitted, although exceptions may be made for direct investments abroad when it is considered that Surinamese inter-

ests will benefit. All borrowing from nonresidents by nonbank residents requires the prior approval of the FEC. The foreign transactions of authorized banks are restricted, in principle, to those undertaken for the account of their customers, and banks are required, in principle, to surrender to the Central Bank any excess of foreign currency purchased.

Authorized banks are permitted to place a part of their liquid funds abroad and to use the short-term credit lines extended by their foreign correspondent banks as a source of operating funds. The Central Bank, the authorized banks, and the correspondent banks have made an arrangement whereby the Central Bank guarantees the letters of credit issued by the authorized banks by pledging its balances up to a specified ceiling, while the authorized banks keep their balances abroad at a minimum level.[6] The authorized banks may place abroad in short-term U.S. dollar assets the amounts corresponding to balances in their nonresident U.S. dollar accounts.

Nonbank residents are allowed to hold foreign exchange; but for exchange transactions exceeding Sf 10,000, they must report to the bank the source of foreign exchange.

Gold

Producers of gold may sell only to the authorized gold buyers (the Central Bank and Grassalco). Locally produced gold must be surrendered to the FEC by sale to the Central Bank. The authorized gold buyers are permitted, however, to sell nuggets at freely agreed prices for industrial and artistic purposes; dealings between residents in gold bars and other forms of unworked gold, with the exception of nuggets, are prohibited. As local production does not meet the demand for industrial purposes, the Central Bank may import some gold.

Three kinds of gold coins with face values of Sf 100, Sf 200, and Sf 250 are legal tender. Residents may hold and acquire gold coins in Suriname for numismatic and investment purposes; authorized banks may freely negotiate gold coins among themselves and with other residents. Residents other than the monetary authorities, producers of gold, and authorized industrial and dental users are not allowed, without special permission, to hold or acquire gold in any form other than nuggets, jewelry, or coins, at home or abroad. Imports and exports of gold in any form other than jewelry require exchange licenses issued by the FEC; licenses

---

[5]Belgium, Canada, France, Germany, Italy, Luxembourg, Netherlands, Netherlands Antilles, United Kingdom, and United States.

[6]This arrangement applies to the nationally controlled Landbouw Bank, De Surinaamsche Bank, and Hakrinbank, but not to the Dutch-owned Algemene Bank Nederland.

are not normally granted except for imports and exports of coins by authorized banks and for imports and exports by or on behalf of the monetary authorities, producers of gold, and industrial users. Residents arriving from abroad, however, may freely bring in gold, subject to declaration and provided that they surrender it to the Central Bank within 20 days. Nonresident travelers may also freely bring in gold, subject to declaration; they may re-export the declared amount freely.

Imports of gold coins are duty free and those of unworked gold are subject to a duty of Sf 1.00 a gram, irrespective of origin. The general tariff for gold ornaments is 60 percent ad valorem. Imports and exports of all forms of gold are subject to a statistical fee of 0.5 percent; in addition, imports are subject to a licensing fee of 1.5 percent.

Changes During 1995

Exports and Export Proceeds

December 31. Rice export proceeds may be surrendered to commercial banks.

SWAZILAND

(Position as of December 31, 1995)

Exchange Arrangement

The currency of Swaziland is the Lilangeni (plural Emalangeni), which is pegged to the South African rand at E 1 per R 1. Exchange rates for the U.S. dollar quoted by the Central Bank of Swaziland are based on the exchange rate of the South African rand against the U.S. dollar. On December 31, 1995, the closing buying and selling rates were E 3.6450 and E 3.6465, respectively, per $1. Rates are also quoted for the Canadian dollar, deutsche mark, French franc, Japanese yen, pound sterling, and Swiss franc, based on the London and New York market quotations for these currencies against the U.S. dollar, and for the European currency unit (ECU).

The Central Bank of Swaziland also quotes rates for the currencies of the member states of the Preferential Trade Area of Eastern and Southern African States (PTA), based on their relationship with the SDR as reported by the PTA clearinghouse. These currencies include the Kenya shilling, the Malawi kwacha, the Zambian kwacha, and the Zimbabwe dollar. There are no taxes or subsidies on purchases or sales of foreign exchange. The Central Bank of Swaziland permits authorized dealers to engage in forward exchange operations. Commercial banks are generally able to meet demands for forward sales of foreign currency against emalangeni. The forward exchange rates are market determined.

Swaziland accepted the obligations of Article VIII, Sections 2, 3, and 4 of the Fund Agreement on December 11, 1989.

Exchange Control Territory

Swaziland is part of the Common Monetary Area (CMA), a single exchange control territory comprising Lesotho, Namibia, South Africa, and Swaziland. No restrictions are applied to payments within the CMA, and, in principle, payments are not controlled. Residents of Swaziland have access to the Johannesburg market in accordance with the terms and conditions ruling in that market. In relations with countries outside the CMA, Swaziland applies exchange controls that are generally similar to those of South Africa.

Administration of Control

The Central Bank of Swaziland, on behalf of the Ministry of Finance, controls all external currency transactions.

Imports and Import Payments

Swaziland is a member of the Southern African Customs Union (SACU) with Botswana, Lesotho, Namibia, and South Africa, and no import restrictions are imposed on goods originating in any country of the customs union. Imports from South Africa do not require licenses and include an unknown quantity of goods originating outside the customs union. Imports from countries outside the customs union are licensed in conformity with specific import regulations. Import licenses granted in Swaziland entitle the holder to buy the foreign exchange required to make the import payment. Ports of entry outside Swaziland may be used, but the Swazi authorities are responsible for controlling import licenses and payments procedures.

Exports and Export Proceeds

All exports are subject to licensing. For those goods that are shipped to any one member of the customs area, licenses are used mainly for tax levy purposes. For goods shipped to countries outside the customs area, licensing is administered to ensure that export proceeds are repatriated in the prescribed manner and within the stipulated period.

Payments for and Proceeds from Invisibles

Payments to nonresidents for current transactions, while subject to control, are not normally restricted. Authority to approve some types of current payments up to established limits is delegated to authorized dealers. The basic exchange allowances for tourist travel are E 25,000 for each adult and E 12,500 for each child, a year. For business travel, the basic allowance is E 2,000 for each person a day, not to exceed E 38,000 a year. Larger amounts are granted upon application supported by proof of bona fide need. Residents traveling to the member countries of the PTA may use traveler's checks denominated in the units of account of the PTA (UAPTAs). The allowance for payment of medical costs abroad is E 4,000 a year. Students undergoing full time courses outside the CMA may be allowed foreign exchange to cover the cost of board and lodging, books, and other expenses up to a maximum of E 3,500 a month for single persons and E 8,000 for married persons accompanied by their spouse. An additional E 6,000 a year for single persons, and up to E 12,000 a year for those accompanied by their spouse may be allowed to cover traveling expenses. To use credit cards outside the CMA, a resident cardholder must complete a letter of undertaking before departure.

Capital

All inward capital transfers require the prior approval of the Central Bank of Swaziland and must be properly documented in order to facilitate the subsequent repatriation of interest, dividends, profits, and other income. No person may borrow foreign currency or register shares in the name of a nonresident, or act as a nominee for a nonresident, without prior approval.

Applications for most outward transfers of capital are considered on their merits. Blocked emalangeni may be invested in quoted securities and other such investments as may be approved by the Central Bank of Swaziland.

Changes During 1995

Exchange Arrangement

March 10. As South Africa abolished the financial rand system and unified the exchange rate for the rand, investments in Swaziland through the financial rand system could no longer be undertaken.

SWEDEN

(Position as of December 31, 1995)

Exchange Arrangement

The currency of Sweden is the Swedish Krona. The Swedish authorities do not maintain margins in respect of exchange transactions, and spot and forward exchange rates are determined on the basis of demand and supply conditions in the exchange market. The Sveriges Riksbank, however, has the discretionary power to intervene in the exchange market. On December 31, 1995, the buying and selling rates for the U.S. dollar were Skr 6.6375 and Skr 6.6975, respectively, per $1. There are no taxes or subsidies on purchases or sales of foreign exchange.

Authorized banks may buy from and sell to other authorized banks and residents any foreign currency on a spot or forward basis against another foreign currency or Swedish kronor. Authorized banks may also purchase (sell) foreign currencies, spot or forward, from (to) foreign banks and other nonresidents against any foreign currency or Swedish kronor credited (debited) to a krona account. Also, currency option contracts may be concluded freely with both residents and nonresidents.

For prudential purposes, net foreign exchange positions (spot, forward, options) in individual foreign currencies and on the total net position in all foreign currencies are subject to limits. The limit for each foreign currency and for the total net position is equal to 10 percent of a bank's capital base. For a bank that is a recognized market maker, the limit is equal to 15 percent of its capital base. Banks may grant overdrafts to nonresidents and may incur foreign exchange net liabilities for which the same limits apply. This enables the banks to borrow foreign currency from nonresidents for on-lending to foreign banks, to other nonresidents, or to residents. Lending abroad in kronor is also freely permitted. Swedish banks may, while observing their limits on net foreign exchange holdings, borrow abroad freely and sell the proceeds against Swedish kronor in the market. A limit also exists on a bank's total net positions calculated as the sum of all liability positions. This limit is equal to 20 percent of the bank's capital base and to 30 percent for recognized market makers.

Sweden accepted the obligations of Article VIII, Sections 2, 3, and 4 of the Fund Agreement on February 15, 1961.

Administration of Control

All current and capital transactions are free from exchange control. When required, import and export licenses are issued by the National Board of Trade, except those for foodstuffs, which are issued by the National Agricultural Market Board.

In accordance with the Fund's Executive Board Decision No. 144-(52/51) adopted on August 14, 1952, Sweden notified the Fund on August 7, 1992, that, in compliance with UN Security Council Resolution No. 757 (1992), certain restrictions had been imposed on the making of payments and transfers for current international transactions in respect of the Federal Republic of Yugoslavia (Serbia/Montenegro). These restrictions were extended on September 23, 1994, to include areas of Bosnia and Herzegovina under the control of Bosnian Serb forces.[1] Certain restrictions were imposed on the Libyan Arab Jamahiriya and Angola, according to UN Security Council Resolution No. 748 (1992) of March 31, 1992, and UN Security Council Resolution No. 864 (1993) of September 15, 1993, respectively. Financial transactions with Iraq are prohibited in accordance with UN Security Council Resolution No. 661 (1990) and other relevant UN resolutions.

Prescription of Currency

Payments to and from foreign countries may be made in any foreign currency or in Swedish kronor through an external krona account (see section on Nonresident Accounts, below).

Nonresident Accounts

External krona accounts may be held by nonresidents domiciled abroad, including persons who have become nonresidents after emigrating. They may be used for payments and transfers and may be converted into any foreign currency.

Imports and Import Payments

As a result of Sweden's membership in the European Union (EU) as of January 1, 1995, import of textiles and clothing from more than 50 countries are subject to restrictions or licensing for surveillance purposes. Agricultural and fishery products are also subject to import licensing.

---

[1]Sanctions against the Federal Republic of Yugoslavia (Serbia/Montenegro) and Bosnia and Herzegovina were lifted on February 26, 1996.

Imports of most iron and steel products from all countries outside the EU, other than countries of the European Free Trade Association (EFTA) or countries that are parties to the Agreement on the European Economic Area (EEA), are subject to import licensing for surveillance purposes. Some iron and steel products from Russia, Ukraine, and Kazakstan are also subject to restrictions.

Imports from China of certain goods such as shoes, porcelain, and toys, are subject to restrictions. Other goods such as fireworks, working gloves, bicycles, and brushes, are subject to licensing for surveillance purposes.

With a few exceptions, imports from Iraq and from areas of the Republic of Bosnia and Herzegovina under the control of Bosnian Serb forces are prohibited.

Payments for imports may be made freely. Importers are also permitted to accept foreign suppliers' credits.

Payments for Invisibles

Payments for invisibles may be made by residents in favor of nonresidents without limit or restriction. Travelers may export any amount of domestic and foreign banknotes or any other means of payment.

While abroad, residents may open accounts, provided that the amounts are reported to the Swedish National Tax Board for tax control and to the Riksbank for statistical purposes.

Exports and Export Proceeds

With a few exceptions, exports to Iraq and to areas of Bosnia and Herzegovina under the control of Bosnian Serb forces are prohibited. Some exports to the Libyan Arab Jamahiriya and Angola are prohibited. Proceeds from exports of goods may be sold for kronor or kept in a foreign currency account in Sweden and used by the holder to make payments abroad.

Proceeds from Invisibles

Receipts from current invisibles are subject to the same treatment as those from exports (see section on Exports and Export Proceeds, above). Travelers may import any amount of domestic and foreign banknotes or any other means of payment.

Capital

All capital transactions are free from restriction. For tax control and statistical purposes, however, residents depositing funds in foreign bank accounts or transacting through such an account must report the amount to the Swedish National Tax Board and to the Riksbank. Transactions in securities may be carried out freely.

Gold

There are no special regulations on trading in gold.

Changes During 1995

Administration of Control

December 31. Sanctions against the Federal Republic of Yugoslavia (Serbia/Montenegro) were suspended.

Imports and Import Payments

January 1. As a result of joining the EU, the import regime was changed; restriction and/or licensing for surveillance purposes on imports of textiles and clothing, iron and steel products, and on certain imports from China (shoes, porcelain, and toys) were introduced.

(See Appendix for a summary of trade measures introduced on an EU-wide basis during 1995.)

Exports and Export Proceeds

January 1. As a result of joining the EU, the export regime was changed.

January 1. The licensing requirements on exports to the Democratic People's Republic of Korea and on exports of scrap metal were removed.

SWITZERLAND

(Position as of December 31, 1995)

Exchange Arrangement

The currency of Switzerland is the Swiss Franc. The Swiss National Bank does not maintain margins in respect of exchange transactions; exchange rates are determined, in principle, on the basis of demand and supply conditions in the exchange markets. However, the National Bank reserves the right to intervene if and when circumstances warrant. The principal intervention currency is the U.S. dollar. On December 31, 1995, the midpoint market rate for the Swiss franc in terms of the U.S. dollar was Sw F 1.1520 per $1.

All settlements may be made at free market rates. Foreign banknotes are negotiated freely in Switzerland at rates determined by the interplay of supply and demand. Residents and nonresidents may freely negotiate foreign exchange contracts with banks in all currencies, in respect of both commercial and financial transactions. No officially fixed premiums and discount rates apply to forward exchange contracts, all of which are negotiated at free market rates. Under the Export Risk Guarantee System, export receipts, excluding exchange rate risks, may be insured by the Government under certain conditions.

Switzerland accepted the obligations of Article VIII, Sections 2, 3, and 4 of the Fund Agreement on May 29, 1992.

Exchange Control Territory

For all purposes of importation and exportation, the Principality of Liechtenstein is included in the Swiss customs territory. For purposes of monetary policy measures, natural persons domiciled in Liechtenstein are considered by Switzerland as residents, as are juridical persons, including banks. However, this rule does not apply to the acquisition of Swiss real estate. Liechtenstein is considered a foreign country for purposes of banking supervision.

Administration of Control

Authority to impose measures for the control of imports, exports, and payments is vested in the Swiss Federal Council, acting on the advice of the Federal Department of Public Economy, the Federal Department of Foreign Affairs, or the Federal Department of Finance. The National Bank is the advisory and executive authority in matters of currency for both Switzerland and Liechtenstein.

In accordance with the Fund's Executive Board Decision No. 144-(52/51) adopted on August 14, 1952, Switzerland notified the Fund that, in accordance with the relevant UN Security Council resolutions, certain payments restrictions were imposed with respect to the Libyan Arab Jamahiriya, Iraq, and regions in Bosnia under Serbian control. Sanctions against the Federal Republic of Yugoslavia (Serbia/Montenegro) were suspended in November 1995.

Prescription of Currency

Settlements may be made or received in any currency.

Imports and Import Payments

With minor exceptions, imports into Switzerland may be made freely. The importation of alcohol, butter, and wheat grain is a partial state monopoly. The most important products subject to licensing, irrespective of their origin, are certain agricultural products. The purpose of the licensing requirements is to administer World Trade Organization-based tariff rate quotas. Payments for imports from all countries may be made freely.

Payments for Invisibles

Payments for invisibles may be made freely. The exportation of Swiss and foreign banknotes is unrestricted.

Exports and Export Proceeds

The exportation (including the re-exportation) of some goods, including weapons and dual-use equipment for the production of conventional weapons or weapons of mass destruction, is controlled through individual licenses. This export-licensing system is operated in part with the assistance of appropriate semiofficial or private organizations. Export proceeds are freely disposable.

Proceeds from Invisibles

Proceeds from invisibles are freely disposable. The importation of Swiss and foreign banknotes is unrestricted.

Capital

Transfers of capital may be made without formality. Foreign and domestic bond issues denominated in Swiss francs must be reported to the National Bank. The physical importation and exportation of Swiss and foreign securities are unrestricted. In case of any disturbances in the capital markets, the federal Government may introduce a permit requirement for certain outward capital transfers (e.g., bond issues).

Selected banks and finance companies are required to report their positions (their own assets and liabilities in foreign currencies, spot and forward) in domestic and foreign currencies on a monthly basis.

Purchases of real estate in Switzerland by or on behalf of persons or firms of foreign nationality who are domiciled or residing abroad require approval by the canton in which the property is situated. The approval of the canton is subject to supervision and appeal by the federal Government.

Gold

Swiss gold coins are not legal tender. Residents may freely purchase, hold, and sell gold in any form, at home or abroad. There is a free gold market in Zurich. Imports and exports of gold in any form by residents and nonresidents are unrestricted and free of license. No customs duties or other charges are levied on exports of gold. Imports of gold bars and of certain gold coins are exempt from customs duty. Import and export licenses, which are issued freely, are required for commercial imports and exports of certain articles containing gold.

Changes During 1995

Administration of Control

November 1. Sanctions against the Federal Republic of Yugoslavia (Serbia/Montenegro) were suspended.

Capital

February 1. The revised banking law abolished the former permit requirement for foreign bond issues exceeding Sw F 10 million each and with a maturity of 12 months or more, and introduced instead a reporting requirement for foreign and domestic bond issues.

SYRIAN ARAB REPUBLIC

(Position as of January 31, 1996)

Exchange Arrangement

The currency of the Syrian Arab Republic is the Syrian Pound, which is pegged to the U.S. dollar, the intervention currency. The exchange rate system consists of the following four rates: (1) the official rate of LS 11.20/11.25 per $1 applies to some government transactions and to repayment of loans and interests arising from bilateral payments agreements and banking arrangements; (2) the rate of LS 22.95/23.00 per $1 applies as an accounting rate to public sector exports of petroleum and some agricultural products, imports of essential subsidized commodities and invisibles, and repayment of loans and interests; (3) the "rate in neighboring countries" of LS 42.43 per $1 applies to all public and private capital inflows, receipts from 25 percent of export proceeds surrendered by the private sector and that part of the 75 percent of export proceeds retained by private sector exporters not used to finance their own imports or those of others, to travel allowances, tourism and medical expenses, student allowances, remittances abroad and payments by the public sector approved by the Committee for Foreign Exchange, and for some government transactions and customs valuation of some imports.[1] Since October 1995, the rate in neighboring countries has been applied to all hotel transactions; and (4) the "government fee rate" (LS 42.95/43.00 per $1), which applies to a number of fees, including those on transit and port services, and as an accounting rate for some government transactions as well as for customs valuation of some imports.

In addition to the above rates, there is also the promotion rate of LS 20.22 per $1, which is used only for payments of allowances to students who started overseas study before January 1, 1991. There is also a neighboring countries free market rate that stood at LS 50.20 per $1 on December 31, 1995, and an "export proceeds" market in which a market-determined rate applies to a number of newly permitted goods that may be imported only with foreign exchange earned through exports; in December 1995, the exchange rate in this market stood at LS 54.00 per $1. Exporters who do not use all of their export earnings to import goods may sell their retained foreign exchange earnings to importers in this market.

Exchange rates between the Syrian pound and other major currencies are set on the basis of the exchange rate between the Syrian pound and the U.S. dollar in relation to the exchange rates of the currencies concerned in the international markets.

There are no arrangements for forward cover against exchange rate risk operating in the official or the commercial banking sector.

Administration of Control

Policy with regard to imports and exports is determined by the Ministry of Economy and Foreign Trade. Under an agreement between the Central Bank of Syria and the Administrative Committee of the Exchange Office, all transactions of the Exchange Office are carried out through the Central Bank. Import licenses are issued by the Ministry of Economy and Foreign Trade, and exchange licenses for invisibles and capital transactions by the Exchange Office. Only the Central Bank and the Commercial Bank of Syria may deal in foreign exchange. The Commercial Bank of Syria opens letters of credit and accepts bills for collection without prior approval, provided that certain conditions are fulfilled.

Arrears are maintained with respect to external payments.

Prescription of Currency

The Exchange Office is empowered to prescribe the currencies that can be obtained for exports. Proceeds from exports to all countries may be obtained in any convertible currency. Prescription of currency requirements are not applied to outgoing payments. All payments to, and receipts from, Israel are prohibited.

The Syrian Arab Republic maintains bilateral payments agreements with the Islamic Republic of Iran, Russia, and Sri Lanka; however, the agreements with Russia and Sri Lanka are inoperative, and payments for imports from the Islamic Republic of Iran may also be made in convertible currencies.

Nonresident and Foreign Currency Accounts

Nonresident accounts in Syrian pounds may be credited with the proceeds of foreign currencies sold

---

[1]In 1994, the "airline rate," which applies to purchases of airline tickets by nonresidents and to transfers abroad by airline companies, was adjusted to LS 42/43 per $1 and was effectively merged with the "rate in neighboring countries."

to the authorized banks and with other receipts; they may be debited without prior approval to pay for Syrian exports to the country of the account holder and for expenses in the Syrian Arab Republic. Non-residents (individuals and corporations) may open accounts in convertible foreign currencies at the Commercial Bank of Syria for the deposit of funds from abroad. Balances in such accounts may be sold to local banks, transferred abroad without restriction, or used to pay for authorized imports. Temporary nonresident accounts may be opened in the name of nonresidents temporarily residing in the Syrian Arab Republic. These accounts may not be used, however, for funds received in settlement currencies, through payment conventions, or by diplomatic and UN missions and their staffs. Diplomatic and UN missions and their staffs are allowed to exchange all their transfers to the Syrian Arab Republic at the rate in neighboring countries. The debiting for expenditures in the Syrian Arab Republic and abroad is free.

Residents not involved in export activities and wishing to open foreign currency accounts are required to present written evidence that they have sources of income from abroad.

Imports and Import Payments

Imports of commodities originating in Israel are prohibited. Many basic commodities (including paper, salt, tobacco, wheat, iron and steel, and certain agricultural machinery) are imported only by state trading agencies or, for their own account, by certain private sector importers. Agencies having the sole authority to import may be required to import certain commodities to meet the raw material needs of the private sector. The list of items that the private sector is permitted to import includes certain agricultural goods, industrial goods, and raw materials.

Imports of goods not on the permitted list are prohibited, with certain exceptions. In principle, imports must come directly from the country of origin, without the intervention of any foreign firm. The Ministry of Economy and Foreign Trade has the authority, however, to permit certain goods to be imported from countries other than the country of origin. Imports from the Syrian free zones are allowed for certain industrial goods and for goods with a free-zone value added of at least 40 percent.

All imports valued at more than LS 2,000 (LS 500 for imports from Lebanon) require licensing.[2] The foreign exchange requirements of the state trading agencies are met from the annual foreign exchange budget; these agencies automatically receive import licenses upon submission of documentation of their import requirements. A fee ranging from LS 25 to LS 200 is charged upon issuing the import license. Additionally, an import surcharge of 2 percent is charged on all imports; government imports and imports of certain essential items (including raw materials, petroleum, and petroleum products) are exempted. Imports for customs duty purposes are valued at the official exchange rate except for items subject to duty at the rate of 75 percent or higher. Import tariffs range from zero to 200 percent, and all the previous special levies on imports have been replaced by a unified import surcharge ranging from 6 percent to 35 percent.[3] Private importers are authorized to import products specified on the permitted list by opening letters of credit at the Commercial Bank of Syria. However, when foreign exchange is not made available, private sector imports must be financed with the importers' own resources through external credit arrangements, foreign currency deposits maintained in the Syrian Arab Republic by nonresidents, the importers' own foreign exchange deposited in the Commercial Bank of Syria under the export proceeds retention regulations, or foreign exchange purchased from other private or mixed sector enterprises through the intermediary of the Commercial Bank of Syria at the rate in neighboring countries. Imports of a number of goods are restricted to specific methods of financing. For example, a number of imports may be imported using only foreign exchange generated through exports.

A non-interest-bearing advance import deposit for public sector imports is required for an amount equal to 100 percent of the value of the imports. These deposits, which are held for six months, range from 10 percent to 40 percent of the value of imports. For several categories of goods, an advance import deposit equal to 100 percent of the value of the import, plus a 3 percent fee, is required.

Payments for Invisibles

Most payments for invisibles must be made at the rate in neighboring countries.

---

[2]In accordance with the Arab Common Market Agreement, certain imports from Jordan, Lebanon, and Saudi Arabia are exempted from the licensing requirement; in these cases, an authorization to import is granted upon written request.

[3]The simple and weighted average (using 1987 import values as weights) of basic tariffs are 19.9 percent and 10.4 percent, respectively. The simple and weighted average of all import duties (defined as the sum of the basic tariffs, unified surcharges, and the 2 percent import license fee) are 35 percent and 22.8 percent, respectively.

Residents traveling abroad may take with them foreign exchange, up to a limit of $2,000 a trip, to all countries except Jordan and Lebanon. Of this amount, up to the equivalent of LS 5,000 a trip may be purchased at the rate in neighboring countries for travel to Arab countries (except Jordan and Lebanon) and up to the equivalent of LS 7,500 a trip for travel to non-Arab countries. Travelers to Jordan and Lebanon are not eligible for a foreign exchange travel allowance but may take with them up to LS 5,000 a trip in Syrian banknotes. With this exception, Syrian banknotes may not be taken out of the country. For children 10 years old or younger, the allowances are 50 percent of these amounts. Workers on secondment to a foreign country may take with them the entire amount of the allocations on producing proof that they have transferred foreign exchange from abroad; otherwise they may take with them only foreign exchange equivalent to 25 percent of the above-mentioned allocations. For travel to countries with which payments agreements are maintained, 50 percent of the travel allocation must be handled through the clearing account concerned (30 percent for travel on official business). On departure, residents of Syrian nationality must pay an exit tax of LS 600 a person if traveling to Arab countries and LS 1,500 a person for other destinations. An airport stamp tax of LS 200 is added to this tax.

Fixed allocations are maintained for other transactions in invisibles. A maximum of 60 percent of the salaries received by foreign technicians and experts employed in the Syrian Arab Republic, and 50 percent of the salaries of personnel of foreign diplomatic and international missions in the Syrian Arab Republic may be transferred. All other transactions require prior approval from the Exchange Office, with the exception of embassies and international organizations; such entities may convert all their transfers at the rate in neighboring countries. The allowance for education abroad is subject to prior authorization from the Ministry of Higher Education. The transfer of funds abroad for family maintenance is limited to LS 250 for each transfer and is effected upon presentation of proof of need. The allowance for medical treatment must be authorized by the Ministry of Health. Remittances of profits from investment must be authorized by the Exchange Office upon documentation (for example, a certificate confirming payment of income tax). Profits from projects approved by the Higher Committee for Investment under the new investment law can be repatriated freely.

Exports and Export Proceeds

Exports of wheat, barley, cotton, cotton yarn, and their derivatives are made by the government organizations dealing in cereals and cotton.[4] Petroleum exports are handled by the Petroleum Marketing Office. Exports of certain other commodities are also reserved for government agencies, state trading agencies, or specified companies. Exports of a few goods to all countries and all exports to Israel are prohibited. Exports under bilateral payments agreements and of all goods of foreign origin require licensing; no repatriation commitment is required, with the exporter repatriating and surrendering the proceeds to the Commercial Bank of Syria within 45 days of the date of shipment to Lebanon, within three months of the date of export shipment to other Arab countries, and within four months of the date of export shipment to other countries.

Public sector enterprises may retain 100 percent of their export proceeds in special foreign currency accounts with the Commercial Bank of Syria to finance imports on the permitted list; the retained portion of foreign exchange earnings can be deposited at the Commercial Bank of Syria in special foreign currency accounts until import payments are made or foreign exchange is voluntarily sold to the Commercial Bank of Syria. In the case of fruits and vegetables, public and private sector exporters may convert 100 percent of the proceeds at the rate in neighboring countries.

Since May 1995, exporters of juice and its concentrate may retain 100 percent of their export proceeds to finance imports on the permitted list.

The Commercial Bank of Syria may accept prepayments for exports of Syrian products by residents and nonresidents without referring to the Central Bank. Subsidies for exports of ginned cotton from the Fund for the Development of Exports of Industrial Products have been suspended. A tax ranging from 9 percent to 12 percent ad valorem is charged on the value of exports of agricultural origin, except fruits and vegetables (which are exempt) and cotton (for which the export tax is 12.5 percent of the value of the exports (f.o.b.), less the cost of transportation within the Syrian Arab Republic). Exports of other agricultural commodities are subject to an ad valorem agricultural tax of 7 percent.

Proceeds from Invisibles

Proceeds from transactions by the public sector must be sold at the official rate and those from trans-

---

[4]The General Organization for Cereals Trade and Production and the General Organization for Cotton Ginning and Marketing.

actions by the private sector must be sold at the rate in neighboring countries. Nonresidents entering the Syrian Arab Republic are permitted to bring in unlimited foreign exchange and Syrian pounds without declaration, if the amount does not exceed $5,000. All Syrian nationals employed by Arab, foreign, or international organizations within the Syrian Arab Republic and paid in full or in part in foreign currencies are required to exchange all such earnings at the Commercial Bank of Syria at the official exchange rate.

With few exceptions, non-Syrians visiting the Syrian Arab Republic are required to settle their bills in foreign exchange. All Syrian employees working abroad are subject to an annual tax of $50–$700, depending on their profession, and are allowed import tax exemptions on luxury items (valued between $500 and $7,000) if the equivalent funds are surrendered at the rate in neighboring countries. Syrian government employees who are on leave and working abroad are required to repatriate and convert a minimum of 25 percent of each year's earnings received in foreign exchange at the rate in neighboring countries.

Capital

All capital transfers to and from the Syrian Arab Republic by the public and private sector take place at the rate in neighboring countries. Exports of capital require the approval of the Exchange Office.

The Syrian Arab Republic provides special facilities for the investment of funds of immigrants and of nationals of Arab states, including a seven-year tax exemption from all taxes in the tourism and agricultural industries. Under Investment Law No. 10, projects with minimum fixed assets of LS 10 million approved by the Government benefit from a number of exemptions from exchange and trade regulations, including exemption from customs duties of imports of required machinery, equipment, and vehicles. Mixed companies with at least 25 percent public participation are exempted from all taxes for seven years and private companies are exempted for five years; exemption periods may be extended by an additional two years if the company exports at least 50 percent of its output. Investors are permitted to hold foreign exchange accounts with the Commercial Bank of Syria to finance convertible currency requirements. These accounts comprise all capital and loans secured in foreign currency and 75 percent of foreign currency exports. Funds from such accounts may be provided on demand and may be used for the compensation of foreign staff. Investors are free to repa-

triate foreign exchange capital after five years from the date of investment. Capital may be repatriated after six months if the project suffers from events beyond the control of the investor. All profits may be transferred freely. Foreign staff are entitled to transfer abroad 60 percent of salaries and 100 percent of severance pay.

The Syrian Arab Republic has investment guarantee agreements with France, the Federal Republic of Germany, Switzerland, and the United States. Nonresidents and foreign nationals may acquire immovable property in the Syrian Arab Republic only after presenting evidence that they have converted into Syrian pounds the foreign exchange equivalent of the price of the property at an authorized local bank.

Gold

Residents may hold, acquire, and sell manufactured gold in the Syrian Arab Republic without restriction. Domestic transactions in manufactured gold take place at free market prices that are in line with free market prices abroad. Imports of gold are exempt from import licensing, but exports are subject to export licensing. Foreign exchange proceeds from exports by residents must be surrendered. Exports of gold previously imported by nonresidents out of their resources abroad are subject to a repatriation commitment covering the cost of manufacturing and the profit earned.

Changes During 1995

Exchange Arrangement

October 23. The exchange rates were unified for all hotel transactions at the rate in neighboring countries.

Imports and Import Payments

April 10. The following products were removed from the negative import list: ceramics, hens, milk and milk products, plastic material, oxygen equipment, cleaning material, glass, and certain trucks. These products may now be imported using export proceeds.

Exports and Export Proceeds

May 27. Decree No. 7 extended Decree No. 2315 (1990) applying to exports of juice and its concentrates. According to Decree No. 2315, exporters may retain 100 percent of their export proceeds to finance imports on the permitted list.

Changes During 1996

Exchange Arrangement

January 2. The Central Bank of Syria and the Commercial Bank of Syria were allowed to buy foreign currency for the public sector export of petroleum at the rate of LS 22.95 per $1 and to sell foreign currency for the import of essential subsidized commodities and repayment of loans and interests at the rate of LS 23.00 per $1.

January 8. The Commercial Bank of Syria was allowed to buy foreign currency from grants at the rate in neighboring countries.

Nonresident and Foreign Currency Accounts

January 8. Diplomatic and UN missions and their staffs were allowed to exchange all their transfers to the Syrian Arab Republic at the rate in neighboring countries.

TAJIKISTAN

(Position as of March 31, 1996)

Exchange Arrangement

The currency of Tajikistan is the Tajik Ruble, which was introduced on May 10, 1995, replacing the post-1993 Russian rubles, which are now treated as foreign currency.[1] The exchange rate system consists of three rates: the official accounting exchange rate based on the outcome of the foreign exchange auctions at the Tajik Interbank Foreign Currency Exchange (TICEX); the buying and selling rates at the official exchange bureaus operated by the National Bank of the Republic of Tajikistan; and the parallel (curb) market rate. The TICEX, which was established by the National Bank and the major commercial banks, holds weekly auctions for the sale of U.S. dollars. However, due primarily to the lack of a steady supply of foreign exchange to the TICEX, the auctions have been frequently halted. After August 2, 1995, only two auctions took place in 1995, one in mid-September and another in late-November, in which the amounts of sales were very small and only in cash.

The National Bank holds Tajikistan's official foreign exchange reserves and acts as an agent for the Government in connection with significant government transactions in the foreign exchange market. However, government ministries and agencies continue to hold foreign exchange accounts with the banking system in which working balances are maintained for small day-to-day requirements.

The principal exchange rate in use in Tajikistan is that determined in the interbank market. Transactions in the interbank market take place via weekly auctions and daily transactions among banks or between banks and enterprises. Since December 1995, enterprises have been permitted to participate directly (as well as indirectly via their banks) in the interbank auctions. Once a week, the National Bank quotes an official representative exchange rate for the Tajik ruble based on the midpoint of buying and selling rates for the Tajik ruble against the U.S. dollar in the TICEX. In the event that an auction does not take place, the National Bank's official rate is set at the average of commercial banks' exchange rates for transactions in the interbank market during the previous week, as reported by the banks to the National Bank. The official exchange rate is used for revaluation of the National Bank's foreign currency balances, for the calculation of customs duties, and for most of the National Bank's foreign exchange transactions. Prior to February 1996, there was a surrender requirement of 30 percent of foreign currency export receipts to the National Bank. The official rate was used for the conversion of those receipts. On February 24, 1996, the surrender requirement was abolished and replaced with a repatriation requirement. In March 1996, the average TICEX rate was 283 Tajik rubles per U.S. dollar.

A freely negotiated market exchange rate may also emerge outside the auction from transactions among authorized commercial banks and/or between banks and enterprises. Fifteen commercial banks are authorized to deal in foreign exchange. However, only three or four banks in addition to the National Bank are active. With the exception of the Vneshekonombank, most banks have only a handful of transactions each week. Authorized banks and the National Bank obtain foreign exchange, inter alia, by purchasing repatriated foreign exchange earnings from exporters. Authorized bank holdings of foreign exchange may be sold to customers to pay for imports of goods and services with the appropriate documentation. The National Bank mandates a maximum service commission or margin of 10 percent between commercial bank buying and selling rates. Exchange rates of authorized banks are published weekly in the business press.

A retail foreign exchange market operates through foreign exchange bureaus, which are owned by authorized banks. Individuals may make purchases and sales in this market without limit. In addition, an informal parallel market in foreign exchange exists. Although, technically, parallel market transactions are illegal, small transactions are tolerated by the authorities. The parallel market exchange rate was within 2 percent of the official rate during March 1996. Commercial banks monitor movements in the parallel market and TICEX rates when setting their own rates. There are no taxes on purchases or sales of foreign exchange, except that banks must pay tax equal to the full amount of any commission or margin in excess of 10 percent.

---

[1]Since January 8, 1994, post-1993 Russian rubles have been in circulation only in cash form, and in very small denominations; other pre-1993 Russian rubles remain frozen in bank accounts.

Administration of Control

Regulations concerning the availability and use of the Tajik ruble are set out in the Law on Foreign Currency Control of May 10, 1995. The Finance Ministry and the Ministry of Economy and Foreign Economic Relations have responsibility for financial relations between Tajikistan and other countries. The Vneshekonombank acts as the agent of the Finance Ministry and the depository of most day-to-day governmental accounts, while the official foreign exchange reserves are held at the National Bank. The National Bank has licensed the 15 commercial banks that are foreign exchange traders and collects information on the foreign currency transactions of these banks.

Commercial banks are allowed to maintain open foreign exchange positions, subject to the limitation that individual and overall net positions do not exceed 5 percent and 20 percent, respectively, of unimpaired capital.

Arrears are maintained with respect to external payments.

Prescription of Currency

Residents of Tajikistan may make and receive payments and transfers in any convertible currency as well as in Tajik rubles, but major transactions are authorized and monitored by the National Bank. Since May 1995, residents and nonresidents are no longer permitted to use foreign exchange for domestic transactions, except for special cases allowed by the authorities. Commercial transactions with nonresident entities from all other countries must take place via correspondent accounts maintained either by authorized commercial banks or by the National Bank. The Vneshekonombank has the most active correspondent accounts with banks abroad. The National Bank has correspondent accounts with the Baltic countries, Russia, and the other countries of the former Soviet Union, but these accounts are effectively inoperative. While in the past the majority of trade transactions were arranged on a barter basis, in November 1995, the Government passed a resolution prohibiting new barter trade contracts, with the exception of contracts for aluminum.

Resident and Nonresident Accounts

Resident individuals may open, maintain, and use foreign currency accounts in authorized banks in Tajikistan. Resident enterprises may open foreign currency accounts in Tajikistan if they are registered foreign traders at the Ministry for Foreign Economic Relations. Documentation, including the relevant import contract, is required any time a resident enterprise desires to buy foreign exchange from an authorized bank. Resident individuals or enterprises may also open foreign exchange bank accounts in banks abroad.[2] The transfer of foreign exchange held in domestic accounts to a resident bank account abroad does not require authorization. Nonresident individuals and enterprises can open foreign exchange accounts with authorized domestic banks in Tajikistan. The amounts in such accounts may be transferred abroad or sold to the local banks for Tajik rubles. Nonresident enterprises and foreign governments and institutions are also permitted to open Tajik ruble accounts.

Inward and outward transfers of Tajik rubles and foreign currency banknotes are regulated by the Customs Committee together with the Ministry of Finance and the National Bank. The physical importation and exportation of foreign currency banknotes and Tajik ruble banknotes are freely permitted, subject only to declaration of amounts over $500.

Imports and Import Payments

Imports are free from all restrictions, including tariffs, licenses, monopoly import rights, and quotas, with the following exceptions. The importation of firearms, narcotics, poisons, chemical weapons, and nuclear material is prohibited. Five product categories (certain alcohol products, tobacco products, photographic items, audio equipment, and motor vehicles) are subject to ad valorem customs import tariffs, which are levied at one of only two rates (2 percent and 5 percent). Certain types of imports are exempt from these customs tariffs (goods imported from trading partners of the Baltic Countries, Russia, and the other countries of the former Soviet Union, goods imported according to barter contracts, and goods imported by certain state agencies).

Payments for imports may be made through authorized commercial bank correspondent accounts. Foreign exchange needed for authorized import transactions may be purchased from commercial banks, taken from a domestic foreign exchange account, or purchased directly by enterprises or their agents in the weekly foreign exchange auction.

---

[2]While this is the case in practice, some legal ambiguity exists with respect to the ability of residents to hold foreign exchange accounts abroad. The ambiguity arises from the fact that while such accounts are permitted under the Law on Foreign Currency Control, they are prohibited under the Monetary Law.

Exports and Export Proceeds

In the past, exports were subject to multiple restrictions, including state orders, quotas, trading directed through government monopoly agencies, licensing, and tariffs. In November 1995, export quotas and state orders were abolished for all goods with the exception of the 1995 cotton crop.[3] Also, barter trade was prohibited, except for the aluminum plant. As for the 1996 cotton crop, the complete abolition of the system of state orders was announced in November 1995, and cotton growers will be free to decide to whom and at what prices they will sell their crops. Exports are currently free from export licensing requirements and, with the exception of the 70 percent of the 1995 cotton crop that is subject to state orders, free from monopoly export rights. On February 24, 1996, the Government abolished all customs duties on exports with effect from March 1, 1996. However, exports of cotton fiber, aluminum and other metal products, tobacco, leather, fertilizers, and certain other products remain subject to a 100 percent prepayment requirement before goods will be shipped. Exports of other products are subject to a requirement for payment within 90 days to be guaranteed by a domestic bank.

On November 1, 1995, the surrender requirement for export proceeds from goods other than cotton and aluminum was reduced to 30 percent from 70 percent. On February 24, 1996, the Government abolished the foreign exchange surrender requirement and replaced it with a requirement that foreign exchange earnings be repatriated. Upon repatriation, foreign exchange proceeds may either be held by exporters in foreign currency accounts with domestic banks or sold in the interbank market. On February 24, 1996, export duties and export licenses were also abolished.

Payments for and Proceeds from Invisibles

There is no limit on the amount of foreign exchange that may be taken out of Tajikistan by residents traveling abroad for tourism purposes, for public or private business, or other travel (e.g., education, medical expenses). There are no minimum spending or conversion requirements for nonresident travelers to Tajikistan. Nonresidents from countries other than the Baltic countries, Russia, and the other countries of the former Soviet Union are not required to pay for transportation and hotel services in foreign currencies. There are no restrictions on the making of interest payments or principal debt-service payments.

Capital

Inward and outward capital transactions do not require licensing by the National Bank. Foreign investors are required to register with the Ministry of Finance, but there are no limits on inward capital transactions. There are no restrictions on the repatriation of foreign investment profits, assuming domestic tax obligations have been fulfilled. Profits may be reinvested in Tajikistan, held in local commercial banks in rubles or foreign currency, or transferred abroad.

Changes During 1995

Exchange Arrangement

May 10. The Tajik ruble was introduced as the sole legal tender in the Republic of Tajikistan.

May 23. Weekly foreign exchange auctions began to be conducted at the TICEX.

Administration of Control

May 10. Commercial banks were allowed to maintain open foreign exchange positions, subject to the limitation that individual and overall net positions do not exceed 5 percent and 20 percent, respectively, of unimpaired capital.

May 10. The Law on Foreign Currency Control was passed.

Exports and Export Proceeds

November 1. The surrender requirement for export proceeds from goods other than cotton and aluminum was reduced to 30 percent from 70 percent.

November 1. Export quotas and state orders, other than for the 1995 cotton crop, were eliminated.

November 1. Barter trade was prohibited, except for aluminum.

Changes During 1996

Exports and Export Proceeds

February 24. Export duties, export licenses, and surrender requirements were abolished, and a repatriation requirement was imposed.

---

[3]However, Government Decree No. 617 of October 10, 1995, instructs producers to give the State Committee for Contracts and Trade and the Tajik Consumer Cooperative priority access to the output of manufactured consumer goods.

TANZANIA

(Position as of April 30, 1996)

Exchange Arrangement

The currency of Tanzania is the Tanzania Shilling, the external value of which is determined in the interbank market. The Bank of Tanzania intervenes in the interbank market only to smooth movements that are caused by transitory factors. The official exchange rate varies according to the rate emerging from the interbank market and remains within a 2 percent band around the current day's market rate. The official exchange rate is used for accounting, taxation, and for settlement of government obligations. The exchange rates for other currencies are determined on the basis of the cross rates of the U.S. dollar against the currencies concerned in international markets.[1] On December 31, 1995, the exchange rate in the interbank market was T Sh 555.92 per $1. Certain transactions may be effected through foreign exchange bureaus that are authorized to buy and sell foreign exchange at freely negotiated rates. Currency convertibility within the East African countries was established on December 31, 1995.

The Bank of Tanzania does not offer forward cover against exchange rate risk. However, authorized dealers may, at their discretion, enter into forward contracts for purchases and sales of foreign currencies with their customers in export and import transactions. There are no taxes or subsidies on purchases or sales of foreign exchange.

Administration of Control

Under the Foreign Exchange Act of 1992, the Bank of Tanzania was vested with the power to administer all matters related to transactions in foreign exchange and gold. The Bank of Tanzania has delegated authority to make payments abroad to all licensed banks. The Bank of Tanzania Act of 1995 empowers the Bank to control exchange operations in the United Republic of Tanzania, including operations in Zanzibar.

Zanzibar has liberalized its foreign trade system.

---

[1]Australian dollars, Austrian schillings, Belgian francs, Canadian dollars, Comorian francs, Danish kroner, deutsche mark, Ethiopian birr, French francs, Indian rupees, Italian lire, Japanese yen, Kenya shillings, Lesotho maloti, Malawian kwacha, Mauritian rupees, Mozambican meticais, Netherlands guilders, Norwegian kroner, Pakistan rupees, pounds sterling, Rwanda francs, Somali shillings, Swaziland emalangeni, Swedish kronor, Swiss francs, Uganda shillings, Zambian kwacha, and Zimbabwe dollars.

Arrears are maintained with respect to external payments.

Prescription of Currency

Settlements between residents of Tanzania and nonresidents must be made either in convertible currencies or in Tanzania shillings by debit or credit to a convertible nonresident account.

Tanzania maintains inoperative bilateral payments agreement with Mozambique. It participates in the payments arrangement of the Preferential Trade Area for Eastern and Southern African States (PTA) and maintains clearing arrangements with Kenya and Uganda.

Foreign Currency Accounts

Tanzanian nationals and foreign nationals who usually reside in Tanzania may maintain foreign exchange accounts in the form of a current, savings, or deposit account.

Imports and Import Payments

With the exception of certain imports to the mainland from any source that are prohibited for reasons of health or security, imports are not subject to licensing requirement. For statistical purposes only, all imports of goods require an import declaration form. Imports of goods with a value exceeding $5,000 have to undergo a preshipment inspection for quality, quantity, and price verification.

Customs tariffs are levied on the c.i.f. value of imports, and the tariff schedule is ad valorem. The tariff regime comprises four bands of 10 percent, 20 percent, 30 percent, and 40 percent. However, a minimum rate of 5 percent is granted by the Minister of Finance for imports considered to be in the public interest. Specific duties are levied on alcoholic beverages, tobacco, and petroleum products. Statutory exemptions are granted for the diplomatic corps; and religious, educational, and welfare institutions. However, low tariffs are charged on machinery and discretionary full or partial exemptions may be allowed by the Minister of Finance if imports are considered to be in the public interest.

There are no regulations governing the means by which imports can be financed. Most imports, irrespective of their origin, are subject to a sales tax at rates ranging up to 30 percent of the c.i.f. value plus import duty. This tax is also assessed on sales of domestic products.

Payments for Invisibles

There are no limits on purchases of foreign exchange for travel, education, and other invisible payments and transfers. Commercial banks and foreign exchange bureaus have the authority to approve remittances abroad of up to one-third of the salary, throughout the period of employment, of foreigners temporarily working in Tanzania under contract and having a firm commitment to leave the country.

A resident traveler may take out of the country up to the equivalent of $50 in domestic currency. No limits are imposed on travelers to Kenya and Uganda. Nonresident travelers may take out foreign currency notes, traveler's checks, and letters of credit for any remaining amount of the foreign exchange brought in.

Exports and Export Proceeds

Export licenses are required for only a few items for health, sanitary, or national heritage reasons.

Export proceeds must be repatriated within 180 days of the date of exportation, but they need not be surrendered. Proceeds from the exportation of traditional goods from Zanzibar are subject to a 100 percent repatriation requirement and exporters are allowed to operate foreign exchange accounts or sell the proceeds to the commercial banks or to the bureaus.

Proceeds from Invisibles

Receipts from invisibles may be retained. Travelers may freely bring in convertible foreign currency notes; a returning traveler may bring in Tanzania shilling notes and coins up to the equivalent of $50.

Capital

Capital transfers to all countries are subject to approval by the Bank of Tanzania.

Repatriation of capital and associated income is done freely through commercial banks upon presentation of audited accounts indicating declared dividends, profits or capital to be repatriated, plus authenticated documents confirming payment of all taxes.

Investment of foreign funds is not restricted in Tanzania, but, to ensure eventual repatriation, these investments must be recognized by the Investment Promotion Center, and a certificate of status as an approved enterprise under the National Investment Promotion Act of 1990 should be obtained from the

Center. The act distinguishes three areas for foreign investments: (1) controlled areas, which are reserved for public investment or joint public and private enterprises; (2) reserved areas, which are reserved exclusively for investment by the public sector; and (3) areas that are reserved exclusively for Tanzanian citizens. Registered foreign investors are permitted to use up to 100 percent of their net foreign exchange earnings for debt servicing or remittances of profits and dividends.

All loans or overdrafts from residents to nonresidents or to foreign-controlled resident bodies require approval from the Bank of Tanzania.

Gold

Commemorative gold coins are legal tender but do not circulate in Tanzania. Residents may hold and acquire raw gold in any form at home or abroad. Import licenses are not required.

Changes During 1995

Exchange Arrangement

December 31. Currency convertibility within the East African countries was established.

Changes During 1996

Exchange Arrangement

January 1. Foreign exchange bureaus not meeting new capital requirements were restricted to over-the-counter money-changing transactions and thereby prohibited from providing trade finance. They were also prohibited from participating in the interbank foreign exchange market. Control over foreign exchange operations in Zanzibar was moved from the Bank of Zanzibar to the Bank of Tanzania.

Nonresident Accounts

January 1. Restrictions on nonresident accounts were removed.

Imports and Import Payments

January 1. The threshold above which imports require a license was raised to $5,000 from $2,000. Restrictions on the payment for insurance were removed as were restrictions on the financial instruments that could be used for payment for imports.

Payments for Invisibles

January 1. All limits on the purchase of foreign exchange for invisibles were replaced by automatic sale for all bona fide requests. The limit on the amount of domestic currency that can be taken out of the country was raised.

April 30. The requirement that nonresidents pay hotel bills and related services in convertible currencies was eliminated.

Proceeds from Invisibles

January 1. Receipts from invisibles were no longer required to be sold to an authorized dealer.

THAILAND

(Position as of December 31, 1995)

Exchange Arrangement

The currency of Thailand is the Thai Baht. The external value of the baht is determined on the basis of a weighted basket of currencies of Thailand's major trading partners and on other considerations. The Exchange Equalization Fund announces the daily buying and selling rates for the U.S. dollar, the intervention currency, for transactions between itself and commercial banks; it also announces daily minimum buying and maximum selling rates that commercial banks must observe when dealing with the public in Brunei dollars, deutsche mark, Hong Kong dollars, Indonesian rupiah, Japanese yen, Malaysian ringgit, Philippine pesos, pounds sterling, Singapore dollars, and U.S. dollars.

On December 29, 1995, the middle official rate for the U.S. dollar was B 25.19 per $1. There are no taxes or subsidies on purchases or sales of foreign exchange. Forward exchange transactions are carried out between commercial banks and customers and among the commercial banks. All forward transactions must be related to underlying trade and financial transactions. The open foreign exchange positions of commercial banks are restricted by the Bank of Thailand. The forward premium in the baht-U.S. dollar rate is freely determined and usually reflects interest rate differentials.

Thailand accepted the obligations of Article VIII, Sections 2, 3, and 4 of the Fund Agreement on May 4, 1990.

Administration of Control

Exchange control is administered by the Bank of Thailand on behalf of the Ministry of Finance; the Bank of Thailand delegates responsibility to authorized banks (commercial banks) for approving most transactions. Apart from authorized banks, authorized companies and authorized persons are also allowed to deal in foreign exchange operations, although their activities are limited to the buying and selling of foreign banknotes and traveler's checks up to a set amount prescribed by the Bank of Thailand. Import and export licenses are issued by the Ministry of Commerce.

Prescription of Currency

There are no special requirements for currencies that can be used in settlements with foreign countries; most payments are made in U.S. dollars.

Nonresident Accounts

No restrictions are placed on the opening of nonresident foreign currency accounts as long as the funds originate abroad. Foreign currency borrowed by nonresidents from authorized banks and foreign currency arising from withdrawals from nonresident baht accounts may be freely deposited in foreign currency accounts. Balances on these accounts earn interest and may be transferred abroad without restriction.

Nonresidents may also open nonresident baht accounts. These accounts may be debited without restriction, and foreign currency arising from withdrawals from these accounts can be freely deposited in foreign currency accounts. Nonresident baht accounts may also be credited freely with payments for goods and services by residents and with funds transferred from other nonresident baht accounts. These accounts may also be freely credited with proceeds from the sale of foreign currency withdrawn from nonresidents' foreign currency accounts, as well as baht proceeds borrowed from authorized banks.

Imports and Import Payments

Most commodities may be imported freely, but import licenses are required for certain goods. Imports of some goods are prohibited for protective or social reasons. Milk producers are required to use locally produced milk in some quantity in the production of skim milk when they import skim milk for domestic sale. In 1995, quantitative restrictions on 22 agricultural products and on tobacco were eliminated and the surcharges on soya bean cakes were removed.

Importers are required to complete foreign exchange transaction forms for transactions where the value exceeds B 500,000 when submitting the import entry form at customs, except for certain goods, such as military equipment imported by the Ministry of Defense, donated goods, and samples. Payments for imports may be made through any authorized bank. Importers may freely purchase foreign currency or draw foreign exchange from their own foreign currency accounts for payments.

A reduction of import tariffs on 3,842 items was initiated as a part of the Uruguay Round. The average tariff rate will be 28 percent by the end of the implementation period, compared to an initial negotiating level of about 30 percent. In addition, Thailand has restructured customs tariffs covering 6,898 items, whereby the average tariff will decrease to about 17 percent from 30 percent by January 1, 1997, with a decline in the number of tariff rates to 6 from 39: zero percent for certain goods, such as medical equipments; 1 percent for raw materials, electronic components, and international transport vehicles; 5 percent for primary and capital goods, including machinery, tools, and computers; 10 percent for intermediate goods; 20 percent for finished products; and 30 percent for those goods designated as requiring additional protection, like silk fabrics, canvas goods, garments, shoes, hats, and leather bags.

Payments for Invisibles

Remittances abroad of service fees, royalties, insurance premiums, educational expenses, and family maintenance are permitted without restriction. Remittances of dividends and profits on all bona fide investments may be made freely. Authorized banks are also permitted to sell up to $100,000 a person a year in foreign exchange for remittances to families and relatives living abroad and up to $1 illion a person a year for remittances from the personal assets of Thai emigrants who have permanent residence permits abroad. Foreign exchange transaction forms must be completed for transactions involving amounts of more than $5,000. Authorized money changers are allowed to sell up to $2,000, or its equivalent, a person in foreign exchange.

Travelers may take out domestic currency up to B 50,000; those traveling to Vietnam and the countries bordering Thailand are allowed to take out or remit a maximum of B 500,000. Authorized banks are permitted to sell foreign exchange in foreign banknotes for purposes of travel without any restriction.

Exports and Export Proceeds

Certain categories of exports are subject to licensing and quantitative restrictions and, in a few cases, to prior approval, irrespective of destination.[1] All other products may be exported freely. Exporters are required to complete foreign exchange transaction forms for transactions involving more than B 500,000 when submitting the export entry form at customs. Export proceeds exceeding B 500,000 must be received within 180 days of shipment. Exporters are required to surrender foreign exchange proceeds to authorized banks or deposit them in foreign currency accounts with authorized banks in Thailand

within 15 days of receipt, except that they are allowed to use foreign exchange proceeds to service external obligations without having to first surrender them to authorized banks or deposit them in domestic banking accounts.

Proceeds from Invisibles

Foreign exchange earnings from invisibles must be surrendered to authorized banks or retained in foreign currency accounts with authorized banks in Thailand within 15 days of receipt. Travelers passing through Thailand, foreign embassies, and international organizations are exempted from this requirement. Authorized money changers are allowed to purchase foreign currency notes and coins or traveler's checks in foreign currencies, but the latter must be resold to authorized banks within 15 days of purchase. Travelers may bring in domestic or foreign banknotes and coins without restriction.

Capital

Foreign investments in Thailand through equity participation or portfolio investments are permitted freely. Investments that receive promotional privileges from the Board of Investment under the Investment Promotion Act (B.E. 2520) are accorded various incentives and special benefits.

Foreign capital may be brought into the country and loans contracted without restriction, but proceeds must be surrendered to authorized banks or deposited in foreign currency accounts with authorized banks in Thailand within 15 days of receipt. Repatriation of investment funds, loan repayments, and interest payments may be made without restriction. Inflows and outflows of funds exceeding $5,000 or its equivalent are subject to completion of foreign exchange transaction forms. External borrowing by the public sector must be approved by the Foreign Debt Committee.

Authorized banks in Thailand may lend to nonresidents in foreign currency without restriction. Foreign currency loans may be extended to residents for outward remittance or domestic use. If loans are used domestically, resident borrowers are required to convert the foreign currency obtained into baht, which they are not allowed to deposit in foreign currency accounts.

Banks are not allowed to count loans in foreign currencies to purchase unused land, or for personal reasons, as foreign assets and only 50 percent of certain other loans may be counted as foreign assets, unless the borrower fully covers his exchange risk by buying the exchange forward at the same bank that extended the loan.

---

[1] These include rice, canned tuna, all types of sugar, and certain types of coal, charcoal, and textile products.

In April 1995, finance and securities companies were required to hold a daily long and short foreign exchange position not exceeding 25 percent and 20 percent, respectively, of first-tier capital funds. In November 1995, the average weekly net long and short foreign exchange position that authorized banks are required to hold was changed to either 20 percent or 15 percent, respectively, of first-tier capital funds, or $5 million, whichever is larger. Direct investments abroad by Thai residents or lending to companies abroad that have at least 25 percent equity participation by Thai residents is permitted up to $10 million a year without authorization from the Bank of Thailand. Portfolio investments and purchases of properties abroad by Thai residents require approval from the Bank of Thailand.

Gold

Residents may hold and negotiate domestically gold jewelry, gold coins, and unworked gold. Purchases or sales of gold on commodity futures exchanges are prohibited. Imports and exports of gold other than gold jewelry are prohibited unless a license has been obtained from the Ministry of Finance or the transaction is made on behalf of the monetary authorities. Foreign tourists may take out precious stones, gold or platinum ornaments, and other articles without restriction. Exports of gold bullion are prohibited. Exporters and importers of gold ornaments exceeding B 500,000 in value must complete foreign exchange transaction forms at customs when submitting import or export entry forms. Gold ornaments are not subject to export duty or taxes.

Changes During 1995

Nonresident Accounts

February 22. The Provincial International Banking Facility (PIBF) was established; PIBF's funding must be from overseas like the Bangkok International Banking Facility (BIBF), but PIBF can extend credit in both baht and foreign currencies.

Imports and Import Payments

January 1. The licensing requirement for 23 agricultural products was eliminated and the surcharge on soya bean cakes were removed. A reduction in import tariffs for 3,842 items was initiated as a part of the Uruguay Round. The average tariff rate will be 28 percent by the end of the implementation period, compared to an initial negotiating level of about 30 percent. In addition, Thailand has restructured customs tariffs covering 6,898 items, whereby the average tariff rate will decrease to about 17 percent from 30 percent by January 1, 1997, with a decline in the number of tariff rates to 6 percent from 39 percent prior to the reforms: zero percent for certain goods, such as medical equipment; 1 percent for raw materials, electronic components, and international transport vehicles; 5 percent for primary and capital goods, including machinery, tools, and computers; 10 percent for intermediate goods; 20 percent for finished products; and 30 percent for those goods designated as requiring additional protection, like silk fabrics, canvas goods, garments, shoes, hats, and leather bags.

Payments for Invisibles

March 21. The Copyright Act went into force.

Capital

March 7. The Bank of Thailand required banks to submit detailed information on risk control measures on trading in foreign exchange and derivatives.

August 8. The Bank of Thailand imposed a reserve requirement of 7 percent on nonresident baht accounts with maturities of less than one year.

September 21. The Bank of Thailand adopted a new method of calculating nontrade net open foreign exchange positions (on which there are limits set as a percent of capital) for foreign and locally incorporated banks. For these banks, foreign-exchange-denominated loans are not to be counted as foreign assets if the loans are used for purchasing unused land or for personal purposes. For certain other categories, only 50 percent of the loan would be allowed to be counted as a foreign asset. Borrowers who fully hedge the foreign exchange risk by buying foreign exchange forward from the bank that extended the loan are exempted from this requirement.

TOGO

(Position as of June 30, 1996)

Exchange Arrangement

The currency of Togo is the CFA Franc,[1] which is pegged to the French franc, the intervention currency, at the fixed rate of CFAF 1 per F 0.01. The official buying and selling rates are CFAF 100 per F 1. Exchange rates for other currencies are derived from the rate for the currency concerned in the Paris exchange market and the fixed rate between the French franc and the CFA franc. Banks levy a proportional commission of 2.50 per mil with a maximum collection of CFAF 100 and a freely determined charge for each transaction; the commission on transfers between member countries of the BCEAO is freely fixed by the banks. The proportional commission must be surrendered to the Treasury. There are no taxes or subsidies on purchases or sales of foreign exchange. The contracting of forward exchange cover requires the prior authorization of the Minister of Economy and Finance, and permission may be granted only in respect of the importation of certain clearly specified goods. The maturity of exchange contracts can be no more than three months for goods deemed essential or strategic and one month for all other goods. There is no official currency swap scheme or guaranteed exchange rate for debt servicing.

With the exception of measures relating to gold; the repatriation of export proceeds; the issuing, advertising, or offering for sale of securities; capital assets; and the soliciting of funds for investments abroad, Togo's exchange controls do not apply to (1) France (and its overseas departments and territories) and Monaco; and (2) all other countries whose bank of issue is linked with the French Treasury by an Operations Account (Benin, Burkina Faso, Cameroon, Central African Republic, Chad, Comoros, the Congo, Côte d'Ivoire, Equatorial Guinea, Gabon, Mali, Niger, and Senegal). Hence, all payments to these countries may be made freely. All other countries are considered foreign countries.

Togo accepted the obligations of Article VIII, Sections 2, 3, and 4 of the Fund Agreement on June 1, 1996.

---

[1]The CFA franc is issued by the Central Bank of West African States (BCEAO) and is the common currency in Benin, Burkina Faso, Côte d'Ivoire, Mali, Niger, Senegal, and Togo.

Administration of Control

Exchange control is administered by the Ministry of Economy and Finance, which also supervises borrowing abroad; the issuing, advertising, or offering for sale of foreign securities in Togo; inward direct investment and all outward investment; and the soliciting of funds in Togo for placement in foreign countries. The Foreign Exchange Legal Commission has been created to advise the Minister of Economy and Finance on requests to settle cases involving violations of foreign exchange regulations for amounts of CFAF 500,000 or more and on specific requests from violators of foreign exchange regulations. Some of the approval authority in respect of exchange control has been delegated to authorized intermediaries and the BCEAO. The BCEAO is authorized to collect, either directly through economic agents or through the banks, financial institutions, Postal and Telecommunications Office (Office des postes et télécommunications), and offices of government ministries, any information necessary to compile balance of payments statistics. The forwarding and receipt through the mail by authorized intermediaries of banknotes, other than those issued by the BCEAO, are subject to control by the BCEAO. The forwarding and receipt through the mail by authorized intermediaries of banknotes issued by the BCEAO are prohibited. All exchange transactions relating to foreign countries must be effected through authorized banks, the Postal and Telecommunications Office, or the BCEAO. All required import licenses and virtually all required export licenses are issued by the Foreign Trade Division in the Ministry of Commerce and Transport, except those for gold, which are granted by the Minister of Economy and Finance. Exports of locally manufactured products, and food crops other than cereals, and imports of most products are not subject to licensing.

Prescription of Currency

Because Togo is an Operations Account country, settlements with France (as defined above), Monaco, and the Operations Account countries are made in CFA francs, French francs, or the currency of any other Operations Account country. Current payments involving The Gambia, Ghana, Guinea, Guinea-Bissau, Liberia, Mauritania, Nigeria, and Sierra Leone are normally effected through the West

African Clearing House. Settlements with all other countries are usually effected through correspondent banks in France, in any of the currencies of those countries, or in French francs through foreign accounts in francs.

Nonresident Accounts

Because the BCEAO has suspended the repurchase of BCEAO banknotes circulating outside the territories of the CFA franc zone, foreign accounts in francs may not be credited or debited with BCEAO banknotes without authorization.

Imports and Import Payments

All imports may be made freely, with the following exceptions for which licenses are required: (1) pharmaceuticals, explosives, and firearms; and (2) imports of potatoes, which may be prohibited during the period when local production is adequate to meet local demand (between August and February).

The following taxes are imposed on all imports: (1) a statistical tax of 3 percent; (2) fiscal import duties of zero, 5 percent, 10 percent, and 20 percent; (3) a value-added tax at rates of zero, 7 percent, and 18 percent. With the exception of the value-added tax, which is assessed on the basis of the c.i.f. value of imports inclusive of fiscal import duties, all other taxes are levied on c.i.f. values.

All import transactions must be domiciled with an authorized bank when their value exceeds CFAF 500,000, with the exception of imports not involving payment or financing through the Postal and Telecommunications Office and certain imports of a private nature. Importers may purchase foreign exchange for import payments after establishing bank payment order accounts (*dossiers de domiciliation*) and submitting supporting documents, but not earlier than eight days before shipment if a documentary credit is opened, or on the due date of payment if the products have already been imported. Purchases of foreign exchange for down payments are subject to prior authorization from the Ministry of Economy and Finance; such authorization may be granted only on the date payment is due and only for up to 30 percent for each transaction involving capital goods and up to 10 percent for other transactions. For all import operations exceeding CFAF 200,000, merchandise insurance must be taken out and domiciled with an approved insurance company in Togo. Inspection of the quality, quantity, and price of imports has been suspended.

Payments for Invisibles

Payments for invisibles to France (as defined above), Monaco, and the Operations Account countries are permitted freely; those to other countries are subject to approval. Payments for invisibles related to trade are permitted by a general authorization when the basic trade transaction has been approved or does not require authorization. Transfers of income accruing to nonresidents in the form of profits, dividends, and royalties are also generally permitted.

Residents traveling for tourism or business purposes to countries in the franc zone that are not members of the West African Economic and Monetary Union (WAEMU) are allowed to take out up to the equivalent of CFAF 2 million in banknotes other than CFA banknotes; amounts in excess of this limit may be taken out in the form of other means of payment. The allowances for travel to countries outside the franc zone are subject to the following regulations: (1) for tourist travel, CFAF 500,000 without limit on the number of trips or differentiation by the age of the traveler; (2) for business travel, CFAF 75,000 a day for up to one month, corresponding to a maximum of CFAF 2.25 million (business travel allowances may be combined with tourist allowances); (3) allowances in excess of these limits must be authorized by the respective ministries of finance or, by delegation, the BCEAO; and (4) credit cards, which must be issued by resident financial intermediaries and authorized by the respective ministers of finance, may be used up to the ceilings indicated above for tourist and business travel. Upon arrival at customs, returning resident travelers are required to declare all means of payment in their possession and must surrender within eight days all means of payment exceeding the equivalent of CFAF 25,000. All resident travelers, when traveling to countries that are not members of the WAEMU, must declare in writing at the time of departure all means of payment at their disposal. Nonresident travelers may re-export means of payment other than banknotes issued abroad and registered in their name, subject to documentation that they had used funds drawn from a foreign account in CFA francs or with other foreign exchange to purchase these means of payment. The re-exportation of foreign banknotes is allowed up to the equivalent of CFAF 250,000; the re-exportation of foreign banknotes above these ceilings requires documentation demonstrating either the importation of foreign banknotes or their purchase against other means of payment registered in the name of the traveler or through the use of nonresident deposits lodged in local banks.

The transfer of the entire net salary of a foreign national working in Togo is permitted upon presentation of the appropriate pay voucher, residence permit, or work permit, provided that the transfer takes place within three months of the pay period.

Exports and Export Proceeds

Exports to all countries require licenses in certain cases. The Office of Togolese Phosphates has a monopoly over the exportation of phosphates, the Office of Togolese Agricultural Products has a monopoly over the exportation of cocoa and coffee, and the Togolese Cotton Company has monopoly over the export of cotton fiber. Exports of cereals have been temporarily suspended by the Technical Committee for Cereal Exports; the Technical Committee meets twice a year—before March to make a determination of whether an exportable surplus exists, and again before November 10 to establish the actual export levels. The due date for payment for exports to foreign countries, including the Operations Account area, may not be later than 180 days after the arrival of the goods at their destination, and the proceeds must be surrendered within a month of the due date to authorized intermediaries; authorized diamond purchasing officers, however, may retain foreign currency proceeds in foreign currency accounts with authorized banks in Togo. All export transactions, including those with the Operations Account countries, must be domiciled with an authorized bank when their value exceeds CFAF 500,000. The domiciling bank is responsible for ensuring effective repatriation of such receipts through the BCEAO.

Proceeds from Invisibles

Proceeds from invisibles transactions with France (as defined above), Monaco, and the Operations Account countries may be retained. All amounts due from residents of other countries in respect of services, and all income earned in those countries from foreign assets, must be collected and surrendered within one month of the due date or the date of receipt. Resident and nonresident travelers may bring in any amount of banknotes and coins issued by the BCEAO, the Bank of France, or any institute of issue maintaining an Operations Account with the French Treasury, as well as any amount of foreign banknotes and coins (except gold coins) of countries outside the Operations Account area. Residents bringing in foreign banknotes and foreign currency traveler's checks in excess of CFAF 25,000 must sell them to an authorized bank within eight days.

Capital

Capital movements between Togo and France (as defined above), Monaco, and the other countries of the Operations Account area are free of exchange control; capital transfers to all other countries require exchange control approval from the Ministry of Economy and Finance, and are restricted, but capital receipts from such countries are permitted freely.

Special controls (in addition to any exchange control requirements that may be applicable) are maintained over borrowing abroad, inward direct investment, and all outward investment; the issuing, advertising, or offering for sale of foreign securities in Togo; and the soliciting of funds in Togo for placement abroad. Such operations require prior authorization from the Ministry of Economy and Finance. Exempt from authorization, however, are operations in connection with (1) loans backed by a guarantee from the Togolese Government; and (2) shares that are identical to, or can be substituted for, securities whose issuing, advertising, or offering for sale in Togo has already been authorized. With the exception of controls relating to foreign securities and the soliciting of funds in Togo, these measures do not apply to relations with France (as defined above), Monaco, member countries of the WAEMU, and the Operations Account countries.

All investments abroad by residents of Togo, including investments made through foreign companies directly or indirectly controlled by persons in Togo and those made by branches or subsidiaries abroad of companies in Togo, require prior authorization from the Ministry of Economy and Finance, and at least 75 percent of such investments must be financed by foreign borrowing. Foreign direct investments in Togo, including those made by companies in Togo directly or indirectly under foreign control and those made by branches or subsidiaries of foreign companies in Togo, must be reported to the Ministry of Economy and Finance before they are made. The Minister may request postponement of the projects within two months of receiving the declaration. Total or partial liquidation of any inward direct investment or any outward investment also requires prior reporting to the Ministry of Economy and Finance. Both the making and the liquidation of investments, whether Togolese investments abroad or foreign investments in Togo, must be reported to the Ministry of Economy and Finance and to the BCEAO within 20 days of each operation. (Direct investments are investments implying control of a company or enterprise. Mere participation is not considered direct investment, provided that it does not exceed 20 percent of the capital of a company whose shares are quoted on a stock exchange.)

Borrowing by residents from nonresidents requires prior authorization from the Ministry of Economy and Finance. The following are, however, exempt from this authorization: (1) loans constituting a direct investment, which are subject to prior declaration, as indicated above; (2) loans contracted by authorized banks; (3) loans taken up either by industrial firms to finance operations abroad or by approved international merchanting houses to finance imports or exports; and (4) in certain circumstances, any other loans, provided that the outstanding amount for any one borrower does not exceed CFAF 100 million. The repayment of any foreign borrowing requires the prior authorization of the Ministry of Economy and Finance; exempt from this requirement are loans constituting a direct investment, loans taken up by authorized banks, and loans exempted by the Minister. Lending abroad is subject only to special authorization from the Directorate of Economy.

Under the provisions of the general tax legislation, certain fiscal benefits are accorded to specified new investment (foreign and domestic) in both new and existing enterprises. In addition, certain enterprises, in accordance with their importance to the economic development of Togo, may, for a specified number of years, be granted special privileges relating to the maintenance of existing taxes and exemption from import duties. Such privileges are negotiated by the Government and the investor.

To obtain the tax benefits provided under the Investment Code adopted in 1989, firms must provide an amount from equity equivalent to at least 25 percent of the amount net of taxes to finance new projects (excluding working capital), and pay at least 60 percent of their wage bill to workers who are nationals of Togo. Tax benefits include primarily exemptions from the minimum *forfait* tax and corporate income taxes for five years for small and medium-size enterprises, seven years for enterprises that process domestic raw materials, and three years for other enterprises. The code guarantees the right of free transfer abroad of capital invested in Togo and of all investment income therefrom.

Gold

Residents are free to hold, acquire, and dispose of gold in any form in Togo. The importation and exportation of gold to or from any other country require prior authorization from the Ministry of Economy and Finance. Exempt from this requirement are (1) imports and exports by or on behalf of the Treasury or the BCEAO; (2) imports and exports of manufactured articles containing a minor quantity of gold (such as gold-filled or gold-plated articles); and (3) imports and exports by travelers of gold objects up to a combined weight of 500 grams. Both licensed and exempt imports of gold are subject to customs declaration.

Changes During 1995

Imports and Import Payments

August 17. Import license requirement for the importation of cement, corrugated iron, concrete reinforcing bars, and wheat flour was eliminated.

Exports and Export Proceeds

February 8. The export of cereals was provisionally suspended.

May 31. The monopoly over the export of cotton fiber was transferred to the Togolese Cotton Company (SOTOCO).

Changes During 1996

Exchange Arrangement

June 1. Togo accepted the obligations of Article VIII, Sections 2, 3, and 4 of the Fund Agreement.

TONGA

(Position as of December 31, 1995)

Exchange Arrangement

The currency of Tonga is the Pa'anga. Its external value is determined on the basis of a weighted basket of currencies, comprising the U.S. dollar, the Australian dollar, and the New Zealand dollar. The National Reserve Bank of Tonga (the central bank) maintains buying and selling rates for the U.S. dollar, the intervention currency. The commercial banks quote daily rates for 16 currencies[1] on the basis of their values against the pa'anga. The spread between the commercial banks' buying and selling rates is approximately 2 percent. Sales of foreign exchange are at a premium of approximately 1.5 percent, and purchases are at a discount of approximately 0.5 percent. On December 31, 1995, the central bank's buying and selling rates for the U.S. dollar were T$1.275 and T$1.277, respectively, per US$1.[2] There are no taxes or subsidies on purchases or sales of foreign exchange. Commercial banks are allowed to provide forward exchange cover, but their gross foreign exchange liabilities must not exceed US$1 million.

Tonga accepted the obligations of Article VIII, Sections 2, 3, and 4 of the Fund Agreement on March 22, 1991.

Administration of Control

Tonga's trade and payments system is relatively free of controls. Foreign exchange transactions are regulated by the National Reserve Bank of Tonga and the Ministry of Finance.

Prescription of Currency

There are no regulations prescribing the currencies that can be used in particular transactions.

Imports and Import Payments

Licenses are required for all imports, although these are generally issued freely. Import quotas apply only to fresh eggs and are intended to protect domestic producers, but the restriction is not enforced. The importation of certain items is restricted for cultural or environmental reasons or to protect the health and safety of residents. Tariffs, which range up to 35 percent and apply to most private sector imports, are aimed primarily at increasing revenues, but protective tariffs are levied on a few items, such as beer, paint, and wire fencing. Tariffs are levied at an ad valorem rate on the c.i.f. value of imports, except for a few items (petroleum, tobacco products, and alcoholic beverages), which are subject to either specific tariffs or ad valorem rates ranging up to 300 percent of the c.i.f. value, whichever is higher. The maximum tariff rate, which is levied on motor vehicles, is 45 percent. Goods imported by the reigning monarch, by the Government and the public sector, and by diplomatic missions, under certain technical assistance agreements, and personal effects are exempt from tariffs. Imports are also subject to a 20 percent port and services tax, except for items under the Industrial Development Incentives (IDI) Act, which qualify for concessional rates, and imports of government and quasi-government organizations, which are exempt.

Exports and Export Proceeds

All export proceeds must be repatriated within 12 months and surrendered to the banking system, but this regulation is not enforced. Commercial banks must surrender all of their foreign exchange, apart from small working balances to the central bank. Licenses are required for all exports, except for shipments weighing less than 10 kilograms. With the exception of squash, which is subject to an export quota,[3] the authorities maintain a liberal attitude toward granting those licenses. Effective January 1, 1992, the monopoly of the Commodities Board over exports of coconut and coconut derivatives, vanilla, and bananas was abolished.

Payments for and Proceeds from Invisibles

Commercial banks are authorized to provide foreign exchange for invisible payments up to T$5,000 a transaction. The Ministry of Finance may approve requests for larger amounts upon submission of sat-

---

[1] Australian dollars, Canadian dollars, deutsche mark, Fiji dollars, French francs, Hong Kong dollars, Indian rupees, Italian lire, Japanese yen, Netherlands guilders, New Zealand dollars, pounds sterling, Singapore dollars, Swedish kronor, Swiss francs, and U.S. dollars.

[2] For transactions with commercial banks, buying and selling rates were T$1.275 and T$1.277, respectively, per US$1 for transactions with other organizations, including the Government.

[3] The export quota applies only to the October–December season and not to the small May crop. The quota for 1996 was eliminated.

isfactory documentary evidence that the underlying transaction is a bona fide current international transaction. Such approvals are routinely granted without undue delay.

Shipping and airline agencies may remit income earned from activities in Tonga upon producing income statements relating to local business activities that have been submitted to their respective head offices.

Capital

The authorities maintain a liberal attitude toward foreign direct investment, although so far such investment remains small. Foreign investors are required to apply for licenses from the Ministry of Labor, Commerce, and Industries, with approval depending on the type of investment. High-technology projects are readily approved; intermediate projects are accepted if there is a local partner; and simple projects that can be readily undertaken by locals are likely to be rejected. The IDI Act prohibits foreign investment in certain sectors, including wholesaling and retailing, transportation, and some tourist-related activities, and all resource-based activities, such as fishing. However, joint ventures may be allowed if the project is deemed beneficial to the country. No time period has been specified for the approval process, which can be quite lengthy, but once licensed, foreign projects in manufacturing and tourism are fully eligible for incentives under the IDI Act. Under the IDI Act, foreign investors involved in manufacturing are allowed duty-free imports of capital inputs, a maximum 15-year tax holiday, and, on a case-by-case basis, repatriation of profits and capital.

In principle, outward investment is restricted. Direct investment abroad requires the approval of the Ministry of Finance, but is usually given if the transaction is considered beneficial to Tongan exports. The acquisition of foreign financial assets is, in principle, prohibited, but in practice, the restriction is not strictly enforced because the repatriation requirement is not enforced.

Banks are permitted to hold only working balances in foreign currencies up to a limit of T$1 million. No explicit limits exist on foreign exchange liabilities, but provision of forward exchange cover for squash exporters requires the approval of the Ministry of Finance. Cover is not permitted for imports.

Changes During 1995

Exports and Export Proceeds

July 1. The quota for squash exports during the October–December season was set at 17,500 tons.

TRINIDAD AND TOBAGO

(Position as of December 31, 1995)

Exchange Arrangement

The currency of Trinidad and Tobago is the Trinidad and Tobago Dollar. The exchange rate of the Trinidad and Tobago dollar is determined in the interbank market on the basis of supply and demand. On December 31, 1995, the buying and selling rates were TT$5.8765 and TT$5.971, respectively, per US$1. Banks are allowed to conduct foreign exchange transactions, both spot and forward, with the public without limitation. Commercial banks must notify the Central Bank of Trinidad and Tobago in advance of any planned significant adjustment to the exchange rate. At the end of each trading day, the Central Bank publishes a nominal rate for the Trinidad and Tobago dollar against each of the major currencies, based on a weighted average of the rates at which these currencies have been trading.

Trinidad and Tobago accepted the obligations of Article VIII, Sections 2, 3, and 4 of the Fund Agreement on December 13, 1993.

Administration of Control

The authority to administer exchange control is vested in the Central Bank, which acts under the authority of the Ministry of Finance.

Commercial banks can purchase foreign currency notes from the public, and the Central Bank in turn buys certain of these currencies from the commercial banks for repatriation to the respective monetary authorities under bilateral arrangements. The Central Bank does not repatriate Trinidad and Tobago currency.

Prescription of Currency

Settlements may be made in U.S. dollars or in specified currencies.[1] Authorized payments, including payments for imports, to all countries may be made in U.S. dollars or in one of the specified currencies. Payments from all countries with which trade is allowed must be received in U.S. dollars or in any of the specified currencies.

Foreign Currency Accounts

Foreign currency accounts denominated in foreign currency may be maintained at local banks by residents and nonresidents.

Imports and Import Payments

All goods, unless excepted for reasons of health and security, may be imported under open general license (OGL) arrangements. Imports of firearms, ammunition, and narcotics are either prohibited or tightly controlled for security and health reasons. Imports of animal feed, flour, rice, petroleum, and edible oil are traded principally by state companies. All imports of food and drugs must satisfy prescribed standards. Imports of meat, live animals, plants, and mining materials are subject to specific regulations.

Duty-free licenses are granted to local concessionaire manufacturers for imports of certain inputs for manufacturing industries. Where goods are subject to import license, a general import license is used in addition to the duty-free license.

Imports from non-CARICOM countries[2] may be paid for in any currency in which goods are satisfactorily invoiced.

The customs duty rates on most goods range from 5 percent to 30 percent; the rate on agricultural produce is 40 percent. The duty rates on consumer goods, such as perfumes, cosmetics, jewelry, clothing, and cotton and silk fabrics, range from 25 percent to 30 percent; the rate on motor vehicles is 35 percent.

Some foodstuffs, fertilizers, and raw materials, and all goods originating from CARICOM countries are exempt from customs duties. Local enterprises producing import substitutes or export goods may be granted exemptions from customs duties by the Minister of Trade and Industry and the Tourism Industrial Development Company Limited (TIDCO).

Payments for Invisibles

Residents and nonresidents may take out of Trinidad and Tobago local currency notes up to the value of TT$20,000. For amounts exceeding TT$20,000,

---

[1] Austrian schillings, Belgian francs, Canadian dollars, Danish kroner, deutsche mark, French francs, Italian lire, Japanese yen, Myanmar kyats, Netherlands guilders, Norwegian kroner, Portuguese escudos, Spanish pesetas, Swedish kronor, Swiss francs, and pounds sterling.

[2] The CARICOM countries are Antigua and Barbuda, The Bahamas, Barbados, Belize, Dominica, Grenada, Guyana, Jamaica, Montserrat, St. Kitts and Nevis, St. Lucia, St. Vincent and the Grenadines, and Trinidad and Tobago.

there is no restriction, but a customs declaration is required.

Exports and Export Proceeds

Exports of certain goods usually require an individual license. These include some foodstuffs, firearms and explosives, animals, gold, and petroleum and petroleum products produced in Trinidad and Tobago, as well as specified products not produced locally. Exports of all other commodities are permitted under OGL. In addition, general licenses may be issued at the discretion of the Ministry of Trade and Industry.

There are no requirements for the repatriation of export proceeds received in foreign currencies. In practice, the foreign-owned petroleum company operating in Trinidad and Tobago repatriates all foreign exchange after providing for the equivalent of its local currency needs.

Proceeds from Invisibles

Residents and nonresidents may bring into Trinidad and Tobago domestic currency notes up to the value of TT$20,000. For larger amounts, a customs declaration is required. Both resident and nonresident travelers may bring in foreign currency notes up to US$5,000 without declaration to the controller of customs.

Capital

Capital transfers abroad do not require prior approval.

The laws of Trinidad and Tobago do not discriminate between nationals and foreigners in the formation and operation of companies in the country. Foreign investors are required, however, to comply with the provisions of the Foreign Investment Act of 1990 in order to hold an interest in real estate or shares in local companies. Following passage of the Central Bank Amendment Act of 1993, exchange control restrictions were removed, and foreign investors are no longer required to obtain approval from the Central Bank to repatriate capital or capital gains. There are no limitations on borrowing by foreign investors on the local financial market.

The Government has enacted basic incentive legislation designed to attract domestic and foreign investment in manufacturing and in import-substitution industries. Since 1973, these policies have been effected within the framework of a CARICOM agreement on the harmonization of fiscal incentives. Certain concessions may be granted to approved enterprises, including temporary relief from import duties and taxes and other privileges outlined in the Investment Policy document issued by the Industrial Development Corporation.

A commercial bank, as an authorized dealer, is allowed to hold an "open" asset or liability position in foreign exchange. Cross-border trading of shares of companies listed on the respective stock exchanges is permitted among the residents of Barbados, Jamaica, and Trinidad and Tobago; residents and companies of the other two countries are designated as residents of Trinidad and Tobago for exchange control purposes in cross-border trading.

Gold

Except with specific exemptions and permissions granted by the Minister of Finance, (1) one party to every transaction in gold between residents must be an authorized bank, and (2) gold (defined by the Exchange Control Act of 1970 as gold coins and bullion) may not be taken or sent out of Trinidad and Tobago. When appropriate, however, residents are permitted to purchase, hold, or sell gold coins in Trinidad and Tobago for numismatic purposes.

Exports of gold are controlled by the Ministry of Trade and Industry. Imports of gold jewelry are subject to an OGL, but imports of other forms of gold are controlled by the Central Bank. Exports of gold in any form are subject to specific export licenses; licenses for gold other than jewelry are not usually granted except to the monetary authorities, who may need to get authorization from the Central Bank.

Changes During 1995

Imports and Import Payments

January 1. The customs duties were reduced to the 5–30 percent range. The stamp duty was removed, and the import surcharge on all nonagricultural goods was removed. Tariffs on agricultural goods are scheduled to be eliminated by 1998.

TUNISIA

(Position as of December 31, 1995)

Exchange Arrangement

The currency of Tunisia is the Tunisian Dinar, the external value of which is determined in the inter-bank market in which commercial banks (including offshore banks acting on behalf of their resident cus-tomers) conduct transactions at freely negotiated rates. The spread between the buying and selling rates, however, may not exceed 0.25 percent. The Central Bank of Tunisia intervenes in the market by buying or selling dinars for foreign exchange. It pub-lishes an indicative interbank exchange rate for for-eign currencies and banknotes by the following day, at the latest. On December 31, 1995, the average interbank spot rates were D 0.19398 for one French franc and D 0.9508 for one U.S. dollar.[1]

Forward rates are published daily by the Central Bank. Forward cover may be requested for a mini-mum of the equivalent of D 10 million in foreign exchange. The forward rates published daily by the Central Bank are merely indicative when cover is requested for amounts equal to or more than the for-eign currency equivalent of D 10 million. Different rates may be set for these requests; the authorized bank is notified thereof prior to the conclusion of the forward contract. Importers and exporters are authorized to obtain forward exchange cover from the authorized banks as of the date the contract is signed or the date on which the foreign commercial paper is domiciled, depending on the arrangements for the product concerned. Forward cover may be established for a maximum of 12 months for imports and a maximum of 9 months for exports. Persons who provide services are eligible for exchange cover for up to 12 months, to be provided within 30 days of the date on which the claim originated. Curren-cies quoted forward are Belgian francs, deutsche mark, French francs, Italian lire, Netherlands guil-ders, pounds sterling, and U.S. dollars. Swaps are permitted among foreign currency operators. Trad-ing on 3-, 6-, and 12-month foreign currency options

on French francs, deutsche mark, and U.S. dollars is available to resident borrowers of foreign exchange under standard contracts. The Central Bank extends exchange rate guarantees to certain officially guar-anteed loans, with risk premiums based on domestic and international interest rates.

Tunisia accepted the obligations of Article VIII, Sections 2, 3, and 4 of the Fund Agreement, on Janu-ary 6, 1993.

Administration of Control

Exchange control is administered by the Central Bank, which delegates authority over payments for imports and most invisibles to the authorized banks. Foreign trade control is administered by the Minis-try of Trade, which issues import and export autho-rization for products when required.

Prescription of Currency

Settlements between Tunisia and foreign countries may be made in any convertible currency (traded in the interbank market) or in convertible Tunisian dinars through foreign accounts. Settlements between Tunisia and Algeria, the Libyan Arab Jamahiriya, Mauritania, and Morocco may be effected through convertible accounts in the national currencies con-cerned at the respective central banks. Payments to Israel are prohibited.

Resident and Nonresident Accounts

Special accounts in foreign currency or convertible dinars may be opened by (1) natural persons of Tuni-sian nationality changing their normal residence to Tunisia from abroad and any other natural or juridi-cal persons of Tunisian nationality for their non-transferable assets legitimately acquired abroad; (2) natural persons of foreign nationality residing in Tunisia; (3) foreign juridical persons for their estab-lishments located in Tunisia; and (4) Tunisian diplo-mats and civil servants stationed abroad. No formalities are required for the opening of these accounts by foreigners; a declaration of holdings, however, is required for Tunisians. Funds legiti-mately acquired abroad, not from the exportation of goods or services from Tunisia, may be credited to these accounts. They may be debited for (1) foreign exchange surrendered to the Central Bank; (2) foreign exchange remitted to the account holder,

---

[1]Currencies quoted spot for account holdings and banknotes are Austrian schillings, Belgian francs, Canadian dollars, Danish kroner, deutsche mark, European currency units (ECUs), Finnish markkaa, French francs, Italian lire, Japanese yen, Kuwaiti dinars, Libyan dinars, Moroccan dirhams, Netherlands guilders, Norwe-gian kroner, pounds sterling, Saudi Arabian riyals, Spanish pese-tas, Swedish kronor, Swiss francs, U.A.E. dirhams, and U.S. dollars. Currencies quoted spot for banknotes only are CFA francs, Luxembourg francs, and Qatar riyals. Algerian dinars are quoted spot only.

his or her spouse, parents, and offspring to undertake foreign travel; (3) amounts credited to another special account in foreign currency or convertible dinars; and (4) any payments abroad (including those for the acquisition of movable or immovable tangible property located abroad, of ownership rights abroad, or of foreign claims and for payments for imports subject to applicable foreign trade formalities).

Foreign accounts in convertible dinars and convertible currencies may be opened freely by all nonresidents regardless of nationality. These accounts may be credited freely with (1) receipts in convertible foreign currencies or the dinar proceeds from sales of convertible currencies to the Central Bank; banknotes must be declared to customs; (2) convertible foreign currencies remitted to the account holder by a nonresident; (3) foreign currency purchased from the Central Bank by debit of a foreign account in convertible dinars; (4) authorized payments by residents in favor of the account holder; (5) interest on balances in these accounts and interest payable by the authorized intermediaries on foreign exchange deposits in the accounts whenever they can use the funds thus deposited at remunerative rates; (6) transfers from other foreign accounts; and (7) proceeds from the cashing of checks, traveler's checks, or drafts expressed in convertible currencies and made out by a nonresident to the order of the account holder. All other credits require prior authorization from the Central Bank, either directly or by delegation. These accounts may be debited freely for (1) payments of any kind in Tunisia (irrespective of the payer's country of residence); (2) transfers to other foreign accounts; (3) the purchase of any foreign currency from, or sales of any foreign exchange to, the Central Bank; and (4) transfers abroad or delivery of foreign currency to the account holder, to any other nonresident beneficiary, or to residents with the status of permanent representatives or salaried employees of the account holder.

Professional accounts in foreign currency may be opened by any natural person residing in Tunisia or by any Tunisian or foreign juridical person for their foreign currency assets in connection with their establishments located in Tunisia. These accounts are essentially designed to allow their holders to cover themselves against exchange risks. They may be credited with (1) up to 40 percent of the export receipts of their holders; (2) the interest generated by the amounts deposited in such accounts; and (3) transfers from another professional account of the holder, either in the same foreign currency or another one. They may be debited for (1) payment of any current operation pertaining to the activity for

which they were opened; and (2) any other transaction with general or specific authorization. Balances may also be placed on the foreign exchange market.

Professional accounts in convertible dinars may be opened by natural or juridical persons residing in Tunisia with resources in foreign exchange, subject to central bank authorization. These accounts may be credited and debited under the terms laid down by the Central Bank in the authorization to open such accounts.

Internal nonresident accounts may be opened freely by authorized intermediaries in the name of nonresident individuals of foreign nationality residing temporarily in Tunisia. These accounts may be credited without authorization from the Central Bank with the following: (1) transfers of funds carried out in convertible currencies from a foreign country; (2) revenue of any kind accruing in Tunisia to the holder of the account (in particular, the nontransferable part of remuneration for services rendered by that person in Tunisia); (3) liquid assets from estates opened in Tunisia; (4) proceeds from the repayment of loans previously granted in dinars with funds from the account holder's internal nonresident account; and (5) transfers from another internal nonresident account opened in the name of the account holder. They may be debited for (1) support of the account holder and his or her family in Tunisia; (2) payment of costs of managing property in Tunisia; (3) lending to residents; and (4) transfers to another internal nonresident account opened in the name of the account holder.

Special dinar accounts may be freely opened by nonresident foreign enterprises holding contracts in Tunisia that have been approved by the Central Bank. Such enterprises are authorized to open, for each contract, a single special account in dinars, in which they may deposit the portion of the contract price payable in dinars to cover their local expenses. Such accounts may also be credited with funds from a foreign account in convertible dinars, the dinar equivalent of foreign currency drawn on a foreign account in convertible foreign currency, the dinar equivalent of any transfer in convertible foreign currency from abroad, and interest accruing on funds deposited in the account. The account may be freely debited for the enterprise's contract-related expenses in Tunisia.

Any transfer operations from such accounts must be authorized by the Central Bank. Interest is paid at rates comparable to those applied to resident accounts in dinars.

Suspense accounts may be opened by all nonresidents regardless of nationality and may be used for crediting all proceeds accruing to nonresidents and awaiting utilization. These proceeds may, upon general or specific approval, be used in Tunisia for specific purposes, transferred abroad, or transferred to other nonresident accounts. Subject to certain conditions, suspense accounts may be debited, without the prior authorization of the Central Bank, for purchases of Tunisian securities, subscriptions to issues of short-term debentures or bonds, portfolio management expenses in respect of certain securities, payments to the Tunisian Government or public institutions, or payments of the expenses of managing securities deposited in a suspense file opened in the name of the account holder. They may also be debited for settlement of living expenses incurred in Tunisia by the account holder and his or her family up to D 100 a person a week, provided that the total withdrawals in any calendar year from one or more accounts do not exceed D 2,000 a family. In addition, a suspense account holder traveling in Tunisia between November 1 and March 31 of the following year may withdraw from the account an amount equal to the foreign exchange imported for the trip and surrendered to the Central Bank, an authorized intermediary, or a subagency, provided that total withdrawals for the living expenses of the account holder and his or her family do not exceed D 2,000 a year. Up to D 50 a person a month may be debited to assist the offspring or parents of the resident account holder. Individuals or juridical persons of French or Italian nationality holding suspense accounts may transfer all funds in their accounts regardless of the date of deposit. These accounts do not pay interest.

Capital accounts may be opened in the name of a nonresident natural person of foreign nationality or by a nonresident juridical person. The opening of these accounts by a nonresident of Tunisian nationality or his or her spouse must be authorized by the Central Bank. Foreign banks may hold global capital accounts for their nonresident customers. Subject to certain conditions, capital accounts may be credited, without the prior approval of the Central Bank, with the proceeds of the sale on the stock exchange, or of the contractual or advance redemption, of transferable Tunisian securities; the sales proceeds of real estate through an attorney at the Supreme Court (Cour de cassation), or rights to real estate situated in Tunisia; and with funds from another capital account. Irrespective of the account holder's country of residence, capital accounts may be freely debited for the living expenses in Tunisia of the account holder and his or her family, up to D 100 a person a week, provided that total withdrawals from one or more capital accounts in a calendar year do not exceed D 2,000 a family for trips to Tunisia between November 1 and March 31 of the subsequent year. In

addition, a capital account holder traveling in Tunisia between November 1 and March 31 may withdraw from the account an amount equal to the foreign exchange imported for the trip and surrendered to the Central Bank, an authorized intermediary, or a subagency, provided that total withdrawals for the living expenses of the account holder and his or her family do not exceed D 2,000 a year.

Such accounts may also be debited, subject to certain conditions, for expenses connected with the management of Tunisian securities; for the maintenance, repair, and insurance of real estate and all taxes; and for transfer to the credit of another capital account. Balances on capital accounts are freely transferable between nonresidents of foreign nationality, with the exception of juridical persons governed by public law. Subject to certain conditions, they may also be debited to assist the account holder's parents and offspring residing in Tunisia, at a maximum rate of D 50 a person a month. These accounts do not pay interest and may not be overdrawn. Individuals and juridical persons of French or Italian nationality holding capital accounts may transfer all funds in their accounts regardless of the date of deposit.

Imports and Import Payments

All imports from Israel are prohibited. All imports are liberalized except those that have an impact on law and order, hygiene, health, morals, protection of flora and fauna, and cultural heritage. Some goods may only be imported temporarily, subject to an import authorization. The list of items not subject to import liberalization is set by decree. Some items, the list of which is drawn up by decree by the Minister of Trade, are subject to technical import controls. A countervailing import duty may be applied to any item that has been dumped or subsidized and that, when used, is or could be detrimental to the national production of a similar product. The importation of liberalized products is effected by an import certificate upon presentation of a contract domiciled with an authorized intermediary. Goods not subject to liberalization are imported under cover of an import authorization issued by the Ministry of Trade.

Imports of raw materials, semifinished products, spare parts, and equipment paid with funds from sources outside Tunisia may be effected without foreign trade formalities by enterprises for their own use up to a value of D 100,000. Furthermore, companies exclusively engaged in exporting goods or services and set up under the Investment Incentives Code promulgated by Law No. 93-120 of December 27, 1993, and companies established in a free trade zone under Law No. 92-81 of August 3, 1992, on free trade zones may import freely without foreign trade formalities any goods required for their production process, subject only to customs declaration.

Importers must receive a customs code number before they can obtain an import certificate. All import documents involving payments must be handled by an authorized intermediary. Foreign currency may be purchased from the Central Bank or a delegated commercial bank for all payments. Resident importers are authorized to buy forward foreign currencies required for future settlement of their merchandise imports, for a maximum term of 12 months, at rates established daily by the Central Bank. In addition to customs duties, imports are subject to the value-added tax and, in some cases, to the consumption tax. In some cases, imports destined for domestic investment projects are eligible for full or partial exemption from import duties.

Payments for Invisibles

Authorized banks are empowered to provide foreign exchange for tourist and business travel, study and educational expenses, expenses related to travel abroad for reasons of health, and salary transfers, up to prescribed limits. The annual limits for tourist travel allowances are D 500 for an adult and D 250 for a child under the age of 10. The annual settlement and the monthly educational expense allowances for a student are D 1,000 and D 600, respectively. Amounts exceeding these limits may be authorized by the Central Bank. Business travel allowances are granted for all exporters of goods and services, all enterprises, including liberal professions, who have declared their business turnover during the previous year to the tax authorities, and promoters of new projects. The allowance for exporters is 10 percent of export proceeds for the current year, with an annual limit of D 80,000. The annual limit on the allowance for business travel by importers ranges from D 5,000 to D 30,000, depending on turnover, and the annual limit on the allowance for business travel by other professions ranges from D 2,000 to D 20,000, depending on turnover declared to the tax authorities. The allowance for promoters of new projects is a maximum of D 5,000, and is granted only once for the duration of the project.

Contractually employed foreign nationals and foreign experts employed by the public sector may transfer up to 50 percent of their earnings; for technical assistants, limits on transfers are specified in their contracts.

Persons traveling abroad for health reasons may transfer up to D 750 a year for travel expenses. Additional amounts may be allowed for this purpose if the state of their health requires several trips abroad during the same year. Persons accompanying patients may transfer up to D 250 a trip in the case of medical or paramedical staff and D 500 in all other cases. Other payments for invisibles may be made freely.

Regardless of nationality, residents traveling abroad by air or sea, except to the countries of the Arab Maghreb Union, are subject to a travel tax of D 45 a trip. Nonresidents, diplomats, persons traveling under the Agence de coopération technique, emigrant workers, a resident of Tunisia whose spouse resides abroad, children living in Tunisia who have one or both parents residing abroad, students, pilgrims to Mecca, and those traveling for medical reasons are exempt from the tax. The exportation of Tunisian dinar banknotes and coins is prohibited.

Exports and Export Proceeds

All exports to Israel are prohibited. All exports are liberalized, except those indicated in a list established by decree. Certain products, the list of which is established by edict of the Ministry of Trade, are subject to technical export control.

Liberalized items are exported upon presentation to customs of the final invoice. The exports must be domiciled within eight days of the date of shipment of the merchandise.

Goods not subject to liberalization are exported upon presentation of an authorization issued by the Minister of Trade. Companies exclusively engaged in exporting goods or services and set up under the Investment Incentives Code and companies established in a free economic zone may export freely without foreign trade formalities, subject only to customs declarations. As a general rule, all export proceeds must be repatriated within ten days of the payment due date. If no credit is extended, payment is due within 30 days of the date of shipment. Under certain conditions, approval from the Central Bank is not required for the extension of export credits of up to 180 days. Resident exporters may sell forward, for a maximum term of 9 months (12 months for providers of services), foreign currencies representing the proceeds from their merchandise exports through authorized intermediaries.

Resident exporters may credit up to 40 percent of their foreign exchange proceeds to their professional accounts (see section on Resident and Nonresident Accounts, above). Balances in these accounts may be used for any foreign exchange transaction with specific or general authorization, such as payments of expenses needed for the enterprise's activities and servicing of external obligations. Nonresident companies exclusively engaged in exporting goods or services and covered by the Investment Incentives Code, nonresident international trading companies, and nonresident enterprises constituted in a free trade zone are not required to repatriate or surrender their export proceeds.

Proceeds from Invisibles

Residents must repatriate and surrender all amounts derived from services rendered to persons residing abroad and all other income or proceeds from invisibles received from foreign countries. However, the facilities associated with professional accounts in foreign exchange and in convertible dinars apply to proceeds from services (see sections on Resident and Nonresident Accounts and Exports and Export Proceeds). Foreign banknotes and coins (except gold coins) may be brought in freely, but importation of Tunisian dinar banknotes and coins is prohibited.

Nonresidents travelers wishing to re-export the foreign exchange equivalent of amounts exceeding D 1,000 must declare to customs the foreign currencies they are importing upon their entry into Tunisia. There is no ceiling on the reconversion of Tunisian banknotes by nonresident travelers. Foreign exchange from dinar reconversion may be re-exported upon presentation of a foreign exchange voucher or receipt if the amount to be re-exported is less than D 1,000 or if the foreign exchange used in the purchase of the dinars was received from abroad in the form of a check, draft, money order, or any other evidence of a claim or by debiting a foreign account in foreign currency or convertible dinars. The foreign exchange import declaration approved by customs is also required if the amount of foreign exchange from dinar reconversion exceeds the equivalent of D 1,000 derived from the surrender of foreign currencies physically imported from abroad.

Capital

All foreign direct investments carried out legitimately in Tunisia with foreign exchange transferred from abroad are guaranteed the right to repatriate the net proceeds from the sale or liquidation of the invested capital, even if the net proceeds exceed the initial value of foreign exchange invested.

Foreign direct investments in agriculture and fisheries, manufacturing, public works, tourism, handicrafts, transport, education and teaching, vocational training, the production of culture and related industries, youth coordination and child supervision, health, environmental conservation, real estate promotion, and other nonfinancial activities and services benefit from the incentives contained in the Investment Incentives Code, promulgated by Law No. 93-120 of December 27, 1993. Foreign direct investments in the financial and banking sector and those carried out in a free trade zone benefit from the incentives provided for in Law No. 85-108 of December 6, 1985 (on incentives for financial and banking establishments conducting business essentially with nonresidents), and in Law No. 92–81 of August 3, 1992 (on free trade zones), respectively. The investment incentives include tax and financial benefits, as well as facilities, with regard to laws and regulations governing foreign exchange and foreign trade that are essentially oriented toward export promotion.

The acquisition of stock by foreign nonresidents in companies established in Tunisia with foreign exchange transferred from abroad is free; however, in case stock has attached voting rights, the approval by the High Investment Commission is required for acquisitions that result in foreign ownership exceeding 10 percent of capital for shares listed in the stock exchange and 30 percent for unlisted shares.

Foreign nationals who have been residents of Tunisia and who leave the country permanently are entitled to transfer the following: 50 percent of their assets (with a minimum of D 1,750 and a maximum of D 3,500) if they left Tunisia before August 20, 1970; D 4,000 if they left between August 20, 1970 and December 31, 1973; D 5,000 if they left between January 1, 1974 and December 31, 1974; D 10,000 if they left after December 31, 1974; D 15,000 if they left Tunisia after December 31, 1978, are over 60 years of age, and are Tunisian nationals; and an unlimited amount if they are French or Italian nationality regardless of their date of departure from Tunisia.

To support their export activities, resident exporters may, depending on their turnover for the previous financial year, transfer abroad amounts ranging from D 20,000 to D 100,000 a calendar year to cover installation, maintenance, and operating costs of branches and subsidiaries or to finance equity participation, and D 10,000 to D 50,000 to cover installation, maintenance, and operating costs of liaison or representative offices.

Resident financial institutions and other resident enterprises may freely contract foreign currency loans from nonresidents up to an annual limit of D 10 million and D 3 million, respectively.

All other transfers by residents, the contracting of foreign loans by residents, and the extension of loans to nonresidents require approval from the Central

Bank, except for investment loans extended by resident banks for nonresident industrial enterprises with funds held abroad.

Gold

Five denominations of commemorative gold coins are legal tender but do not circulate. Residents may acquire and hold gold in any form in Tunisia. Only dentists, artisan jewelers, and cooperatives formed by artisans are eligible to purchase gold from the Central Bank. The Central Bank has a monopoly over the importation and exportation of monetary gold. Other imports of gold require joint authorization from the Central Bank and the Ministry of Trade. The exportation of gold is prohibited.

Changes During 1995

Imports and Import Payments

January 1. The list of products subject to temporary complementary import duties was modified; duty rates previously introduced were modified or eliminated; a new VAT rate category of 10 percent was introduced; VAT rates on certain products were reduced, suspended, or eliminated (Law No. 94-127).

November 13. The list of products excluded from trade liberalization was modified.

Capital

June 28. Inward portfolio investment was partially liberalized.

TURKEY

(Position as of May 31, 1996)

Exchange Arrangement

The currency of Turkey is the Turkish Lira. Turkey follows a flexible exchange rate policy under which the exchange rate for the Turkish lira is market determined. Commercial banks, special finance institutions, authorized institutions, post, telephone, and telegraphic offices (PTT), and precious metal intermediary institutions are free to set their exchange rates according to prevalent market conditions. The lowest and highest rates applied in these transactions are to be reported daily to the Central Bank of Turkey. On each business day, the Central Bank announces an indicative exchange rate that is determined as the average of the buying and selling rates of the ten banks with the largest involvement in foreign exchange trading. On December 29, 1995, the average buying and selling rates in the interbank market for the U.S. dollar were TL 59,501 and TL 59,800, respectively, per $1.

The commercial banks and precious metal brokerage institutions may engage in forward transactions within the framework of open position limits determined by the Central Bank. Forward exchange rates are freely established between the banks and their customers in accordance with international practices. Banks enter into swap transactions with the Central Bank with terms of quarterly periods up to 12 months. On November 27, 1995, the Central Bank announced the establishment of an interbank forward exchange market that would operate alongside the existing interbank spot market.

Turkey accepted the obligations of Article VIII, Sections 2, 3, and 4 of the Fund Agreement on March 22, 1990.

Administration of Control

Exchange and trade controls are the responsibility of the Prime Ministries, to which the Undersecretariat of the Treasury and the Undersecretariat of Foreign Trade are attached. Administration of exchange controls has been delegated to the Central Bank, which regulates all matters related to foreign exchange operations. All commercial banks have been authorized by the Central Bank. Export registration is carried out by trade organizations, according to instructions from the Central Bank.

In accordance with the Fund's Executive Board Decision No. 144-(52/51) adopted on August 14, 1952, Turkey notified the Fund on September 12, 1990 that certain restrictions were imposed on the making of payments and transfers for current international transactions to the Government of Iraq.

Prescription of Currency

Certain commercial transactions with the Baltic countries, Russia, and the other countries of the former Soviet Union, the Czech Republic, Poland, and the Slovak Republic are made through special accounts denominated in U.S. dollars. Settlements with all other countries may be made in convertible currencies.

Resident and Nonresident Accounts

Residents and nonresidents may open foreign exchange and gold deposit accounts with commercial banks. Balances on these accounts may be used freely.

Persons holding valid Turkish passports and having permission or the right to work or reside abroad may open interest-bearing foreign currency deposit accounts or "super" foreign currency accounts, depending on the amount deposited and the maturity, with the head office of the Central Bank in Ankara. These accounts may be maintained upon the return of these persons to Turkey.

Nonresidents may open accounts denominated in foreign exchange and Turkish liras with authorized commercial banks. The holders may dispose of such accounts at their discretion.

Imports and Import Payments

All goods are freely importable, except for those explicitly prohibited by law, such as narcotics, weapons, foreign coins made of metals other than gold, and ammunition. Imports of these goods are allowed only with a special permit from the authorities. Old, used and reconditioned, defective, substandard, soiled, or poor-quality goods may be imported only with special permission from the Undersecretariat of Foreign Trade. But certain used goods that are not older than five years may be imported freely.

In addition to the membership in the European Free Trade Association (EFTA), Turkey has signed a Customs Union agreement with the European Union (EU). The import regime has been revised in line with the EU legislation. According to the free circulation of goods and customs declaration principles of the EU legislation, import licenses and import document practices have been abolished. Since January 1, 1996, customs duties and a Mass Housing Fund deduction from the importation of industrial products from the EU and the EFTA have been reduced to zero, whereas the above-mentioned ratio has been reduced to approximately 6 percent for other countries parallel with the EU Common Customs Tariff.

Value of importation is paid in Turkish lira or in foreign exchange by banks and special finance institutions in conformity with customary banking and international practices. Import payments can be made through foreign exchange deposit accounts held with banks. Exporters and providers of services are freely allowed to use foreign exchange earned from exports of goods and services for payment of their own imports. Residents, individuals, and corporations with a legal number may import goods freely. Individuals may import goods only for their own needs.

Payments for Invisibles

Residents may freely make payments for invisible transactions relating to all services to nonresidents at home or abroad.

All residents traveling abroad may carry foreign currency notes up to the equivalent of $5,000 a person without proof of exchange allocation by commercial banks, and banks are permitted to sell foreign exchange to residents and nonresidents without restriction. Residents are allowed to use credit cards on a revolving basis up to a limit of $10,000 for travel and expenses abroad; balances exceeding $10,000 must be settled within 30 days. The travel tax was abolished on April 1, 1996.

Travelers are permitted to take out up to the equivalent of $5,000 in foreign currency notes and Turkish lira notes and coins. Nonresidents and Turkish citizens working abroad who are considered residents may take out foreign currency notes exceeding the equivalent of $5,000, provided that they have declared the amount upon their arrival; residents may take out foreign currency notes exceeding the equivalent of $5,000, provided that they produce proof of purchase from banks and special financial institutions within the framework of regulations related to invisible transactions.

Exports and Export Proceeds

Exports are generally free of restrictions. The exportation of the goods that is prohibited by laws, decrees, and international agreements is forbidden.

In addition, exportation of some goods requires permission of authorized institutions. The registration requirement on exportation of goods is only for statistical purposes.

All companies are allowed to conduct barter trade in accordance with established procedures.

Foreign exchange receipts from merchandise exports must be surrendered within 180 days of the date of shipment. If exchange receipts are surrendered within 90 days, exporters are entitled to retain 30 percent of proceeds, which they may deposit in foreign exchange accounts with commercial banks, keep abroad, or dispose of freely. Exporters may retain export proceeds abroad up to $50,000. Commercial banks; special financial institutions; and the PTT are required to sell to the Foreign Currency Notes Market and to the Central Bank 4 percent and 10 percent, respectively, of all foreign exchange they obtain from exports, invisible transactions, and gold accounts within a period agreed with the Central Bank.

A system of export incentives in the form of subsidized credits administered by the Turkish Eximbank is in operation. Under the Foreign Trade Companies Rediscount Credit Program (introduced in January 1990), exporters whose annual export turnover exceeds $50 million are eligible to receive credit either in Turkish liras, with the interest rate related to the government bond yields, or in foreign currency, with the interest rate linked to LIBOR. The Eximbank also maintains a program of preshipment credit designed to meet the financing needs of manufacturers and exporters. The credits under this program are extended for up to 120 days (180 days for small- and medium-sized industries) with fixed interest rates of between 25 percent and 50 percent of the f.o.b. value of the export commitment, depending on the maturity. In addition, the Eximbank provides buyers' credit facilities to support Turkish exports to certain countries, including Albania, Algeria, Bulgaria, the Czech Republic, Hungary, Romania, the Slovak Republic, the Syrian Arab Republic, Tunisia, and some of the countries of the former Soviet Union; it provides insurance against commercial and political risks on commercial terms.

A new export credit program was introduced on January 15, 1996, by the Turkish Eximbank. The credits extended under this program mature to ten years. The importing countries are classified in three groups, and OECD Commercial Interest Reference Rates (CIRR), government bond yields, and SDR basket rates are applied to these loans.

Premiums are paid from the Support and Price Stabilization Fund for selected export products.

Proceeds from Invisibles

Residents may accept foreign currency from non-residents for transactions processed in Turkey. Foreign exchange earned by residents in exchange for services they have rendered to nonresidents or on behalf of them in Turkey or abroad (including contracting services), as well as foreign exchange corresponding to expenses incurred in the name, and on behalf of, nonresidents, may be disposed of freely.

Capital

Nonresident individuals and corporations wishing to invest in Turkey must import the required capital in kind or in the form of foreign exchange and must obtain a license from the Undersecretariat of the Treasury. In establishing partnerships or joint companies in the Turkish private sector, foreign investors must bring in a minimum of $50,000 of capital. Certain investments are allowed under the provisions of the Law for the Encouragement of Foreign Investments or the Petroleum Law. For commercial activities other than forming a company or opening a branch in accordance with the Capital and Petroleum Law, foreign investors must obtain the permission of the Undersecretariat of the Treasury. Profits and dividends and the proceeds from sales and liquidation of foreign capital may be transferred abroad and must be reported to the Central Bank.

Resident individuals or corporations may invest abroad and in the free trade zones in Turkey up to the equivalent of $5 million in cash or in kind. The exportation of capital in amounts exceeding the equivalent of $5 million requires the authorization of the ministry to which the Undersecretariat of the Treasury is attached. Nonresidents may transfer abroad proceeds from sales of real estate without restriction. Purchases and sales by nonresidents (including investments, partnerships, and mutual funds abroad) of all kinds of securities and other capital instruments through the banks and intermediary institutions authorized according to the capital legislation may be made freely. The transfer of the income from such securities and instruments as well as the proceeds from their sale may be effected freely through banks and special finance institutions. Purchases and sales by residents of the securities traded in foreign financial markets are also free, provided that the transactions are carried out by banks, special finance institutions, and intermediary institutions authorized according to the capital market legislation and that the transfer of their purchase value abroad is made through banks and special financial institutions. Residents may also issue, introduce, and sell securities and other capital market instruments in the financial markets abroad. Also the issuance, public introduction, and sales of securities and other capital market instruments in Turkey by nonresidents are unrestricted within the provisions of capital market legislation.

Commercial banks may open foreign exchange accounts and gold deposit accounts for residents or nonresidents. Funds in such accounts may be freely disposed of by the holders, and interest rates and other conditions on the above accounts are freely negotiable between the parties. Commercial banks are free to conduct foreign exchange transactions according to their needs, within the margins of certain ratios set by the Central Bank.

Foreign exchange deposit accounts held at the commercial banks are subject to reserve requirements, as follows. The reserve requirement ratio for demand and time deposit balances with one-month maturity, which was subject to the ratio in effect on March 31, 1994, is 18.5 percent, the ratio for these deposits with maturities of longer than one month is 15.5 percent, and the ratio for the deposit balance exceeding the amount that was subject to the reserve requirement in effect on March 31, 1994 is 13 percent irrespective of their maturities.

Gold

Under a decree issued on December 21, 1994, exports and imports of precious metals, stones, and articles have been liberalized within the framework of the Foreign Trade Regime. However, the import and export of unprocessed gold, while declaration to the customs administrations is required, are not subject to the provisions of the import and export regime and related regulation. Unprocessed gold may be imported by the Central Bank and by precious metals intermediary institutions who are members of the Precious Metals Exchange. However, the unprocessed gold imported by precious metals intermediary institutions who are members of the Precious Metals Exchange must be surrendered to the Istanbul Gold Exchange within three days.

The transaction regarding the purchase and sale in Turkey of unprocessed gold imported by the Central Bank and by precious metals intermediary institutions can only be conducted at the Istanbul Gold Exchange.

The Istanbul Gold Exchange began its operations on July 26, 1995.

Banks may open gold deposit accounts in the name of legal and real entities residing in Turkey and abroad. The account holders may freely use balances on their accounts.

Within the framework of the banking regulations, banks may extend gold credits to juridical and natural persons involved in the jewelry business, upon the physical delivery of the gold purchased by their institutions, and against the gold held in the gold deposit accounts.

The buying and selling prices of gold are freely determined by banks.

The purchase and sale of precious metals, stones, and articles are free within the country.

Passengers may bring into and take out of the country articles and made from precious metals and stones carrying the characteristics of ornamental articles that are not used for commercial purposes and of which the value does not exceed $15,000. The taking out of ornamental articles exceeding the said value is dependent on their declaration upon arrival or authenticating that they have been purchased in Turkey.

Changes During 1995

Exchange Arrangement

March 13. The Central Bank revised the implementation of surrender requirements, according to which the daily foreign exchange rates subject to these requirements would no longer be used as a means of monetary policy, but instead will be determined according to market conditions, that is, the upper and lower limits of the foreign exchange rates would remain in a band reflecting market fluctuations.

Resident and Nonresident Accounts

January 27. Communiqué No. 95-32/13 authorizing banks to open gold deposit accounts and credits became effective. Under the communiqué, banks would be authorized to open gold deposit accounts in the name of residents and nonresidents and to extend gold credits to natural and juridical persons and/or persons engaged in the dealing of jewelry in accordance with the principles of banking legislation.

September 12. Turkish nationals working or residing abroad would be permitted to open interest-bearing foreign currency accounts, or "super" foreign currency accounts depending on the amount deposited. Withdrawal before the due date would be allowed, provided that the minimum balance is maintained. The interest rates applicable to the accounts denominated in deutsche mark and Swiss francs were reduced from 7.5 percent and 4 percent to 3.5 percent, respectively.

Exports and Export Proceeds

September 7 and November 19. The rate of surrender of foreign exchange receipts to the Central Bank by commercial banks and special financial institutions, the PTT, and precious metal intermediary institutions was reduced to 20 percent, 18 percent, and 16 percent, respectively (they are planned to be reduced to 14 percent on June 1, 1996).

December 31. The maximum amount of export proceeds not subject to the repatriation requirement was increased from $10,000 to $50,000 for each shipment.

Capital

January 27. The Central Bank modified the regulation on reserve requirements. By accepting the amount of foreign exchange deposit accounts subject to the reserve requirement schedule as of March 31, 1994, the reserve requirements for demand and time deposits with one-month maturity would be 18.5 percent and 15.5, respectively, percent for maturities longer than one month. For the balances exceeding the amount that was subject to the reserve requirement in effect on March 31, 1994, the ratio would be 13 percent, irrespective of their maturities.

February 9. A communiqué was published by the Treasury with the purpose of maintaining banks' capital increases and equity capital at a specific level to meet risks and to reduce risks arising from insufficient capital by taking into consideration the "capital-base/risk-weighted assets, in-kind credits and liabilities" standard ratio. This would be a ratio formulated between banks' equity capital and assets and in-kind credits and liabilities. With another circular published on the same date, banks were subjected to a ceiling on the credits opened for the companies in which they have shares so as to limit the risks arising from capital inadequacy.

March 1. A communiqué regarding the standard ratio of foreign exchange net general position or capital base became effective. The communiqué would require authorized banks to preserve a maximum ratio of 50 percent of their net general position to their capital base.

March 1. Banks authorized to deal in foreign exchange were required to apply a maximum ratio of 50 percent of their net general position to their capital base.

March 11. The definition of foreign currency holdings, claims, and debts that are to be taken into account in calculating the foreign currency liquidity ratio and foreign exchange position ratio was modified also to include gold holdings and liabilities relating to gold transactions.

March 11. The Central Bank issued a circular redefining holdings, claims, and debts that would be taken into account in calculating the foreign currency liquidity ratio and foreign exchange position ratio. Calculation of the liquidity ratio and the foreign exchange ratio would henceforth include gold holdings and liabilities.

May 2. The Foreign Investment Law No. 6224 was amended, according to which foreign investors would not be allowed to own the majority of the shares of establishments operating as monopolies throughout Turkey.

Changes During 1996

Imports and Import Payments

January 1. The rate of Resource Utilization Support Fund applied to credits obtained by banks from abroad was reduced from 6 percent to 4 percent, and the rate applied to imports with credits was reduced from 6 percent to zero percent.

Payments for Invisibles

April 1. The tax on Turkish citizens traveling abroad was abolished.

Capital

January 2. The restriction on the maturity period with respect to government papers denominated in foreign exchange or indexed to foreign exchange that are used to meet the liquidity requirement was abolished.

January 15. A new export credit program was introduced by the Turkish Eximbank. The credits extended under this program would mature to ten years. The importing countries are classified in three groups, and OECD CIRR, government bond yields, and SDR basket rates would be applied to these loans.

Premiums would be paid from the Support and Price Stabilization Fund for selected export products.

Gold

July 26. The Istanbul Gold Exchange began to operate.

TURKMENISTAN

(Position as of April 30, 1996)

Exchange Arrangement

The currency of Turkmenistan is the Manat. The interbank rate is determined by demand and supply, and the official rate is adjusted once a month to reflect the interbank rate. On December 31, 1995, the official exchange rate for the U.S. dollar was manat 200 per $1 and the interbank rate was manat 2,400 per $1. Exchange rates for other currencies are determined on the basis of the cross rates of the U.S. dollar against the currencies concerned in the international market. Authorized banks may charge commissions on exchange transactions not exceeding 5 percent.

Administration of Control

Under existing laws, only the Central Bank of Turkmenistan, alone or together with the Ministry of Economy and Finance and the Tax Authority depending on the type of operation involved, is empowered to issue exchange control regulations.

The Foreign Exchange Regulation Law, which came into effect November 1, 1993, provides for freedom to make payments and transfers for current international transactions and for nonresidents to export previously imported capital. However, this freedom is not granted at present. This law gives the Government the right to acquire foreign exchange according to the exchange arrangements established by the Central Bank. The use of foreign exchange reserves is, to a large extent, controlled by the President of Turkmenistan; since January 1, 1996, a special Presidential Foreign Exchange Committee has had the power to restrict access to foreign exchange auctions. Foreign exchange transactions of individuals must be made through the authorized banks, who may not themselves retain foreign exchange balances. All other transactions take place through the Central Bank.

Arrears are maintained with respect to external payments.

Prescription of Currency

Settlement with some Baltic countries, Russia, and other countries of the former Soviet Union are made through a system of correspondent accounts. Settlements with countries with which Turkmenistan has bilateral payments agreements are effected in accordance with the procedures set forth in these agreements.[1] Transactions with other countries are made in convertible currencies. Barter transactions must take place through the state commodity exchange.

Foreign Exchange Accounts

Authorized banks that have received a general license from the Central Bank to deal in foreign exchange may open foreign exchange accounts for natural and juridical persons if they possess a certificate of registration issued by the Ministry of Foreign Economic Relations. All external payments orders using balances on these accounts must be approved by the Central Bank, but cash withdrawals from these accounts in foreign currency do not require central bank approval. Interest is payable on balances in these accounts in the currency of the account at a rate to be determined by the authorized bank.

Imports and Exports

Trade with some countries is conducted under trade agreements. All goods may be imported and exported without restriction except for those on the negative list. In addition to certain items (such as arms and narcotics, and antiquities) whose trade is prohibited for national security reasons, quantitative and price restrictions are imposed on exports of cotton and other raw materials to protect domestic supplies.

There is a 50 percent surrender requirement on export receipts (20 percent is surrendered to the Central Bank for use in the auctions and 30 percent to the Foreign Exchange Reserve Fund at the official exchange rate); cotton receipts are exempt, and gas receipts are subject to a 70 percent requirement, which is split between the Central Bank (30 percent) and the Foreign Exchange Reserve Fund (40 percent). The retained earnings may be sold to the banks at the market exchange rate.

Payments for and Proceeds from Invisibles

Residents must possess valid passports to purchase foreign exchange for travel abroad. The maximum amount of foreign exchange a person may purchase from authorized banks without approval

---

[1]Turkmenistan has intergovernmental bilateral agreements with Armenia, Azerbaijan, Georgia, and Ukraine, and a trilateral agreement with Armenia and Iran.

from the Central Bank is $1,000; there is no limit on the number of times an individual may purchase foreign exchange during any given day. All other payments for invisibles require approval from the Central Bank.

Proceeds from invisibles not allowed to be retained must be sold to a commercial bank.

Capital

Both inward and outward capital transfers are subject to the approval of the Central Bank. The Law on Foreign Investments in Turkmenistan permits, in principle, foreign direct investments by juridical persons with foreign participation in all sectors. Investors are required to obtain authorization from the Ministry of Foreign Economic Relations.[2] Foreign investments are protected from nationalization. The law provides that, at the request of investors, the law in force at the time of registration will be applied for a period of ten years. After required tax payments have been made, profits may be reinvested in Turkmenistan, held in bank accounts in national or other currencies, or transferred abroad.

Gold

A license is required to engage in international trade in gold. Laws regulating trade in gold are in effect.

Changes During 1995

Exchange Arrangement

February 21. The exchange rate of manat 10 per $1 for gas exports was eliminated.

June 1. Transactions through commercial banks were restricted to individuals; all other transactions were required to take place through the Central Bank. A limit of 5 percent was placed on commercial banks' commissions on foreign transactions.

September 19. The official exchange rate was devalued to manat 200 per $1 from manat 75 per $1, and the commercial (cash) exchange rate was devalued to manat 500 per $1 from manat 200 per $1.

November 27. Commercial banks were allowed to buy and sell foreign exchange at market-determined exchange rates, based on supply and demand conditions, and the commercial rate of manat 500 per $1 was abolished. The limit for each transaction was established at $1,000, but there is no limit on the

number of times an individual or an enterprise might conduct transactions in any given day. The buying of foreign exchange from customers would not require documents stating the source of income. Customers were to be given a certificate during the sale or purchase of foreign exchange, and the customer must produce his or her passport or another identification. The maximum commission allowed to be charged during the sale or purchase of foreign exchange was set at 5 percent.

Payments for and Proceeds from Invisibles

June 1. The maximum amount of foreign exchange that a person may purchase from the authorized banks without approval from the Central Bank was reduced to manat 200 from manat 500 for most purposes other than business travel, for which the allowance remained unchanged.

July 26. Provision of foreign exchange without approval by the Central Bank was withdrawn for tourist travel.

Changes During 1996

Exchange Arrangement

January 1. The official exchange rate was unified at the level of the exchange rate determined by banks.

February 1. The official rate was adjusted to market developments.

February 26. A formal multiple exchange rate system was reintroduced when the official rate was substantially revalued.

April 10. The official rate was again set at the market rate and the authorities announced that henceforth the official rate would be adjusted to the market rate that results from foreign exchange auctions held twice a month.

Imports and Exports

January 1. The surrender requirements were modified whereby 20 percent of proceeds were required to be surrendered to the Central Bank for use in foreign exchange auctions and 30 percent to the Foreign Exchange Reserve Fund at the unified exchange rate, compared to the earlier arrangement of 50 percent surrender to the Foreign Exchange Reserve Fund at the official exchange rate. For oil and gas exports, the surrender requirement was raised to 70 percent from 60 percent, split between the Central Bank (30 percent) and the Foreign Exchange Reserve Fund (40 percent).

---

[2]If the amount of investment is more than $500,000, the approval of the Cabinet of Ministers of Turkmenistan is required.

UGANDA

(Position as of December 31, 1995)

Exchange Arrangement

The currency of Uganda is the Uganda Shilling, the external value of which is determined in the interbank foreign exchange market. Certain transactions may be effected in foreign exchange bureaus that are licensed to buy and sell foreign exchange at freely negotiated rates. On December 31, 1995, the buying and selling rates in the interbank foreign exchange market were U Sh 1,003 and U Sh 1,016, respectively, per $1.

Authorized banks may deal forward with customers in pounds sterling, U.S. dollars, and certain other convertible currencies, provided that there is an underlying approved import or export contract. Authorized foreign exchange dealers may impose a service charge of not more than 1 percent.

There are no taxes or subsidies on purchases or sales of foreign exchange. There are no arrangements for forward cover against exchange rate risk operating in the official sector.

Uganda accepted the obligations of Article VIII, Sections 2, 3, and 4 of the Fund Agreement on April 5, 1994.

Administration of Control

The Bank of Uganda administers exchange controls on behalf of the Minister of Finance but has delegated a broad range of exchange control responsibilities to authorized banks and exchange bureaus. Import and export control regulations are administered by the Ministry of Commerce, which has powers to prohibit imports and exports.

Prescription of Currency

The Bank of Uganda settles accounts in U.S. dollars with the member countries of the Common Market of Eastern and Southern Africa (COMESA) for Eastern and Southern African States through the COMESA clearinghouse. Authorized payments, including payments for imports by residents of Uganda to residents of foreign countries, may be made in Uganda shillings to the credit of an external account in Uganda or in any other currency that is appropriate to the country of residence of the payee. Uganda maintains bilateral clearing arrangements with Burundi, Rwanda, and Zaïre, but these are inoperative. Inoperative bilateral trade and payments agreements are also maintained with Algeria, Cuba, Egypt, the Democratic People's Republic of Korea, and the Libyan Arab Jamahiriya.

External Accounts

Accounts in foreign exchange held by persons with diplomatic status are designated external accounts. They may be credited with authorized payments by residents of Uganda and with transfers from other external accounts or any other external source. They may be debited freely for payments to nonresidents, for transfers to other external accounts in Uganda, and for purchases of foreign currencies from authorized dealers.

Convertible Currency Accounts

Private Ugandan residents who are exporters of goods who are earning commissions, consulting fees, rent, and other incomes in foreign exchange may operate foreign exchange accounts with commercial banks in Uganda. Payments made from these accounts are subject to the same regulations as those governing sales of foreign exchange in the foreign exchange bureaus.

Imports and Import Payments

Most imports are controlled through the import-licensing system. Foreign exchange sales to various ministries and departments must be backed by documents showing the approval of the Central Tender Board.

Importers are provided with a renewable certificate, which is valid for six months and which permits them to import a broad range of goods not on the negative list. The certificate does not prescribe the importation of a specific good. The importation of pornographic materials, beer, and soft drinks is prohibited. Imports of firearms and ammunition require special permission. Private sector importers may purchase foreign exchange in the interbank market or in foreign exchange bureaus to pay for imports without restriction.

Payments for Invisibles

All payments for invisibles, except for debt-service payments, are financed through the interbank foreign exchange market. With the permission of the Director of Exchange Control of the Bank of Uganda, residents of Uganda may transfer abroad profits, fees, and savings. The following limits apply to foreign exchange that may be purchased in the interbank market or in the foreign exchange bureaus without referring to the Bank of Uganda: (1) travel, $4,000 a trip; (2) medical treatment, $20,000 a person to be transferred through a bank with supporting documents; and (3) education, $25,000 a person a year.

Dividends may be transferred through the interbank market without restriction and without reference to the Bank of Uganda.

Payments by the private nonbank sector for all other invisible transactions and for certain capital transfers are subject to a combined limit (see section on Capital, below).

Exports and Export Proceeds

All exports require certificates from the Ministry of Commerce and Trade, which are valid for six months and are renewable; they may be restricted to ensure sufficient supplies for consumption in Uganda. Exporters may retain proceeds from exports and sell them in the interbank foreign exchange market.

Proceeds from Invisibles

Proceeds from invisibles may be sold in the foreign exchange interbank market. Travelers may freely bring in foreign currency banknotes and traveler's checks.

Capital

Capital transfers to all countries require individual exchange control approval.

Principal payments on nonguaranteed overseas loans by resident companies or individuals are transferable. There are no restrictions on nonguaranteed overseas loans by resident companies or individuals. Foreign investment in Uganda is permitted with or without government participation. To secure a guarantee of repatriation, it is necessary to obtain "approved status" for the investment in terms of the Investment Code of 1991. In normal circumstances, approved status is given freely.

All imports and exports of securities require approval. Approval is freely granted for the purchase by nonresidents of Ugandan securities, provided that payment is received in an appropriate manner. The income from such securities is remittable, as are the proceeds on resale in most cases.

Gold

Residents may hold and acquire gold coins in Uganda for numismatic purposes. Only monetary authorities and licensed dealers are allowed to hold or acquire gold in Uganda in any form other than jewelry. Imports and exports of gold in any form other than jewelry constituting the personal effects of a traveler require licenses issued by the Ministry of Mines.

Changes During 1995

No significant changes occurred in the exchange and trade system.

UKRAINE

(Position as of December 31, 1995)

Exchange Arrangement

The currency of the Republic of Ukraine is the Ukrainian Karbovanets. The official exchange rates of the karbovanets against the U.S. dollar, the deutsche mark, the Russian ruble, the Belarussian rubel, and on occasion other major currencies are determined through competitive bidding of commercial banks at daily auctions conducted by the National Bank of Ukraine.[1] The official rates for all other convertible currencies, when not auctioned, are determined daily on the basis of the cross rates of the U.S. dollar for the currencies concerned in the international market. The official rate applies to all external transactions. The National Bank is frequently a major supplier of the U.S. dollar in the auctions, using the funds that it has previously purchased from exporters at earlier auctions. The National Bank may also participate in the auctions to replenish its reserves, depending on supply and demand conditions in the exchange market. Commercial banks may participate in the auctions without limitation provided they hold contracts for import payments; they may not participate in the auction on their own behalf. However, since March 1995, legal restrictions prohibiting interbank transactions in deutsche mark, Russian rubles, and U.S. dollars were removed. Interbank transactions are now permitted to take place within a ±5 percent spread (including fees, charges, and commissions) of the auction exchange rate and, by the end of 1995, the volume of currency trading on the interbank market had grown to exceed that in the exchange auctions. The exchange rate for cash transactions for individuals at commercial banks is freely determined and quoted on a daily basis by commercial banks; the spread between the selling and buying rates for such transactions, however, must not exceed 2.5 percent. On December 29, 1995, the official rate for the U.S. dollar was Krb 179,400 per $1.

There are no taxes or subsidies on purchases or sales of foreign exchange. There are no arrangements for forward cover against exchange rate risk

operating in the official or the commercial banking sector.

Administration of Control

Exchange control is administered by the National Bank. Commercial banks must be licensed by the National Bank to engage in foreign exchange transactions.

Arrears are maintained with respect to external payments.

Restrictions on payments and the provision of financial services to the Federal Republic of Yugoslavia (Serbia/Montenegro) were lifted in November 1995.

Prescription of Currency

Settlements with the Baltic countries, Russia, and the other countries of the former Soviet Union are made through a system of correspondent accounts. Payments to and receipts from countries with which Ukraine has bilateral payments agreements are made in the currencies and in accordance with the procedures set forth in those agreements. At the end of 1995, Ukraine maintained bilateral trade (and in some cases, payments) agreements with Bulgaria, China, Hungary, India, the Islamic Republic of Iran, and Mongolia. Trade with all other countries is settled in convertible currencies. Nonbarter trade with the Baltic countries, Russia, and the other countries of the former Soviet Union is now settled mainly in convertible currencies, especially the U.S. dollar. Some trade is also conducted on a barter basis.

Resident and Nonresident Accounts

Residents and nonresidents may open and operate foreign currency deposits under certain conditions. The opening and operation of accounts in domestic currency by nonresidents is restricted.

Imports and Exports

Licenses issued by the Ministry of Foreign Economic Relations are required for import transactions.[2] There are no quantitative restrictions on imports; nontariff barriers were limited to the standard rules that imported goods must meet national

---

[1]Auctions for U.S. dollars and Russian rubles are held daily, and those for other currencies, less frequently; for example, deutsche mark are auctioned twice a week. The National Bank has also begun auctioning French francs and pounds sterling once a week. Additional foreign exchange auction centers have also been opened; previously, auctions were held only in Kiev.

[2]A license fee of 0.1 percent of the total amount exported or imported is levied on all importers.

safety and environmental standards. The customs tariff regime contains three categories of duty rates, with the average tariff rate, on a trade-weighted basis, being about 5 percent. The first category (preferred duty rates) applies to goods entering from countries that belong, with Ukraine, to customs unions; those imported from developing countries (agricultural and industrial goods); and those imported under intergovernmental preferential agreements. The rate of duty for these goods, except for tobacco and alcohol products, is zero. The second category (concessional duty rates) applies to goods imported from countries that have entered into a most-favored-nation arrangement with Ukraine and to goods imported from developing countries that are not covered under the first category. The average rate in this category is 6 percent. The third category applies to goods imported from all other countries; the average rate in this category is 12 percent. An import duty, equivalent to approximately 15 percent on an ad valorem basis, is imposed on imports of coal and refined oil products. A value-added tax at the rate of 28 percent is levied on all imported goods.

Most goods are exported freely. Exports of grain, ferrous and nonferrous scrap, cast iron, and coal are subject to voluntary export restraint under international agreements. The system of state contracts and orders for contracts has been abolished, and it exists only for fulfilling intergovernmental barter agreements for gas imports. Exports of grain must be undertaken through the agricultural commodity exchange.[3] Certain goods falling under the "special export regime" are subject to quotas and licenses.[4] A system of "export contract preregistration" is limited to goods subject to, or potentially subject to, voluntary export restraints or antidumping actions. A system of "minimum indicative prices" for a wide range of export products, covering as much as one-half of all Ukraine exports, is in operation to allay antidumping actions abroad. The prices, published monthly, are intended to provide information to Ukrainian exporters, but in the past, they have reportedly been interpreted frequently as mandatory minimum export prices by customs officials.

Firms must repatriate all of their foreign exchange proceeds from exports to domestic commercial bank accounts within 30 days of shipment, and sell, within 5 days of repatriation, 50 percent of the for-

eign currency export proceeds. Foreign exchange proceeds from exports by foreign firms are exempt from the surrender requirements. Forty percent of foreign exchange proceeds must be sold at the auctions, and the remaining 10 percent must be sold to the National Bank at the official exchange rate.

Payments for and Proceeds from Invisibles

Exporters of services, such as the tourist industry, are also subject to the surrender requirement. Exemptions from these repatriation and surrender requirements are limited to the following: (1) a few enterprises engaging in international operations, such as the international airline company, are not required to repatriate their foreign exchange earnings; (2) individuals who provide services to nonresidents are not required to hold foreign exchange earnings in domestic foreign currency accounts or surrender them to the Government or the National Bank; (3) exporters who need to service external debt obligations that have been approved by the National Bank, if the maturity exceeds 90 days, may retain foreign exchange needed for external debt-service obligations before surrendering proceeds; and (4) intermediary firms in the foreign trade sector are required to surrender 50 percent of their profits in foreign exchange rather than 50 percent of revenues in foreign exchange.

Residents are permitted to purchase foreign exchange of up to $400 a trip for tourist travel abroad.[5] Foreign exchange for the purpose of medical treatment is made available only if the medical treatment is considered urgent.

Residents may export foreign banknotes up to $400; and with the permission of authorized banks, they may export up to $2,000, and up to $10,000 with the permission of the National Bank.

The Law on Foreign Investment guarantees that foreign investors may, after paying taxes and fees, transfer abroad without restriction dividends, profits, and other foreign exchange assets obtained legally in connection with their investments.

Capital

The contracting of external loans with maturities exceeding 90 days must be approved by the National Bank. The National Bank does not guarantee any loan. Lending to foreign borrowers also requires permission from the National Bank.

---

[3]Access to the commodity exchange, however, is restricted to those farmers who have fulfilled their obligations under the prepaid portion of the state contract.

[4]The licenses required for coal, scrap of precious metals, and alcoholic spirits are, however, freely provided to exporters, except in the case of precious metals.

[5]Where Ukrainian residents hold deposits in foreign currencies, they may, subject to some limitations, use such deposits to pay for tourist travel abroad in addition to the $400 limit.

Foreign investments in Ukraine are governed by the Law on Foreign Economic Activity of April 16, 1991; the Law on Income Tax for Companies and Organizations of February 21, 1992; the Law on Foreign Investment of March 3, 1992; and the Cabinet of Ministers Decree on Foreign Investment Regimes of May 20, 1993.[6] Foreign investments in most types of business are permitted, although licenses are required in some cases. A license from the Ministry of Finance is required for investments in insurance and businesses engaged in intermediation activities. A license from the National Bank is required for investments in the banking sector. In addition, concessions from the Council of Ministers are required for investments in the mining sector; such concessions may be for a maximum of 49 years. Foreign investment in Ukraine must be made in convertible currency or in kind. The Russian ruble is not regarded as convertible currency for this purpose.

Tax relief is granted to enterprises established with foreign capital investments. The nature of the relief depends on the activity of the enterprise or organization, its turnover, and the proportion of foreign equity capital ownership. The basic profit tax rate is 18 percent, although special tax rates apply in certain sectors. For joint ventures whose foreign equity capital ownership is less than 20 percent, the basic tax rate is also 18 percent. Firms other than those engaged in trading and intermediating activities are exempt from the profit tax for five years from the first year in which profit is recorded; thereafter, the profit tax rate is reduced by 50 percent from the rates applicable to domestic enterprises. Moreover, they are granted a further five-year tax exemption from any new taxes imposed in the future. Trading firms are exempt from the profit tax for the first three years, and intermediating firms for the first two years, from the first year in which profit is recorded; thereafter, the profit tax rate is reduced by 30 percent from the applicable tax rate. In cases where the foreign equity capital ownership is 100 percent, taxable profits may be reduced by the amount of capital

actually invested in Ukraine; additional relief may be granted for investments in priority sectors or in special economic zones.

Gold

The National Bank grants permission to commercial banks to export and import gold and other monetary metals. Other residents are required to obtain a license from the Ministry of Finance to deal in precious metals and stones. Permission to export precious metals and precious stones is granted by the Cabinet of Ministers of Ukraine.

Changes During 1995

Exchange Arrangement

March 20. Legal restrictions prohibiting interbank transactions in deutsche mark were eliminated.

March 30. Legal restrictions prohibiting interbank transactions in U.S. dollars and in Russian rubles were eliminated.

March 30. Interbank transactions were permitted to take place within a spread of ±5 percent (including fees, charges, and commissions) of the auction exchange rate. In addition, the frequency of foreign exchange auctions was increased to three times a week from two.

March 30. The frequency of foreign exchange auctions was increased to daily auctions and additional foreign exchange auction centers outside Kiev were opened.

Administration of Control

November 22. Restrictions on payments and the provision of financial services to the Federal Republic of Yugoslavia (Serbia/Montenegro) were lifted.

Imports and Exports

January 1. Import duties equivalent to about 15 percent on an ad valorem basis were imposed on coal and refined oil products.

January 1. Export quotas were abolished, except for grain and goods subject to voluntary export restraint or other international agreements.

September 5. The export quota on grain was abolished.

---

[6]The State Program for Attraction of Foreign Investment of December 17, 1993, came into force on March 1, 1994. The program provides foreign investors with investment incentives on tax, insurance, credit, and depreciation for 32 branches of the Ukrainian economy.

UNITED ARAB EMIRATES[1]

(Position as of December 31, 1995)

Exchange Arrangement

The currency of the United Arab Emirates is the U.A.E. Dirham, which is pegged to the SDR at Dh 4.76190 per SDR 1. The United Arab Emirates has established margins of 7.25 percent around the official rate. Since November 1980, the U.A.E. dirham has maintained an unchanged relationship with the U.S. dollar, which is the intervention currency. The United Arab Emirates Central Bank publishes buying and selling rates for the U.S. dollar only. On December 31, 1995, the official buying and selling rates were Dh 3.673 and Dh 3.669, respectively, per $1. The Central Bank sets no limits on the amount of U.S. dollars that it is prepared to buy from or sell to any commercial bank. Commercial banks are free to enter into foreign exchange transactions, including forward contracts related to commercial and financial transactions, at rates of their own choosing; the rates quoted by commercial banks for currencies other than the U.S. dollar are determined on the basis of international quotations.

The Central Bank maintains a swap facility, which the commercial banks may use to purchase dirhams spot and sell dirhams forward for periods of one week, one month, and three months. For each bank, maximum limits of $20 million outstanding for one-month and three-month swaps and $10 million outstanding for one-week swaps are in effect. There is also a limit of $3 million a day on purchases by each bank for one-month and three-month swaps. Swap facilities are not available to banks having a short position in dirhams, except for the covering of forward transactions for commercial purposes. There are no taxes or subsidies on purchases or sales of foreign exchange.

The United Arab Emirates accepted the obligations of Article VIII, Sections 2, 3, and 4 of the Fund Agreement on February 13, 1974.

Administration of Control

There is neither exchange control legislation nor an exchange control authority in the United Arab Emirates, and there are no registration requirements for inward or outward transfers. There is no regime of export and import licensing.

Prescription of Currency

All settlements with Israel are prohibited. No other prescription of currency requirements are in force.

Nonresident Accounts

Distinction is drawn between accounts held by residents and those held by nonresidents. Nonresident accounts consist of those held with commercial banks on behalf of U.A.E. citizens working abroad; all foreigners working in the United Arab Emirates but who do not have residency; all embassies and diplomatic agencies in the country; all trade and financial companies, banks, and industrial companies incorporated outside the United Arab Emirates that have no local branches; and branches of local institutions in foreign countries.

Imports and Import Payments

In February 1995, the World Trade Organization accepted the United Arab Emirates as a member. The United Arab Emirates joined the General Agreements on Tariffs and Trade (GATT) in March 1994.

Imports from Israel are prohibited, as are imports of products manufactured by foreign companies blacklisted by the Arab League. Imports of a few commodities are prohibited from all sources for health or security reasons, but virtually all other commodities may be freely imported without an individual import permit. However, only licensed parties can enter the import trade, and importers may import only the commodities specified in their license. There are no restrictions on the availability of foreign exchange for payments in respect of permitted imports. With the exception of specified items, imports into the United Arab Emirates are subject to a customs duty of 4 percent of the c.i.f. value. Imports originating from member countries of the Cooperation Council for the Arab States of the Gulf (GCC) are not subject to customs duty.

Exports and Export Proceeds

Exports and re-exports to Israel are prohibited. Virtually all commodities may be exported or re-exported freely and without an export license to any other destination.

Each Emirate establishes its own export regulations. The proceeds from exports need not be repa-

---

[1]The seven federated states of the United Arab Emirates are Abu Dhabi, Dubai, Sharjah, Ajman, Umm al Qaiwain, Ras al Khaimah, and Fujairah.

triated or surrendered and may be disposed of freely, regardless of the currency involved.

Payments for and Proceeds from Invisibles

All payments for current invisibles may be made freely, with the exception of payments to Israel, which are prohibited. There are no requirements governing receipts. Travelers may take out and bring in any amount in foreign or domestic banknotes.

Capital

No exchange control requirements are imposed on capital receipts or payments by residents or nonresidents. Commercial banks operating in the United Arab Emirates are prohibited from engaging in nonbanking operations (as specified in Article 90 of the Central Bank Act of 1980) and from owning real estate except for the purpose of carrying on business and for accommodation. Under the United Arab Emirates Company Law (Law No. 8 of 1984), at least 51 percent of the equity of companies, other than branches of foreign companies, must be held by nationals of the United Arab Emirates. Nationals of the other member countries of the GCC are permitted to hold (1) up to 75 percent of the equity of companies in the industrial, agricultural, fisheries, and construction sectors, and in the consultancy areas

(Law No. 2 of 1984); and (2) up to 100 percent of the equity of companies in the hotel industry. Furthermore, nationals of the other member countries of the GCC are permitted to engage in wholesale and retail trade activities, except in the form of companies, in which case they are subject to the Company Law of 1984. Profits on foreign capital invested in the United Arab Emirates may be remitted freely. Banks operating in the United Arab Emirates are required to maintain special deposits with the Central Bank equal to 30 percent of their placements with, or lending to, nonresident banks in dirhams with a remaining life of one year or less. The profits of certain banks are subject to a fee levied by local authorities at an annual rate of 20 percent.

Gold

Residents and nonresidents may freely purchase, hold, and sell gold in any form, at home or abroad. They may also, without a permit, import and export gold in any form, but only licensed parties may import gold for trade purposes. Gold bullion is exempt from import duty, but jewelry is not.

Changes During 1995

No significant changes occurred in the exchange and trade system.

UNITED KINGDOM

(Position as of December 31, 1995)

Exchange Arrangement

The currency of the United Kingdom is the Pound Sterling. The U.K. authorities do not maintain margins in respect of exchange transactions, and spot and forward exchange rates are determined on the basis of demand and supply in the exchange markets. However, the authorities may intervene at their discretion to moderate undue fluctuations in the exchange rate.[1] On December 31, 1995, the closing buying and selling rates for the pound sterling against the U.S. dollar in foreign exchange markets in London as observed by the Bank of England were $1.5500 and $1.5510, respectively, per £1. Banks are allowed to engage in spot and forward exchange transactions in any currency, and they may deal among themselves and with residents and nonresidents in foreign notes and coins at free market exchange rates.

The United Kingdom accepted the obligations of Article VIII, Sections 2, 3, and 4 of the Fund Agreement on February 15, 1961.

Administration of Control

There are no exchange controls. The licensing of imports and exports is handled mostly by the Department of Trade and Industry, but other departments also issue licenses in specialized fields.

In accordance with the Fund's Executive Board Decision No. 144-(52/51) adopted on August 14, 1952, the United Kingdom notified the IMF on July 26, 1992 that, in compliance with UN Security Council Resolution No. 757 (1992), certain restrictions had been imposed on the making of payments and transfers for current international transactions in respect of the Federal Republic of Yugoslavia (Serbia/Montenegro). These sanctions were suspended on November 22, 1995, pursuant to UN Security Council Resolution No. 1022.

The United Kingdom also notified the IMF on September 22, 1994 that, in compliance with UN Security Council Resolution Nos. 883 and 841 (1993), certain restrictions had been imposed on the making of payments and transfers for current international transactions in respect of the Libyan Arab Jamahiriya and Haiti. Sanctions against the latter were lifted on October 16, 1994, in accordance with UN Security Council Resolution No. 944. Restrictions against Iraq, as reported to the IMF on August 13, 1990, continue to be enforced. Since the passing of UN Security Council Resolution No. 942 in October 1994, there have been sanctions against the Federal Republic of Yugoslavia (Serbia/Montenegro) and areas of Bosnia and Herzegovina.

Prescription of Currency

There are no prescription of currency requirements.

Imports and Import Payments

Most imports are admitted to the United Kingdom under an open general import license. The remaining restrictions concern textiles and clothing under the Multifiber Arrangement (MFA) or other European Union (EU) bilateral agreements, certain steel products from Russia and Ukraine that are subject to EU-wide voluntary restraint agreements, autonomous EU-wide restrictions on certain steel products from Kazakstan, and EU-wide quotas on seven categories of goods originating in China. Imports of cars from Japan are also subject to restraint under a separate agreement (The Elements of Consensus) between the EU and the Japanese Government. Imports of cereals and cereal products, beef and veal, mutton and lamb, poultry meat, and dairy products, other than butter and cheese, are subject to minimum import prices enforced through autonomously imposed variable import levies. Imports of many other agricultural, horticultural, and livestock products are subject to EU regulations. A few articles may be imported under open individual licenses, that is, without limit as to quantity or value.

Exports and Export Proceeds

Most exports are free of export control, and there are no requirements affecting export proceeds.[2] Under the Tender to Contract Facility of the Export Credits Guarantee Department, exporters bidding for major capital projects in Canadian dollars, deutsche mark, Japanese yen, Swiss francs, or U.S. dollars, when the U.K. element of the contract is for the

---

[1]The United Kingdom suspended intervention obligations with respect to the exchange rate and intervention mechanism of the European monetary system (EMS) on September 16, 1992.

[2]Exports of certain products are controlled for reasons of national security, animal welfare, national heritage, and in accordance with international agreements.

equivalent of at least £10 million, may obtain cover against exchange rate fluctuations between the submission of their bid and the awarding of the contract.

Payments for and Proceeds from Invisibles

There are no restrictions on payments for and proceeds from invisibles. Travelers may import or export any amount of domestic and foreign banknotes or any other means of payment.

Capital

There are no restrictions or exchange control requirements on capital transfers by residents or nonresidents. Residents and nonresidents may freely transfer assets to and from the United Kingdom.

Investments, whether direct or portfolio, may be freely made by nonresidents in the United Kingdom or by residents abroad. Investments involving the takeover of existing U.K. companies may be subject to merger control under the Fair Trading Act of 1973. It is for the Secretary of State to decide whether or not qualifying merges should be referred to the Monopolies and Mergers Commission (MMC) for further investigation. U.K. and foreign mergers are treated the same under U.K. merger control procedures. Decisions about whether or not to refer mergers for further investigation are made primarily where there are competition concerns. If the MMC finds that the merger operates against the public interest, the Secretary of State may prohibit the merger or impose conditions. The Secretary of State Department of Trade and Industry also has the power, under the Industry Act of 1975, to prohibit a proposed transfer of an important U.K. manufacturing undertaking to a nonresident when the transfer is considered to be contrary to the interests of the United Kingdom or a substantial part of it. This power has never been used. There are no restrictions

or formalities on transactions in sterling or foreign currency securities. Banks may freely accept foreign currency deposits and employ them in their foreign currency business or convert them to sterling, subject to prudential guidelines issued by the Bank of England concerning the limitation of risks arising from their foreign exchange exposure. Net spot liabilities in foreign currencies (that is, the net amount of foreign currency resources funding sterling assets) form part of a bank's eligible liabilities that are subject to a 0.35 percent non-interest-bearing deposit requirement with the Bank of England and may also be subject to calls for special deposits to be placed with the bank. There is currently no special deposit call.

Gold

Gold bullion and gold coins are not subject to control in the United Kingdom. Gold sovereigns and Britannias are legal tender but do not circulate. Gold coins have also been issued in Jersey and the Isle of Man and are legal tender there. Except under license granted by the Treasury, it is an offense to melt down or break up any metal coin that is for the time being current in the United Kingdom or that, having been current there, has at any time after May 16, 1969 ceased to be so. The exportation of gold in manufactured form over 50 years old and valued at £8,000 and over for each item or matching set of items also requires a license from the Department of Trade and Industry. There is a free gold market in London in which gold bars are freely traded.

Changes During 1995

No significant changes occurred in the exchange and trade system.

(See Appendix for a summary of trade measures introduced and eliminated on an EU-wide basis during 1995.)

UNITED STATES

(Position as of May 31, 1996)

Exchange Arrangement

The currency of the United States is the U.S. Dollar. The U.S. authorities do not maintain margins in respect of exchange transactions, and spot and forward exchange rates are determined on the basis of supply and demand in the exchange markets. However, the authorities intervene when necessary to counter disorderly conditions in the exchange markets or when otherwise deemed appropriate. There are no taxes or subsidies on purchases or sales of foreign exchange.

The United States accepted the obligations of Article VIII, Sections 2, 3, and 4 of the Fund Agreement on December 10, 1946.

Administration of Control

The Department of the Treasury administers economic sanction programs involving direct or indirect financial or commercial transactions with Cuba, the Democratic People's Republic of Korea, Iraq, the Libyan Arab Jamahiriya, designated Middle East terrorists and designated narcotics traffickers centered in Colombia, the Federal Republic of Yugoslavia (Serbia/Montenegro), the areas of Bosnia and Herzegovina controlled by Bosnian Serb forces, and the UN-protected areas of Croatia,[1] as specified respectively under the Cuban Assets Control Regulations, the Foreign Assets Control Regulations, the Libyan Sanctions Regulations, the Iraqi Sanctions Regulations, the Federal Republic of Yugoslavia (Serbia/Montenegro) Sanctions Regulations, and the Terrorism Sanctions Regulations and Executive Order 12978 of October 1995. The Treasury also has administrative responsibility for blocked accounts of the above countries and for assets of the Federal Republic of Yugoslavia (Serbia/Montenegro) blocked prior to December 27, 1995, and assets of the Bosnian Serb forces and authorities.

The Department of the Treasury regulates the trade of goods and services, blocked prior to May 10, 1996, between the United States and the Islamic Republic of Iran under the Iranian Transactions Regulations and restricts the sale or supply of arms and petroleum products, regardless of origin, to UNITA (otherwise known as Armed Forces for the Liberation of Angola) and to the territory of Angola under the UNITA (Angola) Sanctions Regulations.

The Customs Service of the Treasury Department administers import quotas and tariff rate quotas; such quotas, however, are frequently established or allocated by other agencies. The Committee for the Implementation of Textile Agreements, chaired by the Department of Commerce and representing other agencies, decides when to request consultation with exporting countries to limit imports on the basis of the guidelines of the World Trade Organization (WTO) Agreement on Textiles and Clothing and bilateral restraint agreements. For items subject to export control—other than munitions items and items qualified below—the Department of Commerce is, in general, the responsible authority.

There are no restrictions on foreign payments, except those imposed under Treasury Department regulations on transactions involving the government or nationals of Cuba, the Democratic People's Republic of Korea, the Government of Libya, the Government of Iraq, designated Middle East terrorists and designated narcotics traffickers centered in Colombia, entities located in or controlled from the Federal Republic of Yugoslavia (Serbia/Montenegro), as well as trade with, and certain assets of, the Islamic Republic of Iran and on prohibited exports to UNITA or to the territory of Angola. Transfers of funds are also prohibited to persons in Iraq and the Federal Republic of Yugoslavia (Serbia/Montenegro), or to or for the benefit of entities, wherever located, owned or controlled by entities in the Federal Republic of Yugoslavia (Serbia/Montenegro), pursuant to UN Security Council resolutions, or to or through Libyan financial institutions or to entities owned or controlled by the Government of Libya. Certain payments to Cuba and to the Democratic People's Republic of Korea related to authorized travel are permitted, as are certain payments in connection with travel to and in the United States by nationals of these countries.

In accordance with the Fund's Executive Board Decision No. 144-(52/51) adopted on August 14, 1952, the United States notified the Fund on June 26, 1992 that, in compliance with UN Security Council Resolution No. 757 (1992), certain restrictions had been imposed on the making of payments and transfers for current international transactions in respect

---

[1]Sanctions against the Federal Republic of Yugoslavia (Serbia/Montenegro) were suspended on January 16, 1996 and sanctions against the Bosnian Serbs were suspended on May 10, 1996.

of the Federal Republic of Yugoslavia (Serbia/Montenegro).

Imports and Import Payments

The importation of goods and services originating in Cuba, the Islamic Republic of Iran, Iraq, the Democratic People's Republic of Korea, the Libyan Arab Jamahiriya, and the Federal Republic of Yugoslavia (Serbia/Montenegro), and those areas of Bosnia and Herzegovina controlled by the Bosnian Serb forces and the UN-protected areas of Croatia is prohibited unless specifically authorized.

Import quotas imposed under the authority of Section 22 of the Agricultural Adjustment Act of 1993, as amended (including on cotton of specified staple lengths, certain cotton waste and products, certain dairy products, peanuts, and certain products containing sugar), were converted to tariff rate quotas as a result of the Uruguay Round. These quotas are allocated on a country-of-origin basis, except those for peanuts, certain cotton products, butter and certain other dairy products, and certain products containing sugar. Quotas may be imposed on certain types of meat under conditions set forth in the Meat Import Act of 1979. Most dairy products that are subject to tariff rate quotas are also subject to import licensing.

The Generalized System of Preferences (GSP), which provided for duty-free treatment for approximately 4,400 items from 146 beneficiary developing countries and had been in operation since January 1976, expired July 31, 1995. Certain benefits that had been extended to Thailand under the GSP and were removed in 1989 were reinstated in August 1995.

Under the Caribbean Basin Economic Recovery Act, 24 countries and entities[2] were designated to receive preferential tariff treatment on specified imports.

The North American Free-Trade Agreement (NAFTA), which built on the 1989 U.S. Canadian Free Trade Agreement (CFTA), came into force on January 1, 1994. NAFTA incorporates some provisions of CFTA by reference, most importantly CFTA's bilateral tariff phaseout schedule. Upon NAFTA's entry into force, half of NAFTA members' exports to Mexico became eligible for duty-free treatment. Remaining Mexican tariffs on NAFTA

members' goods are scheduled for elimination over 5- 10- or 15-year periods.

The Agreement on Textiles and Clothing (ATC) entered into force on January 1, 1995, superseding the Multifiber Arrangement. The ATC provided for the gradual and complete integration of apparel and textile products into the WTO regime over a ten-year transition period, and the gradual phaseout of quantitative restrictions on textile and apparel exports to the United States. "Integrated products" are removed from the scope of the ATC's special safeguard mechanism and any applicable quotas are eliminated. Integration takes place in four stages: in 1995, 16 percent (by volume) of textile and apparel trade was integrated; at the beginning of year four and year seven an additional 17 and 18 percent, respectively, will be integrated; and after year ten, all remaining products will be integrated. With regard to the phasing out of quotas, the vast majority of quotas affecting imports to the United States will be subject to automatic "growth-on-growth" liberalization each year of the transition period. For example, in 1995, the annual quota growth rate was increased by 16 percent.

Exports and Export Proceeds

Ammunition may be exported only under license issued by the Office of Defense Trade Controls in the Department of State. The Department of Commerce administers controls directly on exports of crime control and detection equipment, as well as on instruments and related technical data to all countries, except other members of the North Atlantic Treaty Organization (NATO), Australia, Japan, and New Zealand. The Department of Commerce administers controls directly on exports of other goods from the United States and on re-exports of goods of U.S. origin from any area.

With the exception of publications and other information materials, personal baggage, and similar items, all exports from the United States to Cuba, the Islamic Republic of Iran, Iraq, the Democratic People's Republic of Korea, the Libyan Arab Jamahiriya, the Federal Republic of Yugoslavia (Serbia/Montenegro), those areas of Bosnia and Herzegovina controlled by the Bosnian Serb forces, and the UN-protected areas of Croatia are prohibited unless licensed by the Department of Commerce and/or the Treasury Department. The Treasury Department administers controls on exports from third countries to Cuba, and to the Democratic People's Republic of Korea, of goods of U.S. or foreign origin by U.S. nationals or by foreign firms that are owned or controlled by U.S. nationals, and on certain third-coun-

---

[2]Antigua and Barbuda, Aruba, The Bahamas, Barbados, Belize, British Virgin Islands, Costa Rica, Dominica, Dominican Republic, El Salvador, Grenada, Guatemala, Guyana, Haiti, Honduras, Jamaica, Montserrat, Netherlands Antilles, Nicaragua, Panama, St. Kitts and Nevis, St. Lucia, St. Vincent and the Grenadines, and Trinidad and Tobago.

try exports by U.S. nationals to the Libyan Arab Jamahiriya. Third-country exports by U.S. nationals to Iraq; and the Federal Republic of Yugoslavia (Serbia/Montenegro), and exports by U.S. nationals of arms and petroleum products, regardless of origin, to UNITA or to the territory of Angola, other than through certain designated points of entry, are also prohibited. Restrictions on exports of certain military equipment to South Africa remain in effect along with a munitions embargo. Exports to all other countries, except Canada, of designated strategic materials and equipment require validated licenses from the Department of Commerce.

Persons subject to U.S. jurisdiction require a Treasury Department license to participate in offshore transactions in strategic goods involving certain countries, regardless of the origin of the goods. For many commodities being exported to countries other than the Islamic State of Afghanistan, former member countries of the Council for Mutual Economic Assistance (CMEA), Cuba, the Democratic People's Republic of Korea, the Lao People's Democratic Republic, the Libyan Arab Jamahiriya, Vietnam, and the Federal Republic of Yugoslavia (Serbia/Montenegro), distribution licenses may be obtained from the Commerce Department to cover multiple shipments.

Under the Export Administration Act of 1979, amended in 1985, the President can suspend the exportation of nonagricultural goods for reasons of national security, foreign policy, or short supply in the domestic economy, although efforts are made to minimize the use of such authority. Export suspension of agricultural commodities may not be imposed for reasons of short supply, foreign policy, or national security unless a national emergency is declared. For agricultural commodities such as wheat, flour, corn, sorghum, rice, soybeans and soybean products, and cotton, exporting companies are required to participate in a reporting system designed to improve market information and allow for more orderly exporting. The proceeds of exports are not subject to exchange control.

Payments for and Proceeds from Invisibles

Payments and transfers abroad may be made freely, except for payments to or for the account of the governments or nationals of Cuba, and the Democratic People's Republic of Korea, or to or for the accounts of the governments and government-controlled entities worldwide, of Iraq, the Libyan Arab Jamahiriya, the Federal Republic of Yugoslavia (Serbia/Montenegro), the military and civilian authorities in those areas of Bosnia and Herzegovina

controlled by Bosnian Serb forces, designated Middle East terrorists, designated narcotics traffickers centered in Colombia, and certain payments relating to the Islamic Republic of Iran.[3]

Transfers of funds to persons in Iraq and in the Federal Republic of Yugoslavia (Serbia/Montenegro) are prohibited. Effective December 19, 1991, the Socialist People's Libyan Arab Jamahiriya was prohibited from clearing funds involving third countries through U.S. banks. Payments and transfers to entities located in or controlled from the Federal Republic of Yugoslavia (Serbia/Montenegro) or those areas of Bosnia and Herzegovina under the control of Bosnian Serb forces are prohibited. Remittances of up to $1,000 to Cuba are allowed to aid a relative's emigration from Cuba to the United States. Receipts of funds from Cuba and the Democratic People's Republic of Korea are subject to blocking, as are payments involving a governmental interest from Iraq, the Libyan Arab Jamahiriya, and the Federal Republic of Yugoslavia (Serbia/Montenegro); payments involving an interest of an entity or undertaking in or controlled from the Federal Republic of Yugoslavia (Serbia/Montenegro); and payments involving designated Middle East terrorists, designated narcotics traffickers centered in Colombia, or those areas of Bosnia and Herzegovina controlled by Bosnia Serb forces. Individuals leaving or entering the United States with more than $10,000 in domestic or foreign currency, traveler's checks, money orders, or bearer-form negotiable securities must declare these to customs at the point of exit or entry.

Capital

Incoming or outgoing capital payments by residents or nonresidents are not subject to exchange control. In addition, inward and outward direct or portfolio investment is generally free of any other form of approval requirement. Investments involving ownership interest in banks are subject to federal and state banking laws and regulations. However, as noted above, there are restrictions on certain transactions with, or involving, Cuba, Iraq, the Democratic People's Republic of Korea, the Libyan Arab Jama-

---

[3]Certain payments and transfers to the Government of the Islamic Republic of Iran, its instrumentalities, and controlled entities involving obligations contracted before January 19, 1981 are subject to restrictions, as are payments for goods or services imported from the Islamic Republic of Iran. On May 6, 1995, a much more comprehensive trade and investment embargo with respect to Iran became effective; although funds are not blocked under the new program, trade in goods and services is prohibited and the transfers of funds to Iran are generally prohibited as an exportation of services.

hiriya, the Federal Republic of Yugoslavia (Serbia/ Montenegro), those areas of Bosnia and Herzegovina controlled by Bosnian Serb forces, designated Middle East terrorists, and designated narcotics traffickers centered in Colombia.

The 1988 Omnibus Trade Act contained a provision authorizing the President to suspend or prohibit foreign acquisitions, mergers, and takeovers in the United States (the Exon-Florio Amendment) if the President determines that the foreign investor might take action that would threaten to impair national security and if existing laws, except the International Emergency Economic Powers Act and the Exon-Florio provision itself, are not, in the President's judgment, adequate or appropriate to protect national security.

Bilateral investment agreements were signed in January 1995 with Albania and Latvia.

The Johnson Act, 18 U.S.C. 955, prohibits, with certain exceptions, persons within the United States from dealing in financial obligations or extending loans to foreign governments that have defaulted on payments of their obligations to the U.S. Government. The act does not apply to those foreign governments that are members of both the IMF and the World Bank.

There is no restriction on the amount of cash or negotiable instruments that may be brought into or taken out of the United States; however, there are certain reporting requirements for travelers entering or leaving the United States when they are carrying more than $10,000 in cash or negotiable instruments (as well as corresponding reporting requirements for shipments of currency or bearer assets through the mails). In addition, ownership of U.S. agricultural land by foreign nationals or by U.S. corporations in which foreign owners have a significant interest (at least 10 percent) or substantial control must be reported to the U.S. Department of Agriculture. Certain states in the United States impose varying restrictions on foreign nationals' purchases of land within their borders.

The foreign currency positions of banks, whether overall or with respect to individual currencies, are not subject to quantitative limitations, but banks are subject to prudential oversight. U.S. agencies and branches of foreign banks, as well as domestic banks, may be subject to reserve requirements by the Federal Reserve system.

U.S. chartered depository institutions, U.S. offices of Edge Act and Agreement Corporations,[4] and U.S.

branches and agencies of foreign banks are allowed to establish international banking facilities (IBFs) in the United States. IBFs may accept deposits only from foreign residents (including foreign offices of domestic banks), from other IBFs, or from the institution establishing the IBF. Such funds are exempt from reserve requirements under Regulation D. For nonbank foreign residents, the minimum maturity or notice requirement is two business days, and the minimum transaction amount is $100,000. Funds raised by an IBF may be used only to extend credit to foreign residents (including foreign offices of domestic banks), to other IBFs, or to the entity establishing the IBF. Credit may be extended to nonbank foreign residents only if the proceeds are used to finance the operations of the borrower or its affiliates outside the United States. Advances from an IBF to its establishing entity in the United States are subject to Eurocurrency reserve requirements (currently set at zero percent) in the same manner as advances to the establishing entity from the entity's foreign branches. A number of individual states (but not the federal Government) have granted favorable tax treatment under state or local law to IBF operations. In addition, federal legislation was enacted to exempt deposits at IBFs from Federal Deposit Insurance Corporation insurance coverage and assessments. U.S. banks are permitted to accept foreign currency deposits.

Gold

U.S. citizens or residents may freely purchase, hold, and sell gold in any form, at home or abroad, except for certain gold transactions (e.g., imports or exports) involving Cuba, the Islamic Republic of Iran, Iraq, the Democratic People's Republic of Korea, the Libyan Arab Jamahiriya, the Federal Republic of Yugoslavia (Serbia/Montenegro), those areas of Bosnia and Herzegovina controlled by Bosnian Serb forces, and the UN-protected areas of Croatia. Commercial banks may deal in gold bullion and gold coins, with the same exceptions. Treasury Department licensing for importers, exporters, producers, refiners, and processors of gold is not required, with the same country exceptions. Gold producers may sell their output in the free market, with the same country exceptions. Gold, but not counterfeit gold coins, may be freely imported, except from the countries mentioned above. U.S. gold coins are legal tender at their face value.

Commercial imports of gold jewelry are free of quantitative restrictions but are subject to import duty at a rate of approximately 12 percent. There is no duty on gold ore, bullion, or coins. All forms of

---

[4]These are defined as domestically chartered corporations authorized to engage in international banking and financial operations.

gold must be declared at the point of entry into the United States.

Changes During 1995

Administration of Control

January 24. The President issued Executive Order 12947, blocking all property and interests in property of foreign terrorists that disrupt the Middle East peace process.

October 21. The President issued Executive Order 12978, blocking all property and interests in property of significant foreign narcotics traffickers centered in Colombia.

Imports and Import Payments

January 1. The ATC entered into force.

February 26. The United States and China reached agreement on intellectual property rights enforcement. Tariffs were suspended on effective date.

March 16. A Trade and Investment Framework Agreement (TIFA) was signed with Morocco.

July 15. The GSP program expired.

August 1. Certain benefits that had been extended to Thailand under the GSP and subsequently removed in 1989 were reinstated.

Capital

January 13. Bilateral investment treaties were signed with Albania and Latvia.

July 3. A bilateral investment treaty was signed with Nicaragua.

Changes During 1996

Administration of Control

January 16. Sanctions against the Federal Republic of Yugoslavia (Serbia/Montenegro) were suspended.

May 10. Sanctions against the Bosnian Serbs were suspended.

URUGUAY

(Position as of December 31, 1995)

Exchange Arrangement

The currency of Uruguay is the Uruguayan Peso. The Central Bank of Uruguay intervenes to ensure that the exchange rate will remain within the higher and lower limits of the exchange rate band (currently 7 percent) and allows market rates to float freely within these limits. The Central Bank periodically announces its intervention buying and selling rates. On December 31, 1995, the buying and selling interbank rates for the U.S. dollar, the intervention currency, were Ur$7.111 and Ur$7.113, respectively, per US$1. Rates for other currencies are based on the cross rate relationship between the U.S. dollar and the currencies concerned in the international market.

Purchases of foreign exchange by public sector institutions are subject to a tax of 2 percent; central bank and official banks' purchases are exempted from the tax. There are no arrangements for forward cover against exchange rate risk operating in the official or the commercial banking sector.

There are no limits on the amount of foreign exchange that the Central Bank may sell to or buy from the state-owned Bank of the Republic, the Mortgage Bank, the private commercial banks, and financial and exchange houses.

Uruguay accepted the obligations of Article VIII, Sections 2, 3, and 4 of the Fund Agreement on May 2, 1980.

Administration of Control

Exchange transactions are carried out through authorized banks, financial houses, exchange houses, and the Bank of the Republic. Any person or firm may conduct exchange transactions in the market, provided this does not become a customary business. Exchange houses also must be authorized by the Central Bank.

Prescription of Currency

Payments between Uruguay and the countries with which Uruguay has concluded reciprocal credit agreements may be made through accounts maintained with each other by the central banks, within the framework of the multilateral clearing system of the Latin American Integration Association (LAIA); these countries are Argentina, Bolivia, Brazil, Chile, Colombia, Dominican Republic, Ecuador, Mexico, Paraguay, Peru, and Venezuela. There are separate arrangements for trade in specified goods with Argentina, Brazil, and Mexico, among other countries. There is a similar arrangement with Cuba, but settlements are effected in a currency other than the U.S. dollar. All settlements of balances under the multilateral clearing system are made in U.S. dollars.

Imports and Import Payments

All imports are subject to registration. The registrations are generally valid for 180 days, and goods must be cleared through customs during this period.

The Treaty of Asunción, signed in 1991 by Argentina, Brazil, Paraguay, and Uruguay, created the Common Market of the South (Mercosur); under the treaty, a customs union began to operate on January 1, 1995. The most important instrument of the customs union is the common external tariff (CET), which consists of the tariffs and a new nomenclature (the *Nomenclatura Arancelaria* Mercosur). There are 11 different tariff levels, ranging from zero to 20 percent. Regionally produced capital goods and telecommunications equipment are subject to a tariff of 14 percent and 16 percent, respectively.

The parties to Mercosur are allowed to exempt up to 300 goods from the CET until the year 2001 (in the case of Paraguay, the number is 399). The tariff rates on these exempted goods are to converge linearly and automatically to the CET by 2001. Uruguay and Paraguay are allowed to converge in the same way to the CET in respect of capital goods and telecommunications equipment until the year 2006, from the zero to 6 percent tariff prior to January 1995. Buses and trucks are subject to a tariff of 20 percent, to which Uruguay may converge by the year 2006. The CET for cars and sugar is still under negotiation.

Except for a precise number of items, which are included in the *Régimen de Adecuación*, there are no remaining import duties among Mercosur countries. The Mercosur treaty allowed Uruguay 950 exemptions to zero-tariff trade during 1995; some products—such as pharmaceuticals, plastics, automobile parts, textiles, and dairy products—may continue to be exempted until the end of 1999.

Duties on the imports of wheat, tires, paper, glass, sugar, textiles, and apparel are computed on the basis of "minimum export prices" (*precios mínimos de exportación*), which, in addition, provide the basis for a sliding surcharge to be paid by the importer, representing the difference between the minimum export and the declared c.i.f. import price. Those minimum export prices are set by government decree but are established transitorily by a decision of the Ministry of Finance.

Imports of used cars are prohibited.

Payments for Invisibles

There are no limitations on payments for invisibles or the exportation of foreign or domestic banknotes. Royalties transferred to a country with no taxation treaty with Uruguay have to pay a tax of 30 percent; dividends and interests are exempted.

Exports and Export Proceeds

From time to time, and for special reasons (for example, stock position, protection, or sanitary considerations), certain exports are prohibited or are subject to special requirements. A simple export document was introduced in mid-1995 to rationalize the trade system.

Exports of dry, salted, and pickled hides are subject to an export tax at the rate of 5 percent.

Access to the market conditions established by the bilateral trade agreements with Argentina (CAUCE) and Brazil (PEC), which allow Uruguay to export limited amounts of specific goods with preferential treatment, will be maintained until the year 2001, within the framework of MERCOSUR.

Proceeds from Invisibles

There are no surrender requirements on the proceeds from invisibles, and there are no limitations on the importation of foreign or domestic banknotes.

Capital

Inward and outward private capital transfers by either residents or nonresidents may be made freely, with the exception of certain inward and outward transfers relating to investments registered under the Foreign Investment Law. The amortization or liquidation proceeds of foreign capital registered under this law cannot normally be transferred abroad until three years after the date on which the investment was approved.

Gold

Residents and nonresidents may freely purchase, hold, and sell financial gold with a fineness of not less than 0.9 in Uruguay or abroad. Gold for industrial purposes is subject to the general policy that governs the exportation, importation, and trading of goods.

Changes During 1995

Imports and Import Payments

January 1. Tariffs on most imports from member countries of MERCOSUR were eliminated and the CET, ranging from zero to 20 percent (with 11 different positions), was applied to most products from non-MERCOSUR countries.

Exports and Export Proceeds

July 1. A simple export document was introduced to rationalize the trade system.

UZBEKISTAN

(Position as of April 30, 1996)

Exchange Arrangement

The currency of the Republic of Uzbekistan is the Sum. The official exchange rate is determined daily on the basis of the weighted average of exchange rates at which authorized banks purchase and sell foreign exchange in the interbank market on days when the rate is not determined in the twice-weekly auction. Exchange rates for currencies not traded at the auction are determined from cross rates in the international market. On December 31, 1995, the official rate for the U.S. dollar quoted by the Central Bank of Uzbekistan was Sum 35.5 per $1. Foreign exchange transactions are conducted by authorized banks, which may not charge a commission in excess of 1 percent of the amount of foreign currency bought or sold, for noncash foreign exchange transactions. Individuals buy and sell foreign exchange cash through exchange bureaus at an exchange rate established by authorized banks on the basis of supply and demand for foreign currency. A commission in sum is collected when selling foreign currency notes. Retail traders and enterprises are required to obtain a patent for a nominal fee of $10 to gain access to the auction in order to purchase foreign exchange for the payment of imports of consumer goods and related services. The priority list of consumer goods and sectorial activities used with respect to the patents system was abolished in October 1995. On December 5, 1995, the maximum spread between the cash and official exchange rates was set at 20 percent. Since April 1996, the spread has not exceeded 3 percent.

As of October 15, 1994, all domestic payments and settlements must be effected in sum. Authorized banks are permitted to maintain an overall open foreign exchange position of up to 20 percent of statutory capital.

Administration of Control

The authority for the control of foreign exchange transactions is vested with the Central Bank, the Ministry of Finance, and the State Tax Committee of the Republic of Uzbekistan.

Prescription of Currency

Settlements with countries with which Uzbekistan maintains bilateral payments agreements are effected in accordance with the terms of the agreements.[1] Transactions with other countries are settled in convertible currencies.

Resident and Nonresident Accounts

Residents may open and maintain accounts in foreign currency with an authorized bank in Uzbekistan. The Central Bank may, on a case-by-case basis, permit residents to open and maintain accounts in foreign currency with banks outside of Uzbekistan. Nonresidents may open and maintain accounts in sum and/or in foreign currency with authorized banks. These accounts may be credited with any amount of sum or foreign currency that has been lawfully acquired by nonresidents. Withdrawals from these accounts are unrestricted.

Imports and Exports

A negative import list was introduced in July 1995 that included publications, manuscripts, video and audio material, and photographs aimed at undermining state and social order or promoting war, violence, nationalism, and racism, as well as pornographic material. A system of import duties was reintroduced beginning July 1995. The new import tariff schedule, which took effect from October 1, 1995, imposes rates ranging from 5 percent to 100 percent on 61 products or product groups with most items in the categories of 5 percent, 10 percent, and 20 percent (47 items). The rate of 100 percent applies to used motor vehicles only.

Export tariffs were modified also with effect from October 1. The new export tariff schedule imposes rates ranging from 5 percent to 100 percent on 102 products or product groups, with most items in the categories of 10 percent, 20 percent, or 50 percent (70 items).

Proceeds from exports in convertible currencies are subject to a 30 percent surrender requirement, and receipts from transactions with the Baltic countries, Russia, and the other countries of the former Soviet Union are subject to a 15 percent surrender requirement.

---

[1]Uzbekistan maintains bilateral payments agreements with Armenia, Belarus, China, Estonia, India, Indonesia, Islamic Republic of Iran, Kazakstan, Kyrgyz Republic, Latvia, Lithuania, Malaysia, Moldova, Russia, Tajikistan, Turkmenistan, and Ukraine.

The Ministry of Foreign Economic Relations is responsible for negotiating trade agreements with nontraditional trading partners as well as those agreements denominated in hard currency with traditional trading partners, and for implementing foreign trade agreements and external trade policy through the issuance of licenses and export quotas.

The Ministry of Foreign Economic Relations must register and review all contracts and agreements by entities requiring licenses for a limited number of goods. Effective July 1995, nonferrous metals, crude oil, gas condensate, gasoline, diesel fuel, lint and cotton fiber, and ferrous metals are subject to export licensing in the amount of established quotas. There is a system of automatic licensing for cotton exports. There are also certain specific goods and services (such as medicines, weapons, precious metals, uranium and other radioactive substances, foreign motion pictures and videos, and research data) that require export and import licenses from the Ministry of Foreign Economic Relations. Quotas do not apply to these goods or services, and licensing requirements are consistent with international procedures. A license is required for each contract. Exports of 13 types of goods, including flour and cereals from state resources, livestock and poultry, meat, dry milk, tea, sugar, ethylene alcohol, and antique items, are prohibited.

At present, Uzbekistan has three types of trade agreements. The first category includes agreements with countries other than the Baltic countries, Russia, and countries of the former Soviet Union that focus only on defining trade regimes (tariffs, duties, etc.). In these agreements, there are no indicative lists of goods, and trade is generally conducted in freely convertible currencies. The second category of trade agreements is based upon convertible currencies and a list of indicative goods that the country is selling. The delivery of such goods is not compulsory, because governments do not agree to supply such goods. Commercial enterprises carry out such transactions through contracts. Agreements in this category are those with the Baltic countries, Belarus, Armenia, and until 1994, Eastern European countries (which are currently in the first category). The third category includes agreements with the Baltic countries, Russia, and other countries of the former Soviet Union, in which there are indicative lists as well as lists of commodities to be supplied on a mutual basis.[2] Under these trade agreements, governments assume responsibility for mutually agreed supplies and are thus guarantors of the contracts, which are set in freely convertible currencies.

Payments for and Proceeds from Invisibles

Restrictions on access by individuals to buy foreign exchange were abolished on July 1, 1995. There are no restrictions on bringing foreign currency into Uzbekistan, and nonresidents are allowed to take freely convertible currency out of Uzbekistan.

Proceeds from invisibles for legal entities are subject to the same surrender requirements as those applicable to proceeds from exports.

Capital

Enterprises may establish joint ventures as foreign direct investment with the approval of the Ministry of Justice. Foreign equity capital participation of up to 100 percent is allowed. Joint ventures are exempt from the profit tax during the first two years after registration; joint ventures with a foreign equity capital share exceeding 50 percent are exempted from the profit tax during the first five years. Joint ventures are allowed to export their products and import inputs without licenses and to retain all of their foreign exchange earnings. Remittance of the foreign investors' share of profits is guaranteed, and the repatriation of capital is not restricted. A guarantee is provided to foreign investors that legislation will not be changed for ten years.

Gold

Trade in gold is prohibited (with the exception of jewelry and collectibles); however, transactions in gold may be conducted by the Central Bank and the Ministry of Finance. Joint ventures operating in the precious metals sector may export without restriction a portion of their output that corresponds to the share of profits of the foreign participant.

Emigrants are allowed to take out of the country 100 grams of gold and 200 grams of silver in the form of jewelry or personal effects.

Changes During 1995

Exchange Arrangement

April 1. The frequency of foreign exchange auctions was increased to twice weekly.

November 1. The official exchange rate of the sum in terms of the U.S. dollar and other currencies was to be determined daily, with the rate based on the weighted average exchange rates at which authorized banks purchase and sell foreign exchange in

---

[2]Clearing arrangements are in effect with Kazakstan, Kyrgyz Republic, Russia, and Ukraine.

the interbank market on days when the rate is not determined at the auction.

December 5. The maximum spread between the cash (both buying and selling) exchange rate and the official exchange rate was set at 20 percent.

Administration of Control

April 1. New foreign exchange regulations were issued by the Central Bank that provided for broad current account convertibility.

Prescription of Currency

April 1. Limits on individuals' purchases of foreign exchange at the commercial rate were increased to $500 from $300.

July 1. Limits on individuals' access for the purchase of foreign exchange were abolished.

October 16. The fee to obtain a patent to purchase foreign exchange in the auction was reduced to $10.

Imports and Exports

July 25. Prohibited exports were increased to 13 from 9 groups of products.

October 1. A system of import duties was reintroduced, and the system of export duties was modified.

October 1. The number of goods subject to export licensing was reduced to 4 from 11, and a system for the automatic granting of licenses for cotton exports was introduced.

November 1. The priority list of consumer imports was replaced with a negative list of imports, and the priority list for sectorial activities was eliminated.

Gold

December 31. All gold reserves and foreign exchange of the Ministry of Finance held as short-term deposits at the National Bank for Foreign Economic Activity were sold to the Central Bank.

Changes During 1996

Imports and Exports

April 1. A new schedule of import tariffs established rates of 5 percent to 100 percent for 56 commodities or groups of commodities, the majority of which (47 items) are in the 5 percent, 10 percent, and 20 percent categories. The 100 percent rate applies solely to used vehicles.

April 1. A new schedule of export tariffs established rates of 5 percent to 100 percent for 83 commodities or groups of commodities, the majority of which (59 items) are in the 5 percent, 10 percent, 15 percent, 20 percent, or 30 percent categories. The 100 percent rate applies only to the exportation of art objects and antiques (with the authorization of the Ministry for Cultural Affairs).

VANUATU

(Position as of December 31, 1995)

Exchange Arrangement

The currency of Vanuatu is the Vatu, the external value of which is determined on the basis of an undisclosed transactions-weighted (trade and tourism receipts) basket of currencies of its major trading partners. The Reserve Bank of Vanuatu buys and sells foreign exchange daily, and buying and selling rates of the vatu against the currencies in the basket are quoted twice a day within margins ranging between 0.25 percent and 0.30 percent around the middle rate. The Reserve Bank deals with the commercial banks only in U.S. dollars on a spot basis and buys and sells foreign exchange only in transactions with commercial banks for the Government's account or for commercial bank operations. On December 29, 1995, the buying and selling rates for the U.S. dollar (for telegraphic transfers) were VT 113.56 and VT 114.12, respectively, per $1. There are no taxes or subsidies on purchases or sales of foreign exchange.

There are no arrangements for forward exchange rate cover facilities operating in the official sector. Commercial banks provide forward exchange rate cover facilities.

Vanuatu accepted the obligations of Article VIII, Sections 2, 3, and 4 of the Fund Agreement on December 1, 1982.

Administration of Control

There are no exchange controls.

Prescription of Currency

There are no prescription of currency requirements.

Nonresident Accounts

No distinction is made between the accounts of residents and nonresidents. Debits and credits to all accounts may be made freely.

Imports and Import Payments

All items may be freely imported with the exception of the following: any goods that are controlled under internal legislation in the interest of national health and well-being, such as explosives and dangerous drugs. The importation of frozen chicken, chicken pieces, T-shirts bearing a Vanuatu motif, firearms and ammunition, animals and plants, and transistor and telephone equipment is restricted through import-licensing arrangements. A similar restriction is applied to the importation of five basic products—rice, sugar, flour, canned mackerel, and tobacco products—under a scheme designed to provide funds for the Vanuatu Cooperative Federation. Currently, about two dozen importers pay a commission of 3 percent (4 percent in the case of tobacco products) to the cooperative for the right to import these five products.

Customs duties are levied mainly on an ad valorem basis on the c.i.f. value of imports. Certain goods, including spirits, wine, beer, tobacco products, and petroleum products, are subject to specific rates of import duty. Imported goods that compete with locally produced equivalents are generally subject to high duty rates. A customs service tax of 5 percent is applied to most imports, based on the duty-inclusive import value. Under a regional trade agreement that came into operation in September 1994, canned tuna from the Solomon Islands and tea from Papua New Guinea may be imported free of import duty. Under an amended agreement, which took effect on December 20, 1995, all goods listed for duty-free trade can originate from any of the three countries—Vanuatu, Solomon Islands, and Papua New Guinea—and the original list of products for duty-free trade (frozen beef, canned tuna, and tea) was expanded to include coffee, yogurt, cheese and curd, wooden furniture, kava, jam, fruit jellies, portland cement, matches, fiberglass boats, toilet paper, iron or steel nails, and plastic shopping bags.

Goods imported for a specified end use may be exempt from import duties. These include goods imported by or on behalf of the Government and funded by external aid, goods imported for sale to and exported by tourists, ships' stores (including fuels), goods imported for processing and re-exportation, and goods imported for investment projects.

Payments for Invisibles

There are no restrictions on payments for invisibles.

Exports and Export Proceeds

With a few exceptions, no restrictions are imposed on exports. The exportation of logs has been banned for environmental reasons since 1990 although exemptions have been granted in certain circumstances. Exports of trochus, green snails, bêches-de-mer, mother-of-pearl, aquarium fish, and crustaceans[1] are subject to authorization by the Minister of Agriculture, Fisheries, and Forestry. Exports of copra, cocoa, and kava are channeled through the Vanuatu Commodities Marketing Board (VCMB); however, exports of kava can be undertaken by individuals subject to authorization from the VCMB. Artifacts having a special value either as a result of ceremonial use or because they are more than ten years old are subject to authorization from the Cultural Center.

Most exports are subject to export duties, mainly on an ad valorem basis (f.o.b.); specific duties are levied on timber products and some other minor exports. There are no surrender requirements for export proceeds.

Proceeds from Invisibles

Exchange proceeds from invisibles need not be surrendered.

---

[1]Including coconut crabs for conservation purposes.

Capital

All inward and outward movements of capital are unrestricted.

Gold

There are no restrictions on gold transactions.

Changes During 1995

Imports and Import Payments

December 20. Under an amended import agreement with the Solomon Islands and New Guinea, all goods listed for duty-free trade can originate from any of the three countries and the original list of products for duty-free trade (frozen beef, canned tuna, and tea) was expanded to include coffee, yogurt, cheese and curd, wooden furniture, kava, jam, fruit jellies, portland cement, matches, fiberglass boats, toilet paper, iron or steel nails, and plastic shopping bags.

VENEZUELA

(Position as of July 31, 1996)

Exchange Arrangement

The currency of Venezuela is the Venezuelan Bolívar, the external value of which is pegged to the U.S. dollar. On December 31, 1995, the official rate of the Central Bank of Venezuela for the U.S. dollar was Bs 290 per $1. On June 22, 1995, a legal parallel market for foreign exchange was created, with the authorized trading on local securities exchanges of foreign-currency-denominated government bonds trading on the secondary market ("Brady bonds"), for settlement in bolívares. An exchange rate applicable to travel and credit card transactions was temporarily introduced in October 1995. On December 11, 1995, the official exchange rate was devalued to Bs 290 per $1, and was made applicable to all transactions, thus effectively eliminating the temporary dual exchange rate system. In January 1996, certain limitations were imposed on domestic trading of Brady bonds. On April 22, 1996, Venezuela unified the exchange rate under a temporary managed float exchange system. During the initial weeks following this measure, the exchange rate was in the range of Bs 460 to Bs 470 per $1; the previous parallel market rate was in the range of Bs 470 to Bs 520 per $1. On July 8, 1996, the Central Bank introduced the system of an exchange rate band; the initial rate was set at Bs 470 per $1, and the width of the band at ±7.5 percent.[1]

Resident commercial banks and exchange houses are designated as authorized foreign exchange dealers. Tourist establishments are allowed to offer their clients foreign exchange services in the form of purchases of foreign currency notes, coins, and traveler's checks.

Venezuela accepted the obligations of Article VIII, Sections 2, 3, and 4 of the Fund Agreement on July 1, 1976.

Administration of Control

Under the system of exchange controls established on July 11, 1994, the newly created Exchange Administration Board (EAB) and the associated Technical Administration Office are responsible for the administration of exchange transactions. The EAB was closed with the elimination of exchange controls in April 22, 1996. These bodies were established initially by presidential decree, but the powers to designate an EAB were formalized subsequently in a new foreign exchange law, dated December 1, 1994, and signed into law in April 1995, under which the President of the Republic may establish exchange restrictions when warranted by the economic and financial conditions of the country. The EAB was closed when exchange controls were eliminated on April 22, 1996. When required, export and import licenses are issued by the Ministry of Agriculture and Livestock, the Ministry of Development, the Ministry of Defense, or the Ministry of Foreign Relations, depending on the product.

The Superintendency of Foreign Investment (SIEX), attached to the Ministry of Finance, oversees the registration of foreign direct investments, contracts involving technology transfers, and the use of foreign patents and trademarks.

Arrears are maintained with respect to certain external payments.

Prescription of Currency

No prescription of currency requirements are in force. Payments between Venezuela and Argentina, Bolivia, Brazil, Chile, Colombia, Cuba, the Dominican Republic, Ecuador, Jamaica, Malaysia, Mexico, Peru, and Uruguay may be settled through accounts maintained with each other by the Central Bank of Venezuela and the central banks of the countries concerned.

Imports and Import Payments

Some imports, irrespective of country of origin, are subject to licensing requirements for environmental, health, or security reasons. The importation of military arms must be authorized by the Ministry of Defense; the importation of nonmilitary weapons and ammunitions must be authorized by the Ministry of Domestic Affairs. At the end of 1995, some 24 tariff items, of which 7 were chemicals used in drug production and approximately 17 were agro-industrial products, were subject to Legal Regime No. 2 and required approval from the import office. Quantitative restrictions apply to a small number of agricultural imports. During 1995, applications for the purchase of foreign exchange for all imports in excess of $5,000 had to be approved by the EAB in accordance with official quarterly targets for net international reserves. Prior to consideration by the

---

[1]During the remainder of 1996, the central rate is to be adjusted in line with the inflation target for the fourth quarter of 1996, i.e., 1.5 percent a month.

EAB, all requests must be processed and verified by the Technical Administration Office. As of October 18, 1995, importers were allowed to purchase only 30 percent of the authorized sale of foreign exchange at the time of customs clearance; the remaining amount is provided in equal parts 90 and 120 days subsequent to customs clearance. As of November 23, 1995, the Central Bank required letters of credit from importers using the ALADI clearing facility.

Most customs tariffs on manufactured goods are on an ad valorem basis; there are four basic rates of 5 percent, 10 percent, 15 percent, and 20 percent, except for motor vehicles, which are subject to a special regime under the Andean Pact. The common external tariff on motor vehicles is 35 percent for passenger cars; 15 percent for cargo and commercial vehicles (except for cargo vehicles under 4,500 kg., such as pickup trucks, for which the rate is 25 percent); and 3 percent for imported components and parts for vehicles assembled in the member countries. The importation of used vehicles is prohibited, with the exception of hearses, prison vans, and ambulances. Specific tariffs apply to agricultural products and to certain products included in Chapter 27 of the tariff code (e.g., mineral fuels, oil, mineral wax, distilled products, and bituminous substances).

Storage charges apply to imports that remain in customs warehouses for more than 12 days. The industrial free zone of Paraguana and the Free Port of Margarita Island enjoy a special customs regime that includes exemptions from customs tariffs.

Colombia, Ecuador, and Venezuela extend duty-free access to each other's imports. Duty-free entry is also granted to certain goods originating from the member countries of the CARICOM region. Venezuela maintains a bilateral trade agreement with Chile, which aims at a gradual reduction of tariffs on each other's imports and at a coordination of the tariff structure with other trading partners. On December 29, 1994, the law approving the Trade Treaty of the Group of Three—Colombia, Mexico, and Venezuela—was passed and became effective on January 1, 1995.

Payments for Invisibles

Until April 22, 1996, when exchange controls were eliminated, all payments for invisibles had to be authorized by the EAB with the exception of purchases of foreign exchange for travel abroad and remittances abroad that were subject to annual limits. For personal travel abroad, the following limits applied: $500 a year for travel to the Caribbean, Colombia, and Panama; $1,000 for travel to Florida,

Central America, Ecuador, Peru, and Bolivia; $1,500 for travel to Mexico; $2,000 for travel to both the United States and Mexico; and $4,000 for travel to other destinations; travelers less than 18 years of age may purchase only one-half of these amounts. Limits on the purchase of foreign exchange for business travel were $3,000 a trip, with a maximum of three trips a calendar year. Monthly remittances to students abroad, in addition to enrollment fees, were allocated according to level of study as follows: $700 for secondary school students; $1,000 for undergraduate students; $1,500 for single postgraduate students; and $2,500 for married postgraduate students. Remittances from senior citizens to individuals were limited to $200 a month, and remittances to pensioners and retirees of Venezuelan institutions were limited to $1,000 a month. Remittances of dividends resulting from investments associated with debt-to-equity conversions could not exceed 10 percent of the total investment for a three-year period from the date it was registered (see section on Capital, below).

In October 1995, the authorities shifted certain tourism-related transactions to the parallel market, but with the December 1995 devaluation of the bolívar, foreign exchange for travel abroad was again sold at the official rate.

Exports and Export Proceeds

There are no controls or restrictions on exports. Export proceeds were subject to surrender requirements and had to be sold to the Central Bank through authorized foreign exchange dealers up to April 22, 1996. However, the state petroleum company (PDVSA) continues to be required to surrender its export proceeds to the Central Bank. PDVSA exports are subject to a surcharge of 8 percent. Exporters may retain up to 10 percent of the foreign exchange to meet commitments abroad; subject to verification, large exporters may retain unlimited amounts of foreign exchange receipts to meet commitments abroad.[2]

Exports of agricultural commodities, with the exception of those exported to Andean Pact member countries, are entitled to a fiscal credit at the rate of 10 percent of the f.o.b. value in the form of a negotiable bond that is issued by the Ministry of Finance.

---

[2]Prior to June 27, 1994, only PDVSA and its Venezuelan affiliates were required to surrender their foreign exchange earnings, although they were allowed to maintain working balances of foreign exchange at a level preapproved by the Board of the Central Bank of Venezuela. Foreign exchange proceeds of loan disbursements to the public sector were also required to be surrendered to the Central Bank of Venezuela.

These bonds may be used for tax payments. Fiscal credits for manufactured exports have been replaced by a system of drawback of customs duties that are paid on imported inputs used in export production. Drawbacks take the form of tax reimbursement certificates issued by the Ministry of Finance.

PDVSA and Ferrominera Orinoco have monopolies over the exportation of hydrocarbons and iron ore, respectively. The tax on exports of hydrocarbons was 4 percent in 1995, and is to be eliminated by the end of 1996.

Proceeds from Invisibles

Proceeds from invisibles were subject to surrender requirements until April 22, 1996. Travelers may freely import domestic and foreign currency, except that foreign coins other than gold coins may not be imported for commercial purposes.

Capital

Capital outflows not related to the amortization of external debt and the repatriation of capital by foreigners were prohibited and foreign direct investments in the petroleum and iron ore sectors were subject to specific regulations up to April 22, 1996.

Mass media, communications, newspapers in Spanish, and security services are reserved for national ownership. New investments do not require prior authorization from the SIEX but must be registered with the SIEX after the fact, and approval is automatically granted if the new investment is consistent with national legislation; purchases of corporate stocks in the Caracas Stock Exchange made from sales of foreign exchange in the parallel exchange market do not require approval from the SIEX. Foreign investments in the financial sector are allowed in accordance with the new banking law. Foreign enterprises may establish subsidiaries in Venezuela without prior authorization as long as they are consistent with the Commerce Code; the SIEX must, however, be notified within 60 working days about newly established subsidiaries. The reinvestment of profits does not require prior authorization and is not restricted. Until April 22, 1996, sales of foreign exchange for the repatriation of capital were subject to the authorization of the EAB. Authorization was not provided for the repatriation of capital originally invested through the parallel exchange market. Foreign investors are allowed to purchase corporate stocks in the Caracas Stock Exchange but must inform the SIEX of such purchases at the end of each calendar year. Until April 22, 1996, foreign investors who purchased corporate stocks in the Caracas Stock Exchange through sales of foreign exchange in the parallel market could not repatriate the capital invested through the official market.

Certain external public debt can be converted into equity. The Central Bank purchases debt instruments at a price fixed at 20 percent above the average price prevailing in the market for those instruments within the ten banking business days before the date of conversion. The eligible areas are infrastructure (ports, bridges, and railways); aqueducts and water treatment plants; terrestrial and fluvial transportation; wholesale markets for agricultural products (including construction, maintenance, and administration); educational institutions; funds for financing research and studies for Venezuelan students in Venezuela or overseas; and medical assistance centers. The maximum component of the investment to be covered by the conversion of the external public debt will be determined by the Ministry of Finance.

To effect a debt conversion, the Central Bank purchases the external debt with domestic currency (or public debt securities denominated in domestic currency), which is then deposited into a trust account opened by the investor with a fiduciary agent (normally a commercial bank) in Venezuela. The agent is responsible for ensuring the proper use of the trust account and releases the funds in step with the implementation of the investment project. (As part of the required documentation, investors must submit in advance a timetable for the investment and its domestic component to be financed through debt conversion.) To further ensure the proper use of the conversion proceeds, investors must deposit with a fiduciary agent a guarantee (equivalent to 5 percent of the total investment), which can be reduced in line with the implementation of the investment.

There are no restrictions on conversions of private external debt into private domestic debt or equity; these conversions may be effected freely through the interbank market.

Gold

Venezuelan gold coins are legal tender but do not circulate. Residents may hold, acquire, and sell gold coins in Venezuela for numismatic and investment purposes. Gold coins, medallions, and bars are freely negotiated among authorized dealers, exchange houses, and the public. Commercial banks may freely negotiate gold coins among themselves and other residents but do not normally deal in gold with the public. Imports and exports of monetary gold and imports of gold coins that are legal tender in Venezuela are reserved for the Central Bank.

The exportation of nonmonetary gold (other than jewelry for personal use) and gold coins eligible as legal tender in Venezuela or abroad are subject to prior authorization from the Central Bank. Under the terms of the agreement between the National Executive and the Central Bank, imports of nonmonetary gold may be regulated. The Central Bank may authorize private exporters to export gold bars, provided that the exported gold bars will be reimported after undergoing processing that is not available in the country and that the reimported gold is used as an input in domestic production.

Changes During 1995

Exchange Arrangement

June 22. A legal parallel market for foreign exchange was established with the trading of Brady bonds on the nation's securities exchanges for settlement in bolívares.

October 26. Sales and purchases of foreign exchange relating to travel and to credit card payments were transferred from the Central Bank to the parallel market.

December 11. The official exchange rate was devalued to Bs 290 per $1. Foreign exchange transactions related to travel and credit card payments were transferred back to the official market.

Imports and Import Payments

October 18. Sales of foreign exchange for imports by the Central Bank would be provided in three installments: 30 percent at the time of customs clearance and the remainder in equal parts 90 and 120 days subsequent to customs clearance.

November 23. The Central Bank required letters of credit from importers using the ALADI clearing facility.

Payments for Invisibles

February 13. Limits on the sale of foreign exchange for personal travel abroad were reduced.

August 2. Limits on the sale of foreign exchange for personal and business travel abroad were reduced.

Changes During 1996

Exchange Arrangement

January 31. Certain limitations were imposed on domestic trading of Brady bonds.

April 22. The exchange rate was unified under a temporary managed float exchange system.

July 8. The Central Bank introduced the system of an exchange rate band, setting the initial central rate at Bs 470 per $1 and the width of the band at ±7.5 percent.

Administration of Control

April 22. The Exchange Administration Board was closed.

Payments for Invisibles

April 22. Controls on payments for invisibles were eliminated.

Exports and Export Proceeds

April 22. Surrender requirements were eliminated, except those applied to PDVSA.

Proceeds from Invisibles

April 22. Surrender requirements were eliminated.

Capital

April 22. Exchange controls were eliminated.

VIETNAM

(Position as of December 31, 1995)

Exchange Arrangement

The currency of Vietnam is the Dong. All foreign exchange transactions are channeled through the interbank market.[1] Spot and forward transactions are permitted between the Vietnamese dong and six other currencies.[2] Trading must take place at exchange rates within ranges stipulated daily by the State Bank of Vietnam. Only the State Bank, state-owned banks, such as the Bank of Investment and Development, shareholding banks, joint-venture banks, and branches of foreign banks may participate in the exchange markets. On December 30, 1995, the average buying and selling rates in the interbank market for the U.S. dollar were D 11,011 and D 11,018, respectively, per $1.

Administration of Control

Exchange control is administered by the State Bank. Foreign trade is administered by the Ministry of Trade, which supervises the operations carried out by the foreign trade organizations and firms with direct foreign trading rights. Import and export licenses, which are required for all trade transactions, are issued by the Ministry of Trade. Foreign trade organizations and firms engaged in international trade must submit annual plans for their imports and exports to the Ministry of Planning and Investment; revisions of the plans may be requested every three months. Most grants in convertible currencies from bilateral official donors and international organizations are under the supervision of the Committee for Reception and Management of Aid, an agency attached to the Ministry of Finance. Foreign investment is monitored and coordinated by the Ministry of Planning and Investment.

Arrears are maintained with respect to external payments.

Prescription of Currency

There is no prescription of currency requirement in place.

Resident and Nonresident Accounts

Nonresidents are permitted to maintain nonresident accounts either in foreign currencies or in convertible dong; however, they may not open interest-yielding bank accounts in dong. Nonresidents can freely reconvert into foreign currency and transfer abroad unused balances in Vietnamese currency that have been acquired against foreign currency. Vietnamese citizens are allowed to sell foreign exchange in their possession to banks, or to deposit it into interest-bearing foreign currency bank accounts. Vietnamese citizens living abroad may also remit foreign exchange to interest-bearing foreign currency accounts. Foreign currency deposited in a bank may be withdrawn for payments or transferred to other units or individuals. Households may maintain savings accounts in foreign currency; the minimum interest rate on these accounts is 3.2 percent for time deposits and 1.5 percent for sight deposits.

Imports and Exports

Manufacturing firms and local authorities are allowed to conduct trade; some export transactions and all import transactions require a license issued by the Ministry of Trade. Trade transactions are carried out by about 700 firms, including 140 foreign trade organizations that produce exportable goods or purchase them from producers, but trade of certain products is regulated by quotas. About 200 producers have temporary or permanent trading rights, which allow them to export and import directly; about 160 foreign-owned or joint-venture firms trade directly with foreign partners. State-owned firms with an annual export turnover of more than $5 million may obtain permanent direct foreign trading rights, whereas those with an annual export turnover in the range of $2–5 million may obtain temporary direct foreign trading rights. Other firms may obtain direct export permits on the basis of shipments or trade with a foreign trade organization. Decree No. 114 entered into force in April 1992; it permits private commercial trading houses to engage in import and export activities.

In 1995, imports of the following products were prohibited: (1) weapons, ammunition and explosives, and military equipment; (2) drugs and toxic chemicals; (3) dangerous and unhealthy cultural products; (4) "reactionary and depraved" cultural products; (5) fireworks and children's toys that det-

---

[1]There is also the foreign exchange trading floor of the auction market located at the branch of the State Bank in Ho Chi Minh City; however, activity in the auction market effectively ceased in 1995.

[2]Deutsche mark, French francs, Hong Kong dollars, Japanese yen, pounds sterling, and U.S. dollars.

rimentally influence personality, education, social order, and safety; (6) most used consumer goods; (7) most used equipment operating at less than 80 percent of original specifications or over ten years old; (8) most left-hand-drive cars; and (9) materials and additives required for making cigarettes. All import quotas are formally approved by the Government. The Ministry of Planning and Investment, in coordination with the Ministry of Trade, may impose ad hoc temporary quantity controls. The following seven commodity groups are subject to quantitative controls: steel, cement, fertilizer, passenger cars (less than 12 seats), motorcycles, petroleum products, and sugar. The issuance of import licenses is on a shipment-by-shipment basis for all products.[3] Import tariffs range up to a maximum of 60 percent. Machinery and equipment as well as medicine are exempt from tariffs. Certain imports of foreign investment enterprises, incorporated under the Law on Foreign Investment are also exempted from duty, including imports for capital construction; first-time imports of instruments, working tools, machine components, assembling devices, and materials destined for initial production and business activities, as described in the Foreign Ministry's Feasibility Study; goods and equipment destined for activities in connection with petroleum exploration or exploitation; and the first-time imports of automobiles for enterprises not in the passenger transportation business. Tariff rates of 50 percent to 60 percent are applied to garments and footwear, soft drinks, cosmetics, and automobiles.

Local foreign trade organizations are permitted to export all commodities, and local firms may import the commodities that they need for production. The procurement of exportable goods is normally unrestricted, except for some sensitive goods (such as rice), for which a minimum export price prevails. Only exports of rice are subject to a quota. For rice, crude oil, products made of wool and rattan, and re-exported goods, export licenses must be obtained for each shipment.

Under Decision No. 188 of the Council of Ministers, export earnings are subject to various surrender requirements, ranging up to 30 percent; however, this regulation is not strictly enforced. In practice, the authorities have tolerated full retention of foreign exchange receipts. All receipts must be repatriated within 30 days, except for special cases authorized by the Governor of the State Bank, such

as for firms with marketing or representative activities abroad. Organizations and enterprises must deposit all foreign exchange proceeds in foreign exchange accounts at domestic commercial banks that are licensed to conduct foreign exchange business in Vietnam. Limits on foreign exchange holdings in such accounts are set by the commercial banks applying rules set by the State Bank. Deposits in excess of those limits must be sold to the commercial banks. While foreign exchange must normally be deposited in banks in Vietnam, firms that are permitted to open branch offices abroad may be granted special permission to deposit these funds in foreign accounts.

Payments for and Proceeds from Invisibles

All transactions in invisibles require individual authorization from the Ministry of Finance. Foreign exchange is made available upon authorization of the transaction. Payments for invisibles related to authorized imports are not restricted. The foreign exchange allocation for travel abroad is $5,000 a trip,[4] but the allocation may be raised to $10,000 for travelers using foreign exchange from their own foreign currency accounts, but banks are required to ensure that the traveler actually possesses resources before engaging in a transaction. Larger allocations of foreign exchange require permission from the State Bank. Remittances of profits are subject to a tax of 5 percent to 10 percent. Receipts from transactions in invisibles must be surrendered to the State Bank.

Organizations and enterprises must deposit all foreign exchange proceeds from invisibles transactions in foreign exchange accounts at domestic commercial banks, according to the same rules and conditions that apply to export proceeds. While such funds must normally be deposited in banks within Vietnam, firms in the aviation, shipping, postal, and insurance sectors, as well as commercial banks, finance companies, and other firms permitted to open branches abroad may be granted special permission to deposit these funds in foreign accounts.

Capital

Foreign direct investment is regulated by a foreign investment code approved by the National Assembly in 1987 and amended in December 1992. The code provides for three forms of foreign investment: (1) contracted business cooperation, such as product-sharing arrangements; (2) joint ventures between a foreign investor and a Vietnamese private enterprise

---

[3]With effect from February 1, 1996, all shipment licenses have been abolished. Import licenses are now issued by the Ministry of Trade for the majority of goods, and for a limited number of specialized goods import certificates are issued by line ministries.

[4]On January 1, 1996, this limit was raised to $7,000.

or state economic organization; and (3) firms wholly owned by foreign investors. The permitted share of foreign capital is no less than 30 percent, and there is no maximum limit. Other provisions in the code include (1) a 50 to 70 year limit on the duration of the enterprise with foreign capital; (2) a tax of 5 percent to 10 percent on the remittance of profits abroad; and (3) profit taxes to be paid at rates of 15 percent to 25 percent, starting two years after the first profit-making year (foreign joint ventures in priority sectors are, however, exempt from the tax in their first two years of eligibility, and the tax rate is halved in the following two years). In 1992, the code was amended to allow domestic private firms to participate with foreign firms in investment projects. Provisions for repatriating profits were also amended to allow the use of domestic currency to purchase and export domestically produced goods and retain the proceeds from these exports abroad.

The authority to grant foreign investment licenses is entrusted to the Ministry of Planning and Investment for projects under $1 million; for projects over $1 million, the provincial authorities concerned are consulted. In principle, 100 percent of profits may be repatriated; however, in practice, the conversion of domestic currency profits into foreign currency for repatriation is governed by the prevailing foreign exchange regulations. Land cannot be owned by foreign investors but must be leased from the state.

Vietnamese organizations and citizens who need foreign currency for production and business purposes have been permitted, upon verification by competent agencies, to borrow foreign currency or obtain a bank guarantee for loans in foreign currency. If allowed to borrow directly from foreign countries under commercial credit, the borrower must report periodically to the State Bank the expenditures in foreign currency from funds deposited abroad, including loan repayments.

Gold

Gold may be brought into the country, provided that required customs declarations are made and a customs tariff is paid; nonresidents are entitled to export gold up to the amount they brought in. The price of gold for domestic transactions is set at auctions organized by the Vietnam Gold and Silver Trading Company. The importation of gold by residents requires a license from the State Bank.

Changes During 1995

Administration of Control

November 1. The State Committee on Cooperation and Investment and the State Planning Committee were combined into the Ministry of Planning and Investment.

Resident and Nonresident Accounts

February 23. Vietnamese citizens living abroad were permitted to remit foreign exchange to interest-bearing foreign currency accounts at banks authorized to deal in foreign exchange.

Imports and Exports

April 1. Circular No. 20/TC/TCT exempted from duty certain imports of Foreign Investment Enterprises, incorporated under the Law on Foreign Investment, including imports for capital construction; first-time imports of instruments, working tools, assembling devices, and materials destined for the initial production and business activities, as described in the Foreign Ministry's Feasibility Study; goods and equipment destined for activities in connection with petroleum exploration or exploitation; and the first-time imports of automobiles for enterprises not in the passenger transportation business machine components.

October 17. Standards for the import of second-hand equipment were issued under Decision No. 1762/QD-PCTN. Under these requirements (1) most equipment over ten years old was excluded; (2) all equipment must be at a technical capacity of no less than 80 percent of its original level; (3) the products produced by the equipment must meet Vietnam's domestic or export standards; and (4) the safety of the users and the environment must be ensured. In addition, foreign investment companies may not import used equipment from developing countries, and imports of equipment required by capital projects, such as aircraft and ships, would be approved on a case-by-case basis.

Payments for and Proceeds from Invisibles

August 24. The foreign exchange allocation for travel abroad was raised to $10,000 a trip from $5,000, if travelers use funds from their own foreign exchange account. Allocations in excess of those limits would require special permission from the State Bank.

WESTERN SAMOA

(Position as of December 31, 1995)

Exchange Arrangement

The currency of Western Samoa is the Western Samoa Tala. Its exchange rate is determined on the basis of a fixed relationship with a weighted basket of currencies of Western Samoa's main trading partners. The Central Bank of Samoa has the authority to make discretionary exchange rate adjustments against the currency basket within a margin of up to 2 percent. On December 31, 1995, the buying and selling rates of the tala in terms of the U.S. dollar, the intervention currency, were US$0.4117 and US$0.4027, respectively, per WS$1. Exchange rates for the tala against other currencies are established on the basis of their daily rates against the U.S. dollar. An exchange levy of 1 percent is charged on gross sales of foreign exchange. There are no arrangements for forward cover against exchange rate risk in the official or the commercial banking sector.

Western Samoa accepted the obligations of Article VIII, Sections 2, 3, and 4 of the Fund Agreement on October 6, 1994.

Administration of Control

Overall responsibility for the administration of exchange control rests with the Central Bank, which delegates part of its powers to authorized banks. In principle, all payments to nonresidents of Western Samoa require the Central Bank's approval. However, the Bank of Western Samoa and the Pacific Commercial Bank—the only authorized banks—are empowered to approve certain payments up to any amount and others up to specified amounts.

Prescription of Currency

There are no prescription of currency requirements that may be used for making or receiving payments to or from nonresidents of Western Samoa.

Nonresident Accounts

Nonresidents and residents who earn foreign exchange in the normal course of their business may open, with the approval of the Central Bank, external or foreign currency accounts with one of the two commercial banks. No distinction is made between the accounts of residents and nonresidents of Western Samoa.

Imports and Import Payments

There are no import licensing requirements. The importation of a few products is prohibited for reasons of security or health. Other products may be imported from any source without restriction, with the exception of used cars, the importation of which requires prior approval from the Central Bank, which does not grant approval for imports of cars more than five years old, for safety reasons. Approvals for the importation of other cars are granted liberally. Imports with a c.i.f. value of more than WS$15,000 must be financed with a letter of credit. Imports with a c.i.f. value of between WS$5,000 and WS$15,000 must be settled with a sight draft. Imports with a c.i.f. value of less than WS$5,000 may be imported under open account, provided that payments are effected within 30 days of their arrival in Western Samoa.

Import duties are applied on an ad valorem basis and assessed on the c.i.f. value of imports. Most products are subject to a tariff of 35 percent. The tariff rates on machinery and agricultural inputs are generally levied at 20 percent or lower, while those on motor vehicles are levied at 50 percent. In addition, an import excise tax is levied on the value of a limited range of imports, inclusive of import duties. That tax is, for example, either 50 percent, 60 percent, or 70 percent on passenger cars, according to engine size. Approved enterprises producing goods for export may receive full or partial exemption from customs duties and excise tax paid on capital equipment, motor vehicles for business use, building materials, and raw materials and components.

Payments for Invisibles

Payments for certain invisibles may be approved by the authorized banks up to specified limits. Payments in excess of these limits, as well as payments for all other invisibles, require the prior approval of the Central Bank, which is granted when applications are supported by documentary proof that capital transactions are not involved. The Central Bank's approval process governing the remittance of invisible payments is concerned only with whether a transaction is bona fide. Residents and expatriates traveling overseas for private purposes are entitled to a foreign currency allowance equivalent to WS$200 a person a day, subject to a limit of WS$3,000 a person a trip; children under 15 years of age are entitled to one half the adult allowances. A daily allowance of WS$300 a person is allotted for business travel, with a limit of WS$4,500 a trip. The Central Bank grants supplementary allocations against evidence that foreign exchange is being used for approved purposes. As part of their foreign currency allowance, resident travelers may take out foreign banknotes equivalent to WS$1,000 a person a trip.

All requests from residents of Western Samoa to remit funds to residents studying abroad to cover their education expenses must be supported by documentary evidence confirming that the beneficiary is enrolled at an educational institution abroad. There is no specific limit for such remittances, but the amount requested must be supported by documentary evidence for costs (e.g., fees, accommodation, and meals) and must be in line with the prevailing costs in the countries of study. Residents of Western Samoa with dependents living abroad may remit, from personal resources, an amount not exceeding WS$2,000 a donor a year to support such dependents. The Central Bank considers requests in excess of this amount on merit. Although no limit is set on remittances to cover expenses for medical treatment abroad, documentary evidence must be provided to support requests for such remittances.

Expatriate workers with local contracts of one year and longer are considered residents and need central bank approval if they wish to repatriate funds in excess of 80 percent of their net earnings on a fortnightly or monthly basis. Earnings not repatriated during the contract may be repatriated at the end of the contract.

Travelers may not take out any domestic currency. A 15 percent withholding tax is levied on remittances of dividends at the source and on interest payments on overseas loans.

Exports and Export Proceeds

All exports require export licenses issued by the Customs Department. Exports may be prohibited by the Director of Agriculture on grounds of low quality, or by order of the head of state to alleviate domestic shortages.

Export proceeds from goods shipped to countries other than American Samoa must be surrendered to the authorized banks within three months of the date of shipment; export proceeds from goods shipped to American Samoa must be surrendered to the authorized bank within four weeks of the date of shipment. Certificates validated by an authorized bank are required for exports in excess of WS$250.

Proceeds from Invisibles

All foreign currencies earned by residents performing services for nonresidents must be surrendered to the authorized banks. Resident travelers must, on their return, sell to the banks all unused foreign currency brought in. Resident and nonresident travelers may bring in any amount in foreign banknotes but may not bring in any domestic banknotes.

Capital

All outward capital transfers by residents require the specific approval of the Central Bank, as does all borrowing abroad by residents, including banks. Inward capital remittances do not normally require approval. Authorized banks may approve transfers of gifts to relatives and dependents, either for special family occasions or for maintenance, up to WS$250 a person a year. Requests for larger amounts may be approved by the Central Bank on a case-by-case basis.

Foreign investment in specified activities in Western Samoa are encouraged. Under the Enterprises Incentive Act, persons engaged in approved enterprises are granted some relief from income tax and business license fees. Both the repatriation of capital and profit remittances on foreign capital must be approved by the Central Bank; such approval is granted when the appropriate documentation is supplied.

Gold

Residents may freely purchase, hold, and sell gold in any form. There are no restrictions on imports or exports of gold.

Changes During 1995

No significant changes occurred in the exchange and trade system.

REPUBLIC OF YEMEN

(Position as of January 31, 1996)

Exchange Arrangement

The currency of the Republic of Yemen is the Yemeni Rial, which is pegged to the U.S. dollar, the intervention currency, at YRls 50.04 per $1 (midpoint rate).[1] On December 31, 1995, the official buying and selling rates for the U.S. dollar were YRls 50.00 and YRls 50.08, respectively, per $1. Buying and selling rates for 12 other currencies[2] are fixed daily by the Central Bank of Yemen on the basis of rates for the U.S. dollar in markets abroad.

There are three exchange rates in the Republic of Yemen. The official rate applies to oil exports, payments of interest and principal on public external debt, government receipts from nonresidents, official travel abroad, limited allocations of foreign exchange for students studying abroad or residents traveling abroad for medical treatment, the Government's transactions with Yemeni embassies, and payments to nonnationals working for the Government. There is a special exchange rate of YRls 12 per $1 applied to the imports of basic foods (wheat and flour). All other foreign exchange transactions take place in the free parallel market where the exchange rate is freely determined by supply and demand. The exchange rate in the parallel market on December 31, 1995, was YRls 127 per $1.

Both banks and moneychangers operate in the free parallel market.[3] The moneychangers operate both inside Yemen and in neighboring countries (mainly in Saudi Arabia), where they acquire foreign exchange primarily from expatriate Yemeni workers, which they remit to their offices in Yemen, which credit the workers' accounts. Most private sector external transactions take place in the parallel market.

There are no arrangements for forward cover against exchange rate risk operating in the official or the commercial banking sector.

---

[1]The dinar of the former People's Democratic Republic of Yemen (YD) is also circulating as legal tender at the rate of YRls 26 per YD 1, but is gradually being withdrawn from circulation.

[2]Deutsche mark, French francs, Italian lire, Japanese yen, Jordan dinars, Kuwaiti dinars, Lebanese pounds, Netherlands guilders, pounds sterling, Saudi Arabian riyals, Swedish kronor, and Swiss francs.

[3]Since December 1995, the commercial banks are permitted to freely compete with moneychangers in the parallel market (Circular No. 5 of November 26, 1995), and may buy and sell foreign exchange at market price on their own account or on behalf of their customers.

Administration of Control

The Central Bank of Yemen establishes a foreign exchange budget in parallel with a commodity budget prepared by the Ministry of Supply and Trade and the Ministry of Industry in consultation with the Central Bank of Yemen. All but a few imports require a license issued by the Ministry of Supply and Trade. Licenses are sent directly to banks opening letters of credit. Commercial banks must provide an implementation guarantee in Yemeni rials equivalent to 2 percent of the value of the import. Transactions in invisibles are supervised by the Central Bank of Yemen.

Prescription of Currency

There are no prescription of currency requirements.[4]

Foreign Exchange Accounts

Commercial banks are permitted to open freely transferable foreign-currency-denominated accounts for residents and nonresidents, provided that the funds in these accounts are derived from (1) foreign currency transfers from abroad; (2) foreign exchange receipts from exports; (3) income from services rendered abroad or to nonresidents; (4) transfers from other freely transferable foreign currency accounts; or (5) foreign currencies, traveler's checks, or bank checks that have been declared to customs. These accounts may be used to (1) finance licensed imports; (2) transfer foreign exchange abroad without prior approval from the Central Bank of Yemen; (3) withdraw foreign currency in cash; (4) make transfers to another freely transferable or nontransferable foreign currency account; and (5) pay expenses and bank commissions.[5]

Imports and Import Payments

An annual foreign exchange budget is prepared by the Central Bank of Yemen and is approved by the Supreme Council for Economic, Oil, and Investment Affairs. In conjunction with the foreign exchange budget, an import program is prepared

---

[4]The requirement to pay hotel bills and airline tickets of nonresidents in foreign currency was abolished on January 1, 1996.

[5]Effective January 1, 1996, the distinction between transferable and nontransferable foreign currency accounts was abolished and these accounts were made free and convertible.

annually by the Ministry of Supply and Trade and the Ministry of Industry. The priority categories are foodstuffs, petroleum products, medicines, and inputs for production.

Imports from Israel and imports of certain types of used machinery for resale are prohibited. Most other imports require licenses and must be processed through local commercial banks. Imports of capital equipment by foreign oil companies do not require a license. Also, all enterprises are permitted to import spare parts up to a maximum value of $5,000 for each unlicensed shipment to meet emergency requirements. The value of imports under this facility is not allowed to exceed $50,000 a year for each enterprise. Yemeni nationals returning from abroad who use their savings in foreign exchange to establish small enterprises or craft shops are allowed to import machinery and spare parts needed for their business activities up to a limit of $40,000 with the authorization of the Ministry of Supply and Trade. In addition, the importation of certain products requires the permission of certain government agencies, and imports of petroleum products are reserved for the Yemen Petroleum Company, a public corporation. With the exception of medical imports, insurance for all imports must be purchased locally.

All importers holding an import license for wheat or flour may obtain the necessary foreign exchange from the Central Bank of Yemen. Imports of other commodities must be self-financed, and foreign exchange may be obtained from any source other than the Central Bank of Yemen. The commercial banks are authorized to open letters of credit for the importation of most goods, provided that such imports are self-financed. The commercial banks are thus authorized to accept import licenses in respect of these imports (which have been issued by the Ministry of Supply and Trade) without approval from the Central Bank of Yemen.

In addition to the applicable customs duty, imports are subject to a tax of 1 percent for reconstruction related to earthquake damage. Imports transported over land routes without a license are subject to a 100 percent surcharge and an advance payment of profits tax equal to 3 percent of their value. A conversion rate of YRls 18 per $1 is applied to all imports for the purpose of customs valuation.

Payments for Invisibles

There is no restriction on invisible payments, although amounts sold by the Central Bank of Yemen at the official exchange rate are limited. The Central Bank of Yemen sells foreign exchange to students studying abroad as well as to individuals seeking medical treatment abroad; the amount allowed for treatment depends on the patient's destination and may not exceed $2,500. Larger amounts are granted on presentation of an official medical report. There are no restrictions on outward remittances in foreign exchange by expatriate workers. The exportation of Yemeni rial banknotes is prohibited.

Exports and Export Proceeds

Exports to Israel are prohibited. All exports must be registered for statistical purposes on forms issued by banks. Exporters of products other than petroleum may use 100 percent of their foreign exchange receipts to finance imports of either their own inputs or any other permitted goods, as long as they have an import license. Exporters do not have to repatriate or surrender their foreign exchange proceeds, which they may retain in free foreign currency accounts with domestic banks.

Proceeds from Invisibles

Proceeds from invisibles need not be repatriated. Travelers may freely bring in any amount in foreign banknotes. The importation of Yemeni rial banknotes is prohibited.

Capital

Inward and outward capital transfers are not restricted.[6]

Foreign direct investment is subject to the provisions of the Investment Law administered by the Public Investment Authority. For approved and registered projects, this law guarantees freedom of investment, equal treatment of foreigners and nationals, the transfer abroad of net profits after taxes attributable to foreign capital, and the repatriation of registered capital on liquidation in the currency of investment. In practice, investors are free to transfer abroad any portion of their share of net profits after taxes and other provisions and to repatriate their capital. Nationalization and confiscation are prohibited, except in cases of urgent public necessity, and then only with compensation and permission to transfer foreign capital abroad. Foreign investments are authorized by the Public Investment Authority for projects deemed to be economically viable and socially acceptable; a reasonable timetable for completion and other conditions must be specified. Certain tax and import duty exemptions and concessions are granted for five years to

---

[6]On January 1, 1996, the Central Bank of Yemen prohibited the banks from granting foreign currency loans.

approved projects that meet specific economic criteria. The registration of direct foreign investments and the authentication of intended profit and capital repatriation are undertaken by the Public Investment Authority. Private capital transactions unrelated to direct investments may also be made without restriction; however, Circular No. 3 of May 7, 1995, prohibits the commercial banks from purchasing foreign exchange for their customers for the purpose of transferring these purchases abroad. External public debt transactions are conducted through the Central Bank of Yemen, which also maintains accounts of outstanding amounts and service payments due.

Commercial banks are required to maintain their overall foreign currency position (short or long) within 20 percent of capital base while the limit in a single currency is 10 percent.

Gold

Residents are free to purchase, hold, and sell gold in any form in the Republic of Yemen.

Changes During 1995

Exchange Arrangement

March 29. The number of exchange rates used in Yemen was reduced from five to three by abolishing the incentive exchange rate of YRls 25 per $1 and the fixed parallel exchange rate of YRls 84 per $1. The official exchange rate that applies to most government, public enterprises, and other agencies transactions was devalued by 76 percent to YRls 50.04 from YRls 12 per $1 (midpoint rate). The "special" exchange rate of YRls 12 per $1 is applied to imports of basic foods (wheat and flour). The third exchange rate is the parallel market exchange rate.

May 7. Commercial banks were allowed to participate in the parallel foreign exchange market, and the official parallel market exchange rate was abolished. The market exchange rate for the commercial banks was set by a committee consisting of the representatives of banks and the Central Bank of Yemen. The limits for the overall foreign currency exposure of banks was set at 20 percent of their capital base, while the limit for any single currency exposure was set at 10 percent of their capital base. In addition, commercial banks were prohibited from purchasing foreign exchange for their customers for the purpose of transferring these purchases to foreign accounts.

December 1. Commercial banks were allowed to buy and sell foreign exchange at freely determined exchange rates in the parallel market and hence compete with moneychangers (Circular No. 5 of November 26, 1995).

Imports and Import Payments

November 27. The Central Bank of Yemen canceled the prohibition on opening letters of credit unless the foreign exchange was purchased from the parallel market using the official parallel exchange rate.

Capital

December 14. The Central Bank of Yemen prohibited banks from granting foreign currency loans. The banks were then given permission to transact on their own account as well as for their customers; banks remit their purchases in foreign currencies to the Central Bank of Yemen.

Changes During 1996

Exchange Arrangement

January 1. Hotels were required to collect all their bills in local currency and convert the balances to foreign exchange using the market exchange rate. The airline companies and agencies were required to collect airline tickets sold domestically only in local currency.

Foreign Exchange Accounts

January 1. The distinction between transferable and nontransferable accounts was eliminated and these accounts became freely transferable.

ZAÏRE

(Position as of December 31, 1995)

Exchange Arrangement

The currency of Zaïre is the New Zaïre. The external value of the new zaïre is determined in daily fixing sessions, in which all financial institutions and the Bank of Zaïre (the central bank) participate. The rates emerging from the fixing session is based on the rate prevailing in the unofficial exchange market. All commercial banks and financial institutions (including 38 exchange bureaus) are permitted to trade in foreign exchange. At the end of each day, all commercial banks and financial institutions are required to determine the total value of purchase and sales transactions in Belgian francs, French francs, and U.S. dollars with customers and with other commercial banks and financial institutions. The banks must also determine the value in new zaïres of the transactions in each of the three currencies and report to the Bank of Zaïre the calculated average effective buying and selling rates of the three currencies as well as the highest and lowest rates quoted in these transactions. The Bank of Zaïre uses this information to arrive at the average effective exchange rate of the new zaïre against 22 other currencies and units, based on the rates provided by the IMF between the U.S. dollar and the currencies concerned.[1] The fixing rate is used as an indicative rate at the opening of trading on the day of their publication and are applied to all government operations, including debt-service payments and the transactions of government-owned enterprises. On December 31, 1995, the rate published by the Bank of Zaïre was NZ 14,830.5 per $1, and the rate emerging from the fixing session was NZ 15,800 per $1.

Charges or commissions are not assessed on interbank market transactions. In their transactions with customers, commercial banks and financial institutions may charge an exchange commission not exceeding 1 percent. The spread between the buying and selling rates for foreign banknotes set by the commercial banks and financial institutions in the foreign exchange market must not exceed 5 percent. Forward transactions may be conducted in the foreign exchange market.

Administration of Control

The Bank of Zaïre has full regulatory authority over all foreign trade and payments, including discretionary power to authorize residents to hold and use foreign exchange abroad and within Zaïre. The Bank of Zaïre may delegate this authority to certain bank or nonbank intermediaries.

The Public Debt Management Office (OGEDEP), operating under the aegis of the Department of Finance, manages the medium- and long-term external and domestic public and publicly guaranteed debt, is responsible for its servicing, and advises the Government on external debt policy, including terms and guarantees extended by the Government on loans contracted by public, semipublic, and private enterprises. In principle, no new external borrowing may be contracted or guaranteed by the Government without the prior advice of OGEDEP and the central bank.

Arrears are maintained with respect to external payments.

Prescription of Currency

Payments from nonresidents to residents must be made in one of the listed convertible currencies whose rates are published daily by the Bank of Zaïre (see footnote 1). Special authorization for the acceptance of any other currency may be given only in respect of currencies that can be exchanged freely without a discount. Residents must make payments to nonresidents in one of the listed convertible currencies or by crediting nonresident accounts in new zaïres or in foreign currency.

Settlements with the member countries of the Economic Community of the Great Lakes Countries (CEPGL), Burundi and Rwanda, and the member countries of the Economic Community of Central African States (CEEAC)[2] are made through convertible accounts established under arrangements concluded by the Bank of Zaïre with the central banks of the countries concerned. Balances on these convertible accounts at the end of settlement periods—each quarter for CEPGL countries and each month for the CEEAC countries—are transferable into the currency stipulated by the creditor. Virtually all settle-

---

[1] Austrian schillings, Belgian francs, Burundi francs, Canadian dollars, CFA francs, Danish kroner, deutsche mark, European currency units, French francs, Italian lire, Japanese yen, Kenya shillings, Netherlands guilders, Norwegian kroner, Portuguese escudos, pounds sterling, Rwanda francs, SDRs, South African rand, Spanish pesetas, Swedish kronor, and Swiss francs.

[2] Burundi, Cameroon, Central African Republic, Chad, the Congo, Equatorial Guinea, Gabon, Rwanda, and São Tomé and Príncipe.

ments (other than for re-exports) with member countries of the CEEAC are effected through the Central African Clearing House (Chambre de compensation de l'Afrique Centrale) through its account with the Bank of Zaïre.

Resident and Nonresident Accounts

There are four categories of nonresident accounts: nonresident foreign currency accounts (*comptes de non-résidents en devises*), nonresident convertible accounts (*comptes étrangers convertibles*), nonresident ordinary accounts (*comptes étrangers ordinaires*), and nonresident special accounts (*comptes étrangers indisponibles*). All nonresident accounts must be maintained as sight deposits and may not show a debit balance.

Nonresident foreign currency accounts, as well as nonresident convertible and special accounts, can be opened at any authorized commercial bank without the prior authorization of the Bank of Zaïre. The opening of nonresident ordinary accounts requires the prior authorization of the Bank of Zaïre. Such authorization is not required when accounts are opened for embassies and other diplomatic missions (including those representing international and official multilateral organizations) or for official civil and military cooperation programs.

Nonresident foreign currency accounts may be credited with foreign currency payments by residents or nonresidents in the following cases: (1) payments authorized by the Bank of Zaïre; (2) transfers of foreign currencies from nonresident convertible accounts; (3) proceeds from arbitrage transactions; (4) inward transfers in foreign currencies from nonresidents and from foreign exchange accounts held abroad; (5) payments in foreign currencies made by nonresidents; and (6) transfers in foreign currencies from other nonresident foreign currency accounts. Nonresident foreign currency accounts may be debited freely for the following purposes: (1) payments authorized by the Bank of Zaïre; (2) sales of foreign currency to any authorized bank against new zaïres; (3) arbitrage of foreign currencies against other foreign currencies authorized by the Bank of Zaïre; (4) outward transfers in foreign currencies; (5) transfers to other nonresident foreign currency accounts; (6) withdrawals of banknotes or traveler's checks by the holder of such accounts; and (7) banking commissions and fees.

Nonresident convertible accounts may be credited with (1) transfers of means of payment in foreign currency at banks or authorized financial institutions; (2) transfers from other nonresident convertible accounts as well as from resident foreign currency accounts; and (3) payments by authorized commercial banks in connection with operations for which the Bank of Zaïre authorizes those banks either to credit nonresident convertible accounts or to deliver foreign currency as stipulated by the exchange regulation. These accounts may be freely debited for (1) payments to residents for operations other than exports of goods and services; (2) purchases in the foreign exchange market of foreign currencies or any other means of payment for travel expenses abroad; (3) transfers to other nonresident convertible accounts and purchases of banknotes or any other means of payment in new zaïres at any authorized commercial bank; and (4) banking commissions and fees.

Nonresident ordinary accounts may be credited with (1) sales of foreign exchange against new zaïres received as down payments or transferred from abroad; (2) transfers in new zaïres from nonresident convertible accounts; and (3) receipts in new zaïres from residents for services rendered in Zaïre, property rentals, transportation fares, consular and chancery fees, and other services as specified by the Bank of Zaïre at the time such accounts are opened. Nonresident ordinary accounts may be debited for (1) payments in new zaïres to residents for local purchases of goods and services, dues, taxes, and banking commissions and fees; (2) transfers to other nonresident ordinary accounts of the same holder; and (3) withdrawals of banknotes or any other means of payment in new zaïres. In addition, assets held in nonresident ordinary accounts are not transferable abroad, nor can they be transferred to nonresident convertible accounts.

Nonresident special accounts can be opened for nonresidents entitled to receive specified payments on account of (1) the sale of, or rental income from, real estate properties and other fixed capital located in Zaïre and owned by nonresidents; and (2) the sale of businesses and goodwill, as well as shares in agricultural, commercial, industrial, and service companies located in Zaïre and owned by nonresidents. In addition, all assets denominated in new zaïres and owned by non-Zaïrian residents permanently leaving Zaïre must be deposited in or transferred to a nonresident special account opened on behalf of or under the name of the respective persons. The same requirements apply to proceeds from the sale of real estate or the rental of fixed capital owned by non-Zaïrian residents who subsequently become nonresidents. Accounts under this category can be debited only for (1) travel expenses incurred by the holders of such accounts; (2) transfers to religious organizations or any nonprofit cultural, philanthropic, or social organizations; (3) banking commissions and fees; (4) local taxes payable to the central Government of Zaïre; (5) insurance and maintenance fees of fixed capital (including real estate properties); and (6) any other payment authorized by the Bank of Zaïre.

Resident foreign currency accounts. Residents are permitted to open foreign currency accounts at local commercial banks. These accounts may be credited with funds arising from capital transactions, receipts from exports of goods and services and prefinancing credits in respect of such exports within the limits established by the Bank of Zaïre. These accounts may be sight or term accounts, may bear interest, and may be denominated in any currency for which the Bank of Zaïre publishes exchange rates. Overdrafts on these accounts are not permitted. Deposits in these accounts may be used to meet virtually any foreign exchange obligation, including import payments, and funds may be transferred from one foreign exchange account to another opened in the name of the same holder, with the exception of accounts opened by artisanal diamond and gold marketing agencies. Existing regulatory and administrative provisions relating to imports apply to imports financed from these accounts. Anyone permitted to make import payments through this method (using Form I) may do so by debiting these accounts. Authorized banks may pay royalties, merchandise transport costs, services, and capital retransfer to nonresidents out of these accounts on the instruction of the account holders, who provide the supporting documents required under the exchange regulations. For account holders with the requisite supporting documentation, Form V is not required for withdrawals to cover travel or living expenses abroad, medical expenses incurred or that will be incurred abroad, educational or training expenses incurred or that will be incurred abroad, and tickets for international travel.

Imports and Import Payments

Certain imports, including arms, explosives and ammunition, narcotics, materials contrary to public morals, and certain alcoholic beverages, are prohibited or require special authorization from the Government. Most other imports are subject only to an import declaration at the authorized banks. In general, import declarations remain valid for 12 months; an importer wishing to extend the validity period must so indicate in the import documents accompanying the declaration. The validity may be extended for the first time by the authorized banks if shipment has begun; if shipment has not begun, extension of the validity period requires authoriza-

tion from the Bank of Zaïre. Imports of goods intended for expansion of a capital base or for the importer's own use may be effected without a declaration to an authorized bank, provided that the value does not exceed SDR 1,000 for each tariff item and SDR 5,000 for each shipment and that the shipments are financed from the importer's own resources.

All goods shipped by sea to Zaïre must be transported on vessels belonging to shipowners that are bonded with the Office zaïrois de gestion des frets maritimes (OGEFREM) and whose freight charges have been negotiated with that office.

Payments for imports may be made either upon arrival or upon shipment (including payments up to 30 days from date of shipment). Banks may pay freight charges only upon presentation of invoices from the carriers or their agents. The mode of payment must be indicated on all import declaration forms. Authorized banks are allowed to pay transportation and insurance costs in foreign exchange only on imports for which they are directly involved in the financing on an f.o.b. basis. With a few exceptions, imports are subjected to a preshipment inspection. The amount, the invoice price, and the quality of imports must be verified and found acceptable by the foreign agents of the Zaïrian Control Office (OZAC); however, in special cases, verification may be effected upon arrival, subject to a waiver from the Bank of Zaïre. Verification certificates are not required for import values (f.o.b.) of SDR 1,000 or less for each tariff item, or of SDR 5,000 or less for each shipment.

Prior approval from the Bank of Zaïre is required for (1) imports in the form of foreign contributions to capital intended for resale; (2) imports financed by suppliers' credits or other interest-bearing foreign financing with a maturity of more than one year, except imports contracted or guaranteed by the Government; (3) imports requiring a down payment in foreign currency before shipment; and (4) imports requiring special authorization from the Government and imports of currency, coins, and articles imitating or bearing the monetary symbols of Zaïrian currency.

Prior approval from the Bank of Zaïre is no longer required for imports by air provided that (1) such imports are of an emergency nature; (2) goods to be imported are fragile or perishable; or (3) the cost to the final destination in Zaïre is less than or equivalent to any other means of transport.

The customs tariff rates range from 15 percent to 50 percent, with a special rate of 5 percent for some equipment. The rate of the turnover tax ranges from zero to 20 percent.

Payments for Invisibles

All payments for invisibles must be made through an authorized bank. When the approval of the Bank of Zaïre is required, it must be requested by the authorized banks concerned. The Bank of Zaïre will not authorize the payment in foreign exchange of commissions in favor of shippers or purchasing agents.

Other payments relating to services performed by nonresidents are, in principle, permitted. However, outward remittances of salaries of expatriate employees are limited to the levels authorized during the preceding year. The transfer abroad of salaries of newly hired expatriates is limited to 50 percent of net salary, provided that the nontransferable amount is sufficient to meet local needs. Transfers pertaining to certain administrative expenses that firms incur abroad, payment of interest on private loans and certain portions of insurance premiums are generally permitted. Transfers of net profits of firms with foreign participation are authorized. Transfers of rental income received by nonresidents and residents who are foreign nationals are suspended. Payments for commissions, brokerage charges and miscellaneous fees, and royalties may be authorized in some cases.

Tickets for travel abroad may be purchased in new zaïres or in foreign currency for trips originating in Zaïre. Zaïrian nationals traveling abroad may buy foreign exchange from banks or authorized financial institutions, including money changers. Residents who are foreign nationals and who are entitled to transfer part of their income abroad are not allowed to obtain foreign currency from authorized banks to pay for their tickets for international travel and their living expenses abroad involving private travel. For trips to Burundi and Rwanda, tourists and households residing in the border area are entitled to purchase the equivalent of SDR 100 in Burundi or Rwanda francs a month.

The exportation of Zaïrian banknotes and coins by residents and nonresidents is permitted only up to the equivalent of $100. However, the exportation of Zaïrian banknotes and coins by travelers from Burundi and Rwanda is authorized within the limits of the agreements concluded between the members of the CEPGL.

Exports and Export Proceeds

Exporters must file an exchange document (declaration of foreign exchange commitment), which banks are normally authorized to validate, for all exports. These declarations must specify the type of merchandise to be exported, its price, and the currency in which payment is to be received. Declarations of foreign exchange commitment are normally valid for 90 days. Exports must be carried out and proceeds must be received and surrendered within this period, which must not exceed 45 days from the date of shipment, except for export earnings from artisanal gold and diamonds which must be repatriated before the declaration of foreign exchange commitment is validated at a bank.

Exporters are authorized to retain the following in their RME accounts at authorized banks: (1) 70 percent of their export-generated revenue from artisanal gold and diamonds, and 40 percent from all other goods, to the extent that repatriation occurs within the legally required period of 45 days from the date of shipment, except for the exports by Gécamine, which are under discussion; and (2) 100 percent of funds received as prefinancing for products intended for exportation. The corresponding ratios are: 45 percent for Générale des carrières et des mines du Zaïre, 50 percent for Société de développement industriel et minier du Zaïre, and 20 percent for Société minière de Bakwanga. The Bank of Zaïre may authorize the holding abroad of a portion of earnings from exports.

The exportation, turnover, and statistical taxes on coffee exports have been suspended. Economic transactors may export coffee, subject to inspection and quality certificates issued respectively by the OZAC and the Zaïrian Office for Coffee (OZACAF). As in the case of other export products, coffee may be exported under prefinancing contracts.

Artisanal gold and diamonds may be exported only through authorized marketing agencies (comptoirs agréés).

The Bank of Zaïre purchases and exports gold on its own account, along with the authorized marketing agencies in the market. Industrial diamonds and gold may be exported directly by the mining companies involved.

Proceeds from Invisibles

Proceeds from invisibles must be repatriated and transferred through authorized banks. A declaration must be made for each transaction and checked by the bank. For some operations, proceeds may be credited to a resident foreign currency account.

An unlimited amount of banknotes and other means of payment in foreign currency may be brought into the country by resident and nonresident travelers. The importation of Zaïrian banknotes and coins is permitted only up to the equivalent of $100.

Capital

The repatriation of foreign capital brought in under the provisions of the Investment Code is permitted only at the time of liquidation, nationalization, or partial or total transfers of shares. Borrowed capital and equity contributions are authorized. Transfers abroad of such contributions made under the Investment Code are guaranteed. The Bank of Zaïre also guarantees transfers abroad of interest, dividends, and profits in respect of foreign capital.

Gold

Only Zaïrian nationals are allowed to purchase, transport, sell, or hold gold within Zaïre outside the boundaries of areas covered by exclusive mining concessions. Foreign individuals or corporate persons and corporate persons under Zaïrian law may do so only on behalf of and for the account of authorized marketing agencies. Exports of gold and diamonds by authorized marketing agencies do not require prior authorization from the Bank of Zaïre.

Changes During 1995

No significant changes occurred in the exchange and trade system.

ZAMBIA

(Position as of December 31, 1995)

Exchange Arrangement

The currency of Zambia is the Zambian Kwacha. All foreign exchange transactions take place at market-determined exchange rates. The official exchange rate of the Bank of Zambia is determined by the weighted-average buying exchange rate quoted by commercial banks through the dealing window of the Bank of Zambia. A spread of ±2 percent is applied to the weighted average dealing rate to arrive at the Bank of Zambia's buying and selling rates. The Bank of Zambia's official rate applies to that portion of foreign exchange purchased from the market, the most important being the Zambia Consolidated Copper Mines (ZCCM), and to government transactions, including donor assistance and debt service.

The Bank of Zambia conducts daily interbank dealing sessions at which it invites bids and offers from authorized dealers (i.e., registered commercial banks). On the basis of the bids and offers received, as well as other budgetary considerations (such as government and Bank of Zambia requirements, donor assistance funds, and export earnings), the Bank of Zambia determines the amount of foreign exchange to be sold to or purchased from the market. In addition to the Bank of Zambia dealing market, there is an emerging interbank market. Exchange rates in this market closely follow those established at the Bank of Zambia's dealing window.

The Bank of Zambia deals with the Government and authorized commercial banks in U.S. dollars, which is also its currency of intervention. However, banks are free to deal in currencies of their choice, on the basis of cross rates with the U.S. dollar prevailing in the major international foreign exchange markets. With the lifting of exchange controls, all fees and charges applied by commercial banks and foreign exchange bureaus are determined competitively.

There are no arrangements for forward cover against exchange rate risk operating in the official or the commercial banking sector. Banks are allowed to maintain open foreign exchange positions. Foreign exchange bureaus are required to maintain open foreign exchange positions of up to 25 percent of their capital. Any breach of the open position limits may be subject to a penalty from the Bank of Zambia.

Administration of Control

All exchange controls were abolished as of January 28, 1994. The only exceptions are the require-

ment that (1) the ZCCM must sell all or part of its foreign exchange earnings to the Bank of Zambia until a more integrated interbank market develops and foreign exchange earnings from nontraditional exports become significant; and (2) prior approval of the Bank of Zambia must be obtained for servicing of private debt incurred prior to January 28, 1994. The Ministry of Commerce, Trade, and Industry is responsible for trade control.

Arrears are maintained with respect to certain external payments.

Prescription of Currency

Authorized payments, including import payments, from residents of Zambia to residents of other countries may be made in any foreign currency. Payments from residents of other countries may be made in pounds sterling or in Zambian kwacha from an external account, or in any currency freely exchangeable for U.S. dollars or pounds sterling.

External Accounts

Both residents and nonresidents are free to establish and maintain foreign currency accounts at commercial banks in Zambia and abroad.

Imports and Import Payments

Imports in general require a license for statistical purposes, which are granted automatically by commercial banks. Personal and household effects, trade samples, diplomatic shipments, and vehicles brought into Zambia temporarily do not require a license.

Imports are subject to preshipment inspection except when the f.o.b. value of each import consignment is less than $10,000.

Imports are subject to a tariff with a minimum rate of 20 percent and a maximum rate of 50 percent (except for a few luxury goods). Some imports are exempt under the provisions of bilateral agreements, and nontraditional exporters and certain competing import firms are exempt under the 1991 Investment Act. In addition, imported goods are subject to an "uplift factor" in computing domestic sales tax.

Payments for Invisibles

All payments for invisibles, except external debt-service payments, may be effected through banks and foreign exchange bureaus without the prior approval of the Bank of Zambia. Remittances of profits and dividends may be made without restriction after payment of all taxes.

Foreign nationals working on contract in Zambia may remit any amount including "inducement allowances" and gratuities without restriction. Payments to expatriates employed by the ZCCM and other exporters may be made from the exporters' exchange holdings or from the foreign exchange market.

Travelers may take out any amount in any currency without prior permission, although they are required to make a declaration if the amounts involved exceed the equivalent of $5,500.

Exports and Export Proceeds

All exports must be declared on the prescribed export declaration form for statistical purposes. Although export licenses are required for most goods, they are administered routinely by commercial banks under the authority delegated by the Ministry of Commerce, Trade, and Industry. Exports of white maize and fertilizers may be subject to quantitative restrictions when domestic supplies are short; exports of ivory are prohibited. Forty-five percent of the foreign exchange earnings of the ZCCM must be surrendered to the Bank of Zambia. Exporters of nontraditional products are allowed to retain all of their foreign exchange earnings without restriction.

Proceeds from Invisibles

Receipts from invisibles may be retained in full. There is no limit on the amount of foreign exchange or domestic currency notes a traveler may bring in, but amounts exceeding the equivalent of $5,000 must be declared at customs.

Capital

All borrowings outside Zambia must be registered with the Bank of Zambia for statistical purposes. Outward transfers of capital are free of controls. Disinvestment and repatriation of capital are also unrestricted, subject to verification that no tax obligations are due. No restrictions apply to the sale of assets between foreigners and between Zambians and foreigners. Local borrowing by companies controlled either directly or indirectly from outside Zambia is unrestricted. Nonresidents may participate in the treasury bill and government bond markets without restriction and are free to remit proceeds from the sales of these instruments after payment of applicable taxes.

Gold

Residents may hold and acquire gold coins in Zambia for numismatic and any other purpose. Imports and exports of gold in any form other than jewelry require approval from the Ministry of Mines.

Changes During 1995

Exchange Arrangement

April 24. The Bank of Zambia began to deal in foreign exchange operations on a daily basis instead of three times a week.

ZIMBABWE

(Position as of December 31, 1995)

Exchange Arrangement

The currency of Zimbabwe is the Zimbabwe Dollar. The external value of the Zimbabwe dollar is determined on the basis of supply and demand in the exchange market. The U.S. dollar is the intervention currency. The spread applied by the Reserve Bank of Zimbabwe between the buying and selling rates is 0.8 percent for all currencies. Authorized dealers (authorized commercial and merchant banks) may charge an additional 0.25 percent on either side of the quoted rates of major currencies. The authorized dealers base their rates for other currencies on current international market rates. On December 31, 1995, the exchange rate quoted by the Reserve Bank was Z$8.3472 per US$1.

Forward exchange contracts are permitted only for trade transactions. There is no limit on the size of such contracts, but their duration must be at least one year, depending on the currencies involved and the type of coverage. The Reserve Bank does not offer forward foreign exchange contracts. Forward sales of foreign exchange take place at the spot preferential telex transfer rate plus a premium loading for six months, depending on the currencies involved and type of coverage. Authorized dealers are expected to quote to their customers the dealers' own telex transfer rates. Authorized dealers are subject to overnight net foreign currency exposure limits, but no other restrictions from the Reserve Bank apply to interbank trading.

Zimbabwe accepted the obligations of Article VIII, Sections 2, 3, and 4 of the Fund Agreement on February 5, 1995.

Administration of Control

Exchange control is administered by the Reserve Bank under powers delegated by the Minister of Finance, in keeping with the Exchange Control Act, Chapter 170, and the Exchange Control Regulations of 1977. Authorized dealers may approve certain foreign exchange transactions in accordance with Exchange Control Instructions Issued to Authorized Dealers (July 1, 1981, as amended) and Exchange Control Circulars (issued periodically).

Prescription of Currency

With the exception of payments otherwise specified or effected through nonresident accounts, all payments by nonresidents to residents must be effected in denominated currencies.[1] Under the Clearing House Agreement, which went into effect on February 1, 1984, within the Preferential Trade Area for Eastern and Southern African States (PTA), residents of member countries may use national currencies in day-to-day payments during a transaction period of two calendar months; the monetary authorities settle net balances at the end of this period in convertible currencies.

Resident and Nonresident Accounts

Nonresident accounts may be opened with the approval of the exchange control authorities by persons who have never been residents of Zimbabwe. Nonresident accounts may be credited with foreign currencies, with payments from other nonresident accounts, or with payments by residents that would be eligible for transfer outside Zimbabwe. Nonresident accounts may be debited for payments to residents, for payments to other nonresident accounts, or for payments abroad. Only former residents now residing outside Zimbabwe may maintain emigrants' accounts in Zimbabwe. Cash assets held in Zimbabwe in the names of emigrants must be blocked in these accounts, and all payments to and from these accounts are subject to various exchange restrictions.

Residents and nonresident individuals may open foreign currency accounts in one of the denominated currencies in local branches of authorized dealers. Funds in these accounts are traded at market-determined exchange rates. Funds withdrawn from these accounts and converted into local currency, however, may not be redeposited in the account, except in the case of the initial investment, and income or capital gains from investments in the stock exchange, unlisted companies, or money markets.

Imports and Import Payments

There are no import-licensing requirements. The negative list for imports includes items restricted for

---

[1]Seventeen denominated currencies are freely convertible through authorized dealers: Austrian schillings, Belgian francs, Canadian dollars, Danish kroner, deutsche mark, French francs, Italian lire, Japanese yen, Netherlands guilders, Norwegian kroner, Portuguese escudos, pounds sterling, South African rand, Spanish pesetas, Swedish kronor, Swiss francs, and U.S. dollars.

health or security reasons as well as textiles and apparel, alcoholic beverages, canned beverages, nonmonetary gold, pearls, precious and semiprecious stones, and some jewelry items. Imports of certain goods (mostly agricultural and processed food products) require a special permit issued by the Ministry of Agriculture. Certain agricultural products (coffee, maize, sorghum, soybeans, and wheat) may be imported only by the Grain Marketing and Cotton Marketing Boards or by others with the permission of the Boards. No quotas are in force, but seasonal restrictions are applied to certain agricultural products.

Authorized dealers may approve applications to effect payments for authorized imports, provided the necessary documentation (including the details of import licenses or open general licenses) is submitted. Payments for imports into Zimbabwe from all countries may be made in Zimbabwean currency to a local nonresident account or in any foreign currency. Authorized dealers may provide foreign exchange for advanced payment for imports up to US$50,000.

The customs duty regime consists mainly of ad valorem duties, which range up to a maximum of 35 percent of the c.i.f. value for most consumer goods (up to 60 percent to 75 percent for vehicles) with a surtax of 10 percent, and specific duties on a number of products. Generally, imports are subject to an additional tax (between 12.5 percent and 20 percent) equivalent to the sales taxes imposed at the same rates on goods sold domestically. Government imports and capital goods for statutory bodies are exempt from customs duties.

Payments for Invisibles

Foreign exchange to pay for invisibles related to imports and, within certain limits, for other purposes is provided by commercial banks under delegated authority. Applications for foreign exchange exceeding the limit established for commercial banks are approved by the Reserve Bank, which deals with each case on its merits.

All dividends declared by foreign investors in the export sector after January 1, 1995 may be remitted to foreign shareholders without restriction after payment of applicable taxes. If direct foreign exchange allocation was used, the following rules apply: (1) a wholly foreign-owned company that meets the criteria to qualify as an export firm, and funds its projects through a combination of foreign exchange, "switched blocked funds," or surplus funds, is permitted to remit the declared dividends from net after-tax profits on a basis proportionate to the level of foreign exchange invested but limited to a maximum of 50 percent for five years from the beginning of operations, after which the company will qualify for 100 percent remittance of dividends (blocked and surplus funds are assets held by foreigners as a result of the limited remittance of dividends; switched blocked funds are blocked funds purchased by a foreigner from the original owner); (2) a wholly foreign-owned company with its own blocked funds is permitted to repatriate 100 percent of its declared dividends, provided it meets all its foreign exchange requirements from external sources; and (3) in the case of a new joint venture that meets the criteria to qualify as an export firm and has at least 30 percent local participation, the foreign partner is allowed to remit 100 percent of its share of declared dividends, provided that it meets its share of foreign exchange requirements from external sources. Outward remittances in respect of services are subject to a 20 percent tax; in cases that fall under double taxation agreements, the tax rate is 10 percent. Foreign companies established prior to September 1979 are permitted to remit 50 percent of net after-tax profits if exports comprise more than 25 percent of total sales.

The following regulations apply to investments in the mining sector: (1) a wholly foreign-owned company that funds its projects through foreign funds is allowed to repatriate 100 percent of its net after-tax profits, provided that it qualifies as an export-oriented project; (2) a wholly foreign-owned company that funds its projects through a combination of foreign funds and either its own blocked funds, switched blocked funds, or surplus funds (subject to a minimum matching formula of 50–50) is allowed to remit dividends of up to 50 percent in proportion to the matching ratio; and (3) the level of dividend remittance for joint ventures subject to the minimum 30 percent local participation criterion is also determined by the matching formula used by the foreign shareholder. After five years, the company can remit 100 percent of its dividends to the foreign shareholder.

The basic foreign exchange allowance for holiday travel is US$5,000 a year. Children under ten years are entitled to one-half this amount. The basic foreign exchange allowance for business travel is US$600 a day. Applications for holiday and business travel allowances exceeding the specified limits are subject to the approval of the Reserve Bank and are granted in bona fide cases.

Foreign exchange is provided for education abroad beyond the secondary school level for certain diploma and degree courses up to US$50,000 a year. All applications for educational allowances must be submitted to the Reserve Bank for approval. For medical treatment, foreign exchange is provided up to US$20,000 a trip for the patient and any necessary accompanying companion. Applications for additional amounts must be submitted to the Reserve Bank for approval.

Applications for emigrant status must be submitted to the Reserve Bank; the settling-in allowance that emigrants may remit abroad is limited to Z$1,000 a family unit. In exceptional and deserving cases, the exchange control authorities will consider applications exceeding this maximum. All those applying for emigrant status are required to take steps to liquidate their assets within six months and to invest the total proceeds, less any settling-in allowance granted, in 4 percent, 12-year Zimbabwean government external bonds. If emigrants are unable to comply with the six-month limit, the matter may be referred to the Reserve Bank. Transferable allowances at the time of emigration are as follows: (1) each person under the age of 40 years, Z$500; (2) each person aged 40–59 years, Z$1,000; (3) family units and single persons (under 60 years of age) with dependents, Z$1,000; (4) family units (husband over 60 years of age) and single persons over 60, Z$7,000; (5) persons over 80 years of age, Z$10,000; and (6) handicapped or disabled persons, Z$10,000. A further release of capital is authorized as an annual allowance on each anniversary of the emigrant's departure, as follows: persons over 65 years of age, Z$2,000; and persons over 70 years of age, Z$3,000.

Travelers leaving Zimbabwe may take out, as part of their travel allowance, up to Z$250 in Zimbabwean currency, together with a maximum of the equivalent of US$500 in foreign banknotes. Nonresident travelers may take out the traveler's checks they brought in, less the amount they sold to authorized dealers. Upon departure from Zimbabwe, nonresident travelers may reconvert unspent Zimbabwean currency into foreign currencies on presentation of exchange certificates.

Exports and Export Proceeds

Exporters must have licenses to export the following: (1) any ore, concentrate, or other manufactured product of chrome, copper, lithium, nickel, tin, or tungsten; (2) petroleum products; (3) jute and hessian bags; (4) road or rail tankers for carrying liquids or semiliquids; (5) bitumen, asphalt, and tar; (6) wild animals and wild animal products; (7) certain wood products; (8) ammonium nitrate; and (9) implements of war. Export-licensing requirements are imposed for reasons of health and social welfare, as well as to

ensure an adequate domestic supply of essential products.

Export permits are required from the Ministry of Lands and Agriculture for some basic agricultural commodities, including maize, oilseeds, cheese, skimmed milk, seeds, potatoes, citrus fruits, apples, bananas, and tomatoes.

Goods may not be exported without permission unless the customs authorities are satisfied that payment has been made in an approved manner or will be made within three months of the date of shipment (or a longer period if permitted by the Reserve Bank). Payments for exports must be received in one of the following ways: (1) in a denominated currency; (2) in Zimbabwean currency from a nonresident account; and (3) in the case of Malawi and Botswana, by checks drawn in Malawi kwacha or Botswana pula. Exporters are permitted to retain 100 percent of proceeds in foreign exchange. Under the PTA arrangement, member countries may use national currencies in the settlement of payments during a transaction period of two months, with net balances at the end of this period to be settled in convertible currencies. Exports to some 50 countries are approved only upon advance payment of export proceeds or if the payment is covered by an irrevocable letter of credit issued or confirmed before exportation by a reputable overseas bank.

Proceeds from Invisibles

Receipts from invisibles must be sold to authorized banks within a reasonable period of time. Residents performing services abroad may also retain a portion of their earnings. Foreign currency and traveler's checks may be imported without restriction but must be sold or exchanged in Zimbabwe only through authorized dealers. A traveler may bring in Zimbabwean currency up to a maximum of Z$250.

Capital

Inward transfers of capital through normal banking channels are not restricted. The limit on foreign borrowing without prior approval of the External Loans Coordinating Committee is US$5 million.

Outward transfers of capital are controlled. However, all foreign investments, irrespective of their source, that have been undertaken through normal banking channels since September 1, 1979 may be considered for repatriation up to the value of capital invested less dividends transferred abroad. The balance may be transferred only through the established medium of six-year external government bonds bearing interest at the rate of 4 percent a year.

Repatriation of net equity may be permitted without restriction if funds are used to acquire foreign exchange and if dividends were not remitted with such funds.

The repatriation of capital invested before September 1, 1979 is prohibited; however, shareholders are allowed, within limits, to apply to the Reserve Bank for the remittance of such capital upon the sale of shares to local residents, and if such application is approved, the capital is invested in external government bonds bearing interest at the rate of 4 percent a year and carrying a maturity of 12 years (for individuals) or 20 years (for firms). Repatriation of net equity at accelerated rates that depend on discounted sales prices is allowed.

Former residents holding blocked assets and new emigrants are allowed to invest their funds in government external bonds with a maturity of 12 years and an annual interest rate of 4 percent. Remittance of a former resident's Zimbabwean pension is guaranteed under the constitution. All other outward transfers of capital are subject to approval by the Reserve Bank, as are dealings in external securities.

Previously blocked funds, whether already converted into government bonds or not, can qualify as new venture capital if they are reinvested in Zimbabwe in an approved project and matched by an inflow of investment funds of up to 50 percent of the reinvested blocked funds, as determined by the Reserve Bank. Blocked funds can be used by third parties, foreign as well as domestic, for investment on freely negotiated terms as new venture capital; the total investment is eligible to be remitted as dividends for up to 50 percent of after-tax profits. However, the "blocked" portion of the new investment, unlike new venture capital, must be reinvested in Zimbabwe for at least five years. Gold producers undertaking new expansion projects are permitted access to offshore financing in the form of gold loans. Foreign investors are permitted to participate in the Zimbabwe Stock Exchange Market using currency received in Zimbabwe through normal banking channels. Purchase of shares by foreign investors is limited to 25 percent of the total equity of the company, with a limit of 5 percent for one investor. These limits are in addition to any existing foreign shareholdings in the companies. The initial investment plus any capital gains and dividend income may be remitted without restriction. Foreign investors may also invest up to a maximum of 15 percent of the assets brought to Zimbabwe in primary issues of bonds and stocks.

Locally owned companies (greater than 75 percent equity owned by residents) may buy blocked funds from the original owners for investment purposes by using funds from the export retention scheme, provided that they export at least 75 percent of their output.

Direct foreign investments up to US$40 million in the preferred areas (mining, agro-industry, manufacturing, tourism, and high-technology services) are approved by the Zimbabwe Investment Centre (ZIC). In the preferred areas, 100 percent foreign ownership is permitted; it is restricted to 25 percent in other areas.

Gold

The exportation of gold in unmanufactured form is controlled and licensed under the Control of Goods (exportation of minerals and metals) Order, 1979, which is administered by the Ministry of Mines. No person may export any precious metal or certain other specified metals and minerals without an export license; no such licenses for gold are issued. These controls do not, however, apply to the Reserve Bank. The importation of gold is controlled by the Gold Trade Act, which requires those intending to import gold into Zimbabwe to meet certain requirements.

No person, either as principal or agent, is entitled to deal in or possess gold unless that person is (1) the holder of a license or permit; (2) the holder or distributor of a registered mining location from which gold is being produced; or (3) the employee or agent of any of the persons mentioned in (1) and (2) above and authorized by an employer or principal to deal in or possess gold that is already in the lawful possession of such employer or principal. A mining commissioner may issue to any person a permit authorizing the acquisition, possession, or disposal of any gold, provided the quantity does not exceed 1 troy ounce. In all other cases, permission can be issued only by the Secretary for Mines. Three types of licenses may be issued under the terms of the Gold Trade Act: a gold dealing license, a gold recovery works license, and a gold assaying license. Barclays Bank of Zimbabwe, Ltd., is the only authorized dealer under the terms of the act. Each holder or distributor of a registered mining location is required to lodge with this bank all gold acquired each month by the tenth day of the following month. Any person intending to smelt gold or any article containing gold must first obtain a license issued by a district commissioner under the terms of the Secondhand Goods Act that authorizes the possession of smelting equipment.

Changes During 1995

Exchange Arrangement

February 5. Zimbabwe accepted the obligations of Article VIII, Sections 2, 3, and 4 of the Articles of Agreement.

Payments for Invisibles

September 6. The maximum amount of foreign currency in cash that Zimbabwean travelers may carry when traveling abroad was increased from US$200 to US$500, or its equivalent in other foreign currencies.

Capital

February 1. A timetable for the liquidation, over a three-year period starting July 1, 1995, of blocked funds relating to profits and dividends earned on foreign investments made prior to May 1993 was established.

September 6. (1) The "switching" of blocked funds, which allowed release of blocked funds under certain conditions if purchased by a foreign investor or local exporter, was discontinued; (2) Foreign investments of up to 25 percent, in aggregate, in primary issues of stocks and bonds were permitted.

APPENDIX
European Union: Selected Trade Measures
Introduced and Eliminated on an EU-Wide Basis During 1995[1]

Common Import Policy

1. Antidumping Activities

May 29. Changes in antidumping and countervailing duty procedures, including new time limits for the procedures, were adopted by the Council and entered into force on September 1, 1995. The changes transposed Uruguay Round rules into EU legislation (Council Regulations Nos. 1251/95 and 1252/95).

The European Union undertook the following numbers of antidumping actions in 1995: investigations, 33; provisional duties, 24; definitive duties, 13; reviews, 26; temporary suspensions, 3; and terminations, 8. Major actions included the following:

March 27. Definitive antidumping duties were imposed on imports of television sets from the People's Republic of China, the Republic of Korea, Malaysia, Singapore, and Thailand (Council Regulation No. 710/95).

August 16. Definitive antidumping duties were imposed on imports of ammonium nitrate from the Russian Federation (Council Regulation No. 2022/95).

October 2. Definitive antidumping duties were imposed on imports of photocopiers from Japan after a review of a case (Council Regulation No. 2380/95).

October 6. Definitive antidumping duties were imposed on imports of ferro-silico-manganese from Brazil, the Russian Federation, South Africa, and Ukraine (Council Regulation No. 2413/95).

October 10. Definitive antidumping duties were imposed on imports of disodium carbonate from the United States (Council Regulation No. 2381/95).

December 22. Definitive antidumping duties were imposed on imports of microwave ovens from the People's Republic of China, the Republic of Korea, Malaysia, and Thailand (Council Regulation No. 5/96).

2. Safeguards

January 16. The Commission adopted a regulation introducing provisional quantitative limits on imports of certain textile products from the People's

Republic of China (Commission Regulation No. 59/95).

February 27. The Commission adopted a regulation introducing modified quantitative limits on imports of certain textile products from Pakistan (Commission Regulation No. 405/95).

March 7. The Commission adopted a regulation imposing definitive quantitative limits on imports of certain textile products from India and Indonesia (Commission Regulation No. 507/95).

3. Preferences

May 22. The Council approved the accession of Zambia to the Protocol on sugar of the fourth Lomé Convention effective January 1, 1995 (Council Decision 95/185/EC).

July 17. The Council adopted agreements on preferential import quotas for unrefined cane sugar with African, Caribbean, and Pacific (ACP) sugar suppliers and India for the period July 1, 1995 to June 30, 2001 (Council Decision No. 95/284/EC).

October 23. The application by the European Union of tariff preferences for imports of certain agricultural goods from South Africa was extended for 1995 (Council Regulation No. 2651/95).

October 30. The Council adopted a decision providing for implementation of the fourth Lomé Convention by the new EU members (Austria, Finland, and Sweden) and the ACP countries (Bulletin 10-1995, Point 1.4.115).

December 22. The Council adopted a regulation extending application of generalized tariff preferences for certain agricultural products for six months (Council Regulation No. 3058/95).

4. Other Import Measures

February 20. The EU Council adopted a decision authorizing provisional implementation of protocols adjusting bilateral textiles agreements with numerous suppliers to take into account the accession to the European Union of Austria, Finland, and Sweden (Bulletin 1/2-1995, Point 1.4.61).

March 1. The European Commission established tariff quotas for banana imports for 1995 in which 2.2 million tons would come from nontraditional (i.e., non-ACP) suppliers.

March 6. The rules governing imports from state-trading countries were amended in order to take account of EU enlargement resulting in changes in

[1]Sources: *Official Journals of the European Communities*; *General Report on the Activities of the European Union*; *1995*; *European Report*.

the system of non-textile import quotas applying to the People's Republic of China.

March 31. The European Commission and the Ministry of Trade and Industry of Japan extended an arrangement regarding Japanese exports of automobiles to the European Union, establishing overall export levels to the European Union and expected levels of exports to five protected markets (France, Italy, Portugal, Spain, and the United Kingdom) for 1995. The export ceilings were also modified to take account of EU enlargement.

April 4. The European Commission approved an increase in imports of bananas under its tariff quota system to take account of the accession to the European Union of Austria, Finland, and Sweden.

April 10. The rules governing imports from state-trading countries were amended to terminate their applicability to the Baltic countries.

April 11. The European Commission adopted a regulation establishing definitive quantitative limits on imports of certain textile products from the People's Republic of China (Commission Regulation No. 810/95).

June 6. The Council adopted a regulation adjusting Community import quotas on textiles with third countries as a result of the accession to the European Union of Austria, Finland, and Sweden (Council Regulation No. 1325/95).

June 13. The Council approved an agreement between the European Union and the People's Republic of China adjusting the rates of increase and flexibility of textile import quotas (Bulletin 6-1995, Point 1.4.38).

June 13. The Council approved a textile trade agreement between the European Union and Mongolia to run through end-1997 (Bulletin 6-1995, Point 1.4.39).

July 24. The Council approved a regulation setting quotas on rum imported from ACP states for the period July 1, 1995–December 31, 1995, prior to the entry into force of a new rum import regime beginning in 1996.

October 6. The European Union reduced the 1995 import targets for automobiles from Japan in order to reflect an expected decline in sales growth.

October 31. The Council adopted a regulation phasing out quotas on rum imported from ACP states by the year 2000.

November 13. The European Union introduced a system for the surveillance of imports of certain textile and clothing items from the United Arab Emirates, pending conclusion of a bilateral textile and clothing agreement (Commission Regulation No. 2635/95).

December 7. The European Commission signed a steel import agreement with the Russian Federation covering 1995 and 1996. Russian quotas were set at 309,000 metric tons in 1995 (Bulletin 12-1995, Point 1.4.37).

December 15. The European Commission signed a steel import agreement with Ukraine covering 1995 and 1996, with Ukrainian quotas set at 131,000 metric tons for 1995 (Bulletin 12-1995, Point 1.4.37).

December 22. The Council adopted a provisional decision implementing a renewal of a bilateral agreement with amendments on textile trade with the People's Republic of China previously covered under the Multifiber Arrangement, which was scheduled to expire at end-1995.

December 22. The Council adopted a regulation extending for three years autonomous arrangements covering textiles imports from Taiwan Province of China, which were scheduled to expire at end-1995 (Council Regulation No. 3060/95).

December 22. The Council decided to implement provisionally amendments to a textile import agreement with Vietnam.

December 22. The Council adopted revised protocols to the European Agreements dealing with textile imports from Bulgaria, the Czech Republic, Hungary, Poland, Romania, and the Slovak Republic.

December 22. The Council adopted a provisional decision implementing a protocol on textile trade with Slovenia, whereby all quantitative restrictions would be eliminated by January 1, 1998, and Slovenia would eliminate all duties on textiles by January 1, 2001.

December 22. The Council adopted a provisional decision to apply renewed agreements on textile trade for two years with Egypt, Malta, Morocco, and Tunisia that were scheduled to expire at end-1995.

December 22. The Council authorized provisional implementation of renewed bilateral textile and clothing trade agreements with Belarus, the Russian Federation, Ukraine, and Uzbekistan, which were scheduled to expire at end-1995.

Multilateral and Regional Developments

1. Multilateral Developments

January 1. The United States and the European Union reached agreement on an interim six-month set of compensating tariffs and quotas to offset increases due to EU enlargement to include Austria, Finland, and Sweden.

February 6. The Council authorized negotiations under Article XXIV:6 of GATT, 1994, to adjust tariff bindings and other commitments as a result of the accession to the European Union of Austria, Finland, and Sweden (Bulletin 1/2-1995, Point 1.4.28).

June 29. The Council adopted a regulation reducing import duties on newsprint earlier than committed to under the Uruguay Round to compensate Canada under GATT Article XXIV:6 for the accession to the European Union of Austria, Finland, and Sweden (Council Regulation No. 1644/95).

July 25. The European Commission and Norway signed an agreement giving Norway duty-free quotas for fish exports to the European Union in compensation for the accession to the European Union of Austria, Finland, and Sweden.

December 22. The Council adopted a regulation applying tariff reductions resulting from negotiations with the European Union's major trading partners under GATT Article XXIV:6 (Bulletin 12-1995, Point 1.4.17).

2. Regional Developments

January 1. The European Union was enlarged to include Austria, Finland, and Sweden.

January 1. Free-trade agreements between the European Union and the Baltic countries (Estonia, Latvia, and Lithuania) entered into force.

January 23. The European Union signed a partnership and cooperation agreement with Kazakstan (Bulletin 1/2-1995, Point 1.4.97).

February 1. The Europe Association Agreements with Bulgaria, the Czech Republic, Romania, and the Slovak Republic entered into force (Bulletin 1/2-1995, Point 1.4.73).

February 9. The European Union signed a partnership and cooperation agreement with Kyrgyzstan (Bulletin 1/2-1995, Point 1.4.99).

March 6. The European Union signed a partnership and cooperation agreement with Belarus (Bulletin 3-1995, Point 1.4.70).

March 6. The EU-Turkey Association Council reached an agreement on the formation of a customs union (Bulletin 3-1995, Point 1.4.65).

June 1. The European Union signed an interim agreement implementing the trade provisions of a partnership and cooperation agreement with Ukraine (Bulletin 6-1995, Point 1.4.93).

June 12. Europe Association Agreements were signed with Estonia, Latvia, and Lithuania (Bulletin 6-1995, Point 1.4.63).

July 17. A Euro-Mediterranean Association Agreement was signed with Tunisia (Bulletin 7/8-1995, Point 1.4.84).

July 17. The European Union signed an interim agreement implementing the trade provisions of a partnership and cooperation agreement with the Russian Federation (Bulletin 7/8-1995, Point 1.4.89).

October 2. The European Union signed an interim agreement implementing the trade provisions of a partnership and cooperation agreement with Moldova (Bulletin 10-1995, Point 1.4.88).

November 20. A Euro-Mediterranean Association Agreement was signed with Israel (Bulletin 11-1995, Point 1.4.69).

December 5. The European Union signed an interim agreement to implement the trade provisions of the partnership and cooperation agreement with Kazakstan (Bulletin 12-1995, Point 1.4.99).

December 15. The European Union and the MERCOSUR countries (Argentina, Brazil, Paraguay, and Uruguay) signed an interregional framework cooperation agreement (Bulletin 12-1995, Point 1.4.111).

December 21. The Council adopted a regulation providing for advanced implementation of EU concessions to Morocco for certain agricultural products under a Euro-Mediterranean Association Agreement (Council Regulation No. 3057/95).

Summary Features of Exchange and Trade Systems in Member Countries

	Albania	Algeria	Angola	Antigua and Barbuda	Argentina	Armenia	Aruba	Australia	Austria	Azerbaijan	Bahamas, The	Bahrain	Bangladesh	Barbados	Belarus	Belgium and Luxembourg	Belize	Benin	Bhutan	Bolivia	Bosnia Herzegovina	Botswana	Brazil	Brunei Darussalam	Bulgaria
A. Acceptance of Article Status																									
1. Article VIII status	—	—	—	●	●	—	●	●	●	—	●	●	●	●	—	●	●	●	—	●	—	●	—	●	—
2. Article XIV status	●	●	●	—	—	●	—	—	—	●	—	—	—	—	●	—	—	—	●	—	●	—	●	—	●
B. Exchange Arrangement³																									
1. Exchange rate determined on the basis of:																									
(a) A peg to:																									
(i) the U.S. dollar	—	—	—	●	●	—	●	—	—	—	●	—	●	—	—	—	●	—	—	—	—	—	—	—	—
(ii) the French franc	—	—	—	—	—	—	—	—	—	—	—	—	—	—	—	—	—	●	—	—	—	—	—	—	—
(iii) other currencies⁴	—	—	—	—	—	—	—	—	—	—	—	—	—	—	—	—	—	—	●	—	●	—	—	●	—
(iv) a composite of currencies	—	—	—	—	—	—	—	—	—	—	—	—	●	—	—	—	—	—	—	—	—	●	—	—	—
(b) Limited flexibility with respect to:																									
(i) single currency	—	—	—	—	—	—	—	—	—	—	—	●	—	—	—	—	—	—	—	—	—	—	—	—	—
(ii) cooperative arrangement	—	—	—	—	—	—	—	—	●	—	—	—	—	—	—	●	—	—	—	—	—	—	—	—	—
(c) More flexible arrangements:																									
(i) adjusted according to a set of indicators	—	—	—	—	—	—	—	—	—	—	—	—	—	—	—	—	—	—	—	—	—	—	—	—	—
(ii) other managed floating	—	●	●	—	—	—	—	—	—	—	—	—	●	—	—	—	—	—	—	—	—	●	—	—	—
(iii) independently floating	●	—	—	—	—	●	—	●	—	●	—	—	—	—	—	—	—	—	—	●	—	—	—	—	●
2. Separate exchange rate(s) for some or all capital transactions and/or some or all invisibles	—	—	●	—	●	—	—	—	●	●	—	—	—	—	●	—	—	—	●	—	●	—	●	—	—
3. More than one rate for imports	—	—	●	—	●	—	—	—	—	●	—	—	—	—	●	—	—	—	●	—	—	—	●	—	—
4. More than one rate for exports	—	—	●	—	●	—	—	—	—	●	—	—	—	—	●	—	—	—	●	—	—	—	●	—	—
5. Import rate(s) different from export rate(s)	—	—	●	—	●	—	—	—	—	●	—	—	—	—	●	—	—	—	●	—	—	—	●	—	—
C. Payments Arrears	●	—	●	●	—	—	—	—	—	●	—	—	—	—	●	—	—	●	—	—	—	—	—	—	—
D. Bilateral Payments Arrangements																									
1. With members	●	●	—	—	●	—	—	—	—	●	—	—	●	—	●	—	—	●	—	—	—	—	●	—	●
2. With nonmembers	●	—	—	—	—	—	—	—	—	—	—	—	—	—	—	—	—	—	—	—	—	—	—	—	—
E. Payments Restrictions																									
1. Restrictions on payments for current transactions⁵	—	●	●	—	—	●	—	—	—	●	—	—	●	—	—	—	—	—	●	—	●	—	●	—	●
2. Restrictions on payments for capital transactions⁵,⁶	●	●	●	—	—	●	●	—	—	●	●	—	●	●	●	—	—	—	●	●	●	●	●	—	●
F. Cost-Related Import Restrictions																									
1. Import surcharges	—	—	—	—	●	—	—	—	—	—	—	●	—	—	—	—	●	—	—	—	—	—	—	—	—
2. Advance import deposits	—	—	—	—	—	—	—	—	—	—	—	—	●	—	—	—	—	—	—	—	—	—	—	—	—
G. Export Proceeds																									
1. Repatriation requirement	●	●	●	—	●	—	—	—	—	●	—	●	—	—	—	—	—	●	●	●	●	●	●	—	●
2. Surrender requirement	—	●	●	—	—	—	●	—	—	●	●	—	●	●	—	—	—	●	●	●	●	●	●	—	—

For key and footnotes, see page 552.

Trade Systems in Member Countries[1]
country page)[2]

	Burkina Faso	Burundi	Cambodia	Cameroon	Canada	Cape Verde	Central African Republic	Chad	Chile	China	Colombia	Comoros	Congo	Costa Rica	Côte d'Ivoire	Croatia	Cyprus	Czech Republic	Denmark	Djibouti	Dominica	Dominican Republic	Ecuador	Egypt	El Salvador	Equatorial Guinea	Eritrea	Estonia	Ethiopia	Fiji	Finland	France	Gabon	Gambia, The	Georgia	Germany
	●	—	—	●	●	—	—	●	●	—	—	—	●	●	●	●	●	●	●	—	●	●	●	—	●	●	—	●	—	●	●	●	●	●	—	●
	—	●	●	—	—	●	●	—	—	●	●	●	—	—	—	—	—	—	—	—	—	—	●	—	—	●	—	●	—	—	—	—	—	—	●	—
	—	—	—	—	—	—	—	—	—	—	—	—	—	—	—	—	—	—	—	●	●	—	—	—	—	—	—	—	—	—	—	—	—	—	—	—
	●	—	—	●	—	●	●	●	—	●	●	—	●	—	●	—	—	—	—	—	—	—	—	—	—	●	—	—	—	—	—	—	●	—	—	—
	—	—	—	—	—	—	—	—	—	—	—	—	—	—	—	—	—	—	—	—	—	—	—	—	—	—	—	●	—	—	—	—	—	—	—	—
	—	●	—	—	—	●	—	—	—	—	—	—	—	—	—	—	●	●	—	—	—	—	—	—	—	—	—	—	—	●	—	—	—	—	—	—
	—	—	—	—	—	—	—	—	—	—	—	—	—	—	—	—	—	—	●	—	—	—	—	—	—	—	—	—	—	—	●	—	—	—	●
	—	—	—	—	—	—	—	—	●	—	—	—	—	—	—	—	—	—	—	—	—	—	—	—	—	—	—	—	—	—	—	—	—	—	—	—
	—	—	●	—	—	—	—	—	—	●	●	—	—	●	●	—	—	—	—	—	—	●	●	●	●	—	—	—	—	—	—	—	—	—	●	—
	—	—	—	—	●	—	—	—	—	—	—	—	—	—	—	—	—	—	—	—	—	—	—	—	—	—	—	●	—	●	—	●	—	—	●	—
	—	—	—	—	—	—	—	—	●	—	—	—	●	—	—	—	—	—	—	—	—	—	●	●	—	—	—	—	—	—	—	—	—	—	●	—
	—	—	—	—	—	—	—	—	—	—	—	—	●	—	—	—	—	—	—	—	—	—	●	●	—	—	—	●	—	—	—	—	—	—	●	—
	—	—	—	—	—	—	—	—	—	—	—	—	●	—	—	—	—	—	—	—	—	—	●	●	—	—	—	●	—	—	—	—	—	—	●	—
	—	—	—	—	—	—	—	—	—	—	—	—	●	—	—	—	—	—	—	—	—	—	●	●	—	—	—	—	—	—	—	—	—	—	●	—
	●	—	—	●	—	●	●	●	—	—	—	—	●	●	—	—	—	—	—	—	—	●	●	●	—	●	—	—	—	—	—	—	—	—	—	—
	●	—	—	—	—	●	—	—	—	●	●	—	—	—	—	—	—	—	—	—	—	●	●	—	—	—	●	—	●	—	—	—	—	●	—
	—	—	—	—	—	—	—	—	—	—	—	●	—	—	—	—	—	—	—	—	—	—	●	—	—	—	—	—	—	—	—	—	—	—	—	—
	—	●	—	—	—	●	—	—	—	●	●	●	—	—	—	●	—	—	—	—	—	—	●	—	—	●	—	●	—	●	—	—	—	—	—	—
	●	●	●	●	—	●	●	●	●	●	●	●	●	●	—	●	●	●	—	—	●	●	●	—	●	●	●	—	●	●	—	—	●	●	●	—
	●	—	—	●	—	—	—	—	●	—	—	—	—	●	●	●	—	—	—	●	—	●	●	—	—	—	—	—	—	—	—	—	●	—	●	—
	—	—	—	—	—	—	—	—	—	—	—	—	—	—	—	—	—	●	—	—	—	—	—	—	—	—	—	—	—	—	—	—	—	—	—	—
	●	●	●	●	—	●	●	●	●	●	●	●	●	●	●	●	●	●	—	●	●	●	—	●	●	●	—	●	●	—	●	●	—	●	●	—
	●	●	●	—	—	●	●	●	●	—	●	●	●	●	—	●	●	●	—	—	●	●	●	—	●	●	—	—	●	●	—	—	●	—	—	—

	Ghana	Greece	Grenada	Guatemala	Guinea	Guinea-Bissau	Guyana	Haiti	Honduras	Hong Kong	Hungary	Iceland	India	Indonesia	Iran, Islamic Rep. of	Ireland	Israel	Italy	Jamaica	Japan	Jordan	Kazakstan	Kenya	Kiribati	Korea
A. Acceptance of Article Status																									
1. Article VIII status	●	●	●	●	●	—	●	●	●	●	●	●	●	●	—	●	●	●	●	●	●	●	●	●	●
2. Article XIV status	—	—	—	—	—	●	—	—	—	—	—	—	—	—	●	—	—	—	—	—	—	—	—	—	—
B. Exchange Arrangement[3]																									
1. Exchange rate determined on the basis of:																									
(a) A peg to:																									
(i) the U.S. dollar	—	—	●	—	—	—	—	—	—	—	—	—	—	—	—	—	—	—	—	—	—	—	—	—	—
(ii) the French franc	—	—	—	—	—	—	—	—	—	—	—	—	—	—	—	—	—	—	—	—	—	—	—	—	—
(iii) other currencies[4]	—	—	—	—	—	—	—	—	—	—	—	—	—	—	—	—	—	—	—	—	—	—	—	●	—
(iv) a composite of currencies	—	—	—	—	—	—	—	—	—	—	—	●	—	—	—	—	—	—	—	—	●	—	—	—	—
(b) Limited flexibility with respect to:																									
(i) single currency	—	—	—	—	—	—	—	—	—	—	—	—	—	—	—	—	—	—	—	—	—	—	—	—	—
(ii) cooperative arrangement	—	—	—	—	—	—	—	—	—	—	—	—	—	—	—	●	—	—	—	—	—	—	—	—	—
(c) More flexible arrangements:																									
(i) adjusted according to a set of indicators	—	—	—	—	—	—	—	—	—	—	—	—	—	—	—	—	—	—	—	—	—	—	—	—	—
(ii) other managed floating	—	●	—	—	—	●	—	—	●	●	●	—	—	●	●	—	●	—	—	—	—	—	—	—	●
(iii) independently floating	●	—	—	●	●	—	●	●	—	—	—	—	●	—	—	—	●	●	●	●	—	●	●	—	—
2. Separate exchange rate(s) for some or all capital transactions and/or some or all invisibles	—	—	—	—	—	●	—	—	—	—	—	—	—	—	●	—	—	—	—	—	●	●	—	—	—
3. More than one rate for imports	—	—	—	—	—	●	—	—	—	—	—	—	—	—	●	—	—	—	—	—	●	●	—	—	—
4. More than one rate for exports	—	—	—	—	—	●	—	—	—	—	—	—	—	—	●	—	—	—	—	—	●	●	—	—	—
5. Import rate(s) different from export rate(s)	—	—	—	—	—	●	—	—	—	—	—	—	—	—	●	—	—	—	—	—	●	●	—	—	—
C. Payments Arrears	—	—	—	●	●	●	—	—	—	—	—	—	—	—	—	—	—	—	—	—	●	—	●	—	—
D. Bilateral Payments Arrangements																									
1. With members	●	—	—	●	—	—	—	—	●	—	●	—	●	—	●	—	●	—	●	●	—	●	—	—	—
2. With nonmembers	●	—	—	—	●	—	—	—	—	—	—	—	—	—	—	—	—	—	—	—	—	●	—	—	—
E. Payments Restrictions																									
1. Restrictions on payments for current transactions[5]	—	—	—	—	●	●	—	—	—	—	—	—	—	●	●	—	—	—	●	—	●	●	●	—	—
2. Restrictions on payments for capital transactions[5,6]	●	●	●	—	●	●	●	●	●	●	●	—	●	●	●	●	●	●	●	●	●	●	●	—	●
F. Cost-Related Import Restrictions																									
1. Import surcharges	—	●	●	—	●	—	—	—	—	—	—	—	●	●	●	—	—	—	●	—	●	—	—	—	—
2. Advance import deposits	—	—	—	—	—	—	—	—	—	—	—	—	—	—	●	—	—	—	—	—	—	—	—	—	—
G. Export Proceeds																									
1. Repatriation requirement	●	●	●	●	●	●	●	●	●	●	—	●	●	—	●	—	●	—	—	●	●	●	●	—	●
2. Surrender requirement	●	●	—	●	●	●	●	—	●	—	●	—	●	—	●	—	●	—	—	—	—	●	●	—	—

For key and footnotes, see page 552.

Trade Systems in Member Countries[1] (continued)

country page)[2]

	Kuwait	Kyrgyz Republic	Lao People's Dem. Rep.	Latvia	Lebanon	Lesotho	Liberia	Libyan Arab Jamahiriya	Lithuania	Macedonia, former Yugoslav Republic of	Madagascar	Malawi	Malaysia	Maldives	Mali	Malta	Marshall Islands	Mauritania	Mauritius	Mexico	Micronesia, Fed. States of	Moldova	Mongolia	Morocco	Mozambique	Myanmar	Namibia	Nepal	Netherlands	Netherlands Antilles	New Zealand	Nicaragua	Niger	Nigeria
	●	●	—	●	●	—	—	—	●	—	●	●	—	●	●	●	—	●	●	●	●	●	●	●	—	—	—	●	●	●	●	●	●	—
	—	—	●	—	—	●	●	●	—	●	●	—	—	●	—	—	—	●	—	—	—	—	—	—	●	●	●	—	—	—	—	—	—	●
	—	—	—	—	—	●	—	—	●	—	—	—	—	—	—	—	●	—	—	—	●	—	—	—	—	—	—	●	—	—	—	—	—	●
	—	—	—	—	—	—	—	—	—	—	—	—	—	—	●	—	—	—	—	—	—	—	—	—	—	—	—	—	—	—	—	—	—	—
	—	—	—	●	—	—	—	—	—	—	—	—	—	—	—	—	—	—	—	—	—	—	—	—	—	—	●	—	—	—	—	—	—	—
	●	—	—	—	—	—	●	—	—	—	—	—	—	—	●	—	—	—	—	—	—	—	—	—	●	●	—	●	—	—	—	—	—	—
	—	—	—	—	—	—	—	—	—	—	—	—	—	—	—	—	—	—	—	—	—	—	—	—	—	—	—	—	—	—	—	—	—	—
	—	—	—	—	—	—	—	—	—	—	—	—	—	—	—	—	—	—	—	—	—	—	—	—	—	—	—	—	—	●	—	—	—	—
	—	—	—	—	—	—	—	—	—	—	—	—	—	—	—	—	—	—	—	—	—	—	—	—	—	—	—	—	—	—	—	—	—	—
	—	—	—	—	—	—	—	—	—	—	—	—	—	—	—	—	—	—	—	—	—	—	—	—	—	—	—	—	—	—	—	—	●	—
	—	●	—	●	—	—	—	—	—	●	—	—	●	●	—	—	—	—	—	—	—	—	—	—	—	—	—	—	—	—	—	—	—	—
	—	—	●	—	●	—	—	—	—	—	●	●	—	—	—	—	—	●	—	●	—	●	●	●	●	—	—	—	—	—	●	—	—	—
	—	—	—	●	—	—	—	—	—	—	—	—	—	—	—	—	—	—	—	—	—	—	—	—	—	—	—	—	—	—	—	—	—	●
	—	—	—	—	—	—	—	—	—	—	—	—	—	—	—	—	—	—	—	—	—	—	—	—	—	—	—	—	—	—	—	—	—	—
	—	—	—	—	—	—	—	—	—	—	—	—	—	—	—	—	—	—	—	—	—	—	—	—	—	—	—	—	—	—	—	—	—	—
	—	—	—	—	—	—	●	—	—	—	—	—	—	—	—	—	—	—	—	—	—	—	—	—	—	—	—	—	—	—	—	—	—	—
	—	●	—	●	—	—	●	●	—	—	●	—	●	●	—	—	—	●	—	—	—	—	●	—	●	—	—	—	—	—	—	—	—	—
	—	—	—	—	—	—	—	—	●	—	—	—	—	—	—	—	—	—	—	—	—	—	●	—	—	—	—	—	—	—	—	—	—	—
	—	—	●	—	—	—	●	—	—	—	●	●	—	—	—	—	—	●	—	—	—	—	●	●	●	●	●	—	—	—	—	—	—	●
	—	●	●	—	—	●	●	●	—	—	●	●	●	—	●	●	—	●	●	●	—	●	●	●	●	●	●	●	—	—	—	●	●	●
	—	—	—	—	—	●	●	—	—	—	●	●	—	—	—	—	—	—	—	—	—	—	—	—	—	—	●	—	—	—	●	—	●	—
	—	—	●	—	—	—	—	●	—	—	—	—	—	—	—	—	—	—	—	—	—	—	●	—	—	—	—	—	—	—	—	—	—	—
	—	●	—	—	●	—	●	●	—	—	●	●	●	●	●	●	—	●	●	●	—	●	●	●	●	●	●	●	—	—	—	—	●	●
	—	—	—	—	—	●	●	●	—	—	●	●	●	●	●	●	—	●	●	—	—	●	●	—	●	●	●	—	—	—	—	—	—	●

549

	Norway	Oman	Pakistan	Panama	Papua New Guinea	Paraguay	Peru	Philippines	Poland	Portugal	Qatar	Romania	Russian Federation	Rwanda	St. Kitts and Nevis	St. Lucia	St. Vincent and the Grenadines	San Marino	São Tomé and Príncipe	Saudi Arabia	Senegal	Seychelles	Sierra Leone	Singapore	Slovak Republic
A. Acceptance of Article Status																									
1. Article VIII status	●	●	●	●	●	●	●	●	●	●	●	—	●	—	●	●	●	●	—	●	●	●	●	●	●
2. Article XIV status	—	—	—	—	—	—	—	—	—	—	—	●	—	●	—	—	—	—	●	—	—	—	—	—	—
B. Exchange Arrangement[3]																									
1. Exchange rate determined on the basis of:																									
(a) A peg to:																									
(i) the U.S. dollar	—	●	—	●	—	—	—	—	—	—	—	—	—	—	●	●	●	—	—	—	—	—	—	—	—
(ii) the French franc	—	—	—	—	—	—	—	—	—	—	—	—	—	—	—	—	—	—	—	—	●	—	—	—	—
(iii) other currencies[4]	—	—	—	—	—	—	—	—	—	—	—	—	—	—	—	—	—	—	●	—	—	—	—	—	—
(iv) a composite of currencies	—	—	—	—	—	—	—	—	—	—	—	—	—	—	—	—	—	—	—	—	—	●	—	—	●
(b) Limited flexibility with respect to:																									
(i) single currency	—	—	—	—	—	—	—	—	—	—	●	—	—	—	—	—	—	—	—	●	—	—	—	—	—
(ii) cooperative arrangement	—	—	—	—	—	—	—	—	—	●	—	—	—	—	—	—	—	—	—	—	—	—	—	—	—
(c) More flexible arrangements:																									
(i) adjusted according to a set of indicators	—	—	—	—	—	—	—	—	—	—	—	—	—	—	—	—	—	—	—	—	—	—	—	—	—
(ii) other managed floating	●	—	●	—	—	—	●	—	—	—	—	—	●	—	—	—	—	—	—	—	—	—	—	●	—
(iii) independently floating	—	—	—	—	●	●	—	●	—	—	—	●	—	●	—	—	—	—	●	—	—	—	●	—	—
2. Separate exchange rate(s) for some or all capital transactions and/or some or all invisibles	—	—	—	—	—	—	—	—	—	—	—	●	—	—	—	—	—	—	—	—	—	—	—	—	—
3. More than one rate for imports	—	—	—	—	—	—	—	—	—	—	—	●	—	—	—	—	—	—	—	—	—	—	—	—	—
4. More than one rate for exports	—	—	—	—	—	—	—	—	—	—	—	●	—	—	—	—	—	—	—	—	—	—	—	—	—
5. Import rate(s) different from export rate(s)	—	—	—	—	—	—	—	—	—	—	—	●	—	—	—	—	—	—	—	—	—	—	—	—	—
C. Payments Arrears	—	—	—	●	—	●	●	—	—	—	—	●	●	—	—	—	—	—	●	—	—	●	●	●	—
D. Bilateral Payments Arrangements																									
1. With members	—	—	—	●	—	—	—	—	—	—	—	●	●	●	—	—	—	—	●	—	—	—	—	—	●
2. With nonmembers	—	—	—	—	—	—	—	—	—	—	—	●	●	—	—	—	—	—	—	—	—	—	—	—	●
E. Payments Restrictions																									
1. Restrictions on payments for current transactions[5]	—	—	●	—	—	—	—	—	—	—	—	●	●	—	—	—	—	—	●	—	—	—	—	—	●
2. Restrictions on payments for capital transactions[5,6]	—	—	●	—	●	●	—	●	●	—	—	●	●	●	●	●	●	—	●	●	●	—	●	—	●
F. Cost-Related Import Restrictions																									
1. Import surcharges	—	—	●	●	—	—	●	—	●	—	—	●	—	—	—	—	—	—	●	—	—	—	—	—	—
2. Advance import deposits	—	—	—	—	—	—	—	—	—	—	—	—	—	—	—	—	—	—	●	—	—	—	—	—	—
G. Export Proceeds																									
1. Repatriation requirement	—	—	●	—	●	●	—	—	●	—	—	●	●	●	●	●	●	—	●	—	—	●	●	—	●
2. Surrender requirement	—	—	●	—	—	—	—	—	●	—	—	●	●	—	—	—	—	—	●	—	—	●	●	—	●

For key and footnotes, see page 552.

Slovenia	Solomon Islands	South Africa	Spain	Sri Lanka	Sudan	Suriname	Swaziland	Sweden	Switzerland	Syrian Arab Republic	Tajikistan	Tanzania	Thailand	Togo	Tonga	Trinidad and Tobago	Tunisia	Turkey	Turkmenistan	Uganda	Ukraine	United Arab Emirates	United Kingdom	United States	Uruguay	Uzbekistan	Vanuatu	Venezuela	Vietnam	Western Samoa	Yemen, Republic of	Zaïre	Zambia	Zimbabwe
•	•	•	•	•	—	•	•	•	•	—	—	—	•	•	•	•	•	•	—	•	—	•	•	•	•	—	•	•	—	•	—	—	—	•
—	—	—	—	—	•	—	—	—	—	•	•	•	—	—	—	—	—	—	•	—	•	—	—	—	—	•	—	—	•	—	•	•	•	—
—	—	—	—	—	—	—	—	—	—	•	—	—	—	—	—	—	—	—	—	—	—	—	—	—	—	—	—	•	—	•	—	—	—	—
—	—	—	—	—	—	—	—	—	—	—	—	—	—	•	—	—	—	—	—	—	—	—	—	—	—	—	—	—	—	—	—	—	—	—
—	—	—	—	—	—	—	•	—	—	—	—	—	—	—	—	—	—	—	—	—	—	—	—	—	—	—	—	—	—	—	—	—	—	—
—	•	—	—	—	—	—	—	—	—	—	—	—	•	—	•	—	—	—	—	—	—	—	—	—	—	—	•	—	—	•	—	—	—	—
—	—	—	—	—	—	—	—	—	—	—	—	—	—	—	—	—	—	—	—	—	—	•	—	—	—	—	—	—	—	—	—	—	—	—
—	—	•	—	—	—	—	—	—	—	—	—	—	—	—	—	—	—	—	—	—	—	—	—	—	—	—	—	—	—	—	—	—	—	—
—	—	—	—	—	—	—	—	—	—	—	—	—	—	—	—	—	—	—	—	—	—	—	—	—	—	—	—	—	—	—	—	—	—	—
•	—	—	•	—	•	—	—	—	—	•	•	—	•	—	—	•	•	—	—	•	—	—	—	—	•	•	—	•	—	—	—	—	—	—
—	—	•	—	—	•	—	—	•	•	•	—	•	•	—	•	•	—	•	—	—	•	—	—	•	•	•	—	—	—	—	—	•	•	•
—	—	—	•	—	—	—	—	•	•	•	—	—	—	—	—	—	—	—	—	•	—	•	—	—	—	—	—	—	—	—	•	—	•	—
—	—	—	•	—	—	—	•	—	—	•	—	•	—	—	—	—	—	—	—	•	—	—	—	—	—	—	—	—	—	—	•	—	•	—
—	—	—	•	—	—	—	—	—	—	•	—	•	—	—	—	—	—	—	—	•	—	—	—	—	—	—	—	—	—	—	•	—	•	—
—	—	—	•	—	•	—	•	—	—	•	—	•	—	—	—	—	—	—	—	•	—	—	—	—	—	—	•	•	—	—	•	—	•	—
•	—	—	—	•	—	—	—	—	—	•	•	—	—	—	—	—	•	•	•	•	•	—	—	—	—	•	—	•	—	—	•	—	•	—
—	—	—	—	—	—	—	—	—	—	—	—	—	—	—	—	—	—	—	•	—	•	—	—	—	•	—	—	•	—	—	—	—	—	—
•	—	—	•	•	—	—	—	•	•	—	•	—	—	•	—	—	•	—	•	—	—	—	—	—	•	—	•	•	—	•	•	•	•	•
•	•	•	—	•	•	•	—	—	•	•	•	•	•	•	•	—	•	•	•	—	—	—	—	•	•	•	•	•	•	•	•	•	•	•
—	—	—	•	—	—	•	—	—	•	—	—	—	—	—	—	—	—	—	—	—	—	—	—	•	•	—	•	—	•	—	—	•	—	—
—	—	—	—	•	—	—	—	—	—	—	—	—	—	—	—	—	—	•	•	—	—	—	—	—	—	—	•	•	—	—	•	—	—	—
•	•	•	—	—	•	•	—	•	—	—	•	•	—	•	—	—	•	•	•	•	—	—	—	—	•	•	—	•	•	•	•	—	•	•
•	•	•	—	•	•	•	—	—	•	—	—	•	•	—	•	•	•	—	—	•	•	—	•	—	—	•	—	•	•	•	•	—	•	—

Summary Features
of Exchange and Trade Systems
in Member Countries

Key and Footnotes

• indicates that the specified practice is a feature of the exchange and trade system.

– indicates that the specified practice is not a feature of the system.

◘ indicates that the composite is the SDR.

[1] The listing includes the nonmetropolitan territory of Hong Kong, for which the United Kingdom has accepted the Fund's Articles of Agreement, and Aruba and the Netherlands Antilles, for which the Kingdom of the Netherlands has accepted the Fund's Articles of Agreement. Exchange practices indicated in individual countries do not necessarily apply to all external transactions.

[2] Usually December 31, 1995.

[3] It should be noted that existence of a separate rate does not necessarily imply a multiple currency practice under Fund jurisdiction. Exchange arrangements involving transactions at a unitary rate with one group of countries and at another unitary rate with a second group of countries are considered, from the viewpoint of the overall economy, to involve two separate rates for similar transactions.

[4] Australian dollar, deutsche mark, Indian rupee, Italian lira, Singapore dollar, or South African rand.

[5] Restrictions (i.e., official actions directly affecting the availability or cost of exchange, or involving undue delay) on payments to member countries, other than restrictions evidenced by external payments arrears and restrictions imposed for security reasons under Executive Board Decision No. 144-(52/51) adopted August 14, 1952.

[6] Resident-owned funds.

Definitions of Acronyms

Note: This list does not include acronyms of purely national institutions mentioned in the country chapters

ACU	Asian Clearing Union
AFTA	ASEAN free trade area (see ASEAN, below)
AMU	Asian monetary unit
ANZCERTA	Australia-New Zealand Closer Economic Relations and Trade Agreement
ASEAN	Association of South East Asian Nations
ATC	Agreement of Textiles and Clothing
BCEAO	Central Bank of West African States (Banque centrale des Etats de l'Afrique de l'Ouest)
BEAC	Bank of Central African States (Banque des Etats de l'Afrique Centrale)
BLEU	Belgian-Luxembourg Economic Union
CACM	Central American Common Market
CAP	Common agricultural policy (of the EU)
CARICOM	Caribbean Common Market
CEEAC	Economic Community of Central African States
CEFTA	Central European free trade area
CEPGL	Economic Community of the Great Lakes Countries
CEPT	Common effective preferential tariff of the ASEAN free trade area
CET	Common external tariff (of CARICOM)
CFA	Communauté financière africaine
CIS	Commonwealth of Independent States
CMA	Common monetary area
CMEA	Council for Mutual Economic Assistance (dissolved)
COCOM	Coordinating Committee for Multilateral Export Controls
ECCB	Eastern Caribbean Central Bank
ECLAC	Economic Commission for Latin America and the Caribbean
ECOWAS	Economic Community of West African States (Cedeao)
ECSC	European Coal and Steel Community
ECU	European currency unit
EEA	European economic area
EFTA	European Free Trade Association
EMS	European monetary system
ERM	Exchange rate mechanism (of the EMS)
EU	European Union (formerly European Community)
GATT	General Agreement on Tariffs and Trade
GCC	Gulf Cooperation Council (Cooperation Council for the Arab States of the Gulf)
GSP	Generalized system of preferences
HCDCS	Harmonized commodity description and coding system
LAIA	Latin American Integration Association
LIBOR	London interbank offered rate
MERCOSUR	Southern Cone Common Market
MFA	Multifiber Arrangement
MFN	Most favored nation
MTN	Multilateral trade negotiations (the Uruguay Round)
NAFTA	North American Free Trade Agreement
NATO	North Atlantic Treaty Organization
OECD	Organization for Economic Cooperation and Development
OECS	Organization of Eastern Caribbean States
OGL	Open general license
PTA	Preferential trade area for Eastern and Southern African states
SACU	Southern African Customs Union
SPARTECA	South Pacific Regional Trade and Economic Cooperation Agreement

Definitions of Acronyms

UAPTA	Unit of account of the PTA
UDEAC	Central African Customs and Economic Union
WAEC	West African Economic Community (CEAO) (dissolved)
WAEMU	West African Economic and Monetary Union (formely WAMU)
WAMU	West African Monetary Union
WTO	World Trade Organization (supercedes GATT)